INTELLECTUAL PROPERTY

CASES AND MATERIALS
Third Edition

By

David Lange

Melvin G. Shimm Professor of Law
Duke University School of Law

Mary LaFrance

William S. Boyd Professor of Law
William S. Boyd School of Law
University of Nevada, Las Vegas

Gary Myers

Professor of Law
University of Mississippi School of Law

AMERICAN CASEBOOK SERIES®

Mat # 40542642

© West, a Thomson business, 1998, 2002
© 2007 Thomson/West
    610 Opperman Drive
    P.O. Box 64526
    St. Paul, MN 55164–0526
    1–800–328–9352

ISBN–13: 978–0–314–17616–5

 TEXT IS PRINTED ON 10% POST CONSUMER RECYCLED PAPER

The authors dedicate this edition to

Tom Blackwell
1961-2002

Gladly wolde he lerne, and gladly teche

*

Authors' Acknowledgments

We are indebted to the respective institutions at which we teach, and to their Deans and administrators, whose support and encouragement in the preparation of this work we gratefully acknowledge.

Professor Lange gratefully acknowledges the numerous helpful contributions by research assistants who have added immeasurably to the preparation of the casebook, teachers' manuals and supplements through the years, and who have been individually identified in these earlier publications. Much of their work continues to find expression in the third edition of this casebook. In the preparation of this edition, he particularly acknowledges the continuing research and editorial assistance of his valued professional colleagues and associates, Jennifer Anderson and David McKenzie, members of the North Carolina Bar.

Professor LaFrance acknowledges with gratitude the efforts of her research assistants, the law librarians at the Boyd School of Law, and her assistant Judy Meyerson. She expresses special appreciation to Dean Richard Morgan upon his retirement from Boyd after a decade of extraordinary leadership and support for faculty scholarship.

Professor Myers gratefully acknowledges the efforts of his research assistants on prior editions of this casebook.

Above all, we are grateful to our many students through the years whose suggestions, arguments, comments and advice have added immeasurably to our collective judgment and insight.

*

Preface to the Third Edition

This casebook offers comprehensive coverage of all of the basic doctrinal areas of study and practice in the field of intellectual property. The book provides both breadth and depth of coverage; its flexible structure allows teachers and students the opportunity, within a topic area, to choose whether to focus purely on fundamentals or to probe more deeply into subtopics of special interest. As a result, the casebook has been used successfully to teach survey courses of 3-6 credits as well as specialized courses on individual topics such as trademark or copyright law. Teachers will find our book thorough and detailed, while remaining remarkably "teachable"; and students will find the materials accessible, yet truly rich in learning.

We have been especially pleased at the increasing number of adoptions of our book since we published the first edition a few years ago. With each edition, we have endeavored to provide not only the most up-to-date materials, but to improve the selection and presentation of materials so that they will complement a variety of teaching styles and subject matter emphases. We hope the present edition, which we believe to be our best effort yet, will continue to find favor among our colleagues.

To stimulate critical thinking, we begin with a Prologue that invites students to reflect on the presuppositions they may bring to their study. We move on through an Introduction that sketches the broad outlines of the field in bold strokes. We turn next to unfair competition and trademarks -- the topics most deeply rooted in the common law – then move on to publicity rights, the law of ideas, and trade secrets. From there we move into the most heavily statutory fields, patent and copyright law, with all of their extraordinary complexity. It is here that the book offers its most flexible coverage options, allowing teachers to choose greater depth of coverage by utilizing the exceptionally rich note materials.

Although we rely heavily on carefully chosen case law as our foundational teaching tool, we encourage students to question the reasoning and conclusions of those cases rather than respond to them with unquestioning acceptance. In addition, with respect to those areas of intellectual property law that are governed in whole or in part by federal statutes, the casebook also seeks to instill in students an appreciation for the primacy of the statutory materials. Many students who enroll in their first intellectual property course will have had limited exposure to statutory interpretation. This text will provide them with a transformative experi-

---

[1] A word about editing: Cases and materials in the text have been edited not only as required in the authors' judgment but also to conform to the style approved by West Group. In particular, citations and footnotes are sometimes omitted without specific indication.

ence. Some of our note materials raise statutory interpretation questions that are not explored in the principal cases which the students have read; these questions require the students to engage in a close and thoughtful reading of the statutes themselves rather than rely on the exegesis provided by a published opinion.

This is a demanding casebook, but one which students and teachers tell us is both rewarding and enjoyable. Intellectual property is complex and fast-paced. It can be fascinating, metaphysical, and quite often fun. We hope this edition has captured our enthusiasm.

Summary of Contents

PART III.   THE RIGHT OF PUBLICITY

PART IV.   TRADE SECRET LAW

PART V.   IDEA PROTECTION

PART VI.   PATENT LAW

*

Table of Contents

Table of Cases

The principal cases are in bold type. Cases cited or discussed in the text are roman type. References are to pages. Cases cited in principal cases and within other quoted materials are not included.

INTELLECTUAL PROPERTY

CASES AND MATERIALS
Third Edition

"Moonrise (Hernandez, New Mexico) 1941"
Photograph by Ansel Adams. Used by permission.

Accompanying text (opposite in Prologue) by Ansel Adams, in Examples: The Making of 40 Photographs (Little Brown and Company Boston 1983). Edited and used by permission.

Prologue

Question: What does it take to create a "Moonrise"?

Question: What should it mean to protect a "Moonrise" once we agree it has been created?

The first question comes from an advertisement for a coffee table book, *Ansel Adams, The Making of 40 Photographs*. The second question is the first among many to be asked by the student of intellectual property. These are the questions, endlessly reiterated in variant forms, that make up the field of law known as "intellectual property."

In the course of our exploration of this subject we will consider numerous doctrines and principles, all of which attempt to furnish answers to these questions from a legal perspective. You will almost certainly find the subject matter of these inquiries intriguing—not because of any magic we will work as guides, but rather because so much of the field itself seems magic.

Or so at least it seems to us. But then, as to that, you can judge for yourselves—all in good time.

Before we begin, take some time to reflect on the two questions posed above. Allow yourself to think first about the nature of creativity and invention as you understand them; and only then turn to the question of rights: of ownership and exclusivity; of the moral claims a creator may make upon a subject; of the conflicts between the creator's claims and the interests others may have in replicating the work; of the interests, if any, the State may claim in the work. Try to recognize the presuppositions you bring to the effort. What do you mean (and whom do you have in mind) when you think of authorship? How firmly committed are you to freedom of expression? Do you believe that plagiarism (or "piracy") is morally wrong? Are you generally comfortable with the concepts of property and commodities as you understand them? Where do you stand in the contemporary debate about the proper role of the individual in relation to society? And so on.

If you take the effort seriously, you may find that it produces an unexpected—at times, an almost painful—ambivalence.

Where, exactly, is the creative work in a photograph like "Moonrise"? In the artist's recognition and appropriation of the moment? In the expression of his ideas? In his mastery of the medium? In the ability of the artist's work to distinguish itself in the marketplace? In the utilitarian processes of photography itself?

In *Ansel Adams, Examples: The Making of 40 Photographs*, Ansel Adams discusses the decisions that went into the production of his work. Here is the artist himself on the creation of "Moonrise, Hernandez, New Mexico, 1941":

> The making of this photograph—it is certainly my most popular single image—combined serendipity and immediate technical recall. [My companions and I] were sailing southward along the highway not far from Española when I glanced to the left and saw an extraordinary situation—an inevitable photograph! I had a clear visualization of the image I wanted, but I was at a loss with the subject luminance values, and I confess I was thinking of bracketing several exposures, when I suddenly realized I knew the luminance of the moon—250 c/ft^2. Using the Exposure Formula [I had previously developed], I placed this luminance on Zone VII; 60 c/ft^2 therefore fell on Zone V, and the exposure with the filter factor of 3x was about *I* second at f/32 with ASA 64 film. Realizing as I released the shutter that I had an unusual photograph which deserved a duplicate negative, I swiftly reversed the film holder, but as I pulled the darkslide the sunlight passed from the white crosses; I was a few seconds too late!
>
> I am sure that the image would command general interest for the subject alone. However, the mood of the scene requires subtle value qualities in the print that I feel are supportive of the original visualization.

Surely, in the teeth of so exact an account of creation, we cannot begrudge Adams recognition as creator. But what of it? That is, what are we to make of his entitlement to recognition? Is it personal, merely, to him? And optional at that, on our part? Or is there some sense in which recognition of individual creativity is obligatory? Does the recognition of creativity or invention inevitably confer some additional status upon the work itself? Why? And if so, to what end?

Consider which, if any, among the following propositions you would agree with (whether or not with modifications):

1. Adams is entitled to create a work of this sort, even though the subject matter of the photograph is public property. Private property? Both?

2. Adams is entitled to acknowledgment as creator from anyone who publishes or circulates the work.

3. Adams is entitled to withhold the work from publication or distribution. Or, once having consented to its publication or

distribution, is entitled subsequently to withdraw it from further circulation upon finding it no longer pleasing or representative of his sensibilities as a creator? Or upon determining that withdrawal will enhance its value in the marketplace?

4. Adams is entitled to prevent excessive criticism of his work.

5. Adams is entitled to prevent destruction or mutilation of the work. (The negative merely? Or copies of the work as well?)

6. Adams is entitled to prevent unauthorized public displays of the work.

7. Adams is entitled to prevent unauthorized copying or reproduction of the work. (Is there a difference between copying and reproduction?)

Let us elaborate on that last question a bit. If you think, as many in our time do, that a creator should be able to prevent unauthorized copying, what should that mean in the case of "Moonrise"? How would you respond in the following situations?

1. The work is copied in a pen-and-ink drawing for private use and enjoyment. Or copied mechanically, at the Fotomat, for example, or with the help of a Xerox copier?

2. The work is copied, whether as a drawing or mechanically, for public use. For commercial public use? For non-profit public use?

3. The work is combined with another work by a second creator, incorporated in a collage, for example. Or reflected in a scene from a motion picture? Or made the basis for a short story? Or the prologue to a law school casebook?

Would it be "copying the work" if someone who saw "Moonrise", and was inspired by it, sought to replicate it in a photograph taken today at the same site and from the same perspective? From a different prospective? Would it bear upon the question of copying if the original site is now changed, so that elements in the original are no longer there, or are altered, or are joined by other elements not in existence in 1941? Would it matter if Adams's admirer exactly followed the technical specifications described in Adams's account of his making of the photograph? Would the admirer's use of a radically different technical medium (computer generated holography, for example) affect your judgment as to copying?

Ask yourself again: Where exactly is "the work" in a setting like this one? In the subject alone? In the "mood of the scene?" In the "original visualization?" In the negative? Adams refers to the need to respect "subtle value qualities" in striking prints from the original negative. What do you think he means? Does this suggest a different or additional standard of creativity or originality than is implicit in the taking of the photograph in the first place? In the last sentence of his essay on how he came to make this photograph he says: "The printed image has varied over the years; I have sought more intensity of light and richness of values as time goes on." What does this suggest about the continuing or evolving nature of creativity and entitlement in a work?

Would it be objectionable if someone who knew nothing of "Moonrise" chanced, through a combination of "serendipity and immediate technical recall", to produce a photograph strikingly similar to Adams's work? What if the second work led to confusion as to authorship? Or as to commercial identity? What, exactly, do these terms mean?

Ansel Adams died April 22, 1984, full of years and honors. He is widely recognized as one of America's foremost photographers. But how many of the rights we have considered above would you be willing to see survive him? How long after his death would you be willing to extend them? And in whom would you be prepared to see those rights vest?

Do not allow yourself to be moved by what you imagine the law to be. Reflect instead upon how you think these questions should be answered.

Part I

INTRODUCTION

Chapter 1

DOCTRINES, ALTERNATIVES, AND DEBATE

A. BASIC INTELLECTUAL PROPERTY DOCTRINES UNDER THE UNITED STATES CONSTITUTION

BAKER v. SELDEN

Supreme Court of the United States, 1879.
101 U.S. (11 Otto) 99, 25 L.Ed. 841.

Mr. Justice Bradley delivered the opinion of the court.

Charles Selden, the testator of the complainant in this case, in the year 1859 took the requisite steps for obtaining the copyright of a book, entitled "Selden's Condensed Ledger, or Book-keeping Simplified," the object of which was to exhibit and explain a peculiar system of book-keeping. In 1860 and 1861, he took the copyright of several other books, containing additions to and improvements upon the said system. The bill of complaint was filed against the defendant, Baker, for an alleged infringement of these copyrights. The latter, in his answer, denied that Selden was the author or designer of the books, and denied the infringement charged, and contends on the argument that the matter alleged to be infringed is not a lawful subject of copyright.

The book or series of books of which the complainant claims the copyright consists of an introductory essay explaining the system of book-keeping referred to, to which are annexed certain forms or blanks, consisting of ruled lines, and headings, illustrating the system and showing how it is to be used and carried out in practice. This system effects the same results as book-keeping by double entry; but, by a peculiar arrangement of columns and headings, presents the entire operation, of a day, a week, or a month, on a single page, or on two pages facing each other, in an account-book. The defendant uses a similar plan so far as results are concerned; but makes a different arrangement of the columns, and uses different headings. If the complainant's testator had the exclusive right to the use of the system explained in his book, it would be difficult to contend that the defendant does not infringe it, notwithstanding the difference in his form of arrangement; but if it be assumed that the system is open to public use, it seems to be equally difficult to contend that the books made and sold by the defendant are a violation of the copyright of the complainant's book considered merely as a book explanatory of the system. Where the truths of a science or the methods of an art are the common property of the whole world, any author has the right to express the one, or explain and use the other, in his own way. As an author, Selden explained the system in a particular way. It may be conceded that Baker makes and uses account-books arranged on substantially the same system; but the proof fails to show that he has violated the copyright of Selden's book, regarding the latter merely as an explanatory work; or that he has infringed Selden's right in any way, unless the latter became entitled to an exclusive right in the system.

The evidence of the complainant is principally directed to the object of showing that Baker uses the same system as that which is explained and illustrated in Selden's books. It becomes important, therefore, to determine whether, in obtaining the copyright of his books, he secured the exclusive right to the use of the system or method of book-keeping which the said books are intended to illustrate and explain. It is contended that he has secured such exclusive right, because no one can use the system without using substantially the same ruled lines and headings which he has appended to his books in illustration of it. In other words, it is contended that the ruled lines and headings, given to illustrate the system, are a part of the book, and, as such, are secured by the copyright; and that no one can make or use similar ruled lines and headings, or ruled lines and headings made and arranged on substantially the same system, without violating the copyright. And this is really the question to be decided in this case. Stated in another form, the question is, whether the exclusive property in a system of book-keeping can be claimed, under the law of copyright, by means of a book in which that system is explained? The complainant's bill, and the case made under it, are based on the hypothesis that it can be.

It cannot be pretended, and indeed it is not seriously urged, that the ruled lines of the complainant's account-book can be claimed under any special class of objects, other than books, named in the law of copyright existing in 1859. The law then in force was that of 1831, and specified only books, maps, charts, musical compositions, prints, and engravings. An account-book, consisting of ruled lines and blank columns, cannot be called by any of these names unless by that of a book.

There is no doubt that a work on the subject of book-keeping, though only explanatory of well-known systems, may be the subject of a copyright; but, then, it is claimed only as a book. Such a book may be explanatory either of old systems, or of an entirely new system; and, considered as a book, as the work of an author, conveying information on the subject of book-keeping, and containing detailed explanations of the

art, it may be a very valuable acquisition to the practical knowledge of
the community. But there is a clear distinction between the book, as
such, and the art which it is intended to illustrate. The mere statement
of the proposition is so evident, that it requires hardly any argument to
support it. The same distinction may be predicated of every other art as
well as that of book-keeping. A treatise on the composition and use of
medicines, be they old or new; on the construction and use of ploughs, or
watches, or churns; or on the mixture and application of colors for
painting or dyeing; or on the mode of drawing lines to produce the effect
of perspective,—would be the subject of copyright; but no one would
contend that the copyright of the treatise would give the exclusive right
to the art or manufacture described therein. The copyright of the book, if
not pirated from other works, would be valid without regard to the
novelty, or want of novelty, of its subject-matter. The novelty of the art
or thing described or explained has nothing to do with the validity of the
copyright. To give to the author of the book an exclusive property in the
art described therein, when no examination of its novelty has ever been
officially made, would be a surprise and a fraud upon the public. That is
the province of letters-patent, not of copyright. The claim to an invention or discovery of an art or manufacture must be subjected to the
examination of the Patent Office before an exclusive right therein can be
obtained; and it can only be secured by a patent from the government.

The difference between the two things, letters-patent and copyright,
may be illustrated by reference to the subjects just enumerated. Take the
case of medicines. Certain mixtures are found to be of great value in the
healing art. If the discoverer writes and publishes a book on the subject
(as regular physicians generally do), he gains no exclusive right to the
manufacture and sale of the medicine; he gives that to the public. If he
desires to acquire such exclusive right, he must obtain a patent for the
mixture as a new art, manufacture, or composition of matter. He may
copyright his book, if he pleases; but that only secures to him the
exclusive right of printing and publishing his book. So of all other
inventions or discoveries.

The copyright of a book on perspective, no matter how many
drawings and illustrations it may contain, gives no exclusive right to the
modes of drawing described, though they may never have been known or
used before. By publishing the book, without getting a patent for the art,
the latter is given to the public. The fact that the art described in the
book by illustrations of lines and figures, which are reproduced in
practice in the application of the art, makes no difference. Those illustrations are the mere language employed by the author to convey his ideas
more clearly. Had he used words of description instead of diagrams
(which merely stand in the place of words), there could not be the
slightest doubt that others, applying the art to practical use, might
lawfully draw the lines and diagrams which were in the author's mind,
and which he thus described by words in his book.

The copyright of a work on mathematical science cannot give to the
author an exclusive right to the methods of operation which he pro-

pounds, or to the diagrams which he employs to explain them, so as to prevent an engineer from using them whenever occasion requires. The very object of publishing a book on science or the useful arts is to communicate to the world the useful knowledge which it contains. But this object would be frustrated if the knowledge could not be used without incurring the guilt of piracy of the book. And where the art it teaches cannot be used without employing the methods and diagrams used to illustrate the book, or such as are similar to them, such methods and diagrams are to be considered as necessary incidents to the art, and given therewith to the public; not given for the purpose of publication in other works explanatory of the art, but for the purpose of practical application.

Of course, these observations are not intended to apply to ornamental designs, or pictorial illustrations addressed to the taste. Of these it may be said, that their form is their essence, and their object, the production of pleasure in their contemplation. This is their final end. They are as much the product of genius and the result of composition, as are the lines of the poet or the historian's period. On the other hand, the teachings of science and the rules and methods of useful art have their final end in application and use; and this application and use are what the public derive from the publication of a book which teaches them. But as embodied and taught in a literary composition or book, their essence consists only in their statement. This alone is what is secured by the copyright. The use by another of the same methods of statement, whether in words or illustrations, in a book published for teaching the art, would undoubtedly be an infringement of the copyright.

Recurring to the case before us, we observe that Charles Selden, by his books, explained and described a peculiar system of book-keeping, and illustrated his method by means of ruled lines and blank columns, with proper headings on a page, or on successive pages. Now, whilst no one has a right to print or publish his book, or any material part thereof, as a book intended to convey instruction in the art, any person may practice and use the art itself which he has described and illustrated therein. The use of the art is a totally different thing from a publication of the book explaining it. The copyright of a book on book-keeping cannot secure the exclusive right to make, sell, and use account-books prepared upon the plan set forth in such book. Whether the art might or might not have been patented, is a question which is not before us. It was not patented, and is open and free to the use of the public. And, of course, in using the art, the ruled lines and headings of accounts must necessarily be used as incident to it.

The plausibility of the claim put forward by the complainant in this case arises from a confusion of ideas produced by the peculiar nature of the art described in the books which have been made the subject of copyright. In describing the art, the illustrations and diagrams employed happen to correspond more closely than usual with the actual work performed by the operator who uses the art. Those illustrations and diagrams consist of ruled lines and headings of accounts; and it is similar ruled lines and headings of accounts which, in the application of the art, the book-keeper makes with his pen, or the stationer with his press; whilst in most other cases the diagrams and illustrations can only be represented in concrete forms of wood, metal, stone, or some other physical embodiment. But the principle is the same in all. The description of the art in a book, though entitled to the benefit of copyright, lays no foundation for an exclusive claim to the art itself. The object of the one is explanation; the object of the other is use. The former may be secured by copyright. The latter can only be secured, if it can be secured at all, by letters-patent.

The remarks of Mr. Justice Thompson in the Circuit Court in Clayton v. Stone & Hall (2 Paine, 392), in which copyright was claimed in a daily price-current, are apposite and instructive. He says: "In determining the true construction to be given to the act of Congress, it is proper to look at the Constitution of the United States, to aid us in ascertaining the nature of the property intended to be protected. 'Congress shall have power to promote the progress of science and useful arts, by securing for limited times to authors and inventors the exclusive right to their writings and discoveries.' The act in question was passed in execution of the power here given, and the object, therefore, was the promotion of science; and it would certainly be a pretty extraordinary view of the sciences to consider a daily or weekly publication of the state of the market as falling within any class of them. They are of a more fixed, permanent, and durable character. The term 'science' cannot, with any propriety, by applied to a work of so fluctuating and fugitive a form as that of a newspaper or price-current, the subject-matter of which is daily changing, and is of mere temporary use. Although great praise may be due to the plaintiffs for their industry and enterprise in publishing this paper, yet the law does not contemplate their being rewarded in this way: it must seek patronage and protection from its utility to the public, and not a work of science. The title of the act of Congress is, 'for the encouragement of learning,' and was not intended for the encouragement of mere industry, unconnected with learning and the sciences.... We are, accordingly, of opinion that the paper in question is not a book the copyright to which can be secured under the act of Congress."

* * *

In Drury v. Ewing (1 Bond, 540), which is much relied on by the complainant, a copyright was claimed in a chart of patterns for cutting dresses and basques for ladies, and coats, jackets, & c., for boys. It is obvious that such designs could only be printed and published for information, and not for use in themselves. Their practical use could only be exemplified in cloth on the tailor's board and under his shears; in other words, by the application of a mechanical operation to the cutting of cloth in certain patterns and forms. Surely the exclusive right to this practical use was not reserved to the publisher by his copyright of the chart. Without undertaking to say whether we should or should not concur in the decision in that case, we think it cannot control the present.

The conclusion to which we have come is, that blank account-books are not the subject of copyright; and that the mere copyright of Selden's book did not confer upon him the exclusive right to make and use account-books, ruled and arranged as designated by him and described and illustrated in said book.

Notes

1. *Baker v. Selden* suggests that copyright protects an author's original expression, but not the utilitarian ends to which that expression may be put. The patent system meanwhile does offer protection to inventive utility. As we will see, these fundamental differences between the two forms of protection give rise to doctrinal distinctions which have separated and divided the fields. Among the most important of these distinctions are differences in the degree to which copyright and patent rights presuppose "originality" or "novelty." In copyright law, originality may mean little more than that the would-be copyright proprietor has not copied the work from an earlier work; historically, no great amount of creativity has been required. *Alfred Bell & Co. v. Catalda Fine Arts*, 191 F.2d 99 (2d Cir.1951). In patent law, on the other hand, protection for inventions has long required proof of both novelty and nonobviousness, as well as utility. *Graham v. John Deere Co.*, 383 U.S. 1, 86 S.Ct. 684, 15 L.Ed.2d 545 (1966).

The distinctions observed in *Baker v. Selden* reflect traditional constitutional thinking in American law, supposedly as is reflected in the Intellectual Property (or Patent and Copyright) Clause. U.S. Const. Art. I, § 8, cl. 8. They are quite widely observed, meanwhile, in other legal systems of the world, though typically without any equivalent "constitutional" significance.

2. Charles Selden actually appears to have understood these distinctions. In an introduction to his original work he offered the following observations:

> The author, though always desirous of promoting the public good, does not in this instance, disclaim a hope of pecuniary reward; to this end he has taken steps to secure his right to some personal compensation, for what he thinks, a valuable discovery. In addition to the copyright of this little book, he has applied for a patent right to cover the forms of the publication, and prevent their indiscriminate use by the public.

Selden's Condensed Ledger, or Bookkeeping Simplified (1859)*

TRADE-MARK CASES:
UNITED STATES v. STEFFENS;
UNITED STATES v. WITTEMANN;
UNITED STATES v. JOHNSON

Supreme Court of the United States, 1879.
100 U.S. (10 Otto) 82, 25 L.Ed. 550.

MR. JUSTICE MILLER delivered the opinion of the court.

The three cases whose titles stand at the head of this opinion are criminal prosecutions for violations of what is known as the trade-mark

---

* First reprinted in Melville B. Nimmer, Copyright and Other Aspects of Laws Pertaining to Literary, Musical, and Artistic Works Illustrated 97 (West Publishing Co. Second Edition 1977).

legislation of Congress. The first two are indictments in the southern district of New York, and the last is an information in the southern district of Ohio. In all of them the judges of the circuit courts in which they are pending have certified to a difference of opinion on what is substantially the same question; namely, are the acts of Congress on the subject of trade-marks founded on any rightful authority in the Constitution of the United States?

The entire legislation of Congress in regard to trade-marks is of very recent origin. It is first seen in sects. 77 to 84, inclusive, of the act of July 8, 1870, entitled "An Act to revise, consolidate, and amend the statutes relating to patents and copyrights." 16 Stat. 198. The part of this act relating to trade-marks is embodied in chap. 2, tit. 60, sects. 4937 to 4947, of the Revised Statutes.

It is sufficient at present to say that they provide for the registration in the Patent Office of any device in the nature of a trade-mark to which any person has by usage established an exclusive right, or which the person so registering intends to appropriate by that act to his exclusive use; and they make the wrongful use of a trade-mark, so registered, by any other person, without the owner's permission, a cause of action in a civil suit for damages. Six years later we have the act of Aug. 14, 1876 (19 Stat. 141), punishing by fine and imprisonment the fraudulent use, sale, and counterfeiting of trademarks registered in pursuance of the statutes of the United States, on which the informations and indictments are founded in the cases before us.

The right to adopt and use a symbol or a device to distinguish the goods or property made or sold by the person whose mark it is, to the exclusion of use by all other persons, has been long recognized by the common law and the chancery courts of England and of this country, and by the statutes of some of the States. It is a property right for the violation of which damages may be recovered in an action at law, and the continued violation of it will be enjoined by a court of equity, with compensation for past infringement. This exclusive right was not created by the act of Congress, and does not now depend upon it for its enforcement. The whole system of trademark property and the civil remedies for its protection existed long anterior to that act, and have remained in full force since its passage.

These propositions are so well understood as to require neither the citation of authorities nor an elaborate argument to prove them.

As the property in trademarks and the right to their exclusive use rest on the laws of the States, and, like the great body of the rights of person and of property, depend on them for security and protection, the power of Congress to legislate on the subject, to establish the conditions on which these rights shall be enjoyed and exercised, the period of their duration, and the legal remedies for their enforcement, if such power exist at all, must be found in the Constitution of the United States, which is the source of all powers that Congress can lawfully exercise.

In the argument of these cases this seems to be conceded, and the advocates for the validity of the acts of Congress on this subject point to two clauses of the Constitution, in one or in both of which, as they assert, sufficient warrant may be found for this legislation.

The first of these is the eighth clause of sect. 8 of the first article. That section, manifestly intended to be an enumeration of the powers expressly granted to Congress, and closing with the declaration of a rule for the ascertainment of such powers as are necessary by way of implication to carry into efficient operation those expressly given, authorizes Congress, by the clause referred to, "to promote the progress of science and useful arts, by securing for limited times, to authors and inventors, the exclusive right to their respective writings and discoveries."

As the first and only attempt by Congress to regulate the right of trade-marks is to be found in the act of July 8, 1870, to which we have referred, entitled "An Act to revise, consolidate, and amend the statutes relating to patents and copyrights," terms which have long since become technical, as referring, the one to inventions and the other to the writings of authors, it is a reasonable inference that this part of the statute also was, in the opinion of Congress, an exercise of the power found in that clause of the Constitution. It may also be safely assumed that until a critical examination of the subject in the courts became necessary, it was mainly if not wholly to this clause that the advocates of the law looked for its support.

Any attempt, however, to identify the essential characteristics of a trade-mark with inventions and discoveries in the arts and sciences, or with the writings of authors, will show that the effort is surrounded with insurmountable difficulties.

The ordinary trade-mark has no necessary relation to invention or discovery. The trade-mark recognized by the common law is generally the growth of a considerable period of use, rather than a sudden invention. It is often the result of accident rather than design, and when under the act of Congress it is sought to establish it by registration, neither originality, invention, discovery, science, nor art is in any way essential to the right conferred by that act. If we should endeavor to classify it under the head of writings of authors, the objections are equally strong. In this, as in regard to inventions, originality is required. And while the word writings may be liberally construed, as it has been, to include original designs for engravings, prints, & c., it is only such as are original, and are founded in the creative powers of the mind. The writings which are to be protected are the fruits of intellectual labor, embodied in the form of books, prints, engravings, and the like. The trade-mark may be, and generally is, the adoption of something already in existence as the distinctive symbol of the party using it. At common law the exclusive right to it grows out of its use, and not its mere adoption. By the act of Congress this exclusive right attaches upon registration. But in neither case does it depend upon novelty, invention, discovery, or any work of the brain. It requires no fancy or imagination, no genius, no laborious thought. It is simply founded on priority of appropriation. We look in vain in the statute for any other qualification or condition. If the symbol, however plain, simple, old, or well-known, has been first appropriated by the claimant as his distinctive trade-mark, he may by registration secure the right to its exclusive use. While such legislation may be a judicious aid to the common law on the subject of trade-marks, and may be within the competency of legislatures whose general powers embrace that class of subjects, we are unable to see any such power in the constitutional provision concerning authors and inventors, and their writings and discoveries.

The other clause of the Constitution supposed to confer the requisite authority on Congress is the third of the same section, which, read in connection with the granting clause, is as follows: "The Congress shall have power to regulate commerce with foreign nations, and among the several States, and with the Indian tribes."

The argument is that the use of a trademark—that which alone gives it any value—is to identify a particular class or quality of goods as the manufacture, produce, or property of the person who puts them in the general market for sale; that the sale of the article so distinguished is commerce; that the trade-mark is, therefore, a useful and valuable aid or instrument of commerce, and its regulation by virtue of the clause belongs to Congress, and that the act in question is a lawful exercise of this power.

Every species of property which is the subject of commerce, or which is used or even essential in commerce, is not brought by this clause within the control of Congress. The barrels and casks, the bottles and boxes in which alone certain articles of commerce are kept for safety and by which their contents are transferred from the seller to the buyer, do not thereby become subjects of congressional legislation more than other property. Nathan v. Louisiana, 8 How. 73. In Paul v. Virginia (8 Wall. 168), this court held that a policy of insurance made by a corporation of one State on property situated in another, was not an article of commerce, and did not come within the purview of the clause we are considering. "They are not," says the court, "commodities to be shipped or forwarded from one State to another, and then put up for sale." On the other hand, in Almy v. State of California (24 How. 169), it was held that a stamp duty imposed by the legislature of California on bills of lading for gold and silver transported from any place in that State to another out of the State, was forbidden by the Constitution of the United States, because such instruments being a necessity to the transaction of commerce, the duty was a tax upon exports.

The question, therefore, whether the trade-mark bears such a relation to commerce in general terms as to bring it within congressional control, when used or applied to the classes of commerce which fall within that control, is one which, in the present case, we propose to leave undecided. We adopt this course because when this court is called on in the course of the administration of the law to consider whether an act of Congress, or of any other department of the government, is within the constitutional authority of that department, a due respect for a co-ordinate branch of the government requires that we shall decide that it has transcended its powers only when that is so plain that we cannot avoid the duty.

In such cases it is manifestly the dictate of wisdom and judicial propriety to decide no more than is necessary to the case in hand. That such has been the uniform course of this court in regard to statutes passed by Congress will readily appear to any one who will consider the vast amount of argument presented to us assailing them as unconstitutional, and he will count, as he may do on his fingers, the instances in which this court has declared an act of Congress void for want of constitutional power.

Governed by this view of our duty, we proceed to remark that a glance at the commerce clause of the Constitution discloses at once what has been often the subject of comment in this court and out of it, that the power of regulation there conferred on Congress is limited to commerce with foreign nations, commerce among the States, and commerce with the Indian tribes. While bearing in mind the liberal construction, that commerce with foreign nations means commerce between citizens of the United States and citizens and subjects of foreign nations, and commerce among the States means commerce between the individual citizens of different States, there still remains a very large amount of commerce, perhaps the largest, which, being trade or traffic between citizens of the same State, is beyond the control of Congress.

When, therefore, Congress undertakes to enact a law, which can only be valid as a regulation of commerce, it is reasonable to expect to find on the face of the law, or from its essential nature, that it is a regulation of commerce with foreign nations, or among the several States, or with the Indian tribes. If not so limited, it is in excess of the power of Congress. If its main purpose be to establish a regulation applicable to all trade, to commerce at all points, especially if it be apparent that it is designed to govern the commerce wholly between citizens of the same State, it is obviously the exercise of a power not confided to Congress.

We find no recognition of this principle in the chapter on trade-marks in the Revised Statutes. We would naturally look for this in the description of the class of persons who are entitled to register a trade-mark, or in reference to the goods to which it should be applied. If, for instance, the statute described persons engaged in a commerce between the different States, and related to the use of trade-marks in such commerce, it would be evident that Congress believed it was acting under the clause of the Constitution which authorizes it to regulate commerce among the States. So if, when the trade-mark has been registered, Congress had protected its use on goods sold by a citizen of one State to another, or by a citizen of a foreign State to a citizen of the United States, it would be seen that Congress was at least intending to exercise the power of regulation conferred by that clause of the Constitution. But no such idea is found or suggested in this statute. Its language is: "Any person or firm domiciled in the United States, and any corporation created by the United States, or of any State or Territory thereof," or any person residing in a foreign country which by treaty or convention affords similar privileges to our citizens, may by registration obtain protection for his trade-mark. Here is no requirement that such person shall be engaged in the kind of commerce which Congress is authorized to regulate. It is a general declaration that anybody in the United States, and anybody in any other country which permits us to do the like, may, by registering a trade-mark, have it fully protected. So, while the person registering is required to "furnish a statement of the class of merchandise, and the particular description of the goods comprised in such class, by which the trade-mark has been or is intended to be appropriated," there is no hint that the goods are to be transported from one State to another, or between the United States and foreign countries. Sect. 4939 is intended to impose some restriction upon the Commissioner of Patents in the matter of registration, but no limitation is suggested in regard to persons or property engaged in the different classes of commerce mentioned in the Constitution. The remedies provided by the act when the right of the owner of the registered trade-mark is infringed, are not confined to the case of a trade-mark used in foreign or inter-state commerce.

It is therefore manifest that no such distinction is found in the act, but that its broad purpose was to establish a universal system of trade-mark registration, for the benefit of all who had already used a trade-mark, or who wished to adopt one in the future, without regard to the character of the trade to which it was to be applied or the residence of the owner, with the solitary exception that those who resided in foreign countries which extended no such privileges to us were excluded from them here.

* * *

In what we have here said we wish to be understood as leaving untouched the whole question of the treaty-making power over trade-marks, and of the duty of Congress to pass any laws necessary to carry treaties into effect.

* * *

Notes

1. *The Trade–Mark Cases* were decided at a relatively early moment in the development of American trademark law when the chief function of a

trademark was to distinguish goods from other similar goods in direct competition, thereby protecting the public from a likelihood of confusion, mistake or deception in the marketplace. Today, trademark doctrines (and their counterparts in the broader arena of unfair competition) extend considerably further, with additional or expanded direct protection for the trademark proprietor against appropriation or dilution of the particular significance in both marks and trade dress. Meanwhile, the Commerce Clause has assumed a leading role in the expansion of Congressional jurisdiction; the Lanham Trademark Act of 1946, 15 U.S.C.A. §§ 1051–1127, is founded upon this greatly expanded Commerce Clause power. These developments have introduced tensions into the law not present in 1879. Some contemporary observers now argue that the Intellectual Property Clause (Article I, section 8, clause 8) must take on an expanded role to constrain unacceptable incursions into copyright or patent law, as well as unwise encroachments upon the public domain. See, e.g., Davis, Copying in the Shadow of the Constitution, 80 Minn. L. Rev. 595 (1996); Pollack, Unconstitutional Incontestability? The Intersection of the Intellectual Property and Commerce Clause of the Constitution, 18 Puget Sound L. Rev. 259 (1995). Others suggest that Congress may now be free to act under the Commerce Clause, essentially without regard for the Intellectual Property clause. See, e.g., Goldstein, Copyright, 55 Law & Contemp. Probs. 79 (1992).

Consider also the final paragraph of the Court's opinion above. Does Congress have Commerce Clause power to effectuate international treaties affecting intellectual property that are inconsistent with the Intellectual Property Clause? See David Nimmer, The End of Copyright, 48 Vand. L. Rev. 1385, 1411–12 (1995). Does the treaty power generally authorize compacts with other nations that violate the Constitution? Could the Executive Branch approve, the Senate ratify, and Congress ultimately effectuate a treaty obliging American citizens to fall upon their knees and worship a Golden Calf?

2. *The Trade–Mark Cases* continue to have considerable vitality as precedent. Justice O'Connor cited the opinion numerous times, for example, in her own seminal opinion in *Feist Publications v. Rural Telephone Service Co.,* 499 U.S. 340, 111 S.Ct. 1282, 113 L.Ed.2d 358 (1991), in which the Court underscored the continuing importance of the originality requirement in copyright on constitutional as well as statutory grounds.

ALFRED C. YEN, A FIRST AMENDMENT PERSPECTIVE ON THE IDEA/EXPRESSION DICHOTOMY AND COPYRIGHT IN A WORK'S "TOTAL CONCEPT AND FEEL"

38 Emory L. J. 393 (1989).*

At first blush, the coexistence of the first amendment and the copyright law poses a puzzling contradiction. The first amendment provides that "Congress shall pass no law abridging the freedom of speech." The Supreme Court has often invoked this passage to prevent the suppression or censorship of written, spoken, symbolic, and artistic expression. By contrast, the copyright law appears to do exactly what the first amendment prohibits by forcing authors not to make unauthorized use of copyrighted material. To the extent that copyright dictates the manner in which an author may express herself, it infringes the author's freedom of expression.

In 1970, separate articles by Professors Melville Nimmer and Paul Goldstein identified this apparent conflict between the first amendment and copyright. However, they also noted that copyright actually encourages speech by granting limited monopolies to authors. Without these incentives, expressive output would presumably decline. Thus, in their view, copyright's promotion of expression was generally consistent with the first amendment. The courts have generally supported this position by referring to a copyright doctrine known as the idea/expression dichotomy. This dichotomy, which is presently embodied in Section 102(b) of the copyright code, is perhaps the most important limit on the unwarranted expansion of copyright. It operates by denying protection to the ideas which underlie copyrightable works. Consequently, only the original "expressions" contained in these works can actually receive copyright protection. This makes certain portions (the "ideas") of every work freely available for others to copy. Such permitted borrowing from copyrighted works ostensibly keeps copyright from unduly restricting speech and running afoul of the first amendment. Under this view, copyright law can be characterized as a facilitator of speech entirely consistent with the first amendment.

Unfortunately, such analysis overlooks the fact that the first amendment guarantees more than just the protection of speech deemed constitutionally valuable. The first amendment also recognizes that laws are sometimes unavoidably vague, thereby making prospective speakers unsure as to whether or not their contemplated expression is prohibited. This uncertainty creates a "chilling effect" which forces individuals to forego exercising their first amendment rights for fear of being prosecuted or sued. In such cases, the first amendment requires clear legal standards which leave breathing room for the exercise of constitutionally valuable speech. This means pulling legal standards back from constitutional limits, so that any speech deterred by vague standards falls on the constitutionally valueless side of the line. However, even though copyright theoretically aims only at constitutionally valueless speech, judicial interpretation of the idea/expression dichotomy has failed to leave ample room for constitutionally valuable expression.

Brief reflection on this state of affairs reveals the important role played by the idea/expression dichotomy in regulating the scope of copyright. On the one hand, if courts adopt a narrow view of idea and a broad view of expression, more and more similarities will be similarities of expression and will therefore support claims of infringement. In turn, this implies a broad scope of copyright. Conversely, if courts adopt a broad view of idea and a narrow view of expression, few similarities will qualify as similarities of expression. This will result in a relatively limited scope of copyright. The above-described analysis is attractive because it indicates how applying the idea/expression dichotomy can prevent overbroad copyright claims. However, the analysis is deficient in that it provides no definition of what constitutes an idea.

Fortunately, some progress has been made in this area. Judge Learned Hand authored the most widely quoted distinction between idea and expression:

> Upon any work, and especially upon a play, a great number of patterns of increasing generality will fit equally well, as more and more of the incident is left out. The last may perhaps be no more than the most general statement of what the play is about, and at times might consist only of its title; but there is a point in this series of abstractions where they are no longer protected, since otherwise the playwright could prevent the use of his "ideas," to which, apart from their expression, his property is never extended.

Presently, the consensus view is that Hand's attempt to solve the idea/expression dichotomy is the best effort to date. Therefore, since Hand himself admitted that his solution rested ultimately upon instinct, the idea/expression dichotomy does not provide a clear, principled separation between the first amendment and copyright law. Instead, the best that can be said is that the idea/expression dichotomy provides a slippery slope on which to slide in our efforts to properly limit copyright law. Furthermore, since courts generally see no need to even consider the first amendment when interpreting the idea/expression dichotomy, there is simply no reason to believe that those slippery slope decisions have fortuitously conformed to first amendment requirements.

Even if the idea/expression dichotomy limits copyright so that it prohibits only copying that is constitutionally valueless, this alone does not necessarily keep copyright law from running afoul of the first amendment. This is because in addition to requiring that laws must avoid suppressing speech that would contribute to the marketplace of ideas, the first amendment further mandates that laws must also not accidentally chill constitutionally valuable speech. The Supreme Court's analysis of libel law provides the best known example of this first amendment principle.

In a line of famous cases beginning with *New York Times v. Sullivan* the Court applied the first amendment to limit the scope of libel actions. Prior to *New York Times,* ordinary state libel law held a defendant strictly liable for all false and defamatory statements. State law also awarded presumed damages to the successful plaintiff. This meant that plaintiffs could sometimes recover huge monetary awards without showing any pecuniary harm. The New York Times (like other libel defendants) contended that these state libel laws unduly suppressed its right of free expression. The Supreme Court agreed, and stated that the application of strict liability and presumed damages created an unacceptable fear of damage awards among certain potential libel defendants. To reduce this chill, the Court raised the standards required to support a libel claim.

For purposes of this Article, the salient feature of the Supreme Court's libel analysis is that the Court applied the first amendment to libel laws even though those laws were aimed only at speech which was false, and therefore constitutionally valueless. This reflected a constitutional judgment that the harm created by the risk of unwarranted libel awards and the attendant chilling effect was greater than the harm created by allowing some libel to go unpunished. By raising the substantive standards required to support libel claims, the Court created a buffer zone protecting constitutionally valuable speech from the uncertain and chilling prohibition of the libel laws. Thus, the Court managed to restrict libel's chilling effect to constitutionally valueless speech. To be sure, the buffer zone also allows some false libelous statements to go unpunished, but this result merely reflects our constitutional judgment that some evil must be tolerated to make sure that all good survives.

The analysis of *New York Times* and the other libel cases points out the flaw in the prevailing judicial approach to the conflict between the first amendment and copyright. Instead of merely satisfying themselves that copyright aims only at constitutionally valueless speech, the courts should make sure that the copyright law does not create an unacceptable chilling effect. Indeed, the courts' failure to undertake such analysis has allowed copyright to create a chilling effect which is fully comparable to that created by libel law.

The first amendment requires us to err on the side of protecting free speech. There is a constitutional preference for minimizing interference with free speech, even when such interference might serve other legitimate government goals. The above analysis demonstrates that the courts' failure to heed first amendment values has allowed copyright to unduly chill basic rights of expression. In light of the first amendment's supremacy over copyright, the courts must begin limiting this trend before it irreversibly pushes copyright beyond its first amendment limits.

* * *

Notes

1. Are you convinced by Yen's implicit argument that the First Amendment ultimately must control doctrines initially subject to the Intellectual Property Clause? Should that be the case? Is there a plausible argument to be made instead that the Intellectual Property Clause and the First Amendment should be read *in pari materia*, each working with the other to achieve ends peculiarly within its own appropriate sphere of influence? See Lange, The Intellectual Property Clause in Contemporary Trademark Law, 59 L. & Contemp. Probs. 213, 239–40 (1996).

2. The relationship between copyright and the First Amendment has been the subject of numerous essays. For three classic early treatments

(cited and discussed by Yen), see Denicola, Copyright and Free Speech: Constitutional Limitations on the Protection of Expression, 67 Calif.L.Rev. 283 (1979); Goldstein, Copyright and the First Amendment, 70 Colum.L.Rev. 983 (1970); Melville B. Nimmer, *Does Copyright Abridge the First Amendment Guarantees to Freedom of Speech and Press?* 12 UCLA L.Rev. 1180 (1970). For still more recent treatments of the subject, see Rubenfeld, The Freedom Of Information 112 Yale L.J. 1 (2002), and Benkler, Free As The Air To Common Use: First Amendment Constraints On The Enclosure Of The Public Domain, 74 N.Y.U. L. Rev. 354 (1999).

3. In *Eldred v. Ashcroft*, 537 U.S. 186, 123 S.Ct. 769, 154 L.Ed.2d 683 (2003), excerpted, *infra*, at p. 903, the Supreme Court said that copyright is not "categorically immune" to First Amendment review, as had been suggested erroneously in the Court of Appeals opinion, *Eldred v. Ashcroft*, 255 F.3d 849 (D.C.Cir.2001), *cert. granted*, 534 U.S. 1126, 122 S.Ct. 1062, 151 L.Ed.2d 966, *and modified*, 534 U.S. 1160, 122 S.Ct. 1170, 152 L.Ed.2d 115 (2002), but held that the First Amendment was not violated by the term extension at issue in the case.

B. "PROPERTY": SIGNIFICANCE AND ALTERNATIVES

INTERNATIONAL NEWS SERVICE v. ASSOCIATED PRESS

Supreme Court of the United States, 1918.
248 U.S. 215, 39 S.Ct. 68, 63 L.Ed. 211.

MR. JUSTICE PITNEY delivered the opinion of the Court.

The parties are competitors in the gathering and distribution of news and its publication for profit in newspapers throughout the United States. The Associated Press, which was complainant in the District Court, is a co-operative organization, incorporated under the Membership Corporations Law of the state of New York, its members being individuals who are either proprietors or representatives of about 950 daily newspapers published in all parts of the United States. * * * Complainant gathers in all parts of the world, by means of various instrumentalities of its own, by exchange with its members, and by other appropriate means, news and intelligence of current and recent events of interest to newspaper readers and distributes it daily to its members for publication in their newspapers. The cost of the service, amounting approximately to $3,500,000 per annum, is assessed upon the members and becomes a part of their costs of operation, to be recouped, presumably with profit, through the publication of their several newspapers. Under complainant's by-laws each member agrees upon assuming membership that news received through complainant's service is received exclusively for publication in a particular newspaper, language, and place specified in the certificate of membership, that no other use of it shall be permitted, and that no member shall furnish or permit any one in his employ or connected with his newspaper to furnish any of complainant's news in advance of publication to any person not a member. And each member is required to gather the local news of his district and supply it to the Associated Press and to no one else.

Defendant is a corporation organized under the laws of the state of New Jersey, whose business is the gathering and selling of news to its customers and clients, consisting of newspapers published throughout the United States, under contracts by which they pay certain amounts at stated times for defendant's service. It has widespread news-gathering agencies; the cost of its operations amounts, it is said, to more than $2,000,000 per annum; and it serves about 400 newspapers located in the various cities of the United States and abroad, a few of which are represented, also, in the membership of the Associated Press.

The parties are in the keenest competition between themselves in the distribution of news throughout the United States; and so, as a rule, are the newspapers that they serve, in their several districts.

Complainant in its bill, defendant in its answer, have set forth in almost identical terms the rather obvious circumstances and conditions under which their business is conducted. The value of the service, and of the news furnished, depends upon the promptness of transmission, as well as upon the accuracy and impartiality of the news; it being essential that the news be transmitted to members or subscribers as early or earlier than similar information can be furnished to competing newspapers by other news services, and that the news furnished by each agency shall not be furnished to newspapers which do not contribute to the expense of gathering it. And further, to quote from the answer: "Prompt knowledge and publication of worldwide news is essential to the conduct of a modern newspaper, and by reason of the enormous expense incident to the gathering and distribution of such news, the only practical way in which a proprietor of a newspaper can obtain the same is, either through co-operation with a considerable number of other newspaper proprietors in the work of collecting and distributing such news, and the equitable division with them of the expenses thereof, or by the purchase of such news from some existing agency engaged in that business."

The bill was filed to restrain the pirating of complainant's news by defendant in three ways: First, by bribing employees of newspapers published by complainant's members to furnish Associated Press news to defendant before publication, for transmission by telegraph and telephone to defendant's clients for publication by them; second, by inducing Associated Press members to violate its by-laws and permit defendant to obtain news before publication; and, third, by copying news from bulletin boards and from early editions of complainant's newspapers and selling this, either bodily or after rewriting it, to defendant's customers.

* * *

The only matter that has been argued before us is whether defendant may lawfully be restrained from appropriating news taken from bulletins issued by complainant or any of its members, or from newspapers published by them, for the purpose of selling it to defendant's clients. Complainant asserts that defendant's admitted course of conduct in this regard both violates complainant's property right in the news and constitutes unfair competition in business. And notwithstanding the case has proceeded only to the stage of a preliminary injunction, we have deemed it proper to consider the underlying questions, since they go to the very merits of the action and are presented upon facts that are not in dispute. As presented in argument, these questions are: (1) whether there is any property in news; (2) whether, if there be property in news collected for the purpose of being published, it survives the instant of its publication in the first newspaper to which it is communicated by the news-gatherer; and (3) whether defendant's admitted course of conduct in appropriating for commercial use matter taken from bulletins or early editions of Associated Press publications constitutes unfair competition in trade.

The federal jurisdiction was invoked because of diversity of citizenship, not upon the ground that the suit arose under the copyright or other laws of the United States. Complainant's news matter is not copyrighted. It is said that it could not, in practice, be copyrighted, because of the large number of dispatches that are sent daily; and, according to complainant's contention, news is not within the operation of the copyright act. Defendant, while apparently conceding this, nevertheless invokes the analogies of the law of literary property and copyright, insisting as its principal contention that, assuming complainant has a right of property in its news, it can be maintained (unless the copyright act by complied with) only by being kept secret and confidential, and that upon the publication with complainant's consent of uncopyrighted news of any of complainant's members in a newspaper or upon a bulletin board, the right of property is lost, and the subsequent use of the news by the public or by defendant for any purpose whatever becomes lawful.

* * *

In considering the general question of property in news matter, it is necessary to recognize its dual character, distinguishing between the substance of the information and the particular form or collocation of words in which the writer has communicated it.

No doubt news articles often possess a literary quality, and are the subject of literary property at the common law; nor do we question that such an article, as a literary production, is the subject of copyright by the terms of the act as it now stands. In an early case at the circuit Mr. Justice Thompson held in effect that a newspaper was not within the protection of the copyright acts of 1790 (1 Stat. 124) and 1802 (2 Stat. 171). Clayton v. Stone, 2 Paine, 382, Fed. Cas. No. 2,872. But the present act is broader; it provides that the works for which copyright may be secured shall include "all the writings of an author," and specifically mentions "periodicals, including newspapers." Act of March 4, 1909, c. 320, §§ 4 and 5, 35 Stat. 1075, 1076 (Comp. St. 1916, §§ 9520, 9521). Evidently this admits to copyright a contribution to a newspaper, notwithstanding it also may convey news; and such is the practice of the copyright office, as the newspapers of the day bear witness. See Copyright Office Bulletin No. 15 (1917) pp. 7, 14, 16, 17.

But the news element—the information respecting current events contained in the literary production—is not the creation of the writer, but is a report of matters that ordinarily are publici juris; it is the history of the day. It is not to be supposed that the framers of the Constitution, when they empowered Congress "to promote the progress of science and useful arts, by securing for limited times to authors and inventors the exclusive right to their respective writings and discoveries" (Const. art. 1, § 8, par. 8), intended to confer upon one who might happen to be the first to report a historic event the exclusive right for any period to spread the knowledge of it.

We need spend no time, however, upon the general question of property in news matter at common law, or the application of the copyright act, since it seems to us the case must turn upon the question of unfair competition in business. And, in our opinion, this does not depend upon any general right of property analogous to the common-law right of the proprietor of an unpublished work to prevent its publication without his consent; nor is it foreclosed by showing that the benefits of the copyright act have been waived. We are dealing here not with restrictions upon publication but with the very facilities and processes of publication. The peculiar value of news is in the spreading of it while it is fresh; and it is evident that a valuable property interest in the news, as news, cannot be maintained by keeping it secret. Besides, except for matters improperly disclosed, or published in breach of trust or confidence, or in violation of law, none of which is involved in this branch of the case, the news of current events may be regarded as common property. What we are concerned with is the business of making it known to the world, in which both parties to the present suit are engaged. That business consists in maintaining a prompt, sure, steady, and reliable service designed to place the daily events of the world at the breakfast table of the millions at a price that, while of trifling moment to each reader, is sufficient in the aggregate to afford compensation for the cost of gathering and distributing it, with the added profit so necessary as an incentive to effective action in the commercial world. The service thus performed for newspaper readers is not only innocent but extremely useful in itself, and indubitably constitutes a legitimate business. The parties are competitors in this field; and, on fundamental principles, applicable here as elsewhere, when the rights or privileges of the one are liable to conflict with those of the other, each party is under a duty so to conduct its own business as not unnecessarily or unfairly to injure that of the other. Hitchman Coal & Coke Co. v. Mitchell, 245 U. S. 229, 254, 38 Sup. Ct. 65, 62 L. Ed. 260, L.R.A. 1918C,497, Ann.Cas. 1918B,461.

Obviously, the question of what is unfair competition in business must be determined with particular reference to the character and circumstances of the business. The question here is not so much the rights of either party as against the public but their rights as between themselves. See Morison v. Moat, 9 Hare, 241, 258. And, although we may and do assume that neither party has any remaining property interest as against the public in uncopyrighted news matter after the moment of its first publication, it by no means follows that there is no remaining property interest in it as between themselves. For, to both of them alike, news matter, however little susceptible of ownership or dominion in the absolute sense, is stock in trade, to be gathered at the cost of enterprise, organization, skill, labor, and money, and to be distributed and sold to those who will pay money for it, as for any other merchandise. Regarding the news, therefore, as but the material out of which both parties are seeking to make profits at the same time and in the same field, we hardly can fail to recognize that for this purpose, and as between them, it must be regarded as quasi property, irrespective of the rights of either as against the public.

* * *

The question, whether one who has gathered general information or news at pains and expense for the purpose of subsequent publication through the press has such an interest in its publication as may be protected from interference, has been raised many times, although never, perhaps, in the precise form in which it is now presented.

* * *

Not only do the acquisition and transmission of news require elaborate organization and a large expenditure of money, skill, and effort; not only has it an exchange value to the gatherer, dependent chiefly upon its novelty and freshness, the regularity of the service, its reputed reliability and thoroughness, and its adaptability to the public needs; but also, as is evident, the news has an exchange value to one who can misappropriate it.

The peculiar features of the case arise from the fact that, while novelty and freshness form so important an element in the success of the business, the very processes of distribution and publication necessarily occupy a good deal of time. Complainant's service, as well as defendant's, is a daily service to daily newspapers; most of the foreign news reaches this country at the Atlantic seaboard, principally at the city of New York, and because of this, and of time differentials due to the earth's rotation, the distribution of news matter throughout the country is principally from east to west; and, since in speed the telegraph and telephone easily outstrip the rotation of the earth, it is a simple matter for defendant to take complainant's news from bulletins or early editions of complainant's members in the eastern cities and at the mere cost of telegraphic transmission caused it to be published in western papers issued at least as early as those served by complainant. Besides this, and irrespective of time differentials, irregularities in telegraphic transmission on different lines, and the normal consumption of time in printing and distributing the newspaper, result in permitting pirated news to be placed in the hands of defendant's readers sometimes simultaneously with the service of competing Associated Press papers, occasionally even earlier.

Defendant insists that when, with the sanction and approval of complainant, and as the result of the use of its news for the very purpose for which it is distributed, a portion of complainant's members communicate it to the general public by posting it upon bulletin boards so that all may read, or by issuing it to newspapers and distributing it indiscriminately, complainant no longer has the right to control the use to be made of it; that when it thus reaches the light of day it becomes the common possession of all to whom it is accessible; and that any purchaser of a newspaper has the right to communicate the intelligence which it contains to anybody and for any purpose, even for the purpose of selling it for profit to newspapers published for profit in competition with complainant's members.

The fault in the reasoning lies in applying as a test the right of the complainant as against the public, instead of considering the rights of complainant and defendant, competitors in business, as between themselves. The right of the purchaser of a single newspaper to spread knowledge of its contents gratuitously, for any legitimate purpose not unreasonably interfering with complainant's right to make merchandise of it, may be admitted; but to transmit that news for commercial use, in competition with complainant—which is what defendant has done and seeks to justify—is a very different matter. In doing this defendant, by its very act, admits that it is taking material that has been acquired by complainant as the result of organization and the expenditure of labor, skill, and money, and which is salable by complainant for money, and that defendant in appropriating it and selling it as its own is endeavoring to reap where it has not sown, and by disposing of it to newspapers that are competitors of complainant's members is appropriating to itself the harvest of those who have sown. Stripped of all disguises, the process amounts to an unauthorized interference with the normal operation of complainant's legitimate business precisely at the point where the profit is to be reaped, in order to divert a material portion of the profit from those who have earned it to those who have not; with special advantage to defendant in the competition because of the fact that it is not burdened with any part of the expense of gathering the news. The transaction speaks for itself and a court of equity ought not to hesitate long in characterizing it as unfair competition in business.

The underlying principle is much the same as that which lies at the base of the equitable theory of consideration in the law of trusts—that he who has fairly paid the price should have the beneficial use of the property. Pom. Eq. Jur. § 981. It is no answer to say that complainant spends its money for that which is too fugitive or evanescent to be the subject of property. That might, and for the purposes of the discussion we are assuming that it would furnish an answer in a common-law controversy. But in a court of equity, where the question is one of unfair competition, if that which complainant has acquired fairly at substantial cost may be sold fairly at substantial profit, a competitor who is misappropriating it for the purpose of disposing of it to his own profit and to the disadvantage of complainant cannot be heard to say that it is too fugitive or evanescent to be regarded as property. It has all the attributes of property necessary for determining that a misappropriation of it by a competitor is unfair competition because contrary to good conscience.

The contention that the news is abandoned to the public for all purposes when published in the first newspaper is untenable. Abandonment is a question of intent, and the entire organization of the Associated Press negatives such a purpose. The cost of the service would be prohibitive if the reward were to be so limited. No single newspaper, no small group of newspapers, could sustain the expenditure. Indeed, it is one of the most obvious results of defendant's theory that, by permitting indiscriminate publication by anybody and everybody for purposes of profit in competition with the news-gatherer, it would render publication profitless, or so little profitable as in effect to cut off the service by rendering the cost prohibitive in comparison with the return. The practical needs and requirements of the business are reflected in complainant's by-laws which have been referred to. Their effect is that publication by each member must be deemed not by any means an abandonment of the news to the world for any and all purposes, but a publication for limited purposes; for the benefit of the readers of the bulletin or the newspaper as such; not for the purpose of making merchandise of it as news, with the result of depriving complainant's other members of their reasonable opportunity to obtain just returns for their expenditures.

It is to be observed that the view we adopt does not result in giving to complainant the right to monopolize either the gathering or the distribution of the news, or, without complying with the copyright act, to prevent the reproduction of its news articles, but only postpones participation by complainant's competitor in the processes of distribution and reproduction of news that it has not gathered, and only to the extent necessary to prevent that competitor from reaping the fruits of complainant's efforts and expenditure, to the partial exclusion of complainant, and in violation of the principle that underlies the maxim "sic utere tuo," etc.

It is said that the elements of unfair competition are lacking because there is no attempt by defendant to palm off its goods as those of the complainant, characteristic of the most familiar, if not the most typical, cases of unfair competition. Howe Scale Co. v. Wyckoff, Seamans, etc., 198 U. S. 118, 140, 25 Sup. Ct. 609, 49 L. Ed. 972. But we cannot concede that the right to equitable relief is confined to that class of cases. In the present case the fraud upon complainant's rights is more direct and obvious. Regarding news matter as the mere material from which these two competing parties are endeavoring to make money, and treating it, therefore, as quasi property for the purposes of their business because they are both selling it as such, defendant's conduct differs from the ordinary case of unfair competition in trade principally in this that, instead of selling its own goods as those of complainant, it substitutes misappropriation in the place of misrepresentation, and sells complainant's goods as its own.

Besides the misappropriation, there are elements of imitation, of false pretense, in defendant's practices. The device of rewriting complainant's news articles, frequently resorted to, carries its own comment. The habitual failure to give credit to complainant for that which is taken is significant. Indeed, the entire system of appropriating complainant's news and transmitting it as a commercial product to defendant's clients and patrons amounts to a false representation to them and to their newspaper readers that the news transmitted is the result of defendant's own investigation in the field. But these elements, although accentuating the wrong, are not the essence of it. It is something more than the advantage of celebrity of which complainant is being deprived.

The doctrine of unclean hands is invoked as a bar to relief; it being insisted that defendant's practices against which complainant seeks an injunction are not different from the practice attributed to complainant, of utilizing defendant's news published by its subscribers. At this point it becomes necessary to consider a distinction that is drawn by complainant, and, as we understand it, was recognized by defendant also in the submission of proofs in the District Court, between two kinds of use that may be made by one news agency of news taken from the bulletins and newspapers of the other. The first is the bodily appropriation of a statement of fact or a news article, with or without rewriting, but without independent investigation or other expense. This form of pirating was found by both courts to have been pursued by defendant systematically with respect to complainant's news, and against it the Circuit Court of Appeals granted an injunction. This practice complainant denies having pursued and the denial was sustained by the finding of the District Court. It is not contended by defendant that the finding can be set aside, upon the proofs as they now stand. The other use is to take the news of a rival agency as a "tip" to be investigated, and if verified by independent investigation the news thus gathered is sold. This practice complainant admits that it has pursued and still is willing that defendant shall employ.

Both courts held that complainant could not be debarred on the ground of unclean hands upon the score of pirating defendant's news, because not shown to be guilty of sanctioning this practice.

* * *

In the case before us, in the present state of the pleadings and proofs, we need go no further than to hold, as we do, that the admitted pursuit by complainant of the practice of taking news items published by defendant's subscribers as tips to be investigated, and, if verified, the result of the investigation to be sold—the practice having been followed by defendant also, and by news agencies generally—is not shown to be such as to constitute an unconscientious or inequitable attitude towards its adversary so as to fix upon complainant the taint of unclean hands, and debar it on this ground from the relief to which it is otherwise entitled.

There is some criticism of the injunction that was directed by the District Court upon the going down of the mandate from the Circuit Court of Appeals. In brief, it restrains any taking or gainfully using of the complainant's news, either bodily or in substance from bulletins issued by the complainant or any of its members, or from editions of their newspapers, "until its commercial value as news to the complainant and all of its members has passed away." The part complained of is the clause we have italicized; but if this be indefinite, it is no more so than the criticism. Perhaps it would be better that the terms of the injunction be made specific, and so framed as to confine the restraint to an extent consistent with the reasonable protection of complainant's newspapers, each in its own area and for a specified time after its publication, against the competitive use of pirated news by defendant's customers. But the case presents practical difficulties; and we have not the materials, either in the way of a definite suggestion of amendment, or in the way of proofs, upon which to frame a specific injunction; hence, while not expressing approval of the form adopted by the District Court, we decline to modify it at this preliminary stage of the case, and will leave that court to deal with the matter upon appropriate application made to it for the purpose.

The decree of the Circuit Court of Appeals will be affirmed.

Mr. Justice Holmes:

When an uncopyrighted combination of words is published there is no general right to forbid other people repeating them—in other words there is no property in the combination or in the thoughts or facts that the words express. Property, a creation of law, does not arise from value, although exchangeable—a matter of fact. Many exchangeable values may be destroyed intentionally without compensation. Property depends upon exclusion by law from interference, and a person is not excluded from using any combination of words merely because some one has used it before, even if it took labor and genius to make it. If a given person is to be prohibited from making the use of words that his neighbors are free to make some other ground must be found. One such ground is vaguely expressed in the phrase unfair trade. This means that the words are repeated by a competitor in business in such a way as to convey a misrepresentation that materially injures the person who first used them, by appropriating credit of some kind which the first user has earned. The ordinary case is a representation by device, appearance, or other indirection that the defendant's goods come from the plaintiff. But the only reason why it is actionable to make such a representation is that it tends to give the defendant an advantage in his competition with the plaintiff and that it is thought undesirable that an advantage should be gained in that way. Apart from that the defendant may use such unpatented devices and uncopyrighted combinations of words as he likes. The ordinary case, I say, is palming off the defendant's product as the plaintiff's but the same evil may follow from the opposite falsehood—from saying whether in words or by implication that the plaintiff's product is the defendant's, and that, it seems to me, is what has happened here.

Fresh news is got only by enterprise and expense. To produce such news as it is produced by the defendant represents by implication that it has been acquired by the defendant's enterprise and at its expense. When it comes from one of the great news collecting agencies like the Associated Press, the source generally is indicated, plainly importing that credit; and that such a representation is implied may be inferred with some confidence from the unwillingness of the defendant to give the credit and tell the truth. If the plaintiff produces the news at the same time that the defendant does, the defendant's presentation impliedly denies to the plaintiff the credit of collecting the facts and assumes that credit to the defendant. If the plaintiff is later in Western cities it naturally will be supposed to have obtained its information from the defendant. The falsehood is a little more subtle, the injury a little more indirect, than in ordinary cases of unfair trade, but I think that the principle that condemns the one condemns the other. It is a question of how strong an infusion of fraud is necessary to turn a flavor into a poison. The dose seems to me strong enough here to need a remedy from the law. But as, in my view, the only ground of complaint that can be recognized without legislation is the implied misstatement, it can be corrected by stating the truth; and a suitable acknowledgment of the source is all that the plaintiff can require. I think that within the limits recognized by the decision of the Court the defendant should be enjoined from publishing news obtained from the Associated Press for [blank] hours after publication by the plaintiff unless it gives express credit to the Associated Press; the number of hours and the form of acknowledgment to be settled by the District Court.

MR. JUSTICE McKENNA concurs in this opinion.

MR. JUSTICE BRANDEIS, dissenting.

There are published in the United States about 2,500 daily papers. More than 800 of them are supplied with domestic and foreign news of general interest by the Associated Press—a corporation without capital stock which does not sell news or earn or seek to earn profits, but serves merely as an instrumentality by means of which these papers supply themselves at joint expense with such news. Papers not members of the Associated Press depend for their news of general interest largely upon agencies organized for profit. Among these agencies is the International News Service which supplies news to about 400 subscribing papers. It has, like the Associated Press, bureaus and correspondents in this and foreign countries; and its annual expenditures in gathering and distributing news is about $2,000,000. Ever since its organization in 1909, it has included among the sources from which it gathers news, copies (purchased in the open market) of early editions of some papers published by members of the Associated Press and the bulletins publicly posted by them. These items, which constitute but a small part of the news transmitted to its subscribers, are generally verified by the International News Service before transmission; but frequently items are transmitted without verification; and occasionally even without being re-written. In no case is the fact disclosed that such item was suggested by or taken from a paper or bulletin published by an Associated Press member.

No question of statutory copyright is involved. The sole question for our consideration is this: Was the International News Service properly enjoined from using, or causing to be used gainfully, news of which it acquired knowledge by lawful means (namely, by reading publicly posted bulletins or papers purchased by it in the open market) merely because the news had been originally gathered by the Associated Press and continued to be of value to some of its members, or because it did not reveal the source from which it was acquired?

The "ticker" cases, the cases concerning literary and artistic compositions, and cases of unfair competition were relied upon in support of the injunction. But it is admitted that none of those cases affords a complete analogy with that before us. The question presented for decision is new, and it is important.

News is a report of recent occurrences. The business of the news agency is to gather systematically knowledge of such occurrences of interest and to distribute reports thereof. The Associated Press contended that knowledge so acquired is property, because it costs money and labor to produce and because it has value for which those who have it not are ready to pay; that it remains property and is entitled to protection as long as it has commercial value as news; and that to protect it effectively, the defendant must be enjoined from making, or causing to be made, any gainful use of it while it retains such value. An essential element of individual property is the legal right to exclude others from enjoying it. If the property is private, the right of exclusion may be absolute; if the property is affected with a public interest, the right of exclusion is qualified. But the fact that a product of the mind has cost its producer money and labor, and has a value for which others are willing to pay, is not sufficient to ensure to it this legal attribute of property. The general rule of law is, that the noblest of human productions—knowledge, truths ascertained, conceptions, and ideas—become, after voluntary communication to others, free as the air to common use. Upon these incorporeal productions the attribute of property is continued after such communication only in certain classes of cases where public policy has seemed to demand it. These exceptions are confined to productions which, in some degree, involve creation, invention, or discovery. But by no means all such are endowed with this attribute of property. The creations which are recognized as property by the common law are literary, dramatic, musical, and other artistic creations; and these have also protection under the copyright statutes. The inventions and discoveries upon which this attribute of property is conferred only by statute, are the few comprised within the patent law. There are also many other cases in which courts interfere to prevent curtailment of plaintiff's enjoyment of incorporeal productions; and in which the right to relief is often called a property right, but is such only in a special sense. In those cases, the plaintiff has no absolute right to the protection of his production; he has merely the qualified right to be protected as against the defendant's acts, because of the special relation in which the latter stands or the wrongful method or means employed in acquiring the knowledge or the manner in which it is used. Protection of this character is afforded where the suit is based upon breach of contract or of trust or upon unfair competition.

The knowledge for which protection is sought in the case at bar is not of a kind upon which the law has heretofore conferred the attributes of property; nor is the manner of its acquisition or use nor the purpose to which it is applied, such as has heretofore been recognized as entitling a plaintiff to relief.

* * *

The rule for which the plaintiff contends would effect an important extension of property rights and a corresponding curtailment of the free use of knowledge and of ideas; and the facts of this case admonish us of the danger involved in recognizing such a property right in news, without imposing upon news-gatherers corresponding obligations. A large majority of the newspapers and perhaps half the newspaper readers of the United States are dependent for their news of general interest upon agencies other than the Associated Press. The channel through which about 400 of these papers received, as the plaintiff alleges, "a large amount of news relating to the European war of the greatest importance and of intense interest to the newspaper reading public" was suddenly closed. The closing to the International News Service of these channels for foreign news (if they were closed) was due not to unwillingness on its part to pay the cost of collecting the news, but to the prohibitions imposed by foreign governments upon its securing news from their respective countries and from using cable or telegraph lines running therefrom. For aught that appears, this prohibition may have been wholly undeserved; and at all events the 400 papers and their readers may be assumed to have been innocent. For aught that appears, the International News Service may have sought then to secure temporarily by arrangement with the Associated Press the latter's foreign news service. For aught that appears, all of the 400 subscribers of the International News Service would gladly have then become members of the Associated Press, if they could have secured election thereto. It is possible, also, that a large part of the readers of these papers were so situated that they could not secure prompt access to papers served by the Associated Press. The prohibition of the foreign governments might as well have been extended to the channels through which news was supplied to the more than a thousand other daily papers in the United States not served by the Associated Press; and a large part of their readers may also be so located that they cannot procure prompt access to papers served by the Associated Press.

A Legislature, urged to enact a law by which one news agency or newspaper may prevent appropriation of the fruits of its labors by another, would consider such facts and possibilities and others which appropriate inquiry might disclose. Legislators might conclude that it was impossible to put an end to the obvious injustice involved in such appropriation of news, without opening the door to other evils, greater than that sought to be remedied. Such appears to have been the opinion of our Senate which reported unfavorably a bill to give news a few hours' protection; and which ratified, on February 15, 1911, the convention adopted at the Fourth International American Conference; and such was evidently the view also of the signatories to the International Copyright Union of November 13, 1908, as both these conventions expressly exclude news from copyright protection.

Or legislators dealing with the subject might conclude, that the right to news values should be protected to the extent of permitting recovery of damages for any unauthorized use, but that protection by injunction should be denied, just as courts of equity ordinarily refuse (perhaps in the interest of free speech) to restrain actionable libels, and for other reasons decline to protect by injunction mere political rights; and as Congress has prohibited courts from enjoining the illegal assessment or collection of federal taxes. If a Legislature concluded to recognize property in published news to the extent of permitting recovery at law, it might, with a view to making the remedy more certain and adequate, provide a fixed measure of damages, as in the case of copyright infringement.

Or again, a Legislature might conclude that it was unwise to recognize even so limited a property right in published news as that above indicated; but that a news agency should, on some conditions, be given full protection of its business; and to that end a remedy by injunction as well as one for damages should be granted, where news collected by it is gainfully used without permission. If a Legislature concluded (as at least one court has held, *New York and Chicago Grain and Stock Exchange v. Board of Trade*, 127 Ill. 153, 19 N. E. 855, 2 L. R. A. 411, 11 Am. St. Rep. 107) that under certain circumstances news-gathering is a business affected with a public interest, it might declare that, in such cases, news should be protected against appropriation, only if the gatherer assumed the obligation of supplying it, at reasonable rates and without discrimination, to all papers which applied therefor. If legislators reached that conclusion, they would probably go further, and prescribe the conditions under which and the extent to which the protection should be afforded; and they might also provide the administrative machinery necessary for insuring to the public, the press, and the news agencies, full enjoyment of the rights so conferred.

Courts are ill-equipped to make the investigations which should precede a determination of the limitations which should be set upon any property right in news or of the circumstances under which news gathered by a private agency should be deemed affected with a public interest. Courts would be powerless to prescribe the detailed regulations essential to full enjoyment of the rights conferred or to introduce the machinery required for enforcement of such regulations. Considerations such as these should lead us to decline to establish a new rule of law in the effort to redress a newly disclosed wrong, although the propriety of some remedy appears to be clear.

HAELAN LABORATORIES, INC. v. TOPPS CHEWING GUM, INC.

United States Court of Appeals, Second Circuit, 1953.
202 F.2d 866.

* * * After a trial without a jury, the trial judge dismissed the complaint on the merits. The plaintiff maintains that defendant invaded plaintiff's exclusive right to use the photographs of leading baseball-players. Probably because the trial judge ruled against plaintiff's legal contentions, some of the facts were not too clearly found. 1. So far as we can now tell, there were instances of the following kind: (a). The plaintiff, engaged in selling chewing-gum, made a contract with a ball-player providing that plaintiff for a stated term should have the exclusive right to use the ball-player's photograph in connection with the sales of plaintiff's gum; the ball-player agreed not to grant any other gum manufacturer a similar right during such term; the contract gave plaintiff an option to extend the term for a designated period. (b). Defendant, a rival chewing-gum manufacturer, knowing of plaintiff's contract, deliberately induced the ball-player to authorize defendant, by a contract with defendant, to use the player's photograph in connection with the sales of defendant's gum either during the original or extended term of plaintiff's contract, and defendant did so use the photograph. Defendant argues that, even if such facts are proved, they show no actionable wrong, for this reason: The contract with plaintiff was no more than a release by the ball-player to plaintiff of the liability which, absent the release, plaintiff would have incurred in using the ball-player's photograph, because such a use, without his consent, would be an invasion of his right of privacy under Section 50 and Section 51 of the New York Civil Rights Law; this statutory right of privacy is personal, not assignable; therefore, plaintiff's contract vested in plaintiff no 'property' right or other legal interest which defendant's conduct invaded. Both parties agree, and so do we, that, on the facts here, New York 'law' governs. And we shall assume, for the moment, that, under the New York decisions, defendant correctly asserts that any such contract between plaintiff and a ball-player, in so far as it merely authorized plaintiff to use the player's photograph, created nothing but a release of liability. On that basis, were there no more to the contract, plaintiff would have no actionable claim against defendant. But defendant's argument neglects the fact that, in the contract, the ball-player also promised not to give similar releases to others. If defendant, knowing of the contract, deliberately induced the ball-player to break that promise, defendant behaved tortiously. Some of defendant's contracts were obtained by it through its agent, Players Enterprise, Inc.; others were obtained by Russell Publishing Co., acting independently, and were then assigned by Russell to defendant. Since Players acted as defendant's agent, defendant is liable for any breach of plaintiff's contracts thus induced by Players. However, as Russell did not act as defendant's agent when Russell, having knowledge of plaintiff's contract with a player, by subsequently contracting with that player, induced a breach of plaintiff's contract, defendant is not liable for any breach so induced; nor did there arise such a liability against defendant for such an induced breach when defendant became the assignee of one of those Russell contracts. 2. The foregoing covers the situations where defendant, by itself or through its agent, induced breaches. But in those instances where Russell induced the breach, we have a different problem; and that problem also confronts us in instances—alleged in one paragraph of the complaint and to which the trial judge in his opinion also (although not altogether clearly) refers—where defendant, 'with knowledge of plaintiff's exclusive rights,' used a photograph of a ball-player without his consent during the term of his contract with plaintiff. With regard to such situations, we must consider defendant's contention that none of plaintiff's contracts created more than a release of liability, because a man has no legal interest in the publication of his picture other than his right of privacy, i.e., a personal and non-assignable right not to have his feelings hurt by such a publication. A majority of this court rejects this contention. We think that, in addition to and independent of that right of privacy (which in New York derives from statute), a man has a right in the publicity value of his photograph, i.e., the right to grant the exclusive privilege of publishing his picture, and that such a grant may validly be made 'in gross,' i.e., without an accompanying transfer of a business or of any-thing else. Whether it be labelled a 'property' right is immaterial; for here, as often elsewhere, the tag 'property' simply symbolizes the fact that courts enforce a claim which has pecuniary worth. This right might be called a 'right of publicity.' For it is common knowledge that many prominent persons (especially actors and ball-players), far from having their feelings bruised through public exposure of their likenesses, would feel sorely deprived if they no longer received money for authorizing advertisements, popularizing their countenances, displayed in newspapers, magazines, busses, trains and subways. This right of publicity would usually yield them no money unless it could be made the subject of an exclusive grant which barred any other advertiser from using their pictures. We think the New York decisions recognize such a right. See, e.g., Wood v. Lucy, Lady Duff-Gordon, 222 N.Y. 88, 118 N.E. 214; Madison Square Garden Corp. v. Universal Pictures Co., 255 App.Div. 459, 465, 7 N.Y.S.2d 845; Cf. Liebig's Extract of Meat Co. v. Liebig Extract Co., 2 Cir., 180 F. 688.

* * *

We said above that defendant was not liable for a breach of any of plaintiff's contracts induced by Russell, and did not become thus liable (for an induced breach) when there was assigned to defendant a contract between Russell and a ball-player, although Russell, in making that contract, knowingly induced a breach of a contract with plaintiff. But plaintiff, in its capacity publicity,' has a valid claim against defendant if defendant used that player's photograph during the term of plaintiff's grant and with knowledge of it. It is no defense to such a claim that defendant is the assignee of a subsequent contract between that player and Russell, purporting to make a grant to Russell or its assignees. For the prior grant to plaintiff renders that subsequent grant invalid during the period of the grant (including an exercised option) to plaintiff, but not thereafter. 3. We must remand to the trial court for a determination (on the basis of the present record and of further evidence introduced by either party) of these facts: (1) the date and contents of each of plaintiff's contracts, and whether plaintiff exercised its option to renew; (2) defendant's or Players' conduct with respect to each such contract. Of course, if defendant made a contract with a ball-player which was not executed- or which did not authorize defendant to use the player's photograph- until the expiration of the original or extended term of plaintiff's contract with that player, or which did not induce a breach of the agreement to renew, then defendant did no legal wrong to plaintiff. The same is true of instances where neither defendant nor Players induced a breach of plaintiff's contract, and defendant did not use the player's photograph until after the expiration of such original or extended or option term. If, upon further exploration of the facts, the trial court, in the light of our opinion, concludes that defendant is liable, it will, of course, ascertain damages and decide what equitable relief is justified. Reversed and remanded. * * *

MELVILLE B. NIMMER, THE RIGHT OF PUBLICITY*

19 Law & Contemporary Problems 203 (1954).

Louis Brandeis and Samuel Warren in their essay "The Right to Privacy"[1] produced what is perhaps the most famous and certainly the most influential law review article ever written. In the words of Roscoe Pound, it did "nothing less than add a chapter to our law."[2] It was primarily due to the persuasiveness of this article that first Georgia[3] and then 14 other states[4] came to recognize a common law right of privacy. Furthermore, when the New York Court of Appeals rejected the Brandeis–Warren arguments and refused to recognize a common law right of privacy,[5] the New York Legislature instituted legislation[6] which in some ways has extended the scope of privacy actions even beyond that envi-

* Copyright 1954 by Law & Contemporary Problems. Edited and used with permission.

1. 4 HARV. L. REV. 193 (1890).

2. Quoted in A.T. Mason, BRANDEIS, A FREE MAN'S LIFE 70 (1946).

3. Pavesich v. New England Life Ins. Co., 122 Ga. 190, 50 S. E. 68 (1904).

4. Alabama, Arizona, California, Florida, Illinois, Indiana, Kansas, Kentucky, Michigan, Missouri, Montana, North Carolina, Oregon, and Pennsylvania.

5. Roberson v. Rochester Folding Box Co., 171 N. Y. 538, 64 N.E. 442 (1902).

6. N.Y. CIVIL RIGHTS LAW §§ 50, 51 (1948).

saged by Brandeis and Warren. Moreover, two states have since adopted privacy statutes substantially similar to the New York statute.[7]

But although the concept of privacy which Brandeis and Warren evolved fulfilled the demands of Beacon Street in 1890, it may seriously be doubted that the application of this concept satisfactorily meets the needs of Broadway and Hollywood in 1954. Brandeis and Warren were concerned with the preservation of privacy against a press "overstepping in every direction the obvious bounds of propriety and of decency," and in which "to satisfy a prurient taste the details of sexual relations are spread broadcast in the columns of the daily papers."[8] Without in any way implying that the right of privacy is less important today than when first suggested by Brandeis and Warren, it is suggested that the doctrine, first developed to protect the sensibilities of nineteenth century Brahmin Boston, is not adequate to meet the demands of the second half of the twentieth century, particularly with respect to the advertising, motion picture, television, and radio industries. Well known personalities connected with these industries do not seek the "solitude and privacy"[9] which Brandeis and Warren sought to protect. Indeed, "privacy is the one thing they do not want, or need."[10] Their concern is rather with publicity, which may be regarded as the reverse side of the coin of privacy. However, although the well known personality does not wish to hide his light under a bushel of privacy, neither does he wish to have his name, photograph, and likeness reproduced and publicized without his consent or without remuneration to him. With the tremendous strides in communications, advertising, and entertainment techniques, the public personality has found that the use of his name, photograph, and likeness has taken on a pecuniary value undreamed of at the turn of the century. Often, however, this important value (which will be referred to in this article as publicity value) cannot be legally protected either under a privacy theory or under any other traditional legal theory.

* * *

Inadequacy of Privacy

Those persons and enterprises in the entertainment and allied industries wishing to control but not prohibit the use by others of their own or their employees' names and portraits will find, for the reasons indicated below, that the right of privacy is generally an unsatisfactory means of assuring such control.

Waiver by Celebrities. It is generally the person who has achieved the somewhat ephemeral status of "celebrity" who must cope with the unauthorized use by others of his name and portrait, since the fact of his

---

7. Utah and Virginia. Wisconsin also gives some protection to the right of privacy. See Yankwich, *The Right of Privacy,* 27 Notre Dame Law. 499, 521 (1952).

8. Warren and Brandeis, *The Right to Privacy* 4 Harv. L. Rev. 193, I 96 (1890).

9. Warren and Brandeis, *supra* note 8, at 196.

10. Gautier v. Pro–Football, 304 N. Y. 354, 361, 107 N. E. 2d 485, 489 (1952).

fame makes such use commercially attractive to others. Yet, when such a person seeks to invoke the right of privacy to protect himself from such unauthorized use, he finds that by the very fact of his being a celebrity "he has dedicated his life to the public and thereby waived his right to privacy."[12] Some courts find this waiver to be absolute so that even aspects of the celebrity's private life which he has never made public no longer command the protection of the law of privacy.[13]

* * *

Non-assignable. In most jurisdictions it is well established that a right of privacy is a personal right rather than a property right[47] and consequently is not assignable.[48] The publicity value of a prominent person's name and portrait is greatly restricted if this value cannot be assigned to others. Moreover, persons willing to pay for such publicity values will usually demand that in return for payment they obtain an exclusive right.[49] Yet since the right of privacy is non-assignable, any agreement purporting to grant the right to use the grantor's name and portrait (as in connection with a commercial endorsement or tie-up) is construed as constituting merely a release as to the purchaser and as not granting the purchaser any right which he can enforce as against a third party.[50]

* * *

INADEQUACY OF UNFAIR COMPETITION

If the well known personality finds that misappropriation of his publicity values cannot be effectively prevented under a privacy theory, he will usually find no greater relief under the traditional theory of unfair competition.

Competition Requirement. The absence of competition between the plaintiff and defendant is in a number of jurisdictions an effective defense to an unfair competition action.[55] In such jurisdictions, it is obvious that publicity values are not effectively protected, since a person's publicity values may be profitably exploited in non-competitive

---

12. Leon R. Yankwich, Chief Judge, United States District Court for the Southern District of California.

13. Donahue v. Warner Bros. Pictures, District Court of the Third Judicial District, State of Utah, No. 87,714 (1952). This case had been transferred from the federal courts after the Court of Appeals for the Tenth Circuit, in the federal district court. See Peay v. Curtis Publishing Co., 78 F.Supp. 305 (D.D.C.1948); and Reed v. Real Detective Publishing Co., 162 P.2d 133 (Sup.Ct. Ariz. 1945).

47. Mau v. Rio Grande Oil, 28 F.Supp. 845 (N.D.Calif. 1939); Metter v. Examiner, 35 Cal.App.2d 304, 95 P.2d 491 (1939).

48. Hanna Manufacturing Co. v. Hillerich & Bradsby, 78 F.2d 763 (5th Cir.1935); Note, 45 YALE L.J. 520 (1936); see Haelan Laboratories v. Topps Chewing Gum, 202 F.2d 866 (2d Cir.1953).

49. *See* Rogers v. Republic Productions, 104 F.Supp. 328, 341 (S.D.Calif. 1952).

50. *Cf.* Haelan Laboratories v. Topps Chewing Gum, 202 F.2d 866 (2d Cir.1953).

55. *E.g.,* Women's Mutual Benefit Society v. Catholic Society Feminine, 304 Mass. 349, 23 N.E.2d 886 (1939); Acme Screen Co. v. Pebbles, 159 Okla. 116, 14 P.2d 366 (1932); Scutt v. Bassett, 86 Cal.App.2d 373, 194 P.2d 781 (1948). *See* Riggs Optical Co. v. Riggs, 132 Neb. 26, 270 N.W. 667 (1937).

fields. Thus, a chewing gum company which includes in its packages pictures of prominent baseball players could hardly be characterized as in competition with the players. Even with respect to business or other enterprises (as distinguished from personalities) which, as has been indicated *supra*,[56] cannot invoke the right of privacy, the defense of no competition will effectively prevent a successful unfair competition action for misappropriation of the enterprise's publicity values.

* * *

Passing Off Requirement. It is generally recognized that "the essence of unfair competition consists in the palming off of the goods or business of one person as that of another."[61]

This requirement of passing off (or palming off), which is probably more universally recognized than the requirement of competition discussed *supra*, serves to limit further the protection available for publicity values under the theory of unfair competition. Publicity values of a person or firm may be profitably appropriated and exploited without the necessity of any imputation that such person or firm is connected with the exploitation undertaken by the appropriator. That is to say, publicity values may be usefully appropriated without the necessity of passing off, and therefore without violating the traditional theory of unfair competition.

* * *

No Assignment in Gross. The pecuniary worth of publicity values will be greatly diminished if not totally destroyed if these values cannot be effectively sold. Yet, under the theory of unfair competition, an assignee cannot acquire the right to use a name except as an incident to his purchase of the business and good will in connection with which the name has been used.[65] Therefore, if the potential purchaser of publicity values must rely upon the law of unfair competition to protect his investment, he will be unwilling to purchase publicity values unconnected with a business. This in effect means that the sale of publicity values will usually be effectively blocked, since the potential seller of publicity values generally has established such value not in connection with his own business but rather through the rendering of personal services for another; he will therefore be unable to sell the business in connection with which his name has achieved fame. Furthermore, even if the potential seller has achieved fame through his own business, if he can only sell his publicity values as an incident to the sale of his business, he will ordinarily prefer not to enter such a transaction.

Unfair Competition Extended. In recent years there has been a marked tendency in a number of jurisdictions to take a broader view of the scope of unfair competition. Many courts have rejected the defense of

56. See p. 210.

61. American Broadcasting Co. v. Wahl Co., 36 F.Supp. 167, 168 (S.D.N.Y.1940). The leading case on this point is Howe

Scale Co. v. Wyckoff, Seamans & Benedict, 198 U.S. 118 (1905).

65. Fisk v. Fisk, 3 F.2d 7 (8th Cir.1924).

lack of competition between the parties.[66] Some other courts no longer require a showing of passing off in order to establish an action in unfair competition.[67] However, even in those jurisdictions which have permitted recovery in the absence of either competition or passing off, the doctrine would generally not appear to be so far extended as to permit recovery where *both* competition and passing off are absent. Thus, in *International News Service v. Associated Press*,[68] a case usually cited by those courts which have extended the doctrine of unfair competition, I.N.S. appropriated news gathered by the Associated Press, and although there was no passing off in that I.N.S. did not represent the appropriated news as emanating from Associated Press, there was, of course, the element of competition between the two major news services.[69] Other instances may be found in which relief was granted under an unfair competition theory upon a showing of passing off although the parties were not in competition.[70] The language contained in *Metropolitan Opera Ass'n v. Wagner–Nichols Recorder Corp.*,[71] however, goes so far as to indicate that relief might be granted although both competition and passing off were not established. * * * "The courts have thus recognized that in the complex pattern of modern business relationships, persons in theoretically noncompetitive fields may, by unethical business practices, inflict as severe and reprehensible injuries upon others as can direct competitors."[73] It will be seen from the above passage that under this view (*i.e.*, discarding the requirements of competition and passing off) the scope of unfair competition covers "any form of commercial immorality," and "unethical business practices." If this loose standard were in fact applied by the courts, the already uncertain field of unfair competition would be reduced to a chaos of complete uncertainty, since what lawyer or business man could predict with any degree of certainty where the courts would find that properly aggressive business practices leave off and "commercial immorality" and "unethical business practices" begin? True, publicity values might be protected under such a broad theory, but in doing so the courts would be adopting a standard which by its uncertainty could prove highly detrimental to orderly commercial intercourse. It is suggested that publicity values can be adequately protected under the right of publicity discussed *infra*, without going to the extremes indicated above.

66. Finchley, Inc. v. Finchly Co., 40 F.2d 736 (D.Md.1929); Horlick's Malted Milk Corp. v. Horluck's, Inc., 43 F.2d 767 (W.D.Wash.1930); Kotabs, Inc. v. Kotex Co., 50 F.2d 810 (3d Cir.1931); Standard Oil Co. of New Mexico v. Standard Oil Co. of California, 56 F.2d 973 (10th Cir.1932); Emerson Electric Mfg. Co. v. Emerson Radio & Phonograph Corp., 105 F.2d 908 (2d Cir. 1939).

67. International News Service v. Associated Press, 248 U.S. 215 (1918); Montegut v. Hickson, 178 App.Div. 94, 164 N.Y.S. 858 (Ist Dep't 1917). See In re Northern Pigment Co., 71 F.2d 447 (C.C.P.A.1934).

68. 248 U.S. 215 (1918).

69. Mutual Broadcasting System v. Muzak, 177 Misc. 489, 30 N.Y.S.2d 419 (Sup. Ct.1941) presented another instance wherein, although passing off could not be established, relief was nevertheless granted on the basis of competition between the parties. See Hanna Mfg. Co. v. Hillerich and Bradsby, 78 F.2d 763 (5th Cir.1935).

70. See Madison Square Garden Corp. v. Universal Pictures Co., 255 App.Div. 459 7 N.Y.S.2d 845 (1st Dep't 1938).

71. 101 N.Y.S.2d 483 (Sup.Ct.1950).

73. 101 N.Y.S.2d 483, 492 (Sup.Ct. 1950).

INADEQUACY OF OTHER THEORIES

Publicity values may to a limited extent be protected by contract,[74] but such protection extends, of course, only to the parties to such contracts. The inadequacy of the contract theory in protecting publicity values is illustrated in *Corliss v. E. W. Walker Co.*,[75] in which plaintiff's deceased husband had his portrait taken by a photographer who agreed by contract not to furnish prints of the photograph to anyone other than plaintiff and plaintiff's husband. Thereafter the defendant purchased a print of the photograph from the photographer and inserted it in a biographical sketch of the deceased husband. The plaintiff sought to obtain an injunction against the use of the photograph, and the court granted the defendant's motion to dissolve the injunction on the ground that defendant was not a party to the contract between the plaintiff's husband and the photographer, and therefore defendant was not bound thereby.[76] However, if the plaintiff can establish a contract restricting use of the publicity values and if defendant although not a party to the contract can be shown to have induced breach of the contract, then relief may be obtained.[77] Thus if *A* purchases the right to use *B*'s publicity values under a contract in which *B* agrees not to grant the right to use such publicity values to anyone else, and if thereafter *C* induces *B* to grant to him the same publicity values and thereby causes *B* to breach his contract with *A*, *C* will be liable to *A* for the tort of inducing breach of contract. However, if *C* having thus acquired the publicity rights from *B* in turn assigns these rights to *D*, *D* in using such publicity rights will not be liable to *A* for the tort of inducing breach of contract since *D* merely benefitted from the breach of contract but did not induce it,[78] and *D* will not be liable for breach of contract since he was not a party to the contract between *A* and *B*. Thus even in the limited situations where appropriation of publicity values involves a breach of contract, a person who is not a party to the contract and who has not induced its breach may not be prevented from using the publicity values on either a contract theory or a theory of inducing breach of contract.

If the use of the plaintiff's publicity values is made in a manner so as to constitute defamation, trade libel or disparagement then, of course, liability will ensue. Thus, in *Paramount Pictures, Inc. v. Leader Press*,[79] although the court found that defendant's practice of producing advertising accessories embodying the publicity value of plaintiff's pictures and stars constituted neither an invasion of privacy nor unfair competition, still relief was granted on the theory of disparagement because of the fact that defendant's advertising accessories depicted plaintiff's stars in an unattractive manner. However, for the reasons discussed in connection with the right of privacy, publicity values are not adequately

---

74. See Wood v. Lucy, Lady Duff–Gordon, 222 N.Y. 88, 118 N.E. 214 (1917).

75. 64 Fed. 280 (C.C.D.Mass.1894).

76. See also Lawrence v. Ylla, 184 Misc. 807, 55 N.Y.S.2d 343 (Sup.Ct.1945).

77. Paramount Pictures v. Leader Press, 106 F.2d 229 (10th Cir.1939).

78. Haelan Laboratories v. Topps Chewing Gum, 202 F.2d 866 (2d Cir.1953).

79. 106 F.2d 229 (10th Cir.1939).

protected if relief can only be granted when the use of the values is made in an offensive manner, since generally an appropriation of publicity values does not involve a disparagement of the values thus appropriated, or of the persons identified with such values.[80]

Substance of and Limitations on the Right of Publicity

The substance and direction of the right of publicity has to some extent been indicated by adjudicated cases which will be discussed later.[81] Before examining the somewhat fragmentary outline embodied in existing case law, it might be well first to attempt some perspective as to the fundamental elements necessary to a workable and socially useful right of publicity. From such a perspective, the meaning and continuity of existing case law will be more apparent.

* * *

The nature of the inadequacy of the traditional legal theories dictates in large measure the substance of the right of publicity. The right of publicity must be recognized as a property (not a personal) right, and as such capable of assignment and subsequent enforcement by the assignee. Furthermore, appropriation of publicity values should be actionable regardless of whether the defendant has used the publicity in a manner offensive to the sensibilities of the plaintiff. Usually the use will be non-offensive, since such a use is more valuable to the defendant as well as to the plaintiff. Likewise, the measure of damages should be computed in terms of the value of the publicity appropriated by defendant rather than, as in privacy, in terms of the injury sustained by the plaintiff. There must be no waiver of the right by reason of the plaintiff being a well known personality. Indeed, the right usually becomes important only when the plaintiff (or potential plaintiff) has achieved in some degree a celebrated status. Moreover, since animals, inanimate objects, and business and other institutions all may be endowed with publicity values, the human owners of these non-human entities should have a right of publicity (although no right of privacy) in such property, and this right should exist (unlike unfair competition) regardless of whether the defendant is in competition with the plaintiff, and regardless of whether he is passing off his own products as those of the plaintiff.

* * *

Recognition of the Right of Publicity

It would be premature to state that the right of publicity has as yet received any substantial degree of judicial recognition. * * * [Yet with Judge Jerome Frank's recent opinion in *Haelan Laboratories v. Topps*

---

80. This section is not intended to exhaust other possible theories under which publicity values may be protected in particular circumstances. For instance, a copyright theory may be invoked if defendant uses a photograph in which plaintiff can claim a common law or statutory copyright.

81. See p. 218, *infra.*

Chewing Gum, Inc.,[110]] the right of a person (or his assignee) to protect the publicity value of his photograph was expressly recognized and designated the "right of publicity." The facts of this case, in so far as they involve the right of publicity, were as follows: The plaintiff and defendant were competitors in that both were manufacturers of candy or chewing gum confections. Plaintiff contracted with certain prominent baseball players for the exclusive right to use their photographs in connection with the sale of plaintiff's products. Thereafter one Russel contracted with the same players for the same purpose. Russell subsequently assigned his rights to the defendant who proceeded to use photographs of the players in connection with his product. In the ensuing litigation, the defendant argued plaintiff could not recover either under a privacy theory since the right of privacy is personal and non-assignable, nor for inducing breach of contract since it was Russell, not the defendant, who induced the breach.[111] The court impliedly recognized the validity of these defenses, but went on to state:[112]

> We think that, in addition to and independent of that right of privacy (which in New York derives from statute), a man has a right in the publicity value of his photograph, i.e., the right to grant the exclusive privilege of publishing his picture, and that such a grant may be validly made "in gross" i.e., without any accompanying transfer of a business or anything else ... This right may be called a "right of publicity." For it is common knowledge that many prominent persons (especially actors and ball-players), far from having their feelings bruised through public exposure of their likenesses, would feel sorely deprived if they no longer received money for authorizing advertisements, popularizing their countenances. This right of publicity would usually yield no money unless it could be made the subject of an exclusive grant which barred any other advertiser from using their pictures.

Thus in the *Haelan* case the highly respected Second Circuit of the Federal Courts of Appeals granted to the right of publicity a recognition and status of a qualitatively higher order than had been accorded in any previous case. The court clearly held that the right of publicity, unlike the right of privacy, is a property right which may be validly assigned and it at least implied that the privacy defenses of waiver by celebrities and of no liability for non-offensive uses are not applicable in a right of publicity action. Yet, by the very nature of our judicial process, a new principle of law can never be completely embodied in any one decision. The *Haelan* case in final analysis is limited to its own facts, and therefore leaves unexplored certain important phases of the right of publicity. It remains for future cases finally to determine that the measure of damages in a publicity action shall be for the value of the use of the appropriated publicity rather than for the injury to the plaintiff's

---

110. *Supra.*

111. Defendant had directly contracted with certain other players who had previously contracted with plaintiff. As to the players, the court found defendant liable for inducing breach of contract.

112. 202 F.2d 866, 868 (2d Cir.1953).

sensibilities. Likewise, the right to recover for misappropriation of publicity values inherent in animals, inanimate objects, and business and other institutions (regardless of competition and passing off) remains to be established. Furthermore, the effect of the *Haelan* case as a precedent is questionable since the Court of Appeals had jurisdiction on grounds of diversity of citizenship and therefore the resulting decision represents the federal court's interpretation and application of New York law,[113] which is of course not binding in other jurisdictions. In fact, although persuasive, it is not even binding on the New York courts. Despite its limitations, the *Haelan* case represents a major step in the inexorable process of reconciling law and contemporary problems.

This raises the final question of the right of our courts, in the absence of legislation, to enforce a right not previously recognized. Here we may return to the essay by Brandeis and Warren discussed at the beginning of this article. The argument was there advanced that "the beautiful capacity for growth which characterizes the common law" would with respect to the right of privacy "enable the judges to afford the requisite protection, without the interposition of the legislature."[114] That this proved true is attested by judicial opinions in fifteen jurisdictions. There is no less reason to believe that the common law can likewise meet the publicity problems created by modern methods of advertising and communications without doing violence to our concept of an independent but limited judiciary. But whether the right of publicity is finally and fully realized by statute or through growth and adaptation of common law principles, eventual recognition of the right seems assured both from the trend of decisions already rendered, and from the more fundamental fact of community needs.

Note

In Professor Nimmer's essay the reader can gain some impression of the traditional significance and utility in common law concepts sounding in "property"—concepts which allow the possessor to transcend certain limitations classically attached to alternative theories, including personal rights (*choses* in action) or contract claims. Perhaps most notably, a property owner enjoys the ability to fence out others while controlling the right freely to convey and assign in gross. In practical terms these rights permit the owner to develop property (by investing time and capital in its production), confident of the ability to recoup the investment without threat from "free riders." In this sense, the theory of misappropriation recognized in *INS*, though nominally an aspect of unfair competition, also recognizably establishes a classic species of "property".

But rights of this character at common law also tend to be protean—i.e., to proliferate easily and quickly—unless carefully checked and circumscribed (as presumably they are, for example, in such statutory systems as copyright and patents). See Lange, Recognizing the Public Domain, 44 Law and

---

113. Erie Railroad v. Tompkins, 304 U.S. 64 (1938).

114. Warren and Brandeis, *supra* note 8, at 195.

Contemp. Probs. 147 (1981). Professor Nimmer himself suggested that the concept of misappropriation recognized in *INS,* if extended, surely would prove too broad and ungovernable to be useful in developing the property rights he favored for the newly emerging right of publicity. In fact, however, just such an extended theory of misappropriation is at the center of the publicity right in contemporary practice. See ALI, Restatement (3d), Unfair Competition §§ 38, 46–49 (1994). Might it have been the better part of judgment had the Second Circuit in *Haelan* waited for some legislative enactment before recognizing a new property right? Would the publicity right have been better confined to the tort-based personal privacy doctrine from which (arguably) it sprang? Is it even possible that contract doctrines, more imaginatively applied, could have furnished the needed protection? *Cf.* Palmer, Intellectual Property: A Non–Posnerian Law and Economics Approach, 12 Hamline L. Rev. 261 (1989).

The movement toward increasing recognition of property-based rights in intangible interests (which is essentially the definition of "intellectual property") has gathered momentum in the years since Professor Nimmer wrote. Ask yourself which side you would have been inclined to take at this early point in your study of the doctrines.

*

Part II

TRADEMARK AND UNFAIR COMPETITION LAW

Chapter 2

THE NATURE
AND ESTABLISHMENT
OF TRADEMARK RIGHTS

A. INTRODUCTION

One broad area of intellectual property involves the protection of good will—brand names and other forms of marketing information—from improper usurpation by competitors or others. The classic claim in this area of intellectual property law is the infringement of a well-known trademark, a brand name such as "Coca–Cola" or "Mercedes–Benz." Common sense would tell us that it is impermissible for an imitator to sell a carbonated beverage using the Coca–Cola brand name or to market an automobile under the name Mercedes–Benz. The firms that manufacture those products have spent considerable resources to develop a high-quality product, which is what consumers now come to expect when they purchase a soft drink or a car bearing those brand names. The firms have also invested considerable resources in marketing their products and increasing the brand recognition of their products. They have been so successful that Coca–Cola and Mercedes–Benz are now household names.

Trademark law traces its origins to medieval times, when skilled artisans and craftsmen formed guilds and applied symbols to their products to signify the identity of their makers. The common law provided protection for trademarks through actions for deceit. "Beginning in about 1803, English and American common law slowly developed an offshoot of the tort of fraud and deceit and called it 'passing off' or 'palming off.' Simply stated, passing off as a tort consists of one passing off his goods as the goods of another. In 1842 Lord Langdale wrote: 'I think that the principle on which both the courts of law and equity proceed is very well understood. A man is not to sell his own goods under the pretense that they are the goods of another man.... ' In 19th century cases, trademark infringement embodied much of the elements

44

of fraud and deceit from which trademark protection developed. That is, the element of fraudulent intent was emphasized over the objective facts of consumer confusion." 1 J. Thomas McCarthy, Trademarks and Unfair Competition § 5.02 (3d ed. 1995) (footnotes omitted).

To this day, trademark owners can assert common law claims to protect their trade identity. These claims are variously asserted as suits for unfair competition, palming off, passing off, or deceit, depending upon the jurisdiction and the extent of the violation. In addition to this common law claim under state law, there is now an extensive scheme of federal statutes governing trademarks that are used in interstate and foreign commerce, as well as counterpart state statutes in nearly all jurisdictions. Congress enacted the first trademark statute in 1870, but the law was soon overturned by the Supreme Court on the ground that it exceeded Congress' constitutional powers. The Trade–Mark Cases, 100 U.S. (10 Otto) 82, 25 L.Ed. 550 (1879). This case is reproduced in the Introduction, supra. Congress soon reenacted new trademark legislation, but expressly based its authority on the Commerce Clause. U.S. Const. art. I, § 8, cl. 3. The current version of federal trademark law was enacted in the Lanham Act of 1946, 15 U.S.C. §§ 1051–1127. The Lanham Act has been amended a number of times since then. Together with state common law claims and state trademark statutes, the Lanham Act today provides extensive protection for trademark owners.

Many states have statutes recognizing an even broader claim for "dilution" of distinctive trademarks. These dilution claims do not require the showing of consumer confusion traditionally made in trademark infringement cases. In 1995, Congress enacted legislation providing for a federal claim for dilution of widely recognized trademarks. These claims of state and federal trademark infringement, unfair competition, and dilution offer overlapping protection. Often, several claims can be asserted on one set of facts. Parties seeking to protect their trademarks thus have a variety of options available in terms of registration and enforcement of their rights.

Trademark and unfair competition law further important interests of both sellers of goods and services and of consumers. First, these areas of law protect the good will that is, for many businesses, their most valuable asset. Sellers of goods and services develop good will through lengthy and reliable production, extensive advertising and marketing, and other expenditures of time, money, and resources. Trademark and unfair competition laws protect prior investments in good will and provide an incentive for further investments. Second, the law in this area prevents counterfeiters, pirates, and other imitators from benefitting from the good will of others; in other words, the law prevents unjust enrichment. Third, trademark and unfair competition law protect consumers from deception or confusion as to the source or origin of goods and services. Permitting an imitator to sell its goods or services as those of a recognized products works a fraud upon the consuming public.

Although there are good reasons to provide protection for trademarks, there is a balance of interests in this field as in other areas of intellectual property law. For example, no one is entitled to a monopoly on the name of a product—such as "cola" or "automobile." These words are necessary to identify the product being sold, and permitting any one producer to monopolize these terms would give that firm an unfair advantage in the market. Similarly, if a firm chooses a highly descriptive word as its trademark, it will be entitled to less protection that if it selects a more distinctive name. Other firms may, in good faith, seek to use the descriptive term to refer to the product—not to usurp good will or confuse consumers. Thus, a balance must be struck in trademark law between the rights of trademark owners and the rights of those who would use the terms for which a monopoly is sought.

WILLIAM R. WARNER & CO. v. ELI LILLY & CO.

Supreme Court of the United States, 1924.
265 U.S. 526, 44 S.Ct. 615, 68 L.Ed. 1161.

MR. JUSTICE SUTHERLAND delivered the opinion of the court:

Respondent is a corporation engaged in the manufacture and sale of pharmaceutical and chemical products. In 1899 it began and has ever since continued to make and sell a liquid preparation of quinine, in combination with other substances, including yerba-santa and chocolate, under the name of Coco–Quinine.

Petitioner also is a pharmaceutical and chemical manufacturer. The Pfeiffer Chemical Company, Searle & Hereth Company, and petitioner are under the same ownership and control. The first-named company, in 1906, began the manufacture of a liquid preparation which is substantially the same as respondent's preparation, and which was put upon the market under the name of Quin–Coco. Two years later the Searle & Hereth Company engaged in the manufacture of the preparation, which ever since has been sold and distributed by petitioner.

This suit was brought in the Federal district court for the eastern district of Pennsylvania by respondent, to enjoin petitioner from continuing to manufacture and sell the preparation if flavored or colored with chocolate; and also from using the name "Quin–Coco," on the ground that it was an infringement of the name "Coco–Quinine," to the use of which respondent had acquired an exclusive right. The district court decided against respondent upon both grounds. 268 Fed. 156. On appeal the court of appeals ruled with the district court upon the issue of infringement, but reversed the decree upon that of unfair competition. 275 Fed. 752.

The entire record is here, and both questions are open for consideration.

First. We agree with the courts below that the charge of infringement was not sustained. The name "Coco–Quinine" is descriptive of the ingredients which enter into the preparation. The same equally true of the name "Quin–Coco." A name which is merely descriptive of the ingredients, qualities, or characteristics of an article of trade cannot be appropriated as a trademark and the exclusive use of it afforded legal protection. The use of a similar name by another to truthfully describe his own product does not constitute a legal or moral wrong, even if its effect be to cause the public to mistake the origin or ownership of the product.

Second. The issue of unfair competition, on which the courts below differed, presents a question of more difficulty. The testimony is voluminous, more than two hundred witnesses having been examined; but, since the question with which we are now dealing is primarily one of fact, we have found it necessary to examine and consider it. Nothing is to be gained by reviewing the evidence at length, and we shall do no more than summarize the facts upon which we have reached our conclusions.

The use of chocolate as an ingredient has a threefold effect: It imparts to the preparation a distinctive color and a distinctive flavor, and, to some extent, operates as a medium to suspend the quinine and prevent its precipitation. It has no therapeutic value, but it supplies the mixture with a quality of palatability for which there is no equally satisfactory substitute. Respondent, by laboratory experiments, first developed the idea of the addition of chocolate to the preparation for the purpose of giving it a characteristic color and an agreeable flavor. There was at the time no liquid preparation of quinine on the market containing chocolate, though there is evidence that it was sometimes so made up by druggists when called for. There is some evidence that petitioner endeavored by experiments to produce a preparation of the exact color and taste of that produced by respondent; and there is evidence in contradiction. We do not, however, regard it as important to determine upon which side lies the greater weight. Petitioner, in fact, did produce a preparation by the use of chocolate so exactly like that of respondent that they were incapable of being distinguished by ordinary sight or taste. By various trade methods an extensive and valuable market for the sale of respondent's preparation already had been established when the preparation of petitioner was put on the market. It is apparent, from a consideration of the testimony, that efforts of petitioner to create a market for Quin–Coco were directed not so much to showing the merits of that preparation as they were to demonstrating its practical identity with Coco–Quinine; and, since it was sold at a lower price, inducing the purchasing druggist, in his own interest, to substitute, as far as he could, the former for the latter. In other words, petitioner sought to avail itself of the favorable repute which had been established for respondent's preparation in order to sell its own. Petitioner's salesmen appeared more anxious to convince the druggists with whom they were dealing that Quin–Coco was a good substitute for Coco–Quinine and was cheaper, than they were to independently demonstrate its merits. The evidence establishes by a fair preponderance that some of petitioner's salesmen suggested that, without danger of detection, prescriptions and orders for Coco–Quinine could be filled by substituting Quin–Coco. More often, however, the feasibility of such a course was brought to the mind of the druggist by pointing out the identity of the two preparations and the enhanced profit to be made by selling Quin–Coco because of its lower price. There is much conflict in the testimony; but, on the whole, it fairly appears that petitioner's agents induced the substitution, either in direct terms or by suggestion or insinuation. Sales to druggists are in original bottles, bearing clearly distinguishing labels, and there is no suggestion of deception in those transactions; but sales to the ultimate purchasers are of the bottle; and the testimony discloses many instances of passing off by retail druggists of petitioner's preparation when respondent's preparation was called for. That no deception was practiced on the retail dealers, and that they knew exactly what they were getting, is of no consequence. The wrong was in designedly enabling the dealers to palm off the preparation as that of the respondent. One who induces another to commit a fraud, and furnishes the means of consummating it, is equally guilty and liable for the injury.

The charge of unfair competition being established, it follows that equity will afford relief by injunction to prevent such unfair competition for the future. Several acts of unfair competition having been shown, we are warranted in concluding that petitioner is willing to continue that course of conduct unless restrained. It remains to consider the character and extent of this relief.

Respondent has no exclusive right to the use of its formula. Chocolate is used as an ingredient not alone for the purpose of imparting a distinctive color, but for the purpose, also, of making the preparation peculiarly agreeable to the palate, to say nothing of its effect as a suspending medium. While it is not a medicinal element in the preparation, it serves a substantial and desirable use, which prevents it from being a mere matter of dress. It does not merely serve the incidental use of identifying the respondent's preparation, and it is doubtful whether it should be called a nonessential. The petitioner or anyone else is at liberty, under the law, to manufacture and market an exactly similar preparation containing chocolate, and to notify the public that it is being done. But the imitator of another's goods must sell them as his own production. He cannot lawfully palm them off on the public as the goods of his competitor. The manufacturer or vendor is entitled to the reputation which his goods have acquired, and the public to the means of distinguishing between them and other goods; and protection is accorded against unfair dealing, whether there be a technical trademark or not. The wrong is in the sale of the goods of one manufacture or vendor as those of another. If petitioner had been content to manufacture the preparation and let it make its own way in the field of open and fair competition, there would be nothing more to be said. It was not thus content, however, but availed itself of unfair means, either expressly or tacitly, to impose its preparation on the ultimate purchaser as and for the product of respondent.

Nevertheless, the right to which respondent is entitled is that of being protected against unfair competition, not of having the aid of a decree to create or support, or assist in creating or supporting, a monopoly of the sale of a preparation which everyone, including petitioner, is free to make and vend. The legal wrong does not consist in the mere use of chocolate as an ingredient, but in the unfair and fraudulent advantage which is taken of such use to pass off the product as that of respondent. The use dissociated from the fraud is entirely lawful, and it is against the petitioner, which has shown by its conduct that it is not to be trusted. Clearly, the relief should extend far enough to enjoin petitioner and its various agents from, directly or indirectly, representing or suggesting to its customers the feasibility or possibility of passing off Quin–Coco for Coco–Quinine. The court of appeals held that petitioner should be unconditionally enjoined from the use of chocolate. We think this goes too far; but, having regard to the past conduct of petitioner, the practices of some druggists to which it has led, and the right of respondent to an effective remedy, we think the decree fairly may require that the original packages sold to druggists shall not only bear labels clearly distinguishing petitioner's bottled product from the bottled product of respondent, but that the preparation is not to be sold or dispensed as Coco–Quinine, or to be used for the latter. With these general suggestions, the details and form of the injunction can be more satisfactorily determined by the district court. The decree of the Court of Appeals is reversed and the cause remanded to the District Court for further proceedings in conformity with this opinion.

Notes

1.   What relief did the plaintiff obtain in this case? Do you think it was satisfied with the relief it obtained? Should it obtain any more extensive relief? How broad is trademark protection as compared to the scope of copyright protection, as illustrated by *Baker v. Selden, supra* Chapter 1?

2.   What might be some policy rationales for protecting trademarks? Are these policies furthered by the decision in this case? For discussion of trademark policies, see 1 J. Thomas McCarthy, Trademarks and Unfair Competition §§ 1.01, 1.02, 2.01 (3d ed. 1995); Restatement (Third) of Unfair Competition § 1, comments a, d–g (1995).

3.   Are consumers harmed by the defendant's conduct in this case?

4.   An action for palming off is defined as follows:

One is subject to liability to another ... if, in connection with the marketing of goods or services, the actor makes a representation likely to deceive or mislead prospective purchasers by causing the mistaken belief that the actor's business is the business of the other, or that the actor is the agent, affiliate, or associate of the other, or that the goods or services that the actor markets are produced, sponsored, or approved by the other.

Restatement (Third) of Unfair Competition § 4 (1995).

B.   VALIDITY OF MARKS—THE "SPECTRUM OF DISTINCTIVENESS"

KING–SEELEY THERMOS CO. v. ALADDIN INDUSTRIES, INC.

United States Court of Appeals, Second Circuit, 1963.
321 F.2d 577.

LEONARD P. MOORE, CIRCUIT JUDGE.

This action brought by appellant King–Seeley Thermos Co. (King–Seeley) to enjoin the defendant, Aladdin Industries, Incorporated from threatened infringement of eight trademark registrations for the word "Thermos" owned by appellant. Defendant answered, acknowledging its intention to sell its vacuum-insulated containers as "thermos bottles", asserted that the term "thermos" or "thermos bottle" is a generic term in the English language, asked that plaintiff's registrations of its trademark "Thermos" be cancelled and that it be adjudicated that plaintiff have no trademark rights in the word "thermos" on its vacuum bottles. The trial court held that plaintiff's registrations were valid but that the word "thermos" had become "a generic descriptive word in the English language * * * as a synonym for 'vacuum insulated' container." 207 F.Supp. 9.

The facts are set out at great length in the comprehensive and well-reasoned opinion of the district court and will not be detailed here. In that opinion, the court reviewed King–Seeley's corporate history and its use of the trademark "Thermos". He found that from 1907 to 1923, King–Seeley undertook advertising and educational campaigns that tended to make "thermos" a generic term descriptive of the product rather than of its origin. This consequence flowed from the corporation's attempt to popularize "Thermos bottle" as the name of that product without including any of the generic terms then used, such as "Thermos vacuum-insulated bottle". The court found that by 1923 the word "thermos" had acquired firm roots as a descriptive or generic word.

At about 1923, because of the suggestion in an opinion of a district court that "Thermos" might be a descriptive word, King–Seeley adopted the use of the word "vacuum" or "vacuum bottle" with the word "Thermos". Although "Thermos" was generally recognized in the trade as a trademark, the corporation did police the trade and notified those using "thermos" in a descriptive sense that it was a trademark. It failed, however, to take affirmative action to seek out generic uses by non-trade publications and protested only those which happened to come to its attention. Between 1923 and the early 1950's the generic use of "thermos" had grown to a marked extent in non-trade publications and by the end of this period there was wide-spread use by the unorganized public of "thermos" as a synonym for "vacuum insulated." The court concluded that King–Seeley had failed to use due diligence to rescue "Thermos" from becoming a descriptive or generic term.

Between 1954 and 1957, plaintiff showed awareness of the widespread generic use of "thermos" and of the need to educate the public to the word's trademark significance. It diversified its products to include those not directly related to containers designed to keep their contents hot or cold. It changed its name from the American Thermos Bottle Company to The American Thermos Products Company and intensified its policing activities of trade and non-trade publications. The court found, however, that the generic use of "thermos" had become so firmly impressed as a part of the everyday language of the American public that plaintiff's extraordinary efforts commencing in the mid–1950's came too late to keep "thermos" from falling into the public domain. The court also held that appellant's trademarks are valid and because there is an appreciable, though minority, segment of the consumer public which knows and recognizes plaintiff's trademarks, it imposed certain restrictions and limitations on the use of the word "thermos" by defendant.

We affirm the district court's decision that the major significance of the word "thermos" is generic. No useful purpose would be served by repeating here what is fully documented in the opinion of the court below.

Appellant's primary protest on appeal is directed at the district court's finding that "The word 'thermos' became a part of the public domain because of the plaintiff's wide dissemination of the word 'thermos' used as a synonym for 'vacuum-insulated' and as an adjectival-noun, 'thermos', through its educational and advertising campaigns and because of the plaintiff's lack of reasonable diligence in asserting and protecting its trademark rights in the word 'Thermos' among the members of the unorganized public, exclusive of those in the trade, from 1907 to the date of this action." 207 F.Supp. at 14.

We are not convinced that the trademark's loss of distinctiveness was the result of some failure on plaintiff's part. Substantial efforts to preserve the trademark significance of the word were made by plaintiff, especially with respect to members of the trade. However, there was little they could do to prevent the public from using "thermos" in a generic rather than a trademark sense. And whether the appropriation by the public was due to highly successful educational and advertising campaigns or to lack of diligence in policing or not is of no consequence; the fact is that the word "thermos" had entered the public domain beyond recall. Even as early as 1910 plaintiff itself asserted that "Thermos had become a household word."

Judge Anderson found that although a substantial majority of the public knows and uses the word "thermos", only a small minority of the public knows that this word has trademark significance. He wrote at 207 F.Supp. 21–22:

"The results of the survey (conducted at the behest of the defendant) were that about 75% of adults in the United States who were familiar with containers that keep the contents hot or cold, call such a container a 'thermos'; about 12% of the adult American public know that 'thermos' has a trade-mark significance, and about 11% use the term 'vacuum bottle'. This is generally corroborative of the court's conclusions drawn from the other evidence, except that such other evidence indicated that a somewhat larger minority than 12% was aware of the trade-mark meaning of 'thermos'; and a somewhat larger minority than 11% used the descriptive term 'vacuum' bottle or other container.''

The record amply supports these findings.

Appellant argues that the court below misapplied the doctrine of the *Aspirin* and *Cellophane* cases. Its primary contention is that in those cases, there was no generic name, such as vacuum bottle, that was suitable for use by the general public. As a result, to protect the use of the only word [that] identified the product in the mind of the public would give the owners of the trademark an unfair competitive advantage. The rule of those cases, however, does not rest on this factor. Judge Learned Hand stated the sole issue in *Aspirin* to be: "What do the buyers understand by the word for whose use the parties are contending? If they understand by it only the kind of goods sold, then, I take it, it makes no difference whatever what efforts the plaintiff has made to get them to understand more." 272 F. at 509. Of course, it is obvious that the fact that there was no suitable descriptive word for either aspirin or cellophane made it difficult, if not impossible, for the original manufacturers to prevent their trademark from becoming generic. But the test is not what is available as an alternative to the public, but what the public's understanding is of the word that it uses. What has happened here is that the public had become accustomed to calling vacuum bottles by the word "thermos". If a buyer walked into a retail store asking for a thermos bottle, meaning any vacuum bottle and not specifically plaintiff's product, the fact that the appellation "vacuum bottle" was available to him is of no significance. The two terms had become synonymous; in fact, defendant's survey showed that the public was far more inclined to use the word "thermos" to describe a container that keeps its contents hot or cold than the phrase "vacuum bottle".

Appellant asserts that the courts in a number of cases have upheld the continued exclusive use of a dual functioning trademark, which both identifies the class of product as well as its source. See, e.g., Standard Brands v. Smidler, 151 F.2d 34 (2 Cir.1945) ("V–8"); Walgreen v. Obear–Nester, 113 F.2d 956 (8 Cir.), cert. denied, 311 U.S. 708, 61 S.Ct. 174, 85 L.Ed. 459 (1940) ("Pyrex"); Marks v. Polaroid Corp., 129 F.Supp. 243 (D.Mass.1955), aff'd 237 F.2d 428 (1 Cir.1956) ("Polaroid"); Q–Tips v. Johnson & Johnson, 108 F.Supp. 845 (D.N.J.1952), aff'd 206 F.2d 144 (3 Cir.), cert. denied, 346 U.S. 867, 74 S.Ct. 106, 98 L.Ed. 377 (1953) ("Q–Tips"); Keebler Weyl Baking Co. v. J. S. Ivins' Son, 7 F.Supp. 211 (E.D.Pa.1934) ("Club Crackers"); Barnes v. Pierce, 164 F. 213 (S.D.N.Y. 1908) ("Argyrol"). As this court recently indicated:

"a mark is not generic merely because it has some significance to the public as an indication of the nature or class of an article. * * *

In order to become generic the principal significance of the word must be its indication of the nature or class of an article, rather than an indication of its origin."

Feathercombs, Inc. v. Solo Products Corp., 306 F.2d 251, 256 (2 Cir.), cert. denied, 371 U.S. 910, 83 S.Ct. 253, 9 L.Ed.2d 170 (1962). But see Marks v. Polaroid Corp., supra, 129 F.Supp. at 270 ("a defendant alleging invalidity of a trademark for genericness must show that to the consuming public as a whole the word has lost all its trademark significance").

Since in this case, the primary significance to the public of the word "thermos" is its indication of the nature and class of an article rather than as an indication of its source, whatever duality of meaning of word still holds for a minority of the public is of little consequence except as a consideration in the framing of a decree. Since the great majority of those members of the public who use the word "thermos" are not aware of any trademark significance, there is not enough dual use to support King–Seeley's claims to monopoly of the word as a trademark.

No doubt, the *Aspirin* and *Cellophane* doctrine can be a harsh one for it places a penalty on the manufacturer who has made skillful use of advertising and has popularized his product. See 3 Callman, Unfair Competition and Trademarks 1149–50 (2d ed. 1950). However, King–Seeley has enjoyed a commercial monopoly of the word "thermos" for over fifty years. During that period, despite its efforts to protect the trademark, the public has virtually expropriated it as its own. The word having become part of the public domain, it would be unfair to unduly restrict the right of a competitor of King–Seeley to use the word.

The court below, mindful of the fact that some members of the public and a substantial portion of the trade still recognize and use the word "thermos" as a trademark, framed an eminently fair decree designed to afford King–Seeley as much future protection as was possible. The decree provides that defendant must invariably precede the use of the word "thermos" by the possessive of the name "Aladdin"; that the defendant must confine its use of "thermos" to the lower-case "t"; and that it may never use the words "original" or "genuine" in describing its product. See Bayer Co. v. United Drug Co., 272 F. 505 (S.D.N.Y. 1921); DuPont Cellophane Co. v. Waxed Products Co., 85 F.2d 75 (2 Cir.1936). In addition, plaintiff is entitled to retain the exclusive right to all of its present forms of the trademark "Thermos" without change. These conditions provide a sound and proper balancing of the competitive disadvantage to defendants arising out of plaintiff's exclusive use of the word "thermos" and the risk that those who recognize "Thermos" as a trademark will be deceived.

The courts should be ever alert, as the district court said, "to eliminate confusion and the possibility of deceit." The purchasing public is entitled to know the source of the article it desires to purchase. It is not within our province to speculate whether the dire predictions made by appellant in forceful appellate argument will come to pass. Certain it is that the district court made every endeavor in its judgment to give as much protection to plaintiff as possible. The use by defendant of the now generic word "thermos" was substantially curtailed. Plaintiff's trademark "thermos" was protected in every style of printing except the lower case "thermos" and then the use of the word must be preceded by the possessive of defendant's name "Aladdin" or the possessive of "Aladdin" plus one of defendant's brand names. Any doubt about plaintiff's position in the field is removed by the prohibition against the use by defendant in labeling, advertising or publication of the words "genuine" or "original" in referring to the word "thermos". Furthermore, the district court has given both parties the opportunity to apply to it for such orders and directions as may be warranted in the light of changed circumstances and for the enforcement of compliance or for the punishment of violations. In our opinion the trial court has reached a most equitable solution which gives appropriate consideration to the law and the facts.

Affirmed.

Notes

1.   What policies underlie the court's rule prohibiting a company from maintaining exclusive rights to a generic name? Is the court's focus primarily on the trademark owner's diligence or on the public perception of product names in the marketplace? Will the court's decision and remedy in this case result in some consumer confusion?

2.   Was King–Seeley, the trademark owner in this case, doomed by its own marketing success? How can a company protect itself from a finding that its mark is generic?

3.   How can one establish that a name is generic? Are such well-known brand names as "Xerox" photocopiers and "Tabasco" brand pepper sauce now generic names as a result of their sales success? What about "the sofa & chair company" for furniture? See In re K–T Zoe Furniture, Inc., 16 F.3d 390 (Fed.Cir.1994). Is the term "self-realization" generic as to the services of a Hindu or yoga spiritual organization? See Self–Realization Fellowship Church v. Ananda Church of Self–Realization, 59 F.3d 902 (9th Cir.1995).

4.   Does success necessarily render a mark generic? In Anti–Monopoly, Inc. v. General Mills Fun Group, Inc., 684 F.2d 1316 (9th Cir.1982), the makers of a game called "Anti–Monopoly" brought suit to have the trademark for the game "Monopoly" invalidated. The court noted that 63 percent of those polled recognized "Monopoly" as a trademark and 55 percent correctly identified Parker Brothers as the manufacturer of the game. Nonetheless, the court relied upon other survey evidence to conclude that the primary significance of "monopoly" was as a type of product rather than a brand name, i.e., that "monopoly" was equivalent to terms such as backgammon or poker. Do you agree? For discussion of generic names, see 2 J. Thomas McCarthy, Trademarks and Unfair Competition §§ 12.01 to 12.18 (3d ed. 1995); Restatement (Third) of Unfair Competition § 15 (1995).

ABERCROMBIE & FITCH CO. v.
HUNTING WORLD, INC.

United States Court of Appeals, Second Circuit, 1976.
537 F.2d 4.

FRIENDLY, CIRCUIT JUDGE:

This action in the District Court for the Southern District of New York by Abercrombie & Fitch Company (A & F), owner of well-known stores at Madison Avenue and 45th Street in New York City and seven places in other states, against Hunting World, Incorporated (HW), operator of a competing store on East 53rd Street, is for infringement of some of A & F's registered trademarks using the word "Safari". It has had a long and, for A & F, an unhappy history. On this appeal from a judgment which not only dismissed the complaint but canceled all of A & F's "Safari" registrations, including several that were not in suit, we relieve A & F of some of its unhappiness but not of all.

I.

The complaint, filed in January, 1970, after describing the general nature of A & F's business, reflecting its motto, "The Greatest Sporting Goods Store in the World," alleged as follows: For many years A & F has used the mark "Safari" on articles "exclusively offered and sold by it." Since 1936 it has used the mark on a variety of men's and women's outer garments. Its United States trademark registrations include:

Trademark	Number	Issued	Goods
Safari	358,781	7/26/38	Men's and Women's outer garments, including hats.
Safari Mills	125,531	5/20/19	Cotton Piece goods.
Safari	652,098	9/24/57	Men's and Women's outer garments, including shoes.
Safari	703,279	8/23/60	Woven cloth, sporting goods, apparel, etc.

A & F has spent large sums of money in advertising and promoting products identified with its mark "Safari" and in policing its right in the mark, including the successful conduct of trademark infringement suits. HW, the complaint continued, has engaged in the retail marketing of sporting apparel including hats and shoes, some identified by use of "Safari" alone or by expressions such as "Minisafari" and "Safariland". Continuation of HW's acts would confuse and deceive the public and impair "the distinct and unique quality of the plaintiff's trademark." A & F sought an injunction against infringement and an accounting for damages and profits.

HW filed an answer and counterclaim. This alleged, inter alia, that "the word 'safari' is an ordinary, common, descriptive, geographic, and generic word" which "is commonly used and understood by the public to mean and refer to a journey or expedition, especially for hunting or exploring in East Africa, and to the hunters, guides, men, animals, and equipment forming such an expedition" and is not subject to exclusive appropriation as a trademark. HW sought cancellation of all of A & F's registrations using the word "Safari" on the ground that A & F had fraudulently failed to disclose the true nature of the term to the Patent Office.

* * *

[The court discussed the procedural history, including a prior remand for a trial on the merits.]

Judge Ryan, before whom the action was tried on remand, ruled broadly in HW's favor. He found there was frequent use of the word "Safari" in connection with wearing apparel, that A & F's policing efforts thus had evidently been unsuccessful, and that A & F had itself used the term in a descriptive sense not covered by its registration, e.g., in urging customers to make a "Christmas Gift Safari" to the A & F store. After referring to statements by Judge Lasker that "Safari" was a "weak" mark, the judge found the mark to be invalid. "Safari," the court held, "is merely descriptive and does not serve to distinguish plaintiff's goods as listed on the registration from anybody else's"; while such terms are afforded protection by the Lanham Act if they come to identify the company merchandising the product, rather than the product itself, A & F had failed to establish that this had become the situation with respect to "Safari".[4] The opinion did not discuss A & F's assertion that some of its marks had become incontestable under § 15 of the Lanham Act, 15 U.S.C. § 1065. The court entered a judgment which dismissed the complaint and canceled not only the four registered trademarks in suit but all A & F's other registered "Safari" trademarks. A & F has appealed.

II.

It will be useful at the outset to restate some basic principles of trademark law, which, although they should be familiar, tend to become lost in a welter of adjectives.

The cases, and in some instances the Lanham Act, identify four different categories of terms with respect to trademark protection. Arrayed in an ascending order which roughly reflects their eligibility to trademark status and the degree of protection accorded, these classes are (1) generic, (2) descriptive, (3) suggestive, and (4) arbitrary or fanciful. The lines of demarcation, however, are not always bright. Moreover, the difficulties are compounded because a term that is in one category for a particular product may be in quite a different one for another,[6] because a term may shift from one category to another in light of differences in usage through time,[7] because a term may have one meaning to one group

4. This finding that A & F did not establish "secondary meaning" for its marks is not here disputed.

6. To take a familiar example "Ivory" would be generic when used to describe a product made from the tusks of elephants but arbitrary as applied to soap.

7. See, e.g., Haughton Elevator Co. v. Seeberger, 85 U.S.P.Q. 80 (1950), in which the coined word "Escalator", originally fan-of users and a different one to others, and because the same term may be put to different uses with respect to a single product. In various ways, all of these complications are involved in the instant case.

A generic term is one that refers, or has come to be understood as referring, to the genus of which the particular product is a species. At common law neither those terms which were generic nor those which were merely descriptive could become valid trademarks, see Delaware & Hudson Canal Co. v. Clark, 80 U.S. (13 Wall.) 311, 323, 20 L.Ed. 581 (1872) ("Nor can a generic name, or a name merely descriptive of an article or its qualities, ingredients, or characteristics, be employed as a trademark and the exclusive use of it be entitled to legal protection"). The same was true under the Trademark Act of 1905, Standard Paint Co. v. Trinidad Asphalt Mfg. Co., 220 U.S. 446, 31 S.Ct. 456, 55 L.Ed. 536 (1911), except for marks which had been the subject of exclusive use for ten years prior to its enactment, 33 Stat. 726.[10] While, as we shall see, the Lanham Act makes an important exception with respect to those merely descriptive terms which have acquired secondary meaning, see § 2(f), 15 U.S.C. § 1052(f), it offers no such exception for generic marks. The Act provides for the cancellation of a registered mark if at any time it "becomes the common descriptive name of an article or substance," § 14(c). This means that even proof of secondary meaning, by virtue of which some "merely descriptive" marks may be registered, cannot transform a generic term into a subject for trademark. As explained in J. Kohnstam, Ltd. v. Louis Marx and Company, 280 F.2d 437, 440, 47 CCPA 1080 (1960), no matter how much money and effort the user of a generic term has poured into promoting the sale of its merchandise and what success it has achieved in securing public identification, it cannot deprive competing manufacturers of the product of the right to call an article by its name. We have recently had occasion to apply this doctrine of the impossibility of achieving trademark protection for a generic term, CES Publishing Corp. v. St. Regis Publications, Inc., 531 F.2d 11 (1975). The pervasiveness of the principle is illustrated by a series of well known cases holding that when a suggestive or fanciful term has become generic as a result of a manufacturer's own advertising efforts, trademark protection will be denied save for those markets where the term still has not become generic and a secondary meaning has been shown to continue. A term may thus be generic in one market and descriptive or suggestive or fanciful in another.

The term which is descriptive but not generic[11] stands on a better basis. Although § 2(e) of the Lanham Act, 15 U.S.C. § 1052, forbids the

ciful, or at the very least suggestive, was held to have become generic.

10. Some protection to descriptive marks which had acquired a secondary meaning was given by the law of unfair competition. The Trademark Act of 1920 permitted registration of certain descriptive marks which had acquired secondary meaning, see Armstrong Paint & Varnish Works v. Nu–Enamel Corp., 305 U.S. 315, 59 S.Ct. 191, 83 L.Ed. 195 (1938).

11. See, e.g., W. E. Bassett Co. v. Revlon, Inc., 435 F.2d 656 (2 Cir.1970). A commentator has illuminated the distinction with an example of the "Deep Bowl Spoon": "Deep Bowl" identifies a significant characteristic of the article. It is "merely descrip-

registration of a mark which, when applied to the goods of the applicant, is "merely descriptive," § 2(f) removes a considerable part of the sting by providing that "except as expressly excluded in paragraphs (a)-(d) of this section, nothing in this chapter shall prevent the registration of a mark used by the applicant which has become distinctive of the applicant's goods in commerce" and that the Commissioner may accept, as prima facie evidence that the mark has become distinctive, proof of substantially exclusive and continuous use of the mark applied to the applicant's goods for five years preceding the application. As indicated in the cases cited in the discussion of the unregistrability of generic terms, "common descriptive name," as used in §§ 14(c) and 15(4), refers to generic terms applied to products and not to terms that are "merely descriptive." In the former case any claim to an exclusive right must be denied since this in effect would confer a monopoly not only of the mark but of the product by rendering a competitor unable effectively to name what it was endeavoring to sell. In the latter case the law strikes the balance, with respect to registration, between the hardships to a competitor in hampering the use of an appropriate word and those to the owner who, having invested money and energy to endow a word with the good will adhering to his enterprise, would be deprived of the fruits of his efforts.

The category of "suggestive" marks was spawned by the felt need to accord protection to marks that were neither exactly descriptive on the one hand nor truly fanciful on the other a need that was particularly acute because of the bar in the Trademark Act of 1905, 33 Stat. 724, 726, (with an exceedingly limited exception noted above) on the registration of merely descriptive marks regardless of proof of secondary meaning. See Orange Crush Co. v. California Crushed Fruit Co., 54 App.D.C. 313, 297 F. 892 (1924). Having created the category the courts have had great difficulty in defining it. Judge Learned Hand made the not very helpful statement: It is quite impossible to get any rule out of the cases beyond this: That the validity of the mark ends where suggestion ends and description begins. Franklin Knitting Mills, Inc. v. Fashionit Sweater Mills, Inc., 297 F. 247, 248 (S.D.N.Y.1923), aff'd per curiam, 4 F.2d 1018 (2 Cir.1925), a statement amply confirmed by comparing the list of terms held suggestive with those held merely descriptive in 3 Callmann, Unfair Competition, Trademarks and Monopolies § 71.2 (3d ed.). Another court has observed, somewhat more usefully, that: A term is suggestive if it requires imagination, thought and perception to reach a conclusion as to the nature of goods. A term is descriptive if it forthwith conveys an immediate idea of the ingredients, qualities or characteristics of the goods. Stix Products, Inc. v. United Merchants & Manufacturers Inc., 295 F.Supp. 479, 488 (S.D.N.Y.1968) a formulation deriving from Gener-

tive" of the goods, because it informs one that they are deep in the bowl portion.... It is not, however, "the common descriptive name" of the article (since) the implement is not a deep bowl, it is a spoon.... "Spoon" is not merely descriptive of the article it identifies the article (and therefore) the term is generic. Fletcher, Actual Confusion as to Incontestability of Descriptive Marks, 64 Trademark Rep. 252, 260 (1974). On the other hand, "Deep Bowl" would be generic as to a deep bowl.

al Shoe Corp. v. Rosen, 111 F.2d 95, 98 (4 Cir.1940). Also useful is the approach taken by this court in Aluminum Fabricating Co. of Pittsburgh v. Season–All Window Corp., 259 F.2d 314 (2 Cir.1958), that the reason for restricting the protection accorded descriptive terms, namely the undesirability of preventing an entrant from using a descriptive term for his product, is much less forceful when the trademark is a suggestive word since, as Judge Lumbard wrote, 259 F.2d at 317: The English language has a wealth of synonyms and related words with which to describe the qualities which manufacturers may wish to claim for their products and the ingenuity of the public relations profession supplies new words and slogans as they are needed. If a term is suggestive, it is entitled to registration without proof of secondary meaning. Moreover, as held in the *Season-All* case, the decision of the Patent Office to register a mark without requiring proof of secondary meaning affords a rebuttable presumption that the mark is suggestive or arbitrary or fanciful rather than merely descriptive.

It need hardly be added that fanciful or arbitrary terms[12] enjoy all the rights accorded to suggestive terms as marks without the need of debating whether the term is "merely descriptive" and with ease of establishing infringement.

In the light of these principles we must proceed to a decision of this case.

III.

We turn first to an analysis of A & F's trademarks to determine the scope of protection to which they are entitled. We have reached the following conclusions: (1) applied to specific types of clothing "safari" has become a generic term and "minisafari" may be used for a smaller brim hat; (2) "safari" has not, however, become a generic term for boots or shoes; it is either "suggestive" or "merely descriptive" and is a valid trademark even if "merely descriptive" since it has become incontestable under the Lanham Act; but (3) in light of the justified finding below that "Camel Safari," "Hippo Safari" and "Safari Chukka" were devoted by HW to a purely descriptive use on its boots, HW has a defense against a charge of infringement with respect to these on the basis of "fair use." We now discuss how we have reached these conclusions.

It is common ground that A & F could not apply "Safari" as a trademark for an expedition into the African wilderness. This would be a clear example of the use of "Safari" as a generic term. What is perhaps less obvious is that a word may have more than one generic use. The word "Safari" has become part of a family of generic terms which,

---

12. As terms of art, the distinctions between suggestive terms and fanciful or arbitrary terms may seem needlessly artificial. Of course, a common word may be used in a fanciful sense; indeed one might say that only a common word can be so used, since a coined word cannot first be put to a bizarre use. Nevertheless, the term "fanciful", as a classifying concept, is usually applied to words invented solely for their use as trademarks. When the same legal consequences attach to a common word, i. e., when it is applied in an unfamiliar way, the use is called "arbitrary."

although deriving no doubt from the original use of the word and reminiscent of its milieu, have come to be understood not as having to do with hunting in Africa, but as terms within the language referring to contemporary American fashion apparel. These terms name the components of the safari outfit well-known to the clothing industry and its customers: the "Safari hat", a broad flat-brimmed hat with a single, large band; the "Safari jacket", a belted bush jacket with patch pockets and a buttoned shoulder loop; when the jacket is accompanied by pants, the combination is called the "Safari suit". Typically these items are khaki-colored.

This outfit, and its components, were doubtless what Judge Ryan had in mind when he found that "the word 'safari' in connection with wearing apparel is widely used by the general public and people in the trade." The record abundantly supports the conclusion that many stores have advertised these items despite A & F's attempts to police its mark. In contrast, a search of the voluminous exhibits fails to disclose a single example of the use of "Safari", by anyone other than A & F and HW, on merchandise for which A & F has registered "Safari" except for the safari outfit and its components as described above.

What has been thus far established suffices to support the dismissal of the complaint with respect to many of the uses of "Safari" by HW. Describing a publication as a "Safariland Newsletter", containing bulletins as to safari activity in Africa, was clearly a generic use which is nonenjoinable, see CES Publishing Corp. v. St. Regis Publications, Inc., supra. A & F also was not entitled to an injunction against HW's use of the word in advertising goods of the kind included in the safari outfit as described above. And if HW may advertise a hat of the kind worn on safaris as a safari hat, it may also advertise a similar hat with a smaller brim as a minisafari. Although the issue may be somewhat closer, the principle against giving trademark protection to a generic term also sustains the denial of an injunction against HW's use of "Safariland" as a name of a portion of its store devoted at least in part to the sale of clothing as to which the term "Safari" has become generic.

A & F stands on stronger ground with respect to HW's use of "Camel Safari", "Hippo Safari" and Chukka "Safari" as names for boots imported from Africa. As already indicated, there is no evidence that "Safari" has become a generic term for boots. Since, as will appear, A & F's registration of "Safari" for use on its shoes has become incontestable, it is immaterial (save for HW's contention of fraud which is later rejected) whether A & F's use of "Safari" for boots was suggestive or "merely descriptive."

HW contends, however, that even if "Safari" is a valid trademark for boots, it is entitled to the defense of "fair use" within § 33(b)(4) of the Lanham Act, 15 U.S.C. § 1115(b)(4). That section offers such a defense even as against marks that have become incontestable when the term charged to be an infringement is not used as a trademark "and is used fairly and in good faith only to describe to users the goods and services of such party, or their geographic origin."

Here, Lee Expeditions, Ltd., the parent company of HW, has been primarily engaged in arranging safaris to Africa since 1959; Robert Lee, the president of both companies, is the author of a book published in 1959 entitled "Safari Today The Modern Safari Handbook" and has, since 1961, booked persons on safaris as well as purchased safari clothing in Africa for resale in America. These facts suffice to establish, absent a contrary showing, that defendant's use of "Safari" with respect to boots was made in the context of hunting and traveling expeditions and not as an attempt to garner A & F's good will. The district court here found the HW's use of "Camel Safari", "Hippo Safari", and "Safari Chukka" as names for various boots imported from Africa constituted "a purely descriptive use to apprise the public of the type of product by referring to its origin and use." The court properly followed the course sanctioned by this court in Venetianaire Corp. of America v. A & P Import Co., 429 F.2d 1079, 1081–82 (1970), by focusing on the "use of words, not on their nature or meaning in the abstract" (emphasis in original). When a plaintiff has chosen a mark with some descriptive qualities, he cannot altogether exclude some kinds of competing uses even when the mark is properly on the register, see 3 Callmann, supra, § 85.1; Kiki Undies Corp. v. Alexander's Dep't Stores, Inc., 390 F.2d 604 (2 Cir.1968); contrast Kiki Undies Corp. v. Promenade Hosiery Mills, Inc., 411 F.2d 1097 (2 Cir.1969), cert. dismissed, 396 U.S. 1054, 90 S.Ct. 707, 24 L.Ed.2d 698 (1970). We do not have here a situation similar to those in *Venetianaire*, supra, and Feathercombs, Inc. v. Solo Products Corp., 306 F.2d 251 (2 Cir.1962), in both of which we rejected "fair use" defenses, wherein an assertedly descriptive use was found to have been in a trademark sense. It is significant that HW did not use "Safari" alone on its shoes, as it would doubtless have done if confusion had been intended.

We thus hold that the district court was correct in dismissing the complaint.

IV.

We find much greater difficulty in the court's broad invalidation of A & F's trademark registrations. Section 37 of the Lanham Act, 15 U.S.C. § 1119, provides authority for the court to cancel those registrations of any party to an action involving a registered mark. The cases cited above, establish that when a term becomes the generic name of the product to which it is applied, grounds for cancellation exist. The relevant registrations of that sort are Nos. 358,781 and 703,279. Although No. 358,751 dates back to July 20, 1938, and No. 703,279 was registered on August 23, 1960, and an affidavit under § 15(3), 15 U.S.C. § 1065(3), was filed on October 13, 1965, cancellation may be decreed at any time if the registered mark has become "the common descriptive name of an article or substance," § 14(c), see also § 15(4), 15 U.S.C. §§ 1064(c) and 1065(4). The whole of Registration No. 358,781 thus was properly canceled. With respect to Registration No. 703,279 only a part has become generic[14] and cancellation on that ground should be correspondingly limited.[15] Such partial cancellation, specifically recognized by § 37, accords with the rationale by which a court is authorized to cancel a registration, viz, to "rectify" the register by conforming it to court judgments which often must be framed in something less than an all-or-nothing way.

There remain eight other registrations and those terms not pared from No. 703,279. Three of these registrations, Nos. 652,098, 768,332 and 770,336, and the non-generic portions of No. 703,279 appear to have become incontestable by virtue of the filing of affidavits under § 15(3), of five years continuous use. There is nothing to suggest that the uses included in these registrations, except the uses described above with respect to 703,279 are the common descriptive names of either current fashion styles or African expeditions. The generic term for A & F's "safari cloth Bermuda shorts", for example, is "Bermuda shorts", not "safari"; indeed one would suppose this garment to be almost ideally unsuited for the forest or the jungle and there is no evidence that it has entered into the family for which "Safari" has become a generic adjective. The same analysis holds for luggage, portable grills, and the rest of the suburban paraphernalia, from swimtrunks and raincoats to belts and scarves, included in these registrations. * * *

We hold also that the registrations which have not become incontestable should not have been canceled. "Safari" as applied to ice chests, axes, tents and smoking tobacco does not describe such items. Rather it is a way of conveying to affluent patrons of A & F a romantic notion of high style, coupled with an attractive foreign allusion. * * * It is even wider of the mark to say that "Safari Mills" "describes" cotton piece goods. Such uses fit into the category of suggestive marks. We need not now decide how valuable they may prove to be; it suffices here that they should not have been canceled.

In sum, we conclude that cancellation should have been directed only with respect to No. 358,781 and portions of No. 703,279 and the New York registration. * * *

[On petition for rehearing by A & F, the court concluded "that footnote 14 was in error in indicating that Safari had become generic with respect to shirts. * * * HW's answer adduces nothing to show that Safari has become the 'common descriptive name' for this type of shirt; indeed, HW admits never having advertised its own shirts as such. While HW asserts that 'the record is clear that the upper garment of the safari suit is referred to interchangeably as a safari bush jacket and as a safari shirt,' the cited pages do not bear this out."]

14. To wit, pants, shirts, jackets, coats and hats.

15. Similar partial cancellation is the proper remedy with respect to the New York registration.

Notes

1. *Fanciful or Arbitrary Marks*. As described in this case, the strength of a trademark is frequently analyzed based upon its distinctiveness. The strongest trademarks are fanciful marks, which are words (or other marks) created to serve as trademarks. See, *e.g.*, Eastman Kodak Co. v. Rakow, 739 F.Supp. 116, 117–18 (W.D.N.Y.1989) (Kodak film and photographic supplies); Exxon Corp. v. Xoil Energy Resources, Inc., 552 F.Supp. 1008, 1014 (S.D.N.Y.1981) (Exxon petroleum); Clorox Chemical Co. v. Chlorit Mfg. Corp., 25 F.Supp. 702, 705 (E.D.N.Y.1938) (Clorox bleach). Nearly as strong are arbitrary marks, which are words that have no association with the underlying product or service being marketed. See, *e.g.*, Fleischmann Distilling Corp. v. Maier Brewing Co., 314 F.2d 149, 153–54 (9th Cir.1963) ("Black & White" scotch whiskey), *cert. denied*, 374 U.S. 830, 83 S.Ct. 1870, 10 L.Ed.2d 1053 (1963); Mustang Motels, Inc. v. Patel, 226 U.S.P.Q. 526, 527–28 (C.D.Cal.1985) (Mustang motel); WGBH Educational Foundation Inc. v. Penthouse Int'l Ltd., 453 F.Supp. 1347, 1350 (S.D.N.Y.1978) (Nova television series), *aff'd*, 598 F.2d 610 (2d Cir.1979).

2. *Suggestive Marks*. Suggestive marks have some association with the underlying product or service, but it requires some imagination to see the connection. See, *e.g.*, Citibank, N.A. v. Citibanc Group, Inc., 724 F.2d 1540, 1545 (11th Cir.1984) (Citibank banking services); Cullman Ventures, Inc. v. Columbian Art Works, Inc., 717 F.Supp. 96, 119–20 (S.D.N.Y.1989) ("At–A–Glance" calendars); Louis Rich, Inc. v. Horace W. Longacre, Inc., 423 F.Supp. 1327, 1337–38 (E.D.Pa.1976) ("Gobble Gobble" turkey meat); Bass Buster, Inc. v. Gapen Manufacturing Co., 420 F.Supp. 144, 157 (W.D.Mo. 1976) ("Beetle" fishing lures); In re Wham–O Mfg. Co., 134 U.S.P.Q. 447, 449 (T.T.A.B. 1962) ("Hula hoop" toys).

3. *Descriptive Marks*. Descriptive marks describe some characteristic of the product or service, and are protectable only upon a showing of secondary meaning. See, *e.g.*, Food Fair Stores, Inc. v. Lakeland Grocery Corp., 301 F.2d 156 (4th Cir.1962) ("Food Fair" supermarkets); beef & brew, inc. v. Beef & Brew, Inc., 389 F.Supp. 179, 184–85 (D.Or.1974) ("Beef & Brew" restaurants); In re Wileswood, Inc., 201 U.S.P.Q. 400, 402–04 (T.T.A.B. 1978) ("America's Best Popcorn!" popcorn snacks); In re Sony Corp., 176 U.S.P.Q. 61 (T.T.A.B. 1972) ("Easyload" tape recorders).

4. Where do the following marks fall in the "spectrum of distinctiveness"?

APPLE computers

ARM & HAMMER baking soda

CAMEL cigarettes

CHICKEN OF THE SEA tuna

COPPERTONE suntan lotion

HOLIDAY INN motels

POLAROID cameras

RAISIN BRAN cereal

RICH 'N CHIPS chocolate chip cookies

SANKA coffee

SHELL gasoline

SUN bank

WRANGLER jeans

YUBAN coffee

For further discussion of "the spectrum of distinctiveness," see 1 J. Thomas McCarthy, Trademarks and Unfair Competition §§ 11.01 to 11.28 (3d ed. 1995); Restatement (Third) of Unfair Competition §§ 13–17 (1995).

5. Consider the following recent cases raising issues of trademark validity. *In re Precision Cuts*, 131 Fed.Appx. 288 (Fed Cir. 2005) (addressing "Precision Cuts" mark for barbershop services); *In re Innovation Development Group*, 126 Fed.Appx. 471 (Fed Cir. 2005) (addressing "Tick Tape" mark for a handtool with an adhesive surface that can remove insects from humans or animals); *In Re Stereotaxis, Inc.*, 429 F.3d 1039 (Fed Cir. 2005) (addressing "stereotaxis" mark for medical devices); *Yellow Cab Co. of Sacramento v. Yellow Cab of Elk Grove, Inc.*, 419 F.3d 925 (9th Cir. 2005) (addressing "Yellow Cab" mark for taxicab services); *In Re Steelbuilding.com*, 415 F.3d 1293 (Fed Cir. 2005) (addressing "steelbuildings.com" mark for on-line services including but not limited to sale of steel buildings); *Blendco, Inc. v. Conagra Foods, Inc.*, 132 Fed. Appx. 520 (5th Cir. 2005) (addressing "Better–N–Butter" mark for butter-flavored oil).

6. Is the name "brick oven" generic as applied to the sale of frozen pizzas? *See Schwan's IP, LLC. v. Kraft Pizza Co.*, 460 F.3d 971 (8th Cir. 2006). What about "yellow cab" for taxicab services? *See Yellow Cab Co. of Sacramento v. Yellow Cab of Elk Grove, Inc.*, 419 F.3d 925 (9th Cir. 2005).

C. DESCRIPTIVE MARKS AND SECONDARY MEANING

INTERNATIONAL KENNEL CLUB OF CHICAGO, INC. v. MIGHTY STAR, INC.

United States Court of Appeals, Seventh Circuit, 1988.
846 F.2d 1079.

COFFEY, CIRCUIT JUDGE.

Plaintiff-appellee International Kennel Club of Chicago, Inc. ("IKC"), brought this action against the defendants-appellants Mighty Star, Inc. ("Mighty Star") and DCN Industries, Inc. ("DCN"), alleging that the defendants' use of the plaintiff's "International Kennel Club" name violates section 43(a) of the Lanham Act, 15 U.S.C. § 1125(a), as well as state statutory and common law. The district court granted the plaintiff's motion for a preliminary injunction against the defendants' use of the name. The defendants appeal. We affirm in part, reverse in part, and remand.

I.

A. *Plaintiff's use of the "International Kennel Club" name*

The IKC is an Illinois business corporation that sponsors dog shows in Chicago, and is a "show giving member club" of the American Kennel

Club ("AKC"), a nationwide organization devoted to furthering the "sport" of showing purebred dogs. In addition to giving dog shows, the IKC serves as an information source for AKC activities in Chicago and provides assistance in the pedigree registration of purebred dogs with the AKC. The IKC also sponsors seminars and contributes funds for animal medical research, the Dog Museum of America, and 4–H programs.

The IKC sponsors two major dog shows each year, with the annual spring show having an attendance of between 20,000 to 30,000 people. An average of 1,500 to 2,000 dogs are entered in plaintiff's shows, and for the spring 1986 show, entries came from 36 different states and various Canadian provinces. Persons who attend the plaintiff's shows are often interested in canine-related paraphernalia. While the IKC does not sell such items, private vendors rent booth space at plaintiff's shows at prices ranging from $600 to $800 per booth and sell dog-related items, including stuffed dogs. In 1985 and 1986, the annual revenue from the rental of booth space averaged $60,000.

In an effort to promote its activities, the IKC spent approximately $60,000 of its total revenue of $231,226 for fiscal year 1986 to hire a full-time staff person to handle the advertising of the dog shows and public relations. The paid advertising of the IKC, consisting of advertisements in magazines with a nationwide circulation such as the American Kennel Club Gazette and Dog World Magazine, as well as advertisements in the Chicago-area media, is primarily designed to reach canine enthusiasts (the dog "fancy" in trade parlance). The activities of the IKC have also been covered in a variety of national and local publications.

B. Defendant's decision to market toy dogs under the name "International Kennel Club"

For almost three decades, defendants DCN and its wholly-owned subsidiary Mighty Star have sold stuffed toys in the United States, Canada, England, Australia and Asia. For many years, defendants used the trademark "Polar Puff" to refer to their top of the line products and prominently displayed the trademark on their products and in their advertisements. In the later part of 1985, the defendants decided to add to their product line of stuffed animals a line of stuffed "pedigree" dogs representing different breeds. The defendants state that at the time they had never heard of the plaintiff, and that they chose the name "International Kennel Club" in part because of the international scope of their business, and also because the products were toy dogs. The defendants utilized a marketing strategy whereby purchasers could "register" their dogs with the "International Kennel Club" and receive an "official International Kennel Club membership and pedigree certificate." Part of the defendants' registration strategy was to emphasize that the stuffed canines represent breeds "sanctioned by the International Kennel Club." Although the defendants' International Kennel Club collection of dogs was marketed in conjunction with their "24K Polar Puff" line of toy animals, the advertising for the stuffed dogs did not always use this second name along with the International Kennel Club name. Defendants' instore advertising included plaques, buttons and counter displays, all of which referred to the "International Kennel Club Center," the "International Kennel Club," or the "IKC" without also referring to the defendants' "Polar Puff" trademark.

After choosing the IKC name for its line of toy dogs, Mighty Star's counsel conducted a search of trade directories in major cities as well as a search of federally registered trademarks. The search disclosed two telephone directory listings in Chicago—one for "international kennel" and one for the "International Kennel Club of Chicago." Nevertheless, counsel advised the defendants that the use of the International Kennel Club name would not infringe upon the plaintiff's name given the local scope of the plaintiff's operations and the fact that the plaintiff did not directly compete with Mighty Star or DCN.[3] Thus, the defendants proceeded to market their line of stuffed dogs under that name without contacting the plaintiff to determine if the use of the International Kennel Club name would present a problem of infringement.

C.   Evidence of confusion allegedly caused by the marketing of the defendants' toy dogs under the "International Kennel Club" name

In late March 1986—six months after learning of the plaintiff's existence—the defendants placed a full-page advertisement for their line of stuffed dogs in the April edition of the Good Housekeeping magazine. This advertisement was followed by ads in the June issues of Better Homes and Gardens, Vogue, and Cosmopolitan magazines that reached the public in mid-May. Following the publication of these ads, IKC officials began receiving telephone calls (at a rate of about one per day), letters, and personal inquiries from people expressing confusion as to the plaintiff's relationship to the International Kennel Club stuffed dogs. Prior to the plaintiff's spring 1986 dog show, the IKC's public relations officer, Ms. Johnson, received telephone calls asking to purchase "International Kennel Club stuffed dogs." Ms. Johnson testified that she thought the callers were referring to the stuffed dogs sold by vendors at the plaintiff's shows, and told the callers that the toy dogs would continue to be sold at the show.

The IKC learned of the defendants' line of International Kennel Club toys at the plaintiff's spring dog show on March 29 through 30, 1986. Mr. Auslander, the Secretary and Treasurer of the IKC, testified that a vendor at the show brought one of the defendants' ads to his attention, and asked "why I was involved or why our club was involved in a venture of that type." Thereafter, in early April, the IKC began to receive letters of inquiry concerning the defendants' toy canines. Eight letters requested information on purchasing the dogs, and another from a vendor expressed concern about the IKC's apparent competition. The

---

3. DCN's president testified that he thought "they ... [The International Kennel Club of Chicago, Inc. and the International Kennel] were kennels. So I didn't visualize them to be anything more than that."

latter wrote that "[w]e are concerned as vendors that this practice [the plaintiff's apparent selling of toy dogs] conflicts with the stated aims of your involvement as a purebred dog club." The defendants' Executive Vice–President Sheldon Bernstein testified that neither Mighty Star nor DCN received any letters indicating confusion as to their relationship with the plaintiff.

After the plaintiff's spring 1986 dog show, Mr. Auslander attended between 15 and 20 other dog shows throughout the country during 1986. Auslander testified that at about half of these shows—including the shows in Florida, Wisconsin, Nebraska, Colorado, Massachusetts, California and Illinois—he was questioned about the relationship between the IKC and Mighty Star's toy dogs. Auslander further recounted that members of the board of directors of the American Kennel Club consulted him, expressing concern that the International Kennel Club might be involved in their sale. According to Auslander's testimony, the President of the American Kennel Club reported to Auslander that it had received questions about whether the toys were a fundraising effort for the Dog Museum of America or the American Kennel Club. Thereafter, at the request of the American Kennel Club, the plaintiff placed an ad disclaiming any relationship to the defendants' toys in the July issue of the American Kennel Club Gazette.

* * *

II.

* * *

A. *Likelihood of success on the merits*

In order to prevail in its action under section 43(a) of the Lanham Act, the IKC must establish: (1) that it has a protectible trademark, and (2) a "likelihood of confusion" as to the origin of the defendant's product. * * *

The first step in determining whether an unregistered mark or name is entitled to the protection of the trademark laws is to categorize the name according to the nature of the term itself. Trademarks that are fanciful, arbitrary [i.e. made-up terms like "Kodak"] or suggestive are fully protected, while "descriptive words (e.g., 'bubbly' champagne) may be trademarked only if they have acquired secondary meaning, that is, only if most consumers have come to think of the word not as descriptive at all but as the name of the product." Blau Plumbing, Inc. v. SOS Fix–It, Inc., 781 F.2d 604, 609 (7th Cir.1986). In *Blau*, the court explained that: "The goal of trademark protection is to allow a firm to affix an identifying mark to its product (or service) offering that will, because it is distinctive and no competitor may use a confusingly similar designation, enable the consumer to discover in the least possible amount of time and with the least possible amount of head scratching whether a particular brand is that firm's brand or a competitor's brand. . . . To allow a firm to use as a trademark a generic word, or a descriptive word still understood by the consuming public to describe, would make it difficult for competitors to market their own brands of the same product. Imagine being forbidden to describe a Chevrolet as a 'car' or an 'automobile' because Ford or Chrysler or Volvo had trademarked these generic words, or an after-shave lotion as 'bracing' because the maker of one brand of after-shave lotion had trademarked this descriptive word." (Emphasis added, citations omitted). Hence, although a term's "primary" meaning is merely descriptive, if through use the public has come to identify the term with a plaintiff's product or service, the words have acquired a "secondary meaning" and would become a protectible trademark. Gimix, Inc. v. JS & A Group, Inc., 699 F.2d 901, 907 (7th Cir.1983); Miller Brewing Co. v. G. Heileman Brewing Co., 561 F.2d 75, 79 (7th Cir.1977), cert. denied, 434 U.S. 1025, 98 S.Ct. 751, 54 L.Ed.2d 772 (1978). In other words, " 'secondary meaning' denotes an association in the mind of the consumer between the trade dress [or name] of a product and a particular producer." Vaughan Manufacturing Co. v. Brikam Intern., Inc., 814 F.2d 346, 348 (7th Cir.1987). We agree with the district court that the phrase "International Kennel Club" fits within the category of descriptive words in that it "specifically describes a characteristic or ingredient of an article [or service]." Miller Brewing Co., 561 F.2d at 79. Thus, the "International Kennel Club" name is entitled to trademark protection only if the name has acquired "secondary meaning," i.e. has become distinctive of the plaintiff's goods and/or services.

The defendants claim that the plaintiff's evidence introduced at the preliminary injunction hearing is insufficient to demonstrate that the plaintiff has better than a negligible chance of establishing that the "International Kennel Club" name acquired secondary meaning among the consuming public. "The factors which this court has indicated it will consider on the issue of secondary meaning include '[t]he amount and manner of advertising, volume of sales, the length and manner of use, direct consumer testimony, and consumer surveys.' " Gimix, Inc., 699 F.2d at 907 (quoting Union Carbide Corp. v. Ever–Ready, Inc., 531 F.2d 366, 380 (7th Cir.), cert. denied, 429 U.S. 830, 97 S.Ct. 91, 50 L.Ed.2d 94 (1976)). "Consumer testimony and consumer surveys are the only direct evidence on this question ... [t]he other factors are relevant in a more circumstantial fashion." Id. Not surprisingly, the defendants attack the absence of a consumer survey in the evidence produced by the plaintiff at the preliminary injunction hearing.

Despite this attack, we are not persuaded that the absence of a consumer survey is per se fatal to the plaintiff's request for a preliminary injunction. As noted previously, the trial court merely granted a preliminary injunction; it did not decide the case on the merits after allowing for full discovery. See Hyatt Corp., 736 F.2d at 1156. The IKC may be in a better position to produce a survey at a full trial on the merits. Thus, while the lack of survey evidence fails to support the plaintiff's request for preliminary relief, we are convinced that it does not necessarily destroy the plaintiff's entitlement to that relief: the existence of a survey is only one of the variety of factors outlined in *Gimix* as being relevant to the issue of secondary meaning, and the plaintiff may resort to evidence other than a survey in attempting to demonstrate a "better than negligible" chance of establishing secondary meaning. Moreover, *Gimix* was decided at the summary judgment stage, after the parties had completed their discovery. In contrast, the plaintiff's motion in this case was decided under the time pressures characteristic of preliminary injunction hearings and without the benefit of extensive discovery. For these reasons, the plaintiff's burden at the preliminary injunction stage is slight, and on two separate occasions this court has declined to mandate a consumer survey at this preliminary stage. See A.J. Canfield, 796 F.2d at 908 ("Although Canfield [the plaintiff] did not introduce its own survey, it was not required to do so in order to prevail on a preliminary injunction motion."); Vaughan Manufacturing Co., 814 F.2d at 346.

The remaining factors articulated in *Gimix* as material to the issue of secondary meaning weigh in favor of the trial court's conclusion that the International Kennel Club of Chicago "has acquired a secondary meaning like that among a small but very well-defined group of people in Chicago and elsewhere." In particular, the "amount and manner of advertising" and the "length and manner of use" of the International Kennel Club name yields a better than negligible chance of establishing secondary meaning. With respect to advertising, the plaintiff introduced evidence supporting the inference that the International Kennel Club has developed and maintained its reputation among canine enthusiasts through advertising carefully targeted to reach persons interested in the sport of showing purebred dogs. It has advertised in publications with a continent-wide circulation that are of interest to dog fanciers, including the American Kennel Club Gazette, Kennel Review, and Dog World. And because its shows are held in Chicago, the plaintiff advertises in regional publications of a more general appeal, including the major Chicago newspapers and magazines, as well as various local periodicals. Moreover, the plaintiff mails out as many as 15,000 "premium lists" prior to each show to persons on its mailing lists, and also employs a full-time public relations professional. In its most recent fiscal year, these advertising and public relations expenses have amounted to almost $60,000, or more than 42 percent of the club's total administrative and operating expenses. Viewed another way, these expenses come to more than 25 percent of the club's total revenues; further, the club's activities are often given extensive free publicity. As an example, both major Chicago newspapers have highlighted the plaintiff's dog shows and have designed and promoted special advertising supplements around those columns.

As evidence of secondary meaning, the International Kennel Club also introduced evidence that the club received a number and a variety of letters and phone calls asking about the defendants' toy dogs. In A.J. Canfield, the court found similar evidence—letters and phone calls to Canfield "all searching for the elusive diet chocolate fudge drink" (after a competitor advertised its own "Chocolate Fudge" drink)—"sufficient to show that when consumers think of diet chocolate fudge soda they think of Canfield." 796 F.2d at 907. Likewise, the correspondence directed to the plaintiff provides support for the inference that when dog fanciers see the "International Kennel Club" name, they think of the plaintiff. Finally, the plaintiff has operated under and advertised the "International Kennel Club" name continuously for over 50 years. In our view, the club's half-century use of the name, combined with their advertising, substantial free publicity, and wide-ranging activities in support of dog groups, clearly renders the plaintiff's chances of establishing that the International Kennel Club name has acquired secondary meaning better than negligible. See A.J. Canfield, 796 F.2d 907 (plaintiff's use of the label "chocolate fudge" for 13 years, combined with substantial advertising and free publicity, is sufficient to establish a likelihood of secondary meaning); Vaughan Manufacturing Company, 814 F.2d at 349 (plaintiff's use of its "trade dress" for over 14 years, combined with extensive advertising and evidence of copying, is sufficient to demonstrate a likelihood of secondary meaning).

The second element of section 43(a) liability is the existence of a "likelihood of confusion" as to the origin of the defendant's product. McGraw–Edison Co. v. Walt Disney Productions, 787 F.2d 1163, 1167 (7th Cir.1986). "Whether or not there is a likelihood of confusion is a question of fact as to the probable or actual actions and reactions of prospective purchasers of the goods or services of the parties. A variety of factors may be material in assessing the likelihood of confusion." American International Group, Inc. v. London American International Corp., Ltd., 664 F.2d 348, 351 (2d Cir.1981). See also Henri's Food Products Co., Inc. v. Kraft, Inc., 717 F.2d 352, 354 (7th Cir.1983). In determining a likelihood of confusion, this circuit, applying a slightly modified version of Judge Friendly's analysis in Polaroid Corp. v. Polarad Electronics Corp., 287 F.2d 492, 495 (2d Cir.), cert. denied, 368 U.S. 820, 82 S.Ct. 36, 7 L.Ed.2d 25 (1961), has considered several factors to be important: "The degree of similarity between the marks in appearance and suggestion; the similarity of the products for which the name is used; the area and manner of concurrent use; the degree of care likely to be exercised by consumers; the strength of the complainant's mark; actual confusion; and intent on the part of the alleged infringer to palm off his products as those of another." McGraw–Edison, 787 F.2d at 1167–68 (quoting Helene Curtis Industries, Inc. v. Church and Dwight Co., Inc., 560 F.2d 1325, 1330 (7th Cir.1977), cert. denied, 434 U.S. 1070, 98 S.Ct. 1252, 55 L.Ed.2d 772 (1978)). * * *

Initially, the plaintiff argues that "[p]erhaps the most blatant evidence of the likelihood of confusion is the fact that the defendants have marketed their pedigree toy dogs under a mark that is not merely similar to plaintiff's name, but is actually indistinguishable from it: The International Kennel Club." The defendants point out, however, that the plaintiff typically uses its full name, "International Kennel Club of Chicago" and that it uses the name in conjunction with a wolfhound head logo. In contrast, the defendants' advertisements display its "24K

Polar Puff'' house mark along with the International Kennel Club name. The defendants urge that these differences serve to clearly distinguish the parties' marks, thereby undercutting any possible confusion. [The court concludes that the defendant's mark is similar to the salient portions of the plaintiff's mark] * * *

The plaintiff next asserts that the likelihood of confusion as to the origin of the defendants' product is increased through the "similarity of the products for which the name is used." McGraw–Edison, 787 F.2d at 1167. But the defendants maintain that the plaintiff, whose business primarily involves the promotion and sponsoring of dog shows, is engaged in a totally different business than the defendants, who merely sell toy stuffed dogs and who use different channels of trade and advertising media. Consequently, the defendants argue that the differences in the parties' businesses weigh against the possibility of consumer confusion. The defendants fail to persuade us that these differences are dispositive: we have specifically noted that a plaintiff need not demonstrate that it is in direct competition with an alleged infringer in order to establish likelihood of confusion. * * *

In the case at hand, the "products" of the litigants, while not identical, certainly cannot be considered as unrelated. As such, it is reasonable to infer the public is likely to be confused as to the source of the defendants' stuffed toys. As the plaintiff properly asserts, it is entirely logical for a dog fancier to believe that a well-known kennel club engaged in various dog-related activities might market or sponsor "pedigree" toy dogs representing "officially sanctioned" breeds. (This is particularly true where the seller of the toy dog informs the customer that he can receive a "pedigree registration certificate" from an entity with the same name as the plaintiff.) * * *

The plaintiff also introduced evidence of actual consumer confusion at the preliminary injunction hearing. Although the evidence of "actual confusion" introduced at the hearing was, as the district court put it, "hardly overwhelming," "[t]here can be no more positive or substantial proof of the likelihood of confusion than proof of actual confusion. Moreover, reason tells us that while very little proof of actual confusion would be necessary to prove the likelihood of confusion, an almost overwhelming amount of proof would be necessary to refute such proof." World Carpets, Inc. v. Dick Littrell's New World Carpets, 438 F.2d 482, 489 (5th Cir.1971) (footnote omitted). Indeed, while likelihood of confusion "can be proven without any evidence of actual confusion, such evidence if available, is entitled to substantial weight." Helene Curtis, 560 F.2d at 1330. Cf. 3A Callman Unfair Competition, Trademarks and Monopolies § 20.06 (4th ed. 1983) ("When equitable relief is sought with due promptness, the use of the defendant's mark will have been of such short duration that even if actual confusion has occurred, proof thereof is virtually unobtainable. . . . It is therefore accurate to say that in every case, even one in which a preliminary injunction is sought, actual confusion is the best evidence of likelihood of confusion").

Hence, plaintiff's evidence of actual confusion—accumulated during the relatively brief period of time between the end of March and mid-June of 1986, when defendants' magazine ads reached the newsstands—is entitled to substantial weight in determining the likelihood of plaintiff's succeeding on the merits. Evidence of actual confusion proffered by the plaintiff consisted of the following: (1) the plaintiff's public relations official (Ms. Johnson) testified that she received calls on an almost daily basis from people who expressed confusion as to the plaintiff's relationship to the defendants' stuffed canines; (2) the plaintiff received eight written requests for information about the defendants' products; (3) the plaintiff's secretary-treasurer testified that he was questioned about the plaintiff's connection to the defendants' toys at dog shows throughout the country; (4) the American Kennel Club indicated that it had been questioned about the plaintiff's relationship to the defendants' product.
* * *

Because the unsolicited letters received by the plaintiff merely requested information about purchasing the defendants' stuffed toy dogs, the letters are competent factual evidence of confusion on the part of the authors, and were properly considered by the trial court as evidence of a likelihood of confusion.[6] Given the similarities in the parties' marks and their products, the testimony of plaintiff's employees as to the instances of actual confusion, as well as letters indicating actual confusion, we agree with the plaintiff that there is more than ample support in the record for the trial court's finding that the plaintiff demonstrated a better than negligible chance of establishing the "likelihood of confusion" prong under section 43(a).[7]

B. Balance of harms and adequate remedy at law

[The court finds first that defendant's "blatant use of the plaintiff's name" in a commercial venture with knowledge of plaintiff's prior use, and the resulting loss of control of the plaintiff's reputation, outweighed

6. The defendants attempt to contrast plaintiff's evidence of actual confusion with the letters they received in response to their national advertising. To the date of the preliminary injunction hearing, the defendants received approximately 4,300 letters, none suggesting that the writer believed there was an affiliation between the defendants' stuffed dogs and the plaintiffs. We question the probative value of this "evidence" because even if the authors of those letters mistakenly assumed that the plaintiff has sponsored or licensed the defendants toy dogs, there would be no reason for the writer to mention this fact in a letter to the defendants whose sole purpose was to request to purchase the toy. Thus, we disagree that the letters received by the defendants in response to their ads can be said to amount to a "survey" of the extent of consumer confusion.

7. The defendants maintain that two other factors listed by McGraw as bearing on the question of confusion—the weakness of the plaintiff's mark and the defendants' lack of intent to infringe—weigh against plaintiff's evidence of confusion. Even assuming the validity of this assertion, we are convinced that the district court properly weighed these factors into the equation, and the judge's finding that plaintiff had demonstrated a better than negligible chance of establishing a likelihood of confusion is not an abuse of discretion. In addition, because the plaintiff's state law claims for unfair competition and trademark dilution are "absorbed in a finding that trademark infringement ... exists," James Burrough, Ltd., 540 F.2d at 274 n. 16, a discussion of those claims is unnecessary.

the burden on the defendant if it were ordered to change the name of its product.] * * *

The defendants also assert that the injunction should not have been issued because the plaintiff has an adequate remedy at law. In fact, the defendants argue, the district court's order requiring them to set aside fifty cents per toy as a "licensing fee" will necessarily ensure that the plaintiff is adequately compensated should the plaintiff prevail on the merits. While we agree that the district court's licensing arrangement provides a small measure of protection for the plaintiff, the court approved the arrangement as much for the defendants' benefit as the plaintiff: its primary purpose was to allow the defendants to unload their inventory of IKC toys without removing all the names on the toys. More importantly, this court has: "[o]ften recognized that the damages occasioned by trademark infringement are by their very nature irreparable and not susceptible of adequate measurement for remedy at law. . . . As this court recently explained in Ideal Industries [v. Gardner Bender, Inc., 612 F.2d 1018 (7th Cir.1979)], this readiness to find irreparable injury arises in part from the realization that 'the most corrosive and irreparable harm attributable to trademark infringement is the inability of the victim to control the nature and quality of the defendants' goods. Even if the infringer's products are of high quality, the plaintiff can properly insist that its reputation should not be imperiled by the acts of another.' . . ." Processed Plastic, 675 F.2d at 858 (emphasis added) (citations omitted). We are convinced that the trial court carefully and properly weighed the extent of harm to each party, and we find no error in the court's balancing process. Because the trial judge properly determined that the plaintiff has a better than negligible chance of prevailing on the merits, and that the possibility of the plaintiff incurring irreparable harm is greater than that of the defendants, there is no support in the record for the defendants' allegation that the trial court abused its discretion in granting the requested preliminary relief.

III.

The defendants also challenge the terms and scope of the district court's injunction. Initially, the defendants attempt to hang their hat on their use of a disclaimer in one of their magazine ads, which they argue, if used consistently, would dispel any confusion that may exist as to the origin of the defendants' toy dogs.[9] They urge this court to overturn the trial judge's rejection of their proposal to use the International Kennel Club name in conjunction with such a disclaimer. In fashioning its relief, the district judge stated that "[f]or a while I considered the idea of a

---

9. At oral argument, the defendants maintained that because the letters and calls indicating confusion ceased after defendants' ads with a disclaimer reached the public, there is evidence in the record that their use of disclaimers has in fact remedied any potential confusion. However, as the plaintiff points out, defendants' advertise-ments containing the disclaimer had not run by the time of the hearing, and it is equally reasonable to assume that the complaints ceased because the defendants halted their advertising of the International Kennel Club line in response to the plaintiff's lawsuit.

disclaimer, which the defendant has actually used, but I, as the plaintiff, agree that it is not workable." While some courts have held that a trial court should adopt less drastic interim remedies than an outright injunction where there is an inadequate showing of irreparable injury due to confusion, see Bell and Howell: Mamiya Co. v. Masel Supply Co., 719 F.2d 42, 45–46 (2d Cir.1983), others have rejected the use of a disclaimer as a remedy where, as here, the plaintiffs have demonstrated a likelihood of confusion and resultant harm. See, e.g., Hyatt Corp., 736 F.2d at 1160 (favoring a name change over the use of a disclaimer); Boston Pro Hockey Association v. Dallas Cap & E. Manufacturing, Inc., 510 F.2d 1004, 1013 (5th Cir.), cert. denied, 423 U.S. 868, 96 S.Ct. 132, 46 L.Ed.2d 98 (1975), (holding a proposed disclaimer "insufficient to remedy the illegal confusion."); Marquis Who's Who v. North American Ad Associates, 426 F.Supp. 139, 143, n. 5 (D.D.C.1976), aff'd, 574 F.2d 637 (D.C.Cir.1978); Volkswagenwerk Aktiengesellschaft v. Karadizian, 170 U.S.P.Q. 565, 567 (C.D.Cal.1971).

Additionally, the record reveals that the trial judge considered the use of a disclaimer as a remedy but did not find the proposal workable. For instance, while the defendants selectively used a disclaimer in their magazine advertisements, they failed to do so on the products themselves, the accompanying literature, or in-store advertisements. The defendants also conceded that it would be difficult to ensure the use of disclaimers by their distributors since the defendants had no direct control over the distributors' advertising. Under the circumstances, we refuse to second-guess the court's conclusion that a disclaimer would neither be workable nor effective in eliminating consumer confusion. Especially where the infringement in issue is a verbatim copying of the plaintiff's name, we are convinced that that plaintiff's reputation and goodwill should not be rendered forever dependent on the effectiveness of fineprint disclaimers often ignored by consumers. As Justice Frankfurter explained over 45 years ago: "The protection of trademarks is the laws' recognition of the psychological function of symbols. If it is true that we live by symbols, it is no less true that we purchase goods by them. A trade-mark is a merchandising short-cut which induces a purchaser to select what he wants, or what he has been led to believe he wants. The owner of a trade-mark exploits this human propensity by making every human effort to impregnate the atmosphere of the market with the drawing power of a congenial symbol. Whatever the means employed, the aim is the same—to convey through the mark, in the minds of potential customers, the desirability of the commodity upon which it appears. Once this is attained, the trade-mark owner has something of value. If another poaches upon the commercial magnetism of the symbol he has created, the owner can obtain legal redress." Mishawaka Rubber and Woolen Manufacturing Co. v. S.S. Kresge Co., 316 U.S. 203, 205, 62 S.Ct. 1022, 1024, 86 L.Ed. 1381 (1942).

* * *

AFFIRMED IN PART, REVERSED IN PART, AND REMANDED.

CUDAHY, CIRCUIT JUDGE, dissenting:

This seems to me a strange case of trademark infringement where likelihood of success on the merits and irreparable harm to the plaintiff are both exceedingly unclear. And the majority's rather selective statement of the facts does little to clarify the picture.

There is a loss to society in permitting one user to appropriate a descriptive term to the exclusion of others through the establishment of "secondary meaning." See R. Callmann, 3 The Law of Unfair Competition Trademarks and Monopolies § 19.29, at 109 (1983). Courts should therefore be adequately demanding in setting secondary meaning standards before issuing injunctions in aid of such appropriations.

In the present case, the majority finds that the plaintiff, "International Kennel Club of Chicago," had "better than a negligible chance" of showing that its name has acquired a secondary meaning by virtue of its use for many years, its advertising of semi-annual dog shows directed to a limited group of dog enthusiasts and its maintenance of a 15,000–person mailing list. The plaintiff spent less than $60,000 on advertising and public relations last year. Here the demands on the plaintiff have been so minimal that in the future almost anything will be susceptible to being claimed under the secondary meaning rubric.

The likelihood of confusion is equally uncertain. The plaintiff, a sponsor of live dog shows in Chicago, seeks to enjoin a national manufacturer of stuffed toy dogs. The plaintiff does not manufacture or distribute toy dogs, or goods of any kind. The closest the plaintiff comes to stuffed dogs is to rent booth space at its shows to merchants who may sell them along with a variety of other dog-related items. Thus, although the defendant's mark bears a high degree of similarity to the plaintiff's name, their respective products and services do not compete and are related only by their connection to the broad theme of "dogs." Further, evidence of actual consumer confusion about the origin of the toy dogs is, in the words of the district court, "hardly overwhelming."

The plaintiff has not suggested any economic harm it may be suffering as a result of confusion with the defendant's operation. There is no complaint, for example, of diminishing participation, by either dog breeders or vendors, in its dog shows. And evidence of potential harm to its reputation seems to center on a few letters and conversations inquiring into its connection with defendant's sales campaigns. The plaintiff alleges in effect that the inquiries are mildly embarrassing (or perhaps gently demeaning) because they taint it with commercialism. It is surely not clear to me, however, how any real harm is being done. In contrast, the defendant has expended hundreds of thousands of dollars advertising its line of stuffed dogs and thus will suffer considerable economic harm from this injunction.

To establish secondary meaning (and the right to appropriate descriptive terms from the public domain) it should be requisite either to show substantial expenditures for advertising—a real investment in the claimed secondary meaning—or actual evidence that consumers associate the descriptive term with the product or service, or both. In lieu of consumer surveys, letters or conversations might be acceptable if genuinely relevant and produced in sufficient volume. Here none of these paths has been followed in any kind of persuasive way. We are thus blazing an uncertain trail, which may allow prior users of the most descriptive of terms to win wide-ranging injunctions with only nominal showings of either harm or confusion. If this case can be a winner, it is difficult to imagine one that could lose.

In addition, I do not understand why a disclaimer would not do the job quite satisfactorily here. It is not necessary to crack walnuts with a sledgehammer. Any ill effects on the plaintiff of the defendant's advertising could be remedied by disclaimer. I do not discount the trial court's discretion in these matters, but I am not persuaded it can justify a preliminary injunction (for which no bond has been posted) here.

I therefore respectfully dissent.

Notes

1. Does the plaintiff in this case have a weak or a strong mark? What role should the strength of the plaintiff's mark play in a trademark case?

2. The "likelihood of confusion" standard for trademark infringement is discussed in detail in Chapter 4. Does the plaintiff's showing in this case seem very strong? What factors favor the defendant? What policies may have motivated the court to rule in the plaintiff's favor?

3. Courts routinely grant injunctive relief in trademark infringement cases. Why are license fees or disclaimers an inadequate remedy in most trademark cases?

4. A descriptive mark can receive trademark protection if it has attained secondary meaning, as illustrated by *International Kennel Club*. See also Car Freshner Corp. v. Turtle Wax, Inc., 268 F.Supp. 162 (S.D.N.Y.1967) (plaintiff seller of automotive products under the descriptive name "CAR FRESHNER" had established secondary meaning and was entitled to enjoin defendants from using that mark to sell competing products); Nissen Trampoline Co. v. International Tram–Po–Line Mfrs., Inc., 190 F.Supp. 238 (E.D.N.Y.1960) (same result in case of "TRAMPOLINE"). At some point, can these terms become generic? For further discussion of descriptive marks and secondary meaning, see 1 J. Thomas McCarthy, Trademarks and Unfair Competition §§ 11.05 to 11.09, 15.01 to 15.27 (3d ed. 1995); Restatement (Third) of Unfair Competition §§ 13–14 (1995).

5. Geographic terms and surnames can also function as trademarks if they have developed secondary meaning, *i.e.*, if their primary significance is to serve as an indication of the source of the goods or services. See In re Nantucket, 677 F.2d 95, 99 (C.C.P.A. 1982) (geographic terms); Interpace Corp. v. Lapp, Inc., 574 F.Supp. 1072 (D.N.J.1982), rev'd on other grounds, 721 F.2d 460 (3d Cir.1983); see generally 2 J. Thomas McCarthy, Trademarks and Unfair Competition §§ 13.01 to 14.14 (3d ed. 1995); Restatement (Third) of Unfair Competition § 14 (1995).

6. How much protection should be given to a car dealer, steak house, or dry cleaning business that adopts a geographic name (such as the name of the city or neighborhood in which it is located) as a trademark?

7. Does registration of a descriptive mark abroad satisfy the acquired distinctiveness requirement? *See In Re Rath*, 402 F.3d 1207 (Fed Cir. 2005). What showing must be made to establish secondary meaning in the context of an internet-based business? *See In Re Steelbuilding.com*, 415 F.3d 1293 (Fed Cir. 2005). What about a non-profit advocacy group? *See Flynn v. Health Advocate, Inc.*, 169 Fed. Appx. 99 (3d Cir. 2006) (group called "Healthcare Advocates").

D. SURNAMES

DAVID B. FINDLAY, INC. v. FINDLAY

Court of Appeals of New York, 1966.
18 N.Y.2d 12, 271 N.Y.S.2d 652, 218 N.E.2d 531.

KEATING, JUDGE.

When should a man's right to use his own name in his business be limited? This is the question before us.

The individual plaintiff David B. Findlay ("David") and the individual defendant Walstein C. Findlay ("Wally") are brothers. The Findlay art business was founded in 1870 by their grandfather in Kansas City. Their father continued and expanded the business with a Chicago branch managed by Wally and a New York branch established and managed by David on East 57th Street. In 1936 the Kansas City gallery was closed and in 1938, after a dispute, the brothers separated. By agreement David, as president of Findlay Galleries, Inc., and owner of nearly all of the stock of the original Missouri corporation, sold to Wally individually the Chicago gallery and allowed Wally to use the name "Findlay Galleries, Inc." in the conduct of his business in Chicago. Wally organized an Illinois corporation under the name "Findlay Galleries, Inc." in 1938 and has since operated his Chicago gallery. He also opened, in 1961, a Palm Beach, Florida, gallery.

David, since the separation, has operated his gallery on East 57th Street in Manhattan. For many years he has conducted his business on the second floor of 11–13 East 57th Street.

In October, 1963, Wally purchased the premises at 17 East 57th Street and informed David of his plans to open an art gallery. David objected to Wally's use of the name "Findlay" on 57th Street and by letter announced he would 'resist any appropriation by you in New York of the name Findlay in connection with a gallery * * * any funds spent by you to establish a gallery at 17 East 57th Street under the name Findlay Galleries, Inc. (or any variation thereof using the name Findlay) are spent at your peril.' David also, in self-defense and in an effort to survive, rented additional space at 15 East 57th Street so as to have a street level entrance.

David's objections and pleas seemed to have some effect on Wally. As renovation on the building was carried on from October, 1963 to September, 1964, a large sign proclaimed the coming opening of "W. C. F. Galleries, Inc." There was also a display and listing in the New York Telephone directory under the same name and similar advertisements in other publications. However, in September, 1964 the sign was suddenly changed to announce the imminent opening of "Wally Findlay Galleries" affiliated with "Findlay Galleries, Inc." David immediately sought an injunction. Wally went ahead with his opening and erected a sidewalk canopy from the curb to the building displaying the name "Wally Findlay Galleries."

The trial court made very detailed findings and, based on them, enjoined defendant from using the names "Wally Findlay Galleries", "Findlay Galleries" and any other designation including the name "Findlay" in the conduct on an art gallery on East 57th Street. The Appellate Division has affirmed on the trial court's findings and we find evidence to sustain them.

The trial court concluded that if injunctive relief were not granted, plaintiff would continue to be damaged by confusion and diversion and would suffer great and irreparable loss in his business and in his name and reputation. In his quarter of a century on East 57th Street David has established a valuable good will and reputation as an art dealer. Through hard work, business ability and expenditure of large sums of money, David has reached the level where a significant portion of his business comes from people who have been referred to him by others and told to go to "Findlay's on 57th St."

The effect of Wally's new gallery, with its long canopy, can only be that those looking for "Findlay's on 57th St." will be easily confused and find their way into Wally's rather than David's gallery. Though Wally perhaps did not deliberately set out to exploit David's good will and reputation, the trial court found, and we agree, that such a result would follow if Wally were permitted to operate a gallery under the name "Wally Findlay Galleries" next door to David.

There were numerous instances of people telephoning or asking at David's for personnel of Wally's or for art work exhibited at Wally's. Many regular customers congratulated David on the opening of "his" new gallery next door. Moreover, advertisements frequently appeared on the same pages of the local press for "Findlay Galleries", "Findlay's", or "Wally Findlay Galleries" thus making it very difficult to tell whose advertisement it was. Even the art editors and reporters referred to Wally as "Findlay Galleries"—the name used for many years by David— or as "the new Findlay Gallery."

It is apparent that confusion has and must result from Wally's opening next to David. This is compounded by the fact that both brothers have for years specialized in French impressionist and post-impressionist painters. Therefore, quite naturally, both brothers have in the past dealt in the works of such famous deceased painters as Modigliani, Degas, Renoir, Gauguin, Bonnard, Braque, Monet and many others.

Although someone seeking a Renoir from David is unlikely to purchase a Degas from Wally, it is likely that with respect to some of the lesser-known impressionists such diversion might happen. More important, someone wishing to own a nude by Modigliani, a dancer by Degas or a portrait of a girl by Renoir would not necessarily have a particular painting in mind and would likely purchase any of these species, whether it be in Wally's or David's. The items sold by the two brothers are not unique, nonsubstitutional works.

Moreover, art, particularly modern art, is sold only to those who see it. Works of art are sold to those who cross the threshold of the art gallery and the more people you get into your gallery, the more art you will sell. To this end David has worked hard to develop the name "Findlay's on 57th St." and bring in customers. Many people who have the finances to purchase art do not necessarily have the knowledge to distinguish between the works of all the various painters represented by galleries such as Wally's or David's. For this reason they rely on the reputation of the gallery. David has spent over 25 years in developing satisfied customers who will tell others to go to "Findlay's on 57th St." This good will brings in customers who look for a work of art that suits their fancy and, if Wally were to continue to use the name Findlay, it is inevitable that some would walk into Wally's by mistake and would have their tastes satisfied there, to David's great harm.

The so-called "sacred right" theory that every man may employ his own name in his business is not unlimited. Moreover, fraud or deliberate intention to deceive or mislead the public are not necessary ingredients to a cause of action. (See Higgins Co. v. Higgins Soap Co., 144 N.Y. 462, 468, 39 N.E. 490, 491, 27 L.R.A. 42.)

The present trend of the law is to enjoin the use even of a family name when such use tends or threatens to produce confusion in the public mind (Sullivan v. Sullivan Radio & T.V., 1 A.D.2d 609, 152 N.Y.S.2d 227). Whether this confusion should be satisfied by misplaced phone calls or confusing advertisements alone we do not decide because there has been a finding that diversion, as well as confusion, will exist if Wally is not enjoined. Thus it is clear that the "confusion" with which we are dealing includes impairment of good will of a business.

In Meneely v. Meneely, 62 N.Y. 427, this court noted that one can use his own name provided he does not resort to any artifice or contrivance for the purpose of producing the impression that the establishments are identical, or do anything calculated to mislead the public.

Thirty-five years later, we noted that, as a general principle of law, one's name is his property and he is entitled to its use. However, it was equally a principle of law that no man can sell his goods as those of another. "He may not through unfairness, artifice, misrepresentation or fraud, injure the business of another, or induce the public to believe his product is the product of that other." (World's Dispensary Medical Ass'n v. Pierce, 203 N.Y. 419, 424, 96 N.E. 738, 740.)

* * *

In the present case Wally knew that David had conducted his business and built a reputation under the names "Findlay Galleries" and "Findlay's on 57th St." and that many years of effort and expenses had gone into promoting the name of "Findlay" in the art business on 57th Street. He also knew that people would come into his gallery looking for "Findlay Galleries" and even instructed his employees on this matter before he opened. Nonetheless he opened his gallery next door to David dealing in substantially similar works and using the name Findlay. The *bona fides* of Wally's intentions do not change the applicable principles. The objective facts of this unfair competition and injury to plaintiff's business are determinative, not the defendant's subjective state of mind. Wally's conduct constituted unfair competition and an unfair trade practice, and it is most inequitable to permit Wally to profit from his brother's many years of effort in promoting the name of "Findlay" on 57th Street. Wally should use any name other than "Findlay" in the operation of his business next door to his brother.

In framing its injunction the trial court went no farther than was necessary to avoid the harm threatened. It prevented the use of the name Findlay but limited this to the particular area in which its use would cause confusion and diversion—East 57th Street. It resolved the conflict with as little injury as possible to Wally. The proof showed and the trial court found that many, if not most of the leading art galleries, are now located on Madison Avenue and in the area of the 60's, 70's and 80's in New York City. Wally could probably have found an appropriate place for his New York gallery other than at 17 East 57th Street and can now either find such another location or remain where he is under some name such as "W. C. F. Galleries".

The decision in this case is in accord with the directions of our court: "The defendant has the right to use his name. The plaintiff has the right to have the defendant use it in such a way as will not injure his business or mislead the public. Where there is such a conflict of rights, it is the duty of the court so to regulate the use of his name by the defendant that, due protection to the plaintiff being afforded, there will be as little injury to him as possible. * * *

Burke, Judge (dissenting).

This court decided in Meneely v. Meneely, 62 N.Y. 427, 431–432 more than 90 years ago—and the rule, well settled then, has been consistently followed ever since—that "every man has the absolute right to use his own name in his own business, even though he may thereby interfere with or injure the business of another person bearing the same name, provided he does not resort to any artifice or contrivance for the purpose of producing the impression that the establishments are identical, or do anything calculated to mislead. Where the only confusion

created is that which results from the similarity of the names the courts will not interfere. A person cannot make a trade mark of his own name, and thus obtain a monopoly of it which will debar all other persons of the same name from using their own names in their own business."
* * *

In the case before us, there is not the slightest support for any claim of dishonesty or deceit, not the slightest suggestion of a design on the part of the defendant to defraud or mislead the public or to palm off his business as that of his brother. And this was the view of the Trial Judge below who granted the injunction solely on the strength of the possible confusion which would result from the defendant's use of his own name. Thus, declaring that he did "not believe that Wally set out to deliberately exploit this goodwill and business reputation of the plaintiffs", (47 Misc.2d 649, 652, 262 N.Y.S.2d 1011) the Judge specifically ruled that it was immaterial "whether defendant *intended* to confuse and mislead, if in fact, his conduct tends or threatens to produce confusion." (47 Misc.2d, p. 656, 262 N.Y.S.2d 1015, italics supplied.)

As the decisions cited above establish, proof of confusion—understandably inevitable when there is a similarity of name—is irrelevant since confusion resulting from the honest use of one's own name is not actionable. This is especially appropriate in a case such as this, where the patrons or customers of the plaintiff and the defendant are discriminating and knowledgeable people usually intent on acquiring a particular work of art, people ordinarily fully aware that a desired painting or other work of art can be purchased only at a particular gallery and not apt to be misled into buying by a similarity of dealers' names. Too, the evidence of confusion which, as stated, is the predicate for the injunction in this case—telephone calls to the wrong gallery, misdeliveries, visitors seeking paintings in one gallery exhibited at the other—is not unlike that presented in Wholesale Serv. Supply Corp. v. Wholesale Bldg. Materials Corp., 304 N.Y. 854, 109 N.E.2d 718, affg. 280 App.Div. 189, 190, 112 N.Y.S.2d 622, 623 and there held to be insufficient to justify the issuance of an injunction.

Moreover, there is no proof in this case of any actual damage suffered by plaintiff and in this respect it is similar to the *Ryan* case (15 N.Y.2d 812, 257 N.Y.S.2d 934, 205 N.E.2d 859, supra) in which this court decided that there must be shown, if not deception or palming off, at least real and substantial confusion *plus* damage resulting therefrom. No such damage appears here although plaintiff seems mostly to fear that its reputation may in the end be somewhat diminished. The *Ryan* rationale is thus directly in point. Plaintiff seems to fear not present damage but damage in the future. It has proved no financial loss at all, shown no injury whatsoever; it has produced no customer or anyone else to testify that he was confused between the two galleries.

Despite the finding of no deceit and in the face of a claim of confusion far weaker than that proven in the cases to which we have referred, the court now refuses to apply the rule of law observed for over a century. The exception rests apparently on the singular circumstance that this competition is between siblings. We are unable to see why that should prompt the court to grant one brother the exclusive right to use the family name in connection with what was originally the family art business. We, therefore, perceive no valid basis for prohibiting the defendant from using his own name in the conduct of his business at 17 East 57th Street in New York City.

We would reverse the order appealed from and dismiss the complaint.

Notes

1. Courts have sometimes extended the rights of trademark owners beyond the immediate market in which they have established good will. In Sullivan v. Ed Sullivan Radio & T.V., Inc., 1 A.D.2d 609, 152 N.Y.S.2d 227 (1956), the court held that Ed Sullivan, the host of a well-known television show, was entitled to enjoin Ed Sullivan Radio & TV from engaging in the business of selling and repairing radio and television sets in Buffalo, New York. The court reached this conclusion despite the fact that the local store was owned primarily by an individual named Edward J. Sullivan. The court noted that the plaintiff had "no objection to use of the name 'Sullivan' as such nor even 'E. J. Sullivan', nor the full name 'Edward J. Sullivan', since he feels that such forms of the name would not induce or result in any confusion in the public mind. The objection here stems from the use of the diminutive form 'Ed' in conjunction with the surname 'Sullivan' in the combined name 'Ed Sullivan' which appellant has continuously used throughout his entire career. In this regard it is to be noted that our courts have, on a number of occasions, enjoined the use even of variants of a name where such use threatened confusion in the public mind." *Id.* The court held that "[a]lthough, in fact, but one isolated store in Buffalo is involved at the present time, nevertheless the state of facts may so change as to encompass a situation wherein there may be a series or a chain of similar stores throughout the country, in which case indeed, unless appellant had taken this present, prompt action, he might at a later date encounter great difficulty in obtaining an injunction because of his own laches. Also, at this stage the corporate enterprise would suffer minimal inconvenience in dropping the diminutive prefix, a situation which might not hold true at some future time." *Id.*

Have the courts struck the proper balance between protecting the good will of well known celebrities and permitting persons to use their own names in trade?

2. What is the relevance of section 2(c) of the Lanham Act, 15 U.S.C. § 1052(c), to questions regarding the use of personal names as trademarks? For further discussion of surnames, see 2 J. Thomas McCarthy, Trademarks and Unfair Competition §§ 13.01 to 13.12 (3d ed. 1995); Restatement (Third) of Unfair Competition § 14 (1995).

3. Ernest and Julio Gallo are brothers who have owned and operated the E. & J. Gallo winery for many years. Their younger brother, Joseph

Gallo, seeks to use the "Gallo" name to sell cheese and meat. What result? See E. & J. Gallo Winery v. Gallo Cattle Co., 967 F.2d 1280 (9th Cir.1992).

4. Should the courts provide relief when an individual sells a business established under his or her own name as an on-going concern to another party and later seeks to establish a new business under the individual's own name? What relief would be appropriate? See Levitt Corp. v. Levitt, 593 F.2d 463 (2d Cir.1979) (founder of Levittown, New York, residential development later establishes a residential development called Levittown, Florida).

5. The owner of a well-known and long-established New Orleans restaurant called "Brennan's" files suit against a new Manhattan restaurant called "Terrance Brennan's Seafood & Chop House," which is named after a New York celebrity chef named Terrance Brennan. What result? *See Brennan's, Inc. v. Brennan's Rest., LLC*, 360 F.3d 125 (2d Cir. 2004). For more litigation involving the Brennan restaurants, see *Brennan's Inc. v. Dickie Brennan & Co.*, 376 F.3d 356 (5th Cir. 2004).

6. Are personal names always descriptive? Consider the case of "Niles," a first name used for a toy camel. *Peaceable Planet, Inc. v. Ty, Inc.*, 362 F.3d 986 (7th Cir. 2004) (finding "Niles" toy camel to be protectable mark despite absence of secondary meaning).

E. COLOR, SOUNDS, SCENTS, AND OTHER MARKS

QUALITEX CO. v. JACOBSON PRODUCTS CO., INC.

Supreme Court of the United States, 1995.
514 U.S. 159, 115 S.Ct. 1300, 131 L.Ed.2d 248.

Justice Breyer delivered the opinion of the Court.

The question in this case is whether the Lanham Trademark Act of 1946 (Lanham Act), 15 U.S.C. §§ 1051–1127 (1988 ed. and Supp. V), permits the registration of a trademark that consists, purely and simply, of a color. We conclude that, sometimes, a color will meet ordinary legal trademark requirements. And, when it does so, no special legal rule prevents color alone from serving as a trademark.

I

The case before us grows out of petitioner Qualitex Company's use (since the 1950's) of a special shade of green-gold color on the pads that it makes and sells to dry cleaning firms for use on dry cleaning presses. In 1989 respondent Jacobson Products (a Qualitex rival) began to sell its own press pads to dry cleaning firms; and it colored those pads a similar green-gold. In 1991 Qualitex registered the special green-gold color on press pads with the Patent and Trademark Office as a trademark. Registration No. 1,633,711 (Feb. 5, 1991). Qualitex subsequently added a trademark infringement count, 15 U.S.C. § 1114(1), to an unfair competition claim, § 1125(a), in a lawsuit it had already filed challenging Jacobson's use of the green-gold color.

Qualitex won the lawsuit in the District Court. 21 U.S.P.Q.2d 1457, 1991 WL 318798 (C.D.Cal.1991). But, the Court of Appeals for the Ninth Circuit set aside the judgment in Qualitex's favor on the trademark infringement claim because, in that Circuit's view, the Lanham Act does not permit Qualitex, or anyone else, to register "color alone" as a trademark. 13 F.3d 1297, 1300, 1302 (1994).

The courts of appeals have differed as to whether or not the law recognizes the use of color alone as a trademark. Compare NutraSweet Co. v. Stadt Corp., 917 F.2d 1024, 1028 (C.A.7 1990) (absolute prohibition against protection of color alone), with In re Owens–Corning Fiberglas Corp., 774 F.2d 1116, 1128 (C.A.Fed.1985) (allowing registration of color pink for fiberglass insulation), and Master Distributors, Inc. v. Pako Corp., 986 F.2d 219, 224 (C.A.8 1993) (declining to establish per se prohibition against protecting color alone as a trademark). Therefore, this Court granted certiorari. 512 U.S. 1287, 115 S.Ct. 40, 129 L.Ed.2d 935 (1994). We now hold that there is no rule absolutely barring the use of color alone, and we reverse the judgment of the Ninth Circuit.

II

The Lanham Act gives a seller or producer the exclusive right to "register" a trademark, 15 U.S.C. § 1052 (1988 ed. and Supp. V), and to prevent his or her competitors from using that trademark, § 1114(1). Both the language of the Act and the basic underlying principles of trademark law would seem to include color within the universe of things that can qualify as a trademark. The language of the Lanham Act describes that universe in the broadest of terms. It says that trademarks "includ[e] any word, name, symbol, or device, or any combination thereof." § 1127. Since human beings might use as a "symbol" or "device" almost anything at all that is capable of carrying meaning, this language, read literally, is not restrictive. The courts and the Patent and Trademark Office have authorized for use as a mark a particular shape (of a Coca–Cola bottle), a particular sound (of NBC's three chimes), and even a particular scent (of plumeria blossoms on sewing thread). See, e.g., Registration No. 696,147 (Apr. 12, 1960); Registration Nos. 523,616 (Apr. 4, 1950) and 916,522 (July 13, 1971); In re Clarke, 17 U.S.P.Q.2d 1238, 1240 (TTAB 1990). If a shape, a sound, and a fragrance can act as symbols why, one might ask, can a color not do the same?

A color is also capable of satisfying the more important part of the statutory definition of a trademark, which requires that a person "us[e]" or "inten[d] to use" the mark "to identify and distinguish his or her goods, including a unique product, from those manufactured or sold by others and to indicate the source of the goods, even if that source is unknown." 15 U.S.C. § 1127. True, a product's color is unlike "fanciful," "arbitrary," or "suggestive" words or designs, which almost automatically tell a customer that they refer to a brand. The imaginary word "Suntost," or the words "Suntost Marmalade," on a jar of orange jam immediately would signal a brand or a product "source"; the jam's orange color does not do so. But, over time, customers may come to treat a particular color on a product or its packaging (say, a color that in context seems unusual, such as pink on a firm's insulating material or red on the head of a large industrial bolt) as signifying a brand. And, if so, that color would have come to identify and distinguish the goods—i.e. to "indicate" their "source"—much in the way that descriptive words on a product (say, "Trim" on nail clippers or "Car–Freshner" on deodorizer) can come to indicate a product's origin. In this circumstance, trademark law says that the word (e.g., "Trim"), although not inherently distinctive, has developed "secondary meaning." See Inwood Laboratories, Inc. v. Ives Laboratories, Inc., 456 U.S. 844, 851, n. 11, 102 S.Ct. 2182, 2187, n. 11, 72 L.Ed.2d 606 (1982) ("secondary meaning" is acquired when "in the minds of the public, the primary significance of a product feature ... is to identify the source of the product rather than the product itself"). Again, one might ask, if trademark law permits a descriptive word with secondary meaning to act as a mark, why would it not permit a color, under similar circumstances, to do the same?

We cannot find in the basic objectives of trademark law any obvious theoretical objection to the use of color alone as a trademark, where that color has attained "secondary meaning" and therefore identifies and distinguishes a particular brand (and thus indicates its "source"). In principle, trademark law, by preventing others from copying a source-identifying mark, "reduce[s] the customer's costs of shopping and making purchasing decisions," 1 J. McCarthy, McCarthy on Trademarks and Unfair Competition § 2.01[2], p. 2–3 (3d ed. 1994) (hereinafter McCarthy), for it quickly and easily assures a potential customer that this item—the item with this mark—is made by the same producer as other similarly marked items that he or she liked (or disliked) in the past. At the same time, the law helps assure a producer that it (and not an imitating competitor) will reap the financial, reputation-related rewards associated with a desirable product. The law thereby "encourage[s] the production of quality products," ibid., and simultaneously discourages those who hope to sell inferior products by capitalizing on a consumer's inability quickly to evaluate the quality of an item offered for sale. * * * It is the source-distinguishing ability of a mark—not its ontological status as color, shape, fragrance, word, or sign—that permits it to serve these basic purposes. See Landes & Posner, Trademark Law: An Economic Perspective, 30 J.Law & Econ. 265, 290 (1987). And, for that reason, it is difficult to find, in basic trademark objectives, a reason to disqualify absolutely the use of a color as a mark.

Neither can we find a principled objection to the use of color as a mark in the important "functionality" doctrine of trademark law. The functionality doctrine prevents trademark law, which seeks to promote competition by protecting a firm's reputation, from instead inhibiting legitimate competition by allowing a producer to control a useful product feature. It is the province of patent law, not trademark law, to encourage invention by granting inventors a monopoly over new product designs or functions for a limited time, 35 U.S.C. §§ 154, 173, after which competitors are free to use the innovation. If a product's functional features could be used as trademarks, however, a monopoly over such features could be obtained without regard to whether they qualify as patents and could be extended forever (because trademarks may be renewed in perpetuity). See Kellogg Co. v. National Biscuit Co., 305 U.S. 111, 119–120, 59 S.Ct. 109, 113–114, 83 L.Ed. 73 (1938) (Brandeis, J.); Inwood Laboratories, Inc., supra, 456 U.S., at 863, 102 S.Ct., at 2193 (White, J., concurring in result) ("A functional characteristic is 'an important ingredient in the commercial success of the product,' and, after expiration of a patent, it is no more the property of the originator than the product itself") (citation omitted). Functionality doctrine therefore would require, to take an imaginary example, that even if customers have come to identify the special illumination-enhancing shape of a new patented light bulb with a particular manufacturer, the manufacturer may not use that shape as a trademark, for doing so, after the patent had expired, would impede competition—not by protecting the reputation of the original bulb maker, but by frustrating competitors' legitimate efforts to produce an equivalent illumination-enhancing bulb. See, e.g., Kellogg Co., supra, 305 U.S., at 119–120, 59 S.Ct., at 113–114 (trademark law cannot be used to extend monopoly over "pillow" shape of shredded wheat biscuit after the patent for that shape had expired). This Court consequently has explained that, "[i]n general terms, a product feature is functional," and cannot serve as a trademark, "if it is essential to the use or purpose of the article or if it affects the cost or quality of the article," that is, if exclusive use of the feature would put competitors at a significant non-reputation-related disadvantage. Inwood Laboratories, Inc., 456 U.S., at 850, n. 10, 102 S.Ct., at 2186, n. 10. Although sometimes color plays an important role (unrelated to source identification) in making a product more desirable, sometimes it does not. And, this latter fact—the fact that sometimes color is not essential to a product's use or purpose and does not affect cost or quality— indicates that the doctrine of "functionality" does not create an absolute bar to the use of color alone as a mark. See Owens–Corning, 774 F.2d, at 1123 (pink color of insulation in wall "performs no nontrademark function").

It would seem, then, that color alone, at least sometimes, can meet the basic legal requirements for use as a trademark. It can act as a symbol that distinguishes a firm's goods and identifies their source, without serving any other significant function. See U.S. Dept. of Commerce, Patent and Trademark Office, Trademark Manual of Examining Procedure § 1202.04(e), p. 1202–13 (2d ed. May, 1993) (hereinafter PTO Manual) (approving trademark registration of color alone where it "has become distinctive of the applicant's goods in commerce," provided that "there is [no] competitive need for colors to remain available in the industry" and the color is not "functional"); see also 1 McCarthy §§ 3.01[1], 7.26 ("requirements for qualification of a word or symbol as a trademark" are that it be (1) a "symbol," (2) "use[d] ... as a mark," (3) "to identify and distinguish the seller's goods from goods made or sold by others," but that it not be "functional"). Indeed, the District Court, in this case, entered findings (accepted by the Ninth Circuit) that show Qualitex's green-gold press pad color has met these requirements. The green-gold color acts as a symbol. Having developed secondary meaning (for customers identified the green-gold color as Qualitex's), it identifies the press pads' source. And, the green-gold color serves no other function. (Although it is important to use some color on press pads to avoid noticeable stains, the court found "no competitive need in the press pad industry for the green-gold color, since other colors are equally usable." 21 U.S.P.Q.2d, at 1460, 1991 WL 318798.) Accordingly, unless there is some special reason that convincingly militates against the use of color alone as a trademark, trademark law would protect Qualitex's use of the green-gold color on its press pads.

III

Respondent Jacobson Products says that there are four special reasons why the law should forbid the use of color alone as a trademark. We shall explain, in turn, why we, ultimately, find them unpersuasive.

First, Jacobson says that, if the law permits the use of color as a trademark, it will produce uncertainty and unresolvable court disputes about what shades of a color a competitor may lawfully use. Because lighting (morning sun, twilight mist) will affect perceptions of protected color, competitors and courts will suffer from "shade confusion" as they try to decide whether use of a similar color on a similar product does, or does not, confuse customers and thereby infringe a trademark. Jacobson adds that the "shade confusion" problem is "more difficult" and "far different from" the "determination of the similarity of words or symbols."

We do not believe, however, that color, in this respect, is special. Courts traditionally decide quite difficult questions about whether two words or phrases or symbols are sufficiently similar, in context, to confuse buyers. They have had to compare, for example, such words as "Bonamine" and "Dramamine" (motion-sickness remedies); "Huggies" and "Dougies" (diapers); "Cheracol" and "Syrocol" (cough syrup); "Cyclone" and "Tornado" (wire fences); and "Mattres" and "1–800–Mattres" (mattress franchisor telephone numbers). See, e.g., G.D. Searle & Co. v. Chas. Pfizer & Co., 265 F.2d 385, 389 (C.A.7 1959); Kimberly–Clark Corp. v. H. Douglas Enterprises, Ltd., 774 F.2d 1144, 1146–1147 (C.A.Fed.1985); Upjohn Co. v. Schwartz, 246 F.2d 254, 262 (C.A.2 1957); Hancock v. American Steel & Wire Co. of New Jersey, 40 C.C.P.A. 931, 935 (Pat.), 203 F.2d 737, 740–741 (1953); Dial–A–Mattress Franchise Corp. v. Page, 880 F.2d 675, 678 (C.A.2 1989). Legal standards exist to guide courts in making such comparisons. See, e.g., 2 McCarthy § 15.08; 1 McCarthy §§ 11.24–11.25 ("[S]trong" marks, with greater secondary meaning, receive broader protection than "weak" marks). We do not see why courts could not apply those standards to a color, replicating, if necessary, lighting conditions under which a colored product is normally sold. See Ebert, Trademark Protection in Color: Do It By the Numbers!, 84 T.M.Rep. 379, 405 (1994). Indeed, courts already have done so in cases where a trademark consists of a color plus a design, i.e., a colored symbol such as a gold stripe (around a sewer pipe), a yellow strand of wire rope, or a "brilliant yellow" band (on ampules). See, e.g., Youngstown Sheet & Tube Co. v. Tallman Conduit Co., 149 U.S.P.Q. 656, 657 (TTAB 1966); Amsted Industries, Inc. v. West Coast Wire Rope & Rigging Inc., 2 U.S.P.Q.2d 1755, 1760 (TTAB 1987); In re Hodes–Lange Corp., 167 U.S.P.Q. 255, 256 (TTAB 1970).

Second, Jacobson argues, as have others, that colors are in limited supply. See, e.g., NutraSweet Co., 917 F.2d, at 1028; Campbell Soup Co. v. Armour & Co., 175 F.2d 795, 798 (C.A.3 1949). Jacobson claims that, if one of many competitors can appropriate a particular color for use as a trademark, and each competitor then tries to do the same, the supply of colors will soon be depleted. Put in its strongest form, this argument would concede that "[h]undreds of color pigments are manufactured and thousands of colors can be obtained by mixing." L. Cheskin, Colors: What They Can Do For You 47 (1947). But, it would add that, in the context of a particular product, only some colors are usable. By the time one discards colors that, say, for reasons of customer appeal, are not usable, and adds the shades that competitors cannot use lest they risk infringing a similar, registered shade, then one is left with only a handful of possible colors. And, under these circumstances, to permit one, or a few, producers to use colors as trademarks will "deplete" the supply of usable colors to the point where a competitor's inability to find a suitable color will put that competitor at a significant disadvantage.

This argument is unpersuasive, however, largely because it relies on an occasional problem to justify a blanket prohibition. When a color serves as a mark, normally alternative colors will likely be available for similar use by others. See, e.g., Owens–Corning, 774 F.2d, at 1121 (pink insulation). Moreover, if that is not so—if a "color depletion" or "color scarcity" problem does arise—the trademark doctrine of "functionality" normally would seem available to prevent the anticompetitive consequences that Jacobson's argument posits, thereby minimizing that argument's practical force.

The functionality doctrine, as we have said, forbids the use of a product's feature as a trademark where doing so will put a competitor at a significant disadvantage because the feature is "essential to the use or purpose of the article" or "affects [its] cost or quality." Inwood Laboratories, Inc., 456 U.S., at 850, n. 10, 102 S.Ct., at 2186, n. 10. The functionality doctrine thus protects competitors against a disadvantage (unrelated to recognition or reputation) that trademark protection might otherwise impose, namely their inability reasonably to replicate important non-reputation-related product features. For example, this Court has written that competitors might be free to copy the color of a medical pill where that color serves to identify the kind of medication (e.g., a type of blood medicine) in addition to its source. See id., at 853, 858, n. 20, 102 S.Ct., at 2188, 2190, n. 20 ("[S]ome patients commingle medications in a container and rely on color to differentiate one from another"); see also J. Ginsburg, D. Goldberg, & A. Greenbaum, Trademark and Unfair Competition Law 194–195 (1991) (noting that drug color cases "have more to do with public health policy" regarding generic drug substitution "than with trademark law"). * * * The Restatement (Third) of Unfair Competition adds that, if a design's "aesthetic value" lies in its ability to "confe[r] a significant benefit that cannot practically be duplicated by the use of alternative designs," then the design is "functional." Restatement (Third) of Unfair Competition § 17, Comment c, pp. 175–176 (1995). The "ultimate test of aesthetic functionality," it explains, "is whether the recognition of trademark rights would significantly hinder competition." Id., at 176.

The upshot is that, where a color serves a significant nontrademark function—whether to distinguish a heart pill from a digestive medicine or to satisfy the "noble instinct for giving the right touch of beauty to common and necessary things," G.K. Chesterton, Simplicity and Tolstoy 61 (1912)—courts will examine whether its use as a mark would permit one competitor (or a group) to interfere with legitimate (nontrademark-related) competition through actual or potential exclusive use of an important product ingredient. That examination should not discourage firms from creating aesthetically pleasing mark designs, for it is open to their competitors to do the same. See, e.g., W.T. Rogers Co. v. Keene, 778 F.2d 334, 343 (C.A.7 1985) (Posner, J.). But, ordinarily, it should prevent the anticompetitive consequences of Jacobson's hypothetical "color depletion" argument, when, and if, the circumstances of a particular case threaten "color depletion."

Third, Jacobson points to many older cases—including Supreme Court cases—in support of its position. * * * [The Court notes that Congress enacted the Lanham Act to "dispense with mere technical prohibitions" and to permit registration of descriptive words if they had acquired secondary meaning.]

Fourth, Jacobson argues that there is no need to permit color alone to function as a trademark because a firm already may use color as part of a trademark, say, as a colored circle or colored letter or colored word, and may rely upon "trade dress" protection, under § 43(a) of the Lanham Act, if a competitor copies its color and thereby causes consumer confusion regarding the overall appearance of the competing products or their packaging, see 15 U.S.C. § 1125(a) (1988 ed., Supp. V). The first part of this argument begs the question. One can understand why a firm might find it difficult to place a usable symbol or word on a product (say, a large industrial bolt that customers normally see from a distance); and, in such instances, a firm might want to use color, pure and simple, instead of color as part of a design. Neither is the second portion of the argument convincing. Trademark law helps the holder of a mark in many ways that "trade dress" protection does not. See 15 U.S.C. § 1124 (ability to prevent importation of confusingly similar goods); § 1072 (constructive notice of ownership); § 1065 (incontestable status);

§ 1057(b) (prima facie evidence of validity and ownership). Thus, one can easily find reasons why the law might provide trademark protection in addition to trade dress protection.

IV

Having determined that a color may sometimes meet the basic legal requirements for use as a trademark and that respondent Jacobson's arguments do not justify a special legal rule preventing color alone from serving as a trademark (and, in light of the District Court's here undisputed findings that Qualitex's use of the green-gold color on its press pads meets the basic trademark requirements), we conclude that the Ninth Circuit erred in barring Qualitex's use of color as a trademark. For these reasons, the judgment of the Ninth Circuit is

Reversed.

Notes

1. Is there any practical or legal limitation of the types of symbols that can be protected under the Lanham Act? Should there be? Consider a trademark application for the following trademark: "The mark is a high impact, fresh, floral fragrance reminiscent of Plumeria blossoms." The mark is used in connection with sewing thread and embroidery yarn. Should it be eligible for trademark protection and registered on the principal register? See In re Clarke, 17 U.S.P.Q.2d 1238 (T.T.A.B. 1990). Would a lemon scent be a protectable trademark for dishwashing detergent? A floral scent for perfume? Is a bubble gum scent a protectable trademark for welding material? A floral scent for pens or markers?

2. Should competitors be able to copy the green color used by a major producer of farm machinery? See Deere & Co. v. Farmhand, Inc., 560 F.Supp. 85, 98 (S.D.Iowa 1982), aff'd, 721 F.2d 253 (8th Cir.1983). Should protection be granted on the color black as a trademark for outboard boat motors? See Brunswick Corp. v. British Seagull Ltd., 35 F.3d 1527, 1532 (Fed.Cir.1994). Is the blue color of a brand of fertilizer functional because it indicates the presence of nitrogen? See Nor–Am Chemical v. O.M. Scott & Sons Co., 4 U.S.P.Q.2d 1316, 1320, 1987 WL 13742 (E.D.Pa.1987). Could the color configuration of fishing rods include functional elements to which competitors are entitled to access? See Shakespeare Co. v. Silstar Corp., 906 F.Supp. 997 (D.S.C.1995), aff'd, 110 F.3d 234 (4th Cir.1997), *cert. denied*, 522 U.S. 1046, 118 S.Ct. 688, 139 L.Ed.2d 634 (1998). Are blue and white colors functional in the swimming pool industry? Polaris Pool Systems, Inc. v. Letro Products, Inc., 886 F.Supp. 1513 (C.D.Cal.1995). Should trademark protection be available for a color used in product packaging, for example on packages of artificial sweeteners?

3. For further discussion, see 1 J. Thomas McCarthy, Trademarks and Unfair Competition §§ 7.01 to 7.38 (3d ed. 1995); Restatement (Third) of Unfair Competition §§ 16–17 (1995).

F. MARKS PRECLUDED FROM REGISTRATION

IN RE OLD GLORY CONDOM CORP.

U.S. Patent and Trademark Office, Trademark Trial and Appeal Board, 1993.
26 U.S.P.Q.2d 1216.

SAMS, MEMBER.

Old Glory Condom Corp. has appealed from the examining attorney's final refusal to register its mark "OLD GLORY CONDOM CORP" (and design), as shown below, for "prophylactics (condoms)." The design feature of applicant's mark consists of a pictorial representation of a condom decorated with stars and stripes in a manner to suggest the American flag.

The drawing of the mark is lined for the colors red and blue.

The examining attorney refused registration, under section 2(a) of the Trademark act, on the grounds that the mark consists of immoral or scandalous matter.[2] In particular, the examining attorney found that the use of the American flag as part of applicant's mark for condoms was scandalous because it was likely to offend "a substantial composite of the general public."

APPLICANT'S USE OF ITS MARK

The record on appeal shows that applicant corporation was formed after Jay Kritchley, applicant's president, participated in an exhibition at the List Visual Arts Center of the Massachusetts Institute of Technology (M.I.T.) in Cambridge, Massachusetts. The exhibition, held in October 1989, was entitled "Trouble in Paradise" and focused on artists' responses to contemporary social and political issues. Mr. Kritchley's exhibit was an adaptation of the symbols of American patriotism to focus attention on the AIDS epidemic and, in particular, to emphasize that Americans have a patriotic duty to fight the AIDS epidemic and other sexually transmitted diseases. Applicant states that, when the exhibition received widespread critical acclaim, Mr. Kritchley decided to turn his theoretical concepts into a corporate enterprise, which now markets condoms under the mark applicant is seeking to register.

While the American flag design appears as a feature of applicant's trademark for condoms, the flag design is not applied to the condoms themselves. Applicant states that on the back of each condom package is the "Old Glory Pledge":

2. Section 2 of the Trademark Act (15 U.S.C. Section 1052) provides, in pertinent part, as follows:

No trademark by which the goods of the applicant may be distinguished from the goods of others shall be refused registration on the principal register on account of its nature unless it—

(a) Consists of or comprises immoral, deceptive, or scandalous matter which may disparage or falsely suggest a connection with persons, living or dead, institutions, beliefs, or national symbols, or bring them into contempt, or disrepute.

We believe it is patriotic to protect and save lives. We offer only the highest quality condoms. Join us in promoting safer sex. Help eliminate AIDS. A portion of Old Glory profits will be donated to AIDS related services.

The Refusal of Registration

In refusing registration of applicant's mark, the examining attorney argues that a majority of the American public would be offended by the use of American flag imagery to promote products associated with sexual activity. She argues that the flag is a sacrosanct symbol whose association with condoms would necessarily give offense.

Applicant characterizes the issue on appeal as one of first impression: whether a trademark may be refused registration as scandalous solely on the basis of its political content. Applicant argues that the Patent and Trademark Office has registered more than a thousand marks for condoms, many of them sexually suggestive and many that might be considered vulgar. Applicant goes on to argue that the Patent and Trademark Office has registered more than one thousand marks in which an image of the American flag appears. Applicant emphasizes that its mark is expressly designed not to offend but to redefine patriotism to include the fight against sexually-transmitted diseases, including AIDS. Applicant points to its exhibit at M.I.T., which employed a frank sense of humor about both condoms and patriotism to encourage people to overcome an aversion to the use of condoms.

In this record, the only direct evidence of the impact of applicant's mark on the public is that described by applicant in its response to the first office action in this case. Applicant alluded to a "marketing study commissioned by applicant from the Simmons College Graduate School of Management." About this study, applicant noted:

The study, which was made completely independent of applicant, which took three months to complete, and which was undertaken by Simmons College without cost to applicant (due to the College's recognition of the pressing social need to encourage the use of condoms), found that there was a negative public reaction of under 5% of those polled to applicant's use of the subject mark with regard to condoms.

We do not know the details of the survey, because applicant did not submit a copy for the record (nor, indeed, did applicant mention the survey in its appeal brief). On the other hand, the examining attorney did not request that applicant submit a copy of the survey, nor did she challenge applicant's summary of the survey results.

"Scandalous" Marks under Section 2(a)

There is relatively little published precedent to guide us in deciding whether a mark is "scandalous" within the meaning of Section 2(a) of the Trademark Act. The examining attorney places principal reliance on In re McGinley, 211 USPQ 668 (CCPA 1981), the most recent decision in which the Board's reviewing court has interpreted the section of the

Trademark Act here at issue. In *McGinley*, the Court was asked to decide the registrability of a mark comprising a photograph of a man and woman kissing and embracing in a manner appearing to expose the man's genitalia. In deciding whether the mark presented for registration was "scandalous" under Section 2(a), the Court first noted that whether a mark is scandalous is to be determined from the standpoint of a substantial composite of the general public. To define "scandalous," under Section 2(a), the Court looked to the "ordinary and common meaning" of the term, which meaning could be established, according to the Court, by reference to Court and Board decisions and to dictionary definitions. The Court went on to cite dictionary definitions of "scandalous" as "shocking to the sense of ... propriety," "[that which gives] offense to the conscience or moral feelings" and "giving offense to the conscience or moral feelings; exciting reprobation, calling out condemnation ... disgraceful to reputation.... " and "shocking to the sense of truth, decency, or propriety; disgraceful, offensive; disreputable.... " In an attempt to put these provisions of Section 2(a) in context, the Court expressed its opinion that this section of the Trademark Act represents not " ... an attempt to legislate morality, but, rather a judgment by the Congress that such marks not occupy the time, services, and use of funds of the federal government." Having set forth its opinion as to the underpinnings of this portion of Section 2(a) of the Trademark Act, the Court (one judge dissenting) concluded that the mark for which registration was sought (i.e., the pictorial representation of an embracing nude couple with exposed male genitalia) was scandalous and, therefore, unregistrable.

In the more than ten years since the *McGinley* decision, this Board has decided only four cases involving the issue of whether marks were "scandalous" under Section 2(a). The first of these cases, In re Tinseltown, Inc., 212 USPQ 863 (TTAB 1981), involved the mark "BULLSHIT" for attache cases, handbags, purses, belts, and wallets. The Board allowed that the registrability of a profane word was a case of first impression and found that "BULLSHIT," the profane word at issue, was scandalous, within the meaning of Section 2(a), and, therefore, unregistrable. In finding the mark unregistrable, the Board relied on the *McGinley* case and, in particular, two of the dictionary definitions of "scandalous" cited by the Court in that case: "[g]iving offense to the conscience or moral feelings ... " and "shocking to the sense of ... decency or propriety.... "

In re Hershey, 6 USPQ2d 1470 (TTAB 1988) involved the mark "BIG PECKER BRAND" for T-shirts. The mark had been refused registration, as scandalous, on the grounds that "pecker" was a vulgar expression for "penis" and that the mark as a whole, therefore, was offensive or shocking to a substantial composite of the general public. The Board reversed the refusal of registration, finding the evidence unpersuasive to demonstrate the vulgarity of the word "pecker" and noted that the specimens of record were labels showing a design of a bird in conjunction with the word mark "BIG PECKER BRAND." The Board concluded that, in view of the context of the mark's use, the mark neither offended morality nor raised a scandal.

In Greyhound Corp. v. Both Worlds Inc., 6 USPQ2d 1635 (TTAB 1988), the Board determined that a design consisting of the silhouette of a defecating dog, as a mark for polo shirts and T-shirts, was scandalous. Citing the definitions of "scandalous" relied on by the Court in *McGinley* and by the Board in *Tinseltown*, the Board found applicant's design mark "vulgar", and, therefore, scandalous. The Board noted in particular the depiction of feces as part of the mark.

The most recent case in which the Board considered whether a mark was "scandalous" under Section 2(a) was In re In Over Our Heads Inc., 16 USPQ2d 1653 (TTAB 1990). In that case, the mark involved was "MOONIES" (and a design feature) for dolls. The particular dolls to which the mark was applied were novelty items which, upon the squeezing of an attached collapsible bulb, dropped their pants to reveal buttocks (an action known as "mooning"). The examining attorney had contended that the mark was lacking in taste and was an affront to an organized religious group, namely, the Unification Church, whose members were sometimes referred to as "Moonies." The Board reversed the refusal of registration, finding that purchasers were more likely to view the mark as an allusion to "mooning" than as a reference to members of the Unification Church. In discussing the Section 2(a) issue presented, the Board noted that the standards for determining whether a mark is scandalous are somewhat vague and the determination of the issue necessarily highly subjective. In view of the subjective nature of the decision, the Board determined that any doubts about whether a mark was scandalous should be resolved in favor of allowing the mark to be published, to permit any party who believes it would be damaged by registration of the mark to file an opposition to registration.

Although we have concentrated our attention on the more recent cases arising under Section 2(a), we are aware of several reported cases decided during the period 1938–1971 by the Court of Customs and Patent Appeals, the Commissioner of Patents, or this Board, where marks were found scandalous and, therefore, unregistrable. We find the latter to be of little precedential value in deciding the case now before us. Most of these older cases involved a perceived offense to religious sensibilities. In re Riverbank Canning Co., supra [the mark "MADONNA" for wines held scandalous]; Ex parte Summit Brass and Bronze Works, Inc., 59 USPQ 22 (Comr. Pats. 1943) [the mark "AGNUS DEI" (and design) for metallic tabernacle safes held scandalous]; * * * In re Reemtsma Cigarettenfabriken GmbH, 122 USPQ 339 (TTAB 1959) [the mark "SENUSSI" for cigarettes held scandalous ("Senussi" being the name of a Moslem sect whose adherents are forbidden the use of cigarettes)]. * * * Moreover, what was considered scandalous as a trademark or service mark twenty, thirty or fifty years ago may no longer be considered so, given the changes in societal attitudes. Marks once thought scandalous may now be thought merely humorous (or even quaint), as we suspect is the case with the marks held scandalous in Ex parte Martha Maid Mfg. Co., 37 USPQ 156 (Comr. Pats. 1938) ["QUEEN MARY" (and design) for women's underwear] and In re Runsdorf, 171 USPQ 443 (TTAB 1971) ["BUBBY TRAP" for brassieres]. The point to be made here is that, in deciding whether a mark is scandalous under Section 2(a), we must consider that mark in the context of contemporary attitudes. * * *

REGISTRABILITY OF APPLICANT'S MARK

Applicant's argument for reversing the refusal to register in this case is essentially two-fold. First, applicant argues that, when viewed in the light of the legal precedent of the Board and the Board's reviewing court, its mark is not scandalous. Second, applicant makes a Constitutional argument that the Board is obligated to apply the provisions of Section 2(a) in a Constitutional manner and that denial of the benefits of registration to applicant's mark because of its political content, even assuming (we presume) the political content of the mark would give offense, would violate the First and Fifth Amendments to the Constitution. Because we are in agreement with applicant's first line of argument, we need not consider the second line of argument in order to allow registration of the mark in this case.

Taking as our starting point the definitions of "scandalous" to which the Board has in previous cases looked for assistance in applying Section 2(a), we have considered whether "OLD GLORY CONDOM CORP" (and flag design) can be characterized as "[g]iving offense to the conscience or moral feelings" or "shocking to the sense of decency or propriety." If any pattern can be discerned from the most recent cases, previously discussed, where the Board or its reviewing court found marks to be scandalous [viz., a mark comprising a photograph of a man and woman kissing and embracing in a manner appearing to expose the man's genitalia, for newsletters (*McGinley*, supra), "BULLSHIT," for handbags, wallets, etc. (*Tinseltown*, supra), and the design of a defecating dog, for shirts (*Greyhound Corp. v. Both Worlds Inc.*, supra)], that pattern seems to describe marks that convey, in words or in pictures, vulgar imagery.

As applicant has asserted (and as the examining attorney seems to concede), this Office has registered many trademarks and service marks that include imagery of the American flag. While we realize that there may be citizens of this country who disapprove of any commercial use of the American flag or American flag imagery, such uses have been sufficiently common that there can be no justification for refusing registration of applicant's mark simply on the basis of the presence in that mark of flag imagery. Nor do we find any evidence in this case that convinces us that a mark containing a pictorial representation of a condom should, simply because of that fact, be refused registration as scandalous. The particular pictorial presentation featured in applicant's composite mark was not found by the examining attorney to be vulgar, nor do we find it so. The examining attorney's objection to applicant's mark seems to be directed to the mark's linking of flag imagery and a pictorial representation of a condom, each of which, in itself, she apparently finds unobjectionable. Precisely why this combination of images is scandalous the examining attorney fails to articulate.[3]

Moreover, the examining attorney offers very little evidence in support of her refusal of registration in this case. Her position is supported mainly by an expression of opinion that a substantial composite of the public would be offended by applicant's mark, which opinion is, in turn, supported by her opinion that the American flag is a "sacrosanct" symbol. To bolster the latter opinion, she alluded to an unsuccessful proposed amendment to the U.S. Constitution to prohibit flag burning and to a comment by Chief Justice Rehnquist in his dissent in Texas v. Johnson, 491 U.S. 397, 428 (1989), that many Americans have an "almost mystical reverence" for the American flag. The examining attorney also made of record printouts, from Mead Data's NEXIS data base, of several news stories referring to a video public service announcement promoting voter registration. The video in question showed rock star Madonna, scantily clad and wrapped in an American flag. The news stories made mention of the disapproval in some quarters of the video's use of the American flag. We are not willing, based solely on the examining attorney's opinion, the evidence of the reaction to the Madonna video, and the unsuccessful effort to amend the U.S. Constitution to prohibit the burning of the flag, to presume that the flag imagery of applicant's mark would give offense in a manner that must be deemed "scandalous" under Section 2(a).

Moreover, whether applicant's mark would be likely to offend must be judged not in isolation but in the entire context of the mark's use. The Board has in other cases looked to the entire context of the use in determining whether the mark in question was scandalous. See In re Hershey, supra ["BIG PECKER BRAND" applied to T-shirts with labels bearing both the trademark and the design of a bird]; In re Leo Quan Inc., 200 USPQ 370 (TTAB 1978) ["BADASS" for bridges for stringed musical instruments found not scandalous, the Board noting that the mark was an acronym derived from the words "Bettencourt Acoustically Designed Audio Sound Systems"]. Here, applicant markets its condoms in packaging which emphasizes applicant's commitment to the sale of high quality condoms as a means of promoting safer sex and eliminating

---

3. In this case, as in others where the issue has been whether a mark is scandalous, we have detected an undercurrent of concern that the issuance of a trademark registration for applicant's mark amounts to the awarding of the U.S. Government's "imprimatur" to the mark. Such a notion is, of course, erroneous. The duty of this Office under the Trademark Act in reviewing applications for registration is nothing more and nothing less than to register those marks that are functioning to identify and distinguish goods and services in the marketplace, as long as those marks do not run afoul of any statutory provision that would prohibit registration. Moreover, the registration scheme of the Trademark Act is one more inclined to inclusion than exclusion, the obvious idea being to give as comprehensive a notice as possible, to those engaged in commerce, of the trademarks and service marks in which others have claimed rights. Just as the issuance of a trademark registration by this Office does not amount to a government endorsement of the quality of the goods to which the mark is applied, the act of registration is not a government imprimatur or pronouncement that the mark is a "good" one in an aesthetic, or any analogous, sense.

AIDS and its belief that the use of condoms is a patriotic act. Although we know that not everyone would share applicant's view that the use of condoms is a patriotic act, the seriousness of purpose surrounding the use of applicant's mark—a seriousness of purpose made manifest to purchasers on the packaging for applicant's goods—is a factor to be taken into account in assessing whether the mark is offensive or shocking. When we consider that factor, along with the others we have discussed, we find that applicant's mark can in no way be considered "scandalous" under Section 2(a).

Decision: The refusal to register is reversed.

OLD GLORY CONDOM CORP

Notes

1.   Should a design mark, consisting of "a cartoon-like representation of a melancholy, unclothed male figure ruefully contemplating an unseen portion of his genitalia," be considered scandalous as applied to "a corrective implement for increasing the size of the human penis"? See In re Thomas Laboratories, Inc., 189 U.S.P.Q. 50 (T.T.A.B.1975). What about the name "Dick Heads" and an accompanying logo for restaurant and bar services? See In re Wilcher Corp., 40 U.S.P.Q.2d 1929 (T.T.A.B.1996). Should a "Buddha beachware" mark and logo be allowed registration? See In re Hines, 32 U.S.P.Q.2d 1376 (T.T.A.B.1994). See generally In re Mavety Media Group, Ltd., 33 F.3d 1367 (Fed.Cir.1994) (setting forth standard for refusal to register mark on ground that it is immoral or scandalous).

2.   To what extent does the First Amendment inform the analysis of whether a mark is scandalous? See In re Thomas Laboratories, Inc., 189 U.S.P.Q. 50 (T.T.A.B.1975) (citing Roth v. United States, 354 U.S. 476, 477, 77 S.Ct. 1304, 1 L.Ed.2d 1498 (1957)) (noting that "the contemporary liberal attitude concerning the question of obscenity as derived from the present understanding of the meaning of the freedoms guaranteed under the First Amendment to the Constitution militates against" refusing registration).

3.   Trademarks can be precluded from registration on grounds of offensiveness. Recent litigation involving the Washington Redskins marks addresses whether the registrations for that mark should be cancelled as disparaging toward Native Americans. See Harjo v. Pro Football, Inc., 30 U.S.P.Q.2d 1828 (T.T.A.B.1994) (denying motion to dismiss suit to cancel registration of Washington Redskins trademark on the ground that it disparages Native Americans and striking defenses based on secondary meaning and equitable considerations), later proceeding, 50 U.S.P.Q.2d 1705

(T.T.A.B.1999) (finding certain marks to be disparaging). The T.T.A.B. found as follows:

> We find petitioners have clearly established, by at least a preponderance of the evidence, that, as of the dates the challenged registrations issued, the word "redskin(s)," as it appears in respondent's marks in those registrations and as used in connection with the identified services, may disparage Native Americans, as perceived by a substantial composite of Native Americans. No single item of evidence or testimony alone brings us to this conclusion; rather, we reach our conclusion based on the cumulative effect of the entire record. We discuss below some of the more significant evidence in the record. We look, first, at the evidence establishing that, in general and during the relevant time periods, the word "redskin(s)" has been a term of disparagement of and to Native Americans. Then we look at the evidence establishing that, during the relevant time periods, the disparaging connotation of "redskin(s)" as a term of reference for Native Americans extend to the word "Redskin(s)" as it appears in respondent's subject marks and as used in connection with respondent's identified services. We have considered the perceptions of both the general public and Native Americans to be probative. For example, we have found that the evidence supports the conclusion that a substantial composite of the general public finds the word "redskin(s)" to be a derogatory term of reference for Native Americans. Thus, in the absence of evidence to the contrary, it is reasonable to infer that a substantial composite of Native Americans would similarly perceive the word. This is consistent with the testimony of the petitioners.

> We look, first, at the evidence often considered in the decisional law concerning Section 2(a) scandalousness and disparagement, namely, dictionary definitions. Both petitioners and respondent have submitted excerpts defining "redskin" from numerous well-established American dictionary publishers from editions covering the time period, variously, from 1966 through 1996. Across the time period, the number of publishers including in their dictionaries a usage label indicating that the word "redskin" is disparaging is approximately equal, on this record, to those who do not include any usage label. * * * Discussing the substantial body of historical documents he reviewed in connection with his testimony herein, Dr. Geoffrey Nunberg, petitioners' linguistics expert, concluded that the word "redskin(s)" first appeared in writing as a reference to Native Americans in 1699 and that, from 1699 to the present, the word "redskin(s),"used as a term of reference for Native Americans, evokes negative associations and is, thus, a term of disparagement. * * *

> Finally, we note petitioners' telephone survey, as described herein, purporting to measure the views, at the time of the survey in 1996, of the general population and, separately, of Native Americans towards the word "redskin" as a reference to Native Americans. When read a list of seven words referring to Native Americans, 46.2% of participants in the general population sample (139 of 301 participants) and 36.6% of participants in the Native American sample (131 of 358 participants) indicated that they found the word "redskin" offensive as a reference to Native Americans. We have discussed, supra, several of the flaws in the survey that limit its probative value. Additionally, the survey is of limited

applicability to the issues in this case as it sought to measure the participants' views only as of 1996, when the survey was conducted, and its scope is limited to the connotation of the word "redskin" as a term of Native Americans, without any reference to respondent's football team. However, considering these limitations, we find that the percentage of participants in each sample who responded positively, i.e., stated they were offended by the word "redskin(s)" for Native Americans, to be significant. While the survey polls a relatively small sample and the positive results reflect less than a majority of that sample, we find these results supportive of the other evidence in the record indicating the derogatory nature of the word "redskin(s)" for the entire period from, at least, the mid–1960's to the present, to substantial composites of both the general population and the Native American population. * * *

The evidence herein shows a parallel development of respondent's portrayal of Native Americans in connection with its services. For example, various covers of respondent's game program guides and other promotional efforts, including public relations stunts presenting players in Native American headdresses, from the 1940's through the middle to late 1950's show caricature-like portrayals of Native Americans as, period, usually, either savage aggressors or buffoons. Similarly, for the same time period, the costumes and antics of the team, the Redskins Marching Band, and the "Redskinettes" cheerleaders reflect a less than respectful portrayal of Native Americans.

During the late 1950's and early 1960's, the evidence shows respondent's game program covers with realistic portraits of actual Native American individuals, reflecting society's increased respect for, and interest in, Native American culture and history. During the 1960's through to the present, the evidence establishes that respondent has largely substituted football imagery for Native American imagery on its game program covers; that it has modified the lyrics of its theme song, "Hail to the Redskins" and modified its cheerleaders' uniforms; and Mr. Cooke testified that respondent has, for several years, had a strict policy mandating a restrained and "tasteful" portrayal of Native American imagery by its licensees. Of course, the allusion to Native Americans in connection with respondent's team has continued unabated, for example, in respondent's name, its trademarks, and through the use of Native American imagery such as the headdresses worn for many years by the Redskins Band.

Both parties have submitted voluminous excerpts from newspapers, including cartoons, headlines, editorials and articles, from the 1940's to the present, that refer to respondent's football team in the context of stories and writings about the game of football. These excerpts show that, despite respondent's more restrained use of its Native American imagery over time, the media has used Native American imagery in connection with respondent's team, throughout this entire time period, in a manner that often portrays Native Americans as either aggressive savages or buffoons. For example, many headlines refer to the "Redskins" team, players or managers "scalping" opponents, seeking "revenge," "on the warpath," and holding "pow wows"; or use pidgin English, such as "Big Chief Choo–He Ponder." Similarly, petitioners have submitted evidence, both excerpts from newspapers and video excerpts of games, showing respondent's team's fans dressed in costumes and engaging in antics that clearly poke fun at Native American culture and portrays Native Americans as savages and buffoons. As we have already stated, we agree with respondent that it is not responsible for the actions of the media or fans; however, the actions of the media and fans are probative of the general public's perception of the word "redskin(s)" as it appears in respondent's marks herein. As such, this evidence reinforces our conclusion that the word "redskin(s)" retains its derogatory character as part of the subject marks and as used in connection with respondent's football team.

Regarding the views of Native Americans in particular, the record contains the testimony of petitioners themselves stating that they have been seriously offended by respondent's use of the word "redskin(s)" as part of its marks in connection with its identified services. The record includes resolutions indicating a present objection to the use of this word in respondent's marks from the NCAI, which the record adequately establishes as a broad-based organization of Native American tribes and individuals; from the Oneida tribe; and from Unity 94, an organization including Native Americans. * * *

The Board also concluded that the Redskins marks should also be cancelled on the ground that they may bring Native Americans into contempt or disrepute. 50 U.S.P.Q.2d at 1743–48. The trademark owner has appealed these determinations. Litigation concerning the Washington Redskins marks continues to proceed through the courts. *See Pro–Football, Inc. v. Harjo*, 415 F.3d 44 (D.C. Cir. 2005) (reversing grant of summary judgment to team based on laches defense and remanding for further consideration).

IN RE BUDGE MANUFACTURING CO., INC.

United States Court of Appeals, Federal Circuit, 1988.
857 F.2d 773.

Nies, Circuit Judge.

Budge Manufacturing Co., Inc., appeals from the final decision of the United States Trademark Trial and Appeal Board refusing registration of LOVEE LAMB for "automotive seat covers," application Serial No. 507,974 filed November 9, 1984. The basis for rejection is that the term LAMB is deceptive matter within the meaning of section 2(a) of the Lanham Act, 15 U.S.C. § 1052(a) (1982), as applied to Budge's goods which are made wholly from synthetic fibers. We affirm.

Opinion

Section 2(a) of the Lanham Act bars registration of a mark which: "Consists of or comprises ... deceptive ... matter.... " As stated in In re Automatic Radio Mfg. Co., 404 F.2d 1391, 1396, 160 USPQ 233, 236 (CCPA 1969): "The proscription [of section 2(a)] is not against misdescriptive terms unless they are also deceptive." Thus, that a mark or part of a mark may be inapt or misdescriptive as applied to an applicant's goods does not make it "deceptive." Id. (AUTOMATIC RADIO not a deceptive mark for air conditioners, ignition systems, and antennas). Recognizing that premise, the Trademark Trial and Appeal Board has sought to articulate a standard by which "deceptive matter" under section 2(a) can be judged. In this case, the board applied the three-part test which was stated in In re Shapely, Inc., 231 USPQ 72, 73 (TTAB 1986): (1) whether the term is misdescriptive as applied to the goods, (2) if so, whether anyone would be likely to believe the misrepresentation, and (3) whether the misrepresentation would materially affect a potential purchaser's decision to buy the goods.

Budge argues that the board was bound to follow the standard articulated in In re Simmons, Inc., 192 USPQ 331 (TTAB 1976). Per Budge, Simmons sets forth a different standard in that it requires as a minimum that "the mark convey some information, upon which an intended customer may reasonably rely, concerning something about the character, quality, function, composition or use of the goods to induce the purchase thereof, but which information, in fact, is misleadingly false." Id. at 332.

The standard applied by the board for determining deceptive matter in section 2(a) cases has not been uniformly articulated in some material respects. For example, in at least one opinion an intent to mislead was required to establish section 2(a) deceptiveness. See Steinberg Bros., Inc. v. Middletown Rubber Corp., 137 USPQ 319, 321 (TTAB 1963). However, while phrased differently, we discern no material difference between the standard set forth in *Shapely* and that in *Simmons*. Budge points to no substantive difference and, indeed, merely quarrels over the different result here from that in Simmons. Thus, we need not address the question of the extent to which panels of the board are required to follow prior decisions of other board panels.

What is more significant, in any event, is that this court is bound only by its own precedent, none of which Budge discusses. Although we will give deference in appropriate circumstances to a board's decision on a question of law, we are, of course, not bound by such rulings. Where the issue relates to deceptive misdescriptiveness within the meaning of 2(a), we are in general agreement with the standard set out by the board in Shapely, with the following amplification in part drawn from *Simmons*: (1) Is the term misdescriptive of the character, quality, function, composition or use of the goods? (2) If so, are prospective purchasers likely to believe that the misdescription actually describes the goods? (3) If so, is the misdescription likely to affect the decision to purchase?

In ex parte prosecution, the burden is initially on the Patent and Trademark Office (PTO) to put forth sufficient evidence that the mark for which registration is sought meets the above criteria of unregistrability. Mindful that the PTO has limited facilities for acquiring evidence—it cannot, for example, be expected to conduct a survey of the marketplace or obtain consumer affidavits—we conclude that the evidence of record here is sufficient to establish a prima facie case of deceptiveness. That evidence shows with respect to the three-pronged test:

(1) Budge admits that its seat covers are not made from lamb or sheep products. Thus, the term LAMB is misdescriptive of its goods. (2) Seat covers for various vehicles can be and are made from natural lambskin and sheepskin. Applicant itself makes automobile seat covers of natural sheepskin. Lambskin is defined, inter alia, as fine-grade sheep skin. See Webster's Third New International Dictionary 639 (unabr. 1976). The board's factual inference is reasonable that purchasers are likely to believe automobile seat covers denominated by the term LAMB or SHEEP are actually made from natural sheep or lamb skins. (3) Evidence of record shows that natural sheepskin and lambskin is more expensive than simulated skins and that natural and synthetic skins have different characteristics. Thus, the misrepresentation is likely to affect the decision to purchase.

Faced with this prima facie case against registration, Budge had the burden to come forward with countering evidence to overcome the rejection. It wholly failed to do so.

Budge argues that its use of LAMB as part of its mark is not misdescriptive when considered in connection with the text in its advertising, which states that the cover is of "simulated sheepskin." Some, but not all, of Budge's specimen labels also have this text. This evidence is unpersuasive. In R. Neumann & Co. v. Overseas Shipments, Inc., 326 F.2d 786, 51 CCPA 946, 140 USPQ 276 (1964), a similar argument was made that the mark DURA–HYDE on shoes was not deceptive as an indication of leather because of tags affixed to the shoes proclaiming the legend "Outwears leather." In discounting the evidence, the court stated: "The legends constitute advertisement material separate and apart from any trademark significance." Id. at 790, 51 CCPA at 951, 140 USPQ at 279. * * *

Thus, we conclude that the board properly discounted Budge's advertising and labeling which indicate the actual fabric content. Misdescriptiveness of a term may be negated by its meaning in the context of the whole mark inasmuch as the combination is seen together and makes a unitary impression. A.F. Gallun & Sons Corp. v. Aristocrat Leather Prods., Inc., 135 USPQ 459, 460 (TTAB 1962) (COPY CALF not misdescriptive, but rather suggests imitation of calf skin). The same is not true with respect to explanatory statements in advertising or on labels which purchasers may or may not note and which may or may not always be provided. The statutory provision bars registration of a mark comprising deceptive matter. Congress has said that the advantages of registration may not be extended to a mark which deceives the public. Thus, the mark standing alone must pass muster, for that is what the applicant seeks to register, not extraneous explanatory statements.

Budge next argues that no reasonable purchaser would expect to purchase lambskin automobile seat covers because none made of lambskin are on the market. Only sheepskin automobile seat covers are being made, per Budge. Not only was no evidence submitted on the point Budge seeks to make, only statements of Budge's attorney, but also the argument is without substance. The board properly equated sheepskin and lambskin based on the dictionary definition which indicates that the terms may be used interchangeably. In addition, while Budge would discount the evidence presented that bicycle and airline seat coverings are made of lambskin, we conclude that it does support the board's finding that there is nothing incongruous about automobile seat covers being made from lambskin. We also agree with the board's conclusion that any differences between sheepskin and lambskin would not be readily apparent to potential purchasers of automobile seat covers. The board's finding here that purchasers are likely to believe the misrepresentation is not clearly erroneous. * * *

Finally, we note the evidence of Budge's extensive sales since 1974 under the mark. However, it is too well established for argument that a mark which includes deceptive matter is barred from registration and cannot acquire distinctiveness.

CONCLUSION

None of the facts found by the board have been shown to be clearly erroneous nor has the board erred as a matter of law. Accordingly, we affirm the board's decision that Budge's mark LOVEE LAMB for automobile seat covers made from synthetic fibers is deceptive within the meaning of 15 U.S.C. § 1052(a) and is, thus, barred from registration.

AFFIRMED.

NICHOLS, SENIOR CIRCUIT JUDGE, concurring.

I agree that the TTAB decision should be affirmed, and with most of what the court well says. There is one matter, however, as to which I do not wholly agree, much as I respect the court's expertise in this field.

* * *

No one can tell what future cases will bring or whether our formula will aid the solution of future cases, or hinder it. *In re Simmons, Inc.*, one of our three cases, well illustrates my point. The mark: "White Sable" for paint brush bristles, is construed in light of the fact that the animal, sable, is extremely dark and that is so well known that "sable" as an adjective, serves as a synonym for black, as in "sable plumage." As the white sable is a fictitious animal, the mark "white sable" cannot deceptively represent that the hairs in the brush came from a real animal. Who could prescribe beforehand how to deal with such a case? To deal with it after it arose, by an unhampered board, was no trick at all.

In the case before us, the board asked itself: "is anyone likely to believe the product is made of lamb or sheepskin?" The question might, perhaps ideally, be "is any reasonable person * * * "because unreasonable persons are likely to believe anything. It is clearly what the board meant. This court transforms that question in its formula to this: If so, are prospective purchasers likely to believe that the misdescription actually describes the goods? Thus "anyone," a single individual, is transmuted into a class of persons. I readily can picture the fun future counsel will have with this. They can demand that the board, with its limited investigative facilities as we acknowledge, first define who are the prospective purchasers, old, young, Ph.D's, illiterates, etc.? Then, what are their tastes, their intellectual quirks, their degree of gullibility?

A simple issue, mostly or wholly of law, is transmuted into a wide-ranging factual inquiry. Is the board to indulge in guesswork and speculation as to this supposititious class, and its mores? * * * Is it to conduct a sweeping inquest, the process known outside the Beltway as "making a federal case out of it." Far better, it seems to me, is not to fix anything when nothing is broke.

Notes

1. What role should intent play in the determination of whether a mark is deceptive? See Daphne Leeds, "Trademarks—The Rationale of Registrability," 26 Geo. Wash. L. Rev. 653, 662–63 (1958).

2. Would the mark "Bahia" be deceptive when used as a trademark for cigars? Bahia is a region in Brazil where cigars are produced, but the cigars in question are not produced in that area. What other information would be pertinent to this determination? See In re House of Windsor, Inc., 221 U.S.P.Q. 53 (T.T.A.B. 1983).

3. Is the mark "Sweden" deceptive as applied to external artificial kidney units not made in Sweden? See In re Sweden Freezer Mfg. Co., 159 U.S.P.Q. 246 (T.T.A.B.1968). What about the mark "Italian Maide," when applied to canned vegetables? In re Amerise, 160 U.S.P.Q. 687, 691 (T.T.A.B. 1969). "Swiss Precision" for watches not made in Switzerland?

4. Section 2 of the Lanham Act, 15 U.S.C.A. § 1052, contains a number of specific prohibitions on registration. The cases illustrate several applications of this rule, but a full review of this provision is necessary to understand which otherwise registrable marks are precluded by operation of section 2. One of the most significant restrictions is section 2(d), which prohibits the registration of marks that are confusingly similar to a mark that is previously registered or used. See Marshall Field & Co. v. Mrs. Fields Cookies, 25 U.S.P.Q.2d 1321 (T.T.A.B. 1992) (holding that cookie producer's brand name was not confusingly similar to department store mark). For further discussion of limitations on trademark registration, see 1 J. Thomas McCarthy, Trademarks and Unfair Competition §§ 11.19, 19.25 to 28 (3d ed. 1995).

IN RE CALIFORNIA INNOVATIONS, INC.

United States Court of Appeals, Federal Circuit, 2003.
329 F.3d 1334.

RADER, CIRCUIT JUDGE.

California Innovations, Inc. (CA Innovations), a Canadian-based corporation, appeals the Trademark Trial and Appeal Board's refusal to register its mark—CALIFORNIA INNOVATIONS. Citing section 2(e)(3) of the Lanham Act, 15 U.S.C. § 1052(e)(3) (2000), the Board concluded that the mark was primarily geographically deceptively misdescriptive. Because the Board applied an outdated standard in its analysis under § 1052(e)(3), this court vacates the Board's decision and remands.

I

CA Innovations filed an intent-to-use trademark application, Serial No. 74/650,703, on March 23, 1995, for the composite mark CALIFORNIA INNOVATIONS and Design. The application sought registration for the following goods: automobile visor organizers, namely, holders for personal effects, and automobile trunk organizers for automotive accessories in International Class 12; backpacks in International Class 18; thermal insulated bags for food and beverages, thermal insulated tote bags for food or beverages, and thermal insulated wraps for cans to keep the containers cold or hot in International Class 21; and nylon, vinyl, polyester and/or leather bags for storage and storage pouches in International Class 22.

The United States Patent and Trademark Office (PTO) initially refused registration based on an alleged likelihood of confusion with some prior registrations. At the PTO's request, applicant disclaimed the CALIFORNIA component of the mark. Applicant also amended its identification and classification of goods to conform to the examiner's suggestions. Thereafter, the PTO issued a notice of publication. The mark was published for opposition on September 29, 1998. No opposition was ever filed. In July 1999, the PTO reasserted jurisdiction over the application under 37 C.F.R. § 2.84(a) and refused registration under § 1052(e)(3), concluding that the mark was primarily geographically deceptively misdescriptive. Applicant filed a timely notice for reconsideration with the PTO and a notice of appeal to the Board in November 2000. After the PTO refused to reconsider its decision, CA Innovations renewed its appeal to the Board. On February 20, 2002, the Board upheld the PTO's refusal to register applicant's mark and concluded that the mark was primarily geographically deceptively misdescriptive.

* * *

II

The Lanham Act addresses geographical marks in three categories. The first category, § 1052(a), identifies geographically deceptive marks:

> No trademark by which the goods of the applicant may be distinguished from the goods of others shall be refused registration on the principal register on account of its nature unless it—(a) Consists of or comprises immoral, deceptive, or scandalous matter; or matter which may disparage or falsely suggest a connection with persons, living or dead, institutions, beliefs, or national symbols, or bring them into contempt, or disrepute.

15 U.S.C. § 1052(a) (2000). Although not expressly addressing geographical marks, § 1052(a) has traditionally been used to reject geographic

marks that materially deceive the public. A mark found to be deceptive under § 1052(a) cannot receive protection under the Lanham Act. To deny a geographic mark protection under § 1052(a), the PTO must establish that (1) the mark misrepresents or misdescribes the goods, (2) the public would likely believe the misrepresentation, and (3) the misrepresentation would materially affect the public's decision to purchase the goods. See In re Budge Mfg. Co., 857 F.2d 773, 775, 8 USPQ2d 1259, 1260 (Fed.Cir.1988). This test's central point of analysis is materiality because that finding shows that the misdescription deceived the consumer. See In re House of Windsor, 221 USPQ 53, 56–57, 1983 WL 51833 (TTAB 1983).

The other two categories of geographic marks are (1) "primarily geographically descriptive" marks and (2) "primarily geographically deceptively misdescriptive" marks under § 1052(e). The North American Free Trade Agreement, see North American Free Trade Agreement, Dec. 17, 1992, art. 1712, 32 I.L.M. 605, 698 [hereinafter NAFTA], as implemented by the NAFTA Implementation Act in 1993, see NAFTA Implementation Act, Pub. L. No. 103–182, 107 Stat. 2057 (1993), has recently changed these two categories. Before the NAFTA changes, § 1052(e) and (f) stated:

> No trademark by which the goods of the applicant may be distinguished from the goods of others shall be refused registration on the principal register on account of its nature unless it—
>
> (e) Consists of a mark which . . .
>
> (2) when used on or in connection with the goods of the applicant is primarily geographically descriptive or deceptively misdescriptive of them.
>
> * * *
>
> (f) Except as expressly excluded in paragraphs (a) (d) of this section, nothing in this chapter shall prevent the registration of a mark used by the applicant which has become distinctive of the applicant's goods in commerce. 15 U.S.C. § 1052(e)(2) and (f) (1988).

The law treated these two categories of geographic marks identically. Specifically, the PTO generally placed a "primarily geographically descriptive" or "deceptively misdescriptive" mark on the supplemental register. Upon a showing of acquired distinctiveness, these marks could qualify for the principal register.

Thus, in contrast to the permanent loss of registration rights imposed on deceptive marks under § 1052(a), pre-NAFTA § 1052(e)(2) only required a temporary denial of registration on the principal register. Upon a showing of distinctiveness, these marks could acquire a place on the principal register. In re Dial–A–Mattress Operating Corp., 240 F.3d 1341, 1347, 57 USPQ2d 1807, 1812 (Fed.Cir.2001). As permitted by pre-NAFTA § 1052(f), a mark could acquire distinctiveness or "secondary meaning" by showing that "in the minds of the public, the primary significance of a product feature or term is to identify the source of the product rather than the product itself." Inwood Labs., Inc. v. Ives Labs., 456 U.S. 844, 851 n. 11, 102 S.Ct. 2182, 72 L.Ed.2d 606 (1982).

In the pre-NAFTA era, the focus on distinctiveness overshadowed the deceptiveness aspect of § 1052(e)(2) and made it quite easy for the PTO to deny registration on the principal register to geographically deceptively misdescriptive marks under § 1052(e)(2). On the other hand, the deception requirement of § 1052(a) protected against fraud and could not be overlooked. Therefore, the PTO had significantly more difficulty denying registration based on that higher standard. See generally Andrew P. Vance, Can't Get There From Here: How NAFTA and GATT Have Reduced Protection for Geographical Trademarks, 26 Brook. J. Int'l L. 1097 (2001).

Before NAFTA, in In re Nantucket, 209 USPQ 868, 870, 1981 WL 48122 (TTAB 1981), the Board used a three-prong test to detect either primarily geographically descriptive or deceptively misdescriptive marks. Under the Board's test, the only substantive inquiry was whether the mark conveyed primarily a geographical connotation. On appeal in In re Nantucket, this court's predecessor rejected that test:

> The board's test rests mechanistically on the one question of whether the mark is recognizable, at least to some large segment of the public, as the name of a geographical area. NANTUCKET is such. That ends the board's test. Once it is found that the mark is the name of a known place, i.e., that it has "a readily recognizable geographic meaning," the next question, whether applicant's goods do or do not come from that place, becomes irrelevant under the board's test, for if they do, the mark is "primarily geographically descriptive"; if they don't, the mark is "primarily geographically deceptively misdescriptive." Either way, the result is the same, for the mark must be denied registration on the principal register unless resort can be had to § 2(f).

In re Nantucket, Inc., 677 F.2d 95, 97–98 (CCPA 1982). Thus In re Nantucket, for the first time, set forth a goods-place association requirement. Id. at 99–100. In other words, this court required a geographically deceptively misdescriptive mark to have more than merely a primary geographic connotation. Specifically, the public must also associate the goods in question with the place identified by the mark—the goods-place association requirement. However, this court did not require a showing that the goods-place association was material to the consumer's decision before rejection under § 1052(e).

In In re Loew's Theatres, Inc., 769 F.2d 764, 767–69 (Fed.Cir.1985), this court expressly permitted a goods-place association without any showing that the place is "well-known" or "noted" for the goods in question. The Loew's court explained: "[I]f the place is noted for the particular goods, a mark for such goods which do not originate there is likely to be deceptive under § 2(a) and not registrable under any circumstances." Id. at 768, n. 6. Clarifying that pre-NAFTA § 1052(e)(2) does not require a "well-known" place, this court noted:

> The PTO's burden is simply to establish that there is a reasonable predicate for its conclusion that the public would be likely to make the particular goods/place association on which it relies. . . . The issue is not the fame or exclusivity of the place name, but the likelihood that a particular place will be associated with particular goods. Id.

As noted, the Lanham Act itself does not expressly require different tests for geographically misleading marks. In order to implement the Lanham Act prior to the NAFTA amendments, the PTO used a low standard to reject marks for geographically deceptive misdescriptiveness under pre-NAFTA § 1052(e), which was relatively simple to meet. In contrast, the PTO required a much more demanding finding to reject for geographical deception under § 1052(a). This distinction was justified because rejection under subsection (a) was final, while rejection under pre-NAFTA subsection (e)(2) was only temporary, until the applicant could show that the mark had become distinctive. The more drastic consequence establishes the propriety of the elevated materiality test in the context of a permanent ban on registration under § 1052(a).

NAFTA and its implementing legislation obliterated the distinction between geographically deceptive marks and primarily geographically deceptively misdescriptive marks. Article 1712 of NAFTA provides:

> 1. Each party [United States, Mexico, Canada] shall provide, in respect of geographical indications, the legal means for interested persons to prevent:
>
> > (a) the use of any means in the designation or presentation of a good that indicates or suggests that the good in question originates in a territory, region or locality other than the true place of origin, in a manner that misleads the public as to the geographical origin of the good. . . .

See NAFTA, Dec. 17, 1992, art. 1712, 32 I.L.M. 605, 698. This treaty shifts the emphasis for geographically descriptive marks to prevention of any public deception. Accordingly, the NAFTA Act amended § 1052(e) to read:

> No trademark by which the goods of the applicant may be distinguished from the goods of others shall be refused registration on the principal register on account of its nature unless it—
>
> > (e) Consists of a mark which (1) when used on or in connection with the goods of the applicant is merely descriptive or deceptively misdescriptive of them, (2) when used on or in connection with the goods of the applicant is primarily geographically descriptive of them, except as indications of regional origin may be registrable under section 4 [15 USCS § 1054], (3) when used on or in connection with the goods of the applicant is primarily geographically deceptively misdescriptive of them, (4) is primari-

ly merely a surname, or (5) comprises any matter that, as a whole, is functional.

(f) Except as expressly excluded in subsections (a), (b), (c), (d), (e)(3), and (e)(5) of this section, nothing herein shall prevent the registration of a mark used by the applicant which has become distinctive of the applicant's goods in commerce. 15 U.S.C. § 1052(e)-(f) (2000).

Recognizing the new emphasis on prevention of public deception, the NAFTA amendments split the categories of geographically descriptive and geographically deceptively misdescriptive into two subsections (subsections (e)(2) and (e)(3) respectively). Under the amended Lanham Act, subsection (e)(3)—geographically deceptive misdescription—could no longer acquire distinctiveness under subsection (f). Accordingly, marks determined to be primarily geographically deceptively misdescriptive are permanently denied registration, as are deceptive marks under § 1052(a).

Thus, § 1052 no longer treats geographically deceptively misdescriptive marks differently from geographically deceptive marks. Like geographically deceptive marks, the analysis for primarily geographically deceptively misdescriptive marks under § 1052(e)(3) focuses on deception of, or fraud on, the consumer. The classifications under the new § 1052 clarify that these two deceptive categories both receive permanent rejection. Accordingly, the test for rejecting a deceptively misdescriptive mark is no longer simple lack of distinctiveness, but the higher showing of deceptiveness. The legislative history of the NAFTA Act confirms the change in standard for geographically deceptively misdescriptive marks. In a congressional record statement, which appears to be the equivalent of a committee report, the Senate Judiciary Committee acknowledges the new standard for these marks:

> [T]he bill creates a distinction in subsection 2(e) of the Trademark Act between geographically "descriptive" and "misdescriptive" marks and amends subsections 2(f) and 23(a) of the Act to preclude registration of "primarily geographically deceptively misdescriptive" marks on the principal and supplemental registers, respectively. The law as it relates to "primarily geographically descriptive" marks would remain unchanged. 139 Cong. Rec. S 16,092 (1993).

The amended Lanham Act gives geographically deceptively misdescriptive marks the same treatment as geographically deceptive marks under § 1052(a). Because both of these categories are subject to permanent denial of registration, the PTO may not simply rely on lack of distinctiveness to deny registration, but must make the more difficult showing of public deception. In other words, by placing geographically deceptively misdescriptive marks under subsection (e)(3) in the same fatal circumstances as deceptive marks under subsection (a), the NAFTA Act also elevated the standards for identifying those deceptive marks.

Before NAFTA, the PTO identified and denied registration to a primarily geographically deceptively misdescriptive mark with a showing that (1) the primary significance of the mark was a generally known geographic location, and (2) "the public was likely to believe the mark identified the place from which the goods originate and that the goods did not come from there." In re Loew's, 769 F.2d at 768. The second prong of the test represents the "goods-place association" between the mark and the goods at issue. This test raised an inference of deception based on the likelihood of a goods-place association that did not reflect the actual origin of the goods. A mere inference, however, is not enough to establish the deceptiveness that brings the harsh consequence of non-registrability under the amended Lanham Act. As noted, NAFTA and the amended Lanham Act place an emphasis on actual misleading of the public.

Therefore, the relatively easy burden of showing a naked goods-place association without proof that the association is material to the consumer's decision is no longer justified, because marks rejected under § 1052(e)(3) can no longer obtain registration through acquired distinctiveness under § 1052(f). To ensure a showing of deceptiveness and misleading before imposing the penalty of non-registrability, the PTO may not deny registration without a showing that the goods-place association made by the consumer is material to the consumer's decision to purchase those goods. This addition of a materiality inquiry equates this test with the elevated standard applied under § 1052(a). See House of Windsor, 221 USPQ at 56–57 (establishing "a 'materiality' test to distinguish marks that fall within the proscription of Section 2(e)(2) from those that fall also within the proscription of Section 2(a)"). This also properly reflects the presence of the deceptiveness criterion often overlooked in the "primarily geographically deceptively misdescriptive" provision of the statute.

The shift in emphasis in the standard to identify primarily geographically deceptively misdescriptive marks under § 1052(e)(3) will bring that section into harmony with § 1052(a). Both sections involve proof of deception with the consequence of non-registrability. The adherence to the pre-NAFTA standard designed to focus on distinctiveness would almost read the term "deceptively" out of § 1052(e)(3), which is the term that the NAFTA amendments to the Lanham Act has reemphasized. Accordingly, under the amended Lanham Act, both subsection (a) and subsection (e)(3) share a similar legal standard.

Since the NAFTA amendments, this court has dealt with two cases involving § 1052(e)(3). Wada, 194 F.3d 1297; In re Save Venice New York, Inc., 259 F.3d 1346, 59 USPQ2d 1778 (Fed.Cir.2001). Although neither of those cases explores the effect of the NAFTA Act on the test for determining geographically deceptive misdescription, both cases satisfy the new NAFTA standard. "[I]f there is evidence that goods like applicant's or goods related to applicant's are a principal product of the geographical area named by the mark, then the deception will most likely be found material and the mark, therefore, deceptive." House of Windsor, 221 USPQ at 57. "[I]f the place is noted for the particular goods, a mark for such goods which do not originate there is likely to be deceptive under § 2(a) and not registrable under any circumstances.'' Loew's Theatres, 769 F.2d at 768, n. 6.

In Save Venice, this court affirmed the Board's refusal to register applicant's marks ''THE VENICE COLLECTION'' and ''SAVE VENICE, INC.'' because of the ''substantial evidence available showing that Venice, Italy is known for glass, lace, art objects, jewelry, cotton and silk textiles, printing and publishing.'' 259 F.3d at 1354 (emphasis added). Although the court in Save Venice did not expressly address the materiality issue, because it was not officially recognized in this context, the court emphasized that ''all of the applicant's goods are associated with traditional Venetian products.'' Id. at 1350 (emphasis added). The court in Save Venice concluded that the public would mistakenly believe they were purchasing ''traditional Venetian products'' because the applicant's products were ''indistinguishable'' from the products traditionally originating in Venice. Id. at 1350–54. Thus, the record in Save Venice satisfies the test for deception.

Similarly, in Wada, this court affirmed the Board's refusal to register applicant's mark ''NEW YORK WAYS GALLERY'' because there was ''evidence that showed ... New York is well-known as a place where leather goods and handbags are designed and manufactured.'' Wada, 194 F.3d at 1299–1300 (emphasis added). Again, the court in Wada did not expressly make a finding that the goods-place association would materially influence the consumer. However, this court noted that the public, ''upon encountering goods bearing the mark NEW YORK WAYS GALLERY, would believe that the goods'' originate in New York, ''a world-renown fashion center ... well-known as a place where goods of this kind are designed, manufactured, or sold.'' Id. This showing that the place was not only well-known, but renowned for the products at issue supports a finding of materiality. See House of Windsor, 221 USPQ at 57.

Thus, due to the NAFTA changes in the Lanham Act, the PTO must deny registration under § 1052(e)(3) if (1) the primary significance of the mark is a generally known geographic location, (2) the consuming public is likely to believe the place identified by the mark indicates the origin of the goods bearing the mark, when in fact the goods do not come from that place, and (3) the misrepresentation was a material factor in the consumer's decision.

As a result of the NAFTA changes to the Lanham Act, geographic deception is specifically dealt with in subsection (e)(3), while deception in general continues to be addressed under subsection (a). Consequently, this court anticipates that the PTO will usually address geographically deceptive marks under subsection (e)(3) of the amended Lanham Act rather than subsection (a). While there are identical legal standards for deception in each section, subsection (e)(3) specifically involves deception involving geographic marks.

III

CA Innovations unequivocally states in its opening brief that its "petition seeks review only of that portion of the [Board's] decision that pertains to 'thermal insulated bags for food and beverages and thermal insulated wraps for cans' " as identified in International Class 21 in the application. Therefore, because of applicant's decision not to challenge the Board's judgment with respect to all goods other than those identified in class 21, that part of the Board's decision is not affected by this opinion.

As a preliminary issue, this court may affirm or reverse a rejection of an application with respect to only a portion of the goods identified. This court discerns no legal limitation on an appeal with respect to a portion of the goods listed in the application. In fact, the Board also perceives no legal restrictions on narrowing the issues in an application. See In re Wielinski, 49 USPQ2d 1754, 1998 WL 998961 (TTAB 1998) (affirming refusal to register only as to class 16 and reversing refusal to register as to all other classes); In re Harry N. Abrams, Inc., 223 USPQ 832, 1984 WL 63592 (TTAB 1984) (affirming refusal to register as to class 14 and reversing refusal to register as to all remaining classes); see also Trademark Manual of Examining Procedure § 1403.05 (3d ed. 2002).

The parties agree that CA Innovations' goods do not originate in California. Under the first prong of the test—whether the mark's primary significance is a generally known geographic location—a composite mark such as the applicant's proposed mark must be evaluated as a whole. . . . It is not erroneous, however, for the examiner to consider the significance of each element within the composite mark in the course of evaluating the mark as a whole.

Save Venice, 259 F.3d at 1352 (citations omitted).

The Board found that "the word CALIFORNIA is a prominent part of applicant's mark and is not overshadowed by either the word INNOVATIONS or the design element." Although the mark may also convey the idea of a creative, laid-back lifestyle or mindset, the Board properly recognized that such an association does not contradict the primary geographic significance of the mark. Even if the public may associate California with a particular life-style, the record supports the Board's finding that the primary meaning remains focused on the state of California. Nonetheless, this court declines to review at this stage the Board's finding that CA Innovations' composite mark CALIFORNIA INNOVATIONS and Design is primarily geographic in nature. Rather the PTO may apply the entire new test on remand.

The second prong of the test requires proof that the public is likely to believe the applicant's goods originate in California. The Board stated that the examining attorney submitted excerpts from the Internet and the NEXIS database showing "some manufacturers and distributors of backpacks, tote bags, luggage, computer cases, and sport bags ... headquartered in California." The Board also acknowledged articles "which make reference to companies headquartered in California which manufacture automobile accessories such as auto organizers," as well as the "very serious apparel and sewn products industry" in California.

A great deal of the evidence cited in this case relates to the fashion industry, which is highly prevalent in California due to Hollywood's influence on this industry. However, clothing and fashion have nothing to do with the products in question. At best, the record in this case shows some general connection between the state of California and backpacks and automobile organizers. However, because CA Innovations has limited its appeal to insulated bags and wraps, the above referenced evidence is immaterial. Therefore, this opinion has no bearing on whether the evidence of record supports a rejection of the application with regard to any goods other than those identified in CA Innovations' application under International Class 21, namely insulated bags and wraps. CA Innovations argues that the examining attorney provided no evidence at all concerning insulated bags for food and wraps for cans in California. The Government contends that the evidence shows some examples of a lunch bag, presumed to be insulated, and insulated backpacks. According to the government, the evidence supports a finding of a goods-place association between California and insulated bags and wraps. This court has reviewed the publications and listings supplied by the examining attorney. At best, the evidence of a connection between California and insulated bags and wraps is tenuous. Even if the evidence supported a finding of a goods-place association, the PTO has yet to apply the materiality test in this case. This court declines to address that issue and apply the new standard in the first instance. Accordingly, this court vacates the finding of the Board that CA Innovations' mark is primarily geographically deceptively misdescriptive, and remands the case for further proceedings. On remand, the Board shall apply the new three-prong standard.

* * *

VACATED and REMANDED.

Note

How would you analyze the use of "Le Marais" for a French kosher restaurant located in New York City? The name is identical to an area of Paris known for having fashionable restaurants (and is known to be the Jewish part of the city). *See In re Les Halles de Paris J.V.*, 334 F.3d 1371 (Fed. Cir. 2003), *remanded*, 2004 WL 839413 (T.T.A.B. Apr. 15, 2004).

G. SERVICE MARKS

IN RE DR. PEPPER CO.

United States Court of Appeals, Federal Circuit, 1987.
836 F.2d 508.

NIES, CIRCUIT JUDGE.

Dr Pepper Company appeals from the decision of the Patent and Trademark Office Trademark Trial and Appeal Board, 1 USPQ2d 1421 (TTAB 1986), affirming the examining attorney's refusal to register the mark PEPPER MAN as a service mark on the ground that applicant's asserted service of sponsoring and operating a particular contest to promote its soft drinks was not a service within the contemplation of sections 3 and 45 of the Trademark Act of 1946, 15 U.S.C. §§ 1053 and 1127 (1982 & Supp. III 1985). We affirm.

I

Appellant filed an application, Serial No. 477,600, seeking registration of PEPPER MAN which it asserts is its "service mark for sponsorship and operation of contest services."[1] To promote its DR PEPPER soft drinks, appellant conducts a promotional contest in which cash prizes are awarded to households found to have on hand certain specified quantities of unopened cans or bottles of DR PEPPER soft drinks, or certain coupons called "I'M A PEPPER" cards, which can be obtained free of charge from Dr. Pepper or its bottlers. Appellant displays the name PEPPER MAN on promotional pieces for the contest.

The examining attorney refused registration, and the board affirmed, on the ground that applicant was not rendering a service within the contemplation of the Act. The crux of the board's reasoning is that where, as here, an activity claimed to be a service is incidental to the sale of goods, the activity cannot be separately recognizable as a service unless it is shown that the activity constitutes something clearly different from, or over and above, any activity normally involved in promoting the sale of such goods. The running of a contest to advertise and promote the sale of one's goods is not a service over and above, or materially different from, what would normally be expected from one engaged in the sale of goods.

II

The sole issue raised on appeal is whether conducting a contest to promote the sale of one's own goods is a "service" within the meaning of

---

1. Specifically, the application states that the mark was used for the services of "sponsorship and operation of contests in which cash awards are presented to selected households based upon the quantity of certain soft drink products present in those households or the quantity of official 'I'm a pepper' cards present in those households." Prizes are also awarded to randomly select- ed shoppers near stores selling DR PEPPER soft drinks if the shoppers have in their possession the required cans, bottles, or "I'M A PEPPER" cards. In either case, the amount of the prize depends on the quantity of soft drinks or cards found. The awards are made by applicant's agent who is called the PEPPER MAN.

sections 3 and 45 of the Trademark Act of 1946, 15 U.S.C. §§ 1053, 1127 (1982).[2] Appellant maintains that sponsorship and operation of a promotional contest is a "service" to the public because some of them will receive the benefit of cash prizes. Thus, it maintains that the name it uses in promoting the contest is registrable as its service mark.

While this court and its predecessor have stated that "services" is a term of "broad scope" under the Lanham Act, In re Advertising & Mktg. Dev., Inc., 821 F.2d 614, 618, 2 USPQ2d 2010, 2013 (Fed.Cir.1987), some business activities which may be described in terms of a "service" to the public do not constitute a service within the intendment of the Act. Appellant does not challenge that general proposition, but urges that contest activities to promote one's products should not be placed in that category, particularly when denominated by a name different from the trademark for the product.

The Act itself provides no definition of a "service" and the legislative history gives no guidance beyond the general principle that, for the first time, marks of businesses engaged in rendering services, such as laundries, were made registrable. Further refinement was left to the administrative agency, now the Patent and Trademark Office, and to the courts.

Through a series of decisions it has become a settled principle that the rendering of a service which is normally "expected or routine" in connection with the sale of one's own goods is not a registrable service whether denominated by the same or a different name from the trademark for its product. This interpretation is a refinement of the basic principle that the service for which registration is sought must be rendered to others. Merely advertising one's own goods, while, in a sense, an "informational" or in some instances an "entertainment" service to others, was early held not to be a "service" within the purview of sections 3 and 45. In re Tampax Inc., 91 USPQ 215 (Dec.Comm'r Pat.1951).

The interpretation that a company's promotional activities are not services to others under the Act was subsequently endorsed in judicial decisions of our predecessor, the Court of Customs and Patent Appeals. In re Radio Corp. of Am., 205 F.2d 180, 182, 98 USPQ 157, 158 (CCPA 1953) (supplying radio stations with packaged radio programs of records is mere advertising of record company, not a "service" to consumers).

---

2. Section 3 of the Trademark Act of 1946, 15 U.S.C. § 1053, provides in pertinent part:

> Service marks registrable Subject to the provisions relating to the registration of trade-marks, so far as they are applicable, service marks used in commerce shall be registrable, in the same manner and with the same effect as are trade-marks, and when registered they shall be entitled to the protection provided in this chapter in the case of trade-marks....

The provision of section 45 of the Trademark Act of 1946, 15 U.S.C. § 1127, relating to service marks states:

> The term "service mark" means a mark used in the sale or advertising of services to identify and distinguish the services of one person, including a unique service, from the services of others and to indicate the source of services, even if that source is unknown.

See also In re Orion Research Inc., 523 F.2d 1398, 1400, 187 USPQ 485, 487 (CCPA 1975) (Orion I) (the repair or replacement of one's own merchandise or "guaranteeing" same held not a registrable "service" because it is normally expected by purchasers from the purveyor of goods); In re Orion Research Inc., 669 F.2d 689, 691, 205 USPQ 688, 690 (CCPA 1980) (Orion II) (same). Thus, our precedent has drawn the line in connection with promotional activities that those which are "ordinary or routine" are not registrable services, despite some extra benefit to the public beyond the existence of the goods themselves. The public does not, per our precedent, perceive such activity as a service to the public but as mere sales activity by and for the benefit of the offerer of the goods.

In several decisions the board has specifically addressed the registrability of the name for a contest promoting the goods of the company conducting the contest. In In re Johnson Publishing Co., 130 USPQ 185 (TTAB 1961), the board held that the publisher of a magazine which offered prizes to readers who submitted at least one paid subscription and solved a puzzle was not providing a registrable service. This interpretation was followed and reaffirmed in In re Loew's Theatres, Inc., 179 USPQ 126, 127 (TTAB 1973), where the board stated:

> The lottery type contest, as conducted by applicant, is incidental to the sale of goods, and it is not a service over and above that normally involved in the promotion and sale of its goods. It is directly related to and tied to applicant's "KENT" cigarettes, and it is nothing more and would not be recognized as anything more than a promotional gimmick or device used to advertise and foster the sale of these cigarettes. Benefits do accrue to winners of the contest, but this is true generally of all promotional devices, but this fact alone cannot serve to obfuscate the true nature and character of applicant's contest.

While the interpretations of the statute by the board are not binding on this court, under general principles of administrative law, deference should be given by a court to the interpretation by the agency charged with its administration. We conclude that the board reasonably has treated promotional contests as "routine" sales activity for a producer's goods.

* * *

Appellant argues that the exclusion of services ordinarily or routinely rendered in connection with the sale of goods will preclude registration of marks for a vast array of activities currently recognized as services under the Act, such as those provided by retail department stores, mail order companies, and gasoline stations. Contrary to appellant's view, this consequence does not follow. Appellant leaves out the key element which is that the activities being questioned here relate to promotion of its own goods. Department stores and gasoline stations are service businesses and provide precisely the types of services intended to be brought under the Act. Indeed, advertising agency services as well as the service of conducting contests for others are within the Act. A parallel nonregistrability situation with a service business would be a refusal to register an asserted service of offering "free" glassware to customers who have made a certain level of purchases at a gasoline station, the service of providing "free" bags for purchasers at a grocery store, or a lottery contest by a new shopping mall. Registration of the marks identifying the services of service businesses is not endangered by continuing to apply the principle that services which are ordinary or routine in the sale of goods (or services), such as promotional activities for one's own business, are not services within the meaning of the Act. As stated by Professor McCarthy:

> The point is that a manufacturer or merchant cannot proliferate registrations by obtaining a trademark registration along with a whole raft of service mark registrations covering each and every "service" which every other competitor also provides as an adjunct to the sale of goods.... Thus, even though a given term may function as both a trademark and a service mark, the service must constitute more than mere promotion and advertising of one's own goods. The difference lies between those services which are mandatory or common in promoting the sale of this type of merchandise, and those services which are not so mandatory or common.

1 J. McCarthy, Trademarks and Unfair Competition § 19.30, at 940 (2d ed. 1984) (footnotes omitted). Such proliferation of registrations by devising ways to describe a sale-of-goods situation as a service has been held not to be within the intendment of the Act. We adhere to that precedent.

Alternatively, appellant seeks to elevate its promotional contest to a service under the Act on the ground that its contest is different from a routine advertising contest in that persons who have not purchased its goods may be contacted. However, it admits that only persons who have full containers for its soft drink or have obtained promotional coupons can win. We see nothing which takes this contest out of the ordinary advertising contest.

III

For the foregoing reasons, we affirm the board's decision refusing registration on the ground that appellant is not rendering a service within the meaning of the Act.

AFFIRMED.

NEWMAN, CIRCUIT JUDGE, dissenting.

I respectfully dissent. Federal registration of the mark PEPPER MAN is squarely within the intended purview of the Lanham Trademark Act. Precedential authority also weighs heavily in support of registration.

The policy underlying federal registration of trade and service marks is to facilitate business activity, not to place unnecessary obstacles in its path. The policy of the Lanham Act is to "conform to legitimate present-day business practices." D. Robert, Commentary on The Lanham Trade–Mark Act, 15 U.S.C.A. 265, 267 (1948). Importantly in connection with the issue at bar, "the Act was designed to ... create an incentive to register all valid marks in use to the end that a complete public record of such marks might be maintained and the rights of all registrants thereby secured." Id. at 268.

* * *

The statute contains the following definition of "service mark":

15 U.S.C. § 1127 ... The term "service mark" means a mark used in the sale or advertising of services to identify and distinguish the services of one person, including a unique service, from the services of others and to indicate the source of the services, even if that source is unknown.

Titles, character names and other distinctive features of radio or television programs may be registered as service marks notwithstanding that they, or the programs, may advertise the goods of the sponsor. * * *

Precedent has implemented this mandate for realistic, rather than constrained, statutory construction. In the case closest on its facts to those at bar, In re Congoleum Corporation, 222 USPQ 452 (TTAB 1984), the applicant conducted contests for customers, using the phrase "The Wonderful World of Congoleum". The board held that the phrase was properly registrable as a service mark, observing that the fact that the mark used for the contests was different from that used with the product tended to show that the promotional activity could support a separate service mark. The board stated: "That an applicant uses, in conjunction with such activity, a mark different from that used in conjunction with its principal goods or services is also a factor to be considered in determining whether the activity is a service for which a service mark registration may issue." Id. at 453–454. The board explained that registration was authorized because the contest activity conducted under the phrase was a service separate from the applicant's principal activity; because the service was not a necessary part of the applicant's primary business; and because the service conferred a benefit different from that normally expected from the sale of the applicant's goods. Id. at 454.

This court's decisions have also favored registration of separate service marks for promotional campaigns. In In re Advertising & Marketing Development, Inc., 821 F.2d 614, 620, 2 USPQ2d 2010, 2014 (Fed.Cir.1987), this court stated that "the standard for service mark registration for advertising and promotional services is the same as that for other services", and held that the term THE NOW GENERATION, used in sales promotion campaigns for financial services and for advertising automobiles, was registrable as a service mark. This court emphasized that the "mark must be used to identify advertising services [the service for which registration was sought], not merely to identify [the] subject of the advertising." Id. at 620, 2 USPQ2d at 2014.

The principle is also illustrated in the board's decision in In re Universal Press Syndicate, 229 USPQ 638 (TTAB 1986), wherein the board approved the registration of "Cathy remembers" for licensing services for the cartoon character "Cathy." No goods are purveyed under the mark "Cathy remembers," although the licensing services bear a continuing relationship to those services provided with the service mark "Cathy." In accord is the board's holding in In re Heavenly Creations, Inc., 168 USPQ 317, 318 (TTAB 1971) ("the fact that a service may be incidental to a principal service or to the sale of goods does not make it any less of a service or make a mark used in the sale or advertising of such service any less of a service mark") (quoting In re John Breuner Co., 136 USPQ 94, 95 (TTAB 1963)).

The decisions on service mark registration have turned on the specific facts of each case. The controlling question has been whether the services were of a nature normally expected based on the applicant's principal activity. Most past decisions denying registration arose in cases wherein the applicant's principal activity was the sale of goods, and the applicant sought further registration, usually of the identical mark, for services undertaken in connection with the sale of the same goods. * * * 1 J. McCarthy, Trademarks and Unfair Competition § 19.30 at 939–40 (2d ed. 1984). See also Ex parte Handmacher–Vogel, Inc., 98 USPQ 413 (Comr.Pats.1953), wherein the mark WEATHERVANE, registered for apparel, was held registrable to the same owner for the service of conducting promotional golf tournaments. In contrast, the board has refused registration to what it called a "promotional gimmick," as in In re Loew's Theatres, Inc., 179 USPQ 126, 127 (TTAB 1973).

When the services are legally required, registration has been denied. In In re Orion Research Inc., 523 F.2d 1398, 187 USPQ 485 (CCPA 1975), our predecessor court held that it was not a "service" to offer a repair or replacement warranty with the sale of goods, and therefore that the words and design associated with that warranty was not a service mark. The court, explaining the basis for its decision, distinguished the service business of repairing instruments, which the court remarked could indeed be conducted in association with a registrable service mark, from the warranty that accompanies the sale of goods, which the court held was a usual and legally required merchandising duty.

* * *

Applicant emphasizes that the PEPPER MAN promotional contests are apart from the normal advertising of "Dr Pepper" soft drinks, and, distinguishing *Orion*, that there is no legal requirement for such promotional activity. Although applicant strains when it argues that the purchaser of "Dr Pepper" soft drinks does not have to drink them to win the contest, federal registration does not depend on so fine a palate. The purpose of federal registration of marks used in business is to provide safeguards for commercial activity, and to provide those public assurances of quality and responsibility that are borne by trade and service marks.

The majority's decision does not bar the use of PEPPER MAN in connection with promotional contests. It only denies the merchant and the public of the benefits and responsibilities of federal registration. The imposition of new restrictions on registration, based on a narrowing interpretation of the statute, is inimical to the public purposes of the Lanham Act. I can not join the majority in its reasoning or conclusion.

Note

For further discussion of service marks, see 2 J. Thomas McCarthy, Trademarks and Unfair Competition §§ 19.29 to 19.31 (3d ed. 1995); Restatement (Third) of Unfair Competition § 9 (1995).

H. CERTIFICATION AND COLLECTIVE MARKS

MIDWEST PLASTIC FABRICATORS, INC. v. UNDERWRITERS LABORATORIES INC.

United States Court of Appeals, Federal Circuit, 1990.
906 F.2d 1568.

Michel, Circuit Judge.

Midwest Plastic Fabricators, Inc. (Midwest) appeals the decision of the United States Patent and Trademark Office, Trademark Trial and Appeal Board (Board), denying Midwest's petition to cancel two certification mark registrations issued to Underwriters Laboratories Inc. (UL). Midwest Plastic Fabricators, Inc. v. Underwriters Laboratories Inc., 12 USPQ2d 1267 (TTAB 1989). Because the Board's findings that UL did not misuse and did control use of its certification marks are not clearly erroneous, we affirm.

Background

UL, a corporation that promulgates and certifies compliance with safety standards for thousands of consumer and other products, is the owner and federal registrant of the two certification marks[1] at issue in this appeal. (Registration No. 782,589, issued Dec. 29, 1964, and Registration No. 1,102,931, issued Sept. 19, 1978). Each registration states, in part, that the certification is used by persons authorized by UL to certify

---

1. A certification mark is a mark "used upon or in connection with the products or services of one or more persons other than the owner of the mark to certify regional or other origin, material, mode of manufacture, quality, accuracy or other characteristics of such goods or services...." 15 U.S.C. § 1127 (1982). The statute defining and providing for cancellation of certifica-

tion mark registrations was amended in 1988, but this case arose prior to the effective date of the amendments, November 16, 1989. See Trademark Law Revision Act of 1988, Pub.L. No. 100–667, 102 Stat. 3935. The Trademark Law Revision Act of 1988 is therefore not relevant to this appeal which we decide under the previous statute.

that representative samplings of the goods conform to the safety standards or requirements established by UL. Id. A manufacturer that wishes to use the UL marks on its products to indicate compliance with UL safety standards must first submit samples to UL for testing and evaluation. Once those samples are determined to comply with UL standards, the products become eligible for listing with UL. Usually the manufacturer will enter into a listing and follow-up service agreement with UL.

This agreement provides, inter alia, that the manufacturer order UL marks through [UL] from an authorized printer; that no UL mark shall be used on products not in compliance with [UL's] requirements; that the manufacturer agrees that it will ensure that the products bearing the UL mark are in compliance with [UL's] requirements; that a testing and inspection program will be maintained by the manufacturer to assure continued compliance ... ; that access to [UL's] inspectors shall be allowed together with providing adequate facilities for the conducting of product testing and that any tests which indicate noncompliance with [UL's] requirements shall result in the manufacturer's being required to either correct the problem or remove the UL mark from the noncomplying products. [The] follow-up service agreement provides for a periodic inspection program whereby [UL's] inspectors will visit factories and plants in which listed products are produced. If an inspector finds a variation from [UL's] requirements, a variation notice is issued ... [and] a manufacturer cannot ship products which are encompassed by the variation notice until the problem is resolved. The record shows that inspectors have discretion to allow products to be shipped with minor variations that do not affect the safety of the product. Inspectors are also authorized to remove the UL mark in appropriate situations. [UL] exercises authority over use of the UL certification marks as described above by employing some 500 inspectors who work out of over 200 inspection centers throughout the United States. In 1987, [UL's] inspectors conducted approximately 438,000 inspections in approximately 38,-900 factories and over 9 billion UL labels were issued covering approximately 12,500 different products. Midwest, 12 USPQ2d at 1271.

Midwest is a manufacturer and seller of polyvinyl chloride (PVC) fittings and elbows for use with PVC conduit which encases electrical wiring. The company entered into a listing and follow-up service agreement with UL which provides, in part, that Midwest "agrees that his use of the Listing Mark constitutes his declaration that the products are Listed by [UL] and have been made in compliance with the requirements of [UL]."

Midwest now seeks reversal of the Board's denial of its petition to cancel UL's registrations on the same two bases it presented to the Board. First, Midwest alleged that UL permits use of the certification marks for purposes other than certification, in violation of 15 U.S.C. § 1064(e)(3) (1982). According to Midwest, UL's president testified that application of UL's mark represents not UL's, but merely the manufacturer's declaration that the products meet UL standards. Midwest argued that the failure of UL itself to certify that the products carrying the UL mark meet UL standards demonstrates that UL permits use of the marks for purposes other than certification.

As the second basis for cancellation, Midwest charged UL fails to control the use of its marks. Specifically, Midwest alleged: (1) certain PVC elbows carrying the UL marks failed impact tests performed by its expert, Professor Charles E. Rogers, of Case Western Reserve University; and (2) certain conduit pipe manufactured by a competitor of Midwest, National Pipe Company (National), carried counterfeit UL marks. If UL fails to control its marks, the registrations are subject to cancellation under 15 U.S.C. § 1064(e)(1) (1982). Alternatively, Midwest argued to the Board that as UL fails to control use of the marks on PVC conduit, the registrations should be cancelled at least as to such conduit. UL controverted these allegations and asserted that Midwest's cancellation petition was barred by the doctrine of licensee estoppel.

ISSUE

Whether either the Board's fact finding that UL does not use the marks other than for certification or that UL does control use of its marks is clearly erroneous.

OPINION

I. *Use of the Marks for Purposes Other Than to Certify*

We have jurisdiction over this appeal under 28 U.S.C. § 1295(a)(4)(B) (1988).

Although our court has not previously addressed either the burden or the standard of proof in cancellation proceedings for certification mark registrations, we discern no reason to make them different than for trademark registration cancellations. See Cerveceria Centroamericana, S.A. v. Cerveceria India, Inc., 892 F.2d 1021, 1023, 13 USPQ2d 1307, 1309 (Fed.Cir.1989) ("[I]n a [trademark registration] cancellation for abandonment, as for any other ground, the petitioner bears the burden of proof. Moreover, the petitioner's burden is to establish the case for cancellation by a preponderance of the evidence.") (emphasis added).

A certification mark registration may be cancelled if the mark is not used exclusively as a certification mark. 15 U.S.C. § 1064(e)(3). For example, if a certification mark's owner also allowed the mark to be used as a trademark, there would be a basis for cancellation of the registration. See In re Florida Citrus Comm'n, 160 USPQ 495, 499 (TTAB 1968) ("[T]he owner of a certification mark cannot use the identical mark as a service mark or a trademark.... A certification mark should be used only to certify."); Consolidated Dairy Prods. Co. v. Gildener & Schimmel Inc., 101 USPQ 465, 467 (Comm'r Pat.1954) (stating that it is incompatible to use a mark as both a trademark and as a certification mark); see generally J. McCarthy, Trademark and Unfair Competition §§ 19:32(D), at 947–49, and 20:15(G), at 1060–61 (2d ed. 1984) [hereinafter J.

McCarthy]; E. Vandenburgh III, Trademark Law & Procedure § 1.40, at 40–42 (1968).

Midwest argues that UL's registrations must be cancelled because the UL certification marks are not UL's own declarations to consumers that the marked products comply with UL standards, but instead are the manufacturer's declarations. Midwest asserts the failure of UL itself to make that declaration is evidence that UL "permits the use of the certification mark for purposes other than to certify" and therefore the registrations must be cancelled. See 15 U.S.C. § 1064(e)(3).

There is an important difference, however, between the mark's use and the user. That others test products and apply UL's certification marks simply is not probative that the marks are used for other than certification. Certainly, on this record, there is no evidence that these certification marks are used, by anyone, as trademarks or service marks. Instead, Midwest merely complains about who applies the mark to the product. Midwest in effect argues that third party application of a certification mark constitutes per se misuse—use for a purpose other than certification. But Midwest offers no authority to support such a proposition.

The statute, however, plainly does not require that, as the registrant, UL itself must test the products and declare to the public that items carrying UL marks meet UL standards. It merely authorizes cancellation of a registration if the registrant allows use of the mark for purposes other than certification. Id. In addition, the general practice, in accord with the statute, allows for a third party to apply the certification mark. See U.S. Patent & Trademark Office, Trademark Manual of Examining Procedures § 1306.01, at 1300–14 (1986) (The certification mark is "applied by other persons, to their goods or services, with authorization from the owner of the mark.") (emphasis added in part).

Thus, both registrations at issue here include a provision that the certification marks may be used by "persons authorized by [UL]" to indicate that "representative samplings" of the products conform to safety standards established by UL. The registrations clearly state what the marks do and do not represent to the public. The registrations certainly do not require UL to represent that UL itself tests the items.

* * *

II.   *Failure to Control Use of the Marks*

Midwest also asserts UL does not control the use of the UL marks as required under 15 U.S.C. § 1064(e)(1), and cancellation is thus necessary. Section 1064(e)(1) provides for cancellation if the certification mark registrant "does not control, or is not able legitimately to exercise control over, the use of such mark."

The purpose of requiring a certification mark registrant to control use of its mark is the same as for a trademark registrant: to protect the public from being misled. Cf. Haymaker Sports, Inc. v. Turian, 581 F.2d

257, 261, 198 USPQ 610, 613 (CCPA 1978) (A trademark licensor "may license his mark if the licensing agreement provides for adequate control by the licensor over the quality of goods or services produced under the mark by a licensee. The purpose of such a requirement is to protect the public from being misled.") (citations omitted). In the case of a certification mark registrant, the risk of misleading the public may be even greater because a certification mark registration sets forth specific representations about the manufacture and characteristics of the goods to which the mark is applied.

As the purpose of the control requirement is to protect the public, the requirement places an affirmative obligation on the certification mark owner to monitor the activities of those who use the mark. Cf. Siegel v. Chicken Delight, Inc., 448 F.2d 43, 51, 171 USPQ 269, 274–75 (9th Cir.1971), cert. denied, 405 U.S. 955, 92 S.Ct. 1172, 31 L.Ed.2d 232 (1972) ("The [trademark] licensor owes an affirmative duty to the public to assure that in the hands of his licensee the trade-mark continues to represent that which it purports to represent."); Dawn Donut Co. v. Hart's Food Stores, Inc., 267 F.2d 358, 367, 121 USPQ 430, 437 (2d Cir.1959) (An "affirmative duty of policing [licensees] in a reasonable manner" is placed on a trademark licensor.).

To obtain cancellation of the UL certification mark registrations, Midwest has the burden to demonstrate by a preponderance of the evidence that UL failed to exercise control over use of its marks. The statute, however, does not define "control" or otherwise indicate the degree of control that it requires. Clearly, the statutory requirement cannot mean absolute control, because it would be impracticable, if not impossible, to satisfy. The Board stated: "The specific degree of control necessary in determining whether or not a certification mark should be cancelled depends, of course, on the particular facts presented in each case." Midwest, 12 USPQ2d at 1273. While interpretation of the statutory term "control" is a question of law which we review de novo, the Board explicated a rule of reasonableness which, because reasonableness cannot be gauged by some abstract standard, will vary depending on the particular facts. The "control" requirement of the statute means the mark owner must take reasonable steps, under all the circumstances of the case, to prevent the public from being misled.

This standard for demonstrating that a registrant has exercised control over the use of its marks is entirely consistent with the precedent of this court, which speaks in terms of "adequate control," see Turian, 581 F.2d at 261, 198 USPQ at 613, as well as "sufficient control," see Stock Pot Restaurant, 737 F.2d at 1578–79, 222 USPQ at 668. See also Dawn Donut, 267 F.2d at 367, 121 USPQ at 437 (where the term "reasonable" is used to delineate the type and extent of control contemplated). We believe the words "adequate" and "sufficient" used in our prior opinions are, in effect, shorthand expressions to denote a flexible standard of reasonableness based on the totality of the facts and circumstances.

* * *

The Board found that UL has "a vast network of inspectors making hundreds of thousands of inspections of thousands of different products across the country" and that UL conducts comprehensive follow-up programs to ensure compliance with UL standards. The Board also stated that UL demonstrated "considerable diligence in controlling the use of its marks; that while [the] inspection and follow-up procedures are not 100% accurate or foolproof, we know of no such requirement.... "

Midwest relies upon two types of evidence to challenge the Board finding on control. First, it relies on the results of impact tests performed on certain conduit and elbows carrying the UL mark. The Board found the tests were not "shown to be reliable and [are] entitled to very little, if any, probative value." We cannot overturn that finding as clearly erroneous because Midwest's testing of PVC conduit and elbows did not account for the age of the elbows tested or their exposure to sunlight, although it is undisputed that age and sunlight make PVC conduit brittle. Also, impact tests were performed on PVC elbows and Midwest concedes "that the [UL] standards for elbows do not require impact tests." The Board, therefore, appropriately discounted the impact tests.

The second type of evidence Midwest employs to demonstrate UL's failure to control use of its marks is the proven use of counterfeit UL marks on certain conduit manufactured by National, a competitor. The Board concluded that this limited counterfeiting problem was not sufficient to cancel UL's registrations and that UL exercised control over subsequent use of its marks by this company, based on findings about UL's responsiveness and the stringency of its corrective action. It included inspections being done solely by UL personnel and inspection of not just a "representative sampling," all that is required by the registrations, but of 100% of the conduit. These findings have not been shown to be clearly erroneous.

Because Midwest has not shown that the findings supporting the reasonableness of UL's control are clearly erroneous, we must sustain the Board's determination that UL's control avoids cancellation of its registrations in these proceedings.

* * *

Notes

1. In addition to certification marks, the Lanham Act provides trademark protection for "collective marks," which are used by members of a cooperative, association, or other collective group to show membership in the group or association. 15 U.S.C.A. §§ 1054, 1127. See Sebastian International v. Longs Drug Stores Corp., 53 F.3d 1073 (9th Cir.1995); Seven–Up Bottling Co. v. Seven–Up Co., 561 F.2d 1275 (8th Cir.1977); Majorica v. Majorca International, Ltd., 687 F.Supp. 92 (S.D.N.Y.1988). For further discussion of certification and collective marks, see 2 J. Thomas McCarthy, Trademarks and Unfair Competition §§ 19.32 to 19.35 (3d ed. 1995); Restatement (Third) of Unfair Competition §§ 10–11 (1995).

2.   Consider whether the following marks are likely to be either certification or collective marks?

—The "Good Housekeeping" seal of approval

—The Professional Golfers' Association (PGA)

—Roquefort cheese

—Sebastian hair salons

Chapter 3

TRADEMARK OWNERSHIP

A. COMMON LAW TRADEMARK USE

GALT HOUSE, INC. v. HOME SUPPLY CO.

Court of Appeals of Kentucky, 1972.
483 S.W.2d 107.

REED, JUDGE.

The plaintiff, Galt House, Inc., instituted this action to enjoin the defendants, Home Supply Company, and its principal officer and stockholder, Al J. Schneider, from operating a new hotel in Louisville, Kentucky, under the assumed trade name "Galt House." The trial judge refused to enjoin the use of the name at the plaintiff's behest. We affirm that decision for the reasons later discussed. No other issue involved in the pending litigation in the trial court is decided. We confine our consideration to the sole issue presented by this appeal.

In February 1964, the plaintiff, Galt House, Inc., incorporated under the laws of this state. In its articles of incorporation it adopted as its corporate name the term "Galt House." The articles required and specified that the minimum capital with which plaintiff would commence business would be the sum of $1,000. This amount has never been paid in. The plaintiff has no assets and no liabilities; neither does it have corporate books or records. Plaintiff's president and sole shareholder is Arch Stallard, Sr., a real estate broker in Louisville, Kentucky, who specializes in hotel and motel real estate. Mr. Stallard has on occasions since the date of the filing of plaintiff's articles of incorporation made a few sporadic inquiries concerning possible locations for a hotel and considered engaging in an enterprise by which a franchise operation would be effected. These few efforts came to naught and Mr. Stallard testified that because of illness and death in his family he had been "laying dormant."

The defendant, Home Supply Company, is a Kentucky corporation organized sometime prior to 1950. The defendant, Al J. Schneider is its president and controlling shareholder. Home Supply Company is active

127

in the business of constructing and operating hotels in this state. It presently operates a hotel on the Kentucky State Fair Board property under the assumed name "Executive Inn." It is presently engaged in the construction and completion of a high-rise hotel on riverfront-development property belonging to an agency of the City of Louisville.

In April 1969, Home Supply Company, through its president Schneider, submitted to the city agency plans of a hotel bearing the name Galt House. This name had been recommended to Schneider by the then mayor of the City of Louisville, Kenneth Schmied, and the chairman of the Riverfront Development Commission, Archibald Cochran. The trial judge found from the evidence that throughout discussions leading up to the bidding, the new hotel was referred to as the Galt House and has been so referred to since. Home Supply Company was the successful bidder, was awarded the contract, and construction commenced in May 1970. A new hotel, 26 stories in height with 714 rooms, is now nearly completed and has affixed a sign bearing the name "The Galt House." The hotel already has scheduled future conventions and room reservations, although it will not open until after May 1972. In April 1971, Home Supply Company applied for and received from the Secretary of State of Kentucky a registration and service mark of the name "The Galt House."

Plaintiff filed suit in August 1971, seeking to enjoin the defendants from any use of the name Galt House. * * *

During the Nineteenth Century the Galt House Hotel was a famous hostelry in Louisville with an excellent and widely recognized reputation. In 1838 the barroom at the Galt House was the scene of a killing as a result of which an attorney and judge and his two companions were indicted for murder. They were tried and acquitted. The trial was held at Harrodsburg, Kentucky, to which venue had been transferred because of the intense public sentiment in Louisville against the defendants who were prominent citizens of Mississippi. The victims of the affray were Louisville residents. The trial itself is famous in the annals of Kentucky history.

In 1842 Charles Dickens toured America. In his account in "American Notes," he was characteristically uncomplimentary in his description of Louisville; he was impressed, however, with the Galt House. He wrote: "We slept at the Galt House; a splendid hotel; and were as handsomely lodged as though we had been in Paris, rather than hundreds of miles beyond the Alleghanies (sic)." In 1858 Charles Mackay, an English writer, passed through Louisville. In his account in "Life and Liberty in America" he remarked: " ... we crossed in the steamer to Louisville, and once more found ourselves in a land of plenty and comfort, in a flourishing city, in an excellent hotel—the Galt House, one of the best conducted establishments in America; .... "

The Galt House, located on Main Street at Second Street, occupied separate buildings during its existence as a hotel. The second Galt House was destroyed by fire in January 1865 at a reported loss of $1,000,000.

The third Galt House, a magnificent structure in its day, was abandoned as a hotel and ceased operations in 1920. Belknap Hardward Company thereafter occupied the site of the last Galt House.

Thus, it would appear that since 1920 there has been no use of the name Galt House in connection with or to describe a hotel. The name doubtless strikes interest when used in the presence of history buffs and among those familiar with the folklore of Louisville. Among such cognoscenti the name encourages remembrance of things past.

As found by the circuit judge, the corporation which operated the last Galt House was formed in 1911 and its formal corporate existence expired in 1961. From 1920 to 1961, however, it did not engage in the hotel business. Therefore, the name Galt House had not been used in connection with a going business for 49 years when defendants undertook to use it as the name of their new hotel in 1969.

The primary argument asserted by the plaintiff actually rests upon a premise that by mere incorporation under a corporate name it retains the right to exclude others from the use of that name so long as the corporation legally exists. In Covington Inn Corp. v. White Horse Tavern, Inc., Ky., 445 S.W.2d 135 (1969), we considered the effect of KRS 271.045, a part of the corporation law of this state, and held that its provision that a corporate name shall not be the same as "nor deceptively similar to" the name of other corporations, constituted an expression by the legislature that stated a policy conforming to the common law of "unfair competition" as applied in Kentucky. Thus, when under subsection (4) of the same statute an equity action is authorized to enjoin the doing of business under a name adopted in violation of this statute, the common law of unfair competition prescribes the standards which the court applies in determining whether to enjoin.

In that same opinion we remarked that perhaps this statute could be reasonably construed to extend to an assumed name of a corporation. That is the situation in this case. The defendant Home Supply Company has undertaken to do business under the assumed trade name Galt House, which is the same as plaintiff's adopted corporate name. In Meredith v. Universal Plumbing & Construction Co., 272 Ky. 283, 114 S.W.2d 94 (1938), we held that under our corporate statutes and other statutory laws applicable to transacting business under an assumed name there was no legal impediment to a corporation using an additional trade name that was different from its adopted corporate name. The pertinent statutes read the same now as they did then. Hence, there is no legal impediment to the defendant Home Supply Company's adoption of the trade name "Galt House", unless the plaintiff by the mere act of incorporation of the same name has precluded this defendant's right to adopt and use the name.

Surely the plaintiff acquires no standing to enjoin under the accepted principles of the law of unfair competition. Under the modern extended scope of the doctrine of unfair competition, its present outer limits afford protection and relief against the unjust appropriation of, or injury to, the good will or business reputation of another, even though he is not a competitor. Plaintiff is concededly a nonuser of the contested name. Plaintiff has no customers, conducts no real or substantial business and has never held its name out to the public in connection with any going business. Therefore, by its inaction, it could not have established either a good will or reputation which the defendants could be legitimately accused of pirating as a competitor or otherwise. Therefore, if plaintiff has standing to enjoin, its status must rest upon the acquisition of a protectable right by its act of incorporation under the contested name.

* * *

The plaintiff, however, relies upon the case of Drugs Consolidated v. Drug Incorporated, 16 Del.Ch. 240, 144 A. 656 (1929). In our view the opinion in that case undertakes to prove too much. There is dictum that the corporation statutes of Delaware, which are substantially similar to the corporation statutes of Kentucky so far as the present point is concerned, assure a right to have the corporate name distinguished from other corporations of like kind subsequently created and that this right does not depend on showing of actual use, in business, of the name, but the right exists as soon as corporate existence is brought into being and as long as it continues; the specific factual findings in the opinion, however, demonstrate that the plaintiff corporation, although it was not yet actually engaged in the business of manufacturing and marketing drugs, had, nevertheless, been engaged in promoting the objects and purposes of its incorporation. Therefore, if this opinion represents a holding that a nonuser of a corporate name retains the right to pre-empt that name during the period of its formal corporate existence without ever having engaged in carrying on any of the objects and purposes of the corporation, it is contrary to the weight of authority concerning that proposition and does not, in our opinion, represent the generally accepted view.

The *Drugs Consolidated* opinion was cited with approval by the Mississippi Supreme Court in Meridian Yellow Cab Co. v. City Yellow Cabs, 206 Miss. 812, 41 So.2d 14 (1949). In this case, however, the plaintiff who first incorporated had actually commenced operations at the time it sought to enjoin the defendant who had later incorporated under a similar name. Although the plaintiff did not commence business until after the defendant, it, nevertheless, did actually start active operations in the taxicab business within three years of the date of its incorporation and within two months after the defendant actually operated taxicabs; whether the plaintiff was theretofore engaged in activities to promote the objects and purposes of the corporation is not mentioned. However misplaced that court's reliance on the *Drugs Consolidated* case may have been, its decision, which granted the plaintiff injunctive relief, does not militate against our conclusion in this case that the plaintiff's act of incorporation in a particular name preempts the use of that name by a subsequent user only for a reasonable period in which to allow plaintiff's business to begin. To this extent, incorporation and registration take the place of user in the case of a trade name. Pre-emption for a reasonable period of time in which to allow the business to begin is not the equivalent of a perpetual monopoly of the trade name without use in trade. * * *

We are also unable to find that plaintiff has any standing to enjoin under the theory that it was placed on the same footing with the former Galt House Corporation whose existence expired by operation of law in 1961. There was no transfer of the name from the expiring Galt House Corporation to plaintiff. The former Galt House Corporation at the end of its corporate term of existence as fixed by its articles terminated its right to do business in 1961. It had not engaged in the hotel business under its corporate name since 1920. The former Corporation was incapable of possessing a business with a good will or a corporate trade name. The name did not survive, for there was nothing to which it could be attached.

In the instant case, the plaintiff possessed neither good will nor a reasonable prospect to acquire it. Its right to preempt the name by the mere act of incorporation had expired because a reasonable period in which to allow business to begin had passed and the plaintiff neither alleged nor could show reasonable prospect to acquire good will through actively engaging in business. * * *

Notes

1. For further discussion of the acquisition of trademark rights, see 2 J. Thomas McCarthy, Trademarks and Unfair Competition §§ 16.01 to 16.16 (3d ed. 1995); Restatement (Third) of Unfair Competition § 18 (1995).

2. A well-advised company will seek registration of its trademarks under the federal Lanham Act and possibly state law, as well as any necessary registration of corporate names under state law. The firm may also seek a distinctive toll-free number, such as 1–800–MATTRES, and a distinctive domain name on the World Wide Web, such as www.mattress. com. Obtaining each of these rights is a somewhat separate matter, although there may be some overlap of rights during the time when a firm is adopting a new trademark. Thus, federal registration requires an application with the United States Patent & Trademark Office; state registration of both a corporate name and a state trademark is typically with the Secretary of State of each jurisdiction; toll-free numbers are assigned by telephone carriers; and domain names are assigned and reserved through companies that have taken on that task. Can Holiday Inn bring a successful trademark infringement claim to prevent a competitor from using the most common misdialed number for its "800" reservation number? See Holiday Inns, Inc. v. 800 Reservation, Inc., 86 F.3d 619 (6th Cir.1996).

3. As a result of the growth of the Internet, most businesses have established websites making use of their trademarks as domain names. This practice, of course, serves as a valuable marketing tool, allowing consumers to identify quickly a company's website by entering the familiar trademark

(rather than making use of somewhat more cumbersome and imprecise search engines). To protect their marks, firms have asserted trademark rights when others have made use of their mark as a domain name. See, e.g., Cardservice International, Inc. v. McGee, 950 F.Supp. 737 (E.D.Va.1997) (finding infringement of registered "Card Service" mark by the defendant's use of "cardservice.com"); Washington Speakers Bureau v. Leading Authorities, Inc., 33 F.Supp.2d 488 (E.D.Va.1999) (finding that defendant's domain name infringed plaintiff's unregistered trademark), aff'd, 217 F.3d 843 (4th Cir.2000). Courts have found that the mere registration of a domain name is insufficient to establish rights in the term as a mark, requiring instead a traditional "first to use" analysis (in the absence of an intent to use application, discussed infra). See, e.g., Brookfield Communications, Inc. v. West Coast Entertainment Corp., 174 F.3d 1036 (9th Cir.1999).

The potential use of a trademarked name as a domain name has led to the practice of "cybersquatting," in which a third party registers a domain name consisting an individual or company name with the eventual hope of turning a profit, usually by selling the domain name to the trademark owner. Courts have used traditional trademark law and dilution analysis to prevent this practice, as illustrated by Panavision International, L.P. v. Toeppen, 141 F.3d 1316 (9th Cir.1998), in which the court found that Toeppen's registration of "panavision.com" diluted Panavision's trademark.

In 1999, Congress enacted the Anticybersquatting Consumer Protection Act, Pub. L. No. 106–113 (1999) (codified at 15 U.S.C. section 1125(d)(1)(A)), in order to provide more effective remedies in this situation. See Sporty's Farm L.L.C. v. Sportsman's Market, Inc., 202 F.3d 489 (2d Cir.2000). The legislation adds a new section 43(d) to the Lanham Act, with remedies for cybersquatting. It makes actionable the registration, trafficking, or use of a domain name when the domain name dilutes a famous mark, or is confusingly similar to the mark of another. The Act requires a showing of a bad faith intent to profit and delineates nine factors for determination of that intent.

Courts have also addressed the use of trademarks as metatags, i.e., lines of code buried in the HTML code used in websites. Metatags are not visible to the consumer or viewer (unless the viewer opts to view the HTML code), but they do serve as "key words" for purposes of many search engines. Should the unlicensed use of a trademark as a metatag be deemed to infringe on a trademark? See, e.g., Brookfield Communications, Inc. v. West Coast Entertainment Corp., 174 F.3d 1036 (9th Cir.1999) (addressing whether use of "moviebuff" as a metatag infringes registered trademark).

4.   Trademark disputes related to internet activities also present knotty jurisdictional issues. See, e.g., Pebble Beach Co. v. Caddy, 453 F.3d 1151 (9th Cir. 2006) (finding no jurisdiction in California in suit by "Pebble Beach" golf resort against operator of British bed & breakfast—located on a pebbly beach—called "Pebble Beach" and marketed with website named www. pebblebeach-uk.com); see also McBee v. Delica Co., 417 F.3d 107 (1st Cir. 2005).

BLUE BELL, INC. v. FARAH MANUFACTURING CO.

United States Court of Appeals, Fifth Circuit, 1975.

508 F.2d 1260.

GEWIN, CIRCUIT JUDGE:

In the spring and summer of 1973 two prominent manufacturers of men's clothing created identical trademarks for goods substantially identical in appearance. Though the record offers no indication of bad faith in the design and adoption of the labels, both Farah Manufacturing Company (Farah) and Blue Bell, Inc. (Blue Bell) devised the mark "Time Out" for new lines of men's slacks and shirts. Both parties market their goods on a national scale, so they agree that joint utilization of the same trademark would confuse the buying public. Thus, the only question presented for our review is which party established prior use of the mark in trade. A response to that seemingly innocuous inquiry, however, requires us to define the chameleonic term "use" as it has developed in trademark law.

After a full development of the facts in the district court both parties moved for summary judgment. The motion of Farah was granted and that of Blue Bell denied. It is not claimed that summary judgment procedure was inappropriate; the controversy presented relates to the application of the proper legal principles to undisputed facts. A permanent injunction was granted in favor of Farah but no damages were awarded, and Blue Bell was allowed to fill all orders for garments bearing the Time Out label received by it as of the close of business on December 5, 1973. For the reasons hereinafter stated we affirm.

Farah conceived of the Time Out mark on May 16, after screening several possible titles for its new stretch menswear. Two days later the firm adopted an hourglass logo and authorized an extensive advertising campaign bearing the new insignia. Farah presented its fall line of clothing, including Time Out slacks, to sales personnel on June 5. In the meantime, patent counsel had given clearance for use of the mark after scrutiny of current federal registrations then on file. One of Farah's top executives demonstrated samples of the Time Out garments to large customers in Washington, D.C. and New York, though labels were not attached to the slacks at that time. Tags containing the new design were completed June 27. With favorable evaluations of marketing potential from all sides, Farah sent one pair of slacks bearing the Time Out mark to each of its twelve regional sales managers on July 3. Sales personnel paid for the pants, and the garments became their property in case of loss.

Following the July 3 shipment, regional managers showed the goods to customers the following week. Farah received several orders and production began. Further shipments of sample garments were mailed to the rest of the sales force on July 11 and 14. Merchandising efforts were fully operative by the end of the month. The first shipments to customers, however, occurred in September.

Blue Bell, on the other hand, was concerned with creating an entire new division of men's clothing, as an avenue to reaching the "upstairs" market. Though initially to be housed at the Hicks–Ponder plant in El Paso, the new division would eventually enjoy separate headquarters. On June 18 Blue Bell management arrived at the name Time Out to identify both its new division and its new line of men's sportswear. Like Farah, it received clearance for use of the mark from counsel. Like Farah, it inaugurated an advertising campaign. Unlike Farah, however, Blue Bell did not ship a dozen marked articles of the new line to its sales personnel. Instead, Blue Bell authorized the manufacture of several hundred labels bearing the words Time Out and its logo shaped like a referee's hands forming a T. When the labels were completed on June 29, the head of the embryonic division flew them to El Paso. He instructed shipping personnel to affix the new Time Out labels to slacks that already bore the "Mr. Hicks" trademark. The new tags, of varying sizes and colors, were randomly attached to the left hip pocket button of slacks and the left hip pocket of jeans. Thus, although no change occurred in the design or manufacture of the pants, on July 5 several hundred pair left El Paso with two tags.

Blue Bell made intermittent shipments of the doubly-labeled slacks thereafter, though the out-of-state customers who received the goods had ordered clothing of the Mr. Hicks variety. Production of the new Time Out merchandise began in the latter part of August, and Blue Bell held a sales meeting to present its fall designs from September 4–6. Sales personnel solicited numerous orders, though shipments of the garments were not scheduled until October.

By the end of October Farah had received orders for 204,403 items of Time Out sportswear, representing a retail sales value of over $2,750,000. Blue Bell had received orders for 154,200 garments valued at over $900,000. Both parties had commenced extensive advertising campaigns for their respective Time Out sportswear.

Soon after discovering the similarity of their marks, Blue Bell sued Farah for common law trademark infringement and unfair competition, seeking to enjoin use of the Time Out trademark on men's clothing. Farah counter-claimed for similar injunctive relief. The district court found that Farah's July 3 shipment and sale constituted a valid use in trade, while Blue Bell's July 5 shipment was a mere "token" use insufficient at law to create trademark rights. While we affirm the result reached by the trial court as to Farah's priority of use, the legal grounds upon which we base our decision are somewhat different from those undergirding the district court's judgment.

Federal jurisdiction is predicated upon diversity of citizenship, since neither party has registered the mark pursuant to the Lanham Act. Given the operative facts surrounding manufacture and shipment from El Paso, the parties agree the Texas law of trademarks controls. In 1967 the state legislature enacted a Trademark Statute. Section 16.02 of the Act explains that a mark is "used" when it is affixed to the goods and "the goods are sold, displayed for sale, or otherwise publicly distributed." Thus the question whether Blue Bell or Farah established priority of trademark use depends upon interpretation of the cited provision. Unfortunately, there are no Texas cases construing 16.02. This court must therefore determine what principles the highest state court would utilize in deciding such a question. In view of the statute's stated purpose to preserve common law rights, we conclude the Texas Supreme Court would apply the statutory provision in light of general principles of trademark law.

A trademark is a symbol (word, name, device or combination thereof) adopted and used by a merchant to identify his goods and distinguish them from articles produced by others. Ownership of a mark requires a combination of both appropriation and use in trade. Thus, neither conception of the mark, nor advertising alone establishes trademark rights at common law. Rather, ownership of a trademark accrues when goods bearing the mark are placed on the market.

The exclusive right to a trademark belongs to one who first uses it in connection with specified goods. McLean v. Fleming, 96 U.S. 245, 24 L.Ed. 828 (1877); 3 R. Callman, Unfair Competition, Trademarks and Monopolies 76.2(c) (3d ed. 1969). Such use need not have gained wide public recognition, Kathreiner's Malzkaffee Fabriken v. Pastor Kneipp Medicine Co., 82 F. 321 (7th Cir.1897); Waldes v. International Manufacturers' Agency, 237 F. 502 (S.D.N.Y.1916), and even a single use in trade may sustain trademark rights if followed by continuous commercial utilization. Ritz Cycle Car Co. v. Driggs–Seabury Ordnance Corp., 237 F. 125 (S.D.N.Y.1916).

The initial question presented for review is whether Farah's sale and shipment of slacks to twelve regional managers constitutes a valid first use of the Time Out mark. Blue Bell claims the July 3 sale was merely an internal transaction insufficiently public to secure trademark ownership. After consideration of pertinent authorities, we agree.

Secret, undisclosed internal shipments are generally inadequate to support the denomination "use." Trademark claims based upon shipments from a producer's plant to its sales office, and vice versa, have often been disallowed. * * * Though none of the cited cases dealt with sales to intra-corporate personnel, we perceive that fact to be a distinction without a difference. The sales were not made to customers, but served as an accounting device to charge the salesmen with their cost in case of loss. The fact that some sales managers actively solicited accounts bolsters the good faith of Farah's intended use, but does not meet out essential objection: that the "sales" were not made to the public.

* * *

Priority of use and ownership of the Time Out mark are the only issues before this court. The language fashioned by the Board clearly indicates a desire to leave the common law of trademark ownership intact. The decision may demonstrate a reversal of the presumption that ownership rights precede registration rights, but it does not affect our analysis of common law use in trade. Farah had undertaken substantial preliminary steps toward marketing the Time Out garments, but it did not establish ownership of the mark by means of the July 3 shipment to its sales managers. The gist of trademark rights is actual use in trade. Though technically a "sale", the July 3 shipment was not "publicly distributed" within the purview of the Texas statute.

Blue Bell's July 5 shipment similarly failed to satisfy the prerequisites of a bona fide use in trade. Elementary tenets of trademark law require that labels or designs be affixed to the merchandise actually intended to bear the mark in commercial transactions. Furthermore, courts have recognized that the usefulness of a mark derives not only from its capacity to identify a certain manufacturer, but also from its ability to differentiate between different classes of goods produced by a single manufacturer. Here customers had ordered slacks of the Mr. Hicks species, and Mr. Hicks was the fanciful mark distinguishing these slacks from all others. Blue Bell intended to use the Time Out mark on an entirely new line of men's sportswear, unique in style and cut, though none of the garments had yet been produced.

While goods may be identified by more than one trademark, the use of each mark must be bona fide. See, e.g., Old Dutch Foods, Inc. v. Dan Dee Pretzel & Potato Chip Co., 477 F.2d 150 (6th Cir.1973) (continuous utilization of the second mark for over thirty years). Mere adoption of a mark without bona fide use, in an attempt to reserve it for the future, will not create trademark rights. Circle Cab Co. v. Springfield Yellow Cab Co., 137 N.E.2d 137 (Ohio App.1954); Western Leather Goods v. Blue Bell, 178 U.S.P.Q. 382 (TTAB 1973). In the instant case Blue Bell's attachment of a secondary label to an older line of goods manifests a bad faith attempt to reserve a mark. We cannot countenance such activities as a valid use in trade. Blue Bell therefore did not acquire trademark rights by virtue of its July 5 shipment.

We thus hold that neither Farah's July 3 shipment nor Blue Bell's July 5 shipment sufficed to create rights in the Time Out mark. Based on a desire to secure ownership of the mark and superiority over a competitor, both claims of alleged use were chronologically premature. Essentially, they took a time out to litigate their differences too early in the game. The question thus becomes whether we should continue to stop the clock for a remand or make a final call from the appellate bench. While a remand to the district court for further factual development would not be improper in these circumstances, we believe the interests of judicial economy and the parties' desire to terminate the litigation demand that we decide, if possible, which manufacturer first used the mark in trade.

Careful examination of the record discloses that Farah shipped its first order of Time Out clothing to customers in September of 1973. Blue Bell, approximately one month behind its competitor at other relevant stages of development, did not mail its Time Out garments until at least

October. Though sales to customers are not the sine qua non of trademark use, they are determinative in the instant case. These sales constituted the first point at which the public had a chance to associate Time Out with a particular line of sportswear. Therefore, Farah established priority of trademark use; it is entitled to a decree permanently enjoining Blue Bell from utilization of the Time Out trademark on men's garments.

The judgment of the trial court is affirmed.

Notes

1. How would a case such as this one likely develop in light of the "intent to use" provision of section 1(b) of the Lanham Act, 15 U.S.C.A. § 1051(b)?

2. An interesting case presenting issues of trademark ownership in connection with state park concession operations in Old Town San Diego State Historical Park, which resulted in litigation involving a nearby restaurant. *See Department of Parks & Recreation for the State of California v. Bazaar Del Mundo, Inc.*, 448 F.3d 1118 (9th Cir. 2006). Another recent case involving disputes regarding priority and ownership is *Quicksilver, Inc. v. Kymsta Corp.*, 466 F.3d 749 (9th Cir. 2006).

3. For further discussion of trademark priority, see 2 J. Thomas McCarthy, Trademarks and Unfair Competition §§ 16.03 to 16.08 (3d ed. 1995); Restatement (Third) of Unfair Competition § 19 (1995).

B. STATUTORY RIGHTS

THRIFTY RENT–A–CAR SYSTEM, INC. v. THRIFT CARS, INC.

United States Court of Appeals, First Circuit, 1987.
831 F.2d 1177.

DAVIS, CIRCUIT JUDGE.

In this trademark infringement suit brought by Thrifty Rent-a-Car System, Inc. (Thrifty), that firm and defendant Thrift Cars, Inc. (Thrift Cars) both appeal the decision of the district court for the District of Massachusetts (Young, J.), 639 F.Supp. 750. After a bench trial, the court enjoined Thrift Cars from conducting a car or truck rental or leasing business outside of Taunton, Massachusetts under the "Thrift Cars" name, and limited Thrift Cars' advertising to those media it had used prior to July 26, 1964, the date that Thrifty obtained federal registration of its own mark. Concomitantly, the court prohibited Thrifty from operating any of its business establishments in East Taunton, Massachusetts or from advertising in any media principally intended to target the East Taunton community. We affirm.

I.

Background

A.   Thrifty Rent-a-Car System, Inc.

Thrifty Rent-a-Car System traces its beginnings to March 3, 1958 when L.C. Crow, an individual, began renting cars in Tulsa, Oklahoma, under the trade name "Thrifty." In 1962, Stemmons, Inc., an Oklahoma corporation, purchased Crow's business and expanded the business to Houston, Texas, renting automobiles to customers under the "Thrifty" trade name. Stemmons subsequently changed its name to The Thrifty Rent-a-Car System, Inc. and expanded the business to Wichita, Kansas, Dallas, Texas and St. Louis, Missouri. On July 30, 1962 Thrifty Rent-a-Car made an application to the United States Patent Office to register the service mark "Thrifty Rent-a-Car System" and was granted that mark in July 1964. Thrifty expanded the business through both franchises and directly-owned rental agencies. In December 1967, a Thrifty Rent-a-Car outlet opened in Massachusetts. By the time of trial, Thrifty had become the fifth largest car rental agency worldwide, and operated car rental outlets in 23 locations in Massachusetts.

B.   Thrift Cars, Inc.

Thrift Cars' rental business began in October 1962 and was incorporated in Massachusetts as Thrift Cars, Inc. Thrift Cars' owner and proprietor, Peter A. Conlon, at first began a modest car-rental service out of his home in East Taunton, Massachusetts. The East Taunton business was largely limited to what the car-rental industry considers a "tertiary market," that is, the market that serves individuals needing replacement cars to bridge the short term car rental and the longer term automobile lease. Thrift Cars provided customized service, arranging delivery of the rental car to the customer as well as pick-up at the termination of the rental period. In the years immediately following 1962, Thrift Cars delivered automobiles to Boston's Logan Airport and to various cities on Cape Cod and to Nantucket. Prior to Thrifty's federal registration in July 1964, Thrift Cars advertised in the Taunton area yellow pages telephone directory, in The Taunton Daily Gazette, The Cape Cod Times (a newspaper of general circulation servicing Cape Cod, Martha's Vineyard, and Nantucket) and in The Anchor (the newspaper of the Roman Catholic Diocese of Fall River). In 1963 Thrift Cars also advertised in the The Inquirer and Mirror, a Nantucket newspaper. In 1970, some six years after Thrifty had obtained federal registration of its mark, Thrift Cars received a license to operate a car rental facility at the Nantucket airport, and Conlon, Thrift Cars' Chief Executive Officer, moved the major portion of the business to Nantucket.

The Nantucket facility, unlike the operation at East Taunton, was operated largely as a traditional car rental service, servicing the resort market. Customers came directly to the airport to arrange for rental and pick-up of the automobile. Thrift Cars' post–1970 Nantucket operation thus came into a direct clash with Thrifty, which was also operating a car rental facility directed to the resort market in the Cape Cod area.

C. Litigation below.

Thrifty brought this action against Thrift Cars in federal district court, alleging trademark infringement and false designation of title under the Lanham Act. 15 U.S.C. § 1125(a) and §§ 1051–1127. The parties stipulated that the Thrift and Thrifty names are confusingly similar—as, of course, they are. The trial court found that Thrift Cars' business activities as of the critical date of July 26, 1964 (the date of Thrifty's registration) did not extend to areas beyond East Taunton, Massachusetts. The district court then enjoined Thrift Cars from using "Thrift" in conducting a car rental business outside of Taunton. The court also enjoined Thrift Cars from advertising in media directed outside of East Taunton, except in publications in which Thrift Cars had advertised prior to July 26, 1964.

Conversely, the court enjoined Thrifty from operating any business establishment in East Taunton and prohibited it from advertising in any media principally intended to target the East Taunton area.

Both parties appealed. Thrift Cars claims that the court erred by limiting its car rental activities under the "Thrift" name to Taunton, urging that this court expand its permissible business activities to southeastern Massachusetts, including Nantucket. Thrifty's cross-appeal argues that the district court erred in allowing Thrift Cars to conduct business in any locality under the Thrift Cars name because the business had not been continuous until trial, as required under the Lanham Act. In the alternative, Thrifty urges that the scope of Thrift Cars' business activities should be limited to East Taunton, not Taunton, because the record indicates that Thrift Cars' business had been limited to East Taunton, not to Taunton, prior to Thrifty's 1964 federal registration. Thrifty also says that the district court allowed Thrift Cars too broad an advertising base since it permitted Thrift Cars to advertise in publications directed outside of East Taunton.

II.

Discussion

As the district court recognized, disposition of this case revolves around geographical market protection and priority afforded to trademark users[3] under the Lanham Act. Congress passed the Lanham Act in 1946 with the primary purpose of providing some nationwide protection for trademark users. Prior to that time, trademark protection was generally governed by state common law. The normal rule was that the first to appropriate a mark had the exclusive right to use that mark in business. 3 Callman, Unfair Competition and Trademarks § 76.1 (3d ed. 1970). Common law exceptions to the general rule developed as to remote users, but with increased interstate commerce, and the greater mobility of society as a whole, a federal scheme with some consistency

---

3. To be technically precise, this case involves service marks rather than trademarks because the marks and trade names identify the source of services rather than vendible commodities. 15 U.S.C. § 1127.

was felt to be necessary. H.R.Rep. No. 219, 79th Cong., 1st Sess. 4 (1945) * * *.

Section 15 of the Lanham Act, 15 U.S.C. § 1065, provides that a party like Thrifty, which has successfully registered and continued using a federal service mark, has an incontestable right to use the mark throughout the United States in connection with the goods or services with which it has been used. Lanham Act registration also puts all would-be users of the mark (or a confusingly similar mark) on constructive notice of the mark. 15 U.S.C. § 1072.

A. *"Limited area exception"*.

However, Lanham Act § 33(b), 15 U.S.C. § 1115(b)(5)[5] declares a "limited area" exception to that general premise of incontestability, an exception which the district court concluded was applicable in this case. The essence of the exception embodied in § 1115(b)(5) is based on common law trademark protection for remote users established by the Supreme Court in Hanover Star Milling Co. v. Metcalf, 240 U.S. 403, 36 S.Ct. 357, 60 L.Ed. 713 (1916), and United Drug Co. v. Theodore Rectanus Co., 248 U.S. 90, 39 S.Ct. 48, 63 L.Ed. 141 (1918). Subsection (5) confers upon a junior user, such as Thrift Cars, the right to continued use of an otherwise infringing mark in a remote geographical area if that use was established prior to the other party's federal registration. The junior user is permitted to maintain a proprietary interest in the mark even though it has no general federal protection through registration. To be able to invoke the § 1115(b)(5) exception, however, the junior user must have used the mark continuously in that location and initially in good faith without notice of an infringing mark. Burger King of Florida, Inc. v. Hoots, 403 F.2d 904, 907 (7th Cir.1968).

To sustain its "limited area" defense of 15 U.S.C. § 1115(b)(5), Thrift Cars was required to demonstrate (1) that it adopted its mark before Thrifty's 1964 registration under the Lanham Act, and without knowledge of Thrifty's prior use; (2) the extent of the trade area in which Thrift Cars used the mark prior to Thrifty's registration; and (3) that Thrift Cars has continuously used the mark in the pre-registration trade area. There is no issue that Thrift Cars had adopted its mark in good faith and without notice prior to Thrifty's registration. Rather, the questions are whether Thrift Cars had established a market presence in any locality, the extent of that market presence, and whether that market presence had been continuous within the meaning of § 1115(b)(5). The district court found that Thrift Cars' use of the service

---

5. Section 1115(b)(5) provides in pertinent part:

> If the right to use the registered mark has become incontestable under § 1065 of this title, the registration shall be conclusive evidence of the registrant's exclusive right to use the registered mark in commerce ... except when one of the following defenses or defects is established: ....
> (5) That the mark whose use is charged

as an infringement was adopted without knowledge of the registrant's prior use and has been continuously used by such party or those in privity with him from a date prior to registration of the mark under this chapter ... : Provided, however, that this defense of defect shall apply only for the area in which such continuous prior use is proved....

mark had been continuous in East Taunton within the meaning of § 1115(b)(5), but also found that it had not established a sufficient market presence outside of East Taunton (i.e., in Nantucket or other areas of southeastern Massachusetts) to establish there a continuous market presence sufficient to confer on Thrift Cars trademark protection under the statute.

As the district court held, the scope of protection afforded by § 1115(b)(5) is limited. A pre-existing good faith user's rights are frozen to the geographical location where the user has established a market penetration as of the date of registration. Such users are unable thereafter to acquire additional protection superior to that obtained by the federal registrant. The district court therefore held that Thrift Cars' expansion into new market areas after the 1964 date of Thrifty's federal registration is not protected under § 1115(b)(5).

* * *

B. *Thrift Cars did not demonstrate a continuous presence outside of East Taunton within the meaning of § 1115(b)(5).*

The district court found that Thrift Cars had not established a continuous presence in any area outside of East Taunton—prior to July 1964—adequate to satisfy the requirements of § 1115(b)(5). That finding was necessarily based on the hard facts and the inferences drawn from the trial evidence. The limited advertising Thrift Cars had done was not deemed sufficient to establish a presence outside East Taunton; nor were Thrift Cars' sporadic rentals in Nantucket and elsewhere in southeastern Massachusetts enough to sustain Thrift Cars' claim that it had already expanded out of East Taunton prior to Thrifty's federal registration.[8] These findings are not clearly erroneous and we do not overturn the district court's findings on this matter.

We also note that the fact that Thrift Cars had desired to expand into the Nantucket market prior to July 1964 by unsuccessfully applying for a license to operate at the airport is not sufficient to meet the requirements of § 1115(b)(5). A mere desire, without more, will not confer upon Thrift Cars the ability to exclude Thrifty from Nantucket. The policy behind the Lanham Act is very strong and the party challenging the federal registrant has the burden of showing a continued and actual market presence in order to qualify for the "limited area" exception under the statute. The trial court permissibly found that Thrift Cars did not meet its burden in this respect.

C. *Thrift Cars' activities in East Taunton fall into the "limited area" defense of § 1115(b)(5).*

The more difficult question is whether Thrift Cars has established and maintained a continuous market presence in East Taunton so as to sustain an injunction against Thrifty in that region. Under § 1115(b)(5),

---

8. At trial, Conlon of Thrift Cars indicated that, prior to Thrifty's federal registration, Thrift Cars maintained no cars on Nantucket and that there had been only three or four Thrift auto rentals directed to Nantucket.

the junior user must show that it has made continuous use of the mark prior to the issuance of the senior user's registration and must further prove continued use up until trial. 2 McCarthy, Trademarks and Unfair Competition § 26:18 (2d ed. 1984). Otherwise, the defense "dries up" and the junior user cannot assert rights in the limited trade area. See, e.g., Casual Corner Assocs., Inc. v. Casual Stores of Nevada, Inc., 493 F.2d 709 (9th Cir.1974) (one-year hiatus in using mark precluded use of the "limited area" defense); Decatur Fed. Savs. & Loan Assn. v. Peach State Fed. Savs. & Loan Assn., 203 U.S.P.Q. 406 (N.D.Ga.1978) (sixteen months of non-use barred use of defense).

Here, the district court properly found that Thrift Cars established a significant enough market share in East Taunton prior to Thrifty's 1964 federal registration to constitute continuous use there at least until May 1970, when Conlon opened business operations in Nantucket. The pivotal issue is, however, whether Thrift Cars continued enough of a market presence in East Taunton after May 1970 (to the time of trial) to qualify for the § 1115(b)(5) defense. The district court made no specific findings on this precise matter (though its opinion reveals an implicit affirmative finding), and we think it is a close call whether Thrift Cars conducted a significant amount of business in East Taunton up until trial. Nevertheless, we believe that on this record Thrift Cars should be entitled to continue doing business in East Taunton and Thrifty should be enjoined from establishing a franchise there. First, the record shows that Thrift Cars continually advertised in media directed specifically to the East Taunton area such as the Taunton area telephone yellow pages, even after opening the Nantucket facility. The record also reveals that Thrift Cars made a showing of general reputation in the East Taunton area throughout the period involved by maintaining an East Taunton address and an East Taunton telephone number. We cannot say that the district court's inherent finding of continuous use should be upset.

Although Thrift Cars' business was solely in East Taunton, the district court prohibited its future conduct of any car or truck rental leasing business outside Taunton, Massachusetts. This was not error or an abuse of discretion. East Taunton is not a separate entity but simply an integral part of Taunton itself. In these circumstances, it is appropriate to direct the injunction to the overall entity. (East Taunton appears to be a popular name for or a colloquial designation for one part of Taunton.)

D. The district court's injunction did not freeze Thrift Cars' business activities.

Thrift Cars argues that the district court's injunction is tantamount to freezing Thrift Cars' business activities rather than limiting the area in which those activities are conducted. We disagree. While we recognize that the automobile rental business, by its very nature, is mobile, and that we cannot, for example, prevent Nantucket residents from seeking out Thrift Cars in its protected East Taunton geographical area, the courts can prevent Thrift Cars from maintaining a rental agency in

Nantucket using the Thrift Cars name. The district court considered East Taunton and Nantucket as two separate market areas, not parts of a single southeastern Massachusetts market, as Thrift Cars would have us believe. It is settled that a junior user can conduct its activities within the market it had carved out for itself before the senior user obtained federal registration. But there was no showing in this case that Nantucket is within the same market area as East Taunton. On the contrary, it seems clear that the major reason that Thrift Cars began to do significant business in Nantucket was because Conlon deliberately moved the major portion of the business there and opened up a rental counter at the Nantucket airport after Thrifty's registration. This action constituted an expansion out of the East Taunton area after the critical date of Thrifty's registration, not a continuation of business activities within the same market area. The result is that the district court's injunction did not freeze Thrift Cars' business activities, but merely confined them, correctly, to the market area it had established prior to Thrifty's federal registration.

E.   *The district court did not abuse its discretion by allowing Thrift Cars to advertise in those publications it had used prior to Thrifty's registration.*

The district court allowed Thrift Cars to continue advertising in those media it had used prior to the critical date of July 26, 1964. Thrifty now urges that the court allowed Thrift Cars too broad an advertising distribution base, because it extended outside East Taunton to Cape Cod and Nantucket. Thrifty says that by permitting both parties to advertise in the major resort area publications, the court abused its discretion because substantial consumer confusion is likely to result.

We reject Thrifty's arguments and agree with the district court that to contract Thrift Cars' advertising base would be a punitive move. The district court did not allow Thrift Cars to advertise in any publications that it had not used prior to Thrifty's registration. On the contrary, the court simply authorized Thrift Cars to use only the same newspapers it had used prior to that critical date. While we recognize that some consumer confusion may result because there will be some overlap in advertising, the Lanham Act does not require the complete elimination of all confusion. Alfred Dunhill of London, Inc. v. Dunhill Tailored Clothes, Inc., 293 F.2d 685 (C.C.P.A.1961), cert. denied, 369 U.S. 864, 82 S.Ct. 1030, 8 L.Ed.2d 84 (1962). We think, moreover, that the confusion spawned as a result of Thrift Cars' advertising will be minimal and should not significantly interfere with Thrifty's proprietary rights in its mark. Each party shall bear its own costs.

AFFIRMED.

Notes

1.   Will the court's division of the trademark rights in this case result in significant consumer confusion in southeastern Massachusetts? If so, why does the court countenance this result?

2.   The "Burger King" chain of restaurants began operations with a single store in Florida, which opened in 1953, and it successfully registered its federal trademark in 1961. Its first Illinois restaurant opened in 1961. Meanwhile, in 1957, a completely independent "Burger King" (hereinafter the "junior user") opened in Mattoon, Illinois. In 1959, the junior user registered the "Burger King" mark under the *Illinois* trademark statute. In 1962, the junior user opened a second restaurant under the same name, this time in Charleston, Illinois. What are the relative rights of the parties? Does the junior user's registration under Illinois law change the analysis? See Burger King of Florida, Inc. v. Hoots, 403 F.2d 904 (7th Cir.1968).

EASTMAN KODAK CO. v. BELL & HOWELL DOCUMENT MANAGEMENT PRODUCTS CO.

United States Court of Appeals, Federal Circuit, 1993.
994 F.2d 1569.

MICHEL, CIRCUIT JUDGE.

Eastman Kodak Company (Kodak) appeals from the decision of the Trademark Trial and Appeal Board (Board) of the Patent and Trademark Office (PTO) in an intent-to-use application proceeding under the Lanham Act, as amended by the Trademark Law Revision Act of 1988, 15 U.S.C. §§ 1051–1127 (1992), Eastman Kodak Co. v. Bell & Howell Document Management Prods. Co., Nos. 86,083, 86,093, and 86,101 (TTAB June 8, 1992). In its decision, the Board denied Kodak's motion for summary judgment, granting summary judgment for Bell & Howell Document Management Products Company (B & H) on the issue of descriptiveness, and dismissing the oppositions "without prejudice to the filing of a petition to cancel the registration issued after a statement of use has been filed," id., slip op. at 6. Because we hold that, in the circumstances of an intent-to-use application proceeding, the Board's actions are permissible under the statute, we affirm.

BACKGROUND

On October 12, 1990, B & H filed intent-to-use applications, under 15 U.S.C. § 1051(b), to register the numbers "6200," "6800" and "8100" on the Principal Register as trademarks for microfilm reader/printers. After initial examination of the applications, the trademark examining attorney approved the applications for publication in the PTO's Official Gazette.

Section 1051(b) allows an applicant who alleges a bona fide intent to use a mark to file an application seeking registration on the Principal Register. If, upon examination, the mark appears registrable, the PTO publishes it for opposition. 15 U.S.C. § 1062(a). If no opposer is successful, the PTO issues a notice of allowance. Id. § 1063(b)(2). The applicant then has six months[2] in which to file a statement that verifies that the

---

2.   The statute also provides for extensions of time for good cause. See 15 U.S.C. § 1051(d)(2).

mark is in use in commerce, the date of first use in commerce, the goods and services in connection with the mark are used in commerce, and the manner in which the mark is being used. Id. § 1051(d)(1). The statement of use is then subject to another examination, in which the PTO considers how the mark is used and, if it is still satisfied that, as used, the mark is registrable, issues a certificate of registration. Id.

Kodak, a competitor of B & H in the manufacture and marketing of business equipment products, including microfilm reader/printers, timely filed a notice of opposition to registration of each of the three marks. Kodak alleged that the marks would be used solely as model designators for the reader/printers and therefore would be merely descriptive. Kodak argued that B & H had not shown that the marks had acquired secondary meaning and that, therefore, registration of the marks would be improper. The three opposition proceedings were consolidated before the Board.

B & H moved for summary judgment on the grounds that there were no genuine issues of material fact regarding the alleged mere descriptiveness of its applied-for number marks and, alternatively, that Kodak had no standing to oppose B & H's applications. Kodak filed a cross-motion for summary judgment. The Board determined that Kodak did have standing to oppose and that conclusion is not contested in this appeal.

On the issue of mere descriptiveness, the Board stated that it "believe[s] that it is possible for a numerical designation, which functions only in part to designate a model or grade, to be inherently distinctive and registrable without a showing of secondary meaning." Eastman Kodak, slip op. at 5 (citing Neapco Inc. v. Dana Corp., 12 USPQ2d 1746, 1748 (TTAB 1989)). Due to the nature of intent-to-use applications, the number marks at issue had not been used at the time of the opposition proceeding. Accordingly, the Board held that it could not determine whether the numerical designations "are merely descriptive or if they are registrable without a showing of secondary meaning." Id. The Board concluded that in such situations, where the descriptiveness issue could not be resolved until use had begun, the opposition should be dismissed without prejudice to the initiation of a cancellation proceeding against the mark if the mark is registered after the statement of use is filed. Consequently, the Board denied Kodak's motion for summary judgment, granted B & H summary judgment on the descriptiveness issue, and dismissed the oppositions without prejudice. As a result, B & H received a notice of allowance.

Discussion

The principal issue in this case is whether the Board's implied creation of a presumption in favor of the applicant for a numerical mark intended for use as more than a model designator is a reasonable interpretation of the Board's authority under the Lanham Act. We hold that it is.

Under the *Chevron* doctrine, established in Chevron U.S.A., Inc. v. Natural Resources Defense Council, Inc., 467 U.S. 837, 104 S.Ct. 2778, 81 L.Ed.2d 694 (1984), "[w]hen a court reviews an [administrative] agency's construction of the statute which it administers, it is confronted with two questions." Id. at 842, 104 S.Ct. at 2781. The first is whether Congress has directly addressed the precise question at issue. If so, then the agency "must give effect to the unambiguously expressed intent of Congress," id. at 843, 104 S.Ct. at 2782, and the court must, of course, review the agency's interpretation accordingly. If, however, "the statute is silent or ambiguous with respect to the specific issue, the question for the court is whether the agency's answer is based on a permissible construction of the statute." Id. (emphasis added). In order to uphold the agency's interpretation, the court need not conclude that it was the only permissible construction or even the construction the court would have reached on its own reading of the statute. Id. n. 11. The agency's interpretation must merely be "reasonable." See id. at 866, 104 S.Ct. at 2793.

I.

In the instant case, the Board's decision to grant B & H summary judgment and dismiss Kodak's opposition without prejudice, necessarily involved the Board's concluding that numerical designators are presumptively not merely descriptive under Lanham Act section 2(e), 15 U.S.C. § 1052(e), when applied for in an intent-to-use application under section 1(b), 15 U.S.C. § 1051(b). Section 1(b) sets forth the requirements for filing an intent-to-use application. See 15 U.S.C. § 1051(b). Section 2(e) precludes registration of a trademark on the Principal Register that, inter alia, "[c]onsists of a mark which, when used on or in connection with the goods of the applicant is merely descriptive or deceptively misdescriptive of them." Id. § 1052(e). The statute on its face neither requires nor precludes the Board's interpretation.

Nor does the legislative history of the Trademark Law Revision Act of 1988 speak directly to this issue. The legislative history does demonstrate that Congress intended most marks applied for in an intent-to-use application (intent-to-use mark) to be reviewed for descriptiveness in the initial examination/pre-use stage of the intent-to-use application process. For example, Senate Report 515 states that "the absence of specimens at the time the application is filed will not affect examination on numerous fundamental issues of registrability (that is, descriptiveness, geographic or surname significance, or confusing similarity)." S.Rep. No. 515, 100th Cong., 2d Sess. 32 (1988), reprinted in 1988 U.S.C.C.A.N. 5577, 5595. With respect to the examination of the statement of use, which is filed after a notice of allowance has been issued, the Report states:

The Patent and Trademark Office's examination of the statement of use will be only for the purpose of determining issues that could not have been fully considered during the initial examination of the application, that is, whether the person filing the statement of use is the applicant, whether the mark as used corresponds to the drawing submitted with the application, whether the goods or services were identified in the application and not subsequently deleted, and *whether the mark, as displayed in the specimens or facsimiles, functions as a mark*.

Id. at 34, 1988 U.S.C.C.A.N. at 5596 (emphasis added). As the highlighted phrase shows, Congress did intend the PTO to confirm, after the filing of the statement of use, that the intent-to-use mark, as displayed and used, actually "functions as a mark." Indeed, the statute provides: "Subject to *examination and acceptance* of the statement of use, the mark shall be registered.... Such examination may include an examination of the factors set forth in subsections (a) through (e) of section 1052." 15 U.S.C. § 1051(d)(1) (emphasis added). And the legislative history itself emphasized that "[t]his provision [of the statute] permits the [PTO] to raise issues of registrability that might not be evident until the applicant makes available specimens showing the mark as used and/or clarifying the nature of the goods or services involved." H.R.Rep. No. 1028, 100th Cong., 2d Sess. 9 (1988). Thus, the statute and legislative history provide for the situation where, as here, the question of mere descriptiveness cannot be answered until after use has begun.

Furthermore, it is clear from the legislative history that Congress, for policy reasons, chose to sequence the opposition process before the use of an intent-to-use mark had commenced. See S.Rep. No. 515 at 32, 1988 U.S.C.C.A.N. at 5595 ("Subjecting an intent-to-use application to the opposition process before the applicant makes use of its mark is essential if the system is to achieve its goal of reducing uncertainty before the applicant invests in commercial use of the mark."). Accordingly, Congress knew that some issues of registrability could not be decided in opposition proceedings and would therefore have to be addressed in the post-use PTO examination or challenged in a cancellation proceeding after the mark was registered.

Thus, under step one of our inquiry under the *Chevron* doctrine, the Board's interpretation does not contravene any clear and unambiguous statutory meaning.

II.

We further conclude, under step two of the *Chevron* doctrine, that the Board's construction is a reasonable interpretation of the Lanham Act.

Kodak argues, however, that the Board's interpretation is unreasonable because it would preclude asserting mere descriptiveness as a basis for denying registration of both word and number marks in intent-to-use applications. This argument is unavailing for several reasons. First, there are words and phrases that, as applied to certain goods, the examining attorney in the initial examination could certainly find to be prima facie merely descriptive. For example, an examining attorney could easily find that the term "reader/printer" applied to the microfilm reader/printers at issue here would be merely descriptive or that the term "slow-cooker" was merely descriptive of a Dutch oven. Furthermore, the examining attorney may also find numbers that are intended for use solely as model designators to be prima facie merely descriptive. Cf. J.M. Huber Corp. v. Lowery Wellheads, Inc., 778 F.2d 1467, 1469, 228 USPQ 206, 207 (10th Cir.1985) (common law trademark infringement action in district court).

Second, Kodak's argument must assume that under circumstances such as these, after a notice of allowance is issued, intent-to-use marks will automatically be passed to registration. However, the statute provides for another examination of the mark after the statement of use is filed. 15 U.S.C. § 1051(d)(1) ("Subject to examination and acceptance of the statement of use, the mark shall be registered in the Patent and Trademark Office. . . . "). Moreover, the statute contemplates the need, in certain circumstances, for a complete reexamination: "Such examination may include an examination of the factors set forth in subsections (a) through (e) of section 1052." Id. In addition, the trademark regulations, promulgated by the PTO pursuant to authority granted by statute, see id. § 1123, provide that "[a] timely filed statement of use which meets the minimum requirements specified in paragraph (e) of this section *will be* examined in accordance with §§ 2.61 through 2.69." 37 C.F.R. § 2.88(f) (emphasis added). Thus, once the examining attorney establishes that the statement of use has met the minimum requirements set forth in 37 C.F.R. § 2.88(e) (the prescribed fee, at least one specimen of use, and a declaration by the applicant that the mark is in use in commerce), the regulation requires that the examining attorney reexamine the mark under the standards of the initial examination (37 C.F.R. §§ 2.61–2.69).

* * *

Notes

1.   Is Kodak's concern that brand names may be "tied up" through the intent-to-use provision a realistic one? Does the intent-to-use process have sufficient constraints to prevent strategic behavior designed to lock up desirable marks? Why have an intent-to-use system at all? See generally Amy B. Cohen, Intent to Use: A Failed Experiment?, 35 U.S.F. L. Rev. 683 (2001); Kenneth L. Port, The Congressional Expansion Of American Trademark Law: A Civil Law System In The Making, 35 Wake Forest Law Review 827 (2000) (criticizing ITU provision as unnecessary).

2.   What is the distinction between numerical product designations that are used as "model numbers" as opposed to numbers that are used as trademarks? Can you think of examples of each? See generally Arrow Fastener Co. v. Stanley Works, 59 F.3d 384 (2d Cir.1995) (noting that "T–50," term used on staple guns, could not function as both a trademark and a model designation).

3. In what circumstances can the descriptiveness of a proposed trademark be determined prior to its actual use? In what circumstances would the descriptiveness of a proposed trademark become evident only after it has been used? How would the PTO handle an intent-to-use application for "Washington apples" or a "Slow–Cooker Dutch Oven" or "McDonald's Restaurant" or a state flag for a product? For further discussion of the "intent to use" provisions of the Lanham Act, see 2 J. Thomas McCarthy, Trademarks and Unfair Competition §§ 16.05, 19.07 to 19.08 (3d ed. 1995).

PARK 'N FLY, INC. v. DOLLAR PARK AND FLY, INC.

Supreme Court of the United States, 1985.
469 U.S. 189, 105 S.Ct. 658, 83 L.Ed.2d 582.

JUSTICE O'CONNOR delivered the opinion of the Court.

In this case we consider whether an action to enjoin the infringement of an incontestable trade or service mark may be defended on the grounds that the mark is merely descriptive. We conclude that neither the language of the relevant statutes nor the legislative history supports such a defense.

I

Petitioner operates long-term parking lots near airports. After starting business in St. Louis in 1967, petitioner subsequently opened facilities in Cleveland, Houston, Boston, Memphis, and San Francisco. Petitioner applied in 1969 to the United States Patent and Trademark Office (Patent Office) to register a service mark consisting of the logo of an airplane and the words "Park 'N Fly." The registration issued in August 1971. Nearly six years later, petitioner filed an affidavit with the Patent Office to establish the incontestable status of the mark.[2] As required by § 15 of the Trademark Act of 1946 (Lanham Act), 60 Stat. 433, as amended, 15 U.S.C. § 1065, the affidavit stated that the mark had been registered and in continuous use for five consecutive years, that there had been no final adverse decision to petitioner's claim of ownership or right to registration, and that no proceedings involving such rights were pending. Incontestable status provides, subject to the provisions of § 15 and § 33(b) of the Lanham Act, "conclusive evidence of the registrant's exclusive right to use the registered mark...." § 33(b), 15 U.S.C. § 1115(b).

Respondent also provides long-term airport parking services, but only has operations in Portland, Oregon. Respondent calls its business "Dollar Park and Fly." Petitioner filed this infringement action in 1978 in the United States District Court for the District of Oregon and requested the court permanently to enjoin respondent from using the words "Park and Fly" in connection with its business. Respondent counterclaimed and sought cancellation of petitioner's mark on the grounds that it is a generic term. See § 14(c), 15 U.S.C. § 1064(c).

---

2. Petitioner also applied in 1977 to register a mark consisting only of the words "Park 'N Fly." That mark issued in 1979, but has not become incontestable. The existence of this mark does not affect our resolution of the issues in this case.

Respondent also argued that petitioner's mark is unenforceable because it is merely descriptive. See § 2(e), 15 U.S.C. § 1052(e). * * *

After a bench trial, the District Court found that petitioner's mark is not generic and observed that an incontestable mark cannot be challenged on the grounds that it is merely descriptive. * * * Finally, the District Court found sufficient evidence of likelihood of confusion. The District Court permanently enjoined respondent from using the words "Park and Fly" and any other mark confusingly similar to "Park 'N Fly."

The Court of Appeals for the Ninth Circuit reversed. 718 F.2d 327 (1983). The District Court did not err, the Court of Appeals held, in refusing to invalidate petitioner's mark. The Court of Appeals noted, however, that it previously had held that incontestability provides a defense against the cancellation of a mark, but it may not be used offensively to enjoin another's use. Petitioner, under this analysis, could obtain an injunction only if its mark would be entitled to continued registration without regard to its incontestable status. Thus, respondent could defend the infringement action by showing that the mark was merely descriptive. Based on its own examination of the record, the Court of Appeals then determined that petitioner's mark is in fact merely descriptive, and therefore respondent should not be enjoined from using the name "Park and Fly."

The decision below is in direct conflict with the decision of the Court of Appeals for the Seventh Circuit in Union Carbide Corp. v. Ever–Ready Inc., 531 F.2d 366, cert. denied, 429 U.S. 830, 97 S.Ct. 91, 50 L.Ed.2d 94 (1976). We granted certiorari to resolve this conflict, 465 U.S. 1078, 104 S.Ct. 1438, 79 L.Ed.2d 760 (1984), and we now reverse.

II

Congress enacted the Lanham Act in 1946 in order to provide national protection for trademarks used in interstate and foreign commerce. S.Rep. No. 1333, 79th Cong., 2d Sess., 5 (1946). Previous federal legislation, such as the Federal Trademark Act of 1905, 33 Stat. 724, reflected the view that protection of trademarks was a matter of state concern and that the right to a mark depended solely on the common law. S.Rep. No. 1333, at 5. Consequently, rights to trademarks were uncertain and subject to variation in different parts of the country. Because trademarks desirably promote competition and the maintenance of product quality, Congress determined that "a sound public policy requires that trademarks should receive nationally the greatest protection that can be given them." Id., at 6. Among the new protections created by the Lanham Act were the statutory provisions that allow a federally registered mark to become incontestable. §§ 15, 33(b), 15 U.S.C. §§ 1065, 1115(b).

The provisions of the Lanham Act concerning registration and incontestability distinguish a mark that is "the common descriptive name of an article or substance" from a mark that is "merely descriptive." §§ 2(e), 14(c), 15 U.S.C. §§ 1052(e), 1064(c). Marks that constitute a common descriptive name are referred to as generic. A generic term is one that refers to the genus of which the particular product is a species. Abercrombie & Fitch Co. v. Hunting World, Inc., 537 F.2d 4, 9 (C.A.2 1976). Generic terms are not registrable, and a registered mark may be canceled at any time on the grounds that it has become generic. See §§ 2, 14(c), 15 U.S.C. §§ 1052, 1064(c). A "merely descriptive" mark, in contrast, describes the qualities or characteristics of a good or service, and this type of mark may be registered only if the registrant shows that it has acquired secondary meaning, i.e., it "has become distinctive of the applicant's goods in commerce." §§ 2(e), (f), 15 U.S.C. §§ 1052(e), (f).

This case requires us to consider the effect of the incontestability provisions of the Lanham Act in the context of an infringement action defended on the grounds that the mark is merely descriptive. Statutory construction must begin with the language employed by Congress and the assumption that the ordinary meaning of that language accurately expresses the legislative purpose. With respect to incontestable trade or service marks, § 33(b) of the Lanham Act states that "registration shall be conclusive evidence of the registrant's exclusive right to use the registered mark" subject to the conditions of § 15 and certain enumerated defenses.[3] Section 15 incorporates by reference subsections (c) and (e) of § 14, 15 U.S.C. § 1064. An incontestable mark that becomes generic may be canceled at any time pursuant to § 14(c). That section also allows cancellation of an incontestable mark at any time if it has been abandoned, if it is being used to misrepresent the source of the goods or services in connection with which it is used, or if it was obtained fraudulently or contrary to the provisions of § 4, 15 U.S.C. § 1054, or §§ 2(a)-(c), 15 U.S.C. §§ 1052(a)–(c).[4]

One searches the language of the Lanham Act in vain to find any support for the offensive/defensive distinction applied by the Court of Appeals. The statute nowhere distinguishes between a registrant's offensive and defensive use of an incontestable mark. On the contrary, § 33(b)'s declaration that the registrant has an "exclusive right" to use the mark indicates that incontestable status may be used to enjoin infringement by others. A conclusion that such infringement cannot be

---

3. Section 33(b) of the Lanham Act, as set forth in 15 U.S.C. § 1115(b), provides: "If the right to use the registered mark has become incontestable under section 1065 of this title, the registration shall be conclusive evidence of the registrant's exclusive right to use the registered mark in commerce or in connection with the goods or services specified in the affidavit filed under the provisions of said section 1065 subject to any conditions or limitations stated therein except when one of the following defenses or defects is established: [listing the following defenses: (1) 'the registration or the incontestable right to use the mark was obtained fraudulently'; (2) abandon-

ment; or (3) 'the registered mark is being used, by or with the permission of the registrant or a person in privity with the registrant, so as to misrepresent the source of the goods or services in connection with which the mark is used'; (4) fair use; (5) prior use; (6) limited-area exception; or (7) '[t]hat the mark has been or is being used to violate the antitrust laws of the United States.']"

4. Sections 2(a)-(c) prohibit registration of marks containing specified subject matter, e.g., the flag of the United States. Sections 4 and 14(e) concern certification marks and are inapplicable to this case.

enjoined renders meaningless the "exclusive right" recognized by the statute. Moreover, the language in three of the defenses enumerated in § 33(b) clearly contemplates the use of incontestability in infringement actions by plaintiffs. See §§ 33(b)(4)-(6), 15 U.S.C. §§ 1115(b)(4)-(6).

The language of the Lanham Act also refutes any conclusion that an incontestable mark may be challenged as merely descriptive. A mark that is merely descriptive of an applicant's goods or services is not registrable unless the mark has secondary meaning. Before a mark achieves incontestable status, registration provides prima facie evidence of the registrant's exclusive right to use the mark in commerce. § 33(a), 15 U.S.C. § 1115(a). The Lanham Act expressly provides that before a mark becomes incontestable an opposing party may prove any legal or equitable defense which might have been asserted if the mark had not been registered. Ibid. Thus, § 33(a) would have allowed respondent to challenge petitioner's mark as merely descriptive if the mark had not become incontestable. With respect to incontestable marks, however, § 33(b) provides that registration is conclusive evidence of the registrant's exclusive right to use the mark, subject to the conditions of § 15 and the seven defenses enumerated in § 33(b) itself. Mere descriptiveness is not recognized by either § 15 or § 33(b) as a basis for challenging an incontestable mark.

* * *

III

Nothing in the legislative history of the Lanham Act supports a departure from the plain language of the statutory provisions concerning incontestability. Indeed, a conclusion that incontestable status can provide the basis for enforcement of the registrant's exclusive right to use a trade or service mark promotes the goals of the statute. The Lanham Act provides national protection of trademarks in order to secure to the owner of the mark the goodwill of his business and to protect the ability of consumers to distinguish among competing producers. See S.Rep. No. 1333, at 3, 5. National protection of trademarks is desirable, Congress concluded, because trademarks foster competition and the maintenance of quality by securing to the producer the benefits of good reputation. Id., at 4. The incontestability provisions, as the proponents of the Lanham Act emphasized, provide a means for the registrant to quiet title in the ownership of his mark. * * * The opportunity to obtain incontestable status by satisfying the requirements of § 15 thus encourages producers to cultivate the goodwill associated with a particular mark. This function of the incontestability provisions would be utterly frustrated if the holder of an incontestable mark could not enjoin infringement by others so long as they established that the mark would not be registrable but for its incontestable status.

* * *

Respondent's argument that enforcing petitioner's mark will not promote the goals of the Lanham Act is misdirected. Arguments similar to those now urged by respondent were in fact considered by Congress in hearings on the Lanham Act. For example, the United States Department of Justice opposed the incontestability provisions and expressly noted that a merely descriptive mark might become incontestable. Hearings on H.R. 82, at 59–60 (statement of the U.S. Dept. of Justice). This result, the Department of Justice observed, would "go beyond existing law in conferring unprecedented rights on trade-mark owners," and would undesirably create an exclusive right to use language that is descriptive of a product. Id., at 60; see also Hearings on H.R. 102, at 106–107, 109–110 (testimony of Prof. Milton Handler); id., at 107, 175 (testimony of attorney Louis Robertson). These concerns were answered by proponents of the Lanham Act, who noted that a merely descriptive mark cannot be registered unless the Commissioner finds that it has secondary meaning. Id., at 108, 113 (testimony of Karl Pohl, U.S. Trade Mark Assn.). Moreover, a mark can be challenged for five years prior to its attaining incontestable status. Id., at 114 (remarks of Rep. Lanham). The supporters of the incontestability provisions further observed that a generic mark cannot become incontestable and that § 33(b)(4) allows the nontrademark use of descriptive terms used in an incontestable mark. Id., at 110–111 (testimony of Wallace Martin, chairman, ABA Committee on Trade Mark Legislation).

* * *

The dissent echoes arguments made by opponents of the Lanham Act that the incontestable status of a descriptive mark might take from the public domain language that is merely descriptive. As we have explained, Congress has already addressed concerns to prevent the "commercial monopolization," of descriptive language. The Lanham Act allows a mark to be challenged at any time if it becomes generic, and, under certain circumstances, permits the nontrademark use of descriptive terms contained in an incontestable mark. Finally, if "monopolization" of an incontestable mark threatens economic competition, § 33(b)(7), 15 U.S.C. § 1115(b)(7), provides a defense on the grounds that the mark is being used to violate federal antitrust laws. At bottom, the dissent simply disagrees with the balance struck by Congress in determining the protection to be given to incontestable marks.

IV

Respondent argues that the decision by the Court of Appeals should be upheld because trademark registrations are issued by the Patent Office after an ex parte proceeding and generally without inquiry into the merits of an application. This argument also unravels upon close examination. The facts of this case belie the suggestion that registration is virtually automatic. The Patent Office initially denied petitioner's application because the examiner considered the mark to be merely descriptive. Petitioner sought reconsideration and successfully persuaded the Patent Office that its mark was registrable.

* * *

VI

We conclude that the holder of a registered mark may rely on incontestability to enjoin infringement and that such an action may not be defended on the grounds that the mark is merely descriptive. * * *

[JUSTICE STEVENS' dissenting opinion is deleted.]

Notes

1.   What policies underlie the "incontestability" doctrine? How can a competitor challenge a descriptive mark that is being used by another firm in the market?

2.   A trademark owner obtains a number of benefits from registration, as this case illustrates. These benefits include incontestability under sections 14 and 33(b); prima facie validity of a mark; constructive notice of registration; and enhanced remedies. In light of the decisions in this chapter, which of these advantages is most important? Do these benefits justify the cost of registration?

3.   Once a mark has become incontestable, on what grounds can it be challenged? Have the Court and Congress sufficiently addressed the danger that some unprotectable marks may attain incontestable status?

Chapter 4

TRADEMARK INFRINGEMENT

A. THE LIKELIHOOD OF CONFUSION STANDARD

CBS INC. v. LIEDERMAN

United States District Court, S.D. New York, 1994.
866 F.Supp. 763, aff'd per curiam, 44 F.3d 174 (2d Cir.1995).

KEVIN THOMAS DUFFY, DISTRICT JUDGE:

CBS Inc. ("CBS") commenced this action against David and William Liederman ("defendants") alleging trademark infringement, unfair competition, and trademark dilution under the Lanham Act, 15 U.S.C. §§ 1114(1) and 1125(a), and New York statutory and common law. CBS moved for a preliminary injunction and a temporary restraining order preventing the defendants from opening their proposed restaurant, named "Television City."

Since 1952, CBS has owned and operated "Television City," a facility located in Los Angeles, California designed for the production of television shows. On January 26, 1988, the service mark "Television City" was registered on the Principal Register in the United States Patent and Trademark Office in the name of CBS Inc., as U.S. Service Mark Registration No. 1,474,506. The mark was granted for the following categories: "for television production services" and "for entertainment services, namely the production and distribution of television programs, rental of television production facilities and the providing of tours of production facilities to the public." The facility has a somewhat storied past within American popular culture, having been the home to many of CBS' best television series. Today, many soap operas and game shows are produced at Television City, and hundreds of people descend upon the facility each day in order to be a member of a studio audience. The name "Television City" is shown numerous times each week in connection with these television shows, and can often be heard in the voice-over accompanying each show's introduction. In addition, there is a small retail operation at the facility which sells such memorabilia as T-shirts, pins, watches and the like, each bearing the name "CBS Television City."

The defendants are restauranteurs, who are in the process of opening a restaurant in New York City using the identical mark, "Television City." The proposed restaurant, which is to be a "theme" restaurant celebrating "the world of television" would be located at Sixth Avenue and 50th Street in Manhattan, directly across the street from Radio City Music Hall. The restaurant would not only serve food, but would have an entire section devoted to the sale of television memorabilia, such as T-shirts, sweatshirts, posters, and the like.

CBS asserts that the continued promotion and eventual opening of the proposed restaurant will mislead the general public and convey a false impression as to the restaurant's affiliation with CBS. Thus, CBS seeks to preliminarily enjoin defendants' use of the "Television City" mark in connection with their restaurant.

DISCUSSION

I.   *Lanham Act Section 32 and Common Law Infringement Claims*

Plaintiff claims trademark infringement under both the Lanham Act and the state common law. Infringement of a registered trademark is prohibited by § 32(1) of the Lanham Act. 15 U.S.C. 1114 (1988). Section 32(1) prohibits the use of a registered trademark without permission, in connection with the sale or advertising of goods or services, in a manner that is likely to cause confusion or mistake or to deceive the purchaser as to the source or sponsorship of the goods. 15 U.S.C. § 1114(1). See Gruner & Jahr USA Pub. v. Meredith Corp., 991 F.2d 1072, 1075 (2d Cir.1993).

There can be no disputing that CBS is the owner of an incontestable, registered service mark—at least with regard to television production services. The strength of the mark within the television production field is not questioned. The central issue is whether this mark extends from the television production arena to the restaurant arena. The Second Circuit has held that "the strength of an incontestable registered trademark could be overcome by the use of a descriptive or weak portion of the mark." Gruner & Jahr, 991 F.2d at 1077. See also W.W.W. Pharmaceutical Co. v. Gillette Co., 984 F.2d 567, 576 (2d Cir.1993) (incontestable registered trademark for "Sportstick" lip balm was not infringed by Gillette's "Sport Stick" deodorant); Western Pub. Co. v. Rose Art Indus. Inc., 910 F.2d 57, 60 (2d Cir.1990); Pirone v. MacMillan, Inc., 894 F.2d 579 (2d Cir.1990) (observing that registration does not remove proper noun from general language or reduce it to exclusive possession of registrant for all purposes). Additionally, "a term that is in one category for a particular product may be in quite a different one for another." Abercrombie & Fitch Co. v. Hunting World, Inc., 537 F.2d 4, 9 (2d Cir.1976).

* * *

(B) Likelihood of Confusion

Likelihood of confusion has been defined as the likelihood that an appreciable number of ordinarily prudent purchasers are likely to be misled, or simply confused, as to the source, sponsorship or affiliation of defendant's goods or services. Western Pub. Co., 910 F.2d at 59. The law of this circuit with respect to likelihood of confusion was set forth in Polaroid Corp. v. Polarad Elecs. Corp., 287 F.2d 492 (2d Cir.), cert. denied, 368 U.S. 820, 82 S.Ct. 36, 7 L.Ed.2d 25 (1961). While not absolutely dispositive, the *Polaroid* factors establish a balancing test consisting of the following factors: (1) the strength of the mark; (2) the degree of similarity between the two marks; (3) the proximity of the two [products]; (4) the likelihood that the senior user of the mark will bridge the gap; (5) evidence of actual confusion; (6) the junior user's bad faith in adopting the mark; (7) the quality of the junior user's [product]; and (8) the sophistication of the relevant consumer group. Id. at 495.

(1) Strength of the Mark

The strength of a mark is "its tendency to identify goods sold as emanating from a particular, even if anonymous source." See Mead Data Central v. Toyota Motor Sales, U.S.A., Inc., 702 F.Supp. 1031, 1035 (S.D.N.Y.1988). The strength of the mark is the central issue as it will determine the breadth of the mark's protection.

CBS established the first facility used exclusively for television production in 1952 and named it "Television City." Pursuant to 15 U.S.C. § 1065, CBS used the mark continuously for five consecutive years following its registration and it has become an incontestable mark. Although the mark covers only the words "Television City," the plaintiff uses it almost exclusively as "CBS Television City." In this regard, it seems that public recognition of the mark, to the extent that it is recognized, would be more for "CBS Television City," rather than for "Television City." Moreover, defendants' restaurant will not be broadcasting or producing any television programs. The mere similarity in the subject matter—that they both necessarily involve television—does not grant CBS protection in every area where television is an underlying theme.

Interestingly, there are various registrations similar to plaintiff's mark for the sale and repair of television sets and appliances. These other uses are no more likely to cause confusion with the plaintiff's mark than the defendants' proposed use.[2] The mark is strong within the field of television production, but it is limited to that and related fields.

(2) Similarity of Marks

Because the two marks are identical, this factor overwhelmingly favors CBS. Defendants argue that CBS uses their mark almost exclusively in conjunction with the "CBS" name and corporate logo. While

2. Plaintiff has never brought suit against any other company for infringement of the mark "Television City." In fact, plaintiff's agents admitted they were not even aware of the existence of such companies bearing similar marks to the plaintiff.

this is true, the fact remains that the registered mark is merely for "Television City," and not for "CBS Television City." The fact that CBS often connects the two marks does not change the fact that defendants are attempting to use the identical mark that CBS has registered and would like to protect.

(3) Proximity

This factor, which is the central issue in this case, measures whether it is likely that consumers will assume either that the junior user's product is associated with the senior user or is a product of the senior user. See Centaur Communications, Ltd. v. A/S/M Communications, Inc., 830 F.2d 1217, 1226 (2d Cir.1987). See Comic Strip, Inc. v. Fox Television Stations, Inc., 710 F.Supp. 976, 979 (S.D.N.Y.1989). In determining the proximity of the two "Television Cities," the court considers "content, geographic distribution, market position, and audience appeal." Major League Baseball v. Sed Non Olet Denarius, 817 F.Supp. 1103, 1120 (S.D.N.Y.1993) (citing W.W.W. Pharmaceutical, 984 F.2d at 573).

CBS produces television shows at Television City in California. The mark is to protect the name in that context. The intended use of defendants' proposed restaurant will primarily be serving food. There simply is little or no overlap between the services provided be each of the parties. Additionally, the production site and the proposed restaurant are on opposite coasts. While it is true that an avid fan of television may be attracted to both places, it does not mean that they would visit one at the expense of the other. The individual would have two entirely different experiences. CBS invites the public into CBS Television City to make up the audiences for its game shows and other television programs produced on site. While there, CBS provides a tour of the facility. However, there was testimony that the public is excluded from CBS Television City for all purposes other than for seeing a show produced. * * * There is little overlap of markets between plaintiff's and defendants' services. Accordingly, this factor favors a finding for defendants.

(4) Bridging the Gap

This factor evaluates "whether the senior user of the mark is likely to enter the market in which the junior user is operating." Centaur Communications, Ltd., 880 F.2d at 1227. Trademark law protects a senior user's right to enter into a related field in the future. Scarves by Vera, Inc. v. Todo Imports Ltd., 544 F.2d 1167, 1172 (2d Cir.1976). CBS claims in its papers that it is currently planning to open a full service restaurant near the Ed Sullivan Theater on West 57th Street in Manhattan. This proposed restaurant, which plaintiff has apparently acquired, is to be a "television theme restaurant ... probably focusing on the history of television." It must be noted that plaintiff's mark is afforded protection in the television production area and related areas only. Plaintiff's announcement that it is looking to enter the restaurant business is irrelevant to this claim. It is a competitive venture to that of the defendants, but since the restaurant business is not "related" to television production, CBS' mark does not necessarily protect this latest endeavor by CBS.

Plaintiff attempts to show that it has already bridged the gap with regard to restaurants because CBS operates an employee cafeteria named "Television City Cafe" at its Los Angeles facility. This establishment is far removed from the type of restaurant proposed by defendants. Additionally, the cafe operated by CBS is located within the CBS' complex in California, and is not open to the public. Defendants' proposed restaurant is in New York City. CBS' maintenance of an on-site cafeteria for its workers is not sufficient to entitle it to protection under its mark. The on-site facility differs dramatically from that of the proposed restaurant, and does not mean that plaintiff has entered the restaurant business. In fact, the cafeteria is not being operated by CBS at all. Rather, it is run by Marriott through a contract with CBS. Clearly, these two eating establishments would not in any way compete with each other, and this argument is without merit.

(5) Actual Confusion

This factor pertains to whether any consumers have actually been misled by the similarity of the two marks. In this case there has been no realistic opportunity for actual confusion because defendants' restaurant has not yet opened. While it was argued that reports of defendants' proposed restaurant have appeared numerous times in the media without mention of CBS' mark, this factor does not seem to favor either side. CBS acted before the restaurant opened and any actual confusion could arise, and it should not be penalized for so doing. Actual confusion is not an essential element in order to prevail under the Lanham Act, since actual confusion is very difficult to prove and the Act requires only a likelihood of confusion as to source. "It would be unfair to penalize appellee for acting to protect its trademark rights before serious damage has occurred." Lois Sportswear, U.S.A., Inc. v. Levi Strauss & Co., 799 F.2d 867, 875 (2d Cir.1986) (citation omitted). Therefore, this factor favors neither party.

(6) Junior User's Bad Faith

This factor looks to whether the defendants "adopted its mark with the intention of capitalizing on plaintiff's reputation and goodwill and any confusion between [defendant's] and the senior user's product." W.W.W. Pharmaceutical, 984 F.2d at 575 (quoting Lang v. Retirement Living Pub. Co., 949 F.2d 576, 583 (2d Cir.1991) (citation omitted)). In the present case, while CBS argues for bad faith to be inferred, it fails to put forth any evidence that defendants chose this particular mark with the intent of capitalizing on any goodwill which CBS had acquired. * * * Without more, it appears that defendants did not act in bad faith and this factor does not favor either side.

(7) Quality of Junior User's Product

While defendants' restaurant is not yet open, there is no evidence to suggest that it will be anything but top quality.[3] CBS acknowledges this fact, yet makes the point that "[A] senior user is entitled 'to protect its reputation even where the infringer's goods are of top quality.' " Berkshire Fashions, Inc. v. Sara Lee Corp., 725 F.Supp. 790, 799 (S.D.N.Y. 1989) (quoting Mobil Oil Corp. v. Pegasus Petroleum Corp., 818 F.2d 254, 259–60 (2d Cir.1987)). However, because defendants' restaurant has not yet been opened, any discussion of the quality of the defendants' product would be speculative and the issue will not be addressed.

(8) Sophistication of the Consumers

"As a general rule, sophistication of the consumer is a factor that will weigh against a finding of likelihood of confusion." Comic Strip, Inc., 710 F.Supp. at 980 (citation omitted). Defendants' potential customers will be drawn from the general public and thus cannot be said to have unique qualities or sophistication. In fact, the only generalization which it would be possible to make regarding the restaurant's clientele is that many of them will undoubtedly be television watchers. * * *

Applying the *Polaroid* factors to the instant case, the court finds that there is no showing of likelihood of confusion sufficient enough to warrant the issuance of a preliminary injunction. The plaintiff has not demonstrated a likelihood of success on the merits nor sufficiently serious questions warranting litigation. CBS's mark protects it in the field of television production services. The mark does not insure its exclusive use of the mark "Television City" in all markets and all products.

* * *

Notes

1. Is the outcome in this case as clear as the district court makes it appear? Which factors in the "likelihood of confusion" test might weigh more heavily in favor of the plaintiff than the court indicates? Can you frame a persuasive argument on behalf of the plaintiff?

2. Can you predict the outcome if the defendants attempted to open a "Television City" restaurant in Los Angeles? Can the defendants market "Television City" mugs, t-shirts, and other memorabilia at their New York location?

3. Consider the use of the term "Louis Kemp" by a seller of wild rice products when a prior user adopted the same name for seafood. *See Kemp v. Bumble Bee Seafoods, Inc.*, 398 F.3d 1049 (8th Cir. 2005). Does it make a difference if the junior user seeks to use his surname?

4. Consider whether the term "Veuve Royale" by a liquor importer is confusingly similar to the "Veuve Clicquot" mark for similar beverages. *See*

---

3. In fact, there is evidence to suggest otherwise. Defendants' lease for the proposed restaurant requires that the establishment be a "first-class restaurant ... serving high quality food." Supposedly, other restaurants run by one of the defendants, including "Mickey Mantle's," are all of the highest quality.

Palm Bay Imports, Inc. v. Veuve Clicquot Ponsardin Maison Fondee En 1772,
396 F.3d 1369 (Fed. Cir. 2005).

FOXWORTHY v. CUSTOM TEES, INC.

United States District Court, N.D. Georgia, 1995.
879 F.Supp. 1200.

RICHARD C. FREEMAN, SENIOR DISTRICT JUDGE.

* * *

Plaintiff is a comedian known throughout the country for his
"redneck" humor. He is probably best known for his "you might be a
redneck if . . ." jokes. Examples of these jokes are:—You might be a
redneck if . . . you've ever financed a tattoo.—You might be a redneck if
. . . your two-year-old has more teeth than you do.—You might be a
redneck if . . . your dog and your wallet are both on a chain.—You might
be a redneck if . . . your dad walks you to school because you're in the
same grade. Plaintiff claims ownership to hundreds of jokes such as
these, as well as a trademark and service mark.[3] His comedy album
entitled "You Might be a Redneck If . . ." has sold more than 1 million
copies, more than any other comedy album in more than a decade.
Plaintiff has also issued a calendar with 365 "you might be a redneck if
. . ." jokes, one for every day of the year. In addition to these products,
he sells t-shirts with his redneck jokes on them at his concerts and
elsewhere.

In December, 1994, plaintiff, through some associates, became aware
that t-shirts bearing exact replications of plaintiff's jokes were being sold
in various stores across the country, including stores in Georgia. The
only difference between plaintiff's jokes and those appearing on the t-
shirts was the format. On one shirt, for example, the copy read "If
you've ever financed a tattoo . . . you might be a redneck."

An investigation by plaintiff's associates ensued, and the source of
the t-shirts was determined to be defendant Custom Tees. Plaintiff's
representatives contacted defendant Stewart R. Friedman, an employee
of Custom Tees who admits to directing the marketing of, and assisting
in the production of, Custom Tees' products. Upon notification that the
jokes violated plaintiff's copyright and/or trademarks, Friedman turned
the matter over to his legal counsel.[4] Subsequent to these events,
Custom Tees changed the copy on its t-shirts to read, to use a different

---

3. When used in connection with plaintiff's entertainment services, the "you
might be a redneck" phrase functions as a
service mark. For ease of discussion, and
because the battleground in this action concerns goods as opposed to services, the
court will discuss the phrase only in terms
of "trademarks." The legal analysis, of
course, is not affected by this designation.

4. There is evidence that Friedman initially offered to pay a licensing fee for the
shirts. Friedman, however, states in an affidavit that this offer was conditioned upon
proof that plaintiff owned a copyright or
trademark in the jokes. Whatever the case,
the fact is that Friedman's legal counsel
intervened and no licensing fee was paid or
arranged.

example, "[W]hen you learn to drive in a car where you were conceived . . . you ain't nothin' but a redneck."

* * *

PRELIMINARY INJUNCTION

A. *Plaintiff Might be Entitled to a Preliminary Injunction If . . .*

To be entitled to a preliminary injunctive relief, a plaintiff must show: (1) a substantial likelihood that he will ultimately prevail on the merits; (2) that he will suffer irreparable injury unless the injunction issues; (3) that the threatened injury to the movant outweighs whatever damage the proposed injunction may cause the opposing party; and (4) that the injunction, if issued, would not be adverse to the public interest. * * * The court will examine these factors seriatim.

B. *Plaintiff Might be Likely to Succeed on the Merits If . . .*

Plaintiff's request for injunctive relief is directed at the two components of his "redneck" jokes—the "you might be a redneck" phrase and the text of the jokes that follow. As to the phrase "you might be a redneck," plaintiff claims a common-law trademark. As to the joke portion, e.g., "you've ever cut your grass and found a car," plaintiff claims a copyright.

1) . . . . He Can Show a Violation of the Lanham Act

Section 43(a) of the Lanham Act, 15 U.S.C. § 1125(a), protects unregistered, common-law trademarks from infringement by unauthorized users where the unauthorized use would likely confuse the consuming public as to the source or sponsorship of goods or services. See Boston Professional Hockey Ass'n v. Dallas Cap & Emblem Mfg., Inc., 510 F.2d 1004, 1010 (5th Cir.), cert. denied, 423 U.S. 868, 96 S.Ct. 132, 46 L.Ed.2d 98 (1975). In order to prove a violation of Section 43(a), a plaintiff must prove "(1) that [he] has trademark rights in the mark or name at issue . . . ; and (2) that the defendant adopted a mark or name that was the same, or confusingly similar, to the plaintiff's mark, such that there was a likelihood of confusion for consumers as to the proper origin of the goods created by the defendant's use of the [mark] in [its] trade or business." Conagra, Inc. v. Singleton, 743 F.2d 1508, 1512 (11th Cir.1984).

(a) *Does plaintiff have a trademark to protect?*

The court must first determine, therefore, whether plaintiff has any trademark to protect. Plaintiff's asserted trademark lies in the use of the "you might be a redneck" device. Defendants agree that a slogan or combination of words can serve a trademark function, but argue that the "you might be a redneck" device does not function as a trademark. Rather, defendants argue that the phrase is purely functional—i.e., that the phrase is a feature " 'essential to the use or purpose of the article.' " Warner Bros., Inc. v. Gay Toys, Inc., 724 F.2d 327, 331 (2d Cir.1983) (quoting Inwood Laboratories, Inc. v. Ives Laboratories, Inc., 456 U.S.

844, 850–51 n. 10, 102 S.Ct. 2182, 2186–87 n. 10, 72 L.Ed.2d 606 (1982)).
* * *

First, the court finds that the phrase "you might be a redneck" does serve as a trademark when used in connection with plaintiff's humor. The evidence before the court indicates that, once plaintiff hit upon the right combination of words, that phrase became his "hook" or "catch phrase" by which he became known. Indeed, there was testimony from one of plaintiff's fans, Michael Steed, that plaintiff is in fact known in the public by that phrase. Further, the evidence before the court indicates that plaintiff's career began its rapid ascent only after he began using the phrase in conjunction with his jokes. That alone, however, does not establish a trademark; it merely lays the foundation for the association of the public of the phrase "you might be a redneck" with plaintiff. In this regard, therefore, it is highly significant that plaintiff has created a number of marketable goods based upon the "you might be a redneck" phrase. Plaintiff's first book was entitled "You Might be a Redneck." The name of his national comedy tour was the "You Might be a Redneck" tour. The tour was promoted in advertising media (radio and print) using this title. The name of his platinum selling album is "You Might be a Redneck." The name of his first comedy special on the Showtime network was "You Might be a Redneck If." The same title was used on the videocassette version of his Showtime special. Plaintiff has a "page-a-day" calendar with 365 different you might be a redneck jokes. Plaintiff has three books on the market filled with "you might be a redneck" jokes. These facts, taken together, lead the court to the conclusion that a substantial segment of the viewing, listening, reading, and laughing public associate the phrase "you might be a redneck" with Jeff Foxworthy.

Defendants argued at the hearing that the popularity of the above items is attributable to plaintiff, and not to the phrase "you might be a redneck," and that, even if the phrase plays a part, it only plays a functional part. The court disagrees in part. The plain fact is that plaintiff has become known by this phrase. That he is known by his jokes as well does nothing to limit the fact that he is also known by the phrase. In this respect, the court finds Carson v. Here's Johnny Portable Toilets, Inc., 498 F.Supp. 71 (E.D.Mich.1980), vacated in part on other grounds, 698 F.2d 831 (6th Cir.1983), significant. In that case, the district court—as well as the Sixth Circuit on appeal—found that the phrase "Here's Johnny," the familiar introduction of the late night talk show host Johnny Carson, had become associated in the public's mind with Johnny Carson the entertainer. Id., 498 F.Supp. at 74; see also Carson v. Here's Johnny Portable Toilets, Inc., 698 F.2d 831, 832–33 (6th Cir.1983) (agreeing with district court on this issue). Carson's efforts to market the phrase were not as extensive as Mr. Foxworthy's. See 498 F.Supp. at 73 (discussing authorized uses of "Here's Johnny" and the Carson persona). If plaintiff had not used the phrase as identifying indicia on so many of his products, or if the phrase had been varied, the court might agree with defendants on this issue. But plaintiff has not, and the court does not.

The court does agree, however, that the phrase is "functional" to a certain extent. The joke "You might be a redneck if ... you consider a six pack of beer and a bug zapper quality entertainment" clearly depends upon the "you might be a redneck" phrase for its delivery. Notwithstanding this facial functionality, however, the court finds the functionality defense insufficient to foreclose protection of plaintiff's phrase. First, it is questionable whether the "functionality" of the phrase fits into the legal description of functionality. In *Warner Bros.*, supra, a case cited by defendants, the Second Circuit also stated that "[a] design feature of a particular article is 'essential' only if the feature is dictated by the functions to be performed; *a feature that merely accommodates a useful function is not enough.*" Id., 724 F.2d at 331 (emphasis added). The telling of a redneck joke does not require an introductory (or conclusory) phrase. Indeed, there are other southern comedians who have their own style of redneck humor and who tell redneck jokes in a different form. Using an introductory phrase simply accommodates the style of plaintiff's humor. * * *

(b) Are defendants likely to cause confusion?

The Eleventh Circuit (and its predecessor, the former Fifth Circuit) has long held that the sine qua non of Section 43(a) actions is a showing that consumers are likely to be confused "with respect to such things as the product's source, its endorsement by plaintiff, or its connection with the plaintiff." * * *

In determining likelihood of confusion, the Eleventh Circuit has held that a court must consider the following factors:

1). The strength of the plaintiff's mark; 2). the similarity between the plaintiff's mark and the allegedly infringing mark; 3). the similarity between the products and services offered by the plaintiff and defendant[s]; 4). the similarity of the sales methods (i.e., retail outlets or customers); 5). the similarity of the advertising methods; 6). defendant[s]' intent, e.g., do[ ] the defendants hope to gain a competitive advantage by associating [their] product with the plaintiff's established mark; and 7). the most persuasive factor on likely confusion[,] ... actual confusion.

Conagra, 743 F.2d at 1514. The court will address each factor in turn.

i). The strength of plaintiff's mark

Although the court has already found that plaintiff's phrase "you might be a redneck," when used in connection with plaintiff's humor, whether in book, video, novelty item, or other form, has attained secondary meaning, the court finds that plaintiff need not make such a showing because plaintiff's phrase is "suggestive" within the legal meaning of that term. As previously noted, a "suggestive" mark "subtly connotes something about the service or product." University of Georgia Athletic Ass'n, 756 F.2d at 1540. The Eleventh Circuit has explained that "[a] suggestive term suggests the characteristics of the service 'and requires an effort of the imagination by the consumer in order to be understood as descriptive' of the service." * * *

Suggestive marks are inherently distinctive, and are to be afforded strong protection. Jellibeans, Inc. v. Skating Clubs of Georgia, Inc., 716 F.2d 833, 840 (11th Cir.1983) ("[T]he more distinctive plaintiff's mark, the stronger it is considered, and the more protection it is accorded from confusingly similar marks."). Of the four categories of marks (i.e., generic, descriptive, suggestive, and arbitrary or fanciful), suggestive marks are second only to arbitrary marks in distinctiveness. Investacorp, 931 F.2d at 1522.

With these principles in mind, the court finds the phrase "you might be a redneck" suggestive of plaintiff's humor. For example, when customers see "you might be a redneck" as the title for a comedy album, the customers must use their imaginations (or buy the album) to discern the content of the humor, because the phrase itself simply suggests the subject matter of the humor. It is true, of course, that in the context of the t-shirts submitted to the court for review, there is no imagination required. That, however, is a practical and unavoidable result of the juxtaposition of the phrase with the humor it suggests. Suppose, however, that the phrase "you might be a redneck if" appeared only on the front of a t-shirt, with the text of the joke appearing only on the back. Someone familiar with plaintiff's humor would likely recognize the shirt by the phrase (because the phrase operates as a trademark), but the person would have to turn the shirt over to get the joke. * * * The court, therefore, finds that this first factor favors plaintiff.

ii). The similarity between the plaintiff's mark and the allegedly infringing mark

In order to assess this factor, the court must assess the "overall impression" created by the two marks. See Jellibeans, 716 F.2d at 842; Armstrong Cork Co. v. World Carpets, Inc., 597 F.2d 496, 502 (5th Cir.1979). The phrases "you might be a redneck" and "you ain't nothin' but a redneck" therefore are not to be simply parsed into separate words, nor are they to be viewed in a vacuum.

The court finds that the two phrases convey a similar overall impression. First, as plaintiff points out, although the words in the middle differ, the phrases both begin and end the same way: "you ... a redneck." Defendants argue that the words in the middle do make a difference, because not only are the "visual and phonetic differences ... substantial," but "the meaning or connotation created by the phrases is clearly quite different (defendants' phrase message being a positive statement, whereas plaintiff's phrase is 'conditional' and raises a mental inquiry)." To the contrary, the message is the same even though the delivery is not. Both phrases provide a "test" to the reader for whether one is a redneck. Plaintiff's idea in creating his phrase was to create "a way for people to tell." Plaintiff chose "might" after rejecting other choices such as "you could be a redneck" or "you know you're a redneck." Whether plaintiff used "might" as opposed to "know" does not change the effect. Using "ain't nothin' but" conveys a similar impression. Again, the issue is the result, not the precise language.

In addition to the language used, the context of the phrases is also similar—indeed, in the shirts shown to the court, identical. When the phrases are used in connection with an example of redneck life, whether contributed by plaintiff or not, the impression conveyed is the same. Divorced from the joke, the phrases may not be terribly similar. The words cannot be divorced from the humor, however, and the court finds that this factor favors plaintiff.

iii). The similarity between the products and services offered by the plaintiff and defendant[s]

This factor obviously supports plaintiff. The litigants are competitors in the humorous t-shirt business.

iv). The similarity of the sales methods

The undisputed testimony at the hearing indicated that both parties sell, or want to sell, their t-shirts to department stores and other retail markets. In fact, there was testimony at the hearing that plaintiff had difficulty marketing his t-shirts to J.C. Penney, a well-known department store chain, because of the presence of defendants' shirts. This factor therefore also supports plaintiff.

v). The similarity of the advertising methods

Though there was little testimony at the hearing concerning this factor, the court finds it significant that Cynthia Robinson, a senior merchandiser at J.C. Penney, testified that someone from the t-shirt company (she thought his name was "Leon") "called and made the reference to I'm sure you're aware by now about the redneck tees, and you know Jeff Foxworthy, he's so funny, blah, blah, blah, and he was just telling me about some of the phrases and quoted a few of the jokes that's on the t-shirts."

The court notes that the record contains an affidavit from Leon Lehrer, who identifies himself as an "independent sales representative" who telemarkets products of Custom Tees, Inc., including the redneck shirts at issue. Lehrer testifies in his supplemental affidavit that he did, in fact, contact Ms. Robinson, but carefully stated that "no one during the period when I was soliciting sales for Custom Tees Redneck shirts ever mentioned Jeff Foxworthy's name or asked if Custom Tees was in any way affiliated with Jeff Foxworthy." Lehrer further states, "I never represented to any individual I called . . . that the shirts were in any way related, endorsed, or otherwise affiliated with Jeff Foxworthy." This affidavit does not contradict the testimony of Ms. Robinson, because Lehrer does not state that he never mentioned Jeff Foxworthy. His statement that "no one mentioned . . . or asked if," when read in conjunction with the next paragraph stating what he himself never did, leaves the court with the clear impression that Lehrer states only that he was never asked and he never told about Foxworthy's sponsorship of the shirts. These statements may indicate that no one ever mentioned the name to him, but he does not state that he never uttered Jeff Foxworthy's name to Ms. Robinson. Given the credible and apparently unbiased demeanor of Ms. Robinson at the hearing, her testimony itself, and Lehrer's "walking-on eggshells" affidavit, the court believes Ms. Robinson's testimony is entitled to substantial weight. In view of this finding, the court concludes that this factor also favors plaintiff.

vi). Defendant[s]' intent

Even though a finding of fraudulent intent and bad faith is not necessary, Tisch Hotels, Inc. v. Americana Inn, Inc., 350 F.2d 609, 613 (7th Cir.1965), the court finds that this factor weighs heavily in favor of plaintiff. At the hearing, the court received in evidence 11 t-shirts sold by defendants bearing the exact same "operative" language used by plaintiff. To explain the content of the language, defendant Friedman submitted conflicting affidavits. In support of defendant Custom Tees' motion to transfer, Friedman testified that the redneck material in the Custom Tees shirts came from "brainstorming" sessions with other people or from informal suggestions from other people. In support of his brief in opposition to plaintiff's motion for a preliminary injunction, Friedman testified that he received several jokes from his son-in-law, who suggested that they be put on t-shirts. Friedman testified in the same affidavit that, at the time, he had never heard of plaintiff. * * *

vii). Actual confusion

As a preliminary matter, the court notes that evidence of actual confusion is not required, although it is especially important when it does exist. See Amstar Corp. v. Domino's Pizza, Inc., 615 F.2d 252, 263 (5th Cir.), cert. denied, 449 U.S. 899, 101 S.Ct. 268, 66 L.Ed.2d 129 (1980). In this regard, at the hearing in this case, there was testimony from Michael Steed, an individual not affiliated with this case in any formal sense.[17] Mr. Steed testified that, a few weeks after having seen plaintiff in concert in late November, Mr. Steed and his wife were at a dinner party with friends when the subject of plaintiff and his humor arose. One of his dinner companions told Mr. Steed that a local J.C. Penney had some of plaintiff's shirts on sale. A few days later, Mr. Steed went to the J.C. Penney to purchase some of the shirts for his children. Mr. Steed testified that he entered J.C. Penney and encountered what he later discovered to be defendants' t-shirts. Although he testified that he was almost certain the shirts were not plaintiff's, Mr. Steed recognized the jokes and the phrases on them as plaintiff's jokes and phrases.

Three things are significant about this testimony. First, according to Mr. Steed, upon hearing about plaintiff's humor at the dinner party, one of the people at the table told Mr. Steed that J.C. Penney had plaintiff's shirts on sale. Though Mr. Steed may not have been confused, this testimony is evidence that someone was confused.[19]

17. Mr. Steed knows Jay Foxworthy, plaintiff's brother; has briefly met plaintiff before; and has attended several of plaintiff's concerts.

19. Defendants at various points in this lawsuit have argued that some of the evidence presented by plaintiff cannot be considered because it is hearsay. Whether that

Second, Mr. Steed, in some respects, is not an ordinary consumer. Not only is he very well acquainted with plaintiff's humor, but he has also been to at least five concerts where he saw plaintiff's official t-shirts for sale. Mr. Steed identified the differences in the t-shirts as the reason for his belief that defendants' shirts were not authorized. Again, as to this point, *Dallas Cowboys Cheerleaders* is instructive. In that case, the defendants argued (much as the defendants here might argue) that no one would possibly believe (just as Mr. Steed did not believe) that the Dallas Cowboy Cheerleaders sponsored the infringing product, the X-rated movie "Debbie Does Dallas."[20] The Second Circuit held that the likelihood of confusion analysis is not to be so narrowly construed. Rather, the court held that the film would cause an association in the minds of the viewers with the cheerleaders, and that "[t]his association results in confusion ..." Id., 604 F.2d at 204.

Similarly, in the present case, Mr. Steed immediately associated the jokes with plaintiff, and was fairly convinced that the shirts were not "the real McCoy" for other reasons. Thus, in one respect, the mere fact that Mr. Steed's suspicions were aroused because of the association indicates confusion on a legally cognizable level. Cf. Grotrian, Helfferich, Schulz, Th. Steinweg Nachf. v. Steinway & Sons, 523 F.2d 1331, 1342 (2d Cir.1975) (even though customers may know the difference between the products, the public may subliminally associate the names, thereby causing confusion).

More important, defendants' t-shirts, though distinguishable in appearance from plaintiff's shirts, utilized the association to gain a competitive advantage. See id. (even though actual purchasers know the difference, "[s]uch initial confusion works an injury to Steinway") * * *.

Finally, Mr. Steed's testimony as to his "lack" of confusion regarding the products implicates another issue: point-of-sale versus post-sale confusion. The Eleventh Circuit has held that the likelihood of confusion analysis does not depend upon confusion of the purchaser at the time of purchase. Rather, the question is whether the public, not the purchaser alone, would be confused by the use of the mark. * * * It is also significant, however, that the placement of the defendants' t-shirts on the market, and in the public after sale, would cause the public viewing the t-shirts to associate the shirts with plaintiff, regardless of whether the purchaser himself or herself was confused. See id.; Ferrari S.P.A. Esercizio Fabriche Automobili E Corse v. Roberts, 944 F.2d 1235, 1244–45 (6th Cir.1991); Lois Sportswear, U.S.A., Inc. v. Levi Strauss & Co., 799 F.2d 867, 871, 872–73 (2d Cir.1986); Rolex Watch U.S.A., Inc. v. Canner, 645 F.Supp. 484, 488, 493–95 (S.D.Fla.1986). Simply stated, the

---

is the case depends upon the individual statements challenged. As to the statement of the dinner companion to Mr. Steed, it clearly is not hearsay because it is not offered for its truth. Rather, the statement was offered to show both Mr. Steed's state of mind and to explain his subsequent trip to J.C. Penney.

20. The facts of that case are set forth in the Second Circuit's opinion, and are better left there.

fact that Mr. Steed was not "actually" confused at the point of sale does not change the likelihood that others would associate defendants' shirts with plaintiff, whether at the point of sale or in the public after sale.

Evidence of actual confusion is often hard to acquire. See, e.g., Lois Sportswear, 799 F.2d at 874. As the Second Circuit has recognized, it is "particularly difficult to make any showing of actual confusion" where, as here, "the plaintiff move[s] for injunctive relief before the allegedly infringing trademark ha[s] been widely disseminated." Lobo Enterprises, Inc. v. Tunnel, Inc., 822 F.2d 331, 333 (2d Cir.1987). The Eleventh Circuit has also noted that, where the products are relatively inexpensive and constitute impulse purchases, evidence of actual confusion can be elusive. See AmBrit, Inc. v. Kraft, Inc., 805 F.2d 974, 987–88 (11th Cir.) * * *. The *AmBrit* court also stated that "it takes little evidence to establish the existence of the actual confusion factor. Moreover, that there were only a few reported instances of actual confusion does not mean that only those individuals were actually confused." Id., 805 F.2d at 987. * * * On this record, and under the totality of the circumstances, the court finds that this factor also favors plaintiff. * * * [The court finds that the plaintiff is likely to prevail on his trademark claim, as well as on the copyright claim involving the specific texts of his jokes.]

Notes

1. Are all phrases associated with well-known entertainers arguably protectable under trademark law in light of this decision, or are the particular facts of this case unusual? To what extent should phrases used in marketing products be protectable as trademarks?

2. Do you agree with the court's findings on all factors in the likelihood of confusion test? What role should "initial interest confusion" or "post-sale" confusion play in the analysis?

3. "Blockbuster" is a widely known chain of movie rental stores. Its trademark has been registered since 1986 and is incontestable. "Video Busters" is also in the movie rental business, having started operations under that name after Blockbuster's registration. Assuming a suit is timely filed, can Blockbuster prevent Video Busters from using its name? See Blockbuster Entertainment Group v. Laylco, Inc., 869 F.Supp. 505 (E.D.Mich.1994). Although it is not required, evidence of actual confusion is a strong indication that a likelihood of confusion exists. Aside from proof of instances in which consumers were in fact confused, survey evidence is often used to prove actual confusion. For instance, in Blockbuster Entertainment Group v. Laylco, Inc., *supra*, Blockbuster introduced a survey purporting to show that 14 percent of the Detroit-area public was confused as to the identity or origin between the two stores. Twenty-two percent of those who had been in both a Blockbuster and Video Busters store were shown to be confused. How persuasive is this survey evidence? How might it be refuted? Survey results showing 15–20 percent confusion has been deemed sufficient to corroborate a finding of likely confusion in other cases. See *e.g,* RJR Foods, Inc. v. White Rock Corp., 603 F.2d 1058 (2d Cir.1979); James Burrough, Ltd. v. Sign of Beefeater, Inc., 540 F.2d 266 (7th Cir.1976). Are

these percentages persuasive? Would the overall analysis be affected by the fact that the Video Busters store offers X-rated films for rental, a practice that is contrary to Blockbuster's store policy? Can Blockbuster prevent the use of the name "Fat Busters" for a health food store? Of "Blockbuster" for a fireworks store?

4. Each federal circuit has articulated its own version of the "likelihood of confusion" factors. The Sixth Circuit, for example, considers the following: "(1) the strength of the plaintiff's mark; (2) the relatedness of the goods; (3) the similarity of the marks; (4) evidence of actual confusion; (5) marketing channels used; (6) the likely degree of purchaser care; (7) the defendants' intent on selecting the its mark; and (8) the likelihood of expansion of the product lines." Frisch's Restaurants, Inc. v. Elby's Big Boy of Steubenville, Inc., 670 F.2d 642 (6th Cir.1982). Is the ultimate analysis likely to differ based on which circuit's test is applied?

5. The rock band known as the "Eagles," which was formed in 1971, owns a registered trademark and service mark in that name. The American Eagle Foundation is a non-profit organization seeking to protect bald eagles. The Foundation seeks to register the name "American Eagle Records." Should it be permitted to do so? See Eagles, Ltd. v. American Eagle Foundation, 356 F.3d 724 (6th Cir. 2004).

6. The owner of the "Beanie Babies" trademark files suit against the seller of a similar product marketed under the name "Screenie Babies." What result? See Ty Inc. v. Softbelly's Inc., 353 F.3d 528 (7th Cir. 2003). For other recent cases on consumer confusion, see Frosty Treats, Inc. v. Sony Computer Entertainment America, Inc., 426 F.3d 1001 (8th Cir. 2005) (no likelihood of confusion engendered by video game company's use of "safety clown" graphic); Playmakers LLC v. ESPN, Inc., 376 F.3d 894 (9th Cir. 2004); In re Majestic Distilling Co., 315 F.3d 1311 (Fed. Cir. 2003).

7. Coors Brewing Company seeks to register a new brand name, "Blue Moon," for a line of beer. "Blue Moon" is also the name of a restaurant that had previously registered its trademark. Should Coors be able to register its mark? See In re Coors Brewing Co., 343 F.3d 1340 (Fed. Cir. 2003). Illustrations and further information are available in the published opinion.

8. For further discussion of the likelihood of confusion test, see 3 J. Thomas McCarthy, Trademarks and Unfair Competition §§ 23.01 to 24.20 (3d ed. 1995); Restatement (Third) of Unfair Competition §§ 20–23 (1995).

PEOPLE FOR THE ETHICAL TREATMENT OF ANIMALS v. DOUGHNEY

United States Court of Appeals, Fourth Circuit, 2001.
263 F.3d 359.

GREGORY, CIRCUIT JUDGE:

People for the Ethical Treatment of Animals ("PETA") sued Michael Doughney ("Doughney") after he registered the domain name peta.org and created a website called "People Eating Tasty Animals." PETA alleged claims of service mark infringement under 15 U.S.C. § 1114 and Virginia common law, unfair competition under 15 U.S.C.

§ 1125(a) and Virginia common law, and service mark dilution and cybersquatting under 15 U.S.C. § 1123(c). Doughney appeals the district court's decision granting PETA's motion for summary judgment and PETA cross-appeals the district court's denial of its motion for attorney's fees and costs. Finding no error, we affirm.

I.

PETA is an animal rights organization with more than 600,000 members worldwide. PETA "is dedicated to promoting and heightening public awareness of animal protection issues and it opposes the exploitation of animals for food, clothing, entertainment and vivisection."

Doughney is a former internet executive who has registered many domain names since 1995. For example, Doughney registered domain names such as dubyadot.com, dubyadot.net, deathbush.com, RandallTerry.org (Not Randall Terry for Congress), bwtel.com (Baltimore–Washington Telephone Company), pmrc.org ("People's Manic Repressive Church"), and ex-cult.org (Ex–Cult Archive). At the time the district court issued its summary judgment ruling, Doughney owned 50–60 domain names.

Doughney registered the domain name peta.org in 1995 with Network Solutions, Inc. ("NSI"). When registering the domain name, Doughney represented to NSI that the registration did "not interfere with or infringe upon the rights of any third party," and that a "non-profit educational organization" called "People Eating Tasty Animals" was registering the domain name. Doughney made these representations to NSI despite knowing that no corporation, partnership, organization or entity of any kind existed or traded under that name. Moreover, Doughney was familiar with PETA and its beliefs and had been for at least 15 years before registering the domain name.

After registering the peta.org domain name, Doughney used it to create a website purportedly on behalf of "People Eating Tasty Animals." Doughney claims he created the website as a parody of PETA. A viewer accessing the website would see the title "People Eating Tasty Animals" in large, bold type.

Under the title, the viewer would see a statement that the website was a "resource for those who enjoy eating meat, wearing fur and leather, hunting, and the fruits of scientific research." The website contained links to various meat, fur, leather, hunting, animal research, and other organizations, all of which held views generally antithetical to PETA's views. Another statement on the website asked the viewer whether he/she was "Feeling lost? Offended? Perhaps you should, like, exit immediately." The phrase "exit immediately" contained a hyperlink to PETA's official website.

Doughney's website appeared at "www.peta.org" for only six months in 1995–96. In 1996, PETA asked Doughney to voluntarily transfer the peta.org domain name to PETA because PETA owned the "PETA" mark ("the Mark"), which it registered in 1992. See U.S.

Trademark Registration No. 1705,510. When Doughney refused to transfer the domain name to PETA, PETA complained to NSI, whose rules then required it to place the domain name on "hold" pending resolution of Doughney's dispute with PETA. Consequently, Doughney moved the website to www.mtd.com/tasty and added a disclaimer stating that "People Eating Tasty Animals is in no way connected with, or endorsed by, People for the Ethical Treatment of Animals."

In response to Doughney's domain name dispute with PETA, The Chronicle of Philanthropy quoted Doughney as stating that, "[i]f they [PETA] want one of my domains, they should make me an offer." Non–Profit Groups Upset by Unauthorized Use of Their Names on the Internet, THE CHRONICLE OF PHILANTHROPY, Nov. 14, 1996. Doughney does not dispute making this statement. Additionally, Doughney posted the following message on his website on May 12, 1996:

> "PeTa" has no legal grounds whatsoever to make even the slightest demands of me regarding this domain name registration. If they disagree, they can sue me. And if they don't, well, perhaps they can behave like the polite ladies and gentlemen that they evidently aren't and negotiate a settlement with me.... Otherwise, "PeTa" can wait until the significance and value of a domain name drops to nearly nothing, which is inevitable as each new web search engine comes on-line, because that's how long it's going to take for this dispute to play out.

PETA sued Doughney in 1999, asserting claims for service mark infringement, unfair competition, dilution and cybersquatting. PETA did not seek damages, but sought only to enjoin Doughney's use of the "PETA" Mark and an order requiring Doughney to transfer the peta.org domain name to PETA.

Doughney responded to the suit by arguing that the website was a constitutionally-protected parody of PETA. Nonetheless, the district court granted PETA's motion for summary judgment on June 12, 2000. People for the Ethical Treatment of Animals, Inc. v. Doughney, 113 F.Supp.2d 915 (E.D.Va.2000). The district court rejected Doughney's parody defense, explaining that

> [o]nly after arriving at the "PETA.ORG" web site could the web site browser determine that this was not a web site owned, controlled or sponsored by PETA. Therefore, the two images: (1) the famous PETA name and (2) the "People Eating Tasty Animals" website was not a parody because [they were not] simultaneous.

Id. at 921.

* * *

II.

* * *

A.　*Trademark Infringement/Unfair Competition*

A plaintiff alleging causes of action for trademark infringement and unfair competition must prove (1) that it possesses a mark; (2) that the defendant used the mark; (3) that the defendant's use of the mark occurred "in commerce"; (4) that the defendant used the mark "in connection with the sale, offering for sale, distribution, or advertising" of goods or services; and (5) that the defendant used the mark in a manner likely to confuse consumers. 15 U.S.C. §§ 1114, 1125(a); Lone Star Steakhouse & Saloon v. Alpha of Virginia, 43 F.3d 922, 930 (4th Cir.1995).

There is no dispute here that PETA owns the "PETA" Mark, that Doughney used it, and that Doughney used the Mark "in commerce." Doughney disputes the district court's findings that he used the Mark in connection with goods or services and that he used it in a manner engendering a likelihood of confusion.

1.

To use PETA's Mark "in connection with" goods or services, Doughney need not have actually sold or advertised goods or services on the www.peta.org website. Rather, Doughney need only have prevented users from obtaining or using PETA's goods or services, or need only have connected the website to other's goods or services.

While sparse, existing caselaw on infringement and unfair competition in the Internet context clearly weighs in favor of this conclusion. For example, in OBH, Inc. v. Spotlight Magazine, Inc., the plaintiffs owned the "The Buffalo News" registered trademark used by the newspaper of the same name. 86 F.Supp.2d 176 (W.D.N.Y.2000). The defendants registered the domain name thebuffalonews.com and created a website parodying The Buffalo News and providing a public forum for criticism of the newspaper. Id. at 182. The site contained hyperlinks to other local news sources and a site owned by the defendants that advertised Buffalo-area apartments for rent. Id. at 183.

The court held that the defendants used the mark "in connection with" goods or services because the defendants' website was "likely to prevent or hinder Internet users from accessing plaintiffs' services on plaintiffs' own web site." Id.

Prospective users of plaintiffs' services who mistakenly access defendants' web site may fail to continue to search for plaintiffs' web site due to confusion or frustration. Such users, who are presumably looking for the news services provided by the plaintiffs on their web site, may instead opt to select one of the several other news-related hyperlinks contained in defendants' web site. These news-related hyperlinks will directly link the user to other news-related web sites that are in direct competition with plaintiffs in providing news-related services over the Internet. Thus, defendants' action in appropriating plaintiff's mark has a connection to plaintiffs' distribution of its services.

Id. Moreover, the court explained that defendants' use of the plaintiffs' mark was in connection with goods or services because it contained a link to the defendants' apartment-guide website. Id.

Similarly, in Planned Parenthood Federation of America, Inc. v. Bucci, the plaintiff owned the "Planned Parenthood" mark, but the defendant registered the domain name plannedparenthood.com. 42 U.S.P.Q.2d 1430, 1997 WL 133313 (S.D.N.Y.1997). Using the domain name, the defendant created a website containing information antithetical to the plaintiff's views. Id. at 1435.

The court ruled that the defendant used the plaintiff's mark "in connection with" the distribution of services because it is likely to prevent some Internet users from reaching plaintiff's own Internet web site. Prospective users of plaintiff's services who mistakenly access defendant's web site may fail to continue to search for plaintiff's own home page, due to anger, frustration, or the belief that plaintiff's home page does not exist. Id.

The same reasoning applies here. As the district court explained, Doughney's use of PETA's Mark in the domain name of his website is likely to prevent Internet users from reaching [PETA's] own Internet web site. The prospective users of [PETA's] services who mistakenly access Defendant's web site may fail to continue to search for [PETA's] own home page, due to anger, frustration, or the belief that [PETA's] home page does not exist.

Doughney, 113 F.Supp.2d at 919 (quoting Bucci, 42 U.S.P.Q.2d at 1435). Moreover, Doughney's web site provides links to more than 30 commercial operations offering goods and services. By providing links to these commercial operations, Doughney's use of PETA's Mark is "in connection with" the sale of goods or services.

  2.

The unauthorized use of a trademark infringes the trademark holder's rights if it is likely to confuse an "ordinary consumer" as to the source or sponsorship of the goods. Anheuser–Busch, Inc. v. L & L Wings, Inc., 962 F.2d 316, 318 (4th Cir.1992) (citing 2 J. McCarthy, Trademarks and Unfair Competition § 23:28 (2d ed.1984)). To determine whether a likelihood of confusion exists, a court should not consider "how closely a fragment of a given use duplicates the trademark," but must instead consider "whether the use in its entirety creates a likelihood of confusion." Id. at 319.

Doughney does not dispute that the peta.org domain name engenders a likelihood of confusion between his web site and PETA. Doughney claims, though, that the inquiry should not end with his domain name. Rather, he urges the Court to consider his website in conjunction with the domain name because, together, they purportedly parody PETA and, thus, do not cause a likelihood of confusion.

A "parody" is defined as a "simple form of entertainment conveyed by juxtaposing the irreverent representation of the trademark with the idealized image created by the mark's owner." L.L. Bean, Inc. v. Drake Publishers, Inc., 811 F.2d 26, 34 (1st Cir.1987). A parody must "convey two simultaneous—and contradictory—messages: that it is the original, but also that it is not the original and is instead a parody." Cliffs Notes, Inc. v. Bantam Doubleday Dell Publ. Group, Inc., 886 F.2d 490, 494 (2d Cir.1989) (emphasis in original). To the extent that an alleged parody conveys only the first message, "it is not only a poor parody but also vulnerable under trademark law, since the customer will be confused." Id. While a parody necessarily must engender some initial confusion, an effective parody will diminish the risk of consumer confusion "by conveying [only] just enough of the original design to allow the consumer to appreciate the point of parody." Jordache Enterprises, Inc. v. Hogg Wyld, Ltd., 828 F.2d 1482, 1486 (10th Cir.1987).

Looking at Doughney's domain name alone, there is no suggestion of a parody. The domain name peta.org simply copies PETA's Mark, conveying the message that it is related to PETA. The domain name does not convey the second, contradictory message needed to establish a parody—a message that the domain name is not related to PETA, but that it is a parody of PETA.

Doughney claims that this second message can be found in the content of his website. Indeed, the website's content makes it clear that it is not related to PETA. However, this second message is not conveyed simultaneously with the first message, as required to be considered a parody. The domain name conveys the first message; the second message is conveyed only when the viewer reads the content of the website. As the district court explained, "an internet user would not realize that they were not on an official PETA web site until after they had used PETA's Mark to access the web page 'www.peta.org.' "Doughney, 113 F.Supp.2d at 921. Thus, the messages are not conveyed simultaneously and do not constitute a parody. See also Morrison & Foerster LLP v. Wick, 94 F.Supp.2d 1125 (D.Co.2000) (defendant's use of plaintiffs' mark in domain name "does not convey two simultaneous and contradictory messages" because "[o]nly by reading through the content of the sites could the user discover that the domain names are an attempt at parody"); Bucci, 42 U.S.P.Q.2d at 1435 (rejecting parody defense because "[s]eeing or typing the 'planned parenthood' mark and accessing the web site are two separate and nonsimultaneous activities"). The district court properly rejected Doughney's parody defense and found that Doughney's use of the peta.org domain name engenders a likelihood of confusion. Accordingly, Doughney failed to raise a genuine issue of material fact regarding PETA's infringement and unfair competition claims.

B. Anticybersquatting Consumer Protection Act

The district court found Doughney liable under the Anticybersquatting Consumer Protection Act ("ACPA"), 15 U.S.C. § 1125(d)(1)(A). To establish an ACPA violation, PETA was required to (1) prove that Doughney had a bad faith intent to profit from using the peta.org domain name, and (2) that the peta.org domain name is identical or confusingly similar to, or dilutive of, the distinctive and famous PETA Mark. 15 U.S.C. § 1125(d)(1)(A).

Doughney makes several arguments relating to the district court's ACPA holding: (1) that PETA did not plead an ACPA claim, but raised it for the first time in its motion for summary judgment; (2) that the ACPA, which became effective in 1999, cannot be applied retroactively to events that occurred in 1995 and 1996; (3) that Doughney did not seek to financially profit from his use of PETA's Mark; and (4) that Doughney acted in good faith.

None of Doughney's arguments are availing. First, PETA raised its ACPA claim for the first time in its summary judgment briefs. Doughney objected, noting that PETA failed to plead the claim in its complaint and failed to seek leave to amend to do so. Doughney also vigorously defended against the claim. PETA acknowledged below that it did not plead the claim, but "respectfully request[ed]" in its summary judgment reply brief "that th[e district] Court apply the [the ACPA] to the case at bar[.]" Nothing in the record suggests that the district court entered an order amending PETA's complaint to include an ACPA claim. However, the district court appears to have ruled on PETA's informal motion, listing the ACPA in its summary judgment order as one of the claims on which PETA seeks summary judgment and rendering judgment as to that claim.

The Federal Rules "allow liberal amendment of pleadings through-out the progress of a case." Elmore v. Corcoran, 913 F.2d 170, 172 (4th Cir.1990) (citing Brandon v. Holt, 469 U.S. 464, 471, 105 S.Ct. 873, 83 L.Ed.2d 878 (1985) (petitioners allowed to amend pleadings before Supreme Court)). A party's failure to amend will not affect a final judgment if the issues resolved were "tried by express or implied consent of the parties." Id. (citing Fed.R.Civ.P. 15(b)). Even without a formal amendment, "a district court may amend the pleadings merely by entering findings on the unpleaded issues." Id. (quoting Galindo v. Stoody Co., 793 F.2d 1502, 1513 n. 8 (9th Cir.1986)).

Here, PETA's summary judgment briefs essentially moved the district court for leave to amend its complaint to include an ACPA claim, and the district court appears to have granted that motion via its summary judgment ruling. While the record would have been clearer had PETA formally filed such a motion and the district court formally entered such an order, they did so in substance if not in form. Thus, we reject Doughney's first contention.

Doughney's second argument—that the ACPA may not be applied retroactively—also is unavailing. The ACPA expressly states that it "shall apply to all domain names registered before, on, or after the date of the enactment of this Act[.]" Pub.L. No. 106–113, § 3010, 113 Stat. 1536. See also Sporty's Farm L.L.C. v. Sportsman's Market, Inc., 202 F.3d 489, 496 (2d Cir.2000) (same). Moreover, while the ACPA precludes the imposition of damages in cases in which domain names were registered, trafficked, or used before its enactment, Pub.L. No. 106–113, § 3010, 113 Stat. 1536 ("damages under subsection (a) or (d) of section 35 of the Trademark Act of 1946 (15 U.S.C. 1117), ... shall not be available with respect to the registration, trafficking, or use of a domain name that occurs before the date of the enactment of this Act"), it does not preclude the imposition of equitable remedies. See also Virtual Works, Inc. v. Volkswagen of America, Inc., 238 F.3d 264, 268 (4th Cir.2001). Here, the district court did not award PETA damages (nor did PETA request damages), but ordered Doughney to relinquish the domain name, transfer its registration to PETA, and limit his use of domain names to those that do not use PETA's Mark. Doughney, 113 F.Supp.2d at 922. Thus, the district court properly applied the ACPA to this case.

Doughney's third argument—that he did not seek to financially profit from registering a domain name using PETA's Mark—also offers him no relief. It is undisputed that Doughney made statements to the press and on his website recommending that PETA attempt to "settle" with him and "make him an offer." The undisputed evidence belies Doughney's argument. Doughney's fourth argument—that he did not act in bad faith—also is unavailing. Under 15 U.S.C. § 1125(d)(1)(B)(i), a court may consider several factors to determine whether a defendant acted in bad faith, including

(I) the trademark or other intellectual property rights of the person, if any, in the domain name;

(II) the extent to which the domain name consists of the legal name of the person or a name that is otherwise commonly used to identify that person;

(III) the person's prior use, if any, of the domain name in connection with the bona fide offering of any goods or services;

(IV) the person's bona fide noncommercial or fair use of the mark in a site accessible under the domain name;

(V) the person's intent to divert consumers from the mark owner's online location to a site accessible under the domain name that could harm the goodwill represented by the mark, either for commercial gain or with the intent to tarnish or disparage the mark, by creating a likelihood of confusion as to the source, sponsorship, affiliation, or endorsement of the site;

(VI) the person's offer to transfer, sell, or otherwise assign the domain name to the mark owner or any third party for financial gain without having used, or having an intent to use, the domain name in the bona fide offering of any goods or services, or the person's prior conduct indicating a pattern of such conduct;

(VII) the person's provision of material and misleading false contact information when applying for the registration of the domain name, the person's intentional failure to maintain accurate contact information, or the person's prior conduct indicating a pattern of such conduct;

(VIII) the person's registration or acquisition of multiple domain names which the person knows are identical or confusingly similar to marks of others that are distinctive at the time of registration of such domain names, or dilutive of famous marks of others that are famous at the time of registration of such domain names, without regard to the goods or services of the parties; and

(IX) the extent to which the mark incorporated in the person's domain name registration is or is not distinctive and famous within the meaning of subsection (c)(1) of this section.

15 U.S.C. § 1125(d)(1)(B)(i). In addition to listing these nine factors, the ACPA contains a safe harbor provision stating that bad faith intent "shall not be found in any case in which the court determines that the person believed and had reasonable grounds to believe that the use of the domain name was fair use or otherwise lawful." 15 U.S.C. § 1225(d)(1)(B)(ii).

The district court reviewed the factors listed in the statute and properly concluded that Doughney (I) had no intellectual property right in peta.org; (II) peta.org is not Doughney's name or a name otherwise used to identify Doughney; (III) Doughney had no prior use of peta.org in connection with the bona fide offering of any goods or services; (IV) Doughney used the PETA Mark in a commercial manner; (V) Doughney "clearly intended to confuse, mislead and divert internet users into accessing his web site which contained information antithetical and therefore harmful to the goodwill represented by the PETA Mark"; (VI) Doughney made statements on his web site and in the press recommending that PETA attempt to "settle" with him and "make him an offer"; (VII) Doughney made false statements when registering the domain name; and (VIII) Doughney registered other domain names that are identical or similar to the marks or names of other famous people and organizations. People for the Ethical Treatment of Animals, 113 F.Supp.2d at 920.

Doughney claims that the district court's later ruling denying PETA's motion for attorney fees triggers application of the ACPA's safe harbor provision. In that ruling, the district court stated that Doughney registered the domain name because he thought that he had a legitimate First Amendment right to express himself this way. The Court must consider Doughney's state of mind at the time he took the actions in question. Doughney thought he was within his First Amendment rights to create a parody of the plaintiff's organization. People for the Ethical Treatment of Animals, Inc. v. Doughney, Civil Action No. 99–1336–A, Order at 4 (E.D.Va. Aug. 31, 2000). With its attorney's fee ruling, the district court did not find that Doughney "had reasonable grounds to believe" that his use of PETA's Mark was lawful. It held only that Doughney thought it to be lawful.

Moreover, a defendant "who acts even partially in bad faith in registering a domain name is not, as a matter of law, entitled to benefit from [the ACPA's] safe harbor provision." Virtual Works, Inc., 238 F.3d at 270. Doughney knowingly provided false information to NSI upon registering the domain name, knew he was registering a domain name identical to PETA's Mark, and clearly intended to confuse Internet users into accessing his website, instead of PETA's official website. Considering the evidence of Doughney's bad faith, the safe harbor provision can provide him no relief.

* * *

Notes

1. On the subject of "initial interest confusion," see *Playboy Enters., Inc. v. Netscape Communications Corp.*, 354 F.3d 1020 (9th Cir. 2004) (internet search engine using trademark owner's name for key-word banner advertising), 354 F.3d 1020 (9th Cir. 2004) (internet search engine using trademark owner's name for key-word banner advertising).

2. Nissan Motor Co. is a large Japanese automaker, which registered the Nissan trademark in 1959. It operates an Internet website at "www. nissan-usa.com." Nissan Computer Corp. is a North Carolina company, formed in 1991, by Uzi Nissan to sell and service computers. Mr. Nissan has used his surname in various businesses since 1980. Nissan is also a term in the Hebrew and Arabic languages. Nissan Computer registered the Internet domain name "nissan.com" in 1994 and used the site for computer-related information. In 1999, Nissan Computer's website began displaying banner advertisements for automobile dealers. What relief, if any, should trademark law provide to Nissan Motors?

B. DILUTION

MEAD DATA CENTRAL, INC. v. TOYOTA MOTOR SALES, U.S.A., INC.

United States Court of Appeals, Second Circuit, 1989.
875 F.2d 1026.

Van Graafeiland, Circuit Judge:

Toyota Motor Sales, U.S.A., Inc. and its parent, Toyota Motor Corporation, appeal from a judgment of the United States District Court for the Southern District of New York (Edelstein, J.) enjoining them from using LEXUS as the name of their new luxury automobile and the division that manufactures it. The district court held that, under New York's antidilution statute, N.Y.Gen.Bus.Law § 368–d, Toyota's use of LEXUS is likely to dilute the distinctive quality of LEXIS, the mark used by Mead Data Central, Inc. for its computerized legal research service, 702 F.Supp. 1031 (1988). On March 8, 1989, we entered an order of reversal, stating that an opinion would follow. This is the opinion.

The Statute

Section 368–d of New York's General Business Law, which has counterparts in at least twenty other states, reads as follows:

Likelihood of injury to business reputation or of dilution of the distinctive quality of a mark or trade name shall be a ground for injunctive relief in cases of infringement of a mark registered or not registered or in cases of unfair competition, notwithstanding the absence of competition between the parties or the absence of confusion as to the source of goods or services.

The Parties and Their Marks

Mead and Lexis

Mead is a corporation organized under the laws of Delaware with its principal place of business in Miamisburg, Ohio. Since 1972, Mead has provided a computerized legal research service under the trademark LEXIS. Mead introduced evidence that its president in 1972 "came up with the name LEXIS based on Lex which was Latin for law and I S for information systems." In fact, however, the word "lexis" is centuries old. It is found in the language of ancient Greece, where it had the meaning of "phrase", "word", "speaking" or "diction". Pinkerton, Word for Word, 179 (1982). "Lexis" subsequently appeared in the Latin where it had a substantially similar meaning, i.e., "word", "speech", or "language". * * *

Moreover, the record discloses that numerous other companies had adopted "Lexis" in identifying their business or its product, e.g., Lexis Ltd., Lexis Computer Systems Ltd., Lexis Language and Export Information Service, Lexis Corp., Maxwell Labs Lexis 3. In sum, we reject Mead's argument that LEXIS is a coined mark which originated in the mind of its former president and, as such, is entitled per se to the greater protection that a unique mark such as "Kodak" would receive. * * *

Nevertheless, through its extensive sales and advertising in the field of computerized legal research, Mead has made LEXIS a strong mark in that field, and the district court so found. In particular, the district court accepted studies proffered by both parties which revealed that 76 percent of attorneys associated LEXIS with specific attributes of the service provided by Mead. However, among the general adult population, LEXIS is recognized by only one percent of those surveyed, half of this one percent being attorneys or accountants. The district court therefore concluded that LEXIS is strong only within its own market.

As appears in the Addendum to this opinion, the LEXIS mark is printed in block letters with no accompanying logo.

Toyota and Lexus

Toyota Motor Corp. has for many years manufactured automobiles, which it markets in the United States through its subsidiary Toyota Motor Sales, U.S.A. On August 24, 1987 Toyota announced a new line of luxury automobiles to be called LEXUS. The cars will be manufactured by a separate LEXUS division of Toyota, and their marketing pitch will be directed to well-educated professional consumers with annual incomes in excess of $50,000. Toyota had planned to spend $18 million to $20 million for this purpose during the first nine months of 1989.

Before adopting the completely artificial name LEXUS for its new automobile, Toyota secured expert legal advice to the effect that "there is absolutely no conflict between 'LEXIS' and 'LEXUS.' " Accordingly, when Mead subsequently objected to Toyota's use of LEXUS, Toyota rejected Mead's complaints. The district court held correctly that Toyota acted without predatory intent in adopting the LEXUS mark. "[T]he absence of predatory intent by the junior user is a relevant factor in assessing a claim under the antidilution statute, ... since relief under the statute is of equitable origin.... " Sally Gee, Inc. v. Myra Hogan, Inc., 699 F.2d 621, 626 (2d Cir.1983) (citations omitted).

However, the district court erred in concluding that Toyota's refusal to acknowledge that its use of LEXUS might harm the LEXIS mark, deprived it of the argument that it acted in good faith. If, as we now hold, Toyota's mark did not dilute Mead's, it would be anomalous indeed to hold Toyota guilty of bad faith in proceeding in reliance on its attorney's correct advice to that effect. See Sweats Fashions, Inc. v. Pannill Knitting Co., 833 F.2d 1560, 1565 (Fed.Cir.1987); E.S. Originals Inc. v. Stride Rite Corp., 656 F.Supp. 484, 490 (S.D.N.Y.1987); Inc. Publishing Corp. v. Manhattan Magazine, Inc., 616 F.Supp. 370, 394–96 (S.D.N.Y.1985), aff'd, 788 F.2d 3 (2d Cir.1986); Procter & Gamble Co. v. Johnson & Johnson, Inc., 485 F.Supp. 1185, 1201–02 (S.D.N.Y.1979), aff'd, 636 F.2d 1203 (2d Cir.1980). Indeed, even if the attorney's professional advice had been wrong, it does not follow that Toyota's reliance on that advice would have constituted bad faith. Information Clearing House, Inc. v. Find Magazine, 492 F.Supp. 147, 161–62 (S.D.N.Y.1980).

The LEXUS mark is in stylized, almost script-like lettering and is accompanied by a rakish L logo. See Addendum.

The Law

The brief legislative history accompanying section 368–d describes the purpose of the statute as preventing "the whittling away of an established trade-mark's selling power and value through *its* unauthorized use by others upon dissimilar products." 1954 N.Y.Legis.Ann. 49 (emphasis supplied). If we were to interpret literally the italicized word "its", we would limit statutory violations to the unauthorized use of the identical established mark. This is what Frank Schechter, the father of the dilution theory, intended when he wrote The Rational Basis of Trademark Protection, 40 Harv.L.Rev. 813 (1927). See id. at 830–33; see also Shire, Dilution Versus Deception—Are State Antidilution Laws an Appropriate Alternative to the Law of Infringement?, 77 Trademark Rep. 273–76 (1987). However, since the use of obvious simulations or markedly similar marks might have the same diluting effect as would an appropriation of the original mark, the concept of exact identity has been broadened to that of substantial similarity. * * *

The district court made several findings on the issue of similarity in its Lanham Act discussion; it made none in its discussion of section 368–d. Assuming that the district court's finding of lack of physical similarity in the former discussion was intended to carry over into the latter, we would find ourselves in complete accord with it since we would make the same finding. See Addendum; see also Blue Bell, Inc. v. Jaymar–Ruby, Inc., 497 F.2d 433, 435 (2d Cir.1974). However, if the district court's statement in its Lanham Act discussion that "in everyday spoken English, LEXUS and LEXIS are virtually identical in pronunciation" was intended to be a finding of fact rather than a statement of opinion, we question both its accuracy and its relevance. The word LEXUS is not yet widely enough known that any definitive statement can be made concerning its pronunciation by the American public. However, the two members of this Court who concur in this opinion use "everyday spoken English", and we would not pronounce LEXUS as if it were spelled LEXIS. Although our colleague takes issue with us on this point, he does not contend that if LEXUS and LEXIS are pronounced correctly, they will sound the same. We liken LEXUS to such words as "census", "focus" and "locus", and differentiate it from such words as "axis", "aegis" and "iris".[2] If we were to substitute the letter "i" for the letter "u" in "census", we would not pronounce it as we now do. Likewise, if we were to substitute the letter "u" for the letter "i" in "axis", we would not pronounce it as we now do. * * *

In addition, we do not believe that "everyday spoken English" is the proper test to use in deciding the issue of similarity in the instant case. * * * "The legitimate aim of the anti-dilution statute is to prohibit the unauthorized use of another's trademark in order to market incompatible products or services", and this constitutes a "legitimate regulation of commercial speech." L.L. Bean, Inc. v. Drake Publishers, Inc., 811 F.2d 26, 32–33 (1st Cir.), cert. denied, 483 U.S. 1013, 107 S.Ct. 3254, 97 L.Ed.2d 753 (1987). * * * We take it as a given that television and radio announcers usually are more careful and precise in their diction than is the man on the street. Moreover, it is the rare television commercial that does not contain a visual reference to the mark and product, which in the instant case would be the LEXUS automobile. We conclude that in the field of commercial advertising, which is the field subject to regulation, there is no substantial similarity between Mead's mark and Toyota's.

There are additional factors that militate against a finding of dilution in the instant case. Such a finding must be based on two elements. First, plaintiff's mark must possess a distinctive quality capable of dilution. Allied Maintenance Corp. v. Allied Mechanical Trades, Inc., 42 N.Y.2d 538, 545, 399 N.Y.S.2d 628, 369 N.E.2d 1162 (1977). Second, plaintiff must show a likelihood of dilution, Sally Gee, Inc. v. Myra Hogan, Inc., supra, 699 F.2d at 625. As section 368–d expressly states, a

2. Similarly, we liken LEXUS to NEXX-US, a nationally known shampoo, and LEX-IS to NEXIS, Mead's trademark for its computerized news service. NEXXUS and NEXIS have co-existed in apparent tranquility for almost a decade.

plaintiff need not show either competition between its product or service and that of the defendant or a likelihood of confusion as to the source of the goods or services. Allied Maintenance Corp. v. Allied Mechanical Trades, Inc., supra, 42 N.Y.2d at 543, 399 N.Y.S.2d 628, 369 N.E.2d 1162.

Distinctiveness for dilution purposes often has been equated with the strength of a mark for infringement purposes. P.F. Cosmetique, S.A. v. Minnetonka Inc., 605 F.Supp. 662, 672 (S.D.N.Y.1985); Allied Maintenance Corp. v. Allied Mechanical Trades, Inc., supra, 42 N.Y.2d at 545, 399 N.Y.S.2d 628, 369 N.E.2d 1162. It also has been defined as uniqueness or as having acquired a secondary meaning. Allied Maintenance, supra, 42 N.Y.2d at 545, 399 N.Y.S.2d 628, 369 N.E.2d 1162. A trademark has a secondary meaning if it "has become so associated in the mind of the public with that entity [Allied] or its product that it identifies the goods sold by that entity and distinguishes them from goods sold by others." Id. In sum, the statute protects a trademark's "selling power." Sally Gee, Inc. v. Myra Hogan, Inc., supra, 699 F.2d at 624–25. However, the fact that a mark has selling power in a limited geographical or commercial area does not endow it with a secondary meaning for the public generally.

The strength and distinctiveness of LEXIS is limited to the market for its services—attorneys and accountants. Outside that market, LEXIS has very little selling power. Because only one percent of the general population associates LEXIS with the attributes of Mead's service, it cannot be said that LEXIS identifies that service to the general public and distinguishes it from others. Moreover, the bulk of Mead's advertising budget is devoted to reaching attorneys through professional journals.

This Court has defined dilution as either the blurring of a mark's product identification or the tarnishment of the affirmative associations a mark has come to convey. Sally Gee, Inc. v. Myra Hogan, Inc., supra, 699 F.2d at 625 (quoting 3A Callman, The Law of Unfair Competition, Trademarks and Monopolies § 84.2 at 954–55). Mead does not claim that Toyota's use of LEXUS would tarnish affirmative associations engendered by LEXIS. The question that remains, therefore, is whether LEXIS is likely to be blurred by LEXUS.

Very little attention has been given to date to the distinction between the confusion necessary for a claim of infringement and the blurring necessary for a claim of dilution. Shire, supra, 77 Trademark Rep. at 293. Although the antidilution statute dispenses with the requirements of competition and confusion, it does not follow that every junior use of a similar mark will dilute the senior mark in the manner contemplated by the New York Legislature.

As already stated, the brief legislative history accompanying section 368–d described the purpose of the statute as preventing "the whittling away of an established trademark's selling power and value through its unauthorized use by others upon dissimilar products." The history disclosed a need for legislation to prevent such "hypothetical anomalies" as "Dupont shoes, Buick aspirin tablets, Schlitz varnish, Kodak pianos, Bulova gowns, and so forth", and cited cases involving similarly famous marks, e.g., Tiffany & Co. v. Tiffany Productions, Inc., 147 Misc. 679, 264 N.Y.S. 459 (1932), aff'd, 237 A.D. 801, 260 N.Y.S. 821, aff'd, 262 N.Y. 482, 188 N.E. 30 (1933); Philadelphia Storage Battery Co. v. Mindlin, 163 Misc. 52, 296 N.Y.S. 176 (1937). 1954 N.Y.Legis.Ann. 49–50.

It is apparent from these references that there must be some mental association between plaintiff's and defendant's marks. * * * This mental association may be created where the plaintiff's mark is very famous and therefore has a distinctive quality for a significant percentage of the defendant's market. Sally Gee, Inc. v. Myra Hogan, Inc., supra, 699 F.2d at 625. However, if a mark circulates only in a limited market, it is unlikely to be associated generally with the mark for a dissimilar product circulating elsewhere. * * * As discussed above, such distinctiveness as LEXIS possesses is limited to the narrow market of attorneys and accountants. Moreover, the process which LEXIS represents is widely disparate from the product represented by LEXUS. For the general public, LEXIS has no distinctive quality that LEXUS will dilute.

The possibility that someday LEXUS may become a famous mark in the mind of the general public has little relevance in the instant dilution analysis since it is quite apparent that the general public associates nothing with LEXIS. On the other hand, the recognized sophistication of attorneys, the principal users of the service, has substantial relevance. See Sally Gee, Inc. v. Myra Hogan, Inc., supra, 699 F.2d at 626. Because of this knowledgeable sophistication, it is unlikely that, even in the market where Mead principally operates, there will be any significant amount of blurring between the LEXIS and LEXUS marks. * * *

ADDENDUM

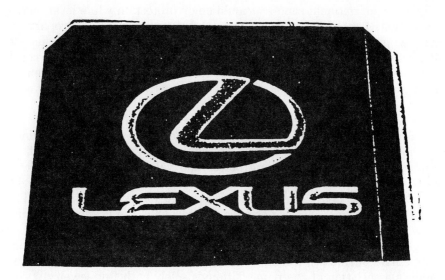

Sᴡᴇᴇᴛ, Dɪsᴛʀɪᴄᴛ Jᴜᴅɢᴇ, concurring:

I concur, but write separately because I disagree with the majority's conclusion that LEXIS is not a strong mark capable of dilution and that LEXIS and LEXUS differ significantly in pronunciation, and I have a different view of the factors that are necessary to a finding of dilution. * * *

The majority concludes that LEXIS is not a strong mark capable of dilution, noting that "the fact that a mark has selling power in a limited geographical or commercial area does not endow it with a secondary meaning for the public generally." Op. at 1030 (citations omitted). * * * This conclusion limits section 368–d's protection to nationally famous marks, because a strong mark capable of dilution is an element of a section 368–d cause of action and a plaintiff can lose on this ground alone. See, e.g., Allied Maintenance Corp. v. Allied Mechanical Trades, Inc., 42 N.Y.2d 538, 369 N.E.2d 1162, 1166, 399 N.Y.S.2d 628, 632–33 (1977).

However, "[t]he interest protected by § 368–d is ... the selling power that a distinctive mark or name with favorable associations has engendered for a product in the mind of the consuming public." Sally Gee, Inc. v. Myra Hogan, Inc., 699 F.2d 621, 624 (2d Cir.1983) (emphasis added). The LEXIS mark has "selling power" among its consuming public—attorneys and accountants. Its lack of selling power among the general public—i.e., the nonconsuming public—should not deprive the company of section 368–d's protection against dilution. See Dreyfus Fund Inc. v. Royal Bank of Canada, 525 F.Supp. 1108, 1125 (S.D.N.Y. 1981) ("The statute should not be read to deprive marks from protection against dilution in limited areas of use, since otherwise it would afford protection only to the most notorious of all marks."); Wedgwood Homes,

Inc. v. Lund, 294 Or. 493, 659 P.2d 377, 381 (1983) ("We see no reason why marks of national renown should enjoy protection while local marks should not. A small local firm may expend efforts and money proportionately as great as those of a large firm in order to establish its mark's distinctive quality."). The renown of a senior mark is a factor a court should assess when evaluating the likelihood of dilution, not the strength of the mark. * * *

LIKELIHOOD OF DILUTION

Several definitions of dilution exist. The legislative history defined the concept as "unlawful injury caused by the whittling away of an established trade-mark's selling power and value through its unauthorized use by others upon dissimilar products." 1954 N.Y.Leg.Ann. 49. The New York Court of Appeals offered the following definition: The harm that section 398–d is designed to prevent is the gradual whittling away of a firm's distinctive trade-mark or name. It is not difficult to imagine the possible effect which the proliferation of various non-competitive businesses utilizing the name Tiffany's would have upon the public's association of the name Tiffany's solely with fine jewelry. * * * Like likelihood of confusion, blurring sufficient to constitute dilution requires a case-by-case factual inquiry. A review of the anti-dilution cases in this Circuit indicates that courts have articulated the following factors in considering the likelihood of dilution caused by blurring: 1) similarity of the marks 2) similarity of the products covered by the marks 3) sophistication of consumers 4) predatory intent 5) renown of the senior mark 6) renown of the junior mark. The application of these factors here requires reversal of the decision below, although on a basis that I believe differs from that stated by the majority.

1. Similarity of the Marks

Dilution is likely only where the junior mark is similar to the senior mark. See McDonald's Corp. v. McBagel's, Inc., 649 F.Supp. 1268, 1281 (S.D.N.Y.1986) ("The similar element that associates defendants' name with plaintiff's family of marks, the use of the 'Mc' prefix with the name of a generic food item, is immediately apparent. New York courts have not hesitated to find 'whittling down' of the identity of the trademark where slogans used by two parties bear such a facial similarity."); Toys R Us, Inc. v. Canarsie Kiddie Shop, Inc., 559 F.Supp. 1189, 1208 (E.D.N.Y.1983) ("although the two names are distinguishable, the identity of the 'R' Us suffixes . . . compels me to conclude that the name Kids 'r' Us is likely to blur Toys 'R' Us' product identification"). [Judge Sweet determined that the product markets were not similar when viewed in context, that Mead's customers are sophisticated parties, that Toyota acted without predatory intent, and that Mead's mark is strong in its market but weak among general consumers.] * * *

6. Renown of the Junior Mark

This case raises an issue that is likely to arise rarely in dilution law—the prospect that a junior mark may become so famous that it will overwhelm the senior mark. * * * Survey evidence revealed that seventy-two percent of the general public associated LEXIS either with Mead's service or with nothing at all. The fact that only two percent of the population recognized LEXIS as being associated with Mead's service indicates that the vast majority of the general public associated LEXIS with nothing at all. The district court noted: The parties have stipulated that in the first nine months of 1989, Toyota expects to spend between $18 million and $23 million on media advertising. Awareness of the LEXUS mark is likely to spread far beyond its potential purchasers through television, radio, billboards and other print advertising. * * *

BALANCING THE FACTORS

* * * Although the district court did not use a balancing test, its findings on the various factors demonstrate that it would have found little likelihood of dilution had it done so. LEXIS and LEXUS are pronounced the same, but the marks differ in physical appearance, they will appear in different contexts, and the products bearing the marks are dissimilar. Moreover, Mead's consumers are sophisticated, Toyota adopted the LEXUS mark without predatory intent, and LEXIS enjoys no national renown. * * * For the reasons set forth above, I concur.

Notes

1. Now that Toyota's Lexus mark has become a household name, can Toyota now bar Mead from continuing to use the Lexis name, in light of the wide brand recognition of its Lexus trademark? Which analytical approach to dilution is more persuasive—the majority or the concurring opinion?

2. In 1995, Congress enacted the federal dilution statute, section 43(c) of the Lanham Act. Does this provision differ substantially from the New York dilution statute quoted in *Mead Data Central*? Would the plaintiff have been successful if this statute was applicable law when *Mead Data Central* was decided? For further discussion of dilution claims involving "blurring" and "tarnishment," see 3 J. Thomas McCarthy, Trademarks and Unfair Competition §§ 24.13 to 24.20 (3d ed. 1995); Restatement (Third) of Unfair Competition § 25 (1995).

3. Coca–Cola has manufactured and sold soft drink beverages under its registered trademark for over one hundred years. Its mark is sometimes displayed in distinctive stylized script lettering in the phrase "Enjoy Coca–Cola." Defendant designs a humorous poster that imitates this stylized script, except that it displays the message "Enjoy Cocaine." Does this poster violate the federal or state dilution statute? Does the claim involve blurring or tarnishment?

MOSELEY v. V SECRET CATALOGUE, INC.
Supreme Court of United States, 2003.
537 U.S. 418, 123 S.Ct. 1115, 155 L.Ed.2d 1.

Petitioners, Victor and Cathy Moseley, own and operate a retail store named "Victor's Little Secret" in a strip mall in Elizabethtown,

Kentucky. They have no employees. Respondents are affiliated corporations that own the VICTORIA'S SECRET trademark, and operate over 750 Victoria's Secret stores, two of which are in Louisville, Kentucky, a short drive from Elizabethtown. In 1998 they spent over $55 million advertising "the VICTORIA'S SECRET brand—one of moderately priced, high quality, attractively designed lingerie sold in a store setting designed to look like a wom[a]n's bedroom." They distribute 400 million copies of the Victoria's Secret catalog each year, including 39,000 in Elizabethtown. In 1998 their sales exceeded $1.5 billion.

In the February 12, 1998, edition of a weekly publication distributed to residents of the military installation at Fort Knox, Kentucky, petitioners advertised the "GRAND OPENING Just in time for Valentine's Day!" of their store "VICTOR'S SECRET" in nearby Elizabethtown. The ad featured "Intimate Lingerie for every woman"; "Romantic Lighting"; "Lycra Dresses"; "Pagers"; and "Adult Novelties/Gifts." Id., at 209. An army colonel, who saw the ad and was offended by what he perceived to be an attempt to use a reputable company's trademark to promote the sale of "unwholesome, tawdry merchandise," sent a copy to respondents. Id., at 210. Their counsel then wrote to petitioners stating that their choice of the name "Victor's Secret" for a store selling lingerie was likely to cause confusion with the well-known Victoria's Secret mark and, in addition, was likely to "dilute the distinctiveness" of the mark. Id., at 190–191. They requested the immediate discontinuance of the use of the name "and any variations thereof." Ibid. In response, petitioners changed the name of their store to "Victor's Little Secret." Because that change did not satisfy respondents, they promptly filed this action in Federal District Court.

* * * After discovery the parties filed cross-motions for summary judgment. The record contained uncontradicted affidavits and deposition testimony describing the vast size of respondents' business, the value of the VICTORIA'S SECRET name, and descriptions of the items sold in the respective parties' stores. Respondents sell a "complete line of lingerie" and related items, each of which bears a VICTORIA'S SECRET label or tag.[3] Petitioners sell a wide variety of items, including adult videos, "adult novelties," and lingerie.[4] Victor Moseley stated in an affidavit that women's lingerie represented only about five percent of their sales. Id., at 131. In support of their motion for summary judgment, respondents submitted an affidavit by an expert in marketing who explained "the enormous value" of respondents' mark. Id., at 195–205. Neither he, nor any other witness,

---

3. Respondents described their business as follows: "Victoria's Secret stores sell a complete line of lingerie, women's undergarments and nightwear, robes, caftans and kimonos, slippers, sachets, lingerie bags, hanging bags, candles, soaps, cosmetic brushes, atomizers, bath products and fragrances." Id., at 168.

4. In answer to an interrogatory, petitioners stated that they "sell novelty action clocks, patches, temporary tattoos, stuffed animals, coffee mugs, leather biker wallets, zippo lighters, diet formula, diet supplements, jigsaw puzzles, whyss, handcufs [sic], hosiery bubble machines, greeting cards, calendars, incense burners, car air fresheners, sunglasses, ball caps, jewelry, candles, lava lamps, blacklights, fiber optic lights, rock and roll prints, lingerie, pagers, candy, adult video tapes, adult novelties, t-shirts, etc." Id., at 87.

expressed any opinion concerning the impact, if any, of petitioners' use of the name "Victor's Little Secret" on that value.

Finding that the record contained no evidence of actual confusion between the parties' marks, the District Court concluded that "no likelihood of confusion exists as a matter of law" and entered summary judgment for petitioners on the infringement and unfair competition claims. Civ. Action No. 3:98CV–395–S, 2000 WL 370525 (WD Ky., Feb. 9, 2000), App. to Pet. for Cert. 28a, 37a. With respect to the FTDA claim, however, the court ruled for respondents. Noting that petitioners did not challenge Victoria Secret's claim that its mark is "famous," the only question it had to decide was whether petitioners' use of their mark diluted the quality of respondents' mark. Reasoning from the premise that dilution "corrodes" a trademark either by " 'blurring its product identification or by damaging positive associations that have attached to it,' " the court first found the two marks to be sufficiently similar to cause dilution, and then found "that Defendants' mark dilutes Plaintiffs' mark because of its tarnishing effect upon the Victoria's Secret mark." Id., at 38a–39a (quoting Ameritech, Inc. v. American Info. Technologies Corp., 811 F.2d 960, 965 (C.A.6 1987)). It therefore enjoined petitioners "from using the mark 'Victor's Little Secret' on the basis that it causes dilution of the distinctive quality of the Victoria's Secret mark." App. to Pet. for Cert. 38a–39a. The court did not, however, find that any "blurring" had occurred. Ibid.

The Court of Appeals for the Sixth Circuit affirmed. 259 F.3d 464 (2001). In a case decided shortly after the entry of the District Court's judgment in this case, the Sixth Circuit had adopted the standards for determining dilution under the FTDA that were enunciated by the Second Circuit in Nabisco, Inc. v. PF Brands, Inc., 191 F.3d 208 (1999). See Kellogg Co. v. Exxon Corp., 209 F.3d 562 (C.A.6 2000). In order to apply those standards, it was necessary to discuss two issues that the District Court had not specifically addressed—whether respondents' mark is "distinctive," and whether relief could be granted before dilution has actually occurred. With respect to the first issue, the court rejected the argument that Victoria's Secret could not be distinctive because "secret" is an ordinary word used by hundreds of lingerie concerns. The court concluded that the entire mark was "arbitrary and fanciful" and therefore deserving of a high level of trademark protection. 259 F.3d, at 470. On the second issue, the court relied on a distinction suggested by this sentence in the House Report: "Confusion leads to immediate injury, while dilution is an infection, which if allowed to spread, will inevitably destroy the advertising value of the mark." H.R.Rep. No. 104–374, p. 1030 (1995), U.S.Code Cong. & Admin.News 1995, pp. 1029, 1030. This statement, coupled with the difficulty of proving actual harm, lent support to the court's ultimate conclusion that the evidence in this case sufficiently established "dilution." 259 F.3d, at 475–477.

* * *

In reaching that conclusion the Court of Appeals expressly rejected the holding of the Fourth Circuit in Ringling Bros.-Barnum & Bailey Combined Shows, Inc. v. Utah Div. of Travel Development, 170 F.3d 449 (1999). In that case, which involved a claim that Utah's use on its license plates of the phrase "greatest *snow* on earth" was causing dilution of the "greatest *show* on earth," the court had concluded "that to establish dilution of a famous mark under the federal Act requires proof that (1) a defendant has made use of a junior mark sufficiently similar to the famous mark to evoke in a relevant universe of consumers a mental association of the two that (2) has caused (3) actual economic harm to the famous mark's economic value by lessening its former selling power as an advertising agent for its goods or services." Id., at 461 (emphasis added). Because other Circuits have also expressed differing views about the "actual harm" issue, we granted certiorari to resolve the conflict. 535 U.S. 985, 122 S.Ct. 1536, 152 L.Ed.2d 463 (2002). * * *

The District Court's decision in this case rested on the conclusion that the name of petitioners' store "tarnished" the reputation of respondents' mark, and the Court of Appeals relied on both "tarnishment" and "blurring" to support its affirmance. Petitioners have not disputed the relevance of tarnishment, presumably because that concept was prominent in litigation brought under state antidilution statutes and because it was mentioned in the legislative history. Whether it is actually embraced by the statutory text, however, is another matter. Indeed, the contrast between the state statutes, which expressly refer to both "injury to business reputation" and to "dilution of the distinctive quality of a trade name or trademark," and the federal statute which refers only to the latter, arguably supports a narrower reading of the FTDA. See Klieger, Trademark Dilution: The Whittling Away of the Rational Basis for Trademark Protection, 58 U. Pitt. L.Rev. 789, 812–813, and n. 132 (1997).

The contrast between the state statutes and the federal statute, however, sheds light on the precise question that we must decide. For those state statutes, like several provisions in the federal Lanham Act, repeatedly refer to a "likelihood" of harm, rather than to a completed harm. The relevant text of the FTDA * * * provides that "the owner of a famous mark" is entitled to injunctive relief against another person's commercial use of a mark or trade name if that use "*causes dilution* of the distinctive quality" of the famous mark. 15 U.S.C. § 1125(c)(1) (emphasis added). This text unambiguously requires a showing of actual dilution, rather than a likelihood of dilution.

This conclusion is fortified by the definition of the term "dilution" itself. That definition provides:

"The term 'dilution' means the lessening of the capacity of a famous mark to identify and distinguish goods or services, regardless of the presence or absence of—

"(1) competition between the owner of the famous mark and other parties, or

"(2) likelihood of confusion, mistake, or deception." § 1127.

The contrast between the initial reference to an actual "lessening of the capacity" of the mark, and the later reference to a "likelihood of confusion, mistake, or deception" in the second caveat confirms the conclusion that actual dilution must be established.

Of course, that does not mean that the consequences of dilution, such as an actual loss of sales or profits, must also be proved. To the extent that language in the Fourth Circuit's opinion in the Ringling Bros. case suggests otherwise, see 170 F.3d, at 460–465, we disagree. We do agree, however, with that court's conclusion that, at least where the marks at issue are not identical, the mere fact that consumers mentally associate the junior user's mark with a famous mark is not sufficient to establish actionable dilution. As the facts of that case demonstrate, such mental association will not necessarily reduce the capacity of the famous mark to identify the goods of its owner, the statutory requirement for dilution under the FTDA. For even though Utah drivers may be reminded of the circus when they see a license plate referring to the "greatest snow on earth," it by no means follows that they will associate "the greatest show on earth" with skiing or snow sports, or associate it less strongly or exclusively with the circus. "Blurring" is not a necessary consequence of mental association. (Nor, for that matter, is "tarnishing.")

The record in this case establishes that an army officer who saw the advertisement of the opening of a store named "Victor's Secret" did make the mental association with "Victoria's Secret," but it also shows that he did not therefore form any different impression of the store that his wife and daughter had patronized. There is a complete absence of evidence of any lessening of the capacity of the Victoria's Secret mark to identify and distinguish goods or services sold in Victoria's Secret stores or advertised in its catalogs. The officer was offended by the ad, but it did not change his conception of Victoria's Secret. His offense was directed entirely at petitioners, not at respondents. Moreover, the expert retained by respondents had nothing to say about the impact of petitioners' name on the strength of respondents' mark.

Noting that consumer surveys and other means of demonstrating actual dilution are expensive and often unreliable, respondents and their amici argue that evidence of an actual "lessening of the capacity of a famous mark to identify and distinguish goods or services," § 1127, may be difficult to obtain. It may well be, however, that direct evidence of dilution such as consumer surveys will not be necessary if actual dilution can reliably be proven through circumstantial evidence—the obvious case is one where the junior and senior marks are identical. Whatever difficulties of proof may be entailed, they are not an acceptable reason for dispensing with proof of an essential element of a statutory violation. The evidence in the present record is not sufficient to support the summary judgment on the dilution count. The judgment is therefore reversed, and the case is remanded for further proceedings consistent with this opinion.

* * *

Notes

1.   In October 2006, in response to this decision, Congress enacted and President Bush signed the Trademark Dilution Revision Act of 2006. Among other things, this revision of trademark dilution law provides a revised definition for dilution. The new definition of dilution states in part:

> the owner of a famous mark that is distinctive, inherently or through acquired distinctiveness, shall be entitled to an injunction against another person who, at any time after the owner's mark has become famous, commences use of a mark or trade name in commerce that is likely to cause dilution by blurring or dilution by tarnishment of the famous mark, regardless of the presence or absence of actual or likely confusion, of competition, or of actual economic injury.

Consider how this amended language changes the federal dilution law.

2.   Consider the evidence presented in *Ringling Bros.–Barnum & Bailey Combined Shows, Inc. v. Utah Division of Travel Development*, 170 F.3d 449 (4th Cir. 1999). In that case, Ringling Bros.–Barnum & Bailey Combined Shows, Inc. ("Ringling") brought a dilution claim under the federal statute with regard to Ringling's famous circus trademark slogan, THE GREATEST SHOW ON EARTH ("GREATEST SHOW mark"). Ringling claimed its slogan had been diluted by the State of Utah's commercial use of its trademark slogan, THE GREATEST SNOW ON EARTH ("GREATEST SNOW mark"), as an advertisement of the state's winter sports attractions. Ringling presented the following survey evidence:

> The survey was conducted by interviewing individuals at seven shopping malls throughout the country, including one in Utah. At each location, randomly selected shoppers were presented with a card containing the fill-in-the-blank statement "THE GREATEST _____ ON EARTH" and were asked what word or words they would use to complete the phrase. If the shoppers completed the statement, they were asked with whom or what they associated the completed statement. And, they were asked further whether they could think of any other way to complete the statement, and with whom or what they associated the resulting statement.

> The survey results showed that in Utah (1) 25% of the respondents completed the statement THE GREATEST _____ ON EARTH with only the word "show" and associated the completed statement with the Circus; (2) 24% completed the statement with only the word "snow" and associated the completed statement with Utah; and (3)21% of respondents completed the statement with "show" and associated the result with the Circus and also completed the statement with "snow" and associated the completed statement with Utah. The survey further showed that outside of Utah (1) 41% of respondents completed the statement THE GREATEST _____ ON EARTH with only the word

"show" and associated the completed statement with the Circus; (2) 0% completed the statement with only the word "snow" and associated the completed statement with Utah; and (3) fewer than 0.5% of respondents completed the statement with "show" and associated the result with the Circus and also completed the statement with "snow" and associated the completed statement with Utah.

Does this evidence suffice to show dilution under any applicable standard?

There have been numerous significant decisions interpreting the Federal Trademark Dilution Act of 1995. Among the successful dilution suits are Anheuser–Busch, Inc. v. Andy's Sportswear Inc., 40 U.S.P.Q.2d 1542 (N.D.Cal.1996) (granting owner of "Budweiser" marks temporary restraining order barring sale of "Buttweiser" t-shirts); Panavision International, L.P. v. Toeppen, 945 F.Supp. 1296 (C.D.Cal.1996) (plaintiff's Panavision and Panaflex marks found to be diluted by defendant's registration those marks as domain names "panavision.com" and "panaflex.com" for specific purpose of obtaining payment), aff'd, 141 F.3d 1316 (9th Cir.1998). See also Toys "R" Us, Inc. v. Akkaoui, 40 U.S.P.Q.2d 1836 (N.D.Cal.1996) (plaintiff owner of "R US" series of trademarks successfully obtained preliminary injunction, on tarnishment theory, against a Website entitled "adultsrus.com"); Hasbro, Inc. v. Internet Entertainment Group, Ltd., 40 U.S.P.Q.2d 1479 (W.D.Wash. 1996) ("Candy Land" toymaker obtained preliminary injunction against x-rated Website "candyland.com").

Good illustrations of unsuccessful dilution cases include Trustees of Columbia University v. Columbia/HCA Healthcare Corp., 964 F.Supp. 733 (S.D.N.Y.1997) (rejecting dilution claim by university against health care provider); American Express Co. v. CFK, Inc., 947 F.Supp. 310, 41 U.S.P.Q.2d 1756 (E.D.Mich.1996) (plaintiff failed to show that its "Don't leave home without it" marks were diluted by defendant's "Don't leave home without me" pocket address book); Dr. Seuss Enterprises, L.P. v. Penguin Books USA, Inc., 924 F.Supp. 1559 (S.D.Cal.1996) (no dilution of "Cat in the Hat" mark by "Cat Not in the Hat" book; defendant's use held to be expressive and non-commercial, and thus exempt from Dilution Act), aff'd, 109 F.3d 1394 (9th Cir.1997), cert. dismissed, 521 U.S. 1146, 118 S.Ct. 27, 138 L.Ed.2d 1057 (1997).

3.   When is a mark sufficiently famous to warrant protection under the federal dilution statute? Consider the case of WAWA Dairy Farms v. Haaf, 40 U.S.P.Q.2d 1629 (E.D.Pa.1996), aff'd per curiam, 116 F.3d 471 (3d Cir.1997). Wawa is a chain of five hundred convenience stores located in five mid-Atlantic states. It was first founded over ninety years earlier. Is Wawa a famous mark? What role should the geographic scope of the trademark owner's activities play in determining fame? What is a mark is very well known, but only in one or two states? See Star Markets, Ltd. v. Texaco, Inc., 950 F.Supp. 1030 (D.Hawai'i 1996) (holding that "Star Markets" chain of markets in Hawai'i was not famous for purposes of its dilution action against Texaco for its use of "Star Mart" for its convenience stores, given nature of the mark and use only in the state of Hawaii). Does it matter that Wawa is relatively unknown in about 45 states? Consider how the Trademark Dilution Revision Act of 2006 affects the analysis. In Enterprise Rent–A–Car Co. v. Advantage Rent–A–Car, Inc., 330 F.3d 1333 (Fed. Cir. 2003), the Federal

Circuit addressed a dilution claim in the context of the trademark registration and opposition process. The court held that when a car rental business had used a service mark in a limited geographic area before its competitor's similar mark became famous, the now-famous competitor was precluded from opposing the car rental agency's federal registration of its mark on the ground that it would dilute the now-famous firm's mark.

4. What if the trademark is known, but only within a niche market. Consider the case of Times Mirror Magazines, Inc. v. Las Vegas Sports News, L.L.C., 212 F.3d 157 (3d Cir.2000), which involved "The Sporting News," a national weekly sports publication. The defendant began publishing a weekly sports-betting publication called the "Las Vegas Sporting News." Is "The Sporting News" sufficiently distinctive and recognizable to warrant protection under the dilution statute? Note again the changes in the Trademark Dilution Revision Act of 2006.

C. INFRINGEMENT ANALYSIS IN PARODY CASES

MUTUAL OF OMAHA INSURANCE CO. v. NOVAK

United States Court of Appeals, Eighth Circuit, 1987.
836 F.2d 397.

BOWMAN, CIRCUIT JUDGE.

Mutual of Omaha Insurance Company (Mutual) brought suit against Franklyn Novak (Novak) alleging trademark infringement and trademark disparagement. The District Court found for Mutual on the infringement issue and granted a permanent injunction, but rejected the disparagement claim. Novak appeals the decision concerning infringement and Mutual appeals the disparagement decision. We affirm the District Court's infringement decision and do not reach the disparagement issue.

Beginning in 1952, Mutual acquired trademark registrations for marks used in connection with its insurance services and a television program it sponsors. These marks include the familiar "Indian head" logo and the designations "Mutual of Omaha" and "Mutual of Omaha's Wild Kingdom."

In 1983 Novak produced a design reminiscent of the Mutual marks. It uses the words "Mutant of Omaha" and depicts a side view of a feather-bonneted, emaciated human head. Novak initially put the design on T-shirts along with the words "Nuclear Holocaust Insurance." Novak marketed approximately 4000 of these shirts before Mutual obtained a preliminary injunction. He also had the design placed on sweatshirts, caps, buttons, and coffee mugs, which he has offered for sale at retail shops, exhibitions, and fairs. Novak also has advertised such merchandise on television and in newspapers and magazines. * * *

In resolving the likelihood of confusion issue, the District Court considered the factors that this Court enumerated in SquirtCo v. Seven–Up Co., 628 F.2d 1086, 1091 (8th Cir.1980): 1) the strength of the trademark; 2) the similarity between the trademark and the defendant's mark; 3) the competitive proximity of the products on which the respective marks are placed; 4) the intent of the alleged infringer to pass off his goods as those of the trademark holder; 5) the incidents of actual confusion; and 6) the degree of care likely to be exercised by potential customers of the trademark holder.[3] * * *

The first factor is undisputed. The parties agree that Mutual's trademarks are strong.

With respect to the second factor, the District Court concluded that Novak's design is "very similar" to Mutual's marks. Mutual of Omaha Ins. Co. v. Novak, 648 F.Supp. 905, 909 (D.Neb.1986). We do not disagree. The letters and styles of the phrases are virtually identical. Novak's "Indian head" logo depicts a side view of a feather-bonneted head similar to Mutual's "Indian head" logo. And use of the word "Mutant" in place of "Mutual" is, in the context of Novak's design, suggestive of Mutual.[4]

Regarding competitive proximity, Novak puts his design on T-shirts and coffee mugs, the same types of items on which Mutual puts its marks. Mutual sells such items to agents and company representatives, who in turn use them as gifts or incentives. While the District Court determined that there was little or no direct competition in these items between the parties, it noted that infringement still could be found. Mutual of Omaha Ins. Co., 648 F.Supp. at 910. This is undoubtedly so, for confusion, not competition, is the touchstone of trademark infringement. See SquirtCo, 628 F.2d at 1091; Hanson v. Triangle Publications, Inc., 163 F.2d 74, 78 (8th Cir.1947), cert. denied, 332 U.S. 855, 68 S.Ct. 387, 92 L.Ed. 424 (1948). It is error to assume that trademark law protects against use of a mark only on directly competitive products. * * * Moreover, by putting his design on items similar to those on which Mutual puts its marks, Novak increased the likelihood of confusion.

With regard to the fourth factor, there is no finding by the District Court that Novak intended to pass off his goods as Mutual's, and it seems clear that he did not. This cuts in Novak's favor, but it is not dispositive, for intent to pass off one's goods as another's is not essential to an infringement claim; rather, its presence or absence is only one

---

3. These are not necessarily the only factors that might be relevant in a particular case. The ultimate inquiry always is whether, under all the circumstances, there exists a likelihood of confusion between the plaintiff's trademark and the allegedly infringing use.

4. The dissent plays down the similarities between Novak's design and Mutual's marks, pointing out specific features that are different and noting that "the differences ... are unmistakable." The issue, however, "is not whether the public would confuse the marks, but whether the viewer

of an [allegedly infringing] mark would be likely to associate the product or service with which it is connected with the source of products or services with which an earlier mark is connected." James Burrough Ltd. v. Sign of the Beefeater, Inc., 540 F.2d 266, 275 (7th Cir.1976) (emphasis in original). The similarity of appearance is to be determined by looking at the total effect of the designation, rather than by comparing individual features. Amstar Corp. v. Domino's Pizza, Inc., 615 F.2d 252, 260–61 (5th Cir.), cert. denied, 449 U.S. 899, 101 S.Ct. 268, 66 L.Ed.2d 129 (1980).

factor to be considered along with the other factors that bear on the issue of likelihood of confusion. SquirtCo, 628 F.2d at 1091.

As to incidents of actual confusion, Mutual produced evidence of actual confusion in the form of a survey conducted by Sorenson Marketing and Management Corporation of New York. We consider this appropriate, for surveys are often used to demonstrate actual consumer confusion. PPX Enters. v. Audiofidelity Enters., 818 F.2d 266, 271 (2d Cir.1987). Sorenson interviewed at random four hundred people over the age of twenty-one in New York, Denver, Chicago, and San Francisco. While viewing Novak's design on a T-shirt, approximately forty-two percent of those surveyed said that Mutual of Omaha came to mind. Plaintiff's Exhibit No. 49, pp. 15, 33. Of that group, twenty-five percent said that they believe Mutual "goes along" with the T-shirts "in order to help make people aware of the nuclear war problem." See id. at 16. Thus, approximately ten percent of all the persons surveyed thought that Mutual "goes along" with Novak's product. Id. at 16, 33. Because manifestations of actual confusion serve as strong evidence of a likelihood of confusion, SquirtCo, 628 F.2d at 1091; World Carpets, Inc. v. Dick Littrell's New World Carpets, 438 F.2d 482, 489 (5th Cir.1971), and may, in fact, be the best such evidence, Jordache Enters., 828 F.2d at 1487, this survey should be given substantial weight unless seriously flawed.

The District Court acknowledged that there may be some ambiguity in the "goes along" question used in the survey, but found the survey as a whole "credible evidence of a likelihood of confusion as to source or sponsorship." Mutual of Omaha Ins. Co., 648 F.Supp. at 911. Novak presents no persuasive reason for overriding the District Court's evaluation of the reliability of the survey.[5] * * *

Concerning the final *SquirtCo* factor, the District Court found that consumers are not likely to exercise the "high degree of care or thought"

---

5. The dissent also attacks the survey's validity, but we remain unpersuaded that we should overrule the District Court's assessment of the weight to be given the survey. The dissent's primary attack focuses on the following survey question: "Would you say that Mutual of Omaha goes along or does not go along with these T-shirts in order to make people aware of the nuclear war problem?" The dissent finds the question "fundamentally flawed" because it "plants the idea of nuclear war in the mind of the interviewee." When during the survey this question is presented, however, the interviewee is already viewing a T-shirt bearing Novak's design along with the phrase "Nuclear Holocaust Insurance." * * * The survey question simply causes the interviewee to focus on one specific kind of nuclear disaster. In our opinion, this reference to nuclear war does not make the survey fatally defective. The dissent also objects to the survey sample. The dissent complains that the survey respondents were not asked whether they were interested in buying a T-shirt or insurance, were not from areas reached, or likely to be reached, by Novak's message, and were not interviewed at places where insurance or T-shirts were "featured." The dissent also criticizes the survey sample size as "miniscule." We do not find the dissent's objections compelling and note that other courts have upheld the validity of surveys against similar attacks. * * * With regard to the survey sample size, without some basis for thinking otherwise, we decline to accept the dissent's assertion that four hundred interviewees is too few. See Exxon, 628 F.2d at 507 (5th Cir.1980) (515 interviewees sufficient); SquirtCo, 628 F.2d at 1089–90 n. 4 (628 survey respondents sufficient); James Burrough Ltd., 540 F.2d at 277 (five hundred interviewees sufficient). * * *

necessary to "distinguish Mutual from the message on [Novak's] products." Mutual of Omaha Ins. Co., 648 F.Supp. at 911. We agree. Nothing in the labeling or packaging of Novak's products indicates that the message and products do not emanate from Mutual. As a result, for consumers to learn that Mutual has no connection with Novak's products requires more than just careful scrutiny of the products, and it is improbable that consumers will engage in further investigation. We believe, as did the District Court, that the degree of care likely to be exercised by consumers does not reduce the likelihood of confusion.

We are satisfied that the District Court properly weighed the *Squirt-Co* factors. The record contains ample support for the District Court's finding of a likelihood of confusion. We therefore cannot say that this pivotal finding is clearly erroneous.

The cases Novak relies upon to support his view that there is no likelihood of confusion here, but merely obvious parody, lack persuasiveness in relation to the situation before us. Those cases either did not involve surveys demonstrating confusion or involved surveys of doubtful validity. For example, in Carson v. Here's Johnny Portable Toilets, Inc., 698 F.2d 831 (6th Cir.1983), the plaintiffs presented no surveys demonstrating confusion, and in Tetley, Inc. v. Topps Chewing Gum, Inc., 556 F.Supp. 785, 793 (E.D.N.Y.1983), the court noted that the plaintiff presented no evidence at all of either the likelihood of or actual confusion. * * * In *Jordache*, there was a survey, but the survey was given little weight because it had been shown to be seriously defective. See Jordache Enters., Inc. v. Hogg Wyld, Ltd., 625 F.Supp. 48, 54 (D.N.M. 1985), aff'd, 828 F.2d 1482 (10th Cir.1987) (court finds problems with survey's setting, sample size, methodology, and computations). Similarly, in *American Footwear*, the Second Circuit affirmed a district court's rejection of survey evidence, finding "numerous deficiencies inherent in the surveys." American Footwear Corp. v. General Footwear Co., 609 F.2d 655, 663 (2d Cir.1979).

Novak argues that his use of the design in question is an exercise of his right of free speech and is protected by the First Amendment. We believe, however, that the protection afforded by the First Amendment does not give Novak license to infringe the rights of Mutual. Mutual's trademarks are a form of property, Hanover Star Milling Co. v. Metcalf, 240 U.S. 403, 413, 36 S.Ct. 357, 360, 60 L.Ed. 713 (1916); Hamilton–Brown Shoe Co. v. Wolf Bros. & Co., 240 U.S. 251, 259, 36 S.Ct. 269, 271, 60 L.Ed. 629 (1916); Dallas Cowboys Cheerleaders, Inc. v. Pussycat Cinema, Ltd., 604 F.2d 200, 206 (2d Cir.1979); J. McCarthy, Trademarks and Unfair Competition § 2:6 (1973), and Mutual's rights therein need not "yield to the exercise of First Amendment rights under circumstances where adequate alternative avenues of communication exist." Lloyd Corp. v. Tanner, 407 U.S. 551, 567, 92 S.Ct. 2219, 2228, 33 L.Ed.2d 131 (1972) * * *. Other avenues for Novak to express his views exist and are unrestricted by the injunction; for example, it in no way infringes upon the constitutional protection the First Amendment would provide were Novak to present an editorial parody in a book, magazine, or film. Because the injunction leaves open many such avenues of expression, it deprives neither Novak nor the public of the benefits of his ideas. * * *

We conclude that the District Court's finding of a likelihood of confusion between Mutual's valid trademarks and Novak's design is not clearly erroneous. That finding warrants the District Court's issuance of a permanent injunction restricting Novak's further use of his infringing design. * * *

HEANEY, CIRCUIT JUDGE, dissenting.

I respectfully dissent. In my view, the trial court's finding that there exists a likelihood of confusion is clearly erroneous. Moreover, the majority's holding sanctions a violation of Novak's first amendment rights. The T-shirts simply expressed a political message which irritated the officers of Mutual, who decided to swat this pesky fly buzzing around in their backyard with a sledge hammer (a federal court injunction). We should not be a party to this effort.

In regard to the majority's interpretation of the six *SquirtCo* factors indicating a likelihood of confusion: The Mutual trademark is no doubt a strong one. There also is a superficial "similarity" between Mutual's mark and the Novak design. Clearly for a parody to be successful, some similarity must be present, but the differences here are unmistakable: an emaciated human replaces the virile "Indianhead" and "Mutant" replaces "Mutual." Moreover, the products on which the design and mark are used are simply not "competitive," indirectly or otherwise. Mutual sells insurance; Novak sells T-shirts—probably to peace activists. Further, Novak had no intent to pass the T-shirts as Mutual's product.

The only *SquirtCo* factor really in dispute in this case is whether consumers could be "actually confused" as to who sponsored or produced the T-shirts.

The evidence on this issue consisted solely of a survey by a nationally recognized firm. Four hundred persons over the age of twenty-one were interviewed at shopping malls in New York, Denver, Chicago and San Francisco. Neither T-shirts nor insurance were featured at the shopping malls where the interviews were conducted. No one was asked whether he or she was interested in buying a T-shirt or insurance.

The interviewees were shown the T-shirts described in the majority opinion and asked: "Does anything come to your mind when you look at this tee shirt?" Ninety-two percent said yes. Those answering yes, were then asked: "What comes to your mind when you see this tee shirt?" Twenty-one percent answered Mutual of Omaha, or the TV program Wild Kingdom sponsored by Mutual. Interviewees were then asked, "anything else," and an additional eight percent then mentioned Mutual of Omaha.

As recognized by the majority, the only possible evidence of actual confusion is contained in the following question: "Would you say that Mutual of Omaha goes along with or does not go along with these tee shirts in order to make people aware of the nuclear war problem?" Twelve percent of those who mentioned Mutual of Omaha in the earlier questions gave an affirmative answer to this question.

This survey question, however, is fundamentally flawed and should be given little evidentiary weight. The question is blatantly suggestive. It plants the idea of nuclear war in the mind of the interviewee. Thus, an interviewee who only casually glances at the T-shirt or who doesn't understand the message in the T-shirt is tipped off by the question that the T-shirt has something to do with nuclear war. But, if the interviewer had not tipped these people off about the message on the T-shirts, many would never have even come to the misconception that Mutual sponsored the message on the T-shirt.

The only class of interviewees that really matter in this case are those who, on their own, recognized the T-shirt contained a message about nuclear war and also believed that Mutual sponsored it. This survey gives us no firm data on how many of these interviewees there were, except that the percentage is somewhere from zero to twelve percent. That is not compelling evidence. See Jordache, 828 F.2d at 1487–88. It is at most an inference of the possibility of confusion, and such a showing is not sufficient to prove infringement. Jordache, 828 F.2d at 1482.

The survey suffers from additional flaws. The sample was miniscule and taken in areas that Novak's message had not reached and had no realistic chance of reaching. His "mom and pop" operation reached a few thousand people, nearly all of whom lived in the Omaha area. Mutual, on the other hand, operates throughout the United States and sells nearly two billion dollars of insurance each year to millions of men and women. * * *

There can be no doubt that Novak used the "Mutant of Omaha" design in a satirical manner. He intended to expose what he considered the folly of nuclear war. He did not intend to harm Mutual's reputation, and there is no evidence that he did so or was likely to do so.

Most importantly, the majority opinion cannot be squared with the first amendment. The Supreme Court has consistently held that prior restraints on publication are presumptively invalid and may be sustained only under the most extraordinary circumstances. Lowe v. SEC, 472 U.S. 181, 204–05, 105 S.Ct. 2557, 2570–71, 86 L.Ed.2d 130 (1985). These are not extraordinary circumstances.

The majority justifies its assault on Novak's first amendment rights by stating that "protection afforded by the first amendment does not give Novak license to violate the [property] rights of Mutual where adequate alternative avenues of communication exist." Unfortunately, neither the district court nor the majority identifies how Mutual's property rights were harmed by the message on the T-shirts—its feelings, yes, but its reputation, highly unlikely. * * * I agree with Professor Robert Denicola that the general approach to trademark parodies should be this:

If the injury to the plaintiff's trademark arises from the ideas that have been expressed through the defendant's use, it is no answer to cite the "shopping center" cases [allowing restrictions on time, place and manner] to justify suppression on the ground that "adequate alternative avenues of communication exist." The issue is not where the defendant may speak, but rather what he may say. The first amendment will not permit the trademark owner the power to dictate the form, and thus the effectiveness, of another's speech simply because his trademark has been used to express ideas that he would prefer to exclude from the public dialogue.

R. Denicola, Trademarks as Speech: Constitutional Implications of the Emerging Rationales for the Protection of Trade Symbols, 1982 Wis. L.Rev. 158, 206.

In sum, the evidence in this case shows at most a possibility of trademark confusion, no real evidence of actual harm to property, and, most importantly, a significant intrusion upon the defendant's first amendment rights. For these reasons, I dissent.

Notes

1.   What analytical framework should courts use in cases of trademark parody or satire? What facts should be particularly decisive or dispositive? What role does survey evidence play in the analysis? Is the likelihood of confusion test well-suited to parody cases? If not, how should it be adapted to address the particular concerns of trademark parodies? Many articles have been written on the subject of trademark parodies. See, *e.g.*, Mark A. Dagitz, Comment, Trademark Parodies and Free Speech: An Expansion of Parodists' First Amendment Rights in L.L. Bean, Inc. v. Drake Publishers, Inc., 73 Iowa L. Rev. 961 (1988); Robert Denicola, Trademarks as Speech: Constitutional Implications of the Emerging Rationales for the Protection of Trade Symbols, 1982 Wis. L. Rev. 158 (1982) (discussing First Amendment implications of laws proscribing the use of trademarks to communicate ideas); J. Steven Gardner, Note, Trademark Infringement, Likelihood of Confusion, and Trademark Parody: Anheuser–Busch, Inc. v. L & L Wings, Inc., 28 Wake Forest L. Rev. 705 (1993); Mary LaFrance, Steam Shovels & Lipstick: Trademarks, Greed, & the Public Domain, 6 Nev. L.J. 44 (2006); Arlen W. Langvardt, Protected Marks and Protected Speech: Establishing the First Amendment Boundaries in Trademark Parody Cases, 36 Vill. L. Rev. 1 (1991); D.V.L. Mastrullo, Trademark Parody Litigation and the Lanham Act: Fitting A Square Peg in a Round Hole, 54 U. Cin. L. Rev. 1311 (1986); Gary Myers, Trademark Parody: Lessons from the Copyright Decision in Campbell v. Acuff–Rose Music, Inc., 60 L. & Contemp. Probs. 181 (1996); Steven M. Perez, Confronting Biased Treatment of Trademark Parody Under the Lanham Act, 44 Emory L.J. 1451, 1451–85 (1995); Robert J. Shaughnessy, Note, Trademark Parody: A Fair Use and First Amendment Analysis, 72 Va. L. Rev. 1079 (1986); Peter W. Smith, Note, Trademarks, Parody, and Consumer Confusion: A Workable Lanhan Act Infringement Standard, 12 Cardozo L. Rev. 1525 (1991); Gene S. Winter & Stuart P. Meyer, The "Merely Descriptive" Term: Is It a Trademark, A Description Protected by

the First Amendment, Or Both?, 31 IDEA: J. Law & Tech. 341, 357–59 (1991).

2. Does a trademark owner attain a litigation advantage by having multiple trademark registrations for any products and services it offers?

3. Is the Supreme Court's analysis of parody in the context of copyright law in *Campbell v. Acuff–Rose Music, Inc.*, discussed *infra* in the copyright materials, pertinent to trademark parodies as well? See *Myers*, *supra*, at 204–11.

4. In Rogers v. Grimaldi, 875 F.2d 994 (2d Cir.1989), Ginger Rogers sued the producers of the film "Ginger and Fred." The movie was about two Italian cabaret performers who imitated Ginger Rogers and Fred Astaire in their performances. Rogers claimed that the title of the film created the false impression that she was the subject of the film or had endorsed it. How should the court analyze such a claim?

5. In Elvis Presley Enterprises, Inc. v. Capece, 141 F.3d 188 (5th Cir.1998), the plaintiff owned the rights to the Elvis Presley name and trademarks, and the defendant operated a nightclub and restaurant in Houston under the name "The Velvet Elvis." The defendant's decor included velvet paintings of Elvis and other celebrities: "Other 'eclectic' decorations include lava lamps, cheap ceramic sculptures, beaded curtains, and vinyl furniture. Playboy centerfolds cover the men's room walls. In addition to the velvet painting of Elvis, the bar's menu and decor include other Elvis references. The menu includes 'Love Me Blenders,' a type of frozen drink; peanut butter and banana sandwiches, a favorite of Elvis's; and 'Your Football Hound Dog,' a hotdog.... Numerous magazine photographs of Elvis, a statuette of Elvis playing the guitar, and a bust of Elvis were also among the decorations. By the time of trial, many of these decorations had been removed from the Defendants' bar and replaced with non-Elvis items. Pictures and references to Elvis Presley appeared in advertising ... and some ads emphasized the "Elvis" portion of the name by "boldly display[ing] the 'Elvis' " portion of "The Velvet Elvis' insignia with an almost unnoticeable 'Velvet' appearing alongside in smaller script.' " Does the Velvet Elvis infringe on the Elvis Presley marks?

4. The Budweiser label design has been used by Anheuser–Busch as a trademark on beer cans since 1876. A t-shirt producer in Myrtle Beach produces a humorous t-shirt that is intentionally patterned after the Budweiser label, but does not make reference to the Budweiser brand. The t-shirt design is depicted on the next page. Should the t-shirt design be enjoined as trademark infringement? See Anheuser–Busch, Inc. v. L. & L. Wings, Inc., 962 F.2d 316 (4th Cir.1992).

T–Shirt Design

Chapter 5

TRADEMARK PROTECTION: DEFENSES AND LIMITATIONS ON RIGHTS

A. ABANDONMENT, DESCRIPTIVE USE, AND EQUITABLE DEFENSES

SANDS, TAYLOR & WOOD COMPANY v. THE QUAKER OATS COMPANY

United States Court of Appeals, Seventh Circuit, 1992.
978 F.2d 947, cert. denied, 507 U.S. 1042, 113 S.Ct. 1879, 123 L.Ed.2d 497 (1993).

CUDAHY, CIRCUIT JUDGE.

Sands, Taylor & Wood Company (STW) brought this action against The Quaker Oats Company (Quaker) for federal trademark infringement and related state-law claims, alleging that Quaker's use of the words "Thirst Aid" in its advertising slogan "Gatorade is Thirst Aid" infringed STW's registered trademark for THIRST–AID. The district court agreed, and entered judgment for STW in the amount of $42,629,399.09, including prejudgment interest and attorney's fees. The court also permanently enjoined Quaker from using the words "Thirst Aid." Not surprisingly, Quaker appeals.

I.

Plaintiff STW is a small, Vermont-based company that for the past 180 years has sold bagged flour at retail under the brand name "King Arthur Flour." In 1973, STW acquired Joseph Middleby, Jr., Inc. (Middleby), a manufacturer of soft drinks, soda fountain syrups and ice cream toppings. STW thereby became the owner of three trademarks registered to Middleby: (1) THIRST–AID "First Aid for Your Thirst," issued October 10, 1950, for use on "nonalcoholic maltless beverages, sold as soft drinks, and syrups therefor"; (2) THIRST–AID, issued August 26, 1952, for use on various ice cream toppings as well as "fruits and sauces used in the making of ice cream"; and (3) THIRST–AID, issued March

203

24, 1953, for use on "soda fountain syrups used in the preparation of maltless soft drinks."

From 1921 to 1973, Middleby used the THIRST–AID mark on a wide variety of beverage products and syrups that it sold to soda fountains, ice cream parlors and food service outlets. Middleby also supplied its THIRST–AID customers with various items displaying the name THIRST–AID, including streamers, banners, glasses and pitchers, for in-store advertising and promotion. STW continued these activities after it acquired Middleby, which it operated as a wholly-owned subsidiary.

In the late 1970s sales of THIRST–AID soft drinks declined as consumers turned increasingly to bottles and cans rather than soda fountains and ice cream parlors for their soft drinks. In addition, between 1979 and 1983 STW underwent a period of severe economic hardship during which its annual gross revenues dropped from $40 million to approximately $3.1 million. In the spring of 1980, Pet, Inc. (Pet) negotiated with STW a nationwide license to use the name THIRST–AID on a new isotonic beverage intended to compete with the very popular Gatorade brand isotonic beverage manufactured by Stokely Van Camp Company (Stokely). Pet began test-marketing the product in twenty stores in Columbia, South Carolina in June of 1980. Pet's THIRST–AID was advertised through the same media as Gatorade, and was sold through the same channels of trade (grocery stores) to the same customers. During the five-month period of the test, Pet's THIRST–AID captured approximately 25% of the isotonic beverage market in the test area. Nevertheless, for reasons that are not important here, Pet decided not to enter the market with the new product and in June of 1981 its license to use the name THIRST–AID expired.

In December of 1981, STW sold the assets of Middleby (now renamed Johnson–Middleby) to L. Karp & Sons (Karp), a distributor of bakery products. As part of the sale, STW assigned to Karp all of the registered THIRST–AID trademarks. STW obtained a simultaneous exclusive license back for retail use of the trademark on certain "Products" defined as "jams, jellies, pie fillings" and various other bakery supplies.

In August of 1983, Stokely, the manufacturer of Gatorade, was acquired by Quaker. Shortly thereafter, Quaker solicited proposals for a new advertising campaign intended to educate consumers about Gatorade's ability to quench thirst and replace fluids and minerals lost by the human body through strenuous exercise. One of the candidates was the slogan "Gatorade is Thirst Aid for That Deep Down Body Thirst."

Pursuant to Quaker's regular practice, the proposed "Thirst Aid" campaign was submitted to the legal department for approval in February or March of 1984. Quaker's in-house counsel, Charles Lannin, concluded that the words "Thirst Aid" did not raise any trademark problems because they were used to describe an attribute of the product rather than as a designation of source or affiliation. Lannin therefore did not conduct a trademark search for the term "Thirst Aid" at this time.

Shortly thereafter, an employee of Quaker's research and development division telephoned Lannin and informed him that Pet had previously test-marketed an isotonic beverage called THIRST–AID. Lannin contacted Pet and was told that Pet had discontinued its isotonic beverage a few years before. Some weeks later, another Quaker employee informed Lannin that he thought a "Thirst Aid" beverage was being marketed in Florida. At this point, on May 2, 1984, Lannin obtained a trademark search of the phrase "Thirst Aid." The search revealed the three THIRST–AID registrations by Middleby as well as the sale of the marks to Karp. Lannin directed a trademark paralegal employed by Quaker to contact Karp in order to determine what products it was selling under the THIRST–AID name; the Karp employee to whom the paralegal spoke[2] stated that "they [sic] didn't think they marketed anything under that name."

On May 12, 1984, the first "Gatorade is Thirst Aid" commercials ran on television. On May 31, 1984, Karp's lawyer, Russell Hattis, called Quaker regarding Quaker's use of "Thirst Aid." Hattis claimed that Quaker was infringing Karp's trademarks, to which Lannin responded that there was no infringement because Quaker was using the words "Thirst Aid" descriptively. * * * On June 4, Lannin was contacted by Frank Sands, the president of STW, who stated that STW owned the rights to use the THIRST–AID mark at retail under a licenseback agreement with Karp. Sands claimed that Quaker was infringing those rights, although he acknowledged that STW did not sell any THIRST–AID products at that time.

Quaker did not hear from either Karp or STW again until the commencement of this litigation. In the interim, STW entered into a written agreement with Karp under which STW paid Karp $1 for an assignment of Karp's trademark registrations. Sands filed suit one week later, alleging that the slogan "Gatorade is Thirst Aid for That Deep Down Body Thirst" infringed its registrations and constituted unfair competition under the Lanham Act, 15 U.S.C. §§ 1051 et seq., state common law and various state statutes. * * *

II.

[T]he district court granted summary judgment in favor of STW on Quaker's defense that it had made a "fair use" of the phrase "Thirst Aid."[3] The fair use doctrine is based on the principle that no one should

---

2. Although the district court stated that Quaker's paralegal spoke only to Karp's receptionist, the paralegal's deposition makes clear that she spoke to two people, only one of whom was the receptionist. The position of the other person is unclear, although the paralegal did testify that she had asked for someone "in sales." Tr. at 941.

3. Because THIRST–AID is a federally registered mark which STW has used continuously for over five years, the validity of the mark itself is incontestable under 15 U.S.C. § 1065. Incontestable marks are subject to only seven defenses, one of which is fair use. Id.

be able to appropriate descriptive language through trademark registration. William R. Warner & Co. v. Eli Lilly & Co., 265 U.S. 526, 528, 44 S.Ct. 615, 616, 68 L.Ed. 1161 (1924). To prevail on the fair use defense, the defendant must establish that its use of a registered "term or device" is "otherwise than as a trade or service mark," that the term or device is "descriptive of" the defendant's goods or services and that the defendant is using the term or device "fairly and in good faith only to describe to users" those goods and services. 15 U.S.C. § 1115(b)(4). The district court found that the term "Thirst Aid" was not descriptive of Gatorade but rather was "suggestive." The court also found that even if "Thirst Aid" were descriptive, Quaker could not prevail on the fair use defense because it had used the term as a trademark in its ads. Quaker challenges both of these conclusions. * * *

A.   Descriptiveness of "Thirst Aid"

* * *

The district court described the difference between a suggestive mark and a descriptive one as follows: " '[I]f the mark imparts information directly it is descriptive. If it stands for an idea which requires some operation of the imagination to connect it with the goods, it is suggestive.' " Mem. Op. at 5, 1985 WL 1567 (May 29, 1985) (quoting Union Carbide Corp. v. Ever–Ready Inc., 531 F.2d 366, 379 (7th Cir.1976)). Purporting to apply this test, the district court found that "Thirst Aid" was suggestive rather than descriptive because it "requires imagination to create the impression of an isotonic beverage." Id. at 9. Quaker argues that the district court erred in reaching this conclusion because it misapplied the relevant legal standard.

We agree. The district court thought that in order to be descriptive the term "Thirst Aid" had to bring to mind the product in question— "create the impression of an isotonic beverage." Our cases, however, hold that "it is not necessary that a descriptive term depict the [product] itself, but only that the term refer to a *characteristic* of the [product]." Forum Corp., 903 F.2d at 444 (emphasis in original); see also Heileman, 873 F.2d at 992 (" 'A merely descriptive term specifically describes a *characteristic* or *ingredient* of the goods.' ") (emphasis added) (quoting Miller Brewing Co. v. G. Heileman Brewing Co., 561 F.2d 75, 79 (7th Cir.1977)). Under that test, the district court's conclusion that "Thirst Aid" is not, as a matter of law, descriptive of Gatorade cannot stand. In support of its opposition to STW's motion for summary judgment, Quaker presented evidence that consumers understand the words "Thirst Aid" to convey the message that Gatorade helps quench thirst— that is, that "Thirst Aid" describes a characteristic of Gatorade. In *Heileman*, we observed that "the true test [of descriptiveness] is one of *consumer perception*—how is [the term] perceived by the average prospective consumer?" 873 F.2d at 994 (emphasis added). Quaker's evidence certainly created a material issue of fact as to whether the average consumer perceives "Thirst Aid" as describing a characteristic of Gatorade—its ability to quench thirst.

The fact that "Thirst Aid" is not a common phrase does not preclude a finding that it is descriptive rather than suggestive. That a term is an "unfamiliar" one which "requires a hearer to think about its meaning does not show that it is suggestive." Forum Corp., 903 F.2d at 443. Nor does the fact that "Thirst Aid" is a play on words which makes one think of "first aid" as well as "thirst quenching" render it suggestive as a matter of law. See, e.g., 20th Century Wear, Inc. v. Sanmark–Stardust, Inc., 747 F.2d 81 (2d Cir.1984) (trademark "Cozy Warm—Energy Savers" for women's pajamas found to be descriptive despite reference to energy crisis); Pizzazz Pizza & Restaurant v. Taco Bell Corp., 642 F.Supp. 88 (N.D.Ohio 1986) (word "pizzazz" to describe pizza found to be descriptive); Pullan v. Fulbright, 287 Ark. 21, 695 S.W.2d 830 (1985) (phrase "shear pleasure" as name for hair salon found to be descriptive). We have stated that "the imagination required to link a suggestive term with the corresponding product 'refers to the mental process required to connect a name that is incongruous or figurative with the product (e.g., "Roach Motel" with an insect trap or "TIDE" with soap)....' " * * * We conclude that the district court erred in finding "Thirst Aid" suggestive as a matter of law.

B.   Use of "Thirst Aid" as a Trademark

The district court also found that, even if "Thirst Aid" were descriptive, Quaker could not prevail on its fair use defense because it used the term as a trademark. A word or phrase functions as a trademark when it is "used by a source of [a product] to identify itself to the public as the source of its [product] and to create in the public consciousness an awareness of the uniqueness of the source and of its [products]." M.B.H. Enterprises, Inc. v. WOKY, Inc., 633 F.2d 50, 54 (7th Cir.1980). The court observed that " 'Gatorade' clearly identifies the product as being from a particular source." The court concluded, however, that "[w]hen defendant uses 'Thirst Aid,' ... it too identifies the product as being from a particular source." The court noted that "Thirst Aid" is "the most prominent feature of some of defendant's advertising. Each of the ads includes the statement 'Gatorade is THIRST AID.' " The court therefore found that "[t]he way in which the defendant uses the words Thirst Aid creates an impression that the slogan is uniquely associated with Gatorade." * * *

Nor is a defendant's use of a term in conjunction with its own trademark per se a use "other than as a trademark." See, e.g., Lindy Pen Co. v. Bic Pen Corp., 725 F.2d 1240, 1248 (9th Cir.1984) (defendant's use of descriptive word "Auditors" on its pen was a trademark use even though the word appeared in conjunction with defendant's brand name on pens, packaging and promotional materials); Beer Nuts, Inc. v. Clover Club Foods Co., 711 F.2d 934, 938 (10th Cir.1983) (no fair use where defendant used "Brew Nuts" as a "secondary trademark" along with its own brand name on packaging). * * * The evidence of

Quaker's advertisements supports the district court's conclusion that Quaker used "Thirst Aid" as a trademark. Quaker's ads do not simply use the words "Thirst Aid" in a sentence describing Gatorade, but as an "attention-getting symbol." 1 McCarthy, supra § 11:17, at 476. In many of the ads, the words "Thirst Aid" appear more prominently and in larger type than does the word "Gatorade." Id. at 476 n. 7 (collecting cases). Further, given the rhyming quality of "Gatorade" and "Thirst Aid," the association between the two terms created by Quaker's ads is likely to be very strong, so that "Thirst Aid" appears as part of a memorable slogan that is uniquely associated with Quaker's product. * * * The district court did not err in concluding that Quaker used "Thirst Aid" as a trademark.

III.

Because trademark rights derive from the use of a mark in commerce and not from mere registration of the mark, the owner of a mark will lose his exclusive rights if he fails actually to use it. 15 U.S.C. § 1127. A mark is deemed to be thus "abandoned" when "its use has been discontinued with intent not to resume such use." Id. Two years of nonuse create a prima facie case of abandonment, which may be rebutted by "evidence explaining the nonuse or demonstrating the lack of an intent not to resume use." Roulo v. Russ Berrie & Co., 886 F.2d 931, 938 (7th Cir.1989). Quaker argues that the district court erred in finding that STW or its predecessors had not abandoned through nonuse the THIRST–AID mark for a beverage sold at retail. Alternatively, Quaker contends that Karp abandoned the THIRST–AID marks through its 1984 assignment of those marks to STW.

A. Nonuse

1. Middleby Abandoned the Mark

Quaker contends that STW has no registration rights covering the use of THIRST–AID on a beverage because the trademark THIRST–AID "First Aid for Your Thirst," the only mark registered for use on "beverages" as opposed to "beverage syrups," has not been used since 1949. We reject this argument for two reasons. First, the fact that STW and its predecessors have not used the entire slogan THIRST–AID "First Aid for Your Thirst" since 1949 does not necessarily mean that the registration has been abandoned. "[M]inor changes in a mark which do not change the basic, overall commercial impression created on buyers will not constitute any abandonment." 1 McCarthy, supra § 17:10, at 787. So long as the owner continues use of the "key element" of the registered mark, courts generally will not find abandonment. Id. Further, "the dropping of a non-essential word from a mark" has been held not to constitute abandonment. Id.; see, e.g., Puritan Sportswear Corp. v. Shure, 307 F.Supp. 377 (W.D.Pa.1969) (change from PURITAN SPORTSWEAR, THE CHOICE OF ALL AMERICANS to PURITAN not abandonment). Certainly, the key element of what Quaker calls the "beverage slogan registration" is the term THIRST–AID. In fact, the trademark registration for the slogan explicitly states that no claim of ownership is made as to the words "First Aid for Your Thirst" apart from the mark as it appears in the registration. * * * Second, even if we were to find that Middleby had abandoned the mark THIRST–AID "First Aid for Your Thirst," we would not conclude that STW therefore had no registration rights covering the use of THIRST–AID on beverages. We do not see the wide gulf between a trademark for beverage syrups and a trademark for beverages, on which Quaker relies. * * *

2. *Intent Not to Resume Use*

Alternatively, Quaker argues that even if Middleby had not abandoned the "beverage slogan registration," any right to use the THIRST–AID marks for a beverage was abandoned by Karp, which acquired the marks in December 1981. Quaker relies on the testimony of Karp's vice president and chief financial officer that Karp did not intend to use THIRST–AID for a beverage when it acquired the marks. This argument misses the point. While it is true that Karp did not use THIRST–AID for a beverage, it is also the case that, approximately 1½ years after acquiring the marks, Karp hired a consultant for the specific purpose of attempting to license THIRST–AID for use on a beverage. "[T]he owner of the trademark need only produce evidence to rebut the presumption [of abandonment] while the ultimate burden of persuasion rests on the defendant." Roulo, 886 F.2d at 938. The district court found that STW's efforts to license THIRST–AID for use on a soft drink during this period were sufficient evidence of intent to resume use to rebut a prima facie case of abandonment. Although the district court erred in focusing on the intent of STW rather than of Karp during the three years that Karp owned the marks, the court at least implicitly found that Karp's efforts to license THIRST–AID to Shasta and Tropicana were sufficient to establish Karp's intent to resume use. Karp did not abandon the right to use THIRST–AID for a beverage.

B. *Abandonment Through Assignment in Gross*

As the district court noted, "[t]he transfer of a trademark apart from the good will of the business which it represents is an invalid 'naked' or 'in gross' assignment," which passes no rights to the assignee. Sands, Taylor & Wood, 18 U.S.P.Q.2d at 1464. Quaker contends that the court erred in concluding that the September 1984 assignment of the THIRST–AID trademarks from Karp to STW was not an invalid assignment in gross. Quaker recognizes that transfer of a mark need not be accompanied by the transfer of any physical or tangible assets in order to be valid. "All that is necessary is the transfer of the goodwill to which the mark pertains." Visa, U.S.A., Inc. v. Birmingham Trust Nat'l Bank, 696 F.2d 1371, 1377 (Fed.Cir.1982). According to Quaker, however, any good will associated with the THIRST–AID mark existed only in the institutional market, and therefore could not support the transfer of the right to use THIRST–AID on a beverage at retail. We disagree with both Quaker's characterization of the facts and its conclusion.

Quaker's argument that any good will associated with THIRST–AID could exist only in the institutional market simply ignores STW's evidence, accepted by the district court, that from 1921 until at least 1976 the THIRST–AID mark was used in retail, in-store advertising and promotional materials provided to soda fountains that sold beverages made from THIRST–AID syrups. As the district court found, this use of the mark, as well as its use on the Pet product, created good will associated with THIRST–AID at the retail level. This good will, built up over more than fifty years, could not dissipate during the three and one-half years between the Pet test-market and the assignment of the marks from Karp to STW. Defiance Button Machine Co. v. C & C Metal Prods. Corp., 759 F.2d 1053, 1061 (2d Cir.1985).

The 1981 agreement between STW and Karp, the validity of which Quaker does not challenge, assigned to Karp "all of [STW's] right, title, ownership and interest in and to the Trademarks *and all goodwill appurtenant thereto*." (Emphasis added.) The agreement then licensed back to STW "the exclusive right and license" to use the marks in connection with certain defined "Products" in the retail trade only. None of the defined products were beverages or beverage-related. Thus, as the district court correctly found, the 1981 agreement conferred on Karp "extremely broad rights of ownership," Sands, Taylor & Wood, 18 U.S.P.Q.2d at 1467–68, including the exclusive right to use THIRST–AID on beverages and the good will associated with that use. Id. at 1466.

Under the 1984 agreement between STW and Karp, Karp assigned to STW "all right, title and interest in and to the trademark and the said registrations including the continued exclusive right to use the trademark THIRST–AID in the retail trade field only, together with any goodwill of the business symbolized by the trademark...." Karp retained the "exclusive right and license in perpetuity to use the trademark THIRST–AID in connection with the manufacture, marketing, sale and other commercialization of the Products in institutional trade only and not in retail trade." Thus, the 1984 agreement transferred back to STW the exclusive right to use THIRST–AID on a beverage, together with the good will associated with that use. As we have already noted, that good will existed at the retail as well as at the institutional level, and it was not dissipated during the three and one-half years between the Pet test-market and the 1984 assignment. The district court did not err in finding that the assignment from Karp to STW was valid.

IV.

A. *Reverse Confusion*

The "keystone" of trademark infringement is "likelihood of confusion" as to source, affiliation, connection or sponsorship of goods or services among the relevant class of customers and potential customers. 2 McCarthy, supra § 23:1, at 42–43, 46–47. Usually, the confusion alleged is "forward confusion," which occurs "when customers mistakenly think that the junior user's goods or services are from the same source as or are connected with the senior user's goods or services." Id. at 48. * * * In this case, however, STW relies not on classic forward confusion but on the doctrine of "reverse confusion." Reverse confusion occurs when a large junior user saturates the market with a trademark similar or identical to that of a smaller, senior user. In such a case, the junior user does not seek to profit from the good will associated with the senior user's mark. Nonetheless, the senior user is injured because

> [t]he public comes to assume that the senior user's products are really the junior user's or that the former has become somehow connected to the latter. The result is that the senior user loses the value of the trademark—its product identity, corporate identity, control over its goodwill and reputation, and ability to move into new markets.

Ameritech, Inc. v. American Information Technologies Corp., 811 F.2d 960, 964 (6th Cir.1987); see also Banff, Ltd., 841 F.2d at 490–91; Big O Tire Dealers, 561 F.2d at 1372. Although this court has not previously recognized reverse confusion as the basis for a claim under the Lanham Act, several other circuits have endorsed the concept.[12] We agree with those courts that "the objectives of the Lanham Act—to protect an owner's interest in its trademark by keeping the public free from confusion as to the source of goods and ensuring fair competition—are as important in a case of reverse confusion as in typical trademark infringement." Banff, Ltd., 841 F.2d at 490. We therefore hold that reverse confusion is a redressable injury under the Lanham Act. [The court upheld the district court's finding of a likelihood of confusion. Its discussion of remedies is reproduced infra.] * * *

Notes

1. For further discussion of trademark fair use, see Rock & Roll Hall of Fame & Museum, Inc. v. Gentile Productions, 134 F.3d 749 (6th Cir.1998) (noting that use of "Rock & Roll Hall of Fame" on poster may be fair use); Cosmetically Sealed Industries, Inc. v. Chesebrough–Pond's USA Co., 125 F.3d 28 (2d Cir.1997) (use of "sealed with a kiss" on promotional display for lipstick); Smith v. Ames Department Stores, Inc., 988 F.Supp. 827 (D.N.J. 1997) (addressing fair use defense of term "big guy" for clothing), aff'd, 172 F.3d 860 (3d Cir.1998); Sports Authority, Inc. v. Abercrombie & Fitch, Inc., 965 F.Supp. 925 (E.D.Mich.1997) (discussing fair use claim involving term "authority"); 1 J. Thomas McCarthy, Trademarks and Unfair Competition § 11.17 (3d ed. 1995); Restatement (Third) of Unfair Competition § 28 (1995) ("In an action for infringement of a trademark, trade name, collective mark, or certification mark, it is a defense that the term used by the actor is descriptive or geographically descriptive of the actor's goods, services, or business, or is the personal name of the actor or a person connected with the

---

12. See, e.g., Banff, Ltd. v. Federated Dep't Stores, Inc., 841 F.2d 486 (2d Cir. 1988); Fuddruckers, Inc. v. Doc's B.R. Others, Inc., 826 F.2d 837 (9th Cir.1987); Ameritech, Inc. v. American Information Technologies Corp., 811 F.2d 960 (6th Cir.1987); Capital Films Corp. v. Charles Fries Productions, Inc., 628 F.2d 387 (5th Cir.1980); Big O Tire Dealers, Inc. v. Goodyear Tire & Rubber Co., 561 F.2d 1365 (10th Cir.1977).

actor, and the actor has used the term fairly and in good faith solely to describe the actor's goods, services, or business or to indicate a connection with the named person.'').

2. *Abandonment*. A trademark owner can unwittingly act in a manner that results in abandonment of its trademark. Abandonment can also occur by deliberate action, as when the owner announces that it is ceasing use of a mark. See General Cigar Co. v. G.D.M. Inc., 988 F.Supp. 647 (S.D.N.Y.1997) (rejecting various defense arguments that plaintiff had abandoned ''Cohiba'' trademark for cigars); Freed v. Farag, 994 F.Supp. 887 (N.D.Ohio 1997) (mark had been abandoned in light of 44 years of non-use). A third way in which abandonment may occur is ''naked licensing,'' when a trademark licensor fails to control adequately the actions of its licensees. Uncontrolled licensing of this type is considered a fraud on the public, which deprives the mark of its source-indicating significance. See generally TMT North America, Inc. v. Magic Touch GmbH, 124 F.3d 876, 885–86 (7th Cir.1997) (rejecting claim of abandonment through naked licensing and discussing inconsistent statements of standard for this form of abandonment); Exxon Corp. v. Oxxford Clothes, Inc., 109 F.3d 1070 (5th Cir.1997) (rejecting claim that Exxon abandoned its trademark through naked licensing), *cert. denied*, 522 U.S. 915, 118 S.Ct. 299, 139 L.Ed.2d 231 (1997); Kentucky Fried Chicken Corp. v. Diversified Packaging Corp., 549 F.2d 368, 387 (5th Cir.1977); Bear U.S.A., Inc. v. Kim, 993 F.Supp. 894 (S.D.N.Y.1998) (fact issues presented regarding whether trademark licensor had abandoned mark by failing to exercise requisite degree of control). Finally, an improper assignment of trademark rights can result in abandonment. An effective assignment occurs when a valid mark is continuously used and is assigned to another party in combination with any goodwill associated with the mark. See generally Money Store v. Harriscorp. Finance, Inc., 689 F.2d 666, 675 (7th Cir.1982). For further discussion of trademark abandonment, see 2 J. Thomas McCarthy, Trademarks and Unfair Competition §§ 17.01 to 17.10 (3d ed. 1995); Restatement (Third) of Unfair Competition § 30 (1995). The Restatement defines abandonment as follows:

> (1) In an action for infringement of a trademark, trade name, collective mark, or certification mark, it is a defense that the designation was abandoned by the party asserting rights in the designation prior to the commencement of use by the actor.

> (2) A trademark, trade name, collective mark, or certification mark is abandoned if:

>> (a) the party asserting rights in the designation has ceased to use the designation with an intent not to resume use; or

>> (b) the designation has lost its significance as a trademark, trade name, collective mark, or certification mark as a result of a cessation of use or other acts or omissions by the party asserting rights in the designation.

3. The Los Angeles Dodgers brought suit against the Brooklyn Dodger Sports Bar & Restaurant challenging use of the words ''The Brooklyn Dodger'' as the name of a restaurant in Brooklyn, New York. The restaurant opened in 1988. Given that the ''Brooklyn Dodgers'' baseball team left Brooklyn in 1958, are the Los Angeles Dodgers entitled to prevent the use of

the restaurant name? Would it matter that the Los Angeles Dodgers licensed t-shirts and advertisements bearing the "Brooklyn Dodgers" name and logo beginning in 1981? See Major League Baseball Properties, Inc. v. Sed Non Olet Denarius, Ltd., 817 F.Supp. 1103 (S.D.N.Y.1993), vacated pursuant to settlement, 859 F.Supp. 80 (S.D.N.Y.1994). See also Indianapolis Colts, Inc. v. Metropolitan Baltimore Football Club Ltd. Partnership, 34 F.3d 410 (7th Cir.1994) (regarding Baltimore Colts); see also Abdul–Jabbar v. General Motors Corp., 85 F.3d 407 (9th Cir.1996) (Lew Alcindor). Recent abandonment cases include *Vais Arms, Inc. v. Vais*, 383 F.3d 287 (5th Cir. 2004) (finding abandonment); *Ritchie v. Williams*, 395 F.3d 283 (6th Cir. 2005) (finding abandonment based on naked licensing by promoter in dispute with "Kid Rock"); *Doeblers' Pennsylvania Hybrids, Inc. v. Doebler*, 442 F.3d 812 (3d Cir. 2006) (fact issues regarding assignment and abandonment).

4. *Generic Marks*. Another affirmative defense in trademark cases is the argument that a particular mark has become generic. See Chapter 1, *supra*.

5. *Consent*. Consent is a defense to trademark infringement. See Restatement (Third) of Unfair Competition § 29 (1995) ("In an action for infringement of a trademark, trade name, collective mark, or certification mark, it is a defense that the actor's use is within the scope of the owner's consent as manifested by an agreement between the parties or by other conduct from which the owner's consent can reasonably be inferred.").

6. *Equitable Defenses*. A number of equitable defenses are also available. Laches is the most common defense, requiring the defendant to prove that (1) the plaintiff had knowledge of the defendant's unauthorized use of a confusingly similar mark; (2) the plaintiff unreasonably delayed taking action; and (3) the defendant was unduly prejudiced as a result of the plaintiff's delay. See Brittingham v. Jenkins, 914 F.2d 447, 456 (4th Cir. 1990); STX, Inc. v. Bauer USA, Inc., 43 U.S.P.Q.2d 1492 (N.D.Cal.1997); Guardian Life Insurance Co. v. American Guardian Life Assurance Co., 943 F.Supp. 509 (E.D.Pa.1996); Warner–Lambert Co. v. Schick U.S.A., Inc., 935 F.Supp. 130 (D.Conn.1996); Restatement (Third) of Unfair Competition § 31 (1995) ("If the owner of a trademark, trade name, collective mark, or certification mark unreasonably delays in commencing an action for infringement or otherwise asserting the owner's rights and thereby causes prejudice to another who may be subject to liability to the owner under the rules stated in this Chapter, the owner may be barred in whole or in part from the relief that would otherwise be available...."). Other recent laches/acquiescence cases include *Tillamook Country Smoker, Inc. v. Tillamook County Creamery Assoc.*, 465 F.3d 1102 (9th Cir. 2006) (laches applied in "beef" between cheese and meat producers, in light of 25 years of knowledge of junior user) and *What–A–Burger of Va., Inc. v. Whataburger, Inc. of Corpus Christi, Tex.*, 357 F.3d 441 (4th Cir. 2004) (rejecting defenses).

Estoppel occurs when the plaintiff knowingly acquiesced or encouraged the defendant's use of a mark. See TMT North America, Inc. v. Magic Touch GmbH, 124 F.3d 876, 885–86 (7th Cir.1997) (discussing acquiescence defense); Guardian Life Insurance Co. v. American Guardian Life Assurance Co., 943 F.Supp. 509 (E.D.Pa.1996) (same). A waiver occurs when the plaintiff knowingly relinquishes an existing legal right. Finally, the plaintiff may be barred by the doctrine of "unclean hands." See Havana Club Holding, S.A. v. Galleon, S.A., 49 U.S.P.Q.2d 1296 (S.D.N.Y.1998), *aff'd on other grounds*, 203 F.3d 116 (2d Cir.2000); Restatement (Third) of Unfair Competition § 32 (1995) ("If a designation used as a trademark, trade name, collective mark, or certification mark is deceptive, or if its use is otherwise in violation of public policy, or if the owner of the designation has engaged in other substantial misconduct directly related to the owner's assertion of rights in the trademark, trade name, collective mark, or certification mark, the owner may be barred in whole or in part from the relief that would otherwise be available...."). See generally Albert Robin & Howard Barnaby, Equitable Defenses in Opposition Proceedings: Where Did They Go? 36 IDEA: J.L. & Tech. 55 (1995); Comment, Incontestable Trademark Rights and Equitable Defenses in Infringement Litigation, 66 Minn. L. Rev. 1067 (1982); 4 J. Thomas McCarthy, Trademarks and Unfair Competition §§ 31.01 to 31.40 (3d ed. 1995) (surveying numerous affirmative defenses).

7. For an additional case on reverse confusion, *see Freedom Card, Inc. v. JPMorgan Chase & Co.*, 432 F.3d 463 (3d Cir. 2005) (addressing claimed reverse confusion between Chase Freedom and Freedom Cards).

8. For a case presenting a unique trademark defense based on the Cuban embargo statute, *see Empresa Cubana del Tobacco v. Culbro Corp.*, 399 F.3d 462 (2d Cir. 2005) (addressing claim involving "Cohiba" mark).

KP PERMANENT MAKE–UP, INC. v. LASTING IMPRESSION I, INC., ET AL.

United States Supreme Court, 2004.
543 U.S. 111, 125 S.Ct. 542, 160 L.Ed.2d 440.

JUSTICE SOUTER delivered the opinion of the Court.

The question here is whether a party raising the statutory affirmative defense of fair use to a claim of trademark infringement, 15 U.S.C. § 1115(b)(4), has a burden to negate any likelihood that the practice complained of will confuse consumers about the origin of the goods or services affected. We hold it does not.

I

Each party to this case sells permanent makeup, a mixture of pigment and liquid for injection under the skin to camouflage injuries and modify nature's dispensations, and each has used some version of the term "micro color" (as one word or two, singular or plural) in marketing and selling its product. Petitioner KP Permanent Make–Up, Inc., claims to have used the single-word version since 1990 or 1991 on advertising flyers and since 1991 on pigment bottles. Respondents Lasting Impression I, Inc., and its licensee, MCN International, Inc. (Lasting, for simplicity), deny that KP began using the term that early, but we accept KP's allegation as true for present purposes; the District and Appeals Courts took it to be so, and the disputed facts do not matter to our resolution of the issue. In 1992, Lasting applied to the United States Patent and Trademark Office (PTO) under 15 U.S.C. § 1051 for registration of a trademark consisting of the words "Micro Colors" in white letters separated by a green bar within a black square. The PTO registered the mark to Lasting in 1993, and in 1999 the registration became incontestable. § 1065.

It was also in 1999 that KP produced a 10–page advertising brochure using "microcolor" in a large, stylized typeface, provoking Lasting to demand that KP stop using the term. Instead, KP sued Lasting in the Central District of California, seeking, on more than one ground, a declaratory judgment that its language infringed no such exclusive right as Lasting claimed. Lasting counterclaimed, alleging, among other things, that KP had infringed Lasting's "Micro Colors" trademark.

KP sought summary judgment on the infringement counterclaim, based on the statutory affirmative defense of fair use, 15 U.S.C. § 1115(b)(4). After finding that Lasting had conceded that KP used the term only to describe its goods and not as a mark, the District Court held that KP was acting fairly and in good faith because undisputed facts showed that KP had employed the term "microcolor" continuously from a time before Lasting adopted the two-word, plural variant as a mark. Without inquiring whether the practice was likely to cause confusion, the court concluded that KP had made out its affirmative defense under § 1115(b)(4) and entered summary judgment for KP on Lasting's infringement claim.

On appeal, 328 F.3d 1061 (2003), the Court of Appeals for the Ninth Circuit thought it was error for the District Court to have addressed the fair use defense without delving into the matter of possible confusion on the part of consumers about the origin of KP's goods. The reviewing court took the view that no use could be recognized as fair where any consumer confusion was probable, and although the court did not pointedly address the burden of proof, it appears to have placed it on KP to show absence of consumer confusion. Id., at 1072 ("Therefore, KP can only benefit from the fair use defense if there is no likelihood of confusion between KP's use of the term 'micro color' and Lasting's mark"). Since it found there were disputed material facts relevant under the Circuit's eight-factor test for assessing the likelihood of confusion, it reversed the summary judgment and remanded the case.

We granted KP's petition for certiorari to address a disagreement among the Courts of Appeals on the significance of likely confusion for a fair use defense to a trademark infringement claim, and the obligation of a party defending on that ground to show that its use is unlikely to cause consumer confusion. *Compare* 328 F.3d, at 1072 (likelihood of confusion bars the fair use defense); PACCAR Inc. v. TeleScan Technologies, L.L.C., 319 F.3d 243, 256 (C.A.6 2003) ("[A] finding of a likelihood of confusion forecloses a fair use defense"); and Zatarains, Inc. v. Oak Grove Smokehouse, 698 F.2d 786, 796 (C.A.5 1983) (alleged infringers were free to use words contained in a trademark "in their ordinary, descriptive sense, so long as such use [did] not tend to confuse customers as to the source of the goods") *with* Cosmetically Sealed Industries, Inc. v. Chesebrough–Pond's USA Co., 125 F.3d 28, 30–31 (C.A.2 1997) (the fair use defense may succeed even if there is likelihood of confusion); Shakespeare Co. v. Silstar Corp. of Am., 110 F.3d 234, 243 (C.A.4 1997) ("[A] determination of likely confusion [does not] preclud[e] considering the fairness of use"); Sunmark, Inc. v. Ocean Spray Cranberries, Inc., 64 F.3d 1055, 1059 (C.A.7 1995) (finding that likelihood of confusion did not preclude the fair use defense). We now vacate the judgment of the Court of Appeals.

II

A

The Trademark Act of 1946, known for its principal proponent as the Lanham Act, 60 Stat. 427, as amended, 15 U.S.C. § 1051 et seq., provides the user of a trade or service mark with the opportunity to register it with the PTO, §§ 1051, 1053. If the registrant then satisfies further conditions including continuous use for five consecutive years, "the right ... to use such registered mark in commerce" to designate the origin of the goods specified in the registration "shall be incontestable" outside certain listed exceptions. § 1065.

The holder of a registered mark (incontestable or not) has a civil action against anyone employing an imitation of it in commerce when "such use is likely to cause confusion, or to cause mistake, or to deceive." § 1114(1). Although an incontestable registration is "conclusive evidence ... of the registrant's exclusive right to use the ... mark in commerce," § 1115(b), the plaintiff's success is still subject to "proof of infringement as defined in section 1114," § 1115(b). And that, as just noted, requires a showing that the defendant's actual practice is likely to produce confusion in the minds of consumers about the origin of the goods or services in question. See Two Pesos, Inc. v. Taco Cabana, Inc., 505 U.S. 763, 780, 112 S.Ct. 2753, 120 L.Ed.2d 615 (1992) (STEVENS, J., concurring); Lone Star Steakhouse and Saloon, Inc. v. Alpha of Virginia, Inc., 43 F.3d 922, 935 (C.A.4 1995); Restatement (Third) of Unfair Competition § 21, Comment a (1995). This plaintiff's burden has to be kept in mind when reading the relevant portion of the further provision for an affirmative defense of fair use, available to a party whose "use of the name, term, or device charged to be an infringement is a use, otherwise than as a mark, ... of a term or device which is descriptive of and used fairly and in good faith only to describe the goods or services of such party, or their geographic origin...." § 1115(b)(4).

Two points are evident. Section 1115(b) places a burden of proving likelihood of confusion (that is, infringement) on the party charging infringement even when relying on an incontestable registration. And Congress said nothing about likelihood of confusion in setting out the elements of the fair use defense in § 1115(b)(4).

Starting from these textual fixed points, it takes a long stretch to claim that a defense of fair use entails any burden to negate confusion. It is just not plausible that Congress would have used the descriptive phrase "likely to cause confusion, or to cause mistake, or to deceive" in

§ 1114 to describe the requirement that a markholder show likelihood of consumer confusion, but would have relied on the phrase "used fairly" in § 1115(b)(4) in a fit of terse drafting meant to place a defendant under a burden to negate confusion. " '[W]here Congress includes particular language in one section of a statute but omits it in another section of the same Act, it is generally presumed that Congress acts intentionally and purposely in the disparate inclusion or exclusion.' " Russello v. United States, 464 U.S. 16, 23, 104 S.Ct. 296, 78 L.Ed.2d 17 (1983) (quoting United States v. Wong Kim Bo, 472 F.2d 720, 722 (C.A.5 1972)) (alteration in original).

Nor do we find much force in Lasting's suggestion that "used fairly" in § 1115(b)(4) is an oblique incorporation of a likelihood-of-confusion test developed in the common law of unfair competition. Lasting is certainly correct that some unfair competition cases would stress that use of a term by another in conducting its trade went too far in sowing confusion, and would either enjoin the use or order the defendant to include a disclaimer. See, e.g., Baglin v. Cusenier Co., 221 U.S. 580, 602, 31 S.Ct. 669, 55 L.Ed. 863 (1911) ("[W]e are unable to escape the conclusion that such use, in the manner shown, was to serve the purpose of simulation ..."); Herring–Hall–Marvin Safe Co. v. Hall's Safe Co., 208 U.S. 554, 559, 28 S.Ct. 350, 52 L.Ed. 616 (1908) ("[T]he rights of the two parties have been reconciled by allowing the use, provided that an explanation is attached"). But the common law of unfair competition also tolerated some degree of confusion from a descriptive use of words contained in another person's trademark. See, e.g., William R. Warner & Co. v. Eli Lilly & Co., 265 U.S. 526, 528, 44 S.Ct. 615, 68 L.Ed. 1161 (1924) (as to plaintiff's trademark claim, "[t]he use of a similar name by another to truthfully describe his own product does not constitute a legal or moral wrong, even if its effect be to cause the public to mistake the origin or ownership of the product"); Canal Co. v. Clark, 13 Wall. 311, 327, 20 L.Ed. 581 (1872) ("Purchasers may be mistaken, but they are not deceived by false representations, and equity will not enjoin against telling the truth"); see also 3 L. Altman, Callmann on Unfair Competition, Trademarks and Monopolies § 18:2, pp. 18–8 to 18–9, n. 1 (4th ed.2004) (citing cases). While these cases are consistent with taking account of the likelihood of consumer confusion as one consideration in deciding whether a use is fair, see Part II–B, infra, they do not stand for the proposition that an assessment of confusion alone may be dispositive. Certainly one cannot get out of them any defense burden to negate it entirely.

Finally, a look at the typical course of litigation in an infringement action points up the incoherence of placing a burden to show nonconfusion on a defendant. If a plaintiff succeeds in making out a prima facie case of trademark infringement, including the element of likelihood of consumer confusion, the defendant may offer rebutting evidence to undercut the force of the plaintiff's evidence on this (or any) element, or raise an affirmative defense to bar relief even if the prima facie case is sound, or do both. But it would make no sense to give the defendant a defense of showing affirmatively that the plaintiff cannot succeed in proving some element (like confusion); all the defendant needs to do is to leave the factfinder unpersuaded that the plaintiff has carried its own burden on that point. A defendant has no need of a court's true belief when agnosticism will do. Put another way, it is only when a plaintiff has shown likely confusion by a preponderance of the evidence that a defendant could have any need of an affirmative defense, but under Lasting's theory the defense would be foreclosed in such a case. "[I]t defies logic to argue that a defense may not be asserted in the only situation where it even becomes relevant." Shakespeare Co. v. Silstar Corp., 110 F.3d, at 243. Nor would it make sense to provide an affirmative defense of no confusion plus good faith, when merely rebutting the plaintiff's case on confusion would entitle the defendant to judgment, good faith or not.

Lasting tries to extenuate the anomaly of this conception of the affirmative defense by arguing that the oddity reflects the "vestigial" character of the fair use defense as a historical matter. Tr. of Oral Arg. 39. Lasting argues that, because it was only in 1988 that Congress added the express provision that an incontestable markholder's right to exclude is "subject to proof of infringement," Trademark Law Revision Act of 1988, § 128(b)(1), 102 Stat. 3944, there was no requirement prior to 1988 that a markholder prove likelihood of confusion. Before 1988, the argument goes, it was sensible to get at the issue of likely confusion by requiring a defendant to prove its absence when defending on the ground of fair use. When the 1988 Act saddled the markholder with the obligation to prove confusion likely, § 1115(b), the revision simply failed to relieve the fair use defendant of the suddenly strange burden to prove absence of the very confusion that a plaintiff had a new burden to show in the first place.

But the explanation does not work. It is not merely that it would be highly suspect in leaving the claimed element of § 1115(b)(4) redundant and pointless. Hibbs v. Winn, 542 U.S. 88, 101, 124 S.Ct. 2276, 2286, 159 L.Ed.2d 172 (2004) (noting "rule against superfluities" in statutory construction). The main problem of the argument is its false premise: Lasting's assumption that holders of incontestable marks had no need to prove likelihood of confusion prior to 1988 is wrong. See, e.g., Beer Nuts, Inc. v. Clover Club Foods Co., 805 F.2d 920, 924–925 (C.A.10 1986) (requiring proof of likelihood of confusion in action by holder of incontestable mark); United States Jaycees v. Philadelphia Jaycees, 639 F.2d 134, 137, n. 3 (C.A.3 1981) ("[I]ncontestability [does not] mak[e] unnecessary a showing of likelihood of confusion ..."); 5 J. McCarthy, Trademarks and Unfair Competition § 32:154, p. 32–247 (4th ed.2004) ("Before the 1988 Trademark Law Revision Act, the majority of courts held that while incontestability grants a conclusive presumption of the 'exclusive right to use' the registered mark, this did not relieve the registrant of proving likelihood of confusion").

B

Since the burden of proving likelihood of confusion rests with the plaintiff, and the fair use defendant has no free-standing need to show confusion unlikely, it follows (contrary to the Court of Appeals's view) that some possibility of consumer confusion must be compatible with fair use, and so it is. The common law's tolerance of a certain degree of confusion on the part of consumers followed from the very fact that in cases like this one an originally descriptive term was selected to be used as a mark, not to mention the undesirability of allowing anyone to obtain a complete monopoly on use of a descriptive term simply by grabbing it first. Canal Co. v. Clark, supra, at 323–324, 327. The Lanham Act adopts a similar leniency, there being no indication that the statute was meant to deprive commercial speakers of the ordinary utility of descriptive words. "If any confusion results, that is a risk the plaintiff accepted when it decided to identify its product with a mark that uses a well known descriptive phrase." Cosmetically Sealed Industries, Inc. v. Chesebrough–Pond's USA Co., 125 F.3d, at 30. See also Park 'N Fly, Inc. v. Dollar Park and Fly, Inc., 469 U.S. 189, 201, 105 S.Ct. 658, 83 L.Ed.2d 582 (1985) (noting safeguards in Lanham Act to prevent commercial monopolization of language); Car–Freshner Corp. v. S.C. Johnson & Son, Inc., 70 F.3d 267, 269 (C.A.2 1995) (noting importance of "protect[ing] the right of society at large to use words or images in their primary descriptive sense"). This right to describe is the reason that descriptive terms qualify for registration as trademarks only after taking on secondary meaning as "distinctive of the applicant's goods," 15 U.S.C. § 1052(f), with the registrant getting an exclusive right not in the original, descriptive sense, but only in the secondary one associated with the markholder's goods, 2 McCarthy, supra, § 11:45 ("The only aspect of the mark which is given legal protection is that penumbra or fringe of secondary meaning which surrounds the old descriptive word").

While we thus recognize that mere risk of confusion will not rule out fair use, we think it would be improvident to go further in this case, for deciding anything more would take us beyond the Ninth Circuit's consideration of the subject. It suffices to realize that our holding that fair use can occur along with some degree of confusion does not foreclose the relevance of the extent of any likely consumer confusion in assessing whether a defendant's use is objectively fair. Two Courts of Appeals have found it relevant to consider such scope, and commentators and amici here have urged us to say that the degree of likely consumer confusion bears not only on the fairness of using a term, but even on the further question whether an originally descriptive term has become so identified as a mark that a defendant's use of it cannot realistically be called descriptive. See Shakespeare Co. v. Silstar Corp., supra, at 243 ("[T]o the degree that confusion is likely, a use is less likely to be found fair ..." (emphasis omitted)); Sunmark, Inc. v. Ocean Spray Cranberries, Inc., 64 F.3d, at 1059; Restatement (Third) of Unfair Competition, § 28.

Since we do not rule out the pertinence of the degree of consumer confusion under the fair use defense, we likewise do not pass upon the

position of the United States, as amicus, that the "used fairly" requirement in § 1115(b)(4) demands only that the descriptive term describe
the goods accurately. Accuracy of course has to be a consideration in
assessing fair use, but the proceedings in this case so far raise no
occasion to evaluate some other concerns that courts might pick as
relevant, quite apart from attention to confusion. The Restatement
raises possibilities like commercial justification and the strength of the
plaintiff's mark. Restatement § 28. As to them, it is enough to say here
that the door is not closed.

III

In sum, a plaintiff claiming infringement of an incontestable mark
must show likelihood of consumer confusion as part of the prima facie
case, 15 U.S.C. § 1115(b), while the defendant has no independent
burden to negate the likelihood of any confusion in raising the affirmative defense that a term is used descriptively, not as a mark, fairly, and
in good faith, § 1115(b)(4).

Because we read the Court of Appeals as requiring KP to shoulder a
burden on the issue of confusion, we vacate the judgment and remand
the case for further proceedings consistent with this opinion.[6]

It is so ordered.

Note

How should this case be resolved on remand? *See KP Permanent Make-
Up, Inc. v. Lasting Impression I, Inc.*, 408 F.3d 596 (9th Cir. 2005) (remanding to address fact issues regarding consumer confusion and fair use).

B. COMPARATIVE ADVERTISING

R.G. SMITH v. CHANEL, INC.

United States Court of Appeals, Ninth Circuit, 1968.
402 F.2d 562.

BROWNING, CIRCUIT JUDGE:

Appellant R. G. Smith, doing business as Ta'Ron, Inc., advertised a
fragrance called "Second Chance" as a duplicate of appellees' "Chanel
No. 5," at a fraction of the latter's price. Appellees were granted a
preliminary injunction prohibiting any reference to Chanel No. 5 in the
promotion or sale of appellants' product. This appeal followed.

---

6. The record indicates that on remand
the courts should direct their attention in
particular to certain factual issues bearing
on the fair use defense, properly applied.
The District Court said that Lasting's motion for summary adjudication conceded
that KP used "microcolor" descriptively
and not as a mark. We think it is arguable
that Lasting made those concessions only as
to KP's use of "microcolor" on bottles and
flyers in the early 1990s, not as to the
stylized version of "microcolor" that appeared in KP's 1999 brochure. We also note
that the fair use analysis of KP's employment of the stylized version of "microcolor"
on its brochure may differ from that of its
use of the term on the bottles and flyers.

The action rests upon a single advertisement published in "Specialty Salesmen," a trade journal directed to wholesale purchasers. The advertisement offered "The Ta'Ron Line of Perfumes" for sale. It gave the seller's address as "Ta'Ron Inc., 26 Harbor Cove, Mill Valley, Calif." It stated that the Ta'Ron perfumes "duplicate 100% Perfect the exact scent of the world's finest and most expensive perfumes and colognes at prices that will zoom sales to volumes you have never before experienced." It repeated the claim of exact duplication in a variety of forms.

The advertisement suggested that a "Blindfold Test" be used "on skeptical prospects," challenging them to detect any difference between a well known fragrance and the Ta'Ron "duplicate." One suggested challenge was, "We dare you to try to detect any difference between Chanel #5 (25.00) and Ta'Ron's 2nd Chance $7.00."

In an order blank printed as part of the advertisement each Ta'Ron fragrance was listed with the name of the well known fragrance which it purportedly duplicated immediately beneath. Below "Second Chance" appeared " *(Chanel #5)." The asterisk referred to a statement at the bottom of the form reading "Registered Trade Name of Original Fragrance House."

Appellees conceded below and concede here that appellants "have the right to copy, if they can, the unpatented formula of appellees' product."[3] Moreover, for the purposes of these proceedings, appellees assume that "the products manufactured and advertised by (appellants) are in fact equivalents of those products manufactured by appellees." Finally, appellees disclaim any contention that the packaging or labeling of appellants' "Second Chance" is misleading or confusing.[4]

I

The principal question presented on this record is whether one who has copied an unpatented product sold under a trademark may use the trademark in his advertising to identify the product he has copied. We hold that he may, and that such advertising may not be enjoined under either the Lanham Act, 15 U.S.C. 1125(a) (1964), or the common law of unfair competition, so long as it does not contain misrepresentations or create a reasonable likelihood that purchasers will be confused as to the source, identity, or sponsorship of the advertiser's product. * * *

In *Saxlehner* the copied product was a "bitter water" drawn from certain privately owned natural springs. The plaintiff sold the natural water under the name "Hunyadi Janos," a valid trademark. The defendant was enjoined from using plaintiff's trademark to designate defen-

---

3. Sears, Roebuck & Co. v. Stiffel Co., 376 U.S. 225, 231–233, 84 S.Ct. 784, 11 L.Ed.2d 661 (1964); Compco Corp. v. Day-Brite Lighting, Inc., 376 U.S. 234, 237–238, 84 S.Ct. 779, 11 L.Ed.2d 669 (1964).

4. Appellants' product was packaged differently from appellees', and the only words appearing on the outside of appellants' packages were "Second Chance Perfume by Ta'Ron." The same words appeared on the front of appellants' bottles; the words "Ta'Ron trademark by International Fragrances, Inc., of Dallas and New York" appeared on the back.

dant's "artificial" water, but was permitted to use it to identify plaintiff's natural water as the product which defendant was copying.

JUSTICE HOLMES wrote:

We see no reason for disturbing the finding of the courts below that there was no unfair competition and no fraud. The real intent of the plaintiff's bill, it seems to us, is to extend the monopoly of such trademark or tradename as she may have to a monopoly of her type of bitter water, by preventing manufacturers from telling the public in a way that will be understood, what they are copying and trying to sell. But the plaintiff has no patent for the water, and the defendants have a right to reproduce it as nearly as they can. They have a right to tell the public what they are doing, and to get whatever share they can in the popularity of the water by advertising that they are trying to make the same article, and think that they succeed. If they do not convey, but, on the contrary, exclude, the notion that they are selling the plaintiff's goods, it is a strong proposition that when the article has a well-known name they have not the right to explain by that name what they imitate. By doing so, they are not trying to get the good will of the name, but the good will of the goods.

216 U.S. at 380–381, 30 S.Ct. at 298, 299.

In *Viavi Co. v. Vimedia Co.*, plaintiff sold unpatented proprietary medicinal preparations under the registered trademark "Viavi," and local sellers of defendant's medicinal preparations represented to prospective purchasers that Vimedia products "were the same or as good as Viavi" preparations. The court held, "in the absence of such a monopoly as a patent confers, any persons may reproduce the articles, if they can, and may sell them under the representation that they are the same article, if they exclude the notion that they are the plaintiff's goods." 245 F. at 292.

* * * The Lanham Act does not prohibit a commercial rival's truthfully denominating his goods a copy of a design in the public domain, though he uses the name of the designer to do so. Indeed it is difficult to see any other means that might be employed to inform the consuming public of the true origin of the design. 299 F.2d at 36.

* * *

We have found no holdings by federal or California appellate courts contrary to the rule of these three cases. Moreover, the principle for which they stand—that use of another's trademark to identify the trademark owner's product in comparative advertising is not prohibited by either statutory or common law, absent misrepresentation regarding the products or confusion as to their source or sponsorship—is also generally approved by secondary authorities.[11] * * *

---

11. See, e.g., Alexander, Honesty and Competition 50–51 (1967); Restatement of Torts 717, comment c, 727, comment a (1938); Livermore, On Uses of a Competi-

Preservation of the trademark as a means of identifying the trademark owner's products, implemented both by the Lanham Act and the common law, serves an important public purpose. It makes effective competition possible in a complex, impersonal marketplace by providing a means through which the consumer can identify products which please him and reward the producer with continued patronage. Without some such method of product identification, informed consumer choice, and hence meaningful competition in quality, could not exist.[14]

On the other hand, it has been suggested that protection of trademark values other than source identification would create serious anticompetitive consequences with little compensating public benefit. This is said to be true for the following reasons.

The object of much modern advertising is "to impregnate the atmosphere of the market with the drawing power of a congenial symbol." Mishawaka Rubber & Woolen Mfg. Co. v. S. S. Kresge Co., 316 U.S. 203, 205, 62 S.Ct. 1022, 1024, 86 L.Ed. 1381 (1942), rather than to communicate information as to quality or price. The primary value of the modern trademark lies in the "conditioned reflex developed in the buyer by imaginative or often purely monotonous selling of the mark itself." Derring, Trademarks on Noncompetitive Products, 36 Or.L.Rev. 1, 2 (1956). To the extent that advertising of this type succeeds, it is suggested, the trademark is endowed with sales appeal independent of the quality or price of the product to which it is attached; economically irrational elements are introduced into consumer choices; and the trademark owner is insulated from the normal pressures of price and quality competition. In consequence the competitive system fails to perform its function of allocating available resources efficiently.

Moreover, the economically irrelevant appeal of highly publicized trademarks is thought to constitute a barrier to the entry of new competition into the market. "The presence of irrational consumer allegiances may constitute an effective barrier to entry. Consumer allegiances built over the years with intensive advertising, trademarks, trade names, copyrights and so forth extend substantial protection to firms already in the market. In some markets this barrier to entry may be insuperable." Papandreou, The Economic Effects of Trademarks, 44

tor's Trademark, 20 Stan.L.Rev. 448, 451–52, 458 (1968); Gaughan, Advertisements Which Identify "Brand X," 35 Fordham L.Rev. 445, 446–47, 456–57 (1967); Symposium, "Honest" Truth or Unfair Competition, 53 Trademark Rep. 225, 233 (1963); cf. Stern & Hoffman, Public Injury and the Public Interest: Secondary Meaning in the Law of Unfair Competition, 110 U.Pa. L.Rev. 935, 950–51, 956, 960 (1962). But see 3 Callmann, Unfair Competition and Trademarks 84.2(b) (2d ed. 1950); Callmann, Trademark Infringement and Unfair Competition, 14 Law & Contemp. Prob. 185, 193 (1949).

14. See generally, Livermore, supra note 11 at 448; Developments in the Law—Competitive Torts, 77 Harv.L.Rev. 888, 890 (1964); Brown Advertising and the Public Interest, 57 Yale L.J. 1165, 1185–86 (1948). On the other hand, it has been argued that these public benefits are outweighed by the monopolistic consequences inherent in the protection of trademarks, and that consumer interests could be better protected by other means. E. Chamberlin, The Theory of Monopolistic Competition 59–62, 270–74 (7th ed. 1960), See also Brown, supra, at 1205–06.

Calif.L.Rev. 503, 508–09 (1956). High barriers to entry tend, in turn, to produce "high excess profits and monopolistic output restriction" and "probably * * * high and possibly excessive costs of sales promotion." J. Bain, Barriers to New Competition 203 (1955). * * *

Against these considerations, two principal arguments are made for protection of trademark values other than source identification.

The first of these, as stated in the findings of the district court, is that the creation of the other values inherent in the trademark require "the expenditure of great effort, skill and ability," and that the competitor should not be permitted "to take a free ride" on the trademark owner's "widespread goodwill and reputation."

A large expenditure of money does not in itself create legally protectable rights. Appellees are not entitled to monopolize the public's desire for the unpatented product, even though they themselves created that desire at great effort and expense. As we have noted, the most effective way (and in some cases the only practical way) in which others may compete in satisfying the demand for the product is to produce it and tell the public they have done so, and if they could be barred from this effort appellees would have found a way to acquire a practical monopoly in the unpatented product to which they are not legally entitled.

Disapproval of the copyist's opportunism may be an understandable first reaction, "but this initial response to the problem has been curbed in deference to the greater public good." American Safety Table Co. v. Schreiber, 269 F.2d at 272. By taking his "free ride," the copyist, albeit unintentionally, serves an important public interest by offering comparable goods at lower prices. On the other hand, the trademark owner, perhaps equally without design, sacrifices public to personal interests by seeking immunity from the rigors of competition.

Moreover, appellees' reputation is not directly at stake. Appellants' advertisement makes it clear that the product they offer is their own. If it proves to be inferior, they, not appellees, will bear the burden of consumer disapproval. Cf. Prestonettes, Inc. v. Coty, 264 U.S. 359, 369, 44 S.Ct. 350, 68 L.Ed. 731 (1924).[25]

The second major argument for extended trademark protection is that even in the absence of confusion as to source, use of the trademark of another "creates a serious threat to the uniqueness and distinctiveness" of the trademark, and "if continued would create a risk of making a generic or descriptive term of the words" of which the trademark is composed.

---

25. In addition, if appellants' specific claims of equivalence are false, appellees may have a remedy under 43(a) of the Lanham Act, 15 U.S.C. 1125(a) (1964), which provides a civil remedy to a person injured by "any false description or representation, including words or other symbols * * *." of goods in interstate commerce. A common-law remedy may also be available. See Restatement (Second) of Torts 712, comment b at 17 (Tent. Draft No. 8, 1963). For discussion of the possible common-law theories, see Developments in the Law, supra, at 892–907. * * *

The contention has little weight in the context of this case. Appellants do not use appellees' trademark as a generic term. They employ it only to describe appellees' product, not to identify their own. They do not label their product "Ta'Ron's Chanel No. 5," as they might if appellees' trademark had come to be the common name for the product to which it is applied. Appellants' use does not challenge the distinctiveness of appellees' trademark, or appellees' exclusive right to employ that trademark to indicate source or sponsorship. For reasons already discussed, we think appellees are entitled to no more. * * *

Reversed and remanded for further proceedings.

Note

Is there a danger of counterfeiting here? What if the Ta'Ron product does not have the same pleasing scent as Chanel? See generally Pebble Beach Co. v. Tour 18 I Limited, 155 F.3d 526 (5th Cir.1998) (golf course asserted nominative use defense); Calvin Klein Cosmetics Corp. v. Lenox Laboratories, Inc., 815 F.2d 500 (8th Cir.1987) ("Obsession" perfume).

C. USED OR RECONDITIONED GOODS

CHAMPION SPARK PLUG CO. v. SANDERS

Supreme Court of the United States, 1947.
331 U.S. 125, 67 S.Ct. 1136, 91 L.Ed. 1386.

Mr. Justice Douglas delivered the opinion of the Court.

Petitioner is a manufacturer of spark plugs which it sells under the trade mark "Champion." Respondents collect the used plugs, repair and recondition them, and resell them. Respondents retain the word "Champion" on the repaired or reconditioned plugs. The outside box or carton in which the plugs are packed has stamped on it the word "Champion," together with the letter and figure denoting the particular style or type. They also have printed on them "Perfect Process Spark Plugs Guaranteed Dependable" and "Perfect Process Renewed Spark Plugs." Each carton contains smaller boxes in which the plugs are individually packed. These inside boxes also carry legends indicating that the plug has been renewed.[1] But respondent company's business name or address is not printed on the cartons. It supplies customers with petitioner's charts containing recommendations for the use of Champion plugs. On each individual plug is stamped in small letters, blue on black, the word "Renewed," which at times is almost illegible.

Petitioner brought this suit in the District Court, charging infringement of its trade mark and unfair competition. The District Court found

---

1. "The process used in renewing this plug has been developed through 10 years continuous experience. This Spark Plug has been tested for firing under compression before packing." "This Spark Plug is guaranteed to be a selected used Spark Plug, thoroughly renewed and in perfect mechanical condition and is guaranteed to give satisfactory service for 10,000 miles."

that respondents had infringed the trade mark. It enjoined them from offering or selling any of petitioner's plugs which had been repaired or reconditioned unless (a) the trade mark and type and style marks were removed, (b) the plugs were repainted with a durable grey, brown, orange, or green paint, (c) the word "Repaired" was stamped into the plug in letters of such size and depth as to retain enough white paint to display distinctly each letter of the word, (d) the cartons in which the plugs were packed carried a legend indicating that they contained used spark plugs originally made by petitioner and repaired and made fit for use up to 10,000 miles by respondent company.[2] The District Court denied an accounting. See 56 F.Supp. 782, 61 F.Supp. 247.

The Circuit Court of Appeals * * * modified the decree in the following respects: (a) it eliminated the provision requiring the trade mark and type and style marks to be removed from the repaired or reconditioned plugs; (b) it substituted for the requirement that the word "Repaired" be stamped into the plug, etc., a provision that the word "Repaired" or "Used" be stamped and baked on the plug by an electrical hot press in a contrasting color so as to be clearly and distinctly visible, the plug having been completely covered by permanent aluminum paint or other paint or lacquer; and (c) it eliminated the provision specifying the precise legend to be printed on the cartons and substituted therefore a more general one.[3] * * *

There is no challenge here to the findings as to the misleading character of the merchandising methods employed by respondents, nor to the conclusion that they have not only infringed petitioner's trade mark but have also engaged in unfair competition. The controversy here relates to the adequacy of the relief granted, particularly the refusal of the Circuit Court of Appeals to require respondents to remove the word "Champion" from the repaired or reconditioned plugs which they resell.

We put to one side the case of a manufacturer or distributor who markets new or used spark plugs of one make under the trade mark of another. Equity then steps in to prohibit defendant's use of the mark which symbolizes plaintiff's good will and "stakes the reputation of the plaintiff upon the character of the goods." * * * We are dealing here with second-hand goods. The spark plugs, though used, are nevertheless Champion plugs and not those of another make. There is evidence to support what one would suspect, that a used spark plug which has been repaired or reconditioned does not measure up to the specifications of a

---

2. The prescribed legend read: "Used spark plug(s) originally made by Champion Spark Plug Company repaired and made fit for use up to 10,000 miles by Perfect Recondition Spark Plug Co., 1133 Bedford Avenue, Brooklyn, N.Y." The decree also provided: "the name and address of the defendants to be larger and more prominent than the legend itself, and the name of plaintiff may be in slightly larger type than the rest of the body of the legend."

3. "The decree shall permit the defendants to state on cartons and containers, selling and advertising material, business records, correspondence and other papers, when published, the original make and type numbers provided it is made clear that any plug referred to therein is used and reconditioned by the defendants, and that such material contains the name and address of defendants."

new one. But the same would be true of a second-hand Ford or Chevrolet car. And we would not suppose that one could be enjoined from selling a car whose valves had been reground and whose piston rings had been replaced unless he removed the name Ford or Chevrolet. Prestonettes, Inc. v. Coty, 264 U.S. 359, 44 S.Ct. 350, 68 L.Ed. 731, was a case where toilet powders had as one of their ingredients a powder covered by a trade mark and where perfumes which were trade marked were rebottled and sold in smaller bottles. The Court sustained a decree denying an injunction where the prescribed labels told the truth. Mr. Justice Holmes stated, "A trade-mark only gives the right to prohibit the use of it so far as to protect the owner's good will against the sale of another's product as his. * * * When the mark is used in a way that does not deceive the public we see no such sanctity in the word as to prevent its being used to tell the truth. It is not taboo." 264 U.S. at page 368, 44 S.Ct. at page 351, 68 L.Ed. 731.

Cases may be imagined where the reconditioning or repair would be so extensive or so basic that it would be a misnomer to call the article by its original name, even though the words "used" or "repaired" were added. Cf. Ingersoll v. Doyle, D.C., 247 F. 620. But no such practice is involved here. The repair or reconditioning of the plugs does not give them a new design. It is no more than a restoration, so far as possible, of their original condition. * * * And there is evidence that the reconditioned plugs are inferior so far as heat range and other qualities are concerned. But inferiority is expected in most second-hand articles. Indeed, they generally cost the customer less. That is the case here. Inferiority is immaterial so long as the article is clearly and distinctively sold as repaired or reconditioned rather than as new. The result is, of course, that the second-hand dealer gets some advantage from the trade mark. But under the rule of Prestonettes, Inc. v. Coty, supra, that is wholly permissible so long as the manufacturer is not identified with the inferior qualities of the product resulting from wear and tear or the reconditioning by the dealer. Full disclosure gives the manufacturer all the protection to which he is entitled.

The decree as shaped by the Circuit Court of Appeals is fashioned to serve the requirements of full disclosure. * * * We are mindful of the fact that this case, unlike Prestonettes, Inc. v. Coty, supra, involves unfair competition as well as trade mark infringement; and that where unfair competition is established, any doubts as to the adequacy of the relief are generally resolved against the transgressor. Warner & Co. v. Lilly & Co., 265 U.S. 526, 532, 44 S.Ct. 615, 618, 68 L.Ed. 1161. But there was here no showing of fraud or palming off. * * * We cannot say that the conduct of respondents in this case, or the nature of the article involved and the characteristics of the merchandising methods used to sell it, called for more stringent controls than the Circuit Court of Appeals provided. * * *

Affirmed.

Notes

1. If a seller represents that goods are new when in fact they are used or reconditioned, a competitor or other injured party may be able to bring suit under section 43(a) of the Lanham Act, discussed *infra*, as well as state statutory or common law. See also Eastman Kodak Co. v. Photaz Imports Ltd., 853 F.Supp. 667 (W.D.N.Y.1993) (misleading repackaging of film), *aff'd*, 28 F.3d 102 (2d Cir.1994); Intel Corp. v. Terabyte International, Inc., 6 F.3d 614 (9th Cir.1993) (remarking and modification of slower computer chips to make them function as faster chips found to infringe Intel trademark); Neles–Jamesbury, Inc. v. Valve Dynamics, Inc., 974 F.Supp. 964 (S.D.Tex. 1997) (fact issues presented regarding reconditioning and resale of valves).

2. Can an independent dealer advertise that it sells new or used trademarked goods by making use of the trademark? *Scott Fetzer Co. v. House of Vacuums Inc.*, 381 F.3d 477 (5th Cir. 2004).

3. To what extent can golf balls be refurbished before the original trademark ought to be removed? *Nitro Leisure Products, L.L.C. v. Acushnet Co.*, 341 F.3d 1356 (Fed. Cir. 2003).

D. IMMUNITY

In College Savings Bank v. Florida Prepaid Postsecondary Education Expense Bd., 527 U.S. 666, 119 S.Ct. 2219, 144 L.Ed.2d 605 (1999), College Savings (a provider of college funding programs) filed an action alleging that Florida Prepaid, a state college savings plan, violated § 43(a) of the Lanham Act. College Savings claimed that the defendant made misstatements about its own tuition savings plans in its marketing brochures and annual reports. Florida Prepaid sought to dismiss the action on the ground that it was barred by Eleventh Amendment sovereign immunity. The Court first rejected the argument that the Lanham Act claim protected the plaintiff's cognizable property interests. In doing so, the Court distinguished between different types of interests protected under the Lanham Act.

> The Lanham Act may well contain provisions that protect constitutionally cognizable property interests—notably, its provisions dealing with infringement of trademarks, which are the "property" of the owner because he can exclude others from using them. See, e.g., K Mart Corp. v. Cartier, Inc., 485 U.S. 176, 185–86, 108 S.Ct. 950, 99 L.Ed.2d 151 (1988) ("Trademark law, like contract law, confers private rights, which are themselves rights of exclusion. It grants the trademark owner a bundle of such rights"). The Lanham Act's false-advertising provisions, however, bear no relationship to any right to exclude; and Florida Prepaid's alleged misrepresentations concerning its own products intruded upon no interest over which petitioner had exclusive dominion.

Id. at 2224–25. The Court then found that because "the sovereign immunity of the State of Florida was neither validly abrogated by the

Trademark Remedy Clarification Act, nor voluntarily waived by the State's activities in interstate commerce, we hold that the federal courts are without jurisdiction to entertain this suit against an arm of the State of Florida.'' Id. at 2233.

What ramifications will this decision have for other types of Lanham Act claims that might be asserted against states or state entities?

Chapter 6

SECONDARY LIABILITY
AND REMEDIES

INWOOD LABORATORIES, INC. v.
IVES LABORATORIES, INC.
Supreme Court of the United States, 1982.
456 U.S. 844, 102 S.Ct. 2182, 72 L.Ed.2d 606.

JUSTICE O'CONNOR delivered the opinion of the Court.

This action requires us to consider the circumstances under which a manufacturer of a generic drug, designed to duplicate the appearance of a similar drug marketed by a competitor under a registered trademark, can be held vicariously liable for infringement of that trademark by pharmacists who dispense the generic drug.

I

In 1955, respondent Ives Laboratories, Inc. (Ives), received a patent on the drug cyclandelate, a vasodilator used in long-term therapy for peripheral and cerebral vascular diseases. Until its patent expired in 1972, Ives retained the exclusive right to make and sell the drug, which it did under the registered trademark CYCLOSPASMOL. Ives marketed the drug, a white powder, to wholesalers, retail pharmacists, and hospitals in colored gelatin capsules. Ives arbitrarily selected a blue capsule, imprinted with "Ives 4124," for its 200 mg dosage and a combination blue-red capsule, imprinted with "Ives 4148," for its 400 mg dosage.

After Ives' patent expired, several generic drug manufacturers, including petitioners Premo Pharmaceutical Laboratories, Inc., Inwood Laboratories, Inc., and MD Pharmaceutical Co., Inc. (collectively the generic manufacturers), began marketing cyclandelate. They intentionally copied the appearance of the CYCLOSPASMOL capsules, selling cyclandelate in 200 mg and 400 mg capsules in colors identical to those selected by Ives.[3]

---

3. Initially, the generic manufacturers did not place any identifying mark on their capsules. After Ives initiated this action, Premo imprinted "Premo" on its capsules and Inwood imprinted "Inwood 258."

230

The marketing methods used by Ives reflect normal industry practice. Because cyclandelate can be obtained only by prescription, Ives does not direct its advertising to the ultimate consumer. Instead, Ives' representatives pay personal visits to physicians, to whom they distribute product literature and "starter samples." Ives initially directed these efforts toward convincing physicians that CYCLOSPASMOL is superior to other vasodilators. Now that its patent has expired and generic manufacturers have entered the market, Ives concentrates on convincing physicians to indicate on prescriptions that a generic drug cannot be substituted for CYCLOSPASMOL.[4]

The generic manufacturers also follow a normal industry practice by promoting their products primarily by distribution of catalogs to wholesalers, hospitals, and retail pharmacies, rather than by contacting physicians directly. The catalogs truthfully describe generic cyclandelate as "equivalent" or "comparable" to CYCLOSPASMOL.[5] In addition, some of the catalogs include price comparisons of the generic drug and CYCLOSPASMOL and some refer to the color of the generic capsules. The generic products reach wholesalers, hospitals, and pharmacists in bulk containers which correctly indicate the manufacturer of the product contained therein.

A pharmacist, regardless of whether he is dispensing CYCLOSPASMOL or a generic drug, removes the capsules from the container in which he receives them and dispenses them to the consumer in the pharmacist's own bottle with his own label attached. Hence, the final consumer sees no identifying marks other than those on the capsules themselves.

II

* * *

Ives' claim under § 32, 15 U.S.C. § 1114, derived from its allegation that some pharmacists had dispensed generic drugs mislabeled as CY-

---

4. Since the early 1970's, most States have enacted laws allowing pharmacists to substitute generic drugs for brand name drugs under certain conditions. The New York statutes involved in this action are typical of these generic substitution laws. New York law requires that prescription forms contain two lines, one of which a prescribing physician must sign. If the physician signs over the words "substitution permissible," substitution is mandatory if a substitute generic drug is on an approved list, N.Y. Educ. Law § 6816–a (McKinney Supp.1981–1982); N.Y.Pub. Health Law § 206.1(o) (McKinney Supp.1981–1982), and permissible if another generic drug is available. Unless the physician directs otherwise, the pharmacist must indicate the name of the generic manufacturer and the strength of the drug dispensed on the label. In addition, the prescription form must specifically state that, unless the physician signs above the line "dispense as written," the prescription will be filled generically. § 6810(6)(a). If a pharmacist mislabels a drug or improperly substitutes, he is guilty of a misdemeanor and subject to a fine, §§ 6811, 6815, 6816, and to revocation of his license. § 6808.

5. Ives conceded that CYCLOSPASMOL and the petitioners' generic equivalents are bioequivalent and have the same bioavailability. See 455 F.Supp. 939, 942 (E.D.N.Y. 1978), and 488 F.Supp. 394, 396 (E.D.N.Y. 1980). * * *

CLOSPASMOL.[8] Ives contended that the generic manufacturers' use of look-alike capsules and of catalog entries comparing prices and revealing the colors of the generic capsules induced pharmacists illegally to substitute a generic drug for CYCLOSPASMOL and to mislabel the substitute drug CYCLOSPASMOL. Although Ives did not allege that the petitioners themselves applied the Ives trademark to the drug products they produced and distributed, it did allege that the petitioners contributed to the infringing activities of pharmacists who mislabeled generic cyclandelate.

Ives' claim under § 43(a), 15 U.S.C. § 1125(a), alleged that the petitioners falsely designated the origin of their products by copying the capsule colors used by Ives and by promoting the generic products as equivalent to CYCLOSPASMOL. In support of its claim, Ives argued that the colors of its capsules were not functional and that they had developed a secondary meaning for the consumers.

Contending that pharmacists would continue to mislabel generic drugs as CYCLOSPASMOL so long as imitative products were available, Ives asked that the court enjoin the petitioners from marketing cyclandelate capsules in the same colors and form as Ives uses for CYCLOSPASMOL. * * *

III

A

As the lower courts correctly discerned, liability for trademark infringement can extend beyond those who actually mislabel goods with the mark of another. Even if a manufacturer does not directly control others in the chain of distribution, it can be held responsible for their infringing activities under certain circumstances. Thus, if a manufacturer or distributor intentionally induces another to infringe a trademark, or if it continues to supply its product to one whom it knows or has reason to know is engaging in trademark infringement, the manufacturer or distributor is contributorially responsible for any harm done as a result of the deceit. See William R. Warner & Co. v. Eli Lilly & Co., supra; Coca–Cola Co. v. Snow Crest Beverages, Inc., supra.

It is undisputed that those pharmacists who mislabeled generic drugs with Ives' registered trademark violated § 32. However, whether these petitioners were liable for the pharmacists' infringing acts depended upon whether, in fact, the petitioners intentionally induced the pharmacists to mislabel generic drugs or, in fact, continued to supply cyclandelate to pharmacists whom the petitioners knew were mislabeling

---

8. The claim involved two types of infringements. The first was "direct" infringement, in which druggists allegedly filled CYCLOSPASMOL prescriptions marked "dispense as written" with a generic drug and mislabeled the product as CYCLOSPASMOL. The second, "intermediate" infringement, occurred when pharma-cists, although authorized by the prescriptions to substitute, allegedly mislabeled a generic drug as CYCLOSPASMOL. The one retail pharmacy originally named as a defendant consented to entry of a decree enjoining it from repeating such actions. 455 F.Supp., at 942.

generic drugs. The District Court concluded that Ives made neither of those factual showings. * * *

IV

In reversing the District Court's judgment, the Court of Appeals initially held that the trial court failed to give sufficient weight to the evidence Ives offered to show a "pattern of illegal substitution and mislabeling in New York...."[16] 638 F.2d, at 543. * * * Because the trial court's findings concerning the significance of the instances of mislabeling were not clearly erroneous, they should not have been disturbed.

Next, after completing its own review of the evidence, the Court of Appeals concluded that the evidence was "clearly sufficient to establish a § 32 violation." Ibid. In reaching its conclusion, the Court of Appeals was influenced by several factors. First, it thought the petitioners reasonably could have anticipated misconduct by a substantial number of the pharmacists who were provided imitative, lower priced products which, if substituted for the higher priced brand name without passing on savings to consumers, could provide an economic advantage to the pharmacists. Ibid.[17] Second, it disagreed with the trial court's finding that the mislabeling which did occur reflected confusion about state law requirements. Id., at 544. Third, it concluded that illegal substitution and mislabeling in New York are neither de minimis nor inadvertent. Ibid. Finally, the Court of Appeals indicated it was further influenced by the fact that the petitioners did not offer "any persuasive evidence of a legitimate reason unrelated to CYCLOSPASMOL" for producing an imitative product. Ibid.[20] * * *

16. As the opinions from the lower courts reveal, more than one inference can be drawn from the evidence presented. Prior to trial, test shoppers hired by Ives gave CYCLOSPASMOL prescriptions on which the "substitution permissible" line was signed to 83 New York pharmacists. Forty-eight of the pharmacists dispensed CYCLOSPASMOL; the rest dispensed a generic drug. Ten of the thirty-five pharmacists who dispensed a generic drug included the word CYCLOSPASMOL on the label, although 5 of those 10 also included some form of the word "generic." Nine of the ten told the consumer of the substitution. Only 1 of the 10 charged the brand name price for the generic drug. 488 F.Supp., at 397. The District Court concluded that that evidence did not justify the inference that the petitioners' catalogs invite pharmacists to mislabel. Ibid. The Court of Appeals, emphasizing that 10 of the 35 druggists who dispensed a generic drug mislabeled it as CYCLOSPASMOL, found a pattern of substitution and mislabeling. 638 F.2d, at 543. The dissenting judge on the appellate panel, emphasizing that only 1 of 83 pharmacists attempted an illegal substitution and

reaped a profit made possible by the color imitation, concluded the facts supported the District Court's finding that mislabeling resulted from confusion about the substitution laws rather than from profit considerations. Id., at 546. On the basis of the record before us, the inferences drawn by the District Court are not, as a matter of law, unreasonable.

17. The Court of Appeals cited no evidence to support its conclusion, which apparently rests upon the assumption that a pharmacist who has been provided an imitative generic drug will be unable to resist the temptation to profit from illegal activity. We find no support in the record for such a far-reaching conclusion. Moreover, the assumption is inconsistent with the District Court's finding that only a "few instances," rather than a substantial number, of mislabelings occurred. 488 F.Supp., at 397.

20. The Court of Appeals reached that conclusion despite the District Court's express finding that, for purposes of § 43(a), the capsule colors were functional. See supra, at 2187–2188. As the dissent below

V

The Court of Appeals erred in setting aside findings of fact that were not clearly erroneous. Accordingly, the judgment of the Court of Appeals that the petitioners violated § 32 of the Lanham Act is reversed. * * *

Notes

1.   What is the statutory basis for contributory infringement liability under the Lanham Act? In the absence of a statutory provision providing for secondary liability, such as that found in the Patent Act, see *infra*, should the courts expand liability beyond what Congress has expressly provided?

2.   For further discussion of contributory infringement and other forms of secondary liability, see 2 J. Thomas McCarthy, Trademarks and Unfair Competition §§ 25.02–25.21 (3d ed. 1995); Restatement (Third) of Unfair Competition §§ 26–27 (1995).

HARD ROCK CAFE LICENSING CORP.
v. CONCESSION SERVICES, INC.

United States Court of Appeals, Seventh Circuit, 1992.
955 F.2d 1143.

CUDAHY, CIRCUIT JUDGE.

The Hard Rock Cafe Licensing Corporation (Hard Rock) owns trademarks on several clothing items, including t-shirts and sweatshirts and apparently attempts to exploit its trademark monopoly to the full. In the summer of 1989, Hard Rock sent out specially trained private investigators to look for counterfeit Hard Rock Cafe merchandise. The investigators found Iqbal Parvez selling counterfeit Hard Rock t-shirts from stands in the Tri–State Swap–O–Rama and the Melrose Park Swap–O–Rama, flea markets owned and operated by Concession Services Incorporated (CSI). The investigators also discovered that Harry's Sweat Shop (Harry's) was selling similar items. Hard Rock brought suit against Parvez, CSI, Harry's and others not relevant to this appeal under the Lanham Trademark Act, 15 U.S.C. § 1051 et seq. (1988). Most of the defendants settled, including Parvez, who paid Hard Rock some $30,000. CSI and Harry's went to trial. * * *

All of the parties who participated in the trial appealed. CSI believes that it is not liable and that, in any event, entry of the injunction was inappropriate. Hard Rock wants attorney's fees from both defendants. Harry's appealed from the finding of liability and the entry of the injunction as well, but filed its appeal one day too late; its appeal has therefore been dismissed. Finding errors of law and a fatal ambiguity in

noted, the Court of Appeals' majority either disregarded the District Court's finding of functionality, see 638 F.2d, at 545, n. 1 (Mulligan, J., dissenting), or implicitly rejected that finding as not "persuasive." See id., at 547. While the precise basis for the Court of Appeals' ruling on this issue is unclear, it is clear that the Court of Appeals erred. * * *

the findings of fact, we vacate the judgment against CSI, vacate the denial of attorney's fees and remand for further proceedings.

I.

* * *

A. *The Parties and Their Practices*

1. *Concession Services, Inc.*

* * *

CSI generates revenue from a flea market in four ways. First, it rents space to vendors for flat fees that vary by the day of the week and the location of the space. Second, CSI charges a reservation and storage fee to those vendors who want to reserve the same space on a month-to-month basis. Third, CSI charges shoppers a nominal 75 cents admission charge. Fourth, CSI runs concession stands inside the market. To promote its business, CSI advertises the markets, announcing "BAR-GAINS" to be had, but does not advertise the presence of any individual vendors or any particular goods.

Supervision of the flea markets is minimal. CSI posts a sign at the Tri–State prohibiting vendors from selling "illegal goods." It also has "Rules For Sellers" which prohibit the sale of food or beverages, alcohol, weapons, fireworks, live animals, drugs and drug paraphernalia and subversive or un-American literature. Other than these limitations, vendors can, and do, sell almost any conceivable item. Two off-duty police officers provide security and crowd control (an arrangement that does not apply to the other markets). These officers also have some duty to ensure that the vendors obey the Sellers' Rules. The manager of the Tri–State, Albert Barelli, walks around the flea market about five times a day, looking for problems and violations of the rules. No one looks over the vendors' wares before they enter the market and set up their stalls, and any examination after that is cursory. Moreover, Barelli does not keep records of the names and addresses of the vendors. The only penalty for violating the Seller's Rules is expulsion from the market.

James Pierski, the vice president in charge of CSI's flea markets, testified that CSI has a policy of cooperating with any trademark owner that notifies CSI of possible infringing activity. But there is no evidence that this policy has ever been carried into effect. * * *

2. *Harry's Sweat Shop*

Harry's is a small store in Darien, Illinois, owned and operated by Harry Spatero. The store sells athletic shoes, t-shirts, jackets with the names of professional sports teams and the like. Spatero testified that the store contains over 20,000 different items. When buying t-shirts, Harry's is somewhat indiscriminate. The store buys seconds, overruns and closeouts from a variety of sources. Harry's buys most of its t-shirts from Supply Brokers of Pennsylvania, a firm which specializes in buying up stocks from stores going out of business. Spatero testified that Supply

Brokers sends him largely unidentified boxes of shirts which he may choose to return after looking them over. But Spatero testified that Harry's also bought shirts from people who came around in unmarked vans, offering shirts at a discount. The store kept no records of the sources of its inventory.

3. Hard Rock Licensing Corp.

Hard Rock owns the rights to a variety of Hard Rock trademarks. The corporation grants licenses to use its trademarks to the limited partnerships that own and operate the various Hard Rock Cafe restaurants. These restaurants are the only authorized distributors of Hard Rock Cafe merchandise, but apparently this practice of exclusivity is neither publicized nor widely known. The shirts themselves are produced by Winterland Productions, which prints logos on blank, first quality t-shirts that it buys from Hanes, Fruit-of-the-Loom and Anvil. According to the manager of the Chicago Hard Rock Cafe, Scott Floersheimer, Winterland has an agreement with Hard Rock to retain all defective Hard Rock shirts. Thus, if Winterland performs as agreed, all legitimate Hard Rock shirts sold to the public are well-made and cleanly printed.

The Chicago Hard Rock Cafe has done very well from its business. Since 1986, it has sold over 500,000 t-shirts at an average gross profit of $10.12 per shirt.

B. The Investigation

* * * The investigators visited both the Melrose Park and the Tri–State Swap–O–Ramas and observed Iqbal Parvez (or his employees) offering more than a hundred Hard Rock t-shirts for sale. Cynthia Myers, the chief investigator on the project, testified that these shirts were obviously counterfeit. The shirts were poor quality stock, with cut labels and were being sold for $3 apiece (a legitimate Hard Rock shirt, we are told, goes for over $14). Harry's had four Hard Rock shirts for sale, sitting on a discount table for $3.99 each. The district court found that these too were of obviously low quality, with cut labels and cracked and worn designs. Nonetheless, both Parvez and Harry's were selling t-shirts made by approved manufacturers. Parvez was selling Hanes t-shirts, and Harry's was selling Fruit-of-the-Loom.

At no point before filing suit did Hard Rock warn Harry's or CSI (or Parvez, whose supplier Hard Rock was trying to track down) that the shirts were counterfeits.

C. The District Court Proceedings

* * * After a bench trial, the district court entered permanent injunctions against both defendants and ordered Harry's to pay treble damages based on Hard Rock's lost profits on four t-shirts (in sum, $120). The court denied Hard Rock's request for attorney's fees.

The court's reasoning is crucial to the resolution of this appeal. Accordingly, we think it appropriate to quote from it at some length. The court concluded that both defendants were "guilty of willful blindness that counterfeit goods were being sold on [their] premises." Another sentence follows, however, which somewhat dilutes the impact of the preceding finding: "Neither defendant took reasonable steps to detect or prevent the sale of Hard Rock Cafe counterfeit T-shirts on its premise [sic]." This suggests mere negligence.

Willful blindness, the court said, "is a sufficient basis for a finding of violation of the Lanham Act. Louis Vuitton S.A. v. Lee, 875 F.2d 584, 590 (7th Cir.1989)." As to CSI's argument that it did not actually sell the offending goods, the court observed that CSI is not "merely a landlord; it also advertises and promotes the activity on its premises, sells admission tickets to buyers and supervises the premises. Under these circumstances it must also take reasonable precautions against the sale of counterfeit products."

II.

* * *

A. *Secondary Liability*

The most interesting issue in this case is CSI's liability for Parvez's sales. Hard Rock argues that CSI has incurred both contributory and vicarious liability for the counterfeits, and we take the theories of liability in that order.

It is well established that "if a manufacturer or distributor intentionally induces another to infringe a trademark, or if it continues to supply its product to one whom it knows or has reason to know is engaging in trademark infringement, the manufacturer or distributor is contributorially responsible for any harm done as a result of the deceit." Id. at 854, 102 S.Ct. at 2188 (footnote omitted). Despite this apparently definitive statement, it is not clear how the doctrine applies to people who do not actually manufacture or distribute the good that is ultimately palmed off as made by someone else. A temporary help service, for example, might not be liable if it furnished Parvez the workers he employed to erect his stand, even if the help service knew that Parvez would sell counterfeit goods. Thus we must ask whether the operator of a flea market is more like the manufacturer of a mislabeled good or more like a temporary help service supplying the purveyor of goods. To answer questions of this sort, we have treated trademark infringement as a species of tort and have turned to the common law to guide our inquiry into the appropriate boundaries of liability. David Berg & Co. v. Gatto Int'l Trading Co., 884 F.2d 306, 311 (7th Cir.1989).

CSI characterizes its relationship with Parvez as that of landlord and tenant. Hard Rock calls CSI a licensor, not a landlord. Either way, the Restatement of Torts tells us that CSI is responsible for the torts of those it permits on its premises "knowing or having reason to know that the other is acting or will act tortiously...." Restatement (Second) of Torts § 877(c) & cmt. d (1979). The common law, then, imposes the same duty on landlords and licensors that the Supreme Court has imposed on manufacturers and distributors. In the absence of any suggestion that a trademark violation should not be treated as a common law tort, we believe that the *Inwood Labs.* test for contributory liability applies. CSI may be liable for trademark violations by Parvez if it knew or had reason to know of them. But the factual findings must support that conclusion.

The district court found CSI to be willfully blind. Since we have held that willful blindness is equivalent to actual knowledge for purposes of the Lanham Act, Lee, 875 F.2d at 590, this finding should be enough to hold CSI liable (unless clearly erroneous). But we very much doubt that the district court defined willful blindness as it should have. To be willfully blind, a person must suspect wrongdoing and deliberately fail to investigate. Id. The district court, however, made little mention of CSI's state of mind and focused almost entirely on CSI's failure to take precautions against counterfeiting. In its conclusions of law, the court emphasized that CSI had a duty to take reasonable precautions. In short, it looks as if the district court found CSI to be negligent, not willfully blind.

This ambiguity in the court's findings would not matter if CSI could be liable for failing to take reasonable precautions. But CSI has no affirmative duty to take precautions against the sale of counterfeits. Although the "reason to know" part of the standard for contributory liability requires CSI (or its agents) to understand what a reasonably prudent person would understand, it does not impose any duty to seek out and prevent violations. Restatement (Second) of Torts § 12(1) & cmt. a (1965). We decline to extend the protection that Hard Rock finds in the common law to require CSI, and other landlords, to be more dutiful guardians of Hard Rock's commercial interests. Thus the district court's findings do not support the conclusion that CSI bears contributory liability for Parvez's transgressions.

Before moving on, we should emphasize that we have found only that the district court applied an incorrect standard. We have not found that the evidence cannot support the conclusion that CSI was in fact willfully blind. At the Tri–State, Barelli saw Parvez's shirts and had the opportunity to note that they had cut labels and were being sold cheap. Further, Barelli testified that he did not ask vendors whether their goods were counterfeit because they were sure to lie to him. One might infer from these facts that Barelli suspected that the shirts were counterfeits but chose not to investigate.

On the other hand, we do not wish to prejudge the matter. For it is undisputed that Hard Rock made no effort to broadcast the information that legitimate Hard Rock t-shirts could only be found in Hard Rock Cafes. Moreover, there does not seem to be any particular reason to believe that inexpensive t-shirts with cut labels are obviously counterfeit, no matter what logo they bear. Cf. Lee, 875 F.2d at 590 (genuine Vuitton and Gucci bags unlikely to display poor workmanship or purple vinyl linings). The circumstantial evidence that Barelli suspected the shirts to be counterfeit is, at best, thin. On remand, the district court may choose to develop this issue more fully.

Perhaps recognizing that the district court's opinion is unclear, Hard Rock urges us to find CSI vicariously liable for Parvez's sales, regardless of its knowledge of the counterfeiting. Indeed, if we accept this theory, CSI is liable for Parvez's sales even if it was not negligent. See, e.g., Shapiro, Bernstein & Co. v. H.L. Green Co., 316 F.2d 304, 309 (2d Cir.1963).

We have recognized that a joint tortfeasor may bear vicarious liability for trademark infringement by another. David Berg, 884 F.2d at 311. This theory of liability requires a finding that the defendant and the infringer have an apparent or actual partnership, have authority to bind one another in transactions with third parties or exercise joint ownership or control over the infringing product. Id. The case before us does not fit into the joint tortfeasor model, and Hard Rock does not argue that it does.

Instead, Hard Rock wants us to apply the more expansive doctrine of vicarious liability applicable to copyright violations. Under the test developed by the Second Circuit, a defendant is vicariously liable for copyright infringement if it has "the right and ability to supervise the infringing activity and also has a direct financial interest in such activities." Gershwin Publishing Corp. v. Columbia Artists Management, Inc., 443 F.2d 1159, 1162 (2d Cir.1971) (hereinafter CAMI). The purpose of the doctrine is to prevent an entity that profits from infringement from hiding behind undercapitalized "dummy" operations when the copyright owner eventually sues. Shapiro, Bernstein, 316 F.2d at 309.

The parties have argued vigorously about the application of this doctrine to the facts.[4] But we need not decide the question; for the Supreme Court tells us that secondary liability for trademark infringement should, in any event, be more narrowly drawn than secondary liability for copyright infringement. Sony Corp. of America v. Universal City Studios, Inc., 464 U.S. 417, 439 n. 19, 104 S.Ct. 774, 787 n. 19, 78 L.Ed.2d 574 (1984) (citing "fundamental differences" between copyright and trademark law). If Hard Rock referred us to some principle of common law that supported its analogy to copyright, we would be more understanding of its claims. But it has not. Further, there is no hint that CSI is playing at the sort of obfuscation that inspired the Second Circuit to develop its more expansive form of vicarious copyright liability. Hard Rock must look to Congress to provide the level of protection it demands of CSI here.

---

4. We are inclined to favor CSI's side of the dispute. CSI neither hired Parvez to entertain its customers, cf. Dreamland Ball Room, 36 F.2d at 355, nor did it take a percentage of his sales, cf. Shapiro, Bernstein, 316 F.2d at 306 (department store took 10%–12% of record department's gross receipts); CAMI, 443 F.2d at 1161 (management company took percentage of infring-er's performance fees). Further, whether CSI is a landlord or a licensor, CSI exercises no more control over its tenants than any landlord concerned with the safety and convenience of visitors and of its tenants as a group. Deutsch v. Arnold, 98 F.2d 686, 688 (2d Cir.1938) (ignorant landlord not liable for copyright infringement by tenant).

In sum, we find that CSI may bear contributory liability for Parvez's unlawful sales, but we see no evidence on the record that would support a finding that CSI is vicariously liable. Accordingly, because the district court's findings fail to establish that CSI knew or had reason to know that Parvez was selling counterfeits, we must vacate the judgment against CSI and remand for further proceedings. * * *

C. Attorney's Fees

Section 35 of the Lanham Act, 15 U.S.C. § 1117 (1988), provides that prevailing plaintiffs may be awarded attorney's fees in two circumstances. If a defendant has sold counterfeit goods by mistake or through negligence, attorney's fees may be awarded "in exceptional circumstances." § 1117(a). But if the violation "consists of intentionally using a mark or designation, knowing such mark or designation is a counterfeit mark," treble damages and attorney's fees must be awarded unless there are "extenuating circumstances." § 1117(b). Willful blindness is sufficient to trigger the mandatory provisions of subsection b.

1. Concession Services, Inc.

In response to Hard Rock's claim for attorney's fees, CSI argues that it cannot be liable for mandatory attorney's fees under subsection b because even if it is a contributory infringer, it did not "intentionally us[e]" a counterfeit mark. We reject this argument. If CSI can bear contributory liability under substantive provisions that impose liability on those who "use[ ]" a counterfeit mark "in commerce," 15 U.S.C. §§ 1114 & 1125 (sections 32 and 43 of the Act), there is no reason to believe that it cannot "intentionally us[e]" a counterfeit within the meaning of section 35(b).

On remand, if the district court finds CSI liable as a contributory infringer, it should consider whether its findings also amount to intentional use. If CSI is liable because it knew that the t-shirts were counterfeit, or because it was willfully blind, an award of attorney's fees is mandatory under section 35(b). If, however, CSI is liable, but only because it had "reason to know" that the shirts were counterfeits,[5] then the district court should award attorney's fees only if it finds that the circumstances were exceptional. * * *

SANDS, TAYLOR & WOOD COMPANY v. THE QUAKER OATS COMPANY
United States Court of Appeals, Seventh Circuit, 1992.
978 F.2d 947, cert. denied, 507 U.S. 1042, 113 S.Ct. 1879, 123 L.Ed.2d 497 (1993).

[The portion of this opinion presenting the facts and discussing liability issues can be found in Chapter 5, *supra.*]

The district court awarded STW ten percent of Quaker's profits on sales of Gatorade for the period during which the "Thirst Aid" campaign

---

5. We realize that finding the line between "willful blindness" and "reason to know" may be like finding the horizon over Lake Michigan in a snowstorm. Nonetheless, we emphasize that the former is a subjective standard—what did Barelli suspect, and what did he do with his suspicion?—whereas the latter is an objective standard—would a reasonably prudent man in Barelli's shoes have known that the t-shirts were counterfeits? See 2 J. Thomas McCarthy, Trademarks and Unfair Competition § 25:2 at 246 (2d ed. 1984).

ran—$24,730,000—based on its finding that Quaker had acted in bad faith. The court also ordered Quaker to pay STW's attorney's fees, again based on the finding of bad faith, as well as prejudgment interest on the award of profits beginning from May 12, 1984. Quaker challenges all three of these rulings.

A. PROFITS

Quaker argues that an award of its profits was inappropriate here because there was no evidence that Quaker intended to trade on STW's good will or reputation; indeed, such an intent is necessarily absent in a reverse confusion case. According to Quaker, an award of the defendant's profits is justified only where the defendant has been unjustly enriched by appropriating the plaintiff's good will. There is some support for this position in the case law. "To obtain an accounting of profits, the courts usually require that defendant's infringement infer some connotation of 'intent,' or a knowing act denoting an intent, to infringe or reap the harvest of another's mark and advertising." 2 McCarthy, supra § 30:25, at 498. The law of this circuit is not, however, so limited. As we stated in *Roulo*:

> The Lanham Act specifically provides for the awarding of profits in the discretion of the judge subject only to principles of equity. As stated by this Court, "The trial court's primary function is to make violations of the Lanham Act unprofitable to the infringing party." Other than general equitable considerations, there is no express requirement that the parties be in direct competition or that the infringer wilfully infringe the trade dress to justify an award of profits. Profits are awarded under different rationales including unjust enrichment, deterrence, and compensation.

886 F.2d at 941. This broader view seems to be more consistent with the language of the Lanham Act than is the narrower (though perhaps more logical) rule espoused by Quaker. 2 McCarthy, supra § 30:28, at 514–15. We decline to adopt Quaker's restrictive interpretation in light of Seventh Circuit precedent.

Nevertheless, we are mindful of the fact that awards of profits are to be limited by "equitable considerations." The district court justified the award of profits based on its finding that Quaker acted in bad faith. The evidence of bad faith in this case, however, is pretty slim. The court based its finding on (1) Quaker's "failure to conduct a basic trademark search until days before the airing of the Thirst Aid commercial," and its "anonymous, cursory investigations" of Karp's use of the mark once it obtained such a search; (2) Quaker's decision to continue with the "Thirst Aid" campaign after it discovered Karp's registrations; (3) the fact that Quaker did not seek a formal legal opinion regarding potential trademark issues until after the first "Thirst Aid" commercials were aired; and (4) Quaker's failure to take "reasonable precautions" to avoid the likelihood of confusion. Sands, Taylor & Wood, 18 U.S.P.Q.2d at 1472–73.

None of these facts is particularly good evidence of bad faith. For example, Quaker's in-house counsel, Lannin, testified at trial that his review of the "Thirst Aid" campaign in February or March of 1984 did not include a trademark search because he concluded that the proposed advertisements used the words "Thirst Aid" descriptively, and not as a trademark, and therefore did not raise any trademark issues. The district court apparently accepted this testimony, but nonetheless found Quaker's failure to investigate indicative of bad faith. Further, the court stated that it is a "close question" whether "Thirst Aid" is a descriptive term. Indeed, this court has found that the district court erred in concluding that "Thirst Aid" was not descriptive as a matter of law. A party who acts in reasonable reliance on the advice of counsel regarding a close question of trademark law generally does not act in bad faith. Cuisinarts, Inc. v. Robot–Coupe Int'l Corp., 580 F.Supp. 634, 637 (S.D.N.Y.1984).

Nor does Quaker's decision to proceed with the "Thirst Aid" campaign once it learned of Karp's registrations necessarily show bad faith. Based both on his earlier conclusion that "Thirst Aid" was descriptive and on his investigation into Karp's use of the term, which revealed that Karp was not currently using the THIRST–AID mark on any products sold at retail, Lannin concluded that Quaker's ads did not infringe Karp's rights in its marks. * * * Even the defendant's refusal to cease using the mark upon demand is not necessarily indicative of bad faith. Absent more, courts should "not make an inference of bad faith from evidence of conduct that is compatible with a good faith business judgment." Munters Corp. v. Matsui America, Inc., 730 F.Supp. 790, 799–800 (N.D.Ill.1989), aff'd, 909 F.2d 250 (7th Cir.1990).

Quaker's failure to obtain a formal legal opinion from outside counsel until after the "Thirst Aid" campaign began is similarly weak evidence of bad faith. Given Lannin's sincere, reasonable conclusion that Quaker's ads used "Thirst Aid" descriptively, so that no trademark issue was raised, Quaker had no reason to seek the opinion of outside trademark counsel. Similarly, Quaker had no reason to take any precautions to avoid likelihood of confusion; Quaker's research had revealed that there was no product about which people were likely to be confused.

A determination of bad faith is a finding of fact subject to the clearly erroneous standard of review. Web Printing Controls Co. v. Oxy–Dry Corp., 906 F.2d 1202, 1205 n. 3 (7th Cir.1990). We cannot say on this record that the district court's conclusion was clearly erroneous. We do think, however, that the evidence of bad faith here is marginal at best. Further, this is not a case where the senior user's trademark is so well-known that the junior user's choice of a confusingly similar mark, out of the infinite number of marks in the world, itself supports an inference that the junior user acted in bad faith. 2 McCarthy, supra § 23:33, at 147. There is no question that Quaker developed the "Thirst Aid" campaign entirely independently, with no knowledge of STW's marks. In such a case, an award of $24 million in profits is not "equitable"; rather, it is a windfall to the plaintiff. Quaker may have been unjustly enriched by using STW's mark without paying for it, but the award of profits bears no relationship to that enrichment. A reasonable royalty, perhaps related in some way to the fee STW was paid by Pet, would more accurately reflect both the extent of Quaker's unjust enrichment and the interest of STW that has been infringed. We therefore reverse the district court's award of profits and remand for a redetermination of damages. * * *

B. ATTORNEY'S FEES

The Lanham Act provides for recovery of attorney's fees by the prevailing party in "exceptional cases." 15 U.S.C. § 1117(a). The district court concluded that this was such an exceptional case based on its finding that Quaker acted in bad faith. Because we affirm that finding, we also affirm the award of attorney's fees. The "equitable considerations" which lead us to reverse the award of profits do not apply to this issue. * * *

VI.

For the foregoing reasons, the decision of the district court is AFFIRMED in part, REVERSED in part and REMANDED for further proceedings.

RIPPLE, CIRCUIT JUDGE, concurring.

I join the judgment of the court and all but part V of Judge Cudahy's comprehensive and thoughtful opinion. In my view, Quaker's corporate conduct in this matter deserves a somewhat less charitable appraisal than that presented in part V. Therefore, in assessing damages, I believe the district court, in the exercise of its discretion, might well place substantial emphasis on deterrence. See Roulo v. Russ Berrie & Co., Inc., 886 F.2d 931, 941 (7th Cir.1989). Therefore, I doubt very much that damages measured by a "reasonable royalty"—a speculative approximation itself—necessarily would suffice in this case. Nevertheless, I agree with Judge Cudahy that the district court's use of a "percentage of profits" benchmark for the award of damages is difficult to sustain. I therefore concur in his conclusion that a more precise determination is appropriate.

FAIRCHILD, SENIOR CIRCUIT JUDGE, dissenting in part.

Twenty-four million dollars ($24 million) is, indeed, a big number. It is, however, only 10% of the profit realized by Quaker out of the product it marketed by using STW's mark. We are affirming the finding that Quaker used the mark in bad faith. The real question, it seems to me, is one of causation. What portion of Quaker's profit resulted from its use of

THIRST AID, and therefore constituted unjust enrichment? I am unable to say that the district court's estimate of 10% was unreasonable or clearly erroneous. Quaker made no showing that it should have been a different number. The 90% ($216 million) of profit which Quaker retains is no paltry reward for everything it contributed to the success of the venture.

Therefore, I respectfully dissent from the decision to reverse the award.

Notes

1. It should be noted that section 35 of the Lanham Act permits recovery of the plaintiff's damages, the infringer's profits, and costs. 15 U.S.C.A. § 1117. There are additional penalties for counterfeiting, *id.*, as well as provisions permitting the destruction of infringing articles and prohibiting the importation of infringing goods. 15 U.S.C.A. §§ 1118, 1124. For further discussion of trademark remedies, see 2 J. Thomas McCarthy, Trademarks and Unfair Competition §§ 30.01 to 30.34 (3d ed. 1995); Restatement (Third) of Unfair Competition §§ 35–37 (1995).

2. Punitive damages may be available under state law for certain forms of unfair competition, although these awards are subject to constitutional constraints. See Cooper Industries, Inc. v. Leatherman Tool Group, Inc., 532 U.S. 424, 121 S.Ct. 1678, 149 L.Ed.2d 674 (2001) (applying de novo review in assessing constitutionality of punitive damage award for unfair competition and false advertising).

Chapter 7

FEDERAL UNFAIR COMPETITION: SECTION 43(A) OF THE LANHAM ACT

A. ATTRIBUTION

DASTAR CORPORATION v. TWENTIETH CENTURY FOX FILM CORPORATION

Supreme Court of the United States, 2003.
539 U.S. 23, 123 S.Ct. 2041, 156 L.Ed.2d 18.

JUSTICE SCALIA delivered the opinion of the Court in which all other Members joined, except Breyer, J., who took no part in the consideration or decision of the case.

In this case, we are asked to decide whether § 43(a) of the Lanham Act, 15 U.S.C. § 1125(a), prevents the unaccredited copying of a work, and if so, whether a court may double a profit award under § 1117(a), in order to deter future infringing conduct.

I

In 1948, three and a half years after the German surrender at Reims, General Dwight D. Eisenhower completed Crusade in Europe, his written account of the allied campaign in Europe during World War II. Doubleday published the book, registered it with the Copyright Office in 1948, and granted exclusive television rights to an affiliate of respondent Twentieth Century Fox Film Corporation (Fox). Fox, in turn, arranged for Time, Inc., to produce a television series, also called Crusade in Europe, based on the book, and Time assigned its copyright in the series to Fox. The television series, consisting of 26 episodes, was first broadcast in 1949. It combined a soundtrack based on a narration of the book with film footage from the United States Army, Navy, and Coast Guard, the British Ministry of Information and War Office, the National Film Board of Canada, and unidentified "Newsreel Pool Cameramen." In 1975, Doubleday renewed the copyright on the book as the " 'proprietor of copyright in a work made for hire.' " App. to Pet for Cert. 9a. Fox, however, did not renew the copyright on the Crusade television series, which expired in 1977, leaving the television series in the public domain.

In 1988, Fox reacquired the television rights in General Eisenhower's book, including the exclusive right to distribute the Crusade television series on video and to sub-license others to do so. Respondents SFM Entertainment and New Line Home Video, Inc., in turn, acquired from Fox the exclusive rights to distribute Crusade on video. SFM obtained the negatives of the original television series, restored them, and repackaged the series on videotape; New Line distributed the videotapes.

Enter petitioner Dastar. In 1995, Dastar decided to expand its product line from music compact discs to videos. Anticipating renewed interest in World War II on the 50th anniversary of the war's end, Dastar released a video set entitled World War II Campaigns in Europe. To make Campaigns, Dastar purchased eight beta cam tapes of the *original* version of the Crusade television series, which is in the public domain, copied them, and then edited the series. Dastar's Campaigns series is slightly more than half as long as the original Crusade television series. Dastar substituted a new opening sequence, credit page, and final closing for those of the Crusade television series; inserted new chapter-title sequences and narrated chapter introductions; moved the "recap" in the Crusade television series to the beginning and retitled it as a "preview;" and removed references to and images of the book. Dastar created new packaging for its Campaigns series and (as already noted) a new title.

Dastar manufactured and sold the Campaigns video set as its own product. The advertising states: "Produced and Distributed by: *Entertainment Distributing*" (which is owned by Dastar), and makes no reference to the Crusade television series. Similarly, the screen credits state "DASTAR CORP presents" and "an ENTERTAINMENT DISTRIBUTING Production," and list as executive producer, producer, and associate producer, employees of Dastar. Supp.App. 2–3, 30. The Campaigns videos themselves also make no reference to the Crusade television series, New Line's Crusade videotapes, or the book. Dastar sells its Campaigns videos to Sam's Club, Costco, Best Buy, and other retailers and mail-order companies for $25 per set, substantially less than New Line's video set.

In 1998, respondents Fox, SFM, and New Line brought this action alleging that Dastar's sale of its Campaigns video set infringes Doubleday's copyright in General Eisenhower's book and, thus, their exclusive television rights in the book. Respondents later amended their complaint to add claims that Dastar's sale of Campaigns "without proper credit" to the Crusade television series constitutes "reverse passing off" in violation of § 43(a) of the Lanham Act, 15 U.S.C. § 1125(a), and in violation of state unfair-competition law. App. to Pet. for Cert. 31a. On cross-motions for summary judgment, the District Court found for respondents on all three counts, *id.*, at 54a–55a, treating its resolution of the

Lanham Act claim as controlling on the state-law unfair-competition claim because "the ultimate test under both is whether the public is likely to be deceived or confused," *id.*, at 54a. The court awarded Dastar's profits to respondents and doubled them pursuant to § 35 of the Lanham Act, 15 U.S.C. § 1117(a), to deter future infringing conduct by petitioner.

The Court of Appeals for the Ninth Circuit affirmed the judgment for respondents on the Lanham Act claim, but reversed as to the copyright claim and remanded. 34 Fed.Appx. 312, 316 (2002). (It said nothing with regard to the state-law claim.) With respect to the Lanham Act claim, the Court of Appeals reasoned that "Dastar copied substantially the entire Crusade in Europe series created by Twentieth Century Fox, labeled the resulting product with a different name and marketed it without attribution to Fox [,and] therefore committed a 'bodily appropriation' of Fox's series." *Id.*, at 314. It concluded that "Dastar's 'bodily appropriation' of Fox's original [television] series is sufficient to establish the reverse passing off." *Ibid.*[2] The court also affirmed the District Court's award under the Lanham Act of twice Dastar's profits. We granted certiorari. 537 U.S. 1099, 123 S.Ct. 816, 154 L.Ed.2d 767 (2003).

II

The Lanham Act was intended to make "actionable the deceptive and misleading use of marks," and "to protect persons engaged in ... commerce against unfair competition." 15 U.S.C. § 1127. While much of the Lanham Act addresses the registration, use, and infringement of trademarks and related marks, § 43(a), 15 U.S.C. § 1125(a) is one of the few provisions that goes beyond trademark protection. As originally enacted, § 43(a) created a federal remedy against a person who used in commerce either "a false designation of origin, or any false description or representation" in connection with "any goods or services." 60 Stat. 441. As the Second Circuit accurately observed with regard to the original enactment, however—and as remains true after the 1988 revision—§ 43(a) "does not have boundless application as a remedy for unfair trade practices," *Alfred Dunhill, Ltd. v. Interstate Cigar Co.*, 499 F.2d 232, 237 (C.A.2 1974). "[B]ecause of its inherently limited wording, § 43(a) can never be a federal 'codification' of the overall law of 'unfair competition,'" 4 J. McCarthy Trademarks and Unfair Competition § 27:7, p.27–14 (4th ed. 2002) (McCarthy), but can apply only to certain unfair trade practices prohibited by its text.

Although a case can be made that a proper reading of § 43(a), as originally enacted, would treat the word "origin" as referring only "to the geographic location in which the goods originated," *Two Pesos, Inc.*

---

2. As for the copyright claim, the Ninth Circuit held that the tax treatment General Eisenhower sought for his manuscript of the book created a triable issue as to whether he intended the book to be a work for hire, and thus as to whether Doubleday properly renewed the copyright in 1976. See 34 Fed.Appx., at 314. The copyright issue is still the subject of litigation, but is not before us. We express no opinion as to whether petitioner's product would infringe a valid copyright in General Eisenhower's book.

v. Taco Cabana, Inc., 505 U.S. 763, 777, 112 S.Ct. 2753, 120 L.Ed.2d 615 (1992) (STEVENS, J. concurring in judgment), the Courts of Appeals considering the issue, beginning with the Sixth Circuit, unanimously concluded that it "does not merely refer to geographical origin, but also to origin of source or manufacture," *Federal–Mogul–Bower Bearings, Inc. v. Azoff*, 313 F.2d 405, 408 (C.A.6 1963), thereby creating a federal cause of action for traditional trademark infringement of unregistered marks. See 4 McCarthy § 27:14; *Two Pesos, supra,* at 768, 112 S.Ct. 2753. Moreover, every Circuit to consider the issue found § 43(a) broad enough to encompass reverse passing off. See, *e.g., Williams v. Curtiss–Wright Corp.*, 691 F.2d 168, 172 (C.A.3 1982); *Arrow United Indus., Inc. v. Hugh Richards, Inc.*, 678 F.2d 410, 415 (C.A.2 1982); *F.E.L. Publications, Ltd. v. Catholic Bishop of Chicago*, 214 USPQ 409, 416, 1982 WL 19198 (C.A.7 1982); *Smith v. Montoro*, 648 F.2d 602, 603 (C.A.9 1981); *Bangor Punta Operations, Inc. v. Universal Marine Co.*, 543 F.2d 1107, 1109 (C.A.5 1976). The Trademark Law Revision Act of 1988 made clear that § 43(a) covers origin of production as well as geographic origin. Its language is amply inclusive, moreover, of reverse passing off—if indeed it does not implicitly adopt the unanimous court-of-appeals jurisprudence on that subject. See, *e.g., ALPO Petfoods, Inc. v. Ralston Purina Co.*, 913 F.2d 958, 963–964, n. 6 (C.A.D.C.1990) (Thomas, J.).

Thus, as it comes to us, the gravamen of respondents' claim is that, in marketing and selling Campaigns as its own product without acknowledging its nearly wholesale reliance on the Crusade television series, Dastar has made a "false designation of origin, false or misleading description of fact, or false or misleading representation of fact, which . . . is likely to cause confusion . . . as to the origin . . . of his or her goods." See, *e.g.*, Brief for Respondents 8, 11. That claim would undoubtedly be sustained if Dastar had bought some of New Line's Crusade videotapes and merely repackaged them as its own. Dastar's alleged wrongdoing, however, is vastly different: it took a creative work in the public domain—the Crusade television series—copied it, made modifications (arguably minor), and produced its very own series of videotapes. If "origin" refers only to the manufacturer or producer of the physical "goods" that are made available to the public (in this case the videotapes), Dastar was the origin. If, however, "origin" includes the creator of the underlying work that Dastar copied, then someone else (perhaps Fox) was the origin of Dastar's product. At bottom, we must decide what § 43(a)(1)(A) of the Lanham Act means by the "origin" of "goods."

III

The dictionary definition of "origin" is "[t]he fact or process of coming into being from a source," and "[t]hat from which anything primarily proceeds; source." Webster's New International Dictionary 1720–1721 (2d ed.1949). And the dictionary definition of "goods" (as relevant here) is "[w]ares; merchandise." *Id.*, at 1079. We think the most natural understanding of the "origin" of "goods"—the source of wares—is the producer of the tangible product sold in the marketplace, in this case the physical Campaigns videotape sold by Dastar. The concept might be stretched (as it was under the original version of § 43(a)) to include not only the actual producer, but also the trademark owner who commissioned or assumed responsibility for ("stood behind") production of the physical product. But as used in the Lanham Act, the phrase "origin of goods" is in our view incapable of connoting the person or entity that originated the ideas or communications that "goods" embody or contain. Such an extension would not only stretch the text, but it would be out of accord with the history and purpose of the Lanham Act and inconsistent with precedent.

Section 43(a) of the Lanham Act prohibits actions like trademark infringement that deceive consumers and impair a producer's goodwill. It forbids, for example, the Coca–Cola Company's passing off its product as Pepsi–Cola or reverse passing off Pepsi–Cola as its product. But the brand-loyal consumer who prefers the drink that the Coca–Cola Company or PepsiCo sells, while he believes that that company produced (or at least stands behind the production of) that product, surely does not necessarily believe that that company was the "origin" of the drink in the sense that it was the very first to devise the formula. The consumer who buys a branded product does not automatically assume that the brand-name company is the same entity that came up with the idea for the product, or designed the product—and typically does not care whether it is. The words of the Lanham Act should not be stretched to cover matters that are typically of no consequence to purchasers.

It could be argued, perhaps, that the reality of purchaser concern is different for what might be called a communicative product—one that is valued not primarily for its physical qualities, such as a hammer, but for the intellectual content that it conveys, such as a book or, as here, a video. The purchaser of a novel is interested not merely, if at all, in the identity of the producer of the physical tome (the publisher), but also, and indeed primarily, in the identity of the creator of the story it conveys (the author). And the author, of course, has at least as much interest in avoiding passing-off (or reverse passing-off) of his creation as does the publisher. For such a communicative product (the argument goes) "origin of goods" in § 43(a) must be deemed to include not merely the producer of the physical item (the publishing house Farrar, Straus and Giroux, or the video producer Dastar) but also the creator of the content that the physical item conveys (the author Tom Wolfe, or—assertedly—respondents).

The problem with this argument according special treatment to communicative products is that it causes the Lanham Act to conflict with the law of copyright, which addresses that subject specifically. The right to copy, and to copy without attribution, once a copyright has expired, like "the right to make [an article whose patent has expired]—including the right to make it in precisely the shape it carried when patented—passes to the public." *Sears, Roebuck & Co. v. Stiffel Co.*, 376 U.S. 225, 230, 84 S.Ct. 784, 11 L.Ed.2d 661 (1964); see also *Kellogg Co. v. National Biscuit Co.*, 305 U.S. 111, 121–122, 59 S.Ct. 109, 83 L.Ed. 73 (1938). "In general, unless an intellectual property right such as a patent or copyright protects an item, it will be subject to copying." *TrafFix Devices, Inc. v. Marketing Displays, Inc.*, 532 U.S. 23, 29, 121 S.Ct. 1255, 149 L.Ed.2d 164 (2001). The rights of a patentee or copyright holder are part of a "carefully crafted bargain," *Bonito Boats, Inc. v. Thunder Craft Boats, Inc.*, 489 U.S. 141, 150–151, 109 S.Ct. 971, 103 L.Ed.2d 118 (1989), under which, once the patent or copyright monopoly has expired, the public may use the invention or work at will and without attribution. Thus, in construing the Lanham Act, we have been "careful to caution against misuse or over-extension" of trademark and related protections into areas traditionally occupied by patent or copyright. *TrafFix*, 532 U.S., at 29, 121 S.Ct. 1255. "The Lanham Act," we have said, "does not exist to reward manufacturers for their innovation in creating a particular device; that is the purpose of the patent law and its period of exclusivity." *Id.*, at 34, 121 S.Ct. 1255. Federal trademark law "has no necessary relation to invention or discovery," *In re Trade–Mark Cases*, 100 U.S. 82, 94, 25 L.Ed. 550 (1879), but rather, by preventing competitors from copying "a source-identifying mark," "reduce[s] the customer's costs of shopping and making purchasing decisions," and "helps assure a producer that it (and not an imitating competitor) will reap the financial, reputation-related rewards associated with a desirable product," *Qualitex Co. v. Jacobson Products Co.*, 514 U.S. 159, 163–164, 115 S.Ct. 1300, 131 L.Ed.2d 248 (1995) (internal quotation marks and citation omitted). Assuming for the sake of argument that Dastar's representation of itself as the "Producer" of its videos amounted to a representation that it originated the creative work conveyed by the videos, allowing a cause of action under § 43(a) for that representation would create a species of mutant copyright law that limits the public's "federal right to 'copy and to use,'" expired copyrights, *Bonito Boats, supra*, at 165, 109 S.Ct. 971.

When Congress has wished to create such an addition to the law of copyright, it has done so with much more specificity than the Lanham Act's ambiguous use of "origin." The Visual Artists Rights Act of 1990, § 603(a), 104 Stat. 5128, provides that the author of an artistic work "shall have the right . . . to claim authorship of that work." 17 U.S.C. § 106A(a)(1)(A). That express right of attribution is carefully limited and focused: It attaches only to specified "work[s] of visual art," § 101, is personal to the artist, §§ 106A(b) and (e), and endures only for "the life of the author," at § 106A(d)(1). Recognizing in § 43(a) a cause of action for misrepresentation of authorship of noncopyrighted works (visual or otherwise) would render these limitations superfluous. A statutory interpretation that renders another statute superfluous is of course to be avoided. *E.g., Mackey v. Lanier Collection Agency & Service, Inc.*, 486 U.S. 825, 837, and n. 11, 108 S.Ct. 2182, 100 L.Ed.2d 836 (1988).

Reading "origin" in § 43(a) to require attribution of uncopyrighted materials would pose serious practical problems. Without a copyrighted work as the basepoint, the word "origin" has no discernable limits. A video of the MGM film Carmen Jones, after its copyright has expired, would presumably require attribution not just to MGM, but to Oscar Hammerstein II (who wrote the musical on which the film was based), to Georges Bizet (who wrote the opera on which the musical was based), and to Prosper Merimee (who wrote the novel on which the opera was based). In many cases, figuring out who is in the line of "origin" would be no simple task. Indeed, in the present case it is far from clear that respondents have that status. Neither SFM nor New Line had anything to do with the production of the Crusade television series—they merely were licensed to distribute the video version. While Fox might have a claim to being in the line of origin, its involvement with the creation of the television series was limited at best. Time, Inc., was the principal if not the exclusive creator, albeit under arrangement with Fox. And of course it was neither Fox nor Time, Inc., that shot the film used in the Crusade television series. Rather, that footage came from the United States Army, Navy, and Coast Guard, the British Ministry of Information and War Office, the National Film Board of Canada, and unidentified "Newsreel Pool Cameramen." If anyone has a claim to being the *original* creator of the material used in both the Crusade television series and the Campaigns videotapes, it would be those groups, rather than Fox. We do not think the Lanham Act requires this search for the source of the Nile and all its tributaries.

Another practical difficulty of adopting a special definition of "origin" for communicative products is that it places the manufacturers of those products in a difficult position. On the one hand, they would face Lanham Act liability for failing to credit the creator of a work on which their lawful copies are based; and on the other hand they could face Lanham Act liability for crediting the creator if that should be regarded as implying the creator's "sponsorship or approval" of the copy, 15 U.S.C. § 1125(a)(1)(A). In this case, for example, if Dastar had simply "copied [the television series] as Crusade in Europe and sold it as Crusade in Europe," without changing the title or packaging (including the original credits to Fox), it is hard to have confidence in respondents' assurance that they "would not be here on a Lanham Act cause of action," Tr. of Oral Arg. 35.

Finally, reading § 43(a) of the Lanham Act as creating a cause of action for, in effect, plagiarism—the use of otherwise unprotected works and inventions without attribution—would be hard to reconcile with our previous decisions. For example, in *Wal-Mart Stores, Inc. v. Samara Brothers, Inc.*, 529 U.S. 205, 120 S.Ct. 1339, 146 L.Ed.2d 182 (2000), we considered whether product-design trade dress can ever be inherently distinctive. . . . We concluded that the designs could not be protected under § 43(a) without a showing that they had acquired "secondary meaning," *id.*, at 214, 120 S.Ct. 1339, so that they " 'identify the source of the product rather than the product itself,' " *id*, at 211, 120 S.Ct. 1339 (quoting *Inwood Laboratories, Inc. v. Ives Laboratories, Inc.*, 456 U.S. 844, 851, n. 11, 102 S.Ct. 2182, 72 L.Ed.2d 606 (1982)). This carefully considered limitation would be entirely pointless if the "original" producer could turn around and pursue a reverse-passing-off claim under exactly the same provision of the Lanham Act. . . .

Similarly under respondents' theory, the "origin of goods" provision of § 43(a) would have supported the suit that we rejected in *Bonito Boats*, 489 U.S. 141, 109 S.Ct. 971, where the defendants had used molds to duplicate the plaintiff's unpatented boat hulls (apparently without crediting the plaintiff). And it would have supported the suit we rejected in *TrafFix*, 532 U.S. 23, 121 S.Ct. 1255: The plaintiff, whose patents on flexible road signs had expired, and who could not prevail on a trade-dress claim under § 43(a) because the features of the signs were functional, would have had a reverse-passing-off claim for unattributed copying of his design.

In sum, reading the phrase "origin of goods" in the Lanham Act in accordance with the Act's common-law foundations (which were *not* designed to protect originality or creativity), and in light of the copyright and patent laws (which were), we conclude that the phrase refers to the producer of the tangible goods that are offered for sale, and not to the author of any idea, concept, or communication embodied in those goods. Cf. 17 U.S.C. § 202 (distinguishing between a copyrighted work and "any material object in which the work is embodied"). To hold otherwise would be akin to finding that § 43(a) created a species of perpetual patent and copyright, which Congress may not do. See *Eldred v. Ashcroft*, 537 U.S. 186, 208, 123 S.Ct. 769, 154 L.Ed.2d 683 (2003).

The creative talent of the sort that lay behind the Campaigns videos is not left without protection. The original film footage used in the Crusade television series could have been copyrighted, see 17 U.S.C. § 102(a)(6), as was copyrighted (as a compilation) the Crusade television series, even though it included material from the public domain, see § 103(a). Had Fox renewed the copyright in the Crusade television series, it would have had an easy claim of copyright infringement. And respondents' contention that Campaigns infringes Doubleday's copyright in General Eisenhower's book is still a live question on remand. If, moreover, the producer of a video that substantially copied the Crusade series were, in advertising or promotion, to give purchasers the impression that the video was quite different from that series, then one or more of the respondents might have a cause of action—not for reverse passing off under the "confusion . . . as to the origin" provision of § 43(a)(1)(A), but for misrepresentation under the "misrepresents the nature, characteristics [or] qualities" provision of § 43(a)(1)(B). For merely saying it is the producer of the video, however, no Lanham Act liability attaches to Dastar.

* * *

Notes

1.   Although *Dastar* is a case about the Lanham Act, it suggests a broad principle—that the Court will not construe legislation undertaken outside of

the Intellectual Property Clause power to provide IP-like protections not available under copyright or patent law. If this conclusion is warranted, it may be sharply limited. *Compare Dastar with Eldred v. Ashcroft*, 537 U.S. 186, 123 S.Ct. 769, 154 L.Ed.2d 683 (2003), *rehearing denied* 538 U.S. 916, 123 S.Ct. 1505, 155 L.Ed.2d 243 (2003). [*Eldred* is excerpted in this casebook in Chapter 17, Section B.]

2. The case of *Gilliam v. ABC*, 538 F.2d 14 (2d Cir. 1976), raises important issues regarding attribution under Section 43(a). *See* Chapter 18. Is *Gilliam* good law after *Dastar*? For a recent application of *Dastar*, see *Williams v. UMG Recordings, Inc.*, 281 F.Supp.2d 1177 (C.D. Ca. 2003) (rejecting trademark claim regarding alleged lack of credit in a film's final credits in light of *Dastar*, but suggesting that copyright law would be the correct law for plaintiff to bring a claim), *aff'd* 2006 WL 1307922 (9th Cir. 2006).

3. A pre-*Dastar* case, *Miramax Films Corp. v. Columbia Pictures Entertainment, Inc.*, 996 F.Supp. 294, 302 (S.D.N.Y.1998), vacated without opinion, 996 F.Supp. 294 (S.D.N.Y.1998), involved a dispute between two movie studios. The plaintiff asserted that Columbia had distributed the film "I Know What You Did Last Summer" and promoted it as being from the "creator" of the plaintiff's film "Scream." The only connection between the two films was an unknown screenwriter who worked on both films. Is this representation actionable under section 43(a)? For further discussion of attribution rights and other claims under section 43(a), see 3 J. Thomas McCarthy, Trademarks and Unfair Competition § 27.08 (3d ed. 1995).

4. What does the "bargain" that Justice Scalia mentions between the public and copyright and patent owners entail? What does it demand of intellectual property owners? What does it imply about the creation or extension of new intellectual property rights? *Compare Dastar with Eldred v. Ashcroft*, 537 U.S. 186, 123 S.Ct. 769, 154 L.Ed.2d 683 (2003).

B.   TRADE DRESS

TWO PESOS, INC. v. TACO CABANA, INC.

Supreme Court of the United States, 1992.
505 U.S. 763, 112 S.Ct. 2753, 120 L.Ed.2d 615.

JUSTICE WHITE delivered the opinion of the Court.

The issue in this case is whether the trade dress[1] of a restaurant may be protected under § 43(a) of the Trademark Act of 1946 (Lanham

---

1. The District Court instructed the jury: " '[T]rade dress' is the total image of the business. Taco Cabana's trade dress may include the shape and general appearance of the exterior of the restaurant, the identifying sign, the interior kitchen floor plan, the decor, the menu, the equipment used to serve food, the servers' uniforms and other features reflecting on the total image of the restaurant." 1 App. 83–84. The Court of Appeals accepted this definition and quoted from Blue Bell Bio–Medical v. Cin–Bad, Inc., 864 F.2d 1253, 1256 (C.A.5 1989): "The 'trade dress' of a product is essentially its total image and overall appearance." See 932 F.2d 1113, 1118 (C.A.5 1991). It "involves the total image of a product and may include features such as size, shape, color or color combinations, texture, graphics, or even particular sales techniques." John H. Harland Co. v. Clarke Checks, Inc., 711 F.2d 966, 980 (C.A.11 1983).

Act), 60 Stat. 441, 15 U.S.C. § 1125(a) (1982 ed.), based on a finding of inherent distinctiveness, without proof that the trade dress has secondary meaning.

I

Respondent Taco Cabana, Inc., operates a chain of fast-food restaurants in Texas. The restaurants serve Mexican food. The first Taco Cabana restaurant was opened in San Antonio in September 1978, and five more restaurants had been opened in San Antonio by 1985. Taco Cabana describes its Mexican trade dress as "a festive eating atmosphere having interior dining and patio areas decorated with artifacts, bright colors, paintings and murals. The patio includes interior and exterior areas with the interior patio capable of being sealed off from the outside patio by overhead garage doors. The stepped exterior of the building is a festive and vivid color scheme using top border paint and neon stripes. Bright awnings and umbrellas continue the theme." 932 F.2d 1113, 1117 (C.A.5 1991).

In December 1985, a Two Pesos, Inc., restaurant was opened in Houston. Two Pesos adopted a motif very similar to the foregoing description of Taco Cabana's trade dress. Two Pesos restaurants expanded rapidly in Houston and other markets, but did not enter San Antonio. In 1986, Taco Cabana entered the Houston and Austin markets and expanded into other Texas cities, including Dallas and El Paso where Two Pesos was also doing business.

In 1987, Taco Cabana sued Two Pesos in the United States District Court for the Southern District of Texas for trade dress infringement under § 43(a) of the Lanham Act, 15 U.S.C. § 1125(a) (1982 ed.), and for theft of trade secrets under Texas common law. The case was tried to a jury, which was instructed to return its verdict in the form of answers to five questions propounded by the trial judge. The jury's answers were: Taco Cabana has a trade dress; taken as a whole, the trade dress is nonfunctional; the trade dress is inherently distinctive; the trade dress has not acquired a secondary meaning in the Texas market; and the alleged infringement creates a likelihood of confusion on the part of ordinary customers as to the source or association of the restaurant's goods or services. Because, as the jury was told, Taco Cabana's trade dress was protected if it either was inherently distinctive or had acquired a secondary meaning, judgment was entered awarding damages to Taco Cabana. In the course of calculating damages, the trial court held that Two Pesos had intentionally and deliberately infringed Taco Cabana's trade dress.[5]

The Court of Appeals ruled that the instructions adequately stated the applicable law and that the evidence supported the jury's findings. In particular, the Court of Appeals rejected petitioner's argument that a

---

5. The Court of Appeals agreed: "The weight of the evidence persuades us, as it did Judge Singleton, that Two Pesos brazenly copied Taco Cabana's successful trade dress, and proceeded to expand in a manner that foreclosed several important markets within Taco Cabana's natural zone of expansion." 932 F.2d, at 1127, n. 20.

finding of no secondary meaning contradicted a finding of inherent distinctiveness. * * * The Court of Appeals noted that this approach conflicts with decisions of other courts, particularly the holding of the Court of Appeals for the Second Circuit in Vibrant Sales, Inc. v. New Body Boutique, Inc., 652 F.2d 299 (1981), cert. denied, 455 U.S. 909, 102 S.Ct. 1257, 71 L.Ed.2d 448 (1982), that § 43(a) protects unregistered trademarks or designs only where secondary meaning is shown. We granted certiorari to resolve the conflict among the Courts of Appeals on the question whether trade dress which is inherently distinctive is protectable under § 43(a) without a showing that it has acquired secondary meaning. We find that it is, and we therefore affirm.

II

* * *

A trademark is defined in 15 U.S.C. § 1127 as including "any word, name, symbol, or device or any combination thereof" used by any person "to identify and distinguish his or her goods, including a unique product, from those manufactured or sold by others and to indicate the source of the goods, even if that source is unknown." * * * Marks are often classified in categories of generally increasing distinctiveness; following the classic formulation set out by Judge Friendly, they may be (1) generic; (2) descriptive; (3) suggestive; (4) arbitrary; or (5) fanciful. See Abercrombie & Fitch Co. v. Hunting World, Inc., 537 F.2d 4, 9 (C.A.2 1976). The Court of Appeals followed this classification and petitioner accepts it. The latter three categories of marks, because their intrinsic nature serves to identify a particular source of a product, are deemed inherently distinctive and are entitled to protection. In contrast, generic marks—those that "refe[r] to the genus of which the particular product is a species," Park 'N Fly, Inc. v. Dollar Park and Fly, Inc., 469 U.S. 189, 194, 105 S.Ct. 658, 661, 83 L.Ed.2d 582 (1985), citing Abercrombie & Fitch, supra, at 9—are not registrable as trademarks. Park 'N Fly, supra, 469 U.S., at 194, 105 S.Ct., at 661–662.

Marks which are merely descriptive of a product are not inherently distinctive. When used to describe a product, they do not inherently identify a particular source, and hence cannot be protected. However, descriptive marks may acquire the distinctiveness which will allow them to be protected under the Act. * * * This acquired distinctiveness is generally called "secondary meaning." The concept of secondary meaning has been applied to actions under § 43(a). See, e.g., University of Georgia Athletic Assn. v. Laite, 756 F.2d 1535 (C.A.11 1985). * * *

* * * There is no persuasive reason to apply to trade dress a general requirement of secondary meaning which is at odds with the principles generally applicable to infringement suits under § 43(a). * * *

Petitioner argues that the jury's finding that the trade dress has not acquired a secondary meaning shows conclusively that the trade dress is not inherently distinctive. The Court of Appeals' disposition of this issue was sound: "Two Pesos' argument—that the jury finding of inherent distinctiveness contradicts its finding of no secondary meaning in the Texas market—ignores the law in this circuit. While the necessarily imperfect (and often prohibitively difficult) methods for assessing secondary meaning address the empirical question of current consumer association, the legal recognition of an inherently distinctive trademark or trade dress acknowledges the owner's legitimate proprietary interest in its unique and valuable informational device, regardless of whether substantial consumer association yet bestows the additional empirical protection of secondary meaning." 932 F.2d, at 1120, n. 7.

Although petitioner makes the above argument, it appears to concede elsewhere in its briefing that it is possible for a trade dress, even a restaurant trade dress, to be inherently distinctive and thus eligible for protection under § 43(a). Recognizing that a general requirement of secondary meaning imposes "an unfair prospect of theft [or] financial loss" on the developer of fanciful or arbitrary trade dress at the outset of its use, petitioner suggests that such trade dress should receive limited protection without proof of secondary meaning. Petitioner argues that such protection should be only temporary and subject to defeasance when over time the dress has failed to acquire a secondary meaning. This approach is also vulnerable for the reasons given by the Court of Appeals. If temporary protection is available from the earliest use of the trade dress, it must be because it is neither functional nor descriptive but an inherently distinctive dress that is capable of identifying a particular source of the product. Such a trade dress, or mark, is not subject to copying by concerns that have an equal opportunity to choose their own inherently distinctive trade dress. To terminate protection for failure to gain secondary meaning over some unspecified time could not be based on the failure of the dress to retain its fanciful, arbitrary, or suggestive nature, but on the failure of the user of the dress to be successful enough in the marketplace. This is not a valid basis to find a dress or mark ineligible for protection. The user of such a trade dress should be able to maintain what competitive position it has and continue to seek wider identification among potential customers.

* * *

The Fifth Circuit was quite right * * * to follow the *Abercrombie* classifications consistently and to inquire whether trade dress for which protection is claimed under § 43(a) is inherently distinctive. If it is, it is capable of identifying products or services as coming from a specific source and secondary meaning is not required. This is the rule generally applicable to trademark, and the protection of trademarks and trade dress under § 43(a) serves the same statutory purpose of preventing deception and unfair competition. There is no persuasive reason to apply different analysis to the two. * * *

It would be a different matter if there were textual basis in § 43(a) for treating inherently distinctive verbal or symbolic trademarks differently from inherently distinctive trade dress. But there is none. The section does not mention trademarks or trade dress, whether they be called generic, descriptive, suggestive, arbitrary, fanciful, or functional. Nor does the concept of secondary meaning appear in the text of § 43(a). Where secondary meaning does appear in the statute, 15 U.S.C. § 1052 (1982 ed.), it is a requirement that applies only to merely descriptive marks and not to inherently distinctive ones. We see no basis for requiring secondary meaning for inherently distinctive trade dress protection under § 43(a) but not for other distinctive words, symbols, or devices capable of identifying a producer's product.

Engrafting onto § 43(a) a requirement of secondary meaning for inherently distinctive trade dress also would undermine the purposes of the Lanham Act. Protection of trade dress, no less than of trademarks, serves the Act's purpose to "secure to the owner of the mark the goodwill of his business and to protect the ability of consumers to distinguish among competing producers. National protection of trademarks is desirable, Congress concluded, because trademarks foster competition and the maintenance of quality by securing to the producer the benefits of good reputation." Park' N Fly, 469 U.S., at 198, 105 S.Ct., at 663, citing S.Rep. No. 1333, 79th Cong., 2d Sess., 3–5 (1946) (citations omitted). By making more difficult the identification of a producer with its product, a secondary meaning requirement for a nondescriptive trade dress would hinder improving or maintaining the producer's competitive position.

Suggestions that under the Fifth Circuit's law, the initial user of any shape or design would cut off competition from products of like design and shape are not persuasive. Only nonfunctional, distinctive trade dress is protected under § 43(a). The Fifth Circuit holds that a design is legally functional, and thus unprotectable, if it is one of a limited number of equally efficient options available to competitors and free competition would be unduly hindered by according the design trademark protection. See Sicilia Di R. Biebow & Co. v. Cox, 732 F.2d 417, 426 (C.A.5 1984). This serves to assure that competition will not be stifled by the exhaustion of a limited number of trade dresses.

On the other hand, adding a secondary meaning requirement could have anticompetitive effects, creating particular burdens on the start-up of small companies. It would present special difficulties for a business, such as respondent, that seeks to start a new product in a limited area and then expand into new markets. Denying protection for inherently distinctive nonfunctional trade dress until after secondary meaning has been established would allow a competitor, which has not adopted a distinctive trade dress of its own, to appropriate the originator's dress in other markets and to deter the originator from expanding into and competing in these areas.

* * *

We agree with the Court of Appeals that proof of secondary meaning is not required to prevail on a claim under § 43(a) of the Lanham Act where the trade dress at issue is inherently distinctive, and accordingly the judgment of that court is affirmed. * * *

Notes

1.   How would a Mexican restaurant that uses "festive colors," sombreros, and murals defend a trade dress infringement action? In what circumstances does a restaurant or an artist lawfully imitate its competitor's successful product and when does it go over the line into unlawful appropriation of trade dress? Can an artist's unique and distinctive style, embodied in a line of fine art posters, be considered trade dress and be protected from imitation by competing artists? See Romm Art Creations Ltd. v. Simcha International, Inc., 786 F.Supp. 1126 (E.D.N.Y.1992) ("Tarkay" posters). To what extent can trade dress exist in an entire product line? See Rose Art Industries, Inc. v. Swanson, 235 F.3d 165 (3d Cir.2000).

2.   At least until *Taco Cabana*, it was unsettled whether trade dress can be registered on the principal register, or whether it is protected solely under section 43(a) and any state law counterparts. This issue seems to have been resolved by implication in *Taco Cabana*'s holding that trade dress questions are analyzed in the same manner as other trademarks under the Lanham Act. Compare Aromatique, Inc. v. Gold Seal, Inc., 28 F.3d 863, 868 (8th Cir.1994) (plurality opinion) ("[T]rade dress may now be registered on the Principal Register of the PTO. The trade dress at issue in this case was so registered.") with Vornado Air Circulation Systems, Inc. v. Duracraft Corp., 58 F.3d 1498, 1499 n. 1 (10th Cir.1995) ("One does not register a product's trade dress—its overall look or image—but trade dress is protected under section 43(a) of the Lanham Act.") (citation omitted), *cert. denied*, 516 U.S. 1067, 116 S.Ct. 753, 133 L.Ed.2d 700 (1996); Vision Sports, Inc. v. Melville Corp., 888 F.2d 609, 613 (9th Cir.1989) (trade dress protection provides broader protection for aspects of packaging and product design that are not registrable as trademarks).

3.   For further discussion of trade dress infringement under section 43(a), see 1 J. Thomas McCarthy, Trademarks and Unfair Competition §§ 7.23 to 8.07 (3d ed. 1995); Restatement (Third) of Unfair Competition §§ 16–17 (1995).

C.   PRODUCT CONFIGURATIONS

WAL–MART STORES, INC. v. SAMARA BROTHERS, INC.

Supreme Court of the United States, 2000.
529 U.S. 205, 120 S.Ct. 1339, 146 L.Ed.2d 182.

SCALIA, J., delivered the opinion for a unanimous Court.

In this case, we decide under what circumstances a product's design is distinctive, and therefore protectible, in an action for infringement of unregistered trade dress under § 43(a) of the Trademark Act of 1946 (Lanham Act), 60 Stat. 441, as amended, 15 U.S.C. § 1125(a).

I

Respondent Samara Brothers, Inc., designs and manufactures children's clothing. Its primary product is a line of spring/summer one-piece seersucker outfits decorated with appliques of hearts, flowers, fruits, and the like. A number of chain stores, including JCPenney, sell this line of clothing under contract with Samara.

Petitioner Wal–Mart Stores, Inc., is one of the nation's best known retailers, selling among other things children's clothing. In 1995, Wal–Mart contracted with one of its suppliers, Judy–Philippine, Inc., to manufacture a line of children's outfits for sale in the 1996 spring/summer season. Wal–Mart sent Judy–Philippine photographs of a number of garments from Samara's line, on which Judy–Philippine's garments were to be based; Judy–Philippine duly copied, with only minor modifications, 16 of Samara's garments, many of which contained copyrighted elements. In 1996, Wal–Mart briskly sold the so-called knockoffs, generating more than $1.15 million in gross profits.

In June 1996, a buyer for JCPenney called a representative at Samara to complain that she had seen Samara garments on sale at Wal–Mart for a lower price than JCPenney was allowed to charge under its contract with Samara. The Samara representative told the buyer that Samara did not supply its clothing to Wal–Mart. Their suspicions aroused, however, Samara officials launched an investigation, which disclosed that Wal–Mart and several other major retailers—Kmart, Caldor, Hills, and Goody's—were selling the knockoffs of Samara's outfits produced by Judy–Philippine.

After sending cease-and-desist letters, Samara brought this action in the United States District Court for the Southern District of New York against Wal–Mart, Judy–Philippine, Kmart, Caldor, Hills, and Goody's for copyright infringement under federal law, consumer fraud and unfair competition under New York law, and—most relevant for our purposes—infringement of unregistered trade dress under § 43(a) of the Lanham Act, 15 U.S.C. § 1125(a). All of the defendants except Wal–Mart settled before trial.

After a weeklong trial, the jury found in favor of Samara on all of its claims. Wal–Mart then renewed a motion for judgment as a matter of law, claiming, inter alia, that there was insufficient evidence to support a conclusion that Samara's clothing designs could be legally protected as distinctive trade dress for purposes of § 43(a). The District Court denied the motion, 969 F.Supp. 895 (S.D.N.Y.1997), and awarded Samara damages, interest, costs, and fees totaling almost $1.6 million, together with injunctive relief. The Second Circuit affirmed the denial of the motion for judgment as a matter of law, 165 F.3d 120 (1998), and we granted certiorari, 528 U.S. 808, 120 S.Ct. 308, 145 L.Ed.2d 35 (1999).

II

The Lanham Act provides for the registration of trademarks, which it defines in § 45 to include "any word, name, symbol, or device, or any combination thereof [used or intended to be used] to identify and distinguish [a producer's] goods ... from those manufactured or sold by others and to indicate the source of the goods.... " 15 U.S.C. § 1127.

Registration of a mark under § 2 of the Act, 15 U.S.C. § 1052, enables the owner to sue an infringer under § 32, 15 U.S.C. § 1114; it also entitles the owner to a presumption that its mark is valid, see § 7(b), 15 U.S.C. § 1057(b), and ordinarily renders the registered mark incontestable after five years of continuous use, see § 15, 15 U.S.C. § 1065. In addition to protecting registered marks, the Lanham Act, in § 43(a), gives a producer a cause of action for the use by any person of "any word, term, name, symbol, or device, or any combination thereof . . . which . . . is likely to cause confusion . . . as to the origin, sponsorship, or approval of his or her goods. . . ." 15 U.S.C. § 1125(a). It is the latter provision that is at issue in this case.

The breadth of the definition of marks registrable under § 2, and of the confusion-producing elements recited as actionable by § 43(a), has been held to embrace not just word marks, such as "Nike," and symbol marks, such as Nike's "swoosh" symbol, but also "trade dress"—a category that originally included only the packaging, or "dressing," of a product, but in recent years has been expanded by many courts of appeals to encompass the design of a product. See, e.g., Ashley Furniture Industries, Inc. v. SanGiacomo N.A. Ltd., 187 F.3d 363 (C.A.4 1999) (bedroom furniture); Knitwaves, Inc. v. Lollytogs Ltd., 71 F.3d 996 (C.A.2 1995) (sweaters); Stuart Hall Co., Inc. v. Ampad Corp., 51 F.3d 780 (C.A.8 1995) (notebooks). These courts have assumed, often without discussion, that trade dress constitutes a "symbol" or "device" for purposes of the relevant sections, and we conclude likewise. "Since human beings might use as a 'symbol' or 'device' almost anything at all that is capable of carrying meaning, this language, read literally, is not restrictive." Qualitex Co. v. Jacobson Products Co., 514 U.S. 159, 162, 115 S.Ct. 1300, 131 L.Ed.2d 248 (1995). This reading of § 2 and § 43(a) is buttressed by a recently added subsection of § 43(a), § 43(a)(3), which refers specifically to "civil action[s] for trade dress infringement under this chapter for trade dress not registered on the principal register." 15 U.S.C.A. § 1125(a)(3) (Oct.1999 Supp.).

The text of § 43(a) provides little guidance as to the circumstances under which unregistered trade dress may be protected. It does require that a producer show that the allegedly infringing feature is not "functional," see § 43(a)(3), and is likely to cause confusion with the product for which protection is sought, see § 43(a)(1)(A), 15 U.S.C. § 1125(a)(1)(A). Nothing in § 43(a) explicitly requires a producer to show that its trade dress is distinctive, but courts have universally imposed that requirement, since without distinctiveness the trade dress would not "cause confusion . . . as to the origin, sponsorship, or approval of [the] goods," as the section requires. Distinctiveness is, moreover, an explicit prerequisite for registration of trade dress under § 2, and "the general principles qualifying a mark for registration under § 2 of the Lanham Act are for the most part applicable in determining whether an unregistered mark is entitled to protection under § 43(a)." Two Pesos, Inc. v. Taco Cabana, Inc., 505 U.S. 763, 768, 112 S.Ct. 2753, 120 L.Ed.2d 615 (1992).

In evaluating the distinctiveness of a mark under § 2 (and therefore, by analogy, under § 43(a)), courts have held that a mark can be distinctive in one of two ways. First, a mark is inherently distinctive if "[its] intrinsic nature serves to identify a particular source." Ibid. In the context of word marks, courts have applied the now-classic test originally formulated by Judge Friendly, in which word marks that are "arbitrary" ("Camel" cigarettes), "fanciful" ("Kodak" film), or "suggestive" ("Tide" laundry detergent) are held to be inherently distinctive. See Abercrombie & Fitch Co. v. Hunting World, Inc., 537 F.2d 4, 10–11 (C.A.2 1976). Second, a mark has acquired distinctiveness, even if it is not inherently distinctive, if it has developed secondary meaning, which occurs when, "in the minds of the public, the primary significance of a [mark] is to identify the source of the product rather than the product itself." Inwood Laboratories, Inc. v. Ives Laboratories, Inc., 456 U.S. 844, 851, n. 11, 102 S.Ct. 2182, 72 L.Ed.2d 606 (1982).

The judicial differentiation between marks that are inherently distinctive and those that have developed secondary meaning has solid foundation in the statute itself. Section 2 requires that registration be granted to any trademark "by which the goods of the applicant may be distinguished from the goods of others"—subject to various limited exceptions. 15 U.S.C. § 1052. It also provides, again with limited exceptions, that "nothing in this chapter shall prevent the registration of a mark used by the applicant which has become distinctive of the applicant's goods in commerce"—that is, which is not inherently distinctive but has become so only through secondary meaning. § 2(f), 15 U.S.C. § 1052(f). Nothing in § 2, however, demands the conclusion that every category of mark necessarily includes some marks "by which the goods of the applicant may be distinguished from the goods of others" without secondary meaning—that in every category some marks are inherently distinctive.

Indeed, with respect to at least one category of mark—colors—we have held that no mark can ever be inherently distinctive. See Qualitex, 514 U.S., at 162–163, 115 S.Ct. 1300. In *Qualitex*, petitioner manufactured and sold green-gold dry-cleaning press pads. * * * We held that a color could be protected as a trademark, but only upon a showing of secondary meaning. Reasoning by analogy to the Abercrombie & Fitch test developed for word marks, we noted that a product's color is unlike a "fanciful," "arbitrary," or "suggestive" mark, since it does not "almost automatically tell a customer that [it] refer[s] to a brand," ibid., and does not "immediately . . . signal a brand or a product 'source.'" * * * Because a color, like a "descriptive" word mark, could eventually "come to indicate a product's origin," we concluded that it could be protected upon a showing of secondary meaning.

It seems to us that design, like color, is not inherently distinctive. The attribution of inherent distinctiveness to certain categories of word marks and product packaging derives from the fact that the very purpose of attaching a particular word to a product, or encasing it in a distinctive packaging, is most often to identify the source of the product. Although the words and packaging can serve subsidiary functions—a suggestive word mark (such as "Tide" for laundry detergent), for instance, may invoke positive connotations in the consumer's mind, and a garish form of packaging (such as Tide's squat, brightly decorated plastic bottles for its liquid laundry detergent) may attract an otherwise indifferent consumer's attention on a crowded store shelf—their predominant function remains source identification. Consumers are therefore predisposed to regard those symbols as indication of the producer, which is why such symbols "almost automatically tell a customer that they refer to a brand," id., at 162–163, 115 S.Ct. 1300, and "immediately ... signal a brand or a product 'source,'" id., at 163, 115 S.Ct. 1300. And where it is not reasonable to assume consumer predisposition to take an affixed word or packaging as indication of source—where, for example, the affixed word is descriptive of the product ("Tasty" bread) or of a geographic origin ("Georgia" peaches)—inherent distinctiveness will not be found. * * * In the case of product design, as in the case of color, we think consumer predisposition to equate the feature with the source does not exist. Consumers are aware of the reality that, almost invariably, even the most unusual of product designs—such as a cocktail shaker shaped like a penguin—is intended not to identify the source, but to render the product itself more useful or more appealing. The fact that product design almost invariably serves purposes other than source identification not only renders inherent distinctiveness problematic; it also renders application of an inherent-distinctiveness principle more harmful to other consumer interests. Consumers should not be deprived of the benefits of competition with regard to the utilitarian and esthetic purposes that product design ordinarily serves by a rule of law that facilitates plausible threats of suit against new entrants based upon alleged inherent distinctiveness. How easy it is to mount a plausible suit depends, of course, upon the clarity of the test for inherent distinctiveness, and where product design is concerned we have little confidence that a reasonably clear test can be devised. Respondent and the United States as amicus curiae urge us to adopt for product design relevant portions of the test formulated by the Court of Customs and Patent Appeals for product packaging in Seabrook Foods, Inc. v. Bar–Well Foods Ltd., 568 F.2d 1342 (1977). That opinion, in determining the inherent distinctiveness of a product's packaging, considered, among other things, "whether it was a 'common' basic shape or design, whether it was unique or unusual in a particular field, [and] whether it was a mere refinement of a commonly-adopted and well-known form of ornamentation for a particular class of goods viewed by the public as a dress or ornamentation for the goods." Id. at 1344. Such a test would rarely provide the basis for summary disposition of an anticompetitive strike suit. Indeed, at oral argument, counsel for the United States quite understandably would not give a definitive answer as to whether the test was met in this very case, saying only that "[t]his is a very difficult case for that purpose." Tr. of Oral Arg. 19.

It is true, of course, that the person seeking to exclude new entrants would have to establish the nonfunctionality of the design feature, see § 43(a)(3), 15 U.S.C.A. § 1125(a)(3) (Oct.1999 Supp.)—a showing that may involve consideration of its esthetic appeal, see Qualitex, 514 U.S., at 170, 115 S.Ct. 1300. Competition is deterred, however, not merely by successful suit but by the plausible threat of successful suit, and given the unlikelihood of inherently source-identifying design, the game of allowing suit based upon alleged inherent distinctiveness seems to us not worth the candle. That is especially so since the producer can ordinarily obtain protection for a design that is inherently source identifying (if any such exists), but that does not yet have secondary meaning, by securing a design patent or a copyright for the design—as, indeed, respondent did for certain elements of the designs in this case. The availability of these other protections greatly reduces any harm to the producer that might ensue from our conclusion that a product design cannot be protected under § 43(a) without a showing of secondary meaning.

Respondent contends that our decision in *Two Pesos* forecloses a conclusion that product-design trade dress can never be inherently distinctive. * * * *Two Pesos* unquestionably establishes the legal principle that trade dress can be inherently distinctive, but it does not establish that product-design trade dress can be. *Two Pesos* is inapposite to our holding here because the trade dress at issue, the decor of a restaurant, seems to us not to constitute product design. It was either product packaging—which, as we have discussed, normally is taken by the consumer to indicate origin—or else some tertium quid that is akin to product packaging and has no bearing on the present case.

Respondent replies that this manner of distinguishing *Two Pesos* will force courts to draw difficult lines between product-design and product-packaging trade dress. There will indeed be some hard cases at the margin: a classic glass Coca–Cola bottle, for instance, may constitute packaging for those consumers who drink the Coke and then discard the bottle, but may constitute the product itself for those consumers who are bottle collectors, or part of the product itself for those consumers who buy Coke in the classic glass bottle, rather than a can, because they think it more stylish to drink from the former. We believe, however, that the frequency and the difficulty of having to distinguish between product design and product packaging will be much less than the frequency and the difficulty of having to decide when a product design is inherently distinctive. To the extent there are close cases, we believe that courts should err on the side of caution and classify ambiguous trade dress as product design, thereby requiring secondary meaning. * * *

We hold that, in an action for infringement of unregistered trade dress under § 43(a) of the Lanham Act, a product's design is distinctive, and therefore protectible, only upon a showing of secondary meaning. The judgment of the Second Circuit is reversed, and the case is remanded for further proceedings consistent with this opinion. * * *

Notes

1. What is the basis for the Court's differing treatment of product configurations and trade dress? Does the Court adequately distinguish *Two Pesos*? What kind of showing must be made in order to protect product configurations?

2. Can the overall shape of a blender be protectable as a trademark? A gold-fish shaped cracker? A bedroom suite? Can a bottle design be protectable? What if the design is useful in placing the bottle on a bicycle? *Talking Rain Beverage Co. v. South Beach Beverage Co.*, 349 F.3d 601 (9th Cir. 2003).

3. Does the overall appearance of a Hummer constitute trade dress or is it a product configuration? *See generally General Motors Corp. v. Lanard Toys, Inc.*, 468 F.3d 405 (6th Cir. 2006) (suit alleging infringement of Hummer appearance by toymaker).

TrafFix DEVICES, INC. v. MARKETING DISPLAYS, INC.

Supreme Court of the United States, 2001.
532 U.S. 23, 121 S.Ct. 1255, 149 L.Ed.2d 164, 58 U.S.P.Q.2d 1001.

Justice Kennedy delivered the opinion of the Court:

Temporary road signs with warnings like "Road Work Ahead" or "Left Shoulder Closed" must withstand strong gusts of wind. An inventor named Robert Sarkisian obtained two utility patents for a mechanism built upon two springs (the dual-spring design) to keep these and other outdoor signs upright despite adverse wind conditions. The holder of the now-expired Sarkisian patents, respondent Marketing Displays, Inc. (MDI), established a successful business in the manufacture and sale of sign stands incorporating the patented feature. MDI's stands for road signs were recognizable to buyers and users (it says) because the dual-spring design was visible near the base of the sign.

This litigation followed after the patents expired and a competitor, TrafFix Devices, Inc., sold sign stands with a visible spring mechanism that looked like MDI's. MDI and TrafFix products looked alike because they were. When TrafFix started in business, it sent an MDI product abroad to have it reverse engineered, that is to say copied. Complicating matters, TrafFix marketed its sign stands under a name similar to MDI's. MDI used the name "WindMaster," while TrafFix, its new competitor, used "WindBuster." * * * [MDI brought a successful action against TrafFix for trademark infringement of its brand name, but the trial court rejected MDI's trade dress infringement claim as to the dual-spring design.]

I

We are concerned with the trade dress question. The District Court ruled against MDI on its trade dress claim. 971 F.Supp. 262 (E.D.Mich. 1997). After determining that the one element of MDI's trade dress at issue was the dual-spring design, it held that "no reasonable trier of fact could determine that MDI has established secondary meaning" in its alleged trade dress, id., at 269. In other words, consumers did not associate the look of the dual-spring design with MDI. As a second, independent reason to grant summary judgment in favor of TrafFix, the District Court determined the dual-spring design was functional. On this rationale secondary meaning is irrelevant because there can be no trade dress protection in any event. In ruling on the functional aspect of the design, the District Court noted that Sixth Circuit precedent indicated that the burden was on MDI to prove that its trade dress was nonfunctional, and not on TrafFix to show that it was functional (a rule since adopted by Congress, see 15 U.S.C. § 1125(a)(3) (1994 ed., Supp. V)), and then went on to consider MDI's arguments that the dual-spring design was subject to trade dress protection. Finding none of MDI's contentions persuasive, the District Court concluded MDI had not "proffered sufficient evidence which would enable a reasonable trier of fact to find that MDI's vertical dual-spring design is *non*-functional." Id., at 276. Summary judgment was entered against MDI on its trade dress claims.

The Court of Appeals for the Sixth Circuit reversed the trade dress ruling. 200 F.3d 929 (1999). The Court of Appeals held the District Court had erred in ruling MDI failed to show a genuine issue of material fact regarding whether it had secondary meaning in its alleged trade dress, id., at 938, and had erred further in determining that MDI could not prevail in any event because the alleged trade dress was in fact a functional product configuration, id., at 940. The Court of Appeals suggested the District Court committed legal error by looking only to the dual-spring design when evaluating MDI's trade dress. Basic to its reasoning was the Court of Appeals' observation that it took "little imagination to conceive of a hidden dual-spring mechanism or a tri or quad-spring mechanism that might avoid infringing [MDI's] trade dress." Ibid. * * * In its criticism of the District Court's ruling on the trade dress question, the Court of Appeals took note of a split among Courts of Appeals in various other Circuits on the issue whether the existence of an expired utility patent forecloses the possibility of the patentee's claiming trade dress protection in the product's design. 200 F.3d, at 939. Compare Sunbeam Products, Inc. v. West Bend Co., 123 F.3d 246 (C.A.5 1997) (holding that trade dress protection is not foreclosed), Thomas & Betts Corp. v. Panduit Corp., 138 F.3d 277 (C.A.7 1998) (same), and Midwest Industries, Inc. v. Karavan Trailers, Inc., 175 F.3d 1356 (C.A.Fed.1999) (same), with Vornado Air Circulation Systems, Inc. v. Duracraft Corp., 58 F.3d 1498, 1500 (C.A.10 1995) ("Where a product configuration is a significant inventive component of an invention covered by a utility patent … it cannot receive trade dress protection"). To resolve the conflict, we granted certiorari.

II

It is well established that trade dress can be protected under federal law. * * * As we explained just last Term, see Wal–Mart Stores, Inc. v.

Samara Brothers, Inc., 529 U.S. 205, 120 S.Ct. 1339, 146 L.Ed.2d 182 (2000), various Courts of Appeals have allowed claims of trade dress infringement relying on the general provision of the Lanham Act which provides a cause of action to one who is injured when a person uses "any word, term name, symbol, or device, or any combination thereof . . . which is likely to cause confusion . . . as to the origin, sponsorship, or approval of his or her goods." 15 U.S.C. § 1125(a)(1)(A). Congress confirmed this statutory protection for trade dress by amending the Lanham Act to recognize the concept. Title 15 U.S.C. § 1125(a)(3) (1994 ed., Supp. V) provides: "In a civil action for trade dress infringement under this chapter for trade dress not registered on the principal register, the person who asserts trade dress protection has the burden of proving that the matter sought to be protected is not functional." * * * And in Wal–Mart, supra, we were careful to caution against misuse or over-extension of trade dress. We noted that "product design almost invariably serves purposes other than source identification." Id., at 213, 120 S.Ct. 1339.

Trade dress protection must subsist with the recognition that in many instances there is no prohibition against copying goods and products. In general, unless an intellectual property right such as a patent or copyright protects an item, it will be subject to copying. As the Court has explained, copying is not always discouraged or disfavored by the laws which preserve our competitive economy. Bonito Boats, Inc. v. Thunder Craft Boats, Inc., 489 U.S. 141, 160, 109 S.Ct. 971, 103 L.Ed.2d 118 (1989). Allowing competitors to copy will have salutary effects in many instances. "Reverse engineering of chemical and mechanical articles in the public domain often leads to significant advances in technology." Ibid.

The principal question in this case is the effect of an expired patent on a claim of trade dress infringement. A prior patent, we conclude, has vital significance in resolving the trade dress claim. A utility patent is strong evidence that the features therein claimed are functional. If trade dress protection is sought for those features the strong evidence of functionality based on the previous patent adds great weight to the statutory presumption that features are deemed functional until proved otherwise by the party seeking trade dress protection. Where the expired patent claimed the features in question, one who seeks to establish trade dress protection must carry the heavy burden of showing that the feature is not functional, for instance by showing that it is merely an ornamental, incidental, or arbitrary aspect of the device.

In the case before us, the central advance claimed in the expired utility patents (the Sarkisian patents) is the dual-spring design; and the dual-spring design is the essential feature of the trade dress MDI now seeks to establish and to protect. The rule we have explained bars the trade dress claim, for MDI did not, and cannot, carry the burden of overcoming the strong evidentiary inference of functionality based on the disclosure of the dual-spring design in the claims of the expired patents.

The dual springs shown in the Sarkisian patents were well apart (at either end of a frame for holding a rectangular sign when one full side is the base) while the dual springs at issue here are close together (in a frame designed to hold a sign by one of its corners). As the District Court recognized, this makes little difference. The point is that the springs are necessary to the operation of the device. The fact that the springs in this very different-looking device fall within the claims of the patents is illustrated by MDI's own position in earlier litigation. In the late 1970's, MDI engaged in a long-running intellectual property battle with a company known as Winn–Proof. Although the precise claims of the Sarkisian patents cover sign stands with springs "spaced apart," U.S. Patent No. 3,646,696, col. 4; U.S. Patent No. 3,662,482, col. 4, the Winn–Proof sign stands (with springs much like the sign stands at issue here) were found to infringe the patents by the United States District Court for the District of Oregon, and the Court of Appeals for the Ninth Circuit affirmed the judgment. Sarkisian v. Winn–Proof Corp., 697 F.2d 1313 (1983). Although the Winn–Proof traffic sign stand (with dual springs close together) did not appear, then, to infringe the literal terms of the patent claims (which called for "spaced apart" springs), the Winn–Proof sign stand was found to infringe the patents under the doctrine of equivalents, which allows a finding of patent infringement even when the accused product does not fall within the literal terms of the claims. Id., at 1321–1322; see generally Warner–Jenkinson Co. v. Hilton Davis Chemical Co., 520 U.S. 17, 117 S.Ct. 1040, 137 L.Ed.2d 146 (1997). In light of this past ruling—a ruling procured at MDI's own insistence—it must be concluded the products here at issue would have been covered by the claims of the expired patents.

The rationale for the rule that the disclosure of a feature in the claims of a utility patent constitutes strong evidence of functionality is well illustrated in this case. The dual-spring design serves the important purpose of keeping the sign upright even in heavy wind conditions; and, as confirmed by the statements in the expired patents, it does so in a unique and useful manner. As the specification of one of the patents recites, prior art "devices, in practice, will topple under the force of a strong wind." U.S. Patent No. 3,662,482, col. 1. The dual-spring design allows sign stands to resist toppling in strong winds. Using a dual-spring design rather than a single spring achieves important operational advantages. For example, the specifications of the patents note that the "use of a pair of springs . . . as opposed to the use of a single spring to support the frame structure prevents canting or twisting of the sign around a vertical axis," and that, if not prevented, twisting "may cause damage to the spring structure and may result in tipping of the device." U.S. Patent No. 3,646,696, col. 3. In the course of patent prosecution, it was said that "[t]he use of a pair of spring connections as opposed to a single spring connection . . . forms an important part of this combination" because it "forc[es] the sign frame to tip along the longitudinal axis of the elongated ground-engaging members." App. 218. The dual-spring design affects the cost of the device as well; it was acknowledged that the device "could use three springs but this would unnecessarily increase the cost of the device." App. 217. These statements made in the patent applications and in the course of procuring the patents demonstrate the functionality of the design. MDI does not assert that any of these representations are mistaken or inaccurate, and this is further strong evidence of the functionality of the dual-spring design.

III

* * * Discussing trademarks, we have said " '[i]n general terms, a product feature is functional,' and cannot serve as a trademark, 'if it is essential to the use or purpose of the article or if it affects the cost or quality of the article.' " Qualitex, 514 U.S., at 165, 115 S.Ct. 1300 (quoting Inwood Laboratories, Inc. v. Ives Laboratories, Inc., 456 U.S. 844, 850, n. 10, 102 S.Ct. 2182, 72 L.Ed.2d 606 (1982)). Expanding upon the meaning of this phrase, we have observed that a functional feature is one the "exclusive use of [which] would put competitors at a significant non-reputation-related disadvantage." 514 U.S., at 165, 115 S.Ct. 1300. The Court of Appeals in the instant case seemed to interpret this language to mean that a necessary test for functionality is "whether the particular product configuration is a competitive necessity." 200 F.3d, at 940. See also Vornado, 58 F.3d, at 1507 ("Functionality, by contrast, has been defined both by our circuit, and more recently by the Supreme Court, in terms of competitive need"). This was incorrect as a comprehensive definition. As explained in Qualitex, supra, and Inwood, supra, a feature is also functional when it is essential to the use or purpose of the device or when it affects the cost or quality of the device. The *Qualitex* decision did not purport to displace this traditional rule. Instead, it quoted the rule as *Inwood* had set it forth. It is proper to inquire into a "significant non-reputation-related disadvantage" in cases of aesthetic functionality, the question involved in *Qualitex*. Where the design is functional under the *Inwood* formulation there is no need to proceed further to consider if there is a competitive necessity for the feature. In *Qualitex*, by contrast, aesthetic functionality was the central question, there having been no indication that the green-gold color of the laundry press pad had any bearing on the use or purpose of the product or its cost or quality.

* * *

There is no need, furthermore, to engage, as did the Court of Appeals, in speculation about other design possibilities, such as using three or four springs which might serve the same purpose. 200 F.3d, at 940. Here, the functionality of the spring design means that competitors need not explore whether other spring juxtapositions might be used. The dual-spring design is not an arbitrary flourish in the configuration of MDI's product; it is the reason the device works. Other designs need not be attempted.

Because the dual-spring design is functional, it is unnecessary for competitors to explore designs to hide the springs, say by using a box or framework to cover them, as suggested by the Court of Appeals. Ibid. The dual-spring design assures the user the device will work. If buyers are assured the product serves its purpose by seeing the operative mechanism that in itself serves an important market need. It would be at cross-purposes to those objectives, and something of a paradox, were we to require the manufacturer to conceal the very item the user seeks.

In a case where a manufacturer seeks to protect arbitrary, incidental, or ornamental aspects of features of a product found in the patent claims, such as arbitrary curves in the legs or an ornamental pattern painted on the springs, a different result might obtain. There the manufacturer could perhaps prove that those aspects do not serve a purpose within the terms of the utility patent. The inquiry into whether such features, asserted to be trade dress, are functional by reason of their inclusion in the claims of an expired utility patent could be aided by going beyond the claims and examining the patent and its prosecution history to see if the feature in question is shown as a useful part of the invention. No such claim is made here, however. MDI in essence seeks protection for the dual-spring design alone. The asserted trade dress consists simply of the dual-spring design, four legs, a base, an upright, and a sign. MDI has pointed to nothing arbitrary about the components of its device or the way they are assembled. The Lanham Act does not exist to reward manufacturers for their innovation in creating a particular device; that is the purpose of the patent law and its period of exclusivity. * * * Whether a utility patent has expired or there has been no utility patent at all, a product design which has a particular appearance may be functional because it is "essential to the use or purpose of the article" or "affects the cost or quality of the article." Inwood, 456 U.S., at 850, n. 10, 102 S.Ct. 2182.

TrafFix and some of its *amici* argue that the Patent Clause of the Constitution, Art. I, § 8, cl. 8, of its own force, prohibits the holder of an expired utility patent from claiming trade dress protection. We need not resolve this question. If, despite the rule that functional features may not be the subject of trade dress protection, a case arises in which trade dress becomes the practical equivalent of an expired utility patent, that will be time enough to consider the matter. The judgment of the Court of Appeals is reversed, and the case is remanded for further proceedings consistent with this opinion.

Notes

1. Can a distinctive, recognizable, and non-functional product configuration be protected under a dilution rationale? See I.P. Lund Trading ApS v. Kohler Co., 163 F.3d 27 (1st Cir.1998) (addressing dilution claim involving Kohler Falling Water faucet, which resembled plaintiff's highly acclaimed VOLA faucet). Can the design and appearance of buildings at Times Square, in New York, be protectable? *Sherwood 48 Assoc. v. Sony Corp. of America*, 76 Fed. Appx. 389 (2d Cir. 2003). What about the shape of a guitar? *Gibson Guitar Corp. v. Paul Reed Smith Guitars, LP*, 423 F.3d 539 (6th Cir. 2005).

2. For a recent case applying the *TrafFix* analysis, see *Fuji Kogyo Co. v. Pacific Bay International, Inc.*, 461 F.3d 675 (6th Cir. 2006).

D. FALSE ADVERTISING

CASTROL, INC. v. QUAKER STATE CORP.

United States Court of Appeals, Second Circuit, 1992.
977 F.2d 57.

WALKER, CIRCUIT JUDGE:

A Quaker State television commercial asserts that "tests prove" its 10W–30 motor oil provides better protection against engine wear at start-up. In a thoughtful opinion reported at 1992 WL 47981 (S.D.N.Y. March 2, 1992), the United States District Court for the Southern District of New York (Charles S. Haight, Judge) held that plaintiff-appellee Castrol, Inc. ("Castrol") had proven this advertised claim literally false pursuant to § 43(a) of the Lanham Act, 15 U.S.C. § 1125(a) (1988). The district court issued a March 20, 1992 Order preliminarily enjoining defendants-appellants Quaker State Corporation, Quaker State Oil Refining Corporation, and Grey Advertising Inc., ("Quaker State"), from airing the commercial. We agree that Castrol has shown a likelihood of success in proving the commercial literally false. We accordingly affirm.

* * *

The voiceover to Quaker State's 10W–30 motor oil commercial states:

> Warning: Up to half of all engine wear can happen when you start your car. At this critical time, tests prove Quaker State 10W–30 protects better than any other leading 10W–30 motor oil. In an overwhelming majority of engine tests, Quaker State 10W–30 flowed faster to all vital parts. In all size engines tested, Quaker State protected faster, so it protected better. Get the best protection against start up wear. Today's Quaker State! It's one tough motor oil.

Visually, the commercial begins with a man entering a car and then shows a bottle of Quaker State 10W–30 motor oil. Large, block letters, superimposed over the bottle, "crawl" across the screen with the words: AT START UP QUAKER STATE 10W–30 PROTECTS BETTER THAN ANY OTHER LEADING 10W–30 MOTOR OIL. Originally, this "crawl" used the words "tests prove" instead of "at start up," but shortly after the filing of the current lawsuit Quaker State revised the message. The commercial then shows an engine, superimposed over which are bottles of Quaker State and four competing motor oils (including Castrol GTX 10W–30) and a bar graph depicting the speed with which each oil flowed to components of a Chrysler engine. The Quaker State bar is higher than all four competitors indicating that it flowed faster. The commercial closes with the words: "ONE TOUGH MOTOR OIL."

Polymethacrylate or "PMA," an additive intended to quicken oil flow to engine parts, is the source of Quaker State's superiority claim. The competitors listed in its commercial use olefin copolymer or "OCP," another additive. Two laboratory tests, the first run in 1987 and the second in 1991, have compared Quaker State's PMA-based oil with competing OCP-based oils. Rohm and Haas, the Pennsylvania corporation which manufactures PMA, conducted both tests.

Rohm and Haas' 1987 tests measured two performance indicators: "oiling time," or the time it takes for oil to reach distant parts in a just-started engine, and engine wear, measured through the amount of metal debris observed in the oil after the engine had run. Rohm and Haas technicians filled engines, in all other respects similar, with either Quaker State's PMA-based 10W–30 oil, or with a generic OCP-based oil known as "Texstar." During numerous engine starts, Quaker State's oil demonstrated a substantially faster oiling time, reaching distant engine parts as much as 100 seconds earlier than the Texstar competitor. Contrary to expectations, however, this did not translate into reduced engine wear. A Rohm and Haas report stated that "[a]fter 64 starts ... the Quaker State oil gave marginally better results, but there was no significant difference in wear metals accumulation between the two oils."

Rohm and Haas initially attributed the poor engine wear results to the presence of "residual oil" remaining from the prior engine starts. They theorized that this oil might be lubricating the engine in the period between ignition and arrival of the new oil, and so might be preventing the faster flowing Quaker State oil from demonstrating better protection that is statistically significant. To address this, they conducted additional engine starts with a warm-up between each run so as to burn off the residual oil. The Rohm and Haas report, however, concluded that "[w]ear metals analysis for this test cycle also failed to differentiate significantly between the two oils.... " Thus, while the 1987 Rohm and Haas tests demonstrated faster oil flow, they could not prove better protection against engine wear that is statistically significant.

The 1991 Rohm and Haas tests compared Quaker State's oiling time with that of four leading OCP-based competitors, including Castrol GTX 10W–30. Again, Quaker State's PMA-based oil flowed significantly faster to engine parts. Using a 1991 2.2 liter Chrysler engine with a sump temperature of minus 20 degrees Fahrenheit, for example, the Quaker State oiling time was 345 seconds, as compared to the competing oils' times of 430, 430, 505 and 510 seconds. In the 1991 tests, as opposed to the 1987 studies, Rohm and Haas made no attempt to measure whether this faster oiling time resulted in reduced engine wear.

Quaker State broadcast their commercial in November, 1991. On December 19, 1991, Castrol initiated the present action. Castrol asserted that no studies supported the commercial's claim that "tests prove" Quaker State's oil provides better protection, and that this claim of test-proven superiority constituted false advertising. * * * At the hearing on the motion for a preliminary injunction, Quaker State relied on the Rohm and Haas tests. It argued that the Rohm and Haas oiling time findings support the advertised claim of better protection because oil which flows faster to engine parts necessarily protects them better. Dr. Elmer Klaus, Quaker State's sole expert witness, * * * concluded that the faster the new oil flows to the engine parts, the better job it does of minimizing this second period of boundary lubrication. Faster oil flow, therefore, means better protection.

Castrol's three experts focused on the role of residual oil. They testified that the small amount of residual oil left from a prior running of an engine provides more than adequate lubrication at the next start-up. Moreover, they asserted that this residual oil remains functional for a significant period of time so that both PMA-based and OCP-based 10W–30 motor oils reach the engine parts before this residual oil burns off. Thus, they maintained, there is no second boundary lubrication period and Quaker State's faster oiling time is irrelevant to engine wear.

* * *

Judge Haight concluded that because residual oil "holds the fort," Rohm and Haas' faster oiling time findings did not necessarily prove better protection. He consequently held that "Castrol has established the likelihood of proving at trial the falsity of Quaker State's claim that tests prove its oil protects better against start-up engine wear." * * *

Section 43(a) of the Lanham Act, 15 U.S.C. § 1125(a) (1988), pursuant to which Castrol brings this false advertising claim, provides that

> Any person who, on or in connection with any goods or services . . . uses in commerce any . . . false or misleading description of fact, or false or misleading representation of fact, which—* * * (2) in commercial advertising or promotion, misrepresents the nature, characteristics, qualities, or geographic origin of his or her or another person's goods, services, or commercial activities, shall be liable in a civil action by any person who believes that he or she is or is likely to be damaged by such act.

To succeed under § 43(a), a plaintiff must demonstrate that "an advertisement is either literally false or that the advertisement, though literally true, is likely to mislead and confuse consumers. . . . Where the advertising claim is shown to be literally false, the court may enjoin the use of the claim 'without reference to the advertisement's impact on the buying public.' " McNeil–P.C.C., Inc. v. Bristol–Myers Squibb Co., 938 F.2d 1544, 1549 (2d Cir.1991) (quoting Coca–Cola, 690 F.2d at 317) (citations omitted). Here, Castrol contends that the challenged advertisement is literally false. It bears the burden of proving this to a "likelihood of success" standard.

As we have on two occasions explained, plaintiff bears a different burden in proving literally false the advertised claim that tests prove defendant's product superior, than it does in proving the falsity of a superiority claim which makes no mention of tests. In Procter & Gamble

Co. v. Chesebrough–Pond's, Inc., 747 F.2d 114 (2d Cir.1984), for example, Chesebrough alleged the literal falsity of Procter's advertised claim that "clinical tests" proved its product superior. Id. at 116. Procter, in return, challenged as literally false a Chesebrough commercial which, making no mention of tests, asserted that its lotion was equal in effectiveness to any leading brand. Id. We explained that in order to prove literally false Procter's claim of "test-proven superiority," Chesebrough bore the burden of "showing that the tests referred to by P & G were not sufficiently reliable to permit one to conclude with reasonable certainty that they established the proposition for which they were cited." Id. at 119. We held that Procter could prove false Chesebrough's advertisement, however, "only upon adducing evidence" that affirmatively showed Chesebrough's claim of parity to be false. Id.

We drew this same distinction in McNeil–P.C.C., Inc. v. Bristol–Myers Squibb Co., 938 F.2d 1544 (2d Cir.1991). Bristol–Myers initially advertised to trade professionals that "clinical studies" had shown its analgesic provided better relief than McNeil's. Id. at 1546. Bristol–Myers' later televised commercial made the product superiority claim but "did not refer to clinical studies." Id. We held that, with respect to the initial trade advertising, "McNeil could ... meet its burden of proof by demonstrating that these studies did not establish that AF Excedrin provided superior pain relief." Id. at 1549. With respect to the televised commercial, however, McNeil bore the burden of generating "scientific proof that the challenged advertisement was false." Id.

A plaintiff's burden in proving literal falsity thus varies depending on the nature of the challenged advertisement. Where the defendant's advertisement claims that its product is superior, plaintiff must affirmatively prove defendant's product equal or inferior. Where, as in the current case, defendant's ad explicitly or implicitly represents that tests or studies prove its product superior, plaintiff satisfies its burden by showing that the tests did not establish the proposition for which they were cited. We have held that a plaintiff can meet this burden by demonstrating that the tests were not sufficiently reliable to permit a conclusion that the product is superior. The *Procter* "sufficiently reliable" standard of course assumes that the tests in question, if reliable, would prove the proposition for which they are cited. If the plaintiff can show that the tests, even if reliable, do not establish the proposition asserted by the defendant, the plaintiff has obviously met its burden. In such a case, tests which may or may not be "sufficiently reliable," are simply irrelevant.

The district court held that Castrol had met this latter burden, stating that "Castrol has established the likelihood of proving at trial the falsity of Quaker State's claim that tests prove its oil protects better.... " In this Lanham Act case, we will reverse the district court's order of preliminary injunctive relief "only upon a showing that it abused its discretion, which may occur when a court bases its decision on clearly erroneous findings of fact or on errors as to applicable law." Procter, 747 F.2d at 118.

I. The district court committed no errors of law.

Quaker State contends that the district court improperly shifted the burden of proof to the defendant when it stated that "the claim that tests demonstrate ... superiority is false because no test does so and [Dr.] Klaus' analysis fails to fill the gap." It argues that plaintiff bears the burden in a false advertising action and there should be no "gap" for defendant to fill.

Where a plaintiff challenges a test-proven superiority advertisement, the defendant must identify the cited tests. Plaintiff must then prove that these tests did not establish the proposition for which they were cited. McNeil, 938 F.2d at 1549. At the hearing, Quaker State cited the 1987 and 1991 Rohm and Haas oiling time tests in conjunction with Dr. Klaus' theory of engine wear at the second boundary lubrication period. Castrol's burden was to prove that neither the Rohm and Haas tests alone, nor the tests in conjunction with Dr. Klaus' theory, permitted the conclusion to a reasonable certainty that Quaker State's oil protected better at start-up. The district court's statement that "no test [demonstrates superiority] and Klaus' analysis fails to fill the gap" is a finding that Castrol, through its residual oil theory, met its burden. It is, in substance, a finding that the Quaker State tests, which proved faster oiling time, are irrelevant to their claim that Quaker State's oil protects better at start-up. Therefore, we need not consider the tests' reliability. The district court's statement does not shift the burden to defendant.
* * *

II. The district court's findings as to the role of residual oil were not clearly erroneous.

Quaker State asserts that the district court's factual findings as to the role of residual oil are clearly erroneous. See Fed.R.Civ.P. 52(a). We disagree. * * *

In this case, the district court heard five days of expert testimony. Its credibility determinations in favor of Castrol's experts and against Quaker State's support its finding that "residual oil holds the fort." This finding also receives support from the videotape of residual oil in an engine, the absence of catastrophic engine failure following the imposition of the J300 standards, and Rohm and Haas' 1987 failure to demonstrate reduced engine wear. Nothing in the record convincingly contradicts the district court's conclusion. Under the applicable legal standards, we are hard pressed to hold Judge Haight's residual oil finding clearly erroneous.

Quaker State argues that the residual oil theory flies in the face of decades of technical literature documenting the existence of start-up wear. It reasons that if residual oil truly lasted until the new oil arrived, start-up wear would not be possible.

Dr. Hoult, a Castrol expert, answered this point. He testified that the term "start-up," as used in the cited technical papers, refers not to the period between ignition and full oil flow but to the time between ignition and the achievement of equilibrium temperature in the engine. The relatively cool engine temperature during the start-up period, thus defined, results in increased wear due to certain chemical properties best described by Dr. Hoult himself:

> When the engine is driven for a short period of time under cold conditions, it never gets fully warm. And in the combustion process of reciprocating engines, there are acids which are formed, typically nitrate acid; if the fuels have sulfur, sulfuric acid. In a cold engine, there is more acids that mix with the lubricants than there is in a hot engine, because in a hot engine, the parts are hot enough that the acid doesn't condense on them. So that when an engine is colder[,] when it's started up from cold conditions, the engine chemistry is different. And the general understanding [in the field] is that that changes engine wear rate.

This credited testimony effectively rebuts Quaker State's objection. Viewing the record as a whole, we are not left with a " 'definite and firm conviction that a mistake has been committed.' " Anderson, 470 U.S. at 573, 105 S.Ct. at 1511 (citation omitted). We accordingly reject Quaker State's contention that Judge Haight's findings on the role of residual oil are clearly erroneous.

III.   Is the district court's injunction overly broad?

In a March 20, 1992 memorandum opinion accompanying its simultaneously-issued Order of Preliminary Injunction, the district court explained its intent "to enjoin preliminarily Quaker State from claiming 'that tests prove its oil protects better against start-up engine wear.' " The injunction, however, goes beyond this limited intent. Paragraph 2 of the injunction states that

> Defendants ... are preliminarily enjoined from broadcasting, publishing or disseminating, in any manner or in any medium, any advertisement, commercial, or promotional matter ... that claims, directly or by clear implication, that: (a) Quaker State 10W–30 motor oil provides superior protection against engine wear at start-up; (b) Quaker State 10W–30 motor oil provides better protection against engine wear at start-up than other leading 10W–30 motor oils, including Castrol GTX 10W–30; or (c) Castrol GTX 10W–30 motor oil provides inferior protection against engine wear at start-up.

This paragraph enjoins Quaker State from distributing any advertisement claiming that its oil provides superior protection against engine wear at start-up, whether or not the ad claims test-proven superiority. As explained above, Castrol bears a different burden of proof with respect to this broader injunction than it does in seeking to enjoin only commercials which make the test-proven superiority claim.

The district court expressly found that Castrol had met its burden with respect to any test-proven superiority advertisement. It stated that "Castrol has established the likelihood of proving at trial the falsity of

Quaker State's claim that tests prove its oil protects better.... " Its injunction would be too broad, however, absent the additional finding that Castrol had met its burden with respect to superiority advertisements that omit the "tests prove" language. As we have noted above, Castrol meets this burden by adducing proof that Quaker State's oil is not, in fact, superior. * * *

Notes

1. What advertising claims can Quaker State still make in light of the injunction? More generally, are claims about a product's "great performance," "superior performance," or "high quality" actionable under section 43(a)?

2. Would a competitor's message asserting that a manufacturer of consumer products funded Satanic causes or was somehow connected with Satan be actionable? See Proctor & Gamble Co. v. Haugen, 222 F.3d 1262 (10th Cir. 2000).

3. For further discussion of false advertising claims under section 43(a), see 3 J. Thomas McCarthy, Trademarks and Unfair Competition §§ 27.01 to 27.12 (3d ed. 1995); Restatement (Third) of Unfair Competition §§ 2–3, 6 (1995).

Part III

THE RIGHT OF PUBLICITY

Chapter 8

PROTECTING PERSONAL IDENTITY

MIDLER v. FORD MOTOR CO.

United States Court of Appeals, Ninth Circuit, 1988.
849 F.2d 460.

Noonan, Circuit Judge:

This case centers on the protectibility of the voice of a celebrated chanteuse from commercial exploitation without her consent. Ford Motor Company and its advertising agency, Young & Rubicam, Inc., in 1985 advertised the Ford Lincoln Mercury with a series of nineteen 30 or 60 second television commercials in what the agency called "The Yuppie Campaign." The aim was to make an emotional connection with Yuppies, bringing back memories of when they were in college. Different popular songs of the seventies were sung on each commercial. The agency tried to get "the original people," that is, the singers who had popularized the songs, to sing them. Failing in that endeavor in ten cases the agency had the songs sung by "sound alikes." Bette Midler, the plaintiff and appellant here, was done by a sound alike.

Midler is a nationally known actress and singer. She won a Grammy as early as 1973 as the Best New Artist of that year. Records made by her since then have gone Platinum and Gold. She was nominated in 1979 for an Academy award for Best Female Actress in The Rose, in which she portrayed a pop singer. Newsweek in its June 30, 1986 issue described her as an "outrageously original singer/comedian." Time hailed her in its March 2, 1987 issue as "a legend" and "the most dynamic and poignant singer-actress of her time."

When Young & Rubicam was preparing the Yuppie Campaign it presented the commercial to its client by playing an edited version of Midler singing "Do You Want To Dance," taken from the 1973 Midler album, "The Divine Miss M." After the client accepted the idea and form of the commercial, the agency contacted Midler's manager, Jerry Edelstein. The conversation went as follows: "Hello, I am Craig Hazen from

Young and Rubicam. I am calling you to find out if Bette Midler would be interested in doing . . . ?" Edelstein: "Is it a commercial?" "Yes." "We are not interested."

Undeterred, Young & Rubicam sought out Ula Hedwig whom it knew to have been one of "the Harlettes" a backup singer for Midler for ten years. Hedwig was told by Young & Rubicam that "they wanted someone who could sound like Bette Midler's recording of [Do You Want To Dance]." She was asked to make a "demo" tape of the song if she was interested. She made an a capella demo and got the job.

At the direction of Young & Rubicam, Hedwig then made a record for the commercial. The Midler record of "Do You Want To Dance" was first played to her. She was told to "sound as much as possible like the Bette Midler record," leaving out only a few "aahs" unsuitable for the commercial. Hedwig imitated Midler to the best of her ability.

After the commercial was aired Midler was told by "a number of people" that it "sounded exactly" like her record of "Do You Want To Dance." Hedwig was told by "many personal friends" that they thought it was Midler singing the commercial. Ken Fritz, a personal manager in the entertainment business not associated with Midler, declares by affidavit that he heard the commercial on more than one occasion and thought Midler was doing the singing.

Neither the name nor the picture of Midler was used in the commercial; Young & Rubicam had a license from the copyright holder to use the song. At issue in this case is only the protection of Midler's voice. The district court described the defendants' conduct as that "of the average thief." They decided, "If we can't buy it, we'll take it." The court nonetheless believed there was no legal principle preventing imitation of Midler's voice and so gave summary judgment for the defendants. Midler appeals.

The First Amendment protects much of what the media do in the reproduction of likenesses or sounds. A primary value is freedom of speech and press. Time, Inc. v. Hill, 385 U.S. 374, 388, 87 S.Ct. 534, 542, 17 L.Ed.2d 456 (1967). The purpose of the media's use of a person's identity is central. If the purpose is "informative or cultural" the use is immune; "if it serves no such function but merely exploits the individual portrayed, immunity will not be granted." Felcher and Rubin, "Privacy, Publicity and the Portrayal of Real People by the Media," 88 Yale L.J. 1577, 1596 (1979). Moreover, federal copyright law preempts much of the area. "Mere imitation of a recorded performance would not constitute a copyright infringement even where one performer deliberately sets out to simulate another's performance as exactly as possible." Notes of Committee on the Judiciary, 17 U.S.C.A. § 114(b). It is in the context of these First Amendment and federal copyright distinctions that we address the present appeal.

Nancy Sinatra once sued Goodyear Tire and Rubber Company on the basis of an advertising campaign by Young & Rubicam featuring "These Boots Are Made For Walkin'," a song closely identified with her;

the female singers of the commercial were alleged to have imitated her voice and style and to have dressed and looked like her. The basis of Nancy Sinatra's complaint was unfair competition; she claimed that the song and the arrangement had acquired "a secondary meaning" which, under California law, was protectible. This court noted that the defendants "had paid a very substantial sum to the copyright proprietor to obtain the license for the use of the song and all of its arrangements." To give Sinatra damages for their use of the song would clash with federal copyright law. Summary judgment for the defendants was affirmed. Sinatra v. Goodyear Tire & Rubber Co., 435 F.2d 711, 717–718 (9th Cir.1970), cert. denied, 402 U.S. 906, 91 S.Ct. 1376, 28 L.Ed.2d 646 (1971). If Midler were claiming a secondary meaning to "Do You Want To Dance" or seeking to prevent the defendants from using that song, she would fail like Sinatra. But that is not this case. Midler does not seek damages for Ford's use of "Do You Want To Dance," and thus her claim is not preempted by federal copyright law. Copyright protects "original works of authorship fixed in any tangible medium of expression." 17 U.S.C. § 102(a). A voice is not copyrightable. The sounds are not "fixed." What is put forward as protectible here is more personal than any work of authorship.

Bert Lahr once sued Adell Chemical Co. for selling Lestoil by means of a commercial in which an imitation of Lahr's voice accompanied a cartoon of a duck. Lahr alleged that his style of vocal delivery was distinctive in pitch, accent, inflection, and sounds. The First Circuit held that Lahr had stated a cause of action for unfair competition, that it could be found "that defendant's conduct saturated plaintiff's audience, curtailing his market." Lahr v. Adell Chemical Co., 300 F.2d 256, 259 (1st Cir.1962). That case is more like this one. But we do not find unfair competition here. One-minute commercials of the sort the defendants put on would not have saturated Midler's audience and curtailed her market. Midler did not do television commercials. The defendants were not in competition with her.

California Civil Code section 3344 is also of no aid to Midler. The statute affords damages to a person injured by another who uses the person's "name, voice, signature, photograph or likeness, in any manner." The defendants did not use Midler's name or anything else whose use is prohibited by the statute. The voice they used was Hedwig's, not hers. The term "likeness" refers to a visual image not a vocal imitation. The statute, however, does not preclude Midler from pursuing any cause of action she may have at common law; the statute itself implies that such common law causes of action do exist because it says its remedies are merely "cumulative." Id. § 3344(g).

* * * Appropriation of common law rights is a tort in California. Motschenbacher v. R.J. Reynolds Tobacco Co., 498 F.2d 821 (9th Cir. 1974). In that case what the defendants used in their television commercial for Winston cigarettes was a photograph of a famous professional racing driver's racing car. The number of the car was changed and a wing-like device known as a "spoiler" was attached to the car; the car's features of white pinpointing, an oval medallion, and solid red coloring were retained. The driver, Lothar Motschenbacher, was in the car but his features were not visible. Some persons, viewing the commercial, correctly inferred that the car was his and that he was in the car and was therefore endorsing the product. The defendants were held to have invaded a "proprietary interest" of Motschenbacher in his own identity. Id. at 825.

Midler's case is different from Motschenbacher's. He and his car were physically used by the tobacco company's ad; he made part of his living out of giving commercial endorsements. But, as Judge Koelsch expressed it in *Motschenbacher*, California will recognize an injury from "an appropriation of the attributes of one's identity." Id. at 824. It was irrelevant that Motschenbacher could not be identified in the ad. The ad suggested that it was he. The ad did so by emphasizing signs or symbols associated with him. In the same way the defendants here used an imitation to convey the impression that Midler was singing for them.

Why did the defendants ask Midler to sing if her voice was not of value to them? Why did they studiously acquire the services of a sound-alike and instruct her to imitate Midler if Midler's voice was not of value to them? What they sought was an attribute of Midler's identity. Its value was what the market would have paid for Midler to have sung the commercial in person.

A voice is more distinctive and more personal than the automobile accoutrements protected in *Motschenbacher*. A voice is as distinctive and personal as a face. The human voice is one of the most palpable ways identity is manifested. We are all aware that a friend is at once known by a few words on the phone. At a philosophical level it has been observed that with the sound of a voice, "the other stands before me." D. Ihde, Listening and Voice 77 (1976). A fortiori, these observations hold true of singing, especially singing by a singer of renown. The singer manifests herself in the song. To impersonate her voice is to pirate her identity.

We need not and do not go so far as to hold that every imitation of a voice to advertise merchandise is actionable. We hold only that when a distinctive voice of a professional singer is widely known and is deliberately imitated in order to sell a product, the sellers have appropriated what is not theirs and have committed a tort in California. Midler has made a showing, sufficient to defeat summary judgment, that the defendants here for their own profit in selling their product did appropriate part of her identity.

Notes

1. Should the right of publicity be deemed a personal right—like defamation—that cannot be asserted upon the individual's death, or a commercial right that can be maintained by an estate or other successor in interest? Would resolution of this issue depend on the policy underpinning of the right of publicity? Cases holding that the right of publicity survives

death include McFarland v. Miller, 14 F.3d 912 (3d Cir.1994) (suit by estate of George "Spanky" McFarland against restaurant using his character's name); Martin Luther King, Jr., Center for Social Change, Inc. v. American Heritage Products, Inc., 694 F.2d 674 (11th Cir.1983); Joplin Enterprises v. Allen, 795 F.Supp. 349 (W.D.Wash.1992) (play making use of Janis Joplin's voice and name); State of Tennessee ex rel. Elvis Presley International Memorial Foundation v. Crowell, 733 S.W.2d 89 (Tenn.App.1987). Cases holding that the right of publicity does not survive death include Pirone v. MacMillan, Inc., 894 F.2d 579 (2d Cir.1990) (Babe Ruth photographs); Southeast Bank, N.A. v. Lawrence, 66 N.Y.2d 910, 498 N.Y.S.2d 775, 489 N.E.2d 744 (N.Y. 1985) (theater named after Tennessee Williams); Reeves v. United Artists Corp. 765 F.2d 79 (6th Cir.1985) (boxer).

2. Would professional baseball players' publicity rights with regard to the broadcast of copyrighted baseball games be preempted by federal copyright law? Is this situation different from *Midler*? See Baltimore Orioles, Inc. v. Major League Baseball Players Association, 805 F.2d 663 (7th Cir.1986), which is excerpted in Chapter 21, Part A *infra*.

3. For further discussion of the right of publicity, see 4 J. Thomas McCarthy, Trademarks and Unfair Competition §§ 28.01 to 28.07 (3d ed. 1995); Restatement (Third) of Unfair Competition §§ 46–49 (1995).

WHITE v. SAMSUNG ELECTRONICS AMERICA, INC.

United States Court of Appeals, Ninth Circuit, 1992.
971 F.2d 1395, cert. denied, 508 U.S. 951, 113 S.Ct. 2443, 124 L.Ed.2d 660 (1993).

GOODWIN, SENIOR CIRCUIT JUDGE:

This case involves a promotional "fame and fortune" dispute. In running a particular advertisement without Vanna White's permission, defendants Samsung Electronics America, Inc. (Samsung) and David Deutsch Associates, Inc. (Deutsch) attempted to capitalize on White's fame to enhance their fortune. White sued, alleging infringement of various intellectual property rights, but the district court granted summary judgment in favor of the defendants. We affirm in part, reverse in part, and remand.

Plaintiff Vanna White is the hostess of "Wheel of Fortune," one of the most popular game shows in television history. An estimated forty million people watch the program daily. Capitalizing on the fame which her participation in the show has bestowed on her, White markets her identity to various advertisers.

The dispute in this case arose out of a series of advertisements prepared for Samsung by Deutsch. The series ran in at least half a dozen publications with widespread, and in some cases national, circulation. Each of the advertisements in the series followed the same theme. Each depicted a current item from popular culture and a Samsung electronic product. Each was set in the twenty-first century and conveyed the message that the Samsung product would still be in use by that time. By hypothesizing outrageous future outcomes for the cultural items, the ads created humorous effects. For example, one lampooned current popular notions of an unhealthy diet by depicting a raw steak with the caption: "Revealed to be health food. 2010 A.D." Another depicted irreverent "news"-show host Morton Downey Jr. in front of an American flag with the caption: "Presidential candidate. 2008 A.D."

The advertisement which prompted the current dispute was for Samsung video-cassette recorders (VCRs). The ad depicted a robot, dressed in a wig, gown, and jewelry which Deutsch consciously selected to resemble White's hair and dress. The robot was posed next to a game board which is instantly recognizable as the Wheel of Fortune game show set, in a stance for which White is famous. The caption of the ad read: "Longest-running game show. 2012 A.D." Defendants referred to the ad as the "Vanna White" ad. Unlike the other celebrities used in the campaign, White neither consented to the ads nor was she paid.

Following the circulation of the robot ad, White sued Samsung and Deutsch in federal district court under: (1) California Civil Code § 3344; (2) the California common law right of publicity; and (3) § 43(a) of the Lanham Act, 15 U.S.C. § 1125(a). The district court granted summary judgment against White on each of her claims. White now appeals.

I.   Section 3344

White first argues that the district court erred in rejecting her claim under section 3344. Section 3344(a) provides, in pertinent part, that "[a]ny person who knowingly uses another's name, voice, signature, photograph, or likeness, in any manner, ... for purposes of advertising or selling, ... without such person's prior consent ... shall be liable for any damages sustained by the person or persons injured as a result thereof."

White argues that the Samsung advertisement used her "likeness" in contravention of section 3344. In Midler v. Ford Motor Co., 849 F.2d 460 (9th Cir.1988), this court rejected Bette Midler's section 3344 claim concerning a Ford television commercial in which a Midler "sound-alike" sang a song which Midler had made famous. In rejecting Midler's claim, this court noted that "[t]he defendants did not use Midler's name or anything else whose use is prohibited by the statute. The voice they used was [another person's], not hers. The term 'likeness' refers to a visual image not a vocal imitation." Id. at 463.

In this case, Samsung and Deutsch used a robot with mechanical features, and not, for example, a manikin molded to White's precise features. Without deciding for all purposes when a caricature or impressionistic resemblance might become a "likeness," we agree with the district court that the robot at issue here was not White's "likeness" within the meaning of section 3344. Accordingly, we affirm the court's dismissal of White's section 3344 claim.

II.   Right of Publicity

White next argues that the district court erred in granting summary judgment to defendants on White's common law right of publicity claim.

In Eastwood v. Superior Court, 149 Cal.App.3d 409, 198 Cal.Rptr. 342 (1983), the California court of appeal stated that the common law right of publicity cause of action "may be pleaded by alleging (1) the defendant's use of the plaintiff's identity; (2) the appropriation of plaintiff's name or likeness to defendant's advantage, commercially or otherwise; (3) lack of consent; and (4) resulting injury." Id. at 417, 198 Cal.Rptr. 342 (citing Prosser, Law of Torts (4th ed. 1971) § 117, pp. 804–807). The district court dismissed White's claim for failure to satisfy *Eastwood*'s second prong, reasoning that defendants had not appropriated White's "name or likeness" with their robot ad. We agree that the robot ad did not make use of White's name or likeness. However, the common law right of publicity is not so confined.

The *Eastwood* court did not hold that the right of publicity cause of action could be pleaded only by alleging an appropriation of name or likeness. *Eastwood* involved an unauthorized use of photographs of Clint Eastwood and of his name. Accordingly, the *Eastwood* court had no occasion to consider the extent beyond the use of name or likeness to which the right of publicity reaches. That court held only that the right of publicity cause of action "may be" pleaded by alleging, inter alia, appropriation of name or likeness, not that the action may be pleaded only in those terms.

The "name or likeness" formulation referred to in *Eastwood* originated not as an element of the right of publicity cause of action, but as a description of the types of cases in which the cause of action had been recognized. The source of this formulation is Prosser, Privacy, 48 Cal. L.Rev. 383, 401–07 (1960), one of the earliest and most enduring articulations of the common law right of publicity cause of action. In looking at the case law to that point, Prosser recognized that right of publicity cases involved one of two basic factual scenarios: name appropriation, and picture or other likeness appropriation. Id. at 401–02, nn. 156–57.

Even though Prosser focused on appropriations of name or likeness in discussing the right of publicity, he noted that "[i]t is not impossible that there might be appropriation of the plaintiff's identity, as by impersonation, without the use of either his name or his likeness, and that this would be an invasion of his right of privacy." Id. at 401, n. 155.[1] At the time Prosser wrote, he noted however, that "[n]o such case appears to have arisen." Id.

Since Prosser's early formulation, the case law has borne out his insight that the right of publicity is not limited to the appropriation of name or likeness. In Motschenbacher v. R.J. Reynolds Tobacco Co., 498 F.2d 821 (9th Cir.1974), the defendant had used a photograph of the plaintiff's race car in a television commercial. Although the plaintiff appeared driving the car in the photograph, his features were not visible. Even though the defendant had not appropriated the plaintiff's name or

---

1. Under Professor Prosser's scheme, the right of publicity is the last of the four categories of the right to privacy. Prosser, 48 Cal.L.Rev. at 389.

likeness, this court held that plaintiff's California right of publicity claim should reach the jury.

In *Midler*, this court held that, even though the defendants had not used Midler's name or likeness, Midler had stated a claim for violation of her California common law right of publicity because "the defendants ... for their own profit in selling their product did appropriate part of her identity" by using a Midler sound-alike. Id. at 463–64.

In Carson v. Here's Johnny Portable Toilets, Inc., 698 F.2d 831 (6th Cir.1983), the defendant had marketed portable toilets under the brand name "Here's Johnny"—Johnny Carson's signature "Tonight Show" introduction—without Carson's permission. The district court had dismissed Carson's Michigan common law right of publicity claim because the defendants had not used Carson's "name or likeness." Id. at 835. In reversing the district court, the sixth circuit found "the district court's conception of the right of publicity ... too narrow" and held that the right was implicated because the defendant had appropriated Carson's identity by using, inter alia, the phrase "Here's Johnny." Id. at 835–37.

These cases teach not only that the common law right of publicity reaches means of appropriation other than name or likeness, but that the specific means of appropriation are relevant only for determining whether the defendant has in fact appropriated the plaintiff's identity. The right of publicity does not require that appropriations of identity be accomplished through particular means to be actionable. It is noteworthy that the *Midler* and *Carson* defendants not only avoided using the plaintiff's name or likeness, but they also avoided appropriating the celebrity's voice, signature, and photograph. The photograph in *Motschenbacher* did include the plaintiff, but because the plaintiff was not visible the driver could have been an actor or dummy and the analysis in the case would have been the same.

Although the defendants in these cases avoided the most obvious means of appropriating the plaintiffs' identities, each of their actions directly implicated the commercial interests which the right of publicity is designed to protect. As the *Carson* court explained:

> [t]he right of publicity has developed to protect the commercial interest of celebrities in their identities. The theory of the right is that a celebrity's identity can be valuable in the promotion of products, and the celebrity has an interest that may be protected from the unauthorized commercial exploitation of that identity....
> If the celebrity's identity is commercially exploited, there has been an invasion of his right whether or not his "name or likeness" is used.

Carson, 698 F.2d at 835. It is not important how the defendant has appropriated the plaintiff's identity, but whether the defendant has done so. *Motschenbacher, Midler*, and *Carson* teach the impossibility of treating the right of publicity as guarding only against a laundry list of specific means of appropriating identity. A rule which says that the right of publicity can be infringed only through the use of nine different methods of appropriating identity merely challenges the clever advertising strategist to come up with the tenth.

Indeed, if we treated the means of appropriation as dispositive in our analysis of the right of publicity, we would not only weaken the right but effectively eviscerate it. The right would fail to protect those plaintiffs most in need of its protection. Advertisers use celebrities to promote their products. The more popular the celebrity, the greater the number of people who recognize her, and the greater the visibility for the product. The identities of the most popular celebrities are not only the most attractive for advertisers, but also the easiest to evoke without resorting to obvious means such as name, likeness, or voice.

Consider a hypothetical advertisement which depicts a mechanical robot with male features, an African–American complexion, and a bald head. The robot is wearing black hightop Air Jordan basketball sneakers, and a red basketball uniform with black trim, baggy shorts, and the number 23 (though not revealing "Bulls" or "Jordan" lettering). The ad depicts the robot dunking a basketball one-handed, stiff-armed, legs extended like open scissors, and tongue hanging out. Now envision that this ad is run on television during professional basketball games. Considered individually, the robot's physical attributes, its dress, and its stance tell us little. Taken together, they lead to the only conclusion that any sports viewer who has registered a discernible pulse in the past five years would reach: the ad is about Michael Jordan.

Viewed separately, the individual aspects of the advertisement in the present case say little. Viewed together, they leave little doubt about the celebrity the ad is meant to depict. The female-shaped robot is wearing a long gown, blond wig, and large jewelry. Vanna White dresses exactly like this at times, but so do many other women. The robot is in the process of turning a block letter on a game-board. Vanna White dresses like this while turning letters on a game-board but perhaps similarly attired Scrabble-playing women do this as well. The robot is standing on what looks to be the Wheel of Fortune game show set. Vanna White dresses like this, turns letters, and does this on the Wheel of Fortune game show. She is the only one. Indeed, defendants themselves referred to their ad as the "Vanna White" ad. We are not surprised.

Television and other media create marketable celebrity identity value. Considerable energy and ingenuity are expended by those who have achieved celebrity value to exploit it for profit. The law protects the celebrity's sole right to exploit this value whether the celebrity has achieved her fame out of rare ability, dumb luck, or a combination thereof. We decline Samsung and Deutch's invitation to permit the evisceration of the common law right of publicity through means as facile as those in this case. Because White has alleged facts showing that Samsung and Deutsch had appropriated her identity, the district court erred by rejecting, on summary judgment, White's common law right of publicity claim.

III.   The Lanham Act

White's final argument is that the district court erred in denying her claim under § 43(a) of the Lanham Act, 15 U.S.C. § 1125(a). The version of section 43(a) applicable to this case[2] provides, in pertinent part, that "[a]ny person who shall ... use, in connection with any goods or services ... any false description or representation ... shall be liable to a civil action ... by any person who believes that he is or is likely to be damaged by the use of any such false description or designation." 15 U.S.C. § 1125(a).

[The court applied its version of the likelihood of confusion test, enunciated in AMF Inc. v. Sleekcraft Boats, 599 F.2d 341 (9th Cir.1979). The court held that White was well known, that her television appearances were closely related to the Samsung television commercial, that the robot identified White although it was not similar to her, that there was no evidence of actual confusion, that similar marketing channels were used, that purchasers are unlikely to exercise great care, and that a jury could conclude that Samsung intended to cause confusion as to product endorsement.]

* * *

Application of the *Sleekcraft* factors to this case indicates that the district court erred in rejecting White's Lanham Act claim at the summary judgment stage. In so concluding, we emphasize two facts, however. First, construing the motion papers in White's favor, as we must, we hold only that White has raised a genuine issue of material fact concerning a likelihood of confusion as to her endorsement. Cohen v. Paramount Pictures Corp., 845 F.2d 851, 852–53 (9th Cir.1988). Whether White's Lanham Act claim should succeed is a matter for the jury. Second, we stress that we reach this conclusion in light of the peculiar facts of this case. In particular, we note that the robot ad identifies White and was part of a series of ads in which other celebrities participated and were paid for their endorsement of Samsung's products.

IV.   The Parody Defense

In defense, defendants cite a number of cases for the proposition that their robot ad constituted protected speech. The only cases they cite which are even remotely relevant to this case are Hustler Magazine v. Falwell, 485 U.S. 46, 108 S.Ct. 876, 99 L.Ed.2d 41 (1988) and L.L. Bean, Inc. v. Drake Publishers, Inc., 811 F.2d 26 (1st Cir.1987). Those cases involved parodies of advertisements run for the purpose of poking fun at Jerry Falwell and L.L. Bean, respectively. This case involves a true advertisement run for the purpose of selling Samsung VCRs. The ad's spoof of Vanna White and Wheel of Fortune is subservient and only tangentially related to the ad's primary message: "buy Samsung VCRs." Defendants' parody arguments are better addressed to non-commercial

2. The statute was amended after White filed her complaint. The amendments would not have altered the analysis in this case however.

parodies.[3] The difference between a "parody" and a "knock-off" is the difference between fun and profit.

V. Conclusion

In remanding this case, we hold only that White has pleaded claims which can go to the jury for its decision.

AFFIRMED IN PART, REVERSED IN PART, and REMANDED.

ALARCON, CIRCUIT JUDGE, concurring in part, dissenting in part:

Vanna White seeks recovery from Samsung based on three theories: the right to privacy, the right to publicity, and the Lanham Act. I concur in the majority's conclusions on the right to privacy. I respectfully dissent from its holdings on the right to publicity and the Lanham Act claims.

I. RIGHT TO PRIVACY (CAL.CIV.CODE § 3344(A))

I agree with the majority's conclusion that no reasonable jury could find that the robot was a "likeness" of Vanna White within the meaning of California Civil Code section 3344(a).

II. RIGHT TO PUBLICITY

I must dissent from the majority's holding on Vanna White's right to publicity claim. The district court found that, since the commercial advertisement did not show a "likeness" of Vanna White, Samsung did not improperly use the plaintiff's identity. The majority asserts that the use of a likeness is not required under California common law. According to the majority, recovery is authorized if there is an appropriation of one's "identity." I cannot find any holding of a California court that supports this conclusion. Furthermore, the record does not support the majority's finding that Vanna White's "identity" was appropriated.

---

3. In warning of a first amendment chill to expressive conduct, the dissent reads this decision too broadly. See Dissent at 1407. This case concerns only the market which exists in our society for the exploitation of celebrity to sell products, and an attempt to take a free ride on a celebrity's celebrity value. Commercial advertising which relies on celebrity fame is different from other forms of expressive activity in two crucial ways. First, for celebrity exploitation advertising to be effective, the advertisement must evoke the celebrity's identity. The more effective the evocation, the better the advertisement. If, as Samsung claims, its ad was based on a "generic" game-show hostess and not on Vanna White, the ad would not have violated anyone's right of publicity, but it would also not have been as humorous or as effective. Second, even if some forms of expressive activity, such as parody, do rely on identity evocation, the first amendment hurdle will bar most right

of publicity actions against those activities. Cf. Falwell, 485 U.S. at 46, 108 S.Ct. at 876. In the case of commercial advertising, however, the first amendment hurdle is not so high. Central Hudson Gas & Electric Corp. v. Public Service Comm'n of New York, 447 U.S. 557, 566, 100 S.Ct. 2343, 2351, 65 L.Ed.2d 341 (1980). Realizing this, Samsung attempts to elevate its ad above the status of garden-variety commercial speech by pointing to the ad's parody of Vanna White. Samsung's argument is unavailing. See Board of Trustees, State Univ. of N.Y. v. Fox, 492 U.S. 469, 474–75, 109 S.Ct. 3028, 3031, 106 L.Ed.2d 388 (1989); Bolger v. Youngs Drug Products Corp., 463 U.S. 60, 67–68, 103 S.Ct. 2875, 2880–81, 77 L.Ed.2d 469 (1983). Unless the first amendment bars all right of publicity actions— and it does not, see Zacchini v. Scripps– Howard Broadcasting Co., 433 U.S. 562, 97 S.Ct. 2849, 53 L.Ed.2d 965 (1977)—then it does not bar this case.

The district court relied on Eastwood v. Superior Court, 149 Cal. App.3d 409, 198 Cal.Rptr. 342, (1983), in holding that there was no cause of action for infringement on the right to publicity because there had been no use of a likeness. In *Eastwood*, the California Court of Appeal described the elements of the tort of "commercial appropriation of the right of publicity" as "(1) the defendant's use of the plaintiff's identity; (2) the appropriation of plaintiff's name or likeness to defendant's advantage, . . . ; (3) lack of consent; and (4) resulting injury." Id. at 417, 198 Cal.Rptr. 342. (Emphasis added).

All of the California cases that my research has disclosed hold that a cause of action for appropriation of the right to publicity requires proof of the appropriation of a name or likeness. See, e.g., Lugosi v. Universal Pictures, 25 Cal.3d 813, 603 P.2d 425, 160 Cal.Rptr. 323 (1979) ("The so-called right of publicity means in essence that the reaction of the public to name and likeness . . . endows the name and likeness of the person involved with commercially exploitable opportunities."); Guglielmi v. Spelling–Goldberg Prods., 25 Cal.3d 860, 603 P.2d 454, 457, 160 Cal. Rptr. 352, 355 (1979) (use of name of Rudolph Valentino in fictional biography allowed); Eastwood v. Superior Court, supra (use of photo and name of actor on cover of tabloid newspaper); In re Weingand, 231 Cal.App.2d 289, 41 Cal.Rptr. 778 (1964) (aspiring actor denied court approval to change name to "Peter Lorie" when famous actor Peter Lorre objected); Fairfield v. American Photocopy Equip. Co., 138 Cal. App.2d 82, 291 P.2d 194 (1955), later app. 158 Cal.App.2d 53, 322 P.2d 93 (1958) (use of attorney's name in advertisement); Gill v. Curtis Publishing Co., 38 C.2d 273, 239 P.2d 630 (1952) (use of photograph of a couple in a magazine).

Notwithstanding the fact that California case law clearly limits the test of the right to publicity to name and likeness, the majority concludes that "the common law right of publicity is not so confined." The majority relies on two factors to support its innovative extension of the California law. The first is that the *Eastwood* court's statement of the elements was permissive rather than exclusive. The second is that Dean Prosser, in describing the common law right to publicity, stated that it might be possible that the right extended beyond name or likeness. These are slender reeds to support a federal court's attempt to create new law for the state of California.

In reaching its surprising conclusion, the majority has ignored the fact that the California Court of Appeal in *Eastwood* specifically addressed the differences between the common law right to publicity and the statutory cause of action codified in California Civil Code section 3344. The court explained that "[t]he differences between the common law and the statutory actions are: (1) Section 3344, subdivision (a) requires knowing use whereas under case law, mistake and inadvertence are not a defense against commercial appropriation and (2) section 3344, subdivision (g) expressly provides that its remedies are cumulative and in addition to any provided by law." Eastwood, 149 Cal.App.3d at n. 6, 198 Cal.Rptr. 342 (emphasis in original). The court did not include appropriations of identity by means other than name or likeness among its list of differences between the statute and the common law.

The majority also relies on Dean Prosser's statement that "[i]t is not impossible that there might be an appropriation of the plaintiff's identity, as by impersonation, without the use of either his name or his likeness, and that this would be an invasion of his right of privacy." Prosser, Privacy, 48 Cal.L.Rev. 383, 401 n. 155 (1960). As Dean Prosser noted, however, "[n]o such case appears to have arisen." Id.

The majority states that the case law has borne out Dean Prosser's insight that the right to publicity is not limited to name or likeness. As noted above, however, the courts of California have never found an infringement on the right to publicity without the use of the plaintiff's name or likeness.

The interest of the California Legislature as expressed in California Civil Code section 3344 appears to preclude the result reached by the majority. The original section 3344 protected only name or likeness. In 1984, ten years after our decision in Motschenbacher v. R.J. Reynolds Tobacco Company, 498 F.2d 821 (9th Cir.1974) and 24 years after Prosser speculated about the future development of the law of the right of publicity, the California legislature amended the statute. California law now makes the use of someone's voice or signature, as well as name or likeness, actionable. Cal.Civ.Code sec. 2233(a) (Deering 1991 Supp.). Thus, California, after our decision in *Motschenbacher* specifically contemplated protection for interests other than name or likeness, but did not include a cause of action for appropriation of another person's identity. The ancient maxim, inclusio unius est exclusio alterius, would appear to bar the majority's innovative extension of the right of publicity. The clear implication from the fact that the California Legislature chose to add only voice and signature to the previously protected interests is that it wished to limit the cause of action to enumerated attributes.

The majority has focused on federal decisions in its novel extension of California Common Law. Those decisions do not provide support for the majority's decision.

In each of the federal cases relied upon by the majority, the advertisement affirmatively represented that the person depicted therein was the plaintiff. In this case, it is clear that a metal robot and not the plaintiff, Vanna White, is depicted in the commercial advertisement. The record does not show an appropriation of Vanna White's identity.

In *Motschenbacher*, a picture of a well-known race driver's car, including its unique markings, was used in an advertisement. Id. at 822. Although the driver could be seen in the car, his features were not visible. Id. The distinctive markings on the car were the only information shown in the ad regarding the identity of the driver. These distinctive markings compelled the inference that Motschenbacher was the person sitting in the racing car. We concluded that "California appellate courts would ... afford legal protection to an individual's proprietary interest in his own identity." Id. at 825. (Emphasis added). Because the distinctive markings on the racing car were sufficient to identify Motschenbacher as the driver of the car, we held that an issue of fact had been raised as to whether his identity had been appropriated. Id. at 827.

In Midler v. Ford Motor Co., 849 F.2d 460 (9th Cir.1988), a singer who had been instructed to sound as much like Bette Midler as possible, sang a song in a radio commercial made famous by Bette Midler. Id. at 461. A number of persons told Bette Midler that they thought that she had made the commercial. Id. at 462. Aside from the voice, there was no information in the commercial from which the singer could be identified. We noted that "[t]he human voice is one of the most palpable ways identity is manifested." Id. at 463. We held that, "[t]o impersonate her voice is to pirate her identity," id., and concluded that Midler had raised a question of fact as to the misappropriation of her identity.

In Carson v. Here's Johnny Portable Toilets, Inc., 698 F.2d 831 (6th Cir.1983), the Sixth Circuit was called upon to interpret Michigan's common-law right to publicity. The case involved a manufacturer who used the words, "Here's Johnny," on portable toilets. Id. at 832–33. These same words were used to introduce the star of a popular late-night television program. There was nothing to indicate that this use of the phrase on the portable toilets was not associated with Johnny Carson's television program. The court found that "[h]ere there was an appropriation of Carson's identity," which violated the right to publicity. Id. at 837.

The common theme in these federal cases is that identifying characteristics unique to the plaintiffs were used in a context in which they were the only information as to the identity of the individual. The commercial advertisements in each case showed attributes of the plaintiff's identities which made it appear that the plaintiff was the person identified in the commercial. No effort was made to dispel the impression that the plaintiffs were the source of the personal attributes at issue. The commercials affirmatively represented that the plaintiffs were involved. See, e.g., Midler at 462 ("The [Motschenbacher] ad suggested that it was he. . . . In the same way the defendants here used an imitation to convey the impression that Midler was singing for them."). The proper interpretation of Motschenbacher, Midler, and Carson is that where identifying characteristics unique to a plaintiff are the only information as to the identity of the person appearing in an ad, a triable issue of fact has been raised as to whether his or her identity as been appropriated.

The case before this court is distinguishable from the factual showing made in Motschenbacher, Midler, and Carson. It is patently clear to anyone viewing the commercial advertisement that Vanna White was not being depicted. No reasonable juror could confuse a metal robot with Vanna White.

The majority contends that "the individual aspects of the advertisement ... [v]iewed together leave little doubt about the celebrity the ad is meant to depict." It derives this conclusion from the fact that Vanna

White is "the only one" who "dresses like this, turns letters, and does this on the Wheel of Fortune game show." In reaching this conclusion, the majority confuses Vanna White, the person, with the role she has assumed as the current hostess on the "Wheel of Fortune" television game show. A recognition of the distinction between a performer and the part he or she plays is essential for a proper analysis of the facts of this case. As is discussed below, those things which Vanna White claims identify her are not unique to her. They are, instead, attributes of the role she plays. The representation of those attributes, therefore, does not constitute a representation of Vanna White. See Nurmi v. Peterson, 10 U.S.P.Q.2d 1775 (C.D.Cal.1989) (distinguishing between performer and role).

Vanna White is a one-role celebrity. She is famous solely for appearing as the hostess on the "Wheel of Fortune" television show. There is nothing unique about Vanna White or the attributes which she claims identify her. Although she appears to be an attractive woman, her face and figure are no more distinctive than that of other equally comely women. She performs her role as hostess on "Wheel of Fortune" in a simple and straight-forward manner. Her work does not require her to display whatever artistic talent she may possess.

The majority appears to argue that because Samsung created a robot with the physical proportions of an attractive woman, posed it gracefully, dressed it in a blond wig, an evening gown, and jewelry, and placed it on a set that resembles the Wheel of Fortune layout, it thereby appropriated Vanna White's identity. But an attractive appearance, a graceful pose, blond hair, an evening gown, and jewelry are attributes shared by many women, especially in Southern California. These common attributes are particularly evident among game-show hostesses, models, actresses, singers, and other women in the entertainment field. They are not unique attributes of Vanna White's identity. Accordingly, I cannot join in the majority's conclusion that, even if viewed together, these attributes identify Vanna White and, therefore, raise a triable issue as to the appropriation of her identity.

The only characteristic in the commercial advertisement that is not common to many female performers or celebrities is the imitation of the "Wheel of Fortune" set. This set is the only thing which might possibly lead a viewer to think of Vanna White. The Wheel of Fortune set, however, is not an attribute of Vanna White's identity. It is an identifying characteristic of a television game show, a prop with which Vanna White interacts in her role as the current hostess. To say that Vanna White may bring an action when another blond female performer or robot appears on such a set as a hostess will, I am sure, be a surprise to the owners of the show. Cf. Baltimore Orioles, Inc. v. Major League Baseball Players Ass'n, 805 F.2d 663 (7th Cir.1986) (right to publicity in videotaped performances preempted by copyright of owner of telecast).

The record shows that Samsung recognized the market value of Vanna White's identity. No doubt the advertisement would have been more effective if Vanna White had appeared in it. But the fact that Samsung recognized Vanna White's value as a celebrity does not necessarily mean that it appropriated her identity. The record shows that Samsung dressed a robot in a costume usually worn by television game-show hostesses, including Vanna White. A blond wig, and glamorous clothing are not characteristics unique to the current hostess of Wheel of Fortune. This evidence does not support the majority's determination that the advertisement was meant to depict Vanna White. The advertisement was intended to depict a robot, playing the role Vanna White currently plays on the Wheel of Fortune. I quite agree that anyone seeing the commercial advertisement would be reminded of Vanna White. Any performance by another female celebrity as a game-show hostess, however, will also remind the viewer of Vanna White because Vanna White's celebrity is so closely associated with the role. But the fact that an actor or actress became famous for playing a particular role has, until now, never been sufficient to give the performer a proprietary interest in it. I cannot agree with the majority that the California courts, which have consistently taken a narrow view of the right to publicity, would extend law to these unique facts.

III.   THE LANHAM ACT

[Judge Alarcon disputes the majority's conclusion that anyone could confuse the robot in the Samsung ad with Vanna White and questions the majority's analysis of several *Sleekcraft* factors. He would hold that White's Lanham Act claim should fail.]

* * *

IV.   SAMSUNG'S FIRST AMENDMENT DEFENSE

The majority gives Samsung's First Amendment defense short shrift because "[t]his case involves a true advertisement run for the purpose of selling Samsung VCRs." I respectfully disagree with the majority's analysis of this issue as well.

The majority's attempt to distinguish this case from Hustler Magazine v. Falwell, 485 U.S. 46, 108 S.Ct. 876, 99 L.Ed.2d 41 (1988), and L.L. Bean, Inc. v. Drake Publishers, Inc., 811 F.2d 26 (1st Cir.1987), is unpersuasive. The majority notes that the parodies in those cases were made for the purpose of poking fun at the Reverend Jerry Falwell and L.L. Bean. But the majority fails to consider that the defendants in those cases were making fun of the Reverend Jerry Falwell and L.L. Bean for the purely commercial purpose of selling soft-core pornographic magazines.

Generally, a parody does not constitute an infringement on the original work if it takes no more than is necessary to "conjure up" the original. Walt Disney Prods. v. Air Pirates, 581 F.2d 751, 756 (9th Cir.1978). The majority has failed to consider these factors properly in deciding that Vanna White may bring an action for damages solely because the popularity of the fame show, Wheel of Fortune.

The effect of the majority's holding on expressive conduct is difficult to estimate. The majority's position seems to allow any famous person or entity to bring suit based on any commercial advertisement that depicts a character or role performed by the plaintiff. Under the majority's view of the law, Gene Autry could have brought an action for damages against all other singing cowboys. Clint Eastwood would be able to sue anyone who plays a tall, soft-spoken cowboy, unless, of course, Jimmy Stewart had not previously enjoined Clint Eastwood. Johnny Weismuller would have been able to sue each actor who played the role of Tarzan. Sylvester Stallone could sue actors who play blue-collar boxers. Chuck Norris could sue all karate experts who display their skills in motion pictures. Arnold Schwarzenegger could sue body builders who are compensated for appearing in public.

The majority's reading of the Lanham Act would provide a basis for "commercial" enterprises to maintain an action for section 43(a) violations even in the absence of confusion or deception. May Black and Decker, maker of the "Dustbuster" portable vacuum, now sue "Bustdusters," the Los Angeles topless cleaning service. Can the Los Angeles Kings hockey team state a cause of action against the City of Las Vegas for its billboards reading "L.A. has the Kings, but we have the Aces."

Direct competitive advertising could also be affected. Will BMW, which advertises its automobiles as "the ultimate driving machine," be able to maintain an action against Toyota for advertising one of its cars as "the ultimate saving machine"? Can Coca Cola sue Pepsi because it depicted a bottle of Coca Cola in its televised "taste test"? Indeed, any advertisement which shows a competitor's product, or any recognizable brand name, would appear to be liable for damages under the majority's view of the applicable law. Under the majority's analysis, even the depiction of an obvious facsimile of a competitor's product may provide sufficient basis for the maintenance of an action for damages.

V. CONCLUSION

The protection of intellectual property presents the courts with the necessity of balancing competing interests. On the one hand, we wish to protect and reward the work and investment of those who create intellectual property. In so doing, however, we must prevent the creation of a monopoly that would inhibit the creative expressions of others. We have traditionally balanced those interests by allowing the copying of an idea, but protecting a unique expression of it. Samsung clearly used the idea of a glamorous female game show hostess. Just as clearly, it avoided appropriating Vanna White's expression of that role. Samsung did not use a likeness of her. The performer depicted in the commercial advertisement is unmistakably a lifeless robot. Vanna White has presented no evidence that any consumer confused the robot with her identity. Indeed, no reasonable consumer could confuse the robot with Vanna White or believe that, because the robot appeared in the advertisement, Vanna White endorsed Samsung's product.

I would affirm the district court's judgment in all respects.

Vanna White

Ms. C3PO?

WHITE v. SAMSUNG ELECTRONICS AMERICA, INC.

United States Court of Appeals, Ninth Circuit, 1993.
989 F.2d 1512.

* * *

The petition for rehearing is DENIED and the suggestion for rehearing en banc is REJECTED.

Kozinski, Circuit Judge, with whom Circuit Judges O'Scannlain and Kleinfeld join, dissenting from the order rejecting the suggestion for rehearing en banc.

I

Saddam Hussein wants to keep advertisers from using his picture in unflattering contexts.[1] Clint Eastwood doesn't want tabloids to write about him.[2] Rudolf Valentino's heirs want to control his film biography.[3] The Girl Scouts don't want their image soiled by association with certain activities.[4] George Lucas wants to keep Strategic Defense Initiative fans from calling it "Star Wars."[5] Pepsico doesn't want singers to use the word "Pepsi" in their songs.[6] Guy Lombardo wants an exclusive proper-

---

1. See Eben Shapiro, Rising Caution on Using Celebrity Images, N.Y. Times, Nov. 4, 1992, at D20 (Iraqi diplomat objects on right of publicity grounds to ad containing Hussein's picture and caption "History has shown what happens when one source controls all the information").

2. Eastwood v. Superior Court, 149 Cal. App.3d 409, 198 Cal.Rptr. 342 (1983).

3. Guglielmi v. Spelling–Goldberg Prods., 25 Cal.3d 860, 160 Cal.Rptr. 352, 603 P.2d 454 (1979) (Rudolph Valentino); see also Maheu v. CBS, Inc., 201 Cal.App.3d 662, 668, 247 Cal.Rptr. 304 (1988) (aide to Howard Hughes). Cf. Frank Gannon, Vanna Karenina, in Vanna Karenina and Other Reflections (1988) (A humorous short story with a tragic ending. "She thought of the first day she had met VR__SKY. How foolish she had been. How could she love a man who wouldn't even tell her all the letters in his name?").

4. Girl Scouts v. Personality Posters Mfg., 304 F.Supp. 1228 (S.D.N.Y.1969) (poster of a pregnant girl in a Girl Scout uniform with the caption "Be Prepared").

5. Lucasfilm Ltd. v. High Frontier, 622 F.Supp. 931 (D.D.C.1985).

6. Pepsico Inc. claimed the lyrics and packaging of grunge rocker Tad Doyle's "Jack Pepsi" song were "offensive to [it] and [. . .] likely to offend [its] customers," in part because they "associate [Pepsico] and its Pepsi marks with intoxication and drunk driving." Deborah Russell, Doyle Leaves Pepsi Thirsty for Compensation, Billboard, June 15, 1991, at 43. Conversely, the Hell's Angels recently sued Marvel Comics to keep it from publishing a comic book called "Hell's Angel," starring a character of the same name. Marvel settled by paying $35,000 to charity and promising never to use the name "Hell's Angel" again in connection with any of its publications. Marvel, Hell's Angels Settle Trademark Suit, L.A. Daily J., Feb. 2, 1993, § II, at 1.

Trademarks are often reflected in the mirror of our popular culture. See Truman Capote, Breakfast at Tiffany's (1958); Kurt Vonnegut, Jr., Breakfast of Champions (1973); Tom Wolfe, The Electric Kool–Aid Acid Test (1968) (which, incidentally, includes a chapter on the Hell's Angels); Larry Niven, Man of Steel, Woman of Kleenex, in All the Myriad Ways (1971); Looking for Mr. Goodbar (1977); The Coca–Cola Kid (1985) (using Coca–Cola as a metaphor for American commercialism); The Kentucky Fried Movie (1977); Harley Davidson and the Marlboro Man (1991); The Wonder Years (ABC 1988–present) ("Wonder Years" was a slogan of Wonder Bread); Tim Rice & Andrew Lloyd Webber, Joseph and the Amazing Technicolor Dream Coat (musical). Hear Janis Joplin, Mercedes Benz, on Pearl (CBS 1971); Paul Simon, Kodachrome, on There Goes Rhymin' Simon (Warner 1973); Leonard Cohen, Chelsea Hotel, on The Best of Leonard Cohen (CBS 1975); Bruce Springsteen, Cadillac Ranch, on The River (CBS 1980); Prince, Little Red Corvette, on 1999 (Warner 1982); dada, Dizz Knee Land, on Puzzle (IRS 1992) ("I just robbed a grocery store—I'm going to Disneyland/I just flipped off President George—I'm going to Disneyland"); Monty Python, Spam, on The Final Rip Off (Virgin 1988); Roy Clark, Thank God and Greyhound [You're Gone], on Roy Clark's Greatest Hits Volume I (MCA 1979); Mel Tillis, Coca–Cola Cowboy, on The Very Best of (MCA 1981) ("You're just a Coca–Cola cowboy/You've got an Eastwood smile and Robert Redford hair . . . ").

Dance to Talking Heads, Popular Favorites 1976–92: Sand in the Vaseline (Sire 1992); Talking Heads, Popsicle, on id. Admire Andy Warhol, Campbell's Soup Can. Cf. REO Speedwagon, 38 Special, and Jello Biafra of the Dead Kennedys.

The creators of some of these works might have gotten permission from the

ty right to ads that show big bands playing on New Year's Eve.[7] Uri Geller thinks he should be paid for ads showing psychics bending metal through telekinesis.[8] Paul Prudhomme, that household name, thinks the same about ads featuring corpulent bearded chefs.[9] And scads of copyright holders see purple when their creations are made fun of.[10]

Something very dangerous is going on here. Private property, including intellectual property, is essential to our way of life. It provides an incentive for investment and innovation; it stimulates the flourishing of our culture; it protects the moral entitlements of people to the fruits of their labors. But reducing too much to private property can be bad medicine. Private land, for instance, is far more useful if separated from other private land by public streets, roads and highways. Public parks, utility rights-of-way and sewers reduce the amount of land in private hands, but vastly enhance the value of the property that remains.

So too it is with intellectual property. Overprotecting intellectual property is as harmful as underprotecting it. Creativity is impossible without a rich public domain. Nothing today, likely nothing since we tamed fire, is genuinely new: Culture, like science and technology, grows by accretion, each new creator building on the works of those who came before. Overprotection stifles the very creative forces it's supposed to nurture.[11]

The panel's opinion is a classic case of overprotection. Concerned about what it sees as a wrong done to Vanna White, the panel majority erects a property right of remarkable and dangerous breadth: Under the majority's opinion, it's now a tort for advertisers to remind the public of a celebrity. Not to use a celebrity's name, voice, signature or likeness; not to imply the celebrity endorses a product; but simply to evoke the celebrity's image in the public's mind. This Orwellian notion withdraws far more from the public domain than prudence and common sense allow. It conflicts with the Copyright Act and the Copyright Clause. It raises serious First Amendment problems. It's bad law, and it deserves a long, hard second look.

trademark owners, though it's unlikely Kool–Aid relished being connected with LSD, Hershey with homicidal maniacs, Disney with armed robbers, or Coca–Cola with cultural imperialism. Certainly no free society can demand that artists get such permission.

7. Lombardo v. Doyle, Dane & Bernbach, Inc., 58 A.D.2d 620, 396 N.Y.S.2d 661 (1977).

8. Geller v. Fallon McElligott, No. 90–Civ–2839 (S.D.N.Y. July 22, 1991) (involving a Timex ad).

9. Prudhomme v. Procter & Gamble Co., 800 F.Supp. 390 (E.D.La.1992).

10. E.g., Acuff–Rose Music, Inc. v. Campbell, 972 F.2d 1429 (6th Cir.1992);

Cliffs Notes v. Bantam Doubleday Dell Publishing Group, Inc., 886 F.2d 490 (2d Cir. 1989); Fisher v. Dees, 794 F.2d 432 (9th Cir.1986); MCA, Inc. v. Wilson, 677 F.2d 180 (2d Cir.1981); Elsmere Music, Inc. v. NBC, 623 F.2d 252 (2d Cir.1980); Walt Disney Prods. v. The Air Pirates, 581 F.2d 751 (9th Cir.1978); Berlin v. E.C. Publications, Inc., 329 F.2d 541 (2d Cir.1964); Lowenfels v. Nathan, 2 F.Supp. 73 (S.D.N.Y.1932).

11. See Wendy J. Gordon, A Property Right in Self Expression: Equality and Individualism in the Natural Law of Intellectual Property, 102 Yale L.J. 1533, 1556–57 (1993).

II

Samsung ran an ad campaign promoting its consumer electronics. Each ad depicted a Samsung product and a humorous prediction: One showed a raw steak with the caption "Revealed to be health food. 2010 A.D." Another showed Morton Downey, Jr. in front of an American flag with the caption "Presidential candidate. 2008 A.D."[12] The ads were meant to convey—humorously—that Samsung products would still be in use twenty years from now.

The ad that spawned this litigation starred a robot dressed in a wig, gown and jewelry reminiscent of Vanna White's hair and dress; the robot was posed next to a Wheel-of-Fortune-like game board. See Appendix. The caption read "Longest-running game show. 2012 A.D." The gag here, I take it, was that Samsung would still be around when White had been replaced by a robot.

Perhaps failing to see the humor, White sued, alleging Samsung infringed her right of publicity by "appropriating" her "identity." Under California law, White has the exclusive right to use her name, likeness, signature and voice for commercial purposes. Cal.Civ.Code § 3344(a); Eastwood v. Superior Court, 149 Cal.App.3d 409, 417, 198 Cal.Rptr. 342, 347 (1983). But Samsung didn't use her name, voice or signature, and it certainly didn't use her likeness. The ad just wouldn't have been funny had it depicted White or someone who resembled her—the whole joke was that the game show host(ess) was a robot, not a real person. No one seeing the ad could have thought this was supposed to be White in 2012.

The district judge quite reasonably held that, because Samsung didn't use White's name, likeness, voice or signature, it didn't violate her right of publicity. 971 F.2d at 1396–97. Not so, says the panel majority: The California right of publicity can't possibly be limited to name and likeness. If it were, the majority reasons, a "clever advertising strategist" could avoid using White's name or likeness but nevertheless remind people of her with impunity, "effectively eviscerat[ing]" her rights. To prevent this "evisceration," the panel majority holds that the right of publicity must extend beyond name and likeness, to any "appropriation" of White's "identity"—anything that "evoke[s]" her personality. Id. at 1398–99.

III

But what does "evisceration" mean in intellectual property law? Intellectual property rights aren't like some constitutional rights, absolute guarantees protected against all kinds of interference, subtle as well as blatant.[13] They cast no penumbras, emit no emanations: The very point of intellectual property laws is that they protect only against

---

12. I had never heard of Morton Downey, Jr., but I'm told he's sort of like Rush Limbaugh, but not as shy.

13. Cf., e.g., Guinn v. United States, 238 U.S. 347, 364–65, 35 S.Ct. 926, 931, 59 L.Ed. 1340 (1915) (striking down grandfather clause that was a clear attempt to evade the Fifteenth Amendment).

certain specific kinds of appropriation. I can't publish unauthorized copies of, say, Presumed Innocent; I can't make a movie out of it. But I'm perfectly free to write a book about an idealistic young prosecutor on trial for a crime he didn't commit.[14] So what if I got the idea from Presumed Innocent? So what if it reminds readers of the original? Have I "eviscerated" Scott Turow's intellectual property rights? Certainly not. All creators draw in part on the work of those who came before, referring to it, building on it, poking fun at it; we call this creativity, not piracy.[15]

The majority isn't, in fact, preventing the "evisceration" of Vanna White's existing rights; it's creating a new and much broader property right, a right unknown in California law.[16] It's replacing the existing balance between the interests of the celebrity and those of the public by a different balance, one substantially more favorable to the celebrity. Instead of having an exclusive right in her name, likeness, signature or voice, every famous person now has an exclusive right to anything that reminds the viewer of her. After all, that's all Samsung did: It used an inanimate object to remind people of White, to "evoke [her identity]." 971 F.2d at 1399.[17]

Consider how sweeping this new right is. What is it about the ad that makes people think of White? It's not the robot's wig, clothes or jewelry; there must be ten million blond women (many of them quasi-

---

14. It would be called "Burden of Going Forward with the Evidence," and the hero would ultimately be saved by his lawyer's adept use of Fed.R.Evid. 301.

15. In the words of Sir Isaac Newton, "[i]f I have seen further it is by standing on [the shoulders] of Giants." Letter to Robert Hooke, Feb. 5, 1675/1676.

Newton himself may have borrowed this phrase from Bernard of Chartres, who said something similar in the early twelfth century. Bernard in turn may have snatched it from Priscian, a sixth century grammarian. See Lotus Dev. Corp. v. Paperback Software Int'l, 740 F.Supp. 37, 77 n. 3 (D.Mass.1990).

16. In fact, in the one California case raising the issue, the three state Supreme Court Justices who discussed this theory expressed serious doubts about it. Guglielmi v. Spelling–Goldberg Prods., 25 Cal.3d 860, 864 n. 5, 160 Cal.Rptr. 352, 355 n. 5, 603 P.2d 454, 457 n. 5 (1979) (Bird, C.J., concurring) (expressing skepticism about finding a property right to a celebrity's "personality" because it is "difficult to discern any easily applied definition for this amorphous term").

Neither have we previously interpreted California law to cover pure "identity." Midler v. Ford Motor Co., 849 F.2d 460 (9th Cir.1988), and Waits v. Frito–Lay, Inc., 978 F.2d 1093 (9th Cir.1992), dealt with appro-

priation of a celebrity's voice. See id. at 1100–01 (imitation of singing style, rather than voice, doesn't violate the right of publicity).

Motschenbacher v. R.J. Reynolds Tobacco Co., 498 F.2d 821 (9th Cir.1974), stressed that, though the plaintiff's likeness wasn't directly recognizable by itself, the surrounding circumstances would have made viewers think the likeness was the plaintiff's. Id. at 827; see also Moore v. Regents of the Univ. of Cal., 51 Cal.3d 120, 138, 271 Cal.Rptr. 146, 157, 793 P.2d 479, 490 (1990) (construing Motschenbacher as "hold[ing] that every person has a proprietary interest in his own likeness").

17. Some viewers might have inferred White was endorsing the product, but that's a different story. The right of publicity isn't aimed at or limited to false endorsements, Eastwood v. Superior Court, 149 Cal.App.3d 409, 419–20, 198 Cal.Rptr. 342, 348 (1983); that's what the Lanham Act is for.

Note also that the majority's rule applies even to advertisements that unintentionally remind people of someone. California law is crystal clear that the common-law right of publicity may be violated even by unintentional appropriations. Id. at 417 n. 6, 198 Cal.Rptr. at 346 n. 6; Fairfield v. American Photocopy Equipment Co., 138 Cal.App.2d 82, 87, 291 P.2d 194 (1955).

famous) who wear dresses and jewelry like White's. It's that the robot is posed near the "Wheel of Fortune" game board. Remove the game board from the ad, and no one would think of Vanna White. See Appendix. But once you include the game board, anybody standing beside it—a brunette woman, a man wearing women's clothes, a monkey in a wig and gown— would evoke White's image, precisely the way the robot did. It's the "Wheel of Fortune" set, not the robot's face or dress or jewelry that evokes White's image. The panel is giving White an exclusive right not in what she looks like or who she is, but in what she does for a living.[18]

This is entirely the wrong place to strike the balance. Intellectual property rights aren't free: They're imposed at the expense of future creators and of the public at large. Where would we be if Charles Lindbergh had an exclusive right in the concept of a heroic solo aviator? If Arthur Conan Doyle had gotten a copyright in the idea of the detective story, or Albert Einstein had patented the theory of relativity? If every author and celebrity had been given the right to keep people from mocking them or their work? Surely this would have made the world poorer, not richer, culturally as well as economically.[19]

This is why intellectual property law is full of careful balances between what's set aside for the owner and what's left in the public domain for the rest of us: The relatively short life of patents; the longer, but finite, life of copyrights; copyright's idea-expression dichotomy; the fair use doctrine; the prohibition on copyrighting facts; the compulsory license of television broadcasts and musical compositions; federal preemption of over broad state intellectual property laws; the nominative use doctrine in trademark law; the right to make sound alike recordings.[20] All of these diminish an intellectual property owner's rights. All

---

18. Once the right of publicity is extended beyond specific physical characteristics, this will become a recurring problem: Outside name, likeness and voice, the things that most reliably remind the public of celebrities are the actions or roles they're famous for. A commercial with an astronaut setting foot on the moon would evoke the image of Neil Armstrong. Any masked man on horseback would remind people (over a certain age) of Clayton Moore. And any number of songs—"My Way," "Yellow Submarine," "Like a Virgin," "Beat It," "Michael, Row the Boat Ashore," to name only a few—instantly evoke an image of the person or group who made them famous, regardless of who is singing.

See also Carlos V. Lozano, West Loses Lawsuit over Batman TV Commercial, L.A. Times, Jan. 18, 1990, at B3 (Adam West sues over Batman-like character in commercial); Nurmi v. Peterson, 10 U.S.P.Q.2d 1775, 1989 WL 407484 (C.D.Cal.1989) (1950s TV movie hostess "Vampira" sues 1980s TV hostess "Elvira"); text accompanying notes 7–8 (lawsuits brought by Guy

Lombardo, claiming big bands playing at New Year's Eve parties remind people of him, and by Uri Geller, claiming psychics who can bend metal remind people of him). Cf. Motschenbacher, where the claim was that viewers would think plaintiff was actually in the commercial, and not merely that the commercial reminded people of him.

19. See generally Gordon, supra note 11; see also Michael Madow, Private Ownership of Public Image: Popular Culture and Publicity Rights, 81 Cal.L.Rev. 125, 201–03 (1993) (an excellent discussion).

20. See 35 U.S.C. § 154 (duration of patent); 17 U.S.C.A. §§ 302–305 (duration of copyright); 17 U.S.C. § 102(b) (idea-expression dichotomy); 17 U.S.C. § 107 (fair use); Feist Pubs., Inc. v. Rural Tel. Serv. Co., 499 U.S. 340, 347, 111 S.Ct. 1282, 1288, 113 L.Ed.2d 358 (1991) (no copyrighting facts); 17 U.S.C. §§ 115, 119(b) (compulsory licenses); Bonito Boats, Inc. v. Thunder Craft Boats, Inc., 489 U.S. 141, 109 S.Ct. 971, 103 L.Ed.2d 118 (1989) (federal preemption); New Kids on the Block v. News America Publishing, Inc., 971 F.2d

let the public use something created by someone else. But all are necessary to maintain a free environment in which creative genius can flourish.

The intellectual property right created by the panel here has none of these essential limitations: No fair use exception; no right to parody; no idea-expression dichotomy. It impoverishes the public domain, to the detriment of future creators and the public at large. Instead of well-defined, limited characteristics such as name, likeness or voice, advertisers will now have to cope with vague claims of "appropriation of identity," claims often made by people with a wholly exaggerated sense of their own fame and significance. See pp. 1512–13 & notes 1–10 supra. Future Vanna Whites might not get the chance to create their personae, because their employers may fear some celebrity will claim the persona is too similar to her own.[21] The public will be robbed of parodies of celebrities, and our culture will be deprived of the valuable safety valve that parody and mockery create.

Moreover, consider the moral dimension, about which the panel majority seems to have gotten so exercised. Saying Samsung "appropriated" something of White's begs the question: Should White have the exclusive right to something as broad and amorphous as her "identity"? Samsung's ad didn't simply copy White's schtick—like all parody, it created something new.[22] True, Samsung did it to make money, but White does whatever she does to make money, too; the majority talks of "the difference between fun and profit," 971 F.2d at 1401, but in the entertainment industry fun is profit. Why is Vanna White's right to exclusive for-profit use of her persona—a persona that might not even be her own creation, but that of a writer, director or producer—superior to Samsung's right to profit by creating its own inventions? Why should she have such absolute rights to control the conduct of others, unlimited by the idea-expression dichotomy or by the fair use doctrine?

To paraphrase only slightly Feist Publications, Inc. v. Rural Telephone Service Co., 499 U.S. 340, 349–350, 111 S.Ct. 1282, 1289–90, 113 L.Ed.2d 358 (1991), it may seem unfair that much of the fruit of a creator's labor may be used by others without compensation. But this is

---

302, 306–308 (9th Cir.1992) (nominative use); 17 U.S.C. § 114(b) (soundalikes); accord G.S. Rasmussen & Assocs. v. Kalitta Flying Serv., Inc., 958 F.2d 896, 900 n. 7 (9th Cir.1992); Daniel A. Saunders, Comment, Copyright Law's Broken Rear Window, 80 Cal.L.Rev. 179, 204–05 (1992). But see Midler v. Ford Motor Co., 849 F.2d 460 (9th Cir.1988).

21. If Christian Slater, star of "Heathers," "Pump up the Volume," "Kuffs," and "Untamed Heart"—and alleged Jack Nicholson clone—appears in a commercial, can Nicholson sue? Of 54 stories on LEXIS that talk about Christian Slater, 26 talk about Slater's alleged similarities to Nicholson. Apparently it's his nasal wisecracks

and killer smiles, St. Petersburg Times, Jan. 10, 1992, at 13, his eyebrows, Ottawa Citizen, Jan. 10, 1992, at E2, his sneers, Boston Globe, July 26, 1991, at 37, his menacing presence, USA Today, June 26, 1991, at 1D, and his sing-song voice, Gannett News Service, Aug. 27, 1990 (or, some say, his insinuating drawl, L.A. Times, Aug. 22, 1990, at F5). That's a whole lot more than White and the robot had in common.

22. Cf. New Kids on the Block v. News America Publishing, Inc., 971 F.2d 302, 307 n. 6 (9th Cir.1992) ("Where the infringement is small in relation to the new work created, the fair user is profiting largely from his own creative efforts rather than free-riding on another's work.").

not some unforeseen byproduct of our intellectual property system; it is the system's very essence. Intellectual property law assures authors the right to their original expression, but encourages others to build freely on the ideas that underlie it. This result is neither unfair nor unfortunate: It is the means by which intellectual property law advances the progress of science and art. We give authors certain exclusive rights, but in exchange we get a richer public domain. The majority ignores this wise teaching, and all of us are the poorer for it.[23]

IV

The panel, however, does more than misinterpret California law: By refusing to recognize a parody exception to the right of publicity, the panel directly contradicts the federal Copyright Act. Samsung didn't merely parody Vanna White. It parodied Vanna White appearing in "Wheel of Fortune," a copyrighted television show, and parodies of copyrighted works are governed by federal copyright law.

Copyright law specifically gives the world at large the right to make "fair use" parodies, parodies that don't borrow too much of the original. Fisher v. Dees, 794 F.2d 432, 435 (9th Cir.1986). Federal copyright law also gives the copyright owner the exclusive right to create (or license the creation of) derivative works, which include parodies that borrow too much to qualify as "fair use." See Acuff–Rose Music, Inc. v. Campbell, 972 F.2d 1429, 1434–35 (6th Cir.1992).[24] When Mel Brooks, for instance, decided to parody Star Wars, he had two options: He could have stuck with his fair use rights under 17 U.S.C. § 107, or he could have gotten a license to make a derivative work under 17 U.S.C. § 106(b) from the holder of the Star Wars copyright. To be safe, he probably did the latter, but once he did, he was guaranteed a perfect right to make his movie.[25]

The majority's decision decimates this federal scheme. It's impossible to parody a movie or a TV show without at the same time "evok[ing]" the "identit[ies]" of the actors.[26] You can't have a mock Star

---

23. The majority opinion has already earned some well-deserved criticisms on this score. Stephen R. Barnett, In Hollywood's Wheel of Fortune, Free Speech Loses a Turn, Wall St. J., Sept. 28, 1992, at A14; Stephen R. Barnett, Wheel of Misfortune for Advertisers: Ninth Circuit Misreads the Law to Protect Vanna White's Image, L.A. Daily J., Oct. 5, 1992, at 6; Felix H. Kent, California Court Expands Celebrities' Rights, N.Y.L.J., Oct. 30, 1992, at 3 ("To speak of the 'evisceration' of such a questionable common law right in a case that has probably gone the farthest of any case in any court in the United States of America is more than difficult to comprehend"); Shapiro, supra note 1 ("A fat chef? A blond robot in an evening gown? How far will this go?" (citing Douglas J. Wood, an advertising lawyer)). See also Mark Alan

Stamaty, Washingtoon, Wash.Post, Apr. 5, 1993, at A21.

24. How much is too much is a hotly contested question, but one thing is clear: The right to make parodies belongs either to the public at large or to the copyright holder, not to someone who happens to appear in the copyrighted work.

25. See Spaceballs (1987). Compare Madonna: Truth or Dare (1991) with Medusa: Dare to Be Truthful (1991); Loaded Weapon I (1993) with Lethal Weapon (1987); Young Frankenstein (1974) with Bride of Frankenstein (1935).

26. 17 U.S.C. § 301(b)(1) limits the Copyright Act's preemptive sweep to subject matter "fixed in any tangible medium of expression," but White's identity—her look as the hostess of Wheel of Fortune—is definitely fixed: It consists entirely of her

Wars without a mock Luke Skywalker, Han Solo and Princess Leia, which in turn means a mock Mark Hamill, Harrison Ford and Carrie Fisher. You can't have a mock Batman commercial without a mock Batman, which means someone emulating the mannerisms of Adam West or Michael Keaton. See Carlos V. Lozano, West Loses Lawsuit over Batman TV Commercial, L.A. Times, Jan. 18, 1990, at B3 (describing Adam West's right of publicity lawsuit over a commercial produced under license from DC Comics, owner of the Batman copyright).[27] The public's right to make a fair use parody and the copyright owner's right to license a derivative work are useless if the parodist is held hostage by every actor whose "identity" he might need to "appropriate."

Our court is in a unique position here. State courts are unlikely to be particularly sensitive to federal preemption, which, after all, is a matter of first concern to the federal courts. The Supreme Court is unlikely to consider the issue because the right of publicity seems so much a matter of state law. That leaves us. It's our responsibility to keep the right of publicity from taking away federally granted rights, either from the public at large or from a copyright owner. We must make sure state law doesn't give the Vanna Whites and Adam Wests of the world a veto over fair use parodies of the shows in which they appear, or over copyright holders' exclusive right to license derivative works of those shows. In a case where the copyright owner isn't even a party—where no one has the interests of copyright owners at heart—the majority creates a rule that greatly diminishes the rights of copyright holders in this circuit.

V

The majority's decision also conflicts with the federal copyright system in another, more insidious way. Under the dormant Copyright Clause, state intellectual property laws can stand only so long as they don't "prejudice the interests of other States." Goldstein v. California, 412 U.S. 546, 558, 93 S.Ct. 2303, 2310, 37 L.Ed.2d 163 (1973). A state law criminalizing record piracy, for instance, is permissible because citizens of other states would "remain free to copy within their borders those works which may be protected elsewhere." Id. But the right of publicity isn't geographically limited. A right of publicity created by one state applies to conduct everywhere, so long as it involves a celebrity domiciled in that state. If a Wyoming resident creates an ad that features a California domiciliary's name or likeness, he'll be subject to California right of publicity law even if he's careful to keep the ad from being shown in California. See Acme Circus Operating Co. v. Kuperstock, 711 F.2d 1538, 1540 (11th Cir.1983); Groucho Marx Prods. v. Day and

appearances in a fixed, copyrighted TV show. See Baltimore Orioles v. Major League Baseball Players Ass'n, 805 F.2d 663, 675 & n. 22 (7th Cir.1986).

27. Cf. Lugosi v. Universal Pictures, 25 Cal.3d 813, 827–28, 160 Cal.Rptr. 323, 331–32, 603 P.2d 425, 433–34 (1979) (Mosk, J., concurring) (pointing out that rights in characters should be owned by the copyright holder, not the actor who happens to play them); Baltimore Orioles, 805 F.2d at 674–79 (baseball players' right of publicity preempted by copyright law as to telecasts of games).

Night Co., 689 F.2d 317, 320 (2d Cir.1982); see also Factors Etc. v. Pro Arts, 652 F.2d 278, 281 (2d Cir.1981).

The broader and more ill-defined one state's right of publicity, the more it interferes with the legitimate interests of other states. A limited right that applies to unauthorized use of name and likeness probably does not run afoul of the Copyright Clause, but the majority's protection of "identity" is quite another story. Under the majority's approach, any time anybody in the United States—even somebody who lives in a state with a very narrow right of publicity—creates an ad, he takes the risk that it might remind some segment of the public of somebody, perhaps somebody with only a local reputation, somebody the advertiser has never heard of. See note 17 supra (right of publicity is infringed by unintentional appropriations). So you made a commercial in Florida and one of the characters reminds Reno residents of their favorite local TV anchor (a California domiciliary)? Pay up.

This is an intolerable result, as it gives each state far too much control over artists in other states. No California statute, no California court has actually tried to reach this far. It is ironic that it is we who plant this kudzu in the fertile soil of our federal system.

VI

Finally, I can't see how giving White the power to keep others from evoking her image in the public's mind can be squared with the First Amendment. Where does White get this right to control our thoughts? The majority's creation goes way beyond the protection given a trademark or a copyrighted work, or a person's name or likeness. All those things control one particular way of expressing an idea, one way of referring to an object or a person. But not allowing any means of reminding people of someone? That's a speech restriction unparalleled in First Amendment law.[28]

What's more, I doubt even a name-and-likeness-only right of publicity can stand without a parody exception. The First Amendment isn't just about religion or politics—it's also about protecting the free development of our national culture. Parody, humor, irreverence are all vital components of the marketplace of ideas. The last thing we need, the last thing the First Amendment will tolerate, is a law that lets public figures keep

---

28. Just compare the majority's holding to the intellectual property laws upheld by the Supreme Court. The Copyright Act is constitutional precisely because of the fair use doctrine and the idea-expression dichotomy, Harper & Row v. Nation Enterprises, 471 U.S. 539, 560, 105 S.Ct. 2218, 2230, 85 L.Ed.2d 588 (1985), two features conspicuously absent from the majority's doctrine. The right of publicity at issue in Zacchini v. Scripps–Howard Broadcasting Co., 433 U.S. 562, 576, 97 S.Ct. 2849, 2857–58, 53 L.Ed.2d 965 (1977), was only the right to "broadcast of petitioner's entire performance," not "the unauthorized use of another's name for purposes of trade." Id. Even the statute upheld in San Francisco Arts & Athletics, Inc. v. United States Olympic Comm., 483 U.S. 522, 530, 107 S.Ct. 2971, 2977, 97 L.Ed.2d 427 (1987), which gave the USOC sweeping rights to the word "Olympic," didn't purport to protect all expression that reminded people of the Olympics.

people from mocking them, or from "evok[ing]" their images in the mind of the public. 971 F.2d at 1399.[29]

The majority dismisses the First Amendment issue out of hand because Samsung's ad was commercial speech. Id. at 1401 & n. 3. So what? Commercial speech may be less protected by the First Amendment than noncommercial speech, but less protected means protected nonetheless. Central Hudson Gas & Elec. Corp. v. Public Serv. Comm'n, 447 U.S. 557, 100 S.Ct. 2343, 65 L.Ed.2d 341 (1980). And there are very good reasons for this. Commercial speech has a profound effect on our culture and our attitudes. Neutral-seeming ads influence people's social and political attitudes, and themselves arouse political controversy.[30] "Where's the Beef?" turned from an advertising catchphrase into the only really memorable thing about the 1984 presidential campaign.[31] Four years later, Michael Dukakis called George Bush "the Joe Isuzu of American politics."[32]

In our pop culture, where salesmanship must be entertaining and entertainment must sell, the line between the commercial and noncommercial has not merely blurred; it has disappeared. Is the Samsung parody any different from a parody on Saturday Night Live or in Spy Magazine? Both are equally profit-motivated. Both use a celebrity's identity to sell things—one to sell VCRs, the other to sell advertising. Both mock their subjects. Both try to make people laugh. Both add something, perhaps something worthwhile and memorable, perhaps not, to our culture. Both are things that the people being portrayed might dearly want to suppress. See notes 1 & 29 supra.

29. The majority's failure to recognize a parody exception to the right of publicity would apply equally to parodies of politicians as of actresses. Consider the case of Wok Fast, a Los Angeles Chinese food delivery service, which put up a billboard with a picture of then-L.A. Police Chief Daryl Gates and the text "When you can't leave the office. Or won't." (This was an allusion to Chief Gates's refusal to retire despite pressure from Mayor Tom Bradley.) Gates forced the restaurant to take the billboard down by threatening a right of publicity lawsuit. Leslie Berger, He Did Leave the Office—And Now Sign Will Go, Too, L.A. Times, July 31, 1992, at B2.

See also Samsung Has Seen the Future: Brace Youself, Adweek, Oct. 3, 1988, at 26 (ER 72) (Samsung planned another ad that would show a dollar bill with Richard Nixon's face on it and the caption "Dollar bill, 2025 A.D .. ," but Nixon refused permission to use his likeness); Madow supra note 19, at 142–46 (discussing other politically and culturally charged parodies).

30. See, e.g., Bruce Horovitz, Nike Does It Again; Firm Targets Blacks with a Spin on "Family Values", L.A. Times, Aug. 25,

1992, at D1 ("The ad reinforces a stereotype about black fathers" (quoting Lawrence A. Johnson of Howard University)); Gaylord Fields, Advertising Awards–Show Mania: CEBA Awards Honors Black–Oriented Advertising, Back Stage, Nov. 17, 1989, at 1 (quoting the Rev. Jesse Jackson as emphasizing the importance of positive black images in advertising); Debra Kaufman, Quality of Hispanic Production Rising to Meet Clients' Demands, Back Stage, July 14, 1989, at 1 (Hispanic advertising professional stresses importance of positive Hispanic images in advertising); Marilyn Elias, Medical Ads Often Are Sexist, USA Today, May 18, 1989, at 1D ("There's lots of evidence that this kind of ad reinforces stereotypes" (quoting Julie Edell of Duke University)).

31. See Wendy's Kind of Commercial; "Where's the Beef" Becomes National Craze, Broadcasting, Mar. 26, 1984, at 57.

32. See Gregory Gordon, Candidates Look for Feedback Today, UPI, Sept. 26, 1988.

Commercial speech is a significant, valuable part of our national discourse. The Supreme Court has recognized as much, and has insisted that lower courts carefully scrutinize commercial speech restrictions, but the panel totally fails to do this. The panel majority doesn't even purport to apply the *Central Hudson* test, which the Supreme Court devised specifically for determining whether a commercial speech restriction is valid.[33] The majority doesn't ask, as *Central Hudson* requires, whether the speech restriction is justified by a substantial state interest. It doesn't ask whether the restriction directly advances the interest. It doesn't ask whether the restriction is narrowly tailored to the interest. See id. at 566, 100 S.Ct. at 2351.[34] These are all things the Supreme Court told us—in no uncertain terms—we must consider; the majority opinion doesn't even mention them.[35]

Process matters. The Supreme Court didn't set out the *Central Hudson* test for its health. It devised the test because it saw lower courts were giving the First Amendment short shrift when confronted with commercial speech. See Central Hudson, 447 U.S. at 561–62, 567–68, 100 S.Ct. at 2348–49, 2352. The *Central Hudson* test was an attempt to constrain lower courts' discretion, to focus judges' thinking on the important issues—how strong the state interest is, how broad the regulation is, whether a narrower regulation would work just as well. If the Court wanted to leave these matters to judges' gut feelings, to nifty lines about "the difference between fun and profit," 971 F.2d at 1401, it could have done so with much less effort.

Maybe applying the test would have convinced the majority to change its mind; maybe going through the factors would have shown that its rule was too broad, or the reasons for protecting White's "identity" too tenuous. Maybe not. But we shouldn't thumb our nose at the Supreme Court by just refusing to apply its test.

VII

For better or worse, we are the Court of Appeals for the Hollywood Circuit. Millions of people toil in the shadow of the law we make, and much of their livelihood is made possible by the existence of intellectual property rights. But much of their livelihood—and much of the vibrancy of our culture—also depends on the existence of other intangible rights:

33. Its only citation to Central Hudson is a seeming afterthought, buried in a footnote, and standing only for the proposition that commercial speech is less protected under the First Amendment. See 971 F.2d at 1401 n. 3.

34. See also Board of Trustees v. Fox, 492 U.S. 469, 476–81, 109 S.Ct. 3028, 3032–35, 106 L.Ed.2d 388 (1989) (reaffirming "narrowly tailored" requirement, but making clear it's not a "least restrictive means" test).

The government has a freer hand in regulating false or misleading commercial speech, but this isn't such a regulation.

Some "appropriations" of a person's "identity" might misleadingly suggest an endorsement, but the mere possibility that speech might mislead isn't enough to strip it of First Amendment protection. See Zauderer v. Office of Disciplinary Counsel, 471 U.S. 626, 644, 105 S.Ct. 2265, 2278, 85 L.Ed.2d 652 (1985).

35. Neither does it discuss whether the speech restriction is unconstitutionally vague. Posadas de P.R. Assocs. v. Tourism Co., 478 U.S. 328, 347, 106 S.Ct. 2968, 2980, 92 L.Ed.2d 266 (1986).

The right to draw ideas from a rich and varied public domain, and the right to mock, for profit as well as fun, the cultural icons of our time.

In the name of avoiding the "evisceration" of a celebrity's rights in her image, the majority diminishes the rights of copyright holders and the public at large. In the name of fostering creativity, the majority suppresses it. Vanna White and those like her have been given something they never had before, and they've been given it at our expense. I cannot agree.

Notes

1. The Ninth Circuit applied and expanded the *Midler* analysis in *White v. Samsung*. Do the decisions in *Midler* or *White* (or both) go too far in expanding the scope of common law right of publicity claims? In light of those decisions, in what manner can an advertiser evoke the image of a well-known celebrity without incurring possible tort liability? What arguments can the lawyers for Samsung make to a jury when the case is remanded for trial? See generally Restatement (Third) of Unfair Competition § 46 (1995) ("One who appropriates the commercial value of a person's identity by using without consent the person's name, likeness, or other indicia of identity for purposes of trade is subject to liability for the relief appropriate under the rules stated in §§ 48 and 49.").

2. Would the right of publicity be implicated when figures resembling characters from the television series "Cheers" are placed in airport bars licensed by the producers of Cheers? See Wendt v. Host International, Inc., 125 F.3d 806 (9th Cir.1997). By use of a basketball star's former name, Lew Alcindor, in an advertisement for automobile? See Abdul–Jabbar v. General Motors Corp., 85 F.3d 407 (9th Cir.1996). By use of the phrase "Here's Johnny" (which was used to introduce talk-show host Johnny Carson) in connection with the sale of portable toilets? See Carson v. Here's Johnny Portable Toilets, Inc., 698 F.2d 831 (6th Cir.1983). By use of a Wilford Brimley look-alike in advertisements for a restaurant chain? See Brimley v. Hardee's Food Systems, Inc., 1995 Westlaw 51177 (S.D.N.Y.1995).

3. The right of publicity is governed almost exclusively by state law. Should a federal statute should be enacted to establish uniformity? See Eric J. Goodman, A National Identity Crisis: The Need for a Federal Right of Publicity Statute, 9 DePaul–LCA J. Art & Ent. L. 227 (1999); Richard S. Robinson, Preemption, the Right of Publicity & a New Federal Statute, 16 Cardozo Arts & Ent. L.J. 183 (1998) (same); J. Eugene Salomon, Jr., Note, The Right of Publicity Run Riot: The Case for a Federal Statute, 60 S. Cal. L. Rev. 1179 (1987). Does either 15 U.S.C. § 1125(c) or 17 U.S.C. § 1101 have any relevance? English law does not recognize a right to control the commercial use of personal names or likenesses. See Bi–Rite Enterprises, Inc. v. Bruce Miner Co., 757 F.2d 440, 442 (1st Cir.1985). Is there a good argument for adopting such a rule?

4. The Supreme Court has addressed possible First Amendment limits on the right of publicity in Zacchini v. Scripps–Howard Broadcasting Co., 433 U.S. 562, 97 S.Ct. 2849, 53 L.Ed.2d 965 (1977). The plaintiff in that case performed a "human cannonball" act, in which he was shot out of a cannon

into a nearby net. The entire act took place in about 15 seconds. A television broadcaster recorded the entire act—despite the plaintiff's request that it not do so—and broadcast it on the evening news. The Court held that "[w]herever the line in particular situations is to be drawn between media reports that are protected and those that are not, we are quite sure that the First and Fourteenth Amendments do not immunize the media when they broadcast a performer's entire act without his consent." *Id.* Consider the following provision of the Restatement: "The name, likeness, and other indicia of a person's identity are used 'for purposes of trade' under the rule stated in § 46 if they are used in advertising the user's goods or services, or are placed on merchandise marketed by the user, or are used in connection with services rendered by the user. However, use 'for purposes of trade' does not ordinarily include the use of a person's identity in news reporting, commentary, entertainment, works of fiction or nonfiction, or in advertising that is incidental to such uses." Restatement (Third) of Unfair Competition § 47 (1995). Would the defendant's actions in *Zacchini* violate this provision?

PARKS v. LaFACE RECORDS
United States Court of Appeals, Sixth Circuit, 2003.
329 F.3d 437.

HOLSCHUH, DISTRICT JUDGE.

This is a dispute over the name of a song. Rosa Parks is a civil rights icon who first gained prominence during the Montgomery, Alabama bus boycott in 1955. She brings suit against LaFace Records, a record producer, and OutKast, a "rap" (or "hip-hop") music duo, as well as several other named affiliates, for using her name as the title of their song, Rosa Parks. Parks contends that Defendants' use of her name constitutes false advertising under § 43(a) of the Lanham Act, 15 U.S.C. § 1125(a), and intrudes on her common law right of publicity under Michigan state law. Defendants argue that they are entitled to summary judgment because Parks has failed to show any violation of the Lanham Act or her right of publicity. Defendants further argue that, even if she has shown such a violation, their First Amendment freedom of artistic expression should be a defense as a matter of law to each of these claims. Parks also contends that Defendants' conduct renders them liable under Michigan law for defamation and tortious interference with a business relationship; Defendants have also denied liability with respect to these claims.

* * *

For the reasons hereafter set forth, we believe that, with respect to Rosa Parks' claims under the Lanham Act and under the common law right of publicity, "the evidence is such that a reasonable jury could return a verdict for the nonmoving party." Anderson v. Liberty Lobby, Inc., 477 U.S. 242, 248, 106 S.Ct. 2505, 91 L.Ed.2d 202 (1986). We therefore conclude that the district court erred in granting Defendants' motion for summary judgment on those claims. We conclude, however, that the district court properly granted summary judgment in favor of Defendants on Rosa Parks' state law claims of defamation and tortious interference with a business relationship.

I. BACKGROUND

A. *Facts*

Rosa Parks is an historical figure who first gained prominence as a symbol of the civil rights movement in the United States during the 1950's and 1960's. In 1955, while riding in the front of a segregated bus in Montgomery, Alabama, she refused to yield her seat to a white passenger and move to the back of the bus as blacks were required to do by the then-existing laws requiring segregation of the races. A 381–day bus boycott in Montgomery flowed from that one event, which eventually became a catalyst for organized boycotts, sit-ins, and demonstrations all across the South. Her single act of defiance has garnered her numerous public accolades and awards, and she has used that celebrity status to promote various civil and human rights causes as well as television programs and books inspired by her life story. She has also approved a collection of gospel recordings by various artists entitled Verity Records Presents: A Tribute to Mrs. Rosa Parks (the "Tribute" album), released in 1995.

Defendants are OutKast, comprised of recording artists André "Dré" Benjamin and Antwan "Big Boi" Patton; their record producers, LaFace, founded by and named after Antonio "L.A." Reid and Kenny "Babyface" Edmonds; and LaFace's record distributors, Arista Records and BMG Entertainment (collectively "Defendants"). In September 1998, Defendants released the album Aquemini. The album's first single release was a song titled Rosa Parks, described as a "hit single" by a sticker on the album. The same sticker that contained the name Rosa Parks also contained a Parental Advisory warning of "explicit content." Because, as later discussed, the critical issue in this case is a determination of the artistic relevance of the title, Rosa Parks, to the content of the song, the lyrics obviously must be considered in their entirety. They are as follows:

(Hook)

> Ah ha, hush that fuss
>
> Everybody move to the back of the bus
>
> Do you wanna bump and slump with us
>
> We the type of people make the club get crunk

Verse 1: (Big Boi)

> Many a day has passed, the night has gone by
>
> But still I find the time to put that bump off in your eye
>
> Total chaos, for these playas, thought we was absent
>
> We takin another route to represent the Dungeon Family

Like Great Day, me and my nigga decide to take the back way

We stabbing every city then we headed to that bat cave

A–T–L, Georgia, what we do for ya

Bull doggin hoes like them Georgetown Hoyas

Boy you sounding silly, thank my Brougham aint sittin pretty

Doing doughnuts round you suckas like then circles around titties

Damn we the committee gone burn it down

But us gone bust you in the mouth with the chorus now

(Hook)

Verse 2: (André)

I met a gypsy and she hipped me to some life game

To stimulate then activate the left and right brain

Said baby boy you only funky as your last cut

You focus on the past your ass'll be a has what

Thats one to live by or either that one to die to

I try to just throw it at you determine your own adventure

Andre, got to her station here's my destination

She got off the bus, the conversation lingered in my head for hours

Took a shower kinda sour cause my favorite group ain't comin with it

But I'm witcha you cause you probably goin through it anyway

But anyhow when in doubt went on out and bought it

Cause I thought it would be jammin but examine all the flawsky-wawsky

Awfully, it's sad and it's costly, but that's all she wrote

And I hope I never have to float in that boat

Up shit creek it's weak is the last quote

That I want to hear when I'm goin down when all's said and done

And we got a new joe in town

When the record player get to skippin and slowin down

All yawl can say is them niggas earned that crown but until then . . .

(Hook)

(Harmonica Solo)

(Hook til fade)

II. Discussion

B. The Lanham Act

Parks contends that Defendants have violated the Lanham Act because the Rosa Parks title misleads consumers into believing that the song is about her or that she is affiliated with the Defendants, or has sponsored or approved the Rosa Parks song and the Aquemini album. She argues that the risk of confusion is enhanced by the fact that her authorized Tribute album is in the marketplace alongside Defendants' album featuring the Rosa Parks single. As additional evidence for her claim, Parks points to Defendants' concession that they have used the Rosa Parks title to advertise and promote both the song and the Aquemini album. She also supplies twenty-one affidavits from consumers affirming that they either believed Defendants' song was about Parks or was connected to the Tribute album authorized by her.

Defendants respond that Parks' Lanham Act claim must fail for two reasons. First, they claim that Parks does not possess a trademark right in her name and Defendants have not made a trademark use of her name, as allegedly required for a cause of action under the Lanham Act. Second, they contend that even if use of the title posed some risk of consumer confusion, the risk is outweighed by Defendants' First Amendment right to free expression.

1. Trademark Right In and Trademark Use of Parks' Name

Citing Rock & Roll Hall of Fame & Museum, Inc. v. Gentile Productions, 134 F.3d 749, 756 (6th Cir.1998), Defendants contend that Parks' § 43(a) claim must fail because they have made no trademark use of her name. However, Defendants misconceive the legal basis of a Lanham Act claim. It is not necessary for them to make a "trademark" use of Rosa Parks' name in order for her to have a cause of action for false advertising under § 43(a) of the Lanham Act.

Rosa Parks clearly has a property interest in her name akin to that of a person holding a trademark. It is beyond question that Parks is a celebrity. The parties have stipulated to her international fame and to her prior authorization of television programs and books. We have already established, supra, that courts routinely recognize a property right in celebrity identity akin to that of a trademark holder under § 43(a). See, e.g., Landham, 227 F.3d at 626; Waits, 978 F.2d at 1110; Allen, 610 F.Supp. at 624–25. We find Parks' prior commercial activities and international recognition as a symbol of the civil rights movement endow her with a trademark interest in her name the same as if she were a famous actor or musician.

Therefore, even though Rosa Parks' name might not be eligible for registration as a trademark, and even though Defendants were not selling Rosa Parks-brand CD's, a viable cause of action also exists under § 43(a) if consumers falsely believed that Rosa Parks had sponsored or approved the song, or was somehow affiliated with the song or the album. We turn then to Defendants' second argument, that even if Parks could establish some likelihood of confusion, the First Amendment protects Defendants' choice of title.

2.   *The First Amendment Defense—Three Approaches*

Defendants allege that even if Parks' evidence demonstrates some likelihood of consumer confusion regarding their song and album, their First Amendment right of artistic expression trumps that concern. Defendants make an arguable point. From ancient times, music has been a means by which people express ideas. As such, music is firmly ensconced within the protections of the First Amendment. See Hurley v. Irish–American Gay, Lesbian & Bisexual Group of Boston, 515 U.S. 557, 569, 115 S.Ct. 2338, 132 L.Ed.2d 487 (1995) (stating that paintings, music and poetry are "unquestionably shielded" by the First Amendment); Ward v. Rock Against Racism, 491 U.S. 781, 790, 109 S.Ct. 2746, 105 L.Ed.2d 661 (1989) ("Music, as a form of expression and communication, is protected under the First Amendment .. "). However, the First Amendment cannot permit anyone who cries "artist" to have carte blanche when it comes to naming and advertising his or her works, art though it may be. As the Second Circuit sagely observed, "[t]he purchaser of a book, like the purchaser of a can of peas, has a right not to be misled as to the source [or endorsement] of the product." Rogers, 875 F.2d at 997; see also Cliffs Notes, Inc. v. Bantam Doubleday Dell Publ'g Group, Inc., 886 F.2d 490, 493 (2d Cir.1989) ("Trademark protection is not lost simply because the allegedly infringing use is in connection with a work of artistic expression." (citation omitted)). Courts have adopted three approaches to balance First Amendment interests with the protections of the Lanham Act: (a) the "likelihood of confusion" test; (b) the "alternative avenues" test; and (c) the *Rogers v. Grimaldi* test. We will examine each one in turn.

a.   *Likelihood of Confusion Factors Used In Commercial Trademark Cases*

One approach is to rely solely on the "likelihood of confusion" factors applied in other, more traditional, trademark cases. That is, we analyze: 1) the strength of the plaintiff's mark; 2) the relatedness of the goods; 3) the similarity of the marks; 4) evidence of actual confusion; 5) the marketing channels used; 6) the likely degree of purchaser care; 7) the defendant's intent in selecting the mark; and 8) the likelihood of expansion in the product lines of the parties. See Frisch's Rests., Inc. v. Elby's Big Boy of Steubenville, Inc., 670 F.2d 642, 648 (6th Cir.1982) (adopting the test from AMF, Inc. v. Sleekcraft Boats, 599 F.2d 341, 348 (9th Cir.1979)); see also Polaroid Corp. v. Polarad Elecs. Corp., 287 F.2d 492, 495 (2d Cir.1961) (creating a variant of the test). Based upon that evidence, we then decide if the plaintiff has raised a genuine issue of material fact as to the likelihood of consumer confusion. Under this approach, we do not pay special solicitude to an asserted First Amendment defense.

This approach has been inferred from the Ninth Circuit case, Dr. Seuss Enterprises, L.P. v. Penguin Books USA, Inc., 109 F.3d 1394 (9th

Cir.1997). See Films of Distinction, Inc. v. Allegro Film Prods., Inc., 12 F.Supp.2d 1068, 1078 (C.D.Cal.1998) ("[I]t appears the Ninth Circuit will not adopt [a] ... test balancing trademark protections against the artistic interest in protecting literary titles.... Dr. Seuss strongly suggests that this 'balancing' has already been adequately accomplished by the statutory framework [of the Lanham Act]."). But see Mattel, Inc. v. MCA Records, Inc., 296 F.3d 894, 901 (9th Cir.2002), cert. denied, 537 U.S. 1171, 123 S.Ct. 993, 154 L.Ed.2d 912 (2003) (distinguishing Dr. Seuss). The Tenth Circuit has obliquely endorsed this approach as well. See Cardtoons, 95 F.3d at 970 (suggesting the "likelihood of confusion" test "serve[s] to avoid First Amendment concerns" in trademark cases).

b. Alternative Avenues Test

A second approach is the "alternative avenues" test. This is the test urged upon us by Parks, and endorsed by a panel of the Eighth Circuit. Under the "alternative avenues" test, a title of an expressive work will not be protected from a false advertising claim if there are sufficient alternative means for an artist to convey his or her idea. See Mutual of Omaha Ins. Co. v. Novak, 836 F.2d 397, 402 (8th Cir.1987) (creator of parody tee-shirts not protected by First Amendment because he could still produce parody editorials in books, magazines, or film); Am. Dairy Queen Corp. v. New Line Prods., Inc., 35 F.Supp.2d 727, 734 (D.Minn. 1998) (no First Amendment protection for an infringing movie title because there were other titles the producers could use); cf. Anheuser–Busch, Inc. v. Balducci Publ'ns, 28 F.3d 769, 776 (8th Cir.1994) (First Amendment protection not available to parodist because the confusing trademark use was "wholly unnecessary" to the parodist's stated purpose).

c. Rogers v. Grimaldi Test

Finally, a third approach is the one developed by the Second Circuit in *Rogers v. Grimaldi* and adopted by the district court in this case. Under *Rogers*, a title will be protected unless it has "no artistic relevance" to the underlying work or, if there is artistic relevance, the title "explicitly misleads as to the source or the content of the work." Rogers, 875 F. 2d at 999. This test was explicitly adopted by the Fifth Circuit in Westchester Media v. PRL USA Holdings, Inc., 214 F.3d 658, 664–65 (5th Cir.2000), and by a panel of the Ninth Circuit in Mattel, 296 F.3d at 902. It was also adopted by a district court in the Third Circuit in Seale v. Gramercy Pictures, 949 F.Supp. 331, 339 (1996).

d. Analysis

We conclude that neither the first nor the second approach accords adequate weight to the First Amendment interests in this case. The first approach—unmodified application of the likelihood of confusion factors in trademark cases—gives no weight to First Amendment concerns. Instead, it treats the name of an artistic work as if it were no different from the name of an ordinary commercial product. However, this approach ignores the fact that the artistic work is not simply a commercial product but is also a means of communication. See Hicks v. Casablanca

Records, 464 F.Supp. 426, 430 (S.D.N.Y.1978) ("[M]ore so than posters, bubble gum cards, or some other such 'merchandise', books and movies are vehicles through which ideas and opinions are disseminated and, as such, have enjoyed certain constitutional protections, not generally accorded 'merchandise.' "); see also Cardtoons, 95 F.3d at 970 ("The fact that expressive materials are sold neither renders the speech unprotected, nor alters the level of protection under the First Amendment.") (citations omitted). The names artists bestow on their art can be part and parcel of the artistic message. See Rogers, 875 F.2d at 998 ("Filmmakers and authors frequently rely on word-play, ambiguity, irony, and allusion in titling their works."). The fact that Defendants use the Rosa Parks title in advertising does not automatically erase the expressive function of the title and render it mere commercial exploitation; if a song is sold, and the title is protected by the First Amendment, the title naturally will be "inextricably intertwined" with the song's commercial promotion. See id.; see also Riley v. Nat'l Fed'n of the Blind, Inc., 487 U.S. 781, 796, 108 S.Ct. 2667, 101 L.Ed.2d 669 (1988) (holding that when protected speech is inextricable from unprotected speech, the court will treat the entire message as protected); Cardtoons, 95 F.3d at 970.

The public has at least as much interest in the free exchange of ideas as it does in avoiding misleading advertising. If Parks possesses a right to police the use of her name, even when that right can be exercised only to prevent consumer confusion, she has the means to restrict the public discourse to some extent. As Judge Kozinski has pointed out, "Intellectual property rights aren't free: They're imposed at the expense of future creators and of the public at large." White v. Samsung Elecs. Am., Inc., 989 F.2d 1512, 1516 (9th Cir.1993) (Kozinski, J., dissenting from denial of rehearing en banc). "Intellectual property . . . includes the words, images, and sounds that we use to communicate, and 'we cannot indulge in the facile assumption that one can forbid particular words without also running a substantial risk of suppressing ideas in the process.' " Cardtoons, 95 F.3d at 971 (quoting Cohen v. California, 403 U.S. 15, 26, 91 S.Ct. 1780, 29 L.Ed.2d 284 (1971)). In sum, we do not find the unmodified likelihood of confusion test applied to commercial products adequate to differentiate between those artists who choose titles for the purpose of legitimate artistic relevancy and those artists who choose misleading titles for the purpose of commercial gain. See Mattel, 296 F.3d at 900 ("[W]hen a trademark owner asserts a right to control how we express ourselves . . . applying the traditional [likelihood of confusion] test fails to account for the full weight of the public's interest in free expression."). Therefore, we reject the first approach.

The second approach, the "alternative avenues" test, is similarly problematic. The "alternative avenues" test was articulated in Dallas Cowboys Cheerleaders, Inc. v. Pussycat Cinema, Ltd., 604 F.2d 200, 206 (2d Cir.1979), and is derived from real property law. The test is premised on the notion that, just as a real property owner may exclude a speaker from a shopping mall so long as other locations exist for the speaker to deliver his message, a celebrity may prohibit use of his or her name so long as alternative ways exist for the artist to communicate his or her idea. See id. (citing Lloyd Corp. v. Tanner, 407 U.S. 551, 567, 92 S.Ct. 2219, 33 L.Ed.2d 131 (1972)). See also Mutual of Omaha Ins. Co., 836 F.2d at 402 (citing Dallas Cowboys, 604 F.2d at 206); Am. Dairy Queen Corp., 35 F.Supp.2d at 734.

More than one court has noted the awkwardness of analogizing property rights in land to property rights in words or ideas. See Westchester Media, 214 F.3d at 672 ("[T]he reasonable alternative avenues approach bears a tenuous relation to communicative and property interests embodied in trademarks."); L.L. Bean, Inc. v. Drake Publishers, Inc., 811 F.2d 26, 29 (1st Cir.1987) ("The first amendment issues involved in this case cannot be disposed of by equating the rights of a trademark owner with the rights of an owner of real property."). Furthermore, the Second Circuit all but retracted its Dallas Cowboys decision in *Rogers*. See 875 F.2d at 999 n. 4 ("We do not read Dallas Cowboys Cheerleaders as generally precluding all consideration of First Amendment concerns whenever an allegedly infringing author has 'alternative avenues of communication.' "). To suggest that other words can be used as well to express an author's or composer's message is not a proper test for weighing First Amendment rights. As Mark Twain observed, "The difference between the almost-right word and the right word is really a large matter—it's the difference between the 'lightning-bug' and the 'lightning.' " J. Bartlett, Familiar Quotations 527 (16th ed.1992); see also New Kids on the Block v. News Am. Publ'g, Inc., 971 F.2d 302, 306 (9th Cir.1992) ("[W]e need not belabor the point that some words, phrases or symbols better convey their intended meanings than others."). Finally, adopting the "alternative avenues" test would needlessly entangle courts in the process of titling works of art; courts would be asked to determine not just whether a title is reasonably "artistic" but whether a title is "necessary" to communicate the idea. We therefore reject the alternative avenues test.

The third approach, the *Rogers* test, was adopted by the district court in this case and has been endorsed by panels in the Second, Fifth, and Ninth Circuits. Although the *Rogers* test has been criticized, see, e.g., 2 J. Thomas McCarthy, McCarthy on Trademarks and Unfair Competition § 10:31 (4th ed.2002), we find it the most appropriate method to balance the public interest in avoiding consumer confusion with the public interest in free expression.

In *Rogers*, the plaintiff was dancer and film star Ginger Rogers. Italian movie maker Federico Fellini made a fictional movie titled Ginger and Fred about the reunion of two erstwhile cabaret dancers who became known to their fans as Fred and Ginger because they imitated Fred Astaire and Ginger Rogers in their act. Rogers, 875 F.2d at 996–97. Rogers' complaint alleged, inter alia, that the title misled viewers into thinking that the movie was about her famous collaboration with Fred Astaire, in violation of the Lanham Act, and that the use of her name infringed her right of publicity. See id. at 997. The *Rogers* court, finding that overextension of Lanham Act restrictions in the area of titles might intrude on First Amendment values and that the "alternative avenues" test is insufficient to accommodate the public's interest in free expression, adopted a two-pronged test:

> In the context of allegedly misleading titles using a celebrity's name, that balance [between avoiding consumer confusion and protecting free expression] will normally not support application of the Act unless [1] the title has no artistic relevance to the underlying work whatsoever, or, if it has some artistic relevance, unless [2] the title explicitly misleads as to the source or the content of the work.

Id. at 999.

Courts in the Second Circuit have routinely applied the *Rogers* test to other Lanham Act cases. See Twin Peaks Prods., Inc. v. Publ'ns Int'l, Ltd., 996 F.2d 1366, 1379 (2d Cir.1993); Cliffs Notes, 886 F.2d at 494; DeClemente v. Columbia Pictures Indus., Inc., 860 F.Supp. 30, 51 (E.D.N.Y.1994); Girl Scouts of U.S. v. Bantam Doubleday Dell Publ'g Group, Inc., 808 F.Supp. 1112, 1119–20 (S.D.N.Y.1992). The Fifth Circuit has followed suit. See Westchester Media, 214 F.3d at 664.

In addition, a panel of the Ninth Circuit recently adopted the *Rogers* test in Mattel, Inc. v. MCA Records, Inc. In *Mattel*, the manufacturer of the well-known "Barbie" doll, sued a Danish band, Aqua, for their song Barbie Girl, which, among other things, contained lines that portrayed Barbie in a negative light. Mattel alleged that Aqua's use of the name "Barbie" in the title had confused consumers into believing that Mattel was affiliated with the song. Mattel, 296 F.3d at 899. Mattel argued that the song was not about "Barbie" and hence could not be protected by the First Amendment. In the district court, as support, Mattel introduced statements by Aqua band members in interviews that "[t]he song isn't about the doll. We're making fun of the glamourous life." Mattel, Inc. v. MCA Records, Inc., 28 F.Supp.2d 1120, 1138 (C.D.Cal.1998). Mattel also supplied evidence that purported to show that individuals were misled into believing Mattel and the song were affiliated in some way. Among the evidence was a survey of 556 persons of various ages in six states, 17% of whom believed that Mattel or "Barbie" was the source of, connected with, or gave permission for the Barbie Girl song. Id. at 1132–33.

On appeal from a summary judgment in favor of the defendant, the Ninth Circuit, applying *Rogers*, concluded that the First Amendment outweighed any risk of confusion between Mattel and the song title. Specifically it found:

> Under the first prong of *Rogers*, the use of Barbie in the song title clearly is relevant to the underlying work, namely, the song itself. . . . [T]he song is about Barbie and the values Aqua claims she represents. The song title does not explicitly mislead as to the source of the work; it does not, explicitly or otherwise, suggest that it was produced by Mattel. The only indication that Mattel might be associated with the song is the use of Barbie in the title; if this were

enough to satisfy this prong of the *Rogers* test, it would render *Rogers* a nullity.

Mattel, 296 F.3d at 902.

The application of *Rogers* in *Mattel*, as well as in cases decided in other circuits, persuades us that *Rogers* is the best test for balancing Defendants' and the public's interest in free expression under the First Amendment against Parks' and the public's interest in enforcement of the Lanham Act. We thus apply the *Rogers* test to the facts before us.

3.   *Application of the Rogers Test*

a.   *Artistic Relevance Prong*

The first prong of *Rogers* requires a determination of whether there is any artistic relationship between the title and the underlying work. Rogers, 875 F.2d at 999. Parks contends that a cursory review of the Rosa Parks title and the lyrics demonstrates that there is no artistic connection between them. Parks also submits two articles in which members of OutKast are purported to have admitted that the song was not about her. As further evidence, she offers a "translation" of the lyrics of the song Rosa Parks, derived from various electronic "dictionaries" of the "rap" vernacular to demonstrate that the song truly has nothing to do with Parks herself. The "translation" of the chorus reads as follows:

> "Be quiet and stop the commotion. OutKast is coming back out [with new music] so all other MCs [mic checkers, rappers, Master of Ceremonies] step aside. Do you want to ride and hang out with us? OutKast is the type of group to make the clubs get hyped-up/excited."

Pl. Br. at 5.

Defendants respond that their use of Parks' name is "metaphorical" or "symbolic." They argue that the historical association between Rosa Parks and the phrase "move to the back of the bus" is beyond dispute and that Parks' argument that the song is not "about" her in a biographical sense is simply irrelevant.

The district court was of the opinion that the artistic relationship between the title and the song was "so obvious that the matter is not open to reasonable debate." Parks, 76 F.Supp.2d at 782. The court said:

> Rosa Parks is universally known for and commonly associated with her refusal ... to ... "move to the back of the bus." The song at issue makes unmistakable reference to that symbolic act a total of ten times. Admittedly, the song is not about plaintiff in a strictly biographical sense, but it need not be. Rather, defendants' use of plaintiff's name, along with the phrase "move to the back of the bus," is metaphorical and symbolic.

Id. at 780.

Contrary to the opinion of the district court, we believe that the artistic relationship between the title and the content of the song is certainly not obvious and, indeed, is "open to reasonable debate" for the following reasons.

It is true that the phrase "move to the back of the bus" is repeatedly used in the "hook" or chorus of the song. When the phrase is considered in the context of the lyrics, however, the phrase has absolutely nothing to do with Rosa Parks. There could be no stronger, no more compelling, evidence of this fact than the admission of "Dré" (André "Dré" Benjamin) that, "We (OutKast) never intended for the song to be about Rosa Parks or the civil rights movement. It was just symbolic, meaning that we comin' back out, so all you other MCs move to the back of the bus." J.A. at 333.

The composers did not intend it to be about Rosa Parks, and the lyrics are not about Rosa Parks. The lyrics' sole message is that Out-Kast's competitors are of lesser quality and, therefore, must "move to the back of the bus," or in other words, "take a back seat." We believe that reasonable persons could conclude that there is no relationship of any kind between Rosa Parks' name and the content of the song—a song that is nothing more and nothing less than a paean announcing the triumph of superior people in the entertainment business over inferior people in that business. Back of the Bus, for example, would be a title that is obviously relevant to the content of the song, but it also would not have the marketing power of an icon of the civil rights movement. Choosing Rosa Parks' name as the title to the song unquestionably enhanced the song's potential sale to the consuming public.

The *Rogers* court made an important point which clearly applies in this case. The court said, "[p]oetic license is not without limits. The purchaser of a book, like the purchaser of a can of peas, has a right not to be misled as to the source of the product." Rogers, 875 F.2d at 997. The same is also true regarding the content of a song. The purchaser of a song titled Rosa Parks has a right not to be misled regarding the content of that song. While the expressive element of titles admittedly requires more protection than the labeling of ordinary commercial products, "[a] misleading title with no artistic relevance cannot be sufficiently justified by a free expression interest," id. at 999, and the use of such a title, as in the present case, could be found to constitute a violation of the Lanham Act. Including the phrase "move to the back of the bus" in the lyrics of this song, in our opinion, does not justify, as a matter of law, the appropriation of Rosa Parks' name for the title to the song, and the fact that the phrase is repeated ten times or fifty times does not affect the question of the relevancy of the title to the lyrics.

The district court made the following correct observation:

Plaintiff Rosa Parks is a well-known public figure who has been recognized as an international symbol of freedom, humanity, dignity and strength for over 43 years. Plaintiff's notoriety arose from her heroic stance against racial inequality in the South when on December 1, 1955, in Montgomery, Alabama, she refused to give up her seat to a white passenger and move to the back of the bus. This one defiant act precipitated a 381–day bus boycott that ended segregation on public transportation and ultimately sparked the Civil Rights Movement of the 1960's.

Parks, 76 F.Supp.2d at 777.

While Defendants' lyrics contain profanity and a great deal of "explicit" language (together with a parental warning), they contain absolutely nothing that could conceivably, by any stretch of the imagination, be considered, explicitly or implicitly, a reference to courage, to sacrifice, to the civil rights movement or to any other quality with which Rosa Parks is identified. If the requirement of "relevance" is to have any meaning at all, it would not be unreasonable to conclude that the title Rosa Parks is not relevant to the content of the song in question. The use of this woman's name unquestionably was a good marketing tool—Rosa Parks was likely to sell far more recordings than Back of the Bus—but its use could be found by a reasonable finder of fact to be a flagrant deception on the public regarding the actual content of this song and the creation of an impression that Rosa Parks, who had approved the use of her name in connection with the Tribute album, had also approved or sponsored the use of her name on Defendants' composition.

It is certainly not dispositive that, in response to an interview following the filing of this lawsuit, one of the OutKast members said that using Rosa Parks' name was "symbolic." Where an artist proclaims that a celebrity's name is used merely as a "symbol" for the lyrics of a song, and such use is highly questionable when the lyrics are examined, a legitimate question is presented as to whether the artist's claim is sincere or merely a guise to escape liability. Our task, it seems to us, is not to accept without question whatever purpose Defendants may now claim they had in using Rosa Parks' name. It is, instead, to make a determination as to whether, applying the law of *Rogers*, there is a genuine issue of material fact regarding the question of whether the title is artistically relevant to the content of the song. As noted above, crying "artist" does not confer carte blanche authority to appropriate a celebrity's name. Furthermore, crying "symbol" does not change that proposition and confer authority to use a celebrity's name when none, in fact, may exist.

It appears that the district court's rendition of summary judgment for OutKast was based on the court's conclusion that Defendants' use of Plaintiff's name as the song's title was "metaphorical and symbolic." Id. at 780. The obvious question, however, is symbolic of what? There is no doubt that Rosa Parks is a symbol. As the parties agree, she is "an international symbol of freedom, humanity, dignity and strength." J.A. at 79. There is not even a hint, however, of any of these qualities in the song to which Defendants attached her name. In lyrics that are laced with profanity and in a "hook" or chorus that is pure egomania, many reasonable people could find that this is a song that is clearly antithetical to the qualities identified with Rosa Parks. Furthermore, the use of Rosa Parks' name in a metaphorical sense is highly questionable. A metaphor is "a figure of speech in which a word or phrase denoting one kind of object or action is used in place of another to suggest a likeness or analogy between them." Webster's Third New International Dictionary 1420 (Phillip Babcock Gove, ed.1976). The use of the phrase "go to the back of the bus" may be metaphorical to the extent that it refers to OutKast's competitors being pushed aside by OutKast's return and being forced to "take a back seat." The song, however, is not titled Back of the Bus. It is titled Rosa Parks, and it is difficult to equate OutKast's feeling of superiority, metaphorically or in any other manner, to the qualities for which Rosa Parks is known around the world. We believe that reasonable people could find that the use of Rosa Parks' name as the title to this song was not justified as being metaphorical or symbolic of anything for which Rosa Parks is famous. To the contrary, reasonable people could find that the name was appropriated solely because of the vastly increased marketing power of a product bearing the name of a national heroine of the civil rights movement.

We do not mean to imply that Rosa Parks must always be displayed in a flattering manner, or that she should have the ability to prevent any other characterization of her. She is a celebrity and, as such, she cannot prevent being portrayed in a manner that may not be pleasing to her. As the court noted in Guglielmi v. Spelling–Goldberg Productions, 25 Cal.3d 860, 160 Cal.Rptr. 352, 603 P.2d 454, 460 (1979) (Bird J., concurring), "[t]he right of publicity derived from public prominence does not confer a shield to ward off caricature, parody and satire." It has been held, for example, that, "[p]arodies of celebrities are an especially valuable means of expression because of the role celebrities play in modern society." Cardtoons, 95 F.3d at 972. The present case, however, does not involve any claim of caricature, parody or satire. It involves, instead, the use of a celebrity's name as the title to a song when it reasonably could be found that the celebrity's name has no artistic relevance to the content of the song. It involves, in short, a reasonable dispute whether the use of Rosa Parks' name was a misrepresentation and false advertising or whether it was a legitimate use of a celebrity's name in some recognized form of artistic expression protected by the First Amendment.

In Rogers, the court, in discussing the title to the movie Ginger and Fred, observed that "there is no doubt a risk that some people looking at the title 'Ginger and Fred' might think the film was about Rogers and Astaire in a direct, biographical sense. For those gaining that impression, the title is misleading." 875 F.2d at 1001. Likewise, in the present case, some people looking at the title Rosa Parks might think the song is about Rosa Parks and for those gaining that impression (as twenty-one consumer affidavits filed in this case indicate happened, J.A. at 342–62), the title is misleading. This, standing alone, may not be sufficient to show a violation of the Lanham Act if the title is nevertheless artistically relevant to the content of the underlying work.

There is a clear distinction, however, between the facts in Rogers and the facts in the present case. In Rogers, the court had no difficulty in finding that the title chosen for the movie Ginger and Fred had artistic relevance to the content of the movie. "The central characters in the film are nicknamed 'Ginger' and 'Fred,' and these names are not arbitrarily chosen just to exploit the publicity value of their real life counterparts but instead have genuine relevance to the film's story." 875 F.2d at 1001. The *Rogers* court further pointed out that the title Ginger and Fred is "entirely truthful as to its content in referring to the film's fictional protagonists who are known to their Italian audience as 'Ginger and Fred.'" Id. In other words, the title in *Rogers* was obviously relevant and truthful as to the film's content, because the film was about the main characters known in the film as Ginger and Fred. In contrast, it cannot be said that the title in the present case, Rosa Parks, is clearly truthful as to the content of the song which, as OutKast admits, is not about Rosa Parks at all and was never intended to be about Rosa Parks, and which does not refer to Rosa Parks or to the qualities for which she is known.

Furthermore, the contrast between the real Ginger and Fred and the fictional Ginger and Fred in the film served the director's purpose of satirizing contemporary television and, in that sense, the title was "an integral element of the film and the film maker's artistic expressions." Id. OutKast's only explanation for the use of Rosa Parks' name in the title of their song, however, is that the name Rosa Parks is "a symbol." It is, indeed, a symbol, but the question presented is how the symbol of Rosa Parks, a symbol of "freedom, humanity, dignity, and strength," is artistically related to the content of a song that appears to be diametrically opposed to those qualities. The song is not claimed to be a satire, a parody or some other form of artistic expression that would be protected under the broad umbrella of the First Amendment. The mere fact that the phrase "move to the back of the bus" is an apt description of OutKast's attitude toward entertainers they regard as lesser human beings is not, in our view, a justification, as a matter of law, for appropriating the name of Rosa Parks.

Mattel, Inc. v. MCA Records, Inc., 296 F.3d 894 (9th Cir.2002) involved facts that are remarkably different from the facts of this case. In applying the first prong of *Rogers*, the Ninth Circuit in *Mattel* stated:

> We expect a title to describe the underlying work, not to identify the producer, and Barbie Girl does just that.

> The Barbie Girl title presages a song about Barbie, or at least a girl like Barbie. The title conveys a message to consumers about what they can expect to discover in the song itself; it's a quick glimpse of Aqua's take on their own song. The lyrics confirm this: The female singer, who calls herself Barbie, is "a Barbie girl, in [her] Barbie world." She tells her male counterpart (named Ken), "Life in plastic, it's fantastic. You can brush my hair, undress me everywhere/Imagination, life is your creation." And off they go to "party." The song pokes fun at Barbie and the values that Aqua contends she represents.

* * *

> *Under the first prong of* Rogers, *the use of Barbie in the song title clearly is relevant to the underlying work, namely, the song itself. As noted, the song is about Barbie and the values Aqua claims she represents.*

Id. at 901–902 (emphasis added).

In sharp contrast to *Mattel*, it is highly questionable that the facts in the present case satisfy the first prong of *Rogers*. Whereas the title Barbie Girl was clearly relevant to the lyrics of the song, ("the song is about Barbie and the values Aqua claims she represents"), it cannot be said that the title Rosa Parks is clearly relevant to the lyrics of the song in this case. While the lyrics of Barbie Girl are certainly not flattering to the wholesome image preferred by the creator of Barbie ("the song pokes fun at Barbie and the values that Aqua contends she represents"), parody is an artistic form of expression protected by the First Amendment. In contrast, there has been no attempt to defend Rosa Parks on the ground that it constitutes a parody of Rosa Parks or a satire of Rosa Parks or some other form of artistic expression involving Rosa Parks herself.

The *Mattel* case, therefore, in our view, is completely distinguishable from the facts of the present case. If anything, we believe its application of *Rogers* and the result of that application to the title and lyrics of Barbie Girl could support a conclusion that the title Rosa Parks has no artistic relevance to the lyrics of Defendants' song. The result would be that Defendants cannot satisfy even the first prong of *Rogers* in order to justify their appropriation of Rosa Parks' name.

A case that is more similar to the present case than *Mattel* is Seale v. Gramercy Pictures, 949 F.Supp. 331 (E.D.Pa.1996). In *Seale*, defendants produced and distributed a movie entitled "Panther," which was a combination of fiction and historical fact involving Bobby Seale and the Black Panther Party, founded by Seale and Huey P. Newton in 1966. Seale, Newton and another leader of the Black Panther Party, Eldridge Cleaver, were all portrayed in the movie by actors. Similar to the stipulation in the present case, it was undisputed that the plaintiff was "a well-known public and historical figure" and that, "[t]he Plaintiff's name and his role in the Black Panther Party may be found in most history books discussing the Civil Rights Movement of the 1960's." Id. at 335.

In addition to the movie, various defendants in the case produced: (1) a book titled Panther: A Pictorial History of the Black Panthers and the Story Behind the Film; (2) a videotape of the movie; and (3) a CD/cassette containing a collection of the songs from the movie. The promotional cover for the home video release of the movie mentioned Seale's name and had a photograph of the actors who portrayed Seale, Newton and Cleaver in the movie. The cover of the musical CD/cassette contained the same photograph that was on the home video, together with another photograph of a scene from the movie. Seale, who had never consented to the use of his name for the movie, the book, the videotape or the CD/cassette, brought suit alleging violations of § 43(a) of the Lanham Act and his common-law right of publicity. The defendants moved for summary judgment on all claims.

The *Seale* court found that defendants were entitled to summary judgment on plaintiff's common-law right of publicity claim as it concerned the movie, the pictorial history book, and the videotape. The court had no trouble finding that the creation of a movie and history book that integrated fictitious people and events with historical people and events surrounding the emergence of the Black Panther Party in the late 1960's was protected by the First Amendment. The court also found that the "use of the Plaintiff's name and likeness on the cover of the pictorial history book and on the cover for the home video are *clearly related to the content of the book and the film*, the subject matter of which deals with the Black Panther Party and the Plaintiff's role as co-founder of the Party." Id. at 337 (emphasis added).

The use of the plaintiff's name and likeness on the cover of the musical CD/cassette, however, was an entirely different matter. The music contained on the CD/cassette consisted of various songs composed by different musicians. The court pointed out:

> Clearly, the use of the Plaintiff's name and likeness on the cover of the musical CD/cassette does not relate to the content in the CD/cassette in the same manner as the use of the Plaintiff's name and likeness on the cover of the home video and pictorial history book relates to the content of the film and pictorial history book— the subject matter of which concerns the Black Panther Party and the Plaintiff's role as co-founder of the Party. The film and pictorial history book tell the story of the Black Panther Party and the Plaintiff's role in that Party in the late 1960's; *the musical CD/cassette is merely a collection of different songs performed by different musicians, which songs have no direct connection to the Plaintiff or the history of the Black Panther Party.* There is a genuine issue of material fact, therefore, whether the use of the Plaintiff's name and likeness on the cover of the musical CD/cassette is clearly related to the content of the film "Panther" and serves as an advertisement for the film, or whether the Defendants' use of the Plaintiff's name and likeness on the cover of the CD/cassette is a disguised advertisement for the sale of the CD/cassette. See Rogers v. Grimaldi, 875 F.2d 994, 1004–05 (2d Cir.1989).

Id. at 337–38 (emphasis added).

The court further noted that, although Section 47 of the Restatement (Third) of Unfair Competition states that use "for purposes of trade" does not ordinarily include "the use of a person's identity in news reporting, commentary, entertainment, works of fiction or non-fiction, or in advertising that is incidental to such uses," comment c to that section states that "if the name or likeness is used solely to attract attention to a work that is not related to the identified person, the user may be subject to liability for a use of the other's identity in advertising." See Seale, 949 F.Supp. at 336.

The court made the same findings in virtually the same language regarding Seale's claim under Section 43(a) of the Lanham Act, again applying *Rogers* and reaching the same result, i.e., that a genuine issue of material fact was presented. Id. at 340. The court, therefore, denied defendants' motion for summary judgment on both the plaintiff's common law right of publicity claim and Lanham Act claim as those claims related to the defendants' use of Bobby Seale's name and likeness on the CD/cassette.

We reach the same conclusion in the present case. There is a genuine issue of material fact whether the use of Rosa Parks' name as a title to the song and on the cover of the album is artistically related to the content of the song or whether the use of the name Rosa Parks is nothing more than a misleading advertisement for the sale of the song.

b. Misleading Prong

In *Rogers*, the court held that if the title of the work is artistically relevant to its content, there is no violation of the Lanham Act unless the "title explicitly misleads as to the source or the content of the work." 875 F.2d at 999. The court noted with reference to the first prong of the *Rogers* analysis:

> A misleading title with no artistic relevance cannot be sufficiently justified by a free expression interest. For example, if a film-maker placed the title "Ginger and Fred" on a film to which it had no artistic relevance at all, the arguably misleading suggestions as to source or content implicitly conveyed by the title could be found to violate the Lanham Act as to such a film.

Id.

In discussing the second prong of its analysis, in the context of using a celebrity's name in the title of some artistic work, the court explained:

> [T]itles with at least minimal artistic relevance to the work may include explicit statements about the content of the work that are seriously misleading. For example, if the characters in the film in this case had published their memoirs under the title "The True Life Story of Ginger and Fred," and if the film-maker had then used that fictitious book title as the title of the film, the Lanham Act could be applicable to such an explicitly misleading description of content. But many titles with a celebrity's name make no explicit statement that the work is about that person in any direct sense; the relevance of the title may be oblique and may become clear only after viewing or reading the work. As to such titles, the consumer interest in avoiding deception is too slight to warrant application of the Lanham Act.... Where a title with at least some artistic relevance to the work is not explicitly misleading as to the content of the work, it is not false advertising under the Lanham Act.

Id. at 1000 (footnote omitted).

We considered all the facts presented to us and concluded that, with reference to the first prong of the *Rogers* analysis, the issue of artistic relevance of the title Rosa Parks to the lyrics of the song is highly questionable and cannot be resolved as a matter of law. However, if, on remand, a trier of fact, after a full evidentiary hearing, concludes that the title is used in some symbolic or metaphorical sense, application of the *Rogers* analysis, under the particular facts of this case, would appear to be complete. In the present case, the title Rosa Parks "make[s] no explicit statement that the work is about that person in any direct sense." In other words, Defendants did not name the song, for example, The True Life Story of Rosa Parks or Rosa Parks' Favorite Rap.

In short, whether the title Rosa Parks has any artistic relevance to the content of the song is an issue that must be resolved by a finder of fact following an evidentiary hearing and not by a judge as a matter of law upon the limited record submitted in support of a motion for summary judgment. If, on remand, the finder of fact determines that OutKast placed the title Rosa Parks on a song to which it had no artistic relevance at all, then this would constitute a violation of the Lanham Act and judgment should be entered in favor of Plaintiff. However, if the finder of fact determines that the title is artistically relevant to the song's content, then the inquiry is at an end because the title "is not explicitly misleading as to the content of the work." In that event, judgment should be entered in favor of Defendants.

C. *Right of Publicity*

1. *Applicable Law*

The right of publicity protects the identity of a celebrity from exploitive commercial use. See Carson v. Here's Johnny Portable Toilets, Inc., 698 F.2d 831, 835 (6th Cir.1983). "The theory of the right is that a celebrity's identity can be valuable in the promotion of products, and the celebrity has an interest that may be protected from the unauthorized commercial exploitation of that identity." Id. As such, the common law right of publicity forms a species of property right. See Zacchini v. Scripps–Howard Broad. Co., 433 U.S. 562, 573, 97 S.Ct. 2849, 53 L.Ed.2d 965 (1977); Herman Miller, Inc. v. Palazzetti Imports & Exports, Inc., 270 F.3d 298, 325 (6th Cir.2001); Cardtoons, 95 F.3d at 967.

The right of publicity is governed by state law. See Landham, 227 F.3d at 622. Michigan has indicated that it would recognize a right of publicity, see Pallas v. Crowley, Milner & Co., 322 Mich. 411, 33 N.W.2d 911, 914 (1948), and the parties have not questioned that Plaintiff has a right of publicity. The dispute is over its application to the facts of this case.

Parks' right of publicity argument tracks that of her Lanham Act claim. She alleges that Defendants have profited from her fame by using her name solely for a commercial purpose. She supplies much the same evidence in support of her right of publicity claim as she did for her Lanham Act claim: the lyrics of Rosa Parks, the "translation," and the press clippings quoting OutKast members. Defendants do not deny that they have used the title Rosa Parks commercially, but argue that Parks has produced no evidence that their use was solely commercial. Instead, they argue that the choice was also artistic, and that they therefore have a complete defense in the First Amendment.The district court agreed with Defendants. The district court applied *Rogers*, which, in addition to the false advertising claim under § 43(a), also dealt with a right of publicity action arising under Oregon state law. Under *Rogers*, with respect to a right of publicity claim, a title that uses a celebrity's name will be protected by the First Amendment unless the title is "wholly unrelated" to the content of the work or was "simply a disguised commercial advertisement for the sale of goods or services." Rogers, 875 F.2d at 1004. The district court found that, as a matter of law, there was an artistic relationship between the title and the content of the song, and therefore it could not be considered "simply a disguised commercial advertisement." Parks, 76 F.Supp.2d at 781. Defendants' use of the title to promote the album did not change this result. Id.

2. Analysis

A right of publicity claim is similar to a false advertising claim in that it grants a celebrity the right to protect an economic interest in his or her name. See Carson, 698 F.2d at 835 ("The right of publicity has developed to protect the commercial interest of celebrities in their identities."). However, a right of publicity claim does differ from a false advertising claim in one crucial respect; a right of publicity claim does not require any evidence that a consumer is likely to be confused. See Herman Miller, 270 F.3d at 319–20 (citing Restatement (Third) of Unfair Competition § 46 cmt. c (1995)); Rogers, 875 F.2d at 1004; Cairns v. Franklin Mint Co., 24 F.Supp.2d 1013, 1030 (C.D.Cal.1998). All that a plaintiff must prove in a right of publicity action is that she has a pecuniary interest in her identity, and that her identity has been commercially exploited by a defendant. See Landham, 227 F.3d at 624; Carson, 698 F.2d at 835.

The parties have stipulated that Parks is famous and that she has used her name to promote other goods and services. She has therefore established an economic interest in her name. See Landham, 227 F.3d at 624. Furthermore, Defendants admit that they have used Parks' name as the name of their song, and have used that name to sell the song and their album. They argue, however, that, as with the Lanham Act claim, their First Amendment right of artistic expression should prevail over Parks' claim.

a. Cognizability of a First Amendment Defense

Because a plaintiff bears a reduced burden of persuasion to succeed in a right of publicity action, courts and commentators have recognized that publicity rights carry a greater danger of impinging on First Amendment rights than do rights associated with false advertising claims. See Rogers, 875 F.2d at 1004; see also Cardtoons, 95 F.3d at 967 (noting that publicity rights offer "substantially broader protection" than laws preventing false endorsement); cf. Roberta Rosenthal Kwall, The Right of Publicity v. The First Amendment: A Property and Liability Rule Analysis, 70 Ind. L.J. 47 (1994).We have recognized the importance of a First Amendment defense to right of publicity actions in a recent case. In Ruffin–Steinback v. dePasse, friends and family members of the Motown group, the "Temptations," sued the makers of a televised mini-series for the manner in which they and the former group members were portrayed in the film. 82 F.Supp.2d 723, 726–27 (E.D.Mich.2000), aff'd, 267 F.3d 457 (6th Cir.2001). The plaintiffs alleged that their likenesses were appropriated to endorse a product, the film, without their permission. Id. at 728. The court found in that case that the plaintiffs could not overcome the defendant's First Amendment defense, even where the portrayal of the plaintiffs was partly fictionalized, and even where the likenesses of the plaintiffs were used to promote a videocassette version of the mini-series. Id. at 730–31; see also Seale, 949 F.Supp. at 337 (holding that the film Panther, which used the name and likeness of Black Panther founder Bobby Seale, was protected by the First Amendment).

As with the Lanham Act, then, we must conduct another balancing of interests—Parks' property right in her own name versus the freedom of artistic expression. See ETW Corp. v. Jireh Publ'g, Inc., 99 F.Supp.2d 829, 834–36 (N.D.Ohio 2000); Pooley v. Nat'l Hole-in-One Ass'n, 89 F.Supp.2d 1108, 1113–14 (D.Ariz.2000); dePasse, 82 F.Supp.2d at 731.

b. Application of a First Amendment Defense

In *Rogers*, the Second Circuit held that movie titles are protected from right of publicity actions unless the title is "wholly unrelated" to the content of the work or was "simply a disguised commercial advertisement for the sale of goods or services." 875 F.2d at 1004. This test is supported in the context of other expressive works by comment c of § 47 of the Restatement (Third) of Unfair Competition. It states that "[u]se of another's identity in a novel, play, or motion picture is ... not ordinarily an infringement [of the right of publicity, unless] the name or likeness is used solely to attract attention to a work that is not related to the identified person." The *Rogers* formulation is also supported by the decision in dePasse. In dePasse, the court cited Seale, 949 F.Supp. at 337, for the proposition that the relationship between a plaintiff's identity and the content of the work is an element of a defense to a right of publicity action. See dePasse, 82 F.Supp.2d at 731. *Seale*, in turn, relied upon *Rogers*. See 949 F.Supp. at 337; see also Rogers, 875 F.2d at 1004–05. We thus apply *Rogers* to the instant case.

For the same reasons we have stated earlier and need not repeat, we believe that Parks' right of publicity claim presents a genuine issue of material fact regarding the question of whether the title to the song is or is not "wholly unrelated" to the content of the song. A reasonable finder of fact, in our opinion, upon consideration of all the evidence, could find the title to be a "disguised commercial advertisement" or adopted "solely to attract attention" to the work. See Rogers, 875 F.2d at 1004–05.

* * *

III.   CONCLUSION

We are not called upon in this case to judge the quality of Defendants' song, and whether we personally regard it as repulsive trash or a work of genius is immaterial to a determination of the legal issues presented to us. Justice Holmes, 100 years ago, correctly observed that, "It would be a dangerous undertaking for persons trained only to the law to constitute themselves final judges of the worth of pictorial illustrations, outside of the narrowest and most obvious limits." George Bleistein v. Donaldson Lithographing Co., 188 U.S. 239, 251, 23 S.Ct. 298, 47 L.Ed. 460 (1903). The same is no less true today and applies with equal force to musical compositions. The point, however, is that while we, as judges, do not presume to determine the artistic quality of the song in question, we have the responsibility, as judges, to apply a legal standard of "artistic relevance" in resolving the rights of Rosa Parks concerning the use of her name and the First Amendment rights of the Defendants in the creation and marketing of a musical composition. Application of that standard involves a recognition that Rosa Parks has no right to control her image by censoring disagreeable portrayals. It also involves a recognition that the First Amendment cannot permit anyone who cries "artist" to have carte blanche when it comes to naming and advertising his works.

In this case, for the reasons set forth above, the fact that Defendants cry "artist" and "symbol" as reasons for appropriating Rosa Parks' name for a song title does not absolve them from potential liability for, in the words of Shakespeare, filching Rosa Parks' good name.[5] The question of that liability, however, should be determined by the trier of fact after a full evidentiary hearing and not as a matter of law on a motion for summary judgment.

* * *

ETW CORP. v. JIREH PUBLISHING, INC.

United States Court of Appeals, Sixth Circuit, 2003.
332 F.3d 915.

GRAHAM, DISTRICT JUDGE.

Plaintiff–Appellant ETW Corporation ("ETW") is the licensing agent of Eldrick "Tiger" Woods ("Woods"), one of the world's most

---

5. Who steals my purse steals trash; 'tis something, nothing;

   'Twas mine, 'tis his, and has been slave to thousands;

   But he that filches from me my good name

Robs me of that which not enriches him

And makes me poor indeed.

   William Shakespeare, Othello, act 3, sc. 3.

famous professional golfers. Woods, chairman of the board of ETW, has assigned to it the exclusive right to exploit his name, image, likeness, and signature, and all other publicity rights. ETW owns a United States trademark registration for the mark "TIGER WOODS" (Registration No. 2,194,381) for use in connection with "art prints, calendars, mounted photographs, notebooks, pencils, pens, posters, trading cards, and unmounted photographs."

Defendant–Appellee Jireh Publishing, Inc. ("Jireh") of Tuscaloosa, Alabama, is the publisher of artwork created by Rick Rush ("Rush"). Rush, who refers to himself as "America's sports artist," has created paintings of famous figures in sports and famous sports events. A few examples include Michael Jordan, Mark McGuire, Coach Paul "Bear" Bryant, the Pebble Beach Golf Tournament, and the America's Cup Yacht Race. Jireh has produced and successfully marketed limited edition art prints made from Rush's paintings.

In 1998, Rush created a painting entitled The Masters of Augusta, which commemorates Woods's victory at the Masters Tournament in Augusta, Georgia, in 1997. At that event, Woods became the youngest player ever to win the Masters Tournament, while setting a 72–hole record for the tournament and a record 12–stroke margin of victory. In the foreground of Rush's painting are three views of Woods in different poses. In the center, he is completing the swing of a golf club, and on each side he is crouching, lining up and/or observing the progress of a putt. To the left of Woods is his caddy, Mike "Fluff" Cowan, and to his right is his final round partner's caddy. Behind these figures is the Augusta National Clubhouse. In a blue background behind the clubhouse are likenesses of famous golfers of the past looking down on Woods. These include Arnold Palmer, Sam Snead, Ben Hogan, Walter Hagen, Bobby Jones, and Jack Nicklaus. Behind them is the Masters leader board.

The limited edition prints distributed by Jireh consist of an image of Rush's painting which includes Rush's signature at the bottom right hand corner. Beneath the image of the painting, in block letters, is its title, "The Masters Of Augusta." Beneath the title, in block letters of equal height, is the artist's name, "Rick Rush," and beneath the artist's name, in smaller upper and lower case letters, is the legend "Painting America Through Sports."

As sold by Jireh, the limited edition prints are enclosed in a white envelope, accompanied with literature which includes a large photograph of Rush, a description of his art, and a narrative description of the subject painting. On the front of the envelope, Rush's name appears in block letters inside a rectangle, which includes the legend "Painting America Through Sports." Along the bottom is a large reproduction of Rush's signature two inches high and ten inches long. On the back of the envelope, under the flap, are the words "Masters of Augusta" in letters that are three-eights of an inch high, and "Tiger Woods" in letters that are one-fourth of an inch high. Woods's name also appears in the narrative description of the painting where he is mentioned twice in twenty-eight lines of text. The text also includes references to the six other famous golfers depicted in the background of the painting as well as the two caddies. Jireh published and marketed two hundred and fifty 22″ x 30″ serigraphs and five thousand 9″ x 11″ lithographs of The Masters of Augusta at an issuing price of $700 for the serigraphs and $100 for the lithographs.

* * *

ETW filed suit against Jireh on June 26, 1998, in the United States District Court for the Northern District of Ohio, alleging trademark infringement in violation of the Lanham Act, 15 U.S.C. § 1114; dilution of the mark under the Lanham Act, 15 U.S.C. § 1125(c); unfair competition and false advertising under the Lanham Act, 15 U.S.C. § 1125(a); unfair competition and deceptive trade practices under Ohio Revised Code § 4165.01; unfair competition and trademark infringement under Ohio common law; and violation of Woods's right of publicity under Ohio common law. Jireh counterclaimed, seeking a declaratory judgment that Rush's art prints are protected by the First Amendment and do not violate the Lanham Act. Both parties moved for summary judgment.

The district court granted Jireh's motion for summary judgment and dismissed the case. See ETW Corp. v. Jireh Pub., Inc., 99 F.Supp.2d 829 (N.D.Ohio 2000). ETW timely perfected an appeal to this court.

* * *

II. TRADEMARK CLAIMS BASED ON THE UNAUTHORIZED USE OF THE REGISTERED TRADEMARK "TIGER WOODS"

* * *

The district court properly granted summary judgment on ETW's claim for violation of its registered mark, "Tiger Woods," on the grounds that the claim was barred by the fair use defense as a matter of law.

III. TRADEMARK CLAIMS UNDER 15 U.S.C. § 1125(A) BASED ON THE UNAUTHORIZED USE OF THE LIKENESS OF TIGER WOODS

* * * Here, ETW claims protection under the Lanham Act for any and all images of Tiger Woods. This is an untenable claim. ETW asks us, in effect, to constitute Woods himself as a walking, talking trademark. Images and likenesses of Woods are not protectable as a trademark because they do not perform the trademark function of designation. * * *

The district court properly granted summary judgment on ETW's claim of trademark rights in all images and likenesses of Tiger Woods.

* * *

D. Right of Publicity Claim

ETW claims that Jireh's publication and marketing of prints of Rush's painting violates Woods's right of publicity. The right of publicity is an intellectual property right of recent origin which has been defined as the inherent right of every human being to control the commercial use of his or her identity. See MCCARTHY ON PUBLICITY AND PRIVACY, § 1:3. The right of publicity is a creature of state law and its violation gives rise to a cause of action for the commercial tort of unfair competition. Id.

The right of publicity is, somewhat paradoxically, an outgrowth of the right of privacy. See Mccarthy On Publicity And Privacy, § 1:4. A cause of action for violation of the right was first recognized in Haelan Laboratories, Inc. v. Topps Chewing Gum, Inc., 202 F.2d 866 (2nd Cir.1953), where the Second Circuit held that New York's common law protected a baseball player's right in the publicity value of his photograph, and in the process coined the phrase "right of publicity" as the name of this right.

The Ohio Supreme Court recognized the right of publicity in 1976 in Zacchini v. Scripps–Howard Broadcasting Co., 47 Ohio St.2d 224, 351 N.E.2d 454 (1976). In *Zacchini*, which involved the videotaping and subsequent rebroadcast on a television news program of plaintiff's human cannonball act, the Ohio Supreme Court held that Zacchini's right of publicity was trumped by the First Amendment. On appeal, the Supreme Court of the United States reversed, holding that the First Amendment did not insulate defendant from liability for violating Zacchini's state law right of publicity where defendant published the plaintiff's entire act. See Zacchini v. Scripps–Howard Broadcasting Co., 433 U.S. 562, 97 S.Ct. 2849, 53 L.Ed.2d 965 (1977). *Zacchini* is the only United States Supreme Court decision on the right of publicity.

* * *

In § 47, Comment c, the authors of the Restatement (Third) Of Unfair Competition note, "The right of publicity as recognized by statute and common law is fundamentally constrained by the public and constitutional interest in freedom of expression." In the same comment, the authors state that "[t]he use of a person's identity primarily for the purpose of communicating information or expressing ideas is not generally actionable as a violation of the person's right of publicity." Various examples are given, including the use of the person's name or likeness in news reporting in newspapers and magazines. The RESTATEMENT recognizes that this limitation on the right is not confined to news reporting but extends to use in "entertainment and other creative works, including both fiction and non-fiction." Id. The authors list examples of protected uses of a celebrity's identity, likeness or image, including unauthorized print or broadcast biographies and novels, plays or motion pictures. Id. According to the RESTATEMENT, such uses are not protected, however, if the name or likeness is used solely to attract attention to a work that is not related to the identified person, and the privilege may be lost if the work contains substantial falsifications. Id.

We believe the courts of Ohio would follow the principles of the RESTATEMENT in defining the limits of the right of publicity. The Ohio Supreme Court's decision in *Zacchini* suggests that Ohio is inclined to give substantial weight to the public interest in freedom of expression when balancing it against the personal and proprietary interests recognized by the right of publicity. This suggestion is reenforced by the decision in Vinci.

This court first encountered the right of publicity in Memphis Development Foundation v. Factors Etc., Inc., 616 F.2d 956 (6th Cir. 1980), where the issue presented was whether the heirs of Elvis Presley retained his right of publicity after his death. We concluded that they did not. We held that under Tennessee law, "[t]he famous have an exclusive legal right during life to control and profit from the commercial use of their name and personality." Id. at 957. Noting that the Tennessee courts had not addressed the issue, we decided the case "in the light of practical and policy considerations, the treatment of other similar rights in our legal system, the relative weight of the conflicting interests of the parties, and certain moral presuppositions concerning death, privacy, inheritability and economic opportunity." Id. at 958.

In Carson v. Here's Johnny Portable Toilets, Inc., 698 F.2d 831 (6th Cir.1983), a majority of this court, with Judge Kennedy dissenting, held that television comedian and talk show host Johnny Carson's right of publicity was invaded when defendant used the phrase with which Carson was commonly introduced on his television program. In *Carson*, we held that "a celebrity has a protected pecuniary interest in the commercial exploitation of his identity." Id. at 835.

In Landham, 227 F.3d at 625–26, this court held that Landham, a fringe actor who played supporting roles in several motion pictures, had failed to show a violation of his right of publicity when defendant marketed an action figure of a character he had played but which did not bear a personal resemblance to him. This court found that Landham had failed to show that his persona had significant value or that the toy invoked his persona as distinct from that of the fictional character he played.

There is an inherent tension between the right of publicity and the right of freedom of expression under the First Amendment. This tension becomes particularly acute when the person seeking to enforce the right is a famous actor, athlete, politician, or otherwise famous person whose exploits, activities, accomplishments, and personal life are subject to constant scrutiny and comment in the public media. In Memphis Development Foundation, 616 F.2d at 959, this court discussed the problems of judicial line drawing that would arise if it should recognize the inheritability of publicity rights, including the question "[a]t what point does the right collide with the right of free expression guaranteed by the First Amendment?" In *Carson*, after noting that the First Amendment protects commercial speech, Judge Kennedy opined in her dissent that "public policy requires that the public's interest in free enterprise and free expression take precedence over any interest Johnny Carson may have in a phrase associated with his person." Carson, 698 F.2d at 841. In *Landham*, we noted "the careful balance that courts have gradually constructed between the right of publicity and the First Amendment [.]" 227 F.3d at 626.

In a series of recent cases, other circuits have been called upon to establish the boundaries between the right of publicity and the First Amendment. In *Rogers*, the Second Circuit affirmed the district court's grant of summary judgment on Rogers' right of publicity claim, noting that commentators have "advocated limits on the right of publicity to accommodate First Amendment concerns." 875 F.2d at 1004 n. 11. That court also cited three cases in which state courts refused to extend the right of publicity to bar the use of a celebrity's name in the title and text of a fictional or semi-fictional book or movie. Id. at 1004.

In *White*, television celebrity Vanna White, brought suit against Samsung Electronics, alleging that its television advertisement which featured a female-shaped robot wearing a long gown, blonde wig, large jewelry, and turning letters in what appeared to be the "Wheel of Fortune" game show set, violated her California common law right of publicity and her rights under the Lanham Act. The Ninth Circuit, with Judge Alarcon dissenting in part, reversed the grant of summary judgment to defendant, holding that White had produced sufficient evidence that defendant's advertisement appropriated her identity in violation of her right of publicity, and that the issue of confusion about White's endorsement of defendant's product created a jury issue which precluded summary judgment on her Lanham Act claim. In so holding, the court rejected the defendant's parody defense which posited that the advertisement was a parody of White's television act and was protected speech.

A suggestion for rehearing en banc failed. Three judges dissented from the order rejecting the suggestion for a rehearing en banc. See White v. Samsung Electronics America, Inc., 989 F.2d 1512 (9th Cir. 1993). Judge Kozinski, writing the dissenting opinion, observed, "Something very dangerous is going on here.... Overprotecting intellectual property is as harmful as underprotecting it. Creativity is impossible without a rich public domain." 989 F.2d at 1513. Later, he commented:

> Intellectual property rights aren't free: They're imposed at the expense of future creators and of the public at large.... This is why intellectual property law is full of careful balances between what's set aside for the owner and what's left in the public domain for the rest of us[.]

Id. at 1516. In *Landham*, this court declined to follow the majority in *White* and, instead, cited Judge Kozinski's dissent with approval. See 227 F.3d at 626.

In Cardtoons, L.C. v. Major League Baseball Players Assoc., 95 F.3d 959 (10th Cir.1996), the Tenth Circuit held that the plaintiff's First

Amendment right to free expression outweighed the defendant's proprietary right of publicity. The plaintiff in *Cardtoons* contracted with a political cartoonist, a sports artist, and a sports author and journalist to design a set of trading cards which featured readily identifiable caricatures of major league baseball players with a humorous commentary about their careers on the back. The cards ridiculed the players using a variety of themes. The cards used similar names, recognizable caricatures, distinctive team colors and commentaries about individual players which left no doubt about their identity. The Tenth Circuit held that the defendant's use of the player's likenesses on its trading cards would violate their rights of publicity under an Oklahoma statute. Addressing the defendant's First Amendment claim, the court held:

> Cardtoons' parody trading cards receive full protection under the First Amendment. The cards provide social commentary on public figures, major league baseball players, who are involved in a significant commercial enterprise, major league baseball. While not core political speech ... this type of commentary on an important social institution constitutes protected expression.

Cardtoons, 95 F.3d at 969. The Tenth Circuit rejected the reasoning of the panel majority in *White*, and expressed its agreement with the dissenting opinions of Judges Alarcon and Kozinski. See 95 F.3d at 970 ("We disagree with the result in [*White*] for reasons discussed in the two dissents that it engendered."). In striking the balance between the players' property rights and the defendant's First Amendment rights, the court in *Cardtoons* commented on the pervasive presence of celebrities in the media, sports and entertainment. The court noted that celebrities are an important part of our public vocabulary and have come to symbolize certain ideas and values:

> As one commentator explained, celebrities are "common points of reference for millions of individuals who may never interact with one another, but who share, by virtue of their participation in a mediated culture, a common experience and a collective memory." John B. Thompson, IDEOLOGY AND MODERN CULTURE: CRITICAL SOCIAL THEORY IN THE ERA OF MASS COMMUNICATION 163 (1990). Through their pervasive presence in the media, sports and entertainment celebrities come to symbolize certain ideas and values.... Celebrities, then, are an important element of the shared communicative resources of our cultural domain.

Cardtoons, 95 F.3d at 972.

* * *

In Comedy III Productions, Inc. v. Gary Saderup, Inc., 25 Cal.4th 387, 106 Cal.Rptr.2d 126, 21 P.3d 797 (2001), the California Supreme Court adopted a transformative use test in determining whether the artistic use of a celebrity's image is protected by the First Amendment. Saderup, an artist with over twenty-five years experience in making charcoal drawings of celebrities, created a drawing of the famous comedy team, The Three Stooges. The drawings were used to create lithographic and silk screen masters, which were then used to produce lithographic prints and silk screen images on T-shirts. Comedy III, the owner of all rights to the former comedy act, brought suit against Saderup under a California statute, which grants the right of publicity to successors in interest of deceased celebrities.

The California Supreme Court found that Saderup's portraits were entitled to First Amendment protection because they were "expressive works and not an advertisement or endorsement of a product." Id. at 396, 106 Cal.Rptr.2d 126, 21 P.3d at 802. In discussing the tension between the right of publicity and the First Amendment, the court observed:

> [B]ecause celebrities take on personal meanings to many individuals in the society, the creative appropriation of celebrity images can be an important avenue of individual expression. As one commentator has stated: "Entertainment and sports celebrities are the leading players in our Public Drama. We tell tales, both tall and cautionary, about them. We monitor their comings and goings, their missteps and heartbreaks. We copy their mannerisms, their styles, their modes of conversation and of consumption. Whether or not celebrities are 'the chief agents of moral change in the United States,' they certainly are widely used—far more than are our institutionally anchored elites—to symbolize individual aspirations, group identities and cultural values. Their images are thus important expressive and communicative resources: the peculiar, yet familiar idiom in which we conduct a fair portion of our cultural business and everyday conversation." (Madow, Private Ownership of Public Image: Popular Culture and Publicity Rights (1993)) 81 Cal. L.Rev. 125, 128 (Madow, italics and fns. omitted).

Id. at 397, 106 Cal.Rptr.2d 126, 21 P.3d at 803.

The court rejected the proposition that Saderup's lithographs and T-shirts lost their First Amendment protection because they were not original single works of art, but were instead part of a commercial enterprise designed to generate profit solely from the sale of multiple reproductions of likenesses of The Three Stooges:

> [T]his position has no basis in logic or authority. No one would claim that a published book, because it is one of many copies, receives less First Amendment protection than the original manuscript.... [A] reproduction of a celebrity image that, as explained above, contains significant creative elements is entitled to as much First Amendment protection as an original work of art.

Id. at 408, 106 Cal.Rptr.2d 126, 21 P.3d at 810.

Borrowing part of the fair use defense from copyright law, the California court proposed the following test for distinguishing between protected and unprotected expression when the right of publicity conflicts with the First Amendment:

> When artistic expression takes the form of a literal depiction or imitation of a celebrity for commercial gain, directly trespassing on the right of publicity without adding significant expression beyond that trespass, the state law interest in protecting the fruits of artistic labor outweighs the expressive interests of the imitative artist.
>
> On the other hand, when a work contains significant transformative elements, it is not only especially worthy of First Amendment protection, but it is also less likely to interfere with the economic interest protected by the right of publicity. . . .
>
> Accordingly, First Amendment protection of such works outweighs whatever interest the state may have in enforcing the right of publicity.

Id. at 405, 106 Cal.Rptr.2d 126, 21 P.3d at 808 (footnote and citations omitted). Later in its opinion, the California court restated the test as follows:

> Another way of stating the inquiry is whether the celebrity likeness is one of the "raw materials" from which an original work is synthesized, or whether the depiction or imitation of the celebrity is the very sum and substance of the work in question.

Id. at 406, 106 Cal.Rptr.2d 126, 21 P.3d at 809.

Finally, citing the art of Andy Warhol, the court noted that even literal reproductions of celebrity portraits may be protected by the First Amendment.

> Through distortion and the careful manipulation of context, Warhol was able to convey a message that went beyond the commercial exploitation of celebrity images and became a form of ironic social comment on the dehumanization of celebrity itself. . . . Although the distinction between protected and unprotected expression will sometimes be subtle, it is no more so than other distinctions triers of fact are called on to make in First Amendment jurisprudence.

Id. at 408–409, 106 Cal.Rptr.2d 126, 21 P.3d at 811 (citations and footnote omitted).

We conclude that in deciding whether the sale of Rush's prints violate Woods's right of publicity, we will look to the Ohio case law and the RESTATEMENT (THIRD) OF UNFAIR COMPETITION. In deciding where the line should be drawn between Woods's intellectual property rights and the First Amendment, we find ourselves in agreement with the dissenting judges in *White*, the Tenth Circuit's decision in *Cardtoons*, and the Ninth Circuit's decision in *Hoffman*, and we will follow them in determining whether Rush's work is protected by the First Amendment. Finally, we believe that the transformative elements test adopted by the Supreme Court of California in *Comedy III Productions*, will assist us in determining where the proper balance lies between the First Amendment and Woods's intellectual property rights. We turn now to a further examination of Rush's work and its subject.

E. *Application of the Law to the Evidence in this Case*

The evidence in the record reveals that Rush's work consists of much more than a mere literal likeness of Woods. It is a panorama of Woods's victory at the 1997 Masters Tournament, with all of the trappings of that tournament in full view, including the Augusta club-house, the leader board, images of Woods's caddy, and his final round partner's caddy. These elements in themselves are sufficient to bring Rush's work within the protection of the First Amendment. The Masters Tournament is probably the world's most famous golf tournament and Woods's victory in the 1997 tournament was a historic event in the world of sports. A piece of art that portrays a historic sporting event communicates and celebrates the value our culture attaches to such events. It would be ironic indeed if the presence of the image of the victorious athlete would deny the work First Amendment protection. Furthermore, Rush's work includes not only images of Woods and the two caddies, but also carefully crafted likenesses of six past winners of the Masters Tournament: Arnold Palmer, Sam Snead, Ben Hogan, Walter Hagen, Bobby Jones, and Jack Nicklaus, a veritable pantheon of golf's greats. Rush's work conveys the message that Woods himself will someday join that revered group.

Turning first to ETW's Lanham Act false endorsement claim, we agree with the courts that hold that the Lanham Act should be applied to artistic works only where the public interest in avoiding confusion outweighs the public interest in free expression. The *Rogers* test is helpful in striking that balance in the instant case. We find that the presence of Woods's image in Rush's painting The Masters Of Augusta does have artistic relevance to the underlying work and that it does not explicitly mislead as to the source of the work. We believe that the principles followed in *Cardtoons*, *Hoffman* and *Comedy III* are also relevant in determining whether the Lanham Act applies to Rush's work, and we find that it does not.

We find, like the court in *Rogers*, that plaintiff's survey evidence, even if its validity is assumed, indicates at most that some members of the public would draw the incorrect inference that Woods had some connection with Rush's print. The risk of misunderstanding, not engendered by any explicit indication on the face of the print, is so outweighed by the interest in artistic expression as to preclude application of the Act. We disagree with the dissent's suggestion that a jury must decide where the balance should be struck and where the boundaries should be drawn between the rights conferred by the Lanham Act and the protections of the First Amendment.

In regard to the Ohio law right of publicity claim, we conclude that Ohio would construe its right of publicity as suggested in the restatement (Third) Of Unfair Competition, Chapter 4, Section 47, Comment d., which articulates a rule analogous to the rule of fair use in copyright law. Under this rule, the substantiality and market effect of the use of the celebrity's image is analyzed in light of the informational and creative content of the defendant's use. Applying this rule, we conclude that Rush's work has substantial informational and creative content which outweighs any adverse effect on ETW's market and that Rush's work does not violate Woods's right of publicity.

We further find that Rush's work is expression which is entitled to the full protection of the First Amendment and not the more limited protection afforded to commercial speech. When we balance the magnitude of the speech restriction against the interest in protecting Woods's intellectual property right, we encounter precisely the same considerations weighed by the Tenth Circuit in *Cardtoons*. These include consideration of the fact that through their pervasive presence in the media, sports and entertainment celebrities have come to symbolize certain ideas and values in our society and have become a valuable means of expression in our culture. As the Tenth Circuit observed "[c]elebrities ... are an important element of the shared communicative resources of our cultural domain." Cardtoons, 95 F.3d at 972.

In balancing these interests against Woods's right of publicity, we note that Woods, like most sports and entertainment celebrities with commercially valuable identities, engages in an activity, professional golf, that in itself generates a significant amount of income which is unrelated to his right of publicity. Even in the absence of his right of publicity, he would still be able to reap substantial financial rewards from authorized appearances and endorsements. It is not at all clear that the appearance of Woods's likeness in artwork prints which display one of his major achievements will reduce the commercial value of his likeness.

While the right of publicity allows celebrities like Woods to enjoy the fruits of their labors, here Rush has added a significant creative component of his own to Woods's identity. Permitting Woods's right of publicity to trump Rush's right of freedom of expression would extinguish Rush's right to profit from his creative enterprise.

After balancing the societal and personal interests embodied in the First Amendment against Woods's property rights, we conclude that the effect of limiting Woods's right of publicity in this case is negligible and significantly outweighed by society's interest in freedom of artistic expression.

Finally, applying the transformative effects test adopted by the Supreme Court of California in *Comedy III*, we find that Rush's work does contain significant transformative elements which make it especially worthy of First Amendment protection and also less likely to interfere with the economic interest protected by Woods' right of publicity. Unlike the unadorned, nearly photographic reproduction of the faces of The Three Stooges in *Comedy III*, Rush's work does not capitalize solely on a literal depiction of Woods. Rather, Rush's work consists of a collage of images in addition to Woods's image which are combined to describe, in artistic form, a historic event in sports history and to convey a message about the significance of Woods's achievement in that event. Because Rush's work has substantial transformative elements, it is entitled to the full protection of the First Amendment. In this case, we find that Woods's right of publicity must yield to the First Amendment.

V. CONCLUSION

In accordance with the foregoing, the judgment of the District Court granting summary judgment to Jireh Publishing is affirmed.

CLAY, CIRCUIT JUDGE, dissenting.

Genuine issues of material fact remain for trial as to the claims brought by Plaintiff, ETW Corporation, under the Lanham Act, 15 U.S.C. § 1114 and § 1125, and Ohio common law for trademark infringement, unfair competition, and dilution; therefore, I would reverse the district court's judgment and remand the case for trial as to these claims. No genuine issue of material fact remains for trial that Defendant, Jireh Publishing, violated Plaintiff's right of publicity under Ohio common law; therefore, I would reverse the district court's judgment on Plaintiff's right of publicity claim and remand with instructions that the district court enter summary judgment in favor of Plaintiff. For these reasons, I respectfully dissent from the majority opinion, and shall address Plaintiff's claims in an order somewhat different than that utilized by the majority.

I. TRADEMARK CLAIMS BASED ON DEFENDANT'S UNAUTHORIZED USE OF THE UNREGISTERED MARK—§ 43(A) OF THE LANHAM ACT, 15 U.S.C. § 1125(A)

At the outset, it should be noted that the majority's characterization of this claim as the "Unauthorized Use of the Likeness of Tiger Woods" is misleading. Such a characterization bolsters the majority's unfounded position that Plaintiff is seeking protection under the Lanham Act for any and all images of Tiger Woods, but, indeed, such is not the case. Plaintiff's amended complaint squarely sets forth Defendant's conduct to which Plaintiff takes issue—Defendant's portrayal of Woods in his famous golf swing at the Masters Tournament in Augusta as set forth in Rush's print. Plaintiff provided evidence that there was a "high incidence" of consumer confusion as to Woods being the origin or sponsor of The Masters of Augusta print by Rick Rush, thus demonstrating, at the very a least, that a question of fact remains for trial as to whether Woods used this image as a trademark and whether Defendant's print infringed upon the mark. See Rock & Roll Hall of Fame & Museum, Inc. v. Gentile Prods., 134 F.3d 749, 753 (6th Cir.1998) (hereinafter "Rock & Roll Hall of Fame" or "Rock & Roll").

* * *

V. OHIO COMMON LAW RIGHT OF PUBLICITY CLAIM

The majority makes a somewhat disjointed holding regarding Plaintiff's right of publicity claim. It first concludes that, under the rule of the Restatement, "Rush's work has substantial informational and creative content which outweighs any adverse effect on ETW's [Plaintiff's] mar-

ket and the Rush's work does not violate Woods's right of publicity."
Then, the majority appears to engage in a separate analysis or balancing
of the interests under the law of various circuits when it takes into
account the degree of First Amendment protection that should be
afforded Rush's print against Woods' "intellectual property right" in
order to conclude that "[p]ermitting Woods' right of publicity to trump
Rush's right of freedom of expression would extinguish Rush's right to
profit from his creative enterprise." Finally, engaging in yet a separate
analysis under the "transformative effects test" pronounced by the
California Supreme Court, the majority concludes that "[b]ecause Rush's
work has substantial transformative elements, it is entitled to the full
protection of the First Amendment. In this case, we find that Woods's
right of publicity must yield to the First Amendment." Thus, it appears
that the majority engages in three separate analyses, and arrives at
three separate holdings, although all of which reach the same result.

The majority's analysis not only fails in its disjointed approach but
in its outcome as well. The approach best suited for addressing Plaintiff's right of publicity claim in this case is that taken by the California
Supreme Court in Comedy III Productions v. Gary Saderup, Inc., 25
Cal.4th 387, 106 Cal.Rptr.2d 126, 21 P.3d 797 (2001). This is so because
the Court in *Comedy III* took account of a celebrity's right of publicity
and the principles of the right in general, as balanced against competing
First Amendment concerns, in arriving at a test for purposes of adjudicating a case that is nearly on all fours with the matter at hand. This
approach takes into account all of the competing interests while allowing
for a single well-determined outcome that provides guidance and adds to
the jurisprudence as a whole. * * *

B. Woods' Right of Publicity Claim in this Case

Zacchini v. Scripps–Howard Broadcasting Company is the sole case
from the Supreme Court to directly address the right of publicity, and
the case came to the Supreme Court by way of certiorari from the Ohio
Supreme Court under Ohio common law. See Zacchini, 47 Ohio St.2d
224, 351 N.E.2d 454 (1976), rev'd on other grounds, 433 U.S. 562, 572,
97 S.Ct. 2849, 53 L.Ed.2d 965 (1977). The plaintiff, Zacchini, was the
performer of a live human cannonball act who subsequently sued a
television station that had videotaped and broadcast his entire performance without his consent. See 433 U.S. at 563–64, 97 S.Ct. 2849. The
Supreme Court found in favor of Zacchini, holding that the First
Amendment did not protect the television station against a right of
publicity claim under Ohio common law. Id. at 565–66, 97 S.Ct. 2849.
The Court explained that the enforcement of the right of publicity claim
was not at odds with the First Amendment inasmuch as "the rationale
for [protecting the right of publicity] is the straightforward one of
preventing unjust enrichment by the theft of good will. No social purpose
is served by having the defendant get free some aspect of the plaintiff
that would have market value and for which he would normally pay." Id.
at 576, 97 S.Ct. 2849.

Indeed, since *Zacchini*, "[t]he right of publicity has often been invoked in the context of commercial speech when the appropriation of a celebrity likeness creates a false and misleading impression that the celebrity is endorsing a product." See Comedy III Prods., Inc. v. Saderup, Inc., 25 Cal.4th 387, 106 Cal.Rptr.2d 126, 21 P.3d 797, 802 (2001) (citing Waits v. Frito–Lay, Inc. 978 F.2d 1093 (9th Cir.1992); Midler v. Ford Motor Co., 849 F.2d 460 (9th Cir.1988)). "Because the First Amendment does not protect false and misleading commercial speech, and because even non-misleading commercial speech is generally subject to somewhat lesser First Amendment protection, see Central Hudson Gas & Elec. Corp. v. Pub. Serv. Com'n, 447 U.S. 557, 563–64 & 566, 100 S.Ct. 2343, 65 L.Ed.2d 341 (1980), the right of publicity often trumps the right of advertisers to make use of celebrity figures." Comedy III, 106 Cal. Rptr.2d 126, 21 P.3d at 802. In this case, to the extent that the district court was correct in characterizing Defendant's prints as expressive works and not as commercial products, even though Defendant was selling the prints for financial gain, the issue becomes what degree of First Amendment protection should be afforded to Defendant's expressive work.

In answering this question, one must look beyond *Zacchini* inasmuch as *Zacchini* has been criticized as being very "narrowly drawn" in that it involved the wholesale reproduction of a live "entire act," which is quite distinguishable from the unauthorized use of a person's identity, particularly when the unauthorized use is in the form of an expressive work, as in the matter at hand. See MCCARTHY, supra at § 8:27 (recognizing that "while the *Zacchini* majority and dissenting opinions have been picked apart word by word by the commentators, no clear message emerges and no general rule is discernible by which to predict the result of conflicts between the right of publicity and the First Amendment.") With that in mind, guidance is provided by the California Supreme Court because it has addressed the specific issue in a case nearly on all fours with that presented here; namely, Comedy III Productions v. Gary Saderup, Inc., 25 Cal.4th 387, 106 Cal.Rptr.2d 126, 21 P.3d 797 (2001). See MCCARTHY, supra at § 8:27 (stating that when deciding *Comedy III*, the California Supreme Court found that when the challenged speech is not in the category of "commercial speech," what *Zacchini* teaches us is that valid interests behind the right of publicity must be balanced against First Amendment policies, and that an accommodation must be reached).

In *Comedy III*, the plaintiff, Comedy III Productions, which is the registered owner of all rights to the former comedy act known as The Three Stooges, filed suit against the defendants, Gary Saderup and Gary Saderup, Inc., seeking damages and injunctive relief for violation of, among other things, California's right of publicity statute in connection with the defendants' sale of T-shirts and lithographs bearing the image of the Three Stooges produced from a charcoal drawing done by Saderup. See 106 Cal.Rptr.2d 126, 21 P.3d at 800. The defendants sold the T-shirts and lithographs without the plaintiff's consent, profiting $75,000 from the sale of these items. Id. at 800–01. The trial court found for the plaintiff, and entered judgment in the amount of $75,000 as well as $150,000 in attorney's fees plus costs. Id. at 801. The court also issued a permanent injunction restraining Saderup from violating the statute by use of any likeness of The Three Stooges in lithographs, T-shirts, "or any other medium by which Saderup's artwork may be sold or marketed." Id. In addition, the trial court enjoined Saderap in several other respects regarding his marketing products in connection with The Three Stooges, but allowed Saderup's original charcoal drawing from which the reproductions were made to be exempt from the injunction. Id. at 801.

The defendants appealed, and the court of appeals modified the judgment by striking the injunction on the basis that the plaintiff had not shown a likelihood of continued violation of the statute, and that the wording of the statute was overbroad. Id. However, the court of appeals affirmed in all other respects, thereby rejecting the defendants' arguments that 1) his conduct did not violate the terms of the statute; and 2) in any event, his conduct was protected by the constitutional guaranty of freedom of speech under the First Amendment. Id. The defendants appealed to the California Supreme Court, which granted leave to address the two arguments raised by the defendants. Id. For purposes of the matter at hand, we focus on the Supreme Court of California's analysis of the First Amendment argument.

The court began by recognizing that the defendants' First Amendment claim presented a difficult issue, in that the works in question were expressive works and not commercial advertisements. See Comedy III, 106 Cal.Rptr.2d 126, 21 P.3d at 802. The court noted that "[a]lthough [the defendants'] work was done for financial gain, the First Amendment is not limited to those who publish without charge.... An expressive activity does not lose its constitutional protection because it is undertaken for profit." See id. (alterations, internal quotation marks, and citation omitted). The court then recognized the high degree of First Amendment protection for noncommercial speech about celebrities, but at the same time noted that not all expression that trenches on the right of publicity receives such protection. See id. Specifically, the court opined:

> The right of publicity, like copyright, protects a form of intellectual property that society deems to have some social utility. Often considerable money, time and energy are needed to develop one's prominence in a particular field. Years of labor may be required before one's skill, reputation, notoriety or virtues are sufficiently developed to permit an economic return through some medium of commercial promotion. For some, the investment may eventually create considerable commercial value in one's identity.

Id. at 804–05 (internal quotation marks and citation omitted).

The court then found that the case before it exemplified that kind of creative labor. Id. According to the California Supreme Court, the three men who came to enjoy celebrity status began their career in vaudeville and it was a "long and arduous" process until the three finally enjoyed the heights of slapstick comic celebrities known as The Three Stooges. See 106 Cal.Rptr.2d 126, 21 P.3d at 805. As the court stated, "[t]hrough their talent and labor, they joined the relatively small group of actors who constructed identifiable, recurrent comic personalities that they brought to the many parts they were scripted to play." Id. As a result, the issue became whether the defendants' First Amendment rights trumped the plaintiff's right of publicity.

Relying on *Zacchini* and several cases from lower courts recognizing a celebrity's right of publicity, the court found that depictions of celebrities which amounted to little more than the appropriation of the celebrity's economic value, were not protected by the First Amendment. See id. at 805. As that premise related to the expressive works at issue, the court opined:

> It is admittedly not a simple matter to develop a test that will unerringly distinguish between forms of artistic expression protected by the First Amendment and those that must give way to the right of publicity. Certainly, any such test must incorporate the principle that the right of publicity cannot, consistent with the First Amendment, be a right to control the celebrity's image by censoring disagreeable portrayals. Once the celebrity thrusts himself or herself forward into the limelight, the First Amendment dictates that the right to comment on, parody, lampoon, and make other expressive uses of the celebrity image must be given broad scope. The necessary implication of this observation is that the right of publicity is essentially an economic right. What the right of publicity holder possesses is not a right of censorship, but a right to prevent others from misappropriating the economic value generated by the celebrity's fame through the merchandising of the "name, voice, signature, photograph, or likeness" of the celebrity.

Comedy III, 21 P.3d at 807–08. Beyond this precept, the court looked to the first factor of copyright's fair use doctrine—"the purpose and character of the use"—for guidance. Id. at 808 (quoting 17 U.S.C. § 107(1)).

The court further looked to the United States Supreme Court regarding the purpose and application of this fair use factor and noted that the inquiry involved " 'whether the new work merely supersede[s] the objects of the original creation, or instead adds something new, with a further purpose or different character, altering the first with new expression, meaning, or message; it asks, in other words, whether and to what extent the new work is transformative.' " Comedy III, 106 Cal. Rptr.2d 126, 21 P.3d at 808 (internal quotation marks and citations omitted) (quoting Campbell v. Acuff–Rose Music, Inc., 510 U.S. 569, 579, 114 S.Ct. 1164, 127 L.Ed.2d 500 (1994)). The court found that looking to whether the work in question possessed any "transformative" elements squared with the Supreme Court's finding in *Zacchini* that "[w]hen artistic expression takes the form of a literal depiction or imitation of a celebrity for commercial gain, directly trespassing on the right of publicity without adding significant expression beyond that trespass, the state law interest in protecting the fruits of artistic labor outweighs the expressive interests of the imitative artist." Id. (citing Zacchini, 433 U.S.

at 575–76, 97 S.Ct. 2849). In other words, although the Supreme Court did not apply the transformative test per se in *Zacchini*, the Court looked to whether the defendant had simply appropriated the plaintiff's performance in its entirety without any further creative effort. In addition, the court noted that the "transformative" test also squared with the First Amendment and the right of publicity inasmuch as "works of parody or other distortions of the celebrity figure are not, from the celebrity fan's viewpoint, good substitutes for conventional depictions of the celebrity and therefore do not generally threaten markets for celebrity memorabilia that the right of publicity is designed to protect." Id. (citing Cardtoons, L.C. v. Major League Baseball Players Assoc., 95 F.3d 959, 974 (10th Cir.1996)). Said differently, "[t]he 'transformative' test ... protect[s] the right-of-publicity holder's core interest in monopolizing the merchandising of celebrity images without unnecessarily impinging on the artists' right of free expression." Id. at 808 n. 10.

Applying the transformative test to an artist's work at issue in *Comedy III*, the charcoal sketch made into lithographs and printed on T-shirts, the court found that the defendants' work was not protected inasmuch as the creative contribution was subordinated to the overall goal of creating a literal image of the Three Stooges to commercially exploit their fame. Id. at 811. In doing so, the court noted that when an "artist's skill and talent is manifestly subordinated to the overall goal of creating a conventional portrait of a celebrity so as to commercially exploit his or her fame, then the artist's right of free expression is outweighed by the right of publicity." Id.

In the instant case, where we are faced with an expressive work and the question of whether that work is protected under the First Amendment, the reasoning and transformative test set forth in *Comedy III* are in line with the Supreme Court's reasoning in *Zacchini* as well as in harmony with the goals of both the right to publicity and the First Amendment. Applying the test here, it is difficult to discern any appreciable transformative or creative contribution in Defendant's prints so as to entitle them to First Amendment protection. "A literal depiction of a celebrity, even if accomplished with great skill, may still be subject to a right of publicity challenge. The inquiry is in a sense more quantitative than qualitative, asking whether the literal and imitative or the creative elements predominate in the work." Comedy III, 106 Cal.Rptr.2d 126, 21 P.3d at 809 (footnote omitted).

Indeed, the rendition done by Rush is nearly identical to that in the poster distributed by Nike. Although the faces and partial body images of other famous golfers appear in blue sketch blending in the background of Rush's print, the clear focus of the work is Woods in full body image wearing his red shirt and holding his famous swing in the pose which is nearly identical to that depicted in the Nike poster. Rush's print does not depict Woods in the same vein as the other golfers, such that the focus of the print is not the Masters Tournament or the other golfers who have won the prestigious green jacket award, but that of Woods holding his famous golf swing while at that tournament. Thus, although it is apparent that Rush is an adequately skilled artist, after viewing the prints in question it is also apparent that Rush's ability in this regard is "subordinated to the overall goal of creating literal, conventional depictions of [Tiger Woods] so as to exploit his . . . fame [such that Rush's] right of free expression is outweighed by [Woods'] right of publicity." See id. at 811.

In fact, the narrative that accompanies the prints expressly discusses Woods and his fame:

> But the center of their [other golfers'] gaze is 1997 winner Tiger Woods, here flanked by his caddie, "Fluff", and final round player partner's (Constantino Rocca) caddie on right, displaying that awesome swing that sends a golf ball straighter and truer than should be humanly possible. Only his uncanny putting ability serves to complete his dominating performance that lifts him alongside the Masters of Augusta.

Accordingly, contrary to the majority's conclusion otherwise, it is clear that the prints gain their commercial value by exploiting the fame and celebrity status that Woods has worked to achieve. Under such facts, the right of publicity is not outweighed by the right of free expression. See Comedy III, 106 Cal.Rptr.2d 126, 21 P.3d at 811 (noting that the marketability and economic value of the defendant's work was derived primarily from the fame of the three celebrities that it depicted and was therefore not protected by the First Amendment).

This conclusion regarding Plaintiff's right of publicity claim is in harmony with that regarding Plaintiff's claims brought under the Lanham Act. As the Restatement explains:

> Proof of deception or confusion is not required in order to establish an infringement of the right of publicity. However, if the defendant's unauthorized use creates a false suggestion of endorsement or a likelihood of confusion as to source or sponsorship, liability may also be imposed for deceptive marketing or trademark or trade name infringement.

RESTATEMENT, supra § 46 cmt. b, 537.

Because Plaintiff has come forward with evidence of consumer confusion as to Woods' sponsorship of the products in question, it is for the jury to decide whether liability should be imposed for Plaintiff's claims brought under the Lanham Act, and this is true whether employing the balancing approach set forth in *Rogers* or simply employing the eight-factor test in the traditional sense. The majority's failure to do so in this case is in complete contravention to the intent of Congress, the principles of trademark law, and the well-established body of jurisprudence in this area. In addition, the jury should also be allowed to consider evidence regarding Plaintiff's federal dilution claim inasmuch as Plaintiff has proffered evidence on each element of this claim. Finally, although Plaintiff is entitled to summary judgment on its right of publicity claim, at the very least, this claim presents a question for the jury as well.

I therefore respectfully dissent from the majority opinion affirming summary judgment to Defendant as to all of Plaintiff's claims.

Part IV

TRADE SECRET LAW

Chapter 9

PROTECTING CONFIDENTIAL INFORMATION

Like the right of publicity, trade secret protection is predominantly a creature of state law, although federal law offers some remedies for intentional usurpation of trade secrets. See Economic Espionage Act of 1996, Pub. L. No. 104–359, 110 Stat. 3488 (1996) (codified as at 18 U.S.C. §§ 1831–39) (establishing criminal penalties for theft of trade secrets). Along with federal patent law, trade secret law is one of the principal ways in which inventions and other proprietary information are protected. As in the case of other areas of intellectual property, trade secret law requires a balancing of interests. It is important to reward and protect research and development efforts, but on the other hand imitation of a competitor's successful products and services is the essence of competition. Trade secret doctrine generally strikes a balance between these competing interests.

Because trade secret law varies from state to state, it is difficult to set forth definitive statements about trade secret law. There are, however, three general sources for trade secret law. The first and oldest is the Restatement (First) of Torts, which until the last decade was the prevailing view in most jurisdictions. The second source is the Uniform Trade Secrets Act (UTSA), which has now been legislatively adopted in more than 40 states. Finally, the recently promulgated Restatement (Third) of Unfair Competition includes provisions on trade secret law. In addition to these sources of law, a leading treatise in the field is R. Milgrim, Milgrim on Trade Secrets (1987).

A. INFORMATION PROTECTABLE UNDER TRADE SECRET LAW

MINUTEMAN, INC. v. ALEXANDER

Supreme Court of Wisconsin, 1989.
147 Wis.2d 842, 434 N.W.2d 773.

DAY, JUSTICE.

This is a review of an unpublished opinion by the court of appeals which affirmed in part and reversed in part a decision by the circuit court for Dane county, Honorable P. Charles Jones, judge. 140 Wis.2d 868, 412 N.W.2d 902. The circuit court denied a motion for a temporary injunction against L.D. Alexander, George Cash, and Amity, Inc., (Defendants) on behalf of Minuteman, Inc. (Minuteman). Minuteman alleged the Defendants had misappropriated trade secrets and computer data. Minuteman sought the temporary injunction to prevent the Defendants from using these materials. * * *

The basic question to be answered in this review is: what is the proper test for determining what is a "trade secret?" The answer is to be found in sec. 134.90, Stats. We do find, however, that our holding in Corroon & Black v. Hosch, 109 Wis.2d 290, 325 N.W.2d 883 (1982), still provides helpful guidance in determining what are trade secrets under sec. 134.90.

Several other issues are raised: (A)(1) What remedy, if any, is available if a trade secret is improperly acquired, but not subsequently used, by a wrongful taker? We conclude that under section 134.90(2)(a), Stats., an improper acquisition is enough to constitute a misappropriation of a trade secret, and therefore, all remedies in sec. 134.90 are available. (2) What effect, if any, does the possibility of reverse engineering[1] the chemical formula of a trade secret have on remedies available under sec. 134.90? We hold the possibility of reverse engineering is not enough to prevent a temporary injunction from being issued, but rather should be considered when determining the length of the temporary injunction.

(B) What is the trade secret status of customer lists and lists of persons who have made inquiries as a result of a businesses' advertisements? We conclude these lists may be eligible for trade secret protection under sec. 134.90, Stats.

(C) Did the circuit court abuse its discretion by refusing to grant a temporary injunction against the use of allegedly misappropriated computer data in violation of sec. 943.70(2), Stats., of the criminal code? We conclude that because the circuit court articulated acceptable reasons as stated in Werner v. A.L. Grootemaat & Sons, Inc., 80 Wis.2d 513, 519,

---

1. "Reverse engineering" is "starting with a known product and working backward to find the method by which [the item] was developed." Note, 1985 Wis.Act 236, sec. 6.

259 N.W.2d 310 (1977), for refusing to issue the temporary injunction, it did not abuse its discretion.

Minuteman and Amity, Inc., (Amity) are both engaged in the furniture stripping business. Both sell products to people in the furniture restoration business, usually small enterprises. Chemicals, tubs for dipping the furniture, and other related products are sold to customers mostly from catalogs. Their products are essentially the same and both companies consider the other a direct competitor.

This case arises out of events occurring during March and April of 1986. Some facts are in dispute. In March, 1986, Defendants L.D. Alexander (Alexander) and George Cash (Cash) were employed by Minuteman. Alexander was vice president and general manager. Cash was the vice president in charge of Research and Development. Both were employees at will and had not signed any form of non-competition or non-disclosure agreement with Minuteman.

In late March, Alexander and Cash met with Jerry Cook, president of Amity. It is unclear what was discussed, but Minuteman alleged that Alexander and Cash discussed the possibility of leaving Minuteman to join Amity.

On April 7, 1986, the president of Minuteman, Jim Gauthier (Gauthier), returned from a two week vacation. Upon his return to work he was allegedly met by Alexander and Cash who gave him their immediate resignations. Gauthier stated he did not take the two seriously and told them to take that day off.

On the morning of April 8, Alexander was observed removing boxes of materials from Minuteman's premises. Shortly thereafter, Minuteman allegedly discovered both Cash's and Alexander's work stations completely empty of normal business materials. Minuteman claimed it was unable to locate various business related items. They thought Cash and Alexander had taken the materials.

Several days later, Alexander and Cash began working for Amity. Immediately thereafter, Minuteman filed a complaint against the Defendants. Minuteman claimed numerous causes of action against the Defendants, four of which are the subject of this review. The first allegation claimed the Defendants had misappropriated the trade secret formula for Minuteman's Stripper '76 (formula). The second allegation claimed the Defendants had misappropriated a list of inquiries made in response to Minuteman's advertisements (Inquiry list). The third allegation claimed the Defendants had misappropriated a list of Minuteman's customers which included information about what and how much each customer had ordered (Customer list). The fourth allegation claimed the Defendants had misappropriated various computer data from Minuteman. None of the items involved were protected by trademarks or patents.
* * *

A three day hearing was later held on the matter which included conflicting testimony about what happened. There was testimony about

Cash's and Alexander's behavior just before they left Minuteman. In early March 1986, Alexander had requested a printout of the entire Inquiry list. Alexander told Minuteman's computer operator he needed the list for promotional reasons. A complete printout of the list had never been prepared for anyone before, nor had there ever been a complete printed copy of the list routinely maintained in the office. There was also testimony that Minuteman took some security measures to protect the contents of the list from being known by those outside the company. The list was provided to Alexander because of his executive position within Minuteman. After Alexander left Minuteman, it is claimed the list was never found.

There was also testimony that in early April of 1986, Cash had contacted one of Minuteman's two suppliers of Stripper '76. Cash asked for a copy of the formula of Stripper '76 and the supplier complied. The supplier had a record that it had sent the formula directly to Cash, but Minuteman claimed it never found the formula in its files. Cash admitted contacting the supplier for the formula, but said he did so at the request of Gauthier and that he left it on Gauthier's desk when he quit. Minuteman's second supplier of Stripper '76 testified that he considered the formula a trade secret and that he would not have disclosed it to Cash. There was evidence that other steps were taken to keep the formula a secret. There was also testimony that Stripper '76 could possibly be reverse engineered and that the elements of Stripper '76 could have been analyzed to discover its ingredients.

Minuteman asserted additional computer data assigned to Cash and Alexander by Minuteman were also discovered missing, including a recent printout of the Customer list.

A list of Amity's business solicitation mailings made by Cash and Alexander, on April 16 and 17, 1986, was also introduced into evidence. Minuteman argued this list was based on the Customer and Inquiry lists allegedly taken by Cash and Alexander. Minuteman's computer manager testified that the list was in the same sequence as Minuteman's Customer and Inquiry lists and that Minuteman's lists were the sources of Amity's list. Both Minuteman's and Amity's lists were basically in the same zip code order with some random additions in Amity's list. There were also similar mistakes in spelling and addressing on each list. Alexander stated he had written a list for his personal use while he was at Minuteman and used this personal list as the basis for the Amity mailings.

At the circuit court's request, the parties agreed to pay for a report from a Professor Vaughan of the University of Wisconsin, a court appointed expert. Professor Vaughan examined Stripper '76 and Amity's equivalent furniture stripper. The circuit court stated that Professor Vaughan found no evidence that Stripper '76 had been used to develop Amity's equivalent stripper. The report, however, was never introduced into evidence at the hearing, never made a part of the record, nor did Professor Vaughan testify at the hearing. Furthermore, the court of appeals noted that counsel for Minuteman claimed he never saw the report. The report is a fugitive document.

* * *

The first question is: what is the proper test for determining what is a trade secret? In *Corroon & Black*, this court established the definition of trade secret based on the 4 Restatement (First) of Torts, sec. 757. In discussing the definition of a trade secret, we quoted with approval the following language from Restatement, 4 Torts, sec. 757, comment b (1939): Some factors to be considered in determining whether given information is one's trade secret are: (1) the extent to which the information is known outside of his business; (2) the extent to which it is known by employees and others involved in his business; (3) the extent of measures taken by him to guard the secrecy of the information; (4) the value of the information to him and to his competitors; (5) the amount of effort or money expended by him in developing the information; (6) the ease or difficulty with which the information could be properly acquired or duplicated by others. Corroon & Black, 109 Wis.2d at 295, 325 N.W.2d 883. This court required that all six of the Restatement elements be met before the material could be defined as a trade secret. Id., 109 Wis.2d at 297, 325 N.W.2d 883.

In 1986, however, the legislature passed the Wisconsin version of the Uniform Trade Secret Act (UTSA). Section 134.90, Stats., created a new definition of trade secret as well as establishing possible remedies available to those injured by trade secret misappropriation. The basic question before this court is how the passage of the UTSA affects this court's decision in *Corroon & Black*, and what is the current definition of "trade secret" in Wisconsin. * * *

The new definition of trade secret is found in sec. 134.90(1)(c), Stats., which states:

Uniform trade secrets act.... (c) 'Trade secret' means information, including a formula, pattern, compilation, program, device, method, technique or process to which all of the following apply:

1.   The information derives independent economic value, actual or potential, from not being generally known to, and not being readily ascertainable by proper means by, other persons who can obtain economic value from its disclosure or use.

2.   The information is the subject of efforts to maintain its secrecy that are reasonable under the circumstances.

The Commissioners of the Uniform Laws Commission who drafted the UTSA, as well as our legislature, noted "[t]hat the definition of 'trade secret' contains a reasonable departure from the Restatement of Torts (first) definition which required that a trade secret be 'continuously used in one's business.'" 1985 Wis.Act. 236, sec. 6, note; Uniform Trade Secrets Act, sec. 1, comment, 14 U.L.A. 543 (1985).

We still find, however, the Restatement's definition helpful. The Restatement was the basic source of the UTSA's definition of trade secret. Klitzke, The Uniform Trade Secrets Act, 64 Marq. L. Rev. 277, 285–86 (1980). In addition, the UTSA's Comments state it "codifies the results of the better reasoned cases concerning the remedies for trade secret misappropriation." 1985 Wis.Act. 236, Prefatory Note; Uniform Trade Secrets Act, sec. 1, comment, 14 U.L.A. 543 (1985). We hold that although all six elements of the Restatement's test are no longer required, the Restatement requirements still provide helpful guidance in deciding whether certain materials are trade secrets under our new definition. See R. Milgrim, Milgrim on Trade Secrets, sec. 201[1] (1987).

* * *

When examining an alleged violation of sec. 134.90, Stats., three questions arise. First, whether the material complained about is a trade secret under sec. 134.90(1)(c), Stats. Second, whether a misappropriation has occurred in violation of sec. 134.90(2). And finally, if both of the above requirements are met, what type of relief is appropriate under sec. 134.90(3) or (4). See also Electro–Craft Corp. v. Controlled Motion, Inc., 332 N.W.2d 890 (Minn.1983) (same analysis is followed).

A.   Stripper '76 Formula

As to Minuteman's first allegation, both the circuit court and court of appeals determined that the formula for Stripper '76 is a trade secret. The Defendants do not challenge this finding. What is in contention is whether the Defendants misappropriated the formula, and if so, what type of relief should be granted to Minuteman.

The circuit court found that "Cash obtained the formula without permission" but that there was insufficient evidence that it was turned over to Amity. Section 134.90(2), Stats., defines misappropriation as: Uniform trade secrets act.... (2) MISAPPROPRIATION. No person, including the state, may misappropriate or threaten to misappropriate a trade secret by doing any of the following: (a) Acquiring the trade secret of another by means which the person knows or has reason to know constitute improper means....

The circuit court's finding that "Cash obtained the formula without permission" constitutes an "improper means" as defined in sec. 134.90(1)(a), Stats.[4] The circuit court acknowledges that this section "may have been violated by Cash in obtaining the formula." The circuit court held, however, that sec. 134.90(2)(b) [(disclosure to another)] also had to be violated. We disagree. The statute only requires a violation of one of the subsections. It states "any of the following" will constitute a misappropriation of a trade secret. See also Uniform Trade Secret Act, sec. 1, 14 U.L.A.1988 pocket part 332 (1985). * * *

---

4. Section 134.90(1)(a), Stats., provides: Uniform trade secrets act. (1) DEFINITIONS. In this section: (a) "Improper means" includes espionage, theft, bribery, misrepresentation and breach or inducement of a breach of duty to maintain secrecy.

This court notes * * * that the possibility of reverse engineering is not enough to deny a temporary injunction as the circuit court had held. The Commissioners' comments to the UTSA note that discovery by reverse engineering is a proper means to discover a trade secret. Note, 1985 Wis.Act. 236, sec. 6.

The possibility of reverse engineering a trade secret, however, is not a factor in determining whether an item is a trade secret, but rather it is a factor in deciding how long the injunctive relief should last:

> The general principle of section 2(a) and (b) is that an injunction should last for as long as is necessary, but no longer than is necessary, to eliminate the commercial advantage of 'lead time' with respect to good faith competitors that a person has obtained through misappropriation. Subject to any additional period of restraint necessary to negate lead time, an injunction accordingly should terminate when a former trade secret becomes either generally known to good faith competitors or generally knowable to them because of the lawful availability of products that can be reverse engineered to reveal a trade secret. * * *

Commissioners' Comments, Uniform Trade Secrets Act, sec. 2, 14 U.L.A. 544–45 (1985). If the trade secret could have been independently developed or discovered by reverse engineering or otherwise, the maximum appropriate duration of the injunction would be that amount of time which the misappropriator would have needed to discover the trade secret using "proper means." In most cases, the amount of lead time that the defendant would have taken is debatable. A comparison can be made of the time taken by other competitors to develop the trade secret independently, if one or more of them had done so. Klitzke, Uniform Trade Secrets Act, 64 Marq.L.Rev. 277, 302–03 (1980).

B. THE CUSTOMER AND INQUIRY LISTS

Although the lists are distinct, both the circuit court and the court of appeals decided the second and third allegations in a similar fashion. Both courts interpreted sec. 134.90, Stats., as still embodying the trade secret definition in *Corroon* which required all six factors of the Restatement test be met before a trade secret could be found. As discussed above, the *Corroon* test no longer embodies the definition of trade secret. We, therefore, reverse the court of appeals' decision and remand for further determination using the statutory definition in sec. 134.90, Stats.

Some customer lists are afforded protection under the UTSA:

> This is not to say that every customer list would be denied trade secret status under the uniform act. We are well aware, for example, ... that in certain sectors of the business community identical or nearly identical products and/or services are sold to a small, fixed group of purchasers. In such an intensely purchaser-oriented market, a supplier's customer list could well constitute a trade secret.

Steenhoven v. College Life Ins. Co. of Am., 460 N.E.2d 973, 974, n. 5 (Ind.Ct.App.1984).

In Kozuch v. CRA–MAR Video Center, Inc., 478 N.E.2d 110 (Ind.Ct. App.1985), the customer list of a video rental club was found to consti- tute a trade secret under the Indiana version of the UTSA. An injunction was permitted to stop the use of the misappropriated trade secret. Others have noted the possibility of trade secret protection for Customer Lists under the UTSA. See American Paper & Packaging Products, Inc. v. Kirgan, 183 Cal.App.3d, 1318, 1324, 228 Cal.Rptr. 713 (1986); Klitzke, The Uniform Trade Secret Act, 64 Marq.L.Rev. 277, 285 (1980). Deci- sions by other jurisdictions on questions involving the UTSA are to be given careful consideration by the courts in Wisconsin. Section 134.90(7), Stats.

The court of appeals is reversed on this issue and the cause is remanded for an inquiry as to whether the lists are trade secrets as defined in sec. 134.90, Stats.

C. COMPUTER DATA

[The court affirmed the lower court's denial of an injunction on this claim in light of the plaintiff's reliance on conclusory allegations.] * * *

Notes

1. Should the customer lists at issue in this case be found protectable on remand? Explain. What types of customer lists qualify for trade secret protection and what types should not? Consider the case of a tailoring shop's customer list. See Elmer Miller, Inc. v. Landis, 253 Ill.App.3d 129, 192 Ill.Dec. 378, 625 N.E.2d 338 (1993). What about a propane dealer's customer list? See AmeriGas Propane, L.P. v. T–Bo Propane, Inc., 972 F.Supp. 685 (S.D.Ga.1997). In *Harvey Barnett, Inc. v. Shidler*, 338 F.3d 1125 (10th Cir. 2003), the court addressed whether a program for infant swimming instruc- tion would qualify as a trade secret and found that a fact issue existed on this point. What considerations should go into resolving this question?

2. When should a duty arise not to disclose trade secrets even in the absence of an express confidentiality agreement?

3. Information that is easily discerned, widely known, or obvious will not satisfy the secrecy requirement. Kewanee Oil Co. v. Bicron Corp., 416 U.S. 470, 94 S.Ct. 1879, 40 L.Ed.2d 315 (1974). Consider whether a compa- ny's customer tracking methods, such as the use of follow-up letters and deletion of customer names after a second failure to respond, can qualify as a trade secret. See Computer Care v. Service Systems Enterprises, Inc., 982 F.2d 1063, 1071–74 (7th Cir.1992). What if an artist develops a concept for a line of "Noah's Ark" figurines? Noah v. Enesco Corp., 911 F.Supp. 299 (N.D.Ill.1995). What about an idea for a magazine advertisement (a "stepped insert") that has been regularly used in the marketing field? See Web Communications Group, Inc. v. Gateway 2000, Inc., 889 F.Supp. 316 (N.D.Ill.1995).

It should be noted, however, that trade secret law requires only relative secrecy—the information must be sufficiently secret that it accords an advantage to those competitors or others who do not possess it. Thus, if several competitors lawfully possess a trade secret, while several others do not, the information can still qualify as a trade secret. The secrecy requirement is satisfied if it would be difficult or costly for others who could exploit the information to obtain it. Put another way, the information need not be completely novel or new. See Kewanee Oil Co. v. Bicron Corp., 416 U.S. 470, 94 S.Ct. 1879, 40 L.Ed.2d 315 (1974); Restatement (Third) of Unfair Competition § 39, comment f.

4. For further discussion of the scope of trade secret rights, see Restatement (Third) of Unfair Competition § 39 (1995) ("A trade secret is any information that can be used in the operation of a business or other enterprise and that is sufficiently valuable and secret to afford an actual or potential economic advantage over others."). For discussion of a proposed federal trade secret statute, see Marina Lao, Federalizing Trade Secrets Law in an Information Economy, 59 Ohio State L.J. 1633 (1998).

B. TRADE SECRETS REVEALED THROUGH BREACH OF CONFIDENTIAL RELATIONSHIPS

LAMB–WESTON, INC. v. McCAIN FOODS, LTD.

United States Court of Appeals, Ninth Circuit, 1991.
941 F.2d 970.

EUGENE A. WRIGHT, CIRCUIT JUDGE:

Lamb–Weston's attempt to spiral ahead of its competitors was allegedly thwarted by the misappropriation by McCain of Lamb–Weston's trade secrets for manufacturing curlicue french fries. To keep Lamb–Weston from being left to twist in the wind before the trial on the merits, an eight-month preliminary injunction was imposed, barring McCain from producing or selling products made with the technology in question. McCain appeals and we affirm.

I

Lamb–Weston, a potato processor, began in 1986 to develop the technology for producing curlicue french fries. The unique process involved a helical blade and water-feed system. McCain, a competitor, began work on a manufacturing process for curlicue fries in 1989.

In January 1990, McCain approached several Lamb–Weston employees to help its development. At that time, Richard Livermore, who had helped create the Lamb–Weston blade and process, allegedly gave McCain a copy of Lamb–Weston's confidential patent application. Livermore later went to work for McCain. Subsequently, Jerry Ross, the independent contractor who fabricated the Lamb–Weston blade, was hired by McCain to craft a helical blade for it. McCain left the decisions about the specifications, materials and manufacturing process to Ross, knowing he was still working on Lamb–Weston's blades.

Lamb–Weston was issued two patents for its blade system on May 22, 1990. In August, after discovering Ross was working for McCain, Lamb–Weston had him sign a confidentiality agreement. Contemporaneously, it sent a letter to McCain asserting concern that McCain was misappropriating its trade secrets. In October, Lamb–Weston insisted Ross sign an exclusivity agreement. McCain then requested and received from Ross all the information he had on the McCain blade.

According to Lamb–Weston, with the help of Ross and Livermore, McCain built a prototype before the patents issued in May 1990. By June, McCain had the blades hooked up to a prototype water-feed system and by December was producing curlicue fries.

During the following month, Lamb–Weston sued for misappropriation of trade secrets. The parties consented to proceedings before a magistrate judge, who entered an eight-month preliminary injunction against McCain in March 1991.

II

McCain * * * contends that it had no reason to know that trade secrets were being transmitted through Ross, as he was an independent contractor who assured McCain that there would be no confidentiality problems.

Misappropriation of trade secrets under Oregon law requires a showing of (1) a valuable commercial design, (2) a confidential relationship between the party asserting trade secret protection and the party who disclosed the information, and (3) the key features of the design that were the creative product of the party asserting protection. * * *

Circumstantial evidence supports the court's preliminary conclusion that despite Ross's assurance he would not breach confidentiality, McCain knew that he would. McCain hired him knowing he was working on Lamb–Weston's blade. McCain told him to build a helical blade but said nothing about how he was to do it. In contrast, Lamb–Weston had specified what materials, dimensions and process to use. As a practical matter, it would be difficult for a person developing the same technology for two clients not to use knowledge gained from the first project in producing the second. This is obviously true here because McCain left the development to Ross.

McCain points to Ross's testimony that he left both the McCain and Lamb–Weston blades in the open where anyone could see them. McCain argues this shows that Lamb–Weston knew Ross was working on a McCain blade but was unconcerned about breaches of confidence. It was not clear error for the court to reject this proposition. Ross's failure to keep the blades segregated suggests he was using the same information to build both blades.

Furthermore, Lamb–Weston employees testified that they did not see the McCain blade at Ross's shop and that, when they learned in August 1990 that Ross was working for McCain, Lamb–Weston had him sign a confidentiality agreement. This demonstrates Lamb–Weston was concerned about protecting its trade secrets.

Probable success in showing misappropriation is also supported by testimony that Livermore gave McCain a copy of the confidential patent application five months before the patent issued. McCain did not challenge this testimony.[2]

* * *

III

McCain argues that the court abused its discretion by imposing a geographically overbroad injunction. The court enjoined it from selling curlicue french fries worldwide even though Lamb–Weston's foreign market is limited.[3] Arguing that Lamb–Weston cannot be harmed in countries where it is not selling, McCain urges this court to limit the injunction to those countries where Lamb–Weston actually sells its product. * * *

McCain's reliance on Mantek Div. of NCH Corp. v. Share Corp., 780 F.2d 702 (7th Cir.1986), is not persuasive. The case involved violations of covenants not to compete signed by the plaintiff's former employees. The injunction barred the defendants from calling on the plaintiff's actual and potential customers. Noting that the injunction was to protect the goodwill the plaintiff had built up with its customers through its sales staff and reasoning that the plaintiff had no goodwill with respect to unsolicited but potential customers, the court held enjoining the defendants from approaching the unsolicited ones was an abuse of discretion. Id. at 710–11.

The interest protected here is fundamentally different. An injunction in a trade secret case seeks to protect the secrecy of misappropriated

---

2. In its reply brief, McCain argues that the Lamb–Weston information Ross had was not confidential. We decline to address arguments not raised in the appellant's opening brief. Were we to view this argument as part of McCain's assertion that it did not know Ross was breaching any confidentiality and address it, we would find no clear error. McCain acknowledges that at the outset Ross orally agreed to keep Lamb–Weston's information confidential. It also does not challenge the finding that the blade and the fabrication process were trade secrets. In addition, Lamb–Weston's efforts to secure first a written confidentiality agreement and then an exclusivity agreement show it believed the information Ross had was confidential. See Holland Dev. v. Manufacturers Consultants, 81 Or.App. 57, 62–63, 724 P.2d 844, 847–48 (1986)

(finding a confidential relationship existed and noting that the employer would not invest time and money to develop a project simply to allow its employee to turn around and use the developed technology for personal benefit); E.V. Prentice Dryer Co. v. Northwest Dryer & Machinery Co., 246 Or. 78, 81–82, 424 P.2d 227, 229 (1967) (finding no confidentiality agreement where the information was not of a confidential nature and there was nothing in the employment relationship indicating that the plaintiff wanted it to be secret).

3. McCain contends that Lamb–Weston's only foreign markets are in England, Japan and Canada. Lamb–Weston claims that it also has sold or attempted to sell its fries in Europe, Australia and Brazil.

information and to eliminate any unfair head start the defendant may have gained. Winston Research Corp. v. Minnesota Mining and Mfg., 350 F.2d 134, 141 (9th Cir.1965). A worldwide injunction here is consistent with those goals because it "place[s the defendant] in the position it would have occupied if the breach of confidence had not occurred prior to the public disclosure, . . . " Id. at 142. * * * The geographic scope of the injunction was not an abuse of discretion.

IV

McCain argues that the court erred by failing to make specific findings about the length of its alleged head start. McCain also contends the injunction was an abuse of discretion because it is too long. * * * "[T]he appropriate duration for the injunction should be the period of time it would have taken [the defendant], either by reverse engineering or by independent development, to develop [the product] legitimately without use of [plaintiff's] trade secrets." K–2 Ski Co. v. Head Ski Co., 506 F.2d 471, 474 (9th Cir.1974).

McCain argues that April 19, 1990 is the only date for which there is evidence of misappropriation and that at most it had a one-year advantage beginning on that date. It asserts that with a one-year head start, the injunction imposed on March 27, 1991, should have ended on April 19, 1991, one year from the misappropriation date.

If we were to accept McCain's argument that the misappropriation was April 19 and the head start should be calculated from that date, the injunction imposed was not an abuse of discretion simply because it ended a year and seven months after that date. Lamb–Weston presented testimony that its development time for the materials, dimensions and fabricating process for the blade was about a year and a half. Additional testimony was given about Lamb–Weston's reputation for ingenuity and its development time for the blade design.

We reject McCain's argument that if the misappropriation through Ross occurred on April 19, it had only a 33–day head start because Lamb–Weston's patents were issued May 22. Although the shape of the blade and the slicing process was public on May 22, the specifications, materials and manufacturing process for making the blade were still trade secrets because they were not included in the patent applications.

Oregon law affords broad protection to trade secrets so public disclosure of the blade shape did not exonerate McCain from previous illegal use of that trade secret or the subsequent illegal use of the remaining trade secrets. Although a defendant may ask the court to vacate an injunction after the trade secret is public, "the injunction may be continued for an additional reasonable period of time in order to eliminate commercial advantage that otherwise would be derived from the misappropriation." 1989 Or.Laws 646.463(1); Kamin v. Kuhnau, 232 Or. 139, 157–59, 374 P.2d 912, 921–22 (1962).

The eight-month injunction was not an abuse of discretion.

AFFIRMED.

Notes

1. Was the plaintiff vigilant in identifying and protecting its trade secrets? Would an injunction be appropriate if good faith competitors had already developed the process at issue?

2. Why might the plaintiff in this case obtain patents for some of its inventions—the cutting blade and the slicing process—while not seeking a patent on the process for making the blade (the specifications, materials, and manufacturing steps involved)?

3. A trade secret violation can also occur if someone receives trade secret information knowing (or having reason to know based on the circumstances) that it is improperly revealed (i.e., revealed as a result of a breach of confidence or use of improper means) or sometimes even accidentally revealed. What purposes does this rule serve? See Lamb v. Turbine Designs, Inc., 207 F.3d 1259 (11th Cir.2000). For further discussion of trade secret violations, see Restatement (Third) of Unfair Competition §§ 40–42 (1995).

C. REASONABLE SECRECY MEASURES

ELECTRO–CRAFT CORP. v. CONTROLLED MOTION, INC.

Supreme Court of Minnesota, 1983.
332 N.W.2d 890.

Coyne, Justice.

Respondent Electro–Craft Corporation ("ECC") sued appellants Controlled Motion, Inc. ("CMI") and CMI's president, John Mahoney, (a former employee of ECC) for misappropriation of trade secrets. ECC claimed that CMI and Mahoney improperly copied the designs of ECC's electric motors. The district court found that misappropriation had occurred and also found appellants in contempt for violating a temporary restraining order. We reverse the order for judgment based on misappropriation and affirm the order finding appellants in contempt. * * *

The Events

In May of 1980, John Mahoney, while employed by ECC, began to explore the possibility of starting his own business. Mahoney already had many contacts in the business, including people at Storage Technology and at IBM—ECC customers for the ECC 1125–03–003 and brushless motors. Mahoney had also guided development of the IBM project and the Ford project. On June 12, 1980, Mahoney hired an attorney as counsel for the proposed new business, and counsel helped Mahoney prepare a prospectus which was circulated to prospective investors. Mahoney met with several prospective investors during June and July but apparently received no investments before August 1980.

The prospectus indicates that Mahoney proposed to compete with ECC in its IBM and Ford applications. Mahoney planned to complete prototypes for IBM in twelve weeks and obtain IBM approval in another week. Mahoney planned to try eventually to enter the market for the Ford systems. The prospectus projected revenues in the third month from sales of the prototype brushless motors but projected no research and development expenses for the first few months.

In June of 1980 Mahoney met with several of his fellow ECC employees about their joining the new business. On August 6, 1980, Mahoney resigned from ECC. Mahoney and ECC's president, Kelen, met briefly regarding trade secrets and Mahoney told Kelen not to worry. On September 16, 1980, four other ECC employees resigned in order to work for Mahoney's company, now called CMI. The four employees were:

(1) William Craighill, a mechanical engineer who worked with ECC on the design of the ECC 1125 and the brushless motor for IBM. Craighill had previously worked for Control Data Corporation. At Control Data, Craighill did not design D.C. electric motors but worked on systems which he testified were similar to D.C. electric motors.

(2) James West, previously Quality Assurance Manager at ECC for electric motors. West was acting plant manager at one ECC plant for six months.

(3) William Anderson, who had worked for ECC as a technician for about two years. Anderson now works for Honeywell.

(4) Lynn Klatt, Buyer's Assistant at ECC, who was familiar with ECC's vendors and with the parts used in ECC's motors.

All of these employees, as well as Mahoney, had signed confidentiality agreements[1] when hired by ECC. None of these agreements, however, included a non-competition clause. When these four employees left ECC, ECC's management conducted exit interviews. The employees were asked to sign acknowledgment forms which outlined the areas that ECC considered confidential; only Anderson signed the acknowledgment. * * *

On September 18, Mahoney traveled to Colorado to meet representatives of Storage Technology Co. Mahoney received the specifications for a moving coil motor to meet Storage Technology's application, at that time supplied by the ECC 1125–03–003 and a Honeywell motor. Mahoney delivered prototypes of a CMI motor, the CMI 440, to Storage Technolo-

---

1. The agreements were part of the employment agreements, reading in part as follows:

FOURTH—Employee shall not directly or indirectly disclose or use at any time, either during or subsequent to the said employment, any secret or confidential information, knowledge, or data of Employer (whether or not obtained, acquired or developed by Employee) unless he shall first secure the written consent of Employer.

Upon termination of his employment Employee shall turn over to Employer all notes, memoranda, notebooks, drawings or other documents made, compiled by or delivered to him concerning any product, apparatus or process manufactured, used or developed or investigated by Employer during the period of his employment; it being agreed that the same and all information contained therein are at all times the property of the Employer.

gy on December 15, 1980; the motor was finally approved on March 1, 1981.

The evidence is conflicting as to how CMI produced the 440. The CMI 440 is almost identical in dimensions and tolerances[2] to the ECC 1125–03–003. William Craighill, the former ECC employee who developed the CMI 440, testified that he did not copy, nor even possess, an ECC 1125 motor when he designed the CMI 440. Craighill claimed that he used only a similar Honeywell motor, the Storage Technology specifications, and his own calculations to develop the CMI 440. On the other hand, circumstantial evidence pointed to the conclusion that CMI employees copied the ECC 1125. The similarity of the motors suggests copying, although the motors are not absolutely identical. Furthermore, the manufacturing processes, adhesives, and other materials are nearly identical. Expert testimony differed as to how long it should have taken CMI to "reverse engineer" the motor by taking apart an ECC 1125, measuring the parts and testing the material, and putting the plans together. A CMI expert estimated that it should have taken two to three months to develop a prototype motor. An expert for ECC estimated that the process would take at least six months to a year. Kelen estimated it would take a year. * * *

The Action

On September 26, 1980, about six weeks after Mahoney's resignation, ECC sued CMI and Mahoney (hereinafter referred to together as "CMI") claiming that CMI misappropriated ECC's trade secrets. * * * After a preliminary hearing Judge Lindsay Arthur of the Hennepin County District Court granted a temporary injunction in favor of ECC on April 16, 1981. CMI was enjoined by this order, pending decision at trial, from "directly or indirectly selling or soliciting sales of any low inertia, DC, electric servo motor for which any component not available on the open market has dimensions closer than 10% to Plaintiff's 1125 motor." It was later established that CMI had continued to produce and sell electric motors after April 16, 1981. On July 9, 1981, Judge Arthur issued an order holding CMI in civil contempt for violating the temporary injunction. CMI was ordered to pay ECC $50.00 damages for each offending motor which CMI had sold since April 16, 1981, plus the premiums on ECC's cost bond. The $50.00 per motor damages were later rescinded for lack of evidentiary foundation, but CMI remained liable for the bond premiums.

A trial was held before Judge Arthur, without a jury, from June 15, 1981 to July 7, 1981. By order of October 19, 1981, Judge Arthur found that CMI had misappropriated ECC's trade secrets and enjoined CMI from producing or selling any "brushless or low inertia electric motor or tachometer" with dimensions within 10% of the dimensions of ECC's 1125 motor or ECC's brushless motor produced for IBM. The injunction

---

2. Tolerances are the allowable manufacturing errors in dimension which still allow a working product. For example, a part may be required to be five one-thousandths of an inch in diameter, plus or minus one ten-thousandth of an inch.

was to be in effect for 12 months after the expiration of the last stay of execution of the order. The court also awarded ECC $50.00 in exemplary damages (but no compensatory damages) for each offending motor sold.
* * *

A. Trade Secret Status

* * * In order to determine the existence of trade secrets, we must first determine what trade secrets are claimed by ECC and what trade secrets were found by the district court. CMI claims that neither ECC nor the district court were specific enough in defining ECC's trade secrets. CMI also claims that ECC's definition of its trade secrets changed during the course of the litigation. Therefore, according to CMI the district court should be reversed due to lack of specificity.

Regarding the brushless motor, we agree with CMI that ECC did not specify its trade secrets at trial. Nor did ECC even introduce the dimensions, tolerances, etc. of the brushless motor into evidence. The trial court found trade secrets in the general "design procedures" for the brushless motor. The court then enjoined CMI with respect to duplication of only the dimensions of the brushless motors. This lack of clarity is fatal to ECC's claim. On the record before us, ECC did not meet its burden of showing that certain features of the brushless motor were protectable trade secrets which might be misappropriated in the future. Furthermore, given ECC's lack of specificity, it was impossible for the district court to fashion a meaningful injunction which would not overly restrict legitimate competition for the IBM project.

With respect to the moving coil motors, however, ECC claims that the dimensions, tolerances, adhesives, and manufacturing processes of the ECC 1125–03–003 motor are trade secrets. The thrust of ECC's claim is that the specific combination of details and processes for the 1125 motor is a trade secret, and the evidence of the specific features of the 1125 motor sold to Storage Technology adequately identifies the information which ECC claims constitutes a trade secret. We believe that ECC's claim was specific enough in identifying its trade secrets to support a misappropriation action with respect to the 1125. * * *

(a) Not generally known, readily ascertainable. The trial court found the information regarding the ECC 1125–03–003 to be secret. This finding was not clearly erroneous. First, the trial court found on conflicting evidence that CMI could not readily (i.e. quickly) reverse engineer a motor with exactly the same dimensions, tolerances, and materials as the ECC 1125–03–003. This finding was not clearly erroneous. Reverse engineering time is certainly a factor in determining whether information is readily ascertainable. ILG Industries, Inc. v. Scott, 49 Ill.2d 88, 94, 273 N.E.2d 393, 396 (1971); Kubik, Inc. v. Hull, 56 Mich.App. 335, 359–60, 224 N.W.2d 80, 92–93 (1974). The complexity and detail of dimensional data also bears on its ascertainability. A.H. Emery Co. v. Marcan Products Corp., 389 F.2d 11, 16 (2d Cir.1968) ("[I]t is well settled that detailed manufacturing drawings and tolerance data are prima facie trade secrets."); Henry Hope X–Ray Products, Inc. v. Marron Carrel, 674 F.2d 1336, 1340–41 (9th Cir.1982) (configuration of gear system and tolerances was secret).

Second, the district court found that the exact combination of features of the 1125–03–003 is unique, even though none of the processes or features are unique in the industry and the 1125–03–003 is not the only way to achieve the required performance. Novelty is not a requirement for trade secrets to the same extent as for patentability. E.g., Clark v. Bunker, 453 F.2d 1006, 1009 (9th Cir.1972). On the other hand, some novelty is required; mere variations on widely used processes cannot be trade secrets. Thus, in *Jostens*, a type of computer system was held not to be secret where it merely combined known subsystems (and where defendant had produced a different system).[10] In the present case the exact combination of features of the 1125–03–003 could be characterized as a unique solution to the needs of one customer in the industry.

* * * Therefore, the finding of the trial court, that the features of the motor are not generally known or readily ascertainable, is supported by substantial evidence and is not clearly erroneous.[11] * * *

(b) Independent economic value from secrecy. * * * [The court upholds the finding that the trade secrets provided a competitive advantage.]

(c) Reasonable efforts to maintain secrecy. It is this element upon which ECC's claim founders. The district court found that, even though ECC had no "meaningful security provisions," ECC showed an intention to keep its data and processes secret. This finding does not bear upon the statutory requirement that ECC use "efforts that are reasonable under the circumstances to maintain . . . secrecy." Minn.Stat. § 325C.01, subd. 5(ii). The "intention" language used by the district court comes from the

---

10. Compare Jostens and Pressure Science, Inc. v. Kramer, 413 F.Supp. 618 (D.Conn.), aff'd, 551 F.2d 301 (2d Cir.1976) (manufacturing processes for metal seals not trade secrets where others in industry used same processes and could easily reproduce seals), with Forest Laboratories, Inc. v. Pillsbury Co., 452 F.2d 621 (7th Cir.1971) (process of "tempering" effervescent tablets, by leaving in a dry room for 24 to 48 hours before packaging, was a trade secret) and Structural Dynamics Research Corp. v. Engineering Mechanics Research Corp., 401 F.Supp. 1102 (E.D.Mich.1975) (combination of known elements in computer software system was a trade secret where unique, and defendant copied almost exactly).

11. The ECC 1125 represents the "state of the art" in low inertia DC motors. Its dimensions, tolerances, and adhesives are easier to determine and its manufacturing processes are more familiar to engineers today than in the mid–1970's when the 1125 was developed. We recognize that, by allowing possible trade secret protection for the features of the 1125, we risk stifling the ability of employees to leave their employment and compete with their former employers (in the absence of a valid non-competition agreement) using "state of the art" knowledge. Nevertheless, we believe that such a result is necessary under the Act. * * * The danger to legitimate competition, mentioned above, will be mitigated by the following factors: (1) plaintiffs' burden of proof respecting this finding and the other elements of trade secret status; (2) plaintiffs' inability, once employees have left plaintiffs' employ, to protect information with respect to which plaintiffs did not make "reasonable efforts to maintain secrecy" during defendants' employment; and (3) the courts' duty to fashion a remedy which will balance employers' rights to protect secrets with employees' rights to compete using "state of the art" knowledge. E.W. Bliss Co. v. Struthers–Dunn, Inc., 408 F.2d 1108, 1112–1113 (8th Cir.1969).

common law test for trade secret status. Cherne Industrial, Inc. v. Grounds & Associates, supra, 278 N.W.2d at 90. However, even under the common law, more than an "intention" was required—the plaintiff was required to show that it had manifested that intention by making some effort to keep the information secret.

This element of trade secret law does not require maintenance of absolute secrecy; only partial or qualified secrecy has been required under the common law. Radium Remedies Co. v. Weiss, 173 Minn. 342, 347–48, 217 N.W. 339, 341 (1928). What is actually required is conduct which will allow a court acting in equity to enforce plaintiff's rights. * * * To put it another way, the employer must come into court with clean hands; the employer cannot complain of the employee's use of information if the employer has never treated the information as secret.

It is this aspect of trade secret law which truly sets it apart from the other two means through which employers can protect information—patents, and employment contracts containing a non-competition clause. The latter two remedies depend on only a single act by the employer. Trade secret protection, on the other hand, depends upon a continuing course of conduct by the employer, a course of conduct which creates a confidential relationship. This relationship, in turn, creates a reciprocal duty in the employee to treat the information as confidential insofar as the employer has so treated it.

In the present case, even viewing the evidence most favorably to the findings below, we hold that ECC did not meet its burden of proving that it used reasonable efforts to maintain secrecy as to the ECC 1125–03–003. We acknowledge that ECC took minimal precautions in screening its handbook and publications for confidential information and by requiring some of its employees to sign a confidentiality agreement,[13] but these were not enough.

First, ECC's physical security measures did not demonstrate any effort to maintain secrecy. By "security" we mean the protection of information from discovery by outsiders. Security was lax in this case. For example, the main plant had a few guarded entrances, but seven unlocked entrances existed without signs warning of limited access. Employees were at one time required to wear badges, but that system was abandoned by the time of the events giving rise to this case. The same was generally true of the Amery, Wisconsin plant where ECC 1125 and brushless motors were manufactured. One sign was posted at each plant, however, marking the research and development lab at Hopkins and the machine shop at Amery as restricted to "authorized personnel." Discarded drawings and plans for motors were simply thrown away, not destroyed. Documents such as motor drawings were not kept in a central or locked location, although some design notebooks were kept locked.

---

13. Thus, this case is not as extreme as was United Wild Rice, Inc. v. Nelson, 313 N.W.2d 628 (Minn.1982), in which plaintiff itself publicly disclosed the supposedly confidential information.

The relaxed security by itself, however, does not preclude a finding of reasonable efforts by ECC to maintain secrecy. Other evidence did not indicate that industrial espionage is a major problem in the servo motor industry. Therefore, "security" measures may not have been needed,[14] and the trial court could have found trade secrets if ECC had taken other reasonable measures to preserve secrecy.

However, ECC's "confidentiality" procedures were also fatally lax, and the district court was clearly in error in finding ECC's efforts to be reasonable. By "confidentiality" in this case we mean the procedures by which the employer signals to its employees and to others that certain information is secret and should not be disclosed. Confidentiality was important in this case, for testimony demonstrated that employees in the servo motor business frequently leave their employers in order to produce similar or identical devices for new employers. ECC has hired many employees from other corporations manufacturing similar products.[16] If ECC wanted to prevent its employees from doing the same thing, it had an obligation to inform its employees that certain information was secret.[17]

ECC's efforts were especially inadequate because of the nonintuitive nature of ECC's claimed secrets here. The dimensions, etc., of ECC's motors are not trade secrets in as obvious a way as a "secret formula" might be. ECC should have let its employees know in no uncertain terms that those features were secret.

Instead, ECC treated its information as if it were not secret. None of its technical documents were marked "Confidential", and drawings, dimensions and parts were sent to customers and vendors without special marking. Employee access to documents was not restricted. ECC never issued a policy statement outlining what it considered to be secret. Many informal tours were given to vendors and customers without warnings as to confidential information. Further, two plants each had an

14. Compare E.I. duPont deNemours & Co., Inc. v. Christopher, 431 F.2d 1012 (5th Cir.1970), cert. denied 400 U.S. 1024, 91 S.Ct. 581, 27 L.Ed.2d 637 (1971) (not reasonably necessary to guard against aerial reconnaissance flight, which showed plaintiff's plant design during construction of plant), with Capsonic Group, Inc. v. Plas–Met Corp., 46 Ill.App.3d 436, 5 Ill.Dec. 41, 361 N.E.2d 41 (1977) (secrecy not reasonably maintained where plant had no guard, no passes were required, drawings were not kept locked, and people on tours were not told that any information was confidential).

16. One ECC employee actually prided himself on the information he had brought with him from his former employer. One day, just before that employee left ECC to join another company, the president of ECC found him copying documents after hours.

ECC never questioned the employee or warned him or his new employer that certain information was confidential.

17. See Future Plastics, Inc. v. Ware Shoals Plastics, Inc., 340 F.Supp. 1376 (D.S.C.1972) (where plaintiff company's engineer had left plaintiff and formed new competing company and plaintiff had never objected, plaintiff had not treated processes as confidential and could not enjoin defendant employee, who joined other competitor); Sun Dial Corp. v. Rideout, 29 N.J.Super. 361, 102 A.2d 90, aff'd. 16 N.J. 252, 108 A.2d 442 (1954) (even though plaintiff conducted limited plant tours and published vague articles about secret process, reasonable confidentiality was maintained where other efforts were taken to protect secret information).

"open house" at which the public was invited to observe manufacturing processes.

The district court relied on certain contrary evidence to show ECC's "intention," but this evidence does not demonstrate reasonable efforts to maintain confidentiality. There was no showing that a 1977 memo from the president of ECC to its managerial employees, warning them to restrict unannounced laboratory tours in the interests of protecting secrets, had ever been enforced. The confidentiality agreements signed by the employees were too vague to apprise the employees of specific "secrets." (See note 1, supra).

The exit interviews also did not constitute reasonable efforts to maintain secrecy. The exit interviews, a procedure initiated by ECC only after it became clear that the employees were about to work for Mahoney, occurred a mere ten days before the commencement of this litigation. These "interviews" were little more than attempts to intimidate or threaten employees, to prevent them from leaving ECC and engaging in legitimate competition using their skill and expertise. Such thinly-veiled threats certainly do not qualify as ongoing efforts to maintain the secrecy of specific information. The law of trade secrets does not condone, and this court certainly will not reward, ECC's conduct.

In summary, ECC has not met its burden of proof in establishing the existence of any trade secrets. The evidence does not show that ECC was ever consistent in treating the information here as secret.

B. *Misappropriation*

Since no trade secrets existed to be misappropriated, we technically need not reach the issue of whether misappropriation occurred. However, as we noted above the concept of trade secret status and the concept of misappropriation should not be artificially separated. * * * Misappropriation involves the acquisition, disclosure, or use of a trade secret through improper means. Minn.Stat. § 325C.01, subd. 3. "Improper means" are defined as "[T]heft, bribery, misrepresentation, breach or inducement of breach of a duty to maintain secrecy, or espionage through electronic or other means." Minn.Stat. § 325C.01, subd. 2. In the employer-employee context of the present case, ECC was required to show some duty on the part of the employee not to disclose the information. ECC claims that the employees' duty here arose from the employee agreements and from a confidential employer-employee relationship.

However, a common law duty of confidentiality arises out of the employer-employee relationship only as to information which the employer has treated as secret: "[T]he employee is entitled to fair notice of the confidential nature of the relationship and what material is to be kept confidential." Jostens, supra, 318 N.W.2d at 702 (citing Ellis, Trade Secrets 79 (1953)). Therefore, in the present case, ECC's failure to make reasonable efforts to maintain secrecy, discussed above, was fatal to its claim of a confidential relationship. The employees were never put on notice of any duty of confidentiality. The employee agreements do not help ECC's claim for the same reason—ECC never treated specific information as secret. Therefore, the agreements' vague language prohibiting the employee from taking "secrets" did not create a duty of confidentiality in the employee, and no misappropriation occurred. * * *

Note

What advice would you give to a company that was seeking to ensure, from both a legal and practical standpoint, that it has taken sufficient measures to protect its trade secrets?

D. IMPROPER MEANS OF ACQUIRING TRADE SECRETS

E.I. DuPONT DeNEMOURS & CO. v. CHRISTOPHER

United States Court of Appeals, Fifth Circuit, 1970.
431 F.2d 1012.

GOLDBERG, CIRCUIT JUDGE:

This is a case of industrial espionage in which an airplane is the cloak and a camera the dagger. The defendants-appellants, Rolfe and Gary Christopher, are photographers in Beaumont, Texas. The Christophers were hired by an unknown third party to take aerial photographs of new construction at the Beaumont plant of E. I. duPont deNemours & Company, Inc. Sixteen photographs of the DuPont facility were taken from the air on March 19, 1969, and these photographs were later developed and delivered to the third party.

DuPont employees apparently noticed the airplane on March 19 and immediately began an investigation to determine why the craft was circling over the plant. By that afternoon the investigation had disclosed that the craft was involved in a photographic expedition and that the Christophers were the photographers. DuPont contacted the Christophers that same afternoon and asked them to reveal the name of the person or corporation requesting the photographs. The Christophers refused to disclose this information, giving as their reason the client's desire to remain anonymous.

Having reached a dead end in the investigation, DuPont subsequently filed suit against the Christophers, alleging that the Christophers had wrongfully obtained photographs revealing DuPont's trade secrets which they then sold to the undisclosed third party. DuPont contended that it had developed a highly secret but unpatented process for producing methanol, a process which gave DuPont a competitive advantage over other producers. This process, DuPont alleged, was a trade secret developed after much expensive and time-consuming research, and a secret which the company had taken special precautions to safeguard. The area photographed by the Christophers was the plant designed to produce methanol by this secret process, and because the plant was still under construction parts of the process were exposed to view from directly above the construction area. Photographs of that area, DuPont alleged, would enable a skilled person to deduce the secret process for making methanol. DuPont thus contended that the Christophers had wrongfully appropriated DuPont trade secrets by taking the photographs and delivering them to the undisclosed third party. * * *

On June 5, 1969, the trial court held a hearing on all pending motions and an additional motion by the Christophers for summary judgment. The court denied the Christophers' motions to dismiss for want of jurisdiction and failure to state a claim and also denied their motion for summary judgment. The court granted DuPont's motion to compel the Christophers to divulge the name of their client. Having made these rulings, the court then granted the Christophers' motion for an interlocutory appeal under 28 U.S.C.A. 1292(b) to allow the Christophers to obtain immediate appellate review of the court's finding that DuPont had stated a claim upon which relief could be granted. Agreeing with the trial court's determination that DuPont had stated a valid claim, we affirm the decision of that court.

This is a case of first impression, for the Texas courts have not faced this precise factual issue, and sitting as a diversity court we must sensitize our *Erie* antennae to divine what the Texas courts would do if such a situation were presented to them. The only question involved in this interlocutory appeal is whether DuPont has asserted a claim upon which relief can be granted. The Christophers argued both at trial and before this court that they committed no "actionable wrong" in photographing the DuPont facility and passing these photographs on to their client because they conducted all of their activities in public airspace, violated no government aviation standard, did not breach any confidential relation, and did not engage in any fraudulent or illegal conduct. In short, the Christophers argue that for an appropriation of trade secrets to be wrongful there must be a trespass, other illegal conduct, or breach of a confidential relationship. We disagree.

It is true, as the Christophers assert, that the previous trade secret cases have contained one or more of these elements. However, we do not think that the Texas courts would limit the trade secret protection exclusively to these elements. On the contrary, in Hyde Corporation v. Huffines, 1958, 158 Tex. 566, 314 S.W.2d 763, the Texas Supreme Court specifically adopted the rule found in the Restatement of Torts which provides:

> 'One who discloses or uses another's trade secret, without a privilege to do so, is liable to the other if (a) he discovered the secret by improper means, or (b) his disclosure or use constitutes a breach of confidence reposed in him by the other in disclosing the secret to him * * *.'

Restatement of Torts 757 (1939).

Thus, although the previous cases have dealt with a breach of a confidential relationship, a trespass, or other illegal conduct, the rule is much broader than the cases heretofore encountered. Not limiting itself to specific wrongs, Texas adopted subsection (a) of the Restatement which recognizes a cause of action for the discovery of a trade secret by any "improper" means.

The defendants, however, read Furr's Inc. v. United Specialty Advertising Co., Tex.Civ.App.1960, 338 S.W.2d 762, writ ref'd n.r.e., as limiting the Texas rule to breach of a confidential relationship. The court in *Furr's* did make the statement that

> The use of someone else's idea is not automatically a violation of the law. It must be something that meets the requirements of a "trade secret" and has been obtained through a breach of confidence in order to entitle the injured party to damages and/or injunction. 338 S.W.2d at 766.

We think, however, that the exclusive rule which defendants have extracted from this statement is unwarranted. In the first place, in *Furr's* the court specifically found that there was no trade secret involved because the entire advertising scheme claimed to be the trade secret had been completely divulged to the public. Secondly, the court found that the plaintiff in the course of selling the scheme to the defendant had voluntarily divulged the entire scheme. Thus the court was dealing only with a possible breach of confidence concerning a properly discovered secret; there was never a question of any impropriety in the discovery or any other improper conduct on the part of the defendant. * * * We do not read *Furr's* as limiting the trade secret protection to a breach of confidential relationship when the facts of the case do raise the issue of some other wrongful conduct on the part of one discovering the trade secrets of another. If breach of confidence were meant to encompass the entire panoply of commercial improprieties, subsection (a) of the Restatement would be either surplusage or persiflage, an interpretation abhorrent to the traditional precision of the Restatement. We therefore find meaning in subsection (a) and think that the Texas Supreme Court clearly indicated by its adoption that there is a cause of action for the discovery of a trade secret by any "improper means." Hyde Corporation v. Huffines, supra.

The question remaining, therefore, is whether aerial photography of plant construction is an improper means of obtaining another's trade secret. We conclude that it is and that the Texas courts would so hold. The Supreme Court of that state has declared that "the undoubted tendency of the law has been to recognize and enforce higher standards of commercial morality in the business world." Hyde Corporation v. Huffines, supra 314 S.W.2d at 773. That court has quoted with approval articles indicating that the proper means of gaining possession of a competitor's secret process is "through inspection and analysis" of the product in order to create a duplicate. K & G Oil Tool & Service Co. v. G & G Fishing Tool Service, 1958, 158 Tex. 594, 314 S.W.2d 782, 783, 788. * * *

We think, therefore, that the Texas rule is clear. One may use his competitor's secret process if he discovers the process by reverse engineering applied to the finished product; one may use a competitor's process if he discovers it by his own independent research; but one may not avoid these labors by taking the process from the discoverer without his permission at a time when he is taking reasonable precautions to maintain its secrecy. To obtain knowledge of a process without spending the time and money to discover it independently is improper unless the holder voluntarily discloses it or fails to take reasonable precautions to ensure its secrecy.

In the instant case the Christophers deliberately flew over the DuPont plant to get pictures of a process which DuPont had attempted to keep secret. The Christophers delivered their pictures to a third party who was certainly aware of the means by which they had been acquired and who may be planning to use the information contained therein to manufacture methanol by the DuPont process. The third party has a right to use this process only if he obtains this knowledge through his own research efforts, but thus far all information indicates that the third party has gained this knowledge solely by taking it from DuPont at a time when DuPont was making reasonable efforts to preserve its secrecy. In such a situation DuPont has a valid cause of action to prohibit the Christophers from improperly discovering its trade secret and to prohibit the undisclosed third party from using the improperly obtained information.

We note that this view is in perfect accord with the position taken by the authors of the Restatement. In commenting on improper means of discovery the savants of the Restatement said:

> 'f. Improper means of discovery. The discovery of another's trade secret by improper means subjects the actor to liability independently of the harm to the interest in the secret. Thus, if one uses physical force to take a secret formula from another's pocket, or breaks into another's office to steal the formula, his conduct is wrongful and subjects him to liability apart from the rule stated in this Section. Such conduct is also an improper means of procuring the secret under this rule. But means may be improper under this rule even though they do not cause any other harm than that to the interest in the trade secret. Examples of such means are fraudulent misrepresentations to induce disclosure, tapping of telephone wires, eavesdropping or other espionage. A complete catalogue of improper means is not possible. In general they are means which fall below the generally accepted standards of commercial morality and reasonable conduct.'

Restatement of Torts 757, comment f at 10 (1939).

In taking this position we realize that industrial espionage of the sort here perpetrated has become a popular sport in some segments of our industrial community. However, our devotion to free wheeling industrial competition must not force us into accepting the law of the jungle as the standard of morality expected in our commercial relations. Our tolerance of the espionage game must cease when the protections required to prevent another's spying cost so much that the spirit of inventiveness is dampened. Commercial privacy must be protected from espionage which could not have been reasonably anticipated or prevented. We do not mean to imply, however, that everything not in plain view is within the protected vale, nor that all information obtained through every extra optical extension is forbidden. Indeed, for our industrial competition to remain healthy there must be breathing room for observing a competing industrialist. A competitor can and must shop his competition for pricing and examine his products for quality, components, and methods of manufacture. Perhaps ordinary fences and roofs must be built to shut out incursive eyes, but we need not require the discoverer of a trade secret to guard against the unanticipated, the undetectable, or the unpreventable methods of espionage now available.

In the instant case DuPont was in the midst of constructing a plant. Although after construction the finished plant would have protected much of the process from view, during the period of construction the trade secret was exposed to view from the air. To require DuPont to put a roof over the unfinished plant to guard its secret would impose an enormous expense to prevent nothing more than a school boy's trick. * * * Reasonable precautions against predatory eyes we may require, but an impenetrable fortress is an unreasonable requirement, and we are not disposed to burden industrial inventors with such a duty in order to protect the fruits of their efforts. "Improper" will always be a word of many nuances, determined by time, place, and circumstances. We therefore need not proclaim a catalogue of commercial improprieties. Clearly, however, one of its commandments does say "thou shall not appropriate a trade secret through deviousness under circumstances in which countervailing defenses are not reasonably available."

Having concluded that aerial photography, from whatever altitude, is an improper method of discovering the trade secrets exposed during construction of the DuPont plant, we need not worry about whether the flight pattern chosen by the Christophers violated any federal aviation regulations. Regardless of whether the flight was legal or illegal in that sense, the espionage was an improper means of discovering DuPont's trade secret. * * *

Notes

1. Does this decision provide a workable standard or guideline for determining when a competitor or other party is using improper means? For further discussion of trade secret violations based upon improper means, see Restatement (Third) of Unfair Competition § 43 (1995).

2. What measures should a company take to protect its trade secrets? Consider the efficacy of patents, confidentiality agreements, non-competition agreements, general trade secret protection, and security measures such as the ones suggested in *Electro-Craft*.

E. NON–COMPETITION AGREEMENTS

COMPREHENSIVE TECHNOLOGIES INTERNATIONAL v. SOFTWARE ARTISANS, INC.

United States Court of Appeals, Fourth Circuit, 1993.
3 F.3d 730.

WILLIAMS, CIRCUIT JUDGE:

Comprehensive Technologies International, Inc. (CTI), brought this action for copyright infringement against former employees Dean Hawkes, Igor A. Filippides, Randall L. Sterba, Richard T. Hennig, and David R. Bixler (the Defendant employees). CTI also named as defendants Alvan S. Bixler and Software Artisans, Inc. (SA), a corporation formed by Alvan Bixler and several of the Defendant employees shortly after their departure from CTI. CTI contended that "Transend," a computer program developed by the Defendants, infringed upon the copyrights CTI held in its "Claims Express" and "EDI Link" computer programs. CTI * * * alleged that Hawkes breached his covenant not to compete with CTI by performing services for SA, soliciting CTI's customers, and hiring CTI's former employees. After a bench trial, the district court entered judgment for the Defendants on all counts. * * * CTI challenges the district court's conclusion that Hawkes's covenant not to compete with CTI is unreasonable and hence unenforceable under Virginia law. * * *

Each of the Defendant employees except Hawkes signed CTI's standard Confidentiality and Proprietary Information Agreement. Under the Agreement, each employee agreed not to disclose or use, directly or indirectly, during his employment and for three years thereafter any confidential, proprietary, or software-related information belonging to CTI. The Agreement specifically identified the Claims Express and EDI Link projects as confidential. Although Hawkes did not sign a Confidentiality and Proprietary Information Agreement, he did sign an Employment Agreement that contained similar but more restrictive provisions. In addition to promising confidentiality, Hawkes agreed that during the term of his employment he would not compete with CTI, solicit CTI's customers, or employ CTI's current or former employees.

The Software Products Group undertook to develop two software packages for personal computers. The first, Claims Express, is an electronic medical billing system. * * * The program has been successfully marketed. CTI's second software package, EDI Link, is not specific to the health care industry. It is designed to permit users to create generic forms, enter data on the forms electronically, test that data for errors, and store both the forms and the data on a computer. Although CTI expended substantial effort on EDI Link, at the time of trial the program had not been completed and had never been sold or marketed. * * *

In February 1991, all of the Defendant employees left CTI. Hawkes executed a formal Termination Agreement with CTI. In that Agreement, Hawkes agreed to rescind his Employment Agreement in return for $50,000 and more than $20,000 worth of equipment. Hawkes also agreed that he would not disclose or use CTI's confidential information, and that, for a period of one year following his departure, he would not (1) compete with CTI, (2) solicit CTI's customers, or (3) hire CTI's employees.

In April 1991, the Defendants incorporated Software Artisans, Inc., located in Fairfax, Virginia. By July 1991, SA had developed and begun to market its own program called Transend. According to its User's Manual, Transend creates a "paperless office environment" by enabling its users to process business forms on a computer. Transend is similar to Claims Express and EDI Link in that it is designed to prepare forms for transmission by EDI. Transend permits the user to input data, check the data for errors, and prepare the data for transmission by EDI. * * *

IV. COVENANT NOT TO COMPETE

CTI next argues that the district court should have enforced Dean Hawkes's covenant not to compete. In his Termination Agreement, Hawkes agreed that, for a period of twelve months following his departure from CTI, he would not

> engage directly or indirectly in any business within the United States (financially as an investor or lender or as an employee, director, officer, partner, independent contractor, consultant or owner or in any other capacity calling for the rendition of personal services or acts of management, operation or control) which is in competition with the business of CTI. For purposes of this Agreement, the "business of CTI" shall be defined as the design, development, marketing, and sales of CLAIMS EXPRESS) and EDI LINK) type PC-based software with the same functionality and methodology. . . .

Virginia has established a three-part test for assessing the reasonableness of restrictive employment covenants. Under the test, the court must ask the following questions:

> "(1) Is the restraint, from the standpoint of the employer, reasonable in the sense that it is no greater than is necessary to protect the employer in some legitimate business interest?

> (2) From the standpoint of the employee, is the restraint reasonable in the sense that it is not unduly harsh and oppressive in curtailing his legitimate efforts to earn a livelihood?

> (3) Is the restraint reasonable from the standpoint of a sound public policy?"

Blue Ridge Anesthesia & Critical Care, Inc. v. Gidick, 239 Va. 369, 389 S.E.2d 467, 469 (1990) (citation omitted); Meissel v. Finley, 198 Va. 577, 95 S.E.2d 186, 188 (1956). If a covenant not to compete meets each of these standards of reasonableness, it must be enforced. Roanoke Eng'g Sales Co. v. Rosenbaum, 223 Va. 548, 290 S.E.2d 882, 884 (1982). As a general rule, however, the Virginia courts do not look favorably upon covenants not to compete, Grant v. Carotek, Inc., 737 F.2d 410, 411 (4th Cir.1984), and will strictly construe them against the employer, Clinch Valley Physicians, Inc. v. Garcia, 243 Va. 286, 414 S.E.2d 599, 601 (1992); Grant, 737 F.2d at 411. The employer bears the burden of demonstrating that the restraint is reasonable. Richardson v. Paxton Co., 203 Va. 790, 127 S.E.2d 113, 117 (1962).

The district court refused to enforce the covenant not to compete because it concluded that the covenant was broader than necessary to protect CTI's legitimate business interests. * * * We review the enforceability of the covenant not to compete de novo. Brunswick Corp. v. Jones, 784 F.2d 271, 274 n. 2 (7th Cir.1986). CTI asserts that under the facts of this case the employment restrictions were reasonably necessary to protect its business interests.

Although the district court believed that the covenant was categorically overbroad because it precluded Hawkes from working for a competitor of CTI in any capacity, the Virginia Supreme Court has enforced similarly broad restrictions. In *Roanoke Engineering*, the Court enforced a three-year restriction on an employee's right to "own, manage, operate, control, *be employed by*, participate in, or be associated in any manner with the ownership, management, operation or control of any business similar to the type of business conducted by" the employer. Roanoke Eng'g, 290 S.E.2d at 882 (emphasis added). In *Blue Ridge*, the Court upheld a three-year covenant under which the employee could not "open or be employed by or act on behalf of any competitor of Employer which renders the same or similar services as Employer". Blue Ridge, 389 S.E.2d at 468 (emphasis added). The covenant in Hawkes's agreement properly restricts him from competitive employment that would, in all likelihood, substantially interfere with CTI's business.

Moreover, as Vice President of CTI's Software Products Group, Hawkes necessarily came in contact with confidential information concerning both CTI's products and its customers. Hawkes's access to such confidential information makes the covenant not to compete more reasonable. As the Virginia Supreme Court has noted,

> [t]he fact that the employment is of such a character as to inform the employee of business methods and trade secrets which, if brought to the knowledge of a competitor, would prejudice the interests of the employer, tends to give an element of reasonableness to a contract that the employee will not engage in a similar business for a limited time after the termination of his employment, and is always regarded as a strong reason for upholding the contract.

Stoneman, 192 S.E. at 819; Meissel, 95 S.E.2d at 191 (possession of trade secrets and confidential information is an "important consideration" in testing the reasonableness of a restrictive covenant); cf. Community Counselling Serv., Inc. v. Reilly, 317 F.2d 239, 244 (4th Cir.1963) (even in absence of covenant not to compete, employee may not appropriate trade secrets and confidential information rightfully belonging to his former employer). Similarly, in *Roanoke Engineering*, an employee had access to confidential financial records, lists of customers and suppliers, and detailed knowledge of overhead factors, pricing policies, and bidding techniques. Roanoke Eng'g, 290 S.E.2d at 885. The Virginia Supreme Court held that this information enabled the employee to become a "formidable competitor" of his former employer, and concluded that a restriction barring the employee from working for competitors in any capacity was no greater than necessary to protect the employer's legitimate business interests. Id.

Hawkes poses a similar danger to CTI's business. As the individual primarily responsible for the design, development, marketing and sale of CTI's software, Hawkes became intimately familiar with every aspect of CTI's operation, and necessarily acquired information that he could use to compete with CTI in the marketplace. * * * On the facts of this case, we conclude that the scope of the employment restrictions is no broader than necessary to protect CTI's legitimate business interests.

As a second ground for invalidating the covenant not to compete, the district court concluded that the geographic scope of the employment restrictions—"within the United States"—was greater than necessary to protect CTI's business. The district court merely noted that CTI had marketed Claims Express in only three states and therefore did not have a national market for its product.

The district court clearly erred in concluding that CTI did not have a national market for Claims Express. See Fed.R.Civ.P. 52(a) (findings of fact are reviewed for clear error). CTI licensed Claims Express in at least ten states: California, Colorado, Connecticut, Florida, Iowa, Kansas, Maryland, Nebraska, New York, and Oregon. This list alone demonstrates that CTI's customers were dispersed throughout the country and not concentrated in any particular geographic area. CTI's operation was neither local nor regional, but national. Other evidence of a national market for Claims Express was similarly compelling. * * * CTI presented Claims Express and EDI Link (albeit in preliminary form) at national EDIA trade shows in both 1989 and 1990. Finally, CTI presented evidence that it faced direct competition from companies located in California, Colorado, Georgia, Idaho, Illinois, Indiana, Kansas, Maryland, Michigan, Minnesota, New Jersey, Ohio, Oregon, South Carolina, Texas, Utah, and Virginia, and that it faced potential competition from companies in Arizona, California, Georgia, Maryland, North Dakota, Ohio, Oklahoma, Tennessee, and Texas. Given the breadth of the market for Claims Express, we cannot see how anything less than a nationwide prohibition could conceivably protect CTI's business interests. Because CTI had a national market for its product, the restrictions on Hawkes's employment throughout the United States were no greater than necessary to protect it from competition by Hawkes. See Roanoke Eng'g, 290 S.E.2d at 885 (restriction geographically coterminous with territory in which employer did business was reasonable); see also National Homes

Corp. v. Lester Indus., Inc., 404 F.2d 225, 227 (4th Cir.1968) (under Virginia law, injunctive relief against former employee should be extended to entire state, even though employer had record of sales in only widely scattered sections of the state). CTI fully satisfied the first test of reasonableness.

Having determined that the covenant not to compete is reasonable from CTI's point of view, we must next determine whether the covenant is reasonable from Hawkes's point of view, i.e., whether the curtailment on Hawkes's ability to earn a living is unduly harsh or oppressive. Although the agreement applies throughout the United States, it restricts Hawkes from engaging in only an extremely narrow category of business. Hawkes may not render personal services to, or perform acts of management, operation, or control for, any business in competition with "the business of CTI," which the agreement defines as "the design, development, marketing and sales of CLAIMS EXPRESSTM and EDI LINKTM type PC-based software with the same functionality and methodology." The agreement therefore permits Hawkes to design, develop, market and sell any software of a type different from Claims Express or EDI Link, any software of the same type having a different functionality or methodology, or any software of the same type having the same functionality and methodology that is not designed to run on personal computers. Hawkes is also free to compete with any other branch of CTI's business. Because Hawkes retains broad employability under the agreement, the agreement is not unduly harsh or oppressive.

In light of the foregoing, we conclude that the covenant not to compete is no greater than necessary to protect CTI's business and is not unduly harsh or oppressive. Hawkes does not suggest, and we do not find, that the covenant is unreasonable from the standpoint of public policy. We therefore hold that the covenant is enforceable. * * *

MURNAGHAN, CIRCUIT JUDGE, concurring in part and dissenting in part:

While I fully concur with the majority opinion insofar as it disallows recovery on a copyright or trade secrets basis, I reluctantly come to another conclusion with respect to whether CTI, as employer, could enforce as reasonable and not unduly harsh or oppressive the Hawkes covenant not to compete. The covenant not to compete held valid by the majority is operable "within the United States." The district court found that a reasonable covenant would restrict competition only in "Virginia, Nebraska and perhaps one other state." The majority has enhanced CTI's claim to proof of reasonableness by naming 31 states in which CTI has licenses, clients, or potential clients, but that still leaves 19 others, every one of which, it seems to me, is "within the United States." While the majority characterizes CTI's business as "national," it has provided no justification for calling it all inclusive.

The question of validity or not of the non-compete undertaking is one to be decided by the law of the Commonwealth of Virginia. The decision announced by the majority, that a company with business in only 31 states may enforce a non-compete clause in all 50, is a mathematically dubious one on a Virginia point of law. However, the same decision, if announced by the Virginia Supreme Court, would carry more authority than any decision on the point announced by the Fourth Circuit. I feel and have suggested that the question should be certified to the Supreme Court of Virginia. Unfortunately, my colleagues on the panel feel otherwise. Hence, I must make as educated a guess as possible as to what the Virginia law is.[2]

A restraint on an employee is unreasonable if it is greater than is necessary to protect the employer in its legitimate business interest and unreasonable from the employee's standpoint as unduly harsh in curtailing his legitimate efforts to earn his livelihood. * * *

> Because restraints of trade are disfavored in Virginia, we must give effect to the language of the agreement, strictly construed. See Linville v. Servisoft of Virginia, Inc., 211 Va. 53, 55, 174 S.E.2d 785 (1970); Richardson v. Paxton Co., 203 Va. 790, 127 S.E.2d 113 (1962). We construe the agreement, reading it literally and construing it favorably to the employee, as an attempt to impose a post-employment restraint upon Gress [employee] without geographic or other limitation. We must therefore decline Alston's [employer's] invitation to read into the agreement limitations which simply are not there.

Alston Studios, Inc. v. Lloyd V. Gress & Associates, 492 F.2d 279, 285 (4th Cir.1974). "Conceivably the non-competition clause could be interpreted more narrowly, but Virginia law requires that it be strictly construed against the employer...." Grant v. Carotek, Inc., 737 F.2d 410, 412 (4th Cir.1984).

The Supreme Court of Virginia has never approved a non-compete clause that restricts employment "within the United States." To the contrary, Virginia courts have repeatedly held that non-compete clauses should be limited to a geographical area no greater than is necessary to protect the employer's legitimate business interests. Where Virginia courts have enforced non-compete contracts, the contracts have restricted competition only within "quite narrow and well defined geographic limitations." Alston Studios, 492 F.2d at 283 n. 5. See, e.g., Blue Ridge Anesthesia & Critical Care, Inc. v. Gidick, 239 Va. 369, 371, 389 S.E.2d 467, 469 (1990) (covenant that prohibited employment only in territories serviced by the former employee, not in the company's entire market area, enforced); Roanoke Eng'g Sales Co., Inc. v. Rosenbaum, 223 Va. 548, 552, 290 S.E.2d 882, 884 (1982) (three year restriction that broadly limited an employee's right to be employed by any similar business

---

2. In that I have the assistance of the district judge, who has had intimate relationship with Virginia law. "As we have noted in the past 'in determining state law in diversity cases where there is no clear precedent,' we accord 'substantial deference to the opinion of a federal district judge because of his familiarity with the state law which must be applied.'" National Bank of Washington v. Pearson, 863 F.2d 322, 327 (4th Cir.1988). My panel colleagues hail from South Carolina and West Virginia and I from Maryland. The district judge, acting in the Eastern District of Virginia, refused to enforce the covenant because it was geographically overbroad and unreasonably curtailed the employee's legitimate efforts to earn a living.

enforced; court specifically noted that the restriction was reasonable because it was geographically co-terminous with the territory in which the employer did business, which involved only two states); Meissel v. Finley, 198 Va. 577, 581, 95 S.E.2d 186, 190 (1956) (covenant with restrictions that applied only within a radius of 50 miles of Norfolk enforced); Worrie v. Boze, 191 Va. 916, 922–26, 62 S.E.2d 876, 879–81 (1951) (covenant that restricted competition within 25 miles of dance studio enforced); Stoneman v. Wilson, 169 Va. 239, 245, 192 S.E. 816, 818 (1938) (agreement of employee not to go into the hardware business for five years within a limited geographical radius enforced); Power Distribution, Inc. v. Emergency Power Eng'g, 569 F.Supp. 54 (E.D.Va. 1983) (non-compete contract that restrained former employee from employment with anyone in competition with employer found too broad because area in which plaintiff competed was not fixed and thus the limitation could extend "to every location where plaintiff might potentially compete, which included at least the entire United States").

Perhaps the Virginia Supreme Court would agree that the noncompete clause applicable to the employee, Hawkes, was reasonable, but in doing so it would have severely to limit, curtail or even contradict what it has said before. I do not accept that we are free to treat a controlling state rule of law applied by the highest court in the Commonwealth of Virginia so cavalierly.

Accordingly, I would hold the non-compete clause overbroad and hence invalid. I would uphold the district court throughout. So to that extent I dissent.

*

Part V

IDEA PROTECTION

Chapter 10

PROTECTING IDEAS

A. EXPRESS AND IMPLIED CONTRACTS

SELLERS v. AMERICAN BROADCASTING CO.

United States Court of Appeals, Eleventh Circuit, 1982.
668 F.2d 1207.

JOHNSON, CIRCUIT JUDGE:

Plaintiff, Larry L. Sellers, filed a three-count complaint against defendants American Broadcasting Co. (ABC) and Geraldo Rivera, alleging breach of contract, copyright infringement and misappropriation. The district court granted summary judgment in favor of the defendants and plaintiff appeals. We affirm.

In June 1978, Sellers informed Rivera, an investigative reporter occasionally employed by ABC, that he had an "exclusive story" concerning rock-and-roll singer Elvis Presley's death. Before revealing the details, however, Sellers demanded that Rivera sign an agreement guaranteeing him all copyright privileges to the story and requiring ABC to publicly credit him with uncovering the true cause of the singer's death.[1] In return, Sellers agreed to provide ABC and Rivera with the "exclusive story" and further agreed not to release the story to any other network or reporter.[2] Upon execution of the contract, Sellers proceeded to articulate his theory. Sellers recorded the entire conversation and a transcript of the meeting has been made part of the record in this case.

---

1. The entire agreement states: I, Larry L. Sellers, do hereby agree not to release this exclusive story to any reporter other than Geraldo Rivera or any network other than ABC until the network has first released said story within a reasonable period of time or thirty days. Once the story has been released, other media forms may be contacted by Larry Sellers. I, Geraldo Rivera, do hereby agree to grant Larry Sellers all copy-write (sic) privileges of the exclusive Elvis Presley story and full claim for the discovery of the story by acknowledgement in any media use made of it from this day forth. If the story is accepted for further investigation, all expenses incurred by Larry Sellers will be reimbursed by ABC. Should the story be proven false, this contract is hereby null and void.

2. Plaintiff did, however, contact the Atlanta Journal and National Enquirer about his "exclusive story." Neither periodical appears to have published the story.

According to Sellers, cortisone was prescribed for Presley during the three-year period prior to his death. Presley's personal physician and personal bodyguard replaced the cortisone with placebos. Deprivation of the cortisone caused a collapse of Presley's cardiovascular system, resulting in death. Sellers hypothesized that the physician and the bodyguard committed the murder in order to prevent Presley from seeking the repayment of a $1.3 million loan to them to be used for the construction of a racquetball center. As an alternative theory, Sellers postulated that the singer might have been suffocated by either the physician or the bodyguard.

Rivera informed the plaintiff that the story could not be used unless verified. He suggested that plaintiff investigate the matter further and contact him in the event that verification was obtained. Following the conversation with Rivera, Sellers traveled to Memphis on two occasions, apparently in an effort to obtain the needed support for his theory. During the second trip, Sellers called Mrs. Rivera and informed her that he had uncovered proof of his theory but refused to relate to her the nature of the new evidence. The phone call constituted the last time Sellers contacted either Rivera or ABC concerning the story.

More than nine months after signing the agreement with Sellers, Rivera and producer Charles Thomsen decided to do a feature story on Presley's death. After a two-month investigation, it was determined that Presley died of polypharmacy (interaction of prescription drugs) and not cardiac arrhythmia as officially listed. ABC broadcast an hour-long special concerning the information uncovered during the "Rivera–Thomsen" investigation. Geraldo Rivera appeared on the program as a correspondent. ABC also did a number of follow-up stories on Presley's death. In neither the hour-long special nor the follow-up stories did the network suggest that Presley was murdered by a withdrawal of cortisone or by suffocation.

Sellers brought suit contending that ABC and Rivera misappropriated his "exclusive story" concerning the singer's death. Sellers also asserted claims for breach of contract and copyright infringement. The district court entered summary judgment for defendants. The court determined that plaintiff's "exclusive story" consisted of the theory that Presley had been murdered by his bodyguard and his personal physician through a deprivation of cortisone. Since ABC and Rivera did not use Sellers' "exclusive story" in any of their broadcasts, the court concluded that there had not been any misappropriation or breach of the written agreement.

On appeal, Sellers contends that a dispute of material fact exists concerning the precise scope of his "exclusive story" and, accordingly, summary judgment was improvidently granted. Sellers asserts that he informed Rivera not only of the possibility that Presley might have been murdered through a deprivation of cortisone, but also that the cause of death might have been the interaction of numerous prescription drugs, that the singer's personal physician may have been grossly negligent in overprescribing drugs for Presley and that there had been a cover-up of the true cause of death. Assuming without deciding that Sellers did present these additional theories to Rivera,[3] we nonetheless conclude that they are so vague and uncertain as to be unenforceable as a matter of law.

Under New York law, a contract will not be enforced if an essential element is vague, indefinite or incomplete. Brown & Guenther v. North Queensview Homes, Inc., 18 A.D.2d 327, 239 N.Y.S.2d 482, 484 (1963); Campbell v. WABC Towing Corp., N.Y.Sup., 356 N.Y.S.2d 455, 457 (S.Ct.1974). See also 1 A. CORBIN, CONTRACTS § 95, at 394 (1950) ("Vagueness of expression, indefiniteness and uncertainty as to any of the essential terms of an agreement, have often been held to prevent the creation of an enforceable duty."). A complete review of the transcribed meeting between the parties shows that at best Sellers made broad, general statements concerning the possibility of overdose, gross negligence by the personal physician and a cover-up. The transcript demonstrates that plaintiff failed to provide any substantiating details for these vague allegations. He did not make clear whether Presley's death resulted from a single drug or a combination of drugs. He made no effort to provide the name of any specific drug that had been overprescribed by the personal physician. Nor did plaintiff show that medication unnecessary for the treatment of the singer's illnesses was prescribed for Presley. Finally, references to books and newspaper articles[5] constituted the only support for these vague and uncertain statements. Sellers' theory that Presley was murdered by a withdrawal of cortisone may well have been specific enough to give rise to an enforceable agreement. The district court, however, concluded that the defendants did not utilize the cortisone-murder theory in any of their broadcasts and did not, therefore, breach the agreement. Plaintiff does not challenge this conclusion on appeal.

As to plaintiff's remaining claim,[6] New York courts will permit recovery for the misappropriation of an idea or theory if (1) the idea is novel; (2) the idea is in a concrete form; and (3) the defendant makes use of the idea. Galanis v. Proctor and Gamble Corp., 153 F.Supp. 34, 38

---

3. A review of the transcribed meeting between the parties reflects that Sellers never specifically told Rivera that the personal physician may have been grossly negligent in overprescribing Presley. Moreover, the lone reference at the meeting to the possibility that Presley died of the interaction of drugs in his body was made by Sellers in passing and appears to be nothing more than background information. * * *

5. We note that at least a portion of plaintiff's "exclusive story", particularly the theory that Presley died from an interaction of drugs, appeared in a number of newspaper articles prior to his discussion with Rivera. Under New York law, an idea

or theory does not constitute property and will not support the right to recover in contract unless original. Downey v. General Foods Corp., 31 N.Y.2d 56, 334 N.Y.S.2d 874, 877, 286 N.E.2d 257 (1972). Thus, to the extent plaintiff's "exclusive story" was already widely disseminated and in the public domain, he cannot recover in contract for the use of his theory by the defendants.

6. The district court concluded that plaintiff had not copyrighted his "exclusive story" and was therefore not entitled to recover for copyright infringement. The plaintiff does not challenge this determination on appeal.

(S.D.N.Y.1957). We conclude that Sellers' theory that Presley died of an interaction of prescription drugs was neither novel, unique nor original. Plaintiff's own exhibits show that a number of newspapers had speculated that Presley's death might have been drug-related long before the meeting between Sellers and Rivera. As to Sellers' other vague theories, we conclude that they were not sufficiently concrete to give rise to a cause of action for misappropriation.

For the reasons stated herein, judgment for the defendants is AFFIRMED.

Notes

1. If ABC and Rivera had used the "Elvis cortisone" conspiracy story in a feature segment, would they have been liable? If so, what legal theory would be available? Would it make a difference if the story were not entirely novel, *i.e.*, if it had been reported elsewhere previously?

2. Given its importance in the entertainment field, California law is particularly important in the area of idea protection. The following excerpt is from Blaustein v. Burton, 9 Cal.App.3d 161, 88 Cal.Rptr. 319 (1970). In that case, the plaintiff had submitted to Richard Burton's agent the idea of making a motion picture based upon William Shakespeare's play, "The Taming of the Shrew". Although the plaintiff was never paid or credited for this idea, the motion picture was produced and exhibited in March 1967. The motion picture used several ideas specifically disclosed by the plaintiff: (1) it was based upon the Shakespearean play, "The Taming of the Shrew"; (2) Elizabeth Taylor and Richard Burton played the roles of Katherine and Petruchio; (3) the director was Franco Zeffirelli; (4) the movie eliminated the "frame", *i.e.*, the-play-within-a-play device found in the original Shakespearean play, and begins with the main body of the story; (5) it includes an enactment of two key scenes suggested by the plaintiff, both of which in Shakespeare's play occur off-stage; and (6) the film was photographed in Italy.

The evidence indicated that the plaintiff's suggestions were not particularly novel or original, and the defendants sought to avoid contract liability on this basis:

> Appellant [the plaintiff] testified in his deposition that there is nothing unique about doing Shakespeare on the screen. It has been done many times. It has been done by leading stars of the calibre of Laurence Olivier. Respondent Richard Burton has himself previously appeared in a motion picture made of Shakespeare's Hamlet. Shakespearean productions in motion picture form have been made in the United States, with leading stars, and also in England, the Soviet Union and other countries of the world.

> Appellant testified that there is nothing unique about the idea of making a motion picture entitled "The Taming of the Shrew," based on Shakespeare's play of that title. Such has been done in the United States before the making of the film here in issue, and the earlier film featured in its leading roles (Petruchio and Katherine) stars who were

then married to each other and who were perhaps the leading idols of the screen at the time, Mary Pickford and Douglas Fairbanks. The Pickford–Fairbanks film "The Taming of the Shrew" was done in the 1930's. The declaration of Norman B. Rudman filed in support of the motion disclosed that the earlier version of the film also (1) eliminated the "frame" (the play within a play device utilized by Shakespeare), and (2) depicted on screen the wedding night scenes which in the Shakespearean original occurs off-stage and are merely described by narration.

Appellant testified in his deposition that there was nothing unique or unusual about doing The Taming of the Shrew with two of the leading actors of the time, in the sense that it had been done once before, but "there was something unusual about the particular notion of doing it under other circumstances." There is nothing unique about a stage director of good repute coming directly from the stage to motion pictures and directing a major motion picture. Such has been done often in the past by such directors as Ruben Mamoulian, Josh Logan, Danny Mann, Orson Welles, Eliah Kazan, and by Mike Nichols, who directed the film "Who's Afraid of Virginia Woolf," which starred the respondents in its leading roles, as his first film production.

The court held that the plaintiff's claim should nonetheless go to the jury:

From what has been shown respecting the law of ideas and of contracts we conclude that conveyance of an idea can constitute valuable consideration and can be bargained for before it is disclosed to the proposed purchaser, but once it is conveyed, i.e., disclosed to him and he has grasped it, it is henceforth his own and he may work with it and use it as he sees fit. In the field of entertainment the producer may properly and validly agree that he will pay for the service of conveying to him ideas which are valuable and which he can put to profitable use. * * * But, assuming legality of consideration, the idea purveyor cannot prevail in an action to recover compensation for an abstract idea unless (a) before or after disclosure he has obtained an express promise to pay, or (b) the circumstances preceding and attending disclosure, together with the conduct of the offeree acting with knowledge of the circumstances, show a promise of the type usually referred to as 'implied' or 'implied-in-fact.' That is, if the idea purveyor has clearly conditioned his offer to convey the idea upon an obligation to pay for it if it is used by the offeree and the offeree, knowing the condition before he knows the idea, voluntarily accepts its disclosure (necessarily on the specified basis) and finds it valuable and uses it, the law will either apply the objective test and hold that the parties have made an express (sometimes called implied-in-fact) contract, or under those circumstances, as some writers view it, the law itself, to prevent fraud and unjust enrichment, will imply a promise to compensate.

Such inferred or implied promise, if it is to be found at all, must be based on circumstances which were known to the producer at and preceding the time of disclosure of the idea to him and he must voluntarily accept the disclosure, knowing the conditions on which it is tendered. Section 1584 of the Civil Code ('[T]he acceptance of the consideration offered with a proposal, is an acceptance of the proposal') can have no application unless the offeree has an opportunity to reject the consideration—the proffered conveyance of the idea—before it is conveyed. Unless the offeree has opportunity to reject he cannot be said to accept. The idea man who blurts out his idea without having first made his bargain has no one but himself to blame for the loss of his bargaining power. The law will not in any event, from demands stated subsequent to the unconditioned disclosure of an abstract idea, imply a promise to pay for the idea, for its use, or for its previous disclosure. The law will not imply a promise to pay for an idea from the mere facts that the idea has been conveyed, is valuable, and has been used for profit; this is true even though the conveyance has been made with the hope or expectation that some obligation will ensue. * * *" (Desny v. Wilder, Supra, 46 Cal.2d 715, 731—739, 299 P.2d 257, 265—270.)

It is held that " * * * if a producer obligates himself to pay for the disclosure of an idea, whether it is for protectible or unprotectible material, in return for a disclosure thereof he should be compelled to hold to his promise. There is nothing unreasonable in the assumption that a producer would obligate himself to pay for the disclosure of an idea which he would otherwise be legally free to use, but which in fact, he would be unable to use but for the disclosure."

"The producer and the writer should be free to make any contract they desire to make with reference to the buying of the ideas of the writer; the fact that the producer may later determine, with a little thinking, that he could have had the same ideas and could thereby have saved considerable money for himself, is no defense against the claim of the writer. This is so even though the material to be purchased is abstract and unprotected material." (Chandler v. Roach, 156 Cal.App.2d 435, 441—442, 319 P.2d 776, 781.) An idea which can be the subject matter of a contract need not be novel or concrete.

See also Desny v. Wilder, 46 Cal.2d 715, 299 P.2d 257 (1956) (prior disclosure of idea can give rise to contractual obligation to pay when promise is made to do so, even though prior disclosure could be considered "past consideration"). More recently, Art Buchwald prevailed in a suit against Paramount Pictures based on his contract providing for payment if Paramount made a film based on his idea, which was concededly not an original one. When Paramount made "Coming to America," it found itself held liable for damages under California contract law. See Gail D. Cox, African Kings, Movie Studios, and Rip-offs?, National Law Journal, Jan. 15, 1990, p. 7.

B. UNJUST ENRICHMENT OR QUASI–CONTRACT

MATARESE v. MOORE–McCORMACK LINES, INC.
United States Court of Appeals, Second Circuit, 1946.
158 F.2d 631.

CLARK, CIRCUIT JUDGE.

This appeal raises the issue whether a corporation may be required to pay the reasonable value of the use of certain inventive ideas disclosed by an employee to an agent of the corporation in the expectation of payment where an express contract fails for want of proof of the agent's authority. Here the plaintiff, being refused compensation, brought suit upon an alleged express contract to pay one-third of the savings realized by the defendants through the use of his devices. * * * During the trial plaintiff abandoned his theory and, over the objections of defendants, amended his complaint by adding a prayer for recovery of quantum meruit upon the theory of unjust enrichment. The court submitted the case to the jury upon this theory, and it returned a verdict for plaintiff for $90,000. This, upon motion, the district judge ordered set aside unless the plaintiff consented to its reduction to the sum of $40,000. The plaintiff so consented, judgment was entered for the latter sum, and defendants appeal.

The plaintiff is a man of little education, who, emigrating to this country from Italy some forty-six years ago, had always worked around the docks and in 1938 was employed as a part-time stevedore on defendants' pier. His case, which the jury quite obviously must have accepted in full, was that in August of that year he informed Furey, defendants' agent in charge of the pier, that he had something which would facilitate cargo loading and unloading, thus saving the defendants much money and preventing the numerous accidents ordinarily occurring at the pier. So, at plaintiff's invitation, Furey made a special trip to plaintiff's home in the Coney Island section of Brooklyn and was there shown models of devices for loading and unloading cargo which the plaintiff had invented. Present were not only plaintiff and Furey, but also plaintiff's son and a friend named Devereaux, all of whom handled the models in an operational demonstration. All of these were witnesses at the trial; and even Furey, testifying for the defendants, admitted the visit to plaintiff's home and the demonstration of the models, while denying any further commitments upon his part. According to plaintiff and his witnesses, however, Furey expressed his satisfaction with the models and promised the plaintiff one-third of what the defendants would save by use of the device. He suggested that plaintiff patent his device and offered to be the plaintiff's partner in exploiting it. He also offered the plaintiff the job of supervising the construction of his devices for defendants on the defendants' premises and with the defendants' materials. Plaintiff accepted the job and continued to receive longshoreman's pay until the end of the year, when, presumably, he received gearman's pay. After a full-scale test of plaintiff's devices, defendants put a great number of them into use at the pier under Furey's charge and at other piers subsequently acquired by them. From time to time plaintiff asked Furey about his money, and Furey always assured him that he would be compensated in the future. In 1941, however, Furey sent plaintiff to another agent of the defendants, who discharged him from his job. This action was commenced in April, 1943.

Meanwhile on January 28, 1939, plaintiff applied for a patent. The application was divided in the patent office in 1940, and on March 18, 1941, plaintiff was issued two patents. One was for a "cargo loading and unloading apparatus," consisting of a reversible 5' x 4' wooden pallet, and a flexible bridle, a guiding frame, a mesh net, and lifting bars to transport the pallet between ship and pier. The other was for a "cargo loading and unloading platform," or stationary wooden platform attached to, and extending out from, the pier. Defendants objected to the admission of these patents in evidence, asserting that they were "secretly after-acquired" grants which were invalid for want of invention and that their admission was highly prejudicial on plaintiff's claim of novel invention. But the question of validity of the patents was not involved, and the court very carefully explained to the jury that it was not. The patents, however, were properly admitted, as part of the history of events between the parties, taken pursuant to Furey's direction and plan of retaining the benefit to defendants alone.

The main legal issue of the appeal turns, therefore, upon the validity of plaintiff's claim of unjust enrichment under the circumstances of this case. * * * Defendants * * * claim that, since Furey was not shown to have been authorized in the premises, none of the negotiations were admissible in evidence. They claim that the admission of the negotiations necessitated "repeated and continuous objections" by them which, when overruled, "seriously prejudiced the defendants in the eyes of the jury." But the showing of grounds for a reasonable expectation of compensation was a necessary part of the plaintiff's case, as he conceived it, and the number and amount of objections needed by defendants to present their own theory was a matter of their own free choice. These subordinate issues therefore simply lead back to the main question of the legal validity of the case submitted by the court to the determination of the jury.

The doctrine of unjust enrichment or recovery in quasi-contract obviously does not deal with situations in which the party to be charged has by word or deed legally consented to assume a duty toward the party seeking to charge him. Instead, it applies to situations where as a matter of fact there is no legal contract, but where the person sought to be charged is in possession of money or property which in good conscience and justice he should not retain, but should deliver to another. Miller v. Schloss, 218 N.Y. 400, 407, 113 N.E. 337; Byxbie v. Wood, 24 N.Y. 607, 610; White v. Continental Nat. Bank, 64 N.Y. 316, 21 Am.Rep. 612; Oneida County v. First Citizens Bank & Trust Co. of Utica, 264 App.Div. 212, 35 N.Y.S.2d 782; 1 Williston on Contracts, Rev. Ed. 1936, Sec. 3, p. 9. Where this is true the courts impose a duty to refund the money or the use value of the property to the person to whom in good conscience it ought to belong. Restatement, Restitution, 1937, Sec. 1(a); Pullman's Palace–Car Co. v. Central Transp. Co., 171 U.S. 138, 152, 18 S.Ct. 808, 43 L.Ed. 108. The doctrine is applicable to a situation where, as here, the product of an inventor's brain is knowingly received and used by another to his own great benefit without compensating the inventor. This is recognized in the leading New York case of Bristol v. Equitable Life Assur. Soc. of United States, 132 N.Y. 264, 267, 30 N.E. 506, 507, 28 Am.St.Rep. 568. In that case the New York Court of Appeals dismissed a complaint based on the use by defendant of an advertising scheme of which plaintiff had apprised it, because the scheme was not original and because it was not alleged to be marketable. The court, however, was careful to distinguish the situation in which an invention is involved, saying: "In such cases (of inventions) there is a production which can by multiplying copies be put to marketable use, * * * . Whoever infringes takes benefits or profits which otherwise would naturally come to the producer." * * *

Courts have justly been assiduous in defeating attempts to delve into the pockets of business firms through spurious claims for compensation for the use of ideas. Thus to be rejected are attempts made by telephoning or writing vague general ideas to business corporations and then seizing upon some later general similarity between their products and the notions propounded as a basis for damages. See Grombach Productions v. Waring, 293 N.Y. 609, 59 N.E.2d 425; Lueddecke v. Chevrolet Motor Co., 8 Cir., 70 F.2d 345. Such schemes are quite different from the situation envisaged in the *Bristol* case, supra, and that at bar. Here the relationship between the parties before and after the disclosure, the seeking of disclosure by Furey, Furey's promise of compensation, the specific character, novelty, and patentability of plaintiff's invention, the subsequent use made of it by defendants, and the lack of compensation given the plaintiff—all indicate that the application of the principle of unjust enrichment is required. Miller v. Schloss, supra.

Defendants, relying upon the concession of lack of proof of Furey's authority to make the contract as originally alleged, claim a like lack of authority to accept the benefit of plaintiff's ideas to such an extent as to make them liable to pay reasonable compensation therefor. Such liability, they assert, could be based only on an extensive and fearsome corporate responsibility to pay for all chance ideas of an employee unwittingly utilized by the corporation. We may pass the interesting question how far an unwitting appropriation of property in ideas may create liability, since the case was presented and submitted to the jury on the theory of valuable services rendered by the plaintiff either to the knowledge of the defendants or "at the instance of someone authorized to obtain such services for the defendant." * * *

This charge, it seems to us, was justified upon the record. There was evidence that plaintiff was authorized by Furey to manufacture his devices using defendants' workmen and materials; that his devices were demonstrated on the pier in the presence of Furey "and all the rest of the officials, foreman and all"; that he was directed to go ahead with the manufacture of the pallets, something with which previously he had nothing to do; that he then went to work full time for defendants; and that Furey was promoted in the fall of 1938 from Stevedore Superintendent to Chief of Operations, an executive position with wide powers and an increase of pay. Furey's denial that these changes and advances were due to the utilization of plaintiff's ideas was of course offset not merely by plaintiff's testimony, but by such matters as Furey's specific written direction to plaintiff on December 20, 1938, for the making up of twenty-four pallets, together with numerous wire nets, frames, and bridles, for delivery by Saturday morning, December 30. Moreover, Commodore Lee, defendants' executive vice-president, visited the docks regularly at least once a week, knew the plaintiff and spoke to him at work, and saw the extensive use of his devices at this period. It would seem that an inference of actual knowledge by Lee would be justifiable under the circumstances; but in any event Furey's position by that time in the corporate structure was surely sufficiently high to justify his accepting for the company the benefits of more efficient stevedoring. It is true that defendants presented some evidence of use by them of pallets and loading platforms similar to plaintiff's on other operations in Philadelphia and perhaps in New York as early as 1937; but the evaluation of this evidence was of course for the jury, who may indeed have been unfavorably impressed by the somewhat halting and vague nature of the testimony from a responsible company official as to a matter which would seem capable of definite and exact proof.

With the issue of unjust enrichment settled in favor of plaintiff, the final major issue was as to the rate of compensation. The judge properly charged that recovery must be based upon the "reasonable value of the use" of the devices and the "reasonable value of the services" rendered by the plaintiff. Pullman's Pallace–Car Co. v. Central Transp. Co., supra; Restatement, Restitution, 1937, Sec. 1(a). Defendants contend that there was not sufficient proof of damages, either in fact or in amount, to justify submission of the case to the jury.

Plaintiff's evidence was, however, adequate to show extensive gross savings earned for the defendants by his devices. Thus the loading platforms attached to the piers saved the defendants expense of additional labor, since they remained stationary and level with the pier, despite the movements of the tide. * * *

[The court then summarized the manner in which the defendant's operations were streamlined and the consequent reduction in labor and materials.] Thus the amount of money saved per pier a year by the use of plaintiff's pallets in the actual loading and unloading operations only could be found to be about $140,000. The defendants in 1941 operated ten piers, and the plaintiff's devices were used on all of them. Moreover, the period of time for which damages were recovered extends to the date on which the verdict was given, in December, 1945. Restatement, Restitution, 1937, Sec. 157(c). The total gross savings from the use of both platforms and unloading apparatus on all piers were obviously much higher than the yearly per pier figures.

Since the amounts thus indicated are much higher than the award as finally made, the only question arises because plaintiff did not offer evidence on the cost to the defendants of producing the plaintiff's devices. Records containing this information were of course in the possession of the defendants. Plaintiff did, however, prove the fact of damages; and the amount of damages could be determined as a matter of just and reasonable inference from the plaintiff's evidence. * * * The rule which proscribes the recovery of uncertain and speculative damages applies where the fact of damages is uncertain, not where the amount is uncertain. Where the fact of damages is certain, the uncertainty of the amount will not prevent their being assessed. * * * [T]he failure of defendants to introduce their cost records as part of their case tends to indicate that the cost of production might not be very high relative to the savings effected through the use of plaintiff's devices. Under the relevant principles of law here stated and the evidence introduced at the trial, the damages ultimately awarded were not excessive.

Affirmed.

Notes

1. What specific showing must a plaintiff make in order to recover under the legal theory presented in this case? Will plaintiffs be able to make this showing very often?

2. What is the relevance of Matarese's patents in this case? Why does patent law not provide him with a remedy against his former employer?

SMITH v. RECRION CORP.

Supreme Court of Nevada, 1975.
91 Nev. 666, 541 P.2d 663.

ZENOFF, JUSTICE:

Gilbert C. Smith, while employed as a keno writer by the Stardust Hotel in Las Vegas, conceived that a recreational vehicle park constructed and operated as a part of the luxury hotel would be a profitable idea. After developing a brochure somewhat detailing his idea, he arranged for and had a meeting with Allan Sachs, General Manager of the Stardust, later to become President. The hotel was owned and operated by Recrion Corporation through its subsidiary Karat, Inc.

After presenting the idea to Sachs, Smith indicated that he desired to be compensated in the form of an unspecified amount of money or by participation in the venture in an executive capacity. Sachs expressed no interest in the proposal except to suggest that Smith contact him at a later date. Smith's subsequent attempts to meet with Sachs were unsuccessful and culminated in a note from Sachs' secretary stating simply that Mr. Sachs was not interested.

Two years later, the Stardust opened a recreational vehicle park known as "Camperland" adjacent to the hotel. The project had been initiated and carried forward by the Stardust Director of Public Relations, Dick Odessky.

After the opening of Camperland, asserting that the hotel had implemented his idea, Smith made several demands for compensation; all of which were refused. Finally, Smith requested a letter from Sachs acknowledging that the Camperland idea was his. The letter was never forthcoming. Smith sued for money damages, claiming he was entitled to compensation upon alternate theories of express contract, implied contract, contract implied in law (quasi contract), common law copyright and fraud. Smith appeals from the summary judgment granted in favor of respondents. * * *

1. The terms of an express contract are stated in words while those of an implied contract are manifested by conduct. Youngman v. Nevada Irrigation District, 70 Cal.2d 240, 74 Cal.Rptr. 398, 449 P.2d 462 (1969). Both types of contracts are founded upon an ascertainable agreement. Horacek v. Smith, 33 Cal.2d 186, 199 P.2d 929 (1948). Here, there is no evidence that the parties expressly contracted for the purchase and sale of Smith's idea. Smith only alleged that he expected compensation, not that he was promised compensation.

In order to prevail on the theory of a contract implied in fact, the court would necessarily have to determine that both parties intended to contract, Horacek v. Smith, supra, and that promises were exchanged; the crucial promise being that of Sachs to compensate Smith. There is no evidence of conduct on the part of Sachs suggesting an intention to enter into a contract with Smith, nor any evidence from which it would be inferred that he promised to compensate Smith.

There being no evidence of contractual intent or the exchange of mutual promises, express or implied, there was no genuine issue of fact.

Prior to the time Smith and Sachs first met to discuss Smith's idea, Sachs had no knowledge of the purpose of the meeting. Smith's idea was entirely unsolicited and he voluntarily disclosed his idea before the subject of compensation had been discussed. Even if Sachs subsequently promised Smith compensation, the promise would be unenforceable for the reason that it would have been unsupported by consideration. Past consideration is the legal equivalent to no consideration. Murray v. Lichtman, 119 U.S.App.D.C. 250, 339 F.2d 749, 752 n. 5 (1964). An abstract idea cannot be protected by an express or implied contract unless the contract was made before the disclosure of the idea. See e.g., Hampton v. La Salle Hat Company, 88 F.Supp. 153 (S.D.N.Y.1949); Oxenhandler v. Dime Savings Bank of Brooklyn, 33 Misc.2d 626, 227 N.Y.S.2d 642 (1962); Desny v. Wilder, 46 Cal.2d 715, 299 P.2d 257 (1956).

2. Neither statutory nor common law copyright protects against the borrowing of ideas as distinguished from the expression of such ideas. 2 M. B. Nimmer, Nimmer on Copyright 715, § 166 (1975). Generally, abstract ideas will not be protected without a showing of 'concreteness' and 'novelty.' Concreteness pertains to the developmental stage of the idea, i.e., the idea must be sufficiently developed as to constitute a protectable interest. An idea in order to meet the test of concreteness must be ready for immediate use without any additional embellishment. Novelty pertains to originality and, in some jurisdictions, the innovative character of the idea. * * *

Smith's idea does not meet the test of concreteness. His brochure was hardly capable of "immediate use without any additional embellishment." The most that can be said is that respondents may have gleaned the raw idea of a recreational vehicle part from Smith. However, to develop that idea to the point where it was ripe for implementation required extensive investigation, research and planning.

3.   An idea must also meet the test of concreteness and novelty before its author is entitled to quasi contractual recovery. Smith is denied compensation on the theory of quasi contract for this reason and for the reason that the idea was entirely unsolicited. One who officiously confers a benefit on another is not entitled to compensation therefor. Weitzenkorn v. Lesser, 40 Cal.2d 778, 256 P.2d 947 (1953); Krisel v. Duran, D.C., 303 F.Supp. 573, aff'd, 2 Cir., 424 F.2d 1367, cert. denied, 400 U.S. 964, 91 S.Ct. 367, 27 L.Ed.2d 384 (1970); Stein v. Simpson, 37 Cal.2d 79, 230 P.2d 816 (1951).

4.   Nor can Smith recover on the ground of fraud. As a necessary element of proving fraud Smith must show that he was deceived by false representations to the effect that he would receive compensation for disclosing his idea. It is clear from the record that his idea was unsolicited and voluntarily disclosed prior to any discussion of compensation by either party. All discussions regarding compensation were initiated by Smith. There was no fraud.

Summary judgment was appropriate. Affirmed.

DOWNEY v. GENERAL FOODS CORP.

Court of Appeals of New York, 1972.
31 N.Y.2d 56, 334 N.Y.S.2d 874, 286 N.E.2d 257.

FULD, CHIEF JUDGE.

The plaintiff, an airline pilot, brought this action against the defendant General Foods Corporation to recover damages for the alleged misappropriation of an idea.[1] It is his claim that he suggested that the defendant's own gelatin product, "Jell–O," be named "Wiggley" or a variation of that word, including "Mr. Wiggle," and that the product be directed towards the children's market; that, although the defendant disclaimed interest in the suggestion, it later offered its product for sale under the name "Mr. Wiggle." The defendant urges—by way of affirmative defense—that the plaintiff's "alleged 'product concept and name' was independently created and developed" by it. * * *

The plaintiff relies chiefly on correspondence between himself and the defendant, or, more precisely, on letters over the signature of a Miss Dunham, vice-president in charge of one of its departments. On February 15, 1965, the plaintiff wrote to the defendant, stating that he had an "excellent idea to increase the sale of your product JELL–O * * * making it available for children". Several days later, the defendant sent the plaintiff an "Idea Submittal Form" (ISF) which included a form

---

1. Although the complainant's demand was for $34,600,000, that amount was changed, by stipulation, to $2,800,000, representing $200,000 of damages for each of the complainant's 14 causes of action.

letter and a space for explaining the idea.[2] In that form, the plaintiff suggested, in essence, that the produce "be packaged & distributed to children under the name 'WIG–L–E' (meaning wiggly or wiggley) or 'WIGGLE–E' or 'WIGGLE–EEE' or 'WIGLEY.' "He explained that, although his children did not "get especially excited about the Name JELL–O, or wish to eat it", when referred to by that name, "the kids really took to it fast" when his wife "called it wiggle-y," noting that they then "associate(d) the name to the 'wiggleing' dessert." Although this is the only recorded proof of his idea, the plaintiff maintains that he sent Miss Dunham two handwritten letters in which he set forth other variations of "Wiggiley," including "Mr. Wiggley, Wiggle, Wiggle-e."[3]

A letter, dated March 8, 1965, over the signature of Miss Dunham, acknowledged the submission of the ISF and informed the plaintiff that it had no interest in promoting his suggestion. However, in July, the defendant introduced into the market a Jell–O product which it called "Mr. Wiggle." The plaintiff instituted the present action some months later. In addition to general denials, the answer contains several affirmative defenses, one of which, as indicated above, recites that the defendant independently created the product's concept and name before the plaintiff's submission to it.

In support of its position, the defendant pointed to depositions taken by the plaintiff from its employees and from employees of Young & Rubicam, the firm which did its advertising. From these it appears that the defendant first began work on a children's gelatin product in May, 1965—three months after the plaintiff had submitted his suggestion—in response to a threat by Pillsbury Company to enter the children's market with a product named "Jiggly." Those employees of the defendant in charge of the project enlisted the aid of Young & Rubicam which, solely on its own initiative, "came up with the name 'Mr. Wiggle' ". In point of fact, Miss Dunham swore in her deposition that she had had no knowledge whatever of the plaintiff's idea until late in 1966, shortly before commencement of his suit; that ideas submitted by the general public were kept in a file by an assistant of hers "under lock and key"; and that no one from any other of the defendant's departments ever asked to research those files. The assistant, who had alone handled the correspondence with the plaintiff over Miss Dunham's signature—reproduced by means of a signature duplicating machine—deposed that she had no contact whatsoever with Young & Rubicam and had never discussed the name "Wiggle" or "Mr. Wiggle" with any one from that firm.

2. The form letter—signed and returned by the plaintiff—recited that "I submit this suggestion with the understanding, which is conclusively evidenced by my use and transmittal to you of this form, that this suggestion is not submitted to you in confidence, that no confidential relationship has been or will be established between us and that the use, if any, to be made of this suggestion by you and the compensation to be paid therefor, if any, if you use it, are matters resting solely in your discretion."

3. Neither of these letters was found in the defendant's files, nor did the plaintiff have the originals or exact copies.

In addition to the depositions of its employees and the employees of its advertising agency, the defendant submitted documentary proof of its prior use of some form of the word "wiggle" in connection with its endeavor to sell Jell–O to children. Thus, it submitted (1) a copy of a report which Young & Rubicam furnished it in June of 1959 proposing "an advertising program directed at children as a means of securing additional sales volume"; (2) a copy of a single dimensional reproduction of a television commercial, prepared in 1959 and used thereafter by the defendant in national and local television broadcasts, which contained the phrase, "ALL THAT WIGGLES IS NOT JELL–O"; and (3) a copy of a newspaper advertisement that appeared in 1960, depicting an Indian "squaw" puppet and her "papoose" preparing Jell–O—the "top favorite in every American tepee"—and suggesting to mothers that they "(m)ake a wigglewam of Jell–O for your tribe tonight!"

The critical issue in this case turns on whether the idea suggested by the plaintiff was original or novel. An idea may be a property right. But, when one submits an idea to another, no promise to pay for its use may be implied, and no asserted agreement enforced, if the elements of novelty and originality are absent, since the property right in an idea is based upon these two elements. See Bram v. Dannon Milk Prods., 33 A.D.2d 1010, 307 N.Y.S.2d 571. * * *

In the case before us, the record indisputably establishes, first, that the idea submitted—use of a word ("wiggley" or "wiggle") descriptive of the most obvious characteristic of Jell–O, with the prefix "Mr." added— was lacking in novelty and originality and, second, that the defendant had envisaged the idea, indeed had utilized it, years before the plaintiff submitted it. As already noted, it had made use of the word "wiggles" in a 1959 television commercial and the word "wigglewam" in a 1960 newspaper advertisement. It was but natural, then, for the defendant to employ some variation of it to combat Pillsbury's entry into the children's market with its "Jiggly." Having relied on its own previous experience, the defendant was free to make use of "Mr. Wiggle" without being obligated to compensate the plaintiff. * * *

Notes

1. In light of this series of decisions, what advice would you give to an individual seeking to submit an idea in return for compensation? What advice would you give to companies seeking to avoid baseless claims from idea submitters?

2. Does trade secret law provide a means of protecting innovative ideas? Do you think that patents or copyrights might solve the problem? What about the misappropriation theory set forth in *INS v. AP, supra* Chapter 1? The Restatement (Third) of Unfair Competition endorses the view that this legal theory should be abolished. See Restatement (Third) of Unfair Competition, § 38, comments b & c; see also Gary Myers, The Restatement's Rejection of the Misappropriation Tort: A Victory for the Public Domain, 47 S.C. L. Rev. 673 (1996). A recent case involving this

theory is National Basketball Association v. Motorola, Inc., 105 F.3d 841 (2d Cir.1997), which is excerpted in Chapter 21 *infra*. The National Basketball Association (NBA) sued for an injunction preventing the manufacturer of a handheld pager from transmitting NBA basketball scores or other data about games in progress via the pagers, absent authorization from the NBA. The district court issued a permanent injunction in the NBA's favor. The Second Circuit reversed and dismissed the NBA's claim for misappropriation, holding that only a narrow "hot news" misappropriation claim survived preemption for actions concerning material within the realm of copyright. The court found the additional elements that allowed a "hot news" claim to survive preemption were: (1) the plaintiff generates or gathers information at some cost; (2) the information is time sensitive; (3) the defendant's use of the information constitutes free riding upon the plaintiff's investment; (4) the defendant is in direct competition with the plaintiff; and (5) the free rider problem will so reduce incentives to produce the information that its existence or quality of the information would be substantially threatened. These factors were not found to be present in the case of the NBA, because the pagers did not in any meaningful way threaten the NBA's ability to continue to provide its primary products (professional basketball games and related products) and the defendant was not free riding on the NBA's proposed pager system.

*

Part VI

PATENT LAW

Chapter 11

PATENT PROTECTION FOR INVENTIONS

A. INTRODUCTION: HISTORICAL PROTECTION FOR INNOVATIONS

Patent law in the United States offers a monopoly to the developer of a useful product or process, an ornamental design, or a plant. In contrast to trade secret law, patent protection requires disclosure of the invention to the public. In return, the inventor enjoys the exclusive right, during the statutory period, to exclude others not only from copying the subject matter of the patent, but from exploiting any independently-developed subject matter which is identical to, or the equivalent of, the patented invention. In contrast, copyright law (the subject of Part VII) protects against copying a work of authorship, but allows the copyright owner no rights against persons who independently create similar or identical subject matter.

Patent protection is broader in scope, but also shorter in duration and more difficult to obtain, than trademark, trade secret, unfair competition, or copyright protection. To be patentable, an innovation must meet stringent statutory requirements. Among the most significant of these is the requirement of novelty. To meet this standard, an invention must differ significantly from any subject matter in the prior art; this stands in sharp contrast to trademark, unfair competition, trade secret, and copyright law (the latter of which requires not novelty but originality, meaning simply that the work must not itself have been copied). Because the statutory standards of patent law are so demanding, the process of obtaining patent protection is more rigorous than the process of obtaining any other form of intellectual property protection, and the patent, once issued, is more vulnerable to legal challenge.

Much of United States patent law derives from English patent law. In sixteenth century England, the Crown issued numerous "letters patent" giving individuals monopolies over production, importation, and/or sales of particular items within the kingdom regardless of their novelty or their previous availability. The resulting shortages and price increases eventually led Parliament to enact the Statute of Monopolies, 21 Jac. I, c. 3 (1623), declaring all monopolies "contrary to the laws of this Realm" and "utterly void and of none Effect." However, Section VI excepted patents of 14 years to "the true and first Inventor and Inventors" of "new Manufactures" that were "not contrary to the Law, nor mischievous to the State, by raising Prices of Commodities at home, or Hurt of Trade, or generally inconvenient...."

The influence of the Statute of Monopolies is apparent in Article I, Section 8, Clause 8 of the United States Constitution, which grants Congress the power "To promote the Progress of Science and useful Arts, by securing for limited Times to Authors and Inventors the exclusive Right to their respective Writings and Discoveries." Congress first exercised its patent authority in the Patent Act of 1790,[1] and broadened these provisions in 1793.[2] In the 1836 Patent Act,[3] Congress undertook a significant revision which created the Patent Office and introduced the rule that no invention could be patented without first being examined to determine that it satisfied the novelty requirement. Patent protection for ornamental designs was added in 1842.[4]

Other significant developments in United States patent law during the nineteenth and early twentieth centuries involved judicial interpretation. In the Patent Act of 1952,[5] Congress codified some of these judicially created doctrines—for example, the nonobviousness requirement now contained in Section 103—and legislatively overruled others. In 1930[6] and 1954,[7] Congress enacted plant patent legislation. In the latter half of the twentieth century, Congress lengthened the term of utility patents and undertook other revisions of the patent statutes in response to the commercialization of new technologies and increasing emphasis on international harmonization of patent policy and practice in connection with international trade negotiations. However, Congress has not attempted, nor have international agreements mandated, complete harmonization with the patent practices of other nations; thus, significant differences remain. In addition, because statutory change usually lags technological change, both the Patent and Trademark Office (PTO) and the federal courts have encountered difficulty in determining how existing patent statutes can be applied to inventions the nature of which was not even contemplated when those statutes were enacted—inventions such as computer software, biotechnological products and processes, and living organisms.

1. Act of April 10, 1790, ch.7, 1 Stat. 109.

2. Patent Act of 1793, ch. 11, 1 Stat. 318.

3. Act of July 4, 1836, ch. 357, 5 Stat. 117.

4. Act of Aug. 29, 1842, ch. 263, sec. 3, 5 Stat. 543.

5. Act of July 19, 1952, ch. 950, 66 Stat. 797.

6. Pub. L. No. 71–245, 46 Stat. 376 (1930).

7. Pub. L. No. 83–775, 68 Stat. 1190 (1954).

B. PATENTABLE SUBJECT MATTER

Statutes: 35 U.S.C.A. §§ 100, 101, 161, 171

1. PRODUCTS

DIAMOND v. CHAKRABARTY

Supreme Court of the United States, 1980.
447 U.S. 303, 100 S.Ct. 2204, 65 L.Ed.2d 144.

MR. CHIEF JUSTICE BURGER delivered the opinion of the Court.

[Respondent Chakrabarty filed a patent application for a human-made, genetically engineered bacterium of the genus Pseudomonas, containing at least two stable plasmids. This bacterium was capable of breaking down multiple components of crude oil so as to aid in cleaning up oil spills more efficiently than existing methods which relied on naturally occurring bacteria. The patent examiner held that the genetically engineered bacteria were not patentable subject matter under 35 U.S.C. § 101 because (1) they were "products of nature" and (2) they were living things. The Patent Office Board of Appeals affirmed, concluding that while the human-made bacteria were not "products of nature" (because their plasmid content was higher than that of naturally occurring bacteria), nonetheless section 101 was not intended to cover living things. The Court of Customs and Patent Appeals reversed, relying on its decision in In re Bergy, 563 F.2d 1031, 1038 (1977), that "the fact that the microorganisms ... are alive" is "without legal significance" for patent law purposes.]

* * *

The Constitution grants Congress broad power to legislate to "promote the Progress of Science and useful Arts, by securing for limited Times to Authors and Inventors the exclusive Right to their respective Writings and Discoveries." Art. I, § 8, cl. 8. The patent laws promote this progress by offering inventors exclusive rights for a limited period as an incentive for their inventiveness and research efforts. Kewanee Oil Co. v. Bicron Corp., 416 U.S. 470, 480–481 (1974); Universal Oil Co. v. Globe Co., 322 U.S. 471, 484 (1944). The authority of Congress is exercised in the hope that "[the] productive effort thereby fostered will have a positive effect on society through the introduction of new products and processes of manufacture into the economy, and the emanations by way of increased employment and better lives for our citizens." Kewanee, supra, at 480.

The question before us in this case is a narrow one of statutory interpretation requiring us to construe 35 U.S.C. § 101 * * *. Specifically, we must determine whether respondent's micro-organism constitutes a "manufacture" or "composition of matter" within the meaning of the statute.

III

* * *

[In the absence of a statutory definition,] this Court has read the term "manufacture" in § 101 in accordance with its dictionary definition to mean "the production of articles for use from raw or prepared materials by giving to these materials new forms, qualities, properties, or combinations, whether by hand-labor or by machinery." American Fruit Growers, Inc. v. Brogdex Co., 283 U.S. 1, 11 (1931). Similarly, "composition of matter" has been construed consistent with its common usage to include "all compositions of two or more substances and ... all composite articles, whether they be the results of chemical union, or of mechanical mixture, or whether they be gases, fluids, powders or solids." Shell Development Co. v. Watson, 149 F.Supp. 279, 280 (D.C.1957) (citing 1 A. Deller, Walker on Patents § 14, p. 55 (1st ed. 1937)). In choosing such expansive terms as "manufacture" and "composition of matter," modified by the comprehensive "any," Congress plainly contemplated that the patent laws would be given wide scope.

The relevant legislative history also supports a broad construction. The Patent Act of 1793, authored by Thomas Jefferson, defined statutory subject matter as "any new and useful art, machine, manufacture, or composition of matter, or any new or useful improvement [thereof]." Act of Feb. 21, 1793, § 1, 1 Stat. 319. The Act embodied Jefferson's philosophy that "ingenuity should receive a liberal encouragement." 5 Writings of Thomas Jefferson 75–76 (Washington ed. 1871). *See* Graham v. John Deere Co., 383 U.S. 1, 7–10 (1966). Subsequent patent statutes in 1836, 1870, and 1874 employed this same broad language. In 1952, when the patent laws were recodified, Congress replaced the word "art" with "process," but otherwise left Jefferson's language intact. The Committee Reports accompanying the 1952 Act inform us that Congress intended statutory subject matter to "include anything under the sun that is made by man." S. Rep. No. 1979, 82d Cong., 2d Sess., 5 (1952); H. R. Rep. No. 1923, 82d Cong., 2d Sess., 6 (1952).

This is not to suggest that § 101 has no limits or that it embraces every discovery. The laws of nature, physical phenomena, and abstract ideas have been held not patentable. *See* Parker v. Flook, 437 U.S. 584 (1978); Gottschalk v. Benson, 409 U.S. 63, 67 (1972); Funk Brothers Seed Co. v. Kalo Inoculant Co., 333 U.S. 127, 130 (1948); O'Reilly v. Morse, 15 How. 62, 112–121 (1854); Le Roy v. Tatham, 14 How. 156, 175 (1853). Thus, a new mineral discovered in the earth or a new plant found in the wild is not patentable subject matter. Likewise, Einstein could not patent his celebrated law that $E=mc^2$; nor could Newton have patented the law of gravity. Such discoveries are "manifestations of ... nature, free to all men and reserved exclusively to none." *Funk, supra*, at 130.

Judged in this light, respondent's micro-organism plainly qualifies as patentable subject matter. His claim is not to a hitherto unknown natural phenomenon, but to a nonnaturally occurring manufacture or composition of matter—a product of human ingenuity "having a distinctive name, character [and] use." Hartranft v. Wiegmann, 121 U.S. 609, 615 (1887). The point is underscored dramatically by comparison of the invention here with that in *Funk*. There, the patentee had discovered that there existed in nature certain species of root-nodule bacteria which did not exert a mutually inhibitive effect on each other. He used that discovery to produce a mixed culture capable of inoculating the seeds of leguminous plants. Concluding that the patentee had discovered "only some of the handiwork of nature," the Court ruled the product nonpatentable:

> "Each of the species of root-nodule bacteria contained in the package infects the same group of leguminous plants which it always infected. No species acquires a different use. The combination of species produces no new bacteria, no change in the six species of bacteria, and no enlargement of the range of their utility. Each species has the same effect it always had. The bacteria perform in their natural way. Their use in combination does not improve in any way their natural functioning. They serve the ends nature originally provided and act quite independently of any effort of the patentee." 333 U.S., at 131.

Here, by contrast, the patentee has produced a new bacterium with markedly different characteristics from any found in nature and one having the potential for significant utility. His discovery is not nature's handiwork, but his own; accordingly it is patentable subject matter under § 101.

IV

Two contrary arguments are advanced, neither of which we find persuasive.

(A)

The petitioner's first argument rests on the enactment of the 1930 Plant Patent Act, which afforded patent protection to certain asexually reproduced plants, and the 1970 Plant Variety Protection Act, which authorized protection for certain sexually reproduced plants but excluded bacteria from its protection. In the petitioner's view, the passage of these Acts evidences congressional understanding that the terms "manufacture" or "composition of matter" do not include living things; if they did, the petitioner argues, neither Act would have been necessary.

We reject this argument. Prior to 1930, two factors were thought to remove plants from patent protection. The first was the belief that plants, even those artificially bred, were products of nature for purposes of the patent law. This position appears to have derived from the decision of the Patent Office in Ex parte Latimer, 1889 Dec. Com. Pat. 123, in which a patent claim for fiber found in the needle of the Pinus australis was rejected. The Commissioner reasoned that a contrary result would permit "patents [to] be obtained upon the trees of the forest and the plants of the earth, which of course would be unreasonable and impossible." *Id.*, at 126. The Latimer case, it seems, came to "[set] forth the general stand taken in these matters" that plants were natural products not subject to patent protection. Thorne, Relation of Patent Law to Natural Products, 6 J. Pat. Off. Soc. 23, 24 (1923). The second obstacle to patent protection for plants was the fact that plants were thought not amenable to the "written description" requirement of the patent law. *See* 35 U.S.C.A. § 112. Because new plants may differ from old only in color or perfume, differentiation by written description was often impossible.

In enacting the Plant Patent Act, Congress addressed both of these concerns. It explained at length its belief that the work of the plant breeder "in aid of nature" was patentable invention. S. Rep. No. 315, 71st Cong., 2d Sess., 6–8 (1930); H. R. Rep. No. 1129, 71st Cong., 2d Sess., 7–9 (1930). And it relaxed the written description requirement in favor of "a description ... as complete as is reasonably possible." 35 U.S.C. § 162. No Committee or Member of Congress, however, expressed the broader view, now urged by the petitioner, that the terms "manufacture" or "composition of matter" exclude living things. * * * The [House and Senate] Reports observe:

> "There is a clear and logical distinction *between the discovery of a new variety of plant and certain inanimate things*, such, for example, as a new and useful natural mineral. The mineral is created wholly by nature unassisted by man.... On the other hand, a plant discovery resulting from cultivation is unique, isolated, and is not repeated by nature, nor can it be reproduced by nature unaided by man.... " S. Rep. No. 315, *supra*, at 6; H. R. Rep. No. 1129, supra, at 7 (emphasis added).

Congress thus recognized that the relevant distinction was not between living and inanimate things, but between products of nature, whether living or not, and human-made inventions. Here, respondent's microorganism is the result of human ingenuity and research. Hence, the passage of the Plant Patent Act affords the Government no support.

Nor does the passage of the 1970 Plant Variety Protection Act support the Government's position. As the Government acknowledges, sexually reproduced plants were not included under the 1930 Act because new varieties could not be reproduced true-to-type through seedlings. By 1970, however, it was generally recognized that true-to-type reproduction was possible and that plant patent protection was therefore appropriate. The 1970 Act extended that protection. There is nothing in its language or history to suggest that it was enacted because § 101 did not include living things.

In particular, we find nothing in the exclusion of bacteria from plant variety protection to support the petitioner's position. The legislative history gives no reason for this exclusion. As the Court of Customs and Patent Appeals suggested, it may simply reflect congressional agreement with the result reached by that court in deciding In re Arzberger, 27 C.C.P.A. (Pat.) 1315, 112 F.2d 834 (1940), which held that bacteria were not plants for the purposes of the 1930 Act. Or it may reflect the fact that prior to 1970 the Patent Office had issued patents for bacteria under § 101. In any event, absent some clear indication that Congress "focused on [the] issues ... directly related to the one presently before the Court," SEC v. Sloan, 436 U.S. 103, 120–121 (1978), there is no basis for reading into its actions an intent to modify the plain meaning of the words found in § 101.

(B)

The petitioner's second argument is that micro-organisms cannot qualify as patentable subject matter until Congress expressly authorizes such protection. His position rests on the fact that genetic technology was unforeseen when Congress enacted § 101. From this it is argued that resolution of the patentability of inventions such as respondent's should be left to Congress. The legislative process, the petitioner argues, is best equipped to weigh the competing economic, social, and scientific considerations involved, and to determine whether living organisms produced by genetic engineering should receive patent protection. In support of this position, the petitioner relies on our recent holding in Parker v. Flook, 437 U.S. 584 (1978), and the statement that the judiciary "must proceed cautiously when ... asked to extend patent rights into areas wholly unforeseen by Congress." *Id.*, at 596.

It is, of course, correct that Congress, not the courts, must define the limits of patentability; but it is equally true that once Congress has spoken it is "the province and duty of the judicial department to say what the law is." Marbury v. Madison, 1 Cranch 137, 177 (1803). Congress has performed its constitutional role in defining patentable subject matter in § 101; we perform ours in construing the language Congress has employed. In so doing, our obligation is to take statutes as we find them, guided, if ambiguity appears, by the legislative history and statutory purpose. Here, we perceive no ambiguity. The subject-matter provisions of the patent law have been cast in broad terms to fulfill the constitutional and statutory goal of promoting "the Progress of Science and the useful Arts" with all that means for the social and economic benefits envisioned by Jefferson. Broad general language is not necessarily ambiguous when congressional objectives require broad terms.

Nothing in *Flook* is to the contrary. That case applied our prior precedents to determine that a "claim for an improved method of calculation, even when tied to a specific end use, is unpatentable subject matter under § 101." 437 U.S., at 595, n. 18. The Court carefully scrutinized the claim at issue to determine whether it was precluded from patent protection under "the principles underlying the prohibition against patents for 'ideas' or phenomena of nature." *Id.*, at 593. We have done that here. *Flook* did not announce a new principle that inventions in areas not contemplated by Congress when the patent laws were enacted are unpatentable per se.

To read that concept into *Flook* would frustrate the purposes of the patent law. This Court frequently has observed that a statute is not to be confined to the "particular [applications] . . . contemplated by the legislators." Barr v. United States, 324 U.S. 83, 90 (1945). This is especially true in the field of patent law. A rule that unanticipated inventions are without protection would conflict with the core concept of the patent law that anticipation undermines patentability. *See* Graham v. John Deere Co., 383 U.S., at 12–17. Mr. Justice Douglas reminded that the inventions most benefiting mankind are those that "push back the frontiers of chemistry, physics, and the like." Great A. & P. Tea Co. v. Supermarket Corp., 340 U.S. 147, 154 (1950) (concurring opinion). Congress employed broad general language in drafting § 101 precisely because such inventions are often unforeseeable.

* * *

Accordingly, the judgment of the Court of Customs and Patent Appeals is

Affirmed.

Notes

1. Would a purified form of a naturally occurring substance be patentable subject matter under Section 101? Why or why not?

2. Suppose an inventor develops a method for producing a sterile oyster. Its utility lies in the fact that a nonreproducing oyster remains edible year-round. Is the oyster patentable subject matter?

3. *Plant Patents*: In *Ex Parte Hibberd*, 227 U.S.P.Q. 443 (P.T.O. Bd. Pat. App. & Int'f 1985), the Board of Patent Appeals and Interferences took *Chakrabarty* one step further, holding that plants, seeds, and plant tissue cultures are patentable subject matter under section 101, even though the same subject matter might also be eligible for a plant patent or a plant variety protection certificate. If the Board is correct, then non-sexually reproduced plants may be patented under either Section 101 or Section 161 (which applies only to non-sexually reproduced plants). An attempt to obtain both forms of protection for the same variety of plant, however, might constitute prohibited double patenting. (See Chapter 12.G.)

Section 161 explicitly incorporates most of the provisions that govern utility patents. Although it precludes protection for plants found in an uncultivated state, it permits the grant of a patent for a plant found in a cultivated state, even if the "inventor" did no more than discover the plant, recognize its patentable characteristics, and asexually reproduce it.

4. *Plant Variety Protection Certificates*: The patent-like protection available for plants under the Plant Variety Protection Act of 1970 (PVPA), 7 U.S.C.A. § 2321 *et seq.*, applies to sexually reproduced plants. Plant variety protection certificates are issued by the Department of Agriculture rather than the PTO. The certificate holder enjoys the exclusive right to market, sell, reproduce, import or export the plant variety, to use it in producing hybrids or different varieties, to tuber propagate it as a step in marketing, to

condition the variety for propagation (except for farmers replanting their own holdings), and to stock the variety for any purpose which would be infringing. Under the most recent amendments to the PVPA, the term of protection is 20 years (25 years for trees and vines).

5. Controversy surrounds the patentability of human gene sequences, cloning methods that could be applied to human beings, and genetic alterations of human beings. In 1999, the PTO rejected claims for a method of combining human and animal material to produce an animal-human embryo. *See* 58 Patent Trademark & Copyright Journal (BNA) 203 (June 17, 1999). In 2004, a one-year ban went into effect, prohibiting the use of federal appropriations for the issuance of "patents on claims directed to or encompassing a human organism." Pub. L. No. 108–199, 118 Stat. 4 (2004). The ban was renewed for an additional year in 2005. Pub. L. No. 109–108, 119 Stat. 2290 (2005). Notwithstanding the appropriations ban, the PTO in 2004 granted a patent on methods for cloning mammals, some of the claims of which could be construed to apply to the cloning of humans. An earlier cloning patent that arguably encompassed humans was granted in 2001. Setting aside the statutory interpretation issues presented by Section 101, what kinds of policy questions are presented by patents involving humans or other animals, and who should resolve them?

2. PROCESSES

STATE STREET BANK & TRUST CO. v. SIGNATURE FINANCIAL GROUP, INC.

United States Court of Appeals, Federal Circuit, 1998.
149 F.3d 1368, *cert. denied*, 525 U.S. 1093, 119 S.Ct. 851, 142 L.Ed.2d 704 (1999).

RICH, CIRCUIT JUDGE.

Signature Financial Group, Inc. (Signature) appeals from the decision of the United States District Court for the District of Massachusetts granting a motion for summary judgment in favor of State Street Bank & Trust Co. (State Street), finding U.S. Patent No. 5,193,056 (the '056 patent) invalid on the ground that the claimed subject matter is not encompassed by 35 U.S.C. § 101 (1994). *See* State Street Bank & Trust Co. v. Signature Financial Group, Inc., 927 F. Supp. 502 (D.Mass.1996). We reverse and remand because we conclude that the patent claims are directed to statutory subject matter.

BACKGROUND

Signature is the assignee of the '056 patent which is entitled "Data Processing System for Hub and Spoke Financial Services Configuration." The '056 patent issued to Signature on 9 March 1993, naming R. Todd Boes as the inventor. The '056 patent is generally directed to a data processing system (the system) for implementing an investment structure which was developed for use in Signature's business as an administrator and accounting agent for mutual funds. In essence, the system, identified by the proprietary name Hub and Spoke (R), facilitates a structure whereby mutual funds (Spokes) pool their assets in an investment portfolio (Hub) organized as a partnership. This investment configuration provides the administrator of a mutual fund with the advantageous combination of economies of scale in administering investments coupled with the tax advantages of a partnership.

State Street and Signature are both in the business of acting as custodians and accounting agents for multi-tiered partnership fund financial services. State Street negotiated with Signature for a license to use its patented data processing system described and claimed in the '056 patent. When negotiations broke down, State Street brought a declaratory judgment action asserting invalidity, unenforceability, and noninfringement in Massachusetts district court, and then filed a motion for partial summary judgment of patent invalidity for failure to claim statutory subject matter under '101. The motion was granted and this appeal followed.

DISCUSSION

On appeal, we are not bound to give deference to the district court's grant of summary judgment, but must make an independent determination that the standards for summary judgment have been met. Vas–Cath, Inc. v. Mahurkar, 935 F.2d 1555, 1560 (Fed.Cir.1991). Summary judgment is properly granted where there are no genuine issues of material fact and the moving party is entitled to judgment as a matter of law. Fed. R. Civ. P. 56(c). The substantive issue at hand, whether the '056 patent is invalid for failure to claim statutory subject matter under '101, is a matter of both claim construction and statutory construction. "We review claim construction de novo including any allegedly fact-based questions relating to claim construction." Cybor Corp. v. FAS Techs., 138 F.3d 1448, 1451 (Fed.Cir.1998) (in banc). We also review statutory construction de novo. See Romero v. United States, 38 F.3d 1204, 1207 (Fed.Cir.1994). We hold that declaratory judgment plaintiff State Street was not entitled to the grant of summary judgment of invalidity of the '056 patent under '101 as a matter of law, because the patent claims are directed to statutory subject matter.

The following facts pertinent to the statutory subject matter issue are either undisputed or represent the version alleged by the nonmovant. The patented invention relates generally to a system that allows an administrator to monitor and record the financial information flow and make all calculations necessary for maintaining a partner fund financial services configuration. As previously mentioned, a partner fund financial services configuration essentially allows several mutual funds, or "Spokes," to pool their investment funds into a single portfolio, or "Hub," allowing for consolidation of, inter alia, the costs of administering the fund combined with the tax advantages of a partnership. In particular, this system provides means for a daily allocation of assets for two or more Spokes that are invested in the same Hub. The system determines the percentage share that each Spoke maintains in the Hub, while taking into consideration daily changes both in the value of the

Hub's investment securities and in the concomitant amount of each Spoke's assets.

In determining daily changes, the system also allows for the allocation among the Spokes of the Hub's daily income, expenses, and net realized and unrealized gain or loss, calculating each day's total investments based on the concept of a book capital account. This enables the determination of a true asset value of each Spoke and accurate calculation of allocation ratios between or among the Spokes. The system additionally tracks all the relevant data determined on a daily basis for the Hub and each Spoke, so that aggregate year end income, expenses, and capital gain or loss can be determined for accounting and for tax purposes for the Hub and, as a result, for each publicly traded Spoke.

It is essential that these calculations are quickly and accurately performed. In large part this is required because each Spoke sells shares to the public and the price of those shares is substantially based on the Spoke's percentage interest in the portfolio. In some instances, a mutual fund administrator is required to calculate the value of the shares to the nearest penny within as little as an hour and a half after the market closes. Given the complexity of the calculations, a computer or equivalent device is a virtual necessity to perform the task.

The '056 patent application was filed 11 March 1991. It initially contained six "machine" claims, which incorporated means-plus-function clauses, and six method claims. According to Signature, during prosecution the examiner contemplated a § 101 rejection for failure to claim statutory subject matter. However, upon cancellation of the six method claims, the examiner issued a notice of allowance for the remaining present six claims on appeal. Only claim 1 is an independent claim.

The district court began its analysis by construing the claims to be directed to a process, with each "means" clause merely representing a step in that process. However, "machine" claims having "means" clauses may only be reasonably viewed as process claims if there is no supporting structure in the written description that corresponds to the claimed "means" elements. *See* In re Alappat, 33 F.3d 1526, 1540–41 (Fed.Cir.1994) (in banc). This is not the case now before us.

When independent claim 1 is properly construed in accordance with § 112, ¶ 6, it is directed to a machine, as demonstrated below, where representative claim 1 is set forth, the subject matter in brackets stating the structure the written description discloses as corresponding to the respective "means" recited in the claims.

1. A data processing system for managing a financial services configuration of a portfolio established as a partnership, each partner being one of a plurality of funds, comprising:

   (a) computer processor means [a personal computer including a CPU] for processing data;

   (b) storage means [a data disk] for storing data on a storage medium;

(c) first means [an arithmetic logic circuit configured to prepare the data disk to magnetically store selected data] for initializing the storage medium;

(d) second means [an arithmetic logic circuit configured to retrieve information from a specific file, calculate incremental increases or decreases based on specific input, allocate the results on a percentage basis, and store the output in a separate file] for processing data regarding assets in the portfolio and each of the funds from a previous day and data regarding increases or decreases in each of the funds, [sic, funds'] assets and for allocating the percentage share that each fund holds in the portfolio;

(e) third means [an arithmetic logic circuit configured to retrieve information from a specific file, calculate incremental increases and decreases based on specific input, allocate the results on a percentage basis and store the output in a separate file] for processing data regarding daily incremental income, expenses, and net realized gain or loss for the portfolio and for allocating such data among each fund;

(f) fourth means [an arithmetic logic circuit configured to retrieve information from a specific file, calculate incremental increases and decreases based on specific input, allocate the results on a percentage basis and store the output in a separate file] for processing data regarding daily net unrealized gain or loss for the portfolio and for allocating such data among each fund; and

(g) fifth means [an arithmetic logic circuit configured to retrieve information from specific files, calculate that information on an aggregate basis and store the output in a separate file] for processing data regarding aggregate year-end income, expenses, and capital gain or loss for the portfolio and each of the funds.

Each claim component, recited as a "means" plus its function, is to be read, of course, pursuant to § 112, ¶ 6, as inclusive of the "equivalents" of the structures disclosed in the written description portion of the specification. Thus, claim 1, properly construed, claims a machine, namely, a data processing system for managing a financial services configuration of a portfolio established as a partnership, which machine is made up of, at the very least, the specific structures disclosed in the written description and corresponding to the means-plus-function elements (a)-(g) recited in the claim. A "machine" is proper statutory subject matter under § 101. We note that, for the purposes of a § 101 analysis, it is of little relevance whether claim 1 is directed to a "machine" or a "process," as long as it falls within at least one of the four enumerated categories of patentable subject matter, "machine" and "process" being such categories.

This does not end our analysis, however, because the court concluded that the claimed subject matter fell into one of two alternative judicially-created exceptions to statutory subject matter.[8] The court refers to the first exception as the "mathematical algorithm" exception and the second exception as the "business method" exception. Section 101 reads:

> Whoever invents or discovers any new and useful process, machine, manufacture, or composition of matter, or any new and useful improvement thereof, may obtain a patent therefor, subject to the conditions and requirements of this title.

The plain and unambiguous meaning of § 101 is that any invention falling within one of the four stated categories of statutory subject matter may be patented, provided it meets the other requirements for patentability set forth in Title 35, i.e., those found in §§ 102, 103, and 112, ¶ 2.[9]

The repetitive use of the expansive term "any" in § 101 shows Congress's intent not to place any restrictions on the subject matter for which a patent may be obtained beyond those specifically recited in § 101. Indeed, the Supreme Court has acknowledged that Congress intended § 101 to extend to "anything under the sun that is made by man." Diamond v. Chakrabarty, 447 U.S. 303, 309, 65 L.Ed.2d 144, 100 S.Ct. 2204 (1980); see also Diamond v. Diehr, 450 U.S. 175, 182, 67 L.Ed.2d 155, 101 S.Ct. 1048 (1981).[10] Thus, it is improper to read limitations into § 101 on the subject matter that may be patented where the legislative history indicates that Congress clearly did not intend such limitations. See Chakrabarty, 447 U.S. at 308 ("We have also cautioned that courts 'should not read into the patent laws limitations and conditions which the legislature has not expressed.'" (citations omitted)).

The "Mathematical Algorithm" Exception

8. Indeed, although we do not make this determination here, the judicially created exceptions, i.e., abstract ideas, laws of nature, etc., should be applicable to all categories of statutory subject matter, as our own precedent suggests. See Alappat, 33 F.3d at 1542; see also In re Johnston, 502 F.2d 765 (Rich, J., dissenting).

9. As explained in In re Bergy, 596 F.2d 952, 960 (CCPA 1979) (emphases and footnote omitted):

The first door which must be opened on the difficult path to patentability is § 101. . . . The person approaching that door is an inventor, whether his invention is patentable or not. . . . Being an inventor or having an invention, however, is no guarantee of opening even the first door. What kind of an invention or discovery is it? In dealing with the question of kind, as distinguished from the qualitative conditions which make the invention patentable, § 101 is broad and general; its language is: "any * * * pro-cess, machine, manufacture, or composition of matter, or any * * * improvement thereof." Section 100(b) further expands "process" to include "art or method, and * * * a new use of a known process, machine, manufacture, composition of matter, or material." If the invention, as the inventor defines it in his claims (pursuant to § 112, second paragraph), falls into any one of the named categories, he is allowed to pass through to the second door, which is § 102; "novelty and loss of right to patent" is the sign on it. Notwithstanding the words "new and useful" in § 101, the invention is not examined under that statute for novelty because that is not the statutory scheme of things or the long-established administrative practice.

10. The Committee Reports accompanying the 1952 Act inform us that Congress intended statutory subject matter to "include anything under the sun that is made by man." S. Rep. No. 82–1979 at 5 (1952); H.R. Rep. No. 82–1923 at 6 (1952).

The Supreme Court has identified three categories of subject matter that are unpatentable, namely "laws of nature, natural phenomena, and abstract ideas." *Diehr*, 450 U.S. at 185. Of particular relevance to this case, the Court has held that mathematical algorithms are not patentable subject matter to the extent that they are merely abstract ideas. *See Diehr*, 450 U.S. 175, 67 L.Ed.2d 155, 101 S.Ct. 1048, *passim;* Parker v. Flook, 437 U.S. 584, 57 L.Ed.2d 451, 98 S.Ct. 2522 (1978); Gottschalk v. Benson, 409 U.S. 63, 34 L.Ed.2d 273, 93 S.Ct. 253 (1972). In *Diehr*, the Court explained that certain types of mathematical subject matter, standing alone, represent nothing more than abstract ideas until reduced to some type of practical application, i.e., "a useful, concrete and tangible result." *Alappat*, 33 F.3d at 1544.[11]

Unpatentable mathematical algorithms are identifiable by showing they are merely abstract ideas constituting disembodied concepts or truths that are not "useful." From a practical standpoint, this means that to be patentable an algorithm must be applied in a "useful" way. In *Alappat,* we held that data, transformed by a machine through a series of mathematical calculations to produce a smooth waveform display on a rasterizer monitor, constituted a practical application of an abstract idea (a mathematical algorithm, formula, or calculation), because it produced "a useful, concrete and tangible result"—the smooth waveform.

Similarly, in Arrhythmia Research Technology Inc. v. Corazonix Corp., 958 F.2d 1053 (Fed.Cir.1992), we held that the transformation of electrocardiograph signals from a patient's heartbeat by a machine through a series of mathematical calculations constituted a practical application of an abstract idea (a mathematical algorithm, formula, or calculation), because it corresponded to a useful, concrete or tangible thing—the condition of a patient's heart.

Today, we hold that the transformation of data, representing discrete dollar amounts, by a machine through a series of mathematical calculations into a final share price, constitutes a practical application of a mathematical algorithm, formula, or calculation, because it produces "a useful, concrete and tangible result"—a final share price momentarily fixed for recording and reporting purposes and even accepted and relied upon by regulatory authorities and in subsequent trades.

The district court erred by applying the *Freeman–Walter–Abele* test to determine whether the claimed subject matter was an unpatentable abstract idea. The *Freeman–Walter–Abele* test was designed by the Court of Customs and Patent Appeals, and subsequently adopted by this court, to extract and identify unpatentable mathematical algorithms in the aftermath of *Benson* and *Flook*. *See* In re Freeman, 573 F.2d 1237 (CCPA 1978) as modified by In re Walter, 618 F.2d 758 (CCPA 1980). The test has been thus articulated:

11. This has come to be known as the mathematical algorithm exception. This designation has led to some confusion, especially given the *Freeman–Walter–Abele* analysis. By keeping in mind that the mathematical algorithm is unpatentable only to the extent that it represents an abstract idea, this confusion may be ameliorated.

First, the claim is analyzed to determine whether a mathematical algorithm is directly or indirectly recited. Next, if a mathematical algorithm is found, the claim as a whole is further analyzed to determine whether the algorithm is "applied in any manner to physical elements or process steps," and, if it is, it "passes muster under § 101."

In re Pardo, 684 F.2d 912, 915 (CCPA 1982) (citing In re Abele, 684 F.2d 902 (CCPA 1982)).[12]

After *Diehr* and *Chakrabarty,* the *Freeman–Walter–Abele* test has little, if any, applicability to determining the presence of statutory subject matter. As we pointed out in *Alappat,* 33 F.3d at 1543, application of the test could be misleading, because a process, machine, manufacture, or composition of matter employing a law of nature, natural phenomenon, or abstract idea is patentable subject matter even though a law of nature, natural phenomenon, or abstract idea would not, by itself, be entitled to such protection.[13] The test determines the presence of, for example, an algorithm. Under *Benson,* this may have been a sufficient indicium of nonstatutory subject matter. However, after *Diehr* and *Alappat,* the mere fact that a claimed invention involves inputting numbers, calculating numbers, outputting numbers, and storing numbers, in and of itself, would not render it nonstatutory subject matter, unless, of course, its operation does not produce a "useful, concrete and tangible result." *Alappat,* 33 F.3d at 1544.[14] After all, as we have repeatedly stated,

12. The test has been the source of much confusion. In In re Abele, 684 F.2d 902 (CCPA 1982), the CCPA upheld claims applying "a mathematical formula within the context of a process which encompasses significantly more than the algorithm alone." *Id.* at 909. Thus, the CCPA apparently inserted an additional consideration—the significance of additions to the algorithm. The CCPA appeared to abandon the application of the test in In re Taner, 681 F.2d 787 (CCPA 1982), only to subsequently "clarify" that the *Freeman–Walter–Abele* test was simply not the exclusive test for detecting unpatentable subject matter. In re Meyer, 688 F.2d 789, 796 (CCPA 1982).

13. *See, e.g.* Parker v. Flook, 437 U.S. 584, 590, 57 L.Ed.2d 451, 98 S Ct. 2522 (1978) ("[A] process is not unpatentable simply because it contains a law of nature or a mathematical algorithm."); Funk Bros. Seed Co. v. Kalo Inoculant Co., 333 U.S. 127, 130, 92 L.Ed. 588, 68 S. Ct. 440 (1948) ("He who discovers a hitherto unknown phenomenon of nature has no claim to a monopoly of it which the law recognizes. If there is to be invention from such a discovery, it must come from the application of the law to a new and useful end."); Mackay Radio & Tel. Co. v. Radio Corp. of Am., 306 U.S. 86, 94, 83 L.Ed. 506, 59 S.Ct. 427

(1939) ("While a scientific truth, or the mathematical expression of it, is not a patentable invention, a novel and useful structure created with the aid of knowledge of scientific truth may be.").

When a claim containing a mathematical formula implements or applies that formula in a structure or process which, when considered as a whole, is performing a function which the patent laws were designed to protect (e.g., transforming or reducing an article to a different state or thing), then the claim satisfies the requirements of § 101.

Diehr, 450 U.S. at 192; *see also* In re Iwahashi, 888 F.2d 1370, 1375 (Fed.Cir.1989); *Taner,* 681 F.2d at 789. The dispositive inquiry is whether the claim as a whole is directed to statutory subject matter. It is irrelevant that a claim may contain, as part of the whole, subject matter which would not be patentable by itself. "A claim drawn to subject matter otherwise statutory does not become nonstatutory simply because it uses a mathematical formula, computer program or digital computer." *Diehr,* 450 U.S. at 187.

14. As the Supreme Court expressly stated in *Diehr,* its own holdings in *Benson*

every step-by-step process, be it electronic or chemical or mechanical, involves an algorithm in the broad sense of the term. Since § 101 expressly includes processes as a category of inventions which may be patented and '100(b) further defines the word "process" as meaning "process, art or method, and includes a new use of a known process, machine, manufacture, composition of matter, or material," it follows that it is no ground for holding a claim is directed to nonstatutory subject matter to say it includes or is directed to an algorithm. This is why the proscription against patenting has been limited to *mathematical* algorithms....

In re Iwahashi, 888 F.2d 1370, 1374 (Fed.Cir.1989) (emphasis in the original).[15]

The question of whether a claim encompasses statutory subject matter should not focus on which of the four categories of subject matter a claim is directed to[16]—process, machine, manufacture, or composition of matter—but rather on the essential characteristics of the subject matter, in particular, its practical utility. Section 101 specifies that statutory subject matter must also satisfy the other "conditions and requirements" of Title 35, including novelty, nonobviousness, and adequacy of disclosure and notice. *See* In re Warmerdam, 33 F.3d 1354, 1359 (Fed.Cir.1994). For purpose of our analysis, as noted above, claim 1 is directed to a machine programmed with the Hub and Spoke software and admittedly produces a "useful, concrete, and tangible result." *Alappat,* 33 F.3d at 1544. This renders it statutory subject matter, even if the useful result is expressed in numbers, such as price, profit, percentage, cost, or loss.

The Business Method Exception

As an alternative ground for invalidating the '056 patent under § 101, the court relied on the judicially-created, so-called "business method" exception to statutory subject matter. We take this opportunity to lay this ill-conceived exception to rest. Since its inception, the "business method" exception has merely represented the application of some general, but no longer applicable legal principle, perhaps arising out of the "requirement for invention"—which was eliminated by § 103. Since the 1952 Patent Act, business methods have been, and should have been, subject to the same legal requirements for patentability as applied to any other process or method.[17]

and *Flook* "stand for no more than these long-established principles" that abstract ideas and natural phenomena are not patentable. *Diehr,* 450 U.S. at 185 (citing *Chakrabarty,* 447 U.S. at 309 and *Funk Bros.,* 333 U.S. at 130.).

15. In In re Pardo, 684 F.2d 912 (CCPA 1982), the CCPA narrowly limited "mathematical algorithm" to the execution of formulas with given data. In the same year, in In re Meyer, 688 F.2d 789 (CCPA 1982), the CCPA interpreted the same term to include

any mental process that can be represented by a mathematical algorithm. This is also the position taken by the PTO in its Examination Guidelines, 61 Fed. Reg. 7478, 7483 (1996).

16. Of course, the subject matter must fall into at least one category of statutory subject matter.

17. As Judge Newman has previously stated,

The business method exception has never been invoked by this court, or the CCPA, to deem an invention unpatentable. Application of this particular exception has always been preceded by a ruling based on some clearer concept of Title 35 or, more commonly, application of the abstract idea exception based on finding a mathematical algorithm. Illustrative is the CCPA's analysis in In re Howard, 394 F.2d 869 (CCPA 1968), wherein the court affirmed the Board of Appeals' rejection of the claims for lack of novelty and found it unnecessary to reach the Board's section 101 ground that a method of doing business is "inherently unpatentable." 394 F.2d at 872.[19]

Similarly, In re Schrader, 22 F.3d 290 (Fed.Cir.1994), while making reference to the business method exception, turned on the fact that the claims implicitly recited an abstract idea in the form of a mathematical algorithm and there was no "transformation or conversion of subject matter representative of or constituting physical activity or objects." 22 F.3d at 294 (emphasis omitted).[20]

State Street argues that we acknowledged the validity of the business method exception in Alappat when we discussed *Maucorps* and *Meyer*:

> *Maucorps* dealt with a business methodology for deciding how salesmen should best handle respective customers and Meyer involved a "system" for aiding a neurologist in diagnosing patients. Clearly, neither of the alleged "inventions" in those cases falls within any § 101 category.

Alappat, 33 F.3d at 1541. However, closer scrutiny of these cases reveals that the claimed inventions in both *Maucorps* and *Meyer* were rejected as abstract ideas under the mathematical algorithm exception, not the business method exception. *See* In re Maucorps, 609 F.2d 481, 484

[The business method exception] is ... an unwarranted encumbrance to the definition of statutory subject matter in section 101, that [should] be discarded as error-prone, redundant, and obsolete. It merits retirement from the glossary of section 101.... All of the "doing business" cases could have been decided using the clearer concepts of Title 35. Patentability does not turn on whether the claimed method does "business" instead of something else, but on whether the method, viewed as a whole, meets the requirements of patentability as set forth in Sections 102, 103, and 112 of the Patent Act.

In re Schrader, 22 F.3d 290, 298 (Fed.Cir. 1994) (Newman, J., dissenting).

19. *See also* Dann v. Johnston, 425 U.S. 219, 47 L. Ed. 2d 692, 96 S. Ct. 1393 (1976) (the Supreme Court declined to discuss the section 101 argument concerning the computerized financial record-keeping system,

in view of the Court's holding of patent invalidity under section 103); In re Chatfield, 545 F.2d 152, 157 (CCPA 1976); Ex parte Murray, 9 U.S.P.Q.2D (BNA) 1819, 1820 (Bd.Pat.App & Interf.1988) ("The claimed accounting method [requires] no more than the entering, sorting, debiting and totaling of expenditures as necessary preliminary steps to issuing an expense analysis statement.... ") states [sic] grounds of obviousness or lack of novelty, not of non-statutory subject matter.

20. Any historical distinctions between a method of "doing" business and the means of carrying it out blur in the complexity of modern business systems. *See* Paine, Webber, Jackson & Curtis v. Merrill Lynch, 564 F. Supp. 1358 (D.Del.1983) (holding a computerized system of cash management was held to be statutory subject matter.)

(CCPA 1979); In re Meyer, 688 F.2d 789, 796 (CCPA 1982).[21]

Even the case frequently cited as establishing the business method exception to statutory subject matter, Hotel Security Checking Co. v. Lorraine Co., 160 F. 467 (2d Cir.1908), did not rely on the exception to strike the patent.[22] In that case, the patent was found invalid for lack of novelty and "invention," not because it was improper subject matter for a patent. The court stated "the fundamental principle of the system is as old as the art of bookkeeping, i.e., charging the goods of the employer to the agent who takes them." *Id.* at 469. "If at the time of [the patent] application, there had been no system of bookkeeping of any kind in restaurants, we would be confronted with the question whether a new and useful system of cash registering and account checking is such an art as is patentable under the statute." *Id.* at 472.

This case is no exception. The district court announced the precepts of the business method exception as set forth in several treatises, but noted as its primary reason for finding the patent invalid under the business method exception as follows:

> If Signature's invention were patentable, any financial institution desirous of implementing a multi-tiered funding complex modelled (sic) on a Hub and Spoke configuration would be required to seek Signature's permission before embarking on such a project. *This is so because the '056 Patent is claimed [sic] sufficiently broadly to foreclose virtually any computer-implemented accounting method necessary to manage this type of financial structure.*

927 F. Supp. 502, 516 (emphasis added). Whether the patent's claims are too broad to be patentable is not to be judged under § 101, but rather under §§ 102, 103 and 112. Assuming the above statement to be correct, it has nothing to do with whether what is claimed is statutory subject matter.

In view of this background, it comes as no surprise that in the most recent edition of the Manual of Patent Examining Procedures (MPEP) (1996), a paragraph of § 706.03(a) was deleted. In past editions it read:

---

21. Moreover, these cases were subject to the *Benson* era *Freeman–Walter–Abele* test—in other words, analysis as it existed before *Diehr* and *Alappat.*

22. *See also* Loew's Drive–In Theatres v. Park–In Theatres, 174 F.2d 547, 552 (1st Cir.1949) (holding that the means for carrying out the system of transacting business lacked "an exercise of the faculty of invention"); In re Patton, 127 F.2d 324, 327–38 (CCPA 1942) (finding claims invalid as failing to define patentable subject matter over the references of record.); Berardini v. Tocci, 190 F. 329, 332 (C.C.S.D.N.Y.1911); In re Wait, 73 F.2d 982, 983 (CCPA 1934) ("Surely these are, and always have been, essential steps in all dealings of this nature, and even conceding, without holding, that

some methods of doing business might present patentable novelty, we think such novelty is lacking here."); In re Howard, 394 F.2d 869 (CCPA 1968) ("We therefore affirm the decision of the Board of Appeals on the ground that the claims do not define a novel process ... [so we find it] unnecessary to consider the issue of whether a method of doing business is inherently unpatentable."). Although a clearer statement was made in In re Patton, 127 F.2d 324, 327 (CCPA 1942) that a system for transacting business, separate from the means for carrying out the system, is not patentable subject matter, the jurisprudence does not require the creation of a distinct business class of unpatentable subject matter.

Though seemingly within the category of process or method, a method of doing business can be rejected as not being within the statutory classes. *See* Hotel Security Checking Co. v. Lorraine Co., 160 F. 467 (2d Cir.1908) and In re Wait, 73 F.2d 982 (CCPA 1934).

MPEP § 706.03(a) (1994). This acknowledgment is buttressed by the U.S. Patent and Trademark 1996 Examination Guidelines for Computer Related Inventions which now read:

> Office personnel have had difficulty in properly treating claims directed to methods of doing business. Claims should not be categorized as methods of doing business. Instead such claims should be treated like any other process claims.

Examination Guidelines, 61 Fed. Reg. 7478, 7479 (1996). We agree that this is precisely the manner in which this type of claim should be treated. Whether the claims are directed to subject matter within § 101 should not turn on whether the claimed subject matter does "business" instead of something else.

Conclusion

The appealed decision is reversed and the case is remanded to the district court for further proceedings consistent with this opinion.

REVERSED and REMANDED.

Notes

1. The Supreme Court was asked to examine the line between patentable subject matter and abstract ideas or laws of nature in *Metabolite Laboratories, Inc. v. Laboratory Corp. of America Holdings*, 370 F.3d 1354 (Fed.Cir. 2004), *cert. granted,* ___ U.S. ___, 126 S.Ct. 601, 163 L.Ed.2d 501 (2005), *cert. dismissed,* ___ U.S. ___, 126 S.Ct. 2921, 165 L.Ed.2d 399 (2006) (mem.), which involved a method patent claiming, inter alia, the mental step of "correlating" elevated homocysteine levels in body fluids with vitamin deficiencies. The Supreme Court granted certiorari in this case to determine "[w]hether a method patent setting forth an indefinite, undescribed, and non-enabling step directing a party simply to 'correlat[e]' test results can validly claim a monopoly over a basic scientific relationship used in medical treatment such that any doctor necessarily infringes the patent merely by thinking about the relationship after looking at a test result." The case thus presented the Court with the opportunity to determine whether the "correlation" step claimed an unpatentable natural phenomenon. In June of 2006, however, the Court dismissed the writ of certiorari as improvidently granted, apparently because the Federal Circuit, in upholding the patent, had not squarely addressed the issue of statutory subject matter under Section 101. Justices Breyer, Stevens, and Souter dissented from the dismissal, arguing that the subject matter was unpatentable.

2. The claims at issue in *State Street* were drafted in "means plus function" language, *see* Chapter 14.A.2, so that rather than claiming a process they claimed an apparatus for carrying out that process (in this case, a programmed personal computer). The district court followed *Alappat* in

holding that this was not determinative of the question whether the claimed invention was an unpatentable abstraction:

> Regardless of whether the claim is drafted as process or apparatus, the Federal Circuit held that the mathematical algorithm/physical transformation test for statutory subject matter under § 101 applies even to "true apparatus" claims. *Alappat,* 33 F.3d at 1542. The C.C.P.A. also adopted this view:
>
>> Labels are not determinative in § 101 inquiries. "Benson applies equally whether an invention is claimed as an apparatus or process, because the form of the claim is often an exercise in drafting." In re Johnson, 589 F.2d 1070, 1077 (C.C.P.A.1978) * * *.
>
> In re Maucorps, 609 F.2d 481, 485 (C.C.P.A.1979). The analysis of the patentability of claimed subject matter therefore does not hinge on whether the claim is drafted in means-plus-function language.

927 F.Supp. at 511 (footnote omitted).

3.   In *AT&T Corp. v. Excel Communications, Inc.,* 172 F.3d 1352 (Fed.Cir.1999), *cert. denied,* 528 U.S. 946, 120 S.Ct. 368, 145 L.Ed.2d 284 (1999), the Federal Circuit held that a billing method which used a mathematical algorithm to calculate values for a database record was patentable subject matter because the process claims that included the algorithm "applied" it to produce a useful, concrete, and tangible result. The court held that process claims may be patentable subject matter even if they do not involve a "physical transformation" or physical limitations. The opinion thus clarifies that *State Street,* which involved claims reciting a machine, applies equally to process claims.

4.   Why does patent law not protect abstract ideas, such as mathematical formulas? If Congress chose to offer such protection, would that exceed Congress's power under the Intellectual Property Clause? Could Congress enact such a law under any other provision of the Constitution?

5.   Although many countries prohibit patents on medical and surgical procedures except where they are a necessary component of a patentable device or product, the United States until recently imposed no special limitations on the patentability of such inventions. Thus, for example, patents have issued for the use of ultrasound (as opposed to the ultrasound apparatus itself) to determine the gender of a fetus by visualizing its genital structure, and for the use of a frown-shaped incision for a particular operation. Patents may even be granted for emergency medical procedures.

In 1996, Congress added subsection (c) to Section 287, denying holders of patents on medical and surgical procedures the right to sue medical practitioners for the unauthorized use of those procedures in medical activities. Pub. L. No. 104–208, 104th Cong., 2d Sess., § 101(a)(1996). A competing bill would have made process patents unavailable for certain medical procedures, but while the American Medical Association supported this proposal, the bill failed in the face of strong opposition, most notably that of the PTO and the pharmaceutical and biotech industries.

Should patent protection be unavailable, or more limited in scope, for certain lifesaving or medically significant inventions? Should the answer be different for products than for processes? Is Section 287(c) an appropriate compromise?

6. Can a process be Section 101 subject matter if it produces a known or naturally occurring product?

7. If an inventor discovers a new use for a public domain device, can the inventor obtain a patent, and if so, on what?

8. Under current law, are tax planning strategies statutory subject matter? Should they be? See U.S. Patents No 6,567,790 (issued May 20, 2003) and No. 6,625,582 (issued Sept. 23, 2003), as well as U.S. Patent Applications No. 2005/0131730 (published June 16, 2005) and No. 2003/0105701 (published June 5, 2003). If tax strategies are patentable, a tax lawyer, accountant, or taxpayer would have to conduct a patent search before implementing a tax planning strategy, or run the risk of being sued for infringement. The owner of a patent on a tax planning strategy could refuse to license others to use that strategy, and could obtain injunctive relief and/or damages (such as a reasonable royalty) against infringers.

3. ORNAMENTAL DESIGNS

Statutes: 35 U.S.C.A. § 171

As explained in the following excerpt, the purpose of design patents is simply to encourage manufacturers to give a pleasing appearance to articles of manufacture. The subject matter of design patents may therefore overlap with the subject matter of copyrights (as illustrated in the *Yardley* excerpt below). It may even overlap with trade dress protection, if the design in question also serves an origin-identifying function.

GORHAM MFG. COMPANY v. WHITE

Supreme Court of the United States, 1871.
81 U.S. (14 Wall.) 511, 20 L.Ed. 731.

MR. JUSTICE STRONG delivered the opinion of the Court.

* * *

The acts of Congress which authorize the grant of patents for designs were plainly intended to give encouragement to the decorative arts. They contemplate not so much utility as appearance, and that, not an abstract impression, or picture, but an aspect given to those objects mentioned in the acts. It is a new and original design for a manufacture, whether of metal or other material; a new and original design for a bust, statue, bas relief, or composition in alto or basso relievo; a new or original impression or ornament to be placed on any article of manufacture; a new and original design for the printing of woollen, silk, cotton, or other fabrics; a new and useful pattern, print, or picture, to be either worked into, or on, any article of manufacture; or a new and original shape or configuration of any article of manufacture—it is one or all of these that the law has in view. And the thing invented or produced, for which a patent is given, is that which gives a peculiar or distinctive appearance to the manufacture, or article to which it may be applied, or to which it gives form. The law manifestly contemplates that giving certain new and original appearances to a manufactured article may enhance its salable value, may enlarge the demand for it, and may be a meritorious service to the public. It therefore proposes to secure for a limited time to the ingenious producer of those appearances the advantages flowing from them. * * *

APPLICATION OF RICHARD Q. YARDLEY

United States Court of Customs and Patent Appeals, 1974.
493 F.2d 1389.

LANE, JUDGE.

[Yardley appeals from the PTO Board of Appeals' decision rejecting his claim for an ornamental design for a watch face. The design comprises a watch face depicting a caricatured figure whose extended arms and hands serve as the watch's hour and minute hands. The basis for the rejection was estoppel in view of prior copyright registrations for the design. The Board took the position that copyright and design patent protection could not be obtained for the same subject matter.]

* * *

Under the power granted to the Congress in Art. I, § 8, cl. 8 of the Constitution, the Congress has enacted the copyright statute as Title 17, United States Code, and the patent statute as Title 35, United States Code. In the two statutes, the Congress has created an area of overlap with regard to at least one type of subject matter.

Thus, the Congress has provided that subject matter of the type involved in the instant appeal is "statutory subject matter" under the copyright statute and "statutory subject matter" under the design patent statute. The statutory language clearly shows the intent of Congress.

* * *

The Supreme Court has recognized that an area of overlapping "statutory subject matter" exists between copyrights and design patents. In Mazer v. Stein, 347 U.S. 201, 217 (1954), the Court stated:

> * * * We do hold that the patentability of the statuettes, fitted as lamps or unfitted, does not bar copyright as works of art. Neither the Copyright Statute nor any other says that because a thing is patentable it may not be copyrighted. We should not so hold. [footnote omitted]

* * *

The existence of an area of overlap was accepted by the examiner and the board. Nevertheless, both held that an author-inventor must elect between securing a copyright or securing a design patent. We disagree.

We believe that the "election of protection" doctrine is in direct conflict with the clear intent of Congress manifested in the two statutory provisions quoted above. The Congress has provided that subject matter of the type involved in this appeal is "statutory subject matter" under the copyright statute and is "statutory subject matter" under the design patent statute, but the Congress has not provided that an author-inventor must elect between securing a copyright or securing a design patent. Therefore, we conclude that it would be contrary to the intent of Congress to hold that an author-inventor must elect between the two available modes of securing exclusive rights.

* * *

[One of the rationales advanced by the Board in affirming the examiner's rejection was] that "[the] framers of the Constitution presumably recognized the difference between the endeavors of authors and inventors, because they used the word 'respective' in reference to their 'writings and discoveries.' "

We agree with the board's view that the framers of the Constitution recognized a distinction between "authors" and "inventors" and "writings" and "discoveries." But, we do not think that the constitutional provision requires an election. The Congress, through its legislation under the authority of the Constitution, has interpreted the Constitution as authorizing an area of overlap where a certain type of creation may be the subject matter of a copyright and the subject matter of a design patent. We see nothing in that legislation which is contradictory and repugnant to the intent of the framers of the Constitution. Congress has not required an author-inventor to elect between the two modes which it has provided for securing exclusive rights on the type of subject matter here involved. If anything, the concurrent availability of both modes of securing exclusive rights aids in achieving the stated purpose of the constitutional provision.

* * *

REVERSED

Note

Although the design patent statutes do not define "design," the PTO employs the following definition:

The design for an article consists of the visual characteristics embodied in or applied to an article.

Since a design is manifested in appearance, the subject matter of a design patent application may relate to the configuration or shape of an article, to the surface ornamentation applied to an article, or to the combination of configuration and surface ornamentation.

Design is inseparable from the article to which it is applied and cannot exist alone merely as a scheme of surface ornamentation. It must be a definite, preconceived thing, capable of reproduction and not merely the chance result of a method.

U.S. Patent & Trademark Office, Manual of Patent Examining Procedure § 1502 (8th ed. 2006).

The term "article of manufacture," also undefined in the statutes, has been broadly construed. *See, e.g.,* In re Hruby, 373 F.2d 997 (CCPA 1967) (reversing PTO's rejection of design patent application for fountain; although design was "a fleeting product of nozzle arrangements," and thus observable only when the water was flowing, "a manufacture is anything made 'by the hands of man' from raw materials, whether literally by hand or by machinery or by art.")

Chapter 12

REQUIREMENTS FOR PATENT PROTECTION

A. UTILITY PATENTS: THE UTILITY REQUIREMENT

Statutes: 35 U.S.C.A. §§ 101, 161

1. DEFINING UTILITY

BRENNER v. MANSON

Supreme Court of the United States, 1966.
383 U.S. 519, 86 S.Ct. 1033, 16 L.Ed.2d 69.

MR. JUSTICE FORTAS delivered the opinion of the Court.

* * *

[The Patent Office rejected Manson's patent application for a chemical process which produces certain known steroids, basing its rejection on Manson's failure "to disclose any utility for" the steroids as required by 35 U.S.C. § 101, even though Manson had established that a closely related steroid had tumor-inhibiting effects in mice. The Board of Appeals stated that "the statutory requirement of usefulness of a product cannot be presumed merely because it happens to be closely related to another compound which is known to be useful." The Court of Customs and Patent Appeals (CCPA) reversed, holding that "where a claimed process produces a known product it is not necessary to show utility for the product," so long as the product is not "detrimental to the public interest."]

* * *

It is not remarkable that differences arise as to how the test of usefulness is to be applied to chemical processes. Even if we knew precisely what Congress meant in 1790 when it devised the "new and useful" phraseology and in subsequent re-enactments of the test, we

424

should have difficulty in applying it in the context of contemporary chemistry where research is as comprehensive as man's grasp and where little or nothing is wholly beyond the pale of "utility"—if that word is given its broadest reach.

Respondent does not—at least in the first instance—rest upon the extreme proposition, advanced by the court below, that a novel chemical process is patentable so long as it yields the intended product and so long as the product is not itself "detrimental." Nor does he commit the outcome of his claim to the slightly more conventional proposition that any process is "useful" within the meaning of § 101 if it produces a compound whose potential usefulness is under investigation by serious scientific researchers, although he urges this position, too, as an alternative basis for affirming the decision of the CCPA. Rather, he begins with the much more orthodox argument that * * * an adjacent homologue of the steroid yielded by his process has been demonstrated to have tumor-inhibiting effects in mice, and that this discloses the requisite utility. We do not accept any of these theories as an adequate basis for overriding the determination of the Patent Office that the "utility" requirement has not been met.

Even on the assumption that the process would be patentable were respondent to show that the steroid produced had a tumor-inhibiting effect in mice,[17] we would not overrule the Patent Office finding that respondent has not made such a showing. The Patent Office held that, despite the reference to the adjacent homologue, respondent's papers did not disclose a sufficient likelihood that the steroid yielded by his process would have similar tumor-inhibiting characteristics. * * *

The second and third points of respondent's argument present issues of much importance. Is a chemical process "useful" within the meaning of § 101 either (1) because it works—i. e., produces the intended product? or (2) because the compound yielded belongs to a class of compounds now the subject of serious scientific investigation? These contentions present the basic problem for our adjudication. Since we find no specific assistance in the legislative materials underlying § 101, we are remitted to an analysis of the problem in light of the general intent of Congress, the purposes of the patent system, and the implications of a decision one way or the other.

In support of his plea that we attenuate the requirement of "utility," respondent relies upon Justice Story's well-known statement that a "useful" invention is one "which may be applied to a beneficial use in society, in contradistinction to an invention injurious to the morals, health, or good order of society, or frivolous and insignificant"[18]—and upon the assertion that to do so would encourage inventors of new

---

17. In light of our disposition of the case, we express no view as to the patentability of a process whose sole demonstrated utility is to yield a product shown to inhibit the growth of tumors in laboratory animals. * * *

18. Note on the Patent Laws, 3 Wheat. App. 13, 24. See also Justice Story's decisions on circuit in Lowell v. Lewis, 15 Fed. Cas. 1018 (No. 8568) (C.C.D.Mass.), and Bedford v. Hunt, 3 Fed.Cas. 37 (No. 1217) (C.C.D.Mass.).

processes to publicize the event for the benefit of the entire scientific community, thus widening the search for uses and increasing the fund of scientific knowledge. Justice Story's language sheds little light on our subject. Narrowly read, it does no more than compel us to decide whether the invention in question is "frivolous and insignificant"—a query no easier of application than the one built into the statute. Read more broadly, so as to allow the patenting of any invention not positively harmful to society, it places such a special meaning on the word "useful" that we cannot accept it in the absence of evidence that Congress so intended. There are, after all, many things in this world which may not be considered "useful" but which, nevertheless, are totally without a capacity for harm.

It is true, of course, that one of the purposes of the patent system is to encourage dissemination of information concerning discoveries and inventions. And it may be that inability to patent a process to some extent discourages disclosure and leads to greater secrecy than would otherwise be the case. The inventor of the process, or the corporate organization by which he is employed, has some incentive to keep the invention secret while uses for the product are searched out. However, in light of the highly developed art of drafting patent claims so that they disclose as little useful information as possible—while broadening the scope of the claim as widely as possible—the argument based upon the virtue of disclosure must be warily evaluated. Moreover, the pressure for secrecy is easily exaggerated, for if the inventor of a process cannot himself ascertain a "use" for that which his process yields, he has every incentive to make his invention known to those able to do so. Finally, how likely is disclosure of a patented process to spur research by others into the uses to which the product may be put? To the extent that the patentee has power to enforce his patent, there is little incentive for others to undertake a search for uses.

Whatever weight is attached to the value of encouraging disclosure and of inhibiting secrecy, we believe a more compelling consideration is that a process patent in the chemical field, which has not been developed and pointed to the degree of specific utility, creates a monopoly of knowledge which should be granted only if clearly commanded by the statute. Until the process claim has been reduced to production of a product shown to be useful, the metes and bounds of that monopoly are not capable of precise delineation. It may engross a vast, unknown, and perhaps unknowable area. Such a patent may confer power to block off whole areas of scientific development, without compensating benefit to the public. The basic quid pro quo contemplated by the Constitution and the Congress for granting a patent monopoly is the benefit derived by the public from an invention with substantial utility. Unless and until a process is refined and developed to this point—where specific benefit exists in currently available form—there is insufficient justification for permitting an applicant to engross what may prove to be a broad field.

These arguments for and against the patentability of a process which either has no known use or is useful only in the sense that it may be an object of scientific research would apply equally to the patenting of the product produced by the process. Respondent appears to concede that with respect to a product, as opposed to a process, Congress has struck the balance on the side of nonpatentability unless "utility" is shown. Indeed, the decisions of the CCPA are in accord with the view that a product may not be patented absent a showing of utility greater than any adduced in the present case. We find absolutely no warrant for the proposition that although Congress intended that no patent be granted on a chemical compound whose sole "utility" consists of its potential role as an object of use-testing, a different set of rules was meant to apply to the process which yielded the unpatentable product. That proposition seems to us little more than an attempt to evade the impact of the rules which concededly govern patentability of the product itself.

This is not to say that we mean to disparage the importance of contributions to the fund of scientific information short of the invention of something "useful," or that we are blind to the prospect that what now seems without "use" may tomorrow command the grateful attention of the public. But a patent is not a hunting license. It is not a reward for the search, but compensation for its successful conclusion. "(A) patent system must be related to the world of commerce rather than to the realm of philosophy. * * * "[25]

The judgment of the CCPA is

Reversed.

JUICY WHIP, INC. v. ORANGE BANG, INC.

United States Court of Appeals, Federal Circuit, 1999.
185 F.3d 1364.

BRYSON, CIRCUIT JUDGE.

The district court in this case held a patent invalid for lack of utility on the ground that the patented invention was designed to deceive customers by imitating another product and thereby increasing sales of a particular good. We reverse and remand.

I

Juicy Whip, Inc., is the assignee of United States Patent No. 5,575,405, which is entitled "Post–Mix Beverage Dispenser With an Associated Simulated Display of Beverage." A "post-mix" beverage dispenser stores beverage syrup concentrate and water in separate locations until the beverage is ready to be dispensed. The syrup and water are mixed together immediately before the beverage is dispensed, which is usually after the consumer requests the beverage. In contrast, in a "pre-mix" beverage dispenser, the syrup concentrate and water are pre-mixed

---

25. Application of Ruschig, 343 F.2d   (Rich, J.).
965, 970, 52 C.C.P.A. (Pat.) 1238, 1245

and the beverage is stored in a display reservoir bowl until it is ready to be dispensed. The display bowl is said to stimulate impulse buying by providing the consumer with a visual beverage display. A pre-mix display bowl, however, has a limited capacity and is subject to contamination by bacteria. It therefore must be refilled and cleaned frequently.

The invention claimed in the '405 patent is a post-mix beverage dispenser that is designed to look like a pre-mix beverage dispenser. The claims require the post-mix dispenser to have a transparent bowl that is filled with a fluid that simulates the appearance of the dispensed beverage and is resistant to bacterial growth. The claims also require that the dispenser create the visual impression that the bowl is the principal source of the dispensed beverage, although in fact the beverage is mixed immediately before it is dispensed, as in conventional post-mix dispensers.

* * *

Juicy Whip sued defendants Orange Bang, Inc., and Unique Beverage Dispensers, Inc., (collectively, "Orange Bang") in the United States District Court for the Central District of California, alleging that they were infringing the claims of the '405 patent. Orange Bang moved for summary judgment of invalidity, and the district court granted Orange Bang's motion on the ground that the invention lacked utility and thus was unpatentable under 35 U.S.C. § 101.

The court concluded that the invention lacked utility because its purpose was to increase sales by deception, *i.e.*, through imitation of another product. The court explained that the purpose of the invention "is to create an illusion, whereby customers believe that the fluid contained in the bowl is the actual beverage that they are receiving, when of course it is not." Although the court acknowledged Juicy Whip's argument that the invention provides an accurate representation of the dispensed beverage for the consumer's benefit while eliminating the need for retailers to clean their display bowls, the court concluded that those claimed reasons for the patent's utility "are not independent of its deceptive purpose, and are thus insufficient to raise a disputed factual issue to present to a jury." The court further held that the invention lacked utility because it "improves the prior art only to the extent that it increases the salability of beverages dispensed from post-mix dispensers"; an invention lacks utility, the court stated, if it confers no benefit to the public other than the opportunity for making a product more salable. Finally, the court ruled that the invention lacked utility because it "is merely an imitation of the pre-mix dispenser," and thus does not constitute a new and useful machine.

II

Section 101 of the Patent Act of 1952, 35 U.S.C. § 101, provides that "[w]hoever invents or discovers any new and useful process, machine, manufacture, or composition of matter, or any new and useful improvement thereof," may obtain a patent on the invention or discovery. The threshold of utility is not high: An invention is "useful" under section 101 if it is capable of providing some identifiable benefit. *See Brenner v. Manson,* 383 U.S. 519, 534, 86 S.Ct. 1033, 16 L.Ed.2d 69 (1966); *Brooktree Corp. v. Advanced Micro Devices, Inc.,* 977 F.2d 1555, 1571 (Fed.Cir.1992) ("To violate § 101 the claimed device must be totally incapable of achieving a useful result"); *Fuller v. Berger,* 120 F. 274, 275 (7th Cir.1903) (test for utility is whether invention "is incapable of serving any beneficial end").

To be sure, since Justice Story's opinion in *Lowell v. Lewis,* 15 F. Cas. 1018 (C.C.D.Mass.1817), it has been stated that inventions that are "injurious to the well-being, good policy, or sound morals of society" are unpatentable. As examples of such inventions, Justice Story listed "a new invention to poison people, or to promote debauchery, or to facilitate private assassination." *Id.* at 1019. Courts have continued to recite Justice Story's formulation, but the principle that inventions are invalid if they are principally designed to serve immoral or illegal purposes has not been applied broadly in recent years. For example, years ago courts invalidated patents on gambling devices on the ground that they were immoral, but that is no longer the law.

In holding the patent in this case invalid for lack of utility, the district court relied on two Second Circuit cases dating from the early years of this century, *Rickard v. Du Bon,* 103 F. 868 (2d Cir.1900), and *Scott & Williams v. Aristo Hosiery Co.,* 7 F.2d 1003 (2d Cir.1925). In the *Rickard* case, the court held invalid a patent on a process for treating tobacco plants to make their leaves appear spotted. At the time of the invention, according to the court, cigar smokers considered cigars with spotted wrappers to be of superior quality, and the invention was designed to make unspotted tobacco leaves appear to be of the spotted— and thus more desirable—type. The court noted that the invention did not promote the burning quality of the leaf or improve its quality in any way; "the only effect, if not the only object, of such treatment, is to spot the tobacco, and counterfeit the leaf spotted by natural causes." *Id.* at 869.

The *Aristo Hosiery* case concerned a patent claiming a seamless stocking with a structure on the back of the stocking that imitated a seamed stocking. The imitation was commercially useful because at the time of the invention many consumers regarded seams in stockings as an indication of higher quality. The court noted that the imitation seam did not "change or improve the structure or the utility of the article," and that the record in the case justified the conclusion that true seamed stockings were superior to the seamless stockings that were the subject of the patent. *See Aristo Hosiery,* 7 F.2d at 1004. "At best," the court stated, "the seamless stocking has imitation marks for the purposes of deception, and the idea prevails that with such imitation the article is more salable." *Id.* That was not enough, the court concluded, to render the invention patentable.

We decline to follow *Rickard* and *Aristo Hosiery,* as we do not regard them as representing the correct view of the doctrine of utility under the Patent Act of 1952. The fact that one product can be altered to make it look like another is in itself a specific benefit sufficient to satisfy the statutory requirement of utility.

It is not at all unusual for a product to be designed to appear to viewers to be something it is not. For example, cubic zirconium is designed to simulate a diamond, imitation gold leaf is designed to imitate real gold leaf, synthetic fabrics are designed to simulate expensive natural fabrics, and imitation leather is designed to look like real leather. In each case, the invention of the product or process that makes such imitation possible has "utility" within the meaning of the patent statute, and indeed there are numerous patents directed toward making one product imitate another. *See, e.g.,* U.S. Pat. No. 5,762,968 (method for producing imitation grill marks on food without using heat); U.S. Pat. No. 5,899,038 (laminated flooring imitating wood); U.S. Pat. No. 5,571,545 (imitation hamburger). Much of the value of such products resides in the fact that they appear to be something they are not. Thus, in this case the claimed post-mix dispenser meets the statutory requirement of utility by embodying the features of a post-mix dispenser while imitating the visual appearance of a pre-mix dispenser.

The fact that customers may believe they are receiving fluid directly from the display tank does not deprive the invention of utility. Orange Bang has not argued that it is unlawful to display a representation of the beverage in the manner that fluid is displayed in the reservoir of the invention, even though the fluid is not what the customer will actually receive. Moreover, even if the use of a reservoir containing fluid that is not dispensed is considered deceptive, that is not by itself sufficient to render the invention unpatentable. The requirement of "utility" in patent law is not a directive to the Patent and Trademark Office or the courts to serve as arbiters of deceptive trade practices. Other agencies, such as the Federal Trade Commission and the Food and Drug Administration, are assigned the task of protecting consumers from fraud and deception in the sale of food products. *Cf. In re Watson,* 517 F.2d 465, 474–76 (CCPA 1975) (stating that it is not the province of the Patent Office to determine, under section 101, whether drugs are safe). As the Supreme Court put the point more generally, "Congress never intended that the patent laws should displace the police powers of the States, meaning by that term those powers by which the health, good order, peace and general welfare of the community are promoted." *Webber v. Virginia,* 103 U.S. (13 Otto) 344, 347–48, 26 L.Ed. 565 (1880).

Of course, Congress is free to declare particular types of inventions unpatentable for a variety of reasons, including deceptiveness. *Cf.* 42 U.S.C. § 2181(a) (exempting from patent protection inventions useful solely in connection with special nuclear material or atomic weapons). Until such time as Congress does so, however, we find no basis in section 101 to hold that inventions can be ruled unpatentable for lack of utility simply because they have the capacity to fool some members of the public. The district court therefore erred in holding that the invention of the '405 patent lacks utility because it deceives the public through imitation in a manner that is designed to increase product sales.

REVERSED and REMANDED.

Notes

1. The broad concept of utility in Section 101 is exemplified by Justice Story's formulation in *Bedford v. Hunt,* 3 Fed.Cas. 37, 37 (No. 1217) (C.C.D.Mass.1817):

> * * * By useful invention, in the statute, is meant such a one as may be applied to some beneficial use in society, in contradistinction to an invention, which is injurious to the morals, the health, or the good order of society. * * * The law, however, does not look to the degree of utility; it simply requires, that it shall be capable of use, and that the use is such as sound morals and policy do not discountenance or prohibit. * * *

See also Lowell v. Lewis, 15 Fed.Cas. 1018 (No. 8568) (C.C.D.Mass.1817) (rejecting the argument that, for a pump to be patentable, "it must be, for the public, a better pump than the common pump"). Justice Story's minimalist approach to utility continues to be cited with approval today. *See, e.g., Tol–O–Matic, Inc. v. Proma Produkt–Und Marketing Gesellschaft m.b.H.,* 945 F.2d 1546, 1552–53 (Fed.Cir.1991).

Does *Brenner v. Manson* impose limits on Justice Story's standard of utility? Does Justice Story's view permit patents on impractical or inefficient inventions? Does *Brenner v. Manson* do so?

2. Evaluate the Supreme Court's response to the disclosure argument in *Brenner v. Manson.* Is it persuasive? What might be the impact of the court's standard of utility on pharmaceutical or biotechnological research?

3. In *In re Brana,* 51 F.3d 1560 (Fed.Cir.1995), the Federal Circuit held that the utility of a drug intended for humans could be adequately demonstrated by animal testing, even if human testing was a prerequisite for approval by the Food and Drug Administration. The court reaffirmed the view asserted by its predecessor, the CCPA, that

> * * * one who has taught the public that a compound exhibits some desirable pharmaceutical property in a standard experimental animal has made a significant and useful contribution to the art, even though it may eventually appear that the compound is without value in the treatment [of] humans.

51 F.3d at 1567 (citing *In re Krimmel,* 292 F.2d 948, 953 (CCPA 1961)). The Federal Circuit added that

> Usefulness in patent law, and in particular in the context of pharmaceutical inventions, necessarily includes the expectation of further research and development. The stage at which an invention in this field becomes useful is well before it is ready to be administered to humans. Were we to require * * * [human] testing in order to prove utility, the associated costs would prevent many companies from obtaining patent protection

on promising new inventions, thereby eliminating an incentive to pursue, through research and development, potential cures in many crucial areas such as the treatment of cancer.

51 F.3d at 1568. Should a patent issue on an invention that is demonstrated to have utility *only* in animals?

4.   Is the utility requirement satisfied where an invention (a) performs some, but not all, of the useful functions which the patent specification asserts that it performs? (b) is a toy or game? (c) is useful for causing injury?

5.   *Utility and Reduction to Practice*: Where an invention has actually been reduced to practice (that is, constructed and made to function in the intended manner), utility is determined by the effects of that reduction to practice. Where there is only a constructive reduction to practice (that is, a complete patent application), utility is determined by the disclosures of the patent. *See Yasuko Kawai v. Metlesics,* 480 F.2d 880 (CCPA 1973). (Reduction to practice is discussed in Section C.4, *infra*.)

6.   For plant patents, 35 U.S.C.A. §§ 161–64, the requirement of utility is replaced by that of "distinctness." (See Section C.5, *infra*.) Why is utility not required?

2.   BIOMEDICAL RESEARCH TOOLS

IN RE FISHER

United States Court of Appeals, Federal Circuit, 2005.
421 F.3d 1365.

MICHEL, CHIEF JUDGE.

[Fisher appealed the PTO's rejection of its claimed nucleic acid sequence for lack of utility.]

* * *

I.   BACKGROUND

A.   *Molecular Genetics and ESTs*

The claimed invention relates to five purified nucleic acid sequences that encode proteins and protein fragments in maize plants. The claimed sequences are commonly referred to as "expressed sequence tags" or "ESTs." Before delving into the specifics of this case, it is important to understand more about the basic principles of molecular genetics and the role of ESTs.

Genes are located on chromosomes in the nucleus of a cell and are made of deoxyribonucleic acid ("DNA"). DNA is composed of two strands of nucleotides in double helix formation. The nucleotides contain one of four bases, adenine ("A"), guanine ("G"), cytosine ("C"), and thymine ("T"), that are linked by hydrogen bonds to form complementary base pairs (i.e., A–T and G–C).

When a gene is expressed in a cell, the relevant double-stranded DNA sequence is transcribed into a single strand of messenger ribonucleic acid ("mRNA"). Messenger RNA contains three of the same bases as DNA (A, G, and C), but contains uracil ("U") instead of thymine. mRNA is released from the nucleus of a cell and used by ribosomes found in the cytoplasm to produce proteins.

Complementary DNA ("cDNA") is produced synthetically by reverse transcribing mRNA. cDNA, like naturally occurring DNA, is composed of nucleotides containing the four nitrogenous bases, A, T, G, and C. Scientists routinely compile cDNA into libraries to study the kinds of genes expressed in a certain tissue at a particular point in time. One of the goals of this research is to learn what genes and downstream proteins are expressed in a cell so as to regulate gene expression and control protein synthesis.

An EST is a short nucleotide sequence that represents a fragment of a cDNA clone. It is typically generated by isolating a cDNA clone and sequencing a small number of nucleotides located at the end of one of the two cDNA strands. When an EST is introduced into a sample containing a mixture of DNA, the EST may hybridize with a portion of DNA. Such binding shows that the gene corresponding to the EST was being expressed at the time of mRNA extraction.

Claim 1 of the '643 application recites:

> A substantially purified nucleic acid molecule that encodes a maize protein or fragment thereof comprising a nucleic acid sequence selected from the group consisting of SEQ ID NO: 1 through SEQ ID NO: 5.

* * * When Fisher filed the '643 application, he claimed ESTs corresponding to genes expressed from the maize pooled leaf tissue at the time of anthesis. Nevertheless, Fisher did not know the precise structure or function of either the genes or the proteins encoded for by those genes.

The '643 application generally discloses that the five claimed ESTs may be used in a variety of ways, including: (1) serving as a molecular marker for mapping the entire maize genome, which consists of ten chromosomes that collectively encompass roughly 50,000 genes; (2) measuring the level of mRNA in a tissue sample via microarray technology to provide information about gene expression; (3) providing a source for primers for use in the polymerase chain reaction ("PCR") process to enable rapid and inexpensive duplication of specific genes; (4) identifying the presence or absence of a polymorphism; (5) isolating promoters via chromosome walking; (6) controlling protein expression; and (7) locating genetic molecules of other plants and organisms.

B. Final Rejection

In a final rejection, dated September 6, 2001, the examiner rejected claim 1 for lack of utility under § 101. The examiner found that the claimed ESTs were not supported by a specific and substantial utility. She concluded that the disclosed uses were not specific to the claimed

ESTs, but instead were generally applicable to any EST. For example, the examiner noted that any EST may serve as a molecular tag to isolate genetic regions. She also concluded that the claimed ESTs lacked a substantial utility because there was no known use for the proteins produced as final products resulting from processes involving the claimed ESTs. The examiner stated: "Utilities that require or constitute carrying out further research to identify or reasonably confirm a 'real world' context of use are not substantial utilities."

[The Board of Patent Appeals and Interferences upheld the examiner's rejection, and Fisher appealed.]

II.   DISCUSSION

Whether an application discloses a utility for a claimed invention is a question of fact. We consequently review the Board's determination that the '643 application failed to satisfy the utility requirement of § 101 for substantial evidence.

A.   *Utility*

1.

Fisher asserts that the Board unilaterally applied a heightened standard for utility in the case of ESTs, conditioning patentability upon "some undefined 'spectrum' of knowledge concerning the corresponding gene function." Fisher contends that the standard is not so high and that Congress intended the language of § 101 to be given broad construction. In particular, Fisher contends that § 101 requires only that the claimed invention "not be frivolous, or injurious to the well-being, good policy, or good morals of society," essentially adopting Justice Story's view of a useful invention from *Lowell v. Lewis*, 15 F. Cas. 1018, 1019, F. Cas. No. 8568 (C.C. Mass. 1817). Under the correct application of the law, Fisher argues, the record shows that the claimed ESTs provide seven specific and substantial uses, regardless whether the functions of the genes corresponding to the claimed ESTs are known. * * * Fisher likewise argues that the general commercial success of ESTs in the marketplace confirms the utility of the claimed ESTs. Hence, Fisher avers that the Board's decision was not supported by substantial evidence and should be reversed.

The government agrees with Fisher that the utility threshold is not high, but disagrees with Fisher's allegation that the Board applied a heightened utility standard. The government contends that a patent applicant need disclose only a single specific and substantial utility pursuant to Brenner, the very standard articulated in the PTO's "Utility Examination Guidelines" ("Utility Guidelines") and followed here when examining the '643 application. It argues that Fisher failed to meet that standard because Fisher's alleged uses are so general as to be meaningless. What is more, the government asserts that the same generic uses could apply not only to the five claimed ESTs but also to any EST derived from any organism. It thus argues that the seven utilities alleged by Fisher are merely starting points for further research, not the end point of any research effort. It further disputes the importance of the commercial success of ESTs in the marketplace, pointing out that Fisher's evidence involved only databases, clone sets, and microarrays, not the five claimed ESTs. Therefore, the government contends that we should affirm the Board's decision.

* * *

The Supreme Court has not defined what the terms "specific" and "substantial" mean per se. Nevertheless, together with the Court of Customs and Patent Appeals, we have offered guidance as to the uses which would meet the utility standard of § 101. From this, we can discern the kind of disclosure an application must contain to establish a specific and substantial utility for the claimed invention.

Courts have used the labels "practical utility" and "real world" utility interchangeably in determining whether an invention offers a "substantial" utility. Indeed, the Court of Customs and Patent Appeals stated that " 'practical utility' is a shorthand way of attributing 'real-world' value to claimed subject matter. In other words, one skilled in the art can use a claimed discovery in a manner which provides some *immediate benefit to the public*." [*Nelson v. Bowler,* 626 F.2d 853, 856 (C.C.P.A. 1980) (emphasis added)]. It thus is clear that an application must show that an invention is useful to the public as disclosed in its current form, not that it may prove useful at some future date after further research. Simply put, to satisfy the "substantial" utility requirement, an asserted use must show that that claimed invention has a significant and presently available benefit to the public.

Turning to the "specific" utility requirement, an application must disclose a use which is not so vague as to be meaningless. * * * Thus, in addition to providing a "substantial" utility, an asserted use must also show that that claimed invention can be used to provide a well-defined and particular benefit to the public.

In 2001, partially in response to questions about the patentability of ESTs, the PTO issued Utility Guidelines governing its internal practice for determining whether a claimed invention satisfies § 101. * * * According to the Utility Guidelines, a specific utility is particular to the subject matter claimed and would not be applicable to a broad class of invention. Manual of Patent Examining Procedure § 2107.01. The Utility Guidelines also explain that a substantial utility defines a "real world" use. In particular, "utilities that require or constitute carrying out further research to identify or reasonably confirm a 'real world' context of use are not substantial utilities." *Id.* Further, the Utility Guidelines discuss "research tools," a term often given to inventions used to conduct research. The PTO particularly cautions that

> an assessment that focuses on whether an invention is useful only in a research setting thus does not address whether the invention is in fact "useful" in a patent sense. [The PTO] must distinguish be-

tween inventions that have a specifically identified substantial utility and inventions whose asserted utility requires further research to identify or reasonably confirm.

Id. The PTO's standards for assessing whether a claimed invention has a specific and substantial utility comport with this court's interpretation of the utility requirement of § 101.

* * *

Regarding the seven uses asserted by Fisher, we observe that each claimed EST uniquely corresponds to the single gene from which it was transcribed ("underlying gene"). As of the filing date of the '643 application, Fisher admits that the underlying genes have no known functions. Fisher, nevertheless, claims that this fact is irrelevant because the seven asserted uses are not related to the functions of the underlying genes. We are not convinced by this contention. Essentially, the claimed ESTs act as no more than research intermediates that may help scientists to isolate the particular underlying protein-encoding genes and conduct further experimentation on those genes. The overall goal of such experimentation is presumably to understand the maize genome—the functions of the underlying genes, the identity of the encoded proteins, the role those proteins play during anthesis, whether polymorphisms exist, the identity of promoters that trigger protein expression, whether protein expression may be controlled, etc. Accordingly, the claimed ESTs are, in words of the Supreme Court, mere "objects of use-testing," to wit, objects upon which scientific research could be performed with no assurance that anything useful will be discovered in the end. *Brenner,* 383 U.S. at 535.

Fisher compares the claimed ESTs to certain other patentable research tools, such as a microscope. Although this comparison may, on first blush, be appealing in that both a microscope and one of the claimed ESTs can be used to generate scientific data about a sample having unknown properties, Fisher's analogy is flawed. As the government points out, a microscope has the specific benefit of optically magnifying an object to immediately reveal its structure. One of the claimed ESTs, by contrast, can only be used to detect the presence of genetic material having the same structure as the EST itself. It is unable to provide any information about the overall structure let alone the function of the underlying gene. Accordingly, while a microscope can offer an immediate, real world benefit in a variety of applications, the same cannot be said for the claimed ESTs. Fisher's proposed analogy is thus inapt. Hence, we conclude that Fisher's asserted uses are insufficient to meet the standard for a "substantial" utility under § 101.

Moreover, all of Fisher's asserted uses represent merely hypothetical possibilities, objectives which the claimed ESTs, or any EST for that matter, could possibly achieve, but none for which they have been used in the real world. Focusing on the two uses emphasized by Fisher at oral argument, Fisher maintains that the claimed ESTs could be used to identify polymorphisms or to isolate promoters. Nevertheless, in the face of a utility rejection, Fisher has not presented any evidence, as the Board well noted, showing that the claimed ESTs have been used in either way. That is, Fisher does not present either a single polymorphism or a single promoter, assuming at least one of each exists, actually identified by using the claimed ESTs. Further, Fisher has not shown that a polymorphism or promoter so identified would have a "specific and substantial" use. The Board, in fact, correctly recognized this very deficiency and cited it as one of the reasons for upholding the examiner's final rejection.

With respect to the remaining asserted uses, there is no disclosure in the specification showing that any of the claimed ESTs were used as a molecular marker on a map of the maize genome. There also is no disclosure establishing that any of the claimed ESTs were used or, for that matter, could be used to control or provide information about gene expression. Significantly, despite the fact that maize leaves produce over two thousand different proteins during anthesis, Fisher failed to show that one of the claimed ESTs translates into a portion of one of those proteins. Fisher likewise did not provide any evidence showing that the claimed ESTs were used to locate genetic molecules in other plants and organisms. What is more, Fisher has not proffered any evidence showing that any such generic molecules would themselves have a specific and substantial utility. Consequently, because Fisher failed to prove that its claimed ESTs can be successfully used in the seven ways disclosed in the '643 application, we have no choice but to conclude that the claimed ESTs do not have a "substantial" utility under § 101.

Furthermore, Fisher's seven asserted uses are plainly not "specific." Any EST transcribed from any gene in the maize genome has the potential to perform any one of the alleged uses. That is, any EST transcribed from any gene in the maize genome may be a molecular marker or a source for primers. Likewise, any EST transcribed from any gene in the maize genome may be used to measure the level of mRNA in a tissue sample, identify the presence or absence of a polymorphism, isolate promoters, control protein expression, or locate genetic molecules of other plants and organisms. Nothing about Fisher's seven alleged uses set the five claimed ESTs apart from the more than 32,000 ESTs disclosed in the '643 application or indeed from any EST derived from any organism. Accordingly, we conclude that Fisher has only disclosed general uses for its claimed ESTs, not specific ones that satisfy § 101.

We agree with the Board that the facts here are similar to those in *Brenner*. There, as noted above, the applicant claimed a process for preparing compounds of unknown use. Similarly, Fisher filed an application claiming five particular ESTs which are capable of hybridizing with underlying genes of unknown function found in the maize genome. The *Brenner* court held that the claimed process lacked a utility because it could be used only to produce a compound of unknown use. The *Brenner* court stated: "We find absolutely no warrant for the proposition that although Congress intended that no patent be granted on a chemical compound whose sole 'utility' consists of its potential role as an object of use-testing, a different set of rules was meant to apply to the process which yielded the unpatentable product." 383 U.S. at 535. Applying that same logic here, we conclude that the claimed ESTs, which do not correlate to an underlying gene of known function, fail to meet the standard for utility intended by Congress.

* * *

* * * Here, granting a patent to Fisher for its five claimed ESTs would amount to a hunting license because the claimed ESTs can be used only to gain further information about the underlying genes and the proteins encoded for by those genes. The claimed ESTs themselves are not an end of Fisher's research effort, but only tools to be used along the way in the search for a practical utility. Thus, while Fisher's claimed ESTs may add a noteworthy contribution to biotechnology research, our precedent dictates that the '643 application does not meet the utility requirement of § 101 because Fisher does not identify the function for the underlying protein-encoding genes. Absent such identification, we hold that the claimed ESTs have not been researched and understood to the point of providing an immediate, well-defined, real world benefit to the public meriting the grant of a patent.

* * *

Fisher's reliance on the commercial success of general EST databases is also misplaced because such general reliance does not relate to the ESTs at issue in this case. Fisher did not present any evidence showing that agricultural companies have purchased or even expressed any interest in the claimed ESTs. And, it is entirely unclear from the record whether such business entities ever will. Accordingly, while commercial success may support the utility of an invention, it does not do so in this case. *See Raytheon Co. v. Roper Corp.*, 724 F.2d 951, 959 (Fed. Cir. 1983) (stating that proof of a utility may be supported when a claimed invention meets with commercial success).

* * *

AFFIRMED.

RADER, CIRCUIT JUDGE, dissenting.

This court today determines that expressed sequence tags (ESTs) do not satisfy 35 U.S.C. § 101 unless there is a known use for the genes from which each EST is transcribed. While I agree that an invention must demonstrate utility to satisfy § 101, these claimed ESTs have such a utility, at least as research tools in isolating and studying other molecules. Therefore, I respectfully dissent.

Several, if not all, of Fisher's asserted utilities claim that ESTs function to study other molecules. In simple terms, ESTs are research tools. Admittedly ESTs have use only in a research setting. However, the value and utility of research tools generally is beyond question, even though limited to a laboratory setting. *See* U.S. Pat. & Trademark Off., Manual of Patent Examining Procedure (MPEP) § 2107.01 at 2100–33 (8th ed. 2001, rev. Feb. 2003) ("Many research tools such as gas chromatographs, screening assays, and nucleotide sequencing techniques have a clear, specific and unquestionable utility (e.g., they are useful in analyzing compounds).''). Thus, if the claimed ESTs qualify as research tools, then they have a "specific" and "substantial" utility sufficient for § 101. If these ESTs do not enhance research, then *Brenner v. Manson* controls and erects a § 101 bar for lack of utility. For the following reasons, these claimed ESTs are more akin to patentable research tools than to the unpatentable methods in *Brenner*.

In *Brenner*, the Court confronted a growing conflict between this court's predecessor, the Court of Customs and Patent Appeals (CCPA), and the Patent Office over the patentability of methods of producing compounds with no known use. * * * *Brenner* put an end to these cases because, in the 1960s, the Court could not distinguish between denying patents to compounds with no known use and denying patents to methods of producing those useless compounds. The Court commented:

> We find absolutely no warrant for the proposition that although Congress intended that no patent be granted on a chemical compound whose sole 'utility' consists of its potential role as an object of use-testing, a different set of rules was meant to apply to the process which yielded the unpatentable product. That proposition seems to us little more than an attempt to evade the impact of the rules which concededly govern patentability of the product itself.

Id. at 535. This court's predecessor later extended *Brenner* to bar patents on compounds as intermediates in the preparation of other compounds having no known use. *See In re Kirk,* 54 C.C.P.A. 1119, 376 F.2d 936 (CCPA 1967) (rejecting intermediaries for steroids with no known use). These cases, however, share a common underpinning—a method of producing a compound with no known use has no more benefit to society than the useless compound itself.

This case is very different. Unlike the methods and compounds in *Brenner* and *Kirk*, Fisher's claimed EST's *are* beneficial to society. As an example, these research tools "may help scientists to isolate the particular underlying protein-encoding genes ... [with the] overall goal of such experimentation ... presumably [being] to understand the maize genome[.]" Majority Opinion, slip op. at 13. They also can serve as a probe introduced into a sample tissue to confirm "that the gene corresponding to the EST was being expressed in the sample tissue at the time of mRNA extraction." *Id.,* slip op. at 3.

These research tools are similar to a microscope; both take a researcher one step closer to identifying and understanding a previously unknown and invisible structure. Both supply information about a molecular structure. Both advance research and bring scientists closer to unlocking the secrets of the corn genome to provide better food production for the hungry world. If a microscope has § 101 utility, so too do these ESTs.

The Board and this court acknowledge that the ESTs perform a function, that they have a utility, but proceed quickly to a value judgment that the utility would not produce enough valuable information. The Board instead complains that the information these ESTs supply is too "insubstantial" to merit protection. Yet this conclusion denies the very nature of scientific advance. Science always advances in small incremental steps. While acknowledging the patentability of research tools generally (and microscopes as one example thereof), this court concludes with little scientific foundation that these ESTs do not qualify as research tools because they do not "offer an immediate, real world benefit" because further research is required to understand the underlying gene. This court further faults the EST research for lacking any "assurance that anything useful will be discovered in the end." These criticisms would foreclose much scientific research and many vital research tools. Often scientists embark on research with no assurance of success and knowing that even success will demand "significant additional research."

Nonetheless, this court, oblivious to the challenges of complex research, discounts these ESTs because it concludes (without scientific evidence) that they do not supply enough information. This court reasons that a research tool has a "specific" and "substantial" utility *only* if the studied object is readily understandable using the claimed tool—that no further research is required. Surely this cannot be the law. Otherwise, only the final step of a lengthy incremental research inquiry gets protection.

Even with a microscope, significant additional research is often required to ascertain the particular function of a "revealed" structure. To illustrate, a cancerous growth, magnified with a patented microscope, can be identified and distinguished from other healthy cells by a properly trained doctor or researcher. But even today, the scientific community still does not fully grasp the reasons that cancerous growths increase in mass and spread throughout the body,[1] or the nature of compounds that interact with them, or the interactions of environmental or genetic conditions that contribute to developing cancer. Significant additional research is required to answer these questions. Even with answers to these questions, the cure for cancer will remain in the distance. Yet the microscope still has "utility" under § 101. Why? Because it takes the researcher one step closer to answering these questions. Each step, even if small in isolation, is nonetheless a benefit to society sufficient to give a viable research tool "utility" under § 101. In fact, experiments that fail still serve to eliminate some possibilities and provide information to the research process.

The United States Patent Office, above all, should recognize the incremental nature of scientific endeavor. Yet, in the interest of easing its administrative load, the Patent Office will eliminate some research tools as providing "insubstantial" advances. How does the Patent Office

---

1. ESTs have already been used to advance cancer research well beyond what is achievable using microscopes alone. *See* Andy J. Minn, Genes That Mediate Breast Cancer Metastisis To Lung, Nature, July 28, 2005 at 518–24 (discussing research to identify genes that mark and mediate breast cancer metastisis to the lung).

know which "insubstantial" research step will contribute to a substantial breakthrough in genomic study? Quite simply, it does not.

* * *

Thus, for the foregoing reasons, I would find that Fisher's asserted utilities qualify the claimed ESTs as research tools useful in the study of other molecules. Because research tools provide a cognizable benefit to society, much like a microscope, the ESTs claimed here have "utility" under § 101. * * *

Note

Should biotechnology research tools such as ESTs be patentable at all? Should they be treated differently from other types of research tools, such as microscopes? Should they be patentable, but subject to different rules regarding enforceability? *Cf.* 35 U.S.C. § 287(c) (immunizing medical practitioners from liability for infringing patents on medical procedures). What types of rules would strike a proper balance between the interests of the inventor and the public interest in making such research tools readily available? *See, e.g.,* Janice M. Mueller, *No "Dilettante Affair": Rethinking the Experimental Use Exception to Patent Infringement for Biomedical Research Tools,* 76 Wash. L. Rev. 1 (2001); Rebecca Eisenberg, *Technology Transfer and the Genome Project: Problems with Patenting Research Tools,* 5 RISK 163 (1994).

B. DESIGN PATENTS: THE ORNAMENTALITY REQUIREMENT

Statutes: 35 U.S.C.A. § 171

AVIA GROUP INTERNATIONAL, INC. v. L.A. GEAR CALIFORNIA, INC.
United States Court of Appeals, Federal Circuit, 1988.
853 F.2d 1557.

Nies, Circuit Judge.

L.A. Gear California, Inc. (LAG) appeals the decision of the United States District Court for the Central District of California, *Pensa, Inc. v. L.A. Gear of California, Inc.,* 4 USPQ2d 1016 (C.D.Cal.1987), granting the motion of Avia Group International, Inc. (formerly Pensa, Inc.) for summary judgment holding United States Design Patent Nos. 284,420 ('420) and 287,301 ('301) valid as between the parties and willfully infringed, and the case exceptional under 35 U.S.C. § 285 (1982). We affirm.

I

BACKGROUND

Avia owns the '420 patent, claiming an ornamental design for an athletic shoe outer sole, and the '301 patent, claiming an ornamental design for an athletic shoe upper, by assignment from the inventor, James Tong. * * * Avia filed suit against LAG alleging, inter alia, that both of LAG's models infringed its '420 design patent and that LAG's Hi–Top model also infringed the '301 design. LAG counterclaimed for a declaratory judgment that the two patents were not infringed and were invalid because the designs were both obvious and functional. Avia moved for partial summary judgment on the patent validity and infringement issues and for attorney fees.

Finding no bona fide dispute as to any material fact and that Avia had shown entitlement to judgment as a matter of law, the court granted Avia's motion after a hearing. * * *

* * *

III

VALIDITY OF '420 AND '301 DESIGN PATENTS

* * *

The patents in suit are design patents. Under 35 U.S.C. § 171 (1982), a patent may be obtained on the design of an article of manufacture which is "new, original and ornamental" and "nonobvious" within the meaning of section 103, which is incorporated by reference into section 171. LAG attacks the validity of the patents for the subject designs covering parts of shoes on the grounds (1) that the designs are primarily functional rather than ornamental and (2) that the designs would have been obvious from the prior art.

A. Ornamental versus Functional Designs

* * *

LAG correctly asserts that if a patented design is "primarily functional," rather than primarily ornamental, the patent is invalid. *See* Power Controls Corp. v. Hybrinetics, Inc., 806 F.2d 234, 238 (Fed.Cir. 1986). When function dictates a design, protection would not promote the decorative arts, a purpose of the design patent statute. *See* 1 D. Chisum, Patents § 1.04[2] at 1–194.1 to 1.195 (1986). There is no dispute that shoes are functional and that certain features of the shoe designs in issue perform functions. However, a distinction exists between the functionality of an article or features thereof and the functionality of the particular design of such article or features thereof that perform a function. Were that not true, it would not be possible to obtain a design patent on a utilitarian article of manufacture, *see, e.g.,* Pacific Furniture Mfg. Co. v. Preview Furniture Corp., 800 F.2d 1111 (Fed.Cir.1986) (design patent for chairs), or to obtain both design and utility patents on the same article, *see, e.g.,* Carman Indus., Inc. v. Wahl, 724 F.2d 932, 938–39 (Fed.Cir.1983); In re Dubois & Will, 262 F.2d 88, 90 (CCPA 1958).

With respect to functionality of the design of the '301 patent, the court stated:

> [LAG] has taken each little aspect of the upper and pointed out that many of the aspects or features of the upper have a function. Even if, arguendo, true[,] that would not make the design primarily functional. If the functional aspect or purpose could be accomplished in many other ways that [sic] is involved in this very design, that fact is enough to destroy the claim that this design is primarily functional. There are many things in the ['301] patent on the upper which are clearly ornamental and nonfunctional such as the location of perforations and how they are arranged, and the stitching and how it's arranged, and the coloration of elements between black and white colors.
>
> The overall aesthetics of the various components and the way they are combined are quite important and are not functional. They are purely aesthetic. . . .

Pensa, Inc., 4 USPQ2d at 1019.

On the design of the '420 patent, the court made a similar analysis of various features and concluded:

> But every function which [LAG] says is achieved by one of the component aspects of the sole in this case could be and has been achieved by different components. And that is a very persuasive rationale for the holding that the design overall is not primarily functional. Moreover, there is no function which even defendant assigns to the swirl effect around the pivot point, which swirl effect is a very important aspect of the design.
>
> . . . .
>
> . . . [T]his is a unique and pleasing design and it's [sic] patentability in my view is not offset or destroyed by the fact that the utility patent is utilized and incorporated in this aesthetically pleasing design.
>
> Plaintiff has given us evidence of other shoes that incorporate the utility patent and its concavity—others of its own shoes—but with a totally different design, and has thus established that the utility patent does not make the design patent invalid in this case.

Pensa, Inc., 4 USPQ2d at 1019–20. We agree that the designs in suit have not persuasively been shown to be functional and that no genuine issue of material fact is present with respect to this issue.

[The court also rejected the argument that Avia's patents were invalid on obviousness grounds, finding no genuine issue of material fact or error of law on the part of the district court, and affirmed the district court's opinion.]

* * *

IN RE CARLETTI
United States Court of Customs and Patent Appeals, 1964.
328 F.2d 1020.

RICH, JUDGE.

This appeal is from the decision of the Patent Office Board of Appeals affirming the rejection of the claim in an application for a design patent, serial No. 56,122, filed May 28, 1959, for "GASKET."

* * *

One of the examiner's principal grounds of rejection was that the differences between appellants' gasket and the prior art, to which differences we must look in deciding whether patentable invention exists, are *dictated by functional requirements*, "i.e., to make the article fit the place where it is to be used and to increase the functional utility thereof rather than to appeal to the esthetic sense." * * * The board affirmed this rejection saying:

> The instant design *differs* from the [prior art] * * * essentially by the plurality of concentric annular ribs and by the recessed groove. These features, however, are added to the Somerville citation [disclosure] essentially for *purely functional purposes*, the ribs to effect better sealing action and the groove primarily to prevent a fileting action in the mold. It has been held in Court decisions including Connecticut Paper Products Co.-vs-New York Paper Co., 127 F.(2d) 423, 53 USPQ 271, that the addition of features placed upon an old design for *purely functional purposes* does not ordinarily render a design patentable. [Emphasis added.]

> The Examiner's rejection of the appealed claim as being unpatentable over the reference is sustained.

It is thus seen that the *functionality* of the elements asserted to *distinguish* the design from the prior art—as distinguished from the obviousness of those features—was a ground, if not a principal ground, of rejection. The Patent Office Solicitor's brief takes the same position.

While it cannot be said that the Patent Office has made out an ironclad case of the functionality of the features relied on for patentability, more than a good case has been made out and the appellants have failed to refute it. In the first place we have in the record the military specification covering this gasket, MIL–P–40068, 9 June 1959, containing engineering drawings in great detail, specifying the exact position, dimensions, and tolerances of the grooves and ribs etc., without the slightest suggestion that they serve in any way as ornamentation. In the second place, appellants' brief says:

> The design was created at the U.S. Army Quartermaster Research and Engineering Center, Natick, Massachusetts, in the course of appellants' employment by the Government of the United States as

technologists. Its intended use is as a component of a closure assembly for containers, such as gasoline drums.

The record further shows such drums to be the common 55 gal. drums and the gasket to be for the threaded plug which closes the bung hole therein.

It seems naive in the extreme to believe that anyone would try to "ornament" the rubber gasket on the under side of the bung cap for a gasoline drum, notwithstanding the seriocomic legal arguments presented by counsel for the Department of the Army. Common sense and but a slight familiarity with the requirements of gaskets both point to the obvious functionality of the groove and ribs on the gasket. In a letter to the Commissioner of Patents in this application on August 1, 1960, appellants' counsel said:

> [T]he current design resulted from a development program which was inaugurated more than a year prior to publication of MIL–P–40068. Numerous gaskets were *designed* and subjected to *severe testing* under all service conditions including tropical and arctic. Only a device which passes all tests and experiments is finally standardized in a procurement specification. [Emphasis added.]

The gasket at bar was standardized in a specification. This does not bespeak the existence of design in anything other than the sense of engineering "design," and certainly contraindicates the existence of the "ornamental design" referred to in 35 U.S.C. § 71 under which a patent is here sought.

It is clear that appellants never invented an "ornamental design." The appearance of appellants' gasket seems as much dictated by functional considerations as is the appearance of a piece of rope, which, too, has ribs and grooves nicely arranged. The fact that it is attractive or pleasant to behold is not enough. Many well-constructed articles of manufacture whose configurations are dictated solely by function are pleasing to look upon, for example a hex-nut, a ball bearing, a golf club, or a fishing rod, the pleasure depending largely on one's interests. But it has long been settled that when a configuration is the result of functional considerations only, the resulting design is not patentable as an ornamental design for the simple reason that it is not "ornamental"— was not created for the purpose of ornamenting. Walker on Patents, Deller Ed., Sec. 138, p. 434; *Connecticut Paper Products* case, cited by the board, *supra,* Hueter v. Compco Corp., 179 F.2d 416; Applied Arts Corp. v. Grand Rapids Metalcraft Corp., 67 F.2d 428; In re Garbo, 48 CCPA 845, 848, 287 F.2d 192. In the latter case this court said:

> It is true * * * that a design may embody functional features and still be patentable, but in order to attain this legal status under these circumstances, the design *must have an unobvious appearance, distinct from that dictated solely by functional considerations.* [Emphasis added.]

That is the principle which is believed to apply here.

Neither does it suffice to argue, as appellants do, that the ribs and grooves *could* have been less gracefully arranged than they are in their actual "balanced relationship." If obviousness enters into this case, it is at this point. If it is desired to employ a groove for flexibility and three concentric ribs to make a good seal on a flat drum head, what is more obvious than to arrange them with approximately equal spacing, as was done? But it was done without thought of ornament. The creation or origination of an ornamental design does not reside in the mere *avoidance* of dissymmetry.

For the foregoing reasons the decision is affirmed.

Notes

1. As *Avia Group International* indicates, for design patents the requirement of ornamentality replaces that of utility. The term "ornamental" in Section 171 has been construed to require not only that ornamentation be the primary purpose of the design, but also that the design have an aesthetically pleasing *effect*; the design, it is sometimes said, must "appeal to the eye as a thing of beauty." *Bentley v. Sunset House Distributing Corp.*, 359 F.2d 140, 145 (9th Cir.1966); *see also Bonito Boats, Inc. v. Thunder Craft Boats, Inc.*, 489 U.S. 141, 148, 109 S.Ct. 971, 976, 103 L.Ed.2d 118 (1989) (ornamental design "must present an aesthetically pleasing appearance that is not dictated by function alone"). Under this standard, an aesthetically poor design, no matter how original or creative, will be ineligible for design patent protection, although it may be copyrightable (see Chapter 15) and/or protectible under trademark and unfair competition law if it acquires secondary meaning (see Chapter 2.B–C). Not surprisingly, courts examining the validity of design patents display considerable variation in their aesthetic judgments. In addition, as a matter of policy the PTO will not grant a design patent for a design which it deems to be "offensive to any race, religion, sex, ethnic group, or nationality." U.S. Patent & Trademark Office, Manual of Patent Examining Procedure § 1504.01 (July 1996). Are these standards consistent with the design patent statutes? Do they represent sound policy? Is it appropriate to ask the PTO and the courts to make these judgments? For example, if a court finds that a design is non-functional, but also aesthetically unappealing, is it appropriate to deny design patent protection?

2. According to the Federal Circuit, the existence of alternative designs is an important factor, but not the sole factor, in determining whether a particular design is primarily ornamental:

> The presence of alternative designs may or may not assist in determining whether the challenged design can overcome a functionality challenge. Consideration of alternative designs, if present, is a useful tool that may allow a court to conclude that a challenged design is not invalid for functionality. As such, alternative designs join the list of other appropriate considerations for assessing whether the patented design as a whole—its overall appearance—was dictated by functional considerations. Other appropriate considerations might include: whether the protected design represents the best design; whether alternative designs would adversely affect the utility of the specified article; wheth-

er there are any concomitant utility patents; whether the advertising touts particular features of the design as having specific utility; and whether there are any elements in the design or an overall appearance clearly not dictated by function.

Berry Sterling Corp. v. Prescor Plastics, Inc., 122 F.3d 1452, 1456 (Fed. Cir. 1997).

     3.   Should design patent protection be available for a decorative design (a) on the outer surface of a mattress? (b) on an artificial hip joint designed to be surgically implanted inside the human body?

C.   NOVELTY

Statutes: 35 U.S.C.A. § 102(a), (e), (f), (g)

     The novelty requirement of patent law, which applies to all varieties of patents, differs from the originality requirement of copyright law. Under copyright law, a work of authorship that displays at least minimal creativity may be copyrighted even if it is similar or identical to another work, as long as it was not the result of copying. In contrast, an invention is not patentable unless it differs from all products and processes in existence at the time it was invented; in patent terminology, the invention must not be "anticipated" by the prior art. Thus, even if the invention was independently created, it will be unpatentable if it is too similar to the prior art.

     "Anticipation under 35 U.S.C.A. § 102 requires the presence in a single prior art disclosure of each and every element of a claimed invention." *Lewmar Marine, Inc. v. Barient, Inc.,* 827 F.2d 744, 747 (Fed.Cir.1987). The test for anticipation, it has been observed, is the same as the test for literal infringement: "That which would literally infringe if later in time anticipates if earlier than the date of invention." *Id.*

     Each of the four *novelty bars,* 35 U.S.C.A. §§ 102(a), (e), (f), and (g), focuses on the state of the art at the moment of invention, and can be triggered only by the activities of persons other than the patent inventor named in the application. Thus, an inventor's own work cannot be prior art for novelty purposes.

     In contrast, subsections (b), (c), and (d) of Section 102 do not address novelty at the time of invention. Instead, these *statutory bars* (also called *loss of rights* provisions) focus on events which occur at any time before the patent application is filed, and which, in effect, cause a forfeiture of the right to receive a patent, regardless of whether the events in question predate the moment of invention. *See* Section E, *infra.*

1.   SECTION 102(A)

(i) *"Known or Used"*

IN RE BORST

United States Court of Customs and Patent Appeals, 1965.
345 F.2d 851.

SMITH, JUDGE.

[The patent applicant appealed from the PTO's rejection of several claims pertaining to a method for safely and effectively controlling a relatively large neutron output by varying a small and easily controlled neutron input source.]

The single reference relied upon by the Patent Office in rejecting the appealed claims is an Atomic Energy Commission document entitled 'KAPL–M–RWS–1, A Stable Fission Pile with High Speed Control.' The document is in the form of an unpublished memorandum authored by one Samsel, and will hereinafter be referred to as 'Samsel.' Samsel is dated February 14, 1947 and was classified as a secret document by the Commission until March 9, 1957, when it was declassified. In essence, Samsel sets forth and discusses the problems present in the control of a nuclear reactor, the concept of use of successive fuel stages to effect such control, and a description of the arrangement, composition and relative proportions of materials required to obtain the sought-for results. Samsel is prefaced by a statement that it was made to record an idea, and it nowhere indicates that the idea had been tested in an operating reactor.

The Patent Office does not invoke Samsel as a publication (which it apparently was not, at any pertinent date). Rather, the contention is that Samsel constitutes evidence of prior knowledge within the meaning of 35 U.S.C. § 102(a).

While there seems to be some disagreement on the part of the solicitor, we think the most reasonable interpretation of the examiner's rejection, and one which is concurred in by the board and by appellant, is that claims 27, 30, 31 and 32 are fully met by Samsel and thus the subject matter defined therein is unpatentable because it was known by another in this country prior to appellant's invention thereof. * * *

Our own independent consideration of Samsel has convinced us that it contains adequate enabling disclosure of the invention of claims 27 and 30–32, and appellant does not appear to contend otherwise. Rather, appellant contends that Samsel is not available as evidence of prior knowledge under sections 102(a) and 103. * * *

In the case of In re Schlittler, 234 F.2d 882, 43 CCPA 986, this court was presented with the following situation: A manuscript containing an anticipatory disclosure of the appellants' claimed invention had been submitted to The Journal of the American Chemical Society and was later published. The date to which the appellants' application was entitled for purposes of constructive reduction to practice was earlier than the publication date of the Journal article, and therefore the Patent Office did not contend that the 'printed publication' portion of section 102(a) was applicable. However, the manuscript bore a notation that it had been received by the publisher on a date prior to the effective filing date of the appellants' application. On the basis of this notation the Patent Office argued that the article constituted sufficient evidence of prior knowledge under section 102(a).

After an exhaustive review of the authorities, and of the legislative history of the Patent Act of 1952, this court rejected the contention of the Patent Office, and concluded that such a document was not proper evidence of prior knowledge. In reversing, the court stated (234 F.2d at 886):

> 'In our opinion, one of the essential elements of the word 'known' as used in 35 U.S.C. § 102(a) is knowledge of an invention which has been completed by reduction to practice, actual or constructive, and is not satisfied by disclosure of a conception only.'

And therefore, since the Journal article, 'at best, could be evidence of nothing more than conception and disclosure of the invention,' the

> ' * * * placing of the Nystrom article in the hands of the publishers did not constitute either prima facie or conclusive evidence of knowledge or use by others in this country of the invention disclosed by the article, within the meaning of Title 35, § 102(a) of the United States Code, since the knowledge was of a conception only and not of a reduction to practice.'

Another aspect of the court's discussion in *Schlittler* involved the well-established principle that 'prior knowledge of a patented invention would not invalidate a claim of the patent unless such knowledge was available to the public.' After reaffirming that principle, the court went on to state:

> 'Obviously, in view of the above authorities, the mere placing of a manuscript in the hands of a publisher does not necessarily make it available to the public within the meaning of said authorities.'

However, the court did not go on to determine whether the Journal article was in fact available to the public, since such determination was deemed unnecessary for disposition of the case, under the court's theory.

We shall consider first the public availability aspect of the *Schlittler* case. Although that portion of the *Schlittler* opinion is clearly dictum, we think it just as clearly represents the settled law. The knowledge contemplated by section 102(a) must be accessible to the public. * * *

In the instant case, Samsel was clearly not publicly available during the period it was under secrecy classification by the Atomic Energy Commission. We note that the date of declassification, however, was prior to appellant's filing date, and it is perhaps arguable that Samsel became accessible to the public upon declassification. But we do not find it necessary to decide that difficult question, for there is a statutory provision which is, we think, dispositive of the question of publicity. Section 155 of the Atomic Energy Act of 1954 (42 U.S.C. 2185) provides:

'In connection with applications for patents covered by this subchapter, the fact that the invention or discovery was known or used before shall be a bar to the patenting of such invention or discovery even though such prior knowledge or use was under secrecy within the atomic energy program of the United States.'

We think the meaning and intent of this provision is so clear as to admit of no dispute: With respect to subject matter covered by the patent provisions of the Atomic Energy Act, prior knowledge or use under section 102(a) need not be accessible to the public. Therefore, Samsel is available as evidence of prior knowledge insofar as the requirement for publicity is concerned.

The remaining consideration regarding the status of Samsel as evidence of prior knowledge directly calls into question the correctness of the unequivocal holding in *Schlittler* that the knowledge must be of a reduction to practice, either actual or constructive. After much deliberation, we have concluded that such a requirement is illogical and anomalous, and to the extent Schlittler is inconsistent with the decision in this case, it is hereby expressly overruled.

The mere fact that a disclosure is contained in a patent or application and thus 'constructively' reduced to practice, or that it is found in a printed publication, does not make the disclosure itself any more meaningful to those skilled in the art (and thus, ultimately, to the public). Rather, the criterion should be whether the disclosure is sufficient to enable one skilled in the art to reduce the disclosed invention to practice. In other words, the disclosure must be such as will give possession of the invention to the person of ordinary skill. Even the act of publication or the fiction of constructive reduction to practice will not suffice if the disclosure does not meet this standard.

Where, as is true of Samsel, the disclosure constituting evidence of prior knowledge contains, in the words of the Board of Appeals, 'a description of the invention fully commensurate with the present patent application,' we hold that the disclosure need not be of an invention reduced to practice, either actually or constructively. We therefore affirm the rejection of claims 27, 30, 31 and 32.

BENNETT REGULATOR GUARDS, INC.
v. CANADIAN METER CO. INC.

United States Court of Appeals, Federal Circuit, 2006.
184 Fed. Appx. 977.

PROST, CIRCUIT JUDGE.

[Bennett's patent claims a spray cover for a natural gas regulator pressure valve. The spray cover prevents the valve from failing due to ice formation. Accused infringer American Meter Co. argued that its own activities prior to the patentholder's 1994 invention date invalidated the claims at issue on the grounds of prior public knowledge and public use under 35 U.S.C. § 102(a).]

I.

* * *

Meter alleged that its own activities relating to the Splash Guard anticipated Bennett's patent. Specifically, in the 1980s, Meter began searching for the cause of a few catastrophic failures of gas regulating valves. As a result of that research, Meter realized that the old style regulators had malfunctioned when, during freezing conditions, water splashed and subsequently froze onto the screens of the regulators. Canadian Meter then developed a product called the Splash Guard that kept water from splashing up onto the screen and thereby prevented malfunctioning due to ice formation. While Meter never patented its Splash Guard, in the early 1990s, Meter undertook a number of activities relating to its Splash Guard product. These efforts are the factual basis for Meter's theories of anticipation upon which Meter filed a motion for summary judgment of invalidity.[1]

* * *

The district court [granted] the motion for summary judgment as to Meter's last two theories, namely that the patent was anticipated by prior public use and public knowledge. First, Meter contended that, in October 1991, it conducted regulatory testing of the Splash Guard with the Canadian Gas Association ("CGA") in Nebraska City, Nebraska to certify that the Splash Guard met CGA safety standards. The testing was evidenced by affidavits describing the tests, by memos discussing the tests, by the certificate resulting from the CGA testing, and by the test results. Meter contended that the testing was not confidential and was accessible to the public and therefore the Nebraska City testing of the Splash Guard constituted an anticipatory public use under 35 U.S.C. § 102(a) and (b).

Second, Meter contended that the Splash Guard was publicly known in the United States, and thus anticipated under 35 U.S.C. § 102(a). In support, Meter submitted statements from employees attesting to their knowledge of the Splash Guard product demonstrating, according to Meter, that the Splash Guard was known in the United States. The statements also state that Meter's knowledge about the Splash Guard was publicly accessible. Furthermore, Meter submitted a letter sent to the Bay State Gas Company, another letter to the Vermont Gas Company, and an inter-office memo. The letters tell the gas companies that Meter would be "pleased to offer any information [they] may require" regarding the Splash Guard. The inter-office memo asks American Meter to relay customer feedback regarding the Splash Guard. Meter contended

---

1. In this case, the accused infringing device, the Splash Guard, is also the device that allegedly provides the anticipatory use or knowledge. Thus, absent a dispute as to whether the complete Splash Guard device was involved in the anticipatory act, we agree with the district court that "[w]hen the anticipatory reference is the accused product, the Defendant's burden [of showing that the anticipatory reference contains each and every claim element] is satisfied by the Plaintiff's infringement allegations in the Complaint that the accused product embodies the claimed invention."

that these documents evidence that American Meter's knowledge about the Splash Guard was publicly accessible and therefore the '029 patent is invalid due to anticipation by public knowledge under 35 U.S.C. § 102(a).

As to these last two theories, the district court found that Meter presented clear and convincing evidence that the Splash Guard was both publicly known and used prior to the earliest potential date of invention for the '029 patent. First, the district court found that the CGA 1991 testing of the Splash Guard in Nebraska City, Nebraska, was a corroborated public use. Reinforcing the testimony relating to the testing, the district court held that "the certification document not only demonstrates public use, but also corroborates the other documents and statements referencing the Nebraska City testing." Second, as to public knowledge, the district court held that "[t]here can be no dispute that the claimed invention, embodied in the Splash Guard product, was known 'in this country'. [Bennett] cannot argue that Defendant American Meter lacked knowledge of the accused product.... The issue, therefore, is whether the Defendants' knowledge ... was 'public.' " The district court found that the letters from [sic] Bay State Gas Company and Vermont Gas Company along with an inter-office memo demonstrated that Meter's knowledge about the Splash Guard was not secret or confidential. The district court concluded that "the corroborative documentary evidence of public knowledge ... is substantial and constitutes clear and convincing evidence of invalidity." As a result, the district court granted Meter's motion for summary judgment of invalidity. Bennett appealed and we have jurisdiction pursuant to 28 U.S.C. § 1295(a)(1).

II.

* * *

A.

Bennett contends that, as to the public use of the Splash Guard, it raised a genuine issue of fact as to the public nature of the Nebraska City testing and that there is a genuine issue of fact as to whether the product tested in Nebraska City possessed each and every element of the asserted claims in the patent. In response, Meter contends that its testing of the Splash Guard in Nebraska City with a team from the CGA was not confidential. Meter contends that the CGA was under no obligations to keep information about the Splash Guard secret and therefore the testing constitutes a public use under § 102(a) or (b). Further, Meter contends that the complete Splash Guard was tested in Nebraska City and therefore there is no question as to the identity of the public use in regards to the claim elements.

We conclude that there exists a genuine issue of material fact as to the public nature of the testing in Nebraska City. As pointed out by Bennett, a Vice President from Meter testified that "I believe in my opinion, the Canadian Gas Association views [the CGA testing] as being proprietary." Read in the light most favorable to Bennett, this testimony raises a genuine issue of material fact as to the publicness of the Nebraska City testing.

Furthermore, there exists a genuine issue of material fact as to whether the device used in the Nebraska City testing contained each and every element of the asserted claims. In particular, there is a question as to whether the tested device included the baffling means element required by the claims. Bennett highlights that an inter-office memo by Meter stated that the Nebraska City tests were performed "with the prototype ... vent shield, and no device or screen installed." Bennett argues that this memo creates a genuine issue of fact as to the identity of the tested device. Bennett points to Meter's drawings it submitted to the CGA. In those drawings, the "Vent Shield" is only the outer skirt of the Splash Guard without the baffling insert. Because the memo suggests that only the Vent Shield was tested, Bennett argues that the memo demonstrates that the device tested in Nebraska City cannot anticipate as a prior use because the tested device did not contain a baffling means as required by the claims. Although it is not clear what device was tested, the memo does create a genuine issue of fact as to whether the device tested in Nebraska City met the claim limitation requiring "a baffle means." Thus, the Nebraska City testing cannot, on summary judgment, support a judgment of invalidity.

B.

There is also a genuine issue of fact underlying Meter's theory of anticipation via 35 U.S.C. § 102(a) public knowledge. There is little dispute that American Meter knew about the Splash Guard. In other words, the Splash Guard was known in the United States prior to the '029 invention date because American Meter certainly knew about its own product. Rather, the parties dispute whether that knowledge was accessible to the public as required by our caselaw. In support of its contention that its knowledge was publicly known, Meter submitted affidavits and testimony describing its efforts at contacting customers in the United States regarding the Splash Guard highlighting that it did not attempt to keep information about the Splash Guard secret and confidential from the public.

As described above, under § 102(a), knowledge must be publicly accessible. In support of its grant of summary judgment of invalidity as to public knowledge, the district court primarily relied on two pieces of evidence. First, the district court relied on a memorandum sent from Canadian Meter to American Meter that referred to the transfer of forty units of the Splash Guard product and that asked for "future requirements and customer feedback" as to the Splash Guard. Because it referenced customer feedback in regards to the Splash Guard, Meter argues that this memorandum shows that Meter was making its knowledge of the Splash Guard publicly accessible. Second, in March of 1992 and April of 1994, Meter sent letters to the Vermont Gas Company and to Bay State Gas Company respectively, telling these gas companies of the Splash Guard. Both letters concluded by stating that the gas companies could contact Meter for "any information you may require" about the Splash Guard. Meter argues that these letters evidence that it was not keeping the Splash Guard secret and Meter's knowledge about the Splash Guard was accessible to the public. Meter argues that the district court properly granted the motion for summary judgment based on these documents.

However, in our view, there does exist a genuine issue of fact as to whether Meter's letters and memos establish that Meter's knowledge was accessible to the public. As argued by Bennett, the reference in the letters to "any information you may require" or the reference to customer feedback could be taken to mean a wide variety of things relating to the Splash Guard—"prices, product availability, or lack thereof, test results, expected standards to be enacted in the United States, etc." Certainly the letter and memo do suggest that Meter intended to publicize the Splash Guard but, in the light most favorable to Bennett, it does not establish that Meter intended to make its technical knowledge about the structure and function of the Splash Guard publicly accessible. One can publicize that a new product exists while still keeping an enabling disclosure of the structure and function of the product secret. Thus, when viewed in the light most favorable to Bennett, the internal memorandum asking for "customer feedback" or the letters to customers offering "any information you may require" do not establish by clear and convincing evidence that Meter's knowledge about the Splash Guard was accessible to the public. Rather, there exists a genuine issue of material fact as to the public accessibility of Meter's knowledge of the Splash Guard and it cannot properly support summary judgment of invalidity.

III.

When viewed in the light most favorable to Bennett, summary judgment was not properly granted. There exist genuine issues of material fact as to the confidentiality of the Nebraska City testing and the identity of the product tested there that preclude a finding of a public use. Further, when all inferences are drawn in favor of Bennett, the memorandum and letters are not enough to establish that Meter's knowledge of the Splash Guard was accessible to the public. Therefore, we find the grant of summary judgment was improper and we vacate the judgment and remand for further proceedings consistent with this opinion.

Notes

1. The district court in *Oak Industries, Inc. v. Zenith Electronics Corp.*, 726 F.Supp. 1525 (N.D.Ill.1989), summarized the prevailing interpretation of "known or used by others" under Section 102(a) as follows:

Courts construe this phrase to mean that the public must have access to the knowledge of the prior art. While there is no per se rule on the number of persons who must have knowledge of, or who used the prior invention, it appears that more than just a few persons must know or use the invention for it to be publicly known. However, where those skilled in the relevant art know of or use an invention, courts may infer the knowledge will become known to a sufficient number of people to become "public." Furthermore, the court may find a public use where there is a "non-secret use of a claimed process in the usual course of producing articles for commercial purposes."

726 F.Supp. at 1537 (citations omitted). If a device is used only in a factory from which the general public is excluded, does this constitute a public use of the device under Section 102(a)?

2. Suppose that a prior art device, containing certain non-evident construction features, is sold to a customer who is not informed of those non-evident features. With respect to a later-conceived invention containing the same features, will this device constitute anticipating public knowledge or use under Section 102(a)?

3. Company A's patent claims an encapsulating compound that protects certain electrical devices from contamination. The user of the product forms the encapsulant on-site by mixing two separate compounds and applying the mixture to the device. When mixed, the compounds react to form a gel-like protective coating. An alleged infringer seeks to invalidate these claims by demonstrating that, before Company A's invention date, Company B shipped free samples of an identical two-part encapsulant to potential customers, along with a marketing brochure, although there is no proof that any of the recipients actually mixed the two parts of the sample or applied the mixture to an electrical device. Is this invalidating prior art under Section 102(a)? *See Minnesota Mining & Mfg. Co. v. Chemque, Inc.,* 303 F.3d 1294 (Fed. Cir. 2002).

4. *Anticipation by Inherency*: It is possible for a product or process to be unpatentable due to anticipation even though the creator of the prior art product or process did not fully appreciate or recognize the utility or properties of that creation; this is known as anticipation by inherency. "In order for a claim to be inherent in the prior art it is not sufficient that a person following the disclosure sometimes obtain the result set forth in the claim, it must invariably happen." *Standard Oil v. Montedison,* 664 F.2d 356, 372 (3d Cir.1981). Where the prior art reference is a written description that is silent about the allegedly inherent characteristic, the Federal Circuit has permitted resort to extrinsic evidence in order to establish that "the missing descriptive matter is necessarily present in the thing described in the reference, and that it would be so recognized by persons of ordinary skill." *Continental Can Co. USA, Inc. v. Monsanto Co.,* 948 F.2d 1264, 1269 (Fed.Cir.1991).

In *Schering Corp. v. Geneva Pharmaceuticals, Inc.,* 339 F.3d 1373 (Fed. Cir. 2003), the Federal Circuit held that anticipation by inherency occurred where the invention sought to be patented was itself a metabolite of a patented pharmaceutical, and was necessarily formed whenever the latter was put to its intended use (ingestion by humans) under normal conditions. Anticipation did not depend on whether a person of ordinary skill in the art would have recognized this inherent disclosure.

(ii) "Patented or Described in a Printed Publication"

The statutory phrase "patented or described in a printed publication" appears in both the novelty bar of Section 102(a) and the statutory bar of Section 102(b). Although *In re Wyer*, reproduced below, involved Section 102(b), the Court of Customs and Patent Appeals drew heavily on a series of Section 102(a) cases (the *Philips Electronic & Pharmaceutical Industries* and *I.C.E. Corp.* cases cited below) in interpreting the statutory phrase. As *In re Wyer* illustrates, courts ascribe the same meaning to this phrase in both contexts.

IN RE WYER

United States Court of Customs and Patent Appeals, 1981.
655 F.2d 221.

RICH, JUDGE.

[The PTO Board of Appeals upheld the examiner's rejection of all claims in appellant Wyer's patent application based on an Australian patent application containing the same disclosure. Microfilmed and diazo copies of the Australian patent application were located at the Australian Patent Office, with additional diazo copies located at the five sub-offices. Upon demand, additional copies were reproduced for sale to the public at each location. The sole issue before the court was whether these circumstances caused the Australian patent application to be available in a "printed publication."]

* * *

OPINION

It has been stated by this and other courts that to constitute a "printed publication," as that term is used in § 102, a reference must be both "printed" and "published." In re Bayer, 568 F.2d 1357, 1359 (CCPA 1978); In re Tenney, 254 F.2d 619, 622 (CCPA 1958); General Tire & Rubber Co. v. Firestone Tire Co., 349 F.Supp. 345, 355 (N.D.Ohio 1972), *modified,* 489 F.2d 1105 (6th Cir. 1973).

With regard to the "printing" requirement, it has been stated that the "only realistic distinction that we can see as between 'handwritten' and 'printed' publications relates to the *method* of producing them." *Tenney,* 254 F.2d at 625 (emphasis in original). In other words, the requirement of printing increases the probability that a reference will be available to the public, for "Congress no doubt reasoned that one would not go to the trouble of printing a given description of a thing unless it was desired to print a number of copies of it." 254 F.2d at 626.

The "publication requirement," said to be "so connected with [the 'printing' requirement] that treatment of the one cannot be satisfactorily done without overstepping into the bounds of the other," 254 F.2d at 622 n.4, has been equated with public accessibility to the "printed document." In re Bayer, *supra* 568 F.2d at 1359.

On the other hand, there are a number of cases which eschew this two-tiered approach and view the unitary concept of "printed publication" in the context of dissemination or accessibility alone. Philips Electronic & Pharmaceutical Industries Corp. v. Thermal & Electronics Industries, Inc., 450 F.2d 1164, 1170 (3d Cir.1971); I.C.E. Corp. v. Armco Steel Corp., 250 F.Supp. 738, 742, 743 (S.D.N.Y.1966). It was reasoned in *Philips* that:

> The traditional process of "printing" is no longer the only process synonymous with "publication." The emphasis, therefore, should be *public dissemination* of the document, *and its availability and accessibility* to persons skilled in the subject matter or art. [Emphasis ours.]

We agree that "printed publication" should be approached as a unitary concept. The traditional dichotomy between "printing" and "publication" is no longer valid. Given the state of technology in document duplication, data storage, and data-retrieval systems, the "probability of dissemination" of an item very often has little to do with whether or not it is "printed" in the sense of that word when it was introduced into the patent statutes in 1836.[19] In any event, interpretation of the words "printed" and "publication" to mean "probability of dissemination" and "public accessibility," respectively, now seems to render their use in the phrase "printed publication" somewhat redundant. This becomes clear upon examination of the purpose of the § 102 printed publication bar.

As this court pointed out in In re Bayer, *supra* 568 F.2d at 1359, the printed publication provision was designed to prevent withdrawal by an inventor, as the subject matter of a patent, of that which was already in the possession of the public. Thus, the question to be examined under section 102(b) is the accessibility to at least the pertinent part of the public, of a perceptible description of the invention, in whatever form it may have been recorded. Access involves such factual inquiries as classification and indexing. In other words, such a reference is a "printed publication" and a bar to patentability

> upon a satisfactory showing that such document has been disseminated or otherwise made available to the extent that persons interested and ordinarily skilled in the subject matter or art, exercising reasonable diligence, can locate it and recognize and comprehend therefrom the essentials of the claimed invention without need of further research or experimentation. [*I.C.E. Corp., supra* (250 F. Supp.) at 743.]

Appellant filed an application for an Australian patent which resulted in copies of that application being classified and laid open to public inspection at the Australian Patent Office and each of its five "sub-

---

19. The "printed publication" bar appears to have been first enacted in § 7 (on examination) of the Patent Act of 1836, 5 Stat. 117, July 4, 1836. Section 6 of the Act of 1793, 1 Stat. 318, listing defenses, used the expression "described in some public work anterior to the supposed discovery of the patentee."

offices'' over one year before he filed his application in the United States.
* * *

Even though no fact appears in the agreed statement respecting actual viewing or dissemination of any copy of the application, there is no dispute that the records were maintained for this purpose. Given that there is also no genuine issue as to whether the application was properly classified, indexed, or abstracted, we are convinced that the contents of the application were sufficiently accessible to the public and to persons skilled in the pertinent art to qualify as a "printed publication," notwithstanding those cases holding that a foreign patent application laid open for public inspection is not a printed publication.

While intent to make public, activity in disseminating information, production of a certain number of copies, and production by a method allowing production of a large number of copies may aid in determining whether an item may be termed a "printed publication," they are neither always conclusive nor requisite. Each case must be decided on the basis of its own facts. Accordingly, whether information is printed, handwritten, or on microfilm or a magnetic disc or tape, etc., the one who wishes to characterize the information, in whatever form it may be, as a "printed publication"

> should produce sufficient proof of its dissemination or that it has otherwise been available and accessible to persons concerned with the art to which the document relates and thus most likely to avail themselves of its contents. [*Philips Electronic Corp., supra* at 1171.]

Through demonstration of the accessibility of reproductions of appellant's application in the Australian Patent Office and in each of its sub-offices, the PTO has met this burden.

In affirming the board's decision, however, we do not approve its rather sweeping statement, quoted at the beginning, that

> * * * the time has come to hold that a microfilm of a foreign patent application maintained in the foreign patent office, accessible to the pertinent part of the public and available for duplication is a "printed publication" * * *.

We are approving its decision on the totality of the facts of this case, several of which are missing from that statement. Decision in this field of statutory construction and application must proceed on a case-by-case basis.

The decision of the board affirming the rejection of claims 1–5 and 7–13 is *affirmed*.

Notes

1. As indicated in *In re Wyer*, the trend is toward liberal interpretation of the "printed publication" requirement. What impact does *Wyer* have on the distinction between references that are merely "known" to the public and those that are "described in a printed publication"? Under what

circumstances, if any, would this distinction be important? Should the distinction be eliminated?

2. What facts in this case explain why *In re Wyer* was decided under Section 102(b) rather than section 102(a)?

3. In order to invalidate a patent under Section 102, a "printed publication" must contain a disclosure that is "enabling"—that is, complete enough to enable a person of ordinary skill in the art to make the invention. *See* 35 U.S.C.A. § 112, paragraph one (discussed in Section F, *infra*); *see, e.g., Paperless Accounting, Inc. v. Bay Area Rapid Transit Sys.*, 804 F.2d 659, 665 (Fed.Cir.1986) (construing section 102(b)), *cert. denied*, 480 U.S. 933, 107 S.Ct. 1573, 94 L.Ed.2d 764 (1987). A non-enabling disclosure, however, may still be considered prior art for purposes of determining obviousness under section 103 (discussed in Section D, *infra*).

4. Anticipation can be predicated on a foreign patent only if the patent is publicly accessible (although it need not be a printed publication). Where novelty is challenged on the basis of a foreign patent, it may be necessary to determine whether the grant in question constitutes a "patent" within the meaning of Section 102. For example, a foreign patent that does not contain an enabling disclosure will not qualify. *United States v. Adams*, 383 U.S. 39, 86 S.Ct. 708, 15 L.Ed.2d 572 (1966). If the foreign patent provides an enabling description of the invention in question but does not claim it, it will still anticipate if the patent has been sufficiently disseminated to constitute a printed publication. If not, most courts have taken the position that unclaimed subject matter does not anticipate, *see, e.g., Carter Products v. Colgate–Palmolive*, 130 F.Supp. 557, 566 (D.Md.1955), *aff'd*, 230 F.2d 855 (4th Cir.1956) (treating publicly available foreign patent as not a "printed publication"), *cert. denied*, 352 U.S. 843, 77 S.Ct. 43, 1 L.Ed.2d 59 (1956), although courts have allowed reference to unclaimed material in the specification for the sole purpose of interpreting the claims, *see, e.g., Bendix Corp. v. Balax, Inc.*, 421 F.2d 809, 812–813 (7th Cir.1970) (treating publicly accessible foreign patent as not a "printed publication"). In some cases, an issue may arise as to the date on which the invention in question became subject to a foreign patent, because the date on which a foreign patent issues may differ from the date on which it becomes accessible to the public, the date from which the patent term is measured, the date on which some or all of the inventor's rights become exclusive, the date on which the patentee is entitled to enforce the patent, and/or the first date on which infringement is remediable in damages. *See In re Monks*, 588 F.2d 308 (CCPA 1978) (date on which invention is "patented" under a foreign patent is same for Sections 102(a) and 102(d)). Finally, where a foreign grant conveys rights which are significantly different from those conveyed by United States patents, courts must determine whether to treat the foreign grant as a patent at all. *See, e.g., In re Carlson*, 983 F.2d 1032 (Fed.Cir.1992) (treating German design patent as anticipatory subject matter even though the rights conveyed more closely resembled a copyright).

Why must prior art merely be known or used "in this country" to anticipate under Section 102(a), while in a *foreign* country only patenting or a printed publication will suffice? (Note that the failed Patent Reform Acts of 2005 and 2006 would have eliminated this distinction.)

5. In the case of a utility patent for a plant, consider which of the following disclosures, if known to the public, would give rise to a novelty bar under Section 102(a): (a) a detailed description of the plant's novel characteristics, with photographs; (b) a description of the steps taken in breeding the plant; (c) availability of seeds for purchase. Would your answers be different in the case of a plant patent under Section 161?

6. In *In re Klopfenstein*, 380 F.3d 1345 (Fed. Cir. 2004), another Section 102(b) case, the Federal Circuit expanded on its approach to determining whether a document is sufficiently publicly accessible to be a "printed publication." While noting that distribution and indexing are helpful "proxies for public accessibility," the court cautioned that these are not the sole measures of public accessibility, and that the determination instead requires "a case-by-case inquiry into the facts and circumstances surrounding the reference's disclosure to members of the public." *Id.* at 1350. In *Klopfenstein*, where the material in question was displayed to members of the public, but never distributed, factors considered by the court included "the length of time the display was exhibited, the expertise of the target audience, the existence (or lack thereof) of reasonable expectations that the material displayed would not be copied, and the simplicity or ease with which the material displayed could have been copied." *Id.*

Recently, in *Bruckelmyer v. Ground Heaters, Inc.*, 445 F.3d 1374 (Fed. Cir. 2006), the Federal Circuit held that a Canadian patent application was an invalidating "printed publication" under Section 102(b) where the invention in question was disclosed in two figures that were contained in the underlying application but not in the issued patent. The court reached this conclusion because the issued patent was classified and indexed, the application was publicly accessible as part of the issued patent's underlying file wrapper, and the issued patent stated a possible use for the claimed invention that was illustrated by the two figures in the application.

The rationales of *Bruckelmyer* and *Klopfenstein* should be equally applicable under Section 102(a).

7. Consider whether the following references should be deemed to anticipate under Section 102(a). (Unless otherwise indicated, you should assume that each contains an enabling disclosure of the invention in question):

(a) a single copy of a document, deposited in a library or archive?

(b) a "classified" or "secret" government document?

(c) a device manufactured for, and delivered to, the federal government under conditions of secrecy?

(d) a United States patent that describes, but does not claim, the subject matter of the invention?

(e) a company's confidential internal memorandum distributed to a small group of researchers and executives?

(f) a manuscript delivered to a publisher but not yet published?

2. SECTION 102(E)

ALEXANDER MILBURN COMPANY v. DAVIS– BOURNONVILLE COMPANY

Supreme Court of the United States, 1926.
270 U.S. 390, 46 S.Ct. 324, 70 L.Ed. 651.

Mr. Justice Holmes delivered the opinion of the Court.

[The infringement defendant challenged the validity of the plaintiff's patent for an improved welding apparatus, claiming that the named inventor, Whitford, was not the first inventor. Whitford's application was filed on March 4, 1911, and issued on June 4, 1912. No evidence carried Whitford's date of invention further back. Clifford, alleged to be the prior inventor, filed his patent application on January 31, 1911, and his patent issued on February 6, 1912. His application gave a complete description of the subject matter claimed by Whitford, but did not claim it. The district court and the court of appeals held that Clifford's failure to claim the subject matter meant that he was not a prior inventor, and thus rejected the invalidity defense.]

* * *

The patent law authorizes a person who has invented an improvement like the present, "not known or used by others in this country, before his invention," & c., to obtain a patent for it. Rev. Sts. § 4886, amended, March 3, 1897, c. 391, § 1, 29 Stat. 692. Among the defences to a suit for infringement the fourth specified by the statute is that the patentee "was not the original and first inventor or discoverer of any material and substantial part of the thing patented." Rev. Sts. § 4920, amended, March 3, 1897, c. 391, § 2, 29 Stat. 692. Taking these words in their natural sense as they would be read by the common man, obviously one is not the first inventor if, as was the case here, somebody else has made a complete and adequate description of the thing claimed before the earliest moment to which the alleged inventor can carry his invention back. But the words cannot be taken quite so simply. In view of the gain to the public that the patent laws mean to secure we assume for purposes of decision that it would have been no bar to Whitford's patent if Clifford had written out his prior description and kept it in his portfolio uncommunicated to anyone. More than that, since the decision in the case of The Cornplanter Patent, 23 Wall. 181, it is said, at all events for many years, the Patent Office has made no search among abandoned patent applications, and by the words of the statute a previous foreign invention does not invalidate a patent granted here if it has not been patented or described in a printed publication. Rev. Sts. § 4923. *See* Westinghouse Machine Co. v. General Electric Co., 207 Fed. 75. These analogies prevailed in the minds of the Courts below.

On the other hand, publication in a periodical is a bar. This as it seems to us is more than an arbitrary enactment, and illustrates, as does the rule concerning previous public use, the principle that, subject to the exceptions mentioned, one really must be the first inventor in order to be entitled to a patent. Coffin v. Ogden, 18 Wall. 120. We understand the Circuit Court of Appeals to admit that if Whitford had not applied for his patent until after the issue to Clifford, the disclosure by the latter would have had the same effect as the publication of the same words in a periodical, although not made the basis of a claim. 1 Fed. 2d 233. The invention is made public property as much in the one case as in the other. But if this be true, as we think that it is, it seems to us that a sound distinction cannot be taken between that case and a patent applied for before but not granted until after a second patent is sought. The delays of the patent office ought not to cut down the effect of what has been done. The description shows that Whitford was not the first inventor. Clifford had done all that he could do to make his description public. He had taken steps that would make it public as soon at the Patent Office did its work, although, of course, amendments might be required of him before the end could be reached. We see no reason in the words or policy of the law for allowing Whitford to profit by the delay and make himself out to be the first inventor when he was not so in fact, when Clifford had shown knowledge inconsistent with the allowance of Whitford's claim, and when otherwise the publication of his patent would abandon the thing described to the public unless it already was old.

The question is not whether Clifford showed himself by the description to be the first inventor. By putting it in that form it is comparatively easy to take the next step and say that he is not an inventor in the sense of the statute unless he makes a claim. The question is whether Clifford's disclosure made it impossible for Whitford to claim the invention at a later date. The disclosure would have had the same effect as at present if Clifford had added to his description a statement that he did not claim the thing described because he abandoned it or because he believed it to be old. It is not necessary to show who did invent the thing in order to show that Whitford did not.

It is said that without a claim the thing described is not reduced to practice. But this seems to us to rest on a false theory helped out by the fiction that by a claim it is reduced to practice. * * * A description that would bar a patent if printed in a periodical or in an issued patent is equally effective in an application so far as reduction to practice goes.

As to the analogies relied upon below, the disregard of abandoned patent applications, however explained, cannot be taken to establish a principle beyond the rule as actually applied. As an empirical rule it no doubt is convenient if not necessary to the Patent Office, and we are not disposed to disturb it, although we infer that originally the practice of the Office was different. The policy of the statute as to foreign inventions obviously stands on its own footing and cannot be applied to domestic affairs. The fundamental rule we repeat is that the patentee must be the first inventor. The qualifications in aid of a wish to encourage improvements or to avoid laborious investigations do not prevent the rule from applying here.

Decree reversed.

Note

In 1952, the holding of *Alexander Milburn Co.* was codified in Section 102(e). Although that section originally treated only successful *United States* patent applications as prior art, a later amendment extended similar treatment to international applications filed under the 1978 Patent Cooperation Treaty (PCT). Legislation in 1999 and 2002 further amended Section 102(e) to treat applications published pursuant to 35 U.S.C. § 122 (as amended in 1999 to require publication of certain applications eighteen months after filing) as prior art as of their earliest effective U.S. filing date, and to provide that PCT applications designating the United States have prior art effect under Section 102(e) only if they have been published in English (pursuant to Article 21(2) of the PCT).

3. SECTION 102(F)

APPLEGATE v. SCHERER

United States Court of Customs and Patent Appeals, 1964.
332 F.2d 571.

RICH, JUDGE.

[The PTO declared an interference between separate patent applications filed by Scherer and Applegate, each of whom had applied for a patent on a method of controlling sea lampreys without harming fish by use of the chemical compound 3–trifluoromethyl–4–nitrophenol. The PTO Board of Patent Interferences awarded priority to Scherer, and Applegate appealed.]

* * *

By way of background, for several decades the sea lamprey had been causing havoc in the Great Lakes to commercial and game fish. The Fish and Wildlife Service of the Department of the Interior, under the direction of Applegate and Howell, was engaged in a large-scale screening program, seeking chemical compounds which would control the sea lamprey without undue harm to desirable fish species. The scheme was to treat streams where the lamprey spawn with a chemical which would destroy the larvae.

Prior to the invention here involved, as the result of examining thousands of compounds, 3–bromo–4–nitrophenol had been found to be efficacious. This fact was disclosed in the December 17, 1955, issue of Chemical Week. Thereafter Progressive Color Company wrote a letter to the Fish and Wildlife Service on December 29, 1955 (Mr. L. C. Balling to Mr. Applegate) * * *. [The letter suggested that 3–trifluoromethyl–4–nitrophenol might be even more effective for lamprey control, and offered a free sample for testing. Applegate accepted this offer by letter dated January 19, 1956.]

* * *

In February, 1956, the sample was delivered, it was tested, found to be effective, the patent applications followed, and the interference was declared.

Both parties are in agreement with the board's view that the sole issue is originality, or, who made the invention. Scherer contends that the subject matter of the count was fully disclosed to Applegate in the letter from Progressive Color Company of December 29, 1955, by reason of which fact Applegate did not make the invention. The board so held. In support of its decision, the board pointed out that Applegate (called as a witness by Scherer, the only party taking testimony) testified that before the date of the letter he did not know of the chemical of the count. The gist of the board's opinion is contained in the following paragraph:

> There is no doubt that the Scherer et al. letter of December 29, 1955 was a conception of the invention of the count. The letter names the chemical as a substitute for the bromo-compound, which had been added to water, for the elimination of sea lampreys. This is all that the count requires. It is sufficient if an inventor is able to make a disclosure which would enable a person of ordinary skill in the art to practice the disclosure without extensive research or experimentation; In re Tansel, 45 CCPA 834, 253 F.2d 241 .. We conclude, therefore, that the aforementioned letter amply meets the test of conception set forth in In re Tansel, supra, and so constitutes a full disclosure of the invention of the count in late December, 1955. This date is well prior to Applegate et al.'s record date.

In view of the disclosure to him of a complete conception of the invention of the count, the board found, as a corollary, that the reduction to practice by Applegate, by the tests which demonstrated effectiveness for the intended purpose, inured to the benefit of Scherer, citing several precedents including this court's decision in Shumaker v. Paulson, 30 CCPA 1156, 136 F.2d 700.

Applegate's attack on the decision below is on the theory that Scherer did not conceive the invention; and to show that Scherer had no conception the further theory is propounded that under the law there could not be a conception until there was a reduction to practice, which reduction to practice was by Applegate who, therefore, was the first to conceive. Not having a conception of the invention, it is argued, Scherer could not communicate the invention to Applegate and therefore Applegate did not derive the invention from Scherer, as the board held he did.
* * *

* * *

Appellants seem to propose that there cannot be a conception of an invention of the type here involved in the absence of knowledge that the invention will work. Such knowledge, necessarily, can rest only on an actual reduction to practice. To adopt this proposition would mean, as a practical matter, that one could never communicate an invention thought up by him to another who is to try it out, for, when the tester succeeds, the one who does no more than exercise ordinary skill would be rewarded and the innovator would not be. Such cannot be the law. A contrary intent is implicit in the statutes and in a multitude of precedents.

Thinking of the matter in this light and asking who made the invention, clearly it was Scherer who had the thought and not Applegate who merely made the test.

The decision of the board is affirmed.

4. SECTION 102(G)

PAULIK v. RIZKALLA

United States Court of Appeals, Federal Circuit, 1985.
760 F.2d 1270.

NEWMAN, CIRCUIT JUDGE.

This appeal is from the decision of the United States Patent and Trademark Office Board of Patent Interferences (Board), awarding priority of invention to the senior party Nabil Rizkalla and Charles N. Winnick (Rizkalla), on the ground that the junior party and de facto first inventors Frank E. Paulik and Robert G. Schultz (Paulik) had suppressed or concealed the invention within the meaning of 35 U.S.C. § 102(g). We vacate this decision and remand to the Board.

I.

Rizkalla's patent application has the effective filing date of March 10, 1975, its parent application. Paulik's patent application was filed on June 30, 1975. * * * Paulik presented deposition testimony and exhibits in support of his claim to priority; Rizkalla chose to rely solely on his filing date.

The Board held and Rizkalla does not dispute that Paulik reduced the invention of the count to practice in November 1970 and again in April 1971. On about November 20, 1970 Paulik submitted a "Preliminary Disclosure of Invention" to the Patent Department of his assignee, the Monsanto Company. The disclosure was assigned a priority designation of "B", which Paulik states meant that the case would "be taken up in the ordinary course for review and filing."

Despite occasional prodding from the inventors, and periodic review by the patent staff and by company management, this disclosure had a lower priority than other patent work. Evidence of the demands of other projects on related technology was offered to justify the patent staff's delay in acting on this invention, along with evidence that the inventors and assignee continued to be interested in the technology and that the invention disclosure was retained in active status.

In January or February of 1975 the assignee's patent solicitor started to work toward the filing of the patent application; drafts of the application were prepared, and additional laboratory experiments were requested by the patent solicitor and were duly carried out by an inventor. The evidentiary sufficiency of these activities was challenged by Rizkalla, but the Board made no findings thereon, on the basis that these activities were not pertinent to the determination of priority. The Board held that "even if Paulik demonstrated continuous activity from prior to the Rizkalla effective filing date to his filing date ... such would have no bearing on the question of priority in this case", and cited 35 U.S.C. § 102(g) as authority for the statement that "while diligence during the above noted period may be relied upon by one alleging prior conception and subsequent reduction to practice, it is of no significance in the case of the party who is not the last to reduce to practice". The Board thus denied Paulik the opportunity to antedate Rizkalla, for the reason that Paulik was not only the first to conceive but he was also the first to reduce to practice.

The Board then held that Paulik's four-year delay from reduction to practice to his filing date was prima facie suppression or concealment under the first clause of section 102(g), that since Paulik had reduced the invention to practice in 1971 and 1972 he was barred by the second clause of section 102(g) from proving reasonable diligence leading to his 1975 filing, and that in any event the intervening activities were insufficient to excuse the delay. The Board refused to consider Paulik's evidence of renewed patent-related activity.

II.

The Board's decision converted the case law's estoppel against reliance on Paulik's early work for priority purposes, into a forfeiture encompassing Paulik's later work, even if the later work commenced before the earliest activity of Rizkalla. According to this decision, once the inference of suppression or concealment is established, this inference cannot be overcome by the junior party to an interference. There is no statutory or judicial precedent that requires this result, and there is sound reason to reject it.

United States patent law embraces the principle that the patent right is granted to the first inventor rather than the first to file a patent application. The law does not inquire as to the fits and starts by which an invention is made. The historic jurisprudence from which 35 U.S.C. § 102(g) flowed reminds us that "the mere lapse of time" will not prevent the inventor from receiving a patent. Mason v. Hepburn, 13 App. D.C. 86, 91, 1898 C.D. 510, 513 (1898). The sole exception to this principle resides in section 102(g) and the exigencies of the priority contest.

There is no impediment in the law to holding that a long period of inactivity need not be a fatal forfeiture, if the first inventor resumes work on the invention before the second inventor enters the field. We deem this result to be a fairer implementation of national patent policy, while in full accord with the letter and spirit of section 102(g).

The Board misapplied the rule that the first inventor does not have to show activity following reduction to practice to mean that the first inventor will not be allowed to show such activity. Such a showing may serve either of two purposes: to rebut an inference of abandonment, suppression, or concealment; or as evidence of renewed activity with respect to the invention. Otherwise, if an inventor were to set an invention aside for "too long" and later resume work and diligently develop and seek to patent it, according to the Board he would always be worse off than if he never did the early work, even as against a much later entrant.

Such a restrictive rule would merely add to the burden of those charged with the nation's technological growth. Invention is not a neat process. The value of early work may not be recognized or, for many reasons, it may not become practically useful, until months or years later. Following the Board's decision, any "too long" delay would constitute a forfeiture fatal in a priority contest, even if terminated by extensive and productive work done long before the newcomer entered the field.

We do not suggest that the first inventor should be entitled to rely for priority purposes on his early reduction to practice if the intervening inactivity lasts "too long," as that principle has evolved in a century of judicial analysis. Precedent did not deal with the facts at bar. There is no authority that would estop Paulik from relying on his resumed activities in order to pre-date Rizkalla's earliest date. We hold that such resumed activity must be considered as evidence of priority of invention. Should Paulik demonstrate that he had renewed activity on the invention and that he proceeded diligently to filing his patent application, starting before the earliest date to which Rizkalla is entitled—all in accordance with established principles of interference practice—we hold that Paulik is not prejudiced by the fact that he had reduced the invention to practice some years earlier.

III.

* * *

There is over a hundred years of judicial precedent on the issue of suppression or concealment due to prolonged delay in filing. From the earliest decisions, a distinction has been drawn between deliberate suppression or concealment of an invention, and the legal inference of suppression or concealment based on "too long" a delay in filing the patent application. Both types of situations were considered by the courts before the 1952 Patent Act, and both are encompassed in 35 U.S.C. § 102(g). The result is consistent over this entire period—loss of the first inventor's priority as against an intervening second inventor—and has consistently been based on equitable principles and public policy as applied to the facts of each case.

* * *

In *Mason v. Hepburn, supra,* the classical case on inferred as contrasted with deliberate suppression or concealment, Hepburn was granted a patent in September 1894. Spurred by this news Mason filed his patent application in December 1894. In an interference, Mason demonstrated that he had built a working model in 1887 but showed no activity during the seven years thereafter. The court held that although Mason may have negligently rather than willfully concealed his invention, the "indifference, supineness, or wilful act" of a first inventor is the basis for "the equity" that favors the second inventor when that person made and disclosed the invention during the prolonged inactivity of the first inventor. 13 App. D.C. at 96, 1898 C.D. at 517.

Other early cases affirmed these principles. Thomson v. Weston, 19 App. D.C.373, 381, 1902 C.D. 521, 527 (1902) discussed the situation where a second inventor appeared "during the period of inactivity and concealment". The decisions are consistent, and were codified in section 102(g) of the 1952 Patent Act.

The legislative history of section 102(g) makes clear that its purpose was not to change the law. As described in H.R. Rep. No. 1923, 82d Cong., 2d Sess. 17–18(1951), section 102(g) "retains the present rules of [the case] law governing the determination of priority of invention". The pre–1952 cases all dealt with situations whereby a later inventor made the same invention during a period of either prolonged inactivity or deliberate concealment by the first inventor, after knowledge of which (usually, but not always, by the issuance of a patent to the second inventor) the first inventor was "spurred" into asserting patent rights, unsuccessfully.

* * *

IV.

The decisions applying section 102(g) balanced the law and policy favoring the first person to make an invention, against equitable considerations when more than one person had made the same invention: in each case where the court deprived the de facto first inventor of the right to the patent, the second inventor had entered the field during a period of either inactivity or deliberate concealment by the first inventor. Often the first inventor had been spurred to file a patent application by news of the second inventor's activities. Although "spurring" is not necessary to a finding of suppression or concealment, *see* Young v. Dworkin, 489 F.2d [1277 (CCPA 1974),] at 1281 and citations therein, the courts' frequent references to spurring indicate their concern with this equitable factor.

Some decisions used the word "forfeiture" to describe the first inventor's loss of priority; but none interpreted section 102(g) as requiring an absolute forfeiture rather than requiring a balance of equities. In *Brokaw v. Vogel,* for example, the court said "the *Mason v. Hepburn* principle is not a forfeiture in the true sense; rather it is a rule according to which the patent right goes to the most deserving. Realistically, it is a forfeiture by the de facto first inventor of the right to rely on his earlier reduction to practice." 429 F.2d at 480. In *Young v. Dworkin* Judge Rich wrote "I cannot agree with the board that the question in this case is whether Young 'forfeited his *right to a patent*'. But for Dworkin's conflicting claim, Young forfeited nothing and would get a patent. All he *forfeited* ... was the right to rely on his prior actual reduction to practice in a priority dispute." 489 F.2d at 1286 (emphases in original).

In no case where the first inventor had waited "too long" did he end his period of inactivity before the second inventor appeared. We affirm the long-standing rule that too long a delay may bar the first inventor from reliance on an early reduction to practice in a priority contest. But we hold that the first inventor will not be barred from relying on later, resumed activity antedating an opponent's entry into the field, merely because the work done before the delay occurred was sufficient to amount to a reduction to practice.

This result furthers the basic purpose of the patent system. The exclusive right, constitutionally derived, was for the national purpose of advancing the useful arts—the process today called technological innovation. As implemented by the patent statute, the grant of the right to exclude carries the obligation to disclose the workings of the invention, thereby adding to the store of knowledge without diminishing the patent-supported incentive to innovate.

But the obligation to disclose is not the principal reason for a patent system; indeed, it is a rare invention that cannot be deciphered more readily from its commercial embodiment than from the printed patent. The reason for the patent system is to encourage innovation and its fruits: new jobs and new industries, new consumer goods and trade benefits. We must keep this purpose in plain view as we consider the consequences of interpretations of the patent law such as in the Board's decision.

A foreseeable consequence of the Board's ruling is to discourage inventors and their supporters from working on projects that had been "too long" set aside, because of the impossibility of relying, in a priority contest, on either their original work or their renewed work. This curious result is neither fair nor in the public interest. We do not see that the public interest is served by placing so severe a sanction on failure to file premature patent applications on immature inventions of unknown value. In reversing the Board's decision we do not hold that such inventions are necessarily entitled to the benefits of their earliest dates in a priority contest; we hold only that they are not barred from entitlement to their dates of renewed activity.

* * *

VACATED AND REMANDED.

Notes

1. Compare Sections 102(g)(1) and 102(g)(2). How do they differ, and why? If two people invent the same device, the first inventor in Australia, and the later inventor in the United States, can the later inventor satisfy the novelty requirements to obtain a U.S. patent?

2. Under Sections 102(a), 102(e), and 102(g), invalidating prior art does not include work by the exact same inventorship entity (that is, the same sole inventor or the same group of co-inventors) as in the later patent application. In contrast, while the matter is not entirely free from doubt, it appears that work by another inventorship entity with overlapping membership *would* constitute prior art under these provisions. *See generally* Donald S. Chisum, 1–3 Chisum on Patents § 3.08[2][a] (collecting cases).

3. Unlike the United States, which awards patent priority to the first inventor, most countries give priority to the inventor who is the first to file a patent application. What arguments can you devise for and against adopting a first-to-file system in the United States?

4. The failed Patent Reform Act of 2005, H.R. 2795 (and its short-lived counterpart, the Patent Reform Act of 2006, S. 3818) would have enacted the most sweeping patent reforms since the 1952 Patent Act, including a shift from the first-to-invent system to a first-to-file system. This proposal has been revived in the Patent Reform Act of 2007, although its prospects remain uncertain. How would Section 102 have to be amended to accomplish this result?

5. Section 104 provides that a patent applicant may not establish a date of conception or reduction to practice by relying on knowledge, use or other activity with respect to the invention in foreign countries which do not belong to the North American Free Trade Agreement (NAFTA) or the World Trade Organization (WTO), except for certain persons performing overseas duties on behalf of the United States or a NAFTA or WTO member, or where a foreign filing qualifies as a constructive reduction to practice under Section 119 (and Section 365, where applicable). What purpose is served by this geographic restriction? Does it unfairly discriminate against foreign inventors? Can an accused infringer challenge the validity of the plaintiff's patent by showing that the same device was previously invented or publicly known or used in a non-NAFTA non-WTO country?

6. *Date of Invention*: To establish priority of invention, a party must either (1) reduce the invention to practice first or (2) conceive the invention first and exercise reasonable diligence in reducing it to practice. *See, e.g., Scott v. Finney,* 34 F.3d 1058 (Fed.Cir.1994). Thus, merely conceiving the invention first does not establish priority. To reduce the invention to practice means to demonstrate that it is "suitable for its intended purpose." *Id.* at 1061.

A reduction to practice may be actual or constructive. An actual reduction to practice requires a physical embodiment which includes all limitations of the claims. *UMC Electronics Co. v. United States,* 816 F.2d 647, 651 (Fed.Cir.1987), *cert. denied,* 484 U.S. 1025, 108 S.Ct. 748, 98 L.Ed.2d 761 (1988); *Correge v. Murphy,* 705 F.2d 1326, 1329 (Fed.Cir.1983) In some cases, actual reduction to practice requires testing the invention to establish that the invention works for its intended purpose; in such a case, a court may examine the quality and quantity of testing to determine its sufficiency. Testing is sufficient if it establishes a "reasonable expectation" that the invention will work under normal conditions for its intended purpose. *Id.* Where a device is intended for human use, testing on laboratory animals may be sufficient. *See, e.g., Engelhardt v. Judd,* 369 F.2d 408, 410–11 (CCPA 1966) (human testing of antihistamine and antiserotonin unnecessary in light of tests on laboratory animals). Some inventions, however, are simple enough that merely constructing the device is a sufficient reduction to practice; no testing is necessary. *King Instrument Corp. v. Otari Corp.,* 767 F.2d 853, 861 (Fed.Cir.1985), *cert. denied,* 475 U.S. 1016, 106 S.Ct. 1197, 89 L.Ed.2d 312 (1986).

If an inventor does not actually construct a complete embodiment of the invention at issue, then a "constructive reduction to practice" is deemed to take place at the time of filing the patent application that eventually leads to issuance of the patent. *See, e.g., Automatic Weighing Machine Co. v. Pneumatic Scale Corp., Ltd.,* 166 F. 288 (1st Cir.1909) (reasoning that sufficient reduction to practice has occurred once an inventor "has done all that he is required to do to obtain a valid patent"). Indeed, the law presumes that the filing date is the date of invention unless the applicant demonstrates that actual reduction to practice preceded the filing date. In the *Telephone Cases,* 126 U.S. 1, 536, 8 S.Ct. 778, 783, 31 L.Ed. 863, 1006 (1888), the Supreme Court rejected the argument that actual reduction to practice is a prerequisite to patentability:

> The law does not require that a discoverer or inventor, in order to get a patent for a process, must have succeeded in bringing his art to the highest degree of perfection; it is enough if he describes his method with sufficient clearness and precision to enable those skilled in the matter to understand what the process is, and if he points out some practicable way of putting it into operation.

7. In *Invitrogen Corp. v. Clontech Laboratories, Inc.*, 429 F.3d 1052 (Fed. Cir. 2005), the Federal Circuit ruled that, in order to find that another inventor conceived an anticipating prior art reference under Section 102(g)(2), it must be shown that the asserted inventor of that prior art reference recognized the inventive aspect of what he created, because "conception requires that the inventor appreciate that which he has invented." *Id.* at 1063. Accordingly, the district court erred by failing to consider whether the asserted prior art inventor had understood his creation to have the features that were claimed in the patent for the later invention.

5. NOVELTY AS APPLIED TO DESIGN AND PLANT PATENTS

The Section 102 novelty bars apply to design and plant patents to the same extent that they apply to utility patents. However, novelty itself must be defined somewhat differently in these contexts. Moreover, plant patents are subject to the additional requirement of "distinctness."

With respect to design patents, courts have reached a consensus on the meaning of novelty under Section 171. The Eighth Circuit's language in

Contico International, Inc. v. Rubbermaid Commercial Products, Inc., 665 F.2d 820 (8th Cir.1981), is typical:

> The novelty of a design patent is to be considered in light of the impact of the design upon the ordinary observer. This condition is met when the "average observer takes the new design for a different, and not a modified already existing design."

Id. at 823 (quoting *Thabet Manufacturing Co. v. Kool Vent Metal Awning Corp.,* 226 F.2d 207, 212 (6th Cir.1955)).

In *Yoder Bros., Inc. v. California–Florida Plant Corp.,* 537 F.2d 1347, 1377 (5th Cir.1976), *cert. denied,* 429 U.S. 1094, 97 S.Ct. 1108, 51 L.Ed.2d 540 (1977), the Fifth Circuit discussed the novelty and distinctness requirements as applied to plant patents under Section 161:

> Normally, the three requirements for patentability are novelty, utility, and non-obviousness. For plant patents, the requirement of distinctness replaces that of utility, and the additional requirement of asexual reproduction is introduced.

> The concept of novelty refers to novelty of conception, rather than novelty of use; no single prior art structure can exist in which all of the elements serve substantially the same function. * * * As applied to plants, the Patent Office Board of Appeals held that a "new" plant had to be one that literally had not existed before, rather than one that had existed in nature but was newly found, such as an exotic plant from a remote part of the earth. Ex parte Foster, 90 U.S.P.Q. 16 (1951). In Application of Greer, Ct.Cust. & Pat.App.1973, 484 F.2d 488, the court indicated that the Board believed that novelty was to be determined by a detailed comparison with other known varieties.

> The legislative history of the Plant Patent Act is of considerable assistance in defining "distinctness." The Senate Report said:

>> In order for the new variety to be distinct it must have characteristics clearly distinguishable from those of existing varieties and it is immaterial whether in the judgment of the Patent Office the new characteristics are inferior or superior to those of existing varieties. Experience has shown the absurdity of many views held as to the value of new varieties at the time of their creation.

>> The characteristics that may distinguish a new variety would include, among others, those of habit; immunity from disease; or soil conditions; color of flower, leaf, fruit or stems; flavor; productivity, including ever-bearing qualities in case of fruits; storage qualities; perfume; form; and ease of asexual reproduction. Within any one of the above or other classes of characteristics the differences which would suffice to make the variety a distinct variety, will necessarily be differences of degree.

> S.Rep. 315, 71st Cong., 2d Sess. (1930). (Emphasis omitted.) A definition of "distinctness" as the aggregate of the plant's distinguishing characteristics seems to us a sensible and workable one.

537 F.2d at 1377–78 (footnote omitted). In a footnote, the court added:

In order for a plant to have "existed" before in nature, we think that it must have been capable of reproducing itself. Thus, we have concluded that the mere fact that a sport [i.e., bud mutation] of a plant had appeared in the past would not be sufficient to preclude the patentability of the plant on novelty grounds, since each sport is a one-time phenomenon absent human intervention. * * *

Id. at 1378 n. 34.

Is a plant patent invalid under Section 102(f) if: (a) the patent claimant discovered the plant growing in another person's cultivated tract and then reproduced the plant asexually? (b) in addition, the claimant did not recognize the distinctive features of the plant until after they were pointed out by another party?

D. NONOBVIOUSNESS

Statutes: 35 U.S.C.A. § 103

GRAHAM v. JOHN DEERE CO.

Supreme Court of the United States, 1966.
383 U.S. 1, 86 S.Ct. 684, 15 L.Ed.2d 545.

Mr. Justice Clark delivered the opinion of the Court.

[In addressing a challenge to patent validity on obviousness grounds, the Court considered the effect of Congress's codification, in Section 103 of the Patent Act of 1952, of the judicially developed test of nonobviousness.]

* * *

At the outset it must be remembered that the federal patent power stems from a specific constitutional provision which authorizes the Congress "To promote the Progress of ... useful Arts, by securing for limited Times to ... Inventors the exclusive Right to their ... Discoveries." Art. I, § 8, cl. 8. The clause is both a grant of power and a limitation. This qualified authority, unlike the power often exercised in the sixteenth and seventeenth centuries by the English Crown, is limited to the promotion of advances in the "useful arts." It was written against the backdrop of the practices—eventually curtailed by the Statute of Monopolies—of the Crown in granting monopolies to court favorites in goods or businesses which had long before been enjoyed by the public. The Congress in the exercise of the patent power may not overreach the restraints imposed by the stated constitutional purpose. Nor may it enlarge the patent monopoly without regard to the innovation, advancement or social benefit gained thereby. Moreover, Congress may not authorize the issuance of patents whose effects are to remove existent knowledge from the public domain, or to restrict free access to materials already available. Innovation, advancement, and things which add to the sum of useful knowledge are inherent requisites in a patent system which by constitutional command must "promote the Progress of . . . useful Arts." * * *

* * *

As a member of the patent board for several years [and the author of the 1793 Patent Act, Thomas] Jefferson saw clearly the difficulty in "drawing a line between the things which are worth to the public the embarrassment of an exclusive patent, and those which are not." * * * Although the Patent Act was amended, revised or codified some 50 times between 1790 and 1950, Congress steered clear of a statutory set of requirements other than the bare novelty and utility tests reformulated in Jefferson's draft of the 1793 Patent Act.

* * *

III.

The difficulty of formulating conditions for patentability was heightened by the generality of the constitutional grant and the statutes implementing it, together with the underlying policy of the patent system that "the things which are worth to the public the embarrassment of an exclusive patent," as Jefferson put it, must outweigh the restrictive effect of the limited patent monopoly. The inherent problem was to develop some means of weeding out those inventions which would not be disclosed or devised but for the inducement of a patent.

This Court formulated a general condition of patentability in 1851 in Hotchkiss v. Greenwood, 11 How. 248. The patent involved a mere substitution of materials—porcelain or clay for wood or metal in doorknobs—and the Court condemned it, holding:

> "[U]nless more ingenuity and skill . . . were required . . . than were possessed by an ordinary mechanic acquainted with the business, there was an absence of that degree of skill and ingenuity which constitute essential elements of every invention. In other words, the improvement is the work of the skilful mechanic, not that of the inventor." At p. 267.

Hotchkiss, by positing the condition that a patentable invention evidence more ingenuity and skill than that possessed by an ordinary mechanic acquainted with the business, merely distinguished between new and useful innovations that were capable of sustaining a patent and those that were not. * * * The language in the case, and in those which followed, gave birth to "invention" as a word of legal art signifying patentable inventions. * * * In practice, *Hotchkiss* has required a comparison between the subject matter of the patent, or patent application, and the background skill of the calling. It has been from this comparison that patentability was in each case determined.

IV.

The 1952 Patent Act.

The Act sets out the conditions of patentability in three sections. An analysis of the structure of these three sections indicates that patentability is dependent upon three explicit conditions: novelty and utility as articulated and defined in § 101 and § 102, and nonobviousness, the new statutory formulation, as set out in § 103. * * *

* * *

The first sentence of [Section 103] * * * is strongly reminiscent of the language in *Hotchkiss*. Both formulations place emphasis on the pertinent art existing at the time the invention was made and both are implicitly tied to advances in that art. The major distinction is that Congress has emphasized "nonobviousness" as the operative test of the section, rather than the less definite "invention" language of *Hotchkiss* that Congress thought had led to "a large variety" of expressions in decisions and writings. In the title itself the Congress used the phrase "Conditions for patentability; *non-obvious subject matter*" (italics added), thus focusing upon "non-obviousness" rather than "invention." The Senate and House Reports, S. Rep. No. 1979, 82d Cong., 2d Sess. (1952); H. R. Rep. No. 1923, 82d Cong., 2d Sess. (1952), reflect this emphasis in these terms:

'Section 103, for the first time in our statute, provides a condition which exists in the law and has existed for more than 100 years, but only by reason of decisions of the courts. An invention which has been made, and which is new in the sense that the same thing has not been made before, may still not be patentable if the difference between the new thing and what was known before is not considered sufficiently great to warrant a patent. That has been expressed in a large variety of ways in decisions of the courts and in writings. Section 103 states this requirement in the title. It refers to the difference between the subject matter sought to be patented and the prior art, meaning what was known before as described in section 102. If this difference is such that the subject matter as a whole would have been obvious at the time to a person skilled in the art, then the subject matter cannot be patented.

'That provision paraphrases language which has often been used in decisions of the courts, and the section is added to the statute for uniformity and definiteness. This section should have a stabilizing effect and minimize great departures which have appeared in some cases.' H. R. Rep., *supra,* at 7; S. Rep., *supra,* at 6.

* * *

We believe that this legislative history, as well as other sources, shows that the revision was not intended by Congress to change the general level of patentable invention. We conclude that the section was intended merely as a codification of judicial precedents embracing the *Hotchkiss* condition, with congressional directions that inquiries into the obviousness of the subject matter sought to be patented are a prerequisite to patentability.

V.

Approached in this light, the § 103 additional condition, when followed realistically, will permit a more practical test of patentability. The emphasis on nonobviousness is one of inquiry, not quality, and, as such, comports with the constitutional strictures.

While the ultimate question of patent validity is one of law, the § 103 condition, which is but one of three conditions, each of which must be satisfied, lends itself to several basic factual inquiries. Under § 103, the scope and content of the prior art are to be determined; differences between the prior art and the claims at issue are to be ascertained; and the level of ordinary skill in the pertinent art resolved. Against this background, the obviousness or nonobviousness of the subject matter is determined. Such secondary considerations as commercial success, long felt but unsolved needs, failure of others, etc., might be utilized to give light to the circumstances surrounding the origin of the subject matter sought to be patented. As indicia of obviousness or nonobviousness, these inquiries may have relevancy.

* * *

Although we conclude here that the inquiry which the Patent Office and the courts must make as to patentability must be beamed with greater intensity on the requirements of § 103, it bears repeating that we find no change in the general strictness with which the overall test is to be applied. We have been urged to find in § 103 a relaxed standard, supposedly a congressional reaction to the "increased standard" applied by this Court in its decisions over the last 20 or 30 years. The standard has remained invariable in this Court. Technology, however, has advanced—and with remarkable rapidity in the last 50 years. Moreover, the ambit of applicable art in given fields of science has widened by disciplines unheard of a half century ago. It is but an evenhanded application to require that those persons granted the benefit of a patent monopoly be charged with an awareness of these changed conditions. The same is true of the less technical, but still useful arts. He who seeks to build a better mousetrap today has a long path to tread before reaching the Patent Office.

VI.

We now turn to the application of the conditions found necessary for patentability to the cases involved here:

A. *The Patent in Issue in No. 11, Graham v. John Deere Co.*

This patent, No. 2,627,798 (hereinafter called the '798 patent) relates to a spring clamp which permits plow shanks to be pushed upward when they hit obstructions in the soil, and then springs the shanks back into normal position when the obstruction is passed over.
* * *

When the chisel hits a rock or other obstruction in the soil, the obstruction forces the chisel and the rear portion of the shank to move upward. * * * When the obstruction is passed over, the upward force on the chisel disappears and the spring pulls the shank and hinge plate back into their original position. * * *

In practical use, a number of spring-hinge-shank combinations are clamped to a plow frame, forming a set of ground-working chisels capable of withstanding the shock of rocks and other obstructions in the soil without breaking the shanks.

Background of the Patent.

Chisel plows, as they are called, were developed for plowing in areas where the ground is relatively free from rocks or stones. Originally, the shanks were rigidly attached to the plow frames. When such plows were used in the rocky, glacial soils of some of the Northern States, they were found to have serious defects. As the chisels hit buried rocks, a vibratory motion was set up and tremendous forces were transmitted to the shank near its connection to the frame. The shanks would break. Graham, one of the petitioners, sought to meet that problem, and in 1950 obtained a patent, U.S. No. 2,493,811 (hereinafter '811), on a spring clamp which solved some of the difficulties. Graham and his companies manufactured and sold the '811 clamps. In 1950, Graham modified the '811 structure and filed for a patent. That patent, the one in issue, was granted in 1953. This suit against competing plow manufacturers resulted from charges by petitioners that several of respondents' devices infringed the '798 patent.

The Prior Art.

Five prior patents indicating the state of the art were cited by the Patent Office in the prosecution of the '798 application. Four of these patents, 10 other United States patents and two prior-use spring-clamp arrangements not of record in the '798 file wrapper were relied upon by respondents as revealing the prior art. The District Court and the Court of Appeals found that the prior art "as a whole in one form or another contains all of the mechanical elements of the 798 Patent." One of the prior-use clamp devices not before the Patent Examiner—Glencoe—was found to have "all of the elements."

We confine our discussion to the prior patent of Graham, '811, and to the Glencoe clamp device, both among the references asserted by respondents. The Graham '811 and '798 patent devices are similar in all elements, save two: (1) the stirrup and the bolted connection of the shank to the hinge plate do not appear in '811; and (2) the position of the shank is reversed, being placed in patent '811 above the hinge plate, sandwiched between it and the upper plate. The shank is held in place by the spring rod which is hooked against the bottom of the hinge plate passing through a slot in the shank. Other differences are of no consequence to our examination. In practice the '811 patent arrangement permitted the shank to wobble or fishtail because it was not rigidly fixed to the hinge plate; moreover, as the hinge plate was below the shank, the latter caused wear on the upper plate, a member difficult to repair or replace.

Graham's '798 patent application contained 12 claims. All were rejected as not distinguished from the Graham '811 patent. The inverted position of the shank was specifically rejected as was the bolting of the shank to the hinge plate. The Patent Office examiner found these to be "matters of design well within the expected skill of the art and devoid of invention." Graham withdrew the original claims and substituted the two new ones which are substantially those in issue here. His contention was that wear was reduced in patent '798 between the shank and the heel or rear of the upper plate. He also emphasized several new features, the relevant one here being that the bolt used to connect the hinge plate and shank maintained the upper face of the shank in continuing and constant contact with the underface of the hinge plate.

Graham did not urge before the Patent Office the greater "flexing" qualities of the '798 patent arrangement which he so heavily relied on in the courts. The sole element in patent '798 which petitioners argue before us is the interchanging of the shank and hinge plate and the consequences flowing from this arrangement. The contention is that this arrangement—which petitioners claim is not disclosed in the prior art—permits the shank to flex under stress for its entire length. * * * Petitioners say that this difference in flex, though small, effectively absorbs the tremendous forces of the shock of obstructions whereas prior art arrangements failed.

The Obviousness of the Differences.

We cannot agree with petitioners. We assume that the prior art does not disclose such an arrangement as petitioners claim in patent '798. Still we do not believe that the argument on which petitioners' contention is bottomed supports the validity of the patent. The tendency of the shank to flex is the same in all cases. If free-flexing, as petitioners now argue, is the crucial difference above the prior art, then it appears evident that the desired result would be obtainable by not boxing the shank within the confines of the hinge. The only other effective place available in the arrangement was to attach it below the hinge plate and run it through a stirrup or bracket that would not disturb its flexing qualities. Certainly a person having ordinary skill in the prior art, given the fact that the flex in the shank could be utilized more effectively if allowed to run the entire length of the shank, would immediately see that the thing to do was what Graham did, *i. e.,* invert the shank and the hinge plate.

* * *

We find no nonobvious facets in the '798 arrangement. The wear and repair claims were sufficient to overcome the patent examiner's original conclusions as to the validity of the patent. However, some of the prior art, notably Glencoe, was not before him. There the hinge plate is below the shank but, as the courts below found, all of the elements in the '798 patent are present in the Glencoe structure. Furthermore, even though the position of the shank and hinge plate appears reversed in Glencoe, the mechanical operation is identical. The shank there pivots about the underside of the stirrup, which in Glencoe is above the shank. In other words, the stirrup in Glencoe serves exactly the same function as the heel of the hinge plate in '798. The mere shifting of the wear point to the heel of the '798 hinge plate from the stirrup of Glencoe— itself a part of the hinge plate—presents no operative mechanical distinctions, much less nonobvious differences.

B.   *The Patent in Issue in No. 37, Calmar, Inc. v. Cook Chemical Co., and in No. 43, Colgate–Palmolive Co. v. Cook Chemical Co.*

The single patent involved in these cases relates to a plastic finger sprayer with a "hold-down" lid used as a built-in dispenser for containers or bottles packaging liquid products, principally household insecticides. * * *

* * *

[For many years, insecticide makers had tried unsuccessfully to develop sprayers that could be integrated with the containers in which the insecticides were marketed. In 1956, Scoggin, an officer of Cook Chemical, developed the finger-operated shipper-sprayer in suit, an integrated sprayer that could be mounted directly on each container during the packaging process and which would not leak during shipment or handling. The patent examiner allowed the claims, based solely on the novelty of the sealing mechanism, and a patent issued to Cook Chemical as Scoggin's assignee in 1959. In the meantime, Calmar also developed a shipper-sprayer, which it began marketing in 1958. When the Scoggin patent issued, Cook Chemical charged Calmar with infringement. The validity of the patent was upheld by the district court and the court of appeals.]

The Invalidity of the Patent.

* * *

The substitution of a rib built into a collar [as a component of the device's sealing mechanism] * * * presents no patentable difference above the prior art. It was fully disclosed and dedicated to the public in the [prior art] Livingstone patent. Cook Chemical argues, however, that Livingstone is not in the pertinent prior art because it relates to liquid containers having pouring spouts rather than pump sprayers. Apart from the fact that respondent made no such objection to similar references cited by the Examiner, so restricted a view of the applicable prior art is not justified. The problems confronting Scoggin and the insecticide industry were not insecticide problems; they were mechanical closure problems. Closure devices in such a closely related art as pouring spouts for liquid containers are at the very least pertinent references.

Cook Chemical insists, however, that the development of a workable shipper-sprayer eluded Calmar, who had long and unsuccessfully sought to solve the problem. And, further, that the long-felt need in the industry for a device such as Scoggin's together with its wide commercial success supports its patentability. These legal inferences or subtests do focus attention on economic and motivational rather than technical issues and are, therefore, more susceptible of judicial treatment than are the highly technical facts often present in patent litigation. Such inquiries may lend a helping hand to the judiciary which, as Mr. Justice Frankfurter observed, is most ill-fitted to discharge the technological duties cast upon it by patent legislation. *Marconi Wireless Co. v. United States,* 320 U.S. 1, 60 (1943). They may also serve to "guard against slipping into use of hindsight," *Monroe Auto Equipment Co. v. Heckethorn Mfg. & Sup. Co.,* 332 F.2d 406, 412 (1964), and to resist the temptation to read into the prior art the teachings of the invention in issue.

However, these factors do not, in the circumstances of this case, tip the scales of patentability. The Scoggin invention, as limited by the Patent Office and accepted by Scoggin, rests upon exceedingly small and quite nontechnical mechanical differences in a device which was old in the art. At the latest, those differences were rendered apparent in 1953 by the appearance of the Livingstone patent, and unsuccessful attempts to reach a solution to the problems confronting Scoggin made before that time became wholly irrelevant. It is also irrelevant that no one apparently chose to avail himself of knowledge stored in the Patent Office and readily available by the simple expedient of conducting a patent search— a prudent and nowadays common preliminary to well organized research. To us, the limited claims of the Scoggin patent are clearly evident from the prior art as it stood at the time of the invention.

We conclude that the claims in issue in the Scoggin patent must fall as not meeting the test of § 103, since the differences between them and the pertinent prior art would have been obvious to a person reasonably skilled in that art.

* * *

Notes

1. *Secondary Considerations*: As the Supreme Court recognized in *Graham v. John Deere Co.,* various secondary considerations can offer relevant, and relatively non-technical, evidence on the question of whether an invention represents a nonobvious solution to the particular problem at issue. The secondary factors which various courts have treated as evidence of nonobviousness include: failure of others to solve the problem in spite of long-felt need for a solution, the commercial success of the invention (or of infringements), acquiescence of competitors through licensing (or, conversely, nonacquiescence through copying), the favorable comments of experts in the field (or, in some cases, of the accused infringer), and an accused infringer's attempt to patent the technology. Obviousness, in contrast, is suggested where several persons independently develop similar solutions at almost the same time.

2. *Analogous arts:* As illustrated by *Graham v. John Deere Co.,* where the Supreme Court found a patented shipper-sprayer device for insecticides to be obvious in light of prior art in the "closely related art" of "pouring spouts for liquid containers," obviousness cases often raise questions of whether subject matter in one field of endeavor can be rendered obvious by prior art in another field. The Federal Circuit employs a "field of endeavor" test to identify such "analogous arts." That test inquires:

> (1) whether the art is from the same field of endeavor, regardless of the problem addressed and, (2) if the reference is not within the field of the inventor's endeavor, whether the reference still is reasonably pertinent to the particular problem.

In re Deminski, 796 F.2d 436, 442 (Fed. Cir. 1986). As the court more recently explained:

> This test for analogous art requires the PTO to determine the appropriate field of endeavor by reference to explanations of the invention's subject matter in the patent application, including the embodiments, function, and structure of the claimed invention.

In re Bigio, 381 F.3d 1320, 1325 (Fed. Cir. 2004). The test is intended to be objective, employing the "person of ordinary skill" standard:

> In that vein, this court has previously "reminded ... the PTO that it is necessary to consider 'the reality of the circumstances'—in other words, common sense—in deciding in which fields a person of ordinary skill would reasonably be expected to look for a solution to the problem facing the inventor." Accordingly, the examiner and the Board must consider the "circumstances" of the application—the full disclosure— and weigh those circumstances from the vantage point of the common sense likely to be exerted by one of ordinary skill in the art in assessing the scope of the endeavor. Those factual determinations are neither unbridled nor wholly subjective. Instead this test rests on an assessment of the nature of the application and claimed invention in addition to the level of ordinary skill in the art.

Id. at 1326 (citations omitted).

Under this test, would a toothbrush and a hairbrush be analogous arts? *Compare id.* at 1327 (Rader, J., for the majority) *with id.* at 1327–28 (Newman, J. dissenting).

3. *The Scope of Section 103 Prior Art:* The statutes do not specify what is "prior art" for Section 103 purposes. Although there has never been any doubt that Section 102(a) subject matter can render an invention obvious (as opposed to rendering it not novel, which requires that the Section 102(a) subject matter anticipate every claimed feature), the application of the other novelty bars has been the subject of extensive judicial interpretation.

In *Hazeltine Research, Inc. v. Brenner,* 382 U.S. 252, 86 S.Ct. 335, 15 L.Ed.2d 304 (1965), the Supreme Court held that prior art under Section 103 included Section 102(e) subject matter—that is, a patent application which was pending in the Patent Office at the time the invention at issue was made—even though the actual prior art patent was not issued (and thus its contents not disclosed) until after the invention date. The Court reasoned that if a pending application could invalidate a subsequent invention on novelty grounds under *Alexander Milburn Co.* (as codified in Section 102(e)), the same reasoning should apply to invalidation on obviousness grounds.

Section 103 prior art also includes Section 102(g) subject matter. Overruling prior case law to the contrary, the Federal Circuit has held in a series of cases that a Section 102(g) reference may constitute Section 103 prior art, regardless of whether the reference was "known to the art or to the patentee before he made the invention." *E.I. du Pont de Nemours & Co. v. Phillips Petroleum Co.*, 849 F.2d 1430, 1436 (Fed.Cir.1988), *cert. denied*, 488 U.S. 986, 109 S.Ct. 542, 102 L.Ed.2d 572 (1988).

However, the circumstances in which Section 103 prior art includes Section 102(g) subject matter were narrowed by the Patent Law Amendments Act of 1984, which added the following sentence to Section 103:

> Subject matter developed by another person, which qualifies as prior art only under subsection (f) or (g) of section 102 of this title, shall not preclude patentability under this section where the subject matter and the claimed invention were, at the time the invention was made, owned by the same person or subject to an obligation of assignment to the same person.

The purpose of this amendment was to overturn case law holding that nonpublic inventions could be Section 102(g)/103 prior art with respect to a later invention by a different employee of the same organization. *See Kimberly–Clark Corp. v. Procter & Gamble Dist. Co., Inc.*, 973 F.2d 911, 917 (Fed.Cir.1992) (discussing history of amendment). In *OddzOn Prods., Inc. v. Just Toys, Inc.*, 122 F.3d 1396 (Fed. Cir. 1997), the Federal Circuit held that, by reverse implication from the 1984 amendment, nonpublic Section 102(f) subject matter constitutes Section 103 prior art except where it falls within the scope of the amendment.

The Patent Reform Act of 1999 amended Section 103(c) to encompass Section 102(e) subject matter as well. This amendment reversed prior law, under which commonly-assigned pending applications (if successful) were prior art for Section 103 purposes, as illustrated in *In re Bartfeld*, 925 F.2d 1450 (Fed.Cir.1991). Thus, as a result of the 1999 amendment, Section 102(e) subject matter now receives the same treatment as Section 102(f) or (g) subject matter for purposes of determining nonobviousness.

In 2004, Congress further amended Section 103(c) to treat inventions arising from joint research and development ventures (for example, between a university and a private entity) the same as inventions that are the subject of commonly-assigned patent applications. This legislation, the Cooperative Research and Technology Enhancement (CREATE) Act of 2004, added subsections (c)(2) and (c)(3) to Section 103. The purpose of this amendment was to encourage and protect research collaborations between private companies and universities or other entities, but critics of the proposed legislation argued that it would permit a form of double-patenting, in which partners in such collaborations could obtain patents on inventions which were not patentably distinct from one another. Advocates for the new legislation responded by proposing that such indistinct patents should include mandatory disclaimers requiring the patent's owner to waive enforcement of that patent separately from the first-issued patent, and permitting enforcement only during the term of the first-issued patent. These recommendations have since been incorporated into the PTO regulations at 37 C.F.R. § 1.321(d).

4. Should Section 103 prior art include (a) subject matter that is neither publicly known nor the subject of a patent application but which is actually known to the patent applicant? (b) an inventor's own prior work (and, if so, under what circumstances)?

KSR INTERNATIONAL CO. v. TELEFLEX INC.

Supreme Court of the United States, 2007.
___ U.S. ___, 127 S.Ct. 1727, ___ L.Ed.2d ___.

JUSTICE KENNEDY delivered the opinion of the Court.

Teleflex Incorporated and its subsidiary Technology Holding Company—both referred to here as Teleflex—sued KSR International Company for patent infringement. The patent at issue, United States Patent No. 6,237,565 B1, is entitled "Adjustable Pedal Assembly With Electronic Throttle Control." The patentee is Steven J. Engelgau, and the patent is referred to as "the Engelgau patent." Teleflex holds the exclusive license to the patent.

Claim 4 of the Engelgau patent describes a mechanism for combining an electronic sensor with an adjustable automobile pedal so the pedal's position can be transmitted to a computer that controls the throttle in the vehicle's engine. When Teleflex accused KSR of infringing the Engelgau patent by adding an electronic sensor to one of KSR's previously designed pedals, KSR countered that claim 4 was invalid under the Patent Act, 35 U.S.C. § 103, because its subject matter was obvious.

Section 103 forbids issuance of a patent when "the differences between the subject matter sought to be patented and the prior art are such that the subject matter as a whole would have been obvious at the time the invention was made to a person having ordinary skill in the art to which said subject matter pertains."

In *Graham v. John Deere Co. of Kansas City,* 383 U.S. 1, 86 S.Ct. 684, 15 L.Ed.2d 545 (1966), the Court set out a framework for applying the statutory language of § 103, language itself based on the logic of the earlier decision in *Hotchkiss v. Greenwood,* 11 How. 248, 13 L.Ed. 683 (1851), and its progeny. *See* 383 U.S., at 15–17. The analysis is objective:

> "Under § 103, the scope and content of the prior art are to be determined; differences between the prior art and the claims at issue are to be ascertained; and the level of ordinary skill in the pertinent art resolved. Against this background the obviousness or nonobviousness of the subject matter is determined. Such secondary considerations as commercial success, long felt but unsolved needs, failure of others, etc., might be utilized to give light to the circumstances surrounding the origin of the subject matter sought to be patented." *Id.,* at 17–18.

While the sequence of these questions might be reordered in any particular case, the factors continue to define the inquiry that controls. If a court, or patent examiner, conducts this analysis and concludes the claimed subject matter was obvious, the claim is invalid under § 103.

Seeking to resolve the question of obviousness with more uniformity and consistency, the Court of Appeals for the Federal Circuit has employed an approach referred to by the parties as the "teaching, suggestion, or motivation" test (TSM test), under which a patent claim is only proved obvious if "some motivation or suggestion to combine the prior art teachings" can be found in the prior art, the nature of the problem, or the knowledge of a person having ordinary skill in the art. *See, e.g., Al–Site Corp. v. VSI Int'l, Inc.,* 174 F.3d 1308, 1323–1324 (C.A.Fed.1999). KSR challenges that test, or at least its application in this case. Because the Court of Appeals addressed the question of obviousness in a manner contrary to § 103 and our precedents, we granted certiorari, 547 U. S. __ (2006). We now reverse.

I

A

In car engines without computer-controlled throttles, the accelerator pedal interacts with the throttle via cable or other mechanical link. The pedal arm acts as a lever rotating around a pivot point. In a cable-actuated throttle control the rotation caused by pushing down the pedal pulls a cable, which in turn pulls open valves in the carburetor or fuel injection unit. The wider the valves open, the more fuel and air are released, causing combustion to increase and the car to accelerate. When the driver takes his foot off the pedal, the opposite occurs as the cable is released and the valves slide closed.

In the 1990's it became more common to install computers in cars to control engine operation. Computer-controlled throttles open and close valves in response to electronic signals, not through force transferred from the pedal by a mechanical link. Constant, delicate adjustments of air and fuel mixture are possible. The computer's rapid processing of factors beyond the pedal's position improves fuel efficiency and engine performance.

For a computer-controlled throttle to respond to a driver's operation of the car, the computer must know what is happening with the pedal. A cable or mechanical link does not suffice for this purpose; at some point, an electronic sensor is necessary to translate the mechanical operation into digital data the computer can understand.

Before discussing sensors further we turn to the mechanical design of the pedal itself. In the traditional design a pedal can be pushed down or released but cannot have its position in the footwell adjusted by sliding the pedal forward or back. As a result, a driver who wishes to be closer or farther from the pedal must either reposition himself in the driver's seat or move the seat in some way. In cars with deep footwells these are imperfect solutions for drivers of smaller stature. To solve the problem, inventors, beginning in the 1970's, designed pedals that could be adjusted to change their location in the footwell. Important for this case are two adjustable pedals disclosed in U.S. Patent Nos. 5,010,782 (filed July 28, 1989) (Asano) and 5,460,061 (filed Sept. 17, 1993) (Redding). The Asano patent reveals a support structure that houses the pedal so that even when the pedal location is adjusted relative to the driver, one of the pedal's pivot points stays fixed. The pedal is also designed so that the force necessary to push the pedal down is the same regardless of adjustments to its location. The Redding patent reveals a different, sliding mechanism where both the pedal and the pivot point are adjusted.

We return to sensors. Well before Engelgau applied for his challenged patent, some inventors had obtained patents involving electronic pedal sensors for computer-controlled throttles. These inventions, such as the device disclosed in U.S. Patent No. 5,241,936 (filed Sept. 9, 1991) ('936), taught that it was preferable to detect the pedal's position in the pedal assembly, not in the engine. The '936 patent disclosed a pedal with an electronic sensor on a pivot point in the pedal assembly. U.S. Patent No. 5,063,811 (filed July 9, 1990) (Smith) taught that to prevent the wires connecting the sensor to the computer from chafing and wearing out, and to avoid grime and damage from the driver's foot, the sensor should be put on a fixed part of the pedal assembly rather than in or on the pedal's footpad.

In addition to patents for pedals with integrated sensors inventors obtained patents for self-contained modular sensors. A modular sensor is designed independently of a given pedal so that it can be taken off the shelf and attached to mechanical pedals of various sorts, enabling the pedals to be used in automobiles with computer-controlled throttles. One such sensor was disclosed in U.S. Patent No. 5,385,068 (filed Dec. 18, 1992) ('068). In 1994, Chevrolet manufactured a line of trucks using modular sensors "attached to the pedal support bracket, adjacent to the pedal and engaged with the pivot shaft about which the pedal rotates in operation." 298 F.Supp.2d 581, 589 (E.D.Mich.2003).

The prior art contained patents involving the placement of sensors on adjustable pedals as well. For example, U.S. Patent No. 5,819,593 (filed Aug. 17, 1995) (Rixon) discloses an adjustable pedal assembly with an electronic sensor for detecting the pedal's position. In the Rixon pedal the sensor is located in the pedal footpad. The Rixon pedal was known to suffer from wire chafing when the pedal was depressed and released.

This short account of pedal and sensor technology leads to the instant case.

B

KSR, a Canadian company, manufactures and supplies auto parts, including pedal systems. Ford Motor Company hired KSR in 1998 to supply an adjustable pedal system for various lines of automobiles with cable-actuated throttle controls. KSR developed an adjustable mechanical pedal for Ford and obtained U.S. Patent No. 6,151,976 (filed July 16, 1999) ('976) for the design. In 2000, KSR was chosen by General Motors Corporation (GMC or GM) to supply adjustable pedal systems for Chevrolet and GMC light trucks that used engines with computer-controlled throttles. To make the '976 pedal compatible with the trucks, KSR merely took that design and added a modular sensor.

Teleflex is a rival to KSR in the design and manufacture of adjustable pedals. As noted, it is the exclusive licensee of the Engelgau patent. Engelgau filed the patent application on August 22, 2000 as a continuation of a previous application for U.S. Patent No. 6,109,241, which was filed on January 26, 1999. He has sworn he invented the patent's subject matter on February 14, 1998. The Engelgau patent discloses an adjustable electronic pedal described in the specification as a "simplified vehicle control pedal assembly that is less expensive, and which uses fewer parts and is easier to package within the vehicle." * * *

We agree with the District Court that [claim 4] discloses "a position-adjustable pedal assembly with an electronic pedal position sensor attached to the support member of the pedal assembly. Attaching the sensor to the support member allows the sensor to remain in a fixed position while the driver adjusts the pedal." 298 F.Supp.2d, at 586–587.

Before issuing the Engelgau patent the U.S. Patent and Trademark Office (PTO) rejected one of the patent claims that was similar to, but broader than, the present claim 4. The claim did not include the requirement that the sensor be placed on a fixed pivot point. The PTO concluded the claim was an obvious combination of the prior art disclosed in Redding and Smith, explaining:

> " 'Since the prior ar[t] references are from the field of endeavor, the purpose disclosed ... would have been recognized in the pertinent art of Redding. Therefore it would have been obvious ... to provide the device of Redding with the ... means attached to a support member as taught by Smith.' " *Id.,* at 595.

In other words Redding provided an example of an adjustable pedal and Smith explained how to mount a sensor on a pedal's support structure, and the rejected patent claim merely put these two teachings together.

Although the broader claim was rejected, claim 4 was later allowed because it included the limitation of a fixed pivot point, which distinguished the design from Redding's. Engelgau had not included Asano among the prior art references, and Asano was not mentioned in the patent's prosecution. Thus, the PTO did not have before it an adjustable pedal with a fixed pivot point. The patent issued on May 29, 2001 and was assigned to Teleflex.

Upon learning of KSR's design for GM, Teleflex sent a warning letter informing KSR that its proposal would violate the Engelgau patent. " 'Teleflex believes that any supplier of a product that combines an adjustable pedal with an electronic throttle control necessarily employs technology covered by one or more' "of Teleflex's patents. KSR refused to enter a royalty arrangement with Teleflex; so Teleflex sued for infringement, asserting KSR's pedal infringed the Engelgau patent and two other patents. Teleflex later abandoned its claims regarding the other patents and dedicated the patents to the public. The remaining contention was that KSR's pedal system for GM infringed claim 4 of the Engelgau patent. Teleflex has not argued that the other three claims of the patent are infringed by KSR's pedal, nor has Teleflex argued that the mechanical adjustable pedal designed by KSR for Ford infringed any of its patents.

C

The District Court granted summary judgment in KSR's favor. After reviewing the pertinent history of pedal design, the scope of the Engelgau patent, and the relevant prior art, the court considered the validity of the contested claim. By direction of 35 U.S.C. § 282, an issued patent is presumed valid. The District Court applied *Graham*'s framework to determine whether under summary-judgment standards KSR had overcome the presumption and demonstrated that claim 4 was obvious in light of the prior art in existence when the claimed subject matter was invented. *See* § 102(a).

The District Court determined, in light of the expert testimony and the parties' stipulations, that the level of ordinary skill in pedal design was " 'an undergraduate degree in mechanical engineering (or an equivalent amount of industry experience) [and] familiarity with pedal control systems for vehicles.' " 298 F.Supp.2d, at 590. The court then set forth the relevant prior art, including the patents and pedal designs described above.

Following *Graham*'s direction, the court compared the teachings of the prior art to the claims of Engelgau. It found "little difference." 298 F.Supp.2d, at 590. Asano taught everything contained in claim 4 except the use of a sensor to detect the pedal's position and transmit it to the computer controlling the throttle. That additional aspect was revealed in sources such as the '068 patent and the sensors used by Chevrolet.

Under the controlling cases from the Court of Appeals for the Federal Circuit, however, the District Court was not permitted to stop there. The court was required also to apply the TSM test. The District Court held KSR had satisfied the test. It reasoned (1) the state of the industry would lead inevitably to combinations of electronic sensors and adjustable pedals, (2) Rixon provided the basis for these developments, and (3) Smith taught a solution to the wire chafing problems in Rixon, namely locating the sensor on the fixed structure of the pedal. This could lead to the combination of Asano, or a pedal like it, with a pedal position sensor.

The conclusion that the Engelgau design was obvious was supported, in the District Court's view, by the PTO's rejection of the broader version of claim 4. Had Engelgau included Asano in his patent application, it reasoned, the PTO would have found claim 4 to be an obvious combination of Asano and Smith, as it had found the broader version an obvious combination of Redding and Smith. As a final matter, the District Court held that the secondary factor of Teleflex's commercial success with pedals based on Engelgau's design did not alter its conclusion. The District Court granted summary judgment for KSR.

With principal reliance on the TSM test, the Court of Appeals reversed. It ruled the District Court had not been strict enough in applying the test, having failed to make " 'finding[s] as to the specific understanding or principle within the knowledge of a skilled artisan that would have motivated one with no knowledge of [the] invention' . . . to attach an electronic control to the support bracket of the Asano assembly." 119 Fed. Appx., at 288 (brackets in original) (quoting *In re Kotzab*, 217 F.3d 1365, 1371 (C.A.Fed.2000)). The Court of Appeals held that the District Court was incorrect that the nature of the problem to be solved satisfied this requirement because unless the "prior art references address[ed] the precise problem that the patentee was trying to solve," the problem would not motivate an inventor to look at those references. 119 Fed. Appx., at 288.

Here, the Court of Appeals found, the Asano pedal was designed to solve the " 'constant ratio problem' "—that is, to ensure that the force required to depress the pedal is the same no matter how the pedal is adjusted—whereas Engelgau sought to provide a simpler, smaller, cheaper adjustable electronic pedal. As for Rixon, the court explained, that pedal suffered from the problem of wire chafing but was not designed to solve it. In the court's view Rixon did not teach anything helpful to Engelgau's purpose. Smith, in turn, did not relate to adjustable pedals and did not "necessarily go to the issue of motivation to attach the electronic control on the support bracket of the pedal assembly." When the patents were interpreted in this way, the Court of Appeals held, they would not have led a person of ordinary skill to put a sensor on the sort of pedal described in Asano.

That it might have been obvious to try the combination of Asano and a sensor was likewise irrelevant, in the court's view, because " ' "[o]bvious to try" has long been held not to constitute obviousness.' " *Id.*, at 289 (quoting *In re Deuel*, 51 F.3d 1552, 1559 (C.A.Fed.1995)).

The Court of Appeals also faulted the District Court's consideration of the PTO's rejection of the broader version of claim 4. The District Court's role, the Court of Appeals explained, was not to speculate regarding what the PTO might have done had the Engelgau patent mentioned Asano. Rather, the court held, the District Court was obliged first to presume that the issued patent was valid and then to render its own independent judgment of obviousness based on a review of the prior art. The fact that the PTO had rejected the broader version of claim 4, the Court of Appeals said, had no place in that analysis.

The Court of Appeals further held that genuine issues of material fact precluded summary judgment. Teleflex had proffered statements from one expert that claim 4 " 'was a simple, elegant, and novel combination of features,' "119 Fed. Appx., at 290, compared to Rixon, and from another expert that claim 4 was nonobvious because, unlike in Rixon, the sensor was mounted on the support bracket rather than the pedal itself. This evidence, the court concluded, sufficed to require a trial.

II

A

We begin by rejecting the rigid approach of the Court of Appeals. Throughout this Court's engagement with the question of obviousness, our cases have set forth an expansive and flexible approach inconsistent with the way the Court of Appeals applied its TSM test here. To be sure, *Graham* recognized the need for "uniformity and definiteness." 383 U.S., at 18. Yet the principles laid down in *Graham* reaffirmed the "functional approach" of *Hotchkiss,* 11 How. 248, 13 L.Ed. 683. *See* 383 U.S., at 12. To this end, *Graham* set forth a broad inquiry and invited courts, where appropriate, to look at any secondary considerations that would prove instructive. *Id.,* at 17.

Neither the enactment of § 103 nor the analysis in *Graham* disturbed this Court's earlier instructions concerning the need for caution in granting a patent based on the combination of elements found in the prior art. For over a half century, the Court has held that a "patent for a combination which only unites old elements with no change in their respective functions . . . obviously withdraws what is already known into the field of its monopoly and diminishes the resources available to skillful men." *Great Atlantic & Pacific Tea Co. v. Supermarket Equipment Corp.,* 340 U.S. 147, 152, 71 S.Ct. 127, 95 L.Ed. 162 (1950). This is a principal reason for declining to allow patents for what is obvious. The combination of familiar elements according to known methods is likely to be obvious when it does no more than yield predictable results. Three cases decided after *Graham* illustrate the application of this doctrine.

In *United States v. Adams,* 383 U.S. 39, 40, 86 S.Ct. 708, 15 L.Ed.2d 572 (1966), a companion case to *Graham,* the Court considered the obviousness of a "wet battery" that varied from prior designs in two ways: It contained water, rather than the acids conventionally employed in storage batteries; and its electrodes were magnesium and cuprous chloride, rather than zinc and silver chloride. The Court recognized that when a patent claims a structure already known in the prior art that is altered by the mere substitution of one element for another known in the field, the combination must do more than yield a predictable result. 383 U.S., at 50–51. It nevertheless rejected the Government's claim that Adams's battery was obvious. The Court relied upon the corollary principle that when the prior art teaches away from combining certain known elements, discovery of a successful means of combining them is more likely to be nonobvious. *Id.,* at 51–52. When Adams designed his battery, the prior art warned that risks were involved in using the types of electrodes he employed. The fact that the elements worked together in an unexpected and fruitful manner supported the conclusion that Adams's design was not obvious to those skilled in the art.

In *Anderson's-Black Rock, Inc. v. Pavement Salvage Co.,* 396 U.S. 57, 90 S.Ct. 305, 24 L.Ed.2d 258 (1969), the Court elaborated on this approach. The subject matter of the patent before the Court was a device combining two pre-existing elements: a radiant-heat burner and a paving machine. The device, the Court concluded, did not create some new synergy: The radiant-heat burner functioned just as a burner was expected to function; and the paving machine did the same. The two in combination did no more than they would in separate, sequential operation. *Id.,* at 60–62. In those circumstances, "while the combination of old elements performed a useful function, it added nothing to the nature and quality of the radiant-heat burner already patented," and the patent failed under § 103. *Id.,* at 62 (footnote omitted).

Finally, in *Sakraida v. AG Pro, Inc.,* 425 U.S. 273, 96 S.Ct. 1532, 47 L.Ed.2d 784 (1976), the Court derived from the precedents the conclusion that when a patent "simply arranges old elements with each performing the same function it had been known to perform" and yields no more than one would expect from such an arrangement, the combination is obvious. *Id.,* at 282.

The principles underlying these cases are instructive when the question is whether a patent claiming the combination of elements of prior art is obvious. When a work is available in one field of endeavor, design incentives and other market forces can prompt variations of it, either in the same field or a different one. If a person of ordinary skill can implement a predictable variation, § 103 likely bars its patentability. For the same reason, if a technique has been used to improve one device, and a person of ordinary skill in the art would recognize that it would improve similar devices in the same way, using the technique is obvious unless its actual application is beyond his or her skill. *Sakraida* and *Anderson's-Black Rock* are illustrative—a court must ask whether the improvement is more than the predictable use of prior art elements according to their established functions.

Following these principles may be more difficult in other cases than it is here because the claimed subject matter may involve more than the simple substitution of one known element for another or the mere application of a known technique to a piece of prior art ready for the improvement. Often, it will be necessary for a court to look to interrelated teachings of multiple patents; the effects of demands known to the design community or present in the marketplace; and the background knowledge possessed by a person having ordinary skill in the art, all in order to determine whether there was an apparent reason to combine the known elements in the fashion claimed by the patent at issue. To facilitate review, this analysis should be made explicit. *See In re Kahn,*

441 F.3d 977, 988 (C.A.Fed.2006) ("[R]ejections on obviousness grounds cannot be sustained by mere conclusory statements; instead, there must be some articulated reasoning with some rational underpinning to support the legal conclusion of obviousness"). As our precedents make clear, however, the analysis need not seek out precise teachings directed to the specific subject matter of the challenged claim, for a court can take account of the inferences and creative steps that a person of ordinary skill in the art would employ.

B

When it first established the requirement of demonstrating a teaching, suggestion, or motivation to combine known elements in order to show that the combination is obvious, the Court of Customs and Patent Appeals captured a helpful insight. *See Application of Bergel,* 48 C.C.P.A. 1102, 292 F.2d 955, 956–957 (1961). As is clear from cases such as *Adams,* a patent composed of several elements is not proved obvious merely by demonstrating that each of its elements was, independently, known in the prior art. Although common sense directs one to look with care at a patent application that claims as innovation the combination of two known devices according to their established functions, it can be important to identify a reason that would have prompted a person of ordinary skill in the relevant field to combine the elements in the way the claimed new invention does. This is so because inventions in most, if not all, instances rely upon building blocks long since uncovered, and claimed discoveries almost of necessity will be combinations of what, in some sense, is already known.

Helpful insights, however, need not become rigid and mandatory formulas; and when it is so applied, the TSM test is incompatible with our precedents. The obviousness analysis cannot be confined by a formalistic conception of the words teaching, suggestion, and motivation, or by overemphasis on the importance of published articles and the explicit content of issued patents. The diversity of inventive pursuits and of modern technology counsels against limiting the analysis in this way. In many fields it may be that there is little discussion of obvious techniques or combinations, and it often may be the case that market demand, rather than scientific literature, will drive design trends. Granting patent protection to advances that would occur in the ordinary course without real innovation retards progress and may, in the case of patents combining previously known elements, deprive prior inventions of their value or utility.

In the years since the Court of Customs and Patent Appeals set forth the essence of the TSM test, the Court of Appeals no doubt has applied the test in accord with these principles in many cases. There is no necessary inconsistency between the idea underlying the TSM test and the *Graham* analysis. But when a court transforms the general principle into a rigid rule that limits the obviousness inquiry, as the Court of Appeals did here, it errs.

C

The flaws in the analysis of the Court of Appeals relate for the most part to the court's narrow conception of the obviousness inquiry reflected in its application of the TSM test. In determining whether the subject matter of a patent claim is obvious, neither the particular motivation nor the avowed purpose of the patentee controls. What matters is the objective reach of the claim. If the claim extends to what is obvious, it is invalid under § 103. One of the ways in which a patent's subject matter can be proved obvious is by noting that there existed at the time of invention a known problem for which there was an obvious solution encompassed by the patent's claims.

The first error of the Court of Appeals in this case was to foreclose this reasoning by holding that courts and patent examiners should look only to the problem the patentee was trying to solve. 119 Fed. Appx., at 288. The Court of Appeals failed to recognize that the problem motivating the patentee may be only one of many addressed by the patent's subject matter. The question is not whether the combination was obvious to the patentee but whether the combination was obvious to a person with ordinary skill in the art. Under the correct analysis, any need or problem known in the field of endeavor at the time of invention and addressed by the patent can provide a reason for combining the elements in the manner claimed.

The second error of the Court of Appeals lay in its assumption that a person of ordinary skill attempting to solve a problem will be led only to those elements of prior art designed to solve the same problem. The primary purpose of Asano was solving the constant ratio problem; so, the court concluded, an inventor considering how to put a sensor on an adjustable pedal would have no reason to consider putting it on the Asano pedal. Common sense teaches, however, that familiar items may have obvious uses beyond their primary purposes, and in many cases a person of ordinary skill will be able to fit the teachings of multiple patents together like pieces of a puzzle. Regardless of Asano's primary purpose, the design provided an obvious example of an adjustable pedal with a fixed pivot point; and the prior art was replete with patents indicating that a fixed pivot point was an ideal mount for a sensor. The idea that a designer hoping to make an adjustable electronic pedal would ignore Asano because Asano was designed to solve the constant ratio problem makes little sense. A person of ordinary skill is also a person of ordinary creativity, not an automaton.

The same constricted analysis led the Court of Appeals to conclude, in error, that a patent claim cannot be proved obvious merely by showing that the combination of elements was "obvious to try." When there is a design need or market pressure to solve a problem and there are a finite number of identified, predictable solutions, a person of ordinary skill has good reason to pursue the known options within his or her technical grasp. If this leads to the anticipated success, it is likely the product not of innovation but of ordinary skill and common sense. In that instance the fact that a combination was obvious to try might show that it was obvious under § 103.

The Court of Appeals, finally, drew the wrong conclusion from the risk of courts and patent examiners falling prey to hindsight bias. A factfinder should be aware, of course, of the distortion caused by hindsight bias and must be cautious of arguments reliant upon *ex post* reasoning. See *Graham,* 383 U.S., at 36 (warning against a "temptation to read into the prior art the teachings of the invention in issue" and instructing courts to " 'guard against slipping into the use of hindsight' " (quoting *Monroe Auto Equipment Co. v. Heckethorn Mfg. & Supply Co.,* 332 F.2d 406, 412 (C.A.6 1964))). Rigid preventative rules that deny factfinders recourse to common sense, however, are neither necessary under our case law nor consistent with it.

We note the Court of Appeals has since elaborated a broader conception of the TSM test than was applied in the instant matter. *See, e.g., DyStar Textilfarben GmbH & Co. Deutschland KG v. C.H. Patrick Co.,* 464 F.3d 1356, 1367 (2006) ("Our suggestion test is in actuality quite flexible and not only permits, but *requires,* consideration of common knowledge and common sense"); *Alza Corp. v. Mylan Labs., Inc.,* 464 F.3d 1286, 1291 (2006) ("There is flexibility in our obviousness jurisprudence because a motivation may be found *implicitly* in the prior art. We do not have a rigid test that requires an actual teaching to combine . . . "). Those decisions, of course, are not now before us and do not correct the errors of law made by the Court of Appeals in this case. The extent to which they may describe an analysis more consistent with our earlier precedents and our decision here is a matter for the Court of Appeals to consider in its future cases. What we hold is that the fundamental misunderstandings identified above led the Court of Appeals in this case to apply a test inconsistent with our patent law decisions.

III

When we apply the standards we have explained to the instant facts, claim 4 must be found obvious. We agree with and adopt the District Court's recitation of the relevant prior art and its determination of the level of ordinary skill in the field. As did the District Court, we see little difference between the teachings of Asano and Smith and the adjustable electronic pedal disclosed in claim 4 of the Engelgau patent. A person having ordinary skill in the art could have combined Asano with a pedal position sensor in a fashion encompassed by claim 4, and would have seen the benefits of doing so.

* * *

The District Court was correct to conclude that, as of the time Engelgau designed the subject matter in claim 4, it was obvious to a person of ordinary skill to combine Asano with a pivot-mounted pedal position sensor. There then existed a marketplace that created a strong incentive to convert mechanical pedals to electronic pedals, and the prior art taught a number of methods for achieving this advance. The Court of Appeals considered the issue too narrowly by, in effect, asking whether a pedal designer writing on a blank slate would have chosen both Asano and a modular sensor similar to the ones used in the Chevrolet truckline and disclosed in the '068 patent. The District Court employed this narrow inquiry as well, though it reached the correct result nevertheless. The proper question to have asked was whether a pedal designer of ordinary skill, facing the wide range of needs created by developments in the field of endeavor, would have seen a benefit to upgrading Asano with a sensor.

In automotive design, as in many other fields, the interaction of multiple components means that changing one component often requires the others to be modified as well. Technological developments made it clear that engines using computer-controlled throttles would become standard. As a result, designers might have decided to design new pedals from scratch; but they also would have had reason to make pre-existing pedals work with the new engines. Indeed, upgrading its own pre-existing model led KSR to design the pedal now accused of infringing the Engelgau patent.

For a designer starting with Asano, the question was where to attach the sensor. The consequent legal question, then, is whether a pedal designer of ordinary skill starting with Asano would have found it obvious to put the sensor on a fixed pivot point. The prior art discussed above leads us to the conclusion that attaching the sensor where both KSR and Engelgau put it would have been obvious to a person of ordinary skill.

The '936 patent taught the utility of putting the sensor on the pedal device, not in the engine. Smith, in turn, explained to put the sensor not on the pedal's footpad but instead on its support structure. And from the known wire-chafing problems of Rixon, and Smith's teaching that "the pedal assemblies must not precipitate any motion in the connecting wires," the designer would know to place the sensor on a nonmoving part of the pedal structure. The most obvious nonmoving point on the structure from which a sensor can easily detect the pedal's position is a pivot point. The designer, accordingly, would follow Smith in mounting the sensor on a pivot, thereby designing an adjustable electronic pedal covered by claim 4.

Just as it was possible to begin with the objective to upgrade Asano to work with a computer-controlled throttle, so too was it possible to take an adjustable electronic pedal like Rixon and seek an improvement that would avoid the wire-chafing problem. Following similar steps to those just explained, a designer would learn from Smith to avoid sensor movement and would come, thereby, to Asano because Asano disclosed an adjustable pedal with a fixed pivot.

Teleflex indirectly argues that the prior art taught away from attaching a sensor to Asano because Asano in its view is bulky, complex, and expensive. The only evidence Teleflex marshals in support of this argument, however, is the Radcliffe declaration, which merely indicates that Asano would not have solved Engelgau's goal of making a small, simple, and inexpensive pedal. What the declaration does not indicate is that Asano was somehow so flawed that there was no reason to upgrade it, or pedals like it, to be compatible with modern engines. Indeed, Teleflex's own declarations refute this conclusion. Dr. Radcliffe states that Rixon suffered from the same bulk and complexity as did Asano. Teleflex's other expert, however, explained that Rixon was itself designed by adding a sensor to a pre-existing mechanical pedal. If Rixon's base pedal was not too flawed to upgrade, then Dr. Radcliffe's declaration does not show Asano was either. Teleflex may have made a plausible argument that Asano is inefficient as compared to Engelgau's preferred embodiment, but to judge Asano against Engelgau would be to engage in the very hindsight bias Teleflex rightly urges must be avoided. Accordingly, Teleflex has not shown anything in the prior art that taught away from the use of Asano.

Like the District Court, finally, we conclude Teleflex has shown no secondary factors to dislodge the determination that claim 4 is obvious. Proper application of *Graham* and our other precedents to these facts therefore leads to the conclusion that claim 4 encompassed obvious subject matter. As a result, the claim fails to meet the requirement of § 103.

We need not reach the question whether the failure to disclose Asano during the prosecution of Engelgau voids the presumption of validity given to issued patents, for claim 4 is obvious despite the presumption. We nevertheless think it appropriate to note that the rationale underlying the presumption—that the PTO, in its expertise, has approved the claim—seems much diminished here.

IV

* * *

We build and create by bringing to the tangible and palpable reality around us new works based on instinct, simple logic, ordinary inferences, extraordinary ideas, and sometimes even genius. These advances, once part of our shared knowledge, define a new threshold from which innovation starts once more. And as progress beginning from higher levels of achievement is expected in the normal course, the results of ordinary innovation are not the subject of exclusive rights under the patent laws. Were it otherwise patents might stifle, rather than promote, the progress of useful arts. *See* U.S. Const., Art. I, § 8, cl. 8. These premises led to the bar on patents claiming obvious subject matter established in *Hotchkiss* and codified in § 103. Application of the bar must not be confined within a test or formulation too constrained to serve its purpose.

KSR provided convincing evidence that mounting a modular sensor on a fixed pivot point of the Asano pedal was a design step well within the grasp of a person of ordinary skill in the relevant art. Its arguments, and the record, demonstrate that claim 4 of the Engelgau patent is obvious. In rejecting the District Court's rulings, the Court of Appeals analyzed the issue in a narrow, rigid manner inconsistent with § 103 and our precedents. The judgment of the Court of Appeals is reversed, and the case remanded for further proceedings consistent with this opinion.

It is so ordered.

Note

Prior to *KSR International*, the Federal Circuit had begun to require the party challenging a patent to present affirmative evidence in the prior art of a "teaching, suggestion or motivation" to combine prior art elements, and its approach had become increasingly formalistic. As noted by the Supreme Court, however, between the granting of the petition for certiorari in *KSR International* and the issuance of the Court's decision, the Federal Circuit had already begun to retreat from this formalism. How much guidance does *KSR International* provide to lower courts and to potential litigants needing to evaluate the validity of a patent under § 103? What does it mean to say that a combination was "obvious to try"?

The *McGinley* case which follows predates *KSR International*. Would the analysis be any different if the case arose today?

McGINLEY v. FRANKLIN SPORTS, INC.
United States Court of Appeals, Federal Circuit, 2001.
262 F.3d 1339.

CLEVENGER, CIRCUIT JUDGE.

[Plaintiff McGinley sued Franklin Sports, Inc. (FSI) for willfully infringing McGinley's patent for an instructional pitching device in the form of a regulation baseball that has specific "finger placement indicia" for teaching students how to grasp a baseball for throwing different types of pitches. Although the jury found that the patent was valid and willfully infringed, the trial court granted FSI's motion for a JMOL, holding that the claims in question were invalid as obvious under Section 103, and McGinley appealed.]

* * *

In the preferred embodiment of the claimed invention, an aspect of which is illustrated in the following figure, three sets of finger placement indicia 11 are positioned on the cover 17 of a regulation baseball 10. Each set of indicia 11 is intended to illustrate the placement of a student pitcher's index and middle fingers so as to throw a particular type of pitch (*e.g.*, two-seam fast ball, slider, curve ball, etc.).

Indicia 11 are presented in two sizes, to allow the indicia intended for a left-handed student to be easily distinguished from the indicia intended for a right-handed student. The smaller indicia, exemplified by indicia 24 and 26, are intended for use by left-handed pitchers, while the larger indicia, as represented by indicia 20 and 22, are intended for use by right-handed pitchers. Moreover, indicia 11 are coded by coloring all indicia which are representative of a certain type of pitch in one color and indicia representative of another type of pitch in a different color. To further assist a student in learning how to throw a particular pitch, the indicia are shaped so as to indicate the relationship of the palm of the hand in grasping the ball. Specifically, the portion of each "egg-shaped" indicium to be situated closest to the palm is slightly tapered so as to indicate the correct orientation of the baseball in the palm. Although the preferred embodiment of the '193 patent makes no provisions for "thumb placement indicia," the written description of the '193 patent repeatedly states that the thumb is generally to be positioned on the baseball at a location opposite the corresponding set of finger placement indicia.

As originally filed in 1991, the claims of the '193 patent required that eight sets of finger placement indicia be provided on a single baseball pitching training device. Specifically, the four original claims all required the presence of indicia demarcating the placement of fingers for four specific types of pitches (*i.e.,* curve ball, two-seam fast ball, slider, and four-seam fast ball), for both left-handed and right-handed students. These claims were rejected on obviousness grounds in view of U.S. Patent No. 2,925,273 ("Pratt"), which had issued on February 16, 1960, more than thirty years before McGinley's filing date. Pratt was brought to the attention of the Patent and Trademark Office ("PTO") via an Information Disclosure Statement ("IDS") filed concurrently with McGinley's priority patent application by McGinley's counsel.

The McGinley Patent

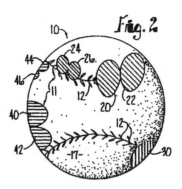

The Pratt Patent   The Morgan Patent

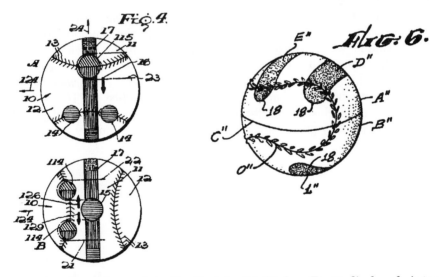

Like the claims originally filed by McGinley, Pratt disclosed, inter alia, a conventional baseball having multiple sets of finger placement indicia for teaching baseball players to throw different types of pitches. Specifically, in the embodiment illustrated in Figure 4 [*supra*], Pratt's written description disclosed the placement of finger and thumb placement indicia for three types of pitches (*i.e.,* fast ball, curve ball, and screw ball). Equatorial band 17 was an important feature of Pratt's claimed invention. When a student threw Pratt's baseball correctly, bands of complementary colors in the equatorial band would blend into a single color to provide a visual indication to the student that the ball had been thrown with proper rotation.

Although the similarities between Pratt's disclosure and McGinley's then-existing claims are striking, there are also a few differences between Pratt's teachings and McGinley's initially claimed invention. First, Pratt did not provide for different sets of indicia on a single ball for distinguishing between left-handed and right-handed students. Also, Pratt's finger placement indicia were described and illustrated as being circular, but "phantom lines" illustrating the placement of fingers 21, 22 and thumb 23 were included in the patent figures. These phantom lines, however, are not described in Pratt as actual markings on the baseball. In contrast, the finger placement indicia in the preferred embodiment of McGinley's invention are actually marked on the ball, and are "egg-shaped" and slightly tapered at one end to indicate the proper orientation of the ball with respect to the student's palm.

Another prior art reference which was brought to the attention of the PTO via McGinley's IDS was U.S. Patent No. 3,110,494 ("Morgan"), which issued on November 12, 1963. In contrast to Pratt and the '193 patent, which are based on using a conventional regulation baseball, Morgan describes a baseball training device using a lightweight and inexpensive baseball "replica" fabricated in the form of plastic or metallic hemispherical shells which occupy a minimum of space before use, but which can be easily assembled by gluing the two hemispherical halves together. In Figure 6 of Morgan [*supra*] and the accompanying written description, a single set of finger-shaped marks D″, E″, and L″ (for teaching proper placement of the forefinger, middle finger, and thumb, respectively) are provided on the baseball training device to teach a student how to throw a baseball with a particular curve or break.

Throughout the prosecution history of the '193 patent, McGinley's claims at issue in this case were rejected in view of Pratt on anticipation grounds. With respect to Morgan, although this reference was before the PTO during the entire pendency of McGinley's patent application, it was never explicitly relied upon as a basis for a rejection based on a prima facie case of anticipation or obviousness.

Ultimately, in 1995, after a series of rejections, amendments, and responses (including a partially successful appeal to the Board of Patent Appeals and Interferences and the filing of a continuation application), the '193 patent issued with 14 claims. Ten of the issued claims (*i.e.,* claims 3–5 and 8–14) explicitly retain the original limitation requiring the inclusion of finger placement indicia on a single baseball pitching training device for both left-handed and right-handed students. These claims were not asserted in this case. Instead, McGinley asserted the remaining four claims (*i.e.,* independent claim 1 and dependent claims 2, 6, and 7) against FSI, alleging willful infringement by making and selling the 2705 baseball.

The asserted claims read as follows in their entirety:

   1. A baseball pitching training device for duplicating finger placement on a baseball by a student comprising:

      a baseball cover;

a plurality of sets of finger placement indicia on said cover, said sets of indicia comprising:

a first set of indicia demarcating the placement of finger [sic] for throwing a first pitch;

a second set of indicia demarcating the placement of fingers for throwing, [sic] a second pitch;

a third set of indicia demarcating the placement of fingers for throwing a third pitch;

means for indicating the orientation of the baseball relative to the palm of the hand; and

means for coding said finger placement indicia sets for identification of each of said indicia associated with any one of said sets.

2. The device as claimed in claim 1 wherein said means for coding comprises a color for association with each indicia of a particular set.

6. The device as claimed in claim 1, wherein said means for indicating orientation comprises shaping said indicia to distinguish that portion of the baseball to be located proximate to the palm of the hand.

7. The device as claimed in claim 1 wherein said indicia are shaped to indicate a correct orientation of the baseball with respect to the palm of the hand.

'193 patent, col. 5, ll. 29–48; col. 5, ll. 61–64; col. 6, ll. 1–3.

[After the jury's verdict in favor of McGinley, the district court granted FSI's motion for JMOL on the ground of invalidity, concluding that "as a matter of law, plaintiff's patent is invalid as obvious in light of Pratt or the combination of Pratt and Morgan," and entered judgment in favor of FSI. This appeal followed.]

* * *

IV

OBVIOUSNESS

A patent is invalid for obviousness if "differences between the subject matter sought to be patented and the prior art are such that the subject matter as a whole would have been obvious at the time the invention was made to a person having ordinary skill in the art to which said subject matter pertains." 35 U.S.C. § 103(a) (1994). "Throughout the obviousness determination, a patent retains its statutory presumption of validity, see 35 U.S.C. § 282, and the movant retains the burden to show the invalidity of the claims by clear and convincing evidence as to underlying facts." *Rockwell Int'l. Corp. v. United States,* 147 F.3d 1358, 1364 (Fed.Cir.1998).

Although it is well settled that the ultimate determination of obviousness is a question of law, it is also well understood that there are factual issues underlying the ultimate obviousness decision. *Richardson–Vicks Inc. v. Upjohn Co.*, 122 F.3d 1476, 1479 (Fed.Cir.1997). Specifically, the obviousness analysis is based on four underlying factual inquiries, the well-known *Graham* factors: (1) the scope and content of the prior art; (2) the differences between the claims and the prior art; (3) the level of ordinary skill in the pertinent art; and (4) secondary considerations, if any, of nonobviousness. *Graham v. John Deere Co.*, 383 U.S. 1, 17–18, 86 S.Ct. 684, 15 L.Ed.2d 545 (1966); *Kegel Co., Inc. v. AMF Bowling, Inc.*, 127 F.3d 1420, 1430 (Fed.Cir.1997).

At trial, FSI argued, inter alia, that the asserted claims of the '193 patent were obvious in view of either Pratt alone, or in view of Pratt in combination with Morgan. FSI's obviousness theories are best summarized in its own words from its opening brief on appeal:

> The only element of the asserted claims that is not clearly anticipated by the Pratt patent is the finger shaped marks that orient the ball with respect to the palm of the user's hand. However, this feature is obvious in light of the lines indicating finger placement on the drawings of the Pratt patent. Moreover, the concept of a set of finger marks to orient the ball is clearly taught in the Morgan patent. It would have been obvious to one of ordinary skill in the art to substitute the finger marks of the Morgan patent for the marks of the Pratt patent. Or, stated another way, it would have been obvious to place three sets of marks on the Morgan ball in light of the teaching of Pratt.

In other words, FSI argued to the jury that the "missing element" in Pratt (*i.e.*, the "means for orientation") can be found either in the "phantom lines" of Pratt or in Figure 6 of Morgan. McGinley argued at trial that there was no motivation to combine the prior art as suggested by FSI, and that even if such a motivation to combine had been demonstrated, that the commercial success of both McGinley's RCIB [baseball] and FSI's accused 2705 baseball constituted sufficient evidence of secondary considerations that would negate any prima facie showing of obviousness.

The jury agreed with McGinley. Specifically, in the special verdict form used in this case, the jury answered three questions that are relevant to this appeal in favor of McGinley. First, the jury found that FSI had not proven by clear and convincing evidence that each of the elements of the invention defined in claims 1, 2, 6 and 7 of the '193 patent is disclosed in Pratt. This was a factual finding. *In re Beattie*, 974 F.2d 1309, 1311 (Fed.Cir.1992) ("What a reference teaches is a question of fact.").

Second, the jury found that FSI had not proven by clear and convincing evidence that any of the asserted claims were invalid as being obvious in view of Pratt alone. Finally, the jury found that FSI had not proven by clear and convincing evidence that any of the asserted claims were invalid as being obvious in view of a combination of Pratt and Morgan. These latter two findings by the jury are directed to the ultimate legal issue of obviousness, and provide no insight as to the jury's findings with respect to the underlying factual underpinnings. The parties do not object to the phrasing of the questions that were posed to the jury in the verdict form, nor do they challenge the district court's comprehensive jury instructions on obviousness.

In its motion for JMOL, FSI argued that no reasonable jury could have concluded that the asserted claims were not obvious in view of either Pratt alone or in view of Pratt in combination with Morgan. The district court agreed, and granted FSI's motion for JMOL. Specifically, the court found that "no reasonable jury could conclude that the motivation to combine Pratt and Morgan did not exist." Moreover, the district court "simply [did] not believe that the evidence regarding secondary considerations [was] sufficient to overcome its firm conclusion that, as a matter of law, plaintiff's patent is invalid as obvious in light of Pratt or the combination of Pratt and Morgan." In sum, the district court concluded that "in light of Pratt alone, as well as in light of Pratt and Morgan in combination, the claims set forth in the '193 patent are invalid as obvious."

We review a grant of JMOL without deference to the district court. Entry of JMOL is inappropriate unless the jury's verdict is unsupported by substantial evidence or premised on incorrect legal standards.

* * *

Whether a patent claim is obvious under section 103 depends upon the answer to several factual questions and how the factual answers meld into the legal conclusion of obviousness vel non. In this case, we think that the central question is whether there is reason to combine the Pratt and Morgan references, because if the references are properly combined, it is certain that the claims are prima facie invalid for obviousness. If the jury was entitled to conclude that these two references should not be combined, then the asserted claims of the '193 patent cannot be invalid for obviousness in the light of the proposed combination. If those claims are not invalid under a combination of Pratt and Morgan, then, as a matter of logic, those claims cannot be invalid in the light of Pratt alone. We thus turn first to the issue of whether Pratt and Morgan must be combined.

The genius of invention is often a combination of known elements which in hindsight seems preordained. To prevent hindsight invalidation of patent claims, the law requires some "teaching, suggestion or reason" to combine cited references. *Gambro Lundia AB v. Baxter Healthcare Corp.*, 110 F.3d 1573, 1579 (Fed.Cir.1997). When the art in question is relatively simple, as is the case here, the opportunity to judge by hindsight is particularly tempting. Consequently, the tests of whether to combine references need to be applied rigorously. *See In re Dembiczak*, 175 F.3d 994, 999 (Fed.Cir.1999), *limited on other grounds by In re Gartside*, 203 F.3d 1305 (2000) (guarding against falling victim to the insidious effect of a hindsight syndrome wherein that which only the inventor taught is used against its teacher).

Whether a motivation to combine prior art references has been demonstrated is a question of fact. *Winner Int'l Royalty Corp. v. Wang,* 202 F.3d 1340, 1348 (Fed.Cir.2000). The assessment of whether to combine references in a given case has sometimes been viewed conceptually as a subset of the first *Graham* factor, the scope and content of the prior art. *See, e.g., id.; Monarch Knitting Mach. Corp.v. Sulzer Morat Gmbh,* 139 F.3d 877, 881–83, 886 (Fed.Cir.1998). Although that view is not incorrect, accurate assessment of whether to combine references may require attention to other *Graham* factors. For example, the level of skill in the art may inform whether the artisan would find a suggestion to combine in the teachings of an exemplar of prior art. Where the level of skill is high, one may assume a keener appreciation of nuances taught by the prior art. Similarly, appreciation of the differences between the claims in suit and the scope of prior art references—a matter itself informed by the operative level of skill in the art—informs the question of whether to combine prior art references. At bottom, in each case the factual inquiry whether to combine references must be thorough and searching.

There is no question here that FSI presented sufficient evidence at trial from which a jury could have decided that one of ordinary skill in this case would have been motivated to combine Pratt and Morgan to produce a prima facie obvious invention. Specifically, FSI argued to the jury that the only elements of the asserted claims that are not clearly anticipated by Pratt are the finger-shaped marks that orient the ball with respect to the palm of the user's hand. Referring to the "phantom lines" in Pratt as suggestive of finger placement on the ball, FSI argued that one of ordinary skill would have been motivated to substitute the finger marks from the Morgan ball for the circular marks on Pratt, or alternatively to place three sets of marks on the Morgan ball in the light of Pratt's teachings. In addition, FSI argued that one of ordinary skill would have known to add the finger orientation means of the Morgan patent to Pratt by "filling in" the phantom lines in Pratt's drawings and treating them as finger orientation means.

But the jury did not hear a one-sided case on the issue of obviousness generally, and in particular on whether to combine Pratt and Morgan. As FSI conceded at oral argument, McGinley presented reasons to the jury to reject a combination of the references. McGinley argued many grounds to support his contention that the asserted claims are not obvious in the light of Pratt and Morgan. To counter FSI's claim that those references should be combined to render McGinley's "means for orientation" obvious, McGinley pointed to specific differences between the prior art and the asserted claims. For example, Morgan does not disclose the required markings for at least three different kinds of pitches, as do the asserted claims. And Morgan does not disclose markings on a real baseball, as do Pratt and the asserted claims. We recount the gist of this testimony below.

The jury heard from Mr. Charles Quinn, FSI's vice president of marketing and corporate representative at trial. Quinn testified in detail as to the express teachings of Pratt and Morgan, and as to the differences between these references and the asserted claims. For example, he conceded that the markings on the baseball in Pratt's invention were circular, and therefore incapable of indicating orientation. He also acknowledged that the "phantom lines" in Pratt's drawings were not actually markings on a baseball. Quinn also pointed out that Morgan did not discuss implementing a baseball training device using a regulation baseball. Moreover, he acknowledged that Morgan taught only the provision of indicia for throwing a single type of pitch on each training device, instead of three sets of indicia as required in the asserted claims.

Trial Tr. Vol. 2, p. 145.

The jury also heard from Mr. Richard Stitt, the attorney who prosecuted the '193 patent. Stitt testified at length about the prosecution history of the '193 patent and the fact that Pratt and Morgan were considered by the PTO throughout the entire pendency of McGinley's application. He confirmed that the "phantom lines" in Pratt's drawings were not actually marked on a baseball. Stitt also pointed out that the PTO never rejected the asserted claims as obvious in view of Pratt, and that it was never suggested by the PTO that the phantom lines of Pratt could easily be transferred to the actual baseball to arrive at McGinley's claimed invention.

Stitt testified that the PTO never rejected McGinley's claims by saying that one could substitute the "elongate finger-shaped markings" shown in Figure 6 of Morgan in place of the "circular dots" in Pratt. He also pointed out that the PTO could have issued an obviousness rejection of the asserted claims based on a theory of transferring Pratt's phantom lines onto the baseball, but never did so. Similarly, he testified that the PTO could have issued an obviousness rejection of the asserted claims based on a theory of combining Pratt with Morgan, but never did so either.

Stitt also testified that he flew to the Patent Office in Washington, D.C., with McGinley for an interview with the Examiner to discuss the differences between Pratt and Morgan and the claimed invention. Finally, he explained in detail why neither Pratt nor Morgan alone or in combination with each other would provide the claimed "means for orientation."

In addition, McGinley relied heavily on the presumption of validity to which his patent is entitled by the terms of 35 U.S.C. § 282, mainly in the context of Stitt's tutorial concerning how McGinley's patent was prosecuted, and in McGinley's opening statement and closing argument to the jury. As noted above, throughout the trial, McGinley pointed out that both the Pratt and Morgan references were before the examiner who tested McGinley's patent for validity. Indeed, those two references were discussed in an interview between the applicant and the examiner.

The examiner rejected McGinley's claims as anticipated by Pratt, and made no mention of any concern as to obviousness in view of Pratt alone or of a combination of Pratt and Morgan.

The Board of Patent Appeals and Interferences reversed the examiner's anticipation rejection, holding that Pratt failed to teach McGinley's means for orienting the baseball relative to the palm of the hand. In due course, McGinley's patent issued and became clothed with the statutory presumption of validity, with no obviousness challenge having been mounted against it, either on the basis of Pratt alone, or of Pratt in combination with Morgan.

The jury in this case was expressly charged that the patent in suit is entitled to the presumption of validity, and that FSI could only overcome that burden with clear and convincing evidence to the contrary. It is well established in our case law that FSI's burden in this case was especially heavy:

> When no prior art other than that which was considered by the PTO examiner is relied on by the attacker [FSI], he has the added burden of overcoming the deference that is due to a qualified government agency presumed to have properly done its job, which includes one or more examiners who are assumed to have some expertise in interpreting the references and to be familiar from their work with the level of skill in the art and whose duty it is to issue only valid patents. In some cases a PTO board of appeals may have approved the issuance of the patent.

American Hoist & Derrick Co. v. Sowa & Sons, Inc., 725 F.2d 1350, 1359 (Fed.Cir.1984), *cert. denied,* 469 U.S. 821, 105 S.Ct. 95, 83 L.Ed.2d 41 (1984).

Perhaps McGinley's best argument to save his claims from prima facie obviousness in the light of Pratt and Morgan is his contention that those references together teach away from their combination. We have noted elsewhere, as a "useful general rule," that references that teach away cannot serve to create a prima facie case of obviousness. *In re Gurley,* 27 F.3d 551, 553 (Fed.Cir.1994). If references taken in combination would produce a "seemingly inoperative device," we have held that such references teach away from the combination and thus cannot serve as predicates for a prima facie case of obviousness. *In re Sponnoble,* 405 F.2d 578, 587 (CCPA 1969) (references teach away from combination if combination produces seemingly inoperative device); *see also In re Gordon,* 733 F.2d 900, 902 (Fed.Cir.1984) (inoperable modification teaches away).

McGinley argues in his brief that Pratt itself teaches away from combining the finger orientation of Morgan, because Pratt, by teaching only the placement of finger tips on the baseball, leads away from placing a full finger orientation on the ball. Such may be the case, but we have no assurance that the jury heard that argument. At oral argument in this court, however, FSI confirmed that McGinley argued to the jury that adding the finger marks of Morgan to Pratt's baseball, by "filling in" the phantom marks to create structure that defines orientation as claimed, would require obliteration of the claimed rotation arrows, a feature that is necessary in order to permit the Pratt invention to operate properly. FSI also confirmed at oral argument that the jury heard McGinley's argument that to combine the finger placements of Morgan onto the Pratt ball would also render the Pratt ball inoperable, by eliminating the multi-colored equatorial band, a claimed feature of the Pratt patent also required for successful operation of Pratt's invention.

We are satisfied that McGinley presented sufficient evidence as well to counter FSI's alternative argument that it would have been obvious to place three sets of marks on the Morgan ball in light of the teaching of Pratt. First, a reasonable jury could have determined from examining the Morgan reference that the finger placement indicia on Morgan are too large to allow the inclusion of more than a single set of markings. This point is important, because Morgan expressly requires markings on the ball to accommodate the placement of two full fingers and a thumb to simulate throwing a single pitch. The jury could have certainly concluded that one of ordinary skill would not attempt to place markings for two additional pitches on Morgan's ball. Two more sets of markings as shown by Morgan itself would require markings for two additional sets of fingers and thumbs.

On the other hand, two sets of markings as shown by Pratt would lead to confusion as to the correct means for orientation on Morgan's ball. Any such configurations, *i.e.,* Morgan's invention with markings for throwing three different pitches, would risk, if not achieve, obliteration of the clear and unmistakable markings shown on Morgan's ball to teach the throwing of a single curving pitch. Moreover, a reasonable jury could have considered that all of the embodiments described and illustrated in the Morgan reference are expressly limited to teaching a student pitcher to throw a baseball with a "particular curve or break," and that none of the embodiments discuss or suggest using a conventional baseball as opposed to a hollow shell comprising two metallic or plastic hemispheres glued or otherwise bonded together. The jury also could have concluded that Morgan—with its full finger and thumb imprint markings on the ball—teaches away from a means for orientation using the smaller teardrop markings disclosed by McGinley or the small truncated finger-shaped markings used in FSI's accused baseballs.

Given the strength of the teaching away point, we think it remarkable that FSI makes no attempt whatsoever in its brief to counter McGinley's argument. The jury's verdict that the claims in suit are not obvious is supported by the evidence brought forward by McGinley to resist FSI's contrary evidence. Here we have the classic example of sufficient evidence to support each position argued to the jury. The key issue, namely what the references teach and whether they teach the necessity of combination or the requirement of separation, is a fact issue. When the jury is supplied with sufficient valid factual information to support the verdict it reaches, that is the end of the matter. In such an instance, the jury's factual conclusion may not be set aside by a JMOL order.

Given the multiple bases upon which the jury's verdict in favor of McGinley can be sustained over FSI's arguments for combining the references, we must conclude that FSI fares no better in arguing a combination of Pratt into Morgan than it does in arguing a combination of Morgan into Pratt. The jury was thus entitled to reach its verdict of nonobviousness on the ground that one of ordinary skill in the art would not deem the asserted claims of the '193 patent obvious in light of Pratt and Morgan in combination. That being the case, it is illogical to think that one of ordinary skill in the art would have deemed McGinley's claims obvious in the light of Pratt alone.

If one of ordinary skill is not taught by Morgan to extend Pratt's circular markings into the phantom lines, that person would not be taught by the phantom lines alone to do so.

Nonetheless, we think the district court erred as well in its decision that McGinley's asserted claims were obvious as a matter of law in view of Pratt alone. According to the district court's reasoning, no reasonable jury could have failed to conclude that an ordinarily skilled artisan would have been motivated to transfer the finger-shaped "phantom lines" shown in the Pratt reference onto the actual Pratt baseball itself, thus providing the missing "means for orientation" that is admittedly otherwise missing in Pratt.

It should be noted that the "phantom lines" shown in Pratt are virtually identical to the finger-shaped markings on Fig. 6 of the Morgan reference, except that the Morgan markings are "filled-in" and actually marked on the ball. Therefore, many of the arguments mentioned above with respect to Morgan apply with equal force with respect to the Pratt phantom lines. Specifically, as FSI conceded at oral argument before this court, the jury heard McGinley's argument that transferring large finger-shaped markings (such as those illustrated in Fig. 6 of Morgan or in the phantom lines of Pratt) would render the Pratt invention inoperable by interfering with the multi-colored equatorial band. Thus, according to this evidence, one of ordinary skill in designing baseballs for use as pitching trainers would not be motivated to modify Pratt by filling in the phantom lines to express palm-oriented finger placement on the ball. As mentioned above, the jury also heard extensive testimony concerning the prosecution history of the '193 patent, including the critical facts that (1) Pratt was before the PTO during the entire pendency of the patent application, and (2) although the PTO continued to reject the asserted claims as anticipated by Pratt until McGinley won an appeal before the Board on that point, the PTO never rejected the asserted claims as obvious in view of Pratt alone. Surely, relying on the presumption of regularity that applies to all administrative agencies such as the PTO, the jury could have reasonably concluded that if the PTO believed that an obviousness rejection based on Pratt alone was warranted, such a rejection would have been promptly been made. Also, just as was the case with the Morgan markings, the jury could have reasonably concluded from an examination of the references that the Pratt phantom lines are so large that it would not be feasible to include three sets of them on a single baseball, as required by the asserted claims. Because substantial evidence supports the jury's implicit factual finding that no motivation to modify Pratt in that manner has been demonstrated in this case, the district court's ruling that Pratt alone renders the asserted claims obvious as a matter of law was erroneous.

Due to the "black box" nature of the jury's verdict, it is impossible to determine which of the above pieces of evidence, alone or in combination, carried the day in the jury room, and how much weight was assigned to each piece. All that can be said with certainty is that—as a whole—the evidence enumerated above (all of which was admittedly before the jury) constitutes substantial evidence to support the jury's verdict. We recognize the concerns of the dissenting opinion that it is difficult to sort out the weight to be given factual determinations in an obviousness inquiry from the degree to which the district court should override permissible found-facts to sum-up the legal conclusion of obviousness vel non. But when a dispositive element of the factual equation, here whether to combine or modify key references, so clearly could have been decided by the jury in McGinley's favor, it is not our place to elide the vagaries of a black box jury verdict by overriding the jury's decision. Our law does not compel the use of special verdicts in these cases, and so long as the parties are content to give the jury unfettered room to operate on dispositive factual issues within the scope of a general verdict request, we must be mindful of our role as an appellate court and respect the verdict reached, notwithstanding what may seem to some to be an invention of little novelty.

For the reasons set forth above, we conclude that the district court erred when it ruled on JMOL that no reasonable juror could have ruled that FSI failed to make out a case of obviousness by clear and convincing evidence.

* * *

VII

CONCLUSION

For the reasons stated above, we reverse the grant of JMOL in favor of FSI and order the jury's verdict reinstated. * * *

MICHEL, CIRCUIT JUDGE, dissenting.

Because I conclude that the Pratt patent, alone, renders the patented invention obvious as a matter of law, I would affirm. I am especially troubled by the implication I see in the majority's opinion that a general jury verdict on the legal question of obviousness is essentially immune from review by the trial court on JMOL, or by this court on appeal.

The issue presented in this appeal derives from the common, if unfortunate, practice of allowing the jury to render a general verdict on the ultimate legal conclusion of obviousness without requiring express findings on the underlying factual issues through a special verdict or special interrogatories under Fed.R.Civ.P. 49. Nevertheless, since the inception of our court, we have recognized that a court may submit this legal question to a jury and that doing so by general verdict rather than by Rule 49 is not ordinarily an abuse of discretion. *Railroad Dynamics, Inc. v. A. Stucki Co.,* 727 F.2d 1506, 1515 (Fed.Cir.1984); *Connell v. Sears, Roebuck & Co.,* 722 F.2d 1542, 1547–48 (Fed.Cir.1983). We have emphasized, however, that "[t]here is no question that the judge must remain the ultimate arbiter on the question of obviousness." *Railroad Dynamics,* 727 F.2d at 1515; *see also Richardson–Vicks Inc. v. Upjohn Co.,* 122 F.3d 1476, 1479 (Fed.Cir.1997) ("That an obviousness determination stands upon the relevant facts of the case does not convert the ultimate conclusion of obviousness from one of law into one of fact.").

The difficulty presented in this appeal is how to separate the role of the jury to find facts (with these findings binding on this court, as well as the trial court, so long as they are supported by at least substantial evidence) from the role of trial judges in reaching, or for us freely reviewing, the ultimate legal conclusion of obviousness, *vel non.* In this case, the verdict form tells us only that the jury found the claimed invention nonobvious in light of Pratt and/or Morgan, with no identification of the jury's resolution of genuine disputes over material factual issues. We must therefore imply such factual findings, under the legal presumption that the jury found all facts necessary to support its verdict in favor of McGinley. *Railroad Dynamics,* 727 F.2d at 1516 ("[W]hen a jury returns a general verdict, the law presumes the existence of fact findings implied from the jury's having reached that verdict.").

When faced with a general verdict of nonobviousness or obviousness, the categories of facts the court must imply concern the scope and content of prior art; what a prior art reference teaches; the differences between the claimed invention and the prior art; the level of ordinary skill in the prior art; and objective evidence of nonobviousness. In cases such as this where a single prior art reference is alleged to render the claimed invention obvious, there must be a sufficient showing of a suggestion or motivation for any modification of the teachings of that reference necessary to reach the claimed invention in order to support the obviousness conclusion. This suggestion or motivation may be derived from the prior art reference itself, from the knowledge of one of ordinary skill in the art, or from the nature of the problem to be solved.

While the trial court must defer to the jury's factual findings, actual or implied, the court nonetheless has the duty, when presented with a motion for JMOL following a general verdict on obviousness, to review the factual findings for substantial evidentiary support, and the ultimate conclusion on obviousness for legal correctness. In the present case, the trial court dutifully performed this analysis, citing our precedent, and concluded that no reasonable jury could find that Pratt did not render McGinley's claimed baseball obvious. I agree.

The only arguable difference between Pratt's and McGinley's claimed marked baseballs for student pitchers is that Pratt purportedly lacks a "means for indicating the orientation of the baseball relative to the palm of the hand," a limitation separately claimed by McGinley. U.S. Patent No. 5,407,193, col. 5, ll. 41–42. There has been no admission, as the majority suggests, that Pratt does not disclose a "means for orienting." The structures corresponding to this means-plus-function limitation in McGinley's claimed baseball are sets of finger markings, shaped like tapered eggs, with the direction of the taper indicating the proper orientation of the ball in the pitcher's hand. That is, the points of the tapers, by extension, lead approximately to the center of the palm. The fingertip placement markings illustrated in Pratt's diagrams, by contrast, are simple circles with no taper, and thus do not point toward the palm.

The jury did indeed hear testimony to the effect that Pratt's rounded fingertip placement indicia would leave a student pitcher confused as to how to grip the ball, as the pitcher would be unsure whether to grip the ball on only one of its hemispheres, or rather to grasp the ball fully across its equator. * * *

Such testimony, in my view, is a nullity because it contradicts the teachings of the Pratt patent, which by its very markings necessarily discloses a means for orienting a pitcher's fingers on the ball "relative to the palm." As illustrated here, Pratt's diagrams show multiple sets of fingertip placement indicia, with a single set comprising two circles situated near each other (described in the specification as markers for the pitcher's forefinger and second finger) and a third spot somewhat removed from the other two (described as a marker for the thumb). As a matter of geometry, there are only two ways for a pitcher to place his or her thumb, forefinger, and second finger on these three spots (barring finger-crossing). One way is to pinch the near hemisphere of the baseball with one's fingertips. The other way is to grasp the ball near the palm of one's hand, wrapping one's fingers across the equator of the ball (*i.e.*, the way a baseball is always thrown).

Pratt's written description tells us that people of ordinary skill in this art (and student pitchers) know generally how to hold and throw baseballs. The patent states that, for a fastball, the ball is thrown with "the usual forearm motion." U.S. Patent No. 2,925,273, col. 2, ll. 25–26. A fingertip grip on only one hemisphere of the ball would be unworkable, as for a curveball, the patent recites using a "tighter grip," and throwing the ball with a "conventional wrist snap," so as to impart a "maximum spin" to the ball. *Id.* at col. 2, ll. 53–54. To do so, the forefinger and second finger must "extend across two sections of the stitches of the seam," such that the thumb "extends along the seam." *Id.* at col. 2, ll. 50–52. These instructions, read in view of the finger placement indicia, reduce the number of possible palm orientations to one: the ball-in-palm grip. Because Mr. Stitt's testimony contradicts the express teachings of Pratt, his testimonial evidence is entitled to no weight. I conclude that the express teachings of Pratt, as a matter of law, disclose to persons of ordinary skill a means for orienting the ball in the pitcher's palm.

Of course, in the context of a means-plus-function claim, the invalidating prior art must disclose not simply *a* means for achieving the desired function, but rather the *particular structure* recited in the written description corresponding to that function, or an equivalent thereof. *In re Donaldson Co., Inc.,* 16 F.3d 1189 (Fed.Cir.1994). To this end, the Pratt patent discloses more than just circular fingertip markings, as his diagrams also display "phantom lines" (which do not appear on the actual ball covered by the patent) extending tangentially from the fingertip placement circles in the direction that a pitcher's fingers should be placed. FSI argues here, as below, that these phantom lines would have taught skilled artisans to extend tangentially Pratt's circular markings to give them directionality.

At trial, Mr. Stitt discounted the importance of these phantom lines, testifying that "[t]hey don't have anything to do with the invention." This remark was legally incorrect, because although the phantom lines do not appear on Pratt's patented ball, they do comprise part of Pratt's disclosure. *See In re Fritch,* 972 F.2d 1260, 1264(Fed.Cir.1992) ("It is well settled that a prior art reference is relevant for all that it teaches to those of ordinary skill in the art."). McGinley also argues in his briefing that adopting the phantom lines from Pratt would be unworkable, because these lines would be too long and would obscure other markings on the baseball. The majority accepts this argument. But absolutely no trial testimony—none—suggests that Pratt's phantom lines are too long, or that their length as shown in the drawings would have dissuaded a skilled artisan from shortening the finger placement indicia as necessary to avoid obscuring any other markings. Mere attorney argument is no substitute for evidence of record. To support its holding (and its statement that the issue of motivation to modify Pratt's lines into McGinley's tapers "so clearly could have been decided by the jury in McGinley's favor"), the majority combines testimony discussing the elongated finger grooves from Morgan with the testimony concerning the circular fingertip placement markings of Pratt. But by importing testimony regarding Morgan into its Pratt analysis, the majority appears to contradict its own holding that these references are not combinable. Moreover, putting aside the lack of evidence on this point, it hardly matters that the phantom lines as shown are longer than they need be if they were actually drawn onto the ball. An artisan need not copy the lines precisely as shown, but instead would know to optimize the length of the lines to fit the constraints of the other marking on the ball. *See In re Baird,* 16 F.3d 380, 383 (Fed.Cir.1994) ("[A] reference must be considered not only for what it expressly teaches, but also for what it fairly suggests.") (quoting *In re Burckel,* 592 F.2d 1175, 1179 (CCPA 1979)). Such a design variation would be routine in the baseball design art.

Presumably, the jury found that the phantom lines depicted in Pratt's diagrams would not have motivated a reasonable artisan to elaborate on Pratt's circular fingertip placement indicia and break their

symmetry. However, the only trial testimony supportive of this finding—
i.e., Stitt's comment that the phantom lines have nothing to do with the
invention—is legally incorrect. Aside from this remark, and testimony
concerning the Morgan patent (which the majority finds to be non-
analogous), there is simply no evidence, let alone substantial evidence, in
support of the jury's implicit finding. Moreover, this implicit finding is
contradicted by the disclosures of Pratt, itself. Pratt clearly contemplated the possibility that the reader of his patent might not immediately
appreciate the proper orientation of a pitcher's fingers—that is why he
added the phantom lines to his drawings. By including these lines in his
disclosure, Pratt imposed directionality on his circular markings in the
drawings and necessarily communicated to those in his field a suggestion
for reshaping the circular fingertip placement indicia accordingly. To the
extent the jury's implicit findings are to the contrary, I find them
unsupported by substantial evidence and contrary to Pratt's express and
graphic disclosures. To the extent the jury rested its conclusion on such
findings, it was legally incorrect.

It is true that the jury found that the Pratt patent does not
anticipate McGinley's invention. I do not dispute that the differences
between Pratt's circular indicia and McGinley's tapered, egg-shaped
indicia, may be sufficient to support the jury's non-anticipation verdict.
But obviousness is different. It remains the province of the court to
determine, whether in light of all the facts properly, if only implicitly,
found by the jury, the claimed invention would have been obvious.
Richardson-Vicks, 122 F.3d at 1479; *Railroad Dynamics,* 727 F.2d at
1515. We of course must view all supportable facts as found in favor of
McGinley, the verdict winner and non-movant. But it is undeniable (by
looking at Pratt's placement of the circular markings, and the accompanying written description that Pratt discloses a means for orienting a
pitcher's fingers around the ball "relative to the palm." Moreover, the
phantom lines suggest altering Pratt's circular markings to provide them
with directionality, and to break the symmetry of the circular fingertip
indicia. I acknowledge that there are differences between the scope and
content of the prior art and the claimed invention. But this is where the
legal analysis, as opposed to the fact analysis, begins. It is the role of the
court to assess whether in light of these differences and the suggestion
to modify the teachings of Pratt, the claimed invention would have been
obvious. Viewing all these factual considerations in context, I cannot
shake the conviction that a ball designer of even minimal skill in the art
would have found it blatantly obvious to modify Pratt's circles (with
their phantom lines), and reshape them into tapered eggs. Nor do
McGinley's purportedly fabulous sales change my conclusion, because
there is no evidence that these sales are due to the markings on the ball,
as opposed to Roger Clemens' endorsement, or advertising. Accordingly,
I conclude that McGinley's patent was proven invalid for obviousness.

I am concerned about far more important effects of today's ruling
than whether McGinley's patent, although invalid, stands to menace still
other baseball competitors. Rather, I am concerned that after reading

the majority opinion, trial courts and our panels will hereafter consider such general verdicts on obviousness immune from meaningful review and that serious legal errors by juries will thus go uncorrected. The result will be that defective patents will remain to threaten all competitors in an industry. Indeed, I think today's appeal represents just such a case. More may follow. It is rare to see such a compelling case of obviousness, and yet more surprising to find our supposedly de novo review so limited, despite our settled case law that a jury's ultimate conclusion on obviousness is a legal question freely reviewable by judges. I therefore respectfully dissent.

Notes

1. *McGinley* involved appellate review of a district court's decision overturning a jury's verdict of nonobviousness. In *Okajima v. Bourdeau,* 261 F.3d 1350 (Fed.Cir.2001), *cert. denied,* 534 U.S. 1128, 122 S.Ct. 1066, 151 L.Ed.2d 969 (2002), the Federal Circuit reviewed a decision of the PTO's Board of Patent Appeals and Interferences rejecting an obviousness challenge by one patent applicant against another who had established an earlier date of invention:

> Whether a claimed invention is unpatentable as obvious under 35 U.S.C. § 103 is a question of law based on underlying findings of fact. *In re Gartside,* 203 F.3d 1305, 1316 (Fed.Cir.2000). The underlying factual inquiries include: (1) the scope and content of the prior art; (2) the level of ordinary skill in the prior art; and (3) the differences between the claimed invention and the prior art. *Graham v. John Deere Co.,* 383 U.S. 1, 17–18, 86 S.Ct. 684, 15 L.Ed.2d 545 (1966). On appeal, the Board's ultimate determination of nonobviousness is reviewed *de novo,* but the Board's underlying factual findings are reviewed for substantial evidence. *Gartside,* 203 F.3d at 1316. Substantial evidence means such relevant evidence as a reasonable mind might accept as adequate to support a conclusion. *Id.*

> * * *

> Okajima * * * contests the Board's factual finding that a person of ordinary skill in the art would not have been motivated to combine the teachings of DE '503 and U.S. '041 with EP '400. Okajima insists that a highly skilled snowboard boot designer would have learned from EP '400 (and its disclosure of two laterally-disposed journals) that a single journal, as disclosed in DE '503 and U.S. '041, could be offset to a position between the Achilles tendon and the internal malleolus, as claimed by Bourdeau. Moreover, Okajima argues that such an artisan would have been motivated to do so to accommodate the need for the snowboarder's leg to incline both laterally and forwardly. Okajima notes that the Board expressly found to the contrary. Indeed, the Board concluded that the use of two journals on opposite sides of the boot disclosed in EP '400 would provide adequate "swiveling action longitudinally," but "would appear to hinder or obstruct most lateral movement by the wearer." The Board found no motivation to combine EP '400 with DE '503 and U.S. '041, as it found that the latter references teach

the desirability of lateral movement by the wearer, as opposed to forward movement, as disclosed in EP '400.

Okajima's argument is essentially a challenge to the Board's factual determinations. However, we may overturn the Board's factual findings only if they are unsupported by substantial evidence. *Gartside,* 203 F.3d at 1316. Here, the Board has done a thorough job of setting forth the basis for its factual findings in its opinion, which contains a review of the scope and content of the prior art references, a description of the differences between Bourdeau's claimed invention and each of the prior art references, and an analysis of the asserted combinability of the references. * * * By explaining its tentative position during the final hearing, giving counsel an opportunity to challenge the Board's imminent holding, and setting forth its findings in detail in its opinion, the Board has provided our court with a well-supported decision. When it sets forth distinct findings of fact, and particularly when it does so in the manner that a district court must under Fed.R.Civ.P. 52(a), the Board's findings are entitled to broad deference. *Gartside,* 203 F.3d at 1316, 53 USPQ2d at 1776. Indeed, such express findings of fact are the key to meaningful appellate review, and obviate the need for us to remand for further proceedings at great cost and inefficiency to the parties. *Gechter v. Davidson,* 116 F.3d 1454, 1457–58 (Fed.Cir.1997). Here, the Board's factual findings are readily sustainable under our deferential standard of review. And we find no legal error in the absence of specific findings as to the level of ordinary skill, nor in the Board's conclusion as to the ultimate determination of nonobviousness.

How does the standard of review in *McGinley* compare with that in *Okajima?*

2. In Pub. L. No. 104–41, 104th Cong., 1st Sess. (1995), Congress added new subsection (b) to Section 103, prohibiting (upon election by the patent applicant) obviousness rejections of process patent applications for biotechnological processes using or resulting in a novel and nonobvious composition of matter if (1) the product and process claims are in the same application and have the same filing date, and (2) the product and process claims were owned by the same person when they were invented. The House Report describes this legislation as a response to the Federal Circuit's "conflicting and irreconcilable decisions" on the nonobviousness of process patent applications in *In re Durden,* 763 F.2d 1406 (Fed.Cir.1985) and *In re Pleuddemann,* 910 F.2d 823 (Fed.Cir.1990) and to delays and inconsistent treatment of process patent applications at the PTO. Section 103(b) is limited to biotechnology processes (that is, processes which use or create naturally occurring compounds that living organisms have been artificially induced to produce in unnaturally large quantities by various techniques), and was motivated by concerns that, without a process patent, domestic biotechnology companies could not invoke 35 U.S.C.A. § 271(g) to prevent overseas parties from making the same unpatentable end products by the same process and importing them into the United States. H.R. Rep. 104–178, 104th Cong., 1st Sess. 397–98 (1995). The legislation does not address the nonobviousness issue with respect to non-biotechnological processes.

Just after Pub. L. 104–41 was enacted, however, the Federal Circuit in *In re Ochiai*, 71 F.3d 1565 (Fed.Cir.1995), rejected the PTO's argument for a per se rule of obviousness where a familiar process was applied to a new and nonobvious starting material to yield a new and nonobvious product. The court observed that the use of any per se rules in section 103 determinations would be inconsistent with the requirement of *Graham v. John Deere Co.* and its progeny that nonobviousness determinations be based on a "fact-specific analysis" comparing the claimed invention, "including all its limitations," with the prior art. *Ochiai*, 71 F.3d at 1572. *Accord In re Brouwer*, 77 F.3d 422 (Fed.Cir.1996). Did Congress create just such a per se rule in Section 103(b)? Does this law represent sound policy?

3. *Design Patents*: Section 171 makes the nonobviousness requirement expressly applicable to design patents. In *In re Borden,* the Federal Circuit reiterated its interpretation of this standard as inquiring "whether the design would have been obvious to 'a designer of ordinary skill who designs articles of the type involved,'" an inquiry which "focuses on the visual impression of the claimed design as a whole and not on selected individual features." 90 F.3d 1570, 1574 (Fed.Cir.1996) (quoting *Avia Group Int'l, Inc. v. L.A. Gear Calif., Inc.,* 853 F.2d 1557, 1564 (Fed.Cir.1988)). Specifically, the court noted:

> In order for a design to be unpatentable because of obviousness, there must first be a basic design reference in the prior art, "a something in existence, the design characteristics of which are basically the same as the claimed design." In re Rosen, 673 F.2d [388 (CCPA 1982)], at 390. A finding of obviousness cannot be based on selecting features from the prior art and assembling them to form an article similar in appearance to the claimed design.

> If the basic reference alone does not render the claimed design unpatentable, design elements from other references in the prior art can be considered in determining whether the claimed design would have been obvious to one of skill in the art. In order for secondary references to be considered, however, there must be some suggestion in the prior art to modify the basic design with features from the secondary references. L.A. Gear, 988 F.2d at 1124; In re Rosen, 673 F.2d at 391. That is, the teachings of prior art designs may be combined only when the designs are "so related that the appearance of certain ornamental features in one would suggest the application of those features to the other." In re Glavas, 43 C.C.P.A. 797, 230 F.2d 447, 450 (CCPA 1956).

90 F.3d at 1574–75.

4. *Plant Patents*: Although nonobviousness is not a requirement under the PVPA, Section 161 appears to make it applicable to plant patents. In *Yoder Bros., Inc. v. California–Florida Plant Corp.,* 537 F.2d 1347 (5th Cir.1976), *cert. denied,* 429 U.S. 1094, 97 S.Ct. 1108, 51 L.Ed.2d 540 (1977), the Fifth Circuit attempted to determine the meaning of nonobviousness with respect to plant patents. The court rejected the argument that obviousness could be established merely by showing that the distinct chrysanthemum "sport" (a bud mutation) claimed in the challenged patent had recurred naturally. The court reasoned that recurrence only indicated that the particular mutation would be predictable to those skilled in the art, and

that the legislative history of the plant patent statutes indicated that Congress intended to extend protection to new plant mutations regardless of whether they were predictable. 537 F.2d at 1381–82. This approach, the court concluded, did not disregard the requirements of the Intellectual Property Clause:

> The only way that the Constitution would be offended by permitting patents on recurring sports would be if such leniency indicated that no "invention" was present. We do not think that sport recurrence would negate invention, however. An infinite number of a certain sized sport could appear on a plant, but until someone recognized its uniqueness and difference and found that the traits could be preserved by asexual reproduction in commercial quantities, no patentable plant would exist. An objective judgment of the value of the sport's new and different characteristics—i.e. nutritive value, ornamental value, hardiness, longevity, etc.—would not depend in any way on whether a similar sport had appeared in the past, or whether that particular sport was predictable. * * *

Id. at 1382 (footnote omitted). The court also attempted to formulate an affirmative statement of what "nonobviousness" means in the context of plant patents:

> Rephrasing the *John Deere* tests for the plant world, we might ask about (1) the characteristics of prior plants of the same general type, both patented and nonpatented, and (2) the differences between the prior plants and the claims at issue. We see no meaningful way to apply the third criterion to plants—*i.e.* the level of ordinary skill in the prior art. Criteria one and two are reminiscent of the "distinctness" requirement already in the Plant Patent Act. Thus, if we are to give obviousness an independent meaning, it must refer to something other than observable characteristics.

> We think that the most promising approach toward the obviousness requirement for plant patents is reference to the underlying constitutional standard that it codifies—namely, invention.

> The general thrust of the "invention" requirement is to ensure that minor improvements will not be granted the protection of a seventeen year monopoly by the state. In the case of plants, to develop or discover a new variety that retains the desirable qualities of the parent stock and adds significant improvements, and to preserve the new specimen by asexually reproducing it constitutes no small feat.

> This Court's case dealing with the patent on the chemical compound commonly known as the drug "Darvon," Eli Lilly & Co. v. Generix Drug Sales, Inc., 5 Cir. 1972, 460 F.2d 1096, provides some insight into the problem of how to apply the "invention" requirement to a new and esoteric subject matter. The court first noted that

> > Analogical reasoning is necessarily restricted in many chemical patent cases because of the necessity for physiological experimentation before any use can be determined.

> > In fact, such lack of predictability of useful result from the making of even the slightest variation in the atomic structure or spatial

arrangement of a complex molecule ... deprives the instant claims of obviousness and anticipation of most of their vitality....

460 F.2d at 1101. The court resolved the apparent dilemma by looking to the therapeutic value of the new drug instead of to its chemical composition:

> [R]eason compels us to agree that novelty, usefulness and non-obviousness inhere in the true discovery that a chemical compound exhibits a new needed medicinal capability, even though it be closely related in structure to a known or patented drug.

460 F.2d at 1103.

The same kind of shift in focus would lead us to a more productive inquiry for plant patents. If the plant is a source of food, the ultimate question might be its nutritive content or its prolificacy. A medicinal plant might be judged by its increased or changed therapeutic value. Similarly, an ornamental plant would be judged by its increased beauty and desirability in relation to the other plants of its type, its usefulness in the industry, and how much of an improvement it represents over prior ornamental plants, taking all of its characteristics together.

Id. at 1379 (footnotes omitted). Compare the *Yoder Bros.* court's discussion of novelty and distinctness, reproduced in Section C.5, *supra*. Do you agree with the court's interpretation of nonobviousness?

E.   STATUTORY BARS

Statutes: 35 U.S.C.A. § 102(b)-(d)

The "loss of rights" provisions in Sections 102(b)-(d) set forth circumstances in which Congress has determined that, because the inventor has not proceeded diligently toward applying for a United States patent, the underlying public purpose of the patent monopoly will not be served by issuing a patent, regardless of the invention's novelty, utility, and nonobviousness at the time of its creation. In order for an event to invalidate a utility or plant patent under Sections 102(b)-(d), the event must take place more than one year before the patent application is filed; in the case of design patents, the statutory period under Section 102(d) is 6 months, *see* 35 U.S.C.A. § 172.

1.   SECTION 102(b)

(i) "Public Use"

METALLIZING ENGINEERING CO., INC. v. KENYON BEARING & AUTO. PARTS CO., INC.
United States Court of Appeals, Second Circuit, 1946.
153 F.2d 516, *cert. denied*, 328 U.S. 840, 66 S.Ct. 1016, 90 L.Ed. 1615 (1946).

L. Hand, Circuit Judge.

[Defendants challenged the validity of the plaintiff's patent on the ground that the inventor had placed the patented process into public use more than one year before the patent application was filed. The district court found that while the inventor's use was commercial, it was also secret, and thus not invalidating, and the defendants appealed.]

* * *

* * * So far as we can find, the first case which dealt with the effect of prior use by the patentee was Pennock v. Dialogue, 2 Pet. 1, 4, 7 L.Ed. 327, in which the invention had been completed in 1811, and the patent granted in 1818 for a process of making hose by which the sections were joined together in such a way that the joints resisted pressure as well as the other parts. It did not appear that the joints in any way disclosed the process; but the patentee, between the discovery of the invention and the grant of the patent, had sold 13,000 feet of hose; and as to this the judge charged: 'If the public, with the knowledge and tacit consent of the inventor, be permitted to use the invention, without opposition, it is a fraud on the public afterwards to take out a patent.' The Supreme Court affirmed a judgment for the defendant, on the ground that the invention had been 'known or used before the application.' 'If an inventor should be permitted to hold back from the knowledge of the public the secrets of his invention; if he should * * * make and sell his invention publicly, and thus gather the whole profits, * * * it would materially retard the progress of science and the useful arts' to allow him fourteen years of legal monopoly 'when the danger of competition should force him to secure the exclusive right' 2 Pet. at page 19, 7 L.Ed. 327. In Shaw v. Cooper, 7 Pet. 292, 8 L.Ed. 689, the public use was not by the inventor, but he had neglected to prevent it after he had learned of it, and this defeated the patent. 'Whatever may be the intention of the inventor, if he suffers his invention to go into public use, through any means whatsoever, without an immediate assertion of his right, he is not entitled to a patent' 7 Pet. at page 323, 8 L.Ed. 689. In Kendall v. Winsor, 21 How. 322, 16 L.Ed. 165, the inventor had kept the machine secret, but had sold the harness which it produced, so that the facts presented the same situation as here. Since the jury brought in a verdict for the defendant on the issue of abandonment, the case adds nothing except for the dicta on page 328 of 21 How., 16 L.Ed. 165: 'the inventor who designedly, and with the view of applying it indefinitely and exclusively for his own profit, withholds his invention for the public, comes not within the policy or objects of the Constitution or acts of Congress.' In Egbert v. Lippmann, 104 U.S. 333, 26 L.Ed. 755, although the patent was for the product which was sold, nothing could be learned about it without taking it apart, yet it was a public use within the statute. In Hall v. Macneale, 107 U.S. 90, 2 S.Ct. 73, 27 L.Ed. 367, the situation was the same.

* * *

Coming now to our own decisions (the opinions in all of which I wrote), the first was Grasselli Chemical Co. v. National Aniline & Chemical Co., 2 Cir., 26 F.2d 305, in which the patent was for a process which had been kept secret, but the product had been sold upon the market for more than two years. We held that, although the process could not have been discovered from the product, the sales constituted a "prior use," relying upon Egbert v. Lippmann, *supra,* 104 U.S. 333, 26 L.Ed. 755, and Hall v. Macneale, *supra,* 107 U.S. 90, 2 S.Ct. 73, 27 L.Ed. 367. There was nothing in this inconsistent with what we are now holding. But in Peerless Roll Leaf Co. v. Griffin & Sons, *supra,* 2 Cir., 29 F.2d 646, where the patent was for a machine, which had been kept secret, but whose output had been freely sold on the market, we sustained the patent on the ground that "the sale of the product was irrelevant, since no knowledge could possibly be acquired of the machine in that way. In this respect the machine differs from a process * * * or from any other invention necessarily contained in a product" 29 F.2d at page 649. So far as we can now find, there is nothing to support this distinction in the authorities, and we shall try to show that we misapprehended the theory on which the prior use by an inventor forfeits his right to a patent. * * * In Gillman v. Stern, *supra,* 2 Cir., 114 F.2d 28, it was not the inventor, but a third person who used the machine secretly and sold the product openly, and there was therefore no question either of abandonment or forfeiture by the inventor. The only issue was whether a prior use which did not disclose the invention to the art was within the statute; and it is well settled that it is not. As in the case of any other anticipation, the issue of invention must then be determined by how much the inventor has contributed any new information to the art. Gayler v. Wilder, 10 How. 477, 496, 497, 13 L.Ed. 504; Tilghman v. Proctor, 102 U.S. 707, 711, 26 L.Ed. 279.

From the foregoing it appears that in Peerless Roll Leaf Co. v. Griffin & Sons, *supra,* 2 Cir., 29 F.2d 646, we confused two separate doctrines: (1) The effect upon his right to a patent of the inventor's competitive exploitation of his machine or of his process; (2) the contribution which a prior use by another person makes to the art. Both do indeed come within the phrase, "prior use"; but the first is a defence for quite different reasons from the second. It had its origin—at least in this country—in the passage we have quoted from Pennock v. Dialogue, *supra,* 2 Pet. 1, 7 L.Ed. 327; *i.e.,* that it is a condition upon an inventor's right to a patent that he shall not exploit his discovery competitively after it is ready for patenting; he must content himself with either secrecy, or legal monopoly. It is true that for the limited period of two years he was allowed to do so, possibly in order to give him time to prepare an application; and even that has been recently cut down by half. But if he goes beyond that period of probation, he forfeits his right regardless of how little the public may have learned about the invention; just as he can forfeit it by too long concealment, even without exploiting the invention at all. Woodbridge v. United States, 263 U.S. 50, 44 S.Ct. 45, 68 L.Ed. 159; Macbeth–Evans Glass Co. v. General Electric Co., *supra,* 6 Cir., 246 F. 695. Such a forfeiture has nothing to do with abandonment, which presupposes a deliberate, though not necessarily an express, surrender of any right to a patent. Although the evidence of both may at times overlap, each comes from a quite different legal source: one, from the fact that by renouncing the right the inventor irrevocably surrenders it; the other, from the fiat of Congress that it is part of the consideration for a patent that the public shall as soon as possible begin to enjoy the disclosure.

It is indeed true that an inventor may continue for more than a year to practice his invention for his private purposes of his own enjoyment and later patent it. But that is, properly considered, not an exception to the doctrine, for he is not then making use of his secret to gain a competitive advantage over others; he does not thereby extend the period of his monopoly. Besides, as we have seen, even that privilege has its limits, for he may conceal it so long that he will lose his right to a patent even though he does not use it at all. With that question we have not however any concern here.

Judgment reversed; complaint dismissed.

Notes

1. The public use bar of Section 102(b) applies to unauthorized activities of parties other than the inventor or the inventor's assignee, regardless of whether the unauthorized use was a pirated use or simply a case of parallel invention, but only if the unauthorized activities disclose the invention to the public. *Lorenz v. Colgate–Palmolive–Peet Co.,* 167 F.2d 423, 429–30 (3d Cir.1948) (pirated public use was a bar); *Electric Storage Battery Co. v. Shimadzu,* 307 U.S. 5, 19–20, 59 S.Ct. 675, 683, 83 L.Ed. 1071 (1939) (unauthorized but non-pirated use of independently developed invention in factory, with no effort at secrecy, was a bar). As noted in *Metallizing Engineering*, where a party acting without the inventor's authority makes secret commercial use of the invention, such as selling articles made by the method or device sought to be patented, courts have generally held that the public use bar will not apply unless the invention is disclosed by the articles sold, even though the bar would have applied to those same activities if undertaken with the inventor's consent.

2. In *Baxter International, Inc. v. Cobe Laboratories, Inc.,* 88 F.3d 1054 (Fed.Cir.1996), the Federal Circuit noted that "[i]n considering whether a particular use was a public use within the meaning of Section 102(b), we consider the totality of the circumstances in conjunction with the policies underlying the public use bar," and reiterated the policies it had identified in *Tone Bros., Inc. v. Sysco Corp.,* 28 F.3d 1192, 1198 (Fed.Cir.1994), *cert. denied,* 514 U.S. 1015, 115 S.Ct. 1356, 131 L.Ed.2d 214 (1995) as the underlying purposes of the public use bar:

(1) discouraging the removal, from the public domain, of inventions that the public reasonably has come to believe are freely available; (2) favoring the prompt and widespread disclosure of inventions; (3) allowing the inventor a reasonable amount of time following sales activity to determine the potential economic value of a patent; and (4) prohibiting the inventor from commercially exploiting the invention for a period greater than the statutorily prescribed time.

Baxter International, 88 F.3d at 1058 (quoting *Tone Bros.*, 28 F.3d at 1198). In light of these purposes, should the public use bar apply where a party other than the inventor, acting independently, develops the same invention and uses it in a research laboratory where the persons observing the invention are under no legal or ethical obligation of confidentiality?

3. *Experimental Uses:* An experimental use of an invention will not trigger the section 102(b) bar even if the use discloses the invention to the public. In *Elizabeth v. American Nicholson Pavement Co.*, 97 U.S. (7 Otto) 126, 24 L.Ed. 1000 (1877), which held that installing pavement on a public street for testing purposes was not an invalidating public use, the Court discussed the scope of "experimental use":

> That the use of the pavement in question was public in one sense cannot be disputed. But can it be said that the invention was in public use? The use of an invention by the inventor himself, or of any other person under his direction, by way of experiment, and in order to bring the invention to perfection, has never been regarded as such a use.

> * * *

> It would not be necessary, in such a case, that the machine should be put up and used only in the inventor's own shop or premises. He may have it put up and used in the premises of another, and the use may inure to the benefit of the owner of the establishment. Still, if used under the surveillance of the inventor, and for the purpose of enabling him to test the machine, and ascertain whether it will answer the purpose intended, and make such alterations and improvements as experience demonstrates to be necessary, it will still be a mere experimental use, and not a public use, within the meaning of the statute.

> Whilst the supposed machine is in such experimental use, the public may be incidentally deriving a benefit from it. If it be a grist-mill, or a carding-machine, customers from the surrounding country may enjoy the use of it by having their grain made into flour, or their wool into rolls, and still it will not be in public use, within the meaning of the law.

> But if the inventor allows his machine to be used by other persons generally, either with or without compensation, or if it is, with his consent, put on sale for such use, then it will be in public use and on public sale, within the meaning of the law.

> * * *

> It is sometimes said that an inventor acquires an undue advantage over the public by delaying to take out a patent, inasmuch as he thereby preserves the monopoly to himself for a longer period than is allowed by the policy of the law; but this cannot be said with justice when the delay is occasioned by a bona fide effort to bring his invention to perfection, or to ascertain whether it will answer the purpose intended. His monopoly only continues for the allotted period, in any event; and it is the interest of the public, as well as himself, that the invention should be perfect and properly tested, before a patent is granted for it. Any attempt to use it for a profit, and not by way of experiment, for a longer period than two

years [now one year] before the application, would deprive the inventor of his right to a patent.

Id. at 134–37.

Subsequent case law has emphasized the degree of control exercised by the inventor over any parties making experimental use of the invention. In *Baxter International,* the Federal Circuit listed the following factors as relevant to the determination whether a particular use is experimental: "the length of the test period, whether the inventor received payment for the testing, any agreement by the user to maintain the use confidential, any records of testing, whether persons other than the inventor performed the testing, the number of tests, and the length of the test period in relation to tests of similar devices." 88 F.3d at 1060 (citing *TP Lab., Inc. v. Professional Positioners, Inc.,* 724 F.2d 965, 971–72 (Fed.Cir.), *cert. denied,* 469 U.S. 826, 105 S.Ct. 108, 83 L.Ed.2d 51 (1984)).

4. Should the experimental use exception apply (1) where the use is by a party, other than the patent applicant, who independently produced the same invention after the applicant's invention date? (2) where the experimentation is directed to non-claimed features of the invention? (3) where the use is for the purpose of ascertaining consumer response to the product?

(ii) "On Sale"

PFAFF v. WELLS ELECTRONICS, INC.

Supreme Court of the United States, 1998.
525 U.S. 55, 119 S.Ct. 304, 142 L.Ed.2d 261.

JUSTICE STEVENS delivered the opinion of the Court.

Section 102(b) of the Patent Act of 1952 provides that no person is entitled to patent an "invention" that has been "on sale" more than one year before filing a patent application. We granted certiorari to determine whether the commercial marketing of a newly invented product may mark the beginning of the 1–year period even though the invention has not yet been reduced to practice.[20]

I

On April 19, 1982, petitioner, Wayne Pfaff, filed an application for a patent on a computer chip socket. Therefore, April 19, 1981, constitutes the critical date for purposes of the on-sale bar of 35 U.S.C. § 102(b); if the 1–year period began to run before that date, Pfaff lost his right to patent his invention.

Pfaff commenced work on the socket in November 1980, when representatives of Texas Instruments asked him to develop a new device for mounting and removing semiconductor chip carriers. In response to this request, he prepared detailed engineering drawings that described

---

20. "A process is reduced to practice when it is successfully performed. A machine is reduced to practice when it is assembled, adjusted and used. A manufacture is reduced to practice when it is completely manufactured. A composition of matter is reduced to practice when it is completely composed." Corona Cord Tire Co. v. Dovan Chemical Corp., 276 U.S. 358, 383, 72 L. Ed. 610, 48 S. Ct. 380 (1928).

the design, the dimensions, and the materials to be used in making the socket. Pfaff sent those drawings to a manufacturer in February or March 1981.

Prior to March 17, 1981, Pfaff showed a sketch of his concept to representatives of Texas Instruments. On April 8, 1981, they provided Pfaff with a written confirmation of a previously placed oral purchase order for 30,100 of his new sockets for a total price of $91,155. In accord with his normal practice, Pfaff did not make and test a prototype of the new device before offering to sell it in commercial quantities.

The manufacturer took several months to develop the customized tooling necessary to produce the device, and Pfaff did not fill the order until July 1981. The evidence therefore indicates that Pfaff first reduced his invention to practice in the summer of 1981. The socket achieved substantial commercial success before Patent No. 4,491,377 (the '377 patent) issued to Pfaff on January 1, 1985.

* * *

[After the patent issued, Pfaff brought an infringement action against respondent, Wells Electronics, Inc., a competing socket manufacturer. The District Court found that claims 7, 10 and 11 of the patent were infringed, and] rejected respondent's § 102(b) defense because Pfaff had filed the application for the '377 patent less than a year after reducing the invention to practice.

The Court of Appeals reversed, finding all six claims invalid. 124 F.3d 1429 (C.A.Fed.1997). Four of the claims (1, 6, 7, and 10) described the socket that Pfaff had sold to Texas Instruments prior to April 8, 1981. Because that device had been offered for sale on a commercial basis more than one year before the patent application was filed on April 19, 1982, the court concluded that those claims were invalid under § 102(b). That conclusion rested on the court's view that as long as the invention was "substantially complete at the time of sale," the 1–year period began to run, even though the invention had not yet been reduced to practice. Id., at 1434. The other two claims (11 and 19) described a feature that had not been included in Pfaff's initial design, but the Court of Appeals concluded as a matter of law that the additional feature was not itself patentable because it was an obvious addition to the prior art. Given the court's § 102(b) holding, the prior art included Pfaff's first four claims.

Because other courts have held or assumed that an invention cannot be "on sale" within the meaning of § 102(b) unless and until it has been reduced to practice, and because the text of § 102(b) makes no reference to "substantial completion" of an invention, we granted certiorari.

II

The primary meaning of the word "invention" in the Patent Act unquestionably refers to the inventor's conception rather than to a physical embodiment of that idea. The statute does not contain any express requirement that an invention must be reduced to practice before it can be patented. Neither the statutory definition of the term in § 100 nor the basic conditions for obtaining a patent set forth in § 101 make any mention of "reduction to practice." The statute's only specific reference to that term is found in § 102(g), which sets forth the standard for resolving priority contests between two competing claimants to a patent. That subsection provides:

> "In determining priority of invention there shall be considered not only the respective dates of conception and reduction to practice of the invention, but also the reasonable diligence of one who was first to conceive and last to reduce to practice, from a time prior to conception by the other."

Thus, assuming diligence on the part of the applicant, it is normally the first inventor to conceive, rather than the first to reduce to practice, who establishes the right to the patent.

It is well settled that an invention may be patented before it is reduced to practice. In 1888, this Court upheld a patent issued to Alexander Graham Bell even though he had filed his application before constructing a working telephone. Chief Justice Waite's reasoning in that case merits quoting at length:

> "It is quite true that when Bell applied for his patent he had never actually transmitted telegraphically spoken words so that they could be distinctly heard and understood at the receiving end of his line, but in his specification he did describe accurately and with admirable clearness his process, that is to say, the exact electrical condition that must be created to accomplish his purpose, and he also described, with sufficient precision to enable one of ordinary skill in such matters to make it, a form of apparatus which, if used in the way pointed out, would produce the required effect, receive the words, and carry them to and deliver them at the appointed place. The particular instrument which he had, and which he used in his experiments, did not, under the circumstances in which it was tried, reproduce the words spoken, so that they could be clearly understood, but the proof is abundant and of the most convincing character, that other instruments, carefully constructed and made exactly in accordance with the specification, without any additions whatever, have operated and will operate successfully. A good mechanic of proper skill in matters of the kind can take the patent and, by following the specification strictly, can, without more, construct an apparatus which, when used in the way pointed out, will do all that it is claimed the method or process will do. . . .

> "The law does not require that a discoverer or inventor, in order to get a patent for a process, must have succeeded in bringing his art to the highest degree of perfection. It is enough if he describes his method with sufficient clearness and precision to enable those skilled in the matter to understand what the process is, and if he

points out some practicable way of putting it into operation." The Telephone Cases, 126 U.S. 1, 31 L. Ed. 863, 8 S. Ct. 778 (1888).[21]

When we apply the reasoning of *The Telephone Cases* to the facts of the case before us today, it is evident that Pfaff could have obtained a patent on his novel socket when he accepted the purchase order from Texas Instruments for 30,100 units. At that time he provided the manufacturer with a description and drawings that had "sufficient clearness and precision to enable those skilled in the matter" to produce the device. The parties agree that the sockets manufactured to fill that order embody Pfaff's conception as set forth in claims 1, 6, 7, and 10 of the '377 patent. We can find no basis in the text of § 102(b) or in the facts of this case for concluding that Pfaff's invention was not "on sale" within the meaning of the statute until after it had been reduced to practice.

III

Pfaff nevertheless argues that longstanding precedent, buttressed by the strong interest in providing inventors with a clear standard identifying the onset of the 1–year period, justifies a special interpretation of the word "invention" as used in § 102(b). We are persuaded that this nontextual argument should be rejected.

As we have often explained, most recently in Bonito Boats, Inc. v. Thunder Craft Boats, Inc., 489 U.S. 141, 151, 103 L. Ed. 2d 118, 109 S. Ct. 971 (1989), the patent system represents a carefully crafted bargain that encourages both the creation and the public disclosure of new and useful advances in technology, in return for an exclusive monopoly for a limited period of time. The balance between the interest in motivating innovation and enlightenment by rewarding invention with patent protection on the one hand, and the interest in avoiding monopolies that unnecessarily stifle competition on the other, has been a feature of the federal patent laws since their inception. As this Court explained in 1871:

> "Letters patent are not to be regarded as monopolies ... but as public franchises granted to the inventors of new and useful improvements for the purpose of securing to them, as such inventors, for the limited term therein mentioned, the exclusive right and liberty to make and use and vend to others to be used their own inventions, as tending to promote the progress of science and the useful arts, and as matter of compensation to the inventors for their labor, toil, and expense in making the inventions, and reducing the same to practice for the public benefit, as contemplated by the Constitution and sanctioned by the laws of Congress." Seymour v. Osborne, 78 U.S. 516, 11 Wall. 516, 533–534, 20 L. Ed. 33.

21. This Court has also held a patent invalid because the invention had previously been disclosed in a prior patent application, although that application did not claim the invention and the first invention apparently had not been reduced to practice. Alexander Milburn Co. v. Davis–Bournonville Co., 270 U.S. 390, 401–402, 70 L. Ed. 651, 46 S. Ct. 324 (1926).

Consistent with these ends, § 102 of the Patent Act serves as a limiting provision, both excluding ideas that are in the public domain from patent protection and confining the duration of the monopoly to the statutory term.

We originally held that an inventor loses his right to a patent if he puts his invention into public use before filing a patent application. "His voluntary act or acquiescence in the public sale and use is an abandonment of his right" Pennock v. Dialogue, 2 Pet. 1, 24 (1829) (Story, J.). A similar reluctance to allow an inventor to remove existing knowledge from public use undergirds the on-sale bar.

Nevertheless, an inventor who seeks to perfect his discovery may conduct extensive testing without losing his right to obtain a patent for his invention—even if such testing occurs in the public eye. The law has long recognized the distinction between inventions put to experimental use and products sold commercially. In 1878, we explained why patentability may turn on an inventor's use of his product.

> "It is sometimes said that an inventor acquires an undue advantage over the public by delaying to take out a patent, inasmuch as he thereby preserves the monopoly to himself for a longer period than is allowed by the policy of the law; but this cannot be said with justice when the delay is occasioned by a bona fide effort to bring his invention to perfection, or to ascertain whether it will answer the purpose intended. His monopoly only continues for the allotted period, in any event; and it is the interest of the public, as well as himself, that the invention should be perfect and properly tested, before a patent is granted for it. *Any attempt to use it for a profit, and not by way of experiment, for a longer period than two years before the application, would deprive the inventor of his right to a patent.*" Elizabeth v. Pavement Co., 97 U.S. 126, 137, 24 L. Ed. 1000 (emphasis added).

The patent laws therefore seek both to protect the public's right to retain knowledge already in the public domain and the inventor's right to control whether and when he may patent his invention. The Patent Act of 1836, 5 Stat. 117, was the first statute that expressly included an on-sale bar to the issuance of a patent. Like the earlier holding in *Pennock,* that provision precluded patentability if the invention had been placed on sale at any time before the patent application was filed. In 1839, Congress ameliorated that requirement by enacting a 2–year grace period in which the inventor could file an application. 5 Stat. 353.

In Andrews v. Hovey, 123 U.S. 267, 274, 31 L. Ed. 160, 8 S. Ct. 101 (1887), we noted that the purpose of that amendment was "to fix a period of limitation which should be certain"; it required the inventor to make sure that a patent application was filed "within two years from the completion of his invention," *ibid.* In 1939, Congress reduced the grace period from two years to one year. 53 Stat. 1212.

Petitioner correctly argues that these provisions identify an interest in providing inventors with a definite standard for determining when a patent application must be filed. A rule that makes the timeliness of an application depend on the date when an invention is "substantially complete" seriously undermines the interest in certainty.[22] Moreover, such a rule finds no support in the text of the statute. Thus, petitioner's argument calls into question the standard applied by the Court of Appeals, but it does not persuade us that it is necessary to engraft a reduction to practice element into the meaning of the term "invention" as used in § 102(b).

The word "invention" must refer to a concept that is complete, rather than merely one that is "substantially complete." It is true that reduction to practice ordinarily provides the best evidence that an invention is complete. But just because reduction to practice is sufficient evidence of completion, it does not follow that proof of reduction to practice is necessary in every case. Indeed, both the facts of the *Telephone Cases* and the facts of this case demonstrate that one can prove that an invention is complete and ready for patenting before it has actually been reduced to practice.[23]

We conclude, therefore, that the on-sale bar applies when two conditions are satisfied before the critical date.

First, the product must be the subject of a commercial offer for sale. An inventor can both understand and control the timing of the first commercial marketing of his invention. The experimental use doctrine, for example, has not generated concerns about indefiniteness,[24] and we

22. The Federal Circuit has developed a multifactor, "totality of the circumstances" test to determine the trigger for the on-sale bar. *See, e. g.,* Micro Chemical, Inc. v. Great Plains Chemical Co., 103 F.3d 1538, 1544 (1997) (stating that, in determining whether an invention is on sale for purposes of 102(b), " 'all of the circumstances surrounding the sale or offer to sell, including the stage of development of the invention and the nature of the invention, must be considered and weighed against the policies underlying section 102(b)' "); *see also* UMC Electronics Co. v. United States, 816 F.2d 647, 656 (1987) (stating the on-sale bar "does not lend itself to formulation into a set of precise requirements"). As the Federal Circuit itself has noted, this test "has been criticized as unnecessarily vague." Seal–Flex, Inc. v. Athletic Track & Court Construction, 98 F.3d 1318, 1323, n. 2 (1996).

23. Several of this Court's early decisions stating that an invention is not complete until it has been reduced to practice are best understood as indicating that the invention's reduction to practice demonstrated that the concept was no longer in an experimental phase. *See, e.g.,* Seymour v. Osborne, 78 U.S. 516, 11 Wall. 516, 552, 20 L. Ed. 33 (1870) ("Crude and imperfect

experiments are not sufficient to confer a right to a patent; but in order to constitute an invention, the party must have proceeded so far as to have reduced his idea to practice, and embodied it in some distinct form"); Clark Thread Co. v. Willimantic Linen Co., 140 U.S. 481, 489, 35 L. Ed. 521, 11 S. Ct. 846 (1891) (describing how inventor continued to alter his thread winding machine until July 1858, when "he put it in visible form in the shape of a machine.... It is evident that the invention was not completed until the construction of the machine"); Corona Cord Tire Co. v. Dovan Chemical Corp., 276 U.S. at 382–383 (stating that an invention did not need to be subsequently commercialized to constitute prior art after the inventor had finished his experimentation. "It was the fact that it would work with great activity as an accelerator that was the discovery, and that was all, and the necessary reduction to use is shown by instances making clear that it did so work, and was a completed discovery").

24. *See, e.g.,* Rooklidge & Jensen, Common Sense, Simplicity and Experimental Use Negation of the Public Use and On Sale Bars to Patentability, 29 John Marshall L. Rev. 1, 29 (1995) (stating that "whether a particular activity is experimental is often clear").

perceive no reason why unmanageable uncertainty should attend a rule that measures the application of the on-sale bar of § 102(b) against the date when an invention that is ready for patenting is first marketed commercially. In this case the acceptance of the purchase order prior to April 8, 1981, makes it clear that such an offer had been made, and there is no question that the sale was commercial rather than experimental in character.

Second, the invention must be ready for patenting. That condition may be satisfied in at least two ways: by proof of reduction to practice before the critical date; or by proof that prior to the critical date the inventor had prepared drawings or other descriptions of the invention that were sufficiently specific to enable a person skilled in the art to practice the invention.[25] In this case the second condition of the on-sale bar is satisfied because the drawings Pfaff sent to the manufacturer before the critical date fully disclosed the invention.

The evidence in this case thus fulfills the two essential conditions of the on-sale bar. As succinctly stated by Learned Hand:

> "It is a condition upon an inventor's right to a patent that he shall not exploit his discovery competitively after it is ready for patenting; he must content himself with either secrecy, or legal monopoly."
> Metallizing Engineering Co. v. Kenyon Bearing & Auto Parts Co., 153 F.2d 516, 520 (C.A.2 1946).

The judgment of the Court of Appeals finds support not only in the text of the statute but also in the basic policies underlying the statutory scheme, including § 102(b). When Pfaff accepted the purchase order for his new sockets prior to April 8, 1981, his invention was ready for patenting. The fact that the manufacturer was able to produce the socket using his detailed drawings and specifications demonstrates this fact. Furthermore, those sockets contained all the elements of the invention claimed in the '377 patent. Therefore, Pfaff's '377 patent is invalid because the invention had been on sale for more than one year in this country before he filed his patent application. Accordingly, the judgment of the Court of Appeals is affirmed.

It is so ordered.

Notes

1. In *Elan Corp., PLC v. Andrx Pharmaceuticals, Inc.*, 366 F.3d 1336 (Fed. Cir. 2004), the Federal Circuit held that the Section 102(b) on-sale bar

---

25. The Solicitor General has argued that the rule governing on-sale bar should be phrased somewhat differently. In his opinion, "if the sale or offer in question embodies the invention for which a patent is later sought, a sale or offer to sell that is primarily for commercial purposes and that occurs more than one year before the application renders the invention unpatentable. Seal–Flex, Inc. v. Athletic Track and Court Constr., 98 F.3d 1318, 1325 (Fed.Cir.1996) (Bryson, J., concurring in part and concurring in the result)." It is true that evidence satisfying this test might be sufficient to prove that the invention was ready for patenting at the time of the sale if it is clear that no aspect of the invention was developed after the critical date. However, the possibility of additional development after the offer for sale in these circumstances counsels against adoption of the rule proposed by the Solicitor General.

was not implicated by an offer to license the right to manufacture an invention:

> Following *Pfaff*, this court held in *Group One[, Ltd. v. Hallmark Cards, Inc.*, 254 F.3d 1041, 1045–46 (Fed.Cir. 2001)] that "[o]nly an offer which rises to the level of a commercial offer for sale, one which the other party could make into a binding contract by simple acceptance ... , constitutes an offer for sale under § 102(b)." 254 F.3d at 1048. We further explained that "a sale of rights in a patent, as distinct from a sale of the invention itself, is not within the scope of the statute, and thus does not implicate the on-sale bar." *Id.* at 1049. In *In re Kollar*, 286 F.3d 1326 (Fed.Cir. 2002), we held that an offer to license a patent claiming an invention after future research and development had occurred, without more, is not an offer to sell the invention.
>
> Based on the principles articulated in *Pfaff, Group One*, and *Kollar,* we conclude that the district court erred in concluding that Elan's product was the subject of a commercial offer for sale based on Elan's letter to Lederle. An offer to enter into a license under a patent for future sale of the invention covered by the patent when and if it has been developed, which is what the Lederle letter was, is not an offer to sell the patented invention that constitutes an on-sale bar. *Kollar,* 286 F.3d at 1331. The letter to Lederle is clear on its face that Elan was not offering to sell naproxen tablets to Lederle, but rather granting a license under the patent and offering Lederle the opportunity to become its partner in the clinical testing and eventual marketing of such tablets at some indefinite point in the future. Although no particular language is required to be present in order for an offer of a license to constitute an offer for sale of the licensed product, a communication that fails to constitute a definite offer to sell the product and to include material terms is not an "offer" in the contract sense. *Restatement (Second) of Contracts* § 33(3) (1981) ("The fact that one or more terms of a proposed bargain are left open or uncertain may show that a manifestation of intention is not intended to be understood as an offer."). The letter to Lederle lacked any mention of quantities, time of delivery, place of delivery, or product specifications beyond the general statement that the potential product would be a 500 mg once-daily tablet containing naproxen. Moreover, the dollar amounts recited in the fourth paragraph of the letter to Lederle are clearly not price terms for the sale of tablets, but rather the amount that Elan was requesting to form and continue a partnership with Lederle. Indeed, the letter explicitly refers to the total as a "licensing fee."
>
> Of course, if Elan had simply disguised a sales price as a licensing fee it would not avoid triggering the on-sale bar. Nonetheless, that is not what Elan did here. If Lederle had accepted Elan's offer, it would have owed Elan $500,000 at contract signing and additional amounts at various milestones in the collaboration. There is no statement in the letter of how many tablets Elan would supply in exchange for those funds, and there is no suggestion that the number of tablets supplied would depend in any way on those payments (although the payments were to be keyed to the number of patients enrolled in clinical trials per the fifth paragraph of the letter).

366 F.3d at 1341.

2. Where the invention in question is a process, the Federal Circuit has held that the on-sale bar is triggered by the sale of a product made by that process, and by performing (or offering to perform) the process itself for consideration, but not by a license of the right to practice the process. *In re Kollar,* 286 F.3d 1326 (Fed. Cir. 2002). The court explained:

> The Board also erred in failing to recognize the distinction between a claim to a product, device, or apparatus, all of which are tangible items, and a claim to a process, which consists of a series of acts or steps. A tangible item is on sale when ... the transaction "rises to the level of a commercial offer for sale" under the Uniform Commercial Code. When money changes hands as a result of the transfer of title to the tangible item, a sale normally has occurred. A process, however, is a different kind of invention; it consists of acts, rather than a tangible item. It consists of doing something, and therefore has to be carried out or performed.

> A process is thus not sold in the same sense as is a tangible item. "Know-how" describing what the process consists of and how the process should be carried out may be sold in the sense that the buyer acquires knowledge of the process and obtains the freedom to carry it out pursuant to the terms of the transaction. However, such a transaction is not a "sale" of the invention within the meaning of § 102(b) because the process has not been carried out or performed as a result of the transaction. The same applies to a license to a patent covering a process. The Board in this case failed to recognize this distinction, and therefore erred in concluding that the license to the process under any future patents, and the accompanying description of that process, constituted a sale of the subject matter of those patents, *viz.,* the process.

Kollar, 286 F.3d at 1332 (citation omitted).

3. Courts generally agree that the on-sale bar also applies to the activities of parties other than the inventor or the inventor's assignee, even where those activities are unauthorized. *See, e.g., In re Epstein,* 32 F.3d 1559, 1564 (Fed.Cir.1994) (collecting cases); *J.A. LaPorte, Inc. v. Norfolk Dredging Co.,* 787 F.2d 1577, 1581 (Fed.Cir.1986). In the case of unauthorized activities, however, courts disagree on whether the bar should apply where an embodiment of the invention is sold under circumstances which prevent disclosure of the invention to the public; the most common example of such sales would be a sale to the federal government under conditions of secrecy. *Compare Wycoff v. Motorola, Inc.,* 502 F.Supp. 77, 88 (N.D.Ill.1980), *aff'd,* 688 F.2d 843 (7th Cir.1982) (finding the bar inapplicable to "secret" sales) *with Hobbs v. United States,* 451 F.2d 849, 860 (5th Cir.1971) (finding secrecy irrelevant). Which approach makes more sense as a matter of policy?

4. Should the "on sale" bar be triggered by: (a) the sale, merger or reorganization of a going concern which includes an invention (or the products thereof)? (b) the transfer of an invention (or the products thereof) by a corporation to its parent, subsidiary, or other corporate affiliate?

5. The experimental use doctrine (discussed in Note 3, Section E.1(i), *supra*) also applies to the "on sale" bar; as in cases involving the "public

use" bar, the doctrine applies only where the evidence demonstrates a bona fide experimental purpose, and factors such as those discussed in *Elizabeth* and *Baxter International* should have equal relevance in the sale context. *See, e.g., In re Hamilton*, 882 F.2d 1576, 1581, 11 U.S.P.Q.2d 1890, 1894 (Fed.Cir.1989) (discussing experimental use in the context of the on-sale bar).

Should the experimental use exception apply where a sale serves both an experimental and a commercial purpose?

6. With respect to subject matter that is "patented or described in a printed publication," courts have interpreted the statutory phrase in Section 102(b) as having the same meaning as the identical phrase in Section 102(a); thus, the same precedents and interpretive problems apply.

For a "printed publication" to occur under Section 102(b) (or, for that matter, Section 102(a)), is it essential that the document in question be publicly distributed or indexed/catalogued in some kind of library or archive? For example, would the Section 102(b) bar be triggered where an applicant disclosed his invention only in the form of a presentation, printed and pasted onto poster boards, at a scientific conference? *See In re Klopfenstein*, 380 F.3d 1345 (Fed. Cir. 2004).

2. SECTION 102(c)

MOORE v. UNITED STATES
United States Court of Claims, 1977.
194 U.S.P.Q. (BNA) 423.

COLAIANNI, TRIAL JUDGE.

* * *

[The infringement defendant argued that patentholder Moore's patent was invalid under section 102(c) because there was a 14–year delay between the plaintiff's 1942 reduction to practice and the filing of his initial patent application in 1955, and this delay constituted either abandonment or forfeiture.]

* * *

ABANDONMENT

Abandonment is an affirmative defense which must be proven by clear and convincing evidence. Petersen v. Fee Int'l, Ltd., 381 F.Supp. 1071, 1079 (W.D.Okla.1974). Abandonment, under 35 U.S.C. § 102(c), presupposes a deliberate, though not necessarily an express, surrender of any rights to a patent. Metallizing Engineer. Co. v. Kenyon Bearing & A.P. Co., 153 F.2d 516, 520, 68 USPQ 54, 58 (2d Cir.1946), *cert. denied*, 328 U.S. 840 (1946). To abandon the invention, the inventor must intend a dedication to the public. Kendall v. Winsor, 21 How. 322, 329 (1858). This intent may be express, as by a declaration by the inventor. U.S. Rifle & Cartridge Co. v. Whitney Arms Co., 118 U.S. 22, 25 (1886), or implied as by the actions or inactions of the inventor, Consolidated

Fruit–Jar Co. v. Wright, 94 U.S. 92, 96 (1876). Delay alone is not a sufficient basis from which to infer the requisite intent. Lovell v. Peer, 148 F.2d 212, 214 (CCPA 1945).

In the present case, abandonment has not been proven. Particularly, defendant has not shown that plaintiff intended to dedicate his invention to the public. To the extent that defendant relies solely upon the mere delay by Moore in filing for a patent, no matter how long, defendant has not shown an express intent by plaintiff to abandon his invention. Moreover, the absence of some other facts, events, or circumstances which make intent to dedicate to the public the only reasonable explanation of Moore's "inaction" is fatal to defendant's position that plaintiff has by implication abandoned his invention.

* * *

Forfeiture

Forfeiture is distinct from abandonment which, it will be recalled, presupposes an intent to surrender all rights to a patent. Although the evidence of both may at times overlap, they come from different sources. The basis for a holding of abandonment results from a renouncing and irrevocable surrender by an inventor to any right he may have to a patent. On the other hand, forfeiture appears to be grounded more on what Judge Learned Hand, in Metallizing Engineer. Co. v. Kenyon Bearing & A.P. Co., *supra,* at 520, characterized as—

[T]he fiat of Congress that it is part of the consideration for a patent that the public shall as soon as possible begin to enjoy the disclosure.

Judge Hand was, of course, concerned in the *Metallizing Engineer. Co.* case with the effect, if any, that a secret commercial use of a process for more than 1 year before the filing date of a patent application would have upon a patent covering the process. He rightly concluded that such use would invalidate the patent. The case at bar is, of course, distinguishable, since defendant has not proven that Mr. Moore was commercially exploiting his invention in secret.

After explaining that the statute then in force permitted an inventor to use or sell his invention for up to 2 years prior to filing for a patent, Judge Hand * * * states by way of obiter dictum (at 520, 68 USPQ at 58–59):

But if he goes beyond that period of probation, he forfeits his right regardless of how little the public may have learned about the invention; just as he can forfeit it by too long concealment, even without exploiting the invention at all. * * *

It is indeed true that an inventor may continue for more than a year to practice his invention for his private purposes or his own enjoyment and later patent it. But that is, properly considered, not an exception to the doctrine, for he is not then making use of his secret to gain a competitive advantage over others; he does not thereby extend the period of his monopoly. Besides, as we have seen, even that privilege has its limits, for he may conceal it so long that he will lose his right to a patent even though he does not use it at all. With that question we have not however any concern here.

* * * [I]t is crucial to point out that the cases cited by Judge Hand as support for the proposition that mere delay may work a forfeiture do not, upon close analysis, support such a conclusion. Moreover, and equally important, Judge Hand's statement is pure dictum and not necessary or relied upon to arrive at a resolution of the issue before him. This is clear from the above quote wherein Judge Hand acknowledged that: "With that question [the effect of a long concealment of an invention in absence of exploitation would have on the right of an inventor to obtain a patent] we have not however any concern here."

* * *

In sum, after reviewing the cases cited, both pro and con, involving abandonment, it must be repeated that defendant has not shown, by clear and convincing evidence, that plaintiff abandoned his invention within the meaning of 35 U.S.C. § 102(c).

Moreover, assuming that forfeiture is a viable doctrine that can be used as a defense to a patent infringement charge, none of the cases cited indicate that it has been applied to a situation which involves pure and simple delay—regardless of the length or duration of the delay—between the time that an inventor reduces his invention to practice and the time that he files for a patent application.

To the contrary, a great number of cases involving both applicants before the Patent Office or patentees in patent infringement actions have recognized the principle that mere delay is not per se bad. This principle was announced in terms which are as accurate and correct today as they were in 1878 when the Supreme Court stated in Bates v. Coe, 98 U.S. 31, 46 (1878):

> Inventors may, if they can, keep their invention secret; and if they do for any length of time, they do not forfeit their right to apply for a patent, unless another in the mean time has made the invention, and secured by patent the exclusive right to make, use, and vend the patented improvement. Within that rule and subject to that condition, inventors may delay to apply for a patent; * * *.

* * *

Finally, and significantly, it is possible to distinguish all of the cases cited by the parties from the case at bar by noting that in each of the cited cases the invention was in the public domain at the time that the first inventor filed his application for a patent. Specifically, the invention was in the public domain because of acts by the inventor which are now proscribed by 35 U.S.C. § 102 or because during the inventor's delay, others working independently made the same or substantially the same invention.

* * *

However, in the case at bar, at least as can best be determined from the record at trial, defendant has not demonstrated that Moore's invention was already in the public domain at the time that he filed for a patent in 1955.

* * *

In sum, defendant has not demonstrated that plaintiff has either abandoned and/or forfeited his right to a patent by merely waiting from 1942 to 1955 to file for a patent.

* * *

Notes

1. Early Supreme Court decisions treated public use of an invention as abandonment of the inventor's patent right.[1] The explicit provision on abandonment, independent of the public use or sale bar, was added in 1870.[2] Although that provision is now embodied in Section 102(c), it is infrequently applied, because most cases in which abandonment could be found also involve events which would trigger the Section 102(b) bar.

2. Abandonment of a patent application does not *by itself* constitute abandonment for purposes of Section 102(c); the inventor who abandons an application loses the benefit of its filing date for priority purposes, but may file a new application. *See, e.g.,* Marvin Glass & Assocs. v. Sears, Roebuck & Co., 318 F.Supp. 1089, 1101–03 (S.D.Tex.1970), *aff'd in part and remanded in part*, 448 F.2d 60 (5th Cir.1971).

3. If an inventor files a patent application which discloses but does not claim an invention, should that disclosure constitute an abandonment of the disclosed invention? *See Toro Co. v. White Consolidated Industries, Inc.*, 383 F.3d 1326 (Fed. Cir. 2004).

3. SECTION 102(d)

IN RE KATHAWALA
United States Court of Appeals, Federal Circuit, 1993.
9 F.3d 942.

LOURIE, CIRCUIT JUDGE.

[Patent applicant Kathawala appealed the patent examiner's final rejection of certain claims as unpatentable under Section 102(d) over his Greek and Spanish patents, both of which issued before Kathawala filed

---

1. *See* Pennock v. Dialogue, 27 U.S. (2 Pet.) 1, 7 L.Ed. 327 (1829); Shaw v. Cooper, 32 U.S. (7 Pet.) 292, 8 L.Ed. 689 (1833).

2. Act of July 8, 1870, ch. 230, § 24, 16 Stat. 201.

his United States application containing the same specifications. Before the PTO Board of Patent Appeals and Interferences ("Board"), Kathawala argued that the Section 102(d) bar should not apply because (1) the Greek patent was invalid under Greek law; (2) the Spanish patent specification was not officially published, and thus not publicly available, until after Kathawala's United States filing date; and (3) the Spanish patent did not claim the same invention as the United States application. The Board rejected these arguments, concluding that the validity of a foreign patent was irrelevant, as long as it contained claims directed to the same invention, that the invention was "patented" in Spain once Kathawala's rights became fixed, and that the invention patented in Spain was the same as that claimed in the United States application. Kathawala appealed.]

* * *

* * * Turning first to the Greek patent, there is no dispute that it contains claims directed to the same invention as that of Kathawala's U.S. application. Kathawala argues, however, that his invention was not first "patented" in Greece under section 102(d) because the compound, composition, and method of use claims are invalid under Greek patent law as directed to non-statutory subject matter. * * *

We disagree. Even assuming that Kathawala's compound, composition, and method of use claims are not enforceable in Greece, a matter on which we will not speculate, the controlling fact for purposes of section 102(d) is that the Greek patent issued containing claims directed to the same invention as that of the U.S. application. When a foreign patent issues with claims directed to the same invention as the U.S. application, the invention is "patented" within the meaning of section 102(d); validity of the foreign claims is irrelevant to the section 102(d) inquiry. * * *

Kathawala does not dispute that the Greek patent issued containing claims directed to the same invention as that of his U.S. application. Kathawala sought and obtained the claims contained in the Greek patent and cannot now avoid the § 102(d) bar by arguing that that which he chose to patent abroad should not have been allowed by the foreign patent office. Acceptance of such a position, as the Board stated, would place an " 'unrealistic burden' on the courts and PTO to resolve 'esoteric legal questions which may arise under the patent laws of numerous foreign countries[.']" The PTO should be able to accept at face value the grant of the Greek patent claiming subject matter corresponding to that claimed in a U.S. application, without engaging in an extensive exploration of fine points of foreign law. The claims appear in the Greek patent because the applicant put them there. He cannot claim exemption from the consequences of his own actions. The Board thus correctly concluded that the validity of the Greek claims is irrelevant for purposes of section 102(d). Accordingly, the Board properly affirmed the examiner's rejection over the Greek patent.

Also before us is the rejection of claims 1 and 2, the compound claims, based on the Spanish patent. * * *

* * * Kathawala concedes that the Spanish patent issued and was enforceable on January 21, 1985, a date prior to the U.S. filing date. Kathawala nevertheless asserts that the effective date of a foreign patent for purposes of § 102(d), the date on which an invention is "patented," is not the date the foreign patent issues and becomes enforceable, but the date on which it becomes publicly available.

The law on this issue was well established by our predecessor court in In re Monks, 588 F.2d 308 (CCPA 1978), and In re Talbott, 443 F.2d 1397 (CCPA 1971). In *Monks,* the court considered the date on which an invention was "patented" in Great Britain under § 102(d), and inquired whether the effective date for purposes of that section was the date on which the complete specification was published, a date prior to the U.S. filing date, or the date on which the patent was "sealed" under British law, which occurred after the U.S. filing date. After reviewing the legislative history of section 102(d), the court concluded that "patented" means "a formal bestowal of patent rights from the sovereign to the applicant such as that which occurs when a British patent is sealed." 588 F.2d at 310. It was on the "sealed" date that the patentee's rights became fixed and settled and the rights of the patent accrued, not the later publication date. * * *

In *Talbott* the court held that a foreign patent need not be publicly available to be "patented" under section 102(d). The court rejected the applicant's argument that the statutory bar did not apply because he had kept his German patent secret until after his U.S. filing date. 443 F.2d 1397 (CCPA 1971). *See also* Duplan Corp. v. Deering Milliken Research Corp., 487 F.2d 459 (4th Cir.1973), *cert. denied,* 415 U.S. 978, 39 L. Ed. 2d 874, 94 S. Ct. 1565 (1974) (An invention is "patented" in France under section 102(d) on its "délivré" date, the date on which the inventor's exclusive rights formally accrue, not on the later publication date when the patent is made publicly available.).

The import of the decisions in *Monks* and *Talbott* is that, contrary to Kathawala's argument, it is irrelevant under section 102(d) whether the Spanish patent was publicly available prior to the U.S. filing date. Rather, the Board correctly concluded that an invention is "patented" in a foreign country under section 102(d) when the patentee's rights under the patent become fixed. In the instant case, Kathawala stipulated that the Spanish patent was enforceable on January 21, 1985, the date the patent was granted and a date prior to the U.S. filing date. Hence, the Board correctly concluded that Kathawala's invention was "patented" in Spain prior to his U.S. filing date.

Kathawala's second argument is that the "invention" patented in Spain is not the same "invention" claimed in claims 1 and 2. Kathawala argues that each claim defines a separate invention, and since the Spanish claims are directed to processes for making the subject compounds, and claims 1 and 2 of the instant application are directed to the compounds themselves, the "invention" patented in Spain is not the same "invention" as that of claims 1 and 2. Hence Kathawala urges that the rejection of claims 1 and 2 under section 102(d) based on the Spanish patent was erroneous.

We do not agree. It is a truism that a claim defines an invention, and a claim to a composition is indeed different from a claim to a process. However, we cannot let rigid definitions be used in situations to which they don't apply to produce absurd results. The word "invention" in the Patent Act has many meanings depending on the context. In the present context, it must have a meaning consistent with the policy and purpose behind section 102(d), which is to require applicants for patent in the United States to exercise reasonable promptness in filing their applications after they have filed and obtained foreign patents.

Kathawala made an "invention" relating to a group of new compounds. He filed applications in Greece and Spain disclosing his invention as consisting of four different aspects: compounds, compositions, methods of use, and processes of making the compounds. While Kathawala had the potential to claim each of those aspects, and did so in his Greek application, he chose to claim only the processes in Spain because, he asserts, pharmaceutical compositions and methods of use were not patentable under Spanish patent law during the relevant time period.

Kathawala's understandable decision not to claim the compounds in Spain, however, does not permit him to evade the statutory bar by arguing that the Spanish Patent Office would not have allowed such claims. Similarly, neither would it have mattered if Kathawala had applied for compound claims and the Spanish Patent Office had rejected them. What is controlling is that the application that Kathawala filed in Spain disclosed and provided the opportunity to claim all aspects of his invention, including the compounds.

It would be contrary to the policy of the statute to permit an applicant to file a foreign application on an invention that may be claimed by four related types of claims, obtain a grant of whatever patent rights were available in the foreign country, and then file an application in the United States, after the foreign patent has issued and more than one year after the foreign filing date on the same invention, with claims directed to those aspects of the invention which were unpatentable in the foreign country. That would permit grant of a U.S. patent on what is essentially the same "invention" as that patented in the foreign country and would frustrate the policy underlying section 102(d), which is to encourage the filing of applications in the United States within a year of the foreign filing of a counterpart patent application. An applicant cannot evade the statutory bar by citing alleged defects of foreign law concerning scope of patentable subject matter.

We thus hold that when an applicant files a foreign application fully disclosing his invention and having the potential to claim his invention in a number of different ways, the reference in section 102(d) to "invention . . . patented" necessarily includes all disclosed aspects of the invention. Thus, the section 102(d) bar applies regardless whether the foreign patent contains claims to less than all aspects of the invention.

* * *

CONCLUSION

Because Kathawala filed Greek and Spanish applications on his "invention" more than one year before he filed an application on the same invention in the United States, and the foreign applications issued as patents prior to his U.S. filing date, Kathawala is barred under 35 U.S.C. § 102(d) from obtaining a U.S. patent. Accordingly, the decision of the Board is affirmed.

Note

Where Section 102(d) does not operate as a bar, under Section 119 an applicant for a United States patent may be able to establish priority based on the filing date of a foreign patent application. See Chapter 13.B.1(iii). Similar problems of interpretation arise under both provisions—*e.g.,* determining when a particular foreign grant constitutes a "patent" or "inventor's certificate," determining the date on which the foreign application was "filed" (which can be problematic when the foreign patent application process differs from the United States process), and determining whether the claimed inventions are the same.

4. OBVIOUSNESS AND STATUTORY BARS

There is some uncertainty on the question whether a reference which would operate as a statutory bar under Sections 102(b), (c), or (d) if it anticipated all the limitations of the invention in question should operate as a bar where it merely renders the invention obvious more than a year before the patent application is filed (rather than at the time of invention, as Section 103 requires). The Court of Customs and Patent Appeals held in *In re Foster,* 343 F.2d 980 (CCPA 1965) that Section 102(b) applies even where the subject matter in public use or on sale merely renders the claimed subject matter obvious. The *Foster* court noted that its conclusion was consistent with the history of both Sections 102(b) and 103:

> As to what the law has been, more particularly what it was prior to 1953, when the new patent act and its section 103 became effective, there is a paucity of direct precedents on the precise problem. We think there is a reason for this. Under the old law (R.S. 4886, where 102(b) finds its origin) patents were refused or invalidated on references dated more than a year before the filing date because the invention was anticipated or, if they were not, then because there was no "invention," the latter rejection being based either on (a) a single non-anticipatory reference plus the skill of the art or (b) on a plurality of references. There was no need to seek out the precise statutory basis because it was R.S. 4886 in any event, read in the light of the Supreme Court's interpretation of the law that there must always be "invention." This issue was determined on the disclosures of the references relied on and if they had dates more than one year before the filing date, it was

assumed they could be relied on to establish a "statutory bar." There was an express prohibition in Rule 131 and in its predecessor Rule 75 against antedating a reference having a date more than a year prior to the filing date and there was no basis on which to contest it. * * *

* * *

* * * [S]ection 103 had but a single purpose which was to add to the statute a provision to take the place of the judge-made "requirement for invention." In doing that, the history also shows, the words "at the time the invention was made" were included for the sole purpose of precluding the use of hindsight in deciding whether an invention is obvious. We are sure Congress had no intent thereby to modify the law respecting loss of right based on the existence of a time-bar. * * * The wrong in such a construction of the statute—beside giving it a meaning that was never intended—is that it permits an inventor to sleep on his rights more than a year after the invention has become entirely obvious to the public, whereby the public has potential possession of it, and still obtain a patent which will take the invention from the public, a result Congress could not possibly have intended in view of its express indication that section 102(b) is merely a continuation of the prior law.

343 F.2d at 988–89, 990 (footnote omitted). Should the obviousness standard apply to the other statutory bars?

F. PATENT SPECIFICATION

Statutes: 35 U.S.C.A. §§ 111–13

CHRISTIANSON v. COLT INDUSTRIES OPERATING CORP.

United States Court of Appeals, Seventh Circuit, 1989.
870 F.2d 1292, *cert. denied*, 493 U.S. 822, 110 S.Ct. 81, 107 L.Ed.2d 47 (1989).

FLAUM, CIRCUIT JUDGE:

* * *

[In the context of an antitrust action against Colt, Christianson challenged the validity of Colt's patents on various components of M–16 rifles, a battlefield weapon used by the U.S. Army. The district court held the patents invalid for failure to meet both the enablement and best mode requirements of Section 112, because they failed to disclose the specifications that would permit the parts to be interchangeable with all other M–16 rifles, an essential feature if the parts were to be marketed successfully as M–16 replacement parts for battlefield use. Colt appealed.]

* * *

A. ENABLEMENT

A patent is enabling when the disclosures made in the patent application are sufficient to allow a person skilled in the art to make and use the claimed invention. The requirement is designed to ensure that the subject matter of the claimed invention is generally in the possession of the public and ready to be reproduced following the expiration of the patent period. To determine whether the disclosure is enabling, a two-part analysis is employed. First, we must delimit the scope of the *claimed* invention. Second, we must look to the disclosures made in the patent to ascertain whether, given that level of disclosure, a person skilled in the art could successfully reproduce the claimed invention in its entire scope. Because only the claimed invention receives patent law protection, the disclosures need generally be no greater than the claim. If the invention can be reproduced in its entire scope, then the patent specifications are enabling.

In this case, the parties hotly contest the issue of the scope of the inventions. Christianson alleges that the inventions are improvements to parts specifically made for an M–16 rifle. As such, Christianson believes that the scope of the inventions includes the ability to use the inventions with every M–16 in existence—*i.e.*, to make the parts "interchangeable." To make the parts in each patent interchangeable, Colt would have had to have disclosed the specifications and tolerances which permit interchangeability. The district court, in granting summary judgment to Christianson, expressly adopted this analysis.

Colt, on the other hand, takes the position that the inventions have nothing to do with the M–16. Colt points out that the patent claims mention neither the M–16 nor interchangeability as features of the inventions. Thus, Colt believes the claims are simply for rifle parts and would delimit the scope of the invention without regard to the ability of the invention to interact with the M–16.

Christianson answers Colt's argument by pointing out that the Federal Circuit has held that the scope of the invention can sometimes exceed the claim actually made in the patent. White Consolidated Industries, Inc. v. Vega Servo–Control, 713 F.2d 788 (Fed.Cir.1983). In *White,* the invention at issue was for a system which controlled the operations performed by automated machinery through the use of a computer program. A key problem for the invention was to translate the language of the computer into a language that the machinery would understand and respond to. At the time the invention was patented, the only language translator available was a computer program called SPLIT, which was a trade secret of the Sundstrand Corporation, White's predecessor in interest. The Federal Circuit, while recognizing that the language translator was not claimed as part of the invention, nevertheless held that the failure to disclose its identity violated the enablement requirement of § 112. According to the court, the translator should have been disclosed since "it [was] an *integral part* of the disclosure necessary to enable those skilled in the art to 'make and use the same.'" *Id.* at 791 (emphasis added); *compare* International Telephone and Telegraph Corp. v. Raychem Corp., 538 F.2d 453, 460 (1st Cir.1976), *cert. denied,* 429 U.S. 886, 50 L. Ed. 2d 167, 97 S. Ct. 238 (1976) (no need to disclose compound which was not claimed to be part of the invention and was not "essential to the production of the patented" invention).

We think that *White* is inapposite to the facts of this case. The disclosure of SPLIT was required because it was an "integral part" of the invention—the invention would not work, even if all other information was disclosed, without disclosure of the program. In the instant case, the specifications and tolerances are not an "integral part" of the inventions. The inventions will work in a rifle, assuming all the other information about the inventions is disclosed, without any data regarding the specifications and tolerances required for commercial utilization of the inventions in the M–16. *See* DeGeorge [v. Bernier, 768 F.2d 1318, 1324 (Fed.Cir.1985)] (claim as to circuitry to be interfaced with word processor was enabling where there was disclosure of "detailed, *claimed* circuitry without requiring detailed disclosure of all related, *unclaimed* circuitry [in the word processor] with which TCCPI might be interfaced") (emphasis in original). Thus, the scope of Colt's inventions cover only the claims actually made, claims involving *rifle* parts, and do not cover the specifications and tolerances required to interchange the inventions with M–16s already in existence.

We now reach the second step of the enablement inquiry, which requires us to determine, given the scope of the inventions, whether sufficient information has been disclosed to allow a person skilled in the art to make and utilize the inventions. Christianson claims, in regard to this part of the analysis, that there is no evidence that enough information was supplied to enable one skilled in the art to use the inventions in *any* weapon. * * *

* * *

* * * It is undisputed that it would be a massive task to reverse engineer the parts so that they would be interchangeable with all other M–16s. But that is not inconsistent with [Colt's witness] Bredbury's testimony that the patent disclosures enable one skilled in the art to put the inventions to use in some other rifle that does not require interchangeable parts. Thus, no evidence in the record supports the plaintiff's assertion, accepted by the district court, that the information provided by Colt in the patents was non-enabling with respect to the claimed inventions. Instead, we agree with Colt that the unrebutted evidence shows that the patent disclosures for the claimed inventions were enabling.

B. BEST MODE

Section 112 requires that "the specification ... set forth the best mode contemplated by the inventor of carrying out the invention." Thus, if the applicant develops specific instrumentalities or techniques which are recognized as the best way to carry out the invention, then the best mode requirement obliges the applicant to disclose that information. The requirement contains a subjective standard; we will find non-compliance only if the patentee has concealed, whether knowingly or unwittingly, *his or her* preferred embodiment of the claimed invention. Again, the focus of the best mode requirement, as it was with the enablement requirement, is on the claimed invention. Thus, before determining whether there is evidence of concealment, the scope of the invention must be delimited.

The district court in this case, again adopting the plaintiff's analysis, determined that the scope of the claims involve inventions which are "fully interchangeable with the corresponding part in every M–16 ever produced." Christianson [v. Colt Industries Operating Corp., 609 F. Supp. 1174 (C.D.Ill.1985)], at 1181. The district court then went on to find that Colt failed to disclose the best mode of using those inventions because it omitted the specifications and tolerances necessary to make the parts interchangeable with M–16 rifles already in existence. However, as we discussed above in relation to the enablement requirement, the district court erred in its definition of the scope of the inventions. Nowhere in the claims is it stated that these inventions purport to be interchangeable with every M–16 ever produced or that the inventions have anything to do with the M–16 at all. The inventions are improvements to parts used in a rifle, any rifle, and we will look to those inventions to determine if the inventor has concealed his or her preferred embodiment.

Given that the claimed inventions involve parts for rifles, without specifying any particular brand of rifle, the district court's determination that Colt failed to disclose the best mode for using these inventions was unsupported by the record. The Federal Circuit [in a prior proceeding in this case] succinctly outlined the district court's error as follows:

> The best mode requirement assures that inventors do not conceal the best mode known to them when they file a patent application, but the "best mode" is that of practicing the *claimed* invention. *It has nothing to do with mass production or sales to customers having particular requirements.* (emphasis added) [*See* Indecor, Inc. v. Fox–Wells, Inc., 642 F.Supp. 1473, 1490 (S.D.N.Y.1986)]. In this case, interchangeability with M–16 parts appears nowhere as a limitation in any claim, and as Christianson concedes, the patents make no reference whatever to the M–16 rifle. Thus the best mode for making and using and carrying out the *claimed inventions* does not entail or involve either the M–16 rifle or interchangeability. The "best mode" for making and using the claimed parts relates to their use in *a* rifle, any rifle. There is nothing anywhere in the present record indicating that any of the patents fail to meet that requirement.

Christianson [v. Colt Industries Operating Corp., 822 F.2d 1544 (Fed.Cir. 1987)], at 1563 (emphasis in original except where otherwise noted). Thus, because this case is unlike cases where the best mode requirement has not been fulfilled because of some sort of concealment—*e.g.,* Union Carbide Corp. v. Borg–Warner Corp., 550 F.2d 355 (6th Cir.1977); Dana Corp. v. IPC Limited Partnership, 860 F.2d 415 (Fed.Cir.1988) (disclosure in patent for valve stem seal inadequate where fluoride surface treatment not disclosed; tests showed that the surface treatment was "necessary" to satisfactory performance of the seal)—we find no evidence in the record to support the district court's determination that Colt failed to disclose its preferred embodiment of these inventions.[8] Again, the evidence of record shows that Colt did disclose the best mode of carrying out its inventions.

* * *

IV.

For all the reasons discussed above, we REVERSE the decision of the district court and REMAND for further proceedings not inconsistent with this opinion.

Notes

1. Although *Christianson* was decided by the Seventh Circuit, its interpretation of Section 112 reflects Federal Circuit precedents.

2. Because the best mode requirement is subjective, and tends to lead to litigation over patent validity, the failed Patent Reform Act of 2005, H.R. 2795, would have eliminated the best mode requirement. Under current law, is the best mode requirement satisfied where: (a) the method disclosed in the application is the best mode known to the inventor, but not the best mode known to others? (b) the assignee of the patent application knows of a better mode at the time of filing, but does not disclose it to the inventor? (c) the inventor learns of a better mode after the application is filed?

3. *Precision Required by Section 112*: In *Georgia–Pacific Corp. v. United States Plywood Corporation,* 258 F.2d 124, 136–37 (2d Cir.1958), the Second Circuit noted that the purposes of Section 112, paragraphs 1 and 2, should determine how strictly the requirement of precision should be applied to a particular patent:

> We think that the district court was too rigorous in applying the requirement of precision. This requirement serves two primary purposes: those skilled in the art must be able to understand and apply the teachings of the invention and enterprise and experimentation must not be discouraged by the creation of an area of uncertainty as to the scope of the invention. On the other hand, the policy of the patent statute

---

8. Christianson objects, quite understandably, that if Colt can validly claim trade secret protection [for the specifications and tolerances which are essential to interchangeability and which were not disclosed in the patents], it will be able to protect its commercial products from competition even after the expiration of its patents. Christianson points out, and we agree, that the best mode requirement is intended to allow the public to compete fairly with the patentee following the expiration of the patents. *See* Phillips Petroleum Co. v. Sid Richardson Carbon & Gasoline Co., 293 F. Supp. 555, 558 n. 2 (N.D.Tex.1968) ("The price an inventor must pay for his seventeen year patent monopoly is a disclosure of the invention which would enable persons skilled in the pertinent art to practice it."). While we sympathize with Christianson's frustration in being unable to compete with Colt, and Christianson may yet prove that Colt has violated the antitrust laws, for the reasons discussed we cannot vindicate its attempt to rectify the situation through an attack on Colt's patent disclosures.

contemplates granting protection to valid inventions, and this policy would be defeated if protection were to be accorded only to those patents which were capable of precise definition. The judicial function requires a balancing of these competing considerations in the individual case.

It is true that the Supreme Court has stated that 'an invention must be capable of accurate definition, and it must be accurately defined, to be patentable,' United Carbon Co. v. Binney & Smith Co., 1942, 317 U.S. 228, 237, 63 S.Ct. 165, 170, 87 L.Ed. 232, and this Court recently stated that ' * * * the requirement of the Act for definiteness in the statement of claims must be strictly construed.' Such general statements, however, must be viewed in the context of circumstances. Objectionable indefiniteness must be determined by the facts in each case, not by reference to an abstract rule. If the subject matter of the patent is such that the patentee cannot verbalize his invention comprehensibly or is incapable of ascribing reasonable limits to his claims, regardless of intrinsic merit his invention cannot be patented. Likewise, the patentee is required to draft his specifications and claims as precisely as the subject matter permits, and his failure to do so may result in judicial invalidation of his patent.

On the other hand, patentable inventions cannot always be described in terms of exact measurements, symbols and formulae, and the applicant necessarily must use the meager tools provided by language, tools which admittedly lack exactitude and precision. If the claims, read in the light of the specifications, reasonably apprise those skilled in the art both of the utilization and scope of the invention, and if the language is as precise as the subject matter permits, the courts can demand no more. That an area of uncertainty necessarily exists in such a situation cannot be denied, but the existence of an inescapable area of uncertainty is not sufficient justification for denying to the patentee the fruits of his invention.

Id. at 136–37 (citations omitted).

Applying the Written Description Requirement to Biotech Patents

Complying with the written description requirement can be problematic in the case of certain types of inventions, such as biological materials. In *Regents of the University of California v. Eli Lilly & Co.,* 119 F.3d 1559 (Fed. Cir. 1997), the Federal Circuit held that the written description of a claimed microorganism containing human insulin cDNA was insufficient where the description failed to provide distinguishing information about the structure or physical characteristics of the claimed DNA sequence. The court noted that the written description requirement "requires a precise definition, such as by structure, formula, chemical name, or physical properties." *Id.* at 1566. By failing to provide such a definition, the patent applicants could not prove that they in fact were in possession of the complete and operative invention.

In 2001, the PTO issued new guidelines for patent examiners to use in applying the written description requirement. The guidelines provide that this requirement can be met by "show[ing] that an invention is complete by disclosure of sufficiently detailed, relevant identifying characteristics ... *i.e.,* complete or partial structure, other physical and/or chemical properties, functional characteristics when coupled with a known or disclosed correlation between function and structure, or some combination of such characteristics." Guidelines for Examination of Patent Applications under the 35 U.S.C. § 112, ¶ 1, "Written Description" Requirement, 66 Fed. Reg. 1099, 1106.

In *Enzo Biochem, Inc. v. Gen–Probe Inc.*, 323 F.3d 956 (Fed. Cir. 2002), the Federal Circuit announced that it would adopt the standard articulated in the new PTO guidelines to determine whether a description of biological materials complies with the written description requirement. In addition, the court held that the written description requirement may in some cases be satisfied by depositing the biological materials in a depository that is accessible to the public:

> Whether reference to a deposit of a nucleotide sequence may adequately describe that sequence is an issue of first impression in this court. In light of the history of biological deposits for patent purposes, the goals of the patent law, and the practical difficulties of describing unique biological materials in a written description, we hold that reference in the specification to a deposit in a public depository, which makes its contents accessible to the public when it is not otherwise available in written form, constitutes an adequate description of the deposited material sufficient to comply with the written description requirement of § 112, ¶ 1.

Id. at 965.

Although *Enzo* held that a deposit of biological materials could satisfy the written description requirement of Section 112 with respect to several of the claims at issue in that case, the court also remanded for a determination whether that requirement was satisfied with respect to other claims. Although the Federal Circuit denied a petition for rehearing en banc in *Enzo*, 323 F.3d 956 (Fed. Cir. 2002), several judges dissented from that denial. The dissenters argued that remand on these other claims was unnecessary, because no question of priority or enablement had been raised. They expressed the view that, absent a question of enablement, the purpose of requiring an adequate written description was merely to determine, in a priority dispute, whether claims added or broadened after the filing of the original patent application should receive the benefit of the earlier filing date because they pertained to an invention already fully disclosed in the original application. The dissenters' view echoes a panel's statement in *Amgen v. Hoechst Marion Roussel*, 314 F.3d 1313 (Fed. Cir. 2003), that "[t]he purpose of the written description requirement is to prevent an applicant from later asserting that he invented that which he did not; the applicant for a patent is therefore required to 'recount his invention in such detail that his future claims can be determined to be encompassed within his original creation.'" *Id.* at 1330 (citation omitted). Further, the dissenters in *Enzo* suggested that *Eli Lilly* itself should have been decided on the basis of non-enablement, rather than on failure to satisfy a written description requirement separate from enablement.

The Federal Circuit continues to be divided on the question whether, outside the context of a priority dispute, a description that is enabling may still be insufficient to satisfy the written description requirement. *Compare University of Rochester v. G.D. Searle & Co.*, 358 F.3d 916 (Fed. Cir. 2004) (panel opinion adhering to *Eli Lilly* and *Enzo*) *with id.*, 375 F.3d 1303, 1307–24 (Fed. Cir. 2004) (Rader, J., dissenting from denial of petition for rehearing en banc) *and id.*, 375 F.3d at 1325–27 (Linn, J., dissenting from denial of petition for rehearing en banc). Patent scholars are divided as well. *See id.*, 375 F.3d at 1314–24 (Rader, J., dissenting) (collecting scholarship).

In *Falko–Gunter Falkner v. Inglis*, 448 F.3d 1357, 1366–68 (Fed. Cir. 2006), the Federal Circuit offered further guidance on the adequacy of written description and enablement in biotech cases, holding that: (1) examples are not required to support the adequacy of a written description; (2) actual reduction to practice is not required in order to satisfy the written description standard; and (3) there is no per se rule that, when a claim limitation is directed to a macromolecular sequence, the specification must always recite the gene or sequence, regardless of whether it is known in the prior art.

G. DOUBLE PATENTING AND TERMINAL DISCLAIMERS

Statutes: 35 U.S.C.A. §§ 101, 253

IN RE LONGI
United States Court of Appeals, Federal Circuit, 1985.
759 F.2d 887.

DAVIS, CIRCUIT JUDGE.

[The PTO Board of Appeals affirmed the examiner's rejection of certain claims in appellants' application based on a holding of "obviousness-type" double patenting over the claims of three commonly-owned applications, and the patent applicants filed this appeal.]

* * *

DOUBLE PATENTING[4]

A. DOUBLE PATENTING—IN GENERAL

A double patenting rejection precludes one person from obtaining more than one valid patent for either (a) the "same invention," or (b) an "obvious" modification of the same invention. A rejection based on double patenting of the "same invention" type finds its support in the language of 35 U.S.C. § 101, which states that "Whoever invents or discovers any new and useful process ... may obtain *a* patent therefor.... " (Emphasis added.) Thus, the term "same invention," in this context means an invention drawn to identical subject matter. In re Vogel, 422 F.2d 438 (CCPA 1970).

---

4. We note that the Board did not make the instant rejection under § 103. However, a double patenting of the obviousness type rejection is "analogous to [a failure to meet] the non-obviousness requirement of 35 U.S.C. § 103," except that the patent principally underlying the double patenting rejection is not considered prior art. In re Braithwaite, 379 F.2d 594, 600 n. 4 (CCPA 1967). * * *

On the other hand, a rejection based upon double patenting of the *obviousness type* ((b), *supra*) is a judicially created doctrine grounded in public policy (a policy reflected in the patent statute) rather than based purely on the precise terms of the statute. The purpose of this rejection is to prevent the extension of the term of a patent, even where an express statutory basis for the rejection is missing, by prohibiting the issuance of the claims in a second patent not patentably distinct from the claims of the first patent. Carman Industries Inc. v. Wahl, 724 F.2d 932 (Fed.Cir.1983); *and* In re Thorington, 418 F.2d 528 (CCPA 1969), *cert. denied,* 397 U.S. 1038, 25 L.Ed.2d 649, 90 S.Ct. 1356 (1970). Fundamental to this doctrine is the policy that:

> The public should ... be able to act on the assumption that upon the *expiration* of the patent it will be free to use not only the invention claimed in the patent but also modifications or variants which would have been *obvious* to those of ordinary skill in the art at the time the invention was made, taking into account the skill of the art and prior art other than the invention claimed in the issued patent. (Emphasis in original.)

In re Zickendraht, 319 F.2d 225, 232 (CCPA 1963) (Rich, J., concurring). Under that facet of the doctrine of double patenting, we must direct our inquiry to whether the claimed invention in the application for the second patent would have been obvious from the subject matter of the claims in the first patent, in light of the prior art. *Carman Industries,* 724 F.2d at 940.

Appellants argue that clear lines of division among the respective groups of claims in the several applications have been maintained. They conclude that because there are no "conflicting claims" and the claims in these applications do not "overlap," double patenting does not exist. However, appellants confuse the difference between the two types of double patenting. Overlapping and conflicting claims are considerations more significant in a § 101 "same invention" double patenting analysis. These are not "significant or controlling" factors in an obviousness type double patenting analysis where a rejection may be applied to "clearly distinct inventions." In re Jentoft, 392 F.2d 633, 640 (CCPA 1968); *see also* In re Siu, 222 F.2d 267 (CCPA 1955). This type of double patenting rejection has been applied where there are separate inventions, each of which is considered patentable over the prior art absent the first patent. In re Bowers, 359 F.2d 886 (CCPA 1966). Thus, appellants' argument that the claimed inventions do not overlap is irrelevant.

Appellants also maintain that the entire doctrine of double patenting of the obviousness type should not apply to commonly-owned applications with different inventive entities. A rejection based upon such a doctrine, appellants say, is unduly restrictive and discourages group research. Moreover, each inventor in a research department should be entitled to separate patents for his or her own independent contribution to the basic objective of the overall research project. Such a broad position has been previously rejected, and it is inconsistent with both our precedents and recent legislation.

Many times our predecessor court, the Court of Customs and Patent Appeals, has treated commonly-owned applications by different inventors as though they were filed by the same inventor, and then relied upon the doctrine of double patenting of the obviousness type to deny a second patent on subject matter not patentably distinct from the claims of the first patent. See * * * In re Rogers, 394 F.2d 566 (CCPA 1968); In re Bowers, 359 F.2d 886 (CCPA 1966) * * *. In fact, the appellant in *In re Rogers* made an argument similar to the one the present appellant makes here. In that case, Rogers asserted that the obviousness type double patenting rejection was "distressing" to corporate practitioners and did not take into account the considerable exchange of information between inventors. The result, as the argument goes, would be that a corporation would find itself in a "box" because patent protection for both inventions would not be possible.

As we declared in that case, appellants, and those in like situations, are not in an inescapable "box." In re Rogers, *supra*, 394 F.2d at 571. A patent may still issue if an applicant faced with such a rejection were to file a terminal disclaimer under 35 U.S.C. § 253, disclaiming "any terminal part of the term ... of the patent," thereby guaranteeing that the second patent would expire at the same time as the first patent. It is well-established that a common assignee is entitled to proceed with a terminal disclaimer to overcome a rejection based on double patenting of the obviousness type. In re Bowers, *supra*, 359 F.2d 886 .. Since the second patent would expire simultaneously with the first, this use of a terminal disclaimer is consistent with the policy that the public should be free to use the invention as well as any obvious modifications at the end of the patent's term. In re Robeson, 331 F.2d 610, 614 (CCPA 1964).

* * *

[The court affirmed the Board's decision upholding rejection of the claims.]

CARMAN INDUSTRIES, INC. v. WAHL

United States Court of Appeals, Federal Circuit, 1983.
724 F.2d 932.

SMITH, CIRCUIT JUDGE.

[Carman Industries sought a declaratory judgment that Wahl's utility patent was invalid on the ground, inter alia, of double patenting, in light of an earlier design patent issued to Wahl and allegedly covering the same subject matter.]

* * *

As a matter of legal theory, double patenting between a design and a utility patent presents significant problems. Judicial and scholarly criticism has been leveled at the concept of applying double patenting between a design and a utility patent. Design and utility patents are based on different statutory provisions and involve different subject matter. The scope of protection afforded by each type of patent is different. It has been asserted that these differences entirely obviate double patenting in the design-utility setting. However, there exists CCPA precedent to the effect that a double patenting rejection of a pending design or utility patent application can be sustained on the basis of a previously issued utility or design patent, respectively.[15]

The Third Circuit in *Wahl [v. Rexnord]* reversed a summary judgment of invalidity which was based on double patenting, because of the existence of material issues of fact regarding the "identity" of the claimed design and utility inventions. In doing so, the court held that double patenting can exist between a design patent and a utility patent despite the differences in subject matter with which each type of patent is concerned. The test applied by the Third Circuit to determine whether double patenting exists is whether the two patents "cross-read," *i.e.*, claim the same thing:[16]

> To say that patents cross-read means that a device embodying the patentable design of the design patent *must* infringe the utility patent; *and* that a device embodying the patentable claims of the utility patent *must* infringe the design patent. * * * [Emphasis in original.]

In adopting the cross-reading standard, the Third Circuit in Wahl followed the decision in *Ropat Corp. v. McGraw–Edison Co.,*[17] in which the Seventh Circuit sought to explain the CCPA holdings in *In re Hargraves*[18] and *In re Dubois:*[19]

> Those cases state that double patenting exists if the feature in which the novel esthetic effect resides is the identical feature which produces the novel function so that a structure embodying the mechanical invention would of necessity embody the design, and vice versa.

We agree with the above analysis that double patenting will be found in a design/utility situation if the two patents cross-read. Further, the precedent of this court supports a broader test of double patenting,

15. [In re Thorington, 418 F.2d 528 (CCPA 1969), *cert. denied* 397 U.S. 1038, 25 L.Ed.2d 649, 90 S.Ct. 1356 (1970)] (affirming rejection of claims for a fluorescent light bulb in view of previously issued design patent for same device); In re Phelan, 205 F.2d 183 (CCPA 1953) (affirming double patenting rejection of utility claims for a finger ring in view of earlier issued design patent); In re Barber, 81 F.2d 231 (CCPA 1936) (affirming double patenting rejection of design claim for a flashlight cap and hanger ring because of lack of patentable distinction between claimed design and earlier utility patent); In re Hargraves, 53 F.2d 900 (CCPA 1931) (affirming double patent-ing rejection of claims covering a balloon tire construction in view of previously is-sued design patent).

16. [Wahl v. Rexnord, 624 F.2d 1169, 1179 (3d Cir.1980).]

17. Ropat Corp. v. McGraw–Edison Co., 535 F.2d 378, 381 (7th Cir.1976). *See also* Transmatic, Inc. v. Gulton Ind., Inc., 601 F.2d 904, 910 (6th Cir.1979); *Wahl,* 624 F.2d at 1179.

18. *Hargraves,* 19 C.C.P.A. 784, 53 F.2d 900.

19. In re Dubois, 46 C.C.P.A. 744, 262 F.2d 88 (CCPA 1958).

encompassing the double patenting of obvious variations as well as of the same invention. However, rather than focusing on the point of novelty, we wish to clarify that double patenting is determined by analysis of the claims as a whole.[20]

Double patenting, as applied between a design and a utility patent, is a judicially created doctrine based purely on the public policy of preventing extension of the term of a patent, even where an express statutory basis for the doctrine is lacking. Double patenting may be found in a design/utility setting "irrespective of whether the patent relied on in the rejection and the application [or patent] on appeal involve the same invention, or whether they involve inventions which are obvious variations of one another."[21] In the former situation ("same invention"-type) the test is whether the design and the utility patent claim the same subject matter. In the latter situation ("obviousness"-type), the test is whether the subject matter of the claims of the patent sought to be invalidated would have been obvious from the subject matter of the claims of the other patent, and vice versa. In considering that question, the disclosure of the "reference" patent may not be used as prior art. In certain situations, however, it may be used to define terms in a claim and to determine whether the embodiment claimed has been modified in an obvious manner.[22]

In applying the above tests, there is a heavy burden of proof on one seeking to show double patenting. Double patenting is rare in the context of utility versus design patents.

We now turn to examine the facts relating to double patenting in terms of the above guidelines. The '068 (design) patent claims the visible external surface configuration of a storage bin flow promoter * * *. The claims of the '508 (utility) patent, on the other hand, are drawn to the interior construction of a flow promoter. The exterior appearance of the invention claimed in the '068 patent does not dictate the interior structure, nor does the exterior appearance disclose the function, of the invention claimed in the '508 patent. It is possible, and fully in accordance with the construction given the claims by the district court, to practice the invention claimed in the '508 patent without utilizing the claimed design. Moreover, the court found that Vibra had indeed practiced the invention claimed in the '508 patent without utilizing the design claimed in the '068 patent. Thus, the '508 patent does not claim the "same" invention as does the '068 patent.

The question then becomes whether one patent claims an obvious variation of that which the other patent claims, and vice versa. With respect to that question, Carman has failed to sustain the heavy burden referred to above. The record is wholly inadequate to establish that it would have been obvious to a person of ordinary skill in the art to make

20. In re Swett, 59 C.C.P.A. 726, 451 F.2d 631 (CCPA 1971).

21. *Thorington*, 418 F.2d at 537. * * *

22. In re Vogel, 57 C.C.P.A. 920, 422 F.2d 438, 441–42 (CCPA 1970) (affirming in part a double patenting rejection in a utility/utility situation).

the interior of the device according to the claims of the '508 (utility) patent simply from knowledge of the exterior configuration of the device claimed in the '068 (design) patent. Thus, even if it would have been obvious to make the invention claimed in the design patent in view of the subject matter claimed in the utility patent by simply designing the exterior and interior walls of the material-receiving member to be parallel, as Carman has attempted to prove, that alone is insufficient to establish double patenting in accordance with the two-way test set forth above.

We hold that, under the above guidelines, the '508 patent does not claim the same invention as, or an obvious variation of, the invention claimed in the '068 patent. Thus, the design patent did not, in effect, extend the beginning of the term of the utility patent. For the above reasons, the '508 patent is not invalid for double patenting. * * *

* * *

Notes

1. The judicially-created doctrine of double-patenting prohibits issuing more than one patent for the same invention (or obvious variations of an invention) either to a single inventorship entity or to the common assignee of several such entities. Although, as *Carman* illustrates, courts have on occasion found utility/design double patenting, the doctrine has been applied more frequently where both patents at issue are utility patents.

Double patenting of the "same invention" type involves patents claiming identical inventions, and is absolutely prohibited. Double patenting of the "obviousness" type involves a patent claiming subject matter that is obvious in light of the subject matter claimed (rather than merely disclosed) in another patent. Either type of double patenting will invalidate a patent, although, as discussed below, the use of a terminal disclaimer may avoid "obviousness" type double patenting.

The double patenting bar has been justified on the ground that it prohibits extending the duration of a patent for a single invention beyond the statutory term. How is this justification affected by the fact that patent terms are now measured from the date of filing rather than the date of issue? See 35 U.S.C.A. § 154(a)(2).

Another justification for the double patenting bar is that it reduces the risk that an accused infringer will be harassed by suits from multiple assignees. How persuasive is this argument?

2. A terminal disclaimer can be used to avoid invalidation of a patent only due to "obviousness-type" double patenting. *See, e.g., Ortho Pharmaceutical Corp. v. Smith,* 959 F.2d 936, 940 (Fed.Cir.1992). One rationale for allowing a terminal disclaimer to "cure" such a double patenting problem is that this approach encourages early filing of a patent application (and thus early disclosure of the invention), because the inventor is less inclined to delay in order to determine if additional claims should be added. Also, by permitting later filings related to that same invention, the terminal disclaimer encourages disclosure of further developments related to the invention.

Were the terminal disclaimer unavailable to avoid invalidation due to double patenting, an inventor might be more likely to delay issuance of a patent by filing a continuation-in-part application. (See Chapter 13.B.1(i).)

PTO Rule 321 requires a terminal disclaimer to include a provision stating that the patents involved will be enforceable only when owned by the same party. What purpose does this requirement serve?

3. If the application of Sections 102 and 103 indicates that a claim is invalid on grounds of novelty, obviousness or a statutory bar, double patenting is not at issue. The double-patenting issue only arises where neither of the patents in question is "prior art" as to the other. Thus, for example, a terminal disclaimer will not avoid a rejection on obviousness grounds. *See, e.g., In re Fong,* 378 F.2d 977, 979–80 n. 1 (CCPA 1967) (a terminal disclaimer "cannot, of course, obviate a rejection based on obviousness in view of prior art under 35 U.S.C. § 103"); *In re Bartfeld,* 925 F.2d 1450 (Fed.Cir.1991) (terminal disclaimer cannot overcome 102(e)/103 rejection despite common ownership).

4. At what point should a patentee no longer be permitted to file a terminal disclaimer? After the patent has issued? After an infringement has occurred? After the infringement suit has been filed? After the double patenting defense has been raised by the accused infringer (or has been raised in a declaratory judgment action)?

5. Would a plant patent and a utility patent for the same plant constitute double patenting? What about a utility patent and a plant variety protection certificate?

6. Where subject matter is disclosed, but not claimed, in a patent, will it support rejection of a later patent application by the same inventor on the grounds of novelty? Obviousness? Double patenting?

Chapter 13

INVENTORSHIP, OWNERSHIP, AND PROSECUTION

A. INVENTORSHIP AND OWNERSHIP

Statutes: 35 U.S.C.A. §§ 101, 115–18, 256, 261–62

1. JOINT INVENTORS

(i) Collaboration

KIMBERLY–CLARK CORP. v. PROCTER & GAMBLE DISTRIBUTING CO., INC.

United States Court of Appeals, Federal Circuit, 1992.
973 F.2d 911.

LOURIE, CIRCUIT JUDGE.

* * *

[A priority dispute under 35 U.S.C. § 291 arose between Kimberly–Clark (K–C) and Proctor & Gamble (P & G), involving their conflicting patents for leakproof diapers with elasticized flaps. The Enloe patent, on which K–C relies, issued in November of 1987 based on an idea which Kenneth Enloe conceived in 1982. The Lawson patent, on which P & G relies, issued in September of 1987 based on an idea which P & G's Michael Lawson conceived in 1985. Lawson worked alone and, until his patent had already issued, was unaware of earlier work done by other P & G employees, including Kenneth Buell, who in 1979 and 1982 had made a disposable diaper with elasticized flaps. The district court awarded priority to the Enloe patent, thus invalidating certain claims of the Lawson patent. The court also denied P & G's request to order the naming of Buell and Blevins (another P & G employee), along with Lawson, as inventors of the Lawson patent pursuant to 35 U.S.C. § 256.]

* * *

P & G argues that the district court erred in holding that P & G was not entitled to priority. In particular, P & G urges that the invention of the Lawson patent was jointly made by Buell, Blevins, and Lawson, satisfying the joint inventor requirements of 35 U.S.C. § 116; through error without any deceptive intention, see 35 U.S.C. § 256, Buell and Blevins were not named as co-inventors along with Lawson. P & G argues that if the district court had corrected the inventorship of the Lawson patent, P & G would then have been given the benefit of the date of Buell's work in March 1979 and February 1982. The Lawson patent would thus have priority over K–C's Enloe patent, which is based on work performed in the spring of 1982.

The district court based its contrary holding, at least in part, on a finding that Lawson knew nothing of the earlier work of Buell upon which P & G now relies * * *.

P & G argues that the 1984 amendment to section 116 defines inventorship more broadly to eliminate any collaboration requirement; it argues that two or more people can be joint inventors even if they know nothing of each others' work.

* * *

Prior to its amendment in 1984, Section 116 provided in pertinent part:

> When an invention is made by two or more persons *jointly*, they shall apply for patent jointly and each sign the application and make the required oath, except as otherwise provided in this title.

(Emphasis added.) It is undisputed that this language required some form of collaboration in order that an "invention" be "made by two or more persons jointly." * * *

After the 1984 amendment, the first sentence of Section 116 remained unchanged, continuing to limit application of the statute to cases in which "an invention is made by two or more persons jointly.... " The amendment added a second sentence to the statute, so that it now reads:

> When an invention is made by two or more persons *jointly*, they shall apply for patent jointly and each make the required oath, except as otherwise provided in this title. *Inventors may apply for a patent jointly even though (1) they did not physically work together or at the same time, (2) each did not make the same type or amount of contribution, or (3) each did not make a contribution to the subject matter of every claim of the patent.*

35 U.S.C. § 116 (1988) (emphasis added). Contrary to P & G's argument, the statute neither states nor implies that two inventors can be "joint inventors" if they have had no contact whatsoever and are completely unaware of each other's work. Indeed, whether inventors "physically work together" would be irrelevant if Congress did not intend that they interact together in some fashion.

P & G also argues that the legislative history of the 1984 amendments to Section 116 shows that collaboration is not a requirement. We disagree, as that history shows that Congress intended to clarify the law of joint inventorship by codifying the principles stated in Monsanto [Co. v. Kamp, 269 F. Supp. 818, 824 (D.D.C.1967)].

* * *

The court in *Monsanto* stated the pertinent principles as follows:

A joint invention is the product of *collaboration* of the inventive endeavors of two or more persons *working toward the same end* and producing an invention by their *aggregate* efforts. To constitute a joint invention, it is necessary that each of the inventors work on the same subject matter and make some contribution to the inventive thought and to the final result. Each needs to perform but a part of the task if an invention emerges from all of the steps taken together. It is not necessary that the entire inventive concept should occur to each of the joint inventors, or that the two should physically work on the project together. One may take a step at one time, the other an approach at different times. One may do more of the experimental work while the other makes suggestions from time to time. The fact that each of the inventors plays a different role and that the contribution of one may not be as great as that of another does not detract from the fact that the invention is joint if each makes some original contribution, though partial, to the final solution of the problem.

Monsanto, 269 F. Supp. at 824 (emphasis added). *Monsanto* clearly contemplated collaboration, working together, even if not physically.

Contrary to P & G's argument, the companion amendment to Section 103 [which added the final sentence of that section] does not indicate that the collaboration requirement of Section 116 was eliminated. A purpose of the 1984 amendment to Section 103 was to overturn a line of cases under which a prior invention which was not public could be treated under Section 102(g) as prior art for purposes of Section 103 with respect to a later invention made by another employee of the same organization. 130 Cong. Rec. H28071 (Oct. 1, 1984), *reprinted in* 1984 U.S.C.C.A.N. 5833–34 (discussing the problems caused by In re Bass, 474 F.2d 1276 (CCPA 1973) and In re Clemens, 622 F.2d 1029 (CCPA 1980)).

The practical consequence of these decisions was that research organizations were given an incentive to discourage information sharing and collaboration among their researchers, thus impeding research, because one inventor's unpublished work might be prior art against another's. Congress amended Section 103 to eliminate this problem and thereby to encourage team research. *Id.*

* * *

What is clear is that the statutory word "jointly" is not mere surplusage. For persons to be joint inventors under Section 116, there must be some element of joint behavior, such as collaboration or working under common direction, one inventor seeing a relevant report and building upon it or hearing another's suggestion at a meeting. Here there was nothing of that nature. Individuals cannot be joint inventors if they are completely ignorant of what each other has done until years after their individual independent efforts. They cannot be totally independent of each other and be joint inventors.

We therefore hold that joint inventorship under Section 116 requires at least some quantum of collaboration or connection. Thus, the district court was correct in finding that Lawson was the sole inventor of P & G's Lawson patent and that P & G was not entitled to the effective priority date of Buell's work. Enloe's earliest effective priority date in the spring of 1982 therefore antedated the earliest date to which Lawson might be entitled, viz., January 1985. We accordingly affirm the district court's judgment with respect to priority, including the invalidity of the claims * * * of the Lawson patent.

* * *

(ii) Conception and Experimentation

BURROUGHS WELLCOME CO. v. BARR LABORATORIES, INC.

United States Court of Appeals, Federal Circuit, 1994.
40 F.3d 1223.

MAYER, CIRCUIT JUDGE.

Barr Laboratories, Inc., Novopharm, Inc., and Novopharm, Ltd., appeal the order of the United States District Court for the Eastern District of North Carolina, *Burroughs Wellcome Co. v. Barr Lab., Inc.*, 828 F.Supp. 1208 (E.D.N.C.1993), granting the motion of Burroughs Wellcome Co. for judgment as a matter of law that six United States patents were not invalid and were infringed. We affirm in part, vacate in part, and remand.

BACKGROUND

Burroughs Wellcome Co. is the owner of six United States patents that cover various preparations of 3'-azidothymidine (AZT) and methods for using that drug in the treatment of persons infected with the human immunodeficiency virus (HIV). Each of these patents names the same five inventors—Janet Rideout, David Barry, Sandra Lehrman, Martha St. Clair, and Phillip Furman (Burroughs Wellcome inventors)—all of whom were employed by Burroughs Wellcome at the time the inventions were alleged to have been conceived. The defendants-appellants concede that all five are properly named as inventors on the patents.

* * *

In the early 1980s, scientists began to see patients with symptoms of an unknown disease of the immune system, now known as AIDS. The disease attacks and destroys certain white blood cells known as CD4 T-lymphocytes or T-cells, which form an important component of the body's immune system. The level of destruction eventually becomes so great that the immune system is no longer able to mount an effective response to infections that pose little threat to a healthy person.

In mid–1984, scientists discovered that AIDS was caused by a retrovirus, known as HTLV III or, more commonly today, HIV. After the identification of HIV, Burroughs Wellcome began to search for a cure, screening compounds for antiretroviral activity using two murine (or mouse) retroviruses, the Friend leukemia virus and the Harvey sarcoma virus.

At about this time, scientists at the National Institutes of Health (NIH), led by Samuel Broder, were looking for effective AIDS therapies as well. Unlike Burroughs Wellcome, Broder and his colleagues used live HIV, and were able to develop a test that could demonstrate a compound's effectiveness against HIV in humans using a unique line of T-cell clones (the ATH8 cell line). The NIH scientists began to seek compounds from private pharmaceutical companies for screening in their cell line. After Burroughs Wellcome contacted Broder in the fall of 1984, he agreed to accept compounds from Burroughs Wellcome under code for testing against live HIV.

Burroughs Wellcome's Rideout selected AZT and a number of other compounds for testing in the murine screens on October 29, 1984. The tests, performed at Burroughs Wellcome facilities by St. Clair, showed that AZT had significant activity against both murine retroviruses at low concentrations.

In light of these positive results, the Burroughs Wellcome inventors met on December 5, 1984, to discuss patenting the use of AZT in the treatment of AIDS. Burroughs Wellcome's patent committee thereafter recommended that the company prepare a patent application for future filing. By February 6, 1985, the company had prepared a draft application for filing in the United Kingdom. The draft disclosed using AZT to treat patients infected with HIV, and set out various pharmaceutical formulations of the compound in an effective dosage range to treat HIV infection.

Two days earlier, on February 4, 1985, Burroughs Wellcome had sent a sample of AZT, identified only as Compound S, to Broder at NIH. In an accompanying letter, Lehrman told Broder of the results of the murine retrovirus tests and asked that he screen the compound for activity against HIV in the ATH8 cell line. Another NIH scientist, Hiroaka Mitsuya, performed the test in mid-February 1985, and found that Compound S was active against HIV. Broder informed Lehrman of the results by telephone on February 20, 1985. Burroughs Wellcome filed its patent application in the United Kingdom on March 16, 1985.

After Burroughs Wellcome learned that AZT was active against HIV, it began the process of obtaining Food and Drug Administration (FDA) approval for AZT as an AIDS therapy. As a part of the clinical trials leading to FDA approval, Broder and another NIH scientist, Robert Yarchoan, conducted a Phase I human patient study which showed that treatment with AZT could result in an increase in the patient's T-cell count. Broder reported this result to Lehrman on July 23, 1985. In 1987, the FDA approved AZT for marketing by Burroughs Wellcome; Burroughs Wellcome markets the drug for treatment of HIV infection under the trademark Retrovir.

On March 19, 1991, Barr Laboratories, Inc. (Barr) sought FDA approval to manufacture and market a generic version of AZT by filing an Abbreviated New Drug Application (ANDA) pursuant to 21 U.S.C. § 355(j) (1988). As part of the process, Barr certified to the FDA that Burroughs Wellcome's patents were invalid or were not infringed by the product described in its ANDA. After Barr informed Burroughs Wellcome of its action, Burroughs Wellcome commenced this case for patent infringement against Barr on May 14, 1991, alleging technical infringement of its patents under 35 U.S.C. § 271(e)(2)(A) (1988).

Barr filed a counterclaim under 35 U.S.C. § 256 (1988) seeking correction of the patents to list Broder and Mitsuya as coinventors. Barr admitted that its AZT product would infringe the patents, but contended that it did not because Barr had obtained a license to manufacture and sell AZT from the government, which should be deemed the owner of the interest of coinventors Broder and Mitsuya in the AZT patents. Burroughs Wellcome denied that Broder and Mitsuya were coinventors and also responded that the assertion of any rights of Broder, Mitsuya, or the government in the patents was barred by laches, estoppel, and waiver.

Thereafter, Novopharm, Ltd. filed an ANDA of its own, seeking approval to manufacture and market its generic version of AZT. Burroughs Wellcome filed infringement suits against Novopharm, Ltd. and its American subsidiary Novopharm, Inc., which were consolidated with the suit against Barr. Like Barr, Novopharm, Ltd. admitted that its AZT product would infringe the claims of the six patents, but for the failure of Burroughs Wellcome to name the NIH scientists as coinventors of the subject matter of the patents. Although Novopharm, Inc. agreed to be bound by any injunction issued against its parent, it argued that it had not infringed the patents because it had not filed an ANDA and had no AZT product of its own. Novopharm contended that Broder and Mitsuya should have been named as inventors on five of the patents, and contended that Broder and Yarchoan were coinventors of the '750 patent. It maintained that the patents were invalid because of the alleged nonjoinder, and because Burroughs Wellcome had omitted the coinventors with deceptive intent, the patents were unenforceable for inequitable conduct.

After more than three weeks of trial, while Burroughs Wellcome was still in the process of presenting its case, the district court granted Burroughs Wellcome's motion for judgment as a matter of law against all of the defendants, concluding that the Burroughs Wellcome inventors had conceived of the subject matter of the inventions at some time before

February 6, 1985, without the assistance of Broder, Mitsuya, or Yarchoan. The court rejected the arguments of Barr and Novopharm that they should be allowed to present evidence that the Burroughs Wellcome inventors had no reasonable belief that the inventions would actually work—that AZT was in fact active against HIV—until they were told the results of the NIH testing.

* * *

DISCUSSION

The arguments of both Barr and Novopharm are directed to when the inventors conceived the invention. Burroughs Wellcome says it was before they learned the results of the NIH tests; Barr and Novopharm say that confirmation of the inventions' operability, which came from the NIH tests, was an essential part of the inventive process. If Burroughs Wellcome is right, then the patents name the proper inventors, they are not invalid, and the appellants are liable for infringement. If Barr and Novopharm are correct, then Broder, Mitsuya, and Yarchoan should have been named as joint inventors and the resolution of Burroughs Wellcome's infringement suits is premature.

* * *

A joint invention is the product of a collaboration between two or more persons working together to solve the problem addressed. 35 U.S.C. § 116 (1988); *Kimberly-Clark Corp. v. Procter & Gamble Distrib. Co.,* 973 F.2d 911, 917 (Fed.Cir.1992). People may be joint inventors even though they do not physically work on the invention together or at the same time, and even though each does not make the same type or amount of contribution. 35 U.S.C. § 116. The statute does not set forth the minimum quality or quantity of contribution required for joint inventorship.

Conception is the touchstone of inventorship, the completion of the mental part of invention. *Sewall v. Walters,* 21 F.3d 411, 415 (Fed.Cir. 1994). It is "the formation in the mind of the inventor, of a definite and permanent idea of the complete and operative invention, as it is hereafter to be applied in practice." *Hybritech Inc. v. Monoclonal Antibodies, Inc.,* 802 F.2d 1367, 1376 (Fed.Cir.1986) (citation omitted). Conception is complete only when the idea is so clearly defined in the inventor's mind that only ordinary skill would be necessary to reduce the invention to practice, without extensive research or experimentation. *Sewall,* 21 F.3d at 415; *see also Coleman v. Dines,* 754 F.2d 353, 359 (Fed.Cir.1985) (conception must include every feature of claimed invention). Because it is a mental act, courts require corroborating evidence of a contemporaneous disclosure that would enable one skilled in the art to make the invention. *Coleman v. Dines,* 754 F.2d at 359.

Thus, the test for conception is whether the inventor had an idea that was definite and permanent enough that one skilled in the art could understand the invention; the inventor must prove his conception by corroborating evidence, preferably by showing a contemporaneous disclosure. An idea is definite and permanent when the inventor has a specific, settled idea, a particular solution to the problem at hand, not just a general goal or research plan he hopes to pursue. *See Fiers v. Revel,* 984 F.2d 1164, 1169 (Fed.Cir.1993); *Amgen, Inc. v. Chugai Pharmaceutical Co.,* 927 F.2d 1200, 1206 (Fed.Cir.1991) (no conception of chemical compound based solely on its biological activity). The conception analysis necessarily turns on the inventor's ability to describe his invention with particularity. Until he can do so, he cannot prove possession of the complete mental picture of the invention. These rules ensure that patent rights attach only when an idea is so far developed that the inventor can point to a definite, particular invention.

But an inventor need not know that his invention will work for conception to be complete. *Applegate v. Scherer,* 332 F.2d 571, 573 (CCPA 1964). He need only show that he had the idea; the discovery that an invention actually works is part of its reduction to practice. *Id.; see also Oka v. Youssefyeh,* 849 F.2d 581, 584 n. 1 (Fed.Cir.1988).

Barr and Novopharm suggest that the inventor's definite and permanent idea must include a reasonable expectation that the invention will work for its intended purpose. They argue that this expectation is of paramount importance when the invention deals with uncertain or experimental disciplines, where the inventor cannot reasonably believe an idea will be operable until some result supports that conclusion. Without some experimental confirmation, they suggest, the inventor has only a hope or an expectation, and has not yet conceived the invention in sufficiently definite and permanent form. But this is not the law. An inventor's belief that his invention will work or his reasons for choosing a particular approach are irrelevant to conception. *MacMillan v. Moffett,* 432 F.2d 1237, 1239 (CCPA 1970).

To support their reasonable expectation rule, Barr and Novopharm point to a line of cases starting with *Smith v. Bousquet,* 111 F.2d 157 (CCPA 1940), establishing the so-called doctrine of simultaneous conception and reduction to practice. *Smith* was an interference priority contest between alleged inventors of the use of two known compounds as insecticides. Both parties asserted priority based on testing of the compounds against selected insect species. Noting the unpredictability of the experimental sciences of chemistry and biology, in particular the uncertain relationship between chemical structure and biological activity, *Smith* declined to find conception until the invention had been reduced to practice by the filing of the first patent application. *Id.* at 162. Barr and Novopharm read this and subsequent cases to establish, or at least support, their rule that conception of an invention in an unpredictable field occurs only when the inventor has reasonable grounds to believe the invention will work.

But these cases do not stand for the proposition that an inventor can never conceive an invention in an unpredictable or experimental field until reduction to practice. In rejecting the asserted evidence of conception, *Smith* said as to one of the compounds:

it is apparent from the record that neither [party] had in mind at the time the suggestions were originally made, nor at any time thereafter, until successful tests, if any, were made, what insects, if any, it might be effective against, or how it might be applied to produce the desired results. Accordingly, neither party had a definite idea of the "complete and operative invention" here involved prior to a successful reduction—actual or constructive—of it to practice.

Id. Thus, in awarding priority to Smith based on his constructive reduction to practice, the court relied not on the inherent unpredictability of the science, but on the absence of any evidence to corroborate an earlier conception for either of the parties.

It is undoubtedly true that "[i]n some instances, an inventor is unable to establish a conception until he has reduced the invention to practice through a successful experiment." *Amgen,* 927 F.2d at 1206; *Alpert v. Slatin,* 305 F.2d 891, 894 (CCPA 1962) (no conception "where results at each step do not follow as anticipated, but are achieved empirically by what amounts to trial and error"). But in such cases, it is not merely because the field is unpredictable; the alleged conception fails because, as in *Smith,* it is incomplete. Then the event of reduction to practice in effect provides the only evidence to corroborate conception of the invention.

Under these circumstances, the reduction to practice can be the most definitive corroboration of conception, for where the idea is in constant flux, it is not definite and permanent. A conception is not complete if the subsequent course of experimentation, especially experimental failures, reveals uncertainty that so undermines the specificity of the inventor's idea that it is not yet a definite and permanent reflection of the complete invention as it will be used in practice. *See Amgen,* 927 F.2d at 1207 (no conception until reduction to practice where others tried and failed to clone gene using suggested strategy); *Rey-Bellet v. Engelhardt,* 493 F.2d 1380, 1387 (CCPA 1974) (focusing on nature of subsequent research as indicator that inventors encountered no perplexing intricate difficulties). It is this factual uncertainty, not the general uncertainty surrounding experimental sciences, that bears on the problem of conception.

Barr and Novopharm argue for a broader reading of *Amgen* and *Fiers* in support of their reasonable expectation rule. Both of these cases involve conception of a DNA encoding a human protein—a chemical compound. Conception of a chemical substance includes knowledge of both the specific chemical structure of the compound and an operative method of making it. *Fiers,* 984 F.2d at 1169; *Amgen,* 927 F.2d at 1206; *Oka,* 849 F.2d at 583. The alleged inventors in *Fiers* and *Amgen* claimed conception of their respective inventions before they knew relevant chemical structure—the nucleotide sequence—so the courts found no conception until experimentation finally revealed that structure. Here, though, Burroughs Wellcome's inventions use a compound of known structure; the method of making the compound is also well known.

We emphasize that we do not hold that a person is precluded from being a joint inventor simply because his contribution to a collaborative effort is experimental. Instead, the qualitative contribution of each collaborator is the key—each inventor must contribute to the joint arrival at a definite and permanent idea of the invention as it will be used in practice.

Nor do we suggest that a bare idea is all that conception requires. The idea must be definite and permanent in the sense that it involves a specific approach to the particular problem at hand. It must also be sufficiently precise that a skilled artisan could carry out the invention without undue experimentation. And, of course, the alleged conception must be supported by corroborating evidence. On the facts before us, it is apparent that the district court correctly ruled against Barr and Novopharm as to five of the patents, but that the court's judgment as to the sixth, the '750 patent, was premature.

The '232, '838, '130, '208, and '538 patents encompass compositions and methods of using AZT to treat AIDS. The Burroughs Wellcome inventors claim conception of these inventions prior to the NIH experiments, based on the draft British patent application. That document is not itself a conception, for conception occurs in the inventors' minds, not on paper. The draft simply corroborates the claim that they had formulated a definite and permanent idea of the inventions by the time it was prepared.

The Burroughs Wellcome inventors set out with the general goal of finding a method to treat AIDS, but by the time Broder confirmed that AZT was active against HIV, they had more than a general hope or expectation. They had thought of the particular antiviral agent with which they intended to address the problem, and had formulated the idea of the inventions to the point that they could express it clearly in the form of a draft patent application, which Barr and Novopharm concede would teach one skilled in the art to practice the inventions. The draft expressly discloses the intended use of AZT to treat AIDS. It sets out the compound's structure, which, along with at least one method of preparation, was already well known. The draft also discloses in detail both how to prepare a pharmaceutical formulation of AZT and how to use it to treat a patient infected with HIV. The listed dosages, dose forms, and routes of administration conform to those eventually approved by the FDA. The draft shows that the idea was clearly defined in the inventors' minds; all that remained was to reduce it to practice—to confirm its operability and bring it to market. *See Haskell v. Colebourne*, 671 F.2d 1362, 1365–66 (CCPA 1982) (enabling draft patent application sufficient to corroborate conception).

An examination of the events that followed the preparation of Burroughs Wellcome's draft confirms the soundness of the conception. Broder and Mitsuya received from Burroughs Wellcome a group of compounds, known to Broder and Mitsuya only by code names, selected for testing by the Burroughs Wellcome inventors. They then tested those compounds for activity against HIV in their patented cell line. The test results revealed for the first time that one of the compounds, later revealed to be AZT, was exceptionally active against the virus.

Here, though, the testing was brief, simply confirming the operability of what the draft application disclosed. True, the science surrounding HIV and AIDS was unpredictable and highly experimental at the time the Burroughs Wellcome scientists made the inventions. But what matters for conception is whether the inventors had a definite and permanent idea of the operative inventions. In this case, no prolonged period of extensive research, experiment, and modification followed the alleged conception. By all accounts, what followed was simply the normal course of clinical trials that mark the path of any drug to the marketplace.

That is not to say, however, that the NIH scientists merely acted as a "pair of hands" for the Burroughs Wellcome inventors. Broder and Mitsuya exercised considerable skill in conducting the tests, using their patented cell line to model the responses of human cells infected with HIV. Lehrman did suggest initial concentrations to Broder, but she hardly controlled the conduct of the testing, which necessarily involved interpretation of results for which Broder and Mitsuya, and very few others, were uniquely qualified. But because the testing confirmed the operability of the inventions, it showed that the Burroughs Wellcome inventors had a definite and permanent idea of the inventions. It was part of the reduction to practice and inured to the benefit of Burroughs Wellcome.

Barr and Novopharm allege error in the district court's refusal to hear their evidence of the poor predictive value of the murine retrovirus screens for activity against HIV. Regardless of the predictive value of the murine tests, however, the record shows that soon after those tests, the inventors determined, for whatever reason, to use AZT as a treatment for AIDS, and they prepared a draft patent application that specifically set out the inventions, including an enabling disclosure. Obviously, enablement and conception are distinct issues, and one need not necessarily meet the enablement standard of 35 U.S.C. § 112 to prove conception. *See Fiers,* 984 F.2d at 1169, 25 USPQ2d at 1605. But the enabling disclosure does suffice in this case to confirm that the inventors had concluded the mental part of the inventive process—that they had arrived at the final, definite idea of their inventions, leaving only the task of reduction to practice to bring the inventions to fruition.

The question is not whether Burroughs Wellcome reasonably believed that the inventions would work for their intended purpose, the focus of the evidence offered by Barr and Novopharm, but whether the inventors had formed the idea of their use for that purpose in sufficiently final form that only the exercise of ordinary skill remained to reduce it to practice. *See MacMillan v. Moffett,* 432 F.2d at 1239 (Inventor's "reasons or lack of reasons for including U–5008 are not relevant to the question of conception. The important thing is that he did think in definite terms of the method claimed."). Whether or not Burroughs

Wellcome believed the inventions would in fact work based on the mouse screens is irrelevant.

We do not know precisely when the inventors conceived their inventions, but the record shows that they had done so by the time they prepared the draft patent application that thoroughly and particularly set out the inventions as they would later be used. The district court correctly ruled that on this record, the NIH scientists were not joint inventors of these inventions.

* * *

Notes

1. *The Inventorship Entity*: A valid patent must name as inventors all persons who participated in the conception of the invention, and no other persons. This rule reflects the fundamental inventorship requirement of Section 102(f). A patent can therefore be found invalid after it issues if it misidentifies the inventor, includes a non-inventor (misjoinder), or omits a co-inventor (nonjoinder). In the absence of deceptive intent on the part of the *true* inventor, Sections 116 and 256 allow for correction of inventorship errors during the application process and after the patent issues, respectively.

2. Another patent at issue in *Burroughs-Wellcome* was a process patent claiming the use of AZT to increase the number of T-lymphocytes in a human infected with HIV. Novopharm argued that the use of AZT to treat HIV by halting the continuing destruction of T-lymphocytes was patentably distinct from the use of AZT to affirmatively *raise* depleted T-lymphocyte counts and restore immune function. Furthermore, it argued, AZT's ability to raise T-lymphocyte counts was unknown to the Burroughs–Wellcome scientists until it was revealed by the Phase I human patient study conducted by NIH scientists. The Federal Circuit remanded this aspect of the case because these arguments, if true, suggested that the Burroughs–Wellcome scientists did not conceive of this invention before they received the results of the NIH tests, and that this patent should therefore have named the NIH scientists as joint inventors. *Burroughs-Wellcome*, 40 F.3d at 1231–32.

3. Why is corroboration important in establishing the date of conception? What form(s) might such corroboration take? How does corroboration differ from reduction to practice? Might they ever coincide?

(iii) The Rights of Joint Inventors

ETHICON, INC. v. UNITED STATES SURGICAL CORP.
United States Court of Appeals, Federal Circuit, 1998.
135 F.3d 1456, *cert. denied*, 525 U.S. 923, 119 S.Ct. 278, 142 L.Ed.2d 229.

RADER, CIRCUIT JUDGE.

In this patent infringement action, Dr. InBae Yoon (Yoon) and his exclusive licensee, Ethicon, Inc. (Ethicon), appeal from the judgment of the United States District Court for the District of Connecticut. In 1989, Yoon and Ethicon sued United States Surgical Corporation (U.S. Surgical) for infringement of U.S. Patent No. 4,535,773 (the '773 patent). In 1993, the parties stipulated to the intervention of Mr. Young Jae Choi (Choi) as defendant-intervenor. Choi claimed to be an omitted co-inventor of the '773 patent and to have granted U.S. Surgical a retroactive license under that patent. On U.S. Surgical's motion to correct inventorship of the '773 patent under 35 U.S.C. § 256, the district court ruled that Choi was an omitted co-inventor of two claims, *see* 937 F.Supp. 1015 (D.Conn.1996), and subsequently granted U.S. Surgical's motion to dismiss the infringement complaint, *see* 954 F.Supp. 51 (D.Conn.1997). Because the district court's determination of co-inventorship was correct, and because Choi is a joint owner of the '773 patent who has not consented to suit against U.S. Surgical, this court affirms.

I. Background

The '773 patent relates to trocars, an essential tool for endoscopic surgery. A trocar is a surgical instrument which makes small incisions in the wall of a body cavity, often the abdomen, to admit endoscopic instruments. Trocars include a shaft within an outer sleeve. One end of the shaft has a sharp blade. At the outset of surgery, the surgeon uses the blade to puncture the wall and extend the trocar into the cavity. The surgeon then removes the shaft, leaving the hollow outer sleeve, through which the surgeon may insert tiny cameras and surgical instruments for the operation.

Conventional trocars, however, pose a risk of damage to internal organs or structures. As the trocar blade punctures the cavity wall, the sudden loss of resistance can cause the blade to lunge forward and injure an internal organ. The '773 patent claims a trocar that alleviates this danger. In one embodiment, the invention equips the trocar with a blunt, spring-loaded rod. As the trocar pierces the cavity wall, the rod automatically springs forward to precede the blade and shield against injury. A second embodiment has a retractable trocar blade that springs back into a protective sheath when it passes through the cavity wall. The patent also teaches the use of an electronic sensor in the end of the blade to signal the surgeon at the moment of puncture.

Yoon is a medical doctor and inventor of numerous patented devices for endoscopic surgery. In the late 1970s, Yoon began to conceive of a safety device to prevent accidental injury during trocar incisions. Yoon also conceived of a device to alert the surgeon when the incision was complete. In 1980, Yoon met Choi, an electronics technician, who had some college training in physics, chemistry, and electrical engineering, but no college degree. Choi had worked in the research and development of electronic devices. After Choi had demonstrated to Yoon some of the devices he had developed, Yoon asked Choi to work with him on several projects, including one for safety trocars. Choi was not paid for his work.

In 1982, after collaborating for approximately eighteen months, their relationship ended. Choi believed that Yoon found his work unsatisfactory and unlikely to produce any marketable product. For these reasons, Choi withdrew from cooperation with Yoon. In the same year, however, Yoon filed an application for a patent disclosing various embodiments of a safety trocar. Without informing Choi, Yoon named himself as the sole inventor. In 1985, the Patent and Trademark Office issued the '773 patent to Yoon, with fifty-five claims. Yoon thereafter granted an exclusive license under this patent to Ethicon. Yoon did not inform Choi of the patent application or issuance.

In 1989, Ethicon filed suit against U.S. Surgical for infringement of claims 34 and 50 of the '773 patent. In 1992, while this suit was still pending, U.S. Surgical became aware of Choi, and contacted him regarding his involvement in Yoon's safety trocar project. When Choi confirmed his role in the safety trocar project, U.S. Surgical obtained from Choi a "retroactive license" to practice "Choi's trocar related inventions." Under the license, Choi agreed to assist U.S. Surgical in any suit regarding the '773 patent. For its part, U.S. Surgical agreed to pay Choi contingent on its ultimate ability to continue to practice and market the invention. With the license in hand, U.S. Surgical moved to correct inventorship of the '773 patent under 35 U.S.C. § 256, claiming that Choi was a co-inventor of claims 23, 33, 46, and 47. Following an extensive hearing, the district court granted U.S. Surgical's motion, finding that Choi had contributed to the subject matter of claims 33 and 47.

U.S. Surgical next moved for dismissal of the infringement suit, arguing that Choi, as a joint owner of the patent, had granted it a valid license under the patent. By its terms, the license purported to grant rights to use the patent extending retroactively back to its issuance. The district court granted U.S. Surgical's motion and dismissed the suit.

Ethicon appeals the district court's finding of co-inventorship and its dismissal of the complaint. Specifically, Ethicon contends that (1) Choi supplied insufficient corroboration for his testimony of co-invention; (2) Choi presented insufficient evidence to show co-invention of claims 33 and 47 clearly and convincingly; (3) Choi accepted illegal payment for his factual testimony which the court should therefore have excluded from the proceedings; (4) the terms of the license agreement limit it to only that part of the invention to which Choi contributed, not the entire patent; and (5) even if the agreement licenses the entire patent, it cannot release U.S. Surgical from liability for past infringement.

II. Co-Inventorship

Patent issuance creates a presumption that the named inventors are the true and only inventors. *See Hess v. Advanced Cardiovascular Sys., Inc.,* 106 F.3d 976, 980 (Fed.Cir.), *cert. denied,* 520 U.S. 1277, 117 S.Ct. 2459, 138 L.Ed.2d 216 (1997). Inventorship is a question of law, which this court reviews without deference. *See Sewall v. Walters,* 21 F.3d 411,

415 (Fed.Cir.1994). However, this court reviews the underlying findings of fact which uphold a district court's inventorship determination for clear error. *See Hess*, 106 F.3d at 980.

A patented invention may be the work of two or more joint inventors. *See* 35 U.S.C. § 116 (1994). Because "[c]onception is the touchstone of inventorship," each joint inventor must generally contribute to the conception of the invention. *Burroughs Wellcome Co. v. Barr Lab., Inc.,* 40 F.3d 1223, 1227–28 (Fed.Cir.1994). "Conception is the 'formation in the mind of the inventor, of a definite and permanent idea of the complete and operative invention, as it is hereafter to be applied in practice.' " *Hybritech, Inc. v. Monoclonal Antibodies, Inc.,* 802 F.2d 1367, 1376 (Fed.Cir.1986) (quoting 1 *Robinson on Patents* 532 (1890)). An idea is sufficiently "definite and permanent" when "only ordinary skill would be necessary to reduce the invention to practice, without extensive research or experimentation." *Burroughs Wellcome,* 40 F.3d at 1228.

The conceived invention must include every feature of the subject matter claimed in the patent. *See Sewall,* 21 F.3d at 415. Nevertheless, for the conception of a joint invention, each of the joint inventors need not "make the same type or amount of contribution" to the invention. 35 U.S.C. § 116. Rather, each needs to perform only a part of the task which produces the invention. On the other hand, one does not qualify as a joint inventor by merely assisting the actual inventor after conception of the claimed invention. *See Sewall,* 21 F.3d at 416–17; *Shatterproof Glass Corp. v. Libbey–Owens Ford Co.,* 758 F.2d 613, 624 (Fed.Cir. 1985) ("An inventor 'may use the services, ideas and aid of others in the process of perfecting his invention without losing his right to a patent.' " (quoting *Hobbs v. U.S. Atomic Energy Comm'n.,* 451 F.2d 849, 864 (5th Cir.1971))). One who simply provides the inventor with well-known principles or explains the state of the art without ever having "a firm and definite idea" of the claimed combination as a whole does not qualify as a joint inventor. *See Hess,* 106 F.3d at 981 (citing *O'Reilly v. Morse,* 56 U.S. (15 How.) 62, 111, 14 L.Ed. 601 (1853)). Moreover, depending on the scope of a patent's claims, one of ordinary skill in the art who simply reduced the inventor's idea to practice is not necessarily a joint inventor, even if the specification discloses that embodiment to satisfy the best mode requirement. *See Sewall,* 21 F.3d at 416.

Furthermore, a co-inventor need not make a contribution to every claim of a patent. *See* 35 U.S.C. § 116. A contribution to one claim is enough. *See SmithKline Diagnostics, Inc. v. Helena Lab. Corp.,* 859 F.2d 878, 888 (Fed.Cir.1988). Thus, the critical question for joint conception is who conceived, as that term is used in the patent law, the subject matter of the claims at issue.

35 U.S.C. § 256 provides that a co-inventor omitted from an issued patent may be added to the patent by a court "before which such matter is called in question." To show co-inventorship, however, the alleged co-inventor or co-inventors must prove their contribution to the conception of the claims by clear and convincing evidence. *See Hess,* 106 F.3d at

980. However, "an inventor's testimony respecting the facts surrounding a claim of derivation or priority of invention cannot, standing alone, rise to the level of clear and convincing proof." *Price v. Symsek*, 988 F.2d 1187, 1194 (Fed.Cir.1993). The rule is the same for an alleged co-inventor's testimony. *See Hess*, 106 F.3d at 980. Thus, an alleged co-inventor must supply evidence to corroborate his testimony. *See Price*, 988 F.2d at 1194. Whether the inventor's testimony has been sufficiently corroborated is evaluated under a "rule of reason" analysis. *Id.* at 1195. Under this analysis, "[a]n evaluation of *all* pertinent evidence must be made so that a sound determination of the credibility of the [alleged] inventor's story may be reached." *Id.*

Corroborating evidence may take many forms. Often contemporaneous documents prepared by a putative inventor serve to corroborate an inventor's testimony. *See id.* at 1195–96. Circumstantial evidence about the inventive process may also corroborate. *See Knorr v. Pearson*, 671 F.2d 1368, 1373 (CCPA 1982) ("[S]ufficient circumstantial evidence of an independent nature can satisfy the corroboration rule."). Additionally, oral testimony of someone other than the alleged inventor may corroborate. *See Price*, 988 F.2d at 1195–96.

A. CLAIM 33

[11] The district court determined that Choi contributed to the conception of the subject matter of claim 33. Claim 33 (with emphasis to highlight relevant elements) reads:

A surgical instrument for providing communication through an anatomical organ structure, comprising:

means having an abutment member and *shaft longitudinally accommodatable within an outer sleeve,* longitudinal movement of said shaft inside said sleeve being limited by contact of said abutment member with said sleeve, said shaft having a distal end with a distal blade surface tapering into a sharp distal point, *said distal blade surface being perforated along one side by an aperture,* for puncturing an anatomical organ structure when subjected to force along the longitudinal axis of said shaft;

means having a blunt distal bearing surface, slidably extending through said aperture, for reciprocating through said aperture while said abutment member is in stationary contact with said sleeve;

means positionable between said puncturing means and said reciprocating means for biasing a distal section of said reciprocating means to protrude beyond said aperture and permitting said distal section of said reciprocating means to recede into said aperture when said bearing surface is subject to force along its axis . . . ; and

means connectible to the proximal end of said puncturing means *for* responding to longitudinal movement of said reciprocating means relative to said puncturing means and *creating a sensible signal* having one state upon recision of said distal section of said reciprocating means into said aperture and another state upon protrusion of said distal section of said reciprocating means from said aperture.

To determine whether Choi made a contribution to the conception of the subject matter of claim 33, this court must determine what Choi's contribution was and then whether that contribution's role appears in the claimed invention. If Choi in fact contributed to the invention defined by claim 33, he is a joint inventor of that claim.

* * *

The district court found that Yoon conceived of the use of a blunt probe. However, the court found that Choi conceived of and thereby contributed two features contained in the embodiment shown in [the specification]: first, Choi conceived of locating the blunt probe in the trocar shaft and allowing it to pass through an aperture in the blade surface; second, Choi conceived of the "means ... for ... creating a sensible signal."

If Choi did indeed conceive of "locating the blunt probe in the shaft and allowing it to pass through an aperture in the blade surface," he contributed to the subject matter of claim 33. Claim 33 requires that the "distal blade surface" be "perforated along one side by an aperture" and requires the "shaft" to be "longitudinally accommodatable within [the] outer sleeve." Properly construed, claim 33 includes the elements that Choi contributed to the invention according to the district court's findings.

* * *

In sum, after full consideration of the relevant evidence, the district court determined that Choi conceived part of the invention recited in claim 33. This court detects no cause to reverse this determination.

B.   CLAIM 47

The district court also determined that Choi contributed to the conception of the subject matter of claim 47. Claim 47 (with emphasis to highlight relevant elements) reads:

A surgical instrument for providing communication through an anatomical organ structure, comprising:

means having an elongate shaft exhibiting a longitudinal axis and terminating in a sharp, distal end, for puncturing the cavity wall of an anatomical organ structure;

means borne by said puncturing means distal end for converting counterforce exerted by said cavity wall against said distal end into transmissible energy;

means connected to said converting means for conveying said transmissible energy toward the proximal end of said puncturing means;

means having an interior bore coaxially aligned with the longitudinal axis of said shaft for receiving said puncturing means proximal end;

means for biasing said puncturing means proximal end to withdraw into said interior bore;

means interposed between said puncturing means proximal end and said interior bore assuming a normally protruding position for determining [sic: detaining][2] said puncturing means proximal end extended from said interior cavity in opposition to said biasing means.

To determine whether Choi made a contribution to the conception of the subject matter of claim 47, this court must determine what Choi's contribution was and then construe the claim language to determine if Choi's contribution found its way into the defined invention.

* * *

The district court concluded that Yoon generally invented the retractable trocar, but that Choi invented both of the detaining means disclosed in the specification. In addition to oral testimony of the parties, the district court cited Choi's sketches, one of which clearly shows the rod detaining means. However, the sketch in which the district court would find the detent detaining means appears to work differently than the embodiment described in the '773 patent. Instead of a detent that extends radially outward through a hole in the sheath, the sketch illustrates the use of the solenoid plunger itself as a detent, extending radially *inward* through a hole in the sheath. Thus, the record does not show that Choi contributed to the detent detaining means. Therefore, this court affirms the district court's finding that Choi contributed the rod detaining means, but determines that the trial court clearly erred in finding that Choi contributed the detent detaining means.

In this instance, however, claim 47 recites a "means ... for [detaining]." The use of the word "means" gives rise to "a presumption that the inventor used the term advisedly to invoke the statutory mandates for means-plus-function clauses." *York Prods., Inc. v. Central Tractor Farm & Family Ctr.,* 99 F.3d 1568, 1574 (Fed.Cir.1996). Although the presumption is not conclusive, *see, e.g., id.* (construing "means" in claim without reference to section 112, paragraph 6), the means language here invokes the interpretation regimens of section 112, paragraph 6. Thus applying section 112, paragraph 6 to interpret this claim, the language adopted the two structures in the specification to define the means for detaining.

2. The prosecution history plainly shows that this is a typesetting error.

Choi showed contribution to one of these alternative structures. The contributor of any disclosed means of a means-plus-function claim element is a joint inventor as to that claim, unless one asserting sole inventorship can show that the contribution of that means was simply a reduction to practice of the sole inventor's broader concept. *See Sewall,* 21 F.3d at 416 (holding that the designer of one disclosed means was not a joint inventor). Although the district court found that Yoon first conceived of a retractable trocar generally, Yoon did not show that Choi's contribution was simply a reduction to practice of the broader concept of using any detaining means commensurate with the scope of claim 47. Thus, Choi showed entitlement to the status of co-inventor for this claim as well.

* * *

IV.   SCOPE OF THE CHOI–U.S. SURGICAL LICENSE

Questions of patent ownership are distinct from questions of inventorship. *See Beech Aircraft Corp. v. EDO Corp.,* 990 F.2d 1237, 1248 (Fed.Cir.1993). In accordance with this principle, this court has nonetheless noted that "an invention presumptively belongs to its creator." *Teets v. Chromalloy Gas Turbine Corp.,* 83 F.3d 403, 406 (Fed.Cir.), *cert. denied,* 519 U.S. 1009, 117 S.Ct. 513, 136 L.Ed.2d 402 (1996).

Indeed, in the context of joint inventorship, each co-inventor presumptively[5] owns a pro rata undivided interest in the entire patent, no matter what their respective contributions. Several provisions of the Patent Act combine to dictate this rule. 35 U.S.C. § 116, as amended in 1984, states that a joint inventor need not make a contribution "to the subject matter of every claim of the patent." In amending section 116 as to joint inventorship, Congress did not make corresponding modifications as to joint ownership. For example, section 261 continues to provide that "patents shall have the attributes of personal property." This provision suggests that property rights, including ownership, attach to patents as a whole, not individual claims. Moreover, section 262 continues to speak of "joint owners of a patent," not joint owners of a claim. Thus, a joint inventor as to even one claim enjoys a presumption of ownership in the entire patent.

This rule presents the prospect that a co-inventor of only one claim might gain entitlement to ownership of a patent with dozens of claims. As noted, the Patent Act accounts for that occurrence: "Inventors *may* apply for a patent jointly even though ... each did not make a contribution to the subject matter of every claim." 35 U.S.C. § 116 (emphasis added). Thus, where inventors choose to cooperate in the inventive process, their joint inventions may become joint property without some express agreement to the contrary. In this case, Yoon must now effectively share with Choi ownership of all the claims, even those which he

---

5.   Ethicon does not claim that Choi had a contractual or other duty to assign his patent rights to Yoon.

invented by himself. Thus, Choi had the power to license rights in the entire patent.

* * *

V. RETROACTIVE LICENSURE

Finally, Ethicon argues that even if the license agreement is enforceable as to the entire patent, it should still be allowed to proceed against U.S. Surgical to recover damages for pre-license infringement. Ethicon contends that to hold otherwise would contravene the decision in *Schering Corp. v. Roussel–UCLAF SA,* 104 F.3d 341 (Fed.Cir.1997). This court agrees with Ethicon's challenge to the retroactive effect of Choi's license, but must affirm the dismissal of the case based on Choi's refusal to join as plaintiff in the suit.

In *Schering,* Roussel and Schering, the two co-owners of the patent in suit, entered into an agreement whereby each granted the other a unilateral right to sue third parties for infringement. Schering then sued to enjoin Zeneca, Inc. from proceeding with planned sales of an allegedly infringing product. Schering joined Roussel in the action as an involuntary plaintiff. Two weeks later, Roussel granted Zeneca a license to practice the patented invention. The district court dismissed Schering's suit. Schering appealed.

On appeal, Schering argued that because Roussel had granted Schering a unilateral right to sue, Roussel could not now grant a license to Zeneca. Schering contended that one grant was incompatible with the other. The court rejected Shering's argument, reasoning that "[t]he right to license and the unilateral right to sue are ... not incompatible, and the granting of one does not necessarily imply the relinquishment of the other." *Id.* at 345. This court acknowledged the critical distinction that a license to a third party only operates prospectively. Absent agreement to the contrary, a co-owner cannot grant a release of another co-owner's right to accrued damages. Consequently, a co-owner who has granted a unilateral right to sue to another co-owner may also license a third party. Nevertheless, by virtue of the unilateral right to sue, the second co-owner can still force the first co-owner to join an infringement action against the licensee to recover the second co-owner's accrued damages for past infringement. Thus, a prospective license is not per se incompatible with a unilateral right to sue, and, barring any other applicable contractual provision, Schering could not prevent Roussel from granting a license to Zeneca:[7]

> [T]he grant of a license by one co-owner cannot deprive the other co-owner of the right to sue for accrued damages for past infringement.

7. A twist provided by the facts of *Schering* was that Schering was seeking only prospective relief. Therefore, the *Schering* court's distinction evaporated under the specific facts of the case—that is, until Schering alleged for the first time on appeal that some of Zeneca's pre-license conduct constituted infringement. The *Schering* court remanded, in part, to allow Schering to pursue these potential pre-license infringement claims. *See Schering,* 104 F.3d at 347.

That would require a release, not a license, and the rights of a patent co-owner, absent agreement to the contrary, do not extend to granting a release that would defeat an action by other co-owners to recover damages for past infringement.

Id. at 345.

Thus, Choi's "retroactive license" to U.S. Surgical attempts to operate as the combination of a release and a prospective license.[8] Nonetheless Choi cannot release U.S. Surgical from its liability for past accrued damages to Ethicon, only from liability to himself.

One more settled principle governs this case, however. An action for infringement must join as plaintiffs all co-owners. *See Waterman v. Mackenzie,* 138 U.S. 252, 255, 11 S.Ct. 334, 335, 34 L.Ed. 923 (1891) ("The patentee or his assigns may, by instrument in writing, assign, grant, and convey, either (1) the whole patent . . . ; or (2) an undivided part or share of that exclusive right; or (3) the exclusive right under the patent within and throughout a specified part of the United States. A transfer of either of these three kinds of interests is an assignment, properly speaking, and vests in the assignee a title in so much of the patent itself, with a right to sue infringers. In the second case, *jointly with the assignor.* In the first and third cases, in the name of the assignee alone." (emphasis added)); *Moore v. Marsh,* 74 U.S. (7 Wall.) 515, 520, 19 L.Ed. 37 (1868) ("[W]here [an] assignment is of an undivided part of the patent, the action should be brought for every infringement committed subsequent to the assignment, in the joint names of the patentee and assignee, as representing the entire interest.").

Further, as a matter of substantive patent law, all co-owners must ordinarily consent to join as plaintiffs in an infringement suit.[9] Consequently, "one co-owner has the right to impede the other co-owner's ability to sue infringers by refusing to voluntarily join in such a suit." *Schering,* 104 F.3d at 345.

This rule finds support in section 262 of the Patent Act:

In the absence of any agreement to the contrary, each of the joint owners of a patent may make, use, offer to sell, or sell the patented invention within the United States, or import the patented invention into the United States, without the consent of and without accounting to the other owners.

8. Although "retroactive licenses" of patent rights have been enforced by the courts without specifically referring to them in this way, all of these cases have involved "retroactive licenses" granted by a sole owner. *See, e.g., Studiengesellschaft Kohle, M.B.H. v. Hercules, Inc.,* 105 F.3d 629 (Fed. Cir.1997).

9. Two established exceptions exist. First, when any patent owner has granted an exclusive license, he stands in a relationship of trust to his licensee and must permit the licensee to sue in his name. *See Independent Wireless Telegraph Co. v. Radio Corp. of Am.,* 269 U.S. 459, 469, 46 S.Ct. 166, 169–70, 70 L.Ed. 357 (1926). Second, the obligation may arise by contract among co-owners. If, by agreement, a co-owner waives his right to refuse to join suit, his co-owners may subsequently force him to join in a suit against infringers. *See Willingham v. Lawton,* 555 F.2d 1340, 1344–45 (6th Cir.1977).

This freedom to exploit the patent without a duty to account to other co-owners also allows co-owners to freely license others to exploit the patent without the consent of other co-owners. *Schering,* 104 F.3d at 344 ("Each co-owner's ownership rights carry with them the right to license others, a right that also does not require the consent of any other co-owner."). Thus, the congressional policy expressed by section 262 is that patent co-owners are "at the mercy of each other." *Willingham v. Lawton,* 555 F.2d 1340, 1344 (6th Cir.1977).

Although in this case, the result is effectively no different than if Choi could grant a release to U.S. Surgical of any liability to Ethicon, it should be emphasized that the principle that governs this case is not incompatible with the principle enunciated in *Schering.* In *Schering,* this court noted that the granting of a unilateral right to sue is not incompatible with the right to grant a license. Similarly, this court notes that the inability to grant a release is not incompatible with the right to refuse to consent to an infringement suit. It is true that, in some circumstances, the decision of one co-owner to not join an infringement suit may have the same effect as granting a release, but this is not true in all cases. For example, when co-owners have granted each other a unilateral right to sue, each has waived his right not to join an infringement suit, and either of them can force the other to join a suit to collect accrued infringement damages.

Because Choi did not consent to an infringement suit against U.S. Surgical and indeed can no longer consent due to his grant of an exclusive license with its accompanying "right to sue," Ethicon's complaint lacks the participation of a co-owner of the patent. Accordingly, this court must order dismissal of this suit.

VI. Conclusion

Accordingly, the judgment of the United States District Court for the District of Connecticut is affirmed.

Pauline Newman, Circuit Judge, dissenting.

I respectfully dissent, for whether or not Mr. Choi made an inventive contribution to two of the fifty-five claims of the '773 patent, he is not a joint owner of the other fifty-three claims of the patent. Neither the law of joint invention nor the law of property so requires, and indeed these laws mandate otherwise.

The district court found that Mr. Choi made a contribution to two claims of the '773 patent. Although precedent would as readily place Mr. Choi's work in the category whereby "an inventor 'may use the services, ideas and aid of others in the process of perfecting his invention without losing his right to a patent,' " *Shatterproof Glass Corp. v. Libbey–Owens Ford Co.,* 758 F.2d 613, 624 (Fed.Cir.1985) (quoting *Hobbs v. United States Atomic Energy Comm'n,* 451 F.2d 849, 864 (5th Cir.1971)), the district court's finding as to the two claims is not clearly in error. That conclusion is not my primary concern. My primary concern is with the failure of the court to recognize, in deciding ownership rights, the effect on these rights of the 1984 amendment of 35 U.S.C. § 116, which markedly changed the law of naming inventors on patents, and authorized the "joint invention" here adjudicated.

Before the statutory change made in 1984 Mr. Choi could not have been named a "joint inventor" of the '773 patent, for he had not jointly conceived and contributed to the entire invention. It is not disputed that his contribution is limited to elements of two of the fifty-five patent claims. Such a person was not a "joint inventor" under pre–1984 law. That law required that joint invention be the "simultaneous production of the genius and labor of both parties." *Stearns v. Barrett,* 22 F. Cas. 1175, 1181 (C.C.D.Mass.1816) (Story, J.). Joint ownership, in turn, was based on this principle of joint invention.

Those assistants who worked on an invention at the behest of the originator of the idea did not achieve the legal status of "joint inventor." Having no legal status as an inventor, such assistants acquired no property right in the invention by virtue of their contributions. *See Collar Co. v. Van Dusen,* 90 U.S. (23 Wall.) 530, 563–64, 23 L.Ed. 128 (1874) (ancillary discoveries of assistant belong to person who conceived original principle unless they "constitute the whole substance of the improvement"); *Agawam Co. v. Jordan,* 74 U.S. (7 Wall.) 583, 602–4, 19 L.Ed. 177 (1868) (same). In *Agawam* the Court explained that one less than a true joint inventor was forbidden from "appropriat[ing] to himself the entire result of the ingenuity and toil of the originator, or put[ting] it in the power of any subsequent infringer to defeat the patent." 74 U.S. at 604.

The 1984 amendment of 35 U.S.C. § 116 permitted the naming as an inventor of all persons who assisted in the development of an idea, or parts thereof, that originated with others. Such naming, however, does not automatically endow the assistant with full and common ownership of the entire invention, including the contributions of all others including the originator. That is not a reasonable consequence of the change in the law of naming inventors that occurred in 1984.

A.   The Law of Joint Invention

The purpose of the amendment of § 116 was to remedy the increasing technical problems arising in team research, for which existing law, deemed to require simultaneous conception as well as shared contribution by each named inventor to every claim, was producing pitfalls for patentees, to no public purpose. As stated in its legislative history, the amendment to 35 U.S.C. § 116 "recognizes the realities of modern team research." 130 Cong. Rec. 28,069–71 (1984) (statement of Rep. Kastenmeier).

Before 1984 precedent did not permit naming as an inventor a person who did not share in the conception of the invention and who did not contribute to all of the claims of the patent. *See In re Sarett,* 51 C.C.P.A. 1180, 327 F.2d 1005, 1010 n. 7 (CCPA 1964) ("It should be clear that the patent could not *legally* contain a claim to Sarett's *sole* invention under existing law because it would not have been the invention of the *joint* patentees." (emphases in original)); *In re Hamilton*, 37 F.2d 758, 759, *op. den. reh'g*, 38 F.2d 889, 890 (CCPA 1930) (joint patent could not issue on portion of invention made by single inventor). If different persons made an inventive contribution to various parts of an invention or to different claims of a patent, the legalistic problems that arose were not readily soluble, even by the complex, expensive, and often confusing expedient of filing separate patent applications on separate claims.

The progress of technology exacerbated the inventorship problems. Patents were invalidated simply because all of the named inventors did not contribute to all the claims; and patents were also invalidated when there were contributors to some of the claims who were not named. Indeed, at the time the '773 patent application was filed in 1982, most practitioners believed that a separate application was required if it was desired to present, for example, the two claims that contain Mr. Choi's contribution.

As team research increased with the growth of technology-based industry, so did the dilemma, for the rules of joint inventorship were not readily adaptable to the development of complex inventions. It became apparent that legislative remedy was needed. The amendment of 35 U.S.C. § 116 provided a simple solution to a complex problem:

> § 116 [second sentence] Inventors may apply for a patent jointly even though (1) they did not physically work together or at the same time, (2) each did not make the same type or amount of contribution, or (3) each did not make a contribution to the subject matter of every claim of the patent.

Pub.L. 98–622, § 104, 98 Stat. 3384, Nov. 8, 1984. The amendment identified the three major pitfalls that had arisen, and removed them.

This amendment did not also deal with the laws of patent ownership, and did not automatically convey ownership of the entire patent to everyone who could now be named as an inventor, whatever the contribution. The amendment simply permitted persons to be named on the patent document, whether as minor contributors to a subordinate embodiment, or full partners in the creation and development of the invention. The ownership relationships among the persons who, under § 116, could now be recognized as contributors to the invention, is irrelevant to the purpose of the amendment of § 116, and to its consequences. Section 116 has nothing to do with patent ownership.

B. The Law of Joint Ownership

The pre–1984 rule of joint ownership of joint inventions can be readily understood in its historical context, for a legally cognizable "joint invention" required mutuality of interaction and a real partnership in the creation and development of the invention. On this foundation, a "joint inventor" was also, justly and legally, an equal owner of the idea and of any patent thereon. *Pointer*, 177 F.2d at 157–58 ("as the cases just cited show clearly, in order that an invention be truly called a joint invention, it must appear by clear and convincing proof that the two inventors collaborated in evolving the patented device"); *see* 1 Donald S. Chisum, *Chisum on Patents* § 202[2] & n.2 (rel. May 1987) ("Only where the same single, unitary idea of means is the product of two or more minds, working *pari passu,* and in communication with each other, is the conception truly joint and the result a joint invention," quoting 1 William C. Robinson, *The Law of Patents for Useful Inventions* § 396 (1890)).

The law of patent ownership has its roots in the common law of property—although a patent has its own peculiar character, for it deals with intangibles. Certain incidents of patent ownership have been created or clarified by statute, *see* 35 U.S.C. § 262, yet the common law provided the basic rules, as manifested in the concepts of tenancy in common and undivided interests that courts have drawn upon in patent ownership disputes.

The jurisprudence governing property interests is generally a matter of state law. Even when the property is the creation of federal statute, private rights are usually defined by state laws of property. This has long been recognized with respect to patent ownership and transfers. *See Jim Arnold Corp. v. Hydrotech Sys., Inc.,* 109 F.3d 1567, 1572, 42 USPQ2d 1119, 1123 (Fed.Cir.1997) ("the question of who owns the patent right and on what terms typically is a question exclusively for state courts"); *Roach v. Crouch,* 524 N.W.2d 400, 33 USPQ2d 1361 (Iowa 1994) (patent ownership issue properly triable in state court). It is equally established that inventorship and patent ownership are separate issues. *Beech Aircraft Corp. v. EDO Corp.,* 990 F.2d 1237, 1248–49, 26 USPQ2d 1572, 1582 (Fed.Cir.1993).

Most of the disputes concerning patent ownership that reached the Supreme Court dealt not with joint invention, but assignments and other transfers. The oft-cited case of *Waterman v. Mackenzie,* 138 U.S. 252, 11 S.Ct. 334, 34 L.Ed. 923 (1891) dealt with a dispute among the inventor's spouse and various assignees concerning ownership of the fountain pen patent, not inventorship. Occasionally an issue of ownership of patent property arose based on whether the claimant actually shared fully in the creation of the invention. In such cases, as cited *supra,* the decision on "joint invention" also decided the issue of ownership, for a person who had fully shared in the creation of the invention was deemed to be a joint owner of the entire patent property. On this premise each joint inventor was deemed to occupy the entirety of the patented subject matter, on a legal theory of tenancy in common. *See* 7 Richard R. Powell, *Powell on Real Property* ¶ 602[5] (1997) ("undivided fractional shares held by tenants in common are usually equal and are presumed equal unless circumstances indicate otherwise"). As patent property became viewed more precisely as personal property, *see* 35 U.S.C. § 261, the concept of tenancy in common was adjusted to that of an undivided interest, although with no substantial change in legal rights.

After the major change that the 1984 amendment to § 116 made in "joint invention," by authorizing the naming of any contributor to any claim of a patent, the legal premise that each named person had made a full and equal contribution to the entire patented invention became obsolete. *See SmithKline Diagnostics, Inc. v. Helena Labs. Corp.*, 859 F.2d 878, 888–89 (Fed.Cir.1988) (collecting cases). It is not an implementation of the common law of property, or its statutory embodiments, to treat all persons, however minor their contribution, as full owners of the entire property as a matter of law. The law had never given a contributor to a minor portion of an invention a full share in the originator's patent.

By amending § 116 in order to remove an antiquated pitfall whereby patents were being unjustly invalidated, the legislators surely did not intend to create another inequity. Apparently no one foresaw that judges might routinely transfer pre–1984 ownership concepts into the changed inventorship law. I have come upon no discussion of this anomaly in various scholarly articles on the amended § 116. *See, e.g.,* David W. Carstens, *Joint Inventorship under 35 U.S.C. § 116*, 73 J. Pat. Off. Soc'y 616 (1991) (discussing amended § 116); W. Fritz Fasse, *The Muddy Metaphysics of Joint Inventorship: Cleaning Up After the 1984 Amendments to 35 U.S.C. § 116*, 5 Harv. J.L. & Tech. 153 (1992), at 201–2 (citing PTO rules implementing amended § 116 and referring to the possibility of lack of common ownership of the subject matter, in the sense of assignment obligations of separately-employed inventors to distinct employers, yet overlooking other divided ownership problems).

In the case at bar, the district court recognized that Dr. Yoon originated the fundamental concept and the major aspects of its implementation. The court, however, construed the law as requiring that since Mr. Choi was named as a "joint inventor" (in accordance with the retroactivity legislated for the amendment to § 116) he automatically owned an undivided interest in the entire patent, and had the unencumbered and unfettered right to alienate an interest in the entire patent. Thus Mr. Choi, who would not pass the pre–1984 test of joint inventor, was nonetheless awarded full property rights in the entire invention and patent, as if he had been a true joint inventor of all the claims.

The panel majority, confirming this error, holds that Mr. Choi's contribution to two claims means and requires that Yoon "must now effectively share with Choi ownership of all the claims, even those which he invented by himself." That is incorrect. As I have discussed, the law of shared ownership was founded on shared invention, a situation that admittedly does not here prevail. Whether or not Mr. Choi is now properly named under § 116 because of his contribution to two claims, he is not a joint owner[1] and he does not have the right to grant a license

---

1. There may indeed be a need for determination of the respective interests of Dr. Yoon and Mr. Choi. Dr. Yoon's attempt to divide the '773 patent by reissue, although rebuffed by the Patent Office because of the ongoing litigation, would have placed the claims to which Mr. Choi contributed into a separate patent, in accor-

under all fifty-five claims. No theory of the law of property supports such a distortion of ownership rights. Thus I must, respectfully, dissent from the decision of the panel majority.

* * *

Notes

1.   In *Ethicon*, which opinion offers the more persuasive construction of the statutes that determine the rights of an inventor who contributed to some but not all of the claims in a patent? Which result would make more sense as a matter of policy?

2.   With respect to patents and patent applications, how does inventorship differ from ownership?

3.   Joint ownership of a patent may arise through joint invention or by assignment. What purpose is served by allowing one owner of a jointly owned patent to exploit the invention without the consent of the other joint owner(s) and without any duty of accounting?

4.   Where a jointly owned patent is infringed, would a release of liability executed by one co-owner bar the other co-owner from suing the infringer for damages for past infringement?

5.   The First Circuit held in *Massachusetts Eye and Ear Infirmary v. QLT Phototherapeutics, Inc.*, 412 F.3d 215 (1st Cir. 2005), *cert. denied*, ___ U.S. ___, 126 S.Ct. 2292, 164 L.Ed.2d 814 (2006), that 35 U.S.C. § 262 did not preempt a state law unjust enrichment claim by one patent co-owner against another, where the defendant co-owner as a practical matter controlled the exploitation of the patent, but failed to provide the compensation which it had promised in order to induce the plaintiff co-owner to broaden the claims of the patent to include the defendant's inventive contributions.

(iv) Inventorship and Design Patents

HOOP v. HOOP

United States Court of Appeals, Federal Circuit, 2002.
279 F.3d 1004.

MAYER, CHIEF JUDGE.

Mark R. and Lisa J. Hoop appeal the preliminary injunction entered by the United States District Court for the Southern District of Ohio enjoining them from acts which would constitute infringement of Jeffrey W. and Stephen E. Hoop's U.S. Design Patent No. 428,831. *Hoop v. Hoop*, No. C–1–00–869 (S.D.Ohio Feb. 28, 2001). Because the district court did not abuse its discretion in determining that Jeffrey and Stephen Hoop would likely succeed in sustaining the validity of their patent, we affirm.

dance with the practice when this patent application was filed. Dividing the patent claims would comport with common law practices.

BACKGROUND

In 1998, Jeffrey and Stephen Hoop ("Hoop brothers") conceived of a pair of eagle-shaped motorcycle fairing guards. Fairings are clear glass or plastic structures mounted above motorcycle handlebars to reduce wind drag. The eagle-shaped guards attach to the fairings to prevent damage to the fairings if the motorcycle tips over. The Hoop brothers created sketches of the eagle design. * * * Lacking drawing and casting expertise, they hired Lisa Hoop, a graphic designer, and Mark Hoop (their cousin and Lisa's ex-husband), a metal die caster, ("Mark and Lisa") to create detailed drawings and three-dimensional models for a patent application. Mark and Lisa signed nondisclosure agreements and prepared sketches and molds. * * *

In November of 1999, the Hoop brothers applied for a design patent. After discussions over a manufacturing agreement between the parties failed, in March of 2000, Mark and Lisa also applied for a design patent, using the same drawings they had prepared for the Hoop brothers. The Hoop brothers' patent issued on August 1, 2000, as U.S. Design Patent No. 428,831, and Mark and Lisa's identical patent issued on September 26, 2000, as U.S. Design Patent No. 431,211. In October of 2000, the Hoop brothers asked to have Mark and Lisa's patent reexamined. During reexamination, the examiner rejected Mark and Lisa's patent as anticipated by the Hoop brothers' patent. Mark and Lisa filed suit in the district court to invalidate the Hoop brothers' patent, and asserted infringement, unfair competition, and tortious interference with prospective economic advantage.

The Hoop brothers counterclaimed and moved to enjoin Mark and Lisa from making, using, selling, or offering for sale, any motorcycle fairing guard containing the design in their patent. The district court found that the Hoop brothers were the true inventors, and therefore held that they would likely succeed in sustaining the validity of their patent, and that Mark and Lisa were likely infringing. The court also held that the Hoop brothers had shown they would suffer irreparable injury absent an injunction. And it reasoned that although a preliminary injunction may cause harm to Mark and Lisa, the public interest favored protection of the patent. The court granted the Hoop brothers' motion for a preliminary injunction. Mark and Lisa appeal.

DISCUSSION

The question here is whether the refinements made by Mark and Lisa rise to the level of inventorship, so as to displace the Hoop brothers as patentees. Mark and Lisa argue that they are the true inventors because they perfected the original design by adding detail to the design sketches and creating the three-dimensional molds. Accordingly, they assert that the trial court erred in finding the Hoop brothers likely to succeed in sustaining the validity of their patent. We do not agree.

Design patents may be obtained by "[w]hoever invents any new, original and ornamental design for an article of manufacture." 35 U.S.C.

§ 171 (1994). We apply the same standard of inventorship to design patents that we require for utility patents. *In re Rousso,* 222 F.2d 729, 731 (CCPA 1955) (rejecting the assertion that a lesser standard of invention applies to design patents than to mechanical patents). An inventor under the patent laws is the "person or persons who conceived the patented invention." *C.R. Bard, Inc. v. M3 Sys.,* 157 F.3d 1340, 1352 (Fed.Cir.1998). An inventor may then "use the services, ideas, and aid of others in the process of perfecting his invention without losing his right to a patent." *Ethicon, Inc. v. United States Surgical Corp.,* 135 F.3d 1456, 1460 (Fed.Cir.1998) (citing *Shatterproof Glass Corp. v. Libbey–Owens Ford Co.,* 758 F.2d 613, 624 (Fed.Cir.1985)). The facts are undisputed that the Hoop brothers were the first to conceive of the eagle-shaped fairing guards, and brought the concept to Mark and Lisa for assistance. Thus in the absence of the inventive quality required for a patentable design on the part of Mark and Lisa, the Hoop brothers remain the true inventors.

One may not qualify as a joint inventor, or as here, a new inventor, by "merely assisting the actual inventor *after conception* of the claimed invention." *Ethicon,* 135 F.3d at 1460, 45 USPQ2d at 1548 (emphasis added). Minor differences between the prior art and the new claim will not suffice. *In re Zemon,* 205 F.2d 317, 320 (CCPA 1953). The differences here must be substantial and not just superficial; the new design must contain an inventive concept. *Id.* The ultimate test for design-patent inventorship, like the test for anticipation and infringement, is whether the second asserted invention is "substantially similar" to the first. *Gorham Mfg. Co. v. White,* 81 U.S. (14 Wall.) 511, 528, 20 L.Ed. 731 (1871); *Payless Shoesource, Inc. v. Reebok Int'l Ltd.,* 998 F.2d 985, 990 (Fed.Cir.1993). Substantial similarity is a question of fact. *L.A. Gear, Inc. v. Thom McAn Shoe Co.,* 988 F.2d 1117, 1124 (Fed.Cir.1993).

The district court found that Mark and Lisa's drawing lacked an "independent," which we read as inventive, concept. The court summarized its improvements over the Hoop brothers' sketch as increased detailed feathering and an overall less triangular shape. Noting the strong similarity between the drawings, the court reasoned that Mark and Lisa merely refined and perfected the Hoop brothers' concept. Therefore, the two designs were not separate inventions. Mark and Lisa did remove the suggestion of the eagle's tail, * * *, but the two eagles have the same proportions, body size, orientation, three rows of feathers, head and beak shape, and eye placement. We agree that the trial court could permissibly conclude at the preliminary injunction stage that the second design was likely to be found to be merely a more refined version of the first. However, final resolution of this factual question must await a trial on the merits. The court's determination that the Hoop brothers are likely to be found to be the true inventors and that they are likely to succeed in sustaining the validity of their patent is sustained.

CONCLUSION

Accordingly, the order of the United States District Court for the Southern District of Ohio is affirmed.

AFFIRMED.

Lourie, Circuit Judge, dissenting.

I respectfully dissent. I would reverse the district court's grant of a preliminary injunction on the ground that the district court applied the wrong legal standard in determining inventorship of a design patent and that the court's determination that the Hoop brothers had proved a likelihood of success on the question of validity was therefore flawed. I would remand for a redetermination of the likelihood of success under the proper standard.

While brought by Mark and Lisa as a § 291 action seeking a determination of priority between two issued patents, the Hoop brothers counterclaimed in this case, asserted infringement by Mark and Lisa, and requested the grant of an injunction. The district court determined that the Hoop brothers were the inventors of the patented fairing design and that Mark and Lisa were infringing the brothers' patent. The court relied on its conclusion that the original drawings made by the brothers and that made by Mark and Lisa do not "evidence an independent concept," and that the brothers hired Mark and Lisa to refine what was their drawing. The majority has affirmed that determination. I disagree.

The undisputed facts are that the Hoop brothers made a sketch of an eagle fairing design and asked Mark and Lisa to make three-dimensional drawings and models of that design. In doing so, Mark and Lisa made a different design, one that differed from the original design of the brothers in several respects. Both parties then filed patent applications and obtained the grant of patents on the design of Mark and Lisa. The majority opinion does not note that the design that accompanied the brothers' patent application and constituted its claim * * * was Mark and Lisa's design.

When one party conceives an invention and then asks a second party to reduce it to practice, the second party is not normally an inventor, or co-inventor, unless the second party has made significant changes in the original proposal necessary to carry out the conception. *See Ethicon, Inc. v. U.S. Surgical Corp.,* 135 F.3d 1456, 1460 (Fed.Cir.1998) ("[D]epending on the scope of a patent's claim, one of ordinary skill in the art who simply reduced the inventor's idea to practice is not necessarily a joint inventor."). The second party's work may constitute a separate invention if it is different in respects that render it nonobvious and the first party did not conceive of those aspects. If the parties worked together, they may be co-inventors, *id.,* but that does not appear to be the case here. What does appear to be the case here is that the second party may have made an invention that is distinct from, and possibly separately patentable from, that of the first party's original design.

Design patents do not claim concepts. They claim specific designs set forth in their claims, which invariably refer to the appearance of what is illustrated in the patent's drawings. 37 C.F.R. § 1.153(a) (2001). Contrary to the conclusion of the district court, as the invention is not the concept of an eagle design, but only the specific claimed representation of that eagle, the "concept" of the design is not what one must look at in determining whether the inventions are one and the same or separate. *See In re Harvey,* 12 F.3d 1061, 1064 [(Fed. Cir. 1993)] (reversing a finding of obviousness under 35 U.S.C. § 103 because it "should have focused on actual appearances, rather than 'design concepts' "). One must look at the differences between the overall appearance of the eagles to determine inventorship of the specific design. *See KeyStone Retaining Wall Sys. v. Westrock, Inc.,* 997 F.2d 1444, 1450 (Fed.Cir.1993) ("[I]t is the appearance of a design as a whole which is controlling in determining questions of patentability and infringement." (quoting *In re Rubinfield,* 270 F.2d 391, 395 (CCPA 1959))). When a design is changed, the result may be a new design. *See In re Mann,* 861 F.2d 1581, 1582 (Fed.Cir.1988) ("[I]f ... the design is changed, the result is a new and different design; the original design remains just what it was. Design patents have almost no scope.").

It is undisputed that both patents claim the same design, a design consisting of the specific appearance of the eagle shown in the patents, which is different from that in the sketch made by the Hoop brothers and identical to that made by Mark and Lisa * * *. Quite possibly, one could reasonably conclude that the changes are significant enough to constitute a new design. The brothers' design has little detail in the eyes and wings, has a fairly straight beak, and has humps in the wings near the head. In contrast, the patented design of Mark and Lisa has substantial eye and wing detail, a curved beak, and nearly straight wings adjacent the head. Without recognizing the specifics of each design, one cannot evaluate the identity or separate patentability of the designs. *See In re Laverne,* 356 F.2d 1003, 1006–07 (CCPA 1966) ("[W]e point out a number of differences ... the cumulative effect of which is unquestionably to create a different appearance.").

The principal question in determining the validity of the Hoop brothers' patent is whether the design claimed in that patent, which is the design Mark and Lisa made and claimed, is the same as or patentably indistinct from the sketch the brothers made and gave to Mark and Lisa, *i.e.,* whether it is the brothers' invention. Contrary to what seemed to impress the district court, it does not matter how much or how little experience the respective parties had in the field of motorcycle fairings. Nor does it matter that the brothers may have hired Mark and Lisa to make a design, or whether, through contract or operation of law, the brothers were entitled to ownership of any invention Mark and Lisa may have made. *See Beech Aircraft Corp. v. EDO Corp.,* 990 F.2d 1237, 1248 (Fed.Cir.1993) ("It is elementary that inventorship and ownership are separate issues."). The issue here is inventorship, not ownership. What matters in determining whether the brothers are the inventors of the claimed design is whether, from the standpoint of an ordinary designer, the claimed design is the same as or different and patentably distinct from the brothers' original design. *See In re Nalbandian,* 661 F.2d 1214, 1215 (CCPA 1981) (adopting an "ordinary designer" standard for patentability of designs, as opposed to an "ordinary observer" test for infringement of design patents).

Because we are not designers of ordinary skill, we cannot make the conclusive factual evaluations necessary to determine whether the original brothers' design and Mark and Lisa's design are patently distinct. I would therefore reverse the grant of the injunction and remand this case for the trial court to focus on the appearance of the respective designs and decide whether they are sufficiently different in a nonobviousness sense that it can be concluded that the brothers are not the inventors of the design claimed in their patent. If so, then they cannot show a likelihood of success in sustaining the validity of their patent under 35 U.S.C. § 102(f) so as to justify the grant of the preliminary injunction.

Note

If the two designs in *Hoop* are not patently distinct, which of the patents is/are valid, and who are the inventors?

2. EMPLOYMENT RELATIONSHIPS

UNITED STATES v. DUBILIER CONDENSER CORP.

Supreme Court of the United States, 1933.
289 U.S. 178, 53 S.Ct. 554, 77 L.Ed. 1114.

Mr. Justice Roberts delivered the opinion of the Court.

[The government sought a declaratory judgment that inventors Dunmore and Lowell and their exclusive licensee were required to assign their rights to the United States because, at the time they made their inventions, Dunmore and Lowell were employed to conduct scientific research in a division of the Department of Commerce. However, the inventions which they developed in the course of their employment, and through the use of their employer's facilities, were not part of their assigned research tasks.]

* * *

Dunmore and Lowell were permitted by their chief, after the discoveries had been brought to his attention, to pursue their work in the laboratory and to perfect the devices embodying their inventions. No one advised them prior to the filing of applications for patents that they would be expected to assign the patents to the United States or to grant the Government exclusive rights thereunder.

The respondent concedes that the United States may practice the inventions without payment of royalty, but asserts that all others are excluded, during the life of the patents, from using them without the respondent's consent. The petitioner insists that the circumstances require a declaration either that the Government has sole and exclusive property in the inventions or that they have been dedicated to the public so that anyone may use them.

* * *

A patent is property and title to it can pass only by assignment. If not yet issued an agreement to assign when issued, if valid as a contract, will be specifically enforced. The respective rights and obligations of employer and employee, touching an invention conceived by the latter, spring from the contract of employment.

One employed to make an invention, who succeeds, during his term of service, in accomplishing that task, is bound to assign to his employer any patent obtained. The reason is that he has only produced that which he was employed to invent. His invention is the precise subject of the contract of employment. A term of the agreement necessarily is that what he is paid to produce belongs to his paymaster. Standard Parts Co. v. Peck, 264 U.S. 52. On the other hand, if the employment be general, albeit it cover a field of labor and effort in the performance of which the employee conceived the invention for which he obtained a patent, the contract is not so broadly construed as to require an assignment of the patent. Hapgood v. Hewitt, 119 U.S. 226; Dalzell v. Dueber Watch–Case Mfg. Co. 149 U.S. 315. In the latter case it was said [p. 320]:

> "But a manufacturing corporation, which has employed a skilled workman, for a stated compensation, to take charge of its works, and to devote his time and services to devising and making improvements in articles there manufactured, is not entitled to a conveyance of patents obtained for inventions made by him while so employed, in the absence of express agreement to that effect."

The reluctance of courts to imply or infer an agreement by the employee to assign his patent is due to a recognition of the peculiar nature of the act of invention, which consists neither in finding out the laws of nature, nor in fruitful research as to the operation of natural laws, but in discovering how those laws may be utilized or applied for some beneficial purpose, by a process, a device or a machine. It is the result of an inventive act, the birth of an idea and its reduction to practice; the product of original thought; a concept demonstrated to be true by practical application or embodiment in tangible form.

Though the mental concept is embodied or realized in a mechanism or a physical or chemical aggregate, the embodiment is not the invention and is not the subject of a patent. This distinction between the idea and its application in practice is the basis of the rule that employment merely to design or to construct or to devise methods of manufacture is not the same as employment to invent. Recognition of the nature of the act of invention also defines the limits of the so-called shop-right, which shortly stated, is that where a servant, during his hours of employment, working with his master's materials and appliances, conceives and perfects an invention for which he obtains a patent, he must accord his master a non-exclusive right to practice the invention. McClurg v.

Kingsland, 1 How. 202; Solomons v. United States, 137 U.S. 342; Lane & Bodley Co. v. Locke, 150 U.S. 193. This is an application of equitable principles. Since the servant uses his master's time, facilities and materials to attain a concrete result, the latter is in equity entitled to use that which embodies his own property and to duplicate it as often as he may find occasion to employ similar appliances in his business. But the employer in such a case has no equity to demand a conveyance of the invention, which is the original conception of the employee alone, in which the employer had no part. This remains the property of him who conceived it, together with the right conferred by the patent, to exclude all others than the employer from the accruing benefits. These principles are settled as respects private employment.

* * *

[The court found nothing in the Constitution or the patent statutes to suggest that the same principles applicable to private employment should not apply equally to federal government employment. In addition, the court found that the government had failed to prove that Dunmore and Lowell were employed specifically for the purpose of inventing.]

The United States is entitled, in the same way and to the same extent as a private employer, to shop-rights, that is, the free and non-exclusive use of a patent which results from effort of its employee in his working hours and with material belonging to the Government.

* * *

The Government is consequently driven to the contention that though the employees were not specifically assigned the task of making the inventions (as in *Standard Parts Co. v. Peck, supra*), still, as the discoveries were "within the general field of their research and inventive work," the United States is entitled to an assignment of the patents. The courts below expressly found that Dunmore and Lowell did not agree to exercise their inventive faculties in their work, and that invention was not within its scope. In this connection it is to be remembered that the written evidence of their employment does not mention research, much less invention; that never was there a word said to either of them, prior to their discoveries, concerning invention or patents or their duties or obligations respecting these matters; that as shown by the records of the patent office, employees of the Bureau of Standards and other departments had, while so employed, received numerous patents and enjoyed the exclusive rights obtained as against all private persons without let or hindrance from the Government. In no proper sense may it be said that the contract of employment contemplated invention; everything that Dunmore and Lowell knew negatived the theory that they were employed to invent; they knew, on the contrary, that the past and then present practice was that the employees of the Bureau were allowed to take patents on their inventions and have the benefits thereby conferred save as to use by the United States. The circumstances preclude the implication of any agreement to assign their inventions or patents.

* * *

The decrees are

Affirmed.

Notes

1.   Although a patent must be issued in the name(s) of the inventor(s) (also called the "inventorship entity" in the case of joint inventors) in order to be valid, under Section 261 the inventor may assign any interest in the patent, or the patent application, by a written instrument. Section 261 requires such an assignment to be recorded in the PTO to establish priority over subsequent conflicting transfers for consideration and without notice. An inventor's employment contract may require that all patent applications be assigned to the employer; such a contract may be enforced by a court order if deemed to be valid and enforceable by the court. A provision in the failed Patent Reform Act of 2005, H.R. 2795, would have allowed assignees to file patent applications directly. This provision has been reintroduced in the proposed Patent Reform Act of 2007. Under current law, what remedy, if any, is available to an assignee if the inventor is unwilling or unable to file a patent application?

2.   State law governs the determination whether the parties to an employment relationship have entered an express or implied contract granting the employer exclusive rights to the employee's inventions. In the case of an implied or express oral assignment of rights to an employee's patentable inventions, if such an assignment is held to be enforceable under state law, does that law conflict with the policy underlying Section 261? Under the general Supremacy Clause principle that federal law preempts conflicting state laws, should these state laws be deemed preempted by Section 261?

3.   State statutes may also restrict the enforceability of employee preinvention assignment agreements, even when they are in writing. For example, a contract which grants an employer exclusive rights in inventions made on the employee's own time, and with his or her own resources, and which do not reasonably pertain to the employer's business, may be held invalid. What policy arguments can you make both for and against such a statute?

4.   A shop right is a defense to infringement, but does not give the holder of the right standing to sue for infringement. Although a shop right is generally not assignable, it has been held to be assignable as part of the entire business of the employer; in addition, there is authority allowing delegation of an employer's shop right to another party acting on the employer's behalf. There is a split of authority on whether shop rights are confined to a true employer/employee relationship or apply as well to independent contractors. What equitable principles underlie the shop right doctrine? *See McElmurry v. Arkansas Power & Light Co.,* 995 F.2d 1576 (Fed.Cir.1993). To what extent would those same principles apply in the case of an independent contractor?

5. How would the common law rules governing employee inventions apply to the facts in *Hoop v. Hoop, supra?*

6. Although *Dubilier* held that the patent rights of federal government employees were no different from those of private sector employees, this holding has been superceded in part by Executive Order 10096, *codified as amended at* 37 C.F.R. § 501.6, which provides that the United States is entitled to the entire domestic rights to any invention which a federal employee makes during working hours, or makes with resources contributed by the government, or which either bears a direct relation to the inventor's official duties or is made in consequence of those duties. The Order establishes a rebuttable presumption that these conditions are satisfied whenever the inventor is employed for the specific purpose of research or invention. Where the conditions are found not to be satisfied, the United States nonetheless is entitled to an irrevocable, royalty-free, nonexclusive license in the invention.

7. The Bayh–Dole University and Small Business Patent Procedure Act of 1980, 35 U.S.C.A. § 200 *et seq.*, which addresses rights in inventions arising from federally funded research, is especially relevant to universities. Under the Act, institutions engaged in federally funded research are required to disclose the resulting inventions to the federal government. The contracting institutions may elect to retain ownership of the inventions, and are free to license them, provided that they (1) share the royalties with their employee-inventors, and (2) use the remaining proceeds to fund further research and development. The government retains an irrevocable paid-up license in such inventions.

B. THE PATENT APPLICATION PROCESS

Statutes: 35 U.S.C.A. §§ 111, 119–22, 131–35, 141, 145–46, 151, 172, 251–52

1. PATENT PROSECUTION

The initial determination of patentability is made by the Patent and Trademark Office ("PTO"). If the patent examiner rejects some or all of the claims, the applicant may amend or cancel those claims, abandon the application, file a *continuation* or *continuation-in-part* application in order to add new claims, amend the patent's disclosures to support the challenged claims (although 35 U.S.C.A. § 132 prohibits adding "new matter," meaning matter unsupported by the original disclosure), or dispute the examiner's grounds for rejection. When co-pending applications, or a patent and an application, claim the same patentable invention(s), the PTO may declare an *interference* under 35 U.S.C.A. § 135, referring the matter to the Board of Patent Appeals and Interferences (the "Board") to determine patent priority (and, where necessary, validity).

If the patent examiner twice rejects the disputed claims, the applicant can appeal to the Board, 35 U.S.C.A. § 134. If that appeal is unsuccessful, the applicant may seek judicial review either by appealing the Board's decision to the United States Court of Appeals for the Federal Circuit[1] (in which case review is limited to the PTO record) or by filing a civil action in the United States District Court for the District of Columbia, which conducts a full trial, the outcome of which is appealable to the Federal Circuit.

In contrast, interferences are appealable only to the Federal Circuit.

In *Dickinson v. Zurko,* 527 U.S. 150, 119 S.Ct. 1816, 144 L.Ed.2d 143 (1999), the Supreme Court held that the standard of review applicable to judicial review of findings of fact made by the PTO in patent examinations is governed by Section 706 of the Administrative Procedure Act (APA), 5 U.S.C. § 706 (1999), which permits a reviewing court to set aside an administrative agency's "actions, findings and conclusions" only where they are found to be "arbitrary, capricious, an abuse of discretion, or otherwise not in accordance with law, [or] unsupported by substantial evidence." Because the Federal Circuit had previously employed the "clearly erroneous" standard, *Zurko* required the Federal Circuit to begin according greater deference to PTO findings of fact than was required by the Federal Circuit's own precedents. However, as the Court itself recognized, 527 U.S. at 163, because the Federal Circuit cannot help but review the agency's fact findings through the lens of its own expertise as a specialized court, it remains to be seen whether in practice the Federal Circuit's application of the APA standard will lead to results that are markedly different from its application of the "clearly erroneous" standard.

Until the Patent Reform Act of 1999 took effect (in November of 2000), a patent application remained confidential (absent special circumstances such as a court order) until the patent issued. However, Section 122 now requires the PTO to publish certain pending patent applications 18 months after filing. Publication is mandatory if the inventor has filed foreign patent applications for the same invention which will be published within 18 months of the foreign filing. Applicants who have not filed such foreign applications (and do not intend to) may elect to avoid PTO publication. (This option would be eliminated under the proposed Patent Reform Act of 2007, under which 18-month publication would apply to all pending applications.) The publication rules do not apply to provisional patent or design patent applications. Section 102(e) treats published applications as anticipating subject matter (and, thus, as prior art for Section 103 purposes) as of their filing dates, and Section 154 grants provisional royalty rights to inventors whose applications are published under the new rule.

Under Sections 133 and 111(a)(4), if an applicant fails to prosecute an application in a timely manner (as specified by the statute), the application will be deemed abandoned, unless the applicant can demonstrate that the delay was unavoidable.

1. The Court of Customs and Patent Appeals and the United States Court of Claims were predecessors of the Federal Circuit, which adopted their decisions as binding precedent.

(i) Continuation and Divisional Applications

Under Section 120, a patent applicant may file a second application containing the same disclosure as the previous (or "parent") application while receiving the benefit of the earlier filing date. Such a "continuation" application is used to add new claims and establish a right to further consideration by the patent examiner. It receives the benefit of the parent application's filing date only if: (1) it contains the same disclosure under Section 112, paragraph 1 (although it may contain new claims); (2) it is filed while the parent application is still pending; (3) it specifically cross-references the parent application; and (4) at least one of the inventors named in the parent application is also named in the later application. However, PTO rules specify that Section 120 applies only if no new inventors are added on the later application; addition of new inventors requires a continuation-in-part application. 37 C.F.R. §§ 1.60(b)–(d), 1.62(c).

A "continuation-in-part" application is one which contains claims unsupported by the disclosure of the parent application. To support the new claims, the applicant adds new matter to the disclosure. Thus, in a priority dispute involving a continuation-in-part application, those claims supported by the disclosure in the parent application receive the benefit of the latter's filing date, but those claims which depend on the new matter that was added in the continuation-in-part application are entitled only to the filing date of the continuation-in-part application.

A "divisional" application under Section 121 is a later application for an invention that was originally included in, but was later separated from, the claims of the parent application. To be entitled to the parent's filing date, the divisional application must disclose or claim only subject matter that was disclosed in the parent application. Both a "continuation-in-part" and a "divisional" application must have at least one inventor in common with their respective parent applications.

A "substitute" application, which duplicates a previously-abandoned application, is not entitled to the latter's filing date because the applications are not co-pending.

(ii) Reissue Applications

When a patent is found to be wholly or partly invalid or inoperative as a result of defects in the specification or drawing(s), or claims that are too broad or too narrow, under Section 251 a patentee may obtain a corrected, or "reissue," patent for the remainder of the patent term, provided that the defects in the original patent were the result of error and not "deceptive intention."[2] However, a patentee may not use this procedure to introduce "new matter" into the patent specification or to claim an invention that was not disclosed in the original patent.

---

2. In addition to revising claims that are too broad or too narrow, reissue patents have been permitted to remedy defects in claims to priority, and to amend claims that are invalid due to ambiguity.

To the extent that the claims in the reissue patent are substantially identical to those in the original patent, the reissue patent is treated like a continuation patent and is effective retroactively to the issue date of the original patent. New or amended claims are effective only from the date of reissue. *See Spectronics Corp. v. H.B. Fuller Co., Inc.,* 940 F.2d 631 (Fed.Cir.1991), *cert. denied,* 502 U.S. 1013, 112 S.Ct. 658, 116 L.Ed.2d 749 (1991). However, where a reissue patent broadens the claims of the original patent, the reissue application must be filed within two years of the granting of the original patent. In addition, the statute protects the "intervening rights" of parties that manufactured, purchased, offered to sell, used or imported anything covered by the reissue patent; those parties may continue to use, sell, or offer to sell that "specific thing"[3] after the reissue, unless those activities would infringe any valid claims of the original patent that carry over into the reissue patent.[4] Where the claims of the reissue patent are narrower than the claims of the original patent, the doctrine of intervening rights also protects a party that relied on the invalidity of the original overbroad claims. *See, e.g., Wayne–Gossard Corp. v. Moretz Hosiery Mills, Inc.,* 539 F.2d 986 (4th Cir.1976).

The reissue application must be for same invention that was disclosed in the original patent. Section 251's prohibition against "new matter" bars use of the reissue procedure where new information must be added to the original specification in order to satisfy the minimum requirements of Section 112, paragraph 1. In *In re Oda,* 443 F.2d 1200, 1206 (CCPA 1971), the Court of Customs and Patent Appeals acknowledged the difficulty of defining "new matter," but permitted the patentee to correct an obvious translation error in the specification. Because "the reissue statute is based on fundamental principles of equity and fairness," the court held that an appropriate standard was whether "one skilled in the art would appreciate not only the existence of error in the specification but what the error is." *Compare In re Hay,* 534 F.2d 917, 919 (CCPA 1976) (where patent is invalid due to inadequate disclosure, reissue is unavailable to cure the defect by "seeking to put into the specification something required to be there when the patent application was originally filed"), *cert. denied,* 429 U.S. 977, 97 S.Ct. 485, 50 L.Ed.2d 585 (1976).

(iii) Establishing Priority by Filing Date of Foreign Application

Under Section 119(a), a patent applicant can establish priority through constructive reduction to practice based on the filing date of the

---

3. The "intervening rights" also apply when the "specific thing" is repaired, but not when it is modified to a different form. *See Cohen v. United States,* 487 F.2d 525, 528 (Ct.Cl.1973).

4. The statute gives courts discretion to recognize a still broader right to engage in activities that infringe the reissued patent, but not the original patent, where "sub-stantial preparation" for the activities was made before the date of reissue, "to such extent and under such terms as the court deems equitable for the protection of investments made or business commenced before the grant of the reissue." 35 U.S.C.A. § 252.

earliest foreign patent application disclosing (even if not claiming) the same invention. The foreign application must have been filed by the same applicant (or the applicant's legal representatives or assigns) in a foreign country which provides reciprocity to United States citizens and patent applications, and may not predate the filing of the United States patent application by more than twelve months (six months for design patents, under Section 172). It is not necessary that the foreign patent actually issue. Under Section 119(c), an applicant can rely on the filing date of a foreign application filed later than the earliest foreign application, but only if it is filed in the same country *and* the earlier foreign application has been terminated without public disclosure of its contents.

Any priority granted under Section 119 can be invoked only in *favor* of a patent applicant. It cannot be used to create an earlier reference date for prior art under Sections 102(e) and 102(g). *See In re Hilmer*, 359 F.2d 859, 862 (CCPA 1966); *In re Hilmer*, 424 F.2d 1108, 1112–13 (CCPA 1970).

(iv) Reexamination of Issued Patents

Sections 301 through 318, as amended in 2002, set forth the procedures for PTO reexamination of the validity of one or more claims in an issued patent. Such reexamination procedures are typically less costly than challenging the validity of a patent through litigation.

Under the *ex parte* reexamination provisions, 35 U.S.C.A. §§ 301–307, any person may petition the PTO for reexamination of an issued patent based on prior art patents or printed publications, or the PTO Director may reexamine the patent on his or her own initiative. The patent owner is entitled to respond to the validity challenge, and to appeal an adverse determination to the Board and ultimately to the Federal Circuit. The party requesting reexamination has a very limited opportunity to participate in the reexamination process, and has no right of appeal.

Alternatively, pursuant to Sections 311–318 (enacted in 1999), any person other than the patent owner may request an *inter partes* reexamination of a patent based on prior art patents or printed publications. Both the requester and the patent owner participate in the reexamination process, and either party may appeal an adverse determination to the Federal Circuit. However, if a claim is finally determined to be valid as a result of inter partes reexamination, then the requester will be estopped from challenging the validity of that claim on any ground which the requester raised or could have raised during the reexamination proceedings.

In both types of reexaminations, the PTO will consider no prior art other than patents and printed publications. However, under the 2002 amendments, the PTO will consider prior art patents and printed publications in a reexamination proceeding regardless of whether it had already considered the same prior art in the original examination.

2. PROVISIONAL PATENT APPLICATIONS

Section 111 allows inventors to file provisional patent applications ("PPAs"), which require specifications and drawings but no claims. If the provisional application is not followed by a complete application within one year, it will be deemed abandoned, unless the applicant has, in the interim, asked for the PPA to be treated as a nonprovisional application under Section 111(a).

Under Section 119(e)(1), the filing date of the provisional application will apply to the complete application, provided the latter is filed within one year and names at least one of the same inventors. Thus, a PPA may be filed to create domestic priority based on the PPA date, although the patent term does not commence until the filing date of the nonprovisional application. A PPA is not entitled to priority based on any other patent application or filing date under Sections 119, 120, 121, 365(a) or 365(c).

The provisional application is not examined for patentability and cannot be placed in interference; it also cannot benefit from the priority or filing date of any earlier application under Sections 119–21 or 365. Under PTO Rule 53(b), 37 C.F.R. § 1.53(b), within one year of filing a complete patent application, an applicant may, for a fee, convert that application to a provisional application, but the applicant then loses the benefit of any earlier-filed applications from which the nonprovisional application had derived its priority or filing date.

Under Section 172, PPA's cannot establish priority for design patents.

3. REFORMING THE PATENT PROCESS

Recent reports by the Federal Trade Commission and the National Research Council have raised serious concerns regarding the quality of issued patents. Patents of questionable validity can have a chilling effect on competition, because of the high cost of challenging a patent in court. The PTO has come under increasing criticism for conducting inadequate prior art searches during the patent examination process, leading to the issuance of patents of doubtful validity. However, the broadening scope of patentable subject matter, the increasing number of patent applications received by the PTO, and a lack of searchable databases in many subject areas have made it difficult for patent examiners to uncover all of the prior art that may be relevant to a particular invention.

In response to these concerns, the Patent Quality Assistance Act (PQAA), H.R. 5299, was introduced in 2004, but not enacted. This proposed legislation would have introduced a number of reforms aimed at improving the quality of issued patents and providing additional mechanisms to challenge patent validity without incurring the expense of litigation. The proposed reforms included (1) establishing a post-grant opposition procedure, (2) permitting third party submissions during a limited time period while a patent application is pending, (3) narrowing the estoppel provision for *inter partes* patent reexamination proceedings, and (4) establishing a presumption of obviousness for certain business method inventions as to which the only point of novelty is the use of computer technology.

Some of the PQAA's proposals for reforming PTO procedures were reintroduced in the Patents Depend on Quality Act of 2006 (PDQA), H.R. 5096 (introduced in April of 2006 but never enacted). Like the PQAA, the PDQA would have established a post-grant opposition procedure within the PTO, allowing submission of opposition requests up to nine months after a patent issues, and up to six months after the requester receives a notice of infringement. It would also have required that *all* patent applications be published 18 months after filing, and would have allowed prior art submissions by third parties during the six-month period following publication of an application, in order to give patent examiners greater access to prior art during the examination process. In addition, the PDQA would have altered the estoppel that arises from *inter partes* reexamination proceedings (and which has discouraged parties from making use of these proceedings) by eliminating the " ... or could have raised ... " estoppel of current law (35 U.S.C. § 315(c)). The PDQA would also have expanded the availability of *inter partes* reexamination to include all subsisting patents, regardless of filing date, and would have limited the ability of parties to invoke *inter partes* reexamination after district court litigation. A number of these provisions have been reintroduced in the proposed Patent Reform Act of 2007.

In an effort to increase the access of patent examiners to relevant prior art, the PTO is collaborating with New York Law School on the Community Patent Review project, with the goal of creating an open web-based network for peer review of patent applications. The initial implementation of this network (which began in May 2007) focuses on software-related patent applications. *See* Beth Simone Noveck, *"Peer to Patent": Collective Intelligence, Open Review, and Patent Reform*, 20 Harv. J. Law & Tech. 123 (2006). The Patent Reform Act of 2007 includes a proposal that would allow third parties to submit relevant information directly to the PTO during the examination process.

An important administrative development is the institution of electronic filing for patent applications and related documents. The PTO's new web-based electronic patent application filing system (EFS–Web) became available for use in March of 2006.

C. TERM OF PATENT PROTECTION

Statutes: 35 U.S.C.A. §§ 119(e), 154, 156, 173

The Uruguay Round Agreements Act ("URAA")[5] amended Section 154 to change the term of protection for utility and plant patents from

---

5. Pub. L. No. 103–465, 108 Stat. 4809 (December 8, 1994). The change is effective for patents with U.S. application dates on or after June 8, 1995, including original, continuation, divisional, and Section 365(c) international applications.

17 years from issuance to 20 years from filing. Limited extensions are permitted where prosecution of a patent is delayed by interferences, appeals, secrecy orders, or PTO processing delays.

The URAA did not alter the term of protection for design patents, which remains 14 years from the date of issue, under Section 173.

Under the Drug Price Competition and Patent Term Restoration Act of 1984 (the Hatch–Waxman Act), codified at 35 U.S.C.A. § 156, the term of a patent involving a drug product, medical device, or food or color additive may be extended once (beyond any extension already granted under Section 154(b)), upon submission of a timely application, if the patentholder did not receive the full benefit of the statutory patent term because the marketing of the product in question was delayed by regulatory review under the Federal Food, Drug and Cosmetic Act. Section 156 contains detailed provisions regarding the length of such extensions. In *Merck & Co. v. Kessler,* 80 F.3d 1543 (Fed.Cir.1996), *cert. denied sub nom. Organon, Inc. v. Kessler,* 519 U.S. 1101, 117 S.Ct. 788, 136 L.Ed.2d 730 (1997), the Federal Circuit held that section 156 extensions may be added to the end of the new URAA-mandated 20–year patent term, except where a patent remained in force on June 8, 1995 only because of a prior Section 156 extension.

Notes

1.   Suppose that a senior inventor's patent issues after a good faith junior inventor (or assignee or licensee thereof) has already begun making or using an identical product or process, with no knowledge of the senior inventor's prior claim. What rights in the invention can the junior inventor assert (a) while the senior inventor's patent application is pending, and (b) after the patent issues? Consider whether this result should be changed through legislation, and if so, how.

2.   What policy arguments support measuring the patent term from (a) the date the application is filed? (b) the date the patent issues?

3.   Suppose that an interference is declared between inventors X and Y, each of whom independently conceived the same invention. X conceived first, but Y filed a patent application while X was still working diligently to reduce the invention to practice. By the time X filed a patent application, Y had been producing and selling the invention for 14 months. If all events took place within the United States, which inventor should be awarded the patent? Does your answer change if any of X's or Y's activities took place overseas?

4.   Suppose that Section 119 permits an applicant for a utility patent to establish constructive reduction to practice by reference to the July 1, 2005 filing date of a foreign application disclosing that invention, and the applicant filed a United States application on June 1, 2006.

(a) If the invention in question had already become known to the public in the U.S. as of January 1, 2005, will the U.S. application be subject to a statutory bar?

(b) If the U.S. patent issued on January 1, 2007, when will the patent term expire?

(c) If another inventor filed a PPA for the same invention (and converted it to nonprovisional status within one year), which applicant would receive priority based on filing date if the PPA was filed on May 1, 2005? On August 1, 2005?

5. In determining whether a statutory bar applies to a patent application which commenced as a PPA, which filing date applies?

Chapter 14

PATENT INFRINGEMENT, DEFENSES AND REMEDIES

A. INFRINGEMENT

Statutes: 35 U.S.C.A. §§ 154(a), 163, 271, 289

During the patent term, the holder of a design or utility patent has the right to exclude others from making, using, selling, or offering to sell the invention throughout the United States, and from importing the invention into this country. Where the invention is a process, the exclusive rights extend also to products produced by that process. A patent holder may, under certain circumstances, exclude others from *exporting* components of a patented combination for assembly abroad (Section 271(f)), and may exclude others from *importing* unpatented products made abroad if those products were made with a process protected by a United States patent (Section 271(g)).

In contrast, under Section 163, the holder of a plant patent has only the right to exclude others from asexually reproducing the plant or selling or using the plant so reproduced.

As discussed in the readings below, to constitute *literal infringement*, an accused product or process must literally embody every limitation in the claim(s) alleged to have been infringed. Under the *doctrine of equivalents*, however, minor departures from the literal claims of a patent will not necessarily bar a finding of infringement. Conversely, even exact correspondence with the literal language of a claim will not lead to a finding of infringement where the accused device or process is not functionally equivalent to what is claimed.

1. COMPARING THE ACCUSED SUBJECT MATTER WITH THE CLAIMS

AUTOGIRO COMPANY OF AMERICA
v. THE UNITED STATES

United States Court of Claims, 1967.
384 F.2d 391.

DURFEE, JUDGE.

* * *

I

The Patent Act of 1952, 35 U.S.C. § 1 et seq., which applies to all patents granted on or before January 1, 1953, is the controlling law in this case. No previous patent act contained a section on infringement. Congress had always allowed the courts to settle the issue without any legislative guidelines. Section 271(a) which covers the type of infringement alleged here was not inserted in the Act to clarify any legal problems, but only as a codification of existing judicial determinations. * * *

The claims of the patent provide the concise formal definition of the invention. They are the numbered paragraphs which "particularly [point] out and distinctly [claim] the subject matter which the applicant regards as his invention." 35 U.S.C. § 112. It is to these wordings that one must look to determine whether there has been infringement. Courts can neither broaden nor narrow the claims to give the patentee something different than what he has set forth. No matter how great the temptations of fairness or policy making, courts do not rework claims. They only interpret them. Although courts are confined by the language of the claims, they are not, however, confined to the language of the claims in interpreting their meaning.

Courts occasionally have confined themselves to the language of the claims. When claims have been found clear and unambiguous, courts have not gone beyond them to determine their content. Courts have also held that the fact that claims are free from ambiguity is no reason for limiting the material which may be inspected for the purpose of better understanding the meaning of claims. We find both approaches to be hypothetical. Claims cannot be clear and unambiguous on their face. A comparison must exist. The lucidity of a claim is determined in light of what ideas it is trying to convey. Only by knowing the idea, can one decide how much shadow encumbers the reality.

The very nature of words would make a clear and unambiguous claim a rare occurrence. Writing on statutory interpretation, Justice Frankfurter commented on the inexactitude of words:

They are symbols of meaning. But unlike mathematical symbols, the phrasing of a document, especially a complicated enactment, seldom attains more than approximate precision. If individual words are inexact symbols, with shifting variables, their configuration can hardly achieve invariant meaning or assured definiteness.

Frankfurter, Some Reflections on the Reading of Statutes, 47 Col.L.Rev. 527, 528 (1947). *See, also,* A Re–Evaluation of the Use of Legislative History in the Federal Courts, 52 Col.L.Rev. 125 (1952).

The inability of words to achieve precision is none the less extant with patent claims than it is with statutes. The problem is likely more acute with claims. Statutes by definition are the reduction of ideas to print. Since the ability to verbalize is crucial in statutory enactment, legislators develop a facility with words not equally developed in inventors. An invention exists most importantly as a tangible structure or a series of drawings. A verbal portrayal is usually an afterthought written to satisfy the requirements of patent law. This conversion of machine to words allows for unintended idea gaps which cannot be satisfactorily filled. Often the invention is novel and words do not exist to describe it. The dictionary does not always keep abreast of the inventor. It cannot. Things are not made for the sake of words, but words for things. To overcome this lag, patent law allows the inventor to be his own lexicographer. Allowing the patentee verbal license only augments the difficulty of understanding the claims. The sanction of new words or hybrids from old ones not only leaves one unsure what a rose is, but also unsure whether a rose is a rose. Thus we find that a claim cannot be interpreted without going beyond the claim itself. No matter how clear a claim appears to be, lurking in the background are documents that may completely disrupt initial views on its meaning.

The necessity for a sensible and systematic approach to claim interpretation is axiomatic. The Alice-in-Wonderland view that something means whatever one chooses it to mean makes for enjoyable reading, but bad law. Claims are best construed in connection with the other parts of the patent instrument and with the circumstances surrounding the inception of the patent application. In utilizing all the patent documents, one should not sacrifice the value of these references by the 'unimaginative adherence to well-worn professional phrases.' Frankfurter, *supra,* at 529. Patent law is replete with major canons of construction of minor value which have seldom provided useful guidance in the unraveling of complex claims. Instead, these canons have only added confusion to the problem of claim interpretation.

* * *

II

In deriving the meaning of a claim, we inspect all useful documents and reach what Justice Holmes called the "felt meaning" of the claim. In seeking this goal, we make use of three parts of the patent: the specification, the drawings, and the file wrapper.

Specification.—Section 112 of the 1952 Patent Act requires the specification to describe the manner and process of making and using the invention so that any person skilled in the patent's art may utilize it. In serving its statutory purpose, the specification aids in ascertaining the scope and meaning of the language employed in the claims inasmuch as words must be used in the same way in both the claims and the specification. U.S. Pat. Off. Rule 75(d). The use of the specification as a concordance for the claims is accepted by almost every court, and is a basic concept of patent law. * * *

The specification "set[s] forth the best mode contemplated by the inventor of carrying out his invention." 35 U.S.C. § 112. This one embodiment of the invention does not restrict the claims. Claim interpretation must not make use of "best mode" terms inasmuch as the patentee need not guard against infringement by listing every possible infringing device in the specification. But where the specification does not refer to an embodiment or a class of embodiments in terms of "best mode," such reference may be of value in claim interpretation. This would be where the patentee describes an embodiment as being the invention itself and not only one way of utilizing it.

Drawings.—The patent may contain drawings. 35 U.S.C. § 113. In those instances where a visual representation can flesh out words, drawings may be used in the same manner and with the same limitations as the specification.

File wrapper.—The file wrapper contains the entire record of the proceedings in the Patent Office from the first application papers to the issued patent. Since all express representations of the patent applicant made to induce a patent grant are in the file wrapper, this material provides an accurate charting of the patent's pre-issuance history. One use of the file wrapper is file wrapper estoppel, which is the application of familiar estoppel principles to Patent Office prosecution and patent infringement litigation. The patent applicant must convince the patent examiner that his invention meets the statutory requirements; otherwise, a patent will not be issued. When the application is rejected, the applicant will insert limitations and restrictions for the purpose of inducing the Patent Office to grant his patent. When the patent is issued, the patentee cannot disclaim these alterations and seek an interpretation that would ignore them. He cannot construe the claims narrowly before the Patent Office and later broadly before the courts. File wrapper estoppel serves two functions in claim interpretation; the applicant's statements not only define terms, but also set the barriers within which the claim's meaning must be kept. These results arise when the file wrapper discloses either what the claim covers or what it does not cover.

The file wrapper also has a broader and more general use. This is its utilization, like the specification and drawings, to determine the scope of claims. For example, the prior art cited in the file wrapper is used in this manner. In file wrapper estoppel, it is not the prior art that provides the guidelines, but the applicant's acquiescence with regard to the prior art.

In its broader use as source material, the prior art cited in the file wrapper gives clues as to what the claims do not cover.

III

The use of the various parts of the patent to determine the meaning of the claims is only half the process of determining patent infringement. The other half is "reading the claims on the accused structures." If the claims read literally on the accused structures, an initial hurdle in the test for infringement has been cleared. The race is not over; it has only started. To allow literality to satisfy the test for infringement would force the patent law to reward literary skill and not mechanical creativity. And since the law is to benefit the inventor's genius and not the scrivener's talents, claims must not only read literally on the accused structures, but also the structures must "do the same work, in substantially the same way, and accomplish substantially the same result." Dominion Magnesium Ltd. v. United States, 162 Ct. Cl. 240, 252, 320 F. 2d 388, 396 (1963). This approach of making literal overlap only a step and not the entire test of infringement has been consistently applied by the courts since Westinghouse v. Boyden Power–Brake Co., 170 U.S. 537 (1898), where Justice Brown stated at 568:

> The patentee may bring the defendant within the letter of his claims, but if the latter has so far changed the principle of the device that the claims of the patent, literally construed, have ceased to represent his actual invention, he is as little subject to be adjudged an infringer as one who has violated the letter of a statute has to be convicted, when he has done nothing in conflict with its spirit and intent.

If the claims do not read literally on the accused structures, infringement is not necessarily ruled out. The doctrine of equivalence casts around a claim a penumbra which also must be avoided if there is to be no infringement. It provides that a structure infringes, without there being literal overlap, if it performs substantially the same function in substantially the same way and for substantially the same purpose as the claims set forth. Equivalence is the obverse of the discounting of literal overlap. The latter is to protect the accused; the former to protect the patentee. The rationale behind equivalence was set forth by the Supreme Court in Graver Tank & Mfg. Co. v. Linde Air Products Co., [339 U.S. 605, 607 (1950)]:

> [T]o permit imitation of a patented invention which does not copy every literal detail would be to convert the protection of the patent grant into a hollow and useless thing. Such a limitation would leave room for—indeed encourage—the unscrupulous copyist to make unimportant and unsubstantial changes and substitutions in the patent which, though adding nothing, would be enough to take the copied matter outside the claim, and hence outside the reach of the law.

Checking the subordination of substance to form and not depriving the inventor of the benefit of his invention cannot be standardized. The range of equivalence varies with each patent; however, some general guidelines can be drawn. One important guide is whether persons reasonably skilled in the art would have known of the interchangeability of an ingredient not contained in the patent with one that was. *Id.* at 609. Another guide is the notion that pioneer patents are to be given wider ranges of equivalence than minor improvement patents. This statement is less a canon of construction and more a shorthand expression for the dictates of the law and the patents themselves. The doctrine of equivalence is subservient to file wrapper estoppel. It may not include within its range anything that would vitiate limitations expressed before the Patent Office. Thus a patent that has been severely limited to avoid the prior art will only have a small range between it and the point beyond which it violates file wrapper estoppel. Similarly a patent which is a major departure from the prior art will have a larger range in which equivalence can function. The scope of the patents also influences the range of equivalence. A pioneer patent which occupies symbolically a six-inch circle will have three inches of equivalence if its range is fifty percent. An improvement patent occupying a two-inch circle has only one inch of equivalence with the same range. Thus with relatively identical ranges, the scope of the patent provides the pioneer patent with absolutely a larger range of equivalence.

IV

In summary, the determination of patent infringement is a two-step process. First, the meaning of the claims in issue must be determined by a study of all relevant patent documents. Secondly, the claims must be read on the accused structures. In doing this, it is of little value that they read literally on the structures. What is crucial is that the structures must do the same work, in substantially the same way, and accomplish substantially the same result to constitute infringement. This is the general approach which this court uses to determine the infringement of all the patent claims properly before it in this case.

* * *

Notes

1. Ordinarily, the test for interpreting the meaning of a claim term is determined from the vantage point of one skilled in the art. *See SmithKline Diagnostics, Inc. v. Helena Lab. Corp.,* 859 F.2d 878, 882 (Fed.Cir.1988). In *Markman v. Westview Instruments, Inc.,* 517 U.S. 370, 116 S.Ct. 1384, 134 L.Ed.2d 577 (1996), the Supreme Court held that the judge, rather than the jury, should decide questions of claim interpretation in an infringement action. The Court emphasized that judges are better trained in "the construction of written instruments," and noted that patent construction, in particular, requires specialized training and discipline. The Court took special note of "the importance of uniformity in the treatment of a given patent:"

As we noted in General Elec. Co. v. Wabash Appliance Corp., 304 U.S. 364, 369, 58 S.Ct. 899, 902, 82 L.Ed. 1402 (1938), "the limits of a patent must be known for the protection of the patentee, the encouragement of the inventive genius of others and the assurance that the subject of the patent will be dedicated ultimately to the public." Otherwise, a "zone of uncertainty which enterprise and experimentation may enter only at the risk of infringement claims would discourage invention only a little less than unequivocal foreclosure of the field," United Carbon Co. v. Binney & Smith Co., 317 U.S. 228, 236, 63 S.Ct. 165, 170, 87 L.Ed. 232 (1942), and "[t]he public [would] be deprived of rights supposed to belong to it, without being clearly told what it is that limits these rights." Merrill v. Yeomans, 94 U.S. 568, 573, 24 L.Ed. 235 (1877).

116 S.Ct. at 1396, 134 L.Ed.2d at 592.

2. *Interpreting Product-by-Process Claims*: Traditionally, the PTO required an applicant for a product patent to describe the claimed product in terms of its structural characteristics. Recognizing, however, that some products resist structural description, the PTO created a narrow exception permitting an applicant for a product patent to claim the product by describing the process by which it was produced, but only where necessitated by the difficulty of describing the product in structural terms. A product-by-process patent was not available for a product that existed in the prior art. In *Merrill v. Yeomans*, 94 U.S. (4 Otto) 568, 24 L.Ed.2d 235 (1877), the Supreme Court held that such product-by-process claims were not infringed by a substantially identical product made by a different process.

In 1974, however, the PTO liberalized its approach and began permitting product-by-process claims even for products for which a structural description was possible, provided the claim in question satisfied the definiteness requirement of Section 112. The proliferation of such patents has led to conflicting Federal Circuit decisions on whether a product-by-process patent is infringed where the defendant makes the same product by a different process. *Compare Scripps Clinic & Research Found. v. Genentech, Inc.*, 927 F.2d 1565 (Fed.Cir.1991), *reh'g en banc denied*, 1991 WL 525082 (Fed.Cir.1991) (product-by-process patent covers product, no matter how produced, because patentability of the product is independent of the process) *with Atlantic Thermoplastics Co. v. Faytex Corp.*, 970 F.2d 834 (Fed.Cir.), *reh'g en banc denied*, 974 F.2d 1299 (Fed.Cir.1992) (patent covers only products produced by the same process, because process is a limitation on the claim).

In *SmithKline Beecham Corp. v. Apotex Corp.*, 439 F.3d 1312 (Fed. Cir. 2006), the Federal Circuit passed up an opportunity to resolve the product-by-process confusion, holding that where a prior art patent claimed a product without regard to the process by which it was made, a future claim to the same product was anticipated even if it involved making the product by a new process. After expressly declining to resolve the conflict between *Scripps* and *Atlantic Thermoplastics*, the court observed: "Regardless of how broadly or narrowly one construes a product-by-process claim, it is clear that such claims are always to a product, not a process. It has long been established that one cannot avoid anticipation by an earlier product disclosure by claiming the same product more narrowly, that is, by claiming the product as produced by a particular process." *Id.* at 1317. Therefore, the court held:

> [A]nticipation by an earlier product patent cannot be avoided by claim-ing the same product more narrowly in a product-process claim. It makes no difference here whether the [disputed] patent's product-by-process claims are construed broadly to cover the product made by any process or narrowly to cover only the product made by a dry admixing process. Either way, anticipation by an earlier product disclosure (which disclosed the product itself) cannot be avoided. While the process set forth in the product-by-process claim may be new, that novelty can only be captured by obtaining a process claim.

Id. at 1318–19. Dissenting from the denial of a petition for rehearing en bank in *Apotex,* 453 F.3d 1346 (Fed. Cir. 2006), three judges argued that the Federal Circuit should address the confusion over *Scripps* and *Atlantic Thermoplastics.*

The *Apotex* decision involved a question of invalidity due to anticipation; does it shed any light on the proper infringement analysis for product-by-process claims? Which approach–*Scripps* or *Atlantic Thermoplastics*—repre-sents better policy? *Compare Tropix, Inc. v. Lumigen,* Inc., 825 F.Supp. 7, 8 (D.Mass.1993) *with Trustees of Columbia University v. Roche Diagnostics GmbH,* 126 F.Supp.2d 16, 32–33 (D.Mass.2000).

3. In *Phillips v. AWH Corp.,* 376 F.3d 1382 (Fed. Cir. 2004), the Federal Circuit granted a petition for rehearing en banc in a case presenting numerous issues of claim construction. The vacated panel opinion in that case had held that the term "baffle" in the claims should be construed in light of the specification to have a narrower meaning than the dictionary definition of that term; the dissent argued that the dictionary definition should govern. *Phillips v. AWH Corp.,* 363 F.3d 1207 (Fed. Cir. 2004). In its order granting the rehearing en banc, the Federal Circuit requested briefing on, *inter alia:*

> (i) The respective weight to be accorded to technical dictionaries, gener-al purpose dictionaries, expert testimony, prosecution history, and the language of the specification in determining the meaning of claim terms;

> (ii) When, if ever, claim language should be construed narrowly for the sole purpose of avoiding invalidity under, *e.g.,* 35 U.S.C. §§ 102, 103, and 112;

> (iii) The degree of deference, if any, which the court should accord to any aspect of trial court claim construction rulings.

Phillips v. AWH Corp., 376 F.3d 1382, 1383 (Fed. Cir. 2004).

In a disappointment to court watchers, however, the en banc decision in *Phillips* offered no new insights, simply reaffirming that the primary sources for claim construction are the language of the claim, the written description, and the prosecution history. The court rejected the suggestion in some earlier case law that dictionaries should be the starting point for claim interpretation, and did not address the question whether any deference should be given to a district court's claim construction. *Phillips v. AWH*

Corp., *415 F.3d 1303 (Fed. Cir. 2005) (en banc),* cert. denied, ___ U.S. ___, *126 S.Ct. 1332, 164 L.Ed.2d 49 (2006).*

4. *De Novo Review of Claim Construction*: According to the Federal Circuit's decision in *Cybor Corp. v. FAS Technologies, Inc.,* 138 F.3d 1448 (Fed.Cir.1998), because claim construction is a question of law a district court's claim construction is always subject to de novo review by the Federal Circuit. This rule has been criticized for adding another layer of uncertainty to patent litigation. *See, e.g., Phillips v. AWH Corp.,* 415 F.3d at 1330–35 (Mayer, J., dissenting). The proposed Patent Reform Act of 2007 would allow interlocutory appeals regarding claim construction.

2. THE DOCTRINE OF EQUIVALENTS AND PROSECUTION HISTORY ESTOPPEL

WARNER–JENKINSON COMPANY, INC. v. HILTON DAVIS CHEMICAL CO.

Supreme Court of the United States, 1997.
520 U.S. 17, 117 S.Ct. 1040, 137 L.Ed.2d 146.

JUSTICE THOMAS delivered the opinion of the Court.

Nearly 50 years ago, this Court in Graver Tank & Mfg. Co. v. Linde Air Products Co., 339 U.S. 605, 70 S.Ct. 854, 94 L.Ed. 1097 (1950), set out the modern contours of what is known in patent law as the "doctrine of equivalents." Under this doctrine, a product or process that does not literally infringe upon the express terms of a patent claim may nonetheless be found to infringe if there is "equivalence" between the elements of the accused product or process and the claimed elements of the patented invention. *Id.,* at 609. Petitioner, which was found to have infringed upon respondent's patent under the doctrine of equivalents, invites us to speak the death of that doctrine. We decline that invitation. The significant disagreement within the Court of Appeals for the Federal Circuit concerning the application of *Graver Tank* suggests, however, that the doctrine is not free from confusion. We therefore will endeavor to clarify the proper scope of the doctrine.

I

* * *

[Respondent Hilton Davis's patent (the '746 patent) claims an "ultrapurification" process for purifying dyes, utilizing a specified range of hydrostatic pressure and a pH range of "approximately 6.0 to 9.0." The upper pH limit of 9.0 was added during patent prosecution to distinguish prior art (the "Booth patent") which used pH levels above 9.0. When Warner–Jenkinson began commercial use of a similar process using a pH of 5.0, Hilton Davis sued for patent infringement.]

As trial approached, Hilton Davis conceded that there was no literal infringement, and relied solely on the doctrine of equivalents. Over Warner–Jenkinson's objection that the doctrine of equivalents was an equitable doctrine to be applied by the court, the issue of equivalence was included among those sent to the jury. The jury found that the '746 patent was not invalid and that Warner–Jenkinson infringed upon the patent under the doctrine of equivalents. * * * A fractured en banc Court of Appeals for the Federal Circuit affirmed.

The majority below held that the doctrine of equivalents continues to exist and that its touchstone is whether substantial differences exist between the accused process and the patented process. The court also held that the question of equivalence is for the jury to decide and that the jury in this case had substantial evidence from which it could conclude that the Warner–Jenkinson process was not substantially different from the ultrafiltration process disclosed in the '746 patent.

There were three separate dissents, commanding a total of 5 of 12 judges. Four of the five dissenting judges viewed the doctrine of equivalents as allowing an improper expansion of claim scope, contrary to this Court's numerous holdings that it is the claim that defines the invention and gives notice to the public of the limits of the patent monopoly. The fifth dissenter, the late Judge Nies, was able to reconcile the prohibition against enlarging the scope of claims and the doctrine of equivalents by applying the doctrine to each element of a claim, rather than to the accused product or process "overall." As she explained it, "[t]he 'scope' is not enlarged if courts do not go beyond the substitution of equivalent elements." All of the dissenters, however, would have found that a much narrowed doctrine of equivalents may be applied in whole or in part by the court.

We granted certiorari, and now reverse and remand.

II

In *Graver Tank* we considered the application of the doctrine of equivalents to an accused chemical composition for use in welding that differed from the patented welding material by the substitution of one chemical element. 339 U.S., at 610. The substituted element did not fall within the literal terms of the patent claim, but the Court nonetheless found that the "question which thus emerges is whether the substitution [of one element for the other] . . . is a change of such substance as to make the doctrine of equivalents inapplicable; or conversely, whether under the circumstances the change was so insubstantial that the trial court's invocation of the doctrine of equivalents was justified." *Ibid.* The Court also described some of the considerations that go into applying the doctrine of equivalents:

> "What constitutes equivalency must be determined against the context of the patent, the prior art, and the particular circumstances of the case. Equivalence, in the patent law, is not the prisoner of a formula and is not an absolute to be considered in a vacuum. It does not require complete identity for every purpose and in every respect. In determining equivalents, things equal to the same thing may not be equal to each other and, by the same token, things for most purposes different may sometimes be equivalents. Consideration

must be given to the purpose for which an ingredient is used in a patent, the qualities it has when combined with the other ingredients, and the function which it is intended to perform. An important factor is whether persons reasonably skilled in the art would have known of the interchangeability of an ingredient not contained in the patent with one that was." *Id.* at 609.

Considering those factors, the Court viewed the difference between the chemical element claimed in the patent and the substitute element to be "colorable only," and concluded that the trial court's judgment of infringement under the doctrine of equivalents was proper.

A

Petitioner's primary argument in this Court is that the doctrine of equivalents, as set out in *Graver Tank* in 1950, did not survive the 1952 revision of the Patent Act, 35 U.S.C. § 100 *et seq.,* because it is inconsistent with several aspects of that Act. In particular, petitioner argues: (1) the doctrine of equivalents is inconsistent with the statutory requirement that a patentee specifically "claim" the invention covered by a patent, 35 U.S.C. § 112; (2) the doctrine circumvents the patent reissue process—designed to correct mistakes in drafting or the like— and avoids the express limitations on that process, 35 U.S.C. §§ 251– 252; (3) the doctrine is inconsistent with the primacy of the Patent and Trademark Office (PTO) in setting the scope of a patent through the patent prosecution process; and (4) the doctrine was implicitly rejected as a general matter by Congress' specific and limited inclusion of the doctrine in one section regarding "means" claiming, 35 U.S.C. § 112, ¶ 6. All but one of these arguments were made in *Graver Tank* in the context of the 1870 Patent Act, and failed to command a majority.

The 1952 Patent Act is not materially different from the 1870 Act with regard to claiming, reissue, and the role of the PTO. *Compare, e.g.,* 35 U.S.C. § 112 ("The specification shall conclude with one or more claims particularly pointing out and distinctly claiming the subject matter which the applicant regards as his invention") *with* The Consolidated Patent Act of 1870, ch. 230, § 26, 16 Stat. 198, 201 (the applicant "shall particularly point out and distinctly claim the part, improvement, or combination which he claims as his invention or discovery"). Such minor differences as exist between those provisions in the 1870 and the 1952 Acts have no bearing on the result reached in *Graver Tank*, and thus provide no basis for our overruling it. * * *

Petitioner's fourth argument for an implied congressional negation of the doctrine of equivalents turns on the reference to "equivalents" in the "means" claiming provision of the 1952 Act. Section 112, ¶ 6, a provision not contained in the 1870 Act, states:

"An element in a claim for a combination may be expressed as a means or step for performing a specified function without the recital of structure, material, or acts in support thereof, and such claim shall be construed to cover the corresponding structure, material, or acts described in the specification *and equivalents thereof.*" (Emphasis added.)

Thus, under this new provision, an applicant can describe an element of his invention by the result accomplished or the function served, rather than describing the item or element to be used (*e.g.,* "a means of connecting Part A to Part B," rather than "a two-penny nail"). Congress enacted § 112, ¶ 6 in response to Halliburton Oil Well Cementing Co. v. Walker, which rejected claims that "do not describe the invention but use 'conveniently functional language at the exact point of novelty,'" 329 U.S. 1, 8, 67 S.Ct. 6, 91 L.Ed. 3 (1946) (citation omitted). Section 112, ¶ 6 now expressly allows so-called "means" claims, with the proviso that application of the broad literal language of such claims must be limited to only those means that are "equivalent" to the actual means shown in the patent specification. This is an application of the doctrine of equivalents in a restrictive role, narrowing the application of broad literal claim elements. We recognized this type of role for the doctrine of equivalents in *Graver Tank* itself. The added provision, however, is silent on the doctrine of equivalents as applied where there is no literal infringement.

Because § 112, ¶ 6 was enacted as a targeted cure to a specific problem, and because the reference in that provision to "equivalents" appears to be no more than a prophylactic against potential side effects of that cure, such limited congressional action should not be overread for negative implications. Congress in 1952 could easily have responded to *Graver Tank* as it did to the *Halliburton* decision. But it did not. Absent something more compelling than the dubious negative inference offered by petitioner, the lengthy history of the doctrine of equivalents strongly supports adherence to our refusal in *Graver Tank* to find that the Patent Act conflicts with that doctrine. Congress can legislate the doctrine of equivalents out of existence any time it chooses. The various policy arguments now made by both sides are thus best addressed to Congress, not this Court.

B

We do, however, share the concern of the dissenters below that the doctrine of equivalents, as it has come to be applied since *Graver Tank*, has taken on a life of its own, unbounded by the patent claims. There can be no denying that the doctrine of equivalents, when applied broadly, conflicts with the definitional and public-notice functions of the statutory claiming requirement. Judge Nies identified one means of avoiding this conflict:

> "[A] distinction can be drawn that is not too esoteric between substitution of an equivalent for a component *in* an invention and enlarging the metes and bounds of the invention *beyond* what is claimed.

* * *

"Where a claim to an invention is expressed as a combination of elements, as here, 'equivalents' in the sobriquet 'Doctrine of Equivalents' refers to the equivalency of an *element* or *part* of the invention with one that is substituted in the accused product or process.

* * *

"This view that the accused device or process must be more than 'equivalent' *overall* reconciles the Supreme Court's position on infringement by equivalents with its concurrent statements that 'the courts have no right to enlarge a patent beyond the scope of its claims as allowed by the Patent Office.' [Citations omitted.] The 'scope' is not enlarged if courts do not go beyond the substitution of equivalent elements." 62 F.3d, at 1573–1574 (Nies, J., dissenting) (emphasis in original).

We concur with this apt reconciliation of our two lines of precedent. Each element contained in a patent claim is deemed material to defining the scope of the patented invention, and thus the doctrine of equivalents must be applied to individual elements of the claim, not to the invention as a whole. It is important to ensure that the application of the doctrine, even as to an individual element, is not allowed such broad play as to effectively eliminate that element in its entirety. So long as the doctrine of equivalents does not encroach beyond the limits just described, or beyond related limits to be discussed infra, * * * we are confident that the doctrine will not vitiate the central functions of the patent claims themselves.

III

Understandably reluctant to assume this Court would overrule *Graver Tank*, petitioner has offered alternative arguments in favor of a more restricted doctrine of equivalents than it feels was applied in this case. We address each in turn.

A

Petitioner first argues that *Graver Tank* never purported to supersede a well-established limit on nonliteral infringement, known variously as "prosecution history estoppel" and "file wrapper estoppel." *See* Bayer Aktiengesellschaft v. Duphar Int'l Research B.V., 738 F.2d 1237, 1238 (C.A.Fed.1984). According to petitioner, any surrender of subject matter during patent prosecution, regardless of the reason for such surrender, precludes recapturing any part of that subject matter, even if it is equivalent to the matter expressly claimed. Because, during patent prosecution, respondent limited the pH element of its claim to pH levels between 6.0 and 9.0, petitioner would have those limits form bright lines beyond which no equivalents may be claimed. Any inquiry into the reasons for a surrender, petitioner claims, would undermine the public's right to clear notice of the scope of the patent as embodied in the patent file.

We can readily agree with petitioner that *Graver Tank* did not dispose of prosecution history estoppel as a legal limitation on the doctrine of equivalents. But petitioner reaches too far in arguing that the reason for an amendment during patent prosecution is irrelevant to any subsequent estoppel. In each of our cases cited by petitioner and by the dissent below, prosecution history estoppel was tied to amendments made to avoid the prior art, or otherwise to address a specific concern—such as obviousness—that arguably would have rendered the claimed subject matter unpatentable. Thus, in Exhibit Supply Co. v. Ace Patents Corp., Chief Justice Stone distinguished inclusion of a limiting phrase in an original patent claim from the "very different" situation in which "the applicant, in order to meet objections in the Patent Office, *based on references to the prior art,* adopted the phrase as a substitute for the broader one" previously used. 315 U.S. 126, 136, 62 S.Ct. 513, 86 L.Ed. 736 (1942) (emphasis added). Similarly, in Keystone Driller Co. v. Northwest Engineering Corp., 294 U.S. 42, 55 S.Ct. 262, 79 L.Ed. 747 (1935), estoppel was applied where the initial claims were "rejected on the prior art," *id.*, at 48, n. 6, and where the allegedly infringing equivalent element was outside of the revised claims and within the prior art that formed the basis for the rejection of the earlier claims, *id.*, at 48.

It is telling that in each case this Court probed the reasoning behind the Patent Office's insistence upon a change in the claims. In each instance, a change was demanded because the claim as otherwise written was viewed as not describing a patentable invention at all—typically because what it described was encompassed within the prior art. But, as the United States informs us, there are a variety of other reasons why the PTO may request a change in claim language. And if the PTO has been requesting changes in claim language without the intent to limit equivalents or, indeed, with the expectation that language it required would in many cases allow for a range of equivalents, we should be extremely reluctant to upset the basic assumptions of the PTO without substantial reason for doing so. Our prior cases have consistently applied prosecution history estoppel only where claims have been amended for a limited set of reasons, and we see no substantial cause for requiring a more rigid rule invoking an estoppel regardless of the reasons for a change.

In this case, the patent examiner objected to the patent claim due to a perceived overlap with the Booth patent, which revealed an ultrafiltration process operating at a pH above 9.0. In response to this objection, the phrase "at a pH from approximately 6.0 to 9.0" was added to the claim. While it is undisputed that the upper limit of 9.0 was added in order to distinguish the Booth patent, the reason for adding the lower limit of 6.0 is unclear. The lower limit certainly did not serve to distinguish the Booth patent, which said nothing about pH levels below 6.0. Thus, while a lower limit of 6.0, by its mere inclusion, became a material element of the claim, that did not necessarily preclude the application of the doctrine of equivalents as to that element. Where the reason for the change was not related to avoiding the prior art, the change may introduce a new element, but it does not necessarily preclude infringement by equivalents of that element.

We are left with the problem, however, of what to do in a case like the one at bar, where the record seems not to reveal the reason for including the lower pH limit of 6.0. In our view, holding that certain reasons for a claim amendment may avoid the application of prosecution history estoppel is not tantamount to holding that the absence of a reason for an amendment may similarly avoid such an estoppel. Mindful that claims do indeed serve both a definitional and a notice function, we think the better rule is to place the burden on the patentholder to establish the reason for an amendment required during patent prosecution. The court then would decide whether that reason is sufficient to overcome prosecution history estoppel as a bar to application of the doctrine of equivalents to the element added by that amendment. Where no explanation is established, however, the court should presume that the PTO had a substantial reason related to patentability for including the limiting element added by amendment. In those circumstances, prosecution history estoppel would bar the application of the doctrine [of] equivalents as to that element. The presumption we have described, one subject to rebuttal if an appropriate reason for a required amendment is established, gives proper deference to the role of claims in defining an invention and providing public notice, and to the primacy of the PTO in ensuring that the claims allowed cover only subject matter that is properly patentable in a proffered patent application. Applied in this fashion, prosecution history estoppel places reasonable limits on the doctrine of equivalents, and further insulates the doctrine from any feared conflict with the Patent Act.

Because respondent has not proffered in this Court a reason for the addition of a lower pH limit, it is impossible to tell whether the reason for that addition could properly avoid an estoppel. Whether a reason in fact exists, but simply was not adequately developed, we cannot say. On remand, the Federal Circuit can consider whether reasons for that portion of the amendment were offered or not and whether further opportunity to establish such reasons would be proper.

B

Petitioner next argues that even if *Graver Tank* remains good law, the case held only that the absence of substantial differences was a necessary element for infringement under the doctrine of equivalents, not that it was sufficient for such a result. Relying on *Graver Tank*'s references to the problem of an "unscrupulous copyist" and "piracy," 339 U.S., at 607, petitioner would require judicial exploration of the equities of a case before allowing application of the doctrine of equivalents. To be sure, *Graver Tank* refers to the prevention of copying and piracy when describing the benefits of the doctrine of equivalents. That the doctrine produces such benefits, however, does not mean that its application is limited only to cases where those particular benefits are obtained.

Elsewhere in *Graver Tank* the doctrine is described in more neutral terms. And the history of the doctrine as relied upon by *Graver Tank* reflects a basis for the doctrine not so limited as petitioner would have it. In Winans v. Denmead, 15 How. 330, 343, 14 L.Ed. 717 (1854), we described the doctrine of equivalents as growing out of a legally implied term in each patent claim that "the claim extends to the thing patented, however its form or proportions may be varied." Under that view, application of the doctrine of equivalents involves determining whether a particular accused product or process infringes upon the patent claim, where the claim takes the form—half express, half implied—of "X and its equivalents."

Machine Co. v. Murphy, 97 U.S. 120, 125, 24 L.Ed. 935 (1878), on which *Graver Tank* also relied, offers a similarly intent-neutral view of the doctrine of equivalents:

> "[T]he substantial equivalent of a thing, in the sense of the patent law, is the same as the thing itself; so that if two devices do the same work in substantially the same way, and accomplish substantially the same result, they are the same, even though they differ in name, form, or shape."

If the essential predicate of the doctrine of equivalents is the notion of identity between a patented invention and its equivalent, there is no basis for treating an infringing equivalent any differently than a device that infringes the express terms of the patent. Application of the doctrine of equivalents, therefore, is akin to determining literal infringement, and neither requires proof of intent.

Petitioner also points to *Graver Tank*'s seeming reliance on the absence of independent experimentation by the alleged infringer as supporting an equitable defense to the doctrine of equivalents. The Federal Circuit explained this factor by suggesting that an alleged infringer's behavior, be it copying, designing around a patent, or independent experimentation, indirectly reflects the substantiality of the differences between the patented invention and the accused device or process. According to the Federal Circuit, a person aiming to copy or aiming to avoid a patent is imagined to be at least marginally skilled at copying or avoidance, and thus intentional copying raises an inference—rebuttable by proof of independent development—of having only insubstantial differences, and intentionally designing around a patent claim raises an inference of substantial differences. This explanation leaves much to be desired. At a minimum, one wonders how ever to distinguish between the intentional copyist making minor changes to lower the risk of legal action, and the incremental innovator designing around the claims, yet seeking to capture as much as is permissible of the patented advance.

But another explanation is available that does not require a divergence from generally objective principles of patent infringement. In both instances in *Graver Tank* where we referred to independent research or experiments, we were discussing the known interchangeability between the chemical compound claimed in the patent and the compound substituted by the alleged infringer. The need for independent experimentation thus could reflect knowledge—or lack thereof—of interchangeability possessed by one presumably skilled in the art. The known interchangeability of substitutes for an element of a patent is one of the express objective factors noted by *Graver Tank* as bearing upon whether the accused device is substantially the same as the patented invention. Independent experimentation by the alleged infringer would not always reflect upon the objective question whether a person skilled in the art would have known of the interchangeability between two elements, but in many cases it would likely be probative of such knowledge.

Although *Graver Tank* certainly leaves room for petitioner's suggested inclusion of intent-based elements in the doctrine of equivalents, we do not read it as requiring them. The better view, and the one consistent with *Graver Tank*'s predecessors and the objective approach to infringement, is that intent plays no role in the application of the doctrine of equivalents.

C

Finally, petitioner proposes that in order to minimize conflict with the notice function of patent claims, the doctrine of equivalents should be limited to equivalents that are disclosed within the patent itself. A milder version of this argument, which found favor with the dissenters below, is that the doctrine should be limited to equivalents that were known at the time the patent was issued, and should not extend to after-arising equivalents.

As we have noted, with regard to the objective nature of the doctrine, a skilled practitioner's knowledge of the interchangeability between claimed and accused elements is not relevant for its own sake, but rather for what it tells the fact-finder about the similarities or differences between those elements. Much as the perspective of the hypothetical "reasonable person" gives content to concepts such as "negligent" behavior, the perspective of a skilled practitioner provides content to, and limits on, the concept of "equivalence." Insofar as the question under the doctrine of equivalents is whether an accused element is equivalent to a claimed element, the proper time for evaluating equivalency—and thus knowledge of interchangeability between elements—is at the time of infringement, not at the time the patent was issued. And rejecting the milder version of petitioner's argument necessarily rejects the more severe proposition that equivalents must not only be known, but must also be actually disclosed in the patent in order for such equivalents to infringe upon the patent.

* * *

V

All that remains is to address the debate regarding the linguistic framework under which "equivalence" is determined. Both the parties and the Federal Circuit spend considerable time arguing whether the so-called "triple identity" test—focusing on the function served by a particular claim element, the way that element serves that function, and the result thus obtained by that element—is a suitable method for determining equivalence, or whether an "insubstantial differences" approach is better. There seems to be substantial agreement that, while the triple identity test may be suitable for analyzing mechanical devices, it often provides a poor framework for analyzing other products or processes. On the other hand, the insubstantial differences test offers little additional guidance as to what might render any given difference "insubstantial."

In our view, the particular linguistic framework used is less important than whether the test is probative of the essential inquiry: Does the accused product or process contain elements identical or equivalent to each claimed element of the patented invention? Different linguistic frameworks may be more suitable to different cases, depending on their particular facts. A focus on individual elements and a special vigilance against allowing the concept of equivalence to eliminate completely any such elements should reduce considerably the imprecision of whatever language is used. An analysis of the role played by each element in the context of the specific patent claim will thus inform the inquiry as to whether a substitute element matches the function, way, and result of the claimed element, or whether the substitute element plays a role substantially different from the claimed element. With these limiting principles as a backdrop, we see no purpose in going further and micro-managing the Federal Circuit's particular word-choice for analyzing equivalence. We expect that the Federal Circuit will refine the formulation of the test for equivalence in the orderly course of case-by-case determinations, and we leave such refinement to that court's sound judgment in this area of its special expertise.

VI

Today we adhere to the doctrine of equivalents. The determination of equivalence should be applied as an objective inquiry on an element-by-element basis. Prosecution history estoppel continues to be available as a defense to infringement, but if the patent-holder demonstrates that an amendment required during prosecution had a purpose unrelated to patentability, a court must consider that purpose in order to decide whether an estoppel is precluded. Where the patentholder is unable to establish such a purpose, a court should presume that the purpose behind the required amendment is such that prosecution history estoppel would apply. Because the Court of Appeals for the Federal Circuit did not consider all of the requirements as described by us today, particularly as related to prosecution history estoppel and the preservation of some meaning for each element in a claim, we reverse and remand for further proceedings consistent with this opinion.

It is so ordered.

Notes

1.   In *Graver Tank & Mfg. Co. v. Linde Air Prods. Co.,* 339 U.S. 605, 70 S.Ct. 854, 94 L.Ed. 1097 (1950), the Supreme Court considered whether a patented welding flux containing magnesium was infringed by the defendant's welding flux, which was identical except that it substituted manganese for magnesium. The Court held that the substitution of manganese infringed the patent under the doctrine of equivalents, based on the trial court's finding that the compositions were "substantially identical in operation and in result." The Court observed:

> It is difficult to conceive of a case more appropriate for application of the doctrine of equivalents. The disclosures of the prior art made clear that manganese silicate was a useful ingredient in welding compositions. Specialists familiar with the problems of welding compositions understood that manganese was equivalent to and could be substituted for magnesium in the composition of the patented flux and their observations were confirmed by the literature of chemistry. * * *

Id. at 612, 70 S.Ct. at 858.

2.   As is true of literal infringement, a finding of infringement by equivalents requires a one-to-one correspondence with respect to *every* limitation in the claim that has been infringed. *See Forest Laboratories, Inc. v. Abbott Laboratories,* 239 F.3d 1305, 1313 (Fed.Cir.2001)(ruling that infringement of a respiratory drug patent is not proved without proving all the elements).

3.   Equivalence is a question of fact. *Graver Tank,* 339 U.S. at 609. Equivalence is generally found where the accused product would have been obvious in light of the plaintiff's patent. For example, equivalence has been found where a patent for a playpen claimed a pair of holes in the side fabric through which two drawstrings could be pulled to adjust the side webbing, and the accused product had a single hole for the drawstrings, *see Tigrett Indus., Inc. v. Standard Indus., Inc.,* 162 U.S.P.Q. 32, 36 (W.D.Tenn.1967), *aff'd,* 411 F.2d 1218 (6th Cir.1969), *aff'd by an equally divided court,* 397 U.S. 586, 90 S.Ct. 1310, 25 L.Ed.2d 590 (1970), and where a patent called for a single application of a particular chemical in solution, and the accused process called for multiple applications of a dry version of the same chemical, *see Noll v. O.M. Scott & Sons,* 467 F.2d 295 (6th Cir.1972), *cert. denied,* 411 U.S. 965, 93 S.Ct. 2143, 36 L.Ed.2d 685 (1973).

4.   It is frequently said that "the range of equivalents depends upon and varies with the degree of invention." *Continental Paper Bag Co. v. Eastern Paper Bag Co.,* 210 U.S. 405, 28 S.Ct. 748, 52 L.Ed. 1122 (1908). Thus, a "pioneer" patent is entitled to a broader range of equivalents than a patent for a narrow improvement.

5.   *Reverse Doctrine of Equivalents*: As noted in *Autogiro,* a product or process that literally reads on the claims of a patent may be found non-

infringing because it is not the "equivalent" of the patented invention. For example, in *Mead Digital Systems, Inc. v. A.B. Dick Co.,* 723 F.2d 455 (6th Cir.1983) the Sixth Circuit affirmed a district court's finding of non-infringement on the ground that, while defendant's ink jet printer was described in the literal language of the plaintiff's claims, the claims should be read as "limited to oscillography—the recording of waveforms of electrical signals" in a continuous path transverse to a moving strip of paper. The court rejected the plaintiff's argument that the claims "disclose[d] a method and apparatus for recording a wide variety of images, including alphanumeric characters[,]" which interpretation would have rendered the defendant's character printer infringing. The court explained the "reverse doctrine of equivalents" as follows:

> [A]s Justice Jackson noted in Graver Mfg. Co. v. Linde Co., 339 U.S. 605, 608–609, 70 S.Ct. 854, 856, 94 L.Ed. 1097 (1950), the doctrine of equivalents is a two-edged sword: "where a device is so far changed in principle from a patented article that it performs the same or similar function in a substantially different way, but nevertheless falls within the literal words of the claim, the doctrine of equivalents may be used to restrict the claim and defeat the patentee's action for infringement." The doctrine thus may be applied in favor of as well as against a patentee. It can be used to hold a device in infringement even though the device does not literally infringe the patent claims; it can be used to hold a device not in infringement even though the device falls within the literal words of the claim.

Id. at 462 (footnotes omitted).

6. *Infringement of "Means Plus Function" Claims*: The concept of "equivalence" performs two different roles in infringement analysis. As seen above, if the accused device contains elements that are literally different from, but nonetheless equivalent to, the limitations of a claim, then the literal differences will not prevent a finding of infringement. However, in certain cases the concept of "equivalence" also plays a role in the analysis of *literal* infringement. These cases involve infringement of "means plus function" claims.

In paragraph six of Section 112, the Patent Act of 1952 added a new provision allowing patent applicants to draft claims in combination patents in a manner that had previously been held overbroad and ambiguous. In *Valmont Indus., Inc. v. Reinke Mfg. Co., Inc.,* 983 F.2d 1039 (Fed.Cir.1993), the Federal Circuit explained the standard for determining whether means-plus-function claims are infringed:

> Congress decided to permit broad means-plus-function language, but provided a standard to make the broad claim language more definite. The 1952 Patent Act included a new section 112. This new language permits a patent applicant to express an element in a combination claim as a means for performing a function. The applicant need not recite structure, material, or acts in the claim's means-plus-function limitation. * * *
>
> The second clause of the new paragraph, however, places a limiting condition on an applicant's use of means-plus-function language. A claim limitation described as a means for performing a function, if read

literally, could encompass any conceivable means for performing the function. This second clause confines the breadth of protection otherwise permitted by the first clause. The applicant must describe in the patent specification some structure which performs the specified function. Moreover, a court must construe the functional claim language "to cover the corresponding structure, material, or acts described in the specification and equivalents thereof." Section 112 thus permits means-plus-function language in a combination claim, but with a "string attached." The "attached string" limits the applicant to the structure, material, or acts in the specification *and their equivalents*. Indeed the section operates more like the reverse doctrine of equivalents than the doctrine of equivalents because it restricts the coverage of literal claim language.

This court has explained:

> In applying the "means plus function" paragraph of § 112, however, the sole question is whether the single means in the accused device which performs the function stated in the claim is the same as or an equivalent of the corresponding structure described in the patentee's specification as performing that function.

D.M.I., Inc. v. Deere & Co., 755 F.2d 1570, 1575 (Fed.Cir.1985). In sum, for a means-plus-function limitation to read on an accused device, the accused device must employ means identical to or the equivalent of the structures, material, or acts described in the patent specification. The accused device must also perform the identical function as specified in the claims.

* * *

Section 112 and the doctrine of equivalents have something in common. The word "equivalent" in section 112 invokes the familiar concept of an insubstantial change which adds nothing of significance. In the context of section 112, however, an equivalent results from an insubstantial change which adds nothing of significance to the structure, material, or acts disclosed in the patent specification. A determination of section 112 equivalence does not involve the equitable tripartite test of the doctrine of equivalents. As this court has stated, "the sole question" under section 112 involves comparison of the *structure* in the accused device which performs the claimed function to the *structure* in the specification.

In sum, section 112, ¶ 6, and the doctrine of equivalents have separate origins and purposes. Section 112, ¶ 6, limits the broad language of means-plus-function limitations in combination claims to equivalents of the structures, materials, or acts in the specification. The doctrine of equivalents equitably expands exclusive patent rights.

Id. at 1042–44 (emphasis added).

WMS Gaming, Inc. v. International Game Technology, 184 F.3d 1339 (Fed. Cir. 1999), illustrates the application of literal infringement and the doctrine of equivalents to a means-plus-function claim. In this case, the means-plus-function claim covered a random number generator that was used to control the operation of casino slot machines. The court held that the accused device did not literally infringe the claim, but that it did infringe under the doctrine of equivalents.

The court held that there was no literal infringement of the means-plus-function claim, because while the claim elements at issue were structurally equivalent, they did not perform identical functions. Specifically, the court held that the first part of the literal infringement test (identity *or* equivalence of structures) was satisfied, because the structure that was described in the patent specification as the "means" referenced in the means-plus-function claim (*i.e.,* a microprocessor that was programmed to randomly generate and assign *single* numbers to the "stop" positions on the slot machine reel) was the *equivalent* of the corresponding structure in the accused device (*i.e.,* a microprocessor that was programmed to randomly generate and assign *combinations* of numbers to the stop positions on the reel). The court based this finding of *structural equivalence* on the fact that the differences between the programmed microprocessor disclosed in the specification and the programmed microprocessor found in the accused device were "insubstantial." However, the second part of the literal infringement test—identity of function—was *not* satisfied, because these structures did not perform identical functions. The means-plus-function claim covered a device which assigned and selected *single* numbers, while the accused device assigned and selected *combinations* of numbers. The literal infringement test could be satisfied only if these functions were *identical*; mere equivalence of function was not sufficient.

Finding no literal infringement of the means-plus-function claim, the court then analyzed whether the claim was infringed under the doctrine of equivalents, which required only that the structures in question perform "substantially the same function," as opposed to identical functions. Because it found that there were only insubstantial differences between the function of assigning single random numbers and the function of assigning combinations of random numbers, the court held that the accused device infringed the means-plus-function claim under the doctrine of equivalents.

3. THE SCOPE OF PROSECUTION HISTORY ESTOPPEL

As noted in *Autogiro* and *Hilton Davis*, the range of equivalents with respect to a particular claim may be limited by the doctrine of prosecution history estoppel (also known as "file wrapper estoppel"). Consider how the scope of prosecution history estoppel has been affected by the Supreme Court's 2002 decision in *Festo Corporation v. Shoketsu Kinzoku Kogyo Kabushiki Co., Ltd.*

FESTO CORPORATION v. SHOKETSU KINZOKU KOGYO KABUSHIKI CO., LTD.

Supreme Court of the United States, 2002.
535 U.S. 722, 122 S.Ct. 1831, 152 L.Ed.2d 944.

JUSTICE KENNEDY delivered the opinion of the Court.

This case requires us to address once again the relation between two patent law concepts, the doctrine of equivalents and the rule of prosecution history estoppel. The Court considered the same concepts in *War-*

ner-Jenkinson Co. v. Hilton Davis Chemical Co., 520 U.S. 17, 117 S.Ct. 1040, 137 L.Ed.2d 146 (1997), and reaffirmed that a patent protects its holder against efforts of copyists to evade liability for infringement by making only insubstantial changes to a patented invention. At the same time, we appreciated that by extending protection beyond the literal terms in a patent the doctrine of equivalents can create substantial uncertainty about where the patent monopoly ends. If the range of equivalents is unclear, competitors may be unable to determine what is a permitted alternative to a patented invention and what is an infringing equivalent.

To reduce the uncertainty, *Warner-Jenkinson* acknowledged that competitors may rely on the prosecution history, the public record of the patent proceedings. In some cases the Patent and Trademark Office (PTO) may have rejected an earlier version of the patent application on the ground that a claim does not meet a statutory requirement for patentability. 35 U.S.C. § 132 (1994 ed., Supp. V). When the patentee responds to the rejection by narrowing his claims, this prosecution history estops him from later arguing that the subject matter covered by the original, broader claim was nothing more than an equivalent. Competitors may rely on the estoppel to ensure that their own devices will not be found to infringe by equivalence.

In the decision now under review the Court of Appeals for the Federal Circuit held that by narrowing a claim to obtain a patent, the patentee surrenders all equivalents to the amended claim element. Petitioner asserts this holding departs from past precedent in two respects. First, it applies estoppel to every amendment made to satisfy the requirements of the Patent Act and not just to amendments made to avoid pre-emption by an earlier invention, *i.e.,* the prior art. Second, it holds that when estoppel arises, it bars suit against every equivalent to the amended claim element. The Court of Appeals acknowledged that this holding departed from its own cases, which applied a flexible bar when considering what claims of equivalence were estopped by the prosecution history. Petitioner argues that by replacing the flexible bar with a complete bar the Court of Appeals cast doubt on many existing patents that were amended during the application process when the law, as it then stood, did not apply so rigorous a standard.

We granted certiorari to consider these questions.

I

Petitioner Festo Corporation owns two patents for an improved magnetic rodless cylinder, a piston-driven device that relies on magnets to move objects in a conveying system. The device has many industrial uses and has been employed in machinery as diverse as sewing equipment and the Thunder Mountain ride at Disney World. Although the precise details of the cylinder's operation are not essential here, the prosecution history must be considered.

Petitioner's patent applications, as often occurs, were amended during the prosecution proceedings. The application for the first patent, the Stoll Patent (U.S. Patent No. 4,354,125), was amended after the patent examiner rejected the initial application because the exact method of operation was unclear and some claims were made in an impermissible way. (They were multiply dependent.) 35 U.S.C. § 112 (1994 ed.). The inventor, Dr. Stoll, submitted a new application designed to meet the examiner's objections and also added certain references to prior art. 37 CFR § 1.56 (2000). The second patent, the Carroll Patent (U.S. Patent No. 3,779,401), was also amended during a reexamination proceeding. The prior art references were added to this amended application as well. Both amended patents added a new limitation—that the inventions contain a pair of sealing rings, each having a lip on one side, which would prevent impurities from getting on the piston assembly. The amended Stoll Patent added the further limitation that the outer shell of the device, the sleeve, be made of a magnetizable material.

After Festo began selling its rodless cylinder, respondents (whom we refer to as SMC) entered the market with a device similar, but not identical, to the ones disclosed by Festo's patents. SMC's cylinder, rather than using two one-way sealing rings, employs a single sealing ring with a two-way lip. Furthermore, SMC's sleeve is made of a nonmagnetizable alloy. SMC's device does not fall within the literal claims of either patent, but petitioner contends that it is so similar that it infringes under the doctrine of equivalents.

SMC contends that Festo is estopped from making this argument because of the prosecution history of its patents. The sealing rings and the magnetized alloy in the Festo product were both disclosed for the first time in the amended applications. In SMC's view, these amendments narrowed the earlier applications, surrendering alternatives that are the very points of difference in the competing devices—the sealing rings and the type of alloy used to make the sleeve. As Festo narrowed its claims in these ways in order to obtain the patents, says SMC, Festo is now estopped from saying that these features are immaterial and that SMC's device is an equivalent of its own.

The United States District Court for the District of Massachusetts disagreed. It held that Festo's amendments were not made to avoid prior art, and therefore the amendments were not the kind that give rise to estoppel. A panel of the Court of Appeals for the Federal Circuit affirmed. 72 F.3d 857 (1995). We granted certiorari, vacated, and remanded in light of our intervening decision in *Warner-Jenkinson v. Hilton Davis Chemical Co.,* 520 U.S. 17, 117 S.Ct. 1040, 137 L.Ed.2d 146 (1997). After a decision by the original panel on remand, 172 F.3d 1361 (1999), the Court of Appeals ordered rehearing en banc to address questions that had divided its judges since our decision in *Warner-Jenkinson,* 187 F.3d 1381 (1999).

The en banc court reversed, holding that prosecution history estoppel barred Festo from asserting that the accused device infringed its patents under the doctrine of equivalents. 234 F.3d 558 (2000). The court held, with only one judge dissenting, that estoppel arises from any amendment that narrows a claim to comply with the Patent Act, not only from amendments made to avoid prior art. More controversial in the Court of Appeals was its further holding: When estoppel applies, it stands as a complete bar against any claim of equivalence for the element that was amended. The court acknowledged that its own prior case law did not go so far. Previous decisions had held that prosecution history estoppel constituted a flexible bar, foreclosing some, but not all, claims of equivalence, depending on the purpose of the amendment and the alterations in the text. The court concluded, however, that its precedents applying the flexible-bar rule should be overruled because this case-by-case approach has proved unworkable. In the court's view a complete-bar rule, under which estoppel bars all claims of equivalence to the narrowed element, would promote certainty in the determination of infringement cases.

Four judges dissented from the decision to adopt a complete bar. In four separate opinions, the dissenters argued that the majority's decision to overrule precedent was contrary to *Warner-Jenkinson* and would unsettle the expectations of many existing patentees. Judge Michel, in his dissent, described in detail how the complete bar required the Court of Appeals to disregard 8 older decisions of this Court, as well as more than 50 of its own cases.

We granted certiorari. 533 U.S. 915 (2001).

II

The patent laws "promote the Progress of Science and useful Arts" by rewarding innovation with a temporary monopoly. U.S. Const., Art. I, § 8, cl. 8. The monopoly is a property right; and like any property right, its boundaries should be clear. This clarity is essential to promote progress, because it enables efficient investment in innovation. A patent holder should know what he owns, and the public should know what he does not. For this reason, the patent laws require inventors to describe their work in "full, clear, concise, and exact terms," 35 U.S.C. § 112, as part of the delicate balance the law attempts to maintain between inventors, who rely on the promise of the law to bring the invention forth, and the public, which should be encouraged to pursue innovations, creations, and new ideas beyond the inventor's exclusive rights. *Bonito Boats, Inc. v. Thunder Craft Boats, Inc.*, 489 U.S. 141, 150, 109 S.Ct. 971, 103 L.Ed.2d 118 (1989).

Unfortunately, the nature of language makes it impossible to capture the essence of a thing in a patent application. The inventor who chooses to patent an invention and disclose it to the public, rather than exploit it in secret, bears the risk that others will devote their efforts toward exploiting the limits of the patent's language:

"An invention exists most importantly as a tangible structure or a series of drawings. A verbal portrayal is usually an afterthought written to satisfy the requirements of patent law. This conversion of machine to words allows for unintended idea gaps which cannot be satisfactorily filled. Often the invention is novel and words do not exist to describe it. The dictionary does not always keep abreast of the inventor. It cannot. Things are not made for the sake of words, but words for things." *Autogiro Co. of America v. United States,* 181 Ct.Cl. 55, 384 F.2d 391, 397 (Ct.Cl.1967).

The language in the patent claims may not capture every nuance of the invention or describe with complete precision the range of its novelty. If patents were always interpreted by their literal terms, their value would be greatly diminished. Unimportant and insubstantial substitutes for certain elements could defeat the patent, and its value to inventors could be destroyed by simple acts of copying. For this reason, the clearest rule of patent interpretation, literalism, may conserve judicial resources but is not necessarily the most efficient rule. The scope of a patent is not limited to its literal terms but instead embraces all equivalents to the claims described. *See Winans v. Denmead,* 15 How. 330, 347, 14 L.Ed. 717 (1854).

It is true that the doctrine of equivalents renders the scope of patents less certain. It may be difficult to determine what is, or is not, an equivalent to a particular element of an invention. If competitors cannot be certain about a patent's extent, they may be deterred from engaging in legitimate manufactures outside its limits, or they may invest by mistake in competing products that the patent secures. In addition the uncertainty may lead to wasteful litigation between competitors, suits that a rule of literalism might avoid. These concerns with the doctrine of equivalents, however, are not new. Each time the Court has considered the doctrine, it has acknowledged this uncertainty as the price of ensuring the appropriate incentives for innovation, and it has affirmed the doctrine over dissents that urged a more certain rule. When the Court in *Winans v. Denmead, supra,* first adopted what has become the doctrine of equivalents, it stated that "[t]he exclusive right to the thing patented is not secured, if the public are at liberty to make substantial copies of it, varying its form or proportions." *Id.,* at 343. The dissent argued that the Court had sacrificed the objective of "[f]ul[l]ness, clearness, exactness, preciseness, and particularity, in the description of the invention." *Id.,* at 347 (opinion of Campbell, J.).

The debate continued in *Graver Tank & Mfg. Co. v. Linde Air Products Co.,* 339 U.S. 605, 70 S.Ct. 854, 94 L.Ed. 1097 (1950), where the Court reaffirmed the doctrine. *Graver Tank* held that patent claims must protect the inventor not only from those who produce devices falling within the literal claims of the patent but also from copyists who "make unimportant and insubstantial changes and substitutions in the patent which, though adding nothing, would be enough to take the copied matter outside the claim, and hence outside the reach of law." *Id.,* at 607. Justice Black, in dissent, objected that under the doctrine of equivalents a competitor "cannot rely on what the language of a patent claims. He must be able, at the peril of heavy infringement damages, to forecast how far a court relatively unversed in a particular technological field will expand the claim's language.... " *Id.*, at 617.

Most recently, in *Warner-Jenkinson,* the Court reaffirmed that equivalents remain a firmly entrenched part of the settled rights protected by the patent. A unanimous opinion concluded that if the doctrine is to be discarded, it is Congress and not the Court that should do so:

> "[T]he lengthy history of the doctrine of equivalents strongly supports adherence to our refusal in *Graver Tank* to find that the Patent Act conflicts with that doctrine. Congress can legislate the doctrine of equivalents out of existence any time it chooses. The various policy arguments now made by both sides are thus best addressed to Congress, not this Court." 520 U.S., at 28.

III

Prosecution history estoppel requires that the claims of a patent be interpreted in light of the proceedings in the PTO during the application process. Estoppel is a "rule of patent construction" that ensures that claims are interpreted by reference to those "that have been cancelled or rejected." *Schriber-Schroth Co. v. Cleveland Trust Co.,* 311 U.S. 211, 220–221, 61 S.Ct. 235, 85 L.Ed. 132 (1940). The doctrine of equivalents allows the patentee to claim those insubstantial alterations that were not captured in drafting the original patent claim but which could be created through trivial changes. When, however, the patentee originally claimed the subject matter alleged to infringe but then narrowed the claim in response to a rejection, he may not argue that the surrendered territory comprised unforeseen subject matter that should be deemed equivalent to the literal claims of the issued patent. On the contrary, "[b]y the amendment [the patentee] recognized and emphasized the difference between the two phrases[,] ... and [t]he difference which [the patentee] thus disclaimed must be regarded as material." *Exhibit Supply Co. v. Ace Patents Corp.,* 315 U.S. 126, 136–137, 62 S.Ct. 513, 86 L.Ed. 736 (1942).

A rejection indicates that the patent examiner does not believe the original claim could be patented. While the patentee has the right to appeal, his decision to forgo an appeal and submit an amended claim is taken as a concession that the invention as patented does not reach as far as the original claim. *See Goodyear Dental Vulcanite Co. v. Davis,* 102 U.S. 222, 228, 26 L.Ed. 149 (1880) ("In view of [the amendment] there can be no doubt of what [the patentee] understood he had patented, and that both he and the commissioner regarded the patent to be for a manufacture made exclusively of vulcanites by the detailed process"); *Wang Laboratories, Inc. v. Mitsubishi Electronics America, Inc.,* 103 F.3d 1571, 1577–1578 (C.A.Fed.1997) ("Prosecution history estoppel ... preclud[es] a patentee from regaining, through litigation, coverage of subject matter relinquished during prosecution of the application for the patent"). Were it otherwise, the inventor might avoid the PTO's gatekeeping role and seek to recapture in an infringement action the very subject matter surrendered as a condition of receiving the patent.

Prosecution history estoppel ensures that the doctrine of equivalents remains tied to its underlying purpose. Where the original application once embraced the purported equivalent but the patentee narrowed his claims to obtain the patent or to protect its validity, the patentee cannot assert that he lacked the words to describe the subject matter in question. The doctrine of equivalents is premised on language's inability to capture the essence of innovation, but a prior application describing the precise element at issue undercuts that premise. In that instance the prosecution history has established that the inventor turned his attention to the subject matter in question, knew the words for both the broader and narrower claim, and affirmatively chose the latter.

A

The first question in this case concerns the kinds of amendments that may give rise to estoppel. Petitioner argues that estoppel should arise when amendments are intended to narrow the subject matter of the patented invention, for instance, amendments to avoid prior art, but not when the amendments are made to comply with requirements concerning the form of the patent application. In *Warner-Jenkinson* we recognized that prosecution history estoppel does not arise in every instance when a patent application is amended. Our "prior cases have consistently applied prosecution history estoppel only where claims have been amended for a limited set of reasons," such as "to avoid the prior art, or otherwise to address a specific concern—such as obviousness—that arguably would have rendered the claimed subject matter unpatentable." 520 U.S., at 30–32. While we made clear that estoppel applies to amendments made for a "substantial reason related to patentability," *id.,* at 33, we did not purport to define that term or to catalog every reason that might raise an estoppel. Indeed, we stated that even if the amendment's purpose were unrelated to patentability, the court might consider whether it was the kind of reason that nonetheless might require resort to the estoppel doctrine. *Id.,* at 40–41.

Petitioner is correct that estoppel has been discussed most often in the context of amendments made to avoid the prior art. Amendment to accommodate prior art was the emphasis, too, of our decision in *Warner-Jenkinson, supra,* at 30. It does not follow, however, that amendments for other purposes will not give rise to estoppel. Prosecution history may rebut the inference that a thing not described was indescribable. That rationale does not cease simply because the narrowing amendment, submitted to secure a patent, was for some purpose other than avoiding prior art.

We agree with the Court of Appeals that a narrowing amendment made to satisfy any requirement of the Patent Act may give rise to an estoppel. As that court explained, a number of statutory requirements must be satisfied before a patent can issue. The claimed subject matter must be useful, novel, and not obvious. 35 U.S.C. § § 101–103 (1994 ed. and Supp. V). In addition, the patent application must describe, enable, and set forth the best mode of carrying out the invention. § 112 (1994 ed.). These latter requirements must be satisfied before issuance of the patent, for exclusive patent rights are given in exchange for disclosing the invention to the public. See *Bonito Boats,* 489 U.S., at 150–151. What is claimed by the patent application must be the same as what is disclosed in the specification; otherwise the patent should not issue. The patent also should not issue if the other requirements of § 112 are not satisfied, and an applicant's failure to meet these requirements could lead to the issued patent being held invalid in later litigation.

Petitioner contends that amendments made to comply with § 112 concern the form of the application and not the subject matter of the invention. The PTO might require the applicant to clarify an ambiguous term, to improve the translation of a foreign word, or to rewrite a dependent claim as an independent one. In these cases, petitioner argues, the applicant has no intention of surrendering subject matter and should not be estopped from challenging equivalent devices. While this may be true in some cases, petitioner's argument conflates the patentee's reason for making the amendment with the impact the amendment has on the subject matter.

Estoppel arises when an amendment is made to secure the patent and the amendment narrows the patent's scope. If a § 112 amendment is truly cosmetic, then it would not narrow the patent's scope or raise an estoppel. On the other hand, if a § 112 amendment is necessary and narrows the patent's scope—even if only for the purpose of better description—estoppel may apply. A patentee who narrows a claim as a condition for obtaining a patent disavows his claim to the broader subject matter, whether the amendment was made to avoid the prior art or to comply with § 112. We must regard the patentee as having conceded an inability to claim the broader subject matter or at least as having abandoned his right to appeal a rejection. In either case estoppel may apply.

B

Petitioner concedes that the limitations at issue—the sealing rings and the composition of the sleeve—were made for reasons related to § 112, if not also to avoid the prior art. Our conclusion that prosecution history estoppel arises when a claim is narrowed to comply with § 112 gives rise to the second question presented: Does the estoppel bar the inventor from asserting infringement against any equivalent to the narrowed element or might some equivalents still infringe? The Court of Appeals held that prosecution history estoppel is a complete bar, and so the narrowed element must be limited to its strict literal terms. Based upon its experience the Court of Appeals decided that the flexible-bar rule is unworkable because it leads to excessive uncertainty and burdens legitimate innovation. For the reasons that follow, we disagree with the decision to adopt the complete bar.

Though prosecution history estoppel can bar challenges to a wide range of equivalents, its reach requires an examination of the subject matter surrendered by the narrowing amendment. The complete bar avoids this inquiry by establishing a *per se* rule; but that approach is inconsistent with the purpose of applying the estoppel in the first place— to hold the inventor to the representations made during the application process and to the inferences that may reasonably be drawn from the amendment. By amending the application, the inventor is deemed to concede that the patent does not extend as far as the original claim. It does not follow, however, that the amended claim becomes so perfect in its description that no one could devise an equivalent. After amendment, as before, language remains an imperfect fit for invention. The narrowing amendment may demonstrate what the claim is not; but it may still fail to capture precisely what the claim is. There is no reason why a narrowing amendment should be deemed to relinquish equivalents unforeseeable at the time of the amendment and beyond a fair interpretation of what was surrendered. Nor is there any call to foreclose claims of equivalence for aspects of the invention that have only a peripheral relation to the reason the amendment was submitted. The amendment does not show that the inventor suddenly had more foresight in the drafting of claims than an inventor whose application was granted without amendments having been submitted. It shows only that he was familiar with the broader text and with the difference between the two. As a result, there is no more reason for holding the patentee to the literal terms of an amended claim than there is for abolishing the doctrine of equivalents altogether and holding every patentee to the literal terms of the patent.

This view of prosecution history estoppel is consistent with our precedents and respectful of the real practice before the PTO. While this Court has not weighed the merits of the complete bar against the flexible bar in its prior cases, we have consistently applied the doctrine in a flexible way, not a rigid one. We have considered what equivalents were surrendered during the prosecution of the patent, rather than imposing a complete bar that resorts to the very literalism the equivalents rule is designed to overcome.

The Court of Appeals ignored the guidance of *Warner-Jenkinson*, which instructed that courts must be cautious before adopting changes that disrupt the settled expectations of the inventing community. In that case we made it clear that the doctrine of equivalents and the rule of prosecution history estoppel are settled law. The responsibility for changing them rests with Congress. Fundamental alterations in these rules risk destroying the legitimate expectations of inventors in their property. The petitioner in *Warner-Jenkinson* requested another bright-line rule that would have provided more certainty in determining when estoppel applies but at the cost of disrupting the expectations of countless existing patent holders. We rejected that approach: "To change so substantially the rules of the game now could very well subvert the various balances the PTO sought to strike when issuing the numerous patents which have not yet expired and which would be affected by our decision." *Id.*, at 32, n. 6; *see also id.*, at 41 (GINSBURG, J., concurring)

("The new presumption, if applied woodenly, might in some instances unfairly discount the expectations of a patentee who had no notice at the time of patent prosecution that such a presumption would apply"). As *Warner-Jenkinson* recognized, patent prosecution occurs in the light of our case law. Inventors who amended their claims under the previous regime had no reason to believe they were conceding all equivalents. If they had known, they might have appealed the rejection instead. There is no justification for applying a new and more robust estoppel to those who relied on prior doctrine.

In *Warner-Jenkinson* we struck the appropriate balance by placing the burden on the patentee to show that an amendment was not for purposes of patentability:

"Where no explanation is established, however, the court should presume that the patent application had a substantial reason related to patentability for including the limiting element added by amendment. In those circumstances, prosecution history estoppel would bar the application of the doctrine of equivalents as to that element." *Id.,* at 33.

When the patentee is unable to explain the reason for amendment, estoppel not only applies but also "bar[s] the application of the doctrine of equivalents as to that element." *Ibid.* These words do not mandate a complete bar; they are limited to the circumstance where "no explanation is established." They do provide, however, that when the court is unable to determine the purpose underlying a narrowing amendment— and hence a rationale for limiting the estoppel to the surrender of particular equivalents—the court should presume that the patentee surrendered all subject matter between the broader and the narrower language.

Just as *Warner-Jenkinson* held that the patentee bears the burden of proving that an amendment was not made for a reason that would give rise to estoppel, we hold here that the patentee should bear the burden of showing that the amendment does not surrender the particular equivalent in question. This is the approach advocated by the United States, and we regard it to be sound. The patentee, as the author of the claim language, may be expected to draft claims encompassing readily known equivalents. A patentee's decision to narrow his claims through amendment may be presumed to be a general disclaimer of the territory between the original claim and the amended claim. There are some cases, however, where the amendment cannot reasonably be viewed as surrendering a particular equivalent. The equivalent may have been unforeseeable at the time of the application; the rationale underlying the amendment may bear no more than a tangential relation to the equivalent in question; or there may be some other reason suggesting that the patentee could not reasonably be expected to have described the insubstantial substitute in question. In those cases the patentee can overcome the presumption that prosecution history estoppel bars a finding of equivalence.

This presumption is not, then, just the complete bar by another name. Rather, it reflects the fact that the interpretation of the patent must begin with its literal claims, and the prosecution history is relevant to construing those claims. When the patentee has chosen to narrow a claim, courts may presume the amended text was composed with awareness of this rule and that the territory surrendered is not an equivalent of the territory claimed. In those instances, however, the patentee still might rebut the presumption that estoppel bars a claim of equivalence. The patentee must show that at the time of the amendment one skilled in the art could not reasonably be expected to have drafted a claim that would have literally encompassed the alleged equivalent.

IV

On the record before us, we cannot say petitioner has rebutted the presumptions that estoppel applies and that the equivalents at issue have been surrendered. Petitioner concedes that the limitations at issue—the sealing rings and the composition of the sleeve—were made in response to a rejection for reasons under § 112, if not also because of the prior art references. As the amendments were made for a reason relating to patentability, the question is not whether estoppel applies but what territory the amendments surrendered. While estoppel does not effect a complete bar, the question remains whether petitioner can demonstrate that the narrowing amendments did not surrender the particular equivalents at issue. On these questions, respondents may well prevail, for the sealing rings and the composition of the sleeve both were noted expressly in the prosecution history. These matters, however, should be determined in the first instance by further proceedings in the Court of Appeals or the District Court.

The judgment of the Federal Circuit is vacated, and the case is remanded for further proceedings consistent with this opinion.

It is so ordered.

Notes

1. How does the *Festo* decision affect the ability of competitors to comprehend the scope of a patent they wish to avoid infringing?

2. After *Festo,* if the patentee in an infringement action fails to establish the reason for a claim amendment, will a court recognize any equivalents with respect to the amended element? If so, what determines the scope of allowable equivalents? Suppose that an applicant responds to a patent examiner's prior art objection to one claim by adding a narrowing limitation to that claim. If other, unamended, claims in the same application already contain that same limitation does prosecution history estoppel bar recognition of equivalents with respect to that element in the unamended claims? *See Intermatic, Inc. v. Lamson & Sessions Co.,* 273 F.3d 1355 (Fed. Cir.2001), *vacated and remanded,* 537 U.S. 1016, 123 S.Ct. 549, 154 L.Ed.2d 423 (2002)(remanding for reconsideration in light of *Festo*).

The Aftermath of Festo

On remand of *Festo* from the Supreme Court, the Federal Circuit issued a new en banc opinion. *Festo Corp. v. Shoketsu Kinzoku Kogyo Kabushiki Co., Ltd.*, 344 F.3d 1359 (Fed. Cir. 2003) (en banc), *cert. denied*, 541 U.S. 988, 124 S.Ct. 2018, 158 L.Ed.2d 492 (2004), *and cert. denied*, 541 U.S. 988, 124 S.Ct. 2019, 158 L.Ed.2d 492 (2004). That opinion first restated those aspects of prior law which survived the Supreme Court's decision in *Festo*:

1. A narrowing amendment made to comply with any provision of the Patent Act, including Section 112, may give rise to prosecution history estoppel.

2. Even a voluntary amendment may give rise to prosecution history estoppel.

3. As the Supreme Court held in *Warner-Jenkinson*, a narrowing amendment will be treated as having been made for a "substantial reason related to patentability," thus triggering estoppel, when the prosecution record does not reveal the reason for the amendment.

The Federal Circuit then outlined the correct post-*Festo* procedure for analyzing the effect of a narrowing amendment:

Although the Supreme Court rejected th[e] "complete bar" approach, it confirmed that a patentee's failure to overcome the *Warner-Jenkinson* presumption gives rise to the new *Festo* presumption of surrender. A patentee is now entitled to rebut the presumption that an "unexplained" narrowing amendment surrendered the entire territory between the original and the amended claim limitations.

Thus, the *Warner-Jenkinson* and *Festo* presumptions operate together in the following manner: The first question in a prosecution history estoppel inquiry is whether an amendment filed in the Patent and Trademark Office ("PTO") has narrowed the literal scope of a claim. If the amendment was not narrowing, then prosecution history estoppel does not apply. But if the accused infringer establishes that the amendment was a narrowing one, then the second question is whether the reason for that amendment was a substantial one relating to patentability. When the prosecution history record reveals no reason for the narrowing amendment, *Warner-Jenkinson* presumes that the patentee had a substantial reason relating to patentability; consequently, the patentee must show that the reason for the amendment was not one relating to patentability if it is to rebut that presumption. In this regard, we reinstate our earlier holding that a patentee's rebuttal of the *Warner-Jenkinson* presumption is restricted to the evidence in the prosecution history record. If the patentee successfully establishes that the amendment was not for a reason of patentability, then prosecution history estoppel does not apply.

If, however, the court determines that a narrowing amendment has been made for a substantial reason relating to patentability—whether based on a reason reflected in the prosecution history record or on the patentee's failure to overcome the *Warner-Jenkinson* presumption—then the third question in a prosecution history estoppel analysis addresses the scope of the subject matter surrendered by the narrowing amendment. At that point *Festo* [] imposes the presumption that the patentee has surrendered all territory between the original claim limitation and the amended claim limitation. The patentee may rebut that presumption of total surrender by demonstrating that it did not surrender the particular equivalent in question according to the criteria discussed below. Finally, if the patentee fails to rebut the *Festo* presumption, then prosecution history estoppel bars the patentee from relying on the doctrine of equivalents for the accused element. If the patentee successfully rebuts the presumption, then prosecution history estoppel does not apply and the question whether the accused element is in fact equivalent to the limitation at issue is reached on the merits.

344 F.3d at 1366–67.

Finally, the Federal Circuit addressed several issues which had been left unresolved by the Supreme Court's decision in *Festo*, including:

1. Whether rebuttal of the presumption of surrender, including issues of foreseeability, tangentialness, or reasonable expectations of those skilled in the art, is a question of law or one of fact; and what role a jury should play in determining whether a patent owner can rebut the presumption.

2. What factors are encompassed by the criteria set forth by the Supreme Court.

The en banc decision answered these questions as follows:

1. Rebuttal of the presumption of surrender is a question of law to be determined by the court, not a jury. 344 F.3d at 1367–68.

2. While leaving the factors encompassed by the rebuttal criteria to case-by-case determination, the court offered the following "general guidance":

> The first criterion requires a patentee to show that an alleged equivalent would have been "unforeseeable at the time of the amendment and thus beyond a fair interpretation of what was surrendered." This criterion presents an objective inquiry, asking whether the alleged equivalent would have been unforeseeable to one of ordinary skill in the art at the time of the amendment. Usually, if the alleged equivalent represents later-developed technology (*e.g.,* transistors in relation to vacuum tubes, or Velcro® in relation to fasteners) or technology that was not known in the relevant art, then it would not have been foreseeable. In contrast, old technology, while not always foreseeable, would more likely have been foreseeable. Indeed, if the alleged equivalent were known in the prior art in the field of the invention, it certainly should have been foreseeable at the time of the amendment. By its very nature, objective unforeseeability depends on underlying factual issues relating to, for example, the state of the art and the understanding of a hypothetical person of ordinary skill in the art at the time of the amendment. Therefore, in determining whether an alleged equivalent would have been unforeseeable, a district court may hear expert testimony and consider other extrinsic evidence relating to the relevant factual inquiries.

The second criterion requires a patentee to demonstrate that "the rationale underlying the narrowing amendment [bore] no more than a tangential relation to the equivalent in question." In other words, this criterion asks whether the reason for the narrowing amendment was peripheral, or not directly relevant, to the alleged equivalent. Although we cannot anticipate the instances of mere tangentialness that may arise, we can say that an amendment made to avoid prior art that contains the equivalent in question is not tangential; it is central to allowance of the claim. Moreover, much like the inquiry into whether a patentee can rebut the *Warner-Jenkinson* presumption that a narrowing amendment was made for a reason of patentability, the inquiry into whether a patentee can rebut the *Festo* presumption under the "tangential" criterion focuses on the patentee's objectively apparent reason for the narrowing amendment. As we have held in the *Warner-Jenkinson* context, that reason should be discernible from the prosecution history record, if the public notice function of a patent and its prosecution history is to have significance. Moreover, whether an amendment was merely tangential to an alleged equivalent necessarily requires focus on the context in which the amendment was made; hence the resort to the prosecution history. Thus, whether the patentee has established a merely tangential reason for a narrowing amendment is for the court to determine from the prosecution history record without the introduction of additional evidence, except, when necessary, testimony from those skilled in the art as to the interpretation of that record.

The third criterion requires a patentee to establish "some other reason suggesting that the patentee could not reasonably be expected to have described the insubstantial substitute in question." This category, while vague, must be a narrow one; it is available in order not to totally foreclose a patentee from relying on reasons, other than unforeseeability and tangentialness, to show that it did not surrender the alleged equivalent. Thus, the third criterion may be satisfied when there was some reason, such as the shortcomings of language, why the patentee was prevented from describing the alleged equivalent when it narrowed the claim. When at all possible, determination of the third rebuttal criterion should also be limited to the prosecution history record. For example, as we recently held in *Pioneer Magnetics, Inc. v. Micro Linear Corp.,* 330 F.3d 1352 (Fed.Cir.2003), a patentee may not rely on the third rebuttal criterion if the alleged equivalent is in the prior art, for then "there can be no other reason the patentee could not have described the substitute in question." *Id.* at 1357. We need not decide now what evidence outside the prosecution history record, if any, should be considered in determining if a patentee has met its burden under this third rebuttal criterion.

344 F.3d at 1368–70 (some citations omitted).

Because the question whether a patentee has rebutted the *Festo* presumption of surrender is a question of law, the Federal Circuit subjects these determinations to *de novo* review. Indeed, the first attempt by a district court to apply the Federal Circuit's post-*Festo* guidance led to reversal by the Federal Circuit, which held that the district court erred in finding that the patentee had rebutted the presumption of surrender. *See Amgen, Inc. v. Hoechst Marion Roussel, Inc.*, 457 F.3d 1293, 1311–16 (Fed. Cir. 2006), *aff'g in part and rev'g in part* 287 F.Supp.2d 126 (D. Mass. 2003). According to the Federal Circuit, the patentee failed to satisfy *any* of the Supreme Court's three alternative conditions for rebutting the presumption: (1) showing that the alleged equivalent was unforeseeable at the time the amendment was made, (2) showing that the alleged equivalent was tangential to the purpose of the amendment, or (3) showing that there was some other reason suggesting that the patentee could not reasonably be expected to have described the insubstantial substitute in question. *Amgen,* 457 F.3d at 1312–13 (citing *Festo,* 535 U.S. at 740–41). If one of the goals of prosecution history estoppel is to provide competitors with greater certainty regarding the scope of patent claims and their range of equivalents, has *Festo* advanced that goal?

In another post-*Festo* development, an the Federal Circuit has held, in a 2004 en banc decision, that *Festo*'s presumptive surrender of equivalents also applies when an original *dependent* claim is rewritten into *independent* form to replace a broader independent claim that was cancelled during prosecution. "[R]ewriting a dependent claim into independent form, coupled with the cancellation of the original independent claim, constitutes a narrowing amendment when the dependent claim includes an additional claim limitation not found in the cancelled independent claim or circumscribes a limitation found in the cancelled independent claim." *Honeywell International, Inc. v. Hamilton Sundstrand Corp.*, 370 F.3d 1131, 1141 (Fed. Cir. 2004) (en banc), *cert. denied,* 545 U.S. 1127, 125 S.Ct. 2928, 162 L.Ed.2d 865 (2005). Thus, "the fact that the scope of the rewritten claim has remained unchanged will not preclude the application of prosecution history estoppel if, by canceling the original independent claim and rewriting the dependent claims into independent form, the scope of subject matter claimed in the independent claim has been narrowed to secure the patent." *Id.* at 1142. The presumption applied even though the dependent claim was not *itself* narrowed by amendment, but in fact remained identical in scope after it was rewritten. As a result, rewriting the narrower dependent claim into independent form gave rise to a presumptive surrender of all equivalents of the narrower limitation.

4. INFRINGING ACTIVITIES

ARO MANUFACTURING CO., INC. v. CONVERTIBLE TOP REPLACEMENT CO., INC.

Supreme Court of the United States, 1961.
365 U.S. 336, 81 S.Ct. 599, 5 L.Ed.2d 592.

Mr. Justice Whittaker delivered the opinion of the Court.

* * *

[Respondent Convertible Top Replacement Co. sued Aro Manufacturing Co. for contributory infringement of its '724 combination patent on a convertible folding top for an automobile, consisting of a flexible fabric top and supporting apparatus. Individual components of the patented combination, such as the fabric, were not covered by the patent. The district court held that the activities of petitioner Aro in making and selling replacement fabric for the convertible tops constituted contributory infringement, because the act of replacing the worn-out fabric was an infringing reconstruction of the patented combination. The court of appeals affirmed, and this appeal followed.]

* * *

Since the patentees never claimed the fabric or its shape as their invention, and the claims made in the patent are the sole measure of the grant, the fabric is no more than an unpatented element of the combination which was claimed as the invention, and the patent did not confer a monopoly over the fabric or its shape. * * *

It follows that petitioners' manufacture and sale of the fabric is not a direct infringement under 35 U.S.C. § 271 (a). But the question remains whether petitioners' manufacture and sale of the fabric constitute a contributory infringement of the patent under 35 U.S.C. § 271 (c). It is admitted that petitioners know that the purchasers intend to use the fabric for replacement purposes on automobile convertible tops which are covered by the claims of respondent's combination patent, and such manufacture and sale with that knowledge might well constitute contributory infringement under § 271 (c), if, but only if, such a replacement by the purchaser himself would in itself constitute a direct infringement under § 271 (a), for it is settled that if there is no direct infringement of a patent there can be no contributory infringement. * * * The determinative question, therefore, comes down to whether the car owner would infringe the combination patent by replacing the worn-out fabric element of the patented convertible top on his car, or even more specifically, whether such a replacement by the car owner is infringing "reconstruction" or permissible "repair."

This Court's decisions specifically dealing with whether the replacement of an unpatented part, in a patented combination, that has worn out, been broken or otherwise spent, is permissible "repair" or infringing "reconstruction," have steadfastly refused to extend the patent monopoly beyond the terms of the grant. Wilson v. Simpson, 9 How. 109—doubtless the leading case in this Court that deals with the distinction—concerned a patented planing machine which included, as elements, certain cutting knives which normally wore out in a few months' use. The purchaser was held to have the right to replace those knives without the patentee's consent. The Court held that, although there is no right to "rebuild" a patented combination, the entity "exists" notwithstanding the fact that destruction or impairment of one of its elements renders it inoperable; and that, accordingly, replacement of that worn-out essential part is permissible restoration of the machine to the original use for which it was bought. 9 How., at 123. The Court explained that it is "the use of the whole" of the combination which a purchaser buys, and that repair or replacement of the worn-out, damaged or destroyed part is but an exercise of the right "to give duration to that which he owns, or has a right to use as a whole." *Ibid.*

The distilled essence of the *Wilson* case was stated by Judge Learned Hand in United States v. Aluminum Co. of America, 148 F.2d 416, 425 (C. A. 2d Cir.): "The [patent] monopolist cannot prevent those to whom he sells from . . . reconditioning articles worn by use, unless they in fact make a new article." * * *

* * *

No element, not itself separately patented, that constitutes one of the elements of a combination patent is entitled to patent monopoly, however essential it may be to the patented combination and no matter how costly or difficult replacement may be. While there is language in some lower court opinions indicating that "repair" or "reconstruction" depends on a number of factors, it is significant that each of the three cases of this Court, cited for that proposition, holds that a license to use a patented combination includes the right "to preserve its fitness for use so far as it may be affected by wear or breakage." Leeds & Catlin Co. v. Victor Talking Machine Co., 213 U.S. 325, 336. We hold that maintenance of the "use of the whole" of the patented combination through replacement of a spent, unpatented element does not constitute reconstruction.

The decisions of this Court require the conclusion that reconstruction of a patented entity, comprised of unpatented elements, is limited to such a true reconstruction of the entity as to "in fact make a new article," United States v. Aluminum Co. of America, *supra*, at 425, after the entity, viewed as a whole, has become spent. In order to call the monopoly, conferred by the patent grant, into play for a second time, it must, indeed, be a second creation of the patented entity * * *. Mere replacement of individual unpatented parts, one at a time, whether of the same part repeatedly or different parts successively, is no more than the lawful right of the owner to repair his property. Measured by this test, the replacement of the fabric involved in this case must be characterized as permissible "repair," not "reconstruction."

Reversed.

ARO MANUFACTURING CO., INC. v. CONVERTIBLE TOP REPLACEMENT CO., INC.

Supreme Court of the United States, 1964.
377 U.S. 476, 84 S.Ct. 1526, 12 L.Ed.2d 457.

MR. JUSTICE BRENNAN delivered the opinion of the Court.

[As in the previous adjudication between these parties (*Aro I*), the plaintiff here alleged that Aro's actions in supplying replacement fabric for use in repairing its patented convertible tops was a contributory infringement, because the repair itself was a direct infringement. However, in this case (*Aro II*) the tops had been installed without a license from the patentee. Thus, the Court was asked to decide whether repair of the infringing tops constituted direct infringement, and whether the manufacture and sale of the replacement fabric used in that repair constituted contributory infringement.]

* * *

Section 271(a) provides that "whoever without authority makes, uses or sells any patented invention . . . infringes the patent." It is not controverted—nor could it be—that Ford infringed by making and selling cars embodying the patented top-structures without any authority from the patentee. If Ford had had such authority, its purchasers would not have infringed by using the automobiles, for it is fundamental that sale of a patented article by the patentee or under his authority carries with it an "implied license to use." Adams v. Burke, 17 Wall. 453, 456; United States v. Univis Lens Co., 316 U.S. 241, 249, 250–251. But with Ford lacking authority to make and sell, it could by its sale of the cars confer on the purchasers no implied license to use, and their use of the patented structures was thus "without authority" and infringing under § 271(a). Not only does that provision explicitly regard an unauthorized user of a patented invention as an infringer, but it has often and clearly been held that unauthorized use, without more, constitutes infringement.

If the owner's *use* infringed, so also did his *repair* of the top-structure, as by replacing the worn-out fabric component. Where use infringes, repair does also, for it perpetuates the infringing use. * * * Consequently replacement of worn-out fabric components with fabrics sold by Aro, held in *Aro I* to constitute "repair" rather than "reconstruction" and thus to be permissible in the case of licensed General Motors cars, was not permissible here in the case of unlicensed Ford cars. Here, as was not the case in *Aro I*, the direct infringement by the car owners that is prerequisite to contributory infringement by Aro was unquestionably established.

We turn next to the question whether Aro, as supplier of replacement fabrics for use in the infringing repair by the Ford car owners, was a contributory infringer under § 271 (c) of the Patent Code. * * * We think Aro was indeed liable under this provision.

Such a result would plainly have obtained under the contributory-infringement case law that § 271 (c) was intended to codify.[1] Indeed, most of the law was established in cases where, as here, suit was brought to hold liable for contributory infringement a supplier of replacement parts specially designed for use in the repair of infringing articles. In Union Tool Co. v. Wilson, [259 U.S. 107, 113–114], the Court held that where use of the patented machines themselves was not authorized,

---

1. The section was designed to "codify in statutory form principles of contributory infringement" which had been "part of our law for about 80 years." H. R. Rep. No. 1923 on H. R. 7794, 82d Cong., 2d Sess., at 9.

"There was, consequently, no implied license to use the spare parts in these machines. As such use, unless licensed, clearly constituted an infringement, the sale of the spare parts to be so used violated the injunction [enjoining infringement]."

As early as 1897, Circuit Judge Taft, as he then was, thought it "well settled" that

"where one makes and sells one element of a combination covered by a patent with the intention and for the purpose of bringing about its use in such a combination he is guilty of contributory infringement and is equally liable to the patentee with him who in fact organizes the complete combination." Thomson–Houston Elec. Co. v. Ohio Brass Co., 80 F. 712, 721 (C.A. 6th Cir. 1897).

While conceding that in the case of a machine purchased from the patentee, one "may knowingly assist in assembling, repairing, and renewing a patented combination by furnishing some of the needed parts," Judge Taft added: "but, when he does so, he must ascertain, if he would escape liability for infringement, that the one buying and using them for this purpose has a license, express or implied, to do so." *Id.*, at 723. * * *

"The right of one, other than the patentee, furnishing repair parts of a patented combination, can be no greater than that of the user, and he is bound to see that no other use of such parts is made than that authorized by the user's license." National Malleable Casting Co. v. American Steel Foundries, 182 F. 626, 641 (C.C.D.N.J.1910).

In enacting § 271 (c), Congress clearly succeeded in its objective of codifying this case law. The language of the section fits perfectly Aro's activity of selling "a component of a patented ... combination ... , constituting a material part of the invention, ... especially made or especially adapted for use in an infringement of such patent, and not a staple article or commodity of commerce suitable for substantial noninfringing use." Indeed, this is the almost unique case in which the component was hardly suitable for *any* noninfringing use.[2] On this basis both the District Court originally, 119 U. S. P. Q., at 124, and the Court of Appeals in the instant case, 312 F.2d, at 57, held that Aro was a contributory infringer within the precise letter of § 271(c). *See also Aro I*, 365 U.S., at 341.

However, the language of § 271 (c) presents a question, apparently not noticed by the parties or the courts below, concerning the element of knowledge that must be brought home to Aro before liability can be imposed. It is only sale of a component of a patented combination *"knowing* the same to be especially made or especially adapted for use in an infringement of such patent" that is contributory infringement under the statute. Was Aro "knowing" within the statutory meaning because—

2. Aro's factory manager admitted that the fabric replacements in question not only were specially designed for the Ford con- vertibles but would not, to his knowledge, fit the top-structures of any other cars.

as it admits, and as the lower courts found—it knew that its replacement fabrics were especially designed for use in the 1952–1954 Ford convertible tops and were not suitable for other use? Or does the statute require a further showing that Aro knew that the tops were patented, and knew also that Ford was not licensed under the patent so that any fabric replacement by a Ford car owner constituted infringement?

On this question a majority of the Court is of the view that § 271 (c) does require a showing that the alleged contributory infringer knew that the combination for which his component was especially designed was both patented and infringing. With respect to many of the replacement-fabric sales involved in this case, Aro clearly had such knowledge. * * *

[The Court instructed the lower court, on remand, to determine whether January 2, 1954 was the date on which Aro first had knowledge that the Ford tops were both patented and infringing, and to vacate its judgment of liability with respect to any sales which took place before Aro acquired this knowledge. As to subsequent sales, however, Aro was liable for contributory infringement.]

* * *

Notes

1.   Would infringing reconstruction occur where sequential repairs to a patented combination led, over time, to replacement of all or substantially all of its unpatented components?

The distinction between infringing reconstruction and permissible repairs under *Aro I* was further explored in *Sandvik Aktiebolag v. E.J. Co.*, 121 F.3d 669 (Fed.Cir.1997), *cert. denied,* 523 U.S. 1040, 118 S.Ct. 1337, 140 L.Ed.2d 499 (1998). In holding that the replacement of a spent drill tip was an infringing reconstruction of the patented drill, the court explained:

> There are a number of factors to consider in determining whether a defendant has made a new article, after the device has become spent, including the nature of the actions by the defendant, the nature of the device and how it is designed (namely, whether one of the components of the patented combination has a shorter useful life than the whole), whether a market has developed to manufacture or service the part at issue and objective evidence of the intent of the patentee. Under the totality of the circumstances, we hold in this case that E.J.'s actions are a reconstruction.

> By E.J.'s own admission, the drill is "spent" when the tip can no longer be resharpened unless it is retipped. In fact, the record reveals that E.J.'s customers may elect not to retip and inform E.J. to discard the drill instead.

> Moreover, the nature of the work done by E.J. shows that retipping is more like reconstruction than repair. E.J. does not just attach a new part for a worn part, but rather must go though several steps to replace, configure and integrate the tip onto the shank. It has to break the worn or damaged tip from the shank by heating it to 1300 degrees Fahrenheit.

It brazes to the shank a new rectangular block of carbide and grinds and machines it to the proper diameter and creates the point. Thereafter, the tip is honed and sharpened, grinding the rake surfaces and the center of the point and honing the edges. These actions are effectively a re-creation of the patented invention after it is spent.

This is not a case where it is clear that the patented device has a useful life much longer than that of certain parts which wear out quickly. * * *

The drill tip in this case is not a part [that must] * * * be replaced periodically over the useful life of the planing machine. The drill tip was not manufactured to be a replaceable part, although it could be resharpened a number of times to extend its life. It was not intended or expected to have a life of temporary duration in comparison to the drill shank. And finally, the tip was not attached to the shank in a manner to be easily detachable.

In *Aro I,* the Supreme Court also noted that "the consequent demand for replacement fabrics has given rise to a substantial industry." Evidence of development in the industry could also be a factor tending to prove that there is a reasonable expectation that the part of the patented combination wears out quickly and requires frequent replacement. *See also* Kendall Co. v. Progressive Medical Tech., Inc., 85 F.3d 1570, 1572 (Fed.Cir.1996) ("The resulting market for replacement sleeves has been substantial."); *Sage Prods.,* 45 F.3d at 1577 (noting that "the sale of replacement inner containers is a sizable market."). In this case, there is no evidence of a substantial market for drill retipping of the sort required for the Sandvik drill. There is no evidence of large numbers of customers retipping these drills or of companies (other than E.J.) offering to retip these drills. No one manufactures replacement tips for Sandvik's drill and although some customers opt to retip the drill only a small percentage of all drills manufactured are retipped.

Finally, there was no intent evidenced by the patentee that would support E.J.'s argument that replacement of the tips is a repair. *See Kendall Co.,* 85 F.3d at 1575, 38 U.S.P.Q.2D (BNA) at 1921 (replacing the sleeve in a medical device which applies pressure to patients' limbs was a repair noting that the manufacturer "clearly intended to permit its customers to replace the sleeves" and actually sold replacement sleeves); *Sage Prods.,* 45 F.3d at 1578–79 (evidence that patentee intended the inner containers to be replaced, that it manufactures replacement parts and instructs customers to replace supports holding such replacement a permissible repair); *Porter,* 790 F.2d at 885–86 (considering that the patentee sold replacement cutting disks for its tomato harvester). The evidence shows that Sandvik never intended for its drills to be retipped. It did not manufacture or sell replacement drill tips. It did not publish instructions on how to retip its patented drills or suggest that the drills could or should be retipped. Sandvik was aware that the drill tip would need occasional resharpening and instructed its customer on how to resharpen the tip. There is, therefore, no objective evidence that Sandvik's drill tip was intended to be a replaceable part. Although the repair or reconstruction issue does not turn on the intention of the patentee alone, the fact that no replacement drill tips have ever been made or sold by the patentee is consistent with the conclusion that replacement of the carbide tip is not a permissible repair.

121 F.3d at 673–74.

2.   Is it an infringement for the owner of a patented canning machine designed for use with one-pound cans to alter the apparatus, without the patent owner's permission, so that it can pack five-ounce cans instead?

3.   Suppose that a patented product is sold with the express understanding that it is to be used only once and then discarded. If the defendant reconditions it for reuse, is the reconditioning or the reuse an infringement?

4.   Suppose that various auto makers install patented intermittent windshield wipers without the consent of the patentee. Does the car dealer infringe the patent by selling the car so equipped? Does the buyer of the car infringe if he or she uses the patented intermittent function of the wipers? What if the buyer operates the car without using the wipers at all? Or just without using their patented intermittent function? Does your answer change if the wipers themselves do not infringe a patent, but are manufactured using an infringing process?

5.   In problem 4, would a car owner who incurred liability for patent infringement by normal operation of the car have any action against the seller of the car?

6.   If the defendant sells a component part specially designed for an infringing use, but the buyer does not in fact use the part in any infringing way, is the seller still liable for contributory infringement?

7.   Must a direct infringer know that a process or product is patented and infringing in order to be held liable? (Compare Section 271(a) with Sections 271(c) and 287(a).) Why should such knowledge be a prerequisite to liability for contributory infringement? Note that the majority in *Aro II* rejected the dissent's suggestion that the knowledge requirement could be satisfied by establishing that the defendant knew ''that the component was especially designed for use in a combination and was not a staple article suitable for substantial other use,'' without necessarily knowing that the combination was either patented or infringing. 377 U.S. at 491 n.8. Which interpretation would better serve the purposes of the patent monopoly? Which would be easier to apply in practice?

8.   Would the analysis in *Aro II* have been different if the replacement fabric were designed to fit both the infringing and the noninfringing convertible tops? Suppose it fit the infringing tops, did not fit the noninfringing tops, but could also be used as a tarp to keep firewood dry?

9.   Suppose parts which the seller knows are suitable for use in an infringing combination are sold before the combination patent issues, and are assembled into the infringing combination after the patent issues? Alternatively, what if such parts are sold shortly before the patent term expires, and are assembled after expiration?

10.   Suppose a seller of parts suitable for use in an infringing device believes, erroneously but in good faith, that the patent is invalid?

11. *Active Inducement*: One who knowingly induces another to infringe a patent may be held personally liable for the resulting infringement under Section 271(b), but only if the inducing party acted with specific intent to encourage the infringement. Liability under Section 271(b) requires proof (1) that an act of direct infringement occurred, (2) that the defendant's conduct actually induced the infringing act, (3) that the defendant knew or should have known that its actions would induce actual infringement, and (4) that the defendant knew of the existence of the patent. The intent requirement specifically requires that the defendant intend to induce *infringement*, and not merely to induce the *acts* which are ultimately determined to constitute infringement. *DSU Medical Corp. v. JMS Co.*, 471 F.3d 1293, 1305–06 (Fed Cir. 2006).

12. Under familiar principles of tort law, a principal (for example, a corporation) can be held liable for patent infringement by its agent (for example, an employee) acting within the scope of the agent-principal relationship. *See, e.g., Westinghouse Elec. & Mfg. Co. v. Independent Wireless Tel. Co.*, 300 F. 748 (S.D.N.Y.1924). Under what circumstances, if any, should corporate officers be held personally liable for a corporation's direct infringement in which they do not individually participate?

13. Suppose a manufacturer makes a drug which, after ingestion by humans, is converted by the human body into a patented compound. Would the manufacturer be liable for patent infringement? What about the consumer?

14. In 1984,[3] Congress created a new, and somewhat artificial, act of infringement, with limited remedies, by adding Sections 271(e)(2) and (e)(4) to the patent statutes. Under section 271(e)(2), it is an infringement of a drug patent to file certain applications for streamlined regulatory approval of generic equivalents which the applicant believes will not infringe the patent on the brand-name drug (for example, because the applicant believes the patent is invalid). If the patentee fails to commence an infringement action within 45 days after the filing of such an application (and timely notice to the patentee), the FDA may approve the generic drug for marketing. 21 U.S.C. § 355(c)(3)(C). Where the generic drug applicant is found liable for infringement under Section 271 (e)(2), the limited remedies set forth in Section (e)(4) are exclusive. Why did Congress create this new act of infringement, and then deny the plaintiff access to the full range of remedies?

15. Pub. L. No. 108–173, Title XI, § 1101(d), 108th Cong., 1st Sess. (2003), added a new section subsection (e)(5) to Section 271 to provide that, if a brand name drug manufacturer does not sue a generic drug maker for infringement arising from the latter's ANDA within 45 days of receiving notice of the ANDA filing, the generic drug maker may seek a declaratory judgment that the patent for the drug is invalid or not infringed. Even where the conditions of Section 271(e)(5) are otherwise satisfied, the Federal Circuit has held that no justiciable controversy exists, and thus no action for declaratory judgment may proceed, unless the brand name manufacturer has taken actions which give rise to a

---

3. Pub. L. No. 98–417, 98 Stat. 1585 (1984).

"reasonable apprehension" that it will sue the generic manufacturer for infringement. *Teva Pharmaceuticals USA, Inc. v. Pfizer, Inc.*, 395 F.3d 1324 (Fed. Cir. 2005), *cert. denied* ___ U.S. ___, 126 S.Ct. 473, 163 L.Ed.2d 359 (2005). However, the Supreme Court's subsequent decision in *MedImmune, Inc. v. Genentech, Inc.*, ___ U.S. ___, 127 S.Ct. 764, 166 L.Ed.2d 604 (2007) (see excerpt in Chapter 14.C.2(ii)) casts doubt on the continuing validity of this decision.

5.   CROSS–BORDER INFRINGEMENT

Sections 271(f) and (g) describe infringing activities that take place partly in the United States and partly overseas. These are exceptions to the prevailing rule of territoriality in patent law, under which liability for infringement of United States patent laws generally arises only when an act of direct infringement takes place within United States territory. Recent case law has examined the scope of Sections 271(f) and (g), as well as the question of what it means to use an invention within the United States under Section 271(a).

The Federal Circuit in *NTP, Inc. v. Research in Motion, Ltd.*, 418 F.3d 1282 (Fed. Cir. 2005), *cert. denied,* ___ U.S. ___, 126 S.Ct. 1174, 163 L.Ed.2d 1141 (2006), examined defendant Research in Motion's ("RIM") Blackberry wireless system, which integrated electronic mail systems ("wireline" systems) with radio frequency ("RF") wireless communication networks so as to enable mobile users to receive email over a wireless network. Some components of the defendant's system were located in the United States, while others were located in Canada. Distinguishing between the system (or "device") claims and the method claims of the patent in question, the court held that, for purposes of Section 271(a), the place where a system is "used" is "the place where control of the system is exercised and beneficial use of the system obtained." *Id.* at 1317. In this case, because the defendant's "customers located within the United States controlled the transmission of the originated information and also benefited from such an exchange of information," the defendant's system was used in the United States. *Id.* However, the court reached a different conclusion with respect to the method claims, holding "that a process cannot be used 'within' the United States as required by Section 271(a) unless each of the steps is performed within this country." *Id.* at 1318. In this case, each of the method claims in question involved a step utilizing an "interface" or "interface switch," which was satisfied only by the use of the defendant's relay, which was located in Canada. The court held, therefore, that the claimed methods were not infringed. *Id.* In addition, the court held that the defendant's sales within the United States of the Blackberry devices used to receive its wireless transmissions did not constitute infringing sales of the patented *method* for purposes of Section 271(a). *Id.* at 1319. The court also rejected the patent holder's argument that the defendant's sales of the Blackberry devices constituted "supplying" a "component" of the patented method for purposes of Section 271(f): "By merely supplying products to its customers in the United States, RIM is not supplying or causing to be supplied in this country any steps of a patented process invention for combination outside the United States and cannot infringe NTP's asserted method claims under Section 271(f) as a matter of law." *Id.* at 1322–23. Finally, the court held that the defendant's activities did not involve the importation of a product made by a patented process under Section 271(g), even though the defendant used a patented method to deliver wireless emails to customers within the United States. Citing its prior holding in *Bayer AG v. Housey Pharmaceuticals, Inc.*, 340 F.3d 1367 (Fed.Cir.2003), which held that Section 271(g) applies only to the production of physical articles, not intangibles such as information, the court held that an email is merely a transmission of information, and is therefore not a "product" within the meaning of Section 271(g). *Id.* at 1323–24.

Shortly after deciding the *NTP* case, the Federal Circuit distinguished it in another case involving cross-border application of Section 271(f) to a patented process. In *Union Carbide Chemicals & Plastics Technology Corp. v. Shell Oil Co.*, 425 F.3d 1366 (Fed. Cir. 2005), the court held that infringement liability under Section 271(f) arises when a defendant exports a catalyst for use in carrying out a claimed chemical process performed abroad. Whereas the Blackberry devices in *NTP* were sold to customers in the United States so that they could use a wireless e-mail system partially operating abroad, the Federal Circuit distinguished *NTP* on the ground that the defendant in *Union Carbide* supplied catalysts from the United States directly to foreign entities. Is this distinction persuasive?

Legislation was introduced in November of 2005 to overrule the Federal Circuit's holding in *Bayer* that Section 271(g) applies only to the importation of physical objects, not information. The Informatics Act of 2005, H.R. 4208, would have made Section 271(g) expressly applicable to information gained from practicing a patented process overseas. Proponents of the legislation argued that patent holders need protection against competitors whose use of U.S.-patented testing methods overseas provides substantial assistance in producing products that are ultimately imported into the United States. H.R. 4208 did not make it out of committee, although its substance could be revived by a future Congress.

In *Pellegrini v. Analog Devices, Inc.*, 375 F.3d 1113 (Fed. Cir. 2004), *cert. denied,* 543 U.S. 1003, 125 S.Ct. 642, 160 L.Ed.2d 464 (2004), the Federal Circuit held that a defendant headquartered in the United States that provided instructions for the overseas assembly of the components of a patented invention did not violate Section 271(f), where the components themselves were not manufactured in the United States, and were never shipped to or from the United States. In contrast, in *Eolas Technologies Inc. v. Microsoft Corp.*, 399 F.3d 1325, 1339 (Fed.Cir. 2005), the Federal Circuit held that software alone may be a "component" of a patented invention for purposes of Section 271(f); furthermore, it held, Section 271(f) applies not only to patented devices but also to patented processes. Shortly thereafter, the Federal Circuit reiterated and extended this analysis in *AT & T Corp. v. Microsoft Corp.*, 414 F.3d

1366 (Fed. Cir. 2005), holding not only that exporting software from the United States to foreign computer manufacturers constitutes "supplying" a patented component in violation of Section 271(f), but also that, when the exported software is replicated abroad, the foreign-made copies are themselves "supplied from" the United States for purposes of Section 271(f). A petition for certiorari in *Microsoft Corp. v. AT & T Corp.* was filed in February of 2006, asking the Supreme Court to determine whether software constitutes a "component of a patented invention" under Section 271(f), and whether foreign-made copies of such code are components supplied from the United States. In April of 2007, the Supreme Court issued the decision which follows.

MICROSOFT CORP. v. AT & T CORP.

Supreme Court of the United States, 2007.
___ U.S. ___, 127 S.Ct. 1746, ___ L.Ed.2d ___.

JUSTICE GINSBURG delivered the opinion of the Court, except as to footnote 14.

It is the general rule under United States patent law that no infringement occurs when a patented product is made and sold in another country. There is an exception. Section 271(f) of the Patent Act, adopted in 1984, provides that infringement does occur when one "supplies ... from the United States," for "combination" abroad, a patented invention's "components." 35 U.S.C. § 271(f)(1). This case concerns the applicability of § 271(f) to computer software first sent from the United States to a foreign manufacturer on a master disk, or by electronic transmission, then copied by the foreign recipient for installation on computers made and sold abroad.

AT & T holds a patent on an apparatus for digitally encoding and compressing recorded speech. Microsoft's Windows operating system, it is conceded, has the potential to infringe AT & T's patent, because Windows incorporates software code that, when installed, enables a computer to process speech in the manner claimed by that patent. It bears emphasis, however, that uninstalled Windows software does not infringe AT & T's patent any more than a computer standing alone does; instead, the patent is infringed only when a computer is loaded with Windows and is thereby rendered capable of performing as the patented speech processor. The question before us: Does Microsoft's liability extend to computers made in another country when loaded with Windows software copied abroad from a master disk or electronic transmission dispatched by Microsoft from the United States? Our answer is "No."

The master disk or electronic transmission Microsoft sends from the United States is never installed on any of the foreign-made computers in question. Instead, copies made abroad are used for installation. Because Microsoft does not export from the United States the copies actually installed, it does not "suppl[y] ... from the United States" "components" of the relevant computers, and therefore is not liable under § 271(f) as currently written.

Plausible arguments can be made for and against extending § 271(f) to the conduct charged in this case as infringing AT & T's patent. Recognizing that § 271(f) is an exception to the general rule that our patent law does not apply extraterritorially, we resist giving the language in which Congress cast § 271(f) an expansive interpretation. Our decision leaves to Congress' informed judgment any adjustment of § 271(f) it deems necessary or proper.

I

Our decision some 35 years ago in *Deepsouth Packing Co. v. Laitram Corp.,* 406 U.S. 518, 92 S.Ct. 1700, 32 L.Ed.2d 273 (1972), a case about a shrimp deveining machine, led Congress to enact § 271(f). In that case, Laitram, holder of a patent on the time-and-expense-saving machine, sued Deepsouth, manufacturer of an infringing deveiner. Deepsouth conceded that the Patent Act barred it from making and selling its deveining machine in the United States, but sought to salvage a portion of its business: Nothing in United States patent law, Deepsouth urged, stopped it from making in the United States the *parts* of its deveiner, as opposed to the machine itself, and selling those *parts* to foreign buyers for assembly and use abroad. *Id.,* at 522–524. We agreed.

Interpreting our patent law as then written, we reiterated in *Deepsouth* that it was "not an infringement to make or use a patented product outside of the United States." *Id.,* at 527; *see* 35 U.S.C. § 271(a) (1970 ed.) ("[W]hoever without authority makes, uses or sells any patented invention, within the United States during the term of the patent therefor, infringes the patent."). Deepsouth's foreign buyers did not infringe Laitram's patent, we held, because they assembled and used the deveining machines outside the United States. Deepsouth, we therefore concluded, could not be charged with inducing or contributing to an infringement. 406 U.S., at 526–527. Nor could Deepsouth be held liable as a direct infringer, for it did not make, sell, or use the patented invention—the fully assembled deveining machine—within the United States. The parts of the machine were not themselves patented, we noted, hence export of those parts, unassembled, did not rank as an infringement of Laitram's patent. *Id.,* at 527–529.

Laitram had argued in *Deepsouth* that resistance to extension of the patent privilege to cover exported parts "derived from too narrow and technical an interpretation of the [Patent Act]." *Id.,* at 529. Rejecting that argument, we referred to prior decisions holding that "a combination patent protects only against the operable assembly of the whole and not the manufacture of its parts." *Id.,* at 528. Congress' codification of patent law, we said, signaled no intention to broaden the scope of the privilege. *Id.,* at 530 ("When, as here, the Constitution is permissive, the sign of how far Congress has chosen to go can come only from Congress."). And we again emphasized that "[o]ur patent system makes no claim to extraterritorial effect; these acts of Congress do not, and were not intended to, operate beyond the limits of the United States; and we correspondingly reject the claims of others to such control over our markets." *Id.*, at 531 (quoting *Brown v. Duchesne,* 19 How. 183, 195, 15 L.Ed. 595 (1857)).

Absent "a clear congressional indication of intent," we stated, courts had no warrant to stop the manufacture and sale of the parts of patented inventions for assembly and use abroad. 406 U.S., at 532.

Focusing its attention on *Deepsouth,* Congress enacted § 271(f). The provision expands the definition of infringement to include supplying from the United States a patented invention's components:

"(1) Whoever without authority supplies or causes to be supplied in or from the United States all or a substantial portion of the components of a patented invention, where such components are uncombined in whole or in part, in such manner as to actively induce the combination of such components outside of the United States in a manner that would infringe the patent if such combination occurred within the United States, shall be liable as an infringer.

"(2) Whoever without authority supplies or causes to be supplied in or from the United States any component of a patented invention that is especially made or especially adapted for use in the invention and not a staple article or commodity of commerce suitable for substantial noninfringing use, where such component is uncombined in whole or in part, knowing that such component is so made or adapted and intending that such component will be combined outside of the United States in a manner that would infringe the patent if such combination occurred within the United States, shall be liable as an infringer." 35 U.S.C. § 271(f).

II

Windows is designed, authored, and tested at Microsoft's Redmond, Washington, headquarters. Microsoft sells Windows to end users and computer manufacturers, both foreign and domestic. Purchasing manufacturers install the software onto the computers they sell. Microsoft sends to each of the foreign manufacturers a master version of Windows, either on a disk or via encrypted electronic transmission. The manufacturer uses the master version to generate copies. Those copies, not the master sent by Microsoft, are installed on the foreign manufacturer's computers. Once assembly is complete, the foreign-made computers are sold to users abroad.

AT & T's patent ('580 patent) is for an apparatus (as relevant here, a computer) capable of digitally encoding and compressing recorded speech. Windows, the parties agree, contains software that enables a computer to process speech in the manner claimed by the '580 patent. In 2001, AT & T filed an infringement suit in the United States District

Court for the Southern District of New York, charging Microsoft with liability for domestic and foreign installations of Windows.

Neither Windows software (*e.g.,* in a box on the shelf) nor a computer standing alone (*i.e.,* without Windows installed) infringes AT & T's patent. Infringement occurs only when Windows is installed on a computer, thereby rendering it capable of performing as the patented speech processor. Microsoft stipulated that by installing Windows on its own computers during the software development process, it directly infringed the '580 patent. Microsoft further acknowledged that by licensing copies of Windows to manufacturers of computers sold in the United States, it induced infringement of AT & T's patent.

Microsoft denied, however, any liability based on the master disks and electronic transmissions it dispatched to foreign manufacturers, thus joining issue with AT & T. By sending Windows to foreign manufacturers, AT & T contended, Microsoft "supplie[d] ... from the United States," for "combination" abroad, "components" of AT & T's patented speech processor; accordingly, AT & T urged, Microsoft was liable under § 271(f). Microsoft responded that unincorporated software, because it is intangible information, cannot be typed a "component" of an invention under § 271(f). In any event, Microsoft urged, the foreign-generated copies of Windows actually installed abroad were not "supplie[d] ... from the United States." Rejecting these responses, the District Court held Microsoft liable under § 271(f). On appeal, a divided panel of the Court of Appeals for the Federal Circuit affirmed. 414 F.3d 1366 (2005). We granted certiorari, 549 U.S. ___ (2006), and now reverse.

III

A

This case poses two questions: First, when, or in what form, does software qualify as a "component" under § 271(f)? Second, were "components" of the foreign-made computers involved in this case "supplie[d]" by Microsoft "from the United States"?[7]

As to the first question, no one in this litigation argues that software can *never* rank as a "component" under § 271(f). The parties disagree, however, over the stage at which software becomes a component. Software, the "set of instructions, known as code, that directs a computer to perform specified functions or operations," *Fantasy Sports Properties, Inc. v. Sportsline.com, Inc.,* 287 F.3d 1108, 1118 (C.A.Fed.2002), can be conceptualized in (at least) two ways. One can speak of software in the abstract: the instructions themselves detached from any medium. (An analogy: The notes of Beethoven's Ninth Symphony.) One can alternatively envision a tangible "copy" of software, the instructions encoded on

---

7. The record leaves unclear which paragraph of § 271(f) AT & T's claim invokes. While there are differences between § 271(f)(1) and (f)(2), the parties do not suggest that those differences are outcome determinative. *Cf. infra,* at 14–15, n. 16 (explaining why both paragraphs yield the same result). For clarity's sake, we focus our analysis on the text of § 271(f)(1).

a medium such as a CD–ROM. (Sheet music for Beethoven's Ninth.) AT & T argues that software in the abstract, not simply a particular copy of software, qualifies as a "component" under § 271(f). Microsoft and the United States argue that only a copy of software, not software in the abstract, can be a component.[8]

The significance of these diverse views becomes apparent when we turn to the second question: Were components of the foreign-made computers involved in this case "supplie[d]" by Microsoft "from the United States"? If the relevant components are the copies of Windows actually installed on the foreign computers, AT & T could not persuasively argue that those components, though generated abroad, were "supplie[d] ... from the United States" as § 271(f) requires for liability to attach.[9] If, on the other hand, Windows in the abstract qualifies as a component within § 271(f)'s compass, it would not matter that the master copies of Windows software dispatched from the United States were not themselves installed abroad as working parts of the foreign computers.[10]

With this explanation of the relationship between the two questions in view, we further consider the twin inquiries.

B

First, when, or in what form, does software become a "component" under § 271(f)? We construe § 271(f)'s terms "in accordance with [their] ordinary or natural meaning." *FDIC v. Meyer*, 510 U.S. 471, 476, 114 S.Ct. 996, 127 L.Ed.2d 308 (1994). Section 271(f) applies to the supply abroad of the "components of a patented invention, where *such components* are uncombined in whole or in part, in such manner as to actively induce the combination of *such components*." § 271(f)(1) (emphasis added). The provision thus applies only to "such components" as are combined to form the "patented invention" at issue. The patented invention here is AT & T's speech-processing computer.

8. Microsoft and the United States stress that to count as a component, the copy of software must be expressed as "object code." "Software in the form in which it is written and understood by humans is called 'source code.' To be functional, however, software must be converted (or 'compiled') into its machine-usable version," a sequence of binary number instructions typed "object code." Brief for United States as *Amicus Curiae* 4, n. 1; 71 USPQ 2d 1118, 1119, n. 5 (S.D.N.Y.2004) (recounting Microsoft's description of the software development process). It is stipulated that object code was on the master disks and electronic transmissions Microsoft dispatched from the United States.

9. On this view of "component," the copies of Windows on the master disks and electronic transmissions that Microsoft sent from the United States could not themselves serve as a basis for liability, because those copies were not installed on the foreign manufacturers' computers. *See* § 271(f)(1) (encompassing only those components "combin[ed] ... outside of the United States in a manner that would infringe the patent if such combination occurred within the United States").

10. The Federal Circuit panel in this case, relying on that court's prior decision in *Eolas Technologies Inc. v. Microsoft Corp.*, 399 F.3d 1325 (2005), held that software qualifies as a component under § 271(f). We are unable to determine, however, whether the Federal Circuit panels regarded as a component software in the abstract, or a copy of software.

Until it is expressed as a computer-readable "copy," *e.g.,* on a CD–ROM, Windows software—indeed any software detached from an activating medium—remains uncombinable. It cannot be inserted into a CD–ROM drive or downloaded from the Internet; it cannot be installed or executed on a computer. Abstract software code is an idea without physical embodiment, and as such, it does not match § 271(f)'s categorization: "components" amenable to "combination." Windows abstracted from a tangible copy no doubt is information—a detailed set of instructions—and thus might be compared to a blueprint (or anything containing design information, *e.g.,* a schematic, template, or prototype). A blueprint may contain precise instructions for the construction and combination of the components of a patented device, but it is not itself a combinable component of that device. AT & T and its *amici* do not suggest otherwise. *Cf. Pellegrini v. Analog Devices, Inc.,* 375 F.3d 1113, 1117–1119 (C.A.Fed.2004) (transmission abroad of instructions for production of patented computer chips not covered by § 271(f)).

AT & T urges that software, at least when expressed as machine-readable object code, is distinguishable from design information presented in a blueprint. Software, unlike a blueprint, is "modular"; it is a stand-alone product developed and marketed "for use on many different types of computer hardware and in conjunction with many other types of software." Software's modularity persists even after installation; it can be updated or removed (deleted) without affecting the hardware on which it is installed. Software, unlike a blueprint, is also "dynamic." After a device has been built according to a blueprint's instructions, the blueprint's work is done (as AT & T puts it, the blueprint's instructions have been "exhausted."). Software's instructions, in contrast, are contained in and continuously performed by a computer.

The distinctions advanced by AT & T do not persuade us to characterize software, uncoupled from a medium, as a combinable component. Blueprints too, or any design information for that matter, can be independently developed, bought, and sold. If the point of AT & T's argument is that we do not see blueprints lining stores' shelves, the same observation may be made about software in the abstract: What retailers sell, and consumers buy, are *copies* of software. Likewise, before software can be contained in and continuously performed by a computer, before it can be updated or deleted, an actual, physical copy of the software must be delivered by CD–ROM or some other means capable of interfacing with the computer.[12]

Because it is so easy to encode software's instructions onto a medium that can be read by a computer, AT & T intimates, that extra step should not play a decisive role under § 271(f). But the extra step is

12. The dissent, embracing AT & T's argument, contends that, "unlike a blueprint that merely instructs a user how to do something, software actually causes infringing conduct to occur." *Post,* at 3 (Stevens, J., dissenting). We have emphasized, however, that Windows can "caus[e] infringing conduct to occur"—*i.e.,* function as part of AT & T's speech-processing computer—only when expressed as a computer-readable copy. Abstracted from a usable copy, Windows code is intangible, uncombinable information, more like notes of music in the head of a composer than "a roller that causes a player piano to produce sound." *Ibid.*

what renders the software a usable, combinable part of a computer; easy or not, the copy-producing step is essential. Moreover, many tools may be used easily and inexpensively to generate the parts of a device. A machine for making sprockets might be used by a manufacturer to produce tens of thousands of sprockets an hour. That does not make the machine a "component" of the tens of thousands of devices in which the sprockets are incorporated, at least not under any ordinary understanding of the term "component." Congress, of course, might have included within § 271(f)'s compass, for example, not only combinable "components" of a patented invention, but also "information, instructions, or tools from which those components readily may be generated." It did not. In sum, a copy of Windows, not Windows in the abstract, qualifies as a "component" under § 271(f).[13]

C

The next question, has Microsoft "supplie[d] ... from the United States" components of the computers here involved? Under a conventional reading of § 271(f)'s text, the answer would be "No," for the foreign-made copies of Windows actually installed on the computers were "supplie[d]" from places outside the United States. The Federal Circuit majority concluded, however, that "for software 'components,' the act of copying is subsumed in the act of 'supplying.'" 414 F.3d, at 1370. A master sent abroad, the majority observed, differs not at all from the exact copies, easily, inexpensively, and swiftly generated from the master; hence "sending a single copy abroad with the intent that it be replicated invokes § 271(f) liability for th[e] foreign-made copies." *Ibid.; cf. post*, at 2 (STEVENS, J., dissenting) ("[A] master disk is the functional equivalent of a warehouse of components ... that Microsoft fully expects to be incorporated into foreign-manufactured computers.").

Judge Rader, dissenting, noted that "supplying" is ordinarily understood to mean an activity separate and distinct from any subsequent "copying, replicating, or reproducing—in effect manufacturing." 414 F.3d, at 1372–1373 (internal quotation marks omitted); *see id.*, at 1373 ("[C]opying and supplying are separate acts with different consequences—particularly when the 'supplying' occurs in the United States and the copying occurs in Dusseldorf or Tokyo. As a matter of logic, one cannot supply one hundred components of a patented invention without first making one hundred copies of the component.... ."). He further observed: "The only true difference between making and supplying software components and physical components [of other patented inventions] is that copies of software components are easier to make and transport." *Id.*, at 1374. But nothing in § 271(f)'s text, Judge Rader maintained, renders ease of copying a relevant, no less decisive, factor in triggering liability for infringement. *See ibid*. We agree.

13. We need not address whether software in the abstract, or any other intangible, can *ever* be a component under § 271(f). If an intangible method or process, for instance, qualifies as a "patented invention" under § 271(f) (a question as to which we express no opinion), the combinable components of that invention might be intangible as well. The invention before us, however, AT & T's speech-processing computer, is a tangible thing.

Section 271(f) prohibits the supply of components "from the United States ... in such manner as to actively induce the combination of *such components*." § 271(f)(1) (emphasis added). Under this formulation, the very components supplied from the United States, and not copies thereof, trigger § 271(f) liability when combined abroad to form the patented invention at issue. Here, as we have repeatedly noted, the copies of Windows actually installed on the foreign computers were not themselves supplied from the United States.[14] Indeed, those copies did not exist until they were generated by third parties outside the United States.[15] Copying software abroad, all might agree, is indeed easy and inexpensive. But the same could be said of other items: "Keys or machine parts might be copied from a master; chemical or biological substances might be created by reproduction; and paper products might be made by electronic copying and printing." Brief for United States as *Amicus Curiae* 24. *See also supra,* at 11–12 (rejecting argument similarly based on ease of copying in construing "component"). Section 271(f) contains no instruction to gauge when duplication is easy and cheap enough to deem a copy in fact made abroad nevertheless "supplie[d] ... from the United States." The absence of anything addressing copying in the statutory text weighs against a judicial determination that replication abroad of a master dispatched from the United States "supplies" the foreign-made copies from the United States within the intendment of § 271(f).[16]

D

Any doubt that Microsoft's conduct falls outside § 271(f)'s compass would be resolved by the presumption against extraterritoriality, on

14. In a footnote, Microsoft suggests that even a disk shipped from the United States, and used to install Windows directly on a foreign computer, would not give rise to liability under § 271(f) if the disk were removed after installation. We need not and do not reach that issue here.

15. The dissent analogizes Microsoft's supply of master versions of Windows abroad to "the export of an inventory of ... knives to be warehoused until used to complete the assembly of an infringing machine." *Post,* at 2. But as we have underscored, foreign-made copies of Windows, not the masters Microsoft dispatched from the United States, were installed on the computers here involved. A more apt analogy, therefore, would be the export of knives for *copying* abroad, with the foreign-made *copies* "warehoused until used to complete the assembly of an infringing machine." *Ibid.* Without stretching § 271(f) beyond the text Congress composed, a copy made entirely abroad does not fit the description "supplie[d] ... from the United States."

16. Our analysis, while focusing on § 271(f)(1), is equally applicable to § 271(f)(2). But *cf. post,* at 1 (STEVENS, J., dissenting) (asserting "paragraph (2) ... best supports AT & T's position here"). While the two paragraphs differ, among other things, on the quantity of components that must be "supplie[d] ... from the United States" for liability to attach, *see infra,* at 18, n. 18, that distinction does not affect our analysis. Paragraph (2), like (1), covers only a "component" amenable to "combination." § 271(f)(2); *see supra,* at 9–12 (explaining why Windows in the abstract is not a combinable component). Paragraph (2), like (1), encompasses only the "[s]uppl[y] ... from the United States" of "such [a] component" as will itself "be combined outside of the United States." § 271(f)(2); *see supra,* at 12–13 and this page (observing that foreign-made copies of Windows installed on computers abroad were not "supplie[d] ... from the United States"). It is thus unsurprising that AT & T does not join the dissent in suggesting that the outcome might turn on whether we view the case under paragraph (1) or (2).

which we have already touched. *See supra,* at 2, 4. The presumption that United States law governs domestically but does not rule the world applies with particular force in patent law. The traditional understanding that our patent law "operate [s] only domestically and d[oes] not extend to foreign activities," is embedded in the Patent Act itself, which provides that a patent confers exclusive rights in an invention within the United States. 35 U.S.C. § 154(a)(1) (patentee's rights over invention apply to manufacture, use, or sale "throughout the United States" and to importation "into the United States"). *See Deepsouth,* 406 U.S., at 531 ("Our patent system makes no claim to extraterritorial effect"; our legislation "d[oes] not, and [was] not intended to, operate beyond the limits of the United States, and we correspondingly reject the claims of others to such control over our markets." (quoting *Brown,* 19 How., at 195, 15 L.Ed. 595)).

As a principle of general application, moreover, we have stated that courts should "assume that legislators take account of the legitimate sovereign interests of other nations when they write American laws." *F. Hoffmann–La Roche Ltd. v. Empagran S. A.,* 542 U.S. 155, 164, 124 S.Ct. 2359, 159 L.Ed.2d 226 (2004); *see EEOC v. Arabian American Oil Co.,* 499 U.S. 244, 248, 111 S.Ct. 1227, 113 L.Ed.2d 274 (1991). Thus, the United States accurately conveyed in this case: "Foreign conduct is [generally] the domain of foreign law," and in the area here involved, in particular, foreign law "may embody different policy judgments about the relative rights of inventors, competitors, and the public in patented inventions." Applied to this case, the presumption tugs strongly against construction of § 271(f) to encompass as a "component" not only a physical copy of software, but also software's intangible code, and to render "supplie[d] . . . from the United States" not only exported copies of software, but also duplicates made abroad.

AT & T argues that the presumption is inapplicable because Congress enacted § 271(f) specifically to extend the reach of United States patent law to cover certain activity abroad. But as this Court has explained, "the presumption is not defeated . . . just because [a statute] specifically addresses [an] issue of extraterritorial application," *Smith v. United States,* 507 U.S. 197, 204, 113 S.Ct. 1178, 122 L.Ed.2d 548 (1993); it remains instructive in determining the *extent* of the statutory exception. *See Empagran,* 542 U.S., at 161–162, 164–165; *Smith,* 507 U.S., at 204.

AT & T alternately contends that the presumption holds no sway here given that § 271(f), by its terms, applies only to domestic conduct, *i.e.,* to the supply of a patented invention's components "from the United States." § 271(f)(1). AT & T's reading, however, "converts a single act of supply from the United States into a springboard for liability each time a copy of the software is subsequently made [abroad] and combined with computer hardware [abroad] for sale [abroad.]" Brief for United States as *Amicus Curiae* 29; see 414 F.3d, at 1373, 1375 (Rader, J., dissenting). In short, foreign law alone, not United States law, currently governs the manufacture and sale of components of patented inventions in foreign countries. If AT & T desires to prevent copying in foreign countries, its remedy today lies in obtaining and enforcing foreign patents.

IV

AT & T urges that reading § 271(f) to cover only those copies of software actually dispatched from the United States creates a "loophole" for software makers. Liability for infringing a United States patent could be avoided, as Microsoft's practice shows, by an easily arranged circumvention: Instead of making installation copies of software in the United States, the copies can be made abroad, swiftly and at small cost, by generating them from a master supplied from the United States. The Federal Circuit majority found AT & T's plea compelling:

> "Were we to hold that Microsoft's supply by exportation of the master versions of the Windows® software—specifically for the purpose of foreign replication—avoids infringement, we would be subverting the remedial nature of § 271(f), permitting a technical avoidance of the statute by ignoring the advances in a field of technology—and its associated industry practices—that developed after the enactment of § 271(f).... Section § 271(f), if it is to remain effective, must therefore be interpreted in a manner that is appropriate to the nature of the technology at issue." 414 F.3d, at 1371.

While the majority's concern is understandable, we are not persuaded that dynamic judicial interpretation of § 271(f) is in order. The "loophole," in our judgment, is properly left for Congress to consider, and to close if it finds such action warranted.

There is no dispute, we note again, that § 271(f) is inapplicable to the export of design tools—blueprints, schematics, templates, and prototypes—all of which may provide the information required to construct and combine overseas the components of inventions patented under United States law. We have no license to attribute to Congress an unstated intention to place the information Microsoft dispatched from the United States in a separate category.

Section 271(f) was a direct response to a gap in our patent law revealed by this Court's *Deepsouth* decision. The facts of that case were undeniably at the fore when § 271(f) was in the congressional hopper. In *Deepsouth*, the items exported were kits containing all the physical, readily assemblable parts of a shrimp deveining machine (not an intangible set of instructions), and those parts themselves (not foreign-made copies of them) would be combined abroad by foreign buyers. Having attended to the gap made evident in *Deepsouth*, Congress did not address other arguable gaps: Section 271(f) does not identify as an infringing act conduct in the United States that facilitates making a component of a patented invention outside the United States; nor does the provision check "suppl[ying] ... from the United States" information, instructions, or other materials needed to make copies abroad.[18] Given that

---

18. Section 271(f)'s text does, in one respect, reach past the facts of *Deepsouth*. While Deepsouth exported kits containing all the parts of its deveining machines,

Congress did not home in on the loophole AT & T describes, and in view of the expanded extraterritorial thrust AT & T's reading of § 271(f) entails, our precedent leads us to leave in Congress' court the patent-protective determination AT & T seeks. *Cf. Sony Corp. of America v. Universal City Studios, Inc.,* 464 U.S. 417, 431, 104 S.Ct. 774, 78 L.Ed.2d 574 (1984) ("In a case like this, in which Congress has not plainly marked our course, we must be circumspect in construing the scope of rights created by a legislative enactment which never contemplated such a calculus of interests.").

Congress is doubtless aware of the ease with which software (and other electronic media) can be copied, and has not left the matter untouched. In 1998, Congress addressed "the ease with which pirates could copy and distribute a copyrightable work in digital form." *Universal City Studios, Inc.* v. *Corley,* 273 F.3d 429, 435 (C.A.2 2001). The resulting measure, the Digital Millennium Copyright Act, 17 U.S.C. § 1201 *et seq.,* "backed with legal sanctions the efforts of copyright owners to protect their works from piracy behind digital walls such as encryption codes or password protections." *Universal City Studios,* 273 F.3d, at 435. If the patent law is to be adjusted better "to account for the realities of software distribution," 414 F.3d, at 1370, the alteration should be made after focused legislative consideration, and not by the Judiciary forecasting Congress' likely disposition.

* * *

For the reasons stated, the judgment of the Court of Appeals for the Federal Circuit is

Reversed.

THE CHIEF JUSTICE took no part in the consideration or decision of this case.

JUSTICE ALITO, with whom JUSTICE THOMAS and JUSTICE BREYER join, concurring as to all but footnote 14.

I agree with the Court that no "component[s]" of the foreign-made computers involved in this case were "supplie[d]" by Microsoft "from the United States." 35 U.S.C. § 271(f)(1). I write separately because I reach this conclusion through somewhat different reasoning.

I

Computer programmers typically write programs in a "human read-able" programming language. This " 'source code' "is then generally converted by the computer into a "machine readable code" or "machine language" expressed in a binary format. During the Windows writing

§ 271(f)(1) applies to the supply abroad of "all or a substantial portion of" a patented invention's components. And § 271(f)(2) applies to the export of even a single compo-nent if it is "especially made or especially adapted for use in the invention and not a staple article or commodity of commerce suitable for substantial noninfringing use."

process, the program exists in the form of machine readable code on the magnetic tape fields of Microsoft's computers' hard drives.

When Microsoft finishes writing its Windows program in the United States, it encodes Windows onto CD–ROMs known as " 'golden masters' " in the form of machine readable code. This is done by engraving each disk in a specific way such that another computer can read the engravings, understand what they mean, and write the code onto the magnetic fields of its hard drive.

Microsoft ships these disks (or sends the code via electronic transmission) abroad, where the code is copied onto other disks that are then placed into foreign-made computers for purposes of installing the Windows program. No physical aspect of a Windows CD–ROM—original disk or copy—is ever incorporated into the computer itself. *See Stenograph L.L.C. v. Bossard Assocs., Inc.,* 144 F.3d 96, 100 (C.A.D.C.1998) (noting that, within the context of the Copyright Act, "installation of software onto a computer results in 'copying' "). The intact CD–ROM is then removed and may be discarded without affecting the computer's implementation of the code. The parties agree for purposes of this litigation that a foreign-made computer containing the Windows code would violate AT & T's patent if present in the United States.

II

A

I agree with the Court that a component of a machine, whether a shrimp deveiner or a personal computer, must be something physical. This is because the word "component," when concerning a physical device, is most naturally read to mean a physical part of the device. Furthermore, § 271(f) requires that the component be "combined" with other components to form the infringing device, meaning that the component must remain a part of the device. For these reasons, I agree with the Court that a set of instructions on how to build an infringing device, or even a template of the device, does not qualify as a component.

B

As the parties agree, an inventor can patent a machine that carries out a certain process, and a computer may constitute such a machine when it executes commands—given to it by code—that allow it to carry out that process. Such a computer would not become an infringing device until enough of the code is installed on the computer to allow it to execute the process in question. The computer would not be an infringing device prior to the installation, or even during the installation. And the computer remains an infringing device after the installation process because, even though the original installation device (such as a CD–ROM) has been removed from the computer, the code remains on the hard drive.

III

Here, Windows software originating in the United States was sent abroad, whether on a master disk or by means of an electronic transmission, and eventually copied onto the hard drives of the foreign-made computers. Once the copying process was completed, the Windows program was recorded in a physical form, *i.e.*, in magnetic fields on the computers' hard drives. The physical form of the Windows program on the master disk, *i.e.*, the engravings on the CD–ROM, remained on the disk in a form unchanged by the copying process. There is nothing in the record to suggest that any physical part of the disk became a physical part of the foreign-made computer, and such an occurrence would be contrary to the general workings of computers.

Because no physical object originating in the United States was combined with these computers, there was no violation of § 271(f). Accordingly, it is irrelevant that the Windows software was not copied onto the foreign-made computers *directly* from the master disk or from an electronic transmission that originated in the United States. To be sure, if these computers could not run Windows without inserting and keeping a CD–ROM in the appropriate drive, then the CD–ROMs might be components of the computer. But that is not the case here.

* * *

Because the physical incarnation of code on the Windows CD–ROM supplied from the United States is not a "component" of an infringing device under § 271(f), it logically follows that a copy of such a CD–ROM also is not a component. For this reason, I join the Court's opinion, except for footnote 14.

JUSTICE STEVENS, dissenting.

As the Court acknowledges, "[p]lausible arguments can be made for and against extending § 271(f) to the conduct charged in this case as infringing AT & T's patent." Strong policy considerations, buttressed by the presumption against the application of domestic patent law in foreign markets, support Microsoft Corporation's position. I am, however, persuaded that an affirmance of the Court of Appeals' judgment is more faithful to the intent of the Congress that enacted § 271(f) than a reversal.

The provision was a response to our decision in *Deepsouth Packing Co. v. Laitram Corp.*, 406 U.S. 518, 92 S.Ct. 1700, 32 L.Ed.2d 273 (1972), holding that a patent on a shrimp deveining machine had not been infringed by the export of components for assembly abroad. Paragraph (1) of § 271(f) would have been sufficient on its own to overrule *Deepsouth*, but it is paragraph (2) that best supports AT & T's position here.* * *

Under this provision, the export of a specially designed knife that has no use other than as a part of a patented deveining machine would constitute infringement. It follows that § 271(f)(2) would cover the export of an inventory of such knives to be warehoused until used to complete the assembly of an infringing machine.

The relevant component in this case is not a physical item like a knife. Both Microsoft and the Court think that means it cannot be a "component." But if a disk with software inscribed on it is a "component," I find it difficult to understand why the most important ingredient of that component is not also a component. Indeed, the master disk is the functional equivalent of a warehouse of components—components that Microsoft fully expects to be incorporated into foreign-manufactured computers. Put somewhat differently: On the Court's view, Microsoft could be liable under § 271(f) only if it sends individual copies of its software directly from the United States with the intent that each copy would be incorporated into a separate infringing computer. But it seems to me that an indirect transmission via a master disk warehouse is likewise covered by § 271(f).

I disagree with the Court's suggestion that because software is analogous to an abstract set of instructions, it cannot be regarded as a "component" within the meaning of § 271(f). Whether attached or detached from any medium, software plainly satisfies the dictionary definition of that word. And unlike a blueprint that merely instructs a user how to do something, software actually causes infringing conduct to occur. It is more like a roller that causes a player piano to produce sound than sheet music that tells a pianist what to do. Moreover, it is surely not "a staple article or commodity of commerce suitable for substantial noninfringing use" as that term is used in § 271(f)(2). On the contrary, its sole intended use is an infringing use.

I would therefore affirm the judgment of the Court of Appeals.

Notes

1. If parts with no substantial noninfringing use are sold in the United States, and assembled into an infringing device overseas, is the seller of the parts liable for contributory infringement? Does it matter whether the seller knows what they are to be used for?

2. If parts are sold overseas for assembly into infringing devices in the United States, can the foreign seller be held liable for contributory infringement?

3. If a French drug manufacturer makes an unpatented compound using a process which is patented in the United States but not in France, is the process patent infringed by importation of that compound into the United States without the patentee's permission? What if the process is patented in France as well as the United States, and the manufacturer has a license from the patentee to use the process in France?

6. INFRINGEMENT OF DESIGN PATENTS

(i) Ordinary Observer Test

ARMINAK & ASSOCIATES, INC. v. SAINT–GOBAIN CALMAR, INC.

United States District Court, C.D. California, 2006.
424 F.Supp.2d 1188.

CARNEY, DISTRICT JUDGE.

[Calmar sued Arminak for infringement of its two design patents for a trigger sprayer shroud, which is a plastic cover that fits over the pump mechanism used in plastic spray bottles. Arminak moved for partial summary judgment, on the ground that no reasonable jury could find that its device infringed either of Calmar's patents.]

* * *

A. THE TEST FOR INFRINGEMENT OF A DESIGN PATENT

"A design patent protects the nonfunctional aspects of an ornamental design as shown in the patent." *Elmer v. ICC Fabricating, Inc.,* 67 F.3d 1571 (Fed.Cir.1995) (*citing KeyStone,* 997 F.2d at 1450). A design patent is infringed by the "unauthorized manufacture, use, or sale of the article embodying the patented design or any colorable imitation thereof." *Goodyear Tire & Rubber Co. v. Hercules Tire & Rubber Co.,* 162 F.3d 1113, 1116–17 (Fed.Cir.1998). 35 U.S.C. Section 289 provides in relevant part:

> Whoever during the term of a patent for a design, without license of the owner, (1) applies the patented design, or any colorable imitation thereof, to any article of manufacture for the purpose of sale, or (2) sells or exposes for sale any article of manufacture to which such design or colorable imitation has been applied shall be liable to the owner to the extent of his total profit, but not less than $250, recoverable in any United States district court having jurisdiction of the parties.

The first step in determining whether a design patent has been infringed is to construe its claims to determine their meaning and scope. *Markman v. Westview Instruments, Inc.,* 52 F.3d 967, 976 (Fed.Cir.1995) (en banc), *aff'd,* 517 U.S. 370, 116 S.Ct. 1384, 134 L.Ed.2d 577, 38 U.S.P.Q.2d 1461 (1996); *OddzOn Products, Inc. v. Just Toys, Inc.,* 122 F.3d 1396, 1404 (Fed.Cir.1997) ("Whether a design patent is infringed is determined by first construing the claim to the design ... "). Claim construction is a question of law for the court. In construing patent claims, courts consider the patent's claims, the specification, and the prosecution history. Courts may also consider "expert testimony, including evidence of how those skilled in the art would interpret the claims," as well as other extrinsic evidence. As design patents typically are claimed as shown in drawings, without any written description, the court's claim construction must be adapted accordingly.

Once the court has construed the patent's claims, it must compare the accused item to the patented design for overall visual similarity, to determine whether infringement has occurred. The test for infringement has long been known as the "ordinary observer" test:

> [I]f, in the eye of an ordinary observer, giving such attention as a purchaser usually gives, two designs are substantially the same, if the resemblance is such as to deceive such an observer, inducing him to purchase one supposing it to be the other, the first one patented is infringed by the other.

Gorham Co. v. White, 81 U.S. (14 Wall.) 511, 528, 20 L.Ed. 731 (1871).

Infringement of a design patent occurs if "the designs have the same general visual appearance, such that it is likely that the purchaser would be deceived into confusing the design of the accused article with the patented design." *Goodyear,* 162 F.3d at 1118. Complete similarity is not required to find infringement, and "minor changes in a design are often readily made without changing its overall appearance." *Id.* at 1117. However, if the overall impression of the designs are dissimilar, infringement cannot be found based on similarity of specific features. *OddzOn,* 122 F.3d at 1405. In applying the ordinary observer test, the court's analysis "is not limited to the ornamental features of a subset of the [design patent's] drawings, but instead must encompass the claimed ornamental features of all figures of a design patent." *Contessa Food Products, Inc. v. Conagra, Inc.,* 282 F.3d 1370, 1379 (Fed.Cir.2002). The court must consider the features of the design that would be visible during normal and intended use throughout the article's entire lifetime, not only those features visible at the time of sale. *Id.* The period of consideration is that "beginning after completion of manufacture or assembly and ending with the ultimate destruction, loss, or disappearance of the article." *Id.* at 1379.

Finally, the similarity between the accused device and the patented design must stem from the points of novelty that distinguish the patented invention from the prior art. *Bernhardt, L.L.C. v. Collezione Europa U.S.A., Inc.,* 386 F.3d 1371, 1383 (Fed.Cir.2004); *Contessa,* 282 F.3d at 1377; *Goodyear,* 162 F.3d at 1113. This "point of novelty" test is distinct from the "ordinary observer" test, and it is legal error to merge them by, for example, taking the overall claimed design to be the point of novelty. *Bernhardt,* 386 F.3d at 1383 ("[I]n determining infringement, the 'point of novelty' test is distinct from the 'ordinary observer' test and requires proof that the accused design appropriates the novelty which distinguishes the patented design from the prior art."); *Contessa,* 282 F.3d at 1377. "While it is the design as a whole that is patented ... the distinctions from prior designs inform the court's understanding of the patent." *Goodyear,* 162 F.3d at 1118 (citation omitted). If the overall visual impression of the accused device and the patented design are dissimilar, and would not deceive the ordinary observer, there is no need to address the "point of novelty" test.

B. APPLICATION

1. Claim Construction

The '581 and '602 Patents are each titled "Sprayer Shroud," and the claim of each patent is represented by five drawings showing different views of the shroud. The drawings show, respectively, a side view (figure 1), front view (figure 2), top view (figure 3), back view (figure 4), and bottom view (figure 5). Based on its review of the '581 and '602 Patents, the parties' proposed claim constructions, and examples of prior art submitted by the parties, the Court construes the Patents' claims as follows:

[Here the court provided detailed verbal descriptions of the drawings.]

* * *

2.   The Ordinary Observer Test

a.   Who is the "Ordinary Observer"?

Having construed the patents' claims, the Court now considers whether the overall visual similarity between the AA Trigger and the patented designs would likely deceive an ordinary observer. As an initial matter, the parties differ as to the ordinary observer's identity. Arminak argues that the ordinary observer is a buyer for an industrial purchaser or contract filler, because only such buyers purchase trigger sprayers directly. Calmar counters that retail consumers are the "ordinary observer" because they purchase the end products that incorporate the shrouds.

The focus of the "ordinary observer" test "is on the actual product that is presented for purchase, and the ordinary purchaser of that product." *Goodyear,* 162 F.3d at 1117. "[T]he ordinary observer is not any observer but one who, with less than the trained faculties of the expert, is 'a purchaser of things of similar design,' or 'one interested in the subject.' " *Applied Arts Corp. v. Grand Rapids Metalcraft Corp.,* 67 F.2d 428, 430 (6th Cir.1933). Such an observer is not a person who has never seen the type of item the patent describes, "but one who, though not an expert, has reasonable familiarity with such objects, and is capable of forming a reasonable judgment when confronted with a design therefor as to whether it presents to his eye distinctiveness from or similarity with those which have preceded it." *Id. See also Goodyear,* 162 F.3d at 1116 ("[D]eception concerning the patented design is determined from the viewpoint of the person who is the ordinary purchaser of the article charged to be an infringement.")

The question is whether, where a patented article is only sold to consumers as incorporated into a larger product, the "ordinary observer" is the consumer or the upstream purchaser of the patented item. The Federal Circuit addressed a similar issue in *KeyStone,* which involved a design patent for blocks used in retaining walls. *KeyStone Retaining Wall Systems, Inc. v. Westrock,* Inc., 997 F.2d 1444 (Fed.Cir.1993). After the district court granted the defendant's motion for partial summary judgment on the issue of noninfringement, the patentee appealed. On appeal, the patentee argued that the district court had improperly failed to credit evidence that visitors to trade shows were confused between the patentee's blocks and the accused blocks. *Id.* at 1451. The Federal Circuit disagreed, stating that the patentee's evidence improperly focused on the blocks as incorporated into a larger product:

> Even crediting [the patentee's] evidence, it did not create a genuine issue for trial on the issue of overall similarity of the accused design with the patented block design because it primarily related to the unpatented wall, not the blocks. Although the blocks when aligned in a retaining wall may create a similar wall appearance, *the patented design is of an individual block, not an assembled wall, and the 'ordinary observer' for the purpose of the block design patent is a purchaser of the patented block, not of the unpatented wall.*

KeyStone, 997 F.2d at 1451 (emphasis added.)

In *Goodyear,* 162 F.3d at 1113, the Federal Circuit addressed a design patent for a tire tread design used on truck tires. *Goodyear,* 162 F.3d at 1115. Following the district court's determination of noninfringement, the patentee appealed. *Id.* On appeal, it argued that the district court had erred in its claim construction by construing the word "tire" in the patent's claim language, "the ornamental design for a tire tread," to mean "truck tire." *Id.* at 1116. The patentee further argued that the district court had erred by taking the "ordinary observer" to be a purchaser of truck tires, when the patent was not so limited. *Id.* at 1117. Although the Federal Circuit agreed that the patent was not limited to truck tires, it held that the "ordinary observer" was a trucker or truck fleet operator, because "both the accused tire and the [patentee's] commercial embodiment are truck tires." *Id.* at 1117. The Federal Circuit held that the focus must be on the "actual use of the accused infringing tread," the "actual product that is presented for purchase, and the ordinary purchaser of that product." *Id.* It based this holding on the fact that "the standard [annunciated in *Gorham*] is whether ... a purchaser [of the patented] item would be misled, by the design similarity imparted to the article by the copier, to think that it is the patentee's design that is being purchased." *Id.*

That the "ordinary observer" is the purchaser in danger of being misled was confirmed in *Puritan-Bennett Corp. v. Penox Technologies Inc.,* 2004 WL 866618 (S.D.Ind., March 2, 2004). That case presented the issue whether, when a product is purchased by institutional entities for use by individuals, the ordinary observer is the institutional entity or the end user. The patentee, Puritan–Bennett, sued for infringement of its design patent for portable liquid oxygen tanks. Patients could only obtain the tanks by prescription, and typically rented them from equipment dealers, medical suppliers, or hospitals. The court granted summary judgment for the defendant, holding that there was no infringement as a matter of law because the overall visual impression of the accused device was dramatically different than that of the patented design. The court reached its holding despite Puritan–Bennett's presentation of a survey of hospital patients who used the oxygen tanks, which purported to show consumer confusion. The court stated that the study failed to present a genuine issue of material fact because the surveyed patients did not represent the "ordinary observer." The ordinary observer, the court held, was a medical equipment distributor and not a patient, because it was the distributors who actually purchased the oxygen tanks. The court declined to hold that patients were the ordinary observers, despite the fact that the patentee presented substantial evidence that it marketed its products directly to patients and that its marketing created substantial interest and demand from those patients.

To similar effect is *Spotless Enterprises, Inc. v. A & E Products Group, L.P.,* 294 F.Supp.2d 322 (E.D.N.Y.2003), which involved a design patent for lingerie hangers. Garment manufacturers purchased the hangers from the hanger manufacturer, and then resold them with the garments to stores such as Wal–Mart, Target, and Mervyns. *Spotless Enterprises,* 294 F.Supp.2d at 329. The court held the "ordinary observer" to be "not the general public, but the sophisticated buyer for the garment manufacturer." *Id.* at 347.

In light of the above cases, "ordinary observers," of sprayer shrouds must be buyers for companies that purchase trigger sprayers. It is undisputed that those buyers are the only people who buy trigger sprayers that are not already incorporated into a bottled product. Calmar's Vice President of Sales, Anthony Mirocke, testified in his deposition that Calmar had never sold a single item to a consumer directly. Ed Rodden, a former Calmar customer service manager, stated that it was "accurate" to say that "Calmar's customers are not consumers." Although an end user necessarily obtains the shrouds when she buys the complete household product, she is not the "ordinary observer" because she purchases a product into which the patented item is incorporated. *KeyStone,* 997 F.2d at 1451 ("the 'ordinary observer' for the purpose of the block design patent is a purchaser of the patented block, not of the unpatented wall.") *See also Spotless Enterprises,* 294 F.Supp.2d 322 (purchaser was buyer of hangers, not consumer of lingerie sold on the hangers).

Calmar argues that consumers must be the ordinary observers because consumers notice differences among different types of trigger[] sprayers and the sprayer design affects the user's physical comfort while using the product. * * *

The fact that consumers notice differences in quality between different sprayers, and may have preferences among various types of sprayers, does not establish that they are the "ordinary observer" of sprayer shrouds. The product they purchase is not a trigger sprayer or shroud, but an entire bottle of cleaning solution. *See KeyStone,* 997 F.2d at 1451 (ordinary observer is purchaser of patented block, not unpatented wall incorporating the block.) As in *Puritan-Bennett,* consumer preferences and even direct marketing to consumers do not convert those consumers into "ordinary observers." Indeed, there is much less evidence of marketing to the end consumer in this case than there was in *Puritan-Bennett,* where the court held that consumers were not ordinary observers despite evidence that some consumers actually called the manufacturer seeking information about the tanks.[4]

Calmar cites *Gorham* for the principle that the "ordinary observer" cannot be an expert, because if experts were the ordinary observer there could never be design patent infringement. It points out that the *Gorham* court criticized the district court's reference to experts as the ordinary observer, stating that "[s]uch a test would destroy all the protection which the act of Congress intended to give. There could never be piracy of a patented design, for human ingenuity has never yet produced a design, in all its details, exactly like another, so like, that an expert could not distinguish them." *Gorham*, 81 U.S. at 527, 14 Wall. 511. This argument fails for several reasons. First, Calmar itself argues that purchasers of trigger sprayers do not necessarily qualify as "experts" on trigger shroud design. Several Calmar employees testified that the companies that buy trigger sprayers range from large, sophisticated entities to relatively unsophisticated operations for whom price is the primary consideration. * * *

Even assuming that trigger sprayer buyers are "experts," however, they still are the proper "ordinary observers" in this case. *Gorham's* statement that experts should not be the ordinary observer where they are not the buyers of the relevant product does not preclude sophisticated buyers from being the ordinary observer where they are the only ones who purchase the patented product directly.[5] The reason *Gorham* cautioned against using experts as ordinary observers in most cases was that experts in most cases are *not* purchasers of the relevant items: *"It is [ordinary consumers] who are the principal purchasers* of the articles to which designs have given novel appearances, and if they are misled, and induced to purchase what is not the article they supposed it to be ... the patentees are injured." *Gorham*, 81 U.S. at 528, 14 Wall. 511.[6] Thus, *Gorham* counsels that the likelihood of deception must be judged by reference to the people who actually purchase the patented article, and who could be misled by excessive similarity.

Consumers' purchasing decisions are unlikely to hinge on the appearance of sprayer shrouds. Calmar's own evidence shows that consumers base their decisions on other factors, such as the brand and product characteristics. [Here the court summarized Calmar's survey evidence.]

* * *

In short, consumers are not at risk of being confused into buying the wrong product by visual similarities between sprayer shrouds. The only

---

4. Although Calmar argues that consumers are the "end user," the "end user" test was rejected in *Puritan-Bennett*, in which the patients, though "end users" of the oxygen tanks, were held not to be the ordinary observer.

5. Indeed, courts have so held. *See, e.g., Spotless Enterprises, Inc. v. A & E Products Group L.P.*, 294 F.Supp.2d 322 (E.D.N.Y.

2003) ("The ordinary observer in this case is not the general public, but the sophisticated buyer for the garment manufacturer, who purchases the hangers."); *Puritan-Bennett*, 2004 WL 866618.

6. Indeed, the patented design in *Gorham* was used on retail items, spoons and forks, primarily purchased by consumers.

people likely to base their purchasing decisions to a significant degree on the shrouds' appearance, or to experience confusion if shrouds are overly similar, are buyers of trigger sprayers. To effectuate *Gorham's* purpose of preventing purchasing decisions based on confusion, it is those buyers who must be taken as the ordinary observer.[8]

Calmar also cites *Contessa* for the proposition that the "ordinary observer" includes all people who will purchase the product throughout its lifetime, including consumers. Calmar is incorrect. *Contessa* referred to the lifespan of a product in annunciating the correct standard for determining *whether deception is likely,* not in annunciating the test for the ordinary observer. The Federal Circuit held the district court had erred in failing to consider all views of the patented design that the purchaser was likely to see over the product's lifespan.[9] *Contessa,* 282 F.3d at 1379, 62 U.S.P.Q.2d at 1069. The Federal Circuit did not state that the product's entire lifespan must be considered to determine *who purchases* the patented item.

For the foregoing reasons, the Court concludes that the ordinary observer of trigger sprayer shrouds is the purchaser of trigger sprayers.

b. Would the Ordinary Purchaser of Trigger Sprayer Shrouds be Deceived by the Similarities Between the AA Trigger and the Patented Designs?

[The court found that Calmar's own evidence demonstrated that buyers for companies that purchase sprayer shrouds were not in fact deceived by the similarities between the AA Trigger and the patented designs.]

* * *

Even apart from Calmar's admission that most of its customers would not be deceived, the Court's independent comparison of the patented designs and the AA shroud convinces it that no reasonable buyer of trigger sprayers would confuse them. Calmar urges the Court to

---

8. Calmar argues that, under *Goodyear,* the ordinary observer is the purchaser of the item into which the patented design is incorporated, because the truckers and fleet operators in *Goodyear* purchased tires that incorporated the patented tread. Like purchasers of tires that incorporate tread, Calmar argues, consumers purchase household products that incorporate sprayer shrouds. Calmar's analogy is inapposite, however, because the focus of the *Gorham* test must be on the purchaser who is at risk of being confused and making the wrong purchase. Whereas a purchaser of truck tires is likely to consider the tread one of the main attributes of the tire, and thus to base his purchasing decision on the tread's appearance, a purchaser of a bottle of cleaning fluid is unlikely to consider the appearance of the sprayer shroud as a major factor in the purchasing decision, as Calmar's own evidence shows. Thus, a more apt analogy to the purchaser of tires incorporating patented tread is a buyer of trigger *sprayers* incorporating a patented shroud.

9. Specifically, the district court failed to consider the appearance of the underside of the patented shrimp tray, because the underside was "at least partially obscured in the accused product at the point of sale." *Id.* at 1379. The Federal Circuit held that was error because the ordinary observer test must consider "all ornamental features visible during normal use of the product, *i.e.* beginning after completion of manufacture or assembly and ending with the ultimate destruction, loss, or disappearance of the article." *Id.* at 1380.

focus only on the side views of the accused product and the designs, because shoppers in a supermarket are most likely to view the products from the side, standing a substantial distance away, and are unlikely to look at the triggers from the front or bottom. Calmar also urges the Court to disregard aspects of the AA Trigger and patented designs that do not appropriate the "points of novelty" that Calmar asserts. Arminak counters that all views claimed in the patent are relevant, and that the Court should focus on all aspects of the design and accused article rather than simply the asserted points of novelty.

The Court's comparison takes into consideration all the views included in the design patents, not simply those views that a customer would likely see when viewing cleaning products on a store shelf at the point of sale. *Contessa,* 282 F.3d at 1379 (district court erred in considering only the views of the patented shrimp tray design that a consumer likely would see at the point of sale.) Also, at this stage the Court declines to consider only the asserted points of novelty in the patented designs, because the "point of novelty" test is separate from the ordinary observer inquiry. *Bernhardt,* 386 F.3d at 1383. Indeed, there is no need even to consider the point of novelty test if the overall visual impression of the two articles is dissimilar. *KeyStone,* 997 F.2d at 1451.

* * *

[The court found that "the overall differences in shape and surface elevation create a striking degree of dissimilarity between the patented designs and the accused device, such that no reasonable jury could find that an ordinary purchaser of trigger sprayers would be deceived."]

3. *Point of Novelty*

Even if an ordinary observer could be deceived by the similarities between the accused shroud and the patented designs, whatever similarities exist do not stem from the points of novelty claimed in the '581 and '602 Patents. Calmar contends that those points of novelty are:

● There is a prominent horizontal line extending along each side [of the shroud], parallel to the top surface of the shroud, all the way to the sloped rear surface; and

● The sides of the shroud first go straight downwardly, and then, as viewed from the rear, at the horizontal lines on each side, bulge outwardly in a bulbous fashion, to the bottom rear of the shroud.

* * *

Those points of novelty, however, do not create an overall impression of similarity. The AA Trigger's sides do not "bulge outwardly in a bulbous fashion," but instead flare out in straight lines before converging slightly inward towards the bottom of the shroud. While the "bulbous" portion of the patented designs begins approximately halfway down the back of the shroud, the flare in the AA Trigger occurs more than halfway down. Overall, the AA Trigger and the patented designs are significantly dissimilar when viewed from the back. The only similarity is in the shrouds' general outline when viewed from the side, and the horizontal line running along the side from the nozzle to the rear edge. Although the line is a point of novelty, it is insufficient to lead to an overall impression of similarity, especially since the line on the AA Trigger is intersected by a slanted line defining a raised surface. Consequently, the Court concludes that the "point of novelty" test would not be met even if overall visual similarity did exist.

III.   CONCLUSION

For the foregoing reasons, Arminak's motion for partial summary judgment on the issue of noninfringement is GRANTED.

(ii) Points of Novelty

SUN HILL INDUSTRIES, INC. v. EASTER UNLIMITED, INC.

United States Court of Appeals, Federal Circuit, 1995.
48 F.3d 1193.

RADER, CIRCUIT JUDGE.

[Fun World appeals the trial court's finding that it infringed Sun Hill's design patent by appropriating certain novel features of the claimed design.]

* * *

Background

The patent, titled "Bag," claims "the ornamental design for a bag, as shown and described" in fifteen patent drawings. The drawings show a bag tied at the top and having one of three bottom closures. The drawings show a bag with vertical stripes and Halloween-style "happy" and "scary" jack-o-lantern faces on opposing sides:

Sun Hill markets an embodiment of the patented design called the GIANT STUFF–A–PUMPKIN. The GIANT STUFF–A–PUMPKIN is a large, orange, plastic lawn bag. It displays the claimed features of vertical stripes, opposing happy and scary faces, and one of the claimed bottom closures. When stuffed with leaves or other debris and tied at the top, it resembles a huge Halloween pumpkin.

The prior art includes the Noteworthy bag, a yellow plastic Halloween trick-or-treat bag sold by Noteworthy Industries Inc. The two sides of the Noteworthy bag are identical. The following illustration appears at the upper right corner of each side:

As the illustration shows, the Noteworthy bag can be stuffed with paper and tied at the top. The resulting "decorative pumpkin" has vertical stripes and opposing identical happy jack-o-lantern faces.

[Fun World's competing lawn bag has a jack-o-lantern face on only one side, no stripes, a bottom closure different from that claimed in Sun Hill's patent, and facial features copied from its own prior art products. In Sun Hill's suit for patent and copyright infringement, the trial court found no infringement of Sun Hill's copyright in the facial features of its GIANT STUFF–A–PUMPKIN.]

* * *

In its opinion on the patent issues, the trial court found that the design patent recites "a shiny, stuffed bag which has jack-o-lantern faces on either side." [Sun Hill Indus., Inc. v. Easter Unlimited, Inc., 831 F.Supp. 1024 (E.D.N.Y.1993),] at 1035. The patent, the trial court observed, does not show other features of the GIANT STUFF–A–PUMP-KIN:

The patent never mentions color or size or material—despite standard ways to include such information, see Manual of Patent Examining Procedures [section 608.02 (5th ed. latest rev. 1994)]. . . .

Id. at 1035–36.

In assessing infringement, however, the trial court relied on color, size, and material—features not shown in the patent. *See id.* at 1036. The trial court found that the larger Fun World bags infringe both literally and under the doctrine of equivalents, *id.* at 1037, even though

Fun World's product [sic] has only one face, no vertical lines, and a different bottom tuck.

Id. at 1036. In its judgment, the trial court found that the smaller Fun World bags, which are indistinguishable except in size from the larger bags, do not infringe. The trial court also found the patent nonobvious over the asserted prior art.

Fun World appeals the trial court's infringement and validity findings. Sun Hill appeals the finding that Fun World's smaller bags do not infringe.

DISCUSSION

I.

Design patent infringement occurs only when the accused design is "substantially the same" as the claimed design. Gorham Co. v. White, 81 U.S. (14 Wall.) 511, 528, 20 L.Ed. 731 (1871); L.A. Gear, Inc. v. Thom McAn Shoe Co., 988 F.2d 1117, 1124 (Fed.Cir.), *cert. denied,* 510 U.S. 908, 114 S.Ct. 291, 126 L.Ed.2d 240 (1993). The patent claim measures the invention. Therefore, "to find infringement, the accused [product] must be compared to the claimed design to determine whether the two designs are substantially the same." Unette Corp. v. Unit Pack Co., 785 F.2d 1026, 1028 (Fed.Cir.1986).

The test for infringement is not whether the accused product is substantially similar to the patentee's commercial embodiment of the claimed design. Such a test risks relying on unclaimed and therefore irrelevant features as grounds for similarity or difference. It is legal error to base an infringement finding on features of the commercial embodiment not claimed in the patent.

The trial court committed legal error by relying on unclaimed features of Sun Hill's commercial embodiment. The trial court recognized that "the patent never mentions color or size or material." *Sun Hill,* 831 F.Supp. at 1035. But the court erroneously relied on these unclaimed features of Sun Hill's GIANT STUFF–A–PUMPKIN in finding infringement:

> [T]here is no question that [one of the Fun World bags] and [the GIANT STUFF–A–PUMPKIN] have a nearly identical overall appearance: both products are *oversized* and suitable for stuffing and displaying on a lawn; the lower portion of each pumpkin bag is tucked inward in order to take on a rounded shape when stuffed; both bags are formed of *orange plastic*; and both are imprinted with black graphics although the precise facial features differ. In sum, when used as intended, each product resembles a *giant* jack-o-lantern.

Id. at 1036 (emphasis added). Color, size, and material are the primary grounds of similarity in the trial court's analysis. Moreover, the trial court erroneously relied on size alone in finding that Fun World's larger bags infringe, while its otherwise indistinguishable smaller bags do not.

* * *

II.

Beyond the substantial similarity requirement of *Gorham* and *L.A. Gear*, design patent infringement requires that the accused product "appropriate the novelty in the patented device which distinguishes it from the prior art." Litton Sys., Inc. v. Whirlpool Corp., 728 F.2d 1423, 1444 (Fed.Cir.1984) (quoting Sears, Roebuck & Co. v. Talge, 140 F.2d 395, 396 (8th Cir.1944)). The patentee must prove both substantial similarity and appropriation of the "point of novelty." Shelcore, Inc. v. Durham Indus., Inc., 745 F.2d 621, 628 n. 16 (Fed.Cir.1984).

Although the trial court recognized the point of novelty test, *Sun Hill*, 831 F.Supp. at 1034–35, the trial court did not consider whether Fun World had appropriated the specific novel features of Sun Hill's claimed design. The trial court instead asserted that "the essence of the product's design" controls. *Id.* at 1035. The trial court then concluded that "if a product has some function which, combined with its [overall] design, justifies its protection, that may be its point of novelty." *Id.*

Both steps in the trial court's reasoning are flawed. First, *Litton* and *Shelcore* establish that the fact finder must consider both the claimed overall design and the point of novelty in assessing infringement. This the trial court failed to do. Second, the trial court cannot evade the point of novelty test by relying on the claimed overall design as the point of novelty:

> To consider the overall appearance of a design without regard to prior art would eviscerate the purpose of the "point of novelty" approach, which is to focus on those aspects of a design which render the design different from prior art designs.

Winner Int'l Corp. v. Wolo Mfg. Corp., 905 F.2d 375, 376 (Fed.Cir.1990). The trial court's choice of the overall design as the point of novelty, and its consequent collapsing of the point of novelty test into the substantial similarity test, constitute legal error.

III.

This court need not, however, remand for an infringement assessment under the correct legal standard, because "nothing of record warrants a further exercise of the fact-finding function." The record demonstrates that Fun World has not appropriated the point of novelty of Sun Hill's claimed design. The point of novelty of Sun Hill's claimed design is narrow. The trial court identified the claimed features in its description of the patent:

> The drawings that make up the '023 patent show six views of the same ornamental object which has facial features on both sides, a [bottom] closure, and a shiny surface as demonstrated by the shading; nothing in the patent mentions color or size or material.

Sun Hill, 831 F.Supp. at 1027–28. The facial features consist of vertical stripes and contrasting jack-o-lantern faces.

The Noteworthy bag discloses several of these claimed features. The illustration on the Noteworthy bag, reproduced above, teaches stuffing the bag with paper and tying it at the top. The resulting "decorative pumpkin" has vertical stripes and opposing identical happy jack-o-lantern faces. The record does not show whether the plastic used in the Noteworthy bag has a shiny surface.

The only differences between the trial court's description of Sun Hill's claimed design and the Noteworthy bags are the contrasting jack-o-lantern faces, the bottom closure, the specific features of the jack-o-lantern faces, and the shiny surface. The point of novelty therefore consists at most of these four features. This court assumes, without deciding, that none of these features are functional, and therefore all qualify as valid points of novelty of the claimed ornamental design. *Cf.* Lee [v. Dayton–Hudson Corp., 838 F.2d 1186, 1188 (Fed.Cir.1988)] ("it is the non-functional, design aspects that are pertinent to determinations of infringement").

The trial court mistakenly asserted two additional differences between the claimed design and the Noteworthy bag. *Sun Hill,* 831 F.Supp. at 1033. First, the trial court clearly erred by finding that the Noteworthy bag does not "represent a pumpkin":

> While the [Noteworthy] bag is rounded, it differs from the products in question in that it contains a jack-o-lantern, but itself does not represent a pumpkin. . . .

Id. The illustration on the Noteworthy bag itself contradicts this statement. As the trial court also recognized, the illustration on the Noteworthy bag shows that it can be stuffed and tied at the top to make a "decorative pumpkin."

The trial court also clearly erred by relying on unclaimed features to distinguish the Noteworthy bag from the patented design:

> [T]he latter is unique because it transforms an ordinary trash or leaf bag into a lawn ornament by furnishing that old article of manufacture with a new ornamental and decorative aspect.

Id. This statement asserts the size and function of Sun Hill's commercial embodiment as distinguishing features. But as the trial court correctly observed, "nothing in the patent mentions . . . size." *Id.* at 1028. As for function, the patent is simply titled "Bag." Neither the patent nor the prosecution history limits Sun Hill's claimed bag to lawn bags. Size and function are not points of novelty of the claimed design.

As mentioned above, Sun Hill's claimed design has at most four points of novelty. The accused Fun World products have none of these features. As the parties stipulated, and the trial court recognized, *id.* at 1028, each Fun World bag has a jack-o-lantern face on only one side and has a different bottom closure. The trial court concluded on summary judgment, furthermore, that Fun World has not usurped the specific facial features Sun Hill claims. *Id.* at 1026. Finally, neither the trial court nor the record indicates that the accused Fun World bags have a shiny surface.

Because Fun World has not appropriated any of the features that make up the point of novelty of Sun Hill's claimed design, Fun World cannot, as a matter of law, infringe. This case is similar to *Litton*, where this court reversed an infringement finding because the accused design had none of the novel claimed design features. *Litton*, 728 F.2d at 1444. This court's reasoning in that case applies equally here:

> We recognize that minor differences between a patented design and an accused article's design cannot, and shall not, prevent a finding of infringement. In this case, however, "while there is some similarity between the patented and alleged infringing designs, which without consideration of the prior art might seem important, yet such similarity as is due to common external configuration is no greater, if as great, between the patented and challenged designs as between the former and the designs of the prior art." Applied Arts Corp. v. Grand Rapids Metalcraft Corp., 67 F.2d 428, 430, 19 U.S.P.Q. (BNA) 266, 268 (6th Cir.1933).

Litton, 728 F.2d at 1444. This court concluded in *Litton* that the trial court had clearly erred in finding infringement. *Id.* The trial court clearly erred here as well.

The result is the same under the doctrine of equivalents. While the doctrine of equivalents applies to design patent cases, *Lee*, 838 F.2d at 1190, it applies only when the accused product includes features equivalent to the novel claimed design features. A patentee cannot invoke the doctrine to evade scrutiny of the point of novelty, because to do so would "eviscerate the purpose of the 'point of novelty' approach, which is to focus on those aspects of a design which render the design different from prior art designs." *Winner*, 905 F.2d at 376 (citing *Litton*, 728 F.2d at 1444). Thus, when faced in *Litton* with an accused product that appropriated none of the novel claimed features, this court reversed the infringement finding without separate consideration of the doctrine of equivalents. *Litton*, 728 F.2d at 1444. The doctrine of equivalents cannot apply here either.

* * *

CONCLUSION

None of Fun World's products appropriate the novel features of Sun Hill's claimed design. Therefore, Fun World does not infringe. The district court correctly found that Fun World's smaller bags do not infringe, but clearly erred by finding that Fun World's larger bags infringe.

* * *

7. INFRINGEMENT OF PLANT PATENTS

IMAZIO NURSERY, INC. v. DANIA GREENHOUSES

United States Court of Appeals, Federal Circuit, 1995.
69 F.3d 1560, *cert. denied*, 518 U.S. 1018, 116
S.Ct. 2549, 135 L.Ed.2d 1069 (1996).

RICH, CIRCUIT JUDGE.

[Plaintiff filed a patent infringement suit alleging that defendants' Holiday Heather infringed plaintiff's U.S. Plant Patent No. 5,336 (the '336 patent), which claimed an early-blooming variety of heather named Erica Sunset, which the plaintiff had discovered in a cultivated field. Defendants appeal the district court's decision granting the plaintiff's motion for summary judgment of infringement, and specifically rejecting the defense of independent creation.]

* * *

B.   Scope of a Plant Patent

* * *

The parties dispute the meaning of the term "variety" in section 161. The meaning of that term may inform the scope of protection of plant patents inasmuch as such patents are granted to "whoever invents or discovers and asexually reproduces any distinct and new *variety* of plant." 35 U.S.C. § 161 (emphasis added). Imazio argues that in providing plant patent protection for "any distinct and new variety of plant," it was intended that a plant patent cover "all plants of that new and distinct variety, i.e., all plants having the same essential and distinctive characteristics." Thus, argues Imazio, "variety" should be construed in its technical, taxonomical sense and should be interpreted to encompass more than just clones of a single plant. [Defendant] Coastal, on the other hand, contends that "variety" should be construed in the vernacular sense as "something different from others of the same general kind." Coastal maintains that by use of the term "variety" Congress did not intend to afford plant patent protection to a range of plants but intended only to protect a single plant.

* * *

Although the legislative history does not answer the question of what "variety" means in terms of whether a single plant or a range of plants is protected by a plant patent, in addition to being distinct and new, a patentable plant must also be asexually reproduced. 35 U.S.C. § 161; *see* Yoder Bros., Inc. v. California–Florida Plant Corp., 537 F.2d 1347, 1377, 193 USPQ 264, 291 (5th Cir.1976) ("For plant patents ... the additional requirement of asexual reproduction is introduced."), *cert. denied,* 429 U.S. 1094, 97 S.Ct. 1108, 51 L.Ed.2d 540 (1977); Senate Report [No. 315, 71st Cong., 2d Sess. (1930) (hereinafter "Senate Report")] at 5 ("It is not only necessary that the new and distinct variety of plant shall have been invented or discovered, but it is also necessary that it shall have been asexually reproduced prior to the application for patent."). As discussed below, this additional requirement informs the scope of protection of plant patents and hence directs the meaning of "variety" in § 161.

* * *

It is clear from the legislative history that as a result of the asexual reproduction requirement, only a single plant, *i.e.,* reproduction from one original specimen in the words of Congress, is protected by a plant patent. At the time of enactment, Congress recognized that the asexual reproduction prerequisite greatly narrowed the scope of protection of plant patents but found such a limitation necessary to ensure that the characteristics of the plant to be patented were maintained. Additionally, it has since been recognized that as intimated by Congress, asexual reproduction confirms the existence of a new variety by separating variations resulting from fluctuations in environmental conditions from true plant variations. The Supreme Court also recognized the significance of the asexual reproduction requirement of the Plant Patent Act. In *Diamond v. Chakrabarty,* the Court indicated that asexual reproduction was required in the Plant Patent Act because it was believed that new varieties could not be reproduced true-to-type through seed. 447 U.S. at 312, 100 S.Ct. at 2209.

* * *

Due to the asexual reproduction prerequisite, plant patents cover a single plant and its asexually reproduced progeny. *See* Senate Report at 6 (Plant patent protection encourages "those who own the single specimen to reproduce it asexually and create an adequate supply."). Thus, the term "variety" in section 161 must be interpreted consistently with this requirement. Accordingly, "variety" in section 161 cannot be read as affording plant patent protection to a range of plants, as asserted by Imazio.

* * *

V. INFRINGEMENT

A. *The Trial Court's Analysis*

[The trial court granted the plaintiff's motion for summary judgment of infringement, adopting] the standard set forth in Pan–American Plant Co. v. Matsui, 433 F.Supp. 693, 694 n. 2 (N.D.Cal.1977) that the Plant Patent Act "bars the asexual reproduction and sale of any plant which is the same variety (*i.e.,* has the same essential characteristics) as the patented plant, whether or not the infringing plant was originally cloned from the patented plant." [Imazio Nursery Inc. v. Dania Greenhouse, 29 U.S.P.Q.2d (BNA) 1217, 1219 (N.D.Cal.1992).] The district court also addressed whether independent creation could be a defense to plant patent infringement as discussed in *Yoder,* 537 F.2d 1347. The district court stated that "independent creation is [not] a proper defense to patent infringement" and asserted that "the courts' recognition of an independent creation defense would inadvertently entice deliberate infringement, with a fraudulent defense of independent creation asserted." *Id.*

* * *

C. Infringement of a Plant Patent

* * *

Section 163 grants to plant patentees the right to exclude others from asexually reproducing the plant or selling or using the plant so reproduced. As stated above, the trial court held that asexual reproduction is shown if the patentee can prove that the alleged infringing plant has the same essential characteristics as the patented plant. We disagree.

* * *

The "asexual reproduction question" * * * is critical to the infringement analysis. In construing section 161, we held above that the scope of a plant patent is the asexual reproduction of the plant shown and described in the specification. Asexual reproduction, in terms of section 161, means the progeny of the patented plant via "grafting, budding, cuttings, layering, division and the like, but not by seeds." Senate Report at 1.

We must construe the term "asexual reproduction" in section 163 in the same way as we did in section 161. Thus, for purposes of plant patent infringement, the patentee must prove that the alleged infringing plant is an asexual reproduction, that is, that it is the progeny of the patented plant. *Yoder,* 537 F.2d at 1380 ("It is quite possible that infringement of a plant patent would occur only if stock obtained is used, given the extreme unlikelihood that any other plant could actually infringe.").

* * *

1. Independent creation as a defense to plant patent infringement

Below, the parties disputed whether independent creation is a proper defense to plant patent infringement. The trial court refused to recognize such a defense stating that the "patent holder would have great difficulties enforcing his patent rights if a defendant were allowed to raise independent creation as an affirmative defense." The trial court reasoned that it would be hard for the patentee to refute evidence of independent creation because all such evidence would be in the defendant's control.

We must reject the trial court's analysis of the independent creation defense because it is contrary to the plain meaning of the statute. The statute requires asexual reproduction of the patented plant for there to be infringement. It is necessarily a defense to plant patent infringement that the alleged infringing plant is not an asexual reproduction of the patented plant. Part of this proof could be, thus, that the defendant independently developed the allegedly infringing plant. However, the sine qua non is asexual reproduction. That is what the patentee must prove and what the defendant will seek to disprove.

D. Conclusion as to Infringement

In this case, therefore, in order for there to be infringement of the '336 patent, the infringing plant must be an asexual reproduction of the plant claimed, *i.e.,* the Heather persoluta shown and described in the '336 patent. The trial court erred as a matter of law when it held that infringement of the '336 patent was shown by proof merely of asexual reproduction of a plant having the same essential characteristics as the patented plant. Accordingly, we reverse the holding of infringement. * * *

Notes

1. Although the plant patent statutes do not define "variety," the *Imazio* court declined to import the definition assigned to that term under the Plant Variety Protection Act of 1970, 7 U.S.C.A. § 2401(a)(9) (defining a variety as a group of plants sharing certain genetically-dictated characteristics and capable of being propagated unchanged):

It is true that both the Plant Patent Act and the PVPA use the term "variety" and grant some form of intellectual property protection. However, the two statutes differ significantly in their purposes. The Plant Patent Act grants a plant patent to one who "invents or discovers and asexually reproduces any distinct and new variety of plant." 35 U.S.C.A. § 161. Conversely, one is entitled to plant variety protection under the PVPA if he has sexually reproduced the variety and has otherwise met the requirements of 7 U.S.C.A. § 2402(a). The term "variety" in both statutes cannot be read divorced from the very different circumstances in which that term is used.

Those circumstances, asexual reproduction in the case of plant patents, and sexual reproduction in the case of plant variety protection, mandate the protection afforded under these different statutory provisions. Asexual reproduction is the cornerstone of plant patent protection, while sexual reproduction is the distinguishing feature of plant variety protection. Indeed, this is why the PVPA was enacted, to afford protection for sexually reproduced plants. The result of asexual reproduction is a plant that is genetically identical to its parent. The result of sexual reproduction is a plant that combines the characteristics of the parents, but is a different plant.

It follows from this that the scope of protection afforded as a result of sexual versus asexual reproduction must be different; in the case of asexual reproduction, the same plant is produced, but in the case of sexual reproduction, a different plant, albeit like the parent plants, is produced. Given this, we reject Imazio's contention that the meaning of variety in the Plant Patent Act and the PVPA must be the same.

69 F.3d at 1568.

2. At what point in the asexual reproduction process should infringement of a plant patent be deemed to occur: When cuttings are first taken? When the cuttings mature into adult plants? When the resulting plants are first offered for sale? Would it be an infringement to propagate a plant asexually for personal noncommercial use only?

B. DEFENSES

Statutes: 35 U.S.C.A. §§ 271(e), 282, 296

Defenses available to a patent infringement defendant include: invalidity of the claims in question (Chapter 12), shop rights (Chapter 13.A.2), implied license, patent misuse, de minimis use, inequitable conduct in procuring the patent, laches, and estoppel. The plaintiff's rights will also be subject to special limitations where the defendant is acting on behalf of the federal government or a state government, or, in the case of medical procedure patents, where the defendant is a medical practitioner (35 U.S.C.A. § 287(c)).

In some cases, the doctrine of assignor estoppel will bar an infringement defendant from raising otherwise valid defenses. Under this doctrine, a party that has assigned a patent right for valid consideration may submit evidence to help construe or narrow the claims of the assigned patent, but may not challenge the patent's validity. In *Diamond Scientific Co. v. Ambico, Inc.,* 848 F.2d 1220, 1224 (Fed.Cir.1988), *cert. dismissed,* 487 U.S. 1265, 109 S.Ct. 28, 101 L.Ed.2d 978 (1988), the Federal Circuit discussed the rationale behind this doctrine:

> Assignor estoppel is an equitable doctrine that prevents one who has assigned the rights to a patent (or patent application) from later contending that what was assigned is a nullity. The estoppel also operates to bar other parties in privity with the assignor, such as a corporation founded by the assignor. The estoppel historically has applied to invalidity challenges based on "novelty, utility, patentable invention, anticipatory matter, and the state of the art."

* * *

> Courts that have expressed the estoppel doctrine in terms of unfairness and injustice have reasoned that an assignor should not be permitted to sell something and later to assert that what was sold is worthless, all to the detriment of the assignee. Justice Frankfurter's dissent in *Scott Paper* explained that the doctrine was rooted in the notion of fair dealing. "The principle of fair dealing as between assignor and assignee of a patent whereby the assignor will not be allowed to say that what he has sold as a patent was not a patent has been part of the fabric of our law throughout the life of this nation." Scott Paper Co. v. Marcalus Mfg. Co., 326 U.S. 249, 260, 66 S.Ct. 101, 106, 90 L.Ed. 47 (1945) (Frankfurter, J., dissenting). "The essence of the principle of fair dealing which binds the assignor of a

patent in a suit by the assignee, even though it turns out that the patent is invalid or lacks novelty, is that in this relation the assignor is not part of the general public but is apart from the general public." *Id.* at 261–62. In other words, it is the implicit representation by the assignor that the patent rights that he is assigning (presumably for value) are not worthless that sets the assignor apart from the rest of the world and can deprive him of the ability to challenge later the validity of the patent. To allow the assignor to make that representation at the time of the assignment (to his advantage) and later to repudiate it (again to his advantage) could work an injustice against the assignee.

The application of assignor estoppel, however, is less certain where a defendant assigns the rights to an invention *before* the patent issues. As noted by the Supreme Court in *Westinghouse Elec. & Mfg. Co. v. Formica Insulation Co.,* 266 U.S. 342, 352–53, 45 S.Ct. 117, 121, 69 L.Ed. 316 (1924):

> It is apparent that the scope of the right conveyed in such an assignment is much less certainly defined than that of a granted patent, and the question of the extent of the estoppel against the assignor of such an inchoate right is more difficult to determine than in the case of a patent assigned after its granting. When the assignment is made before patent, the claims are subject to change by curtailment or enlargement by the Patent Office with the acquiescence or at the instance of the assignee, and the extent of the claims to be allowed may ultimately include more than the assignor intended to claim. This difference might justify the view that the range of relevant and competent evidence in fixing the limits of the subsequent estoppel should be more liberal than in the case of an assignment of a granted patent. * * *

See also Diamond Scientific Co., 848 F.2d at 1226 (noting that *Westinghouse* may permit defendants to introduce prior art evidence to narrow the scope of the patent's claims, "to the extent that [patentholder] Diamond may have broadened the claims in the patent applications (after the assignments) beyond what could be validly claimed in light of the prior art"); *Q.G. Products, Inc. v. Shorty, Inc.,* 992 F.2d 1211 (Fed.Cir.1993) (where defendant assigned rights in patent application, but challenged patent issued from subsequent continuation-in-part application, significance of the differences between the two applications determined the scope of the estoppel), *cert. denied,* 510 U.S. 868, 114 S.Ct. 192, 126 L.Ed.2d 150 (1993). The Federal Circuit has adopted a "presumption" that assignor estoppel applies, rebuttable only by a showing of "exceptional circumstances." *Mentor Graphics Corp. v. Quickturn Design Systems, Inc.,* 150 F.3d 1374 (Fed.Cir.1998).

In contrast, the Supreme Court in *Lear, Inc. v. Adkins,* 395 U.S. 653, 89 S.Ct. 1902, 23 L.Ed.2d 610 (1969), abolished the doctrine of licensee estoppel, under which a patent licensee was estopped from contesting the validity of the licensed patent as a defense to infringement.

Why are patent assignors and licensees subject to different estoppel rules?

1. INVALIDITY

Under 35 U.S.C.A. § 282, a patent is presumed valid. Thus, the burden of proving invalidity falls on the infringement defendant, who must show by "clear and convincing evidence" that the claims in question are invalid.

In *Blonder–Tongue Laboratories, Inc. v. University of Illinois Foundation*, 402 U.S. 313, 91 S.Ct. 1434, 28 L.Ed.2d 788 (1971), the Supreme Court held that once a federal court had ruled a particular patent invalid the patentee was estopped from relitigating the issue of patent validity unless the patentee had not had "a full and fair chance to litigate the validity of his patent" in the earlier case. *Id.* at 333. Overruling the contrary holding of *Triplett v. Lowell*, 297 U.S. 638, 56 S.Ct. 645, 80 L.Ed. 949 (1936), the Court observed:

> [T]he expense of patent litigation has two principal consequences if the *Triplett* rule is maintained. First, assuming that a perfectly sound judgment of invalidity has been rendered in an earlier suit involving the patentee, a second infringement action raising the same issue and involving much of the same proof has a high cost to the individual parties. The patentee is expending funds on litigation to protect a patent which is by hypothesis invalid. These moneys could be put to better use, such as further research and development. The alleged infringer—operating as he must against the presumption of validity—is forced to divert substantial funds to litigation that is wasteful.
>
> The second major economic consideration is far more significant. Under *Triplett*, only the comity restraints flowing from an adverse prior judgment operate to limit the patentee's right to sue different defendants on the same patent. In each successive suit the patentee enjoys the statutory presumption of validity, and so may easily put the alleged infringer to his expensive proof. As a consequence, prospective defendants will often decide that paying royalties under a license or other settlement is preferable to the costly burden of challenging the patent.

* * *

The tendency of Triplett to multiply the opportunities for holders of invalid patents to exact licensing agreements or other settlements from alleged infringers must be considered in the context of other decisions of this Court. Although recognizing the patent system's desirable stimulus to invention, we have also viewed the patent as a monopoly which, although sanctioned by law, has the economic consequences attending other monopolies. A patent yielding returns for a device that fails to meet the congressionally imposed criteria of patentability is anomalous. * * *

402 U.S. at 338, 343, 91 S.Ct. at 1447–48, 1450 (footnotes omitted).

2. IMPLIED LICENSE

MET–COIL SYSTEMS CORPORATION v. KORNERS UNLIMITED, INC.

United States Court of Appeals, Federal Circuit, 1986.
803 F.2d 684.

NIES, CIRCUIT JUDGE.

The determinative issue in this appeal is whether a patent owner's unrestricted sale of a machine useful only in practicing the claimed inventions presumptively carries with it an implied license under the patent. The United States District Court for the Western District of Pennsylvania decided that legal issue in the affirmative.[1] We affirm.

I.

[Met–Coil, the assignee of a patent claiming an apparatus and method for connecting sections of metal ducts, sells roll-forming machines for practicing the patented process of bending metal ducts to produce the patented integral flanges. It also sells specially shaped but unpatented corner pieces for use with the flanges. Korners also sells corner pieces for use with Met–Coil's flanges. Met–Coil sued Korners for inducing infringement of its patent by selling these corner pieces. Korners raised the defense of implied license, arguing that Met–Coil, by selling the roll-forming machines, granted its buyers an implied license to use the patented method.]

* * *

The district court recognized that "the integral flanges are an essential part of Met–Coil's patented duct connecting system" and that the "flanges have no use other than in the practice of the duct connecting system." 628 F.Supp. at 133. Applying the holding of United States v. Univis Lens Co., 316 U.S. 241, 86 L. Ed. 1408, 62 S. Ct. 1088 (1942), to those facts, the court held that purchasers of Met–Coil's machines enjoyed an implied license under the patent.

In *Univis,* the patent covered multifocal eyeglass lenses, and the patent owner sold blank eyeglass lenses to its licensees. The Court held that the sale of the blanks carried a license to complete the lenses:

But in any case it is plain that where the sale of the blank is by the patentee or his licensee—here the Lens Company—to a finisher, the only use to which it could be put and the only object of the sale is to

---

1. Met–Coil Systems Corp. v. Korners   (W.D.Penn.1986) (Teitelbaum, J.).
Unlimited, Inc., 628 F.Supp. 130

enable the latter to grind and polish it for use as a lens by the prospective wearer. An incident to the purchase of any article, whether patented or unpatented, is the right to use and sell it, and upon familiar principles the authorized sale of an article which is capable of use only in practicing the patent is a relinquishment of the patent monopoly with respect to the article sold. Sale of a lens blank by the patentee or by his licensee is thus in itself both a complete transfer of ownership of the blank, which is within the protection of the patent law, and a license to practice the final stage of the patent procedure.

* * *

... [W]here one has sold an uncompleted article which, because it embodies essential features of his patented invention, is within the protection of his patented invention, and has destined the article to be finished by the purchaser in conformity to the patent, he has sold his invention so far as it is or may be embodied in that particular article. The reward he has demanded and received is for the article and the invention which it embodies and which his vendee is to practice upon it.

316 U.S. at 249–51. The trial court recognized that *Univis* was factually distinct from the instant case, but found the distinction to be of no effect:

It should be noted, however, that unlike *Univis* ... , the practice of the final stage of Met–Coil's patented system requires not just "finishing" the element sold, *i.e.* forming the integral flanges, but also the purchase of an additional element of the patented system, i.e. the corner pieces. Met–Coil cites no authority which suggests that this difference takes the present case out of the rule of Univis.

628 F.Supp. at 133. Met–Coil appealed the district court's judgment of noninfringement to this court. 28 U.S.C. § 1295(a)(1) (1982).

III.

On appeal, Met–Coil urges that the district court erred in relying on *Univis*. To support that proposition, Met–Coil cites Bandag, Inc. v. Al Bolser's Tire Stores, Inc., 750 F.2d 903 (Fed.Cir.1984). In that case, the owner of a patent claiming a method for retreading tires sued a retreader who had purchased retreading equipment from a former licensee of the patent owner. This court set out two requirements for the grant of an implied license by virtue of a sale of nonpatented equipment used to practice a patented invention. First, the equipment involved must have no noninfringing uses. *Id.* at 924. In *Bandag*, the retreading equipment had noninfringing uses, so no license could be implied. To the contrary, Met–Coil's machines have no noninfringing use. Second, the circumstances of the sale must "plainly indicate that the grant of a license should be inferred." *Id.* at 925, quoting Hunt v. Armour & Co., 185 F.2d 722, 729 (7th Cir.1950). The circumstances of the sale in *Bandag*, purchase of the equipment from the former licensee of the patent owner, did not plainly indicate that the grant of a license should be inferred.

Met–Coil contends that this case does not meet the two-part test set out in *Bandag*, that is, although the machines sold have no noninfringing use, the circumstances do not plainly indicate that the grant of a license should be inferred. In this connection Met–Coil introduced certain written notices to customers with respect to the purchase of corner pieces from unlicensed sources.[4] Met–Coil relies on cases holding that no implied license arises where the original sale was accompanied by an express notice negating the grant of an implied license. Those cases, however, are inapposite. Met–Coil does not assert that its customers were notified at the time of the sale of the machine. Rather, the customers were notified after they purchased the machine. The subsequent notices are not a part of the circumstances at the time of the sale, when the implied license would have arisen. After the fact notices are of no use in ascertaining the intent of Met–Coil and its customers at the time of the sales.

Met–Coil urges that, even though it has not shown that the sales were accompanied by an express disclaimer of license, Korners has not met its burden of proof. As the alleged infringer, Korners has the burden of showing the establishment of an implied license. *Bandag,* 750 F.2d at 924. We agree with the district court that Korners met that burden. A patent owner's unrestricted sales of a machine useful only in performing the claimed process and producing the claimed product "plainly indicate that the grant of a license should be inferred." Korners established a prima facie case, thereby shifting the burden of going forward to Met–Coil. Met–Coil offered nothing to carry its burden. Absent any circumstances tending to show the contrary, we see no error in the district court's holding that Met–Coil's customers enjoyed an implied license under the patent.

* * *

AFFIRMED.

Notes

1.   If Met–Coil notified the buyers of its machine, at the time of purchase, that their implied license did not extend to the use of the machine with corner pieces other than Met–Coil's, should Met–Coil be permitted to enforce that restriction?

2.   Under the "first sale" or "exhaustion of rights" doctrine of patent law, the authorized sale of a patented article is said to "exhaust" the patentholder's rights in that item. Thus, use or resale of that article by the

---

4.   Met–Coil's subsidiary Iowa Precision Industries, Inc. sent a letter to owners of Lockformer machines and distributors of Iowa Precision's corner pieces, notifying them that "as long as you are a customer of ours, you are automatically licensed to use the [claimed invention] insofar as your use involves forming rolls and corners purchased from us but not from other unauthorized sources."

purchaser does not infringe. *See, e.g., Adams v. Burke,* 84 U.S. (17 Wall.) 453, 21 L.Ed. 700 (1873) (use); *Keeler v. Standard Folding–Bed Co.,* 157 U.S. 659, 15 S.Ct. 738, 39 L.Ed. 848 (1895) (resale). However, the Federal Circuit takes the position that the exhaustion doctrine applies only if the first sale takes place in the United States. *See, e.g., Fuji Photo Film Co. v. Jazz Photo Corp.,* 394 F.3d 1368, 1376 (Fed. Cir. 2005) (holding that patent holder's authorization of foreign sale of its patented camera did not exhaust its patent rights in the United States).

If a patentholder sells a patented article under a sales contract which states that the seller is prohibited from reselling or repairing the article, should a court enforce that contract?

3.   Assume that the patentee owns a valid combination patent in a television remote control system, consisting of a remote transmitter, a receiver, and a signaling protocol. The patent claims do not cover the transmitter itself. If the defendant makes a transmitter that is compatible with the patented system, is it infringement for the owners of the televisions that incorporate the patented invention to use the defendant's transmitters? Is the defendant liable for contributory infringement?

4.   If patented machines are lawfully seized by a patentee's creditors, does infringement occur when the creditors sell the machines? When the buyers use them? Is the answer different where the creditors seize infringing machines from an infringer?

5.   Suppose a patentholder enters a contract with a manufacturer to mass produce articles embodying the patented invention. When the manufacturer delivers the products in compliance with the contract, the patentholder refuses delivery in breach of their contract. If the manufacturer then sells the articles to a distributor, who then sells them at retail, is the patent infringed by the actions of the manufacturer or the distributor?

3.   PATENT MISUSE

IN RE RECOMBINANT DNA TECHNOLOGY PATENT AND CONTRACT LITIGATION
United States District Court, S. D. of Indiana, 1994.
850 F.Supp. 769.

DILLIN, DISTRICT JUDGE.

[In this infringement action, defendant Eli Lilly sought a summary judgment that the doctrine of patent misuse prohibited plaintiff Genentech from enforcing its patents.]

* * *

Lilly alleges that Genentech has included in the Insulin and hGH Agreements a provision that illegally restrains competition and impermissibly extends the statutory scope of Genentech's patent monopoly. Such inclusion constitutes per se patent misuse and unclean hands, Lilly argues, and renders Genentech's patents in issue unenforceable.* * *

* * *

Additionally, Lilly argues that the 1988 Patent Misuse Reform Act (alternatively, the Act) is inapplicable to its patent misuse defense. Conversely, Genentech contends that the Act should govern Lilly's recently added defense. We begin by addressing the issue of patent misuse.

"The grant to the inventor of the special privilege of a patent monopoly carries out a public policy adopted by the Constitution and laws of the United States, 'to promote the Progress of Science and useful Arts, by securing for limited Times to ... Inventors the exclusive Right ... ' to their 'new and useful' inventions." Morton Salt Co. v. G.S. Suppiger Co., 314 U.S. 488, 492, 86 L. Ed. 363, 365–66, 62 S. Ct. 402 (1942) (quoting United States Constitution, Art. I, § 8, Cl. 8, 35 U.S.C.A. § 31). "But the public policy which includes inventions within the granted monopoly excludes from it all that is not embraced in the invention. It equally forbids the use of the patent to secure an exclusive right or limited monopoly not granted by the Patent Office and which it is contrary to public policy to grant." Morton Salt Co., 314 U.S. 488, 492, 86 L. Ed. 363, 366, 62 S. Ct. 402 (1942).

To ensure that the patentee does not prosper from an impermissible broadening of the "physical or temporal scope" of the patent grant, the courts long have recognized the doctrine of patent misuse as an affirmative defense to a suit for patent infringement. Windsurfing Int'l, Inc. v. AMF, Inc., 782 F.2d 995, 1001 (Fed.Cir.1986) (quoting Blonder–Tongue Labs. Inc. v. University of Ill. Found., 402 U.S. 313, 343, 28 L. Ed. 2d. 788, 91 S. Ct. 1434 (1971)). Traditionally, some forms of inappropriate action have been deemed per se patent misuse. Thus, if a patentee has used his patent as leverage to fix resale prices, see, e.g., Bauer & Cie. v. O'Donnell, 229 U.S. 1, 57 L. Ed. 1041, 33 S. Ct. 616 (1913), or has tied another product to his patent (a practice referred to as a tying arrangement), see, e.g., Morton Salt Co., 314 U.S. 488, 86 L. Ed. 363, 62 S. Ct. 402, the patentee has been precluded as a matter of law from maintaining an infringement action, at least until the illegal restraint is removed.

In the past, courts have found per se patent misuse whenever the patentee conditioned the licensee's right to use his patent "on the licensee's agreement to purchase, use or sell, or not to purchase use or sell, another article of commerce not within the scope of his patent monopoly." Zenith Radio Corp. v. Hazeltine Research, 395 U.S. 100, 136, 23 L. Ed. 2d 129, 155, 89 S. Ct. 1562 (1969). For example, the Court in Morton Salt found per se patent misuse where the patentee permitted the licensee to use with the patented machines only salt tablets sold by the patentee. Morton Salt, 314 U.S. 488, 86 L. Ed. 363, 62 S. Ct. 402. And, the Court in National Lockwasher v. George K. Garrett Co. found per se patent misuse in a provision stipulating that the licensee would not manufacture any non-tangling spring washers except those covered by the licensor's patent. National Lockwasher, 137 F.2d 255 (3d Cir. 1943).

Furthermore, agreements that implicitly rather than explicitly forbid the licensee from using the products or devices of a competitor also have been condemned. For example, in United Shoe Mach. Corp. v. United States, the lessor of patented shoe machinery included several restrictive provisions in his leases. 258 U.S. 451, 66 L. Ed. 708, 42 S. Ct. 363 (1922). Among these provisions was one stipulating " . . . that if the lessee fails to use exclusively machinery of certain kinds made by the lessor, the lessor shall have the right to cancel the right to use all such machinery so leased . . . " *United Shoe*, 258 U.S. 451, 456, 66 L. Ed. 708, 716–17, 42 S. Ct. 363. The Court held that although the agreement specifically did not prohibit lessees from using the machinery of a competitor or lessor, " . . . the practical effect of these drastic provisions is to prevent such use." *Id.* at 456, 66 L. Ed. at 717. The Court determined that the restrictions and tying arrangements in the leases "must necessarily lessen competition and tend to monopoly. . . . " *Id.* The Court found lessor's retention of a right to cancel as effective a method of tying as express covenants could be. *Id.* at 458, 66 L. Ed. at 717.

Lilly argues that the holdings in *Morton Salt, United Shoe* and *National Lockwasher*, among others, illustrate that a finding of per se patent misuse is appropriate in this case. Lilly alleges that provisions in two license agreements entered by Genentech support such a finding. * * *

* * *

Lilly's patent misuse charge focuses on Genentech's retention of a right to terminate the agreement should [licensees] Lilly or Kabi sell recombinant insulin or hGH, respectively, produced or derived without using either Genentech microorganisms or Genentech patented technology. Lilly argues that this right to terminate presents a continual, inchoate threat. Specifically, if Lilly should use materials and services of others for the production of human insulin or develop its own rather than use those of Genentech, Genentech can terminate Lilly's right both to Genentech's materials and patented technology. This threat, Lilly contends, counters the public interest by stifling both competition and innovation. Thus, Lilly argues, the provisions are Genentech's attempt by means other than that of free competition to extend the bounds of its lawful monopoly such that Lilly and Kabi are forced to use solely " . . . Genentech patented technology and/or Genentech materials in their production of insulin and hGH, respectively." Lilly Memo. at 3.

Were it not for the 1988 Patent Misuse Reform Act, we believe precedent would dictate a finding in Lilly's favor. Although the Insulin and hGH Agreements grant Lilly and Kabi, respectively, both unpatented materials and patented technology, we do not believe this sufficiently distinguishes the instant case from others in which per se patent misuse historically has been found. It is clear that Genentech's contractual right to terminate the agreements should the licensees sell recombinant insulin or hGH for which Genentech receives no royalty includes the right to cancel the patent license of the licensee. The retention of such a right appears to use the patent as leverage to insure that the licensee will not use the microorganisms and the technology of competitors. This type of tying arrangement previously has been condemned as per se patent misuse.

Moreover, the fact that the provisions are rights to terminate rather than explicit prohibitions on the licensees' use of competitors' products does not lessen their impact. As noted earlier in this Entry, the Supreme Court has found that such a tying method is as effective as an express covenant not to use competitor's products or technology. *See United Shoe,* 258 U.S. at 458, 66 L. Ed. at 717.

However, the 1988 Patent Misuse Reform Act has placed limitations on the finding of patent misuse in tying arrangements. The Act eliminates per se findings of patent misuse in such situations. When the Act governs, a finding of patent misuse is prohibited unless the patentee is shown to have market power in the relevant market for the patent involved in the tying arrangement. The relevant part of the Act stipulates:

> (d) No patent owner otherwise entitled to relief for infringement or contributory infringement of a patent shall be denied relief or deemed guilty of misuse or illegal extension of the patent right by reason of his having done one or more of the following:

> . . . (5) conditioned the license of any rights to the patent or the sale of the patented product on the acquisition of a license to rights in another patent or purchase of a separate product, unless, in view of the circumstances, the patent owner has market power in the relevant market for the patent or patented product on which the license or sale is conditioned.

35 U.S.C. § 271(d)(5).

* * *

* * * Lilly argues that the tying arrangement involved in the instant action is not included within the language of the Act and, thus, the Act does not prevent a summary resolution of this motion. Conversely, Genentech argues that summary judgment is improper because the language of the Act includes the tying arrangement presently under consideration.

This issue is a difficult one to resolve. The difficulty arises in interpreting the relevant section of the 1988 Patent Misuse Reform Act in light of the history of the doctrine of patent misuse. Through the years, courts have found per se patent misuse in varying forms of tying arrangements. In some cases, the patentee is conditioning the license of his patent on the licensee agreeing to use some specific unpatented product. *See, e.g., Morton Salt,* 314 U.S 488, 86 L. Ed. 363, 62 S. Ct. 402. In other cases, the patentee is conditioning the license of his patent on the licensee agreeing not to use the products or devices of a competitor. *See e.g., National Lockwasher,* 137 F.2d 255.

Courts have recognized that the two situations involve slightly different factual situations, but generally refer to both situations as tying arrangements. We cannot find an instance in which a court has indicated that the two tying arrangements should be treated differently. Some commentators, however, have referred to the former situations as "tie-ins" and the latter as "tie-outs." This is important to Lilly's argument in that Lilly insists that the above-quoted language of the Act refers only to "tie-in" arrangements. The tying arrangements challenged in the instant actions, Lilly contends, are "tie-outs" and, thus, unaffected by the Act.

* * *

An examination of the legislative history of the Act leads us to conclude that the language of the Act is meant to encompass both types of tying situations. For example, the Congressional Record of the Senate regarding the Act indicates that Congress' intention was to deal with " . . . a small piece of the patent misuse problem—tying arrangements— and leaves the rest for us to address in the future." 134 Cong. Rec. S17146–02 (daily ed. Oct. 21, 1988) (statement of Sen. Deconcini). Certainly, this passage does not suggest that some tying arrangements were not included in the statutory language. Moreover, the Congressional Record of the Senate reads: "Reform of patent misuse will ensure that the harsh misuse sanction of unenforceability is imposed only against those engaging in truly anticompetitive conduct." *Id.* (statement of Sen. Leahy). We are convinced that Congress would not have fashioned a "rule-of-reason type" approach for one form of tying arrangement and excluded from that approach another intimately related tying situation, especially in light of its clear purpose of permitting a misuse defense only when the patentee has acted anticompetitively. Contrary to Lilly's argument, we do not believe that Congress recognizes a difference between "tie-ins" and "tie-outs."

For these reasons, we find that 35 U.S.C. § 271(d)(5) is applicable to the instant motion, requires a rule of reason approach to the issue of Genentech's market power, and prevents summary resolution of this action. * * *

* * *

Notes

1.   Although Sections 271(d)(4) and (5) have eliminated some problems in interpreting the scope of the the patent misuse defense, they fall short of providing a clear rule for determining which tying arrangements or other restrictions imposed on patent licensees constitute "misuse or illegal extension of the patent right." Courts therefore must rely on the substantial body of case law in this area. Although not entirely consistent with one another, these precedents indicate that a finding of misuse can be predicated on a wide variety of anticompetitive activities. In addition, although courts frequently state that an activity need not violate antitrust laws to constitute

patent misuse, in most cases courts look for the same kind of abuse of market power. *See, e.g., Automatic Radio Mfg. Co. v. Hazeltine Research, Inc.*, 339 U.S. 827, 70 S.Ct. 894, 94 L.Ed. 1312 (1950) (refusing to find per se misuse where patent royalties were based on percentage of all of licensee's sales, not just sales of products embodying the patent); *Zenith Radio v. Hazeltine Research, Inc.*, 395 U.S. 100, 89 S.Ct. 1562, 23 L.Ed.2d 129 (1969) (finding misuse where patentee conditioned license on payment of royalties based on sales of all products, not just those embodying the licensed patent, and distinguishing *Automatic Radio Mfg. Co.* as non-coercive); *USM Corp. v. SPS Technologies, Inc.*, 694 F.2d 505 (7th Cir.1982), *cert. denied*, 462 U.S. 1107, 103 S.Ct. 2455, 77 L.Ed.2d 1334 (1983) (finding no misuse where patentee required licensee to remit higher sublicensing royalties for some sublicensees than for others); *Laitram Corp. v. King Crab, Inc.*, 244 F.Supp. 9 (D.Alaska 1965) (finding misuse where patentee charged different royalty rates to licensees in different geographic areas).

2. Should patent misuse be found where a license requires payment of royalties to continue even after the patent term expires? Where a license is entered into while the patent application is pending, and specifies that royalties will be payable even if the patent does not issue? Where a condition of the license is that the licensor receive a license to exploit any improvements on the invention which are developed by the licensee?

3. Should an infringement defendant be entitled to invoke the patent misuse defense based on anticompetitive provisions contained in patent licenses by which the defendant was not bound?

4. Reconsider questions 1 and 2 following *Met-Coil, supra*, at pages 680–81: does the patent misuse doctrine affect your answers?

5. The principles of the Patent Misuse Reform Act of 1988 are reflected in the Supreme Court's recent antitrust decision in *Illinois Tool Works Inc. v. Independent Ink, Inc.*, 547 U.S. 28, 126 S.Ct. 1281, 164 L.Ed.2d 26 (2006), where the Court held unanimously that, for purposes of a tying claim under Section 1 of the Sherman Act, courts may no longer presume that a patent confers monopoly power, and that in all tying cases a plaintiff must prove that the defendant has market power in the tying product.

4. EXPERIMENTAL USE

Although the unauthorized use of a patented product or process even for noncommercial purposes is an infringement, courts have often recognized a nonstatutory de minimis privilege. Most courts have limited this privilege to making or using the patented invention purely for purposes of experimentation or research, with no purpose of commercial advantage, and on a small enough scale to qualify as truly de minimis. In 2002, the Federal Circuit's decision in *Madey v. Duke University* gave a narrow interpretation to this common law "experimental use" exception.

MADEY v. DUKE UNIVERSITY

United States Court of Appeals, Federal Circuit, 2002.
307 F.3d 1351, *cert. denied,* 539 U.S. 958, 123 S.Ct. 2639, 156 L.Ed.2d 656.

GAJARSA, CIRCUIT JUDGE.

[After he was removed from his position as a lab director at Duke University, plaintiff Madey sued the university for infringement when it continued to use his patented laser technology in its research lab. The district court granted summary judgment in favor of the university, holding that the experimental use defense applied, and Madey appealed.]

* * *

The Patent Motion and the Experimental Use Defense

The district court acknowledged a common law "exception" for patent infringement liability for uses that, in the district court's words, are "solely for research, academic or experimental purposes." The district court recognized the debate over the scope of the experimental use defense, but cited this court's opinion in *Embrex, Inc. v. Service Engineering Corp.,* 216 F.3d 1343, 1349 (Fed.Cir.2000) to hold that the defense was viable for experimental, non-profit purposes. *Summary Judgment Opinion* at 9 (citing *Embrex,* 216 F.3d at 1349 (noting that courts should not "construe the experimental use rule so broadly as to allow a violation of the patent laws in the guise of 'scientific inquiry,' when that inquiry has definite, cognizable, and not insubstantial commercial purposes" (quoting *Roche Prods., Inc. v. Bolar Pharm. Co.,* 733 F.2d 858, 863 (Fed.Cir.1984))[3])).

After having recognized the experimental use defense, the district court then fashioned the defense for application to Madey in the passage set forth below.

> Given this standard [for experimental use], for [Madey] to overcome his burden of establishing actionable infringement in this case, he must establish that [Duke] has not used the equipment at issue "solely for an experimental or other non-profit purpose." 5 Donald S. Chisum, *Chisum on Patents* § 16.03[1] (2000). More specifically, [Madey] must sufficiently establish that [Duke's] use of the patent had "definite, cognizable, and not insubstantial commercial purposes." *Roche Prods., Inc. v. Bolar Pharm. Co.,* 733 F.2d 858, 863 (Fed.Cir.1984), *cert. denied,* 469 U.S. 856, 105 S.Ct. 183, 83 L.Ed.2d 117 (1984).

Summary Judgment Opinion at 10.

On appeal, Madey attacks this passage as improperly shifting the burden to the plaintiff to allege and prove that the defendant's use was not experimental.

---

3. The accused infringer in *Roche* sought to assert the experimental use defense to allow early development of a generic drug. After the *Roche* decision, however, Congress changed the law, overruling *Roche* in part, but without impacting the experimental use doctrine. Congress provided limited ability for a company to practice a patent in furtherance of a drug approval application.

Before the district court, Madey argued that Duke's research in its FEL lab was commercial in character and intent. *Id.* Madey relied on *Pitcairn v. United States,* 212 Ct.Cl. 168, 547 F.2d 1106 (Ct. Cl. 1976), where the government used patented rotor structures and control systems for a helicopter to test the "lifting ability" and other attributes of the patented technology. *Pitcairn,* 547 F.2d at 1125–26. The *Pitcairn* court held that the helicopters were not built solely for experimental purposes because they were also built to benefit the government in its legitimate business. *Id.* Based on language in Duke's patent policy, Madey argues that Duke is in the business of "obtaining grants and developing possible commercial applications for the fruits of its 'academic research.' "

The district court rejected Madey's argument, relying on another statement in the preamble of the Duke patent policy which stated that Duke was "dedicated to teaching, research, and the expansion of knowledge . . . [and] does not undertake research or development work principally for the purpose of developing patents and commercial applications." *Id.* The district court reasoned that these statements from the patent policy refute any contention that Duke is "in the business" of developing technology for commercial applications. *Id.* at 12. According to the district court, Madey's "evidence" was mere speculation,[4] and thus Madey did not meet his burden of proof to create a genuine issue of material fact.[5] *Id.* The court went on to state that "[w]ithout more concrete evidence to rebut [Duke's] stated purpose with respect to its research in the FEL lab, Plaintiff has failed to meet its burden of establishing patent infringement by a preponderance of the evidence." *Id.* at 13.

* * *

On appeal, Madey asserts three primary errors related to experimental use. First, Madey claims that the district court improperly shifted the burden to Madey to prove that Duke's use was not experimental. Second, Madey argues that the district court applied an overly broad version of the very narrow experimental use defense inconsistent with our precedent. Third, Madey attacks the supporting evidence relied on by the district court as overly general and not indicative of the specific propositions and findings required by the experimental use defense, and further

4. Madey also argued that Duke's acceptance of funding from the government and private foundations was evidence of developing patented devices with commercial intent. The district court also rejected this proposition. *Summary Judgment Opinion* at 13 (citing *Ruth v. Stearns–Roger Mfg. Co.,* 13 F.Supp. 697, 713 (D.Colo.1935) (concluding that the experimental use defense applies when a university uses a patented device in furtherance of its educational purpose); Ronald D. Hartman, *Experimental Use as an Exception to Patent Infringement,* 67 J. Pat. Off. Soc'y 617, 633 (1985) (concluding that *Ruth* supports application of the experimental use defense to a university's operations in furtherance of its educational function)).

5. The district court discussed and dismissed in a footnote other evidence suggested by Madey, including the fact that Duke had established (but not yet applied) an hourly fee for industrial users wishing to use the FEL lab's resources, and statements from Duke's website for the FEL lab indicating an interest in corporate partnerships. *Id.* at 15 n. 2.

argues that there is no support in the record before us to allow any court to apply the very narrow experimental use defense to Duke's ongoing FEL lab operation. We substantially agree with Madey on all three points. * * *

[The appellate court held that the district court erred in placing on Madey the burden of establishing that the university was not entitled to the experimental use defense. The non-experimental nature of a defendant's use is not part of a plaintiff's prima facie case of infringement; rather, the burden is on the defendant to establish that the defense applies.]

* * *

The District Court's Overly Broad Conception of Experimental Use

Madey argues, and we agree, that the district court had an overly broad conception of the very narrow and strictly limited experimental use defense. The district court stated that the experimental use defense inoculated uses that "were solely for research, academic, or experimental purposes," and that the defense covered use that "is made for experimental, non-profit purposes only." *Id.* at 9. Both formulations are too broad and stand in sharp contrast to our admonitions in *Embrex* and *Roche* that the experimental use defense is very narrow and strictly limited. In *Embrex,* we followed the teachings of *Roche* and *Pitcairn* to hold that the defense was very narrow and limited to actions performed "for amusement, to satisfy idle curiosity, or for strictly philosophical inquiry." *Embrex,* 216 F.3d at 1349. Further, use does not qualify for the experimental use defense when it is undertaken in the "guise of scientific inquiry" but has "definite, cognizable, and not insubstantial commercial purposes." *Id.* (quoting *Roche,* 733 F.2d at 863). The concurring opinion in *Embrex* expresses a similar view: use is disqualified from the defense if it has the "slightest commercial implication." *Id.* at 1353, 216 F.3d 1343. Moreover, use in keeping with the legitimate business of the alleged infringer does not qualify for the experimental use defense. *See Pitcairn,* 547 F.2d at 1125–26. The district court supported its conclusion with a citation to *Ruth v. Stearns–Roger Mfg. Co.,* 13 F.Supp. 697, 713 (D.Colo.1935), a case that is not binding precedent for this court.

The *Ruth* case represents the conceptual dilemma that may have led the district court astray. Cases evaluating the experimental use defense are few, and those involving non-profit, educational alleged infringers are even fewer. In *Ruth,* the court concluded that a manufacturer of equipment covered by patents was not liable for contributory infringement because the end-user purchaser was the Colorado School of Mines, which used the equipment in furtherance of its educational purpose. *Id.* Thus, the combination of apparent lack of commerciality, with the non-profit status of an educational institution, prompted the court in *Ruth,* without any detailed analysis of the character, nature and effect of the use, to hold that the experimental use defense applied. *Id.* This is not consistent with the binding precedent of our case law postulated by *Embrex, Roche* and *Pitcairn.*

Our precedent clearly does not immunize use that is in any way commercial in nature. Similarly, our precedent does not immunize any conduct that is in keeping with the alleged infringer's legitimate business, regardless of commercial implications. For example, major research universities, such as Duke, often sanction and fund research projects with arguably no commercial application whatsoever. However, these projects unmistakably further the institution's legitimate business objectives, including educating and enlightening students and faculty participating in these projects. These projects also serve, for example, to increase the status of the institution and lure lucrative research grants, students and faculty.

In short, regardless of whether a particular institution or entity is engaged in an endeavor for commercial gain, so long as the act is in furtherance of the alleged infringer's legitimate business and is not solely for amusement, to satisfy idle curiosity, or for strictly philosophical inquiry, the act does not qualify for the very narrow and strictly limited experimental use defense. Moreover, the profit or non-profit status of the user is not determinative.

In the present case, the district court attached too great a weight to the non-profit, educational status of Duke, effectively suppressing the fact that Duke's acts appear to be in accordance with any reasonable interpretation of Duke's legitimate business objectives.[7] On remand, the district court will have to significantly narrow and limit its conception of the experimental use defense. The correct focus should not be on the non-profit status of Duke but on the legitimate business Duke is involved in and whether or not the use was solely for amusement, to satisfy idle curiosity, or for strictly philosophical inquiry.

* * *

III. CONCLUSION

The district court erred in its application of the common law experimental use defense, and, consequently, incorrectly found that there was no genuine issue of material fact upon which Madey could prevail. * * * Accordingly, we affirm-in-part and reverse-in-part the district court's decision and remand for additional proceedings consistent with this opinion.

AFFIRMED-IN–PART, REVERSED–IN–PART, AND REMANDED.

Notes

1. Is it possible to craft an experimental use provision that would shelter at least some academic activities? Which activities should be covered, and which should be excluded?

---

7. Duke's patent and licensing policy may support its primary function as an educational institution. Duke, however, like other major research institutions of higher learning, is not shy in pursuing an aggressive patent licensing program from which it derives a not insubstantial revenue stream.

2. In *Roche Products, Inc. v. Bolar Pharmaceutical Co.*, 733 F.2d 858 (Fed.Cir.1984), *cert. denied*, 469 U.S. 856, 105 S.Ct. 183, 83 L.Ed.2d 117 (1984), the Federal Circuit held that the defendant's commercial purpose made the experimental use privilege inapplicable where a generic drug maker used samples of a patented drug (acquired from a foreign source) in connection with FDA-required testing of the generic equivalent which it intended to market when the patent expired. Concerned that this result would delay the marketing of many generic drugs, Congress immediately enacted the narrowly defined experimentation privilege of section 271(e)(1),[1] which the Supreme Court later held applicable to both drugs and medical devices in *Eli Lilly & Co. v. Medtronic, Inc.*, 496 U.S. 661, 110 S.Ct. 2683, 110 L.Ed.2d 605 (1990). (This is the legislation described in footnote 3 of *Madey*.) At the same time, Congress enacted Sections 271(e)(2) and (e)(4), discussed at page 640 *supra*.

The Section 271(e)(1) safe harbor provision makes it lawful to make, use, import, sell, or offer to sell certain patented inventions "solely for uses reasonably related to the development and submission of information under a Federal law which regulates the manufacture, use, or sale of drugs or veterinary biological products." The safe harbor applies only to patented inventions that are manufactured through certain genetic manipulation techniques, such as recombinant DNA. The chief purpose and effect of Section 271(e)(1) is to enable generic drug makers to establish bioequivalence with patented drugs as part of the FDA approval process without having to delay their testing activities until the expiration of the patent term. *Eli Lilly*, 496 U.S. at 676. However, the safe harbor is not limited to drugs, and extends to medical devices, food additives, color additives, new drugs, antibiotic drugs, and human biological products. *Eli Lilly*, 496 U.S. at 674. *See also Merck KGAA v. Integra Lifesciences I, Ltd.*, 545 U.S. 193, 125 S.Ct. 2372, 162 L.Ed.2d 160 (2005) (holding that Section 271(e)(1) applies to both clinical and preclinical trials, and that it applies to experimentation on compounds regardless of whether or not the compound or the results of the particular experiment are ultimately submitted to the FDA).

5. INEQUITABLE CONDUCT

A patent applicant has a duty of candor in dealing with the Patent and Trademark Office. Intentional misrepresentations, omissions, or misleading statements violate that duty and constitute "inequitable conduct" or "fraud," provided they pertain to subject matter that is material to patentability. Some examples of material subject matter include the identity of the inventor, prior art, existence of any facts constituting a statutory bar, and date of invention. Clear and convincing evidence is required to establish inequitable conduct.

The consequences of finding that a patent was procured through inequitable conduct may include rejection of the application if it is still pending, invalidity or unenforceability of the patent (which differ in concept but not in practical effect) in an infringement proceeding, cancellation of the patent in a suit brought by the United States, liability under the securities or antitrust laws or under the Federal Trade

---

1. Pub. L. No. 98–417, 98 Stat. 1585 (1984).

Commission Act, and liability for the prevailing defendant's attorney's fees in an infringement action.

6. LACHES AND ESTOPPEL

Laches: The defense of laches applies if there is an unreasonable and inexcusable delay in filing suit after the patentee knows or reasonably should know of the infringement, and the delay materially prejudices the infringer. *Jamesbury Corp. v. Litton Industrial Prods., Inc.,* 839 F.2d 1544 (Fed.Cir.1988), *cert. denied,* 488 U.S. 828, 109 S.Ct. 80, 102 L.Ed.2d 57 (1988); *see, e.g., Cobe Laboratories, Inc. v. Baxter Healthcare Corp.,* 34 U.S.P.Q.2d (BNA) 1472 (D.Colo.1994) (laches bars action brought eight years after learning of infringement); *Cover v. Hydramatic Packing Co., Inc.,* 34 U.S.P.Q.2d (BNA) 1128 (E.D.Pa.1994) (laches defense unavailable where defendant received timely notice of infringement and failed to conduct reasonable inquiry into patent's validity); *Valutron N.V. v. NCR Corp.,* 33 U.S.P.Q.2d (BNA) 1986 (S.D.Ohio 1992) (plaintiff's actual notice of possible infringement warranted presumption of unreasonable delay and material prejudice which plaintiff failed to rebut). Whether a delay is unreasonable depends on the circumstances. After a delay of six years, however, courts have held that the burden shifts to the plaintiff to establish reasonableness.

Laches will bar recovery of damages for infringements prior to filing the infringement action, but will not bar injunctive relief or damages for post-filing infringements.

Estoppel: Equitable estoppel bars all relief for both pre-and postfiling infringements where the patent owner has represented to the defendant that no infringement claim will be brought, and the defendant has reasonably and detrimentally relied on that representation.

7. INFRINGEMENT BY GOVERNMENT ENTITIES

Federal government: Under 28 U.S.C.A. § 1498, a patentholder's exclusive remedy for infringing use by or for the federal government (including use by a government contractor where authorized by the federal government) is a suit for reasonable compensation in the United States Court of Federal Claims. The same rule applies to infringement suits under the PVPA and the Semiconductor Chip Protection Act, 17 U.S.C. §§ 901–14 (2007).

State governments: After a series of conflicting court rulings on the question whether states were immune from suit for patent infringement, Congress passed the Patent and Plant Variety Protection Remedy Clarification Act of 1992, Pub. L. No. 102–560, 106 Stat. 4230, in order to clarify its intent to abrogate state immunity from patent and PVPA infringement suits, *see* 35 U.S.C.A. §§ 271(h), 296(a), specifying that in doing so it was acting upon its authority under the Intellectual Property Clause, the Commerce Clause, and Section 5 of the Fourteenth Amendment. However, the Supreme Court's subsequent decision in *Seminole Tribe v. Florida,* 517 U.S. 44, 116 S.Ct. 1114, 134 L.Ed.2d 252 (1996), suggested that only the last of these constitutional provisions is a valid source of authority for such abrogation, thus placing the validity of the 1992 amendments in question.

This issue was resolved in 1999, when the Supreme Court held the 1992 amendments invalid in *Florida Prepaid Postsecondary Education Expense Board v. College Savings Bank,* 527 U.S. 627, 119 S.Ct. 2199, 144 L.Ed.2d 575 (1999). The Court held that Congress was not acting within the scope of its authority under Section 5 of the Fourteenth Amendment when it abrogated Eleventh Amendment immunity for purposes of patent infringement suits, because there was no evidence that states had engaged in a historical pattern of infringing patents and providing inadequate remedies for those infringements. Because the federal courts have exclusive jurisdiction over patent infringement suits (under 28 U.S.C. § 1338(a)), this holding appears to immunize states from damages liability for patent infringement. However, the Eleventh Amendment allows federal courts to enjoin individual state actors from continuing to infringe. *Pennington Seed Inc. v. Produce Exchange No. 299,* 457 F.3d 1334 (Fed. Cir. 2006). Moreover, when a state actor initiates a patent infringement suit, thus voluntarily subjecting itself to federal court jurisdiction, this constitutes a waiver of its immunity with respect to any compulsory counterclaims. *Regents of Univ. of New Mexico v. Knight,* 321 F.3d 1111 (Fed. Cir. 2003). Proposed legislation, considered but not yet enacted, would respond to *College Savings* by denying certain federal intellectual property rights to states which fail to waive their immunity to infringement suits.

Note: Good Faith Prior Users

The Patent Reform Act of 1999, Pub. L. No. 106–113, 106th Cong., 1st Sess. (1999), added a new Section 273 to Title 35, establishing a first inventor—or "prior user"—defense against patent infringement claims involving "methods of doing or conducting business." The defense applies when the alleged infringer has, acting in good faith, reduced the accused subject matter to practice in the United States at least one year before the patentee's effective filing date, *and* commercially used the invention before that filing date. The defense is available only for infringement claims filed after the enactment date, and only to a defendant who did not derive the subject matter from the patentee or from persons in privity with the patentee, and who has not abandoned the commercial use. The legislative history implies that the defense is available only to one who has *invented* (rather than merely *used*) the patented subject matter, H.R. Rep. No. 106–464, 106th Cong., 1st Sess. (1999), but the statute does not include this restriction (outside of a single caption referring to an "earlier inventor") and subsection (b)(3)(B) implies that the defense is available to a non-inventor who derived the idea from an independent third party. The defense may not be licensed or assigned except with the transfer of the entire enterprise or line of business to which the accused subject matter relates.

Congress chose not to enact a broader prior user defense which would have applied to subject matter other than business methods, because of significant opposition by parties concerned about the conflict between trade secret rights and the patent policy favoring prompt disclosure of new technology. A broad prior user defense could discourage some inventors from filing patent applications, and encourage them to rely on trade secret protection instead, by insulating them from the risk of infringement liability where another inventor later obtains a patent on the same invention. Should these concerns preclude a broad prior user defense? Why did Congress not view them as preclusive with respect to business methods?

The House Report indicates that Congress viewed the "prior user" issue as particularly urgent with respect to business methods after the Federal Circuit's 1998 *State Street* decision (*see supra* Chapter 11.B.2.), because that decision made it likely that patents would be sought for a wide range of business-related methods that might previously have been considered unpatentable, and which might therefore already be in use by prior inventors who had chosen to rely on trade secret protection.

However, Section 273 does not limit the defense to users whose use predates the decision in *State Street*, or even the effective date of the statute. Is this consistent with the purpose of Section 273?

The failed Patent Reform Act of 2005, H.R. 2795, would have expanded the good faith prior user defense to apply to all statutory subject matter, not just business methods. This amendment has been reintroduced in the proposed Patent Reform Act of 2007.

C. INFRINGEMENT ADJUDICATION

1. JURISDICTION

Under 28 U.S.C.A. § 1338(a), the federal district courts have exclusive original jurisdiction over claims of patent or plant variety infringements and suits for declaratory judgments of invalidity or non-infringement regarding patents or plant variety protection. Under 28 U.S.C.A. § 1295(a)(1), the Federal Circuit has exclusive appellate jurisdiction over cases in which the district court's jurisdiction was based "in whole or in part" on a claim arising under the patent or plant variety statutes.

However, in 2002 the Supreme Court held in *Holmes Group, Inc. v. Vornado Air Circulation Systems,* 535 U.S. 826, 122 S.Ct. 1889, 153 L.Ed.2d 13 (2002), that the Federal Circuit does not have appellate jurisdiction over a case in which an issue of federal patent law arises only in a *counterclaim,* because such a case is not one "arising under" the federal patent laws. Applying the "well-pleaded complaint" rule, the Court held that the Federal Circuit has jurisdiction over a patent appeal only if an issue of federal patent law was raised in the plaintiff's complaint, rather than in a counterclaim by the defendant.

In *Chamberlain Group, Inc. v. Skylink Techs., Inc.,* 381 F.3d 1178 (Fed. Cir. 2004), *cert. denied,* 544 U.S. 923, 125 S.Ct. 1669, 161 L.Ed.2d 481 (2005), the Federal Circuit applied *Vornado* to hold that a district court's dismissal of all patent claims in a case divested the Federal Circuit of appellate jurisdiction only where the claims were dismissed without prejudice. The court reasoned that "[d]ismissals *without prejudice* are de facto amendments to the complaint," 381 F.3d at 1189 (emphasis in original), thus divesting the Federal Circuit of appellate jurisdiction when the dismissal eliminates all of the patent claims in the complaint. In contrast, "dismissals *with prejudice* are adjudications on the merits" of the patent claims, *id.* (emphasis in original), which confer appellate jurisdiction on the Federal Circuit.

The Intellectual Property Jurisdiction Clarification Act of 2005, H.R. 2955, would have restored the Federal Circuit's jurisdiction over patent counterclaims, thus legislatively overruling *Vornado*. The bill was amended to clarify that the Federal Circuit would be required to transfer to the appropriate regional circuit court any case that did not raise a patent claim on appeal, even if a patent counterclaim had initially been asserted. Although the bill was approved by the House Judiciary Committee in 2006, no further action was taken.

At its creation in 1982, the Federal Circuit adopted as binding precedent the decisions of its predecessor courts, the United States Court of Claims and the Court of Customs and Patent Appeals. Although the Federal Circuit follows these and its own precedents regarding matters over which it has exclusive jurisdiction, in cases involving a mix of patent and nonpatent issues, with regard to the nonpatent matters it follows the precedents of the United States Court of Appeals for the Circuit which would otherwise have had jurisdiction over the appeal.

2. JUSTICIABILITY

(i) *Standing to Bring Infringement Actions*

Under 35 U.S.C. § 281, standing to bring an infringement claim is limited to patent owners (unless they have assigned all significant rights under the patent), their assignees, and, in some cases, their exclusive licensees. Ordinarily, an exclusive licensee has standing to bring suit independently only when the licensee holds all substantial rights in the patent; otherwise, the licensee may sue only by joining the patent owner as an indispensable co-plaintiff. However, an exception is recognized where the infringer is the patent owner. *See Mentor H/S, Inc. v. Medical Device Alliance, Inc.*, 240 F.3d 1016, 1017 (Fed.Cir.2001). Furthermore, an exclusive licensee has standing to sue an infringer only if the rights infringed are within the scope of the license. Where patent rights have been transferred, standing belongs to the party that owned the infringed rights at the time of the infringement.

The question whether a patent owner has transferred all substantial rights, and is thus deprived of standing to sue for infringement, can be difficult and fact-specific. For example, in *Aspex Eyewear, Inc. v. Miracle Optics, Inc.*, 434 F.3d 1336 (Fed. Cir. 2006), the Federal Circuit vacated a district court's decision that the owner of a patent for eyeglass frames had transferred all substantial rights to its U.S. distributor. The appellate court held that the distributor was merely an exclusive licensee and not an assignee, regardless of the scope of the rights conveyed in the agreement, because the agreement granted rights to the distributor only for a fixed term of years, rather than for the remaining term of the patent. At the expiration of the fixed term, all rights to the invention would revert to the patent owner.

Where parties share undivided co-ownership of patent rights (as joint inventors, for example), the traditional rule is that an infringement action can proceed only if all co-owners join voluntarily as plaintiffs. A few decisions, however, have departed from that rule. *See, e.g., Willingham v. Lawton*, 555 F.2d 1340 (6th Cir.1977) (allowing action to proceed where co-owner was joined as involuntary plaintiff, and where co-owners had agreed by contract that either could sue an infringer even if the other did not join). The same joinder rules generally apply in determining the proper defendants in an action for a declaratory judgment of invalidity or non-infringement of a patent.

(ii) Declaratory Judgment Actions

On the principle that the best defense is a good offense, a party that anticipates being sued for patent infringement may seek to take the offensive by asking a federal court to issue a declaratory judgment that the claims in question are invalid and/or are not infringed. Such a determination may help a potential infringer decide whether or not to make a substantial investment in the technology necessary to produce the product or service in question.

Under what circumstances should a federal court exercise jurisdiction over such an action? Pursuant to Article III of the Constitution and the Declaratory Judgment Act, federal courts will not rule on hypothetical scenarios, requiring instead that an actual case or controversy exist. In the case that follows, the Supreme Court in 2007 clarified the standards for determining when a potential patent infringer may obtain a declaratory judgment, articulating a more liberal policy than the Federal Circuit had embraced in its most recent decisions.

MedIMMUNE, INC. v. GENENTECH, INC.

Supreme Court of the United States, 2007.
___ U.S. ___, 127 S.Ct. 764, 166 L.Ed.2d 604.

JUSTICE SCALIA delivered the opinion of the Court.

We must decide whether Article III's limitation of federal courts' jurisdiction to "Cases" and "Controversies," reflected in the "actual controversy" requirement of the Declaratory Judgment Act, 28 U.S.C. § 2201(a), requires a patent licensee to terminate or be in breach of its license agreement before it can seek a declaratory judgment that the underlying patent is invalid, unenforceable, or not infringed.

I

[Respondent Genentech entered an agreement to license its then-pending patent (the "Cabilly II" patent) to petitioner MedImmune in which the latter agreed to pay royalties on sales of products which would, in the absence of the license, infringe one or more claims in respondent's patent until the patent expired or the claims were held invalid. The licensing agreement gave petitioner the right to terminate upon six months' written notice. When the patent issued, respondent demanded that petitioner begin paying royalties. Although petitioner believed that the patent was invalid, it paid the royalties "under protest and with reservation of all of [its] rights." Petitioner then commenced this declaratory judgment action.]

* * *

Petitioner sought the declaratory relief discussed in detail in Part II below. Petitioner also requested damages and an injunction with respect to other federal and state claims not relevant here. The District Court granted respondents' motion to dismiss the declaratory-judgment claims for lack of subject-matter jurisdiction, relying on the decision of the United States Court of Appeals for the Federal Circuit in *Gen-Probe Inc. v. Vysis, Inc.,* 359 F.3d 1376 (2004). *Gen-Probe* had held that a patent licensee in good standing cannot establish an Article III case or controversy with regard to validity, enforceability, or scope of the patent because the license agreement "obliterate[s] any reasonable apprehension" that the licensee will be sued for infringement. *Id.,* at 1381. The Federal Circuit affirmed the District Court, also relying on *Gen-Probe.* 427 F.3d 958 (2005). We granted certiorari. 546 U.S. 1169 (2006).

* * *

III

The Declaratory Judgment Act provides that, "[i]n a case of actual controversy within its jurisdiction ... any court of the United States ... may declare the rights and other legal relations of any interested party seeking such declaration, whether or not further relief is or could be sought." 28 U.S.C. § 2201(a). There was a time when this Court harbored doubts about the compatibility of declaratory-judgment actions with Article III's case-or-controversy requirement. We dispelled those doubts, however, in *Nashville, C. & St. L.R. Co. v. Wallace,* 288 U.S. 249, 53 S.Ct. 345, 77 L.Ed. 730 (1933), holding (in a case involving a declaratory judgment rendered in state court) that an appropriate action for declaratory relief *can* be a case or controversy under Article III. The federal Declaratory Judgment Act was signed into law the following year, and we upheld its constitutionality in *Aetna Life Ins. Co. v. Haworth,* 300 U.S. 227, 57 S.Ct. 461, 81 L.Ed. 617 (1937). Our opinion explained that the phrase "case of actual controversy" in the Act refers to the type of "Cases" and "Controversies" that are justiciable under Article III. *Id.,* at 240.

Aetna and the cases following it do not draw the brightest of lines between those declaratory-judgment actions that satisfy the case-or-controversy requirement and those that do not. Our decisions have required that the dispute be "definite and concrete, touching the legal relations of parties having adverse legal interests"; and that it be "real and substantial" and "admi[t] of specific relief through a decree of a conclusive character, as distinguished from an opinion advising what the law would be upon a hypothetical state of facts." *Id.,* at 240–241. In *Maryland Casualty Co. v. Pacific Coal & Oil Co.,* 312 U.S. 270, 273, 61 S.Ct. 510, 85 L.Ed. 826 (1941), we summarized as follows: "Basically, the question in each case is whether the facts alleged, under all the circumstances, show that there is a substantial controversy, between parties having adverse legal interests, of sufficient immediacy and reality to warrant the issuance of a declaratory judgment."

There is no dispute that these standards would have been satisfied if petitioner had taken the final step of refusing to make royalty payments under the 1997 license agreement. Respondents claim a right to royalties under the licensing agreement. Petitioner asserts that no royalties are owing because the Cabilly II patent is invalid and not infringed; and alleges (without contradiction) a threat by respondents to enjoin sales if royalties are not forthcoming. The factual and legal dimensions of the dispute are well defined and, but for petitioner's continuing to make royalty payments, nothing about the dispute would render it unfit for judicial resolution. Assuming (without deciding) that respondents here could not claim an anticipatory breach and repudiate the license, the continuation of royalty payments makes what would otherwise be an imminent threat at least remote, if not nonexistent. As long as those payments are made, there is no risk that respondents will seek to enjoin petitioner's sales. Petitioner's own acts, in other words, eliminate the imminent threat of harm. The question before us is whether this causes the dispute no longer to be a case or controversy within the meaning of Article III.

Our analysis must begin with the recognition that, where threatened action by *government* is concerned, we do not require a plaintiff to expose himself to liability before bringing suit to challenge the basis for the threat—for example, the constitutionality of a law threatened to be enforced. The plaintiff's own action (or inaction) in failing to violate the law eliminates the imminent threat of prosecution, but nonetheless does not eliminate Article III jurisdiction. For example, in *Terrace v. Thompson,* 263 U.S. 197, 44 S.Ct. 15, 68 L.Ed. 255 (1923), the State threatened the plaintiff with forfeiture of his farm, fines, and penalties if he entered into a lease with an alien in violation of the State's anti-alien land law. Given this genuine threat of enforcement, we did not require, as a prerequisite to testing the validity of the law in a suit for injunction, that the plaintiff bet the farm, so to speak, by taking the violative action. *Id.,* at 216. Likewise, in *Steffel v. Thompson,* 415 U.S. 452, 94 S.Ct. 1209, 39 L.Ed.2d 505 (1974), we did not require the plaintiff to proceed to distribute handbills and risk actual prosecution before he could seek a declaratory judgment regarding the constitutionality of a state statute prohibiting such distribution. *Id.,* at 458–460. As then-Justice Rehnquist put it in his concurrence, "the declaratory judgment procedure is an alternative to pursuit of the arguably illegal activity." *Id.,* at 480. In each of these cases, the plaintiff had eliminated the imminent threat of harm by simply not doing what he claimed the right to do (enter into a lease, or distribute handbills at the shopping center). That did not preclude subject-matter jurisdiction because the threat-eliminating behavior was effectively coerced. See *Terrace, supra,* at 215–216; *Steffel, supra,* at 459. The dilemma posed by that coercion—putting the challenger to the choice between abandoning his rights or risking prosecution—is "a dilemma that it was the very purpose of the Declaratory Judgment Act to ameliorate." *Abbott Laboratories v. Gardner,* 387 U.S. 136, 152, 87 S.Ct. 1507, 18 L.Ed.2d 681 (1967).

Supreme Court jurisprudence is more rare regarding application of the Declaratory Judgment Act to situations in which the plaintiff's self-avoidance of imminent injury is coerced by threatened enforcement action of *a private party* rather than the government. Lower federal courts, however (and state courts interpreting declaratory judgment Acts requiring "actual controversy"), have long accepted jurisdiction in such cases.

The only Supreme Court decision in point is, fortuitously, close on its facts to the case before us. *Altvater v. Freeman,* 319 U.S. 359, 63 S.Ct. 1115, 87 L.Ed. 1450 (1943), held that a licensee's failure to cease its payment of royalties did not render nonjusticiable a dispute over the validity of the patent. In that litigation, several patentees had sued their licensees to enforce territorial restrictions in the license. The licensees filed a counterclaim for declaratory judgment that the underlying patents were invalid, in the meantime paying "under protest" royalties required by an injunction the patentees had obtained in an earlier case. The patentees argued that "so long as [licensees] continue to pay royalties, there is only an academic, not a real controversy, between the parties." *Id.,* at 364. We rejected that argument and held that the declaratory-judgment claim presented a justiciable case or controversy: "The fact that royalties were being paid did not make this a 'difference or dispute of a hypothetical or abstract character.' " *Ibid.* (quoting *Aetna,* 300 U.S., at 240). The royalties "were being paid under protest and under the compulsion of an injunction decree," and "[u]nless the injunction decree were modified, the only other course [of action] was to defy it, and to risk not only actual but treble damages in infringement suits." 319 U.S., at 365. We concluded that "the requirements of [a] case or controversy are met where payment of a claim is demanded as of right and where payment is made, but where the involuntary or coercive nature of the exaction preserves the right to recover the sums paid or to challenge the legality of the claim." *Ibid.*

The Federal Circuit's *Gen-Probe* decision distinguished *Altvater* on the ground that it involved the compulsion of an injunction. But *Altvater* cannot be so readily dismissed. Never mind that the injunction had been privately obtained and was ultimately within the control of the patentees, who could permit its modification. More fundamentally, and contrary to the Federal Circuit's conclusion, *Altvater* did not say that the coercion dispositive of the case was governmental, but suggested just the opposite. The opinion acknowledged that the licensees had the option of stopping payments in defiance of the injunction, but explained that the *consequence* of doing so would be to risk "actual [and] treble damages in infringement suits" by the patentees. 319 U.S., at 365. It significantly did not mention the threat of prosecution for contempt, or any other sort of governmental sanction. Moreover, it cited approvingly a treatise which said that an "actual or threatened serious injury to business or employment" by a private party can be as coercive as other forms of coercion supporting restitution actions at common law; and that "[t]o imperil a man's livelihood, his business enterprises, or his solvency, [was] ordinarily quite as coercive" as, for example, "detaining his property." F. Woodward, The Law of Quasi Contracts § 218 (1913), cited in *Altvater, supra,* at 365.[11]

Jurisdiction over the present case is not contradicted by *Willing v. Chicago Auditorium Association,* 277 U.S. 274, 48 S.Ct. 507, 72 L.Ed. 880. There a ground lessee wanted to demolish an antiquated auditorium and replace it with a modern commercial building. The lessee believed it had the right to do this without the lessors' consent, but was unwilling to drop the wrecking ball first and test its belief later. Because there was no declaratory judgment act at the time under federal or applicable state law, the lessee filed an action to remove a "cloud" on its lease. This Court held that an Article III case or controversy had not arisen because "[n]o defendant ha[d] wronged the plaintiff or ha[d] threatened to do so." *Id.,* at 288, 290. It was true that one of the colessors had disagreed with the lessee's interpretation of the lease, but that happened in an "informal, friendly, private conversation," *id.,* at 286, a year before the lawsuit was filed; and the lessee never even bothered to approach the other co-lessors. The Court went on to remark that "[w]hat the plaintiff seeks is simply a declaratory judgment," and "[t]o grant that relief is beyond the power conferred upon the federal judiciary." *Id.,* at 289. Had *Willing* been decided after the enactment (and our upholding) of the Declaratory Judgment Act, and had the legal disagreement between the parties been as lively as this one, we are confident a different result would have obtained. The rule that a plaintiff must destroy a large

---

11. Even if *Altvater* could be distinguished as an "injunction" case, it would still contradict the Federal Circuit's "reasonable apprehension of suit" test (or, in its evolved form, the "reasonable apprehension of *imminent* suit" test, *Teva Pharm. USA, Inc. v. Pfizer, Inc.,* 395 F.3d 1324, 1333 (2005)). A licensee who pays royalties under compulsion of an injunction has no more apprehension of imminent harm than a licensee who pays royalties for fear of treble damages and an injunction fatal to his business. The reasonable-apprehension-of-suit test also conflicts with our decisions in *Maryland Casualty Co. v. Pacific Coal & Oil Co.,* 312 U.S. 270, 273, 61 S.Ct. 510, 85 L.Ed. 826 (1941), where jurisdiction obtained even though the collision-victim de-

fendant could not have sued the declaratory-judgment plaintiff-insurer without first obtaining a judgment against the insured; and *Aetna Life Ins. Co. v. Haworth,* 300 U.S. 227, 239, 57 S.Ct. 461, 81 L.Ed. 617 (1937), where jurisdiction obtained even though the very reason the insurer sought declaratory relief was that the insured had given no indication that he would file suit. It is also in tension with *Cardinal Chemical Co. v. Morton Int'l, Inc.,* 508 U.S. 83, 98, 113 S.Ct. 1967, 124 L.Ed.2d 1 (1993), which held that appellate affirmance of a judgment of noninfringement, eliminating any apprehension of suit, does not moot a declaratory judgment counterclaim of patent invalidity.

building, bet the farm, or (as here) risk treble damages and the loss of 80 percent of its business, before seeking a declaration of its actively contested legal rights finds no support in Article III.

Respondents assert that the parties in effect settled this dispute when they entered into the 1997 license agreement. When a licensee enters such an agreement, they contend, it essentially purchases an insurance policy, immunizing it from suits for infringement so long as it continues to pay royalties and does not challenge the covered patents. Permitting it to challenge the validity of the patent without terminating or breaking the agreement alters the deal, allowing the licensee to continue enjoying its immunity while bringing a suit, the elimination of which was part of the patentee's *quid pro quo*. Of course even if it were valid, this argument would have no force with regard to petitioner's claim that the agreement does not call for royalties because their product does not infringe the patent. But even as to the patent invalidity claim, the point seems to us mistaken. To begin with, it is not clear where the prohibition against challenging the validity of the patents is to be found. It can hardly be implied from the mere promise to pay royalties on patents "which have neither expired nor been held invalid by a court or other body of competent jurisdiction from which no appeal has been or may be taken," App. 399. Promising to pay royalties on patents that have not been held invalid does not amount to a promise *not to seek* a holding of their invalidity.

Respondents appeal to the common-law rule that a party to a contract cannot at one and the same time challenge its validity and continue to reap its benefits, citing *Commodity Credit Corp. v. Rosenberg Bros. & Co.*, 243 F.2d 504, 512 (C.A.9 1957), and *Kingman & Co. v. Stoddard*, 85 F. 740, 745 (C.A.7 1898). *Lear*, they contend, did not suspend that rule for patent licensing agreements, since the plaintiff in that case had already repudiated the contract. Even if *Lear*'s repudiation of the doctrine of licensee estoppel was so limited (a point on which, as we have said earlier, we do not opine), it is hard to see how the common-law rule has any application here. Petitioner is not repudiating or impugning the contract while continuing to reap its benefits. Rather, it is asserting that the contract, properly interpreted, does not prevent it from challenging the patents, and does not require the payment of royalties because the patents do not cover its products and are invalid. Of course even if respondents were correct that the licensing agreement or the common-law rule precludes this suit, the consequence would be that respondents win this case *on the merits*—not that the very genuine contract dispute disappears, so that Article III jurisdiction is somehow defeated. In short, Article III jurisdiction has nothing to do with this "insurance-policy" contention.

* * *

We hold that petitioner was not required, insofar as Article III is concerned, to break or terminate its 1997 license agreement before seeking a declaratory judgment in federal court that the underlying patent is invalid, unenforceable, or not infringed. The Court of Appeals erred in affirming the dismissal of this action for lack of subject-matter jurisdiction.

The judgment of the Court of Appeals is reversed, and the cause is remanded for proceedings consistent with this opinion.

It is so ordered.

Notes

1. After *MedImmune*, are patent licensees more likely to seek declaratory judgments? What factors might influence a licensee's decision?

2. If a patent license contains a clause in which the licensee expressly agrees not to seek a declaratory judgment of invalidity or non-infringement, is the clause enforceable?

3. How might *MedImmune* affect a potential licensor's decisions to seek a running royalty (*e.g.,* an annual royalty based on the licensee's annual revenues from use of the patented product or process during the term of the license) as opposed to a one-time lump sum royalty payable upon execution of the licensing agreement?

4. Like an action for infringement, a declaratory judgment action can involve expensive and protracted litigation. Should Congress provide greater opportunities for administrative challenges to the validity of issued patents– *e.g.,* post-grant oppositions?

5. The Federal Circuit applied *MedImmune* in *Sandisk Corp.* v. *STMicroelectronics, Inc.,* 480 F.3d 1372 (Fed. Cir. 2007), where it allowed an action for declaratory judgment of patent invalidity and non-infringement to proceed even before the parties had entered into a licensing agreement. It was sufficient, the court held, that the parties had engaged in licensing negotiations, and that the party seeking the declaratory judgment was engaged in an activity that could give rise to an infringement action:

> In the context of conduct prior to the existence of a license, declaratory judgment jurisdiction generally will not arise merely on the basis that a party learns of the existence of a patent owned by another or even perceives such a patent to pose a risk of infringement, without some affirmative act by the patentee. But Article III jurisdiction may be met where the patentee takes a position that puts the declaratory judgment plaintiff in the position of either pursuing arguably illegal behavior or abandoning that which he claims a right to do. We need not define the outer boundaries of declaratory judgment jurisdiction, which will depend on the application of the principles of declaratory judgment jurisdiction to the facts and circumstances of each case. We hold only that where a patentee asserts rights under a patent based on certain identified ongoing or planned activity of another party, and where that party contends that it has the right to engage in the accused activity without license, an Article III case or controversy will arise and the party need not risk a suit for infringement by engaging in the identified activity before seeking a declaration of its legal rights.

Id. at 1380–81. The court held further that a patentee's declaration that it has no intent to sue for infringement does not eliminate the justiciable controversy, if the patentee has "engaged in a course of conduct that shows a preparedness and willingness to enforce its patent rights." *Id.* at 1383.

D. REMEDIES

Statutes: 35 U.S.C.A. §§ 283–86, 287(a), 289, 292

1. INJUNCTIONS

eBAY, INC. v. MercEXCHANGE, L.L.C.
Supreme Court of the United States, 2006.
___ U.S. ___, 126 S.Ct. 1837, 164 L.Ed.2d 641.

JUSTICE THOMAS delivered the opinion of the Court.

Ordinarily, a federal court considering whether to award permanent injunctive relief to a prevailing plaintiff applies the four-factor test historically employed by courts of equity. Petitioners eBay Inc. and Half.com, Inc., argue that this traditional test applies to disputes arising under the Patent Act. We agree and, accordingly, vacate the judgment of the Court of Appeals.

I

Petitioner eBay operates a popular Internet Web site that allows private sellers to list goods they wish to sell, either through an auction or at a fixed price. Petitioner Half.com, now a wholly owned subsidiary of eBay, operates a similar Web site. Respondent MercExchange, L.L.C., holds a number of patents, including a business method patent for an electronic market designed to facilitate the sale of goods between private individuals by establishing a central authority to promote trust among participants. *See* U.S. Patent No. 5,845,265. MercExchange sought to license its patent to eBay and Half.com, as it had previously done with other companies, but the parties failed to reach an agreement. MercExchange subsequently filed a patent infringement suit against eBay and Half.com in the United States District Court for the Eastern District of Virginia. A jury found that MercExchange's patent was valid, that eBay and Half.com had infringed that patent, and that an award of damages was appropriate.

Following the jury verdict, the District Court denied MercExchange's motion for permanent injunctive relief. 275 F.Supp.2d 695 (2003). The Court of Appeals for the Federal Circuit reversed, applying its "general rule that courts will issue permanent injunctions against patent infringement absent exceptional circumstances." 401 F.3d 1323, 1339 (2005). We granted certiorari to determine the appropriateness of this general rule.

II

According to well-established principles of equity, a plaintiff seeking a permanent injunction must satisfy a four-factor test before a court may grant such relief. A plaintiff must demonstrate: (1) that it has suffered an irreparable injury; (2) that remedies available at law, such as monetary damages, are inadequate to compensate for that injury; (3) that, considering the balance of hardships between the plaintiff and defendant, a remedy in equity is warranted; and (4) that the public interest would not be disserved by a permanent injunction. *See, e.g., Weinberger v. Romero–Barcelo,* 456 U.S. 305, 311–313, 102 S.Ct. 1798, 72 L.Ed.2d 91 (1982); *Amoco Production Co. v. Gambell,* 480 U.S. 531, 542, 107 S.Ct. 1396, 94 L.Ed.2d 542 (1987). The decision to grant or deny permanent injunctive relief is an act of equitable discretion by the district court, reviewable on appeal for abuse of discretion. *See, e.g., Romero–Barcelo,* 456 U.S., at 320, 102 S.Ct. 1798.

These familiar principles apply with equal force to disputes arising under the Patent Act. As this Court has long recognized, "a major departure from the long tradition of equity practice should not be lightly implied." *Ibid; see also Amoco, supra,* at 542, 107 S.Ct. 1396. Nothing in the Patent Act indicates that Congress intended such a departure. To the contrary, the Patent Act expressly provides that injunctions "may" issue "in accordance with the principles of equity." 35 U.S.C. § 283.

To be sure, the Patent Act also declares that "patents shall have the attributes of personal property," § 261, including "the right to exclude others from making, using, offering for sale, or selling the invention," § 154(a)(1). According to the Court of Appeals, this statutory right to exclude alone justifies its general rule in favor of permanent injunctive relief. 401 F.3d, at 1338. But the creation of a right is distinct from the provision of remedies for violations of that right. Indeed, the Patent Act itself indicates that patents shall have the attributes of personal property "[s]ubject to the provisions of this title," 35 U.S.C. § 261, including, presumably, the provision that injunctive relief "may" issue only "in accordance with the principles of equity," § 283.

This approach is consistent with our treatment of injunctions under the Copyright Act. Like a patent owner, a copyright holder possesses "the right to exclude others from using his property." *Fox Film Corp. v. Doyal,* 286 U.S. 123, 127, 52 S.Ct. 546, 76 L.Ed. 1010 (1932); *see also id.,* at 127–128, 52 S.Ct. 546 ("A copyright, like a patent, is at once the equivalent given by the public for benefits bestowed by the genius and meditations and skill of individuals, and the incentive to further efforts for the same important objects" (internal quotation marks omitted)). Like the Patent Act, the Copyright Act provides that courts "may" grant injunctive relief "on such terms as it may deem reasonable to prevent or restrain infringement of a copyright."17 U.S.C. § 502(a). And as in our decision today, this Court has consistently rejected invitations to replace traditional equitable considerations with a rule that an injunction automatically follows a determination that a copyright has been infringed. *See, e.g., New York Times Co. v. Tasini,* 533 U.S. 483, 505, 121 S.Ct. 2381, 150 L.Ed.2d 500 (2001) (citing *Campbell v. Acuff–Rose Music, Inc.,* 510 U.S. 569, 578, n. 10, 114 S.Ct. 1164, 127 L.Ed.2d 500 (1994)); *Dun v.*

Lumbermen's Credit Assn., 209 U.S. 20, 23–24, 28 S.Ct. 335, 52 L.Ed. 663 (1908).

Neither the District Court nor the Court of Appeals below fairly applied these traditional equitable principles in deciding respondent's motion for a permanent injunction. Although the District Court recited the traditional four-factor test, 275 F.Supp.2d, at 711, it appeared to adopt certain expansive principles suggesting that injunctive relief could not issue in a broad swath of cases. Most notably, it concluded that a "plaintiff's willingness to license its patents" and "its lack of commercial activity in practicing the patents" would be sufficient to establish that the patent holder would not suffer irreparable harm if an injunction did not issue. *Id.,* at 712. But traditional equitable principles do not permit such broad classifications. For example, some patent holders, such as university researchers or self-made inventors, might reasonably prefer to license their patents, rather than undertake efforts to secure the financing necessary to bring their works to market themselves. Such patent holders may be able to satisfy the traditional four-factor test, and we see no basis for categorically denying them the opportunity to do so. To the extent that the District Court adopted such a categorical rule, then, its analysis cannot be squared with the principles of equity adopted by Congress. The court's categorical rule is also in tension with *Continental Paper Bag Co. v. Eastern Paper Bag Co.,* 210 U.S. 405, 422–430, 28 S.Ct. 748, 52 L.Ed. 1122 (1908), which rejected the contention that a court of equity has no jurisdiction to grant injunctive relief to a patent holder who has unreasonably declined to use the patent.

In reversing the District Court, the Court of Appeals departed in the opposite direction from the four-factor test. The court articulated a "general rule," unique to patent disputes, "that a permanent injunction will issue once infringement and validity have been adjudged." 401 F.3d, at 1338. The court further indicated that injunctions should be denied only in the "unusual" case, under "exceptional circumstances" and " 'in rare instances . . . to protect the public interest.' " *Id.,* at 1338–1339. Just as the District Court erred in its categorical denial of injunctive relief, the Court of Appeals erred in its categorical grant of such relief. *Cf. Roche Products v. Bolar Pharmaceutical Co.,* 733 F.2d 858, 865 (C.A.Fed.1984) (recognizing the "considerable discretion" district courts have "in determining whether the facts of a situation require it to issue an injunction").

Because we conclude that neither court below correctly applied the traditional four-factor framework that governs the award of injunctive relief, we vacate the judgment of the Court of Appeals, so that the District Court may apply that framework in the first instance. In doing so, we take no position on whether permanent injunctive relief should or should not issue in this particular case, or indeed in any number of other disputes arising under the Patent Act. We hold only that the decision whether to grant or deny injunctive relief rests within the equitable discretion of the district courts, and that such discretion must be exercised consistent with traditional principles of equity, in patent disputes no less than in other cases governed by such standards.

Accordingly, we vacate the judgment of the Court of Appeals, and remand for further proceedings consistent with this opinion.

It is so ordered.

CHIEF JUSTICE ROBERTS, with whom JUSTICE SCALIA and JUSTICE GINSBURG join, concurring.

I agree with the Court's holding that "the decision whether to grant or deny injunctive relief rests within the equitable discretion of the district courts, and that such discretion must be exercised consistent with traditional principles of equity, in patent disputes no less than in other cases governed by such standards," *ante,* at 1841, and I join the opinion of the Court. That opinion rightly rests on the proposition that "a major departure from the long tradition of equity practice should not be lightly implied." *Weinberger v. Romero–Barcelo,* 456 U.S. 305, 320, 102 S.Ct. 1798, 72 L.Ed.2d 91 (1982); see *ante,* at 1839.

From at least the early 19th century, courts have granted injunctive relief upon a finding of infringement in the vast majority of patent cases. This "long tradition of equity practice" is not surprising, given the difficulty of protecting a right to *exclude* through monetary remedies that allow an infringer to *use* an invention against the patentee's wishes- a difficulty that often implicates the first two factors of the traditional four-factor test. This historical practice, as the Court holds, does not *entitle* a patentee to a permanent injunction or justify a *general rule* that such injunctions should issue. The Federal Circuit itself so recognized in *Roche Products, Inc. v. Bolar Pharmaceutical Co.,* 733 F.2d 858, 865–867 (1984). At the same time, there is a difference between exercising equitable discretion pursuant to the established four-factor test and writing on an entirely clean slate. "Discretion is not whim, and limiting discretion according to legal standards helps promote the basic principle of justice that like cases should be decided alike." *Martin v. Franklin Capital Corp.,* 546 U.S. 132, ___, 126 S.Ct. 704, 710, 163 L.Ed.2d 547 (2005). When it comes to discerning and applying those standards, in this area as others, "a page of history is worth a volume of logic." *New York Trust Co. v. Eisner,* 256 U.S. 345, 349, 41 S.Ct. 506, 65 L.Ed. 963 (1921) (opinion for the Court by Holmes, J.).

JUSTICE KENNEDY, with whom JUSTICE STEVENS, JUSTICE SOUTER, and JUSTICE BREYER join, concurring.

The Court is correct, in my view, to hold that courts should apply the well-established, four-factor test-without resort to categorical rules- in deciding whether to grant injunctive relief in patent cases. The Chief Justice is also correct that history may be instructive in applying this test. *Ante,* at 1841–1842 (concurring opinion). The traditional practice of issuing injunctions against patent infringers, however, does not seem to rest on "the difficulty of protecting a right to *exclude* through monetary remedies that allow an infringer to *use* an invention against the patentee's wishes." *Ante,* at 1841 (ROBERTS, C.J., concurring). Both the terms of the Patent Act and the traditional view of injunctive relief accept that the existence of a right to exclude does not dictate the remedy for a violation of that right. *Ante,* at 1839–1840 (opinion of the Court). To the extent earlier cases establish a pattern of granting an injunction against patent infringers almost as a matter of course, this pattern simply illustrates the result of the four-factor test in the contexts then prevalent. The lesson of the historical practice, therefore, is most helpful and instructive when the circumstances of a case bear substantial parallels to litigation the courts have confronted before.

In cases now arising trial courts should bear in mind that in many instances the nature of the patent being enforced and the economic function of the patent holder present considerations quite unlike earlier cases. An industry has developed in which firms use patents not as a basis for producing and selling goods but, instead, primarily for obtaining licensing fees. *See* FTC, To Promote Innovation: The Proper Balance of Competition and Patent Law and Policy, ch. 3, pp. 38–39 (Oct.2003), available at http://www.ftc.gov/os/2003/ 10/innovationrpt.pdf (as visited May 11, 2006, and available in Clerk of Court's case file). For these firms, an injunction, and the potentially serious sanctions arising from its violation, can be employed as a bargaining tool to charge exorbitant fees to companies that seek to buy licenses to practice the patent. *See ibid.* When the patented invention is but a small component of the product the companies seek to produce and the threat of an injunction is employed simply for undue leverage in negotiations, legal damages may well be sufficient to compensate for the infringement and an injunction may not serve the public interest. In addition injunctive relief may have different consequences for the burgeoning number of patents over business methods, which were not of much economic and legal significance in earlier times. The potential vagueness and suspect validity of some of these patents may affect the calculus under the four-factor test.

The equitable discretion over injunctions, granted by the Patent Act, is well suited to allow courts to adapt to the rapid technological and legal developments in the patent system. For these reasons it should be recognized that district courts must determine whether past practice fits the circumstances of the cases before them. With these observations, I join the opinion of the Court.

Notes

1.   Compare the majority and concurring opinions in *eBay v. MercExchange.* Do they offer consistent guidance to lower courts?

2.   Under what circumstances would it be appropriate to withhold permanent injunctive relief against a patent infringer?

3.   *eBay v. MercExchange* involved a patent holder which (1) had not practiced or licensed the patent invention, and (2) had probably acquired the patent only for the purpose of suing infringers. Such patent holders are often

referred to as "patent trolls." Under the Court's decision, should the availability of a permanent injunction depend on whether the patent holder is exploiting the patent?

4. How might the decision in *eBay v. MercExchange* influence settlement negotiations between patent holders and alleged infringers?

5. The Patents Depend on Quality Act of 2006, H.R. 5096 (introduced in April of 2006), which was already under consideration when the Court issued its opinion in *eBay v. MercExchange,* would have amended 35 U.S.C. § 283 to provide that:

> In determining equity, the court shall consider the fairness of the remedy in light of all the facts and the relevant interest of the parties associated with the invention. Unless an injunction is entered pursuant to a nonappealable judgment of infringement, a court shall stay the injunction pending an appeal upon an affirmative showing that the stay would not result in irreparable harm to the owner of the patent and that the balance of hardships from the stay does not favor the owner of the patent.

No action was taken on this bill in the 109th Congress. How does this proposed standard for injunctive relief compare with the holding in *eBay v. MercExchange*?

6. Where the term of a patent expires during the infringement litigation, should an injunction be awarded in order to effectively extend the patent term?

7. *Preliminary Injunctions*: In determining when to grant a preliminary injunction (as opposed to a permanent injunction) in a patent infringement proceeding, a court must evaluate: (1) whether the plaintiff has demonstrated a reasonable likelihood of success on the merits, (2) whether irreparable harm will occur if injunctive relief is denied, (3) whether the balance of hardships tips in the plaintiff's favor, and (4) whether issuing an injunction is in the public interest. No one factor is dispositive. *See, e.g., Chrysler Motors Corp. v. Auto Body Panels of Ohio, Inc.,* 908 F.2d 951, 953 (Fed.Cir.1990). In a case where the defendant challenges the validity of the patent in suit, the plaintiff seeking a preliminary injunction cannot rely solely on the statutory presumption of patent validity under Section 282; according to the Federal Circuit, the plaintiff must make a "clear showing" that the defendant's challenge to the patent's validity will fail. *See, e.g., Chrysler Motors,* 908 F.2d at 954; *Atlas Powder Co. v. Ireco Chemicals,* 773 F.2d 1230, 1232–33 (Fed.Cir.1985).

2. MONETARY RELIEF

RITE–HITE CORPORATION v. KELLEY COMPANY, INC.

United States Court of Appeals, Federal Circuit, 1995.
56 F.3d 1538, *cert. denied,* 516 U.S. 867, 116 S.Ct. 184, 133 L.Ed.2d 122 (1995).

LOURIE, CIRCUIT JUDGE.

[Kelley appeals the district court's award of damages for infringement of Rite–Hite's '847 patent for a device (the MDL–55) that secures a vehicle to a loading dock. The district court held that Rite–Hite was entitled to lost profits for lost sales not only of the MDL–55 truck restraint but also of Rite–Hite's ADL–100 truck restraint, an older model which did not incorporate the patented invention but which directly competed with Kelley's infringing "Truk Stop" product, and which incorporated one or more patents other than the '847 patent. Kelley also appeals the court's award of lost profits for lost sales of Rite–Hite's dock levelers, which did not compete directly with Kelley's infringing device but which were often sold in a package with the ADL–100 and MDL–55 devices. Kelley argues that the patent statute does not provide for damages for lost sales of products not covered by the patent in suit.]

* * *

I.   Lost Profits on the ADL–100 Restraints

The district court's decision to award lost profits damages pursuant to 35 U.S.C. § 284 turned primarily upon the quality of Rite–Hite's proof of actual lost profits. The court found that, "but for" Kelley's infringing Truk Stop competition, Rite–Hite would have sold 3,243 additional ADL–100 restraints and 80 additional MDL–55 restraints. The court reasoned that awarding lost profits fulfilled the patent statute's goal of affording complete compensation for infringement and compensated Rite–Hite for the ADL–100 sales that Kelley "anticipated taking from Rite–Hite when it marketed the Truk Stop against the ADL–100." *Rite–Hite,* 774 F.Supp. at 1540. The court stated, "the rule applied here therefore does not extend Rite–Hite's patent rights excessively, because Kelley could reasonably have foreseen that its infringement of the '847 patent would make it liable for lost ADL–100 sales in addition to lost MDL–55 sales." *Id.* The court further reasoned that its decision would avoid what it referred to as the "whip-saw" problem, whereby an infringer could avoid paying lost profits damages altogether by developing a device using a first patented technology to compete with a device that uses a second patented technology and developing a device using the second patented technology to compete with a device that uses the first patented technology.

Kelley maintains that Rite–Hite's lost sales of the ADL–100 restraints do not constitute an injury that is legally compensable by means of lost profits. It has uniformly been the law, Kelley argues, that to recover damages in the form of lost profits a patentee must prove that, "but for" the infringement, it would have sold a product covered by the patent in suit to the customers who bought from the infringer. Under the circumstances of this case, in Kelley's view, the patent statute provides only for damages calculated as a reasonable royalty. Rite–Hite, on the other hand, argues that the only restriction on an award of actual lost profits damages for patent infringement is proof of causation-in-fact. A patentee, in its view, is entitled to all the profits it would have made on any of its products "but for" the infringement. Each party argues that a judgment in favor of the other would frustrate the purposes of the patent statute. Whether the lost profits at issue are legally compensable is a question of law, which we review de novo.

Our analysis of this question necessarily begins with the patent statute. *See* General Motors Corp. v. Devex Corp., 461 U.S. 648, 653–54, 76 L. Ed. 2d 211, 103 S. Ct. 2058 (1983). Implementing the constitutional power under Article I, section 8, to secure to inventors the exclusive right to their discoveries, Congress has provided in 35 U.S.C. § 284 as follows:

> Upon finding for the claimant the court shall award the claimant damages adequate to compensate for the infringement, but in no event less than a reasonable royalty for the use made of the invention by the infringer, together with interest and costs as fixed by the court.

35 U.S.C. § 284 (1988). The statute thus mandates that a claimant receive damages "adequate" to compensate for infringement. Section 284 further instructs that a damage award shall be "in no event less than a reasonable royalty"; the purpose of this alternative is not to direct the form of compensation, but to set a floor below which damage awards may not fall. Del Mar Avionics, Inc. v. Quinton Instrument Co., 836 F.2d 1320, 1326 (Fed.Cir.1987). Thus, the language of the statute is expansive rather than limiting. It affirmatively states that damages must be adequate, while providing only a lower limit and no other limitation.

The Supreme Court spoke to the question of patent damages in *General Motors*, stating that, in enacting § 284, Congress sought to "ensure that the patent owner would in fact receive full compensation for 'any damages' [the patentee] suffered as a result of the infringement." *General Motors*, 461 U.S. at 654; *see also* H.R. Rep. No. 1587, 79th Cong., 2d Sess., 1 (1946) (the Bill was intended to allow recovery of "any damages the complainant can prove"); S. Rep. No. 1503, 79th Cong., 2d Sess., 2 (1946) (same). Thus, while the statutory text states tersely that the patentee receive "adequate" damages, the Supreme Court has interpreted this to mean that "adequate" damages should approximate those damages that will fully compensate the patentee for infringement. Further, the Court has cautioned against imposing limitations on patent infringement damages, stating: "When Congress wished to limit an element of recovery in a patent infringement action, it said so explicitly." *General Motors*, 461 U.S. at 653 (refusing to impose limitation on court's authority to award interest).

In Aro Mfg. Co. v. Convertible Top Replacement Co., 377 U.S. 476, 141 U.S.P.Q. (BNA) 681, 12 L. Ed. 2d 457, 84 S. Ct. 1526 (1964), the Court discussed the statutory standard for measuring patent infringement damages, explaining:

> The question to be asked in determining damages is "how much had the Patent Holder and Licensee suffered by the infringement. And that question [is] primarily: had the Infringer not infringed, what would the Patentee Holder–Licensee have made?"

377 U.S. at 507 (plurality opinion) (citations omitted). This surely states a "but for" test. In accordance with the Court's guidance, we have held that the general rule for determining actual damages to a patentee that is itself producing the patented item is to determine the sales and profits lost to the patentee because of the infringement. *Del Mar,* 836 F.2d at 1326; *see* State Indus., Inc. v. Mor–Flo Indus., Inc., 883 F.2d 1573, 1577 (Fed.Cir.1989), *cert. denied,* 493 U.S. 1022 (1990) (award of damages may be split between lost profits as actual damages to the extent they are proven and a reasonable royalty for the remainder). To recover lost profits damages, the patentee must show a reasonable probability that, "but for" the infringement, it would have made the sales that were made by the infringer. *Id.*; King Instrument Corp. v. Otari Corp., 767 F.2d 853, 863 (Fed.Cir.1985), *cert. denied,* 475 U.S. 1016, 89 L. Ed. 2d 312, 106 S. Ct. 1197 (1986).

Panduit Corp. v. Stahlin Bros. Fibre Works, Inc., 575 F.2d 1152 (6th Cir.1978), articulated a four-factor test that has since been accepted as a useful, but non-exclusive, way for a patentee to prove entitlement to lost profits damages. *State Indus.,* 883 F.2d at 1577. The *Panduit* test requires that a patentee establish: (1) demand for the patented product; (2) absence of acceptable non-infringing substitutes; (3) manufacturing and marketing capability to exploit the demand; and (4) the amount of the profit it would have made. *Panduit,* 575 F.2d at 1156. A showing under *Panduit* permits a court to reasonably infer that the lost profits claimed were in fact caused by the infringing sales, thus establishing a patentee's prima facie case with respect to "but for" causation. Kaufman Co. v. Lantech, Inc., 926 F.2d 1136, 1141 (Fed.Cir.1991). A patentee need not negate every possibility that the purchaser might not have purchased a product other than its own, absent the infringement. *Id.* The patentee need only show that there was a reasonable probability that the sales would have been made "but for" the infringement. *Id.* When the patentee establishes the reasonableness of this inference, *e.g.,* by satisfying the *Panduit* test, it has sustained the burden of proving entitlement to lost profits due to the infringing sales. *Id.* at 1141. The burden then shifts to the infringer to show that the inference is unreasonable for some or all of the lost sales. *Id.*

Applying *Panduit*, the district court found that Rite–Hite had established "but for" causation. In the court's view, this was sufficient to prove entitlement to lost profits damages on the ADL–100. Kelley does not challenge that Rite–Hite meets the *Panduit* test and therefore has proven "but for" causation; rather, Kelley argues that damages for the ADL–100, even if in fact caused by the infringement, are not legally compensable because the ADL–100 is not covered by the patent in suit.

Preliminarily, we wish to affirm that the "test" for compensability of damages under § 284 is not solely a "but for" test in the sense that an infringer must compensate a patentee for any and all damages that proceed from the act of patent infringement. Notwithstanding the broad language of § 284, judicial relief cannot redress every conceivable harm that can be traced to an alleged wrongdoing. *See* Associated General

Contractors, Inc. v. California State Council of Carpenters, 459 U.S. 519, 536, 74 L. Ed. 2d 723, 103 S. Ct. 897 (1983). For example, remote consequences, such as a heart attack of the inventor or loss in value of shares of common stock of a patentee corporation caused indirectly by infringement are not compensable. Thus, along with establishing that a particular injury suffered by a patentee is a "but for" consequence of infringement, there may also be a background question whether the asserted injury is of the type for which the patentee may be compensated.

* * *

We believe that under § 284 of the patent statute, the balance between full compensation, which is the meaning that the Supreme Court has attributed to the statute, and the reasonable limits of liability encompassed by general principles of law can best be viewed in terms of reasonable, objective foreseeability. If a particular injury was or should have been reasonably foreseeable by an infringing competitor in the relevant market, broadly defined, that injury is generally compensable absent a persuasive reason to the contrary. Here, the court determined that Rite–Hite's lost sales of the ADL–100, a product that directly competed with the infringing product, were reasonably foreseeable. We agree with that conclusion. Being responsible for lost sales of a competitive product is surely foreseeable; such losses constitute the full compensation set forth by Congress, as interpreted by the Supreme Court, while staying well within the traditional meaning of proximate cause. Such lost sales should therefore clearly be compensable.

Recovery for lost sales of a device not covered by the patent in suit is not of course expressly provided for by the patent statute. Express language is not required, however. Statutes speak in general terms rather than specifically expressing every detail. Under the patent statute, damages should be awarded "where necessary to afford the plaintiff full compensation for the infringement." *General Motors,* 461 U.S. at 654. Thus, to refuse to award reasonably foreseeable damages necessary to make Rite–Hite whole would be inconsistent with the meaning of § 284.

* * *

Kelley further asserts that, as a policy matter, inventors should be encouraged by the law to practice their inventions. This is not a meaningful or persuasive argument, at least in this context. A patent is granted in exchange for a patentee's disclosure of an invention, not for the patentee's use of the invention. There is no requirement in this country that a patentee make, use, or sell its patented invention. *See* Continental Paper Bag Co. v. Eastern Paper Bag Co., 210 U.S. 405, 424–30, 52 L. Ed. 1122, 28 S. Ct. 748 (1908) (irrespective of a patentee's own use of its patented invention, it may enforce its rights under the patent). If a patentee's failure to practice a patented invention frustrates an important public need for the invention, a court need not enjoin infringement of the patent. *See* 35 U.S.C. § 283 (1988) (courts may grant injunctions in accordance with the principles of equity). Accordingly, courts have in rare instances exercised their discretion to deny injunctive relief in order to protect the public interest. *See, e.g.,* Hybritech Inc. v. Abbott Lab., 4 U.S.P.Q.2D (BNA) 1001 (C.D.Cal.1987) (public interest required that injunction not stop supply of medical test kits that the patentee itself was not marketing), *aff'd,* 849 F.2d 1446 (Fed.Cir.1988); Vitamin Technologists, Inc. v. Wisconsin Alumni Research Found., 64 U.S.P.Q. (BNA) 285 (9th Cir.1944) (public interest warranted refusal of injunction on irradiation of oleomargarine); City of Milwaukee v. Activated Sludge, Inc., 21 U.S.P.Q. (BNA) 69 (7th Cir.1934) (injunction refused against city operation of sewage disposal plant because of public health danger). Whether a patentee sells its patented invention is not crucial in determining lost profits damages. Normally, if the patentee is not selling a product, by definition there can be no lost profits. However, in this case, Rite–Hite did sell its own patented products, the MDL–55 and the ADL–100 restraints.

Kelley next argues that to award lost profits damages on Rite–Hite's ADL–100s would be contrary to precedent. Citing *Panduit,* Kelley argues that case law regarding lost profits uniformly requires that "the intrinsic value of the patent in suit is the only proper basis for a lost profits award." Kelley argues that each prong of the Panduit test focuses on the patented invention; thus, Kelley asserts, Rite–Hite cannot obtain damages consisting of lost profits on a product that is not the patented invention.

Generally, the *Panduit* test has been applied when a patentee is seeking lost profits for a device covered by the patent in suit. However, *Panduit* is not the sine qua non for proving "but for" causation. If there are other ways to show that the infringement in fact caused the patentee's lost profits, there is no reason why another test should not be acceptable. Moreover, other fact situations may require different means of evaluation, and failure to meet the *Panduit* test does not ipso facto disqualify a loss from being compensable.

In any event, the only *Panduit* factor that arguably was not met in the present fact situation is the second one, absence of acceptable non-infringing substitutes. Establishment of this factor tends to prove that the patentee would not have lost the sales to a non-infringing third party rather than to the infringer. That, however, goes only to the question of proof. Here, the only substitute for the patented device was the ADL–100, another of the patentee's devices. Such a substitute was not an "acceptable, non-infringing substitute" within the meaning of *Panduit* because, being patented by Rite–Hite, it was not available to customers except from Rite–Hite. *Cf. State Indus.,* 883 F.2d at 1578. Rite–Hite therefore would not have lost the sales to a third party. The second *Panduit* factor thus has been met. If, on the other hand, the ADL–100 had not been patented and was found to be an acceptable substitute, that would have been a different story, and Rite–Hite would have had to prove that its customers would not have obtained the ADL–100 from a third party in order to prove the second factor of *Panduit*.

Kelley's conclusion that the lost sales must be of the patented invention thus is not supported. Kelley's concern that lost profits must relate to the "intrinsic value of the patent" is subsumed in the "but for" analysis; if the patent infringement had nothing to do with the lost sales, "but for" causation would not have been proven. However, "but for" causation is conceded here. The motive, or motivation, for the infringement is irrelevant if it is proved that the infringement in fact caused the loss. We see no basis for Kelley's conclusion that the lost sales must be of products covered by the infringed patent.

Kelley has thus not provided, nor do we find, any justification in the statute, precedent, policy, or logic to limit the compensability of lost sales of a patentee's device that directly competes with the infringing device if it is proven that those lost sales were caused in fact by the infringement. Such lost sales are reasonably foreseeable and the award of damages is necessary to provide adequate compensation for infringement under 35 U.S.C. § 284. Thus, Rite–Hite's ADL–100 lost sales are legally compensable and we affirm the award of lost profits on the 3,283 sales lost to Rite–Hite's wholesale business in ADL–100 restraints.

II. Damages on the Dock Levelers

Based on the "entire market value rule," the district court awarded lost profits on 1,692 dock levelers that it found Rite–Hite would have sold with the ADL–100 and MDL–55 restraints. Kelley argues that this award must be set aside because Rite–Hite failed to establish that the dock levelers were eligible to be included in the damage computation under the entire market value rule. We agree.

When a patentee seeks damages on unpatented components sold with a patented apparatus, courts have applied a formulation known as the "entire market value rule" to determine whether such components should be included in the damage computation, whether for reasonable royalty purposes, *see* Leesona Corp. v. United States, 220 Ct. Cl. 234, 599 F.2d 958, 974 (Ct. Cl.), *cert. denied,* 444 U.S. 991, 62 L. Ed. 2d 420, 100 S. Ct. 522 (1979), or for lost profits purposes, *see* Paper Converting Machine Co. v. Magna–Graphics Corp., 745 F.2d 11, 23 (Fed.Cir.1984). Early cases invoking the entire market value rule required that for a patentee owning an "improvement patent" to recover damages calculated on sales of a larger machine incorporating that improvement, the patentee was required to show that the entire value of the whole machine, as a marketable article, was "properly and legally attributable" to the patented feature. *See* Garretson v. Clark, 111 U.S. 120, 121, 28 L. Ed. 371, 4 S. Ct. 291 (1884); Westinghouse Elec. & Mfg. Co. v. Wagner Elec. & Mfg. Co., 225 U.S. 604, 615, 56 L. Ed. 1222, 32 S. Ct. 691 (1912). Subsequently, our predecessor court held that damages for component parts used with a patented apparatus were recoverable under the entire market value rule if the patented apparatus "was of such paramount importance that it substantially created the value of the component parts." Marconi Wireless Telegraph Co. v. United States, 99 Ct.Cl. 1, 53 U.S.P.Q. (BNA) 246, 250 (Ct. Cl. 1942), *aff'd in part and vacated in part,* 320 U.S. 1 (1943). We have held that the entire market value rule permits recovery of damages based on the value of a patentee's entire apparatus containing several features when the patent-related feature is the "basis for customer demand." *State Indus.,* 883 F.2d at 1580; TWM Mfg. Co. v. Dura Corp., 789 F.2d 895, 900–01 (Fed.Cir.), *cert. denied,* 479 U.S. 852, 93 L. Ed. 2d 117, 107 S. Ct. 183 (1986).

The entire market value rule has typically been applied to include in the compensation base unpatented components of a device when the unpatented and patented components are physically part of the same machine. *See, e.g.,* Western Elec. Co. v. Stewart–Warner Corp., 631 F.2d 333 (4th Cir.1980), *cert. denied,* 450 U.S. 971, 67 L. Ed. 2d 622, 101 S. Ct. 1492 (1981). The rule has been extended to allow inclusion of physically separate unpatented components normally sold with the patented components. *See, e.g., Paper Converting,* 745 F.2d at 23. However, in such cases, the unpatented and patented components together were considered to be components of a single assembly or parts of a complete machine, or they together constituted a functional unit. *See, e.g.,* Velo–Bind, Inc. v. Minnesota Mining & Mfg. Co., 647 F.2d 965 (9th Cir.), *cert. denied,* 454 U.S. 1093, 70 L. Ed. 2d 631, 102 S. Ct. 658 (1981).

* * *

Thus, the facts of past cases clearly imply a limitation on damages, when recovery is sought on sales of unpatented components sold with patented components, to the effect that the unpatented components must function together with the patented component in some manner so as to produce a desired end product or result. All the components together must be analogous to components of a single assembly or be parts of a complete machine, or they must constitute a functional unit. Our precedent has not extended liability to include items that have essentially no functional relationship to the patented invention and that may have been sold with an infringing device only as a matter of convenience or business advantage. We are not persuaded that we should extend that liability. Damages on such items would constitute more than what is "adequate to compensate for the infringement."

The facts of this case do not meet this requirement. The dock levelers operated to bridge the gap between a loading dock and a truck. The patented vehicle restraint operated to secure the rear of the truck to the loading dock. Although the two devices may have been used together, they did not function together to achieve one result and each could effectively have been used independently of each other. The parties had established positions in marketing dock levelers long prior to developing the vehicle restraints. Rite–Hite and Kelley were pioneers in that industry and for many years were primary competitors. Although following Rite–Hite's introduction of its restraints onto the market, customers frequently solicited package bids for the simultaneous installation of restraints and dock levelers, they did so because such bids facilitated contracting and construction scheduling, and because both Rite–Hite and Kelley encouraged this linkage by offering combination discounts. The dock levelers were thus sold by Kelley with the restraints only for marketing reasons, not because they essentially functioned together. We distinguish our conclusion to permit damages based on lost sales of the unpatented (not covered by the patent in suit) ADL–100 devices, but not on lost sales of the unpatented dock levelers, by emphasizing that the Kelley Truk Stops were devices competitive with the ADL–100s, whereas the dock levelers were merely items sold together with the restraints for convenience and business advantage. It is a clear purpose of the patent law to redress competitive damages resulting from infringement of the patent, but there is no basis for extending that recovery to include damages for items that are neither competitive with nor function with the patented invention. Promotion of the useful arts, *see* U.S. Const., art. I, § 8, cl. 8, requires one, but not the other. These facts do not establish the functional relationship necessary to justify recovery under the entire market value rule. Therefore, the district court erred as a matter of law in including them within the compensation base. Accordingly, we vacate the court's award of damages based on the dock leveler sales.

* * *

Notes

1. In *Juicy Whip, Inc. v. Orange Bang, Inc.*, 382 F.3d 1367 (Fed. Cir. 2004), the Federal Circuit applied the "entire market value rule" to hold that Juicy Whip's damages for infringement of its patented beverage dispenser could include lost sales of the unpatented syrup products that were sold for use in the dispenser. The dispenser's patented design included a transparent bowl which made it appear that the beverage was pre-mixed, when in fact the syrup and water were in separate vessels and were not mixed until the beverage was dispensed. The court held that *Rite-Hite*'s "functional unit" test was satisfied even though the patentee's dispenser and syrups were sold separately and other syrups could be used in the dispenser. The court explained:

> In the present case, the district court held that Juicy Whip's patented dispenser and the syrup did not share a functional relationship because the dispenser had been sold separately from the syrup on occasion and because other syrups could be used in Juicy Whip's dispenser. Furthermore, the court stated that the two items were sold together "only as a matter of convenience or business advantage." While Orange Bang maintains that Juicy Whip's claim for lost profits failed for lack of persuasive evidence, it is clear from the district court's opinion that such evidence was excluded because of its belief that no functional relationship existed between the patented dispenser and the syrup. We disagree with the district court in its analysis.

> The dispenser and the syrup are in fact analogous to parts of a single assembly or a complete machine, as the syrup functions together with

the dispenser to produce the visual appearance that is central to Juicy Whip's '405 patent. Despite some limited interchangeability—other syrups may be used in Juicy Whip's dispenser and, likewise, other dispensers could use Juicy Whip's syrups—the two items do "function together to achieve one result," *Rite-Hite,* 56 F.3d at 1551. The dispenser needs syrup and the syrup is mixed in a dispenser. Such is indeed a functional relationship, and a functional relationship between a patented device and an unpatented material used with it is not precluded by the fact that the device can be used with other materials or that the unpatented material can be used with other devices. We therefore conclude that the district court erred as a matter of law by denying Juicy Whip the opportunity to present to the jury evidence for its theory of lost profits on lost syrup sales. . . .

382 F.3d at 1372–73 (citation omitted). Do you agree with the court's finding of a "functional relationship"?

2. In *King Instruments Corp. v. Perego,* 65 F.3d 941 (Fed.Cir.1995), *cert. denied,* 517 U.S. 1188, 116 S.Ct. 1675, 134 L.Ed.2d 778 (1996), the Federal Circuit extended the reasoning of *Rite-Hite* to award lost profits where the defendant's infringing product competed *only* with the patentee's unpatented product, because the patentee had opted not to exploit its patented invention at all:

> The 1952 Act, § 154, clarified that a patent empowered its owner "to *exclude others* from making, using, or selling" the invention. 35 U.S.C. § 154 (1952) (emphasis added). The 1952 amendment should have corrected any mistaken belief that patent rights somehow hinged upon the patentee's exploitation of the invention. Inventors possess the natural right to exploit their inventions (subject to the patent rights of others in a dominant patent) apart from any Government grant. Therefore, patent rights do not depend upon the exercise of rights already in the patentee's possession. Thus, the 1952 Act clarified that a patent confers the right to exclude others from exploiting an invention. It does not confer the right to exploit the invention already possessed by the inventor.

> This understanding of the right protected by section 284 informs the purpose and scope of the damages provision. Section 284 protects the right to exclude others from exploiting an invention. To invoke that protection, a patentee need not have exercised its natural right to itself make, use, or sell the invention. The damages section, section 284, protects the right to exclude, not the right to exploit. A patentee qualifies for damages adequate to compensate for infringement without exploiting its patent.

* * *

> The potential for increasing the complexity of patent litigation is especially disturbing. The inventor would have to prove that its own product falls under the patent. Infringers would escape lost profits and acquire a mandatory license by showing the inventor's product is not within the claims. The length, cost, and complexity of an infringement trial would conceivably double. The damages phase of a trial would feature an entire

new issue of "reverse infringement." The inventor would have to show that the patent's claims read on the inventor's own product, while the infringer would try to show they do not. Once again, as a precondition for lost profits, the parties would parse the claims and call on experts to apply the claim language to an unaccused device.

The language of the 1952 Act did not contemplate creation of an entire new issue of "reverse infringement." The language of the Patent Act recognizes that the value of a claim to the patentee, and the extent of harm from infringement, do not depend on whether the patentee markets the claimed device. To adequately compensate for infringement of the right to exclude, as section 284 requires, "damages" includes lost profits on competing products not covered by the infringed claims.

* * *

65 F.3d at 949–52.

3. As noted in *Rite-Hite*, the *Panduit* test is not the exclusive test of lost profits. Lost profits may be awarded in any situation where the patentee establishes that the infringement caused economic harm. For example, even if the patentee does not establish that particular sales were lost to the infringer, lost profits may be awarded where the infringer's competition forces the patentee to lower its prices or forego a price increase. In a case where the second *Panduit* factor is not satisfied—for example, where a third party offers acceptable noninfringing substitutes—lost profits may be established by showing that the infringement caused a drop in the patentee's market share.

4. *Reasonable royalty*: Even where a patentee cannot prove lost profits due to infringement (for example, where the patentee does not sell a competing product, or where the defendant's customers might have purchased noninfringing substitute goods if the infringing goods had not been offered), under Section 284 courts must still award the patentee, at a minimum, a reasonable royalty on sales of the infringing goods. A reasonable royalty may be determined by examining existing licensing agreements or by considering a hypothetical negotiation between the patentee and a potential licensee.

(a) Would it be appropriate for a district court to increase a reasonable royalty award by an amount reflecting the patentee's litigation expenses?

(b) Could a reasonable royalty award ever exceed the infringer's net profits from sales of the infringing item? Could it ever exceed the patentee's lost profits (assuming that the patentee could demonstrate lost profits)?

(c) On the facts of *Rite-Hite*, should the lost sales of dock levelers have any relevance in the reasonable royalty calculation?

The failed Patent Reform Act of 2005, H.R. 2795, would have amended Section 284 to require courts, in determining a reasonable royalty, to consider how much of the value of an accused combination derives from the inventive elements and how much derives from other features of the combination, the manufacturing process, business risks, or significant features or improvements added by the infringer. The proposed Patent Reform Act of 2007 contains a similar provision.

5. *Marking*: Section 287(a) imposes a duty to mark patented articles; if the patentee does not satisfy the marking requirement, then damages may be recovered only for infringements that occur after the infringer receives notice of the infringement (a requirement which may be satisfied by filing the infringement suit).

"[O]nce marking has begun, it must be substantially consistent and continuous in order for the party to avail itself of the constructive notice provisions of the statute." *American Medical Sys., Inc. v. Medical Eng'g Corp.*, 6 F.3d 1523, 1537 (Fed.Cir.1993), *cert. denied*, 511 U.S. 1070, 114 S.Ct. 1647, 128 L.Ed.2d 366 (1994). In *Maxwell v. J. Baker, Inc.*, 86 F.3d 1098 (Fed.Cir.1996), the Federal Circuit applied a "rule of reason" test to determine whether a third party's failure to mark should affect the patentee's damages entitlement:

> When the failure to mark is caused by someone other than the patentee, the court may consider whether the patentee made reasonable efforts to ensure compliance with the marking requirements. The rule of reason is consistent with the purpose of the constructive notice provision—to encourage patentees to mark their products in order to provide notice to the public of the existence of the patent and to prevent innocent infringement.

86 F.3d at 1111–12 (citing *American Medical*, 6 F.3d at 1538).

The marking requirement does not guarantee that a particular defendant encounters the marked article (for example, where the defendant independently produces the same invention or acquires the infringing article without knowledge that it is infringing). Is it fair to hold a defendant liable in damages for use or sale of an infringing article without knowledge that it infringes?

Is the marking prerequisite inconsistent with the holding of *Rite-Hite* that lost profits may be awarded even where the patentee has not exploited the infringed patent?

Penalties for false marking are set forth in Section 292. Although case law interpreting this statute is sparse, in *Clontech Labs., Inc. v. Invitrogen Corp.*, 406 F.3d 1347 (Fed. Cir. 2005), the Federal Circuit clarified that false marking is not a strict liability offense, and that liability under the statute requires a showing of intent to deceive the public. Such intent must be proved by a preponderance of the evidence.

6. *Time Limit on Damages Awards*: Section 286 bars damages awards for infringements occurring more than six years before commencement of the infringement suit. In determining whether the six–year time limit for damages awards has expired in a case of contributory infringement, should the determinative date be that of the direct infringement or the action constituting contributory infringement?

7. Where a patentee sues both a direct and a contributory infringer on the same underlying infringement, how should a monetary settlement or damages award from one infringer affect the liability of, and/or amount recoverable from, the other infringer? Consider the same question where one infringer makes, and the other sells, the infringing article.

8. Section 284 authorizes enhanced damages, up to a total of three times the plaintiff's actual damages, and Section 285 permits courts in "exceptional cases" to award attorneys' fees to prevailing infringement litigants. In general, both awards are limited to cases of willful infringement or bad faith litigation.

9. Although not mandatory, prejudgment interest is normally awarded in order to ensure that the total damages award satisfies Section 284. However, courts have held that it is not appropriate to award prejudgment interest on enhanced damages.

10. *Remedies for Infringement by United States*: Under 28 U.S.C.A. § 1498, an infringement plaintiff may not obtain an injunction against unauthorized use or manufacture of the patented invention "by or for the United States" (including use or manufacture by a government contractor or subcontractor "with the authorization or consent" of the government). The plaintiff's remedies are limited to a suit for "reasonable and entire compensation" in the United States Court of Federal Claims. Under a new rule enacted in 1996, independent inventors, nonprofit organizations and companies with fewer than 500 employees may collect expert witness and attorney fees unless the defendant's position is "substantially justified" or such an award would be unjust, but these exceptions do not apply if the case has been pending more than 10 years. Pub. L. No. 104–308 (1996) (amending 28 U.S.C.A. § 1498(a)).

In *Zoltek Corp. v. United States*, 442 F.3d 1345, 1350 (Fed. Cir. 2006), the Federal Circuit held that the United States is not liable under 28 U.S.C. § 1498(a) for its unauthorized use of a method patent unless it practices every step of the claimed process within the United States. The court relied on its prior holding in *NTP, Inc. v. Research in Motion, Ltd.*, 418 F.3d 1282 (Fed. Cir. 2005), that "direct infringement under section 271(a) is a necessary predicate for government liability under section 1498," 418 F.3d at 1316, and that "a process cannot be used 'within' the United States as required by section 271(a) unless each of the steps is performed within this country," *id.* at 1318. The *Zoltek* court also rejected the patent holder's argument that the United States' unauthorized use of its patent constituting a "taking" in violation of the Fifth Amendment. 442 F.3d at 1351–53.

11. *Remedies for Infringement of Design or Plant Patents*: The same remedial provisions which apply to utility patents apply equally to plant patents. Those same remedies apply also to design patents. In addition, however, the design patentee may recover the infringer's total profit, with a minimum award of $250. 35 U.S.C.A. § 289.

12. *Remedies under the Plant Variety Protection Act*: The remedial rules of the PVPA closely parallel those of the patent statutes, including a six-year time limit on damages awards, a requirement of actual notice as a prerequisite to damages where the certificate holder has not complied with the PVPA's marking provisions, and a prohibition against false marking. *See* 7 U.S.C.A. §§ 2561–68.

13. *Section 337 Proceedings*: In a case involving importation of infringing goods into the United States, an additional remedy may be obtained in a Section 337 proceeding before the U.S. International Trade Commission. Authorized by the Tariff Act of 1930, 19 U.S.C.A. § 1337 (as amended by the

URAA in 1994), Section 337 relief may be pursued in place of, or in addition to, an infringement action in district court. Where infringement is found, the ITC is empowered to issue an exclusion order instructing the U.S. Customs Service to prevent the infringing goods from entering the country.

Note: Willful Infringement

Overruling its own precedent to the contrary, in *Knorr–Bremse Systeme Fuer Nutzfahrzeuge GmbH v. Dana Corp.*, 383 F.3d 1337 (Fed. Cir. 2004) (en banc), the Federal Circuit held that neither a defendant's failure to seek legal advice regarding a potential infringement, nor a defendant's invocation of attorney-client privilege or work-product privilege with respect to any such legal advice, should give rise to the inference that such legal advice was, or would have been, unfavorable. Under prior law, such an inference could provide one basis for a finding of bad faith.

In *Golden Blount, Inc. v. Robert H. Peterson Co.*, 438 F.3d 1354 (Fed. Cir. 2006), the Federal Circuit held that *Knorr-Bremse* does not prevent a patent owner from proving willful infringement by challenging the competence of opinions of counsel when the attorney-privilege is not asserted. Affirming an award of treble damages and attorneys' fees for willful patent infringement, the appellate court held that when an accused infringer voluntarily submits opinions of counsel as a defense to willful infringement, the district court may consider the competence of those opinions without violating *Knorr-Bremse*'s prohibition against drawing an adverse inference from the defendant's failure to obtain or produce an exculpatory opinion of counsel.

The Patents Depend on Quality Act of 2006 (PDQA), H.R. 5096, which was introduced but not enacted in the 109th Congress, would have amended Section 284 to limit the availability of enhanced damages for willful infringement. Specifically, the bill would have redesignated the three paragraphs of Section 284 as subsections (a), (b), and (c), and would have amended the second paragraph (redesignated as subsection (b)) to provide as follows:

"(b) WILLFUL INFRINGEMENT.—

"(1) INCREASED DAMAGES.—A court that has determined that the infringer has willfully infringed a patent or patents may increase the damages up to three times the amount of damages found or assessed under subsection (a), except that increased damages under this paragraph shall not apply to provisional rights under section 154(d) of this title.

"(2) PERMITTED GROUNDS FOR WILLFULNESS.—A court may find that an infringer has willfully infringed a patent only if the patent owner presents clear and convincing evidence that—

"(A) after receiving written notice from the patentee—

"(i) alleging acts of infringement in a manner sufficient to give the infringer an objectively reasonable apprehension of suit on such patent, and

"(ii) identifying with particularity each claim of the patent, each product or process that the patent owner alleges infringes the patent, and the relationship of such product or process to such claim,

the infringer, after a reasonable opportunity to investigate, thereafter performed one or more of the alleged acts of infringement;

"(B) the infringer intentionally copied the patented invention with knowledge that it was patented; or

"(C) after having been found by a court to have infringed that patent, the infringer engaged in conduct that was not colorably different from the conduct previously found to have infringed the patent, and which resulted in a separate finding of infringement of the same patent.

"(3) LIMITATIONS ON WILLFULNESS.—(A) A court shall not find that an infringer has willfully infringed a patent under paragraph (2) for any period of time during which the infringer had an informed good faith belief that the patent was invalid or unenforceable, or would not be infringed by the conduct later shown to constitute infringement of the patent.

"(B) An informed good faith belief within the meaning of subparagraph (A) may be established by reasonable reliance on advice of counsel.

"(C) The decision of the infringer not to present evidence of advice of counsel shall have no relevance to a determination of willful infringement under paragraph (2).

"(4) LIMITATION ON PLEADING.—Before the date on which a determination has been made that the patent in suit is not invalid, is enforceable, and has been infringed by the infringer, a patentee may not plead, and a court may not determine, that an infringer has willfully infringed the patent. The court's determination of an infringer's willfulness shall be made without a jury."

These provisions of the PDQA were partly a response to certain abusive practices in which patent owners send vague letters to third parties stating that the third parties are infringing a patent, and offering to license the patent for a fee. These letters often fail to identify the patent allegedly being infringed, but a recipient that ignores such a letter may become liable for treble damages on the ground of willful infringement under the existing version of Section 284.

A similar provision is included in the proposed Patent Reform Act of 2007.

Part VII

COPYRIGHT LAW

Chapter 15

INTRODUCTION AND A SHORT HISTORY

Copyright law in the United States grants limited exclusive exploitation rights to the authors of a wide variety of expressive and creative works. Though some rights (sometimes called "common law copyright", or the right of first publication) can arise under state law, most forms of copyright today are governed by federal law. Under current federal law, when an original work of authorship eligible for copyright (such as a novel) is fixed in a tangible medium of embodiment (such as a written manuscript or book), its author automatically enjoys the exclusive rights available to that category of work under the copyright statute. Rights can vary somewhat by categories, as we will see. For example, musical compositions carry performance rights that are unavailable to many sound recordings. What this means is that the DJ who plays a recording of a song at a rave needs a license to play the song itself but not to play the recording of the song. In this sense (and many others) copyright can seem wonderfully complex. And yet there is a certain simplicity to the subject as well. In contrast to a patent, for example, no formalities are required to obtain a copyright, and the examination process that leads to a registration is relatively uncomplicated; the scope and duration of the exclusive rights in copyright differ significantly from patent rights as well.

As the following short history reveals, Anglo–American copyright law began as a response to revolutionary changes in the instruments and practices of authorship and expression: notably, first, in the introduction of the printing press into late fifteenth century England; and then, some two centuries later, in the insistence of the English Parliament upon cessation of the licensing system that had enabled the Tudor monarchs to control dissent by controlling the press. Copyright law has been struggling to keep pace with developments in technology and with evolving understandings of freedom of expression ever since.

A. ENGLISH LAW

Our federal copyright law owes its origins to the copyright laws of England. Until 1709, copyright as such did not exist in England, and certainly not in statutory form, although the English common law was credited somewhat later with having previously recognized the right of authors to prevent the publication of their unpublished manuscripts. Once copies of a work were circulated to the public, however, the author's common law right was exhausted. Thanks to the invention of the printing press, which made it possible to copy works cheaply and quickly, a loss of exclusive rights upon publication would mean that after its initial publication a work could be mass produced without generating any financial return to its author or publisher.

The press itself is said to have been brought to England from Mainz, Germany, in 1476 by William Caxton, perhaps acting upon the authority of a Royal Warrant issued by Edward IV. Caxton established the press at Westminster Abbey under "The Sign of the Red Pale" (still there to this very day along the exterior wall to the right, above the transept), where for a number of years (which saw, among other published works, the appearance of the celebrated Caxton edition of Malory's *Le Morte d'Arthur*) he operated without effective oversight or legal constraint. The succession of the Tudors to the English Crown would change that. In 1529, Henry VIII promulgated an *Index Librorum Prohibitum* (or list of proscribed works), an effort to consolidate his role as head of the newly-established Anglican Catholic Church. By 1556 the Crown had subjected all printing to royal control, this through an evolving system of Warrants, Charters and Monopolies. Eventually the privilege of printing was granted exclusively to a group of publishers known as the Stationers' Company. Any member of the Company wishing to publish a work was required to register it with the Company itself, and upon doing so received in return the exclusive right to publish that work in perpetuity. But these Crown-sponsored privileges and monopolies were repressive and even brutal in practice (the infamous Star Chamber was but one of many instruments of suppression that grew out of these on-going efforts to control the press), and over time the system grew to be much despised. At last, in 1694, in a time of revolutionary fervor and dissent, Parliament allowed the final English Printing Act to expire.[1]

When the restrictions on printing ended at the end of the seventeenth century, members of the Stationers' Company discovered that this newfound freedom of the press had also cost them their exclusive publication rights and, they insisted, their very livelihood. In a dramatic appeal to Parliament that included a parade of wives and children dressed in rags, the erstwhile Stationers asked for statutory protection to restore some of the constraints upon the press that had expired with

---

1. This account of the origins of the press in England is drawn mainly from Lange, *The Speech and Press Clauses*, 23 U.C.L.A. L. Rev. 77, 94–6 (1976), and especially from authorities cited therein.

the Printing Act. Parliament responded in 1709 by enacting the Statute of Anne, 8 Anne c.19 (effective 1710), which bore the title "An Act for the Encouragement of Learning, by Vesting the Copies of Printed Books in the Authors or Purchasers of such Copies, during the Times therein mentioned." The preamble reveals the intent of the act:

> Whereas Printers, Booksellers and other Persons have of late frequently taken the Liberty of Printing, Reprinting, and Publishing . . . Books and other Writings without the Consent of the Authors or Proprietors . . . to their very great Detriment, and too often to the Ruin of them and their Families:
>
> For Preventing therefore such Practices for the future, and for the Encouragement of Learned men to Compose and write useful Books . . .

To accomplish these goals, the Statute of Anne gave the authors of new works the exclusive right to publish them for an initial term of fourteen years, measured from the date of first publication, at the expiration of which a second fourteen-year term would vest in the author if he or she were still living (even if the original term had been conveyed). However, enforcement of these rights was conditioned on registering the work and depositing copies at official libraries. Printing, reprinting or importing a protected work without the author's permission was punishable by a fine and by forfeiture and destruction of the unlawful copies.

This was the state of English copyright law when the American colonies broke away. At the instance of the Continental Congress, and at the urging of Noah Webster, most of the new states enacted copyright statutes shortly after Independence. Most resembled the English Statute of Anne, which had emphasized (in "the encouragement of learned men to compose and write useful books") the public benefits of granting limited monopolies to authors. Others, however, adopted the Continental view of copyright as a "natural right," arising as a moral entitlement in acknowledgment of the very fact of authorship itself. Whatever the underlying jurisprudence might be, as a practical matter lack of uniformity in these copyright laws made it difficult to protect works widely disseminated beyond the borders of an individual state.

B. THE ADVENT OF FEDERAL COPYRIGHT LAW

When the Constitution replaced the Articles of Confederation in 1787, the enactment of federal copyright (and patent) law was facilitated by Article I, section 8, clause 8, which grants Congress the power "to Promote the Progress of Science and useful Arts, by securing for limited Times to Authors and Inventors the exclusive Right to their respective Writings and Discoveries." James Madison summarized the goals of the Intellectual Property Clause in The Federalist No. 43:

> The utility of this power will scarcely be questioned. The copyright of authors has been solemnly adjudged, in Great Britain,

to be a right of common law. The right to useful inventions seems with equal reason to belong to inventors. The public good fully coincides in both cases with the claims of individuals. The States cannot separately make effectual provision for either of the cases, and most of them have anticipated the decision of this point, by laws passed at the instance of Congress.

Despite some hint of a dual purpose in this passage from Madison, it is the English view that has come to prevail as the accepted jurisprudence in American copyright under the Constitution. Thus, copyright in the United States is generally said to be justified as a means for encouraging the creation of new works for the benefit of the public, rather than to recognize the more personal natural, or moral, rights of authors. In the conventional understanding, copyright is said to reflect a kind of *"quid pro quo"*: authors receive exclusive rights for a limited time, in exchange for eventual contributions of their works to the public domain.

Congress passed the first federal copyright statute in 1790. Since then, the copyright laws have undergone significant changes. These changes generally fall into four categories: (1) broadening the scope of copyrightable subject matter (often in response to technological change, from photography to the internet); (2) lengthening the term of protection; (3) broadening the array of exclusive rights that comprise copyright; and (4) reducing formalities and other barriers to protection. Changes in the fourth category have been particularly important to the internationalization of commerce in copyrights, which in itself may be said to amount to a fifth category of change, especially in the past two decades.

Copyright scholars and practitioners must be mindful of the changes that have taken place in copyright law since its first enactment. Many contemporary controversies require an understanding of the law as it existed prior to the current (1976) Act, since events taking place decades ago (for example, the public distribution of copies lacking adequate copyright notice) can affect the copyright status of a work today. In particular, no student of copyright can afford to give short shrift to the provisions of the 1909 Act, as well as any subsequent legislation.

C. FEDERAL LEGISLATION PRIOR TO THE 1976 ACT

Subject matter: The 1790 Act provided copyright protection to a narrow range of subject matter—"any map, chart, book or books already printed."[2] Congress soon expanded this list, adding designs, prints, etchings and engravings in 1802, musical compositions in 1831, dramatic compositions in 1856, "photographs and the negatives thereof" in 1865, and "statuary" and "models or designs intended to be perfected as

2. Act of May 31, 1790, ch. 15, § 1, 1 Stat. 124, 124 (repealed 1831).

works of the fine arts" in 1870.[3] Not until 1891, however, were works of foreign origin protected.[4]

In the Copyright Act of 1909, Congress took a different approach to defining copyrightable subject matter. Instead of trying to list exhaustively all works eligible for copyright, Congress simply provided that "[t]he works for which copyright may be secured under this title shall include all the writings of an author."[5] The 1909 Act also contained a non-exhaustive list of eligible works in order simply to clarify the meaning of "all the writings of an author."[6] When the advent of motion pictures made further clarification necessary, Congress in 1912 added "motion pictures" to the list of examples.[7] In 1971, Congress added "sound recordings".[8] As discussed in Chapter 18, the chief significance of these categories today lies in defining the scope of the exclusive rights that attach to certain types of copyrighted works that do not enjoy the full panoply of rights afforded to other works.

Prior to the Copyright Act of 1976, federal statutory copyright was unavailable for unpublished works, except for certain works designed for exhibition, performance or oral delivery rather than reproduction (for example, motion pictures), and then only if the works were registered. For other unpublished works, only common law protection was available.

Duration: As Congress broadened the scope of copyrightable subject matter, it also lengthened the term of protection. Under the 1790 Act, the duration of copyright was the same as it had been under the Statute of Anne—fourteen years, renewable for another fourteen if the author was alive at the end of the first term. The 1831 Act lengthened the first term to 28 years, and extended the renewal privilege to the author's surviving spouse and children. The 1909 Act extended the renewal term to 28 years, and starting in 1962 this term was repeatedly extended in order to prevent renewal terms from expiring on the eve of the comprehensive copyright revision that became the Copyright Act of 1976.

Formalities: The 1790 Act had conditioned protection on registering the work and publishing a copy of this registration in a newspaper. The

3. Act of Apr. 29, 1802, ch. 36, § 2, 2 Stat. 171, 171, repealed by Act of Feb. 3, 1831, ch. 16, §§ 1, 14, 4 Stat. 436, 436, 439, amended by Act of Aug. 18, 1856, ch. 169, 11 Stat. 138, 139, amended by Act of Mar. 3, 1865, ch. 126, §§ 1, 2, 13 Stat. 540, 540, repealed by Act of July 8, 1870, ch. 180, § 86, 16 Stat. 198, 212 (repealed 1909).

4. Act of March 3, 1891, 26 U.S.C.A. § 1106.

5. Act of Mar. 4, 1909, ch. 320, § 4, 35 Stat. 1075, 1076 (emphasis added) (previously codified at 17 U.S.C.A. § 4, reprinted in 17 U.S.C.A. App. § 4 (West Supp. 1990); recodified 1947; repealed 1976). *See Goldstein v. California,* 412 U.S. 546, 562, 93 S.Ct. 2303, 2312, 37 L.Ed.2d 163 (1973) (footnote omitted):

* * * The history of federal copyright statutes indicates that the congressional de-

termination to consider specific classes of writings is dependent, not only on the character of the writing, but also on the commercial importance of the product to the national economy. As our technology has expanded the means available for creative activity and has provided economical means for reproducing manifestations of such activity, new areas of federal protection have been initiated.

6. Id. at § 5.

7. Act of Aug. 24, 1912, ch. 356, § 5(1)-(m), 37 Stat. 488, 488 (previously codified at 17 U.S.C.A. § 5(1)-(m), reprinted in 17 U.S.C.A. App. § 5(1)-(m); recodified 1947; repealed 1976).

8. Act of Oct. 15, 1971, Pub. L. 92–140, § 1(b), 85 Stat. 391, 391 (previously codified at 17 U.S.C.A. § 5(n), reprinted in 17 U.S.C.A. App. § 5(n); repealed 1976).

copyright claimant was also required to deposit a copy of the work with the Secretary of State within six months of publication.[9] The 1802 revisions replaced the requirement that the notice of registration be published in a newspaper with the requirement that copyright notice be inserted in each copy of the published work. Although protection was extended to foreign works in 1891, foreign authors were not exempt from these formalities, and often forfeited their U.S. copyrights through inadvertence. The 1909 Act also changed the law to provide that copyright protection for *published* works would commence upon publication with notice, rather than upon registration. Publication without notice led to forfeiture of copyright. The 1909 Act also introduced the rule, still in effect today, that a certificate of registration constitutes prima facie evidence of the facts recorded in the registration—that is, the validity of the registrant's copyright. The 1909 Act also added, in section 16, the now-defunct manufacturing clause, a protectionist provision which required printed books and periodicals in the English language, or by an American author, to be manufactured in the United States rather than imported. Copyright in some works was forfeited for noncompliance.

Rights: The early copyright statutes did not include the full panoply of rights afforded by copyright today. The 1790 Act included only the rights to print, reprint, publish, and sell. It did not include an exclusive right of public performance; this right was added in 1856 for dramatic compositions, in 1897 for musical compositions, and in 1952 for nondramatic literary works. The exclusive right to create derivative works was added in 1870.

D. COMPREHENSIVE REVISION: THE COPYRIGHT ACT OF 1976

The most significant rewrite of the federal copyright law, however, was the Copyright Act of 1976,[10] the culmination of twenty years of studies, hearings, debates, reports and revisions.[11] Among other things, the 1976 Act abrogated common law copyright in unpublished works and replaced it with statutory copyright, providing a single federal system of copyright for most works of authorship commencing as soon as they were fixed in a tangible medium of expression. The Act relaxed the rule that publication without proper copyright notice resulted in forfeiture of copyright, prescribing steps by which an author could "cure" a publication without notice. The Act eliminated the renewal term in favor of a single term of copyright protection, measured in most cases by the life of

9. In *Wheaton v. Peters*, 33 U.S. (8 Pet.) 591, 8 L.Ed. 1055 (1834), the Supreme Court held that deposit was mandatory under the 1790 Act. Thus, noncompliance would lead to forfeiture of copyright.

10. Act of Oct. 19, 1976, Pub. L. 94–553, 90 Stat. 2541 (codified at 17 U.S.C.A. §§ 101 et seq.).

11. The legislative history of the 1976 Act is vital to understanding the statutory language; consequently, excerpts from that history are found throughout this textbook and play a significant role in many of the judicial opinions excerpted herein.

the author plus 50 years, but measured as a fixed term from the date of creation (100 years) or publication (75 years), whichever first occurred, in the case of works made for hire and pseudonymous or anonymous works. The Act codified for the first time the judicially created doctrine of fair use, and further limited the copyright owner's exclusive rights by expressly permitting specific nonprofit uses and providing for compulsory licenses in certain other situations. The Act also expressly provided for federal preemption of state laws "equivalent" to copyright, and recognized the concept of divisibility of copyright ownership, which allowed assignees and exclusive licensees of portions of a copyright to sue for infringement of their rights. The 1976 Act introduced the exclusive right of public display, and provided for four copyright compulsory licenses (the cable television license of sec. 111, the mechanical recording license of sec. 115, the jukebox license of sec. 116 (since replaced with a negotiated license), and the public broadcasting license of sec. 118). It also modified the much-criticized manufacturing clause and provided for its eventual repeal (which took effect in 1986).

E.   POST–1976 REVISIONS

Although it dramatically altered the copyright landscape, the 1976 Act was by no means the last significant revision of federal copyright. Indeed, compared with the evolution of copyright law prior to 1976, revisions since 1976 have been fast and furious, in keeping with—and, in large part, resulting from—technological change and the increasing internationalization of the marketplace for intellectual property.

Technological Change: While preparing the 1976 revisions, Congress established the National Commission on New Technological Uses of Copyrighted Works (CONTU) to study and make recommendations regarding the provisions needed to make copyright law responsive to significant technological developments such as computers and photocopying. CONTU submitted its final report in 1978, and Congress implemented most of its recommendations soon after—for example, in 1980 revising section 117 to address the copying of computer software.[12]

In 1990, Congress banned the commercial rental of computer software, fearing the ease with which software could be copied by those who rented it; in this legislation Congress echoed earlier concerns that had led it (in 1987) to forbid record rentals on similar grounds. Concerns as to copying grew ever more intense as digital technologies displaced earlier analog technologies, particularly in the case of video and sound recordings. The older technology might well allow for rapid copying, but generally at a considerable cost in quality (measured by the declining signal to noise ratio) in each succeeding generation. In contrast, a digital copy is for most practical purposes indistinguishable from its predecessor in any medium. In the Audio Home Recording Act of 1992, responding to

---

12. Congress also amended section 101 to ensure that the definition of "literary works" was broad enough to include com- puter programs. Act of Dec. 12, 1980, Pub. L. 96–517, 94 Stat. 3015, 3028.

the concerns of music publishers and record companies that digital audio recordings would be widely copied, Congress clarified the permissibility of home audio taping while imposing a royalty on the sale of digital recording media and devices, and requiring all such devices to be equipped with copying controls to prevent serial copying of digital works. In 1995, responding to concerns that digital transmission of sound recordings would supplant many record purchases, Congress enacted a limited public performance right for sound recordings performed by means of digital subscription services.[13]

Even greater pressures have been brought to bear upon the copyright system by the rapid growth of the internet, which enables copyrighted works to be disseminated instantly in digital format throughout the world. It is difficult to exaggerate the number or the complexity of issues this new fact of life raises for copyright proprietors, to whom the net is an unprecedented medium for the exploitation of their works, but a medium in which the threat of digital copying is omnipresent and exponentially magnified. Meanwhile, every issue to be seen from the perspective of proprietors raises a corresponding issue from the perspective of the public domain. In essence the question for the public domain is this: how to realize the enormous possibilities for freedom of expression, creativity and cultural exchange which inhere in the internet, without unnecessarily undermining copyright as an incentive for continuing intellectual productivity? What is ultimately at issue in these differing perspectives is the continued viability of copyright's fundamental *quid pro quo.*

Because the stakes are high, and there are no easy answers to these questions, copyright today can resemble a battlefield in which the contest is desperate and the outcome still uncertain. On the one hand proprietors appear at times to have the edge in Congress, where effective lobbying efforts have led to new legislation aimed at curtailing the worst excesses of digital copying. A number of early successful efforts in this direction have been mentioned above. Perhaps the crowning achievement to date, however, is the Digital Millennium Copyright Act of 1998, a major piece of legislation designed principally to deal with efforts by hackers to circumvent digital security measures (such as the motion picture industry's CSS encryption system, intended to protect on-line movies from unauthorized copying), as well as certain issues affecting the liability of online service providers (such as AOL) for copyright infringement arising from postings by others. Against these advances, however, the forces of the public domain can claim some victories as well, though not always victories at law. The achievement of 15–year-old Jon Johanssen, the Norwegian lad who deconstructed the CSS code and then posted his results on the internet so that others might make use of his work, suggests the guerrilla nature of some of the public domain resistance. Napster, Gnutella, and Grockster, systems for unauthorized downloads of recorded music well known to most persons under the age

---

13. Pub. L. 104–39, 109 Stat. 336 (1995).

of twenty-five, are additional examples of the guerrilla movement at work. Other efforts, somewhat more systematically aimed at creating a viable commons, are reflected in the advancing fortunes of the Linux operating system, an alternative to Microsoft's operating systems which, unlike Microsoft's copyrighted computer codes, depends on a so-called "general public license" (or GPL) that is meant to be a deliberate alternative to copyright protection. And meanwhile a growing movement, particularly among copyright academics, to develop and advance the jurisprudence of the public domain at large has gained ground in the past two decades, and gives some promise of securing a greater place in conventional law for this once-neglected alternative to copyright.

There are at least two ways to present these latest developments in a casebook. One is to deal with the issues arising from the so-called Digital Millennium, or with the movement toward affirmative recognition of the public domain, as subjects unto themselves. A second is to treat each of these developments thoroughly, but to incorporate each treatment into a more systematic exposition of the law at large. There is something to be said for either approach. We have opted for the second, however, because we think it is how the most sophisticated professionals who practice in the field of copyright must come to understand these issues. To fully grasp the importance of the public domain movement in the context of copyright, one must first understand the basic tenets of copyright itself, and then see how they have evolved; and this is equally true of the issues arising from the advent of the digital technologies. In this casebook, then, you will find the new developments carefully woven into the larger fabric of our subject matter. When your study is completed, we think your understanding of the entire field will be enhanced by this approach.

Internationalization: The United States first participated in a multilateral copyright treaty in 1952, when it signed the Universal Copyright Convention (UCC). UCC members were required to protect, on a nondiscriminatory basis, works authored by nationals of member nations or first published in member nations. Formalities were waived for unpublished works and works published with proper notice. The UCC was especially attractive to the United States (which had been instrumental in its development) because it demanded little in the way of recognition of moral rights. For that very reason, however, it proved less than successful in attracting adherents. In recent decades its importance has dwindled as the vast majority of its signatories have ratified the more sweeping, moral rights-based Berne Convention for the Protection of Literary and Artistic Works. In 1988 the United States itself finally adhered to the Berne Convention, a move that has had a major impact on U.S. copyright law.

The Berne Convention was originally formed in 1886 and has been periodically revised (most recently in the 1971 Paris revision) with ever-expanding membership. The treaty is not self-executing, and therefore Congress has had to make several significant changes in domestic law in order to satisfy the treaty requirements—for example, eliminating the notice requirement (for works first published on or after March 1, 1989), removing registration as a prerequisite to suit for infringement of works originating in Berne countries, eliminating altogether the requirement that copyright transfers be recorded in the Copyright Office as a prerequisite to suit, and phasing out the compulsory license for jukeboxes in favor of negotiated licenses (which were finally eliminated in 1993).

The post-Berne period has seen numerous other changes in federal copyright law, of which some, though by no means all, were inspired, if not strictly required, by the Berne Convention. In 1988, Congress doubled the limits for statutory damages. In 1990, Congress expressly recognized "moral rights" in certain works of visual art (sec. 106A), recognized copyright in architectural works,[14] and added language to the copyright statutes expressly abrogating the sovereign immunity of states from infringement suits (although it is unclear whether the constitutionality of this abrogation will be upheld). In 1992, copyright renewal (still relevant for works published before the effective date of the 1976 Act) became automatic, the fair use doctrine was clarified with respect to unpublished works, and broader criminal penalties for infringement were imposed. 1993 saw the elimination of the Copyright Royalty Tribunal (which had administered the compulsory licensing provisions) and its replacement by Copyright Arbitration Panels (CARPS).

When the United States signed the North American Free Trade Agreement (NAFTA) in 1993, and then subscribed to the results of the Uruguay Round of the General Agreement on Tariffs and Trade (GATT) (which established the World Trade Organization, or WTO, and included for the first time specific provisions on Trade Related Aspects of Intellectual Property, or TRIPS) in 1994, yet another round of revisions to the Copyright Act of 1976 also ensued. Some of these revisions were merely technical and of small account, but others were of considerable significance. Particularly notable among the latter, Section 104A, enacted in 1993[15] and expanded in 1994,[16] restored copyright protection to works originating in countries belonging to the World Trade Organization (WTO) or the Berne Convention which prematurely entered the public domain in the United States (often through failure to comply with formalities). Certain protections were built in, however, for parties that relied on such a work's uncopyrighted status. In another significant departure from traditional American copyright law, the GATT-inspired revisions to Title 17 also recognize certain rights in unfixed works, providing civil and criminal penalties for making or "trafficking in" bootleg recordings of live musical performances.

In 1998, the United States Senate ratified two new international treaties, one on Copyright itself, and the other on Performances and

---

14. Architectural Works Protection Copyright Act of 1990, Pub. L. No. 101–650, 104 Stat. 5133 (1990).

15. North American Free Trade Agreement Act, Pub. L. No. 103–182, 107 Stat. 2057 (1993).

16. Uruguay Round Agreements Act, Pub. L. No. 103–465, 108 Stat. 4809 (1994).

Phonograms, with both to be administered by the World Intellectual Property Organization (WIPO).[17] These treaties had been proposed at an international meeting convened by the WIPO at its headquarters in Geneva late in 1996, and were considered by some observers to reflect concern on the part of WIPO officials that the new provisions of GATT–TRIPS, as well as the administrative structure of the WTO, were displacing WIPO influence and jurisdiction over copyright and neighboring rights. Be that as it may, the Digital Millennium Copyright Act of 1998 (DMCA), discussed above, did further amend the 1976 Copyright Act to bring the signatories to the two WIPO treaties into approximate parity under American law with the signatories to Berne and GATT–TRIPS. Of particular note, the DMCA effectively extended the copyright restoration provisions of section 104A to signatories to the new WIPO treaties.

Meanwhile, the WIPO Copyright treaty actually calls for further legislative action, particularly in the area of data protection. Stiff resistance from diverse interests has stalled this legislation, however. Some who oppose efforts to deal with data sense threats to their accustomed manner of doing business. Others see threats to the public domain, and particularly to efforts to engage in scientific research. Legislation continues to be advanced, but as of May 1, 2007, no final results appear to be in sight.

A final note on post–1976 developments: The Sonny Bono Copyright Term Extension Act (SBCTEA), Pub. L. No. 105–298 (signed Oct. 27, 1998), added 20 years to the terms of most subsisting U.S. copyrights, thus making it possible for U.S. copyright owners to enjoy the maximum term of copyright protection provided by countries belonging to the European Union. The SBCTEA resulted in litigation challenging the constitutionality of the extension. Among the most contested issues in the case was the provision of the Act which retrospectively extends the copyright term so as to benefit works already under copyright—as in the case, for example, of Disney's Mickey Mouse. The argument against doing so is that, by definition, no incentive to create can be seen in the case of works already under copyright—which is to say that the Constitutional justification for copyright (the fundamental *quid pro quo*) cannot be demonstrated in at least this much of the legislation. In *Eldred v. Ashcroft*, 537 U.S. 186, 123 S.Ct. 769, 154 L.Ed.2d 683 (2003), excerpted, *infra*, at p. 903, the legislation was upheld in its entirety. The Court also stated in dictum that while copyright is not "categorically immune" to First Amendment review, as suggested by the Court of Appeals opinion in *Eldred v. Ashcroft*, 255 F.3d 849 (D.C.Cir.2001), the First Amendment was not violated by the term extension at issue in the case, including retroactivity.

---

17. The Senate's ratification of the Phonograms Treaty is subject to one reservation limiting the implementation of Article 15(1) to "certain acts of broadcasting and communications to the public by digital means for which a direct or indirect fee is charged for reception, and for other transmissions and digital phonorecord deliveries, as provided under United States Law."

Chapter 16

THE SUBJECT MATTER
OF COPYRIGHT

A. INTRODUCTION

Statutes: 17 U.S.C.A. §§ 101 (as needed, for definitions of material terms), 102–03

BURROW–GILES LITHOGRAPHIC CO. v. SARONY

Supreme Court of the United States, 1884.
111 U.S. 53, 4 S.Ct. 279, 28 L.Ed. 349.

MR. JUSTICE MILLER delivered the opinion of the Court.

* * *

Plaintiff is a lithographer and defendant a photographer, with large business in those lines in the city of New York.

The suit was commenced by an action at law in which Sarony was plaintiff and the lithographic company was defendant, the plaintiff charging the defendant with violating his copyright in regard to a photograph, the title of which is "Oscar Wilde No. 18." A jury being waived, the court made a finding of facts on which a judgment in favor of the plaintiff was rendered * * *.

* * *

The eighth section of the first article of the Constitution is the great repository of the powers of Congress, and by the eighth clause of that section Congress is authorized:

"To promote the progress of science and useful arts, by securing, for limited times to authors and inventors, the exclusive right to their respective writings and discoveries."

The argument here is, that a photograph is not a writing nor the production of an author. Under the acts of Congress designed to give effect to this section, the persons who are to be benefited are divided into two classes, authors and inventors. The monopoly which is granted to the former is called a copyright, that given to the latter, letters patent, or, in the familiar language of the present day, patent right.

We have, then, copyright and patent right, and it is the first of these under which plaintiff asserts a claim for relief.

It is insisted in argument, that a photograph being a reproduction on paper of the exact features of some natural object or of some person, is not a writing of which the producer is the author.

Section 4952 of the Revised Statutes places photographs in the same class as things which may be copyrighted with "books, maps, charts, dramatic or musical compositions, engravings, cuts, prints, paintings, drawings, statues, statuary, and models or designs intended to be perfected as works of the fine arts." * * *

* * *

Unless, therefore, photographs can be distinguished in the classification on this point from the maps, charts, designs, engravings, etchings, cuts, and other prints, it is difficult to see why Congress cannot make them the subject of copyright as well as the others.

These statutes certainly answer the objection that books only, or writing in the limited sense of a book and its author, are within the constitutional provision. Both these words are susceptible of a more enlarged definition than this. An author in that sense is "he to whom anything owes its origin; originator; maker; one who completes a work of science or literature." Worcester. So, also, no one would now claim that the word writing in this clause of the Constitution, though the only word used as to subjects in regard to which authors are to be secured, is limited to the actual script of the author, and excludes books and all other printed matter. By writings in that clause is meant the literary productions of those authors, and Congress very properly has declared these to include all forms of writing, printing, engraving, etching, & c., by which the ideas in the mind of the author are given visible expression. The only reason why photographs were not included in the extended list in the act of 1802 is probably that they did not exist, as photography as an art was then unknown, and the scientific principle on which it rests, and the chemicals and machinery by which it is operated, have all been discovered long since that statute was enacted.

* * *

We entertain no doubt that the Constitution is broad enough to cover an act authorizing copyright of photographs, so far as they are representatives of original intellectual conceptions of the author.

But it is said that an engraving, a painting, a print, does embody the intellectual conception of its author, in which there is novelty, invention, originality, and therefore comes within the purpose of the Constitution in securing its exclusive use or sale to its author, while the photograph is the mere mechanical reproduction of the physical features or outlines of some object animate or inanimate, and involves no originality of thought or any novelty in the intellectual operation connected with its visible reproduction in shape of a picture. That while the effect of light on the prepared plate may have been a discovery in the production of these pictures, and patents could properly be obtained for the combination of the chemicals, for their application to the paper or other surface, for all the machinery by which the light reflected from the object was thrown on the prepared plate, and for all the improvements in this machinery, and in the materials, the remainder of the process is merely mechanical, with no place for novelty, invention or originality. It is simply the manual operation, by the use of these instruments and preparations, of transferring to the plate the visible representation of some existing object, the accuracy of this representation being its highest merit.

This may be true in regard to the ordinary production of a photograph, and, further, that in such case a copyright is no protection. On the question as thus stated we decide nothing.

In regard, however, to the kindred subject of patents for invention, they cannot by law be issued to the inventor until the novelty, the utility, and the actual discovery or invention by the claimant have been established by proof before the Commissioner of Patents; and when he has secured such a patent, and undertakes to obtain redress for a violation of his right in a court of law, the question of invention, of novelty, of originality, is always open to examination. Our copyright system has no such provision for previous examination by a proper tribunal as to the originality of the book, map, or other matter offered for copyright. A deposit of two copies of the article or work with the Librarian of Congress, with the name of the author and its title page, is all that is necessary to secure a copyright. It is, therefore, much more important that when the supposed author sues for a violation of his copyright, the existence of those facts of originality, of intellectual production, of thought, and conception on the part of the author should be proved, than in the case of a patent right.

In the case before us we think this has been done.

The third finding of facts says, in regard to the photograph in question, that it is a "useful, new, harmonious, characteristic, and graceful picture, and that plaintiff made the same ... entirely from his own original mental conception, to which he gave visible form by posing the said Oscar Wilde in front of the camera, selecting and arranging the costume, draperies, and other various accessories in said photograph, arranging the subject so as to present graceful outlines, arranging and disposing the light and shade, suggesting and evoking the desired expression, and from such disposition, arrangement, or representation, made entirely by plaintiff, he produced the picture in suit."

These findings, we think, show this photograph to be an original work of art, the product of plaintiff's intellectual invention, of which plaintiff is the author, and of a class of inventions for which the Constitution intended that Congress should secure to him the exclusive right to use, publish and sell, as it has done by section 4952 of the Revised Statutes.

* * *

COPYRIGHT ACT OF 1976

H.R. Rep. No. 94–1476.
94th Cong., 2d Sess. 51–54 (1976).

* * *

Section 102. General Subject Matter of Copyright

"Original Works of Authorship"

The two fundamental criteria of copyright protection—originality and fixation in tangible form—are restated in the first sentence of this cornerstone provision. The phrase "original works of authorship," which is purposely left undefined, is intended to incorporate without change the standard of originality established by the courts under the present copyright statute. This standard does not include requirements of novelty, ingenuity, or esthetic merit, and there is no intention to enlarge the standard of copyright protection to require them.

In using the phrase "original works of authorship," rather than "all the writings of an author" now in section 4 of the statute, the committee's purpose is to avoid exhausting the constitutional power of Congress to legislate in this field, and to eliminate the uncertainties arising from the latter phrase. * * *

The history of copyright law has been one of gradual expansion in the types of works accorded protection * * *.

Authors are continually finding new ways of expressing themselves, but it is impossible to foresee the forms that these new expressive methods will take. The bill does not intend either to freeze the scope of copyrightable subject matter at the present stage of communications technology or to allow unlimited expansion into areas completely outside the present congressional intent. Section 102 implies neither that that subject matter is unlimited nor that new forms of expression within that general area of subject matter would necessarily be unprotected. * * *

* * * [T]here are unquestionably other areas of existing subject matter that this bill does not propose to protect but that future Congresses may want to.

* * *

Categories of copyrightable works

The second sentence of section 102 lists seven broad categories which the concept of "works" of ["]authorship" is said to "include." The use of the word "include," as defined in section 101, makes clear that the listing is "illustrative and not limitative," and that the seven categories do not necessarily exhaust the scope of "original works of authorship" that the bill is intended to protect. Rather, the list sets out the general area of copyrightable subject matter, but with sufficient flexibility to free the courts from rigid or outmoded concepts of the scope of particular categories. The items are also overlapping in the sense that a work falling within one class may encompass works coming within some or all of the other ca[t]egories. * * *

* * * The term "literary works" does not connote any criterion of literary merit or qualitative value: it includes catalogs, directories, and similar factual, reference, or instructional works and compilations of data. It also includes computer data bases, and computer programs to the extent that they incorporate authorship in the programmer's expression of original ideas, as distinguished from the ideas themselves.

* * *

Notes

1. The Supreme Court has discussed the scope of the constitutional terms "Authors" and "Writings" on several occasions when it has been called upon to address the scope of Congress's power to define copyrightable subject matter. In the *Trade–Mark Cases*, 100 U.S. (10 Otto) 82, 94, 25 L.Ed. 550 (1879) (see page 7, *supra*), the Court defined "Writings" as "the fruits of intellectual labor," but only those that "are original, and are founded in the creative powers of the mind." After the *Burrow-Giles* decision, the Court held in *Bleistein v. Donaldson Lithographing Co.*, 188 U.S. 239, 249, 23 S.Ct. 298, 299, 47 L.Ed. 460 (1903), that Congress was empowered to extend copyright protection to chromolithographs used in printing circus posters, even where the depictions in question were realistic rather than fanciful:

It is obvious also that the plaintiffs' case is not affected by the fact, if it be one, that the pictures represent actual groups—visible things. They seem from the testimony to have been composed from hints or description, not from sight of a performance. But even if they had been drawn from the life, that fact would not deprive them of protection. The opposite proposition would mean that a portrait by Velasquez or Whistler was common property because others might try their hand on the same face. Others are free to copy the original. They are not free to copy the copy. * * * The copy is the personal reaction of an individual upon nature. Personality always contains something unique. It expresses its singularity even in handwriting, and a very modest grade of art has in it something irreducible, which is one man's alone. That something he may copyright unless there is a restriction in the words of the act.

* * *

It would be a dangerous undertaking for persons trained only to the law to constitute themselves final judges of the worth of pictorial illustrations, outside of the narrowest and most obvious limits. At the one extreme some works of genius would be sure to miss appreciation. Their very novelty would make them repulsive until the public had learned the new language in which their author spoke. It may be more than doubted, for instance, whether the etchings of Goya or the paintings of Manet would have been sure of protection when seen for the first time. At the other end, copyright would be denied to pictures which appealed to a public less educated than the judge. Yet if they command the interest of any public, they have a commercial value—it would be bold to say that they have not an aesthetic and educational value—and the taste of any public is not to be treated with contempt. It is an ultimate fact for the moment, whatever may be our hopes for a change.

In 1973, the Supreme Court determined that the Intellectual Property Clause empowered Congress to extend copyright protection to audio recordings of musical performances:

> By Art. I, § 8, cl. 8, of the Constitution, the States granted to Congress the power to protect the "Writings" of "Authors." These terms have not been construed in their narrow literal sense but, rather, with the reach necessary to reflect the broad scope of constitutional principles. While an "author" may be viewed as an individual who writes an original composition, the term, in its constitutional sense, has been construed to mean an "originator," "he to whom anything owes its origin." *Burrow–Giles Lithographic Co. v. Sarony*, 111 U.S. 53, 58 (1884). Similarly, although the word "writings" might be limited to script or printed material, it may be interpreted to include any physical rendering of the fruits of creative intellectual or aesthetic labor. Ibid.; Trade–Mark Cases, 100 U.S. 82, 94 (1879). Thus, recordings of artistic performances may be within the reach of Clause 8.

> While the area in which Congress may act is broad, the enabling provision of Clause 8 does not require that Congress act in regard to all categories of materials which meet the constitutional definitions. Rather, whether any specific category of "Writings" is to be brought within the purview of the federal statutory scheme is left to the discretion of the Congress. The history of federal copyright statutes indicates that the congressional determination to consider specific classes of writings is dependent, not only on the character of the writing, but also on the commercial importance of the product to the national economy. As our technology has expanded the means available for creative activity and has provided economical means for reproducing manifestations of such activity, new areas of federal protection have been initiated.

Goldstein v. California, 412 U.S. 546, 561–62, 93 S.Ct. 2303, 2312, 37 L.Ed.2d 163 (1973) (footnotes omitted).

Does the Intellectual Property Clause authorize Congress to extend copyright protection to unposed snapshots? Videotapes or film footage of real-life events? A recording of the sounds of nature? The title "Gone With the Wind"? The name "Coca–Cola"? An invented word, such as "supercalifragilisticexpialidocious"? A simple commercial logo (for example, the Nike "swoosh" symbol)? A federal statute? A typeface? A recipe? A questionnaire? A halloween costume? The design of a sports car? The design of a golf course? If a category of subject matter is eligible for copyright under the Intellectual Property Clause, may Congress refuse to extend protection to that subject matter? See *Graham v. John Deere Co.*, 383 U.S. 1, 86 S.Ct. 684,

15 L.Ed.2d 545 (1966). *Cf.,* Copyright Office Regulations, 37 C.F.R. § 202.1 (listing material not subject to copyright).

2. Consider Holmes' observations in *Bleistein* as to the question of copyright and aesthetics. Does the Intellectual Property Clause *require* Congress to extend copyright without regard to the merits of an individual work? Does the Clause allow Congress to extend copyright protection to works which arguably do not "promote the progress of science and useful arts"? See Heald & Sherry, *Implied Limits on the Legislative Power: The Intellectual Property Clause as an Absolute Constraint on Congress,* 2000 U.Ill.L.Rev. 1119 (2000).

MANNION v. COORS BREWING CO.

United States District Court, S.D. New York, 2005.
377 F.Supp.2d 444.

KAPLAN, DISTRICT JUDGE.

The parties dispute whether a photograph used in billboard advertisements for Coors Light beer infringes the plaintiff's copyright in a photograph of a basketball star. The defendants almost certainly imitated the plaintiff's photograph. The major question is whether and to what extent what was copied is protected. The case requires the Court to consider the nature of copyright protection in photographs. The matter is before the Court on cross motions for summary judgment.

FACTS

Jonathan Mannion is a freelance photographer who specializes in portraits of celebrity athletes and musicians in the rap and rhythm-and-blues worlds.... In 1999 he was hired by SLAM, a basketball magazine, to photograph basketball star Kevin Garnett in connection with an article that the magazine planned to publish about him. The article, entitled "Above the Clouds," appeared as the cover story of the December 1999 issue of the magazine. It was accompanied by a number of Mannion's photographs of Garnett, including the one at issue here (the "Garnett Photograph"), which was printed on a two-page spread introducing the article.

The Garnett Photograph is a three-quarter-length portrait of Garnett against a backdrop of clouds with some blue sky shining through. The view is up and across the right side of Garnett's torso, so that he appears to be towering above earth. He wears a white T-shirt, white athletic pants, a black close-fitting cap, and a large amount of platinum, gold, and diamond jewelry ("bling bling" in the vernacular), including several necklaces, a Rolex watch and bracelet on his left wrist, bracelets on his right wrist, rings on one finger of each hand, and earrings. His head is cocked, his eyes are closed, and his heavily-veined hands, nearly all of which are visible, rest over his lower abdomen, with the thumbs hooked on the waistband of the trousers. The light is from the viewer's left, so that Garnett's right shoulder is the brightest area of the photograph and his hands cast slight shadows on his trousers. As reproduced in the magazine, the photograph cuts off much of Garnett's left arm.

In early 2001, defendant Carol H. Williams Advertising ("CHWA") began developing ideas for outdoor billboards that would advertise Coors Light beer to young black men in urban areas. One of CHWA's "comp boards"—a "comp board" is an image created by an advertising company to convey a proposed design—used a manipulated version of the Garnett Photograph and superimposed on it the words "Iced Out" ("ice" being slang for diamonds) and a picture of a can of Coors Light beer (the "Iced Out Comp Board"). CHWA obtained authorization from Mannion's representative to use the Garnett Photograph for this purpose. The authorization was for "[u]sage in internal corporate merchandising catalog," which Mannion concedes extended to the Iced Out Comp Board. The Iced Out Comp Board ... used a black-and-white, mirror image of the Garnett Photograph, but with the head cropped out on top and part of the fingers cropped out below. CHWA forwarded its comp boards to, and solicited bids for the photograph for the Coors advertising from, various photographers including Mannion, who submitted a bid but did not receive the assignment.

Coors and CHWA selected for a Coors billboard a photograph (the "Coors Billboard"), reproduced below, that resembles the Iced Out Comp Board. The Coors Billboard depicts, in black-and-white, the torso of a muscular black man, albeit a model other than Garnett, shot against a cloudy backdrop. The pose is similar to that in the Garnett Photograph, and the view also is up and across the left side of the torso. The model in the billboard photograph also wears a white T-shirt and white athletic pants. The model's jewelry is prominently depicted; it includes a necklace of platinum or gold and diamonds, a watch and two bracelets on the right wrist, and more bracelets on the left wrist. The light comes from the viewer's right, so that the left shoulder is the brightest part of the photograph, and the right arm and hand cast slight shadows on the trousers.

Mannion subsequently noticed the Coors Billboard at two locations in the Los Angeles area. He applied for registration of his copyright of the Garnett Photograph in 2003 and brought this action for infringement in February of 2004. The registration was completed in May 2004. The parties each move for summary judgment.

DISCUSSION

* * *

Mannion concededly owns a valid copyright in the Garnett photograph. Access is undisputed. There is ample evidence from which a trier of fact could find that CHWA actually copied the Garnett Photograph for the Coors Billboard. Thus, the major questions presented by these motions are whether a trier of fact could or must find substantial similarity between protected elements of the Garnett Photograph and the Coors Billboard. If no reasonable trier could find such similarity, the defendants' motion must be granted and the plaintiff's denied. If any reasonable trier would be obliged to find such similarity (along with actual copying), the plaintiff's motion must be granted and the defendants' denied. If a reasonable trier could, but would not be required to, find substantial similarity (and actual copying), both motions must be denied.

* * *

C. Determining the Protectible Elements of the Garnett Photograph

The first question must be: in what respects is the Garnett Photograph protectible?

1. Protectible Elements of Photographs

It is well-established that "[t]he sine qua non of copyright is originality" and, accordingly, that "copyright protection may extend only to those components of a work that are original to the author." "Original" in the copyright context "means only that the work was independently created by the author (as opposed to copied from other works), and that it possesses at least some minimal degree of creativity."

It sometimes is said that "copyright in the photograph conveys no rights over the subject matter conveyed in the photograph." But this is not always true. It of course is correct that the photographer of a building or tree or other pre-existing object has no right to prevent others from photographing the same thing. That is because originality depends upon independent creation, and the photographer did not create that object. By contrast, if a photographer arranges or otherwise creates the subject that his camera captures, he may have the right to prevent others from producing works that depict that subject.

Almost any photograph "may claim the necessary originality to support a copyright." Indeed, ever since the Supreme Court considered an 1882 portrait by the celebrity photographer Napoleon Sarony of the 27–year-old Oscar Wilde, courts have articulated lists of potential components of a photograph's originality.

[*The so-called "lists", from an otherwise deleted footnote:* See Burrow–Giles Lithographic Co., 111 U.S. at 60, 4 S.Ct. at 282 (originality of Wilde portrait founded upon overall composition, including pose, clothing, background, light, and shade, "suggesting and evoking the desired expression"); Leibovitz v. Paramount Pictures Corp., 137 F.3d 109, 116 (2d Cir.1998) ("Leibovitz is entitled to protection for such artistic elements as the particular lighting, the resulting skin tone of the subject, and the camera angle that she selected."); Rogers v. Koons, 960 F.2d 301, 307 (2d Cir.1992) ("Elements of originality in a photograph may include posing the subjects, lighting, angle, selection of film and camera, evoking the desired expression, and almost any other variant involved."); Gross v. Seligman, 212 F. 930, 931 (2d Cir.1914) ("exercise of artistic talent" reflected in "pose, light, and shade, etc."); SHL Imaging, Inc. v. Artisan House, Inc., 117 F.Supp.2d 301, 311 (S.D.N.Y.2000) ("What makes plaintiff's photographs original is the totality of the precise lighting selection, angle of the camera, lens and filter selection."); Eastern Am. Trio Prods., Inc. v. Tang Elec. Corp., 97 F.Supp.2d 395, 417 (S.D.N.Y.2000) ("The necessary originality for a photograph may be founded upon, among other things, the photographer's choice of subject matter, angle of photograph, lighting, determination of the precise time when the photograph is to be taken, the kind of camera, the kind of film, the kind of lens, and the area in which the pictures are taken."); Kisch v. Ammirati & Puris Inc., 657 F.Supp. 380, 382 (S.D.N.Y.1987) (copyrightable elements of a photograph "include such features as the photographer's selection of lighting, shading, positioning and timing."). Even these lists are not complete. They omit such features as the amount of the image in focus, its graininess, and the level of contrast.]

These lists, however, are somewhat unsatisfactory. First, they do not deal with the issue, alluded to above, that the nature and extent of a photograph's protection differs depending on what makes that photograph original. Second, courts have not always distinguished between decisions that a photographer makes in creating a photograph and the originality of the final product. Several cases, for example, have included in lists of the potential components of photographic originality "selection of film and camera," "lens and filter selection," and "the kind of camera, the kind of film, [and] the kind of lens." Having considered the matter fully, however, I think this is not sufficiently precise. Decisions about film, camera, and lens, for example, often bear on whether an image is original. But the fact that a photographer made such choices does not alone make the image original. "Sweat of the brow" is not the touchstone of copyright. Protection derives from the features of the work itself, not the effort that goes into it. This point is illustrated by Bridgeman Art Library, Ltd. v. Corel Corp., 36 F.Supp.2d 191 (S.D.N.Y. 1999), in which this Court held that there was no copyright in photographic transparencies that sought to reproduce precisely paintings in the public domain. To be sure, a great deal of effort and expertise may have been poured into the production of the plaintiff's images, including decisions about camera, lens, and film. But the works were "slavish copies." They did not exhibit the originality necessary for copyright.

The Court therefore will examine more closely the nature of originality in a photograph. In so doing, it draws on the helpful discussion in a leading treatise on United Kingdom copyright law, [Hon. Sir Hugh Laddie et al., The Modern Law of Copyright and Designs (3d ed. Butterworths 2000)] which is similar to our own with respect to the requirement of originality.

A photograph may be original in three respects. They are not mutually exclusive.

a. Rendition

First, "there may be originality which does not depend on creation of the scene or object to be photographed ... and which resides [instead] in such specialties as angle of shot, light and shade, exposure, effects achieved by means of filters, developing techniques etc." I will refer to this type of originality as originality in the rendition because, to the extent a photograph is original in this way, copyright protects not what is depicted, but rather how it is depicted.

It was originality in the rendition that was at issue in SHL Imaging, Inc. v. Artisan House, Inc., 117 F.Supp. 2d 301 (S.D.N.Y 2000). That case concerned photographs of the defendants' mirrored picture frames that the defendants commissioned from the plaintiff. The photographs were to be used by the defendants' sales force for in-person pitches. When the defendants reproduced the photographs in their catalogues and brochures, the court found infringement: "Plaintiff cannot prevent others from photographing the same frames, or using the same lighting techniques and blue sky reflection in the mirrors. What makes plaintiff's photographs original is the totality of the precise lighting selection, angle of the camera, lens and filter selection." Again, what made the photographs original was not the lens and filter selection themselves. It was the effect produced by the lens and filters selected, among other things. In any case, those effects were the basis of the originality of the works at issue in SHL Imaging. By contrast, in Bridgeman Art Library, the goal was to reproduce exactly other works. The photographs were entirely unoriginal in the rendition, an extremely unusual circumstance. Unless a photograph replicates another work with total or near-total fidelity, it will be at least somewhat original in the rendition.

b. Timing

A photograph may be original in a second respect. "[A] person may create a worthwhile photograph by being at the right place at the right time." I will refer to this type of originality as originality in timing.

One case that concerned originality in timing, among other things, was Pagano v. Chas. Beseler Co., 234 F. 963 (S.D.N.Y.1916), which addressed the copyrightability of a photograph of a scene in front of the New York Public Library at Fifth Avenue and Forty–Second Street: "The question is not, as defendant suggests, whether the photograph of a public building may properly be copyrighted. Any one may take a photograph of a public building and of the surrounding scene. It undoubtedly requires originality to determine just when to take the photograph, so as to bring out the proper setting for both animate and inanimate objects.... The photographer caught the men and women in not merely lifelike, but artistic, positions, and this is especially true of the traffic policeman.... There are other features, which need not be discussed in detail, such as the motor cars waiting for the signal to proceed." 234 F.Supp.2d at 964.

A modern work strikingly original in timing might be Catch of the Day, by noted wildlife photographer Thomas Mangelsen, which depicts a salmon that appears to be jumping into the gaping mouth of a brown bear at Brooks Falls in Katmai National Park, Alaska. An older example is Alfred Eisenstaedt's photograph of a sailor kissing a young woman on

VJ Day in Times Square, the memorability of which is attributable in significant part to the timing of its creation.

Copyright based on originality in timing is limited by the principle that copyright in a photograph ordinarily confers no rights over the subject matter. Thus, the copyright in Catch of the Day does not protect against subsequent photographs of bears feasting on salmon in the same location. Furthermore, if another photographer were sufficiently skilled and fortunate to capture a salmon at the precise moment that it appeared to enter a hungry bear's mouth—and others have tried, with varying degrees of success—that photographer, even if inspired by Mangelsen, would not necessarily have infringed his work because Mangelsen's copyright does not extend to the natural world he captured.

In practice, originality in timing gives rise to the same type of protection as originality in the rendition. In each case, the image that exhibits the originality, but not the underlying subject, qualifies for copyright protection.

c. Creation of the Subject

The principle that copyright confers no right over the subject matter has an important limitation. A photograph may be original to the extent that the photographer created "the scene or subject to be photographed." This type of originality, which I will refer to as originality in the creation of the subject, played an essential role in Rogers v. Koons, 960 F.2d 301 (2d Cir.1992), and Gross v. Seligman, 212 F. 930 (2d Cir.1914).

In Rogers, the court held that the copyright in the plaintiff's photograph Puppies, which depicted a contrived scene of the photographer's acquaintance, Jim Scanlon, and his wife on a park bench with eight puppies on their laps, protected against the defendants' attempt to replicate precisely, albeit in a three dimensional sculpture, the content of the photograph. Although the Circuit noted that Puppies was original because the artist "made creative judgments concerning technical matters with his camera and the use of natural light"—in other words, because it was original in the rendition—its originality in the creation of the subject was more salient. The same is true of the works at issue in Gross v. Seligman, in which the Circuit held that the copyright in a photograph named Grace of Youth was infringed when the same artist created a photograph named Cherry Ripe using "the same model in the identical pose, with the single exception that the young woman now wears a smile and holds a cherry stem between her teeth."

To conclude, the nature and extent of protection conferred by the copyright in a photograph will vary depending on the nature of its originality. Insofar as a photograph is original in the rendition or timing, copyright protects the image but does not prevent others from photographing the same object or scene. Thus, the copyright at issue in SHL Imaging does not protect against subsequent photographs of the picture frames because the originality of the plaintiffs' photographs was almost purely in the rendition of those frames, not in their creation or the timing of the scene captured. In Pagano, the timing of the capture of the scene in front of the New York Public Library and its rendition were original, but the copyright in the Pagano photograph does not protect against future attempts to capture a scene in front of the same building, just as a copyright in Catch of the Day would not protect against other photographers capturing images of salmon-eating bears.

By contrast, to the extent that a photograph is original in the creation of the subject, copyright extends also to that subject. Thus, an artist who arranges and then photographs a scene often will have the right to prevent others from duplicating that scene in a photograph or other medium. [*From an otherwise deleted footnote:* I recognize that the preceding analysis focuses on a medium—traditional print photography—that is being supplanted in significant degree by digital technology. These advancements may or may not demand a different analytical framework.]

2. *Originality of the Garnett Photograph*

There can be no serious dispute that the Garnett Photograph is an original work. The photograph does not result from slavishly copying another work and therefore is original in the rendition. Mannion's relatively unusual angle and distinctive lighting strengthen that aspect of the photograph's originality. His composition—posing man against sky—evidences originality in the creation of the subject. Furthermore, Mannion instructed Garnett to wear simple and plain clothing and as much jewelry as possible, and "to look 'chilled out.' " His orchestration of the scene contributes additional originality in the creation of the subject.

Of course, there are limits to the photograph's originality and therefore to the protection conferred by the copyright in the Garnett Photograph. For example, Kevin Garnett's face, torso, and hands are not original with Mannion, and Mannion therefore may not prevent others from creating photographic portraits of Garnett. Equally obviously, the existence of a cloudy sky is not original, and Mannion therefore may not prevent others from using a cloudy sky as a backdrop.

The defendants, however, take this line of reasoning too far. They argue that it was Garnett, not Mannion, who selected the specific clothing, jewelry, and pose. In consequence, they maintain, the Garnett Photograph is not original to the extent of Garnett's clothing, jewelry, and pose. They appear to be referring to originality in the creation of the subject.

The defendants complain as well that Mannion's declaration does not mention, among other things, the type of film, camera, and filters that he used to produce the Garnett Photograph.... These omissions are irrelevant. As discussed above, originality in the rendition is assessed with respect to the work, not the artist's specific decisions in producing it.

There are two problems with the defendants' argument. The first is that Mannion indisputably orchestrated the scene, even if he did not plan every detail before he met Garnett, and then made the decision to capture it. The second difficulty is that the originality of the photograph extends beyond the individual clothing, jewelry, and pose viewed in isolation. It is the entire image—depicting man, sky, clothing, and jewelry in a particular arrangement—that is at issue here, not its individual components. The Second Circuit has rejected the proposition that: "in comparing designs for copyright infringement, we are required to dissect them into their separate components, and compare only those elements which are in themselves copyrightable.... [I]f we took this argument to its logical conclusion, we might have to decide that 'there can be no originality in a painting because all colors of paint have been used somewhere in the past.' Knitwaves, Inc. v. Lollytogs Ltd., 71 F.3d 996, 1003 (2d Cir.1995) (citation omitted).

3. The Idea/Expression Difficulty

Notwithstanding the originality of the Garnett Photograph, the defendants argue that the Coors Billboard does not infringe because the two, insofar as they are similar, share only "the generalized idea and concept of a young African American man wearing a white T-shirt and a large amount of jewelry." It is true that an axiom of copyright law is that copyright does not protect "ideas," only their expression. Furthermore, when "a given idea is inseparably tied to a particular expression" so that "there is a 'merger' of idea and expression," courts may deny protection to the expression in order to avoid conferring a monopoly on the idea to which it inseparably is tied. But the defendants' reliance on these principles is misplaced. The "idea" (if one wants to call it that) postulated by the defendants does not even come close to accounting for all the similarities between the two works, which extend at least to angle, pose, background, composition, and lighting. It is possible to imagine any number of depictions of a black man wearing a white T-shirt and "bling bling" that look nothing like either of the photographs at issue here.

This alone is sufficient to dispose of the defendants' contention that Mannion's claims must be rejected because he seeks to protect an idea rather than its expression. But the argument reveals an analytical difficulty in the case law about which more ought to be said. One of the main cases upon which the defendants rely is Kaplan v. Stock Market Photo Agency, Inc.,133 F.Supp.2d 317 (S.D.N.Y.2001), in which two remarkably similar photographs of a businessman's shoes and lower legs, taken from the top of a tall building looking down on a street below (the plaintiff's and defendants' photographs are reproduced below), were held to be not substantially similar as a matter of law because all of the similarities flowed only from an unprotected idea rather than from the expression of that idea.

But what is the "idea" of Kaplan's photograph? Is it (1) a business-man contemplating suicide by jumping from a building, (2) a businessman contemplating suicide by jumping from a building, seen from the vantage point of the businessman, with his shoes set against the street far below, or perhaps something more general, such as (3) a sense of desperation produced by urban professional life?

If the "idea" is (1) or, for that matter, (3), then the similarities between the two photographs flow from something much more than that idea, for it have would been possible to convey (1) (and (3)) in any number of ways that bear no obvious similarities to Kaplan's photograph. (Examples are a businessman atop a building seen from below, or the entire figure of the businessman, rather than just his shoes or pants, seen from above.) If, on the other hand, the "idea" is (2), then the two works could be said to owe much of their similarity to a shared idea.

[*From a related footnote:* The Kaplan decision itself characterized the "idea" as "a businessperson contemplating a leap from a tall building onto the city street below," see id. at 323, but this characterization does not fully account for the disposition of the case. The court agreed with the defendants that: "in order to most accurately express th[is] idea . . . , the photograph must be taken from the 'jumper's' own viewpoint, which would (i) naturally include the sheer side of the building and the traffic below, and (ii) logically restrict the visible area of the businessperson's body to his shoes and a certain portion of his pants legs. . . . Thus, the angle and viewpoint used in both photographs are essential to, commonly associated with, and naturally flow from the photograph's unprotectable subject matter. . . . [T]he most common, and most effective, viewpoint from which the convey the idea of the 'jumper'. . . . remains that of the 'jumper' himself." Id. at 326. The Kaplan court's observations about the angle and viewpoint "essential to" and "commonly associated with," that "naturally flow from," "most accurately express," and "most effective[ly]" convey the "idea of a businessperson's contemplation of a leap" are unpersuasive. Thus, the opinion is best read to hold that the "idea" expressed was that of a businessperson contemplating suicide as seen from his own vantage point because only this reading explains the outcome.]

To be sure, the difficulty of distinguishing between idea and expression long has been recognized. Judge Learned Hand famously observed in 1930: "Upon any work, and especially upon a play, a great number of patterns of increasing generality will fit equally well, as more and more of the incident is left out. The last may perhaps be no more than the most general statement of what the play is about, and at times might consist only of its title; but there is a point in this series of abstractions where they are no longer protected, since otherwise the playwright could prevent the use of his 'ideas,' to which, apart from their expression, his property is never extended. Nobody has ever been able to fix that boundary, and nobody ever can." Nichols v. Universal Pictures Corp., 45 F.2d 119, 121 (2d Cir.1930).

This passage is often referred to as the abstractions test, but it is no such thing. Judge Newman has lamented this parlance and the underlying difficulty it elides: "Judge Hand manifestly did not think of his observations as the enunciation of anything that might be called a 'test.' His disclaimer (for himself and everyone else) of the ability to 'fix the boundary' should have been sufficient caution that no 'test' capable of yielding a result was intended." Hon. Jon O. Newman, New Lyrics for an Old Melody: The Idea/Expression Dichotomy in the Computer Age, 17 Cardozo Arts & Ent. L.J. 691, 694 (1999).

Three decades later, Judge Hand's views were essentially the same: "The test for infringement of a copyright is of necessity vague.... Obviously, no principle can be stated as to when an imitator has gone beyond copying the 'idea,' and has borrowed its 'expression.' Decisions must therefore inevitably be ad hoc." Peter Pan Fabrics, Inc. v. Martin Weiner Corp., 274 F.2d 487, 489 (2d Cir.1960). Since then, the Second Circuit and other authorities repeatedly have echoed these sentiments.

But there is a difference between the sort of difficulty Judge Hand identified in Nichols and Peter Pan Fabrics and the one presented by the Kaplan rationale and the defendants' argument about ideas in this case. The former difficulty is essentially one of line-drawing, and, as Judge Hand taught, is common to most cases in most areas of the law. The latter difficulty, however, is not simply that it is not always clear where to draw the line; it is that the line itself is meaningless because the conceptual categories it purports to delineate are ill-suited to the subject matter.

The idea/expression distinction arose in the context of literary copyright. For the most part, the Supreme Court has not applied it outside that context. The classic Hand formulations reviewed above also were articulated in the context of literary works. And it makes sense to speak of the idea conveyed by a literary work and to distinguish it from its expression. To take a clear example, two different authors each can describe, with very different words, the theory of special relativity. The words will be protected as expression. The theory is a set of unprotected ideas.

In the visual arts, the distinction breaks down. For one thing, it is impossible in most cases to speak of the particular "idea" captured, embodied, or conveyed by a work of art because every observer will have a different interpretation. Furthermore, it is not clear that there is any real distinction between the idea in a work of art and its expression. An artist's idea, among other things, is to depict a particular subject in a particular way. As a demonstration, a number of cases from this Circuit have observed that a photographer's "conception" of his subject is copyrightable. By "conception," the courts must mean originality in the rendition, timing, and creation of the subject-for that is what copyright protects in photography. But the word "conception" is a cousin of "concept," and both are akin to "idea." In other words, those elements of a photograph, or indeed, any work of visual art protected by copyright, could just as easily be labeled "idea" as "expression."

In cases dealing with toys or products that have both functional and design aspects, courts sometimes use "idea" to refer to a gimmick embodied in the product. See, e.g., Mazer v. Stein, 347 U.S. 201, 217–18, 74 S.Ct. 460, 98 L.Ed. 630 (1954) (court, after introducing idea/expression dichotomy, stated that plaintiffs, who had copyrights in statuettes of human figures used as table lamps, "may not exclude others from using statuettes of human figures in table lamps; they may only prevent use of copies of their statuettes as such or as incorporated in some other article."); Herbert Rosenthal Jewelry Corp. v. Kalpakian, 446 F.2d 738, 742 (9th Cir.1971) (bejeweled gold pin in the shape of a bee was an unprotected "idea"); Herbert Rosenthal Jewelry Corp. v. Honora Jewelry Co., 509 F.2d 64, 65–66 (2d Cir.1974) (same for turtle pins); Great Importations, Inc. v. Caffco Int'l, Inc., No. 95 Civ. 0514, 1997 WL 414111, at *4 (S.D.N.Y. July 24, 1997) (M.J.) ("To the degree the similarities between the two sculptures herein are simply because they are both three-piece sets of candleholders in the shape of the letters J, O and Y with baby angels and holly, those similarities are non-copyrightable ideas. . . .").

This case does not concern any kind of gimmick, and the Court ventures no opinion about the applicability of the idea/expression dichotomy to any product that embodies a gimmick, including toys or other objects that combine function and design.

This Court is not the first to question the usefulness of the idea/expression terminology in the context of non-verbal media. Judge Hand pointed out in Peter Pan Fabrics that whereas "[i]n the case of verbal 'works', it is well settled that. . . . there can be no copyright in the 'ideas' disclosed but only in their 'expression[,]'" "[i]n the case of designs, which are addressed to the aesthetic sensibilities of the observer, the test is, if possible, even more intangible." 274 F.2d at 489. Moreover, Judge Newman has written: "I do not deny that all of these subject matters [computer programs, wooden dolls, advertisements in a telephone directory] required courts to determine whether the first work was copyrightable and whether the second infringed protectable elements. What I question is whether courts should be making those determinations with the same modes of analysis and even the same vocabulary that was appropriate for writings. . . . [I]t is not just a matter of vocabulary. Words convey concepts, and if we use identical phrases from one context to resolve issues in another, we risk failing to notice that the relevant concepts are and ought to be somewhat different." Newman, New Lyrics for an Old Melody, supra, at 697. . . .

For all of these reasons, I think little is gained by attempting to distinguish an unprotectible "idea" from its protectible "expression" in a photograph or other work of visual art. It remains, then, to consider just what courts have been referring to when they have spoken of the "idea" in a photograph.

A good example is Rogers v. Koons, in which the court observed that "[i]t is not . . . the idea of a couple with eight small puppies seated on a bench that is protected, but rather Rogers' expression of this idea-as caught in the placement, in the particular light, and in the expressions of the subjects...." 960 F.2d at 308. But "a couple with eight small puppies seated on a bench" is not necessarily the idea of Puppies, which just as easily could be "people with dogs on their laps," "the bliss of owning puppies," or even a sheepishly ironic thought such as "Ha ha! This might look cute now, but boy are these puppies going to be a lot of work!"

Rather, "a couple with eight small puppies seated on a bench" is nothing more or less than what "a young African American man wearing a white T-shirt and a large amount of jewelry" is: a description of the subject at a level of generality sufficient to avoid implicating copyright protection for an original photograph. Other copyright cases that have referred to the "idea" of a photograph also used "idea" to mean a general description of the subject or subject matter. The Kaplan decision even used these terms interchangeably: "The subject matter of both photographs is a businessperson contemplating a leap from a tall building onto the city street below. As the photograph's central idea, rather than Kaplan's expression of the idea, this subject matter is unprotectable in and of itself." Thus another photographer may pose a couple with eight puppies on a bench, depict a businessman contemplating a leap from an office building onto a street, or take a picture of a black man in white athletic wear and showy jewelry. In each case, however, there would be infringement (assuming actual copying and ownership of a valid copyright) if the subject and rendition were sufficiently like those in the copyrighted work.

It is interesting to note that United Kingdom law faces a similar terminological problem and that the solution of Laddie and supporting authorities is to conclude that the generality of an "idea" is what determines its protectability: "Confusion is caused in the law of copyright because of the use of the catchphrase 'There is no copyright in ideas but only in the form of their expression'. Unless one understands what this means its utility is non-existent, or it is positively misleading. An artistic work of the imagination presupposes two kinds of ingredients: the conception of one or more ideas, and artistic dexterity and skill in their representation in the chosen medium. It is not the law that copyright protects the second kind of ingredient only. If that were so a debased copy which failed to capture the artist's dexterity and skill would not infringe, which plainly is not the case. Unless an artist is content merely to represent a pre-existent object (eg a building) or scene, it is part of his task as artist to exercise his imagination and in so doing he may create a pattern of ideas for incorporation in his finished work. This idea-pattern may be as much part of his work, and deserving of copyright protection, as the brushstrokes, pencil-lines, etc. The true proposition is that there is no copyright in a general idea, but that an original combination of ideas may [be protected]." 1 Laddie § 4.43, at 212 (footnote omitted).

This discussion of course prompts the question: at what point do the similarities between two photographs become sufficiently general that there will be no infringement even though actual copying has occurred? But this question is precisely the same, although phrased in the opposite way, as one that must be addressed in all infringement cases, namely whether two works are substantially similar with respect to their protected elements. It is nonsensical to speak of one photograph being substantially similar to another in the rendition and creation of the subject but somehow not infringing because of a shared idea. Conversely, if the two photographs are not substantially similar in the rendition and creation of the subject, the distinction between idea and expression will be irrelevant because there can be no infringement. The idea/expression distinction in photography, and probably the other visual arts, thus achieves nothing beyond what other, clearer copyright principles already accomplish.

I recognize that those principles sometimes may pose a problem like the one that Judge Hand identified with distinguishing idea from expression in the literary context. As Judge Hand observed, however, such line-drawing difficulties appear in all areas of the law. The important thing is that the categories at issue be useful and relevant, even if their precise boundaries are sometimes difficult to delineate. In the context of photography, the idea/expression distinction is not useful or relevant.

D.   Comparison of the Coors Billboard and the Garnett Photograph

The next step is to determine whether a trier of fact could or must find the Coors Billboard substantially similar to the Garnett Photograph with respect to their protected elements.

Substantial similarity ultimately is a question of fact. "The standard test for substantial similarity between two items is whether an 'ordinary observer, unless he set out to detect the disparities, would be disposed to overlook them, and regard [the] aesthetic appeal as the same.'" The Second Circuit sometimes has applied a "more discerning observer" test when a work contains both protectible and unprotectible elements. The test "requires the court to eliminate the unprotectible elements from its consideration and to ask whether the protectible elements, standing alone, are substantially similar." The Circuit, however, is ambivalent about this test. In several cases dealing with fabric and garment designs, the Circuit has cautioned that: "a court is not to dissect the works at issue into separate components and compare only the copyrightable elements.... To do so would be to take the 'more discerning' test to an extreme, which would result in almost nothing being copyrightable because original works broken down into their composite parts would usually be little more than basic unprotectible elements like letters, colors and symbols."

Dissecting the works into separate components and comparing only the copyrightable elements, however, appears to be exactly what the "more discerning observer" test calls for. The Circuit indirectly spoke to this tension in the recent case of Tufenkian Import/Export Ventures, Inc. v. Einstein Moomjy, Inc., 338 F.3d 127 (2d Cir.2003). There the trial court purported to use the more discerning observer test but nonetheless compared the "total-concept-and-feel" of carpet designs. The Circuit observed that the more discerning observer test is "intended to emphasize that substantial similarity must exist between the defendant's allegedly infringing design and the protectible elements in the plaintiff's design." In making its own comparison, the Circuit did not mention the "more discerning observer" test at all, but it did note that: "the total-concept-and-feel locution functions as a reminder that, while the infringement analysis must begin by dissecting the copyrighted work into its component parts in order to clarify precisely what is not original, infringement analysis is not simply a matter of ascertaining similarity between components viewed in isolation.... The court, confronted with an allegedly infringing work, must analyze the two works closely to figure out in what respects, if any, they are similar, and then determine whether these similarities are due to protected aesthetic expressions original to the allegedly infringed work, or whether the similarity is to something in the original that is free for the taking."

In light of these precedents, the Court concludes that it is immaterial whether the ordinary or more discerning observer test is used here because the inquiries would be identical. The cases agree that the relevant comparison is between the protectible elements in the Garnett Photograph and the Coors Billboard, but that those elements are not to be viewed in isolation.

The Garnett Photograph is protectible to the extent of its originality in the rendition and creation of the subject. Key elements of the Garnett Photograph that are in the public domain—such as Kevin Garnett's likeness—are not replicated in the Coors Billboard. Other elements arguably in the public domain—such as the existence of a cloudy sky, Garnett's pose, his white T-shirt, and his specific jewelry—may not be copyrightable in and of themselves, but their existence and arrangement in this photograph indisputably contribute to its originality. Thus the fact that the Garnett Photograph includes certain elements that would not be copyrightable in isolation does not affect the nature of the comparison. The question is whether the aesthetic appeal of the two images is the same.

The two photographs share a similar composition and angle. The lighting is similar, and both use a cloudy sky as backdrop. The subjects are wearing similar clothing and similar jewelry arranged in a similar way. The defendants, in other words, appear to have recreated much of the subject that Mannion had created and then, through imitation of angle and lighting, rendered it in a similar way. The similarities here thus relate to the Garnett Photograph's originality in the rendition and the creation of the subject and therefore to its protected elements.

There of course are differences between the two works. The similarity analysis may take into account some, but not all, of these. It long has been the law that "no plagiarist can excuse the wrong by showing how much of his work he did not pirate." Thus the addition of the words "Iced Out" and a can of Coors Light beer may not enter into the similarity analysis.

Other differences, however, are in the nature of changes rather than additions. One image is black and white and dark, the other is in color and bright. One is the mirror image of the other. One depicts only an unidentified man's torso, the other the top three-fourths of Kevin Garnett's body. The jewelry is not identical. One T-shirt appears to fit more tightly than the other. These changes may enter the analysis because "[i]f the points of dissimilarity not only exceed the points of similarity, but indicate that the remaining points of similarity are, within the context of plaintiff's work, of minimal importance . . . then no infringement results."

The parties have catalogued at length and in depth the similarities and differences between these works. In the last analysis, a reasonable jury could find substantial similarity either present or absent. As in Kisch v. Ammirati & Puris Inc., 657 F.Supp. 380, 384 (S.D.N.Y.1987), which presents facts as close to this case as can be imagined, the images are such that infringement cannot be ruled out-or in-as a matter of law.

Conclusion

The defendants' motion for summary judgment dismissing the complaint is granted to the extent that the complaint seeks relief for violation of the plaintiff's exclusive right to prepare derivative works and otherwise denied. The plaintiff's cross motion for summary judgment is denied.

Notes

1.   The opinion in *Mannion* suggests how far the law of photography has traveled in the years since *Burrow–Giles*. How should Ansel Adams's "Moonrise: Hernandez (1941)" be analyzed in light of the discussion in *Burrow–Giles* and *Mannion*?

2.   Consider whether *Mannion* clarifies the law or provides useful guidance to practitioners and their clients? As we will see in our study of copyright, the stakes are enormous in a case like this: in addition to the threat of damages, the losing party is at risk of paying the winner's attorneys' fees. If the defendant loses it may be enjoined against further dissemination of its work; the work itself may even be seized and destroyed. Thus, the operation of a regime like the one advanced in this case means that freedom of expression and creativity itself are also decidedly at risk when weighed against copyright. Should copyright law have been permitted to develop in this fashion? Should we tolerate a rule of such admitted indeterminacy where expression and creativity are at stake? As we will also see, a so-called "merger doctrine" requires that copyright be set aside when idea and expression merge in a work. Why does the merger doctrine (or at least a suitably adapted version of it) not apply in a case like *Mannion*?

Would it be helpful if all doubtful cases were simply resolved for or against a finding of infringement? Could a court adopt such a presumption without Congressional approval? Which presumption would you favor?

B. THE FIXATION REQUIREMENT

COPYRIGHT ACT OF 1976

H.R. Rep. No. 94–1476.
94th Cong., 2d Sess. 52–53 (1976).

Fixation in tangible form

As a basic condition of copyright protection, the bill perpetuates the existing requirement that work be fixed in a "tangible medium of expression," and adds that this medium may be one "now known or later developed," and that the fixation is sufficient if the work "can be perceived, reproduced, or otherwise communicated, either directly or with the aid of a machine or device." This broad language is intended to avoid the artificial and largely unjustifiable distinctions, derived from cases such as *White-Smith Publishing Co. v. Apollo Co.*, 209 U.S. 1 (1908), under which statutory copyrightability in certain cases has been made to depend upon the form or medium in which the work is fixed. Under the bill it makes no difference what the form, manner, or medium of fixation may be—whether it is in words, numbers, notes, sounds, pictures, or any other graphic or symbolic indicia, whether embodied in a physical object in written, printed, photographic, sculptural, punched, magnetic, or any other stable form, and whether it is capable of perception directly or by means of any machine or device "now known or later developed."

Under the bill, the concept of fixation is important since it not only determines whether the provisions of the statute apply to a work, but it also represents the dividing line between common law and statutory protection. As will be noted in more detail in connection with section 301, an unfixed work of authorship, such as an improvisation or an unrecorded choreographic work, performance, or broadcast, would continue to be subject to protection under State common law or statute, but would not be eligible for Federal statutory protection under section 102.

The bill seeks to resolve, through the definition of "fixation" in section 101, the status of live broadcasts—sports, news coverage, live performances of music, etc.—that are reaching the public in unfixed form but that are simultaneously being recorded. When a football game is being covered by four television cameras, with a director guiding the activities of the four cameramen and choosing which of their electronic images are sent out to the public and in what order, there is little doubt that what the cameramen and the director are doing constitutes "authorship." The further question to be considered is whether there has been a fixation. If the images and sounds to be broadcast are first recorded (on a video tape, film, etc.) and then transmitted, the recorded work would be considered a "motion picture" subject to statutory protection against unauthorized reproduction or retransmission of the broadcast. If the program content is transmitted live to the public while being recorded at the same time, the case would be treated the same; the copyright owner would not be forced to rely on common law rather than statutory rights in proceeding against an infringing user of the live broadcast.

Thus, assuming it is copyrightable—as a "motion picture" or "sound recording," for example—the content of a live transmission should be regarded as fixed and should be accorded statutory protection if it is being recorded simultaneously with its transmission. On the other hand, the definition of "fixation" would exclude from the concept purely evanescent or transient reproductions such as those projected briefly on a screen, shown electronically on a television or other cathode ray tube, or captured momentarily in the "memory" of a computer.

Under the first sentence of the definition of "fixed" in section 101, a work would be considered "fixed in a tangible medium of expression" if there has been an authorized embodiment in a copy or phonorecord and if that embodiment "is sufficiently permanent or stable" to permit the work "to be perceived, reproduced, or otherwise communicated for a period of more than transitory duration." The second sentence makes clear that, in the case of "a work consisting of sounds, images, or both, that are being transmitted," the work is regarded as "fixed" if a fixation is being made at the same time as the transmission.

Under this definition "copies" and "phonorecords" together will comprise all of the material objects in which copyrightable works are capable of being fixed. * * * Two essential elements—original work and tangible object—must merge through fixation in order to produce subject matter copyrightable under the statute.

* * *

STERN ELECTRONICS, INC. v. KAUFMAN

United States Court of Appeals, Second Circuit, 1982.
669 F.2d 852.

NEWMAN, CIRCUIT JUDGE:

[Defendants appeal the district court's grant of a preliminary injunction barring Omni Video Games, Inc., its distributor, and two of its officers, from infringing Stern Electronics' copyright in the electronic video game "Scramble," on the ground that "the visual images and accompanying sounds of the video game fail to satisfy the fixation and originality requirements of the Copyright Act, 17 U.S.C.App. § 102(a) (1976)."]

* * *

* * * To satisfy the statutory requirement for deposit of copies of a work to be copyrighted, 17 U.S.C.App. § 408(b) (1976), [Stern's licensor]

Konami submitted video tape recordings of the "Scramble" game, both in its "attract mode" and in its "play mode."[1]

* * * In April 1981 Omni began to sell a video game called "Scramble" that not only bears the same name as the "Scramble" game Stern was then marketing, but also is virtually identical in both sight and sound. It sold this copy of Stern's "Scramble" game, known in the trade as a "knock-off," for several hundred dollars less than Stern's game.

1. COPYRIGHT ISSUES

In challenging the preliminary injunction that bars distribution of its "Scramble" game, Omni does not dispute that Konami and its sublicensee Stern are entitled to secure some copyright protection for their "Scramble" game. Omni contends that Konami was entitled to copyright only the written computer program that determines the sights and sounds of the game's audiovisual display. While that approach would have afforded some degree of protection, it would not have prevented a determined competitor from manufacturing a "knock-off" of "Scramble" that replicates precisely the sights and sounds of the game's audiovisual display. This could be done by writing a new computer program that would interact with the hardware components of a video game to produce on the screen the same images seen in "Scramble," accompanied by the same sounds. Such replication is possible because many different computer programs can produce the same "results," whether those results are an analysis of financial records or a sequence of images and sounds. A program is simply "a set of statements (i.e., data) or instructions to be used directly or indirectly in a computer in order to bring about a certain result," Pub.L.No. 96–517, § 10(a), 94 Stat. 3015, 3028 (1980) (amending 17 U.S.C.App. § 101 (1976)). To take an elementary example, the result of displaying a "4" can be achieved by an instruction to add 2 and 2, subtract 3 from 7, or in a variety of other ways. Obviously, writing a new program to replicate the play of "Scramble" requires a sophisticated effort, but it is a manageable task.

To secure protection against the risk of a "knock-off" of "Scramble" based upon an original program, Konami eschewed registration of its program as a literary work and chose instead to register the sights and sounds of "Scramble" as an audiovisual work. See 17 U.S.C.App. § 102(a)(6) (1976). The Act defines "audiovisual works" as "works that consist of a series of related images which are intrinsically intended to be shown by the use of machines, or devices such as projectors, viewers, or electronic equipment, together with accompanying sounds, if any, regardless of the nature of the material objects, such as films or tapes, in which the works are embodied." 17 U.S.C.App. § 101 (1976). Omni contends that Konami is not entitled to secure a copyright in the sights and sounds of its "Scramble" game because the audiovisual work is

---

1. "Attract mode" refers to the audiovisual display seen and heard by a prospective customer contemplating playing the game; the video screen displays some of the essential visual and sound characteristics of the game. "Play mode" refers to the audiovisual display seen and heard by a person playing the game.

neither "fixed in any tangible medium of expression" nor "original" within the meaning of § 102(a). Both contentions arise from the fact that the sequence of some of the images appearing on the screen during each play of the game will vary depending upon the actions taken by the player. For example, if he fails to avoid enemy fire, his spaceship will be destroyed; if he fails to destroy enough fuel depots, his own fuel supply will run out, and his spaceship will crash; if he succeeds in destroying missile sites and enemy planes, those images will disappear from the screen; and the precise course travelled by his spaceship will depend upon his adjustment of the craft's altitude and velocity.

If the content of the audiovisual display were not affected by the participation of the player, there would be no doubt that the display itself, and not merely the written computer program, would be eligible for copyright. The display satisfies the statutory definition of an original "audiovisual work," and the memory devices of the game satisfy the statutory requirement of a "copy" in which the work is "fixed."[4] The Act defines "copies" as "material objects ... in which a work is fixed by any method now known or later developed, and from which the work can be perceived, reproduced, or otherwise communicated, either directly or with the aid of a machine or device" and specifies that a work is "fixed" when "its embodiment in a copy ... is sufficiently permanent or stable to permit it to be perceived, reproduced, or otherwise communicated for a period of more than transitory duration." 17 U.S.C.App. § 101 (1976). The audiovisual work is permanently embodied in a material object, the memory devices, from which it can be perceived with the aid of the other components of the game.

We agree with the District Court that the player's participation does not withdraw the audiovisual work from copyright eligibility. No doubt the entire sequence of all the sights and sounds of the game are different each time the game is played, depending upon the route and speed the player selects for his spaceship and the timing and accuracy of his release of his craft's bombs and lasers. Nevertheless, many aspects of the sights and the sequence of their appearance remain constant during each play of the game. These include the appearance (shape, color, and size) of the player's spaceship, the enemy craft, the ground missile bases and fuel depots, and the terrain over which (and beneath which) the player's ship flies, as well as the sequence in which the missile bases, fuel depots, and terrain appears. Also constant are the sounds heard whenever the player successfully destroys an enemy craft or installation or fails to avoid an enemy missile or laser. It is true, as appellants contend, that

---

4. In arguing that the permanent "imprinting" of the computer program in the game's memory devices satisfies the requirement of fixation in a tangible medium, appellees direct our attention to the PROM ["Programmable Read Only Memory"], which contains, in electronically usable form, the computer program for the game. While the PROM device contains the program specifically written for the "Scram- ble" game, there are undoubtedly some items of program stored in memory devices located in other components of the game. Whether located in the PROM prepared for this particular game or elsewhere in the total assembly, all portions of the program, once stored in memory devices anywhere in the game, are fixed in a tangible medium within the meaning of the Act.

some of these sights and sounds will not be seen and heard during each play of the game in the event that the player's spaceship is destroyed before the entire course is traversed. But the images remain fixed, capable of being seen and heard each time a player succeeds in keeping his spaceship aloft long enough to permit the appearances of all the images and sounds of a complete play of the game. The repetitive sequence of a substantial portion of the sights and sounds of the game qualifies for copyright protection as an audiovisual work.

* * *

Notes

1. In certain countries, fixation is not a copyright prerequisite. Under United States law, however, fixation generally is conceded (though not entirely without dissent) to be a constitutional requirement under the Intellectual Property Clause, as well as a statutory requirement? See Nimmer on Copyright § 1.08[C][2]. What purpose does fixation serve?

2. The Uruguay Round Agreements Act of 1994 added 17 U.S.C. § 1101 and 18 U.S.C. § 2319A, providing civil and criminal remedies for making or trafficking in unauthorized recordings of live musical performances. Does this exceed Congress's power under the Intellectual Property Clause? Is the statute therefore unconstitutional? See Nimmer, *The End of Copyright*, 48 Vand. L. Rev. 1385 (1985). Should other types of live performances receive similar protection?

In *United States v. Martignon*, 346 F.Supp.2d 413 (S.D.N.Y. 2004), the court held section 2319A unconstitutional on the ground that the statute represented an essentially "copyright-like" enactment, and therefore was in excess of congressional power under the Copyright Clause by virtue of its failure to impose a limit on the term of protection. The court acknowledged, but declined to follow, an earlier Eleventh Circuit decision upholding the statute in circumstances that failed to present the issue raised in *Martignon*. See *United States v. Moghadam*, 175 F.3d 1269 (11th Cir. 1999). Note that (as the Court observed in *Martignon*) section 1101 is the civil law counterpart of section 2319A. It would seem to follow that section 1101 should be held unconstitutional as well—unless, perhaps, the limitation in section 1101 to damages might be seen to lend strength to a claim that this section is more plausibly to be seen as touching upon "commerce". Such an argument can be imagined; but whether plausibly so (as against the larger reasoning in *Martignon*) seems doubtful.

3. Outside the context of sections 1101 and 2319A, is it possible to obtain copyright (or similar) protection for a live event (for example, a live stage performance, or a news or sporting event), or any portion thereof? If so, how? (Consider the definition of "fixed" in Section 101 of the Copyright Act.) Who would own the copyright?

4. If material is entered into a computer but not saved on the hard drive or a floppy disk, is it sufficiently fixed to be copyrightable? For example, does copyright law protect material in an on-line "chat room" conversation that is typed onto the screen but not "saved" by its author?

C. "ORIGINAL WORKS OF AUTHORSHIP"

1. ORIGINALITY: THE MINIMUM REQUIREMENT

Absent a statutory definition of the term, courts have labored to determine which works constitute "original works of authorship." The statutes do not define the quantum of originality required. It is clear, in principle, that an erstwhile "author" cannot obtain copyright protection for any portions of a work which consist entirely of material that is copied from a work in the public domain or from another copyrighted work. However, since all works of authorship necessarily are made up of public domain components—such as ideas, facts, words, musical notes, and naturally occurring images and sounds, as well as preexisting works of authorship—applying this general principle in particular cases can be difficult.

FEIST PUBLICATIONS v. RURAL
TELEPHONE SERVICE

Supreme Court of the United States, 1991.
499 U.S. 340, 111 S.Ct. 1282, 113 L.Ed.2d 358.

Justice O'Connor delivered the opinion of the Court.

This case requires us to clarify the extent of copyright protection available to telephone directory white pages.

I

Rural Telephone Service Company, Inc., is a certified public utility that provides telephone service to several communities in northwest Kansas. It is subject to a state regulation that requires all telephone companies operating in Kansas to issue annually an updated telephone directory. Accordingly, as a condition of its monopoly franchise, Rural publishes a typical telephone directory, consisting of white pages and yellow pages. The white pages list in alphabetical order the names of Rural's subscribers, together with their towns and telephone numbers. The yellow pages list Rural's business subscribers alphabetically by category and feature classified advertisements of various sizes. Rural distributes its directory free of charge to its subscribers, but earns revenue by selling yellow pages advertisements.

Feist Publications, Inc., is a publishing company that specializes in area-wide telephone directories. Unlike a typical directory, which covers only a particular calling area, Feist's area-wide directories cover a much larger geographical range, reducing the need to call directory assistance or consult multiple directories. The Feist directory that is the subject of this litigation covers 11 different telephone service areas in 15 counties and contains 46,878 white pages listings—compared to Rural's approximately 7,700 listings. Like Rural's directory, Feist's is distributed free of charge and includes both white pages and yellow pages. Feist and Rural compete vigorously for yellow pages advertising.

As the sole provider of telephone service in its service area, Rural obtains subscriber information quite easily. Persons desiring telephone service must apply to Rural and provide their names and addresses; Rural then assigns them a telephone number. Feist is not a telephone company, let alone one with monopoly status, and therefore lacks independent access to any subscriber information. To obtain white pages listings for its area-wide directory, Feist approached each of the 11 telephone companies operating in northwest Kansas and offered to pay for the right to use its white pages listings.

Of the 11 telephone companies, only Rural refused to license its listings to Feist. Rural's refusal created a problem for Feist, as omitting these listings would have left a gaping hole in its area-wide directory, rendering it less attractive to potential yellow pages advertisers. In a decision subsequent to that which we review here, the District Court determined that this was precisely the reason Rural refused to license its listings. The refusal was motivated by an unlawful purpose "to extend its monopoly in telephone service to a monopoly in yellow pages advertising." Rural Telephone Service Co. v. Feist Publications, Inc., 737 F.Supp. 610, 622 (D.Kan.1990).

Unable to license Rural's white pages listings, Feist used them without Rural's consent. Feist began by removing several thousand listings that fell outside the geographic range of its area-wide directory, then hired personnel to investigate the 4,935 that remained. These employees verified the data reported by Rural and sought to obtain additional information. As a result, a typical Feist listing includes the individual's street address; most of Rural's listings do not. Notwithstanding these additions, however, 1,309 of the 46,878 listings in Feist's 1983 directory were identical to listings in Rural's 1982–1983 white pages. * * * Four of these were fictitious listings that Rural had inserted into its directory to detect copying.

Rural sued for copyright infringement in the District Court for the District of Kansas taking the position that Feist, in compiling its own directory, could not use the information contained in Rural's white pages. Rural asserted that Feist's employees were obliged to travel door-to-door or conduct a telephone survey to discover the same information for themselves. Feist responded that such efforts were economically impractical and, in any event, unnecessary because the information copied was beyond the scope of copyright protection. The District Court granted summary judgment to Rural, explaining that "[c]ourts have consistently held that telephone directories are copyrightable" and citing a string of lower court decisions. In an unpublished opinion, the Court of Appeals for the Tenth Circuit affirmed "for substantially the reasons given by the district court." We granted certiorari, 498 U.S. 808 (1990), to determine whether the copyright in Rural's directory protects the names, towns, and telephone numbers copied by Feist.

II

A

This case concerns the interaction of two well-established propositions. The first is that facts are not copyrightable; the other, that compilations of facts generally are. Each of these propositions possesses an impeccable pedigree. That there can be no valid copyright in facts is universally understood. The most fundamental axiom of copyright law is that "no author may copyright his ideas or the facts he narrates." Harper & Row, Publishers, Inc. v. Nation Enterprises, 471 U.S. 539, 556 (1985). Rural wisely concedes this point, noting in its brief that "facts and discoveries, of course, are not themselves subject to copyright protection." Brief for Respondent 24. At the same time, however, it is beyond dispute that compilations of facts are within the subject matter of copyright. Compilations were expressly mentioned in the Copyright Act of 1909, and again in the Copyright Act of 1976.

There is an undeniable tension between these two propositions. Many compilations consist of nothing but raw data—i. e., wholly factual information not accompanied by any original written expression. On what basis may one claim a copyright in such a work? Common sense tells us that 100 uncopyrightable facts do not magically change their status when gathered together in one place. Yet copyright law seems to contemplate that compilations that consist exclusively of facts are potentially within its scope.

The key to resolving the tension lies in understanding why facts are not copyrightable. The sine qua non of copyright is originality. To qualify for copyright protection, a work must be original to the author. See Harper & Row, supra, at 547–549. Original, as the term is used in copyright, means only that the work was independently created by the author (as opposed to copied from other works), and that it possesses at least some minimal degree of creativity. 1 M. Nimmer & D. Nimmer, Copyright §§ 2.01[A], [B] (1990) (hereinafter Nimmer). To be sure, the requisite level of creativity is extremely low; even a slight amount will suffice. The vast majority of works make the grade quite easily, as they possess some creative spark, "no matter how crude, humble or obvious" it might be. Id., § 1.08[C][1]. Originality does not signify novelty; a work may be original even though it closely resembles other works so long as the similarity is fortuitous, not the result of copying. To illustrate, assume that two poets, each ignorant of the other, compose identical poems. Neither work is novel, yet both are original and, hence, copyrightable. See Sheldon v. Metro–Goldwyn Pictures Corp., 81 F. 2d 49, 54 (C.A.2 1936).

Originality is a constitutional requirement. The source of Congress' power to enact copyright laws is Article I, § 8, cl. 8, of the Constitution, which authorizes Congress to "secure for limited Times to Authors ... the exclusive Right to their respective Writings." In two decisions from the late 19th century—The Trade–Mark Cases, 100 U.S. 82 (1879); and Burrow–Giles Lithographic Co. v. Sarony, 111 U.S. 53 (1884)—this Court defined the crucial terms "authors" and "writings." In so doing, the Court made it unmistakably clear that these terms presuppose a degree of originality.

In The Trade–Mark Cases, the Court addressed the constitutional scope of "writings." For a particular work to be classified "under the head of writings of authors," the Court determined, "originality is required." 100 U.S., at 94. The Court explained that originality requires independent creation plus a modicum of creativity: "[W]hile the word *writings* may be liberally construed, as it has been, to include original designs for engraving, prints, & c., it is only such as are *original,* and are founded in the creative powers of the mind. The writings which are to be protected are *the fruits of intellectual labor,* embodied in the form of books, prints, engravings, and the like." Ibid. (emphasis in original).

In Burrow–Giles, the Court distilled the same requirement from the Constitution's use of the word "authors." The Court defined "author," in a constitutional sense, to mean "he to whom anything owes its origin; originator; maker." 111 U.S., at 58 (internal quotation marks omitted). As in The Trade–Mark Cases, the Court emphasized the creative component of originality. It described copyright as being limited to "original intellectual conceptions of the author," 111 U.S., at 58, and stressed the importance of requiring an author who accuses another of infringement to prove "the existence of those facts of originality, of intellectual production, of thought, and conception." Id., at 59–60.

The originality requirement articulated in The Trade–Mark Cases and Burrow–Giles remains the touchstone of copyright protection today. See Goldstein v. California, 412 U.S. 546, 561–562 (1973). It is the very "premise of copyright law." Miller v. Universal City Studios, Inc., 650 F. 2d 1365, 1368 (C.A.5 1981). Leading scholars agree on this point. As one pair of commentators succinctly puts it: "The originality requirement is *constitutionally mandated* for all works." Patterson & Joyce, Monopolizing the Law: The Scope of Copyright Protection for Law Reports and Statutory Compilations, 36 UCLA L. Rev. 719, 763, n. 155 (1989) (emphasis in original) (hereinafter Patterson & Joyce). Accord, id., at 759–760, and n. 140; Nimmer § 1.06[A] ("Originality is a statutory as well as a constitutional requirement"); id., § 1.08[C][1] ("[A] modicum of intellectual labor ... clearly constitutes an essential constitutional element").

It is this bedrock principle of copyright that mandates the law's seemingly disparate treatment of facts and factual compilations. "No one may claim originality as to facts." Id., § 2.11[A], p. 2–157. This is because facts do not owe their origin to an act of authorship. The distinction is one between creation and discovery: The first person to find and report a particular fact has not created the fact; he or she has merely discovered its existence. To borrow from Burrow–Giles, one who discovers a fact is not its "maker" or "originator." 111 U.S., at 58. "The discoverer merely finds and records." Nimmer § 2.03[E]. Census takers, for example, do not "create" the population figures that emerge from their efforts; in a sense, they copy these figures from the world around them. Denicola, Copyright in Collections of Facts: A Theory for the Protection of Nonfiction Literary Works, 81 Colum. L. Rev. 516, 525 (1981) (hereinafter Denicola). Census data therefore do not trigger copyright because these data are not "original" in the constitutional sense. Nimmer § 2.03[E]. The same is true of all facts—scientific, historical, biographical, and news of the day. "They may not be copyrighted and are part of the public domain available to every person." Miller, supra, at 1369.

Factual compilations, on the other hand, may possess the requisite originality. The compilation author typically chooses which facts to include, in what order to place them, and how to arrange the collected data so that they may be used effectively by readers. These choices as to selection and arrangement, so long as they are made independently by the compiler and entail a minimal degree of creativity, are sufficiently original that Congress may protect such compilations through the copyright laws. Nimmer §§ 2.11[D], 3.03; Denicola 523, n. 38. Thus, even a directory that contains absolutely no protectible written expression, only facts, meets the constitutional minimum for copyright protection if it features an original selection or arrangement. See Harper & Row, 471 U.S., at 547. Accord, Nimmer § 3.03.

This protection is subject to an important limitation. The mere fact that a work is copyrighted does not mean that every element of the work may be protected. Originality remains the sine qua non of copyright; accordingly, copyright protection may extend only to those components of a work that are original to the author. Patterson & Joyce 800–802; Ginsburg, Creation and Commercial Value: Copyright Protection of Works of Information, 90 Colum. L. Rev. 1865, 1868, and n. 12 (1990) (hereinafter Ginsburg). Thus, if the compilation author clothes facts with an original collocation of words, he or she may be able to claim a copyright in this written expression. Others may copy the underlying facts from the publication, but not the precise words used to present them. In Harper & Row, for example, we explained that President Ford could not prevent others from copying bare historical facts from his autobiography, see 471 U.S., at 556–557, but that he could prevent others from copying his "subjective descriptions and portraits of public figures." Id., at 563. Where the compilation author adds no written expression but rather lets the facts speak for themselves, the expressive element is more elusive. The only conceivable expression is the manner in which the compiler has selected and arranged the facts. Thus, if the selection and arrangement are original, these elements of the work are eligible for copyright protection. See Patry, Copyright in Compilations of Facts (or Why the "White Pages" Are Not Copyrightable), 12 Com. & Law 37, 64 (Dec. 1990) (hereinafter Patry). No matter how original the format, however, the facts themselves do not become original through association. See Patterson & Joyce 776.

This inevitably means that the copyright in a factual compilation is thin. Notwithstanding a valid copyright, a subsequent compiler remains free to use the facts contained in another's publication to aid in preparing a competing work, so long as the competing work does not feature the same selection and arrangement. As one commentator explains it: "No matter how much original authorship the work displays, the facts and ideas it exposes are free for the taking.... The very same facts and ideas may be divorced from the context imposed by the author, and restated or reshuffled by second comers, even if the author was the first to discover the facts or to propose the ideas." Ginsburg 1868.

It may seem unfair that much of the fruit of the compiler's labor may be used by others without compensation. As Justice Brennan has correctly observed, however, this is not "some unforeseen byproduct of a statutory scheme." Harper & Row, 471 U.S. 539, at 589 (dissenting opinion). It is, rather, "the essence of copyright," ibid., and a constitutional requirement. The primary objective of copyright is not to reward the labor of authors, but "to promote the Progress of Science and useful Arts." Art. I, § 8, cl. 8. Accord, Twentieth Century Music Corp. v. Aiken, 422 U.S. 151, 156 (1975). To this end, copyright assures authors the right to their original expression, but encourages others to build freely upon the ideas and information conveyed by a work. Harper & Row, supra, at 556–557. This principle, known as the idea/expression or fact/expression dichotomy, applies to all works of authorship. As applied to a factual compilation, assuming the absence of original written expression, only the compiler's selection and arrangement may be protected; the raw facts may be copied at will. This result is neither unfair nor unfortunate. It is the means by which copyright advances the progress of science and art.

This Court has long recognized that the fact/expression dichotomy limits severely the scope of protection in fact-based works. More than a century ago, the Court observed: "The very object of publishing a book on science or the useful arts is to communicate to the world the useful knowledge which it contains. But this object would be frustrated if the knowledge could not be used without incurring the guilt of piracy of the book." Baker v. Selden, 101 U.S. 99, 103 (1880). We reiterated this point in Harper & Row:

"[N]o author may copyright facts or ideas. The copyright is limited to those aspects of the work—termed 'expression'—that display the stamp of the author's originality.

"[C]opyright does not prevent subsequent users from copying from a prior author's work those constituent elements that are not original—for example ... facts, or materials in the public domain— as long as such use does not unfairly appropriate the author's original contributions." 471 U.S., at 547–548 (citation omitted).

This, then, resolves the doctrinal tension: Copyright treats facts and factual compilations in a wholly consistent manner. Facts, whether alone or as part of a compilation, are not original and therefore may not be copyrighted. A factual compilation is eligible for copyright if it features an original selection or arrangement of facts, but the copyright is limited to the particular selection or arrangement. In no event may copyright extend to the facts themselves.

B

As we have explained, originality is a constitutionally mandated prerequisite for copyright protection. The Court's decisions announcing this rule predate the Copyright Act of 1909, but ambiguous language in the 1909 Act caused some lower courts temporarily to lose sight of this requirement.

The 1909 Act embodied the originality requirement, but not as clearly as it might have. See Nimmer § 2.01. The subject matter of copyright was set out in §§ 3 and 4 of the Act. Section 4 stated that copyright was available to "all the writings of an author." 35 Stat. 1076. By using the words "writings" and "author"—the same words used in Article I, § 8, of the Constitution and defined by the Court in The Trade–Mark Cases and Burrow–Giles—the statute necessarily incorporated the originality requirement articulated in the Court's decisions. It did so implicitly, however, thereby leaving room for error.

Section 3 was similarly ambiguous. It stated that the copyright in a work protected only "the copyrightable component parts of the work." It thus stated an important copyright principle, but failed to identify the specific characteristic—originality—that determined which component parts of a work were copyrightable and which were not.

* * *

[Because of these ambiguities, some courts adopted the view that factual compilations were protectible regardless of their originality.] Making matters worse, these courts developed a new theory to justify the protection of factual compilations. Known alternatively as "sweat of the brow" or "industrious collection," the underlying notion was that copyright was a reward for the hard work that went into compiling facts. The classic formulation of the doctrine appeared in Jeweler's Circular Publishing Co. [v. Keystone Publishing Co., 281 F. 83 (2d Cir.1922)], at 88:

> "The right to copyright a book upon which one has expended labor in its preparation does not depend upon whether the materials which he has collected consist or not of matters which are publici juris, or whether such materials show literary skill *or originality*, either in thought or in language, or anything more than industrious collection. The man who goes through the streets of a town and puts down the names of each of the inhabitants, with their occupations and their street number, acquires material of which he is the author" (emphasis added).

The "sweat of the brow" doctrine had numerous flaws, the most glaring being that it extended copyright protection in a compilation beyond selection and arrangement—the compiler's original contributions—to the facts themselves. Under the doctrine, the only defense to infringement was independent creation. A subsequent compiler was "not entitled to take one word of information previously published," but rather had to "independently wor[k] out the matter for himself, so as to arrive at the same result from the same common sources of information." Id., at 88–89 (internal quotations omitted). "Sweat of the brow" courts thereby eschewed the most fundamental axiom of copyright law—that no one may copyright facts or ideas. See Miller v. Universal City Studios, Inc., 650 F.2d, at 1372 (criticizing "sweat of the brow" courts because "ensur[ing] that later writers obtain the facts independently ... is precisely the scope of protection given ... copyrighted matter, and the law is clear that facts are not entitled to such protection").

Decisions of this Court applying the 1909 Act make clear that the statute did not permit the "sweat of the brow" approach. The best example is International News Service v. Associated Press, 248 U.S. 215 (1918). In that decision, the Court stated unambiguously that the 1909 Act conferred copyright protection only on those elements of a work that were original to the author. International News Service had conceded taking news reported by Associated Press and publishing it in its own newspapers. Recognizing that § 5 of the Act specifically mentioned " 'periodicals, including newspapers,' " § 5(b), the Court acknowledged that news articles were copyrightable. Id., at 234. It flatly rejected, however, the notion that the copyright in an article extended to the factual information it contained: "[T]he news element—the information respecting current events contained in the literary production—is not the creation of the writer, but is a report of matters that ordinarily are publici juris; it is the history of the day." Ibid.*

Without a doubt, the "sweat of the brow" doctrine flouted basic copyright principles. Throughout history, copyright law has "recognize[d] a greater need to disseminate factual works than works of fiction or fantasy." Harper & Row, 471 U.S. 539, at 563. Accord, Gorman, Fact or Fancy: The Implications for Copyright, 29 J. Copyright Soc. 560, 563 (1982). But "sweat of the brow" courts took a contrary view; they handed out proprietary interests in facts and declared that authors are absolutely precluded from saving time and effort by relying upon the facts contained in prior works. In truth, "[i]t is just such wasted effort that the proscription against the copyright of ideas and facts ... [is] designed to prevent." Rosemont Enterprises, Inc. v. Random House, Inc., 366 F.2d 303, 310 (C.A.2 1966), cert. denied, 385 U.S. 1009 (1967). "Protection for the fruits of such research ... may in certain circumstances be available under a theory of unfair competition. But to accord copyright protection on this basis alone distorts basic copyright principles in that it creates a monopoly in public domain materials without the necessary justification of protecting and encouraging the creation of 'writings' by 'authors.' " Nimmer § 3.04, p. 3–23 (footnote omitted).

C

* * *

---

* The Court ultimately rendered judgment for Associated Press on non-copyright grounds that are not relevant here. See 248 U.S., at 235, 241–242.

* * * In enacting the Copyright Act of 1976, Congress dropped the reference to "all the writings of an author" and replaced it with the phrase "original works of authorship." 17 U. S. C. § 102(a). In making explicit the originality requirement, Congress announced that it was merely clarifying existing law * * *.

* * *

To ensure that the mistakes of the "sweat of the brow" courts would not be repeated, Congress took additional measures. For example, § 3 of the 1909 Act had stated that copyright protected only the "copyrightable component parts" of a work, but had not identified originality as the basis for distinguishing those component parts that were copyrightable from those that were not. The 1976 Act deleted this section and replaced it with § 102(b), which identifies specifically those elements of a work for which copyright is not available: "In no case does copyright protection for an original work of authorship extend to any idea, procedure, process, system, method of operation, concept, principle, or discovery, regardless of the form in which it is described, explained, illustrated, or embodied in such work." Section 102(b) is universally understood to prohibit any copyright in facts. Harper & Row, supra, at 547, 556. Accord, Nimmer § 2.03[E] (equating facts with "discoveries"). As with § 102(a), Congress emphasized that § 102(b) did not change the law, but merely clarified it: "Section 102(b) in no way enlarges or contracts the scope of copyright protection under the present law. Its purpose is to restate ... that the basic dichotomy between expression and idea remains unchanged." H. R. Rep., at 57; S. Rep., at 54.

Congress took another step to minimize confusion by deleting the specific mention of "directories ... and other compilations" in § 5 of the 1909 Act. * * * In its place, Congress enacted two new provisions. First, to make clear that compilations were not copyrightable per se, Congress provided a definition of the term "compilation." Second, to make clear that the copyright in a compilation did not extend to the facts themselves, Congress enacted § 103.

The definition of "compilation" is found in § 101 of the 1976 Act. It defines a "compilation" in the copyright sense as "a work formed by the collection and assembling of preexisting materials or of data *that* are selected, coordinated, or arranged *in such a way that* the resulting work as a whole constitutes an original work of authorship" (emphasis added).

The purpose of the statutory definition is to emphasize that collections of facts are not copyrightable per se. It conveys this message through its tripartite structure, as emphasized above by the italics. The statute identifies three distinct elements and requires each to be met for a work to qualify as a copyrightable compilation: (1) the collection and assembly of pre-existing material, facts, or data; (2) the selection, coordination, or arrangement of those materials; and (3) the creation, by virtue of the particular selection, coordination, or arrangement, of an "original" work of authorship. "This tripartite conjunctive structure is self-evident, and should be assumed to 'accurately express the legislative purpose.' " Patry 51, quoting Mills Music[, Inc. v. Snyder, 469 U.S. 153, 164, 105 S.Ct. 638, 83 L.Ed.2d 556 (1985)].

At first glance, the first requirement does not seem to tell us much. It merely describes what one normally thinks of as a compilation—a collection of pre-existing material, facts, or data. What makes it significant is that it is not the sole requirement. It is not enough for copyright purposes that an author collects and assembles facts. To satisfy the statutory definition, the work must get over two additional hurdles. In this way, the plain language indicates that not every collection of facts receives copyright protection. Otherwise, there would be a period after "data."

The third requirement is also illuminating. It emphasizes that a compilation, like any other work, is copyrightable only if it satisfies the originality requirement ("an original work of authorship"). Although § 102 states plainly that the originality requirement applies to all works, the point was emphasized with regard to compilations to ensure that courts would not repeat the mistake of the "sweat of the brow" courts by concluding that fact-based works are treated differently and measured by some other standard. As Congress explained it, the goal was to "make plain that the criteria of copyrightable subject matter stated in section 102 apply with full force to works ... containing preexisting material." H. R. Rep. [No. 94–1476], at 57; S. Rep. [No. 94–473], at 55.

The key to the statutory definition is the second requirement. It instructs courts that, in determining whether a fact-based work is an original work of authorship, they should focus on the manner in which the collected facts have been selected, coordinated, and arranged. This is a straight-forward application of the originality requirement. Facts are never original, so the compilation author can claim originality, if at all, only in the way the facts are presented. To that end, the statute dictates that the principal focus should be on whether the selection, coordination, and arrangement are sufficiently original to merit protection.

Not every selection, coordination, or arrangement will pass muster. This is plain from the statute. It states that, to merit protection, the facts must be selected, coordinated, or arranged "in such a way" as to render the work as a whole original. This implies that some "ways" will trigger copyright, but that others will not. * * * Otherwise, the phrase "in such a way" is meaningless and Congress should have defined "compilation" simply as "a work formed by the collection and assembly of preexisting materials or data that are selected, coordinated, or arranged." That Congress did not do so is dispositive. In accordance with "the established principle that a court should give effect, if possible, to every clause and word of a statute," Moskal v. United States, 498 U.S. 103, 109–110 (1990) (internal quotation marks omitted), we conclude that the statute envisions that there will be some fact-based works in which the selection, coordination, and arrangement are not sufficiently original to trigger copyright protection.

As discussed earlier, however, the originality requirement is not particularly stringent. A compiler may settle upon a selection or arrangement that others have used; novelty is not required. Originality requires only that the author make the selection or arrangement independently (i. e., without copying that selection or arrangement from another work), and that it display some minimal level of creativity. Presumably, the vast majority of compilations will pass this test, but not all will. There remains a narrow category of works in which the creative spark is utterly lacking or so trivial as to be virtually nonexistent. See generally Bleistein v. Donaldson Lithographing Co., 188 U.S. 239, 251 (1903) (referring to "the narrowest and most obvious limits"). Such works are incapable of sustaining a valid copyright. Nimmer § 2.01[B].

Even if a work qualifies as a copyrightable compilation, it receives only limited protection. This is the point of § 103 of the Act. Section 103 explains that "the subject matter of copyright … includes compilations," § 103(a), but that copyright protects only the author's original contributions—not the facts or information conveyed * * *.

As § 103 makes clear, copyright is not a tool by which a compilation author may keep others from using the facts or data he or she has collected. "The most important point here is one that is commonly misunderstood today: copyright … has no effect one way or the other on the copyright or public domain status of the preexisting material." [H.R. Rep. No. 94–1476, 94th Cong., 2d Sess. 57 (1976); S. Rep. No. 94–473, 94th Cong., 1st Sess. 55 (1975)]. The 1909 Act did not require, as "sweat of the brow" courts mistakenly assumed, that each subsequent compiler must start from scratch and is precluded from relying on research undertaken by another. See, e. g., Jeweler's Circular Publishing Co. 281 F., at 88–89. Rather, the facts contained in existing works may be freely copied because copyright protects only the elements that owe their origin to the compiler—the selection, coordination, and arrangement of facts.

In summary, the 1976 revisions to the Copyright Act leave no doubt that originality, not "sweat of the brow," is the touchstone of copyright protection in directories and other fact-based works. * * * The revisions explain with painstaking clarity that copyright requires originality, § 102(a); that facts are never original, § 102(b); that the copyright in a compilation does not extend to the facts it contains, § 103(b); and that a compilation is copyrightable only to the extent that it features an original selection, coordination, or arrangement, § 101.

* * *

III

* * *

The selection, coordination, and arrangement of Rural's white pages do not satisfy the minimum constitutional standards for copyright protection. As mentioned at the outset, Rural's white pages are entirely typical. Persons desiring telephone service in Rural's service area fill out an application and Rural issues them a telephone number. In preparing its white pages, Rural simply takes the data provided by its subscribers and lists it alphabetically by surname. The end product is a garden-variety white pages directory, devoid of even the slightest trace of creativity.

Rural's selection of listings could not be more obvious: It publishes the most basic information—name, town, and telephone number—about each person who applies to it for telephone service. This is "selection" of a sort, but it lacks the modicum of creativity necessary to transform mere selection into copyrightable expression. Rural expended sufficient effort to make the white pages directory useful, but insufficient creativity to make it original.

We note in passing that the selection featured in Rural's white pages may also fail the originality requirement for another reason. Feist points out that Rural did not truly "select" to publish the names and telephone numbers of its subscribers; rather, it was required to do so by the Kansas Corporation Commission as part of its monopoly franchise. See 737 F.Supp., at 612. Accordingly, one could plausibly conclude that this selection was dictated by state law, not by Rural.

Nor can Rural claim originality in its coordination and arrangement of facts. The white pages do nothing more than list Rural's subscribers in alphabetical order. This arrangement may, technically speaking, owe its origin to Rural; no one disputes that Rural undertook the task of alphabetizing the names itself. But there is nothing remotely creative about arranging names alphabetically in a white pages directory. It is an age-old practice, firmly rooted in tradition and so commonplace that it has come to be expected as a matter of course. * * * It is not only unoriginal, it is practically inevitable. This time-honored tradition does not possess the minimal creative spark required by the Copyright Act and the Constitution.

We conclude that the names, towns, and telephone numbers copied by Feist were not original to Rural and therefore were not protected by the copyright in Rural's combined white and yellow pages directory. As a constitutional matter, copyright protects only those constituent elements of a work that possess more than a de minimis quantum of creativity. Rural's white pages, limited to basic subscriber information and arranged alphabetically, fall short of the mark. As a statutory matter, 17 U. S. C. § 101 does not afford protection from copying to a collection of facts that are selected, coordinated, and arranged in a way that utterly lacks originality. Given that some works must fail, we cannot imagine a more likely candidate. Indeed, were we to hold that Rural's white pages pass muster, it is hard to believe that any collection of facts could fail.

Because Rural's white pages lack the requisite originality, Feist's use of the listings cannot constitute infringement. This decision should not be construed as demeaning Rural's efforts in compiling its directory, but rather as making clear that copyright rewards originality, not effort. As this Court noted more than a century ago, " 'great praise may be due to the plaintiffs for their industry and enterprise in publishing this paper, yet the law does not contemplate their being rewarded in this way.' " Baker v. Selden, 101 U.S., at 105.

The judgment of the Court of Appeals is

Reversed.

Notes

1. Why did the Court find it necessary to discuss the constitutional standards for copyright protection in *Feist*? Is this discussion part of the holding in the case? Could the decision have been grounded entirely in section 102 of the Act? Should it have been?

2. In *Feist*, the Supreme Court articulated two components of the constitutional requirement of "originality"—independent creation and creativity. How do these concepts differ? Are randomly generated symbols (such as arbitrary paint splatters) copyrightable after *Feist*? Is the standard of originality in copyright law too low? Should greater creativity be required? Should a standard approaching novelty be required? Why should copyright be different from patent law?

SILVERSTEIN v. PENGUIN PUTNAM, INC.

United States Court of Appeals, Second Circuit, 2004.
368 F.3d 77.

JACOBS, CIRCUIT JUDGE.

* * *

BACKGROUND

Dorothy Parker, a prolific American poet, short-story writer, screen-writer, and critic, published three volumes of poetry in her lifetime: *Enough Rope* (1926), *Sunset Gun* (1928), and *Death and Taxes* (1931). They have been continuously in print since 1944 within *The Portable Dorothy Parker*....

[Silverstein collected Mrs. Parker's unpublished poems, and published the 122 he identified in a book called *Not Much Fun: The Lost Poems of Dorothy Parker*. He sent the book to Penguin for consideration. Penguin offered to include the works in a larger compilation, which Silverstein declined.]

[Three years later, Penguin published a compilation entitled *Dorothy Parker: Complete Poems*. It included 121 of the 122 poems printed in Silverstein's book, ordered chronologically. Penguin concedes that the editor who prepared that section cut the poems from Silverstein's book, then pasted them into the new section in the new order. Penguin did not reference Silverstein in the compilation.]

[Silverstein sued alleging that Penguin infringed his copyright, and other claims. The United States District Court for the Southern District of New York granted Silverstein's motion for summary judgment and permanently enjoined Penguin from further sales or distribution of *Complete Poems*.]

DISCUSSION

I

* * *

It is well settled that compilations of fact may be copyrightable even though facts themselves are not protected. 17 U.S.C. § § 102, 103 (2003); *Feist Publ'ns v. Rural Tel. Serv. Co.*, 499 U.S. 340, 344, 111 S.Ct. 1282, 113 L.Ed.2d 358 (1991). Because "the sine qua non of copyright is originality," a compilation must possess "at least some minimal degree of creativity" to warrant copyright protection. *Id.* at 346, 111 S.Ct. 1282.

Mrs. Parker herself created the category of uncollected Parker poems by collecting fewer than all her poems in her lifetime; so that principle of selection owes nothing to Silverstein. Silverstein claims as his creative contribution the weeding out of works that he did not consider to be poems and of works he believed Mrs. Parker did not write. He undertakes to demonstrate his selectivity by identifying (A) differences in classification between *Not Much Fun* and bibliographies prepared by a Parker biographer; and (B) additions and omissions made to Silverstein's manuscript between the time it was offered to Penguin and the time it was published. Silverstein further claims that his copyediting changes reflect subjective judgment.

A.

Silverstein claims that he and Professor Randall Calhoun—a foremost Parker scholar and bibliographer—disagree as to whether certain uncollected Parker works should be considered poems. In particular, Silverstein cites six works that he labeled as poems or verses and included in *Not Much Fun*, but that do not appear on the list of poems published in Calhoun's "bio-bibliography" of Mrs. Parker . . . .

Silverstein claims that he classified six items as poems that Calhoun "concluded" were not. However, Professor Calhoun does not seem to be a party to this scholarly dispute. Silverstein has never communicated with Calhoun and has no direct knowledge of what, if anything, he "concluded." Moreover, Calhoun undertakes to list only poems that were published in certain specified periodicals, and he acknowledges that the list may be incomplete even as to those periodicals: "the primary bibliography is as complete as I could make it, given the limitation of time."

As to the six allegedly disputed poems, two of them—"The Passionate Screenwriter to His Love" and "Letter to Robert Benchley"—were, according to Silverstein, never before published; so there is no basis for assuming that Calhoun was aware of them, or that he would have omitted those works if he was.

Little judgment inheres in Silverstein's classification of "Monody" and "Men I'm Not Married To" as (i) poems (ii) written by Mrs. Parker. Both were published as poems, in metered lines and stanzas. "Monody" was signed by Mrs. Parker; "Men I'm Not Married To" was signed by Helen Wells (a near-homophone of "hell on wheels"), a well-known Parker pseudonym. Calhoun's omission of these items does not remotely suggest a scholarly conclusion that they are not poems written by Dorothy Parker. . . .

"Chris–Cross" and "After Dawn" are verses that were published within book reviews that are listed in the "Book Review" section of Calhoun's bibliography. This classification is not indicative of whether he considered the embedded verses to be "poems." Calhoun did not double-count any items published by Mrs. Parker within his bibliography; each work that he found appeared in one section only. Thus, Calhoun may have pegged "Book Reviews" as the best overall category for these works, whether or not he recognized the embedded verses as poems.

As further evidence of his exercise of judgment and disagreement with Calhoun, Silverstein cites seven works listed as poems in Calhoun's bibliography that Silverstein omitted from *Not Much Fun*. Six of them are classified by Calhoun as one work—"Standardized Song Sheet for Get–Together Meetings"—appearing on a single page in Life. The "Song Sheet" is a set of six famous songs to which Mrs. Parker provided alternative words ("Marching Through Georgia"; "A Long, Long Trail"; "Dear Old Pal of Mine"; "Tipperary"; "K-k-k-Katy"; and "Auld Lang Syne"). It is possible that Silverstein omitted the "Song Sheet" because he considered it pastiche or parody rather than Mrs. Parker's own verses. On the other hand, there is a question as to whether Silverstein was aware of the existence of the "Song Sheet" (or of the remaining poem listed by Calhoun) before publication of *Not Much Fun*.

Silverstein has no high regard for the accuracy and reliability of Calhoun's work. He only discovered Calhoun's book "about midway through" his research, and stated that he "used it after I went through and found all the poems myself[;] I went through it to find out if I missed anything." Silverstein culled "two or three items" from Calhoun's book that he had not discovered on his own, all of which had been published in the Saturday Evening Post under one of Mrs. Parker's pseudonyms. He also used the book to locate one uncollected poem called "Balto." But Silverstein seems not to have carefully cross-checked the "Complete Chronology" section of *Not Much Fun* against Calhoun's bibliography. Silverstein lists at the end of his chronology the poems for which he could not find the original publication date; yet Calhoun's bibliography listed original publication dates for at least three of those poems ("The Dramatists"; "Ballade of a Well–Earned Weariness"; and "The False Friends"). Silverstein also omitted from his "Complete Chronology" one previously-collected poem that Calhoun had listed in his bibliography complete with source and publication date ("To a Lady Who Must Write Verse," *The New Yorker*, June 18, 1928).

In short, the inclusion of two (or seven) poems in Calhoun's bibliography does not establish that Silverstein's omission of them reflects a dispute on classification between scholars, or that Silverstein actually knew that the poems he omitted even existed. If Silverstein did not find these poems before submitting the *Not Much Fun* manuscript, there could be no creativity in their exclusion. Moreover, even if Silverstein knowingly omitted these poems, a question still remains as to whether that decision (alone or together with others) imbued his selection with sufficient creativity to warrant copyright protection.

B.

As further evidence of his creativity in selection, Silverstein points to twenty-five poems in the final manuscript of *Not Much Fun* that were added after his 1994 submission to Penguin. However, there is no evidence as to when Silverstein discovered those twenty-five items, or when (or why) he decided to exclude (or add) them. For example, there seems to be no evident reason Silverstein would withhold recognition of "Rosemary [1]" as a poem by Mrs. Parker; it is in iambic pentameter, in two stanzas each composed of two rhyming quatrains, and it appeared originally in the Saturday Evening Post under Mrs. Parker's Helen Wells pseudonym. Silverstein stated in his deposition that he had not flagged any works written under Mrs. Parker's pseudonyms before he saw them listed in Calhoun's book; it is therefore possible that he found "Rosemary [1]" and other pseudonymous poems after much of his research had been completed.

Most of the twenty-five "initially excluded" poems appear originally to have been published as poetry, in metered lines arranged in rhymed stanzas. It is unexplained why Silverstein would have deliberately excluded them if he had discovered them prior to 1994; and if Silverstein did not find all or most of these twenty-five poems until after he had submitted the manuscript to Penguin, he would be hard pressed to argue that their subsequent inclusion reflects creative judgment. In any event, there are issues of fact as to the timing of Silverstein's discovery of these poems, and whether his decision to ultimately include them in *Not Much Fun* reflects creative judgment.

Silverstein also cites as evidence of creative selection his ultimate exclusion of four works that had initially been included in the manuscript of *Not Much Fun*. In the 1994 manuscript, the table of contents was divided into two categories, poems and verse, and the four works in question were set apart and listed together approximately four lines below the end of the "verse" category. The removal of these works may reflect a creative judgment that the works are not poems. Calhoun's bibliography categorized the works, called "Figures in American Folk Lore," as prose. There are questions as to whether these items were excluded because Silverstein decided they were prose, or for some other reason; if so, whether their classification as prose entailed creativity; and if so, whether that example of creativity (alone or with others) fuels a spark sufficient to sustain copyright.

C.

Silverstein claims to have made 600 copy edits, mainly changes in punctuation, capitalization, indentation, and titling, in order to standardize the text. The district court did not conclude that these emendations were entitled to copyright protection, and Silverstein reasserts infringement of these aspects on appeal.

There is a question as to whether copyediting changes of this kind are sufficiently creative to merit copyright protection. *See Matthew Bender & Co. v. West Publishing Co.*, 158 F.3d 674, 681 n. 4 (2d Cir.1998) (noting that corrections to the text, including punctuation or spelling, may be trivial); *Torah Soft Ltd. v. Drosnin*, 136 F.Supp.2d 276, 287 (S.D.N.Y.2001) (Scheindlin, J.) (holding that "functional, as opposed to creative, alteration[s]" are not protectible). Moreover, even assuming these changes were protectible, Silverstein is estopped from asserting infringement on this basis. *Not Much Fun* contains no "Note on the Text" or other advice to the reader that changes were made in punctuation, titling, or formatting, let alone what those changes were. The introduction and dust jacket both imply that the works appear as originally published by Mrs. Parker. A reasonable reader would conclude that Silverstein was reproducing Mrs. Parker's own work. Silverstein cannot now claim that Penguin infringed his selection by copying textual alterations of which he gave no notice. *See Arica Inst., Inc. v. Palmer*, 970 F.2d 1067 (2d Cir.1992) (plaintiff estopped from arguing that copyrighted work is creative if work represented as completely factual).

D.

A compiler of material previously published by others certainly may enjoy a copyright in the selection if "some minimal level" of creativity has been exercised in the selection process. *See Feist*, 499 U.S. at 348, 358–59, 111 S.Ct. 1282. And if the selection process imbues a compilation with the requisite creative spark, the compilation may be protected so long as there are indicia that principles of selection (other than all-inclusiveness) have been employed. *See Matthew Bender & Co.*, 158 F.3d at 687 (finding West's decision to include every record of Supreme Court opinions in a database constituted "no 'selection' at all" for copyright purposes). As discussed, material questions of fact exist as to whether Silverstein exercised creativity in selecting the works for his compilation. Those questions must be answered before the creativity, if any, in his selection process can be assessed. We therefore reverse the grant of summary judgment on the copyright claim and remand for further findings, which in turn will determine whether monetary relief is warranted.

* * *

Notes

1.   Plaintiff publishes a yellow pages directory. Defendant copies the names, subject matter headings, addresses, and phone numbers from plaintiff's directory for its competing directory. Has defendant copied protectible subject matter? Does it matter whether defendant's directory deletes or adds to the plaintiff's listings? Does it matter whether defendant changes some of plaintiff's subject matter headings (for example, consolidating several into one)? See, *e.g., BellSouth Advertising & Publishing Corp. v. Donnelley Info. Publishing, Inc.*, 999 F.2d 1436 (11th Cir.1993)(en banc).

2.   Is a color, by itself, original enough to satisfy the constitutional standards for copyright protection? What about a simple geometric shape such as a circle, depicted in a single color?

3.   Copyright Office regulations state that "words and short phrases such as names, titles, and slogans" are not copyrightable under current law. 37 C.F.R. § 202.1(a) (1994); see also Copyright Office Compendium II, § 202.021; Copyright Office Circular No. 34. Are these exclusions correct as a matter of statutory interpretation? As a matter of policy?

Words, phrases and titles that are denied copyright protection may, under appropriate circumstances, enjoy protection of a different sort under trademark and/or unfair competition law. See Chapter 2.

4.   The Ninth Circuit held that elements of glass-in-glass sculptures of jellyfish that followed from the type of medium used or jellyfish physiology were not copyrightable. In *Satava v. Lowry*, 323 F.3d 805, 811 (9th Cir. 2003), the court held that "a combination of unprotectable elements is eligible for copyright protection only if those elements are numerous enough and their selection and arrangement original enough that their combination constitutes an original work of authorship." *Id*. at 811.

5.   In *Mattel, Inc. v. Goldberger Doll Manufacturing Co.*, 365 F.3d 133 (2nd Cir. 2004), the Second Circuit held that the particular "upturned nose, bow lips, and widely spaced eyes," 365 F.3d at 136, of a Barbie doll are sufficiently original to deserve copyright protection.

WEST PUBLISHING CO. v. MEAD DATA CENTRAL, INC.

United States Court of Appeals, Eighth Circuit, 1986.
799 F.2d 1219. *cert. denied*, 479 U.S. 1070, 107 S.Ct. 962, 93 L.Ed.2d 1010 (1987).

ARNOLD, CIRCUIT JUDGE:

* * *

For more than a century, West has been compiling and reporting opinions of state and federal courts. West publishes these opinions in a series of books known as the "National Reporter System." * * *

* * * [Mead Data Central (MDC)] developed, owns, and operates LEXIS, a computer-assisted, on-line legal-research service first marketed in 1973. LEXIS, like West's National Reporter System, reports the decisions of state and federal courts. Since LEXIS's inception, MDC has included on the first computer screen of each LEXIS case report the citation to the first page of West's report of the opinion. West concedes that citation to the first page of its reports is a noninfringing "fair use" under 17 U.S.C. § 107, so these citations are not at issue here.

On June 24, 1985, MDC announced that it planned to add "star pagination" to the text of opinions stored in the LEXIS database. This new service, named the LEXIS Star Pagination Feature, was to be available to LEXIS users by September or October of 1985. This feature would insert page numbers from West's National Reporter System publications into the body of LEXIS reports, providing "jump" or "pinpoint" citations to the location in West's reporter of the material viewed on LEXIS. Thus, with the LEXIS Star Pagination Feature, LEXIS users would be able to determine the West page number corresponding to the portion of an opinion viewed on LEXIS without ever physically referring to the West publication in which the opinion appears.

In response to MDC's announcement, West brought this action, claiming, inter alia, that the LEXIS Star Pagination Feature is an appropriation of West's comprehensive arrangement of case reports in violation of the Copyright Act of 1976, 17 U.S.C. §§ 101–810. West sought, and was granted, a preliminary injunction. * * * The District Court held that there is a substantial likelihood that West's arrangements of case reports are protected by copyright law, [and] that MDC's copying of West's pagination constitutes copyright infringement * * *. We affirm.

* * *

I.

MDC's principal contention here is that there is no likelihood that West will succeed on the merits of its copyright claim. MDC readily concedes that portions of West's National Reporter System publications that are not at issue here, such as headnotes prepared by West, merit copyright protection.[2] Yet, MDC maintains that any aspects of West's reporters affected by the LEXIS Star Pagination Feature are not copyrightable. The dominant chord of MDC's argument is that West claims copyright in mere page numbers. MDC adds that in any event, whether West claims copyright in its case arrangement or simply in its pagination, West's claim must fail because neither case arrangement nor pagination can ever qualify as the original work of an author. Even were this possible, MDC goes on, West's case arrangement and pagination do not in fact meet this standard. Finally, MDC contends that even were West's arrangement of cases protected by copyright, the proposed use of West's page numbers in LEXIS reports would not constitute infringement.

2. West does not and could not claim any copyright in the judicial opinions themselves. See Wheaton v. Peters, 33 U.S. (8 Pet.) 591, 668, 8 L.Ed. 1055 (1834) ("no reporter . . . can have any copyright in the written opinions delivered by this court").

We do not agree with MDC that West's claim here is simply one for copyright in its page numbers. Instead, we concur in the District Court's conclusion that West's arrangement is a copyrightable aspect of its compilation of cases, that the pagination of West's volumes reflects and expresses West's arrangement, and that MDC's intended use of West's page numbers infringes West's copyright in the arrangement.

A. COPYRIGHT PROTECTION

* * *

To be the original work of an author, a work must be the product of some "creative intellectual or aesthetic labor." Goldstein v. California, 412 U.S. 546, 561, 37 L.Ed. 2d 163, 93 S. Ct. 2303 (1973). However, "a very slight degree of such labor[,] ... almost any ingenuity in selection, combination or expression, no matter how crude, humble or obvious, will be sufficient" to make the work copyrightable. M. Nimmer, 1 Nimmer on Copyright, supra, § 1.08[C][1]; id., § 1.06. * * *

MDC argues that case arrangement is per se uncopyrightable because it cannot meet these standards. However, it is apparent on the face of the Copyright Act that it is possible for an arrangement of pre-existing materials to be an independently produced work of intellectual creation. Section 103 of the Act, 17 U.S.C. § 103, establishes that "the subject matter of copyright ... includes compilations and derivative works." * * * An arrangement of opinions in a case reporter, no less than a compilation and arrangement of Shakespeare's sonnets, can qualify for copyright protection.

* * *

For the proposition that case arrangement and pagination cannot, as a matter of law, meet originality and intellectual-creation requirements, MDC relies heavily upon Banks Law Publishing Co. v. Lawyers' Co–Operative Publishing Co., 169 F. 386 (2d Cir.1909) (per curiam), appeal dismissed by stipulation, 223 U.S. 738, 32 S.Ct. 530, 56 L.Ed. 636 (1911). The plaintiff in Banks was the successor to the copyrights of an official reporter of the United States Supreme Court in published volumes of opinions compiled by the reporter. The defendant published a competing edition of the Supreme Court's decisions. The plaintiff claimed copyright infringement based on the defendant's reproduction of the plaintiff's arrangement of cases and on the defendant's star pagination to the plaintiff's reports. The trial court rejected the plaintiff's claim that its case arrangement and pagination merited copyright protection; the Second Circuit, in a per curiam opinion, reproduced the trial court's opinion in full, adopting the opinion as its own.

In our view, Banks does not support MDC's claim that case arrangement is uncopyrightable per se; we agree with the District Court that instead, the denial of copyright protection in Banks was based upon the official status of the reporter. See 616 F.Supp. at 1577. The plaintiff in Banks argued that its case arrangements were the product of sufficient intellectual labor to be copyrightable because the reporter's general, though not unalterable, approach in arranging cases was to begin each volume with what he considered to be the most important cases on hand and to group cases on the same subject matter together. The Banks court responded by noting that the official reporter was required by statute to prepare reports of Supreme Court decisions, gather them into volumes, and have them printed and published. To fulfill this duty, the court continued, the reporter must of necessity provide an orderly arrangement of cases and pagination for the volumes. The court concluded that "no valid copyright for these elements or details alone can be secured to the official reporter." 169 Fed. at 390. Although it acknowledged that "the trend of some of the decisions and of the text-writers indicates that an arrangement of the material matter of a book may be the subject of a valid copyright," the court rejoined that,

> Any principle upon which such cases are based is not thought applicable where the arrangement of the cases, though involving some merit, so obviously was necessary to produce the volumes required by the statute. Such labor, under the circumstances presented, like the decisions and opinions of the court, became the property of the public.

Id. We conclude that the ultimate rationale for the Banks decision was that while * * * the official reporter could copyright any material that was the product of his intellectual labor, because the reporter's statutory duties required case arrangement and pagination, these should not be considered the product of the reporter's intellectual labor.

* * *

MDC argues, citing, e.g., Order of June 7, 1978, Minnesota Supreme Court (unreported), that West is the "official reporter" for some states, and that, therefore, even a narrow reading of Banks supports its position. We are inclined to think that the term "official reporter" in orders discontinuing, for example, the Minnesota Reports, and providing that the Northwestern Reporter should henceforth be the "official reporter" for the opinions of the Supreme Court of Minnesota, means something quite different from the title "official reporter" held by Messrs. Wheaton and Peters. We do not believe that West is employed by any State, with a salary and duties fixed by statute, and with the details of its work controlled by statute or rule. But even if it is, the facts of this case, as found on the present record by the District Court, convince us that West has used sufficient talent and industry in compiling and arranging cases to entitle it to copyright protection under the 1976 Act as construed by the more recent cases.

Having determined that there is no per se rule that case arrangements are not copyrightable, we turn to examine the District Court's findings that West's arrangements in fact meet originality and intellectual-creation requirements.

West publishes opinions not from just one court, but from every state and all the federal courts in the United States. As it collects these opinions, West separates the decisions of state courts from federal-court decisions. West further divides the federal opinions and the state opinions and then assigns them to the appropriate West reporter series. State court decisions are divided by geographic region and assigned to West's corresponding regional reporter. Federal decisions are first divided by the level of the court they come from into district court decisions, court of appeals decisions, and Supreme Court decisions; Court of Claims and military court decisions are also separated out. Before being assigned to a reporter, district court decisions are subdivided according to subject matter into bankruptcy decisions, federal rules decisions, and decisions on other topics. After an opinion is assigned to a reporter, it is assigned to a volume of the reporter and then arranged within the volume. Federal court of appeals decisions, for example, are arranged according to circuit within each volume of West's Federal Reporter, Second Series, though there may be more than one group of each circuit's opinions in each volume.

We conclude, as did the District Court, that the arrangement West produces through this process is the result of considerable labor, talent, and judgment. As discussed above, * * * to meet intellectual-creation requirements a work need only be the product of a modicum of intellectual labor; West's case arrangements easily meet this standard. Further, since there is no allegation that West copies its case arrangements from some other source, the requirement of originality poses no obstacle to copyrighting the arrangements. In the end, MDC's position must stand or fall on its insistence that all West seeks to protect is numbers on pages. If this is a correct characterization, MDC wins: two always comes after one, and no one can copyright the mere sequence of Arabic numbers. As MDC points out, the specific goal of this suit is to protect some of West's page numbers, those occurring within the body of individual court opinions. But protection for the numbers is not sought for their own sake. It is sought, rather, because access to these particular numbers—the "jump cites"—would give users of LEXIS a large part of what West has spent so much labor and industry in compiling, and would pro tanto reduce anyone's need to buy West's books. The key to this case, then, is not whether numbers are copyrightable, but whether the copyright on the books as a whole is infringed by the unauthorized appropriation of these particular numbers. On the record before us (and subject to reconsideration if materially new evidence comes in at the plenary trial on the merits), the District Court's findings of fact relevant to this issue are supportable. We therefore hold (again subject to reexamination after the record has closed) that West's case arrangements, an important part of which is internal page citations, are original works of authorship entitled to copyright protection.

B. Infringement

We further hold (with a similar qualification) that MDC's proposed use of West page numbers will infringe West's copyright in the arrangement. * * * With the LEXIS Star Pagination Feature, a LEXIS user could summon up the first case in a West Volume, page through it until he or she reaches the end of the case, and discern from the "jump cite" for the final page of the case the citation for the first page of the next case in the volume. The LEXIS user could then use LEXSEE to call up the next case. By repeating this procedure, the LEXIS user would be able to page through each succeeding case in the West reporter. * * *

Even if the LEXIS Star Pagination Feature did not make it possible to use LEXIS to page through cases as they are arranged in West volumes, we would still hold that MDC's use of West's page numbers infringes West's copyright in the arrangement. Jump cites to West volumes within a case on LEXIS are infringing because they enable LEXIS users to discern the precise location in West's arrangement of the portion of the opinion being viewed. MDC contends that these page numbers communicate nothing about West's arrangement. This might be true if MDC proposed to use the numbers in some way unconnected to their position in West's reporters, for example by simply printing a list of the numbers. However, MDC understandably has no interest in making such a use of the numbers; instead, it plans to replicate on LEXIS every page break in West's volumes and to note the corresponding West page number. Communication to LEXIS users of the location in West's arrangement of specific portions of text is precisely what the LEXIS Star Pagination Feature is designed to do.

With MDC's star pagination, consumers would no longer need to purchase West's reporters to get every aspect of West's arrangement. * * *

MDC asserts that enjoining its use of West page numbers is tantamount to giving West a copyright in the Arabic numbering system. West cannot, MDC argues, claim that its use of the numbering system is an original work of authorship. It is true that some uses of a numbering system cannot meet originality requirements for copyright. See Toro Co. v. R & R Products Co., 787 F.2d 1208 (8th Cir.1986) (arbitrary assignment of random numbers to replacement parts did not qualify for copyright protection). However, as already noted, the copyright we recognize here is in West's arrangement, not in its numbering system; MDC's use of West's page numbers is problematic because it infringes West's copyrighted arrangement, not because the numbers themselves are copyrighted.

MDC also argues that the LEXIS Star Pagination Feature does not infringe West's copyright because its citations to page numbers in West reporters are merely statements of pure fact. The flaw in this argument is that it does not distinguish between isolated use of the factual aspects of a compilation or arrangement and wholesale appropriation of the arrangement. "Isolated instances of minor infringements, when multiplied many times, become in the aggregate a major inroad on copyright that must be prevented." S. Rep. No. 473, 94th Cong., 1st Sess. 65 (1975), quoted in Harper & Row, 105 S.Ct. at 2235. The names, addresses, and phone numbers in a telephone directory are "facts"; though isolated use of these facts is not copyright infringement, copying each and every listing is an infringement. See Hutchinson Telephone Co. v. Fronteer Directory, 770 F.2d 128 (8th Cir.1985). Similarly, MDC's wholesale appropriation of West's arrangement and pagination for a competitive, commercial purpose is an infringement.

We hold that West's arrangement of cases in its National Reporter System publications is entitled to copyright protection and that the LEXIS Star Pagination feature infringes West's copyright in the arrangement. * * *

* * *

Notes

1. *Wheaton v. Peters*, 33 U.S. (8 Pet.) 591, 8 L.Ed. 1055 (1834), was the first case addressing the status of judicial opinions under U.S. copyright law. Until West sued Mead Data for infringing its copyright in case arrangements, the most significant post-Wheaton cases on this subject were *Banks v. Manchester*, 128 U.S. 244, 9 S.Ct. 36, 32 L.Ed. 425 (1888); *Callaghan v. Myers*, 128 U.S. 617, 9 S.Ct. 177, 32 L.Ed. 547 (1888); and *Banks Law Publishing Co. v. Lawyers' Co–Operative Publishing Co.*, 169 Fed. 386 (2d Cir.1909).

The question of West's copyright in its case arrangements remains controversial. In Matthew Bender & Co. v. West Pub. Co., 158 F.3d 693 (2d Cir.1998), the Second Circuit declined to follow *Mead*, holding that the Eighth Circuit's reasoning reflected the "sweat of the brow" doctrine rejected by *Feist*, and therefore a competitor's interpolation of West page numbers in a CD–ROM compilation of cases did not infringe West's copyrights because it did not reproduce West's selection and arrangement:

> * * * [W]e conclude that a CD–ROM disc infringes a copyrighted arrangement when a machine or device that reads it perceives the embedded material in the copyrighted arrangement or in a substantially similar arrangement. At least absent some invitation, incentive, or facilitation not in the record here, a copyrighted arrangement is not infringed by a CD–ROM disc if a machine can perceive the arrangement only after another person uses the machine to re-arrange the material into the copyrightholder's arrangement.

* * *

The Eighth Circuit in West Publishing Co. adduces no authority for protecting pagination as a "reflection" of arrangement, and does not explain how the insertion of star pagination creates a "copy" featuring an arrangement of cases substantially similar to West's—rather than a dissimilar arrangement that simply references the location of text in West's case reporters and incidentally simplifies the task of someone who wants to reproduce West's arrangement of cases. It is true that star pagination enables users to locate (as closely as is useful) a piece of text within the West volume. But this location does not result in any proximate way from West's original arrangement of cases (or any other exercise of original creation) and may be lawfully copied.

158 F.3d 693, at 708.

The majority criticized the contrary holding in *Oasis Pub. Co. v. West Pub. Co.*, 924 F.Supp. 918 (D.Minn.1996) (granting West's motion for partial summary judgment), in which a federal district court refused to find that *Feist* implicitly overruled *Mead* or that *Mead* relied on a "sweat of the brow" theory of copyright, and found instead that West's pagination was sufficiently creative to satisfy *Feist*. The district court in *Oasis* found fair use only with respect to the defendant's citations of the first page of each West opinion.

Dissenting from the Second Circuit's opinion in *Matthew Bender & Co.*, Judge Sweet argued that the *Mead* opinion was based on West's originality and creativity (rather than "sweat of the brow") and therefore survived *Feist*. He also questioned the majority's conclusion that star pagination did not involve "copying," and argued that the defendant should be liable at least for contributory infringement since its inclusion of star pagination made it possible for the user of the CD–ROM disks to recreate West's arrangement of cases:

> In my view West's case arrangements, an essential part of which is page citations, are original works of authorship entitled to copyright protection. Comprehensive documentation of West's selection and arrangement of judicial opinions infringes the copyright in that work.
>
> * * *
>
> * * * Clearly, plaintiffs' CD–ROM disks are not "copies" in the traditional sense. Yet, plaintiffs provide the ability for a user to push a button or two and obtain West's exact selection and arrangement. This technological capacity presents a new question. The majority's answer threatens to eviscerate copyright protection for compilations.

158 F.3d 693, at 710.

In another opinion issued the same day, the Second Circuit held that certain of West's enhancements of court opinions, including (1) the arrangement of information specifying the parties, court, and date of decision, (2) the selection of parallel and alternative case citations, (3) the selection and arrangement of attorney information, and (4) the arrangement of information pertaining to subsequent procedural history, were not sufficiently original or creative to warrant copyright protection. (West's headnotes and key numbers were not at issue in this case.). *Matthew Bender & Co., Inc. v. West Publishing Co.*, 158 F.3d 674 (1998). The majority explained:

> West's editorial work entails considerable scholarly labor and care, and is of distinct usefulness to legal practitioners. Unfortunately for West, however, creativity in the task of creating a useful case report can only proceed in a narrow groove. Doubtless, that is because for West or any other editor of judicial opinions for legal research, faithfulness to the public-domain original is the dominant editorial value, so that the creative is the enemy of the true.

Our decision in this case does not mean that an editor seeking to create the most accurate edition of another work never exercises creativity. As West argues, our decisions establish a low threshold of creativity, even in works involving selection from among facts. But those cases involved the exercise of judgments more evaluative and creative than West exercises in the four elements of the case reports that HyperLaw intends to copy. * * *

158 F.3d 774, at 688 (footnotes omitted). Again, Judge Sweet dissented, finding West's annotations sufficiently creative to satisfy *Feist*. *Id*.

See also *United States v. Thomson Corp.*, 949 F.Supp. 907 (D.D.C.1996) (in reviewing proposed licensing of West's star pagination as part of anti-trust settlement, court expresses doubt as to copyrightability of West pagination, finding district court's reasoning in *Oasis* unpersuasive and agreeing with lower court opinion in *Matthew Bender & Co.* that *Feist* casts serious doubt on continuing validity of *Mead*); Georgia v. Harrison, 548 F.Supp. 110 (N.D.Ga.1982), *vacated* 559 F.Supp. 37 (N.D.Ga.1983) (headings and section numbers applied to statutes are not copyrightable).

In analyzing copyrightability, should it matter whether the West Reporter series is the "official" state or federal reporter? Compare *CCC Information Services, Inc. v. Maclean Hunter Market Reports, Inc.*, *infra*, p. 810.

ASSESSMENT TECHNOLOGIES OF WI, LLC v. WIREDATA, INC.

United States Court of Appeals, Seventh Circuit, 2003.
350 F.3d 640.

POSNER, CIRCUIT JUDGE.

This case is about the attempt of a copyright owner to use copyright law to block access to data that not only are neither copyrightable nor copyrighted, but were not created or obtained by the copyright owner. The owner is trying to secrete the data in its copyrighted program—a program the existence of which reduced the likelihood that the data would be retained in a form in which they would have been readily accessible. It would be appalling if such an attempt could succeed.

Assessment Technologies (AT, we'll call it) brought suit for copyright infringement and theft of trade secrets against WIREdata, and the district court after an evidentiary hearing issued a permanent injunction on the basis of AT's copyright claim alone, without reaching the trade secret claim. A sample database in the demo version of AT's product—a version freely distributed for promotional purposes—reveals the entire structure of the database, thus making the trade secret claim incomprehensible to us. But we shall not make a formal ruling on the claim. It was not addressed either by the district court or by the parties in their submissions in this court, and conceivably if improbably it has more merit than we can find in it.

The copyright case seeks to block WIREdata from obtaining noncopyrighted data. AT claims that the data can't be extracted without infringement of its copyright. The copyright is of a compilation format, and the general issue that the appeal presents is the right of the owner of such a copyright to prevent his customers (that is, the copyright licensees) from disclosing the compiled data even if the data are in the public domain.

WIREdata, owned by Multiple Listing Services, Inc., wants to obtain, for use by real estate brokers, data regarding specific properties—address, owner's name, the age of the property, its assessed valuation, the number and type of rooms, and so forth—from the southeastern Wisconsin municipalities in which the properties are located. The municipalities collect such data in order to assess the value of the properties for property-tax purposes. Ordinarily they're happy to provide the data to anyone who will pay the modest cost of copying the data onto a disk. Indeed, Wisconsin's "open records" law, Wis. Stat. § § 19.31–.39; *State ex rel. Milwaukee Police Ass'n v. Jones*, 237 Wis.2d 840, 615 N.W.2d 190, 194–96 (2000), which is applicable to data in digital form, *see id.* at 195–96; Wis. Stat. § 19.32(2), requires them to furnish such data to any person who will pay the copying cost. However, three municipalities refused WIREdata's request. They (or the contractors who do the actual tax assessment for them) are licensees of AT. The open-records law contains an exception for copyrighted materials, *id.*, and these municipalities are afraid that furnishing WIREdata the requested data would violate the copyright. WIREdata has sued them in the state courts of Wisconsin in an attempt to force them to divulge the data, and those suits are pending. Alarmed by WIREdata's suits, AT brought the present suit to stop WIREdata from making such demands of the municipalities and seeking to enforce them by litigation.

The data that WIREdata wants are collected not by AT but by tax assessors hired by the municipalities. The assessors visit the property and by talking to the owner and poking around the property itself obtain the information that we mentioned in the preceding paragraph—the age of the property, the number of rooms, and so forth. AT has developed and copyrighted a computer program, called "Market Drive," for compiling these data. The assessor types into a computer the data that he has obtained from his visit to the property or from other sources of information and then the Market Drive program, in conjunction with a Microsoft database program (Microsoft Access), automatically allocates the data to 456 fields (that is, categories of information) grouped into 34 master categories known as tables. Several types of data relating to a property, each allocated to a different field, are grouped together in a table called "Income Valuations," others in a table called "Residential Buildings," and so on. The data collected by the various assessors and inputted in the manner just described are stored in an electronic file, the database. The municipality's tax officials can use various queries in Market Drive or [Microsoft] Access to view the data in the file.

WIREdata's appeal gets off on the wrong foot, with the contention that Market Drive lacks sufficient originality to be copyrightable. Copyright law unlike patent law does not require substantial originality. *Feist Publications, Inc. v. Rural Telephone Service Co.*, 499 U.S. 340, 345–48,

111 S.Ct. 1282, 113 L.Ed.2d 358 (1991). In fact, it requires only enough originality to enable a work to be distinguished from similar works that are in the public domain, *Bucklew v. Hawkins, Ash, Baptie & Co.*, 329 F.3d 923, 929 (7th Cir.2003); *Alfred Bell & Co. v. Catalda Fine Arts, Inc.*, 191 F.2d 99, 102–03 (2d Cir.1951), since without some discernible distinction it would be impossible to determine whether a subsequent work was copying a copyrighted work or a public-domain work. This modest requirement is satisfied by Market Drive because no other real estate assessment program arranges the data collected by the assessor in these 456 fields grouped into these 34 categories, and because this structure is not so obvious or inevitable as to lack the minimal originality required, *Key Publications, Inc. v. Chinatown Today Publishing Enterprises, Inc.*, 945 F.2d 509, 513–14 (2d Cir.1991), as it would if the compilation program simply listed data in alphabetical or numerical order. *Feist Publications, Inc. v. Rural Telephone Service Co., supra*, 499 U.S. at 362–64. The obvious orderings, the lexical and the numeric, have long been in the public domain, and what is in the public domain cannot be appropriated by claiming copyright. Alternatively, if there is only one way in which to express an idea—for example, alphabetical order for the names in a phone book—then form and idea merge, and in that case since an idea cannot be copyrighted the copying of the form is not an infringement. *Ets-Hokin v. Skyy Spirits, Inc.*, 225 F.3d 1068, 1082 (9th Cir.2000); *Kregos v. Associated Press*, 937 F.2d 700, 705–07 (2d Cir. 1991). That is not the situation here.

So AT has a valid copyright; and if WIREdata said to itself, "Market Drive is a nifty way of sorting real estate data and we want the municipalities to give us their data in the form in which it is organized in the database, that is, sorted into AT's 456 fields grouped into its 34 tables," and the municipalities obliged, they would be infringing AT's copyright because they are not licensed to make copies of Market Drive for distribution to others; and WIREdata would be a contributory infringer (subject to a qualification concerning the fair-use defense to copyright infringement, including contributory infringement, that we discuss later). But WIREdata doesn't want the compilation as structured by Market Drive. It isn't in the business of making tax assessments, which is the business for which Market Drive is designed. It only wants the raw data, the data the assessors inputted into Market Drive. Once it gets those data it will sort them in accordance with its own needs, which have to do with providing the information about properties that is useful to real estate brokers as opposed to taxing authorities.

But how are the data to be extracted from the database without infringing the copyright? Or, what is not quite the same question, how can the data be separated from the tables and fields to which they are allocated by Market Drive? One possibility is to use tools in the Market Drive program itself to extract the data and place it in a separate electronic file; this can be done rapidly and easily with just a few keystrokes. But the municipalities may not have the program, because the inputting of the data, which did of course require its use, was done by assessors employed by firms to do this work as independent contractors of the municipalities. And if the municipalities do have the program, still their license from AT forbids them to disseminate the data collected by means of it—a restriction that may or may not be in violation of the state's open-records law, a question we come back to later. A second extraction possibility, which arises from the fact that the database is a Microsoft file accessible by Microsoft Access, is to use Access to extract the data and place it in a new file, bypassing Market Drive. But there is again the scope of the license to be considered and also whether the method of extraction is so cumbersome that it would require more effort than the open-records law requires of the agencies subject to it. It might take a programmer a couple of days to extract the data using Microsoft Access, and the municipalities might lack the time, or for that matter the programmers, to do the extraction. But that should not be a big problem, because WIREdata can hire programmers to extract the data from the municipalities' computers at its own expense.

From the standpoint of copyright law all that matters is that the process of extracting the raw data from the database does not involve copying Market Drive, or creating, as AT mysteriously asserts, a derivative work; all that is sought is raw data, data created not by AT but by the assessors, data that are in the public domain. A derivative work is a translation or other transformation of an original work and must itself contain minimum originality for the same evidentiary reason that we noted in discussing the requirement that a copyrighted work be original. *Pickett v. Prince*, 207 F.3d 402, 405 (7th Cir.2000); *Gracen v. Bradford Exchange*, 698 F.2d 300, 304–05 (7th Cir.1983). A work that merely copies uncopyrighted material is wholly unoriginal and the making of such a work is therefore not an infringement of copyright. The municipalities would not be infringing Market Drive by extracting the raw data from the databases by either method that we discussed and handing those data over to WIREdata; and since there would thus be no direct infringement, neither would there be contributory infringement by WIREdata. It would be like a Westlaw licensee's copying the text of a federal judicial opinion that he found in the Westlaw opinion database and giving it to someone else. Westlaw's compilation of federal judicial opinions is copyrighted and copyrightable because it involves discretionary judgments regarding selection and arrangement. But the opinions themselves are in the public domain (federal law forbids assertion of copyright in federal documents, 17 U.S.C. § 105), and so Westlaw cannot prevent its licensees from copying the opinions themselves as distinct from the aspects of the database that are copyrighted. *See Matthew Bender & Co. v. West Publishing Co.*, 158 F.3d 693 (2d Cir.1998); *Matthew Bender & Co. v. West Publishing Co.*, 158 F.3d 674 (2d Cir.1998).

AT would lose this copyright case even if the raw data were so entangled with Market Drive that they could not be extracted without making a copy of the program. The case would then be governed by *Sega Enterprises Ltd. v. Accolade, Inc.*, 977 F.2d 1510, 1520–28 (9th Cir.1992).

Sega manufactured a game console, which is a specialized computer, and copyrighted the console's operating system, including the source code. Accolade wanted to make computer games that would be compatible with Sega's console, and to that end it bought a Sega console and through reverse engineering reconstructed the source code, from which it would learn how to design its games so that they would activate the operating system. For technical reasons, Accolade had to make a copy of the source code in order to be able to obtain this information. It didn't want to sell the source code, produce a game-console operating system, or make any other use of the copyrighted code except to be able to sell a noninfringing product, namely a computer game. The court held that this "intermediate copying" of the operating system was a fair use, since the only effect of enjoining it would be to give Sega control over noninfringing products, namely Accolade's games. *See also Sony Computer Entertainment, Inc. v. Connectix Corp.*, 203 F.3d 596, 602–08 (9th Cir.2000); *Bateman v. Mnemonics, Inc.*, 79 F.3d 1532, 1539–40 n. 18 (11th Cir.1996); *Atari Games Corp. v. Nintendo of America, Inc.*, 975 F.2d 832, 842–44 (Fed.Cir.1992). Similarly, if the only way WIREdata could obtain public-domain data about properties in southeastern Wisconsin would be by copying the data in the municipalities' databases as embedded in Market Drive, so that it would be copying the compilation and not just the compiled data only because the data and the format in which they were organized could not be disentangled, it would be privileged to make such a copy, and likewise the municipalities. For the only purpose of the copying would be to extract noncopyrighted material, and not to go into competition with AT by selling copies of Market Drive. We emphasize this point lest AT try to circumvent our decision by reconfiguring Market Drive in such a way that the municipalities would find it difficult or impossible to furnish the raw data to requesters such as WIREdata in any format other than that prescribed by Market Drive. If AT did that with that purpose it might be guilty of copyright misuse, of which more shortly.

AT argues that WIREdata doesn't need to obtain the data in digital form because they exist in analog form, namely in the handwritten notes of the assessors, notes that all agree are not covered by the Market Drive copyright. But we were told at argument without contradiction that some assessors no longer make handwritten notes to copy into a computer at a later time. Instead they take their laptop to the site and type the information in directly. So WIREdata could not possibly obtain all the data it wants (all of which data are in the public domain, we emphasize) from the handwritten notes. But what is more fundamental is that since AT has no ownership or other legal interest in the data collected by the assessor, it has no legal ground for making the acquisition of that data more costly for WIREdata. AT is trying to use its copyright to sequester uncopyrightable data, presumably in the hope of extracting a license fee from WIREdata.

We are mindful of pressures, reflected in bills that have been pending in Congress for years, Jonathan Band & Makoto Kono, "The Database Protection Debate in the 106th Congress," 62 *Ohio St. L.J.* 869

(2001), to provide legal protection to the creators of databases, as Europe has already done. Jane C. Ginsburg, "Copyright, Common Law, and Sui Generis Protection of Databases in the United States and Abroad," 66 *U. Cinc. L.Rev.* 151 (1997). (Ironically, considering who owns WIREdata, the multiple-listing services are pressing for such protection. Ron Eckstein, "The Database Debate," *Legal Times*, Jan. 24, 2000, p. 16.) The creation of massive electronic databases can be extremely costly, yet if the database is readily searchable and the data themselves are not copyrightable (and we know from *Feist* that mere data are indeed not copyrightable) the creator may find it difficult or even impossible to recoup the expense of creating the database. Legal protection of databases as such (as distinct from programs for arranging the data, like Market Drive) cannot take the form of copyright, as the Supreme Court made clear in *Feist* when it held that the copyright clause of the Constitution does not authorize Congress to create copyright in mere data. But that is neither here nor there; what needs to be emphasized in this case is that the concerns (whether or not valid, as questioned in Ginsburg, *supra*, and also J.H. Reichman & Pamela Samuelson, "Intellectual Property Rights in Data?" 50 *Vand. L.Rev.* 51 (1997), and Stephen M. Maurer & Suzanne Scotchmer, "Database Protection: Is It Broken and Should We Fix It?" 284 *Sci.* 1129 (1999)) that actuate the legislative proposals for database protection have no relevance because AT is not the collector of the data that go into the database. All the data are collected and inputted by the assessors; it is they, not AT, that do the footwork, the heavy lifting.

AT points to the terms of its license agreements with the municipalities, which though ambiguous might be interpreted to forbid the licensees to release the raw data, even without the duplication, or revelation of any copyrighted feature, of Market Drive. But AT is not suing for breach of the terms of the agreements—it can't, since WIREdata is not a party to them. Nor is it suing for intentional interference with contract, *Frandsen v. Jensen–Sundquist Agency, Inc.*, 802 F.2d 941, 947–48 (7th Cir.1986) (Wisconsin law); *Dorr v. Sacred Heart Hospital*, 228 Wis.2d 425, 597 N.W.2d 462, 478 (1999); *Cudd v. Crownhart*, 122 Wis.2d 656, 364 N.W.2d 158, 160–61 (1985), which would be the logical route for complaining about WIREdata's inviting the municipalities that are AT's licensees to violate the terms of their license. The licenses do nothing for AT in this case.

So it is irrelevant that *ProCD, Inc. v. Zeidenberg*, 86 F.3d 1447, 1453–55 (7th Cir.1996), holds that a copyright owner can by contract limit copying beyond the right that a copyright confers. *See also Bowers v. Baystate Technologies, Inc.*, 320 F.3d 1317, 1323–26 (Fed.Cir.2003). Like other property rights, a copyright is enforceable against persons with whom the owner has no contractual relations; so a property owner can eject a trespasser even though the trespasser had not contractually bound himself to refrain from entering the property. That is why AT is suing WIREdata for copyright infringement rather than for breach of contract. The scope of a copyright is given by federal law, but the scope of contractual protection is, at least prima facie, whatever the parties to the contract agreed to. The existence of contractual solutions to the problem of copying the contents of databases is one of the reasons that Professor Ginsburg and others are skeptical about the need for legislative protection of databases. But our plaintiff did not create the database that it is seeking to sequester from WIREdata; or to be more precise, it created only an empty database, a bin that the tax assessors filled with the data. It created the compartments in the bin and the instructions for sorting the data to those compartments, but those were its only innovations and their protection by copyright law is complete. To try by contract or otherwise to prevent the municipalities from revealing their own data, especially when, as we have seen, the complete data are unavailable anywhere else, might constitute copyright misuse.

* * *

[The court discusses copyright misuse. This portion of the case is reprinted in Chapter 20, Section E.]

* * *

To summarize, there are at least four possible methods by which WIRE data can obtain the data it is seeking without infringing AT's copyright; which one is selected is for the municipality to decide in light of applicable trade-secret, open-records, and contract laws. The methods are: (1) the municipalities use Market Drive to extract the data and place it in an electronic file; (2) they use Microsoft Access to create an electronic file of the data; (3) they allow programmers furnished by WIREdata to use their computers to extract the data from their database—this is really just an alternative to WIREdata's paying the municipalities' cost of extraction, which the open-records law requires; (4) they copy the database file and give it to WIREdata to extract the data from.

The judgment is reversed with instructions to vacate the injunction and dismiss the copyright claim.

* * *

Notes

1. Consider the following facts: A state legislature revises its statutes without assigning any section numbers to indicate where in the state code the new provisions should appear. A publisher of state codes determines the proper placement of the new provisions, and identifies them by the section number of the immediately preceding code section followed by an identifier (such as A or AA) generated by the publisher. To what extent, if any, can the publisher assert a copyright in its compilation of the state laws? Does it matter whether the state adopts that compilation as the "official" code? What if, for all practical purposes, the only sources of the state code to which most persons have access are copyrighted works? See *Texas v. West Pub. Co.*, 882 F.2d 171 (5th Cir.1989). See also Hyatt, *That "Government Code" May Be Protected By Copyright*, ABA Section on Intellectual Property Newsletter, Spring 2002, at page 1.

2.   Could a state legislature adopt legislation that would have the effect of placing existing compilations of state judicial opinions or statutes in the public domain? Which, if any, of these constitutional provisions might come into play in answering the question: the Copyright Clause? the Takings Clause? the Supremacy Clause? the First Amendment? the Fifth Amendment? the Eleventh Amendment? the Fourteenth Amendment? Are there others?

2.   DISTINGUISHING EXPRESSION FROM IDEAS AND FACTS

The leading case distinguishing copyrightable expression from non-copyrightable ideas is *Baker v. Selden*, 101 U.S. (11 Otto) 99, 25 L.Ed. 841 (1879), excerpted *supra* at page 2. The principles of *Baker v. Selden* are reflected in section 102(b), as noted in the House Report accompanying the 1976 Act:

> Copyright does not preclude others from using the ideas or information revealed by the author's work. It pertains to the literary, musical, graphic, or artistic form in which the author expressed intellectual concepts. Section 102(b) makes clear that copyright protection does not extend to any idea, procedure, process, system, method of operation, concept, principle, or discovery, regardless of the form in which it is described, explained, illustrated, or embodied in such work. Some concern has been expressed lest copyright in computer programs should extend protection to the methodology or processes adopted by the programmer, rather than merely to the 'writing' expressing his ideas. Section 102(b) is intended, among other things, to make clear that the expression adopted by the programmer is the copyrightable element in a computer program, and that the actual processes or methods embodied in the program are not within the scope of the copyright law. Section 102(b) in no way enlarges or contracts the scope of copyright protection under the present law. Its purpose is to restate, in the context of the new single Federal system of copyright, that the basic dichotomy between expression and idea remains unchanged.

H.R. Rep. No. 94–1476, 94th Cong., 2d Sess. 56–57 (1976).

After reviewing the Supreme Court's analysis in *Baker*, consider how the principles articulated there apply in the materials which follow.

HOEHLING v. UNIVERSAL CITY STUDIOS, INC.

United States Court of Appeals, Second Circuit, 1980.
618 F.2d 972. *cert. denied*, 449 U.S. 841, 101 S.Ct. 121, 66 L.Ed.2d 49 (1980).

KAUFMAN, CHIEF JUDGE:

A grant of copyright in a published work secures for its author a limited monopoly over the expression it contains. The copyright provides a financial incentive to those who would add to the corpus of existing knowledge by creating original works. Nevertheless, the protection afforded the copyright holder has never extended to history, be it documented fact or explanatory hypothesis. The rationale for this doctrine is that the cause of knowledge is best served when history is the common property of all, and each generation remains free to draw upon the discoveries and insights of the past. Accordingly, the scope of copyright in historical accounts is narrow indeed, embracing no more than the author's original expression of particular facts and theories already in the public domain. As the case before us illustrates, absent wholesale usurpation of another's expression, claims of copyright infringement where works of history are at issue are rarely successful.

I.

This litigation arises from three separate accounts of the triumphant introduction, last voyage, and tragic destruction of the Hindenburg, the colossal dirigible constructed in Germany during Hitler's reign. The zeppelin, the last and most sophisticated in a fleet of luxury airships, which punctually floated its wealthy passengers from the Third Reich to the United States, exploded into flames and disintegrated in 35 seconds as it hovered above the Lakehurst, New Jersey Naval Air Station at 7:25 p. m. on May 6, 1937. Thirty-six passengers and crew were killed but, fortunately, 52 persons survived. Official investigations conducted by both American and German authorities could ascertain no definitive cause of the disaster, but both suggested the plausibility of static electricity or St. Elmo's Fire, which could have ignited the highly explosive hydrogen that filled the airship. Throughout, the investigators refused to rule out the possibility of sabotage.

The destruction of the Hindenburg marked the concluding chapter in the chronicle of airship passenger service, for after the tragedy at Lakehurst, the Nazi regime permanently grounded the Graf Zeppelin I and discontinued its plan to construct an even larger dirigible, the Graf Zeppelin II.

The final pages of the airship's story marked the beginning of a series of journalistic, historical, and literary accounts devoted to the Hindenburg and its fate. * * *

Appellant A. A. Hoehling published *Who Destroyed the Hindenburg?*, a full-length book based on his exhaustive research in 1962. Mr. Hoehling studied the investigative reports, consulted previously published articles and books, and conducted interviews with survivors of the crash as well as others who possessed information about the Hindenburg. His book is presented as a factual account, written in an objective, reportorial style.

The first half recounts the final crossing of the Hindenburg, from Sunday, May 2, when it left Frankfurt, to Thursday, May 6, when it exploded at Lakehurst. Hoehling describes the airship, its role as an instrument of propaganda in Nazi Germany, its passengers and crew, the danger of hydrogen, and the ominous threats received by German officials, warning that the Hindenburg would be destroyed. The second portion, headed The Quest, sets forth the progress of the official investigations, followed by an account of Hoehling's own research. In the final chapter, spanning eleven pages, Hoehling suggests that all proffered explanations of the explosion, save deliberate destruction, are unconvincing. He concludes that the most likely saboteur is one Eric Spehl, a "rigger" on the Hindenburg crew who was killed at Lakehurst.

According to Hoehling, Spehl had motive, expertise, and opportunity to plant an explosive device, constructed of dry-cell batteries and a flashbulb, in "Gas Cell 4," the location of the initial explosion. An amateur photographer with access to flashbulbs, Spehl could have destroyed the Hindenburg to please his ladyfriend, a suspected communist dedicated to exploding the myth of Nazi invincibility.

Ten years later appellee Michael MacDonald Mooney published his book, *The Hindenburg*. Mooney's endeavor might be characterized as more literary than historical in its attempt to weave a number of symbolic themes through the actual events surrounding the tragedy. His dominant theme contrasts the natural beauty of the month of May, when the disaster occurred, with the cold, deliberate progress of "technology." The May theme is expressed not simply by the season, but also by the character of Spehl, portrayed as a sensitive artisan with needle and thread. The Hindenburg, in contrast, is the symbol of technology, as are its German creators and the Reich itself. The destruction is depicted as the ultimate triumph of nature over technology, as Spehl plants the bomb that ignites the hydrogen. Developing this theme from the outset, Mooney begins with an extended review of man's efforts to defy nature through flight, focusing on the evolution of the zeppelin. This story culminates in the construction of the Hindenburg, and the Nazis' claims of its indestructibility. Mooney then traces the fateful voyage, advising the reader almost immediately of Spehl's scheme. The book concludes with the airship's explosion.

Mooney acknowledges, in this case, that he consulted Hoehling's book, and that he relied on it for some details. He asserts that he first discovered the "Spehl-as-saboteur" theory when he read * * * [another account of the disaster authored by Dale Titler, and entitled] *Wings of Mystery*. Indeed, Titler concludes that Spehl was the saboteur, for essentially the reasons stated by Hoehling. Mooney also claims to have studied the complete National Archives and New York Times files concerning the Hindenburg, as well as all previously published material. Moreover, he traveled to Germany, visited Spehl's birthplace, and conducted a number of interviews with survivors.

After Mooney prepared an outline of his anticipated book, his publisher succeeded in negotiations to sell the motion picture rights to appellee Universal City Studios. Universal then commissioned a screen story by writers Levinson and Link, best known for their television series, *Columbo*, in which a somewhat disheveled, but wise detective unravels artfully conceived murder mysteries. In their screen story, Levinson and Link created a Columbo-like character who endeavored to identify the saboteur on board the Hindenburg. Director Robert Wise, however, was not satisfied with this version, and called upon Nelson Gidding to write a final screenplay. Gidding * * * had engaged in preliminary work on a film about the Hindenburg almost twenty years earlier.

The Gidding screenplay follows what is known in the motion picture industry as a "Grand Hotel" formula, developing a number of fictional characters and subplots involving them. This formula has become standard fare in so-called "disaster" movies, which have enjoyed a certain popularity in recent years. In the film, which was released in late 1975, a rigger named "Boerth," who has an anti-Nazi ladyfriend, plans to destroy the airship in an effort to embarrass the Reich. Nazi officials, vaguely aware of sabotage threats, station a Luftwaffe intelligence officer on the zeppelin, loosely resembling a Colonel Erdmann who was aboard the Hindenburg. This character is portrayed as a likable fellow who soon discovers that Boerth is the saboteur. Boerth, however, convinces him that the Hindenburg should be destroyed and the two join forces, planning the explosion for several hours after the landing at Lakehurst, when no people would be on board. In Gidding's version, the airship is delayed by a storm, frantic efforts to defuse the bomb fail, and the Hindenburg is destroyed. The film's subplots involve other possible suspects, including a fictional countess who has had her estate expropriated by the Reich, two fictional confidence men wanted by New York City police, and an advertising executive rushing to close a business deal in America.

Upon learning of Universal's plans to release the film, Hoehling instituted this action against Universal for copyright infringement and common law unfair competition in the district court for the District of Columbia in October 1975. Judge Smith declined to issue an order restraining release of the film in December, and it was distributed throughout the nation.

[In subsequent litigation, the district court granted summary judgment in favor of defendants Universal and Mooney, concluding that all similarities between the plaintiff's and the defendants' works pertained to various categories of non-copyrightable material.]

* * *

II.

* * *

A

Hoehling's principal claim is that both Mooney and Universal copied the essential plot of his book i.e., Eric Spehl, influenced by his girlfriend, sabotaged the Hindenburg by placing a crude bomb in Gas Cell 4. In their briefs, and at oral argument, appellees have labored to convince us that their plots are not substantially similar to Hoehling's. While Hoehling's Spehl destroys the airship to please his communist girlfriend,

Mooney's character is motivated by an aversion to the technological age. Universal's Boerth, on the other hand, is a fervent anti-fascist who enlists the support of a Luftwaffe colonel who, in turn, unsuccessfully attempts to defuse the bomb at the eleventh hour.

Although this argument has potential merit when presented to a fact finder adjudicating the issue of substantial similarity, it is largely irrelevant to a motion for summary judgment where the issue of substantial similarity has been eliminated by the judge's affirmative assumption. Under Rule 56(c), summary judgment is appropriate only when "there is no genuine issue as to any material fact." * * * Perhaps recognizing this, appellees further argue that Hoehling's plot is an "idea," and ideas are not copyrightable as a matter of law. See Sheldon v. Metro–Goldwyn Pictures Corp., 81 F.2d 49, 54 (2d Cir.), cert. denied, 298 U.S. 669, 56 S. Ct. 835, 80 L. Ed. 1392 (1936).

Hoehling, however, correctly rejoins that while ideas themselves are not subject to copyright, his "expression" of his idea is copyrightable. Id. at 54. He relies on Learned Hand's opinion in Sheldon, supra, at 50, holding that *Letty Lynton* infringed *Dishonored Lady* by copying its story of a woman who poisons her lover, and Augustus Hand's analysis in Detective Comics, Inc. v. Bruns Publications, Inc., 111 F.2d 432 (2d Cir.1940), concluding that the exploits of "Wonderman" infringed the copyright held by the creators of "Superman," the original indestructible man. Moreover, Hoehling asserts that, in both these cases, the line between "ideas" and "expression" is drawn, in the first instance, by the fact finder.

Sheldon and Detective Comics, however, dealt with works of fiction,[4] where the distinction between an idea and its expression is especially elusive. But, where, as here, the idea at issue is an interpretation of an historical event, our cases hold that such interpretations are not copyrightable as a matter of law. In Rosemont Enterprises, Inc. v. Random House, Inc., 366 F.2d 303 (2d Cir.1966), cert. denied, 385 U.S. 1009, 87 S. Ct. 714, 17 L. Ed. 2d 546 (1967), we held that the defendant's biography of Howard Hughes did not infringe an earlier biography of the reclusive alleged billionaire. Although the plots of the two works were necessarily similar, there could be no infringement because of the "public benefit in encouraging the development of historical and biographical works and their public distribution." Id. at 307; accord, Oxford Book Co. v. College Entrance Book Co., 98 F.2d 688 (2d Cir.1938). To avoid a chilling effect on authors who contemplate tackling an historical issue or event, broad latitude must be granted to subsequent authors who make use of historical subject matter, including theories or plots. Learned Hand counseled in Myers v. Mail & Express Co., 36 C.O.Bull.

---

4. In Sheldon, both works were loosely based on an actual murder committed by a young Scottish girl. Judge Hand, however, clearly dealt only with the fictional plots conceived by the respective authors. See Sheldon v. Metro–Goldwyn Pictures Corp., 81 F.2d 49, 54 (2d Cir.), cert. denied, 298 U.S. 669, 56 S. Ct. 835, 80 L. Ed. 1392 (1936).

478, 479 (S.D.N.Y.1919), "(t)here cannot be any such thing as copyright in the order of presentation of the facts, nor, indeed, in their selection."[5]

In the instant case, the hypothesis that Eric Spehl destroyed the Hindenburg is based entirely on the interpretation of historical facts, including Spehl's life, his girlfriend's anti-Nazi connections, the explosion's origin in Gas Cell 4, Spehl's duty station, discovery of a dry-cell battery among the wreckage, and rumors about Spehl's involvement dating from a 1938 Gestapo investigation. Such an historical interpretation, whether or not it originated with Mr. Hoehling, is not protected by his copyright and can be freely used by subsequent authors.

B

The same reasoning governs Hoehling's claim that a number of specific facts, ascertained through his personal research, were copied by appellees.[6] The cases in this circuit, however, make clear that factual information is in the public domain. See, e. g., Rosemont Enterprises, Inc., supra, 366 F.2d at 309; Oxford Book Co., supra, 98 F.2d at 691. Each appellee had the right to "avail himself of the facts contained" in Hoehling's book and to "use such information, whether correct or incorrect, in his own literary work." Greenbie v. Noble, 151 F.Supp. 45, 67 (S.D.N.Y.1957). Accordingly, there is little consolation in relying on cases in other circuits holding that the fruits of original research are copyrightable. See, e. g., Toksvig v. Bruce Publishing Co., 181 F.2d 664, 667 (7th Cir.1950); Miller v. Universal City Studios, Inc., 460 F.Supp. 984 (S.D.Fla.1978). Indeed, this circuit has clearly repudiated Toksvig and its progeny. In Rosemont Enterprises, Inc., supra, 366 F.2d at 310, we refused to "subscribe to the view that an author is absolutely precluded from saving time and effort by referring to and relying upon prior published material.... It is just such wasted effort that the proscription against the copyright of ideas and facts.... are designed to prevent." Accord, 1 Nimmer on Copyright § 2.11 (1979).

---

5. This circuit has permitted extensive reliance on prior works of history. See, e. g., Gardner v. Nizer, 391 F.Supp. 940 (S.D.N.Y.1975) (the story of the Rosenberg trial not copyrightable); Fuld v. National Broadcasting Co., 390 F.Supp. 877 (S.D.N.Y.1975) ("Bugsy" Siegel's life story not copyrightable); Greenbie v. Noble, 151 F.Supp. 45 (S.D.N.Y.1957) (the life of Anna Carroll, a member of Lincoln's cabinet, not copyrightable). The commentators are in accord with this view. See, e. g. 1 Nimmer on Copyright § 2.11(A) (1979); Chafee, Reflections on the Law of Copyright: I, 45 Colum.L.Rev. 503, 511 (1945).

6. In detailed comparisons of his book with Mooney's work and Universal's motion picture, Hoehling isolates 266 and 75 alleged instances of copying, respectively. Judge Metzner correctly pointed out that many of these allegations are patently frivolous. The vast majority of the remainder deals with alleged copying of historical facts. It would serve no purpose to review Hoehling's specific allegations in detail in this opinion. The following ten examples, however, are illustrative: (1) Eric Spehl's age and birthplace; (2) Crew members had smuggled monkeys on board the Graf Zeppelin; (3) Germany's ambassador to the United States dismissed threats of sabotage; (4) A warning letter had been received from a Mrs. Rauch; (5) The Hindenburg's captain was constructing a new home in Zeppelinheim; (6) Eric Spehl was a photographer; (7) The airship flew over Boston; (8) The Hindenburg was "tail heavy" before landing; (9) A member of the ground crew had etched his name in the zeppelin's hull; and (10) The navigator set the Hindenburg's course by reference to various North Atlantic islands.

C

The remainder of Hoehling's claimed similarities relate to random duplications of phrases and sequences of events. For example, all three works contain a scene in a German beer hall, in which the airship's crew engages in revelry prior to the voyage. Other claimed similarities concern common German greetings of the period, such as "Heil Hitler," or songs, such as the German National anthem. These elements, however, are merely scenes a faire, that is, "incidents, characters or settings which are as a practical matter indispensable, or at least standard, in the treatment of a given topic." Alexander, supra, 460 F.Supp. at 45; accord, Bevan v. Columbia Broadcasting System, Inc., 329 F.Supp. 601, 607 (S.D.N.Y.1971). Because it is virtually impossible to write about a particular historical era or fictional theme without employing certain "stock" or standard literary devices, we have held that scenes a faire are not copyrightable as a matter of law. See Reyher v. Children's Television Workshop, 533 F.2d 87, 91 (2d Cir.), cert. denied, 429 U.S. 980, 97 S. Ct. 492, 50 L. Ed. 2d 588 (1976).

D

All of Hoehling's allegations of copying, therefore, encompass material that is non-copyrightable as a matter of law, rendering summary judgment entirely appropriate. We are aware, however, that in distinguishing between themes, facts, and scenes a faire on the one hand, and copyrightable expression on the other, courts may lose sight of the forest for the trees. By factoring out similarities based on non-copyrightable elements, a court runs the risk of overlooking wholesale usurpation of a prior author's expression. A verbatim reproduction of another work, of course, even in the realm of nonfiction, is actionable as copyright infringement. See Wainwright Securities, Inc. v. Wall Street Transcript Corp., 558 F.2d 91 (2d Cir.1977), cert. denied, 434 U.S. 1014, 98 S. Ct. 730, 54 L. Ed. 2d 759 (1978). Thus, in granting or reviewing a grant of summary judgment for defendants, courts should assure themselves that the works before them are not virtually identical. In this case, it is clear that all three authors relate the story of the Hindenburg differently.

In works devoted to historical subjects, it is our view that a second author may make significant use of prior work, so long as he does not bodily appropriate the expression of another. Rosemont Enterprises, Inc., supra, 366 F.2d at 310. This principle is justified by the fundamental policy undergirding the copyright laws the encouragement of contributions to recorded knowledge. The "financial reward guaranteed to the copyright holder is but an incident of this general objective, rather than an end in itself." Berlin v. E. C. Publications, Inc., 329 F.2d 541, 543–44 (2d Cir.), cert. denied, 379 U.S. 822, 85 S. Ct. 46, 13 L. Ed. 2d 33 (1964). Knowledge is expanded as well by granting new authors of historical works a relatively free hand to build upon the work of their predecessors.

III.

Finally, we affirm Judge Metzner's rejection of Hoehling's claims based on the common law of "unfair competition." Where, as here, historical facts, themes, and research have been deliberately exempted from the scope of copyright protection to vindicate the overriding goal of encouraging contributions to recorded knowledge, the states are pre-empted from removing such material from the public domain. See, e. g., Sears, Roebuck & Co. v. Stiffel Co., 376 U.S. 225, 84 S.Ct. 784, 11 L.Ed.2d 661 (1964); Compco Corp. v. Day–Brite Lighting, Inc., 376 U.S. 234, 84 S. Ct. 779, 11 L. Ed. 2d 669 (1964). "To forbid copying" in this case, "would interfere with the federal policy . . . of allowing free access to copy whatever the federal patent and copyright laws leave in the public domain." Id. at 237, 84 S. Ct. at 782.

The judgment of the district court is affirmed.

WALT DISNEY PRODUCTIONS v. AIR PIRATES
United States Court of Appeals, Ninth Circuit, 1978.
581 F.2d 751. *cert. denied*, 439 U.S. 1132, 99 S.Ct. 1054, 59 L.Ed.2d 94 (1979).

CUMMINGS, CIRCUIT JUDGE:

This case involves the admitted copying of plaintiff Walt Disney Productions' ("Disney") cartoon characters in defendants' adult "counter-culture" comic books. * * *

* * *

The essence of defendants' argument is that characters are never copyrightable and therefore cannot in any way constitute a copyrightable component part. That argument flies in the face of a series of cases dating back to 1914 that have held comic strip characters protectable under the old Copyright Act. See Detective Comics, Inc. v. Bruns Publications Inc., 111 F.2d 432 (2d Cir.1940); Fleischer Studios v. Freundlich, 73 F.2d 276 (2d Cir.1934), certiorari denied, 294 U.S. 717, 55 S. Ct. 516, 79 L. Ed. 1250; King Features Syndicate v. Fleischer, 299 F. 533 (2d Cir.1924); Detective Comics, Inc. v. Fox Publications, Inc., 46 F.Supp. 872 (S.D.N.Y.1942); Hill v. Whalen & Martell, Inc., 220 F. 359 (S.D.N.Y.1914); 1 Nimmer on Copyright § 30.

It is true that this Court's opinion in Warner Brothers Pictures v. Columbia Broadcasting System, 216 F.2d 945 (9th Cir.1954), certiorari denied, 348 U.S. 971, 75 S. Ct. 532, 99 L. Ed. 756, lends some support to the position that characters ordinarily are not copyrightable. There the mystery writer Dashiell Hammett and his publisher entered into a 1930 contract with Warner Brothers giving the movie production company copyright and various other rights to a "certain story * * * entitled Maltese Falcon" involving the fictional detective Sam Spade. In 1946, Hammett and other defendants used the Maltese Falcon characters in other writings, causing Warner Brothers to sue for copyright infringement and "unfair use and competition." After pointing out the sophisticated nature of the plaintiff, we construed the contracts between the parties and held:

> "We are of the opinion that since the use of characters and character names are nowhere specifically mentioned in the agreements (including the assignment of copyright instrument), but that other items, including the title, 'The Maltese Falcon', and their use are specifically mentioned as being granted (to Warner Brothers), that the character rights with the names cannot be held to be within the grants, and that under the doctrine of Ejusdem generis, general language cannot be held to include them." (Footnote omitted.)

After so holding, Judge Stephens' opinion considered "whether it was ever intended by the copyright statute that characters with their names should be under its protection."[10] In that context he concluded that such a restriction on Hammett's future use of a character was unreasonable, at least when the characters were merely vehicles for the story and did not "really constitute" the story being told. Judge Stephens' reasons for that conclusion provide an important indication of the applicability of that conclusion to comic book characters as opposed to literary characters. In reasoning that characters "are always limited and always fall into limited patterns," Judge Stephens recognized that it is difficult to delineate distinctively a literary character. Cf. Nichols v. Universal Pictures Corp., 45 F.2d 119 (2d Cir.1930), certiorari denied, 282 U.S. 902, 51 S. Ct. 216, 75 L. Ed. 795. When the author can add a visual image, however, the difficulty is reduced. See generally 1 Nimmer on Copyright § 30. Put another way, while many literary characters may embody little more than an unprotected idea (see Sid & Marty Krofft Television v. McDonald's Corp., 562 F.2d 1157 (9th Cir.1977)), a comic book character, which has physical as well as conceptual qualities, is more likely to contain some unique elements of expression. Because comic book characters therefore are distinguishable from literary characters, the Warner Brothers language does not preclude protection of Disney's characters.[11]

* * *

10. Judge Wollenberg's opinion viewed this language as an alternate holding rather than dicta, rekindling an old dispute about the status of the language. See 1 Nimmer on Copyright § 30 n. 587. For the reasons that follow, either characterization of the language would not affect the result in this case.

11. Because this conclusion is sufficient to justify protection of the characters, we need not endorse the district court's conclusion that Disney's characters fell within the Warner Brothers exception for characters who "really constitute" the story. The district judge did not state which Disney sto-

ries were the basis of the protection for any character, nor did it state which characters were so protected. Apart from failing to recognize that this exception seems to be limited to a "story devoid of plot" (1 Nimmer on Copyright § 30), the district court's conclusion may have been based on the incorrect assumption that Disney's characters could be protected if together they constitute a whole story. Obviously the larger the group of characters that is selected, the easier it is to say that they "constitute" the entire story, particularly when only a general abstraction and not a particular story is analyzed.

Notes

1. To what extent, if any, should copyright protect the following characters: Mickey Mouse, Superman, Tarzan, Sam Spade (from "The Maltese Falcon"), James Bond, R2D2 (from "Star Wars"), Austin Powers (International Man of Mystery)? If copyright does not protect a particular character against copying, would protection be available under any other doctrine?

See *Rice v. Fox Broadcasting Company*, 330 F.3d 1170 (9th Cir. 2003) (holding that a masked magician who reveals the secrets behind magic tricks was too generic a character to warrant copyright protection).

2. Recall the facts of *Stern Electronics, Inc. v. Kaufman*, 669 F.2d 852 (2d Cir.1982), at page 757, *supra*. The court discussed the application of the "originality" requirement to the "Scramble" videogame as follows:

> Appellants' claim that the work lacks originality proceeds along two lines. Repeating their attack on fixation, they assert that each play of the game is an original work because of the player's participation. The videotape of a particular play of the game, they assert, secured protection only for that one "original" display. However, the repeated appearance of the same sequence of numerous sights and sounds in each play of the game defeats this branch of the argument. Attacking from the opposite flank, appellants contend that the audiovisual display contains no originality because all of its reappearing features are determined by the previously created computer program. This argument is also without merit. The visual and aural features of the audiovisual display are plainly original variations sufficient to render the display copyrightable even though the underlying written program has an independent existence and is itself eligible for copyright. Nor is copyright defeated because the audiovisual work and the computer program are both embodied in the same components of the game. The same thing occurs when an audio tape embodies both a musical composition and a sound recording. Moreover, the argument overlooks the sequence of the creative process. Someone first conceived what the audiovisual display would look like and sound like. Originality occurred at that point. Then the program was written. Finally, the program was imprinted into the memory devices so that, in operation with the components of the game, the sights and sounds could be seen and heard. The resulting display satisfies the requirement of an original work.

> We need not decide at what point the repeating sequence of images would form too insubstantial a portion of an entire display to warrant a copyright, nor the somewhat related issue of whether a sequence of images (e.g., a spaceship shooting down an attacking plane) might contain so little in the way of particularized form of expression as to be only an abstract idea portrayed in noncopyrightable form, see *Nichols v. Universal Pictures Corp.*, 45 F.2d 119, 121 (2d Cir.1930), cert. denied, 282 U.S. 902, 51 S.Ct. 216, 75 L.Ed. 795 (1931). Assessing the entire effect of the game as it appears and sounds, we conclude that its repetitive sequence of images is copyrightable as an audiovisual display.
> * * *

Consider whether a screen display which displays a black-and-white checkerboard or tic-tac-toe pattern satisfies the *Stern* court's originality test. What about a similar display using two or more colors (*i.e.,* to demarcate the playing spaces, and/or to differentiate the opponents' positions on the board)? What about the screen display of words typed on a word processing program?

3. In *Baker v. Selden, supra,* page 2, if the defendant had copied the plaintiff's arrangement of "ruled lines and headings" in a competing *text-book*, would the Court court have found that Baker had infringed Selden's copyright? Would that be an appropriate result?

4. Should copyright protection extend more readily to the expression of fanciful ideas such as plots and characters than to the expression of more fact-oriented ideas such as bookkeeping methods or scientific theories?

MASON v. MONTGOMERY DATA, INC.

United States Court of Appeals, Fifth Circuit, 1992.
967 F.2d 135.

REAVLEY, CIRCUIT JUDGE:

[Plaintiff Mason sued MDI, Landata, and Conroe Title for infringing Mason's copyrights in 233 real estate maps.] * * * The district court initially held that * * * Mason's maps are not copyrightable under the idea expression merger doctrine, and granted summary judgment for the defendants. We agree with Mason that the maps are copyrightable, so we reverse * * *.

I. BACKGROUND

* * * [Mason's] maps, which display copyright notices, pictorially portray the location, size, and shape of surveys, land grants, tracts, and various topographical features within the county. Numbers and words on the maps identify deeds, abstract numbers, acreage, and the owners of the various tracts. Mason obtained the information that he included on the maps from a variety of sources. * * * Mason testified that he used substantial judgment and discretion to reconcile inconsistencies among the various sources, to select which features to include in the final map sheets, and to portray the information in a manner that would be useful to the public. * * *

Mason's infringement claims are based on the defendants' use of his maps as part of a geographical indexing system that Landata created to continuously organize and store ever-changing title information on each tract in Montgomery County. To create this system, Landata purchased a set of Mason's maps and reorganized them by cutting and pasting them into 72 map sheets. Landata then attached a transparent overlay to each of the 72 sheets, and depicted on these overlays numerous updates and corrections to the information on Mason's maps. * * * Landata then made sepia copies of the master overlays * * *.

* * *

II. Discussion

A. *The Copyrightability of Mason's Maps*

1. *The Idea Expression Merger Doctrine*

The Copyright Act extends copyright protection to "original works of authorship fixed in any tangible medium of expression." 17 U.S.C.A. § 102(a) (West Supp. 1992). The scope of that protection, however, is not unlimited. "In no case does copyright protection for an original work of authorship extend to any *idea*, ... regardless of the form in which it is described, explained, illustrated, or embodied in such work." Id. § 102(b) (emphasis added). Thus, while a copyright bars others from copying an author's original expression of an idea, it does not bar them from using the idea itself. "Others are free to utilize the 'idea' so long as they do not plagiarize its 'expression.'" Herbert Rosenthal Jewelry Corp. v. Kalpakian, 446 F.2d 738, 741 (9th Cir.1971). In some cases, however, it is so difficult to distinguish between an idea and its expression that the two are said to merge. Thus, when there is essentially only one way to express an idea, "copying the 'expression' will not be barred, since protecting the 'expression' in such circumstances would confer a monopoly of the 'idea' upon the copyright owner free of the conditions and limitations imposed by the patent law." Id. at 742. By denying protection to an expression that is merged with its underlying idea, we "prevent an author from monopolizing an idea merely by copyrighting a few expressions of it." Toro Co. v. R & R Products Co., 787 F.2d 1208, 1212 (8th Cir.1986).

The district court applied these principles to the present case and concluded that "the problem with the Hodge Mason maps is ... that [they] express the only pictorial presentation which could result from a correct interpretation of the legal description and other factual information relied upon by the plaintiffs in producing the maps." Mason, 765 F.Supp. at 355. The court believed that, to extend copyright protection to the Hodge Mason maps, which resulted from facts essentially in the public domain, would give the plaintiffs a monopoly over the facts. * * * The court thus concluded that "the plaintiffs' idea to create the maps, based on legal and factual public information, is inseparable from its expression embodied within the maps, and hence not subject to copyright protection." Id.

We agree with Mason that the district court erred in applying the merger doctrine in this case. To determine whether the doctrine is applicable in any case, the court must "focus on whether the idea is capable of various modes of expression." Apple Computer, [Inc. v. Franklin Computer Corp., 714 F.2d 1240 (3d Cir.1983), *cert. dismissed,* 464 U.S. 1033, 104 S.Ct. 690, 79 L.Ed.2d 158 (1984),] at 1253. Thus, the court must first identify the idea that the work expresses, and then attempt to distinguish that idea from the author's expression of it. If the court concludes that the idea and its expression are inseparable, then the merger doctrine applies and the expression will not be protected. Conversely, if the court can distinguish the idea from its expression, then the expression will be protected because the fact that one author has copyrighted one expression of that idea will not prevent other authors from creating and copyrighting their own expressions of the same idea. In all cases, "the guiding consideration in drawing the line is the preservation of the balance between competition and protection reflected in the patent and copyright laws." Herbert Rosenthal Jewelry, 446 F.2d at 742.

The district court determined that Mason's idea, "which includes drawing the abstract and tract boundaries, indicating the ownership name, the tract size, and the other factual information" on a map of Montgomery County, was "to create the maps, based on legal and factual public information." Mason, 765 F.Supp. at 356 . Mason argues that the court clearly erred in finding that this idea can be expressed in only one or a limited number of ways. We agree. The record in this case contains copies of maps created by Mason's competitors that prove beyond dispute that the idea embodied in Mason's maps is capable of a variety of expressions. Although the competitors' maps and Mason's maps embody the same idea, they differ in the placement, size, and dimensions of numerous surveys, tracts, and other features. The record also contains affidavits in which licensed surveyors and experienced mapmakers explain that the differences between Mason's maps and those of his competitors are the natural result of each mapmaker's selection of sources, interpretation of those sources, discretion in reconciling inconsistencies among the sources, and skill and judgment in depicting the information.

* * * By selecting different sources, or by resolving inconsistencies among the same sources differently, or by coordinating, arranging, or even drawing the information differently, other mapmakers may create—and indeed have created—expressions of Mason's idea that differ from those that Mason created.

Finally, the defendants contend that this court's decision in Kern River Gas Transmission Co. v. Coastal Corp., [899 F.2d 1458 (5th Cir.1990),] requires application of the merger doctrine in this case. Kern River concerned the copyrightability of maps on which Kern River Gas Transmission Company (Kern River) depicted the location that it proposed for construction of a gas pipeline. The idea at issue in Kern River was simply the placing on a map of Kern River's certain "proposed location for a prospective pipeline." Id. at 1464. This court concluded that that idea merged with Kern River's expression because there was only one way to effectively express that idea. Id.

The defendants argue that the merger doctrine applies in this case because drawing lines on a public map is the only way to depict the locations of surveys and boundary lines in Montgomery County, just as it was the only way to depict the location of a pipeline in Kern River. But the distinction between Kern River and this case is not in the methods available for depicting an object's location on a map, but in the ideas that the maps in the two cases embody. We cannot determine whether an idea is capable of a variety of expressions until we first identify what that idea is. A court's decision whether to apply the merger doctrine often depends on how it defines the author's idea. For this reason, in defining the idea the court should be guided by "the balance between competition and protection reflected in the patent and copyright laws." Herbert Rosenthal Jewelry, 446 F.2d at 742.[8]

We focus in this case on an earlier point in the mapping process, a point prior to the selection of information and decisions where to locate tract lines. The idea here was to bring together the available information on boundaries, landmarks, and ownership, and to choose locations and an effective pictorial expression of those locations. That idea and its final expression are separated by Mason's efforts and creativity that are entitled to protection from competitors. The evidence in this case demonstrates that a mapmaker who desires to express the idea of depicting the location and ownership of property in Montgomery County in map form must select information from numerous sources, reconcile inconsistencies among those sources, and depict the information according to the mapmaker's skill and judgment. Although Mason sought to depict the information accurately, the conflicts among the sources and the limitations inherent in the process of representing reality in pictorial map form required him to make choices that resulted in independent expression. Extending protection to that expression will not grant Mason a monopoly over the idea, because other mapmakers can express the same idea differently. The protection that each map receives extends only to its original expression, and neither the facts nor the idea embodied in the maps is protected. "[T]he facts and ideas ... are free for the taking.... " "[T]he very same facts and ideas may be divorced from the context imposed by the author, and restated or reshuffled by second comers, even if the author was the first to discover the facts or to propose the ideas." Feist, 111 S.Ct. at 1289 (quoting Jane C. Ginsburg, Creation and Commercial Value: Copyright Protection of Works of Information, 90 Colum.L.Rev. 1865, 1868 (1990)).

For these reasons, we conclude that the district court erred by applying the merger doctrine in this case. Because the idea embodied in Mason's maps can be expressed in a variety of ways, the merger doctrine does not render Mason's expression of that idea uncopyrightable.

2. The "Originality" Requirement

Landata contends that, even if the merger doctrine does not apply, Mason's maps are uncopyrightable because they are not "original" under Feist. Although the district court applied the merger doctrine to

---

8. Thus, as one commentator states:

In copyright law, an "idea" is not an epistemological concept, but a legal conclusion prompted by notions—often unarticulated and unproven—of appropriate competition. Thus, copyright doctrine attaches the label "idea" to aspects of works which, if protected, would (or, we fear, might) preclude, or render too expensive, subsequent authors' endeavors.

Jane C. Ginsburg, No "Sweat"? Copyright and Other Protection of Works of Information after Feist v. Rural Telephone, 92 Colum.L.Rev. 338, 346 (1992) (footnotes omitted).

hold that Mason's maps are not copyrightable, it found that "the problem with the Hodge Mason maps is not a lack of originality." Mason, 765 F.Supp. at 355. We agree that Mason's maps are original. Originality does not require "novelty, ingenuity, or aesthetic merit." H.R.Rep. No. 1476, 94th Cong., 2d Sess. 51 (1976), reprinted in 1976 U.S.C.C.A.N. 5659, 5664; see also Feist, 111 S. Ct. at 1287. Instead, originality "means only that the work was independently created by the author (as opposed to copied from other works), and that it possesses at least some minimal degree of creativity." Feist, 111 S. Ct. at 1287 (citing 1 M. Nimmer & D. Nimmer, Copyright § 2.01A-[B] (1990)). The parties do not dispute Mason's claim that he independently created his maps, but Landata contends that they do not possess the degree of creativity necessary to qualify them as original under Feist.

Mason's maps pass muster under Feist because Mason's selection, coordination, and arrangement of the information that he depicted are sufficiently creative to qualify his maps as original "compilations" of facts. Under the originality standard, bare facts are never copyrightable "because facts do not owe their origin to an act of authorship." Id. at 1288. A compilation of facts, however, may be copyrightable if the author made choices as to "which facts to include, in what order to place them, and how to arrange the collected data so that they may be used effectively by readers." Id. at 1289. The author's selection, coordination, and arrangement of facts, however, are protected only if they were "made independently . . . and entail a minimal degree of creativity." Id.

* * *

But the evidence in this case demonstrates that Mason exercised sufficient creativity when he created his maps. In his deposition and affidavit, Mason explained the choices that he independently made to select information from numerous and sometimes conflicting sources, and to depict that information on his maps.[10] Mason's compilation of the information on his maps involved creativity that far exceeds the required minimum level.

---

10. Mason explained in his deposition:
In 1967, I placed all of the survey lines in the county on the [United States Geological Survey] topographical maps. Now, you just don't draw it on there. I placed each corner of each survey separately; each line of each survey separately . . . , and each—the positioning of each survey corner, each survey line was a matter of judgment. You just can't buy a map, of any source I know, that has them all on there correctly. . . . So, each line was placed on there. I made a judgment on each corner, each line for every survey. Then, the same system worked for the tracts within the survey; and I detailed on the topo map the individual real property lines within each survey.

In his affidavit, Mason explained that he chose to "locate each individual survey on the topographic maps independently of each of the other surveys," to place the oldest titled grants on the topographic maps first, and then add the more recent surveys proceeding from the earliest grants, and to position the surveys on the USGS maps "not only by examining the record facts, but also by using topographic features shown on U.S.G.S. maps, especially the features from the U.S.G.S. map commonly found at property boundaries as a check on [his] placement of the survey and real property boundaries." Mason Aff. at 2.

Mason's maps also possess sufficient creativity to merit copyright protection as pictorial and graphic works of authorship. Historically, most courts have treated maps solely as compilations of facts. * * * The Copyright Act, however, categorizes maps not as factual compilations but as "pictorial, graphic, and sculptural works"—a category that includes photographs and architectural plans. 17 U.S.C.A. § 101 (West Supp. 1992). Some courts have recognized that maps, unlike telephone directories and other factual compilations, have an inherent pictorial or photographic nature that merits copyright protection. See, e.g., Rockford Map Publishers, Inc. v. Directory Service Co., 768 F.2d 145, 149 (7th Cir. 1985) ("Teasing pictures from the debris left by conveyancers is a substantial change in the form of the information. The result is copyrightable. . . . "), cert. denied, 474 U.S. 1061, 106 S. Ct. 806, 88 L. Ed. 2d 781 (1986); United States v. Hamilton, 583 F.2d 448, 451 (9th Cir.1978) ("Expression in cartography is not so different from other artistic forms seeking to touch upon external realities that unique rules are needed to judge whether the authorship is original."). We agree with these courts. As Wolf explains in his article:

> It is true that maps are factual compilations insofar as their subject matter is concerned. Admittedly, most maps present information about geographic relationships, and the "accuracy" of this presentation, with its utilitarian aspects, is the reason most maps are made and sold. Unlike most other factual compilations, however, maps translate this subject-matter into pictorial or graphic form. . . . Since it is this pictorial or graphic form, and not the map's subject matter, that is relevant to copyright protection, maps must be distinguished from non-pictorial fact compilations. . . . A map does not present objective reality; just as a photograph's pictorial form is central to its nature, so a map transforms reality into a unique pictorial form central to its nature.

[David B. Wolf, Is There any Copyright Protection for Maps After Feist?, 39 J. Copyr. Soc'y 224 (1992),] at 239–40.

The level of creativity required to make a work of authorship original "is extremely low; even a slight amount will suffice." Feist, 111 S. Ct. at 1287. We think that the process by which Mason, using his own skill and judgment, pictorially portrayed his understanding of the reality in Montgomery County by drawing lines and symbols in particular relation to one another easily exceeds that level.

Because Mason's maps possess sufficient creativity in both the selection, coordination, and arrangement of the facts that they depict, and as in the pictorial, graphic nature of the way that they do so, we find no error in the district court's determination that Mason's maps are original.

* * *

REVERSED and REMANDED.

Notes

1.   The court in *Mason* emphasizes that the differences in the maps of Montgomery County arise from the use of different sources, and the mapmakers' skill and judgment. If a mapmaker were to produce a map that was an indisputably complete and accurate depiction of a geographic area, would the map be copyrightable? *Cf., County of Suffolk v. First American Real Estate Solutions*, 261 F.3d 179 (2d Cir.2001)(reversing lower court's dismissal of complaint for infringement, and remanding for proof of originality).

2.   In *Mason* the court notes that the mapmaker exercised judgment in reconciling conflicting information. Would it be more accurate to say that this mental effort was expended in acquiring information, or in expressing it? How does this affect the copyright analysis?

3.   If *Mason* had used copyrighted source maps as his source materials without the permission of their copyright owners, but had exercised a high degree of selectivity and judgment in selecting information from those maps and reconciling conflicting information, would the resulting work be copyrightable?

4.   In *Kern River Gas Transmission Co. v. Coastal Corp.*, 899 F.2d 1458 (5th Cir.1990), *cert. denied*, 498 U.S. 952, 111 S.Ct. 374, 112 L.Ed.2d 336 (1990), discussed by the *Mason* court, two contractors were competing for the same contract to build an oil pipeline. The first submitted a proposal which included the location of its proposed pipeline, drawn on USGS topographic maps, after compiling information about the pipeline's route by undertaking independent field work. An environmental consulting group then completed an Environmental Impact Statement (EIS) covering a mile-wide corridor along the proposed route. The second competitor's proposal initially deviated from this mile-wide corridor in several locations. In the process of correcting these deviations, the second competitor copied the center line of the EIS corridor from the first competitor's maps onto their own maps. The first competitor sued for copyright infringement, but the district court and the Fifth Circuit found no infringement by virtue of the merger doctrine:

> [T]he district court held that the idea of the location of the pipeline and its expression embodied in the 1:250,000 maps are inseparable and not subject to protection. We agree. The idea of the proposed location of a prospective pipeline is not copyrightable. The 1:250,000 maps consisted of lines representing the proposed location of the pipeline drawn on maps sold to the general public. Such map markings are certainly the only effective way to convey the idea of the proposed location of a pipeline across 1,000 miles of terrain. To extend protection to the lines would be to grant [plaintiff] Kern River a monopoly of the idea for locating a proposed pipeline in the chosen corridor, a foreclosure of competition that Congress could not have intended to sanction through copyright law, especially given the ALJ's finding in the Mojave–Kern River proceedings that the southern California enhanced oil recovery market could support only one pipeline.

The quad maps, drawn on a scale of 1:24,000, do not differ from the larger-scale maps to such a degree that copyright protection should attach. They also consist of lines representing the proposed location of a pipeline on standard reference, publicly available maps. Only the scale differs. And, just as with the 1:250,000 maps, the lines Kern River created express in the only effective manner the idea of the pipeline's location. Kern River's principal planning engineer testified that he could think of no other way to portray the idea of the pipeline's proposed location. The Commission's environmental approval of the route proposed by Kern River was neither private nor exclusive. Rather, it extended similar environmental approval to any applicant otherwise qualified to build a pipeline within the approved corridor. Just as with the 1:250,000 maps, Kern River may not invoke the Copyright Act to monopolize this proposed location for a pipeline.

The district court did find that Kern River conducted expensive and detailed field work to acquire the information needed to formulate mile-by-mile the precise location of their pipeline. Clearly, the consequent placement of locating lines on the 1:24,000 maps met the originality requirement of the Act. The problem for the copyrightability of the resulting maps, however, is not a lack of originality, but rather that the maps created express in the only effective way the idea of the location of the pipeline.

899 F.2d at 1463–64. Does *Kern River* properly apply the merger doctrine? Does *Mason* persuasively distinguish *Kern River*?

5. Is a contract for the sale of goods copyrightable? What about forms containing blanks to be filled in? Rules for a contest?

6. Consider whether a particular color is copyrightable, assuming that the originality requirement is satisfied.

7. In *Gentieu v. Tony Stone Images/Chicago*, 255 F.Supp.2d 838 (N.D. Ill. 2003), the court held that the pictures Penny Gentieu takes substantially mix idea with expression, and therefore can only be infringed by exact duplication. The idea of a naked baby, a bright white background and sharp focus are not original elements of expression that can be protected by copyright. Gentieu cannot claim a monopoly over these abstract ideas.

CCC INFORMATION SERVICES, INC. v. MACLEAN HUNTER MARKET REPORTS, INC.

United States Court of Appeals, Second Circuit, 1994.
44 F.3d 61. *cert. denied*, 516 U.S. 817, 116 S.Ct. 72, 133 L.Ed.2d 32 (1995).

LEVAL, CIRCUIT JUDGE:

The appellant, publisher of a compendium of its projections of used car valuations, seeks to establish copyright infringement on the part of a competitor, which copied substantial portions of appellant's compendium into the computer data base of used car valuations it offers to its customers. * * *

BACKGROUND

The Red Book. The appellant is Maclean Hunter Market Reports, Inc. ("Maclean"). Since 1911, Maclean, or its predecessors, have published the *Automobile Red Book—Official Used Car Valuations* (the "Red Book"). The Red Book, which is published eight times a year, in different versions for each of three regions of the United States (as well as a version for the State of Wisconsin), sets forth the editors' projections of the values for the next six weeks of "average" versions of most of the used cars (up to seven years old) sold in that region. These predicted values are set forth separately for each automobile make, model number, body style, and engine type. Red Book also provides predicted value adjustments for various options and for mileage in 5,000 mile increments.

The valuation figures given in the Red Book are not historical market prices, quotations, or averages; nor are they derived by mathematical formulas from available statistics. They represent, rather, the Maclean editors' predictions, based on a wide variety of informational sources and their professional judgment, of expected values for "average" vehicles for the upcoming six weeks in a broad region. * * *

CCC's computer services. Appellee CCC Information Services, Inc. ("CCC"), is also in the business of providing its customers with information as to the valuation of used vehicles. Rather than publishing a book, however, CCC provides information to its customers through a computer data base. Since at least 1988, CCC has itself been systematically loading major portions of the Red Book onto its computer network and republishing Red Book information in various forms to its customers.

CCC utilizes and resells the Red Book valuations in several different forms. CCC's "VINguard Valuation Service" ("VVS") provides subscribers with the average of a vehicle's Red Book valuation and its valuation in the NADA Official Used Car Guide (the "Bluebook"), the other leading valuation book, published by the National Automobile Dealers Association ("NADA"). The offer of this average of Red Book and Bluebook satisfies a market because the laws of certain states use that average figure as a minimum for insurance payments upon the "total loss" of a vehicle. CCC's "Computerized Valuation Service" ("CVS"), while it primarily provides its subscribers with CCC's independent valuation of used cars, also provides customers with the Red Book/Bluebook average and the Red Book values standing alone.

* * *

DISCUSSION

1. *Does the Red Book manifest originality so as to be protected by the copyright laws?* The first significant question raised by this appeal is whether Maclean holds a protected copyright interest in the Red Book. CCC contends, and the district court held, that the Red Book is nothing more than a compilation of unprotected facts, selected and organized without originality or creativity, and therefore unprotected under the Supreme Court's teachings in Feist [Publications, Inc. v. Rural Tele-

phone Serv. Co., 499 U.S. 340, 111 S.Ct. 1282, 113 L.Ed.2d 358 (1991)]. We disagree.

* * *

The thrust of the Supreme Court's ruling in Feist was not to erect a high barrier of originality requirement. It was rather to specify, rejecting the strain of lower court rulings that sought to base protection on the "sweat of the brow," that some originality is essential to protection of authorship, and that the protection afforded extends only to those original elements. Because the protection is so limited, there is no reason under the policies of the copyright law to demand a high degree of originality. To the contrary, such a requirement would be counterproductive. The policy embodied into law is to encourage authors to publish innovations for the common good—not to threaten them with loss of their livelihood if their works of authorship are found insufficiently imaginative.

In recognition of these considerations, we have several times since Feist upheld copyright claims for compilations and similar works where the originality component was extremely modest. In Kregos v. Associated Press, 937 F.2d 700, 706–07 (2d Cir.1991), for example, we reversed a ruling of the district court that the selection of nine statistical categories for use on a baseball pitching form failed to demonstrate the necessary originality. In Key Publications, Inc. v. Chinatown Today Publishing Enterprises, Inc., 945 F.2d 509, 514 (2d Cir.1991), we held, inter alia, that the selection, from a more general list, of businesses of special interest to Chinese–Americans also merited copyright protection. Several years before Feist, in Eckes v. Card Prices Update, 736 F.2d 859, 863 (2d Cir.1984), we held that an author's subjective decision as to which baseball cards are "premium" is entitled to protection.[5]

In our view, the district court misapplied these precedents. It interpreted Feist and our subsequent holdings as erecting a high barrier of originality as a prerequisite to copyright protection, rather than, as Feist so emphatically stated, a minimal requirement.

---

5. By contrast, we found no infringement in Victor Lalli Enters. Inc. v. Big Red Apple, Inc., 936 F.2d 671 (2d Cir.1991), because the charts at issue were " 'purely functional grids that offered no opportunity for variation,' " and the author exercised "neither selectivity in what he reports nor creativity in how he reports it." Id. at 673 (quoting district court in part).

For other examples of cases upholding data selection as meeting copyright's originality requirement, see 1 William F. Patry, Copyright Law and Practice (1994). They include:

the choice of categories of Medicaid data to include in charts; the "judgement and knowledge of the author respecting the social standing and societal relations of a limited class of the general public;" a daily time organizer; the choice of "true" public relations firms to include in a directory; a list of state tariffs on pay telephones; selection of the most important and helpful cross-streets and assignment of address numbers for the streets; information about cable television systems throughout the United States.... The key factor is the exercise of some editorial judgment in the selection of data.

Id. at 199–200.

The district court gave several reasons for its ruling that the Red Book failed the test for originality. First, the court stated, "Maclean Hunter has not persuasively demonstrated that the values published in the Red Book are anything more than interpretations or analyses of factual information.... While Maclean Hunter may have been the first to discover and report this material, the material does not 'owe its origin' to Maclean Hunter." (Citing Feist, 499 U.S. at 361 * * *)

The district court was simply mistaken in its conclusion that the Red Book valuations were, like the telephone numbers in Feist, pre-existing facts that had merely been discovered by the Red Book editors. To the contrary, Maclean's evidence demonstrated without rebuttal that its valuations were neither reports of historical prices nor mechanical derivations of historical prices or other data. Rather, they represented predictions by the Red Book editors of future prices estimated to cover specified geographic regions. According to Maclean's evidence, these predictions were based not only on a multitude of data sources, but also on professional judgment and expertise. The testimony of one of Maclean's deposition witnesses indicated that fifteen considerations are weighed; among the considerations, for example, is a prediction as to how traditional competitor vehicles, as defined by Maclean, will fare against one another in the marketplace in the coming period. The valuations themselves are original creations of Maclean.

Recognizing that "originality may also be found in the selection and ordering of particular facts or elements," the district court concluded that none had been shown. * * * This was because the Red Book's selection and arrangement of data represents "a logical response to the needs of the vehicle valuation market." * * * In reaching this conclusion, the district court applied the wrong standard. The fact that an arrangement of data responds logically to the needs of the market for which the compilation was prepared does not negate originality. To the contrary, the use of logic to solve the problems of how best to present the information being compiled is independent creation. See Feist, 499 U.S. at 359 (originality is to be found unless the creative spark is so utterly lacking as to be "virtually nonexistent").

We find that the selection and arrangement of data in the Red Book displayed amply sufficient originality to pass the low threshold requirement to earn copyright protection. This originality was expressed, for example, in Maclean's division of the national used car market into several regions, with independent predicted valuations for each region depending on conditions there found. * * * In furnishing a single number to cover vast regions that undoubtedly contain innumerable variations, the Red Book expresses a loose judgment that values are likely to group together with greater consistency within a defined region than without. The number produced is necessarily both approximate and original. Several other aspects of the Red Book listings also embody sufficient originality to pass Feist's low threshold. These include: (1) the selection and manner of presentation of optional features for inclusion;[7] (2) the adjustment for mileage by 5,000 mile increments (as opposed to using some other breakpoint and interval); (3) the use of the abstract concept of the "average" vehicle in each category as the subject of the valuation; and (4) the selection of the number of years' models to be included in the compilation.

We conclude for these reasons that the district court erred in ruling that the Red Book commands no copyright protection by reason of lack of originality.[8]

2. The idea-expression dichotomy and the merger of necessary expression with the ideas expressed.

CCC's strongest argument is that it took nothing more than ideas, for which the copyright law affords no protection to the author. According to this argument, (1) each entry in the Red Book expresses the authors' idea of the value of a particular vehicle; (2) to the extent that "expression" is to be found in the Red Book's valuations, such expression is indispensable to the statement of the idea and therefore merges with the idea, so that the expression is also not protectible, and; (3) because each of Red Book's valuations could freely be taken without infringement, all of them may be taken without infringement. This was one of the alternate bases of the district court's ruling in CCC's favor.

The argument is not easily rebutted, for it does build on classically accepted copyright doctrine. It has been long accepted that copyright protection does not extend to ideas; it protects only the means of expression employed by the author. * * *

It is also well established that, in order to protect the immunity of ideas from private ownership, when the expression is essential to the statement of the idea, the expression also will be unprotected, so as to insure free public access to the discussion of the idea. See Kregos, 937 F.2d at 705; Herbert Rosenthal Jewelry Corp. v. Kalpakian, 446 F.2d 738, 742 (9th Cir.1971) ("When the 'idea' and its 'expression' are ... inseparable, copying the 'expression' will not be barred, since protecting the 'expression' in such circumstances would confer a monopoly of the 'idea' upon the copyright owner free of the conditions and limitations imposed by the patent law.").

We nonetheless believe the district court erred in granting judgment to CCC. We reach this conclusion based on the need to balance the

7. This selection includes far fewer than all extant options, and presents them in a manner that furnishes a single valuation to cover the particular option in numerous different vehicles. The editors make these choices to accommodate the practical space limitations imposed by the book's format, while providing the information most likely to satisfy customers' needs.

8. The district court also believed that CCC did not infringe Red Book's original protected elements because CCC included Red Book's selection in a more extensive data base. We disagree. Original aspects of Red Book's ordination and arrangement were inextricably present whenever CCC copied and republished any Red Book valuation, because each valuation incorporated the Red Book editors' original judgment concerning the predicted value of that automobile, as well as their judgment as to geographic consistency within a region.

conflicts and contradictions that pervade the law of copyright, and the need, where elements of the copyright law conflict, to determine, as a policy judgment, which of its commands prevails over the other.

* * *

Given the nature of compilations, it is almost inevitable that the original contributions of the compilers will consist of ideas. Originality in selection, for example, will involve the compiler's idea of the utility to the consumer of a limited selection from the particular universe of available data. One compiler might select out of a universe of all businesses those that he believes will be of interest to the Chinese–American community, see Key Publications, 945 F.2d at 514, another will select those statistics as to racehorses or pitchers that are believed to be practical to the consumer in helping to pick winners, see Kregos, 937 F.2d at 706–07; Wabash Publishing Co. v. Flanagan, No. 89 Civ. 1923, 1989 WL 32939, 1989 U.S. Dist. LEXIS 3546 (N.D. Ill. Mar. 31, 1989) (particular selection and arrangement of information relevant to horse races found copyrightable); Triangle Publications, Inc. v. New England Newspaper Publishing Co., 46 F.Supp. 198, 201–02 (D.Mass. 1942) (same); another will offer a list of restaurants he suggests are the best, the most elegant, or offer the best value within a price range. Each of these exercises in selection represents an idea.

In other compilations, the original contribution of the compiler will relate to ideas for the coordination, or arrangement of the data. Such ideas for arrangement are generally designed to serve the consumers' needs, making the data more useful by increasing the ease of access to those data that answer the needs of the targeted customers, or dividing the data in ways that will efficiently serve the needs of more diverse groups of customers. For example, a listing of New York restaurants might be broken down by geographic areas of the city, specialty or type (e.g., seafood, steaks and chops, vegetarian, kosher, Chinese, Indian); (price range; handicapped accessibility, etc.).

It is apparent that virtually any independent creation of the compiler as to selection, coordination, or arrangement will be designed to add to the usefulness or desirability of his compendium for targeted groups of potential customers, and will represent an idea. In the case of a compilation, furthermore, such structural ideas are likely to be expressed in the most simple, unadorned, and direct fashion. If, as CCC argues, the doctrine of merger permits the wholesale copier of a compilation to take the individual expression of such ideas, so as to avoid the risk that an idea will improperly achieve protection, then the protection explicitly conferred on compilations by Section 103 of the U.S. Copyright Act will be illusory.

We addressed precisely this problem in Kregos, 937 F.2d 700. The plaintiff Kregos had created a form to be used to help predict the outcome of a baseball game by filling in nine statistics of the competing pitchers. The defendant contended, in terms similar to CCC's argument, that the copyright owner's idea was the utility of the nine selected statistics in helping a fan predict the outcome, and that the idea was merged in the expression of it—in the copyrighted form that listed those nine statistics. Judge Newman wrote:

> In one sense, every compilation of facts can be considered to represent a merger of an idea with its expression. Every compiler of facts has the idea that his particular selection of facts is useful. If the compiler's idea is identified at that low level of abstraction, then the idea would always merge into the compiler's expression of it. Under that approach, there could never be a copyrightable compilation of facts.[20]

Kregos, 937 F.2d at 706.

Recognizing that the purpose of the doctrine of merger of expression with idea is to insure that protection not extend to ideas, the Kregos opinion went on to describe different categories of ideas. It distinguished between, on the one hand, those ideas that undertake to advance the understanding of phenomena or the solution of problems, such as the identification of the symptoms that are the most useful in identifying the presence of a particular disease; and those, like the pitching form there at issue, that do not undertake to explain phenomena or furnish solutions, but are infused with the author's taste or opinion. Kregos postulated that the importance of keeping ideas free from private ownership is far greater for ideas of the first category, directed to the understanding of phenomena or the solving of problems, than for those that merely represent the author's taste or opinion and therefore do not materially assist the understanding of future thinkers.[21] As to the latter category, the opinion asserted that, so long as the selections reflected in the compilation "involve matters of taste and personal opinion, there is no serious risk that *withholding the merger doctrine*," 937 F.2d at 707 (emphasis added), would inflict serious injury on the policy underlying the rule that forbids granting protection to an idea. This was in contrast to analyses belonging to the first category—building blocks of understanding—as to which "protecting the [necessary] 'expression' of the selection would clearly risk protecting the idea of the analysis." Id. at 707. Because Kregos's idea was of the soft type infused with taste or opinion, the court withheld application of the merger doctrine, permitting Kregos to exercise ownership. It accomplished this by assigning to the idea a different level of abstraction from the expression of it, so that the merger doctrine would not apply and the copyright owner would not lose protection.[23] ("His 'idea,' for purposes of the merger doctrine,

---

20. Judge Newman might have omitted the last two words. For the reasoning he discusses would destroy all protection for compilations of ideas as well as for compilations of facts.

21. See also Eckes [v. Card Prices Update, 736 F.2d 859 (2d Cir.1984)] at 863 (upholding finding of infringement because list of premium cards "subjectively based").

23. Professor Robert Gorman has written that protection of compilations is more strongly suggested where the "works are more fanciful than functional, and where the selection criteria are driven by subjective and evaluative judgement . . . " Robert A. Gorman, The Feist Case: Reflections on a Pathbreaking Copyright Decision, 18 Rutgers Computer & Tech. L.J. 731, 751 (1992). * * * Compare Hoehling v. Univer-

remains the general idea that statistics can be used to assess pitching performance rather than the precise idea that his selection yields a determinable probability of outcome." 937 F.2d at 707.)

Kregos, thus, makes a policy judgment as between two evils. Unbridled application of the merger doctrine would undo the protection the copyright law intends to accord to compilations. Complete failure to apply it, however, would result in granting protection to useful ideas.[24] Kregos adopts a middle ground. In cases of wholesale takings of compilations, a selective application of the merger doctrine, withholding its application as to soft ideas infused with taste and opinion, will carry out the statutory policy to protect innovative compilations without impairing the policy that requires public access to ideas of a more important and useful kind.[25]

Application of the Kregos approach to our facts leads us to the conclusion that the district court should, as in Kregos, have "withheld" the merger doctrine. As a matter of copyright policy, this was not an appropriate instance to apply the merger doctrine so as to deprive Red Book of copyright protection. The consequences of giving CCC the benefit of the merger doctrine are too destructive of the protection the Act intends to confer on compilations, without sufficient benefit to the policy of copyright that seeks to preserve public access to ideas.

In the first place, the takings by CCC from the Red Book are of virtually the entire compendium. This is not an instance of copying of a few entries from a compilation. This copying is so extensive that CCC effectively offers to sell its customers Maclean's Red Book through CCC's data base. CCC's invocation of the merger doctrine to justify its conten-

sal City Studios, Inc., 618 F.2d 972 (2d Cir.), cert. denied, 449 U.S. 841, 66 L. Ed. 2d 49, 101 S. Ct. 121 (1980) (denying protection to historical theory explaining destruction of Hindenburg dirigible) with Eckes, 736 F.2d at 863 (granting protection to identification of "premium" baseball cards because of personal subjectivity of the selection). The Hoehling opinion justified the denial of protection to historical analysis on the theory that "knowledge is expanded ... by granting new authors of historical works a relatively free hand to build upon the work of their predecessors." 618 F.2d at 980.

24. Discussing merger in the context of computer programs, Nimmer points out that "this line [for determining when an idea has become sufficiently delineated to warrant copyright protection] is a pragmatic one, drawn not on the basis of some metaphysical property of 'ideas,' but by balancing the need to protect the labors of authors with the desire to assure free access to ideas." Nimmer, § 13.03[F] at 13–128.

25. See Herbert Rosenthal Jewelry Corp. v. Kalpakian, 446 F.2d 738, 742 (9th Cir.1971) ("The guiding consideration in drawing the line is the preservation of the balance between competition and protection reflected in the patent and copyright laws. What is basically at stake is the extent of the copyright owner's monopoly—from how large an area of activity did Congress intend to allow the copyright owner to exclude others?") * * *.

Indeed, courts have consistently ruled in a manner that supports the distinction made in Kregos. Compare Baker v. Selden, 101 U.S. 99, 25 L. Ed. 841 (1880), and Kern River, supra, (copyright protection denied, based on merger doctrine, respectively to a system of double entry bookkeeping and the designation of the best available pipeline route from Wyoming to California), with Eckes, supra, and Key, supra, (granting protection to the identification of premium baseball cards and business establishments likely to be of interest to the Chinese–American community).

tion that it has taken no protectible matter would effectively destroy all protection for Maclean's compilation.

Secondly, the valuations copied by CCC from the Red Book are not ideas of the first, building-block, category described in Kregos, but are rather in the category of approximative statements of opinion by the Red Book editors. To the extent that protection of the Red Book would impair free circulation of any ideas, these are ideas of the weaker category, infused with opinion; the valuations explain nothing, and describe no method, process or procedure. Maclean Hunter makes no attempt, for example, to monopolize the basis of its economic forecasting or the factors that it weighs; the Red Book's entries are no more than the predictions of Red Book editors of used car values for six weeks on a rough regional basis. As noted above, Red Book specifies in its introduction that "you, the subscriber, must be the final judge of the actual value of a particular vehicle. Any guide book is a supplement to and not a substitute for expertise in the complex field of used vehicle valuation." This language is remarkably similar to our observation in Kregos, that the author "has been content to select categories of data that he obviously believes have some predictive power, but has left it to all sports page readers to make their own judgments as to the likely outcomes from the sets of data he has selected." 937 F.2d at 707.

The balancing of interests suggested by Kregos leads to the conclusion that we should reject CCC's argument seeking the benefit of the merger doctrine. Because the ideas contained in the Red Book are of the weaker, suggestion-opinion category, a withholding of the merger doctrine would not seriously impair the policy of the copyright law that seeks to preserve free public access to ideas. If the public's access to Red Book's valuations is slightly limited by enforcement of its copyright against CCC's wholesale copying, this will not inflict injury on the opportunity for public debate, nor restrict access to the kind of idea that illuminates our understanding of the phenomena that surround us or of useful processes to solve our problems.[28] In contrast, if the merger doctrine were applied so as to bar Maclean's enforcement of its copyright against CCC's wholesale takings, this would seriously undermine the protections guaranteed by § 103 of the Copyright Act to compilations that employ original creation in their selection, coordination, or arrangement. It would also largely vitiate the inducements offered by the copyright law to the makers of original useful compilations.

3.   Public domain. We disagree also with the district court's ruling sustaining CCC's affirmative defense that the Red Book has fallen into the public domain. The district court reasoned that, because the insurance statutes or regulations of several states establish Red Book values as an alternative standard, i.e., by requiring that insurance payments for total losses be at least equal either to Red Book value or to an average of

---

28. Others, including CCC, remain free to value used cars and to profit from their valuations. They are barred only from wholesale copying of what is original to the authors of the Red Book. * * *

Red Book and Bluebook values (unless another approved valuation method is employed), the Red Book has passed into the public domain. The argument is that the public must have free access to the content of the laws that govern it; if a copyrighted work is incorporated into the laws, the public need for access to the content of the laws requires the elimination of the copyright protection.

No authority cited by CCC directly supports the district court's view. It relied on Building Officials & Code Adm. v. Code Tech., Inc., 628 F.2d 730 (1st Cir.1980) ("BOCA"), which the Magistrate Judge found "virtually indistinguishable" from our case. Although the First Circuit Court of Appeals, in BOCA, indeed expressed sympathy with the arguments here advanced by CCC, its ruling is not a holding to that effect. The Court of Appeals merely vacated a preliminary injunction, expressing doubts as to the plaintiff copyright holder's likelihood of success, and remanding for a full hearing on whether the plaintiff had lost its copyright protection by reason of the adoption of its previously protected work (a construction code) as part of the laws of Massachusetts.

We are not prepared to hold that a state's reference to a copyrighted work as a legal standard for valuation results in loss of the copyright. While there are indeed policy considerations that support CCC's argument, they are opposed by countervailing considerations. For example, a rule that the adoption of such a reference by a state legislature or administrative body deprived the copyright owner of its property would raise very substantial problems under the Takings Clause of the Constitution. We note also that for generations, state education systems have assigned books under copyright to comply with a mandatory school curriculum. It scarcely extends CCC's argument to require that all such assigned books lose their copyright—as one cannot comply with the legal requirements without using the copyrighted works. Yet we think it unlikely courts would reach this conclusion. Although there is scant authority on CCC's argument, Nimmer's treatise opposes such a suggestion as antithetical to the interests sought to be advanced by the Copyright Act. See Nimmer § 5.06[C] at 5–60.[30]

Conclusion

Because Maclean has demonstrated a valid copyright, and an infringement thereof, we direct the entry of judgment in Maclean's favor. We remand to the district court for further proceedings.

Notes

1. Would the court in *CCC* have reached the same conclusion if the plaintiff's data consisted not of car valuations but of the insurance rates assigned to each type of car by auto insurance companies?

---

30. Nimmer argues that the adoption of a private work into law might well justify a fair use defense for personal use, but should not immunize a competitive commercial publisher from liability since this would "prove destructive of the copyright interest in encouraging creativity in connection with the increasing trend toward state and federal adoptions of model codes." Nimmer, § 5.06[C] at 5–60.

2.   Does *CCC* correctly apply the merger doctrine?

3.   In each of the following scenarios, consider whether the defendant has copied protectible expression:

a.   Plaintiff prepares and administers standardized multiple-choice tests. These tests are required for admission to many state schools. Plaintiff maintains the secrecy of each test until it "retires" that test. Plaintiff registers its copyright in each test under Register of Copyright's "secure test" regulations. (See Chapter 17.A.2(ii)(Note 7).) Defendant, a company which offers a "prep" course to help students score higher on plaintiff's tests, acquired a stolen copy of one of plaintiff's tests, and incorporated between 200 and 300 of the questions in a series of practice tests for defendant's students. Many of the questions were copied "verbatim or nearly verbatim." See *Educational Testing Services v. Katzman,* 793 F.2d 533 (3d Cir.1986).

b.   Plaintiff publishes a list of thousands of medical procedures and assigns to each of them a 5–digit numerical code with a 2–digit modifier. The codes are listed in numerical order, except that the most frequently used numbers, which begin with "99," are listed first. Federal and state governments have mandated use of the plaintiff's codes by medical care providers seeking government reimbursement for their services (for example, services covered by Medicaid). The defendant publishes an improved, pocket-sized version of the plaintiff's work which copies the plaintiff's list of procedures and identifying numbers in the same order, but corrects certain errors. See *Practice Management Information Corp. v. American Medical Ass'n,* 877 F.Supp. 1386 (C.D.Cal.1994), aff'd in part and rev'd in part 121 F.3d 516 (9th Cir.1997).

c.   Plaintiff publishes a comprehensive daily listing of called municipal bonds. The list identifies the issuer, the series, the redemption date and price, and the name of the paying agent. Plaintiff obtains this information from "tombstone" ads in newspapers. Defendant, a provider of bond rating and other financial information services, publishes biweekly news reports on the municipal bonds which it rates. When preparing a report on a particular bond that has been called, the defendant copies the redemption information published by plaintiff and adds certain additional information of interest to its subscribers. See *Financial Information, Inc. v. Moody's Investors Service, Inc.,* 751 F.2d 501 (2d Cir.1984).

d.   Plaintiff, the star of a television cooking show, periodically publishes his recipes in paperback compilations for sale to the public. Each compilation contains a dozen or so recipes. Defendant, a cookbook publisher, reproduces three of these recipes, each from a different compilation, in a new cookbook. Defendant copies the ingredients lists virtually verbatim, but rewrites the directions in the simplest terms possible in order to eliminate the plaintiff's distinctive phrasings and appeal to a broader audience. See *Publications, Int'l Ltd. v. Meredith Corp.,* 88 F.3d 473 (7th Cir.1996)

e.   Plaintiff, a physician, has prepared "symptom guides," which are list of symptoms which she has found helpful in diagnosing particular diseases. She distributes them to her staff and occasionally her patients. Defendant, a publishing house, obtains copies of the guides and reproduces them in a monthly health magazine without the physician's consent. See *Kregos v. Associated Press*, 937 F.2d 700 (2d Cir.1991).

f.   Plaintiffs publish several indexes to the New York Times: an annual index, and four cumulative indexes (obituaries, film reviews, theatre reviews, and book reviews). The indexes use topical headings, many of which are personal names. Plaintiffs also operate a computerized subject index to the Times which, for a fee, allows subscribers to locate topics by entering "key words," many of which are personal names.

Defendants wish to publish an index to all the personal names that have ever appeared in the plaintiffs' annual index? The names will be listed alphabetically, and each name will be followed by citations to the pages of the New York Times Index on which the name appears. Some names will be accompanied by additional information (*e.g.,* years of birth and death, and titles held) most, if not all, of which was taken from the Times Index. See *New York Times Co. v. Roxbury Interface, Inc.*, 434 F.Supp. 217 (D.N.J.1977).

Alternatively, suppose that (a) defendants published a general cumulative index to the New York Times, which they compiled largely by copying entries from the plaintiffs' indexes, or (b) that plaintiffs publish the New York Times itself, and that defendants seek to publish a cumulative index to the Times.

g.   Plaintiff is the author of two books on trivia. Each consists of a compilation of facts, alphabetically arranged under headings that are followed by explanations of the particular entry. Each book contains 6,000 entries. Plaintiff gathered the information from books, films, and television shows after extensive research. Defendant makes and sells trivia games using many facts copied from plaintiff's books. See *Worth v. Selchow & Righter Co.*, 827 F.2d 569 (9th Cir.1987).

h.   Plaintiff's college-level physics book contains problems designed to allow students to test their understanding of the principles taught in each chapter. Plaintiff's text does not contain solutions to the problems, although an appendix provides numerical answers to the odd-numbered questions. Defendant publishes a book containing complete solutions to the problems. Defendant's solutions do not literally copy plaintiff's questions, although they contain formulas, equations, and diagrams illustrating the problems and the steps for solving them. Each solution is identified by two numbers, which correspond to the chapter and problem number in plaintiff's text. See *Addison–Wesley Publishing Co., Inc. v. Brown*, 223 F.Supp. 219 (E.D.N.Y.1963).

i.   Plaintiff, an amateur videographer, captures footage of a crime in progress. No other footage, and no still photographs, are available which record the event. Defendant wishes to incorporate that footage in a documentary about the crime. See *Time, Inc. v. Bernard Geis Assocs.*, 293 F.Supp. 130 (S.D.N.Y.1968)

j.   Plaintiff, a Scrabble champion, wrote a handbook describing his systematic strategy for winning at Scrabble. Defendant, the owner of the

Scrabble trademark and manufacturer of the Scrabble game, obtains and reads a copy of plaintiff's manuscript under false pretenses, and publishes its own handbook revealing plaintiff's strategy. See *Landsberg v. Scrabble Crossword Game Players, Inc.*, 736 F.2d 485 (9th Cir.1984), *cert. denied*, 469 U.S. 1037, 105 S.Ct. 513, 83 L.Ed.2d 403 (1984).

k.　Plaintiff publisher is the creator of a widely used stock market index. At any given time, this index is a number derived by adding together the current stock prices of a carefully selected list of 30 publicly traded companies, and dividing this sum by a divisor. The companies are selected because they possess certain characteristics which satisfy plaintiff's selection criteria. Plaintiff constantly scrutinizes this list, so that companies can be added to or deleted from the list as their characteristics change. Defendant wishes to sell certain financial products (called "futures contracts") whose value at any given time is based on the plaintiff's index at that time. In order to sell this product, defendant must make and distribute copies of a list identifying the 30 stocks that comprise plaintiff's index. Can defendant copy and distribute the list of 30 stocks? Can defendant copy and distribute the number that represents plaintiff's index? See *Dow Jones & Co., Inc. v. Board of Trade*, 546 F.Supp. 113 (S.D.N.Y.1982).

l.　Plaintiff publishes the Social Register, which lists the most socially prominent families in the community. Defendant copies the entire list for its competing publication. See *Social Register Ass'n v. Murphy*, 128 Fed. 116 (C.C.D.R.I.1904).

4.　Some countries have enacted legislation protecting owners of certain databases against unauthorized copying, and similar legislation has been proposed (as yet, unsuccessfully) in the United States. One such proposal would have defined a database as "a collection, assembly or compilation, in any form or medium now or later known or developed, of works, data, or other materials, arranged in a systematic or methodical way," but excludes computer programs. Under this proposal, no one would be permitted, without the database owner's consent, to "extract, use or reuse all or a substantial part [on a single instance or cumulatively] * * * of the contents of a database * * * in a manner that conflicts with the database owner's normal exploitation of the database or adversely affects the actual or potential market for the database." To "extract" would mean to transfer the contents; to "use" or "reuse" would mean to make available in any fashion or by any means.

Could Congress enact such a proposal under the Intellectual Property Clause? Under the Commerce Clause or other lawmaking authority? How significantly would such a proposal change the law regarding data compilations? Is such legislation advisable?

3. ORIGINALITY IN DERIVATIVE WORKS

ALFRED BELL & CO. LTD. v. CATALDA
FINE ARTS, INC.

United States Court of Appeals, Second Circuit, 1951.
191 F.2d 99.

FRANK, CIRCUIT JUDGE:

[Plaintiff commissioned mezzotint engravings of well-known public domain paintings. Mezzotint engraving was a difficult, expensive, and time-consuming process, requiring substantial skill and judgment. It produced realistic and fairly accurate reproductions of the original works, although no two engravings of the same work would be identical. Plaintiff sued for copyright infringement when defendants produced and sold color lithographs of plaintiff's mezzotints. The district court found that the copyrights were valid and infringed, and the defendants appealed.]

* * *

1.   Congressional power to authorize both patents and copyrights is contained in Article 1, Sec. 8 of the Constitution. In passing on the validity of patents, the Supreme Court recurrently insists that this constitutional provision governs. On this basis, pointing to the Supreme Court's consequent requirement that, to be valid, a patent must disclose a high degree of uniqueness, ingenuity and inventiveness, the defendants assert that the same requirement constitutionally governs copyrights. As several sections of the Copyright Act—e.g., those authorizing copyrights of "reproductions of works of art," maps, and compilations—plainly dispense with any such high standard, defendants are, in effect, attacking the constitutionality of those sections. But the very language of the Constitution differentiates (a) "authors" and their "writings" from (b) "inventors" and their "discoveries." Those who penned the Constitution, of course, knew the difference. * * *

* * *

The defendants' contention apparently results from the ambiguity of the word "original". It may mean startling, novel or unusual, a marked departure from the past. Obviously this is not what is meant when one speaks of "the original package," or the "original bill," or (in connection with the "best evidence" rule) an "original" document; none of those things is highly unusual in creativeness. "Original" in reference to a copyrighted work means that the particular work "owes its origin" to the "author." No large measure of novelty is necessary. Said the Supreme Court in Baker v. Selden, 101 U.S. 99, 102–103, 25 L.Ed. 841: "The copyright of the book, if not pirated from other works, would be valid without regard to the novelty, or want of novelty, of its subject-matter. The novelty of the art or thing described or explained has nothing to do with the validity of the copyright. To give to the author of the book an exclusive property in the art described therein, when no examination of its novelty has ever been officially made, would be a surprise and a fraud upon the public. That is the province of letters-patent, not of copyright. The claim to an invention or discovery of an art or manufacture must be subjected to the examination of the Patent Office before an exclusive right therein can be obtained; and it can only be secured by a patent from the government. * * * "

In Bleistein v. Donaldson Lithographing Co., 188 U.S. 239, 250, 252, 23 S.Ct. 298, 47 L.Ed. 460, the Supreme Court cited with approval Henderson v. Tompkins, C.C., 60 F. 758, where it was said, 60 F. at page 764: "There is a very broad distinction between what is implied in the word 'author,' found in the constitution, and the word 'inventor.' The latter carries an implication which excludes the results of only ordinary skill, while nothing of this is necessarily involved in the former. Indeed, the statutes themselves make broad distinctions on this point. So much as relates to copyrights * * * is expressed, so far as this particular is concerned, by the mere words, 'author, inventor, designer or proprietor,' with such aid as may be derived from the words 'written, composed or made,' * * *. But a multitude of books rest safely under copyright, which show only ordinary skill and diligence in their preparation. Compilations are noticeable examples of this fact. With reference to this subject, the courts have not undertaken to assume the functions of critics, or to measure carefully the degree of originality, or literary skill or training involved."

It is clear, then, that nothing in the Constitution commands that copyrighted matter be strikingly unique or novel. Accordingly, we were not ignoring the Constitution when we stated that a "copy of something in the public domain" will support a copyright if it is a "distinguishable variation";[10] or when we rejected the contention that "like a patent, a copyrighted work must be not only original, but new", adding, "That is not * * * the law as is obvious in the case of maps or compendia, where later works will necessarily be anticipated."[11] All that is needed to satisfy both the Constitution and the statute is that the "author" contributed something more than a "merely trivial" variation, something recognizably "his own."[12] Originality in this context "means little more than a prohibition of actual copying."[13] No matter how poor artistically the "author's" addition, it is enough if it be his own. Bleistein v. Donaldson Lithographing Co., 188 U.S. 239, 250, 23 S.Ct. 298, 47 L.Ed. 460.

On that account, we have often distinguished between the limited protection accorded a copyright owner and the extensive protection granted a patent owner. So we have held that "independent reproduc-

---

10. Gerlach–Barklow Co. v. Morris & Bendien, 2 Cir., 23 F.2d 159, 161.

11. Sheldon v. Metro–Goldwyn Pictures Corp., 2 Cir., 81 F.2d 49, 53. See also Ricker v. General Electric Co., 2 Cir., 162 F.2d 141, 142.

12. Chamberlin v. Uris Sales Corp., 2 Cir., 150 F.2d 512; cf. Gross v. Seligman, 2 Cir., 212 F. 930.

13. Hoague–Sprague Corp. v. Frank C. Meyer Co., Inc., D.C.N.Y., 31 F.2d 583, 586. * * *

tion of a copyrighted * * * work is not infringement", whereas it is vis a vis a patent. Correlative with the greater immunity of a patentee is the doctrine of anticipation which does not apply to copyrights: The alleged inventor is chargeable with full knowledge of all the prior art, although in fact he may be utterly ignorant of it. The "author" is entitled to a copyright if he independently contrived a work completely identical with what went before; similarly, although he obtains a valid copyright, he has no right to prevent another from publishing a work identical with his, if not copied from his. A patentee, unlike a copyrightee, must not merely produce something "original"; he must also be "the first inventor or discoverer." "Hence it is possible to have a plurality of valid copyrights directed to closely identical or even identical works. Moreover, none of them, if independently arrived at without copying, will constitute an infringement of the copyright of the others."

* * *

2. We consider untenable defendants' suggestion that plaintiff's mezzotints could not validly be copyrighted because they are reproductions of works in the public domain. Not only does the Act include "Reproductions of a work of art",[19] but—while prohibiting a copyright of "the original text of any work * * * in the public domain"[20]—it explicitly provides for the copyrighting of "translations, or other versions of works in the public domain".[21] The mezzotints were such "versions." They "originated" with those who make them, and—on the trial judge's findings well supported by the evidence—amply met the standards imposed by the Constitution and the statute.[22] There is evidence that they were not intended to, and did not, imitate the paintings they reproduced. But even if their substantial departures from the paintings were inadvertent, the copyrights would be valid. A copyist's bad eyesight or defective musculature, or a shock caused by a clap of thunder, may yield sufficiently distinguishable variations. Having hit upon such a variation unintentionally, the "author" may adopt it as his and copyright it.

Accordingly, defendants' arguments about the public domain become irrelevant. * * *

* * *

19.   17 U.S.C. § 5.

20.   17 U.S.C. § 8 (formerly Sec. 7).

21.   17 U.S.C. § 7 (formerly Sec. 6). * * *

22.   See Copinger, The Law of Copyrights (7th ed. 1936) 46: "Again, an engraver is almost invariably a copyist, but although his work may infringe copyright in the original painting if made without the consent of the owner of the copyright therein, his work may still be original in the sense that he has employed skill and judgment in its production. He produces the resemblance he is desirous of obtaining by means very different from those employed by the painter or draughtsman from whom he copies: means which require great labour and talent. The engraver produces his effects by the management of light and shade, or, as the term of his art expresses it, the chiaroscuro. The due degrees of light and shade are produced by different lines and dots; he who is the engraver must decide on the choice of the different lines or dots for himself, and on his choice depends the success of his print."

L. BATLIN & SON, INC. v. SNYDER

United States Court of Appeals, Second Circuit, 1976.

536 F.2d 486. *cert. denied*, 429 U.S. 857, 97 S.Ct. 156, 50 L.Ed.2d 135 (1976).

OAKES, CIRCUIT JUDGE:

[Appellants, who obtained copyright registration for a plastic replica of an antique cast metal "Uncle Sam" bank, appeal from the district court's decision enjoining them from enforcing their copyright.]

Uncle Sam mechanical banks have been on the American scene at least since June 8, 1886, when Design Patent No. 16,728, issued on a toy savings bank of its type. The basic delightful design has long since been in the public domain. The banks are well documented in collectors' books and known to the average person interested in Americana. A description of the bank is that Uncle Sam, dressed in his usual stove pipe hat, blue full dress coat, starred vest and red and white striped trousers, and leaning on his umbrella, stands on a four-or five-inch wide base, on which sits his carpetbag. A coin may be placed in Uncle Sam's extended hand. When a lever is pressed, the arm lowers, and the coin falls into the bag, while Uncle Sam's whiskers move up and down. The base has an embossed American eagle on it with the words "Uncle Sam" on streamers above it, as well as the word "Bank" on each side. Such a bank is listed in a number of collectors' books, the most recent of which may be F. H. Griffith, Mechanical Banks (1972 ed.) where it was listed as No. 280, and is said to be not particularly rare.

[Appellant Snyder commissioned a foreign manufacturer to make a plastic version of the public domain Uncle Sam Bank. The plastic bank was shorter than the cast iron original] "in order to fit into the required price range and quality and quantity of material to be used." The figure of Uncle Sam was thus shortened from 11 to nine inches, and the base shortened and narrowed. It was also decided, Snyder averred, to change the shape of the carpetbag and to include the umbrella in a one-piece mold for the Uncle Sam figure, "so as not to have a problem with a loose umbrella or a separate molding process." * * *

[Appellee Batlin also commissioned a foreign manufacturer to make both cast iron and plastic versions of the public domain bank. However, the Customs Service refused to allow importation of those banks on the ground that they infringed Snyder's copyright.] Thus Batlin instituted suit for a judgment declaring appellants' copyright void and for damages for unfair competition and restraint of trade. * * *

This court has examined both the appellants' plastic Uncle Sam bank made under Snyder's copyright and the uncopyrighted model cast iron mechanical bank which is itself a reproduction of the original public domain Uncle Sam bank. Appellant Snyder claims differences not only of size but also in a number of other very minute details: the carpetbag shape of the plastic bank is smooth, the iron bank rough; the metal bank bag is fatter at its base; the eagle on the front of the platform in the metal bank is holding arrows in his talons while in the plastic bank he clutches leaves, this change concededly having been made, however, because "the arrows did not reproduce well in plastic on a smaller size." The shape of Uncle Sam's face is supposedly different, as is the shape and texture of the hats, according to the Snyder affidavit. In the metal version the umbrella is hanging loose while in the plastic item it is included in the single mold. The texture of the clothing, the hairline, shape of the bow ties and of the shirt collar and left arm as well as the flag carrying the name on the base of the statute are all claimed to be different, along with the shape and texture of the eagles on the side. Many of these differences are not perceptible to the casual observer. Appellants make no claim for any difference based on the plastic mold lines in the Uncle Sam figure which are perceptible.

Our examination of the banks results in the same conclusion as that of Judge Metzner in Etna Products, the earlier case enjoining Snyder's copyright, that the Snyder bank is "extremely similar to the cast iron bank, save in size and material" with the only other differences, such as the shape of the satchel and the leaves in the eagle's talons being "by all appearances, minor." Similarities include, more importantly, the appearance and number of stripes on the trousers, buttons on the coat, and stars on the vest and hat, the attire and pose of Uncle Sam, the decor on his base and bag, the overall color scheme, the method of carpetbag opening, to name but a few. After seeing the banks and hearing conflicting testimony from opposing expert witnesses as to the substantiality or triviality of the variations and as to the skill necessary to make the plastic model, the court below stated:

> I am making a finding of fact that as far as I'm concerned, it is practically an exact copy and whatever you point to in this [sic] differences are so infinitesimal they make no difference. All you have proved here by the testimony today is that if you give a man a seven-inch model and you say I want this to come out in a five-inch model, and he copies it, the fact that he has to have some artistic ability to make a model by reducing the seven to the five adds something to it. That is the only issue in this case.

* * *

As Judge Metzner went on to say in his opinion, the appellants' plastic version "reproduces" the cast iron bank "except that it proportionately reduces the height from approximately 11 inches to approximately nine inches with trivial variations." 394 F.Supp. at 1390. The court noted that appellants "went to great pains on the hearing to prove that there were substantial differences between the iron and the plastic articles," id. at 1391, and found that there had been no "level of input" such as in Alva Studios, Inc. v. Winninger, 177 F.Supp. 265, 267 (S.D.N.Y.1959) ("great skill and originality" called for in producing an exact scale reduction of Rodin's famous "Hand of God," to museum specifications). The substance of appellee's expert's testimony on which the district judge evidently relied was that the variations found in appellants' plastic bank were merely "trivial" and that it was a reproduction of the metal bank made as simply as possible for the purposes of manufacture. In other words, there were no elements of difference that amounted to significant alteration or that had any purpose other than the functional one of making a more suitable (and probably less expensive) figure in the plastic medium.

* * *

The test of originality is concededly one with a low threshold in that "all that is needed ... is that the 'author' contributed something more than a 'merely trivial' variation, something recognizably 'his own.' " Alfred Bell & Co. v. Catalda Fine Arts, Inc., 191 F.2d at 103. But as this court said many years ago, "while a copy of something in the public domain will not, if it be merely a copy, support a copyright, a distinguishable variation will...." Gerlach–Barklow Co. v. Morris & Bendien, Inc., 23 F.2d 159, 161 (2d Cir.1927).

Necessarily, none of these underlying principles is different in the case of "reproductions of a work of art," 17 U.S.C. § 5(h), from the case of "works of art ... ," 17 U.S.C. § 5(g). The requirement of substantial as opposed to trivial variation and the prohibition of mechanical copying, both of which are inherent in and subsumed by the concept of originality, apply to both statutory categories. There is implicit in that concept a "minimal element of creativity over and above the requirement of independent effort." 1 M. Nimmer, supra § 10.2, at 36. While the quantum of originality that is required may be modest indeed, Herbert Rosenthal Jewelry Corp. v. Grossbardt, 436 F.2d 315, 316 (2d Cir.1970), we are not inclined to abandon that requirement, even if in the light of the constitutional and statutory bases therefor and our precedents we could do so.

A reproduction of a work of art obviously presupposes an underlying work of art. * * * The underlying work of art may as here be in the public domain. But even to claim the more limited protection given to a reproduction of a work of art (that to the distinctive features contributed by the reproducer), the reproduction must contain "an original contribution not present in the underlying work of art" and be "more than a mere copy." 1 M. Nimmer, supra, § 20.2, at 93.

According to Professor Nimmer, moreover, "the mere reproduction of a work of art in a different medium should not constitute the required originality for the reason that no one can claim to have independently evolved any particular medium." Id. at 94. See Millworth Converting Corp. v. Slifka, 276 F.2d 443, 444–45 (2d Cir.1960). Cf. Gardenia Flowers, Inc. v. Joseph Markovits, Inc., 280 F.Supp. 776, 781 (S.D.N.Y.1968). Professor Nimmer refers to Doran v. Sunset House Distributing Corp., 197 F.Supp. 940 (S.D.Cal.1961), aff'd, 304 F.2d 251 (9th Cir.1962), as suggesting "the ludicrous result that the first person to execute a public domain work of art in a different medium thereafter obtains a monopoly on such work in such medium, at least as to those persons aware of the first such effort." 1 M. Nimmer, supra, § 20.2, at 94. We do not follow the Doran case. We do follow the school of cases in this circuit and elsewhere supporting the proposition that to support a copyright there must be at least some substantial variation, not merely a trivial variation such as might occur in the translation to a different medium.

Nor can the requirement of originality be satisfied simply by the demonstration of "physical skill" or "special training" which, to be sure, Judge Metzner found was required for the production of the plastic molds that furnished the basis for appellants' plastic bank. A considerably higher degree of skill is required, true artistic skill, to make the reproduction copyrightable. Thus in Alfred Bell & Co. v. Catalda Fine Arts, Inc., supra, 191 F.2d at 104–05 n.22, Judge Frank pointed out that the mezzotint engraver's art there concerned required "great labour and talent" to effectuate the "management of light and shade ... produced by different lines and dots ... ," means "very different from those employed by the painter or draughtsman from whom he copies.... " See also Millworth Converting Corp. v. Slifka, [276 F.2d 443 (2d Cir.1960)] (fabric designer required one month of work to give three-dimensional color effect to flat surface). Here on the basis of appellants' own expert's testimony it took the Unitoy representative "about a day and a half, two days work" to produce the plastic mold sculpture from the metal Uncle Sam bank. If there be a point in the copyright law pertaining to reproductions at which sheer artistic skill and effort can act as a substitute for the requirement of substantial variation, it was not reached here.

Appellants rely heavily upon Alva Studios, Inc. v. Winninger, supra, the "Hand of God" case, where the court held that "great skill and originality [were required] to produce a scale reduction of a great work with exactitude." 177 F.Supp. at 267. There, the original sculpture was "one of the most intricate pieces of sculpture ever created" with "innumerable planes, lines and geometric patterns ... interdependent in [a] multi-dimensional work." Id. Originality was found by the district court to consist primarily in the fact that "it takes 'an extremely skilled sculptor' many hours working directly in front of the original" to effectuate a scale reduction. Id. at 266. The court, indeed, found the exact replica to be so original, distinct, and creative as to constitute a work of art in itself. The complexity and exactitude there involved distinguishes that case amply from the one at bar. As appellants themselves have pointed out, there are a number of trivial differences or deviations from the original public domain cast iron bank in their plastic reproduction. Thus concededly the plastic version is not, and was scarcely meticulously produced to be, an exactly faithful reproduction. Nor is the creativity in the underlying work of art of the same order of magnitude as in the case of the "Hand of God." Rodin's sculpture is, furthermore, so unique and rare, and adequate public access to it such a problem that a significant public benefit accrues from its precise, artistic reproduction. No such benefit can be imagined to accrue here from the "knock-off" reproduction of the cast iron Uncle Sam bank. Thus appellants' plastic bank is neither in the category of exactitude required by

Alva Studios nor in a category of substantial originality; it falls within what has been suggested by the amicus curiae is a copyright no-man's land.

Absent a genuine difference between the underlying work of art and the copy of it for which protection is sought, the public interest in promoting progress in the arts—indeed, the constitutional demand, Chamberlin v. Uris Sales Corp., [150 F.2d 512 (2d Cir.1945)]—could hardly be served. To extend copyrightability to minuscule variations would simply put a weapon for harassment in the hands of mischievous copiers intent on appropriating and monopolizing public domain work. Even in Mazer v. Stein, [347 U.S. 201, 98 L.Ed. 630, 74 S.Ct. 460 (1954)], which held that the statutory terms "works of art" and "reproduction of works of art" (terms which are clearly broader than the earlier term "works of the fine arts") permit copyright of quite ordinary mass-produced items, the Court expressly held that the objects to be copyrightable, "must be original, that is, the author's tangible expression of his ideas." 347 U.S. at 214. No such originality, no such expression, no such ideas here appear. * * *

* * *

WOODS v. BOURNE CO.

United States Court of Appeals, Second Circuit, 1995.
60 F.3d 978.

FEINBERG, CIRCUIT JUDGE:

[Defendant Bourne was the successor in interest to music publisher Berlin, which had prepared and commercially exploited various arrangements of a song ("When the Red, Red, Robin Comes Bob, Bob, Bobbin' Along") after acquiring the rights to the song from its author Harry Woods. Several decades later, when Woods' heirs exercised their statutory right under 17 U.S.C. § 304 to terminate the grant, Bourne argued that it was entitled to continue to exploit these arrangements because they constituted derivative works and thus were excluded from the termination provisions under section 304(c)(6)(A). (For a discussion of these provisions, see Chapter 17.C.2.)]

In the district court and again on appeal, Bourne has argued that all of the pre-termination arrangements prepared under its authority qualify as derivative works. This argument stems from the premise that the first published piano-vocal arrangement of the Song was itself a Bourne-authorized derivative work. The original grant from Woods to Berlin, according to Bourne, was just a "lead sheet"—a very simple, handwritten rendering of the lyrics and melody of the composition without harmonies or other embellishments. Bourne argues that Berlin modified the lead sheet by adding harmonies and other elements to create a commercially exploitable piano-vocal arrangement that qualifies as a derivative work. Bourne also argues that the 1981 arrangement allegedly used in the Delta Faucet commercial, as well as all other Bourne-authorized arrangements, were derivative works. * * *

The district court rejected both aspects of this argument—that the piano-vocal or any other Bourne-authorized arrangements were derivative works and that all relevant performances were in fact performances of Bourne-authorized arrangements. In finding that the piano-vocal arrangement is not a derivative work, the court relied on a close reading of the statutory definition of a derivative work and inferences regarding industry practice. 841 F.Supp. at 121. For convenience, we repeat the Copyright Act's definition of a derivative work as

> a work based upon one or more preexisting works, such as a ... musical arrangement ... motion picture version, sound recording ... or any other form in which a work may be recast, transformed, or adapted. A work consisting of editorial revisions, annotations, elaborations, or other modifications which, as a whole, represent an original work of authorship, is a "derivative work."

17 U.S.C. § 101.

The district court found that the first sentence of that definition, which plainly identifies a "musical arrangement" as one type of derivative work, must be read in conjunction with the second sentence's requirement of "modifications which, as a whole, represent an original work of authorship." 841 F.Supp. at 121. Therefore, according to the district court, not every musical arrangement is entitled to derivative work status. The arrangement must be an original work of authorship. The court then asserted that Bourne's claim that Berlin's arrangers somehow exercised authorship by turning the lead sheet into a commercially exploitable piano-vocal arrangement was "contrary to the ways of the trade." Id. The court inferred that Woods "doubtless played the song for Berlin when he brought it into the firm," id., and that, at the very least, he must have approved the piano-vocal arrangement before it was published and made available to the public. The court concluded that, "accordingly, the very first piano and voice version that was sold could not possibly be a 'musical arrangement' making it a 'derivative work' of the lead sheet." Id. The court went on to find that none of the printed or (with one minor exception) performed arrangements were derivative works. Id. at 122–23.

1. THE STANDARD OF ORIGINALITY

In order for a work to qualify as a derivative work it must be independently copyrightable. Weissmann v. Freeman, 868 F.2d 1313, 1320–21 (2d Cir.), cert. denied, 493 U.S. 883, 107 L. Ed. 2d 172, 110 S. Ct. 219 (1989). The basis for copyright protection contained in both the constitution and the Copyright Act is originality of authorship. L. Batlin & Son, Inc. v. Snyder, 536 F.2d 486, 490 (2d Cir.) (in banc), cert. denied, 429 U.S. 857, 50 L. Ed. 2d 135, 97 S. Ct. 156 (1976). While a certificate of copyright registration, such as the one that Berlin obtained for the piano-vocal arrangement, creates a presumption of copyrightability, the existence of a registration certificate is not dispositive. Weissmann, 868 F.2d at 1320.

We thoroughly discussed the standard of originality in a derivative work in our in banc decision in Batlin. There we held that "there must be at least some substantial variation [from the underlying work], not merely a trivial variation." Batlin, 536 F.2d at 491; accord Durham Indus., Inc. v. Tomy Corp., 630 F.2d 905, 909 (2d Cir.1980) ("To support a copyright the original aspects of a derivative work must be more than trivial."). Further, "the requirement of originality [cannot] be satisfied simply by the demonstration of 'physical skill' or 'special training'.... " Batlin, 536 F.2d at 491; see also Tempo Music, Inc. v. Famous Music Corp., 838 F.Supp. 162, 170 (S.D.N.Y.1993) (discussing Batlin). Our discussions of the originality standard in recent decisions, such as Weissmann, 868 F.2d at 1321, and Gaste v. Kaiserman, 863 F.2d 1061, 1066 (2d Cir.1988), upon which Bourne relies, do not render the Batlin standard inapplicable. See Waldman Publishing Corp. v. Landoll, Inc., 43 F.3d 775, 782 (2d Cir.1994) (relying on Batlin as authoritative statement of originality requirement).

In Batlin we warned that "to extend copyrightability to minuscule variations would simply put a weapon for harassment in the hands of mischievous copiers intent on appropriating and monopolizing public domain work." 536 F.2d at 492. At least one other circuit, relying on this court's opinion in Batlin, has advised special caution in analyzing originality in derivative works, since too low a threshold will "giv[e] the first [derivative work] creator a considerable power to interfere with the creation of subsequent derivative works from the same underlying work." Gracen v. Bradford Exchange, 698 F.2d 300, 305 (7th Cir.1983). As the Gracen court explained in discussing the originality requirement for a painting derived from a photograph, there must be "sufficiently gross difference between the underlying and the derivative work to avoid entangling subsequent artists depicting the underlying work in copyright problems." 698 F.2d at 305. This observation may be particularly relevant in the musical context. While it is easy enough to describe the threshold of originality as being low, it is difficult to translate this standard from one medium to another. See Tempo Music, 838 F.Supp. at 170 ("The risk of copyright confusion seems particularly significant in music cases given that finders of fact often lack musical expertise."); 1 Nimmer § 2.05[C] at 2–57 (noting "tendency to require a somewhat greater degree of originality in order to accord copyright in a musical arrangement"). But see 1 William F. Patry, Copyright Law and Practice 237 (1994).

Bourne argues that the district court overstated the degree of originality required for an arrangement of a song to merit derivative work status. Bourne focuses on the court's statement that "there must be such things as unusual vocal treatment, additional lyrics of consequence, unusual altered harmonies, novel sequential uses of themes.... " 841 F.Supp. at 121. We agree that the sentence that Bourne quotes does overstate the standard for derivative work originality. As we have observed on several occasions, the requirement of originality is not the same as the requirement of novelty, the higher standard usually applied to patents. E.g., Batlin, 536 F.2d at 490 ("There must be independent creation, but it need not be invention in the sense of striking uniqueness, ingeniousness, or novelty.... "); Alfred Bell & Co. v. Catalda Fine Arts, Inc., 191 F.2d 99, 102–03 (2d Cir.1951). However, we read the district court's statement as brief dictum within a discussion that otherwise does identify the correct standard.

Earlier in its opinion, the district court correctly cited the statutory definition of a derivative work, which the court said required "the 'modification' to the composition to be an original work of authorship." 841 F.Supp. at 121. Following its apparent exaggeration of the standard for derivative work originality, the court explained that

> [there must be] something of substance added making the piece to some extent a new work with the old song embedded in it but from which the new has developed. It is not merely a stylized version of the original song where a major artist may take liberties with the lyrics or the tempo, the listener hearing basically the original tune. It is, in short, the addition of such new material as would entitle the creator to a copyright on the new material.

Id.

This, we believe, is a correct statement of the originality standard as set out in Batlin. The first and third sentences simply reiterate Batlin's "substantial variation" requirement. The second sentence, disqualifying "stylized versions of the original song," as well as the district court's earlier dismissal of "cocktail pianist variations of the piece that are standard fare in the music trade by any competent musician," id., merely express, in terms relevant to the musical context, our explanation in Batlin that "the demonstration of 'physical skill' or 'special training,'" 536 F.2d at 491, is insufficient to satisfy the requirement of originality. Because we conclude that the district court articulated the correct standard of originality, we turn to consider the application of the standard to the facts of this case.

2. APPLICATION OF THE ORIGINALITY STANDARD

To determine whether a work is sufficiently original to be a derivative work, the judge in a bench trial must make findings of fact based upon a comparison of two works. The judge must then apply the legal standard of originality to the facts to determine whether the standard has been met. * * *

a. *The piano-vocal arrangement*

* * *

* * * [T]he district court found that the piano-vocal arrangement is not sufficiently original compared with the lead sheet to be considered a derivative work. A side-by-side comparison of the two printed documents

quickly reveals that they are not literally identical. But it is not readily apparent whether the differences between the two documents are "substantial." At trial, both Callicoon and Bourne presented expert testimony on whether the differences were "substantial variations" reflecting deliberate aesthetic choices or merely "trivial" changes dictated, for instance, by applying conventional rules of harmony to the melody in the lead sheet. The district court was ultimately persuaded by Callicoon's expert, Thomas Shepard, that the variations in the piano-vocal arrangement were insubstantial.

We have considered the record before the district court, and we cannot say that on the particular facts before it the court erred in making this determination. * * *

* * *

b. The 1981 arrangement

A new arrangement of the Song was made under license from Bourne in 1981. * * * The district court found that the 1981 arrangement "in no way exhibits the degree of creativity required to make it a derivative work." Id. at 123.

According to both parties' experts, the principal variation in the 1981 arrangement as compared with the piano-vocal arrangement concerns the bass line in the piano part. While the bass line in the first piano-vocal arrangement consists primarily of quarter notes on the first and third beat of each measure, there is a so-called "moving bass line" in the 1981 arrangement.

As with the piano-vocal arrangement, we have considered the record before the district court, and we are unable to conclude that the court erred in finding the 1981 arrangement * * * insufficiently original to be called a derivative work. * * *

c. Other printed and performed arrangements

We have reviewed the evidence concerning other recorded and printed arrangements and find that the district court did not err in its determinations regarding the originality of any of these arrangements.

* * *

Notes

1. Were *Batlin* and *Alva Studios* (cited in *Batlin*) correctly decided? Do they both survive *Feist*? Are these cases consistent with *Alfred Bell & Co.*?

2. In *Batlin*, if Snyder had designed and produced a sculpture depicting only the cluster of leaves that were to be held in the eagle's talons, would that sculpture have been copyrightable? Does your answer change when the leaves are placed in the eagle's talons?

3. If a musician transposes existing music into a different key, is the result copyrightable as a derivative work?

4.   Is a colorized film copyrightable?

5.   Suppose that a writer publishes an unauthorized English-language translation of a copyrighted French novel. Can she claim a copyright in her translation? *Cf.,* section 103(a) of the Act.

6.   Suppose that a short story was adapted into a motion picture with the consent of the story's copyright owner. Some years later, the motion picture enters the public domain because the movie studio failed to comply with certain copyright formalities. Does the owner of copyright in the short story have a copyright claim against parties that make and distribute copies of the public domain motion picture? See *Russell v. Price,* 612 F.2d 1123 (9th Cir.1979). Alternatively, suppose the short story enters the public domain before the motion picture. Does the owner of the motion picture copyright have a copyright claim against the maker of a second motion picture based on the same story?

7.   In *Gracen v. Bradford Exchange,* 698 F.2d 300, 304–05 (7th Cir. 1983), discussed in *Woods v. Bourne,* Judge Posner found that an artist's drawings and paintings based on movie stills from "The Wizard of Oz" were insufficiently original to merit copyright protection:

> Miss Gracen reminds us that judges can make fools of themselves pronouncing on aesthetic matters. But artistic originality is not the same thing as the legal concept of originality in the Copyright Act. Artistic originality indeed might inhere in a detail, a nuance, a shading too small to be apprehended by a judge. A contemporary school of art known as "Super Realism" attempts with some success to make paintings that are indistinguishable to the eye from color photographs. * * * A portrait is not unoriginal for being a good likeness.

> But especially as applied to derivative works, the concept of originality in copyright law has as one would expect a legal rather than aesthetic function—to prevent overlapping claims. See *L. Batlin & Son, Inc. v. Snyder,* supra, 536 F.2d at 491–92. Suppose Artist A produces a reproduction of the Mona Lisa, a painting in the public domain, which differs slightly from the original. B also makes a reproduction of the Mona Lisa. A, who has copyrighted his derivative work, sues B for infringement. B's defense is that he was copying the original, not A's reproduction. But if the difference between the original and A's reproduction is slight, the difference between A's and B's reproductions will also be slight, so that if B had access to A's reproductions the trier of fact will be hard-pressed to decide whether B was copying A or copying the Mona Lisa itself. Miss Gracen's drawings illustrate the problem. They are very similar both to the photographs from the movie and to the plates designed by [accused infringer] Auckland. Auckland's affidavit establishes that he did not copy or even see her drawings. But suppose he had seen them. Then it would be very hard to determine whether he had been copying the movie stills, as he was authorized to do, or copying her drawings.

> We are speaking, however, only of the requirement of originality in derivative works. If a painter paints from life, no court is going to hold that his painting is not copyrightable because it is an exact photographic likeness. If that were the rule photographs could not be copyrighted—

the photographs of Judy Garland in "The Wizard of Oz," for example—but of course they can be, 1 Nimmer on Copyright § 2.08[E] (1982). The requirement of originality is significant chiefly in connection with derivative works, where if interpreted too liberally it would paradoxically inhibit rather than promote the creation of such works by giving the first creator a considerable power to interfere with the creation of subsequent derivative works from the same underlying work.

Is this passage from *Gracen* consistent with any conventional understanding of copyright doctrine, or is it the opinion, rather, of a copyright innocent in the person of Judge Posner? Is it defensible nevertheless on policy grounds? Is there a better doctrinal response to the dilemma Judge Posner imagines in the example of the Mona Lisa than the response he offers? Do you understand Judge Feinberg's opinion (in *Bourne*) to "follow" the opinion in *Gracen*? Is *Bourne* consistent with *Alfred Bell & Co.*?

8. The U.S. Court of Appeals for the Ninth Circuit ruled that a commercial photograph of a vodka bottle lacked sufficient originality to qualify for copyright protection as a derivative work. See *Ets–Hokin v. Skyy Spirits, Inc.*, 225 F.3d 1068 (9th Cir.2000)(reversing summary judgment, the court also noted that the vodka bottle is a utilitarian object that fails to qualify as a preexisting work). See also *SHL Imaging, Inc. v. Artisan House, Inc.*, 117 F.Supp.2d 301 (S.D.N.Y.2000)(court granted partial summary judgment for the plaintiff, concluding that photographs of picture frames were not derivative works because no transformative authorship existed). The district court distinguished its reasoning from the Ninth Circuit decision in the determination that the mirrored frames were copyrightable. Why is it relevant whether the antecedent work (the bottle or the frame) is copyrightable? Should not copyright in the photographs be judged according to the originality in each photograph itself? Is it relevant to the question of originality in the photograph that the photograph is (or is not) a derivative work? Consider the definition of a "derivative work" in section 101 of the Act.

4.　ORIGINALITY IN SPECIALIZED SUBJECT MATTER

(i) Computer Software

(1) Literal Code and Screen Displays

Should computer software be considered copyrightable "expression", or is it rather an uncopyrightable extension of the computer itself, or perhaps otherwise uncopyrightable as a "method of operation"? And what of the images that appear on the computer screen—the so-called user interface? Do these images gain additional, separate copyright beyond the copyright in the software? These questions vexed copyright specialists in the early years following enactment of the 1976 Act.

Section 101 of the 1976 Act and its legislative history indicated early on that computer software was to be considered copyrightable as a "literary work," *see* H.R.Rep.No. 1476, 94th Cong., 2d Sess. 54, *reprinted in* 1976 U.S. Code Cong. & Ad. News 5659, 5667 (" 'literary works' ... includes ... computer programs"). This policy was clarified by the 1980 amendments revising section 117 and defining "computer program" in section 101. *See* H.R.Rep.No. 1307, 96th Cong., 2d Sess. 23, *reprinted in* 1980 U.S. Code Cong. & Ad. News 6460, 6482; *see also Williams Electronics, Inc. v. Artic International, Inc.*, 685 F.2d 870, 875 (3d Cir.1982) (holding that "the copyrightability of computer programs is firmly established after the 1980 amendment to the Copyright Act").

Meanwhile, in *Apple Computer, Inc. v. Franklin Computer Corp.*, 714 F.2d 1240, 1251 (3d Cir.1983), the Third Circuit rejected the argument that operating systems software, as distinguished from applications software, was an uncopyrightable "method of operation" under section 102(b):

> Franklin's attack on operating system programs as "methods" or "processes" seems inconsistent with its concession that application programs are an appropriate subject of copyright. Both types of programs instruct the computer to do something. Therefore, it should make no difference for purposes of section 102(b) whether these instructions tell the computer to help prepare an income tax return (the task of an application program) or to translate a high level language program from source code into its binary language object code form (the task of an operating system program such as "Applesoft" * * *). Since it is only the instructions which are protected, a "process" is no more involved because the instructions in an operating system program may be used to activate the operation of the computer than it would be if instructions were written in ordinary English in a manual which described the necessary steps to activate an intricate complicated machine. There is, therefore, no reason to afford any less copyright protection to the instructions in an operating system program than to the instructions in an application program.

These early authorities dealt only with the copyrightability of the actual (literal) codes (both source and object) in which the computer program was expressed. Other authorities held that screen displays (and accompanying sounds) were additionally protectable as audiovisual works, separate from the underlying software, so that copying the screen display without copying the software would still constitute literal infringement. See, *e.g., Stern Electronics, Inc. v. Kaufman*, 669 F.2d 852, 855–57 (2d Cir.1982). There remained, however, the question of whether and to what extent copyright could subsist in the "nonliteral" aspects of software—*i.e.*, in the outlines, patterns and expressive structure of the software.

(2) Nonliteral Elements of Software

COMPUTER ASSOCIATES INTERNATIONAL, INC. v. ALTAI, INC.

United States Court of Appeals, Second Circuit, 1992.
982 F.2d 693.

WALKER, CIRCUIT JUDGE.

[The subject of this litigation is Computer Associates' ("CA" 's) job scheduling program, CA–SCHEDULER, and its sub-program ADAPTER, which acts as a translator and allows CA–SCHEDULER to be used on different operating systems. In an effort to create a competing job scheduler, Altai hired a former CA employee who was familiar with ADAPTER and who, unknown to Altai, copied large portions of the ADAPTER source code in order to create the new program, OSCAR 3.4. Upon learning this, Altai rewrote the program, using a completely different source code. The result was OSCAR 3.5. The district court held that OSCAR 3.5 did not infringe ADAPTER. On appeal, CA contends that the district court failed to consider the copyrightability of a computer program's non-literal elements.]

Among other things, this case deals with the challenging question of whether and to what extent the "non-literal" aspects of a computer program, that is, those aspects that are not reduced to written code, are protected by copyright. While a few other courts have already grappled with this issue, this case is one of first impression in this circuit. As we shall discuss, we find the results reached by other courts to be less than satisfactory. Drawing upon long-standing doctrines of copyright law, we take an approach that we think better addresses the practical difficulties embedded in these types of cases. In so doing, we have kept in mind the necessary balance between creative incentive and industrial competition.

* * *

As a general matter, and to varying degrees, copyright protection extends beyond a literary work's strictly textual form to its non-literal components. As we have said, "it is of course essential to any protection of literary property ... that the right cannot be limited literally to the text, else a plagiarist would escape by immaterial variations." Nichols v. Universal Pictures Corp., 45 F.2d 119, 121 (2d Cir.1930) (L. Hand, J.), cert. denied, 282 U.S. 902, 75 L. Ed. 795, 51 S. Ct. 216 (1931). Thus, where "the fundamental essence or structure of one work is duplicated in another," 3 Nimmer, § 13.03[A][1], at 13–24, courts have found copyright infringement. * * *

A. Copyright Protection for the Non-literal Elements of Computer Programs

* * *

CA argues that, despite Altai's rewrite of the OSCAR code, the resulting program remained substantially similar to the structure of its ADAPTER program. * * * [A] program's structure includes its nonliteral components such as general flow charts as well as the more specific organization of inter-modular relationships, parameter lists, and macros. In addition to these aspects, CA contends that OSCAR 3.5 is also substantially similar to ADAPTER with respect to the list of services that both ADAPTER and OSCAR obtain from their respective operating systems. We must decide whether and to what extent these elements of computer programs are protected by copyright law.

* * *

The syllogism that follows from the foregoing premises is a powerful one: if the non-literal structures of literary works are protected by copyright; and if computer programs are literary works, as we are told by the legislature; then the non-literal structures of computer programs are protected by copyright. See Whelan [Associates, Inc. v. Jaslow Dental Laboratory, Inc., 797 F.2d 1222 (3d Cir.1986),] at 1234 ("By analogy to other literary works, it would thus appear that the copyrights of computer programs can be infringed even absent copying of the literal elements of the program."). We have no reservation in joining the company of those courts that have already ascribed to this logic. See, e.g., Johnson Controls, Inc. v. Phoenix Control Sys., Inc., 886 F.2d 1173, 1175 (9th Cir.1989) * * *. However, that conclusion does not end our analysis. We must determine the scope of copyright protection that extends to a computer program's non-literal structure.

* * *

(1) Idea vs. Expression Dichotomy

It is a fundamental principle of copyright law that a copyright does not protect an idea, but only the expression of the idea. * * *

Congress made no special exception for computer programs. To the contrary, the legislative history explicitly states that copyright protects computer programs only "to the extent that they incorporate authorship in programmer's expression of original ideas, as distinguished from the ideas themselves." [H.R.Rep. No. 1476, 94th Cong., 2d Sess. 54, reprinted in 1976 U.S.C.C.A.N. 5659, 5667 (hereinafter "House Report")]; see also id. at 5670 ("Section 102(b) is intended . . . to make clear that the expression adopted by the programmer is the copyrightable element in a computer program, and that the actual processes or methods embodied in the program are not within the scope of copyright law.").

* * *

Drawing the line between idea and expression is a tricky business. Judge Learned Hand noted that "nobody has ever been able to fix that boundary, and nobody ever can." Nichols, 45 F.2d at 121. Thirty years later his convictions remained firm. "Obviously, no principle can be stated as to when an imitator has gone beyond copying the 'idea,' and has borrowed its 'expression,'" Judge Hand concluded. "Decisions must therefore inevitably be ad hoc." Peter Pan Fabrics, Inc. v. Martin Weiner Corp., 274 F.2d 487, 489 (2d Cir.1960).

The essentially utilitarian nature of a computer program further complicates the task of distilling its idea from its expression. * * * In order to describe both computational processes and abstract ideas, its content "combines creative and technical expression." * * * The variations of expression found in purely creative compositions, as opposed to those contained in utilitarian works, are not directed towards practical application. For example, a narration of Humpty Dumpty's demise, which would clearly be a creative composition, does not serve the same ends as, say, a recipe for scrambled eggs—which is a more process oriented text. Thus, compared to aesthetic works, computer programs hover even more closely to the elusive boundary line described in § 102(b).

The doctrinal starting point in analyses of utilitarian works, is the seminal case of Baker v. Selden, 101 U.S. 99, 25 L. Ed. 841 (1879). In Baker, the Supreme Court faced the question of "whether the exclusive property in a system of bookkeeping can be claimed, under the law of copyright, by means of a book in which that system is explained?" Id. at 101. * * *

The Supreme Court found nothing copyrightable in Selden's bookkeeping system, and rejected his infringement claim regarding the ledger sheets. * * *

To the extent that an accounting text and a computer program are both "a set of statements or instructions ... to bring about a certain result," 17 U.S.C. § 101, they are roughly analogous. In the former case, the processes are ultimately conducted by human agency; in the latter, by electronic means. In either case, as already stated, the processes themselves are not protectable. But the holding in Baker goes farther. The Court concluded that those aspects of a work, which "must necessarily be used as incident to" the idea, system or process that the work describes, are also not copyrightable. 101 U.S. at 104. Selden's ledger sheets, therefore, enjoyed no copyright protection because they were "necessary incidents to" the system of accounting that he described. Id. at 103. From this reasoning, we conclude that those elements of a computer program that are necessarily incidental to its function are similarly unprotectable.

While Baker v. Selden provides a sound analytical foundation, it offers scant guidance on how to separate idea or process from expression, and moreover, on how to further distinguish protectable expression from that expression which "must necessarily be used as incident to" the work's underlying concept. In the context of computer programs, the Third Circuit's noted decision in Whelan has, thus far, been the most thoughtful attempt to accomplish these ends.

The court in Whelan faced substantially the same problem as is presented by this case. There, the defendant was accused of making off with the non-literal structure of the plaintiff's copyrighted dental lab management program, and employing it to create its own competitive version. In assessing whether there had been an infringement, the court had to determine which aspects of the programs involved were ideas, and which were expression. In separating the two, the court settled upon the following conceptual approach:

> The line between idea and expression may be drawn with reference to the end sought to be achieved by the work in question. In other

words, the purpose or function of a utilitarian work would be the work's idea, and everything that is not necessary to that purpose or function would be part of the expression of the idea.... Where there are various means of achieving the desired purpose, then the particular means chosen is not necessary to the purpose; hence, there is expression, not idea.

797 F.2d at 1236 (citations omitted). The "idea" of the program at issue in Whelan was identified by the court as simply "the efficient management of a dental laboratory." Id. at n.28.

* * *

Whelan['s] * * * standard for distinguishing idea from expression has been widely criticized for being conceptually overbroad. * * * The leading commentator in the field has stated that, "the crucial flaw in [Whelan's] reasoning is that it assumes that only one 'idea,' in copyright law terms, underlies any computer program, and that once a separable idea can be identified, everything else must be expression." 3 Nimmer § 13.03[F], at 13–62.34. This criticism focuses not upon the program's ultimate purpose but upon the reality of its structural design. As we have already noted, a computer program's ultimate function or purpose is the composite result of interacting subroutines. Since each subroutine is itself a program, and thus, may be said to have its own "idea," Whelan's general formulation that a program's overall purpose equates with the program's idea is descriptively inadequate.

Accordingly, we think that Judge Pratt wisely declined to follow Whelan. See Computer Assocs. [Int'l, Inc. v. Altai, 775 F.Supp. 544 (E.D.N.Y.1991)], at 558–60. In addition to noting the weakness in the Whelan definition of "program-idea," mentioned above, Judge Pratt found that Whelan's synonymous use of the terms "structure, sequence, and organization," see Whelan, 797 F.2d at 1224 n.1, demonstrated a flawed understanding of a computer program's method of operation. See Computer Assocs., 775 F.Supp. at 559–60 (discussing the distinction between a program's "static structure" and "dynamic structure"). Rightly, the district court found Whelan's rationale suspect because it is so closely tied to what can now be seen—with the passage of time—as the opinion's somewhat outdated appreciation of computer science.

(2) Substantial Similarity Test for Computer Program Structure: Abstraction–Filtration–Comparison

We think that Whelan's approach to separating idea from expression in computer programs relies too heavily on metaphysical distinctions and does not place enough emphasis on practical considerations. Cf. Apple Computer, [Inc. v. Franklin Computer Corp., 714 F.2d 1240 (3d Cir. 1983)] at 1253 (rejecting certain commercial constraints on programming as a helpful means of distinguishing idea from expression because they did "not enter into the somewhat metaphysical issue of whether particular ideas and expressions have merged"). As the cases that we shall discuss demonstrate, a satisfactory answer to this problem cannot be reached by resorting, a priori, to philosophical first principals.

As discussed herein, we think that district courts would be well-advised to undertake a three-step procedure, based on the abstractions test utilized by the district court, in order to determine whether the non-literal elements of two or more computer programs are substantially similar. This approach breaks no new ground; rather, it draws on such familiar copyright doctrines as merger, scenes a faire, and public domain. In taking this approach, however, we are cognizant that computer technology is a dynamic field which can quickly outpace judicial decision-making. Thus, in cases where the technology in question does not allow for a literal application of the procedure we outline below, our opinion should not be read to foreclose the district courts of our circuit from utilizing a modified version.

In ascertaining substantial similarity under this approach, a court would first break down the allegedly infringed program into its constituent structural parts. Then, by examining each of these parts for such things as incorporated ideas, expression that is necessarily incidental to those ideas, and elements that are taken from the public domain, a court would then be able to sift out all non-protectable material. Left with a kernel, or possibly kernels, of creative expression after following this process of elimination, the court's last step would be to compare this material with the structure of an allegedly infringing program. * * *

Step One: Abstraction

As the district court appreciated, see Computer Assocs., 775 F.Supp. at 560, the theoretic framework for analyzing substantial similarity expounded by Learned Hand in the Nichols case is helpful in the present context. In Nichols, we enunciated what has now become known as the "abstractions" test for separating idea from expression:

> Upon any work ... a great number of patterns of increasing generality will fit equally well, as more and more of the incident is left out. The last may perhaps be no more than the most general statement of what the [work] is about, and at times might consist only of its title; but there is a point in this series of abstractions where they are no longer protected, since otherwise the [author] could prevent the use of his "ideas," to which, apart from their expression, his property is never extended.

Nichols, 45 F.2d at 121.

While the abstractions test was originally applied in relation to literary works such as novels and plays, it is adaptable to computer programs. In contrast to the Whelan approach, the abstractions test "implicitly recognizes that any given work may consist of a mixture of numerous ideas and expressions." 3 Nimmer § 13.03[F] at 13–62.34–63.

As applied to computer programs, the abstractions test will comprise the first step in the examination for substantial similarity. Initially, in a manner that resembles reverse engineering on a theoretical plane, a court should dissect the allegedly copied program's structure and isolate each level of abstraction contained within it. This process begins with the code and ends with an articulation of the program's ultimate function. Along the way, it is necessary essentially to retrace and map each of the designer's steps—in the opposite order in which they were taken during the program's creation. * * *

As an anatomical guide to this procedure, the following description is helpful:

> At the lowest level of abstraction, a computer program may be thought of in its entirety as a set of individual instructions organized into a hierarchy of modules. At a higher level of abstraction, the instructions in the lowest-level modules may be replaced conceptually by the functions of those modules. At progressively higher levels of abstraction, the functions of higher-level modules conceptually replace the implementations of those modules in terms of lower-level modules and instructions, until finally, one is left with nothing but the ultimate function of the program.... A program has structure at every level of abstraction at which it is viewed. At low levels of abstraction, a program's structure may be quite complex; at the highest level it is trivial.

[Steven R. Englund, Note, Idea, Process, or Protected Expression?: Determining the Scope of Copyright Protection of the Structure of Computer Programs, 88 MICH. L. REV. 866, 897–98 (1990)]. * * *

Step Two: Filtration

Once the program's abstraction levels have been discovered, the substantial similarity inquiry moves from the conceptual to the concrete. Professor Nimmer suggests, and we endorse, a "successive filtering method" for separating protectable expression from non-protectable material. See generally 3 Nimmer § 13.03[F]. This process entails examining the structural components at each level of abstraction to determine whether their particular inclusion at that level was "idea" or was dictated by considerations of efficiency, so as to be necessarily incidental to that idea; required by factors external to the program itself; or taken from the public domain and hence is nonprotectable expression. * * * The structure of any given program may reflect some, all, or none of these considerations. Each case requires its own fact specific investigation.

Strictly speaking, this filtration serves "the purpose of defining the scope of plaintiff's copyright." Brown Bag Software v. Symantec Corp., 960 F.2d 1465, 1475 (9th Cir.) (endorsing "analytic dissection" of computer programs in order to isolate protectable expression), cert. denied, 113 S. Ct. 198, 121 L. Ed. 2d 141 (1992). By applying well developed doctrines of copyright law, it may ultimately leave behind a "core of protectable material." 3 Nimmer § 13.03[F][5], at 13–72. Further explication of this second step may be helpful.

(a) Elements Dictated by Efficiency

The portion of Baker v. Selden, discussed earlier, which denies copyright protection to expression necessarily incidental to the idea being expressed, appears to be the cornerstone for what has developed into the doctrine of merger. See Morrissey v. Procter & Gamble Co., 379 F.2d 675, 678–79 (1st Cir.1967) (relying on Baker for the proposition that expression embodying the rules of a sweepstakes contest was inseparable from the idea of the contest itself, and therefore were not protectable by copyright) * * *. The doctrine's underlying principle is that "when there is essentially only one way to express an idea, the idea and its expression are inseparable and copyright is no bar to copying that expression." Concrete Machinery Co. v. Classic Lawn Ornaments, Inc., 843 F.2d 600, 606 (1st Cir.1988). Under these circumstances, the expression is said to have "merged" with the idea itself. In order not to confer a monopoly of the idea upon the copyright owner, such expression should not be protected. See Herbert Rosenthal Jewelry Corp. v. Kalpakian, 446 F.2d 738, 742 (9th Cir.1971).

[The National Commission on New Technological Uses of Copyrighted Works ("CONTU")] recognized the applicability of the merger doctrine to computer programs. In its report to Congress it stated that:

> Copyrighted language may be copied without infringing when there is but a limited number of ways to express a given idea.... In the computer context, this means that when specific instructions, even though previously copyrighted, are the only and essential means of accomplishing a given task, their later use by another will not amount to infringement.

[CONTU Final Report 20 (1979)]. * * * While this statement directly concerns only the application of merger to program code, that is, the textual aspect of the program, it reasonably suggests that the doctrine fits comfortably within the general context of computer programs.

Furthermore, when one considers the fact that programmers generally strive to create programs "that meet the user's needs in the most efficient manner," [Peter S. Menell, An Analysis of the Scope of Copyright Protection for Application Programs, 41 STAN. L. REV. 1045, 1052 (1989) (hereinafter "Menell")], the applicability of the merger doctrine to computer programs becomes compelling. In the context of computer program design, the concept of efficiency is akin to deriving the most concise logical proof or formulating the most succinct mathematical computation. Thus, the more efficient a set of modules are, the more closely they approximate the idea or process embodied in that particular aspect of the program's structure.

While, hypothetically, there might be a myriad of ways in which a programmer may effectuate certain functions within a program,—i.e., express the idea embodied in a given subroutine—efficiency concerns may so narrow the practical range of choice as to make only one or two forms of expression workable options. See 3 Nimmer § 13.03[F][2], at 13–63; see also Whelan, 797 F.2d at 1243 n.43 ("It is true that for certain tasks there are only a very limited number of file structures available, and in such cases the structures might not be copyrighta- ble.... "). Of course, not all program structure is informed by efficiency concerns. See Menell, at 1052 (besides efficiency, simplicity related to user accommodation has become a programming priority). It follows that in order to determine whether the merger doctrine precludes copyright protection to an aspect of a program's structure that is so oriented, a court must inquire "whether the use of this particular set of modules is necessary efficiently to implement that part of the program's process" being implemented. Englund, at 902. If the answer is yes, then the expression represented by the programmer's choice of a specific module or group of modules has merged with their underlying idea and is unprotected. Id. at 902–03.

Another justification for linking structural economy with the appli- cation of the merger doctrine stems from a program's essentially utilita- rian nature and the competitive forces that exist in the software market- place. * * * Working in tandem, these factors give rise to a problem of proof which merger helps to eliminate.

Efficiency is an industry-wide goal. Since, as we have already noted, there may be only a limited number of efficient implementations for any given program task, it is quite possible that multiple programmers, working independently, will design the identical method employed in the allegedly infringed work. Of course, if this is the case, there is no copyright infringement. See Roth Greeting Cards v. United Card Co., 429 F.2d 1106, 1110 (9th Cir.1970); Sheldon [v. Metro–Goldwyn Pictures Corp., 81 F.2d 49 (2d Cir.1936)], at 54.

* * *

We find support for applying the merger doctrine in cases that have already addressed the question of substantial similarity in the context of computer program structure. Most recently, in Lotus Dev. Corp. [v. Paperback Software Int'l, 740 F.Supp. 37 (D.Mass.1990)], at 66, the district court had before it a claim of copyright infringement relating to the structure of a computer spreadsheet program. The court observed that "the basic spreadsheet screen display that resembles a rotated 'L' ..., if not present in every expression of such a program, is present in most expressions." Id. Similarly, the court found that "an essential detail present in most if not all expressions of an electronic spread- sheet—is the designation of a particular key that, when pressed, will invoke the menu command system." Id. Applying the merger doctrine, the court denied copyright protection to both program elements.

In Manufacturers Technologies, Inc. v. Cams, Inc., 706 F.Supp. 984, 995–99 (D.Conn.1989), the infringement claims stemmed from various alleged program similarities "as indicated in their screen displays." Id. at 990. Stressing efficiency concerns in the context of a merger analysis, the court determined that the program's method of allowing the user to navigate within the screen displays was not protectable because, in part, "the process or manner of navigating internally on any specific screen displays ... is limited in the number of ways it may be simply achieved to facilitate user comfort." Id. at 995.

The court also found that expression contained in various screen displays (in the form of alphabetical and numerical columns), was not the proper subject of copyright protection because it was "necessarily incident to the ideas" embodied in the displays. Id. at 996–97. Cf. Digital Communications [Assocs. v. Softklone Distrib. Corp., 659 F.Supp. 449 (N.D.Ga.1987)], at 460 (finding no merger and affording copyright protection to program's status screen display because "modes of expression chosen ... are clearly not necessary to the idea of the status screen").

We agree with the approach taken in these decisions, and conclude that application of the merger doctrine in this setting is an effective way to eliminate non-protectable expression contained in computer programs.

(b) Elements Dictated By External Factors

We have stated that where "it is virtually impossible to write about a particular historical era or fictional theme without employing certain 'stock' or standard literary devices," such expression is not copyrightable. Hoehling v. Universal City Studios, Inc., 618 F.2d 972, 979 (2d Cir.), cert. denied, 449 U.S. 841, 66 L. Ed. 2d 49, 101 S. Ct. 121 (1980). * * * This is known as the scenes a faire doctrine, and like "merger," it has its analogous application to computer programs. Cf. Data East USA, [Inc. v. Epyx, Inc., 862 F.2d 204 (9th Cir.1988),] at 208 (applying scenes a faire to a home computer video game).

Professor Nimmer points out that "in many instances it is virtually impossible to write a program to perform particular functions in a specific computing environment without employing standard techniques." 3 Nimmer § 13.03[F][3], at 13–65. This is a result of the fact that a programmer's freedom of design choice is often circumscribed by extrinsic considerations such as (1) the mechanical specifications of the computer on which a particular program is intended to run; (2) compatibility requirements of other programs with which a program is designed to operate in conjunction; (3) computer manufacturers' design standards; (4) demands of the industry being serviced; and (5) widely accepted programming practices within the computer industry. Id. at 13–66–71.

Courts have already considered some of these factors in denying copyright protection to various elements of computer programs. In the Plains Cotton case, the Fifth Circuit refused to reverse the district court's denial of a preliminary injunction against an alleged program infringer because, in part, "many of the similarities between the ... programs [were] dictated by the externalities of the cotton market." [Plains Cotton Coop. Assn. v. Goodpasture Computer Serv., 807 F.2d 1256 (5th Cir.1987),] at 1262.

In Manufacturers Technologies, the district court noted that the program's method of screen navigation "is influenced by the type of hardware that the software is designed to be used on." 706 F.Supp. at 995. Because, in part, "the functioning of the hardware package impacted and constrained the type of navigational tools used in plaintiff's screen displays," the court denied copyright protection to that aspect of the program. Cf. Data East USA, 862 F.2d at 209 (reversing a district court's finding of audiovisual work infringement because, inter alia, "the use of the Commodore computer for a karate game intended for home consumption is subject to various constraints inherent in the use of that computer").

Finally, the district court in Q–Co Industries rested its holding on what, perhaps, most closely approximates a traditional scenes a faire rationale. There, the court denied copyright protection to four program modules employed in a teleprompter program. This decision was ultimately based upon the court's finding that "the same modules would be an inherent part of any prompting program." [Q–Co. Indus. v. Hoffman, 625 F.Supp. 608 (S.D.N.Y.1985),] at 616.

Building upon this existing case law, we conclude that a court must also examine the structural content of an allegedly infringed program for elements that might have been dictated by external factors.

(c) Elements taken From the Public Domain

Closely related to the non-protectability of scenes a faire, is material found in the public domain. Such material is free for the taking and cannot be appropriated by a single author even though it is included in a copyrighted work. See E.F. Johnson Co. v. Uniden Corp. of America, 623 F.Supp. 1485, 1499 (D.Minn.1985); see also Sheldon, 81 F.2d at 54. We see no reason to make an exception to this rule for elements of a computer program that have entered the public domain by virtue of freely accessible program exchanges and the like. See 3 Nimmer § 13.03[F][4]; see also Brown Bag Software, 960 F.2d at 1473 (affirming the district court's finding that " 'plaintiffs may not claim copyright protection of an ... expression that is, if not standard, then commonplace in the computer software industry.' "). Thus, a court must also filter out this material from the allegedly infringed program before it makes the final inquiry in its substantial similarity analysis.

Step Three: Comparison

The third and final step of the test for substantial similarity that we believe appropriate for non-literal program components entails a comparison. Once a court has sifted out all elements of the allegedly infringed program which are "ideas" or are dictated by efficiency or external factors, or taken from the public domain, there may remain a core of protectable expression. In terms of a work's copyright value, this is the golden nugget. See Brown Bag Software, 960 F.2d at 1475. At this point, the court's substantial similarity inquiry focuses on whether the defendant copied any aspect of this protected expression, as well as an assessment of the copied portion's relative importance with respect to the plaintiff's overall program. See 3 Nimmer § 13.03[F][5]; Data East USA, 862 F.2d at 208 ("To determine whether similarities result from unprotectable expression, analytic dissection of similarities may be performed. If ... all similarities in expression arise from use of common ideas, then no substantial similarity can be found.'').

(3) Policy Considerations

We are satisfied that the three step approach we have just outlined not only comports with, but advances the constitutional policies underlying the Copyright Act. Since any method that tries to distinguish idea from expression ultimately impacts on the scope of copyright protection afforded to a particular type of work, "the line [it draws] must be a pragmatic one, which also keeps in consideration 'the preservation of the balance between competition and protection.... ' " Apple Computer, 714 F.2d at 1253 (citation omitted).

CA and some amici argue against the type of approach that we have set forth on the grounds that it will be a disincentive for future computer program research and development. At bottom, they claim that if programmers are not guaranteed broad copyright protection for their work, they will not invest the extensive time, energy and funds required to design and improve program structures. While they have a point, their argument cannot carry the day. The interest of the copyright law is not in simply conferring a monopoly on industrious persons, but in advancing the public welfare through rewarding artistic creativity, in a manner that permits the free use and development of non-protectable ideas and processes.

In this respect, our conclusion is informed by Justice Stewart's concise discussion of the principles that correctly govern the adaptation of the copyright law to new circumstances. In Twentieth Century Music Corp. v. Aiken, he wrote:

> The limited scope of the copyright holder's statutory monopoly, like the limited copyright duration required by the Constitution, reflects a balance of competing claims upon the public interest: Creative work is to be encouraged and rewarded, but private motivation must ultimately serve the cause of promoting broad public availability of literature, music, and the other arts.

> The immediate effect of our copyright law is to secure a fair return for an "author's" creative labor. But the ultimate aim is, by this incentive, to stimulate artistic creativity for the general public good.... When technological change has rendered its literal terms ambiguous, the Copyright Act must be construed in light of this basic purpose.

422 U.S. 151, 156, 95 S. Ct. 2040, 45 L. Ed. 2d 84 (1975) (citations and footnotes omitted).

Recently, the Supreme Court has emphatically reiterated that "the primary objective of copyright is not to reward the *labor* of authors.... " Feist Publications, Inc. v. Rural Tel. Serv. Co., 499 U.S. 340, 349, 113 L. Ed. 2d 358, 111 S. Ct. 1282, 1290 (1991) (emphasis added). While the Feist decision deals primarily with the copyrightability of purely factual compilations, its underlying tenets apply to much of the work involved in computer programming. Feist put to rest the "sweat of the brow" doctrine in copyright law. Id. at 1295. The rationale of that doctrine "was that copyright was a reward for the hard work that went into compiling facts." Id. at 1291. The Court flatly rejected this justification for extending copyright protection, noting that it "eschewed the most fundamental axiom of copyright law—that no one may copyright facts or ideas." Id.

Feist teaches that substantial effort alone cannot confer copyright status on an otherwise uncopyrightable work. As we have discussed, despite the fact that significant labor and expense often goes into computer program flow-charting and debugging, that process does not always result in inherently protectable expression. Thus, Feist implicitly undercuts the Whelan rationale, "which allowed copyright protection beyond the literal computer code . . . [in order to] provide the proper incentive for programmers by protecting their most valuable efforts. . . . " Whelan, 797 F.2d at 1237 (footnote omitted). We note that Whelan was decided prior to Feist when the "sweat of the brow" doctrine still had vitality. In view of the Supreme Court's recent holding, however, we must reject the legal basis of CA's disincentive argument.

Furthermore, we are unpersuaded that the test we approve today will lead to the dire consequences for the computer program industry that plaintiff and some amici predict. To the contrary, serious students of the industry have been highly critical of the sweeping scope of copyright protection engendered by the Whelan rule, in that it "enables first comers to 'lock up' basic programming techniques as implemented in programs to perform particular tasks." [Peter S. Menell, An Analysis of the Scope of Copyright Protection for Application Programs, 41 STAN. L. REV. 1045, 1087 (1989)]; see also [Peter G. Spivack, Comment, Does Form Follow Function? The Idea/Expression Dichotomy In Copyright Protection of Computer Software, 35 U.C.L.A. L. REV. 723, 765 (1988)] (Whelan "results in an inhibition of creation by virtue of the copyright owner's quasi-monopoly power").

To be frank, the exact contours of copyright protection for non-literal program structure are not completely clear. We trust that as future cases are decided, those limits will become better defined. Indeed, it may well be that the Copyright Act serves as a relatively weak barrier against public access to the theoretical interstices behind a program's source and object codes. This results from the hybrid nature of a computer program, which, while it is literary expression, is also a highly functional, utilitarian component in the larger process of computing.

Generally, we think that copyright registration—with its indiscriminating availability—is not ideally suited to deal with the highly dynamic technology of computer science. Thus far, many of the decisions in this area reflect the courts' attempt to fit the proverbial square peg in a round hole. The district court, see Computer Assocs., 775 F.Supp. at 560, and at least one commentator have suggested that patent registration, with its exacting up-front novelty and non-obviousness requirements, might be the more appropriate rubric of protection for intellectual property of this kind. See Randell M. Whitmeyer, Comment, A Plea for Due Processes: Defining the Proper Scope of Patent Protection for Computer Software, 85 NW. U. L. REV. 1103, 1123–25 (1991); see also Lotus Dev. Corp. v. Borland Int'l, Inc., 788 F.Supp. 78, 91 (D.Mass.1992) (discussing the potentially supplemental relationship between patent and copyright protection in the context of computer programs). In any event, now that more than 12 years have passed since CONTU issued its final report, the resolution of this specific issue could benefit from further legislative investigation—perhaps a CONTU II.

In the meantime, Congress has made clear that computer programs are literary works entitled to copyright protection. Of course, we shall abide by these instructions, but in so doing we must not impair the overall integrity of copyright law. While incentive based arguments in favor of broad copyright protection are perhaps attractive from a pure policy perspective, see Lotus Dev. Corp., 740 F.Supp. at 58, ultimately, they have a corrosive effect on certain fundamental tenets of copyright doctrine. If the test we have outlined results in narrowing the scope of protection, as we expect it will, that result flows from applying, in accordance with Congressional intent, long-standing principles of copyright law to computer programs. Of course, our decision is also informed by our concern that these fundamental principles remain undistorted.

* * *

Notes

1. In *Softel, Inc. v. Dragon Medical & Scientific Communications, Inc.*, 118 F.3d 955 (2d Cir.1997), *cert. denied*, 523 U.S. 1020, 118 S.Ct. 1300, 140 L.Ed.2d 466 (1998), the Second Circuit clarified its *Altai* methodology by observing that even though individual elements of a computer program might be found to be unprotectible, nevertheless *Feist* requires the court to consider whether the selection and arrangement of these individually uncopyrightable elements might itself be copyrightable as a compilation.

2. What is the essential difference between the *Whelan* and *Altai* approaches? Which approach is more consistent with the copyright statutes? With precedents such as *Baker v. Selden*? Which approach better serves the purposes of copyright law? Is there a better way to encourage creation of new software?

3. Is the merger analysis in *Altai* persuasive? Is it consistent with that of *Mason v. Montgomery Data*?

4. *Further applications of Altai*: In *Bateman v. Mnemonics, Inc.*, 79 F.3d 1532 (11th Cir.1996), the Eleventh Circuit held the *Altai* test applicable to both literal and nonliteral copying. The court also noted that computer interface commands, while copyrightable, should be excluded from the infringement analysis at the filtration step because they were elements necessary to compatibility.

In contrast, in *Lotus Development Corp. v. Borland International, Inc.,* 49 F.3d 807 (1st Cir.1995), *aff'd by an equally divided court,* 516 U.S. 233, 116 S.Ct. 804, 133 L.Ed.2d 610 (1996), the First Circuit declined to apply the *Altai* test. *Lotus* concerned the copyrightability of a menu command hierarchy used in the Lotus 1–2–3 computer spreadsheet program. The hierarchy consisted of 469 commands, such as "copy," "print," and "quit," which were arranged into more than 50 menus and submenus. Lotus 1–2–3 also permitted users to create "macros," each of which was a series of commands strung together so that, with a single keystroke, the user could instruct the computer to execute all of the commands. Although defendant Borland had copied none of Lotus's computer code, it did copy the words, commands, and ordering of Lotus's menu hierarchy, including all the menus and submenus. The First Circuit declined to apply the *Altai* test, because the court considered it applicable only to nonliteral copying:

> We think that abstracting menu command hierarchies down to their individual word and menu levels and then filtering idea from expression at that stage, as both the Altai and the district court tests require, obscures the more fundamental question of whether a menu command hierarchy can be copyrighted at all. The initial inquiry should not be whether individual components of a menu command hierarchy are expressive, but rather whether the menu command hierarchy as a whole can be copyrighted. But see *Gates Rubber Co. v. Bando Chem. Indus., Ltd.,* 9 F.3d 823 (10th Cir.1993) (endorsing *Altai's* abstraction-filtration-comparison test as a way of determining whether "menus and sorting criteria" are copyrightable).

49 F.3d at 815.

The *Lotus* court instead held that the menu command hierarchy was an uncopyrightable "method of operation" under section 102(b):

> The district court held that the Lotus menu command hierarchy, with its specific choice and arrangement of command terms, constituted an "expression" of the "idea" of operating a computer program with commands arranged hierarchically into menus and submenus. Borland II, 799 F.Supp. at 216. Under the district court's reasoning, Lotus's decision to employ hierarchically arranged command terms to operate its program could not foreclose its competitors from also employing hierarchically arranged command terms to operate their programs, but it did foreclose them from employing the specific command terms and arrangement that Lotus had used. In effect, the district court limited Lotus 1–2–3's "method of operation" to an abstraction.
>
> Accepting the district court's finding that the Lotus developers made some expressive choices in choosing and arranging the Lotus command terms, we nonetheless hold that that expression is not copyrightable because it is part of Lotus 1–2–3's "method of operation." We do not think that "methods of operation" are limited to abstractions; rather, they are the means by which a user operates something. If specific words are essential to operating something, then they are part of a "method of operation" and, as such, are unprotectable. This is so whether they must be highlighted, typed in, or even spoken, as computer programs no doubt will soon be controlled by spoken words.

The fact that Lotus developers could have designed the Lotus menu command hierarchy differently is immaterial to the question of whether it is a "method of operation." In other words, our initial inquiry is not whether the Lotus menu command hierarchy incorporates any expression. Rather, our initial inquiry is whether the Lotus menu command hierarchy is a "method of operation." Concluding, as we do, that users operate Lotus 1–2–3 by using the Lotus menu command hierarchy, and that the entire Lotus menu command hierarchy is essential to operating Lotus 1–2–3, we do not inquire further whether that method of operation could have been designed differently. The "expressive" choices of what to name the command terms and how to arrange them do not magically change the uncopyrightable menu command hierarchy into copyrightable subject matter.

Id. at 816. The court cited *Baker v. Selden,* 101 U.S. (11 Otto) 99, 25 L.Ed. 841 (1879), in support of this holding. It then drew an analogy between the menu command hierarchy and the buttons on a VCR:

Just as one could not operate a buttonless VCR, it would be impossible to operate Lotus 1–2–3 without employing its menu command hierarchy. Thus the Lotus command terms are not equivalent to the labels on the VCR's buttons, but are instead equivalent to the buttons themselves. Unlike the labels on a VCR's buttons, which merely make operating a VCR easier by indicating the buttons' functions, the Lotus menu commands are essential to operating Lotus 1–2–3. Without the menu commands, there would be no way to "push" the Lotus buttons, as one could push unlabeled VCR buttons. While Lotus could probably have designed a user interface for which the command terms were mere labels, it did not do so here. Lotus 1–2–3 depends for its operation on use of the precise command terms that make up the Lotus menu command hierarchy.

* * *

That the Lotus menu command hierarchy is a "method of operation" becomes clearer when one considers program compatibility. Under Lotus's theory, if a user uses several different programs, he or she must learn how to perform the same operation in a different way for each program used. For example, if the user wanted the computer to print material, then the user would have to learn not just one method of operating the computer such that it prints, but many different methods. We find this absurd. The fact that there may be many different ways to operate a computer program, or even many different ways to operate a computer program using a set of hierarchically arranged command terms, does not make the actual method of operation chosen copyrightable; it still functions as a method for operating the computer and as such is uncopyrightable.

49 F.3d at 817–18. The First Circuit acknowledged the contrary holdings of *Autoskill, Inc. v. National Educational Support Systems, Inc.,* 994 F.2d 1476, 1495 n. 23 (10th Cir.1993) (rejecting the argument that computer program's keying procedure was uncopyrightable under section 102(b), on the ground that even though the procedure only required the user to select one of three keys, the procedure nonetheless reflected the minimal "creativity" required

by *Feist*), *cert. denied*, 510 U.S. 916, 114 S.Ct. 307, 126 L.Ed.2d 254 (1993), and *Brown Bag Software v. Symantec Corp.*, 960 F.2d 1465, 1477 (9th Cir.) (stating in dicta that "menus, and keystrokes" may be copyrightable), *cert. denied sub nom. BB Asset Management, Inc. v. Symantec Corp.*, 506 U.S. 869, 113 S.Ct. 198, 121 L.Ed.2d 141 (1992).

In evaluating the reasoning in *Lotus*, consider the following questions: Did the *Lotus* court correctly apply *Baker v. Selden*? Would the *Altai* analysis have led to a different result? Can the menu commands and macros be meaningfully distinguished from the medical codes in problem 3(b) on page 820?

5. During the copyright law revision process which culminated in the Copyright Act of 1976, Congress created the National Commission on New Technological Uses of Copyrighted Works (CONTU) to evaluate what changes would be necessary to update the copyright laws to reflect emerging technologies. In its report on the roles of copyright and patent law in protecting computer software, the Software Subcommittee distinguished the patentable aspects of software from the copyrightable aspects:

> A computer program is a writing which sets forth instructions which can direct the operation of an automatic system capable of storing, processing, retreiving [sic] or transferring information. It is an explanation of a process and not the process itself. The distinction between the process and the writing which describes it is of critical importance to understanding how copyright applies to computer programs. With a computer program as with all forms of creative endeavor, there are three different phenomena:
>
> (1) A description of the activity (process);
>
> (2) The activity (process) itself; and
>
> (3) The results of the activity (process).
>
> Descriptions of a process are protectable through copyright without regard to whether they are narrative descriptions or lists of instructions. Processes or principles of operation—indicated by the second category—are protectable, if at all, through patents or trade secrecy.

Report of the Software Subcommittee to the National Commission on New Technological Uses of Copyrighted Works 3–4 (July 13, 1978) (footnote omitted). Compare the scope of the monopolies granted to software under patent, trade secret, and copyright law. What policies are served by these differences?

(ii) Useful Articles

MAZER v. STEIN

Supreme Court of the United States, 1954.
347 U.S. 201, 74 S.Ct. 460, 98 L.Ed. 630.

Mr. Justice Reed delivered the opinion of the Court.

This case involves the validity of copyrights obtained by respondents for statuettes of male and female dancing figures made of semivitreous china. The controversy centers around the fact that although copyright-ed as "works of art," the statuettes were intended for use and used as bases for table lamps, with electric wiring, sockets and lamp shades attached.

[The defendant contended that the statuettes were not copyrightable because plaintiff intended to, and did, mass produce them and use them as lamp bases.]

* * *

This Court once essayed to fix the limits of the fine arts. That effort need not be appraised in relation to this copyright issue. It is clear Congress intended the scope of the [1909] copyright statute to include more than the traditional fine arts. Herbert Putnam, Esq., then Librari-an of Congress and active in the movement to amend the copyright laws, told the joint meeting of the House and Senate Committees:

> * * * "The term 'works of art' is deliberately intended as a broader specification than 'works of the fine arts' in the present statute with the idea that there is subject-matter (for instance, of applied design, not yet within the province of design patents), which may properly be entitled to protection under the copyright law."

The successive acts, the legislative history of the 1909 Act and the practice of the Copyright Office unite to show that "works of art" and "reproductions of works of art" are terms that were intended by Con-gress to include the authority to copyright these statuettes. Individual perception of the beautiful is too varied a power to permit a narrow or rigid concept of art. * * *

* * *

But petitioners assert that congressional enactment of the design patent laws should be interpreted as denying protection to artistic articles embodied or reproduced in manufactured articles. They say:

> "Fundamentally and historically, the Copyright Office is the repository of what each claimant considers to be a cultural treasure, whereas the Patent Office is the repository of what each applicant considers to be evidence of the advance in industrial and technologi-cal fields."

Their argument is that design patents require the critical examination given patents to protect the public against monopoly. Attention is called to Gorham Mfg. Co. v. White, 14 Wall. 511, 20 L.Ed. 731, interpreting the design patent law of 1842, 5 Stat. 544, granting a patent to anyone who by "their own industry, genius, efforts, and expense, may have invented or produced any new and original design for a manufacture * * *." A pattern for flat silver was there upheld. The intermediate and present law differs little. "Whoever invents any new, original and ornamental design for an article of manufacture may obtain a patent therefor, . . ." subject generally to the provisions concerning patents for invention. § 171, 66 Stat. 805. As petitioner sees the effect of the design patent law:

> "If an industrial designer can not satisfy the novelty requirements of the design patent laws, then his design as used on articles of manufacture can be copied by anyone."

Petitioner has furnished the Court a booklet of numerous design patents for statuettes, bases for table lamps and similar articles for manufacture, quite indistinguishable in type from the copyrighted statuettes here in issue. Petitioner urges that overlapping of patent and copyright legislation so as to give an author or inventor a choice between patents and copyrights should not be permitted. We assume petitioner takes the position that protection for a statuette for industrial use can only be obtained by patent, if any protection can be given.

As we have held the statuettes here involved copyrightable, we need not decide the question of their patentability. Though other courts have passed upon the issue as to whether allowance by the election of the author or patentee of one bars a grant of the other, we do not. We do hold that the patentability of the statuettes, fitted as lamps or unfitted, does not bar copyright as works of art. Neither the Copyright Statute nor any other says that because a thing is patentable it may not be copyrighted. We should not so hold.

* * * The copyright protects originality rather than novelty or invention—conferring only "the sole right of multiplying copies." Absent copying there can be no infringement of copyright. Thus, respondents may not exclude others from using statuettes of human figures in table lamps; they may only prevent use of copies of their statuettes as such or as incorporated in some other article. [Copyright Office] Regulation § 202.8, supra, makes clear that artistic articles are protected in "form but not their mechanical or utilitarian aspects." See Stein v. Rosenthal, 103 F.Supp. 227, 231. The dichotomy of protection for the aesthetic is not beauty and utility but art for the copyright and the invention of original and ornamental design for design patents. We find nothing in the copyright statute to support the argument that the intended use or use in industry of an article eligible for copyright bars or invalidates its registration. We do not read such a limitation into the copyright law.

* * *

"The copyright law, like the patent statutes, makes reward to the owner a secondary consideration." United States v. Paramount Pictures, 334 U.S. 131, 158. However, it is "intended definitely to grant valuable, enforceable rights to authors, publishers, etc., without burdensome requirements; 'to afford greater encouragement to the production of literary [or artistic] works of lasting benefit to the world.'" Washingtonian Co. v. Pearson, 306 U.S. 30, 36.

The economic philosophy behind the clause empowering Congress to grant patents and copyrights is the conviction that encouragement of individual effort by personal gain is the best way to advance public welfare through the talents of authors and inventors in "Science and useful Arts." Sacrificial days devoted to such creative activities deserve rewards commensurate with the services rendered.

Affirmed.

BRANDIR INTERNATIONAL, INC. v. CASCADE PACIFIC LUMBER CO.

United States Court of Appeals, Second Circuit, 1987.
834 F.2d 1142.

OAKES, CIRCUIT JUDGE.

In passing the Copyright Act of 1976 Congress attempted to distinguish between protectable "works of applied art" and "industrial designs not subject to copyright protection." See H.R. Rep. No. 1476, 94th Cong., 2d Sess. 54, reprinted in 1976 U.S. Code Cong. & Admin. News 5659, 5667 (hereinafter H.R. Rep. No. 1476). The courts, however, have had difficulty framing tests by which the fine line establishing what is and what is not copyrightable can be drawn. Once again we are called upon to draw such a line, this time in a case involving the "RIBBON Rack," a bicycle rack made of bent tubing that is said to have originated from a wire sculpture. * * *

Against the history of copyright protection well set out in the majority opinion in Carol Barnhart Inc. v. Economy Cover Corp., 773 F.2d 411, 415–18 (2d Cir.1985), and in Denicola, Applied Art and Industrial Design: A Suggested Approach to Copyright in Useful Articles, 67 Minn. L. Rev. 707, 709–17 (1983), Congress adopted the Copyright Act of 1976. The "works of art" classification of the Copyright Act of 1909 was omitted and replaced by reference to "pictorial, graphic, and sculptural works," 17 U.S.C. § 102(a)(5). According to the House Report, the new category was intended to supply "as clear a line as possible between copyrightable works of applied art and uncopyrighted works of industrial design." H.R. Rep. No. 1476, at 55. The statutory definition of "pictorial, graphic, and sculptural works" states that "the design of a useful article, as defined in this section, shall be considered a pictorial, graphic, or sculptural work only if, and only to the extent that, such design incorporates pictorial, graphic, or sculptural features that can be identified separately from, and are capable of existing independently of, the utilitarian aspects of the article." 17 U.S.C. § 101. The legislative history added gloss on the criteria of separate identity and independent existence in saying:

> On the other hand, although the shape of an industrial product may be aesthetically satisfying and valuable, the Committee's intention is not to offer it copyright protection under the bill. Unless the shape of an automobile, airplane, ladies' dress, food processor, television set, or any other industrial product contains some element that, physically or conceptually, can be identified as separable from the

utilitarian aspects of that article, the design would not be copyrighted under the bill.

H.R. Rep. No. 1476, at 55.

As courts and commentators have come to realize, however, the line Congress attempted to draw between copyrightable art and noncopyrightable design "was neither clear nor new." Denicola, supra, 67 Minn. L. Rev. at 720. One aspect of the distinction that has drawn considerable attention is the reference in the House Report to "physically *or conceptually*" (emphasis added) separable elements. The District of Columbia Circuit in Esquire, Inc. v. Ringer, 192 U.S. App. D.C. 187, 591 F.2d 796, 803–04 (D.C.Cir.1978) (holding outdoor lighting fixtures ineligible for copyright), cert. denied, 440 U.S. 908, 59 L. Ed. 2d 456, 99 S. Ct. 1217 (1979), called this an "isolated reference" and gave it no significance. Professor Nimmer, however, seemed to favor the observations of Judge Harold Leventhal in his concurrence in Esquire, who stated that "the overall legislative policy ... sustains the Copyright Office in its effort to distinguish between the instances where the aesthetic element is conceptually severable and the instances where the aesthetic element is inextricably interwoven with the utilitarian aspect of the article." 591 F.2d at 807; see 1 Nimmer on Copyright § 2.08[B] at 2–93 to 2–96.2 (1986). But see Gerber, Book Review, 26 U.C.L.A. L. Rev. 925, 938–43 (1979) (criticizing Professor Nimmer's view on conceptual separability). Looking to the section 101 definition of works of artistic craftsmanship requiring that artistic features be "capable of existing independently of the utilitarian aspects," Professor Nimmer queries whether that requires physical as distinguished from conceptual separability, but answers his query by saying "there is reason to conclude that it does not." See 1 Nimmer on Copyright § 2.08[B] at 2–96.1. In any event, in Kieselstein–Cord v. Accessories by Pearl, Inc., 632 F.2d 989, 993 (2d Cir.1980), this court accepted the idea that copyrightability can adhere in the "conceptual" separation of an artistic element. Indeed, the court went on to find such conceptual separation in reference to ornate belt buckles that could be and were worn separately as jewelry. Kieselstein–Cord was followed in Norris Industries, Inc. v. International Telephone & Telegraph Corp., 696 F.2d 918, 923–24 (11th Cir.), cert. denied, 464 U.S. 818, 78 L. Ed. 2d 89, 104 S. Ct. 78 (1983), although there the court upheld the Register's refusal to register automobile wire wheel covers, finding no "conceptually separable" work of art. See also Trans–World Mfg. Corp. v. Al Nyman & Sons, Inc., 95 F.R.D. 95 (D.Del.1982) (finding conceptual separability sufficient to support copyright in denying summary judgment on copyrightability of eyeglass display cases).

In Carol Barnhart Inc. v. Economy Cover Corp., 773 F.2d 411 (2d Cir.1985), a divided panel of this circuit affirmed a district court grant of summary judgment of noncopyrightability of four life-sized, anatomically correct human torso forms. Carol Barnhart distinguished Kieselstein–Cord, but it surely did not overrule it. The distinction made was that the ornamented surfaces of the Kieselstein–Cord belt buckles "were not in any respect required by their utilitarian functions," but the features claimed to be aesthetic or artistic in the Carol Barnhart forms were "inextricably intertwined with the utilitarian feature, the display of clothes." 773 F.2d at 419. But cf. Animal Fair, Inc. v. AMFESCO Indus., Inc., 620 F.Supp. 175, 186–88 (D.Minn.1985) (holding bear-paw design conceptually separable from the utilitarian features of a slipper), aff'd mem., 794 F.2d 678 (8th Cir.1986). As Judge Newman's dissent made clear, the Carol Barnhart majority did not dispute "that 'conceptual separability' is distinct from 'physical separability' and, when present, entitles the creator of a useful article to a copyright on its design." 773 F.2d at 420.

"Conceptual separability" is thus alive and well, at least in this circuit. The problem, however, is determining exactly what it is and how it is to be applied. Judge Newman's illuminating discussion in dissent in Carol Barnhart, see 773 F.2d at 419–24, proposed a test that aesthetic features are conceptually separable if "the article ... stimulate[s] in the mind of the beholder a concept that is separate from the concept evoked by its utilitarian function." Id. at 422. This approach has received favorable endorsement by at least one commentator, W. Patry, Latman's The Copyright Law 43–45 (6th ed. 1986), who calls Judge Newman's test the "temporal displacement" test. It is to be distinguished from other possible ways in which conceptual separability can be tested, including whether the primary use is as a utilitarian article as opposed to an artistic work, whether the aesthetic aspects of the work can be said to be "primary," and whether the article is marketable as art, none of which is very satisfactory. But Judge Newman's test was rejected outright by the majority as "a standard so ethereal as to amount to a 'nontest' that would be extremely difficult, if not impossible, to administer or apply." 773 F.2d at 419 n.5.

Perhaps the differences between the majority and the dissent in Carol Barnhart might have been resolved had they had before them the Denicola article on Applied Art and Industrial Design: A Suggested Approach to Copyright in Useful Articles, supra. There, Professor Denicola points out that although the Copyright Act of 1976 was an effort " 'to draw as clear a line as possible,' " in truth "there is no line, but merely a spectrum of forms and shapes responsive in varying degrees to utilitarian concerns." 67 Minn. L. Rev. at 741. Denicola argues that "the statutory directive requires a distinction between works of industrial design and works whose origins lie outside the design process, despite the utilitarian environment in which they appear." He views the statutory limitation of copyrightability as "an attempt to identify elements whose form and appearance reflect the unconstrained perspective of the artist," such features not being the product of industrial design. Id. at 742. "Copyrightability, therefore, should turn on the relationship between the proffered work and the process of industrial design." Id. at 741. He suggests that "the dominant characteristic of industrial design is the influence of nonaesthetic, utilitarian concerns" and hence concludes that copyrightability "ultimately should depend on the extent to which the work reflects artistic expression uninhibited by functional considerations."[2] Id. To state the Denicola test in the language of conceptual separability, if design elements reflect a merger of aesthetic and functional considerations, the artistic aspects of a work cannot be said to be conceptually separable from the utilitarian elements. Conversely, where design elements can be identified as reflecting the designer's artistic judgment exercised independently of functional influences, conceptual separability exists.

We believe that Professor Denicola's approach provides the best test for conceptual separability and, accordingly, adopt it here for several reasons. First, the approach is consistent with the holdings of our previous cases. In Kieselstein–Cord, for example, the artistic aspects of the belt buckles reflected purely aesthetic choices, independent of the buckles' function, while in Carol Barnhart the distinctive features of the torsos—the accurate anatomical design and the sculpted shirts and collars—showed clearly the influence of functional concerns. Though the torsos bore artistic features, it was evident that the designer incorporated those features to further the usefulness of the torsos as mannequins. Second, the test's emphasis on the influence of utilitarian concerns in the design process may help, as Denicola notes, to "alleviate the de facto discrimination against nonrepresentational art that has regrettably accompanied much of the current analysis." Id. at 745.[3] Finally, and perhaps most importantly, we think Denicola's test will not be too difficult to administer in practice. The work itself will continue to give "mute testimony" of its origins. In addition, the parties will be required to present evidence relating to the design process and the nature of the work, with the trier of fact making the determination whether the aesthetic design elements are significantly influenced by functional considerations.

Turning now to the facts of this case, we note first that Brandir contends, and its chief owner David Levine testified, that the original design of the RIBBON Rack stemmed from wire sculptures that Levine had created, each formed from one continuous undulating piece of wire. These sculptures were, he said, created and displayed in his home as a

---

2. Professor Denicola rejects the exclusion of all works created with some utilitarian application in view, for that would not only overturn Mazer v. Stein, 347 U.S. 201, 98 L. Ed. 630, 74 S. Ct. 460 (1954), on which much of the legislation is based, but also "a host of other eminently sensible decisions, in favor of an intractable factual inquiry of questionable relevance." 67 Minn. L. Rev. at 741. He adds that "any such categorical approach would also undermine the legislative determination to preserve an artist's ability to exploit utilitarian markets." Id. (citing 17 U.S.C. § 113(a) (1976)).

3. We are reminded not only by Judge Gesell in the district court in Esquire, 414 F.Supp. 939, 941 (D.D.C.1976), but by Holmes in Bleistein v. Donaldson Litho-graphing Co., 188 U.S. 239, 251–52, 47 L. Ed. 460, 23 S. Ct. 298 (1903), by Mazer v. Stein, 347 U.S. at 214, and by numerous other opinions, that we judges should not let our own view of styles of art interfere with the decisionmaking process in this area. Denicola suggests that the shape of a Mickey Mouse telephone is copyrightable because its form is independent of function, and "[a] telephone shape owing more to Arp, Brancusi, or Moore than Disney may be equally divorced from utilitarian influence." 67 Minn. L. Rev. at 746. This is true, of course, of the artist Christo's "Running Fence," approved (following Professor Nimmer) as an example of conceptual separability in Keiselstein–Cord, 632 F.2d at 993.

means of personal expression, but apparently were never sold or displayed elsewhere. He also created a wire sculpture in the shape of a bicycle and states that he did not give any thought to the utilitarian application of any of his sculptures until he accidentally juxtaposed the bicycle sculpture with one of the self-standing wire sculptures. It was not until November 1978 that Levine seriously began pursuing the utilitarian application of his sculptures, when a friend, G. Duff Bailey, a bicycle buff and author of numerous articles about urban cycling, was at Levine's home and informed him that the sculptures would make excellent bicycle racks, permitting bicycles to be parked under the overloops as well as on top of the underloops. Following this meeting, Levine met several times with Bailey and others, completing the designs for the RIBBON Rack by the use of a vacuum cleaner hose, and submitting his drawings to a fabricator complete with dimensions. The Brandir RIBBON Rack began being nationally advertised and promoted for sale in September 1979.

In November 1982 Levine discovered that another company, Cascade Pacific Lumber Co., was selling a similar product. Thereafter, beginning in December 1982, a copyright notice was placed on all RIBBON Racks before shipment and on December 10, 1982, five copyright applications for registration were submitted to the Copyright Office. The Copyright Office refused registration by letter, stating that the RIBBON Rack did not contain any element that was "capable of independent existence as a copyrightable pictorial, graphic or sculptural work apart from the shape of the useful article." * * *

Between September 1979 and August 1982 Brandir spent some $38,500 for advertising and promoting the RIBBON Rack, including some 85,000 pieces of promotional literature to architects and landscape architects. Additionally, since October 1982 Brandir has spent some $66,000, including full-, half-, and quarter-page advertisements in architectural magazines such as Landscape Architecture, Progressive Architecture, and Architectural Record, indeed winning an advertising award from Progressive Architecture in January 1983. The RIBBON Rack has been featured in Popular Science, Art and Architecture, and Design 384 magazines, and it won an Industrial Designers Society of America design award in the spring of 1980. In the spring of 1984 the RIBBON Rack was selected from 200 designs to be included among 77 of the designs exhibited at the Katonah Gallery in an exhibition entitled "The Product of Design: An Exploration of the Industrial Design Process," an exhibition that was written up in the New York Times.

* * *

Applying Professor Denicola's test to the RIBBON Rack, we find that the rack is not copyrightable. It seems clear that the form of the rack is influenced in significant measure by utilitarian concerns and thus any aesthetic elements cannot be said to be conceptually separable from the utilitarian elements. This is true even though the sculptures which inspired the RIBBON Rack may well have been—the issue of originality aside—copyrightable.

Brandir argues correctly that a copyrighted work of art does not lose its protected status merely because it subsequently is put to a functional use. The Supreme Court so held in Mazer v. Stein, 347 U.S. 201, 98 L. Ed. 630, 74 S. Ct. 460 (1954), and Congress specifically intended to accept and codify Mazer in section 101 of the Copyright Act of 1976. See H.R. Rep. No. 1476 at 54–55. The district court thus erred in ruling that, whatever the RIBBON Rack's origins, Brandir's commercialization of the rack disposed of the issue of its copyrightability.

Had Brandir merely adopted one of the existing sculptures as a bicycle rack, neither the application to a utilitarian end nor commercialization of that use would have caused the object to forfeit its copyrighted status. Comparison of the RIBBON Rack with the earlier sculptures, however, reveals that while the rack may have been derived in part from one of more "works of art," it is in its final form essentially a product of industrial design. In creating the RIBBON Rack, the designer has clearly adapted the original aesthetic elements to accommodate and further a utilitarian purpose. These altered design features of the RIBBON Rack, including the spacesaving, open design achieved by widening the upper loops to permit parking under as well as over the rack's curves, the straightened vertical elements that allow in-and above-ground installation of the rack, the ability to fit all types of bicycles and mopeds, and the heavy-gauged tubular construction of rustproof galvanized steel, are all features that combine to make for a safe, secure, and maintenance-free system of parking bicycles and mopeds. Its undulating shape is said in Progressive Architecture, January 1982, to permit double the storage of conventional bicycle racks. Moreover, the rack is manufactured from 2 ⅜–inch standard steam pipe that is bent into form, the six-inch radius of the bends evidently resulting from bending the pipe according to a standard formula that yields bends having a radius equal to three times the nominal internal diameter of the pipe.

Brandir argues that its RIBBON Rack can and should be characterized as a sculptural work of art within the minimalist art movement. Minimalist sculpture's most outstanding feature is said to be its clarity and simplicity, in that it often takes the form of geometric shapes, lines, and forms that are pure and free of ornamentation and void of association. As Brandir's expert put it, "The meaning is to be found in, within, around and outside the work of art, allowing the artistic sensation to be experienced as well as intellectualized." People who use Foley Square in New York City see in the form of minimalist art the "Tilted Arc," which is on the plaza at 26 Federal Plaza. Numerous museums have had exhibitions of such art, and the school of minimalist art has many admirers.

It is unnecessary to determine whether to the art world the RIBBON Rack properly would be considered an example of minimalist sculpture. The result under the copyright statute is not changed. Using the test we have adopted, it is not enough that, to paraphrase Judge Newman, the rack may stimulate in the mind of the reasonable observer a concept separate from the bicycle rack concept. While the RIBBON Rack may be worthy of admiration for its aesthetic qualities alone, it remains nonetheless the product of industrial design. Form and function are inextricably intertwined in the rack, its ultimate design being as much the result of utilitarian pressures as aesthetic choices. Indeed, the visually pleasing proportions and symmetricality of the rack represent design changes made in response to functional concerns. Judging from the awards the rack has received, it would seem in fact that Brandir has achieved with the RIBBON Rack the highest goal of modern industrial design, that is, the harmonious fusion of function and aesthetics. Thus there remains no artistic element of the RIBBON Rack that can be identified as separate and "capable of existing independently of, the utilitarian aspects of the article." Accordingly, we must affirm * * *.

* * *

APPENDIX

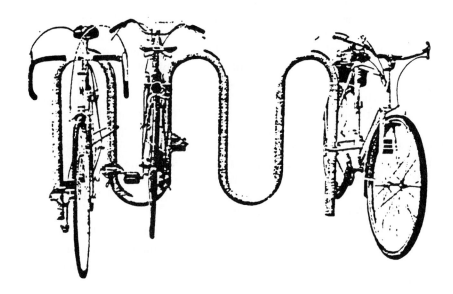

THE BRANDIR "RIBBON RACK"

Notes

1. The *Brandir* court refers in passing to this discussion of Christo's "Running Fence" sculpture in Kieselstein–Cord v. Accessories by Pearl, Inc., 632 F.2d 989, 993 (2d Cir.1980):

* * * As the late Judge Harold Leventhal observed in his concurrence in *Esquire, Inc. v. Ringer*, 192 U.S.App.D.C. 187, 591 F.2d 796, 807 (D.C.Cir.1978), cert. denied, 440 U.S. 908, 99 S.Ct. 1217, 59 L.Ed.2d 456 (1979), legislative policy supports the Copyright Office's "effort to

distinguish between the instances where the aesthetic element is conceptually severable and the instances where the aesthetic element is inextricably interwoven with the utilitarian aspect of the article.'' Examples of conceptual separateness as an artistic notion may be found in many museums today and even in the great outdoors. Professor Nimmer cites Christo's ''Running Fence'' as an example of today's ''conceptual art'': it ''did not contain sculptural features that were physically separable from the utilitarian aspects of the fence, but the whole point of the work was that the artistic aspects of the work were conceptually separable.'' 1 Nimmer, supra, § 2.08(B) at 2–94.

''Running Fence'' consisted of an 18–foot tall ''fence'' made of white nylon fabric, stretched over 24.5 miles of undulating hillside terrain, where the appearance of the fence was affected by wind and light. What if Christo were a property owner who placed his ''Running Fence'' around his property in order to delineate its boundaries and discourage trespassers? Would the resulting work be copyrightable?

2. If a ''fence'' such as Christo's can have conceptually separable artistic aspects, can a bicycle rack? Can another sort of bicycle rack perform the rack function as well as the RIBBON Rack can?

3. Suppose that the plaintiff in *Brandir* had designed the ''RIBBON Rack'' sculpture so that the lowest points in the downward loops stood two feet off the ground, thus making it useless as a bicycle rack. Would it then be copyrightable? What if the plaintiff designed it exactly as it is described in the case, but had no idea that it could function as a bicycle rack until the defendant copied it?

4. Consider the copyrightability of the following: A seamstress's mannequin shaped like a male or female torso? A taxidermist's mannequins shaped like a fish, a deer's head, or the full body of a bear? A soft chair shaped like a baseball glove? A teddy bear? A toy truck? A board game (*e.g.*, Monopoly)? Fashion designs? Theatrical or halloween costumes?

5. Copyright scholar Howard B. Abrams credits fellow scholar J. Thomas McCarthy for suggesting the following as an alternative test for conceptual separability: Inquire whether the feature in question makes the article function, or function better. If so, it is not a copyrightable design element. If the feature does not contribute to functionality, it is copyrightable. See Abrams, *The Law of Copyright* (1995), § 3.04[B][3], at n. 135. What result would this test dictate if applied to the RIBBON Rack? To Christo's Running Fence? To the examples listed in problem 4, above?

6. In *Lamps Plus, Inc. v. Seattle Lighting Fixture Co.*, 345 F.3d 1140 (9th Cir. 2003), the Second Circuit held that merely combining several useful, unprotectable elements does not rise to the level of originality that affords copyright protection, stating:

Lamps Plus's mechanical combination of four preexisting ceiling-lamp elements with a preexisting table-lamp base did not result in the expression of an original work of authorship as required by § 101. Lamps Plus did not create any of the ''design ... features that can be identified separately from, and are capable of existing independently of, the utilitarian aspects'' of any of the lamp's component parts.

345 F.3d at 1147.

7. Could the RIBBON Rack be protected by a design patent? A utility patent?

8. In *Pivot Point International Inc. v. Charlene Products Inc.*, 372 F.3d 913 (7th Cir. 2004) the court held that a beauty school mannequin head with the "hungry-look" of a runway model had physically and conceptually separable sculptural and utilitarian features and was therefore copyrightable.

(iii) Sui Generis Protection for Boat Hull Designs

The Digital Millenium Copyright Act, Pub. L. No. 105–304 (signed Oct. 28, 1998), introduced *sui generis* protection for boat hull designs, to replace the type of state law protection which the Supreme Court held to be preempted in *Bonito Boats, Inc. v. Thunder Craft Boats, Inc.*, 489 U.S. 141, 109 S.Ct. 971, 103 L.Ed.2d 118 (1989) (see *infra*, Chapter 21.B.2.). Title V of the Act, titled the "Vessel Hull Design Protection Act," adds a new Chapter 13 to Title 17 which gives the owner of an original boat hull design the exclusive right for 10 years to make, import, sell or distribute articles embodying that design for sale or use in trade, notwithstanding the intrinsic utilitarian function of the design. The new provision imposes a marking requirement, limits infringement liability to cases in which the infringing article was created with knowledge that its design was copied from a protected design, exempts copying that is solely for teaching or evaluative purposes, and requires that a design be registered with the Copyright Office before an infringement suit can be filed. Infringement remedies include injunctions, seizure and/or destruction of the infringing articles, attorneys' fees, and either damages (including enhanced damages) or the infringer's profits. Issuance of a design patent for a vessel hull design preempts Chapter 13 protection for that design, but Chapter 13 does not preempt either (a) federal or state protection for unregistered designs or (b) trademark or unfair competition laws. The new provision was initially scheduled to expire after two years, but has subsequently been extended.

(iv) Architectural Works

Prior to 1990, drawings and blueprints depicting architectural works had been copyrightable in the "pictorial, graphic, and sculptural works category." However, it was not clear whether copying such a design from the building itself infringed the copyright. The Architectural Works Copyright Protection Act of 1990 attempted to resolve this issue.

ARCHITECTURAL WORKS COPYRIGHT
PROTECTION ACT OF 1990

H.R. Rep. No. 101–735.
101st Cong., 2d Sess. 11, 18–21 (1990).

* * *

Article 2(1) of the Berne Convention requires member countries to provide copyright for "works of architecture"—the constructed design of buildings. This category of subject matter is distinct from "illustrations, plans, sketches and three-dimensional works relative to architecture," which are also required to be protected under Article 2(1). The current U.S. Copyright Act expressly includes "diagrams, models, and technical drawings, including architectural plans" as a species of protected "pictorial, graphic, and sculptural work." It does not, however, expressly protect "works of architecture," although this Committee's Report accompanying the 1976 Copyright Act contemplated that at least selected works of architecture—those containing elements physically or conceptually separable from their utilitarian function—would be protected to the extent of their separability. * * *

* * *

Section 202. Definitions

Section 202 adds a new definition ("architectural work") to the Copyright Act and amends an existing definition ("Berne Convention work").

Subsection (a) amends section 101 of title 17, United States Code, to provide a definition of the subject matter protected by the bill, "architectural works." * * *

* * * The protected work i[s] the design of a building. The term "design" includes the overall form as well as the arrangement and composition of spaces and elements in the design. The phrase "arrangement and composition of spaces and elements" recognizes that: (1) creativity in architecture frequently takes the form of a selection, coordination, or arrangement of unprotectible elements into an original, protectible whole; (2) an architect may incorporate new, protectible design elements into otherwise standard, unprotectible building features; and (3) interior architecture may be protected.

Consistent with other provis[i]ons of the Copyright Act and Copyright Office regul[a]tions, the definition makes clear that protection does not extend to individual standard features, such as common windows, doors, and other staple building components. A grant of exclusive rights in such features would impede, rather than promote, the progress of architectural innovation. The provision is not, however, intended to ex[c]lude from the copyright in the architectural work any individual features that reflect the [a]rchitect's creativity.

* * *

During the Subcommittee's 1990 hearing, testimony was received that a potential gap in protection may exist where an architectural work has been depicted in plans or drawings, but has not yet been constructed. Since the original definition of architectural work in H.R. 3990 referred only to architectural works "as embodied in" buildings, there was concern that a defendant with access to the plans or drawings could construct an identical building but escape liability so long as the plans or drawings were not copied.

The Register of Copyright disagrees that liability could be avoided in such circumstances, arguing that the witnesses misconstrued the access prong of infringement analysis. The Register's position, based on general principles of copyright law, is that where a three-dimensional work meets the standard for protection, infringement may lie regardless of whether access to the three-dimensional work is obtained from a two-dimensional or three-dimensional depiction thereof.

In order to resolve this debate, subsection 202(a) of title II of H.R. 5498 modifies the definition of architectural work so that a work of architecture may be embodied in the built design—the constructed three-dimensional building—or in plans, drawings, or in "any tangible medium of expression," such as a blueprint or computer disk. Protection for architectural plans, drawings, and models as pictorial, graphic, or sculptural works under section 102(a)(5), title 17, United States Code, is unaffected by this bill.

This change does, however, raise questions regarding the relationship between copyright in the architectural work and copyright in plans and drawings. The bill's intention is to keep these two forms of protection separate. An individual creating an architectural work by depicting that work in plans or drawing will have two separate copyrights, one in the architectural work (section 102(a)(8)), the other in the plans or drawings (section 102(a)(5)). * * *

The Subcommittee made a second amendment in the definition of architectural work: the deletion of the phrase "or three-dimensional structure." This phrase was included in H.R. 3990 to cover cases where architectural works embodied in innovative structures that defy easy classification. Unfortunately, the phrase also could be interpreted as covering interstate highway bridges, cloverleafs, canals, dams, and pedestrian walkways. The Subcommittee examined protection for these works, some of which form important elements of this nation's transportation system, and determined that copyright protection is not necessary to stimulate creativity or prohibit unauthorized reproduction.

The sole purpose of legislating at this time is to place the United States unequivocally in compliance with its Berne Convention obligations. Protection for bridges and related nonhabitable three-dimensional structures is not required by the Berne Convention. Accordingly, the question of copyright protection for these works can be deferred to another day. As a consequence, the phrase "or other three-dimensional structures" was deleted from the definition of architectural work and from all other places in the bill.

This deletion, though, raises more sharply the question of what is meant by the term "building." Obviously, the term encompassed habitable structures such as houses and office buildings. It also covers structures that are used, but not inhabited, by human beings, such as churches, pergolas, gazebos, and garden pavilions.

Subsection (b) amends the definitions of "Berne Convention work" in section 101, title 17, United States Code, to provide a point of attachment for national eligibility purposes. An architectural work is a "Berne Convention work" if the building in which the architectural work is embodied "is erected in a country adhering to the Berne Convention." This amendment is necessitated by United States membership in the Berne Union.

Section 203. Subject Matter of Copyright

* * * By creating a new category of protectible subject matter in new section 102(a)(8), and, therefore, by deliberately not encompassing architectural works as pictorial, graphic, or sculptural works in existing section 102(a)(5), the copyrightability of architectural works shall not be evaluated under the separability test applicable to pictorial, graphic, or sculptural works embodied in useful articles. There is considerable scholarly and judicial disagreement over how to apply the separability test, and the principal reason for not treating architectural works as pictorial, graphic, or sculptural works is to avoid entangling architectural works in this disagreement.

The Committee does not suggest, though, that in evaluating the copyrightability or scope of protection for architectural works, the Copyright Office or the courts should ignore functionality. A two-step analysis is envisioned. First, an architectural work should be examined to determine whether there are original design elements present, including overall shape and interior architecture. If such design elements are present, a second step is reached to examine whether the design elements are functionally required. If the design elements are not functionally required, the work is protectible without regard to physical or conceptual separability. As a consequence, contrary to the Committee's report accompanying the 1976 Copyright Act with respect to industrial products, the aesthetically pleasing overall shape of an architectural work could be protected under this bill.

The proper scope of protection for architectural works is distinct from registrability. Functional considerations may, for example, determine only particular design elements. Protection would be denied for the functionally determined elements, but would be available for the nonfunctionally determined elements. Under such circumstances, the Copyright Office should issue a certificate of registration, letting the courts determine the scope of protection. In each case, the courts must be free to decide the issue upon the facts presented, free of the separability conundrum presented by the useful articles doctrine applicable for pictorial, graphic, and sculptural works. Evidence that there is more than one method of obtaining a given functional result may be considered in evaluating registrability or the scope of protection.

The proposed legislation incorporates the general standards of originality applicable for all other copyrightable subject matter. * * *

* * * The references in the definition of "architectural work" to "overall form," and to the nonprotectibility of "individual standard features" are not intended to indicate that a higher standard of similari-

ty is required to prove infringement of an architectural work, or that the scope of protection of architectural works is limited to verbatim or near-verbatim copying. These definitional provisions are intended merely to give the courts some guidance regarding the nature of the protected matter. The extent of protection is to be made on an ad hoc basis.

* * *

Notes

1. What kinds of architectural design elements are sufficiently non-functional to be copyrightable under current law but would not have been copyrightable before the effective date of the 1990 amendments?

2. At the hearings preceding enactment of the 1990 architectural works provisions, several experts testified that the designs of buildings were already copyrightable under the 1976 Act regardless of whether they were embodied in drawings or in three-dimensional structures, and that further legislation was therefore unnecessary in order to comply with the requirements of the Berne Convention. Do you agree? If so, does copyright already extend to the types of structures that Congress intended to exclude from the definition of "architectural works"? For example, would a design for a bridge or a highway overpass be copyrightable? Should it be?

3. Most pre–1990 case law indicated that, despite *Baker v. Selden*, copying architectural plans was an infringement even if the purpose of copying them was to construct the building they depicted, *see Imperial Homes Corp. v. Lamont*, 458 F.2d 895 (5th Cir.1972); *Demetriades v. Kaufmann*, 680 F.Supp. 658 (S.D.N.Y.1988); *contra* Scholz Homes, Inc. v. Maddox, 379 F.2d 84 (6th Cir.1967) (applying *Baker* to reach contrary holding). However, the same opinions distinguished the situation where the only copying that took place was the actual construction of the building depicted in the plans, finding that copyright should not exclude others from implementing the ideas revealed in the plans. Do the 1990 amendments overrule this line of cases?

4. In *Leicester v. Warner Brothers*, 232 F.3d 1212 (9th Cir.2000), the court affirmed a lower court decision that the producers of a feature film did not infringe an artist's copyrightable streetwall design in three dimensions, held to be conceptually inseparable from an urban work of architecture, when they captured and then displayed the design in their film. The court concluded that Congress intended photographs of public architectural works to be exempt from charges of infringement; the exemption must logically extend to such conceptually inseparable three-dimensional works of visual art as may be incorporated into the architectural work.

5. For additional perspectives on the history and effect of the 1990 amendments, see Jane Ginsburg, Copyright in the 101st Congress: Commentary on the Visual Artists Rights Act and the Architectural Works Protection Act of 1990, 14 Colum.-VLA J.L. & Arts 477 (1990); Todd Hixon, Note: The Architectural Works Copyright Protection Act of 1990: At Odds with the Traditional Limitations of American Copyright Law, 37 Ariz. L.Rev. 629 (1995); Vanessa N. Scaglione, Building Upon the Architectural Works Pro-

tection Copyright Act of 1990, 61 Fordham L.Rev. 193 (1992); Raphael Winick, Copyright Protection for Architecture after the Architectural Works Copyright Protection Act of 1990, 41 Duke L.J. 1598 (1992).

6.   The inclusion of architectural drawings in a restrictive covenant did not put them in the public domain. *John G. Danielson, Inc. v. Winchester–Conant Props., Inc.,* 322 F.3d 26 (1st Cir. 2003). Determining that a restrictive covenant is a private agreement rather than a generally applicable law, the court rejected defendant's argument that the drawings had lost their copyright protection by becoming "laws." After its efforts to alter the covenant failed, the real estate developer infringed the architect's plans by developing land in compliance with the covenant.

5.   SUBJECT MATTER EXCLUDED DUE TO ORIGIN

(i)   United States Government Works

Statutes: 17 U.S.C.A. § 105

COPYRIGHT ACT OF 1976

H.R. Rep. No. 94–1476.
94th Cong., 2d Sess. 58–59 (1976).

* * *

Section 105. U.S. Government Works

Scope of the prohibition

* * *

The general prohibition against copyright in section 105 applies to "any work of the United States Government," which is defined in section 101 as "a work prepared by an officer or employee of the United States Government as part of that person's official duties." Under this definition a Government official or employee would not be prevented from securing copyright in a work written at that person's own volition and outside his or her duties, even though the subject matter involves the Government work or professional field of the official or employee. Although the wording of the definition of "work of the United States Government" differs somewhat from that of the definition of "work made for hire," the concepts are intended to be construed in the same way.

A more difficult and far-reaching problem is whether the definition should be broadened to prohibit copyright in works prepared under U.S. Government contract or grant. As the bill is written, the Government agency concerned could determine in each case whether to allow an independent contractor or grantee to secure copyright in works prepared in whole or in part with the use of Government funds. * * *

* * *

The prohibition on copyright protection for United States Government works is not intended to have any effect on protection of these works abroad. Works of the governments of most other countries are copyrighted. There are no valid policy reasons for denying such protection to United States Government works in foreign countries, or for precluding the Government from making licenses for the use of its works abroad.

* * *

Notes

1. Does section 105 mean that the federal government can never own a copyright?

2. Suppose that a federal official writes and delivers a speech at a college graduation, a National Press Club luncheon, an academic conference, or a trade association gathering. In which case(s), if any, is the speech copyrightable, and by whom?

3. To what extent can a state, local or foreign government own copyrights?

In *Veeck v. Southern Bldg. Code Cong. Int'l, Inc.*, 293 F.3d 791 (5th Cir.2002), a website operator who posted municipal building codes, developed by a private defendant, on a website sought a declaration that he did not violate the Copyright Act. In finding that the "law" was not subject to federal copyright protection, the court said the defendant's copyrights were valid until the cities adopted the codes. Upon adoption, the codes became "facts" and thus entered the public domain.

4. What are the arguments for and against allowing an independent contractor to own the copyright in a work prepared under a federal government grant? In *Assessment Technologies Of WI, LLC v. Wiredata, Inc.*, 350 F.3d 640 (2003), excerpted *infra*, p. 786, Judge Posner expressed doubt about the ability of a local governmental entity or its subcontractor to control information via the manipulation of copyright, suggesting (inter alia) the possibility of a finding of misuse.

(ii) National Origin Restrictions on Copyright
Statutes: 17 U.S.C.A. § 104

Although United States copyright has applied to many works by foreign authors since 1891, some restrictions based on national origin remain. Under current law, copyright in unpublished works exists regardless of the author's nationality or domicile. In the case of published works, however, copyright exists only if the work fits within at least one of the five categories set forth in section 104(b)(1)-(5). Generally speaking, the works that fail this test are works which are first published outside the United States or any other nation that is a member of the Berne Convention or the Universal Copyright Convention (a pre-Berne international copyright convention to which the United States is a signatory), *and* which do not have at least one author that is a stateless person, a national or domiciliary of the United States or a national, domiciliary or sovereign authority of one of our copyright treaty partners. Protection extends to architectural works and pictorial, graphic or sculptural works that are incorporated in buildings located in countries belonging to the Berne convention, to works first published by the United Nations or the Organization of American States, and to works simultaneously first published in a Berne country and in a non-Berne country. The President is authorized to extend protection to other foreign works only upon finding that the nation of authorship or first publication extends nondiscriminatory protection to United States works. Thus, in general, the United States does not extend its copyright protection to published works originating in countries that fail to provide nondiscriminatory protection to works originating in the United States.

The WIPO Copyright and Performances and Phonograms Treaties Implementation Act of 1998, contained in Title I of the Digital Millennium Copyright Act, Pub. L. No. 105–304 (1998), revised the copyright statutes to conform to the requirements of the WIPO Copyright Treaty the WIPO Performances and Phonograms Treaty. Section 102 of the Act revised §§ 101, 104, and 104A of Title 17 to reflect the United States' adherence to those treaties.

Chapter 17

OWNERSHIP, ASSIGNMENT, AND LICENSING OF COPYRIGHTS

A. INITIAL OWNERSHIP

1. IDENTIFYING THE AUTHOR

Statutes: 17 U.S.C.A. §§ 101 (as needed), 201–02

(i) Joint Works

CHILDRESS v. TAYLOR

United States Court of Appeals, Second Circuit, 1991.
945 F.2d 500.

NEWMAN, CIRCUIT JUDGE.

This appeal requires consideration of the standards for determining when a contributor to a copyrighted work is entitled to be regarded as a joint author. The work in question is a play about the legendary Black comedienne Jackie "Moms" Mabley. The plaintiff-appellee Alice Childress claims to be the sole author of the play. Her claim is disputed by defendant-appellant Clarice Taylor, who asserts that she is a joint author of the play. * * *

FACTS

[Actress Taylor asked playwright Childress to write her a play based on the life of legendary black comedienne Jackie "Moms" Mabley. While Childress was writing the play, the two spoke regularly about its progress, and Taylor contributed her own research and ideas. Childress registered the script's copyright in her own name, and declined to enter an agreement for co-ownership with Taylor. Taylor then hired another writer, Caldwell, to revise the play without Childress's consent.]

* * *

Taylor identifies the following as her major contributions to the play: (1) she learned through interviews that "Moms" Mabley called all

872

of her piano players "Luther," so Taylor suggested that the play include such a character; (2) Taylor and Childress together interviewed Carey Jordan, "Moms" Mabley's housekeeper, and upon leaving the interview they came to the conclusion that she would be a good character for the play, but Taylor could not recall whether she or Childress suggested it; (3) Taylor informed Childress that "Moms" Mabley made a weekly trip to Harlem to do ethnic food shopping; (4) Taylor suggested a street scene in Harlem with speakers because she recalled having seen or listened to such a scene many times; (5) the idea of using a minstrel scene came out of Taylor's research; (6) the idea of a card game scene also came out of Taylor's research, although Taylor could not recall who specifically suggested the scene; (7) some of the jokes used in the play came from Taylor's research; and (8) the characteristics of "Moms" Mabley's personality portrayed in the play emerged from Taylor's research. Essentially, Taylor contributed facts and details about "Moms" Mabley's life and discussed some of them with Childress. However, Childress was responsible for the actual structure of the play and the dialogue.

* * *

Childress sued Taylor and other defendants alleging violations of the Copyright Act, 17 U.S.C. § 101 et seq. (1988) * * *. Taylor contended that she was a joint author with Childress, and therefore shared the rights to the play. Childress moved for summary judgment, which the District Court granted. The Court concluded that Taylor was not a joint author of Childress's play and that Caldwell's play was substantially similar to and infringed Childress's play. In rejecting Taylor's claim of joint authorship, Judge Haight ruled (a) that a work qualifies as a "joint work" under the definition section of the Copyright Act, 17 U.S.C. § 101, only when both authors intended, at the time the work was created, "that their contributions be merged into inseparable or interdependent parts of a unitary whole," id., and (b) that there was insufficient evidence to permit a reasonable trier to find that Childress had the requisite intent. The Court further ruled that copyright law requires the contributions of both authors to be independently copyrightable, and that Taylor's contributions, which consisted of ideas and research, were not copyrightable.

Discussion

In common with many issues arising in the domain of copyrights, the determination of whether to recognize joint authorship in a particular case requires a sensitive accommodation of competing demands advanced by at least two persons, both of whom have normally contributed in some way to the creation of a work of value. Care must be taken to ensure that true collaborators in the creative process are accorded the perquisites of co-authorship and to guard against the risk that a sole author is denied exclusive authorship status simply because another person rendered some form of assistance. Copyright law best serves the interests of creativity when it carefully draws the bounds of "joint authorship" so as to protect the legitimate claims of both sole authors and co-authors.

* * *

The Copyright Act defines a "joint work" as

a work prepared by two or more authors with the intention that their contributions be merged into inseparable or interdependent parts of a unitary whole.

17 U.S.C. § 101. As Professor Nimmer has pointed out, this definition is really the definition of a work of joint authorship. See 1 Nimmer on Copyright § 6.01 (1991). The definition concerns the creation of the work by the joint authors, not the circumstances, in addition to joint authorship, under which a work may be jointly owned, for example, by assignment of an undivided interest. The distinction affects the rights that are acquired. Joint authors hold undivided interests in a work, like all joint owners of a work, but joint authors, unlike other joint owners, also enjoy all the rights of authorship, including the renewal rights applicable to works in which a statutory copyright subsisted prior to January 1, 1978. See 17 U.S.C. § 304.

Some aspects of the statutory definition of joint authorship are fairly straightforward. Parts of a unitary whole are "inseparable" when they have little or no independent meaning standing alone. That would often be true of a work of written text, such as the play that is the subject of the pending litigation. By contrast, parts of a unitary whole are "interdependent" when they have some meaning standing alone but achieve their primary significance because of their combined effect, as in the case of the words and music of a song. Indeed, a novel and a song are among the examples offered by the legislative committee reports on the 1976 Copyright Act to illustrate the difference between "inseparable" and "interdependent" parts. See H.R. Rep. No. 1476, 94th Cong., 2d Sess. 120 (1976) ("House Report"), reprinted in 1976 U.S.C.C.A.N. 5659, 5736; S. Rep. No. 473, 94th Cong., 2d Sess. 103–04 (1975) ("Senate Report").

The legislative history also clarifies other aspects of the statutory definition, but leaves some matters in doubt. Endeavoring to flesh out the definition, the committee reports state:

[A] work is "joint" if the authors collaborated with each other, or if *each* of the authors prepared his or her contribution with the knowledge and *intention* that it would be merged with the contributions of other authors as "inseparable or interdependent parts of a unitary whole." The touchstone here is the *intention, at the time the writing is done,* that the parts be absorbed or combined into an integrated unit. . . .

House Report at 120; Senate Report at 103 (emphasis added). This passage appears to state two alternative criteria—one focusing on the act of collaboration and the other on the parties' intent. However, it is hard to imagine activity that would constitute meaningful "collaboration" unaccompanied by the requisite intent on the part of both participants that their contributions be merged into a unitary whole, and the case law has read the statutory language literally so that the intent requirement applies to all works of joint authorship. See, e.g., Weissmann v. Freeman, 868 F.2d 1313, 1317–19 (2d Cir.1989); Eckert v. Hurley Chicago Co., Inc., 638 F. Supp. 699, 702–03 (N.D.Ill.1986).

A more substantial issue arising under the statutory definition of "joint work" is whether the contribution of each joint author must be copyrightable or only the combined result of their joint efforts must be copyrightable. The Nimmer treatise argues against a requirement of copyrightability of each author's contribution, see 1 Nimmer on Copyright § 6.07; Professor Goldstein takes the contrary view, see 1 Paul Goldstein, Copyright: Principles, Law and Practice § 4.2.1.2 (1989), with the apparent agreement of the Latman treatise, see William F. Patry, Latman's The Copyright Law 116 (6th ed. 1986) (hereinafter "Latman"). The case law supports a requirement of copyrightability of each contribution. * * * The Register of Copyrights strongly supports this view, arguing that it is required by the statutory standard of "authorship" and perhaps by the Constitution. See Moral Rights in Our Copyright Laws: Hearings on S. 1198 and S. 1253 Before the Subcomm. on Patents, Copyrights and Trademarks of the Senate Comm. on the Judiciary, 101st Cong., 1st Sess. 210–11 (1989) (statement of Ralph Oman).

The issue, apparently open in this Circuit, is troublesome. If the focus is solely on the objective of copyright law to encourage the production of creative works, it is difficult to see why the contributions of all joint authors need be copyrightable. An individual creates a copyrightable work by combining a non-copyrightable idea with a copyrightable form of expression; the resulting work is no less a valuable result of the creative process simply because the idea and the expression came from two different individuals. Indeed, it is not unimaginable that there exists a skilled writer who might never have produced a significant work until some other person supplied the idea. The textual argument from the statute is not convincing. The Act surely does not say that each contribution to a joint work must be copyrightable, and the specification that there be "authors" does not necessarily require a copyrightable contribution. "Author" is not defined in the Act and appears to be used only in its ordinary sense of an originator. The "author" of an uncopyrightable idea is nonetheless its author even though, for entirely valid reasons, the law properly denies him a copyright on the result of his creativity. And the Register's tentative constitutional argument seems questionable. It has not been supposed that the statutory grant of "authorship" status to the employer of a work made for hire exceeds the Constitution, though the employer has shown skill only in selecting employees, not in creating protectable expression.

Nevertheless, we are persuaded to side with the position taken by the case law and endorsed by the agency administering the Copyright Act. The insistence on copyrightable contributions by all putative joint authors might serve to prevent some spurious claims by those who might otherwise try to share the fruits of the efforts of a sole author of a copyrightable work, even though a claim of having contributed copyrightable material could be asserted by those so inclined. More important, the prevailing view strikes an appropriate balance in the domains of both copyright and contract law. In the absence of contract, the copyright remains with the one or more persons who created copyrightable material. Contract law enables a person to hire another to create a copyrightable work, and the copyright law will recognize the employer as "author." 17 U.S.C. § 201(b). Similarly, the person with non-copyrightable material who proposes to join forces with a skilled writer to produce a copyrightable work is free to make a contract to disclose his or her material in return for assignment of part ownership of the resulting copyright. Id. § 201(d). And, as with all contract matters, the parties may minimize subsequent disputes by formalizing their agreement in a written contract. Cf. 17 U.S.C. § 101 ("work made for hire" definition of "specially ordered" or "commissioned" work includes requirement of written agreement). It seems more consistent with the spirit of copyright law to oblige all joint authors to make copyrightable contributions, leaving those with non-copyrightable contributions to protect their rights through contract.

There remains for consideration the crucial aspect of joint authorship—the nature of the intent that must be entertained by each putative joint author at the time the contribution of each was created. The wording of the statutory definition appears to make relevant only the state of mind regarding the unitary nature of the finished work—an intention "that their contributions be merged into inseparable or interdependent parts of a unitary whole." However, an inquiry so limited would extend joint author status to many persons who are not likely to have been within the contemplation of Congress. For example, a writer frequently works with an editor who makes numerous useful revisions to the first draft, some of which will consist of additions of copyrightable expression. Both intend their contributions to be merged into inseparable parts of a unitary whole, yet very few editors and even fewer writers would expect the editor to be accorded the status of joint author, enjoying an undivided half interest in the copyright in the published work. Similarly, research assistants may on occasion contribute to an author some protectable expression or merely a sufficiently original selection of factual material as would be entitled to a copyright, yet not be entitled to be regarded as a joint author of the work in which the contributed material appears. What distinguishes the writer-editor relationship and the writer-researcher relationship from the true joint author relationship is the lack of intent of both participants in the venture to regard themselves as joint authors.

Focusing on whether the putative joint authors regarded themselves as joint authors is especially important in circumstances, such as the instant case, where one person (Childress) is indisputably the dominant author of the work and the only issue is whether that person is the sole author or she and another (Taylor) are joint authors. * * * This concern requires less exacting consideration in the context of traditional forms of collaboration, such as between the creators of the words and music of a song.

In this case, appellant contends that Judge Haight's observation that "Childress never shared Taylor's notion that they were co-authors of the play" misapplies the statutory standard by focusing on whether Childress "intended the legal consequences which flowed from her prior acts." * * * We do not think Judge Haight went so far. He did not inquire whether Childress intended that she and Taylor would hold equal undivided interests in the play. But he properly insisted that they entertain in their minds the concept of joint authorship, whether or not they understood precisely the legal consequences of that relationship. Though joint authorship does not require an understanding by the co-authors of the legal consequences of their relationship, obviously some distinguishing characteristic of the relationship must be understood in order for it to be the subject of their intent. In many instances, a useful test will be whether, in the absence of contractual agreements concerning listed authorship, each participant intended that all would be identified as co-authors. Though "billing" or "credit" is not decisive in all cases and joint authorship can exist without any explicit discussion of this topic by the parties,[1] consideration of the topic helpfully serves to focus the fact-finder's attention on how the parties implicitly regarded their undertaking.

* * *

Examination of whether the putative co-authors ever shared an intent to be co-authors serves the valuable purpose of appropriately confining the bounds of joint authorship arising by operation of copyright law, while leaving those not in a true joint authorship relationship with an author free to bargain for an arrangement that will be recognized as a matter of both copyright and contract law. Joint authorship entitles the co-authors to equal undivided interests in the work, see 17 U.S.C. § 201(a); Community for Creative Non–Violence v. Reid, 270 U.S. App. D.C. 26, 846 F.2d 1485, 1498 (D.C.Cir.1988), aff'd without consideration of this point, 490 U.S. 730, 109 S. Ct. 2166, 104 L. Ed. 2d 811, 10 U.S.P.Q.2d (BNA) 1985 (1989). That equal sharing of rights should be reserved for relationships in which all participants fully intend to be joint authors. The sharing of benefits in other relationships involving assistance in the creation of a copyrightable work can be more precisely calibrated by the participants in their contract negotiations regarding division of royalties or assignment of shares of ownership of the copyright, see 17 U.S.C. § 201(d).

In this case, the issue is not only whether Judge Haight applied the correct standard for determining joint authorship but also whether he

---

1. Obviously, consideration of whether the parties contemplated listed co-authorship (or would have accepted such billing had they thought about it) is not a helpful inquiry for works written by an uncredited "ghost writer," either as a sole author, as a joint author, or as an employee preparing a work for hire.

was entitled to conclude that the record warranted a summary judgment in favor of Childress. We are satisfied that Judge Haight was correct as to both issues. We need not determine whether we agree with his conclusion that Taylor's contributions were not independently copyrightable since, even if they were protectable as expression or as an original selection of facts, we agree that there is no evidence from which a trier could infer that Childress had the state of mind required for joint authorship. As Judge Haight observed, whatever thought of co-authorship might have existed in Taylor's mind "was emphatically not shared by the purported co-author." There is no evidence that Childress ever contemplated, much less would have accepted, crediting the play as "written by Alice Childress and Clarice Taylor."

Childress was asked to write a play about "Moms" Mabley and did so. To facilitate her writing task, she accepted the assistance that Taylor provided, which consisted largely of furnishing the results of research concerning the life of "Moms" Mabley. As the actress expected to portray the leading role, Taylor also made some incidental suggestions, contributing ideas about the presentation of the play's subject and possibly some minor bits of expression. But there is no evidence that these aspects of Taylor's role ever evolved into more than the helpful advice that might come from the cast, the directors, or the producers of any play. A playwright does not so easily acquire a co-author.

* * *

Notes

1. In *Erickson v. Trinity Theatre, Inc.*, 13 F.3d 1061 (7th Cir.1994), the Seventh Circuit followed *Childress* in concluding that joint authorship required both separate copyrightability and intent to be co-authors. In finding intent necessary, the court observed:

> [T]he "collaboration alone" standard would frustrate the goal of the Act "to promote the Progress of Science and the useful Arts." U.S. CONST. art. I, § 8, cl. 8. Seldom would an author subject his work to preregistration peer review if this were the applicable test. Those seeking copyrights would not seek further refinement that colleagues may offer if they risked losing their sole authorship. * * *

13 F.3d at 1069.

Does *Childress* require that *both* collaborators think of themselves as co-authors in order to create a joint work? Is this requirement appropriate? Supported by the statutes?

2. In *Thomson v. Larson*, 147 F.3d 195 (2d Cir.1998), the Second Circuit followed *Childress* in affirming a district court's rejection of a dramaturg's claim that she was a co-author of the musical "Rent". Although the plaintiff's contributions appeared to be both copyrightable and substantial, the Second Circuit agreed with the lower court that the musical could not be a joint work because the principal author had never intended to share authorship with her. Is this a reasonable interpretation of the concept of

"joint works"? Does it represent sound policy? If not, what legal standard would best distinguish true joint works? For a particularly thoughtful treatment of these issues, see Kwall, "Author–Stories": Narrative's Implications for Moral Rights and Copyright's Joint Authorship Doctrine, 75 So. Cal. L. Rev. 1 (2001).

3. In *Matthew Fisher v. Gary Brooker and Onward Music*, [2006] EWHC 3239 (Ch. D. 2006), England's High Court acknowledged Mattew Fisher, the organist for the popular 1967 Procol Harum song, *A Whiter Shade of Pale,* as a joint author some 40 years after the song was written. Joint authorship had originally appeared to reside in Gary Brooker, the singer and pianist, and co-manager, Keith Reid, who wrote the lyrics for the work. While Mr. Justice Blackborne found that Fisher's memorable organ solo was a product of labor and skill, and also a distinctive and significant authorial contribution to the overall composition, the Judge's comments in the case do not appear to rule out joint author status even if the claimant had not written the solo at all, and had only provided accompaniment to the verses and chorus. Does this serve as a warning to artists who hire session musicians, or where contributions are made by producers, arrangers or engineers at a recording session?

Compare, in addition, the discussion with respect to Section 1011D of the Satellite Home Viewer Improvement Act of 1999, at note 8, *infra,* p. 889.

4. The *Erickson* court noted that Professor Melville Nimmer rejected the rule that a co-author's contribution must be separately copyrightable:

> Professor Nimmer, the late scholar on copyright, took the position that all that should be required to achieve joint author status is more than a de minimis contribution by each author. "De minimis" requires that "more than a word or line must be added by one who claims to be a joint author." Nimmer § 6.07, at 6–21. Professor Nimmer distinguishes his de minimis standard from the standard for copyrightability. Id. As an example, Professor Nimmer asserts that if two authors collaborate, with one contributing only uncopyrightable plot ideas and another incorporating those ideas into a completed literary expression, the two authors should be regarded as joint authors of the resulting work. Id.

13 F.3d at 1069–70. Does the Goldstein or the Nimmer standard better serve the goals of copyright? If an actor or producer provides detailed character and plot elements to a writer who supplies the dialogue, are they co-authors under Nimmer's standard? Under the Goldstein standard?

5. In *Erickson,* the court repeatedly emphasized that Erickson (whom it ultimately found to be the sole author) had the final say as to which of the other contributors' suggestions would be included in the final work (a play). How is this relevant to the question of joint authorship? How much weight should this factor receive?

The Seventh Circuit modified the separate copyrightability requirement from *Erickson* in *Gaiman v. McFarlane,* 360 F.3d 644 (7th Cir. 2004). Gaiman, a writer, and McFarlane, an illustrator, collaborated on Spawn comic books together. Jointly, Gaiman and McFarlane created the characters "Medieval Spawn," "Angela," and "Count Nicholas Cogliostro." Based on the nature of comic book creation, the court observed:

[T]he decisions that say, rightly in the generality of cases, that each contributor to a joint work must make a contribution that if it stood alone would be copyrightable weren't thinking of the case in which it couldn't stand alone because of the nature of the particular creative process that had produced it.

360 F.3d at 659.

Therefore, Gaiman's contribution of character traits and dialogue was sufficiently original for him to be considered a joint author.

6.   The legislative history of the 1976 Act includes the following discussion of the rights of co-authors:

There is also no need for a specific statutory provision concerning the rights and duties of the coowners of a work; court-made law on this point is left undisturbed. Under the bill, as under the present law, coowners of a copyright would be treated generally as tenants in common, with each coowner having an independent right to use or license the use of a work, subject to a duty of accounting to the other coowners for any profits.

H.R. Rep. No. 94–1476, 94th Cong., 2d Sess. 121 (1976). Can one author of a co-authored work give a third party a non-exclusive license in that work? An exclusive license? Can a single co-owner transfer ownership of the copyright? In each case, what are the rights of the non-granting co-author? Of the transferee? Suppose that, for nominal consideration, one of two co-authors grants a third party a nonexclusive license to exploit a work in all media for the duration of the copyright. If these rights were in fact worth a great deal more, what are the rights of the non-licensing co-author?

7.   If two co-authors agree between themselves that neither one may license their copyright without the consent of the other, what are the rights of a licensee who receives the consent of only one of the co-authors to exploit the work?

8.   If two parties intend to create a joint work, and each makes a separately copyrightable contribution, but one makes a significantly greater contribution than the other, have they created a joint work? If so, what share of the copyright will be owned by each contributor? Is there any way they can alter this result?

9.   Suppose one author writes a poem, and a composer later obtains the lyricist's permission to set the poem to music. Who is the author of the resulting song? Would it matter if the first author wrote the poem as a lyric, anticipating that someone eventually might set it to music?

10.   If a composer writes the music and lyrics of a song, then later agrees to allow new lyrics to be substituted, is the composer a joint author of the new song?

11.   If two authors collaborate on a joint work, and one of them independently creates a derivative work based on the joint work, does the other co-author become a co-author of the derivative work?

12.   Suppose that a homeowner hires an architect to design a home, and the homeowner provides the architect with a general description of the

desired features. Is the homeowner a joint author of the resulting design? What if the homeowner contributes sketches which illustrate those features?

13. Assuming that the fixation requirement is satisfied, who owns the copyright in an interview? In an on-line "chat room" conversation?

14. Besides joint authorship, in what other ways might a person become a joint copyright owner? Where a copyright has multiple owners, can their ownership take a form other than ownership of joint undivided interests?

15. Can an editor be a co-author? Did *Larson* (note 2, *supra*) present essentially the same question in considering the claim to co-authorship by a dramaturg?

16. How do the rights of joint copyright owners differ from those of joint patent owners? What accounts for the difference?

(ii) Works Made for Hire

COMMUNITY FOR CREATIVE NON–VIOLENCE ET AL. v. REID

Supreme Court of the United States, 1989.
490 U.S. 730, 109 S.Ct. 2166, 104 L.Ed.2d 811.

JUSTICE MARSHALL delivered the opinion of the Court.

In this case, an artist and the organization that hired him to produce a sculpture contest the ownership of the copyright in that work. To resolve this dispute, we must construe the "work made for hire" provisions of the Copyright Act of 1976 (Act or 1976 Act), 17 U.S.C. §§ 101 and 201(b), and in particular, the provision in § 101, which defines as a "work made for hire" a "work prepared by an employee within the scope of his or her employment" (hereinafter § 101(1)).

I

[Petitioners are the Community for Creative Non–Violence ("CCNV"), an organization dedicated to helping the homeless, and Mitch Snyder, a member and trustee of CCNV. CCNV conceived the idea of commissioning, as a Christmastime display, a modern Nativity scene titled "Third World America," which featured a sculpture of a homeless family on a steam grate.]

* * *

Snyder made inquiries to locate an artist to produce the sculpture. He was referred to respondent James Earl Reid, a Baltimore, Maryland, sculptor. In the course of two telephone calls, Reid agreed to sculpt the three human figures. CCNV agreed to make the steam grate and pedestal for the statue. Reid proposed that the work be cast in bronze, at a total cost of approximately $100,000 and taking six to eight months to complete. Snyder rejected that proposal because CCNV did not have sufficient funds, and because the statue had to be completed by December 12 to be included in the pageant. Reid then suggested, and Snyder agreed, that the sculpture would be made of a material known as "Design Cast 62," a synthetic substance that could meet CCNV's monetary and time constraints, could be tinted to resemble bronze, and could withstand the elements. The parties agreed that the project would cost no more than $15,000, not including Reid's services, which he offered to donate. The parties did not sign a written agreement. Neither party mentioned copyright.

After Reid received an advance of $3,000, he made several sketches of figures in various poses. At Snyder's request, Reid sent CCNV a sketch of a proposed sculpture showing the family in a crechelike setting: the mother seated, cradling a baby in her lap; the father standing behind her, bending over her shoulder to touch the baby's foot. Reid testified that Snyder asked for the sketch to use in raising funds for the sculpture. Snyder testified that it was also for his approval. Reid sought a black family to serve as a model for the sculpture. Upon Snyder's suggestion, Reid visited a family living at CCNV's Washington shelter but decided that only their newly born child was a suitable model. While Reid was in Washington, Snyder took him to see homeless people living on the streets. Snyder pointed out that they tended to recline on steam grates, rather than sit or stand, in order to warm their bodies. From that time on, Reid's sketches contained only reclining figures.

Throughout November and the first two weeks of December 1985, Reid worked exclusively on the statue, assisted at various times by a dozen different people who were paid with funds provided in installments by CCNV. On a number of occasions, CCNV members visited Reid to check on his progress and to coordinate CCNV's construction of the base. CCNV rejected Reid's proposal to use suitcases or shopping bags to hold the family's personal belongings, insisting instead on a shopping cart. Reid and CCNV members did not discuss copyright ownership on any of these visits.

On December 24, 1985, 12 days after the agreed-upon date, Reid delivered the completed statue to Washington. There it was joined to the steam grate and pedestal prepared by CCNV and placed on display near the site of the pageant. Snyder paid Reid the final installment of the $15,000. * * *

[When a dispute over copyright in the statue arose, both Reid and CCNV filed certificates of copyright registration, and petitioners commenced this action. The District Court held that CCNV owned the copyright under the "work made for hire" doctrine, because Reid had acted as an employee of CCNV.]

The Court of Appeals for the District of Columbia Circuit reversed and remanded, holding that Reid owned the copyright because "Third World America" was not a work for hire. 270 U.S.App.D.C. 26, 35, 846 F.2d 1485, 1494 (1988). Adopting what it termed the "literal interpretation" of the Act as articulated by the Fifth Circuit in Easter Seal Society for Crippled Children & Adults of Louisiana, Inc. v. Playboy Enterprises, 815 F.2d 323, 329 (1987), cert. denied, 485 U.S. 981 (1988), the court read § 101 as creating "a simple dichotomy in fact between employees and independent contractors." 270 U.S.App.D.C., at 33, 846 F.2d, at 1492. Because, under agency law, Reid was an independent contractor, the court concluded that the work was not "prepared by an employee" under § 101(1). Id., at 35, 846 F. 2d, at 1494. Nor was the sculpture a "work made for hire" under the second subsection of § 101 (hereinafter § 101(2)): sculpture is not one of the nine categories of works enumerated in that subsection, and the parties had not agreed in writing that the sculpture would be a work for hire. Ibid. The court suggested that the sculpture nevertheless may have been jointly authored by CCNV and Reid, id., at 36, 846 F.2d, at 1495, and remanded for a determination whether the sculpture is indeed a joint work under the Act, id., at 39–40, 846 F.2d, at 1498–1499.

We granted certiorari to resolve a conflict among the Courts of Appeals over the proper construction of the "work made for hire" provisions of the Act. * * * We now affirm.

II

A

The Copyright Act of 1976 provides that copyright ownership "vests initially in the author or authors of the work." 17 U.S.C. § 201(a). As a general rule, the author is the party who actually creates the work, that is, the person who translates an idea into a fixed, tangible expression entitled to copyright protection. § 102. The Act carves out an important exception, however, for "works made for hire." If the work is for hire, "the employer or other person for whom the work was prepared is considered the author" and owns the copyright, unless there is a written agreement to the contrary. § 201(b). Classifying a work as "made for hire" determines not only the initial ownership of its copyright, but also the copyright's duration, § 302(c), and the owners' renewal rights, § 304(a), termination rights, § 203(a), and right to import certain goods bearing the copyright, § 601(b)(1). See 1 M. Nimmer & D. Nimmer, Nimmer on Copyright § 5.03 [A], pp. 5–10 (1988). The contours of the work for hire doctrine therefore carry profound significance for freelance creators—including artists, writers, photographers, designers, composers, and computer programmers—and for the publishing, advertising, music, and other industries which commission their works.

Section 101 of the 1976 Act provides that a work is "for hire" under two sets of circumstances * * *. Petitioners do not claim that the statue satisfies the terms of § 101(2). Quite clearly, it does not. Sculpture does not fit within any of the nine categories of "specially ordered or commissioned" works enumerated in that subsection, and no written agreement between the parties establishes "Third World America" as a work for hire.

The dispositive inquiry in this case therefore is whether "Third World America" is "a work prepared by an employee within the scope of his or her employment" under § 101(1). The Act does not define these terms. In the absence of such guidance, four interpretations have emerged. The first holds that a work is prepared by an employee whenever the hiring party retains the right to control the product. See Peregrine v. Lauren Corp., 601 F.Supp. 828, 829 (D.Colo.1985); Clarkstown v. Reeder, 566 F.Supp. 137, 142 (S.D.N.Y.1983). Petitioners take this view. * * * A second, and closely related, view is that a work is prepared by an employee under § 101(1) when the hiring party has actually wielded control with respect to the creation of a particular work. This approach was formulated by the Court of Appeals for the Second Circuit, Aldon Accessories Ltd. v. Spiegel, Inc., 738 F.2d 548, cert. denied, 469 U.S. 982 (1984), and adopted by the Fourth Circuit, Brunswick Beacon, Inc. v. Schock–Hopchas Publishing Co., 810 F.2d 410 (1987), the Seventh Circuit, Evans Newton Inc. v. Chicago Systems Software, 793 F.2d 889, cert. denied, 479 U.S. 949 (1986), and, at times, by petitioners * * *. A third view is that the term "employee" within § 101(1) carries its common-law agency law meaning. This view was endorsed by the Fifth Circuit in Easter Seal Society for Crippled Children & Adults of Louisiana, Inc. v. Playboy Enterprises, 815 F.2d 323 (1987), and by the Court of Appeals below. Finally, respondent and numerous amici curiae contend that the term "employee" only refers to "formal, salaried" employees. * * * The Court of Appeals for the Ninth Circuit recently adopted this view. See Dumas v. Gommerman, 865 F.2d 1093 (1989).

The starting point for our interpretation of a statute is always its language. Consumer Product Safety Comm'n v. GTE Sylvania, Inc., 447 U.S. 102, 108 (1980). The Act nowhere defines the terms "employee" or "scope of employment." It is, however, well established that "[w]here Congress uses terms that have accumulated settled meaning under ... the common law, a court must infer, unless the statute otherwise dictates, that Congress means to incorporate the established meaning of these terms." NLRB v. Amax Coal Co., 453 U.S. 322, 329 (1981) * * *. In the past, when Congress has used the term "employee" without defining it, we have concluded that Congress intended to describe the conventional master-servant relationship as understood by common-law agency doctrine. See, e.g., Kelley v. Southern Pacific Co., 419 U.S. 318, 322–323 (1974); Baker v. Texas & Pacific R. Co., 359 U.S. 227, 228 (1959) (per curiam); Robinson v. Baltimore & Ohio R. Co., 237 U.S. 84, 94 (1915). Nothing in the text of the work for hire provisions indicates that Congress used the words "employee" and "employment" to describe anything other than " 'the conventional relation of employer and employee.' " Kelley, supra, at 323, quoting Robinson, supra, at 94 * * *.

In past cases of statutory interpretation, when we have concluded that Congress intended terms such as "employee," "employer," and "scope of employment" to be understood in light of agency law, we have relied on the general common law of agency, rather than on the law of any particular State, to give meaning to these terms. See, e.g., Kelley, 419 U.S., at 323–324, and n. 5; id., at 332 (Stewart, J., concurring in judgment); Ward v. Atlantic Coast Line R. Co., 362 U.S. 396, 400 (1960);

Baker, supra, at 228. This practice reflects the fact that "federal statutes are generally intended to have uniform nationwide application." Mississippi Band of Choctaw Indians v. Holyfield, [490 U.S. 30 (1989)] at 43. Establishment of a federal rule of agency, rather than reliance on state agency law, is particularly appropriate here given the Act's express objective of creating national, uniform copyright law by broadly pre-empting state statutory and common-law copyright regulation. See 17 U.S.C. § 301(a). We thus agree with the Court of Appeals that the term "employee" should be understood in light of the general common law of agency.

In contrast, neither test proposed by petitioners is consistent with the text of the Act. The exclusive focus of the right to control the product test on the relationship between the hiring party and the product clashes with the language of § 101(1), which focuses on the relationship between the hired and hiring parties. The right to control the product test also would distort the meaning of the ensuing subsection, § 101(2). Section 101 plainly creates two distinct ways in which a work can be deemed for hire: one for works prepared by employees, the other for those specially ordered or commissioned works which fall within one of the nine enumerated categories and are the subject of a written agreement. The right to control the product test ignores this dichotomy by transforming into a work for hire under § 101(1) any "specially ordered or commissioned" work that is subject to the supervision and control of the hiring party. Because a party who hires a "specially ordered or commissioned" work by definition has a right to specify the characteristics of the product desired, at the time the commission is accepted, and frequently until it is completed, the right to control the product test would mean that many works that could satisfy § 101(2) would already have been deemed works for hire under § 101(1). Petitioners' interpretation is particularly hard to square with § 101(2)'s enumeration of the nine specific categories of specially ordered or commissioned works eligible to be works for hire, e.g., "a contribution to a collective work," "a part of a motion picture," and "answer material for a test." The unifying feature of these works is that they are usually prepared at the instance, direction, and risk of a publisher or producer. By their very nature, therefore, these types of works would be works by an employee under petitioners' right to control the product test.

The actual control test, articulated by the Second Circuit in Aldon Accessories, fares only marginally better when measured against the language and structure of § 101. Under this test, independent contractors who are so controlled and supervised in the creation of a particular work are deemed "employees" under § 101(1). Thus work for hire status under § 101(1) depends on a hiring party's *actual* control of, rather than *right to* control, the product. Aldon Accessories, 738 F.2d, at 552. Under the actual control test, a work for hire could arise under § 101(2), but not under § 101(1), where a party commissions, but does not actually control, a product which falls into one of the nine enumerated categories. Nonetheless, we agree with the Court of Appeals for the Fifth Circuit that "[t]here is simply no way to milk the 'actual control' test of Aldon Accessories from the language of the statute." Easter Seal Society, 815 F.2d, at 334. Section 101 clearly delineates between works prepared by an employee and commissioned works. Sound though other distinctions might be as a matter of copyright policy, there is no statutory support for an additional dichotomy between commissioned works that are actually controlled and supervised by the hiring party and those that are not.

We therefore conclude that the language and structure of § 101 of the Act do not support either the right to control the product or the actual control approaches.[8] The structure of § 101 indicates that a work for hire can arise through one of two mutually exclusive means, one for employees and one for independent contractors, and ordinary canons of statutory interpretation indicate that the classification of a particular hired party should be made with reference to agency law.

[The Court also examined the legislative history of the "work made for hire" definition and found no support there for a "control" test of employment status.]

* * *

Finally, petitioners' construction of the work for hire provisions would impede Congress' paramount goal in revising the 1976 Act of enhancing predictability and certainty of copyright ownership. See H. R. Rep. No. 94–1476, supra, at 129. In a "copyright marketplace," the parties negotiate with an expectation that one of them will own the copyright in the completed work. Dumas, 865 F.2d, at 1104–1105, n. 18. With that expectation, the parties at the outset can settle on relevant contractual terms, such as the price for the work and the ownership of reproduction rights.

To the extent that petitioners endorse an actual control test, CCNV's construction of the work for hire provisions prevents such planning. Because that test turns on whether the hiring party has closely monitored the production process, the parties would not know until late in the process, if not until the work is completed, whether a work will ultimately fall within § 101(1). Under petitioners' approach, therefore, parties would have to predict in advance whether the hiring party will sufficiently control a given work to make it the author. "If they guess incorrectly, their reliance on 'work for hire' or an assignment may give them a copyright interest that they did not bargain for." Easter Seal Society, 815 F.2d, at 333; accord, Dumas, supra, at 1103. This under-

---

8. We also reject the suggestion of respondent and amici that the § 101(1) term "employee" refers only to formal, salaried employees. While there is some support for such a definition in the legislative history, * * * the language of § 101(1) cannot support it. The Act does not say "formal" or "salaried" employee, but simply "employee." Moreover, respondent and those amici who endorse a formal, salaried employee test do not agree upon the content of this test. * * * Even the one Court of Appeals to adopt what it termed a formal, salaried employee test in fact embraced an approach incorporating numerous factors drawn from the agency law definition of employee which we endorse. See Dumas, 865 F.2d, at 1104.

standing of the work for hire provisions clearly thwarts Congress' goal of ensuring predictability through advance planning. Moreover, petitioners' interpretation "leaves the door open for hiring parties, who have failed to get a full assignment of copyright rights from independent contractors falling outside the subdivision (2) guidelines, to unilaterally obtain work-made-for-hire rights years after the work has been completed as long as they directed or supervised the work, a standard that is hard not to meet when one is a hiring party." Hamilton, Commissioned Works as Works Made for Hire Under the 1976 Copyright Act: Misinterpretation and Injustice, 135 U. Pa. L. Rev. 1281, 1304 (1987).

In sum, we must reject petitioners' argument. Transforming a commissioned work into a work by an employee on the basis of the hiring party's right to control, or actual control of, the work is inconsistent with the language, structure, and legislative history of the work for hire provisions. To determine whether a work is for hire under the Act, a court first should ascertain, using principles of general common law of agency, whether the work was prepared by an employee or an independent contractor. After making this determination, the court can apply the appropriate subsection of § 101.

B

We turn, finally, to an application of § 101 to Reid's production of "Third World America." In determining whether a hired party is an employee under the general common law of agency, we consider the hiring party's right to control the manner and means by which the product is accomplished. Among the other factors relevant to this inquiry are the skill required; the source of the instrumentalities and tools; the location of the work; the duration of the relationship between the parties; whether the hiring party has the right to assign additional projects to the hired party; the extent of the hired party's discretion over when and how long to work; the method of payment; the hired party's role in hiring and paying assistants; whether the work is part of the regular business of the hiring party; whether the hiring party is in business; the provision of employee benefits; and the tax treatment of the hired party. See Restatement § 220(2) (setting forth a nonexhaustive list of factors relevant to determining whether a hired party is an employee). No one of these factors is determinative. See Ward, 362 U.S., at 400; Hilton Int'l Co. v. NLRB, 690 F.2d 318, 321 (C.A.2 1982).

Examining the circumstances of this case in light of these factors, we agree with the Court of Appeals that Reid was not an employee of CCNV but an independent contractor. 270 U.S.App.D.C., at 35, n. 11, 846 F.2d, at 1494, n. 11. True, CCNV members directed enough of Reid's work to ensure that he produced a sculpture that met their specifications. 652 F.Supp., at 1456. But the extent of control the hiring party exercises over the details of the product is not dispositive. Indeed, all the other circumstances weigh heavily against finding an employment relationship. Reid is a sculptor, a skilled occupation. Reid supplied his own tools. He worked in his own studio in Baltimore, making daily supervision of his activities from Washington practicably impossible. Reid was retained for less than two months, a relatively short period of time. During and after this time, CCNV had no right to assign additional projects to Reid. Apart from the deadline for completing the sculpture, Reid had absolute freedom to decide when and how long to work. CCNV paid Reid $15,000, a sum dependent on "completion of a specific job, a method by which independent contractors are often compensated." Holt v. Winpisinger, 258 U.S.App.D.C. 343, 351, 811 F.2d 1532, 1540 (1987). Reid had total discretion in hiring and paying assistants. "Creating sculptures was hardly 'regular business' for CCNV." 270 U.S.App.D.C., at 35, n. 11, 846 F.2d, at 1494, n. 11. Indeed, CCNV is not a business at all. Finally, CCNV did not pay payroll or Social Security taxes, provide any employee benefits, or contribute to unemployment insurance or workers' compensation funds.

Because Reid was an independent contractor, whether "Third World America" is a work for hire depends on whether it satisfies the terms of § 101(2). This petitioners concede it cannot do. Thus, CCNV is not the author of "Third World America" by virtue of the work for hire provisions of the Act. However, as the Court of Appeals made clear, CCNV nevertheless may be a joint author of the sculpture if, on remand, the District Court determines that CCNV and Reid prepared the work "with the intention that their contributions be merged into inseparable or interdependent parts of a unitary whole." 17 U.S.C. § 101. In that case, CCNV and Reid would be co-owners of the copyright in the work. See § 201(a).

For the aforestated reasons, we affirm the judgment of the Court of Appeals for the District of Columbia Circuit.

Notes

1. Should the list of commissioned works that can be treated as works made for hire be expanded, and if so, what categories should be included?

2. Based on the facts presented in *Reid*, how strong is CCNV's argument for joint authorship?

3. Should each of the *Reid* factors receive equal weight in any given case? Why or why not?

4. Where it is unclear that an employment relationship exists for purposes of the work-made-for-hire doctrine, to what extent, if any, can the parties reduce the resulting legal uncertainties?

5. To ensure work-made-for-hire status under clause (2) of the statutory definition:

    (a) Must the work-made-for-hire agreement be executed before the work is produced?

    (b) Would a pre-production oral agreement or implied agreement be sufficient if it were reduced to writing after the work was produced?

    (c) Must the agreement use the phrase "work made for hire"?

If no legally sufficient writing is ever executed, why did Congress decide that the commissioned party should be entitled to the copyright?

6. When university professors write articles or books, or prepare their classroom lectures, who owns the copyright in these works? Who owns the copyright in material authored by their research assistants? Would a college or university have standing (as a copyright owner) to bring an infringement suit if a company hired students to tape professors' lectures and then sold transcripts of those lectures?

In *Foraste v. Brown University,* 290 F.Supp.2d 234 (D.R.I. 2003), photographer John Foraste claimed that he held the copyrights of the photographs he took for Brown University, based on a copyright policy written in Brown staff and faculty handbooks, which stated: *"Ownership:* It is the University's position that, as a general premise, ownership of copyrightable property which results from performance of one's University duties and activities will belong to the author or originator. This applies to books, art works, software, etc." 290 F.Supp.2d at 236. Yet the court held that in order for copyright ownership to be transferred from an employer to an employee in a "work made for hire" situation, the strict requirements of section 201(b) of the 1976 Copyright Act must be met. Even assuming these requirements were met, the policy set out in the Brown handbooks was too vague to constitute a valid transfer pursuant to section 204(a) because none of the particular details about the transfer appeared in the policy. This result is clearly the product of erroneous reasoning, is it not?

7. Assume that a greeting card and novelty manufacturer executes a contract with an artist under which the artist agrees to provide artwork to the manufacturer. The manufacturer is free to accept or reject any of the artwork. The parties' contract states that "Any work created by the Artist during the period of this contract shall be the sole property of the Company." Comment on the legal effect of this language.

8. Section 1011(d) of the Satellite Home Viewer Improvement Act of 1999, which was enacted in section 1000(a)(9) of Pub. L. No. 106–113, 106th Cong., 1st Sess. (1999), amended the definition of "work made for hire" in 17 U.S.C. § 101 to add sound recordings to the list of enumerated works which can be works made for hire if created pursuant to a written work made for hire agreement.

Under prior law, it was unclear whether "work made for hire" contract clauses were enforceable against artists performing as independent contractors on sound recordings. The recording industry had taken the position that a sound recording was a "contribution to a collective work," and thus included in the enumerated list even prior to this amendment, but recent federal decisions have held that sound recordings do not fit the enumerated categories. *E.g., Lulirama Ltd. v. Axcess Broad. Servs., Inc.,* 128 F.3d 872, 878 (5th Cir.1997); *Staggers v. Real Authentic Sound,* 77 F.Supp.2d 57, 62–64 (D.D.C.1999); *Ballas v. Tedesco,* 41 F.Supp.2d 531, 541 (D.N.J.1999). If the works in question are not works made for hire, then they are in most cases joint works. The earliest opportunity for authors of such works to exercise their termination rights arises in 2013 (for sound recordings created during 1978).

Because most record companies have routinely required recording artists to sign "work made for hire" agreements (as well as copyright transfer agreements) with respect to their recorded performances, it was unclear whether this "technical" amendment might affect authorship determinations with respect to *existing* as well as future recordings, in which case many recording artists would be unable to reclaim their copyrights in existing recordings under the section 203 termination provisions.

Although described in the legislation as a "technical" amendment, the addition of sound recordings to the list of enumerated works was characterized as a substantial change in the law by recording artists and their representatives, as well as by Register of Copyrights Marybeth Peters and many copyright scholars, who criticized Congress for enacting this change with no hearings, debate, or input from musical performers. In response to the outrage expressed by recording artists, H.R. 5107 was enacted in October of 2000. Specifically, Section 2(a)(1) strikes the phrase "as a sound recording" from Section 101(2) of Title 17. For an excellent analysis of these events, see Nimmer & Menell, Sound Recordings, Works for Hire, and the Termination-of-Transfers Time Bomb, 49 J. Copyright Soc'y 387 (2001). The authors write: "As a result of this 'millennial flipflop,' the issue [whether sound recordings can qualify as specially commissioned works for hire] is now left squarely indeterminate. . . . After analyzing the issue in depth, the conclusion reached . . . is a definite *maybe*."

In this context, reflect again upon the potential implications of Justice Blackborne's finding of authorship in the Procol Harum matter discussed *Supra*, at note 3, p. 879.

9.   In *Marvel Characters, Inc. v. Simon*, 310 F.3d 280 (2d Cir. 2002), excerpted, *infra*, at p. 953, the court considered whether an agreement made after the creation of a work that stated that the work was one for hire was sufficient to guarantee to the putative employer the renewal term in a copyright at the expense of the creator's termination interest. The Court decided in the circumstances that it was not. [*Marvel Characters, Inc.* is excerpted in this casebook supplement in Chapter 17, Section C.]

10.   In *Estate of Burne Hogarth v. Edgar Rice Burroughs, Inc. (ERB)*, 342 F.3d 149 (2d Cir. 2003), ERB commissioned Hogarth to illustrate pictorial versions of Tarzan books in 1971. The court found that the Tarzan Books were made at the "instance and expense" of ERB and thus were works for hire under the 1909 Act.

11.   In *Martha Graham School and Dance Foundation, Inc. v. Martha Graham Center of Contemporary Dance, Inc.*, 380 F.3d 624 (2d Cir. 2004), the court ruled that the work for hire status of dance choreography depended on the details of the employment contracts between choreographer Martha Graham and the non-profit organizations she established.

12.   On remand, after the Supreme Court's opinion in *Dastar* (see Chapter Seven on "Trademarks", *supra*), the Ninth Circuit subsequently upheld a lower court ruling that the Eisenhower biography ("Crusade in Europe") had been undertaken as a work-for-hire. See *Twentieth Century Fox Film Corp. v. Entertainment Distributing*, 429 F.3d 869 (9th Cir. 2005). In applying the 1909 Copyright Act the court noted that the work had been financed by the publisher, which had also exercised substantial editorial

control over the completion of the manuscript. The result was that, despite the adverse ruling by the Supreme Court as to the plaintiff's Lanham Act Section 43(a) claim, liability followed on copyright grounds.

2. FORMALITIES: NOTICE, REGISTRATION, AND DEPOSIT

Statutes: 17 U.S.C.A. §§ 101 (as needed), 401–12

The Copyright Act of 1909 required copyright owners to take affirmative steps to prevent their works from entering the public domain. In many cases those steps were not taken, through ignorance, error or inadvertence, and valuable property rights disappeared. Beginning with the 1976 Copyright Act, however, the significance of formalities in federal copyright law has been greatly reduced.

(i) Notice

Under the 1909 Act, publication marked the dividing line between common law copyright protection and federal copyright protection. Once a work was published, it either enjoyed federal copyright protection or it entered the public domain in the United States. To prevent the work from entering the public domain upon publication, section 10 required the copyright owner to affix copyright notice "to each copy thereof published or offered for sale in the United States by authority of the copyright proprietor."[4] Sections 19 and 20 spelled out the required form, content and placement of the copyright notice. The work would enter the public domain if notice were omitted from even a single copy of the work. In some cases, minor deviations from the required form had the same consequence, although courts displayed varying degrees of tolerance where the copyright claimant demonstrated good faith. Where the copyright owner sought to comply with the notice requirement, but notice was omitted from one or more copies "by accident or mistake," section 21 provided that the copyright would not be deemed invalid in an action against an infringer that undertook the infringing conduct after receiving actual notice of the copyright; however, "accident or mistake" was generally interpreted narrowly, including omissions resulting from mechanical failures in the printing process but excluding omissions due to negligence or oversight.

The significance of copyright notice changed dramatically beginning with the 1976 Act, which provided that a copyright owner who failed to affix copyright notice on a published work could avoid forfeiting the copyright by undertaking the steps outlined in 17 U.S.C.A. § 405(a). For works first published on or after March 1, 1989 (the effective date of the Berne Convention Implementation Act of 1988[5]), omission of notice does not lead to loss of copyright at all. However, notice may still be advisable to preclude a defendant from invoking the "innocent infringement"

---

4. Sections 22 and 23 exempted English-language books and periodicals first published abroad, giving them a 5–year interim copyright (convertible into the full term after publication with notice in the United States) if the author complied with certain deposit and registration requirements.

5. Pub. L. 100–568, 102 Stat. 2853.

defense in mitigation of statutory damages under 17 U.S.C.A. § 504 (c)(2).

Notes

1. In *Charles Garnier, Paris v. Andin International, Inc.*, 36 F.3d 1214 (1st Cir. 1994), the First Circuit addressed the proper application of the copyright law cure provision, 17 U.S.C. § 405(a) holding that the plaintiff did not make sufficient efforts to remedy a prior failure to affix notice of copyright to copies of its creative work sufficient to avoid forfeiture of copyright protection.

2. Suppose that the plaintiff, a United States toy manufacturer, acquired the copyright in certain toys from a party that had, before 1989, distributed the toys without notice overseas. Assuming that the toys would be otherwise eligible for copyright in the United States, would this omission trigger the forfeiture/cure provisions of the 1976 Act? If so, when should the United States copyright owner be found to have "discovered" the omission? Would the plaintiff's obligation to affix notice (to cure the omission) extend to copies distributed in the United States by a foreign distributor? See *Hasbro Bradley, Inc. v. Sparkle Toys, Inc.*, 780 F.2d 189 (2d Cir.1985).

3. When the cure provisions of section 405(a) apply and the copyright owner complies with them, does the original omission of notice have any effect on the copyright owner's rights?

4. When the cure provisions of section 405(a) apply and the copyright owner fails to comply with them, is copyright forfeited retroactively to the date of publication, or only prospectively?

5. What year should be included in a copyright notice? What is the effect of an erroneous name or date in the copyright notice affixed to a work distributed after March 1, 1989? Before that date?

6. Suppose that a book was published in 1987 under the authority of the copyright owner but without notice, and the omission was cured by complying with section 405(a)(2). If the work went out of print in 1989, and a second printing of the book (with no alteration of the copyrighted material) commenced in 1994, what would be the legal effect, if any, of omitting copyright notice from the copies published in 1994 and thereafter?

7. In the case of certain foreign works that entered the public domain in the United States due to noncompliance with formalities such as the notice requirement, copyright may be restored pursuant to section 104A. See Section B.2, *infra.*

8. Besides the "cure" provisions of section 405(a)(2), the 1976 Act contains two additional exceptions to copyright forfeiture. Application of the section 405(a)(1) exception for omission of copyright notice on a "relatively small" number of copies or phonorecords has led one court to conclude that 1% of publicly distributed copies is relatively small, and another to conclude that 2.4% is too many. (Compare section 21 of the 1909 Act.) Section 405(a)(3) creates a more complex ambiguity: If notice is omitted in violation of an implied or oral condition of publication, is the publication not "by authority of the copyright owner" under section 405(a)? However this

question is resolved, should the answer be the same for purposes of unnoticed publication under section 10 of the 1909 Act?

9. If two persons own the copyright in a work, and only one of them authorizes the public distribution of the work without notice, what effect does this have on the work's copyright (a) under the 1909 Act? (b) under the 1976 Act? Would it matter whether the distribution without notice took place in the United States or exclusively overseas? Would it matter whether they each owned undivided interests in the entire copyright, or distinct and separate pieces of the copyright?

10. If a compilation was published without notice under the 1909 or 1976 Acts, did the underlying works enter the public domain? *Cf., Shoptalk, Ltd. v. Concorde–New Horizons Corp.*, 168 F.3d 586 (2d Cir.1999) (dealing with unpublished underlying works).

(ii) Registration and Deposit

Under section 12 of the 1909 Act, registration and deposit were essential to statutory copyright protection of unpublished works. Under section 13, registration and deposit were not essential to obtaining a copyright in published works (since this was accomplished by publication with notice) but they were prerequisites to filing an infringement claim. In addition, registration was a prerequisite to filing a renewal registration. (The significance of renewal registration is discussed in Section B.1, *infra*.)

Registration has taken on a different significance under the 1976 Act. Because statutory copyright now commences with fixation rather than publication, registration is no longer a prerequisite to statutory copyright protection of unpublished works. Except for works published without proper notice between January 1, 1978, and March 1, 1989, which entered the public domain unless they were registered within the five-year window specified by section 405(a)(2), registration under the 1976 Act was, and remains, permissive for all works. However, under section 411 it continues to be a prerequisite to filing an infringement claim under section 106 (except in the case of Berne Convention works, as defined in section 101, and certain live transmissions under section 411(b) if they are registered within three months of the initial transmission). Registration is not, however, a prerequisite to an infringement claim under section 106A. Registration, if timely, is also prima facie evidence of a claimant's valid copyright (section 410(c)). Registration has further evidentiary value in helping to establish the date on which a work was created, which can support or rebut circumstantial evidence of copying (see Chapter 20). In addition, section 412 specifies that no statutory damages or attorney's fees can be recovered for a pre-registration infringement of an unpublished work; where a work is infringed after publication, statutory damages and attorney's fees are available for a pre-registration infringement only if the work is registered within three months of publication. Registration must take place in order to establish priority through recordation under section 205 in the event of conflicting transfers, and, in the case of nondramatic musical works, compulsory license fees under section 115 can only be collected by the copyright owner identified in the registration or other public records of the copyright office. Finally, registration is a prerequisite to obtaining relief against importation of infringing items through the U.S. Customs service under section 603, or in an action before the International Trade Commission, under 19 U.S.C.A. § 1337(a)(1)(B)(i), (a)(1)(D). Thus, while reducing the significance of registration, Congress retained certain incentives to encourage copyright owners to register their works.

Copyright registrants are required to deposit one complete copy or phonorecord (two, in the case of published works) under section 408(b). In addition, a separate deposit requirement applies to published works (whether or not registered) under section 407. Although noncompliance with section 407 may lead to a fine, it does not lead to loss of copyright protection.

Notes

1.   Is an infringement suit barred if the plaintiff's application to register the work is refused?

2.   Suppose a producer plans a live pay-per-view broadcast (with simultaneous fixation) of a major sporting event. Two days before the broadcast, she learns that several sports bars with de-scrambling devices plan to intercept the broadcast for the benefit of their patrons without paying for it. Can she get injunctive relief before the broadcast?

3.   Suppose that a composer who resides outside the United States in a country that is a Berne signatory writes a song but does not register it in the United States because she has no thought of exploiting it here. Without her knowledge or consent, her song is recorded by an American record company. The composer learns of this shortly before the record's scheduled release and would like to obtain immediate injunctive relief. What obstacles is the composer likely to encounter in filing her suit? Would your answer change if the infringement took place after she filed her registration papers but before she received her registration certificate?

4.   What public purposes are served by registration and deposit?

5.   What if a copyright plaintiff wishes to register a work in order to initiate an infringement action, but no longer has access to a copy of the work—for example, because the plaintiff's copy was lost or destroyed, or because the defendant has lawful possession of the only copy?

6.   The Copyright Office regulations exempt "secure tests" from the deposit requirement of section 408. 37 C.F.R. § 202.20(c)(2)(vi). A "secure test" is "a nonmarketed test administered under supervision at specified centers on specific dates, all copies of which are accounted for and either destroyed or returned to restricted locked storage following each administration." 37 C.F.R. § 202.20(b)(4). Where a test meets this definition, the registrant need only deposit a portion or description of the test that is sufficient to identify it. Id. § 202.20(c)(2)(vi). Does this exemption conflict with any of the policies behind the copyright statutes or the copyright clause of the Constitution? Note that the regulations exempt from the deposit requirement of section 407 (but not section 408) several other categories of

works—three-dimensional sculptural works, individual contributions to collective works, and most advertisements. See 17 U.S.C.A. § 407(c); 37 C.F.R. §§ 202.19.

7. In *Raquel v. Education Management Corp.*, 196 F.3d 171 (3d Cir. 1999), the Third Circuit invalidated a copyright registration because it misidentified the registered work—a song—as an "audiovisual work". What types of errors, if any, should invalidate a copyright registration, and why?

8. In *Morris v. Business Concepts, Inc.*, 259 F.3d 65 (2d Cir.2001), the Second Circuit ruled as a matter of first impression that a magazine publisher's collective work registration does not fulfill the author's registration requirement under 17 U.S.C. Section 114 (a). The defendant Morris had written several articles, and had conferred exclusive license to publish the articles to Conde Nast Publications. Conde Nast registered each issue of its magazine and obtained collective work registrations but Morris did not obtain registrations as copyright owner of the work. Defendant Business Concepts copied 24 of Morris's articles and the plaintiff sued for infringement. The court affirmed a summary judgment for the defendant finding no subject matter jurisdiction over the copyright claims because the defendant had not registered the work. Although the plaintiff argued that the exclusive license to publish the articles gave Conde Nast copyright ownership over them, the court disagreed, stating that Section 201 (d)(2) addresses the divisibility of rights only and that copyright ownership itself is not divisible.

9. In *Murray Hill Publ'ns, Inc. v. ABC Communs., Inc.*, 264 F.3d 622 (6th Cir.2001), the Sixth Circuit held that a derivative work must be registered to support subject matter jurisdiction over an infringement claim. In this case, musician Robert Laurel had produced a movie and created and used a registered song in the soundtrack. Laurel later reworked the song for use as a theme for his radio DJ friend McCarthy, but did not register the derivative work. After McCarthy's death, a compilation of his programs were made that included the theme song written by Laurel. Acknowledging the unsettled state of the law in this area, the court affirmed a lower court ruling dismissing plaintiff's action for copyright infringement, noting that while "the registration of a derivative work would relate back to include the original work," the "registration of the original material would not carry forward to new, derivative material."

3. THE CHANGED SIGNIFICANCE OF PUBLICATION

INTELLECTUAL PROPERTY AND THE NATIONAL INFORMATION INFRASTRUCTURE

The Report of the Working Group on Intellectual Property Rights,
Information Infrastructure Task Force 28–30 (1995).

* * *

Historically, the concept of publication has been a major underpinning of copyright law. Under the dual system of protection which existed until the 1976 Copyright Act took effect, unpublished works were generally protected under state law. Published works, on the other hand, were protected under Federal copyright law.[68] On the effective date of the 1976 Act [January 1, 1978], Federal copyright protection became available for unpublished as well as published works.[69] The concept of publication thus lost its "all-embracing importance" as the threshold to Federal statutory protection.[70]

However, while the importance of publication has been reduced through amendment to the law (e.g., granting Federal protection to unpublished works and removing the notice requirement for published works), the status of a work as either published or unpublished still has significance under the Copyright Act. For example:

> only works that are published in the United States are subject to mandatory deposit in the Library of Congress;[71] deposit requirements for registration with the Copyright Office differ depending on whether a work is published or unpublished;[72] the scope of the fair use defense may be narrower for unpublished works;[73] unpublished works are eligible for protection without regard to the nationality or domicile of the author;[74] published works must bear a copyright notice if published before March 1, 1989;[75] and certain limitations on the exclusive rights of a copyright owner are applicable only to published works.[76]

* * *

4. THE MEANING OF PUBLICATION

The meaning of "publication" was somewhat different under the 1909 Act than under the 1976 Act. Whether a particular event constitutes "publication" depends in part on which of these Acts was in effect when that event took place. Thus, the uncertainties surrounding the

68. See Wheaton v. Peters, 33 U.S. (8 Pet.) 591, 662–63 (1834).

69. See 17 U.S.C. § 104 (1988 & Supp. V 1993). Prior to 1978, certain unpublished works, particularly dramatic works and musical compositions, could obtain Federal copyright protection through registration with the Copyright Office. Since 1978, all otherwise eligible unpublished works are protected under Federal law. See 17 U.S.C. § 104(a) (1988 & Supp. V 1993).

70. House Report [H.R. Rep. No. 94–1476, 94th Cong., 2d Sess. (1976)] at 129, reprinted in 1976 U.S.C.C.A.N. 5745.

71. 17 U.S.C. § 407 (1988). * * * The deposit requirements are not conditions of copyright protection, but failure to deposit copies of a published work may subject the copyright owner to significant fines. See 17 U.S.C. § 407(a), (d) (1988).

72. See 17 U.S.C. § 408(b) (1988) * * *.

73. The first factor of the fair use analysis—the nature of the copyrighted work—generally weighs against a finding of fair use if the work is unpublished. See Harper & Row [v. Nation Enterprises, 471 U.S. 539, 105 S. Ct. 2218, 85 L. Ed. 2d 588 (1985)] * * *.

74. 17 U.S.C. § 104(a) (1988 & Supp. V 1993); House Report at 58, reprinted in 1976 U.S.C.C.A.N. 5671 (Section 104(a) "imposes no qualification of nationality and domicile with respect to unpublished works"); see also 17 U.S.C. § 104(b) (1988 & Supp. V 1993) (national origin requirements for published works).

75. 17 U.S.C. § 405 (1988 & Supp. V 1993).

76. See generally 17 U.S.C. §§ 107–120 (1988 & Supp. V 1993). See, e.g., 17 U.S.C. § 118 (1988 & Supp. V 1993) (compulsory license is available for the use of certain published works in connection with non-commercial broadcasting).

meaning of "publication" under the 1909 Act will remain problematic until all works published before 1978 have entered the public domain.

Because the 1909 Act provided little guidance as to what constituted "publication," defining this term was left largely to the courts.[1] The question whether a work had been published was often a crucial one since, prior to January 1, 1978, publication without proper copyright notice could inject a work into the public domain. In addition, publication was, for most works,[2] a prerequisite to obtaining federal copyright protection under section 10 of the 1909 Act, and thus was necessary if a copyright plaintiff wished to invoke the federal court's subject matter jurisdiction and obtain federal remedies. Therefore, copyright plaintiffs whose disseminated works bore the required copyright notice often sought a ruling that their works had been published. This was known as "investive" publication. In contrast, where a work had been disseminated without notice, the copyright owner would argue that the dissemination was not a publication and that the work therefore retained its perpetual common law copyright under section 2 of the 1909 Act. A publication without notice, which caused the work to enter the public domain, was known as a "divestive" publication. Because the last works published under the 1909 Act will not enter the public domain until the end of 2072, in many cases courts are still required to resolve questions of investive or divestive publication.

Although section 101 of the 1976 Act includes an explicit definition of "publication," it does not resolve all of the uncertainties that arose under prior law. The 1976 Act is silent on the question whether, under any circumstances, an unauthorized public distribution can constitute publication; courts interpreting the 1909 Act found publication only where the copyright owner had consented to the distribution. For the most part, the 1976 Act does not reject the case law interpreting "publication" under prior law; thus, those authorities help to define "publication" even under current law. Under both the 1909 and 1976 Acts, for example, a "publication" without notice will not be found where the work is distributed without the authority of the copyright owner. See, *e.g., Twentieth Century–Fox Film Corp. v. Dunnahoo,* 637 F.2d 1338 (9th Cir.1981) (applying 1909 Act); *Midway Manufacturing Co. v. Artic International, Inc.,* 547 F.Supp. 999 (N.D.Ill.1982), *aff'd,* 704 F.2d 1009 (7th Cir.1983) (applying 1976 Act).

According to case law interpreting the 1909 Act, a mere offer to sell or otherwise distribute a work (either the original or copies) to the public, if authorized by the copyright owner, was a publication. This interpretation was at least partially codified in the definition of "publication" contained in section 101 of the 1976 Act; however, because of the ambiguous language of that section, the codified rule appears to be

---

1. Section 26 defined the "date of publication" as the date on which copies were first "placed on sale, sold, or publicly distributed" under the copyright owner's authority.

2. Section 22 provided an exception for certain works not reproduced for sale, provided the author satisfied the registration and deposit requirements of that section.

narrower than that adopted by courts applying the 1909 Act, because the codified rule refers only to an offer to distribute "for purposes of further distribution, public performance, or public display," thus creating uncertainty as to the status of offers to distribute works to the public for their private use.

Significant issues in interpreting "publication" under the 1909 Act have included: (1) whether a particular distribution was private or public; (2) whether a public performance or display was a publication; and (3) whether publication of a derivative work (such as a sound recording or a motion picture) constituted publication of the underlying work (a musical composition or a story or screenplay, respectively). Some, but not all, of these questions were addressed in the 1976 Act.

(i) General versus Limited Distributions

Courts interpreting the 1909 Act distinguished general distributions, which constituted publication, from "limited" distributions, which did not. "Limited" distributions were made to "a definitely selected group for a limited purpose, and without the right of diffusion, reproduction, distribution or sale.... [T]he circulation must be restricted both as to persons and purpose, or it cannot be called a private or limited publication." *White v. Kimmell*, 193 F.2d 744 (9th Cir.1952) (holding that distribution of no more than 20 copies of a manuscript lacking copyright notice to persons author did not know, with no restriction on further distribution, was general publication), *rev'g* 94 F.Supp. 502 (S.D.Cal. 1950), *cert. denied*, 343 U.S. 957, 72 S.Ct. 1052, 96 L.Ed. 1357 (1952). The precedents distinguishing limited from general distributions under the 1909 Act continue to be relevant in construing "publication" under the 1976 Act. See, *e.g., Vane v. The Fair, Inc.*, 676 F.Supp. 133 (E.D.Tex. 1987).

In general, it appears that courts interpreting the 1909 Act were especially reluctant to find that a distribution constituted divestive publication; indeed, some courts explicitly stated that a broader dissemination was necessary to prove divestive publication than investive publication. See, *e.g., Hirshon v. United Artists Corp.*, 243 F.2d 640 (D.C.Cir. 1957); *American Visuals v. Holland*, 239 F.2d 740 (2d Cir.1956).

It is nonetheless difficult to reconcile some of these decisions.

In one notable case, *Academy of Motion Picture Arts & Sciences v. Creative House Promotions, Inc.*, 944 F.2d 1446 (9th Cir.1991), *rev'g in part, aff'g in part, and remanding* 728 F.Supp. 1442 (C.D.Cal.1989), the Ninth Circuit ruled that the Oscar statuette was not injected into the public domain when the Academy distributed 158 Oscars without copyright notice and with no express restriction on further distribution by the recipients; the court went to some trouble to find an "implied" restriction.

In *King v. Mister Maestro*, 224 F.Supp. 101 (S.D.N.Y.1963), the district court found only a "limited" distribution where Martin Luther King gave advance copies of his "I Have a Dream" speech to reporters, with no restriction on further distribution or copying, even though this enabled the media to reproduce and distribute numerous copies to the public. There were also sharply conflicting decisions on whether distributing copies of motion pictures and television programs for the purpose of public performance was a publication under the 1909 Act; most courts found only a limited distribution. Years later, in *Estate of Martin Luther King, Jr., Inc. v. CBS, Inc.*, 13 F.Supp.2d 1347 (N.D.Ga.1998), a federal district court expressly disagreed with the holding of *King v. Mister Maestro* and granted summary judgment that King's "I Have a Dream" speech entered the public domain because it was publicly distributed without notice during the 1963 March on Washington, but the court of appeals reversed, finding genuine issues of material fact as to whether the alleged instances of distribution were controlled and/or unauthorized. See *Estate of Martin Luther King, Jr. v. CBS, Inc.*, 194 F.3d 1211 (11th Cir.1999). The case was subsequently settled.

In 2003, a District Court in the Southern District of New York invalidated a pre–1976 copyright for publication without notice. *Penguin Books U.S.A., Inc. v. New Christian Church of Full Endeavor, Ltd.*, 288 F.Supp.2d 544 (S.D.N.Y. 2003). The court found a pattern of distribution of the religious text to anyone who expressed an interest in the text, including people who were unknown to the author and publisher.

(ii) Public Performances and Displays

In *Ferris v. Frohman*, 223 U.S. 424, 32 S.Ct. 263, 56 L.Ed. 492 (1912), the Supreme Court concluded that public performance of a work did not constitute publication under the 1909 Act. Public displays were the subject of numerous precedents, including one Supreme Court decision that predated the 1909 Act. See *American Tobacco Co. v. Werckmeister*, 207 U.S. 284, 28 S.Ct. 72, 52 L.Ed. 208 (1907) (divestive publication did not occur when a picture was publicly displayed without a copyright notice, because the rules of the exhibition prohibited copying, but such publication might be found where the artist took "no measure to protect" against copying). The courts generally agreed that no publication would be found where a work was publicly displayed without notice, as long as the circumstances evidenced that the author did not intend to forfeit copyright. This was usually established by showing that the viewers were subject to restrictions on copying. See, *e.g., Letter Edged in Black Press, Inc. v. Public Building Commission*, 320 F.Supp. 1303 (N.D.Ill.1970).

The 1976 Act expressly excludes public performances and displays from the definition of "publication" in section 101.

(iii) Public Distributions of Sound Recordings and Other Derivative Works as Publication of Underlying Work

A persistent question under the 1909 Act was whether public distribution of a sound recording or motion picture (or, for that matter, any other derivative work) amounted to publication of the underlying musical, dramatic or literary composition.[3]

In the case of sound recordings, cases interpreting the 1909 Act reached conflicting conclusions until Congressional action finally resolved the matter in 1997. Compare *Rosette v. Rainbo Record Mfg. Corp.,* 354 F.Supp. 1183 (S.D.N.Y.1973), *aff'd per curiam,* 546 F.2d 461 (2d Cir.1976) (sale of phonograph records did not constitute "publication" of the musical composition, based on the holding in *White–Smith Music Pub. Co. v. Apollo Co.,* 209 U.S. 1, 17–18, 28 S.Ct. 319, 323, 52 L.Ed. 655 (1908), that for copyright purposes only an object from which a musical composition was visually perceptible could be a "copy" of the composition, a decision which Congress did not expressly overrule in the 1909 Act) *with La Cienega Music Co. v. ZZ Top,* 53 F.3d 950 (9th Cir.1995) (expressly rejecting *Rosette*), *cert. denied,* 516 U.S. 927, 116 S.Ct. 331, 133 L.Ed.2d 231 (1995). The consequence of finding publication was highly significant; the phonorecords in question typically bore no copyright notice for the underlying composition; indeed, sound recordings fixed before February 15, 1972 did not bear a copyright notice at all, because they were not eligible for federal copyright. If distribution of the phonorecords published the underlying works, then these works entered the public domain. Otherwise, assuming that the underlying compositions had not also been distributed as sheet music, they retained their perpetual common law copyright (until January 1, 1978, at which time unpublished works became subject to the statutory term, as discussed in Section B, *infra*). In 1997, an amendment to the Copyright Act (prompted by the result in *La Cienega*) provided that the distribution of a phonorecord is not a publication of the underlying musical work. The U.S. Court of Appeals for the Ninth Circuit has subsequently held that the new Section 303(b) applies retroactively because it is not a change in the law, merely a clarification. See *ABKCO Music, Inc. v. LaVere,* 217 F.3d 684 (9th Cir.2000) (reversing a summary judgement, the court held that the legislation explicitly applies to conduct occurring before January 1, 1978).

With respect to derivative works other than sound recordings—motion pictures, for example—the resolution does not involve the distinction between copies and phonorecords, and yet, until recently, there was surprisingly little direct authority on the question whether publishing the derivative work also publishes the underlying work. In *Shoptalk Ltd. v. Concorde–New Horizons Corp.,* 168 F.3d 586 (2d Cir.1999), *cert. denied,* 527 U.S. 1038, 119 S.Ct. 2399, 144 L.Ed.2d 798 (1999), the Second Circuit held that publication in 1960 of a film constituted publication of the previously-unpublished screenplay, which as a result entered the public domain. The court rejected the argument that section

3. Under the 1976 Act, before notice became optional, this question was addressed by requiring notice on "copies" but not on "phonorecords" of musical works. See H.R. Rep. No. 1476, 94th Cong., 2d Sess. 145 (1976); 17 U.S.C.A. § 402 (prior to amendment by Berne Convention Implementation Act of 1988); 17 U.S.C.A. § 101 (definition of "copies").

7 of the 1909 Act preserved common law rights in unpublished works incorporated in derivative works. Should the same result follow in the case of films published between January 1, 1978 and March 1, 1989?

Note

If a work is made available to the public only by digital transmission (for example, by "posting" it on a computer bulletin board or including it in an electronic library or other database available to the public in general or to participants in a subscriber service), does this constitute publication under current law? Should it?

B. DURATION

Statutes: 17 U.S.C.A. §§ 101 (as needed), 302–05

1. 1909 AND 1976 ACTS COMPARED

COPYRIGHT ACT OF 1976

H.R. Rep. No. 94–1476.
94th Cong., 2d Sess. 133–35 (1976).

* * *

Section 302. Duration of Copyright in Works Created After Effective Date

In general

The debate over how long a copyright should last is as old as the oldest copyright statute and will doubtless continue as long as there is a copyright law. * * *

Under the present law statutory copyright protection begins on the date of publication (or on the date of registration in unpublished form) and continues for 28 years from that date; it may be renewed for a second 28 years, making a total potential term of 56 years in all cases. The principal elements of this system—a definite number of years, computed from either publication or registration, with a renewal feature—have been a part of the U.S. copyright law since the first statute in 1790. The arguments for changing this system to one based on the life of the author can be summarized as follows:

1. The present 56–year term is not long enough to insure an author and his dependents the fair economic benefits from his works. Life expectancy has increased substantially, and more and more authors are seeing their works fall into the public domain during their lifetimes, forcing later works to compete with their own early works in which copyright has expired.

2. The tremendous growth in communications media has substantially lengthened the commercial life of a great many works. A

short term is particularly discriminatory against serious works of music, literature, and art, whose value may not be recognized until after many years.

3. Although limitations on the term of copyright are obviously necessary, too short a term harms the author without giving any substantial benefit to the public. * * * In some cases the lack of copyright protection actually restrains dissemination of the work, since publishers and other users cannot risk investing in the work unless assured of exclusive rights.

4. A system based on the life of the author would go a long way toward clearing up the confusion and uncertainty involved in the vague concept of "publication," and would provide a much simpler, clearer method for computing the term. The death of the author is a definite, determinable event, and it would be the only date that a potential user would have to worry about. All of a particular author's works, including successive revisions of them, would fall into the public domain at the same time, thus avoiding the present problems of determining a multitude of publication dates and of distinguishing "old" and "new" matter in later editions. The bill answers the problems of determining when relatively obscure authors died, by establishing a registry of death dates and a system of presumptions.

5. One of the worst features of the present copyright law is the provision for renewal of copyright. A substantial burden and expense, this unclear and highly technical requirement results in incalculable amounts of unproductive work. In a number of cases it is the cause of inadvertent and unjust loss of copyright. Under a life-plus–50 system the renewal device would be inappropriate and unnecessary.

6. Under the preemption provisions of section 301 and the single Federal system they would establish, authors will be giving up perpetual, unlimited exclusive common law rights in their unpublished works, including works that have been widely disseminated by means other than publication. A statutory term of life-plus–50 years is no more than a fair recompense for the loss of these perpetual rights.

7. A very large majority of the world's countries have adopted a copyright term of the life of the author and 50 years after the author's death. * * * Without this change, the possibility of future United States adherence to the Berne Copyright Union would evaporate * * *.

* * *

Based on sentiments like the ones reflected in the passage excerpted above from the legislative history, Congress enacted the 1976 General Copyright Revision with provisions establishing a statutory term of life plus 50 years for individually authored works, and alternative provisions establishing terms of 75 years from publication or 100 years from creation (whichever occurred first) for all other works, including works for hire as well as anonymous and pseudonymous works.

Meanwhile, most European countries began to move toward providing a copyright term of life plus 70 years—while limiting protection of U.S. works to life plus 50 years because that remained the maximum protection which U.S. law afforded to works originating in those countries. Pressure in the United States to match the European terms mounted accordingly, and Congress finally responded in 1998.

The Sony Bono Copyright Term Extension Act (SBCTEA), Pub. L. No. 105–298 (signed Oct. 27, 1998) added 20 years to U.S. copyright terms, effective October 27, 1998. Although section 304(b) was amended to grant the additional 20 years of protection to older works whose renewal terms had not yet expired, works whose renewal terms had expired as of that date received no additional term of protection. The new law also amended section 301(c) to postpone preemption of state copyright laws protecting pre-February 15, 1972 sound recordings for an additional 20 years, until February 15, 2067, and amended section 303 to add another 20 years to the minimum copyright terms of works that were created before 1978 and first published between January 1, 1978 and December 31, 2002.

In *Eldred v. Reno,* 74 F.Supp.2d 1, 3 (D.D.C.1999), the district court refused to hold that the SBCTEA was invalid under either the "limited times" language of the Intellectual Property Clause or the First Amendment, or that Congress had exceeded its authority under the clause by giving the benefit of the extended term to copyright assignees rather than solely to authors. The D.C. Circuit affirmed the decision in favor of the government. See *Eldred v. Reno*, 239 F.3d 372 (D.C.Cir.2001) (holding, inter alia, that copyright is "categorically immune" to First Amendment challenges). The Supreme Court thereafter granted certiorari in *Eldred v. Ashcroft*, 122 S.Ct. 1062, *modified*, 122 S.Ct. 1170 (2002), a grant limited to two issues: first, whether Congress has the power under the Intellectual Property Clause to extend terms of copyright retrospectively in unexpired works; and second, whether that extension is categorically immune to First Amendment challenge.

ELDRED v. ASHCROFT

Supreme Court of the United States, 2003.
537 U.S. 186, 123 S.Ct. 769, 154 L.Ed.2d 683, *rehearing denied*
538 U.S. 916, 123 S.Ct. 1505, 155 L.Ed.2d 243 (2003).

JUSTICE GINSBURG delivered the opinion of the court.

* * *

... Under the CTEA, most copyrights now run from creation until 70 years after the author's death. 17 U.S.C. § 302(a). Petitioners do not challenge the "life-plus–70–years" timespan itself.... Congress went awry, petitioners maintain, not with respect to newly created works, but in enlarging the term for published works with existing copyrights. The "limited Tim[e]" in effect when a copyright is secured, petitioners urge, becomes the constitutional boundary, a clear line beyond the power of Congress to extend. *See* [Brief of Petitioners 14]. As to the First Amendment, petitioners contend that the CTEA is a content-neutral regulation of speech that fails inspection under the heightened judicial scrutiny appropriate for such regulations.

* * *

I

A

We evaluate petitioners' challenge to the constitutionality of the CTEA against the backdrop of Congress' previous exercises of its authority under the Copyright Clause. [The Court reviewed the copyright terms under the 1790 Act (14 years with a 14 year renewal term), 1831 act (28 years with a 14 year renewal term), the 1909 Act (28 years with a 28 year renewal term), and the 1976 Act (author's life plus 50 years).]

* * *

The measure at issue here, the CTEA, installed the fourth major duration extension of federal copyrights.... Retaining the general structure of the 1976 Act, the CTEA enlarges the terms of all existing and future copyrights by 20 years. For works created by identified natural persons, the term now lasts from creation until 70 years after the author's death. 17 U.S.C. § 302(a). This standard harmonizes the baseline United States copyright term with the term adopted by the European Union in 1993. See Council Directive 93/98/EEC of 29 October 1993 Harmonizing the Term of Protection of Copyright and Certain Related Rights, 1993 Official J. Eur. Coms. (L290), p.9 (EU Council Directive 93/98). For anonymous works, pseudonymous works, and works made for hire, the term is 95 years from publication or 120 years from creation, whichever expires first. 17 U.S.C. § 302(c).

Paralleling the 1976 Act, the CTEA applies these new terms to all works not published by January 1, 1978. §§ 302(a), 303(a). For works published before 1978 with existing copyrights as of the CTEA's effective date, the CTEA extends the term to 95 years from publication. §§ 304(a) and (b). Thus, in common with the 1831, 1909, and 1976 Acts, the CTEA's new terms apply to both future and existing copyrights....

* * *

II

A

We address first the determination of the courts below that Congress has authority under the Copyright Clause to extend the terms of existing copyrights. Text, history, and precedent, we conclude, confirm that the Copyright Clause empowers Congress to prescribe "limited

Times" for copyright protection and to secure the same level and duration of protection for all copyright holders, present and future.

The CTEA's baseline term of life plus 70 years, petitioners concede, qualifies as a "limited Tim[e]" as applied to future copyrights.... Petitioners contend, however, that existing copyrights extended to endure for that same term are not "limited." Petitioners' argument essentially reads into the text of the Copyright Clause the command that a time prescription, once set, becomes forever "fixed" or "inalterable." The word "limited," however, does not convey a meaning so constricted. At the time of the Framing, that word meant what it means today: "confine[d] within certain bounds," "restrain[ed]," or "circumscribe[d]." S. Johnson, A Dictionary of the English Language (7th ed. 1785); see T. Sheridan, A Complete Dictionary of the English Language (6th ed. 1796) ("confine[d] within certain bounds"); Webster's Third New International Dictionary 1312 (1976) ("confined within limits"; "restricted in extent, number, or duration"). Thus understood, a timespan appropriately "limited" as applied to future copyrights does not automatically cease to be "limited" when applied to existing copyrights. And as we observe, *infra* ... , there is no cause to suspect that a purpose to evade the "limited Times" prescription prompted Congress to adopt the CTEA.

To comprehend the scope of Congress' power under the Copyright Clause, "a page of history is worth a volume of logic." *New York Trust Co. v. Eisner*, 256 U.S. 345, 349, 41 S.Ct. 506, 65 L.Ed. 963 (1921) (Holmes, J.). History reveals an unbroken congressional practice of granting to authors of works with existing copyrights the benefit of term extensions so that all under copyright protection will be governed evenhandedly under the same regime. As earlier recounted, see *supra* ... , the First Congress accorded the protections of the Nation's first federal copyright statute to existing and future works alike. 1790 Act § 1. Since then, Congress has regularly applied duration extensions to both existing and future copyrights. 1831 Act §§ 1, 16; 1909 Act §§ 23–24; 1976 Act §§ 302–303; 17 U.S.C. §§ 302–304.[1]

Because the Clause empowering Congress to confer copyrights also authorizes patents, congressional practice with respect to patents informs our inquiry. We count it significant that early Congresses extended the duration of numerous individual patents as well as copyrights. See, e.g., Act of Jan. 7, 1808, ch. 6, 6 Stat. 70 (patent); Act of Mar. 3,

---

1. Moreover, the precise duration of a federal copyright has never been fixed at the time of the initial grant. The 1790 Act provided a federal copyright term of 14 years from the work's publication, renewable for an additional 14 years if the author survived and applied for an additional term. § 1. Congress retained that approach in subsequent statutes. See *Stewart v. Abend*, 495 U.S. 207, 217, 110 S.Ct. 1750, 109 L.Ed.2d 184 (1990) ("Since the earliest copyright statute in this country, the copyright term of ownership has been split between an original term and a renewal term."). Similarly, under the method for measuring copyright terms established by the 1976 Act and retained by the CTEA, the baseline copyright term is measured in part by the life of the author, rendering its duration indeterminate at the time of the grant. See 1976 Act § 302(a); 17 U.S.C. § 302(a).

1809, ch. 35, 6 Stat. 80 (patent); Act of Feb. 7, 1815, ch. 36, 6 Stat. 147 (patent); Act of May 24, 1828, ch. 145, 6 Stat. 389 (copyright); Act of Feb. 11, 1830, ch. 13, 6 Stat. 403 (copyright); see generally Ochoa, Patent and Copyright Term Extension and the Constitution: A Historical Perspective, 49 J. Copyright Soc. 19 (2001). The courts saw no "limited Times" impediment to such extensions; renewed or extended terms were upheld in the early days, for example, by Chief Justice Marshall and Justice Story sitting as circuit justices. See *Evans v. Jordan*, 8 F. Cas. 872, 874 (No. 4,564) (CC Va. 1813) (Marshall, J.) ("Th[e] construction of the constitution which admits the renewal of a patent, is not controverted. A renewed patent ... confers the same rights, with an original."), aff'd, 9 Cranch 199, 3 L.Ed. 704 (1815); *Blanchard v. Sprague*, 3 F. Cas. 648, 650 (No. 1,518) (CC Mass. 1839) (Story, J.) ("I never have entertained any doubt of the constitutional authority of congress" to enact a 14–year patent extension that "operates retrospectively"); see also *Evans v. Robinson*, 8 F. Cas. 886, 888 (No. 4,571) (CC Md. 1813) (Congresses "have the exclusive right ... to limit the times for which a patent right shall be granted, and are not restrained from renewing a patent or prolonging" it.).

Further, although prior to the instant case this Court did not have occasion to decide whether extending the duration of existing copyrights complies with the "limited Times" prescription, the Court has found no constitutional barrier to the legislative expansion of existing patents. *McClurg v. Kingsland*, 1 How. 202, 11 L.Ed. 102 (1843), is the pathsetting precedent. The patentee in that case was unprotected under the law in force when the patent issued because he had allowed his employer briefly to practice the invention before he obtained the patent. Only upon enactment, two years later, of an exemption for such allowances did the patent become valid, retroactive to the time it issued. *McClurg* upheld retroactive application of the new law. The Court explained that the legal regime governing a particular patent "depend[s] on the law as it stood at the emanation of the patent, together with such changes as have been since made; for though they may be retrospective in their operation, that is not a sound objection to their validity." *Id.*, at 206. Neither is it a sound objection to the validity of a copyright term extension, enacted pursuant to the same constitutional grant of authority, that the enlarged term covers existing copyrights.

Congress' consistent historical practice of applying newly enacted copyright terms to future and existing copyrights reflects a judgment stated concisely by Representative Huntington at the time of the 1831 Act: "[J]ustice, policy, and equity alike forb[id]" that an "author who had sold his [work] a week ago, be placed in a worse situation than the author who should sell his work the day after the passing of [the] act." 7 Cong. Deb. 424 (1831); accord, Symposium, The Constitutionality of Copyright Term Extension, 18 Cardozo Arts & Ent. L.J. 651, 694 (2000) (Prof.Miller) ("[S]ince 1790, it has indeed been Congress's policy that the author of yesterday's work should not get a lesser reward than the author of tomorrow's work just because Congress passed a statute lengthening the term today.''). The CTEA follows this historical practice by keeping the duration provisions of the 1976 Act largely in place and simply adding 20 years to each of them. Guided by text, history, and precedent, we cannot agree with petitioners' submission that extending the duration of existing copyrights is categorically beyond Congress' authority under the Copyright Clause.

Satisfied that the CTEA complies with the "limited Times" prescription, we turn now to whether it is a rational exercise of the legislative authority conferred by the Copyright Clause. On that point, we defer substantially to Congress. *Sony Corp. of America v. Universal City Studios, Inc.*, 464 U.S. 417, 429, 104 S.Ct. 774 ("[I]t is Congress that has been assigned the task of defining the scope of the limited monopoly that should be granted to authors . . . in order to give the public appropriate access to their work product.").

The CTEA reflects judgments of a kind Congress typically makes, judgments we cannot dismiss as outside the Legislature's domain. As respondent describes, see Brief for Respondent 37–38, a key factor in the CTEA's passage was a 1993 European Union (EU) directive instructing EU members to establish a copyright term of life plus 70 years. EU Council Directive 93/98, Art. 1(1), p. 11; see 144 Cong. Rec. S12377–S12378 (daily ed. Oct. 12, 1998) (statement of Sen. Hatch). Consistent with the Berne Convention, the EU directed its members to deny this longer term to the works of any non-EU country whose laws did not secure the same extended term. See Berne Conv. Art. 7(8); P. Goldstein, International Copyright § 5.3, p. 239 (2001). By extending the baseline United States copyright term to life plus 70 years, Congress sought to ensure that American authors would receive the same copyright protection in Europe as their European counterparts. . . . The CTEA may also provide greater incentive for American and other authors to create and disseminate their work in the United States. See Perlmutter, Participation in the International Copyright System as a Means to Promote the Progress of Science and Useful Arts, 36 Loyola (LA) L.Rev. 323, 330 (2002) ("[M]atching th[e] level of [copyright] protection in the United States [to that in the EU] can ensure stronger protection for U.S. works abroad and avoid competitive disadvantages vis à vis foreign rightholders."); see also *id.*, at 332 (the United States could not "play a leadership role" in the give-and-take evolution of the international copyright system, indeed it would "lose all flexibility," "if the only way to promote the progress of science were to provide incentives to create new works").

In addition to international concerns, Congress passed the CTEA in light of demographic, economic, and technological changes, Brief for Respondent 25–26, 33, and nn. 23 and 24,[5] and rationally credited

---

5. Members of Congress expressed the view that, as a result of increases in human longevity and in parents' average age when their children are born, the pre-CTEA term did not adequately secure "the right to profit from licensing one's work during one's lifetime and to take pride and comfort in knowing that one's children—and perhaps their children—might also benefit from one's posthumous popularity." 141 Cong. Rec. 6553 (1995) (statement of Sen. Feinstein); see 144 Cong. Rec. S12377 (daily

projections that longer terms would encourage copyright holders to invest in the restoration and public distribution of their works, id., at 34–37; see H.R.Rep. No. 105–452, p. 4 (1998) (term extension "provide[s] copyright owners generally with the incentive to restore older works and further disseminate them to the public").…

In sum, we find that the CTEA is a rational enactment; we are not at liberty to second-guess congressional determinations and policy judgments of this order, however debatable or arguably unwise they may be. Accordingly, we cannot conclude that the CTEA—which continues the unbroken congressional practice of treating future and existing copyrights in parity for term extension purposes—is an impermissible exercise of Congress' power under the Copyright Clause.

B

Petitioners' Copyright Clause arguments rely on several novel readings of the Clause. We next address these arguments and explain why we find them unpersuasive.

1

Petitioners contend that even if the CTEA's 20–year term extension is literally a "limited Tim[e]," permitting Congress to extend existing copyrights allows it to evade the "limited Times" constraint by creating effectively perpetual copyrights through repeated extensions. We disagree.

As the Court of Appeals observed, a regime of perpetual copyrights "clearly is not the situation before us." 239 F.3d, at 379. Nothing before this Court warrants construction of the CTEA's 20–year term extension as a congressional attempt to evade or override the "limited Times" constraint. Critically, we again emphasize, petitioners fail to show how the CTEA crosses a constitutionally significant threshold with respect to "limited Times" that the 1831, 1909, and 1976 Acts did not. See Austin, Does the Copyright Clause Mandate Isolationism? 26 Colum.J.L. & Arts 17, 56 (2002) ("If extending copyright protection to works already in existence is constitutionally suspect," so is "extending the protections of U. S copyright law to works by foreign authors that had already been created and even first published when the federal rights attached."). Those earlier Acts did not create perpetual copyrights, and neither does the CTEA.

ed. Oct. 12, 1998) (statement of Sen. Hatch) ("Among the main developments [compelling reconsideration of the 1976 Act's term] is the effect of demographic trends, such as increasing longevity and the trend toward rearing children later in life, on the effectiveness of the life-plus–50 term to provide adequate protection for American creators and their heirs."). Also cited was "the failure of the U.S. copyright term to keep pace with the substantially increased commercial life of copyrighted works resulting from the rapid growth in communications media." *Ibid.* (statement of Sen. Hatch); cf. *Sony*, 464 U.S., at 430–431, 104 S.Ct. 774 ("From its beginning, the law of copyright has developed in response to significant changes in technology.… [A]s new developments have occurred in this country, it has been the Congress that has fashioned the new rules that new technology made necessary.").

2

Petitioners dominantly advance a series of arguments all premised on the proposition that Congress may not extend an existing copyright absent new consideration from the author. They pursue this main theme under three headings. Petitioners contend that the CTEA's extension of existing copyrights (1) overlooks the requirement of "originality," (2) fails to "promote the Progress of Science," and (3) ignores copyright's quid pro quo.

Petitioners' "originality" argument draws on *Feist Publications, Inc. v. Rural Telephone Service Co.*, 499 U.S. 340, 111 S.Ct. 1282, 113 L.Ed.2d 358 (1991). In *Feist*, we observed that "[t]he *sine qua non* of copyright is originality," *id.*, at 345, 111 S.Ct. 1282, and held that copyright protection is unavailable to "a narrow category of works in which the creative spark is utterly lacking or so trivial as to be virtually nonexistent," *id.*, at 359, 111 S.Ct. 1282. Relying on *Feist*, petitioners urge that even if a work is sufficiently "original" to qualify for copyright protection in the first instance, any extension of the copyright's duration is impermissible because, once published, a work is no longer original.

Feist, however, did not touch on the duration of copyright protection. Rather, the decision addressed the core question of copyrightability, i.e., the "creative spark" a work must have to be eligible for copyright protection at all. Explaining the originality requirement, *Feist* trained on the Copyright Clause words "Authors" and "Writings." *Id.*, at 346–347, 111 S.Ct. 1282. The decision did not construe the "limited Times" for which a work may be protected, and the originality requirement has no bearing on that prescription.

More forcibly, petitioners contend that the CTEA's extension of existing copyrights does not "promote the Progress of Science" as contemplated by the preambular language of the Copyright Clause. Art. I, § 8, cl. 8. To sustain this objection, petitioners do not argue that the Clause's preamble is an independently enforceable limit on Congress' power. See 239 F.3d, at 378 (Petitioners acknowledge that "the preamble of the Copyright Clause is not a substantive limit on Congress' legislative power." (internal quotation marks omitted)). Rather, they maintain that the preambular language identifies the sole end to which Congress may legislate; accordingly, they conclude, the meaning of "limited Times" must be "determined in light of that specified end." Brief for Petitioners 19. The CTEA's extension of existing copyrights categorically fails to "promote the Progress of Science," petitioners argue, because it does not stimulate the creation of new works but merely adds value to works already created.

As petitioners point out, we have described the Copyright Clause as "both a grant of power and a limitation," *Graham v. John Deere Co. of Kansas City*, 383 U.S. 1, 5, 86 S.Ct. 684, 15 L.Ed.2d 545 (1966), and have said that "[t]he primary objective of copyright" is "[t]o promote the Progress of Science," *Feist*, 499 U.S., at 349, 111 S.Ct. 1282. The "constitutional command," we have recognized, is that Congress, to the extent it enacts copyright laws at all, create a "system" that "promote[s] the Progress of Science." *Graham*, 383 U.S., at 6, 86 S.Ct. 684.[6]

We have also stressed, however, that it is generally for Congress, not the courts, to decide how best to pursue the Copyright Clause's objectives. See *Stewart v. Abend*, 495 U.S., at 230, 110 S.Ct. 1750 ("Th[e] evolution of the duration of copyright protection tellingly illustrates the difficulties Congress faces.... [I]t is not our role to alter the delicate balance Congress has labored to achieve."); *Sony*, 464 U.S., at 429, 104 S.Ct. 774 ("[I]t is Congress that has been assigned the task of defining the scope of [rights] that should be granted to authors or to inventors in order to give the public appropriate access to their work product."); *Graham*, 383 U.S., at 6, 86 S.Ct. 684 ("Within the limits of the constitutional grant, the Congress may, of course, implement the stated purpose of the Framers by selecting the policy which in its judgment best effectuates the constitutional aim."). The justifications we earlier set out for Congress' enactment of the CTEA, *supra* ... , provide a rational basis for the conclusion that the CTEA "promote[s] the Progress of Science."

On the issue of copyright duration, Congress, from the start, has routinely applied new definitions or adjustments of the copyright term to both future works and existing works not yet in the public domain.... Such consistent congressional practice is entitled to "very great weight, and when it is remembered that the rights thus established have not been disputed during a period of [over two] centur[ies], it is almost conclusive." *Burrow-Giles Lithographic Co. v. Sarony*, 111 U.S., at 57, 4 S.Ct. 279. Indeed, "[t]his Court has repeatedly laid down the principle that a contemporaneous legislative exposition of the Constitution when the founders of our Government and framers of our Constitution were actively participating in public affairs, acquiesced in for a long term of years, fixes the construction to be given [the Constitution's] provisions." *Myers v. United States*, 272 U.S. 52, 175, 47 S.Ct. 21, 71 L.Ed. 160 (1926). Congress' unbroken practice since the founding generation thus overwhelms petitioners' argument that the CTEA's extension of existing copyrights fails per se to "promote the Progress of Science."

---

6. Justice STEVENS' characterization of reward to the author as "a secondary consideration" of copyright law, *post* [], n. 4 (internal quotation marks omitted), understates the relationship between such rewards and the "Progress of Science." As we have explained, "[t]he economic philosophy behind the [Copyright] [C]lause ... is the conviction that encouragement of individual effort by personal gain is the best way to advance public welfare through the talents of authors and inventors." *Mazer v. Stein*, 347 U.S. 201, 219, 74 S.Ct. 460, 98 L.Ed. 630 (1954). Accordingly, "copyright law celebrates the profit motive, recognizing that the incentive to profit from the exploitation of copyrights will redound to the public benefit by resulting in the proliferation of knowledge.... The profit motive is the engine that ensures the progress of science." *American Geophysical Union v. Texaco Inc.*, 802 F.Supp. 1, 27 (S.D.N.Y.1992), aff'd, 60 F.3d 913 (C.A.2 1994). Rewarding authors for their creative labor and "promot[ing] ... Progress" are thus complementary; as James Madison observed, in copyright "[t]he public good fully coincides ... with the claims of individuals." The Federalist No. 43, p. 272 (C. Rossiter ed.1961). Justice BREYER's assertion that "copyright statutes must serve public, not private, ends," *post* [], similarly misses the mark. The two ends are not mutually exclusive; copyright law serves public ends by providing individuals with an incentive to pursue private ones.

Closely related to petitioners' preambular argument, or a variant of it, is their assertion that the Copyright Clause "imbeds a quid pro quo." Brief for Petitioners 23. They contend, in this regard, that Congress may grant to an "Autho[r]" an "exclusive Right" for a "limited Tim[e]," but only in exchange for a "Writin[g]." Congress' power to confer copyright protection, petitioners argue, is thus contingent upon an exchange: The author of an original work receives an "exclusive Right" for a "limited Tim[e]" in exchange for a dedication to the public thereafter. Extending an existing copyright without demanding additional consideration, petitioners maintain, bestows an unpaid-for benefit on copyright holders and their heirs, in violation of the quid pro quo requirement.

We can demur to petitioners' description of the Copyright Clause as a grant of legislative authority empowering Congress "to secure a bargain—this for that." *Id.*, at 16; see *Mazer v. Stein*, 347 U.S. 201, 219, 74 S.Ct. 460, 98 L.Ed. 630 (1954) ("The economic philosophy behind the clause empowering Congress to grant patents and copyrights is the conviction that encouragement of individual effort by personal gain is the best way to advance public welfare through the talents of authors and inventors in 'Science and useful Arts.'"). But the legislative evolution earlier recalled demonstrates what the bargain entails. Given the consistent placement of existing copyright holders in parity with future holders, the author of a work created in the last 170 years would reasonably comprehend, as the "this" offered her, a copyright not only for the time in place when protection is gained, but also for any renewal or extension legislated during that time.[7] Congress could rationally seek to "promote ... Progress" by including in every copyright statute an express guarantee that authors would receive the benefit of any later legislative extension of the copyright term. Nothing in the Copyright Clause bars Congress from creating the same incentive by adopting the same position as a matter of unbroken practice. See Brief for Respondent 31–32.

* * *

We note, furthermore, that patents and copyrights do not entail the same exchange, and that our references to a quid pro quo typically appear in the patent context. See, e.g., *J.E.M. Ag Supply, Inc. v. Pioneer Hi–Bred International, Inc.*, 534 U.S. 124, 142, 122 S.Ct. 593, 151 L.Ed.2d 508 (2001) ("The disclosure required by the Patent Act is 'the

---

7. Standard copyright assignment agreements reflect this expectation. See, e.g., A. Kohn & B. Kohn, Music Licensing 471 (3d ed.1992–2002) (short form copyright assignment for musical composition, under which assignor conveys all rights to the work, "including the copyrights and proprietary rights therein and in any and all versions of said musical composition(s), and any renewals and extensions thereof (whether presently available or *subsequently available as a result of intervening legislation*)" (emphasis added)); 5 M. Nimmer & D. Nimmer, Copyright § 21.11[B], p. 21–305 (2002) (short form copyright assignment under which assignor conveys all assets relating to the work, "including without limitation, copyrights and renewals and/or extensions thereof"); 6 id., § 30.04[B][1], p. 30–325 (form composer-producer agreement under which composer "assigns to Producer all rights (copyrights, rights under copyright and otherwise, whether now or hereafter known) and all renewals and extensions (as may now or hereafter exist)").

quid pro quo of the right to exclude.'" (quoting *Kewanee Oil Co. v. Bicron Corp.*, 416 U.S. 470, 484, 94 S.Ct. 1879, 40 L.Ed.2d 315 (1974))); *Bonito Boats, Inc. v. Thunder Craft Boats, Inc.*, 489 U.S. 141, 161, 109 S.Ct. 971 (1989) ("the quid pro quo of substantial creative effort required by the federal [patent] statute"); *Brenner v. Manson*, 383 U.S. 519, 534, 86 S.Ct. 1033, 16 L.Ed.2d 69 (1966) ("The basic quid pro quo ... for granting a patent monopoly is the benefit derived by the public from an invention with substantial utility."); *Pennock v. Dialogue*, 2 Pet. 1, 23, 7 L.Ed. 327 (1829) (If an invention is already commonly known and used when the patent is sought, "there might be sound reason for presuming, that the legislature did not intend to grant an exclusive right," given the absence of a "quid pro quo."). This is understandable, given that immediate disclosure is not the objective of, but is exacted from, the patentee. It is the price paid for the exclusivity secured. See *J.E.M. Ag Supply*, 534 U.S., at 142, 122 S.Ct. 593. For the author seeking copyright protection, in contrast, disclosure is the desired objective, not something exacted from the author in exchange for the copyright. Indeed, since the 1976 Act, copyright has run from creation, not publication. See 1976 Act § 302(a); 17 U.S.C. § 302(a).

Further distinguishing the two kinds of intellectual property, copyright gives the holder no monopoly on any knowledge. A reader of an author's writing may make full use of any fact or idea she acquires from her reading. See § 102(b). The grant of a patent, on the other hand, does prevent full use by others of the inventor's knowledge. See Brief for Respondent 22; *Alfred Bell & Co. v. Catalda Fine Arts*, 191 F.2d 99, 103, n. 16 (C.A.2 1951) (The monopoly granted by a copyright "is not a monopoly of knowledge. The grant of a patent does prevent full use being made of knowledge, but the reader of a book is not by the copyright laws prevented from making full use of any information he may acquire from his reading." (quoting W. Copinger, Law of Copyright 2 (7th ed.1936))). In light of these distinctions, one cannot extract from language in our patent decisions—language not trained on a grant's duration—genuine support for petitioners' bold view. Accordingly, we reject the proposition that a quid pro quo requirement stops Congress from expanding copyright's term in a manner that puts existing and future copyrights in parity.

* * *

For the several reasons stated, we find no Copyright Clause impediment to the CTEA's extension of existing copyrights.

III

Petitioners separately argue that the CTEA is a content-neutral regulation of speech that fails heightened judicial review under the First Amendment.... We reject petitioners' plea for imposition of uncommonly strict scrutiny on a copyright scheme that incorporates its own speech-protective purposes and safeguards. The Copyright Clause and First Amendment were adopted close in time. This proximity indicates that, in the Framers' view, copyright's limited monopolies are compatible with free speech principles. Indeed, copyright's purpose is to promote the creation and publication of free expression. As *Harper & Row* observed: "[T]he Framers intended copyright itself to be the engine of free expression. By establishing a marketable right to the use of one's expression, copyright supplies the economic incentive to create and disseminate ideas." 471 U.S., at 558, 105 S.Ct. 2218.

In addition to spurring the creation and publication of new expression, copyright law contains built-in First Amendment accommodations. See *id.*, at 560, 105 S.Ct. 2218. First, it distinguishes between ideas and expression and makes only the latter eligible for copyright protection. Specifically, 17 U.S.C. § 102(b) provides: "In no case does copyright protection for an original work of authorship extend to any idea, procedure, process, system, method of operation, concept, principle, or discovery, regardless of the form in which it is described, explained, illustrated, or embodied in such work." As we said in *Harper & Row*, this "idea/expression dichotomy strike[s] a definitional balance between the First Amendment and the Copyright Act by permitting free communication of facts while still protecting an author's expression." 471 U.S., at 556, 105 S.Ct. 2218 (internal quotation marks omitted). Due to this distinction, every idea, theory, and fact in a copyrighted work becomes instantly available for public exploitation at the moment of publication. See *Feist*, 499 U.S., at 349–350, 111 S.Ct. 1282.

Second, the "fair use" defense allows the public to use not only facts and ideas contained in a copyrighted work, but also expression itself in certain circumstances. Codified at 17 U.S.C. § 107, the defense provides: "[T]he fair use of a copyrighted work, including such use by reproduction in copies ..., for purposes such as criticism, comment, news reporting, teaching (including multiple copies for classroom use), scholarship, or research, is not an infringement of copyright." The fair use defense affords considerable "latitude for scholarship and comment," *Harper & Row*, 471 U.S., at 560, 105 S.Ct. 2218, and even for parody, see *Campbell v. Acuff–Rose Music, Inc.*, 510 U.S. 569, 114 S.Ct. 1164, 127 L.Ed.2d 500 (1994) (rap group's musical parody of Roy Orbison's "Oh, Pretty Woman" may be fair use).

The CTEA itself supplements these traditional First Amendment safeguards. First, it allows libraries, archives, and similar institutions to "reproduce" and "distribute, display, or perform in facsimile or digital form" copies of certain published works "during the last 20 years of any term of copyright ... for purposes of preservation, scholarship, or research" if the work is not already being exploited commercially and further copies are unavailable at a reasonable price. 17 U.S.C. § 108(h); see Brief for Respondent 36. Second, Title II of the CTEA, known as the Fairness in Music Licensing Act of 1998, exempts small businesses, restaurants, and like entities from having to pay performance royalties on music played from licensed radio, television, and similar facilities. 17 U.S.C. § 110(5)(B); see Brief for Representative F. James Sensenbrenner, Jr., et al. as Amici Curiae 5–6, n. 3.

Finally, the case petitioners principally rely upon for their First Amendment argument, *Turner Broadcasting System, Inc. v. FCC*, 512 U.S. 622, 114 S.Ct. 2445, 129 L.Ed.2d 497 (1994), bears little on copyright. The statute at issue in Turner required cable operators to carry and transmit broadcast stations through their proprietary cable systems. Those "must-carry" provisions, we explained, implicated "the heart of the First Amendment," namely, "the principle that each person should decide for himself or herself the ideas and beliefs deserving of expression, consideration, and adherence." *Id.*, at 641, 114 S.Ct. 2445.

The CTEA, in contrast, does not oblige anyone to reproduce another's speech against the carrier's will. Instead, it protects authors' original expression from unrestricted exploitation. Protection of that order does not raise the free speech concerns present when the government compels or burdens the communication of particular facts or ideas. The First Amendment securely protects the freedom to make—or decline to make—one's own speech; it bears less heavily when speakers assert the right to make other people's speeches. To the extent such assertions raise First Amendment concerns, copyright's built-in free speech safeguards are generally adequate to address them. We recognize that the D.C. Circuit spoke too broadly when it declared copyrights "categorically immune from challenges under the First Amendment." 239 F.3d, at 375. But when, as in this case, Congress has not altered the traditional contours of copyright protection, further First Amendment scrutiny is unnecessary. See *Harper & Row*, 471 U.S., at 560, 105 S.Ct. 2218; cf. *San Francisco Arts & Athletics, Inc. v. United States Olympic Comm.*, 483 U.S. 522, 107 S.Ct. 2971, 97 L.Ed.2d 427 (1987)....

IV

If petitioners' vision of the Copyright Clause held sway, it would do more than render the CTEA's duration extensions unconstitutional as to existing works. Indeed, petitioners' assertion that the provisions of the CTEA are not severable would make the CTEA's enlarged terms invalid even as to tomorrow's work. The 1976 Act's time extensions, which set the pattern that the CTEA followed, would be vulnerable as well.

As we read the Framers' instruction, the Copyright Clause empowers Congress to determine the intellectual property regimes that, overall, in that body's judgment, will serve the ends of the Clause. See *Graham*, 383 U.S., at 6, 86 S.Ct. 684 (Congress may "implement the stated purpose of the Framers by selecting the policy which in its judgment best effectuates the constitutional aim." (emphasis added)). Beneath the facade of their inventive constitutional interpretation, petitioners forcefully urge that Congress pursued very bad policy in prescribing the CTEA's long terms. The wisdom of Congress' action, however, is not within our province to second guess. Satisfied that the legislation before us remains inside the domain the Constitution assigns to the First Branch, we affirm the judgment of the Court of Appeals.

* * *

JUSTICE STEVENS, dissenting.

Writing for a unanimous Court in 1964, Justice Black stated that it is obvious that a State could not "extend the life of a patent beyond its expiration date," *Sears, Roebuck & Co. v. Stiffel Co.*, 376 U.S. 225, 231, 84 S.Ct. 784, 11 L.Ed.2d 661 (1964).... [T]he reasons why a State may not extend the life of a patent apply to Congress as well. If Congress may not expand the cope of a patent monopoly, it also may not extend the life of a copyright beyond its expiration date. Accordingly, insofar as the 1998 Sonny Bono Copyright Term Extension Act, 112 Stat. 2827, purported to extend the life of unexpired copyrights, it is invalid. Because the majority's contrary conclusion rests on the mistaken premise that this Court has virtually no role in reviewing congressional grants of monopoly privileges to authors, inventors, and their successors, I respectfully dissent.

I

The authority to issue copyrights stems from the same Clause in the Constitution that created the patent power. * * * Almost two centuries ago the Court plainly stated that public access to inventions at the earliest possible date was the essential purpose of the Clause:

> "While one great object was, by holding out a reasonable reward to inventors and giving them an exclusive right to their inventions for a limited period, to stimulate the efforts of genius; the main object was 'to promote the progress of science and useful arts;' and this could be done best, by giving the public at large a right to make, construct, use, and vend the thing invented, at as early a period as possible, having a due regard to the rights of the inventor. If an inventor should be permitted to hold back from the knowledge of the public the secrets of his invention; if he should for a long period of years retain the monopoly, and make, and sell his invention publicly, and thus gather the whole profits of it, relying upon his superior skill and knowledge of the structure; and then, and then only, when the danger of competition should force him to secure the exclusive right, he should be allowed to take out a patent, and thus exclude the public from any farther use than what should be derived under it during his fourteen years; it would materially retard the progress of science and the useful arts, and give a premium to those, who should be least prompt to communicate their discoveries." *Pennock v. Dialogue*, 2 Pet. 1, 18, 7 L.Ed. 327 (1829).

* * *

The issuance of a patent is appropriately regarded as a *quid pro quo*—the grant of a limited right for the inventor's disclosure and subsequent contribution to the public domain. See, *e.g., Pfaff v. Wells Electronics, Inc.*, 525 U.S. 55, 63, 119 S.Ct. 304, 142 L.Ed.2d 261 (1998) ("[T]he patent system represents a carefully crafted bargain that encourages both the creation and the public disclosure of new and useful advances in technology, in return for an exclusive monopoly for a limited period of time"). It would be manifestly unfair if, after issuing a patent, the Government as a representative of the public sought to modify the bargain by shortening the term of the patent in order to accelerate public access to the invention.... [The considerations protecting against shortening of patent terms] should protect members of the public who make plans to exploit an invention as soon as it enters the public domain from a retroactive modification of the bargain that extends the term of the patent monopoly....

Neither the purpose of encouraging new inventions nor the overriding interest in advancing progress by adding knowledge to the public domain is served by retroactively increasing the inventor's compensation for a completed invention and frustrating the legitimate expectations of members of the public who want to make use of it in a free market. Because those twin purposes provide the only avenue for congressional action under the Copyright/Patent Clause of the Constitution, any other action is manifestly unconstitutional.

II

We have recognized that these twin purposes ... apply to copyrights as well as patents.... [A]s with patents, we have emphasized that the overriding purpose of providing a reward for authors' creative activity is to motivate that activity and "to allow the public access to the products of their genius after the limited period of exclusive control has expired." *Sony Corp. of America v. Universal City Studios, Inc.*, 464 U.S. 417, 429, 104 S.Ct. 774, 78 L.Ed.2d 574 (1984). *Ex post facto* extensions of copyrights result in a gratuitous transfer of wealth from the public to authors, publishers, and their successors in interest. Such retroactive extensions do not even arguably serve either of the purposes of the Copyright/Patent Clause. The reasons why such extensions of the patent monopoly are unconstitutional apply to copyrights as well.

* * *

VII

The express grant of a perpetual copyright would unquestionably violate the textual requirement that the authors' exclusive rights be only "for limited Times." Whether the extraordinary length of the grants authorized by the 1998 Act are invalid because they are the functional equivalent of perpetual copyrights is a question that need not be answered in this case because the question presented by the certiorari petition merely challenges Congress' power to extend retroactively the terms of existing copyrights. Accordingly, there is no need to determine whether the deference that is normally given to congressional policy judgments may save from judicial review its decision respecting the appropriate length of the term.... It is important to note, however, that a categorical rule prohibiting retroactive extensions would effectively preclude perpetual copyrights. More importantly, as the House of Lords recognized when it refused to amend the Statute of Anne in 1735, unless the Clause is construed to embody such a categorical rule, Congress may extend existing monopoly privileges *ad infinitum* under the majority's analysis.

By failing to protect the public interest in free access to the products of inventive and artistic genius—indeed, by virtually ignoring the central purpose of the Copyright/Patent Clause—the Court has quitclaimed to Congress its principal responsibility in this area of the law. Fairly read, the Court has stated that Congress' actions under the Copyright/Patent Clause are, for all intents and purposes, judicially unreviewable. That result cannot be squared with the basic tenets of our constitutional structure. It is not hyperbole to recall the trenchant words of Chief Justice John Marshall: "It is emphatically the province and duty of the judicial department to say what the law is." *Marbury v. Madison*, 1 Cranch 137, 177, 2 L.Ed. 60 (1803). We should discharge that responsibility as we did in *Chadha*.

I respectfully dissent.

JUSTICE BREYER, dissenting.

The Constitution's Copyright Clause grants Congress the power to "promote the Progress of Science ... by securing for limited Times to Authors ... the exclusive Right to their respective Writings." Art. I, § 8, cl. 8 (emphasis added). The statute before us, the 1998 Sonny Bono Copyright Term Extension Act, extends the term of most existing copyrights to 95 years and that of many new copyrights to 70 years after the author's death. The economic effect of this 20–year extension—the longest blanket extension since the Nation's founding—is to make the copyright term not limited, but virtually perpetual. Its primary legal effect is to grant the extended term not to authors, but to their heirs, estates, or corporate successors. And most importantly, its practical effect is not to promote, but to inhibit, the progress of "Science"—by which word the Framers meant learning or knowledge, E. Walterscheid, The Nature of the Intellectual Property Clause: A Study in Historical Perspective 125–126 (2002).

The majority believes these conclusions rest upon practical judgments that at most suggest the statute is unwise, not that it is unconstitutional. Legal distinctions, however, are often matters of degree. *Panhandle Oil Co. v. Mississippi ex rel. Knox*, 277 U.S. 218, 223, 48 S.Ct. 451, 72 L.Ed. 857 (1928) (Holmes, J., dissenting), overruled in part by *Alabama v. King & Boozer*, 314 U.S. 1, 8–9, 62 S.Ct. 43, 86 L.Ed. 3 (1941); accord, *Walz v. Tax Comm'n of City of New York*, 397 U.S. 664, 678–679, 90 S.Ct. 1409, 25 L.Ed.2d 697 (1970). And in this case the failings of degree are so serious that they amount to failings of constitutional kind. Although the Copyright Clause grants broad legislative power to Congress, that grant has limits. And in my view this statute falls outside them.

I

The "monopoly privileges" that the Copyright Clause confers "are neither unlimited nor primarily designed to provide a special private benefit." *Sony Corp. of America v. Universal City Studios, Inc.*, 464 U.S. 417, 429, 104 S.Ct. 774, 78 L.Ed.2d 574 (1984); cf. *Graham v. John Deere Co. of Kansas City*, 383 U.S. 1, 5, 86 S.Ct. 684, 15 L.Ed.2d 545 (1966). This Court has made clear that the Clause's limitations are judicially enforceable. *E.g., Trade–Mark Cases*, 100 U.S. 82, 93–94, 25 L.Ed. 550 (1879). And, in assessing this statute for that purpose, I would take into account the fact that the Constitution is a single document, that it contains both a Copyright Clause and a First Amendment, and that the two are related.

The Copyright Clause and the First Amendment seek related objectives—the creation and dissemination of information. When working in tandem, these provisions mutually reinforce each other, the first serving as an "engine of free expression," *Harper & Row, Publishers, Inc. v. Nation Enterprises*, 471 U.S. 539, 558, 105 S.Ct. 2218, 85 L.Ed.2d 588 (1985), the second assuring that government throws up no obstacle to its dissemination. At the same time, a particular statute that exceeds proper Copyright Clause bounds may set Clause and Amendment at cross-purposes, thereby depriving the public of the speech-related benefits that the Founders, through both, have promised.

Consequently, I would review plausible claims that a copyright statute seriously, and unjustifiably, restricts the dissemination of speech somewhat more carefully than reference to this Court's traditional Copyright Clause jurisprudence might suggest, ... There is no need in this case to characterize that review as a search for " 'congruence and proportionality,' " . . . or as some other variation of what this Court has called "intermediate scrutiny," e.g., *San Francisco Arts & Athletics, Inc. v. United States Olympic Comm.*, 483 U.S. 522, 536–537, 107 S.Ct. 2971, 97 L.Ed.2d 427 (1987) (applying intermediate scrutiny to a variant of normal trademark protection). Cf. *Nixon v. Shrink Missouri Government PAC*, 528 U.S. 377, 402–403, 120 S.Ct. 897, 145 L.Ed.2d 886 (2000) (BREYER, J., concurring) (test of proportionality between burdens and benefits "where a law significantly implicates competing constitutionally protected interests"). Rather, it is necessary only to recognize that this statute involves not pure economic regulation, but regulation of expression, and what may count as rational where economic regulation is at issue is not necessarily rational where we focus on expression—in a Nation constitutionally dedicated to the free dissemination of speech, information, learning, and culture. In this sense only, and where line-drawing among constitutional interests is at issue, I would look harder than does the majority at the statute's rationality—though less hard than precedent might justify, see, e.g., *Cleburne v. Cleburne Living Center, Inc.*, 473 U.S. 432, 446–450, 105 S.Ct. 3249, 87 L.Ed.2d 313 (1985); *Plyler v. Doe*, 457 U.S. 202, 223–224, 102 S.Ct. 2382, 72 L.Ed.2d 786 (1982); *Department of Agriculture v. Moreno*, 413 U.S. 528, 534–538, 93 S.Ct. 2821, 37 L.Ed.2d 782 (1973).

Thus, I would find that the statute lacks the constitutionally necessary rational support (1) if the significant benefits that it bestows are private, not public; (2) if it threatens seriously to undermine the expressive values that the Copyright Clause embodies; and (3) if it cannot find justification in any significant Clause-related objective. Where, after examination of the statute, it becomes difficult, if not impossible, even to dispute these characterizations, Congress' "choice is clearly wrong." *Helvering v. Davis*, 301 U.S. 619, 640, 57 S.Ct. 904, 81 L.Ed. 1307 (1937).

II

A

Because we must examine the relevant statutory effects in light of the Copyright Clause's own purposes, we should begin by reviewing the basic objectives of that Clause. The Clause authorizes a "tax on readers for the purpose of giving a bounty to writers." 56 Parl. Deb. (3d Ser.) (1841) 341, 350 (Lord Macaulay). Why? What constitutional purposes does the "bounty" serve?

For present purposes ... we should take the following as well established: that copyright statutes must serve public, not private, ends; that they must seek "to promote the Progress" of knowledge and learning; and that they must do so both by creating incentives for authors to produce and by removing the related restrictions on dissemination after expiration of a copyright's "limited Tim[e]"—a time that (like "a *limited* monarch") is "restrain[ed]" and "circumscribe[d]," "not [left] at large," 2 S. Johnson, A Dictionary of the English Language 1151 (4th rev. ed. 1773). I would examine the statute's effects in light of these well-established constitutional purposes.

B

This statute, like virtually every copyright statute, imposes upon the public certain expression-related costs in the form of (1) royalties that may be higher than necessary to evoke creation of the relevant work, and (2) a requirement that one seeking to reproduce a copyrighted work must obtain the copyright holder's permission. The first of these costs translates into higher prices that will potentially restrict a work's dissemination. The second means search costs that themselves may prevent reproduction even where the author has no objection. Although these costs are, in a sense, inevitable concomitants of copyright protection, there are special reasons for thinking them especially serious here.

First, the present statute primarily benefits the holders of existing copyrights, *i.e.*, copyrights on works already created. And a Congressional Research Service (CRS) study prepared for Congress indicates that the added royalty-related sum that the law will transfer to existing copyright holders is large. E. Rappaport, CRS Report for Congress, Copyright Term Extension: Estimating the Economic Values (1998) (hereinafter CRS Report). In conjunction with official figures on copyright renewals, the CRS Report indicates that only about 2% of copyrights between 55 and 75 years old retain commercial value—*i.e.*, still generate royalties after that time. Brief for Petitioners 7 (estimate, uncontested by respondent, based on data from the CRS, Census Bureau, and Library of Congress). But books, songs, and movies of that vintage still earn about $400 million per year in royalties. CRS Report 8, 12, 15. Hence, (despite declining consumer interest in any given work over time) one might conservatively estimate that 20 extra years of copyright protection will mean the transfer of several billion extra royalty dollars to holders of existing copyrights—copyrights that, together, already will have earned many billions of dollars in royalty "reward." See *id.*, at 16.

The extra royalty payments will not come from thin air. Rather, they ultimately come from those who wish to read or see or hear those classic books or films or recordings that have survived. Even the $500,000 that United Airlines has had to pay for the right to play George Gershwin's 1924 classic Rhapsody in Blue represents a cost of doing business, potentially reflected in the ticket prices of those who fly. See Ganzel, Copyright or Copywrong? 39 Training 36, 42 (Dec. 2002). Further, the likely amounts of extra royalty payments are large enough to suggest that unnecessarily high prices will unnecessarily restrict distribution of classic works (or lead to disobedience of the law)—not just in theory but in practice. Cf. CRS Report 3 ("[N]ew, cheaper editions can be expected when works come out of copyright"); Brief for College Art Association et al. as Amici Curiae 24 (One year after expiration of copyright on Willa Cather's My Antonia, seven new editions appeared at prices ranging from $2 to $24); Ganzel, *supra*, at 40–41, 44 (describing later abandoned plans to charge individual Girl Scout camps $257 to $1,439 annually for a license to sing songs such as God Bless America around a campfire).

A second, equally important, cause for concern arises out of the fact that copyright extension imposes a "permissions" requirement—not only upon potential users of "classic" works that still retain commercial value, but also upon potential users of *any other work* still in copyright. Again using CRS estimates, one can estimate that, by 2018, the number of such works 75 years of age or older will be about 350,000. See Brief for Petitioners 7. Because the Copyright Act of 1976 abolished the requirement that an owner must renew a copyright, such still-in-copyright works (of little or no commercial value) will eventually number in the millions. See Pub.L. 94–553, §§ 302–304, 90 Stat. 2572–2576; U.S. Dept. of Commerce, Bureau of Census, Statistical History of the United States: From Colonial Times to the Present 956 (1976) (hereinafter Statistical History).

The potential users of such works include not only movie buffs and aging jazz fans, but also historians, scholars, teachers, writers, artists, database operators, and researchers of all kinds—those who want to make the past accessible for their own use or for that of others. The permissions requirement can inhibit their ability to accomplish that task. Indeed, in an age where computer-accessible databases promise to facilitate research and learning, the permissions requirement can stand as a significant obstacle to realization of that technological hope.

The reason is that the permissions requirement can inhibit or prevent the use of old works (particularly those without commercial value): (1) because it may prove expensive to track down or to contract with the copyright holder, (2) because the holder may prove impossible to find, or (3) because the holder when found may deny permission either outright or through misinformed efforts to bargain. The CRS, for example, has found that the cost of seeking permission "can be prohibitive." CRS Report 4. And amici, along with petitioners, provide examples of the kinds of significant harm at issue.

Thus, the American Association of Law Libraries points out that the clearance process associated with creating an electronic archive, Documenting the American South, "consumed approximately a dozen man-hours" per work. Brief for American Association of Law Libraries et al. as *Amici Curiae* 20. The College Art Association says that the costs of obtaining permission for use of single images, short excerpts, and other short works can become prohibitively high; it describes the abandonment of efforts to include, e.g., campaign songs, film excerpts, and documents exposing "horrors of the chain gang" in historical works or archives; and it points to examples in which copyright holders in effect have used their control of copyright to try to control the content of historical or cultural works. Brief for College Art Association et al. as *Amici Curiae* 7–13. The National Writers Union provides similar examples. Brief for National Writers Union et al. as Amici Curiae 25–27. Petitioners point to music fees that may prevent youth or community orchestras, or church choirs, from performing early 20th-century music. Brief for Petitioners 3–5; see also App. 16–17 (Copyright extension caused abandonment of plans to sell sheet music of Maurice Ravel's Alborada Del Gracioso). *Amici* for petitioners describe how electronic databases tend to avoid adding to their collections works whose copyright holders may prove difficult to contact, see, e.g., Arms, Getting the Picture: Observations from the Library of Congress on Providing Online Access to Pictorial Images, 48 Library Trends 379, 405 (1999) (describing how this tendency applies to the Library of Congress' own digital archives).

As I have said, to some extent costs of this kind accompany any copyright law, regardless of the length of the copyright term. But to extend that term, preventing works from the 1920's and 1930's from falling into the public domain, will dramatically increase the size of the costs just as—perversely—the likely benefits from protection diminish.... The older the work, the less likely it retains commercial value, and the harder it will likely prove to find the current copyright holder. The older the work, the more likely it will prove useful to the historian, artist, or teacher. The older the work, the less likely it is that a sense of authors' rights can justify a copyright holder's decision not to permit reproduction, for the more likely it is that the copyright holder making the decision is not the work's creator, but, say, a corporation or a great-grandchild whom the work's creator never knew. Similarly, the costs of obtaining permission, now perhaps ranging in the millions of dollars, will multiply as the number of holders of affected copyrights increases from several hundred thousand to several million.... The costs to the users of nonprofit databases, now numbering in the low millions, will multiply as the use of those computer-assisted databases becomes more prevalent. See, *e.g.*, Brief for Internet Archive et al. as *Amici Curiae* 2, 21, and n. 37 (describing nonprofit Project Gutenberg). And the qualitative costs to education, learning, and research will multiply as our children become ever more dependent for the content of their knowledge upon computer-accessible databases—thereby condemning that which is not so accessible, say, the cultural content of early 20th-century history, to a kind of intellectual purgatory from which it will not easily emerge.

* * *

Because this subsection concerns only costs, not countervailing benefits, I shall simply note here that, with respect to films as with respect to other works, extension does cause substantial harm to efforts to preserve and to disseminate works that were created long ago. And I shall turn to the second half of the equation: Could Congress reasonably have found that the extension's toll-related and permissions-related harms are justified by extension's countervailing preservationist incentives or in other ways?

C

What copyright-related benefits might justify the statute's extension of copyright protection? First, no one could reasonably conclude that copyright's traditional economic rationale applies here. The extension will not act as an economic spur encouraging authors to create new works. See *Mazer*, 347 U.S., at 219, 74 S.Ct. 460 (The "economic philosophy" of the Copyright Clause is to "advance public welfare" by "encourag[ing] individual effort" through "personal gain") ... No potential author can reasonably believe that he has more than a tiny chance of writing a classic that will survive commercially long enough for the copyright extension to matter. After all, if, after 55 to 75 years, only 2% of all copyrights retain commercial value, the percentage surviving after 75 years or more (a typical pre-extension copyright term)—must be far smaller. See *supra* ... ; CRS Report 7 (estimating that, even after copyright renewal, about 3.8% of copyrighted books go out of print each year). And any remaining monetary incentive is diminished dramatically by the fact that the relevant royalties will not arrive until 75 years or more into the future, when, not the author, but distant heirs, or shareholders in a successor corporation, will receive them. Using assumptions about the time value of money provided us by a group of economists (including five Nobel prize winners), Brief for George A. Akerlof et al. as *Amici Curiae* 5–7, it seems fair to say that, for example, a 1% likelihood of earning $100 annually for 20 years, starting *75 years into the future*, is worth less than seven cents today. See *id.*, App. 3a; see also CRS Report 5. See generally Appendix, Part A, *infra*.

What potential Shakespeare, Wharton, or Hemingway would be moved by such a sum? What monetarily motivated Melville would not realize that he could do better for his grandchildren by putting a few dollars into an interest-bearing bank account? The Court itself finds no evidence to the contrary. It refers to testimony before Congress (1) that the copyright system's incentives encourage creation, and (2) (referring to Noah Webster) that income earned from one work can help support an artist who " 'continue[s] to create.' " ... But the first of these amounts to no more than a set of undeniably true propositions about the value of incentives *in general*. And the applicability of the second to *this* Act is mysterious. How will extension help today's Noah Webster create new works 50 years after his death? Or is that hypothetical Webster supposed to support himself with the extension's present discounted value, *i.e.*, a few pennies? Or (to change the metaphor) is the argument that Dumas *fils* would have written more books had Dumas *pére's* Three Musketeers earned more royalties?

Regardless, even if this cited testimony were meant more specifically to tell Congress that somehow, somewhere, some potential author might be moved by the thought of great-grandchildren receiving copyright royalties a century hence, so might some potential author also be moved by the thought of royalties being paid for two centuries, five centuries, 1,000 years, " 'til the End of Time." And from a rational economic perspective the time difference among these periods *makes no real difference*. The present extension will produce a copyright period of protection that, even under conservative assumptions, is worth more than *99.8%* of protection in *perpetuity* (more than *99.99%* for a songwriter like Irving Berlin and a song like Alexander's Ragtime Band). See Appendix, Part A, *infra*. The lack of a practically meaningful distinction from an author's ex ante perspective between (a) the statute's extended terms and (b) an infinite term makes this latest extension difficult to square with the Constitution's insistence on "limited Times." Cf. Tr. of Oral Arg. 34 (Solicitor General's related concession).

I am not certain why the Court considers it relevant in this respect that "[n]othing ... warrants construction of the [1998 Act's] 20–year term extension as a congressional attempt to evade or override the 'limited Times' constraint." ... Of course Congress did not intend to act unconstitutionally. But it may have sought to test the Constitution's limits. After all, the statute was named after a Member of Congress, who, the legislative history records, "wanted the term of copyright protection to last forever." 144 Cong. Rec. H9952 (daily ed. Oct. 7, 1998) (statement of Rep. Mary Bono). See also Copyright Term, Film Labeling, and Film Preservation Legislation: Hearings on H.R. 989 et al. before the Subcommittee on Courts and Intellectual Property of the House Judiciary Committee, 104th Cong., 1st Sess., 94 (1995) (hereinafter House Hearings) (statement of Rep. Sonny Bono) (questioning why copyrights should ever expire); *ibid.* (statement of Rep. Berman) ("I guess we could ... just make a permanent moratorium on the expiration of copyrights"); *id.*, at 230 (statement of Rep. Hoke) ("Why 70 years? Why not forever? Why not 150 years?"); cf. *ibid.* (statement of the Register of Copyrights) (In Copyright Office proceedings, "[t]he Songwriters Guild suggested a perpetual term''); *id.*, at 234 (statement of Quincy Jones) (''I'm particularly fascinated with Representative Hoke's statement.... [W]hy not forever?''); *id.*, at 277 (statement of Quincy Jones) (''If we can start with 70, add 20, it would be a good start''). And the statute ended up creating a term so long that (were the vesting of 19th-century real property at issue) it would typically violate the traditional rule against perpetuities. See 10 R. Powell, Real Property §§ 71.02[2]-[3], p. 71–11 (M. Wolf ed. 2002) (traditional rule that estate must vest, if at all, within lives in being plus 21 years); cf. *id.*, § 71.03, at 71–15 (modern statutory perpetuity term of 90 years, 5 years shorter than 95–year copyright terms).

In any event, the incentive-related numbers are far too small for Congress to have concluded rationally, even with respect to new works, that the extension's economic-incentive effect could justify the serious expression-related harms earlier described. See Part II–B, *supra*. And, of course, in respect to works already created—the source of many of the harms previously described—the statute creates no economic incentive at all. See *ante*, . . . (STEVENS, J., dissenting).

Second, the Court relies heavily for justification upon international uniformity of terms.... Although it can be helpful to look to international norms and legal experience in understanding American law, cf. Printz v. U.S., 521 U.S. 898, 977, 117 S.Ct. 2365, 138 L.Ed.2d 914 (1997) (BREYER, J., dissenting), in this case the justification based upon foreign rules is surprisingly weak. Those who claim that significant copyright-related benefits flow from greater international uniformity of terms point to the fact that the nations of the European Union have adopted a system of copyright terms uniform among themselves. And the extension before this Court implements a term of life plus 70 years that appears to conform with the European standard. But how does ''uniformity'' help to justify this statute?

Despite appearances, the statute does not create a uniform American–European term with respect to the lion's share of the economically significant works that it affects—all works made ''for hire'' and all existing works created prior to 1978. See Appendix, Part B, *infra*. With respect to those works the American statute produces an extended term of 95 years while comparable European rights in ''for hire'' works last for periods that vary from 50 years to 70 years to life plus 70 years. Compare 17 U.S.C. §§ 302(c), 304(a)-(b) with Council Directive 93/98/EEC of 29 October 1993 Harmonizing the Term of Protection of Copyright and Certain Related Rights, Arts. 1–3, 1993 Official J. Eur. Coms. (L290), pp. 11–12 (hereinafter EU Council Directive 93/98). Neither does the statute create uniformity with respect to anonymous or pseudonymous works. Compare 17 U.S.C. §§ 302(c), 304(a)-(b) with EU Council Directive 93/98, Art. 1, p. 11.

The statute does produce uniformity with respect to copyrights in new, post–1977 works attributed to natural persons. Compare 17 U.S.C. § 302(a) with EU Council Directive 93/98, Art. 1(1), p. 11. But these works constitute only a subset … [a]nd the fact that uniformity comes so late, if at all, means that bringing American law into conformity with this particular aspect of European law will neither encourage creation nor benefit the long-dead author in any other important way.

What benefit, then, might this partial future uniformity achieve? * * * [T]he partial, future uniformity that the 1998 Act promises cannot reasonably be said to justify extension of the copyright term for new works. And concerns with uniformity cannot possibly justify the extension of the new term to older works, for the statute there creates no uniformity at all.

Third, several publishers and filmmakers argue that the statute provides incentives to those who act as publishers to republish and to redistribute older copyrighted works. This claim cannot justify this statute, however, because the rationale is inconsistent with the basic purpose of the Copyright Clause—as understood by the Framers and by this Court. The Clause assumes an initial grant of monopoly, designed primarily to encourage creation, followed by termination of the monopoly grant in order to promote dissemination of already-created works. It assumes that it is the disappearance of the monopoly grant, not its perpetuation, that will, on balance, promote the dissemination of works already in existence. This view of the Clause does not deny the empirical possibility that grant of a copyright monopoly to the heirs or successors of a long-dead author could on occasion help publishers resurrect the work, say, of a long-lost Shakespeare. But it does deny Congress the Copyright Clause power to base its actions primarily upon that empirical possibility—lest copyright grants become perpetual, lest on balance they restrict dissemination, lest too often they seek to bestow benefits that are solely retroactive.

* * *

Given this support, it is difficult to accept the conflicting rationale that the publishers advance, namely, that extension, rather than limitation, of the grant will, by rewarding publishers with a form of monopoly, promote, rather than retard, the dissemination of works already in existence. Indeed, given these considerations, this rationale seems constitutionally perverse—unable, constitutionally speaking, to justify the blanket extension here at issue. Cf. *ante*, … (STEVENS, J., dissenting).

Fourth, the statute's legislative history suggests another possible justification. That history refers frequently to the financial assistance the statute will bring the entertainment industry, particularly through the promotion of exports. See, e.g., S.Rep. No. 104–315, p. 3 (1996) ("The purpose of the bill is to ensure adequate copyright protection for American works in foreign nations and the continued economic benefits of a healthy surplus balance of trade"); 144 Cong. Rec., at H9951 (statement of Rep. Foley) (noting "the importance of this issue to America's creative community," "[w]hether it is Sony, BMI, Disney," or other companies). I recognize that Congress has sometimes found that suppression of competition will help Americans sell abroad—though it has simultaneously taken care to protect American buyers from higher domestic prices. See, *e.g.*, Webb–Pomerene Act (Export Trade), 40 Stat. 516, as amended, 15 U.S.C. §§ 61–65; see also IA P. Areeda & H. Hovenkamp, Antitrust Law 251a, pp. 134–137 (2d ed.2000) (criticizing export cartels). In doing so, however, Congress has exercised its commerce, not its copyright, power. I can find nothing in the Copyright Clause that would authorize Congress to enhance the copyright grant's monopoly power, likely leading to higher prices both at home and abroad, *solely* in order to produce higher foreign earnings. That objective is not a *copyright* objective. Nor, standing alone, is it related to any other objective more closely tied to the Clause itself. Neither can higher corporate profits alone justify the grant's enhancement. The Clause seeks public, not private, benefits.

Finally, the Court mentions as possible justifications "demographic, economic, and technological changes"—by which the Court apparently means the facts that today people communicate with the help of modern technology, live longer, and have children at a later age.... The first fact seems to argue not for, but instead against, extension. See Part II–B, *supra*. The second fact seems already corrected for by the 1976 Act's life-plus–50 term, which automatically grows with lifespans. Cf. Department of Health and Human Services, Centers for Disease Control and Prevention, Deaths: Final Data for 2000 (2002) (Table 8) (reporting a 4–year increase in expected lifespan between 1976 and 1998). And the third fact—that adults are having children later in life—is a makeweight at best, providing no explanation of why the 1976 Act's term of 50 years after an author's death—a longer term than was available to authors themselves for most of our Nation's history—is an insufficient potential bequest. The weakness of these final rationales simply underscores the conclusion that emerges from consideration of earlier attempts at justification: There is no legitimate, serious copyright-related justification for this statute.

* * *

IV

This statute will cause serious expression-related harm. It will likely restrict traditional dissemination of copyrighted works. It will likely inhibit new forms of dissemination through the use of new technology. It threatens to interfere with efforts to preserve our Nation's historical and cultural heritage and efforts to use that heritage, say, to educate our Nation's children. It is easy to understand how the statute might benefit the private financial interests of corporations or heirs who own existing copyrights. But I cannot find any constitutionally legitimate, copyright-related way in which the statute will benefit the public. Indeed, in respect to existing works, the serious public harm and the virtually nonexistent public benefit could not be more clear.

I have set forth the analysis upon which I rest these judgments. This analysis leads inexorably to the conclusion that the statute cannot be understood rationally to advance a constitutionally legitimate interest.

The statute falls outside the scope of legislative power that the Copyright Clause, read in light of the First Amendment, grants to Congress. I would hold the statute unconstitutional.

I respectfully dissent.

* * *

Notes

1. Justice Ginsburg, in her majority opinion in *Eldred*, states that the copyright is not "categorically immune" to First Amendment challenges, but that the SBCTEA did not violate the First Amendment. Ginsburg does analyze the SBCTEA's speech protections, however. What level of scrutiny is Ginsburg applying? Under what circumstances would the First Amendment be implicated in such a way as to trigger heightened scrutiny?

In *Prelinger Associates, Inc. v. Gonzales*, 474 F.3d 665 (9th Cir. 2007), the United States District Court for the Northern District of California, relying on the Supreme Court's decision in *Eldred*, rejected a claim that the Copyright Renewal Act and the Sony Bono Term extension Act are unconstitutional as applied to pre–1978 works.

2. During the last 20 years of the term in published works, a new subsection 108 privilege (§ 108(h)), added by the SBCTEA, permits libraries and archives to make, distribute, display or perform copies or phonorecords of the work (in facsimile or digital form) for purposes of preservation, scholarship, or research, under circumstances in which copies or phonorecords cannot otherwise be obtained at a reasonable price. Subsection 108(i), however, limits the reproduction and distribution rights granted by section 108 in the case of "musical works, pictorial, graphic or sculptural works, or a motion picture or other audiovisual work other than an audiovisual work dealing with news.... " Why this limitation? What does it mean in practice?

3. The SBCTEA added 20 years to all copyright terms, not just to the terms of works individually authored. Why?

4. What copyright term applies to works by joint authors? What about a work that is jointly authored by some persons who are acting under work-made-for-hire arrangements and other persons who are not?

5. In the case of manuscripts that were unpublished (and thus entitled to perpetual copyright under common law) when the 1976 Act took effect, what copyright term now applies under the Act?

6. In the case of a copyright that is measured by the life-plus-seventy term, how can a potential user determine whether a particular author is still living, or what was the author's date of death? Does it matter if the work is unregistered and unpublished?

7. In addition to replacing initial and renewal copyright terms of the 1909 Act with a single copyright term, the 1976 Act added an additional 19 years to the renewal terms of all copyrights subsisting as of January 1, 1978; this is known as the "extended renewal term." Because Congress passed interim legislation extending the renewal terms of subsisting copyrights during the years preceding enactment of the 1976 Act, any copyright that

was timely renewed under the 1909 Act subsisted for a total of 75 years. (The SBCTEA extends the term of copyrights unexpired as of the date of its enactment by another 20 years.)

8. Can trademark law extend protection even beyond the term offered by copyright? See *Dastar Corp. v. Twentieth Century Fox Film Corp.*, 539 U.S. 23, 123 S.Ct. 2041, 156 L.Ed.2d 18 (2003), [*Dastar*, excerpted, Supra, at p. 245, in this casebook supplement in Chapter 7, Section A.] Subsequently, in *Williams v. UMG Recordings, Inc.*, 281 F.Supp.2d 1177 (C.D. Cal. 2003) the District Court rejected a trademark lawsuit for lack of credit, relying on the Supreme Court's holding in *Dastar*. In dicta, the court suggested that a suit might properly be grounded in copyright law. Does copyright law guarantee a right of credit?

STEWART v. ABEND

Supreme Court of the United States, 1990.
495 U.S. 207, 110 S.Ct. 1750, 109 L.Ed.2d 184.

JUSTICE O'CONNOR delivered the opinion of the Court.

The author of a pre-existing work may assign to another the right to use it in a derivative work. In this case the author of a pre-existing work agreed to assign the rights in his renewal copyright term to the owner of a derivative work, but died before the commencement of the renewal period. The question presented is whether the owner of the derivative work infringed the rights of the successor owner of the pre-existing work by continued distribution and publication of the derivative work during the renewal term of the pre-existing work.

I

[Cornell Woolrich's short story "It Had to Be Murder" was published in 1942. In 1945, for consideration of $9,250, Woolrich assigned the film rights, together with a promise to renew the copyright and to assign the renewal term to the grantee. The film version, titled "Rear Window," was released in 1954. Woolrich died in 1968 before the renewal term commenced. He left no surviving spouse or child, but the executor of his estate renewed the story's copyright pursuant to section 24 of the 1909 Act, and assigned the renewal term to plaintiff-respondent Abend. When petitioners rereleased "Rear Window" after the renewal term commenced in 1970, Abend sued for copyright infringement, arguing that he owned the exclusive film rights during the renewal term.]

* * *

II

A

Petitioners would have us read into the Copyright Act a limitation on the statutorily created rights of the owner of an underlying work. They argue in essence that the rights of the owner of the copyright in the derivative use of the pre-existing work are extinguished once it is incorporated into the derivative work, assuming the author of the pre-existing work has agreed to assign his renewal rights. Because we find no support for such a curtailment of rights in either the 1909 Act or the 1976 Act, or in the legislative history of either, we affirm the judgment of the Court of Appeals.

Petitioners and amicus Register of Copyrights assert, as the Court of Appeals assumed, that § 23 of the 1909 Act, 17 U.S.C. § 24 (1976 ed.), and the case law interpreting that provision, directly control the disposition of this case. Respondent counters that the provisions of the 1976 Act control, but that the 1976 Act re-enacted § 24 in § 304 and, therefore, the language and judicial interpretation of § 24 are relevant to our consideration of this case. Under either theory, we must look to the language of and case law interpreting § 24.

The right of renewal found in § 24 provides authors a second opportunity to obtain remuneration for their works. Section 24 provides:

"[T]he author of [a copyrighted] work, if still living, or the widow, widower, or children of the author, if the author be not living, or if such author, widow, widower, or children be not living, then the author's executors, or in the absence of a will, his next of kin shall be entitled to a renewal and extension of the copyright in such work for a further term of twenty-eight years when application for such renewal and extension shall have been made to the copyright office and duly registered therein within one year prior to the expiration of the original term of copyright." 17 U.S.C. § 24 (1976 ed.)

* * *

In its debates leading up to the Copyright Act of 1909, Congress elaborated upon the policy underlying a system comprised of an original term and a completely separate renewal term. See G. Ricordi & Co. v. Paramount Pictures, Inc., 189 F.2d 469, 471 (CA2) (the renewal right "creates a new estate, and the . . . cases which have dealt with the subject assert that the new estate is clear of all rights, interests or licenses granted under the original copyright"), cert. denied, 342 U.S. 849 (1951). "It not infrequently happens that the author sells his copyright outright to a publisher for a comparatively small sum." H.R. Rep. No. 2222, 60th Cong., 2d Sess., 14 (1909). The renewal term permits the author, originally in a poor bargaining position, to renegotiate the terms of the grant once the value of the work has been tested. "[U]nlike real property and other forms of personal property, [a copyright] is by its very nature incapable of accurate monetary evaluation prior to its exploitation." 2 M. Nimmer & D. Nimmer, Nimmer on Copyright § 9.02, p. 9–23 (1989) (hereinafter Nimmer). "If the work proves to be a great success and lives beyond the term of twenty-eight years, . . . it should be the exclusive right of the author to take the renewal term, and the law should be framed . . . so that [the author] could not be deprived of that right." H.R. Rep. No. 2222, supra, at 14. With these purposes in mind, Congress enacted the renewal provision of the Copyright Act of 1909, 17 U.S.C. § 24 (1976 ed.). With respect to works in their original or renewal term as of January 1, 1978, Congress retained the two-term system of copyright protection in the 1976 Act. See 17 U.S.C. §§ 304(a) and (b) (1988 ed.) (incorporating language of 17 U.S.C. § 24 (1976 ed.)).

Applying these principles in Miller Music Corp. v. Charles N. Daniels, Inc., 362 U.S. 373 (1960), this Court held that when an author dies before the renewal period arrives, his executor is entitled to the renewal rights, even though the author previously assigned his renewal rights to another party. "An assignment by an author of his renewal rights made before the original copyright expires is valid against the world, if the author is alive at the commencement of the renewal period. [Fred] Fisher Co. v. [M.] Witmark & Sons, 318 U.S. 643, so holds." Id., at 375. If the author dies before that time, the "next of kin obtain the renewal copyright free of any claim founded upon an assignment made by the author in his lifetime. These results follow not because the author's assignment is invalid but because he had only an expectancy to assign; and his death, prior to the renewal period, terminates his interest in the renewal which by § 24 vests in the named classes." Ibid. The legislative history of the 1909 Act echoes this view: "The right of renewal is contingent. It does not vest until the end [of the original term]. If [the author] is alive at the time of renewal, then the original contract may pass it, but his widow or children or other persons entitled would not be bound by that contract." 5 Legislative History of the 1909 Copyright Act, Part K, p. 77 (E. Brylawski & A. Goldman eds. 1976) (statement of Mr. Hale). Thus, the renewal provisions were intended to give the author a second chance to obtain fair remuneration for his creative efforts and to provide the author's family a "new estate" if the author died before the renewal period arrived.

An author holds a bundle of exclusive rights in the copyrighted work, among them the right to copy and the right to incorporate the work into derivative works. By assigning the renewal copyright in the work without limitation, as in Miller Music, the author assigns all of these rights. After Miller Music, if the author dies before the commencement of the renewal period, the assignee holds nothing. If the assignee of all of the renewal rights holds nothing upon the death of the assignor before arrival of the renewal period, then, a fortiori, the assignee of a portion of the renewal rights, e.g., the right to produce a derivative work, must also hold nothing. See also Brief for Register of Copyrights as Amicus Curiae 22 ("[A]ny assignment of renewal rights made during the original term is void if the author dies before the renewal period"). Therefore, if the author dies before the renewal period, then the assignee may continue to use the original work only if the author's successor transfers the renewal rights to the assignee. This is the rule adopted by the Court of Appeals below and advocated by the Register of Copyrights. See 863 F. 2d, at 1478; Brief for Register of Copyrights as Amicus Curiae 22. Application of this rule to this case should end the inquiry. Woolrich died before the commencement of the renewal period in the story, and, therefore, petitioners hold only an unfulfilled expectancy. Petitioners have been "deprived of nothing. Like all purchasers of contingent interests, [they took] subject to the possibility that the contingency may not occur." Miller Music, supra, at 378.

B

The reason that our inquiry does not end here, and that we granted certiorari, is that the Court of Appeals for the Second Circuit reached a contrary result in Rohauer v. Killiam Shows, Inc., 551 F.2d 484 (1977). Petitioners' theory is drawn largely from Rohauer. The Court of Appeals in Rohauer attempted to craft a "proper reconciliation" between the owner of the pre-existing work, who held the right to the work pursuant to Miller Music, and the owner of the derivative work, who had a great deal to lose if the work could not be published or distributed. 551 F.2d, at 490. Addressing a case factually similar to this case, the court concluded that even if the death of the author caused the renewal rights in the pre-existing work to revert to the statutory successor, the owner of the derivative work could continue to exploit that work. The court reasoned that the 1976 Act and the relevant precedents did not preclude such a result and that it was necessitated by a balancing of the equities:

> "[T]he equities lie preponderantly in favor of the proprietor of the derivative copyright. In contrast to the situation where an assignee or licensee has done nothing more than print, publicize and distribute a copyrighted story or novel, a person who with the consent of the author has created an opera or a motion picture film will often have made contributions literary, musical and economic, as great as or greater than the original author.... [T]he purchaser of derivative rights has no truly effective way to protect himself against the eventuality of the author's death before the renewal period since there is no way of telling who will be the surviving widow, children or next of kin or the executor until that date arrives." Id., at 493.

The Court of Appeals for the Second Circuit thereby shifted the focus from the right to use the pre-existing work in a derivative work to a right inhering in the created derivative work itself. By rendering the renewal right to use the original work irrelevant, the court created an exception to our ruling in Miller Music and, as petitioners concede, created an "intrusion" on the statutorily created rights of the owner of the pre-existing work in the renewal term. * * *

Though petitioners do not, indeed could not, argue that its language expressly supports the theory they draw from Rohauer, they implicitly rely on § 6 of the 1909 Act, 17 U.S.C. § 7 (1976 ed.), which states that "dramatizations ... of copyrighted works when produced with the consent of the proprietor of the copyright in such works ... shall be regarded as new works subject to copyright under the provisions of this title." Petitioners maintain that the creation of the "new," i.e., derivative, work extinguishes any right the owner of rights in the pre-existing work might have had to sue for infringement that occurs during the renewal term.

We think, as stated in Nimmer, that "[t]his conclusion is neither warranted by any express provision of the Copyright Act, nor by the rationale as to the scope of protection achieved in a derivative work. It is moreover contrary to the axiomatic copyright principle that a person may exploit only such copyrighted literary material as he either owns or is licensed to use." 1 Nimmer § 3.07[A], pp. 3–23 to 3–24 (footnotes omitted). The aspects of a derivative work added by the derivative author are that author's property, but the element drawn from the pre-existing work remains on grant from the owner of the pre-existing work. See Russell v. Price, 612 F.2d 1123, 1128 (C.A.9 1979) (reaffirming "well-established doctrine that a derivative copyright protects only the new material contained in the derivative work, not the matter derived from the underlying work"), cert. denied, 446 U.S. 952 (1980); see also Harper & Row, Publishers, Inc. v. Nation Enterprises, 471 U.S. 539, 547 (1985) ("The copyright is limited to those aspects of the work—termed 'expression'—that display the stamp of the author's originality"). So long as the pre-existing work remains out of the public domain, its use is infringing if one who employs the work does not have a valid license or assignment for use of the pre-existing work. Russell v. Price, supra, at 1128 ("[E]stablished doctrine prevents unauthorized copying or other infringing use of the underlying work or any part of that work contained in the derivative product so long as the underlying work itself remains copyrighted"). It is irrelevant whether the pre-existing work is inseparably intertwined with the derivative work. See Gilliam v. American Broadcasting Cos., 538 F.2d 14, 20 (C.A.2 1976) ("[C]opyright in the underlying script survives intact despite the incorporation of that work into a derivative work"). Indeed, the plain language of § 7 supports the view that the full force of the copyright in the pre-existing work is preserved despite incorporation into the derivative work. See 17 U.S.C. § 7 (1976 ed.) (publication of the derivative work "shall not affect the force or validity of any subsisting copyright upon the matter employed"); see also 17 U.S.C. § 3 (1976 ed.) (copyright protection of a work extends to "all matter therein in which copyright is already subsisting, but without extending the duration or scope of such copyright"). This well-settled rule also was made explicit in [section 103(b) of] the 1976 Act * * *.

* * *

Moreover, although dissemination of creative works is a goal of the Copyright Act, the Act creates a balance between the artist's right to control the work during the term of the copyright protection and the public's need for access to creative works. The copyright term is limited so that the public will not be permanently deprived of the fruits of an artist's labors. See Sony Corp. of America v. Universal City Studios, Inc., 464 U.S. 417, 429 (1984) (the limited monopoly conferred by the Copyright Act "is intended to motivate creative activity of authors and inventors by the provision of a special reward, and to allow the public access to the products of their genius after the limited period of exclusive control has expired"). But nothing in the copyright statutes would prevent an author from hoarding all of his works during the term of the copyright. In fact, this Court has held that a copyright owner has the capacity arbitrarily to refuse to license one who seeks to exploit the work. See Fox Film Corp. v. Doyal, 286 U.S. 123, 127 (1932).

The limited monopoly granted to the artist is intended to provide the necessary bargaining capital to garner a fair price for the value of the works passing into public use. * * * When an author produces a work which later commands a higher price in the market than the original bargain provided, the copyright statute is designed to provide the author the power to negotiate for the realized value of the work. That is how the separate renewal term was intended to operate. See Ringer, Renewal of Copyright (1960), reprinted as Copyright Law Revision Study No. 31, prepared for the Senate Committee on the Judiciary, 86th Cong., 2d. Sess., 125 (1961) ("Congress wanted to give [the author] an opportunity to benefit from the success of his work and to renegotiate disadvantageous bargains ... made at a time when the value of the work [wa]s unknown or conjectural and the author ... necessarily in a poor bargaining position"). At heart, petitioners' true complaint is that they will have to pay more for the use of works they have employed in creating their own works. But such a result was contemplated by Congress and is consistent with the goals of the Copyright Act.

* * *

COPYRIGHT RENEWAL ACT OF 1992
S.Rep. No. 102–194.
102nd Cong., 1st Sess. 4–7, 21–22 (1991).

* * *

A. COPYRIGHT REGISTRATION RENEWAL

* * *

Because of its complexities, the Copyright Office, book and music publishers, authors, filmmakers and other copyright organizations criticized the registration renewal provision for being burdensome and unfair to thousands of copyright holders and their heirs. * * *

* * * Witnesses also maintained that the present renewal provisions are even more puzzling for foreign authors, who are even less familiar with this formality because it is unique to U.S. law. * * *

* * * The domestic laws of most developed countries contain very few formalities conditioning copyright protection. Compliance with formalities is antithetical to the major international treaty on copyright relations, the Berne Convention for the Protection of Literary and Artistic Works. In the 1976 general revision, Congress dispensed with many of the formalities contained in the 1909 copyright law, and in 1988, the United States adhered to the Berne Convention (Paris, 1971). However, Congress declined to modify the renewal provision in the

Berne Convention Implementation Act (Public Law 100–568) because it felt that the cutting off or altering [of] existing expectancies at that time would be unfair and the safer course would be to allow the renewal provisions to phase out by the year 2005. * * *

Opponents of the bill argue that mandatory registration renewal should be retained because it * * * serves an important public purpose: increasing the volume of works that fall into the public domain, free of copyright protection. This argument is contrary to the real public purpose for copyright protection: our copyright law grants authors exclusive, limited rights to exploit their creations for a sufficient time so they will be encouraged to continue creating works that entertain, educate, and fire our imaginations.

The committee believes that the public domain should consist of works which have enjoyed a full and fair term of protection and should not be enlarged because of an author's error in recordkeeping, or any other innocent failure to comply with overly technical formalities in the copyright law. * * *

* * *

The automatic renewal provisions will apply only to those works that are still in their first, 28–year term of protection on the date this bill becomes law. Under the bill, works that acquired a first-term of copyright protection between 1963 and December 31, 1977, and that are eligible for registration renewal between 1991 and 2005, will benefit from the automatic renewal provisions. Consequently, the bill provides only prospective protection; it does not restore protection to works that have already fallen into the public domain, nor extend the term of protection to qualifying works beyond what they are already entitled to receive if a renewal registration is made. The committee concludes that these amendments to the registration renewal provisions will restore a measure of equity and fairness to the copyright law.

* * *

* * * Paragraphs (4)(A) and (B) of Section 101(a) provide incentives for making a renewal registration within the last year of the first term. Paragraph (4)(A) permits the continued use during the renewal term of derivative works prepared under a grant of a transfer or license of copyright made before the expiration of the original term of copyright if a renewal registration is not made during the last year of the first term. Currently such grants do not automatically extend into the second term. This amendment does not authorize the preparation of other derivative works based upon the copyrighted work which is the subject of the grant. This incentive to make a renewal registration parallels the derivative works clause of the termination provisions of section 203 (relating to post–1977 copyrighted works) and 304(c) (relating only to the 19–year period at the end of the extended term for pre–1978 copyrighted works). The bill leaves undisturbed the decision of the Supreme Court in Stewart et al. v. Abend, 110 S.Ct. 1750 (1990). Renewal registration is mandatory

under existing law. If renewal registration is made under the amended section 304(a) in the last year of the original term, the derivative works clause of this bill will not be triggered. In any event, moreover, the bill makes no change in the persons entitled to claim the renewal copyright. Whoever is entitled under existing law, remains entitled to claim the renewal under the bill.

Paragraph (4)(B) provides that if registration of copyright in the renewal term is made during the last year of the first term, the certificate of renewal registration shall constitute prima facie evidence as to the validity of the copyright during its renewed term and of the facts stated in the certificate. The evidentiary weight to be accorded the certificate of renewal registration made after the end of that 1–year period will be within the discretion of the court. The possibility of making registration after the renewal term commences is a change in the law, which should provide an incentive to register works whose copyright is automatically extended under this bill. Works registered for the first time during the renewal term will enjoy statutory damages and attorney's fees, in accordance with section 412.

* * *

Notes

1. A footnote in *Stewart v. Abend* expressly left open the question of when the renewal term became vested under the 1909 Act. How is that question answered under the automatic renewal provisions (which apply to works first copyrighted between January 1, 1964, and December 31, 1977, inclusive)? How should this question be answered for works that reached the end of their first term before the effective date of automatic renewal? See *Marascalco v. Fantasy, Inc.*, 953 F.2d 469 (9th Cir.1991).

2. Under the automatic renewal provisions, who owns the renewal term if an author conveys both the initial term and the renewal term to a producer, then dies in the 27th year of the first term, leaving a spouse and two children, and:

   (a) the spouse files a timely renewal registration?

   (b) neither the spouse nor the children file a timely renewal registration?

   (c) the author's will leaves both the first term of copyright and the renewal term to the producer?

   (d) the author's will leaves both the first term of copyright and the renewal term to the children?

   (e) while the author was still living, the spouse and children executed a contract conveying their interests in the copyright to the producer?

   (f) while the author was still living, the spouse and one child executed a contract conveying their interests in the copyright to the producer, but the second child refused?

(g) while the author was still living, the spouse and two children executed a contract conveying their interests in the copyright to the producer, but the spouse and children die before the end of the first term?

3. In the case of a work made for hire, if the employee-author dies during the first term of copyright, who owns the renewal term?

4. Suppose that a film producer wishes to acquire the right to use a song in her film's soundtrack. The music publisher that owns the copyright is willing to grant her the rights. Evaluate the potential impact of *Stewart v. Abend* on her ability to exploit these rights, and discuss what, if anything, she can do to minimize her risk, if:

(a) The song was published with notice in 1979, and the author is still living.

(b) The song was published with notice in 1977, and the author is still living.

(c) The song was published with notice in 1977, and was created as a work-made-for-hire. (Does it matter whether the employee-author is still living?)

(d) The work was published with notice in 1977, and the author has since died intestate, leaving a spouse but no children.

5. At what date will potential acquirers of renewal expectancies no longer face the risk that their expectancies will lapse under the *Abend* rule?

6. Suppose that a motion picture producer has made a film based on a short story published in 1977. The contract for the film rights conveys both the initial and the renewal terms. If short story's author is still living at the start of the 28th year of the first term, should the producer make an effort to ensure that a renewal registration is promptly filed? What if the author is already dead? Does it matter whether the possible renewal claimants have executed contracts conveying their expectancies to the producer?

7. Where the renewal claimants are a widower and two children, how should the renewal term be allocated among them?

2. COPYRIGHT RESTORATION

Statutes: 17 U.S.C.A. § 104A

URUGUAY ROUND AGREEMENTS ACT
S.Rep. No. 103–412.
103d Cong., 2d Sess. 225–26 (1994).

The legislation includes language to restore copyright protection to certain foreign works from countries that are members of the Berne Convention or WTO that have fallen into the public domain for reasons other than the normal expiration of their term of protection.

The Agreement requires WTO countries to comply with Article 18 of the Berne Convention. While the United States declared its compliance with the Berne Convention in 1989, it never addressed or enacted legislation to implement Article 18 of the Convention. Article 18 requires that the terms of the convention apply to all works that have fallen into the public domain by reasons other than the expiration of its term of protection. (Examples include failure to file a timely renewal application and failure to affix a copyright notice).

The bill would automatically restore copyright protection for qualifying works of authors from Berne or WTO countries one year after the WTO comes into being. In order for the restored copyright to be enforced against a "reliance party," it is necessary for the author or copyright owner (rightholder) of the foreign work to either file a "notice of intent" with the Copyright Office during the 24 months after the effective date of the Uruguay Round Agreement or provide actual notice (for the life of the copyright term) directly by notifying the reliance party. Reliance parties then have one year from publication of the constructive notice or receipt of the actual notice to continue to use or sell off copies of the work that have been restored to a foreign author or rightholder. Reproduction of the work during this period is not permitted. After this period, reliance parties are subject to remedies for infringement, except in certain cases.

Section 104A(d)(3) provides additional protection to a reliance party who used a restored foreign work to create a derivative work because a one year sell off period might be an inadequate period to recoup the investment. In the case of a derivative work that was created based upon a foreign work that was in the public domain but has been restored, the reliance party may continue to sell the derivative work in exchange for providing reasonable compensation to the owner of the restored copyright. In the event that an agreement cannot be reached regarding compensation a district court may determine reasonable compensation, based upon the contribution made by the reliance party as well as the author of the underlying restored work. The court is to take into consideration any damage to the market for the restored work.

* * *

Notes

1. The Uruguay Round Agreements Act (URAA), Pub.L. 103–465, became law on Dec. 8, 1994. The copyright restoration provisions are contained in section 514 of the URAA, and codified at 17 U.S.C.A. § 104A.

For a work to qualify for copyright restoration: (1) it must be an original work of authorship; (2) its copyright term in its country of origin must not have expired; (3) it must have entered the public domain in the United States because of lack of national eligibility (see 17 U.S.C.A. § 104), noncompliance with formalities (such as notice, renewal, or the manufacturing clause under 17 U.S.C.A. § 601), or ineligible subject matter (in the case of a sound recording fixed before February 15, 1972); and (4) at the time the work was created, at least one of its authors or rightholders must have been a national or domiciliary of an eligible country, meaning a country (other than the United States) that is a member of the Berne Convention or the World Trade Organization, or that is subject to a presidential proclamation extending copyright protection to works of that country based on reciprocal treatment. If the work is published, it must not have been published in the United States within 30 days of first publication in the eligible country.

According to the Copyright Office, the date on which reliance parties are required to stop reproducing or preparing derivative works based on any restored work is the earlier of (1) the date on which they receive actual notice of the owner's intent to enforce the restored copyright, or (2) the date on which the Copyright Office publishes in the Federal Register a list identifying works as to which notices of intent to enforce have been filed. After receiving either form of notice, reliance parties have a 12–month grace period during which they may sell off existing inventory, publicly perform or display the work, or authorize others to do so.

Notices of intent to enforce could be filed beginning January 1, 1996. Beginning in May, 1996, and at regular intervals thereafter, the Copyright Office was required to publish lists of those notices of intent.

2. During the interval between the effective date of the North American Free Trade Agreement legislation and the effective date of the URAA, a narrower version of section 104A restored the remaining term of copyright to certain Mexican and Canadian motion pictures (and works included in such motion pictures and first fixed or published therein) which had entered the public domain in the United States due to publication without adequate copyright notice between January 1, 1978 and March 1, 1989. To benefit from these provisions, the copyright claimant had to file a notice of intent with the Copyright Office during 1994, after which the Copyright Office was required to publish a list of the restored works. Restoration was effective January 1, 1995. Existing copies of restored works could still be distributed and publicly performed for one year thereafter. *See* North American Free Trade Agreement Act, Pub. L. No. 103–182, 107 Stat. 2057 (1993).

3. In *Alameda Films SA de CV v. Authors Rights Restoration Corp. Inc.*, 331 F.3d 472 (5th Cir. 2003), Mexican film production companies sued U.S. distributors for copyright violations on 88 Mexican films, most of which had lost their U.S. copyrights for failure of the authors to comply with formalities. The trial court found the defendants liable for infringement on 81 films and dropped seven other films from consideration. At issue on appeal was whether corporations could own copyrights under Mexican law and whether the copyrights in the seven remaining films had also been restored by the URAA. The defendants, who had begun obtaining "rights" to the films from individual screenwriters and composers, claimed corporations could not be authors under Mexican law. The URAA and 17 U.S.C. § 104A(2)(b) provide that a restored work vests in the author or initial rightholder of the work as determined by the law of the source country. Interpreting Mexican law, the court determined that companies can have "author's rights" and hold copyrights. On the second issue, the court found that the seven films were produced before the effective date of a Mexican statute removing the requirement of copyright registration. Because they were never registered, the seven films were thrust into the public domain in Mexico and were not eligible for U.S. copyright restoration.

4. Affirming a lower court decision (321 F. Supp. 2d 107 (D.D.C. 2004)) that had rejected arguments by music publishing and film preservation firms wishing to exploit erstwhile public domain works, the U.S. Court of Appeals for the District of Columbia Circuit held that restoration of copyright to foreign holders under the URAA is not overreaching and does not violate the copyright clause of the U.S. Constitution. *See Luck's Music Library, Inc. v. Gonzales,* 407 F.3d 1262 (D.C. Cir. 2005). *Accord, Golan v. Gonzales,* 74 USPQ2d 1808, 2005 WL 914754 (D. Colo. 2005).

C. ALIENABILITY OF COPYRIGHT

1. ASSIGNMENTS AND LICENSES

Statutes: 17 U.S.C.A. §§ 201–05

COPYRIGHT ACT OF 1976
H.R. Rep. No. 94–1476.
94th Cong., 2d Sess. 123 (1976).

* * *

TRANSFER OF OWNERSHIP

The principle of unlimited alienability of copyright is stated in clause (1) of section 201(d). Under that provision the ownership of a copyright, or of any part of it, may be transferred by any means of conveyance or by operation of law, and is to be treated as personal property upon the death of the owner. * * *

Clause (2) of subsection (d) contains the first explicit statutory recognition of the principle of divisibility of copyright in our law. This provision, which has long been sought by authors and their representatives, and which has attracted wide support from other groups, means that any of the exclusive rights that go to make up a copyright, including those enumerated in section 106 and any subdivision of them, can be transferred and owned separately. The definition of "transfer of copyright ownership" in section 101 makes clear that the principle of divisibility applies whether or not the transfer is "limited in time or place of effect," and another definition in the same section provides that the term "copyright owner," with respect to any one exclusive right, refers to the owner of that particular right.

* * *

Notes

1. Suppose that a copyright owner attempts an oral assignment of his rights to a second party. Some time after that, an infringement occurs. Does the second party have standing to sue the infringer? Suppose the parties confirm the transfer in writing after the infringement occurs? See *Imperial Residential Design, Inc. v. Palms Dev. Group, Inc.,* 70 F.3d 96 (11th Cir.1995).

But see Silvers v. Sony Pictures Entertainment, Inc., 402 F.3d 881 (9th Cir. 2005) (copyright owner cannot assign an accrued right to sue infringer).

2.   Is an exclusive license a "transfer" for copyright purposes? What about a nonexclusive license? Which must be in writing to be valid? Why?

3.   What purposes are served by the recording provisions of section 205? What kinds of transactions can be recorded? What kinds should *always* be recorded?

4.   Which party prevails where:

a.   An exclusive licensee fails to record, and the licensor makes a subsequent gift of the entire copyright, which is promptly recorded?

b.   An exclusive license takes place, followed by the licensor's grant of a conflicting nonexclusive license (in a written instrument signed by the licensor)? Assume that the exclusive transferee records within 30 days, but this recordation takes place 5 days *after* the nonexclusive license was granted.

c.   The first exclusive licensee records 90 days after the transfer, and a conflicting transfer for valid consideration occurs 100 days after the first transfer, where the second transferee acts in good faith and is unaware of the prior transfer?

d.   Same facts as (c), but the work was never registered.

5.   Section 28 of the 1909 Act required a written instrument for any assignment of a statutory copyright in its entirety, but not for an exclusive license of a statutory copyright, and not for any assignment or license of a common law copyright. What impact, if any, does this have on copyright interests today? Should the 1976 Act be applied retroactively to pre–1978 assignments and exclusive licenses? See Roth v. Pritikin, 710 F.2d 934 (2d Cir.1983).

6.   In *Gardner v. Nike, Inc.,* 279 F.3d 774 (9th Cir.2002), the U.S. Court of Appeals for the Ninth Circuit, affirming a summary judgment for the defendant, found that the 1976 Copyright Act does not permit an exclusive copyright licensee to transfer its rights without the licensor's consent. In 1996, Sony Music Entertainment Corp had assigned to the plaintiff Gardner the rights Sony had been granted by an exclusive and perpetual license to use a cartoon character created by Nike. The court noted that while the agreement between Sony and Nike did not address Sony's power to transfer its rights under the license, and neither the 1909 Act nor the 1976 Act expressly considers the matter, the plain language of Section 201(d)(2) limits an exclusive licensee's rights to only those "protections and remedies" granted to the copyright owner.

7.   In *Random House, Inc. v. Rosetta Books LLC,* 283 F.3d 490 (2d Cir.2002) the Second Circuit affirmed the lower court's ruling denying the plaintiff's motion for a preliminary injunction. The court found mixed questions of law and fact regarding the defendant's sale of e-books despite the plaintiff's licensing agreement granting Random House the exclusive right to publish the author's works "in book form." The court pointed to evolving technology as well as to the reasonable expectations of the parties

in concluding that the licensing agreement did not extend to the right to publish the author's works as e-books.

8.   In *Foad Consulting Group v. Musil Govan Azzalino*, 270 F.3d 821 (9th Cir.2001), the Ninth Circuit ruled that while the Copyright Act determines the transferability of implied copyright licenses, state law governs whether such a license was in fact granted. In this case, the Plaintiff, engineering firm Foad Consulting Group, granted a nonexclusive implied license to GenCom Inc. to use copyrighted plans to complete a work, to hire others to create derivative works, and to publish a final work. Musil Govan Azzolli was ultimately hired to complete the plans for the shopping center development project and used much of the plaintiff's preliminary development plan in the final engineering drawings. The court disagreed with Foad's claim that use of the revised plan without permission was an infringement of its reproduction rights and stated that GenCom had been granted an implied license under state contract law.

9.   In *Meisner Brem Corp. v. Mitchell*, 313 F.Supp.2d 13 (D.N.H. 2004), the plaintiff was hired to design a subdivision, but was terminated over a fee payment dispute. The property owners gave the defendants, who were retained after the plaintiff was fired, the subdivision plans prepared by plaintiff to use in creating the final plans. The plaintiff then sued for copyright infringement. In granting summary judgment to the defendants, the district court stated that because of the language of the contract between the plaintiff and the property owners, "an implied nonexclusive license exists that extended to defendants' work on the [p]roject," 313 F.Supp.2d at 20, and therefore the plaintiff's plans could be used without the plaintiff's future involvement.

EFFECTS ASSOCIATES, INC. v. COHEN

United States Court of Appeals, Ninth Circuit, 1990.
908 F.2d 555, *cert. denied*, 498 U.S. 1103, 111
S.Ct. 1003, 112 L.Ed.2d 1086 (1991).

KOZINSKI, CIRCUIT JUDGE.

What we have here is a failure to compensate. Larry Cohen, a low-budget horror movie mogul, paid less than the agreed price for special effects footage he had commissioned from Effects Associates. Cohen then used this footage without first obtaining a written license or assignment of the copyright; Effects sued for copyright infringement. We consider whether a transfer of copyright without a written agreement, an arrangement apparently not uncommon in the motion picture industry, conforms with the requirements of the Copyright Act.

[When Effects orally agreed to provide special effects footage for Cohen's film, the parties never discussed who would own the copyright in the commissioned footage. When Effects sued Cohen for infringement (after Cohen failed to tender full payment), the district court granted summary judgment, holding that Effects had granted Cohen an implied license to use the footage. On appeal, the Ninth Circuit held that Effects (which both parties agree is the initial copyright owner) had not transferred the copyright to Cohen, because an oral transfer of copyright ownership is invalid under 17 U.S.C. § 204(a). However, because a "transfer" of copyright is defined by 17 U.S.C. § 101 to include an exclusive license but not a nonexclusive license, the court then addressed the question whether Cohen had acquired an oral nonexclusive license to use the footage.]

* * *

Although we reject any suggestion that moviemakers are immune to section 204, we note that there is a narrow exception to the writing requirement that may apply here. Section 204 provides that all transfers of copyright ownership must be in writing; section 101 defines transfers of ownership broadly, but expressly removes from the scope of section 204 a "nonexclusive license." * * *. The sole issue that remains, then, is whether Cohen had a nonexclusive license to use plaintiff's special effects footage.

The leading treatise on copyright law states that "[a] nonexclusive license may be granted orally, or may even be implied from conduct." 3 M. Nimmer & D. Nimmer, Nimmer on Copyright § 10.03[A], at 10–36 (1989). Cohen relies on the latter proposition; he insists that, although Effects never gave him a written or oral license, Effects's conduct created an implied license to use the footage in "The Stuff."

Cohen relies largely on our decision in Oddo v. Ries, 743 F.2d 630 (9th Cir.1984). There, we held that Oddo, the author of a series of articles on how to restore Ford F–100 pickup trucks, had impliedly granted a limited non-exclusive license to Ries, a publisher, to use plaintiff's articles in a book on the same topic. We relied on the fact that Oddo and Ries had formed a partnership to create and publish the book, with Oddo writing and Ries providing capital. Id. at 632 & n. 1. Oddo prepared a manuscript consisting partly of material taken from his prior articles and submitted it to Ries. Id. at 632. Because the manuscript incorporated pre-existing material, it was a derivative work; by publishing it, Ries would have necessarily infringed the copyright in Oddo's articles, unless Oddo had granted him a license. Id. at 634. We concluded that, in preparing and handing over to Ries a manuscript intended for publication that, if published, would infringe Oddo's copyright, Oddo "impliedly gave the partnership a license to use the articles insofar as they were incorporated in the manuscript, for without such a license, Oddo's contribution to the partnership venture would have been of minimal value." Id.[5]

The district court agreed with Cohen, and we agree with the district court: Oddo controls here. Like the plaintiff in Oddo, Effects created a work at defendant's request and handed it over, intending that defen-

---

5. Oddo did nevertheless prevail, but on other grounds. Ries was unhappy with Oddo's manuscript and hired another writer to do the job right. This writer added much new material, but also used large chunks of Oddo's manuscript, thereby incorporating portions of Oddo's pre-existing articles. 743 F.2d at 632. By publishing the other writer's book, Ries exceeded the scope of his implied license to use Oddo's articles and was liable for copyright infringement. Id. at 634.

dant copy and distribute it.[6] To hold that Effects did not at the same time convey a license to use the footage in "The Stuff" would mean that plaintiff's contribution to the film was "of minimal value," a conclusion that can't be squared with the fact that Cohen paid Effects almost $56,000 for this footage. Accordingly, we conclude that Effects impliedly granted nonexclusive licenses to Cohen and his production company to incorporate the special effects footage into "The Stuff" and to New World Entertainment to distribute the film.

Nor can we construe payment in full as a condition precedent to implying a license. Conditions precedent are disfavored and will not be read into a contract unless required by plain, unambiguous language. Sulmeyer v. United States (In re Bubble Up Delaware, Inc.), 684 F.2d 1259, 1264 (9th Cir.1982). The language of the October 29, 1984, agreement doesn't support a conclusion that full payment was a condition precedent to Cohen's use of the footage. Moreover, Effects's president conceded at his deposition that he never told Cohen that a failure to pay would be viewed as copyright infringement. * * *

CONCLUSION

We affirm the district court's grant of summary judgment in favor of Cohen and the other defendants. We note, however, that plaintiff doesn't leave this court empty-handed. Copyright ownership is comprised of a bundle of rights; in granting a nonexclusive license to Cohen, Effects has given up only one stick from that bundle—the right to sue Cohen for copyright infringement. It retains the right to sue him in state court on a variety of other grounds, including breach of contract. Additionally, Effects may license, sell or give away for nothing its remaining rights in the special effects footage. * * *

Notes

1.   Consider the provisions of Section 201(c) of the Act with respect to "contributions to collective works." In *New York Times v. Tasini*, 533 U.S. 483, 121 S.Ct. 2381, 150 L.Ed.2d 500 (2001), the Supreme Court held that these provisions do not have the effect of creating a statutory license to republish a freelance author's work in subsequent internet compilations. The holding means that publishers (like the New York Times) can bundle works previously published in the pages of the paper only with each author's consent and, presumably, upon payment.

6. As the district court found, "every objective fact concerning the transaction at issue supports a finding that an implied license existed." Order Granting Summary Judgment (Aug. 26, 1988) at 2. Effects's copyright registration certificate states that the footage is to be used in "The Stuff," so does the letter agreement of October 29, 1984, and Effects's President James Danforth agreed at his deposition that this was his understanding. * * * Also, Effects delivered the film negatives to Cohen, never warning him that cutting the negatives into the film would constitute copyright infringement. * * * While delivery of a copy "does not *of itself* convey any rights in the copyrighted work," 17 U.S.C. § 202 (1988) (emphasis added), it is one factor that may be relied upon in determining that an implied license has been granted.

As a practical matter, how significant is *Tasini* likely to be in shaping future practices in the area of copyright transfers and assignments like the ones involved in the case? How are publishers likely to respond?

Will the result in *Tasini* have a significant impact on internet research?

2. In *Greenberg v. National Geographic Soc'y*, 244 F.3d 1267 (11th Cir.2001), the Eleventh Circuit decided that the publisher had no Section 201(c) privilege to republish a photographic contribution in a CD–Rom compilation. In this case, the defendants had added material to the copyrighted work in the course of preparing the CD–Rom. Thus, there was some suggestion that, in addition to the Section 201(c) issue, a derivative works infringement might also be involved.

3. In *Faulkner v. National Geographic Soc'y*, 294 F.Supp.2d 523 (S.D.N.Y. 2003), freelance photographers and writers claimed that the defendant magazine's archived issues on DVD and CD–ROM infringed their copyrights. The plaintiffs owned copyrights in their separate contributions to each magazine issue, while the defendants owned the copyrights in the individual print issues. The court held that the digital archive was a "revision" of the collective work under 17 U.S.C. § 201(c); thus, the plaintiffs' infringement claims were precluded. In distinguishing a new collection from a revision, the court followed *Tasini* and looked at whether the context of the original contribution had changed. In this case, each page was digitally scanned exactly as it appeared in the original edition so that the relationship between the digital and print versions was apparent. Rejecting the contention that the digital version was an "entirely different" work, the court said the appearance of the product in a new medium was irrelevant ("... media neutrality is a fundamental principle of the Copyright Act"). *Id.* at 541. Also, the addition of elements in the digital version that were not in the original was not sufficient to foreclose the § 201(c) privilege. *Affirmed, Faulkner v. National Geographic Enterprises Inc.,* 409 F.3d 26 (2d Cir. 2005).

2. TERMINATION PROVISIONS

Statutes: 17 U.S.C.A. §§ 203, 304(c)

It is important to distinguish the two termination provisions created by the 1976 Act. The termination provision of section 304(c) applies only to pre–1978 grants of the renewal term for works copyrighted under the 1909 Act. The termination provision of section 203 applies only to grants executed after 1977. Both provisions contain a "derivative works exception."

COPYRIGHT ACT OF 1976

H.R. Rep. No. 94–1476.
94th Cong., 2d Sess. 124–27, 140–41 (1976).

* * *

THE PROBLEM IN GENERAL

The provisions of section 203 are based on the premise that the reversionary provisions of the present section on copyright renewal (17

U.S.C. sec. 24) should be eliminated, and that the proposed law should substitute for them a provision safeguarding authors against unremunerative transfers. A provision of this sort is needed because of the unequal bargaining position of authors, resulting in part from the impossibility of determining a work's value until it has been exploited. Section 203 reflects a practical compromise that will further the objectives of the copyright law while recognizing the problems and legitimate needs of all interests involved.

SCOPE OF THE PROVISION

Instead of being automatic, as is theoretically the case under the present renewal provision, the termination of a transfer or license under section 203 would require the serving of an advance notice within specified time limits and under specified conditions. However, although affirmative action is needed to effect a termination, the right to take this action cannot be waived in advance or contracted away. Under section 203(a) the right of termination would apply only to transfers and licenses executed after the effective date of the new statute, and would have no retroactive effect.

The right of termination would be confined to inter vivos transfers or licenses executed by the author, and would not apply to transfers by the author's successors in interest or to the author's own bequests. The scope of the right would extend not only to any "transfer of copyright ownership," as defined in section 101, but also to nonexclusive licenses. The right of termination would not apply to "works made for hire," which is one of the principal reasons the definition of that term assumed importance in the development of the bill.

* * *

WHEN A GRANT CAN BE TERMINATED

Section 203 draws a distinction between the date when a termination becomes effective and the earlier date when the advance notice of termination is served. With respect to the ultimate effective date, section 203(a)(3) provides, as a general rule, that a grant may be terminated during the 5 years following the expiration of a period of 35 years from the execution of the grant. As an exception to this basis 35-year rule, the bill also provides that "if the grant covers the right of publication of the work, the period begins at the end of 35 years from the date of publication of the work under the grant or at the end of 40 years from the date of execution of the grant, whichever term ends earlier." * * *

* * *

EFFECT OF TERMINATION

Section 203(b) makes clear that, unless effectively terminated within the applicable 5-year period, all rights covered by an existing grant will continue unchanged, and that rights under other Federal, State, or foreign laws are unaffected. * * *

* * *

An important limitation on the rights of a copyright owner under a terminated grant is specified in section 203(b)(1). This clause provides that, notwithstanding a termination, a derivative work prepared earlier may "continue to be utilized" under the conditions of the terminated grant; the clause adds, however, that this privilege is not broad enough to permit the preparation of other derivative works. In other words, a film made from a play could continue to be licensed for performance after the motion picture contract had been terminated but any remake rights covered by the contract would be cut off. * * *

* * *

Termination of Grants Covering Extended Term

An issue underlying the 19–year extension of renewal terms under both subsections (a) and (b) of section 304 is whether, in a case where their rights have already been transferred, the author or the dependents of the author should be given a chance to benefit from the extended term. The arguments for granting rights of termination are even more persuasive under section 304 than they are under section 203; the extended term represents a completely new property right, and there are strong reasons for giving the author, who is the fundamental beneficiary of copyright under the Constitution, an opportunity to share in it.

Subsection (c) of section 304 is a close but not exact counterpart of section 203. In the case of either a first-term or renewal copyright already subsisting when the new statute becomes effective, any grant of rights covering the renewal copyright in the work, executed before the effective date, may be terminated under conditions and limitations similar to those provided in section 203. Except for transfers and licenses covering renewal copyrights already extended under Public Laws 87–668, 89–142, 90–141, 90–416, 91–147, 91–555, 92–170, 92–566, and 93–573, which would become subject to termination immediately upon the coming into effect of the revised law, the 5–year period during which termination could be made effective would start 56 years after copyright was originally secured.

The bill distinguishes between the persons who can terminate a grant under section 203 and those entitled to terminate a grant covering an extended term under section 304. Instead of being limited to transfers and licenses executed by the author, the right of termination under section 304(c) also extends to grants executed by those beneficiaries of the author who can claim renewal under the present law: his or her widow or widower, children, executors, or next of kin.

* * *

* * * [I]n connection with section 203, the bill adopts the principle that, where a transfer or license by the author is involved, termination may be effected by a per stirpes majority of those entitled to terminate, and this principle also applies to the ownership of rights under a termination and to the making of further grants of reverted rights. In general, this principle has also been adopted with respect to the termination of rights under an extended renewal copyright in section 304, but with several differences made necessary by the differences between the legal status of transfers and licenses made after the effective date of the new law (governed by section 203) and that of grants of renewal rights made earlier and governed by section 304(c). * * *

Notes

1. Note that termination rights apply to assignments affecting individually authored works, but not to assignments of works made for hire–another factor to be considered when parties have the opportunity to proceed under either arrangement.

2. Compare the derivative works exceptions in section 203 and 304 with that of section 104A: they have a similar purpose–to protect investments in new creative works that were made in reliance on an underlying work having a particular legal status. But the section 104A exception protects a party that relied on the underlying work's public domain status at a time when there was little reason to believe that its copyright would someday be restored, whereas the section 203 exception protects reliance on rights acquired under a post–1978 grant even though the possibility of the grant being terminated was foreseeable at the time of the grant (and thus this exception encourages parties to enter into such grants by eliminating the risk of losing their investment in the derivative work); and the section 304 exception protects reliance on a pre–1978 grant which was entered into with the expectation that the underlying work would enter the public domain at the end of 56 years so that continued exploitation of the derivative work after that time would not infringe.

3. In *Fred Ahlert Music Corp. v. Warner/Chappell Music, Inc.*, 155 F.3d 17 (2d Cir.1998), the Second Circuit held that the scope of the derivative works exception to the termination rights of a music copyright owner depends not only on the scope of the original author-publisher grant, but also on the scope of that publisher's grant to a record company authorizing the creation of a derivative work sound recording. Thus, where the first publisher had (prior to termination) granted a record company a license that was limited to making and distributing a single sound recording (the derivative work at issue) of the plaintiff's musical composition, after termination of the original author-publisher grant the first publisher could not authorize a second record company to distribute that same sound recording on a movie soundtrack, because such a license would exceed the scope of the original grant under which the derivative work was created.

4. The Sonny Bono Copyright Term Extension Act, Pub. L. No. 105–298 (signed Oct. 27, 1998), which added 20 years to U.S. copyright terms, also added a new termination right at 17 U.S.C. § 304(d), permitting

termination with respect to the new 20–year term extension, but only with respect to pre–1978 grants pertaining to works which are not works made for hire, which are in their renewal term as of Oct. 27, 1998, which have not previously been the subject of a termination under section 304(c), and with respect to which the section 304(c) termination rights granted under prior law expired on or before Oct. 27, 1998.

The new law also extends section 203 and 304 termination rights to an author's executor, administrator, personal representative, or trustee if the author is not survived by a spouse, children or grandchildren.

WOODS v. BOURNE CO.

United States Court of Appeals, Second Circuit, 1995.
60 F.3d 978.

FEINBERG, CIRCUIT JUDGE:

This appeal requires us to address conflicting claims to royalties generated by various uses of the song "When the Red, Red, Robin Comes Bob, Bob, Bobbin' Along" (the Song) during what is known in copyright law as an extended renewal term. Plaintiffs [doing business as Callicoon Music], heirs of song composer Harry Woods, and defendant Bourne, Inc., Woods's music publisher, both claim the right to receive certain royalties generated during this period. Essentially, plaintiffs claim that they are entitled to the royalties because they have exercised their statutory right to terminate the publisher's interests in the Song pursuant to 17 U.S.C. § 304(c). Bourne maintains that the royalties belong to it because all the disputed post-termination uses of the Song are attributable to so-called derivative works, which were prepared under its authority prior to termination and which therefore do not revert to the author. 17 U.S.C. § 304(c)(6)(A).

The royalties at issue were generated by several different uses of the Song following termination. These uses include (1) television performances of movies and television programs that incorporate the Song (hereafter sometimes referred to collectively as "audiovisual works"); (2) radio performances of sound recordings of the Song; and (3) sales of reprints of published arrangements. * * *

The district court essentially reached its determination by analyzing whether any of the musical arrangements of the Song contained in the movies, television shows, sound recordings and printed arrangements were sufficiently original to qualify as derivative works. Finding that, with one minor exception, no version of the Song was sufficiently original, the district court granted judgment for the plaintiffs. The district court did not consider it relevant that some of the disputed royalties were generated by performances of audiovisual works, such as movies containing the Song, which are conceded to be original enough to qualify as derivative works.

For reasons set forth below, we hold that when a musical arrangement is contained within an audiovisual work produced under license from a publisher prior to termination, the publisher is entitled to receive royalties from post-termination performances of the audiovisual work under the terms of pre-termination licenses governing performance rights. It is irrelevant to disposition of those royalties whether the musical arrangement in the audiovisual work would qualify independently as a derivative work. * * *

* * *

B.   THE EXTENDED RENEWAL TERM

[In 1926, composer Woods assigned the copyright and renewal term in the Song to music publisher Berlin. During the original and renewal copyright terms, Berlin and its successor Bourne issued "synchronization" (or "synch") licenses authorizing others to incorporate the Song in movies and television programs.]

Under the Copyright Act of 1909, in effect at the time of Woods's grant to Berlin, the original term of a copyright was 28 years, followed by a renewal term of another 28 years. Pub. L. No. 349, 35 Stat. 1075, § 23 (1909). Thus, the grant from Woods to Berlin in the Songwriter's Agreement, which included renewal rights, was to endure for up to 56 years, ending in 1982.

The reason for including a renewal term in the Copyright Act was to permit an author who sold the rights in his work for little consideration, when measured against the work's subsequent success, to enjoy a second opportunity with more bargaining power to reap the full value of the work. See 2 Melville B. Nimmer & David Nimmer, Nimmer on Copyright § 9.02 at 9–28 to 9–29 (1994). Thus, Congress attempted to alleviate the problem of the inability of authors to know the true monetary value of their works prior to commercial exploitation. Id. at 9–30. That purpose, however, was largely eroded by a subsequent Supreme Court decision holding that renewal rights were assignable along with original term rights in a work. Fisher Music Co. v. M. Witmark & Sons, 318 U.S. 643, 87 L. Ed. 1055, 63 S. Ct. 773 (1943); see 2 Nimmer § 9.06[B][1] at 9–108.

When the Copyright Act was thoroughly revised in 1976, Pub. L. No. 94–553, 90 Stat. 2541 (1976), Congress attempted to restore a second chance to authors or their heirs. Among other changes, Congress prolonged the duration of copyrights then in the renewal term so that they would continue for an additional 19 years. 17 U.S.C. § 304(b). At the end of the 28th year of the renewal term, the author (if alive) or the author's surviving spouse or children may terminate the rights of a grantee, usually a publisher, to whom the author had transferred rights in the original work. 17 U.S.C. § 304(c)(1)-(3). During the 19–year extended renewal term, a copyrighted work does not enter the public domain but continues to generate royalties. If the author or heirs elect to terminate the publisher's rights, royalties become payable to them rather than to the publisher. 17 U.S.C. § 304(c)(6). The author or heirs thus "recapture" rights in the copyrighted work and may thereby be relieved "of the consequences of ill-advised and unremunerative grants that had been made before the author had a fair opportunity to appreciate the [work's] true value." Mills Music, Inc. v. Snyder, 469 U.S. 153, 172–73, 83 L. Ed. 2d 556, 105 S. Ct. 638 (1985).

There is an important exception to the reversion rights of the author or heirs for derivative works produced by an authorized party during the original and renewal copyright terms. The Copyright Act of 1976 provides that

> [a] derivative work prepared under authority of the grant before its termination may continue to be utilized under the terms of the grant after its termination, but this privilege does not extend to the preparation after the termination of other derivative works based upon the copyrighted work covered by the terminated grant.

17 U.S.C. § 304(c)(6)(A) (referred to hereafter as "the Derivative Works Exception" or simply "the Exception"). * * *

The renewal term for Bourne's copyright in the Song came to an end in April 1982, and Callicoon terminated Bourne's rights immediately thereafter.

* * *

D. PERFORMANCE RIGHTS

* * *

During the original and renewal terms, Bourne received royalties from ASCAP for television broadcasts of movies and television programs containing the Song and radio broadcasts of the Song. A typical synch license issued by Bourne for the production of an audiovisual work required a producer to pay a flat fee but provided that any broadcast entity performing the Song as contained in the audiovisual work must obtain a performance license from ASCAP or Bourne. Thus, for each pre-recorded audiovisual work incorporating the Song, Bourne had two sources of income: royalties from the producer for the right to incorporate the Song in the audiovisual work and royalties from television stations, via ASCAP, for each performance of the Song contained in the work. * * *

* * *

The district court determined that Callicoon was entitled to all of the royalties generated by post-termination performances of the Song, including performances contained in pre-termination derivative audiovisual works. The court acknowledged, and the parties do not dispute, that the works in which the Song was incorporated—for example, movies— were by definition derivative. Nevertheless, the court found the controlling issue, as to all categories of performance, to be whether the underlying arrangement of the Song itself is a derivative work. Only then would performance royalties continue to go to Bourne during the extended renewal term. * * *

* * *

A. ROYALTIES FROM TELEVISION PERFORMANCES

We consider first the basis for determining entitlement to royalties from post-termination performances of the Song as contained in pre-termination movies and television programs.

The Derivative Works Exception preserves the right of owners of derivative works to continue to exploit their works during the extended renewal term under previously negotiated terms. Without such an exception, authors might use their reversion rights to extract prohibitive fees from owners of successful derivative works or to bring infringement actions against them. See Mills Music, 469 U.S. at 172–74 (discussing legislative history of termination right and Derivative Works Exception); id. at 183–84 n.8 (White, J., dissenting) (explaining that under the 1909 Act, films had been removed from public circulation during renewal periods for fear of infringement actions).

The goal of keeping derivative works in public circulation does not require that publishers rather than authors receive royalties for their use. As long as the royalties paid by a derivative work user remain unchanged, the user should be indifferent as to whether an author or publisher receives the payment. See Mills Music, 469 U.S. at 177. The royalties generated during the extended renewal term will be a windfall to either authors (and their heirs) or publishers since, at the time the rights at issue were originally established, neither group expected to get royalties for more than 56 years. The question, therefore, is: Who is the beneficiary of this windfall?

1. The Mills Music Decision

The answer, according to the decision of the Supreme Court in Mills Music, Inc. v. Snyder, is found in the phrase "under the terms of the grant," as used in the Derivative Works Exception. We quote its text again for convenience:

> A derivative work prepared under authority of the grant before its termination may continue to be utilized *under the terms of the grant* after its termination, but this privilege does not extend to the preparation after the termination of other derivative works based upon the copyrighted work covered by the terminated grant.

17 U.S.C. § 304(c)(6)(A) (emphasis supplied); see Mills Music, 469 U.S. at 156.

Mills Music posed circumstances similar to those of the instant case. Snyder, treated for purposes of that case as the sole author of the song "Who's Sorry Now," had assigned renewal rights in the song to a publisher, Mills, in 1940 in exchange for, among other things, a 50% share in mechanical royalties, that is, royalties from sales of copies of sound recordings. Mills in turn licensed record companies to produce copies of sound recordings of the song. Upon termination of the grant from Snyder to Mills, Snyder's heirs claimed the right to 100%, rather than just 50%, of future mechanical royalties. Harry Fox Agency, Inc. v. Mills Music, Inc., 543 F.Supp. 844, 850 (S.D.N.Y.1982), rev'd, 720 F.2d 733 (2d Cir.1983), rev'd sub nom. Mills Music, Inc. v. Snyder, 469 U.S. 153, 105 S.Ct. 638, 83 L.Ed.2d 556 (1985). Mills claimed that the sound recordings at issue were derivative works created under the terms of the grant from Snyder to Mills and that, therefore, Mills should continue to share in mechanical royalties according to the terms of that grant. 543 F.Supp. at 850.

In the district court, Judge Edward Weinfeld held that the sound recordings produced before termination were derivative works and that the terms of the grant required payment of mechanical royalties to Mills. Id. at 852. This court reversed, holding that upon termination only the grant from Mills to the record companies remained in effect. Since the basis for Mills's retention of half the mechanical royalties was the grant from Snyder, and since that grant was now terminated, all mechanical royalties should revert to Snyder's heirs. 720 F.2d at 739.

The Supreme Court reversed. It found that the phrase "terminated grant," the last two words in the Derivative Works Exception, must refer to the original grant from author to publisher. The Court reasoned that the other two uses of the word "grant" in the single sentence of the Derivative Works Exception must logically refer to the same grant. 469 U.S. at 164–65. The Court noted that "[t]he 1940 grant from Snyder to Mills expressly gave Mills the authority to license others to make derivative works." Id. at 165. It then concluded that "a fair construction of the phrase 'under the terms of the grant' as applied to any particular licensee would necessarily encompass both the [original] grant [from author to publisher] and the individual license [to record producers] executed pursuant thereto." Id. at 166–67. Because the combination of the two grants directed record companies to pay royalties to Mills, and Mills in turn to pay 50% of the amount collected to Snyder, the Court held that Mills was entitled to retain its 50% share of mechanical royalties on sales of records produced before termination but sold during the extended renewal term. Id. at 178.

Mills Music is, of course, binding upon us. Mills Music appears to require that where multiple levels of licenses govern use of a derivative work, the "terms of the grant" encompass the original grant from author to publisher and each subsequent grant necessary to enable the particular use at issue. See Howard B. Abrams, Who's Sorry Now? Termination Rights and the Derivative Works Exception, 62 U. Det. L. Rev. 181, 234–35 (1985) (describing holding in Mills Music as "preserving the entire paper chain that defines the entire transaction"). If one of those grants requires payment of royalties by licensees to an intermediary, such as a publisher, then continued utilization of derivative works "under the terms of the grant" requires continued payments to the intermediary. See Mills Music, 469 U.S. at 167. The effect of Mills Music, then, is to preserve during the post-termination period the panoply of contractual obligations that governed pre-termination uses of derivative works by derivative work owners or their licensees.

2. Applying the Mills Music Decision

The derivative works involved in Mills Music were sound recordings, and the use there was the sale of copies. The concededly derivative works we now address are audiovisual works and the use in question is public performance. We believe that the reasoning of Mills Music also applies in this situation.

There is no question that the owners of the copyrights in audiovisual works have the right to perform the works publicly. They typically exercise this right by licensing television stations to broadcast their works. In this case, the terms of the synch licenses issued by Bourne to the producers required the television stations performing the audiovisual works to obtain a second grant from either Bourne or ASCAP, licensing the stations to perform the Song contained in the audiovisual works. In practice, this license is always obtained from ASCAP, which then remits the publisher's share of fees to Bourne pursuant to the agreement between Bourne and ASCAP. Under our reading of Mills Music, the "terms of the grant" include the provisions of the grants from Bourne to ASCAP and from ASCAP to television stations. This pair of licenses is contemplated in the grant of the synch licenses from Bourne to film and television producers.

* * *

We therefore reverse the decision of the district court as to royalties from post-termination performances of pre-termination audiovisual works. On remand, the court should enter judgment ordering defendant ASCAP to pay these royalties to Bourne in accordance with the terms of the grants in effect immediately prior to the effective date of Callicoon's termination.

* * *

MARVEL CHARACTERS, INC. v. SIMON

United States Court of Appeals, Second Circuit, 2002.
310 F.3d 280.

Batchelder, Circuit Judge.

This appeal requires us to examine the scope of the termination provision of the Copyright Act of 1976 (the "1976 Act"). 17 U.S.C. § 304(c). Section 304(c) grants authors (or if deceased, their statutory heirs) an inalienable right to terminate a grant in a copyright fifty-six years after the original grant "notwithstanding any agreement to the contrary." 17 U.S.C. § 304(c)(3), (5). The termination provision, however, has one salient exception: copyright grants in works created for hire cannot be terminated. 17 U.S.C. § 304(c).

The question of first impression raised here is whether a settlement agreement, entered into long after a work's creation, stipulating that a work was created for hire constitutes "any agreement to the contrary" under the 1976 Act. We conclude that it does and, therefore, reverse.

BACKGROUND

This being an appeal from a grant of summary judgment to plaintiff Marvel Comics, Inc. ("Marvel"), we view the deposition testimony, affidavits, and documentary evidence in the light most favorable to defendant Joseph H. Simon, the non-moving party. *Roge v. NYP Holdings, Inc.*, 257 F.3d 164, 165 (2d Cir. 2001).

* * *

[In December 1940, Martin and Jean Goodman, doing business as Timely Publications and Timely Comics, Inc. began publishing *Captain America Comics*. Authorship of the comic book and characters was attributed to Simon and Jack Kirby. According to Simon, he created Captain America as an independent, freelance project. Simon sold the story to Timely for a fixed page rate and a profit share. Throughout 1941, Simon maintains that he created the subsequent issues as a freelance artist and sold them to Timely. The second through tenth issues were published during this time. Timely applied for and received the certificates of registration of copyright for each issue.]

[As the initial copyright term in Captain America Works neared its end, Simon sued the Goodmans and their affiliates. He sued in 1966 in New York State Supreme Court for unfair competition and misappropriation. One year later, he sued in United States District Court for the Southern District of New York, seeking a declaratory judgment that he had the sole right to the renewal term of the copyright in the Works.]

[The actions were contested, and a cross-suit was filed. Meanwhile, Timely's successor in interest applied for renewal of the copyrights in the Works.]

* * *

In November 1969, after two years of discovery, the parties to the Prior Actions entered into a settlement agreement (the "Settlement Agreement"). In the Settlement Agreement, Simon acknowledged that his contribution to the Works "was done as an employee for hire of the Goodmans." (R. at 185). Pursuant to this Settlement Agreement, Simon assigned "any and all right, title and interest he may have or control or which he has had or controlled in [the Works] (without warranty that he has had or controlled any such right, title or interest)" to the Goodmans and their affiliates. (R. at 179–80). The parties to both actions filed stipulations with the respective courts dismissing with prejudice "all claims and matters alleged, threatened, implied or set forth in any of the pleadings filed by [Simon]." (R. at 188–91).

* * *

In December 1999, recognizing an opportunity created by § 304(c) to reclaim his copyright in the Works, Simon filed Notices of Termination (the "Termination Notices") with the Copyright Office purporting to terminate his transfers of the copyrights to Timely pursuant to § 304(c). In the Termination Notices, Simon claimed that he independently created the Captain America character and authored the first issue in the Captain America comic book series, and that he was "neither an employee for hire nor a creator of a work for hire."

Thereafter, Marvel—as Timely's successor in interest in all rights, title, and interest to the Works by virtue of a series of assignments—commenced this action in the United States District Court for the Southern District of New York (Casey, J.) seeking a declaratory judgment that the Termination Notices were invalid and that Marvel remains the sole owner of the copyrights in the Works. Simon in turn filed a counterclaim for a declaratory judgment that: (1) he is the sole author of the Works; (2) the Termination Notices are valid; and (3) all copyrights in the Works revert to him on the effective date of the Notices of Termination.

After discovery, Marvel moved for summary judgment on its claim for a declaration that Simon's Termination Notices were invalid. Marvel argued that it was entitled to summary judgment on three separate grounds: (1) equitable estoppel; (2) res judicata; and (3) fundamental principles of contract law. Each argument was bottomed on the premise that the new termination right granted to authors under § 304(c) of the 1976 Act did not apply to Simon because the Settlement Agreement expressly stated that he was not the author of the Works for copyright purposes.

* * *

Discussion

* * *

[The Court considered and rejected that the prior actions or the Settlement Agreement had preclusive effect. It then turned to the application of Section 304(c) of the 1976 Act.]

Having concluded that Simon is not precluded from asserting that he is the author of the Works for purposes of exercising his statutory termination right, we turn, at length, to the issue of first impression presented by this case: whether an agreement made subsequent to a work's creation that declares that it is a work created for hire constitutes an "agreement to the contrary" under § 304(c) of the 1976 Act. The district court never addressed this question. Instead, it simply assumed that because Simon had conceded in the unambiguous Settlement Agreement that the Works were created for hire, he could not now assert that he was the Works' author for purposes of exercising the termination right in this action. While the district court was undoubtedly correct that the Settlement Agreement is not ambiguous—a contention disputed by the amici curiae—this is not the relevant analysis on this issue. Instead, we must analyze the legislative intent and purpose of § 304(c) of the 1976 Act to determine its application to this case.

Simon contends that the district court's failure to give effect to § 304(c)'s mandate that authors can terminate copyright grants "notwithstanding any agreement to the contrary" contravenes the legislative intent and purpose of § 304(c). Further, because Simon has submitted testimony that he was not in fact an employee for hire when he created the Captain Marvel character, he maintains that a genuine issue of material fact exists regarding Marvel's claims that the Termination Notices are invalid and it is the sole owner of the copyright in the Works. Marvel's only response to Simon's contentions is that if Simon's reading of the statute is upheld, no litigation concerning a claim to authorship could ever be resolved by settlement. We find Simon's arguments persuasive and Marvel's prediction unfounded.

In order to determine the meaning of § 304(c), we apply the well established canons of statutory construction. In interpreting a statute, we look first to the language of the statute itself. *See, e.g., Cmty. for Creative Non–Violence v. Reid*, 490 U.S. 730, 739, 109 S.Ct. 2166, 104 L.Ed.2d 811 (1989); *Auburn Housing Auth. v. Martinez*, 277 F.3d 138, 143 (2d Cir. 2002). When the language of a statute is unambiguous, "judicial inquiry is complete." *Connecticut Nat'l Bank v. Germain*, 503 U.S. 249, 254, 112 S.Ct. 1146, 117 L.Ed.2d 391 (1992). When the terms of a statute are ambiguous, however, we may seek guidance in the legislative history and purpose of the statute. *See Novak v. Kasaks*, 216 F.3d 300, 310 (2d Cir. 2000). In so doing, we must "construct an interpretation that comports with [the statute's] primary purpose and does not lead to anomalous or unreasonable results." *Connecticut v. United States Dep't of the Interior*, 228 F.3d 82, 89 (2d Cir. 2000).

Here, whether § 304(c)(5)'s phrase "any agreement to the contrary" includes a settlement agreement stating that a work was created for hire is not clear from the test of the statute itself. Generally speaking, the Settlement Agreement is an agreement to the contrary. But without more specific or compelling evidence from the text, we find it necessary to go beyond the mere text and consider the legislative intent and purpose of § 304(c) to ascertain the statute's meaning.

The Supreme Court has elucidated the intent and purpose behind the termination provision of the 1976 Act:

> The principal purpose of the amendments in § 304 was to provide added benefits to authors. The ... concept of a termination right itself, w[as] obviously intended to make the rewards for the creativity of authors more substantial. More particularly, the termination right was expressly intended to relieve authors of the consequences of ill-advised and unremunerative grants that had been made before the author had a fair opportunity to appreciate the true value of his work product. That general purpose is plainly defined in the legisla-

tive history and, indeed, is fairly inferable from the text of § 304 itself.

Mills Music, 469 U.S. at 172–73, 105 S.Ct. 638 (footnote omitted) (interpreting the derivative works exception to the termination clause of § 304(c)). Furthermore, the legislative history of the termination provision reflects Congress's intent to protect authors from unequal bargaining positions. See H.R.Rep. No. 94–1476, at 124 (1976), reprinted in 1976 U.S.C.C.A.N. 5659, 5740 ("A provision of this sort is needed because of the unequal bargaining position of authors, resulting in part from the impossibility of determining a work's value until it has been exploited."); see also *Mills Music*, 469 U.S. at 173 n. 39, 105 S.Ct. 638. As these statements suggest, the clear Congressional purpose behind § 304(c) was to prevent authors from waiving their termination right by contract. Accord *Stewart*, 495 U.S. at 230, 110 S.Ct. 1750 ("The 1976 Copyright Act provides ... an inalienable termination right.").

When examining the legislative intent and purpose of § 304(c), it becomes clear that an agreement made after a work's creation stipulating that the work was created as a work for hire constitutes an "agreement to the contrary" which can be disavowed pursuant to the statute. Any other construction of § 304(c) would thwart the clear legislative purpose and intent of the statute. If an agreement between an author and publisher that a work was created for hire were outside the purview of § 304(c)(5), the termination provision would be rendered a nullity; litigation-savvy publishers would be able to utilize their superior bargaining position to compel authors to agree that a work was created for hire in order to get their works published. In effect, such an interpretation would likely ... provide a blueprint by which publishers could effectively eliminate an author's termination right. We conclude that Congress included the "notwithstanding any agreement to the contrary" language in the termination provision precisely to avoid such a result.

This view finds support in Nimmer on Copyright:

> The parties to a grant may not agree that a work shall be deemed one made "for hire" in order to avoid the termination provisions if a "for hire" relationship ... does not in fact exist between them. Such an avoidance device would be contrary to the statutory provision that "[t]ermination of the grant may be effected notwithstanding any agreement to the contrary." ... [I]t is the relationship that in fact exists between the parties, and not their description of that relationship, that is determinative.

3 Melville B. Nimmer & David Nimmer, *Nimmer on Copyright* § 11.02[A][2] (2000 ed.) (footnote omitted). This reading of the statute also explains why copyright grants in works created for hire are not subject to termination. *See* 17 U.S.C. § 304(c). Under the 1909 Act, the statutory author of a work created for hire was the employer-publisher. *See, e.g.,* 17 U.S.C. § 26 (repealed 1976); *Cmty. for Creative Non-Violence*, 490 U.S. at 743–44 & n. 9, 109 S.Ct. 2166. Because an employer-publisher does not face the same potential unequal bargaining

position as an individual author, it follows that an employer-publisher does not need the same protections as an individual author.

This reading of § 304(c) is also consistent with the way in which courts have interpreted the 1909 Act's "work for hire" provision. Courts engaging in such an analysis have focused on the actual relationship between the parties, rather than the language of their agreements, in determining authorship of the work. *See, e.g., Donaldson Pub. Co. v. Bregman, Vocco & Conn, Inc.*, 375 F.2d 639, 640–42 (2d Cir.1967) (holding that a composer's work was not created as a work for hire for defendant even though his contract with defendant provided him with a drawing account during his "employment"); *see also Murray v. Gelderman*, 566 F.2d 1307, 1310–11 (5th Cir.1978) (holding that a writer was not the "author" of a book produced by the defendant even though she expressly contracted for "exclusive control" of its contents).

Additionally, this Court has looked to agency law to determine whether a work is created "for hire" under the 1909 Act. *See Aldon Accessories Ltd. v. Spiegel, Inc.*, 738 F.2d 548, 552 (2d Cir.1984). And under agency law, "[t]he manner in which the parties designate the relationship is not controlling, and if an act done by one person in behalf of another is in its essential nature one of agency, the one is the agent of such other notwithstanding that he or she is not so called. Conversely, the mere use of the word 'agent' by parties in their contract does not make one an agent who, in fact, is not such." 3 Am.Jur.2d Agency § 19 (2002) (footnotes omitted).

Contrary to Marvel's dire prediction about an expansive interpretation of § 304(c), we believe that parties will still be able to resolve their authorship disputes by settlement. If parties intend to preclude any future litigation regarding authorship by settling their claims, they need only comply with the requirements of collateral estoppel by filing a detailed stipulation of settlement, complete with sufficient factual findings on authorship, with the court. Furthermore, when the relationship between parties has deteriorated to the point of litigation, presumably all parties are represented by counsel. Accordingly, the need to protect "ill-advised" authors from publishers or other more sophisticated entities— the policy concern underlying § 304(c)—is no longer present.

In sum, we hold that an agreement made subsequent to a work's creation which retroactively deems it a "work for hire" constitutes an "agreement to the contrary" under § 304(c)(5) of the 1976 Act. Therefore, Simon is not bound by the statement in the Settlement Agreement that he created the Works as an employee for hire. Because Simon has proffered admissible evidence that he did not create the Works as an employee for hire, the district court's grant of summary judgment to Marvel was erroneous. It will be up to a jury to determine whether Simon was the author of the Works and, therefore, whether he can exercise § 304(c)'s termination right. *See, e.g., Medforms, Inc. v. Healthcare Mgmt. Solutions, Inc.*, 290 F.3d 98, 110 (2d Cir.2002) (noting that authorship is a jury question).

* * *

Chapter 18

EXCLUSIVE RIGHTS

A. THE SECTION 106 RIGHTS

Statutes: 17 U.S.C.A. §§ 101 (as needed), 106, 109, 114, 602–03

1. REPRODUCTION

HORGAN v. MACMILLAN, INC.

United States Court of Appeals, Second Circuit, 1986.
789 F.2d 157.

FEINBERG, CHIEF JUDGE:

This appeal presents the novel question whether still photographs of a ballet can infringe the copyright on the choreography for the ballet. Barbara Horgan, executrix of the estate of the renowned choreographer George Balanchine, appeals from a judgment of the United States District Court for the Southern District of New York, Richard Owen, J., denying her motion for a preliminary injunction. Appellant Horgan sought to enjoin the publication of a book entitled "The Nutcracker: A Story & a Ballet," which portrays, in text and photographs, the New York City Ballet Company's production of The Nutcracker ballet, choreographed by Balanchine. Defendant Macmillan is the publisher, and defendant Ellen Switzer the author, of the book; defendants Steven Caras and Costas provided the photographs. The district court held that the book did not infringe Balanchine's copyright because choreography is the flow of steps in a ballet, which could not be reproduced from the still photographs in the book. 621 F. Supp. 1169 (S.D.N.Y.1985). * * *

I.

[In 1954, Balanchine choreographed his now-classic version of the ballet The Nutcracker, an adaptation of a folk tale set to music by Tchaikovsky. Balanchine's version of the ballet also incorporates elements of a previous version by Russian choreographer Ivanov. The New York City Ballet Company and other entities pay Balanchine's estate a

959

royalty or other consideration in exchange for a license to publicly perform his copyrighted choreography.]

In December 1981, Balanchine registered his claim to copyright in the choreography of The Nutcracker with the United States Copyright Office. As part of his claim, he deposited with the Copyright Office a videotape of a New York City Ballet Company dress rehearsal of the ballet. * * *

In early April 1985, appellant Horgan learned for the first time that Macmillan was planning to publish, under its Atheneum imprint, a book about the New York City Ballet/Balanchine version of The Nutcracker. * * *

The book is designed primarily for an audience of young people. The title page displays three black and white photographs of George Balanchine directing a rehearsal of the ballet. The book begins with a 15–page text by defendant Switzer regarding the origins of The Nutcracker as a story and as a ballet. The remainder of the book is introduced by a second title page, as follows:

THE BALANCHINE BALLET

As Performed by the Dancers of the New York City Ballet Company

The principal section of the book consists of 60 color photographs by Caras and Costas of scenes from the New York City Ballet Company production of The Nutcracker, following the sequence of the ballet's story and dances. The photographs are interspersed with Switzer's narration of the story, including those portions not portrayed visually. The final section of the book contains interviews with ten of the dancers, with black and white photographs of them out of costume. Defendants Switzer, Caras and Costas obtained this material through their access to company rehearsals and performances. Switzer is a free lance journalist who was apparently given such access by the press liaison for the Company. Caras and Costas are considered "official photographers" of the New York City Ballet. According to appellant, this means that Balanchine authorized them to take photographs of the Company, some of which might be purchased by the Company for publicity and related purposes.

* * *

On October 11, 1985, Horgan brought suit on behalf of the estate, seeking declaratory relief and both a preliminary and permanent injunction against publication of the book. At the same time, Horgan applied for a temporary restraining order. The district court denied the application in a memorandum endorsement dated October 17, 1985. Some five weeks later, after receiving additional papers and hearing argument, the judge denied Horgan's motion for a preliminary injunction. The judge stated, in an opinion and order substantially similar to his earlier memorandum, that the book did not infringe the copyright on Balanchine's choreography because choreography has to do with the flow of the steps in a ballet. The still photographs in the Nutcracker book, numerous though they are, catch dancers in various attitudes at specific instants of time; they do not, nor do they intend to, take or use the underlying choreography. The staged performance could not be recreated from them.

621 F. Supp. at 1170 [(adding in a footnote: "Just as a Beethoven symphony could not be recreated from a document containing only every twenty-fifth chord of the symphony.")]. * * *

II.

The principal question on appeal, whether still photographs of a ballet can infringe the copyright on the choreography for the ballet, is a matter of first impression. Explicit federal copyright protection for choreography is a fairly recent development, and the scope of that protection is an uncharted area of the law. The 1976 Copyright Act (the Act), 17 U.S.C. § 101 et seq., was the first federal copyright statute expressly to include "choreographic works" as a subject of protection. * * *

* * *

The Act does not define choreography, and the legislative reports on the bill indicate only that "social dance steps and simple routines" are not included. See, e.g., H.R. Rep. No. 1476, 94th Cong., 2d Sess. 53–54, reprinted in 1976 U.S. Code Cong. & Ad. News 5659, 5666–67. The Compendium of Copyright Office Practices, Compendium II (1984), which is issued by that office, defines choreographic works as follows:

> Choreography is the composition and arrangement of dance movements and patterns, and is usually intended to be accompanied by music. Dance is static and kinetic successions of bodily movement in certain rhythmic and spatial relationships. Choreographic works need not tell a story in order to be protected by copyright.

Section 450.01. Under "Characteristics of choreographic works," Compendium II states that

> Choreography represents a related series of dance movements and patterns organized into a coherent whole.

Section 450.03(a). * * * The Act grants the owner of a copyrighted original work that is "fixed in any tangible medium of expression," 17 U.S.C. § 102(a), the exclusive right "to reproduce the copyrighted work in copies ... ," "to prepare derivative works based upon the copyrighted work" and, "in the case of ... choreographic works, ... to display the copyrighted work publicly." 17 U.S.C. § 106(1), (2) & (5). Appellant claims that the Switzer book is a "copy" of Balanchine's copyrighted work because it portrays the essence of the Balanchine Nutcracker, or, in the alternative, that the book is an infringing "derivative work." * * *

In response, appellees assert that the photographs in the Switzer book do not capture the flow of movement, which is the essence of dance, and thus cannot possibly be substantially similar to the choreographic component of the production of the ballet. Appellees rely on the various definitions of choreography in Compendium II, quoted above, to support their position that the central characteristic of choreography is "movement." According to appellees, since each photograph in the book captures only a fraction of an instant, even the combined effect of 60 color photographs does not reproduce the choreography itself, nor provide sufficient details of movement to enable a choreographic work to be reproduced from the photographs.

* * *

* * * [T]he district judge took a far too limited view of the extent to which choreographic material may be conveyed in the medium of still photography. A snapshot of a single moment in a dance sequence may communicate a great deal. It may, for example, capture a gesture, the composition of dancers' bodies or the placement of dancers on the stage. Such freezing of a choreographic moment is shown in a number of the photographs in the Switzer book * * *. A photograph may also convey to the viewer's imagination the moments before and after the split second recorded. On page 76–77 of the Switzer book, for example, there is a two-page photograph of the "Sugar Canes," one of the troupes that perform in The Nutcracker. In this photograph, the Sugar Canes are a foot or more off the ground, holding large hoops above their heads. One member of the ensemble is jumping through a hoop, which is held extended in front of the dancer. The dancer's legs are thrust forward, parallel to the stage and several feet off the ground. The viewer understands instinctively, based simply on the laws of gravity, that the Sugar Canes jumped up from the floor only a moment earlier, and came down shortly after the photographed moment. An ordinary observer, who had only recently seen a performance of The Nutcracker, could probably perceive even more from this photograph. The single instant thus communicates far more than a single chord of a Beethoven symphony—the analogy suggested by the district judge.

It may be that all of the photographs mentioned above are of insufficient quantity or sequencing to constitute infringement; it may also be that they do copy but also are protected as fair use. But that is not what the district judge said in denying a preliminary injunction. The judge erroneously held that still photographs cannot infringe choreography. Since the judge applied the wrong test in evaluating appellant's likelihood of success on the preliminary injunction, we believe that a remand is appropriate. * * *

* * *

We reverse and remand for further proceedings consistent with this opinion.

WALT DISNEY PRODUCTIONS v. FILMATION ASSOCIATES

United States District Court, C. D. of California, 1986.
628 F.Supp. 871.

STOTLER, UNITED STATES DISTRICT JUDGE:

INTRODUCTION

* * *

[Plaintiff Walt Disney Productions ("Disney") alleges that Filmation Associates ("Filmation") copied cartoon figures from Disney's animated film "Pinocchio" and has begun to use them in producing an animated film entitled "The New Adventures of Pinocchio."]

* * * In the course of production, Filmation has produced a script, "story board," "story reel,"[5] models, and designs, which are said to be tangible and permanent reproductions of characters and scenes, "constituting copies of material" copyrighted by Disney. Id., para. 61.

It is undisputed that Filmation has generated a substantial body of work preliminary to a "finished film." It is also undisputed, however, that it has not completed its film "The New Adventures of Pinocchio." Filmation contends that Count Six is not actionable until it has completed work on its motion picture. Alternatively, Filmation asserts it is entitled to judgment because any articles so far produced are not substantially similar to Disney's copyrighted expressions.

1. Actionable "Copies"

Filmation argues that the materials so far created are only transitory steps en route to a fixed product, and that until its film is completed and ready for distribution, there exists no article that could be said to infringe any of Disney's copyrights.

Filmation's argument is refuted by the provisions of the 1976 Copyright Act, 17 U.S.C. §§ 101–914 (the "Act"). Under the Act, " 'copies' are material objects ... in which a work is fixed by any method now known or later developed, and from which the work can be perceived, reproduced, or otherwise communicated, either directly or with the aid of a machine or device." 17 U.S.C. § 101. The definition "includes the material object ... in which the work is first fixed." Id. Further, a work is " 'fixed' in a tangible medium of expression when its embodiment in a copy ... is sufficiently permanent or stable to permit it to be perceived, reproduced, or otherwise communicated for a period of more than

---

5. A "story reel" is a working model used to create the final animated product. To create a story reel, Filmation first records a reading of the script. It then creates a "story board" comprising sketches of the various scenes in the film set in the order in which they will be portrayed and "shoots" the sketches to synchronize with the recorded dialogue track and a rough music track. By viewing the reel, the director can get a "feel" for the story line and pacing of the anticipated picture and can begin allocating responsibility for its animation. * * *

transitory duration." Id. When the work is "prepared over a period of time, the portion of it that has been fixed at any particular time constitutes the work as of that time, and where the work has been prepared in different versions, each version constitutes a separate work." Id. To constitute an actionable copy, therefore, an expression need only be a material object permanently cast in some intelligible form. See 2 Nimmer on Copyrights, § 8.02(B), pp. 8–22—8–25 (1985).

The articles created by Filmation in the production of its film, including a script, story board, story reel, and promotional "trailer," satisfy this definition, and thus can constitute copies for purposes of the Act. Because the right of reproduction affords a copyright owner protection against an infringer even if he does not also infringe the § 106(3) right of distribution, Sony Corp. v. Universal City Studios, Inc., 464 U.S. 417, 474, 78 L.Ed. 2d 574, 104 S.Ct. 774 (1984) (Blackmun, J., dissenting); House Report No. 94–1476, 94th Cong., 2d Sess. (1976), p. 61, the fact that the articles may never be published or, indeed, may be prepared only for the use of Filmation's animators, does not obviate the possibility of infringement. See Harper & Row v. Nation Enterprises, 471 U.S. 539, 105 S.Ct. 2218, 2226, 85 L.Ed. 2d 588, 602(1985) (noting that the Act "eliminated publication 'as a dividing line between common law and statutory protection,' ... extending statutory protection to all works from the time of their creation"). As explained by Professor Nimmer, "subject to the privilege of fair use, and subject to certain other exemptions, copyright infringement occurs whenever an unauthorized copy ... is made, even if it is used solely for the private purposes of the reproducer." 2 Nimmer, § 8.02(C), p. 8–26. It is thus irrelevant that Filmation has not concluded or "realized" what it considers to be a final motion picture: the Act prohibits the creation of copies, even if the creator considers those copies mere interim steps toward some final goal.

It is similarly no defense to copying that some of Filmation's expressions may be embodied in a medium different from that of plaintiff's. Berkic v. Crichton, 761 F.2d 1289, 1292 (9th Cir.1985) ("in comparing ... a film with a written work, the proper question ... is whether the ordinary, reasonable audience would recognize the defendant's work as a 'dramatization' or 'picturization' of the plaintiff's work"). See also Eden Toys, Inc. v. Florelee Undergarment Co., 697 F.2d 27 (2d Cir.1982) (copying from gift wrapping paper to clothing actionable). But see Sid & Marty Krofft Television v. McDonald's Corp., 562 F.2d 1157, 1164 (9th Cir.1977) (observing, in dicta, that a painting of a nude would not infringe a statue of a nude). Thus, Filmation's materials, including scripts and story outlines, can infringe Disney's copyright on "Pinocchio" even though they are not rendered as a motion picture.

This had been the law in the Ninth Circuit even under the Copyright Act of 1909. In Walker v. University Books, Inc., 602 F.2d 859 (9th Cir.1979), plaintiff had copyrighted a set of fortune telling cards. She attempted unsuccessfully to strike a marketing deal with defendants, submitting to them a sample of her deck in the process. Afterward, she assigned her copyright to a third party. Plaintiff subsequently discovered that defendant planned to market a deck of cards similar to the ones she had supplied them in the course of negotiations. She received from defendants "certain blueprints," which were produced before the date of the assignment (id. at 863), but could adduce no evidence of a completed deck of cards produced and sold during the period in which she owned the copyright.

On appeal from summary judgment in defendant's favor, the court of appeals rejected defendant's argument that the blueprints were not themselves copies:

> The district court viewed the making of the blueprints as merely a preliminary step or process directed towards the manufacture of [defendants'] finished product, their set of [cards].... However, the fact that an allegedly infringing copy of a protected work may itself be only an inchoate representation of some final product to be marketed commercially does not in itself negate the possibility of infringement.

Walker, 602 F.2d at 864. According to the Walker court, the operative question was not whether defendants considered the article a final product, but "whether they unauthorizedly utilized [plaintiff's] work in the manufacture of their blueprints." Id.

Finally, the absence of a completed motion picture does not preclude meaningful comparison of Disney's character depictions and film with Filmation's materials. Although Filmation contends that copyright infringement of a cartoon character cannot be based on a mere sketch that is not part of a story, there is no support for this proposition. It is true that courts generally have considered "not only the visual resemblances but also the totality of the characters' attributes and traits," 1 Nimmer § 2.12, p. 175, n. 16.2, and, thus, that the trier of fact would ordinarily evaluate a character in the context of a story. But where the work sued upon is not a "completed" story, but a series of depictions and other works, comparison of the expressions may be made in the form in which they are presented. Walt Disney Productions v. Air Pirates, 581 F.2d 751, 756 (9th Cir.1978) (comparison of graphic images of cartoon characters sufficient to allow action for copyright infringement).

* * *

Notes

1. In *Sega Enterprises Ltd. v. Accolade, Inc.*, 977 F.2d 1510 (9th Cir.1992), the Ninth Circuit reaffirmed its holding in *Walker v. University Books* that a copyright holder's exclusive rights under section 106 extended to copying undertaken as a preliminary step to creating a non-infringing finished product. See also *DSC Communications Corp. v. DGI Techs., Inc.*, 898 F.Supp. 1183, 1188 (N.D.Tex.1995) (following *Sega*), aff'd, 81 F.3d 597 (5th Cir.1996). Citing *Filmation* with approval, the *Sega* court distinguished several cases which had refused to consider evidence of intermediate copying, noting that in each case the plaintiff had alleged infringement only by the

final, publicly distributed version of the defendant's work. See, *e.g., Walker v. Time Life Films, Inc.,* 784 F.2d 44, 52 (2d Cir.1986); *See v. Durang,* 711 F.2d 141, 142 (9th Cir.1983).

In determining whether liability should arise from such intermediate copying, should it matter whether a final version of the defendant's work has been completed and/or distributed, and whether the final version itself infringes the plaintiff's work? Suppose the defendant abandons or delays the project after the intermediate copying, or, as happened in *Walker v. University Books*, the plaintiff assigns her copyright after the intermediate copy has been made, but before the defendant's final version is completed and distributed? What remedies should be available in a case involving intermediate copying but a non-infringing final product?

2. In *Amsinck v. Columbia Pictures Industries*, 862 F.Supp. 1044, 1047–48 (S.D.N.Y.1994), the district court defined the reproduction right narrowly, refusing to find infringement of that right where the the plaintiff's copyrighted mobile was clearly visible in the background of certain scenes in the defendants' motion picture:

> The term "copy" was defined in the old English case West v. Francis, 5 Barn. & Ald. 743; this definition has been cited with approval by the United States Supreme Court in *White–Smith Music Publishing Co. v. Apollo Co.*, 209 U.S. 1, 17, 28 S.Ct. 319, 323, 52 L.Ed. 655 (1908), and by this district in Mura v. Columbia Broadcasting System, Inc., 245 F.Supp. 587, 589 (S.D.N.Y.1965): "A copy is that which comes so near the original as to give to every person seeing it the idea created by the original."

> To establish "copying", the plaintiff must prove that the defendant "mechanically copied the plaintiff's work." II Goldstein, Copyright, § 7.2, at 7. There must be some degree of permanence or the maxim "de minimis" applies, requiring a finding of no liability. Weil, American Copyright Law, at 1406. In determining whether a use constitutes a copy, the courts look to a functional test to see whether the use has "the intent or the effect of fulfilling the demand for the original." 3 M. Nimmer, Nimmer on Copyright, § 13.05 [B], 13–192, quoting Berlin v. E.C. Publications, Inc., 329 F.2d 541, 545 (2d Cir.1964).

* * *

> The issue of whether the defendants' use of plaintiff's work constituted a copy is disputed in this action. While it is obvious that a copyright of a work of art may be infringed by reproduction of the object itself, see, *Home Art Inc. v. Glensder Textile Corp.*, 81 F.Supp. 551 (S.D.N.Y.1948) (oil painting reproduced on a scarf), that is not the nature of the copying here alleged. In this case, the defendants have not sold, manufactured, or even used an article simulating the copyrighted work. Rather, the defendants have used the genuine artwork (on the Mobile) in a film. The plaintiff argues that this use is an infringement of her copyright. The question is whether this use constitutes a copy.

> In a situation similar to the one at bar, a court in this District has found that the broadcasting of copyrighted hand puppets on a television show was not a copy for the purposes of copyright infringement. *Mura v.*

Columbia Broadcasting System, Inc., 245 F.Supp. 587, 590 (S.D.N.Y. 1965). That Court determined that the act of broadcasting altered the copyrighted items to such a degree that they became so "different in nature from the actual copyrighted design" that the use was not a copy. See id. Here, as in Mura, the defendants' display of the Mobile bearing Amsinck's work is different in nature from her copyrighted design. In this matter, the defendants' use was not meant to supplant demand for Amsinck's work; nor does the film have the effect of diminishing interest in Amsinck's work. Defendant's [sic] use was not a mechanical copy. Defendants' use, which appears for only seconds at a time and can be seen only by viewing a film, is fleeting and impermanent. This Court therefore concludes that the defendants' use is not a copy for the purposes of a copyright infringement action.

Can this analysis be reconciled with *Horgan* and *Filmation*? Is it relevant that *Mura* was decided under the 1909 Act, whereas the events in *Amsinck* were governed by the 1976 Act? Consider the following discussion in *Walker v. University Books*:

> * * * Although the 1909 Act contains no definition of the term of art "copy" and there exists no precedent which precisely supports the assertion of the Appellant [that intermediate copying may constitute infringement], the 1909 Act does specifically enumerate those exclusive rights granted to the copyright holder and our inquiry begins at this point. The Act grants to the copyright holder the exclusive rights to "print, reprint, publish, copy and vend the copyrighted work." 17 U.S.C.A. § 1(a) (1909 Act).
>
> Given that the Appellant possessed, prior to March 2, 1972, the exclusive right to "print" and "copy" her work, the question thus before us is whether the blueprints can constitute a copy for purposes of the Act. A copy must of necessity consist of some tangible material object upon which the work is "fixed". See C. M. Paula v. Logan, 355 F.Supp. 189 (N.D.Tex.1973); 2 Nimmer § 8.02(b). The notion of "fixation" requires that the material object must, in some manner, take on the physical aspects of the protected work such that the "copy" of that work may be perceived by an observer. Clearly, a blueprint, which consists of visible printed markings on paper, is sufficiently tangible and permanent in nature to permit "fixation" under the above definition, particularly in a case such as this where the protected work, like the blueprints themselves, is perceived by the observer via a two dimensional printed presentation.

Walker, 602 F.2d at 863–64; see also *Woods v. Universal City Studios*, 920 F.Supp. 62 (S.D.N.Y.1996) (holding that drawing of apparatus was reproduced where apparatus was constructed and used as scenery in motion picture). *Cf., Ringgold v. Black Entertainment Television, Inc.*, 126 F.3d 70 (2d Cir.1997) (reversing the lower court's grant of summary judgment on fair use grounds where the defendants had included shots of a copyrighted poster in the background of a television program: the reproduction was not de minimis under section 106, and the question of fair use required redetermination).

3. How permanent must a fixation be in order to "reproduce" the copyrighted work in "copies"? How relevant is the language of the 1976 House Report (page 738, *supra*) discussing the question of when a work is sufficiently fixed to be copyrightable?

In the 1976 Act, Congress authorized the creation of a National Commission on New Technological Uses of Copyrighted Works (CONTU) to study copyright questions pertaining to computer software and photocopying. CONTU's 1978 report to Congress stated that "[t]he text of the new [1976] copyright law makes it clear that the placement of a copyrighted work into a computer * * * is the preparation of a copy," and added, with respect to the "fixation" language in the 1976 House Report:

> Insofar as a contrary conclusion is suggested in one report accompanying the new law, this should be regarded as incorrect and should not be followed, since legislative history need not be perused in the construction of an unambiguous statute.

Final Report of the National Commission on New Technological Uses of Copyrighted Works 55 & n. 131 (July 31, 1978) ("CONTU Report"); see also *id.* at 98 & n. 169 (noting that section 106 "seemingly would prohibit the unauthorized storage of a work within a computer memory, which would be merely one form of reproduction * * *," and the process of "inputting" material into a computer is one in which "a reproduction is created within the computer memory").

In *MAI Systems Corp. v. Peak Computer, Inc.*, 991 F.2d 511 (9th Cir.1993), *cert. dismissed*, 510 U.S. 1033, 114 S.Ct. 671, 126 L.Ed.2d 640 (1994), the Ninth Circuit concluded that the loading of a program into a computer's random access memory (RAM) was sufficient to constitute reproduction even though the program would be lost when the computer's power was turned off. The *Peak* court relied in part on language in *Apple Computer, Inc. v. Formula Int'l, Inc.*, 594 F.Supp. 617, 622 (C.D.Cal.1984), which described the loading of a program into RAM as a "temporary fixation":

> RAM can be simply defined as a computer component in which data and computer programs can be temporarily recorded. Thus, the purchaser of [software] desiring to utilize all of the programs on the diskette could arrange to copy [the software] into RAM. This would only be a temporary fixation. It is a property of RAM that when the computer is turned off, the copy of the program recorded in RAM is lost.

Accord Religious Technology Center v. Netcom On–Line Communication Services, Inc., 907 F.Supp. 1361 (N.D.Cal.1995) (following *MAI v. Peak*); *Advanced Computer Services of Michigan, Inc. v. MAI Systems Corp.*, 845 F.Supp. 356 (E.D.Va.1994) ("loading" or "booting" a program—that is, transferring a program from a computer's hard drive or a floppy disk to its random access memory ("RAM")—constitutes copying under section 106); *Triad Systems Corp. v. Southeastern Express Co.*, 64 F.3d 1330 (9th Cir. 1995); but see *NLFC, Inc. v. Devcom Mid–America, Inc.*, 45 F.3d 231, 236 (7th Cir.) (implying that remote access to a document through a dedicated phone line from a "dumb terminal" does not involve copying the document into the computer's memory), *cert. denied*, 515 U.S. 1104, 115 S.Ct. 2249, 132 L.Ed.2d 257 (1995). Regardless of whether copying into RAM is a sufficient fixation for copyrightability, should it be sufficient for purposes of determining whether an infringing reproduction has occurred?

In *Stenograph L.L.C. v. Bossard Associates, Inc.*, 144 F.3d 96 (D.C.Cir. 1998), the D.C. Circuit agreed with the Ninth Circuit's holding in *MAI Systems Corp.* that loading software into a computer's random access memory constitutes copying for purposes of section 106.

Congress appears to have acquiesced in the conclusion that loading software into RAM constitutes copying, but has not resolved the question directly. Title III of the DMCA revised section 117 to permit "the owner or lessee" of a computer to authorize computer repair services to copy software into RAM in the course of activating the computer for servicing. The Conference Report states that such a clarification is "necessary in light of judicial decisions holding that such copying is a 'reproduction' under section 106," and adds that "this section does not in any way alter the law with respect to the scope of the term 'reproduction' as it is used in the Copyright Act." H.R. Rep. No. 105–796, 105th Cong., 2d Sess. (1998).

On the limited privilege to copy computer software, see 17 U.S.C.A. § 117 (discussed at Section B.3, *infra*).

4. As more copyrighted works are made available by digital transmission, more people will seek access to such works, even if they do not seek to obtain permanent copies. How does the meaning of "reproduce" in section 106 affect the rights of those persons who wish to access a digitized work? Can electronic libraries serve the public without impairing the rights of copyright owners?

5. Suppose an artist produces a painting of a model, and then sells the painting and its copyright. Is the exclusive reproduction right infringed where an artist subsequently places the same model in the same pose and thereby produces a nearly identical painting? Does your answer change if it is the same artist? Would it matter if the painting were a landscape, and the artist duplicated it from memory by standing in the same place and waiting for the same lighting conditions?

6. Consider whether the following activities involve "reproduction" of a copyrighted work within the meaning of section 106(1):

a. Defendant records her performance of a copyrighted musical composition for which she acquired a copy of the sheet music.

b. Defendant, who is impressed with a low-budget student film, but convinced that in its current form it is not commercially viable, produces a big-budget remake which incorporates all of the plot and character details of the original without using any of the literal dialogue or original footage.

c. A building is constructed from copyrighted architectural plans.

d. A tourist photographs a newly constructed historical monument.

e. On request, a bakery decorates birthday cakes with the same design that appears on the customers' birthday party invitations.

f. A publisher downloads cases from WESTLAW, then edits out the headnotes and page numbers, as well as any other original content added by West, then publishes the cases (organized by subject matter) in digital and print media for distribution to law students and practitioners.

g. Plaintiff makes and sells both videogame hardware and videogames, and defendant wishes to make its videogames compatible with plaintiff's hardware. To accomplish this, defendant copies the object code from plaintiff's cartridges, and "reverse engineers" this information to construct its own object code, which provides the compatibility needed without containing any of the plaintiff's code.

7. A passerby who observed the assassination of President John F. Kennedy in 1963 captured the event on film. Because it is the only known film footage of the assassination, and the best known photographic evidence, it was studied extensively by the FBI and the Warren Commission. A few years later, an author writing a book about the assassination and the investigation was denied permission to reproduce portions of the footage in his book. Instead, he used sketches which accurately depicted the most significant aspects of those individual frames. Assuming that there had been no divestive publication of the footage, did the author of the book make unauthorized copies of a copyrighted work? What remedy, if any, should be available to the filmmaker? See *Time, Inc. v. Bernard Geis Associates*, 293 F.Supp. 130 (S.D.N.Y.1968).

8. Does "reproduction" necessarily mean "copying" for the purposes of section 106? Conventional copyright opinion generally holds that it does, though the legislative history does not say so. In the usages of language, however, "to reproduce" may mean "to produce again", an understanding of the term that would suggest that not every act of copying would necessarily amount to a "reproduction". Private copying for personal use, for example, might be excused under this interpretation of section 106 if there were no further dissemination or "production" of the copied work. Is this a plausible reading of the reproduction right?

The late Professor Alan Latman, in a study of fair use conducted for the Copyright Office prior to the adoption of the 1976 Act, observed that some students of copyright under the 1909 Act believed that such private copying was simply beyond the reach of copyright. Latman concluded that one could neither dismiss this view out of hand nor sustain it with case law, and the 1909 Act itself did not define either copying or reproduction. See Latman, Copyright Office Study No. 14, "Fair Use of Copyrighted Works", March, 1958, at pages 11–12, in Volume 1, Omnibus Copyright Revision Legislative History (Grossman, ed., 1976).

Meanwhile, the most authoritative Legislative History accompanying the adoption of the 1976 Act, states:

> Read together with the relevant definitions in section 101, the right "to reproduce the copyrighted work in copies or phonorecords" means the right to produce a material object in which the work is duplicated, transcribed, imitated, or simulated in a fixed form from it can be "perceived, reproduced, or otherwise communicated, either directly or with the aid of a machine or device." *As under the present law,* a copyrighted work would be infringed by reproducing it in whole or in

any substantial part, and by duplicating it exactly or by imitation or simulation.

Copyright Act of 1976, H. R. Rep. 94–1476, 94th Cong., 2d Sess., p. 61 (emphasis added).

Does this passage (especially the italicized language) from the Legislative History suggest that the meaning of the term "to reproduce" in section 106 should be governed by the meaning of reproduction or copying under the 1909 Act? What consequences would follow?

2. PREPARATION OF DERIVATIVE WORKS

COPYRIGHT ACT OF 1976
H.R. Rep. No. 94–1476.
94th Cong., 2d Sess. 62 (1976).

* * *

Preparation of derivative works.—The exclusive right to prepare derivative works, specified separately in clause (2) of section 106, overlaps the exclusive right of reproduction to some extent. It is broader than that right, however, in the sense that reproduction requires fixation in copies or phonorecords, whereas the preparation of a derivative work, such as a ballet, pantomime, or improvised performance, may be an infringement even though nothing is ever fixed in tangible form.

To be an infringement the "derivative work" must be "based upon the copyrighted work," and the definition in section 101 refers to "a translation, musical arrangement, dramatization, fictionalization, motion picture version, sound recording, art reproduction, abridgment, condensation, or any other form in which a work may be recast, transformed, or adapted." Thus, to constitute a violation of section 106(2), the infringing work must incorporate a portion of the copyrighted work in some form; for example, a detailed commentary on a work or a programmatic musical composition inspired by a novel would not normally constitute infringements under this clause. * * *

NB: As we begin to consider the derivative works right in the context of Section 106(2) of the Act, be sure also to recall the cases on originality in derivative works we considered earlier, especially including *Alfred Bell; L. Batlin & Son, Inc.; Woods v. Bourne; and Gracen.*

MIDWAY MANUFACTURING CO. v. ARTIC INTERNATIONAL, INC.
United States Court of Appeals, Seventh Circuit, 1983.
704 F.2d 1009, *cert. denied*, 464 U.S. 823, 104 S.Ct. 90, 78 L.Ed.2d 98 (1983).

Cummings, Chief Judge:

* * *

Plaintiff manufactures video game machines. * * *

Defendant sells printed circuit boards for use inside video game machines. One of the circuit boards defendant sells speeds up the rate of play—how fast the sounds and images change—of "Galaxian," one of plaintiff's video games, when inserted in place of one of the "Galaxian" machine's circuit boards. * * *

* * *

[Although an expert witness concluded that portions of the source code in defendant's speed-up kits had been copied from the plaintiff's Galaxian memory board, *see* 547 F. Supp. 999, 1004 (N.D.Ill.1982), the district court concluded that "the copyrighted work at issue in this case is the audiovisual display that appears on the video game's screen. The speed-up kit sold by Artic clearly changes that display during the play mode." *Id.* at 1013. The district court concluded that the plaintiff was likely to succeed on the merits of its claim that defendant "induced others to prepare a derivative work" by using the speed-up kits to alter the plaintiff's copyrighted audiovisual displays. *Id.*]

[Defendant appeals from the district court's order enjoining defendant from making or distributing its speed-up kits, arguing] that selling plaintiff's licensees circuit boards that speed up the rate of play of plaintiff's video games is not an infringement of plaintiff's copyrights. Speeding up the rate of play of a video game is a little like playing at 45 or 78 revolutions per minute ("RPM's") a phonograph record recorded at 33 RPM's. If a discotheque licensee did that, it would probably not be an infringement of the record company's copyright in the record. One might argue by analogy that it is not a copyright infringement for video game licensees to speed up the rate of play of video games, and that it is not a contributory infringement for the defendant to sell licensees circuit boards that enable them to do that.

There is this critical difference between playing records at a faster than recorded speed and playing video games at a faster than manufactured rate: there is an enormous demand for speeded-up video games but there is little if any demand for speeded-up records. Not many people want to hear 33 RPM records played at 45 and 78 RPM's so that record licensors would not care if their licensees play them at that speed. But there is a big demand for speeded-up video games. Speeding up a video game's action makes the game more challenging and exciting and increases the licensee's revenue per game. Speeded-up games end sooner than normal games and consequently if players are willing to pay an additional price-per-minute in exchange for the challenge and excitement of a faster game, licensees will take in greater total revenues. Video game copyright owners would undoubtedly like to lay their hands on some of that extra revenue and therefore it cannot be assumed that licensees are implicitly authorized to use speeded-up circuit boards in the machines plaintiff supplies.

Among a copyright owner's exclusive rights is the right "to prepare derivative works based upon the copyrighted work." 17 U.S.C. § 106(2). If, as we hold, the speeded-up "Galaxian" game that a licensee creates with a circuit board supplied by the defendant is a derivative work based upon "Galaxian," a licensee who lacks the plaintiff's authorization to create a derivative work is a direct infringer and the defendant is a contributory infringer through its sale of the speeded-up circuit board. See, e.g., Gershwin Publishing Corp. v. Columbia Artists Mgmt., Inc., 443 F.2d 1159, 1162 (2d Cir.1971); Universal City Studios, Inc. v. Sony Corp. of America, 659 F.2d 963, 975 (9th Cir.1981), certiorari granted, 457 U.S. 1116, 102 S.Ct. 2926, 73 L.Ed. 2d 1328 (1982).

Section 101 of the 1976 Copyright Act defines a derivative work as "a work based upon one or more preexisting works, such as a translation, musical arrangement, dramatization, fictionalization, motion picture version, sound recording, art reproduction, abridgment, condensation, or any other form in which a work may be recast, transformed, or adapted." It is not obvious from this language whether a speeded-up video game is a derivative work. A speeded-up phonograph record probably is not. Cf. Shapiro, Bernstein & Co. v. Jerry Vogel Music Co., 73 F. Supp. 165, 167 (S.D.N.Y.1947) ("The change in time of the added chorus, and the slight variation in the base of the accompaniment, there being no change in the tune or lyrics, would not be 'new work' "); 1 Nimmer on Copyright § 3.03 (1982). But that is because the additional value to the copyright owner of having the right to market separately the speeded-up version of the recorded performance is too trivial to warrant legal protection for that right. A speeded-up video game is a substantially different product from the original game. As noted, it is more exciting to play and it requires some creative effort to produce. For that reason, the owner of the copyright on the game should be entitled to monopolize it on the same theory that he is entitled to monopolize the derivative works specifically listed in Section 101. The current rage for video games was not anticipated in 1976, and like any new technology the video game does not fit with complete ease the definition of derivative work in Section 101 of the 1976 Act. But the amount by which the language of Section 101 must be stretched to accommodate speeded-up video games is, we believe, within the limits within which Congress wanted the new Act to operate. * * *

* * *

AFFIRMED.

LEWIS GALOOB TOYS, INC. v. NINTENDO OF AMERICA, INC.

United States Court of Appeals, Ninth Circuit, 1992.
964 F.2d 965.

FARRIS, CIRCUIT JUDGE:

Nintendo of America appeals the district court's judgment following a bench trial (1) declaring that Lewis Galoob Toys' Game Genie does not violate any Nintendo copyrights and dissolving a temporary injunction and (2) denying Nintendo's request for a permanent injunction enjoining Galoob from marketing the Game Genie. * * * We affirm.

FACTS

The Nintendo Entertainment System is a home video game system marketed by Nintendo. To use the system, the player inserts a cartridge containing a video game that Nintendo produces or licenses others to produce. By pressing buttons and manipulating a control pad, the player controls one of the game's characters and progresses through the game. The games are protected as audiovisual works under 17 U.S.C. § 102(a)(6).

The Game Genie is a device manufactured by Galoob that allows the player to alter up to three features of a Nintendo game. For example, the Game Genie can increase the number of lives of the player's character, increase the speed at which the character moves, and allow the character to float above obstacles. The player controls the changes made by the Game Genie by entering codes provided by the Game Genie Programming Manual and Code Book. The player also can experiment with variations of these codes.

The Game Genie functions by blocking the value for a single data byte sent by the game cartridge to the central processing unit in the Nintendo Entertainment System and replacing it with a new value. If that value controls the character's strength, for example, then the character can be made invincible by increasing the value sufficiently. The Game Genie is inserted between a game cartridge and the Nintendo Entertainment System. The Game Genie does not alter the data that is stored in the game cartridge. Its effects are temporary.

DISCUSSION

1. Derivative work

The Copyright Act of 1976 confers upon copyright holders the exclusive right to prepare and authorize others to prepare derivative works based on their copyrighted works. See 17 U.S.C. § 106(2). Nintendo argues that the district court erred in concluding that the audiovisual displays created by the Game Genie are not derivative works. * * *

A derivative work must incorporate a protected work in some concrete or permanent "form." The Copyright Act defines a derivative work as follows:

> A "derivative work" is a work based upon one or more preexisting works, such as a translation, musical arrangement, dramatization, fictionalization, motion picture version, sound recording, art reproduction, abridgment, condensation, *or any other form in which a work may be recast, transformed, or adapted.* A work consisting of editorial revisions, annotations, elaborations, or other modifications which, as a whole, represent an original work of authorship, is a "derivative work."

17 U.S.C. § 101 (emphasis added).

The examples of derivative works provided by the Act all physically incorporate the underlying work or works. The Act's legislative history similarly indicates that "the infringing work must incorporate a portion of the copyrighted work in some form." 1976 U.S. Code Cong. & Admin. News 5659, 5675. See also Mirage Editions, Inc. v. Albuquerque A.R.T. Co., 856 F.2d 1341, 1343–44 (9th Cir.1988) (discussing same), cert. denied, 489 U.S. 1018 (1989).

Our analysis is not controlled by the Copyright Act's definition of "fixed." The Act defines copies as "material objects, other than phonorecords, in which a work is *fixed* by any method." 17 U.S.C. § 101 (emphasis added). The Act's definition of "derivative work," in contrast, lacks any such reference to fixation. See id. Further, we have held in a copyright infringement action that "it makes no difference that the derivation may not satisfy certain requirements for statutory copyright registration itself." Lone Ranger Television v. Program Radio Corp., 740 F.2d 718, 722 (9th Cir.1984). See also Paul Goldstein, Derivative Rights and Derivative Works in Copyright, 30 J. Copyright Soc'y U.S.A. 209, 231 n.75 (1983) ("the Act does not require that the derivative work be protectable for its preparation to infringe"). Cf. Kalem Co. v. Harper Bros., 222 U.S. 55, 61 (1911) (finding the movie "Ben Hur" infringed copyright in the book Ben Hur even though Copyright Act did not yet include movies as protectable works). A derivative work must be fixed to be *protected* under the Act, see 17 U.S.C. § 102(a), but not to *infringe*.

The argument that a derivative work must be fixed because "[a] 'derivative work' is a work," 17 U.S.C. § 101, and "[a] work is 'created' when it is fixed in a copy or phonorecord for the first time," id., relies on a misapplication of the Copyright Act's definition of "created":

> A work is 'created' when it is fixed in a copy or phonorecord for the first time; where a work is prepared over a period of time, the portion of it that has been fixed at any particular time constitutes the work as of that time, and where the work has been prepared in different versions, each version constitutes a separate work.

Id. The definition clarifies the *time* at which a work is *created*. If the provision were a definition of "work," it would not use that term in such a casual manner. The Act does not contain a definition of "work." Rather, it contains specific definitions: "audiovisual works," "literary works," and "pictorial, graphic and sculptural works," for example. The definition of "derivative work" does not require fixation.

The district court's finding that no independent work is created, see Galoob, 780 F. Supp. at 1291, is supported by the record. The Game Genie merely enhances the audiovisual displays (or underlying data bytes) that originate in Nintendo game cartridges. The altered displays do not incorporate a portion of a copyrighted work in some concrete or permanent form. Nintendo argues that the Game Genie's displays are as fixed in the hardware and software used to create them as Nintendo's original displays. Nintendo's argument ignores the fact that the Game

Genie cannot produce an audiovisual display; the underlying display must be produced by a Nintendo Entertainment System and game cartridge. Even if we were to rely on the Copyright Act's definition of "fixed," we would similarly conclude that the resulting display is not "embodied," see 17 U.S.C. § 101, in the Game Genie. It cannot be a derivative work.

Mirage Editions is illustrative. Albuquerque A.R.T. transferred artworks from a commemorative book to individual ceramic tiles. See Mirage Editions, 856 F.2d at 1342. We held that "by borrowing and mounting the preexisting, copyrighted individual art images without the consent of the copyright proprietors ... [Albuquerque A.R.T.] has prepared a derivative work and infringed the subject copyrights." Id. at 1343. The ceramic tiles *physically* incorporated the copyrighted works in a form that could be sold. Perhaps more importantly, sales of the tiles supplanted purchasers' demand for the underlying works. Our holding in Mirage Editions would have been much different if Albuquerque A.R.T. had distributed lenses that merely enabled users to view several artworks simultaneously.

Nintendo asserted at oral argument that the existence of a $150 million market for the Game Genie indicates that its audiovisual display must be fixed. We understand Nintendo's argument; consumers clearly would not purchase the Game Genie if its display was not "sufficiently permanent or stable to permit it to be perceived ... for a period of more than transitory duration." 17 U.S.C. § 101. But, Nintendo's reliance on the Copyright Act's definition of "fixed" is misplaced. Nintendo's argument also proves too much; the existence of a market does not, and cannot, determine conclusively whether a work is an infringing derivative work. For example, although there is a market for kaleidoscopes, it does not necessarily follow that kaleidoscopes create unlawful derivative works when pointed at protected artwork. The same can be said of countless other products that enhance, but do not replace, copyrighted works.

Nintendo also argues that our analysis should focus exclusively on the audiovisual displays created by the Game Genie, i.e., that we should compare the altered displays to Nintendo's original displays. Nintendo emphasizes that " 'audiovisual works' are works that consist of a series of related images ... *regardless of the nature of the material objects ... in which the works are embodied.*" 17 U.S.C. § 101 (emphasis added). The Copyright Act's definition of "audiovisual works" is inapposite; the *only* question before us is whether the audiovisual displays created by the Game Genie are "derivative works." The Act does not similarly provide that a work can be a derivative work regardless of the nature of the material objects in which the work is embodied. A derivative work must incorporate a protected work in some concrete or permanent form. We cannot ignore the actual source of the Game Genie's display.

Nintendo relies heavily on Midway Mfg. Co. v. Artic Int'l, Inc., 704 F.2d 1009 (7th Cir.), cert. denied, 464 U.S. 823 (1983). Midway can be distinguished. The defendant in Midway, Artic International, marketed a computer chip that could be inserted in Galaxian video games to speed up the rate of play. The Seventh Circuit held that the speeded-up version of Galaxian was a derivative work. Id. at 1013–14. Artic's chip substantially copied and replaced the chip that was originally distributed by Midway. Purchasers of Artic's chip also benefited economically by offering the altered game for use by the general public. The Game Genie does not physically incorporate a portion of a copyrighted work, nor does it supplant demand for a component of that work. The court in Midway acknowledged that the Copyright Act's definition of "derivative work" "must be stretched to accommodate speeded-up video games." Id. at 1014. Stretching that definition further would chill innovation and fail to protect "society's competing interest in the free flow of ideas, information, and commerce." Sony Corp. of America v. Universal Studios, Inc., 464 U.S. 417, 429 (1984).

In holding that the audiovisual displays created by the Game Genie are not derivative works, we recognize that technology often advances by improvement rather than replacement. * * * Some time ago, for example, computer companies began marketing spell-checkers that operate within existing word processors by signalling the writer when a word is misspelled. These applications, as well as countless others, could not be produced and marketed if courts were to conclude that the word processor and spell-checker combination is a derivative work based on the word processor alone. The Game Genie is useless by itself. It can only enhance, and cannot duplicate or recast, a Nintendo game's output. It does not contain or produce a Nintendo game's output in some concrete or permanent form, nor does it supplant demand for Nintendo game cartridges. Such innovations rarely will constitute infringing derivative works under the Copyright Act. * * *

* * *

Galoob has not violated the Copyright Act. Nintendo therefore is not entitled to a temporary or permanent injunction.

AFFIRMED.

Notes

1. *Midway* and *Lewis Galoob Toys* both emphasize the impact of the defendant's product on the market for the plaintiff's copyrighted work. Is this the "correct" test for determining whether the plaintiff's right to create derivative works has been infringed? If not, is it perhaps a better test? Is it consistent with the Copyright Act?

2. *Lewis Galoob Toys* repeatedly states that the infringing work must incorporate the plaintiff's work in a "concrete or permanent" form, but rejects the suggestion that a derivative work must be "fixed". How can a copyrighted work be incorporated in a concrete or permanent but unfixed form? How would this analysis apply to a defendant who, in rendering a live performance of a copyrighted work, improvises substantial variations on the original work without the copyright owner's permission?

3. If the altered visual display of the video games in *Lewis Galoob Toys* is processed through the computer's RAM before it appears on the screen, is this a sufficient fixation to constitute a "reproduction" under section 106(1)? (See Section A.1, *supra.*) Is it a sufficient "incorporation" in "concrete or permanent form" to be a derivative work under *Lewis Galoob Toys*?

4. In *Vault Corp. v. Quaid Software Ltd.*, 847 F.2d 255 (5th Cir.1988), defendant Quaid had created and marketed a computer program ("RAM-KEY") designed to "unlock" the plaintiff's program which was designed to prevent copying of software contained on floppy disks. Although the earlier version of the defendant's software incorporated some of the plaintiff's code, the court held that the amount copied was so insignificant that the works could not be found to be "substantially similar," and thus the defendant's work was not an infringing derivative work even though it incorporated a portion of the plaintiff's work. With respect to a later version of the defendant's program which did not incorporate any of the plaintiff's code, the court again found no derivative work:

> While Vault acknowledges that the latest version of RAMKEY does not contain a sequence of characters from Vault's program, Vault contends that this version is also a derivative work because it "alters" Vault's program. Vault cites Midway for the proposition that a product can be a derivative work where it alters, rather than copies, the copyrighted work. The court in Midway, however, held that the sale of a product which speeded-up plaintiff's programs constituted contributory infringement because the speeded-up programs were derivative works. 704 F.2d at 1013–14. The court did not hold, as Vault asserts, that defendant's product itself was a derivative work. We therefore reject Vault's contention that the latest version of RAMKEY constitutes a derivative work.

847 F.2d at 268. Note that both *Lewis Galoob Toys* and *Vault* distinguish *Midway*. Are the distinctions persuasive? Consistent?

The *Vault* court also held that the defendant's RAMKEY programs could not be infringing derivative works because the function they performed was the opposite of the function performed by the plaintiff's software: "[W]hile Vault's program is designed to prevent the duplication of its customers' programs, RAMKEY is designed to facilitate the creation of copies of Vault's customers' programs." *Id.* at 268. Is this rationale persuasive? Supported by the statutes?

5. The holding in *Lewis Galoob Toys* has since been applied to a series of cases involving Internet "pop-up" ads. "Pop-up" ads are advertisements which suddenly appear during web browsing on the Internet. In *U-Haul International, Inc. v. WhenU.com, Inc.*, 279 F.Supp.2d 723 (E.D.Va. 2003) and *Wells Fargo & Co. v. WhenU.com, Inc.*, 293 F.Supp.2d 734 (E.D.Mich. 2003), the courts held that "pop-up" ads do not infringe the copyright of the underlying website because the original website is not altered, but merely placed in the computer's background when the advertisement appears in the foreground.

LEE v. A.R.T. CO.

United States Court of Appeals, Seventh Circuit, 1997.
125 F.3d 580.

EASTERBROOK, CIRCUIT JUDGE.

Annie Lee creates works of art, which she sells through her firm Annie Lee & Friends. Deck the Walls, a chain of outlets for modestly priced art, is among the buyers of her works, which have been registered with the Register of Copyrights. One Deck the Walls store sold some of Lee's notecards and small lithographs to A.R.T. Company, which mounted the works on ceramic tiles (covering the art with transparent epoxy resin in the process) and resold the tiles. Lee contends that these tiles are derivative works, which under 17 U.S.C. § 106(2) may not be prepared without the permission of the copyright proprietor. She seeks both monetary and injunctive relief. Her position has the support of two cases holding that A.R.T.'s business violates the copyright laws. Munoz v. Albuquerque A.R.T. Co., 38 F.3d 1218 (9th Cir.1994), affirming without published opinion, 829 F. Supp. 309 (D.Alaska 1993); Mirage Editions, Inc. v. Albuquerque A.R.T. Co., 856 F.2d 1341 (9th Cir.1988). Mirage Editions, the only full appellate discussion, dealt with pages cut from books and mounted on tiles; the court of appeals' brief order in Munoz concludes that the reasoning of Mirage Editions is equally applicable to works of art that were sold loose. Our district court disagreed with these decisions and entered summary judgment for the defendant. 925 F.Supp. 576 (N.D.Ill.1996).

Now one might suppose that this is an open and shut case under the doctrine of first sale, codified at 17 U.S.C. § 109(a). A.R.T. bought the work legitimately, mounted it on a tile, and resold what it had purchased. Because the artist could capture the value of her art's contribution to the finished product as part of the price for the original transaction, the economic rationale for protecting an adaptation as "derivative" is absent. See William M. Landes & Richard A. Posner, An Economic Analysis of Copyright Law, 17 J. Legal Studies 325, 353–57 (1989). An alteration that includes (or consumes) a complete copy of the original lacks economic significance. One work changes hands multiple times, exactly what sec. 109(a) permits, so it may lack legal significance too. But sec. 106(2) creates a separate exclusive right, to "prepare derivative works", and Lee believes that affixing the art to the tile is "preparation," so that A.R.T. would have violated sec. 106(2) even if it had dumped the finished tiles into the Marianas Trench. For the sake of argument we assume that this is so and ask whether card-on-a-tile is a "derivative work" in the first place.

"Derivative work" is a defined term:

A "derivative work" is a work based upon one or more preexisting works, such as a translation, musical arrangement, dramatization, fictionalization, motion picture version, sound recording, art repro-

duction, abridgment, condensation, or any other form in which a
work may be recast, transformed, or adapted. A work consisting of
editorial revisions, annotations, elaborations, or other modifications
which, as a whole, represent an original work of authorship, is a
"derivative work".

17 U.S.C. § 101. The district court concluded that A.R.T.'s mounting of
Lee's works on tile is not an "original work of authorship" because it is
no different in form or function from displaying a painting in a frame or
placing a medallion in a velvet case. No one believes that a museum
violates sec. 106(2) every time it changes the frame of a painting that is
still under copyright, although the choice of frame or glazing affects the
impression the art conveys, and many artists specify frames (or pedestals
for sculptures) in detail. Munoz and Mirage Editions acknowledge that
framing and other traditional means of mounting and displaying art do
not infringe authors' exclusive right to make derivative works. Nonetheless, the ninth circuit held, what A.R.T. does creates a derivative work
because the epoxy resin bonds the art to the tile. Our district judge
thought this a distinction without a difference, and we agree. If changing
the way in which a work of art will be displayed creates a derivative
work, and if Lee is right about what "prepared" means, then the
derivative work is "prepared" when the art is mounted; what happens
later is not relevant, because the violation of the sec. 106(2) right has
already occurred. If the framing process does not create a derivative
work, then mounting art on a tile, which serves as a flush frame, does
not create a derivative work. What is more, the Ninth Circuit erred in
assuming that normal means of mounting and displaying art are easily
reversible. A painting is placed in a wooden "stretcher" as part of the
framing process; this leads to some punctures (commonly tacks or
staples), may entail trimming the edges of the canvas, and may affect the
surface of the painting as well. Works by Jackson Pollock are notoriously
hard to mount without damage, given the thickness of their paint. As a
prelude to framing, photographs, prints, and posters may be mounted on
stiff boards using wax sheets, but sometimes glue or another more
durable substance is employed to create the bond.

Lee wages a vigorous attack on the district court's conclusion that
A.R.T.'s mounting process cannot create a derivative work because the
change to the work "as a whole" is not sufficiently original to support a
copyright. Cases such as Gracen v. The Bradford Exchange, Inc., 698
F.2d 300 (7th Cir.1983), show that neither A.R.T. nor Lee herself could
have obtained a copyright in the card-on-a-tile, thereby not only extending the period of protection for the images but also eliminating competition in one medium of display. After the ninth circuit held that its
mounting process created derivative works, A.R.T. tried to obtain a
copyright in one of its products; the Register of Copyrights sensibly
informed A.R.T. that the card-on-a-tile could not be copyrighted independently of the note card itself. But Lee says that this is irrelevant—that a
change in a work's appearance may infringe the exclusive right under
sec. 106(2) even if the alteration is too trivial to support an independent

copyright. Pointing to the word "original" in the second sentence of the statutory definition, the district judge held that "originality" is essential to a derivative work. This understanding has the support of both cases and respected commentators. E.g., L. Batlin & Son, Inc. v. Snyder, 536 F.2d 486 (2d Cir.1976); Melville B. Nimmer & David Nimmer, 1 Nimmer on Copyrights sec. 3.03 (1997). Pointing to the fact that the first sentence in the statutory definition omits any reference to originality, Lee insists that a work may be derivative despite the mechanical nature of the transformation. This view, too, has the support of both cases and respected commentators. E.g., Lone Ranger Television, Inc. v. Program Radio Corp., 740 F.2d 718, 722 (9th Cir.1984); Paul Goldstein, Copyright: Principles, Law and Practice sec. 5.3.1 (2d ed.1996) (suggesting that a transformation is covered by sec. 106(2) whenever it creates a "new work for a different market").

Fortunately, it is not necessary for us to choose sides. Assume for the moment that the first sentence recognizes a set of non-original derivative works. To prevail, then, Lee must show that A.R.T. altered her works in one of the ways mentioned in the first sentence. The tile is not an "art reproduction"; A.R.T. purchased and mounted Lee's original works. That leaves the residual clause: "any other form in which a work may be recast, transformed, or adapted." None of these words fits what A.R.T. did. Lee's works were not "recast" or "adapted". "Transformed" comes closer and gives the ninth circuit some purchase for its view that the permanence of the bond between art and base matters. Yet the copyrighted note cards and lithographs were not "transformed" in the slightest. The art was bonded to a slab of ceramic, but it was not changed in the process. It still depicts exactly what it depicted when it left Lee's studio. See William F. Patry, Copyright Law and Practice 823–24 (1994) (disapproving Mirage Editions on this ground).[1] If mounting works a "transformation," then changing a painting's frame or a photograph's mat equally produces a derivative work. Indeed, if Lee is right about the meaning of the definition's first sentence, then any alteration of a work, however slight, requires the author's permission. We asked at oral argument what would happen if a purchaser jotted a note on one of the note cards, or used it as a coaster for a drink, or cut it in half, or if a collector applied his seal (as is common in Japan); Lee's counsel replied that such changes prepare derivative works, but that as a practical matter artists would not file suit. A definition of derivative work that makes criminals out of art collectors and tourists is jarring despite Lee's gracious offer not to commence civil litigation.

If Lee (and the Ninth Circuit) are right about what counts as a derivative work, then the United States has established through the back door an extraordinarily broad version of authors' moral rights, under which artists may block any modification of their works of which

1. Scholarly disapproval of Mirage Editions has been widespread. Goldstein[, Copyright Law] sec. 5.3 at 5:81–82; Nimmer & Nimmer[, Nimmer on Copyright] sec. 3.03; Wendy J. Gordon, On Owning Information: Intellectual Property and the Restitutionary Impulse, 78 Va. L. Rev. 149, 255 n. 401 (1992).

they disapprove. No European version of droit moral goes this far. Until recently it was accepted wisdom that the United States did not enforce any claim of moral rights; even bowdlerization of a work was permitted unless the modifications produced a new work so different that it infringed the exclusive right under sec. 106(2). Compare WGN Continental Broadcasting Co. v. United Video, Inc., 693 F.2d 622 (7th Cir.1982), with Gilliam v. American Broadcasting Companies, Inc., 538 F.2d 14, 24 (2d Cir.1976). The Visual Artists Rights Act of 1990, Pub.L. 101–650, 104 Stat. 5089, 5123–33, moves federal law in the direction of moral rights, but the cornerstone of the new statute, 17 U.S.C. § 106A, does not assist Lee. Section 106A(a)(3)(A) gives an artist the right to "prevent any intentional distortion, mutilation, or other modification of that work which would be prejudicial to his or her honor or reputation". At oral argument Lee's lawyer disclaimed any contention that the sale of her works on tile has damaged her honor or reputation. What is more, sec. 106A applies only to a "work of visual art", a new term defined in sec. 101 to mean either a unique work or part of a limited edition (200 copies or fewer) that has been "signed and consecutively numbered by the author". Lee's note cards and lithographs are not works of visual art under this definition, so she could not invoke sec. 106A even if A.R.T.'s use of her works to produce kitsch had damaged her reputation. It would not be sound to use sec. 106(2) to provide artists with exclusive rights deliberately omitted from the Visual Artists Rights Act. We therefore decline to follow Munoz and Mirage Editions.

Affirmed.

Notes

1. In *Mirage Editions, Inc. v. Albuquerque A.R.T. Co.*, 856 F.2d 1341 (9th Cir.1988), the Ninth Circuit found that infringing derivative works were created where the defendant removed individual pictures from the plaintiff's book of art reproductions, then glued each picture on a black plastic sheet so that a black margin showed on all sides, glued this onto a white ceramic tile, covered it with a transparent plastic film, and then offered the mounted artwork for resale:

> What appellant has clearly done here is to make another version of Nagel's art works, * * * and that amounts to preparation of a derivative work. By borrowing and mounting the preexisting, copyrighted individual art images without the consent of the copyright proprietors—Mirage and Dumas as to the art works and Van Der Marck as to the book—appellant has prepared a derivative work and infringed the subject copyrights. * * *

> Appellant's contention that since it has not engaged in "art reproduction" and therefore its tiles are not derivative works is not fully dispositive of this issue. Appellant has ignored the disjunctive phrase "or any other form in which a work may be recast, transformed or adapted." The legislative history of the Copyright Act of 1976 indicates that Congress intended that for a violation of the right to prepare

derivative works to occur "the infringing work must incorporate a portion of the copyrighted work in *some form*." 1976 U.S. Code Cong. & Admin. News 5659, 5675 (emphasis added). The language "recast, transformed or adapted" seems to encompass other alternatives besides simple art reproduction. By removing the individual images from the book and placing them on the tiles, perhaps the appellant has not accomplished reproduction. We conclude, though, that appellant has certainly recast or transformed the individual images by incorporating them into its tile-preparing process.

Id. at 1343–44. Were the defendant's actions in *Mirage* protected by section 109(a) or (c)? Why or why not?

2. Can *Mirage, Deck The Walls*, and *Munoz* be reconciled? Suppose that a defendant simply removed pictures from a book and sold them unmounted? Or reassembled them in separate groupings, in a collage, or in a different sequence than they appeared in the plaintiff's book? In *Peker v. Masters Collection*, 96 F.Supp.2d 216 (E.D.N.Y.2000), the court found that the first sale doctrine was no defense where posters of the plaintiff's paintings were transferred to canvas and replicated. The court held that the use of the lawfully acquired posters in an attempt to reproduce the exact colors and stye of the original was unlawful copying.

3. Would the *Deck The Walls* court have reached a different conclusion if the defendant had added hour and minute hands to the front of each mounted notecard, and a battery-powered motor to the back, and sold them as clocks?

4. In *Lone Ranger Television, Inc. v. Program Radio Corp.*, 740 F.2d 718, 721–22 (9th Cir.1984), the Ninth Circuit adopted Professor Paul Goldstein's distinction between the right to copy and the right to create a derivative work:

> * * * As one commentator distinguishes between such a derivative right and a right to copy: "It is that point at which the contribution of independent expression to an existing work effectively creates a new work for a different market." (quoting Goldstein, Derivative Rights and Derivative Works in Copyright, 30 J. Copyright Soc'y U.S.A. 209, 217 (1983). Cf. Sony, 104 S.Ct. at 811 (Blackmun, J., dissenting).

> * * *

> As Russell [v. Price, 612 F.2d 1123 (9th Cir.1979)] makes clear, the protection of derivative rights extends beyond mere protection against unauthorized copying to include the right to "make other versions of, perform or exhibit the work." 612 F.2d at 1128 n.16. It makes no difference that the derivation may not satisfy certain requirements for statutory copyright registration itself. See Goldstein, supra, 30 J. Copyright Soc'y U.S.A. at 229–32 & 231 n.75 (discussing 1909 and 1976 Acts collectively) ("the Act does not require that the derivative work be protectable for its preparation to infringe"); see also Kalem Co. v. Harper Brothers, 222 U.S. 55, 61, 32 S.Ct. 20, 21, 56 L.Ed. 92 (1911) (a year before the 1909 Act's 1912 amendment, which specifically included

movies as protectable works, * * * the Court found the movie "Ben Hur" infringed the copyright in the book Ben Hur). * * *

Do you agree? Or should the copyright owner who sells copies of her work be required to tolerate certain alterations in those copies? (For example, should the seller of software be required to permit users to customize the software for their needs? See 17 U.S.C.A. § 117). If copyright law does not allow the copyright owner to prohibit purchasers from making such changes to the purchased copies, can she assert this right under any other legal doctrine?

5. Plaintiff owns the copyrights in a line of baseball cards. Defendant purchases the cards and assembles them in groups of three by using one card as a backdrop, then cutting the players out of two other cards and staggering these cut-outs in front of the rear card, creating a three-dimensional effect. This assemblage is then mounted in a plastic frame and offered for sale. Has the defendant infringed the plaintiff's exclusive right to create derivative works? Would infringement occur if the defendant simply tore the cards in half? See *Major League Baseball Players Ass'n v. Dad's Kid Corp.*, 806 F.Supp. 458 (S.D.N.Y.1992).

6. Would the owner of copyright in a motion picture have a copyright infringement claim if the film were edited for television broadcasting without the copyright owner's consent? What about the author of the underlying script? See *Gilliam v. American Broadcasting Companies, Inc.*, 538 F.2d 14 (2d Cir.1976).

7. Suppose an entrepreneur purchases videotapes of popular motion pictures, and inserts paid advertising throughout the tape without cutting out any of the original film. Is this a derivative work (a) for purposes of the infringement analysis? (b) for purposes of copyrightability?

8. Why should a copyright owner's monopoly include the market for derivative works? Is this inquiry relevant to determining whether the test of infringement should be the same as the test of a derivative work's copyrightability? In answering the first question, does it matter whether the accused infringer's contribution to the derivative work is as creative as the original author's work (or more so)?

9. How far does the right to create derivative works extend? In *Well-Made Toy Mfg. Corp. v. Goffa Int'l Corp.*, 354 F.3d 112 (2d Cir. 2003), the plaintiff held the copyright in its 20–inch "Sweetie Mine" doll. Plaintiff had also created a 48–inch version of "Sweetie Mine" as a derivative work of the original 20–inch version. Defendants based their own doll on the 48–inch version. The Second Circuit concluded that, after removing the elements of the doll which were in the public domain, there were enough differences between plaintiff's 20–inch doll and the defendant's doll that defendants did not violate the derivative right of the "Sweetie Mine" doll. Additionally, the court held that even if the defendant's doll was found to be a derivative of the plaintiff's 48–inch doll the court lacked subject matter jurisdiction because the plaintiffs had not registered the copyright in the 48–inch doll.

3. PUBLIC DISTRIBUTION

COPYRIGHT ACT OF 1976

H.R. Rep. No. 94–1476.
94th Cong., 2d Sess. 62 (1976).

* * *

Public distribution.—Clause (3) of section 106 establishes the exclusive right of publication: The right "to distribute copies or phonorecords of the copyrighted work to the public by sale or other transfer of ownership, or by rental, lease, or lending." Under this provision the copyright owner would have the right to control the first public distribution of an authorized copy or phonorecord of his work, whether by sale, gift, loan, or some rental or lease arrangement. Likewise, any unauthorized public distribution of copies or phonorecords that were unlawfully made would be an infringement. As section 109 makes clear, however, the copyright owner's rights under section 106(3) cease with respect to a particular copy or phonorecord once he has parted with ownership of it.

* * *

WALT DISNEY CO. v. VIDEO 47, INC.

United States District Court, S. D. Florida, 1996.
972 F.Supp. 595, 40 U.S.P.Q.2d (BNA) 1747.

UNGARO-BENAGES, UNITED STATES DISTRICT JUDGE.

* * *

[Upon learning that defendants' video stores rented to the public unauthorized copies of plaintiffs' copyrighted motion picture videocassettes, plaintiffs filed an action for infringement. Pursuant to a court order, the videotapes were seized and, upon examination, were determined to be counterfeit. The district court then entered a Consent Decree and Final Judgment pursuant to a settlement agreement. Upon learning that the defendants were continuing to rent counterfeit tapes, the plaintiffs filed this action for contempt.]

FINDINGS OF FACT

* * *

3. Plaintiffs are the lawful owners of the exclusive right under the United States Copyright Act to reproduce, to distribute and to authorize the reproduction and distribution of thirteen (13) motion picture titles at issue in this action. * * *

4. Plaintiffs are members of the Motion Picture Association of America (MPAA), a trade association whose film security office investigates unlawful duplication and distribution of videocassette tapes whose copyrights are owned by members of the MPAA.

5. Based upon a tip to the MPAA, an investigation of Defendants was conducted from October 10, 1995 to October 11, 1995 as testified to by Robert W. Butler ("Butler"), presently a field representative for the Film Security office of the MPAA and formerly a Special Agent in Charge of the Tampa Office for the Federal Bureau of Investigation ("FBI").

6. The investigation of VIDEO 47 was conducted by Patrick R. Cooney ("Cooney"), a former FBI agent who currently works for the anti-piracy office of the MPAA. Cooney employed a "stringer" from the neighborhood to rent tapes from VIDEO 47. Initially, six (6) tapes were rented and five (5) were counterfeit * * *.

* * *

14. Defendants did not produce any documentation that showed any authorization by Plaintiffs or any of their distributors to distribute copies of the Plaintiffs' copyrighted motion pictures.

15. Defendant Eduardo Celorio testified and stated that he * * * purchased tapes from individuals who sold videocassettes from their cars and that he contacted his distributors by beeper.

16. Defendant Eduardo Celorio testified that the 16 videocassettes at issue were not available for rental to the public, whereas Mr. Cooney testified that these videocassettes were seized from the portion of the store where the videocassettes were available for rental. The Court rejects the testimony of Defendant Eduardo Celorio and accepts the testimony of Mr. Cooney on this factual issue.

* * *

CONCLUSIONS OF LAW

* * *

* * * [T]his Court entered a Consent Decree and Final Judgment in this case on or about August 4, 1994, pursuant to which the Defendants were permanently enjoined from infringing or participating in the infringement by others of Plaintiffs' rights in any motion pictures as to which Plaintiffs own the copyrights or other exclusive interests. * * * Plaintiffs now move to hold the Defendants in contempt for violation of such Final Judgment. Therefore, the Court must determine whether Defendants have violated Plaintiffs' rights under the copyright laws, and whether Defendants are liable for contempt for violation of this Court's prior Orders.

1. Copyright

* * *

* * * Plaintiffs' copyright registrations give Plaintiffs the exclusive right to reproduce, distribute and sell videocassette tapes of the movie titles at issue in this litigation. 17 U.S.C. § 106. The Court finds that

Defendants infringed Plaintiffs' rights in the titles at issue in this litigation by renting counterfeit videocassette tapes without Plaintiffs' authorization to do so. 17 U.S.C. § 501. Plaintiffs need not demonstrate knowledge or intent on the part of the Defendants. * * *

As the Court finds that Defendants have violated Plaintiffs' rights in the motion pictures at issue here, it follows that Defendants are in direct violation of this Court's Consent Decree and Final Judgment dated August 4, 1994, which permanently enjoined Defendants from:

> (a) manufacturing, duplicating or performing publicly, without authorization, any motion picture as to which any Plaintiff holds legal or beneficial ownership of the copyright or other exclusive interest;
> (b) in any manner infringing or contributing to or participating in the infringement by others of any copyright or other exclusive interest owned by any Plaintiff in, for or to any motion picture; or
> (c) acting in concert or confederacy with, or aiding or abetting others to infringe in any way any copyright or other exclusive interest owned by any Plaintiff.

* * *

[The court therefore held the defendants in contempt.]

RELIGIOUS TECHNOLOGY CENTER v. NETCOM ON-LINE COMMUNICATION SERVICES, INC.

United States District Court, N.D. California, 1995.
907 F.Supp. 1361.

WHYTE, UNITED STATES DISTRICT JUDGE.

* * *

Plaintiffs Religious Technology Center ("RTC") and Bridge Publications, Inc. ("BPI") hold copyrights in the unpublished and published works of L. Ron Hubbard, the late founder of the Church of Scientology ("the Church"). Defendant Dennis Erlich ("Erlich") is a former minister of Scientology turned vocal critic of the Church, whose pulpit is now the Usenet newsgroup alt.religion.scientology ("a.r.s."), an on-line forum for discussion and criticism of Scientology. Plaintiffs maintain that Erlich infringed their copyrights when he posted portions of their works on a.r.s. Erlich gained his access to the Internet through defendant Thomas Klemesrud's ("Klemesrud's") BBS[*] "support.com." Klemesrud is the operator of the BBS, which is run out of his home and has approximately 500 paying users. Klemesrud's BBS is not directly linked to the Internet, but gains its connection through the facilities of defendant Netcom On-Line Communications, Inc. ("Netcom"), one of the largest providers of Internet access in the United States.

After failing to convince Erlich to stop his postings, plaintiffs contacted defendants Klemesrud and Netcom. Klemesrud responded to

---

* BBS stands for "bulletin board service."

plaintiffs' demands that Erlich be kept off his system by asking plaintiffs to prove that they owned the copyrights to the works posted by Erlich. However, plaintiffs refused Klemesrud's request as unreasonable. Netcom similarly refused plaintiffs' request that Erlich not be allowed to gain access to the Internet through its system. Netcom contended that it would be impossible to prescreen Erlich's postings and that to kick Erlich off the Internet meant kicking off the hundreds of users of Klemesrud's BBS. Consequently, plaintiffs named Klemesrud and Netcom in their suit against Erlich, although only on the copyright infringement claims.

On June 23, 1995, this court heard the parties' arguments on eight motions, three of which relate to Netcom and Klemesrud and are discussed in this order: (1) Netcom's motion for summary judgment: (2) Klemesrud's motion for judgment on the pleadings; and (3) plaintiffs' motion for a preliminary injunction against Netcom and Klemesrud. For the reasons set forth below, the court grants in part and denies in part Netcom's motion for summary judgment and Klemesrud's motion for judgment on the pleadings and denies plaintiffs' motion for a preliminary injunction.

I. NETCOM'S MOTION FOR SUMMARY JUDGMENT OF NONINFRINGEMENT

* * *

B. *Copyright Infringement*

* * *

a. *Undisputed Facts*

The parties do not dispute the basic processes that occur when Erlich posts his allegedly infringing messages to a.r.s. Erlich connects to Klemesrud's BBS using a telephone and a modem. Erlich then transmits his messages to Klemesrud's computer, where they are automatically briefly stored. According to a prearranged pattern established by Netcom's software, Erlich's initial act of posting a message to the Usenet results in the automatic copying of Erlich's message from Klemesrud's computer onto Netcom's computer and onto other computers on the Usenet. In order to ease transmission and for the convenience of Usenet users, Usenet servers maintain postings from newsgroups for a short period of time—eleven days for Netcom's system and three days for Klemesrud's system. Once on Netcom's computers, messages are available to Netcom's customers and Usenet neighbors, who may then download the messages to their own computers. Netcom's local server makes available its postings to a group of Usenet servers, which do the same for other servers until all Usenet sites worldwide have obtained access to the postings, which takes a matter of hours. * * *

Unlike some other large on-line service providers, such as CompuServe, America Online, and Prodigy, Netcom does not create or control the content of the information available to its subscribers. It also does not monitor messages as they are posted. It has, however, suspended the accounts of subscribers who violated its terms and conditions, such as where they had commercial software in their posted files. Netcom admits that, although not currently configured to do this, it may be possible to reprogram its system to screen postings containing particular words or coming from particular individuals. Netcom, however, took no action after it was told by plaintiffs that Erlich had posted messages through Netcom's system that violated plaintiffs' copyrights, instead claiming that it could not shut out Erlich without shutting out all of the users of Klemesrud's BBS.

* * *

c.   *Is Netcom Directly Liable for Making the Copies?*

* * *

Playboy Enterprises, Inc. v. Frena involved a suit against the operator of a small BBS whose system contained files of erotic pictures. 839 F. Supp. 1552, 1554 (M.D.Fla.1993). A subscriber of the defendant's BBS had uploaded files containing digitized pictures copied from the plaintiff's copyrighted magazine, which files remained on the BBS for other subscribers to download. Id. The court did not conclude, as plaintiffs suggest in this case, that the BBS is itself liable for the unauthorized reproduction of plaintiffs' work; instead, the court concluded that the BBS operator was liable for violating the plaintiff's right to publicly distribute and display copies of its work. Id. at 1556–57.

In support of their argument that Netcom is directly liable for copying plaintiffs' works, plaintiffs cite to the court's conclusion that "there is no dispute that [the BBS operator] supplied a product containing unauthorized copies of a copyrighted work. It does not matter that [the BBS operator] claims he did not make the copies himself." Id. at 1556. It is clear from the context of this discussion[14] that the Playboy court was looking only at the exclusive right to distribute copies to the public, where liability exists regardless of whether the defendant makes copies. Here, however, plaintiffs do not argue that Netcom is liable for its public distribution of copies. Instead, they claim that Netcom is liable because its computers in fact made copies. Therefore, the above-quoted language has no bearing on the issue of direct liability for unauthorized reproductions. Notwithstanding Playboy's holding that a BBS operator may be directly liable for distributing or displaying to the public copies of

---

14. The paragraph in Playboy containing the quotation begins with a description of the right of public distribution. Id. Further, the above quoted language is followed by a citation to a discussion of the right of public distribution in Jay Dratler, Jr., INTELLECTUAL PROPERTY LAW: COMMERCIAL, CREATIVE AND INDUSTRIAL PROPERTY § 6.01[3], at 6–15 (1991). This treatise states that "the distribution right may be decisive, if, for example, a distributor supplies products containing unauthorized copies of a copyrighted work but has not made the copies itself." Id. (citing to Williams Electronics, Inc. v. Artic International, Inc., 685 F.2d 870, 876 (3d Cir. 1982)). In any event, the Williams holding regarding public distribution was dicta, as the court found that the defendant had also made copies. Id.

protected works,[15] this court holds that the storage on a defendant's system of infringing copies and retransmission to other servers is not a direct infringement by the BBS operator of the exclusive right to reproduce the work where such copies are uploaded by an infringing user. Playboy does not hold otherwise.[16]

* * *

f. Public Distribution and Display?

Plaintiffs allege that Netcom is directly liable for making copies of their works. * * * They also allege that Netcom violated their exclusive rights to publicly display copies of their works. * * * There are no allegations that Netcom violated plaintiffs' exclusive right to publicly distribute their works. However, in their discussion of direct infringement, plaintiffs insist that Netcom is liable for "maintaining copies of [Erlich's] messages on its server for eleven days for access by its subscribers and 'USENET neighbors'" and they compare this case to the Playboy case, which discussed the right of public distribution. * * * Plaintiffs also argued this theory of infringement at oral argument. * * * Because this could be an attempt to argue that Netcom has infringed plaintiffs' rights of public distribution and display, the court will address these arguments.

Playboy concluded that the defendant infringed the plaintiff's exclusive rights to publicly distribute and display copies of its works. 839 F. Supp. at 1556–57. The court is not entirely convinced that the mere possession of a digital copy on a BBS that is accessible to some members of the public constitutes direct infringement by the BBS operator. Such a holding suffers from the same problem of causation as the reproduction argument. Only the subscriber should be liable for causing the distribution of plaintiffs' work, as the contributing actions of the BBS provider are automatic and indiscriminate. Erlich could have posted his messages through countless access providers and the outcome would be the same: anyone with access to Usenet newsgroups would be able to read his messages. There is no logical reason to draw a line around Netcom and Klemesrud and say that they are uniquely responsible for distributing Erlich's messages. Netcom is not even the first link in the chain of distribution—Erlich had no direct relationship with Netcom but dealt solely with Klemesrud's BBS, which used Netcom to gain its Internet access. Every Usenet server has a role in the distribution, so plaintiffs' argument would create unreasonable liability. Where the BBS merely stores and passes along all messages sent by its subscribers and others,

15. Given the ambiguity in plaintiffs' reference to a violation of the right to "publish" and to Playboy, it is possible that plaintiffs are also claiming that Netcom infringed their exclusive right to publicly distribute their works. The court will address this argument infra.

16. The court further notes that Playboy has been much criticized. See, e.g., L. Rose, NETLAW 91–92 (1995). The finding of direct infringement was perhaps influenced by the fact that there was some evidence that defendants in fact knew of the infringing nature of the works, which were digitized photographs labeled "Playboy" and "Playmate."

the BBS should not be seen as causing these works to be publicly distributed or displayed.

Even accepting the Playboy court's holding, the case is factually distinguishable. Unlike the BBS in that case, Netcom does not maintain an archive of files for its users. Thus, it cannot be said to be "supplying a product." In contrast to some of its larger competitors, Netcom does not create or control the content of the information available to its subscribers; it merely provides access to the Internet, whose content is controlled by no single entity. Although the Internet consists of many different computers networked together, some of which may contain infringing files, it does not make sense to hold the operator of each computer liable as an infringer merely because his or her computer is linked to a computer with an infringing file. It would be especially inappropriate to hold liable a service that acts more like a conduit, in other words, one that does not itself keep an archive of files for more than a short duration. Finding such a service liable would involve an unreasonably broad construction of public distribution and display rights. No purpose would be served by holding liable those who have no ability to control the information to which their subscribers have access, even though they might be in some sense helping to achieve the Internet's automatic "public distribution" and the users' "public" display of files.

g. *Conclusion*

The court is not persuaded by plaintiffs' argument that Netcom is directly liable for the copies that are made and stored on its computer. Where the infringing subscriber is clearly directly liable for the same act, it does not make sense to adopt a rule that could lead to the liability of countless parties whose role in the infringement is nothing more than setting up and operating a system that is necessary for the functioning of the Internet. Such a result is unnecessary as there is already a party directly liable for causing the copies to be made. Plaintiffs occasionally claim that they only seek to hold liable a party that refuses to delete infringing files after they have been warned. However, such liability cannot be based on a theory of direct infringement, where knowledge is irrelevant. The court does not find workable a theory of infringement that would hold the entire Internet liable for activities that cannot reasonably be deterred. Billions of bits of data flow through the Internet and are necessarily stored on servers throughout the network and it is thus practically impossible to screen out infringing bits from noninfringing bits. Because the court cannot see any meaningful distinction (without regard to knowledge) between what Netcom did and what every other Usenet server does, the court finds that Netcom cannot be held liable for direct infringement. Cf. [Information Infrastructure Task Force, Intellectual Property and the National Information Infrastructure: The Report of the Working Group on Intellectual Property Rights (1995) ("IITF Report")] at 69 (noting uncertainty regarding whether

BBS operator should be directly liable for reproduction or distribution of files uploaded by a subscriber).[19]

* * *

Notes

1. Were the defendants in *Video 47* subjected to a different liability standard than the defendants in *Netcom*? Is this appropriate? If a merchant distributes a work (such as a videocassette) without knowing that it incorporates an infringing component (such as a piece of soundtrack music), is the merchant liable? What if the defendant is a public lending library?

2. In determining what constitutes an infringing distribution of a work, courts have applied the same criteria that determine whether a work has been "published" for copyright purposes (distinguishing between private and public distributions, for example). See Chapter 17.A.4(i), *supra*. In this regard, the 1976 House Report advises:

> * * * Under the definition in section 101, a work is "published" if one or more copies or phonorecords embodying it are distributed to the public—that is, generally to persons under no explicit or implicit restrictions with respect to disclosure of its contents—without regard to the manner in which the copies or phonorecords changed hands. The definition clears up the question of whether the sale of phonorecords constitutes publication, and it also makes plain that any form or dissemination in which a material object does not change hands—performances or displays on television, for example—is not a publication no matter how many people are exposed to the work. On the other hand, the definition also makes clear that, when copies or phonorecords are offered to a group of wholesalers, broadcasters, motion picture theaters, etc., publication takes place if the purpose is "further distribution, public performance, or public display."

* * *

H.R. Rep. No. 94–1476, 94th Cong., 2d Sess. 138 (1976). If this legislative history is treated as an authoritative construction of the meaning of "public distribution," should the exclusive distribution right be interpreted to include electronic transmissions?

Although the *Netcom* court characterized *Frena* as holding "that a BBS operator may be directly liable for distributing or displaying to the public copies of protected works", the *Frena* court's actual language was more ambiguous, stating that the exclusive public distribution right was "implicated" when works were uploaded to and downloaded from a computer bulletin

---

19. Despite that uncertainty, the IITF Report recommends a strict liability paradigm for BBS operators. See IITF Report at 122–24. It recommends that Congress not exempt on-line service providers from strict liability because this would prematurely deprive the system of an incentive to get providers to reduce the damage to copyright holders by reducing the chances that users will infringe by educating them, requiring indemnification, purchasing insurance, and, where efficient, developing technological solutions to screening out infringement. Denying strict liability in many cases would leave copyright owners without an adequate remedy since direct infringers may act anonymously or pseudonymously or may not have the resources to pay a judgment. Id. * * *.

board service, because the defendant BBS operator "supplied a product containing unauthorized copies of a copyrighted work." Playboy Enterprises v. Frena, 839 F.Supp. 1552, 1555–56 (M.D.Fla.1993).

In *Sega Enterprises Ltd. v. MAPHIA*, 857 F.Supp. 679 (N.D.Cal.1994), the operator of an on-line bulletin board system encouraged subscribers to upload and download copies of Sega's video games. In its conclusions of law, the district court held that these activities infringed the plaintiff's exclusive reproduction right. While the court did not clearly hold that the exclusive distribution right had also been infringed, the court's findings of fact repeatedly refer to the defendant's activities as an unauthorized "distribution" of copies. On these facts, can *MAPHIA* be meaningfully distinguished from *Frena* and/or *Netcom*?

In its 1995 White Paper, the Information Infrastructure Task Force noted that "[i]t is not clear under the current law that a transmission can constitute a distribution of copies or phonorecords of a work." Information Infrastructure Task Force, Intellectual Property and the National Information Infrastructure: The Report of the Working Group on Intellectual Property Rights 213 (1995). The White Paper recommended amending the copyright statutes to treat certain electronic transmissions as public distributions (while exempting certain private transmissions, such as private email, as well as "restricted" transmissions, meaning those with respect to which no retransmission is authorized). *Id.* at 213–17. Is such a change necessary? Advisable? If the copyright statutes are amended to make clear that copyright includes an exclusive electronic transmission right, how would this affect public access to electronic libraries?

Since the decision in *Netcom*, the Digital Millennium Copyright Act has introduced limits on the infringement liability of internet service providers. (These limits are addressed and more fully discussed in Chapter 20.D.1.). The DMCA did not clarify the meaning of publication or distribution in the internet context, however.

3. When a teacher distributes materials to students, is this a public distribution?

4. The exclusive importation right, 17 U.S.C.A. §§ 602–03, is closely related to the exclusive distribution right and the first sale rule. See Section B, *infra*.

4. PUBLIC PERFORMANCE AND PUBLIC DISPLAY

COPYRIGHT ACT OF 1976
H.R. Rep. No. 94–1476.
94th Cong., 2d Sess. 62–65 (1976).

* * *

Under the definitions of "perform," "display," "publicly," and "transmit" in section 101, the concepts of public performance and public display cover not only the initial rendition or showing, but also any further act by which that rendition or showing is transmitted or communicated to the public. * * *

* * * A performance may be accomplished "either directly or by means of any device or process," including all kinds of equipment for reproducing or amplifying sounds or visual images, any sort of transmitting apparatus, any type of electronic retrieval system, and any other techniques and systems not yet in use or even invented.

* * *

Under clause (1) of the definition of "publicly" in section 101, a performance or display is "public" if it takes place "at a place open to the public or at any place where a substantial number of persons outside of a normal circle of a family and its social acquaintances is gathered." One of the principal purposes of the definition was to make clear that, contrary to the decision in *Metro-Goldwyn–Mayer Distributing Corp. v. Wyatt*, 21 C.O.Bull. 203 (D. Md. 1932), performances in "semipublic" places such as clubs, lodges, factories, summer camps, and schools are "public performances" subject to copyright control. The term "a family" in this context would include an individual living alone, so that a gathering confined to the individual's social acquaintances would normally be regarded as private. Routine meetings of businesses and governmental personnel would be excluded because they do not represent the gathering of a "substantial number of persons."

Clause (2) of the definition of "publicly" in section 101 makes clear that the concepts of public performance and public display include not only performances and displays that occur initially in a public place, but also acts that transmit or otherwise communicate a performance or display of the work to the public by means of any device or process. The definition of "transmit"—to communicate a performance or display "by any device or process whereby images or sound are received beyond the place from which they are sent"—is broad enough to include all conceivable forms and combinations of wires and wireless communications media, including but by no means limited to radio and television broadcasting as we know them. Each and every method by which the images or sounds comprising a performance or display are picked up and conveyed is a "transmission," and if the transmission reaches the public in [any] form, the case comes within the scope of clauses (4) or (5) of section 106.

Under the bill, as under the present law, a performance made available by transmission to the public at large is "public" even though the recipients are not gathered in a single place, and even if there is no proof that any of the potential recipients was operating his receiving apparatus at the time of the transmission. The same principles apply whenever the potential recipients of the transmission represent a limited segment of the public, such as the occupants of hotel rooms or the subscribers of a cable television service.

* * *

COLUMBIA PICTURES INDUSTRIES, INC. v. REDD HORNE, INC.

United States Court of Appeals, Third Circuit, 1984.
749 F.2d 154.

RE, CHIEF JUDGE:

* * *

Maxwell's Video Showcase, Ltd., operates two stores in Erie, Pennsylvania. At these two facilities, Maxwell's sells and rents video cassette recorders and prerecorded video cassettes, and sells blank video cassette cartridges. These activities are not the subject of the plaintiffs' complaint. The copyright infringement issue in this case arises from defendants' exhibition of video cassettes of the plaintiffs' films, or what defendants euphemistically refer to as their "showcasing" or "in-store rental" concept.

Each store contains a small showroom area in the front of the store, and a "showcase" or exhibition area in the rear. The front showroom contains video equipment and materials for sale or rent, as well as dispensing machines for popcorn and carbonated beverages. Movie posters are also displayed in this front area. In the rear "showcase" area, patrons may view any of an assortment of video cassettes in small, private booths with space for two to four people. There are a total of eighty-five booths in the two stores. Each booth or room is approximately four feet by six feet and is carpeted on the floor and walls. In the front there is a nineteen inch color television and an upholstered bench in the back.

The procedure followed by a patron wishing to utilize one of the viewing booths or rooms is the same at both facilities. The customer selects a film from a catalogue which contains the titles of available films. The fee charged by Maxwell's depends on the number of people in the viewing room, and the time of day. The price is $5.00 for one or two people before 6 p.m., and $6.00 for two people after 6 p.m. There is at all times a $1.00 surcharge for the third and fourth person. The fee also entitles patrons to help themselves to popcorn and soft drinks before entering their assigned rooms. Closing the door of the viewing room activates a signal in the counter area at the front of the store. An employee of Maxwell's then places the cassette of the motion picture chosen by the viewer into one of the video cassette machines in the front of the store and the picture is transmitted to the patron's viewing room. The viewer may adjust the light in the room, as well as the volume, brightness, and color levels on the television set.

Access to each room is limited to the individuals who rent it as a group. Although no restriction is placed on the composition of a group, strangers are not grouped in order to fill a particular room to capacity. Maxwell's is open to any member of the public who wishes to utilize its facilities or services.

Maxwell's advertises on Erie radio stations and on the theatre pages of the local newspapers. Typically, each advertisement features one or more motion pictures, and emphasizes Maxwell's selection of films, low prices, and free refreshments. The advertisements do not state that these motion pictures are video cassette copies. At the entrance to the two Maxwell's facilities, there are also advertisements for individual films, which resemble movie posters.

Infringement of Plaintiffs' Copyright

It may be stated at the outset that this is not a case of unauthorized taping or video cassette piracy. The defendants obtained the video cassette copies of plaintiffs' copyrighted motion pictures by purchasing them from either the plaintiffs or their authorized distributors. The sale or rental of these cassettes to individuals for home viewing is also not an issue. Plaintiffs do not contend that in-home use infringes their copyright.

The plaintiffs' complaint is based on their contention that the exhibition or showing of the video cassettes in the private booths on defendants' premises constitutes an unauthorized public performance in violation of plaintiffs' exclusive rights under the federal copyright laws.

It is acknowledged that it is the role of the Congress, not the courts, to formulate new principles of copyright law when the legislature has determined that technological innovations have made them necessary. See, e.g., Sony Corp. v. Universal City Studios, Inc., 464 U.S. 417, 104 S.Ct. 774, 783, 78 L.Ed. 2d 574 (1984); Teleprompter Corp. v. CBS, 415 U.S. 394, 414, 39 L.Ed. 2d 415, 94 S.Ct. 1129 (1974). In the words of Justice Stevens, "Congress has the constitutional authority and the institutional ability to accommodate fully the varied permutations of competing interests that are inevitably implicated by such new technology." Sony Corp., supra, 104 S.Ct. at 783. A defendant, however, is not immune from liability for copyright infringement simply because the technologies are of recent origin or are being applied to innovative uses. Although this case involves a novel application of relatively recent technological developments, it can nonetheless be readily analyzed and resolved within the existing statutory framework.

* * *

It is undisputed that the defendants were licensed to exercise the right of distribution. Id. § 106(3). A copyright owner, however, may dispose of a copy of his work while retaining all underlying copyrights which are not expressly or impliedly disposed of with that copy. Id. § 202. Thus, it is clear that the plaintiffs have retained their interest in the other four enumerated rights. * * * Since the rights granted by section 106 are separate and distinct, and are severable from one another, the grant of one does not waive any of the other exclusive rights. Thus, plaintiffs' sales of video cassette copies of their copyrighted motion pictures did not result in a waiver of any of the other exclusive rights enumerated in section 106, such as the exclusive right to perform their motion pictures publicly. In essence, therefore, the fundamental question is whether the defendants' activities constitute a public performance of the plaintiffs' motion pictures. We agree with the conclusion of the district court that these activities constitute a public performance, and are an infringement.

"To perform a work means ... in the case of a motion picture or other audiovisual work, to show its images in any sequence or to make the sounds accompanying it audible." 17 U.S.C. § 101 (1982). Clearly, playing a video cassette results in a sequential showing of a motion picture's images and in making the sounds accompanying it audible. Thus, Maxwell's activities constitute a performance under section 101.

The remaining question is whether these performances are public. Section 101 also states that to perform a work "publicly" means "to perform ... it at a place open to the public or at any place where a substantial number of persons outside of a normal circle of a family and its social acquaintances is gathered." Id. The statute is written in the disjunctive, and thus two categories of places can satisfy the definition of "to perform a work publicly." The first category is self-evident; it is "a place open to the public." The second category, commonly referred to as a semi-public place, is determined by the size and composition of the audience.

The legislative history indicates that this second category was added to expand the concept of public performance by including those places that, although not open to the public at large, are accessible to a significant number of people. See H.R. Rep. No. 1476, 94th Cong., 2d Sess. 64, reprinted in, 1976 U.S. Code Cong. & Ad. News 5659, 5677–78 (hereinafter cited as House Report). Clearly, if a place is public, the size and composition of the audience are irrelevant. However, if the place is not public, the size and composition of the audience will be determinative.

We find it unnecessary to examine the second part of the statutory definition because we agree with the district court's conclusion that Maxwell's was open to the public. On the composition of the audience, the district court noted that "the showcasing operation is not distinguishable in any significant manner from the exhibition of films at a conventional movie theater." 568 F. Supp. at 500. Any member of the public can view a motion picture by paying the appropriate fee. The services provided by Maxwell's are essentially the same as a movie theatre, with the additional feature of privacy. The relevant "place" within the meaning of section 101 is each of Maxwell's two stores, not each individual booth within each store. Simply because the cassettes can be viewed in private does not mitigate the essential fact that Maxwell's is unquestionably open to the public.

The conclusion that Maxwell's activities constitute public performances is fully supported by subsection (2) of the statutory definition of public performance [in section 101.] * * * As explained in the House

Report which accompanies the Copyright Revision Act of 1976, "a performance made available by transmission to the public at large is 'public' even though the recipients are not gathered in a single place.... The same principles apply whenever the potential recipients of the transmission represent a limited segment of the public, such as the occupants of hotel rooms.... " House Report, supra, at 64–65. Thus, the transmission of a performance to members of the public, even in private settings such as hotel rooms or Maxwell's viewing rooms, constitutes a public performance. As the statutory language and legislative history clearly indicate, the fact that members of the public view the performance at different times does not alter this legal consequence.

Professor Nimmer's examination of this definition is particularly pertinent: "*if the same copy* ... of a given work is repeatedly played (i.e., 'performed') by different members of the public, albeit at different times, this constitutes a 'public' performance." 2 M. Nimmer, § 8.14[C][3], at 8–142 (emphasis in original). Indeed, Professor Nimmer would seem to have envisaged Maxwell's when he wrote:

> one may anticipate the possibility of theaters in which patrons occupy separate screening rooms, for greater privacy, and in order not to have to await a given hour for commencement of a given film. These too should obviously be regarded as public performances within the underlying rationale of the Copyright Act.

Id. at 8–142. Although Maxwell's has only one copy of each film, it shows each copy repeatedly to different members of the public. This constitutes a public performance.

[The court also rejected the defendants' contention that their activities were protected by the first sale doctrine, 17 U.S.C. § 109(a). The court noted that the first sale doctrine permits distribution, not public performance, and on these facts there was a performance rather than a distribution.]

* * *

* * * Maxwell's maintained physical dominion and control over the tapes. Its employees actually played the cassettes on its machines. The charges or fees received for viewing the cassettes at Maxwell's facilities are analytically indistinguishable from admission fees paid by patrons to gain admission to any public theater. Plainly, in their showcasing operation, the appellants do not sell, rent, or otherwise dispose of the video cassette. On the facts presented, Maxwell's "showcasing" operation is a public performance, which, as a matter of law, constitutes a copyright infringement.

* * *

ON COMMAND VIDEO CORPORATION v. COLUMBIA PICTURES INDUSTRIES

United States District Court, N. D. California, 1991.
777 F.Supp. 787.

WEIGEL, DISTRICT JUDGE:

Plaintiff seeks a declaratory judgment that its hotel video-movie viewing system does not infringe defendants' copyrights in the movies shown through the system. * * * Plaintiff, the designer and builder of an innovative video viewing system currently installed in a number of hotels, insists that a hotel occupant's viewing of one or more of defendants' movies through its system does not constitute a "public performance" under the 1976 Copyright Act, 17 U.S.C. § 101 et seq. Defendants, seven major United States movie companies, contend that such viewings do constitute public performances and that plaintiff's system therefore violates defendants' exclusive right of public performance under § 106(4) of the Act.

I. FACTS

The material facts of this case are not in dispute. On Command has developed a system for the electronic delivery of movie video tapes. The system consists of a computer program, a sophisticated electronic switch, and a bank of video cassette players ("VCPs"), all of which are centrally located in a hotel equipment room. The VCPs are connected to the hotel's guest rooms by wiring. The computer program directs the electronic switches so that a particular VCP will be dedicated to the guest room where a particular movie is requested. Each VCP contains a video tape. When a guest requests a particular movie, the computer identifies the VCP containing that movie, switches the VCP to that particular room, and starts the movie video.

A hotel guest operates the system from his or her room by remote control. After the television is turned on, the screen lists a menu of available movies. The guest selects a movie by entering the appropriate code on the remote control. Once a particular video is selected, that video selection disappears from the menu of available videos displayed on all other television sets in the hotel. The video is seen only in the room where it was selected by the guest. It cannot be seen in any other guest room or in any other location in the hotel. The viewer cannot pause, rewind, or fast-forward the video. When the movie ends, it is automatically rewound and then immediately available for viewing by another hotel guest.

The only components of the system installed in the guest rooms are the hand-held remote control and a microprocessor in the television set. When a guest checks in to the hotel, the hotel clerk uses a front-desk terminal connected to the On Command computer program to activate movie transmission to the appropriate room. At the guest's request, the clerk can prevent the transmission of adult movies to a room or deactivate service to a room altogether. The apparent advantages On Command's system enjoys over existing closed-circuit hotel video systems with pre-set movie times, such as "Spectravision," are the larger variety of movies available for viewing and the guests' freedom to watch them on their own schedule. On Command's system also eliminates the effort and potential guest embarrassment of in-house hotel video rental programs, in which VCPs are installed in individual rooms and guests must physically rent videos from the hotel staff.

II. Discussion

A copyright owner has the exclusive right "to perform the copyrighted work publicly" or to authorize any such public performance. 17 U.S.C. § 106(4). What constitutes a public performance is defined by the Copyright Act in two clauses. Under clause (1), the "public place" clause, a performance is public if it occurs

> at a place open to the public or at any place where a substantial number of persons outside of a normal circle of a family and its social acquaintances is gathered.

17 U.S.C. § 101. Under clause (2), the "transmit" clause, a performance is public if someone

> transmits or otherwise communicates a performance or display of the work to a place specified by clause (1) or to the public, by means of any device or process.

Id. Under the transmit clause, a performance is public "whether the members of the public capable of receiving the performance or display receive it in the same place or in separate places and at the same time or at different times." Id.

Both plaintiff and defendants base their motions for summary judgment on favorable interpretations of these clauses. Both also rely heavily on the Ninth Circuit's decision in Columbia Pictures v. Professional Real Estate, 866 F.2d 278 (9th Cir.1989). This Court must therefore determine whether On Command's system results in the public performance of defendants' movies under the statutory clauses and Professional Real Estate.

A. The Public Place Clause.

Professional Real Estate held that hotel guest rooms are not "public places" for the purposes of the Copyright Act. 866 F.2d at 280. Defendants do not challenge this holding. Rather, defendants argue that because On Command's system comprises components dispersed throughout a hotel—i.e., the command center is located in a hotel equipment room, the hotel operator's terminal is in the front lobby, the transmission wiring is installed throughout the walls and ceilings—the relevant place of performance is not the individual hotel rooms but the entire hotel, which defendants contend is a public place under the language of the Act. This argument is unavailing. At least for the purposes of public place analysis, a performance of a work does not occur every place a wire carrying the performance passes through; a performance occurs where it is received. Accepting defendants' argument would eviscerate both the concepts of "performance" and "public place." The Act defines the performance of a motion picture as the "showing of its images in any sequence or to make the sounds accompanying it audible." 17 U.S.C. § 101. A movie video is thus performed only when it is visible and audible. In On Command's system, this viewing and hearing occurs only in an individual guest room. That can be the only relevant place of performance for public place analysis. Since hotel guest rooms are indisputably not public places for copyright purposes, On Command's system results in no public performances under the public place clause.

B. The Transmit Clause.

Public performance of defendants' movies under this clause occurs if On Command "transmits" the movies "to the public." Under the Copyright Act, to "transmit" a performance is

> to communicate it by any device or process whereby images or sounds are received beyond the place from which they are sent.

Id. Plaintiff's argument that On Command's system involves not "transmissions" but "electronic rentals" similar to patrons' physical borrowing of videotapes is without merit. On Command transmits movie performances directly under the language of the definition. The system "communicates" the motion picture "images and sounds" by a "device or process"—the equipment and wiring network—from a central console in a hotel to individual guest rooms, where the images and sounds are received "beyond the place from which they are sent." See also Professional Real Estate, 866 F.2d at 282 n.7. The fact that hotel guests initiate this transmission by turning on the television and choosing a video is immaterial.

On Command's video transmissions are also "to the public" for the purposes of the transmit clause. Hotel guests watching a video movie in their room through On Command's system are not watching it in a "public place" but they are nonetheless members of "the public." See Columbia Pictures Industries, Inc. v. Redd Horne, 568 F.Supp. 494, 219 U.S.P.Q. (BNA) 995 (W.D.Pa.1983), aff'd 749 F.2d 154, 159, 224 U.S.P.Q. (BNA) 641 (3d Cir.1984) ("the transmission of a performance to members of the public, even in private settings such as hotel rooms . . . constitutes a public performance") (citing H.R. Rep. No. 1476, 94th Cong., 2d Sess. at 64 (1976) ("1976 House Report")); ESPN Inc. v. Edinburg Community Hotel, Inc., 735 F.Supp. 1334, 1340 (S.D.Tex.1986) ("The [1976] House Report . . . on the Copyright Act makes explicit that performances to occupants of hotel rooms fall within the definition of a public performance"). This is because the relationship between the transmitter of the performance, On Command, and the audience, hotel guests, is a commercial, "public" one regardless of where the viewing takes place. The non-public nature of the place of the performance has no bearing on whether or not those who enjoy the performance constitute "the public" under the transmit clause.

A performance may still be public under the transmit clause "whether the members of the public ... receive it in the same place or in separate places and at the same time or at different times." 17 U.S.C. § 101. A 1967 Report by the House of Representatives reveals that Congress added this language to the transmit clause to cover precisely the sort of single-viewer system developed by plaintiff:

> [This language makes doubly clear that] a performance made available by transmission to the public at large is "public" even though the recipients are not gathered in a single place, and even if there is no direct proof that any of the potential recipients was operating his receiving apparatus at the time of the transmission. The same principles apply whenever the potential recipients of the transmission represent a limited segment of the public, such as the occupants of hotel rooms. . . . ; they are also applicable where the transmission is capable of reaching different recipients at different times, as in the case of sounds or images stored in an information system and capable of being performed or displayed at the initiative of individual members of the public.

H.R. Rep. No. 83, 90th Cong., 1st Sess. at 29 (1967). Thus, whether the number of hotel guests viewing an On Command transmission is one or one hundred, and whether these guests view the transmission simultaneously or sequentially, the transmission is still a public performance since it goes to members of the public. See also Redd Horne, 749 F.2d at 159 (transmissions of videos to private viewing booths occupied by one to four persons infringing under transmit clause); Paramount Pictures Corp. v. Labus, 16 U.S.P.Q. 2d (BNA) 1142, 1147 (W.D. Wisc.1990) (hotel's distribution of unauthorized copies of video cassettes to single guest violated copyright owner's exclusive right to distribute work to "the public"). On Command therefore "publicly performs" defendants' movies under the meaning of the transmit clause.

* * *

Notes

1. Do you agree with *On Command Video*'s interpretation of the "transmit" clause? Was the performance in *Redd Horne* a transmission? Does the existence of a "transmission" depend on whether the videocassette player is in the same room as the television set to which it is attached?

2. Consider whether a public performance occurs in the following scenarios:

(a) Defendants operate a hotel which rents videodiscs to its guests. Each hotel room is equipped with a videodisc player and a large-screen television. Guests operate the videodisc players themselves, although the hotel staff is available to answer questions. See *Columbia Pictures*

Industries, Inc. v. Professional Real Estate Investors, Inc., 866 F.2d 278 (9th Cir.1989).

(b) Defendant rents both private rooms and videos. Customers may rent a video and take it elsewhere for viewing, may rent a room for viewing a videotape which they have obtained elsewhere, or may rent a room and a tape from defendant. Each viewing room contains a videocassette player, which the customers themselves operate (although defendant's employees will assist upon request). Defendant's policy is to allow individuals renting rooms to be accompanied only by members of their family or social acquaintances. See *Columbia Pictures Industries, Inc. v. Aveco, Inc.*, 800 F.2d 59 (3d Cir.1986).

From a copyright policy perspective, can a hotel room be meaningfully distinguished from a rented booth at a video store?

3. Consider whether a public performance occurs when (a) a state penitentiary shows movies once a week to prisoners in the prison's dining hall; (b) a university shows movies once a week in the recreation room of each dormitory; (c) a corporation shows a movie to employees at the company's annual retreat; (d) same as (c), except that the employees may be accompanied by guests; (e) videocassettes are played for military personnel on a military base or on a ship at sea; (f) a movie theatre shows free movies every Friday at midnight; (g) a music or video store plays music videos or other videotaped performances on a large screen for their customers; (h) a retail store plays background music for its customers; (i) a person plays a portable CD player loudly in a street or shopping mall?

4. In order to enforce their public performance rights, owners of copyrighted musical compositions normally designate a performance rights organization to act as as their nonexclusive agent for the purpose of licensing and monitoring nondramatic public performances and collecting the associated royalties. The three principal performance rights organizations operating in the United States are the American Society of Composers, Authors and Publishers (ASCAP), Broadcast Music, Inc. (BMI), and SESAC. Performance rights organizations exist in other nations as well. See generally 2 Melville B. Nimmer & David Nimmer, Nimmer on Copyright § 8.19, at 8–264 to 8–273.

Television networks, clubs, restaurants and other enterprises that perform large numbers of musical works can, for a fee, obtain a "blanket" license covering the entire catalog of works represented by a particular performance rights organization. "Per program licenses" are also available for individual television programs. Each performing rights organization monitors the frequency with which particular works in its repertoire are performed in order to determine how to allocate its receipts among the various copyright owners it represents. Where a publisher owns the copyright in a work, the organization distributes half of the collected fees to the publisher and half to the composer, unless the contract between those parties calls for a different allocation. See generally Al Kohn & Bob Kohn, The Art of Music Licensing 863–84 (1996).

5. Suppose that a nightclub which performed recorded music transformed itself into a private club, allowing people to become members only if they filed an application form, submitted to an interview, and paid an

initiation fee and membership dues. How would this affect the "public performance" analysis?

6. When someone makes a copyrighted artistic, musical or audiovisual work available on the Internet, does this constitute a public display? A public performance? What about when someone else downloads the work from the Internet?

7. In *Amsinck, supra* page 966, can it be argued that any of the mobile creator's exclusive section 106 rights *other than* the reproduction right were infringed? If so, which one(s)?

8. If a transmission originates overseas, but is received in the United States, does this implicate the federal public performance right? See *Los Angeles News Service v. Conus Communications*, 969 F.Supp. 579 (C.D.Cal. 1997).

9. If a defendant receives a satellite transmission and transmits it to a cable television system, but not directly to the public, does this implicate the public performance right? Compare *Allarcom Pay Television v. General Instrument Corp.*, 69 F.3d 381 (9th Cir.1995) *with NFL v. Primetime 24 Joint Venture*, 211 F.3d 10 (2d Cir.2000) *and WGN Continental Broadcasting Co. v. United Video*, 693 F.2d 622 (7th Cir.1982).

KELLY v. ARRIBA SOFT CORPORATION

United States Court of Appeals, Ninth Circuit, 2002.
280 F.3d 934.

NELSON, CIRCUIT JUDGE:

* * * The defendant, Arriba Soft Corp., operates an internet search engine that displays its results in the form of small pictures rather than the more usual form of text. Arriba obtained its database of pictures by copying images from other web sites. By clicking on one of these small pictures, called "thumbnails," the user can then view a large version of that same picture within the context of the Arriba web page.

[The plaintiff is a photographer whose copyrighted pictures have appeared in the defendant's web site. The court found fair use in the creation of the thumbnails, but not in the production of the large versions of the pictures. The fair use portions of the opinion are reproduced in Chapter 19 on Fair Use, *infra*, page 975.]

* * *

The second part of our analysis concerns Arriba's inline linking to and framing of Kelly's full-sized images. This use of Kelly's images does not entail copying them but, rather, importing them directly from Kelly's web site. Therefore, it cannot be copyright infringement based on the reproduction of copyrighted works as in the previous discussion. Instead, this use of Kelly's images infringes upon Kelly's exclusive right to "display the copyrighted work publicly."[20]

20. 17 U.S.C. § 106(5).

1. Public display right.

In order for Kelly to prevail, Arriba must have displayed Kelly's work without his permission and made that display available to the public. The Copyright Act defines "display" as showing a copy of a work.[21] This would seem to preclude Kelly from arguing that showing his original images was an infringement. However, the Act defines a copy as a material object in which a work is fixed, including the material object in which the work is first fixed. The legislative history of the Act makes clear that "[s]ince 'copies' are defined as including the material object 'in which the work is first fixed,' the right of public display applies to original works of art as well as to reproductions of them."[22] By inline linking and framing Kelly's images, Arriba is showing Kelly's original works without his permission.

The legislative history goes on to state that " 'display' would include the projection of an image on a screen or other surface by any method, the transmission of an image by electronic or other means, and the showing of an image on a cathode ray tube, or similar viewing apparatus connected with any sort of information storage and retrieval system."[23] This language indicates that showing Kelly's images on a computer screen would constitute a display.

The Act's definition of the term "publicly" encompasses a transmission of a display of a work to the public "by means of any device or process, whether the members of the public capable of receiving the performance or display receive it in the same place or in separate places and at the same time or at different times." A display is public even if there is no proof that any of the potential recipients was operating his receiving apparatus at the time of the transmission.[24] By making Kelly's images available on its web site, Arriba is allowing public access to those images. The ability to view those images is unrestricted to anyone with a computer and internet access.

The legislative history emphasizes the broad nature of the display right, stating that "[e]ach and every method by which the images or sounds comprising a performance or display are picked up and conveyed is a 'transmission,' and if the transmission reaches the public in [any] form, the case comes within the scope of [the public performance and display rights] of section 106." Looking strictly at the language of the Act and its legislative history, it appears that when Arriba imports Kelly's images into its own web page, Arriba is infringing upon Kelly's public display right. The limited case law in this area supports this conclusion.

No cases have addressed the issue of whether inline linking or framing violates a copyright owner's public display rights. However, in

21. *Id.* § 101.

22. H.R.Rep. No. 94–1476, at 64 (1976), *reprinted in* 1976 U.S.C.C.A.N. 5659, 5677.

23. *Id.*

24. H.R.Rep. No. 94–1476, at 64–65 (1976), *reprinted in* 1976 U.S.C.C.A.N. 5659, 5678.

Playboy Enterprises, Inc. v. Webbworld, Inc.,[25] the court found that the owner of an internet site infringed a magazine publisher's copyrights by displaying copyrighted images on its web site.[26] The defendant, Webbworld, downloaded material from certain newsgroups, discarded the text and retained the images, and made those images available to its internet subscribers. Playboy owned copyrights to many of the images Webbworld retained and displayed. The court found that Webbworld violated Playboy's exclusive right to display its copyrighted works, noting that allowing subscribers to view copyrighted works on their computer monitors while online was a display. The court also discounted the fact that no image existed until the subscriber downloaded it. The image existed in digital form, which made it available for decoding as an image file by the subscriber, who could view the images merely by visiting the Webbworld site.

Although Arriba does not download Kelly's images to its own server but, rather, imports them directly from other web sites, the situation is analogous to *Webbworld.* By allowing the public to view Kelly's copyrighted works while visiting Arriba's web site, Arriba created a public display of Kelly's works. Arriba argues that Kelly offered no proof that anyone ever saw his images and, therefore, there can be no display. We dispose of this argument, as did the court in *Webbworld,* because Arriba made the images available to any viewer that merely visited Arriba's site. Allowing this capability is enough to establish an infringement; the fact that no one saw the images goes to the issue of damages, not liability.

In a similar case, *Playboy Enterprises, Inc. v. Russ Hardenburgh, Inc.,*[27] the court held that the owner of an electronic bulletin board system infringed Playboy's copyrights by displaying copyrighted images on its system. The bulletin board is a central system that stores information, giving home computer users the opportunity to submit information to the system (upload) or retrieve information from the system (download). In this case, the defendant encouraged its subscribers to upload adult photographs, screened all submitted images, and moved some of the images into files from which general subscribers could download them. Because these actions resulted in subscribers being able to download copyrighted images, it violated Playboy's right of public display.[28] Again, the court noted that adopting a policy that allowed the defendants to place images in files available to subscribers entailed a display. This conclusion indicates that it was irrelevant whether anyone actually saw the images.

Both of these cases highlighted the fact that the defendants took an active role in creating the display of the copyrighted images. The reason for this emphasis is that several other cases held that operators of bulletin board systems and internet access providers were not liable for

25. 991 F.Supp. 543 (N.D.Texas 1997).   **27.** 982 F.Supp. 503 (N.D.Ohio 1997).

26. *Id.* at 552–53.   **28.** *Id.*

copyright infringement.[29] These cases distinguished direct infringement from contributory infringement and held that where the defendants did not take any affirmative action that resulted in copying copyrighted works, but only maintained a system that acted as a passive conduit for third parties' copies, they were not liable for direct infringement.

The courts in *Webbworld* and *Hardenburgh* specifically noted that the defendants did more than act as mere providers of access or passive conduits. In *Webbworld,* the web site sold images after actively trolling the internet for them and deciding which images to provide to subscribers. The court stated that "Webbworld exercised total dominion over the content of its site and the product it offered its clientele." Likewise, in *Hardenburgh,* the court found that by encouraging subscribers to upload images and then screening those images and selecting ones to make available for downloading, the defendants were more than passive conduits.

Like the defendants in *Webbworld* and *Hardenburgh,* Arriba is directly liable for infringement. Arriba actively participated in displaying Kelly's images by trolling the web, finding Kelly's images, and then having its program inline link and frame those images within its own web site. Without this program, users would not have been able to view Kelly's images within the context of Arriba's site. Arriba acted as more than a passive conduit of the images by establishing a direct link to the copyrighted images. Therefore, Arriba is liable for publicly displaying Kelly's copyrighted images without his permission.

* * *

5.　THE SCOPE OF EXCLUSIVE RIGHTS IN SOUND RECORDINGS

Statutes: 17 U.S.C.A. §§ 106(6), 114–15

In the case of sound recordings, section 114 defines the exclusive rights to reproduce a work and to incorporate it in derivative works more narrowly than in the case of other copyrightable works. In addition, section 114(a) clarifies that there is no exclusive public performance right in sound recordings. Sound recordings are one instance in which

---

29.　*See e.g. Religious Tech. Ctr. v. Net-com On–Line Communication Servs., Inc.,* 907 F.Supp. 1361, 1372–73 (N.D.Cal.1995) (holding that operator of a computer bulletin board system that forwarded messages from subscribers to other subscribers was not liable for displaying copyrighted works because it took no role in controlling the content of the information but only acted as passive conduit of the information); *Marobie-Fl, Inc. v. Nat'l. Ass'n of Fire and Equip. Distribs.,* 983 F.Supp. 1167, 1176–79 (N.D.Ill.1997) (holding that company that provided a host computer for web page and access link to internet users was not directly liable for copyright infringement when administrator of web page posted copyrighted works on the page, because it only provided the means to display the works but did not engage in the activity itself); *Costar Group Inc. v. Loopnet, Inc.,* 164 F.Supp.2d 688, 695–96 (D.Md.2001) (holding that operator of a web site that hosted real estate listings and photos was not directly liable for copyright infringement because it did not actively participate in copying or displaying the images).

the classification of a work under section 102(a) significantly affects the scope of the copyright owner's rights.

Until recently, the United States did not recognize performance rights in sound recordings. However, the Digital Performance Right in Sound Recordings Act of 1995, Pub. L. 104–39, added new section 106(6), giving the owners of copyrights in sound recordings a public performance right limited to performances via transmission by digital subscription services. The Act does not extend the right to any other digital or analog performance media. The Act reflects the concern that digital subscription services have the potential to supplant phonorecord sales, thus reducing the revenues which those sales previously generated for the owners of sound recording copyrights. In addition, any decrease in phonorecord sales will reduce the royalties payable by record companies to composers, publishers, and performers according to their contracts.

The new law benefits recording artists regardless of whether they own copyright interests in the recordings on which they perform; new section 114(g) requires the owners of sound recording copyrights to allocate specified portions of their digital subscription licensing revenues to the artists who perform on their recordings. It also amends the section 115 compulsory licensing provisions (discussed at Section B.5, *infra*) to require payment of compulsory licensing fees for each digital "delivery" of a musical composition, just as those fees are payable for each sale of a phonorecord embodying a copyrighted musical work. Thus, even if digital deliveries completely supplant record sales, under section 106(6) the revenues payable to copyright owners and recording artists should not be diminished.

New section 114(d)(3) limits the right of the sound recording copyright owner to grant exclusive licenses of the section 106(6) right to interactive subscription services (such as "audio-on-demand" services), in response to the concern expressed by composers and music copyright owners "that the copyright owners of sound recordings might become 'gatekeepers' and limit opportunities for public performances of the musical works embodied in the sound recordings." S. Rep. No. 104–128, 104th Cong., 1st Sess. 25 (1995). No restrictions are imposed on the granting of nonexclusive licenses for section 106(6) rights. New sections 114(e) through (i) establish licensing rules and royalty rates for digital performance rights.

Nations that recognize broader performance rights in sound recordings have in the past refused to allow United States persons owning copyrighted sound recordings to collect royalties for performances in those countries because the United States did not reciprocate. Such nations may continue this practice in spite of the enactment of Pub. L. 104–39, since, at least for now, it applies to only a narrow range of performances.

Notes

1. If someone wishes to make a "soundalike" recording that closely imitates an existing recording of a copyrighted musical work, can this be done without seeking the consent of any copyright owners? If not, whose consent is required? Does it matter whether the existing recording is part of a motion picture soundtrack?

2. If a soundalike recording is authorized by section 114, would a featured musician or singer have a cause of action against the maker of the soundalike recording?

3. Why did Congress define the reproduction right so narrowly in the case of sound recordings?

4. Should Congress revise the copyright laws to recognize a public performance right in sound recordings that is broader than section 106(6)? (Compare Article 15 of the 1996 WIPO Performances and Phonograms Treaty.)

5. If digitization constitutes reproduction under section 106(1), why is section 106(6) necessary to protect the rights of copyright owners? Is section 106(6) necessary if a temporary fixation in RAM constitutes reproduction?

6. Will section 114(i) succeed in preventing sound recording performance royalties from reducing performance royalties payable to the owners of copyright in the underlying musical works? In the case of books-on-tape or other sound recordings of literary works, what impact will sound recording performance royalties have on the performance royalties payable to the owners of the copyright in the underlying literary works?

7. Title IV of the DMCA amended section 114(d)(1) to clarify which transmissions of sound recordings are excluded from section 106(6), and amended section 114(d)(2) to extend the statutory licensing provisions for nonexempt subscription transmissions to include certain eligible nonsubscription transmissions (defined in a new subsection (j)(6) to exclude interactive services and most advertising). The statutory licensing scheme and royalty distribution scheme is thus broadened to include many Internet music transmissions.

B.   SPECIFIC LIMITATIONS ON THE SECTION 106 RIGHTS

Statutes: 17 U.S.C.A. §§ 101 (as needed), 108–22, 1001–10

The exclusive rights of the copyright owner under section 106 are subject to a a number of narrowly-tailored limitations and compulsory licenses, which are set forth in sections 108–122 and 1001–1010. In addition, as discussed in Chapter 15, all of the rights under section 106 are subject to the more broadly-framed fair use provisions of section 107. The limitations under section 114 have already been discussed. Limitations applicable to Title 17 rights other than those embodied in section 106 are discussed in Section C, *infra*.

1.   SECTION 109: THE FIRST SALE RULE

Statutes: 17 U.S.C.A. §§ 109, 602

QUALITY KING DISTRIBUTORS, INC. v. L'ANZA
RESEARCH INTERNATIONAL, INC.

Supreme Court of the United States, 1998.
523 U.S. 135, 118 S.Ct. 1125, 140 L.Ed.2d 254.

JUSTICE STEVENS delivered the opinion of the Court.

Section 106(3) of the Copyright Act of 1976 (Act), 17 U.S.C. § 106(3), gives the owner of a copyright the exclusive right to distribute copies of a copyrighted work. That exclusive right is expressly limited, however, by the provisions of §§ 107 through 120. Section 602(a) gives the copyright owner the right to prohibit the unauthorized importation of copies. The question presented by this case is whether the right granted by § 602(a) is also limited by §§ 107 through 120. More narrowly, the question is whether the "first sale" doctrine endorsed in § 109(a) is applicable to imported copies.

I

Respondent, L'anza Research International, Inc. (L'anza), is a California corporation engaged in the business of manufacturing and selling shampoos, conditioners, and other hair care products. L'anza has copyrighted the labels that are affixed to those products. In the United States, L'anza sells exclusively to domestic distributors who have agreed to resell within limited geographic areas and then only to authorized retailers such as barber shops, beauty salons, and professional hair care colleges. L'anza has found that the American "public is generally unwilling to pay the price charged for high quality products, such as L'anza's products, when they are sold along with the less expensive lower quality products that are generally carried by supermarkets and drug stores." App. 54 (declaration of Robert Hall). L'anza promotes the domestic sales of its products with extensive advertising in various trade magazines and at point of sale, and by providing special training to authorized retailers.

L'anza also sells its products in foreign markets. In those markets, however, it does not engage in comparable advertising or promotion; its prices to foreign distributors are 35% to 40% lower than the prices charged to domestic distributors. In 1992 and 1993, L'anza's distributor in the United Kingdom arranged the sale of three shipments to a distributor in Malta; each shipment contained several tons of L'anza products with copyrighted labels affixed. The record does not establish whether the initial purchaser was the distributor in the United Kingdom or the distributor in Malta, or whether title passed when the goods were delivered to the carrier or when they arrived at their destination, but it is undisputed that the goods were manufactured by L'anza and first sold by L'anza to a foreign purchaser.

It is also undisputed that the goods found their way back to the United States without the permission of L'anza and were sold in California by unauthorized retailers who had purchased them at discounted prices from Quality King Distributors, Inc. (petitioner). There is some uncertainty about the identity of the actual importer, but for the purpose of our decision we assume that petitioner bought all three shipments from the Malta distributor, imported them, and then resold them to retailers who were not in L'anza's authorized chain of distribution.

After determining the source of the unauthorized sales, L'anza brought suit against petitioner and several other defendants. The complaint alleged that the importation and subsequent distribution of those products bearing copyrighted labels violated L'anza's "exclusive rights under 17 U.S.C. §§ 106, 501 and 602 to reproduce and distribute the copyrighted material in the United States." App. 32. The District Court rejected petitioner's defense based on the "first sale" doctrine recognized by § 109 and entered summary judgment in favor of L'anza. Based largely on its conclusion that § 602 would be "meaningless" if § 109 provided a defense in a case of this kind, the Court of Appeals affirmed. 98 F.3d 1109, 1114 (C.A.9 1996). Because its decision created a conflict with the Third Circuit, see Sebastian Int'l, Inc. v. Consumer Contacts (PTY) Ltd., 847 F.2d 1093 (1988), we granted the petition for certiorari. 520 U.S. 1250, 117 S.Ct. 2406, 138 L.Ed.2d 173 (1997).

II

This is an unusual copyright case because L'anza does not claim that anyone has made unauthorized copies of its copyrighted labels. Instead, L'anza is primarily interested in protecting the integrity of its method of marketing the products to which the labels are affixed. Although the labels themselves have only a limited creative component, our interpretation of the relevant statutory provisions would apply equally to a case involving more familiar copyrighted materials such as sound recordings or books. Indeed, we first endorsed the first sale doctrine in a case involving a claim by a publisher that the resale of its books at discounted prices infringed its copyright on the books. Bobbs–Merrill Co. v. Straus, 210 U.S. 339, 28 S.Ct. 722, 52 L.Ed. 1086 (1908).

In that case, the publisher, Bobbs–Merrill, had inserted a notice in its books that any retail sale at a price under $1.00 would constitute an infringement of its copyright. The defendants, who owned Macy's department store, disregarded the notice and sold the books at a lower price without Bobbs–Merrill's consent. We held that the exclusive statutory right to "vend"[5] applied only to the first sale of the copyrighted work:

> "What does the statute mean in granting 'the sole right of vending the same'? Was it intended to create a right which would permit the holder of the copyright to fasten, by notice in a book or upon one of the articles mentioned within the statute, a restriction upon the subsequent alienation of the subject-matter of copyright after the owner had parted with the title to one who had acquired full

---

5. In 1908, when Bobbs–Merrill was decided, the copyright statute provided that copyright owners had "the sole liberty of printing, reprinting, publishing, completing, copying, executing, finishing, and *vending*" their copyrighted works. Copyright Act of 1891, § 4952, 26 Stat. 1107 (emphasis added).

dominion over it and had given a satisfactory price for it? It is not denied that one who has sold a copyrighted article, without restriction, has parted with all right to control the sale of it.' The purchaser of a book, once sold by authority of the owner of the copyright, may sell it again, although he could not publish a new edition of it.

"In this case the stipulated facts show that the books sold by the appellant were sold at wholesale, and purchased by those who made no agreement as to the control of future sales of the book, and took upon themselves no obligation to enforce the notice printed in the book, undertaking to restrict retail sales to a price of one dollar per copy." Id., at 349–350, 28 S.Ct., at 726.

The statute in force when Bobbs–Merrill was decided provided that the copyright owner had the exclusive right to "vend" the copyrighted work. Congress subsequently codified our holding in Bobbs–Merrill that the exclusive right to "vend" was limited to first sales of the work.[7] Under the 1976 Act, the comparable exclusive right granted in 17 U.S.C. § 106(3) is the right "to distribute copies ... by sale or other transfer of ownership." The comparable limitation on that right is provided not by judicial interpretation, but by an express statutory provision. Section 109(a) provides:

"Notwithstanding the provisions of section 106(3), the owner of a particular copy or phonorecord lawfully made under this title, or any person authorized by such owner, is entitled, without the authority of the copyright owner, to sell or otherwise dispose of the possession of that copy or phonorecord...."[9]

The Bobbs–Merrill opinion emphasized the critical distinction between statutory rights and contract rights.[10] In this case, L'anza relies on the terms of its contracts with its domestic distributors to limit their sales to authorized retail outlets. Because the basic holding in Bobbs–Merrill is now codified in § 109(a) of the Act, and because those domestic distributors are owners of the products that they purchased from L'anza (the labels of which were "lawfully made under this title"), L'anza does not, and could not, claim that the statute would enable L'anza to treat unauthorized resales by its domestic distributors as an infringement of its exclusive right to distribute copies of its labels. L'anza does claim,

---

7. Congress codified the first sale doctrine in § 41 of the Copyright Act of 1909, ch. 320, 35 Stat. 1084, and again in § 27 of the 1947 Act, ch. 391, 61 Stat. 660.

9. The comparable section in the 1909 and 1947 Acts provided that "nothing in this Act shall be deemed to forbid, prevent, or restrict the transfer of any copy of a copyrighted work the possession of which has been lawfully obtained." Copyright Act of 1909, ch. 320, § 41, 35 Stat. 1084; see also Copyright Act of 1947, ch. 391, § 27, 61 Stat. 660. It is noteworthy that § 109(a)

of the 1978 Act does not apply to "any copy"; it applies only to a copy that was "lawfully made under this title."

10. "We do not think the statute can be given such a construction, and it is to be remembered that this is purely a question of statutory construction. There is no claim in this case of contract limitation, nor license agreement controlling the subsequent sales of the book." Bobbs–Merrill Co. v. Straus, 210 U.S. 339, 350, 28 S.Ct. 722, 726, 52 L.Ed. 1086 (1908).

however, that contractual provisions are inadequate to protect it from the actions of foreign distributors who may resell L'anza's products to American vendors unable to buy from L'anza's domestic distributors, and that § 602(a) of the Act, properly construed, prohibits such unauthorized competition. To evaluate that submission, we must, of course, consider the text of § 602(a).

III

The most relevant portion of § 602(a) provides:

"Importation into the United States, without the authority of the owner of copyright under this title, of copies or phonorecords of a work that have been acquired outside the United States is an infringement of the exclusive right to distribute copies or phonorecords under section 106, actionable under section 501.... "

It is significant that this provision does not categorically prohibit the unauthorized importation of copyrighted materials.

Instead, it provides that such importation is an infringement of the exclusive right to distribute copies "under section 106." Like the exclusive right to "vend" that was construed in Bobbs–Merrill, the exclusive right to distribute is a limited right.

The introductory language in § 106 expressly states that all of the exclusive rights granted by that section—including, of course, the distribution right granted by subsection (3)—are limited by the provisions of §§ 107 through 120.

One of those limitations, as we have noted, is provided by the terms of § 109(a), which expressly permit the owner of a lawfully made copy to sell that copy "[n]otwithstanding the provisions of section 106(3)."

After the first sale of a copyrighted item "lawfully made under this title," any subsequent purchaser, whether from a domestic or from a foreign reseller, is obviously an "owner" of that item. Read literally, § 109(a) unambiguously states that such an owner "is entitled, without the authority of the copyright owner, to sell" that item. Moreover, since § 602(a) merely provides that unauthorized importation is an infringement of an exclusive right "under section 106," and since that limited right does not encompass resales by lawful owners, the literal text of § 602(a) is simply inapplicable to both domestic and foreign owners of L'anza's products who decide to import them and resell them in the United States.[14]

Notwithstanding the clarity of the text of §§ 106(3), 109(a), and 602(a), L'anza argues that the language of the Act supports a construction of the right granted by § 602(a) as "distinct from the right under Section 106(3) standing alone," and thus not subject to § 109(a). Brief

---

14. Despite L'anza's contention to the contrary, see Brief for Respondent 26–27, the owner of goods lawfully made under the Act is entitled to the protection of the first sale doctrine in an action in a United States court even if the first sale occurred abroad. Such protection does not require the extraterritorial application of the Act any more than § 602(a)'s "acquired abroad" language does.

for Respondent 15. Otherwise, L'anza argues, both the § 602(a) right itself and its exceptions would be superfluous. Moreover, supported by various amici curiae, including the Solicitor General of the United States, L'anza contends that its construction is supported by important policy considerations. We consider these arguments separately.

IV

L'anza advances two primary arguments based on the text of the Act: (1) that § 602(a), and particularly its three exceptions, are superfluous if limited by the first sale doctrine; and (2) that the text of § 501 defining an "infringer" refers separately to violations of § 106, on the one hand, and to imports in violation of § 602. The short answer to both of these arguments is that neither adequately explains why the words "under section 106" appear in § 602(a). The Solicitor General makes an additional textual argument: he contends that the word "importation" in § 602(a) describes an act that is not protected by the language in § 109(a) authorizing a subsequent owner "to sell or otherwise dispose of the possession of" a copy. Each of these arguments merits separate comment.

The Coverage of § 602(a)

Prior to the enactment of § 602(a), the Act already prohibited the importation of "piratical," or unauthorized, copies.[16] Moreover, that earlier prohibition is retained in § 602(b) of the present act.[17] L'anza therefore argues (as do the Solicitor General and other amici curiae) that § 602(a) is superfluous unless it covers non-piratical ("lawfully made") copies sold by the copyright owner, because importation nearly always implies a first sale. There are several flaws in this argument.

First, even if § 602(a) did apply only to piratical copies, it at least would provide the copyright holder with a private remedy against the importer, whereas the enforcement of § 602(b) is vested in the Customs Service. Second, because the protection afforded by § 109(a) is available only to the "owner" of a lawfully made copy (or someone authorized by the owner), the first sale doctrine would not provide a defense to a § 602(a) action against any non-owner such as a bailee, a licensee, a consignee, or one whose possession of the copy was unlawful.[19] Third,

---

16. See 17 U.S.C. §§ 106, 107 (1970).

17. Section 602(b) provides in relevant part: "In a case where the making of the copies or phonorecords would have constituted an infringement of copyright if this title had been applicable, their importation is prohibited.... " The first sale doctrine of § 109(a) does not protect owners of piratical copies, of course, because such copies were not "lawfully made."

19. In its opinion in this case, the Court of Appeals quoted a statement by a representative of the music industry expressing the need for protection against the importa-

tion of stolen motion picture prints: "We've had a similar situation with respect to motion picture prints, which are sent all over the world—legitimate prints made from the authentic negative. These prints get into illicit hands. They're stolen, and there's no contractual relationship.... Now those are not piratical copies." Copyright Law Revision Part 2: Discussion and Comments on Report of the Register of Copyrights on General Revision of the U.S. Copyright Law, 88th Cong., 1st Sess., 213 (H.R. Judiciary Comm. Print 1963) (statement of Mr.

§ 602(a) applies to a category of copies that are neither piratical nor "lawfully made under this title." That category encompasses copies that were "lawfully made" not under the United States Copyright Act, but instead, under the law of some other country.

The category of copies produced lawfully under a foreign copyright was expressly identified in the deliberations that led to the enactment of the 1976 Act. We mention one example of such a comment in 1961 simply to demonstrate that the category is not a merely hypothetical one. In a report to Congress, the Register of Copyrights stated, in part:

> "When arrangements are made for both a U.S. edition and a foreign edition of the same work, the publishers frequently agree to divide the international markets. The foreign publisher agrees not to sell his edition in the United States, and the U.S. publisher agrees not to sell his edition in certain foreign countries. It has been suggested that the import ban on piratical copies should be extended to bar the importation of the foreign edition in contravention of such an agreement." Copyright Law Revision: Report of the Register of Copyrights on the General Revision of the U.S. Copyright Law, 87th Cong., 1st Sess., 125–126 (H.R. Judiciary Comm. Print 1961).

Even in the absence of a market allocation agreement between, for example, a publisher of the U.S. edition and a publisher of the British edition of the same work, each such publisher could make lawful copies. If the author of the work gave the exclusive U.S. distribution rights— enforceable under the Act—to the publisher of the U.S. edition and the exclusive British distribution rights to the publisher of the British edition,[20] however, presumably only those made by the publisher of the U.S. edition would be "lawfully made under this title" within the meaning of § 109(a). The first sale doctrine would not provide the publisher of the British edition who decided to sell in the American market with a defense to an action under § 602(a) (or, for that matter, to an action under § 106(3), if there was a distribution of the copies).

The argument that the statutory exceptions to § 602(a) are superfluous if the first sale doctrine is applicable rests on the assumption that the coverage of that section is co-extensive with the coverage of § 109(a). But since it is, in fact, broader because it encompasses copies that are not subject to the first sale doctrine—e.g., copies that are lawfully made under the law of another country—the exceptions do protect the traveler who may have made an isolated purchase of a copy of a work that could

---

Sargoy), quoted in 98 F.3d 1109, 1116 (C.A.9 1996).

20. A participant in a 1964 panel discussion expressed concern about this particular situation. Copyright Law Revision Part 4: Further Discussion and Comments on Preliminary Draft for Revised U.S. Copyright Law, 88th Cong., 2d Sess., 119 (H.R. Judiciary Comm. Print 1964) (statement of Mrs. Pilpel) ("For example, if someone were to import a copy of the British edition of an American book and the author had transferred exclusive United States and Canadian rights to an American publisher, would that British edition be in violation so that this would constitute an infringement under this section?"); see also id., at 209 (statement of Mr. Manges) (describing similar situation as "a troublesome problem that confronts U.S. book publishers frequently").

not be imported in bulk for purposes of resale. As we read the Act, although both the first sale doctrine embodied in § 109(a) and the exceptions in § 602(a) may be applicable in some situations, the former does not subsume the latter; those provisions retain significant independent meaning.

Section 501's Separate References to §§ 106 and 602

The text of § 501 does lend support to L'anza's submission. In relevant part, it provides:

"(a) Anyone who violates any of the exclusive rights of the copyright owner as provided by sections 106 through 118 or of the author as provided in section 106A(a), or who imports copies or phonorecords into the United States in violation of section 602, is an infringer of the copyright or right of the author, as the case may be. . . ."

The use of the words "or who imports," rather than words such as "including one who imports," is more consistent with an interpretation that a violation of § 602 is distinct from a violation of § 106 (and thus not subject to the first sale doctrine set out in § 109(a)) than with the view that it is a species of such a violation. Nevertheless, the force of that inference is outweighed by other provisions in the statutory text.

Most directly relevant is the fact that the text of § 602(a) itself unambiguously states that the prohibited importation is an infringement of the exclusive distribution right "under section 106, actionable under section 501." Unlike that phrase, which identifies § 602 violations as a species of § 106 violations, the text of § 106A, which is also cross-referenced in § 501, uses starkly different language. It states that the author's right protected by § 106A is "independent of the exclusive rights provided in Section 106." The contrast between the relevant language in § 602 and that in § 106A strongly implies that only the latter describes an independent right.[21]

Of even greater importance is the fact that the § 106 rights are subject not only to the first sale defense in § 109(a), but also to all of the other provisions of "sections 107 through 120." If § 602(a) functioned independently, none of those sections would limit its coverage. For example, the "fair use" defense embodied in § 107 would be unavailable to importers if § 602(a) created a separate right not subject to the limitations on the § 106(3) distribution right. Under L'anza's interpretation of the Act, it presumably would be unlawful for a distributor to import copies of a British newspaper that contained a book review quoting excerpts from an American novel protected by a United States

---

21. The strength of the implication created by the relevant language in § 106A is not diminished by the fact that Congress enacted § 106A more recently than § 602(a), which is part of the Copyright Act of 1976. Section 106A was passed as part of the Visual Artists Rights Act of 1990 in order to protect the moral rights of certain visual artists. Section 106A is analogous to Article 6bis of the Berne Convention for the Protection of Literary and Artistic Works, but its coverage is more limited. See 2 P. Goldstein, Copyright § 5.12, p. 5:225 (2d ed. 1996) (§ 106A encompasses aspects of the moral rights guaranteed by Article 6bis of the Berne Convention, "but effectively gives these rights a narrow subject matter and scope").

copyright.[23] Given the importance of the fair use defense to publishers of scholarly works, as well as to publishers of periodicals, it is difficult to believe that Congress intended to impose an absolute ban on the importation of all such works containing any copying of material protected by a United States copyright.

In the context of this case, involving copyrighted labels, it seems unlikely that an importer could defend an infringement as a "fair use" of the label. In construing the statute, however, we must remember that its principal purpose was to promote the progress of the "useful Arts," U.S.Const., Art. I, § 8, cl. 8, by rewarding creativity, and its principal function is the protection of original works, rather than ordinary commercial products that use copyrighted material as a marketing aid. It is therefore appropriate to take into account the impact of the denial of the fair use defense for the importer of foreign publications. As applied to such publications, L'anza's construction of § 602 "would merely inhibit access to ideas without any countervailing benefit." Sony Corp. of America v. Universal City Studios, Inc., 464 U.S. 417, 450–451, 104 S.Ct. 774, 793, 78 L.Ed.2d 574 (1984).[24]

Does an importer "sell or otherwise dispose" of copies as those words are used in § 109(a)?

Whether viewed from the standpoint of the importer or from that of the copyright holder, the textual argument advanced by the Solicitor General—that the act of "importation" is neither a sale nor a disposal of a copy under § 109(a)—is unpersuasive. Strictly speaking, an importer could, of course, carry merchandise from one country to another without surrendering custody of it. In a typical commercial transaction, however, the shipper transfers "possession, custody, control and title to the products" to a different person, and L'anza assumes that petitioner's importation of the L'anza shipments included such a transfer. An ordinary interpretation of the statement that a person is entitled "to sell or otherwise dispose of the possession" of an item surely includes the right to ship it to another person in another country.

More important, the Solicitor General's cramped reading of the text of the statutes is at odds not only with § 602(a)'s more flexible treatment of unauthorized importation as an infringement of the distribution right (even when there is no literal "distribution"), but also with the necessarily broad reach of § 109(a). The whole point of the first sale doctrine is that once the copyright owner places a copyrighted item in the stream of commerce by selling it, he has exhausted his exclusive statutory right to control its distribution. As we have recognized, the codification of that doctrine in § 109(a) makes it clear that the doctrine applies only to copies that are "lawfully made under this title," but that

---

23. The § 602(a) exceptions, which are substantially narrower than § 107, would not permit such importation. See n. 11, supra.

24. L'anza's reliance on § 602(a)(3)'s reference to § 108(g)(2), see n. 11, supra, to demonstrate that all of the other limitations set out in §§ 107 through 120—including the first sale and fair use doctrines—do not apply to imported copies is unavailing for the same reasons.

was also true of the copies involved in the Bobbs–Merrill case, as well as those involved in the earlier cases applying the doctrine. There is no reason to assume that Congress intended either § 109(a) or the earlier codifications of the doctrine to limit its broad scope.[27]

In sum, we are not persuaded by either L'anza's or the Solicitor General's textual arguments.

V

The parties and their amici have debated at length the wisdom or unwisdom of governmental restraints on what is sometimes described as either the "gray market" or the practice of "parallel importation." In K Mart Corp. v. Cartier, Inc., 486 U.S. 281, 108 S.Ct. 1811, 100 L.Ed.2d 313 (1988), we used those terms to refer to the importation of foreign-manufactured goods bearing a valid United States trademark without the consent of the trademark holder. Id., at 285–286, 108 S.Ct., at 1814–1815. We are not at all sure that those terms appropriately describe the consequences of an American manufacturer's decision to limit its promotional efforts to the domestic market and to sell its products abroad at discounted prices that are so low that its foreign distributors can compete in the domestic market.[29] But even if they do, whether or not we think it would be wise policy to provide statutory protection for such price discrimination is not a matter that is relevant to our duty to interpret the text of the Copyright Act.

Equally irrelevant is the fact that the Executive Branch of the Government has entered into at least five international trade agreements that are apparently intended to protect domestic copyright owners from the unauthorized importation of copies of their works sold in those five countries.[30] The earliest of those agreements was made in 1991; none has been ratified by the Senate. Even though they are of course consistent with the position taken by the Solicitor General in this litigation, they shed no light on the proper interpretation of a statute that was enacted in 1976.[31]

The judgment of the Court of Appeals is reversed.

It is so ordered.

27. See, e.g., H.R. Rep. No. 1476, 94th Cong., 2d Sess., 79 (1979) ("Section 109(a) restates and confirms" the first sale doctrine established by prior case law); S.Rep. No. 473, 94th Cong., 1st Sess., 71 (1975) (same).

29. Presumably L'anza, for example, could have avoided the consequences of that competition either (1) by providing advertising support abroad and charging higher prices, or (2) if it was satisfied to leave the promotion of the product in foreign markets to its foreign distributors, to sell its products abroad under a different name.

30. The Solicitor General advises us that such agreements have been made with Cambodia, Trinidad and Tobago, Jamaica, Ecuador, and Sri Lanka.

31. We also note that in 1991, when the first of the five agreements was signed, the Third Circuit had already issued its opinion in Sebastian Int'l, Inc. v. Consumer Contacts (PTY) Ltd., 847 F.2d 1093 (1988), adopting a position contrary to that subsequently endorsed by the Executive Branch.

JUSTICE GINSBURG, concurring.

This case involves a "round trip" journey, travel of the copies in question from the United States to places abroad, then back again. I join the Court's opinion recognizing that we do not today resolve cases in which the allegedly infringing imports were manufactured abroad. See W. Patry, Copyright Law and Practice 166–170 (1997 Supp.) (commenting that provisions of Title 17 do not apply extraterritorially unless expressly so stated, hence the words "lawfully made under this title" in the "first sale" provision, 17 U.S.C. § 109(a), must mean "lawfully made in the United States"); see generally P. Goldstein, Copyright § 16.0, pp. 16:1–16:2 (2d ed. 1998) ("Copyright protection is territorial. The rights granted by the United States Copyright Act extend no farther than the nation's borders.").

Notes

1. Does the first sale rule:

(a) allow the owner of an original work of art (*e.g.*, a handwritten manuscript, a film negative, a master sound recording, or a work of architecture) to alter, mutilate or destroy that article? (Assume that section 106A does not apply.)

(b) permit the owner of a copy of a copyrighted work to display that copy publicly in a museum? on television? on the Internet?

(c) permit the owner of a videotape copy of a motion picture to publicly perform the videotape?

(d) allow a defendant to transmit electronically a lawfully acquired copy of a work? Should it?

2. The first sale rule is subject to two important exceptions, applicable to phonorecords and computer software. The phonorecords exception was introduced in the Record Rental Amendment of 1984, Pub. L. 98–450, 98 Stat. 1727 (1984), and the software exception was added several years later by the Computer Software Rental Amendments Act of 1990, Pub. L. 101–650, tit. 8, sec. 802, 104 Stat. 5089, 5134–35 (1990). Those exceptions are codified in section 109(b). Why did Congress carve out exceptions only for these categories of works, and why is there no comparable exception for videocassettes of motion pictures? Are the current provisions consistent with Article 7 of the 1996 WIPO Copyright Treaty? Do they apply to commercial rental of books on tape?

3. Suppose that a software retailer permits its customers to return software within one week even if the package has been opened, and provides full refunds minus a $5.00 handling fee. Is this activity infringing?

4. Defendant is a computer servicing company which provides "loaner" equipment to its customers whenever their computers must be serviced off-premises. Plaintiff owns the copyright in the operating system software contained in those computers. Does the plaintiff have an infringement claim?

2. THE SECTION 110 LIMITATIONS

Statutes: 17 U.S.C.A. § 110

Section 110 exempts a variety of public performances and displays from the reach of section 106. In contrast to the 1909 Act, which treated nonprofit public performances as noninfringing, in section 106 the 1976 Act broadened the public performance right to include nonprofit performances. Section 110 preserves a number of narrowly defined nonprofit exemptions. However, section 110 also exempts some for-profit activities. One of these for-profit exemptions is the "homestyle exemption" of section 110(5).

COPYRIGHT ACT OF 1976

H.R. Rep. No. 94–1476.
94th Cong., 2d Sess. 62–63, 86–87 (1976).

* * *

Right of Public Performance and Display

Performing rights and the "for profit" limitation.—The right of public performance under section 106(4) extends to "literary, musical, dramatic, and choreographic works, pantomimes, and motion pictures and other audiovisual works and sound recordings" and, unlike the equivalent provisions now in effect, is not limited by any "for profit" requirement. The approach of the bill, as in many foreign laws, is first to state the public performance right in broad terms, and then to provide specific exemptions for educational and other nonprofit uses.

This approach is more reasonable than the outright exemption of the 1909 statute. The line between commercial and "nonprofit" organizations is increasingly difficult to draw. Many "non-profit" organizations are highly subsidized and capable of paying royalties, and the widespread public exploitation of copyrighted works by public broadcasters and other noncommercial organizations is likely to grow. In addition to these trends, it is worth noting that performances and displays are continuing to supplant markets for printed copies and that in the future a broad "not for profit" exemption could not only hurt authors but could dry up their incentive to write.

* * *

MERE RECEPTION IN PUBLIC

Unlike the first four clauses of section 110, clause (5) is not to any extent a counterpart of the "for profit" limitation of the present statute. It applies to performances and displays of all types of works, and its purpose is to exempt from copyright liability anyone who merely turns on, in a public place, an ordinary radio or television receiving apparatus of a kind commonly sold to members of the public for private use.

The basic rationale of this clause is that the secondary use of the transmission by turning on an ordinary receiver in public is so remote and minimal that no further liability should be imposed. In the vast majority of these cases no royalties are collected today, and the exemption should be made explicit in the statute. This clause has nothing to do with cable television systems and the exemptions would be denied in any case where the audience is charged directly to see or hear the transmission.

On June 17, 1975, the Supreme Court handed down a decision in Twentieth Century Music Corp. v. Aiken, 95 S.Ct. 2040, that raised fundamental questions about the proper interpretation of section 110(5). The defendant, owner and operator of a fast-service food shop in downtown Pittsburgh, had "a radio with outlets to four speakers in the ceiling," which he apparently turned on and left on throughout the business day. Lacking any performing license, he was sued for copyright infringement by two ASCAP members. He lost in the District Court, won a reversal in the Third Circuit Court of Appeals, and finally prevailed, by a margin of 7–2, in the Supreme Court.

* * *

The majority of the Supreme Court in the Aiken case based its decision on a narrow construction of the word "perform" in the 1909 statute. This basis for the decision is completely overturned by the present bill and its broad definition of "perform" in section 101. The Committee has adopted the language of section 110(5), with an amendment expressly denying the exemption in situations where "the performance or display is further transmitted beyond the place where the receiving apparatus is located"; in doing so, it accepts the traditional, pre-Aiken, interpretation of the *Jewell-LaSalle* decision, under which public communication by means other than a home receiving set, or further transmission of a broadcast to the public, is considered an infringing act.

Under the particular fact situation in the Aiken case, assuming a small commercial establishment and the use of a home receiver with four ordinary loudspeakers grouped within a relatively narrow circumference from the set, it is intended that the performances would be exempt from clause (5). However, the Committee considers this fact situation to represent the outer limit of the exemption, and believes that the line should be drawn at that point. Thus, the clause would exempt small commercial establishments whose proprietors merely bring onto their premises standard radio or television equipment and turn it on for their customers' enjoyment, but it would impose liability where the proprietor has a commercial "sound system" installed or converts a standard home receiving apparatus (by augmenting it with sophisticated or extensive amplification equipment) into the equivalent of a commercial sound system. Factors to consider in particular cases would include the size, physical arrangement, and noise level of the areas within the establishment where the transmissions are made audible or visible, and the extent to which the receiving apparatus is altered or augmented for the purpose of improving the aural or visual quality of the performance for individual members of the public using those areas.

* * *

Notes

1. The Conference Report on section 110(5) added that "the intent of the conferees [is] that a small commercial establishment of the type involved in *Aiken*, which merely augmented a home-type receiver and which was not of sufficient size to justify, as a practical matter, a subscription to a commercial background music service, would be exempt." H.R. Rep. 1733, 94th Cong., 2d Sess. 75 (1976). Why should small businesses enjoy an exemption from the public performance rules?

2. In determining whether section 110(5) should apply to a particular establishment, courts had difficulty determining which factors to consider, and what relative weights to assign them. Factors that courts considered include: the revenues of the business, the square footage of the establishment, the nature of the receiving apparatus and/or the speaker system, whether the receiver and speakers are located in different rooms, and whether the business is independent or part of a chain. Representative appellate opinions include *Broadcast Music, Inc. v. Claire's Boutiques, Inc.*, 949 F.2d 1482 (7th Cir.1991); *Broadcast Music, Inc. v. United States Shoe Corp.*, 678 F.2d 816 (9th Cir.1982); and *Sailor Music v. Gap Stores, Inc.*, 668 F.2d 84 (2d Cir.1981), *cert. denied*, 456 U.S. 945, 102 S.Ct. 2012, 72 L.Ed.2d 468 (1982); there are numerous district court cases as well.

The difficulty in applying section 110(5) in its original form led to numerous amendment proposals. Some of these would have broadened the exemption to reach any situation in which music is merely "incidental" to the main purpose of the business, while others would simply clarify the scope of the exemption—by specifying, for example, the maximum number of speakers permitted, the maximum square footage of the store, or the maximum level of annual revenues. Some proposals would have incorporated specific guidelines in the statute, while others would delegate this task to the Copyright Office.

Title II of the SBCTEA, titled the "Fairness in Music Licensing Act of 1998," amended section 110(5) by redesignating the existing 110(5) exemption as section 110(5)(A) and adding a new section 110(5)(B) which provides safe harbors for certain establishments that communicate "a transmission embodying a performance or display of a nondramatic musical work intended to be received by the general public." New subsection (B) limits the safe harbor to transmissions that are originated by an FCC-licensed radio or television broadcast station, or, in the case of audiovisual transmissions, by a cable system or satellite carrier. To qualify for the safe harbor, the establishment must either (a) be smaller than 2,000 square feet (except for a food service or drinking establishment, which must be smaller than 3,750 square feet), or (b) use no more than six loudspeakers (with no more than four in one room) for the audio portion of any performances, and no more than four audiovisual devices (with screens no larger than than fifty-five inches diagonal, and no more than one such device per room) for any visual component. The exemption does not apply at all if a direct charge is made to see or hear the transmission, if the establishment transmits the performance or display to any other location, or if the transmission was not authorized by the copyright owner of the work performed or displayed therein.

Title II also revised 17 U.S.C. § 504 to double the amount of damages a plaintiff can collect from a defendant that invokes section 110(5) without reasonable grounds for doing so, and broadened the section 110(7) exemption to include in-store public performances of nondramatic musical works for the purpose of selling audiovisual or other devices used for those performances.

Finally, Title II added section 513 to Title 17, providing certain small business owners with an alternative means to resolve their licensing fee disputes with ASCAP and BMI. Whereas the antitrust decree binding those organizations requires that such disputes be adjudicated in the federal district court for the Southern District of New York, the bill permits an individual proprietor who owns or operates fewer than seven non-publicly-traded establishments to seek a reasonable license fee determination from a federal district court in the circuit where his or her establishment is located.

In the summer of 2000, a World Trade Organization (WTO) Dispute Panel ruled that the revised version of section 110(5)(B) violated Articles 9.1 and 13 of the TRIPS (Trade–Related Aspects of Intellectual Property) provisions of the WTO Agreement (previously known as the General Agreement on Tarriffs and Trade, or "GATT"), because it created too broad an exception to the public performance right in musical compositions. If Congress does not repeal or amend section 110(5)(B) to bring it into compliance with TRIPS, the WTO may impose trade sanctions against the United States. The amount of damages owed to foreign copyright owners is being determined through arbitration.

3.　What is the meaning of "further transmitted" in section 110(5)? For example, does a "further transmission" occur where speakers are located in a different room from the receiver? In *Claire's Boutiques*, 949 F.2d at 1495 & n.14, the Seventh Circuit rejected that interpretation, but noted the existence of substantial contrary authority. Consider the court's reasoning in *On Command Video* (see Section A.4, *supra*); how does this affect the "further transmission" analysis?

4.　Does section 110(5) permit the playing of tapes, CD's, or videocassettes in a small business establishment? Does it permit a restaurant to use a satellite dish to receive transmissions of football games that are blacked out in that vicinity?

5.　Under sections 106 and 110(5), is there an infringing public performance where music is played on a radio or cassette player in a taxi? Where a store selling television sets turns them on while customers are in the store? Where a store places a television in its window so that passers-by can view the programs? Where a bar plays free or pay-per-view television for its patrons?

6.　*Other Section 110 Exemptions*: Although the homestyle exemption is the most often litigated, section 110 recognizes a number of other specific exemptions, of which most, though not all, are limited to nonprofit uses. Consider whether the actions described below are protected by section 110:

> (a) A church choir director makes twenty copies of the sheet music for a Christmas carol, which the choir then performs at the Christmas Eve mass.

(b) A college dormitory director plays videotapes of popular movies for students in one of the dorm's public areas every Friday night, with no admission charge.

(c) A college professor tapes an episode of a popular television show off the air, plays it for students in his Modern Literature class, and engages those students in a discussion of its theme and dramatic structure.

(d) A civic organization performs a popular song in the course of a musical revue to which admission is charged, and the profits from which are devoted to the organization's civic activities.

(e) A traveling nonprofit theatre troupe performs a play, translated into American Sign Language, at a school for deaf students.

3. SECTION 117: COPYING COMPUTER SOFTWARE

Statutes: 17 U.S.C.A. § 117

VAULT CORP. v. QUAID SOFTWARE LTD.

United States Court of Appeals, Fifth Circuit, 1988.
847 F.2d 255.

REAVLEY, CIRCUIT JUDGE:

[Plaintiff Vault manufactured and marketed PROLOK computer diskettes containing Vault's copyrighted copy-protection software, which prevented persons from making fully functional copies of any other computer programs contained on those diskettes. Vault sold its diskettes to software makers who would place their own copyrighted programs on the copy-protected diskettes in order to prevent unauthorized copying. Defendant Quaid manufactured and sold CopyWrite diskettes, which contained software with a feature known as "RAMKEY" that could "unlock" the PROLOK copy protection. Buyers of Copywrite diskettes could use them to make fully functional copies of any software contained in a PROLOK diskette.]

* * *

* * * Vault claims that Quaid infringed its copyright under § 501(a) by: (1) directly copying Vault's program into the memory of Quaid's computer; (2) contributing to the unauthorized copying of Vault's program and the programs Vault's customers place on PROLOK diskettes; and (3) preparing derivative works of Vault's program.

Section 117 of the Copyright Act limits a copyright owner's exclusive rights under § 106 by permitting an owner of a computer program to make certain copies of that program without obtaining permission from the program's copyright owner. With respect to Vault's first two claims of copyright infringement, Quaid contends that its activities fall within the § 117 exceptions and that it has, therefore, not infringed Vault's exclusive rights under § 501(a). To appreciate the arguments of the parties, we examine the legislative history of § 117.

A. BACKGROUND

In 1974 Congress established the National Commission on New Technological Uses of Copyrighted Works (the "CONTU") to perform research and make recommendations concerning copyright protection for computer programs. Before receiving the CONTU's recommendations, Congress amended the Copyright Act in 1976 to include computer programs in the definition of protectable literary works and to establish that a program copied into a computer's memory constitutes a reproduction.[6] * * *

In 1978 the CONTU issued its final report[8] in which it recognized that "the cost of developing computer programs is far greater than the cost of their duplication," CONTU Report at 26, and concluded that "some form of protection is necessary to encourage the creation and broad distribution of computer programs in a competitive market," id. at 27. After acknowledging the importance of balancing the interest of proprietors in obtaining "reasonable protection" against the risks of "unduly burdening users of programs and the general public," id. at 29, the Report recommended * * * the enactment of a new section 117 which would proscribe the unauthorized copying of computer programs but permit a "rightful possessor" of a program

> to make or authorize the making of another copy or adaptation of that computer program *provided*:
>
> (1) that such a new copy or adaptation is created as an essential step in the utilization of the computer program in conjunction with a machine and that it is used in no other manner, or
>
> (2) that such new copy or adaptation is for archival purposes only and that all archival copies are destroyed in the event that continued possession of the computer program should cease to be rightful.

Id. at 30 (emphasis in original).

Because the act of loading a program from a medium of storage into a computer's memory creates a copy of the program, the CONTU reasoned that "one who rightfully possesses a copy of a program ... should be provided with a legal right to copy it to that extent which will permit its use by the possessor," and drafted proposed § 117(1) to "provide that persons in rightful possession of copies of programs be able to use them freely without fear of exposure to copyright liability." Id. at 31. With respect to proposed section 117(2), the "archival exception," the Report explained that a person in rightful possession of a program should have the right "to prepare archival copies of it to guard against destruction or damage by mechanical or electrical failure. But this permission would not extend to other copies of the program. Thus one

---

6. Section 102(a) was amended to protect original works of authorship which can be reproduced "either directly or with the aid of a machine or device." 17 U.S.C. § 102(a) (1977).

8. Final Report of the National Commission on New Technological Uses of Copyrighted Works (July 31, 1978) (the "CONTU Report" or the "Report").

could not, for example, make archival copies of a program and later sell some to another while retaining some for use." Id.

In 1980, Congress enacted the Computer Software Copyright Act which adopted the recommendations contained in the CONTU Report. Section 117[11] * * * was enacted, and the proposed definition of "computer program" was added to section 101. The Act's legislative history, contained in a short paragraph in a committee report, merely states that the Act, "embodies the recommendations of [the CONTU] with respect to clarifying the law of copyright of computer software." H.R.Rep. No. 1307, 96th Cong., 2d Sess., pt. 1, at 23, reprinted in 1980 U.S.Code Cong. & Admin.News 6460, 6482. The absence of an extensive legislative history and the fact that Congress enacted proposed section 117 with only one change have prompted courts to rely on the CONTU Report as an expression of legislative intent. See Micro–Sparc, Inc. v. Amtype Corp., 592 F. Supp. 33, 35 (D.Mass.1984); Atari, Inc. v. JS & A Group, Inc., 597 F. Supp. 5, 9 (N.D.Ill.1983); Midway Mfg. Co. v. Strohon, 564 F. Supp. 741, 750 n. 6 (N.D.Ill.1983).

B.   Direct Copying

In order to develop RAMKEY, Quaid analyzed Vault's program by copying it into its computer's memory. Vault contends that, by making this unauthorized copy, Quaid directly infringed upon Vault's copyright. The district court held that "Quaid's actions clearly fall within [the § 117(1)] exemption. The loading of [Vault's] program into the [memory] of a computer is an 'essential step in the utilization' of [Vault's] program. Therefore, Quaid has not infringed Vault's copyright by loading [Vault's program] into [its computer's memory]." Vault, 655 F. Supp. at 758.

Section 117(1) permits an owner of a program to make a copy of that program provided that the copy "is created as an essential step in the utilization of the computer program in conjunction with a machine and that it is used in no other manner." Congress recognized that a computer program cannot be used unless it is first copied into a computer's memory, and thus provided the § 117(1) exception to permit copying for this essential purpose. See CONTU Report at 31. Vault contends that, due to the inclusion of the phrase "and that it is used in no other manner," this exception should be interpreted to permit only the copying of a computer program for the purpose of using it for its intended purpose. Because Quaid copied Vault's program into its computer's memory for the express purpose of devising a means of defeating its protective function, Vault contends that § 117(1) is not applicable.

We decline to construe § 117(1) in this manner. Even though the copy of Vault's program made by Quaid was not used to prevent the copying of the program placed on the PROLOK diskette by one of

---

11. In enacting the new section 117, Congress adopted the proposed section with only one change. The final version grants "owners," as opposed to "rightful possessors," a limited right to copy and adapt their software. * * *

Vault's customers (which is the purpose of Vault's program), and was, indeed, made for the express purpose of devising a means of defeating its protective function, the copy made by Quaid was "created as an essential step in the utilization" of Vault's program. Section 117(1) contains no language to suggest that the copy it permits must be employed for a use intended by the copyright owner, and, absent clear congressional guidance to the contrary, we refuse to read such limiting language into this exception. We therefore hold that Quaid did not infringe Vault's exclusive right to reproduce its program in copies under § 106(1).

* * *

C. Contributory Infringement

Vault contends that, because purchasers of programs placed on PROLOK diskettes use the RAMKEY feature of CopyWrite to make unauthorized copies, Quaid's advertisement and sale of CopyWrite diskettes with the RAMKEY feature violate the Copyright Act by contributing to the infringement of Vault's copyright and the copyrights owned by Vault's customers. Vault asserts that it lost customers and substantial revenue as a result of Quaid's contributory infringement because software companies which previously relied on PROLOK diskettes to protect their programs from unauthorized copying have discontinued their use.

* * *

[The court reviewed the test for contributory copyright infringement (see Chapter 20.C.2, *infra*) and determined that Quaid could not be held liable for the infringing acts of RAMKEY customers if RAMKEY also had substantial "commercially significant" noninfringing uses.]

[Quaid contends that] the RAMKEY portion of its CopyWrite diskettes serves a substantial noninfringing use by allowing purchasers of programs on PROLOK diskettes to make archival copies as permitted under 17 U.S.C. § 117(2), and thus that it is not liable for contributory infringement. The district court held that * * * CopyWrite is capable of "commercially significant noninfringing uses" because the RAMKEY feature permits the making of archival copies of copy-protected software, and CopyWrite diskettes (without the RAMKEY feature) are used to make copies of unprotected software and as a diagnostic tool to analyze the quality of new computer programs. Id. Therefore, the court held that the sale of CopyWrite did not constitute contributory infringement.

* * *

2. *Substantial Noninfringing Uses of RAMKEY*

* * *

Quaid asserts that RAMKEY serves the legitimate purpose of permitting purchasers of programs recorded on PROLOK diskettes to make archival copies under § 117(2) and that this purpose constitutes a substantial noninfringing use. At trial, witnesses for Quaid testified that software programs placed on floppy diskettes are subject to damage by physical and human mishap[18] and that RAMKEY protects a purchaser's investment by providing a fully functional archival copy that can be used if the original program on the PROLOK protected diskette, or the diskette itself, is destroyed. Quaid contends that an archival copy of a PROLOK protected program, made without RAMKEY, does not serve to protect against these forms of damage because a computer will not read the program into its memory from the copy unless the PROLOK diskette containing the original undamaged program is also in one of its disk drives, which is impossible if the PROLOK diskette, or the program placed thereon, has been destroyed due to physical or human mishap.

> Computer programs can be stored on a variety of mediums, including floppy diskettes, hard disks, non-erasable read only memory ("ROM") chips, and a computer's random access memory, and may appear only as printed instructions on a sheet of paper. Vault contends that the archival exception was designed to permit *only* the copying of programs which are subject to "destruction or damage by *mechanical or electrical failure.*" CONTU Report at 31 (emphasis added). While programs stored on all mediums may be subject to damage due to physical abuse or human error, programs stored on certain mediums are not subject to damage by mechanical or electrical failure.[19] Therefore, Vault argues, the medium of storage determines whether the archival exception applies, thus providing only owners of programs, placed on mediums of storage which subject them to damage by mechanical or electrical failure, the right to make back-up copies. To support its construction of § 117(2), Vault notes that one court has held that the archival exception does not apply to the copying of programs stored on ROM chips where there was no evidence that programs stored on this medium were subject to damage by mechanical or electrical failure, Atari[, Inc. v. JS & A Group, Inc., 597 F. Supp. 5, 9–10 (N.D.Ill.1983)],[20] and another court

---

18. John Kurko, a technical support engineer, testified that he used CopyWrite to protect against physical mishaps such as house fires and other catastrophes. Trial Record ("T.R.") at 323. Warren Steinke, an administrative assistant at an insurance brokerage business, testified that back-up copies of computer programs were important to protect against damage due to experimentation with the original program and physical mishaps such as bending the diskette. T.R. at 325 & 331. Michael Kirk–Duggan, a professor at the University of Texas, testified that he makes back-up copies to protect against human error, T.R. at 335, and Peter Stone, a copy protection consultant, testified that a PROLOK diskette is subject to damage by liquids, severe heat and sharp objects. T.R. at 422. Finally, Robert McQuaid, in his deposition, testified that floppy diskettes can wear out and pro-

grams placed on floppy diskettes can be erased by human error. McQuaid Deposition at 16 & 18.

19. The CONTU Report did not define the term "mechanical or electrical failure." At trial, Ray Strackbein, the head of Vault's engineering department, testified that "mechanical failure" results from damage to a storage medium's recording surface, while "electrical failure" results from the erasure or reformatting of the program. T.R. at 255–56. A program recorded on a floppy diskette would be subject to mechanical or electrical failure, if subject to this type of failure at all, only while the diskette upon which it is recorded is in a computer's disk drive. Strackbein, T.R. at 256–57.

20. The court in Atari held that:

The dangers to ROMs presented by [defendant] are *physical* dangers not unlike

has likewise held that the archival exception does not apply to the copying of programs which appear only in the form of printed instructions in a magazine, Micro–Sparc[, Inc. v. Amtype Corp., 592 F. Supp. 33, 35–36 (D.Mass.1984)].[21]

Vault contends that the district court's finding that programs stored on floppy diskettes are subject to damage by mechanical or electrical failure is erroneous because there was insufficient evidence presented at trial to support it, and, based on this contention, Vault asserts that the archival exception does not apply to permit the unauthorized copying of these programs. Vault performed a trial demonstration to prove that even if a program on an original PROLOK diskette, and Vault's protective program, were completely erased from this diskette, these programs could be restored on the original diskette using a copy made without RAMKEY. Therefore, Vault argues that even if a program recorded on a PROLOK diskette is subject to damage by mechanical or electrical failure, the non-operational copy of a PROLOK protected program made without RAMKEY is sufficient to protect against this type of damage. Vault concludes that, in light of the fact that RAMKEY facilitates the making of unauthorized copies and owners of PROLOK protected programs can make copies to protect against damage by mechanical and electrical failure without RAMKEY, the RAMKEY feature is not capable of substantial noninfringing uses.

---

the risk that a handwritten computer program will be shredded accidentally. Virtually every copy of a copyrighted work, be it a book, a phonograph record, or a videotape, faces that kind of risk. Yet Congress did not enact a general rule that making back-up copies of copyrighted works would not infringe. Rather, according to the CONTU report, it limited its exception to computer programs which are subject to "destruction or damage by mechanical or electrical failure." Some media must be especially susceptible to this danger. [Defendant] has simply offered no evidence that a ROM in a 2600–compatible video game cartridge is such a medium.

597 F. Supp. at 9–10 (emphasis in original) (footnote omitted). The court noted that, other than the § 117 exceptions, the Copyright Act contains only three other exceptions for "archival" copying:

> Libraries and archives may copy an unpublished work "for purposes of preservation and security.... " 17 U.S.C. § 108(b). These institutions may also make a replacement copy of a published work that is "damaged, deteriorating, lost, or stolen, if the library or archives has, after a reasonable effort, determined that an unused replacement cannot be obtained at a fair price." 17 U.S.C. § 108(c). Finally, § 112 provides several

exceptions for archival copying of various "ephemeral" works, such as the broadcast of a live performance of a copyrighted play. See 2 Nimmer on Copyright § 806.

Id. at 10 n. 2.

21. In Micro–Sparc, the plaintiff published a weekly magazine containing computer programs which subscribers could type into their computers. The defendant typed programs contained in plaintiff's magazine into a computer and then transferred these programs onto a "master disk." From the master disk, the defendant copied the programs onto blank diskettes and then sold these diskettes to subscribers of plaintiff's magazine. 592 F.Supp. at 34.

In response to plaintiff's claim that defendant's "typing service" constituted copyright infringement, defendant contended that it was making back-up copies of programs which appeared in plaintiff's magazine and that its activity therefore fell within the "archival exception." The court rejected this defense, holding that when a subscriber to plaintiff's magazine "orders a disk from the defendant, he possesses the programs as they appear in the magazine. In this printed form, the programs are susceptible only to physical dangers, such as accidental shredding." Id. at 35.

The narrow construction of the archival exception, advanced by Vault and accepted in the Atari and Micro–Sparc decisions, has undeniable appeal. This construction would leave the owner of a protected software program free to make back-up copies of the software to guard against erasures, which is probably the primary concern of owners as well as the drafters of the CONTU Report. Software producers should perhaps be entitled to protect their product from improper duplication, and Vault's PROLOK may satisfy producers and most purchasers on this score—if PROLOK cannot be copied by the purchaser onto a CopyWrite diskette without infringing the PROLOK copyright. That result does have appeal, but we believe it is an appeal that must be made to Congress. "It is not our job to apply laws that have not yet been written." Sony, 464 U.S. at 456, 104 S.Ct. at 796. We read the statute as it is now written to authorize the owner of the PROLOK diskette to copy both the PROLOK program and the software program for any reason[23] so long as the owner uses the copy for archival purposes only and not for an unauthorized transfer.

The CONTU Report's words of "mechanical or electrical failure" are contained in a paragraph quoted in the footnote.[24] We read the stated causes of damage to be illustrative only, and not exclusive. Similarly, the statement follows with the prohibited use of the archival copies which does not include a prohibition against copying for purposes other than to protect against "mechanical or electrical failure." The Report, or Congress, could have easily limited the scope of § 117(2) to authorize the making of archival copies of programs subject to damage, and to guard against, only mechanical or electrical failure. CONTU did not recommend that language, nor did Congress enact it. Congress, following CONTU's advice, provided that an owner of a computer program may

23. The trial court found:

It is an ordinary practice of computer users to purchase computer software and immediately make archival backup copies of that software. This is done in order to assure the user that in the event of mechanical, electrical or physical damage to the software program or disks, a functional backup copy is available for use.

Vault, 655 F. Supp. at 754.

24. Because the placement of a work into a computer is the preparation of a copy, the law should provide that persons in rightful possession of copies of programs be able to use them freely without fear of exposure to copyright liability. Obviously, creators, lessors, licensors and vendors of copies of programs intend that they be used by their customers, so that rightful users would but rarely need a legal shield against potential copyright problems. It is easy to imagine, however, a situation in which the copyright owner might desire, for good reason or none at all, to force a lawful owner

or possessor of a copy to stop using a particular program. One who rightfully possesses a copy of a program, therefore, should be provided with a legal right to copy it to that extent which will permit its use by that possessor. This would include the right to load it into a computer and to prepare archival copies of it to guard against destruction or damage by mechanical or electrical failure. But this permission would not extend to other copies of the program. Thus one could not, for example, make archival copies of a program and later sell some to another while retaining some for use. The sale of a copy of a program by a rightful possessor to another must be of all rights in the program, thus creating a new rightful possessor and destroying that status as regards the seller. This is in accord with the intent of that portion of the law which provides that owners of authorized copies of a copyrighted work may sell those copies without leave of the copyright proprietor.

CONTU Report at 31–32 (footnote omitted).

make a copy of that program provided that "such new copy . . . is for archival purposes only." 17 U.S.C. § 117(2). Congress did not choose to spell out detailed restrictions on the copying as was done in sections 108 and 112. Congress imposed no restriction upon the purpose or reason of the owner in making the archival copy; only the use made of that copy is restricted. See CONTU Report at 31 ("one could not, for example, make archival copies of a program and later sell some to another while retaining some for use"). An owner of a program is entitled, under § 117(2), to make an archival copy of that program in order to guard against all types of risks, including physical and human mishap as well as mechanical and electrical failure.

A copy of a PROLOK protected program made with RAMKEY protects an owner from all types of damage to the original program, while a copy made without RAMKEY only serves the limited function of protecting against damage to the original program by mechanical and electrical failure. Because § 117(2) permits the making of fully functional archival copies, it follows that RAMKEY is capable of substantial noninfringing uses. Quaid's advertisement and sale of CopyWrite diskettes with the RAMKEY feature does not constitute contributory infringement.

* * *

Notes

1. The enactment of the narrowed version of section 117 has led to findings of infringement in cases where the defendant acted under authority of the lawful possessor, but not the owner, of a copy of the plaintiff's software. See *MAI Systems Corp. v. Peak Computer, Inc.*, 991 F.2d 511, 519 n. 5 (9th Cir.1993) (computer service company infringed when it loaded MAI software into RAM for servicing purposes, where customer was licensee rather than owner of the copy of the software); *accord Triad Systems Corp. v. Southeastern Express Co.*, 64 F.3d 1330 (9th Cir.1995) (following *MAI*, and rejecting fair use defense); *Advanced Computer Services of Michigan, Inc. v. MAI Systems Corp.*, 845 F.Supp. 356 (E.D.Va.1994) (similar). Should section 117 be amended to apply to rightful possessors as well as owners?

Title III of the DMCA, titled the "Computer Maintenance Competition Assurance Act," amended 17 U.S.C. § 117 to permit an authorized computer repair service to utilize copyrighted software in a computer during servicing, thus legislatively overruling *MAI Systems Corp. v. Peak Computer, Inc.*, 991 F.2d 511 (9th Cir.1993), *cert. dismissed,* 510 U.S. 1033, 114 S.Ct. 671, 126 L.Ed.2d 640 (1994), which held that such a repair company infringed copyrighted software by loading it into RAM for servicing purposes (thereby "copying" it), because the section 117 privilege applied only to purchasers of software, not to licensees.

In *DSC Communications Corp. v. Pulse Communications, Inc.*, 170 F.3d 1354 (Fed.Cir.1999), *cert. denied,* 528 U.S. 923, 120 S.Ct. 286, 145 L.Ed.2d 240 (1999), the Federal Circuit addressed the meaning of the term "owner" in section 117. Reversing the district court's finding that ownership was established where a single payment entitled the payor to possession of the software for an unlimited period of time, the court held that the ownership determination depends on the specific restrictions imposed by the software license.

2. Consider the following scenarios:

(a) Defendant manufactures and sells kits which can be assembled into computers. Plaintiff is a manufacturer of computers and software. Defendant purchases authorized copies of two of the plaintiff's most valuable programs on diskettes. Defendant then copies these programs, without the plaintiff's consent, onto silicon chips which are included with the computer kits and which enable the computers, when assembled, to utilize the plaintiff's other software. Is the defendant's copying authorized by section 117?

(b) Plaintiff manufactures and sells video games. The game cartridges store the videogame programs in ROM ("read only memory"), a form of memory that can neither be reprogrammed nor erased. However, they could be mechanically destroyed—e.g., by crushing or liquid spillage. Defendant manufactures and sells a device which enables users to copy plaintiff's games. Defendant may be held contributorily liable (see Chapter 20.C.2, *infra*) for copyright infringement only if the users' copying infringes the plaintiff's copyright in its games. Does section 117 help the defendant?

3. Suppose a person purchases software for use in a business, but finds it necessary to modify the software to suit the particular characteristics of that business. If this is done without the copyright owner's permission, is this an infringing derivative work? When the business is sold, is the copyright owner's permission required to include the modified software in the sale?

4. Computer software makers often include "shrinkwrap licenses" in the packaging of their software products sold to the public. The following language is typical, and is based on the license employed by the plaintiff in *Vault*:

[MAKER] IS PROVIDING THE ENCLOSED MATERIALS TO YOU ON THE EXPRESS CONDITION THAT YOU ASSENT TO THIS SOFTWARE LICENSE. BY USING ANY OF THE ENCLOSED DISKETTE(S), YOU AGREE TO THE FOLLOWING PROVISIONS. IF YOU DO NOT AGREE WITH THESE LICENSE PROVISIONS, RETURN THESE MATERIALS TO YOUR DEALER, IN ORIGINAL PACKAGING WITHIN 3 DAYS FROM RECEIPT, FOR A REFUND.

This copy of the [MAKER'S] Software Protection System and this [MAKER'S] Software Protection Diskette (the "Licensed Software") are licensed to you, the end-user, for your own internal use. Title to the Licensed Software and all copyrights and proprietary rights in the Licensed Software shall remain with [MAKER]. You may not transfer, sublicense, rent, lease, convey, copy, modify, translate, convert to another programming language, decompile or disassemble the Licensed Software for any purpose without [MAKER's] prior written consent.

(a) How are the rights of a retail software buyer affected by this language?

(b) If these restrictions are binding on the initial retail buyer of the software, are they also enforceable against a subsequent acquirer who lacks notice of the license?

(c) Could similar licenses be enforced against purchasers of other copyrightable works, such as books or videotapes? Against users of on-line services? Against recipients of television or radio broadcasts?

4. SECTION 108: LIBRARY AND ARCHIVAL COPYING

Statutes: 17 U.S.C.A. § 108

Section 108 reflects Congress's decision that libraries and archives should be free to make copies or phonorecords of copyrighted works for such legitimate purposes as repairing damaged works, making archival copies of works that would be difficult to replace if lost or damaged, and making interlibrary loans, but not for such purposes as avoiding the cost of purchases or subscriptions. The number of copies made, and the purpose and frequency of copying, must be within the statutory limits. No distribution for direct or indirect commercial advantage is permitted, and to qualify under section 108 the library or archives must be open to the public or to persons conducting research in a specialized field even if not affiliated with the institution of which the library or archives is a part. All copies must bear a copyright notice. Subsections (d) and (e) spell out the limitations on user-initiated copying requests, and require that copyright warnings be placed on self-service copying equipment.

Notes

1. Does section 108 allow a university library to make copies of reading materials assigned by a professor for a large class, where the library has only one or two copies of each reading? Suppose the professor places the materials on reserve, and the students make their own copies on self-service copiers?

2. Suppose that over a 30–day period seven different patrons enter a university library with a request for a copy of the same article. At what point, if any, does the copying exceed the scope of section 108?

3. Suppose the Bigleaf Tobacco Company has a library of research material relevant to addictive drugs and carcinogens. Does section 108 apply to the library if it is open to the public? Open only to Bigleaf employees? Open only to persons doing research on the health effects of smoking?

4. Does section 108 allow the central branch of the local public library to make copies of certain materials and send them to the other branches so that the branches will not have to purchase those materials?

5. Does section 108 allow a university library to electronically scan a rare book in its entirety and download it onto a floppy disk to be lent to a patron? Can it do so in order to preserve a copy of the book to guard against loss, theft, damage or deterioration?

6. Does section 108 allow a university library to make copies of film footage for a researcher?

7. The 1998 copyright legislation made several changes to section 108. The DMCA broadened the exemptions for libraries and archives found in section 108(a)-(c) to allow digital as well as facsimile copying, and to extend this exemption to a published work when its existing format has become obsolete. The SBCTEA, which added 20 years to the terms of most subsisting copyrights, also revised section 108 to provide that, during the last 20 years of a published work's copyright term, libraries and archives may make, distribute, display or perform copies or phonorecords of selected works (in facsimile or digital form) for purposes of preservation, scholarship, or research, under circumstances in which copies or phonorecords cannot otherwise be obtained at a reasonable price.

8. The Registrar of Copyright has appointed a Study Group to examine section 108 for the purpose of reconsidering the exceptions and limitations that should be made applicable to libraries and archives. The Study Group called for public discussion at the end of January 2007. Its report is expected later in the year.

5. SECTION 115: COMPULSORY LICENSING OF MUSICAL COMPOSITIONS FOR REPRODUCTION ON PHONO-RECORDS

Statutes: 17 U.S.C.A. § 115

The oldest compulsory licensing provision in United States copyright law, section 115 of the 1976 Act, is based on section 1(e) of the 1909 Act. This provision concerns "mechanical licensing" of nondramatic musical works for the manufacture and distribution of phonorecords. Although the term "nondramatic musical works" is nowhere defined in the Copyright Act, it is generally understood to refer to music (together with lyrics, if any) which was not created as part of a dramatic work.

Section 115(a) provides that once a nondramatic musical work has been recorded on phonorecords and these have been distributed to the public in the United States under the authority of the copyright owner, any other persons may record that work on phonorecords for the primary purpose of distributing those recordings to the public for private use, provided that they notify the copyright owner as required by section 115(b), and provided that they pay the royalty specified in section 115(c)(2) on each phonorecord that is made and distributed. Under the Digital Performance Right in Sound Recordings Act of 1995, *see* Section A.5, *supra,* the compulsory licensing provisions now apply to digital audio subscription transmissions as well.

Notes

1. Consider whether the following actions may be undertaken under section 115(a) without seeking the consent of a copyright owner, assuming that the musical composition for which the compulsory license is sought was originally fixed on phonorecords and distributed to the public in the United

States under the authority of the copyright owner, that the requirements of sections 115(b) and (c) are satisfied, and that the musical composition is nondramatic, unless otherwise indicated:

(a) recording a musical composition onto the soundtrack of a motion picture or television program

(b) arranging the music (originally written for a male singer) to accommodate the higher vocal range of a female singer and recording the resulting arrangement on phonorecords for retail sale

(c) recording on phonorecords, for retail sale, an "easy listening" version of a rap song

(d) recording on phonorecords, for retail sale, an instrumental version of a musical composition that was originally written and recorded with lyrics

(e) recording a musical composition, with few alterations, for use as background music at a roller rink

(f) copying an existing sound recording of a musical composition onto phonorecords to be sold at retail establishments

(g) recording on phonorecords, for retail sale, songs from the musical "Phantom of the Opera"

(h) recording on phonorecords, for retail sale, a musical composition that was previously distributed on phonorecords only in Europe and Japan

(i) recording on phonorecords, for retail sale, an instrumental composition from a movie soundtrack

(j) recording a musical composition, previously distributed on phonorecords, onto a multimedia format which causes a video display of the song's lyrics while the song is being played.

2. If a dramatic musical work is later recorded separately (that is, not as part of the dramatic work itself) on phonorecords, does that work become subject to compulsory licensing under section 115?

3. If the music and lyrics of a song were created separately, rather than as a joint work, does section 115 apply to the song?

4. On October 16, 2006, the Registrar of Copyright held that cell phone ringtones can qualify as falling within the scope of the compulsory license provided by Section 115:

> Ringtones that are merely excerpts of a preexisting sound recording fall squarely within the scope of the statutory license, whereas those that contain additional material may actually be considered original derivative works and therefore outside the scope of the Section 115 license. Moreover, we decide that a ringtone is made and distributed for private use even though some consumers may purchase them for the purpose of identifying themselves in public. We also conclude that if a newly created ringtone is considered a derivative work, and the work has been first distributed with the authorization of the copyright owner, then any person may use the statutory license to make and distribute the musical work in the ringtone. For those ringtones that are covered by Section

115 of the Copyright Act, all of the rights, conditions, and requirements in the Act would apply. For those ringtones that fall outside the scope of Section 115, the rights at issue must be acquired through voluntary licenses. See Compulsory License for Musical Works: Mobile phone ringtones may fall under Section 115 Statutory License, BNA Patent, Trademark & Copyright Journal (October 20, 2006).

6. THE AUDIO HOME RECORDING ACT

Statutes: 17 U.S.C.A. §§ 1001–10

The growth of digital audio technology has made it possible to make durable, high quality, inexpensive copies of sound recordings. These results could not be obtained through the analog recording technology that was previously available. Music publishers and record companies understandably became concerned that widespread unauthorized copying of their copyrighted works onto digital media would lead to substantial lost revenues. In response to these concerns, Congress enacted the Audio Home Recording Act of 1992, Pub. L. 102–563, 106 Stat. 4237, a compromise measure that allows home audio taping for private use while providing compensation to copyright owners.

Section 1008 of the Act bars any infringement action "based on the noncommercial use by a consumer" of digital audio recording devices or media, or analog recording devices or media, for making digital or analog musical recordings. It also bars infringement actions based on the manufacture, importation, or distribution of such devices or media. However, section 1002 prohibits the manufacture, distribution or importation of any digital audio recording device that fails to incorporate an effective means of preventing serial copying of digital works. *See* 17 U.S.C.A. § 1001(11) (defining "serial copying"); H.R. Rep. No. 102–873, pt. 1, 102d Cong., 2d Sess. 14 (1992) (defining the statutory term "Serial Copy Management System" by reference to a Technical Reference Document). In addition, section 1003 imposes a royalty, payable to the Register of Copyrights, on each digital audio recording device or medium distributed in the United States. Under sections 1006–1007, these royalties are allocated to various funds payable to the parties most likely to be affected by consumer copying—composers, music publishers, performers, and owners of sound recording copyrights. Section 1002 prohibits importing, manufacturing or distributing devices, or offering or performing services, that are designed to circumvent the serial copying controls mandated by that section.

Under section 1009, remedies for violations of section 1002 or 1003 include injunctions, statutory damages, costs, and attorney's fees, and the impounding, remedial modification and/or destruction of the offending devices and recordings; actual damages are also available for violations of section 1002. Actions under sections 1002 or 1003 may be brought by any "interested copyright party" as defined in section 1001; other injured parties may bring suit as well, but they are limited to actual damages. 17 U.S.C.A. § 1009(a), (b).

Note

In *Recording Industry Association of America v. Diamond Multimedia Systems, Inc.*, 180 F.3d 1072 (9th Cir.1999), the Ninth Circuit held that the "Rio," a portable device that plays digital music downloaded by a computer from the Internet, is not a "digital audio recording device" within the meaning of the Audio Home Recording Act of 1992, and thus need not incorporate a Serial Copy Management System. The court reasoned that music on a computer's hard drive is not a "digital musical recording" as that term is used in section 1001(5)(A)–(B). Do you agree?

7. SECTION 120: ARCHITECTURAL WORKS

Statutes: 17 U.S.C.A. § 120

Although the Architectural Works Copyright Protection Act of 1990 extended copyright protection to works of architecture in the form of buildings rather than only in the form of drawings, blueprints or other nonfunctional depictions, the right to reproduce architectural works is limited by section 120.

ARCHITECTURAL WORKS COPYRIGHT PROTECTION ACT OF 1990

H.R Rep. No. 101–735.
101st Cong., 2d Sess. 21–23 (1990).

* * *

Section 204. Scope of Exclusive Rights on Architectural Works

Section 204 creates a new section 120 of title 17, United States Code, limiting the exclusive rights in architectural works.

Subsection (a) of new section 120 permits the unauthorized "making, distributing, or public display of pictures, paintings, photographs, or other pictorial representations of the work, if the building in which the work is embodied is located in or ordinarily visible from a public place." Similar exceptions are found in many Berne member countries, and serve to balance the interests of authors and the public. Architecture is a public art form and is enjoyed as such. Millions of people visit our cities every year and take back home photographs, posters, and other pictorial representations of prominent works of architecture as a memory of their trip. Additionally, numerous scholarly books on architecture are based on the ability to use photographs of architectural works.

These uses do not interfere with the normal exploitation of architectural works. Given the important public purpose served by these uses and the lack of harm to the copyright owner's market, the Committee chose to provide an exemption, rather than rely on the doctrine of fair use, which requires ad hoc determinations. After a careful examination of the provisions of the Berne Convention, the laws of other Berne member countries, and expert opinion, the Committee concluded that this exemption is consistent with our obligations under the Convention.

Subsection (b) provides a limitation on the copyright owner's right—under section 106(2) of title 17, United States Code—to prepare derivative works. Subsection (b) permits the owner of a building embodying a protected architectural work to "make or authorize the making of alterations to such building, and to destroy or authorize the destruction of such building" without the copyright owner's consent. With respect to the right to destroy a building embodying a protected architectural work, the provision is consistent with existing section 109(a) of title 17, United States Code. Section 109(a) permits the owner of a particular copy or phonorecord lawfully made to "sell or otherwise dispose of the possession of that copy of phonorecord." While the provisions of section 109(a) apply to architectural works, in light of the fact that architectural works represent a new category of protected subject matter, and unlike other forms of subject matter are habitable, the Committee believed it advisable to spell out expressly the limitations contained in section 120(b).

* * *

Notes

1. In *Leicester v. Warner Brothers*, 232 F.3d 1212 (9th Cir.2000) the Ninth Circuit affirmed a lower court decision that a graphic embodied on a building's streetwall which appeared in the defendant's film did not infringe the plaintiff artist's rights. The court concluded that Congress intended public photographing of architectural works to be exempt from protection; this exemption extended to the graphic depicted on the architectural work.

2. Would section 120(a) permit the manufacture and sale of such souvenirs as snow globes, key chains, refrigerator magnets, and small statuettes depicting protected works of architecture?

8. SECTION 112: EPHEMERAL RECORDINGS

Statutes: 17 U.S.C.A. § 112

Section 112 allows broadcasters to make temporary fixations, and more limited archival fixations, of their transmissions to the public which embody authorized performances or displays of certain copyrighted works. In the case of nonprofit or governmental transmissions, subsections 112(b)-(d) permit, under specified conditions, more liberal copying than is allowed under the general rule of section 112(a). Generally speaking, these liberalized copying rules apply to educational transmissions, transmissions of religious music, and transmissions directed to handicapped persons under section 110(8).

Title IV of the DMCA broadened the section 112(a) exemption for ephemeral reproduction of sound recordings during radio or television broadcast transmissions so that it now explicitly includes both subscription and nonsubscription digital audio transmissions (thus including FCC-licensed broadcasters as well as subscription music services, Internet "webcasters," satellite digital audio radio services and others with statutory licenses to perform sound recordings under section 114(f)).

Title IV also added a new section 112(a)(2) exempting transmitting organizations from liability under the new anti-circumvention provisions of section 1201(a)(1) to the extent necessary to exercise their ephemeral recording privilege.

Notes

1. In *Agee v. Paramount Communications, Inc.*, 59 F.3d 317 (2d Cir. 1995), the Second Circuit ruled that the ephemeral recording exemption of section 112(a) protected individual television stations from liability for certain infringements of copyrighted sound recordings. In this case, the infringement occurred when the producer of a syndicated television program incorporated the sound recordings into its program without the consent of the copyright owner. The producer recorded the program on videotape and then delivered it by satellite feed to the individual stations, which taped the feed for later rebroadcast. Was this a proper application of section 112(a)?

2. Does section 112 permit ephemeral recordings of a transmission embodying a performance or display that was not authorized by the copyright owner but falls within the bounds of fair use?

3. Once a broadcaster has made copies under section 112, how may the copies be used?

9. OTHER SPECIFIC LIMITATIONS ON SECTION 106

Statutes: 17 U.S.C.A. §§ 111, 113(a)-(c), 116, 118–19, 121–22

(a) *Secondary Transmissions: Exemptions and Compulsory Licenses for Cable Systems and Satellite Carriers (Sections 111 and 119).* Although the growth of cable television and satellite systems has made it possible for more consumers to be served by television broadcasters, it has also raised questions of copyright liability, since allowing cable and satellite systems to carry television programming for free into subscribers' homes would enable them to perform and display copyrighted material to a large audience without compensating the copyright owners. In addition, these retransmitters often compete directly with the broadcasters who have paid to carry the same copyrighted material. However, it would be impracticable to require such simultaneous retransmitters to separately negotiate copyright licensing for all the programming they retransmit. Finding that the provisions of the 1909 Act were inadequate to resolve these problems, Congress enacted and periodically has revised the secondary transmission provisions of Title 17, beginning with the enactment of section 111 in the 1976 Act, which exempted certain narrowly-defined retransmissions (*see* § 111(a)-(b)) while subjecting most cable television retransmissions to a compulsory licensing scheme. The emergence of satellite delivery systems during the 1980s led to enactment of the Satellite Home Viewer Act of 1988, which revised section 111 and added section 119 to make the scheme of exemptions and compulsory licensing applicable to satellite systems. Originally scheduled to expire in 1994, the compulsory licensing scheme for satellite systems was extended through 1999 by the Satellite Home Viewer Act of 1994.

To make the satellite industry more competitive with the cable industry, the Satellite Home Viewer Improvement Act of 1999, Pub. L. No. 106–113, 106th Cong., 1st Sess. (1999), created a new section 122 compulsory license permitting satellite retransmission of broadcast signals from local stations, and renewed the satellite compulsory license of section 119 through Dec. 31, 2004. Section 119 was also amended to revise the definition of "unserved households" eligible for satellite coverage and to reduce the compulsory license fees for retransmission of network and superstation broadcasts.

During 1999, Congress also considered, but did not adopt, provisions addressing the eligibility of Internet companies for satellite and/or cable compulsory licenses for purposes of retransmitting ("webcasting") radio and television signals. In *National Football League v. TVRadioNow Corp.*, 2000 WL 255989 (W.D.Pa.2000) and *Twentieth Century Fox Film Corp. v. iCraveTV*, No. 00–121, 2000 WL 255989 (W.D.Pa. Feb. 8, 2000), a group of broadcasters, film studios, and sports leagues won a preliminary injunction prohibiting an Internet service from "streaming" television broadcasts to subscribers over its website until the company establishes effective security measures to restrict the service to Canadian subscribers.

(b) *Sections 113(a)-(c): Useful Articles.* Subsections (a) through (c) of section 113 address the rights of the various interested parties when copyrighted artwork is incorporated in a useful article that is manufactured, displayed and distributed in commerce, or when a copyrighted work depicts a useful article. Section 113(d), which addresses the rights of an author whose work of visual art may be damaged or destroyed in removing it from a building, is discussed in Section C.2, *infra*.

(c) *Section 116: Jukebox Licenses.* Section 1(e) of the 1909 Act gave jukebox operators an outright exemption from copyright liability unless the establishment charged admission. Intense criticism led Congress to replace this exemption with a compulsory license in the 1976 Act, applicable only to nondramatic musical works. Further change became necessary, however, when the United States joined the Berne Convention, Article 11(1) of which provides that the authors of musical works "shall enjoy the exclusive right of authorizing: (i) the public performance of their works, including such public performance by any means or process." *See* Final Report of the Ad Hoc Working Group on United States Adherence to the Berne Convention 24, *reprinted in* 10 Col.-VLA J. L. & ARTS 536 (1986) (concluding that former section 116 was incompatible with Article 11(1)). While retaining the compulsory license provisions (embodied at that time in section 116), Congress added section 116A, which encouraged copyright owners and jukebox operators to negotiate licenses and provided for arbitration where needed. Berne Convention Implementation Act of 1988, Pub. L. 100–568, sec. 4(a)(4), 102 Stat. 2853, 2855–57. Congress also provided that the compulsory licensing rules of section 116 would take effect if the negotiation and arbitration processes failed to make enough musical works available for jukebox performances. *Id.* In 1990, however, the musical performing rights societies reached an agreement with the chief trade association representing jukebox operators, *see* Agreement Dated March 1, 1990, between the American Society of Composers, Authors and Publishers, Broadcast Music, Inc., and SESAC, Inc., and the Amusement and Music Operators Association, *reprinted in* 1 Copyright L. Rep. (CCH) para. 16,077. The Copyright Royalty Tribunal Reform Act of 1993 (Pub. L. 103–198) repealed the compulsory license and renumbered the new negotiation and arbitration provisions as section 116.

(d) *Section 118: Noncommercial Educational Broadcasting.* The compulsory license under section 118 provides that owners of copyright in published nondramatic musical works and published pictorial, graphic and sculptural works may negotiate with noncommercial educational broadcasters to reach agreement on royalties to be paid for producing and transmitting a program in which such a work is performed or displayed, as well as for reproducing and distributing copies of such a program for the purpose of future qualifying transmissions. The statute calls for binding arbitration where voluntary negotiations fail. The license also allows a nonprofit or government entity to copy the program during its transmission, and temporarily retain the copies, solely for purposes of a performance or display that meets the requirements of section 110(1).

(e) *Section 121: Special Formats for the Disabled.* Section 121, which was added in 1996,[1] permits authorized nonprofit organizations, under specified conditions, to distribute copies or phonorecords of published nondramatic literary works in specialized braille, audio and digitized formats, for persons who are blind or have other disabilities, without obtaining the copyright owner's consent.

C.   BEYOND COPYRIGHT: PERFORMERS' RIGHTS, MORAL RIGHTS, AND RESALE ROYALTIES

1.   PERFORMERS' RIGHTS

Statutes: 17 U.S.C.A. §§ 106(6), 114(d), 502–05, 1101; 18 U.S.C.A. § 2319A

Until recently, Title 17 gave performers no rights in their performances except to the extent that those performances constituted copyrightable works authored by the performers. Other performers asserting a protectable interest in their performances were, and in many cases still are, limited to remedies under the Lanham Act and state law doctrines such as unfair competition and the right of publicity. However, recent legislation has granted certain additional federal rights to musical performers.

---

1. H.R. 3754, Pub. L. 104–197 (1996).

Under the Digital Performance Right in Sound Recordings Act of 1995,[2] discussed in Section A.5, *supra*, owners of copyrights in sound recordings enjoy a right to receive negotiated or statutory royalties for certain public performances of their works through digital subscription transmissions. Section 114 requires that portions of those royalties be allocated to the featured and nonfeatured musicians and vocalists who performed on those recordings.

In addition, recent legislation has addressed the problem of unauthorized recording (or "bootlegging") of live musical performances. The United States enacted an anti-bootlegging law in order to meet its obligations under the TRIPS provisions of the Uruguay Round of the General Agreement on Tariffs and Trade (GATT). Sections 512 and 513 of the Uruguay Round Agreements Act of 1994 ("URAA")[3] amended Titles 17 and 18 to impose civil, and in some cases, criminal penalties for unauthorized transmission or recording of live musical performances, and for reproduction and distribution of such unauthorized recordings. The Senate Report notes, however, that "[i]t is intended that the legislation will not apply in cases where First Amendment principles are implicated, such as where small portions of an unauthorized fixation of a sound recording are used without permission in a news broadcast or for other purposes of comment or criticism." S. Rep. No. 412, 103d Cong., 2d Sess. 225 (1994). The federal courts have exclusive jurisdiction over actions arising under section 1101.

Section 1101 applies regardless whether the unauthorized fixation occurred before or after the law's enactment date (Dec. 8, 1994), but liability will arise only for acts taken after enactment. Users of pre–1995 recordings must therefore be mindful of any potential liability.

As you read section 1101, try to answer the following questions:

    a.　Do the work-made-for-hire provisions apply to section 1101?

    b.　Are the rights assignable?

    c.　Where several performers render a single performance, will the consent of one performer, or of a majority of the performers, satisfy section 1101 with respect to the entire performance?

    d.　If all performers consent to recording of their performance in return for compensation, how should that compensation be divided among them?

    e.　Do the rights created by section 1101 apply to federal government employees rendering performances within the scope of their employment?

    f.　Must consent under 1101 be in a signed writing?

    g.　What is a "live musical performance"? Where a live performance integrates music, dance, literary and dramatic elements,

---

2. P.L. 104–39, 109 Stat. 336 (Nov. 1, 1995).

3. Pub. L. 103–465, 103d Cong., 2d Sess. (Act of Dec. 8, 1994), 108 Stat. 4809.

does section 1101 apply to the entire performance or only to its musical components?

h. Whereas the criminal provisions under 18 U.S.C.A. § 2319A(a) do have a scienter requirement, most of the civil remedies under 17 U.S.C.A. §§ 502–05 are available without regard to the defendant's state of mind. How can a person wishing to reproduce or distribute a musical recording (or a work incorporating such a recording) acquired from another party protect himself or herself from liability under these provisions?

i. Does section 1101 apply to performances by non-U.S. performers? Does it apply to performances outside the United States?

j. How long do a performer's rights endure under section 1101? Can the spouse or children of a deceased performer bring suit under section 1101?

k. Is originality a prerequisite to protection under section 1101?

l. Do sections 1101 and 2319A satisfy our obligations under Article 14 of TRIPS? Do they exceed those obligations? (Also compare Article 6 of the 1996 WIPO Performances and Phonograms Treaty.)

m. Does section 1101 exceed Congress's authority under the Intellectual Property Clause? If so, is it defensible nevertheless under the Commerce Clause? At this point, reconsider the implications in *United States v. Martignon*, 346 F.Supp.2d. 413 (S.D.N.Y. 2004)(holding 2319A unconstitutional for failure to comply with the limited terms provision of the Clause), discussed in connection with the fixation requirement at note 2, *supra,* at page 760. Do differences in the nature of the statutory aims of the two sections justify a different interpretation of the constitutionality of 1101?

n. Is there a "fair use" exception to section 1101?

For an excellent overview of section 1101 and its legislative history, see William F. Patry, Copyright and the GATT (BNA) (1995 Supp. to Copyright Law and Practice).

2. MORAL RIGHTS

Statutes: 17 U.S.C.A. §§ 101 (as needed), 106A, 113(d), 412, 501(a); 15 U.S.C.A. § 1125(a)

CARTER v. HELMSLEY–SPEAR, INC.

United States Court of Appeals, Second Circuit, 1995.
71 F.3d 77, *cert. denied*, 517 U.S. 1208, 116 S.Ct. 1824, 134 L.Ed.2d 930 (1996).

CARDAMONE, CIRCUIT JUDGE.

[In this opinion, the Second Circuit reversed and vacated a district court decision enjoining destruction of a work of visual art under 17

U.S.C. § 106A; the appellate court ultimately found section 106A inapplicable because it concluded that the work in question, a sculpture, was a work made for hire. Its opinion included this discussion of the background and legislative history of section 106A.]

* * *

On this appeal we deal with an Act of Congress that protects the rights of artists to preserve their works. One of America's most insightful thinkers observed that a country is not truly civilized "where the arts, such as they have, are all imported, having no indigenous life." 7 Works of Ralph Waldo Emerson, Society and Solitude, Chapt. II Civilization 34 (AMS. ed. 1968). From such reflection it follows that American artists are to be encouraged by laws that protect their works. Although Congress in the statute before us did just that, it did not mandate the preservation of art at all costs and without due regard for the rights of others.

* * *

The term "moral rights" has its origins in the civil law and is a translation of the French le droit moral, which is meant to capture those rights of a spiritual, non-economic and personal nature. The rights spring from a belief that an artist in the process of creation injects his spirit into the work and that the artist's personality, as well as the integrity of the work, should therefore be protected and preserved. See Ralph E. Lerner & Judith Bresler, Art Law 417 (1989) (Art Law). Because they are personal to the artist, moral rights exist independently of an artist's copyright in his or her work. See, e.g., 2 Nimmer on Copyright 8D–4 & n.2 (1994) (Nimmer).

While the rubric of moral rights encompasses many varieties of rights, two are protected in nearly every jurisdiction recognizing their existence: attribution and integrity. See Art Law at 420. The right of attribution generally consists of the right of an artist to be recognized by name as the author of his work or to publish anonymously or pseudonymously, the right to prevent the author's work from being attributed to someone else, and to prevent the use of the author's name on works created by others, including distorted editions of the author's original work. See, e.g., id. at 419–20; Nimmer at 8D–5. The right of integrity allows the author to prevent any deforming or mutilating changes to his work, even after title in the work has been transferred. See, e.g., Art Law at 420.

In some jurisdictions the integrity right also protects artwork from destruction. Whether or not a work of art is protected from destruction represents a fundamentally different perception of the purpose of moral rights. If integrity is meant to stress the public interest in preserving a nation's culture, destruction is prohibited; if the right is meant to emphasize the author's personality, destruction is seen as less harmful than the continued display of deformed or mutilated work that misrepresents the artist and destruction may proceed. See Art Law at 421; see also 2 William F. Patry, Copyright Law and Practice 1044 n.128 (1994) (Copyright Law) (noting the different models but suggesting that "destruction of a work shows the utmost contempt for the artist's honor or reputation").

Although moral rights are well established in the civil law, they are of recent vintage in American jurisprudence. Federal and state courts typically recognized the existence of such rights in other nations, but rejected artists' attempts to inject them into U.S. law. See, e.g., Vargas v. Esquire, Inc., 164 F.2d 522, 526 (7th Cir.1947); Crimi v. Rutgers Presbyterian Church, 194 Misc. 570, 573–76, 89 N.Y.S.2d 813 (N.Y.Sup.Ct. 1949). Nonetheless, American courts have in varying degrees acknowledged the idea of moral rights, cloaking the concept in the guise of other legal theories, such as copyright, unfair competition, invasion of privacy, defamation, and breach of contract. See Nimmer at 8D–10; Art Law at 423.

In the landmark case of Gilliam v. American Broadcasting Companies, Inc., 538 F.2d 14 (2d Cir.1976), we relied on copyright law and unfair competition principles to safeguard the integrity rights of the "Monty Python" group, noting that although the law "seeks to vindicate the economic, rather than the personal rights of authors ... the economic incentive for artistic ... creation ... cannot be reconciled with the inability of artists to obtain relief for mutilation or misrepresentation of their work to the public on which the artists are financially dependent." Id. at 24. Because decisions protecting artists rights are often "clothed in terms of proprietary right in one's creation," we continued, "they also properly vindicate the author's personal right to prevent the presentation of his work to the public in a distorted form." Id.

Artists fared better in state legislatures than they generally had in courts. California was the first to take up the task of protecting artists with the passage in 1979 of the California Art Preservation Act, Cal. Civ. Code § 987 et seq. (West 1982 & Supp. 1995), followed in 1983 by New York's enactment of the Artist's Authorship Rights Act, N.Y. Arts & Cult. Aff. Law § 14.03 (McKinney Supp. 1995). Nine other states have also passed moral rights statutes, generally following either the California or New York models. See generally Art Law at 430–35; id. at 301–09 (Supp. 1992) (describing the different states' laws).

B. Visual Artists Rights Act of 1990

Although bills protecting artists' moral rights had first been introduced in Congress in 1979, they had drawn little support. See Copyright Law at 1018 n.1. The issue of federal protection of moral rights was a prominent hurdle in the debate over whether the United States should join the Berne Convention, the international agreement protecting literary and artistic works. Article 6bis of the Berne Convention protects attribution and integrity, stating in relevant part:

> Independently of the author's economic rights, and even after the transfer of the said rights, the author shall have the right to claim

authorship of the work and to object to any distortion, mutilation or other modification of, or other derogatory action in relation to, the said work, which would be prejudicial to his honor or reputation.

Berne Convention for the Protection of Literary and Artistic Works, September 9, 1886, art. 6bis, S. Treaty Doc. No. 27, 99th Cong., 2d Sess. 41 (1986).

The Berne Convention's protection of moral rights posed a significant difficulty for U.S. adherence. See Copyright Law at 1022 ("The obligation of the United States to provide droit moral . . . was the single most contentious issue surrounding Berne adherence."); Nimmer at 8D–15 ("During the debate over [the Berne Convention Implementation Act], Congress faced an avalanche of opposition to moral rights, including denunciations of moral rights by some of the bill's most vociferous advocates."); H.R. Rep. No. 514, 101st Cong., 2d Sess. 7 (1990), reprinted in 1990 U.S.C.C.A.N. 6915, 6917 ("After almost 100 years of debate, the United States joined the Berne Convention. . . . Consensus over United States adherence was slow to develop in large part because of debate over the requirements of Article 6bis.").

Congress passed the Berne Convention Implementation Act of 1988, Pub. L. No. 100–568, 102 Stat. 2853 (1988), and side-stepped the difficult question of protecting moral rights. It declared that the Berne Convention is not self-executing, existing law satisfied the United States' obligations in adhering to the Convention, its provisions are not enforceable through any action brought pursuant to the Convention itself, and neither adherence to the Convention nor the implementing legislation expands or reduces any rights under federal, state, or common law to claim authorship of a work or to object to any distortion, mutilation, or other modification of a work. See id. §§ 2, 3; see also S. Rep. No. 352, 100th Cong., 2d Sess. 9–10 (1988), reprinted in 1988 U.S.C.C.A.N. 3706, 3714–15.

Two years later Congress enacted the Visual Artists Rights Act of 1990 (VARA or Act), Pub. L. No. 101–650 (tit. VI), 104 Stat. 5089, 5128–33 (1990). * * * The Act

protects both the reputations of certain visual artists and the works of art they create. It provides these artists with the rights of "attribution" and "integrity." . . .

These rights are analogous to those protected by Article 6bis of the Berne Convention, which are commonly known as "moral rights." The theory of moral rights is that they result in a climate of artistic worth and honor that encourages the author in the arduous act of creation.

H.R. Rep. No. 514 at 5 (internal quote omitted). * * *

* * *

GILLIAM v. AMERICAN BROADCASTING COMPANIES, INC.

United States Court of Appeals, Second Circuit, 1976.
538 F.2d 14.

LUMBARD, CIRCUIT JUDGE.

[Plaintiffs Gilliam et al., known as the "Monty Python" group, were the authors and copyright owners of certain television scripts which they licensed to BBC for production and public performance. The plaintiffs retained their copyright in the scripts, however, and the licensing agreement expressly reserved to them the right to object to any alterations of the recorded programs. BBC sublicensed the American television rights to Time–Warner. When Time–Warner granted broadcast rights to ABC, ABC edited the programs extensively in order to fit time constraints and insert commercials. After determining that the plaintiffs were likely to succeed on their claim that this unauthorized editing violated the plaintiffs' exclusive right under 17 U.S.C. § 106(2) to create derivative works, the court of appeals addressed the plaintiffs' claims under section 43(a) of the Lanham Act, 15 U.S.C. § 1125(a).]

* * *

It also seems likely that appellants will succeed on the theory that, regardless of the right ABC had to broadcast an edited program, the cuts made constituted an actionable mutilation of Monty Python's work. This cause of action, which seeks redress for deformation of an artist's work, finds its roots in the continental concept of droit moral, or moral right, which may generally be summarized as including the right of the artist to have his work attributed to him in the form in which he created it. See 1 M. Nimmer, supra, at § 110.1.

American copyright law, as presently written, does not recognize moral rights or provide a cause of action for their violation, since the law seeks to vindicate the economic, rather than the personal, rights of authors. Nevertheless, the economic incentive for artistic and intellectual creation that serves as the foundation for American copyright law, Goldstein v. California, 412 U.S. 546, 37 L.Ed. 2d 163, 93 S.Ct. 2303 (1973); Mazer v. Stein, 347 U.S. 201, 98 L.Ed. 630, 74 S.Ct. 460 (1954), cannot be reconciled with the inability of artists to obtain relief for mutilation or misrepresentation of their work to the public on which the artists are financially dependent. Thus courts have long granted relief for misrepresentation of an artist's work by relying on theories outside the statutory law of copyright, such as contract law, Granz v. Harris, 198 F.2d 585 (2d Cir.1952) (substantial cutting of original work constitutes misrepresentation), or the tort of unfair competition, Prouty v. National Broadcasting Co., 26 F. Supp. 265 (D.Mass.1939). See Strauss, The Moral Right of the Author 128–138, in Studies on Copyright (1963). Although such decisions are clothed in terms of proprietary right in one's creation, they also properly vindicate the author's personal right to prevent the presentation of his work to the public in a distorted form. See Gardella v. Log Cabin Products Co., 89 F.2d 891, 895–96 (2d Cir.1937); Roeder, The Doctrine of Moral Right, 53 Harv. L. Rev. 554, 568 (1940).

Here, the appellants claim that the editing done for ABC mutilated the original work and that consequently the broadcast of those programs as the creation of Monty Python violated the Lanham Act § 43(a), 15 U.S.C. § 1125(a).[10] This statute, the federal counterpart to state unfair competition laws, has been invoked to prevent misrepresentations that may injure plaintiff's business or personal reputation, even where no registered trademark is concerned. See Mortellito v. Nina of California, 335 F. Supp. 1288, 1294 (S.D.N.Y.1972). It is sufficient to violate the Act that a representation of a product, although technically true, creates a false impression of the product's origin. See Rich v. RCA Corp., 390 F. Supp. 530 (S.D.N.Y.1975) (recent picture of plaintiff on cover of album containing songs recorded in distant past held to be a false representation that the songs were new); Geisel v. Poynter Products, Inc., 283 F. Supp. 261, 267 (S.D.N.Y.1968).

These cases cannot be distinguished from the situation in which a television network broadcasts a program properly designated as having been written and performed by a group, but which has been edited, without the writer's consent, into a form that departs substantially from the original work. "To deform his work is to present him to the public as the creator of a work not his own, and thus makes him subject to criticism for work he has not done." Roeder, supra at 569. In such a case, it is the writer or performer, rather than the network, who suffers the consequences of the mutilation, for the public will have only the final product by which to evaluate the work.[11] Thus, an allegation that a defendant has presented to the public a "garbled," Granz v. Harris, supra (Frank, J., concurring), distorted version of plaintiff's work seeks to redress the very rights sought to be protected by the Lanham Act, 15 U.S.C. § 1125(a), and should be recognized as stating a cause of action under that statute. See Autry v. Republic Productions, Inc., 213 F.2d 667 (9th Cir.1954); Jaeger v. American Intn'l Pictures, Inc., 330 F. Supp. 274 (S.D.N.Y.1971), which suggest the violation of such a right if mutilation could be proven.

During the hearing on the preliminary injunction, Judge Lasker viewed the edited version of the Monty Python program broadcast on December 26 and the original, unedited version. After hearing argument of this appeal, this panel also viewed and compared the two versions. We find that the truncated version at times omitted the climax of the skits

---

10. That statute provides in part:

Any person who shall affix, apply, or annex, or use in connection with any goods or services, ... a false designation of origin, or any false description or representation ... and shall cause such goods or services to enter into commerce ... shall be liable to a civil action by any person

... who believes that he is or is likely to be damaged by the use of any such false description or representation.

11. This result is not changed by the fact that the network, as here, takes public responsibility for editing. See Rich v. RCA Corp., supra.

to which appellants' rare brand of humor was leading and at other times deleted essential elements in the schematic development of a story line. We therefore agree with Judge Lasker's conclusion that the edited version broadcast by ABC impaired the integrity of appellants' work and represented to the public as the product of appellants what was actually a mere caricature of their talents. We believe that a valid cause of action for such distortion exists and that therefore a preliminary injunction may issue to prevent repetition of the broadcast prior to final determination of the issues.[13]

* * *

For these reasons we direct that the district court issue the preliminary injunction sought by the appellants.

GURFEIN, CIRCUIT JUDGE, concurring:

* * *

The misdescription of origin can be dealt with, as Judge Lasker did below, by devising an appropriate legend to indicate that the plaintiffs had not approved the editing of the ABC version.[1] With such a legend, there is no conceivable violation of the Lanham Act. If plaintiffs complain that their artistic integrity is still compromised by the distorted version, their claim does not lie under the Lanham Act, which does not protect the copyrighted work itself but protects only against the misdescription or mislabelling.

So long as it is made clear that the ABC version is not approved by the Monty Python group, there is no misdescription of origin. So far as the content of the broadcast itself is concerned, that is not within the proscription of the Lanham Act when there is no misdescription of the authorship.

I add this brief explanation because I do not believe that the Lanham Act claim necessarily requires the drastic remedy of permanent injunction. That form of ultimate relief must be found in some other fountainhead of equity jurisprudence.

---

13. Judge Gurfein's concurring opinion suggests that since the gravamen of a complaint under the Lanham Act is that the origin of goods has been falsely described, a legend disclaiming Monty Python's approval of the edited version would preclude violation of that Act. We are doubtful that a few words could erase the indelible impression that is made by a television broadcast, especially since the viewer has no means of comparing the truncated version with the complete work in order to determine for himself the talents of plaintiffs. Furthermore, a disclaimer such as the one originally suggested by Judge Lasker in the exigencies of an impending broadcast last December would go unnoticed by viewers who tuned into the broadcast a few minutes after it began.

We therefore conclude that Judge Gurfein's proposal that the district court could find some form of disclaimer would be sufficient might not provide appropriate relief.

1. I do not imply that the appropriate legend be shown only at the beginning of the broadcast. That is a matter for the District Court.

Notes

1. In its fullest realization (as legislated in France, for example), the artist's droit moral includes, in addition to the rights of attribution and integrity, a right of disclosure (meaning a right to control the first public distribution of a work), and the right of withdrawal (meaning the right to remove one's work from public circulation). Are any of these rights protected under federal law? Should they be?

2. Although Article 6bis of the Berne Convention requires signatory nations to recognize the rights of attribution and integrity, it leaves the "means of redress for safeguarding the rights granted by this Article" to the legislation of each member nation. The Senate Report which accompanied the Berne Convention Implementation Act of 1988 states that:

> [P]rotection is provided under existing U.S. law for the rights of authors listed in Article 6bis: (1) to claim authorship of their works ("the right of paternity"); and (2) to object to distortion, mutilation or other modification of their works, or other derogatory action with respect thereto, that would prejudice their honor or reputation (the "right of integrity"). This existing U.S. law includes various provisions of the Copyright Act and Lanham Act, various state statutes, and common law principles such as libel, defamation, misrepresentation, and unfair competition, which have been applied by courts to redress authors' invocation of the right to claim authorship or the right to object to distortion.

S. Rep. No. 100–352, 100th Cong., 2d Sess. 9–10 (1988). The report concluded that these sources of existing law were adequate to satisfy the requirements of Article 6bis. *Id.* Do you agree?

3. If individual states adopt moral rights laws, to the extent that those laws are not preempted by federal copyright (see Chapter 22, discussing preemption), what are the policy implications of having different moral rights laws in each state?

4. In spite of its statement in 1988 that no federal moral rights legislation was necessary to comply with Article 6bis, in 1990 Congress enacted the Visual Artists Rights Act ("VARA"), codified in 17 U.S.C.A. § 106A, granting certain inalienable rights of attribution and integrity to the creators of "works of visual art" as newly defined in section 101. In reading section 106A, consider the following questions:

> (a) For a waiver of section 106A rights to be effective with respect to a joint work, must all the authors agree to the waiver? What rights would one co-author have against the other co-author if the latter signed a moral rights waiver with respect to their joint work?

> (b) Are rights under VARA inheritable? If so, by whom?

> (c) Suppose an artist grants someone "the right to create a derivative work of any kind, without reservation," based on the artist's work of visual art, but the grant instrument does not expressly waive the artist's rights under section 106A. Does section 106A provide a remedy if the artist finds the derivative work offensive?

> (d) Why did Congress enact special moral rights legislation for works of visual art, but not for literary, musical, or audio-visual works?

Other western countries, such as France, extend moral rights to a wider array of works of authorship. See, *e.g.*, Loi du 11 mars 1957 Sur la Propriete Litteraire et Artistique, 1957 Journal Officiel de la Republique Francaise [J.O.] 2723, *translated in* UNESCO, Copyright Laws and Treaties of the World (1976). To what other works of authorship, if any, should the United States extend VARA-like protection? Should protection extend only to originals, or to copies as well?

(e) If an office building's management places Christmas wreaths, "Santa" hats, and red-and-green ribbons on a sculpture in its lobby, does the sculptor have a claim under section 106A? Does it matter whether the sculpture depicts a flight of geese or victims of the Nazi Holocaust?

(f) What remedies are available for violations of section 106A?

(g) Would an artist's rights under section 106A be violated where his or her work was destroyed in (1) a fire caused by someone forgetting to turn off a coffee pot? (2) a fire started for the purpose of collecting insurance on the work?

(h) In section 106A, what is meant by the terms "work of recognized stature," "prejudicial," "honor," and "reputation"? How should a district court approach the problem of making these factual determinations?

(i) Compare the standards for protecting a work against (1) alteration and (2) destruction. How and why do they differ? Is this approach appropriate?

(j) What rights, if any, does VARA give an artist to repair a work of visual art if it begins to deteriorate or suffers accidental damage?

(k) Where a work is installed in a building and the work is likely to be damaged in the course of renovating or destroying the building, which party's rights receive more protection under section 113(d)(1)—the artist or the building's owner? Why did Congress draft the statute in this way? Would it matter whether the party undertaking the damaging activity had purchased the building?

(*l*) Suppose that, without the consent of the building's owner, the tenant of an office building authorizes the installation of a sculpture in the building's lobby. Does section 106A bar alteration or destruction of the sculpture by the owner?

(m) Compare the terms of protection for works created before and after the effective date of section 106A. Why is there a difference?

(n) Would section 106A provide a cause of action for a public display, after section 106A's effective date, of a work that was mutilated *before* that date? *Should* there be such a cause of action?

(o) Under current law, does VARA apply to a work of visual art created before June 1, 1991 (VARA's effective date), but sold before that date? What if the copyright, rather than the work itself, was transferred before that date? Would it matter if only a portion of the copyright was transferred? Consider the following passage from the legislative history of VARA:

> Consistent with current law on preemption for economic rights, the new Federal law will not preempt State causes of action relating to works that are not covered by the law, such as audiovisual works, photographs produced for non-exhibition purposes, and works in which the copyright has been transferred before the effective date.
>
> * * *

H.R. Rep. No. 101–514, 101st Cong., 2d Sess. 21 (1990). Can you reconcile the statutory language with this legislative history? Does the "correct" answer according to the statute and/or its legislative history make sense as a matter of policy?

5. Does Article 6bis of the Berne Convention require that moral rights be non-assignable? Non-waivable? What approach is best from a policy perspective? What policies are served by the waiver provisions in section 106A?

6. In *Pollara v. Seymour*, 344 F.3d 265 (2d Cir. 2003), the court held that a banner which cost $1800 and took over 100 man hours to complete was not protected under VARA because it was created for the purpose of drawing attention to an informational desk and conveying a political message, and VARA expressly excludes promotional and advertisement materials from its protection. Are there other examples of artistic advertisements which, under this court's ruling, would not receive VARA protection?

3. RESALE ROYALTIES (DROIT DE SUITE)

The European doctrine of the droit de suite recognizes an artist's right to participate in the revenues from subsequent sales of his or her work. In the United States, however, there is no federal resale royalty provision, and state legislation has been adopted only in California. The California Resale Royalties Act, Cal. Civ. Code § 986 (West Supp. 1994), gives the artist a five percent royalty on sales of "fine art" for $1000 or more which take place within California or involve state residents; the right expires 20 years after the artist's death.

In response to a request from Congress, the United States Copyright Office in 1992 issued a report on the question whether a federal resale royalty law should be enacted. The report concluded that there was as yet insufficient evidence of the effect of resale royalties on artists and art markets, and recommended that no federal resale royalty legislation be enacted until the European Union reaches a decision on similar legislation for its members. United States Copyright Office, Droit de Suite: The Artist's Resale Royalty 149 (1992).

What public interests are served by resale royalty legislation? Should Congress enact a federal resale royalties statute? If individual states follow California's lead, what are the potential economic effects of imposing resale royalty obligations only on transactions taking place within certain states or involving state residents? Does California's law frustrate the purposes of the first sale rule?

Chapter 19

FAIR USE

Statutes: 17 U.S.C.A. § 107

When "fair use" was finally codified in the 1976 Act as a statutory offset against copyright infringement, this judicially-created concept already had a lengthy history. English courts applying the Statute of Anne of 1710 had recognized that in some instances a "fair abridgement" of a work should not be deemed to infringe the author's rights, and though Congress did not mention fair use in the Copyright Act of 1790, the doctrine was recognized shortly thereafter in two opinions by Justice Story, *Folsom v. Marsh*, 9 F. Cas. 342 (C.C.D.Mass.1841), and *Gray v. Russell,* 10 F. Cas. 1035 (C.C.D.Mass.1839). It received broad judicial acceptance thereafter as an affirmative defense.

Unlike the rights-specific limitations spelled out in sections 108–120 and 1008 of Title 17, section 107 can be applied to limit any of the rights contained in sections 106 and 106A. Reflecting Congress's intent to preserve the historic flexibility of this judge-made doctrine, the codification of fair use in section 107 is remarkably brief. The 1976 House Report lists examples, "by no means exhaustive," of

> the sort of activities the courts might regard as fair use under the circumstances: "Quotation of excerpts in a review or criticism for purposes of illustration or comment; quotation of short passages in a scholarly or technical work, for illustration or clarification of the author's observations; use in a parody of some of the content of the work parodied; summary of an address or article, with brief quotations, in a news report; reproduction by a library of a portion of a work to replace part of a damaged copy; reproduction by a teacher or student of a small part of a work to illustrate a lesson; reproduction of a work in legislative or judicial proceedings or reports; incidental and fortuitous reproduction, in a newsreel or broadcast, of a work located in the scene of an event being reported." * * *

H.R. Rep. No. 94–1476, 94th Cong., 2d Sess. 65 (1976) (quoting p. 24 of 1961 Register of Copyright's Report).

The function of fair use in copyright law was summarized in the House Report accompanying the most recent amendment of section 107:

> * * * As United States District Judge Pierre Leval has written, the purpose of fair use is to "serve the copyright objective of stimulating productive thought and public instruction without excessively diminishing the incentives for creativity." * * * Section 107 contains criteria derived from earlier court decisions. The preamble to Section 107 lists six illustrative types of uses that may be analyzed under the doctrine: criticism, comment, news reporting, teaching, scholarship, and research. These uses are not, however, presumptively fair. Instead, the courts are directed to examine the use according to four statutory factors * * *. While all four factors must be considered in each fair use case, additional factors may also be considered in the court's discretion. All claims of fair use must be judged on the totality of the facts in the particular case by balancing all the factors. For this reason, fair use litigation will always be piecemeal: no legislative solution can answer in advance the outcome of a given dispute.

H.R. Rep. No. 102–836, 102d Cong., 2d Sess. 3–4 (1992).

SONY CORP. OF AMERICA v. UNIVERSAL CITY STUDIOS, INC.
Supreme Court of the United States, 1984.
464 U.S. 417, 104 S.Ct. 774, 78 L.Ed.2d 574.

JUSTICE STEVENS delivered the opinion of the Court.

[Respondents Universal City Studios and Walt Disney Productions, which owned copyrights in various motion pictures broadcast on television, brought this action against petitioner Sony for damages, an accounting and an injunction preventing further manufacture and marketing of its home videotape recorders (Betamax VTRs). Respondents argued that selling the VTRs made Sony a contributory copyright infringer because some of Sony's customers used the devices to record respondents' programs off the air. At trial, the evidence showed that the customers' primary use of their VTRs was for "time-shifting"—that is, recording a television program in order to view it at a later, more convenient, time, and then erasing the tape for reuse. The evidence also, showed, however, that a substantial number of VTR users retained the recorded tapes. There was no evidence of decreased television viewing by VTR owners. After a trial, the district court entered judgment for petitioners. The Ninth Circuit reversed, holding petitioners liable for contributory infringement. On appeal, the Supreme Court held that, by analogy to patent law, Sony could be held liable for contributory copyright infringement only if the VTR were not capable of any "substantial noninfringing use." See Chapter 20.C.2, *infra* (discussing the showing required to establish liability for contributory copyright infringement). The Court then turned to the question of whether the VTRs were capable of a substantial noninfringing use.]

* * *

Even unauthorized uses of a copyrighted work are not necessarily infringing. An unlicensed use of the copyright is not an infringement unless it conflicts with one of the specific exclusive rights conferred by the copyright statute. Twentieth Century Music Corp. v. Aiken, 422 U.S., at 154–155. Moreover, the definition of exclusive rights in § 106 of the present Act is prefaced by the words "subject to sections 107 through 118." Those sections describe a variety of uses of copyrighted material that "are not infringements of copyright" "notwithstanding the provisions of section 106." The most pertinent in this case is § 107, the legislative endorsement of the doctrine of "fair use."[29]

That section identifies various factors that enable a court to apply an "equitable rule of reason" analysis to particular claims of infringement.[31] Although not conclusive, the first factor requires that "the commercial or nonprofit character of an activity" be weighed in any fair use decision.[32] If the Betamax were used to make copies for a commercial

29. The Copyright Act of 1909, 35 Stat. 1075, did not have a "fair use" provision. Although that Act's compendium of exclusive rights "to print, reprint, publish, copy, and vend the copyrighted work" was broad enough to encompass virtually all potential interactions with a copyrighted work, the statute was never so construed. The courts simply refused to read the statute literally in every situation. When Congress amended the statute in 1976, it indicated that it "intended to restate the present judicial doctrine of fair use, not to change, narrow, or enlarge it in any way." H. R. Rep. No. 94–1476, p. 66 (1976).

31. The House Report expressly stated that the fair use doctrine is an "equitable rule of reason" in its explanation of the fair use section:

"Although the courts have considered and ruled upon the fair use doctrine over and over again, no real definition of the concept has ever emerged. Indeed, since the doctrine is an equitable rule of reason, no generally applicable definition is possible, and each case raising the question must be decided on its own facts. . . .

. . .

"General intention behind the provision

"The statement of the fair use doctrine in section 107 offers some guidance to users in determining when the principles of the doctrine apply. However, the endless variety of situations and combinations of circumstances that can rise in particular cases precludes the formulation of exact rules in the statute. The bill endorses the purpose and general scope of the judicial doctrine of fair use, but there is no disposition to freeze the doctrine in the stat-

ute, especially during a period of rapid technological change. Beyond a very broad statutory explanation of what fair use is and some of the criteria applicable to it, the courts must be free to adapt the doctrine to particular situations on a case-by-case basis." H. R. Rep. No. 94–1476, supra, at 65–66.

The Senate Committee similarly eschewed a rigid, bright-line approach to fair use. The Senate Report endorsed the view "that off-the-air recording for convenience" could be considered "fair use" under some circumstances, although it then made it clear that it did not intend to suggest that off-the-air recording for convenience should be deemed fair use under any circumstances imaginable. S. Rep. No. 94–473, pp. 65–66 (1975). The latter qualifying statement is quoted by the dissent, post, at 481, and if read in isolation, would indicate that the Committee intended to condemn all off-the-air recording for convenience. Read in context, however, it is quite clear that that was the farthest thing from the Committee's intention.

32. "The Committee has amended the first of the criteria to be considered—'the purpose and character of the use'—to state explicitly that this factor includes a consideration of 'whether such use is of a commercial nature or is for non-profit educational purposes.' This amendment is not intended to be interpreted as any sort of not-for-profit limitation on educational uses of copyrighted works. It is an express recognition that, as under the present law, the commercial or non-profit character of an activity, while not conclusive with respect to fair use, can and should be weighed along with other factors in fair use decisions." H. R. Rep. No. 94–1476, supra, at 66.

or profit-making purpose, such use would presumptively be unfair. The contrary presumption is appropriate here, however, because the District Court's findings plainly establish that time-shifting for private home use must be characterized as a noncommercial, nonprofit activity. Moreover, when one considers the nature of a televised copyrighted audiovisual work, see 17 U. S. C. § 107(2) (1982 ed.), and that time-shifting merely enables a viewer to see such a work which he had been invited to witness in its entirety free of charge, the fact that the entire work is reproduced, see § 107(3), does not have its ordinary effect of militating against a finding of fair use.

This is not, however, the end of the inquiry because Congress has also directed us to consider "the effect of the use upon the potential market for or value of the copyrighted work." § 107(4). The purpose of copyright is to create incentives for creative effort. Even copying for noncommercial purposes may impair the copyright holder's ability to obtain the rewards that Congress intended him to have. But a use that has no demonstrable effect upon the potential market for, or the value of, the copyrighted work need not be prohibited in order to protect the author's incentive to create. The prohibition of such noncommercial uses would merely inhibit access to ideas without any countervailing benefit.

Thus, although every commercial use of copyrighted material is presumptively an unfair exploitation of the monopoly privilege that belongs to the owner of the copyright, noncommercial uses are a different matter. A challenge to a noncommercial use of a copyrighted work requires proof either that the particular use is harmful, or that if it should become widespread, it would adversely affect the potential market for the copyrighted work. Actual present harm need not be shown; such a requirement would leave the copyright holder with no defense against predictable damage. Nor is it necessary to show with certainty that future harm will result. What is necessary is a showing by a preponderance of the evidence that some meaningful likelihood of future harm exists. If the intended use is for commercial gain, that likelihood may be presumed. But if it is for a noncommercial purpose, the likelihood must be demonstrated.

In this case, respondents failed to carry their burden with regard to home time-shifting. * * *

On the question of potential future harm from time-shifting, the District Court * * * rejected respondents' "fear that persons 'watching' the original telecast of a program will not be measured in the live audience and the ratings and revenues will decrease," by observing that current measurement technology allows the Betamax audience to be reflected. Id., at 466. It rejected respondents' prediction "that live television or movie audiences will decrease as more people watch Betamax tapes as an alternative," with the observation that "[there] is no factual basis for [the underlying] assumption." Ibid. It rejected respondents' "fear that time-shifting will reduce audiences for telecast reruns," and concluded instead that "given current market practices, this should aid plaintiffs rather than harm them." Ibid.[38] And it declared that respondents' suggestion that "theater or film rental exhibition of a program will suffer because of time-shift recording of that program" "lacks merit." Id., at 467.[39]

After completing that review, the District Court [concluded that] * * * "Harm from time-shifting is speculative and, at best, minimal." Ibid. * * *

The District Court's conclusions are buttressed by the fact that to the extent time-shifting expands public access to freely broadcast television programs, it yields societal benefits. In Community Television of Southern California v. Gottfried, 459 U.S. 498, 508, n. 12 (1983), we acknowledged the public interest in making television broadcasting more available. Concededly, that interest is not unlimited. But it supports an interpretation of the concept of "fair use" that requires the copyright holder to demonstrate some likelihood of harm before he may condemn a private act of time-shifting as a violation of federal law.

When these factors are all weighed in the "equitable rule of reason" balance, we must conclude that this record amply supports the District Court's conclusion that home time-shifting is fair use. In light of the findings of the District Court regarding the state of the empirical data, it is clear that the Court of Appeals erred in holding that the statute as presently written bars such conduct.[40]

38. "The underlying assumptions here are particularly difficult to accept. Plaintiffs explain that the Betamax increases access to the original televised material and that the more people there are in this original audience, the fewer people the rerun will attract. Yet current marketing practices, including the success of syndication, show just the opposite. Today, the larger the audience for the original telecast, the higher the price plaintiffs can demand from broadcasters from rerun rights. There is no survey within the knowledge of this court to show that the rerun audience is comprised of persons who have not seen the program. In any event, if ratings can reflect Betamax recording, original audiences may increase and, given market practices, this should aid plaintiffs rather than harm them." Ibid.

39. " * * * By definition, time-shift recording entails viewing and erasing, so the program will no longer be on tape when the later theater run begins. * * * It should also be noted that there is no evidence to suggest that the public interest in later theatrical exhibitions of motion pictures will be reduced any more by Betamax recording than it already is by the television broadcast of the film." Id., at 467.

40. The Court of Appeals chose not to engage in any "equitable rule of reason" analysis in this case. Instead, it assumed that the category of "fair use" is rigidly circumscribed by a requirement that every such use must be "productive." It therefore concluded that copying a television program merely to enable the viewer to receive information or entertainment that he would otherwise miss because of a personal scheduling conflict could never be fair use. That understanding of "fair use" was erroneous.

Congress has plainly instructed us that fair use analysis calls for a sensitive balancing of interests. The distinction between "productive" and "unproductive" uses may be helpful in calibrating the balance, but it cannot be wholly determinative. Although copying to promote a scholarly endeavor certainly has a stronger claim to fair use than copying to avoid interrupting a poker game, the question is not simply two-dimensional. For one thing, it is not true that all copyrights are fungible. Some copyrights govern material with broad potential secondary markets. Such material may well have a broader claim to protection because of the greater potential for commercial harm. Copying a news broadcast may have a stronger claim to fair use than copying a motion picture. And, of course, not all uses are fungible. Copying for commercial gain has a much weaker claim to fair use than copying for personal enrichment. But the

In summary, * * * respondents failed to demonstrate that time-shifting would cause any likelihood of nonminimal harm to the potential market for, or the value of, their copyrighted works. The Betamax is, therefore, capable of substantial noninfringing uses. Sony's sale of such equipment to the general public does not constitute contributory infringement of respondents' copyrights.

* * *

V

"The direction of Art. I is that Congress shall have the power to promote the progress of science and the useful arts. When, as here, the Constitution is permissive, the sign of how far Congress has chosen to go can come only from Congress." Deepsouth Packing Co. v. Laitram Corp., 406 U.S. 518, 530 (1972).

One may search the Copyright Act in vain for any sign that the elected representatives of the millions of people who watch television every day have made it unlawful to copy a program for later viewing at home, or have enacted a flat prohibition against the sale of machines that make such copying possible.

It may well be that Congress will take a fresh look at this new technology, just as it so often has examined other innovations in the past. But it is not our job to apply laws that have not yet been written. Applying the copyright statute, as it now reads, to the facts as they have been developed in this case, the judgment of the Court of Appeals must be reversed.

It is so ordered.

Notes

1. Suppose that television ratings (which influence the price of commercial time during a program's initial and rerun broadcasts) distinguished between the number of "viewers" who were recording the television broadcast rather than viewing it. Alternatively, suppose that *Sony* were decided years later, when pay-per-view and subscription cable television represented a large part of the television market. How should these factors influence the fair use analysis?

notion of social "productivity" cannot be a complete answer to this analysis. A teacher who copies to prepare lecture notes is clearly productive. But so is a teacher who copies for the sake of broadening his personal understanding of his specialty. Or a legislator who copies for the sake of broadening her understanding of what her constituents are watching; or a constituent who copies a news program to help make a decision on how to vote.

Making a copy of a copyrighted work for the convenience of a blind person is expressly identified by the House Committee Report as an example of fair use, with no suggestion that anything more than a purpose to entertain or to inform need motivate the copying. In a hospital setting, using a VTR to enable a patient to see programs he would otherwise miss has no productive purpose other than contributing to the psychological well-being of the patient. Virtually any time-shifting that increases viewer access to television programming may result in a comparable benefit. The statutory language does not identify any dichotomy between productive and nonproductive time-shifting, but does require consideration of the economic consequences of copying.

2. How would the fair use analysis apply to each of the following instances of copying, assuming that the copy in each case is retained permanently for the purpose of noncommercial, personal use: (a) recording television or radio broadcasts off the air? (b) copying prerecorded videocassettes? (c) copying digitized music off of a computer bulletin board? Note that the fair use defense is no longer necessary to avoid infringement liability for most noncommercial copying of phonorecords since the enactment of the Audio Home Recording Act of 1992, see 17 U.S.C.A. § 1008 (discussed at Chapter 18.B.6, *supra*); this interesting fair use question never reached the federal courts.

3. In *Sony*, the only individual defendant named in the complaint was a client of the plaintiffs' law firm who consented to be sued; the remaining defendants (who were accused of contributory or vicarious infringement) were all business enterprises engaged in manufacturing or marketing the Betamax. The principal target of the suit was clearly the machine itself and the degree to which it lent itself to infringements, and not the supposed infringements by individual defendants themselves. How is it that section 107 applies in a case of this sort? By what authority? Is it appropriate to consider copyright infringement and fair use at large, as if the underlying question of liability were akin to the issues in mass tort litigation? Doesn't the legislative history quoted above make it clear that in applying the fair use section a court must evaluate each alleged infringement individually, taking into close account the actual facts in each case?

4. Consider the nature of the alleged infringement: in essence, the complaint alleges private recording for personal use. Recall our earlier discussion of section 106. Does private appropriation for personal use violate the reproduction right? Is it appropriate for a court to apply section 107 to what is, in effect, a request for clarification as to the scope of the section 106 reproduction right? Note that the Court does not address this issue directly. Why not?

HARPER & ROW v. NATION ENTERPRISES

Supreme Court of the United States, 1985.
471 U.S. 539, 105 S.Ct. 2218, 85 L.Ed.2d 588.

JUSTICE O'CONNOR delivered the opinion of the Court.

* * *

I

In February 1977, shortly after leaving the White House, former President Gerald R. Ford contracted with petitioners Harper & Row and Reader's Digest, to publish his as yet unwritten memoirs. The memoirs were to contain "significant hitherto unpublished material" concerning the Watergate crisis, Mr. Ford's pardon of former President Nixon and "Mr. Ford's reflections on this period of history, and the morality and personalities involved." * * * In addition to the right to publish the Ford memoirs in book form, the agreement gave petitioners the exclusive right to license prepublication excerpts, known in the trade as "first serial rights." Two years later, as the memoirs were nearing completion, petitioners negotiated a prepublication licensing agreement with Time, a weekly news magazine. Time agreed to pay $25,000, $12,500 in advance and an additional $12,500 at publication, in exchange for the right to excerpt 7,500 words from Mr. Ford's account of the Nixon pardon. The issue featuring the excerpts was timed to appear approximately one week before shipment of the full length book version to bookstores. Exclusivity was an important consideration; Harper & Row instituted procedures designed to maintain the confidentiality of the manuscript, and Time retained the right to renegotiate the second payment should the material appear in print prior to its release of the excerpts.

Two to three weeks before the Time article's scheduled release, an unidentified person secretly brought a copy of the Ford manuscript to Victor Navasky, editor of The Nation, a political commentary magazine. Mr. Navasky knew that his possession of the manuscript was not authorized and that the manuscript must be returned quickly to his "source" to avoid discovery. 557 F.Supp. 1067, 1069 (S.D.N.Y.1983). He hastily put together what he believed was "a real hot news story" composed of quotes, paraphrases, and facts drawn exclusively from the manuscript. Ibid. Mr. Navasky attempted no independent commentary, research or criticism, in part because of the need for speed if he was to "make news" by "[publishing] in advance of publication of the Ford book." * * * The 2,250–word article * * * appeared on April 3, 1979. As a result of The Nation's article, Time canceled its piece and refused to pay the remaining $12,500.

[Petitioners brought an action for, inter alia, copyright infringement. The district court awarded actual damages of $12,500, rejecting the respondents' fair use defense because, although the facts and memoranda included in the memoirs were not copyrightable, "the totality of these facts and memoranda collected together with Ford's reflections" was protected by copyright.]

* * *

A divided panel of the Court of Appeals for the Second Circuit reversed. The majority recognized that Mr. Ford's verbatim "reflections" were original "expression" protected by copyright. But it held that the District Court had erred in assuming the "coupling [of these reflections] with uncopyrightable fact transformed that information into a copyrighted 'totality.'"723 F.2d 195, 205 (1983). The majority noted that copyright attaches to expression, not facts or ideas. It concluded that, to avoid granting a copyright monopoly over the facts underlying history and news, " 'expression' [in such works must be confined] to its barest elements—the ordering and choice of the words themselves." Id., at 204. Thus similarities between the original and the challenged work traceable to the copying or paraphrasing of uncopyrightable material, such as historical facts, memoranda and other public documents, and quoted remarks of third parties, must be disregarded in evaluating whether the second author's use was fair or infringing.

"When the uncopyrighted material is stripped away, the article in The Nation contains, at most, approximately 300 words that are copyrighted. These remaining paragraphs and scattered phrases are all verbatim quotations from the memoirs which had not appeared previously in other publications. They include a short segment of Ford's conversations with Henry Kissinger and several other individuals. Ford's impressionistic depictions of Nixon, ill with phlebitis after the resignation and pardon, and of Nixon's character, constitute the major portion of this material. It is these parts of the magazine piece on which [the court] must focus in [its] examination of the question whether there was a 'fair use' of copyrighted matter." Id., at 206.

Examining the four factors enumerated in § 107, * * * the majority found the purpose of the article was "news reporting," the original work was essentially factual in nature, the 300 words appropriated were insubstantial in relation to the 2,250–word piece, and the impact on the market for the original was minimal as "the evidence [did] not support a finding that it was the very limited use of expression per se which led to Time's decision not to print the excerpt." The Nation's borrowing of verbatim quotations merely "[lent] authenticity to this politically significant material ... complementing the reporting of the facts." 723 F.2d, at 208. The Court of Appeals was especially influenced by the "politically significant" nature of the subject matter and its conviction that it is not "the purpose of the Copyright Act to impede that harvest of knowledge so necessary to a democratic state" or "chill the activities of the press by forbidding a circumscribed use of copyrighted words." Id., at 197, 209.

II

We agree with the Court of Appeals that copyright is intended to increase and not to impede the harvest of knowledge. But we believe the Second Circuit gave insufficient deference to the scheme established by the Copyright Act for fostering the original works that provide the seed and substance of this harvest. The rights conferred by copyright are designed to assure contributors to the store of knowledge a fair return for their labors. Twentieth Century Music Corp. v. Aiken, 422 U.S. 151, 156 (1975).

* * *

* * * The Nation has admitted to lifting verbatim quotes of the author's original language totaling between 300 and 400 words and constituting some 13% of The Nation article. In using generous verbatim excerpts of Mr. Ford's unpublished manuscript to lend authenticity to its account of the forthcoming memoirs, The Nation effectively arrogated to itself the right of first publication, an important marketable subsidiary right. For the reasons set forth below, we find that this use of the copyrighted manuscript, even stripped to the verbatim quotes conceded by The Nation to be copyrightable expression, was not a fair use within the meaning of the Copyright Act.

III

A

Fair use was traditionally defined as "a privilege in others than the owner of the copyright to use the copyrighted material in a reasonable manner without his consent." H. Ball, Law of Copyright and Literary Property 260 (1944) (hereinafter Ball). The statutory formulation of the defense of fair use in the Copyright Act reflects the intent of Congress to codify the common-law doctrine. 3 Nimmer § 13.05. Section 107 requires a case-by-case determination whether a particular use is fair, and the statute notes four nonexclusive factors to be considered. This approach was "intended to restate the [pre-existing] judicial doctrine of fair use, not to change, narrow, or enlarge it in any way." H. R. Rep. No. 94–1476, p. 66 (1976) (hereinafter House Report).

"[The] author's consent to a reasonable use of his copyrighted works [had] always been implied by the courts as a necessary incident of the constitutional policy of promoting the progress of science and the useful arts, since a prohibition of such use would inhibit subsequent writers from attempting to improve upon prior works and thus ... frustrate the very ends sought to be attained." Ball 260. Professor Latman, in a study of the doctrine of fair use commissioned by Congress for the revision effort, see Sony Corp. of America v. Universal City Studios, Inc., 464 U.S., at 462–463, n. 9 (dissenting opinion), summarized prior law as turning on the "importance of the material copied or performed from the point of view of the reasonable copyright owner. In other words, would the reasonable copyright owner have consented to the use?" Latman 15.

As early as 1841, Justice Story gave judicial recognition to the doctrine in a case that concerned the letters of another former President, George Washington.

"[A] reviewer may fairly cite largely from the original work, if his design be really and truly to use the passages for the purposes of fair and reasonable criticism. On the other hand, it is as clear, that if he thus cites the most important parts of the work, with a view, not to criticise, but to supersede the use of the original work, and substitute the review for it, such a use will be deemed in law a piracy." Folsom v. Marsh, 9 F.Cas. 342, 344–345 (No. 4,901) (C.C.Mass.)

As Justice Story's hypothetical illustrates, the fair use doctrine has always precluded a use that "[supersedes] the use of the original." Ibid. Accord, S. Rep. No. 94–473, p. 65 (1975) (hereinafter Senate Report).

* * * [I]t has never been seriously disputed that "the fact that the plaintiff's work is unpublished ... is a factor tending to negate the defense of fair use." [3 Nimmer § 13.05, at 13–62, n. 2.] Publication of an author's expression before he has authorized its dissemination seriously infringes the author's right to decide when and whether it will be made public, a factor not present in fair use of published works. Respondents contend, however, that Congress, in including first publication among the rights enumerated in § 106, which are expressly subject

to fair use under § 107, intended that fair use would apply in pari materia to published and unpublished works. The Copyright Act does not support this proposition.

* * *

Though the right of first publication, like the other rights enumerated in § 106, is expressly made subject to the fair use provision of § 107, fair use analysis must always be tailored to the individual case. * * * The right of first publication implicates a threshold decision by the author whether and in what form to release his work. First publication is inherently different from other § 106 rights in that only one person can be the first publisher; as the contract with Time illustrates, the commercial value of the right lies primarily in exclusivity. Because the potential damage to the author from judicially enforced "sharing" of the first publication right with unauthorized users of his manuscript is substantial, the balance of equities in evaluating such a claim of fair use inevitably shifts.

The Senate Report confirms that Congress intended the unpublished nature of the work to figure prominently in fair use analysis. In discussing fair use of photocopied materials in the classroom the Committee Report states:

"A key, though not necessarily determinative, factor in fair use is whether or not the work is available to the potential user. If the work is 'out of print' and unavailable for purchase through normal channels, the user may have more justification for reproducing it.... The applicability of the fair use doctrine to unpublished works is narrowly limited since, although the work is unavailable, this is the result of a deliberate choice on the part of the copyright owner. Under ordinary circumstances, the copyright owner's 'right of first publication' would outweigh any needs of reproduction for classroom purposes." Senate Report, at 64.

* * *

We also find unpersuasive respondents' argument that fair use may be made of a soon-to-be-published manuscript on the ground that the author has demonstrated he has no interest in nonpublication. This argument assumes that the unpublished nature of copyrighted material is only relevant to letters or other confidential writings not intended for dissemination. It is true that common-law copyright was often enlisted in the service of personal privacy. See Brandeis & Warren, The Right to Privacy, 4 Harv. L. Rev. 193, 198–199 (1890). In its commercial guise, however, an author's right to choose when he will publish is no less deserving of protection. The period encompassing the work's initiation, its preparation, and its grooming for public dissemination is a crucial one for any literary endeavor. The Copyright Act, which accords the copyright owner the "right to control the first public distribution" of his work, House Report, at 62, echo[e]s the common law's concern that the author or copyright owner retain control throughout this critical stage.

* * * Under ordinary circumstances, the author's right to control the first public appearance of his undisseminated expression will outweigh a claim of fair use.

B

Respondents, however, contend that First Amendment values require a different rule under the circumstances of this case. The thrust of the decision below is that "[t]he scope of [fair use] is undoubtedly wider when the information conveyed relates to matters of high public concern." Consumers Union of the United States, Inc. v. General Signal Corp., 724 F.2d 1044, 1050 (C.A.2 1983) (construing 723 F.2d 195 (1983) (case below) as allowing advertiser to quote Consumer Reports), cert. denied, 469 U.S. 823 (1984). Respondents advance the substantial public import of the subject matter of the Ford memoirs as grounds for excusing a use that would ordinarily not pass muster as a fair use—the piracy of verbatim quotations for the purpose of "scooping" the authorized first serialization. Respondents explain their copying of Mr. Ford's expression as essential to reporting the news story it claims the book itself represents. In respondents' view, not only the facts contained in Mr. Ford's memoirs, but "the precise manner in which [he] expressed himself [were] as newsworthy as what he had to say." * * * Respondents argue that the public's interest in learning this news as fast as possible outweighs the right of the author to control its first publication.

The Second Circuit noted, correctly, that copyright's idea/expression dichotomy "strike[s] a definitional balance between the First Amendment and the Copyright Act by permitting free communication of facts while still protecting an author's expression." 723 F.2d, at 203. No author may copyright his ideas or the facts he narrates. 17 U. S. C. § 102(b). * * *

Respondents' theory, however, would expand fair use to effectively destroy any expectation of copyright protection in the work of a public figure. Absent such protection, there would be little incentive to create or profit in financing such memoirs, and the public would be denied an important source of significant historical information. The promise of copyright would be an empty one if it could be avoided merely by dubbing the infringement a fair use "news report" of the book. See Wainwright Securities Inc. v. Wall Street Transcript Corp., 558 F.2d 91 (C.A.2 1977), cert. denied, 434 U.S. 1014 (1978).

Nor do respondents assert any actual necessity for circumventing the copyright scheme with respect to the types of works and users at issue here. Where an author and publisher have invested extensive resources in creating an original work and are poised to release it to the public, no legitimate aim is served by pre-empting the right of first publication. The fact that the words the author has chosen to clothe his narrative may of themselves be "newsworthy" is not an independent justification for unauthorized copying of the author's expression prior to publication. * * *

In our haste to disseminate news, it should not be forgotten that the Framers intended copyright itself to be the engine of free expression. By establishing a marketable right to the use of one's expression, copyright supplies the economic incentive to create and disseminate ideas. This Court stated in Mazer v. Stein, 347 U.S. 201, 209 (1954):

> "The economic philosophy behind the clause empowering Congress to grant patents and copyrights is the conviction that encouragement of individual effort by personal gain is the best way to advance public welfare through the talents of authors and inventors in 'Science and useful Arts.' "

And again in Twentieth Century Music Corp. v. Aiken:

> "The immediate effect of our copyright law is to secure a fair return for an 'author's' creative labor. But the ultimate aim is, by this incentive, to stimulate [the creation of useful works] for the general public good." 422 U.S., at 156.

It is fundamentally at odds with the scheme of copyright to accord lesser rights in those works that are of greatest importance to the public. Such a notion ignores the major premise of copyright and injures author and public alike. * * *

* * *

In view of the First Amendment protections already embodied in the Copyright Act's distinction between copyrightable expression and uncopyrightable facts and ideas, and the latitude for scholarship and comment traditionally afforded by fair use, we see no warrant for expanding the doctrine of fair use to create what amounts to a public figure exception to copyright. Whether verbatim copying from a public figure's manuscript in a given case is or is not fair must be judged according to the traditional equities of fair use.

IV

Fair use is a mixed question of law and fact. Pacific & Southern Co. v. Duncan, 744 F.2d 1490, 1495, n. 8 (C.A.11 1984). Where the district court has found facts sufficient to evaluate each of the statutory factors, an appellate court "need not remand for further factfinding ... [but] may conclude as a matter of law that [the challenged use] do[es] not qualify as a fair use of the copyrighted work." Id., at 1495. Thus whether The Nation article constitutes fair use under § 107 must be reviewed in light of the principles discussed above. The factors enumerated in the section are not meant to be exclusive: "[S]ince the doctrine is an equitable rule of reason, no generally applicable definition is possible, and each case raising the question must be decided on its own facts." House Report, at 65. The four factors identified by Congress as especially relevant in determining whether the use was fair are: (1) the purpose and character of the use; (2) the nature of the copyrighted work; (3) the substantiality of the portion used in relation to the copyrighted work as a whole; (4) the effect on the potential market for or value of the copyrighted work. We address each one separately.

Purpose of the Use. The Second Circuit correctly identified news reporting as the general purpose of The Nation's use. News reporting is one of the examples enumerated in § 107 to "give some idea of the sort of activities the courts might regard as fair use under the circumstances." Senate Report, at 61. This listing was not intended to be exhaustive, see ibid.; § 101 (definition of "including" and "such as"), or to single out any particular use as presumptively a "fair" use. The drafters resisted pressures from special interest groups to create presumptive categories of fair use, but structured the provision as an affirmative defense requiring a case-by-case analysis. See H. R. Rep. No. 83, 90th Cong., 1st Sess., 37 (1967); Patry 477, n. 4. "[W]hether a use referred to in the first sentence of section 107 is a fair use in a particular case will depend upon the application of the determinative factors, including those mentioned in the second sentence." Senate Report, at 62. The fact that an article arguably is "news" and therefore a productive use is simply one factor in a fair use analysis.

We agree with the Second Circuit that the trial court erred in fixing on whether the information contained in the memoirs was actually new to the public. As Judge Meskill wisely noted, "[c]ourts should be chary of deciding what is and what is not news." 723 F.2d, at 215 (dissenting). Cf. Gertz v. Robert Welch, Inc., 418 U.S. 323, 345–346 (1974). "The issue is not what constitutes 'news,' but whether a claim of news reporting is a valid fair use defense to an infringement of *copyrightable expression.*" Patry 119. The Nation has every right to seek to be the first to publish information. But The Nation went beyond simply reporting uncopyrightable information and actively sought to exploit the headline value of its infringement, making a "news event" out of its unauthorized first publication of a noted figure's copyrighted expression.

The fact that a publication was commercial as opposed to nonprofit is a separate factor that tends to weigh against a finding of fair use. "[E]very commercial use of copyrighted material is presumptively an unfair exploitation of the monopoly privilege that belongs to the owner of the copyright." Sony Corp. of America v. Universal City Studios, Inc., 464 U.S., at 451. In arguing that the purpose of news reporting is not purely commercial, The Nation misses the point entirely. The crux of the profit/nonprofit distinction is not whether the sole motive of the use is monetary gain but whether the user stands to profit from exploitation of the copyrighted material without paying the customary price. See Roy Export Co. Establishment v. Columbia Broadcasting System, Inc., 503 F.Supp., at 1144; 3 Nimmer § 13.05[A][1], at 13–71, n. 25.3.

In evaluating character and purpose we cannot ignore The Nation's stated purpose of scooping the forthcoming hardcover and Time abstracts. * * * The Nation's use had not merely the incidental effect but the *intended purpose* of supplanting the copyright holder's commercially valuable right of first publication. * * * Also relevant to the "character" of the use is "the propriety of the defendant's conduct." 3 Nimmer § 13.05[A], at 13–72. "Fair use presupposes 'good faith' and 'fair dealing.' " Time Inc. v. Bernard Geis Associates, 293 F.Supp. 130, 146 (S.D.N.Y.1968), quoting Schulman, Fair Use and the Revision of the Copyright Act, 53 Iowa L. Rev. 832 (1968). The trial court found that The Nation knowingly exploited a purloined manuscript. * * * Unlike the typical claim of fair use, The Nation cannot offer up even the fiction of consent as justification. Like its competitor newsweekly, it was free to bid for the right of abstracting excerpts from "A Time to Heal." Fair use "distinguishes between 'a true scholar and a chiseler who infringes a work for personal profit.' " Wainwright Securities Inc. v. Wall Street Transcript Corp., 558 F.2d, at 94, quoting from Hearings on Bills for the General Revision of the Copyright Law before the House Committee on the Judiciary, 89th Cong., 1st Sess., ser. 8, pt. 3, p. 1706 (1966) (statement of John Schulman).

Nature of the Copyrighted Work. Second, the Act directs attention to the nature of the copyrighted work. "A Time to Heal" may be characterized as an unpublished historical narrative or autobiography. The law generally recognizes a greater need to disseminate factual works than works of fiction or fantasy. See Gorman, Fact or Fancy? The Implications for Copyright, 29 J. Copyright Soc. 560, 561 (1982).

> "[E]ven within the field of fact works, there are gradations as to the relative proportion of fact and fancy. One may move from sparsely embellished maps and directories to elegantly written biography. The extent to which one must permit expressive language to be copied, in order to assure dissemination of the underlying facts, will thus vary from case to case." Id., at 563.

Some of the briefer quotes from the memoirs are arguably necessary adequately to convey the facts; for example, Mr. Ford's characterization of the White House tapes as the "smoking gun" is perhaps so integral to the idea expressed as to be inseparable from it. Cf. 1 Nimmer § 1.10[C]. But The Nation did not stop at isolated phrases and instead excerpted subjective descriptions and portraits of public figures whose power lies in the author's individualized expression. Such use, focusing on the most expressive elements of the work, exceeds that necessary to disseminate the facts.

The fact that a work is unpublished is a critical element of its "nature." 3 Nimmer § 13.05[A]; Comment, 58 St. John's L. Rev., at 613. Our prior discussion establishes that the scope of fair use is narrower with respect to unpublished works. While even substantial quotations might qualify as fair use in a review of a published work or a news account of a speech that had been delivered to the public or disseminated to the press, see House Report, at 65, the author's right to control the first public appearance of his expression weighs against such use of the work before its release. The right of first publication encompasses not only the choice whether to publish at all, but also the choices of when, where, and in what form first to publish a work.

In the case of Mr. Ford's manuscript, the copyright holders' interest in confidentiality is irrefutable; the copyright holders had entered into a contractual undertaking to "keep the manuscript confidential" and required that all those to whom the manuscript was shown also "sign an agreement to keep the manuscript confidential." * * * While the copyright holders' contract with Time required Time to submit its proposed article seven days before publication, The Nation's clandestine publication afforded no such opportunity for creative or quality control. * * * It was hastily patched together and contained "a number of inaccuracies." * * * A use that so clearly infringes the copyright holder's interests in confidentiality and creative control is difficult to characterize as "fair."

Amount and Substantiality of the Portion Used. Next, the Act directs us to examine the amount and substantiality of the portion used in relation to the copyrighted work as a whole. In absolute terms, the words actually quoted were an insubstantial portion of "A Time to Heal." The District Court, however, found that "[T]he Nation took what was essentially the heart of the book." 557 F.Supp., at 1072. We believe the Court of Appeals erred in overruling the District Judge's evaluation of the qualitative nature of the taking. See, e. g., Roy Export Co. Establishment v. Columbia Broadcasting System, Inc., 503 F.Supp., at 1145 (taking of 55 seconds out of 1 hour and 29–minute film deemed qualitatively substantial). A Time editor described the chapters on the pardon as "the most interesting and moving parts of the entire manuscript." Reply Brief for Petitioners 16, n. 8. The portions actually quoted were selected by Mr. Navasky as among the most powerful passages in those chapters. He testified that he used verbatim excerpts because simply reciting the information could not adequately convey the "absolute certainty with which [Ford] expressed himself," * * * or show that "this comes from President Ford," * * * or carry the "definitive quality" of the original * * *. In short, he quoted these passages precisely because they qualitatively embodied Ford's distinctive expression.

As the statutory language indicates, a taking may not be excused merely because it is insubstantial with respect to the *infringing* work. As Judge Learned Hand cogently remarked, "no plagiarist can excuse the wrong by showing how much of his work he did not pirate." Sheldon v. Metro–Goldwyn Pictures Corp., 81 F.2d 49, 56 (CA2), cert. denied, 298 U.S. 669 (1936). Conversely, the fact that a substantial portion of the infringing work was copied verbatim is evidence of the qualitative value of the copied material, both to the originator and to the plagiarist who seeks to profit from marketing someone else's copyrighted expression.

Stripped to the verbatim quotes, the direct takings from the unpublished manuscript constitute at least 13% of the infringing article. See Meeropol v. Nizer, 560 F.2d 1061, 1071 (C.A.2 1977) (copyrighted letters constituted less than 1% of infringing work but were prominently featured). The Nation article is structured around the quoted excerpts which serve as its dramatic focal points. * * * In view of the expressive value of the excerpts and their key role in the infringing work, we cannot agree with the Second Circuit that the "magazine took a meager, indeed an infinitesimal amount of Ford's original language." 723 F.2d, at 209.

Effect on the Market. Finally, the Act focuses on "the effect of the use upon the potential market for or value of the copyrighted work." This last factor is undoubtedly the single most important element of fair use.[9] See 3 Nimmer § 13.05[A], at 13–76, and cases cited therein. "Fair use, when properly applied, is limited to copying by others which does not materially impair the marketability of the work which is copied." 1 Nimmer § 1.10[D], at 1–87. The trial court found not merely a potential but an actual effect on the market. Time's cancellation of its projected serialization and its refusal to pay the $12,500 were the direct effect of the infringement. The Court of Appeals rejected this fact-finding as clearly erroneous, noting that the record did not establish a causal relation between Time's nonperformance and respondents' unauthorized publication of Mr. Ford's *expression* as opposed to the facts taken from the memoirs. We disagree. Rarely will a case of copyright infringement present such clear-cut evidence of actual damage. Petitioners assured Time that there would be no other authorized publication of any portion of the unpublished manuscript prior to April 23, 1979. Any publication of material from chapters 1 and 3 would permit Time to renegotiate its final payment. Time cited The Nation's article, which contained verbatim quotes from the unpublished manuscript, as a reason for its nonperformance. With respect to apportionment of profits flowing from a copyright infringement, this Court has held that an infringer who commingles infringing and noninfringing elements "must abide the consequences, unless he can make a separation of the profits so as to assure to the injured party all that justly belongs to him." Sheldon v. Metro–Goldwyn Pictures Corp., 309 U.S. 390, 406 (1940). Cf. 17 U. S. C. § 504(b) (the infringer is required to prove elements of profits attributable to other than the infringed work). Similarly, once a copyright holder establishes with reasonable probability the existence of a causal connection between the infringement and a loss of revenue, the burden properly shifts to the infringer to show that this damage would have occurred had there been no taking of copyrighted expression. See 3 Nimmer § 14.02, at 14–7—14–8.1. Petitioners established a prima facie case of actual damage that respondents failed to rebut. See Stevens Linen Associates, Inc. v. Mastercraft Corp., 656 F.2d 11, 15 (C.A.2 1981). The trial court properly awarded actual damages and accounting of profits. See 17 U. S. C. § 504(b).

---

9. Economists who have addressed the issue believe the fair use exception should come into play only in those situations in which the market fails or the price the copyright holder would ask is near zero. See, e.g., T. Brennan, Harper & Row v. The Nation, Copyrightability and Fair Use, Dept. of Justice Economic Policy Office Discussion Paper 13–17 (1984); Gordon, Fair Use as Market Failure: A Structural and Economic Analysis of the Betamax Case and its Predecessors, 82 Colum. L. Rev. 1600, 1615 (1982). As the facts here demonstrate, there is a fully functioning market that encourages the creation and dissemination of memoirs of public figures. In the economists' view, permitting "fair use" to displace normal copyright channels disrupts the copyright market without a commensurate public benefit.

More important, to negate fair use one need only show that if the challenged use "should become widespread, it would adversely affect the *potential* market for the copyrighted work." Sony Corp. of America v. Universal City Studios, Inc., 464 U.S., at 451 (emphasis added); id., at 484, and n. 36 (collecting cases) (dissenting opinion). This inquiry must take account not only of harm to the original but also of harm to the market for derivative works. See Iowa State University Research Foundation, Inc. v. American Broadcasting Cos., 621 F.2d 57 (C.A.2 1980); Meeropol v. Nizer, supra, at 1070; Roy Export v. Columbia Broadcasting System, Inc., 503 F.Supp., at 1146. "If the defendant's work adversely affects the value of any of the rights in the copyrighted work (in this case the adaptation [and serialization] right) the use is not fair." 3 Nimmer § 13.05[B], at 13–77—13–78 (footnote omitted).

It is undisputed that the factual material in the balance of The Nation's article, besides the verbatim quotes at issue here, was drawn exclusively from the chapters on the pardon. The excerpts were employed as featured episodes in a story about the Nixon pardon—precisely the use petitioners had licensed to Time. The borrowing of these verbatim quotes from the unpublished manuscript lent The Nation's piece a special air of authenticity—as Navasky expressed it, the reader would know it was Ford speaking and not The Nation. * * * Thus it directly competed for a share of the market for prepublication excerpts. The Senate Report states:

"With certain special exceptions . . . a use that supplants any part of the normal market for a copyrighted work would ordinarily be considered an infringement." Senate Report, at 65.

Placed in a broader perspective, a fair use doctrine that permits extensive prepublication quotations from an unreleased manuscript without the copyright owner's consent poses substantial potential for damage to the marketability of first serialization rights in general. "Isolated instances of minor infringements, when multiplied many times, become in the aggregate a major inroad on copyright that must be prevented." Ibid.

V

The Court of Appeals erred in concluding that The Nation's use of the copyrighted material was excused by the public's interest in the subject matter. It erred, as well, in overlooking the unpublished nature of the work and the resulting impact on the potential market for first serial rights of permitting unauthorized prepublication excerpts under the rubric of fair use. Finally, in finding the taking "infinitesimal," the Court of Appeals accorded too little weight to the qualitative importance of the quoted passages of original expression. In sum, the traditional doctrine of fair use, as embodied in the Copyright Act, does not sanction the use made by The Nation of these copyrighted materials. Any copyright infringer may claim to benefit the public by increasing public access to the copyrighted work. See Pacific & Southern Co. v. Duncan, 744 F.2d, at 1499–1500. But Congress has not designed, and we see no warrant for judicially imposing, a "compulsory license" permitting unfettered access to the unpublished copyrighted expression of public figures.

The Nation conceded that its verbatim copying of some 300 words of direct quotation from the Ford manuscript would constitute an infringement unless excused as a fair use. Because we find that The Nation's use of these verbatim excerpts from the unpublished manuscript was not a fair use, the judgment of the Court of Appeals is reversed, and the case is remanded for further proceedings consistent with this opinion.

It is so ordered.

Notes

1. The dissenters in *Harper & Row* (Justices Brennan, White and Marshall) argued that the majority had extended copyright protection to ideas and historical information under the guise of protecting expression. In *Wright v. Warner Books,* 953 F.2d 731 (2d Cir.1991), the concurrence criticized the *Harper & Row* majority for leaping to the fair use analysis without "attempt[ing] to separate the copyrightable from the uncopyrightable * * *." *Id.* at 743 (Van Graafeiland, C.J., concurring). Do you agree with either of these views?

2. After the Supreme Court's decision in *Harper & Row*, the Second Circuit issued two opinions which, to many observers, appeared to conclude that *Harper & Row* had established a *per se* rule that there could be no fair use of an unpublished work. See *Salinger v. Random House, Inc.,* 811 F.2d 90 (2d Cir.1987); *New Era Publications Int'l v. Henry Holt & Co.,* 873 F.2d 576 (2d Cir.1989). Although the Second Circuit later appeared to retreat from this position in *Wright v. Warner Books, supra,* the intense concern sparked by the two prior decisions led Congress in 1992 to expressly disavow such a *per se* rule by adding what is now the final sentence of section 107.

The House Report accompanying Pub. L. No. 102–492 emphasized that "in making any evaluation of a claim of fair use of unpublished material, the Supreme Court's holding that for purposes of the second statutory factor, the unpublished nature of the work is a ' "key, though not necessarily determinative" factor tending to negate a defense of fair use,' remains the law." H.R. Rep. No. 102–836, 102d Cong., 2d Sess. 9 (1992).

In *NXCIVM Corp. v. The Ross Institute,* 364 F.3d 471 (2d Cir. 2004), the Second Circuit did find fair use of an unpublished work. Using the four-part test set out in 17 U.S.C. § 107, the court concluded that even though the "nature of the copyrighted work" factor weighed in favor of the plaintiffs because the work was never published, the other three factors did not weigh in favor of the plaintiffs. The "effect on the market" test weighed heavily in favor of the defendants. Therefore, the plaintiffs' request for a preliminary injunction against defendants was denied.

3. In evaluating the amount of copyrighted expression that was taken, the quantitative analysis asks what percentage of the plaintiff's copyrighted work was taken. But how should the "work" be defined? Suppose the plaintiff owns the copyright in a series of photographs or short stories, which are compiled in a single book? What about individual chapters in a nonfic-

tion text, or entries in an encyclopedia? Which is more probative of the "amount taken" under the fair use analysis—the quantitative measure or the qualitative measure? Is it necessary to analyze both?

In *Elvis Presley Enterprises v. Passport Video,* 349 F.3d 622 (9th Cir. 2003), the court affirmed a preliminary injunction against a filmmaker who used the plaintiff's copyrighted Elvis Presley videos and photographs in a documentary. In some cases copyrighted materials were shown nearly in their entirety. The quantity copied was small but often the heart of the work. The majority court stated that adverse impact on the film market can be assumed from commercial use.

Dissenting, Judge Noonan described the ruling as "a miscarriage of justice," *Id.* at 634 and criticized the majority for ignoring the public interest in approving a preliminary injunction.

4. In *Atari Games Corp. v. Nintendo*, 975 F.2d 832, 843–44 (Fed.Cir. 1992), the Federal Circuit held that the fair use defense was inapplicable where the defendant made false statements to the Copyright Office in order to obtain a copy of plaintiff's source code as an aid to "reverse engineering" those portions of plaintiff's object code that were essential to making defendant's videogames compatible with plaintiff's videogame console. Comment on the following proposition, which the court purported to derive from *Harper & Row*: "To invoke the fair use exception, an individual must possess an authorized copy of a literary work."

CAMPBELL v. ACUFF–ROSE MUSIC, INC.

Supreme Court of the United States, 1994.
510 U.S. 569, 114 S.Ct. 1164, 127 L.Ed.2d 500.

JUSTICE SOUTER delivered the opinion of the Court.

We are called upon to decide whether 2 Live Crew's commercial parody of Roy Orbison's song, "Oh, Pretty Woman," may be a fair use within the meaning of the Copyright Act of 1976, 17 U.S.C. § 107 (1988 ed. and Supp. IV). Although the District Court granted summary judgment for 2 Live Crew, the Court of Appeals reversed, holding the defense of fair use barred by the song's commercial character and excessive borrowing. Because we hold that a parody's commercial character is only one element to be weighed in a fair use enquiry, and that insufficient consideration was given to the nature of parody in weighing the degree of copying, we reverse and remand.

I

In 1964, Roy Orbison and William Dees wrote a rock ballad called "Oh, Pretty Woman" and assigned their rights in it to respondent Acuff–Rose Music, Inc. See Appendix A * * *. Acuff–Rose registered the song for copyright protection.

[Petitioners, a rap music group collectively known as "2 Live Crew," wrote and recorded a song called "Pretty Woman," which one member of the group later described as intended, "through comical lyrics, to satirize the original work." Although the group requested permission to use the respondent's song, offering to pay for it and to afford appropriate credit to the respondent and the authors of the original, respondent refused. Petitioners released the recording anyway, accompanied by the promised credits, on a collection of songs entitled "As Clean As They Wanna Be."]

* * *

Almost a year later, after nearly a quarter of a million copies of the recording had been sold, Acuff–Rose sued 2 Live Crew and its record company, Luke Skywalker Records, for copyright infringement. The District Court granted summary judgment for 2 Live Crew, reasoning that the commercial purpose of 2 Live Crew's song was no bar to fair use; that 2 Live Crew's version was a parody, which "quickly degenerates into a play on words, substituting predictable lyrics with shocking ones" to show "how bland and banal the Orbison song" is; that 2 Live Crew had taken no more than was necessary to "conjure up" the original in order to parody it; and that it was "extremely unlikely that 2 Live Crew's song could adversely affect the market for the original." 754 F. Supp. 1150, 1154–1155, 1157–1158 (M.D.Tenn.1991). The District Court weighed these factors and held that 2 Live Crew's song made fair use of Orbison's original. Id., at 1158–1159.

The Court of Appeals for the Sixth Circuit reversed and remanded. 972 F.2d 1429, 1439 (1992). Although it assumed for the purpose of its opinion that 2 Live Crew's song was a parody of the Orbison original, the Court of Appeals thought the District Court had put too little emphasis on the fact that "every commercial use . . . is presumptively . . . unfair," Sony Corp. of America v. Universal City Studios, Inc., 464 U.S. 417, 451 (1984), and it held that "the admittedly commercial nature" of the parody "requires the conclusion" that the first of four factors relevant under the statute weighs against a finding of fair use. 972 F.2d, at 1435, 1437. Next, the Court of Appeals determined that, by "taking the heart of the original and making it the heart of a new work," 2 Live Crew had, qualitatively, taken too much. Id., at 1438. Finally, after noting that the effect on the potential market for the original (and the market for derivative works) is "undoubtedly the single most important element of fair use," Harper & Row, Publishers, Inc. v. Nation Enterprises, 471 U.S. 539, 566 (1985), the Court of Appeals faulted the District Court for "refusing to indulge the presumption" that "harm for purposes of the fair use analysis has been established by the presumption attaching to commercial uses." 972 F.2d, at 1438–1439. In sum, the court concluded that its "blatantly commercial purpose . . . prevents this parody from being a fair use." Id., at 1439.

We granted certiorari, 507 U.S. 1003 (1993), to determine whether 2 Live Crew's commercial parody could be a fair use.

II

It is uncontested here that 2 Live Crew's song would be an infringement of Acuff–Rose's rights in "Oh, Pretty Woman," under the Copyright Act of 1976, 17 U.S.C. § 106 (1988 ed. and Supp. IV), but for a finding of fair use through parody. From the infancy of copyright protection, some opportunity for fair use of copyrighted materials has been thought necessary to fulfill copyright's very purpose, "to promote the Progress of Science and useful Arts.... " U.S. Const., Art. I, § 8, cl. 8. For as Justice Story explained, "in truth, in literature, in science and in art, there are, and can be, few, if any, things, which in an abstract sense, are strictly new and original throughout. Every book in literature, science and art, borrows, and must necessarily borrow, and use much which was well known and used before." Emerson v. Davies, 8 F. Cas. 615, 619 (No. 4,436) (CCD Mass. 1845). * * *

In Folsom v. Marsh, Justice Story distilled the essence of law and methodology from the earlier cases: "look to the nature and objects of the selections made, the quantity and value of the materials used, and the degree in which the use may prejudice the sale, or diminish the profits, or supersede the objects, of the original work." 9 F. Cas. 342, 348 (No. 4,901) (CCD Mass. 1841). Thus expressed, fair use remained exclusively judge-made doctrine until the passage of [section 107 of] the 1976 Copyright Act, in which Story's summary is discernible[.] * * * Congress meant § 107 "to restate the present judicial doctrine of fair use, not to change, narrow, or enlarge it in any way" and intended that courts continue the common law tradition of fair use adjudication. H. R. Rep. No. 94–1476, p. 66 (1976) (hereinafter House Report); S. Rep. No. 94–473, p. 62 (1975) (hereinafter Senate Report). The fair use doctrine thus "permits [and requires] courts to avoid rigid application of the copyright statute when, on occasion, it would stifle the very creativity which that law is designed to foster." Stewart v. Abend, 495 U.S. 207, 236 (1990) (internal quotation marks and citation omitted).

The task is not to be simplified with bright-line rules, for the statute, like the doctrine it recognizes, calls for case-by-case analysis. Harper & Row, 471 U.S., at 560; Sony, 464 U.S., at 448, and n. 31; House Report, pp. 65–66; Senate Report, p. 62. The text employs the terms "including" and "such as" in the preamble paragraph to indicate the "illustrative and not limitative" function of the examples given, § 101; see Harper & Row, supra, at 561, which thus provide only general guidance about the sorts of copying that courts and Congress most commonly had found to be fair uses.[9] Nor may the four statutory factors be treated in isolation, one from another. All are to be explored, and the results weighed together, in light of the purposes of copyright. * * *

A

The first factor in a fair use enquiry is "the purpose and character of the use, including whether such use is of a commercial nature or is for nonprofit educational purposes." § 107(1). This factor draws on Justice Story's formulation, "the nature and objects of the selections made." Folsom v. Marsh, 9 F. Cas., at 348. The enquiry here may be guided by

9. See Senate Report, p. 62 ("Whether a use referred to in the first sentence of section 107 is a fair use in a particular case will depend upon the application of the determinative factors.")

the examples given in the preamble to § 107, looking to whether the use is for criticism, or comment, or news reporting, and the like, see § 107. The central purpose of this investigation is to see, in Justice Story's words, whether the new work merely "supersedes the objects" of the original creation, Folsom v. Marsh, supra, at 348; accord, Harper & Row, supra, at 562 ("supplanting" the original), or instead adds something new, with a further purpose or different character, altering the first with new expression, meaning, or message; it asks, in other words, whether and to what extent the new work is "transformative." [Leval, Toward a Fair Use Standard, 103 Harv. L. Rev. 1105, 1111 (1990) (hereinafter Leval)] * * *. Although such transformative use is not absolutely necessary for a finding of fair use, Sony, supra, at 455, n.40,[11] the goal of copyright, to promote science and the arts, is generally furthered by the creation of transformative works. Such works thus lie at the heart of the fair use doctrine's guarantee of breathing space within the confines of copyright, see, e.g., Sony, supra, at 478–480 (BLACKMUN, J., dissenting), and the more transformative the new work, the less will be the significance of other factors, like commercialism, that may weigh against a finding of fair use.

This Court has only once before even considered whether parody may be fair use, and that time issued no opinion because of the Court's equal division. Benny v. Loew's Inc., 239 F.2d 532 (C.A.9 1956), aff'd sub nom. Columbia Broadcasting System, Inc. v. Loew's Inc., 356 U.S. 43 (1958). Suffice it to say now that parody has an obvious claim to transformative value, as Acuff–Rose itself does not deny. Like less ostensibly humorous forms of criticism, it can provide social benefit, by shedding light on an earlier work, and, in the process, creating a new one. We thus line up with the courts that have held that parody, like other comment or criticism, may claim fair use under § 107. See, e.g., Fisher v. Dees, 794 F.2d 432 (C.A.9 1986) ("When Sonny Sniffs Glue," a parody of "When Sunny Gets Blue," is fair use); Elsmere Music, Inc. v. National Broadcasting Co., 482 F. Supp. 741 (S.D.N.Y.), aff'd, 623 F.2d 252 (C.A.2 1980) ("I Love Sodom," a "Saturday Night Live" television parody of "I Love New York" is fair use); see also House Report, p. 65; Senate Report, p. 61 ("Use in a parody of some of the content of the work parodied" may be fair use).

The germ of parody lies in the definition of the Greek parodeia, quoted in Judge Nelson's Court of Appeals dissent, as "a song sung alongside another." 972 F.2d, at 1440, quoting 7 Encyclopedia Britannica 768 (15th ed. 1975). Modern dictionaries accordingly describe a parody as a "literary or artistic work that imitates the characteristic style of an author or a work for comic effect or ridicule,"[12] or as a "composition in prose or verse in which the characteristic turns of thought and phrase in an author or class of authors are imitated in such

---

11. The obvious statutory exception to this focus on transformative uses is the straight reproduction of multiple copies for classroom distribution.

12. The American Heritage Dictionary 1317 (3d ed. 1992).

a way as to make them appear ridiculous."[13] For the purposes of copyright law, the nub of the definitions, and the heart of any parodist's claim to quote from existing material, is the use of some elements of a prior author's composition to create a new one that, at least in part, comments on that author's works. See, e.g., Fisher v. Dees, supra, at 437; MCA, Inc. v. Wilson, 677 F.2d 180, 185 (C.A.2 1981). If, on the contrary, the commentary has no critical bearing on the substance or style of the original composition, which the alleged infringer merely uses to get attention or to avoid the drudgery in working up something fresh, the claim to fairness in borrowing from another's work diminishes accordingly (if it does not vanish), and other factors, like the extent of its commerciality, loom larger.[14] Parody needs to mimic an original to make its point, and so has some claim to use the creation of its victim's (or collective victims') imagination, whereas satire can stand on its own two feet and so requires justification for the very act of borrowing.[15] See Ibid.; Bisceglia, Parody and Copyright Protection: Turning the Balancing Act Into a Juggling Act, in ASCAP, Copyright Law Symposium, No. 34, p. 25 (1987).

The fact that parody can claim legitimacy for some appropriation does not, of course, tell either parodist or judge much about where to draw the line. Like a book review quoting the copyrighted material criticized, parody may or may not be fair use, and petitioner's suggestion that any parodic use is presumptively fair has no more justification in law or fact than the equally hopeful claim that any use for news reporting should be presumed fair, see Harper & Row, 471 U.S., at 561. The Act has no hint of an evidentiary preference for parodists over their victims, and no workable presumption for parody could take account of the fact that parody often shades into satire when society is lampooned through its creative artifacts, or that a work may contain both parodic and non-parodic elements. Accordingly, parody, like any other use, has to work its way through the relevant factors, and be judged case by case, in light of the ends of the copyright law.

Here, the District Court held, and the Court of Appeals assumed, that 2 Live Crew's "Pretty Woman" contains parody, commenting on

---

13. 11 The Oxford English Dictionary 247 (2d ed. 1989).

14. A parody that more loosely targets an original than the parody presented here may still be sufficiently aimed at an original work to come within our analysis of parody. If a parody whose wide dissemination in the market runs the risk of serving as a substitute for the original or licensed derivatives (see infra, discussing factor four), it is more incumbent on one claiming fair use to establish the extent of transformation and the parody's critical relationship to the original. By contrast, when there is little or no risk of market substitution, whether because of the large extent of transformation of the earlier work, the new work's minimal dis-

tribution in the market, the small extent to which it borrows from an original, or other factors, taking parodic aim at an original is a less critical factor in the analysis, and looser forms of parody may be found to be fair use, as may satire with lesser justification for the borrowing than would otherwise be required.

15. Satire has been defined as a work "in which prevalent follies or vices are assailed with ridicule," 14 The Oxford English Dictionary 500 (2d ed. 1989), or are "attacked through irony, derision, or wit," The American Heritage Dictionary 1604 (3d ed. 1992).

and criticizing the original work, whatever it may have to say about society at large. As the District Court remarked, the words of 2 Live Crew's song copy the original's first line, but then "quickly degenerate into a play on words, substituting predictable lyrics with shocking ones ... [that] derisively demonstrate how bland and banal the Orbison song seems to them." 754 F. Supp., at 1155 (footnote omitted). Judge Nelson, dissenting below, came to the same conclusion, that the 2 Live Crew song "was clearly intended to ridicule the white-bread original" and "reminds us that sexual congress with nameless streetwalkers is not necessarily the stuff of romance and is not necessarily without its consequences. The singers (there are several) have the same thing on their minds as did the lonely man with the nasal voice, but here there is no hint of wine and roses." 972 F.2d, at 1442. Although the majority below had difficulty discerning any criticism of the original in 2 Live Crew's song, it assumed for purposes of its opinion that there was some. Id., at 1435–1436, and n. 8.

We have less difficulty in finding that critical element in 2 Live Crew's song than the Court of Appeals did, although having found it we will not take the further step of evaluating its quality. The threshold question when fair use is raised in defense of parody is whether a parodic character may reasonably be perceived.[16] Whether, going beyond that, parody is in good taste or bad does not and should not matter to fair use. As Justice Holmes explained, "it would be a dangerous undertaking for persons trained only to the law to constitute themselves final judges of the worth of [a work], outside of the narrowest and most obvious limits. At the one extreme some works of genius would be sure to miss appreciation. Their very novelty would make them repulsive until the public had learned the new language in which their author spoke." Bleistein v. Donaldson Lithographing Co., 188 U.S. 239, 251 (1903) (circus posters have copyright protection); cf. Yankee Publishing Inc. v. News America Publishing, Inc., 809 F. Supp. 267, 280 (S.D.N.Y. 1992) (Leval, J.) ("First Amendment protections do not apply only to those who speak clearly, whose jokes are funny, and whose parodies succeed") (trademark case).

While we might not assign a high rank to the parodic element here, we think it fair to say that 2 Live Crew's song reasonably could be perceived as commenting on the original or criticizing it, to some degree. 2 Live Crew juxtaposes the romantic musings of a man whose fantasy comes true, with degrading taunts, a bawdy demand for sex, and a sigh of relief from paternal responsibility. The later words can be taken as a comment on the naivete of the original of an earlier day, as a rejection of its sentiment that ignores the ugliness of street life and the debasement that it signifies. It is this joinder of reference and ridicule that marks off

---

16. The only further judgment, indeed, that a court may pass on a work goes to an assessment of whether the parodic element is slight or great, and the copying small or extensive in relation to the parodic element, for a work with slight parodic element and extensive copying will be more likely to merely "supersede the objects" of the original. * * *

the author's choice of parody from the other types of comment and criticism that traditionally have had a claim to fair use protection as transformative works.[17]

The Court of Appeals, however, immediately cut short the enquiry into 2 Live Crew's fair use claim by confining its treatment of the first factor essentially to one relevant fact, the commercial nature of the use. The court then inflated the significance of this fact by applying a presumption ostensibly culled from Sony, that "every commercial use of copyrighted material is presumptively ... unfair.... " Sony, 464 U.S., at 451. In giving virtually dispositive weight to the commercial nature of the parody, the Court of Appeals erred.

The language of the statute makes clear that the commercial or nonprofit educational purpose of a work is only one element of the first factor enquiry into its purpose and character. Section 107(1) uses the term "including" to begin the dependent clause referring to commercial use, and the main clause speaks of a broader investigation into "purpose and character." As we explained in Harper & Row, Congress resisted attempts to narrow the ambit of this traditional enquiry by adopting categories of presumptively fair use, and it urged courts to preserve the breadth of their traditionally ample view of the universe of relevant evidence. 471 U.S., at 561; House Report, p. 66. Accordingly, the mere fact that a use is educational and not for profit does not insulate it from a finding of infringement, any more than the commercial character of a use bars a finding of fairness. If, indeed, commerciality carried presumptive force against a finding of fairness, the presumption would swallow nearly all of the illustrative uses listed in the preamble paragraph of § 107, including news reporting, comment, criticism, teaching, scholarship, and research, since these activities "are generally conducted for profit in this country." Harper & Row, supra, at 592 (Brennan, J., dissenting). Congress could not have intended such a rule, which certainly is not inferable from the common-law cases, arising as they did from the world of letters in which Samuel Johnson could pronounce that "no man but a blockhead ever wrote, except for money." 3 Boswell's Life of Johnson 19 (G. Hill ed. 1934).

Sony itself called for no hard evidentiary presumption. There, we emphasized the need for a "sensitive balancing of interests," 464 U.S., at 455, n. 40, noted that Congress had "eschewed a rigid, bright-line approach to fair use," id., at 449, n. 31, and stated that the commercial or nonprofit educational character of a work is "not conclusive," id., at 448–449, but rather a fact to be "weighed along with others in fair use decisions." Id., at 449, n. 32 (quoting House Report, p. 66). The Court of

---

17. We note in passing that 2 Live Crew need not label its whole album, or even this song, a parody in order to claim fair use protection, nor should 2 Live Crew be penalized for this being its first parodic essay. Parody serves its goals whether labeled or not, and there is no reason to require paro-dy to state the obvious, (or even the reasonably perceived). See [Patry & Perlmutter, Fair Use Misconstrued: Profit, Presumptions, and Parody, 11 Cardozo Arts & Ent. L. J. 667, 716–17 (1993) (hereinafter Patry & Perlmutter)] * * *.

Appeals's elevation of one sentence from Sony to a per se rule thus runs as much counter to Sony itself as to the long common-law tradition of fair use adjudication. Rather, as we explained in Harper & Row, Sony stands for the proposition that the "fact that a publication was commercial as opposed to nonprofit is a separate factor that tends to weigh against a finding of fair use." 471 U.S., at 562. But that is all, and the fact that even the force of that tendency will vary with the context is a further reason against elevating commerciality to hard presumptive significance. The use, for example, of a copyrighted work to advertise a product, even in a parody, will be entitled to less indulgence under the first factor of the fair use enquiry, than the sale of a parody for its own sake, let alone one performed a single time by students in school.[18]
* * *

B

The second statutory factor, "the nature of the copyrighted work," § 107(2), draws on Justice Story's expression, the "value of the materials used." Folsom v. Marsh, 9 F. Cas., at 348. This factor calls for recognition that some works are closer to the core of intended copyright protection than others, with the consequence that fair use is more difficult to establish when the former works are copied. See, e.g., Stewart v. Abend, 495 U.S., at 237–238 (contrasting fictional short story with factual works); Harper & Row, 471 U.S., at 563–564 (contrasting soon-to-be-published memoir with published speech); Sony, 464 U.S., at 455, n. 40 (contrasting motion pictures with news broadcasts); Feist, 499 U.S., at 348–351 (contrasting creative works with bare factual compilations); 3 M. Nimmer & D. Nimmer, Nimmer on Copyright § 13.05[A][2] (1993) (hereinafter Nimmer); Leval 1116. We agree with both the District Court and the Court of Appeals that the Orbison original's creative expression for public dissemination falls within the core of the copyright's protective purposes. 754 F. Supp., at 1155–1156; 972 F.2d, at 1437. This fact, however, is not much help in this case, or ever likely to help much in separating the fair use sheep from the infringing goats in a parody case, since parodies almost invariably copy publicly known, expressive works.

C

The third factor asks whether "the amount and substantiality of the portion used in relation to the copyrighted work as a whole," § 107(3)

---

18. Finally, regardless of the weight one might place on the alleged infringer's state of mind, compare Harper & Row, 471 U.S., at 562 (fair use presupposes good faith and fair dealing) (quotation marks omitted), with Folsom v. Marsh, 9 F.Cas. 342, 349 (No. 4,901) (CCD Mass. 1841) (good faith does not bar a finding of infringement); Leval 1126–1127 (good faith irrelevant to fair use analysis), we reject Acuff–Rose's argument that 2 Live Crew's request for permission to use the original should be weighed against a finding of fair use. Even if good faith were central to fair use, 2 Live Crew's actions do not necessarily suggest that they believed their version was not fair use; the offer may simply have been made in a good faith effort to avoid this litigation. If the use is otherwise fair, then no permission need be sought or granted. Thus, being denied permission to use a work does not weigh against a finding of fair use. See Fisher v. Dees, 794 F.2d 432, 437 (C.A.9 1986).

(or, in Justice Story's words, "the quantity and value of the materials used," Folsom v. Marsh, supra, at 348) are reasonable in relation to the purpose of the copying. Here, attention turns to the persuasiveness of a parodist's justification for the particular copying done, and the enquiry will harken back to the first of the statutory factors, for, as in prior cases, we recognize that the extent of permissible copying varies with the purpose and character of the use. See Sony, 464 U.S., at 449–450 (reproduction of entire work "does not have its ordinary effect of militating against a finding of fair use" as to home videotaping of television programs); Harper & Row, 471 U.S., at 564 ("Even substantial quotations might qualify as fair use in a review of a published work or a news account of a speech" but not in a scoop of a soon-to-be-published memoir). The facts bearing on this factor will also tend to address the fourth, by revealing the degree to which the parody may serve as a market substitute for the original or potentially licensed derivatives. See Leval 1123.

The District Court considered the song's parodic purpose in finding that 2 Live Crew had not helped themselves overmuch. 754 F. Supp., at 1156–1157. The Court of Appeals disagreed, stating that "while it may not be inappropriate to find that no more was taken than necessary, the copying was qualitatively substantial.... We conclude that taking the heart of the original and making it the heart of a new work was to purloin a substantial portion of the essence of the original." 972 F.2d, at 1438.

The Court of Appeals is of course correct that this factor calls for thought not only about the quantity of the materials used, but about their quality and importance, too. In Harper & Row, for example, the Nation had taken only some 300 words out of President Ford's memoirs, but we signalled the significance of the quotations in finding them to amount to "the heart of the book," the part most likely to be newsworthy and important in licensing serialization. 471 U.S., at 564–566, 568 (internal quotation marks omitted). We also agree with the Court of Appeals that whether "a substantial portion of the infringing work was copied verbatim" from the copyrighted work is a relevant question, see id., at 565, for it may reveal a dearth of transformative character or purpose under the first factor, or a greater likelihood of market harm under the fourth; a work composed primarily of an original, particularly its heart, with little added or changed, is more likely to be a merely superseding use, fulfilling demand for the original.

Where we part company with the court below is in applying these guides to parody, and in particular to parody in the song before us. Parody presents a difficult case. Parody's humor, or in any event its comment, necessarily springs from recognizable allusion to its object through distorted imitation. Its art lies in the tension between a known original and its parodic twin. When parody takes aim at a particular original work, the parody must be able to "conjure up" at least enough of that original to make the object of its critical wit recognizable. See, e.g., Elsmere Music, 623 F.2d, at 253, n. 1; Fisher v. Dees, 794 F.2d, at

438–439. What makes for this recognition is quotation of the original's most distinctive or memorable features, which the parodist can be sure the audience will know. Once enough has been taken to assure identification, how much more is reasonable will depend, say, on the extent to which the song's overriding purpose and character is to parody the original or, in contrast, the likelihood that the parody may serve as a market substitute for the original. But using some characteristic features cannot be avoided.

We think the Court of Appeals was insufficiently appreciative of parody's need for the recognizable sight or sound when it ruled 2 Live Crew's use unreasonable as a matter of law. It is true, of course, that 2 Live Crew copied the characteristic opening bass riff (or musical phrase) of the original, and true that the words of the first line copy the Orbison lyrics. But if quotation of the opening riff and the first line may be said to go to the "heart" of the original, the heart is also what most readily conjures up the song for parody, and it is the heart at which parody takes aim. Copying does not become excessive in relation to parodic purpose merely because the portion taken was the original's heart. If 2 Live Crew had copied a significantly less memorable part of the original, it is difficult to see how its parodic character would have come through. See Fisher v. Dees, 794 F.2d, at 439.

This is not, of course, to say that anyone who calls himself a parodist can skim the cream and get away scot free. In parody, as in news reporting, see Harper & Row, supra, context is everything, and the question of fairness asks what else the parodist did besides go to the heart of the original. It is significant that 2 Live Crew not only copied the first line of the original, but thereafter departed markedly from the Orbison lyrics for its own ends. 2 Live Crew not only copied the bass riff and repeated it,[19] but also produced otherwise distinctive sounds, interposing "scraper" noise, overlaying the music with solos in different keys, and altering the drum beat. See 754 F. Supp., at 1155. This is not a case, then, where "a substantial portion" of the parody itself is composed of a "verbatim" copying of the original. It is not, that is, a case where the parody is so insubstantial, as compared to the copying, that the third factor must be resolved as a matter of law against the parodists.

Suffice it to say here that, as to the lyrics, we think the Court of Appeals correctly suggested that "no more was taken than necessary," 972 F.2d, at 1438, but just for that reason, we fail to see how the copying can be excessive in relation to its parodic purpose, even if the portion taken is the original's "heart." As to the music, we express no opinion whether repetition of the bass riff is excessive copying, and we remand to permit evaluation of the amount taken, in light of the song's parodic purpose and character, its transformative elements, and considerations of the potential for market substitution sketched more fully below.

---

19. This may serve to heighten the comic effect of the parody, as one witness stated * * *; see also Elsmere Music, Inc. v. National Broadcasting Co., 482 F. Supp. 741, 747 (S.D.N.Y.1980) (repetition of "I Love Sodom"), or serve to dazzle with the original's music, as Acuff–Rose now contends.

D

The fourth fair use factor is "the effect of the use upon the potential market for or value of the copyrighted work." § 107(4). It requires courts to consider not only the extent of market harm caused by the particular actions of the alleged infringer, but also "whether unrestricted and widespread conduct of the sort engaged in by the defendant ... would result in a substantially adverse impact on the potential market" for the original. Nimmer § 13.05[A][4], p. 13–102.61 (footnote omitted); accord Harper & Row, 471 U.S., at 569; Senate Report, p. 65; Folsom v. Marsh, 9 F. Cas., at 349. The enquiry "must take account not only of harm to the original but also of harm to the market for derivative works." Harper & Row, supra, at 568.

Since fair use is an affirmative defense,[20] its proponent would have difficulty carrying the burden of demonstrating fair use without favorable evidence about relevant markets.[21] In moving for summary judgment, 2 Live Crew left themselves at just such a disadvantage when they failed to address the effect on the market for rap derivatives, and confined themselves to uncontroverted submissions that there was no likely effect on the market for the original. They did not, however, thereby subject themselves to the evidentiary presumption applied by the Court of Appeals. In assessing the likelihood of significant market harm, the Court of Appeals quoted from language in Sony that " 'if the intended use is for commercial gain, that likelihood may be presumed. But if it is for a noncommercial purpose, the likelihood must be demonstrated.' " 972 F.2d, at 1438, quoting Sony, 464 U.S., at 451. The court reasoned that because "the use of the copyrighted work is wholly commercial, ... we presume a likelihood of future harm to Acuff–Rose exists." 972 F.2d, at 1438. In so doing, the court resolved the fourth factor against 2 Live Crew, just as it had the first, by applying a presumption about the effect of commercial use, a presumption which as applied here we hold to be error.

No "presumption" or inference of market harm that might find support in Sony is applicable to a case involving something beyond mere duplication for commercial purposes. Sony's discussion of a presumption contrasts a context of verbatim copying of the original in its entirety for commercial purposes, with the non-commercial context of Sony itself (home copying of television programming). In the former circumstances, what Sony said simply makes common sense: when a commercial use amounts to mere duplication of the entirety of an original, it clearly "supersedes the objects," Folsom v. Marsh, 9 F. Cas., at 348, of the

20. Harper & Row, 471 U.S., at 561; H. R. Rep. No. 102–836, p. 3, n. 3 (1992).

21. Even favorable evidence, without more, is no guarantee of fairness. Judge Leval gives the example of the film producer's appropriation of a composer's previously unknown song that turns the song into a commercial success; the boon to the song does not make the film's simple copying fair. Leval 1124, n. 84. This factor, no less than the other three, may be addressed only through a "sensitive balancing of interests." Sony, 464 U.S., at 455, n. 40. Market harm is a matter of degree, and the importance of this factor will vary, not only with the amount of harm, but also with the relative strength of the showing on the other factors.

original and serves as a market replacement for it, making it likely that cognizable market harm to the original will occur. Sony, 464 U.S., at 451. But when, on the contrary, the second use is transformative, market substitution is at least less certain, and market harm may not be so readily inferred. Indeed, as to parody pure and simple, it is more likely that the new work will not affect the market for the original in a way cognizable under this factor, that is, by acting as a substitute for it ("superseding [its] objects"). See Leval 1125; Patry & Perlmutter 692, 697–698. This is so because the parody and the original usually serve different market functions. Bisceglia, ASCAP, Copyright Law Symposium, No. 34, p. 23.

We do not, of course, suggest that a parody may not harm the market at all, but when a lethal parody, like a scathing theater review, kills demand for the original, it does not produce a harm cognizable under the Copyright Act. Because "parody may quite legitimately aim at garroting the original, destroying it commercially as well as artistically," B. Kaplan, An Unhurried View of Copyright 69 (1967), the role of the courts is to distinguish between "biting criticism [that merely] suppresses demand [and] copyright infringement[, which] usurps it." Fisher v. Dees, 794 F.2d, at 438.

This distinction between potentially remediable displacement and unremediable disparagement is reflected in the rule that there is no protectable derivative market for criticism. The market for potential derivative uses includes only those that creators of original works would in general develop or license others to develop. Yet the unlikelihood that creators of imaginative works will license critical reviews or lampoons of their own productions removes such uses from the very notion of a potential licensing market. "People ask ... for criticism, but they only want praise." S. Maugham, Of Human Bondage 241 (Penguin ed. 1992). Thus, to the extent that the opinion below may be read to have considered harm to the market for parodies of "Oh, Pretty Woman," see 972 F.2d, at 1439, the court erred. Accord, Fisher v. Dees, 794 F.2d, at 437; Leval 1125; Patry & Perlmutter 688–691.[22]

In explaining why the law recognizes no derivative market for critical works, including parody, we have, of course, been speaking of the later work as if it had nothing but a critical aspect (i.e., "parody pure and simple," supra, at 22). But the later work may have a more complex character, with effects not only in the arena of criticism but also in protectable markets for derivative works, too. In that sort of case, the law looks beyond the criticism to the other elements of the work, as it does here. 2 Live Crew's song comprises not only parody but also rap music, and the derivative market for rap music is a proper focus of enquiry, see Harper & Row, 471 U.S., at 568; Nimmer § 13.05[B]. Evidence of substantial harm to it would weigh against a finding of fair

---

22. We express no opinion as to the derivative markets for works using elements of an original as vehicles for satire or amusement, making no comment on the original or criticism of it.

use,[23] because the licensing of derivatives is an important economic incentive to the creation of originals. See 17 U.S.C. § 106(2) (copyright owner has rights to derivative works). Of course, the only harm to derivatives that need concern us, as discussed above, is the harm of market substitution. The fact that a parody may impair the market for derivative uses by the very effectiveness of its critical commentary is no more relevant under copyright than the like threat to the original market.[24]

Although 2 Live Crew submitted uncontroverted affidavits on the question of market harm to the original, neither they, nor Acuff–Rose, introduced evidence or affidavits addressing the likely effect of 2 Live Crew's parodic rap song on the market for a non-parody, rap version of "Oh, Pretty Woman." * * * [I]t is impossible to deal with the fourth factor except by recognizing that a silent record on an important factor bearing on fair use disentitled the proponent of the defense, 2 Live Crew, to summary judgment. The evidentiary hole will doubtless be plugged on remand.

III

It was error for the Court of Appeals to conclude that the commercial nature of 2 Live Crew's parody of "Oh, Pretty Woman" rendered it presumptively unfair. No such evidentiary presumption is available to address either the first factor, the character and purpose of the use, or the fourth, market harm, in determining whether a transformative use, such as parody, is a fair one. The court also erred in holding that 2 Live Crew had necessarily copied excessively from the Orbison original, considering the parodic purpose of the use. We therefore reverse the judgment of the Court of Appeals and remand for further proceedings consistent with this opinion.

It is so ordered.

Appendix A

"Oh, Pretty Woman" by Roy Orbison and William Dees

Pretty Woman, walking down the street,
Pretty Woman, the kind I like to meet,
Pretty Woman, I don't believe you, you're not the truth,
No one could look as good as you
Mercy
Pretty Woman, won't you pardon me,
Pretty Woman, I couldn't help but see,

---

23. See Nimmer § 13.05[A][4], p. 13–102.61 ("a substantially adverse impact on the potential market"); Leval 1125 ("reasonably substantial" harm); Patry & Perlmutter 697–698 (same).

24. In some cases it may be difficult to determine whence the harm flows. In such cases, the other fair use factors may provide some indicia of the likely source of the harm. A work whose overriding purpose and character is parodic and whose borrowing is slight in relation to its parody will be far less likely to cause cognizable harm than a work with little parodic content and much copying.

Pretty Woman, that you look lovely as can be
Are you lonely just like me?
Pretty Woman, stop a while,
Pretty Woman, talk a while,
Pretty Woman give your smile to me
Pretty Woman, yeah, yeah, yeah
Pretty Woman, look my way,
Pretty Woman, say you'll stay with me
'Cause I need you, I'll treat you right
Come to me baby, Be mine tonight
Pretty Woman, don't walk on by,
Pretty Woman, don't make me cry,
Pretty Woman, don't walk away,
Hey, O. K.
If that's the way it must be, O. K.
I guess I'll go on home, it's late
There'll be tomorrow night, but wait!
What do I see
Is she walking back to me?
Yeah, she's walking back to me!
Oh, Pretty Woman.

Appendix B

"Pretty Woman" as Recorded by 2 Live Crew

Pretty woman walkin' down the street
Pretty woman girl you look so sweet
Pretty woman you bring me down to that knee
Pretty woman you make me wanna beg please
Oh, pretty woman
Big hairy woman you need to shave that stuff
Big hairy woman you know I bet it's tough
Big hairy woman all that hair it ain't legit
'Cause you look like 'Cousin It'
Big hairy woman
Bald headed woman girl your hair won't grow
Bald headed woman you got a teeny weeny afro
Bald headed woman you know your hair could look nice
Bald headed woman first you got to roll it with rice
Bald headed woman here, let me get this hunk of biz for ya
Ya know what I'm saying you look better than rice a roni
Oh bald headed woman
Big hairy woman come on in
And don't forget your bald headed friend
Hey pretty woman let the boys
Jump in
Two timin' woman girl you know you ain't right
Two timin' woman you's out with my boy last night
Two timin' woman that takes a load off my mind
Two timin' woman now I know the baby ain't mine

Oh, two timin' woman
Oh pretty woman

Notes

1. Concurring in *Campbell*, but expressing some doubt as to whether 2 Live Crew's song was "a legitimate parody," Justice Kennedy stated that:

> * * * [P]arody may qualify as fair use only if it draws upon the original composition to make humorous or ironic commentary about that same composition. It is not enough that the parody use the original in a humorous fashion, however creative that humor may be. The parody must target the original, and not just its general style, the genre of art to which it belongs, or society as a whole (although if it targets the original, it may target those features as well). * * *

> * * *

> * * * Almost any revamped modern version of a familiar composition can be construed as a "comment on the naivete of the original," *ante*, at 1173, because of the difference in style and because it will be amusing to hear how the old tune sounds in the new genre. Just the thought of a rap version of Beethoven's Fifth Symphony or "Achy, Breaky Heart" is bound to make people smile. If we allow any weak transformation to qualify as parody, however, we weaken the protection of copyright. * * *

510 U.S. at 597, 599, 114 S.Ct. at 1180, 1181. How does this view of the scope of fair use protection for parody compare with the views expressed by the majority?

2. The *Campbell* majority distinguishes between parody and satire for purposes of the fair use analysis. Is this distinction persuasive? Practicable? How should the court resolve the question reserved in note 22? Consider the following specific examples in your response:

> (a) Defendant, a professional political humorist, writes and performs a humorous song, containing pointed social commentary about the United States military establishment, which uses the music and some of the lyrics of the well-known Marine Corps Hymn.

> (b) Defendant writes a song that is intended as a parody but is not perceived as one because where the consumers who purchase the sound recording of the parody are either unfamiliar with the original version (and simply want to listen to the parodic version for its own sake), or else simply do not perceive the intended criticism of the original.

> (c) Defendant writes a song that is intended simply as a humorous or irreverent variation on another work but is perceived by at least some listeners as a parody, satire, or other form of criticism.

3. Compare *Sony*, *Harper & Row*, and *Campbell* in answering the following: (a) In a fair use case, which party bears the burden of establishing the presence or absence of injury to the market for the plaintiff's work? (b) Once injury to the market for the plaintiff's work has been established, which party must prove the cause of the injury—that is, must the defendant

prove that the injury was caused by factors other than substitution of the defendant's work for the plaintiff's work, or must the plaintiff prove that no other factors caused the injury?

4. The *Campbell* majority defines the "market" for a work narrowly for purposes of evaluating the fourth factor: "The market for potential derivative uses includes only those that creators of original works would in general develop or license others to develop." Is this akin to a "reasonable copyright owner" standard? Is it circular? Does—and should—the standard take account of different levels of entrepreneurship between different copyright owners? Does this standard make allowance for future technological and market developments? (Consider, for example, whether the market for articles in a daily financial newspaper should be considered to include the use of those articles as teaching materials in a business school.)

5. In *American Geophysical Union v. Texaco, Inc.*, 60 F.3d 913, 926 (2d Cir.1994), the Second Circuit observed:

> Prior to Campbell, the Supreme Court had characterized the fourth factor as "the single most important element of fair use," *Harper & Row*, 471 U.S. at 566 * * *. However, Campbell's discussion of the fourth factor conspicuously omits this phrasing. Apparently abandoning the idea that any factor enjoys primacy, Campbell instructs that "all [four factors] are to be explored, and the results weighed together, in light of the purposes of copyright." 114 S.Ct. at 1171.

Do you agree with the Second Circuit's interpretation of *Campbell*? Can such a shift in emphasis improve the fair use analysis?

SUNTRUST BANK v. HOUGHTON MIFFLIN COMPANY

United States Court of Appeals, Eleventh Circuit, 2001.
268 F.3d 1257.

BIRCH, CIRCUIT JUDGE:

In this opinion, we decide whether publication of The Wind Done Gone ("*TWDG*"), a fictional work admittedly based on Margaret Mitchell's Gone With the Wind ("*GWTW*"), should be enjoined from publication based on alleged copyright violations. The district court granted a preliminary injunction against publication of *TWDG* because it found that Plaintiff–Appellee Suntrust Bank ("Suntrust") met the four-part test governing preliminary injunctions. * * *

I. BACKGROUND

A. *Procedural History*

Suntrust is the trustee of the Mitchell Trust, which holds the copyright in *GWTW*. Since its publication in 1936, *GWTW* has become one of the best-selling books in the world, second in sales only to the Bible. The Mitchell Trust has actively managed the copyright, authorizing derivative works and a variety of commercial items. It has entered into a contract authorizing, under specified conditions, a second sequel to *GWTW* to be published by St. Martin's Press. The Mitchell Trust maintains the copyright in all of the derivative works as well. *See* 17 U.S.C. § 103.[1]

Alice Randall, the author of *TWDG*, persuasively claims that her novel is a critique of *GWTW*'s depiction of slavery and the Civil–War era American South. To this end, she appropriated the characters, plot and major scenes from *GWTW* into the first half of *TWDG*. According to Suntrust, *TWDG* "(1) explicitly refers to [*GWTW*] in its foreword; (2) copies core characters, character traits, and relationships from [*GWTW*]; (3) copies and summarizes famous scenes and other elements of the plot from [*GWTW*]; and (4) copies verbatim dialogues and descriptions from [*GWTW*]." *Suntrust Bank v. Houghton Mifflin Co.,* 136 F.Supp.2d 1357, 1364 (N.D.Ga.2001), *vacated,* 252 F.3d 1165 (11th Cir.2001). Defendant–Appellant Houghton Mifflin, the publisher of *TWDG*, does not contest the first three allegations,[2] but nonetheless argues that there is no substantial similarity between the two works or, in the alternative, that the doctrine of fair use protects *TWDG* because it is primarily a parody of *GWTW*.

After discovering the similarities between the books, Suntrust asked Houghton Mifflin to refrain from publication or distribution of *TWDG*, but Houghton Mifflin refused the request. Subsequently, Suntrust filed an action alleging copyright infringement, violation of the Lanham Act, and deceptive trade practices, and immediately filed a motion for a temporary restraining order and a preliminary injunction. * * *

II. DISCUSSION

Our primary focus at this stage of the case is on the appropriateness of the injunctive relief granted by the district court. In our analysis, we must evaluate the merits of Suntrust's copyright infringement claim, including Houghton Mifflin's affirmative defense of fair use.[3] As we assess the fair-use defense, we examine to what extent a critic may use a work to communicate her criticism of the work without infringing the copyright in that work. To approach these issues in the proper framework, we should initially review the history of the Constitution's Copyright Clause and understand its relationship to the First Amendment.

---

1. Hereafter, the Copyright Act of 1976 shall be referred to by only the section number of the Act.

2. Houghton Mifflin denies that there are passages from *GWTW* copied verbatim in *TWDG*.

3. I believe that fair use should be considered an affirmative *right* under the 1976 Act, rather than merely an affirmative defense, as it is defined in the Act as a use that is not a violation of copyright. *See Bateman v. Mnemonics, Inc.,* 79 F.3d 1532, 1542 n. 22 (11th Cir.1996). However, fair use is commonly referred to as an affirma-tive defense, *see Campbell v. Acuff–Rose Music, Inc.,* 510 U.S. 569, 590, 114 S.Ct. 1164, 1177, 127 L.Ed.2d 500 (1994), and, as we are bound by Supreme Court precedent, we will apply it as such. *See also* David Nimmer, *A Riff on Fair Use in the Digital Millennium Copyright Act,* 148 U. PA. L. REV. 673, 714 n. 227 (2000) (citing *Bateman*). Nevertheless, the fact that the fair use right must be procedurally asserted as an affirmative defense does not detract from its constitutional significance as a guarantor to access and use for First Amendment purposes.

A. History and Development of the Copyright Clause

The Copyright Clause finds its roots in England, where, in 1710, the Statute of Anne "was designed to destroy the booksellers' monopoly of the booktrade and to prevent its recurrence." L. Ray Patterson, *Understanding the Copyright Clause,* 47 J. COPYRIGHT SOC'Y USA 365, 379 (2000). This Parliamentary statute assigned copyright in books to authors, added a requirement that only a new work could be copyrighted, and limited the duration, which had been perpetual, to two fourteen-year terms. 8 Anne, C.19 (1710), *reprinted in* 8 Melville B. Nimmer & David Nimmer, *Nimmer on Copyright* § 7–5 (2001). It is clear that the goal of the Statute of Anne was to encourage creativity and ensure that the public would have free access to information by putting an end to "the continued use of copyright as a device of censorship." Patterson at 379.[4] The Framers of the U.S. Constitution relied on this statute when drafting the Copyright Clause of our Constitution,[5] which reads,

> The Congress shall have Power ... to promote the Progress of Science ... by securing for limited Times to Authors ... the exclusive Right to their respective Writings....

U.S. CONST. art. 1, § 8, cl. 8. Congress directly transferred the principles from the Statute of Anne into the copyright law of the United States in 1783, first through a recommendation to the states to enact similar copyright laws,[6] and then in 1790, with the passage of the first American federal copyright statute.[7]

The Copyright Clause was intended "to be the engine of free expression." *Harper & Row Publishers, Inc. v. Nation Enters.,* 471 U.S. 539, 558, 105 S.Ct. 2218, 2229, 85 L.Ed.2d 588 (1985). To that end, copyright laws have been enacted to achieve three main goals: the promotion of learning, the protection of the public domain, and the granting of an exclusive right to the author.

1. Promotion of Learning

In the United States, copyright has always been used to promote learning by guarding against censorship.[8] Throughout the nineteenth

4. The Statute of Anne providing for copyright is introduced as "[a]n act for the encouragement of learning," and has a preamble that states one of the purposes as "the encouragement of learned men to compose and write useful books." 8 Anne, C.19 (1710), *reprinted in* 8 Nimmer § 7–5.

5. *See* Edward C. Walterscheid, *The Remarkable-and-Irrational-Disparity Between the Patent Term and the Copyright Term,* 83 J. PAT. & TRADEMARK OFF. SOC'Y 233, 235 (2001) ("The American Copyright Act of 1790 simply copied this same basic scheme [from the Statute of Anne] into the new American copyright law."); Pierre N. Leval, *Nimmer Lecture: Fair Use Rescued,* 44 UCLA L. REV. 1449, 1450 (1997) ("The law of copyright, [was] fashioned by the

Statute of Anne in 1710 and recognized in our Constitution.").

6. "Resolution of the Continental Congress Respecting Copyright" (1783), *reprinted in* 8 Nimmer § 7–11.

7. 1 Stat. 124 (May 31, 1790), *reprinted in* 8 Nimmer § 7–41 ("AN ACT for the encouragement of learning ...").

8. *See* Jane C. Ginsburg, *Creation and Commercial Value: Copyright Protection in Works of Information,* 90 COLUM. L. REV. 1865, 1873 (1990) ("[T]he 1710 English Statute of Anne, the 1787 United States Constitution, and the 1790 United States federal copyright statute all characterized copyright as a device to promote the advancement of knowledge.").

century, the copyright in literature was limited to the right "to publish and vend books." Patterson, at 383. The term "copy" was interpreted literally; an author had the right only to prevent others from copying and selling her particular literary work. See Stowe v. Thomas, 23 F. Cas. 201 (C.C.E.D.Pa.1853) (holding that a translation of *Uncle Tom's Cabin* into German was not a copyright infringement because it was not a copy of the work as it was published).[9] This limited right ensured that a maximum number of new works would be created and published. It was not until the 1909 Act, which codified the concept of a derivative work, that an author's right to protect his original work against imitation was established. This change more closely represents current statutory copyright law and is consistent with copyright's constitutional mandate.

As a further protection of the public interest, until 1976, statutory copyright law required that a work be published before an author was entitled to a copyright in that work. Therefore, in order to have the sole right of publication for the statutory period, the author was first required to make the work available to the public. In 1976, copyright was extended to include any work "fixed in any tangible medium of expression" in order to adapt the law to technological advances. § 102(a). Thus, the publication requirement was removed, but the fair use right was codified to maintain the constitutionally mandated balance to ensure that the public has access to knowledge.

The Copyright Act promotes public access to knowledge because it provides an economic incentive for authors to publish books and disseminate ideas to the public. *Harper & Row,* 471 U.S. at 558, 105 S.Ct. at 2229 ("By establishing a marketable right to the use of one's expression, copyright supplies the economic incentive to create and disseminate ideas."). The Supreme Court has recognized that "[t]he monopoly created by copyright thus rewards the individual author in order to benefit the public." *Id.* at 546, 105 S.Ct. at 2223 (quoting *Sony Corp. of America v. Univ. City Studios, Inc.,* 464 U.S. 417, 477, 104 S.Ct. 774, 807, 78 L.Ed.2d 574 (1984) (Blackmun, J., dissenting)). Without the limited monopoly, authors would have little economic incentive to create and publish their work. Therefore, by providing this incentive, the copyright law promotes the public access to new ideas and concepts.

2. Protection of the Public Domain

The second goal of the Copyright Clause is to ensure that works enter the public domain after an author's rights, exclusive, but limited, have expired. Parallel to the patent regime, the limited time period of the copyright serves the dual purpose of ensuring that the work will enter the public domain and ensuring that the author has received "a fair return for [her] labors." *Harper & Row,* 471 U.S. at 546, 105 S.Ct. at 2223. This limited grant "is intended to motivate the creative activity

---

9. Under modern copyright, such a right to translate would enjoy protection as a "derivative work." §§ 101 and 106. In *Folsom v. Marsh,* 9 F.Cas. 342 (C.C.Mass. 1841), Justice Story created the concept of "fair use," which actually expanded the copyright monopoly, since until that time a translation or abridgement was not considered an infringement.

of authors ... by the provision of a special reward, and to allow the public access to the products of their genius after the limited period of exclusive control has expired." *Sony,* 464 U.S. at 429, 104 S.Ct. at 782. The public is protected in two ways: the grant of a copyright encourages authors to create new works, as discussed in section II.A.1., and the limitation ensures that the works will eventually enter the public domain, which protects the public's right of access and use.[10]

3. *Exclusive Rights of the Author*

Finally, the Copyright Clause grants the author limited exclusive rights in order to encourage the creation of original works. Before our copyright jurisprudence developed, there were two separate theories of copyright in England—the natural law copyright, which was the right of perpetual publication, and the statutory copyright, which was the limited-time copyright. The natural law copyright, which is not a part of our system, implied an ownership in the work itself, and thus was preferred by the booksellers and publishers striving to maintain their monopoly over literature as well as by the Crown to silence "seditious" writings. Even after passage of the Statute of Anne, the publishers and booksellers resisted the loss of their monopoly in the courts for more than sixty years. Finally, in 1774, the House of Lords ruled that the natural law copyright, that is, the ownership of the work itself, expires upon publication of the book, when the statutory copyright attaches. Patterson at 382.

This bifurcated system was carried over into our copyright law. As of the 1909 Act, an author had "state common law protection [that] persisted until the moment of general publication." *Estate of Martin Luther King, Jr. v. CBS, Inc.,* 194 F.3d 1211, 1214 (11th Cir.1999). After the work was published, the author was entitled to federal statutory copyright protection if she had complied with certain federal requirements (i.e. publication with notice). If not, the work was released into the public domain. *Id.* The system illustrates that the author's ownership is in the copyright, and not in the work itself, for if the author had an ownership interest in the work itself, she would not lose that right if she published the book without complying with federal statutory copyright requirements. Compliance with the copyright law results in the guarantee of copyright to the author for a limited time, but the author never owns the work itself. § 202 ("Ownership of a copyright, or of any of the exclusive rights under a copyright, is distinct from ownership of any material object in which the work is embodied.").

This has an important impact on modern interpretation of copyright, as it emphasizes the distinction between ownership of the work, which an author does not possess, and ownership of the copyright, which an author enjoys for a limited time. In a society oriented toward property ownership, it is not surprising to find many that erroneously equate the

---

10. *See Feist Publications, Inc. v. Rural Tel. Serv. Co.,* 499 U.S. 340, 349, 111 S.Ct. 1282, 1290, 113 L.Ed.2d 358 (1991) ("The primary objective of copyright is not to reward the labor of authors, but '[t]o promote the Progress of Science and useful Arts.' ").

work with the copyright in the work and conclude that if one owns the copyright, they must also own the work. However, the fallacy of that understanding is exposed by the simple fact that the work continues to exist after the term of copyright associated with the work has expired. "The copyright is not a natural right inherent in authorship. If it were, the impact on market values would be irrelevant; any unauthorized taking would be obnoxious." Pierre Leval, Towards a Fair Use Standard, 105 Harv. L.Rev. 1105, 1124 (1990).

B. The Union of Copyright and the First Amendment

The Copyright Clause and the First Amendment,[11] while intuitively in conflict,[12] were drafted to work together to prevent censorship; copyright laws were enacted in part to prevent private censorship and the First Amendment was enacted to prevent public censorship.[13] There are "[c]onflicting interests that must be accommodated in drawing a definitional balance" between the Copyright Clause and the First Amendment. 1 Nimmer § 1.10[B][1]. In establishing this balance "[o]n the copyright side, economic encouragement for creators must be preserved and the privacy of unpublished works recognized. Freedom of speech[, on the other hand,] requires the preservation of a meaningful public or democratic dialogue, as well as the uses of speech as a safety valve against violent acts, and as an end in itself." *Id.*

In copyright law, the balance between the First Amendment and copyright is preserved, in part, by the idea/expression dichotomy and the doctrine of fair use. *See Eldred v. Reno,* 239 F.3d 372, 375 (D.C.Cir.2001) ("The first amendment objection ... was misplaced '[i]n view of the First Amendment protections already embodied in the Copyright Act's distinction between copyrightable expression and uncopyrightable facts and ideas, and the latitude for scholarship and comment traditionally afforded by fair use.' ") (quoting *Harper & Row,* 471 U.S. at 560, 105 S.Ct. at 2218).

1. The Idea/ Expression Dichotomy

Copyright cannot protect an idea, only the expression of that idea. *Baker v. Selden,* 101 U.S. 99, 25 L.Ed. 841 (1879) * * * Holding an infringer liable in copyright for copying the expression of another author's ideas does not impede First Amendment goals because the public purpose has been served—the public already has access to the idea or the concepts.[14] A new author may use or discuss the idea, but must do so using her own original expression.

---

11. "Congress shall make no law ... abridging the freedom of speech ..." U.S. CONST. amend. I.

12. While the First Amendment disallows laws that abridge the freedom of speech, the Copyright Clause calls specifically for such a law.

13. *See* Rebecca Tushnet, *Copyright as a Model for Free Speech Law: What Copyright Has in Common with Anti–Pornogra-*

phy Laws, Campaign Finance Reform, and Telecommunications Regulation, 42 B.C.L. REV. 1, 2 (2000) ("The First Amendment gets government off speakers' backs, while the Copyright Act enables speakers to make money from speaking and thus encourages them to enter the public marketplace of ideas.").

14. *See* 1 Nimmer § 1.10[B][2] ("It is exposure to ideas, and not to their particu-

2. *Fair Use*

First Amendment privileges are also preserved through the doctrine of fair use.[15] Until codification of the fair-use doctrine in the 1976 Act, fair use was a judge-made right developed to preserve the constitutionality of copyright legislation by protecting First Amendment values. Had fair use not been recognized as a right under the 1976 Act, the statutory abandonment of publication as a condition of copyright that had existed for over 200 years would have jeopardized the constitutionality of the new Act because there would be no statutory guarantee that new ideas, or new expressions of old ideas, would be accessible to the public. Included in the definition of fair use are "purposes such as criticism, comment, news reporting, teaching . . . , scholarship, or research." § 107. The exceptions carved out for these purposes are at the heart of fair use's protection of the First Amendment, as they allow later authors to use a previous author's copyright to introduce new ideas or concepts to the public. Therefore, within the limits of the fair-use test,[16] any use of a copyright is permitted to fulfill one of the important purposes listed in the statute.

Because of the First Amendment principles built into copyright law through the idea/expression dichotomy and the doctrine of fair use, courts often need not entertain related First Amendment arguments in a copyright case. *See, e.g., Eldred,* 239 F.3d at 376 (where the works in question "are by definition under copyright; that puts the works on the latter half of the 'idea/expression dichotomy' and makes them subject to fair use. This obviates further inquiry under the First Amendment."); *Nihon Keizai Shimbun, Inc. v. Comline Bus. Data, Inc.,* 166 F.3d 65, 74 (2d Cir.1999) ("We have repeatedly rejected First Amendment challenges to injunctions from copyright infringement on the ground that First Amendment concerns are protected by and coextensive with the fair use doctrine."); *Los Angeles News Serv. v. Tullo,* 973 F.2d 791, 795 (9th Cir.1992) ("First Amendment concerns are also addressed in the copyright field through the 'fair use' doctrine.").[17]

The case before us calls for an analysis of whether a preliminary injunction was properly granted against an alleged infringer who, relying largely on the doctrine of fair use, made use of another's copyright for comment and criticism. As discussed herein, *copyright does not immunize a work from comment and criticism.* Therefore, the narrower question in this case is to what extent a critic may use the protected elements of an original work of authorship to communicate her criticism without infringing the copyright in that work. As will be discussed below, this becomes essentially an analysis of the fair use factors. As we

---

lar expression, that is vital if self-governing people are to make informed decisions.").

15. § 107 ("[F]air use of a copyrighted work . . . for purposes such as criticism [or] comment . . . is not an infringement of copyright.").

16. See discussion section II.C.1.b.

17. For a more policy-based discussion, *see* 1 Nimmer § 1.10[D].

turn to the analysis required in this case, we must remain cognizant of the First Amendment protections interwoven into copyright law.

C. *Appropriateness of Injunctive Relief*

"The chief function of a preliminary injunction is to preserve the status quo until the merits of the controversy can be fully and fairly adjudicated." *Northeastern Fl. Chapter of Ass'n of Gen. Contractors of Am. v. City of Jacksonville, Fl.,* 896 F.2d 1283, 1284 (11th Cir.1990). The Copyright Act specifically vests the federal courts with power to grant injunctions "to prevent or restrain infringement of a copyright." § 502(a). While injunctive relief may be particularly appropriate in cases involving simple copying or "piracy" of a copyrighted work, the Supreme Court has cautioned that such relief may not be consistent with the goals of copyright law in cases in which the alleged infringer of the copyright has a colorable fair-use defense. *Campbell v. Acuff–Rose Music, Inc.,* 510 U.S. 569, 578 n. 10, 114 S.Ct. 1164, 1171 n. 10, 127 L.Ed.2d 500 (1994).[18]

The basic framework for our analysis remains, however, the standard test governing the issuance of preliminary injunctions. Suntrust is not entitled to relief in the form of a preliminary injunction unless it has proved each of the following four elements: "(1) a substantial likelihood of success on the merits, (2) a substantial threat of irreparable injury if the injunction were not granted, (3) that the threatened injury to the plaintiff outweighs the harm an injunction may cause the defendant, and (4) that granting the injunction would not disserve the public interest." *Am. Red Cross v. Palm Beach Blood Bank, Inc.,* 143 F.3d 1407, 1410 (11th Cir.1998).

1. *Substantial Likelihood of Success on the Merits*

a. *Prima Facie Copyright Infringement*

The first step in evaluating the likelihood that Suntrust will succeed on the merits is to determine whether it has established the *prima facie* elements of a copyright infringement claim: (1) that Suntrust owns a valid copyright in *GWTW* and (2) that Randall copied *original* elements of *GWTW* in *TWDG. Feist,* 499 U.S. at 361, 111 S.Ct. at 1296; *Leigh v. Warner Bros., Inc.,* 212 F.3d 1210, 1214 (11th Cir.2000). The district court found that Suntrust had carried its burden on both of these elements.

The first element, Suntrust's ownership of a valid copyright in *GWTW,* is not disputed. Houghton Mifflin does assert, however, that Suntrust did not establish the second element of infringement, that *TWDG* appropriates copyright-protected expression from *GWTW.* In order to prove copying, Suntrust was required to show a "substantial similarity" between the two works such that "an average lay observer would recognize the alleged copy as having been appropriated from the copyrighted work." *Leigh,* 212 F.3d at 1214 (quoting *Original Appala-*

---

18. The Supreme Court reiterated this point in *New York Times v. Tasini,* 533 U.S. 483, 121 S.Ct. 2381, 2393, 150 L.Ed.2d 500 (2001).

chian Artworks, Inc. v. Toy Loft, Inc., 684 F.2d 821, 829 (11th Cir.1982)). Not all copying of a work is actionable, however, for, as discussed in section II.B.1., "no author may copyright facts or ideas. The copyright is limited to those aspects of the work—termed 'expression'—that display the stamp of the author's originality." *Harper & Row,* 471 U.S. at 547, 105 S.Ct. at 2224 (citation omitted). Thus, we are concerned with substantial similarities between *TWDG* and *GWTW* only to the extent that they involve the copying of original, protected expression. *Leigh,* 212 F.3d at 1214.[19]

There is no bright line that separates the protectable expression from the nonprotectable idea in a work of fiction. While often referred to as a test for distinguishing the idea from the expression, Judge Learned Hand's famous statement in *Nichols v. Universal Pictures Corp.,* 45 F.2d 119 (2d Cir.1930), is actually nothing more than a concise restatement of the problem facing the courts:

> Upon any work, and especially upon a play, a great number of patterns of increasing generality will fit equally well, as more and more of the incident is left out. The last may perhaps be no more than the most general statement of what the play is about, and at times might consist only of its title; but there is a point in this series of abstractions where they are no longer protected, since otherwise the playwright could prevent the use of his "ideas," to which, apart from their expression, his property is never extended.

Id. at 121. At one end of the spectrum, *scenes a faire*—the stock scenes and hackneyed character types that "naturally flow from a common theme"—are considered "ideas," and therefore are not copyrightable. *Beal v. Paramount Pictures Corp.,* 20 F.3d 454, 459–60 (11th Cir.1994). But as plots become more intricately detailed and characters become more idiosyncratic, they at some point cross the line into "expression" and are protected by copyright. *See* 1 Nimmer § 2.12 (2001).

After conducting a thorough comparison of the two works, the district court found that *TWDG* copied far more than unprotected *scenes a faire* from *GWTW:* "[*TWDG*] uses fifteen fictional characters from [*GWTW*], incorporating their physical attributes, mannerisms, and the distinct features that Ms. Mitchell used to describe them, as well as their complex relationships with each other. Moreover, the various [fictional] locales, ... settings, characters, themes, and plot of [*TWDG*] closely mirror those contained in [*GWTW*]." *Suntrust,* 136 F.Supp.2d at 1367.

Our own review of the two works reveals substantial use of *GWTW. TWDG* appropriates numerous characters, settings, and plot twists from *GWTW.* For example, Scarlett O'Hara, Rhett Butler, Bonnie Butler,

---

19. Originally the word "copie" was a noun, indicating the manuscript. Ownership of the "copie" thus meant ownership of the manuscript for the purposes of publishing it. Today, "copy" has become a verb, meaning the act of reproduction of a work. But in the development of copyright law it was intended to be a term of art, indicating a reproduction of a work for publication. Failure to understand and apply this distinction has confused many courts (assisted by overzealous advocates) into too expansive a view of the scope of the copyright monopoly.

Melanie Wilkes, Ashley Wilkes, Gerald O'Hara, Ellen O'Hara, Mammy, Pork, Dilcey, Prissy, Belle Watling, Carreen O'Hara, Stuart and Brenton Tarleton, Jeems, Philippe, and Aunt Pittypat, all characters in *GWTW*, appear in *TWDG*. Many of these characters are renamed in *TWDG*: Scarlett becomes "Other," Rhett Butler becomes "R.B.," Pork becomes "Garlic," Prissy becomes "Miss Priss," Philippe becomes "Feleepe," Aunt Pittypat becomes "Aunt Pattypit," etc. In several instances, Randall renamed characters using Mitchell's descriptions of those characters in *GWTW*: Ashley becomes "Dreamy Gentleman," Melanie becomes "Mealy Mouth," Gerald becomes "Planter." The fictional settings from *GWTW* receive a similarly transparent renaming in *TWDG*: Tara becomes "Tata," Twelve Oaks Plantation becomes "Twelve Slaves Strong as Trees." *TWDG* copies, often in wholesale fashion, the descriptions and histories of these fictional characters and places from *GWTW*, as well as their relationships and interactions with one another. *TWDG* appropriates or otherwise explicitly references many aspects of *GWTW*'s plot as well, such as the scenes in which Scarlett kills a Union soldier and the scene in which Rhett stays in the room with his dead daughter Bonnie, burning candles. After carefully comparing the two works, we agree with the district court that, particularly in its first half, *TWDG* is largely "an encapsulation of [*GWTW*] [that] exploit[s] its copyrighted characters, story lines, and settings as the palette for the new story." *Suntrust*, 136 F.Supp.2d at 1367.

Houghton Mifflin argues that there is no substantial similarity between *TWDG* and *GWTW* because the retelling of the story is an inversion of *GWTW*: the characters, places, and events lifted from *GWTW* are often cast in a different light, strong characters from the original are depicted as weak (and vice-versa) in the new work, the institutions and values romanticized in *GWTW* are exposed as corrupt in *TWDG*. While we agree with Houghton Mifflin that the characters, settings, and plot taken from *GWTW* are vested with a new significance when viewed through the character of Cynara[20] in *TWDG*, it does not change the fact that they are the very same copyrighted characters, settings, and plot.

b. Fair Use

Randall's appropriation of elements of *GWTW* in *TWDG* may nevertheless not constitute infringement of Suntrust's copyright if the taking is protected as a "fair use." * * * In assessing whether a use of a copyright is a fair use under the statute, we bear in mind that the examples of possible fair uses given are illustrative rather than exclusive, and that "[a]ll [of the four factors] are to be explored, and the results weighed together in light of the purposes of copyright." *Campbell*, 510 U.S. at 577–78, 114 S.Ct. at 1170–71.[22] In light of the discussion in

---

20. "Cynara" is the name of the poem by Ernest Dowson, from which *GWTW* 's title is derived ("I have forgot much, Cynara! gone with the wind, . . .").

22. See section II.A. for a discussion of the purposes of copyright.

§§ IIA and B, one of the most important purposes to consider is the free flow of ideas—particularly criticism and commentary.

Houghton Mifflin argues that *TWDG* is entitled to fair-use protection as a parody of *GWTW.* In *Campbell,* the Supreme Court held that parody, although not specifically listed in § 107, is a form of comment and criticism that may constitute a fair use of the copyrighted work being parodied. *Id.* at 579, 114 S.Ct. at 1171. Parody, which is directed toward a particular literary or artistic work, is distinguishable from satire, which more broadly addresses the institutions and mores of a slice of society. *Id.* at 580–81, 581 n. 15, 114 S.Ct. at 1172, 1172 n. 15. Thus, "[p]arody needs to mimic an original to make its point, and so has some claim to use the creation of its victim's . . . imagination, whereas satire can stand on its own two feet and so requires justification for the very act of borrowing." *Id.* at 580–81, 114 S.Ct. at 1172.

The fact that parody by definition must borrow elements from an existing work, however, does not mean that every parody is shielded from a claim of copyright infringement as a fair use. "The [Copyright] Act has no hint of an evidentiary preference for parodists over their victims, and no workable presumption for parody could take account of the fact that parody often shades into satire when society is lampooned through its creative artifacts, or that a work may contain both parodic and nonparodic elements." *Id.* at 581, 114 S.Ct. at 1172. Therefore, Houghton Mifflin's fair-use defense of parody, like any other claim of fair use, must be evaluated in light of the factors set out in § 107 and the constitutional purposes of copyright law. *Id.,* 114 S.Ct. at 1172.

Before considering a claimed fair-use defense based on parody, however, the Supreme Court has required that we ensure that "a parodic character may reasonably be perceived" in the allegedly infringing work. *Id.* at 582, 114 S.Ct. at 1173. The Supreme Court's definition of parody in *Campbell,* however, is somewhat vague. On the one hand, the Court suggests that the aim of parody is "comic effect or ridicule," but it then proceeds to discuss parody more expansively in terms of its "commentary" on the original. *Id.* at 580, 114 S.Ct. at 1172. In light of the admonition in *Campbell* that courts should not judge the quality of the work or the success of the attempted humor in discerning its parodic character, we choose to take the broader view. For purposes of our fair-use analysis, we will treat a work as a parody if its aim is to comment upon or criticize a prior work by appropriating elements of the original in creating a new artistic, as opposed to scholarly or journalistic, work.[23] Under this definition, the parodic character of *TWDG* is clear. *TWDG* is

---

23. The benefit of our approach to "parody," which requires no assessment of whether or not a work is humorous, is apparent from the arguments made by the parties in this case. Suntrust quotes Michiko Kakutani's review of *TWDG* in the *New York Times,* in which she states that the work is "decidedly unfunny." Houghton Mifflin, on the other hand, claims that

TWDG is an example of "African–American humor," which, Houghton Mifflin strongly implies, non-African–American judges are not permitted to evaluate without assistance from "experts." Under our approach, we may ignore Houghton Mifflin's questionable argument and simply bypass what would always be a wholly subjective inquiry.

not a general commentary upon the Civil–War-era American South, but a specific criticism of and rejoinder to the depiction of slavery and the relationships between blacks and whites in *GWTW*. The fact that Randall chose to convey her criticisms of *GWTW* through a work of fiction, which she contends is a more powerful vehicle for her message than a scholarly article, does not, in and of itself, deprive *TWDG* of fair-use protection. We therefore proceed to an analysis of the four fair-use factors.

i. Purpose and Character of the Work

The first factor in the fair-use analysis, the purpose and character of the allegedly infringing work, has several facets. The first is whether *TWDG* serves a commercial purpose or nonprofit educational purpose. § 107(1). Despite whatever educational function *TWDG* may be able to lay claim to, it is undoubtedly a commercial product.[24] As the Supreme Court has stated, "[t]he crux of the profit/nonprofit distinction is not whether the sole motive of the use is monetary gain but whether the user stands to profit from exploitation of the copyrighted material without paying the customary price." *Harper & Row,* 471 U.S. at 562, 105 S.Ct. at 2231. The fact that *TWDG* was published for profit is the first factor weighing against a finding of fair use. *Id.,* 105 S.Ct. at 2231. However, *TWDG*'s for-profit status is strongly overshadowed and outweighed in view of its highly transformative use of *GWTW's* copyrighted elements. "[T]he more transformative the new work, the less will be the significance of other factors, like commercialism, that may weigh against a finding of fair use." *Campbell,* 510 U.S. at 579, 114 S.Ct. at 1171. "[T]he goal of copyright, to promote science and the arts, is generally furthered by the creation of transformative works." *Id.* A work's transformative value is of special import in the realm of parody, since a parody's aim is, by nature, to transform an earlier work.

The second factor in the "purpose and character" analysis relevant to this case is to what extent *TWDG*'s use of copyrighted elements of *GWTW* can be said to be "transformative." The inquiry is "whether the new work merely supersedes the objects of the original creation, or instead adds something new, with a further purpose or different character, altering the first with new expression, meaning, or message." *Campbell,* 510 U.S. at 579, 114 S.Ct. at 1171 (citations and internal punctuation omitted). The issue of transformation is a double-edged sword in this case. On the one hand, the story of Cynara and her perception of the events in *TWDG* certainly adds new "expression, meaning, [and] message" to *GWTW*. From another perspective, however, *TWDG*'s success as a pure work of fiction depends heavily on copyrighted elements appropriated from *GWTW* to carry its own plot forward.

However, as noted above, *TWDG* is more than an abstract, pure fictional work. It is principally and purposefully a critical statement that

---

24. Randall did not choose to publish her work of fiction on the internet free to all the world to read; rather, she chose a method of publication designed to generate economic profit.

seeks to rebut and destroy the perspective, judgments, and mythology of *GWTW*. Randall's literary goal is to explode the romantic, idealized portrait of the antebellum South during and after the Civil War. In the world of *GWTW*, the white characters comprise a noble aristocracy whose idyllic existence is upset only by the intrusion of Yankee soldiers, and, eventually, by the liberation of the black slaves. Through her characters as well as through direct narration, Mitchell describes how both blacks and whites were purportedly better off in the days of slavery: "The more I see of emancipation the more criminal I think it is. It's just ruined the darkies," says Scarlett O'Hara. *GWTW* at 639. Free blacks are described as "creatures of small intelligence ... [l]ike monkeys or small children turned loose among treasured objects whose value is beyond their comprehension, they ran wild—either from perverse pleasure in destruction or simply because of their ignorance." *Id.* at 654. Blacks elected to the legislature are described as spending "most of their time eating goobers and easing their unaccustomed feet into and out of new shoes." *Id.* at 904.

As the district court noted: "The earlier work is a third-person epic, whereas the new work is told in the first-person as an intimate diary of the life of Cynara. Thematically, the new work provides a different viewpoint of the antebellum world." 136 F.Supp.2d at 1367. While told from a different perspective, more critically, the story is transformed into a very different tale, albeit much more abbreviated. Cynara's very language is a departure from Mitchell's original prose; she acts as the voice of Randall's inversion of *GWTW*. She is the vehicle of parody; she is its means—not its end. It is clear within the first fifty pages of Cynara's fictional diary that Randall's work flips *GWTW*'s traditional race roles, portrays powerful whites as stupid or feckless,[25] and generally sets out to demystify *GWTW* and strip the romanticism from Mitchell's specific account of this period of our history. Approximately the last half of *TWDG* tells a completely new story that, although involving characters based on *GWTW* characters, features plot elements found nowhere within the covers of *GWTW*.

Where Randall refers directly to Mitchell's plot and characters, she does so in service of her general attack on *GWTW*. In *GWTW*, Scarlett O'Hara often expresses disgust with and condescension towards blacks; in *TWDG*, Other, Scarlett's counterpart, is herself of mixed descent. In *GWTW*, Ashley Wilkes is the initial object of Scarlett's affection; in *TWDG*, he is homosexual.[26] In *GWTW*, Rhett Butler does not consort

---

25. On pages 62–63 of *TWDG*, for example, Miss Priss explains that Mammy killed white male heirs to the plantation dynasty when they were babies in order to seal Garlic's and the other African–Americans' control over the drunken Planter. "What would we a done with a sober white man on this place?" Says Miss Priss. *TWDG* at 63.

26. Randall's parodic intent vis-a-vis Ashley becomes manifest when the two

works are read side-by-side. Mitchell has Gerald describe Ashley Wilkes: "The Wilkes are different from any of our neighbors— different from any family I ever knew. They are queer folk, and it's best that they marry their cousins and keep their queerness to themselves ... And when I say queer, it's not crazy I'm meaning ... there's no understanding him at all.... tell me true, do you understand his folderol about books

with black female characters and is portrayed as the captain of his own destiny. In *TWDG*, Cynara ends her affair with Rhett's counterpart, R., to begin a relationship with a black Congressman; R. ends up a washed out former cad. In *TWDG*, nearly every black character is given some redeeming quality—whether depth, wit, cunning, beauty, strength, or courage—that their *GWTW* analogues lacked.

In light of this, we find it difficult to conclude that Randall simply tried to "avoid the drudgery in working up something fresh." *Campbell,* 510 U.S. at 580, 114 S.Ct. at 1172. It is hard to imagine how Randall could have specifically criticized *GWTW* without depending heavily upon copyrighted elements of that book. A parody is a work that seeks to comment upon or criticize another work by appropriating elements of the original. "Parody needs to mimic an original to make its point, and so has some claim to use the creation of its victim's (or collective victims') imagination." *Campbell,* 510 U.S. at 580–81, 114 S.Ct. at 1172. Thus, Randall has fully employed those conscripted elements from *GWTW* to make war against it. Her work, *TWDG,* reflects transformative value because it "can provide social benefit, by shedding light on an earlier work, and, in the process, creating a new one." *Campbell,* 510 U.S. at 579, 114 S.Ct. at 1171.

While "transformative use is not absolutely necessary for a finding of fair use, . . . the more transformative the new work, the less will be the significance of other factors." *Id.,* 114 S.Ct. at 1171 (internal citations omitted). In the case of *TWDG,* consideration of this factor certainly militates in favor of a finding of fair use, and, informs our analysis of the other factors, particularly the fourth, as discussed below.

ii. Nature of the Copyrighted Work

The second factor, the nature of the copyrighted work, recognizes that there is a hierarchy of copyright protection in which original, creative works are afforded greater protection than derivative works or factual compilations. *Id.* at 586, 114 S.Ct. at 1175; *Microdos,* 115 F.3d at 1515 n. 16. *GWTW* is undoubtedly entitled to the greatest degree of protection as an original work of fiction. This factor is given little weight in parody cases, however, "since parodies almost invariably copy publicly known, expressive works." *Campbell,* 510 U.S. at 586, 114 S.Ct. at 1175.

iii. Amount and Substantiality of the Portion Used

The third fair-use factor is "the amount and substantiality of the portion used in relation to the copyrighted work as a whole." § 107(3). It is at this point that parody presents uniquely difficult problems for courts in the fair-use context, for "[p]arody's humor, or in any event its

and poetry and music and oil paintings and such foolishness?" *GWTW* at 34. Later, Mitchell describes how "Scarlett turned her prettiest smile on Ashley, but for some reason he was not looking at her. He was looking at Charles . . ." *GWTW* at 113. This particular element of Randall's parody takes on special relevance in the market-harm analysis of the case, because it is evident from the record evidence that Suntrust makes a practice of requiring authors of its licensed derivatives to make no references to homosexuality.

comment, necessarily springs from recognizable allusion to its object through distorted imitation.... When parody takes aim at a particular original work, the parody must be able to 'conjure up' at least enough of that original to make the object of its critical wit recognizable." *Campbell*, 510 U.S. at 588, 114 S.Ct. at 1176. Once enough has been taken to "conjure up" the original in the minds of the readership, any further taking must specifically serve the new work's parodic aims. *Id.*, 114 S.Ct. at 1176.

GWTW is one of the most famous, popular, and enduring American novels ever written. Given the fame of the work and its primary characters, Suntrust argues that very little reference is required to conjure up *GWTW*. As we have already indicated in our discussion of substantial similarity, *TWDG* appropriates a substantial portion of the protected elements of *GWTW*. Houghton Mifflin argues that *TWDG* takes nothing from *GWTW* that does not serve a parodic purpose, the crux of the argument being that a large number of characters had to be taken from *GWTW* because each represents a different ideal or stereotype that requires commentary, and that the work as a whole could not be adequately commented upon without revisiting substantial portions of the plot, including its most famous scenes. Houghton Mifflin's argument is similar to that made by the defendants in *Harper & Row,* who argued for "expanding the doctrine of fair use to create what amounts to a public figure exception to copyright." 471 U.S. at 560, 105 S.Ct. at 2230. To the extent Houghton Mifflin argues for extra latitude in copying from *GWTW* because of its fame, the Supreme Court has squarely foreclosed any such privilege:

> It is fundamentally at odds with the scheme of copyright to accord lesser rights in those works that are of greatest importance to the public.... To propose that fair use be imposed whenever the social value of dissemination outweighs any detriment to the artist, would be to propose depriving copyright owners of their right in the property precisely when they encounter those users who could afford to pay for it.

Id. at 559, 105 S.Ct. at 2229–30 (internal quotations and punctuation omitted). Notably, however, the Court did not go so far as to grant well-known works a special, higher copyright status either.

There are numerous instances in which *TWDG* appropriates elements of *GWTW* and then transforms them for the purpose of commentary. *TWDG* uses several of *GWTW*'s most famous lines, but vests them with a completely new significance. For example, the final lines of *GWTW*, "Tomorrow, I'll think of some way to get him back. After all, tomorrow is another day," are transformed in *TWDG* into "For all those we love for whom tomorrow will not be another day, we send the sweet prayer of resting in peace." Another such recasting is Rhett's famous quip to Scarlett as he left her in *GWTW*, "My dear, I don't give a damn." In *TWDG,* the repetition of this line (which is paraphrased) changes the reader's perception of Rhett/R.B.—and of black-white relations—because he has left Scarlett/Other for Cynara, a former slave. Another clear instance in which a memorable scene from *GWTW* is taken primarily for the purpose of parody is Gerald/Planter's acquisition of Pork/Garlic. In *GWTW*, Gerald won Pork in a card game with a man from St. Simons Island. In *TWDG*, Planter wins Garlic in a card game with a man from St. Simons Island, but Garlic, far from being the passive "chattel" in *GWTW*, is portrayed as being smarter than either white character by orchestrating the outcome of the card game and determining his own fate. There are many more such transformative uses of elements of *GWTW* in *TWDG*.

On the other hand, however, we are told that not all of *TWDG*'s takings from *GWTW* are clearly justified as commentary. We have already determined that *TWDG* is a parody, but not every parody is a fair use. Suntrust contends that *TWDG*, at least at the margins, takes more of the protected elements of *GWTW* than was necessary to serve a parodic function.

For example, in a sworn declaration to the district court, Randall stated that she needed to reference the scene from *GWTW* in which Jeems is given to the Tarleton twins as a birthday present because she considers it "perhaps the single most repellent paragraph in Margaret Mitchell's novel: a black child given to two white children as a birthday present . . . as if the buying and selling of children thus had no moral significance." Clearly, such a scene is fair game for criticism. However, in this instance, Suntrust argues that *TWDG* goes beyond commentary on the occurrence itself, appropriating such nonrelevant details as the fact that the twins had red hair and were killed at Gettysburg. There are several other scenes from *GWTW*, such as the incident in which Scarlett threw a vase at Ashley while Rhett was hidden on the couch, that are retold or alluded to without serving any apparent parodic purpose. Similar taking of the descriptions of characters and the minor details of their histories and interactions that arguably are not essential to the parodic purpose of the work recur throughout: Melanie/Mealy Mouth is flat-chested, Mammy is described as being like an elephant and is proud of Scarlett/Other's small waist, Gerald/Planter had been run out of Ireland for committing murder and is an excellent horseman, Bonnie/Precious wears a blue velvet riding habit and is afraid of the dark, Belle/Beauty has red hair and lives in Atlanta, Ellen/Lady likes lemon verbena, Carreen/Kareen ends up in a convent in Charleston. Clearly, *TWDG* uses these idiosyncratic characters. But we must determine whether the use is fair. In doing so, we are reminded that literary relevance is a highly subjective analysis ill-suited for judicial inquiry. Thus we are presented with conflicting and opposing arguments relative to the amount taken and whether it was too much or a necessary amount.

The Supreme Court in *Campbell* did not require that parodists take the bare minimum amount of copyright material necessary to conjure up the original work. Parody "must be able to conjure up *at least* enough of [the] original to make the object of its critical wit recognizable." *Camp-*

bell, 510 U.S. at 588, 114 S.Ct. at 1176 (emphasis added; quotations omitted). "Parody frequently needs to be more than a fleeting evocation of an original in order to make its humorous point.... [E]ven more extensive use [than necessary to conjure up the original] would still be fair use, provided the parody builds upon the original, using the original as a known element of modern culture and contributing something new for humorous effect or commentary." *Elsmere Music, Inc. v. National Broad'g Co.,* 623 F.2d 252, 253 n. 1 (2d Cir.1980).

A use does not necessarily become infringing the moment it does more than simply conjure up another work. Rather, "[o]nce enough has been taken to assure identification, how much more is reasonable will depend, say, [1] on the extent to which the [work's] *overriding purpose and character is to parody* the original or, in contrast, [2] the likelihood that the parody may serve as *a market substitute* for the original." *Campbell,* 510 U.S. at 588, 114 S.Ct. at 1176 (numeration and emphasis added). As to the first point, it is manifest that *TWDG's raison d'etre* is to parody *GWTW.*[27] The second point indicates that any material we suspect is "extraneous" to the parody is unlawful only if it negatively effects the potential market for or value of the original copyright. Based upon this record at this juncture, we cannot determine in any conclusive way whether " 'the quantity and value of the materials used' are reasonable in relation to the purpose of the copying." *Id.,* 510 U.S. at 586, 114 S.Ct. at 1175 (quoting *Folsom,* 9 F.Cas. at 348).

iv. Effect on the Market Value of the Original

The final fair-use factor requires us to consider the effect that the publication of *TWDG* will have on the market for or value of Suntrust's copyright in *GWTW,* including the potential harm it may cause to the market for derivative works based on *GWTW. Campbell,* 510 U.S. at 590, 114 S.Ct. at 1177. In addressing this factor, we must "consider not only the extent of market harm caused by the particular actions of the alleged infringer, but also whether unrestricted and widespread conduct of the sort engaged in by the defendant [ ] would result in a substantially adverse impact on the potential market." *Id.,* 114 S.Ct. at 1177 (quotations omitted). More specifically, the *Campbell* Court continued: "[T]he only harm to derivatives that need concern us ... is the harm of market substitution. The fact that a parody may impair the market for deriva-

---

27. Suntrust suggests that Houghton Mifflin decided-as a legalistic afterthought-to market *TWDG* as a "parody." We are mindful of Justice Kennedy's admonition that courts "ensure that not just any commercial takeoff is rationalized post hoc as a parody." *Campbell,* 510 U.S. at 600, 114 S.Ct. at 1182 (Kennedy, J., concurring). Justice Kennedy's concurrence simply underscores the danger of relying upon facile, formalistic labels, and encourages us to march this alleged infringement through fair use's four-pronged analysis as we would any other such work. Randall and Houghton–Mifflin may label their book a "paro-

dy," or a "novel," or whatever they like, and that fact would be largely irrelevant to our task. Defendants "need not label their [work] ... a parody in order to claim fair use protection ... Parody serves its goals whether labeled or not, and there is no reason to require parody to state the obvious ..." *Campbell,* 510 U.S. at 583 n. 17, 114 S.Ct. at 1173 n. 17. The only way in which Houghton Mifflin's marketing strategy might be relevant is if it diverted consumers from *GWTW*-related products to its own. In any case, such a practice, if it were found to exist, would likely fall under the market harm fair use factor.

tive uses by the very effectiveness of its critical commentary is no more relevant under copyright that the like threat to the original market." *Id.*, 510 U.S. at 593, 114 S.Ct. at 1178.[28] *See also Nimmer on Copyright,* § 1305[A][4] at 181 (Vol.4) (citing *Consumers Union of U.S., Inc. v. General Signal Corp.*, 724 F.2d 1044 (2d Cir.1993)) ("The fourth factor looks to adverse impact only by reason of usurpation of the demand for plaintiff's work through defendant's copying of protectible expression from such work.").

As for the potential market, Suntrust proffered evidence in the district court of the value of its copyright in *GWTW*. Several derivative works of *GWTW* have been authorized, including the famous movie of the same name and a book titled *Scarlett: The Sequel*.[29] *GWTW* and the derivative works based upon it have generated millions of dollars for the copyright holders. Suntrust has negotiated an agreement with St. Martin's Press permitting it to produce another derivative work based on *GWTW,* a privilege for which St. Martin's paid "well into seven figures." Part of this agreement was that Suntrust would not authorize any other derivative works prior to the publication of St. Martin's book.

An examination of the record, with its limited development as to relevant market harm due to the preliminary injunction status of the case, discloses that Suntrust focuses on the value of *GWTW* and its derivatives, but fails to address and offers little evidence or argument to demonstrate that *TWDG* would supplant demand for Suntrust's licensed derivatives. However, the Supreme Court and other appeals courts have made clear that, particularly in cases of parody, evidence of harm to the potential market for or value of the original copyright is crucial to a fair use determination. "[E]vidence about relevant markets" is also crucial to the fair use analysis. *Campbell,* 510 U.S. at 590, 114 S.Ct. at 1177. "Evidence of substantial harm to [a derivative market] would weigh against a finding of fair use." *Id.* at 593, 114 S.Ct. at 1178. "What is necessary is a showing by a preponderance of the evidence that *some* meaningful likelihood of future harm exits." *Sony,* 464 U.S. at 451, 104 S.Ct. at 793 (emphasis in original).[30] It should also be remembered that

---

28. "Whereas a work that merely supplants or supersedes another is likely to cause a substantially adverse impact on the potential market of the original, a transformative work is less likely to do so." *Sony Computer Entertainment, Inc. v. Connectix Corp.*, 203 F.3d 596, 607 (9th Cir.2000) (citing *Campbell,* 510 U.S. at 591, 114 S.Ct. at 1177, and *Harper & Row, Publishers, Inc. v. Nation Enters., Inc.*, 471 U.S. 539, 567–69, 105 S.Ct. 2218, 85 L.Ed.2d 588 (1985)).

29. *See generally, Trust Co. Bank v. MGM/UA Entertainment Co.*, 772 F.2d 740 (11th Cir.1985).

30. *See also Worldwide Church of God v. Philadelphia Church of God, Inc.*, 227 F.3d 1110, 1119 (9th Cir.2000) (noting, in

market harm analysis, that "undisputed evidence shows that individuals who received copies of [defendant's work] from [defendant] are present or could be potential adherents of [plaintiff's]"); *Leibovitz v. Paramount Pictures Corp.*, 137 F.3d 109, 116 n. 6 (2d Cir.1998) (where plaintiff conceded lack of market harm for derivative works, "defendant had no obligation to present evidence to present evidence showing lack of harm"); *Ringgold v. Black Entertainment Television, Inc.*, 126 F.3d 70, 81 (2d Cir. 1997) ("[I]n view of what Ringgold has averred is prepared to prove, the record on the fourth fair use factor is inadequate to permit summary judgment for the defendants."); *Dr. Seuss Enter., L.P. v. Penguin Books USA, Inc.*, 109 F.3d 1394, 1403 (9th

with a work as old as *GWTW* on which the original copyright may soon expire, creation of a derivative work only serves to protect that which is original to the latter work and does not somehow extend the copyright in the copyrightable elements of the *original* work. *See* § 103(b) ("The copyright in a ... derivative work extends only to the material contributed by the author of such work, as distinguished from the preexisting material employed in the work, and does not imply *any* exclusive right in the preexisting material.").

In contrast, the evidence proffered in support of the fair use defense[31] specifically and correctly focused on market substitution and demonstrates why Randall's book is unlikely to displace sales of *GWTW*.[32] Thus, we conclude, based on the current record, that Suntrust's evidence falls far short of establishing that *TWDG* or others like it will act as market substitutes for *GWTW* or will significantly harm its derivatives. Accordingly, the fourth fair use factor weighs in favor of *TWDG*.

* * *

We reject the district court's conclusion that Suntrust has established its likelihood of success on the merits. To the contrary, based upon our analysis of the fair use factors we find, at this juncture, *TWDG* is entitled to a fair-use defense. * * *

Notes

1. In an earlier minute order (not reproduced here) the court had dissolved the lower court's preliminary injunction on first amendment grounds alone, apparently the first time such action had ever been taken in the history of copyright. How important is the role of the first amendment in either of the two opinions here?

Cir.1997) (parties "must bring forward favorable evidence about relevant markets.").

31. "Since fair use is an affirmative defense, its proponent would have difficulty carrying the burden of demonstrating fair use without favorable evidence about relevant markets." *Campbell,* 510 U.S. at 590, 114 S.Ct. at 1177. At the injunction stage, the burden remains in the party seeking restraint to demonstrate the likelihood of success on the merits. Thus, in a copyright infringement case, the copyright owner must demonstrate (after establishing copyright ownership and the taking of *original* elements), where a *prima facie* fair use defense is presented, that the fair use factors are insufficient to support such a defense. As a practical matter, the fair use proponent will anticipate its burden on the merits and counter with evidence to support its claim of fair use. That is often why district courts invoke Fed.R.Civ.P. 65(a)(2) to consolidate the trials of the action on the merits with the hearing on the application for preliminary injunction. The record in this case reflects that such a consolidation was not accomplished.

32. It is worth noting that in the several months since we lifted the injunction against publication of *TWDG* there have been sales of both *GWTW* and *TWDG* which may assist the district court in evaluating the economic harm fair use factor. The Court in *Campbell* did acknowledge that "[e]ven favorable evidence, without more, is no guarantee of fairness," and that the market harm factor, "no less than the other three, may be addressed only through a 'sensitive balancing of interests' "510 U.S. at 590, n. 21, 114 S.Ct. at 1177, n. 21 (quoting *Sony Corp.,* 464 U.S. at 455, n. 40, 104 S.Ct. at 795, n. 40). That the market harm factor may not always be a purely factual or evidentiary matter, however, does not mean that it is a purely legal matter. It is, like fair use generally, a mixed question of law and fact.

2.   Note carefully this passage from footnote 3 in Judge Birch's opinion:

"I believe that fair use should be considered an affirmative *right* under the 1976 Act, rather than merely an affirmative defense, as it is defined in the Act as a use that is not a violation of copyright." (Emphasis in original.)

What exactly does he mean? What difference would it make if section 107 were construed as he suggests it ought to be? Does the text of the section support such a construction?

3.   Are you persuaded that *The Wind Done Gone* is a parody of *Gone With The Wind*? Is this a factor of vital significance in the court's decision? Should it be under the holding in *Campbell*?

4.   Is it plausible to interpret the standard established in *Campbell* so as to extend a presumption of fair use to any creative or critical appropriation of copyrighted work? How might such a presumption work? What impact would it be likely to have upon the copyright system?

5.   The Ninth Circuit found that pictures taken by defendant Tom Forsythe depicting a naked Barbie doll being attacked by vintage kitchen appliances constituted fair use in *Mattel, Inc. v. Walking Mountain Productions*, 353 F.3d 792 (9th Cir. 2003). In granting the defendant's summary judgment motion, the court stated:

Forsythe's work constitutes fair use under § 107's exception. His work is a parody of Barbie and highly transformative. The amount of Mattel's figure that he used was justified. His infringement had no discernable impact on Mattel's market for derivative uses. Finally, the benefits to the public in allowing such use—allowing artistic freedom and expression and criticism of a cultural icon—are great. Allowing Forsythe's use serves the aims of the Copyright Act by encouraging the very creativity and criticism that the Act protects.

353 F.3d at 806.

BILL GRAHAM ARCHIVES v. DORLING KINDERSLEY LTD.

United States Court of Appeals, Second Circuit, 2006.
448 F.3d 605, 78 U.S.P.Q.2d 1764.

RESTANI, JUDGE.

This appeal concerns the scope of copyright protection afforded artistic concert posters reproduced in reduced size in a biography of the musical group the Grateful Dead. Asserted copyright holder Bill Graham Archives, LLC ("BGA" or "Appellant") appeals from a judgment of the District Court for the Southern District of New York dismissing, on motion for summary judgment, its copyright infringement action against Dorling Kindersley Limited, Dorling Kindersley Publishing, Inc., and R.R. Donnelley & Sons Company (collectively "DK" or "Appellees"). We review the district court's grant of summary judgment *de novo,* and we agree with the court that DK's reproduction of BGA's images is protected by the fair use exception to copyright infringement.

BACKGROUND

In October of 2003, DK published *Grateful Dead: The Illustrated Trip* ("*Illustrated Trip*"), in collaboration with Grateful Dead Productions, intended as a cultural history of the Grateful Dead. The resulting 480–page coffee table book tells the story of the Grateful Dead along a timeline running continuously through the book, chronologically combining over 2000 images representing dates in the Grateful Dead's history with explanatory text. A typical page of the book features a collage of images, text, and graphic art designed to simultaneously capture the eye and inform the reader. Plaintiff BGA claims to own the copyright to seven images displayed in *Illustrated Trip,* which DK reproduced without BGA's permission.

Initially, DK sought permission from BGA to reproduce the images. In May of 2003, the CEO of Grateful Dead Productions sent a letter to BGA seeking permission for DK to publish the images. BGA responded by offering permission in exchange for Grateful Dead Productions' grant of permission to BGA to make CDs and DVDs out of concert footage in BGA's archives. Next, DK directly contacted BGA seeking to negotiate a license agreement, but the parties disagreed as to an appropriate license fee. Nevertheless, DK proceeded with publication of *Illustrated Trip* without entering a license fee agreement with BGA. Specifically, DK reproduced seven artistic images originally depicted on Grateful Dead event posters and tickets.... BGA's seven images are displayed in significantly reduced form and are accompanied by captions describing the concerts they represent.

When DK refused to meet BGA's post-publication license fee demands, BGA filed suit for copyright infringement. BGA sought to enjoin further publication of *Illustrated Trip,* the destruction of all unsold books, and actual and statutory damages. The parties cross-moved for summary judgment.... After applying the statutory fair use balancing test, the district court determined that DK's reproduction of the images was fair use and granted DK's motion for summary judgment.

DISCUSSION

* * *

In this case, the district court concluded that the balance of fair use factors weighs in favor of DK. Although the issue of fair use is a mixed question of law and fact, the court may resolve issues of fair use at the summary judgment stage where there are no genuine issues of material fact as to such issues.... As there are no genuine issues of material fact here, we review the district court's legal conclusions *de novo*.... We agree with the district court that DK's use of the copyrighted images is protected as fair use.

I. *Purpose and Character of Use*

We first address "the purpose and character of the use, including whether such use is of a commercial nature or is for nonprofit educational purposes." 17 U.S.C. § 107(1). Most important to the court's analysis of the first factor is the "transformative" nature of the work. *See* Pierre N. Leval, *Toward a Fair Use Standard,* 103 Harv. L.Rev. 1105, 1111 (1990). The question is "whether the new work merely supersede[s] the objects of the original creation, or instead adds something new, with a further purpose or different character, altering the first with new expression, meaning, or message." *Campbell v. Acuff–Rose Music, Inc.,* 510 U.S. 569, 579, 114 S.Ct. 1164, 127 L.Ed.2d 500 (1994) (internal citations and quotation marks omitted) (alteration in original).

Here, the district court determined that *Illustrated Trip* is a biographical work, and the original images are not, and therefore accorded a strong presumption in favor of DK's use. In particular, the district court concluded that DK's use of images placed in chronological order on a timeline is transformatively different from the mere expressive use of images on concert posters or tickets. Because the works are displayed to commemorate historic events, arranged in a creative fashion, and displayed in significantly reduced form, the district court held that the first fair use factor weighs heavily in favor of DK.

Appellant challenges the district court's strong presumption in favor of fair use based on the biographical nature of *Illustrated Trip.* Appellant argues that based on this purported error the district court failed to examine DK's justification for its use of each of the images. Moreover, Appellant argues that as a matter of law merely placing poster images along a timeline is not a transformative use. Appellant asserts that each reproduced image should have been accompanied by comment or criticism related to the artistic nature of the image.

We disagree with Appellant's limited interpretation of transformative use and we agree with the district court that DK's actual use of each image is transformatively different from the original expressive purpose. Preliminarily, we recognize, as the district court did, that *Illustrated Trip* is a biographical work documenting the 30–year history of the Grateful Dead. While there are no categories of presumptively fair use, *see Campbell v. Acuff–Rose Music, Inc.,* 510 U.S. at 584, courts have frequently afforded fair use protection to the use of copyrighted material in biographies, recognizing such works as forms of historic scholarship, criticism, and comment that require incorporation of original source material for optimum treatment of their subjects. *See* 17 U.S.C. § 107 (stating that fair use of a copyrighted work "for purposes such as criticism, comment ... [or] scholarship ... is not an infringement of copyright"); Am. Geophysical Union v. Texaco, Inc., 60 F.3d 913, 932 (2d Cir.1994) (Jacobs, J., dissenting) (noting that "[m]uch of our fair use case law has been generated by the use of quotation in biographies, a practice that fits comfortably within the[ ] statutory categories of uses illustrative of uses that can be fair") (internal quotation marks omitted) (alteration in original).... No less a recognition of biographical value is warranted in this case simply because the subject made a mark in pop culture rather than some other area of human endeavor. *See Twin Peaks Prods., Inc. v. Publ'ns Int'l, Ltd.,* 996 F.2d 1366, 1374 (2d Cir.1993) (noting that a work that comments about "pop culture" is not removed from the scope of Section 107 simply because it is not erudite).

In the instant case, DK's purpose in using the copyrighted images at issue in its biography of the Grateful Dead is plainly different from the original purpose for which they were created. Originally, each of BGA's images fulfilled the dual purposes of artistic expression and promotion. The posters were apparently widely distributed to generate public interest in the Grateful Dead and to convey information to a large number people about the band's forthcoming concerts. In contrast, DK used each of BGA's images as historical artifacts to document and represent the actual occurrence of Grateful Dead concert events featured on *Illustrated Trip*'s timeline.

In some instances, it is readily apparent that DK's image display enhances the reader's understanding of the biographical text.... In other instances, the link between image and text is less obvious; nevertheless, the images still serve as historical artifacts graphically representing the fact of significant Grateful Dead concert events selected by the *Illustrated Trip*'s author for inclusion in the book's timeline.... We conclude that both types of uses fulfill DK's transformative purpose of enhancing the biographical information in *Illustrated Trip,* a purpose separate and distinct from the original artistic and promotional purpose for which the images were created. *See Elvis Presley Enters., Inc. v. Passport Video,* 349 F.3d 622, 628–29 (9th Cir.2003) (finding the use of television clips to be transformative where "the clips play for only a few seconds and are used for reference purposes while a narrator talks over them or interviewees explain their context in Elvis' career," but not to be transformative where the clips "play without much interruption, [and t]he purpose of showing these clips likely goes beyond merely making a reference for a biography, but instead serves the same intrinsic entertainment value that is protected by Plaintiffs' copyrights"); *see also Hofheinz v. A & E Television Networks, Inc.,* 146 F.Supp.2d 442, 446–47 (S.D.N.Y.2001) (ruling that unauthorized inclusion of copyrighted film clips in actor's biographical film was protected fair use because the biography "was not shown to recreate the creative expression reposing in plaintiff's [copyrighted] film, [but] for the transformative purpose of enabling the viewer to understand the actor's modest beginnings in the film business"). In sum, because DK's use of the disputed images is transformative both when accompanied by referencing commentary and when standing alone, we agree with the district court that DK was not required to discuss the artistic merits of the images to satisfy this first factor of fair use analysis.

This conclusion is strengthened by the manner in which DK displayed the images. First, DK significantly reduced the size of the reproductions. *See Kelly v. Arriba Soft Corp.,* 336 F.3d 811, 818–20 (9th Cir.2003) (finding online search engine's use of thumbnail-sized images to be highly transformative). While the small size is sufficient to permit readers to recognize the historical significance of the posters, it is inadequate to offer more than a glimpse of their expressive value. In short, DK used the minimal image size necessary to accomplish its transformative purpose.

Second, DK minimized the expressive value of the reproduced images by combining them with a prominent timeline, textual material, and original graphical artwork, to create a collage of text and images on each page of the book. To further this collage effect, the images are displayed at angles and the original graphical artwork is designed to blend with the images and text. Overall, DK's layout ensures that the images at issue are employed only to enrich the presentation of the cultural history of the Grateful Dead, not to exploit copyrighted artwork for commercial gain. . . .

Third, BGA's images constitute an inconsequential portion of *Illustrated Trip*. The extent to which unlicensed material is used in the challenged work can be a factor in determining whether a biographer's use of original materials has been sufficiently transformative to constitute fair use. *See Craft v. Kobler,* 667 F.Supp. 120, 129 (S.D.N.Y.1987) (Leval, J.) (finding biography of Stravinsky to be unfair in part because the takings were numerous and were the "liveliest and most entertaining part of the biography"). Although our circuit has counseled against considering the percentage the allegedly infringing work comprises of the copyrighted work in conducting *third-factor* fair use analysis, *see NXIVM Corp. v. Ross Inst.,* 364 F.3d 471, 480 (2d Cir.2004), several courts have done so, *see, e.g., Harper,* 471 U.S. at 565–66 (finding the fact that quotes from President Ford's unpublished memoirs played a central role in the allegedly infringing magazine article, constituting 13% of that article, weighed against a finding of fair use). . . . We find this inquiry more relevant in the context of *first-factor* fair use analysis.

In the instant case, the book is 480 pages long, while the BGA images appear on only seven pages. Although the original posters range in size from 13″ x 19″ to more than 19″ x 27,″ the largest reproduction of a BGA image in *Illustrated Trip* is less than 3″ x 4 1/2″, less than 1/20 the size of the original. And no BGA image takes up more than one-eighth of a page in a book or is given more prominence than any other image on the page. In total, the images account for less than one-fifth of one percent of the book. This stands in stark contrast to the wholesale takings in cases such as those described above, and we are aware of no case where such an insignificant taking was found to be an unfair use of original materials.

Finally, as to this first factor, we briefly address the commercial nature of *Illustrated Trip*. *See Harper,* 471 U.S. at 562 (stating that the fact that the purpose of a new use is commercial weighs against finding fair use). Even though *Illustrated Trip* is a commercial venture, we recognize that "nearly all of the illustrative uses listed in the preamble paragraph of § 107 . . . are generally conducted for profit. . . . " *Campbell,* 510 U.S. at 584 (internal quotation marks omitted). Moreover, "[t]he crux of the profit/nonprofit distinction is not whether the sole motive of the use is monetary gain but whether the user stands to profit from exploitation of the copyrighted material without paying the customary price." *Harper,* 471 U.S. at 562. Here, *Illustrated Trip* does not exploit the use of BGA's images as such for commercial gain. Significantly, DK has not used any of BGA's images in its commercial advertising or in any other way to promote the sale of the book. *Illustrated Trip* merely uses pictures and text to describe the life of the Grateful Dead. By design, the use of BGA's images is incidental to the commercial biographical value of the book.

Accordingly, we conclude that the first fair use factor weighs in favor of DK because DK's use of BGA's images is transformatively different from the images' original expressive purpose and DK does not seek to exploit the images' expressive value for commercial gain.

II. *Nature of the Copyrighted Work*

The second factor in a fair use determination is "the nature of the copyrighted work." 17 U.S.C. § 107(2). To resolve this inquiry the court considers "the protection of the reasonable expectations of one who engages in the kinds of creation/authorship that the copyright seeks to encourage." Leval, *supra,* at 1122. "[C]reative expression for public dissemination falls within the core of the copyright's protective purposes." *Campbell,* 510 U.S. at 586.

The district court determined that the second factor weighs against DK because the images are creative artworks, which are traditionally the core of intended copyright protection. Nevertheless, the court limited the weight it placed on this factor because the posters have been published extensively. Appellant agrees that the district court properly weighed the second factor against DK, although it questions the lesser protection given to published works. Appellees counter that because the images are mixed factual and creative works and have been long and extensively published, the second factor tilts toward fair use.

We agree with the district court that the creative nature of artistic images typically weighs in favor of the copyright holder. We recognize, however, that the second factor may be of limited usefulness where the creative work of art is being used for a transformative purpose. *See Campbell,* 510 U.S. at 586 (stating that the second factor is not "likely to help much in separating the fair use sheep from the infringing goats" in cases involving transformative copying of "publicly known, expressive works"). This is not a case such as *Ringgold v. Black Entm't Television, Inc.,* 126 F.3d 70 (2d Cir.1997), in which we held that the creative work was being used for the same decorative purpose as the original. Here, we conclude that DK is using BGA's images for the transformative purpose of enhancing the biographical information provided in *Illustrated Trip.* Accordingly, we hold that even though BGA's images are creative works, which are a core concern of copyright protection, the second factor has limited weight in our analysis because the purpose of DK's use was to emphasize the images' historical rather than creative value.

III. Amount and Substantiality of the Portion Used

The third fair use factor asks the court to examine "the amount and substantiality of the portion used in relation to the copyrighted work as a whole." 17 U.S.C. § 107(3). We review this factor with reference to the copyrighted work, not the infringing work. . . . The court must examine the quantitative and qualitative aspects of the portion of the copyrighted material taken. *Campbell*, 510 U.S. at 586.

The district court determined that even though the images are reproduced in their entirety, the third fair use factor weighs in favor of DK because the images are displayed in reduced size and scattered among many other images and texts. In faulting this conclusion, Appellant contends that the amount used is substantial because the images are copied in their entirety. Neither our court nor any of our sister circuits has ever ruled that the copying of an entire work *favors* fair use. At the same time, however, courts have concluded that such copying does not necessarily weigh against fair use because copying the entirety of a work is sometimes necessary to make a fair use of the image. *See Kelly*, 336 F.3d at 821 (concluding that images used for a search engine database are necessarily copied in their entirety for the purpose of recognition); *Nunez v. Caribbean Int'l News Corp.*, 235 F.3d 18, 24 (1st Cir.2000) (concluding that to copy any less than the entire image would have made the picture useless to the story). Adopting this reasoning, we conclude that the third-factor inquiry must take into account that the "the extent of permissible copying varies with the purpose and character of the use." *Campbell*, 510 U.S. at 586–87.

Here, DK used BGA's images because the posters and tickets were historical artifacts that could document Grateful Dead concert events and provide a visual context for the accompanying text. To accomplish this use, DK displayed reduced versions of the original images and intermingled these visuals with text and original graphic art. As a consequence, even though the copyrighted images are copied in their entirety, the visual impact of their artistic expression is significantly limited because of their reduced size. *See Kelly*, 336 F.3d at 821 (concluding that thumbnails are not a substitute for full-size images). We conclude that such use by DK is tailored to further its transformative purpose because DK's reduced size reproductions of BGA's images in their entirety displayed the minimal image size and quality necessary to ensure the reader's recognition of the images as historical artifacts of Grateful Dead concert events. Accordingly, the third fair use factor does not weigh against fair use.

IV. Effect of the Use upon the Market for or Value of the Original

The fourth factor is "the effect of the use upon the potential market for or value of the copyrighted work." 17 U.S.C. § 107(4). The court looks to not only the market harm caused by the particular infringement, but also to whether, if the challenged use becomes widespread, it will adversely affect the potential market for the copyrighted work.

Harper, 471 U.S. at 568. This analysis requires a balancing of "the benefit the public will derive if the use is permitted and the personal gain the copyright owner will receive if the use is denied." *MCA, Inc. v. Wilson,* 677 F.2d 180, 183 (2d Cir.1981).

In the instant case, the parties agree that DK's use of the images did not impact BGA's primary market for the sale of the poster images. Instead, we look to whether DK's unauthorized use usurps BGA's potential to develop a derivative market. Appellant argues that DK interfered with the market for licensing its images for use in books. Appellant contends that there is an established market for licensing its images and it suffered both the loss of royalty revenue directly from DK and the opportunity to obtain royalties from others.

"It is indisputable that, as a general matter, a copyright holder is entitled to demand a royalty for licensing others to use its copyrighted work, and that the impact on potential licensing revenues is a proper subject for consideration in assessing the fourth factor." *Texaco,* 60 F.3d at 929 (citations omitted). We have noted, however, that "were a court automatically to conclude in every case that potential licensing revenues were impermissibly impaired simply because the secondary user did not pay a fee for the right to engage in the use, the fourth fair use factor would *always* favor the copyright holder." *Id.* at 930 n. 17 (emphasis added); *see Princeton Univ. Press v. Mich. Document Servs.,* 99 F.3d 1381, 1387 (6th Cir.1996) (stating that a copyright holder must have a right to copyright revenues before finding that a failure to pay a license fee equals market harm); Leval, *supra,* at 1124 (stating that "[b]y definition every fair use involves some loss of royalty revenue because the secondary user has not paid royalties"); 4 Melville B. Nimmer & David Nimmer, *Nimmer on Copyright* § 13.05[A][4] (2005) (stating that "it is a given in every fair use case that plaintiff suffers a loss of a potential market if that potential is defined as the theoretical market for licensing the very use at bar"). Accordingly, we do not find a harm to BGA's license market merely because DK did not pay a fee for BGA's copyrighted images.

Instead, we look at the impact on potential licensing revenues for "traditional, reasonable, or likely to be developed markets." *Texaco,* 60 F.3d at 930. In order to establish a traditional license market, Appellant points to the fees paid to other copyright owners for the reproduction of their images in *Illustrated Trip.* Moreover, Appellant asserts that it established a market for licensing its images, and in this case expressed a willingness to license images to DK. Neither of these arguments shows impairment to a traditional, as opposed to a transformative market.... *See* Leval, *supra,* at 1125 (explaining that "[t]he fourth factor disfavors a finding of fair use only when the market is impaired because the ... material serves the consumer as a substitute, or, ... supersedes the use of the original") (internal quotation marks omitted).

Here, unlike in *Texaco,* we hold that DK's use of BGA's images is transformatively different from their original expressive purpose.... In a case such as this, a copyright holder cannot prevent others from entering fair use markets merely "by developing or licensing a market for parody, news reporting, educational or other transformative uses of its own creative work." *Castle Rock,* 150 F.3d at 146 n. 11. "[C]opyright owners may not preempt exploitation of transformative markets.... " *Id.* Moreover, a publisher's willingness to pay license fees for reproduction of images does not establish that the publisher may not, in the alternative, make fair use of those images. *Campbell,* 510 U.S. at 585 n. 18 (stating that "being denied permission to use [or pay license fees for] a work does not weigh against a finding of fair use"). Since DK's use of BGA's images falls within a transformative market, BGA does not suffer market harm due to the loss of license fees.

V. Balance of Factors

On balance, we conclude, as the district court did, that the fair use factors weigh in favor of DK's use. For the first factor, we conclude that DK's use of concert posters and tickets as historical artifacts of Grateful Dead performances is transformatively different from the original expressive purpose of BGA's copyrighted images. While the second factor favors BGA because of the creative nature of the images, its weight is limited because DK did not exploit the expressive value of the images. Although BGA's images are copied in their entirety, the third factor does not weigh against fair use because the reduced size of the images is consistent with the author's transformative purpose. Finally, we conclude that DK's use does not harm the market for BGA's sale of its copyrighted artwork, and we do not find market harm based on BGA's hypothetical loss of license revenue from DK's transformative market.

* * *

Notes

1. Evaluate the strength of the defendants' fair use arguments in infringement cases arising out of the following examples:

(a) A former member of a controversial church wishes to discredit the church by revealing the contents of its secret "scriptures"—various training documents instructing church ministers in the indoctrination of new members—and therefore scans the documents electronically and uploads them onto a computer bulletin board, from which various newspapers download them and print substantial excerpts in related news stories. The former church member, the computer bulletin board, and the newspapers are all named as defendants. (Would it matter whether the documents in question were obtained from official court records or from sources within the church?) See *Religious Technology Center v. Netcom On–Line Communication Services, Inc.,* 907 F.Supp. 1361 (N.D.Cal.1995), *supra* page 987.

(b) Defendant, a contemporary artist, finds a postcard with a black-and-white photo of a smiling husband and wife seated on a bench and holding a litter of cute puppies. The artist produces a sculpture which reproduces the photograph in precise detail, except that it leaves out the original copyright notice. The artist includes this sculpture in a collection of his works which he calls "Banality," and which features sculptures depicting various commodities and images that, in his view, reflect something about modern American culture. The literature accompanying the exhibit describes the puppy sculpture as a "satire or parody" of society at large and as "social criticism," reflecting his belief that there has been an aesthetic decline in American culture. He describes himself as belonging to an artistic tradition traceable to Cubism, Dadaism, and the work of Marcel Duchamp. This tradition incorporates manufactured objects into works of art as a critical commentary both on the incorporated object and on the political and economic system that created it. See *Rogers v. Koons*, 960 F.2d 301 (2d Cir.1992).

(c) Defendants, members of a city council, surreptitiously record adult films being shown at plaintiff's theatre in order to obtain evidence for determining whether the plaintiff's theatre is a public nuisance. See *Jartech, Inc. v. Clancy*, 666 F.2d 403 (9th Cir.1982).

(d) Defendant, a controversial religious and political figure, is the subject of an obscene satire in plaintiff's magazine. He makes numerous copies of the satire and sends them to his supporters with a request for contributions to defray the cost of his defamation suit. See *Hustler Magazine, Inc. v. Moral Majority, Inc.*, 796 F.2d 1148 (9th Cir.1986).

(e) Defendant, a college professor, copies plaintiff's copyrighted music videos off of television and edits clips of the videos together into a videotape, which he narrates, analyzing the depiction of women as sex objects in rock music videos. He also offers the video for sale to colleges, libraries and individuals.

(f) Defendant, a political candidate who is challenging the incumbent in a local election, distributes campaign flyers reproducing headlines, excerpts from articles, and in some cases entire articles, all critical of the incumbent, and all from different issues of the same local newspaper.

(g) Defendant makes an unauthorized copy of a physically deteriorating motion picture or sound recording for preservation purposes. Would it matter if the defendant exhibited the resulting works in restored form in order to recoup the expenses of restoration? See H.R. Rep. No 94–1476, at 73. Compare Brief of Amicus Curiae Michael Agee, in *Eldred v. Ashcroft*, cert. granted and modified, 122 S.Ct. 1062, 122 S.Ct. 1170, No. 01–618.

(h) Defendant uses short excerpts and individual frames of an audiovisual work for purposes of criticism or commentary in an educational broadcast. See H.R. Rep. No. 94–1476 at 72.

(i) Defendant runs a news clipping service, which collects newspapers and magazines, and records television and radio news broadcasts and "news magazine" programs, and sorts out the news items, and sends copies to the persons or entities to whom each item pertains, provided that the person or entity subscribes to defendant's service. The publishers and broadcasters that originate the news stories do not provide such a service. *Cf., Pacific & Southern Co. v. Duncan,* 744 F.2d 1490 (11th Cir.1984).

(j) Plaintiff's copyrighted artwork is visible in the background of a scene in defendant's motion picture. *Cf. Amsinck v. Columbia Pictures Industries,* 862 F.Supp. 1044 (S.D.N.Y.1994), *supra* page 966.

(k) Defendant "reads" plaintiff's work in digitized form by loading it (from a diskette or from a computer network) into the RAM of a computer. (For purposes of this question, assume that loading into RAM involves reproducing the work within the meaning of section 106(1).)

(l) Defendant digitizes various medical and scientific journals and provides its customers with the digitized copies as well as software enabling the customers to conduct key word searches of the material. However, defendant supplies this material only to customers who already subscribe to the journals in hard copy.

(m) Recall the facts of *Time, Inc. v. Bernard Geis Assoc.,* summarized at page 821, *supra,* and evaluate the merits of a fair use defense in that case.

2. *Photocopying for Research Purposes*: Consider the following scenarios:

(a) A large for-profit corporation, which employs hundreds of research scientists and engineers to develop and test its products, subscribes to numerous scientific and technical journals. In some cases, it purchases several subscriptions to a single journal. The corporation routes these journals to all interested employees, and photocopies articles for them on request. The scientists and engineers frequently request copies of articles relevant to their research areas. Although in some cases the employees take the copied articles into the lab for convenient reference, in many cases they do not use the articles immediately, but file them away for future reference. Over time, thousands of pages of photocopied material accumulate in these files.

The publishers of the journals do not solicit or pay for the articles they publish. Their revenues come entirely from subscriptions and reprints. It is time-consuming and expensive for subscribers to purchase reprints of individual articles, and normally reprints are only sold in bulk (*e.g.,* in lots of 50).

However, many (though not all) of the publishers have registered their journals with the Copyright Clearance Center (CCC), a clearinghouse which establishes fees (on a per-copy basis or through blanket licensing) for photocopying of works belonging to its member publishers. The process of obtaining permission to copy an individual article through the CCC is less cumbersome than negotiating directly with the publisher. In the case of a blanket license, negotiation is unnecessary but the licensee must still determine whether the journals from which the articles will be copied are covered by the license (that is, whether they participate in the CCC). Alternatively, the party wishing to copy articles may pay a document delivery service to negotiate with the publisher and deliver the requested copies.

In a class action infringement suit by the journal publishers against the corporation, evaluate the strength of the defendant's fair use defense. See *American Geophysical Union v. Texaco, Inc.*, 60 F.3d 913 (2d Cir.1994).

(i) On the facts of (a), how is the fair use analysis affected if the journals are published by academic institutions, which also provide part of their funding?

(ii) On the facts of (a), how is the fair use analysis affected if the defendant is an individual researcher or a nonprofit institution such as a university (assuming that the copying is still for research purposes)?

(iii) On the facts of (a), how is the fair use analysis affected if the journal publishers pay flat fees and/or royalties to the authors of the articles they publish?

(b) Suppose that a law firm subscribes to various journals, newsletters, periodicals, and advance sheets of interest to its attorneys, and photocopies articles at the attorneys' request. Some of the publications are produced for profit, while others are produced by nonprofit institutions such as universities; some, but not all, subscribe to the CCC. Evaluate the potential for a successful fair use defense.

3. Suppose that plaintiff and defendant are competing manufacturers of videogame software. Plaintiff also manufactures a videogame console which is designed to accept only plaintiff's own videogame cartridges. Defendant wishes to make its own cartridges compatible with the plaintiff's console. To accomplish this, defendant copies plaintiff's software, "decompiles" it into source code, and identifies the specific and very short code sequence that is necessary for compatibility. Is defendant's copying fair use if (1) defendant's videogame software incorporates this same code sequence? or (2) after identifying the plaintiff's compatibility code sequence, defendant "designs around" it by writing a different code sequence that makes the software compatible? See *Sega Enterprises, Ltd. v. Accolade, Inc.*, 977 F.2d 1510 (9th Cir.1992).

4. Defendant, a computer servicing company, is sued for copyright infringement by the company that manufactured the computers defendant services. The plaintiff computer maker licenses its software to purchasers of its computers under a licensing agreement that bars the customers from letting any other parties copy the software for any purpose, including maintenance of the computers. Defendant is not licensed by the manufacturer to copy its software, but necessarily does so in the course of servicing the computers. Defendant services plaintiff's computers at a lower cost to customers than does the plaintiff, and points out that many of the plaintiff's customers would not have bought the plaintiff's computers if they did not have access to the lower-cost servicing that defendant provides. If defendant can prove that plaintiff's revenues have in fact been enhanced as a result of defendant's unauthorized copying, does the fourth fair use factor favor the defendant? See, e.g., *Triad Systems Corp. v. Southeastern Express Co.*, 64 F.3d 1330 (9th Cir.1995).

5. Defendant writes a biography of a deceased novelist, and includes excerpts from the novelist's letters, unpublished manuscripts, and private journals (to which defendant had access through a university library) as well as from some of the published novels. In an infringement suit by the novelist's estate, what facts would be important in determining the strength of the defendant's fair use argument? Compare *Salinger v. Random House, Inc.*, 811 F.2d 90 (2d Cir.1987) with *Wright v. Warner Books*, 953 F.2d 731 (2d Cir.1991). (Recall that Congress amended section 107 in 1992, adding the last sentence to that section particularly in response to the opinion in *Salinger*.)

6. What weight, if any, should be given to a defendant's good or bad faith in the fair use analysis?

7. Does "fair use" apply to section 1101? Should it?

Note: Fair Use and Section 106A

The legislative history of the Visual Artists Rights Act of 1990 makes the following comment on fair use:

> Fair Use.—Section 7 of the bill amends 17 U.S.C.A. § 107, and states that section 107's fair use provisions apply to violations of new section 106A as well as to violations of section 106. The Committee does not want to preclude fair use claims in this context. However, it recognizes that it is unlikely that such claims will be appropriate given the limited number of works covered by the Act, and given that the modification of a single copy or limited edition of a work of visual art has different implications for the fair use doctrine than does an act involving a work reproduced in potentially unlimited copies.

H.R. Rep. 101–514, 101st Cong., 2d Sess. 22 (1990).

Note: Educational Copying

In drafting the 1976 Act, Congress chose not to enact a specific exemption for educational copying. H.R. Rep. 1476, 94th Cong., 2d Sess. 66–67 (1976). However, in an effort to provide greater certainty with regard to copying for classroom use, the House Report incorporates a set of guidelines which resulted from negotiations among the Ad Hoc Committee of Educational Institutions and Organizations on Copyright Law Revision, the Authors League of America, Inc., and the Association of American Publishers, Inc. *See* Agreement on Guidelines for Classroom Copying in Not–For–Profit Educational Institutions, *in* H.R. Rep. 1476, 94th Cong., 2d Sess. 68–70 (1976). The House Report also incorporates a separate set of guidelines for educational copying of musical works (not limited to photocopying), developed as a result of negotiations between representatives of music publishers, music teachers, and music schools. *See id.* at 70–72. However, in each case the guidelines note that their purpose is to state the minimum, rather than the maximum, standards of educational fair use. *Id.* at 68, 70.

The scope of "fair use" with respect to classroom photocopying has been litigated on only a few occasions. See *Princeton University Press v. Michigan Document Services*, 99 F.3d 1381 (6th Cir.1996) (en banc) (holding commercial copy center liable for infringement where it exceeded the House Report's guidelines in preparing course packs for university professors), *rev'g* 74 F.3d 1512 (6th Cir.1996), *cert. denied*, 520 U.S. 1156, 117 S.Ct. 1336, 137 L.Ed.2d 495 (1997); *Basic Books, Inc. v. Kinko's Graphics Corp.*, 758 F.Supp. 1522 (S.D.N.Y.1991) (similar); *Addison–Wesley Publishing v. New York University*, 1983 Copyright L. Dec. (CCH) para. 25,544 (S.D.N.Y.1983) (consent decree requiring defendant university to follow House Report's guidelines in future).

Under what circumstances should unauthorized copying of materials for teaching purposes be considered fair use? Consider not only photocopying but downloading and/or printing of digitized works, copying of phonorecords, duplicating videocassettes and sound recordings, and off-the-air taping of broadcast works. Should the fair use analysis depend on whether the copying is done for graduate, undergraduate, or pre-university education? Should it matter how the copying is carried out—*e.g.*, whether all copies are made at the teacher's request by a university copy center, or by a for-profit copy shop, or whether each individual student is instructed to make his or her own copy of a work placed on reserve at a university library? Should it matter whether the copyright owners participate in the CCC or a similar agency arrangement whereby permission can be obtained promptly, without negotiation, at a reasonable price, and cannot be refused? Should the increasing use of electronic publishing affect the analysis?

Is there an argument for adopting a bright-line test for identifying permissible educational uses of copyrighted works? Alternatively, should Congress adopt a compulsory licensing scheme?

A & M RECORDS, INC. v. NAPSTER, INC.

United States Court of Appeals, Ninth Circuit, 2001.
239 F.3d 1004.

BEEZER, CIRCUIT JUDGE:

Plaintiffs are engaged in the commercial recording, distribution and sale of copyrighted musical compositions and sound recordings. The complaint alleges that Napster, Inc. ("Napster") is a contributory and vicarious copyright infringer. On July 26, 2000, the district court granted plaintiffs' motion for a preliminary injunction. The injunction was slightly modified by written opinion on August 10, 2000. A & M Records, Inc. v. Napster, Inc., 114 F.Supp.2d 896 (N.D.Cal.2000). The district court preliminarily enjoined Napster "from engaging in, or facilitating others in copying, downloading, uploading, transmitting, or distributing plaintiffs' copyrighted musical compositions and sound recordings, protected by either federal or state law, without express permission of the rights owner." Id. at 927. Federal Rule of Civil Procedure 65(c) requires successful plaintiffs to post a bond for damages incurred by the enjoined party in the event that the injunction was wrongfully issued. The district court set bond in this case at $5 million.

We entered a temporary stay of the preliminary injunction pending resolution of this appeal. We have jurisdiction pursuant to 28 U.S.C. § 1292(a)(1). We affirm in part, reverse in part and remand.

I

We have examined the papers submitted in support of and in response to the injunction application and it appears that Napster has designed and operates a system which permits the transmission and retention of sound recordings employing digital technology.

In 1987, the Moving Picture Experts Group set a standard file format for the storage of audio recordings in a digital format called MPEG–3, abbreviated as "MP3." Digital MP3 files are created through a process colloquially called "ripping." Ripping software allows a computer owner to copy an audio compact disk ("audio CD") directly onto a computer's hard drive by compressing the audio information on the CD into the MP3 format. The MP3's compressed format allows for rapid transmission of digital audio files from one computer to another by electronic mail or any other file transfer protocol.

Napster facilitates the transmission of MP3 files between and among its users. Through a process commonly called "peer-to-peer" file sharing, Napster allows its users to: (1) make MP3 music files stored on individual computer hard drives available for copying by other Napster users; (2) search for MP3 music files stored on other users' computers; and (3) transfer exact copies of the contents of other users' MP3 files from one computer to another via the Internet. These functions are made possible by Napster's MusicShare software, available free of charge from Napster's Internet site, and Napster's network servers and server-side software. Napster provides technical support for the indexing and searching of MP3 files, as well as for its other functions, including a "chat room," where users can meet to discuss music, and a directory where participating artists can provide information about their music.

A. ACCESSING THE SYSTEM

In order to copy MP3 files through the Napster system, a user must first access Napster's Internet site and download the MusicShare software to his individual computer. *See http://www.Napster.com.* Once the software is installed, the user can access the Napster system. A first-time user is required to register with the Napster system by creating a "user name" and password.

B. LISTING AVAILABLE FILES

If a registered user wants to list available files stored in his computer's hard drive on Napster for others to access, he must first create a "user library" directory on his computer's hard drive. The user then saves his MP3 files in the library directory, using self-designated file names. He next must log into the Napster system using his user name and password. His MusicShare software then searches his user library and verifies that the available files are properly formatted. If in the correct MP3 format, the names of the MP3 files will be uploaded from the user's computer to the Napster servers. The content of the MP3 files remains stored in the user's computer.

Once uploaded to the Napster servers, the user's MP3 file names are stored in a server-side "library" under the user's name and become part of a "collective directory" of files available for transfer during the time the user is logged onto the Napster system. The collective directory is fluid; it tracks users who are connected in real time, displaying only file names that are immediately accessible.

C. Searching For Available Files

Napster allows a user to locate other users' MP3 files in two ways: through Napster's search function and through its "hotlist" function.

Software located on the Napster servers maintains a "search index" of Napster's collective directory. To search the files available from Napster users currently connected to the network servers, the individual user accesses a form in the MusicShare software stored in his computer and enters either the name of a song or an artist as the object of the search. The form is then transmitted to a Napster server and automatically compared to the MP3 file names listed in the server's search index. Napster's server compiles a list of all MP3 file names pulled from the search index which include the same search terms entered on the search form and transmits the list to the searching user. The Napster server does not search the contents of any MP3 file; rather, the search is limited to "a text search of the file names indexed in a particular cluster. Those file names may contain typographical errors or otherwise inaccurate descriptions of the content of the files since they are designated by other users." Napster, 114 F.Supp.2d at 906.

To use the "hotlist" function, the Napster user creates a list of other users' names from whom he has obtained MP3 files in the past. When logged onto Napster's servers, the system alerts the user if any user on his list (a "hotlisted user") is also logged onto the system. If so, the user can access an index of all MP3 file names in a particular hotlisted user's library and request a file in the library by selecting the file name. The contents of the hotlisted user's MP3 file are not stored on the Napster system.

D. Transferring Copies of an MP3 file

To transfer a copy of the contents of a requested MP3 file, the Napster server software obtains the Internet address of the requesting user and the Internet address of the "host user" (the user with the available files). *See generally* Brookfield Communications, Inc. v. West Coast Entm't Corp., 174 F.3d 1036, 1044 (9th Cir.1999) (describing, in detail, the structure of the Internet). The Napster servers then communicate the host user's Internet address to the requesting user. The requesting user's computer uses this information to establish a connection with the host user and downloads a copy of the contents of the MP3 file from one computer to the other over the Internet, "peer-to-peer." A downloaded MP3 file can be played directly from the user's hard drive using Napster's MusicShare program or other software. The file may also be transferred back onto an audio CD if the user has access to equipment designed for that purpose. In both cases, the quality of the original sound recording is slightly diminished by transfer to the MP3 format.

This architecture is described in some detail to promote an understanding of transmission mechanics as opposed to the content of the transmissions. The content is the subject of our copyright infringement analysis.

* * *

III

Plaintiffs claim Napster users are engaged in the wholesale reproduction and distribution of copyrighted works, all constituting direct infringement. The district court agreed. We note that the district court's conclusion that plaintiffs have presented a prima facie case of direct infringement by Napster users is not presently appealed by Napster. We only need briefly address the threshold requirements.

A. INFRINGEMENT

Plaintiffs must satisfy two requirements to present a prima facie case of direct infringement: (1) they must show ownership of the allegedly infringed material and (2) they must demonstrate that the alleged infringers violate at least one exclusive right granted to copyright holders under 17 U.S.C. § 106. *See* 17 U.S.C. § 501(a) (infringement occurs when alleged infringer engages in activity listed in § 106); *see also* Baxter v. MCA, Inc., 812 F.2d 421, 423 (9th Cir.1987); *see, e.g.,* S.O.S., Inc. v. Payday, Inc., 886 F.2d 1081, 1085 n. 3 (9th Cir.1989) ("The word 'copying' is shorthand for the infringing of any of the copyright owner's five exclusive rights.... "). Plaintiffs have sufficiently demonstrated ownership. The record supports the district court's determination that "as much as eighty-seven percent of the files available on Napster may be copyrighted and more than seventy percent may be owned or administered by plaintiffs." Napster, 114 F.Supp.2d at 911.

The district court further determined that plaintiffs' exclusive rights under § 106 were violated: "here the evidence establishes that a majority of Napster users use the service to download and upload copyrighted music.... And by doing that, it constitutes—the uses constitute direct infringement of plaintiffs' musical compositions, recordings." A & M Records, Inc. v. Napster, Inc., Nos. 99–5183, 00–0074, 2000 WL 1009483, at *1 (N.D.Cal. July 26, 2000) (transcript of proceedings). The district court also noted that "it is pretty much acknowledged ... by Napster that this is infringement." Id. We agree that plaintiffs have shown that Napster users infringe at least two of the copyright holders' exclusive rights: the rights of reproduction, § 106(1); and distribution, § 106(3). Napster users who upload file names to the search index for others to copy violate plaintiffs' distribution rights. Napster users who download files containing copyrighted music violate plaintiffs' reproduction rights.

Napster asserts an affirmative defense to the charge that its users directly infringe plaintiffs' copyrighted musical compositions and sound recordings.

B. FAIR USE

Napster contends that its users do not directly infringe plaintiffs' copyrights because the users are engaged in fair use of the material. *See* 17 U.S.C. § 107 ("[T]he fair use of a copyrighted work ... is not an infringement of copyright."). Napster identifies three specific alleged fair uses: sampling, where users make temporary copies of a work before purchasing; space-shifting, where users access a sound recording through the Napster system that they already own in audio CD format; and permissive distribution of recordings by both new and established artists.

The district court considered factors listed in 17 U.S.C. § 107, which guide a court's fair use determination. These factors are: (1) the purpose and character of the use; (2) the nature of the copyrighted work; (3) the "amount and substantiality of the portion used" in relation to the work as a whole; and (4) the effect of the use upon the potential market for the work or the value of the work. *See* 17 U.S.C. § 107. The district court first conducted a general analysis of Napster system uses under § 107, and then applied its reasoning to the alleged fair uses identified by Napster. The district court concluded that Napster users are not fair users. We agree. We first address the court's overall fair use analysis.

1. *Purpose and Character of the Use*

This factor focuses on whether the new work merely replaces the object of the original creation or instead adds a further purpose or different character. In other words, this factor asks "whether and to what extent the new work is 'transformative.'" *See* Campbell v. Acuff–Rose Music, Inc., 510 U.S. 569, 579, 114 S.Ct. 1164, 127 L.Ed.2d 500 (1994).

The district court first concluded that downloading MP3 files does not transform the copyrighted work. Napster, 114 F.Supp.2d at 912. This conclusion is supportable. Courts have been reluctant to find fair use when an original work is merely retransmitted in a different medium. *See, e.g.,* Infinity Broadcast Corp. v. Kirkwood, 150 F.3d 104, 108 (2d Cir.1998) (concluding that retransmission of radio broadcast over telephone lines is not transformative); UMG Recordings, Inc. v. MP3.Com, Inc., 92 F.Supp.2d 349, 351 (S.D.N.Y.) (finding that reproduction of audio CD into MP3 format does not "transform" the work), *certification denied,* 2000 WL 710056 (S.D.N.Y. June 1, 2000) ("Defendant's copyright infringement was clear, and the mere fact that it was clothed in the exotic webbing of the Internet does not disguise its illegality.").

This "purpose and character" element also requires the district court to determine whether the allegedly infringing use is commercial or noncommercial. *See* Campbell, 510 U.S. at 584–85, 114 S.Ct. 1164. A commercial use weighs against a finding of fair use but is not conclusive on the issue. Id. The district court determined that Napster users engage in commercial use of the copyrighted materials largely because (1) "a host user sending a file cannot be said to engage in a personal use when distributing that file to an anonymous requester" and (2) "Napster users get for free something they would ordinarily have to buy." Napster, 114 F.Supp.2d at 912. The district court's findings are not clearly erroneous.

Direct economic benefit is not required to demonstrate a commercial use. Rather, repeated and exploitative copying of copyrighted works, even if the copies are not offered for sale, may constitute a commercial use. *See* Worldwide Church of God v. Philadelphia Church of God, 227 F.3d 1110, 1118 (9th Cir.2000) (stating that church that copied religious text for its members "unquestionably profit[ed]" from the unauthorized "distribution and use of [the text] without having to account to the copyright holder"); American Geophysical Union v. Texaco, Inc., 60 F.3d 913, 922 (2d Cir.1994) (finding that researchers at for-profit laboratory gained indirect economic advantage by photocopying copyrighted scholarly articles). In the record before us, commercial use is demonstrated by a showing that repeated and exploitative unauthorized copies of copyrighted works were made to save the expense of purchasing authorized copies. *See* Worldwide Church, 227 F.3d at 1117–18; Sega Enters. Ltd. v. MAPHIA, 857 F.Supp. 679, 687 (N.D.Cal.1994) (finding commercial use when individuals downloaded copies of video games "to avoid having to buy video game cartridges"); *see also* American Geophysical, 60 F.3d at 922. Plaintiffs made such a showing before the district court.

We also note that the definition of a financially motivated transaction for the purposes of criminal copyright actions includes trading infringing copies of a work for other items, "including the receipt of other copyrighted works." *See* No Electronic Theft Act ("NET Act"), Pub.L. No. 105–147, 18 U.S.C. § 101 (defining "Financial Gain").

2.   *The Nature of the Use*

Works that are creative in nature are "closer to the core of intended copyright protection" than are more fact-based works. *See* Campbell, 510 U.S. at 586, 114 S.Ct. 1164. The district court determined that plaintiffs' "copyrighted musical compositions and sound recordings are creative in nature ... which cuts against a finding of fair use under the second factor." Napster, 114 F.Supp.2d at 913. We find no error in the district court's conclusion.

3.   *The Portion Used*

"While 'wholesale copying does not preclude fair use per se,' copying an entire work 'militates against a finding of fair use.' " Worldwide Church, 227 F.3d at 1118 (quoting Hustler Magazine, Inc. v. Moral Majority, Inc., 796 F.2d 1148, 1155 (9th Cir.1986)). The district court determined that Napster users engage in "wholesale copying" of copyrighted work because file transfer necessarily "involves copying the entirety of the copyrighted work." Napster, 114 F.Supp.2d at 913. We agree. We note, however, that under certain circumstances, a court will conclude that a use is fair even when the protected work is copied in its entirety. *See, e.g.,* Sony Corp. v. Universal City Studios, Inc., 464 U.S. 417, 449–50, 104 S.Ct. 774, 78 L.Ed.2d 574 (1984) (acknowledging that fair use of time-shifting necessarily involved making a full copy of a protected work).

4. *Effect of Use on Market*

"Fair use, when properly applied, is limited to copying by others which does not materially impair the marketability of the work which is copied." Harper & Row Publishers, Inc. v. Nation Enters., 471 U.S. 539, 566–67, 105 S.Ct. 2218, 85 L.Ed.2d 588 (1985). "[T]he importance of this [fourth] factor will vary, not only with the amount of harm, but also with the relative strength of the showing on the other factors." Campbell, 510 U.S. at 591 n. 21, 114 S.Ct. 1164. The proof required to demonstrate present or future market harm varies with the purpose and character of the use:

> A challenge to a noncommercial use of a copyrighted work requires proof either that the particular use is harmful, or that if it should become widespread, it would adversely affect the potential market for the copyrighted work.... *If the intended use is for commercial gain, that likelihood [of market harm] may be presumed. But if it is for a noncommercial purpose, the likelihood must be demonstrated.*

Sony, 464 U.S. at 451, 104 S.Ct. 774 (emphases added).

Addressing this factor, the district court concluded that Napster harms the market in "at least" two ways: it reduces audio CD sales among college students and it "raises barriers to plaintiffs' entry into the market for the digital downloading of music." Napster, 114 F.Supp.2d at 913. The district court relied on evidence plaintiffs submitted to show that Napster use harms the market for their copyrighted musical compositions and sound recordings. In a separate memorandum and order regarding the parties' objections to the expert reports, the district court examined each report, finding some more appropriate and probative than others. A & M Records, Inc. v. Napster, Inc., Nos. 99–5183 & 00–0074, 2000 WL 1170106 (N.D.Cal. August 10, 2000). Notably, plaintiffs' expert, Dr. E. Deborah Jay, conducted a survey (the "JayReport") using a random sample of college and university students to track their reasons for using Napster and the impact Napster had on their music purchases. Id. at *2. The court recognized that the Jay Report focused on just one segment of the Napster user population and found "evidence of lost sales attributable to college use to be probative of irreparable harm for purposes of the preliminary injunction motion." Id. at *3.

Plaintiffs also offered a study conducted by Michael Fine, Chief Executive Officer of Soundscan, (the "Fine Report") to determine the effect of online sharing of MP3 files in order to show irreparable harm.

Fine found that online file sharing had resulted in a loss of "album" sales within college markets. After reviewing defendant's objections to the Fine Report and expressing some concerns regarding the methodology and findings, the district court refused to exclude the Fine Report insofar as plaintiffs offered it to show irreparable harm. Id. at *6.

Plaintiffs' expert Dr. David J. Teece studied several issues ("Teece Report"), including whether plaintiffs had suffered or were likely to suffer harm in their existing and planned businesses due to Napster use. Id. Napster objected that the report had not undergone peer review. The district court noted that such reports generally are not subject to such scrutiny and overruled defendant's objections. Id.

As for defendant's experts, plaintiffs objected to the report of Dr. Peter S. Fader, in which the expert concluded that Napster is *beneficial* to the music industry because MP3 music file-sharing stimulates more audio CD sales than it displaces. Id. at *7. The district court found problems in Dr. Fader's minimal role in overseeing the administration of the survey and the lack of objective data in his report. The court decided the generality of the report rendered it "of dubious reliability and value." The court did not exclude the report, however, but chose "not to rely on Fader's findings in determining the issues of fair use and irreparable harm." Id. at *8.

The district court cited both the Jay and Fine Reports in support of its finding that Napster use harms the market for plaintiffs' copyrighted musical compositions and sound recordings by reducing CD sales among college students. The district court cited the Teece Report to show the harm Napster use caused in raising barriers to plaintiffs' entry into the market for digital downloading of music. Napster, 114 F.Supp.2d at 910. The district court's careful consideration of defendant's objections to these reports and decision to rely on the reports for specific issues demonstrates a proper exercise of discretion in addition to a correct application of the fair use doctrine. Defendant has failed to show any basis for disturbing the district court's findings.

We, therefore, conclude that the district court made sound findings related to Napster's deleterious effect on the present and future digital download market. Moreover, lack of harm to an established market cannot deprive the copyright holder of the right to develop alternative markets for the works. *See* L.A. Times v. Free Republic, 54 U.S.P.Q.2d 1453, 1469–71 (C.D.Cal.2000) (stating that online market for plaintiff newspapers' articles was harmed because plaintiffs demonstrated that "[defendants] are attempting to exploit the market for viewing their articles online"); *see also* UMG Recordings, 92 F.Supp.2d at 352 ("Any allegedly positive impact of defendant's activities on plaintiffs' prior market in no way frees defendant to usurp a further market that directly derives from reproduction of the plaintiffs' copyrighted works."). Here, similar to L.A. Times and UMG Recordings, the record supports the district court's finding that the "record company plaintiffs have already expended considerable funds and effort to commence Internet sales and licensing for digital downloads." 114 F.Supp.2d at 915. Having digital downloads available for free on the Napster system necessarily harms the copyright holders' attempts to charge for the same downloads.

Judge Patel did not abuse her discretion in reaching the above fair use conclusions, nor were the findings of fact with respect to fair use considerations clearly erroneous. We next address Napster's identified uses of sampling and space-shifting.

5. Identified Uses

Napster maintains that its identified uses of sampling and space-shifting were wrongly excluded as fair uses by the district court.

a. Sampling

Napster contends that its users download MP3 files to "sample" the music in order to decide whether to purchase the recording. Napster argues that the district court: (1) erred in concluding that sampling is a commercial use because it conflated a noncommercial use with a personal use; (2) erred in determining that sampling adversely affects the market for plaintiffs' copyrighted music, a requirement if the use is noncommercial; and (3) erroneously concluded that sampling is not a fair use because it determined that samplers may also engage in other infringing activity.

The district court determined that sampling remains a commercial use even if some users eventually purchase the music. We find no error in the district court's determination. Plaintiffs have established that they are likely to succeed in proving that even authorized temporary downloading of individual songs for sampling purposes is commercial in nature. *See* Napster, 114 F.Supp.2d at 913. The record supports a finding that free promotional downloads are highly regulated by the record company plaintiffs and that the companies collect royalties for song samples available on retail Internet sites. Id. Evidence relied on by the district court demonstrates that the free downloads provided by the record companies consist of thirty-to-sixty second samples or are full songs programmed to "time out," that is, exist only for a short time on the downloader's computer. Id. at 913–14. In comparison, Napster users download a full, free and permanent copy of the recording. Id. at 914–15. The determination by the district court as to the commercial purpose and character of sampling is not clearly erroneous.

The district court further found that both the market for audio CDs and market for online distribution are adversely affected by Napster's service. As stated in our discussion of the district court's general fair use analysis: the court did not abuse its discretion when it found that, overall, Napster has an adverse impact on the audio CD and digital download markets. Contrary to Napster's assertion that the district court failed to specifically address the market impact of sampling, the district court determined that "[e]ven if the type of sampling supposedly done on Napster were a non-commercial use, plaintiffs have demonstrated a substantial likelihood that it would adversely affect the potential market for their copyrighted works if it became widespread." Napster, 114 F.Supp.2d at 914. The record supports the district court's preliminary determinations that: (1) the more music that sampling users download, the less likely they are to eventually purchase the recordings on audio CD; and (2) even if the audio CD market is not harmed, Napster has adverse effects on the developing digital download market.

Napster further argues that the district court erred in rejecting its evidence that the users' downloading of "samples" increases or tends to increase audio CD sales. The district court, however, correctly noted that "any potential enhancement of plaintiffs' sales ... would not tip the fair use analysis conclusively in favor of defendant." Id. at 914. We agree that increased sales of copyrighted material attributable to unauthorized use should not deprive the copyright holder of the right to license the material. *See* Campbell, 510 U.S. at 591 n. 21, 114 S.Ct. 1164 ("Even favorable evidence, without more, is no guarantee of fairness. Judge Leval gives the example of the film producer's appropriation of a composer's previously unknown song that turns the song into a commercial success; the boon to the song does not make the film's simple copying fair."); *see also* L.A. Times, 54 U.S.P.Q.2d at 1471–72. Nor does positive impact in one market, here the audio CD market, deprive the copyright holder of the right to develop identified alternative markets, here the digital download market. *See* id. at 1469–71.

We find no error in the district court's factual findings or abuse of discretion in the court's conclusion that plaintiffs will likely prevail in establishing that sampling does not constitute a fair use.

b. *Space–Shifting*

Napster also maintains that space-shifting is a fair use. Space-shifting occurs when a Napster user downloads MP3 music files in order to listen to music he already owns on audio CD. *See* id. at 915–16. Napster asserts that we have already held that space-shifting of musical compositions and sound recordings is a fair use. *See* Recording Indus. Ass'n of Am. v. Diamond Multimedia Sys., Inc., 180 F.3d 1072, 1079 (9th Cir.1999) ("Rio [a portable MP3 player] merely makes copies in order to render portable, or 'space-shift,' those files that already reside on a user's hard drive.... Such copying is a paradigmatic noncommercial personal use."). *See also generally* Sony, 464 U.S. at 423, 104 S.Ct. 774 (holding that "time-shifting," where a video tape recorder owner records a television show for later viewing, is a fair use).

We conclude that the district court did not err when it refused to apply the "shifting" analyses of Sony and Diamond. Both Diamond and Sony are inapposite because the methods of shifting in these cases did not also simultaneously involve distribution of the copyrighted material to the general public; the time or space-shifting of copyrighted material exposed the material only to the original user. In Diamond, for example, the copyrighted music was transferred from the user's computer hard drive to the user's portable MP3 player. So too Sony, where "the majority of VCR purchasers ... did not distribute taped television broadcasts, but merely enjoyed them at home." Napster, 114 F.Supp.2d at 913. Conversely, it is obvious that once a user lists a copy of music he already owns on the Napster system in order to access the music from another location, the song becomes "available to millions of other individuals," not just the original CD owner. *See* UMG Recordings, 92 F.Supp.2d at 351–52 (finding space-shifting of MP3 files not a fair use even when previous ownership is demonstrated before a download is allowed); *cf.* Religious Tech. Ctr. v. Lerma, No. 95–1107A, 1996 WL 633131, at *6 (E.D.Va. Oct.4, 1996) (suggesting that storing copyrighted material on computer disk for later review is not a fair use).

c. *Other Uses*

Permissive reproduction by either independent or established artists is the final fair use claim made by Napster. The district court noted that plaintiffs did not seek to enjoin this and any other noninfringing use of the Napster system, including: chat rooms, message boards and Napster's New Artist Program. Napster, 114 F.Supp.2d at 917. Plaintiffs do not challenge these uses on appeal.

We find no error in the district court's determination that plaintiffs will likely succeed in establishing that Napster users do not have a fair use defense.

* * *

Notes

1. How are the issues in *Napster* different from the issues in *Sony,* as perceived by the Ninth Circuit? How would you yourself distinguish the two cases? Are the alleged individual infringements significantly different? How is downloading via Napster different from recording with a VCR? Is the difference to be seen primarily in Napster's greater potential for destructiveness to the interests of the copyright proprietors? Consider the fact that the motion picture industry's dire predictions in *Sony* proved to be utterly unfounded: in fact, the VCR turned out to be the industry's single greatest source of revenues for theatrical release feature films, thanks to the emergence of new rental markets for home viewing. Does Napster offer any similar promise of new markets? Is it significant that Bertelsmann, the German entertainment mega-consortium (which was among the plaintiffs in *Napster*), initiated negotiations toward some form of co-venture with Napster while the case was pending? (As of this writing, however, the CEO of Bertelsmann has been fired, and the future of any such co-venture appears to be in doubt.) Is it significant that Napster is an innovative new service? Should the fourth factor in fair use be reinterpreted to reward those whose innovation enhances the markets for copyrighted works—even if the innovators are not the copyright proprietors?

2. Note that section 107 is being used once again in *Napster* to decide the fair use question for tens of millions of individuals who are neither present nor represented in the case. *Quo warranto*? Can you think of one or more plausible instances of individual downloading via Napster clearly

amounting to fair use? Can you see downloading as a transformative act? As an act amounting to creative appropriation?

3. Are there first amendment issues in *Napster*? If so, what are they? Do you agree with those who say (as the Court did in *Harper & Row*) that "copyright is the engine of free expression"?

4. In *UMG Recordings, Inc. v. MP3.Com, Inc.*, 92 F.Supp.2d 349 (S.D.N.Y.2000), the district court granted a partial summary judgment of copyright infringement with respect to defendant's "My.MP3.com" service, finding that the defendant infringed the plaintiffs' copyrights in their sound recordings by copying those recordings onto its servers (in MP3 format) in order to replay them for its subscribers. Although the defendant would play a requested recording only for a requester who already possessed a copy of the relevant CD, or purchased one on-line, the court rejected the fair use defense, among others, and held that unauthorized copying was an infringement. The court said: "Here, although defendant recites that MyMP3.com provides a transformative 'space shift' by which subscribers can enjoy the sound recordings contained in their CDs without lugging around the physical discs themselves, this is simply another way of saying the unauthorized copies are being transmitted in another medium—an insufficient basis for any legitimate claim of transformation." Settlements followed among most major litigants.

5. Two additional cases (excerpted in succession, *infra* at page 1189) should be considered in the context of fair use as well. In *Re Aimster Copyright Litigation*, 334 F.3d 643 (7th Cir. 2004), *cert. denied*, 540 U.S. 1107, 124 S.Ct. 1069, 157 L.Ed.2d 893 (2004), Judge Posner suggested several ways in which peer-to-peer file sharing might be justified (though without ultimately endorsing any of them, and in fact affirming a preliminary finding of contributory infringement); while in *Metro–Goldwyn–Mayer Studios, Inc. v. Grockster, Ltd.*, 545 U.S. 913, 125 S.Ct. 2764, 162 L.Ed.2d 781 (2005), the Supreme Court rejected fair use arguments (distinguishing *Sony*) in an opinion that emphasized the defendant's deliberate efforts to encourage infringing appropriations.

KELLY v. ARRIBA SOFT CORPORATION
United States Court of Appeals, Ninth Circuit, 2002.
280 F.3d 934.

NELSON, CIRCUIT JUDGE:

This case involves the application of copyright law to the vast world of the internet and internet search engines. The plaintiff, Leslie Kelly, is a professional photographer who has copyrighted many of his images of the American West. Some of these images are located on Kelly's web site or other web sites with which Kelly has a license agreement. The defendant, Arriba Soft Corp., operates an internet search engine that displays its results in the form of small pictures rather than the more usual form of text. Arriba obtained its database of pictures by copying images from other web sites. By clicking on one of these small pictures, called "thumbnails," the user can then view a large version of that same picture within the context of the Arriba web page.

When Kelly discovered that his photographs were part of Arriba's search engine database, he brought a claim against Arriba for copyright infringement. The district court found that Kelly had established a prima facie case of copyright infringement based on Arriba's unauthorized reproduction and display of Kelly's works, but that this reproduction and display constituted a non-infringing "fair use" under Section 107 of the Copyright Act. Kelly appeals that decision, and we affirm in part and reverse in part. * * *

I.

The search engine at issue in this case is unconventional in that it displays the results of a user's query as "thumbnail" images. When a user wants to search the internet for information on a certain topic, he or she types a search term into a search engine, which then produces a list of web sites that have information relating to the search term. Normally, the list of results is in text format. The Arriba search engine, however, produces its list of results as small pictures.

To provide this functionality, Arriba developed a computer program that "crawls" the web looking for images to index. This crawler downloads full-sized copies of the images onto Arriba's server. The program then uses these copies to generate smaller, lower-resolution thumbnails of the images. Once the thumbnails are created, the program deletes the full-sized originals from the server. Although a user could copy these thumbnails to his computer or disk, he cannot increase the resolution of the thumbnail; any enlargement would result in a loss of clarity of the image.

The second component of the Arriba program occurs when the user double-clicks on the thumbnail. From January 1999 to June 1999, clicking on the thumbnail produced the "Images Attributes" page. This page contained the original full-sized image imported directly from the originating web site, along with text describing the size of the image, a link to the originating web site, the Arriba banner, and Arriba advertising. The process of importing an image from another web site is called inline linking. The image imported from another web site is displayed as though it is part of the current web page, surrounded by the current web page's text and advertising. As a result, although the image in Arriba's Image Attributes page was directly from the originating web site, and not copied onto Arriba's site, the user typically would not realize that the image actually resided on another web site.

From July 1999 until sometime after August 2000, the results page contained thumbnails accompanied by two links: "Source" and "Details." The "Details" link produced a screen similar to the Images Attributes page but with a thumbnail rather than the full-sized image. Alternatively, by clicking on the "Source" link or the thumbnail from the results page, the site produced two new windows on top of the Arriba page. The window in the forefront contained the full-sized image, imported directly from the originating web site. Underneath that was another window displaying the originating web page. This technique is known as framing. The image from a second web site is viewed within a frame that is pulled into the primary site's web page.

In January 1999, Arriba's crawler visited web sites that contained Kelly's photographs. The crawler copied thirty-five of Kelly's images to the Arriba database. Kelly had never given permission to Arriba to copy his images and objected when he found out that Arriba was using them. Arriba deleted the thumbnails of images that came from Kelly's own web sites and placed those sites on a list of sites that it would not crawl in the future. Several months later, Arriba received Kelly's complaint of copyright infringement, which identified other images of his that came from third-party web sites. * * *

II.

* * * An owner of a copyright has the exclusive right to reproduce, distribute, and publicly display copies of the work. To establish a claim of copyright infringement by reproduction, the plaintiff must show ownership of the copyright and copying by the defendant. As to the thumbnails, there is no dispute that Kelly owned the copyright to the images and that Arriba copied those images. Therefore, Kelly established a prima facie case of copyright infringement.

A claim of copyright infringement is subject to certain statutory exceptions, including the fair use exception.[8] This exception "permits courts to avoid rigid application of the copyright statute when, on occasion, it would stifle the very creativity which that law is designed to foster."[9] The statute sets out four factors to consider in determining whether the use in a particular case is a fair use. We must balance these factors, in light of the objectives of copyright law, rather than view them as definitive or determinative tests. We now turn to the four fair use factors.

1. *Purpose and character of the use.*

The Supreme Court has rejected the proposition that a commercial use of the copyrighted material ends the inquiry under this factor.[12] Instead,

> [t]he central purpose of this investigation is to see ... whether the new work merely supersede[s] the objects of the original creation, or instead adds something new, with a further purpose or different character, altering the first with new expression, meaning, or message; it asks, in other words, whether and to what extent the new work is transformative.[13]

---

8. 17 U.S.C. §§ 106, 107.

9. *Dr. Seuss Enters., L.P. v. Penguin Books USA, Inc.,* 109 F.3d 1394, 1399 (9th Cir.1997) (internal quotation marks and citation omitted). [Footnotes omitted.]

12. *Campbell v. Acuff–Rose Music, Inc.,* 510 U.S. 569, 579, 114 S.Ct. 1164, 127 L.Ed.2d 500 (1994).

13. *Id.* (internal quotation marks and citation omitted) (alteration in original).

The more transformative the new work, the less important the other factors, including commercialism, become.[14]

There is no dispute that Arriba operates its web site for commercial purposes and that Kelly's images were part of Arriba's search engine database. As the district court found, while such use of Kelly's images was commercial, it was more incidental and less exploitative in nature than more traditional types of commercial use. Arriba was neither using Kelly's images to directly promote its web site nor trying to profit by selling Kelly's images. Instead, Kelly's images were among thousands of images in Arriba's search engine database. Because the use of Kelly's images was not highly exploitative, the commercial nature of the use only slightly weighs against a finding of fair use.

The second part of the inquiry as to this factor involves the transformative nature of the use. We must determine if Arriba's use of the images merely superseded the object of the originals or instead added a further purpose or different character. We find that Arriba's use of Kelly's images for its thumbnails was transformative.

Despite the fact that Arriba made exact replications of Kelly's images, the thumbnails were much smaller, lower-resolution images that served an entirely different function than Kelly's original images. Kelly's images are artistic works used for illustrative purposes. His images are used to portray scenes from the American West in an esthetic manner. Arriba's use of Kelly's images in the thumbnails is unrelated to any esthetic purpose. Arriba's search engine functions as a tool to help index and improve access to images on the internet and their related web sites. In fact, users are unlikely to enlarge the thumbnails and use them for artistic purposes because the thumbnails are of much lower resolution than the originals; any enlargement results in a significant loss of clarity of the image, making them inappropriate as display material.

Kelly asserts that because Arriba reproduced his exact images and added nothing to them, Arriba's use cannot be transformative. It is true that courts have been reluctant to find fair use when an original work is merely retransmitted in a different medium.[17] Those cases are inapposite, however, because the resulting use of the copyrighted work in those cases was the same as the original use. For instance, reproducing music CD's into computer MP3 format does not change the fact that both formats are used for entertainment purposes. Likewise, reproducing news footage into a different format does not change the ultimate purpose of informing the public about current affairs.

Even in *Infinity Broadcast Corp. v. Kirkwood,*[18] where the retransmission of radio broadcasts over telephone lines was for the purpose of

---

14. *Id.*

17. *See Infinity Broad. Corp. v. Kirkwood,* 150 F.3d 104, 108 (2d Cir.1998) (concluding that retransmission of radio broadcast over telephone lines is not transformative); *UMG Recordings, Inc. v. MP3.Com, Inc.,* 92 F.Supp.2d 349, 351 (S.D.N.Y.2000) (finding that reproduction

of audio CD into computer MP3 format does not transform the work); *Los Angeles News Serv.,* 149 F.3d at 993 (finding that reproducing news footage without editing the footage was not very transformative).

18. 150 F.3d 104.

allowing advertisers and radio stations to check on the broadcast of commercials or on-air talent, there was nothing preventing listeners from subscribing to the service for entertainment purposes. Even though the intended purpose of the retransmission may have been different from the purpose of the original transmission, the result was that people could use both types of transmissions for the same purpose.

This case involves more than merely a retransmission of Kelly's images in a different medium. Arriba's use of the images serves a different function than Kelly's use-improving access to information on the internet versus artistic expression. Furthermore, it would be unlikely that anyone would use Arriba's thumbnails for illustrative or esthetic purposes because enlarging them sacrifices their clarity. Because Arriba's use is not superseding Kelly's use but, rather, has created a different purpose for the images, Arriba's use is transformative.

Comparing this case to two recent cases in the Ninth and First Circuits reemphasizes the functionality distinction. In *Worldwide Church of God v. Philadelphia Church of God,*[19] we held that copying a religious book to create a new book for use by a different church was not transformative.[20] The second church's use of the book merely superseded the object of the original book, which was to serve religious practice and education. The court noted that "where the use is for the same intrinsic purpose as [the copyright holder's] . . . such use seriously weakens a claimed fair use."[21]

On the other hand, in *Nunez v. Caribbean International News Corp.,*[22] the First Circuit found that copying a photograph that was intended to be used in a modeling portfolio and using it instead in a news article was a transformative use.[23] By putting a copy of the photograph in the newspaper, the work was transformed into news, creating a new meaning or purpose for the work. The use of Kelly's images in Arriba's search engine is more analogous to the situation in *Nunez* because Arriba has created a new purpose for the images and is not simply superseding Kelly's purpose.

The Copyright Act was intended to promote creativity, thereby benefitting the artist and the public alike. To preserve the potential future use of artistic works for purposes of teaching, research, criticism, and news reporting, Congress made the fair use exception. Arriba's use of Kelly's images promotes the goals of the Copyright Act and the fair use exception. The thumbnails do not stifle artistic creativity because they are not used for illustrative or artistic purposes and therefore do not supplant the need for the originals. In addition, they benefit the public by enhancing information gathering techniques on the internet.

---

19. 227 F.3d 1110 (9th Cir.2000).

20. *Id.* at 1117.

21. *Id.* (internal quotation and citation omitted) (alteration and ellipses in original).

22. 235 F.3d 18 (1st Cir.2000).

23. *Id.* at 22–23.

In *Sony Computer Entertainment America, Inc. v. Bleem,*[25] we held that when Bleem copied "screen shots" from Sony computer games and used them in its own advertising, it was a fair use.[26] In finding that the first factor weighed in favor of Bleem, we noted that "comparative advertising redounds greatly to the purchasing public's benefit with very little corresponding loss to the integrity of Sony's copyrighted material."[27] Similarly, this first factor weighs in favor of Arriba due to the public benefit of the search engine and the minimal loss of integrity to Kelly's images.

2. *Nature of the copyrighted work.*

"Works that are creative in nature are closer to the core of intended copyright protection than are more fact-based works."[28] Photographs used for illustrative purposes, such as Kelly's, are generally creative in nature. The fact that a work is published or unpublished also is a critical element of its nature.[29] Published works are more likely to qualify as fair use because the first appearance of the artist's expression has already occurred. Kelly's images appeared on the internet before Arriba used them in its search image. When considering both of these elements, we find that this factor only slightly weighs in favor of Kelly.

3. *Amount and substantiality of portion used.*

"While wholesale copying does not preclude fair use per se, copying an entire work militates against a finding of fair use."[31] However, the extent of permissible copying varies with the purpose and character of the use. If the secondary user only copies as much as is necessary for his or her intended use, then this factor will not weigh against him or her.

This factor will neither weigh for nor against either party because, although Arriba did copy each of Kelly's images as a whole, it was reasonable to do so in light of Arriba's use of the images. It was necessary for Arriba to copy the entire image to allow users to recognize the image and decide whether to pursue more information about the image or the originating web site. If Arriba only copied part of the image, it would be more difficult to identify it, thereby reducing the usefulness of the visual search engine.

4. *Effect of the use upon the potential market for or value of the copyrighted work.*

This last factor requires courts to consider "not only the extent of market harm caused by the particular actions of the alleged infringer, but also 'whether unrestricted and widespread conduct of the sort

25. 214 F.3d 1022 (9th Cir.2000).

26. *Id.* at 1029.

27. *Id.* at 1027.

28. *A & M Records,* 239 F.3d at 1016 (citing *Campbell,* 510 U.S. at 586, 114 S.Ct. 1164) (internal quotation marks omitted).

29. *Harper & Row, Publishers, Inc. v. Nation Enters.,* 471 U.S. 539, 564, 105 S.Ct. 2218, 85 L.Ed.2d 588 (1985) (noting that the scope of fair use is narrower with respect to unpublished works because the author's right to control the first public appearance of his work weighs against the use of his work before its release).

31. *Worldwide Church of God,* 227 F.3d at 1118 (internal quotation marks and citation omitted).

engaged in by the defendant ... would result in a substantially adverse impact on the potential market for the original.' "[33] A transformative work is less likely to have an adverse impact on the market of the original than a work that merely supersedes the copyrighted work.[34]

Kelly's images are related to several potential markets. One purpose of the photographs is to attract internet users to his web site, where he sells advertising space as well as books and travel packages. In addition, Kelly could sell or license his photographs to other web sites or to a stock photo database, which then could offer the images to its customers.

Arriba's use of Kelly's images in its thumbnails does not harm the market for Kelly's images or the value of his images. By showing the thumbnails on its results page when users entered terms related to Kelly's images, the search engine would guide users to Kelly's web site rather than away from it. Even if users were more interested in the image itself rather than the information on the web page, they would still have to go to Kelly's site to see the full-sized image. The thumbnails would not be a substitute for the full-sized images because when the thumbnails are enlarged, they lose their clarity. If a user wanted to view or download a quality image, he or she would have to visit Kelly's web site. This would hold true whether the thumbnails are solely in Arriba's database or are more widespread and found in other search engine databases.

Arriba's use of Kelly's images also would not harm Kelly's ability to sell or license his full-sized images. Arriba does not sell or license its thumbnails to other parties. Anyone who downloaded the thumbnails would not be successful selling the full-sized images because of the low-resolution of the thumbnails. There would be no way to view, create, or sell a clear, full-sized image without going to Kelly's web sites. Therefore, Arriba's creation and use of the thumbnails does not harm the market for or value of Kelly's images. This factor weighs in favor of Arriba.

Having considered the four fair use factors and found that two weigh in favor of Arriba, one is neutral, and one weighs slightly in favor of Kelly, we conclude that Arriba's use of Kelly's images as thumbnails in its search engine is a fair use.

B.

* * *

[In this portion of its opinion the court found that Arriba's inline linking to and framing of Kelly's full sized images violated Kelly's public

33. *Id.* at 590, 114 S.Ct. 1164 (quoting 3 M. Nimmer & D. Nimmer, *Nimmer on Copyright* § 13.05[A][4], at 13–102.61 (1993)) (ellipses in original).

34. *See id.* at 591, 114 S.Ct. 1164 (stating that a work that supersedes the object of the original serves as a market replacement for it, making it likely that market harm will occur, but when the second use is transformative, market substitution is less certain).

display right under section 106. The opinion on this point is excerpted *supra*, at page 1130.]

    2.   *Fair use of full-sized images.*

The last issue we must address is whether Arriba's display of Kelly's full-sized images was a fair use. Although Arriba did not address the use of the full-sized images in its fair use argument, the district court considered such use in its analysis, and we will consider Arriba's fair use defense here.

Once again, to decide whom the first factor, the purpose and character of the use, favors, we must determine whether Arriba's use of Kelly's images was transformative. Unlike the use of the images for the thumbnails, displaying Kelly's full-sized images does not enhance Arriba's search engine. The images do not act as a means to access other information on the internet but, rather, are likely the end product themselves. Although users of the search engine could link from the full-sized image to Kelly's web site, any user who is solely searching for images would not need to do so. Because the full-sized images on Arriba's site act primarily as illustrations or artistic expression and the search engine would function the same without them, they do not have a purpose different from Kelly's use of them.

Not only is the purpose the same, but Arriba did not add new expression to the images to make them transformative. Placing the images in a "frame" or locating them near text that specifies the size and originating web site is not enough to create new expression or meaning for the images. In sum, Arriba's full-sized images superseded the object of Kelly's images. Because Arriba has not changed the purpose or character of the use of the images, the first factor favors Kelly.

The analysis of the second factor, the nature of the copyrighted work, is the same as in the previous fair use discussion because Kelly's images are still the copyrighted images at issue. Therefore, as before, this factor slightly weighs in favor of Kelly.

The third fair use factor turns on the amount of the work displayed and the reasonableness of this amount in light of the purpose for the display. Arriba displayed the full images, which cuts against a finding of fair use. And while it was necessary to provide whole images to suit Arriba's purpose of giving users access to the full-sized images without having to go to another site, such a purpose is not legitimate, as we noted above. Therefore, it was not reasonable to copy the full-sized display. The third factor favors Kelly.

The fourth factor often depends upon how transformative the new use is compared to the original use. A work that is very transformative will often be in a different market from the original work and therefore is less likely to cause harm to the original work's market. Works that are not transformative, however, have the same purpose as the original work and will often have a negative effect on the original work's market.

As discussed in the previous fair use analysis, Kelly's markets for his images include using them to attract advertisers and buyers to his web site, and selling or licensing the images to other web sites or stock photo databases. By giving users access to Kelly's full-sized images on its own web site, Arriba harms all of Kelly's markets. Users will no longer have to go to Kelly's web site to see the full-sized images, thereby deterring people from visiting his web site. In addition, users would be able to download the full-sized images from Arriba's site and then sell or license those images themselves, reducing Kelly's opportunity to sell or license his own images. If the display of Kelly's images became widespread across other web sites, it would reduce the number of visitors to Kelly's web site even further and increase the chance of others exploiting his images. These actions would result in substantial adverse effects to the potential markets for Kelly's original works. For this reason, the fourth factor weighs heavily in favor of Kelly.

In conclusion, all of the fair use factors weigh in favor of Kelly. Therefore, the doctrine of fair use does not sanction Arriba's display of Kelly's images through the inline linking or framing processes that puts Kelly's original images within the context of Arriba's web site.

* * *

Notes

1. If those who encounter Kelly's images do so first because they engage Arriba's web-crawler to find images like Kelly's, how realistic is it to think that Kelly's web site is being deprived of hits because of Arriba's service?

2. Could the problem the court sees with the full-size image and the frame be adequately resolved through precautionary labeling and disclaimers? Should devices such as these play any role in copyright?

3. Many observers of the digital millennium have suggested that copyright should be reconsidered in light of the internet and its myriad new possibilities. Do *Napster* and *Kelly v. Arriba Soft* persuade you to that view? How might fair use be altered to give adequate protection to the legitimate interests of the copyright proprietor while at the same time encouraging innovative new uses of the internet itself?

4. In *Field v. Google, Inc.*, 412 F.Supp.2d 1106 (D. Nev. 2006), Google's web crawler visited thousands of sites, taking pictures of each page it visited, then stored the picture in a database called "Google cache". Google offered the proprietor of each site an option to exclude Google's crawler, thereby placing the burden on the web site proprietor to prevent a visit if that was the proprietor's wish. Field sued Google, alleging that this practice violated its 106 rights. Google responded with two arguments, both of which the judge accepted: (1) that by not using a meta-tag to tell Google to stay away, the site owner was granting Google an implied license to reproduce and distribute the page; and (2) that Google's crawling, capturing/photographing, and storing of the page(s) was sufficiently transformative to be fair use, particularly in that Google was offering a version of the work that was of

social importance, while not superseding the objectives of the original creations.

Consider whether the first of Google's two arguments may not also be more than ordinarily consistent with the proper relationship between sections 106 and 107. In particular, consider the introductory language to each section. Fair use is customarily characterized as an affirmative defense. But should it rather be considered as in the nature of an entitlement, and perhaps even an entitlement presumptively superior to the exclusive rights allocated in section 106? (Make no mistake, however: the interpretations suggested in this paragraph are not in accord with the main body of the law of fair use.)

Meanwhile, ask yourself in what sense Google's activities are "transformative"? Compare the *Bill Graham* case, supra, with *Perfect 10 v. Google, Inc.,* 416 F.Supp.2d 828 (C.D. Cal. 2006) (holding, in the context of preliminary motions, that Google's "creation and public display of 'thumbnail'" copies of photographs "likely do directly infringe" the plaintiff's copyrights; and distinguishing *Kelly v. Arriba* on the ground that the defendant's activities in that case were "less exploitative" than Google's activities in this case).

Chapter 20

INFRINGEMENT, DEFENSES, AND REMEDIES

Statutes: 17 U.S.C.A. §§ 101 (as needed), 501–11, 602–03, 1001–10

Copyright infringement is the unauthorized exercise of one of the rights reserved to the copyright owner under sections 106 and 106A, unless the activity in question falls within the exceptions set forth in sections 107–121 and 1008. "A prima facie case of infringement consists of ownership of the right asserted and unauthorized appropriation by the defendant of a material amount of expression. The copying of facts or of a de minimis amount of expression will not support a prima facie case of infringement." H.R. Rep. No. 102–836, 102nd Cong., 2nd Sess. 3 (1992).

A certain amount of common ground in infringement theory and practice is generally understood and accepted by all who know the field. The plaintiff may establish actual appropriation by direct evidence; alternatively, the plaintiff's proof may consist in demonstrating (through circumstantial or direct evidence) the defendant's access to the plaintiff's work plus some similarity between that work and the defendant's work. These attempts at proof ordinarily raise questions of fact. Given adequate proof of appropriation, the materiality of the appropriation—in other words, its ultimate actionability—is a separate, additional issue of fact. Summary disposition is generally disfavored in infringement practice, but a defendant who is confronted with neither evidence of access nor appropriation may move successfully to dismiss the complaint or for summary judgment. Conversely, striking similarity between the works is sometimes accepted as equivalent to proof of both access and appropriation, and may even be sufficient to justify summary judgment or a directed verdict for the plaintiff. In theory and practice alike, however, the existence of similarity (even striking similarity) may be misleading: it is entirely possible that the defendant may have created a work like the plaintiff's, either without copying at all, as in the classic case of independent creation envisioned by Judge Hand in *Sheldon* (*infra*), or without copying from the plaintiff. (As to the latter possibility, if the defendant copies from a third work under copyright, the plaintiff will have no action against the defendant absent ownership or ⌐n exclusive license as to that work—though of course the owner of the third work may have an action unless the defendant has copied under license or some other claim of right such as fair use. In such a case, one will wonder whether the plaintiff may also be liable to the third party owner.) Meanwhile, alternatively, if the third work is in the public domain there can be no action against the defendant at all under copyright law.

Courts frequently use the term "copying" as shorthand for the exercise of any of the exclusive rights described in section 106. *S.O.S., Inc. v. Payday, Inc.*, 886 F.2d 1081, 1085 n. 3 (9th Cir.1989). In some infringement cases, the sole issue is whether the defendant's *activity* is of a type proscribed by section 106 or 106A. (For example, was the defendant's performance of the plaintiff's work public or private?) In other cases, the parties may dispute the threshold question of whether the material exploited by the defendant incorporated the plaintiff's copyrighted material in the first place. In the latter case, absent direct evidence of copying (such as a witness or an admission), a prima facie case of copying may be established by circumstantial evidence. See Section B, *infra*.

Federal district courts have exclusive jurisdiction over actions "arising under" the federal copyright statutes, 28 U.S.C.A. § 1338(a), except that the United States Court of Federal Claims has exclusive jurisdiction over infringement actions brought against the United States government or a person acting on its behalf, 28 U.S.C.A. § 1498(b). Under 17 U.S.C.A. § 411(a), except for actions brought under section 106A or alleging infringement of Berne Convention works whose country of origin is not the United States, copyright registration is a prerequisite to filing suit for infringement.[1]

A.   THE CONCEPT OF INFRINGEMENT

NICHOLS v. UNIVERSAL PICTURES CORP.

United States Court of Appeals, Second Circuit, 1930.
45 F.2d 119. *cert. denied*, 282 U.S. 902, 51 S.Ct. 216, 75 L.Ed. 795 (1931).

L. HAND, CIRCUIT JUDGE.

The plaintiff is the author of a play, "Abie's Irish Rose," which it may be assumed was properly copyrighted under section five, subdivision (d), of the Copyright Act, 17 USCA § 5(d). The defendant produced publicly a motion picture play, "The Cohens and The Kellys," which the plaintiff alleges was taken from it. As we think the defendant's play too unlike the plaintiff's to be an infringement, we may assume, arguendo,

---

1. Before March 1, 1989, recordation was also a prerequisite to an infringement   suit by an assignee. 17 U.S.C. § 205(d).

that in some details the defendant used the plaintiff's play, as will subsequently appear, though we do not so decide. It therefore becomes necessary to give an outline of the two plays.

"Abie's Irish Rose" presents a Jewish family living in prosperous circumstances in New York. The father, a widower, is in business as a merchant, in which his son and only child helps him. The boy has philandered with young women, who to his father's great disgust have always been Gentiles, for he is obsessed with a passion that his daughter-in-law shall be an orthodox Jewess. When the play opens the son, who has been courting a young Irish Catholic girl, has already married her secretly before a Protestant minister, and is concerned to soften the blow for his father, by securing a favorable impression of his bride, while concealing her faith and race. To accomplish this he introduces her to his father at his home as a Jewess, and lets it appear that he is interested in her, though he conceals the marriage. The girl somewhat reluctantly falls in with the plan; the father takes the bait, becomes infatuated with the girl, concludes that they must marry, and assumes that of course they will, if he so decides. He calls in a rabbi, and prepares for the wedding according to the Jewish rite.

Meanwhile the girl's father, also a widower, who lives in California, and is as intense in his own religious antagonism as the Jew, has been called to New York, supposing that his daughter is to marry an Irishman and a Catholic. Accompanied by a priest, he arrives at the house at the moment when the marriage is being celebrated, but too late to prevent it and the two fathers, each infuriated by the proposed union of his child to a heretic, fall into unseemly and grotesque antics. The priest and the rabbi become friendly, exchange trite sentiments about religion, and agree that the match is good. Apparently out of abundant caution, the priest celebrates the marriage for a third time, while the girl's father is inveigled away. The second act closes with each father, still outraged, seeking to find some way by which the union, thus trebly insured, may be dissolved.

The last act takes place about a year later, the young couple having meanwhile been abjured by each father, and left to their own resources. They have had twins, a boy and a girl, but their fathers know no more than that a child has been born. At Christmas each, led by his craving to see his grandchild, goes separately to the young folks' home, where they encounter each other, each laden with gifts, one for a boy, the other for a girl. After some slapstick comedy, depending upon the insistence of each that he is right about the sex of the grandchild, they become reconciled when they learn the truth, and that each child is to bear the given name of a grandparent. The curtain falls as the fathers are exchanging amenities, and the Jew giving evidence of an abatement in the strictness of his orthodoxy.

"The Cohens and The Kellys" presents two families, Jewish and Irish, living side by side in the poorer quarters of New York in a state of perpetual enmity. The wives in both cases are still living, and share in the mutual animosity, as do two small sons, and even the respective dogs. The Jews have a daughter, the Irish a son; the Jewish father is in the clothing business; the Irishman is a policeman. The children are in love with each other, and secretly marry, apparently after the play opens. The Jew, being in great financial straits, learns from a lawyer that he has fallen heir to a large fortune from a great-aunt, and moves into a great house, fitted luxuriously. Here he and his family live in vulgar ostentation, and here the Irish boy seeks out his Jewish bride, and is chased away by the angry father. The Jew then abuses the Irishman over the telephone, and both become hysterically excited. The extremity of his feelings make the Jew sick, so that he must go to Florida for a rest, just before which the daughter discloses her marriage to her mother.

On his return the Jew finds that his daughter has borne a child; at first he suspects the lawyer, but eventually learns the truth and is overcome with anger at such a low alliance. Meanwhile, the Irish family who have been forbidden to see the grandchild, go to the Jew's house, and after a violent scene between the two fathers in which the Jew disowns his daughter, who decides to go back with her husband, the Irishman takes her back with her baby to his own poor lodgings. The lawyer, who had hoped to marry the Jew's daughter, seeing his plan foiled, tells the Jew that his fortune really belongs to the Irishman, who was also related to the dead woman, but offers to conceal his knowledge, if the Jew will share the loot. This the Jew repudiates, and, leaving the astonished lawyer, walks through the rain to his enemy's house to surrender the property. He arrives in great dejection, tells the truth, and abjectly turns to leave. A reconciliation ensues, the Irishman agreeing to share with him equally. The Jew shows some interest in his grandchild, though this is at most a minor motive in the reconciliation, and the curtain falls while the two are in their cups, the Jew insisting that in the firm name for the business, which they are to carry on jointly, his name shall stand first.

It is of course essential to any protection of literary property, whether at common-law or under the statute, that the right cannot be limited literally to the text, else a plagiarist would escape by immaterial variations. That has never been the law, but, as soon as literal appropriation ceases to be the test, the whole matter is necessarily at large, so that, as was recently well said by a distinguished judge, the decisions cannot help much in a new case. Fendler v. Morosco, 253 N.Y. 281, 292, 171 N.E. 56. When plays are concerned, the plagiarist may excise a separate scene (Daly v. Webster, 56 F. 483 (C.C.A.2); Chappell v. Fields, 210 F. 864 (C.C.A.2); Chatterton v. Cave, L.R. 3 App.Cas. 483); or he may appropriate part of the dialogue (Warne v. Seebohm, L.R. 39 Ch.D. 73). Then the question is whether the part so taken is "substantial," and therefore not a "fair use" of the copyrighted work; it is the same question [as] arises in the case of any other copyrighted work. Marks v. Feist, 290 F. 959 (C.C.A.2); Emerson v. Davies, Fed. Cas. No. 4436, 3 Story, 768, 795–797. But when the plagiarist does not take out a block in suit, but an abstract of the whole, decision is more troublesome. Upon any work, and especially upon a play, a great number of patterns of increasing generality will fit equally well, as more and more of the incident is left out. The last may perhaps be no more than the most general statement of what the play is about, and at times might consist only of its title; but there is a point in this series of abstractions where they are no longer protected, since otherwise the playwright could prevent the use of his "ideas," to which, apart from their expression, his property is never extended. Holmes v. Hurst, 174 U.S. 82, 86, 19 S.Ct. 606, 43 L.Ed. 904; Guthrie v. Curlett, 36 F.(2d) 694 (C.C.A.2). Nobody has ever been able to fix that boundary, and nobody ever can. In some cases the question has been treated as though it were analogous to lifting a portion out of the copyrighted work (Rees v. Melville, MacGillivray's Copyright Cases (1911–1916), 168); but the analogy is not a good one, because, though the skeleton is a part of the body, it pervades and supports the whole. In such cases we are rather concerned with the line between expression and what is expressed. As respects plays, the controversy chiefly centers upon the characters and sequence of incident, these being the substance.

We did not in Dymow v. Bolton, 11 F.(2d) 690, hold that a plagiarist was never liable for stealing a plot; that would have been flatly against our ruling in Dam v. Kirk La Shelle Co., 175 F. 902, 41 L.R.A.(N.S.) 1002, 20 Ann.Cas. 1173, and Stodart v. Mutual Film Corp., 249 F. 513, affirming my decision in (D.C.) 249 F. 507; neither of which we meant to overrule. We found the plot of the second play was too different to infringe, because the most detailed pattern, common to both, eliminated so much from each that its content went into the public domain; and for this reason we said, "this mere subsection of a plot was not susceptible of copyright." But we do not doubt that two plays may correspond in plot closely enough for infringement. How far that correspondence must go is another matter. Nor need we hold that the same may not be true as to the characters, quite independently of the "plot" proper, though, as far as we know such a case has never arisen. If Twelfth Night were copyrighted, it is quite possible that a second comer might so closely imitate Sir Toby Belch or Malvolio as to infringe, but it would not be enough that for one of his characters he cast a riotous knight who kept wassail to the discomfort of the household, or a vain and foppish steward who became amorous of his mistress. These would be no more than Shakespeare's "ideas" in the play, as little capable of monopoly as Einstein's Doctrine of Relativity, or Darwin's theory of the Origin of Species. It follows that the less developed the characters, the less they can be copyrighted; that is the penalty an author must bear for marking them too indistinctly.

In the two plays at bar we think both as to incident and character, the defendant took no more—assuming that it took anything at all— than the law allowed. The stories are quite different. One is of a religious zealot who insists upon his child's marrying no one outside his faith; opposed by another who is in this respect just like him, and is his foil.

Their difference in race is merely an obbligato to the main theme, religion. They sink their differences through grandparental pride and affection. In the other, zealotry is wholly absent; religion does not even appear. It is true that the parents are hostile to each other in part because they differ in race; but the marriage of their son to a Jew does not apparently offend the Irish family at all, and it exacerbates the existing animosity of the Jew, principally because he has become rich, when he learns it. They are reconciled through the honesty of the Jew and the generosity of the Irishman; the grandchild has nothing whatever to do with it. The only matter common to the two is a quarrel between a Jewish and an Irish father, the marriage of their children, the birth of grandchildren and a reconciliation.

If the defendant took so much from the plaintiff, it may well have been because her amazing success seemed to prove that this was a subject of enduring popularity. Even so, granting that the plaintiff's play was wholly original, and assuming that novelty is not essential to a copyright, there is no monopoly in such a background. Though the plaintiff discovered the vein, she could not keep it to herself; so defined, the theme was too generalized an abstraction from what she wrote. It was only a part of her "ideas."

Nor does she fare better as to her characters. It is indeed scarcely credible that she should not have been aware of those stock figures, the low comedy Jew and Irishman. The defendant has not taken from her more than their prototypes have contained for many decades. If so, obviously so to generalize her copyright, would allow her to cover what was not original with her. But we need not hold this as matter of fact, much as we might be justified. Even though we take it that she devised her figures out of her brain de novo, still the defendant was within its rights.

There are but four characters common to both plays, the lovers and the fathers. The lovers are so faintly indicated as to be no more than stage properties. They are loving and fertile; that is really all that can be said of them, and anyone else is quite within his rights if he puts loving and fertile lovers in a play of his own, wherever he gets the cue. The Plaintiff's Jew is quite unlike the defendant's. His obsession in his religion, on which depends such racial animosity as he has. He is affectionate, warm and patriarchal. None of these fit the defendant's Jew, who shows affection for his daughter only once, and who has none but the most superficial interest in his grandchild. He is tricky, ostentatious and vulgar, only by misfortune redeemed into honesty. Both are grotesque, extravagant and quarrelsome; both are fond of display; but these common qualities make up only a small part of their simple pictures, no more than any one might lift if he chose. The Irish fathers are even more unlike; the plaintiff's a mere symbol for religious fanaticism and patriarchal pride, scarcely a character at all. Neither quality appears in the defendant's, for while he goes to get his grandchild, it is rather out of a truculent determination not to be forbidden, than from pride in his progeny. For the rest he is only a grotesque hobbledehoy, used for low comedy of the most conventional sort, which any one might borrow, if he chanced not to know the exemplar.

The defendant argues that the case is controlled by my decision in Fisher v. Dillingham (D.C.) 298 F. 145. Neither my brothers nor I wish to throw doubt upon the doctrine of that case, but it is not applicable here. We assume that the plaintiff's play is altogether original, even to an extent that in fact it is hard to believe. We assume further that, so far as it has been anticipated by earlier plays of which she knew nothing, that fact is immaterial. Still, as we have already said, her copyright did not cover everything that might be drawn from her play; its content went to some extent into the public domain. We have to decide how much, and while we are as aware as any one that the line, wherever it is drawn, will seem arbitrary, that is no excuse for not drawing it; it is a question such as courts must answer in nearly all cases. Whatever may be the difficulties a priori, we have no question on which side of the line this case falls. A comedy based upon conflicts between Irish and Jews, into which the marriage of their children enters, is no more susceptible of copyright than the outline of Romeo and Juliet.

The plaintiff has prepared an elaborate analysis of the two plays, showing a "quadrangle" of the common characters, in which each is represented by the emotions which he discovers. She presents the resulting parallelism as proof of infringement, but the adjectives employed are so general as to be quite useless. Take for example the attribute of "love" ascribed to both Jews. The plaintiff has depicted her father as deeply attached to his son, who is his hope and joy; not so, the defendant, whose father's conduct is throughout not actuated by any affection for his daughter, and who is merely once overcome for the moment by her distress when he has violently dismissed her lover. "Anger" covers emotions aroused by quite different occasions in each case; so do "anxiety," "despondency" and "disgust." It is unnecessary to go through the catalogue for emotions are too much colored by their causes to be a test when used so broadly. This is not the proper approach to a solution; it must be more ingenuous, more like that of a spectator, who would rely upon the complex of his impressions of each character.

We cannot approve the length of the record, which was due chiefly to the use of expert witnesses. Argument is argument whether in the box or at the bar, and its proper place is the last. The testimony of an expert upon such issues, especially his cross-examination, greatly extends the trial and contributes nothing which cannot be better heard after the evidence is all submitted. It ought not to be allowed at all; and while its admission is not a ground for reversal, it cumbers the case and tends to confusion, for the more the court is led into the intricacies of dramatic craftsmanship, the less likely it is to stand upon the firmer, if more naive, ground of its considered impressions upon its own perusal. We hope that in this class of cases such evidence may in the future be entirely excluded, and the case confined to the actual issues; that is, whether the defendant copied it, so far as the supposed infringement is identical.

* * *

Decree affirmed.

SHELDON v. METRO–GOLDWYN PICTURES CORPORATION

United States Court of Appeals, Second Circuit, 1936.
81 F.2d 49. *cert. denied*, 298 U.S. 669, 56 S.Ct. 835, 80 L.Ed. 1392 (1936).

L. HAND, CIRCUIT JUDGE.

The suit is to enjoin the performance of the picture play, "Letty Lynton," as an infringement of the plaintiffs' copyrighted play, "Dishonored Lady." The plaintiffs' title is conceded, so too the validity of the copyright; the only issue is infringement. The defendants say that they did not use the play in any way to produce the picture; the plaintiffs discredit this denial because of the negotiations between the parties for the purchase of rights in the play, and because the similarities between the two are too specific and detailed to have resulted from chance. The judge thought that, so far as the defendants had used the play, they had taken only what the law allowed, that is, those general themes, motives, or ideas in which there could be no copyright. Therefore he dismissed the bill.

An understanding of the issue involves some description of what was in the public demesne, as well as of the play and the picture. In 1857 a Scotch girl, named Madeleine Smith, living in Glasgow, was brought to trial upon an indictment in three counts; two for attempts to poison her lover, a third for poisoning him. The jury acquitted her on the first count, and brought in a verdict of "Not Proven" on the second and third. The circumstances of the prosecution aroused much interest at the time not only in Scotland but in England; so much indeed that it became a cause célèbre, and that as late as 1927 the whole proceedings were published in book form. An outline of the story so published, which became the original of the play here in suit, is as follows: The Smiths were a respectable middle-class family, able to send their daughter to a "young ladies' boarding school"; they supposed her protected not only from any waywardness of her own, but from the wiles of seducers. In both they were mistaken, for when at the age of twenty-one she met a young Jerseyman of French blood, Emile L'Angelier, ten years older, and already the hero of many amorous adventures, she quickly succumbed and poured out her feelings in letters of the utmost ardor and indiscretion, and at times of a candor beyond the standards then, and even yet, permissible for well-nurtured young women. They wrote each other as though already married, and he assuming to dictate her conduct and even her feelings; both expected to marry, she on any terms, he with the approval of her family. Nevertheless she soon tired of him and engaged herself to a man some twenty years older who was a better match, but for whom she had no more than a friendly complaisance. L'Angelier was not, however, to be fobbed off so easily; he threatened to expose her to her father by showing her letters. She at first tried to dissuade him by appeals to their tender memories, but finding this useless and thinking herself otherwise undone, she affected a return of her former passion and invited him to visit her again. Whether he did, was the turning point of the trial; the evidence, though it really left the issue in no doubt, was too indirect to satisfy the jury, perhaps in part because of her advocate's argument that to kill him only insured the discovery of her letters. It was shown that she had several times bought or tried to buy poison,— prussic acid and arsenic,—and that twice before his death L'Angelier became violently ill, the second time on the day after her purchase. He died of arsenical poison, which the prosecution charged that she had given him in a cup of chocolate. At her trial, Madeleine being incompetent as a witness, her advocate proved an alibi by the testimony of her younger sister that early on the night of the murder as laid in the indictment, she had gone to bed with Madeleine, who had slept with her throughout the night. As to one of the attempts her betrothed swore that she had been with him at the theatre.

This was the story which the plaintiffs used to build their play. As will appear they took from it but the merest skeleton, the acquittal of a wanton young woman, who to extricate herself from an amour that stood in the way of a respectable marriage, poisoned her lover. The incidents, the characters, the mis[e] en scène, the sequence of events, were all changed; nobody disputes that the plaintiffs were entitled to their copyright. All that they took from the story they might probably have taken, had it even been copyrighted. Their heroine is named Madeleine Cary; she lives in New York, brought up in affluence, if not in luxury; she is intelligent, voluptuous, ardent and corrupt; but, though she has had a succession of amours, she is capable of genuine affection. Her lover and victim is an Argentinian, named Moreno, who makes his living as a dancer in night-clubs. Madeleine has met him once in Europe before the play opens, has danced with him, has excited his concupiscence; he presses presents upon her. The play opens in his rooms, he and his dancing partner who is also his mistress, are together; Madeleine on the telephone recalls herself to him and says she wishes to visit him, though it is already past midnight. He disposes of his mistress by a device which does not deceive her and receives Madeleine; at once he falls to wooing her, luring her among other devices by singing a Gaucho song. He finds her facile and the curtain falls in season.

The second act is in her home, and introduces her father, a bibulous dotard, who has shot his wife's lover in the long past; Laurence Brennan, a self-made man in the fifties, untutored, self-reliant and reliable, who has had with Madeleine a relation, half paternal, half-amorous since she grew up; and Denis Farnborough, a young British labor peer, a mannekin to delight the heart of well ordered young women. Madeleine loves him; he loves Madeleine; she will give him no chance to declare himself, remembering her mottled past and his supposedly immaculate standards. She confides to Brennan, who makes clear to her the imbecility of her self-denial; she accepts this enlightenment and engages herself to her high-minded paragon after confessing vaguely her evil life and being assured that to post-war generations all such lapses are peccadillos.

In the next act Moreno, who has got wind of the engagement, comes to her house. Disposing of Farnborough, who chances to be there, she admits Moreno, acknowledges that she is to marry Farnborough, and asks him to accept the situation as the normal outcome of their intrigue. He refuses to be cast off, high words pass, he threatens to expose their relations, she raves at him, until finally he knocks her down and commands her to go to his apartment that morning as before. After he leaves full of swagger, her eye lights on a bottle of strychnine which her father uses as a drug; her fingers slowly close upon it; the audience understands that she will kill Moreno. Farnborough is at the telephone; this apparently stiffens her resolve, showing her the heights she may reach by its execution.

The scene then shifts again to Moreno's apartment; his mistress must again be put out, most unwillingly for she is aware of the situation; Madeleine comes in; she pretends once more to feel warmly, she must wheedle him for he is out of sorts after the quarrel. Meanwhile she prepares to poison him by putting the strychnine in coffee, which she asks him to make ready. But in the course of these preparations during which he sings her again his Gaucho song, what with their proximity, and this and that, her animal ardors are once more aroused and drag her, unwillingly and protesting, from her purpose. The play must therefore wait for an hour or more until, relieved of her passion, she appears from his bedroom and while breakfasting puts the strychnine in his coffee. He soon discovers what has happened and tries to telephone for help. He does succeed in getting a few words through, but she tears away the wire and fills his dying ears with her hatred and disgust. She then carefully wipes away all traces of her finger prints and manages to get away while the door is being pounded in by those who have come at his call.

The next act is again at her home on the following evening. Things are going well with her and Farnborough and her father, when a district attorney comes in, a familiar of the household, now in stern mood; Moreno's mistress and a waiter have incriminated Madeleine, and a cross has been found in Moreno's pocket, which he superstitiously took off her neck the night before. The district attorney cross-questions her, during which Farnborough several times fatuously intervenes; she is driven from point to point almost to an avowal when as a desperate plunge she says she spent the night with Brennan. Brennan is brought to the house and, catching the situation after a moment's delay, bears her out. This puts off the district attorney until seeing strychnine brought to relieve the father, his suspicions spring up again and he arrests Madeleine. The rest of the play is of no consequence here, except that it appears in the last scene that at the trial where she is acquitted, her father on the witness stand accounts for the absence of the bottle of strychnine which had been used to poison Moreno.

At about the time that this play was being written an English woman named Lowndes wrote a book called Letty Lynton, also founded on the story of Madeleine Smith. Letty Lynton lives in England; she is eighteen years old, beautiful, well-reared and intelligent, but wayward. She has had a more or less equivocal love affair with a young Scot, named McLean, who worked in her father's chemical factory, but has discarded him, apparently before their love-making had gone very far. Then she chances upon a young Swede—half English—named Ekebon, and their acquaintance quickly becomes a standardized amour, kept secret from her parents, especially her mother, who is an uncompromising moralist, and somewhat estranged from Letty anyway. She and her lover use an old barn as their place of assignation; it had been fitted up as a play house for Letty when she was a child. Like Madeleine Smith she had written her lover a series of indiscreet letters which he has kept, for though he is on pleasure bent Ekebon has a frugal mind, and means to marry his sweetheart and set himself up for life. They are betrothed and he keeps pressing her to declare it to her parents, which she means never to do. While he is away in Sweden Letty meets an unmarried peer considerably older than she, poor, but intelligent and charming; he falls in love with her and she accepts him, more because it is a good match than for any other reason, though she likes him well enough, and will make him suppose that she loves him.

Thereupon Ekebon reappears, learns of Letty's new betrothal, and threatens to disclose his own to her father, backing up his story with her letters. She must at once disown her peer and resume her engagement with him. His motive, like L'Angelier's, is ambition rather than love, though conquest is a flattery and Letty a charming morsel. His threats naturally throw Letty into dismay; she has come to loathe him and at any cost must get free, but she has no one to turn to. In her plight she thinks of her old suitor, McLean, and goes to the factory only to find him gone. He has taught her how to get access to poisons in his office and has told of their effect on human beings. At first she thinks of jumping out the window, and when she winces at that, of poisoning herself; that would be easier. So she selects arsenic which is less painful and goes away with it; it is only when she gets home that she thinks of poisoning Ekebon. Her mind is soon made up, however, and she makes an appointment with him at the barn; she has told her father, she writes, and Ekebon is to see him on Monday, but meanwhile on Sunday they will meet secretly once more. She has prepared to go on a week-end party and conceals her car near the barn. He comes; she welcomes him with a pretence of her former ardors, and tries to get back her letters. Unsuccessful in this she persuades him to drink a cup of chocolate into which she puts the arsenic. After carefully washing the pans and cups, she leaves with him, dropping him from her car near his home; he being still unaffected. On her way to her party she pretends to have broken down and by asking the help of a passing cyclist establishes an alibi.

Ekebon dies at his home attended by his mistress; the letters are discovered and Letty is brought before the coroner's inquest and acquitted chiefly through the alibi, for things look very bad for her until the cyclist appears.

The defendants, who are engaged in producing speaking films on a very large scale in Hollywood, California, had seen the play and wished to get the rights. They found, however, an obstacle in an association of motion picture producers presided over by Mr. Will Hays, who thought the play obscene; not being able to overcome his objections, they returned the copy of the manuscript which they had had. That was in the spring of 1930, but in the autumn they induced the plaintiffs to get up a scenario, which they hoped might pass moral muster. Although this did not suit them after the plaintiffs prepared it, they must still have thought in the spring of 1931 that they could satisfy Mr. Hays, for they then procured an offer from the plaintiffs to sell their rights for $30,000. These negotiations also proved abortive because the play continued to be objectionable, and eventually they cried off on the bargain. Mrs. Lowndes' novel was suggested to Thalberg, one of the vice-presidents of the Metro–Goldwyn Company, in July, 1931, and again in the following November, and he bought the rights to it in December. At once he assigned the preparation of a play to Stromberg, who had read the novel in January, and thought it would make a suitable play for an actress named, Crawford, just then not employed. Stromberg chose Meehan, Tuchock and Brown to help him, the first two with the scenario, the third with the dramatic production. All these four were examined by deposition; all denied that they had used the play in any way whatever; all agreed that they had based the picture on the story of Madeleine Smith and on the novel, "Letty Lynton." All had seen the play, and Tuchock had read the manuscript, as had Thalberg, but Stromberg, Meehan and Brown swore that they had not; Stromberg's denial being however worthless, for he had originally sworn the contrary in an affidavit. They all say that work began late in November or early in December, 1931, and the picture was finished by the end of March. To meet these denials, the plaintiffs appeal to the substantial identity between passages in the picture and those parts of the play which are original with them.

The picture opens in Montevideo where Letty Lynton is recovering from her fondness for Emile Renaul. She is rich, luxurious and fatherless, her father having been killed by his mistress's husband; her mother is seared, hard, selfish, unmotherly, and Letty has left home to escape her, wandering about in search of excitement. Apparently for the good part of a year she has been carrying on a love affair with Renaul; twice before she has tried to shake loose, has gone once to Rio where she lit another flame, but each time she has weakened and been drawn back. Though not fully declared as an amour, there can be no real question as to the character of her attachment. She at length determines really to break loose, but once again her senses are too much for her and it is indicated, if not declared, that she spends the night with Renaul. Though he is left a vague figure only indistinctly associated with South America somewhere or other, the part was cast for an actor with a marked foreign accent, and it is plain that he was meant to be understood, in origin anyway, as South American, like Moreno in the play. He is violent, possessive and sensual; his power over Letty lies in his strong animal attractions. However, she escapes in the morning while he is asleep, whether from his bed or not is perhaps uncertain; and with a wax figure in the form of a loyal maid—Letty in the novel had one—boards a steamer for New York. On board she meets Darrow, a young American, the son of a rich rubber manufacturer, who is coming back from a trip to Africa. They fall in love upon the faintest provocation and become betrothed before the ship docks, three weeks after she left Montevideo. At the pier she finds Renaul who has flown up to reclaim her. She must in some way keep her two suitors apart, and she manages to dismiss Darrow and then to escape Renaul by asking him to pay her customs duties, which he does. Arrived home her mother gives her a cold welcome and refuses to concern herself with the girl's betrothal. Renaul is announced; he has read of the betrothal in the papers and is furious. He tries again to stir her sensuality by the familiar gambit, but this time he fails; she slaps his face and declares that she hates him. He commands her to come to his apartment that evening; she begs him to part with her and let her have her life; he insists on renewing their affair. She threatens to call the police; he rejoins that if so her letters will be published, and then he leaves. Desperate, she chances on a bottle of strychnine, which we are to suppose is an accouterment of every affluent household, and seizes it; the implication is of intended suicide, not murder. Then she calls Darrow, tells him that she will not leave with him that night for his parents' place in the Adirondacks as they had planned; she renews to him the pledge of her love, without him she cannot live, an intimation to the audience of her purpose to kill herself.

That evening she goes to Renaul's apartment in a hotel armed with her strychnine bottle, for use on the spot; she finds him cooling champagne, but in bad temper. His caresses which he bestows plentifully enough, again stir her disgust not her passions, but he does not believe it and assumes that she will spend the night with him. Finding that he will not return the letters, she believes herself lost and empties the strychnine into a wine glass. Again he embraces her; she vilifies him; he knocks her down; she vilifies him again. Ignorant of the poison he grasps her glass, and she, perceiving it, lets him drink. He woos her again, this time with more apparent success, for she is terrified; he sings a Gaucho song to her, the same one that has been heard at Montevideo. The poison begins to work and, at length supposing that she has meant to murder him, he reaches for the telephone; she forestalls him, but she does not tear out the wire. As he slowly dies, she stands over him and vituperates him. A waiter enters; she steps behind a curtain; he leaves thinking Renaul drunk; she comes out, wipes off all traces of her fingerprints and goes out, leaving however her rubbers which Renaul had taken from her when she entered.

Next she and Darrow are found at his parents' in the Adirondacks; while there a detective appears, arrests Letty and takes her to New York; she is charged with the murder of Renaul; Darrow goes back to New York with her. The finish is at the district attorney's office; Letty and Darrow, Letty's mother, the wax serving maid are all there. The letters appear incriminating to an elderly rather benevolent district attorney; also the customs slip and the rubbers. Letty begins to break down; she admits that she went to Renaul's room, not to kill him but to get him to release her. Darrow sees that that story will not pass, and volunteers that she came to his room at a hotel and spent the night with him. Letty confirms this and mother, till then silent, backs up their story; she had traced them to the hotel and saw the lights go out, having ineffectually tried to dissuade them. The maid still further confirms them and the district attorney, not sorry to be discomfited, though unbelieving, discharges Letty.

We are to remember that it makes no difference how far the play was anticipated by works in the public demesne which the plaintiffs did not use. The defendants appear not to recognize this, for they have filled the record with earlier instances of the same dramatic incidents and devices, as though, like a patent, a copyrighted work must be not only original, but new. That is not however the law as is obvious in the case of maps or compendia, where later works will necessarily be anticipated. At times, in discussing how much of the substance of a play the copyright protects, courts have indeed used language which seems to give countenance to the notion that, if a plot were old, it could not be copyrighted. London v. Biograph Co. (C.C.A.) 231 F. 696; Eichel v. Marcin (D.C.) 241 F. 404. But we understand by this no more than that in its broader outline a plot is never copyrightable, for it is plain beyond peradventure that anticipation as such cannot invalidate a copyright. Borrowed the work must indeed not be, for a plagiarist is not himself pro tanto an "author"; but if by some magic a man who had never known it were to compose anew Keats's Ode on a Grecian Urn, he would be an "author," and, if he copyrighted it, others might not copy that poem, though they might of course copy Keats's. Bleistein v. Donaldson Lithographing Co., 188 U.S. 239, 249, 23 S.Ct. 298, 47 L.Ed. 460; Gerlach–Barklow Co. v. Morris & Bendien, Inc., 23 F.(2d) 159, 161 (C.C.A.2); Weil, Copyright Law, p. 234. But though a copyright is for this reason less vulnerable than a patent, the owner's protection is more limited, for just as he is no less an "author" because others have preceded him, so another who follows him, is not a tort-feasor unless he pirates his work. Jeweler's Circular Publishing Co. v. Keystone Co., 281 F. 83, 92, 26 A.L.R. 571 (C.C.A. 2); General Drafting Co. v. Andrews, 37 F.(2d) 54, 56 (C.C.A.2); Williams v. Smythe (C.C.) 110 F. 961; American, etc., Directory Co. v. Gehring Pub. Co. (D.C.) 4 F.(2d) 415; New Jersey, etc., Co. v. Barton Business Service (D.C.) 57 F.(2d) 353. If the copyrighted work is therefore original, the public demesne is important only on the issue of infringement; that is, so far as it may break the force of the inference to be drawn from likenesses between the work and the putative piracy. If the defendant has had access to other material which would have served him as well, his disclaimer becomes more plausible.

In the case at bar there are then two questions: First, whether the defendants actually used the play; second, if so, whether theirs was a "fair use." The judge did not make any finding upon the first question, as we said at the outset, because he thought the defendants were in any case justified; in this following our decision in Nichols v. Universal Pictures Corporation, 45 F.(2d) 119. The plaintiffs challenge that opinion because we said that "copying" might at times be a "fair use"; but it is convenient to define such a use by saying that others may "copy" the "theme," or "ideas," or the like, of a work, though not its "expression." At any rate so long as it is clear what is meant, no harm is done. In the case at bar the distinction is not so important as usual, because so much of the play was borrowed from the story of Madeleine Smith, and the plaintiffs' originality is necessarily limited to the variants they introduced. Nevertheless, it is still true that their whole contribution may not be protected; for the defendants were entitled to use, not only all that had gone before, but even the plaintiffs' contribution itself, if they drew from it only the more general patterns; that is, if they kept clear of its "expression." We must therefore state in detail those similarities which seem to us to pass the limits of "fair use." Finally, in concluding as we do that the defendants used the play pro tanto, we need not charge their witnesses with perjury. With so many sources before them they might quite honestly forget what they took; nobody knows the origin of his inventions; memory and fancy merge even in adults. Yet unconscious plagiarism is actionable quite as much as deliberate. Buck v. Jewell–La Salle Realty Co., 283 U.S. 191, 198. 51 S.Ct. 410, 75 L.Ed. 971, 76 A.L.R. 1266; Harold Lloyd Corporation v. Witwer, 65 F.(2d) 1, 16 (C.C.A.9); Fred Fisher, Inc. v. Dillingham (D.C.) 298 F. 145.

The defendants took for their mis[e] en scène the same city and the same social class; and they chose a South American villain. The heroines had indeed to be wanton, but Letty Lynton "tracked" Madeleine Cary more closely than that. She is overcome by passion in the first part of the picture and yields after announcing that she hates Renaul and has made up her mind to leave him. This is the same weakness as in the murder scene of the play, though transposed. Each heroine's waywardness is suggested as an inherited disposition; each has had an errant parent involved in scandal; one killed, the other becoming an outcast. Each is redeemed by a higher love. Madeleine Cary must not be misread; it is true that her lust overcomes her at the critical moment, but it does not extinguish her love for Farnborough; her body, not her soul, consents to the lapse. Moreover, her later avowal, which she knew would finally lose her her lover, is meant to show the basic rectitude of her nature. Though it does not need Darrow to cure Letty of her wanton ways, she too is redeemed by a nobler love. Neither Madeleine Smith, nor the Letty of the novel, were at all like that; they wished to shake off a clandestine intrigue to set themselves up in the world; their love as distinct from their lust, was pallid. So much for the similarity in character.

Coming to the parallelism of incident, the threat scene is carried out with almost exactly the same sequence of event and actuation; it has no prototype in either story or novel. Neither Ekebon nor L'Angelier went to his fatal interview to break up the new betrothal; he was beguiled by the pretence of a renewed affection. Moreno and Renaul each goes to his sweetheart's home to detach her from her new love; when he is there, she appeals to his better side, unsuccessfully; she abuses him, he returns the abuse and commands her to come to his rooms; she pretends to agree, expecting to finish with him one way or another. True, the assault is deferred in the picture from this scene to the next, but it is the same dramatic trick. Again, the poison in each case is found at home, and the girl talks with her betrothed just after the villain has left and again pledges him her faith. Surely the sequence of these details is pro tanto the very web of the authors' dramatic expression; and copying them is not "fair use."

The death scene follows the play even more closely; the girl goes to the villain's room as he directs; from the outset he is plainly to be poisoned while they are together. (The defendants deny that this is apparent in the picture, but we cannot agree. It would have been an impossible denouement on the screen for the heroine, just plighted to the hero, to kill herself in desperation, because the villain has successfully enmeshed her in their mutual past; yet the poison is surely to be used on some one.) Moreno and Renaul each tries to arouse the girl by the memory of their former love, using among other aphrodisiacs the Gaucho song; each dies while she is there, incidentally of strychnine not arsenic. In extremis each makes for the telephone and is thwarted by the girl; as he dies, she pours upon him her rage and loathing. When he is dead, she follows the same ritual to eradicate all traces of her presence, but forgets telltale bits of property. Again these details in the same sequence embody more than the "ideas" of the play; they are its very raiment.

Finally in both play and picture in place of a trial, as in the story and the novel, there is substituted an examination by a district attorney; and this examination is again in parallel almost step by step. A parent is present; so is the lover; the girl yields progressively as the evidence accumulates; in the picture, the customs slip, the rubbers and the letters; in the play, the cross and the witnesses, brought in to confront her. She is at the breaking point when she is saved by substantially the same most unexpected alibi; a man declares that she has spent the night with him. That alibi there introduced is the turning point in each drama and alone prevents its ending in accordance with the classic canon of tragedy; i.e., fate as an inevitable consequence of past conduct, itself not evil enough to quench pity. It is the essence of the authors' expression, the very voice with which they speak.

We have often decided that a play may be pirated without using the dialogue. Daly v. Palmer, Fed. Cas. No. 3,552, 6 Blatch. 256; Daly v. Webster, 56 F. 483, 486, 487; Dam v. Kirk La Shelle Co., 175 F. 902, 907, 41 L.R.A.(N.S.) 1002, 20 Ann.Cas. 1173; Chappell & Co. v. Fields, 210 F. 864. Dymow v. Bolton, 11 F.(2d) 690; and Nichols v. Universal Pictures Corporation, supra, 45 F.(2d) 119, do not suggest otherwise. Were it not so, there could be no piracy of a pantomime, where there cannot be any dialogue; yet nobody would deny to pantomime the name of drama. Speech is only a small part of a dramatist's means of expression; he draws on all the arts and compounds his play from words and gestures and scenery and costume and from the very looks of the actors themselves. Again and again a play may lapse into pantomime at its most poignant and significant moments; a nod, a movement of the hand, a pause, may tell the audience more than words could tell. To be sure, not all this is always copyrighted, though there is no reason why it may not be, for those decisions do not forbid which hold that mere scenic tricks will not be protected. Serrana v. Jefferson (C.C.) 33 F. 347; Barnes v. Miner (C.C.) 122 F. 480; Bloom et al. v. Nixon (C.C.) 125 F. 977. The play is the sequence of the confluents of all these means, bound together in an inseparable unity; it may often be most effectively pirated by leaving out the speech, for which a substitute can be found, which keeps the whole dramatic meaning. That as it appears to us is exactly what the defendants have done here; the dramatic significance of the scenes we have recited is the same, almost to the letter. True, much of the picture owes nothing to the play; some of it is plainly drawn from the novel; but that is entirely immaterial; it is enough that substantial parts were lifted; no plagiarist can excuse the wrong by showing how much of his work he did not pirate. We cannot avoid the conviction that, if the picture was not an infringement of the play, there can be none short of taking the dialogue.

The decree will be reversed and an injunction will go against the picture together with a decree for damages and an accounting. * * *

Notes

1. The opinions in *Nichols* and *Sheldon* are classic sources of infringement theory, as influential in computer program and Internet contexts today as they were in their own time. The original manuscripts are preserved under glass in the Copyright Office.

2. For an enlightening "out of textbook" experience, view the films "Shane" and "Pale Rider" and consider whether the nonliteral similarities between them would satisfy the test for copyright infringement.

B. THE PRIMA FACIE CASE

ARNSTEIN v. PORTER

United States Court of Appeals, Second Circuit, 1946.
154 F.2d 464.

FRANK, CIRCUIT JUDGE:

* * *

[Plaintiff alleged that several of defendant's musical compositions were copied from plaintiff's works, of which some, but not all, had been published, publicly performed on the radio, or distributed to a limited group. Plaintiff offered no direct evidence that defendant had ever seen or heard these compositions, and defendant denied having any acquaintance with them. The district court granted the defendant's motion for summary judgment, and the plaintiff appealed.]

2.   The principal question on this appeal is whether the lower court * * * properly deprived plaintiff of a trial of his copyright infringement action. The answer depends on whether 'there is the slightest doubt as to the facts.' * * * In applying that standard here, it is important to avoid confusing two separate elements essential to a plaintiff's case in such a suit: (a) that defendant copied from plaintiff's copyrighted work and (b) that the copying (assuming it to be proved) went so far as to constitute improper appropriation.

As to the first—copying—the evidence may consist (a) of defendant's admission that he copied or (b) of circumstantial evidence—usually evidence of access—from which the trier of the facts may reasonably infer copying. Of course, if there are no similarities, no amount of evidence of access will suffice to prove copying. If there is evidence of access and similarities exist, then the trier of the facts must determine whether the similarities are sufficient to prove copying. On this issue, analysis ("dissection") is relevant, and the testimony of experts may be received to aid the trier of the facts. If evidence of access is absent, the similarities must be so striking as to preclude the possibility that plaintiff and defendant independently arrived at the same result.

If copying is established, then only does there arise the second issue, that of illicit copying (unlawful appropriation). On that issue (as noted more in detail below) the test is the response of the ordinary lay hearer; accordingly, on that issue, "dissection" and expert testimony are irrelevant.

In some cases, the similarities between the plaintiff's and defendant's work are so extensive and striking as, without more, both to justify an inference of copying and to prove improper appropriation. But such double-purpose evidence is not required; that is, if copying is otherwise shown, proof of improper appropriation need not consist of similarities which, standing alone, would support an inference of copying.

Each of these two issues—copying and improper appropriation—is an issue of fact. If there is a trial, the conclusions on those issues of the trier of the facts—of the judge if he sat without a jury, or of the jury if there was a jury trial—bind this court on appeal, provided the evidence supports those findings, regardless of whether we would ourselves have reached the same conclusions. But a case could occur in which the similarities were so striking that we would reverse a finding of no access, despite weak evidence of access (or no evidence thereof other than the similarities); and similarly as to a finding of no illicit appropriation.

3. We turn first to the issue of copying. After listening to the compositions as played in the phonograph recordings submitted by defendant, we find similarities; but we hold that unquestionably, standing alone, they do not compel the conclusion, or permit the inference, that defendant copied. The similarities, however, are sufficient so that, if there is enough evidence of access to permit the case to go to the jury, the jury may properly infer that the similarities did not result from coincidence.

Summary judgment was, then, proper if indubitably defendant did not have access to plaintiff's compositions. Plainly that presents an issue of fact. On that issue, the district judge, who heard no oral testimony, had before him the depositions of plaintiff and defendant. The judge characterized plaintiff's story as "fantastic"; and, in the light of the references in his opinion to defendant's deposition, the judge obviously accepted defendant's denial of access and copying. Although part of plaintiff's testimony on deposition * * * does seem "fantastic," yet plaintiff's credibility, even as to those improbabilities, should be left to the jury. * * *

But even if we were to disregard the improbable aspects of plaintiff's story, there remain parts by no means "fantastic." On the record now before us, more than a million copies of one of his compositions were sold; copies of others were sold in smaller quantities or distributed to radio stations or band leaders or publishers, or the pieces were publicly performed. If, after hearing both parties testify, the jury disbelieves defendant's denials, it can, from such facts, reasonably infer access. It follows that, as credibility is unavoidably involved, a genuine issue of material fact presents itself. * * *

With all that in mind, we cannot now say—as we think we must say to sustain a summary judgment—that at the close of a trial the judge could properly direct a verdict.

* * *

4. Assuming that adequate proof is made of copying, that is not enough; for there can be "permissible copying," copying which is not illicit. Whether (if he copied) defendant unlawfully appropriated presents, too, an issue of fact. The proper criterion on that issue is not an analytic or other comparison of the respective musical compositions as

they appear on paper or in the judgment of trained musicians.[19] The plaintiff's legally protected interest is not, as such, his reputation as a musician but his interest in the potential financial returns from his compositions which derive from the lay public's approbation of his efforts. The question, therefore, is whether defendant took from plaintiff's works so much of what is pleasing to the ears of lay listeners, who comprise the audience for whom such popular music is composed, that defendant wrongfully appropriated something which belongs to the plaintiff.

Surely, then, we have an issue of fact which a jury is peculiarly fitted to determine.[22] * * *

We should not be taken as saying that a plagiarism case can never arise in which absence of similarities is so patent that a summary judgment for defendant would be correct. Thus suppose that Ravel's "Bolero" or Shostakovitch's "Fifth Symphony" were alleged to infringe "When Irish Eyes Are Smiling."[23] But this is not such a case. For, after listening to the playing of the respective compositions, we are, at this time, unable to conclude that the likenesses are so trifling that, on the issue of misappropriation, a trial judge could legitimately direct a verdict for defendant.

At the trial, plaintiff may play, or cause to be played, the pieces in such manner that they may seem to a jury to be inexcusably alike, in terms of the way in which lay listeners of such music would be likely to react. The plaintiff may call witnesses whose testimony may aid the jury in reaching its conclusion as to the responses of such audiences. Expert testimony of musicians may also be received, but it will in no way be controlling on the issue of illicit copying, and should be utilized only to assist in determining the reactions of lay auditors. The impression made on the refined ears of musical experts or their views as to the musical excellence of plaintiff's or defendant's works are utterly immaterial on the issue of misappropriation; for the views of such persons are caviar to the general—and plaintiff's and defendant's compositions are not caviar.

* * *

SHAW v. LINDHEIM
United States Court of Appeals, Ninth Circuit, 1990.
919 F.2d 1353.

Alarcon, Circuit Judge.

Lou Shaw and Eastbourne Productions, Inc. (Shaw) appeal from a grant of summary judgment in favor of Richard Lindheim, Michael

---

19. Where plaintiff relies on similarities to prove copying (as distinguished from improper appropriation) paper comparisons and the opinions of experts may aid the court.

22. It would, accordingly, be proper to exclude tone-deaf persons from the jury, cf.

Chatterton v. Cave, 3 A.C. 483, 499–501, 502–504.

23. In such a case, the complete absence of similarity would negate both copying and improper appropriation.

Sloan, and three entertainment corporations (defendants). On appeal, Shaw argues that the district court erred in finding that, as a matter of law, there was no substantial similarity between his script entitled "The Equalizer" and defendants' pilot script for their "Equalizer" television series. Because a reasonable trier of fact could have found that the two works are substantially similar, Shaw argues, the district court erred in dismissing his copyright * * * claims on summary judgment. We reverse and remand.

* * *

DISCUSSION

I. Copyright Claim

Copyright law protects an author's expression; facts and ideas within a work are not protected. Narell [v. Freeman, 872 F.2d 907 (9th Cir.1989),] at 910. To establish a successful copyright infringement claim, Shaw must show that he owns the copyright and that defendant copied protected elements of the work. Id. Because, in most cases, direct evidence of copying is not available, a plaintiff may establish copying by showing that the infringer had access to the work and that the two works are substantially similar. Id. The defendants conceded Shaw's ownership of the original Equalizer script and their access to the script for purposes of the summary judgment motion. As a result, the only issue before the district court on the copyright claim was whether defendants' version of the Equalizer is substantially similar to Shaw's original script.

Any test for substantial similarity is necessarily imprecise:

"Upon any work, and especially upon a play, a great number of patterns of increasing generality will fit equally well, as more and more of the incident is left out. The last may perhaps be no more than the most general statement of what the play is about and at times might consist of only its title; but there is a point in this series of abstractions where they are no longer protected, since otherwise the playwright could prevent the use of his 'ideas,' to which, apart from their expression, his property is never extended."

Sid & Marty Krofft Television Prods., Inc. v. McDonald's Corp., 562 F.2d 1157, 1163 (9th Cir.1977) (quoting Nichols v. Universal Pictures Corp., 45 F.2d 119, 121 (2d Cir.1930), cert. denied, 282 U.S. 902, 75 L. Ed. 795, 51 S.Ct. 216 (1931)). It is thus impossible to articulate a definitive demarcation that measures when the similarity between works involves copying of protected expression; decisions must inevitably be ad hoc. Id. at 1164 (citing Peter Pan Fabrics, Inc. v. Martin Weiner Corp., 274 F.2d 487, 489 (2d Cir.1960) (L. Hand, J.)); see also Comment, Does Form Follow Function?, 35 UCLA L. Rev. 723 (1988) (discussing the difficulty of demarcating the idea-expression line).

A. The Krofft Framework

The Ninth Circuit employs a two-part test for determining whether one work is substantially similar to another. Narell, 872 F.2d at 912; Olson v. National Broadcasting Co., 855 F.2d 1446, 1448 (9th Cir.1988). Established in Sid & Marty Krofft Television Prods., Inc. v. McDonald's Corp., 562 F.2d 1157, 1164 (9th Cir.1977), the test permits a finding of infringement only if a plaintiff proves both substantial similarity of general ideas under the "extrinsic test" and substantial similarity of the protectable expression of those ideas under the "intrinsic test." Olson, 855 F.2d at 1449; Krofft, 562 F.2d at 1164.

1. Scope of the Krofft Tests

Krofft defined the extrinsic test as a "test for similarity of ideas" under which "analytic dissection and expert testimony are appropriate." 562 F.2d at 1164. The intrinsic test, according to Krofft, should measure "substantial similarity in expressions . . . depending on the response of the ordinary reasonable person. . . . It does not depend on the type of external criteria and analysis which marks the extrinsic test." Id. In decisions under the intrinsic test, "analytic dissection and expert testimony are not appropriate." Id.

Relying on this language, panels applying Krofft to literary works have included a lengthy list of concrete elements under the extrinsic test. Whereas Krofft listed "the type of artwork involved, the materials used, the subject matter, and the setting for the subject" as criteria for consideration under the extrinsic test, id., a series of opinions beginning with the district court opinion in Jason v. Fonda, 526 F.Supp. 774 (C.D.Cal.1981), aff'd and incorporated by reference, 698 F.2d 966 (9th Cir.1982), have listed "plot, themes, dialogue, mood, setting, pace, and sequence" as extrinsic test criteria. 526 F.Supp. at 777; see also Litchfield v. Spielberg, 736 F.2d 1352, 1356 (9th Cir.1984) (repeating this list), cert. denied, 470 U.S. 1052, 84 L.Ed.2d 817, 105 S.Ct. 1753 (1985); Berkic v. Crichton, 761 F.2d 1289, 1293 (9th Cir.) (same), cert. denied, 474 U.S. 826, 88 L.Ed.2d 69, 106 S. Ct. 85 (1985); Olson, 855 F.2d at 1450 (same); Narell, 872 F.2d at 912 (adding "characters" to the list and transforming "sequence" into "sequence of events").

Now that it includes virtually every element that may be considered concrete in a literary work, the extrinsic test as applied to books, scripts, plays, and motion pictures can no longer be seen as a test for mere similarity of ideas. Because the criteria incorporated into the extrinsic test encompass all objective manifestations of creativity, the two tests are more sensibly described as objective and subjective analyses of expression, having strayed from Krofft's division between expression and ideas. See Narell, 872 F.2d at 912 (referring to an objective, extrinsic test and a subjective, intrinsic test); Berkic, 761 F.2d at 1292 (same); Litchfield, 736 F.2d at 1356 (same). But see Olson, 855 F.2d at 1448–49 (adhering to Krofft's idea/expression distinction). Indeed, a judicial determination under the intrinsic test is now virtually devoid of analysis, for the intrinsic test has become a mere subjective judgment as to whether two literary works are or are not similar. See Berkic, 761 F.2d at 1294 (reaching a result under the intrinsic test in one paragraph); Olson, 855 F.2d at 1453 (same).

2. The District Court's Application of Krofft

An example of how the absence of legal analysis may frustrate appellate review of the intrinsic test is the district court's order in this matter. The district court found, after extensive analysis, that reasonable minds might conclude that plaintiffs' and defendants' works were substantially similar as to the objective characteristics of theme, plot, sequence of events, characters, dialogue, setting, mood, and pace. Nevertheless, the court made a subjective determination under the intrinsic test that no reasonable juror could determine that the works had a substantially similar total concept and feel. * * *

* * *

The district court's decision to grant summary judgment solely on a subjective assessment under Krofft's intrinsic test conflicts with the prescriptions of Krofft. In Krofft, this court stated that the outcome of the extrinsic test "may often be decided as a matter of law." 562 F.2d at 1164. In contrast "[i]f there is substantial similarity in ideas, then *the trier of fact* must decide [under the intrinsic test] whether there is substantial similarity in the expressions of the ideas so as to constitute infringement." Id. (emphasis added); see also id. at 1166 ("[T]he intrinsic test for expression is uniquely suited for determination by *the trier of fact*." (emphasis added)). Professor Nimmer has also noted that "the second step in the [Krofft] analytic process requires that *the trier of fact* then decide 'whether there is substantial similarity in the expressions of the ideas so as to constitute infringement.' " 3 M. Nimmer, Nimmer on Copyright § 13.03[E][3], at 62.14 (1989) [hereinafter Nimmer on Copyright].

3. Krofft and the Summary Judgment Standard

* * *

We must determine in this matter whether a party that demonstrates a triable issue of fact under the extrinsic test has made a sufficient showing of substantial similarity to defeat a summary judgment motion. As noted above, the extrinsic test focuses on "specific similarities between the plot, theme, dialogue, mood, setting, pace, characters, and sequence of events.... 'the actual concrete elements that make up the total sequence of events and the relationships between the major characters.' " Narell, 872 F.2d at 912 (quoting Berkic, 761 F.2d at 1293). These are the measurable, objective elements that constitute a literary work's expression. Because these elements are embodied in the extrinsic test, we hold that it is improper for a court to find, as the district court did, that there is no substantial similarity as a matter of law after a writer has satisfied the extrinsic test. To conclude otherwise would allow a court to base a grant of summary judgment on a purely subjective determination of similarity. * * *

The rule we announce today—that satisfaction of the extrinsic test creates a triable issue of fact in a copyright action involving a literary work—is in harmony with our prior decisions. Although various panels of this circuit have affirmed grants of summary judgment on the issue of substantial similarity between books, scripts, films, or plays, none of these decisions have rested on application of the intrinsic test alone. * * *

* * *

* * * A comparison of literary works * * * generally requires the reader or viewer to engage in a two-step process. The first step involves the objective comparison of concrete similarities; the second employs the subjective process of comprehension, reasoning, and understanding. The imagery presented in a literary work may also engage the imagination of the audience and evoke an emotional response. Because each of us differs, to some degree, in our capability to reason, imagine, and react emotionally, subjective comparisons of literary works that are objectively similar in their expression of ideas must be left to the trier of fact.

For these reasons, a showing of substantial similarity with reference to the eight objective components of expression in the extrinsic test applied to literary works creates a genuine issue for trial. If a district court concludes, after analyzing the objective criteria under the extrinsic test, that reasonable minds might differ as to whether there is substantial similarity between the protected expression of ideas in two literary works, and the record supports the district court's conclusion, there is a triable issue of fact that precludes summary judgment. This rule is necessary because our expansion of the extrinsic test as applied to literary works has incorporated all objective elements of expression, leaving a mere subjective assessment of similarity for the intrinsic test. Because such an assessment may not properly be made as a matter of law, it is for the trier of fact to determine whether the intrinsic test is satisfied.[2] Accordingly, our decision in this matter turns on whether Shaw has raised a triable issue of fact under Krofft's extrinsic test.

B.   The Extrinsic Test

1.   Role of Access

Although access was not an issue before the district court for purposes of the defendants' summary judgment motion, we must consider defendants' access to Shaw's script in determining substantial similarity. The holding in Krofft itself rested in part on a finding that the defendants' "degree of access justifies a lower standard of proof to show substantial similarity." 562 F.2d at 1172. As we stated in Krofft:

---

2. This is not to say that summary judgment on the issue of expression is never proper. * * * When a plaintiff demonstrates an issue of fact as to the objective components of expression now embodied in the extrinsic test, however, it is improper to grant summary judgment based on a subjective assessment under the intrinsic test alone.

No amount of proof of access will suffice to show copying if there are no similarities. This is not to say, however, that where clear and convincing evidence of access is presented, the quantum of proof required to show substantial similarity may not be lower than when access is shown merely by a preponderance of the evidence. As Professor Nimmer has observed:

> "[C]lear and convincing evidence of access will not avoid the necessity of also proving substantial similarity since access without similarity cannot create an inference of copying. However this so-called 'Inverse Ratio Rule' ... would seem to have some limited validity. That is, since a very high degree of similarity is required in order to dispense with proof of access, it must logically follow that *where proof of access is offered, the required degree of similarity may be somewhat less* than would be necessary in the absence of such proof."

Id. (quoting 2 M. Nimmer, Nimmer on Copyright § 143.4, at 634 (1976) (citations omitted)) (emphasis added). But see Aliotti [v. R. Dakin & Co., 831 F.2d 898 (9th Cir.1987),] at 902 (questioning, in dictum, the "continuing viability of Professor Nimmer's proposal"). Because no subsequent decision has disturbed the access rule established in Krofft, we believe that it is the law of this circuit. Thus, defendants' admission that they had access to Shaw's script is a factor to be considered in favor of Shaw.

* * *

3. *The Extrinsic Test Applied*

[The appellate court then applied the extrinsic text to determine the extent of objective similarities in the plot, theme, dialogue, mood, setting, pace, characters, and sequence of events in each of the two works.]

* * *

4. *Conclusion*

We conclude that Shaw has satisfied the extrinsic test for literary works and thus has presented a triable issue of fact regarding substantial similarity of protected expression. "Even if a copied portion be relatively small in proportion to the entire work, if qualitatively important, the finder of fact may properly find substantial similarity." Baxter [v. MCA, Inc., 812 F.2d 421 (9th Cir.1987),] at 425. A reasonable trier of fact could find that the similarity between Shaw's script and defendants' pilot is not so general as to be beyond the protections of copyright law. Because Shaw has produced a triable issue of fact under the extrinsic test, we reverse the district court's grant of summary judgment on Shaw's copyright claim.

* * *

LEIGH v. WARNER BROTHERS, INC.

United States Court of Appeals, Eleventh Circuit, 2000.
212 F.3d 1210.

Kravitch, Senior Circuit Judge.

This appeal concerns the scope of a photographer's copyright and trademark rights in his work, the role of the court in determining whether images are "substantially similar" for purposes of copyright, and the power of the court to rule on dispositive motions without first allowing broad discovery. Jack Leigh took the now-famous photograph of the Bird Girl statue in Savannah's Bonaventure Cemetery that appears on the cover of the best-selling novel *Midnight in the Garden of Good and Evil*. Warner Brothers made a film version of the novel and used images of the Bird Girl both in promotional materials and in the movie itself. Leigh sued Warner Brothers, asserting that it infringed his copyright and trademark rights in the Bird Girl photograph. *See* 17 U.S.C. §§ 101–1101 (1999) (copyright); 15 U.S.C. §§ 1051–1127 (1999) (trademark). The district court granted summary judgment for Warner Brothers on all claims, except one that the parties now have settled, and Leigh appeals.

The district court correctly ascertained the elements of Leigh's photograph protected by copyright and determined that the Warner Brothers film sequences are not substantially similar to those protected elements. Copyright infringement is generally a question of fact for the jury to decide, however, and the court erred in holding as a matter of law that no reasonable jury could find that the Warner Brothers promotional single-frame images were substantially similar to the aspects of Leigh's work protected by copyright.

As for Leigh's Lanham Act claims, the evidence that Leigh used the Bird Girl photograph to identify the source of his other work prior to the Warner Brothers movie is insufficient to establish the photograph as a trademark. We therefore affirm the district court's grant of summary judgment to Warner Brothers on Leigh's trademark claims.

Finally, Leigh contends that the district court abused its discretion by granting summary judgment without first allowing more discovery. Additional discovery, however, would not help prove Leigh's use of his photograph as a trademark, and it could not overcome the substantial *dis* similarity between Leigh's photograph and the film sequences. Additional discovery could well be appropriate on remand for Leigh's remaining copyright claim.

I. Background

In 1993, Random House commissioned Jack Leigh to take a photograph for the cover of *Midnight in the Garden of Good and Evil* ("*Midnight*"), a novel by John Berendt. After reading a manuscript of the novel, Leigh explored appropriate settings in Savannah and ultimately selected a photograph of a sculpture in the Bonaventure Cemetery known as the Bird Girl. Sylvia Shaw Judson had sculpted the Bird Girl in 1938, and she produced three copies of the statue. The Trosdal family had purchased one of the statues and placed it in their plot at Bonaventure Cemetery. The novel does not mention the Bird Girl statue. Leigh granted Random House permission to use the photo, but retained ownership and registered his claim of copyright.

In 1997, Warner Brothers produced a movie based on *Midnight* and decided to use the Bird Girl statue on promotional materials and at the beginning and end of the movie. Because the Trosdals had removed the statue from their cemetery plot after the book's publication, Warner Brothers made a replica of the Bird Girl with the permission of Sylvia Shaw Judson's heir. The company then took photographs and film footage of the replica in a new location in Bonaventure Cemetery. Those images are the subject of this lawsuit.

Three segments of film footage depict the Bird Girl statue. One is a promotional clip, and the others appear at the beginning and end of the Warner Brothers movie. Six still images feature the Bird Girl: a promotional photograph and nearly identical picture on the "goodandevil" web site, a movie poster, a newspaper advertisement, the cover for the movie's soundtrack, and an internet icon. Leigh alleges that these images infringed his copyright and trademark rights in his Bird Girl photograph. The district court granted Warner Brothers' motion to stay all discovery, and later granted summary judgment for Warner Brothers on all claims except a copyright claim pertaining to the internet icon. The parties subsequently settled all claims pertaining to that internet icon.

We review the district court's grant of summary judgment *de novo,* construing all evidence in the light most favorable to the non-moving party. *See* Beal v. Paramount Pictures Corp., 20 F.3d 454, 458–59 (11th Cir.1994). Summary judgment is only proper when there are no genuine issues of material fact. *See* id. We review the court's decision to rule on the summary judgment motion without allowing the plaintiff to complete desired discovery for abuse of discretion. *See* Carmical v. Bell Helicopter Textron, Inc., 117 F.3d 490, 493 (11th Cir.1997).

* * *

II. LEIGH'S COPYRIGHT CLAIMS

To establish a claim of copyright infringement, a plaintiff must prove, first, that he owns a valid copyright in a work and, second, that the defendant copied original elements of that work. *See* Feist Publications, Inc. v. Rural Tel. Serv. Co., 499 U.S. 340, 361, 111 S.Ct. 1282, 1296, 113 L.Ed.2d 358 (1991). The plaintiff can prove copying either directly or indirectly, by establishing that the defendant had access, and produced something "substantially similar," to the copyrighted work. *See* Original Appalachian Artworks, Inc. v. Toy Loft, Inc., 684 F.2d 821, 829 (11th Cir.1982). Substantial similarity, in this sense, "exists where an average lay observer would recognize the alleged copy as having been appropriated from the copyrighted work." Id. (internal quotation omitted).

"Substantial similarity" also is important in a second, more focused way. No matter how the copying is proved, the plaintiff also must establish specifically that the allegedly infringing work is substantially similar to the plaintiff's work *with regard to its protected elements. See* Herzog v. Castle Rock Entertainment, 193 F.3d 1241, 1248, 1257 (11th Cir.1999) (per curiam, adopting the district court opinion in its entirety); Beal, 20 F.3d at 459 & n. 4; William F. Patry, *Latman's The Copyright Law* 193 & n. 18, 196–97 (6th ed.1986). Even in the rare case of a plaintiff with direct evidence that a defendant attempted to appropriate his original expression, there is no infringement unless the defendant succeeded to a meaningful degree. *See* Fisher–Price, Inc. v. Well–Made Toy Mfg. Corp., 25 F.3d 119, 122–23 (2d Cir.1994).

For the purposes of its motion for summary judgment and this appeal, Warner Brothers does not contest Leigh's ownership of a valid copyright in the Bird Girl photograph. Leigh, on the other hand, takes issue both with the district court's view of the scope of his copyright and with the court's analysis of the similarities between the Bird Girl images.

Leigh's copyright does not cover the appearance of the statue itself or of Bonaventure Cemetery, for Leigh has no rights in the statue or its setting. *See* Franklin Mint Corp. v. National Wildlife Art Exch., Inc., 575 F.2d 62, 65 (3d Cir.1978) (artists have no copyright in the "reality of [their] subject matter"); 4 Melville B. Nimmer & David Nimmer, *Nimmer on Copyright* § 13:03[B][2][b] (1999) (noting that appearance of objects in the public domain or as they occur in nature is not protected by copyright). Nor does the copyright protect the association of the statue with the *Midnight* story. Leigh may have been the first to think of the statue as evocative of the novel's mood and as an appropriate symbol of the book's themes, but copyright law protects only original expression, not ideas. *See* 17 U.S.C. § 102(a)-(b); Feist, 499 U.S. at 345, 111 S.Ct. at 1287 (citation omitted); Herzog, 193 F.3d at 1248 (citation omitted).

Thus, the district court correctly identified the elements of artistic craft protected by Leigh's copyright as the selection of lighting, shading, timing, angle, and film. *See* Rogers v. Koons, 960 F.2d 301, 307 (2d Cir.1992). Leigh suggests that the court also should have considered the overall combination of these protected elements as well as the mood they convey. The court determined that the "eerie," "spiritual" mood was *scenes a faire,* expression commonly associated with the subject matter (cemeteries) and thus non-original and unprotectable. *See* Beal, 20 F.3d at 459–60 (describing the *scenes a faire* doctrine). Leigh contests the notion that cemeteries are typically portrayed in an eerie, spiritual manner, but there is no need to determine whether *scenes a faire* applies in this case.

Analyzing relatively amorphous characteristics of the picture as a whole (such as the "mood" or "combination of elements") creates a danger of unwittingly extending copyright protection to unoriginal aspects of the work. *See* 4 Nimmer & Nimmer, *supra,* § 13:03[A][1][c] (criticizing the use of "amorphous referent[s]" such as the "feel" of a work in copyright analysis because it threatens to erode the line between what is and is not protectable). This danger is especially acute in a case such as this, in which the unprotected elements of the plaintiff's work— the haunting pose and expression of the Bird Girl and the cemetery setting—are so significant.

Although some cases have evaluated the "mood" of a work independently, *see, e.g.,* Beal, 20 F.3d at 461–62, in this case it is safest to focus on the more concrete elements of the photographer's craft. Even as Leigh describes it, the mood is not so much an independent aspect of his photograph protected by copyright, as the effect created by the lighting, shading, timing, angle, and film. The same holds true for the overall combination of elements in the photograph. As long as the analysis is not overly detached and technical, it can adequately address both the effect of the protected, original elements of Leigh's photograph on the viewer and the contribution of those elements to the work as a whole.

In its order granting summary judgment, the court methodically and accurately details a number of differences in the compositional elements between Leigh's photograph and the Warner Brothers images. This circuit has noted, however, that lists of similarities between works are inherently subjective and unreliable, *see* Beal, 20 F.3d at 460, and the same can be true of lists of distinguishing characteristics.

The court was correct to hold as a matter of law that the film sequences featuring the Bird Girl statue are not substantially similar to the protected elements of Leigh's photograph. In one sequence, the cemetery is shrouded in fog, revealing only the Bird Girl and a Celtic cross, a decoration absent from Leigh's photograph. The camera frame also crops the head of the Bird Girl statue. A second sequence is shot at least partly in color and in broad daylight. The statue's plinth is never shown, and as the camera pans up it shows only the upper portions of the statue on the left side of the screen. In the final sequence, the camera rotates around the statue, beginning with a side shot, and captures only the head and shoulders before panning back to show the Bird Girl's torso. Again, the statue is on the left side of the screen and the sequence is shot in daylight. The film sequences were not shot in the same section of the Bonaventure Cemetery as Leigh's photograph, so the surrounding gravestones and greenery are different. These film sequences have nothing substantial in common with Leigh's photograph except the statue itself.

The same cannot be said for Warner Brothers' photographic images. There are, undeniably, significant differences between the pictures. The statue is smaller and more distant in most of the Warner Brothers pictures than in Leigh's photograph, and as a result the vegetation and headstones in the foreground are more prominent. The Bird Girl is approximately the same size only on the soundtrack cover. Although both the Leigh photograph and the soundtrack cover have diffuse light that "glows" about the statue, the lighting contrast is more extreme in most of the Warner Brothers pictures, with beams of light piercing the tree canopy like spotlights. The shafts of light and surrounding shadows obscure details of the statue and the cemetery setting. Finally, Warner Brothers has added elements to some of its images that are absent from Leigh's photo: some have a green or orange tint; some prominently feature a Celtic cross and tree; and the movie poster includes pictures of the cast along its left side.

Although it may be easy to identify differences between the Warner Brothers still shots and Leigh's photograph, however, the Warner Brothers images also have much in common with the elements protected by Leigh's copyright. All of the photographs are taken from a low position, angled up slightly at the Bird Girl so that the contents of the bowls in her hands remain hidden. Hanging Spanish moss borders the tops of all the photographs except the soundtrack cover. The statue is close to centered in all of the pictures except one newspaper advertisement for the movie, which places the Bird Girl in the left third of the frame. Light shines down and envelopes the statue in all of the images, leaving the surrounding cemetery in relative darkness. All of the photographs are monochromatic.

These expressive elements all make the pictures more effective. The Spanish moss provides a top border to the images. The location of the statue and the lighting in the pictures together draw the viewer's attention. The lighting also lends a spiritual air to the Bird Girl. Finally, by keeping the contents of the Bird Girl's bowls hidden, the angle contributes to the mystery and symbolic meaning of the images.

A jury ultimately may conclude that the similarities between the protected elements of the Leigh photograph and the Warner Brothers still shots are not "substantial." The similarities are significant enough, however, to preclude summary judgment. "Substantial similarity" is a question of fact, and summary judgment is only appropriate if no reasonable jury could differ in weighing the evidence. *See* Beal, 20 F.3d at 459; Donald Frederick Evans & Assocs. v. Continental Homes, Inc., 785 F.2d 897, 904 (11th Cir.1986).

IV.   DISCOVERY

In addition to claiming that the court erred in its application of copyright and trademark law to the evidence before it, Leigh argues that the court abused its discretion in granting summary judgment without allowing him to conduct additional discovery. The court granted a protective order staying all discovery early in the litigation, and did not lift the stay before ruling on Warner Brothers' summary judgment motions.

Leigh cites numerous cases for the proposition that it generally is inappropriate for a court to rule on a summary judgment motion when the non-moving party has not been able to obtain discovery. *See* Fernandez v. Bankers Nat'l Life Ins. Co., 906 F.2d 559, 570 (11th Cir.1990); Snook v. Trust Co. of Georgia Bank, 859 F.2d 865, 870–71 (11th Cir.1988). Federal Rule of Civil Procedure 56(f) allows courts to defer ruling on summary judgment motions until the non-moving party has been able to conduct all necessary discovery.

We review the court's management of discovery in this context for abuse of discretion, however, and a party must be able to show substantial harm to its case from the denial of its requests for additional discovery. *See* Carmical, 117 F.3d at 493. In this case, the court had an adequate record to grant Warner Brothers' motion for summary judgment on Leigh's trademark claims and the copyright claim concerning the film footage. Any evidence of Leigh's use of the Bird Girl photograph as a trademark would have been in his possession, not Warner Brothers'. Similarly, no evidence that Warner Brothers could have produced would change the fact that its film sequences are not substantially similar to the copyrighted elements of Leigh's photograph.

Because the substantial similarity of the Warner Brothers still shots to Leigh's photograph remains an open question of fact, additional discovery for Leigh's copyright claim could well be appropriate.

V. Conclusion

We AFFIRM the grant of summary judgment for the Defendant on Leigh's trademark claims and the copyright claim as it relates to the film sequences. We REVERSE the grant of summary judgment for the Defendant on Leigh's copyright claim as it relates to Warner Brothers' single-frame images, and we REMAND for proceedings consistent with this decision.

APPLE COMPUTER, INC. v. MICROSOFT CORP.

United States Court of Appeals, Ninth Circuit, 1994.
35 F.3d 1435. *cert. denied*, 513 U.S. 1184, 115
S.Ct. 1176, 130 L.Ed.2d 1129 (1995).

Rymer, Circuit Judge.

[Apple Computer owns the copyright in the graphical user interface ("GUI") for its Lisa and Macintosh computers. Each GUI is based on a desktop metaphor with windows, icons and pull-down menus. In 1985 Apple licensed Microsoft to use and sublicense certain elements of this GUI, but later sued Microsoft for copyright infringement, alleging that certain of Microsoft's derivative works (the Windows and NewWave GUIs) exceeded the scope of the license. The district court applied the concepts of idea versus expression, originality, functionality, standardization, public domain, scenes a faire and merger to identify the copyrightable components of Apple's GUI, and concluded that, once the licensed components were excluded from consideration, the copyrightable components of the two works were not substantially similar. Apple appealed.]

* * *

Apple makes a number of related arguments challenging the district court's copyright analysis. It contends that the district court deprived its works of meaningful protection by dissecting them into individual elements and viewing each element in isolation. Because the Macintosh GUI is a dynamic audiovisual work, Apple argues that the "total concept and feel" of its works—that is, the selection and arrangement of related images and their animation—must be compared with that of the Windows and NewWave GUIs for substantial similarity. * * *

* * *

Although this litigation has raised difficult and interesting issues about the scope of copyright protection for a graphical user interface, resolving this appeal is a matter of applying well-settled principles. In this, as in other cases, the steps we find helpful to follow are these:

(1) The plaintiff must identify the source(s) of the alleged similarity between his work and the defendant's work.

(2) Using analytic dissection, and, if necessary, expert testimony, the court must determine whether any of the allegedly similar features are protected by copyright. Where, as in this case, a license agreement is involved, the court must also determine which features the defendant was authorized to copy. Once the scope of the license is determined, unprotectable ideas must be separated from potentially protectable expression; to that expression, the court must then apply the relevant limiting doctrines in the context of the particular medium involved, through the eyes of the ordinary consumer of that product.

(3) Having dissected the alleged similarities and considered the range of possible expression, the court must define the scope of the plaintiff's copyright—that is, decide whether the work is entitled to "broad" or "thin" protection. Depending on the degree of protection, the court must set the appropriate standard for a subjective comparison of the works to determine whether, as a whole, they are sufficiently similar to support a finding of illicit copying.

* * *

* * * [T]he district court's analytic dissection was appropriately conducted under the extrinsic portion of our test for whether sufficient copying to constitute infringement has taken place. We are not persuaded to the contrary by Apple's arguments that the district court shouldn't have dissected at all, or dissected too much; that it "filtered out" unprotectable and licensed elements instead of viewing the Macintosh interface as a whole; and that it should have recognized protectability of arrangements and the "total concept and feel" of the works under a substantial similarity standard.

First, graphical user interface audiovisual works are subject to the same process of analytical dissection as are other works. We have dissected videogames, which are audiovisual works and therefore closely analogous, see, e.g., Data East [USA, Inc. v. Epyx, Inc., 862 F.2d 204 (9th Cir.1988),] at 208–09 (performing analytic dissection of similarities to determine whether similarities resulted from unprotectable expression); Frybarger [v. International Business Machines Corp., 812 F.2d 525 (9th Cir.1987),] at 529–30 (district court correctly concluded that similar features in videogames were unprotectable ideas and that no reasonable jury could find expressive elements substantially similar), and we have dissected nonliteral elements of computer programs, which are some- what analogous, see, e.g., Brown Bag [Software v. Symantec Corp., 960 F.2d 1465 (9th Cir.1992),] at 1475–77 (rejecting argument similar to Apple's about propriety of analytic dissection of computer program components such as screens, menus and keystrokes); Johnson Controls, Inc. v. Phoenix Control Sys., Inc., 886 F.2d 1173, 1176 (9th Cir.1989) (noting special master's detailed analysis of similarities). Other courts perform the same analysis, although articulated differently. See, e.g., Computer Assocs. Int'l, Inc. v. Altai, Inc., 982 F.2d 693, 706–11 (2d Cir.1992) (adopting "abstraction-filtration-comparison" test for analyz- ing nonliteral structure of computer program, relying in part on our own approach); Gates Rubber Co. v. Bando Chem. Indus., 9 F.3d 823, 834, 841 (10th Cir.1993) (adopting Altai test, but suggesting that comparison of works as a whole may be appropriate as preliminary step before filtering out unprotected elements); Engineering Dynamics, Inc. v. Struc- tural Software, Inc., 26 F.3d 1335, 1342–43 (5th Cir.1994) (adopting Gates Rubber/Altai test to analyze scope of copyright protection for user interface, input formats and output reports); Lotus Dev. Corp. v. Borland Int'l, Inc., 788 F.Supp. 78, 90, 93 (D.Mass.1992) (describing similar three-part test); cf. Whelan Assocs. v. Jaslow Dental Lab., Inc., 797 F.2d 1222, 1236 (3d Cir.1986) (defining idea of utilitarian work as its purpose or function, and everything not necessary to that purpose as expression), cert. denied, 479 U.S. 1031, 93 L.Ed.2d 831, 107 S.Ct. 877 (1987).

* * *

As we made clear in Aliotti [v. R. Dakin & Co., 831 F.2d 898, 901 (9th Cir.1987),] the party claiming infringement may place "*no* reliance upon any similarity in expression resulting from" unprotectable ele- ments. Id. (emphasis added) (similarities between competing stuffed dinosaur toys on account of posture and body design, and being cuddly, stem from the physiognomy of dinosaurs or from the nature of stuffed animals and are thus unprotectable). Otherwise, there would be no point to the extrinsic test, or to distinguishing ideas from expression. In this case, it would also effectively rescind the 1985 Agreement. This does not mean that at the end of the day, when the works are considered under the intrinsic test, they should not be compared as a whole. See McCul- loch v. Albert E. Price, Inc., 823 F.2d 316, 321 (9th Cir.1987) (contrast- ing artistic work at issue, where decorative plates were substantially similar in more than the one unprotectable element (text), with factual works which have many unprotectable elements and very little protectable expression). Nor does it mean that infringement cannot be based on original selection and arrangement of unprotected elements. However, the unprotectable elements have to be identified, or filtered, before the works can be considered as a whole. * * *

C

The district court's conclusion that the works as a whole are entitled only to limited protection and should be compared for virtual identity follows from its analytic dissection. By virtue of the licensing agreement, Microsoft and HP were entitled to use the vast majority of features that Apple claims were copied. Of those that remain, the district court found no unauthorized, protectable similarities of expression in Windows 2.03 and 3.0, and only a handful in NewWave. Thus, any claim of infringement that Apple may have against Microsoft must rest on the copying of Apple's unique selection and arrangement of all of these features. Under Harper House and Frybarger, there can be no infringement unless the works are virtually identical.

Apple, however, contends that its audiovisual work with animation and icon design cannot be analogized to factual works such as game strategy books, see Landsberg v. Scrabble Crossword Game Players, Inc., 736 F.2d 485, 488 (9th Cir.) ("Similarity of expression may have to amount to verbatim reproduction or very close paraphrasing before a factual work will be deemed infringed."), cert. denied, 469 U.S. 1037, 83 L.Ed.2d 403, 105 S.Ct. 513 (1984), accounting systems, see [Baker v.] Selden, 101 U.S. at 104 (copyright in book describing new accounting system not infringed when defendant copied ledger sheets used in system), or organizers, see Harper House[, Inc. v. Thomas Nelson, Inc., 889 F.2d 197 (9th Cir.1989),] at 205 (as compilations consisting largely of uncopyrightable elements, plaintiff's organizers entitled only to protection against "bodily appropriation of expression"), which are afforded only "thin" protection because the range of possible expression is narrow. See Feist [Publications v. Rural Telephone Service,] 499 U.S. at 349. Rather, it submits that the broader protection accorded artistic works is more appropriate. See, e.g., McCulloch, 823 F.2d at 321 (artistic work like a decorative plate receives broader protection because of endless variations of expression available to artist).

Which end of the continuum a particular work falls on is a call that must be made case by case. We are satisfied that this case is closer to Frybarger than to McCulloch. See also Atari Games Corp. v. Oman, 298 U.S. App. D.C. 303, 979 F.2d 242, 245 (D.C.Cir.1992) (analogizing audiovisual work like a videogame to compilation of facts). Accordingly, since Apple did not contest summary judgment under the virtual identity standard on the merits, judgment was properly entered.

* * *

We therefore hold that the district court properly identified the sources of similarity in Windows and NewWave, determined which were licensed, distinguished ideas from expression, and decided the scope of Apple's copyright by dissecting the unauthorized expression and filtering out unprotectable elements. Having correctly found that almost all the similarities spring either from the license or from basic ideas and their obvious expression, it correctly concluded that illicit copying could occur only if the works as a whole are virtually identical.

* * *

Notes

1. "Striking similarity" refers to a degree of similarity so great "as to preclude coincidence." *Heim v. Universal Pictures Co.*, 154 F.2d 480, 488 (2d Cir.1946). Striking similarity might be found, for example, where two works have the same errors or the same highly idiosyncratic or whimsical elements. Where such similarities are found, could a finding of infringement be proper even if the evidence showed that access was highly improbable?

2. In some cases, a defendant is found to have copied the plaintiff's work unconsciously; in other cases, the defendant has copied a work in the erroneous belief that it is in the public domain. Is the defendant's state of mind relevant to the question of infringement liability? Should it be?

3. In *Litchfield v. Spielberg*, 736 F.2d 1352, 1357 (9th Cir.1984), *cert. denied*, 470 U.S. 1052, 105 S.Ct. 1753, 84 L.Ed.2d 817 (1985), the Ninth Circuit held that the substantial similarity test applies to infringement claims involving the right to create derivative works under section 106(2), and not just those claims involving the right to reproduce under section 106(1), noting that "[a] work will be considered a derivative work *only if it would be considered an infringing work if* the material which it has derived from a prior work had been taken without the consent of a copyright proprietor of such prior work." *Id.* (quoting *United States v. Taxe*, 540 F.2d 961, 965 n. 2 (9th Cir.1976) (emphasis added)). Accord *Reyher v. Children's Television Workshop*, 533 F.2d 87 (2d Cir.1976) (no substantial similarity found where where defendant's work copied only uncopyrightable ideas from plaintiff's work).

4. In *Tufenkian Import/Export Ventures, Inc. v. Einstein Moomjy, Inc.*, 338 F.3d 127 (2d Cir. 2003), the court found infringement in the defendant's oriental rugs. The plaintiff's rug design was taken from two patterns in the public domain. However, the court found that the plaintiff had significantly altered the public domain designs (addition of certain details, removal of details, and changing one design from symmetrical to asymmetrical) and the defendant had copied each and every one of these changes. In this decision, the court reversed the District Court's finding that the defendant had made additions which changed the "overall concept and feel" of the design. Circuit Judge Calabresi stated that even though the "overall concept and feel" of the defendant's design was different, there was still infringement from the use of a substantial portion of the plaintiff's protectable design.

5. Should expert testimony be considered under the extrinsic test? Under the intrinsic test?

6. In *Sandoval v. New Line Cinema Corp.*, 147 F.3d 215 (2d Cir.1998), the Second Circuit found no substantial similarity between the plaintiff's photographs and scenes from the defendant's motion picture, in which those photographs were used as set decoration, because the copying was "de minimis." The photos that appeared in the film were never in focus, were seen at a distance, and were often obstructed by actors or props in the foreground. The Second Circuit held that it was error for the district court to undertake a fair use analysis without first determining whether the defendant's use of the plaintiff's copyrighted work was so minimal as to be "de minimis as a matter of law" and therefore not actionable. *Id.* at 217. The court thus approved its previous dicta in *Ringgold v. Black Entertainment Television, Inc.*, 126 F.3d 70 (2d Cir.1997), that where "the allegedly infringing work makes such a quantitatively insubstantial use of the copyrighted work as to fall below the threshold required for actionable copying, it makes more sense to reject the claim on that basis and find no infringement, rather than undertake an elaborate fair use analysis." 126 F.3d at 76 (finding nonetheless that the copying at issue was not de minimis), quoted at 147 F.3d at 217.

7. In *Scholastic, Inc. v. Stouffer*, 221 F.Supp.2d 425 (S.D.N.Y. 2002), defendant Stouffer, author of *Larry Potter and His Best Friend Lilly*, claimed the cover illustrations of the *Harry Potter* books, authored by J.K. Rowling, infringed the copyrights on an illustration in the Larry Potter story. The Larry Potter stories were published nine years before the first Harry Potter book. Ruling for the plaintiff, the court found that the similarities in the character illustrations (young boys with dark hair and glasses) involved generic elements which are not copyrightable. Protectable elements of the Larry Potter drawing (facial features, eyeglass shape and color, and hairstyle) were absent in plaintiff's illustrations. Since the allegedly copied elements were not protectable, the court did not analyze whether the illustrations were substantially similar. The court noted that there was no proof that Rowling or her illustrator had access to the defendant's work. Defendant was sanctioned $50,000 for falsifying evidence by altering copies of *Larry Potter and His Best Friend Lilly* and for altering drawings of "Muggles" characters in a trademark claim in the same suit.

8. The United States Court of Appeals for the Fourth Circuit has held that when a copyrighted work has a targeted audience, the substantial similarity inquiry must focus on the perspective of that particular audience. See *Lyons Partnership, L.P. v. Morris Costumes, Inc.*, 243 F.3d 789 (4th Cir.2001)(holding that the infringement analysis concerning Barney the purple dinosaur and similar costumes must consider the perspective of the intended audience of children rather than the adult purchaser).

Note: Music Sampling and Appropriation

Music sampling has become a source of some controversy when considered from the perspective of infringement theory. Sampling is the practice of copying a previously released portion of music, digitally altering it (through pitch, repetition or other variances), and then using it in a new sound recording; it is omnipresent in today's music, and is particularly common in hip-hop. In 2004, Judge Guy of the Sixth Circuit in *Bridgeport Music, Inc. v.*

Dimension Films, 383 F.3d 390 (6th Cir. 2004), addressed the issues raised in this context and attempted to "approximate a bright-line test." In this case, the sampled music was a two-second chord consisting of three notes which were digitally edited by the defendant. The court held that this was not *de minimis* and that there was infringement.

In *Newton v. Diamond*, 349 F.3d 591 (9th Cir. 2003), the Ninth Circuit held that the Beastie Boys' sampling of a three-note sequence from a composition was *de minimis* and therefore affirmed summary judgment of noninfringement. Because the amount sampled is very small and was a very common three-note sequence, it did not meet the substantial similarity requirement necessary for a finding of infringement.

In *Johnson v. Gordon*, 409 F.3d 12 (1st Cir. 2005), the plaintiff contended that he provided the copyrighted song, 'You're the One (For Me),' to a music distributor who in turn provided the song to a popular vocal group, and that the group (with others) reworked the song to create a hit song entitled 'You're the One.' The plaintiff argued that the similarity of the songs was evident in a melody supporting a lyrical phrase common to both songs, a two-bar harmonic progression, a certain three-bar melody, and the use of the phrase 'You're the One for Me' in the title and lyrics of each song. The court held, however, that the plaintiff failed to show that the songs were sufficiently similar to support an inference that defendants copied the plaintiff's song: the melodies supporting the common lyric in the songs were different, and the defendants' version was in fact a very common melodic pattern. The common harmonic pattern was stereotypical and lacked originality, and the similarity of a brief melodic segment was nothing more than coincidence. Meanwhile, the title lyric captured only a common sentiment in common verbiage and was too trite to warrant copyright protection.

C. THE PROPER PARTIES

Statutes: 17 U.S.C.A. § 501

1. PLAINTIFF: STANDING TO SUE

COPYRIGHT ACT OF 1976

H.R. Rep. No. 94–1476.
94th Cong., 2d Sess. 123, 158–59 (1976).

* * *

[Under section 201(d)(2)] any of the exclusive rights that go to make up a copyright, including those enumerated in section 106 and any subdivision of them, can be transferred and owned separately. The definition of "transfer of copyright ownership" in section 101 makes clear that the principle of divisibility applies whether or not the transfer is "limited in time or place of effect," and another definition in the same section provides that the term "copyright owner," with respect to any one exclusive right, refers to the owner of that particular right. The last sentence of section 201(d)(2) adds that the owner, with respect to the particular exclusive right he or she owns, is entitled "to all of the protection and remedies accorded to the copyright owner by this title." It is thus clear, for example, that a local broadcasting station holding an exclusive license to transmit a particular work within a particular geographic area and for a particular period of time, could sue, in its own name as copyright owner, someone who infringed that particular exclusive right. * * *

* * *

The principle of the divisibility of copyright ownership, established by section 201(d), carries with it the need in infringement actions to safeguard the rights of all copyright owners and to avoid a multiplicity of suits. Subsection (b) of section 501 enables the owner of a particular right to bring an infringement action in that owner's name alone, while at the same time insuring to the extent possible that the other owners whose rights may be affected are notified and given a chance to join the action.

The first sentence of subsection (b) empowers the "legal or beneficial owner of an exclusive right" to bring suit for "any infringement of that particular right committed while he or she is the owner of it." A "beneficial owner" for this purpose would include, for example, an author who had parted with legal title to the copyright in exchange for percentage royalties based on sales or license fees.

* * *

Notes

1. Different standing rules apply to infringement cases that do not involve rights under section 106. Under section 106A, the plaintiff is the artist whose right of attribution or integrity has been violated, even if the artist no longer owns any interest in the copyright. Under section 1101, the plaintiff is the live musical performer whose performance has been unlawfully exploited.

Who would be the plaintiff in a posthumous cause of action under section 106A(d)(2)? Could there be a posthumous cause of action under section 1101, and if so, who would be the plaintiff?

2. Under sections 111(c) and 501(c)–(e), the general rule for standing to bring an infringement claim is broadened in the case of secondary cable or satellite transmissions which fail to comply with the section 111 requirements for compulsory licensing. In some cases, the plaintiff can be a broadcaster that does not have an exclusive license, or even a nonexclusive license, to broadcast the work in question in the local broadcast area where the infringing secondary transmission occurred. The remedies available to plaintiffs whose standing is based on sections 501(c)–(e) are set forth in section 510.

3. In *Walker v. DC Comics, Inc.*, 67 Fed.Appx. 736 (3d Cir. 2003), a writer approached DC Comics with the idea of reversing the Superman story

by making Superman the Last Son of Earth and describing Superman's adventures as an orphan on the planet Krypton. DC Comics later used the idea for the "Elseworlds" series of comic books and entitled the book, "Superman: Last Son of Earth." In this case, the court ruled that Walker had no standing to sue because the written "springboard" of his idea was itself a violation of DC Comics' copyright in Superman and the right to create derivative works. Because Walker's "springboard" was unable to be copyrighted, there could be no violation by DC Comics of his copyright.

2. DEFENDANT: DIRECT, CONTRIBUTORY AND VICARIOUS LIABILITY FOR INFRINGEMENT

SONY CORP. OF AMERICA v. UNIVERSAL CITY STUDIOS, INC.

Supreme Court of the United States, 1984.
464 U.S. 417, 104 S.Ct. 774, 78 L.Ed.2d 574.

[Plaintiffs/respondents, the owners of copyrights in various recorded programs shown on television, brought suit against Sony, the maker of Betamax videotape recorders (VTRs), alleging that Sony was liable for contributory copyright infringement because it sold VTRs to television viewers who used the VTRs to make infringing recordings of those works.]

* * *

The two respondents in this case do not seek relief against the Betamax users who have allegedly infringed their copyrights. Moreover, this is not a class action on behalf of all copyright owners who license their works for television broadcast, and respondents have no right to invoke whatever rights other copyright holders may have to bring infringement actions based on Betamax copying of their works. As was made clear by their own evidence, the copying of the respondents' programs represents a small portion of the total use of VTR's. It is, however, the taping of respondents' own copyrighted programs that provides them with standing to charge Sony with contributory infringement. To prevail, they have the burden of proving that users of the Betamax have infringed their copyrights and that Sony should be held responsible for that infringement.

III

The Copyright Act does not expressly render anyone liable for infringement committed by another. In contrast, the Patent Act expressly brands anyone who "actively induces infringement of a patent" as an infringer, 35 U.S.C. § 271(b), and further imposes liability on certain individuals labeled "contributory" infringers, § 271(c). The absence of such express language in the copyright statute does not preclude the imposition of liability for copyright infringements on certain parties who have not themselves engaged in the infringing activity. For vicarious liability is imposed in virtually all areas of the law, and the concept of contributory infringement is merely a species of the broader problem of identifying the circumstances in which it is just to hold one individual accountable for the actions of another.

* * *

* * * The only contact between Sony and the users of the Betamax that is disclosed by this record occurred at the moment of sale. The District Court expressly found that "no employee of Sony * * * had either direct involvement with the allegedly infringing activity or direct contact with purchasers of Betamax who recorded copyrighted works off-the-air." 480 F.Supp., at 460. And it further found that "there was no evidence that any of the copies made by Griffiths or the other individual witnesses in this suit were influenced or encouraged by [Sony's] advertisements." Ibid.

* * *

If vicarious liability is to be imposed on Sony in this case, it must rest on the fact that it has sold equipment with constructive knowledge of the fact that its customers may use that equipment to make unauthorized copies of copyrighted material. There is no precedent in the law of copyright for the imposition of vicarious liability on such a theory. The closest analogy is provided by the patent law cases to which it is appropriate to refer because of the historic kinship between patent law and copyright law.[19]

In the Patent Act both the concept of infringement and the concept of contributory infringement are expressly defined by statute [in 35 U.S.C. § 271]. The prohibition against contributory infringement is confined to the knowing sale of a component especially made for use in connection with a particular patent. There is no suggestion in the statute that one patentee may object to the sale of a product that might be used in connection with other patents. Moreover, the Act expressly provides that the sale of a "staple article or commodity of commerce suitable for substantial noninfringing use" is not contributory infringement. 35 U.S.C. § 271(c).

When a charge of contributory infringement is predicated entirely on the sale of an article of commerce that is used by the purchaser to infringe a patent, the public interest in access to that article of commerce is necessarily implicated. A finding of contributory infringement does not, of course, remove the article from the market altogether; it does, however, give the patentee effective control over the sale of that item. Indeed, a finding of contributory infringement is normally the

---

19. E.g., United States v. Paramount Pictures, Inc., 334 U.S., at 158; Fox Film Corp. v. Doyal, 286 U.S., at 131; Wheaton v. Peters, 8 Pet. 591, 657–658 (1834). The two areas of the law, naturally, are not identical twins, and we exercise the caution which we have expressed in the past in applying doctrine formulated in one area to the other. See generally Mazer v. Stein, 347 U.S. 201, 217–218 (1954); Bobbs–Merrill Co. v. Straus, 210 U.S., at 345.

* * *

functional equivalent of holding that the disputed article is within the monopoly granted to the patentee.[21]

For that reason, in contributory infringement cases arising under the patent laws the Court has always recognized the critical importance of not allowing the patentee to extend his monopoly beyond the limits of his specific grant. These cases deny the patentee any right to control the distribution of unpatented articles unless they are "unsuited for any commercial noninfringing use." Dawson Chemical Co. v. Rohm & Haas Co., 448 U.S. 176, 198 (1980). Unless a commodity "has no use except through practice of the patented method," id., at 199, the patentee has no right to claim that its distribution constitutes contributory infringement. "To form the basis for contributory infringement the item must almost be uniquely suited as a component of the patented invention." P. Rosenberg, Patent Law Fundamentals § 17.02[2] (2d ed. 1982). "[A] sale of an article which though adapted to an infringing use is also adapted to other and lawful uses, is not enough to make the seller a contributory infringer. Such a rule would block the wheels of commerce." Henry v. A. B. Dick Co., 224 U.S. 1, 48 (1912), overruled on other grounds, Motion Picture Patents Co. v. Universal Film Mfg. Co., 243 U.S. 502, 517 (1917).

We recognize there are substantial differences between the patent and copyright laws. But in both areas the contributory infringement doctrine is grounded on the recognition that adequate protection of a monopoly may require the courts to look beyond actual duplication of a device or publication to the products or activities that make such duplication possible. The staple article of commerce doctrine must strike a balance between a copyright holder's legitimate demand for effective— not merely symbolic—protection of the statutory monopoly, and the rights of others freely to engage in substantially unrelated areas of commerce. Accordingly, the sale of copying equipment, like the sale of other articles of commerce, does not constitute contributory infringement if the product is widely used for legitimate, unobjectionable purposes. Indeed, it need merely be capable of substantial noninfringing uses.

IV

The question is thus whether the Betamax is capable of commercially significant noninfringing uses. In order to resolve that question, we need not explore all the different potential uses of the machine and determine whether or not they would constitute infringement. Rather, we need only consider whether on the basis of the facts as found by the

---

21. It seems extraordinary to suggest that the Copyright Act confers upon all copyright owners collectively, much less the two respondents in this case, the exclusive right to distribute VTR's simply because they may be used to infringe copyrights. That, however, is the logical implication of their claim. The request for an injunction below indicates that respondents seek, in effect, to declare VTR's contraband. Their suggestion in this Court that a continuing royalty pursuant to a judicially created compulsory license would be an acceptable remedy merely indicates that respondents, for their part, would be willing to license their claimed monopoly interest in VTR's to Sony in return for a royalty.

District Court a significant number of them would be noninfringing. Moreover, in order to resolve this case we need not give precise content to the question of how much use is commercially significant. For one potential use of the Betamax plainly satisfies this standard, however it is understood: private, noncommercial time-shifting in the home. It does so both (A) because respondents have no right to prevent other copyright holders from authorizing it for their programs, and (B) because the District Court's factual findings reveal that even the unauthorized home time-shifting of respondents' programs is legitimate fair use.

A.   *Authorized Time–Shifting*

Each of the respondents owns a large inventory of valuable copyrights, but in the total spectrum of television programming their combined market share is small. The exact percentage is not specified, but it is well below 10%. If they were to prevail, the outcome of this litigation would have a significant impact on both the producers and the viewers of the remaining 90% of the programming in the Nation. No doubt, many other producers share respondents' concern about the possible consequences of unrestricted copying. Nevertheless the findings of the District Court make it clear that time-shifting may enlarge the total viewing audience and that many producers are willing to allow private time-shifting to continue, at least for an experimental time period.

The District Court found:

"Even if it were deemed that home-use recording of copyrighted material constituted infringement, the Betamax could still legally be used to record noncopyrighted material or material whose owners consented to the copying. An injunction would deprive the public of the ability to use the Betamax for this noninfringing off-the-air recording.

"Defendants introduced considerable testimony at trial about the potential for such copying of sports, religious, educational and other programming. This included testimony from representatives of the Offices of the Commissioners of the National Football, Basketball, Baseball and Hockey Leagues and Associations, the Executive Director of National Religious Broadcasters and various educational communications agencies. Plaintiffs attack the weight of the testimony offered and also contend that an injunction is warranted because infringing uses outweigh noninfringing uses.

"Whatever the future percentage of legal versus illegal home-use recording might be, an injunction which seeks to deprive the public of the very tool or article of commerce capable of some noninfringing use would be an extremely harsh remedy, as well as one unprecedented in copyright law." 480 F.Supp., at 468.

Although the District Court made these statements in the context of considering the propriety of injunctive relief, the statements constitute a finding that the evidence concerning "sports, religious, educational and other programming" was sufficient to establish a significant quantity of broadcasting whose copying is now authorized, and a significant potential for future authorized copying. That finding is amply supported by the record. In addition to the religious and sports officials identified explicitly by the District Court, two items in the record deserve specific mention.

First is the testimony of John Kenaston, the station manager of Channel 58, an educational station in Los Angeles affiliated with the Public Broadcasting Service. He explained and authenticated the station's published guide to its programs. For each program, the guide tells whether unlimited home taping is authorized, home taping is authorized subject to certain restrictions (such as erasure within seven days), or home taping is not authorized at all. The Spring 1978 edition of the guide described 107 programs. Sixty-two of those programs or 58% authorize some home taping. Twenty-one of them or almost 20% authorize unrestricted home taping.

Second is the testimony of Fred Rogers, president of the corporation that produces and owns the copyright on Mister Rogers' Neighborhood. The program is carried by more public television stations than any other program. Its audience numbers over 3,000,000 families a day. He testified that he had absolutely no objection to home taping for noncommercial use and expressed the opinion that it is a real service to families to be able to record children's programs and to show them at appropriate times.

If there are millions of owners of VTR's who make copies of televised sports events, religious broadcasts, and educational programs such as Mister Rogers' Neighborhood, and if the proprietors of those programs welcome the practice, the business of supplying the equipment that makes such copying feasible should not be stifled simply because the equipment is used by some individuals to make unauthorized reproductions of respondents' works. The respondents do not represent a class composed of all copyright holders. Yet a finding of contributory infringement would inevitably frustrate the interests of broadcasters in reaching the portion of their audience that is available only through time-shifting.

Of course, the fact that other copyright holders may welcome the practice of time-shifting does not mean that respondents should be deemed to have granted a license to copy their programs. Third-party conduct would be wholly irrelevant in an action for direct infringement of respondents' copyrights. But in an action for contributory infringement against the seller of copying equipment, the copyright holder may not prevail unless the relief that he seeks affects only his programs, or unless he speaks for virtually all copyright holders with an interest in the outcome. In this case, the record makes it perfectly clear that there are many important producers of national and local television programs who find nothing objectionable about the enlargement in the size of the television audience that results from the practice of time-shifting for private home use.[28] The seller of the equipment that expands those

---

28. It may be rare for large numbers of copyright owners to authorize duplication of their works without demanding a fee from the copier. In the context of public

producers' audiences cannot be a contributory infringer if, as is true in this case, it has had no direct involvement with any infringing activity.

B.   Unauthorized Time–Shifting

Even unauthorized uses of a copyrighted work are not necessarily infringing. An unlicensed use of the copyright is not an infringement unless it conflicts with one of the specific exclusive rights conferred by the copyright statute. * * * Moreover, the definition of exclusive rights in § 106 of the present Act is prefaced by the words "subject to sections 107 through 118." Those sections describe a variety of uses of copyrighted material that "are not infringements of copyright" "notwithstanding the provisions of section 106." The most pertinent in this case is § 107, the legislative endorsement of the doctrine of "fair use."

[The Court undertook a fair use analysis under section 107 and concluded that "private noncommercial time-shifting in the home" was a non-infringing use. For the Court's discussion of this aspect of the case, see Chapter 19, *supra*.]

* * *

In summary, the record and findings of the District Court lead us to two conclusions. First, Sony demonstrated a significant likelihood that substantial numbers of copyright holders who license their works for broadcast on free television would not object to having their broadcasts time-shifted by private viewers. And second, respondents failed to demonstrate that time-shifting would cause any likelihood of nonminimal harm to the potential market for, or the value of, their copyrighted works. The Betamax is, therefore, capable of substantial noninfringing uses. Sony's sale of such equipment to the general public does not constitute contributory infringement of respondents' copyrights.

* * *

broadcasting, however, the user of the copyrighted work is not required to pay a fee for access to the underlying work. The traditional method by which copyright owners capitalize upon the television medium—commercially sponsored free public broadcast over the public airwaves—is predicated upon the assumption that compensation for the value of displaying the works will be received in the form of advertising revenues.

In the context of television programming, some producers evidently believe that permitting home viewers to make copies of their works off the air actually enhances the value of their copyrights. Irrespective of their reasons for authorizing the practice, they do so, and in significant enough numbers to create a substantial market for a noninfringing use of the Sony VTR's. No one could dispute the legitimacy of that market if the producers had authorized home taping of their programs in exchange for a license fee paid directly by the home user. The legitimacy of that market is not compromised simply because these producers have authorized home taping of their programs without demanding a fee from the home user. The copyright law does not require a copyright owner to charge a fee for the use of his works, and as this record clearly demonstrates, the owner of a copyright may well have economic or noneconomic reasons for permitting certain kinds of copying to occur without receiving direct compensation from the copier. It is not the role of the courts to tell copyright holders the best way for them to exploit their copyrights: even if respondents' competitors were ill-advised in authorizing home videotaping, that would not change the fact that they have created a substantial market for a paradigmatic noninfringing use of Sony's product.

FONOVISA, INC. v. CHERRY AUCTION, INC.

United States Court of Appeals, Ninth Circuit, 1996.
76 F.3d 259.

SCHROEDER, CIRCUIT JUDGE:

This is a copyright and trademark enforcement action against the operators of a swap meet, sometimes called a flea market, where third-party vendors routinely sell counterfeit recordings that infringe on the plaintiff's copyrights and trademarks. The district court dismissed on the pleadings, holding that the plaintiffs, as a matter of law, could not maintain any cause of action against the swap meet for sales by vendors who leased its premises. * * * We reverse.

BACKGROUND

The plaintiff and appellant is Fonovisa, Inc., a California corporation that owns copyrights and trademarks to Latin/Hispanic music recordings. Fonovisa filed this action in district court against defendant-appellee, Cherry Auction, Inc., and its individual operators (collectively "Cherry Auction"). For purposes of this appeal, it is undisputed that Cherry Auction operates a swap meet in Fresno, California, similar to many other swap meets in this country where customers come to purchase various merchandise from individual vendors. * * * The vendors pay a daily rental fee to the swap meet operators in exchange for booth space. Cherry Auction supplies parking, conducts advertising and retains the right to exclude any vendor for any reason, at any time, and thus can exclude vendors for patent and trademark infringement. In addition, Cherry Auction receives an entrance fee from each customer who attends the swap meet.

There is also no dispute for purposes of this appeal that Cherry Auction and its operators were aware that vendors in their swap meet were selling counterfeit recordings in violation of Fonovisa's trademarks and copyrights. Indeed, it is alleged that in 1991, the Fresno County Sheriff's Department raided the Cherry Auction swap meet and seized more than 38,000 counterfeit recordings. The following year, after finding that vendors at the Cherry Auction swap meet were still selling counterfeit recordings, the Sheriff sent a letter notifying Cherry Auction of the on-going sales of infringing materials, and reminding Cherry Auction that they had agreed to provide the Sheriff with identifying information from each vendor. In addition, in 1993, Fonovisa itself sent an investigator to the Cherry Auction site and observed sales of counterfeit recordings.

* * *

The copyright claims are brought pursuant to 17 U.S.C. §§ 101 et seq. Although the Copyright Act does not expressly impose liability on anyone other than direct infringers, courts have long recognized that in certain circumstances, vicarious or contributory liability will be imposed.

See Sony Corp. of America v. Universal City Studios, Inc., 464 U.S. 417, 435, 78 L.Ed.2d 574, 104 S. Ct. 774 (1984) (explaining that "vicarious liability is imposed in virtually all areas of the law, and the concept of contributory infringement is merely a species of the broader problem of identifying circumstances in which it is just to hold one individually accountable for the actions of another").

Similar principles have also been applied in the trademark field. See Inwood Laboratories v. Ives Laboratories, 456 U.S. 844, 102 S.Ct. 2182, 2184, 72 L. Ed. 2d 606 (1982). The Seventh Circuit, for example, has upheld the imposition of liability for contributory trademark infringement against the owners of a flea market similar to the swap meet operated by Cherry Auction. Hard Rock Cafe Licensing Corp. v. Concession Services, Inc., 955 F.2d 1143 (7th Cir.1992). The district court in this case, however, expressly rejected the Seventh Circuit's reasoning on the contributory trademark infringement claim. Contributory and vicarious copyright infringement, however, were not addressed in Hard Rock Cafe, making this the first case to reach a federal appeals court raising issues of contributory and vicarious copyright infringement in the context of swap meet or flea market operations.

We analyze each of the plaintiff's claims in turn.

Vicarious Copyright Infringement

The concept of vicarious copyright liability was developed in the Second Circuit as an outgrowth of the agency principles of respondeat superior. The landmark case on vicarious liability for sales of counterfeit recordings is Shapiro Bernstein and Co. v. H. L. Green Co., 316 F.2d 304 (2d Cir.1963). In Shapiro, the court was faced with a copyright infringement suit against the owner of a chain of department stores where a concessionaire was selling counterfeit recordings. Noting that the normal agency rule of respondeat superior imposes liability on an employer for copyright infringements by an employee, the court endeavored to fashion a principle for enforcing copyrights against a defendant whose economic interests were intertwined with the direct infringer's, but who did not actually employ the direct infringer.

The Shapiro court looked at the two lines of cases it perceived as most clearly relevant. In one line of cases, the landlord-tenant cases, the courts had held that a landlord who lacked knowledge of the infringing acts of its tenant and who exercised no control over the leased premises was not liable for infringing sales by its tenant. See e.g. Deutsch v. Arnold, 98 F.2d 686 (2d Cir.1938); c.f. Fromont v. Aeolian Co., 254 F. 592 (S.D.N.Y.1918). In the other line of cases, the so-called "dance hall cases," the operator of an entertainment venue was held liable for infringing performances when the operator (1) could control the premises and (2) obtained a direct financial benefit from the audience, who paid to enjoy the infringing performance. See e.g. Buck v. Jewell–LaSalle Realty Co., 283 U.S. 191, 198–199, 75 L. Ed. 971, 51 S.Ct. 410 (1931);

Dreamland Ball Room, Inc. v. Shapiro, Bernstein & Co., 36 F.2d 354 (7th Cir.1929).

From those two lines of cases, the Shapiro court determined that the relationship between the store owner and the concessionaire in the case before it was closer to the dance-hall model than to the landlord-tenant model. It imposed liability even though the defendant was unaware of the infringement. Shapiro deemed the imposition of vicarious liability neither unduly harsh nor unfair because the store proprietor had the power to cease the conduct of the concessionaire, and because the proprietor derived an obvious and direct financial benefit from the infringement. 316 F.2d at 307. The test was more clearly articulated in a later Second Circuit case as follows: "even in the absence of an employer-employee relationship one may be vicariously liable if he has the right and ability to supervise the infringing activity and also has a direct financial interest in such activities." Gershwin Publishing Corp. v. Columbia Artists Management, Inc., 443 F.2d 1159, 1162 (2d Cir.1971). See also 3 Melville Nimmer & David Nimmer, Nimmer on Copyright § 1204(A)[1],at 1270–72 (1995). The most recent and comprehensive discussion of the evolution of the doctrine of vicarious liability for copyright infringement is contained in Judge Keeton's opinion in Polygram Intern. Pub., Inc. v. Nevada/TIG, Inc., 855 F.Supp. 1314 (D.Mass. 1984).

The district court in this case agreed with defendant Cherry Auction that Fonovisa did not, as a matter of law, meet either the control or the financial benefit prong of the vicarious copyright infringement test articulated in Gershwin, supra. Rather, the district court concluded that based on the pleadings, "Cherry Auction neither supervised nor profited from the vendors' sales." 847 F.Supp. at 1496. In the district court's view, with respect to both control and financial benefit, Cherry Auction was in the same position as an absentee landlord who has surrendered its exclusive right of occupancy in its leased property to its tenants.

This analogy to absentee landlord is not in accord with the facts as alleged in the district court and which we, for purposes of appeal, must accept. The allegations below were that vendors occupied small booths within premises that Cherry Auction controlled and patrolled. According to the complaint, Cherry Auction had the right to terminate vendors for any reason whatsoever and through that right had the ability to control the activities of vendors on the premises. In addition, Cherry Auction promoted the swap meet and controlled the access of customers to the swap meet area. In terms of control, the allegations before us are strikingly similar to those in Shapiro and Gershwin.

In Shapiro, for example, the court focused on the formal licensing agreement between defendant department store and the direct infringer-concessionaire. There, the concessionaire selling the bootleg recordings had a licensing agreement with the department store (H. L. Green Company) that required the concessionaire and its employees to "abide by, observe and obey all regulations promulgated from time to time by the H. L. Green Company," and H. L. Green Company had the "unre-viewable discretion" to discharge the concessionaires' employees. 316 F.2d at 306. In practice, H. L. Green Company was not actively involved in the sale of records and the concessionaire controlled and supervised the individual employees. Id. Nevertheless, H. L. Green's ability to police its concessionaire—which parallels Cherry Auction's ability to police its vendors under Cherry Auction's similarly broad contract with its ven-dors—was sufficient to satisfy the control requirement. Id. at 308.

In Gershwin, the defendant lacked the formal, contractual ability to control the direct infringer. Nevertheless, because of defendant's "perva-sive participation in the formation and direction" of the direct infring-ers, including promoting them (i.e. creating an audience for them), the court found that defendants were in a position to police the direct infringers and held that the control element was satisfied. 443 F.2d at 1163. As the promoter and organizer of the swap meet, Cherry Auction wields the same level of control over the direct infringers as did the Gershwin defendant. See also Polygram, 855 F.Supp. at 1329 (finding that the control requirement was satisfied because the defendant (1) could control the direct infringers through its rules and regulations; (2) policed its booths to make sure the regulations were followed; and (3) promoted the show in which direct infringers participated).

The district court's dismissal of the vicarious liability claim in this case was therefore not justified on the ground that the complaint failed to allege sufficient control.

We next consider the issue of financial benefit. The plaintiff's allegations encompass many substantive benefits to Cherry Auction from the infringing sales. These include the payment of a daily rental fee by each of the infringing vendors; a direct payment to Cherry Auction by each customer in the form of an admission fee, and incidental payments for parking, food and other services by customers seeking to purchase infringing recordings.

Cherry Auction nevertheless contends that these benefits cannot satisfy the financial benefit prong of vicarious liability because a commis-sion, directly tied to the sale of particular infringing items, is required. They ask that we restrict the financial benefit prong to the precise facts presented in Shapiro, where defendant H. L. Green Company received a 10 or 12 per cent commission from the direct infringers' gross receipts. Cherry Auction points to the low daily rental fee paid by each vendor, discounting all other financial benefits flowing to the swap meet, and asks that we hold that the swap meet is materially similar to a mere landlord. The facts alleged by Fonovisa, however, reflect that the defen-dants reap substantial financial benefits from admission fees, concession stand sales and parking fees, all of which flow directly from customers who want to buy the counterfeit recordings at bargain basement prices. The plaintiff has sufficiently alleged direct financial benefit.

Our conclusion is fortified by the continuing line of cases, starting with the dance hall cases, imposing vicarious liability on the operator of a business where infringing performances enhance the attractiveness of the venue to potential customers. In Polygram, for example, direct infringers were participants in a trade show who used infringing music to communicate with attendees and to cultivate interest in their wares. 855 F.Supp. at 1332. The court held that the trade show participants "derived a significant financial benefit from the attention" that attendees paid to the infringing music. Id.; See also Famous Music Corp. v. Bay State Harness Horse Racing and Breeding Ass'n, 554 F.2d 1213, 1214 (1st Cir.1977) (race track owner vicariously liable for band that entertained patrons who were not "absorbed in watching the races"); Shapiro, 316 F.2d at 307 (dance hall cases hold proprietor liable where infringing "activities provide the proprietor with a source of customers and enhanced income"). In this case, the sale of pirated recordings at the Cherry Auction swap meet is a "draw" for customers, as was the performance of pirated music in the dance hall cases and their progeny.

Plaintiffs have stated a claim for vicarious copyright infringement.

CONTRIBUTORY COPYRIGHT INFRINGEMENT

Contributory infringement originates in tort law and stems from the notion that one who directly contributes to another's infringement should be held accountable. See Sony v. Universal City, 464 U.S. at 417; 1 Niel Boorstyn, Boorstyn On Copyright § 10.06[2], at 10–21 (1994) ("In other words, the common law doctrine that one who knowingly participates in or furthers a tortious act is jointly and severally liable with the prime tortfeasor, is applicable under copyright law"). Contributory infringement has been described as an outgrowth of enterprise liability, see 3 Nimmer § 1204[a][2], at 1275; Demetriades v. Kaufmann, 690 F.Supp. 289, 292 (S.D.N.Y.1988), and imposes liability where one person knowingly contributes to the infringing conduct of another. The classic statement of the doctrine is in Gershwin, 443 F.2d 1159, 1162: "One who, with knowledge of the infringing activity, induces, causes or materially contributes to the infringing conduct of another, may be held liable as a 'contributory' infringer." See also Universal City Studios v. Sony Corp. of America, 659 F.2d 963, 975 (9th Cir.1981), rev'd on other grounds, 464 U.S. 417, 78 L.Ed.2d 574, 104 S.Ct. 774 (1984) (adopting Gershwin in this circuit).

There is no question that plaintiff adequately alleged the element of knowledge in this case. The disputed issue is whether plaintiff adequately alleged that Cherry Auction materially contributed to the infringing activity. We have little difficulty in holding that the allegations in this case are sufficient to show material contribution to the infringing activity. Indeed, it would be difficult for the infringing activity to take place in the massive quantities alleged without the support services provided by the swap meet. These services include, inter alia, the provision of space, utilities, parking, advertising, plumbing, and customers.

Here again Cherry Auction asks us to ignore all aspects of the enterprise described by the plaintiffs, to concentrate solely on the rental of space, and to hold that the swap meet provides nothing more. Yet Cherry Auction actively strives to provide the environment and the market for counterfeit recording sales to thrive. Its participation in the sales cannot be termed "passive," as Cherry Auction would prefer.

The district court apparently took the view that contribution to infringement should be limited to circumstances in which the defendant "expressly promoted or encouraged the sale of counterfeit products, or in some manner protected the identity of the infringers." 847 F.Supp. 1492, 1496. Given the allegations that the local sheriff lawfully requested that Cherry Auction gather and share basic, identifying information about its vendors, and that Cherry Auction failed to comply, the defendant appears to qualify within the last portion of the district court's own standard that posits liability for protecting infringers' identities. Moreover, we agree with the Third Circuit's analysis in Columbia Pictures Industries, Inc. v. Aveco, Inc., 800 F.2d 59 (3d Cir.1986) that providing the site and facilities for known infringing activity is sufficient to establish contributory liability. See 2 William F. Patry, Copyright Law & Practice 1147 ("Merely providing the means for infringement may be sufficient" to incur contributory copyright liability).

* * *

The judgment of the district court is REVERSED and the case is REMANDED FOR FURTHER PROCEEDINGS.

IN RE: AIMSTER COPYRIGHT LITIGATION

United States Court of Appeals, Seventh Circuit, 2003.
334 F.3d 643, *cert. denied,* 540 U.S. 1107, 124 S.Ct. 1069, 157 L.Ed.2d 893 (2004).

POSNER, CIRCUIT JUDGE.

Owners of copyrighted popular music filed a number of closely related suits, which were consolidated and transferred to the Northern District of Illinois by the Multidistrict Litigation Panel, against John Deep and corporations that are controlled by him and need not be discussed separately. The numerous plaintiffs, who among them appear to own most subsisting copyrights on American popular music, claim that Deep's "Aimster" Internet service (recently renamed "Madster") is a contributory and vicarious infringer of these copyrights. The district judge entered a broad preliminary injunction, which had the effect of shutting down the Aimster service until the merits of the suit are finally resolved, from which Deep appeals. Aimster is one of a number of enterprises (the former Napster is the best known) that have been sued for facilitating the swapping of digital copies of popular music, most of it copyrighted, over the Internet. (For an illuminating discussion, see Tim Wu, "When Code Isn't Law," 89 Va. L. Rev. 679 (2003), esp. 723–41; and with special reference to Aimster, see Alec Klein, "Going Napster One Better; Aimster Says Its File–Sharing Software Skirts Legal Quagmire,"

Wash. Post, Feb. 25, 2001, p. A1.) To simplify exposition, we refer to the appellant as "Aimster" and to the appellees (the plaintiffs) as the recording industry.

Teenagers and young adults who have access to the Internet like to swap computer files containing popular music. If the music is copyrighted, such swapping, which involves making and transmitting a digital copy of the music, infringes copyright. The swappers, who are ignorant or more commonly disdainful of copyright and in any event discount the likelihood of being sued or prosecuted for copyright infringement, are the direct infringers. But firms that facilitate their infringement, even if they are not themselves infringers because they are not making copies of the music that is shared, may be liable to the copyright owners as contributory infringers. Recognizing the impracticability or futility of a copyright owner's suing a multitude of individual infringers ("chasing individual consumers is time consuming and is a teaspoon solution to an ocean problem," Randal C. Picker, "Copyright as Entry Policy: The Case of Digital Distribution," 47 *Antitrust Bull.* 423, 442 (2002)), the law allows a copyright holder to sue a contributor to the infringement instead, in effect as an aider and abettor. Another analogy is to the tort of intentional interference with contract, that is, inducing a breach of contract. *See, e.g., Sufrin v. Hosier*, 128 F.3d 594, 597 (7th Cir.1997). If a breach of contract (and a copyright license is just a type of contract) can be prevented most effectively by actions taken by a third party, it makes sense to have a legal mechanism for placing liability for the consequences of the breach on him as well as on the party that broke the contract.

The district judge ruled that the recording industry had demonstrated a likelihood of prevailing on the merits should the case proceed to trial. He so ruled with respect to vicarious as well as contributory infringement; we begin with the latter, the more familiar charge.

The Aimster system has the following essential components: proprietary software that can be downloaded free of charge from Aimster's Web site; Aimster's server (a server is a computer that provides services to other computers, in this case personal computers owned or accessed by Aimster's users, over a network), which hosts the Web site and collects and organizes information obtained from the users but does not make copies of the swapped files themselves and that also provides the matching service described below; computerized tutorials instructing users of the software on how to use it for swapping computer files; and "Club Aimster," a related Internet service owned by Deep that users of Aimster's software can join for a fee and use to download the "top 40" popular-music files more easily than by using the basic, free service. The "AIM" in "Aimster" stands for AOL instant-messaging service. Aimster is available only to users of such services (of which AOL's is the most popular) because Aimster users can swap files only when both are online and connected in a chat room enabled by an instant-messaging service.

Someone who wants to use Aimster's basic service for the first time to swap files downloads the software from Aimster's Web site and then registers on the system by entering a user name (it doesn't have to be his real name) and a password at the Web site. Having done so, he can designate any other registrant as a "buddy" and can communicate directly with all his buddies when he and they are online, attaching to his communications (which are really just e-mails) any files that he wants to share with the buddies. All communications back and forth are encrypted by the sender by means of encryption software furnished by Aimster as part of the software package downloadable at no charge from the Web site, and are decrypted by the recipient using the same Aimster-furnished software package. If the user does not designate a buddy or buddies, then all the users of the Aimster system become his buddies; that is, he can send or receive from any of them.

Users list on their computers the computer files they are willing to share. (They needn't list them separately, but can merely designate a folder in their computer that contains the files they are willing to share.) A user who wants to make a copy of a file goes online and types the name of the file he wants in his "Search For" field. Aimster's server searches the computers of those users of its software who are online and so are available to be searched for files they are willing to share, and if it finds the file that has been requested it instructs the computer in which it is housed to transmit the file to the recipient via the Internet for him to download into his computer. Once he has done this he can if he wants make the file available for sharing with other users of the Aimster system by listing it as explained above. In principle, therefore, the purchase of a single CD could be levered into the distribution within days or even hours of millions of identical, near-perfect (depending on the compression format used) copies of the music recorded on the CD—hence the recording industry's anxiety about file-sharing services oriented toward consumers of popular music. But because copies of the songs reside on the computers of the users and not on Aimster's own server, Aimster is not a direct infringer of the copyrights on those songs. Its function is similar to that of a stock exchange, which is a facility for matching offers rather than a repository of the things being exchanged (shares of stock). But unlike transactions on a stock exchange, the consummated "transaction" in music files does not take place in the facility, that is, in Aimster's server.

What we have described so far is a type of Internet file-sharing system that might be created for innocuous purposes such as the expeditious exchange of confidential business data among employees of a business firm. *See* Daniel Nasaw, "Instant Messages Are Popping Up All Over," *Wall St. J.*, June 12, 2003, p. B4; David A. Vise, "AOL Makes Instant–Messaging Deal," *Wash. Post*, June 12, 2003, p. E5. The fact that copyrighted materials might sometimes be shared between users of such a system without the authorization of the copyright owner or a fair-use privilege would not make the firm a contributory infringer. Otherwise AOL's instant-messaging system, which Aimster piggybacks on, might be deemed a contributory infringer. For there is no doubt that some of the attachments that AOL's multitudinous subscribers transfer are copyrighted, and such distribution is an infringement unless authorized by the owner of the copyright. The Supreme Court made clear in the *Sony* decision that the producer of a product that has substantial noninfringing uses is not a contributory infringer merely because some of the uses actually made of the product (in that case a machine, the predecessor of today's videocassette recorders, for recording television programs on tape) are infringing. *Sony Corp. of America, Inc. v. Universal City Studios, Inc.*, 464 U.S. 417, 104 S.Ct. 774, 78 L.Ed.2d 574 (1984); *see also Vault Corp. v. Quaid Software Ltd.*, 847 F.2d 255, 262–67 (5th Cir.1988). How much more the Court held is the principal issue that divides the parties; and let us try to resolve it, recognizing of course that the Court must have the last word.

* * *

[The Court discusses the facts of the *Sony* case, asserting three uses for Betamax technology that involve copying, and reviewing the holding of the case.]

In our case the recording industry, emphasizing the reference to "articles of commerce" ... in the Court's opinion ... , and emphasizing as well the Court's evident concern that the copyright holders were trying to lever their copyright monopolies into a monopoly over video recorders ... , and also remarking Sony's helplessness to prevent infringing uses of its recorders once it sold them, argues that *Sony* is inapplicable to services. With regard to services, the industry argues, the test is merely whether the provider knows it's being used to infringe copyright. The industry points out that the provider of a service, unlike the seller of a product, has a continuing relation with its customers and therefore should be able to prevent, or at least limit, their infringing copyright by monitoring their use of the service and terminating them when it is discovered that they are infringing. Although Sony could have engineered its video recorder in a way that would have reduced the likelihood of infringement, as by eliminating the fast-forward capability, or, as suggested by the dissent ... by enabling broadcasters by scrambling their signal to disable the Betamax from recording their programs (for that matter, it could have been engineered to have only a play, not a recording, capability), the majority did not discuss these possibilities and we agree with the recording industry that the ability of a service provider to prevent its customers from infringing is a factor to be considered in determining whether the provider is a contributory infringer. Congress so recognized in the Digital Millennium Copyright Act, which we discuss later in this opinion.

It is not necessarily a controlling factor, however, as the recording industry believes. If a service facilitates both infringing and noninfringing uses, as in the case of AOL's instant-messaging service, and the detection and prevention of the infringing uses would be highly burdensome, the rule for which the recording industry is contending could result in the shutting down of the service or its annexation by the copyright owners (contrary to the clear import of the *Sony* decision), because the provider might find it impossible to estimate its potential damages liability to the copyright holders and would anyway face the risk of being enjoined. The fact that the recording industry's argument if accepted might endanger AOL's instant-messaging service (though the service might find shelter under the Digital Millennium Copyright Act— a question complicated, however, by AOL's intention, of which more later, of offering an encryption option to the visitors to its chat rooms) is not only alarming; it is paradoxical, since subsidiaries of AOL's parent company (AOL Time Warner), such as Warner Brothers Records and Atlantic Recording Corporation, are among the plaintiffs in this case and music chat rooms are among the facilities offered by AOL's instant-messaging service.

We also reject the industry's argument that *Sony* provides no defense to a charge of contributory infringement when, in the words of the industry's brief, there is anything "more than a mere showing that a product may be used for infringing purposes." Although the fact was downplayed in the majority opinion, it was apparent that the Betamax was being used for infringing as well as noninfringing purposes—even the majority acknowledged that 25 percent of Betamax users were fast forwarding through commercials ... —yet Sony was held not to be a contributory infringer. The Court was unwilling to allow copyright holders to prevent infringement effectuated by means of a new technology at the price of possibly denying noninfringing consumers the benefit of the technology. We therefore agree with Professor Goldstein that the Ninth Circuit erred in *A & M Records, Inc. v. Napster, Inc.*, 239 F.3d 1004, 1020 (9th Cir.2001), in suggesting that actual knowledge of specific infringing uses is a sufficient condition for deeming a facilitator a contributory infringer. 2 Paul Goldstein, *Copyright* § 6.1.2, p. 6:12–1 (2d ed. 2003).

The recording industry's hostility to the *Sony* decision is both understandable, given the amount of Internet-enabled infringement of music copyrights, and manifest—the industry in its brief offers five reasons for confining its holding to its specific facts. But it is being articulated in the wrong forum.

Equally, however, we reject Aimster's argument that to prevail the recording industry must prove it has actually lost money as a result of the copying that its service facilitates. It is true that the Court in *Sony* emphasized that the plaintiffs had failed to show that they had sustained substantial harm from the Betamax. *Sony*, 464 U.S. at 494, 104 S.Ct. 774. But the Court did so in the context of assessing the argument that time shifting of television programs was fair use rather than infringement. One reason time shifting was fair use, the Court believed, was that it wasn't hurting the copyright owners because it was enlarging the audience for their programs. But a copyright owner who can prove infringement need not show that the infringement caused him a financial loss. Granted, without such a showing he cannot obtain compensatory damages; but he can obtain statutory damages, or an injunction, just as the owner of physical property can obtain an injunction against a trespasser without proving that the trespass has caused him a financial loss.

What is true is that when a supplier is offering a product or service that has noninfringing as well as infringing uses, some estimate of the respective magnitudes of these uses is necessary for a finding of contributory infringement. The Court's action in striking the cost-benefit trade-off in favor of Sony came to seem prescient when it later turned out that the principal use of video recorders was to allow people to watch at home movies that they bought or rented rather than to tape television programs.... An enormous new market thus opened for the movie industry—which by the way gives point to the Court's emphasis on potential as well as actual noninfringing uses. But the balancing of costs and benefits is necessary only in a case in which substantial noninfringing uses, present or prospective, are demonstrated.

We also reject Aimster's argument that because the Court said in *Sony* that mere "constructive knowledge" of infringing uses is not enough for contributory infringement ... , and the encryption feature of Aimster's service prevented Deep from knowing what songs were being copied by the users of his system, he lacked the knowledge of infringing uses that liability for contributory infringement requires. Willful blindness is knowledge, in copyright law (where indeed it may be enough that the defendant should have known of the direct infringement, *Casella v. Morris*, 820 F.2d 362, 365 (11th Cir.1987); 2 Goldstein, *supra*, § 6.1, p. 6:6), as it is in the law generally. *See, e.g., Louis Vuitton S.A. v. Lee*, 875 F.2d 584, 590 (7th Cir.1989) (contributory trademark infringement). One who, knowing or strongly suspecting that he is involved in shady dealings, takes steps to make sure that he does not acquire full or exact knowledge of the nature and extent of those dealings is held to have a criminal intent, *United States v. Giovannetti*, 919 F.2d 1223, 1228 (7th Cir.1990), because a deliberate effort to avoid guilty knowledge is all that the law requires to establish a guilty state of mind. *United States v. Josefik*, 753 F.2d 585, 589 (7th Cir.1985); *AMPAT/Midwest, Inc. v. Illinois Tool Works Inc.*, 896 F.2d 1035, 1042 (7th Cir.1990) ("to know, and to want not to know because one suspects, may be, if not the same state of mind, the same degree of fault)." In *United States v. Diaz*, 864 F.2d 544, 550 (7th Cir.1988), the defendant, a drug trafficker, sought "to insulate himself from the actual drug transaction so that he could deny knowledge of it," which he did sometimes by absenting himself from the scene of the actual delivery and sometimes by pretending to be fussing under the hood of his car. He did not escape liability by this maneuver; no more can Deep by using encryption software to prevent himself from learning what surely he strongly suspects to be the case: that the users of his service—maybe all the users of his service—are copyright infringers.

This is not to say that the provider of an encrypted instant-messaging service or encryption software is ipso factor a contributory infringer should his buyers use the service to infringe copyright, merely because encryption, like secrecy generally, facilitates unlawful transactions. ("Encryption" comes from the Greek word for concealment.) Encryption fosters privacy, and privacy is a social benefit though also a source of social costs. "AOL has begun testing an encrypted version of AIM [AOL Instant Messaging]. Encryption is considered critical for widespread adoption of IM in some industries and federal agencies." Vise, *supra*. Our point is only that a service provider that would otherwise be a contributory infringer does not obtain immunity by using encryption to shield itself from actual knowledge of the unlawful purposes for which the service is being used.

We also do not buy Aimster's argument that since the Supreme Court distinguished, in the long passage from the *Sony* opinion that we quoted earlier, between actual and potential noninfringing uses, all Aimster has to show in order to escape liability for contributory infringement is that its file-sharing system could be used in noninfringing ways, which obviously it could be. Were that the law, the seller of a product or service used solely to facilitate copyright infringement, though it was capable in principle of noninfringing uses, would be immune from liability for contributory infringement. That would be an extreme result, and one not envisaged by the Sony majority. Otherwise its opinion would have had no occasion to emphasize the fact (at least the majority thought it a fact—the dissent disagreed, ...) that Sony had not in its advertising encouraged the use of the Betamax to infringe copyright.... Nor would the Court have thought it important to say that the Betamax was used "principally" for time shifting, ... which as we recall the Court deemed a fair use, or to remark that the plaintiffs owned only a small percentage of the total amount of copyrighted television programming and it was unclear how many of the other owners objected to home taping....

There are analogies in the law of aiding and abetting, the criminal counterpart to contributory infringement. A retailer of slinky dresses is not guilty of aiding and abetting prostitution even if he knows that some of his customers are prostitutes—he may even know which ones are. *See United States v. Giovannetti, supra*, 919 F.2d at 1227; *People v. Lauria*, 251 Cal.App.2d 471, 59 Cal.Rptr. 628 (1967); Rollin M. Perkins & Ronald N. Boyce, *Criminal Law* 746–47 (3d ed.1982). The extent to which his activities and those of similar sellers actually promote prostitution is likely to be slight relative to the social costs of imposing a risk of prosecution on him. But the owner of a massage parlor who employs women who are capable of giving massages, but in fact as he knows sell only sex and never massages to their customers, is an aider and abettor of prostitution (as well as being guilty of pimping or operating a brothel). *See United States v. Sigalow*, 812 F.2d 783, 784, 785 (2d Cir.1987); *State v. Carpenter*, 122 Ohio App.3d 16, 701 N.E.2d 10, 13, 18–19 (1997); *cf. United States v. Luciano–Mosquera*, 63 F.3d 1142, 1149–50 (1st Cir. 1995). The slinky-dress case corresponds to *Sony*, and, like *Sony*, is not inconsistent with imposing liability on the seller of a product or service that, as in the massage-parlor case, is capable of noninfringing uses but in fact is used only to infringe. To the recording industry, a single known infringing use brands the facilitator as a contributory infringer. To the Aimsters of this world, a single noninfringing use provides complete immunity from liability. Neither is correct.

To situate Aimster's service between these unacceptable poles, we need to say just a bit more about it. In explaining how to use the Aimster software, the tutorial gives as its only examples of file sharing the sharing of copyrighted music, including copyrighted music that the recording industry had notified Aimster was being infringed by Aimster's users. The tutorial is the invitation to infringement that the Supreme Court found was missing in *Sony*. In addition, membership in Club Aimster enables the member for a fee of $4.95 a month to download with a single click the music most often shared by Aimster users, which turns out to be music copyrighted by the plaintiffs. Because Aimster's software is made available free of charge and Aimster does not sell paid advertising on its Web site, Club Aimster's monthly fee is the only means by which Aimster is financed and so the club cannot be separated from the provision of the free software. When a member of the club clicks on "play" next to the name of a song on the club's Web site, Aimster's server searches through the computers of the Aimster users who are online until it finds one who has listed the song as available for sharing, and it then effects the transmission of the file to the computer of the club member who selected it. Club Aimster lists only the 40 songs that are currently most popular among its members; invariably these are under copyright.

The evidence that we have summarized does not exclude the possibility of substantial noninfringing uses of the Aimster system, but the evidence is sufficient, especially in a preliminary-injunction proceeding, which is summary in character, to shift the burden of production to Aimster to demonstrate that its service has substantial noninfringing uses. (On burden-shifting in preliminary-injunction proceedings, *see FTC v. University Health, Inc.*, 938 F.2d 1206, 1218–19 (11th Cir.1991); *cf. Johnson v. Cambridge Industries, Inc.*, 325 F.3d 892, 897 (7th Cir.2003); *SEC v. Lipson*, 278 F.3d 656, 661 (7th Cir.2002); *Liu v. T & H Machine, Inc.*, 191 F.3d 790, 795 (7th Cir.1999).) As it might:

> 1. Not all popular music is copyrighted. Apart from music on which the copyright has expired (not much of which, however, is of interest to the teenagers and young adults interested in swapping music), start-up bands and performers may waive copyright in the hope that it will encourage the playing of their music and create a following that they can convert to customers of their subsequent works.

> 2. A music file-swapping service might increase the value of a recording by enabling it to be used as currency in the music-sharing community, since someone who only downloads and never uploads, thus acting as a pure free rider, will not be very popular.

> 3. Users of Aimster's software might form select (as distinct from all-comers) "buddy" groups to exchange noncopyrighted information

about popular music, or for that matter to exchange ideas and opinions about wholly unrelated matters as the buddies became friendlier. Some of the chat-room messages that accompany the listing of music files offered or requested contain information or opinions concerning the music; to that extent, though unremarked by the parties, some noninfringing use is made of Aimster's service, though it is incidental to the infringement.

4. Aimster's users might appreciate the encryption feature because as their friendship deepened they might decide that they wanted to exchange off-color, but not copyrighted, photographs, or dirty jokes, or other forms of expression that people like to keep private, rather than just copyrighted music.

5. Someone might own a popular-music CD that he was particularly fond of, but he had not downloaded it into his computer and now he finds himself out of town but with his laptop and he wants to listen to the CD, so he uses Aimster's service to download a copy. This might be a fair use rather than a copyright infringement, by analogy to the time shifting approved as fair use in the *Sony* case. *Recording Industry Ass'n of America v. Diamond Multimedia Systems, Inc.*, 180 F.3d 1072, 1079 (9th Cir.1999); *cf. Vault Corp. v. Quaid Software Ltd.*, *supra*, 847 F.2d at 266–67. The analogy was sidestepped in *A&M Records, Inc. v. Napster, Inc.*, *supra*, 239 F.3d at 1019, because Napster's system did not limit downloading to music on CDs owned by the downloader. The analogy was rejected in *UMG Recordings v. MP3.Com, Inc.*, 92 F.Supp.2d 349 (S.D.N.Y. 2000), on the ground that the copy on the defendant's server was an unauthorized derivative work; a solider ground, in light of *Sony'* s rejection of the parallel argument with respect to time shifting, would have been that the defendant's method for requiring that its customers "prove" that they owned the CDs containing the music they wanted to download was too lax.

All five of our examples of actually or arguably noninfringing uses of Aimster's service are possibilities, but as should be evident from our earlier discussion the question is how probable they are. It is not enough, as we have said, that a product or service be physically capable, as it were, of a noninfringing use. Aimster has failed to produce any evidence that its service has ever been used for a noninfringing use, let alone evidence concerning the frequency of such uses. In the words of the district judge, "defendants here have provided no evidence whatsoever (besides the unsupported declaration of Deep) that Aimster is *actually* used for any of the stated non-infringing purposes. Absent is any indication from real-life Aimster users that their primary use of the system is to transfer non-copyrighted files to their friends or identify users of similar interests and share information. Absent is any indication that even a single business without a network administrator uses Aimster to exchange business records as Deep suggests." *In re Aimster Copyright Litigation*, 252 F.Supp.2d 634, 653 (N.D.Ill.2002) (emphasis in original). We have to assume for purposes of deciding this appeal that no such evidence exists; its absence, in combination with the evidence presented by the recording industry, justified the district judge in concluding that the industry would be likely to prevail in a full trial on the issue of contributory infringement. Because Aimster failed to show that its service is ever used for any purpose other than to infringe the plaintiffs' copyrights, the question (as yet unsettled, *see* Wu, *supra*, at 708 and nn. 95 and 98) of the net effect of Napsterlike services on the music industry's income is irrelevant to this case. If the only effect of a service challenged as contributory infringement is to enable copyrights to be infringed, the magnitude of the resulting loss, even whether there is a net loss, becomes irrelevant to liability.

Even when there are noninfringing uses of an Internet file-sharing service, moreover, if the infringing uses are substantial then to avoid liability as a contributory infringer the provider of the service must show that it would have been disproportionately costly for him to eliminate or at least reduce substantially the infringing uses. Aimster failed to make that showing too, by failing to present evidence that the provision of an encryption capability effective against the service provider itself added important value to the service or saved significant cost. Aimster blinded itself in the hope that by doing so it might come within the rule of the *Sony* decision.

It complains about the district judge's refusal to hold an evidentiary hearing. But his refusal was consistent with our decision in *Ty, Inc. v. GMA Accessories, Inc., supra*, 132 F.3d at 1171 (citations omitted), where we explained that "if genuine issues of material fact are created by the response to a motion for a preliminary injunction, an evidentiary hearing is indeed required. But as in any case in which a party seeks an evidentiary hearing, he must be able to persuade the court that the issue is indeed genuine and material and so a hearing would be productive—he must show in other words that he has and intends to introduce evidence that if believed will so weaken the moving party's case as to affect the judge's decision on whether to issue an injunction." Aimster hampered its search for evidence by providing encryption. It must take responsibility for that self-inflicted wound.

Turning to the second issue presented by the appeal, we are less confident than the district judge was that the recording industry would also be likely to prevail on the issue of vicarious infringement should the case be tried, though we shall not have to resolve our doubts in order to decide the appeal. "Vicarious liability" generally refers to the liability of a principal, such as an employer, for the torts committed by his agent, an employee for example, in the course of the agent's employment. The teenagers and young adults who use Aimster's system to infringe copyright are of course not Aimster's agents. But one of the principal rationales of vicarious liability, namely the difficulty of obtaining effective relief against an agent, who is likely to be impecunious, Alan O. Sykes, "The Economics of Vicarious Liability," 93 *Yale L.J.* 1231, 1241–42, 1272 (1984), has been extended in the copyright area to cases in which the only effective relief is obtainable from someone who bears a relation to the direct infringers that is analogous to the relation of a principal to an agent. *See* 2 Goldstein, *supra*, § 6.2, pp. 6:17 to 6:18. The canonical illustration is the owner of a dance hall who hires dance bands that sometimes play copyrighted music without authorization. The bands are not the dance hall's agents, but it may be impossible as a practical matter for the copyright holders to identify and obtain a legal remedy against the infringing bands yet quite feasible for the dance hall to prevent or at least limit infringing performances. And so the dance hall that fails to make reasonable efforts to do this is liable as a vicarious infringer. *Dreamland Ball Room v. Shapiro, Bernstein & Co.*, 36 F.2d 354, 355 (7th Cir.1929), and other cases cited in *Sony Corp. of America, Inc. v. Universal City Studios, Inc.*, *supra*, 464 U.S. at 437 n. 18, 104 S.Ct. 774; 2 Goldstein, *supra*, § 6.2, pp. 6:18 to 6:20. The dance hall could perhaps be described as a contributory infringer. But one thinks of a contributory infringer as someone who benefits directly from the infringement that he encourages, and that does not seem an apt description of the dance hall, though it does benefit to the extent that competition will force the dance band to charge the dance hall a smaller fee for performing if the band doesn't pay copyright royalties and so has lower costs than it would otherwise have.

How far the doctrine of vicarious liability extends is uncertain. It could conceivably have been applied in the *Sony* case itself, on the theory that while it was infeasible for the producers of copyrighted television fare to sue the viewers who used the fast-forward button on Sony's video recorder to delete the commercials and thus reduce the copyright holders' income, Sony could have reduced the likelihood of infringement, as we noted earlier, by a design change. But the Court, treating vicarious and contributory infringement interchangeably, *see id.* [], held that Sony was not a vicarious infringer either. By eliminating the encryption feature and monitoring the use being made of its system, Aimster could like Sony have limited the amount of infringement. Whether failure to do so made it a vicarious infringer notwithstanding the outcome in *Sony* is academic, however; its ostrich-like refusal to discover the extent to which its system was being used to infringe copyright is merely another piece of evidence that it was a contributory infringer.

* * *

[The court discusses the Digital Millennium Copyright Act. This portion of the case is excerpted in Chapter 20, Section D.]

[The court then discusses harm, and determines that Aimster is less likely to be permanently harmed by a disruption of its services than are the copyright owners by infringements pending the outcome of the case. Finally, the court discusses the scope of the injunction and decides that it is not excessive and does not violate the First Amendment.]

* * *

METRO–GOLDWYN–MAYER STUDIOS, INC. v. GROKSTER, LTD.

Supreme Court of the United States, 2005.
545 U.S. 913, 125 S.Ct. 2764, 162 L.Ed.2d 781.

JUSTICE SOUTER delivered the opinion of the Court.

The question is under what circumstances the distributor of a product capable of both lawful and unlawful use is liable for acts of copyright infringement by third parties using the product. We hold that one who distributes a device with the object of promoting its use to infringe copyright, as shown by clear expression or other affirmative steps taken to foster infringement, is liable for the resulting acts of infringement by third parties.

I

A

Respondents, Grokster, Ltd., and StreamCast Networks, Inc., defendants in the trial court, distribute free software products that allow computer users to share electronic files through peer-to-peer networks, so called because users' computers communicate directly with each other, not through central servers. The advantage of peer-to-peer networks over information networks of other types shows up in their substantial and growing popularity. Because they need no central computer server to mediate the exchange of information or files among users, the high-bandwidth communications capacity for a server may be dispensed with, and the need for costly server storage space is eliminated. Since copies of a file (particularly a popular one) are available on many users' computers, file requests and retrievals may be faster than on other types of networks, and since file exchanges do not travel through a server, communications can take place between any computers that remain connected to the network without risk that a glitch in the server will disable the network in its entirety. Given these benefits in security, cost, and efficiency, peer-to-peer networks are employed to store and distribute electronic files by universities, government agencies, corporations, and libraries, among others.

Other users of peer-to-peer networks include individual recipients of Grokster's and StreamCast's software, and although the networks that they enjoy through using the software can be used to share any type of digital file, they have prominently employed those networks in sharing copyrighted music and video files without authorization. A group of copyright holders (MGM for short, but including motion picture studios, recording companies, songwriters, and music publishers) sued Grokster and StreamCast for their users' copyright infringements, alleging that they knowingly and intentionally distributed their software to enable users to reproduce and distribute the copyrighted works in violation of the Copyright Act, 17 U.S.C. § 101 et seq. (2000 ed. and Supp. II). MGM sought damages and an injunction.

Discovery during the litigation revealed the way the software worked, the business aims of each defendant company, and the predilections of the users. Grokster's eponymous software employs what is known as FastTrack technology, a protocol developed by others and licensed to Grokster. StreamCast distributes a very similar product except that its software, called Morpheus, relies on what is known as Gnutella technology. A user who downloads and installs either software possesses the protocol to send requests for files directly to the computers of others using software compatible with FastTrack or Gnutella. On the FastTrack network opened by the Grokster software, the user's request goes to a computer given an indexing capacity by the software and designated a supernode, or to some other computer with comparable power and capacity to collect temporary indexes of the files available on the computers of users connected to it. The supernode (or indexing computer) searches its own index and may communicate the search request to other supernodes. If the file is found, the supernode discloses its location to the computer requesting it, and the requesting user can download the file directly from the computer located. The copied file is placed in a designated sharing folder on the requesting user's computer, where it is available for other users to download in turn, along with any other file in that folder.

In the Gnutella network made available by Morpheus, the process is mostly the same, except that in some versions of the Gnutella protocol there are no supernodes. In these versions, peer computers using the protocol communicate directly with each other. When a user enters a search request into the Morpheus software, it sends the request to computers connected with it, which in turn pass the request along to other connected peers. The search results are communicated to the requesting computer, and the user can download desired files directly from peers' computers. As this description indicates, Grokster and StreamCast use no servers to intercept the content of the search requests or to mediate the file transfers conducted by users of the software, there being no central point through which the substance of the communications passes in either direction.

Although Grokster and StreamCast do not therefore know when particular files are copied, a few searches using their software would show what is available on the networks the software reaches. MGM commissioned a statistician to conduct a systematic search, and his study showed that nearly 90% of the files available for download on the FastTrack system were copyrighted works. Grokster and StreamCast dispute this figure, raising methodological problems and arguing that free copying even of copyrighted works may be authorized by the rightholders. They also argue that potential noninfringing uses of their software are significant in kind, even if infrequent in practice. Some musical performers, for example, have gained new audiences by distributing their copyrighted works for free across peer-to-peer networks, and some distributors of unprotected content have used peer-to-peer networks to disseminate files, Shakespeare being an example. Indeed,

StreamCast has given Morpheus users the opportunity to download the briefs in this very case, though their popularity has not been quantified.

As for quantification, the parties' anecdotal and statistical evidence entered thus far to show the content available on the FastTrack and Gnutella networks does not say much about which files are actually downloaded by users, and no one can say how often the software is used to obtain copies of unprotected material. But MGM's evidence gives reason to think that the vast majority of users' downloads are acts of infringement, and because well over 100 million copies of the software in question are known to have been downloaded, and billions of files are shared across the FastTrack and Gnutella networks each month, the probable scope of copyright infringement is staggering.

Grokster and StreamCast concede the infringement in most downloads ... and it is uncontested that they are aware that users employ their software primarily to download copyrighted files, even if the decentralized FastTrack and Gnutella networks fail to reveal which files are being copied, and when. From time to time, moreover, the companies have learned about their users' infringement directly, as from users who have sent e-mail to each company with questions about playing copyrighted movies they had downloaded, to whom the companies have responded with guidance. And MGM notified the companies of 8 million copyrighted files that could be obtained using their software.

Grokster and StreamCast are not, however, merely passive recipients of information about infringing use. The record is replete with evidence that from the moment Grokster and StreamCast began to distribute their free software, each one clearly voiced the objective that recipients use it to download copyrighted works, and each took active steps to encourage infringement.

After the notorious file-sharing service, Napster, was sued by copyright holders for facilitation of copyright infringement, A & M Records, Inc. v. Napster, Inc., 114 F.Supp.2d 896 (N.D.Cal.2000), aff'd in part, rev'd in part, 239 F.3d 1004 (C.A.9 2001), StreamCast gave away a software program of a kind known as OpenNap, designed as compatible with the Napster program and open to Napster users for downloading files from other Napster and OpenNap users' computers. Evidence indicates that "[i]t was always [StreamCast's] intent to use [its Open-Nap network] to be able to capture email addresses of [its] initial target market so that [it] could promote [its] StreamCast Morpheus interface to them," App. 861; indeed, the OpenNap program was engineered " 'to leverage Napster's 50 million user base,' " id., at 746.

StreamCast monitored both the number of users downloading its OpenNap program and the number of music files they downloaded. Id., at 859, 863, 866. It also used the resulting OpenNap network to distribute copies of the Morpheus software and to encourage users to adopt it. Id., at 861, 867, 1039. Internal company documents indicate that StreamCast hoped to attract large numbers of former Napster users if that company was shut down by court order or otherwise, and that

StreamCast planned to be the next Napster. Id., at 861. A kit developed by StreamCast to be delivered to advertisers, for example, contained press articles about StreamCast's potential to capture former Napster users, id., at 568–572, and it introduced itself to some potential advertisers as a company "which is similar to what Napster was," id., at 884. It broadcast banner advertisements to users of other Napster-compatible software, urging them to adopt its OpenNap. Id., at 586. An internal e-mail from a company executive stated: " 'We have put this network in place so that when Napster pulls the plug on their free service . . . or if the Court orders them shut down prior to that . . . we will be positioned to capture the flood of their 32 million users that will be actively looking for an alternative.' " Id., at 588–589, 861.

Thus, StreamCast developed promotional materials to market its service as the best Napster alternative. One proposed advertisement read: "Napster Inc. has announced that it will soon begin charging you a fee. That's if the courts don't order it shut down first. What will you do to get around it?" Id., at 897. Another proposed ad touted StreamCast's software as the "#1 alternative to Napster" and asked "[w]hen the lights went off at Napster . . . where did the users go?" Id., at 836 (ellipsis in original). StreamCast even planned to flaunt the illegal uses of its software; when it launched the OpenNap network, the chief technology officer of the company averred that "[t]he goal is to get in trouble with the law and get sued. It's the best way to get in the new[s]." Id., at 916.

The evidence that Grokster sought to capture the market of former Napster users is sparser but revealing, for Grokster launched its own OpenNap system called Swaptor and inserted digital codes into its Web site so that computer users using Web search engines to look for "Napster" or "[f]ree filesharing" would be directed to the Grokster Web site, where they could download the Grokster software. Id., at 992–993. And Grokster's name is an apparent derivative of Napster.

StreamCast's executives monitored the number of songs by certain commercial artists available on their networks, and an internal communication indicates they aimed to have a larger number of copyrighted songs available on their networks than other file-sharing networks. Id., at 868. The point, of course, would be to attract users of a mind to infringe, just as it would be with their promotional materials developed showing copyrighted songs as examples of the kinds of files available through Morpheus. Id., at 848. Morpheus in fact allowed users to search specifically for "Top 40" songs, id., at 735, which were inevitably copyrighted. Similarly, Grokster sent users a newsletter promoting its ability to provide particular, popular copyrighted materials. Brief for Motion Picture Studio and Recording Company Petitioners 7–8.

In addition to this evidence of express promotion, marketing, and intent to promote further, the business models employed by Grokster and StreamCast confirm that their principal object was use of their software to download copyrighted works. Grokster and StreamCast receive no revenue from users, who obtain the software itself for nothing. Instead, both companies generate income by selling advertising space, and they stream the advertising to Grokster and Morpheus users while they are employing the programs. As the number of users of each program increases, advertising opportunities become worth more. Cf. App. 539, 804. While there is doubtless some demand for free Shakespeare, the evidence shows that substantive volume is a function of free access to copyrighted work. Users seeking Top 40 songs, for example, or the latest release by Modest Mouse, are certain to be far more numerous than those seeking a free Decameron, and Grokster and StreamCast translated that demand into dollars.

Finally, there is no evidence that either company made an effort to filter copyrighted material from users' downloads or otherwise impede the sharing of copyrighted files. Although Grokster appears to have sent e-mails warning users about infringing content when it received threatening notice from the copyright holders, it never blocked anyone from continuing to use its software to share copyrighted files. Id., at 75–76. StreamCast not only rejected another company's offer of help to monitor infringement, id., at 928–929, but blocked the Internet Protocol addresses of entities it believed were trying to engage in such monitoring on its networks, id., at 917–922.

B

After discovery, the parties on each side of the case cross-moved for summary judgment. The District Court limited its consideration to the asserted liability of Grokster and StreamCast for distributing the current versions of their software, leaving aside whether either was liable "for damages arising from past versions of their software, or from other past activities." 259 F.Supp.2d 1029, 1033 (C.D.Cal.2003). The District Court held that those who used the Grokster and Morpheus software to download copyrighted media files directly infringed MGM's copyrights, a conclusion not contested on appeal, but the court nonetheless granted summary judgment in favor of Grokster and StreamCast as to any liability arising from distribution of the then current versions of their software. Distributing that software gave rise to no liability in the court's view, because its use did not provide the distributors with actual knowledge of specific acts of infringement. Case No. CV 01 08541 SVW (PJWx) (CD Cal., June 18, 2003), App. 1213.

The Court of Appeals affirmed. 380 F.3d 1154 (C.A.9 2004). In the court's analysis, a defendant was liable as a contributory infringer when it had knowledge of direct infringement and materially contributed to the infringement. But the court read Sony Corp. of America v. Universal City Studios, Inc., 464 U.S. 417, 104 S.Ct. 774, 78 L.Ed.2d 574 (1984), as holding that distribution of a commercial product capable of substantial noninfringing uses could not give rise to contributory liability for infringement unless the distributor had actual knowledge of specific instances of infringement and failed to act on that knowledge. The fact that the software was capable of substantial noninfringing uses in the

Ninth Circuit's view meant that Grokster and StreamCast were not liable, because they had no such actual knowledge, owing to the decentralized architecture of their software. The court also held that Grokster and StreamCast did not materially contribute to their users' infringement because it was the users themselves who searched for, retrieved, and stored the infringing files, with no involvement by the defendants beyond providing the software in the first place.

The Ninth Circuit also considered whether Grokster and StreamCast could be liable under a theory of vicarious infringement. The court held against liability because the defendants did not monitor or control the use of the software, had no agreed-upon right or current ability to supervise its use, and had no independent duty to police infringement. We granted certiorari.

II

A

MGM and many of the amici fault the Court of Appeals's holding for upsetting a sound balance between the respective values of supporting creative pursuits through copyright protection and promoting innovation in new communication technologies by limiting the incidence of liability for copyright infringement. The more artistic protection is favored, the more technological innovation may be discouraged; the administration of copyright law is an exercise in managing the trade-off. See Sony Corp. v. Universal City Studios, supra, at 442, 104 S.Ct. 774; see generally Ginsburg, Copyright and Control Over New Technologies of Dissemination, 101 Colum. L.Rev. 1613 (2001); Lichtman & Landes, Indirect Liability for Copyright Infringement: An Economic Perspective, 16 Harv. J.L. & Tech. 395 (2003).

The tension between the two values is the subject of this case, with its claim that digital distribution of copyrighted material threatens copyright holders as never before, because every copy is identical to the original, copying is easy, and many people (especially the young) use file-sharing software to download copyrighted works. This very breadth of the software's use may well draw the public directly into the debate over copyright policy, Peters, Brace Memorial Lecture: Copyright Enters the Public Domain, 51 J. Copyright Soc. 701, 705–717 (2004) (address by Register of Copyrights), and the indications are that the ease of copying songs or movies using software like Grokster's and Napster's is fostering disdain for copyright protection, Wu, When Code Isn't Law, 89 Va. L.Rev. 679, 724–726 (2003). As the case has been presented to us, these fears are said to be offset by the different concern that imposing liability, not only on infringers but on distributors of software based on its potential for unlawful use, could limit further development of beneficial technologies. See, e.g., Lemley & Reese, Reducing Digital Copyright Infringement Without Restricting Innovation, 56 Stan. L.Rev. 1345, 1386–1390 (2004); Brief for Innovation Scholars and Economists as

Amici Curiae 15–20; Brief for Emerging Technology Companies as Amici Curiae 19–25; Brief for Intel Corporation as Amicus Curiae 20–22.

The argument for imposing indirect liability in this case is, however, a powerful one, given the number of infringing downloads that occur every day using StreamCast's and Grokster's software. When a widely shared service or product is used to commit infringement, it may be impossible to enforce rights in the protected work effectively against all direct infringers, the only practical alternative being to go against the distributor of the copying device for secondary liability on a theory of contributory or vicarious infringement. See In re Aimster Copyright Litigation, 334 F.3d 643, 645–646 (C.A.7 2003).

One infringes contributorily by intentionally inducing or encouraging direct infringement, see Gershwin Pub. Corp. v. Columbia Artists Management, Inc., 443 F.2d 1159, 1162 (C.A.2 1971), and infringes vicariously by profiting from direct infringement while declining to exercise a right to stop or limit it, Shapiro, Bernstein & Co. v. H.L. Green Co., 316 F.2d 304, 307 (C.A.2 1963). Although "[t]he Copyright Act does not expressly render anyone liable for infringement committed by another," Sony Corp. v. Universal City Studios, 464 U.S., at 434, 104 S.Ct. 774, these doctrines of secondary liability emerged from common law principles and are well established in the law, id., at 486, 104 S.Ct. 774 (Blackmun, J., dissenting); Kalem Co. v. Harper Brothers, 222 U.S. 55, 62–63, 32 S.Ct. 20, 56 L.Ed. 92 (1911); Gershwin Pub. Corp. v. Columbia Artists Management, supra, at 1162; 3 M. Nimmer & D. Nimmer, Copyright, § 12.04[A] (2005).

B

Despite the currency of these principles of secondary liability, this Court has dealt with secondary copyright infringement in only one recent case, and because MGM has tailored its principal claim to our opinion there, a look at our earlier holding is in order. In Sony Corp. v. Universal City Studios, supra, this Court addressed a claim that secondary liability for infringement can arise from the very distribution of a commercial product. There, the product, novel at the time, was what we know today as the videocassette recorder or VCR. Copyright holders sued Sony as the manufacturer, claiming it was contributorily liable for infringement that occurred when VCR owners taped copyrighted programs because it supplied the means used to infringe, and it had constructive knowledge that infringement would occur. At the trial on the merits, the evidence showed that the principal use of the VCR was for " 'time-shifting,' " or taping a program for later viewing at a more convenient time, which the Court found to be a fair, not an infringing, use. Id., at 423–424, 104 S.Ct. 774. There was no evidence that Sony had expressed an object of bringing about taping in violation of copyright or had taken active steps to increase its profits from unlawful taping. Id., at 438, 104 S.Ct. 774. Although Sony's advertisements urged consumers to buy the VCR to " 'record favorite shows' " or " 'build a library' " of recorded programs, id., at 459, 104 S.Ct. 774 (Blackmun, J., dissenting), neither of these uses was necessarily infringing, id., at 424, 454–455, 104 S.Ct. 774.

On those facts, with no evidence of stated or indicated intent to promote infringing uses, the only conceivable basis for imposing liability was on a theory of contributory infringement arising from its sale of VCRs to consumers with knowledge that some would use them to infringe. Id., at 439, 104 S.Ct. 774. But because the VCR was "capable of commercially significant noninfringing uses," we held the manufacturer could not be faulted solely on the basis of its distribution. Id., at 442, 104 S.Ct. 774.

This analysis reflected patent law's traditional staple article of commerce doctrine, now codified, that distribution of a component of a patented device will not violate the patent if it is suitable for use in other ways. 35 U.S.C. § 271(c); Aro Mfg. Co. v. Convertible Top Replacement Co., 377 U.S. 476, 485, 84 S.Ct. 1526, 12 L.Ed.2d 457 (1964) (noting codification of cases); id., at 486, n. 6, 84 S.Ct. 1526 (same). The doctrine was devised to identify instances in which it may be presumed from distribution of an article in commerce that the distributor intended the article to be used to infringe another's patent, and so may justly be held liable for that infringement. "One who makes and sells articles which are only adapted to be used in a patented combination will be presumed to intend the natural consequences of his acts; he will be presumed to intend that they shall be used in the combination of the patent." New York Scaffolding Co. v. Whitney, 224 F. 452, 459 (C.A.8 1915)....

In sum, where an article is "good for nothing else" but infringement ... there is no legitimate public interest in its unlicensed availability, and there is no injustice in presuming or imputing an intent to infringe.... Conversely, the doctrine absolves the equivocal conduct of selling an item with substantial lawful as well as unlawful uses, and limits liability to instances of more acute fault than the mere understanding that some of one's products will be misused. It leaves breathing room for innovation and a vigorous commerce....

The parties and many of the amici in this case think the key to resolving it is the Sony rule and, in particular, what it means for a product to be "capable of commercially significant noninfringing uses." Sony Corp. v. Universal City Studios, supra, at 442, 104 S.Ct. 774. MGM advances the argument that granting summary judgment to Grokster and StreamCast as to their current activities gave too much weight to the value of innovative technology, and too little to the copyrights infringed by users of their software, given that 90% of works available on one of the networks was shown to be copyrighted. Assuming the remaining 10% to be its noninfringing use, MGM says this should not qualify as "substantial," and the Court should quantify Sony to the extent of holding that a product used "principally" for infringement does not qualify. See Brief for Motion Picture Studio and Recording Company Petitioners 31. As mentioned before, Grokster and StreamCast reply by citing evidence that their software can be used to reproduce public domain works, and they point to copyright holders who actually encourage copying. Even if infringement is the principal practice with their software today, they argue, the noninfringing uses are significant and will grow.

We agree with MGM that the Court of Appeals misapplied Sony, which it read as limiting secondary liability quite beyond the circumstances to which the case applied. Sony barred secondary liability based on presuming or imputing intent to cause infringement solely from the design or distribution of a product capable of substantial lawful use, which the distributor knows is in fact used for infringement. The Ninth Circuit has read Sony's limitation to mean that whenever a product is capable of substantial lawful use, the producer can never be held contributorily liable for third parties' infringing use of it; it read the rule as being this broad, even when an actual purpose to cause infringing use is shown by evidence independent of design and distribution of the product, unless the distributors had "specific knowledge of infringement at a time at which they contributed to the infringement, and failed to act upon that information." 380 F.3d, at 1162 (internal quotation marks and alterations omitted). Because the Circuit found the StreamCast and Grokster software capable of substantial lawful use, it concluded on the basis of its reading of Sony that neither company could be held liable, since there was no showing that their software, being without any central server, afforded them knowledge of specific unlawful uses.

This view of Sony, however, was error, converting the case from one about liability resting on imputed intent to one about liability on any theory. Because Sony did not displace other theories of secondary liability, and because we find below that it was error to grant summary judgment to the companies on MGM's inducement claim, we do not revisit Sony further, as MGM requests, to add a more quantified description of the point of balance between protection and commerce when liability rests solely on distribution with knowledge that unlawful use will occur. It is enough to note that the Ninth Circuit's judgment rested on an erroneous understanding of Sony and to leave further consideration of the Sony rule for a day when that may be required.

C

Sony's rule limits imputing culpable intent as a matter of law from the characteristics or uses of a distributed product. But nothing in Sony requires courts to ignore evidence of intent if there is such evidence, and the case was never meant to foreclose rules of fault-based liability derived from the common law. Sony Corp. v. Universal City Studios, 464 U.S., at 439, 104 S.Ct. 774 ("If vicarious liability is to be imposed on Sony in this case, it must rest on the fact that it has sold equipment with constructive knowledge" of the potential for infringement). Thus, where evidence goes beyond a product's characteristics or the knowledge that it may be put to infringing uses, and shows statements or actions directed to promoting infringement, Sony's staple-article rule will not preclude liability.

The classic case of direct evidence of unlawful purpose occurs when one induces commission of infringement by another, or "entic[es] or persuad[es] another" to infringe, Black's Law Dictionary 790 (8th ed.2004), as by advertising. Thus at common law a copyright or patent defendant who "not only expected but invoked [infringing use] by advertisement" was liable for infringement "on principles recognized in every part of the law." Kalem Co. v. Harper Brothers, 222 U.S., at 62–63, 32 S.Ct. 20 (copyright infringement). See also Henry v. A.B. Dick Co., 224 U.S., at 48–49, 32 S.Ct. 364 (contributory liability for patent infringement may be found where a good's "most conspicuous use is one which will co-operate in an infringement when sale to such user is invoked by advertisement" of the infringing use); Thomson–Houston Electric Co. v. Kelsey Electric R. Specialty Co., 75 F. 1005, 1007–1008 (C.A.2 1896) (relying on advertisements and displays to find defendant's "willingness ... to aid other persons in any attempts which they may be disposed to make towards [patent] infringement"); Rumford Chemical Works v. Hecker, 20 F.Cas. 1342, 1346 (No. 12,133) (C.C.D.N.J.1876) (demonstrations of infringing activity along with "avowals of the [infringing] purpose and use for which it was made" supported liability for patent infringement).

The rule on inducement of infringement as developed in the early cases is no different today. Evidence of "active steps ... taken to encourage direct infringement," Oak Industries, Inc. v. Zenith Electronics Corp., 697 F.Supp. 988, 992 (N.D.Ill.1988), such as advertising an infringing use or instructing how to engage in an infringing use, show an affirmative intent that the product be used to infringe, and a showing that infringement was encouraged overcomes the law's reluctance to find liability when a defendant merely sells a commercial product suitable for some lawful use, see, e.g., Water Technologies Corp. v. Calco, Ltd., 850 F.2d 660, 668 (C.A.Fed.1988) (liability for inducement where one "actively and knowingly aid[s] and abet[s] another's direct infringement" (emphasis omitted)); Fromberg, Inc. v. Thornhill, 315 F.2d 407, 412–413 (C.A.5 1963) (demonstrations by sales staff of infringing uses supported liability for inducement); Haworth Inc. v. Herman Miller Inc., 37 U.S.P.Q.2d 1080, 1090, 1994 WL 875931 (W.D.Mich.1994) (evidence that defendant "demonstrate[d] and recommend[ed] infringing configurations" of its product could support inducement liability); Sims v. Mack Trucks, Inc., 459 F.Supp. 1198, 1215 (E.D.Pa.1978) (finding inducement where the use "depicted by the defendant in its promotional film and brochures infringes the ... patent"), overruled on other grounds, 608 F.2d 87 (C.A.3 1979). Cf. W. Keeton, D. Dobbs, R. Keeton, & D. Owen, Prosser and Keeton on Law of Torts 37 (5th ed. 1984) ("There is a definite tendency to impose greater responsibility upon a defendant whose conduct was intended to do harm, or was morally wrong").

For the same reasons that Sony took the staple-article doctrine of patent law as a model for its copyright safe-harbor rule, the inducement rule, too, is a sensible one for copyright. We adopt it here, holding that one who distributes a device with the object of promoting its use to infringe copyright, as shown by clear expression or other affirmative steps taken to foster infringement, is liable for the resulting acts of infringement by third parties. We are, of course, mindful of the need to keep from trenching on regular commerce or discouraging the development of technologies with lawful and unlawful potential. Accordingly, just as Sony did not find intentional inducement despite the knowledge of the VCR manufacturer that its device could be used to infringe, 464 U.S., at 439, n. 19, 104 S.Ct. 774, mere knowledge of infringing potential or of actual infringing uses would not be enough here to subject a distributor to liability. Nor would ordinary acts incident to product distribution, such as offering customers technical support or product updates, support liability in themselves. The inducement rule, instead, premises liability on purposeful, culpable expression and conduct, and thus does nothing to compromise legitimate commerce or discourage innovation having a lawful promise.

III

A

The only apparent question about treating MGM's evidence as sufficient to withstand summary judgment under the theory of inducement goes to the need on MGM's part to adduce evidence that Stream-Cast and Grokster communicated an inducing message to their software users. The classic instance of inducement is by advertisement or solicitation that broadcasts a message designed to stimulate others to commit violations. MGM claims that such a message is shown here. It is undisputed that StreamCast beamed onto the computer screens of users of Napster-compatible programs ads urging the adoption of its OpenNap program, which was designed, as its name implied, to invite the custom of patrons of Napster, then under attack in the courts for facilitating massive infringement. Those who accepted StreamCast's OpenNap program were offered software to perform the same services, which a factfinder could conclude would readily have been understood in the Napster market as the ability to download copyrighted music files. Grokster distributed an electronic newsletter containing links to articles promoting its software's ability to access popular copyrighted music. And anyone whose Napster or free file-sharing searches turned up a link to Grokster would have understood Grokster to be offering the same file-sharing ability as Napster, and to the same people who probably used Napster for infringing downloads; that would also have been the understanding of anyone offered Grokster's suggestively named Swaptor software, its version of OpenNap. And both companies communicated a clear message by responding affirmatively to requests for help in locating and playing copyrighted materials.

In StreamCast's case, of course, the evidence just described was supplemented by other unequivocal indications of unlawful purpose in the internal communications and advertising designs aimed at Napster users ("When the lights went off at Napster ... where did the users go?" App. 836 (ellipsis in original)). Whether the messages were communicated is not to the point on this record. The function of the message in the theory of inducement is to prove by a defendant's own statements that his unlawful purpose disqualifies him from claiming protection (and incidentally to point to actual violators likely to be found among those who hear or read the message).... Proving that a message was sent out, then, is the preeminent but not exclusive way of showing that active steps were taken with the purpose of bringing about infringing acts, and of showing that infringing acts took place by using the device distributed. Here, the summary judgment record is replete with other evidence that Grokster and StreamCast, unlike the manufacturer and distributor in Sony, acted with a purpose to cause copyright violations by use of software suitable for illegal use....

Three features of this evidence of intent are particularly notable. First, each company showed itself to be aiming to satisfy a known source of demand for copyright infringement, the market comprising former Napster users. StreamCast's internal documents made constant reference to Napster, it initially distributed its Morpheus software through an OpenNap program compatible with Napster, it advertised its OpenNap program to Napster users, and its Morpheus software functions as Napster did except that it could be used to distribute more kinds of files, including copyrighted movies and software programs. Grokster's name is apparently derived from Napster, it too initially offered an OpenNap program, its software's function is likewise comparable to Napster's, and it attempted to divert queries for Napster onto its own Web site. Grokster and StreamCast's efforts to supply services to former Napster users, deprived of a mechanism to copy and distribute what were overwhelmingly infringing files, indicate a principal, if not exclusive, intent on the part of each to bring about infringement.

Second, this evidence of unlawful objective is given added significance by MGM's showing that neither company attempted to develop filtering tools or other mechanisms to diminish the infringing activity using their software. While the Ninth Circuit treated the defendants' failure to develop such tools as irrelevant because they lacked an independent duty to monitor their users' activity, we think this evidence underscores Grokster's and StreamCast's intentional facilitation of their users' infringement.

Third, there is a further complement to the direct evidence of unlawful objective. It is useful to recall that StreamCast and Grokster make money by selling advertising space, by directing ads to the screens of computers employing their software. As the record shows, the more the software is used, the more ads are sent out and the greater the advertising revenue becomes. Since the extent of the software's use determines the gain to the distributors, the commercial sense of their enterprise turns on high-volume use, which the record shows is infringing. This evidence alone would not justify an inference of unlawful intent, but viewed in the context of the entire record its import is clear. The unlawful objective is unmistakable.

B

In addition to intent to bring about infringement and distribution of a device suitable for infringing use, the inducement theory of course requires evidence of actual infringement by recipients of the device, the software in this case. As the account of the facts indicates, there is evidence of infringement on a gigantic scale, and there is no serious issue of the adequacy of MGM's showing on this point in order to survive the companies' summary judgment requests. Although an exact calculation of infringing use, as a basis for a claim of damages, is subject to dispute, there is no question that the summary judgment evidence is at least adequate to entitle MGM to go forward with claims for damages and equitable relief.

* * *

In sum, this case is significantly different from Sony and reliance on that case to rule in favor of StreamCast and Grokster was error. Sony dealt with a claim of liability based solely on distributing a product with alternative lawful and unlawful uses, with knowledge that some users would follow the unlawful course. The case struck a balance between the interests of protection and innovation by holding that the product's capability of substantial lawful employment should bar the imputation of fault and consequent secondary liability for the unlawful acts of others.

MGM's evidence in this case most obviously addresses a different basis of liability for distributing a product open to alternative uses. Here, evidence of the distributors' words and deeds going beyond distribution as such shows a purpose to cause and profit from third-party acts of copyright infringement. If liability for inducing infringement is ultimately found, it will not be on the basis of presuming or imputing fault, but from inferring a patently illegal objective from statements and actions showing what that objective was.

There is substantial evidence in MGM's favor on all elements of inducement, and summary judgment in favor of Grokster and Stream-Cast was error. On remand, reconsideration of MGM's motion for summary judgment will be in order.

The judgment of the Court of Appeals is vacated, and the case is remanded for further proceedings consistent with this opinion.

Notes

1. Plaintiff manufactures and sells computer video game systems. The software for plaintiff's games is contained in "Read Only Memory" ("ROM") chips which can neither be reprogrammed nor erased. The cartridges sell for around $40. Defendant sells a device the sole function of which is to copy video games that are compatible with the plaintiff's system. The device sells for $119, and blank cartridges cost $10 each. At the same time defendant began selling its copying device, the defendant also began selling a small number of video games that are compatible with the plaintiff's system.

Defendant expressly gives its customers permission to copy its games. Is defendant contributorily liable for its customers' copying of plaintiff's copyrighted games?

2. Should a party that makes and sells a device that copies videotapes be held contributorily liable for infringement?

3. Suppose that the defendant ships copyrighted videotapes from the United States to a recipient overseas, where the tapes are unavailable. If the defendant knows that the recipient intends to make and distribute unauthorized copies, is the defendant contributorily liable for infringement? Does it matter whether the unauthorized copies are distributed in the United States or only overseas?

D. DISCRETE ISSUES AFFECTING LIABILITY UNDER THE DMCA

1. SAFE HARBORS UNDER SECTION 512

Prior to the enactment of the Digital Millennium Copyright Act in 1998, a recurring question was whether an internet service provider or the operator of a bulletin board service should be held contributorily or vicariously liable for infringing acts by subscribers, and if so, under what circumstances. Conventional analysis, under such cases as *Netcom* and *Fonovisa,* appeared to provide only partially satisfactory responses.

Title II of the DMCA, known as the "Online Copyright Infringement Liability Limitation Act," added new section 512 to Title 17. Section 512 addresses the infringement liability of internet service providers (ISPs), and reflects an agreement between copyright owners and ISPs which (1) creates safe harbors within which ISPs are exempt from monetary damages and (2) limits the availability and scope of injunctive relief against ISPs. The liability limitations apply only if the ISP accommodates standard copy protection measures used by copyright owners and implements a policy of terminating the use of its services by repeat infringers. Under those circumstances, an ISP enjoys limited liability for:

1) serving as a mere conduit for the infringing transmission;

2) temporary storage, through "system caching," of infringing material, provided that the caching incorporates prescribed features which protect the rights of the copyright owner;

3) storing infringing material, provided that (a) the ISP either is unaware of the infringing activity or promptly removes or disables access to the material after becoming aware of the infringing activity, (b) where the ISP has the right and ability to control the infringing activity, it derives no financial benefit from this activity, and (c) the ISP acts promptly to remove or disable access to the infringing material upon receiving notification of the claimed infringement that conforms with certain statutory requirements; and

4) using information location tools to refer or link users to a site containing infringing material, provided that (a) the ISP is

unaware of the infringement or promptly removes or disables access to the material upon becoming aware of the infringement, (b) where the ISP has the right and ability to control the infringing activity, it derives no financial benefit therefrom, and (c) the ISP acts promptly to remove or disable access to the infringing material upon receiving notice that conforms with the statutory requirements.

New section 512 also limits the injunctive relief available against nonprofit educational institutions acting as ISPs, and spells out the circumstances under which institutions acting in such capacity will *not* have imputed to them the knowledge or activities of faculty or graduate student-employees engaged in teaching or research activities.

In *A & M Records, Inc. v. Napster, Inc.*, 114 F.Supp.2d 896 (N.D.Cal. 2000), plaintiffs were allowed to proceed with their copyright infringement action against defendant Napster, an Internet-based service which allegedly infringed the plaintiffs' sound recording copyrights by providing Internet users with a device (consisting of user-side and server-side software, plus the Napster servers) for locating, requesting, and copying MP3 music files located on the hard drives of other Napster users. The MP3 files were transferred from one user's hard drive to another through the Internet, and were not stored on, or transmitted through, Napter's own servers. The court denied the defendant's motion for summary judgment under the section 512(a) safe harbor because Napster failed to establish that it was a "service provider" within the meaning of that section, which applies only where the defendant acts as a conduit by "transmitting, routing, or providing connections" through its own system (as opposed to facilitating such activities through the Internet). In addition, Napster failed to establish that it had complied with the section 512(i) provisions which are prerequisite to all of the section 512 safe harbors, and which require the service provider to adopt, reasonably implement, and inform its users of a policy for terminating repeat infringers. (Public and private university defendants who were threatened with similar litigation acceded to the record companies' demand that they block or limit student access to Napster through university networks.)

On appeal, the Ninth Circuit affirmed. See *A&M Records, Inc. v. Napster, Inc.*, 239 F.3d 1004 (2001). The Circuit Court agreed with the District Court's finding that Napster's clients were engaging in numerous acts of direct infringement, and concurred in rejecting Napster's fair use claims as well. The court further held that the plaintiffs had established the likelihood of Napster's liability for copyright infringement on both contributory and vicarious grounds, along conventional lines of analysis. In a subsequent section of its opinion, the Ninth Circuit also addressed section 512, at greater length than had the District Court:

> Napster also interposes a statutory limitation on liability by asserting the protections of the "safe harbor" from copyright infringement suits for "Internet service providers" contained in the Digital Millennium Copyright Act, 17 U.S.C. § 512. See *Napster*, 114

F.Supp.2d at 919 n. 24. The district court did not give this statutory limitation any weight favoring a denial of temporary injunctive relief. The court concluded that Napster "has failed to persuade this court that subsection 512(d) shelters contributory infringers." *Id.*

We need not accept a blanket conclusion that § 512 of the Digital Millennium Copyright Act will never protect secondary infringers. *See* S. Rep. 105–190, at 40 (1998) ("The limitations in subsections (a) through (d) protect qualifying service providers from liability for all monetary relief for direct, vicarious, and contributory infringement."), *reprinted in* Melville B. Nimmer & David Nimmer, Nimmer on Copyright: Congressional Committee Reports on the Digital Millennium Copyright Act and Concurrent Amendments (2000); *see also* Charles S. Wright, Actual Versus Legal Control: Reading Vicarious Liability for Copyright Infringement Into the Digital Millennium Copyright Act of 1998, 75 Wash. L.Rev. 1005, 1028–31 (July 2000) ("[T]he committee reports leave no doubt that Congress intended to provide some relief from vicarious liability").

We do not agree that Napster's potential liability for contributory and vicarious infringement renders the Digital Millennium Copyright Act inapplicable per se. We instead recognize that this issue will be more fully developed at trial. At this stage of the litigation, plaintiffs raise serious questions regarding Napster's ability to obtain shelter under § 512, and plaintiffs also demonstrate that the balance of hardships tips in their favor. *See Prudential Real Estate*, 204 F.3d at 874; *see also* Micro Star v. Formgen, Inc. 154 F.3d 1107, 1109 (9th Cir.1998) ("A party seeking a preliminary injunction must show . . . 'that serious questions going to the merits were raised and the balance of hardships tips sharply in its favor.' ").

Plaintiffs have raised and continue to raise significant questions under this statute, including: (1) whether Napster is an Internet service provider as defined by 17 U.S.C. § 512(d); (2) whether copyright owners must give a service provider "official" notice of infringing activity in order for it to have knowledge or awareness of infringing activity on its system; and (3) whether Napster complies with § 512(i), which requires a service provider to timely establish a detailed copyright compliance policy. *See* A & M Records, Inc. v. Napster, Inc., No. 99–05183, 2000 WL 573136 (N.D.Cal. May 12, 2000) (denying summary judgment to Napster under a different subsection of the Digital Millennium Copyright Act, § 512(a)).

The district court considered ample evidence to support its determination that the balance of hardships tips in plaintiffs' favor:

> Any destruction of Napster, Inc. by a preliminary injunction is speculative compared to the statistical evidence of massive, unauthorized downloading and uploading of plaintiffs' copyrighted works-as many as 10,000 files per second by defendant's own admission. *See* Kessler Dec. ¶ 29. The court has every reason to believe that, without a preliminary injunction, these

numbers will mushroom as Napster users, and newcomers attracted by the publicity, scramble to obtain as much free music as possible before trial.

114 F.Supp.2d at 926.

239 F.3d at 1025.

In their pursuit of possible copyright infringers, the record industry has attempted to get the names of internet users through their service providers. The D.C. Circuit ruled that an Internet Service Provider (ISP) only has to divulge that information if the alleged violations of copyright are stored on the ISP's servers. Otherwise, the only connection of the ISP to the lawsuit is acting as a conduit for the allegedly illegal activity, which is a protected practice from copyright suits under the DMCA. The court explained:

> We are not unsympathetic either to the RIAA's concern regarding the widespread infringement of its members' copyrights, or to the need for legal tools to protect those rights. It is not the province of the courts, however, to rewrite the DMCA in order to make it fit a new and unforeseen internet architecture, no matter how damaging that development has been to the music industry or threatens being to the motion picture and software industries.

Recording Industry Association of America, Inc. v. Verizon Internet Services, Inc., 351 F.3d 1229 (D.C. Circuit 2003).

ALS SCAN, INC. v. REMARQ COMMUNITIES, INC.
United States Court of Appeals, Fourth Circuit, 2001.
239 F.3d 619.

NIEMEYER, CIRCUIT JUDGE:

We are presented with an issue of first impression—whether an Internet service provider enjoys a safe harbor from copyright infringement liability as provided by Title II of the Digital Millennium Copyright Act ("DMCA") when it is put on notice of infringement activity on its system by an imperfect notice. Because we conclude that the service provider was provided with a notice of infringing activity that *substantially* complied with the Act, it may not rely on a claim of defective notice to maintain the immunity defense provided by the safe harbor. * * *

ALS Scan, Inc., a Maryland corporation, is engaged in the business of creating and marketing "adult" photographs. It displays these pictures on the Internet to paying subscribers and also sells them through the media of CD ROMs and videotapes. ALS Scan is holder of the copyrights for all of these photographs.

RemarQ Communities, Inc., a Delaware corporation, is an online Internet service provider that provides access to its subscribing members. It has approximately 24,000 subscribers to its newsgroup base and provides access to over 30,000 newsgroups which cover thousands of subjects. These newsgroups, organized by topic, enable subscribers to participate in discussions on virtually any topic, such as fine arts, politics, religion, social issues, sports, and entertainment. For example, RemarQ provides access to a newsgroup entitled "Baltimore Orioles," in which users share observations or materials about the Orioles. It claims that users post over one million articles a day in these newsgroups, which RemarQ removes after about 8–10 days to accommodate its limited server capacity. In providing access to newsgroups, RemarQ does not monitor, regulate, or censor the content of articles posted in the newsgroup by subscribing members. It does, however, have the ability to filter information contained in the newsgroups and to screen its members from logging onto certain newsgroups, such as those containing pornographic material.

Two of the newsgroups to which RemarQ provides its subscribers access contain ALS Scan's name in the titles. These newsgroups— "alt.als" and "alt.binaries.pictures.erotica.als"—contain hundreds of postings that infringe ALS Scan's copyrights. These postings are placed in these newsgroups by RemarQ's subscribers.

Upon discovering that RemarQ databases contained material that infringed ALS Scan's copyrights, ALS Scan sent a letter, dated August 2, 1999, to RemarQ, stating:

> Both of these newsgroups ["alt.als" and "alt.binaries.pictures.erotica.als"] were created for the sole purpose of violating our Federally filed Copyrights and Tradename. These newsgroups contain virtually all Federally Copyrighted images.... Your servers provide access to these illegally posted images and enable the illegal transmission of these images across state lines.

> This is a cease and desist letter. You are hereby ordered to cease carrying these newsgroups within twenty-four (24) hours upon receipt of this correspondence.... America Online, Erol's, Mindspring, and others have all complied with our cease and desist order and no longer carry these newsgroups.

* * *

> Our ALS Scan models can be identified at *http:// www.alsscan.com/ modlinf2.html*[.] Our copyright information can be reviewed at *http://www.alsscan.com/ copyrite.html*[.]

RemarQ responded by refusing to comply with ALS Scan's demand but advising ALS Scan that RemarQ would eliminate individual infringing items from these newsgroups if ALS Scan identified them "with sufficient specificity." ALS Scan answered that RemarQ had included over 10,000 copyrighted images belonging to ALS Scan in its newsgroups over the period of several months and that

> [t]hese newsgroups have apparently been created by individuals for the express sole purpose of illegally posting, transferring and disseminating photographs that have been copyrighted by my client through both its websites and its CD–ROMs. The newsgroups, on

their face from reviewing messages posted thereon, serve no other purpose.

When correspondence between the parties progressed no further to resolution of the dispute, ALS Scan commenced this action, alleging violations of the Copyright Act and Title II of the DMCA, as well as unfair competition. In its complaint, ALS Scan alleged that RemarQ possessed actual knowledge that the newsgroups contained infringing material but had "steadfastly refused to remove or block access to the material." ALS Scan also alleged that RemarQ was put on notice by ALS Scan of the infringing material contained in its database. In addition to injunctive relief, ALS Scan demanded actual and statutory damages, as well as attorneys fees. It attached to its complaint affidavits establishing the essential elements of its claims.

In response, RemarQ filed a motion to dismiss the complaint or, in the alternative, for summary judgment, and also attached affidavits, stating that RemarQ was prepared to remove articles posted in its newsgroups if the allegedly infringing articles were specifically identified. It contended that because it is a provider of access to news-groups, ALS Scan's failure to comply with the DMCA notice requirements provided it with a defense to ALS Scan's copyright infringement claim.

The district court ruled on RemarQ's motion, stating, "[RemarQ's] motion to dismiss or for summary judgment is treated as one to dismiss and, as such, is granted." In making this ruling, the district court held: (1) that RemarQ could not be held liable for *direct* copyright infringement merely because it provided access to a newsgroup containing infringing material; and (2) that RemarQ could not be held liable for *contributory* infringement because ALS Scan failed to comply with the notice requirements set forth in the DMCA, 17 U.S.C. § 512(c)(3)(A). This appeal followed.

II

ALS Scan contends first that the district court erred in dismissing its *direct* copyright infringement claim. It contends that it stated a cause of action for copyright infringement when it alleged (1) the "ownership of valid copyrights," and (2) RemarQ's violation of its copyrights "by allowing its members access to newsgroups containing infringing material."[1] *See generally Keeler Brass Co. v. Continental Brass Co.,* 862 F.2d 1063, 1065 (4th Cir.1988) (describing the requirements of a direct infringement claim). In rejecting ALS Scan's direct infringement claim, the district court relied on the decision in *Religious Technology Center v. Netcom On–Line Communication Services, Inc.,* 907 F.Supp. 1361, 1368– 73 (N.D.Cal.1995), which concluded that when an Internet provider serves, without human intervention, as a passive conduit for copyrighted

---

1. It would appear that ALS Scan's allegations amount more to a claim of contributory infringement in which a defendant, "with knowledge of the infringing activity, induces, causes or materially contributes to the infringing conduct of another," *Gershwin Pub. Corp. v. Columbia Artists Management, Inc.,* 443 F.2d 1159, 1162 (2d Cir. 1971), than to a claim of direct infringement.

material, it is not liable as a direct infringer. The *Netcom* court reasoned that "it does not make sense to adopt a rule that could lead to liability of countless parties whose role in the infringement is nothing more than setting up and operating a system that is necessary for the functioning of the Internet." *Id.* at 1372. That court observed that it would not be workable to hold "the entire Internet liable for activities that cannot reasonably be deterred." *Id.; see also Marobie–Fl, Inc. v. National Ass'n of Fire and Equipment Distributors,* 983 F.Supp. 1167, 1176–79 (N.D.Ill. 1997) (agreeing with *Netcom*'s reasoning). ALS Scan argues, however, that the better reasoned position, contrary to that held in *Netcom,* is presented in *Playboy Enterprises, Inc. v. Frena,* 839 F.Supp. 1552, 1555–59 (M.D.Fla.1993), which held a computer bulletin board service provider liable for the copyright infringement when it failed to prevent the placement of plaintiff's copyrighted photographs in its system, despite any proof that the provider had any knowledge of the infringing activities.

Although we find the *Netcom* court reasoning more persuasive, the ultimate conclusion on this point is controlled by Congress' codification of the *Netcom* principles in Title II of the DMCA. As the House Report for that Act states,

> The bill distinguishes between direct infringement and secondary liability, treating each separately. This structure is consistent with evolving case law, and appropriate in light of the different legal bases for and policies behind the different forms of liability. As to direct infringement, liability is ruled out for passive, automatic acts engaged in through a technological process initiated by another. Thus the bill essentially codifies the result in the leading and most thoughtful judicial decision to date: *Religious Technology Center v. Netcom On–Line Communication Services, Inc.,* 907 F.Supp. 1361 (N.D.Cal.1995). In doing so, it overrules these aspects of *Playboy Enterprises, Inc. v. Frena,* 839 F.Supp. 1552 (M.D.Fla.1993), insofar as that case suggests that such acts by service providers could constitute direct infringement, and provides certainty that *Netcom* and its progeny, so far only a few district court cases, will be the law of the land.

H.R.Rep. No. 105–551(I), at 11 (1998). Accordingly, we address only ALS Scan's claims brought under the DMCA itself.

III

For its principal argument, ALS Scan contends that it substantially complied with the notification requirements of the DMCA and thereby denied RemarQ the "safe harbor" from copyright infringement liability granted by that Act. *See* 17 U.S.C. § 512(c)(3)(A) (setting forth notification requirements). It asserts that because its notification was sufficient to put RemarQ on notice of its infringement activities, RemarQ lost its service-provider immunity from infringement liability. It argues that the district court's application of the DMCA was overly strict and that

Congress did not intend to permit Internet providers to avoid copyright infringement liability "merely because a cease and desist notice failed to technically comply with the DMCA."

RemarQ argues in response that it did not have "knowledge of the infringing activity as a matter of law," stating that the DMCA protects it from liability because "ALS Scan failed to identify the infringing works in compliance with the Act, and RemarQ falls within the 'safe harbor' provisions of the Act." It notes that ALS Scan never provided RemarQ or the district court with the identity of the pictures forming the basis of its copyright infringement claim.

These contentions of the parties present the issue of whether ALS Scan complied with the notification requirements of the DMCA so as to deny RemarQ the safe-harbor defense to copyright infringement liability afforded by that Act.

Title II of the DMCA, designated the "Online Copyright Infringement Limitation Act," DMCA, § 201, Pub.L. 105–304, 112 Stat. 2877 (1998) (codified at 17 U.S.C. § 101 note), defines limitations of liability for copyright infringement to which Internet service providers might otherwise be exposed. The Act defines a service provider broadly to include any provider of "online services or network access, or the operator of facilities therefor," including any entity providing "digital online communications, between or among points specified by user, of material of the user's choosing, without modification to the content of the material as sent or received." 17 U.S.C. § 512(k). Neither party to this case suggests that RemarQ is not an Internet service provider for purposes of the Act.

The liability-limiting provision applicable here, 17 U.S.C. § 512(c), gives Internet service providers a safe harbor from liability for "infringement of copyright by reason of the storage at the direction of a user of material that resides on a system or network controlled or operated by or for the service provider" as long as the service provider can show that: (1) it has neither actual knowledge that its system contains infringing materials nor an awareness of facts or circumstances from which infringement is apparent, or it has expeditiously removed or disabled access to infringing material upon obtaining actual knowledge of infringement; (2) it receives no financial benefit directly attributable to infringing activity; *and* (3) it responded expeditiously to remove or disable access to material claimed to be infringing after receiving from the copyright holder a notification conforming with requirements of § 512(c)(3). *Id.* § 512(c)(1).[2] Thus, to qualify for this safe harbor protec-

---

2. Section 512(c)(1) provides in full:

(c) Information residing on systems or networks at direction of users.—

(1) In general.—A service provider shall not be liable for monetary relief, or, except as provided in subsection (j), for injunctive or other equitable relief, for infringement of copyright by reason of the storage at the direction of a user of material that resides on a system or network controlled or operated by or for the service provider, if the service provider—

(A)(i) does not have actual knowledge that the material or an activity using the

tion, the Internet service provider must demonstrate that it has met all three of the safe harbor requirements, and a showing under the first prong—the lack of actual or constructive knowledge—is prior to and separate from the showings that must be made under the second and third prongs.

In this case, the district court evaluated the adequacy given to RemarQ under the third prong only. Despite the fact the district court stated it was treating RemarQ's motion as a motion to dismiss, rather than as a motion for summary judgment, the court's memorandum opinion fails to mention the allegation made in ALS Scan's complaint that RemarQ had *actual* knowledge of the infringing nature of the two subject newsgroups even before being contacted by ALS Scan, an allegation denied by RemarQ. Clearly, had the court truly been evaluating ALS Scan's complaint under a 12(b)(6) standard of review, it would necessarily have had to accept ALS Scan's allegation as proven for purposes of testing the adequacy of the complaint, *see Eastern Shore Markets, Inc. v. J.D. Associates Ltd. Partnership, WWM,* 213 F.3d 175, 180 (4th Cir. 2000), and consequently been required to rule in favor of ALS Scan under the first prong.

Even if we were to treat the district court's order as disposing of a motion for summary judgment, and not a motion to dismiss, the court still could not, as a matter of law, have resolved the conflicting affidavits about actual knowledge. Resolving whether the court actually treated the motion as one to dismiss or for summary judgment is not necessary, however, because we conclude that ALS Scan substantially complied with the third prong, thereby denying RemarQ its safe harbor defense.

In evaluating the third prong, requiring RemarQ to remove materials following "notification," the district court concluded that ALS Scan's notice was defective in failing to comply strictly with two of the six requirements of a notification—(1) that ALS Scan's notice include "a list of [infringing] works" contained on the RemarQ site and (2) that the notice identify the infringing works in sufficient detail to enable RemarQ to locate and disable them. 17 U.S.C. § 512(c)(3)(A)(ii), (iii).[3]

---

material on the system or network is infringing;

(ii) in the absence of such actual knowledge, is not aware of facts or circumstances from which infringing activity is apparent; or

(iii) upon obtaining such knowledge or awareness, acts expeditiously to remove, or disable access to, the material;

(B) does not receive a financial benefit directly attributable to the infringing activity, in a case in which the service provider has the right and ability to control such activity; and

(C) upon notification of claimed infringement as described in paragraph (3), responds expeditiously to remove, or dis-

able access to, the material that is claimed to be infringing or to be the subject of infringing activity.

3. Section 512(c)(3)(A)(ii), (iii) provides:

(3) Elements of notification.—

(A) To be effective under this subsection, a notification of claimed infringement must be a written communication provided to the designated agent of a service provider that includes substantially the following:

* * *

(ii) Identification of the copyrighted work claimed to have been infringed, or, if multiple copyrighted works at a

In support of the district court's conclusion, RemarQ points to the fact that ALS Scan never provided it with a "representative list" of the infringing photographs, as required by § 512(c)(3)(A)(ii), nor did it identify those photographs with sufficient detail to enable RemarQ to locate and disable them, as required by § 512(c)(3)(A)(iii). RemarQ buttresses its contention with the observation that not all materials at the offending sites contained material to which ALS Scan held the copyrights. RemarQ's affidavit states in this regard:

> Some, but not all, of the pictures users have posted on these sites appear to be ALS Scan pictures. It also appears that users have posted other non-ALS Scan's erotic images on these newsgroups. The articles in these newsgroups also contain text messages, many of which discuss the adult images posted on the newsgroups.

ALS Scan responds that the two sites in question—"alt.als" and "alt.binaries.pictures.erotica.als"–were created solely for the purpose of publishing and exchanging ALS Scan's copyrighted images. It points out that the address of the newsgroup is defined by ALS Scan's name. As one of its affidavits states:

> [RemarQ's] subscribers going onto the two offending newsgroups for the purpose of violating [ALS Scan's] copyrights, are actually aware of the copyrighted status of [ALS Scan's] material because (1) each newsgroup has "als" as part of its title, and (2) each photograph belonging to [ALS Scan] has [ALS Scan's] name and/or the copyright symbol next to it.

> Each of these two newsgroups was created by unknown persons for the illegal purpose of trading the copyrighted pictures of [ALS Scan] to one another without the need for paying to either (1) become members of [ALS Scan's] web site(s) or (2) purchasing the CD ROMs produced by[ALS Scan].

ALS Scan presses the contention that these two sites serve no other purpose than to distribute ALS Scan's copyrighted materials and therefore, by directing RemarQ to these sites, it has directed RemarQ to a representative list of infringing materials.

The DMCA was enacted both to preserve copyright enforcement on the Internet and to provide immunity to service providers from copyright infringement liability for "passive," "automatic" actions in which a service provider's system engages through a technological process initiated by another without the knowledge of the service provider. H.R. Conf. Rep. No. 105–796, at 72 (1998), *reprinted in* 1998 U.S.C.C.A.N. 649; H.R.Rep. No. 105–551(I), at 11 (1998). This immunity, however, is not presumptive, but granted only to "innocent" service providers who can prove they do not have actual or constructive knowledge of the

single online site are covered by a single notification, a representative list of such works at that site.

(iii) Identification of the material that is claimed to be infringing or to be

the subject of infringing activity and that is to be removed or access to which is to be disabled, and information reasonably sufficient to permit the service provider to locate the material.

infringement, as defined under any of the three prongs of 17 U.S.C. § 512(c)(1). The DMCA's protection of an innocent service provider disappears at the moment the service provider loses its innocence, i.e., at the moment it becomes aware that a third party is using its system to infringe. At that point, the Act shifts responsibility to the service provider to disable the infringing matter, "preserv[ing] the strong incentives for service providers and copyright owners to cooperate to detect and deal with copyright infringements that take place in the digital networked environment." H.R. Conf. Rep. No. 105–796, at 72 (1998), *reprinted in* 1998 U.S.C.C.A.N. 649. In the spirit of achieving a balance between the responsibilities of the service provider and the copyright owner, the DMCA requires that a copyright owner put the service provider on notice in a detailed manner but allows notice by means that comport with the prescribed format only "substantially," rather than perfectly. The Act states: "To be effective under this subsection, a notification of claimed infringement must be a written communication provided to the designated agent of a service provider that includes *substantially* the following. . . ." 17 U.S.C. § 512(c)(3)(A) (emphasis added). In addition to substantial compliance, the notification requirements are relaxed to the extent that, with respect to multiple works, not all must be identified—only a "representative" list. *See id.* § 512(c)(3)(A)(ii). And with respect to location information, the copyright holder must provide information that is "*reasonably* sufficient" to permit the service provider to "locate" this material. *Id.* § 512(c)(3)(A)(iii) (emphasis added). This subsection specifying the requirements of a notification does not seek to burden copyright holders with the responsibility of identifying every infringing work—or even most of them—when multiple copyrights are involved. Instead, the requirements are written so as to reduce the burden of holders of multiple copyrights who face extensive infringement of their works. Thus, when a letter provides notice equivalent to a list of representative works that can be easily identified by the service provider, the notice substantially complies with the notification requirements.

In this case, ALS Scan provided RemarQ with information that (1) identified two sites created for the sole purpose of publishing ALS Scan's copyrighted works, (2) asserted that virtually all the images at the two sites were its copyrighted material, and (3) referred RemarQ to two web addresses where RemarQ could find pictures of ALS Scan's models and obtain ALS Scan's copyright information. In addition, it noted that material at the site could be identified as ALS Scan's material because the material included ALS Scan's "name and/or copyright symbol next to it." We believe that with this information, ALS Scan substantially complied with the notification requirement of providing a representative list of infringing material as well as information reasonably sufficient to enable RemarQ to locate the infringing material. To the extent that ALS Scan's claims about infringing materials prove to be false, RemarQ has remedies for any injury it suffers as a result of removing or disabling noninfringing material. *See* 17 U.S.C. § 512(f), (g).

Accordingly, we reverse the district court's ruling granting summary judgment in favor of RemarQ on the basis of ALS Scan's non-compliance with the notification provisions of 17 U.S.C. § 512(c)(3)(A)(ii) and (iii). Because our ruling only removes the safe harbor defense, we remand for further proceedings on ALS Scan's copyright infringement claims and any other affirmative defenses that RemarQ may have. * * * *

Notes

1.   Does section 512 add measurably to the security of an online service provider? Is it superior to the conventional analysis of indirect or vicarious liability (under such cases as *Netcom* and *Fonovisa*) in striking a balance between the interests of service providers and their clients on the one hand, and copyright proprietors on the other?

2.   In *Hendrickson v. eBay, Inc.*, 165 F.Supp.2d 1082 (C.D.Cal.2001) (summary judgment for defendant), the producer of the documentary *Manson*, sued online auction site provider eBay for unauthorized sale of the documentary. The court found that the plaintiff's pre-suit notice was improper, and therefore did not satisfy the notice requirement necessary to trigger an affirmative duty to obtain 512 safe harbor protection. The court also found voluntary monitoring of the web service inadequate to constitute "right and ability to control."

3.   In *Costar Group Inc. v. LoopNet, Inc.*, 172 F.Supp.2d 747 (D.Md. 2001)(summary judgment for defendant denied), plaintiff Costar Group Inc. charged that the defendant Loopnet, an online service provider, improperly allowed its users to post Costar's real estate listings. The court found that Loopnet had received notification of the alleged infringement and that material issues of fact remained as to the adequacy of Loopnet's removal policy.

After additional proceedings, however, and on stipulation by the parties, the district court dismissed all claims against Loop–Net except direct infringement, as to which the court had previously granted summary judgment in favor of Loop–Net, relying on the analysis in *Netcom* (excerpted in the main text at page 987). On appeal, the Fourth Circuit affirmed the district court's ruling. The Fourth Circuit held that the DMCA is not preemptive as to issues of direct infringement under sections 106 and 501 of the Copyright Act, and does not preclude *Netcom* analysis. Instead, Congress enacted the DMCA to provide a "safe harbor" to internet service providers who comply with its terms:

> As provided in subsection (*l*), Section 512 is not intended to imply that a service provider is or is not liable as an infringer either for conduct for conduct that qualifies for a limitation of liability or for conduct that fails to so qualify. Rather, the limitations of liability apply if the provider is found to be liable under existing principles of law.

Costar Group, Inc. v. Loopnet, Inc., 373 F.3d 544, 553 (2004).

4.   In *Ellison v. Robertson*, 357 F.3d 1072 (9th Cir. 2004), author Harlan Ellison sued America Online when AOL subscribers accessed copies of his copyrighted stories posted on a peer-to-peer file sharing network by a

third party. Plaintiff claimed vicarious and contributory copyright infringement. AOL claimed safe harbor under the DMCA. AOL kept the postings on its servers for two weeks. The appellate court said that AOL was not vicariously liable but that there were issues of fact as to contributory infringement and whether the AOL qualified for safe harbor under 17 U.S.C. § 512(i). The court ruled out vicarious infringement because there was insufficient evidence of direct financial benefit to AOL. Because of evidence of telephone notification and the fact AOL unreasonably changed its email address for reporting copyright violations, the court said a jury could find that AOL should have known of the direct infringement yet contributorily infringed by not blocking access to the stories.

At issue regarding safe harbor was whether AOL reasonably implemented a policy for terminating repeat infringers as required by § 512(i). By not providing a working email address to receive infringement complaints a reasonable jury could conclude that AOL failed to fulfill the requirements of § 512(i). If a jury were to find that AOL met this threshold, the court said AOL would qualify for safe harbor under § 512(a) which limits liability for "transitory digital network communications." The court held that fourteen days qualified as "intermediate or transient."

5. In *Perfect 10, Inc. v. Cybernet Ventures, Inc.*, 213 F.Supp.2d 1146 (C.D.Cal.2002)(motion to dismiss denied), the court held that the complaint need not state every copyright infringed, and rejected the defendant's safe harbor defense under Section 512 (c)(3). Perfect 10, an adult magazine that maintained an Internet web site, alleged infringement of a large number of its copyrighted images by defendant Cybernet, an online service provider serving as a gateway assurance site for other web sites. The court held that Cybernet had fair notice of the allegations and type of infringement alleged in the complaint. The court rejected Cybernet's argument that it could not be held liable for direct infringement committed by users of its service, distinguishing *Religious Technology Center v. Netcom On–Line Communication Services, Inc.*, 923 F.Supp. 1231 (N.D.Cal.1995), and Bernstein v. J.C. Penney Inc., 50 U.S.P.Q.2d 1063 (C.D.Cal.1998). In this case, the court noted, Cybernet was a partner with the allegedly infringing sites and could therefore be liable for infringement based on its links to other sites.

6. In contrast to an internet service provider such as AOL, Aimster is not entitled to the safe harbor provision of the DMCA. The Seventh Circuit stated that:

> [t]he common element of [the DMCA's] safe harbors is that the service provider must do what it can reasonably be asked to do to prevent the use of its service by 'repeat infringers' 17 U.S.C. § 512(i)(1)(A). Far from doing anything to discourage repeat infringers of the plaintiff's copyrights, Aimster invited them to do so, showed them how they could do so with ease using its system, and by teaching its users how to encrypt their unlawful distribution of copyrighted materials disabled itself from doing anything to prevent infringement.

In Re Aimster, 334 F.3d 643 (7th Cir. 2003). [Excerpts from this case dealing with other issues appear in Chapter 20, Section C.]

7. In *Gordon v. Nextel Communications*, 345 F.3d 922 (6th Cir. 2003), the Sixth Circuit held that Nextel's use of Gordon's dental illustrations were

de minimis, and therefore did not violate his copyright, because they appeared in the advertisements only briefly and mainly out of focus. Nextel also did not violate sections 1202(b)(1) and (3) of the DMCA because there was no proof that Nextel, nor anyone for whom they were vicariously liable, intentionally removed the copyright management information or knew that the copyright management information had been removed without the permission of the author.

2. CIRCUMVENTING ANTI–COPYING TECHNOLOGY OR ALTERING COPYRIGHT MANAGEMENT INFORMATION

In order to bring the United States into compliance with the 1996 WIPO treaties, Congress also included in the DMCA new provisions establishing liability for circumventing anti-copying technology. Title I of the DMCA, the "WIPO Copyright and Performances and Phonograms Treaties Implementation Act of 1998," created a new Chapter 12 of Title 17 which prohibits circumvention of anti-copying technology (new 17 U.S.C. § 1201) and also prohibits falsification, removal or alteration of "copyright management information" which identifies a copyrighted work on computer networks (new 17 U.S.C. § 1202). The liability standards and remedies contained in these provisions are grounded alternatively in Commerce Clause power, and differ from those found in the current copyright provisions of Title 17. The anti-circumvention provisions are subject to narrow limitations and exemptions applicable to reverse engineering, lawful government investigations, encryption research, security testing, investigations relating to personal privacy, activities of nonprofit libraries, archives, educational institutions, and (with respect to remedies only) "innocent" violations. The anti-circumvention provisions also prohibit the manufacturing or distribution of consumer-oriented analog video cassette recording devices which fail to incorporate devices that give effect to the copy protection features contained in prerecorded videocassettes and television broadcasts. The prohibitions of Title I are enforced by civil remedies as well as criminal penalties (17 U.S.C. §§ 1203 and 1204, respectively).

In an early case construing the new copyright management information provisions (*Kelly v. Arriba Soft Corp.*, 77 F.Supp.2d 1116 (C.D.Cal. 1999)), the district court granted the defendant's motion for summary judgment on a section 1202(b) claim, holding that this provision of the DMCA was not violated by a "visual search engine" that produced thumbnail images of photographs appearing on the plaintiff's website without including the plaintiff's copyright management information— which, in this case, consisted of standard copyright notices appearing in the text that accompanied the images on the plaintiff's website (and thus had not been incorporated into the images themselves). The court held that section 1202(b)(1) "applies only to the removal of copyright management information on a plaintiff's product or original work," and that the defendant's removal of this information was not "intentional" within the meaning of that section. The court also found no liability under section 1202(b)(3), which applies only if a defendant "knows or should know" that its actions "will lead to infringement of Plaintiff's copyrights." *Id.* at 1122. This portion of the court's decision was affirmed by the Ninth Circuit. See *Kelly v. Arriba Soft Corp.*, 280 F.3d 934 (9th Cir.2002)(affirming and reversing on other issues).

The DMCA's anti-circumvention provisions were challenged in major litigation that required an intricate construction of the provisions themselves, while also squarely raising substantial constitutional questions. On appeal, the Second Circuit paid particular attention to the First Amendment issues:

UNIVERSAL CITY STUDIOS, INC. v. CORLEY

United States Court of Appeals, Second Circuit 2001.
273 F.3d 429.

NEWMAN, CIRCUIT JUDGE.

When the Framers of the First Amendment prohibited Congress from making any law "abridging the freedom of speech," they were not thinking about computers, computer programs, or the Internet. But neither were they thinking about radio, television, or movies. Just as the inventions at the beginning and middle of the 20th century presented new First Amendment issues, so does the cyber revolution at the end of that century. This appeal raises significant First Amendment issues concerning one aspect of computer technology—encryption to protect materials in digital form from unauthorized access. The appeal challenges the constitutionality of the Digital Millennium Copyright Act ("DMCA"), 17 U.S.C. § 1201 *et seq.* (Supp. V 1999) and the validity of an injunction entered to enforce the DMCA. * * *

[The defendant Corley, proprietor and editor of defendant *2600* Magazine] renews his constitutional challenges on appeal. Specifically, he argues primarily that: (1) the DMCA oversteps limits in the Copyright Clause on the duration of copyright protection; (2) the DMCA as applied to his dissemination of DeCSS violates the First Amendment because computer code is "speech" entitled to full First Amendment protection and the DMCA fails to survive the exacting scrutiny accorded statutes that regulate "speech"; and (3) the DMCA violates the First Amendment and the Copyright Clause by unduly obstructing the "fair use" of copyrighted materials. Corley also argues that the statute is susceptible to, and should therefore be given, a narrow interpretation that avoids alleged constitutional objections. * * *

In November 1999, Corley wrote and placed on his web site, 2600.com, an article about the DeCSS phenomenon. His web site is an auxiliary to the print magazine, *2600: The Hacker Quarterly*, which Corley has been publishing since 1984.[7] As the name suggests, the magazine is designed for "hackers," as is the web site. While the magazine and the web site cover some issues of general interest to

---

7. Defendant 2600 Enterprises, Inc., is the company Corley incorporated to run the magazine, maintain the web site, and manage related endeavors like merchandising.

computer users—such as threats to online privacy—the focus of the publications is on the vulnerability of computer security systems, and more specifically, how to exploit that vulnerability in order to circumvent the security systems. Representative articles explain how to steal an Internet domain name and how to break into the computer systems at Federal Express. *Universal I,* 111 F.Supp.2d at 308–09.

Corley's article about DeCSS detailed how CSS was cracked, and described the movie industry's efforts to shut down web sites posting DeCSS. It also explained that DeCSS could be used to copy DVDs. At the end of the article, the Defendants posted copies of the object and source code of DeCSS. In Corley's words, he added the code to the story because "in a journalistic world, ... [y]ou have to show your evidence ... and particularly in the magazine that I work for, people want to see specifically what it is that we are referring to," including "what evidence ... we have" that there is in fact technology that circumvents CSS. Trial Tr. at 823. Writing about DeCSS without including the DeCSS code would have been, to Corley, "analogous to printing a story about a picture and not printing the picture." *Id.* at 825. Corley also added to the article links that he explained would take the reader to other web sites where DeCSS could be found. *Id.* at 791, 826, 827, 848.

2600.com was only one of hundreds of web sites that began posting DeCSS near the end of 1999. The movie industry tried to stem the tide by sending cease-and-desist letters to many of these sites. These efforts met with only partial success; a number of sites refused to remove DeCSS. In January 2000, the studios filed this lawsuit.[8] * * *

DISCUSSION

I. Narrow Construction to Avoid Constitutional Doubt

The Appellants first argue that, because their constitutional arguments are at least substantial, we should interpret the statute narrowly so as to avoid constitutional problems. They identify three different instances of alleged ambiguity in the statute that they claim provide an opportunity for such a narrow interpretation.

First, they contend that subsection 1201(c)(1), which provides that "[n]othing in this section shall affect rights, remedies, limitations or defenses to copyright infringement, including fair use, under this title," can be read to allow the circumvention of encryption technology protecting copyrighted material when the material will be put to "fair uses" exempt from copyright liability.[12] We disagree that subsection 1201(c)(1) permits such a reading. Instead, it simply clarifies that the DMCA targets the *circumvention* of digital walls guarding copyrighted material

---

8. The lawsuit was filed against Corley, Shawn C. Reimerdes, and Roman Kazan. 2600 Enterprises, Inc., was later added as a defendant. At an earlier stage of the litigation, the action was settled as to Reimerdes and Kazan. *See Universal II,* 111 F.Supp.2d at 346.

12. In Part IV, *infra,* we consider the Appellants' claim that the DMCA is unconstitutional because of its effect on opportunities for fair use of copyrighted materials.

(and trafficking in circumvention tools), but does not concern itself with the *use* of those materials after circumvention has occurred. Subsection 1201(c)(1) ensures that the DMCA is not read to prohibit the "fair use" of information just because that information was obtained in a manner made illegal by the DMCA. The Appellants' much more expansive interpretation of subsection 1201(c)(1) is not only outside the range of plausible readings of the provision, but is also clearly refuted by the statute's legislative history.[13] *See Commodity Futures Trading Commission v. Schor,* 478 U.S. 833, 841, 106 S.Ct. 3245, 92 L.Ed.2d 675 (1986) (constitutional doubt canon "does not give a court the prerogative to ignore the legislative will").

Congress also sought to implement a balanced approach through statutory provisions that leave limited areas of breathing space for fair use. A good example is subsection 1201(d), which allows a library or educational institution to circumvent a digital wall in order to determine whether it wishes legitimately to obtain the material behind the wall. *See* H.R.Rep. No. 105–551, pt. 2, at 41. It would be strange for Congress to open small, carefully limited windows for circumvention to permit fair use in subsection 1201(d) if it then meant to exempt in subsection 1201(c)(1) *any* circumvention necessary for fair use.

Second, the Appellants urge a narrow construction of the DMCA because of subsection 1201(c)(4), which provides that "[n]othing in this section shall enlarge or diminish any rights of free speech or the press for activities using consumer electronics, telecommunications, or computing products." This language is clearly precatory: Congress could not "diminish" constitutional rights of free speech even if it wished to, and the fact that Congress also expressed a reluctance to "enlarge" those rights cuts against the Appellants' effort to infer a narrowing construction of the Act from this provision.

Third, the Appellants argue that an individual who buys a DVD has the "authority of the copyright owner" to view the DVD, and therefore is exempted from the DMCA pursuant to subsection 1201(a)(3)(A) when the buyer circumvents an encryption technology in order to view the DVD on a competing platform (such as Linux). The basic flaw in this argument is that it misreads subsection 1201(a)(3)(A). That provision exempts from liability those who would "decrypt" an encrypted DVD

---

13. The legislative history of the enacted bill makes quite clear that Congress intended to adopt a "balanced" approach to accommodating both piracy and fair use concerns, eschewing the quick fix of simply exempting from the statute all circumventions for fair use. H.R.Rep. No. 105–551, pt. 2, at 25 (1998). It sought to achieve this goal principally through the use of what it called a "fail-safe" provision in the statute, authorizing the Librarian of Congress to exempt certain users from the anti-circumvention provision when it becomes evident that in practice, the statute is adversely affecting certain kinds of fair use. *See* 17 U.S.C. § 1201(a)(1)(C); H.R.Rep. No. 105–551, pt. 2, at 36 ("Given the threat of a diminution of otherwise lawful access to works and information, the Committee on Commerce believes that a 'fail-safe' mechanism is required. This mechanism would ... allow the ... [waiver of the anti-circumvention provisions], for limited time periods, if necessary to prevent a diminution in the availability to individual users of a particular category of copyrighted materials.").

with the authority of a copyright owner, not those who would "view" a DVD with the authority of a copyright owner.[14] In any event, the Defendants offered no evidence that the Plaintiffs have either explicitly or implicitly authorized DVD buyers to circumvent encryption technology to support use on multiple platforms.[15]

We conclude that the anti-trafficking and anti-circumvention provisions of the DMCA are not susceptible to the narrow interpretations urged by the Appellants. We therefore proceed to consider the Appellants' constitutional claims.

II.   Constitutional Challenge Based on the Copyright Clause

In a footnote to their brief, the Appellants appear to contend that the DMCA, as construed by the District Court, exceeds the constitutional authority of Congress to grant authors copyrights for a "limited time," U.S. Const. art. I, § 8, cl. 8, because it "empower[s] copyright owners to effectively secure perpetual protection by mixing public domain works with copyrighted materials, then locking both up with technological protection measures." Brief for Appellants at 42 n.30. This argument is elaborated in the *amici curiae* brief filed by Prof. Julie E. Cohen on behalf of herself and 45 other intellectual property law professors. *See also* David Nimmer, *A Riff on Fair Use in the Digital Millennium Copyright Act*, 148 U. Pa. L. Rev. 673, 712 (2000). For two reasons, the argument provides no basis for disturbing the judgment of the District Court.

First, we have repeatedly ruled that arguments presented to us only in a footnote are not entitled to appellate consideration. *Concourse Rehabilitation & Nursing Center Inc. v. DeBuono*, 179 F.3d 38, 47 (2d Cir.1999); *United States v. Mapp*, 170 F.3d 328, 333 n. 8 (2d Cir.1999); *United States v. Restrepo*, 986 F.2d 1462, 1463 (2d Cir.1993). Although an *amicus* brief can be helpful in elaborating issues properly presented by the parties, it is normally not a method for injecting new issues into an appeal, at least in cases where the parties are competently represented by counsel. *See, e.g., Concourse Center,* 179 F.3d at 47.

Second, to whatever extent the argument might have merit at some future time in a case with a properly developed record, the argument is entirely premature and speculative at this time on this record. There is not even a claim, much less evidence, that any Plaintiff has sought to

---

14. This is actually what subsection 1201(a)(3)(A) means when read in conjunction with the *anti-circumvention* provisions. When read together with the *anti-trafficking* provisions, subsection 1201(a)(3)(A) frees an individual to traffic in encryption technology designed or marketed to circumvent an encryption measure if the owner of the material protected by the encryption measure authorizes that circumvention.

15. Even if the Defendants had been able to offer such evidence, and even if they could have demonstrated that DeCSS was

"primarily designed . . . for the purpose of" playing DVDs on multiple platforms (and therefore not for the purpose of "circumventing a technological measure"), a proposition questioned by Judge Kaplan, *see Universal I,* 111 F.Supp.2d at 311 n. 79, the Defendants would defeat liability only under subsection 1201(a)(2)(A). They would still be vulnerable to liability under subsection 1201(a)(2)(C), because they "marketed" DeCSS for the copying of DVDs, not just for the playing of DVDs on multiple platforms. *See, e.g.,* Trial Tr. at 820.

prevent copying of public domain works, or that the injunction prevents the Defendants from copying such works. As Judge Kaplan noted, the possibility that encryption would preclude access to public domain works "does not yet appear to be a problem, although it may emerge as one in the future." *Universal I*, 111 F.Supp.2d at 338 n. 245.

III. Constitutional Challenges Based on the First Amendment

A. Applicable Principles

Last year, in one of our Court's first forays into First Amendment law in the digital age, we took an "evolutionary" approach to the task of tailoring familiar constitutional rules to novel technological circumstances, favoring "narrow" holdings that would permit the law to mature on a "case-by-case" basis. *See Name.Space, Inc. v. Network Solutions, Inc.*, 202 F.3d 573, 584 n. 11 (2d Cir.2000). In that spirit, we proceed, with appropriate caution, to consider the Appellants' First Amendment challenges by analyzing a series of preliminary issues the resolution of which provides a basis for adjudicating the specific objections to the DMCA and its application to DeCSS. These issues, which we consider only to the extent necessary to resolve the pending appeal, are whether computer code is speech, whether computer programs are speech, the scope of First Amendment protection for computer code, and the scope of First Amendment protection for decryption code. Based on our analysis of these issues, we then consider the Appellants' challenge to the injunction's provisions concerning posting and linking.

1. Code as Speech

Communication does not lose constitutional protection as "speech" simply because it is expressed in the language of computer code. Mathematical formulae and musical scores are written in "code," *i.e.,* symbolic notations not comprehensible to the uninitiated, and yet both are covered by the First Amendment. If someone chose to write a novel entirely in computer object code by using strings of 1's and 0's for each letter of each word, the resulting work would be no different for constitutional purposes than if it had been written in English. The "object code" version would be incomprehensible to readers outside the programming community (and tedious to read even for most within the community), but it would be no more incomprehensible than a work written in Sanskrit for those unversed in that language. The undisputed evidence reveals that even pure object code can be, and often is, read and understood by experienced programmers. And source code (in any of its various levels of complexity) can be read by many more. *See Universal I*, 111 F.Supp.2d at 326. Ultimately, however, the ease with which a work is comprehended is irrelevant to the constitutional inquiry. If computer code is distinguishable from conventional speech for First Amendment purposes, it is not because it is written in an obscure language. *See Junger v. Daley*, 209 F.3d 481, 484 (6th Cir.2000).

2. Computer Programs as Speech

Of course, computer code is not likely to be the language in which a work of literature is written. Instead, it is primarily the language for programs executable by a computer. These programs are essentially instructions to a computer. In general, programs may give instructions either to perform a task or series of tasks when initiated by a single (or double) click of a mouse or, once a program is operational ("launched"), to manipulate data that the user enters into the computer.[16] Whether computer code that gives a computer instructions is "speech" within the meaning of the First Amendment requires consideration of the scope of the Constitution's protection of speech.

The First Amendment provides that "Congress shall make no law ... abridging the freedom of speech.... " U.S. Const. amend. I. "Speech" is an elusive term, and judges and scholars have debated its bounds for two centuries. Some would confine First Amendment protection to political speech. *E.g.,* Robert Bork, *Neutral Principles and Some First Amendment Problems,* 47 Ind. L.J. 1 (1971). Others would extend it further to artistic expression. *E.g.,* Marci A. Hamilton, *Art Speech,* 49 Vand. L. Rev. 73 (1996).

Whatever might be the merits of these and other approaches, the law has not been so limited. Even dry information, devoid of advocacy, political relevance, or artistic expression, has been accorded First Amendment protection. *See Miller v. California,* 413 U.S. 15, 34, 93 S.Ct. 2607, 37 L.Ed.2d 419 (1973) ("The First Amendment protects works which, taken as a whole, have serious literary, artistic, political, or *scientific* value.... " (emphasis added)); *Roth v. United States,* 354 U.S. 476, 484, 77 S.Ct. 1304, 1 L.Ed.2d 1498 (1957) (First Amendment embraces "[a]ll ideas having even the slightest redeeming social importance," including the " 'advancement of truth, science, morality, and arts in general.' "(quoting 1 Journals of the Continental Congress 108 (1774))); *Board of Trustees of Leland Stanford Junior University v. Sullivan,* 773 F.Supp. 472, 474 (D.D.C.1991) ("It is ... settled ... that the First Amendment protects scientific expression and debate just as it protects political and artistic expression."); *see also* Kent Greenawalt, *Speech, Crime and the Uses of Language* 85 (1989) ("[A]ssertions of fact generally fall within a principle of freedom of speech.... "); *cf. Virginia State Board of Pharmacy v. Virginia Citizens Consumer Council, Inc.,* 425 U.S. 748, 763, 96 S.Ct. 1817, 48 L.Ed.2d 346 (1976) ("prescription drug price information" is "speech" because a consumer's interest in "the free flow of commercial information" may be "keener by far" than "his interest in the day's most urgent political debate").

Thus, for example, courts have subjected to First Amendment scrutiny restrictions on the dissemination of technical scientific information,

---

16. For example, a program (or part of a program) will give a computer the direction to "launch" a word-processing program like WordPerfect when the icon for WordPerfect is clicked; a program like WordPerfect will give the computer directions to display letters on a screen and manipulate them according to the computer user's preferences whenever the appropriate keys are struck.

United States v. Progressive, Inc., 467 F.Supp. 990 (W.D.Wis.1979), and scientific research, *Stanford University,* 773 F.Supp. at 473, and attempts to regulate the publication of instructions,[17] *see, e.g., United States v. Raymond,* 228 F.3d 804, 815 (7th Cir.2000) (First Amendment does not protect instructions for violating the tax laws); *United States v. Dahlstrom,* 713 F.2d 1423, 1428 (9th Cir.1983) (same); *Herceg v. Hustler Magazine, Inc.,* 814 F.2d 1017, 1020–25 (5th Cir.1987) (First Amendment protects instructions for engaging in a dangerous sex act); *United States v. Featherston,* 461 F.2d 1119, 1122–23 (5th Cir.1972) (First Amendment does not protect instructions for building an explosive device); *see also Bernstein v. United States Department of State,* 922 F.Supp. 1426, 1435 (N.D.Cal.1996) ("Instructions, do-it-yourself manuals, [and] recipes" are all "speech").[18]

Computer programs are not exempted from the category of First Amendment speech simply because their instructions require use of a computer. A recipe is no less "speech" because it calls for the use of an oven, and a musical score is no less "speech" because it specifies performance on an electric guitar. Arguably distinguishing computer programs from conventional language instructions is the fact that programs are executable on a computer. But the fact that a program has the capacity to direct the functioning of a computer does not mean that it lacks the additional capacity to convey information, and it is the conveying of information that renders instructions "speech" for purposes of the First Amendment.[19] The information conveyed by most "instructions" is how to perform a task.

Instructions such as computer code, which are intended to be executable by a computer, will often convey information capable of comprehension and assessment by a human being.[20] A programmer

---

17. We note that instructions are of varied types. *See Vartuli,* 228 F.3d at 111. "Orders" from one member of a conspiracy to another member, or from a superior to a subordinate, might resemble instructions but nonetheless warrant less or even no constitutional protection because their capacity to inform is meager, and because it is unlikely that the recipient of the order will engage in the "intercession of . . . mind or . . . will" characteristic of the sort of communication between two parties protected by the Constitution, *see id.* at 111–12 (noting that statements in the form of orders, instructions, or commands cannot claim "talismanic immunity from constitutional limitations" but "should be subjected to careful and particularized analysis to ensure that no speech entitled to First Amendment protection fails to receive it"); Kent Greenawalt, *Speech and Crime,* Am. B. Found. Res. J. 645, 743–44 (1980).

18. These cases almost always concern instructions on how to commit illegal acts. Several courts have concluded that such instructions fall outside the First Amend-

ment. However, these conclusions never rest on the fact that the speech took the form of instructions, but rather on the fact that the instructions counseled the listener how to commit illegal acts. *See, e.g., Rice v. Paladin Enterprises, Inc.,* 128 F.3d 233, 247–49 (4th Cir.1997); *United States v. Barnett,* 667 F.2d 835, 842 (9th Cir.1982). None of these opinions even hints that instructions are a form of speech categorically outside the First Amendment.

19. Of course, we do not mean to suggest that the communication of "information" is a prerequisite of protected "speech." Protected speech may communicate, among other things, ideas, emotions, or thoughts. We identify "information" only because this is what computer programs most often communicate, in addition to giving directions to a computer.

20. However, in the rare case where a human's mental faculties do not intercede in executing the instructions, we have withheld protection. *See Vartuli,* 228 F.3d at 111.

reading a program learns information about instructing a computer, and might use this information to improve personal programming skills and perhaps the craft of programming. Moreover, programmers communicating ideas to one another almost inevitably communicate in code, much as musicians use notes.[21] Limiting First Amendment protection of programmers to descriptions of computer code (but not the code itself) would impede discourse among computer scholars,[22] just as limiting protection for musicians to descriptions of musical scores (but not sequences of notes) would impede their exchange of ideas and expression. Instructions that communicate information comprehensible to a human qualify as speech whether the instructions are designed for execution by a computer or a human (or both).

Vartuli is not to the contrary. The defendants in *Vartuli* marketed a software program called "Recurrence," which would tell computer users when to buy or sell currency futures contracts if their computers were fed currency market rates. The Commodity Futures Trading Commission charged the defendants with violating federal law for, among other things, failing to register as commodity trading advisors for their distribution of the Recurrence software. The defendants maintained that Recurrence's cues to users to buy or sell were protected speech, and that the registration requirement as applied to Recurrence was a constitutionally suspect prior restraint. We rejected the defendants' constitutional claim, holding that Recurrence "in the form it was sold and marketed by the defendants" did not generate speech protected by the First Amendment. *Vartuli,* 228 F.3d at 111.

Essential to our ruling in *Vartuli* was the *manner* in which the defendants marketed the software and intended that it be used: the defendants told users of the software to follow the software's cues "with no second-guessing," *id.,* and intended that users follow Recurrence's commands "mechanically" and "without the intercession of the mind or the will of the recipient," *id.* We held that the values served by the First Amendment were not advanced by these instructions, even though the

---

21. Programmers use snippets of code to convey their ideas for new programs; economists and other creators of computer models publish the code of their models in order to demonstrate the models' vigor. Brief of *Amici Curiae* Dr. Harold Abelson *et al.* at 17; Brief of *Amici Curiae* Steven Bellovin *et al.* at 12–13; *see also Bernstein v. United States Department of Justice,* 176 F.3d 1132, 1141 (9th Cir.) (concluding that computer source code is speech because it is "the preferred means" of communication among computer programmers and cryptographers), *reh'g in banc granted and opinion withdrawn,* 192 F.3d 1308 (9th Cir.1999).

22. Reinforcing the conclusion that software programs qualify as "speech" for First Amendment purposes—even though they instruct computers—is the accelerated blurring of the line between "source code" and

conventional "speech." There already exist programs capable of translating English descriptions of a program into source code. Trial Tr. at 1101–02 (Testimony of Professor Andrew Appel). These programs are functionally indistinguishable from the compilers that routinely translate source code into object code. These new programs (still apparently rudimentary) hold the potential for turning "prose" instructions on how to write a computer program into the program itself. Even if there were an argument for exempting the latter from First Amendment protection, the former are clearly protected for the reasons set forth in the text. As technology becomes more sophisticated, instructions to other humans will increasingly be executable by computers as well.

instructions were expressed in words. *Id.* We acknowledged that some users would, despite the defendants' marketing, refuse to follow Recurrence's cues mechanically but instead would use the commands as a source of information and advice, and that, as to these users, Recurrence's cues might very "well have been 'speech.' "*Id.* at 111–12. Nevertheless, we concluded that the Government could require registration for Recurrence's intended use because such use was devoid of any constitutionally protected speech. *Id.* at 112.

Vartuli considered two ways in which a programmer might be said to communicate through code: to the user of the program (not necessarily protected) and to the computer (never protected).[23] However, this does not mean that *Vartuli* denied First Amendment protection to all computer programs. Since *Vartuli* limited its constitutional scrutiny to the code "as marketed," *i.e.,* as an automatic trading system, it did not have occasion to consider a third manner in which a programmer might communicate through code: to another programmer.

For all of these reasons, we join the other courts that have concluded that computer code, and computer programs constructed from code can merit First Amendment protection, *see Junger,* 209 F.3d at 484;[24] *Bernstein,* 922 F.Supp. at 1434–36; *see also Bernstein,* 176 F.3d at 1140–41; *Karn v. United States Department of State,* 925 F.Supp. 1, 9–10 (D.D.C.1996) (assuming, without deciding, that source code with English comments interspersed throughout is "speech"), although the scope of such protection remains to be determined.

3.   The Scope of First Amendment Protection for Computer Code

Having concluded that computer code conveying information is "speech" within the meaning of the First Amendment, we next consider, to a limited extent, the scope of the protection that code enjoys. As the District Court recognized, *Universal I,* 111 F.Supp.2d at 327, the scope of protection for speech generally depends on whether the restriction is imposed because of the content of the speech. Content-based restrictions

---

23. *Vartuli* reasoned that the interaction between "programming commands as triggers and semiconductors as a conduit," even though communication, is not "speech" within the meaning of the First Amendment and that the communication between Recurrence and a customer using it as intended was similarly not "speech." *Vartuli,* 228 F.3d at 111.

24. The reasoning of *Junger* has recently been criticized. *See* Orin S. Kerr, *Are We Overprotecting Code? Thoughts on First–Generation Internet Law,* 57 Wash. & Lee L. Rev. 1287 (2000). Prof. Kerr apprehends that if encryption code is First Amendment speech because it conveys "ideas about cryptography," *Junger,* 209 F.3d at 484, all code will be protected "because code will always convey information about itself." Kerr, *supra,* at 1291. That should not suf-

fice, he argues, because handing someone an object, for example, a padlock, is a good way of communicating how that object works, yet a padlock is not speech. *Id.* at 1291–92. However, code does not cease to be speech just because some objects that convey information are not speech. Both code and a padlock can convey information, but only code, because it uses a notational system comprehensible by humans, is communication that qualifies as speech. Prof. Kerr might be right that making the communication of ideas or information the test of whether code is speech provides First Amendment coverage to many, perhaps most, computer programs, but that is a consequence of the information-conveying capacity of the programs, not a reason for denying them First Amendment coverage.

are permissible only if they serve compelling state interests and do so by the least restrictive means available. *See Sable Communications of California, Inc. v. FCC,* 492 U.S. 115, 126, 109 S.Ct. 2829, 106 L.Ed.2d 93 (1989). A content-neutral restriction is permissible if it serves a substantial governmental interest, the interest is unrelated to the suppression of free expression, and the regulation is narrowly tailored, which "in this context requires ... that the means chosen do not 'burden substantially more speech than is necessary to further the government's legitimate interests.'" *Turner Broadcasting System, Inc. v. FCC,* 512 U.S. 622, 662, 114 S.Ct. 2445, 129 L.Ed.2d 497 (1994) (quoting *Ward v. Rock Against Racism,* 491 U.S. 781, 799, 109 S.Ct. 2746, 105 L.Ed.2d 661 (1989)).[25]

"[G]overnment regulation of expressive activity is 'content neutral' if it is justified without reference to the content of regulated speech." *Hill v. Colorado,* 530 U.S. 703, 720, 120 S.Ct. 2480, 147 L.Ed.2d 597 (2000). "The government's purpose is the controlling consideration. A regulation that serves purposes unrelated to the content of expression is deemed neutral, even if it has an incidental effect on some speakers or messages but not others." *Ward,* 491 U.S. at 791, 109 S.Ct. 2746. The Supreme Court's approach to determining content-neutrality appears to be applicable whether what is regulated is expression, *see id.* at 791–93, 109 S.Ct. 2746 (regulation of volume of music), conduct, *see O'Brien,* 391 U.S. at 377, 88 S.Ct. 1673, or any "activity" that can be said to combine speech and non-speech elements, *see Spence v. Washington,* 418 U.S. 405, 410–11, 94 S.Ct. 2727, 41 L.Ed.2d 842 (1974) (applying *O'Brien* to "activity" of displaying American flag hung upside down and decorated with a peace symbol).

To determine whether regulation of computer code is content-neutral, the initial inquiry must be whether the regulated activity is "sufficiently imbued with elements of communication to fall within the scope of the First ... Amendment[]." *Id.* at 409, 94 S.Ct. 2727; *see also Name.Space,* 202 F.3d at 585. Computer code, as we have noted, often conveys information comprehensible to human beings, even as it also directs a computer to perform various functions. Once a speech compo-

---

25. The Supreme Court has used slightly different formulations to express the narrow tailoring requirement of a content-neutral regulation. In *O'Brien,* the formulation was "if the incidental restriction on alleged First Amendment freedoms is no greater than is essential to the furtherance of that interest." 391 U.S. at 377, 88 S.Ct. 1673. In *Ward,* the formulation was " 'so long as the ... regulation promotes a substantial government interest that would be achieved less effectively absent the regulation.' "491 U.S. at 799, 109 S.Ct. 2746 (quoting *United States v. Albertini,* 472 U.S. 675, 689, 105 S.Ct. 2897, 86 L.Ed.2d 536 (1985)). *Ward* added, however, that the regulation may not "burden *substantially more* speech than

is necessary to further the government's legitimate interests." *Id.* (emphasis added). *Turner Broadcasting* quoted both the "no greater than is essential" formulation from *O'Brien, see Turner Broadcasting,* 512 U.S. at 662, 114 S.Ct. 2445, and the "would be achieved less effectively" formulation from *Ward, see id. Turner Broadcasting* made clear that the narrow tailoring requirement is less demanding than the least restrictive means requirement of a content-specific regulation, *id.,* and appears to have settled on the "substantially more" phrasing from *Ward* as the formulation that best expresses the requirement, *id.* That is the formulation we will apply.

nent is identified, the inquiry then proceeds to whether the regulation is "justified without reference to the content of regulated speech." *Hill*, 530 U.S. at 720, 120 S.Ct. 2480.

The Appellants vigorously reject the idea that computer code can be regulated according to any different standard than that applicable to pure speech, *i.e.,* speech that lacks a nonspeech component. Although recognizing that code is a series of instructions to a computer, they argue that code is no different, for First Amendment purposes, than blueprints that instruct an engineer or recipes that instruct a cook. *See* Supplemental Brief for Appellants at 2, 3.[26] We disagree. Unlike a blueprint or a recipe, which cannot yield any functional result without human comprehension of its content, human decision-making, and human action, computer code can instantly cause a computer to accomplish tasks and instantly render the results of those tasks available throughout the world via the Internet. The only human action required to achieve these results can be as limited and instantaneous as a single click of a mouse. These realities of what code is and what its normal functions are require a First Amendment analysis that treats code as combining nonspeech and speech elements, *i.e.,* functional and expressive elements. *See Red Lion Broadcasting Co. v. FCC*, 395 U.S. 367, 386, 89 S.Ct. 1794, 23 L.Ed.2d 371 (1969) ("[D]ifferences in the characteristics of new media justify differences in the First Amendment standards applied to them." (footnote omitted)).

We recognize, as did Judge Kaplan, that the functional capability of computer code cannot yield a result until a human being decides to insert the disk containing the code into a computer and causes it to perform its function (or programs a computer to cause the code to perform its function). Nevertheless, this momentary intercession of human action does not diminish the nonspeech component of code, nor render code entirely speech, like a blueprint or a recipe. Judge Kaplan, in a passage that merits extensive quotation, cogently explained why this is especially so with respect to decryption code:

> [T]he focus on functionality in order to determine the level of scrutiny is not an inevitable consequence of the speech-conduct distinction. Conduct has immediate effects on the environment. Computer code, on the other hand, no matter how functional, causes a computer to perform the intended operations only if someone uses the code to do so. Hence, one commentator, in a thoughtful article, has maintained that functionality is really "a proxy for effects or harm" and that its adoption as a determinant of the level of scrutiny slides over questions of causation that intervene between the dissemination of a computer program and any harm caused by its use.

The characterization of functionality as a proxy for the consequences of use is accurate. But the assumption that the chain of

26. This argument is elaborated by some of the *amici curiae*. "In the absence of human intervention, code does not func- tion, it engages in no conduct. It is as passive as a cake recipe." Brief of *Amici Curiae* Dr. Harold Abelson *et al.* at 26.

causation is too attenuated to justify the use of functionality to determine the level of scrutiny, at least in this context, is not.

Society increasingly depends upon technological means of controlling access to digital files and systems, whether they are military computers, bank records, academic records, copyrighted works or something else entirely. There are far too many who, given any opportunity, will bypass security measures, some for the sheer joy of doing it, some for innocuous reasons, and others for more malevolent purposes. Given the virtually instantaneous and worldwide dissemination widely available via the Internet, the only rational assumption is that once a computer program capable of bypassing such an access control system is disseminated, it will be used. And that is not all.

There was a time when copyright infringement could be dealt with quite adequately by focusing on the infringing act. If someone wished to make and sell high quality but unauthorized copies of a copyrighted book, for example, the infringer needed a printing press. The copyright holder, once aware of the appearance of infringing copies, usually was able to trace the copies up the chain of distribution, find and prosecute the infringer, and shut off the infringement at the source.

In principle, the digital world is very different. Once a decryption program like DeCSS is written, it quickly can be sent all over the world. Every recipient is capable not only of decrypting and perfectly copying plaintiffs' copyrighted DVDs, but also of retransmitting perfect copies of DeCSS and thus enabling every recipient to do the same. They likewise are capable of transmitting perfect copies of the decrypted DVD. The process potentially is exponential rather than linear.

These considerations drastically alter consideration of the causal link between dissemination of computer programs such as this and their illicit use. Causation in the law ultimately involves practical policy judgments. Here, dissemination itself carries very substantial risk of imminent harm because the mechanism is so unusual by which dissemination of means of circumventing access controls to copyrighted works threatens to produce virtually unstoppable infringement of copyright. In consequence, the causal link between the dissemination of circumvention computer programs and their improper use is more than sufficiently close to warrant selection of a level of constitutional scrutiny based on the programs' functionality.

Universal I, 111 F.Supp.2d at 331–32 (footnotes omitted). The functionality of computer code properly affects the scope of its First Amendment protection.

4.   The Scope of First Amendment Protection for Decryption Code

In considering the scope of First Amendment protection for a decryption program like DeCSS, we must recognize that the essential purpose of encryption code is to prevent unauthorized access. Owners of all property rights are entitled to prohibit access to their property by unauthorized persons. Homeowners can install locks on the doors of their houses. Custodians of valuables can place them in safes. Stores can attach to products security devices that will activate alarms if the products are taken away without purchase. These and similar security devices can be circumvented. Burglars can use skeleton keys to open door locks. Thieves can obtain the combinations to safes. Product security devices can be neutralized.

Our case concerns a security device, CSS computer code, that prevents access by unauthorized persons to DVD movies. The CSS code is embedded in the DVD movie. Access to the movie cannot be obtained unless a person has a device, a licensed DVD player, equipped with computer code capable of decrypting the CSS encryption code. In its basic function, CSS is like a lock on a homeowner's door, a combination of a safe, or a security device attached to a store's products.

DeCSS is computer code that can decrypt CSS. In its basic function, it is like a skeleton key that can open a locked door, a combination that can open a safe, or a device that can neutralize the security device attached to a store's products.[27] DeCSS enables anyone to gain access to a DVD movie without using a DVD player.

The initial use of DeCSS to gain access to a DVD movie creates no loss to movie producers because the initial user must purchase the DVD. However, once the DVD is purchased, DeCSS enables the initial user to copy the movie in digital form and transmit it instantly in virtually limitless quantity, thereby depriving the movie producer of sales. The advent of the Internet creates the potential for instantaneous worldwide distribution of the copied material.

At first glance, one might think that Congress has as much authority to regulate the distribution of computer code to decrypt DVD movies as it has to regulate distribution of skeleton keys, combinations to safes, or devices to neutralize store product security devices. However, despite the evident legitimacy of protection against unauthorized access to DVD movies, just like any other property, regulation of decryption code like DeCSS is challenged in this case because DeCSS differs from a skeleton key in one important respect: it not only is capable of performing the function of unlocking the encrypted DVD movie, it also is a form of communication, albeit written in a language not understood by the general public. As a communication, the DeCSS code has a claim to being "speech," and as "speech," it has a claim to being protected by the First Amendment. But just as the realities of what any computer code can accomplish must inform the scope of its constitutional protection, so the capacity of a decryption program like DeCSS to accomplish unauthorized—indeed, unlawful—access to materials in which the Plaintiffs have intellectual property rights must inform and limit the scope of its First Amendment protection. *Cf. Red Lion,* 395 U.S. at 386, 89 S.Ct. 1794

---

27. More dramatically, the Government calls DeCSS "a digital crowbar." Brief for Intervenor United States at 19.

("[D]ifferences in the characteristics of new media justify differences in the First Amendment standards applied to them.").

With all of the foregoing considerations in mind, we next consider the Appellants' First Amendment challenge to the DMCA as applied in the specific prohibitions that have been imposed by the District Court's injunction.

B. First Amendment Challenge

The District Court's injunction applies the DMCA to the Defendants by imposing two types of prohibition, both grounded on the anti-trafficking provisions of the DMCA. The first prohibits posting DeCSS or any other technology for circumventing CSS on any Internet web site. *Universal II,* 111 F.Supp.2d at 346–47, ¶ 1(a), (b). The second prohibits knowingly linking any Internet web site to any other web site containing DeCSS. *Id.* at 347, ¶ 1(c). The validity of the posting and linking prohibitions must be considered separately.

1. POSTING

The initial issue is whether the posting prohibition is content-neutral, since, as we have explained, this classification determines the applicable constitutional standard. The Appellants contend that the anti-trafficking provisions of the DMCA and their application by means of the posting prohibition of the injunction are content-based. They argue that the provisions "specifically target . . . scientific expression based on the particular topic addressed by that expression—namely, techniques for circumventing CSS." Supplemental Brief for Appellants at 1. We disagree. The Appellants' argument fails to recognize that the target of the posting provisions of the injunction—DeCSS—has both a nonspeech and a speech component, and that the DMCA, as applied to the Appellants, and the posting prohibition of the injunction target only the nonspeech component. Neither the DMCA nor the posting prohibition is concerned with whatever capacity DeCSS might have for conveying information to a human being, and that capacity, as previously explained, is what arguably creates a speech component of the decryption code. The DMCA and the posting prohibition are applied to DeCSS solely because of its capacity to instruct a computer to decrypt CSS. That functional capability is not speech within the meaning of the First Amendment. The Government seeks to "justif[y]," *Hill,* 530 U.S. at 720, 120 S.Ct. 2480, both the application of the DMCA and the posting prohibition to the Appellants solely on the basis of the functional capability of DeCSS to instruct a computer to decrypt CSS, *i.e.,* "without reference to the content of the regulated speech," *id.* This type of regulation is therefore content-neutral, just as would be a restriction on trafficking in skeleton keys identified because of their capacity to unlock jail cells, even though some of the keys happened to bear a slogan or other legend that qualified as a speech component.

As a content-neutral regulation with an incidental effect on a speech component, the regulation must serve a substantial governmental interest, the interest must be unrelated to the suppression of free expression, and the incidental restriction on speech must not burden substantially more speech than is necessary to further that interest. *Turner Broadcasting*, 512 U.S. at 662, 114 S.Ct. 2445. The Government's interest in preventing unauthorized access to encrypted copyrighted material is unquestionably substantial, and the regulation of DeCSS by the posting prohibition plainly serves that interest. Moreover, that interest is unrelated to the suppression of free expression. The injunction regulates the posting of DeCSS, regardless of whether DeCSS code contains any information comprehensible by human beings that would qualify as speech. Whether the incidental regulation on speech burdens substantially more speech than is necessary to further the interest in preventing unauthorized access to copyrighted materials requires some elaboration.

Posting DeCSS on the Appellants' web site makes it instantly available at the click of a mouse to any person in the world with access to the Internet, and such person can then instantly transmit DeCSS to anyone else with Internet access. Although the prohibition on posting prevents the Appellants from conveying to others the speech component of DeCSS, the Appellants have not suggested, much less shown, any technique for barring them from making this instantaneous worldwide distribution of a decryption code that makes a lesser restriction on the code's speech component.[28] It is true that the Government has alternative means of prohibiting unauthorized access to copyrighted materials. For example, it can create criminal and civil liability for those who gain unauthorized access, and thus it can be argued that the restriction on posting DeCSS is not absolutely necessary to preventing unauthorized access to copyrighted materials. But a content-neutral regulation need not employ the least restrictive means of accomplishing the governmental objective. *Id.* It need only avoid burdening "substantially more speech than is necessary to further the government's legitimate interests." *Id.* (internal quotation marks and citation omitted). The prohibition on the Defendants' posting of DeCSS satisfies that standard.[29]

---

28. Briefs of some of the *amici curiae* discuss the possibility of adequate protection against copying of copyrighted materials by adopting the approach of the Audio Home Recording Act of 1992, 17 U.S.C. § 1002(a), which requires digital audio tape recorders to include a technology that prevents serial copying, but permits making a single copy. *See, e.g.,* Brief of *Amici Curiae* Benkler and Lessig at 15. However, the Defendants did not present evidence of the current feasibility of a similar solution to prevent serial copying of DVDs over the Internet. Even if the Government, in defending the DMCA, must sustain a burden of proof in order to satisfy the standards for content-neutral regulation, the Defendants must adduce enough evidence to create fact issues concerning the current availability of less intrusive technological solutions. They

did not do so in the District Court. Moreover, we note that when Congress opted for the solution to serial copying of digital audio tapes, it imposed a special royalty on manufacturers of digital audio recording devices to be distributed to appropriate copyright holders. *See* 17 U.S.C. §§ 1003–1007. We doubt if the First Amendment required Congress to adopt a similar technology/royalty scheme for regulating the copying of DVDs, but in any event the record in this case provides no basis for invalidating the anti-trafficking provisions of the DMCA or the injunction for lack of such an alternative approach.

29. We have considered the opinion of a California intermediate appellate court in *DVD Copy Control Ass'n v. Bunner,* 93 Cal. App.4th 648, 113 Cal.Rptr.2d 338 (2001), declining, on First Amendment grounds, to

2. LINKING

In considering linking, we need to clarify the sense in which the injunction prohibits such activity. Although the injunction defines several terms, it does not define "linking." Nevertheless, it is evident from the District Court's opinion that it is concerned with "hyperlinks," *Universal I*, 111 F.Supp.2d at 307; *see id.* at 339.[30] A hyperlink is a cross-reference (in a distinctive font or color) appearing on one web page that, when activated by the point-and-click of a mouse, brings onto the computer screen another web page. The hyperlink can appear on a screen (window) as text, such as the Internet address ("URL") of the web page being called up or a word or phrase that identifies the web page to be called up, for example, "DeCSS web site." Or the hyperlink can appear as an image, for example, an icon depicting a person sitting at a computer watching a DVD movie and text stating "click here to access DeCSS and see DVD movies for free!" The code for the web page containing the hyperlink includes a computer instruction that associates the link with the URL of the web page to be accessed, such that clicking on the hyperlink instructs the computer to enter the URL of the desired web page and thereby access that page. With a hyperlink on a web page, the linked web site is just one click away.[31]

In applying the DMCA to linking (via hyperlinks), Judge Kaplan recognized, as he had with DeCSS code, that a hyperlink has both a speech and a nonspeech component. It conveys information, the Internet address of the linked web page, and has the functional capacity to bring the content of the linked web page to the user's computer screen (or, as Judge Kaplan put it, to "take one almost instantaneously to the desired destination." *Id.*). As he had ruled with respect to DeCSS code, he ruled that application of the DMCA to the Defendants' linking to web sites containing DeCSS is content-neutral because it is justified without regard to the speech component of the hyperlink. *Id.* The linking prohibition applies whether or not the hyperlink contains any information, comprehensible to a human being, as to the Internet address of the web page being accessed. The linking prohibition is justified solely by the functional capability of the hyperlink.

Applying the *O'Brien/Ward/Turner Broadcasting* requirements for content-neutral regulation, Judge Kaplan then ruled that the DMCA, as applied to the Defendants' linking, served substantial governmental interests and was unrelated to the suppression of free expression. *Id.* We

issue a preliminary injunction under state trade secrets law prohibiting a web site operator from posting DeCSS. To the extent that *DVD Copy Control* disagrees with our First Amendment analysis, we decline to follow it.

30. "Hyperlinks" are also called "hypertext links" or "active links."

31. "Linking" not accomplished by a hyperlink would simply involve the posting of the Internet address ("URL") of another

web page. A "link" of this sort is sometimes called an "inactive link." With an inactive link, the linked web page would be only four clicks away, one click to select the URL address for copying, one click to copy the address, one click to "paste" the address into the text box for URL addresses, and one click (or striking the "enter" key) to instruct the computer to call up the linked web site.

agree. He then carefully considered the "closer call," *id.,* as to whether a linking prohibition would satisfy the narrow tailoring requirement. In an especially carefully considered portion of his opinion, he observed that strict liability for linking to web sites containing DeCSS would risk two impairments of free expression. Web site operators would be inhibited from displaying links to various web pages for fear that a linked page might contain DeCSS, and a prohibition on linking to a web site containing DeCSS would curtail access to whatever other information was contained at the accessed site. *Id.* at 340.

To avoid applying the DMCA in a manner that would "burden substantially more speech than is necessary to further the government's legitimate interests," *Turner Broadcasting,* 512 U.S. at 662, 114 S.Ct. 2445 (internal quotation marks and citation omitted), Judge Kaplan adapted the standards of *New York Times Co. v. Sullivan,* 376 U.S. 254, 283, 84 S.Ct. 710, 11 L.Ed.2d 686 (1964), to fashion a limited prohibition against linking to web sites containing DeCSS. He required clear and convincing evidence that those responsible for the link (a) know at the relevant time that the offending material is on the linked-to site, (b) know that it is circumvention technology that may not lawfully be offered, and (c) create or maintain the link for the purpose of disseminating that technology. *Universal I,* 111 F.Supp.2d at 341. He then found that the evidence satisfied his three-part test by his required standard of proof. *Id.*

In response to our post-argument request for the parties' views on various issues, including specifically Judge Kaplan's test for a linking prohibition, the Appellants replied that his test was deficient for not requiring proof of intent to cause, or aid or abet, harm, and that the only valid test for a linking prohibition would be one that could validly apply to the publication in a print medium of an address for obtaining prohibited material. Supplemental Brief for Appellants at 14. The Appellees and the Government accepted Judge Kaplan's criteria for purposes of asserting the validity of the injunction as applied to the Appellants, with the Government expressing reservations as to the standard of clear and convincing evidence. Supplemental Brief for Appellees at 22–23; Supplemental Brief for Government at 19–21.

Mindful of the cautious approach to First Amendment claims involving computer technology expressed in *Name.Space,* 202 F.3d at 584 n. 11, we see no need on this appeal to determine whether a test as rigorous as Judge Kaplan's is required to respond to First Amendment objections to the linking provision of the injunction that he issued. It suffices to reject the Appellants' contention that an intent to cause harm is required and that linking can be enjoined only under circumstances applicable to a print medium. As they have throughout their arguments, the Appellants ignore the reality of the functional capacity of decryption computer code and hyperlinks to facilitate instantaneous unauthorized access to copyrighted materials by anyone anywhere in the world. Under the circumstances amply shown by the record, the injunction's linking prohibition validly regulates the Appellants' opportunity instantly to enable anyone anywhere to gain unauthorized access to copyrighted movies on DVDs.[32]

At oral argument, we asked the Government whether its undoubted power to punish the distribution of obscene materials would permit an injunction prohibiting a newspaper from printing addresses of bookstore locations carrying such materials. In a properly cautious response, the Government stated that the answer would depend on the circumstances of the publication. The Appellants' supplemental papers enthusiastically embraced the arguable analogy between printing bookstore addresses and displaying on a web page links to web sites at which DeCSS may be accessed. Supplemental Brief for Appellants at 14. They confidently asserted that publication of bookstore locations carrying obscene material cannot be enjoined consistent with the First Amendment, and that a prohibition against linking to web sites containing DeCSS is similarly invalid. *Id.*

Like many analogies posited to illuminate legal issues, the bookstore analogy is helpful primarily in identifying characteristics that *distinguish* it from the context of the pending dispute. If a bookstore proprietor is knowingly selling obscene materials, the evil of distributing such materials can be prevented by injunctive relief against the unlawful distribution (and similar distribution by others can be deterred by punishment of the distributor). And if others publish the location of the bookstore, preventive relief against a distributor can be effective before any significant distribution of the prohibited materials has occurred. The digital world, however, creates a very different problem. If obscene materials are posted on one web site and other sites post hyperlinks to the first site, the materials are available for instantaneous worldwide distribution before any preventive measures can be effectively taken.

This reality obliges courts considering First Amendment claims in the context of the pending case to choose between two unattractive alternatives: either tolerate some impairment of communication in order to permit Congress to prohibit decryption that may lawfully be prevented, or tolerate some decryption in order to avoid some impairment of communication. Although the parties dispute the extent of impairment of communication if the injunction is upheld and the extent of decryption if it is vacated, and differ on the availability and effectiveness of techniques for minimizing both consequences, the fundamental choice between impairing some communication and tolerating decryption cannot be entirely avoided.

In facing this choice, we are mindful that it is not for us to resolve the issues of public policy implicated by the choice we have identified. Those issues are for Congress. Our task is to determine whether the

---

32. We acknowledge that the prohibition on linking restricts more than Corley's ability to facilitate instant access to DeCSS on linked web sites; it also restricts his ability to facilitate access to whatever protected speech is available on those sites. However, those who maintain the linked sites can instantly make their protected material available for linking by Corley by the simple expedient of deleting DeCSS from their web sites.

legislative solution adopted by Congress, as applied to the Appellants by the District Court's injunction, is consistent with the limitations of the First Amendment, and we are satisfied that it is.

IV. Constitutional Challenge Based on Claimed Restriction of Fair Use

Asserting that fair use "is rooted in and required by both the Copyright Clause and the First Amendment," Brief for Appellants at 42, the Appellants contend that the DMCA, as applied by the District Court, unconstitutionally *"eliminates* fair use" of copyrighted materials, *id.* at 41 (emphasis added). We reject this extravagant claim.

Preliminarily, we note that the Supreme Court has never held that fair use is constitutionally required, although some isolated statements in its opinions might arguably be enlisted for such a requirement. In *Stewart v. Abend,* 495 U.S. 207, 110 S.Ct. 1750, 109 L.Ed.2d 184 (1990), cited by the Appellants, the Court merely noted that fair use " 'permits courts to avoid rigid application of the copyright statute when, on occasion, it would stifle the very creativity which that law is designed to foster,' " *id.* (quoting *Iowa State University Research Foundation, Inc. v. American Broadcasting Cos.,* 621 F.2d 57, 60 (2d Cir.1980)); *see also Harper & Row, Publishers, Inc. v. Nation Enterprises,* 471 U.S. 539, 560, 105 S.Ct. 2218, 85 L.Ed.2d 588 (1985) (noting "the First Amendment protections already embodied in the Copyright Act's distinction between copyrightable expression and uncopyrightable facts and ideas, and the latitude for scholarship and comment traditionally afforded by fair use"). In *Campbell v. Acuff–Rose Music, Inc.,* 510 U.S. 569, 114 S.Ct. 1164, 127 L.Ed.2d 500 (1994), the Court observed, "From the infancy of copyright protection, some opportunity for fair use of copyrighted materials has been thought necessary to fulfill copyright's very purpose, '[t]o promote the Progress of Science and useful Arts.... ' "[33] *Id.* at 575, 114 S.Ct. 1164 (citation omitted); *see generally* William F. Patry, *The Fair Use Privilege in Copyright Law* 573–82 (2d ed. 1995) (questioning First Amendment protection for fair use).

We need not explore the extent to which fair use might have constitutional protection, grounded on either the First Amendment or the Copyright Clause, because whatever validity a constitutional claim might have as to an application of the DMCA that impairs fair use of copyrighted materials, such matters are far beyond the scope of this lawsuit for several reasons. In the first place, the Appellants do not claim to be making fair use of any copyrighted materials, and nothing in the injunction prohibits them from making such fair use. They are barred from trafficking in a decryption code that enables unauthorized access to copyrighted materials.

---

33. Although we have recognized that the First Amendment provides no entitlement to use copyrighted materials beyond that accorded by the privilege of fair use, except in "an extraordinary case," *Twin Peaks Productions, Inc. v. Publications In-* *ternational, Ltd.,* 996 F.2d 1366, 1378 (2d Cir.1993), we have not ruled that the Constitution guarantees any particular formulation or minimum availability of the fair use defense.

Second, as the District Court properly noted, to whatever extent the anti-trafficking provisions of the DMCA might prevent others from copying portions of DVD movies in order to make fair use of them, "the evidence as to the impact of the anti-trafficking provision[s] of the DMCA on prospective fair users is scanty and fails adequately to address the issues." *Universal I,* 111 F.Supp.2d at 338 n. 246.

Third, the Appellants have provided no support for their premise that fair use of DVD movies is constitutionally required to be made by copying the original work in its original format.[34] Their examples of the fair uses that they believe others will be prevented from making all involve copying in a digital format those portions of a DVD movie amenable to fair use, a copying that would enable the fair user to manipulate the digitally copied portions. One example is that of a school child who wishes to copy images from a DVD movie to insert into the student's documentary film. We know of no authority for the proposition that fair use, as protected by the Copyright Act, much less the Constitution, guarantees copying by the optimum method or in the identical format of the original. Although the Appellants insisted at oral argument that they should not be relegated to a "horse and buggy" technique in making fair use of DVD movies,[35] the DMCA does not impose even an arguable limitation on the opportunity to make a variety of traditional fair uses of DVD movies, such as commenting on their content, quoting excerpts from their screenplays, and even recording portions of the video images and sounds on film or tape by pointing a camera, a camcorder, or a microphone at a monitor as it displays the DVD movie. The fact that the resulting copy will not be as perfect or as manipulable as a digital copy obtained by having direct access to the DVD movie in its digital form, provides no basis for a claim of unconstitutional limitation of fair use. A film critic making fair use of a movie by quoting selected lines of dialogue has no constitutionally valid claim that the review (in print or on television) would be technologically superior if the reviewer had not been prevented from using a movie camera in the theater, nor has an art student a valid constitutional claim to fair use of a painting by photographing it in a museum. Fair use has never been held to be a guarantee of access to copyrighted material in order to copy it by the fair user's preferred technique or in the format of the original.

* * *

34. As expressed in their supplemental papers, the position of the Appellants is that "fair use extends to works in whatever form they are offered to the public," Supplemental Brief for Appellants at 20, by which we understand the Appellants to contend not merely that fair use may be made of DVD movies but that the fair user must be permitted access to the digital version of the DVD in order to directly copy excerpts for fair use in a digital format.

35. In their supplemental papers, the Appellants contend, rather hyperbolically, that a prohibition on using copying machines to assist in making fair use of texts could not validly be upheld by the availability of "monks to scribe the relevant passages." Supplemental Brief for Appellants at 20.

Notes

1. How is *Corley* different from *Sony* and *Napster*? How is it similar? Clearly one difference is in the statutory texts: section 107's fair use provisions are very general; the provisions of the DMCA at issue in *Corley* are extremely detailed and precisely tailored to the issues raised in the litigation. Does this difference contribute usefully to the courts' ability to thread their way among the constitutional issues? Is it relevant to the First Amendment questions (or should it be) that the DMCA is derived from Commerce Clause power?

2. How important in practice is the outcome in *Corley*? As the opinion acknowledges, DeCSS is now available on hundreds of websites and in numerous print forums as well; at least one printed version of the DeCSS code is available on the backs of T-shirts. What exactly has been gained as a result of this litigation? Consider the implications of these opinions for criminal prosecutions, as in *Elcom* in the next note.

3. In *United States v. Elcom Ltd.,* 203 F.Supp.2d 1111 (N.D.Cal.2002), the defendant, Elcom, a software developer and marketer, was indicted for alleged violation of 17 U.S.C. § 1201 (b)(1)(A) and (C). Elcom's software, Advanced eBook Processor, enabled users of eBook Reader programs to circumvent the purchaser's use restrictions on printing, copying and distributing the program's material. Elcom challenged the statute on vagueness grounds under the First Amendment, but failed in this attempt. The court also rejected Elcom's argument that Congress exceeded its constitutional authority in enacting the DMCA under the Commerce Clause, and observed that the legislation was consistent with the Intellectual Property Clause's grant of authority to provide protection of the exclusive rights of copyright holders.

4. In *DVD Copy Control Assn. v. Bunner,* 113 Cal.Rptr.2d 338, 60 U.S.P.Q.2d 1803 (Cal.App.2001), the California Court of Appeals reversed the trial court's issuance of a preliminary injunction against the defendant. The trial court granted an injunction prohibiting the defendant from posting DeCSS. The plaintiff had argued that the encryption code that protects against unauthorized use contains confidential information that the defendant posted on a website in violation of the California Uniform Trade Secrets Act, and the trial court had accepted that argument. The appellate court disagreed, however, and held that an injunction was an improper prior restraint on defendant's First Amendment right to free speech. The California Supreme Court reversed and remanded. See *DVD Copy Control Assn. v. Bunner,* 31 Cal.4th 864, 4 Cal.Rptr.3d 69, 75 P.3d 1 (2003). 116 Cal.App.4th 241, 10 Cal.Rptr.3d 185, *review denied.*

5. In *Chamberlain Group v. Skylink Technologies,* 381 F.3d 1178 (Fed. Cir. 2004), the plaintiff created a garage door opener which was activated by a computer-generated rotating signal. The defendant developed a universal garage door opener remote which had the ability to crack the plaintiff's rotating code. Plaintiff brought suit under the DMCA for the circumvention of its technological measure to access a copyrighted work (the computer program within the garage door opener). The Federal Circuit concluded that

the DMCA did not override the reasonable expectations of consumers. Instead, in purchasing the garage door opener, the user had received the Plaintiff's permission to decode the opener exactly the way that the defendant's product decoded the opener.

6. Vacating a preliminary injunction and remanding the case for further fact finding, the Sixth circuit held that a manufacturer's claim that a product allowing the use of third-party replacement toner cartridges violated the DMCA's anti-circumvention provisions was not likely to succeed. See *Lexmark International, Inc. v. Static Control Components, Inc.*, 387 F.3d 522 (6th Cir. 2004) (stating that the control measure merely prevented use of the printer and did not control access to the computer program's content).

7. In *Davidson & Assocs. v. Jung*, 422 F.3d 630 (8th Cir. 2005), the court held that reverse engineering in violation of an end user license agreement also amounted to a violation of sections 1201(a) and (b). The court rejected the defendant's argument that the DMCA's interoperability exception applied, as well as an argument that the agreement amounted to copyright misuse.

E.   AFFIRMATIVE DEFENSES

A copyright infringement defendant may attack the validity of the plaintiff's copyright, may argue that the challenged use falls within one of the specific limitations on the exclusive rights discussed in Chapter 18, may assert rights under an assignment or license, or may raise the affirmative defense of fair use, discussed in Chapter 19. Other affirmative defenses include copyright misuse, abandonment, the statute of limitations, and such equitable defenses as laches, estoppel and unclean hands (including, but not limited to fraudulent registration), and possibly, in cases involving a state defendant, the Eleventh Amendment.

LASERCOMB AMERICA, INC. v. REYNOLDS

United States Court of Appeals, Fourth Circuit, 1990.
911 F.2d 970.

SPROUSE, CIRCUIT JUDGE.

[Defendants/appellants Holliday Steel and its principals were licensed to use plaintiff/appellee Lasercomb's computer assisted design and computer assisted manufacture ("CAD/CAM") die-making software known as Interact. Appellant made and marketed unauthorized copies of the Interact software. In finding the appellants liable for copyright infringement, the district court rejected their affirmative defense of copyright misuse. Although Lasercomb's standard licensing agreement contained a clause which prevented the licensee from participating in any manner in the creation of computer-assisted die-making software for a term of 99 years, the district court found that appellants had not agreed to the terms of that clause, and that, even if they had, Lasercomb's use of that clause did not constitute copyright misuse. Finally, the district court questioned whether a defense of copyright misuse should even be recognized.]

* * *

A. DOES A "MISUSE OF COPYRIGHT" DEFENSE EXIST?

We agree with the district court that much uncertainty engulfs the "misuse of copyright" defense. We are persuaded, however, that a misuse of copyright defense is inherent in the law of copyright just as a misuse of patent defense is inherent in patent law.

The misuse of a patent is a potential defense to suit for its infringement, and both the existence and parameters of that body of law are well established. * * * The origins of patent and copyright law in England, the treatment of these two aspects of intellectual property by the framers of our Constitution, and the later statutory and judicial development of patent and copyright law in this country persuade us that parallel public policies underlie the protection of both types of intellectual property rights. We think these parallel policies call for application of the misuse defense to copyright as well as patent law.

* * *

2. The Misuse of Patent Defense

Although a patent misuse defense was recognized by the courts as early as 1917,[14] most commentators point to Morton Salt Co. v. G. S. Suppiger, 314 U.S. 488, 86 L. Ed. 363, 62 S.Ct. 402 (1942), as the foundational patent misuse case. In that case, the plaintiff Morton Salt brought suit on the basis that the defendant had infringed Morton's patent in a salt-depositing machine. The salt tablets were not themselves a patented item, but Morton's patent license required that licensees use only salt tablets produced by Morton. Morton was thereby using its patent to restrain competition in the sale of an item which was not within the scope of the patent's privilege. The Supreme Court held that, as a court of equity, it would not aid Morton in protecting its patent when Morton was using that patent in a manner contrary to public policy. Id. at 490–92. * * *

Since Morton Salt, the courts have recognized patent misuse as a valid defense and have applied it in a number of cases in which patent owners have attempted to use their patents for price fixing, tie-ins, territorial restrictions, and so forth. * * *

3. The "Misuse of Copyright" Defense

Although the patent misuse defense has been generally recognized since Morton Salt, it has been much less certain whether an analogous copyright misuse defense exists. * * * This uncertainty persists because

---

14. Motion Picture Patents Co. v. Universal Film Mfg. Co., 243 U.S. 502, 61 L. Ed. 871, 37 S.Ct. 416 (1917). * * *

no United States Supreme Court decision has firmly established a copyright misuse defense in a manner analogous to the establishment of the patent misuse defense by Morton Salt. The few courts considering the issue have split on whether the defense should be recognized * * *.

We are of the view, however, that since copyright and patent law serve parallel public interests, a "misuse" defense should apply to infringement actions brought to vindicate either right. As discussed above, the similarity of the policies underlying patent and copyright is great and historically has been consistently recognized. Both patent law and copyright law seek to increase the store of human knowledge and arts by rewarding inventors and authors with the exclusive rights to their works for a limited time. At the same time, the granted monopoly power does not extend to property not covered by the patent or copyright. Morton Salt, 314 U.S. at 492; Paramount Pictures, 334 U.S. at 156–58;[16] cf. Baker v. Selden, 101 U.S. 99, 101–04, 25 L. Ed. 841 (1880).

* * *

B.   The District Court's Finding that the Anticompetitive Clauses Are Reasonable

In declining to recognize a misuse of copyright defense, the district court found "reasonable" Lasercomb's attempt to protect its software copyright by using anticompetitive clauses in their licensing agreement. In briefly expressing its reasoning, the court referred to the "delicate and sensitive" nature of software. It also observed that Lasercomb's president had testified that the noncompete language was negotiable.

If, as it appears, the district court analogized from the "rule of reason" concept of antitrust law, we think its reliance on that principle was misplaced. * * * [T]here is an understandable association of antitrust law with the misuse defense. Certainly, an entity which uses its patent as the means of violating antitrust law is subject to a misuse of patent defense. However, Morton Salt held that it is not necessary to prove an antitrust violation in order to successfully assert patent misuse * * *.

So while it is true that the attempted use of a copyright to violate antitrust law probably would give rise to a misuse of copyright defense,

---

16.   In Paramount Pictures, the Court in an antitrust context stated:

Block-booking [of feature films] prevents competitors from bidding for single features on their individual merits. The District Court held it illegal for that reason and for the reason that it "adds to the monopoly of a single copyrighted picture that of another copyrighted picture which must be taken and exhibited in order to secure the first." That enlargement of the monopoly of the copyright was condemned below in reliance on the principle which forbids the owner of a patent to condition its use on the purchase or use of patented or unpatented materials. The court enjoined defendants from performing or entering into any license in which the right to exhibit one feature is conditioned upon the licensee's taking one or more other features.

We approve that restriction.

334 U.S. at 156–58 (citations and footnote omitted). Citing Paramount, the Fifth Circuit has opined in dicta that "it is ... likely that the public monopoly extension rationale of Morton Salt ... is applicable to copyright." Mitchell, 604 F.2d at 865 n. 27.

the converse is not necessarily true—a misuse need not be a violation of antitrust law in order to comprise an equitable defense to an infringement action. The question is not whether the copyright is being used in a manner violative of antitrust law (such as whether the licensing agreement is "reasonable"), but whether the copyright is being used in a manner violative of the public policy embodied in the grant of a copyright.

Lasercomb undoubtedly has the right to protect against copying of the Interact code. Its standard licensing agreement, however, goes much further and essentially attempts to suppress any attempt by the licensee to independently implement the idea which Interact expresses [for 99 years]. * * * Although one or another licensee might succeed in negotiating out the noncompete provisions, this does not negate the fact that Lasercomb is attempting to use its copyright in a manner adverse to the public policy embodied in copyright law, and that it has succeeded in doing so with at least one licensee. * * *

* * *

We think the anticompetitive language in Lasercomb's licensing agreement * * * amounts to misuse of its copyright. * * * The misuse arises from Lasercomb's attempt to use its copyright in a particular expression, the Interact software, to control competition in an area outside the copyright, i.e., the idea of computer-assisted die manufacture, regardless of whether such conduct amounts to an antitrust violation.

C.   THE EFFECT OF APPELLANTS NOT BEING PARTY
TO THE ANTICOMPETITIVE CONTRACT

In its rejection of the copyright misuse defense, the district court emphasized that Holiday Steel was not explicitly party to a licensing agreement containing the offending language. However, again analogizing to patent misuse, the defense of copyright misuse is available even if the defendants themselves have not been injured by the misuse. * * *

Therefore, the fact that appellants here were not parties to one of Lasercomb's standard license agreements is inapposite to their copyright misuse defense. The question is whether Lasercomb is using its copyright in a manner contrary to public policy, which question we have answered in the affirmative.

In sum, we find that misuse of copyright is a valid defense, that Lasercomb's anticompetitive clauses in its standard licensing agreement constitute misuse of copyright, and that the defense is available to appellants even though they were not parties to the standard licensing agreement. Holding that Lasercomb should have been barred by the defense of copyright misuse from suing for infringement of its copyright in the Interact program, we reverse the injunction and the award of damages for copyright infringement.[22]

* * *

22. This holding, of course, is not an invalidation of Lasercomb's copyright. Lasercomb is free to bring a suit for infringement once it has purged itself of the misuse. * * *

ASSESSMENT TECHNOLOGIES OF WI, LLC v. WIREDATA, INC.

United States Court of Appeals, Seventh Circuit, 2003.
350 F.3d 640.

[Portions of this case are excerpted in Chapter 16, Section C.]

POSNER, CIRCUIT JUDGE.

* * *

The doctrine of misuse "prevents copyright holders from leveraging their limited monopoly to allow them control of areas outside the monopoly." *A&M Records, Inc. v. Napster, Inc.*, 239 F.3d 1004, 1026–27 (9th Cir.2001); *see Alcatel USA, Inc. v. DGI Technologies, Inc.*, 166 F.3d 772, 792–95 (5th Cir.1999); *Practice Management Information Corp. v. American Medical Ass'n*, 121 F.3d 516, 520–21 (1997), *amended*, 133 F.3d 1140 (9th Cir.1998); *DSC Communications Corp. v. DGI Technologies, Inc.*, 81 F.3d 597, 601–02 (5th Cir.1996); *Lasercomb America, Inc. v. Reynolds*, 911 F.2d 970, 976–79 (4th Cir.1990). The data in the municipalities' tax-assessment databases are beyond the scope of AT's copyright. It is true that in *Reed-Union Corp. v. Turtle Wax, Inc.*, 77 F.3d 909, 913 (7th Cir.1996), we left open the question whether copyright misuse, unless it rises to the level of an antitrust violation, is a defense to infringement; our earlier decision in *Saturday Evening Post Co. v. Rumbleseat Press, Inc.*, 816 F.2d 1191, 1200 (7th Cir.1987), had intimated skepticism. No effort has been made by WIREdata to show that AT has market power merely by virtue of its having a copyright on one system for compiling valuation data for real estate tax assessment purposes. Cases such as *Lasercomb*, however, cut misuse free from antitrust, pointing out that the cognate doctrine of patent misuse is not so limited, ... though a difference is that patents tend to confer greater market power on their owners than copyrights do, since patents protect ideas and copyrights, as we have noted, do not. The argument for applying copyright misuse beyond the bounds of antitrust, besides the fact that confined to antitrust the doctrine would be redundant, is that for a copyright owner to use an infringement suit to obtain property protection, here in data, that copyright law clearly does not confer, hoping to force a settlement or even achieve an outright victory over an opponent that may lack the resources or the legal sophistication to resist effectively, is an abuse of process.

We need not run this hare to the ground; nor decide whether the licenses interpreted as AT would have us interpret them—as barring municipalities from disclosing noncopyrighted data—would violate the state's open-records law. *Cf. Antisdel v. City of Oak Creek Police & Fire Comm'n*, 229 Wis.2d 433, 600 N.W.2d 1, 3 (App.1999); *Gordie Boucher*

Lincoln–Mercury Madison, Inc. v. J & H Landfill, Inc., 172 Wis.2d 333, 493 N.W.2d 375, 378 (App.1992); *State ex rel. Sun Newspapers v. Westlake Board of Education*, 76 Ohio App.3d 170, 601 N.E.2d 173, 175 (1991); *but cf. Pierce v. St. Vrain Valley School District*, 981 P.2d 600, 605–06 (Colo.1999). WIREdata is not a licensee of AT, and AT is not suing to enforce any contract it might have with WIREdata. It therefore had no cause to drag the licenses before us. But since it did, we shall not conceal our profound skepticism concerning AT's interpretation. If accepted, it would forbid municipalities licensed by AT to share the data in their tax-assessment databases with each other even for the purpose of comparing or coordinating their assessment methods, though all the data they would be exchanging would be data that their assessors had collected and inputted into the databases. That seems an absurd result.

* * *

Notes

1. Early case law largely rejected the notion of a copyright misuse defense. Even before *Lasercomb*, however, the defense had begun to achieve greater acceptance, although in most cases that have permitted the defense the plaintiff has nonetheless prevailed because the defendant failed to establish sufficiently egregious conduct by the plaintiff. Typically the misuse defense requires the defendant to show that the plaintiff has violated an important legal rule, and that this violation is related to the infringement claim. In 1996, the Fifth Circuit followed *Lasercomb* in recognizing the possibility of a copyright misuse defense where the plaintiff's copyright claims arguably prevented the defendant from developing a competing microprocessor card. *DSC Communications Corp. v. DGI Technologies*, 81 F.3d 597, 600–02 (5th Cir.1996). In 1997, the Ninth Circuit followed *Lasercomb* and *DSC Communications* in finding copyright misuse where the American Medical Association (AMA) licensed its medical coding system to a federal agency on the condition that the agency not use any competing coding system; the agency in turn required applicants for Medicaid reimbursement to use the AMA's copyrighted coding system in submitting their claims. *Practice Management Information Corp. v. American Medical Ass'n*, 121 F.3d 516, 43 U.S.P.Q.2d 1611 (9th Cir.1997). The court held that the misuse defense rendered the copyright unenforceable even though the AMA's conduct did not violate antitrust laws. In *Alcatel USA, Inc. v. DGI Technologies, Inc.*, 166 F.3d 772 (5th Cir.1999), the Fifth Circuit found copyright misuse where a license permitted use of the licensor's copyrighted operating system software only in conjunction with the licensor's hardware.

Consider the shrinkwrap license reproduced in the notes following *Vault v. Quaid*, in Chapter 18.B.3. Could the imposition of such a license constitute copyright misuse? Can you think of other activities which might constitute copyright misuse?

2. *Unclean Hands*: Courts sometimes use the terms "copyright misuse" and "unclean hands" interchangeably; however, in addition to antitrust violations and other conventionally anticompetitive behavior, activity supporting an unclean hands defense can include misleading conduct or bad

faith in dealing with the defendant, and fraud or failure to disclose required information in the copyright application.

3. *Statute of Limitations*: Section 507 bars both civil and criminal actions for copyright infringement unless initiated within three years of the date of the infringing activity. Although section 507(a) (the criminal provision) refers to the date on which the cause of action "arose" and section 507(b) (the civil provision) refers to the date on which the claim "accrued," the reason for this different terminology is unclear. Courts disagree on whether infringing activities preceding this three-year period can be included in an infringement action if found to be part of a "continuing wrong." *Compare Taylor v. Meirick*, 712 F.2d 1112 (7th Cir.1983) (copying which preceded the limitations period was actionable in combination with distribution which took place during that period) with *Roley v. New World Pictures, Ltd.*, 19 F.3d 479 (9th Cir.1994) (rejecting *Taylor*). A defendant may be estopped from raising the statute of limitations defense if the defendant misleads the plaintiff into believing that litigation is unnecessary. The statute may be tolled in cases of fraudulent concealment, duress, and coercion, and, in addition, one court has held that the statute should also be tolled where the plaintiff could not reasonably have been expected to discover the infringement within the limitations period. *Taylor v. Meirick, supra*.

4. *Abandonment*: Abandonment differs from forfeiture of copyright, which could occur under pre–1989 law as a result of publication without notice. Abandonment, in contrast, requires intent to surrender copyright. Most courts impose the additional requirement of an overt act evidencing that intent, such as an explicit statement renouncing all claims to copyright. Courts have not recognized a defense of partial abandonment (*e.g.*, abandonment in a particular region or medium).

5. *Laches*: Inexcusable delay in pursuing an infringement claim (either before or after filing the complaint) may bar recovery of damages if the defendant detrimentally relies on that delay, unless the defendant is not engaging in the infringing activity during the period of delay. Laches will not, however, preclude injunctive relief. Courts have extended the laches period where parties were engaging in good faith efforts to settle.

In *Chirco v. Crosswinds Communities, Inc.*, 474 F.3d 227 (6th Cir.2007), real estate developers brought suit against defendants whose condominiums had infringed their original design. The action was filed within the three years statute of limitations, but because construction had already begun, the U.S. District Court for the Eastern District of Michigan ruled the action was barred due to prejudicial delay.

6. *Equitable Estoppel*: Traditional principles of equitable estoppel preclude copyright relief for a plaintiff where (1) the plaintiff knows of the defendant's infringing activity, (2) the plaintiff's conduct with respect to the infringing activity is such that the defendant has a right to rely on that conduct, (3) the defendant is unaware of the truth, and (4) the defendant detrimentally relies on the plaintiff's conduct.

Suppose that a defendant creates a derivative work incorporating non-literal portions of a plaintiff's copyrighted work which the plaintiff had represented as factual. In a subsequent infringement action, however, the plaintiff asserts that these portions of the work were fictional. Who should prevail, and why?

7. *Innocent Infringement*: If an infringer relies in good faith on a purported transfer or license from a person wrongly identified in the copyright notice as the owner of the copyright in the work, and if that copy was publicly distributed by authority of the copyright owner before March 1, 1989, the infringer has a complete defense unless, before the infringement took place, either (1) the work was registered by the copyright owner, or (2) a document showing the ownership of the copyright had been executed by the person named in the notice, and had been recorded. 17 U.S.C.A. § 406(a).

Two other "innocent infringement" defenses, in sections 405(b) and 504(c), affect only the availability of certain damages remedies, not the underlying question of liability. How do sections 401 and 402 affect the availability of these defenses? Why?

8. *Eleventh Amendment*: Prior to 1990, Congress had not addressed the question whether states were immune from liability for copyright infringement under the Eleventh Amendment; most courts concluded that immunity applied. In the Copyright Remedy Clarification Act, Pub. L. 101–553, 102 Stat. 2749, § 1 (1990), Congress amended section 501 (a) and added section 511 to expressly abrogate states' sovereign immunity for such claims.

The validity of section 511(a) appeared doubtful, however, in light of the Supreme Court's decision in *Seminole Tribe v. Florida*, 517 U.S. 44, 116 S.Ct. 1114, 134 L.Ed.2d 252 (1996), in which the Court held that Congress could not abrogate a state's sovereign immunity pursuant to its authority under the Commerce Clause. The Court suggested that Congress's abrogation power was limited to laws enacted pursuant to section 5 of the Fourteenth Amendment. Dissenting, Justice Stevens expressed concern that this reasoning would insulate the states from liability for copyright infringement. The majority responded:

> * * * [C]ontrary to the implication of JUSTICE STEVENS' conclusion, it has not been widely thought that the federal antitrust, bankruptcy, or copyright statutes abrogated the States' sovereign immunity. This Court never has awarded relief against a State under any of those statutory schemes * * *. Although the copyright and bankruptcy laws have existed practically since our nation's inception, and the antitrust laws have been in force for over a century, there is no established tradition in the lower federal courts of allowing enforcement of those federal statutes against the States. * * *

517 U.S. at 44 n. 16, 116 S.Ct. at 1131 n. 16.

The *Seminole Tribe* majority added that even where the Eleventh Amendment bars a suit against a state, normally "an individual may obtain injunctive relief under Ex parte Young in order to remedy a state officer's ongoing violation of federal law." 116 S.Ct. at 1131 n.14 (citing *Ex parte Young*, 209 U.S. 123, 28 S.Ct. 441, 52 L.Ed. 714 (1908)). However, the legislative history of the Copyright Remedy Clarification Act expresses Congress's concern that injunctive relief against state officials is typically an inadequate remedy, because (1) unless plaintiffs can recover attorneys' fees, injunctive relief may not be affordable, and (2) an injunction against one state official does not prohibit the state from continuing the infringing activity through another official. H.R. Rep. No. 101–305, 101st Cong., 2d Sess. 8–12 (1990).

Immediately after *Seminole Tribe*, moreover, the Supreme Court vacated and remanded a Fifth Circuit opinion which had invoked section 511 in holding a state liable for copyright infringement. See *University of Houston v. Chavez*, 517 U.S. 1184, 116 S.Ct. 1667, 134 L.Ed.2d 772 (1996), *vacating and remanding Chavez v. Arte Publico Press*, 59 F.3d 539 (5th Cir.1995).

The Supreme Court's subsequent holding in *Florida Prepaid Postsecondary Education Expense Board v. College Savings Bank*, 527 U.S. 627, 119 S.Ct. 2199, 144 L.Ed.2d 575 (1999), invalidating Congress's abrogaton of states' sovereign immunity with respect to claims of patent infringement and violations of the Lanham Act's false advertising provisions, strengthens the inference that the Court would probably reach a conclusion similar to *Seminole Tribe* with regard to states' liability for copyright infringement. If so, then because the federal courts have exclusive jurisdiction over copyright infringement suits (under 28 U.S.C. § 1338(a)), the states will be immune to ordinary liability for copyright infringement. During 1999, Congress considered, but did not adopt, legislation that would have responded to *College Savings* by denying certain federal intellectual property rights to states which fail to waive their sovereign immunity to intellectual property infringement suits.

In *Bassett v. Mashantucket Pequot Tribe*, 204 F.3d 343 (2d Cir.2000), the Second Circuit held that Native American tribal immunity from copyright infringement liability was not explicitly abrogated by Congress in the Copyright Act, and was not waived by a tribe's off-reservation commercial activity.

9. *Manufacturing Clause*: Under section 601(d), a defendant who copied or distributed certain works that were imported or publicly distributed in the United States, under the authority of the copyright owner, in violation of the manufacturing clause of section 601(a) had a complete defense in the case of infringing copies made in the United States before the registration of copyright in an edition of that work which complied with the manufacturing clause. The purpose of the manufacturing clause was to protect United States printers against foreign competition. Because the section 601(a) ban on importation and distribution was lifted for works imported or distributed on or after July 1, 1986, today the manufacturing clause defense will rarely apply.

10. *First Amendment*: Courts through the years have generally resisted the argument that copyright law, either on its face or as applied to a specific infringement claim, violates the First Amendment; but as we have seen the question is by no means free from doubt. Some important recent cases— including *Suntrust Bank* (the *Wind Done Gone* case) and *Corley*—have supposed that the First Amendment does apply to copyright in some fashion and to some not altogether inconsiderable degree. The Supreme Court's opinion in *Eldred v. Ashcroft* (excerpted supra, at page 903) suggests that a majority of the present Court believes that copyright, "as traditionally configured," does not violate the First Amendment. Despite the opinions in

Eldred and *Harper & Row* (excerpted at page 1059), however, it seems both accurate and fair to say that no opinion of the Court has yet addressed the First Amendment question squarely or at length. Meanwhile, as you read the next section, ask yourself whether First Amendment considerations should ever affect the choice of infringement *remedies*.

11.   Should a defendant be held liable for exploitation of an infringing item if the defendant had no reason to know of the infringement? For example, what if a defendant distributes a film based on a script which, unknown to the defendant, infringes the copyright in a novel? What planning techniques should a defendant undertake to avoid such a situation?

12.   Note that fair use is generally regarded as an affirmative defense (as Judge Burch noted in acquiescent disapproval in the *Wind Done Gone* case). The text of section 107 does suggest, however, that the status of fair use should perhaps be regarded as equal (or perhaps even superior) to the section 106 exclusive rights. We have chosen to present it in this casebook as a discrete subject.

F.   REMEDIES

Statutes: 17 U.S.C.A. §§ 412, 502–06, 509–10, 18 U.S.C.A. §§ 2318–19A

1.   INJUNCTIONS

Although section 502(a) of the 1976 Act authorizes a court to "grant temporary and final injunctions on such terms as it may deem reasonable to prevent or restrain infringement of a copyright," it does not mandate injunctive relief. See H.R. Rep. No. 94–1476, 94th Cong., 2d Sess. 160 (1976) ("Section 502(a) reasserts the discretionary power of courts to grant injunctions and restraining orders, whether 'preliminary,' 'temporary,' 'interlocutory,' 'permanent,' or 'final,' to prevent or stop infringements of copyright."). Note, however, that injunctive relief against the United States is barred by 28 U.S.C.A. § 1498.

Courts and commentators often recite the general rule that a permanent injunction should issue against the defendant when liability for copyright infringement has been established and there is a threat of continuing violations. Although courts continue to follow this general rule in practice, a number of authorities have suggested that equitable considerations may sometimes require departures from the rule.

In *Abend v. MCA, Inc.*, 863 F.2d 1465 (9th Cir.1988), *aff'd sub nom.* Stewart v. Abend, 495 U.S. 207, 110 S.Ct. 1750, 109 L.Ed.2d 184 (1990), the Ninth Circuit adopted a commentator's suggestion that "where great public injury would be worked by an injunction, the courts might ... award damages or a continuing royalty instead of an injunction in such special circumstances." *Id.* at 1479 (quoting 3 M. Nimmer, Nimmer on Copyright § 14.06[B] (1988)). It found such circumstances to exist where the defendant's continued exploitation of its motion picture, a derivative work prepared during the initial copyright term of the underlying short story, infringed the story's copyright during the renewal term, because the short story's author died before the renewal term could vest, thus invalidating the author's previous grant of renewal term rights to the defendant:

> * * * The "Rear Window" film resulted from the collaborative efforts of many talented individuals other than Cornell Woolrich, the author of the underlying story. The success of the movie resulted in large part from factors completely unrelated to the underlying story, "It Had To Be Murder." It would cause a great injustice for the owners of the film if the court enjoined them from further exhibition of the movie. An injunction would also effectively foreclose defendants from enjoying legitimate profits derived from exploitation of the "new matter" comprising the derivative work, which is given express copyright protection by section 7 of the 1909 Act. Since defendants could not possibly separate out the "new matter" from the underlying work, their right to enjoy the renewal copyright in the derivative work would be rendered meaningless by the grant of an injunction. We also note that an injunction could cause public injury by denying the public the opportunity to view a classic film for many years to come.

863 F.2d at 1479 (citing *Universal City Studios, Inc. v. Sony Corp. of Amer.*, 659 F.2d 963, 976 (9th Cir.1981) (approving Nimmer's suggestion that damages or a continuing royalty would constitute an acceptable resolution for infringement caused by in-home taping of television programs), *rev'd on other grounds,* 464 U.S. 417, 104 S.Ct. 774, 78 L.Ed.2d 574 (1984); and *Sony Corp. v. Universal City Studios*, 464 U.S. 417, 499–500, 104 S.Ct. 774, 817–18, 78 L.Ed.2d 574 (1984) (Blackmun, J., dissenting) (agreeing with the appellate court that "an award of damages, or continuing royalties, or even some form of limited injunction, may well be an appropriate means of balancing the equities in this case," and noting that if such remedies were not feasible, "[t]he Studios then would be relegated to statutory damages for proven instances of infringement.").

Since *Abend*, a number of authorities have joined the Ninth Circuit in suggesting that injunctive relief should not be viewed as an entitlement of prevailing infringement plaintiffs. See H.R. Rep. No. 101–735, 101st Cong., 2d Sess. 14 (1990) (accompanying the Architectural Works Copyright Protection Act of 1990) ("[A]ll would agree, the Committee believes, that 'equitable considerations, in this as in all fields of law, are pertinent to the appropriateness of injunctive relief. The public interest is always a relevant consideration for a court deciding whether to issue an injunction.'") (quoting, with an omission, *New Era Publications Int'l v. Henry Holt Co.,* 884 F.2d 659, 664 (2d Cir.1989) (Newman, J., dissenting) (denying petition for rehearing en banc), *cert. denied,* 493 U.S. 1094, 110 S.Ct. 1168, 107 L.Ed.2d 1071 (1990)); see also *New Era,* 884 F.2d at 661 (Miner, J., concurring) ("All now agree that injunction is not the automatic consequence of infringement and that equitable considerations always are germane to the determination of whether an injunction is appropriate.").

In *Campbell v. Acuff–Rose*, 510 U.S. 569, 114 S.Ct. 1164, 127 L.Ed.2d 500 (1994), the Supreme Court suggested in dicta that it agreed with the Ninth Circuit's approach in *Abend*:

> Because the fair use enquiry often requires close questions of judgment as to the extent of permissible borrowing in cases involving parodies (or other critical works), courts may also wish to bear in mind that the goals of the copyright law, "to stimulate the creation and publication of edifying matter," [Leval, Toward a Fair Use Standard, 103 Harv. L. Rev. 1105, 1134 (1990)] are not always best served by automatically granting injunctive relief when parodists are found to have gone beyond the bounds of fair use.

510 U.S. at 578 n. 10, 114 S.Ct. at 1171 n.10 (citing *Abend*, 863 F.2d at 1479); see also H.R. Rep. No. 103–826(I), 103d Cong., 2d Sess. 998 (1994) (Uruguay Round Agreements Act, Statement of Administrative Action) (citing footnote 10 of *Acuff-Rose* with approval, and noting that a court deciding whether to enjoin infringement of a restored copyright under section 104A should "apply all of the traditional canons of equity").

Still more recently, in *New York Times Company, Inc. v. Tasini*, 533 U.S. 483, 121 Sup. Ct. 2381, 150 L.Ed.2d 500 (2001), the Court observed that copyright infringement does not automatically lead to injunctive relief, citing *Acuff-Rose* and other authorities.

Notes

1. In determining whether to deny injunctive relief once infringement has been established, consider how much weight, if any, should be given to each of the following factors: (1) the defendant's creative contribution to the infringing work; (2) the defendant's financial investment in the infringing work; (3) other injuries, such as harm to reputation or business relationships, which the defendant might suffer if an injunction were granted; (4) the omission of copyright notice on the plaintiff's work; (5) the defendant's efforts to locate the copyright owner in order to obtain consent; (6) other evidence of the defendant's good faith, such as crediting the copyright owner. If, as *Abend* suggests, "public injury" is a factor, what does it mean?

2. Consider the appropriateness of injunctive relief where:

    (a) the copyright in an architectural design is infringed by construction of a building;

    (b) a defendant copies protectible elements of the plaintiff's work as a preliminary step in creating a finished work from which all infringing material has been expunged.

3. Consider the facts of the *Napster* case, *supra* pages 1119–1129. Would this be an appropriate scenario for awarding continuing damages (such as a compulsory royalty) in place of injunctive relief? For the Ninth Circuit's answer, see *A&M Records, Inc. v. Napster*, Inc., 239 F.3d 1004, 1028–1029 (9th Cir.2001).

4. Would denial of injunctive relief be consistent with the United States' obligations under Arts. 8–14bis of the Berne Convention? *Cf.* Art. 6bis.

5.   Once infringement has been established, courts have issued permanent injunctions that extend to works which the defendant has not yet
infringed, and even those which the plaintiff has not yet created. See, *e.g.,*
Walt Disney Co. v. Powell, 897 F.2d 565, 568 (D.C.Cir.1990) (collecting
authorities). Can this approach be reconciled with the requirement that a
copyright be registered as a prerequisite to an infringement suit?

6.   *Preliminary Injunctions:* Courts will generally grant a preliminary
injunction where the plaintiff shows "either a likelihood of success on the
merits and the possibility of irreparable injury, or that serious questions
going to the merits [are] raised and the balance of hardships tips sharply in
its favor." *Johnson Controls, Inc. v. Phoenix Control Sys., Inc.,* 886 F.2d
1173, 1174 (9th Cir.1989). The prevailing view is "that a showing of a prima
facie case of copyright infringement, or reasonable likelihood of success on
the merits, raises a presumption of irreparable harm." *Id.* Should a plaintiff's delay in bringing suit be relevant to this analysis?

7.   *Infringement by the United States:* Under 28 U.S.C.A. § 1498(b), the
exclusive remedy for copyright infringement by the United States or its
contractors is a suit in the United States Court of Federal Claims for
reasonable compensation, including statutory damages under section 504(c).
Injunctive relief is unavailable.

2.   ACTUAL DAMAGES AND PROFITS

FRANK MUSIC CORP. v. METRO–GOLDWYN–MAYER, INC.

United States Court of Appeals, Ninth Circuit, 1985.
772 F.2d 505.

FLETCHER, CIRCUIT JUDGE:

This copyright infringement suit arises out of defendants' use of five
songs from plaintiffs' dramatico-musical play *Kismet* in a musical revue
staged at defendant MGM Grand Hotel in 1974–76. After a bench trial,
the district court found infringement and awarded the plaintiffs $22,000
as a share of defendants' profits. Plaintiffs appeal and defendants cross-
appeal. We affirm in part, reverse in part, and remand.

I.   FACTS

[The original version of *Kismet* was a dramatic play by Edward
Knoblock; its copyright expired in 1967. A musical adaptation of that
play was copyrighted in 1953 and 1954, and in 1954 the musical's
authors licensed a predecessor of MGM to produce a motion picture
version of the musical. The plaintiffs in this action are the authors and
assignee of the copyright in the musical stage play.]

* * *

The story presented in the MGM film and in plaintiffs' dramatico-
musical play is essentially the same as that told in Knoblock's dramatic
play. It is the tale of a day in the life of a poetic beggar named Hajj and
his daughter, Marsinah. The story is set in ancient Baghdad, with major

scenes in the streets of Baghdad, the Wazir's palace, an enchanted garden, and the Wazir's harem.

On April 26, 1974, defendant MGM Grand Hotel premiered a musical revue entitled *Hallelujah Hollywood* in the hotel's Ziegfield Theatre. The show was staged, produced, and directed by defendant Donn Arden. It featured ten acts of singing, dancing, and variety performances. Of the ten acts, four were labeled as "tributes" to MGM motion pictures of the past, and one was a tribute to the "Ziegfield Follies." The remaining acts were variety numbers, which included performances by a live tiger, a juggler, and the magicians, Siegfried and Roy.

* * *

Act IV of *Hallelujah Hollywood*, the subject of this lawsuit, was entitled "Kismet," and was billed as a tribute to the MGM movie of that name. Comprised of four scenes, it was approximately eleven and one-half minutes in length. It was set in ancient Baghdad, as was plaintiffs' play, and the characters were called by the same or similar names to those used in plaintiffs' play. Five songs were taken in whole or in part from plaintiffs' play. No dialogue was spoken during the act, and, in all, it contained approximately six minutes of music taken directly from plaintiffs' play.

The total running time of *Hallelujah Hollywood* was approximately 100 minutes, except on Saturday nights when two acts were deleted, shortening the show to 75 minutes. The show was performed three times on Saturday evenings, twice on the other evenings of the week.

* * *

1. *Actual Damages*

"Actual damages" are the extent to which the market value of a copyrighted work has been injured or destroyed by an infringement. 3 M. Nimmer, Nimmer on Copyright § 14.02, at 14–6 (1985). In this circuit, we have stated the test of market value as "what a willing buyer would have been reasonably required to pay to a willing seller for plaintiffs' work." [Sid & Marty Krofft Television Prods., Inc. v. McDonald's Corp., 562 F.2d 1157 (9th Cir.1977),] at 1174.

The district court declined to award actual damages. The court stated that it was "unconvinced that the market value of plaintiffs' work was in any way diminished as a result of defendant's infringement." * * *

Plaintiffs contend the district court's finding is clearly erroneous in light of the evidence they presented concerning the royalties *Kismet* could have earned in a full Las Vegas production. Plaintiffs did offer evidence of the royalties *Kismet* had earned in productions around the country. They also introduced opinion testimony, elicited from plaintiff Lester and from *Kismet*'s leasing agent, that a full production of *Kismet* could have been licensed in Las Vegas for $7,500 per week. And they introduced other opinion testimony to the effect that *Hallelujah Hollywood* had destroyed the Las Vegas market for a production of plaintiffs' *Kismet.*

In a copyright action, a trial court is entitled to reject a proffered measure of damages if it is too speculative. See Peter Pan Fabrics, Inc. v. Jobela Fabrics, Inc., 329 F.2d 194, 196–97 (2d Cir.1964). Although uncertainty as to the amount of damages will not preclude recovery, uncertainty as to the fact of damages may. Universal Pictures Co. v. Harold Lloyd Corp., 162 F.2d at 369; see also 3 M. Nimmer, supra, § 14.02, at 14–8 to–9. It was the *fact* of damages that concerned the district court. The court found that plaintiffs "failed to establish *any* damages attributable to the infringement." (emphasis in original). This finding is not clearly erroneous.

Plaintiffs offered no disinterested testimony showing that *Hallelujah Hollywood* precluded plaintiffs from presenting *Kismet* at some other hotel in Las Vegas. It is not implausible to conclude, as the court below apparently did, that a production presenting six minutes of music from *Kismet,* without telling any of the story of the play, would not significantly impair the prospects for presenting a full production of that play.[7] Based on the record presented, the district court was not clearly erroneous in finding that plaintiffs' theory of damages was uncertain and speculative.

2. *Infringer's Profits*

As an alternative to actual damages, a prevailing plaintiff in an infringement action is entitled to recover the infringer's profits to the

---

7. Another panel of this court considered a similar problem recently in Cream Records, Inc. v. Jos. Schlitz Brewing Co., 754 F.2d 826 (9th Cir.1985) (interpreting the 1976 Act). In Cream Records, the jury found that Schlitz and its advertising agency infringed Cream's copyright in "The Theme from Shaft", by using a ten-note ostinato from the song in a television commercial. The district court awarded $12,000 as actual damages for loss of licensing fees. We concluded that the award was insufficient, stating:

> The only evidence before the court was that unauthorized use of the Shaft theme music in Schlitz's commercial ended Cream's opportunity to license the music for this purpose. There was no evidence that Schlitz sought, or Cream was willing to grant, a license for use of less than the entire copyrighted work, that a license limited to the portion used in the commercial would have had less value, or that use limited to this portion would have had a less devastating effect upon Cream's opportunity to license to anoth-

er. Since defendants' unauthorized use destroyed the value of the copyrighted work for this purpose, plaintiff was entitled to recover that value as damages.

Id. at 827–28 (citation omitted).

In Cream Records, the evidence showed that another advertiser had approached Cream for a license for the song, but withdrew when the Schlitz commercial was aired. "There was testimony that use of a well-known popular song in a commercial destroys its value to other advertisers for that purpose." 754 F.2d 826, 827.

The evidence concerning the effect of defendants' infringement is far less convincing in our case. Plaintiffs did introduce testimony that the infringement had destroyed the Las Vegas market for a full production of *Kismet,* but that testimony came from *Kismet*'s leasing agent, not a disinterested party. We agree with the district court's characterization of this evidence as "meager," and we cannot conclude that the court clearly erred in discrediting it.

extent they are attributable to the infringement. 17 U.S.C. § 101(b); Krofft, 562 F.2d at 1172. In establishing the infringer's profits, the plaintiff is required to prove only the defendant's sales; the burden then shifts to the defendant to prove the elements of costs to be deducted from sales in arriving at profit. 17 U.S.C. § 101(b). Any doubt as to the computation of costs or profits is to be resolved in favor of the plaintiff. Shapiro, Bernstein & Co. v. Remington Records, Inc., 265 F.2d 263 (2d Cir.1959). If the infringing defendant does not meet its burden of proving costs, the gross figure stands as the defendant's profits. Russell v. Price, 612 F.2d 1123, 1130–31 (9th Cir.1979), cert. denied, 446 U.S. 952, 100 S.Ct. 2919, 64 L.Ed.2d 809 (1980).

The district court, following this approach, found that the gross revenue MGM Grand earned from the presentation of *Hallelujah Hollywood* during the relevant time period was $24,191,690. From that figure, the court deducted direct costs of $18,060,084 and indirect costs (overhead) of $3,641,960, thus arriving at a net profit of $2,489,646.

* * * Plaintiffs claim the district court erred in allowing deductions for overhead expenses for two reasons: because the infringement was "conscious and deliberate," and because defendants failed to show that each item of claimed overhead assisted in the production of the infringement. Plaintiffs also contend the court erred in not including in gross profits some portion of MGM's earnings on its hotel and gaming operations.

A portion of an infringer's overhead properly may be deducted from gross revenues to arrive at profits, at least where the infringement was not willful, conscious, or deliberate. Kamar International, Inc. v. Russ Berrie & Co., 752 F.2d 1326, 1331 (9th Cir.1984); Sammons v. Colonial Press, Inc., 126 F.2d 341, 351 (1st Cir.1942); 3 M. Nimmer, supra, § 14.03[B], at 14–16.1. Plaintiffs argue that the infringement here was conscious and deliberate, but the district court found to the contrary. The court's finding is not clearly erroneous. Defendants believed their use of *Kismet* was protected under MGM Grand's ASCAP license. Although their contention ultimately proved to be wrong, it was not implausible. Defendants reasonably could have believed that their production was not infringing plaintiffs' copyrights, and, therefore, the district court was not clearly erroneous in finding that their conduct was not willful. See Kamar International, Inc. v. Russ Berrie & Co., 752 F.2d at 1331.

We find more merit in plaintiffs' second challenge to the deduction of overhead costs. They argue that defendants failed to show that each item of claimed overhead assisted in the production of the infringement. The evidence defendants introduced at trial segregated overhead expenses into general categories, such as general and administrative costs, sales and advertising, and engineering and maintenance. Defendants then allocated a portion of these costs to the production of *Hallelujah Hollywood* based on a ratio of the revenues from that production as compared to MGM Grand's total revenues. The district court adopted this approach.

* * *

We do not doubt that some of defendants' claimed overhead contributed to the production of *Hallelujah Hollywood*. The difficulty we have, however, is that defendants offered no evidence of what costs were included in general categories such as "general and administrative expenses," nor did they offer any evidence concerning how these costs contributed to the production of *Hallelujah Hollywood*. The defendants contend their burden was met when they introduced evidence of their total overhead costs allocated on a reasonable basis. The district court apparently agreed with this approach. That is not the law of this circuit. Under Kamar International, a defendant additionally must show that the categories of overhead actually contributed to sales of the infringing work. 752 F.2d at 1332. We can find no such showing in the record before us. Therefore, we conclude the district court's finding that "defendants have established that these items of general expense [the general categories of claimed overhead] contributed to the production of 'Hallelujah Hollywood' " was clearly erroneous.

Plaintiffs next challenge the district court's failure to consider MGM Grand's earnings on hotel and gaming operations in arriving at the amount of profits attributable to the infringement. The district court received evidence concerning MGM Grand's total net profit during the relevant time period, totaling approximately $395,000,000, but its memorandum decision does not mention these indirect profits and computes recovery based solely on the revenues and profits earned on the production of *Hallelujah Hollywood* (approximately $24,000,000 and $2,500,000 respectively). We surmise from this that the district court determined plaintiffs were not entitled to recover indirect profits, but we have no hint as to the district court's reasons.

Whether a copyright proprietor may recover "indirect profits" is one of first impression in this circuit. We conclude that under the 1909 Act indirect profits may be recovered.

The 1909 Act provided that a copyright proprietor is entitled to "all the profits which the infringer shall have made from such infringement.... " 17 U.S.C. § 101(b). The language of the statute is broad enough to permit recovery of indirect as well as direct profits. See 3 M. Nimmer, supra, § 14.03[A], at 14–15; cf. Nucor Corp. v. Tennessee Forging Steel Service, Inc., 513 F.2d 151, 153 (8th Cir.1975) (common law copyright infringement action; issue of whether infringing use of copyrighted architectural plans resulted in lower manufacturing costs to defendants was properly put to jury). At the same time, a court may deny recovery of a defendant's profits if they are only remotely or speculatively attributable to the infringement. See 3 M. Nimmer, supra, § 14.03[A]; see, e.g., Roy Export Co. v. Columbia Broadcasting System, Inc., 503 F.Supp. 1137, 1156–57 (S.D.N.Y.1980) (profits from an infringing unsponsored television broadcast could not be ascertained since benefit received by CBS "consists of unmeasurable good-will with affiliates and increased stature and prestige vis-a-vis competitors."), aff'd, 672 F.2d 1095 (2d Cir.), cert. denied, 459 U.S. 826, 74 L.Ed.2d 63, 103 S.Ct. 60 (1982).

The allowance of indirect profits was considered in Sid & Marty Krofft Television Productions, Inc. v. McDonald's Corp., 1983 Copyright L. Rep. (CCH) P25,572 at 18,381 (C.D. Cal. 1983) (Krofft II), on remand from 562 F.2d 1157 (9th Cir.1977), a case involving facts analogous to those presented here. The plaintiffs, creators of the "H.R. Pufnstuf" children's television program, alleged that they were entitled to a portion of the profits McDonald's earned on its food sales as damages for the "McDonaldland" television commercials that infringed plaintiffs' copyright. The district court rejected as speculative the plaintiffs' formula for computing profits attributable to the infringement. However, the court's analysis and award of in lieu damages indicate that it considered indirect profits recoverable. The court stated, in awarding $1,044,000 in statutory damages, that "because a significant portion of defendants' profits made from the infringement are not ascertainable, a higher award of [statutory] in lieu damages is warranted." Id. at 18,384; see also Cream Records Inc. v. Jos. Schlitz Brewing Co., 754 F.2d 826, 828–29 (9th Cir.1985) (discussed supra note 7) (awarding profits from the sale of malt liquor for Schlitz's infringing use of plaintiff's song in television commercial).

Like the television commercials in Krofft II, *Hallelujah Hollywood* had promotional value. Defendants maintain that they endeavor to earn profits on all their operations and that *Hallelujah Hollywood* was a profit center. However, that fact does not detract from the promotional purposes of the show—to draw people to the hotel and the gaming tables. MGM's 1976 annual report states that "the hotel and gaming operations of the MGM Grand—Las Vegas continue to be materially enhanced by the popularity of the hotel's entertainment[, including] 'Hallelujah Hollywood', the spectacularly successful production revue.... " Given the promotional nature of *Hallelujah Hollywood,* we conclude indirect profits from the hotel and gaming operations, as well as direct profits from the show itself, are recoverable if ascertainable.

3. *Apportionment of Profits*

How to apportion profits between the infringers and the plaintiffs is a complex issue in this case. Apportionment of direct profits from the production as well as indirect profits from the hotel and casino operations are involved here, although the district court addressed only the former at the first trial.

When an infringer's profits are attributable to factors in addition to use of plaintiff's work, an apportionment of profits is proper. Sheldon v. Metro–Goldwyn Pictures Corp., 309 U.S. 390, 405–06, 84 L.Ed. 825, 60 S.Ct. 681 (1939) (Sheldon II); Universal Pictures Co. v. Harold Lloyd Corp., 162 F.2d at 377. The burden of proving apportionment, (i.e., the contribution to profits of elements other than the infringed property), is the defendant's. Lottie Joplin Thomas Trust v. Crown Publishers, Inc., 592 F.2d 651, 657 (2d Cir.1978). We will not reverse a district court's findings regarding apportionment unless they are clearly erroneous. See Shapiro, Bernstein & Co. v. 4636 S. Vermont Ave., Inc., 367 F.2d at 241–42.

After finding that the net profit earned by *Hallelujah Hollywood* was approximately $2,500,000, the district court offered the following explanation of apportionment:

> While no precise mathematical formula can be applied, the court concludes in light of the evidence presented at trial and the entire record in this case, a fair approximation of the profits of Act IV attributable to the infringement is $22,000.

The district court was correct that mathematical exactness is not required. However, a reasonable and just apportionment of profits is required. Sheldon II, 309 U.S. at 408; Universal Pictures Co. v. Harold Lloyd Corp., 162 F.2d at 377.

Arriving at a proper method of apportionment and determining a specific amount to award is largely a factual exercise. Defendants understandably argue that the facts support the district court's award. They claim that the infringing material, six minutes of music in Act IV, was an unimportant part of the whole show, that the unique features of the Ziegfield Theater contributed more to the show's success than any other factor. This is proved, they argue, by the fact that when the music from *Kismet* was removed from *Hallelujah Hollywood* in 1976, the show suffered no decline in attendance and the hotel received no complaints.

Other evidence contradicts defendants' position. For instance, defendant Donn Arden testified that *Kismet* was "a very important part of the show" and "[he] hated to see it go." Moreover, while other acts were deleted from the shortened Saturday night versions of the show, Act IV "Kismet" never was.

We reject defendants' contention that the relative unimportance of the *Kismet* music was proved by its omission and the show's continued success thereafter. *Hallelujah Hollywood* was a revue, comprised of many different entertainment elements. Each element contributed significantly to the show's success, but no one element was the sole or overriding reason for that success. Just because one element could be omitted and the show goes on does not prove that the element was not important in the first instance and did not contribute to establishing the show's initial popularity.

The difficulty in this case is that the district court has not provided us with any reasoned explanation of or formula for its apportionment. We know only the district court's bottom line: that the plaintiffs are entitled to $22,000. Given the nature of the infringement, the character of the infringed property, the success of defendants' show, and the magnitude of the defendants' profits, the amount seems to be grossly inadequate. It amounts to less than one percent of MGM Grand's profits from the show, or roughly $13 for each of the 1700 infringing perform-ances.

On remand, the district court should reconsider its apportionment of profits, and should fully explain on the record its reasons and the resulting method of apportionment it uses. Apportionment of indirect profits may be a part of the calculus. If the court finds that a reasonable, nonspeculative formula cannot be derived, or that the amount of profits a reasonable formula yields is insufficient to serve the purposes underly-ing the statute, then the court should award statutory damages. * * *

* * *

Notes

1. In calculating a damages award based on defendant's profits, should an infringer be permitted to subtract taxes paid on those profits?

2. Should an infringer's profits be reduced by the cost of infringing inventory that has not been sold?

3. Two federal courts in 1999 permitted copyright infringers to deduct certain overhead expenses in calculating an award of the defendant's profits resulting from the infringement. See *Hamil America, Inc. v. GFI*, 193 F.3d 92 (2d Cir.1999) (requiring a "nexus" between the overhead category and the infringing item); *ZZ Top v. Chrysler Corp.*, 70 F.Supp.2d 1167 (W.D.Wash.1999) (allowing willful infringer to deduct overhead, finding this an open question in the Ninth Circuit, and rejecting contrary authorities from other circuits).

4. In *Los Angeles News Service v. Reuters Television International, Ltd.*, 149 F.3d 987 (9th Cir.1998), *cert. denied*, 525 U.S. 1141, 119 S.Ct. 1032, 143 L.Ed.2d 41 (1999), the Ninth Circuit held that a copyright owner could recover infringement damages "flowing from" overseas exploitation of the defendant's domestic infringements. The court expressly adopted the reason-ing of the Second Circuit in *Sheldon v. Metro–Goldwyn Pictures Corp.*, 106 F.2d 45 (2d Cir.1939), *aff'd*, 309 U.S. 390, 60 S.Ct. 681, 84 L.Ed. 825 (1940), which allowed recovery of damages from infringing uses abroad where a domestic infringing act made the foreign exploitation possible. The court distinguished cases such as *Subafilms, Ltd. v. MGM–Pathe Communications Co.*, 24 F.3d 1088, 1094 (9th Cir.1994) (en banc) and *Allarcom Pay Televi-sion, Ltd. v. General Instrument Corp.*, 69 F.3d 381, 387 (9th Cir.1995), in which no *liability* was found because there was no direct infringement within the United States.

In 2003, the Ninth Circuit again looked at the issue of damages and profits from overseas infringing activity in *Los Angeles News Service v. Reuters Television International Ltd.*, 340 F.3d 926 (9th Cir. 2003). The court narrowed its previous holding, stating that the Copyright Act does not provide recovery of actual damages resulting from overseas infringement, but only the profits that the infringer derived from these infringements.

5. The U.S. Court of Appeals for the Second Circuit held that actual damages for infringement of a copyrighted work may be based on the fair market value of a license fee. See *On Davis v. The Gap, Inc.*, 246 F.3d 152 (2d Cir.2001)(court held that a reasonable license fee theory was not too speculative as a measure of damages for the use of an image of plaintiff's copyrighted design in Gap store advertisements).

3. ADDITIONAL REMEDIES

(i) Statutory Damages and Attorneys' Fees

Although a plaintiff may elect to recover statutory damages in place of actual damages and profits, in most cases involving infringement of exclusive rights under section 106, section 412 precludes an award of statutory damages or attorneys' fees for infringements which precede registration of the copyright in the infringed work. An exception applies to *published* works that are registered within three months of publication, but which are infringed *between* publication and registration. 17 U.S.C.A. § 412(2). Where statutory damages are recoverable, section 504 establishes a wide range of discretion in the amount that may be awarded, but permits only a *single* award of statutory damages for *each* work infringed by the defendant, regardless of how many times the infringing activity was repeated.

The amounts recoverable have increased substantially since 1976. The Digital Theft Deterrence and Copyright Damages Improvement Act of 1999, P.L. 106–160, 106th Cong., 1st Sess. (1999), amended section 504(c) to increase minimum statutory damages for copyright infringements from $500 to $750, and maximum statutory damages from $20,000 to $30,000, per infringed work. However, the minimum award of $200 under prior law remains in effect where the infringer was not aware and had no reason to believe his or her acts constituted infringement. Maximum statutory damages for willful infringement have increased from $100,000 to $150,000.

Meanwhile, in *Feltner v. Columbia Pictures Television, Inc.*, 523 U.S. 340, 118 S.Ct. 1279, 140 L.Ed.2d 438 (1998), the Supreme Court held that, while section 504(c) itself does not provide a right to a jury trial on the question of statutory damages, the Seventh Amendment "provides a right to a jury trial on all issues pertinent to an award of statutory damages under § 504(c) of the Copyright Act, including the amount itself." 523 U.S. at 355.

Innocent and Willful Infringements: Section 504(c)(1) prescribes the normal maximum and minimum amounts of statutory damages, but subsection (c)(2) allows an award above this range where the infringer's conduct is willful (that is, carried out with knowledge that the conduct was infringing), and below this range where the defendant reasonably and in good faith believed that the infringing activities did not infringe. Statutory damages are remitted altogether in the case of certain activities by nonprofit entities and public broadcasters when they believe their actions constitute fair use, and this rule overrides the provisions of section 401 and 402 which make the innocent infringement defense unavailable with respect to works bearing a copyright notice.

Under section 405(b), if copyright notice was omitted from copies or phonorecords distributed before March 1, 1989 (the effective date of the Berne Convention Implementation Act (BCIA)), an infringer who reasonably and in good faith believed that his or her conduct was noninfringing, and who was misled by the omission of notice, will incur no liability for actual or statutory damages for infringing acts undertaken before receiving actual notice of the copyright registration. Note, however, that section 405(b) permits a court to award other remedies, such as the defendant's profits, a reasonable royalty, or injunctive relief.

Standards for Awarding Attorney's Fees: Section 505 permits a court at its discretion to award "full costs" and "a reasonable attorney's fee" to the prevailing party in infringement litigation. In Fogerty v. Fantasy, Inc., 510 U.S. 517, 114 S.Ct. 1023, 127 L.Ed.2d 455 (1994), the defendant successfully defended against a claim that his song infringed the plaintiff's copyright, but the district court refused to award him attorney's fees, finding that the suit was not frivolous or in bad faith. The Supreme Court rejected the argument that attorney's fees should be recovered automatically by the prevailing party. The Court then addressed the split of authority on whether, in determining whether attorney's fees should be awarded, the same standards should apply to prevailing plaintiffs as to prevailing defendants, or whether fees should be awarded to prevailing plaintiffs as a matter of course and to prevailing defendants only if the suit was frivolous or brought in bad faith. The Court held that the 1976 Act required an "evenhanded" approach, finding no support in section 505 or its legislative history for treating plaintiffs and defendants differently. The Court rejected the reasoning of the Ninth Circuit that the "dual" standard was necessary "to avoid chilling a copyright holder's incentive to sue on colorable claims, and thereby to give full effect to the broad protection for copyrights intended by the Copyright Act," *id.* at 521 (quoting Fantasy v. Fogerty, 984 F.2d 1524, 1532 (9th Cir.1993)), and explained:

> * * * [T]he policies served by the Copyright Act are more complex, more measured, than simply maximizing the number of meritorious suits for copyright infringement. * * * We have often recognized the monopoly privileges that Congress has authorized, while "intended to motivate the creative activity of authors and inventors by the provision of a special reward," are limited in nature and must ultimately serve the public good. Sony Corp. of America v. Universal City Studios, Inc., 464 U.S. 417, 429 (1984). * * *

> Because copyright law ultimately serves the purpose of enriching the general public through access to creative works, it is peculiarly important that the boundaries of copyright law be demarcated as clearly as possible. To that end, defendants who seek to advance a variety of meritorious copyright defenses should be encouraged to litigate them to the same extent that plaintiffs are encouraged to

litigate meritorious claims of infringement. In the case before us, the successful defense of "The Old Man Down the Road" increased public exposure to a musical work that could, as a result, lead to further creative pieces. Thus a successful defense of a copyright infringement action may further the policies of the Copyright Act every bit as much as a successful prosecution of an infringement claim by the holder of a copyright.

Id. at 526–27, 114 S.Ct. at 1029–30. Noting that there was "no precise rule or formula" for determining when an award was appropriate, the Court nonetheless took note of certain nonexclusive factors that had been applied by courts in following the evenhanded approach:

> These factors include "frivolousness, motivation, objective unreasonableness (both in the factual and in the legal components of the case) and the need in particular circumstances to advance considerations of compensation and deterrence." Lieb v. Topstone Industries, Inc., 788 F.2d 151, 156 (C.A.3 1986). We agree that such factors may be used to guide courts' discretion, so long as such factors are faithful to the purposes of the Copyright Act and are applied to prevailing plaintiffs and defendants in an evenhanded manner.

Id. at 534 n.19, 114 S.Ct. at 1033 n. 19. Although bad faith is not a statutory prerequisite, in practice most courts have awarded attorney's fees in copyright actions only against a party that has demonstrated some moral culpability, such as willful infringement or bad faith litigation.

Notes

1. In a case involving continuing infringements of a plaintiff's copyrighted maps, where the infringements commenced before registration of most of those works and continued after registration, the Fifth Circuit held that a plaintiff could not recover, for the *same* infringed work, both actual damages for pre-registration infringements and statutory damages and attorneys' fees for post-registration infringements by the same defendant. *Mason v. Montgomery Data, Inc.*, 967 F.2d 135 (5th Cir.1992). Note, however, that where a single action involves infringement of some unregistered and some registered works, the plaintiff may elect actual damages for the unregistered works and statutory damages (plus attorneys' fees) for the registered works.

2. In a suit for a pre-registration infringement under section 106, section 412 provides that, with one exception, prevailing plaintiffs may not recover attorneys' fees or statutory damages. Is this appropriate in the case of works that have only been published abroad and/or have entered the United States only through digital transmissions? What about unpublished foreign works?

3. Where no other actual damages can be established, is it appropriate to award a copyright owner actual damages based on a reasonable estimate of the licensing fees that defendant avoided paying to the plaintiff by

infringing the plaintiff's copyrighted work? Does it matter whether the infringement preceded registration?

4. What impact might *Fogerty* have on potential plaintiffs and defendants in close cases, such as those involving colorable claims of fair use? Should the court's discretion be narrowed to give litigants a better opportunity to assess their risks?

5. How should a court decide the question of attorney's fees where: (a) a party prevails on some, but not all, of the infringement claims (or against some, but not all, of the infringement defendants), (b) some, but not all, infringement claims are litigated in bad faith, (c) the suit involves both copyright and noncopyright claims, or (d) the plaintiff prevails on infringement claims involving both registered and unregistered works?

6. In a case of first impression, the First Circuit held that statutory damages under 504 (c) of the Copyright Act are awarded for the number of songs infringed, rather than the number of infringing albums. *Venegas-Hernandez v. Sonolux Records*, 370 F.3d 183 (1st Cir. 2004).

7. In *BMG Music v. Gonzalez*, 430 F.3d 888 (7th Cir. 2005), in which the defendant had downloaded and saved more than 1300 songs, with notice that they were copyrighted, the court approved an award of unreduced statutory damages, despite the fact that the defendant also owned all but a handful of the songs in other formats. The court further held that the district court's entry of summary judgment as to the minimum statutory damages claim did not deny her right to a jury trial.

(ii) Impounding, Importation Relief, Prejudgment Interest, and Costs

Impounding: A prevailing copyright plaintiff may obtain a court order impounding and ordering the disposition of the infringing articles. Typically the court will order that they be turned over to the plaintiff, although outright destruction may also be ordered. 17 U.S.C.A. § 503.

Importation Relief: Under section 337 of the Tariff Act of 1930, a copyright owner may bring an action before the International Trade Commission to obtain an order barring importation of infringing goods, provided the plaintiff's copyright has been registered. See 19 U.S.C.A. § 1337 (discussed at page 894, *supra*). Exclusion of goods that infringe registered copyrights is also available under 17 U.S.C.A. § 603.

Prejudgment Interest: Although the copyright statutes are silent on the availability of prejudgment interest, a number of courts have allowed it. See, *e.g., Kleier Advertising v. Premier Pontiac*, 921 F.2d 1036 (10th Cir.1990); Computer Associates International, Inc. v. Altai, Inc., 982 F.2d 693 (2d Cir.1992); *Data General Corp. v. Grumman Systems Support Corp.*, 825 F.Supp. 340 (D.Mass.1993), *later opinion* 825 F.Supp. 361, 368 (D.Mass.1993) (prejudgment interest allowed on damages but not on attorney fees); *Bourne Co. v. Walt Disney Co.*, 31 U.S.P.Q. 2d BNA 1858 (S.D.N.Y.1994).

Costs: Section 505 permits a court to award "full costs" to any party "other than the United States or an officer thereof," but provides no guidelines for the exercise of this discretion. In practice, most courts have awarded costs only against a party that demonstrates some degree of moral culpability. Note that section 505, on its face, would allow an award of costs even to a losing party.

(iii) Criminal Penalties

Under sections 506 and 509, some instances of copyright infringement (as well as certain acts other than infringement, as specified in section 506(c)-(f)) may give rise to criminal prosecution and penalties. Prior to 1997, criminal penalties applied only where an infringement was both willful and "for purposes of commercial advantage." 17 U.S.C.A. § 506. In United States v. LaMacchia, 871 F.Supp. 535 (D.Mass.1994), the "commercial advantage" requirement prevented the government from prosecuting a defendant for criminal copyright infringement where he made Internet sites available for others to receive and transmit copyrighted commercial software; as a result, the government unsuccessfully attempted to prosecute the defendant for wire fraud. *LaMacchia* prompted the following response from the Working Group on Intellectual Property Rights in its 1995 report on Intellectual Property and the National Information Infrastructure (NII):

> Although the Copyright Act provides criminal penalties when the infringement is willful and is for purposes of commercial advantage or private financial gain, the dismissal of the criminal charges in United States v. LaMacchia demonstrates a serious lacuna in the criminal copyright provisions: it does not now reach even the most wanton and malicious large-scale endeavors to copy and provide on the NII limitless numbers of unauthorized copies of valuable copyrighted works unless the copier seeks profits. Since there is virtually no cost to the infringer, certain individuals are willing to make such copies (or assist others in making them) for reasons other than monetary reward. For example, someone who believes that all works should be free in Cyberspace can easily make and distribute thousands of copies of a protected work and may have no desire for commercial advantage or private financial gain.

The Working Group agrees with the LaMacchia court:

> Criminal as well as civil penalties should probably attach to willful, multiple infringements of copyrighted software even absent a commercial motive on the part of the infringer. One could envision ways that the copyright law could be modified to permit such prosecution. But, "[i]t is the legislature, not the Court[,] which is to define a crime, and ordain its punishment."

Information Infrastructure Task Force, Intellectual Property and the National Information Infrastructure, The Report of the Working Group on Intellectual Property Rights 228–29 (1995). The Working Group indicated its support for proposed amendments which would make it a criminal offense to willfully infringe a copyright by reproducing or distributing copies with a retail value of $5,000 or more, reasoning that this approach would "ensure that merely casual or careless conduct resulting in distribution of only a few copies will not be subject to criminal prosecution and that criminal charges will not be brought unless there is a significant level of harm to the copyright owner's rights." *Id.* at 229.

In 1997, Congress responded to these concerns by enacting the No Electronic Theft Act, Pub. L. 105–147, 105th Cong., 1st Session (1997), which revised section 506(a) to reach willful copying or distribution that amounts to a retail value of $1,000 or more within a 6–month period, regardless of whether it is undertaken for the purpose of commercial advantage or private financial gain. The Act also defines "financial gain" to include the "receipt, or expectation of receipt, of anything of value, including the receipt of other copyrighted works." The new definition appears in section 101.

* * *

*

Part VIII

PREEMPTION

Chapter 21

PREEMPTION OF STATE LAW BY FEDERAL PATENT AND COPYRIGHT LAW

State laws protecting various forms of intellectual property will in some cases be unenforceable because they interfere with the functioning of the federal copyright or patent regime. Under the Supremacy Clause of the Constitution, federal law must prevail when such a conflict arises. Because it is not always clear whether the operation of a particular state doctrine contravenes the intent of Congress, in section 301 of the Copyright Act of 1976 Congress specified certain conditions under which state laws would be preempted by federal copyright law. A comparable provision appears in the Semiconductor Chip Protection Act of 1984. See 17 U.S.C.A. § 912(c). In patent law, by contrast, there is no statutory preemption standard.

A. STATUTORY COPYRIGHT PREEMPTION: SECTION 301

Statutes: 17 U.S.C.A. § 301

In the excerpt from H.Rep. No. 94–1476 which follows, note that the specific examples cited from 17 U.S.C.A. § 301(b)(3) of the 1976 Act were deleted prior to its passage. See H.R. Rep. No. 94–1733, 94th Cong., 2d Sess. 79 (1976). What impact does this have on your analysis of the scope of preemption under section 301?

COPYRIGHT ACT OF 1976
H.R. Rep. No. 94–1476.
94th Cong., 2d Sess. 129–33 (1976).

* * *

Section 301, one of the bedrock provisions of the bill, would accomplish a fundamental and significant change in the present law. Instead of a dual system of "common law copyright" for unpublished works and statutory copyright for published works, which has been the system in effect in the United States since the first copyright statute in 1790, the bill adopts a single system of Federal statutory copyright from creation. * * *

By substituting a single Federal system for the present anachronistic, uncertain, impractical, and highly complicated dual system, the bill would greatly improve the operation of the copyright law and would be much more effective in carrying out the basic constitutional aims of uniformity and the promotion of writing and scholarship. * * *

* * * One of the fundamental purposes behind the copyright clause of the Constitution, as shown in Madison's comments in The Federalist, was to promote national uniformity and to avoid the practical difficulties of determining and enforcing an author's rights under the differing laws and in the separate courts of the various States. Today, when the methods for dissemination of an author's work are incomparably broader and faster than they were in 1789, national uniformity in copyright protection is even more essential than it was then to carry out the constitutional intent. * * *

* * *

PREEMPTION OF STATE LAW

The intention of section 301 is to preempt and abolish any rights under the common law or statutes of a State that are equivalent to copyright and that extend to works coming within the scope of the Federal copyright law. The declaration of this principle in section 301 is intended to be stated in the clearest and most unequivocal language possible, so as to foreclose any conceivable misinterpretation of its unqualified intention that Congress shall act preemptively, and to avoid the development of any vague borderline areas between State and Federal protection.

* * * Regardless of when the work was created and whether it is published or unpublished, disseminated or undisseminated, in the public domain or copyrighted under the Federal statute, the States cannot offer it protection equivalent to copyright. * * * The preemptive effect of section 301 is limited to State laws; as stated expressly in subsection (d) of section 301, there is no intention to deal with the question of whether Congress can or should offer the equivalent of copyright protection under some constitutional provision other than the patent-copyright clause of article 1, section 8.

As long as a work fits within one of the general subject matter categories of sections 102 and 103, the bill prevents the States from protecting it even if it fails to achieve Federal statutory copyright because it is too minimal or lacking in originality to qualify, or because it has fallen into the public domain. * * * [U]nfixed works are not included in the specified "subject matter of copyright." They are therefore not affected by the preemption of section 301, and would continue to be subject to protection under State statute or common law until fixed in tangible form.

The preemption of rights under State law is complete with respect to any work coming within the scope of the bill, even though the scope of exclusive rights given the work under the bill is narrower than the scope of common law rights in the work might have been.

* * *

In a general way subsection (b) of section 301 represents the obverse of subsection (a). It sets out, in broad terms and without necessarily being exhaustive, some of the principal areas of protection that preemption would not prevent the States from protecting. Its purpose is to make clear, consistent with the 1964 Supreme Court decisions in *Sears, Roebuck & Co. v. Stiffel Co.*, 376 U.S. 225, and *Compco Corp. v. Day–Brite Lighting, Inc.*, 376 U.S. 234, that preemption does not extend to causes of action, or subject matter outside the scope of the revised Federal copyright statute.

* * *

The examples in clause (3), while not exhaustive, are intended to illustrate rights and remedies that are different in nature from the rights comprised in a copyright and that may continue to be protected under State common law or statute. The evolving common law rights of "privacy," "publicity," and trade secrets, and the general laws of defamation and fraud, would remain unaffected as long as the causes of action contain elements, such as an invasion of personal rights or a breach of trust or confidentiality, that are different in kind from copyright infringement. Nothing in the bill derogates from the rights of parties to contract with each other and to sue for breaches of contract; however, to the extent that the unfair competition concept known as "interference with contract relations" is merely the equivalent of copyright protection, it would be preempted.

The last example listed in clause (3)—"deceptive trade practices such as passing off and false representation"—represents an effort to distinguish between those causes of action known as "unfair competition" that the copyright statute is not intended to preempt and those that it is. Section 301 is not intended to preempt common law protection in cases involving activities such as false labeling, fraudulent representation, and passing off even where the subject matter involved comes within the scope of the copyright statute.

"Misappropriation" is not necessarily synonymous with copyright infringement, and thus a cause of action labeled as "misappropriation" is not preempted if it is in fact based neither on a right within the general scope of copyright as specified by section 106 nor on a right equivalent thereto. For example, state law should have the flexibility to afford a remedy (under traditional principles of equity) against a consistent pattern of unauthorized appropriation by a competitor of the facts (i.e., not the literary expression) constituting "hot" news, whether in the traditional mold of *International News Service v. Associated Press*, 248 U.S. 215 (1918), or in the newer form of data updates from scientific, business, or financial data bases. Likewise, a person having no trust or other relationship with the proprietor of a computerized data base should not be immunized from sanctions against electronically or crypto-graphically breaching the proprietor's security arrangements and assess-ing proprietor's data. The unauthorized data access which should be remediable might also be achieved by the intentional interception of data transmissions by wire, microwave or laser transmissions, or by the common unintentional means of "crossed" telephone lines occasioned by errors in switching.

The proprietor of data displayed on the cathode ray tube of a computer terminal should be afforded protection against unauthorized printouts by third parties (with or without improper access), even if the data are not copyrightable. For example, the data may not be copyright-ed because they are not fixed in a tangible medium of expression (i.e., the data are not displayed for a period [of] * * * more than transitory duration).

Nothing contained in section 301 precludes the owner of a material embodiment of a copy or a phonorecord from enforcing a claim of conversion against one who takes possession of the copy or phonorecord without consent.

* * *

COMPUTER ASSOCIATES INTERNATIONAL, INC. v. ALTAI, INC.

United States Court of Appeals, Second Circuit, 1992.
982 F.2d 693.

[Plaintiff Computer Associates (CA) alleged that defendant Altai had copied portions of its ADAPTER software in creating Altai's competing OSCAR software; CA's complaint charged both copyright infringement and misappropriation of its trade secrets. The portion of the opinion addressing the copyright cause of action appears in Chapter 16.C.4(i)(2), *supra*.]

* * *

II. Trade Secret Preemption

In its complaint, CA alleged that Altai misappropriated the trade secrets contained in the ADAPTER program. Prior to trial, while the proceedings were still before Judge Mishler, Altai moved to dismiss and for summary judgment on CA's trade secret misappropriation claim. Altai argued that section 301 of the Copyright Act preempted CA's state law cause of action. Judge Mishler denied Altai's motion, reasoning that " 'the elements of the tort of appropriation of trade secrets through the breach of contract or confidence by an employee are not the same as the elements of a claim of copyright infringement.' '' Computer Assocs., 775 F.Supp. at 563.

The parties addressed the preemption issue again, both in pre-and post-trial briefs. Judge Pratt then reconsidered and reversed Judge Mishler's earlier ruling. The district court concluded that CA's trade secret claims were preempted because "CA—which is the master of its own case—has pleaded and proven facts which establish that one act constituted both copyright infringement and misappropriation of trade secrets [namely, the] copying of ADAPTER into OSCAR 3.4.... '' Computer Assocs., 775 F.Supp. at 565.

In our original opinion, Computer Assocs. Int'l, Inc. v. Altai, Inc., 1992 WL 139364 (2d Cir.1992), we affirmed Judge Pratt's decision. * * * Upon reconsideration, we have granted the petition for rehearing, withdrawn our initial opinion, and conclude in this amended opinion that the district court's preemption ruling on CA's trade secret claims should be vacated. We accordingly vacate the judgment of the district court on this point and remand CA's trade secret claims for a determination on the merits.

A. General Law of Copyright Preemption Regarding Trade Secrets and Computer Programs

Congress carefully designed the statutory framework of federal copyright preemption. In order to insure that the enforcement of these rights remains solely within the federal domain, section 301(a) of the Copyright Act expressly preempts

> all legal or equitable rights that are equivalent to any of the exclusive rights within the general scope of copyright as specified by section 106 in works of authorship that are fixed in a tangible medium of expression and come within the subject matter of copyright as specified by sections 102 and 103....

17 U.S.C. § 301(a). This sweeping displacement of state law is, however, limited by section 301(b), which provides, in relevant part, that

> nothing in this title annuls or limits any rights or remedies under the common law or statutes of any State with respect to ... activities violating legal or equitable rights that are not equivalent to any of the exclusive rights within the general scope of copyright as specified by section 106....

17 U.S.C. § 301(b)(3). * * *

Section 301 thus preempts only those state law rights that "may be abridged by an act which, in and of itself, would infringe one of the exclusive rights" provided by federal copyright law. See Harper & Row, Publishers, Inc. v. Nation Enters., 723 F.2d 195, 200 (2d Cir.1983), rev'd on other grounds, 471 U.S. 539, 85 L.Ed.2d 588, 105 S.Ct. 2218 (1985). But if an "extra element" is "required instead of or in addition to the acts of reproduction, performance, distribution or display, in order to constitute a state-created cause of action, then the right does not lie 'within the general scope of copyright,' and there is no preemption." 1 Nimmer § 1.01[B], at 1–14–15; see also Harper & Row, Publishers, Inc., 723 F.2d at 200 (where state law right "is predicated upon an act incorporating elements beyond mere reproduction or the like, the [federal and state] rights are not equivalent" and there is no preemption).

A state law claim is not preempted if the "extra element" changes the "nature of the action so that it is qualitatively different from a copyright infringement claim." Mayer v. Josiah Wedgwood & Sons, Ltd., 601 F.Supp. 1523, 1535 (S.D.N.Y.1985); see Harper & Row, Publishers, Inc., 723 F.2d at 201. To determine whether a claim meets this standard, we must determine "what plaintiff seeks to protect, the theories in which the matter is thought to be protected and the rights sought to be enforced." 1 Roger M. Milgrim, Milgrim on Trade Secrets § 2.06A[3], at 2–150 (1992) (hereinafter "Milgrim"). An action will not be saved from preemption by elements such as awareness or intent, which alter "the action's scope but not its nature.... " Mayer, 601 F.Supp. at 1535.

Following this "extra element" test, we have held that unfair competition and misappropriation claims grounded solely in the copying of a plaintiff's protected expression are preempted by section 301. See, e.g., Walker v. Time Life Films, Inc., 784 F.2d 44, 53 (2d Cir.), cert. denied, 476 U.S. 1159, 90 L.Ed.2d 721, 106 S.Ct. 2278 (1986); Warner Bros. Inc. v. American Broadcasting Cos., 720 F.2d 231, 247 (2d Cir. 1983); Durham Indus., Inc. v. Tomy Corp., 630 F.2d 905, 919 & n. 15 (2d Cir.1980). We also have held to be preempted a tortious interference with contract claim grounded in the impairment of a plaintiff's right under the Copyright Act to publish derivative works. See Harper & Row, Publishers, Inc., 723 F.2d at 201.

However, many state law rights that can arise in connection with instances of copyright infringement satisfy the extra element test, and thus are not preempted by section 301. These include unfair competition claims based upon breach of confidential relationship, breach of fiduciary duty and trade secrets. Balboa Ins. Co. v. Trans Global Equities, 218 Cal. App. 3d 1327, 1339–53, 267 Cal. Rptr. 787, 793–803 (Ct.App. 3d Dist.), cert. denied, 111 S. Ct. 347, 112 L.Ed.2d 311 (1990).

Trade secret protection, the branch of unfair competition law at issue in this case, remains a "uniquely valuable" weapon in the defensive arsenal of computer programmers. See 1 Milgrim § 2.06A[5][c], at 2–172.4. Precisely because trade secret doctrine protects the discovery of ideas, processes, and systems which are explicitly precluded from coverage under copyright law, courts and commentators alike consider it a necessary and integral part of the intellectual property protection extended to computer programs. See id.; Integrated Cash Management Servs., Inc. v. Digital Transactions, Inc., 920 F.2d 171, 173 (2d Cir.1990) (while plaintiff withdrew copyright infringement claim for misappropriation of computer program, relief for theft of trade secret sustained); Healthcare Affiliated Servs., Inc. v. Lippany, 701 F.Supp. 1142, 1152–55 (W.D.Pa.1988) (finding likelihood of success on trade secret claim, but not copyright claim); Q–Co Indus., Inc., 625 F.Supp. at 616–18 (finding likelihood of success on trade secret claim, but no merit to copyright claim); Kretschmer, at 847–49.

The legislative history of section 301 states that "the evolving common law rights of ... trade secrets ... would remain unaffected as long as the causes of action contain elements, such as ... a breach of trust or confidentiality, that are different in kind from copyright infringement." House Report, at 5748. Congress did not consider the term "misappropriation" to be "necessarily synonymous with copyright infringement," or to serve as the talisman of preemption. Id.

Trade secret claims often are grounded upon a defendant's breach of a duty of trust or confidence to the plaintiff through improper disclosure of confidential material. See, e.g., Mercer v. C.A. Roberts Co., 570 F.2d 1232, 1238 (5th Cir.1978); Brignoli v. Balch Hardy and Scheinman, Inc., 645 F.Supp. 1201, 1205 (S.D.N.Y.1986). The defendant's breach of duty is the gravamen of such trade secret claims, and supplies the "extra element" that qualitatively distinguishes such trade secret causes of action from claims for copyright infringement that are based solely upon copying. See, e.g., Warrington Assoc., Inc. v. Real–Time Eng'g Sys., Inc., 522 F.Supp. 367, 369 (N.D.Ill.1981); Brignoli, 645 F.Supp. at 1205; see also generally Balboa Ins. Co., 218 Cal. App. 3d at 1346–50, 267 Cal. Rptr. at 798–802 (reviewing cases).

B. Preemption in this Case

The district court stated that:

> Were CA's [trade secret] allegations premised on a theory of illegal acquisition of a trade secret, a charge that might have been alleged against Arney [its former employee who used the trade secrets in his new position working for defendant], who is not a defendant in this case, the preemption analysis might be different, for there seems to be no corresponding right guaranteed to copyright owners by § 106 of the copyright act.

Computer Assocs., 775 F.Supp. at 565. However, the court concluded that CA's trade secret claims were not grounded in a theory that Altai violated a duty of confidentiality to CA. Rather, Judge Pratt stated that CA proceeded against Altai solely "on a theory that the misappropriation took place by Altai's use of ADAPTER—the same theory as the copyright infringement count." Id. The district court reasoned that "the right to be free from trade secret misappropriation through 'use', and the right to exclusive reproduction and distribution of a copyrighted work are not distinguishable." Id. Because he concluded that there was no qualitative difference between the elements of CA's state law trade secret claims and a claim for federal copyright infringement, Judge Pratt ruled that CA's trade secret claims were preempted by section 301.

We agree with CA that the district court failed to address fully the factual and theoretical bases of CA's trade secret claims. The district court relied upon the fact that Arney—not Altai—allegedly breached a duty to CA of confidentiality by stealing secrets from CA and incorporating those secrets into OSCAR 3.4. However, under a wrongful acquisition theory based on Restatement (First) of Torts § 757 (1939), Williams and Altai may be liable for violating CA's right of confidentiality. Section 757 states in relevant part:

> One who discloses or uses another's trade secret, without a privilege to do so, is liable to another if.... (c) he learned the secret from a third person with notice of the fact that it was a secret and that the third person discovered it by improper means or that the third person's disclosure of it was otherwise a breach of his duty to the other....

Actual notice is not required for such a third party acquisition claim; constructive notice is sufficient. A defendant is on constructive notice when, "from the information which he has, a reasonable man would infer [a breach of confidence], or if, under the circumstances, a reasonable man would be put on inquiry and an inquiry pursued with reasonable intelligence and diligence would disclose the [breach]." Id., comment 1 [.] * * *

We agree with the district court that New Jersey's governing governmental interest choice of law analysis directs the application of Texas law to CA's trade secret misappropriation claim. See Computer Assocs., 775 F.Supp. at 566. Texas law recognizes trade secret misappropriation claims grounded in the reasoning of Restatement section 757(c), see, e.g., Fourtek, 790 F.2d at 1204, and the facts alleged by CA may well support such a claim.

It is undisputed that, when [Altai employee, and former CA employee,] Arney stole the ADAPTER code and incorporated it into his design of OSCAR 3.4, he breached his confidentiality agreement with CA. The district court noted that while such action might constitute a valid claim against Arney, CA is the named defendant in this lawsuit. Additionally, the district court found, as a matter of fact, that "no one at Altai, other than Arney, knew that Arney had the ADAPTER code.... " Computer Assocs., 775 F.Supp. at 554. However, the district court did not consider fully Altai's potential liability for improper trade secret acquisition. It did not consider the question of Altai's trade secret liability in connection with OSCAR 3.4 under a constructive notice theory, or Altai's potential liability under an actual notice theory in connection with OSCAR 3.5.

* * *

In response to CA's complaint, Altai rewrote OSCAR 3.4, creating OSCAR 3.5. While we agree with the district court that OSCAR 3.5 did not contain any expression protected by copyright, it may nevertheless still have embodied many of CA's trade secrets that Arney brought with him to Altai. Since Altai's rewrite was conducted with full knowledge of Arney's prior misappropriation, in breach of his duty of confidentiality, it follows that OSCAR 3.5 was created with actual knowledge of trade secret violations. Thus, with regard to OSCAR 3.5, CA has a viable trade secret claim against Altai that must be considered by the district court on remand. This claim is grounded in Altai's alleged use of CA's trade secrets in the creation of OSCAR 3.5, while on actual notice of Arney's theft of trade secrets and incorporation of those secrets into OSCAR 3.4. The district court correctly stated that a state law claim based solely upon Altai's "use", by copying, of ADAPTER's non-literal elements could not satisfy the governing "extra element" test, and would be preempted by section 301. However, where the use of copyrighted expression is simultaneously the violation of a duty of confidentiality established by state law, that extra element renders the state right qualitatively distinct from the federal right, thereby foreclosing preemption under section 301.

* * *

Accordingly, we vacate the judgment of the district court and remand for reconsideration of those aspects of CA's trade secret claims related to Altai's alleged constructive notice of Arney's theft of CA's trade secrets and incorporation of those secrets into OSCAR 3.4. We note, however, that CA may be unable to recover damages for its trade secrets which are embodied in OSCAR 3.4 since Altai has conceded copyright liability and damages for its incorporation of ADAPTER into OSCAR 3.4. CA may not obtain a double recovery where the damages for copyright infringement and trade secret misappropriation are coextensive.

* * *

NATIONAL BASKETBALL ASS'N
v. MOTOROLA, INC.

United States Court of Appeals for the Second Circuit, 1997.
105 F.3d 841.

Winter, Circuit Judge:

Motorola, Inc. and Sports Team Analysis and Tracking Systems ("STATS") appeal from a permanent injunction entered by Judge Preska. The injunction concerns a handheld pager sold by Motorola and marketed under the name "SportsTrax," which displays updated information of professional basketball games in progress. The injunction prohibits appellants, absent authorization from the National Basketball Association and NBA Properties, Inc. (collectively the "NBA"), from transmitting scores or other data about NBA games in progress via the pagers, STATS's site on America On–Line's computer dial-up service, or "any equivalent means."

The crux of the dispute concerns the extent to which a state law "hot-news" misappropriation claim based on International News Service v. Associated Press, 248 U.S. 215, 63 L. Ed. 211, 39 S.Ct. 68 (1918) ("INS"), survives preemption by the federal Copyright Act and whether the NBA's claim fits within the surviving INS-type claims. We hold that a narrow "hot-news" exception does survive preemption. However, we also hold that appellants' transmission of "real-time" NBA game scores and information tabulated from television and radio broadcasts of games in progress does not constitute a misappropriation of "hot news" that is the property of the NBA.

* * *

I. BACKGROUND

The facts are largely undisputed. Motorola manufactures and markets the SportsTrax paging device while STATS supplies the game information that is transmitted to the pagers. The product became available to the public in January 1996, at a retail price of about $200. SportsTrax's pager has an inch-and-a-half by inch-and-a-half screen and operates in four basic modes: "current," "statistics," "final scores" and "demonstration." It is the "current" mode that gives rise to the present dispute. In that mode, SportsTrax displays the following information on NBA games in progress: (i) the teams playing; (ii) score changes; (iii) the team in possession of the ball; (iv) whether the team is in the free-throw bonus; (v) the quarter of the game; and (vi) time remaining in the quarter. The information is updated every two to three minutes, with more frequent updates near the end of the first half and the end of the game. There is a lag of approximately two or three minutes between events in the game itself and when the information appears on the pager screen.

SportsTrax's operation relies on a "data feed" supplied by STATS reporters who watch the games on television or listen to them on the radio. The reporters key into a personal computer changes in the score and other information such as successful and missed shots, fouls, and clock updates. The information is relayed by modem to STATS's host computer, which compiles, analyzes, and formats the data for retransmission. The information is then sent to a common carrier, which then sends it via satellite to various local FM radio networks that in turn emit the signal received by the individual SportsTrax pagers.

Although the NBA's complaint concerned only the SportsTrax device, the NBA offered evidence at trial concerning STATS's America On-Line ("AOL") site. Starting in January, 1996, users who accessed STATS's AOL site, typically via a modem attached to a home computer, were provided with slightly more comprehensive and detailed real-time game information than is displayed on a SportsTrax pager. On the AOL site, game scores are updated every 15 seconds to a minute, and the player and team statistics are updated each minute. The district court's original decision and judgment, National Basketball Ass'n v. Sports Team Analysis and Tracking Sys. Inc., 931 F.Supp. 1124 (S.D.N.Y.1996), did not address the AOL site, because "NBA's complaint and the evidence proffered at trial were devoted largely to SportsTrax." National Basketball Ass'n v. Sports Team Analysis and Tracking Sys. Inc., 939

F.Supp. 1071, 1074 n. 1 (S.D.N.Y.1996). Upon motion by the NBA, however, the district court amended its decision and judgment and enjoined use of the real-time game information on STATS's AOL site. Id. at 1075 n.1. Because the record on appeal, the briefs of the parties, and oral argument primarily addressed the SportsTrax device, we similarly focus on that product. However, we regard the legal issues as identical with respect to both products, and our holding applies equally to SportsTrax and STATS's AOL site.

[The district court found Motorola and STATS liable for state law unfair competition by misappropriation, and entered a permanent injunction. Motorola and STATS appealed.]

* * *

II. The State Law Misappropriation Claim

A. *Summary of Ruling*

Because our disposition of the state law misappropriation claim rests in large part on preemption by the Copyright Act, our discussion necessarily goes beyond the elements of a misappropriation claim under New York law, and a summary of our ruling here will perhaps render that discussion—or at least the need for it—more understandable.

The issues before us are ones that have arisen in various forms over the course of this century as technology has steadily increased the speed and quantity of information transmission. Today, individuals at home, at work, or elsewhere, can use a computer, pager, or other device to obtain highly selective kinds of information virtually at will. International News Service v. Associated Press, 248 U.S. 215, 63 L. Ed. 211, 39 S.Ct. 68 (1918) ("INS") was one of the first cases to address the issues raised by these technological advances, although the technology involved in that case was primitive by contemporary standards. INS involved two wire services, the Associated Press ("AP") and International News Service ("INS"), that transmitted news stories by wire to member newspapers. Id. INS would lift factual stories from AP bulletins and send them by wire to INS papers. Id. at 231. INS would also take factual stories from east coast AP papers and wire them to INS papers on the west coast that had yet to publish because of time differentials. Id. at 238. The Supreme Court held that INS's conduct was a common-law misappropriation of AP's property. Id. at 242.

With the advance of technology, radio stations began "live" broadcasts of events such as baseball games and operas, and various entrepreneurs began to use the transmissions of others in one way or another for their own profit. In response, New York courts created a body of misappropriation law, loosely based on INS, that sought to apply ethical standards to the use by one party of another's transmissions of events.

Federal copyright law played little active role in this area until 1976. Before then, it appears to have been the general understanding—there being no case law of consequence—that live events such as baseball games were not copyrightable. Moreover, doubt existed even as to whether a recorded broadcast or videotape of such an event was copyrightable. In 1976, however, Congress passed legislation expressly affording copyright protection to simultaneously-recorded broadcasts of live performances such as sports events. See 17 U.S.C. § 101. Such protection was not extended to the underlying events.

The 1976 amendments also contained provisions preempting state law claims that enforced rights "equivalent" to exclusive copyright protections when the work to which the state claim was being applied fell within the area of copyright protection. See 17 U.S.C. § 301. Based on legislative history of the 1976 amendments, it is generally agreed that a "hot-news" INS-like claim survives preemption. H.R. No. 94–1476 at 132 (1976), reprinted in 1976 U.S.C.C.A.N. 5659, 5748. However, much of New York misappropriation law after INS goes well beyond "hot-news" claims and is preempted.

We hold that the surviving "hot-news" INS-like claim is limited to cases where: (i) a plaintiff generates or gathers information at a cost; (ii) the information is time-sensitive; (iii) a defendant's use of the information constitutes free-riding on the plaintiff's efforts; (iv) the defendant is in direct competition with a product or service offered by the plaintiffs; and (v) the ability of other parties to free-ride on the efforts of the plaintiff or others would so reduce the incentive to produce the product or service that its existence or quality would be substantially threatened. We conclude that SportsTrax does not meet that test.

B.   Copyrights in Events or Broadcasts of Events

The NBA asserted copyright infringement claims with regard both to the underlying games and to their broadcasts. The district court dismissed these claims, and the NBA does not appeal from their dismissal. Nevertheless, discussion of the infringement claims is necessary to provide the framework for analyzing the viability of the NBA's state law misappropriation claim in light of the Copyright Act's preemptive effect.

1.   Infringement of a Copyright in the Underlying Games

In our view, the underlying basketball games do not fall within the subject matter of federal copyright protection because they do not constitute "original works of authorship" under 17 U.S.C. § 102(a). Section 102(a) lists eight categories of "works of authorship" covered by the act, including such categories as "literary works," "musical works," and "dramatic works." The list does not include athletic events, and, although the list is concededly non-exclusive, such events are neither similar nor analogous to any of the listed categories.

Sports events are not "authored" in any common sense of the word. There is, of course, at least at the professional level, considerable preparation for a game. However, the preparation is as much an expression of hope or faith as a determination of what will actually happen. Unlike movies, plays, television programs, or operas, athletic events are competitive and have no underlying script. Preparation may even cause mistakes to succeed, like the broken play in football that gains yardage because the opposition could not expect it. Athletic events may also result in wholly unanticipated occurrences, the most notable recent event being in a championship baseball game in which interference with a fly ball caused an umpire to signal erroneously a home run.

What "authorship" there is in a sports event, moreover, must be open to copying by competitors if fans are to be attracted. If the inventor of the T-formation in football had been able to copyright it, the sport might have come to an end instead of prospering. Even where athletic preparation most resembles authorship—figure skating, gymnastics, and, some would uncharitably say, professional wrestling—a performer who conceives and executes a particularly graceful and difficult-or, in the case of wrestling, seemingly painful—acrobatic feat cannot copyright it without impairing the underlying competition in the future. A claim of being the only athlete to perform a feat doesn't mean much if no one else is allowed to try.

For many of these reasons, Nimmer on Copyright concludes that the "far more reasonable" position is that athletic events are not copyrightable. 1 M. Nimmer & D. Nimmer, Nimmer on Copyright § 2.09[F] at 2–170.1 (1996). Nimmer notes that, among other problems, the number of joint copyright owners would arguably include the league, the teams, the athletes, umpires, stadium workers and even fans, who all contribute to the "work." Concededly, case law is scarce on the issue of whether organized events themselves are copyrightable, but what there is indicates that they are not. See Prod. Contractors, Inc. v. WGN Continental Broadcasting Co., 622 F.Supp. 1500 (N.D.Ill.1985) (Christmas parade is not a work of authorship entitled to copyright protection). In claiming a copyright in the underlying games, the NBA relied in part on a footnote in Baltimore Orioles, Inc. v. Major League Baseball Players Assn., 805 F.2d 663, 669 n. 7 (7th Cir.1986), cert. denied, 480 U.S. 941, 94 L.Ed.2d 782, 107 S.Ct. 1593 (1987), which stated that the "players' performances" contain the "modest creativity required for copyrightability." However, the court went on to state, "Moreover, even if the players' performances were not sufficiently creative, the players agree that the cameramen and director contribute creative labor to the telecasts." Id. This last sentence indicates that the court was considering the copyrightability of telecasts—not the underlying games, which obviously can be played without cameras.

We believe that the lack of case law is attributable to a general understanding that athletic events were, and are, uncopyrightable. Indeed, prior to 1976, there was even doubt that broadcasts describing or depicting such events, which have a far stronger case for copyrightability than the events themselves, were entitled to copyright protection. Indeed, as described in the next subsection of this opinion, Congress found it necessary to extend such protection to recorded broadcasts of live events. The fact that Congress did not extend such protection to the events themselves confirms our view that the district court correctly held that appellants were not infringing a copyright in the NBA games.

2. *Infringement of a Copyright in the Broadcasts of NBA Games*

As noted, recorded broadcasts of NBA games—as opposed to the games themselves—are now entitled to copyright protection. The Copyright Act was amended in 1976 specifically to insure that simultaneously-recorded transmissions of live performances and sporting events would meet the Act's requirement that the original work of authorship be "fixed in any tangible medium of expression." 17 U.S.C. § 102(a). Accordingly, Section 101 of the Act, containing definitions, was amended to read:

> A work consisting of sounds, images, or both, that are being transmitted, is "fixed" for purposes of this title if a fixation of the work is being made simultaneously with its transmission.

17 U.S.C. § 101. Congress specifically had sporting events in mind:

> The bill seeks to resolve, through the definition of "fixation" in section 101, the status of live broadcasts—sports, news coverage, live performances of music, etc.—that are reaching the public in unfixed form but that are simultaneously being recorded.

H.R. No. 94–1476 at 52, reprinted in 1976 U.S.C.C.A.N. at 5665.

The House Report also makes clear that it is the broadcast, not the underlying game, that is the subject of copyright protection. In explaining how game broadcasts meet the Act's requirement that the subject matter be an "original work[] of authorship," 17 U.S.C. § 102(a), the House Report stated:

> When a football game is being covered by four television cameras, with a director guiding the activities of the four cameramen and choosing which of their electronic images are sent out to the public and in what order, there is little doubt that what the cameramen and the director are doing constitutes "authorship."

H.R. No. 94–1476 at 52, reprinted in 1976 U.S.C.C.A.N. at 5665.

Although the broadcasts are protected under copyright law, the district court correctly held that Motorola and STATS did not infringe NBA's copyright because they reproduced only facts from the broadcasts, not the expression or description of the game that constitutes the broadcast. The "fact/expression dichotomy" is a bedrock principle of copyright law that "limits severely the scope of protection in fact-based works." Feist Publications, Inc. v. Rural Tel. Service Co., 499 U.S. 340, 350, 113 L.Ed.2d 358, 111 S.Ct. 1282 (1991). " 'No author may copyright facts or ideas. The copyright is limited to those aspects of the work—termed 'expression'—that display the stamp of the author's originality.' " Id. (quoting Harper & Row, Inc. v. Nation Enterprises, 471 U.S. 539, 547–48, 85 L.Ed.2d 588, 105 S.Ct. 2218 (1985)).

We agree with the district court that the "defendants provide purely factual information which any patron of an NBA game could acquire from the arena without any involvement from the director, cameramen, or others who contribute to the originality of a broadcast." 939 F.Supp.

at 1094. Because the SportsTrax device and AOL site reproduce only factual information culled from the broadcasts and none of the copyrightable expression of the games, appellants did not infringe the copyright of the broadcasts.

C. The State–Law Misappropriation Claim

The district court's injunction was based on its conclusion that, under New York law, defendants had unlawfully misappropriated the NBA's property rights in its games. The district court reached this conclusion by holding: (i) that the NBA's misappropriation claim relating to the underlying games was not preempted by Section 301 of the Copyright Act; and (ii) that, under New York common law, defendants had engaged in unlawful misappropriation. Id. at 1094–1107. We disagree.

1. Preemption Under the Copyright Act

a) Summary

When Congress amended the Copyright Act in 1976, it provided for the preemption of state law claims that are interrelated with copyright claims in certain ways. Under 17 U.S.C. § 301, a state law claim is preempted when: (i) the state law claim seeks to vindicate "legal or equitable rights that are equivalent" to one of the bundle of exclusive rights already protected by copyright law under 17 U.S.C. § 106—styled the "general scope requirement"; and (ii) the particular work to which the state law claim is being applied falls within the type of works protected by the Copyright Act under Sections 102 and 103—styled the "subject matter requirement."

The district court concluded that the NBA's misappropriation claim was not preempted because, with respect to the underlying games, as opposed to the broadcasts, the subject matter requirement was not met. 939 F.Supp. at 1097. The court dubbed as "partial preemption" its separate analysis of misappropriation claims relating to the underlying games and misappropriation claims relating to broadcasts of those games. Id. at 1098, n.24. The district court then relied on a series of older New York misappropriation cases involving radio broadcasts that considerably broadened INS. We hold that where the challenged copying or misappropriation relates in part to the copyrighted broadcasts of the games, the subject matter requirement is met as to both the broadcasts and the games. We therefore reject the partial preemption doctrine and its anomalous consequence that "it is possible for a plaintiff to assert claims both for infringement of its copyright in a broadcast and misappropriation of its rights in the underlying event." Id. We do find that a properly-narrowed INS "hot-news" misappropriation claim survives preemption because it fails the general scope requirement, but that the broader theory of the radio broadcast cases relied upon by the district court were preempted when Congress extended copyright protection to simultaneously-recorded broadcasts.

b) "Partial Preemption" and the Subject Matter Requirement

The subject matter requirement is met when the work of authorship being copied or misappropriated "falls within the ambit of copyright protection." Harper & Row, Inc. v. Nation Enterprises, 723 F.2d 195, 200 (1983), rev'd on other grounds, 471 U.S. 539, 85 L.Ed.2d 588, 105 S.Ct. 2218 (1985). We believe that the subject matter requirement is met in the instant matter and that the concept of "partial preemption" is not consistent with Section 301 of the Copyright Act. Although game broadcasts are copyrightable while the underlying games are not, the Copyright Act should not be read to distinguish between the two when analyzing the preemption of a misappropriation claim based on copying or taking from the copyrightable work. We believe that:

> Once a performance is reduced to tangible form, there is no distinction between the performance and the recording of the performance for the purposes of preemption under § 301(a). Thus, if a baseball game were not broadcast or were telecast without being recorded, the Players' performances similarly would not be fixed in tangible form and their rights of publicity would not be subject to preemption. By virtue of being videotaped, however, the Players' performances are fixed in tangible form, and any rights of publicity in their performances that are equivalent to the rights contained in the copyright of the telecast are preempted.

Baltimore Orioles, 805 F.2d at 675 (citation omitted).

Copyrightable material often contains uncopyrightable elements within it, but Section 301 preemption bars state law misappropriation claims with respect to uncopyrightable as well as copyrightable elements. In Harper & Row, for example, we held that state law claims based on the copying of excerpts from President Ford's memoirs were preempted even with respect to information that was purely factual and not copyrightable. We stated:

> The [Copyright] Act clearly embraces "works of authorship," including "literary works," as within its subject matter. The fact that portions of the Ford memoirs may consist of uncopyrightable material ... does not take the work as a whole outside the subject matter protected by the Act. Were this not so, states would be free to expand the perimeters of copyright protection to their own liking, on the theory that preemption would be no bar to state protection of material not meeting federal statutory standards.

723 F.2d at 200 (citation omitted). The legislative history supports this understanding of Section 301(a)'s subject matter requirement. The House Report stated:

> As long as a work fits within one of the general subject matter categories of sections 102 and 103, the bill prevents the States from protecting it even if it fails to achieve Federal statutory copyright because it is too minimal or lacking in originality to qualify, or because it has fallen into the public domain.

H.R. No. 94–1476 at 131, reprinted in 1976 U.S.C.C.A.N. at 5747. See also Baltimore Orioles, 805 F.2d at 676 (citing excerpts of House Report 94–1476).

Adoption of a partial preemption doctrine—preemption of claims based on misappropriation of broadcasts but no preemption of claims based on misappropriation of underlying facts—would expand significantly the reach of state law claims and render the preemption intended by Congress unworkable. It is often difficult or impossible to separate the fixed copyrightable work from the underlying uncopyrightable events or facts. Moreover, Congress, in extending copyright protection only to the broadcasts and not to the underlying events, intended that the latter be in the public domain. Partial preemption turns that intent on its head by allowing state law to vest exclusive rights in material that Congress intended to be in the public domain and to make unlawful conduct that Congress intended to allow. This concern was recently expressed in ProCD, Inc. v. Zeidenberg, 86 F.3d 1447 (7th Cir.1996), a case in which the defendants reproduced non-copyrightable facts (telephone listings) from plaintiffs' copyrighted software. In discussing preemption under Section 301(a), Judge Easterbrook held that the subject matter requirement was met and noted:

> ProCD's software and data are "fixed in a tangible medium of expression", and the district judge held that they are "within the subject matter of copyright". The latter conclusion is plainly right for the copyrighted application program, and the judge thought that the data likewise are "within the subject matter of copyright" even if, after Feist, they are not sufficiently original to be copyrighted. 908 F.Supp. at 656–57. Baltimore Orioles, Inc. v. Major League Baseball Players Ass'n, 805 F.2d 663, 676 (7th Cir.1986), supports that conclusion, with which commentators agree.... One function of § 301(a) is to prevent states from giving special protection to works of authorship that Congress has decided should be in the public domain, which it can accomplish only if "subject matter of copyright" includes all works of a type covered by sections 102 and 103, even if federal law does not afford protection to them.

ProCD, 86 F.3d at 1453 (citation omitted). We agree with Judge Easterbrook and reject the separate analysis of the underlying games and broadcasts of those games for purposes of preemption.

c) The General Scope Requirement

Under the general scope requirement, Section 301 "preempts only those state law rights that 'may be abridged by an act which, in and of itself, would infringe one of the exclusive rights' provided by federal copyright law." Computer Assoc. Int'l, Inc. v. Altai, Inc., 982 F.2d 693, 716 (2d Cir.1992) (quoting Harper & Row, 723 F.2d at 200). However, certain forms of commercial misappropriation otherwise within the general scope requirement will survive preemption if an "extra-element" test is met. As stated in Altai:

But if an "extra element" is "required instead of or in addition to the acts of reproduction, performance, distribution or display, in order to constitute a state-created cause of action, then the right does not lie 'within the general scope of copyright,' and there is no preemption."

Id. (quoting 1 Nimmer on Copyright § 1.01[B] at 1–15).

ProCD was in part an application of the extra-element test. Having held the misappropriation claims to be preempted, Judge Easterbrook went on to hold that the plaintiffs could bring a state law contract claim. The court held that the defendants were bound by the software's shrink-wrap licenses as a matter of contract law and that the private contract rights were not preempted because they were not equivalent to the exclusive rights granted by copyright law. In other words, the contract right claims were not preempted because the general scope requirement was not met. ProCD, 86 F.3d at 1455.

We turn, therefore, to the question of the extent to which a "hot-news" misappropriation claim based on INS involves extra elements and is not the equivalent of exclusive rights under a copyright. Courts are generally agreed that some form of such a claim survives preemption. Financial Information, Inc. v. Moody's Investors Service, Inc., 808 F.2d 204, 208 (2d Cir.1986), cert. denied, 484 U.S. 820, 98 L.Ed.2d 42, 108 S.Ct. 79 (1987) ("FII"). This conclusion is based in part on the legislative history of the 1976 amendments. The House Report stated:

"Misappropriation" is not necessarily synonymous with copyright infringement, and thus a cause of action labeled as "misappropriation" is not preempted if it is in fact based neither on a right within the general scope of copyright as specified by section 106 nor on a right equivalent thereto. For example, state law should have the flexibility to afford a remedy (under traditional principles of equity) against a consistent pattern of unauthorized appropriation by a competitor of the facts (i.e., not the literary expression) constituting "hot" news, whether in the traditional mold of International News Service v. Associated Press, 248 U.S. 215, 63 L. Ed. 211, 39 S.Ct. 68 (1918), or in the newer form of data updates from scientific, business, or financial data bases.

H.R. No. 94–1476 at 132, reprinted in 1976 U.S.C.C.A.N. at 5748 (footnote omitted),[5] see also FII, 808 F.2d at 209 (" 'misappropriation' of 'hot' news, under International News Service, [is] a branch of the unfair competition doctrine not preempted by the Copyright Act according to the House Report") (citation omitted). The crucial question, therefore, is the breadth of the "hot-news" claim that survives preemption.

In INS, the plaintiff AP and defendant INS were "wire services" that sold news items to client newspapers. AP brought suit to prevent

---

5. Although this passage implies that INS survives preemption because it fails the general scope requirement, Nimmer apparently takes the view adopted by the district court, namely that INS survives preemption because the subject matter requirement is not met. Nimmer § 1.01[B][2][b] at 1–44.2.

INS from selling facts and information lifted from AP sources to INS-affiliated newspapers. One method by which INS was able to use AP's news was to lift facts from AP news bulletins. INS, 248 U.S. at 231. Another method was to sell facts taken from just-published east coast AP newspapers to west coast INS newspapers whose editions had yet to appear. Id. at 238. The Supreme Court held (prior to Erie R. Co. v. Tompkins, 304 U.S. 64, 82 L. Ed. 1188, 58 S.Ct. 817 (1938)), that INS's use of AP's information was unlawful under federal common law. It characterized INS's conduct as

> amounting to an unauthorized interference with the normal operation of complainant's legitimate business precisely at the point where the profit is to be reaped, in order to divert a material portion of the profit from those who have earned it to those who have not; with special advantage to defendant in the competition because of the fact that it is not burdened with any part of the expense of gathering the news.

INS, 248 U.S. at 240.

The theory of the New York misappropriation cases relied upon by the district court is considerably broader than that of INS. For example, the district court quoted at length from Metropolitan Opera Ass'n v. Wagner–Nichols Recorder Corp., 199 Misc. 786, 101 N.Y.S.2d 483 (N.Y.Sup.Ct.1950), aff'd, 279 A.D. 632, 107 N.Y.S.2d 795 (1st Dep't 1951). Metropolitan Opera described New York misappropriation law as standing for the "broader principle that property rights of commercial value are to be and will be protected from any form of commercial immorality"; that misappropriation law developed "to deal with business malpractices offensive to the ethics of [ ] society"; and that the doctrine is "broad and flexible." 939 F.Supp. at 1098–1110 (quoting Metropolitan Opera, 101 N.Y.S.2d at 492, 488–89). However, we believe that Metropolitan Opera's broad misappropriation doctrine based on amorphous concepts such as "commercial immorality" or society's "ethics" is preempted. Such concepts are virtually synonymous for wrongful copying and are in no meaningful fashion distinguishable from infringement of a copyright. The broad misappropriation doctrine relied upon by the district court is, therefore, the equivalent of exclusive rights in copyright law.

Indeed, we said as much in FII. That decision involved the copying of financial information by a rival financial reporting service and specifically repudiated the broad misappropriation doctrine of Metropolitan Opera. We explained:

> We are not persuaded by FII's argument that misappropriation is not "equivalent" to the exclusive rights provided by the Copyright Act. . . . Nor do we believe that a possible exception to the general rule of preemption in the misappropriation area—for claims involving "any form of commercial immorality," . . . quoting Metropolitan Opera Ass'n v. Wagner–Nichols Recorder Corp., 199 Misc. 786, 101 N.Y.S.2d 483, . . . —should be applied here. We believe that no such exception exists and reject its use here. Whether or not reproduction

of another's work is "immoral" depends on whether such use of the work is wrongful. If, for example, the work is in the public domain, then its use would not be wrongful. Likewise, if, as here, the work is unprotected by federal law because of lack of originality, then its use is neither unfair nor unjustified.

FII, 808 F.2d at 208. In fact, FII only begrudgingly concedes that even narrow "hot news" INS-type claims survive preemption. Id. at 209.

Moreover, Computer Associates Intern., Inc. v. Altai Inc. indicated that the "extra element" test should not be applied so as to allow state claims to survive preemption easily. 982 F.2d at 717. "An action will not be saved from preemption by elements such as awareness or intent, which alter 'the action's scope but not its nature'.... Following this 'extra element' test, we have held that unfair competition and misappropriation claims grounded solely in the copying of a plaintiff's protected expression are preempted by section 301." Id. (citation omitted).

In light of cases such as FII and Altai that emphasize the narrowness of state misappropriation claims that survive preemption, most of the broadcast cases relied upon by the NBA are simply not good law. Those cases were decided at a time when simultaneously-recorded broadcasts were not protected under the Copyright Act and when the state law claims they fashioned were not subject to federal preemption. For example, Metropolitan Opera, 199 Misc. 786, 101 N.Y.S.2d 483, involved the unauthorized copying, marketing, and sale of opera radio broadcasts. As another example, in Mutual Broadcasting System v. Muzak Corp., 177 Misc. 489, 30 N.Y.S.2d 419 (Sup. Ct. 1941), the defendant simultaneously retransmitted the plaintiff's baseball radio broadcasts onto telephone lines. As discussed above, the 1976 amendments to the Copyright Act were specifically designed to afford copyright protection to simultaneously-recorded broadcasts, and Metropolitan Opera and Muzak could today be brought as copyright infringement cases. Moreover, we believe that they would have to be brought as copyright cases because the amendments affording broadcasts copyright protection also preempted the state law misappropriation claims under which they were decided.

Our conclusion, therefore, is that only a narrow "hot-news" misappropriation claim survives preemption for actions concerning material within the realm of copyright.[6] See also 1 McCarthy on Trademarks and Unfair Competition (4th ed. 1996), § 10:69, at 10–134 (discussing National Exhibition Co. v. Fass, 133 N.Y.S.2d 379 (Sup. Ct. 1954), Muzak, 177 Misc. 489, 30 N.Y.S.2d 419, and other cases relied upon by NBA that pre-date the 1976 amendment to the Copyright Act and concluding that after the amendment, "state misappropriation law would be unnecessary and would be preempted: protection is solely under federal copyright").[7]

---

6. State law claims involving breach of fiduciary duties or trade-secret claims are not involved in this matter and are not addressed by this discussion. These claims are generally not preempted because they pass the "extra elements" test. See Altai, 982 F.2d at 717.

7. Quite apart from Copyright Act preemption, INS has long been regarded with skepticism by many courts and scholars and

In our view, the elements central to an INS claim are: (i) the plaintiff generates or collects information at some cost or expense, see FII, 808 F.2d at 206; INS, 248 U.S. at 240; (ii) the value of the information is highly time-sensitive, see FII, 808 F.2d at 209; INS, 248 U.S. at 231; Restatement (Third) Unfair Competition, § 38 cmt. c.; (iii) the defendant's use of the information constitutes free-riding on the plaintiff's costly efforts to generate or collect it, see FII, 808 F.2d at 207; INS, 248 U.S. at 239–40; Restatement § 38 at cmt. c.; McCarthy, § 10:73 at 10–139; (iv) the defendant's use of the information is in direct competition with a product or service offered by the plaintiff, FII, 808 F.2d at 209, INS, 248 U.S. at 240; (v) the ability of other parties to free-ride on the efforts of the plaintiff would so reduce the incentive to produce the product or service that its existence or quality would be substantially threatened, FII, 808 F.2d at 209; Restatement, § 38 at cmt. c.; INS, 248 U.S. at 241 ("[INS's conduct] would render [AP's] publication profitless, or so little profitable as in effect to cut off the service by rendering the cost prohibitive in comparison with the return.")[8]

INS is not about ethics; it is about the protection of property rights in time-sensitive information so that the information will be made available to the public by profit-seeking entrepreneurs. If services like AP were not assured of property rights in the news they pay to collect, they would cease to collect it. The ability of their competitors to

often confined strictly to its facts. In particular, Judge Learned Hand was notably hostile to a broad reading of the case. He wrote:

We think that no more was covered than situations substantially similar to those then at bar. The difficulties of understanding it otherwise are insuperable. We are to suppose that the court meant to create a sort of common-law patent or copyright for reasons of justice. Either would flagrantly conflict with the scheme which Congress has for more than a century devised to cover the subject-matter.

Cheney Bros. v. Doris Silk Corp., 35 F.2d 279, 280 (2d Cir.1929), cert. denied, 281 U.S. 728, 74 L. Ed. 1145, 50 S.Ct. 245 (1930). See also Restatement (Third) of Unfair Competition § 38 cmt. c (1995):

The facts of the INS decision are unusual and may serve, in part, to limit its rationale.... The limited extent to which the INS rationale has been incorporated into the common law of the states indicate that the decision is properly viewed as a response to unusual circumstances rather than as a statement of generally applicable principles of common law. Many subsequent decisions have expressly limited the INS case to its facts.

8. Some authorities have labeled this element as requiring direct competition between the defendant and the plaintiff in a primary market. "In most of the small number of cases in which the misappropriation doctrine has been determinative, the defendant's appropriation, like that in INS, resulted in direct competition in the plaintiffs' primary market ... Appeals to the misappropriation doctrine are almost always rejected when the appropriation does not intrude upon the plaintiff's primary market.", Restatement (Third) of Unfair Competition, § 38 cmt. c, at 412–13; see also National Football League v. Delaware, 435 F.Supp. 1372 (D.Del.1977). In that case, the NFL sued Delaware over the state's lottery game which was based on NFL games. In dismissing the wrongful misappropriation claims, the court stated:

While courts have recognized that one has a right to one's own harvest, this proposition has not been construed to preclude others from profiting from demands for collateral services generated by the success of one's business venture.

Id. at 1378. The court also noted, "It is true that Delaware is thus making profits it would not make but for the existence of the NFL, but I find this difficult to distinguish from the multitude of charter bus companies who generate profit from servicing those of plaintiffs' fans who want to go to the stadium or, indeed, the sidewalk popcorn salesman who services the crowd as it surges towards the gate." Id.

appropriate their product at only nominal cost and thereby to disseminate a competing product at a lower price would destroy the incentive to collect news in the first place. The newspaper-reading public would suffer because no one would have an incentive to collect "hot news."

We therefore find the extra elements—those in addition to the elements of copyright infringement—that allow a "hot news" claim to survive preemption are: (i) the time-sensitive value of factual information, (ii) the free-riding by a defendant, and (iii) the threat to the very existence of the product or service provided by the plaintiff.

2. The Legality of SportsTrax

We conclude that Motorola and STATS have not engaged in unlawful misappropriation under the "hot-news" test set out above. To be sure, some of the elements of a "hot-news" INS claim are met. The information transmitted to SportsTrax is not precisely contemporaneous, but it is nevertheless time-sensitive. Also, the NBA does provide, or will shortly do so, information like that available through SportsTrax. It now offers a service called "Gamestats" that provides official play-by-play game sheets and half-time and final box scores within each arena. It also provides such information to the media in each arena. In the future, the NBA plans to enhance Gamestats so that it will be networked between the various arenas and will support a pager product analogous to SportsTrax. SportsTrax will of course directly compete with an enhanced Gamestats.

However, there are critical elements missing in the NBA's attempt to assert a "hot-news" INS-type claim. As framed by the NBA, their claim compresses and confuses three different informational products. The first product is generating the information by playing the games; the second product is transmitting live, full descriptions of those games; and the third product is collecting and retransmitting strictly factual information about the games. The first and second products are the NBA's primary business: producing basketball games for live attendance and licensing copyrighted broadcasts of those games. The collection and retransmission of strictly factual material about the games is a different product: e.g., box-scores in newspapers, summaries of statistics on television sports news, and real-time facts to be transmitted to pagers. In our view, the NBA has failed to show any competitive effect whatsoever from SportsTrax on the first and second products and a lack of any free-riding by SportsTrax on the third.

With regard to the NBA's primary products—producing basketball games with live attendance and licensing copyrighted broadcasts of those games—there is no evidence that anyone regards SportsTrax or the AOL site as a substitute for attending NBA games or watching them on television. In fact, Motorola markets SportsTrax as being designed "for those times when you cannot be at the arena, watch the game on TV, or listen to the radio ... "

The NBA argues that the pager market is also relevant to a "hot-news" INS-type claim and that SportsTrax's future competition with

Gamestats satisfies any missing element. We agree that there is a separate market for the real-time transmission of factual information to pagers or similar devices, such as STATS's AOL site. However, we disagree that SportsTrax is in any sense free-riding off Gamestats.

An indispensable element of an INS "hot-news" claim is free-riding by a defendant on a plaintiff's product, enabling the defendant to produce a directly competitive product for less money because it has lower costs. SportsTrax is not such a product. The use of pagers to transmit real-time information about NBA games requires: (i) the collecting of facts about the games; (ii) the transmission of these facts on a network; (iii) the assembling of them by the particular service; and (iv) the transmission of them to pagers or an on-line computer site. Appellants are in no way free-riding on Gamestats. Motorola and STATS expend their own resources to collect purely factual information generated in NBA games to transmit to SportsTrax pagers. They have their own network and assemble and transmit data themselves.

To be sure, if appellants in the future were to collect facts from an enhanced Gamestats pager to retransmit them to SportsTrax pagers, that would constitute free-riding and might well cause Gamestats to be unprofitable because it had to bear costs to collect facts that SportsTrax did not. If the appropriation of facts from one pager to another pager service were allowed, transmission of current information on NBA games to pagers or similar devices would be substantially deterred because any potential transmitter would know that the first entrant would quickly encounter a lower cost competitor free-riding on the originator's transmissions.[9]

However, that is not the case in the instant matter. SportsTrax and Gamestats are each bearing their own costs of collecting factual information on NBA games, and, if one produces a product that is cheaper or otherwise superior to the other, that producer will prevail in the marketplace. This is obviously not the situation against which INS was intended to prevent: the potential lack of any such product or service because of the anticipation of free-riding.

For the foregoing reasons, the NBA has not shown any damage to any of its products based on free-riding by Motorola and STATS, and the NBA's misappropriation claim based on New York law is preempted.

* * *

IV. Conclusion

We vacate the injunction entered by the district court and order that the NBA's claim for misappropriation be dismissed. * * *

---

9. It may well be that the NBA's product, when enhanced, will actually have a competitive edge because its Gamestats system will apparently be used for a number of in-stadium services as well as the pager market, resulting in a certain amount of cost-sharing. Gamestats might also have a temporal advantage in collecting and transmitting official statistics. Whether this is so does not affect our disposition of this matter, although it does demonstrate the gulf between this case and INS, where the free-riding created the danger of no wire service being viable.

Notes

1. In a footnote, the *Baltimore Orioles* court had rejected the players' argument that copyright law does not preempt the right of publicity "because the work that it protects—a public figure's persona—cannot be fixed in a tangible medium of expression," finding that "a performance is fixed in tangible form when it is recorded." 805 F.2d at 677 n.26. It also rejected the argument that the right of publicity is not the equivalent of any right under section 106 because it requires an "extra element" other than the "reproduction, performance, distribution or display of a copyrighted work," adding:

> [T]he right of publicity does not require an invasion of personal privacy to make out a cause of action. It is true that the rights of publicity and of privacy evolved from similar origins; however, whereas the right of privacy protects against intrusions on seclusion, public disclosure of private facts, and casting an individual in a false light in the public eye, the right of publicity protects against the unauthorized exploitation of names, likenesses, personalities, and performances that have acquired value for the very reason that they are known to the public.

Id. Was the court correct to reject these arguments?

2. Suppose that a well-known professional singer with a distinctive voice and performance style records a song which becomes popular. An advertising agency obtains permission from the owner of the copyright in the music and lyrics of the song to use that song in a television commercial, but the record company refuses to license the actual recording, and the singer refuses to perform the song for the commercial. The agency hires a "sound-alike" singer to imitate the original recording as closely as possible. On these facts, if state law gives the original singer a cause of action for infringement of her right of publicity or commercial misappropriation of her likeness, would that law be preempted by section 301?

3. Under the commercial code of State X, a security interest in mortgaged property can be perfected only by filing a UCC–1 filing statement with the secretary of state. Where the property in question is an exclusive interest in a copyright, section 205 of the 1976 Copyright Act allows the mortgagee to record the mortgage with the Copyright Office. Suppose that a creditor has a security interest in all the assets of a corporation; these assets include several copyright interests. Under section 301, if the creditor records the mortgage only with State X's secretary of state, has the security interest been perfected?

4. Computer software is often sold subject to a "shrinkwrap license" which states that, by opening the package, or by loading the software onto a computer's memory, the purchaser agrees to certain limitations in exchange for the privilege of possessing that copy of the software. Consider the example of such a license in Note 4 on page 1032. Assuming that the license is enforceable under state law, is enforcement barred under section 301?

Controversial proposals to clarify the validity of electronic agreements (such as electronic shrinkwrap licenses), and to increase their enforceability, by amending Article 2B of the Uniform Commercial Code led to the equally controversial Uniform Computer Information Transactions Act (UCITA), which was proposed for adoption by individual states. Although UCITA was strongly endorsed by the software industry, opponents argued that it would allow intellectual property owners to restrict unduly the federal intellectual property rights of consumers. In the Seventh Circuit, the controversial 1996 decision in *ProCD v. Zeidenberg,* 86 F.3d 1447 (7th Cir. 1996) upheld a shrink-wrap license on standard contract grounds, holding that the burden of refusing to accept the terms of the license by returning the shrink-wrapped object to the point of sale was not unduly burdensome. No fully acceptable compromise among the issues raised in settings like these has yet been advanced.

Bowers v. Baystate Techs., Inc., 320 F.3d 1317 (Fed. Cir. 2003), involved two competitors who sold marketing templates to improve CAD (computer aided design) software. In response to an action for declaratory judgment that plaintiff's products did not infringe Bowers' patent, Bowers counterclaimed for copyright infringement, patent infringement, and breach of shrink-wrap license.

Baystate reverse-engineered Bowers' product, which was sold with a shrink-wrap license prohibiting reverse engineering. The Federal Circuit held that the Copyright Act did not preempt the contract claim under First Circuit law, as long as the state claim contained an additional element not present in the copyright claim. The court said its holding did not affect the decision in *Atari Games v. Nintendo,* 975 F.2d 832 (Fed. Cir. 1992), that reverse engineering was a fair use exception to copyright infringement.

The dissent endorsed the decision in *Vault Corp. v. Quaid Software Ltd.,* 847 F.2d 255 (5th Cir. 1988), which held that a state law permitting enforcement of a shrinkwrap license that prohibited all copying of computer programs was preempted by the Copyright Act. The dissent stated that shrink-wrap licenses should not trump fair use and that preemption should apply only to freely negotiated contracts. By the majority reasoning, state law could be used to eliminate fair use and other copyright protection limitations such as the first sale doctrine.

5. Would section 301 preempt

(a) a state law protecting data compilations against unauthorized copying of their informational content (as opposed to their arrangement)?

(b) a state resale royalty law?

(c) a state law allowing minors or incompetent persons to disaffirm written assignments of copyright?

(d) a state law enforcing oral transfers of copyright?

(e) a state law requiring motion picture distributors to provide free screenings when requested by theatrical exhibitors prior to bidding on the right to exhibit those films?

(f) a state law unfair competition claim against a publisher that publishes a work without properly crediting its author?

6. Suppose that bar and restaurant owners in a particular state persuade their legislature that it is unfair to require them to enter into blanket licenses with performing rights organizations without knowing which musi-

cal compositions are included in each license. As a result, the legislature enacts a law requiring ASCAP, BMI and SESAC to provide a printed list of their entire music repertoire to each licensee annually, upon request and at no charge. Because of the size of their repertoires, and the printing, handling and mailing costs, the cost to each organization of complying with such request would substantially increase their expenses and could in some cases equal or exceed the licensing fee ultimately collected. In addition, the statute prohibits representatives of performing rights organizations from asking merchants about their usage of copyrighted music without first revealing their affiliation with the organization, and requires the organizations to promptly notify any merchant that is under investigation.

7. In section 301, did Congress achieve its stated goal of establishing clear and unequivocal rules regarding preemption?

8. In *Rodrigue v. Rodrigue*, 218 F.3d 432 (5th Cir.2000), the Fifth Circuit held that state community property is not preempted by federal copyright law, noting that "even though the author's copyright arises at the moment of creation of the work, the Act explicitly allows for subsequent vesting in non-authors, either jointly with the author or subsequent to him by virtue of transfer of all or lesser portions of the copyright." *Id*. at 436.

9. Note that § 301(b)(4) preserves states' rights to enact laws regarding state and local landmarks as well as preservation, zoning or building codes relating to architectural works otherwise protected under section 102(a)(8). Subsection (4), not originally part of the law as enacted in 1976, was added in 1995 as part of the Architectural Works Protection Act (AWPA). Would preemption under section 301 necessarily have followed the AWPA in the absence of subsection (4)?

10. *Statutory Preemption of Moral Rights Laws*: The Visual Artists Rights Act of 1990 (VARA), which became effective June 1, 1991, added section 301(f) preempting state laws providing equivalent rights. Consider the following questions:

(a) Would section 301 preempt a state law giving an artist a cause of action where the artist's name was removed from a work of visual art without his or her consent?

(b) Would section 301 preempt a state law granting creators of works of visual art a right of integrity, if the state law allowed that right to be exercised by a deceased artist's estate?

(c) Would section 301 preempt a state law granting novelists a right of integrity?

11. In *Lowry's Reports, Inc. v. Legg Mason, Inc.*, 271 F.Supp.2d 737 (D. Md. 2003), Legg Mason's broadcasting of Lowry's stock market numbers to all of its employees constituted a "public performance" under the Copyright Act, which is an exclusive right of the copyright holder. Therefore, the district court held that the Copyright Act preempted Lowry's "hot news" claim.

WRENCH LLC v. TACO BELL CORP.

United States Court Of Appeals, Sixth Circuit, 2001.
256 F.3d 446.

GRAHAM, DISTRICT JUDGE.

This case raises a question of first impression in this circuit regarding the extent to which the Copyright Act preempts state law claims based on breach of an implied-in-fact contract.

* * *

I. BACKGROUND

Appellants Thomas Rinks and Joseph Shields are creators of the "Psycho Chihuahua" cartoon character which they promote, market, and license through their wholly-owned Michigan limited liability company, Wrench LLC. The parties have described Psycho Chihuahua as a clever, feisty dog with an attitude; a self-confident, edgy, cool dog who knows what he wants and will not back down.

In June 1996, Shields and Rinks attended a licensing trade show in New York City, where they were approached by two Taco Bell employees, Rudy Pollak, a vice president, and Ed Alfaro, a creative services manager. Pollak and Alfaro expressed interest in the Psycho Chihuahua character, which they thought would appeal to Taco Bell's core consumers, males aged eighteen to twenty-four. Pollak and Alfaro obtained some Psycho Chihuahua materials to take with them back to Taco Bell's headquarters in California.

Upon returning to California, Alfaro began promoting the Psycho Chihuahua idea within Taco Bell. Alfaro contacted Rinks and asked him to create art boards combining Psycho Chihuahua with the Taco Bell name and image. Rinks and Shields prepared the art boards and sent them to Alfaro along with Psycho Chihuahua T-shirts, hats, and stickers for Alfaro to use in promoting the character. Because Alfaro was not part of the marketing group at Taco Bell, he first sought to gain support for Psycho Chihuahua from top executives outside of the marketing department. After several meetings with non-marketing executives, Alfaro showed the Psycho Chihuahua materials to Vada Hill, Taco Bell's vice president of brand management, as well as to Taco Bell's then-outside advertising agency, Bozell Worldwide. Alfaro also tested the Psycho Chihuahua marketing concept with focus groups to gauge consumer reaction to the designs submitted by Rinks and Shields.

During this time period, Rinks told Alfaro that instead of using the cartoon version of Psycho Chihuahua in its television advertisements, Taco Bell should use a live dog, manipulated by computer graphic imaging, with the personality of Psycho Chihuahua and a love for Taco Bell food. Rinks and Alfaro also discussed what it was going to cost for Taco Bell to use appellants' character, and although no specific numbers were mentioned, Alfaro understood that if Taco Bell used the Psycho Chihuahua concept, it would have to pay appellants.

In September 1996, Rinks and Shields hired Strategy Licensing ("Strategy"), a licensing agent, to represent Wrench in its dealings with Taco Bell. Representatives from Strategy contacted Alfaro about Taco Bell's interest in the Psycho Chihuahua concept, and presented him with additional materials for presentation to Taco Bell's advertising agency. These materials described Psycho Chihuahua as "irreverent," "edgy," and "spicy," with an "over-the-top" attitude and an "insatiable craving" for Taco Bell food. Throughout the late summer and fall of 1996, Alfaro continued his discussions with Wrench about developing Psycho Chihuahua for Taco Bell's use.

On November 18, 1996, Strategy representatives forwarded a licensing proposal to Alfaro. The proposal provided that Taco Bell would pay Wrench a fee based upon a percentage of the money spent on advertising; a percentage of Taco Bell's retail licensing sales; and a percentage of the cost of premiums, such as toys sold at Taco Bell restaurants. Taco Bell did not accept this proposal, although it did not explicitly reject it or indicate that it was ceasing further discussions with Wrench.

On December 5, 1996, Alfaro met with Hill, who had been promoted to the position of chief marketing officer, and others, to present various licensing ideas, including Psycho Chihuahua. On February 6, 1997, Alfaro again met with appellants and representatives of Strategy to review and finalize a formal presentation featuring Psycho Chihuahua that was to be given to Taco Bell's marketing department in early March 1997. At this meeting, appellants exhibited examples of possible Psycho Chihuahua promotional materials and also orally presented specific ideas for television commercials featuring a live dog manipulated by computer graphics imaging. These ideas included a commercial in which a male dog passed up a female dog in order to get to Taco Bell food. While Alfaro was meeting with appellants, another marketing firm, TLP Partnership ("TLP"), was also promoting appellants' Psycho Chihuahua to Taco Bell marketing executives. TLP presented several ideas, including the Psycho Chihuahua concept, to Taco Bell in anticipation of an upcoming summer promotion. TLP had discovered Psycho Chihuahua at a trade show in New York and had received Strategy's consent to use the image in its presentation. Alfaro was not aware of TLP's presentation. Following the presentation, Taco Bell conducted a series of focus groups to research the reaction to TLP's proposals. Psycho Chihuahua was received positively by consumers, but Taco Bell decided not to use any of TLP's ideas.

Alfaro was unable to arrange a meeting with the marketing department during March 1997 to present the Psycho Chihuahua materials. On April 4, 1997, however, Strategy made a formal presentation to Alfaro and his group using samples of uniform designs, T-shirts, food wrappers, posters, and cup designs based on the ideas discussed during the February 6, 1997, meeting. Alfaro and his group were impressed with Strategy's presentation.

On March 18, 1997, Taco Bell hired a new advertising agency, TBWA Chiat/Day ("Chiat/Day"). Taco Bell advised Chiat/Day that it wanted a campaign ready to launch by July 1997 that would reconnect Taco Bell with its core group of consumers. Chuck Bennett and Clay Williams were designated as the creative directors of Taco Bell's account.

On June 2, 1997, Bennett and Williams proposed a commercial to Taco Bell in which a male Chihuahua would pass up a female Chihuahua to get to a person seated on a bench eating Taco Bell food. Bennett and Williams say that they conceived of the idea for this commercial one day as they were eating Mexican food at a sidewalk cafe and saw a Chihuahua trotting down the street, with no master or human intervention, "on a mission." Bennett and Williams contend that this image caused them jointly to conceive of the idea of using a Chihuahua as a way of personifying the intense desire for Taco Bell food. Williams subsequently wrote an advertisement script using a Chihuahua, which Taco Bell decided to produce as a television commercial.

When, in June 1997, Alfaro learned that Chiat/Day was planning to use a Chihuahua in a commercial, he contacted Hill again about the possibility of using Psycho Chihuahua. Hill passed Alfaro on to Chris Miller, a Taco Bell advertising manager and the liaison between Taco Bell's marketing department and Chiat/Day. On June 27, 1997, Alfaro gave Psycho Chihuahua materials to Miller along with a note suggesting that Taco Bell consider using Psycho Chihuahua as an icon and as a character in its advertising. Miller sent these materials to Chiat/Day, which received them sometime between June 28 and July 26.

Taco Bell aired its first Chihuahua commercial in the northeastern United States in July 1997, and received a very positive consumer reaction. On that basis, Taco Bell decided that the Chihuahua would be the focus of its 1998 marketing efforts, and launched a nationwide advertising campaign featuring Chihuahua commercials in late December 1997.

Appellants brought suit in January 1998, alleging breach of implied-in-fact contract as well as various tort and statutory claims under Michigan and California law. Appellee filed a motion to dismiss, which the district court granted in part and denied in part. Although the district court dismissed appellants' unjust enrichment, conversion, and dilution claims on the basis that they were preempted by the Copyright Act, the court held that appellants' misappropriation and unfair competition claims were not preempted because they required appellants to prove an "extra element" not required for a copyright infringement claim, namely, the existence of a legal relationship arising from an implied contract. * * * The district court also granted appellants leave to amend their conversion claim so that it might survive preemption.

* * *

A. *Preemption*

Section 301 of the Copyright Act provides that:

On and after January 1, 1978, all legal or equitable rights that are equivalent to any of the exclusive rights within the general scope of copyright as defined by section 106 in works of authorship that are fixed in a tangible medium of expression and come within the subject matter of copyright as specified by sections 102 and 103, whether created before or after that date and whether published or unpublished, are governed exclusively by this title. Thereafter, no person is entitled to any such right or equivalent right in any such work under the common law or statutes of any State.

In sum, under § 301, a state common law or statutory claim is preempted if: (1) the work is within the scope of the "subject matter of copyright," as specified in 17 U.S.C. §§ 102, 103; and, (2) the rights granted under state law are equivalent to any exclusive rights within the scope of federal copyright as set out in 17 U.S.C. § 106. * * *

1. *Subject Matter Requirement*

Appellants contend that the district court erred in finding that their claims fell within the subject matter provisions of the Copyright Act. Appellants argue that their state law claims are based on ideas and concepts that were conveyed to Taco Bell in both tangible and intangible form. They conclude that their claims do not come within the subject matter of copyright, and are thus not preempted, because § 102(b) expressly excludes intangible ideas and concepts from the subject matter of copyright.

In Wrench I, the district court found that appellants' claims fell within the subject matter of copyright "because they are premised upon ideas and concepts fixed in a tangible medium of expression, namely, 'storyboards' and 'presentation materials' furnished by Plaintiffs." The district court reasoned that appellants' state law claims depended substantially upon works subject to the copyright protection, and did not arise solely out of intangible concepts that were orally conveyed to Taco Bell. Id.

In reaching this conclusion, the district court relied on the Fourth Circuit's decision in [United States ex rel. Berge v. Board of Trustees of the Univ. of Ala., 104 F.3d 1453 (4th Cir.1997)], in which a plaintiff brought a state law conversion action claiming that defendants had used ideas and methods contained in plaintiff's dissertation without her permission. The plaintiff contended that because ideas and methods are excluded from copyright protection under § 102, her state law claims could not be preempted under § 301. The court rejected this argument on the ground that the scope of protection afforded under copyright law is not the same as the scope of preemption. Rather, the court concluded that "the shadow actually cast by the [Copyright] Act's preemption is notably broader than the wing of its protection."

Appellants urge this court to reject this conclusion for the same reason urged by the plaintiff in Berge. Specifically, appellants argue that Berge does not comport with a literal reading of § 102(b), which expressly excludes ideas and other intangible forms of expression from copyright protection. Appellants rely on several district court cases which have held that because ideas and concepts are not afforded copyright protection, they are not within the subject matter of copyright. The appellate courts that have addressed this question have disagreed with the reasoning of the decisions cited by appellants, however. The Second, Fourth, and Seventh Circuits have held that the scope of the Copyright Act's subject matter extends beyond the tangible expressions that can be protected under the Act to elements of expression which themselves cannot be protected. See, e.g., National Basketball Ass'n, 105 F.3d at 849–850 (holding that subject matter of copyright under § 301 includes "uncopyrightable" as well as "copyrightable" elements); Berge, 104 F.3d at 1463 (finding that "scope and protection are not synonyms," and holding that uncopyrightable ideas that make up copyrightable works are within subject matter of copyright); ProCD, Inc. v. Zeidenberg, 86 F.3d 1447, 1453 (7th Cir.1996) (finding that uncopyrightable data underlying a copyrightable computer program are within subject matter of copyright). As the Second Circuit reasoned, the fact that copyrightable material contains uncopyrightable expressions should not remove the work from the subject matter of copyright under § 301, because otherwise "states would be free to expand the perimeters of copyright protection to their own liking, on the theory that preemption would be no bar to state protection of material not meeting federal statutory standards." Harper & Row, 723 F.2d at 200 (quoting H.R. Rep. No. 94–1476 at 130 (1976), reprinted in 1976 U.S.C.C.A.N. 5659, 5746).

We join our sister circuits in holding that the scope of the Copyright Act's subject matter is broader than the scope of the Act's protections. The record demonstrates that appellants expended considerable effort preparing and presenting tangible expressions of their Psycho Chihuahua concept for appellee, which expressions included storyboards, scripts, drawings, clothing designs, and packaging. The position now urged by appellants would require us to separate out appellants' intangible ideas from these tangible expressions, and would afford appellants a state law claim in the face of clear congressional intent to preempt such action. As the Seventh Circuit has noted, "[o]ne function of § 301(a) is to prevent states from giving special protection to works of authorship that Congress has decided should be in the public domain, which it can accomplish only if 'subject matter of copyright' includes all works of a type covered by sections 102 and 103, even if federal law does not afford protection to them." Zeidenberg, 86 F.3d at 1453. Thus, we conclude that the district court did not err with respect to the subject matter prong of its preemption analysis.

2. Equivalency Requirement

The second prong of the preemption analysis—the so-called "equivalency" or "general scope" requirement—augments the subject matter inquiry by asking whether the state common law or statutory action at issue asserts rights that are the same as those protected under § 106 of the Copyright Act. Under § 301(a), even if appellants' state law claims concern works within the subject matter of copyright, such claims will only be preempted if they assert rights that are "equivalent to any of the exclusive rights within the general scope of copyright as specified by section 106[.]" 17 U.S.C. § 301(a).

Equivalency exists if the right defined by state law may be abridged by an act which in and of itself would infringe one of the exclusive rights. See Harper & Row, 723 F.2d at 200. Conversely, if an extra element is required instead of or in addition to the acts of reproduction, performance, distribution or display in order to constitute a state-created cause of action, there is no preemption, provided that the extra element changes the nature of the action so that it is qualitatively different from a copyright infringement claim. See id.; Rosciszewski v. Arete Associates, Inc., 1 F.3d 225, 230 (4th Cir.1993); National Car Rental Sys., Inc. v. Computer Assocs. Intn'l, Inc., 991 F.2d 426, 431 (8th Cir.1993). We find that appellants' state law implied-in-fact contract claim survives preemption under these rules.

Under Michigan law, "[a]n implied contract, like other contracts, requires mutual assent and consideration." Spruytte v. Dep't of Corr., 82 Mich.App. 145, 266 N.W.2d 482, 483 (1978). Michigan draws a clear distinction between contracts implied in fact and contracts implied in law:

> The first does not exist, unless the minds of the parties meet, by reason of words or conduct. The second is quasi or constructive, and does not require a meeting of minds, but is imposed by fiction of law[.]

The gist of appellants' state law implied-in-fact contract claim is breach of an actual promise to pay for appellants' creative work. It is not the use of the work alone but the failure to pay for it that violates the contract and gives rise to the right to recover damages. Thus, the state law right is not abridged by an act which in and of itself would infringe one of the exclusive rights granted by § 106, since the right to be paid for the use of the work is not one of those rights.

An extra element is required instead of or in addition to the acts of reproduction, performance, distribution or display, in order to constitute the state-created cause of action. The extra element is the promise to pay. This extra element does change the nature of the action so that it is qualitatively different from a copyright infringement claim. The qualitative difference includes the requirement of proof of an enforceable promise and a breach thereof which requires, inter alia, proof of mutual assent and consideration, as well as proof of the value of the work and appellee's use thereof.

This qualitative difference is further reflected by the difference in the remedy afforded by the state law claim. Under Michigan law, a plaintiff's remedy for breach of an implied-in-fact contract includes recovery of the reasonable value of the services rendered, considering factors such as the general practice of the industry. * * *

Under the Copyright Act, remedies for infringement are limited to injunctions; impounding and destruction of infringing articles; recovery of the copyright owner's actual damages and any additional profits of the infringer or statutory damages; and costs and attorneys fees. See 17 U.S.C. §§ 502, 503, 504 and 505. The remedies available under copyright law do not include damages for the reasonable value of the defendants' use of the work. See Business Trends Analysts, Inc. v. Freedonia Group, Inc., 887 F.2d 399, 406–07 (2d Cir.1989).

The proposition that a state law breach of contract claim based upon a promise to pay for the use of the work is not preempted is supported by an eminent authority on copyright law. See 1 Nimmer on Copyright § 1.01[B][1][a] at 1–15 to 1–16, which states:

[a] Breach of Contract. Adverting first to contract rights, an author's right to royalties under a publication contract may be conditioned upon the publisher's acts of reproduction and distribution of copies of the work, but there is also another crucial act that stands as a condition to the publisher's liability: the publisher's promise to pay the stated royalty. Without a promise there is no contract, while a promise on the part of one who engages in unlicensed reproduction or distribution is not required in order to constitute him a copyright infringer. Certainly, pre-emption should be denied, to the extent that a breach of contract cause of action alleges more than reproduction, adaptation, etc. simplicter of a copyrighted work. (Footnotes omitted).

Here, as in the example given in Nimmer on Copyright, there is another crucial act that stands as a condition to the appellee's liability, to wit: its promise to pay for the use of the work. Thus, this is a case in which the breach of contract cause of action alleges more than reproduction, adaptation, etc., simplicter.

In finding that appellants' state law contract claim is not preempted, we do not embrace the proposition that all state law contract claims survive preemption simply because they involve the additional element of promise. See, e.g., Zeidenberg, 86 F.3d at 1454; Taquino v. Teledyne Monarch Rubber, 893 F.2d 1488, 1501 (5th Cir.1990) (appendix). Under that rationale, a contract which consisted only of a promise not to reproduce the copyrighted work would survive preemption even though it was limited to one of the exclusive rights enumerated in 17 U.S.C. § 106. If the promise amounts only to a promise to refrain from reproducing, performing, distributing or displaying the work, then the contract claim is preempted. The contrary result would clearly violate the rule that state law rights are preempted when they would be abridged by an act which in and of itself would infringe one of the exclusive rights of § 106. As the authors note in 1 Nimmer on Copyright § 1.01[B][1][a] at 1–22: "Although the vast majority of contract claims will presumably survive scrutiny ... nonetheless pre-emption should continue to strike down claims that, though denominated 'contract,' nonetheless complain directly about the reproduction of expressive materials."

* * *

The authors of Nimmer on Copyright warn against confusing contracts implied in law (quasi-contract) and contracts implied in fact:

> Unfortunately, many courts in dealing with idea cases fail to distinguish between a contract implied in law and a contract implied in fact. An action in quasi contract is not a true contract since " 'quasi contracts, unlike true contracts, are not based upon the apparent intention of the parties to undertake the performances in question, nor are they promises. They are obligations created by law for reasons of justice.' … Quasi contractual recovery is based upon benefit accepted or derived from which the law implies an obligation to pay." An implied in fact contract on the other hand is a consensual agreement presenting the same elements as are found in an express contract except that in an implied in fact contract the promise is not expressed in words but is rather implied from the promisor's conduct. 4 Nimmer on Copyright § 16.03 at 10–10 to 16–11 (quoting Weitzenkorn v. Lesser, 40 Cal.2d 778, 794, 256 P.2d 947, 959 (1953)) (footnotes omitted).

For the purpose of the preemption analysis, there is a crucial difference between a claim based on quasi-contract, i.e., a contract implied in law, and a claim based upon a contract implied in fact. In the former, the action depends on nothing more than the unauthorized use of the work. Thus, an action based on a contract implied in law requires no extra element in addition to an act of reproduction, performance, distribution or display, whereas an action based on a contract implied in fact requires the extra element of a promise to pay for the use of the work which is implied from the conduct of the parties. The authors of Nimmer on Copyright explain the significance of this difference in their analysis of the Ninth Circuit's decision in Del Madera Props. v. Rhodes & Gardner, Inc., 820 F.2d 973 (9th Cir.1987), in which the court held that an unjust enrichment claim based on California law was preempted:

> In Del Madera, however, the court's disposition of the preemption argument may have been dictum, given the court's alternative holding that, under the facts there presented, an essential element for unjust enrichment was lacking under California law. Id. at 978. Further, had that essential element—namely, expectation of compensation by both parties—been present, it would seem that the California cause of action for unjust enrichment could be assimilable to a cause of action sounding in contract, for it would then contain an essential element not envisioned by Section 106. In that event, the unjust enrichment cum contract claim would not be pre-empted. See § 1.01 [B][1][a] supra.

Here, appellants' implied-in-fact contract claim contains the essential element of expectation of compensation which is an element not envisioned by § 106. See Cascaden, 225 N.W. at 511–12 ("Plaintiffs cannot recover on the theory of a contract implied in fact, for the work was not done . . . under circumstances authorizing plaintiffs to entertain an expectation of pay from defendants.").

We conclude that the district court erred with respect to the equivalency prong of the preemption analysis and find that appellants' state law implied-in-fact contract claim is not preempted by the Copyright Act.

* * *

Note

Preemption cases abound under Section 301. Among the more interesting recent cases are: *Sturdza v. United Arab Emirates,* 281 F.3d 1287 (D.C.Cir.2002) (state claims in architectural concepts not preempted); *Lipscher v. LRP Publications, Inc.,* 266 F.3d 1305 (11th Cir.2001) (state claims challenging use of published jury verdict reports preempted). *Lowry's Reports, Inc. v. Legg Mason, Inc.,* 186 F.Supp.2d 592 (D.Md.2002) (state claims alleging the unauthorized copying and distribution of plaintiff's publication established a "private law" governing fair use of the published work); *Archie Comic Publications, Inc. v. DeCarlo,* 141 F.Supp.2d 428 (S.D.N.Y.2001) (state claims for rights in comic book characters preempted); *Design Art Inc. v. National Football League Properties Inc.,* 2000 WL 33151646 (S.D.Cal.2000) (state claims challenging use of logo are preempted); *Information Handling Services, Inc. v. LRP Publications Inc.,* 2000 WL 1468535 (E.D.Pa.2000) (state claim that fact compilation was misappropriated is preempted); *Chicago Style Productions, Inc. v. Chicago Sun Times, Inc.,* 313 Ill.App.3d 45, 245 Ill.Dec. 847, 728 N.E.2d 1204 (2000) (state law claim for the theft of an idea is preempted).

In *ATC Distribution Group, Inc. v. Whatever It Takes Transmissions & Parts, Inc.,* 402 F.3d 700 (6th Cir. 2005), an automobile transmission parts seller's state law claims against a competitor for unfair competition, unjust enrichment, and misappropriation, based on the competitor's copying of the seller's parts catalog, were preempted by federal copyright law. Even though the catalog was found to be insufficiently original to warrant copyright protection, the catalog was nevertheless within the scope of copyrightable subject matter.

B. PREEMPTION UNDER THE INTELLECTUAL PROPERTY CLAUSE

1. THE SEARS/COMPCO DECISIONS

SEARS, ROEBUCK & CO. v. STIFFEL COMPANY

Supreme Court of the United States, 1964.
376 U.S. 225, 84 S.Ct. 784, 11 L.Ed.2d 661.

MR. JUSTICE BLACK delivered the opinion of the Court.

The question in this case is whether a State's unfair competition law can, consistently with the federal patent laws, impose liability for or prohibit the copying of an article which is protected by neither a federal patent nor a copyright. The respondent, Stiffel Company, secured design and mechanical patents on a "pole lamp"—a vertical tube having lamp fixtures along the outside, the tube being made so that it will stand upright between the floor and ceiling of a room. Pole lamps proved a decided commercial success, and soon after Stiffel brought them on the market Sears, Roebuck & Company put on the market a substantially identical lamp, which it sold more cheaply, Sears' retail price being about the same as Stiffel's wholesale price. Stiffel then brought this action against Sears in the United States District Court for the Northern District of Illinois, claiming in its first count that by copying its design Sears had infringed Stiffel's patents and in its second count that by selling copies of Stiffel's lamp Sears had caused confusion in the trade as to the source of the lamps and had thereby engaged in unfair competition under Illinois law. There was evidence that identifying tags were not attached to the Sears lamps although labels appeared on the cartons in which they were delivered to customers, that customers had asked Stiffel whether its lamps differed from Sears', and that in two cases customers who had bought Stiffel lamps had complained to Stiffel on learning that Sears was selling substantially identical lamps at a much lower price.

The District Court, after holding the patents invalid for want of invention, went on to find as a fact that Sears' lamp was "a substantially exact copy" of Stiffel's and that the two lamps were so much alike, both in appearance and in functional details, "that confusion between them is likely, and some confusion has already occurred." On these findings the court held Sears guilty of unfair competition, enjoined Sears "from unfairly competing with [Stiffel] by selling or attempting to sell pole lamps identical to or confusingly similar to" Stiffel's lamp, and ordered an accounting to fix profits and damages resulting from Sears' "unfair competition."

The Court of Appeals affirmed. * * * That court held that, to make out a case of unfair competition under Illinois law, there was no need to show that Sears had been "palming off" its lamps as Stiffel lamps; Stiffel had only to prove that there was a "likelihood of confusion as to the source of the products"—that the two articles were sufficiently identical that customers could not tell who had made a particular one. Impressed by the "remarkable sameness of appearance" of the lamps, the Court of Appeals upheld the trial court's findings of likelihood of confusion and some actual confusion, findings which the appellate court construed to mean confusion "as to the source of the lamps." The Court of Appeals thought this enough under Illinois law to sustain the trial court's holding of unfair competition, and thus held Sears liable under Illinois law for doing no more than copying and marketing an unpatented article. We granted certiorari to consider whether this use of a State's law of unfair competition is compatible with the federal patent law. * * *

* * *

* * * [T]he patent system is one in which uniform federal standards are carefully used to promote invention while at the same time preserving free competition.[7] Obviously a State could not, consistently with the Supremacy Clause of the Constitution,[8] extend the life of a patent beyond its expiration date or give a patent on an article which lacked the level of invention required for federal patents. To do either would run counter to the policy of Congress of granting patents only to true inventions, and then only for a limited time. Just as a State cannot encroach upon the federal patent laws directly, it cannot, under some other law, such as that forbidding unfair competition, give protection of a kind that clashes with the objectives of the federal patent laws.

In the present case the "pole lamp" sold by Stiffel has been held not to be entitled to the protection of either a mechanical or a design patent. An unpatentable article, like an article on which the patent has expired, is in the public domain and may be made and sold by whoever chooses to do so. What Sears did was to copy Stiffel's design and to sell lamps almost identical to those sold by Stiffel. This it had every right to do under the federal patent laws. That Stiffel originated the pole lamp and made it popular is immaterial. "Sharing in the goodwill of an article unprotected by patent or trade-mark is the exercise of a right possessed by all—and in the free exercise of which the consuming public is deeply interested." Kellogg Co. v. National Biscuit Co., [305 U.S. 111 (1938),] at 122. To allow a State by use of its law of unfair competition to prevent the copying of an article which represents too slight an advance to be patented would be to permit the State to block off from the public something which federal law has said belongs to the public. The result would be that while federal law grants only 14 or 17 years' protection to

7. The purpose of Congress to have national uniformity in patent and copyright laws can be inferred from such statutes as that which vests exclusive jurisdiction to hear patent and copyright cases in federal courts, 28 U. S. C. § 1338 (a), and that section of the Copyright Act which expressly saves state protection of unpublished writings but does not include published writings, 17 U. S. C. § 2.

8. U.S. Const., Art. VI.

genuine inventions, see 35 U. S. C. §§ 154, 173, States could allow perpetual protection to articles too lacking in novelty to merit any patent at all under federal constitutional standards. This would be too great an encroachment on the federal patent system to be tolerated.

Sears has been held liable here for unfair competition because of a finding of likelihood of confusion based only on the fact that Sears' lamp was copied from Stiffel's unpatented lamp and that consequently the two looked exactly alike. Of course there could be "confusion" as to who had manufactured these nearly identical articles. But mere inability of the public to tell two identical articles apart is not enough to support an injunction against copying or an award of damages for copying that which the federal patent laws permit to be copied. Doubtless a State may, in appropriate circumstances, require that goods, whether patented or unpatented, be labeled or that other precautionary steps be taken to prevent customers from being misled as to the source, just as it may protect businesses in the use of their trademarks, labels, or distinctive dress in the packaging of goods so as to prevent others, by imitating such markings, from misleading purchasers as to the source of the goods. But because of the federal patent laws a State may not, when the article is unpatented and uncopyrighted, prohibit the copying of the article itself or award damages for such copying. Cf. G. Ricordi & Co. v. Haendler, 194 F.2d 914, 916 (C.A. 2d Cir.1952). The judgment below did both and in so doing gave Stiffel the equivalent of a patent monopoly on its unpatented lamp. That was error, and Sears is entitled to a judgment in its favor.

Reversed.

Note

Simultaneously with *Sears*, the Supreme Court decided *Compco Corp. v. Day–Brite Lighting, Inc.*, 376 U.S. 234, 84 S.Ct. 779, 11 L.Ed.2d 669 (1964), which involved a claim under the same Illinois unfair competition law, again based on the copying of a lamp design—specifically, "a reflector having cross-ribs claimed to give both strength and attractiveness to the fixture" for which a design patent had been issued. Although the district court found the plaintiff's design patent invalid, it also found that the design was distinctive and was not the only one available to the defendant, and that defendant's copying was likely to confuse the public. The court of appeals upheld the award of an injunction and damages. The Supreme Court reversed, noting that even if there was a likelihood of confusion, the state law could not be enforced on these facts:

> Notwithstanding the thinness of the evidence to support findings of likely and actual confusion among purchasers, we do not find it necessary in this case to determine whether there is "clear error" in these findings. They, like those in *Sears, Roebuck & Co. v. Stiffel Co.*, supra, were based wholly on the fact that selling an article which is an exact copy of another unpatented article is likely to produce and did in this case produce confusion as to the source of the article. Even accepting the

findings, we hold that the order for an accounting for damages and the injunction are in conflict with the federal patent laws. Today we have held in *Sears, Roebuck & Co. v. Stiffel Co.*, supra, that when an article is unprotected by a patent or a copyright, state law may not forbid others to copy that article. To forbid copying would interfere with the federal policy, found in Art. I, § 8, cl. 8, of the Constitution and in the implementing federal statutes, of allowing free access to copy whatever the federal patent and copyright laws leave in the public domain. Here Day–Brite's fixture has been held not to be entitled to a design or mechanical patent. Under the federal patent laws it is, therefore, in the public domain and can be copied in every detail by whoever pleases. It is true that the trial court found that the configuration of Day–Brite's fixture identified Day–Brite to the trade because the arrangement of the ribbing had, like a trademark, acquired a "secondary meaning" by which that particular design was associated with Day–Brite. But if the design is not entitled to a design patent or other federal statutory protection, then it can be copied at will.

As we have said in Sears, while the federal patent laws prevent a State from prohibiting the copying and selling of unpatented articles, they do not stand in the way of state law, statutory or decisional, which requires those who make and sell copies to take precautions to identify their products as their own. A State of course has power to impose liability upon those who, knowing that the public is relying upon an original manufacturer's reputation for quality and integrity, deceive the public by palming off their copies as the original. That an article copied from an unpatented article could be made in some other way, that the design is "nonfunctional" and not essential to the use of either article, that the configuration of the article copied may have a "secondary meaning" which identifies the maker to the trade, or that there may be "confusion" among purchasers as to which article is which or as to who is the maker, may be relevant evidence in applying a State's law requiring such precautions as labeling; however, and regardless of the copier's motives, neither these facts nor any others can furnish a basis for imposing liability for or prohibiting the actual acts of copying and selling. *Cf. Kellogg Co. v. National Biscuit Co.*, 305 U.S. 111, 120 (1938). And of course a State cannot hold a copier accountable in damages for failure to label or otherwise to identify his goods unless his failure is in violation of valid state statutory or decisional law requiring the copier to label or take other precautions to prevent confusion of customers as to the source of the goods.

Compco, 376 U.S. at 237–39, 84 S.Ct. at 782. Do *Sears* and *Compco* invalidate state unfair competition laws that provide a cause of action for copying nonfunctional design elements that acquire secondary meaning?

2. DEVELOPMENTS AFTER SEARS/COMPCO

GOLDSTEIN v. CALIFORNIA

Supreme Court of the United States, 1973.
412 U.S. 546, 93 S.Ct. 2303, 37 L.Ed.2d 163.

MR. CHIEF JUSTICE BURGER delivered the opinion of the Court.

[Petitioners were convicted of violating California's "record piracy" law, Calif. Penal Code § 653h, which forbids making unauthorized copies of any musical recordings, regardless of the age of the recording. Although, after this case commenced, Congress amended the copyright statutes to grant copyright protection to sound recordings fixed on or after February 15, 1972, all of the recordings at issue in this case were fixed prior to that date.]

* * *

Petitioners' attack on the constitutionality of § 653h has many facets. First, they contend that the statute establishes a state copyright of unlimited duration, and thus conflicts with Art. I, § 8, cl. 8, of the Constitution. Second, petitioners claim that the state statute interferes with the implementation of federal policies inherent in the federal copyright statutes. 17 U. S. C. § 1 et seq. According to petitioners, it was the intention of Congress, as interpreted by this Court in Sears, Roebuck & Co. v. Stiffel Co., 376 U.S. 225 (1964), and Compco Corp. v. Day–Brite Lighting, 376 U.S. 234 (1964), to establish a uniform law throughout the United States to protect original writings. As part of the federal scheme, it is urged that Congress intended to allow individuals to copy any work which was not protected by a federal copyright. Since § 653h effectively prohibits the copying of works which are not entitled to federal protection, petitioners contend that it conflicts directly with congressional policy and must fall under the Supremacy Clause of the Constitution. * * *

* * *

II

Petitioners' first argument rests on the premise that the state statute under which they were convicted lies beyond the powers which the States reserved in our federal system. If this is correct, petitioners must prevail, since the States cannot exercise a sovereign power which, under the Constitution, they have relinquished to the Federal Government for its exclusive exercise.

A

* * * The clause of the Constitution granting to Congress the power to issue copyrights does not provide that such power shall vest exclusive-

ly in the Federal Government. Nor does the Constitution expressly provide that such power shall not be exercised by the States.

* * *

The question whether exclusive federal power must be inferred is not a simple one, for the powers recognized in the Constitution are broad and the nature of their application varied. * * * We must also be careful to distinguish those situations in which the concurrent exercise of a power by the Federal Government and the States or by the States alone may possibly lead to conflicts and those situations where conflicts will necessarily arise. "It is not ... a mere possibility of inconvenience in the exercise of powers, but an immediate constitutional repugnancy that can by implication alienate and extinguish a pre-existing right of [state] sovereignty." The Federalist No. 32, p. 243 (B. Wright ed. 1961).

* * *

The objective of the Copyright Clause was clearly to facilitate the granting of rights national in scope. * * *

Although the Copyright Clause thus recognizes the potential benefits of a national system, it does not indicate that all writings are of national interest or that state legislation is, in all cases, unnecessary or precluded. * * * [I]t is unlikely that all citizens in all parts of the country place the same importance on works relating to all subjects. Since the subject matter to which the Copyright Clause is addressed may thus be of purely local importance and not worthy of national attention or protection, we cannot discern such an unyielding national interest as to require an inference that state power to grant copyrights has been relinquished to exclusive federal control.

The question to which we next turn is whether, in actual operation, the exercise of the power to grant copyrights by some States will prejudice the interests of other States. As we have noted, a copyright granted by a particular State has effect only within its boundaries. If one State grants such protection, the interests of States which do not are not prejudiced since their citizens remain free to copy within their borders those works which may be protected elsewhere. * * * We do not see here the type of prejudicial conflicts which would arise, for example, if each State exercised a sovereign power to impose imposts and tariffs; nor can we discern a need for uniformity such as that which may apply to the regulation of interstate shipments.

Similarly, it is difficult to see how the concurrent exercise of the power to grant copyrights by Congress and the States will necessarily and inevitably lead to difficulty. At any time Congress determines that a particular category of "writing" is worthy of national protection and the incidental expenses of federal administration, federal copyright protection may be authorized. Where the need for free and unrestricted distribution of a writing is thought to be required by the national interest, the Copyright Clause and the Commerce Clause would allow Congress to eschew all protection. In such cases, a conflict would develop if a State attempted to protect that which Congress intended to be free from restraint or to free that which Congress had protected. However, where Congress determines that neither federal protection nor freedom from restraint is required by the national interest, it is at liberty to stay its hand entirely.[16] Since state protection would not then conflict with federal action, total relinquishment of the States' power to grant copyright protection cannot be inferred.

As we have seen, the language of the Constitution neither explicitly precludes the States from granting copyrights nor grants such authority exclusively to the Federal Government. The subject matter to which the Copyright Clause is addressed may at times be of purely local concern. No conflict will necessarily arise from a lack of uniform state regulation, nor will the interest of one State be significantly prejudiced by the actions of another. No reason exists why Congress must take affirmative action either to authorize protection of all categories of writings or to free them from all restraint. We therefore conclude that, under the Constitution, the States have not relinquished all power to grant to authors "the exclusive Right to their respective Writings."

* * *

III

Our conclusion that California did not surrender its power to issue copyrights does not end the inquiry. We must proceed to determine whether the challenged state statute is void under the Supremacy Clause. No simple formula can capture the complexities of this determination; the conflicts which may develop between state and federal action are as varied as the fields to which congressional action may apply. "Our primary function is to determine whether, under the circumstances of this particular case, [the state] law stands as an obstacle to the accomplishment and execution of the full purposes and objectives of Congress." Hines v. Davidowitz, 312 U.S. 52, 67 (1941). * * *

* * *

[The Court reviewed the historical context and legislative history of the 1909 Act and concluded that Congress in enacting those provisions had not decided to deny copyright protection to sound recordings, but had simply not considered the question.]

Petitioners' argument does not rest entirely on the belief that Congress intended specifically to exempt recordings of performances from state control. Assuming that no such intention may be found, they argue that Congress so occupied the field of copyright protection as to pre-empt all comparable state action. * * *

* * *

---

16. For example, Congress has allowed writings which may eventually be the subject of a federal copyright, to be protected under state law prior to publication. 17 U. S. C. § 2.

Sears and Compco, on which petitioners rely, do not support their position. In those cases, the question was whether a State could, under principles of a state unfair competition law, preclude the copying of mechanical configurations which did not possess the qualities required for the granting of a federal design or mechanical patent. The Court stated:

"The patent system is one in which uniform federal standards are carefully used to promote invention while at the same time preserving free competition. Obviously a State could not, consistently with the Supremacy Clause of the Constitution, extend the life of a patent beyond its expiration date or give a patent on an article which lacked the level of invention required for federal patents. To do either would run counter to the policy of Congress of granting patents only to true inventions, and then only for a limited time. Just as a State cannot encroach upon the federal patent laws directly, it cannot, under some other law, such as that forbidding unfair competition, give protection of a kind that clashes with the objectives of the federal patent laws." Sears, Roebuck & Co. v. Stiffel Co., 376 U.S., at 230–231 (footnotes omitted).

In regard to mechanical configurations, Congress had balanced the need to encourage innovation and originality of invention against the need to insure competition in the sale of identical or substantially identical products. The standards established for granting federal patent protection to machines thus indicated not only which articles in this particular category Congress wished to protect, but which configurations it wished to remain free. The application of state law in these cases to prevent the copying of articles which did not meet the requirements for federal protection disturbed the careful balance which Congress had drawn and thereby necessarily gave way under the Supremacy Clause of the Constitution. No comparable conflict between state law and federal law arises in the case of recordings of musical performances. In regard to this category of "Writings," Congress has drawn no balance; rather, it has left the area unattended, and no reason exists why the State should not be free to act.

IV

* * *

In sum, we have shown that § 653h does not conflict with the federal copyright statute enacted by Congress in 1909. Similarly, no conflict exists between the federal copyright statute passed in 1971 and the present application of § 653h, since California charged petitioners only with copying recordings fixed prior to February 15, 1972. Finally, we have concluded that our decisions in Sears and Compco, which we reaffirm today, have no application in the present case, since Congress has indicated neither that it wishes to protect, nor to free from protection, recordings of musical performances fixed prior to February 15, 1972.

We conclude that the State of California has exercised a power which it retained under the Constitution, and that the challenged statute, as applied in this case, does not intrude into an area which Congress has, up to now, pre-empted. Until and unless Congress takes further action with respect to recordings fixed prior to February 15, 1972, the California statute may be enforced against acts of piracy such as those which occurred in the present case.

Affirmed.

KEWANEE OIL CO. v. BICRON CORP.

Supreme Court of the United States, 1974.
416 U.S. 470, 94 S.Ct. 1879, 40 L.Ed.2d 315.

MR. CHIEF JUSTICE BURGER delivered the opinion of the Court.

We granted certiorari to resolve a question on which there is a conflict in the courts of appeals: whether state trade secret protection is pre-empted by operation of the federal patent law. In the instant case the Court of Appeals for the Sixth Circuit held that there was pre-emption. The Courts of Appeals for the Second, Fourth, Fifth and Ninth Circuits have reached the opposite conclusion.

I

Harshaw Chemical Co., an unincorporated division of petitioner, is a leading manufacturer of a type of synthetic crystal which is useful in the detection of ionizing radiation. In 1949 Harshaw commenced research into the growth of this type crystal and was able to produce one less than two inches in diameter. By 1966, as the result of expenditures in excess of $1 million, Harshaw was able to grow a 17–inch crystal, something no one else had done previously. Harshaw had developed many processes, procedures, and manufacturing techniques in the purification of raw materials and the growth and encapsulation of the crystals which enabled it to accomplish this feat. Some of these processes Harshaw considers to be trade secrets.

The individual respondents former employees of Harshaw who formed or later joined respondent Bicron. While at Harshaw the individual respondents executed, as a condition of employment, at least one agreement each, requiring them not to disclose confidential information or trade secrets obtained as employees of Harshaw. Bicron was formed in August 1969 to compete with Harshaw in the production of the crystals, and by April 1970, had grown a 17–inch crystal.

Petitioner brought this diversity action in United States District Court for the Northern District of Ohio seeking injunctive relief and damages for the misappropriation of trade secrets. The District Court, applying Ohio trade secret law, granted a permanent injunction against the disclosure or use by respondents of 20 of the 40 claimed trade secrets until such time as the trade secrets had been released to the public, had otherwise generally become available to the public, or had been obtained by respondents from sources having the legal right to convey the information.

The Court of Appeals for the Sixth Circuit held that the findings of fact by the District Court were not clearly erroneous, and that it was evident from the record that the individual Respondents appropriated to the benefit of Bicron secret information on processes obtained while they were employees at Harshaw. Further, the Court of Appeals held that the District Court properly applied Ohio law relating to trade secrets. Nevertheless, the Court of Appeals reversed the District Court, finding Ohio's trade secret law to be in conflict with the patent laws of the United States. The Court of Appeals reasoned that Ohio could not grant monopoly protection to processes and manufacturing techniques that were appropriate subjects for consideration under 35 U.S.C. § 101 for a federal patent but which had been in commercial use for over one year and so were no longer eligible for patent protection under 35 U.S.C. § 102(b).

We hold that Ohio's law of trade secrets is not preempted by the patent laws of the United States, and, accordingly, we reverse.

II

Ohio has adopted the widely relied-upon definition of a trade secret found at Restatement of Torts § 757, comment b (1939). B. F. Goodrich Co. v. Wohlgemuth, 117 Ohio App. 493, 498, 192 N.E.2d 99, 104 (1963); W. R. Grace & Co. v. Hargadine, 392 F.2d 9, 14 (C.A.6 1968). According to the Restatement, "(a) trade secret may consist of any formula, pattern, device or compilation of information which is used in one's business, and which gives him an opportunity to obtain an advantage over competitors who do not know or use it. It may be a formula for a chemical compound, a process of manufacturing, treating or preserving materials, a pattern for a machine or other device, or a list of customers."

The subject of a trade secret must be secret, and must not be of public knowledge or of a general knowledge in the trade or business. B. F. Goodrich Co. v. Wohlgemuth, supra, 117 Ohio App., at 499, 192 N.E.2d, at 104; National Tube Co. v. Eastern Tube Co., 3 Ohio Cir.Ct.R., N.S., 459, 462 (1902), aff'd, 69 Ohio St. 560, 70 N.E. 1127 (1903). This necessary element of secrecy is not lost, however, if the holder of the trade secret reveals the trade secret to another "in confidence, and under an implied obligation not to use or disclose it." Cincinnati Bell Foundry Co. v. Dodds, 10 Ohio Dec.Reprint 154, 156, 19 Weekly Law Bull. 84 (Super.Ct.1887). These others may include those of the holder's "employes to whom it is necessary to confide it, in order to apply it to the uses for which it is intended." National Tube Co. v. Eastern Tube Co, supra, 3 Ohio Cir.Ct.R., N.S., at 462. Often the recipient of confidential knowledge of the subject of a trade secret is a licensee of its holder. See Lear, Inc. v. Adkins, 395 U.S. 653, 89 S.Ct. 1902, 23 L.Ed.2d 610 (1969).

The protection accorded the trade secret holder is against the disclosure or unauthorized use of the trade secret by those to whom the secret has been confided under the express or implied restriction of nondisclosure or nonuse. The law also protects the holder of a trade secret against disclosure or use when the knowledge is gained, not by the owner's volition, but by some "improper means," Restatement of Torts § 757(a), which may include theft, wiretapping, or even aerial reconnaissance. A trade secret law, however, does not offer protection against discovery by fair and honest means, such as by independent invention, accidental disclosure, or by so-called reverse engineering, that is by starting with the known product and working backward to divine the process which aided in its development or manufacture.

Novelty, in the patent law sense, is not required for a trade secret, W. R. Grace & Co. v. Hargadine, 392 F.2d, at 14. "Quite clearly discovery is something less than invention." A. O. Smith Corp. v. Petroleum Iron Works Co., 73 F.2d 531, 538 (C.A.6 1934), modified to increase scope of injunction, 74 F.2d 934 (1935). However, some novelty will be required if merely because that which does not possess novelty is usually known; secrecy, in the context of trade secrets, thus implies at least minimal novelty.

The subject matter of a patent is limited to a "process, machine, manufacture, or composition of matter, or . . . improvement thereof," 35 U.S.C. § 101, which fulfills the three conditions of novelty and utility as articulated and defined in 35 U.S.C. §§ 101 and 102, and nonobviousness, as set out in 35 U.S.C. § 103. If an invention meets the rigorous statutory tests for the issuance of a patent, the patent is granted, for a period of 17 years, giving what has been described as the "right of exclusion," R. Ellis, Patent Assignments and Licenses § 4, p. 7 (2d ed. 1943).[9] This protection goes not only to copying the subject matter, which is forbidden under the Copyright Act, 17 U.S.C. § 1 et seq., but also to independent creation.

III

The first issue we deal with is whether the States are forbidden to act at all in the area of protection of the kinds of intellectual property which may make up the subject matter of trade secrets.

Article I, § 8, cl. 8, of the Constitution grants to the Congress the power "(t)o promote the Progress of Science and useful Arts, by securing for limited Times to Authors and Inventors the exclusive Right to their respective Writings and Discoveries . . . " In the 1972 Term, in Goldstein v. California, 412 U.S. 546, 93 S.Ct. 2303, 37 L.Ed.2d 163 (1973), we held that the cl. 8 grant of power to Congress was not exclusive and that, at

---

9. Title 35 U.S.C. § 154 provides: "Every patent shall contain a short title of the invention and a grant to the patentee, his heirs or assigns, for the term of seventeen years, subject to the payment of issue fees as provided for in this title, of the right to exclude others from making, using, or selling the invention throughout the United States, referring to the specification for the particulars thereof. A copy of the specification and drawings shall be annexed to the patent and be a part thereof."

least in the case of writings, the States were not prohibited from encouraging and protecting the efforts of those within their borders by appropriate legislation. The States could, therefore, protect against the unauthorized rerecording for sale of performances fixed on records or tapes, even though those performances qualified as "writings" in the constitutional sense and Congress was empowered to legislate regarding such performances and could pre-empt the area if it chose to do so. This determination was premised on the great diversity of interests in our Nation—the essentially non-uniform character of the appreciation of intellectual achievements in the various States. Evidence for this came from patents granted by the States in the 18th century. 412 U.S., at 557, 93 S.Ct., at 2310.

Just as the States may exercise regulatory power over writings so may the States regulate with respect to discoveries. States may hold diverse viewpoints in protecting intellectual property to invention as they do in protecting the intellectual property relating to the subject matter of copyright. The only limitation on the States is that in regulating the area of patents and copyrights they do not conflict with the operation of the laws in this area passed by Congress, and it is to that more difficult question we now turn.

IV

The question of whether the trade secret law of Ohio is void under the Supremacy Clause involves a consideration of whether that law "stands as an obstacle to the accomplishment and execution of the full purposes and objectives of Congress." Hines v. Davidowitz, 312 U.S. 52, 67, 61 S.Ct. 399, 404, 85 L.Ed. 581 (1941). See Florida Lime & Avocado Growers, Inc. v. Paul, 373 U.S. 132, 141, 83 S.Ct. 1210, 1216, 10 L.Ed.2d 248 (1963). We stated in Sears, Roebuck & Co. v. Stiffel Co., 376 U.S. 225, 229, 84 S.Ct. 784, 11 L.Ed.2d 661 (1964), that when state law touches upon the area of federal statutes enacted pursuant to constitutional authority, "it is 'familiar doctrine' that the federal policy 'may not be set at naught, or its benefits denied' by the state law. Sola Elec. Co. v. Jefferson Elec. Co., 317 U.S. 173, 173, 176, 63 S.Ct. 172, 173, 87 L.Ed. 165 (1942). This is true, of course, even if the state law is enacted in the exercise of otherwise undoubted state power.''

The laws which the Court of Appeals in this case held to be in conflict with the Ohio law of trade secrets were the patent laws passed by the Congress in the unchallenged exercise of its clear power under Art. I, § 8, cl. 8, of the Constitution. The patent law does not explicitly endorse or forbid the operation of trade secret law. However, as we have noted, if the scheme of protection developed by Ohio respecting trade secrets "clashes with the objectives of the federal patent laws," Sears, Roebuck & Co. v. Stiffel Co., supra, 376 U.S., at 231, 84 S.Ct. at 789, then the state law must fall. To determine whether the Ohio law "clashes" with the federal law it is helpful to examine the objectives of both the patent and trade secret laws.

The stated objective of the Constitution in granting the power to Congress to legislate in the area of intellectual property is to "promote the Progress of Science and useful Arts." The patent laws promote this progress by offering a right of exclusion for a limited period as an incentive to inventors to risk the often enormous costs in terms of time, research, and development. The productive effort thereby fostered will have a positive effect on society through the introduction of new products and processes of manufacture into the economy, and the emanations by way of increased employment and better lives for our citizens. In return for the right of exclusion—this "reward for inventions," Universal Oil Co. v. Globe Co., 322 U.S. 471, 484, 64 S.Ct. 1110, 1116, 88 L.Ed. 1399 (1944)—the patent laws impose upon the inventor a requirement of disclosure. To insure adequate and full disclosure so that upon the expiration of the 17–year period "the knowledge of the invention enures to the people, who are thus enabled without restriction to practice it and profit by its use," United States v. Dubilier Condenser Corp., 289 U.S. 178, 187, 53 S.Ct. 554, 77 L.Ed. 1114 (1933), the patent laws require[10] that the patent application shall include a full and clear description of the invention and "of the manner and process of making and using it" so that any person skilled in the art may make and use the invention. 35 U.S.C. § 112. When a patent is granted and the information contained in it is circulated to the general public and those especially skilled in the trade, such additions to the general store of knowledge are of such importance to the public weal that the Federal Government is willing to pay the high price of 17 years of exclusive use for its disclosure, which disclosure, it is assumed, will stimulate ideas and the eventual development of further significant advances in the art. The Court has also articulated another policy of the patent law: that which is in the public domain cannot be removed therefrom by action of the States.

"(F)ederal laws requires that all ideas in general circulation be dedicated to the common good unless they are protected by a valid patent." Lear, Inc. v. Adkins, 395 U.S., at 668, 89 S.Ct., at 1910. See also Goldstein v. California, 412 U.S., at 570–571, 93 S.Ct., at 2316–2317; Sears, Roebuck & Co. v. Stiffel Co., supra; Compco Corp. v. Day–Brite Lighting, Inc., 376 U.S. 234, 237–238, 84 S.Ct. 779, 781–782, 11 L.Ed.2d 669 (1964); International News Service v. Associated Press, 248 U.S. 215, 250, 39 S.Ct. 68, 76, 63 L.Ed. 211 (1918) (Brandeis, J., dissenting).

The maintenance of standards of commercial ethics and the encouragement of invention are the broadly stated policies behind trade secret law. "The necessity of good faith and honest, fair dealing, is the very life and spirit of the commercial world." National Tube Co. v. Eastern Tube Co., 3 Ohio Cir.Cr.R., N.S. at 462. In A. O. Smith Corp. v. Petroleum Iron Works Co., 73 F.2d, at 539, the Court emphasized that even though a discovery may not be patentable, that does not "destroy the value of the discovery to one who makes it, or advantage the competitor who by unfair means, or as the beneficiary of a broken faith, obtains the desired

---

10. 35 U.S.C. § 111.

knowledge without himself paying the price in labor, money, or machines expended by the discover." In Wexler v. Greenberg, 399 Pa. 569, 578–579, 160 A.2d 430, 434–435 (1960), the Pennsylvania Supreme Court noted the importance of trade secret protection to the subsidization of research and development and to increased economic efficiency within large companies through the dispersion of responsibilities for creative developments.

Having now in mind the objectives of both the patent and trade secret law, we turn to an examination of the interaction of these systems of protection of intellectual property—one established by the Congress and the other by a State—to determine whether and under what circumstances the latter might constitute "too great an encroachment on the federal patent system to be tolerated." Sears, Roebuck & Co. v. Stiffel Co., 376 U.S., at 232, 84 S.Ct., at 789.

As we noted earlier, trade secret law protects items which would not be proper subjects for consideration for patent protection under 35 U.S.C. § 101. As in the case of the recordings in Goldstein v. California, Congress, with respect to nonpatentable subject matter, "has drawn no balance; rather, it has left the area unattended, and no reason exists why the State should not be free to act." Goldstein v. California, supra, 412 U.S., at 570, 93 S.Ct. at 2316 (footnote omitted).

Since no patent is available for a discovery, however useful, novel, and nonobvious, unless it falls within one of the express categories of patentable subject matter of 35 U.S.C. § 101, the holder of such a discovery would have no reason to apply for a patent whether trade secret protection existed or not. Abolition of trade secret protection would, therefore, not result in increased disclosure to the public of discoveries in the area of nonpatentable subject matter. Also, it is hard to see how the public would be benefited by disclosure of customer lists or advertising campaigns; in fact, keeping such items secret encourages businesses to initiate new and individualized plans of operation, and constructive competition results. This, in turn, leads to a greater variety of business methods than would otherwise be the case if privately developed marketing and other data were passed illicitly among firms involved in the same enterprise.

Congress has spoken in the area of those discoveries which fall within one of the categories of patentable subject matter of 35 U.S.C. § 101 and which are, therefore, of a nature that would be subject to consideration for a patent. Processes, machines, manufactures, compositions of matter and improvements thereof, which meet the tests of utility, novelty, and nonobviousness are entitled to be patented, but those which do not, are not. The question remains whether those items which are proper subjects for consideration for a patent may also have available the alternative protection accorded by trade secret law.

Certainly the patent policy of encouraging invention is not disturbed by the existence of another form of incentive to invention. In this respect the two systems are not and never would be in conflict. Similarly, the policy that matter once in the public domain must remain in the public domain is not incompatible with the existence of trade secret protection. By definition a trade secret has not been placed in the public domain.

The more difficult objective of the patent law to reconcile with trade secret law is that of disclosure, the quid pro quo of the right to exclude. Universal Oil Co. v. Globe Co., 322 U.S., at 484, 64 S.Ct. at 1116. We are helped in this stage of the analysis by Judge Henry Friendly's opinion in Painton & Co. v. Bourns, Inc., 442 F.2d 216 (C.A.2 1971). There the Court of Appeals thought it useful, in determining whether inventors will refrain because of the existence of trade secret law from applying for patents, thereby depriving the public from learning of the invention, to distinguish between three categories of trade secrets: "(1) the trade secret believed by its owner to constitute a validly patentable invention; (2) the trade secret known to its owner not to be so patentable; and (3) the trade secret whose valid patentability is considered dubious." Id., at 224. Trade secret protection in each of these categories would run against breaches of confidence—the employee and licensee situations— and theft and other forms of industrial espionage.

As to the trade secret known not to meet the standards of patentability, very little in the way of disclosure would be accomplished by abolishing trade secret protection. With trade secrets of nonpatentable subject matter, the patent alternative would not reasonably be available to the inventor. "There can be no public interest in stimulating developers of such (unpatentable) knowhow to flood an overburdened Patent Office with applications (for) what they do not consider patentable." Ibid. The mere filing of applications doomed to be turned down by the Patent Office will bring forth no new public knowledge or enlightenment, since under federal statute and regulation patent applications and abandoned patent applications are held by the Patent Office in confidence and are not open to public inspection. 35 U.S.C. § 122; 37 CFR § 1.14(b).

Even as the extension of trade secret protection to patentable subject matter that the owner knows will not meet the standards of patentability will not conflict with the patent policy of disclosure, it will have a decidedly beneficial effect on society. Trade secret law will encourage invention in areas where patent law does not reach, and will prompt the independent innovator to proceed with the discovery and exploitation of his invention. Competition is fostered and the public is not deprived of the use of valuable, if not quite patentable, invention.

Even if trade secret protection against the faithless employee were abolished, inventive and exploitive effort in the area of patentable subject matter that did not meet the standards of patentability would continue, although at a reduced level. Alternatively with the effort that remained, however, would come an increase in the amount of self-help that innovative companies would employ. Knowledge would be widely dispersed among the employees of those still active in research. Security precautions necessarily would be increased, and salaries and fringe benefits of those few officers or employees who had to know the whole of the secret invention would be fixed in an amount thought sufficient to assure their loyalty. Smaller companies would be placed at a distinct economic disadvantage, since the costs of this kind of self-help could be great, and the cost to the public of the use of this invention would be increased. The innovative entrepreneur with limited resources would tend to confine his research efforts to himself and those few he felt he could trust without the ultimate assurance of legal protection against breaches of confidence. As a result, organized scientific and technological research could become fragmented, and society, as a whole, would suffer.

Another problem that would arise if state trade secret protection were precluded is in the area of licensing others to exploit secret processes. The holder of a trade secret would not likely share his secret with a manufacturer who cannot be placed under binding legal obligation to pay a license fee or to protect the secret. The result would be to hoard rather than disseminate knowledge. Painton & Co. v. Bourns, Inc., 442 F.2d, at 223. Instead, then, of licensing others to use his invention and making the most efficient use of existing manufacturing and marketing structures within the industry, the trade secret holder would tend either to limit his utilization of the invention, thereby depriving the public of the maximum benefit of its use, or engage in the time-consuming and economically wasteful enterprise of constructing duplicative manufacturing and marketing mechanisms for the exploitation of the invention. The detrimental misallocation of resources and economic waste that would thus take place if trade secret protection were abolished with respect to employees or licensees cannot be justified by reference to any policy that the federal patent law seeks to advance.

Nothing in the patent law requires that States refrain from action to prevent industrial espionage. In addition to the increased costs for protection from burglary, wire-tapping, bribery, and the other means used to misappropriate trade secrets, there is the inevitable cost to the basic decency of society when one firm steals from another. A most fundamental human right, that of privacy, is threatened when industrial espionage is condoned or is made profitable; the state interest in denying profit to such illegal ventures is unchallengeable.

The next category of patentable subject matter to deal with is the invention whose holder has a legitimate doubt as to its patentability. The risk of eventual patent invalidity by the courts and the costs associated with that risk may well impel some with a good-faith doubt as to patentability not to take the trouble to seek to obtain and defend patent protection for their discoveries, regardless of the existence of trade secret protection. Trade secret protection would assist those inventors in the more efficient exploitation of their discoveries and not conflict with the patent law. In most cases of genuine doubt as to patent validity the potential rewards of patent protection are so far superior to those accruing to holders of trade secrets, that the holders of such inventions will seek patent protection, ignoring the trade secret route. For those inventors "on the line" as to whether to seek patent protection, the abolition of trade secret protection might encourage some to apply for a patent who otherwise would not have done so. For some of those so encouraged, no patent will be granted and the result "will have been an unnecessary postponement in the divulging of the trade secret to persons willing to pay for it. If (the patent does issue), it may well be invalid, yet many will prefer to pay a modest royalty than to contest it, even though *Lear* allows them to accept a license and pursue the contest without paying royalties while the fight goes on. The result in such a case would be unjustified royalty payments from many who would prefer not to pay them rather than agreed fees from one or a few who are entirely willing to do so." Painton & Co. v. Bourns, Inc., 442 F.2d, at 225. The point is that those who might be encouraged to file for patents by the absence of trade secret law will include inventors possessing the chaff as well as the wheat. Some of the chaff—the nonpatentable discoveries—will be thrown out by the Patent Office, but in the meantime society will have been deprived of use of those discoveries through trade secret-protected licensing. Some of the chaff may not be thrown out. This Court has noted the difference between the standards used by the Patent Office and the courts to determine patentability. Graham v. John Deere Co., 383 U.S. 1, 18, 86 S.Ct. 684, 694, 15 L.Ed.2d 545 (1966). In Lear, Inc. v. Adkins, 395 U.S. 653, 89 S.Ct. 1902, 23 L.Ed.2d 610 (1969), the Court thought that an invalid patent was so serious a threat to the free use of ideas already in the public domain that the Court permitted licensees of the patent holder to challenge the validity of the patent. Better had the invalid patent never issued. More of those patents would likely issue if trade secret law were abolished. Eliminating trade secret law for the doubtfully patentable invention is thus likely to have deleterious effects on society and patent policy which we cannot say are balanced out by the speculative gain which might result from the encouragement of some inventors with doubtfully patentable inventions which deserve patent protection to come forward and apply for patents. There is no conflict, then, between trade secret law and the patent law policy of disclosure, at least insofar as the first two categories of patentable subject matter are concerned.

The final category of patentable subject matter to deal with is the clearly patentable invention, i.e., that invention which the owner believes to meet the standards of patentability. It is here that the federal interest in disclosure is at its peak; these inventions, novel, useful and nonobvious, are "the things which are worth to the public the embarrassment of an exclusive patent." Graham v. John Deere Co., supra, at 9, 86 S.Ct., at 689 (quoting Thomas Jefferson). The interest of the public is that the bargain of 17 years of exclusive use in return for disclosure be accepted. If a State, through a system of protection, were to cause a substantial risk that holders of patentable inventions would not seek patents, but rather would rely on the state protection, we would be compelled to hold that such a system could not constitutionally continue to exist. In the case of trade secret law no reasonable risk of deterrence from patent application by those who can reasonably expect to be granted patents exists.

Trade secret law provides far weaker protection in many respects than the patent law. While trade secret law does not forbid the discovery of the trade secret by fair and honest means, e.g., independent creation or reverse engineering, patent law operates "against the world," forbidding any use of the invention for whatever purpose for a significant length of time. The holder of a trade secret also takes a substantial risk that the secret will be passed on to his competitors, by theft or by breach of a confidential relationship, in a manner not easily susceptible of discovery or proof. Painton & Co. v. Bourns, Inc., 442 F.2d, at 224. Where patent law acts as a barrier, trade secret law functions relatively as a sieve. The possibility that an inventor who believes his invention meets the standards of patentability will sit back, rely on trade secret law, and after one year of use forfeit any right to patent protection, 35 U.S.C. § 102(b), is remote indeed.

Nor does society face much risk that scientific or technological progress will be impeded by the rare inventor with a patentable invention who chooses trade secret protection over patent protection. The ripeness-of-time concept of invention, developed from the study of the many independent multiple discoveries in history, predicts that if a particular individual had not made a particular discovery others would have, and in probably a relatively short period of time. If something is to be discovered at all very likely it will be discovered by more than one person. Singletons and Multiples in Science (1961), in R. Merton, The Sociology of Science 343 (1973); J. Cole & S. Cole, Social Stratification in Science 12–13, 229–230 (1973); Ogburn & Thomas, Are Inventions Inevitable?, 37 Pol.Sci.Q. 83 (1922).[19] Even were an inventor to keep his discovery completely to himself, something that neither the patent nor trade secret laws forbid, there is a high probability that it will be soon independently developed. If the invention, though still a trade secret, is put into public use, the competition is alerted to the existence of the inventor's solution to the problem and may be encouraged to make an extra effort to independently find the solution thus known to be possible. The inventor faces pressures not only from private industry, but from the skilled scientists who work in our universities and our other great publicly supported centers of learning and research.

We conclude that the extension of trade secret protection to clearly patentable inventions does not conflict with the patent policy of disclosure. Perhaps because trade secret law does not produce any positive effects in the area of clearly patentable inventions, as opposed to the beneficial effects resulting from trade secret protection in the areas of the doubtfully patentable and the clearly unpatentable inventions, it has been suggested that partial pre-emption may be appropriate, and that

19. See J. Watson, The Double Helix (1968). If Watson and Crick had not discovered the structure of DNA it is likely that Linus Pauling would have made the discovery soon. Other examples of multiple discovery are listed at length in the Ogburn and Thomas article.

courts should refuse to apply trade secret protection to inventions which the holder should have patented, and which would have been, thereby, disclosed. However, since there is no real possibility that trade secret law will conflict with the federal policy favoring disclosure of clearly patentable inventions partial pre-emption is inappropriate. Partial pre-emption, furthermore, could well create serious problems for state courts in the administration of trade secret law. As a preliminary matter in trade secret actions, state courts would be obliged to distinguish between what a reasonable inventor would and would not correctly consider to be clearly patentable, with the holder of the trade secret arguing that the invention was not patentable and the misappropriator of the trade secret arguing its undoubted novelty, utility, and nonobviousness. Federal courts have a difficult enough time trying to determine whether an invention, narrowed by the patent application procedure and fixed in the specifications which describe the invention for which the patent has been granted, is patentable.[22] Although state courts in some circumstances must join federal courts in judging whether an issued patent is valid, Lear, Inc. v. Adkins, supra, it would be undesirable to impose the almost impossible burden on state courts to determine the patentability—in fact and in the mind of a reasonable inventor—of a discovery which has not been patented and remains entirely uncircumscribed by expert analysis in the administrative process. Neither complete nor partial pre-emption of state trade secret law is justified.

Our conclusion that patent law does not pre-empt trade secret law is in accord with prior cases of this Court. Trade secret law and patent law have co-existed in this country for over one hundred years. Each has its particular role to play, and the operation of one does not take away from the need for the other. Trade secret law encourages the development and exploitation of those items of lesser or different invention than might be accorded protection under the patent laws, but which items still have an important part to play in the technological and scientific advancement of the Nation. Trade secret law promotes the sharing of knowledge, and the efficient operation of industry; it permits the individual inventor to reap the rewards of his labor by contracting with a company large enough to develop and exploit it. Congress, by its silence over these many years, has seen the wisdom of allowing the States to enforce trade secret protection. Until Congress takes affirmative action to the contrary, States should be free to grant protection to trade secrets.

* * *

MR. JUSTICE MARSHALL, concurring in the result.

Unlike the Court, I do not believe that the possibility that an inventor with a patentable invention will rely on state trade secret law rather than apply for a patent is "remote indeed." Ante, at ___. State trade secret law provides substantial protection to the inventor who

---

22. See Judge L. Hand's lament in Harries v. Air King Products Co., 183 F.2d 158, 162 (C.A.2 1950).

intends to use or sell the invention himself rather than license it to others, protection which in its unlimited duration is clearly superior to the 17–year monopoly afforded by the patent laws. I have no doubt that the existence of trade secret protection provides in some instances a substantial disincentive to entrance into the patent system, and thus deprives society of the benefits of public disclosure of the invention which it is the policy of the patent laws to encourage. This case may well be such an instance.

But my view of sound policy in this area does not dispose of this case. Rather, the question presented in this case is whether Congress, in enacting the patent laws, intended merely to offer inventors a limited monopoly in exchange for disclosure of their invention, or instead to exert pressure on inventors to enter into this exchange by withdrawing any alternative possibility of legal protection for their inventions. I am persuaded that the former is the case. State trade secret laws and the federal patent laws have co-existed for many, many years. During this time, Congress has repeatedly demonstrated its full awareness of the existence of the trade secret system, without any indication of disapproval. Indeed, Congress has in a number of instances given explicit federal protection to trade secret information provided to federal agencies. See, e.g., 5 U.S.C. § 552(b)(4); 18 U.S.C. § 1905. Because of this, I conclude that there is "neither such actual conflict between the two schemes of regulation that both cannot stand in the same area, nor evidence of a congressional design to pre-empt the field." Florida Lime & Avocado Growers v. Paul, 373 U.S. 132, 141, 83 S.Ct. 1210, 1217, 10 L.Ed.2d 248 (1963). I therefore concur in the result reached by the majority of the Court.

Mr. Justice Douglas, with whom Mr. Justice Brennan concurs, dissenting.

Today's decision is at war with the philosophy of Sears, Roebuck & Co. v. Stiffel Co., 376 U.S. 225, 84 S.Ct. 784, 11 L.Ed.2d 661 and Compco Corp. v. Day–Brite Lighting, Inc., 376 U.S. 234, 84 S.Ct. 779, 11 L.Ed.2d 669. Those cases involved patents—one of a pole lamp and one of fluorescent lighting fixtures each of which was declared invalid. The lower courts held, however, that though the patents were invalid the sale of identical or confusingly similar products to the products of the patentees violated state unfair competition laws. We held that when an article is unprotected by a patent, state law may not forbid others to copy it, because every article not covered by a valid patent is in the public domain. Congress in the patent laws decided that where no patent existed, free competition should prevail; that where a patent is rightfully issued, the right to exclude others should obtain for no longer than 17 years, and that the States may not "under some other law, such as that forbidding unfair competition, give protection of a kind that clashes with the objectives of the federal patent laws," 376 U.S., at 231, 84 S.Ct. at 789.

The product involved in this suit, sodium iodide synthetic crystals, was a product that could be patented but was not. Harshaw the inventor apparently contributed greatly to the technology in that field by developing processes, procedures, and techniques that produced much larger crystals than any competitor. These processes, procedures, and techniques were also patentable; but no patent was sought. Rather Harshaw sought to protect its trade secrets by contracts with its employees. And the District Court found that, as a result of those secrecy precautions, "not sufficient disclosure occurred so as to place the claimed trade secrets in the public domain"; and those findings were sustained by the Court of Appeals.

The District Court issued a permanent injunction against respondents, ex-employees, restraining them from using the processes used by Harshaw. By a patent which would require full disclosure Harshaw could have obtained a 17–year monopoly against the world. By the District Court's injunction, which the Court approves and reinstates, Harshaw gets a permanent injunction running into perpetuity against respondents. In *Sears*, as in the present case, an injunction against the unfair competitor issued. We said: "To allow a State by use of its law of unfair competition to prevent the copying of an article which represents too slight an advance to be patented would be to permit the State to block off from the public something which federal law has said belongs to the public. The result would be that while federal law grants only 14 or 17 years' protection to genuine inventions, see 35 U.S.C. §§ 154, 173, States could allow perpetual protection to articles too lacking in novelty to merit any patent at all under federal constitutional standards. This would be too great an encroachment on the federal patent system to be tolerated." 376 U.S., at 231–232, 84 S.Ct. at 789.

* * *

BONITO BOATS, INC. v. THUNDER CRAFT BOATS, INC.

Supreme Court of the United States, 1989.
489 U.S. 141, 109 S.Ct. 971, 103 L.Ed.2d 118.

JUSTICE O'CONNOR delivered the opinion of the Court.

We must decide today what limits the operation of the federal patent system places on the States' ability to offer substantial protection to utilitarian and design ideas which the patent laws leave otherwise unprotected. * * *

I

[Bonito Boats, Inc., sued respondent Thunder Craft Boats, Inc., for using the direct molding process to duplicate the hull design of Bonito's Model 5VBR fiberglass recreational boat, and selling the duplicates, in violation of Florida Statute § 559.94 (1987), which made it unlawful "to use the direct molding process to duplicate for the purpose of sale any manufactured vessel hull or component part of a vessel made by another'' or to "knowingly sell" such an unlawfully duplicated hull or component. The trial court dismissed the suit on the ground that the Florida statute was invalid under Sears, Roebuck & Co. v. Stiffel Co., 376 U.S. 225 (1964) and Compco Corporation v. Day–Brite Lighting, Inc., 376 U.S. 234 (1964), because it impermissibly interfered with the scheme of the federal patent laws. The state court of appeal affirmed.]

* * *

On appeal, a sharply divided Florida Supreme Court agreed with the lower courts' conclusion that the Florida law impermissibly interfered with the scheme established by the federal patent laws. * * * The majority read our decisions in Sears and Compco for the proposition that "when an article is introduced into the public domain, only a patent can eliminate the inherent risk of competition and then but for a limited time." * * * [T]he three dissenting judges argued that the Florida anti-direct molding provision "does not prohibit the copying of an unpatented item. It prohibits one method of copying; the item remains in the public domain." * * *

II

* * *

* * * [O]ur past decisions have made clear that state regulation of intellectual property must yield to the extent that it clashes with the balance struck by Congress in our patent laws. The tension between the desire to freely exploit the full potential of our inventive resources and the need to create an incentive to deploy those resources is constant. Where it is clear how the patent laws strike that balance in a particular circumstance, that is not a judgment the States may second-guess. We have long held that after the expiration of a federal patent, the subject matter of the patent passes to the free use of the public as a matter of federal law. * * * Where the public has paid the congressionally mandated price for disclosure, the States may not render the exchange fruitless by offering patent-like protection to the subject matter of the expired patent. * * *

In our decisions in Sears, Roebuck & Co. v. Stiffel Co., 376 U.S. 225 (1964), and Compco Corp. v. Day–Brite Lighting, Inc., 376 U.S. 234 (1964), we found that publicly known design and utilitarian ideas which were unprotected by patent occupied much the same position as the subject matter of an expired patent. * * *

* * *

The pre-emptive sweep of our decisions in Sears and Compco has been the subject of heated scholarly and judicial debate. See, e. g., Symposium, Product Simulation: A Right or a Wrong?, 64 Colum. L. Rev. 1178 (1964); Lear, Inc. v. Adkins, 395 U.S. 653, 676 (1969) (Black, J., concurring in part and dissenting in part). Read at their highest level of generality, the two decisions could be taken to stand for the proposition that the States are completely disabled from offering any form of protection to articles or processes which fall within the broad scope of patentable subject matter. See id., at 677. Since the potentially patentable includes "anything under the sun that is made by man," Diamond v. Chakrabarty, 447 U.S. 303, 309 (1980) (citation omitted), the broadest reading of Sears would prohibit the States from regulating the deceptive simulation of trade dress or the tortious appropriation of private information.

That the extrapolation of such a broad pre-emptive principle from Sears is inappropriate is clear from the balance struck in Sears itself. The Sears Court made it plain that the States "may protect businesses in the use of their trademarks, labels, or distinctive dress in the packaging of goods so as to prevent others, by imitating such markings, from misleading purchasers as to the source of the goods." Sears, supra, at 232 (footnote omitted). Trade dress is, of course, potentially the subject matter of design patents. See W. T. Rogers Co. v. Keene, 778 F. 2d 334, 337 (C.A.7 1985). Yet our decision in Sears clearly indicates that the States may place limited regulations on the circumstances in which such designs are used in order to prevent consumer confusion as to source. Thus, while Sears speaks in absolutist terms, its conclusion that the States may place some conditions on the use of trade dress indicates an implicit recognition that all state regulation of potentially patentable but unpatented subject matter is not ipso facto pre-empted by the federal patent laws.

What was implicit in our decision in Sears, we have made explicit in our subsequent decisions concerning the scope of federal pre-emption of state regulation of the subject matter of patent. Thus, in Kewanee Oil Co. v. Bicron Corp., 416 U.S. 470 (1974), we held that state protection of trade secrets did not operate to frustrate the achievement of the congressional objectives served by the patent laws. Despite the fact that state law protection was available for ideas which clearly fell within the subject matter of patent, the Court concluded that the nature and degree of state protection did not conflict with the federal policies of encouragement of patentable invention and the prompt disclosure of such innovations.

Several factors were critical to this conclusion. First, because the public awareness of a trade secret is by definition limited, the Court noted that "the policy that matter once in the public domain must remain in the public domain is not incompatible with the existence of trade secret protection." Id., at 484. Second, the Kewanee Court emphasized that "[t]rade secret law provides far weaker protection in many respects than the patent law." Id., at 489–490. This point was central to the Court's conclusion that trade secret protection did not conflict with either the encouragement or disclosure policies of the federal patent law. The public at large remained free to discover and exploit the trade secret through reverse engineering of products in the public domain or by independent creation. Id., at 490. Thus, the possibility that trade secret protection would divert inventors from the creative effort necessary to satisfy the rigorous demands of patent protection was remote indeed. Ibid. Finally, certain aspects of trade secret law operated to protect noneconomic interests outside the sphere of congressional concern in the patent laws. As the Court noted, "[A] most fundamental human right, that of privacy, is threatened when industrial espionage is condoned or is made profitable." Id., at 487 (footnote omitted). There was no indication that Congress had considered this interest in the balance struck by the patent laws, or that state protection for it would interfere with the policies behind the patent system.

We have since reaffirmed the pragmatic approach which Kewanee takes to the pre-emption of state laws dealing with the protection of intellectual property. See Aronson [v. Quick Point Pencil Co., 440 U.S. 257, 262, 99 S.Ct. 1096, 59 L.Ed.2d 296 (1979)] ("State law is not displaced merely because the contract relates to intellectual property which may or may not be patentable; the states are free to regulate the use of such intellectual property in any manner not inconsistent with federal law"). At the same time, we have consistently reiterated the teaching of Sears and Compco that ideas once placed before the public without the protection of a valid patent are subject to appropriation without significant restraint. Aronson, supra, at 263.

At the heart of Sears and Compco is the conclusion that the efficient operation of the federal patent system depends upon substantially free trade in publicly known, unpatented design and utilitarian conceptions. In Sears, the state law offered "the equivalent of a patent monopoly," 376 U.S., at 233, in the functional aspects of a product which had been placed in public commerce absent the protection of a valid patent. While, as noted above, our decisions since Sears have taken a decidedly less rigid view of the scope of federal pre-emption under the patent laws, e. g., Kewanee, supra, at 479–480, we believe that the Sears Court correctly concluded that the States may not offer patent-like protection to intellectual creations which would otherwise remain unprotected as a matter of federal law. Both the novelty and the nonobviousness requirements of federal patent law are grounded in the notion that concepts within the public grasp, or those so obvious that they readily could be, are the tools of creation available to all. They provide the baseline of free competition upon which the patent system's incentive to creative effort depends. A state law that substantially interferes with the enjoyment of an unpatented utilitarian or design conception which has been freely disclosed by its author to the public at large impermissibly contravenes the ultimate goal of public disclosure and use which is the centerpiece of federal patent policy. Moreover, through the creation of patent-like rights, the States could essentially redirect inventive efforts away from the careful criteria of patentability developed by Congress over the last 200 years. We understand this to be the reasoning at the core of our decisions in Sears and Compco, and we reaffirm that reasoning today.

III

We believe that the Florida statute at issue in this case so substantially impedes the public use of the otherwise unprotected design and utilitarian ideas embodied in unpatented boat hulls as to run afoul of the teaching of our decisions in Sears and Compco. It is readily apparent that the Florida statute does not operate to prohibit "unfair competition" in the usual sense that the term is understood. The law of unfair competition has its roots in the common-law tort of deceit: its general concern is with protecting consumers from confusion as to source. * * *

With some notable exceptions, including the interpretation of the Illinois law of unfair competition at issue in Sears and Compco, * * *, the common-law tort of unfair competition has been limited to protection against copying of nonfunctional aspects of consumer products which have acquired secondary meaning such that they operate as a designation of source. * * *

In contrast to the operation of unfair competition law, the Florida statute is aimed directly at preventing the exploitation of the design and utilitarian conceptions embodied in the product itself. * * * Like the patentee, the beneficiary of the Florida statute may prevent a competitor from "making" the product in what is evidently the most efficient manner available and from "selling" the product when it is produced in that fashion. Compare 35 U. S. C. § 154. The Florida scheme offers this protection for an unlimited number of years to all boat hulls and their component parts, without regard to their ornamental or technological merit. Protection is available for subject matter for which patent protection has been denied or has expired, as well as for designs which have been freely revealed to the consuming public by their creators.

In this case, the Bonito 5VBR fiberglass hull has been freely exposed to the public for a period in excess of six years. For purposes of federal law, it stands in the same stead as an item for which a patent has expired or been denied: it is unpatented and unpatentable. See 35 U.S.C. § 102(b). Whether because of a determination of unpatentability or other commercial concerns, petitioner chose to expose its hull design to the public in the marketplace, eschewing the bargain held out by the federal patent system of disclosure in exchange for exclusive use. Yet, the Florida statute allows petitioner to reassert a substantial property right in the idea, thereby constricting the spectrum of useful public knowledge. Moreover, it does so without the careful protections of high standards of innovation and limited monopoly contained in the federal scheme. We think it clear that such protection conflicts with the federal policy "that all ideas in general circulation be dedicated to the common good unless they are protected by a valid patent." Lear, Inc. v. Adkins, 395 U.S., at 668.

That the Florida statute does not remove all means of reproduction and sale does not eliminate the conflict with the federal scheme. * * * In essence, the Florida law prohibits the entire public from engaging in a form of reverse engineering of a product in the public domain. This is clearly one of the rights vested in the federal patent holder, but has never been a part of state protection under the law of unfair competition or trade secrets. * * * Reverse engineering of chemical and mechanical articles in the public domain often leads to significant advances in technology. If Florida may prohibit this particular method of study and recomposition of an unpatented article, we fail to see the principle that would prohibit a State from banning the use of chromatography in the reconstitution of unpatented chemical compounds, or the use of robotics in the duplication of machinery in the public domain.

Moreover, as we noted in Kewanee, the competitive reality of reverse engineering may act as a spur to the inventor, creating an incentive to develop inventions that meet the rigorous requirements of patentability. 416 U.S., at 489–490. The Florida statute substantially reduces this competitive incentive, thus eroding the general rule of free competition upon which the attractiveness of the federal patent bargain depends. The protections of state trade secret law are most effective at the developmental stage, before a product has been marketed and the threat of reverse engineering becomes real. During this period, patentability will often be an uncertain prospect, and to a certain extent, the protection offered by trade secret law may "dovetail" with the incentives created by the federal patent monopoly. See Goldstein, Kewanee Oil Co. v. Bicron Corp.: Notes on a Closing Circle, 1974 S.Ct. Rev. 81, 92. In contrast, under the Florida scheme, the would-be inventor is aware from the outset of his efforts that rights against the public are available regardless of his ability to satisfy the rigorous standards of patentability. Indeed, it appears that even the most mundane and obvious changes in the design of a boat hull will trigger the protections of the statute. See Fla. Stat. § 559.94(2) (1987) (protecting "any manufactured vessel hull or component part"). Given the substantial protection offered by the Florida scheme, we cannot dismiss as hypothetical the possibility that it will become a significant competitor to the federal patent laws, offering investors similar protection without the quid pro quo of substantial creative effort required by the federal statute. The prospect of all 50 States establishing similar protections for preferred industries without the rigorous requirements of patentability prescribed by Congress could pose a substantial threat to the patent system's ability to accomplish its mission of promoting progress in the useful arts.

Finally, allowing the States to create patent-like rights in various products in public circulation would lead to administrative problems of no small dimension. The federal patent scheme provides a basis for the public to ascertain the status of the intellectual property embodied in any article in general circulation. Through the application process, detailed information concerning the claims of the patent holder is compiled in a central location. See 35 U. S. C. §§ 111–114. The availability of damages in an infringement action is made contingent upon affixing a notice of patent to the protected article. 35 U. S. C. § 287. The notice requirement is designed "for the information of the public," Wine Railway Appliance Co. v. Enterprise Railway Equipment Co., 297 U.S.

387, 397 (1936), and provides a ready means of discerning the status of the intellectual property embodied in an article of manufacture or design. The public may rely upon the lack of notice in exploiting shapes and designs accessible to all. See Devices for Medicine, Inc. v. Boehl, 822 F. 2d 1062, 1066 (C.A.Fed.1987) ("Having sold the product unmarked, [the patentee] could hardly maintain entitlement to damages for its use by a purchaser uninformed that such use would violate [the] patent").

The Florida scheme blurs this clear federal demarcation between public and private property. One of the fundamental purposes behind the Patent and Copyright Clauses of the Constitution was to promote national uniformity in the realm of intellectual property. See The Federalist No. 43, p. 309 (B. Wright ed. 1961). * * * This purpose is frustrated by the Florida scheme, which renders the status of the design and utilitarian "ideas" embodied in the boat hulls it protects uncertain. Given the inherently ephemeral nature of property in ideas, and the great power such property has to cause harm to the competitive policies which underlay the federal patent laws, the demarcation of broad zones of public and private right is "the type of regulation that demands a uniform national rule." Ray v. Atlantic Richfield Co., 435 U.S. 151, 179 (1978). Absent such a federal rule, each State could afford patent-like protection to particularly favored home industries, effectively insulating them from competition from outside the State.

* * *

* * * [T]he federal standards for patentability, at a minimum, express the congressional determination that patent-like protection is unwarranted as to certain classes of intellectual property. The States are simply not free in this regard to offer equivalent protections to ideas which Congress has determined should belong to all. * * *

Our decisions since Sears and Compco have made it clear that the Patent and Copyright Clauses do not, by their own force or by negative implication, deprive the States of the power to adopt rules for the promotion of intellectual creation within their own jurisdictions. See Aronson, 440 U.S., at 262; Goldstein v. California, 412 U.S. 546, 552–561 (1973); Kewanee, 416 U.S., at 478–479. Thus, where "Congress determines that neither federal protection nor freedom from restraint is required by the national interest," Goldstein, supra, at 559, the States remain free to promote originality and creativity in their own domains.

Nor does the fact that a particular item lies within the subject matter of the federal patent laws necessarily preclude the States from offering limited protection which does not impermissibly interfere with the federal patent scheme. As Sears itself makes clear, States may place limited regulations on the use of unpatented designs in order to prevent consumer confusion as to source. In Kewanee, we found that state protection of trade secrets, as applied to both patentable and unpatentable subject matter, did not conflict with the federal patent laws. In both situations, state protection was not aimed exclusively at the promotion of invention itself, and the state restrictions on the use of unpatented ideas were limited to those necessary to promote goals outside the contemplation of the federal patent scheme. Both the law of unfair competition and state trade secret law have coexisted harmoniously with federal patent protection for almost 200 years, and Congress has given no indication that their operation is inconsistent with the operation of the federal patent laws. See Florida Lime & Avocado Growers, Inc. v. Paul, 373 U.S. 132, 144 (1963); United States v. Bass, 404 U.S. 336, 349 (1971).

Indeed, there are affirmative indications from Congress that both the law of unfair competition and trade secret protection are consistent with the balance struck by the patent laws. Section 43(a) of the Lanham Act, 60 Stat. 441, 15 U. S. C. § 1125(a), creates a federal remedy for making "a false designation of origin, or any false description or representation, including words or other symbols tending falsely to describe or represent the same. . . . " Congress has thus given federal recognition to many of the concerns that underlie the state tort of unfair competition, and the application of Sears and Compco to nonfunctional aspects of a product which have been shown to identify source must take account of competing federal policies in this regard. Similarly, as Justice Marshall noted in his concurring opinion in Kewanee: "State trade secret laws and the federal patent laws have co-existed for many, many, years. During this time, Congress has repeatedly demonstrated its full awareness of the existence of the trade secret system, without any indication of disapproval. Indeed, Congress has in a number of instances given explicit federal protection to trade secret information provided to federal agencies." Kewanee, supra, at 494 (concurring in result) (citation omitted). The case for federal pre-emption is particularly weak where Congress has indicated its awareness of the operation of state law in a field of federal interest, and has nonetheless decided to "stand by both concepts and to tolerate whatever tension there [is] between them." Silkwood v. Kerr–McGee Corp., 464 U.S. 238, 256 (1984). The same cannot be said of the Florida statute at issue here, which offers protection beyond that available under the law of unfair competition or trade secret, without any showing of consumer confusion, or breach of trust or secrecy.

The Florida statute is aimed directly at the promotion of intellectual creation by substantially restricting the public's ability to exploit ideas that the patent system mandates shall be free for all to use. Like the interpretation of Illinois unfair competition law in Sears and Compco, the Florida statute represents a break with the tradition of peaceful coexistence between state market regulation and federal patent policy. The Florida law substantially restricts the public's ability to exploit an unpatented design in general circulation, raising the specter of state-created monopolies in a host of useful shapes and processes for which patent protection has been denied or is otherwise unobtainable. It thus enters a field of regulation which the patent laws have reserved to Congress. The patent statute's careful balance between public right and private monopoly to promote certain creative activity is a "scheme of federal regulation . . . so pervasive as to make reasonable the inference that Congress left no room for the States to supplement it." *Rice v. Santa Fe Elevator Corp.*, 331 U.S. 218, 230 (1947).

Congress has considered extending various forms of limited protection to industrial design either through the copyright laws or by relaxing the restrictions on the availability of design patents. See generally Brown, Design Protection: An Overview, 34 UCLA L. Rev. 1341 (1987). Congress explicitly refused to take this step in the copyright laws, see 17 U. S. C. § 101; H. R. Rep. No. 94–1476, p. 55 (1976), and despite sustained criticism for a number of years, it has declined to alter the patent protections presently available for industrial design. See Report of the President's Commission on the Patent System, S. Doc. No. 5, 90th Cong., 1st Sess., 20–21 (1967); Lindgren, The Sanctity of the Design Patent: Illusion or Reality?, 10 Okla. City L. Rev. 195 (1985). It is for Congress to determine if the present system of design and utility patents is ineffectual in promoting the useful arts in the context of industrial design. By offering patent-like protection for ideas deemed unprotected under the present federal scheme, the Florida statute conflicts with the "strong federal policy favoring free competition in ideas which do not merit patent protection." *Lear, Inc.*, 395 U.S., at 656. We therefore agree with the majority of the Florida Supreme Court that the Florida statute is preempted by the Supremacy Clause, and the judgment of that court is hereby affirmed.

It is so ordered.

Note

The DMCA introduced *sui generis* protection for boat hull designs, to replace the type of state law protection which the Supreme Court held to be preempted in *Bonito Boats*. Title V of the Act, titled the "Vessel Hull Design Protection Act," added a new Chapter 13 to Title 17 which gives the owner of an original boat hull design the exclusive right for 10 years to make, import, sell or distribute articles embodying that design for sale or use in trade, notwithstanding the intrinsic utilitarian function of the design. The new provision imposes a marking requirement, limits infringement liability to cases in which the infringing article was created with knowledge that its design was copied from a protected design, exempts copying that is solely for teaching or evaluative purposes, and requires that a design be registered with the Copyright Office before an infringement suit can be filed. Infringement remedies include injunctions, seizure and/or destruction of the infringing articles, attorneys' fees, and either damages (including enhanced damages) or the infringer's profits. Issuance of a design patent for a vessel hull design preempts Chapter 13 protection for that design, but Chapter 13 does not preempt either (a) federal or state protection for unregistered designs or (b) trademark or unfair competition laws.

Section 5005 of the Satellite Home Viewer Improvement Act of 1999, Pub. L. No. 106–113, 106th Cong., 1st Sess. (1999), removed the sunset date of the vessel hull design protection provisions added to Title 17 by the DMCA, 17 U.S.C. § 1301 *et seq.*, and revised the definition of "vessel" in section 1301(b)(3) thereof.

BALADEVON, INC. v. ABBOTT LABORATORIES, INC.

United States District Court, D. Massachusetts, 1994.
871 F.Supp. 89.

SARIS, DISTRICT JUDGE:

This case marks the crossroads of patent and contract law. Plaintiff seeks to enforce an agreement which assigned patent, trademark and other non-patent rights in a device which was potentially patentable, but not yet patented. When the patents which subsequently issued on the device became generally recognized as invalid, defendant terminated payment of the royalties due under the assignment, but continued manufacturing the device and exercising other non-patent rights, notably trademark rights.

Both sides have filed cross-motions for summary judgment. After hearing, the Court ALLOWS plaintiff's motion in part, and DENIES defendant's motion.

BACKGROUND

* * *

[Radiologists Sacks and Vine invented an "enteral feeding device," used for feeding patients directly through the stomach. Plaintiff Baladevon, Inc. is a corporation owned by the Sacks family and is the assignee of Dr. Vine's claims. While an application for one patent on the device was still pending, and before the application for a second patent had been filed, Baladevon and Vine assigned to Microvasive, Inc. (a division of Boston Scientific, Inc.) the following rights of the two inventors:]

> any rights they may have to [the device and the method for using it which were conceived and developed by Microvasive with their help], to any improvements therein, to the use of the names "Sacks" and "Vine" with respect thereto and to any other rights they may have with respect to the manufacture, use or sale of products that incorporate such concepts, developments or improvements.

In return, Baladevon and Dr. Vine were each to receive 2.5% in royalties through the end of the decade, with the amount to be renegotiated six months before the beginning of 1990, or sooner in the case of certain enumerated events. Most notably, if "a device of comparable design is sold in direct competition," Baladevon and Vine agreed to "consider a reasonable reduction in royalty in order to share the burdens of such events and ensure that Microvasive may continue to sell products without a competitive disadvantage." For the period January 1, 1990 to December 31, 1990, the parties agreed to negotiate over a royalty no less than 1¼ percent or more than 3¾ percent, taking into account, among other things, "devices which are of comparable design and operation and sold in direct competition with products." Any disputes were to be resolved by binding arbitration.

The agreement gave Microvasive the right, but not the legal obligation, to seek and enforce patents for the inventions and improvements, and gave it the "perpetual royalty free" right to use the names Sacks or Vine as a trademark. (Article 4). Microvasive agreed to pay all costs and expenses incurred in connection with all United States and foreign patent applications and patents. The agreement explicitly applies to inventions and improvements "whether patentable or not."

This litigation hinges on the termination provision, article 9(a), which provides as follows:

> This Agreement shall be terminable in whole *or in part* by Microvasive by giving written notice thereof and by assigning to Baladevon and Vine any patents included in Subject Patent Rights which pertain to the part of the Agreement being terminated and neither party shall thereafter have further obligations to the other party with respect to such part of the Agreement. (Emphasis added).

The term of the agreement was August 1, 1984 to December 31, 1994. On August 13, 1987, the defendant, Abbott Laboratories, Inc., entered the picture for the first time. On that day, the Ross Laboratories division of Abbott acquired the enteral feeding device product line from the Microvasive division of Boston Scientific. In the process, defendant acquired all of the original assignee's rights and obligations under the agreement.

The initial patent application resulted in the issuance of a patent in July, 1988. Defendant also applied for a second patent, which issued. Baladevon and Vine (the assignors) did not own or have any interest in the patents; rather Boston Scientific's employees and Dr. Sacks (who is not a party to the agreement) were the inventors listed in the patent application. Then the unexpected occurred. It came to light that Dr. Sacks had published an article containing the ideas embodied in the enteral feeding device over a year before the first application, a fact that rendered both patents invalid per se. See 35 U.S.C. § 102(b). Competitive devices appeared on the market.

On July 14, 1989, defendant notified plaintiff by letter of its intent to "terminate *in part*" (emphasis added) and to assign the patents back under the agreement's termination clause, citing concerns "regarding the validity and enforceability of these patents." Plaintiff's Exh. S. Defendant continued to produce and sell enteral feeding devices under the names "Sacks" and "Vine," without paying plaintiff any royalties. Abbott's registration of the Sacks–Vine trademark became effective on September 26, 1989, two months after Abbott terminated the agreement "in part."

Plaintiff filed suit in this court under a variety of contract theories. A cogent memorandum, issued by Judge Woodlock on July 6, 1992, dismissed all claims except those for breach of contract and for an accounting. With regard to the remaining claims, the court found that two key provisions of the contract are ambiguous: those governing trademark rights and termination rights. The court concluded that, because these two provisions, read in context, were each susceptible of different reasonable interpretations, they presented questions of fact that could not be resolved on a motion to dismiss. * * *

DISCUSSION

* * *

* * * Defendant argues that plaintiff's interpretation of the termination clause—which would obligate defendant, upon termination, to either cease production of the enteral feeding device or pay royalties to plaintiff, despite the invalidity of the patents—is fatally inconsistent with patent law policy.

2. *Lear and its Family*

The seminal case is Lear, Inc. v. Adkins, 395 U.S. 653, 89 S.Ct. 1902, 23 L. Ed. 2d 610 (1969). There, the inventor sued the licensee for using his invention after ceasing royalty payments; the licensee filed a counterclaim for patent invalidity. Two landmark holdings resulted. First, in allowing the licensee to challenge the validity of the patent, the Lear Court abolished the state law doctrine of licensee estoppel. Second, the Lear Court held that the licensee was not liable for royalties on invalid patents from the moment it challenged their validity.

The Lear court characterized the question presented as "whether federal patent law policy bars a State from enforcing a contract regulating access to an unpatented secret idea." 395 U.S. at 672, 89 S.Ct. at 1912. With respect to royalties accruing after the patent issued, the answer was "yes," because "federal law requires that all ideas in general circulation be dedicated to the common good unless they are protected by a valid patent." 395 U.S. at 668, 89 S.Ct. at 1910. More specifically, the Court reasoned that the relegation of unpatentable ideas to the public domain was necessary to ensure that inventors did not reap benefits from an invalid patent; and the only way to put such ideas where they belonged was to give licensees the incentive to make validity challenges. 395 U.S. at 670, 89 S.Ct. at 1911. However, the Court declined to address the claim to royalties before the patent issued "since it squarely raises the question whether, and to what extent, the States may protect the owners of unpatented inventions who are willing to disclose their ideas to manufacturers only upon payments of royalties." 395 U.S. at 674, 89 S.Ct. at 1913.

Lear is conventionally grouped with two other Supreme Court cases that grappled with conflicts between patent law and contract law. In Brulotte v. Thys Co., 379 U.S. 29, 32, 85 S.Ct. 176, 179, 13 L.Ed.2d 99 (1964), the Court held that a contract requiring a licensee to pay royalties after a patent expired was per se unlawful because the patent owner had abused the leverage of the monopoly to project royalties into the period after expiration.

A different principle is embodied in Aronson v. Quick Point Pencil Co., 440 U.S. 257, 259, 99 S.Ct. 1096, 1097, 59 L.Ed.2d 296 (1979), a case decided ten years after Lear. In Quick Point, which involved a royalty agreement covering patent rights and trade secrets, the Court considered "whether federal patent law preempts state contract law so as to preclude enforcement of a contract to pay royalties to a patent applicant, on sales of articles embodying the putative invention, for so long as the contracting party sells them, if a patent is not granted." Pointing out that the parties contracted with "full awareness of both the pendency of a patent application and the possibility that a patent might not issue," it held:

> Commercial agreements traditionally are the domain of state law. State law is not displaced merely because the contract relates to intellectual property which may or may not be patentable; the states are free to regulate the use of such intellectual property in any manner not inconsistent with federal law.

440 U.S. at 261–262, 99 S.Ct. at 1099. The Court found no merit in the contention that enforcement of the agreement withdrew any idea from the public domain because the design, although not patentable, entered the public domain as a result of the manufacture and sale of the design under the contract. The Court also pointed out that the agreement set two different royalty fees, depending on whether or not the patent issued. Although a pending patent application gives the applicant some additional bargaining power, the court stated the "amount of leverage depends on how likely the parties consider it to be that a valid patent will issue." 440 U.S. at 265, 99 S.Ct. at 1101.

The Court distinguished Lear as not controlling "when no patent has issued, and no ideas have been withdrawn from the market place." 440 U.S. at 264, 99 S.Ct. at 1100. Brulotte was distinguished on the grounds that the patent owner in Quick Point had not attempted to use her monopoly as leverage during negotiation of the licensing contract. The Court concluded that federal patent law is not a barrier to enforcement of "contractual obligations, freely undertaken in arm's-length negotiation and with no fixed reliance on a patent or a probable patent grant." 440 U.S. at 266, 99 S.Ct. at 1101.

The Federal Circuit has been leery of a blind application of Lear. In an extensive discussion, the court essentially confined the case to its facts:

> Lear ... precluded the award of royalties to the licensor under the facts of *that case* from the date the patent issued if the patent were later held invalid. Lear does not in fact ... deal with a licensor's right to terminate or rescind a license agreement, or dictate what *must* be held a breach of contract, or what damages *must* be awarded for a breach, or under what circumstances, if any, a licensee can recover royalties paid. Those questions continue to be matters dependent on particular fact situations, contract provisions and state contract law, albeit they must be resolved in harmony with general principles discernible from Lear.

RCA Corp. v. Data General Corp., 887 F.2d 1056, 1064 (Fed.Cir.1989) (emphasis in original). Thus, the public policy expressed in Lear is not so overpowering that it may overcome the especially strong countervailing policy in favor of enforcing contracts that take the form of judicial settlements, Hemstreet v. Spiegel, Inc., 851 F.2d 348, 350–51 (Fed.Cir. 1988), or consent judgments, Foster v. Hallco Mfg. Co., 947 F.2d 469, 477 (Fed.Cir.1991). It is also possible, at least by some means, to contract around the Lear doctrine. See Sun Studs, Inc. v. ATA Equipment Leasing, Inc., 872 F.2d 978, 991–93 (Fed.Cir.1989) (holding that Lear policy of encouraging challenges to patent validity does not require court to void contract provision obligating assignee to protect, defend and enforce the patent and to preserve the confidentiality of information).

3. Hybrid Royalty Agreements

Defendant argues that the agreement here is unenforceable after Lear. Four Circuits have struggled with the question of the enforceability of "hybrid royalty agreements"—agreements, such as the one before the court, that exchange royalties for a mix of patent and non-patent rights—after Lear, Brulotte and Quick Point. A consensus has emerged. Where a licensing agreement fails to distinguish between patent and non-patent rights in royalty payments, and a patent is invalidated, Lear precludes enforcement of the contract according to its terms but does not preclude compensation for the non-patent rights. Chromalloy v. Fischmann, 716 F.2d 683, 685 (9th Cir.1983)(where a royalty agreement was part of a sale of ongoing business, seller was not entitled to compensation for royalty payments on the invalid patent although court could award compensation on transfer and use of non-patent assets); Span–Deck, Inc. v. Fab–Con, Inc., 677 F.2d 1237, 1246–1249 (8th Cir.), cert. denied, 459 U.S. 981, 103 S.Ct. 318, 74 L.Ed.2d 294 (1982) (although hybrid royalty agreement was unenforceable because there was no allocation of the percentage of royalties attributable to trade secrets and know-how, licensor was entitled to compensation for non-patent rights to prevent unjust enrichment); St. Regis Paper Co. v. Royal Inds., 552 F.2d 309, 315 (9th Cir.), cert. denied, 434 U.S. 996, 98 S.Ct. 633, 54 L.Ed.2d 490 (1977) (although court could not enforce royalty agreement which failed to distinguish between patent rights and non-patent rights such as know-how, it could award compensation for non-patent rights).

Moreover, two federal courts have suggested that agreements which specifically provide for separate allocation of payments of royalties for patent and non-patent rights may well survive after expiration or invalidity of the patents despite the Brulotte rule of per se invalidity. See Boggild v. Kenner Prods. Div., 776 F.2d 1315, 1319 (6th Cir.1985) (holding that Brulotte rule of per se invalidity precludes enforcement of license agreement which was developed in "clear contemplation" of patent protection, which requires royalty payments for use, sale or manufacture of patented item for twenty five years, and which "contains neither provisions for reduction of royalties in the event valid patents never issued nor terms for reduction of post-expiration royalties"); Pitney Bowes, Inc. v. Mestre, 701 F.2d 1365, 1372 (11th Cir.1983) (holding Brulotte was applicable to hybrid agreements concerning patent and trade secret rights, and that non-issuance of the pending patent precluded enforcement where there was no allocation in the agreement between trade secrets and patent rights).

Neither the First Circuit nor the Supreme Court has ever addressed the question whether a hybrid agreement in which patents issue can ever survive the expiration or invalidation of the patents where there is a provision for allocation of payments between patent and non-patent rights.

4. The Application of Lear to this Case

There are two crucial factors which support enforceability of this hybrid royalty agreement under this line of cases. First, the contract here took the form of an assignment rather than a licensing arrangement. Second, the assignment agreement provided a mechanism for reducing the royalties to reflect competition in the marketplace should the patent not issue or prove invalid.

a. The assignment

No party disputes that the agreement is, both in form and substance, an assignment. An assignment is a conveyance of a complete bundle of rights, including title to the invention and the right to sue infringers. See CMS Indus. Inc. v. L.P.S. Int'l, Ltd., 643 F.2d 289, 294 (5th Cir.1981) (defining an assignment as a conveyance which "effectively transfers the entire bundle of common law rights presiding in a patent"). An agreement which grants the "exclusive right to make, use and vend the invention" is an assignment, not a license. Waterman v. Mackenzie, 138 U.S. 252, 255–56, 11 S.Ct. 334, 335, 34 L. Ed. 923 (1891).

A license "merely grants a party permission to do something which would otherwise be unlawful; it grants immunity from suit rather than a proprietary interest in the patent." Public Varieties of Mississippi, Inc. v. Sun Valley Seed Co., 734 F.Supp. 250, 252 (N.D.Miss.1990); see also Sybron Transition Corp. v. Nixon Hargrave, et al., 770 F.Supp. 803, 808–09 (W.D.N.Y.1991).

Outside of licensee estoppel, which is commonly understood to have been abolished by Lear, the status of estoppel doctrines in patent law has not been definitively settled. The weight of authority holds that the doctrine of assignee estoppel survived Lear. See Sybron, 770 F.Supp. at 811 ("the policy reasons which justify allowing a licensee to assert patent invalidity against the licensor and to escape the duty to pay royalties do not justify allowing an assignee to avoid its contractual duty to the assignor to make full payment for what it has received"); Roberts v. Sears, Roebuck & Co., 573 F.2d 976, 982 (7th Cir.1978), cert. denied, 439 U.S. 860, 99 S.Ct. 179, 58 L.Ed.2d 168 (1978) ("the primary evil that the Court in Lear sought to end, that the public might have to pay tribute to a 'would-be monopolist' is completely irrelevant to this case [involving a complete assignment of rights])"; Coast Metals, 205 U.S.P.Q. (BNA) 154 (applying assignee estoppel where assignee got the benefit of the bargain). See also Diamond Scientific Co. v. Ambico, Inc., 848 F.2d 1220, 1224–25 (Fed.Cir.), cert. dismissed 487 U.S. 1265, 109 S.Ct. 28, 101 L.Ed.2d 978 (1988) ("if an assignee of a patent were allowed to challenge the patent, it would be placed in the legally awkward position of simultaneously attacking and defending the validity of the same patent"). On the other hand, some courts have refused to apply assignor estoppel. See, e.g., Interconnect Planning Corp. v. Feil, 543 F.Supp. 610 (S.D.N.Y.1982) (rejecting assignor-inventor estoppel when assignee sues assignor for infringement). Whether estoppel should be applied in a particular case, the Federal Circuit has suggested, should be determined by balancing the equities. See Diamond Scientific, 848 F.2d at 1224–25 (justifying application of the generally disfavored doctrine of assignor estoppel).

The equities strongly favor the application of estoppel in this case. There is no evidence that plaintiff exercised the increased leverage of an anticipated patent monopoly based on the parties' expectation of a high likelihood that valid patents would issue. Contrast Boggild, 776 F.2d at 1321. To the contrary, the undisputed evidence is that the issuance of the patents was not a significant factor in the agreement (see undisputed fact #35). Moreover, the terms of the agreement reflect an equality of bargaining power; for example, there is a provision that plaintiff's fees would be reduced in the event of a challenge to the patent or market competition. Finally, the agreement does not purport to extend a royalty agreement beyond the life of the patent.

Furthermore, neither of the two policy rationales supporting the abrogation of estoppel in Lear are relevant to the weighing of equities in this case. The two concerns, it will be recalled, were that a patent's validity might go unchallenged, and that the public would continue to pay tribute for an invalid patent. See 395 U.S. at 670, 89 S.Ct. at 1911. By the time of defendant's termination in this case, the patents had already been widely revealed as invalid and competitive products were on the market. Thus, there is obviously no concern, as there was in Lear, that the patent monopoly would continue to be honored lest the defendant be given an incentive to challenge patent validity.

A little thought about the nature of assignments reveals that the other concern of Lear is equally invalid here. Royalties in a licensing agreement are an ongoing obligation, continually exchanged for an ongoing right. By contrast, royalties in an assignment agreement are properly conceived as deferred consideration for the original conveyance of rights, with the amount of consideration pegged to the commercial success of the product. See Sybron, 770 F.Supp. at 809; Coast Metals, 205 U.S.P.Q. (BNA) at 157.

At the time of the agreement in this case, the assigned bundle of rights included the rights to use and sell an invention that was potentially but not certainly patentable. It also included the right to use Sachs' and Vine's names and to obtain trademark registration for these names. In return, the assignors received payment in the form of royalties. Under plaintiff's interpretation of the agreement, Baladevon would be entitled to some amount of royalties throughout the contract term as long as the defendant continued to manufacture—regardless of whether the inventions or improvements were "patentable," regardless of whether patents issued or not, regardless of the patents' validity, regardless of whether defendant retained ownership of the patents or chose to return them under the termination clause. Unlike those barred by Lear, the payments plaintiff demands would not be benefits derived from ownership of invalid patents. Rather, they would be deferred, contingent consideration for the commercially useful, potentially patentable ideas that a sophisticated, self-interested firm contracted to buy in 1986, in order to get the right to be first in the market and in order to use the names of Sacks and Vine. This court concludes that the defendant should in this case be estopped from challenging the enforceability of the agreement based on patent invalidity.

b.   The royalty renegotiation clause

There is a second, even more significant, distinction between this case and the line of cases extending Lear to the context of hybrid royalty agreements. In each of those cases, the court was compelled to invalidate the whole agreement, because it was impossible to disentangle the consideration given for the invalid patent from the consideration given for nonpatent rights. Each court recognized, however, that the plaintiff was still entitled, on the theory of unjust enrichment, to that portion of the consideration (if any) that was designed to compensate it for nonpatent rights. See Chromalloy, 716 F.2d at 685; Span–Deck, 677 F.2d at 1247; St. Regis, 552 F.2d at 315.

In this case, as in Quick Point, the parties anticipated that the device might not be patentable by providing for renegotiation of the royalty if a competitive product entered the marketplace, and mandatory arbitration if the parties failed to agree. Although the contract itself does not set forth distinct royalty rates depending on the validity of the patent, it takes the more flexible, and equally valid approach, of requiring the parties to renegotiate a fee depending on the validity of the patent. If this court were to invalidate the assignment agreement, then it would be obliged—under the logic of the hybrid royalty cases—to award plaintiff relief tantamount to the renegotiation mechanism provided by the agreement. The assignment contract in this case is not a classic hybrid agreement—it is not an agreement wherein patent and non-patent consideration are hopelessly entangled. On the contrary, the contract fixes the value of the non-patent rights precisely, at the amount of the royalty rate that would be renegotiated in the event of patent invalidity. This court concludes that Lear does not bar enforcement of the agreement as interpreted by plaintiffs.

* * *

In light of the undisputed extrinsic evidence considered at the summary judgment stage, there is no genuine issue of material fact as to the parties' intent. Heavily swayed by the contracting parties unanimity, this Court heeds the plaintiff's entreaty.

6. Relief

Plaintiff asks this Court to assess damages by mandating a royalty fee of 7.5 percent (the upper range of the royalties permitted in the agreement after 1990) and ordering an accounting. The agreement, however, requires the parties to renegotiate the royalty fee in the event a competitive product enters the market place. Accordingly, the royalty rate requested in Count II is inappropriate. The request for an accounting is allowed.

* * *

Notes

1. Consider the questions raised in the Notes following the Section 301 preemption cases, *supra*. Would any of the state laws in question which were *not* preempted under 17 U.S.C.A. § 301 nevertheless be preempted on the ground that they are fundamentally incompatible with federal copyright policy?

2. Plaintiff agrees to license her copyright to defendant, on a nonexclusive basis, in return for a royalty. The contract does not specify the duration of the license. Under the applicable state law, a contract that is silent as to duration is terminable at will. The plaintiff terminates the contract after 8 years. The defendant, however, contends that the license is not terminable for at least 35 years, under 17 U.S.C.A. § 203, and continues to exercise the rights specified in the license. Plaintiff sues for copyright infringement. The court rules, however, that the plaintiff's termination of the license was invalid because the state law permitting termination-at-will is preempted by section 203. Is this ruling correct?

3. Where Congress has enacted statutory provisions defining the scope of federal preemption of state law, such as 17 U.S.C.A. §§ 301, 912(c), should this be interpreted as an acquiescence to state laws which are not preempted by those provisions but might be deemed preempted under a constitutional preemption analysis?

4. When a copyrighted work that contains a person's likeness (such as a motion picture) enters the public domain, can the person depicted therein bring a cause of action for infringement of his or her right of publicity against a person who exploits the public domain work? What about the title of a copyrighted work that enters the public domain—could an unfair competition suit be premised on another person's use of the same title, assuming it has acquired secondary meaning?

5. Does section 1101 preempt state laws? Why did Congress so decide?

6. Do the same standards apply to preemption of state laws by both patent and copyright laws? How can one determine whether Congress made

a deliberate choice to deny protection to a particular kind or work, or simply left the area unattended?

7. If Congress chose to withdraw all federal copyright or patent legislation, would the Supremacy Clause bar states from enacting equivalent statutes on their own?

8. Should trade dress protection be available for a product configuration that is described but not claimed in a patent? Should it matter whether the patent has expired?

9. Would the Supremacy Clause permit a state to offer copyright-or patent-like protection to an idea that was not expressed in any copyrightable or patentable form? To a fixed work that was neither novel nor original? What about a database or other noncopyrightable factual compilation?

10. Does the Lanham Act, 15 U.S.C.A. §§ 1051–1127, preempt any state laws governing trademarks and unfair competition? Is it possible that the Lanham Act itself is preempted by the Intellectual Property Clause?

In *Alameda Films SA de CV v. Authors Rights Restoration Corp. Inc.*, 331 F.3d 472 (5th Cir. 2003), Mexican film production companies sued U.S. distributors for copyright infringement of Mexican films. The jury awarded damages for copyright infringement and unfair competition under the Lanham Act. On appeal, the defendants argued that unfair competition claims are preempted by the 1976 Copyright Act. The court held that the Copyright Act preempts certain state tort claims but it does not preempt the federal Lanham Act. Recovery for both unfair competition under the Lanham Act and infringement under the Copyright Act is permissible.

11. In *Dow Chemical Co. v. Exxon Corp.*, 139 F.3d 1470 (Fed.Cir.1998), *cert. denied,* 525 U.S. 1138, 119 S.Ct. 1026, 143 L.Ed.2d 37 (1999), the Federal Circuit held that federal patent law does not preempt a state law tort claim for intentional interference with actual and prospective contractual relations where that claim implicates the question of inequitable conduct before the PTO and thus raises the issue of patent validity. The patentee in that case had allegedly threatened the plaintiff's customers with infringement suits if they continued to use the plaintiff's products. Tracing the development of preemption doctrine from *Sears/Compco* to *Bonito Boats*, the court explained:

> Under the standard mandated by the Supreme Court, the state law cause of action at issue here does not present an "obstacle" to the execution and accomplishment of the patent laws. None of the three factors identified in *Kewanee* are implicated by a state tort remedy for intentional interference with actual and prospective contractual relations in instances where the tortfeasor's threats to sue were based upon infringement of a patent obtained by inequitable conduct. It is difficult to fathom how such a state law cause of action could have any discernible effect on the incentive to invent, the full disclosure of ideas, or the principle that ideas in the public domain remain in the public domain. Indeed, it seems most improbable that an inventor would choose to forfeit the benefits of patent protection because of fear of the risk of being found tortiously liable based upon attempting to enforce a patent obtained by inequitable conduct. Moreover, a key purpose behind this

tort is the protection of the integrity of commercial contracts which, as noted above, "traditionally are the domain of state law." *Aronson*, 440 U.S. at 262, 99 S.Ct. at 1099; see generally, W. Page Keeton et al., Prosser and Keeton on the Law of Torts 978 (1984) ("The law of interference with contract is thus one part of a larger body of tort law aimed at protection of relationships, some economic and some personal." (footnotes omitted)). The tort plainly does not seek to offer patent-like protection to intellectual property inconsistent with the federal scheme.

While it is true that, under the facts of this case, the "state court" would be required to make a determination of an issue of patent law in reaching its judgment on the underlying tort, this determination would only be ancillary to its central purpose. In any case, it is well established that a state court has authority to adjudicate patent questions so long as the action itself does not arise under the patent laws. See, e.g., Hathorn v. Lovorn, 457 U.S. 255, 266 n. 18, 102 S.Ct. 2421, 2429 n. 18, 72 L.Ed.2d 824 (1982) ("We frequently permit state courts to decide 'collaterally' issues that would be reserved for the federal courts if the cause of action arose directly under federal law. For example, the state courts may decide a variety of questions involving the federal patent laws."); Jacobs Wind Electric Co. v. Florida Dep't of Transp., 919 F.2d 726, 728, 16 USPQ2d 1972, 1974 (Fed.Cir.1990) ("[A]lthough a state court is without power to invalidate an issued patent, there is no limitation on the ability of a state court to decide the question of validity when properly raised in a state court proceeding."); Intermedics Infusaid, Inc. v. Regents of the Univ. of Minn., 804 F.2d 129, 132–33, 231 U.S.P.Q. 653, 656 (Fed.Cir.1986) ("[T]here are no policies reflected in acts of Congress which require that the federal courts enjoin ... a state court contract suit seeking royalties payable under a patent license wherein the state court is or could be asked by the defendant to rule on the validity of the patent."). This analysis remains unchanged regardless of whether the state law claim is grounded in contract or tort. See, e.g., American Well Works v. Layne & Bowler Co., 241 U.S. 257, 259, 36 S.Ct. 585, 586, 60 L.Ed. 987 (1916) (suit for libel or slander based upon an allegation of infringement sounded in tort and did not arise under the patent laws); Gilson v. Republic of Ir., 787 F.2d 655, 657–58, 229 U.S.P.Q. 460, 462 (D.C.Cir.1986) (claim for misappropriation of rights under a patent license sounded in tort and did not arise under the patent laws).

* * *

Nor do we agree with Exxon that the disputed cause of action is an impermissible alternative state law remedy for inequitable conduct before the PTO as prohibited by Abbott Laboratories v. Brennan, 952 F.2d 1346, 21 U.S.P.Q.2d 1192 (Fed.Cir.1991). In *Abbott Laboratories*, we held that a state tort action for abuse of process could not "be invoked as a remedy for inequitable or other unsavory conduct of parties to proceedings in the Patent and Trademark Office." Id. at 1355, 21 USPQ2d at 1200. Such a tort claim "would be an inappropriate collateral intrusion on the regulatory procedures of the PTO ... and is contrary to Congress' preemptive regulation in the area of patent law." Id. at

1357, 21 USPQ2d at 1201 (citation omitted). However unlike the common law abuse of process claim at issue in Abbott, the tort claim asserted here for intentional interference with actual and prospective contractual relations is not an alternative or additional remedy for inequitable conduct before the PTO. In *Abbott*, the abuse of process claim at issue was based entirely upon bad faith misconduct before the PTO. Indeed, the wrong alleged and for which state law tort damages were sought was no more than bad faith misconduct before the PTO. However, the tort claim at issue here is not premised upon bad faith misconduct in the PTO, but rather is premised upon bad faith misconduct in the marketplace. Unlike the abuse of process claim in dispute in *Abbott*, a tort claim for intentional interference with contractual relations requires elements entirely different to those required for inequitable conduct before the PTO. Thus, for example, it requires that the tortfeasor have knowledge of the contractual relationship with which he is interfering and that he commit an act of intentional inducement to harm that relationship. See Restatement (Second) of Torts § 766, cmts. h, i. These required elements take place in the marketplace, not before the PTO. Indeed, the tort can be made out without there being any misconduct whatsoever in the PTO. Thus, for example, a holder of a valid and enforceable patent who knowingly brings baseless infringement actions against a competitor's customers might also be subject to such tort liability. Accordingly, because it requires entirely different elements to establish a prima facie state tort action for intentional interference with contractual relations, it plainly is not a preempted alternative or additional state law remedy for inequitable conduct. Rather it is a long-established independent tort remedy for improprieties in the marketplace.

* * *

The dissent suggests that the state tort of interference with contractual relations is based essentially on an assertion of inequitable conduct and amounts to little more than an attempt to use state law to derive a damages remedy for inequitable conduct. Although acknowledging that the tort has additional elements, the dissent posits that to focus on such differences "merely masks the real issue." In our judgment, however, these different elements are the primary issue. The tort occurs not in the PTO, but later in the marketplace.

A state has every right to protect its citizens and residents in their contractual relations from acts of wrongful interference inside its borders by any party, including a patentee. Moreover, as noted earlier, the Supreme Court has recognized that the protection of commercial, contractual relations is primarily the concern of state law. Any award of damages, then, would be based on local conduct that the state has a right to regulate; proof of acts before the PTO in such a trial are merely evidence of a patentee's bad faith in its subsequent contacts with customers.

Bad faith in turn is only one of three elements that must be established to make out the tort. As noted earlier, the other two are the interfering communications themselves and the disruption and damages therefrom. Nor does the tort simply duplicate federal remedies under patent law as urged by the dissent. The remedy available for proven inequitable conduct is a holding of unenforceability of the patent in federal court; the remedy at law for tortious interference is money damages in state court. Thus, the wrongful acts, the remedies and the forum are all different. In short, we cannot agree with the dissent's characterization of the tort asserted here as based essentially on an assertion of inequitable conduct. Rather, we see the tort as based essentially on bad faith communications that interfere with contractual relations. It is true, however, that in this case without the alleged inequitable conduct before the PTO there would likely be inadequate proof of bad faith. Nevertheless, that the source of proof of bad faith, just one element of the tort, was purported inequitable conduct before the PTO, does not make this tort a patent issue preempted by federal law.

The dissent further suggests that it is undesirable for inequitable conduct to be addressed during trial of a state law cause of action. However, that cannot trump the right of the state to consider inequitable conduct as evidence of wrongful intent in a tort case, any more than it would preclude the state court from addressing the validity of a patent in a contract case. We simply do not see how the "bright line rule" desired by the dissent is either plain in application or possible under our federal patent system and settled case law.

Any argument that this state law cause of action provides a duplication of federal remedies that could lead to conflicting results is similarly unfounded. The tort of intentional interference with contractual relations is a remedy of money damages for improper behavior by competitors in the marketplace. The tort at issue covers all types of commercial actors and does not single out patent-holders for either increased deference or additional scrutiny. Inequitable conduct, however, provides a defense to those accused by a patent-holder whose patent was obtained by improper conduct in the PTO and provides the specific relief of making the patent unenforceable. Far from being a duplication of remedies, the state tort and the federal defense address entirely different wrongs and also provide different forms of relief. In addition, given that, as discussed earlier, it is well-established that issues of validity and enforceability may be adjudicated in licensing disputes governed by state law and thus yield conflicting results, it seems somewhat unpersuasive to suggest that the possibility of conflicting results raised by this case is an adequate ground for preemption.

* * *

Exxon, 139 F.3d at 1475–78 (footnotes omitted).

12.   Does federal patent law preempt a state law regulating the prices of patented prescription medications? See Biotechnology Industry Org. v. District of Columbia et al., 406 F.Supp.2d 56 (D.D.C. 2005), *appeal pending,* No. 2006–1593 (Fed. Cir. 2006).

Index

References are to Pages

---

†